musicHound

ROCK

musicHound

ROCK

The
Essential
Album
Guide

edited by Gary Graff
and Daniel Durchholz

VISIBLE INK PRESS

DETROIT • LONDON

musicHound® ROCK
The
Essential
Album
Guide

Copyright © 1999 Visible Ink Press®

A Cunning Canine Production®

Published by Visible Ink Press
a division of Gale Research
27500 Drake Rd.
Farmington Hills, MI 48331-3535

Cover photo of Bruce Springsteen © Ken Settle

Library of Congress Cataloging-in-Publication Data

MusicHound rock: the essential album guide / edited by Gary Graff and
    Daniel Durchholz — 2nd ed.
        p.   cm.
    Includes bibliographical references (p.   ) and index.
    ISBN 1-57859-061-2 (softcover)
    1. Rock music—Discography. I. Graff, Gary.   II. Durchholz,
Daniel.
    ML156.4.R6M87   1998
    781.66'0266—dc21   98-40006
                                        CIP
                                        MN

ISBN 1-57859-061-2
Printed in the United States of America
All rights reserved

10 9 8 7 6 5 4 3 2 1

musicHound **CONTENTS**

musicHound **SIDEBARS: WHAT ALBUM CHANGED YOUR LIFE?**

I learned how to speak listening to pop records. My mother, not having the time to watch me or the funds to hire a baby-sitter, would sit me in my high chair in front of a record player with a large stack of 45s of the day—records by Dean Martin, Patti Page, Frankie Laine, Julius LaRosa . . . and leave me to be hypnotized by the sounds emanating from this brightly colored box. When the A-sides were finished, she would turn the records over and my trance would begin anew. Day in, day out. Over and over again. By the time I was eight months old, I was singing: "How much is that doggy in the window . . . ," "When the moon hits your eye like a big pizza pie . . . ," "Mule Train . . . ," "Hey Joe, where'd you get that pearly girly. . . . "

I haven't stopped singing since.

The word "pop" has since acquired an undeserved pejorative connotation in the circles of hipdom, but it was once only meant to differentiate popular music from classical. Even with the advent of rock 'n' roll, the term would be used interchangeably to describe the music of Little Richard as well as Little Anthony, even though their styles were certainly different. But labels aside, the music I heard first on a cheap record player, then on a transistor radio pressed to my ear or under my pillow at night, and later on the stereo of my teen years, opened up to me a universe of wonder, romance, heartbreak, power, mystery, passion, and, most of all, fun. Exclusive fun. Serious fun.

Records were the first possessions that I could purchase and own by myself, and the pop of my adolescence was the secret language that my pals and I shared. For me it also became my obsession and my life, but I just took to the extreme what had possessed and moved a whole generation. Pop became the universal language of the young and gained an importance out of proportion to its simple truth.

But perhaps it is important *because* of its simplicity, and since pop music can plumb the depths of the soul and ascend to godhead in three minutes and 27 seconds, it may possess the essence of truth. I don't know. Like my producer, Jimmy Miller, used to say, "When in doubt, turn it up!"

Doug Fieger has been the singer, guitarist, and frontman with the Knack since the group's formation in 1978 in Los Angeles. A native of Detroit, Fieger was raised in suburban Oak Park, Michigan, where he attended school and played in bands with future Was (Not Was) founders Don Fagenson and David Weiss. Fieger continues to lead the Knack, whose latest album, Zoom, *was released during 1998.*

You have in your hands the second edition of *MusicHound Rock: The Essential Album Guide.* You might have noticed that it's a mutha, and we certainly apologize for any injuries incurred while lifting it or accidentally dropping it on your foot. (When we got our first page count, the lawyers told us this kind of disclaimer would be useful.)

Of course, we also hope you find it a muthaload of information—and useful information at that. When we inaugurated the MusicHound series two years ago with our first edition of *MusicHound Rock,* we had in mind guidebooks that would not only educate and enlighten but also help our readers to buy good music. We love music and we want to share our expertise and passion in a way that is more useful than the single-minded pontification that's all too common in these kinds of books.

Two years have passed quickly, but with a great deal of work in between. We've compiled MusicHound volumes on country, blues, R&B, folk, lounge, and jazz. World music is on the horizon, and we have several other ideas currently being put into play, not to mention plans to update all of our books at regular intervals. You can find MusicHound as a reference guide on Amazon.com and at the Borders Books and Music Web site (www.borders.com). The Hound is clearly leaving its mark, and it's not the kind neighborhood ordinances make you sweep up. We hope that along the way our regular readers have noticed the evolution of the series, in both appearance and content. The first *MusicHound Rock* did not have photos. It was also half as large as this volume. The paper stock is better now, and with this book we're introducing a series index to all the MusicHound books to further assist your purchasing decisions. The entries—written by what we can safely call the most talented

assemblage of music writers in a single volume—are sharper and more direct, with a sense of mission and irreverent reverence (trust us on this one) that makes for great entertainment, whether you're reading one entry or the whole (whew!) book.

The second take on any guidebook presents a set of unique challenges, of course. Not only did this edition grow considerably, but it once again made us address the question of "What is rock 'n' roll?" It's always tempting to fall back on the most famous definition of pornography—I know it when I see it (or, in this case, hear it)—but while that's in some ways wickedly appropriate, it's surely not enough. In the nearly 45 years since "Delta 88" blasted out of Memphis and made a whole new music form by fusing together hillbilly country and delta blues, rock has become an umbrella term for an impossibly wide array of approaches. Just look at the Rock and Roll Hall of Fame, which has seen fit to honor seminal bluesmen such as Willie Dixon and Muddy Waters and R&B legends like James Brown and Aretha Franklin alongside guitar slingers Chuck Berry and Jimi Hendrix, piano pounders Little Richard and Jerry Lee Lewis, British invaders the Beatles and the Rolling Stones, and the psychedelic platoon of Jefferson Airplane and the Grateful Dead.

Rock has established sub-genres for any marginally new sound that comes along. We've had surf and garage, punk and new wave, disco and arena rock, grunge and alternative rock (we still laugh at that one), New Romantic and retro. You can also use a hyphen to blend anything—funk-rock, country-rock, rap-rock, etc. And then there are musical forms that aren't necessarily in the rock mainstream but still find their way into the rock universe. The aforementioned R&B, for instance, where its raw sexual energy seems as much a part of the rock mix as screaming electric guitars. Rap's in-your-face attitude (and plethora of rock samples) also puts it in the same realm. Hell, rock is big and forgiving enough to embrace Tony Bennett and—much to his horror—Frank Sinatra as kindred spirits, and it bends enough to allow a hit or two to TV-generated hacks such as the Brady Bunch and the Partridge Family.

Most of all, rock has become a business, a lifestyle soundtrack that's not so subtly exploited to sell product—and that includes far more than rock CDs. Every movie, every advertisement, every sporting event seems to draw on rock to set the tone and convey a message of freshness and vitality. That, in the end, seems to be the best definition of rock: a music that conveys a particular aura of potency. And that can be done with a voice, a guitar, a synthesizer, or the simple creation of a languid mood that sends you to a particular place of being.

Of course, not all artists do this equally well, and that's where *MusicHound Rock* comes in. We hope that in the following pages you re-affirm some of your opinions, re-evaluate others, and discover things you'd never heard of before. We also hope you find stuff that pisses you off; after all, what good is a guidebook if you agree with everything it has to say. But be forewarned: this Hound is one scrappy pup, and it doesn't give up without a good fight. Rock on.

So how do you use *MusicHound Rock*? Here's what you'll find in the entries, and what we intend to accomplish with each point:

• An introductory paragraph, which will give you not only biographical information but also a sense of the artist's or group's sound and its stature in the rock—and overall music—pantheon.

• **what to buy:** The album or albums that we feel are essential purchases for consuming this act. It may be a greatest hits set, or it may be a particular album that captures the essence of the artist in question. In any event, this is where you should start—and don't think it wasn't hard to make these choices when eyeballing the catalogs of the Rolling Stones, the Grateful Dead, Bob Dylan, and some of the other rock titans. Note that for acts with a limited catalog, **what's available** may take the place of **what to buy** and the other sections.

• **what to buy next:** In other words, once you're hooked, these will be the most rewarding next purchases.

• **what to avoid:** This category could include albums the world would be better off without, or it may designate work that newcomers to the particular artist are better off saving for later. Checking the bone ratings—and of course the writer's comments—usually makes it clear whether we're saying "avoid this forever, and cover your ears if anybody plays it in your vicinity," or merely indicating that it's "for completists."

• **the rest:** Everything else that's available for this act, rated with the Hound's trusty bone scale (see below for more on this). Note that for some artists with sizable catalogs, we've condensed this section down to **best of the rest.**

• **worth searching for:** An out-of-print gem. A bootleg. A guest appearance on another artist's album or a film soundtrack. Something that may require some looking but will reward you for the effort.

• ◄◄ : The crucial influences on this act's music.

• ►► : The acts that have been influenced by this artist or group. Used only where applicable; it's a little early for Third Eye Blind, Matchbox 20, or Hanson to have influenced anybody.

We should also remind you that *MusicHound Rock* is a *buyer's* guide. Therefore, for the most part we only discuss CDs that are currently in print and available in the United States.

Now, you ask, what's with those bones? (Down, boy! Sheesh. . . .) It's not hard to figure out—🦴🦴🦴🦴🦴 is nirvana (not Nirvana), a **woof!** is dog food. Keep in mind that the bone ratings don't pertain just to the act's own catalog, but to its worth in the whole music realm. Therefore a lesser act's **what to buy** choice might rate no more than 🦴🦴🦴; some even rate 🦴🦴, a not-so-subtle sign that you might want to think twice about that act. Note that for recent releases that were not available to be reviewed before press time, "N/A" will appear instead of a bone rating.

As with any opinions, all of what you're about to read is subjective and personal. MusicHound has a bit of junkyard dog in it, too; it likes to start fights. We hope it does, too. Ultimately, we think the Hound will point you in the right direction, and if you buy the 🦴🦴🦴🦴🦴 and 🦴🦴🦴🦴 choices, you'll have an album collection to howl about. But if you've got a bone to pick, the Hound wants to hear about it—and promises not to bite (but maybe bark a little bit). If you think we're wagging our tails in the wrong direction or lifting our leg at something that doesn't deserve it, let us know. If you think an act has been capriciously excluded—or charitably included—tell us. Your comments and suggestions will serve the greater MusicHound audience and future projects, so don't be shy.

Editors

Gary Graff is an award-winning music journalist and supervising editor of the MusicHound album guide series. A native of Pittsburgh, Pennsylvania, his work is published regularly by Reuters, *Guitar World, ICE,* the *San Francisco Chronicle,* the *Cleveland Plain Dealer,* Michigan's *Oakland Press,* SW Radio Networks, *Country Song Roundup,* and other publications. A regular contributor to the Web sites Mr. Showbiz/Wall of Sound, JAMTV, and Electric Village, his weekly "Rock 'n' Roll Insider" report airs on Detroit rock station WRIF-FM (101.1). He also appears on public TV station WTVS' *Backstage Pass* program and is a board member of the North American Music Critics Association and co-producer of the annual Detroit Music Awards. He lives in the Detroit suburbs with his wife, daughter, and two stepsons.

Daniel Durchholz never sold his soul for rock 'n' roll. He did, however, put it in escrow. An academic-in-training when journalism came calling, Durchholz began his career at the St. Louis alternative weekly *Riverfront Times,* where he became associate arts editor. He joined *Request* magazine in Minneapolis, serving as associate editor and eventually founding editor of *Request*'s sister publication, *Replay.* He contributed to the first edition of *MusicHound Rock* as well as MusicHound guides on country, folk, lounge, R&B, blues, and jazz. Currently a freelance writer and editor, his work has appeared in numerous magazines, newspapers, and Web publications, including *Pulse!, Guitar, Stereophile,* the *Chicago Tribune,* the *San Francisco Chronicle,* the *St. Louis Post Dispatch,* Wall of Sound, JAMTV, *Rolling Stone* Online, *St. Louis Magazine,* and *Country Song Roundup,* among others. He lives in suburban St. Louis with his wife, Mary, and children, Wolfgang, Eva, Stefan, and Hans.

Managing Editor

Dean Dauphinais is an obsessive-compulsive senior editor at Visible Ink Press and managing editor of several MusicHound titles. His love of music spans all genres and he's been known to crank Led Zeppelin and Aerosmith on his PC during crunch time (much to the delight of his co-workers). He first started to feel old when he took his oldest son, Sam, to his first concert (Hanson, of course). The co-author of two books, *Astounding Averages!* and *Car Crazy,* Dauphinais lives in suburban Detroit with his wife, Kathy, and two sons, Sam and Josh.

Associate Managing Editor

Judy Galens, possessor of a rock and roll heart, is a senior editor at Visible Ink Press and the managing editor of *MusicHound Jazz* and *MusicHound Folk.* She lives in a suburb of Detroit with her growing family and some pets.

Copy Editors

Brigham Narins freelances editorially and studies academically in Motown, Michigan. He doesn't play his mid-'70s fathead Stratocaster enough, he urges people to listen to more instrumental rock (see the entries on the Mermen, Pell Mell, and Friends of Dean Martinez), and he feels real lucky to be sharing a portion of eternity with his lovely wife, who's expecting their soon-to-be-first child.

Pamela Shelton is a freelance writer and copy editor living in Connecticut. She used to write a bluegrass column for *Country in the City News.*

Publisher
Martin Connors

MusicHound Staff

Michelle Banks, Christa Brelin, Jim Craddock, Beth Fhaner, Jeff Hermann, Heather Mack, Brad Morgan, Matt Nowinski, Carol Schwartz, Devra Sladics, Christine Tomassini

Proofreading

Terri Schell, Beth A. Baker, Kathy Dauphinais, Les Stone, Allison Jones, Andy BeDell

Art Direction

Tracey Rowens, Michelle DiMercurio, Cindy Baldwin

Contributing Photographers

Ken Settle is a Detroit-area photographer who has specialized in music photography for over 17 years. His photos have been published worldwide in magazines such as *Rolling Stone, People, Guitar Player, Playboy, Audio,* Japan's *Player,* France's *Guitarist,* and Australia's *Who Weekly,* as well as major newspapers like the *Atlanta Journal Constitution* and the *Arizona Republic.* The Hard Rock Cafe recently acquired 67 of his exhibition prints for their international collection, and several of his images were exhibited in *People* magazine's traveling exhibition, "Through the Years with *People.*" His work also appears in *MusicHound Country, MusicHound Blues, MusicHound R&B, MusicHound Lounge, MusicHound Folk,* and *MusicHound Jazz.* Ken dedicates his photo contributions to the memory of his beloved cats, Angie and Squeaky.

Jack Vartoogian grew up in late 1950s Detroit and heard, but did not get to see, some of the best performers in music. To compensate, he and his wife, Linda, have devoted themselves to photographing musicians (and dancers) from across the country and around the world. While their New York City home virtually guarantees that, eventually, most acts come to them, they continue to seek opportunities to discover new talent and new venues—the farther from home the better. Their images appear regularly in *The New York Times, Time, Newsweek, Living Blues,* and *JazzTimes,* among many others, as well as in innumerable books, including their own *Afropop!* (Chartwell Books, 1995) and *The Living World of Dance* (Smithmark, 1997), and *MusicHound Blues, MusicHound R&B, MusicHound Lounge, MusicHound Folk,* and *MusicHound Jazz.*

Graphic Services

Randy Bassett, Pam Reed, Barbara Yarrow

Permissions

Sarah Chesney

Production

Mary Beth Trimper, Dorothy Maki, Deborah Milliken, Evi Seoud, Wendy Blurton

Technology Wizard

Jeffrey Muhr

Typesetting Virtuoso

Marco Di Vita of the Graphix Group

Marketing & Promotion

Marilou Carlin, Kim Marich, Lauri Taylor, Betsy Rovegno, Nancy Hammond

MusicHound Development

Julia Furtaw

Contributors

Grant Alden is a Nashville-based freelance writer and co-editor of *No Depression* magazine.

Gil Asakawa is an online writer and editor for TheTrip.com and is active in the Japanese American community. Oh yeah, he likes music, too.

Steve Baltin is currently rock & pop editor for CDnow. He has peddled his knowledge of music in exchange for cool swag for almost a decade now.

Brandon Barber writes and produces online music content for www.jamtv.com and www.rollingstone.com.

Ari Bendersky is an editor with JAMTV and the *Rolling Stone* Network. When he's not busy chasing down music news scoops, he can generally be found scarfing sushi, listening to the Grateful Dead, or ironically dodging city traffic on his mountain bike.

Mike Bieber is a music journalist whose work has appeared in several publications, including *Guitar World* and *Jazziz.*

Tracey Birkenhauer is a freelance writer and copy editor living in Ann Arbor, Michigan.

Peter Blackstock is co-editor of the alternative bimonthly *No Depression,* a senior editor at the northwestern music biweekly *The Rocket,* a weekly columnist for the daily *Seattle Post-Intelligencer,* and a contributor to *MusicHound Country* and *MusicHound Folk.*

Steve Braun is a national correspondent with the *Los Angeles Times* based in Washington, D.C. He has poked through Sammy Davis Jr.'s crimson-walled Las Vegas hotel suite and knows how to wield an applause hammer. But as far as listening goes, Jack, Sinatra is where he draws his line in the Sands.

Mike Brown is a DJ, a rave organizer, and a system administrator for Hyperreal, an Internet Web site that provides a home for alternative culture expression.

Ken Burke is a singer/songwriter whose column "The Continuing Saga of Dr. Iguana" has run in numerous small press publications since 1985. His contributions to the *MusicHound Country, MusicHound Blues, MusicHound R&B, MusicHound Folk, MusicHound Jazz,* and *MusicHound Lounge* guides ensure that more people than ever before will have the opportunity to ignore his work.

Carl Cafarelli is a frequent contributor to *Goldmine* and the *Syracuse New Times,* and he wrote the liner notes to Rhino's *Poptopia! Power Pop Classics of the '90s.* He is currently teaching his three-year-old daughter to do the Freddie.

J.D. Cantarella is a music writer and publicist.

Salvatore Caputo is a freelance writer living in metropolitan Phoenix with his wife, three kids, and assorted pets. They've all been known to crank the stereo up to 11 (well, not the pets). Caputo was the rock critic for the *Arizona Republic* from 1990 to 1997, which is something like being the political correspondent for the circus.

Norene Cashen writes for *Alternative Press,* Detroit's *Metro Times,* and *Etch.*

Roger Catlin is the pop music critic at the *Hartford Courant.*

Jeff "DJ Zen" Chang is a writer, a record company hack, and, most shockingly, a father living in the Bay Area on little more than rice and water. He has written for more magazines than you've ever heard of.

Thor Christensen is the pop music critic for the *Dallas Morning News* and has written for *Spin, Billboard,* and other music publications. He blows a lame blues harmonica.

Brian Coleman is a freelance writer and DJ from Boston who feels that Sun Ra, Lee "Scratch" Perry, Rahsaan Roland Kirk, and Kool Keith should have made beautiful music together, not apart.

Martin Connors has contributed to a variety of MusicHound and VideoHound books, and he is especially fond of Celtic music and that country/folk/alternative/guitar-strumming/high-lonesome sound emanating from a lot of places, but especially Texas. He is thankful for the Ark in Ann Arbor, Michigan, his access to Canadian radio and television, and great record stores on land and on the Web.

Jim Craddock is the editor of *VideoHound's Golden Movie Retriever* and just wants to ride his machine without getting hassled by The Man.

Logan Creed is a freelance writer based in Florida. His work has appeared in too many music publications to list.

Jim Cummer manages Madhatter Music Co., a record store in Bowling Green, Ohio.

Spence D., a.k.a. Spencer Abbott, tends to miss deadlines a lot and subsequently angers quite a few editors. Aside from that he's a pretty good writer. His work has appeared in *Bikini, Option, Paper, Raygun, Slap, The Source, URB, Vibe,* and online at Grid Magazine and Wall of Sound. He also writes about film and soundtracks for Roughcut.com. He is currently the associate editor of alternative music at *Gavin,* a San Francisco–based radio and record industry trade publication.

Cary Darling is an entertainment editor at the *Orange County Register* in California, where he also writes a weekly world music column. Rumors that he likes music only in languages other than English are greatly exaggerated.

Dean Dauphinais is managing editor of *MusicHound Rock,* co-managing editor of the MusicHound series, and a contributor to *MusicHound R&B* and *MusicHound Jazz.*

Darren Davis is a reporter for SW Radio Networks in New York City.

Tim Davis is a consultant with Jacobs Media, a suburban Detroit firm that created the modern rock format "The Edge" as well as the "Classic Rock" format.

Eric Deggans is TV and pop culture critic for the *St. Petersburg Times* newspaper in Florida. His work has also appeared in *The Village Voice, Vibe,* the *Chicago Sun-Times,* the *Seattle Times,* and *Rockrgrl* magazine. He's inspired by a wife, three kids, two cats, and one mortgage payment. Not necessarily in that order.

Michael Dixon is a contributor to *Blues Access* magazine and writes for various Maine publications, including the *Southern Maine Blues Society Newsletter* and Lewiston's *Sun-Journal.* He also hosts a weekly blues show on the Bates College radio station, WRBC.

Tom Ellis III has been writing about blues and playing harmonica since 1968. From 1995 to 1997 he authored a five-part series on the life of Paul Butterfield for *Blues Access* magazine and is currently at work on a book about Butterfield. He lives in Dallas,

Texas, and owns Tom's Mics, selling vintage microphones to professional and amateur harmonica players worldwide.

Brian Escamilla is a freelance editor and writer and the former editor of *Contemporary Musicians.*

Shane Faubert played in a band called the Cheepskates during the '80s and is presently a solo artist in Montvale, New Jersey.

Marc Fenton handles public relations for Manhattan PBS affiliate WNET and was a publicist with Razor & Tie Records.

Kim Forster is editor of *WTCA World Business Directory* and the *Companies International* CD-ROM.

Josh Freedom du Lac was born on Haight Street three years and two full seasons after the Summer of Love and has grown to hate patchouli oil, drum-n-space music, questions about his middle name, and one-dimensional wines. The co-editor of *MusicHound R&B* and a budding cork dork, du Lac has been the pop music critic for the *Sacramento Bee* since 1994—incidentally, a great year for California Cabernet Sauvignon.

Bill Friskics-Warren is a Nashville-based writer whose work appears in the *Washington Post*, the *Nashville Scene, Option, Request,* and *No Depression.* He has also contributed to *The Oxford American* and *The Journal of Country Music.*

Christina Fuoco is the music reporter for the *Observer & Eccentric Newspapers* chain based in Livonia, Michigan. She frequently boasts of her Spice Girls dolls collection she got as a gift for her 30th birthday. She lives in Berkley, Michigan, with her cat, Spedliann.

Lawrence Gabriel is a Detroit-based writer, poet, and musician who is also editor of Detroit's *Metro Times.*

David Galens is the editor of Gale Research's *Drama for Students* print series and *Contemporary Authors* on CD, and he's a regular contributor to Gale's *Contemporary Theatre, Film and Television* and *Contemporary Authors* print series. He is also a member of the Detroit-based band the Civilians.

Anna Glen is the former managing editor of *URB* magazine in Los Angeles. Currently she is freelancing and working on her first novel.

Simon Glickman is lead singer and lyricist for the L.A. band Spanish Kitchen. He has written for several MusicHound volumes, *Contemporary Musicians, Uncommon Heroes, Entertainment Today, Rockrgrl,* and other publications, and he served as co-editor of *Native North American Biography.*

Gary Pig Gold, a proud contributor to *MusicHound Country, MusicHound R&B, MusicHound Lounge,* and *MusicHound Folk,* has been publishing his own *Pig Paper* fanzine since 1975 and is a member in good standing of Hoboken, New Jersey's only "maximum rhythm 'n' bluegrass" combo, the Ghost Rockets. He has been listening to rock 'n' roll ever since first encountering the Ran-Dells' immortal "Martian Hop" during the summer of '63 and has no intention of stopping anytime soon.

David Goldberg is executive vice president and co-founder of JAMtv based in Chicago.

Alex Gordon is a former associate editor of *Inside Sports* magazine and the co-author of the book *College: The Best Five Years of Your Life,* published by Hysteria Press.

David Greenberger has been publishing *The Duplex Planet* since 1979. His commentaries and music reviews are heard regularly on National Public Radio's *All Things Considered.*

Mike Greenfield works in advertising, marketing, and public relations in Youngstown, Ohio. In real life, he's a singer, songwriter, guitarist, and lifelong music freak.

Bob Gulla, when he can find a moment of solace amid the sturm und drang of raising three cacophonous (but well-adjusted) children, has snared writing credits in *Rolling Stone, People, Musician,* and *Guitar* magazines.

Jill Hamilton has had her smart-alecky writings appear in *Rolling Stone, Entertainment Weekly, Games, Swing,* and *Mad* magazine. She lives in an okay neighborhood in L.A.

Chris Handyside is a music writer, columnist, and editor for Detroit's *Metro Times.* He also enjoys beating up his drum kit by night and the occasional bout of gardening.

William Hanson works for the Mott Foundation in Flint, Michigan.

William Harmer is an editor at Gale Research and a budding superstar playwright. He knows how to cook up a mean musical stew.

Jeff Hatch is a writer for Ross Roy Communications in Detroit and boasts an extensive musical background, having served on the writing staff for the Palace of Auburn Hills and its associated venues as well as freelancing for numerous publications.

Scott Hess is the program director for JAMtv and the *Rolling Stone* Network, not to mention a die-hard Detroit Red Wings and Chicago Cubs fan.

Seth Hindin is a native of Chicago and promoted all-ages concerts for several years before venturing into music journalism. He has since written for the online edition of *Rolling Stone*, the Illinois alternative weekly *The Octopus*, and the JAMTV music Web site.

Steve Holtje is co-editor of *MusicHound Jazz* and is classical, jazz/blues, and world/soundtracks/new age editor of CDnow. He also freelances for *The Wire*, *Jazziz*, *The Big Takeover*, and various other publications. Though currently living primarily in Lansdale, Pennsylvania, he returns to Brooklyn every weekend to maintain his reputation as a feared softball player.

Pete Howard is editor and publisher of *ICE* magazine.

Michael Isabella is a radio account manager in Detroit whose love of music was nurtured in his native Cleveland.

Brian Ives is a reporter with SW Radio Networks in New York City.

Mike Joiner is an advertising copywriter and music collector in New York City.

Isaac Josephson is an editor at JAMTV and co-founder of *Centerstage Chicago*. In his spare time, he avoids his past, incurs parking fines, and spends money in bicycle shops.

Keith Klingensmith is an avid power pop fan and a member of the Detroit-area group the Phenomenal Cats.

Steve Knopper is a Chicago-based freelance writer whose stories have run in *Rolling Stone*, *George*, *Newsday*, *Chicago*, the *Chicago Tribune*, *Request*, *Billboard*, *Yahoo! Internet Life*, and many other publications. He also writes a regular column, "Blues," for the Knight-Ridder Newspapers wire service, edited *MusicHound Lounge*, and has contributed hundreds of entries for *MusicHound Country*, *MusicHound Blues*, and *MusicHound R&B*.

Greg Kot is the rock critic for the *Chicago Tribune* and has contributed to *Rolling Stone*, *Guitar World*, *Request*, *Details*, *Vibe*, and his daughters' college fund.

George W. Krieger, a.k.a. "The Rock 'n' Roll Dentist," is a general dentist in Elizabeth, Colorado, and has written articles for *Goldmine*, *Colorado Heritage*, the *Pueblo Chieftain*, the *Roundup of Denver Westerners*, and the *Journal of the Colorado Dental Association*.

Bryan Lassner is a student at the University of Michigan and, in his spare time, enjoys playing and composing on the piano and keyboard.

Rob Levine is the music editor of *Details*. He lives and listens to music in New York City.

Elizabeth Lynch is an Evanston, Illinois, writer and novelist who has written for *MusicHound Country*, *MusicHound Folk*, the *Chicago Sun-Times*, the *Fort Lauderdale Sun-Sentinel*, and *Replay* magazine.

Garaud MacTaggart is a Buffalo, New York–based freelance writer with 20 years of experience in music retailing (management/buyer). His work has appeared in newspapers such as the *Buffalo News*, the *Royal Oak* (Michigan) *Tribune*, Detroit's *Metro Times*, the *Orlando Weekly*, the *Columbus Guardian*, and Chicago's *In These Times*.

Billy Manes is a freelance music journalist living in Orlando, Florida, currently published in *Orlando Weekly* and *Jam* magazine. Additionally, Billy writes for RCA Records in New York. He spent two years as editor of *Break* magazine in Tallahassee, Florida, following initial publication in Yale's infamous *Nadine* music rag.

Brian Mansfield has co-edited *MusicHound Country* and *MusicHound Folk*. He lives in Nashville, Tennessee, and writes regularly for *USA Today*, *ICE*, and CountryNow.com. His work has also appeared in *Request*, *Pulse!*, *Country America*, and *Daily Variety*.

Lynne Margolis masquerades as the pop music critic for the *Pittsburgh Tribune-Review* because her dream job—publicist for Spinal Tap—was stolen out from under her by that Bobbi Fleckman!

Patrick McCarty has written about rock 'n' roll for the past 22 years for various publications, including *MusicHound R&B*, *MusicHound Folk*, Richmond, Virginia's *Times-Dispatch* and *News Leader*, and *Style Weekly*. He is a classically trained musician, producer, and songwriter.

Jim McFarlin is co-editor of *MusicHound R&B*, a former nationally known pop music critic and media columnist, and currently senior editor for publications at the Aegis Group Publishers in suburban Detroit.

Adam McGovern deflates the mainstream as senior editor of *Smug* magazine and exalts cheese as a weekly cult-show correspondent for Total TV Online. In addition to editing the forthcoming *MusicHound World*, he's been allowed to produce his state's Arts Council's newsletter. And they wonder why people don't trust the government.

David Menconi is the war correspondent for the *News & Observer* in Raleigh, North Carolina, where he covers the local music scene. He has written for *Spin, Billboard, Request, No Depression,* and *MusicHound Country, MusicHound R&B, MusicHound Lounge,* and *MusicHound Folk.* Someday (but not anytime soon), he swears he will begin acting his age.

Matthew Merta has written for *Home and Studio Recording* and Detroit's *Metro Times.* He is also a music promoter, booking agent, and member of the Detroit band the Masons.

Judy Miller is a publicist who runs Motormouth Media in Los Angeles.

Lisa M. Moore is a freelance writer based in Boston. She writes about music and technology under the watchful eye of her Chow Chow, Chouli, who thoroughly approved of the MusicHound rating system.

Brad Morgan is a senior editor with Visible Ink Press who will listen to anything once (twice, if he likes it). He is editor of *The Vampire Book,* among others, and currently kills time surfing the Internet.

J. Christopher Newberg is a member of the Detroit rock band the Vudu Hippies.

John Nieman works for Ticketmaster's Chicago office.

Jordan Oakes, from St. Louis, is on the music staff of the *Riverfront Times,* publishes *Yellow Pills* magazine, and compiles an ongoing power-pop CD series of the same name. He's also contributed to *Rolling Stone*'s *Alt-Rock-a-Rama* and the *Trouser Press Guide to '90s Rock.* But his real goal is to be an extra in the next Austin Powers movie.

David Okamoto is the music editor for the *Dallas Morning News* and a contributing editor to *ICE* magazine. In between writing for *MusicHound Lounge, MusicHound Folk, MusicHound Country,* and *MusicHound Jazz,* he helped produce a compilation of Martin Mull's music for Razor & Tie Records. Really.

Allan Orski has written extensively for the MusicHound series, as well as *Rolling Stone* Online and a number of other publications, many of which have mysteriously gone belly up shortly after Allan began writing for them. This, of course, is mere coincidence.

Tamara Palmer is an associate editor of *URB* magazine in Los Angeles. Her work has appeared in *Rolling Stone, Wired, Option,* MTV Online, *Raygun,* and the *LA Weekly.*

Joseph Patel is a San Francisco–based music journalist and writer who contributes to several print and Internet publications, including *Rap Pages, The Source, URB* magazine, and Wall of Sound.

Alan Paul is an associate editor of *Guitar World* and the editor of *Guitar World* Online (www.guitarworld.com). He likes piña coladas and making love at midnight.

Mark J. Petracca is the former editor-in-chief of *Creem* magazine and a contributor to *MusicHound Folk.*

Rick Petreycik lives in Bridgeport, Connecticut, and has written for *Guitar Player, New Country, Keyboard, Musician,* and *Live.* He is also a contributor to *The Comprehensive Country Music Encyclopedia* and *MusicHound Country.*

Doug Pippin is an advertising copywriter in New York City and a drummer who ran the band music practice facility Jamland. He is a contributor to *MusicHound Folk, MusicHound Country, MusicHound R&B,* and *MusicHound Lounge.*

Randy Pitts is a contributor to *MusicHound Country* who has labored in the vineyards of traditional music in various circumstances for nearly 20 years, most recently as artistic director of the Freight and Salvage in Berkeley, California, where he worked from 1989 to 1996.

Gary Plochinski is an advertising copy editor at the Bozell agency in suburban Detroit and was a founding member of the Polish Muslims.

Bryan Powell is a musician and journalist who lives in Lawrenceville, Georgia, with his wife, Susan, and daughter, Emily. Bryan contributed to the *MusicHound Blues, MusicHound Folk,* and *MusicHound Lounge* album guides and writes for *Blues Access, Acoustic Guitar, Creative Loafing,* and others. His blues band, Rough Draft, performs frequently around Atlanta.

Barry M. Prickett is a Sacramento, California–based freelance music writer, editor of children's books, and drummer (thus not a musician). He enjoys counting past four, battling sucker MCs, and posing for muscle mag covers in his spare time.

Doug Pullen is the music and media writer for the *Flint* (Michigan) *Journal* and Booth Newspapers. He is a regular contributor to the MusicHound series.

Carl Quintanilla is a Chicago-based staff reporter for *The Wall Street Journal* and a contributor to *MusicHound Lounge.*

Jack Rabid is founder, editor, and publisher of the underground magazine *The Big Takeover* and is currently penning his first book. He is also the drummer for the (newly re-formed) Springhouse and formerly played and toured in Even Worse and the Leaving Trains.

Bob Remstein writes on popular music for several Web sites (Wall of Sound, E! Online) as well as for less high-tech media (*Musician* magazine). An active keyboardist and composer, his "Theme for the Children" can be found on the Qwest/Warner Bros. album *Love Shouldn't Hurt.*

Chris Richards is a music buyer for a large retail chain, and when not buying music, he's fronting his two pop bands, the ultra-famous Phenomenal Cats and the lesser-known Pantookas.

Randall Roberts was born with a silver spoon in his mouth and a full head of hair, humming the melody to "Low Rider." He lives and writes in St. Louis and is the music editor of the city's weekly paper, the *Riverfront Times.*

Leland Rucker is editor of *Musichound Blues* and contributor to every other Musichound volume. He is managing editor of *Blues Access,* a quarterly journal of blues music, and co-author of *The Toy Book: A Celebration of Slinky and G.I. Joe, Tinkertoys, Hula Hoops, Barbie Dolls, Snoot-Flutes, Coonskin Caps, Slot Cars, Frisbees, Yo-Yos, Betsy Wetsy and Much Much More* (Alfred Knopf, 1992). He lives in Boulder, Colorado.

Melissa Ruggieri is the pop music critic for the *Richmond Times-Dispatch.* Other writing gigs include *Billboard, Contemporary Christian* magazine, and the *Fort Lauderdale Sun-Sentinel.* She's also picked up a bunch of awards for music journalism but, then again, who hasn't?

Christopher Scanlon is the former editor of *The Video Source Book* and a MusicHound contributor. He is pursuing his master's degree in social work.

Christopher Scapelliti is a writer based in New York City and an editor with *Guitar World* and *Guitar World Acoustic* magazines.

Tim Schuller was a factory worker/Teamster/rock musician in Ohio and Chicago before moving to Texas in 1977. He presently writes for the *Dallas Observer* and *Blues Access* magazine. His sidebar passions include European horror videos, guns, and Mexican beer.

Jeff Schwager is the executive producer in charge of entertainment for ABCNEWS.com, and oversees the Web sites Mr. Showbiz, CelebSite, and Wall of Sound. The first record he ever bought was the Beatles' *Yellow Submarine.*

Joel Selvin has covered pop music for the *San Francisco Chronicle* since 1970 and is the author of several books on the subect. He co-produced Dick Dale's *Tribal Thunder* album.

Howard Shih is a programmer during the day and writes about electronica, art-rock, avant-jazz, and other types of music that have no words for *Smug* magazine by night.

Greg Siegel is a freelance music critic and graduate student in media and cultural studies at the University of North Carolina, Chapel Hill. A former editor at *ICE* and *Album Network,* his work has appeared in numerous publications, including *Request, Raygun, Audio, Modern Drummer, No Depression,* and *Maximum Guitar.*

David Simons is a New England–based writer/editor who has contributed to *Musician, New Country, Guitar, Country Songwriter,* and other publications, in addition to *MusicHound Country* and *MusicHound Folk.*

Jared Snyder is a graduate of Boston University who currently lives in Philadelphia. He has published articles on music from the United States, the Caribbean, and Africa. His current project is a book of images of accordion players from around the world. He plays diatronic accordion and electric guitar professionally in the Philadelphia area.

David Sokol, senior editor at *Disney Magazine,* served as editor in chief of *New Country* magazine from 1994 to 1997. His writing appears in *MusicHound Country, MusicHound Folk, Stereophile,* and various other publications.

Corey Takahashi is the associate editor of *Blaze* magazine. His work has appeared in publications ranging from *Vibe* to *The Wall Street Journal.*

Coqui Toyoda is a Los Angeles–based music expert.

Brandon Trenz is a contributing editor to Gale Research's *Contemporary Authors* series, as well as a freelance writer and film reviewer.

Philippe Varlet is a performer and teacher of Irish traditional music as well as an ethnomusicologist doing research on many aspects of that tradition. He has produced several CD anthologies, including *From Galway to Dublin* (Rounder), *Milestone at the Garden* (Rounder), and *Joe Derrane—Irish Accordion* (Rego/Copley). Varlet resides near Washington, D.C., where he performs regularly and provides private tuition on Irish fiddle playing.

Aidin Vaziri is the breakdancing world champion and a night manager of KFC #617.

Polly Vedder is an associate editor at Gale Research as well as a singer and sometime guitarist who is practically famous at her church and rather less well known at a local coffeehouse. Her musical tastes run from classical to Scottish folk to off-the-beaten-track pop/rock and contemporary Christian.

Oliver Wang is a contributing editor at *URB* magazine. His work has also appeared in the *San Francisco Bay Guardian, Vinyl Exchange, A.Magazine, Asian Week,* and *Yolk.*

Dan Weber is an advertising copywriter in Detroit.

Hilary Weber is an actress who recently made her first Hollywood picture. She also contributes movie reviews to *Magill's Cinema Annual* and *VideoHound's Golden Movie Retriever.*

Sarah Weber is a freelance writer who frequently contributes to Gale Research and Visible Ink Press publications.

Marc Weingarten is a freelance writer living in Los Angeles.

Amy Weivoda is assistant editor at *Request* magazine.

Ben Wener is the pop music critic for the *Orange County Register* and a contributor to *MusicHound Lounge.* He is currently at work on his first novel and a collection of critical essays on forgotten albums.

Sam Wick is editor-in-chief of *Lounge* magazine and a contributor to *MusicHound Lounge.* In addition to penning books, Wick is a frequent contributor to *Drink, Grammy,* and just about every bartender's pension plan.

Todd Wicks is a copy editor at the Campbell-Ewald Advertising agency in Warren, Michigan, and a member of the hard-pop group Sensitive Clown.

Deborah Wilker is a national correspondent for the Fox News Channel, reporting on entertainment, business, and social issues. From 1987 to 1996 she was music critic for the *Fort Lauderdale Sun-Sentinel* and a frequent contributor to the Knight-Ridder/Tribune wire service and to Tribune newspapers.

Anders Wright is the co-founder and news editor of Wall of Sound, an online music magazine. He lives in Seattle and is a hell of a hoofer.

David Yonke has been the music critic for the *Toledo Blade* for six years, where his memorable moments include golfing with Hootie & the Blowfish, getting kicked by Patti Smith, and mistaking makeup-less Ace Frehley for Gene Simmons.

Josh Zarov is the project manager for Ticketmaster Multimedia. He is also a contributor to Live Vibes Online.

musicHound ACKNOWLEDGMENTS

Another MusicHound book done. Yawn. . . .

That's from exhaustion, not boredom.

The reality, of course, is that the second edition of *MusicHound Rock* was as enjoyable and rewarding to work on as any of the previous seven volumes we've published. A big reason for that was the chance to work with my co-editor, Dan Durchholz, a dear friend since college and a valued colleague over the years, whether I was working for him or he was working for me or we were both grousing about the same editor. Dan's expertise and relentless work ethic were deeply appreciated, as was his resilience as he changed cities, started a new career, and welcomed three more members to his family (at once!) while we were putting this book together. And he's still my brother, in every aspect of the word. Thanks also to Mary, Wolf, Eva, Hans, and Stefan for their indulgences, conscious or otherwise, during the process, and to Mom and Dad Durchholz—particularly for the Beanies.

The Visible Ink Press crew remains a pleasure to work with; they are valuable contributors whose work goes above and beyond what their prescribed duties are. Dean Dauphinais is not only an exceptional managing editor but has a passion for MusicHound that gives us a standard to shoot for. Martin Connors is a valued boss/supporter/combatant/friend, a good Jiminy Cricket for the bunch of us Pinocchios putting these books together. Special thanks also to Judy Galens, Carol Schwartz, Christa Brelin, Marilou Carlin, Kim Marich, Lauri Taylor, Betsy Rovegno, and—last but not least—Jeffrey Muhr, who continues to dazzle us with his technological wizardry.

There are far too many contributors, record company personnel, and artist management folks who are part of the Music-Hound operation to thank by name—at least not without missing somebody important. My gratitude goes to all of them. Special thanks, however, to some folks who put themselves out even further for this book: Ken Burke, Steve Knopper, Josh du Lac, and Christopher Scapelliti. Also a nod to Christina Fuoco, who gave us a lot of good, hard work during a particularly difficult time in her life. Thanks also to Melanie Mahaffey at BIA Research Inc. for the radio station listings and to Brian McCafferty at EMI-Capitol for helping us secure the CD sampler.

During the past two years I've enjoyed the support of a solid network of friends and professional associates whose interest in MusicHound helps keeps me focused. Stephen Scapelliti, my friend and will-work-for-free-books attorney, is never at a loss for ideas about how to refine the MusicHound arrangement. Kent Woodman, Jeff Brown, Jim Lynch, Alan Paul, and Panfilo Garcia provided good ears throughout the making of this book, which I deeply appreciate. Paul Jacobs and Fred Jacobs of Jacobs Media, Doug Podell, Dave Wellington, the morning crew at WRIF, and the assorted concert promoters and venue operators in the Detroit area are friends/business associates whose insights were numerous and valuable.

Thanks also go to my network of editors who exhibited great patience and support during the busiest times: Steve Gorman at Reuters/*Variety;* John Loscalzo, Barry Jeckell, and Matt Sager at SW Radio Networks; Marylynn Hewitt and Patty Bazzani at the *Oakland Press;* Erik Flanigan at Wall of Sound; Brad Tolinski and Jeff Kitts at *Guitar World;* Isaac Josephson and Scott Hess at JAMTv; Joel Selvin and James Sullivan at the *San Francisco Chronicle;* Michael Norman at the *Cleveland Plain Dealer;* and Shelton Ivany at *Country Song Roundup.*

Sadly—but with pride—I again acknowledge the strength and courage of my brothers and sisters in the Detroit Metropolitan Council of Newspaper Unions, who continue our struggle against an illegal and heartless lockout. Nothing is too hard when I consider the sacrifices many of you have made during the past three-and-a-half years. Emily Everett and Susan Watson continue to lay themselves on the line to make sure the *Detroit Sunday Journal* happens each week. And Tom Schram, my hat's off to you, too; you could easily have walked away from all this and instead remain a rock that inspires the rest of us.

Finally, my deepest appreciation to my family, both extended and immediate. Thanks to the assorted Galantys, Brysks, and Graffs for being interested and supportive. For my parents, Ruthe and Milt, here's another one for the mantle. My stepsons, Josh and Ben, now won't be home to hear the assorted mumbling and cursing as we put these things together; congratulations and Go Blue! Hannah gets to bear the brunt of it now, but I promise I'll help you take out the trash. And my wife, Judy, has watched each of these books come to life and boxes of them pile up in the foyer of the house, giving me all the love and encouragement I could want. The Hounds are hard, but these folks make sure I stay a happy puppy.

Gary Graff

This book was completed during the most tumultuous year of my life, and a lot of people deserve credit for keeping me both sane and focused on the task at hand. As this edition came into being, our family increased exponentially with the addition of triplets, we moved from Minneapolis to St. Louis, and I went from working stiff to freelance writer/editor pretty much in one fell swoop. In the face of all that, bringing a 1200-page-plus manuscript to completion was almost a piece of cake.

Almost.

First among equals in my camp is Mary Durchholz, the most wonderful wife, friend, and confidant one could hope for. Married now for 14 years and together for almost a decade longer than that, we've been through a lot, but when it comes to tolerating my chosen profession, Mary has proven herself infinitely patient, kind, and understanding, whether the task at hand was my going on the road to interview Soundgarden four days after the birth of our first child, or my staying up 'til 5 A.M. for nights on end, running down minutiae on the artists represented in this book. My everlasting love goes to her.

Then, too, there are my kids—four-year-old Wolfgang and nine-month-old triplets Eva, Stefan, and Hans. I love you more than words can say, and the fact that you're here at all is proof that miracles do occur in this world. I dedicate this book to you.

My parents, Eric and Annie Durchholz, have been nothing but help in this year of transition, to say nothing of the 37 years that preceded it. The best way I know to say thanks for the love and support you've given me over the years is to try and do the same for my kids. But the question remains: What kind of music will they blare on their stereos or what musical instruments will they take up to bug me? Whatever the answer, I hope I handle it as well as you did.

My partner in this endeavor, Gary Graff, is not a member of my immediate family, but he might as well be. A friend now for 18 years, Gary has been a constant source of inspiration professionally and a rock upon which to lean for personal advice and counsel. He should have been a juggler, for God knows, no one keeps as many balls in the air as he does. But we're all lucky that he chose music journalism instead, because 1) nobody goes to the circus anymore, and 2) it turns out he's the best at what he does in that field, too. I was a proud contributor to the first *MusicHound Rock* volume (as well as the volumes on country, blues, R&B, lounge, folk, and jazz that followed it) and was honored to be brought into this book as co-editor. Thanks for everything, brother.

Many personal friends have kept me going throughout this project thanks to their interest and encouragement. These include Jerome Peirick, a terrific sounding board for ideas, turns of phrase, random facts and quotes, and computer advice. I have more interesting and wide-ranging phone conversations with Jim Lynch than I do with any other human—thanks for keeping us in your thoughts and prayers, Jim. Greg Halling and I crossed paths in college working for the school newspaper, and we've been friends and crack (as opposed to crack-addled) journalists ever since. Attn: Greg—send lawyers, guns, and money. Other friends in need and in deed include Lori Witthaus, Dana Collins and Rich Melvin, Tom and Diane Burke, Joe and Patti Voda, Kevin Baker, and Rob "Jammypac" Schneider.

More family shout-outs go to the O'Donnells—Bill, Peggy, Megan, Tim, and Erin—and the Oswalds—Ralph, Susie, Melissa, Amy, and Emily—for all the baby-sitting. Attn: Linda Clark—keep those cans of formula coming. Thanks in general to all of Mary's many brothers and sisters and their families, as well as to Papa John. Also to my side of the aisle—the Zoellers, the Himmelbergs, and especially Otto Durchholz and Elizabeth Himmelberg.

Many editors helped me through this project in various ways and cut me some slack when I needed it, including Erik Flannigan at Wall of Sound; Cliff Froehlich and Randall Roberts at the *Riverfront Times;* Robert Baird at *Stereophile;* Keith Moerer, formerly of *Request* and now at Amazon.com; Steve Stolder at Amazon.com; Shelton Ivaney at *Country Song Roundup;* Greg Kot at the *Chicago Tribune;* Joel Selvin and James Sullivan at the *San Francisco Chronicle;* Bob Gulla at *Guitar;* Isaac Josephson at JAMtv; and Hans Eisenbeis at Requestline and Samgoody.com. And special thanks to Jim Creighton, formerly of the *St. Louis Post Dispatch.*

I'd also like to acknowledge the influence of several teachers who helped turn me from a potentially bad accountant into a reasonably serviceable writer. These include Deborah Peters, OSB, Mary Faith Schuster, OSB, Jeremy Dempsey, OSB, and the late Celine Carrigan, OSB, all of Benedictine College; and Carter Revard of Washington University.

Publicists too numerous to mention contributed time, information, and, importantly, CDs to the cause, but also friendship and moral support. Heartfelt thanks to all of you, but especially to Bill Bentley, Rick Gershon, Kevin Kennedy, Steve Karras, and Paula Donner, who were (and are) thoughtful and caring far beyond the call of duty. Also, there were many writers, only some of whom are in this book, that I miss working with from my days at *Replay* and *Request.* To Tom Lanham, Amy Linden, Amy Weivoda, Elysa Gardner, Geoffrey Himes, Bob Allen, j. poet, Chris Nickson, Will Hermes, Eric Lindbom, Havelock Nelson, Larry Flick, Alan Paul, Liz Lynch, David Sprague, Don McLeese, Don Kaye, Britt Robson, Billy Altman, Pleasant Gehman, Jon Bream, and so many others—we'll meet again someday on the avenue. . . .

At Visible Ink, Dean Dauphinais has been a paragon of patience and an incisive judge of our material. Thanks, Dean, and I will take your advice now by signing off of AOL and getting a life. Thanks to Martin Connors, the Lord of the Hound, and to Judy Galens for everything, including the gingerbread pancakes.

Finally, thanks to the many contributors to this book. Some of you I only know through random e-mails, and others not at all. I hope to rectify that situation someday, and if you're ever in St. Louis, lunch is on me—but not everybody at once, eh? And last, but certainly not least, to the Brothers of the Hound—Steve Knopper, Brian Mansfield, Leland Rucker, Josh du Lac, and Steve Holtje, who provided plenty of advice before, during, and hopefully after, my joining the club—my profound thanks.

Daniel Durchholz

A

a-ha

Formed 1982, in Oslo, Norway.

Morton Harket, vocals; Magne "Mags" Furuholmen, keyboards; Pal Waaktaar, guitar.

a-ha is living proof that the world is a really big market. The band emerged rapidly with a cutting edge video for the single "Take on Me," a technological marvel that depicted a romantic adventure starring lead singer Morton Harket as a comic book hero who comes to life (the song was rediscovered during 1998 when Reel Big Fish covered it for the *BASEketball* soundtrack). The combination of live action and animation garnered heavy MTV airplay and success in the U.S. during the summer of 1985. Although a-ha made a valiant effort to sustain that level of success, its commercial status in North America diminished as quickly as it came—though a-ha remained popular around the world. Subsequent albums continued to demonstrate a-ha's pop hooks blended with Harket's poetic vocals over a layer of synthesizer-heavy electropop. Other highlights included the theme song for the 1987 James Bond Film *The Living Daylights* and record-breaking crowds at the 1991 "Rock in Rio" festival.

what to buy: *Hunting High and Low* ♪♪♪♪ (Warner Bros., 1985, prod. Alan Tarney) features "Take on Me" as well as other strong material such as the title track and "The Sun Always Shines on T.V.," which demonstrates Harket's magnificent vocal range. *Scoundrel Days* ♪♪♪♪ (Warner Bros., 1986, prod. Alan Tarney, a-ha) continues in the same vein, putting a slightly softer and more soothing varnish on the group's characteristically engaging melodies.

what to buy next: *Headlines and Deadlines: The Hits of a-ha* ♪♪♪ (Warner Bros., 1991, prod. various) is a best-of package that culls all the singles released worldwide, along with some remixes, for a complete taste of a-ha.

what to avoid: On *Memorial Beach* ♪ (Warner Bros., 1993, prod. David Z, a-ha), a-ha tries to be U2 and it does not work.

the rest:
Stay on These Roads ♪♪ (Warner Bros., 1988)
East of the Sun, West of the Moon ♪♪ (Warner Bros., 1991)

worth searching for: The 45 rpm single for "Take on Me" (Warner Bros., 1985, prod. Alan Tarney), complete with the comic book and storyboards from the song's celebrated video.

influences:
 Simple Minds, Duran Duran, Roxy Music, David Bowie

▶▶ Ace of Base

John Nieman

A House

Formed 1985, in Dublin, Ireland.

Dave Couse, vocals, guitar; Fergal Bunbury, guitar; Martin Nealy, bass; Dermot Wylie, drums.

Although not quite as popular as their Irish brethren U2, A House also can write catchy, tuneful pop with a Celtic flavor. Their four-man lineup cuts to the chase in creating standard guitar rock with interesting lyrics that often touch upon a variety of meaningful or at least potentially controversial issues. Their first single was titled "Kick Me Again, Jesus" while another song, "That's Not the Truth," attacks journalists. Some songs paint a violent picture—"I Want to Kill Something," "Violent Love"—yet the band isn't afraid to show some emotion, as on "My Little Lighthouse." Ireland's literary heritage and folk legacy are readily apparent in this band's work.

what to buy: *I Am the Greatest* 𝄞𝄞𝄞 (Radioactive, 1992) is more diverse than the band's previous two albums, containing some melodious tracks and other more noisy cuts. The arrogant-sounding title is actually a song about the price of fame; not that these guys would necessarily know about that. Look for the import version, though, as the U.S. offers only a truncated version of the album.

what to buy next: Their strong first album, *On Our Big Fat Merry-Go-Round* 𝄞𝄞𝄞 (Sire, 1988), proved that Ireland has more to offer than just that other band. It shows off the band's pop and rock chops before it headed for a folkier sound on later releases. *I Want Too Much* 𝄞𝄞𝄞 (Sire, 1990) offers catchy guitar hooks and witty lyrics that translate to meaningful pop tunes such as "The Patron Saint of Mediocrity."

the rest:
Wide Eyed and Ignorant 𝄞𝄞𝄞 (Radioactive, 1995)

influences:
◀◀ The Pogues, Mekons, Violent Femmes

Christopher Scanlon

ABBA

Formed 1971, in Sweden. Disbanded 1982.

Benny Andersson, keyboards, vocals; Bjorn Ulvaeus, guitar, vocals; Agnetha "Anna" Faltskog, vocals; Anni-Frid "Frida" Lyngstad, vocals.

Like the Volvo of the band's homeland—the only Swedish export bigger than this group during the '70s—ABBA's well-oiled pop machine was very nearly a perfectly manufactured product. Heavily layered vocals and synthesizers delivering conversely simple lyrics and melodies made the band's music enormously successful around the world. ABBA was bigger abroad, though it charted 14 Top 20 hits in the U.S. Anna, Benny, Bjorn, and Anni-Frid were individual stars in Sweden before they joined forces (and first initials) to form ABBA, which first drew worldwide attention with "Waterloo," the winner of the 1974 Eurovision Song Contest. After the group's 1982 breakup (said to be necessitated by the members' wealth, which drew death and kidnapping threats), ABBA nostalgia only grew. A decade later, greatest hits compilations topped the charts worldwide, while the music was covered by all manner of artists and frequently popped up on film soundtracks. It may be slick and sugary, but the very optimism of their voices and the tunefulness of their songs makes ABBA's music very hard to dislike.

what to buy: Because it was a singles band, ABBA's *Gold* 𝄞𝄞𝄞𝄞 (Polydor, 1992, prod. Benny Andersson, Bjorn Ulvaeus) is a glit-

tering array of highlights and party sure-things, with 19 tracks ranging from "Dancing Queen" and "Knowing Me, Knowing You" to "S.O.S" and "Waterloo." So sweet you may feel your teeth start to decay. Most of the same hits sung in Spanish are available on *Oro* (PolyGram Latino, 1993).

what to buy next: For those who need more, get *Thank You for the Music* 𝄞𝄞𝄞𝄞 (A&M, 1995, prod. Benny Andersson, Bjorn Ulvaeus), a four-disc box set with one full disc of unreleased tracks, B-sides, and foreign language versions. *More ABBA Gold* 𝄞𝄞𝄞 (Polydor, 1996, prod. Benny Andersson, Bjorn Ulvaeus) features a lot of wonderful and overlooked ABBA ditties, including a few hits such as "I Do, I Do, I Do, I Do, I Do"; the Spanish equivalent is not quite as direct on *Mas Oro* (PolyGram Latino, 1994). For those who wonder what an original ABBA album sounds like, *Arrival* 𝄞𝄞𝄞 (Polydor, 1977, prod. Benny Andersson, Bjorn Ulvaeus), timed to concur with ABBA's first international tour, finds the band at its peak, with the hits "Dancing Queen" and "Knowing Me, Knowing You."

what to avoid: *Ring Ring* 𝄞𝄞 (Atlantic, 1973/Polydor, 1995, prod. Benny Andersson, Bjorn Ulvaeus) begins the story a little too early. The band hasn't quite found itself yet.

the rest:
Waterloo 𝄞𝄞𝄞 (Atlantic, 1974/Polydor, 1995)
ABBA 𝄞𝄞𝄞 (Atlantic, 1975/Polydor, 1995)
The Album 𝄞𝄞𝄞 (Atlantic, 1977/Polydor, 1995)
Voulez-Vous 𝄞𝄞 (Atlantic, 1979/Polydor, 1995)
Super Trouper 𝄞𝄞 (Atlantic, 1980/Polydor, 1995)
The Visitors 𝄞𝄞 (Atlantic, 1981/Polydor, 1995)
The Collection 𝄞𝄞𝄞 (Chronicles, 1998)

worth searching for: *Selections from "Thank You for the Music"* (Polydor, 1995, prod. Benny Andersson, Bjorn Ulvaeus), a promotional sampler from the box set, features "Abba Undeleted," a specially crafted 23-minute "Stars on Abba" medley of hits.

influences:
◀◀ Blue Swede, 1910 Fruitgum Co., the Archies, the Fifth Dimension

▶▶ Ace of Base, the Real McCoy, Bjorn Again, Erasure, Los Umbrellos, Robyn

Roger Catlin

ABC

Formed 1980, in Sheffield, England.

Martin Fry, vocals; Mark White, guitar, keyboards; Mark Lickley, bass (1980); David Robinson, drums (1980); Stephen Singleton, saxo-

phone (1980–84); David Palmer, drums (1980–83); Eden, vocals (1983–90); David Yarritu, keyboards (1983–90).

Amid the fashion-conscious music scene of post-punk England, ABC matched luxuriant pop writing with its wardrobe, crafting one bona fide classic of the period before shifting gears awkwardly to rock, then back to campy pop, then over to dance. The band's career has been in limbo since its stylish frontman and mainstay, Martin Fry, was diagnosed with Hodgkin's disease a decade ago.

what to buy: *The Lexicon of Love* ♫♫♫♫ (Mercury, 1982, prod. ABC) holds up in an era of very flimsy fashion music as a self-assured, tuneful, classy stab into heartfelt emotion tied up with a lot of strings—literal and metaphoric.

what to buy next: *Absolutely* ♫♫♫♫ (Mercury, 1990, prod. various) is a greatest hits album that seems a little premature but captures the high points nicely.

what to avoid: *Beauty Stab* ♫♫ (Mercury, 1983, prod. ABC), the follow-up to *Lexicon of Love*, suffers for the decision to turn ABC into a heavier guitar band.

the rest:
How to Be a Zillionaire ♫♫♫ (Mercury, 1985)
Abracadabra ♫♫ (Mercury, 1991)

worth searching for: *Alphabet City* (Mercury, 1987, prod. Martin Fry, Mark White), now out of print, is a return to form that featured "When Smokey Sings," an infectious tribute to Smokey Robinson.

influences:
◀◀ Roxy Music, David Bowie, Motown

▶▶ George Michael, Pulp, Babybird, Edwyn Collins

Roger Catlin

Paula Abdul

Born June 19, 1962, in Los Angeles, CA.

Chosen as a choreographer for the Los Angeles Lakers basketball team's cheerleaders at age 17, Paul Abdul found herself rubbing shoulders with the town's most famous citizens—eventually attracting interest from the Jacksons, who hired her to choreograph a video. From there, she guided Janet Jackson's dance-heavy breakthrough videos, becoming a star herself when the clips exploded on MTV. After doing similar work for the Pointer Sisters, ZZ Top, and *The Tracey Ullman Show,* among others, Abdul signed a recording deal herself, releasing a critically drubbed but commercially successful debut album filled with disposable dance/pop. Most potshots regarding that and subsequent albums centered on Abdul's singing—a thin, nasal wail that needed lots of processing to sound listenable.

Still, her stylized videos saturated MTV, pushing her into the pop stratosphere. A second record also did well, but trouble loomed when a backup singer on Abdul's first record claimed to have sung lead vocals on all the tunes. Given Abdul's lack of vocal talent, it was a serious charge, but a Los Angeles court eventually decided in Abdul's favor. But by the time the suit was resolved, younger, hip-hop–influenced dance divas were ruling the charts, and Abdul's 1995 album came and went without much notice.

what to buy: Her debut, *Forever Your Girl* ♫♫♫ (Virgin, 1988, prod. various), perfectly distills the tenor of the MTV-fed pop market of the time. It's basically a record featuring a boatload of producers and even more studio musicians, crafting a raft of tracks designed to provide a sonic artifact to go along with an incredibly videogenic star. The songs seem like an afterthought, momentarily enjoyable but ultimately forgettable.

what to avoid: *Shut Up and Dance (The Dance Mixes)* **woof!** (Virgin, 1990, prod. various) merely provided another excuse for MTV to put an Abdul video in heavy rotation.

the rest:
Spellbound ♫♫ (Virgin, 1991)
Head Over Heels ♫♫♫ (Virgin, 1995)

worth searching for: The collection of videos from her debut disc, also called *Straight Up* (Virgin, 1990), is worth a look if only to see the real reason why she got a record deal: videogenic dance moves and well-packaged video showcases.

influences:
◀◀ Janet Jackson, Madonna, Donna Summer, All Saints

▶▶ Mariah Carey, Brandy, Mary J. Blige, Spice Girls

Eric Deggans

Absolute Zeros

See: Chopper

AC/DC

Formed 1973, in Sydney, Australia.

Angus Young, guitar; Malcolm Young, guitar; Dave Evans, vocals (1973–74); Ronald Belford "Bon" Scott (died February 19, 1980), vocals (1974–80); Brian Johnson, vocals (1980–present); Peter Clark, drums (1973–74); Phillip Rudd, drums (1974–82, 1995–present); Simon Wright, drums (1982–89); Chris Slade, drums (1989–95); Rob Bailey, bass (1973–74); Mark Evans, bass (1974–77); Cliff Williams, bass (1977–present).

One of the most popular and influential hard rock bands in the world, AC/DC has enjoyed success for more than two decades without straying from the brand of straightforward, electrified boogie it began with during the mid-'70s. Founding members

Angus Young of AC/DC (© Ken Settle)

and brothers Angus and Malcolm Young were influenced at an early age by their uncle George, a member of the Easybeats (known for the hit "Friday on My Mind"). With George's musicianship and music industry savvy to guide them, the Young brothers soon assembled a group that was filling the Australian bar circuit. Many of AC/DC's fans came to witness Angus's hyperkinetic onstage antics: clad in his signature schoolboy uniform and clutching a Gibson SG (the only guitar he ever plays), little Angus would thrash, bob, crawl, and duck-walk his way through the band's sets, pausing occasionally to moon the audience. After two Australian albums, the band scored overseas and quickly became a worldwide sensation, seemingly immune to even the greatest adversity: in 1980, at the peak of their success, singer Bon Scott died, choking on his own vomit in the back seat of a friend's car. The band pressed on, adding ex-Geordie vocalist Brian Johnson to the lineup; the first album with Johnson, *Back in Black*, was its best-seller yet. AC/DC has since churned out a succession of popular albums that remain true to its raunchy, guitar-fueled formula, for which it's been rewarded with a steadily increasing army of fans and a string of successful world tours.

what to buy: For many fans, there are two AC/DCs: the Bon Scott band and the Brian Johnson band. For fans of Scott's bluesy style, *Let There Be Rock* ♪♪♪♪ (Atlantic, 1977, prod. Harry Vanda, George Young) and *Powerage* ♪♪♪♪♪ (Atlantic, 1978, prod. Harry Vanda, George Young) reign supreme, showcasing both Scott's solid lyrics and Angus's crunching guitar. However, even fans who prefer Scott can't deny the power of *Back in Black* ♪♪♪♪♪ (Atlantic, 1980, prod. Robert John "Mutt" Lange), by far the best of the albums that feature Johnson's whiskey-soaked growl.

what to buy next: The live *If You Want Blood . . . You've Got It* ♪♪♪♪♪ (Atlantic, 1978, prod. Harry Vanda, George Young) finds the Scott-fronted band in fine form; and Johnson's sophomore effort, *For Those about to Rock, We Salute You* ♪♪♪♪ (Atlantic, 1981, prod. Robert John "Mutt" Lange), is one of AC/DC's most solid recordings. If you've got the money, the box set *Bonfire* ♪♪♪♪♪ (Atlantic, 1997, prod. various) gives fans a number of heretofore unreleased demo tracks and live performances, as well as the soundtrack from AC/DC's concert film, *Let There Be Rock,* and a digitally remastered *Back in Black*. Pricey, but worth it.

what to avoid: *Flick of the Switch* ♪♪ (Atlantic, 1983, prod. AC/DC) is one of the group's more lackluster albums.

the rest:
High Voltage ♪♪♪ (Atlantic, 1976)
Dirty Deeds Done Dirt Cheap ♪♪♪♪ (Atlantic, 1976)
Highway to Hell ♪♪♪♪♪ (Atlantic, 1979)
'74 Jailbreak ♪♪♪ (Atlantic EP, 1984)

Fly on the Wall ♪♪ (Atlantic, 1984)
Who Made Who ♪♪♪ (Atlantic, 1986)
Blow up Your Video ♪♪♪ (Atlantic, 1988)
The Razor's Edge ♪♪♪ (Atlantic, 1990)
Live ♪♪♪♪ (Atlantic, 1992)
Ballbreaker ♪♪♪ (EastWest, 1995)

worth searching for: A sampler from *Bonfire* (EastWest, 1997) culls eight songs from the box set for a taste of the rarities involved. But be forewarned—it may whet your appetite for the whole set.

influences:
◀◀ Led Zeppelin, the Yardbirds, Cream, the Who, the Easybeats

▶▶ Soundgarden, Guns N' Roses, the Cult, Joan Jett, Rhino Bucket

Brandon Trenz

The Accelerators

Formed 1983, in Raleigh, NC.

Gerald Duncan, vocals, guitar; Chris Moran, guitar (1983–87); Brad Rice, guitar, vocals (1988–91); Doug Welchel, drums (1983–90); Jon Wurster, drums (1990–91); Skip Anderson, bass (1983–87); Mike Johns, bass, vocals (1988–91).

From the Georgia Satellites to Webb Wilder, most '80s roots rock bands got by on good intentions more than actual songcraft. The underrated Gerald Duncan is slyer than most, a songwriter equipped with enough smarts and droll humor to pull off songs as emotionally outlandish as "Two Girls in Love" (which is about exactly what the title implies). But that never helped Duncan's roots-pop band the Accelerators find an audience, despite making some fine records. At the time of this writing, a version of the band is still together, although Duncan is the lone original member left. From the lineups above, drummer Jon Wurster went on to play in Superchunk, while lead guitarist Brad Rice later resurfaced in the hardcore honkytonk band the Backsliders.

what to buy: By far the best Accelerators album is *Dream Train* ♪♪♪ (Profile, 1991, prod. Dick Hodgin)—a dozen sharp songs, including the best-ever theft of T. Rex's "Bang a Gong (Get It On)" riff on the shoulda-been-a-hit single "Boy & Girl."

what to buy next: The group's middle album, *The Accelerators* ♪♪♪ (Profile, 1988, prod. Dick Hodgin, Don Dixon, Rod Abernethy), is better than its predecessor but worse than its successor, with one too many throwaway covers.

what to avoid: The band's uneven debut album, *Leave My Heart* ♪♪♪ (Dolphin, 1983, prod. Don Dixon), wears its period power pop uneasily and has not aged particularly well, though it does have a great version of the aforementioned "Two Girls in Love."

influences:

◄◄ Don Dixon, the dB's

►► The Georgia Satellites, the Bottle Rockets, the Backsliders

David Menconi

Ace

See: Paul Carrack

Johnny Ace

Born John Marshall Alexander Jr., June 9, 1929. Died December 25, 1954, in Houston, TX.

During his lifetime, Johnny Ace was just a popular R&B balladeer. After his death, he became a tragic, romantic icon for teenagers who found added resonance in his posthumously released hit "Pledging My Love." Before he officially became "Rock 'n' Roll's First Fatality," John Alexander worked in Adolph Duncan's popular Memphis band and played piano on recordings with B.B. King's Beale Street Boys. After King and Bobby "Blue" Bland left, Alexander renamed the group the Beale Streeters and took over the lead vocal spot. When Alexander signed with Duke Records in 1952, he changed his stage name to Johnny Ace so as not to embarrass his father, a Memphis preacher. Ace's first release, "My Song," sounds poorly recorded and off-pitch today, but the vocal was warm and vibrant, and the record was a #1 R&B hit for nine weeks. (Johnny Otis and his orchestra were eventually brought in to supplement Ace's recording sessions.) In 1953, "Cross My Heart" was a Top 5 single, and its echo-laden follow-up, "The Clock," stayed in the #1 spot for five weeks. Ace's winning streak with cozy, vibe-accented ballads continued into 1954 with "Saving My Love for You," "Please Forgive Me," and "Never Let Me Go," prompting disc jockeys to vote him the year's Most Programmed Artist in a *Cashbox Magazine* poll. Ace dealt with the pressure of stardom one time by sticking the barrel of an empty .32 revolver in his mouth, pulling the trigger, and, after the weapon sounded an empty click, laughing at the horrified expressions of those around him. On Christmas Eve in 1954, backstage at a Houston concert, Ace pulled the same stunt with a loaded pistol and died. He was only 25 years old. The wave of publicity surrounding the death of Johnny Ace resulted in "Pledging My Love" not only hitting #1 on the R&B charts for 10 weeks, but peaking at #17 on the pop charts as well. A second posthumous single, "Anymore," was Ace's final Top 10 R&B hit and was all Duke Records had left to issue. Johnny Ace tribute songs became an R&B vogue for awhile, and Duke Records tried to cash in by hiring Ace's younger brother, St. Clair Alexander, to record under the name Buddy Ace. "Pledging My Love"

remains a staple of oldies radio and '50s rock 'n' roll compilations, where Ace's is the one pleadingly heartfelt voice in a sea of frivolity.

what's available: Currently, there are two versions of the *Johnny Ace Memorial Album*: *Johnny Ace Memorial Album* ♪♪♪♪ (MCA, 1973, prod. various) has 12 tracks; its evil twin, *Johnny Ace Memorial Album* ♪♪♪♫ (MCA Special Products, 1987, prod. various) (a.k.a. *Pledging My Love*), is a budget version containing only eight tracks. The 12-song version is an exact reproduction of the LP Duke released in 1955. Ace's work seems ripe for a major repackaging; he recorded 10 singles for Duke, usually coupling a ballad with a rocking jump blues number. Of the 12 songs available, most are ballads, with "Please Forgive Me" being conspicuously absent, and there are no useful session or liner notes.

worth searching for: Some import outlets are carrying *Johnny Ace Memorial Album* (MCA Europe, 1998, prod. various), which contains Ace's entire recorded output for Duke, including his hit duet with Big Mama Thornton. The anthology *The Best of Duke-Peacock Blues* (MCA, 1992) contains one tune currently unavailable elsewhere, "How Can You Be So Mean," a rockin' jump blues. Also, for some background into Johnny Ace's life and times, hunt down a copy of Nick Tosches's *Unsung Heroes of Rock 'n' Roll* (Harmony Books, 1984/1991), an informative, occasionally irreverent collection that also features pieces on the likes of Ella Mae Morse, Merrill Moore, Roy Brown, Amos Milburn, the Treniers, Jackie Brenston, Big Joe Turner, and many others who paved the way for the '50s rock music explosion.

influences:

◄◄ Bobby "Blue" Bland, B.B. King

►► Chuck Willis, Jessie Belvin

Ken Burke

Ace of Base

Formed 1990, in Gothenburg, Sweden.

Jenny Cecilia Berggren, vocals; Malin Sofia Datarina "Linn" Berggren, vocals; Jonas Petter "Joker" Berggren, keyboards; Ulf Gunnar "Buddha" Ekberg, keyboards.

It's appropriate that you can file Ace of Base's albums right after ABBA's in your collection, for like the Swedish Europop pioneer that preceded it, Ace of Base consists of two men and two women playing insidiously catchy songs that are guilty pleasures, pure and simple. The group came together when keyboardists/songwriters "Joker" Berggren and "Buddha" Ekberg tapped Berggren's sisters to front a dance band that played in their native city of Gothenburg, Sweden. Within a year they signed a record deal and scored a Scandinavian hit,

"Wheel of Fortune," which gave way to the even bigger smash "All That She Wants," which topped the charts in 10 countries. The group's momentum carried over the Atlantic, and when their debut, *The Sign* (known as *Happy Nation* in its European version), was released in the U.S., it spawned a number of hit singles, including "All That She Wants," "Don't Turn Around," and the title track, selling over eight million copies of the album and earning three Grammy nominations. The follow-up, 1995's *The Bridge*—sonically a carbon copy of *The Sign*—featured plenty of catchy songs like "Beautiful Life," but, though it did go platinum, the album failed to capture nearly as much attention or acclaim. A third album is due from the quartet before the end of 1998.

what to buy: Percolating along at 95 BPM or so, the intoxicating mix of toy reggae, Eurodisco, and new wave synth-pop that comprises *The Sign* 𝄞𝄞𝄞 (Arista, 1993, prod. Joker/Buddha) produced a trio of international hits, each of which is impossible to dislodge from the frontal lobe. The music doesn't vary much but, in the case of *The Sign*, familiarity somehow breeds contentment.

what to buy next: Despite, or perhaps because of, its adherence to the group's hit formula, *The Bridge* 𝄞𝄞𝄞 (Arista, 1995, prod. Joker/Buddha) failed to ignite much excitement stateside. Still, "Beautiful Life," "Never Gonna Say I'm Sorry," "Lucky Love," and "Blooming 18" offer seamless popcraft as fine as anything on *The Sign*, and fans drawn in by the debut album should give this one a chance, too.

the rest:
Every Time It Rains 𝄞𝄞𝄞𝄞 (Arista, 1998)

worth searching for: The 1995 remix album *Aced! The Unreleased Mixes* is available as an import.

influences:
◄◄ ABBA
►► Aqua

Daniel Durchholz

Acetone
Formed 1987, in Los Angeles, CA.

Richie Lee, vocals, bass; Mark Lightcap, guitar; Steve Hadley, drums.

The sway and drone of the melodic minimum—a shimmering guitar swell and a suggestive high-hat shuffle, all atop a grounding bass drop—is where, quite often, the beauty of music is reminded of its more subtle, reflective origins. Like the Velvet Underground or, more recently, Luna and Low, Acetone hold ambiance in the highest esteem. Aesthetic moodiness reigns over any direct inclination to simply sing along; this is the sound of stewing in it. Acetone formed from the failing art school aspirations of Richie Lee (a painter) and Mark Lightcap (a composer and tuba player). Adding the drums of high school friend Steve Hadley, the band slowly began to formulate its influences into a distinctive blend of postmodern misery and pleasant resignation. It released two full lengths and two EPs on Vernon Yard before catching the notice of Neil Young's fledgling Vapor imprint, for which the group recorded its eponymous and most satisfying release.

what to buy: *Acetone* 𝄞𝄞𝄞𝄞 (Vapor, 1997, prod. Acetone, Scott Campbell) finds the band at a creative peak. Alternately draining and invigorating, the sheer listlessness of songs such as "Might as Well" and "Good Life" is resuscitated by the drunk and confident stare of jazz-bar reflection. Consistent, but never boring, these are songs to live the night by.

what to buy next: *If You Only Knew* 𝄞𝄞𝄞 (Vernon Yard, 1996) is sort of a bridge for the band, connecting its less confident, rougher-edged guitar rock evident on its debut to the mature strains of *Acetone*. "I've Enjoyed As Much of This As I Can Stand" and "Final Say" are as brutally honest as their titles indicate.

the rest:
Acetone 𝄞𝄞𝄞 (Vernon Yard EP, 1993)
Cindy 𝄞𝄞𝄞 (Vernon Yard, 1993)
I Guess I Would 𝄞𝄞𝄞𝄞 (Vernon Yard, 1995)

influences:
◄◄ The Velvet Underground, Luna, Low
►► Mysteries of Life, Elliott Smith

Billy Manes

Adam & the Ants
See: Adam Ant

Bryan Adams
Born Bryan Guy Adams, November 5, 1959, in Kingston, Ontario, Canada.

Bryan Adams started out like everybody's kid brother—nice enough, harmless, but kind of an annoyance. Dressed in blue jeans, T-shirts, and leather jackets, he was a younger, radio-friendly alternative to the era's true heartland-rock hitmakers, Bruce Springsteen and John Mellencamp. Yet there's something to be said for Adams's hooky, unpretentious singles; they stick in your head so readily that you can probably still sing along to "Cuts Like a Knife" and "Summer of '69," which now are nearly 15 years old. Adams will never be accused of being a great artist, but give him this: he knows the craft. In recent years, his image and material have undergone two major shifts: once a rocker, his hits now are frequently ballads, and movie themes at that. And he has thrown off the jeans-and-T-shirt look for expensive suits, greasy hair, and an unshaven face, looking disturbingly like Kurt Cobain if the late Nirvana leader lived and then sold out to the idea of playing the aging, dissolute pop star. As the saying goes, know thyself.

what to buy: From his third album on, Adams has enjoyed enviable success on the singles chart. *So Far So Good* ✍✍✍ (A&M, 1993, prod. various) does a pretty good job of summarizing his career to that point. And since Adams is a hitmaker, not an album-oriented artist, this is the only essential purchase.

what to buy next: The disc on which Adams found his mission as a man with a dependable hook, simple lyric, and memorable chorus was *Cuts Like a Knife* ✍✍✍ (A&M, 1983, prod. Bryan Adams, Bob Clearmountain), which features the singles "This Time," "Straight from the Heart," and the memorable title cut. *Reckless* ✍✍✍ (A&M, 1984, prod. Bryan Adams, Bob Clearmountain) is Adams's best album overall, mostly thanks to a plethora of hits such as "Heaven," "Summer of '69," and "Run to You." After a disappointing half-decade, Adams came roaring back with *Waking up the Neighbours* ✍✍✍ (A&M, 1991, prod. Robert John "Mutt" Lange, Bryan Adams), a worldwide smash that produced still more hits, including "(Everything I Do) I Do It for You" from the film *Robin Hood, Prince of Thieves*.

what to avoid: The overblown, hamhanded *Into the Fire* ✍✍ (A&M, 1987, prod. Bryan Adams, Bob Clearmountain) offered ample proof that Adams should be making singles, not statements.

the rest:
You Want It, You Got It ✍✍✍ (A&M, 1981)
Live! Live! Live! ✍✍✍ (A&M, 1986)
18 'til I Die ✍✍✍ (A&M, 1996)
MTV Unplugged ✍✍✍ (A&M, 1997)
On a Day Like Today N/A (A&M, 1998)

worth searching for: His debut, *Bryan Adams* (A&M, 1980, prod. Bryan Adams, Jim Vallance), can only be found these days in the Great White North.

influences:

◄◄ Joe Cocker, Bruce Springsteen, John Mellencamp, the Beatles, the Guess Who, Fleetwood Mac

►► Steve Perry, Michael McDermott, Bon Jovi, Skid Row

Daniel Durchholz

Barry Adamson

Born June 1, 1958, in England.

Barry Adamson initially honed his skills as the bassist for avant popsters Magazine from 1977 until the band's demise in 1981.

Following this, he linked up with Nick Cave, playing bass for Cave's "backing band," the Bad Seeds, in 1984. By 1987 Adamson had opted for the solo route and embarked upon a career that would yield a wide array of works, including numerous EPs, LPs, and soundtrack contributions. Yet it was his stints in both Magazine and the Bad Seeds that laid the groundwork for the dark, moody atmospheria that would eventually saturate the sonic landscape of his numerous solo albums. Given the inherent cinematic scope of his music, it was only natural that Adamson delve into the soundtrack arena. To date he has composed scores for the films *Delusion*, *Gas Food Lodging* (for which he shares co-scoring credits with Dinosaur Jr.'s J Mascis), and *Lost Highway*.

what to buy: *Moss Side Story* ✍✍✍ (Mute, 1988, prod. Barry Adamson) is Adamson's debut full-length album, and it's the best place to start in order to grasp his sonic modus operandi. Essentially a soundtrack to a non-existent film, it's divided into three acts, each containing four musical movements. The musical scope ranges from Stygian jazz to neo-classical to clammoring organic industrial and showcases Adamson as a diverse composer. Less a soundtrack to a forgotten movie than a sonic trip through Adamson's psyche, *Soul Murder* ✍✍✍ (Mute, 1988, prod. Barry Adamson) revels in a more bebop/dark swing-oriented approach than its predecessor, yet it also includes electric disco spy themes ("Suspicion") and smoky vocal excursions in which Adamson "scats" cryptical lyrics ("Split"). *Oedipus Schmoedipus* ✍✍✍✍ (Mute, 1996, prod. Barry Adamson) is the third entry in Adamson's "unconscious trilogy" and further extends his foray into the polysonic realms of soundtrack symphonia, danceteria rave-out, smoke filled grooveology, and found sound consolidation. Pulp's Jarvis Cocker pops up on "Set the Controls for the Heart of the Pelvis," while "Something Wicked This Way Comes" is a po-mo update on the classic blaxploitation grooves pioneered by the likes of Isaac Hayes.

what to buy next: *The Negro Inside Me* ✍✍✍ (Mute, 1993, prod. Barry Adamson) continues Adamson's descent into up-tempo groove terrain while still retaining a firm hold in both the dark jazz and cinemascopically inclined sonic realms. *As Above So Below* ✍✍✍ (Mute, 1998, prod. Barry Adamson) presents somewhat of a departure for the composer. Tracks run the gamut from spoken work lushness ("Come Hell or High Water") to shuffle jazzadelia ("Jazz Devil") to weird rock permutations ("The Monkey Speaks His Mind"), and while the album as a whole retains all of the deep, atmospheric musicality of Adamson's previous efforts, it's more traditionally song-based in that every song features Adamson's rich, baritone vocals. *Taming of the Shrewd* ✍✍✍ (Mute, 1989, prod. Barry Adamson) is a tight little four-song EP that includes the epic "Diamonds" as well as some solid jazz extrapolations.

what to avoid: *Gas Food Lodging* ♫♫ (Mute, 1992, prod. various) works best as a companion to the film rather than as a separate listening experience.

the rest:
The Man with the Golden Arm ♫♫♫ (Mute, 1988)
Delusion ♫♫♫ (Mute, 1991)
Cinema Is King ♫♫♫ (Mute EP, 1992)
The Big Bamboozle ♫♫♫ (Mute EP, 1995)

worth searching for: Adamson contributed four songs to the soundtrack of *Lost Highway* (nothing, 1996, prod. Trent Reznor).

influences:
◀◀ John Barry, Suicide, Nick Cave & the Bad Seeds, Magazine
▶▶ Portishead, Tricky, the Chemical Brothers, Propellerheads

Spence D.

WHAT ALBUM CHANGED YOUR LIFE?

Abbey Road. I just think it's a brilliant record. I love the sort of eclecticness of it. My favorite song of all time is on that record, 'Because.' You never hear it on the radio, and it's just the most beautiful song.

Bryan Adams

C.C. Adcock

Born Charles Clinton Adcock, 1970, in Lafayette, LA.

One of the most promising roots artists in recent years, C.C. Adcock plays an intoxicating, rhythmic blend of R&B, rockabilly, and foot-stompin' zydeco. As a vocalist, Adcock alternates between joyously shouting lyrics rife with Cajun patois in one breath and emoting moody, sexy rockers in the next. He punctuates his catchy songs (many of which he writes himself) with guitar work that fairly shudders with menacing vibrato and Hoo-Doo twang. During his teenage years, Adcock toured behind such legends as Bo Diddley, Bobby Charles, and Buckwheat Zydeco. Though he has yet to make an impact nationally, C.C. Adcock is a constant presence on the festival circuit and at roots rock venues, where he never fails to get the audiences up on their feet and dancing.

what's available: On his only disc thus far, *C.C. Adcock* ♫♫♫♫ (Island Records, 1994, prod. Tarka Cordell), Adcock rocks up some strong cover versions of Arthur Alexander's "Cindy Lou" and "Sally Sue Brown," as well as Bo Diddley's "Beaux's Bounce." Adcock adds his own "Couchmeal," "Do Right Li'l Baby," and "Done Most Everything" to the mix, and the result is one helluva debut LP. Check it out.

worth searching for: Adcock adds some tasty rhythm guitar hooks to Steve Riley & the Mamou Playboys' *La Toussaint* (Rounder, 1995, prod. Scott Billington), a solid collection of zydeco tunes well worth hearing for its own merits.

influences:
◀◀ Bo Diddley, Bobby Charles, Buckwheat Zydeco, Al Ferrier
▶▶ Steve Riley & the Mamou Playboys, Bayou Hot Sauce

Ken Burke

Hasil Adkins

Born April 29, 1937, in Madison, WV.

Hasil Adkins is proof positive that if you ignore the critics and keep at something long enough, you will finally make it. Adkins is a one-man band who plays drums, guitar, and sometimes harmonica. His recordings are riddled with missed chords, sour guitar leads, out-of-time drumming, and craggy, off-key vocals. Further, there are few politically correct moments on an Adkins record, particularly the early ones. He's written songs about cannibals, sleeping with extraterrestrials, and cutting off his girlfriend's head and hanging it on a wall because she eats too many hot dogs. Yet for all his perceived shortcomings, Adkins is revered by some as a great artist and the Godfather of Psychobilly music. Supporters don't champion Adkins because he is musically accomplished or a good singer (he is neither); they dig his intensity, improvisational creativity, and his cut-to-the bone weirdness—after all, this is the guy who during the late '50s called himself "Elvis" Hasil Adkins, played to any gathering that wouldn't assult him, and cranked out tunes such as "Chicken Walk," "The Hunch," and "She Said." (Of all rock bands, it seems appropriate that the Cramps would cover an Adkins song, in this case "She Said.") Whether he is wailing some mournful ode to a broken heart or spewing eccentric, uptempo nonsense, no one throws himself more completely into a performance than Adkins.

what to buy: To understand Adkins's schtick, you must start with *Out to Hunch* ♫♫♫ (Norton, 1986, compilation prod. Billy Miller), a 16-track collection of his most distinctive one-man band recordings from the mid-'50s through the mid-'60s. If "She Said," "No More Hot Dogs," "I Need Your Head (This Ain't No

Rock 'n' Roll Show)," "Chicken Walk," and the non-dance craze of the title track don't send you screaming from the room, chances are you're ready for the rest of this zany maniac's catalog.

what to buy next: Culled from several live shows, *Look at That Cave Man Go!!* 𝄞𝄞𝄞 (Norton, 1993, prod. Billy Miller) is a surprisingly entertaining (and in spots danceable) compilation featuring such manic one-man band rockers as "Mean Mean Woman," "Devonna Rock," "She Goes Like This," and the wonderfully incoherent blues strut "Boo Boo the Cat." Those curious about Adkins's abilities as a mostly straight old-time style country singer are well-advised to check out *Achy Breaky Ha-Ha-Ha* 𝄞𝄞𝄞 (Norton, 1994, prod. Billy Miller). The mournful Appalachian tone of "Leaves in Autumn," "Gonna Have Me a Garage Sale," "Song of Death," and "Twenty Eight Years" is really quite moving—in a bizarre, other-universe fashion.

what to avoid: With an artist of Adkins's peculiar gifts and style, one either loves everything he does or loathes it on principle. So you should avoid either all of it or none of it.

the rest:
Chicken Walk 𝄞𝄞𝄞 (Buffalo Bop, 1986/1995)
The Wild Man 𝄞𝄞𝄞 (Norton, 1987)
Peanut Butter Rock and Roll 𝄞𝄞𝄟 (Norton, 1990)
Moon Over Madison 𝄞𝄞 (Norton, 1990)
Live in Chicago 𝄞𝄞𝄟 (Bughouse, 1993)
What the Hell Was I Thinking? 𝄞𝄞𝄟 (Fat Possum Records, 1998)

worth searching for: Adkins's wonderfully warped version of "Wooly Bully" is on *Turban Renewal: A Tribute to Sam the Sham & the Pharaohs* (Norton, 1994, compilation prod. Billy Miller). Also, he makes a slicker-than-usual guest appearance on Robert Shafer's *Hillbilly Fever* (Upstart, 1997, prod. Michael Lipton).

influences:
◀◀ Jimmie Rodgers, Hank Williams, George Jones, Elvis Presley, Jerry Lee Lewis, Slim Harpo, Lightning Slim, Fats Domino, Shel Silverstein

▶▶ The Cramps, the A-Bones, King Uszniewicz & the Uszniewicztones, Flat Duo Jets, Wesley Willis

Ken Burke

The Adverts

Formed 1976, in London, England. Disbanded 1979.

Tim "T.V." Smith, vocals; Howard Pickup, guitar; Gaye Advert, bass; Laurie Driver, drums (1976–78); John Towe, drums (1978); Rod Latter, drums (1978–79); Tim Cross, keyboards (1979).

Whenever someone wants to know about the intellectual edge that even the crudest English punk of 1976 to 1978 had, the Adverts are the best place to start. The group's songs were skillfully catchy, despite the raw edges and sometimes tattered sound. More importantly, in T.V. Smith it had perhaps the keenest social critic in a time that was overflowing with them. And for such a short-lived band, with only two proper LPs to its credit, the Adverts produced some of the most fondly remembered, enduring classics of the genre in the incredible "Gary Gilmour's Eyes," "No Time to Be 21," and "One Chord Wonders"—the first two of which were even Top 40 hits in the U.K., despite their contentious subject matter.

what to buy: Fortunately, all three of the aforementioned songs are found on the reissued versions of the band's fabulous U.K. Top 40 debut LP that truly captures those times, *Crossing the Red Sea with the Adverts* 𝄞𝄞𝄞𝄞 (Bright Records U.K., 1978, prod. John Leckie). These songs, and the equally thought-provoking societal analysis/distaste found in the killer "Bombsight Boy," "New Church," and "The Great British Mistake," have held up over nearly two decades. One other single from the LP, "Safety in Numbers," even has the foresight and temerity to criticize the punk scene itself, prophetic when one considers how punk eventually lost its way.

worth searching for: The follow-up, *Cast of Thousands* (RCA U.K., 1979, prod. Tom Newman) doesn't match the immediacy of *Crossing the Red Sea*, but that in no way obscures Smith's first-rate songwriting and typically strong lyrical prowess. Years after the group's demise, two live documents—*The Peel Sessions* (Strange Fruit U.K. EP, 1987) and *Live at the Roxy* (Receiver U.K., 1990)—paid tribute to the Adverts' spark and energy.

solo outings:
T.V. Smith:
(With T.V. Smith's Explorers) *Last Words of the Great Explorer* 𝄞𝄞𝄞 (Epic, 1981)
Channel Five 𝄞𝄞𝄞𝄞 (Expulsion U.K., 1983)
March of the Giants 𝄞𝄞𝄞 (Cooking Vinyl U.K., 1992)
(With T.V. Smith's Cheap) *RIP . . . Everything Must Go* 𝄞𝄞𝄞𝄞 (Griffin, 1994)
Immortal Rich 𝄞𝄞𝄟 (Thirsty Ear, 1996)

influences:
◀◀ The Stooges, the MC5, the Ramones, the Sex Pitols

▶▶ Nirvana, Bad Religion, the Offspring

Jack Rabid

Aerosmith

Formed 1970, in Sunapee, NH.

Steven Tyler, vocals, keyboards; Joe Perry, guitar (1970–79, 1984–present); Brad Whitford, guitar (1970–81, 1984–present); Jimmy Crespo,

Steven Tyler of Aerosmith (© Ken Settle)

guitar (1979–84); Rick Dufay, guitar (1982–84); Tom Hamilton, bass; Joey Kramer, drums.

When Aerosmith released its first album in 1973, there was little to distinguish the band from a hundred other hard rock outfits that could cover old Yardbirds tunes (which Aerosmith did with "Train Kept a Rollin'"). Within three years, however, the Boston quintet had infused a bit more soul and swing into its crunch and evolved from just another blues 'n' boogie band into arguably America's most important hard rockers. But by the '80s, the group had all but flushed its career down the toilet; some of its members had turned into junkies (Tyler and Perry weren't nicknamed "The Toxic Twins" for nothing), ego problems threatened to tear the group apart, and the music went limp. Yet in the late '80s, Aerosmith—buoyed by a Run-D.M.C. remake of its hit "Walk This Way"—detoxed, reunited, and launched one of the most impressive comebacks in rock history, which lasted well into the '90s.

what to buy: *Rocks* ♪♪♪♪ (Columbia, 1976, prod. Jack Douglas, Aerosmith) didn't spawn any big hits, but raunchy rave-ups like "Last Child" and "Rats in the Cellar" make it the mother of all American hard rock albums. *Toys in the Attic* ♪♪♪♪ (Columbia, 1975, prod. Jack Douglas) is almost as nasty, thanks to unapologetically raunchy rave-ups such as "Walk This Way," "Sweet Emotion," and "Big Ten Inch."

what to buy next: *Pump* ♪♪♪♪ (Geffen, 1989, prod. Bruce Fairbairn) gave Aerosmith another shot at packing arenas, and rightfully so: "Janie's Got a Gun" and "What It Takes" are as good as anything the band has done.

what to avoid: Recorded after Perry and Whitford first quit, *Rock in a Hard Place* ♪♪ (Columbia, 1982, prod. Jack Douglas, Steven Tyler, Tony Bongiovi) was more like schlock in soft space.

the rest:
Aerosmith ♪♪♪ (Columbia, 1973)
Get Your Wings ♪♪♪ (Columbia, 1974)
Draw the Line ♪♪♪ (Columbia, 1977)
Live Bootleg ♪♪♪ (Columbia, 1978)
A Night in the Ruts ♪♪ (Columbia, 1979)
Aerosmith's Greatest Hits ♪♪♪♪ (Columbia, 1980)
Done with Mirrors ♪♪ (Geffen, 1985)
Classics Live ♪♪♪ (Columbia, 1986)
Classics Live II ♪♪ (Columbia, 1987)
Permanent Vacation ♪♪♪ (Geffen, 1987)
Gems ♪♪♪ (Columbia, 1988)
Pandora's Box ♪♪♪♪ (Columbia, 1991)
Get a Grip ♪♪♪♪ (Geffen, 1993)
Big Ones ♪♪♪♪ (Geffen, 1994)
Nine Lives ♪♪♪ (Columbia, 1997)
A Little South of Sanity ♪♪♪♪ (Geffen, 1998)

worth searching for: *Train Kept a Rollin'* (Pluto, 1991) is a powerful bootleg of a British concert that featured Jimmy Page on versions of "Train Kept a Rollin' " and "Walk This Way."

solo outings:
Joe Perry Project:
Let the Music Do the Talking ♪♪♪ (Columbia, 1980)
I've Got the Rock 'n' Rolls Again ♪♪ (Columbia, 1981)
Once a Rocker, Always a Rocker ♪♪ (MCA, 1983)

Whitford–St. Holmes:
Whitford–St. Holmes ♪♪♪ (Columbia, 1981)

influences:
◀◀ The Rolling Stones, Led Zeppelin, the Yardbirds

▶▶ Die Kreuzen, Tesla, Ratt, Guns N' Roses

Thor Christensen

The Afghan Whigs

Formed 1986, in Cincinnati, OH.

Greg Dulli, vocals, guitar; Rick McCollum, guitars; John Curley, bass; Steve Earle, drums (1986–95); Paul Buchignani, drums (1995–present).

Often labeled the bastard son of Sub Pop, the Afghan Whigs didn't exactly fit the pre-grunge profile of its Seattle-based label's artistic repertoire. The Whigs almost always relied on an organic formula of passionate rock and soul, a far cry from the Marshall-stacked guitar pummelings of soon-to-be-famous labelmates Nirvana and Soundgarden. It has been long rumored that scratchy-throated vocalist Greg Dulli met guitarist Rick McCollum in an Ohio jail cell, and the pair later became acquainted with bassist John Curley and drummer Steve Earle, thus rounding out what would be the Whigs' permanent lineup until 1995. Despite early detractors, the Whigs recorded heroic garage music that often payed homage to the amorous sounds of soul. As a frontman, Dulli—who sang on the soundtrack for the film *Backbeat*, about the early days of the Beatles—developed a tortured persona that won him a legion of female fans who swooned over his Midwestern, demented boy-next-door charm and lyrical honesty (see *Gentlemen*). Most notably, the Whigs should be listened to for their sense of cinematic adventure; their best is like the soundtrack of your secret desires. During 1998 the Whigs signed with Columbia, signaling a new era in the group's career.

what to buy: *Congregation* ♪♪♪♪ (Sub Pop, 1992, prod. Ross Ian Stein, Greg Dulli) begins what is essentially the Whigs' foray into climactic orchestration, with each song contributing to a larger thematic picture and exhibiting a fearless musical passion and skill that no earlier releases matched. *Gentlemen* ♪♪♪♪ (Sub Pop/Elektra, 1993, prod. Greg Dulli), the Whigs' major label debut, again highlights the group's own special brand of guitar-driven angst, this time with cleaner production. *Gentlemen* glides the listener through a shocking landscape of fear ("What Jail Is Like"), abuse ("Fountain and Fairfax"), and rejection ("Now You Know"), dressing up the group's guitar attack with touches of mellotron and piano.

what to buy next: Punky, grungey, and lots of fun, *Up In It* 𝄞𝄞𝄞𝄞 (Sub Pop, 1990, prod. Jack Endino) exposes the garage glory of the early Whigs. Songs such as "White Trash Party" and "Retarded" are anthemic rockers, though they bear little resemblance to the Whigs' later, more sophisticated work. *Black Love* 𝄞𝄞𝄞𝄎 (Sub Pop/Elektra, 1996, prod. Greg Dulli) is infinitely more sinister and less accessible than previous works. Still, the Whigs' propensity for storytelling remains intact and songs such as "Honkey's Ladder" and "My Enemy" are notable. *The Uptown Avondale* 𝄞𝄞𝄞 (Sub Pop EP, 1992, prod. Afghan Whigs) is a pleasing four-song diversion that finds the Whigs covering soul classics by the Supremes ("Come See about Me"), Freda Payne ("Band of Gold"), and Al Green ("Beware").

what to avoid: The EP *What Jail Is Like* 𝄞𝄎 (Sub Pop/Elektra, 1994, prod. Greg Dulli) is merely a bone-throw to Whigs fans after *Gentlemen* began attracting attention, a hodgepodge of live tracks, covers, and previously released material.

the rest:
1965 𝄞𝄞𝄞𝄎 (Columbia, 1998)

worth searching for: *Big Top Halloween* (Ultrasuede, 1988, prod. Afghan Whigs) is the Whigs' first release, chock-full of fuzzy guitars and garagey glory but burdened by raw, amateurish production.

influences:

◀◀ The Beatles, the Replacements, Hüsker Dü, Motown

▶▶ Howlin' Maggie, Jonny Polonsky, D Generation, Super 8

Judy Miller

A.F.I.
/Asking for It
Formed 1991, in Ukiah, CA.

Davey Havok, vocals; Markus Stopholese, guitar; Vic Chalker, bass (1991); Geoff Kresge, bass, vocals (1991–97); Hunter Burgan, bass (1997–present); Adam Carson, drums.

The melodic straightedge punk/hardcore band A.F.I. (short for "Asking for It") first formed in Ukiah, California, in 1991 when its members were still in high school. After releasing a split 7" with local heroes Loo$e Change and a four-song EP (*Behind the Times*), A.F.I. broke up in mid-1993 when its members graduated and left town. Within six months they were back together,

this time based out of Berkeley, where frontman Davey Havok was attending college. A 1994 tour with the Swingin' Utters quickly expanded A.F.I.'s following beyond the East Bay; its first full-length album, *Answer That and Stay Fashionable*, followed. Signing to the Offspring's Nitro Records label, A.F.I. returned with 1996's *Very Proud of Ya*, which established them as the most popular Bay Area punk band since Green Day. After tours with the Offspring, Rancid, and Guttermouth, bassist Geoff Kresge left the group and was replaced by Hunter Burgan from the Force. A.F.I.'s next effort, 1997's *Shut Your Mouth and Open Your Eyes*, was supported by a U.S. tour with Sick of It All.

what to buy: *Answer That and Stay Fashionable* 𝄞𝄞𝄞 (Wingnut, 1995/Nitro, 1997, prod. Andy Ernst) sports a clever *Reservoir Dogs* parody cover and features numerous A.F.I. classics like "I Wanna Get a Mohawk (But Mom Won't Let Me Get One)," "Yurf Rendemein," and "Two of a Kind."

what to buy next: *Very Proud of Ya* 𝄞𝄞 (Nitro, 1996, prod. Michael Rosen), although not quite as consistent as *Answer That*, is still a respectable sophomore effort, as well as A.F.I.'s debut on Offspring's Nitro Records label.

what to avoid: *Shut Your Mouth and Open Your Eyes* 𝄞 (Nitro, 1997, prod. Andy Ernst) is a clear step backwards for the band, failing to produce any standout cuts like those found on *Answer That*.

worth searching for: Serious A.F.I. fans might want to look for the out-of-print A.F.I./Heckle split 7-inch, released by Wingnut in 1995. It features "Aspirin Free" and "Advances in Modern Technology" on the A.F.I. side, and "Lemmings" and "Something Real" on the Heckle side. It's probably A.F.I.'s best non-album release, and the Heckle tunes aren't bad either.

influences:

◀◀ Bad Religion, Descendents, Misfits, Minor Threat, 7 Seconds, Dag Nasty, Rancid

Seth Hindin

Agent Orange
Formed 1979, in Fullerton, CA.

Mike Palm, vocals, guitars; Steve Soto, bass, vocals; James Levesque, bass, vocals; Brent Liles, bass; Scott Miller, drums (1979–85); Derek O'Brien, drums (1985–present).

One of the first bands to pair punk sensibilities with '60s surf music, Agent Orange often sounds as close to "Wipeout" as it does to "Anarchy in the U.K."—but at the same time it's more melodic and easily accessible than either. A little too rough for the surf dudes on the beach, Agent Orange was adopted by landlubbing skate punks, who found its twangy guitars and unusually harmonious punk vocals a perfect soundtrack for their brand of surfing.

what to buy: *This Is the Voice* 🎵🎵🎵🎵 (Restless, 1986, prod. Daniel Van Patten) remains Agent Orange's best and most accessible release, a bit mellower than its predecessors, with touches of everything from '80s pop to '60s psychedelic guitar solos.

what to buy next: *Living in Darkness* 🎵🎵🎵 (Rhino, 1981, prod. Robbie Fields, Jay Lansford, Daniel Van Patten) is a solid album on its own, but the CD version adds the songs from the 1982 EP *Bitchen' Summer.* Don't miss the band's terrific take on Dick Dale's "Misirlou."

the rest:
When You Least Expect It 🎵🎵🎵 (Restless EP, 1984)
Real Live Sound 🎵🎵🎵 (Restless, 1991)

influences:
◄◄ Fear, Minor Threat, the Jefferson Airplane, the Ventures, the Sex Pistols

►► The Adolescents, Christian Death, Game Theory

Bryan Lassner

Agents of Good Roots

Formed 1995, in Richmond, VA.

Andrew Winn, vocals, guitar, piano; Stewart Myers, bass, vocals; J.C. Kuhl, saxophone; Brian Jones, drums, vocals.

The success of the Dave Matthews Band and Hootie & the Blowfish sent major label talent scouts streaming into the American Southeast to find out if there were more where that came from. There was. And from a rich cache, Agents of Good Roots was one of the gems. Blending soul, jazz, and touches of gospel with its rock, the Agents sound is unique and refreshing—light enough to make for delightful hit singles ("Smiling up the Frown") but still with enough heft to frame some of chief writer Andrew Winn's darker and more contemplative lyrics. The group—whose name comes from the Spanish word for real estate agent, which, literally translated, means "an agent of good roots"—built a grass roots following through gigs in college towns and at frat houses, eventually hooking up with Matthews's managers and, after two indpendent releases, signing up with Matthews's label, RCA. The response was immediately positive, making Agents of Good Roots a likely—and recommended—band to watch in the coming years.

what to buy: Thanks to the band's abundant seasoning before it signed with a major label, the striking *One by One* 🎵🎵🎵🎵 (RCA, 1998, prod. Paul Fox) presents Agents as a confident, fully formed group that makes good use of its good roots. J.C.

Kuhl's sax provides an edgy, otherworldly texture to the songs. The difference from the independent albums is presence; the sound here is bigger and broader, incorporating dense layers of guitars, female backing vocals, and melancholy strings on the appropriately titled closing track, "I'll Be Back." We certainly hope so.

the rest:
Where'd You Get That Vibe? 🎵🎵🎵 (Conflict, 1996)
Straightaround 🎵🎵🎵 (Conflict, 1997)

influences:
◄◄ Sea Level, Muscle Shoals Rhythm Section, the Dave Matthews Band

Gary Graff

Agnes Gooch

Formed 1995, in Los Angeles, CA.

Mat Baker, vocals; Nathan Ehrenfeld, guitars; Scott Bushkin, drums; Johnny Lonely, bass.

Within two years of forming, Agnes Gooch had a major label CD out, a spot on Lollapalooza '97, a debut video for "Baby in Green"—directed by Mark Pellington, who did Pearl Jam's "Jeremy" clip—and a slot on a tour supporting Stabbing Westward and Sponge. Not bad for a group that had gone through the L.A. club scene relatively anonymously, at least from a hype perspective. However, the members had all paid their dues with relatively anonymous local groups and were "due" by the time Nathan Ehrenfeld and Mat Baker met and decided to start the trio.

what's available: *Agnes Gooch* 🎵🎵🎵 (Revolution, 1997) has moments of inspired rock humor such as "Cool Beans," a love song to Frances Bean, the daughter of Courtney Love and the late Kurt Cobain, and the downright disturbed "Mom's Secret." In addition, the quartet displays its technical mettle with the heavy psychedelic opening of "Pretty" and the surprisingly sweet mid-tempo arrangement of "Movie."

influences:
◄◄ Pearl Jam, Soundgarden, the Ramones

Steve Baltin

Air

Formed 1996, in Paris, France.

Nicolas Godin, bass, guitars, keyboards; Jean Benoit Dunckel, keyboards.

In France, young pop musicians get inspiration wherever they can find it. Air clearly grew up with the easy-listening music of

Francis "Un Homme Et Une Femme" Lai, chanteuse Claudine Longet, and the synthesizer experiments of Perrey and Kingsley. The experimental French duo's debut album, *Moon Safari*, focuses mostly on techno-style dance music, but spacey sounds constantly swirl overhead, approximating a wind tunnel one second and a mambo party the next. The music press, always searching for a global trend, lumped the band with DJ Dimitri from Paris as part of "the new French pop movement," but Air has none of Dimitri's kitschy, make-fun-of-France irony. Partners Nicolas Godin and Jean Benoit Dunckel mess around with glockenspiels, Moog synthesizers, strings, Wurlitzer organs, and other strange instruments, but they take their '70s music extremely seriously.

what to buy: *Moon Safari* ♪♪♪♪ (Source/Caroline, 1998, prod. Jean Benoit Dunckel, Nicolas Godin) is excellent mood music, whether Dunckel and Godin program their machines to play in an aggressive hip-hop style ("Sexy Boy") or an elevator-music sleepiness ("Ce Matin La"). Sultry singer Beth Hirsch makes "You Make It Easy" possibly the first original French lounge classic since the days of Claudine Longet. The album works both as a gimmick (two guys from France making strange noises!) and a sustained listening experience.

worth searching for: The band recorded several tracks and remixes before *Moon Safari*, some of which landed on dance-music compilations. *Excursions in Ambience: Third Dimension* (Astralwerks, 1994, prod. various) fits Air's "Trip #2" along with techno tracks by the Future Sound of London and Aphex Twin.

influences:
◄◄ Francis Lai, Michel Legrand, Claudine Longet, the Orb, Brian Eno, Kraftwerk

Steve Knopper

Air Miami

Formed 1995, in Washington, DC.

Mark Robinson, guitars, vocals; Bridget Cross, guitar, bass, vocals; Gabriel Stout, drums, programming.

After five albums, dozens of singles and a legion of devoted fans, seminal indie-pop group Unrest decided to call it quits in 1994. It was not for a lack of musical enthusiasm, frontman Mark Robinson said then, just time to work with new ideas. Thus was born, out of the ashes of Unrest, the group Air Miami, which featured both Robinson and fellow Unrest member Bridget Cross. Air Miami's sound resembled Unrest only in the execution of wonderfully catchy ditties, though Air Miami reveled in the melodic madness of '80s new wave hits. Though Air Miami never officially broke up, it has yet to record any new music since 1997.

what to buy: Air Miami's first full-length album is indeed a treat. *Me, Me, Me* ♪♪♪ (4AD/Teen Beat Records, 1995, prod. Mark Robinson) doesn't have the giddiness of the Unrest work, but it is sweet to listen to.

what to buy next: The group's follow-up EP, *Fuck You, Tiger* ♪♪♪♥ (4AD/Teen Beat Records, 1995), appeases the pop appetite of Air Miami fans taken in by their debut.

worth searching for: The group's first piece of work was the song "Pucker" from the 4AD Records compilation *All Virgos Are Mad*. Perhaps the group's best song, a modernized new wave track, is "Airplane Rider," available only as a 7-inch single on Teen Beat Records.

influences:
◄◄ Unrest, Blake Babies

Joseph Patel

Air Supply

Formed 1976, in Melbourne, Australia. Disbanded 1988. Re-formed 1991.

Graham Russell, vocals, guitar; Russell Hitchcock, vocals.

Air Supply warbled out highly produced, sugary love ballads to massive radio play at the turn of the decade. By the early '80s, a syrupy string of hits made the group an MOR radio staple. The millions of Air Supply records sold are into double digits, proving there may, in fact, be no limit to the public's appetite for schmaltz.

what to buy: If it's sugar you want, then plunge into *Greatest Hits* ♪ (Arista, 1983, prod Robie Porter) and slurp it down in one quick gulp. "Lost in Love," "Every Woman in the World," "Making Love Out of Nothing at All" are here for your romantic nights in front of the Duraflame log.

what to buy next: Thanks to the title track, *Lost in Love* ♪ (Arista, 1980, prod. Robie Porter) is the album that sent upper-middle class 7th grade girls lip synching down the hallways.

what to avoid: Stay away from *The Christmas Album* **woof!** (Arista, 1987). Wasn't giving ballads a bad name enough?

the rest:
Love and Other Bruises ♪ (Columbia, 1977)
Now and Forever ♥ (Arista, 1982)
The Earth Is ♥ (Giant, 1991)
The Vanishing Race ♥ (Giant, 1993)
News from Nowhere ♥ (Giant, 1995)
Greatest Hits Live . . . Now And . . . ♪ (Giant, 1996)
The Book of Love ♥ (Giant, 1997)

worth searching for: Ha!

influences:

◀◀ The Bee Gees, the Captain & Tennille

▶▶ Christopher Cross, Mariah Carey

Allan Orski

The Alarm

Formed 1978, in Rhyl, Wales. Disbanded 1992.

Mike Peters, vocals; Eddie McDonald, bass; Dave Sharp, guitar; Nigel Twist, drums.

With idealistic ambitions and stadium-sized rock tunes, the Alarm initially sought to bring punk's spirit to its acoustic strumming. Inspired by U2 and the Clash, the lofty political messages were vague and unrealized compared with the output of those bands. Eventually, they plugged in and cranked out some admirably fervid mainstream rock, but they never shook the U2 comparisons, and, of course, never surpassed them. Mike Peters and Dave Sharp have pursued solo projects, and in 1998 Peters formed the band Colorsound with the Cult's Billy Duffy.

what to buy: The Alarm was most effective on its singles, and *Standards* 🎵🎵🎵 (I.R.S., 1990, prod. various) has them all. "The Stand" and "Sixty-Eight Guns" are early blazers; the partly successful commercial bid of the highly produced "Rain in the Summertime" and the blues-edged "Sold Me Down the River" are also represented, along with three new tracks recorded for the disc.

what to buy next: *Strength* 🎵🎵🎵 (I.R.S., 1985, prod. Mike Howlett) is one of the band's most consistent albums, featuring the title track and "Spirit of '76." *Change* 🎵🎵🎵 (IRS, 1989, prod. Tony Visconti) is a harbinger of change indeed, revealing a tougher sound with more electric guitar bite than anything the Alarm had recorded previously.

what to avoid: *Raw* 🎵🎵 (IRS, 1991) is the result of the dreary business of fulfilling contractual obligations. And why cover Neil Young's "Rockin' in the Free World"—to point arrows at the band's own lack of depth?

the rest:

The Alarm 🎵🎵🎵 (I.R.S., 1983)
Declaration 🎵🎵🎵 (I.R.S., 1984)
Eye of the Hurricane 🎵🎵🎵 (I.R.S., 1987)
Electric Folklore: Live 🎵🎵 (I.R.S., 1988)
Newid 🎵🎵 (I.R.S., 1989)

worth searching for: The career-spanning *The Best of the Alarm and Mike Peters* (EMI U.K) is available as an import. *Second Generation: Rare Songs of the Alarm* (MPO, 1995) is a collection of re-recorded Alarm rarities and B-sides that Peters recorded and distributed through the band's fan club after the Alarm broke up. Peters's solo disc, *Breathe* (Crai, 1994), was released in a limited edition.

solo outings:

Mike Peters:
Feel Free 🎵🎵🎵 (Select, 1996)
Rise N/A (Velvel, 1998)

Dave Sharp:
Downtown America 🎵🎵 (Dinosaur Entertainment, 1996)

influences:

◀◀ U2, the Clash, the Sex Pistols

▶▶ Hothouse Flowers, Midnight Oil

Allan Orski

Albion Country Band

See: Martin Simpson

Alcatrazz

See: Yngwie Malmsteen

Arthur Alexander

Born May 10, 1940, in Florence, AL. Died June 9, 1993, in Nashville, TN.

Arthur Alexander wrote songs that helped define early '60s popular music, yet he never achieved the wide or sustaining notoriety that his talent deserved. With a smooth and plaintive vocal style, Alexander wedded country with soul to create music that was unique, affecting, and enduring. His first hit, 1962's "You Better Move On," was recorded in Muscle Shoals, Alabama, and helped to establish that locale as a hotbed of soul and R&B talent. Alexander's music was also an early influence on John Lennon and Paul McCartney, who covered his biggest hit, "Anna (Go to Him)," on the Beatles's 1963 debut album; two years later, the Rolling Stones used Alexander's "You Better Move On" on *December's Children*. Bob Dylan ("Sally Sue Brown"), Elvis Presley ("Burning Love"), and Otis Redding ("Johnny Heartbreak") were among the other pop luminaries who recorded Alexander's works. But his own career languished, due mainly to substance abuse and a record industry that insisted on pegging him as a country artist. Disillusioned, he retired from recording and moved to Cleveland, Ohio, where he drove a bus for a social services agency. Marshall Crenshaw kept Alexander's music alive by covering "Soldier of Love (Lay Down Your Arms)" on his 1982 debut album, and in 1991, Alexander was coaxed into performing at a songwriters workshop at the Bottom Line in New York. That sparked him to record a new album and resume his career; tragically, though, he suffered a fatal heart attack on the eve of a concert tour to celebrate his return.

what to buy: *The Ultimate Arthur Alexander* 𝄞𝄞𝄞𝄞 (Razor & Tie, 1993, prod. various) is an outstanding compilation of Alexander's original versions of the songs covered by so many influential artists of the '60s. These are mostly mid-tempo ballads featuring great melodies and lyrics that are hauntingly personal and direct, with a recurring theme of relationships gone wrong.

what to buy next: *Lonely Just Like Me* 𝄞𝄞𝄞 (Elektra Nonesuch, 1993, prod. Ben Vaughn, Thomas Cain) was recorded shortly before Alexander's death and offers some great new originals in the style of his best work, along with some updated versions of his older songs. This was an unexpected treasure for fans who had assumed Alexander would never record again. *Adios Amigo: A Tribute to Arthur Alexander* 𝄞𝄞𝄞𝄞 (Razor & Tie, 1994, prod. various) is a memorable tribute from a wide range of artists paying their respects in song. Elvis Costello's burning version of "Sally Sue Brown" is itself worth the price of admission.

what to avoid: While there are some great moments, *Rainbow Road: Arthur Alexander: The Warner Bros. Recordings* 𝄞𝄞 (Warner Bros., 1994, prod. Tommy Cogbill) is inconsistent and recommended for major fans and completists only.

the rest:
Soldier of Love 𝄞𝄞𝄞 (Ace, 1987)

worth searching for: *A Shot of Rhythm and Soul* (Ace, 1982) is a well-annotated vinyl-only collection that contains all the big hits and some great songs such as "Sally Sue Brown," which are not represented on *The Ultimate Arthur Alexander*.

influences:
◄◄ Eddy Arnold, Hank Williams, Elmore James, Jimmy Reed, B.B. King, Junior Parker, the Drifters, the Clovers, Billy Ward & the Dominos

►► The Beatles, Marshall Crenshaw, Elvis Costello, the Rolling Stones, Otis Redding, Ike & Tina Turner, Humble Pie, Ry Cooder, the Bee Gees, Rod Stewart

Michael Isabella

Alice in Chains

Formed 1987, in Seattle, WA.

Jerry Cantrell, guitar; Layne Staley, vocals; Sean Kinney, drums; Mike Starr, bass (1987–92); Mike Inez, bass (1992–present).

Drugs, sad to say, are what make Alice in Chains stand out from its more conventional contemporaries in grunge and metal bands. Layne Staley airs his private battle with addiction publicly in the band's gloomy songs and layers his vocals so they sound like the moaning you might hear in a haunted house. And when they're wrapped around "Junkhead," "Hate to Feel,"

and "Sickman," they sound positively frightening. Otherwise, Alice in Chains—which began as a hard rock band opening shows for Anthrax, Metallica, and Slayer—is simply Pearl Jam with shorter hair. As the commercial market shifted from speed metal to grunge, Alice in Chains shifted, too, lodging "Would?" on the lucrative *Singles* soundtrack and eventually following Nirvana to the top of the alternative-rock mountain—even taking its own turn on *MTV Unplugged* in 1996.

what to buy: Despite its mopey metallic sound, *Dirt* 𝄞𝄞𝄞 (Columbia, 1992, prod. Bryan Carlstrom) builds the hits "Rooster," "Junkhead," and "Would?" around transfixingly dark melodies.

what to buy next: The EP *Jar of Flies* 𝄞𝄞𝄞 (Columbia, 1993, prod. Alice in Chains) is most notable for its doo-wop vocals from Hell—which sound, oddly enough, like the vocals on a couple of Hootie & the Blowfish hits.

what to avoid: The band's debut, *Facelift* 𝄞𝄞 (Columbia, 1990, prod. Dave Jerden), gave the band a crucial commercial buzz, but it sure sounds bland in retrospect.

the rest:
Sap 𝄞𝄞 (Columbia EP, 1991)
Alice in Chains 𝄞𝄞𝄞 (Columbia, 1995)
MTV Unplugged 𝄞𝄞𝄞 (Columbia, 1996)

worth searching for: *We Die Young* (Columbia EP, 1990) is a promotional EP that predicted the grunge trend long before Alice in Chains joined it.

solo outings:
Jerry Cantrell:
Boggy Depot 𝄞𝄞𝄞 (Sony, 1998)

influences:
◄◄ Nirvana, Pearl Jam, Led Zeppelin, Black Sabbath, Metallica

►► Stone Temple Pilots, Bush, KoЯn, Hootie & the Blowfish

Tracey Birkenhauer and Steve Knopper

All

Formed 1987, in Los Angeles, CA.

Dave Smalley, vocals (1987–89); Scott Reynolds, vocals (1989–93); Chad Price, vocals (1993–present); Stephen Egerton, guitar; Karl Alvarez, bass; Bill Stevenson, drums.

Simply put, All is the Descendents with someone else filling in for that band's legendary bespectacled frontman-cum-grad-student, Milo Aukerman. When Aukerman left the Descendents in 1987 to pursue a PhD in biochemistry at the University of Wisconsin, the remaining Descendents elected to continue under the name All (also the title of a 1987 Descendents album), without substantially changing their melodic, pop-punk sound or their goofy lyrics, which typically revolve around love gone wrong, caffeine over-consumption, and the semi-

Layne Staley of Alice in Chains (© Ken Settle)

mystical slacker concept called All. All's spiky-haired, yellow mascot, Allroy, provided the album title and cover art for several of its releases and is rumored to be the inspiration for Bart Simpson. Ex-D.Y.S./Dag Nasty vocalist Dave Smalley was All's first frontman, though he only lasted until early 1989; he later formed the Epitaph Records band Down by Law. Smalley was succeeded in 1989 by former Three Car Pileup singer Scott Reynolds, who left All in 1993 and went on to release two albums of All-style pop-punk under the name Goodbye Harry. Reynolds was replaced by current All lead singer Chad Price, formerly of Appletree. (All fans are divided over who is their favorite frontman, with the plurality favoring Reynolds.) Throughout the late '80s/early '90s, All was an omnipresent force in the underground punk scene, completing more than 30 tours and releasing an average of one full-length album each year, most of which didn't stray far from their upbeat pop-punk pattern. Aukerman made occasional cameos with All—always highly anticipated by fans—before deciding to permanently rejoin his bandmates in 1996 for a tour and new studio album under the Descendents name. After much speculation by fans as to the fate of All, Stephen Egerton, Karl Alvarez, and Bill Stevenson announced that they would henceforth divide their time between recording and touring as the Descendents (with Aukerman) and as All (with Price). Sure enough, All released a new album, *Mass Nerder*, in the spring of 1998. In addition to All, Egerton and Stevenson produce other pop-punk bands at their own recording studio, the Blasting Room, located in Ft. Collins, Colorado. In his spare time, Price also performs in the country-punk band Armchair Martian.

what to buy: *Allroy's Revenge* ♫♫♫♫ (Cruz, 1989, prod. Bill Stevenson), All's second full-length and the first to feature Scott Reynolds on lead vocals, captures All at its creative peak. This is the blueprint for numerous '90s underground pop-punk bands. (The CD and cassette formats include two extra songs.)

what to buy next: *Breaking Things* ♫♫♫♪ (Cruz, 1993, prod. Stephen Egerton, Bill Stevenson) is the first All album with current vocalist Chad Price. A bit less slick and more serious than previous efforts, songs such as the power pop gem "Shreen" make this an All essential.

what to avoid: *Allroy Saves* ♫♪ (Cruz, 1990, prod. Stephen Egerton, Bill Stevenson), but nobody scores on the rebound of this weak effort.

the rest:
Allroy Sez ♫♫♫ (Cruz, 1988)
Allroy for Prez ♫♫♫ (Cruz, 1988)
Trailblazer: Live ♫♫ (Cruz, 1989)
Percolater ♫♫♫ (Cruz, 1992)
Pummel ♫♫ (Interscope, 1995)
Mass Nerder ♫♫ (Epitaph, 1998)

influences:
◀◀ The Descendents, the Beach Boys
▶▶ Big Drill Car, Goodbye Harry, Wax, Hagfish, Weston

see also: *The Descendents*

Seth Hindin

All Saints

Formed 1995, in London, England.

Shaznay Lewis, vocals; Melanie Blatt, vocals; Simone Rainford, vocals (1995–96); Nicole Appleton, vocals (1996–present); Natalie Appleton (1996–present).

Rather transparently promoted as another label's Spice Girls, the four ladies of All Saints have nonetheless met with fantastic success in the locker shrines and teen rags of their native England. Perhaps more alarming is the amount of credible discourse afforded them in the more fickle and literate music presses—they are the Rolling Stones to Spice's early Beatles, to hear them talk—and, what's worse, they can actually sing! Born of the struggles of four pretty backup singers from the London scene, All Saints had a rocky start with its original lineup. Lewis and Blatt, joined then by Simone Rainford, were signed to Trevor Horn's over-the-top ZTT label and rushed on to the scene with a quickly disposable pop-soul ditty that never even charted. In a short time the band was dropped and back at square one. The inclusion of globe-trotting sisters Nicole and Natalie Appleton, as well as the sudden success of the likewise candy-coated Spice Girls, saw the band quickly roped into the sudden success machine. The splash granted by the initial single, "I Know Where It's At," a raunchy girls-only club romp, sealed their collective fate as the edgier-side of the she-teen market, rushing the production of a passable, self-titled debut for London Records.

what's available: *All Saints* ♫♫♪ (London, 1998, prod. Cameron McVey, Magnus Fiennes, Karl Gordon, Johnny Douglas, Neville Henry) introduces the world to the flip and funky world of All Saints somewhat auspiciously. The nasty winks of such obvious lyrical fare as "Bootie Call" and "Beg" are balanced with a slick, if innocuous, batch of overwrought slippery electro-funk (note the step-too-far inclusion of Labelle's "Lady Marmalade" in wretched urban radio wash). But the faults don't run deep enough to spoil the winsome quartet's well-funded party. This is pop for the populace, after all, and it rarely ceases to charm the banality it decorates.

Influences:
◀◀ Expose, TLC, Bananarama, Spice Girls

Billy Manes

Amy Allison /Parlor James

Born June 24, 1958, in New York, NY.

The daughter of jazz great Mose Allison, Amy Allison puts contemporary twists on the lyin'/cheatin'/drinkin' themes made popular during the '60s, often by playing the remorseful antagonist rather than the victim: she's the one pouring a shot and pouring her heart into an apology letter in the waltzing "Cheater's World" and sorting through the foggy details of a one-night stand in the hangover-nursing "The Whiskey Makes You Sweeter." Her quavering, nasal alto and humorous viewpoints—marked by daring, deliberately awkward rhymes ("If you cared just a smidgen/you'd walk through that kitchen")—sometimes paint her as a satirist rather than a backhanded traditionalist. But Allison's pure-hearted intentions shine through via her deeply rooted affection for country music's heritage—in this case, Loretta Lynn's late 1960s declarations of independence. In between East Coast club shows with her band, the Maudlins, Allison collaborates with former Lone Justice guitarist Ryan Hedgecock in a promising gothic-country-rock duo called Parlor James.

what to buy: Allison's *The Maudlin Years* ♪♪♪♪ (Koch, 1996, prod. various) is drawn from demo sessions recorded between 1987–93, but the twangy, low-fi performances hold together remarkably well. In between such trademark ballads as "Cheater's World" and "The Whiskey Makes You Sweeter," Allison tackles society's bias against interracial dating in the deceptively catchy "Hate at First Sight," and she drowns her sorrows in "Garden State Mall" by replacing an alcoholic bender with a shopping binge ("I bought some perfume at Saks/Blue jeans at the Gap/And a whole album for just one song").

what to buy next: Parlor James's debut, *Dreadful Sorry* ♪♪♪♪ (Discovery, 1996, prod. Malcolm Burn, Parlor James), is a six-song collection of fleshed-out four-track recordings that echo the gothic blues of Gillian Welch and the spooky soundscapes of Lisa Germano.

the rest:
Parlor James:
Old Dreams ♪♪♪ (Sire, 1998)

worth searching for: A country-rock compilation of 7" truck-stop jukebox singles called *Rig Rock Truck Stop* (Diesel Only, 1993, prod. various) includes a different recording of "Cheater's World," discernable mainly by a clearer, more forceful Allison vocal.

influences:
◀◀ Loretta Lynn, Syd Straw

David Okamoto

The Allman Brothers Band

Formed 1969, Jacksonville, FL. Disbanded 1980. Re-formed 1989.

Duane Allman (died October 29, 1971), guitar (1969–71); Gregg Allman, keyboards, vocals; Dickey Betts, guitar, vocals; Berry Oakley (died November 11, 1972), bass (1969–72); Butch Trucks, drums; Jaimoe Johanson, drums; Chuck Leavell, keyboards (1972–76); Lamar Williams (died January 25, 1983), bass (1972–76); Bonnie Bramlett, vocals (1979–80); Dan Toler, guitar (1979–82); David Goldflies, bass (1979–82); David "Frankie" Toler, drums (1981–82); Johnny Neel, keyboards (1989–90); Warren Haynes, guitar (1989–97); Allen Woody, bass (1989–97); Marc Quiñones, percussion (1991–present); Jack Pearson, guitar (1997–present); Oteil Burbridge, bass (1997–present).

The Allman Brothers Band was formed in 1969 by Duane Allman, a young session guitarist who had recorded with Wilson Pickett, Aretha Franklin, King Curtis, and other R&B greats. Returning to Jacksonville, Florida, to strike out on his own, Allman enlisted a collection of players with a wide range of experiences: bassist Berry Oakley and guitarist Dickey Betts led the psychedelic band the Second Coming; drummer J. Johnny "Jaimoe" Johnson was an R&B veteran who had toured with Otis Redding and Percy Sledge; drummer Butch Trucks played with the Jacksonville folk-rock band the 31st of February; and organist/vocalist Gregg Allman had recorded two albums with his brother Duane in the Los Angeles–based blues-rock band Hourglass. Together, this eclectic bunch created an utterly distinct, highly improvisational style that rocked hard while reflecting a profound understanding of virtually every American musical form: blues, country, R&B, jazz, and rock. Driven by Trucks's and Jaimoe's relentlessly propulsive, inventive twin drumming, Gregg Allman's bluesy organ comping, and Oakley's free-range basslines, Betts and Duane Allman crafted a remarkable twin lead guitar approach. Taking cues from jazz horn players, particularly Miles Davis and John Coltrane, and the twin fiddles of Western Swing music, they rewrote the rule book on how rock guitarists can play together, paving the way for every two-guitar band that has followed. But Hall of Fame careers are not built on instrumental virtuosity alone, and the root of the Allman Brothers' success has been a strong, varied songbook. The band has overcome a variety of obstacles, most notably the deaths of Duane and Oakley and two breakups, to return to nearly peak form during the '90s. It is a development few could have predicted.

what to buy: *At Fillmore East* ♪♪♪♪♪ (Capricorn, 1971/1997, prod. Tom Dowd) captured the band's instrumental glory and improvisatory magic remarkably well. Arguably rock's greatest record, the double album holds only seven very long songs—and nary a wasted note. *Eat a Peach* ♪♪♪♪ (PolyGram, 1972, prod. Tom Dowd) includes more tunes from the Fillmore shows, including the 33-minute "Mountain Jam"—which back in the days of vinyl consumed two sides!—as well as great new tunes such as "Melissa" and "Blue Sky." *Brothers and Sisters* ♫♫♫ (Capricorn, 1975/1997, prod. Johnny Sandlin, the Allman Brothers Band), the Allmans's first post-Duane album, includes the band's biggest hits—"Ramblin' Man," "Jessica," and "Southbound." If you want to see what the band's up to now, *An Evening With: First Set* ♫♫♫ (Epic, 1992, prod. Tom Dowd) provides a pretty good overview.

what to buy next: *Beginnings* ♫♫♫ (Capricorn, 1973/1997, prod. Joel Dunn, Tom Dowd) combines the band's first two albums in full. Once you're hooked, you won't want to be without *Dreams* ♫♫♫♫ (Polydor, 1989, prod. various), a four-disc collection that does everything a box set should. *Where It All Begins* ♫♫♫♫ (Epic, 1994, prod. Tom Dowd), while somewhat inconsistent, contains the best material the new Brothers have produced.

what to avoid: Though previously out of print, the Allmans's two worst albums—*Brothers of the Road* **woof!** (Arista, 1981/Razor & Tie, 1997, prod. John Ryan) and *Reach for the Sky* ♫♫ (Arista, 1980/Razor & Tie, 1997, prod. the Allman Brothers Band, Lawler & Cobb)—were recently reissued.

the rest:
The Allman Brothers Band ♫♫♫ (Capricorn, 1969/1997)
Idlewild South ♫♫♫ (Capricorn, 1970/1997)
Win, Lose or Draw ♫♫ (Capricorn, 1975/1997)
The Road Goes on Forever ♫♫♫ (Capricorn, 1976/1998)
Wipe the Windows, Check the Oil, Dollar Gas ♫♫ (Capricorn, 1976/1998)
Enlightened Rogues ♫♫♫ (Capricorn/PolyGram, 1979)
Best of the Allman Brothers Band ♫♫♫ (Polydor, 1981)
Live at Ludlow Garage, 1970 ♫♫♫ (Polydor, 1990)
Seven Turns ♫♫♫ (Epic, 1990)
Shades of Two Worlds ♫♫♫ (Epic, 1991)
Decade of Hits (1969–79) ♫♫♫ (Polydor, 1991)
The Fillmore Concerts ♫♫♫♫ (PolyGram, 1992)
Hell and High Water ♫♫ (Arista, 1994)
An Evening With: Second Set ♫♫♫ (Epic, 1995)
Fillmore East, 2/70 ♫♫♫ (Grateful Dead Records, 1997)
Mycology ♫♫♫ (Epic, 1998)

worth searching for: *The Allman Brothers Band at the R&R Cafe* (Epic, 1992) was a promo-only acoustic performance that is well worth the effort to find. Excellent live bootlegs abound, but *New York City Blues*, recorded in 1970, is exceptional.

solo outings:
Gregg Allman:
Laid Back ♫♫♫ (Capricorn/PolyGram, 1973)
The Gregg Allman Tour ♫♫♫ (Capricorn/PolyGram, 1974)
Playin' up a Storm ♫♫♫ (Capricorn, 1977/Razor & Tie, 1996)
I'm No Angel ♫♫♫♫ (Epic, 1987)
Just Before the Bullets Fly ♫♫♫ (Epic, 1988)

One More Try: The Gregg Allman Anthology ♫♫♫♫ (Polydor, 1997)
Searching for Simplicity ♫♫♫ (Sony 550, 1997)

Dickey Betts:
Highway Call ♫♫♫♫ (Capricorn/PolyGram, 1974)
Pattern Disruptive ♫♫♫ (Epic, 1988)

Jack Pearson:
Step Out! ♫♫♫ (Candlefly Songs, 1994)

influences:
◄◄ Albert King, Cream, Miles Davis, Bob Wills & the Texas Playboys

►► The Eagles, Lynyrd Skynyrd, Little Feat, the Black Crowes

see also: *Gov't Mule*

Alan Paul

Alphaville

Formed 1981, in Berlin, Germany.

Marian Gold, vocals; Bernhard Lloyd, rhythms; others.

This atrocious mid-'80s synthesizer art group fronted by singer Marian Gold is of no consequence save its appalling attempts to craft egocentric dance music. At one time the band boasted 31 musicians (in addition to the core members), lending new meaning to the word bombast.

what to buy: If you've gotta have one Alphaville album—and this is by no means necessary—go for *The Breathtaking Blue* ♫ (Atlantic, 1989, prod. Klaus Shulze), a slightly more stylized effort than the other three.

what to avoid: *The Singles Collection* **woof!** (Atlantic, 1988) is a mindless collection of remixes that natters on endlessly.

the rest:
Forever Young ♫ (Atlantic, 1984)
Afternoon in Utopia ♫ (Atlantic, 1986)

influences:
◄◄ Ultravox, Tangerine Dream, David Bowie

Allan Orski

Alt

See: Split Enz

Altan

Formed 1987, in Gaoth Dobhair, County Donegal, Ireland.

Mairéad Ní Mhaonaigh, fiddle, vocals (1987–present); Frankie Kennedy, flute, whistle, vocals (1987–94); Ciarán Curran, bouzouki (1987–present); Mark Kelly, guitar, vocals (1987–present); Paul O'Shaughnessy, fiddle (1988–92); Cíarán Tourish, fiddle, whistle, vo-

cals (1990–present); Dáithí Sproule, guitar, vocals (1992–present); Dermot Byrne, accordion (1994–present).

As sure as Planxty and the Bothy Band were the Irish supergroups of the '70s, Altan has dominated the traditional scene since the end of the '80s. What is somewhat unusual about it is that the band's music is deeply rooted in the Donegal tradition, one which had received little attention before Altan's commercial success popularized the Gaelic songs and Scottish-tinged highlands, strathspeys, and reels that give the band its unique sound. From the start, the two main ingredients at the core of that sound were the dynamic interplay of the flute and fiddle, played by husband and wife Frankie Kennedy and Mairéad Ní Mhaonaigh, and Ní Mhaonaigh's magical soprano. Weathering personnel changes and Frankie Kennedy's death from cancer in 1994, Altan eventually signed with Virgin for an inauspicious start, though subsequent work offered more exciting instrumental flash and gives us hope that, indeed, they will carry on.

what to buy: Although not strictly an Altan album, *Ceol Aduaidh* 𝄢𝄢𝄢𝄢 (Gael-Linn, 1983/Green Linnet, 1994, prod. Nicky Ryan) is the first commercial recording made by Mairéad Ní Mhaonaigh and Frankie Kennedy. However, the magical sound of their fiddle and flute duets, and of Ní Mhaonaigh's singing, already accompanied by Ciarán Curran's cittern, are just as you can hear them on later albums by the group. *Altan* 𝄢𝄢𝄢𝄢 (Green Linnet, 1987, prod. Dónal Lunny), the first official band album, is very similar in some ways, but the accompaniments and the song arrangements in particular have become quite sophisticated thanks to the addition of Mark Kelly's guitar. However, it is the magnificent *Horse with a Heart* 𝄢𝄢𝄢𝄢 (Green Linnet, 1989, prod. Phil Cunningham) that established Altan as a new force on the Irish traditional music scene. Instrumental medleys such as the opening reel set "The Curlew" or the jig "The Road to Durham" were learned and repeated at many a session during the early '90s, while quieter moments of the album—such as Ní Mhaonaigh's achingly beautiful vocals on "The Lass of Glenshee" or Kennedy's flute solo on Tommy Peoples's air "An Feochán"—are likely to be remembered as well.

what to buy next: The addition to the lineup of yet another fiddler, in the person of Cíarán Tourish, could have been a mixed blessing, but the opening track of *Harvest Storm* 𝄢𝄢𝄢𝄢 (Green Linnet, 1992, prod. P.J. Curtis) dispels all doubts. The powerful sound of the band's three fiddles on the reel medley "Pretty Peg" is simply breathtaking. *Island Angel* 𝄢𝄢𝄢𝄢 (Green Linnet, 1993, prod. Brian Masterson, Altan) continues in the same vein. The band got around to recording some tunes Ní Mhaonaigh and Kennedy had been performing for years, such as their friend Fintan McManus's reel, known to many as "The Guns of the Magnificent Seven," or Charlie O'Neill's highland. There are also two well-produced anthologies, *The First Ten Years*,

1986–1995 𝄢𝄢𝄢𝄢 (Green Linnet, 1995, prod. Dónal Lunny) and *The Best of Altan* 𝄢𝄢𝄢𝄢 (Green Linnet, 1997, prod. various), both based on the band's first five albums.

what to avoid: *Blackwater* 𝄢𝄢𝄢 (Virgin, 1996, prod. Altan, Brian Masterson) was the band's first album after Frankie Kennedy's untimely death, and what may have been a cathartic experience for the musicians did not necessarily translate into their best work.

the rest:
The Red Crow 𝄢𝄢𝄢𝄢 (Green Linnet, 1990)
Ireland 𝄢𝄢𝄢𝄢 (WDR, 1993)
Altan 𝄢𝄢𝄢𝄢 (K-Tel, 1996)
Runaway Sunday 𝄢𝄢𝄢 (Virgin, 1997)

worth searching for: The most devoted fans of Mairéad Ní Mhaonaigh's playing and singing may want to look for the first LP recorded by the Irish all-woman band Macalla, *Mná na hÉireann (Women of Ireland)* (Gael-Linn, 1984, prod. Nicky Ryan). Alongside Ní Mhaonaigh is Paul O'Shaughnessy's mother, Pearl, on fiddle, and a host of other terrific musicians.

influences:

◄◄ John Doherty, Con Cassidy, Proinsias Ó Maonaigh, Tommy Peoples, Clannad, Planxty, the Bothy Band, Macalla

►► Four Men & a Dog, Déanta, Dervish, Craobh Rua

Philippe Varlet

Altered Images

Formed 1979, in Glasgow, Scotland. Disbanded 1984.

Clare Grogan, vocals; Tony McDaid, guitar; Jim McKinnon, guitar (1979–83); Stephen Lironi, keyboards (1984); Johnny McElhone, bass; Tich Anderson, drums (1979–83); Gerry McElhone, drums (1984).

Rising out of the working-class burg of Glasgow at the height of new wave, Altered Images embodied that genre's most (and least) successful characteristics: punky dance music, charmingly novice musicianship, and, most importantly, youthful exuberance. With her cutesy, boop-de-boop voice, Clare Grogan sounded a tad too much like Shirley Temple to be awakening young men's libidos; she could be both coquettishly alluring and childishly annoying. Neither Grogan nor any of the other band members showed especially strong musical talent, but for two years Altered Images spun out a steady string of plucky tunes in the most saccharine style of new wave. The group broke up in 1984, with Grogan pursuing a film career and Johnny McElhone forming the more earnest group Texas.

what to buy: The best of its lot is *Bite* 𝄢𝄢𝄢𝄢 (Epic, 1983, prod. Tony Visconti, Mike Chapman), a plush disco collection that predated that genre's revival by nearly a decade. Grogan's voice is at its least cloying, and most of the songs ("Change of Heart," "Thinking about You," "Another Lost Look," and the U.K. hit "Don't Talk to Me about Love") still shimmer and pop.

what to buy next: *Pinky Blue* ♪♪♪ (Epic, 1982, prod. Martin Rushent) shows Altered Images at its most enjoyable level of pop silliness. The bulk of the songs ("I Could Be Happy," "See Those Eyes") leap about, screaming "hit single," and Rushent's kicky production is appropriate to the band's quirky style.

what to avoid: *Happy Birthday* ♪ (Epic, 1981, prod. Steve Severin) is a befuddled mess. Aside from the title track, which was a minor breakthrough single for the group, there's little here to suggest the band would be more than a one-hit novelty act.

the rest:
Collected Images ♪♪♪ (Epic, 1984)
Best Of ♪♪♪ (Pinnacle, 1994)
I Could Be Happy ♪♪♪ (Epic/Legacy, 1997)

worth searching for: The 12" single "Don't Talk to Me about Love" (Epic, 1983, prod. Mike Chapman) features a great non-album B-side called "Last Goodbye," a bouncy dance track that shows the group skillfully making the transition from silly pop band to sophisticated club act.

influences:
◀◀ Shirley Temple, the Chipmunks, the Fifth Dimension
▶▶ Cyndi Lauper, Björk

see also: *Texas*

Christopher Scapelliti

Dave Alvin
Born November 11, 1955, in Los Angeles, CA.

As a member of the Blasters, guitarist Dave Alvin coined the term "American Music," and he has spent the rest of his career defining the term, crafting a distinctive brand of music now most commonly known as roots—drawing on such solidly domestic forms as country, vintage R&B, rockabilly, and blues. After a split with his brother Phil ended the Blasters's too-brief run, Alvin joined X for one album, then began a solo career that has been defined by songs with a gift for narrative and a fine poetic sense that cuts through Alvin's brusk delivery. He plays a mean lead guitar, too. Of late Alvin has gained a reputation as producer of West Coast roots music and has published a volume of his poetry.

what to buy: *Blue Blvd.* ♪♪♪♪ (HighTone, 1991, prod. Chris Silagyi, Dave Alvin, Bruce Bromberg) reads like a book of short stories and rocks like nobody's business. "Haley's Comet," co-written with Tom Russell, recounts the dubious end of rock 'n' roll legend Bill Haley, while "Andersonville" is the most vivid

song about the Civil War since "The Night They Drove Old Dixie Down." *King of California* ♪♪♪♪ (HighTone, 1994, prod. Greg Leisz) is an acoustic-based album on which Alvin finally grew into his voice, allowing the quieter arrangements to show off its distinctiveness rather than its limitations. You could carp about Alvin taking still another run at "Fourth of July," which has appeared on several albums now, but songs such as "Barn Burning," which rolls like a freight train, and the lush title track, Alvin's best ballad ever, more than make up for the repetition.

what to buy next: *Romeo's Escape* ♪♪♪♪ (Epic, 1987/Razor & Tie, 1995, prod. Steve Berlin, Mark Linnett) contains some of Alvin's finest songs, including several reprised from the Blasters' albums. And while some of the arrangements, notably "Border Radio," cast the songs in new light, Alvin's limited vocal abilities hold him back. *Museum of Heart* ♪♪♪♪ (HighTone, 1993, prod. Chris Silagyi, Bruce Bromberg, Dave Alvin) is a wrenching album of heartbreak and sifting through the shards of a shattered relationship. The best of the lot, "Don't Talk about Her" and "A Woman's Got a Right," could be seen as the laments of a man smart enough to see both sides of the story.

the rest:
(With the Guilty Men) *Interstate City* ♪♪♪♪ (HighTone, 1996)
Blackjack David ♪♪♪♪ (HighTone, 1998)

worth searching for: *The Pleasure Barons Live in Las Vegas* (HighTone, 1993, prod. Mark Linnett, Country Dick Montana) is recommended to serious fans of any one of the principals— Alvin, Mojo Nixon, and the late Country Dick Montana—than to the general populace. Alvin's cover versions of "Closing Time" and "Gangster of Love" stand out, but Country Dick's Tom Jones medley has to be heard to be believed.

influences:
◀◀ Big Joe Turner, Jerry Lee Lewis, Elvis Presley, Sonny Burgess, Hank Williams
▶▶ Big Sandy & His Fly-Rite Boys, the Reverend Horton Heat, Jason & the Scorchers, Tom Russell, Chris Gaffney, Jim Lauderdale, the Derailers

see also: *The Blasters, X*

Daniel Durchholz

Phil Alvin
See: The Blasters

Eric Ambel
See: The Del Lords

Ambitious Lovers

Formed 1984, in New York, NY.

Arto Lindsay, vocals, guitar; Peter Scherer, keyboards, synthesizer bass, drum programming, sampling.

DNA visionary Arto Lindsay and musical renaissance man Peter Scherer combined their disparate talents to produce a polyglot sound unlike anything in the music scene of the time. The gnarled, compact songs bursting with jack-in-the-box energy that typified DNA rested alongside coiled funk and languid Brazilian music—Lindsay was raised in Brazil and sang the latter material in Portuguese. After albums named for three of the Seven Deadly Sins, the duo (always joined on album by an array of guests) split due to a desire to pursue differing musical interests and the economic burden of paying hired guns rather than working with a cooperative band.

what's available: *Lust* 𝄞𝄞𝄞𝄢 (Elektra, 1991, prod. Peter Scherer) is currently the only Ambitious Lovers album in print. It avoids the overtly avant-garde snippets of the earlier albums in favor of a smoother sound, though Lindsay's guitar squiggles remain prominent. A cover of Jorge Ben's soccer tribute "Umbaba-rauma" (which can also be found in an extended version on a 12-inch vinyl) was a local club hit.

worth searching for: Those who assume Scherer was a moderating influence on Lindsay should check import bins for the Belgian release *Pretty Ugly* (Made to Measure, 1990, prod. Peter Scherer, Arto Lindsay). Jointly credited to Lindsay and Scherer rather than being billed as an Ambitious Lovers project, it's largely comprised of instrumental ballet and theater music that's as raw and uncompromised as DNA. *Greed* (Virgin, 1988, prod. Peter Scherer) contains the best funk track this group ever released, "Love Overlap," plus the most impressive roster of guests—including Vernon Reid, Bill Frisell, John Zorn, John Lurie, and Nana Vasconcelos. The group's debut album, *Envy* (EG, 1984, prod. Peter Scherer, M.E. Miller, Arto Lindsay), was shocking in its juxtapositions, with some of Lindsay's most twisted guitar fragments followed by romantic, poignant ballads.

influences:

◄◄ Caetano Veloso, Gilberto Gil, James Brown, Derek Bailey

►► David Byrne, Cameo

see also: *DNA, Golden Palominos, Arto Lindsay, Peter Scherer*

Steve Holtje

Ambrosia

Formed 1971, in Los Angeles, CA. Disbanded 1983. Reunited 1996.

David Pack, guitar; Joe Puerta, bass; Christopher North, keyboards (1971–77); Burleigh Drummond, drums (1977–83); David Lewis, keyboards (1980–82); Royce Jones, percussion, vocals (1980–82).

Until 1975, Britain had the art rock music scene pretty much to itself. Enter Ambrosia, four accomplished vocalists and multi-instrumentalists who performed a rock-fusion debut of Leonard Bernstein's "Mass" with the L.A. Philharmonic in 1973, well before they began recording as a group. Ambrosia's early albums showed a successful synthesis of rock and classical training, often with intentionally humorous results (as on the comically baroque track "Dance with Me George," from the group's 1976 album *Somewhere I've Never Traveled*). Christopher North's keyboard contributions on the first two albums did much to broaden Ambrosia's sound and made the group sound more like an ensemble than a typical four-piece rock band. Following his departure in 1977, the group's music became more slick and mainstream, with mellow hits such as "How Much I Feel," "You're the Only Woman," and "The Biggest Part of Me." Of Ambrosia's work, its earliest tongue-in-cheek recordings are the most enduring. But wherever you look in the band's catalog there is excellent musicianship and spot-on composition.

what to buy: Having deleted the essential albums from Ambrosia's catalog, Warner Bros. makes up for it with *Anthology* 𝄞𝄞𝄞𝄢 (Warner Bros., 1997, prod. David Pack), a better-than-average retrospective that serves up a little something from each of the group's incarnations.

what to avoid: *One Eighty* 𝄞𝄢 (Warner Bros., 1980, prod. Freddie Piro, Ambrosia) is a scattershot effort that suggests the group wasn't quite ready to leave behind its tongue-in-cheek art rock farces or to fully embrace its new status as an adult contemporary light-rock band. "The Biggest Part of Me" and "You're the Only Woman" are the only worthwhile entries here, and they're duly assembled on *Anthology*.

worth searching for: Ambrosia's third album, *Life Beyond L.A.* (Warner Bros., 1978, prod. Freddie Piro, Ambrosia), was a successful hybrid of sardonic humor ("Angola") and mainstream pop ("How Much I Feel," "If Heaven Could Find Me"). It's currently available as a Japanese import.

influences:

◄◄ The Beatles, King Crimson, Yes, Emerson, Lake & Palmer, Sparks, Traffic, Pink Floyd, Genesis, Todd Rundgren, Daryl Hall & John Oates

►► XTC, Toto

Christopher Scapelliti

America

Formed 1969, in London, England.

Dewey Bunnell, vocals, guitar, drums; Gerry Beckley, guitar, vocals; Dan Peek, guitar, vocals (1969–77).

America was folk-rock's Fabian—tuneful and easy on the ears, not terribly subversive, and, therefore, more commercial. The trio, which formed on a U.S. armed forces base, enjoyed a string of hit singles during the '70s, beginning by aping Neil Young on "A Horse with No Name" and hitting a few other high points—including some sides produced by Beatles collaborator George Martin—along with the drivel of "Muskrat Love." After Dan Peek left, however, the bottom seemed to drop out. With the exception of the 1982 hit "You Can Do Magic," Bunnell and Beckley simply soldier along on the oldies circuit, pairing up with fellow travelers such as the Beach Boys and Three Dog Night.

what to buy: *History: America's Greatest Hits* ♫♫♫♧ (Warner Bros., 1975, prod. various) has everything you'd want—and need—from the group's peak period.

what to buy next: *Encore! More Greatest Hits* ♫♫♫ (Rhino, 1990, prod. various) provides a nice addendum for those who want more of the story.

what to avoid: *Alibi* **woof!** (Capitol, 1980, prod.) is the worst of myriad sub-par albums America, as a duo, has recorded during '80s and '90s.

the rest:
America ♫♫♧ (Warner Bros., 1972)
Homecoming ♫♫♧ (Warner Bros., 1972)
Hat Trick ♫♫ (Warner Bros., 1973)
Holiday ♫♫♧ (Warner Bros., 1974)
Hearts ♫♫ (Warner Bros., 1975)
Hideaway ♫♫ (Warner Bros., 1976)
Harbor ♫♫ (Warner Bros., 1976)
Silent Letter ♫♧ (Capitol, 1979)
View from the Ground ♫♫ (Capitol, 1982)
Your Move ♫ (Capitol, 1983)
Perspective ♫♧ (Capitol, 1984)
Hourglass ♫♫ (American Gramophone, 1994)
King Biscuit Flower Hour Presents America ♫♫♫ (KBFH Records, 1995)
Human Nature ♫♫♧ (Oxygen, 1998)

influences:
⏪ James Taylor, the Eagles, Jackson Browne, Crosby, Stills, Nash & Young, Poco, the Kingston Trio

⏩ Firefall, McGuinn, Clark & Hillman

Gary Graff

The American Breed

Formed early 1960s, in Chicago, IL. Disbanded 1969.

Al Ciner, guitar, vocals; Charles Colbert Jr., bass, vocals; Lee Graziano, drums, trumpet, vocals; Gary Loizzo, vocals, guitar, organ; Kevin Murphy, keyboards (1968–69); Paulette McWilliams, vocals (1968–69).

If you were a kid growing up during the '60s, the American Breed was the sort of pop-rock act that your parents may have liked: a clean-cut, peppy alternative to grungy, hide-your-daughters rumpus-raisers like, oh, say, the Rolling Stones. This is an observation, not a criticism; the American Breed was certainly capable of creating well-produced pop records that sounded great on AM radio. The group is best remembered for "Bend Me, Shape Me," its biggest and best hit. Al Ciner, Kevin Murphy, and Paulette McWilliams went on to form a group called Ask Rufus, which later shortened its name to Rufus and, with Chaka Khan replacing McWilliams as lead singer, returned to the Top 40 during the '70s.

what's available: *Bend Me, Shape Me: The Best of the American Breed* ♫♫♫ (Varese Sarabande, 1994, compilation prod. Cary E. Mansfield) collects just about all the Breed you need, kicking off with a nice take on the Gerry Goffin–Carole King gem, "I Don't Think You Know Me," a tune also recorded (but then-unreleased) by the Monkees. "Bend Me, Shape Me" is the high point, but "Step Out of Your Mind," "Don't Forget about Me," "Don't Make Me Leave You," and "Ready, Willing and Able" are likewise agreeable, toe-tappin' tunes. "Keep the Faith" is an uncharacteristic rocker. The ballads (including a cover of the Troggs' "Anyway That You Want Me") are, well, strictly for ballad fans. Or their parents.

influences:
⏪ The Four Seasons, Jay & the Americans, the Monkees, the Vogues

⏩ The Cowsills, Bill Deal & the Rhondels, Chicago, Air Supply

Carl Cafarelli

American Flyer

Formed 1976, in Los Angeles, CA. Disbanded 1978.

Craig Fuller, guitar, vocals; Eric Kaz, keyboard, vocals; Doug Yule, bass, guitar, vocals; Steve Katz, guitar, vocals.

The lineup was impressive enough: Craig Fuller had penned "Aimee" and a handful of other winners for Pure Prairie League's *Bustin' Out* LP; Eric Kaz, a Blues Magoos alumnus, had scored with "Love Has No Pride"; and Steve Katz and Doug Yule hailed from Blood, Sweat & Tears and the Velvet Underground, respectively. Despite the abundance of talent, American Flyer's self-titled debut, though pleasant-enough singer-songwriter fare (and produced by the mighty George Martin), didn't really live up to the grand expectations. This amalgam should have remained a decent one-shot, but the group turned in a forgettable second effort before disbanding. Fuller would make waves a decade later as the Lowell George replacement for a re-formed Little Feat; Kaz continues to lead a successful songwriting career in Nashville and elsewhere.

what to buy: *American Flyer* 🎵🎵🎵 (United Artists, 1976, prod. George Martin), though typically smooth mid-'70s stuff, has its moments, including a decent reading of Kaz's "Love Has No Pride," as well a slightly over-the-top revival of Fuller's Pure Prairie League gem "Call Me, Tell Me."

the rest:
Spirit of a Woman 🎵🎵 (United Artists, 1977)

influences:
◀◀ The Beatles, Buffalo Springfield, Crosby, Stills & Nash

▶▶ Blackhawk, Dan Fogelberg

see also: *Pure Prairie League, Blood, Sweat & Tears, the Velvet Underground*

David Simons

American Music Club
See: Mark Eitzel

aMiniature
Formed 1988, in San Diego, CA.

John Lee, vocals, guitar; Kevin Wells, guitar (1993); Tony Rotter, guitar (1994); Devon Goldberg, guitar (1992–94); Mark Monteith, guitar (1995–present); Colin Watson, bass; Christian Hoffman, drums (1992–94); Mark Trombino, drums (1995); Johnny Schier, drums (1995–present).

aMiniature—the a is silent; it's there to differentiate the group from a jazz ensemble named Miniature—is Korean-American John Lee's baby. He writes all the music and is the only original member still in the group, which undergoes a dizzying number of personnel changes every year, with bassist Colin Watson the only other constant. The dark energy and tempered hope of Lee's densely layered songs are built with two or three hooks going at once; the bass parts alone would make some songs memorable. Equally adept at building a memorable sound and solid structures, Lee fluctuates a song's intensity by thickening or paring down the arrangement, intertwining simple but distinctive guitar riffs that provide an irresistible momentum. Lee's vocals are like another instrument equal to the guitar, nearly shouted yet at the same time melodic in a blunt, minimal way.

what to buy: *Murk Time Cruiser* 🎵🎵🎵🎵 (Restless, 1995, prod. John Lee, Mark Trombino) surpasses the group's other efforts due to perfectly proportioned and paced material from start to finish; the hooks are all knockout punches, and the sound is distinctive and instantly classic.

the rest:
Plexiwatt 🎵🎵🎵 (Scheming Intelligentsia, 1991)
Depth Five Rate Six 🎵🎵🎵🎵 (Restless, 1994)

influences:
◀◀ Elvis Costello, Wire, Band of Susans, Mission of Burma, the Replacements, Pixies

Steve Holtje

Tori Amos
Born Myra Ellen Amos, August 22, 1963, in Newton, NC.

A singer, pianist, and songwriter, Tori Amos is Barbra Streisand by way of Wendy O. Williams; her confessional piano-fired ballads can be sweet and delicate, but what Amos really wants to do is raise hell. The daughter of a Methodist preacher, the classically-trained Amos writes weird, compelling tunes about sex, religion, and all points in between. Her idiosyncratic style borders on the annoying at times, but at its best, Amos's piano-rock is every bit as good Elton John's mid-'70s work, and she's particularly adept at individualizing other artists' songs (she's recorded versions of Nirvana's "Smells Like Teen Spirit" and the Rolling Stones' "Angie").

what to buy: *Little Earthquakes* 🎵🎵🎵🎵 (Atlantic, 1991, prod. Davitt Sigerson, Eric Rosse, Ian Stanley, Tori Amos) remains her benchmark, a 12-song act of high drama. "Me and a Gun," "Crucify," and "Silent All These Years" are the aural equivalent of reading someone's diary a week after a suicide.

what to buy next: *Under the Pink* 🎵🎵🎵🎵 (Atlantic, 1994, prod. Eric Rosse, Tori Amos) boasts a slew of bona fide pop gems in "Cornflake Girl," "Past the Mission," and the sardonic "God." *from the choirgirl hotel* 🎵🎵🎵🎵 (Atlantic, 1998, prod. Tori Amos) finds Amos dabbling in industrial and techno, but she's at her best mining familiar operatic ballad turf in songs such as "Northern Lad."

what to avoid: *Y Kant Tori Read* **woof!** (Atlantic, 1988) is a forgettable new wave–cum–hard rock effort.

the rest:
Crucify 🎵🎵🎵🎵 (Atlantic EP, 1992)
Boys for Pele 🎵🎵🎵 (Atlantic, 1996)
Hey Jupiter 🎵🎵🎵🎵 (Atlantic, 1996)

influences:
◀◀ Elton John, Kate Bush, Joni Mitchell

▶▶ Sarah McLachlan, Tara MacLean, Natlie Merchant

Thor Christensen

The Amps
See: The Breeders

Tori Amos (© Jack Vartoogian)

Eric Andersen
/Andersen, Danko, Fjeld
Born February 14, 1943, in Pittsburgh, PA.

Andersen hit the folk circuit during the '60s, becoming one of the first "new" Dylans, a label that is both daunting and somewhat misleading. Andersen is similar to Dylan only in his phrasing; but where Dylan is elusive and biting, Andersen is open and thoughtful. His vision is nowhere near as far reaching, however, as he prefers to stick to more romantic themes. His career was thrown off track in the '70s after the master tapes the his follow-up to his masterful *Blue River* album were inexplicably lost. After meandering for a decade or so, Andersen appears to be back on track, recently joining forces in a trio with Jonas Fjeld and Band bassist Rick Danko and releasing some of the most focused work of his career.

what to buy: *Blue River* ♫♫♫ (Columbia, 1972) is undoubtedly his greatest work and stands alongside anything that the singer-songwriter movement produced during the '70s. Once located, the tapes for *Stages: The Lost Album* ♫♫♫ (Columbia, 1991, prod. Norbert Putnam) proved as complete and substantial as the rumors indicated. Certainly "Baby, I'm Lonesome" is one of the more moving love songs he's recorded. Also included are some strong new recordings with guests Garth Hudson, Rick Danko, Shawn Colvin, and Eric Bazilian of the Hooters.

what to buy next: *Ghosts upon the Road* ♫♫♫ (Gold Castle, 1988, prod. Steve Addabbo, Eric Andersen) marks a full-force comeback. It's a mature, vast record with vivid, literate songs including the 10-minute title track. *The Best of Eric Andersen* ♫♫♫ (Vanguard, 1970, prod. various) is a solid intro to his coffee house folk beginnings, containing his signature "Thirsty Boots."

what to avoid: *More Hits from Tin Can Alley* ♫♫♫ (Vanguard, 1968, prod. Al Gorgoni) is not without its moments, but the Beatle-esque production will seem a bit florid to the purists and is certainly incongruous with anything else in his catalog.

the rest:
Today Is the Highway ♫♫♫ (Vanguard, 1965)
'Bout Changes and Things ♫♫♫ (Vanguard, 1966)
(With Andersen, Danko, Fjeld) *Andersen, Danko, Fjeld* ♫♫♫♫ (Rykodisc, 1993)
Ridin' on the Blinds ♫♫♫♫ (Rykodisc, 1997)
The Collection ♫♫♫ (Archive, 1997)

influences:
◄◄ Bob Dylan, Woody Guthrie, Hank Williams

►► James Taylor, Jackson Browne, Bruce Springsteen, John Mellencamp, Tom Petty, James McMurtry

Allan Orski

Ian Anderson
See: Jethro Tull

Laurie Anderson
Born June 5, 1947, in Chicago, IL.

Laurie Anderson has challenged the conventions of musical performance with thematic stage shows that employ dramatic lighting, theatrical pacing, and a variety of media (including film, video, and written text) to get her ideas across. Her impressive list of collaborators includes beat author William S. Burroughs, photographer Robert Mapplethorpe, and progressive classical composer Philip Glass. Her themes encompass—but are not limited to—women's rights, the place of art in society, issues of censorship, and myriad variations on the mysteries of human relations; her landmark stage show *United States* sought to delve into nothing less than the collective American consciousness. Impressive credentials, but with all this conceptual stuff going on, Anderson's music could easily get lost in the shuffle. Because she is commonly referred to as a "performance artist"—a label that inspires as much audience dread as the word "mime"—Anderson's music is often written off as merely one element in the patchworks that are her multimedia presentations. While much of her work does benefit from both seeing *and* hearing, her recordings have much to offer.

what to buy: Anderson's early recordings strongly rely on her trademark spoken/sung vocal delivery, a technique best described as monologues with musical accompaniment. Of these, *Mr. Heartbreak* ♫♫♫ (Warner Bros., 1984, prod. Bill Laswell) fares the best. This is due in large part to her collaborators—which include Burroughs, guitarist Adrian Belew, and former Material bassist Bill Laswell. The well-chosen musicians on *Mr. Heartbreak* flesh out Anderson's typically cold electronic soundscapes, adding a welcome warmth to the palette. Peter Gabriel also turns up for two duets, "Gravity's Angel" and "Excellent Birds," a song that appears on his *So* album—with a slightly different arrangement—as the song "This Is the Picture." On *Strange Angels* ♫♫♫ (Warner Bros., 1989, prod. Laurie Anderson), Anderson's vocals are more musical and she pursues more conventional song structures—particularly on the title track and "Beautiful Red Dress."

what to buy next: If *Mr. Heartbreak* is to your liking, the next logical step is the live album *Home of the Brave* ♫♫♫ (Warner Bros., 1986, prod. Laurie Anderson), which features many of the same players from *Mr. Heartbreak*. The concert setting allows the musicians a chance to stretch out a bit, and the results—particularly Belew's guitar playing and singing—are decidedly looser and more groove-oriented than any of Anderson's studio fare. For more of the musical stylings of *Strange*

Angels, *Bright Red* ♫♫♫ (Warner Bros., 1994, prod. Laurie Anderson, Brian Eno) is a good choice.

what to avoid: While impressive in its scope and Herculean length, *United States Live* ♫♫ (Warner Bros., 1984, prod. Laurie Anderson, Roma Baran) is definitely one of those "you had to be there" experiences. The version of "O Superman" is quite good, but the four-plus hours of music here really need the complement of Anderson's arresting visual style to get the maximum bang.

the rest:
Big Science ♫♫♫ (Warner Bros., 1982)
The Ugly One with Jewels ♫♫♫ (Warner Bros., 1995)

worth searching for: While there is no authorized audio version of *Stories from the Nerve Bible* (the piece initially appeared in print and was followed by a Voyager CD-ROM), Anderson did a performance tour of the work, which has cropped up on various bootlegs.

influences:
◀◀ William S. Burroughs, experimental theater, Talking Heads, Brian Eno
▶▶ Adrian Belew, Mae Moore

David Galens

Andersen, Danko, Fjeld
See: Eric Andersen

Leah Andreone
Born 1973, in San Diego, CA.

The mythic propulsion of struggling shy-girl poet/waitress-type into struggling shy-girl poet/songwriter-type has admittedly lost some of its push over the past few years. With the increasing complexity and volume of indulgent, pop-feminist singer-songwriters, sing-by-numbers heart-rendering has necessarily lost much of its potency. Sincerity may just have turned in on itself in its sore-throated search for attention. Following industry discovery as a Los Angeles waitress, Leah Andreone showed herself prone to indulgent whoops of open-mouthed nonsense and a generally unappealing splash of ill-advised California Girl metaphoria.

what to avoid: *Veiled* ♫ (RCA, 1996, prod. Rick Neigher) is a horrific reminder of the vanity of mirrored expression—if only for being so awkwardly unveiled in its shoddiness. Flow charts of recovery abound here, frothed about with some unwelcome production gimickry (at least Kate Bush takes her time). Andreone sounds like the girl next door practicing her Gwen Stefani arpeggios to the tune of her sister's Heart karaoke tape. Guitar solos, loopy candle-lit production, and a naive, unre-

fined sense of artistry help to make this an almost comedically unlikeable affair.

influences:
◀◀ Tori Amos, Kate Bush, Heart

Billy Manes

Horace Andy
See: Massive Attack

Angel
Formed 1975, in Washington, DC. Disbanded 1981.

Frank DiMino, vocals; Gregg Giuffria, keyboards; Punky Meadows, guitar; Mickey Jones, bass (1975–77); Barry Brandt, drums; Felix Robinson, bass (1975–81).

Angel was something of a mess, with its glammy, all-white attire and albums full of bloated pomp-rock that was intended to sound majestic but instead came off as Grade B Genesis or Yes. The group, which was discovered by Kiss' Gene Simmons, released seven albums in its seven years together, none of which made substantial impact on the masses. Keyboardist Greg Giuffria went on to minor success with his own band and later joined the group House of Lords.

what's available: *An Anthology* ♫♫♫ (Mercury, 1992, prod. various) preserves the best of the albums—which, unfortunately, isn't saying much. It also includes the group's title theme for the film *Foxes*.

influences:
◀◀ Yes, Kiss, Genesis
▶▶ Dream Theater

Gary Graff

The Angels
Formed 1961, in Orange, NJ. Disbanded 1967.

Linda Jansen, lead vocalist (1961–62); Peggy Santiglia, lead vocalist (1962–67); Barbara Allibut, vocals; Phyllis "Jiggs" Allibut, vocals.

The Angels began as a more or less standard issue female doo-wop group, scoring a Top 15 hit with "Till" in 1961 and a more modest but still fondly-remembered follow-up, "Thank You and Good Night," the next year. Further success eluded them, and their original lead singer, Linda Jansen, left the group in 1962. Her replacement, Peggy Santiglia, brought a tougher, sexier sound to the group with her raspy vocals. Renowned producers Feldman, Goldstein, and Gotterher (a.k.a. the Strangeloves) soon put it to good use on their classic "My Boyfriend's Back," which shot to #1 during the summer of 1963. (The Beatles themselves appropriated the song's opening handclaps beat for beat just a few months later in "I Want to Hold Your Hand.") A couple of follow-up singles garnered some radio play, but the Angels never again ascended to this height. Nevertheless, they didn't want for work, as they were among the mid-'60s busiest session singers before breaking up in 1967.

what to buy: *The Best of the Angels* 𝄞𝄞𝄞𝄞 (PolyGram, 1996, prod. Feldman, Goldstein, Gotterher) features "My Boyfriend's Back," their earlier hits, and worthy later releases such as the high-energy "Wow, Wow, Wee (He's the Boy for Me)" and "I Adore Him."

what to buy next: Also available is a straight reissue of the album released in the wake of their #1 hit, *My Boyfriend's Back* 𝄞𝄞𝄞 (Collectables, 1991, prod. Feldman, Goldstein, Gotterher).

influences:

◄◄ The McGuire Sisters, Frankie Lymon & the Teenagers

►► Blondie, the B-52's, the Darling Buds

Mike Greenfield

The Animals
/Eric Burdon & the Animals
/Eric Burdon
/Alan Price

Formed 1962, in Newcastle upon Tyne, England. Disbanded 1969. Reformed 1976 and 1983.

Eric Burdon, vocals; Alan Price, keyboards (1962–65); Bryan "Chas" Chandler, bass (1962–66); John Steel, drums (1962–66); Hilton Valentine, guitar (1962–66); Dave Rowberry, keyboards (1965–66); Barry Jenkins, drums (1966); John Weider, guitar (1966); Danny McCullough, bass (1966–68); Tom Parker, organ (1966–67); Vic Briggs, guitar (1967–68); Zoot Money, keyboards (1968–69); Andrew Somers, guitar (1968–69).

During the early '60s British Invasion, the Animals prided themselves on being one of the stalwarts of the blues, even after the Rolling Stones went pop. Yet the band will be remembered as one of the first to marry a folk song to a rock beat for its breakthrough hit, "House of the Rising Sun." Frontman Eric Burdon was one of the great vocalists of the era, with gritty, soulful delivery and his James Brown–style collapse routine on stage. The original Animals split up in 1966, but an altered band—billed with Burdon's name out front—was at the front line of West Coast psychedelia, having been to the Monterey Pop Festival (and writing a hit single about it) and later singing convincingly of such American concerns as Vietnam and San Francisco nights. As they left, the individual Animals made their marks elsewhere in rock: Chas Chandler was Jimi Hendrix's first manager; Alan Price hung around Bob Dylan during the 1965 tour

captured in the documentary *Don't Look Back* and scored the soundtrack to *O Lucky Man!*; Andrew Somers became Andy Summers and joined the Police; and Burdon went on to a solo career, with War as his first backing band. The Animals' reunions have never stuck, but the group's performances showed it could still call up the ferocious attack of its '60s peak at will.

what to buy: There's never been a fully satisfying Animals collection—at least not on these shores. But *The Best of the Animals* 𝄞𝄞𝄞𝄞𝄞 (MGM, 1966/Abkco, 1987, prod. Mickie Most) covers the extraordinary early singles, the Abkco set in digitally remastered sound.

what to buy next: *The Best of Eric Burdon and the Animals, Vol. 2* 𝄞𝄞𝄞𝄞 (MGM, 1967, prod. various) captures the later, psychedelicized version of the band. *Animalization* 𝄞𝄞𝄞𝄞 (MGM, 1966, prod. Mickie Most) is the most fully realized early album.

what to avoid: Of Burdon's many mediocre solo albums, *Black Man's Burdon* 𝄞𝄞 (MGM, 1971/Avenue, 1993, prod. Jerry Goldstein)—his second with War—was incredibly indulgent and self-consciously arty.

the rest:

The Animals 𝄞𝄞𝄞𝄞 (MGM, 1964)
The Animals on Tour 𝄞𝄞𝄞 (MGM, 1965)
Animal Tracks 𝄞𝄞𝄞 (MGM, 1965)
Animalism 𝄞𝄞𝄞 (MGM, 1966)
Winds of Change 𝄞𝄞 (MGM, 1967/One Way, 1995)
Every One of Us 𝄞𝄞𝄞 (MGM, 1968/One Way, 1994)
Love Is 𝄞𝄞 (MGM, 1969/One Way, 1994)
The Greatest Hits of Eric Burdon and the Animals 𝄞𝄞𝄞 (MGM, 1969)
Ark 𝄞𝄞𝄞 (I.R.S., 1983)
Rip It to Shreds: Greatest Hits Live 𝄞𝄞𝄞 (I.R.S., 1984)
The Animals with Sonny Boy Williamson 𝄞𝄞𝄞𝄞 (Griffin Music, 1994)
Best of the Animals 𝄞𝄞𝄞𝄞 (Dominion/K-Tel, 1997)

worth searching for: That elusive, aforementioned 1962 to 1969 Animals collection exists in the form of the strong Australian import *The Most of the Animals* (Raven, 1989, prod. various), which tracks the hits from "House of the Rising Sun" through the group's resurrections of Johnny Cash's "Ring of Fire" and Traffic's "Coloured Rain."

solo outings:

Eric Burdon:

Eric Is Here 𝄞𝄞 (MGM, 1967/One Way, 1995)
Eric Burdon Declares War 𝄞𝄞𝄞𝄞 (Polydor, 1970/Rhino, 1995)
Love Is All Around 𝄞𝄞𝄞 (Avenue, 1976/1993)
That's Live 𝄞𝄞 (Inakustik, 1985)
Wicked Man 𝄞𝄞 (GNP/Crescendo, 1988)
Eric Burdon Sings the Animals Greatest Hits 𝄞𝄞𝄞 (Rhino, 1988/1994)
Unreleased Burdon 𝄞𝄞 (Blue Wave, 1993)
Sun Secrets/Stop 𝄞𝄞𝄞 (Avenue, 1993)
The Best of Eric Burdon and War 𝄞𝄞𝄞𝄞 (Avenue, 1995)
I'm Ready—The Unreleased Burdon, Vol. 2 𝄞𝄞 (Blue Wave, 1997)

Alan Price:
The Price to Play 𝄞𝄞𝄞 (Decca, 1966)
A Price on His Head 𝄞𝄞𝄞 (Decca, 1967)
The Price Is Right 𝄞𝄞𝄞 (Parrot, 1968)
Fame and Price 𝄞𝄞𝄞𝄞 (Columbia, 1971)
O Lucky Man! 𝄞𝄞𝄞𝄞 (Warner Bros., 1973/1995)
Between Yesterday and Today 𝄞𝄞𝄞𝄞 (Warner Bros., 1974)

influences:
◀◀ John Lee Hooker, Alexis Korner

▶▶ Bruce Springsteen, John Mellencamp, Blue Öyster Cult

see also: *War*

Roger Catlin

Paul Anka
Born July 30, 1941, in Ottawa, Ontario, Canada.

One of the few '50s teen idols with a long career in music, Paul Anka has proven resilient and resourceful. He broke through in 1957 with the #1 hit "Diana," a song he wrote about a babysitter, and became a heartthrob almost immediately. He had a few more hits during this era, including "Lonely Boy" and "Puppy Love," before he tried acting in such movies as "The Longest Day," for which he wrote the theme song. Anka has had some hits since then, including the controversial "(You're) Having My Baby," which some took as sexist, others as anti-abortion (others as just really, really bad). Today he is mostly known for his songwriting and business dealings; he'll forever be an asterisk in the Frank Sinatra story for taking a French song and re-arranging it into the lounge-lizard standard "My Way."

what to buy: Most of Anka's albums are either collections of hits or live recordings, and most of them are out of print. The most exhaustive of his several anthologies is the *30th Anniversary Collection* 𝄞𝄞𝄞 (Rhino, 1989, prod. various), which spans his career evolution from a sweet-voiced teen star to a suave crooner who can write. All the hits and near hits, from "Diana" to "My Way," are included on this thoughtfully assembled package.

what to avoid: Anka's chart resurgence during the early '70s was good for his bank account, bad for our ears. Most of that swill was released during his years with United Artists, and it was all collected on the anthology *The Best of the United Artists Years* 𝄞 (EMI, 1996, prod. various).

the rest:
21 Golden Hits 𝄞𝄞 (RCA, 1963)
Classic Hits 𝄞𝄞 (Curb, 1992)
Paul Anka Sings His Big Ten, Vol. 1 and *Vol. 2* 𝄞𝄞𝄞 (Curb, 1992)
Amigos 𝄞𝄞 (Globo, 1996)

influences:
◀◀ Frank Sinatra, Nat King Cole

▶▶ Neil Diamond, Barry Manilow, Julio Iglesias

Doug Pullen

Another Girl
Formed 1995, in Vancouver, British Columbia, Canada.

Despite the band name, Lynne Kellman is not just another girl in the music business: The Canadian singer-songwriter-multi-instrumentalist wrote all of the songs and played nearly all the instruments on her debut album, a seamless blend of mild art-rock and breezy pop.

what's available: *In the Galaxy* 𝄞𝄞𝄞 (RCA, 1997, prod. Lynne Kellman) clocks in at less than 40 minutes, but for a change the issue is quality, not quantity on a CD. Kellman's vocals are more sweet than challenging, but she pulls the cork out of the melody bottle, letting the songs such as "Sometimes," "Favorite," and "Holiday" spill into all different areas.

influences:
◀◀ The Darling Buds, Lush, the Bangles, Liz Phair

Jordan Oakes

Adam Ant
/Adam & the Ants
Born Stuart Leslie Goddard, November 3, 1954, in London, England.

One of the more colorful figures on the British new wave scene, Adam Ant has made dashing forays into post-punk, mainstream pop, and even adult alternative. Under the auspices of former Sex Pistols manager Malcolm McClaren, Adam & the Ants were a gimmicky cartoon outfit dressed in pirate clothes and war paint, hawking itself in self-promoting songs such as "Antmusic" and "Antrap." Replete with tribal double drumming and yodels, the Ants made the British charts but were never taken seriously in the U.S. In a bid for more commercial acceptance, Ant went solo and took passing shots at sex symboldom with sophomoric odes to the flesh. He also built a modest acting career.

what to buy: *Super Hits* 𝄞𝄞𝄞𝄞 (Epic, 1998, prod. various) is the compilation that casual fans will want to start with. As for individual albums, the Ants' *Kings of the Wild Frontier* 𝄞𝄞𝄞𝄞 (Epic, 1980, prod. Chris Hughes) is driven by pounding rhythms and Adam Ant's fantasy world of pirates and Indians rifling through Marco Pirroni's '50s-influenced guitar. Cheap thrills abound on "Jolly Roger," "Los Rancheros," and the signature tune, "Antmusic." *Friend or Foe* 𝄞𝄞𝄞 (Epic, 1982, prod. Chris Hughes) is Ant's first and best solo effort, with a more restrained pop feel that helps "A Place in the Country" and "Goody Two Shoes." *Wonderful* ♫♫♫ (Capitol, 1995, prod. David Tickle) is a solid return to his recording career. Marked by a more adult approach and a focused pop sound, Ant still calls attention to his libido and all its needs, but isn't quite as crass as on his previous efforts.

what to buy next: The Ants' *Prince Charming* ♫♫♫ (Epic, 1981, prod. Chris Hughes) follows the same path as *Kings*, with some of the group's finest moments in the title track and "Stand and Deliver." *Antics in the Forbidden Zone* ♫♫♫ (Epic, 1990, prod. various) compiles all the hits for a decent if occasionally tedious sampler.

what to avoid: *Vive Le Rock* ♫ (Epic, 1985, prod. Tony Visconte) is a faceless trash-heap release that finds Ant in black leather, vainly trying to rock—without memorable tunes, a decent backing band, or even a good gimmick to push it over.

the rest:
Dirk Wears White Sox ♫♫ (Epic, 1979)
Strip ♫♫♫ (Epic, 1983)
Manners & Physique ♫♫♫ (Epic, 1988)
Peel Sessions ♫♫ (Dutch East India, 1991)
B-side Babes ♫♫♫ (Epic/Legacy, 1994)

worth searching for: The import *Antmusic: The Very Best of Adam Ant* (Arcade, 1993, prod. various) is a generous and wide-ranging compilation that comes with a live disc recorded at a 1992 radio concert.

influences:
◄◄ The New York Dolls, Kiss

►► Sigue Sigue Sputnik, Elastica, the Bogmen

see also: *Bow Wow Wow*

Allan Orski

Antenna /Velo-Deluxe /The Mysteries of Life /John P. Strohm & the Hello Strangers

Formed 1991.

Antenna: John Strohm, guitar, vocals; Jake Smith, guitar, vocals; Freda Love, drums; Patrick Spurgeon, drums; Vess Ruhtenberg, guitar (1992); Ed Ackerson, guitar (1993). Velo-Deluxe: John Strohm, guitar, vocals, piano, loops; Lenny Childers, bass, baritone guitar, vocals; Mitch Harris, drums. The Mysteries of Life: Jake Smith, vocals, guitar; Freda Love, drums, vocals; Geraldine Haas, cello; Tina Barbieri, bass, vocals (1996); Lenny Childers, bass, vocals (1997–present). Hello

Strangers: John Strohm, guitar, vocals; Steve Woods, guitar, vocals; Dennis Scoville, pedal steel guitar, fiddle; Glenn Hicks, bass; Mitch Harris, drums.

After the demise of the Blake Babies, as Juliana Hatfield moved on to a successful, tumultuous solo career, John Strohm and Freda Love formed Antenna with Jacob "Jake" Smith (Love's husband), with Strohm strongly in the spotlight. Love, who had been frequently spelled by Patrick Spurgeon, and Smith then took time off for further college studies and to have a child, while Strohm formed Velo-Deluxe to pursue the perfect indie guitar sound and then went country. Love and Smith reappeared in the Mysteries of Life, a quartet distinguished by its inclusion of cello.

what to buy: Antenna's *Sway* ♫♫♫♫ (Mammoth, 1991, prod. Paul Mahern) is as anthemic as any Blake Babies album while covering a broader stylistic range. John P. Strohm & the Hello Strangers's *Caledonia* ♫♫♫ (Flat Earth, 1997, prod. John P. Strohm) is country-rock, which seems to bring out the best in Strohm's songwriting talent. It rocks hard enough that you don't have to like country to enjoy most of it (a few tracks are very twangy, though). And even in this context he experiments with his guitar sounds, which sets this album subtly apart from the rest of the burgeoning field. Love, Ruhtenberg, Childers, Ackerson, and Lisa Germano are among the many guests. Most of the Mysteries of Life's *Come Clean* ♫♫♫ (RCA, 1998, prod. Paul Mahern, Jake Smith) is a bit louder and much peppier than the two EPs that preceded it, although the same general aesthetic applies: stripped down and largely acoustic, with the electric guitar light and undistorted, although they rock out on a few tracks. There's also an imaginatively reworked cover of the Otis Redding classic "That's How Strong My Love Is."

what to buy next: Velo-Deluxe's *Superelastic* ♫♫♫ (Mammoth, 1994, prod. John Strohm, Anjali Dutt) has lots of guests playing with the core trio, including Smith on two tracks (he wrote "Alibi"), a horn section, and a pedal steel guitarist. The sound is generally darker, denser, and practically psychedelic at times thanks to Strohm's guitar textures. The Mysteries of Life's debut, *Keep a Secret* ♫♫♫ (RCA, 1996, prod. Paul Mahern, the Mysteries of Life), is janglier than Blake Babies or Antenna, with a sunnier disposition. The prominent cello is a nice touch, well-integrated into the sound. "Alibi" resurfaces.

the rest:
Antenna:
Sleep ♫♫ (Mammoth, 1992)
Hideout ♫♫♫ (Mammoth, 1993)
(For Now) ♫♫♫ (Mammoth EP, 1993)

The Mysteries of Life:
Focus on the Background ♫♫♫♫ (Flat Earth EP, 1997)
Anonymous Tip ♫♫♫ (Flat Earth EP, 1997)

influences:

◀◀ R.E.M., Keith Richards, Buffalo Tom, the Velvet Underground, the Feelies, Buddy Holly

see also: *Blake Babies, Juliana Hatfield*

Steve Holtje

Anthrax

Formed 1981, in New York, NY.

Scott Ian, guitar; Dan Spitz, guitar; Dan Lilker, bass (1981–84); Charles Benante, drums; Neil Turbin, vocals (1981–84); Joey Belladonna, vocals (1984–92); Frank Bello, bass (1984–present); John Bush, vocals (1992–present).

Along with Slayer, Metallica, and Megadeth, Anthrax was once at the forefront of thrash metal—a much-accelerated version of Ted Nugent, Alice Cooper, Kiss, Black Sabbath, and Led Zeppelin. But thrash changed in the mid-'90s, first as grunge bands like Nirvana and Soundgarden pushed it out of the marketplace, then as even harder bands such as Pantera and Fear Factory seized the commercial baton from Anthrax and Megadeth and wouldn't let go. At its peak, Anthrax was always more interesting in theory than in practice, and its early albums were average despite the funky bass creeping in to make their relentless fury swing. Public Enemy, the influential hardcore rap band, sampled an Anthrax song on its 1988 hit "Bring Tha Noise," which brought respect, a powerful collaborative version of that song, and a national Anthrax-P.E. tour. The band gradually tightened its sound under the leadership of Scott Ian, but as it started to gain commercial clout, personnel problems flared and high-pitched singer Joey Belladonna was forced out in 1992. Despite a couple of strong albums with the more monotone singer John Bush, the band slipped off the charts.

what to buy: *Among the Living* ✧✧✧✧ (Island, 1987, prod. Eddie Kramer, Anthrax) is the band's funniest and most diverse album, with songs based on Stephen King's novels, rhythms that lurch from fast to slow, the headbanging classic "Caught in a Mosh," and language borrowed from hip-hop culture.

what to buy next: The first albums, *Fistful of Metal* ✧✧✧ (Megaforce, 1984, prod. Carl Cannedy) and *Spreading the Disease* ✧✧✧ (Island, 1985, prod. Anthrax, Carl Cannedy), are solid, if one-dimensional, thrash records, perfect for headbanging. The EP *Attack of the Killer B's* ✧✧✧ (Island, 1991, prod. Anthrax, Mark Dodson, Charles Benante) is full of interesting scraps, including "N.F.B. (Dallabnikufesin)," which ends with the satirical sound of a pop-metal band crying through a power ballad and Ian sniffing, "Joey, pass me a tissue."

what to avoid: *State of Euphoria* ✧✧ (Island, 1988, prod. Anthrax, Mark Dodson) is strong evidence that a band can go only

so far with thrash-metal, no matter what weird things it tries to add to it, before the whole business goes stale.

the rest:

I'm the Man ✧✧▽ (Island EP, 1987)
Armed and Dangerous ✧✧▽ (Megaforce, 1989)
Persistence of Time ✧✧▽ (Island, 1990)
Sound of White Noise ✧✧▽ (Elektra, 1993)
Live: The Island Years ✧✧ (Island, 1994)
Stomp 442 ✧✧ (Elektra, 1995)
Vol. 8: The Threat Is Real ✧✧✧▽ (Tommy Boy, 1998)

solo outings:

Joey Belladonna:
Belladonna ✧✧ (Mausoleum, 1995)

Scott Ian:
(With Stormtroopers of Death) *Speak English or Die* ✧✧✧ (Megaforce, 1985/1995)

influences:

◀◀ Black Sabbath, Public Enemy, Alice Cooper, the Sex Pistols, the Ramones, Parliament/Funkadelic, Kiss, Ted Nugent, Motörhead, Metallica, Fishbone

▶▶ Type O Negative, Gravity Kills, Pantera, GWAR, Slayer, Megadeth, the Red Hot Chili Peppers

Steve Knopper

Anti-Nowhere League

Formed early 1980s, in Tunbridge Wells, England. Disbanded in 1988.

Mike "Animal" Kramer, vocals; Magoo, guitar; Winston, bass; P.J., drums.

In the aftermath of the initial punk explosion, various mutant bands sprung up like deformed ironweeds. Amidst England's debris stood the Anti-Nowhere League, a bile-spitting, goofy hate machine. Fueled with raucous energy and noxious diatribes, the band brought their Sex Pistols influence into the distilled but free-floating hate inherent of '80s punk.

what to buy: *We Are . . . the League* ♫♫♫ (Dojo 1996/1984), the group's first album, is the definitive document. Obnoxious, misogynistic, and funny, it's like vandalism with a backbeat. Play it loud. Offend the neighbors.

what to avoid: *The Best of the Anti-Nowhere League* ♫♫♫ (Cleopatra, 1993, prod. varous) is something of a misnomer as it contains material pulled mainly from the band's debut.

influences:

◄◄ The Sex Pistols, the Damned

►► Black Flag, NOFX

Allan Orski

Any Trouble

Formed late 1970s, in England.

Clive Gregson, vocals, guitar; Phil Barnes, bass; Chris Parks, guitar; Mel Harley, drums.

Any Trouble may be the least-known band to hail from Stiff Records, the celebrated new wave label that launched the careers of Elvis Costello, Graham Parker, Nick Lowe, and Ian Dury. Why Any Trouble failed to make a dent in the marketplace may be explained by Clive Gregson's resemblance to Costello in sight and sound. Less caustic but just as geeky looking, perhaps one bespectacled nerd playing hyper pop was all the public could take. And it's a shame, because Any Trouble whipped out pop corkers that stand up against anything released on Stiff. Gregson has gone on to play with Richard Thompson as well as developing an acclaimed solo career, but in 1980 he was just a guy in a band cranking out crazed and melodic pop to anyone that would listen.

what to buy: The reissue of *Where Are All the Nice Girls* ♫♫♫♫ (Stiff, 1980/Compass, 1997, prod. John Wood) finds the band's startling debut on CD for the first time, and not a moment too soon. In a world of dreary mopers and power poppers who have no power, this jolt of melody and rushing beats is a lost treasure.

influences:

◄◄ Elvis Costello, Graham Parker, Nick Lowe

►► Clive Gregson, Tommy Keene, Ben Folds Five

see also: *Clive Gregson*

Allan Orski

Aphex Twin

Born Richard D. James, November 23, 1968, in England.

Aphex Twin, a.k.a. Richard D. James, is one of the most influential electronic music artists of our generation. Since 1987, the extra-prolific James has released a barrage of music under several monikers—Caustic Window, AFX, Polygon Window, Universal Indicator, Joyrex—on a variety of different labels, including his own Rephlex Records in the U.K. In James's music, ambient textures absorb refracted beats that pass through the prism of his own existence. His often disruptive musical vision is matched in its intensity only by his appreciation for the pristine. In fact, many admirers consider James to be a present day Karlheinz Stockhausen or another Philip Glass.

what to buy: James only has four full-length albums available in the U.S., all under the Aphex Twin guise. His third and fourth titles, *Richard D. James* ♫♫♫♫ (Warp/Elektra, 1997, prod. Richard D. James) and the spin-off *Come to Daddy* ♫♫♫♫ (Warp/Sire EP, 1997, prod. Richard D. James), delve into a whirlwind of precisely constructed drum and bass beats. The latter is almost mockingly sinister in its posturing. Both mark a slight departure from *I Care Because You Do* ♫♫♫♫ (Warp/Elektra, 1995, prod. Richard D. James), which strings together beautiful ambient melodies and found sounds.

what to buy next: *Selected Ambient Works, Volume 2* ♫♫♫♫ (Warp/Elektra, 1994, prod. Richard D. James) is, as its name implies, more ambient in its nature. Though some of the tracks can be a bit too long, at its best James's work allows you to see and hear things that you never thought were there.

worth searching for: Available as an import is *Classics* (Bel. R&S, 1995), which includes all of James's early ambient works as well as some more experimental 12-inch single tracks. *Donkey Rhubarb* (Warp EP, 1995) features a track, "Icct Hedral," that James composed with Philip Glass.

influences:

◄◄ Brian Eno, Philip Glass

►► Autechre, Squarepusher, nine inch nails

Joseph Patel

Fiona Apple

Born September 13, 1977, in New York, NY.

One of the few new alternative acts with a unique sound to debut during the mid-'90s, Fiona Apple is the rare artist to capture the public's imagination with both her music and her hype. Apple's actions—complaining during an acceptance speech at the MTV Music Awards, recording phone messages for People for the Ethical Treatment of Animals just in time for Thanksgiving—are always good for a few headlines, but it's the disarming beauty and rawness of her music that really makes her worthy of attention. Her sexy and emotional style have led to comparisons with early jazz singers such as Billie Holiday, but by combining timeless songs with current production values, Apple manages to avoid the retro tag. While record companies scurried to find the next Alanis Morissette, and legions of singer-songwriters strove to be more Alanis-like, Apple got a record contract practically by accident when a three-song demo fell into the hands of a record label bigwig; she had been in the right place (babysitting for a friend of a music industry insider) at the right time (right after the industry realized that female solo artists could sell records but before they signed every last one in the country). A few years later, her debut had sold millions, her fan base included Marilyn Manson, Elton John, and Howard Stern, and her unsmiling face had graced the cover of most every major music and fashion magazine, with her second album being one of the most eagerly anticipated releases of the decade.

what to buy: *Tidal* ♫♫♫♫ (Clean Slate/Work/Columbia, 1996, prod. Andrew Slater) is Apple's only album at this point, but with hits such as "Sleep to Dream," "Shadowboxer," and "Criminal," not to mention such strong tracks as "Sullen Girl" and "Never Is a Promise," the album is certainly a keeper. The only possible complaint could be that too many of the songs are downbeat. But "Criminal" shows that Fiona can get funkier when she wants to.

influences:

◄◄ Billie Holiday, Ella Fitzgerald, Elton John, Sarah McLachlan

Brian Ives

Apples in Stereo

Formed 1993, in Denver, CO.

John Hill, guitar, vocals; Eric Allen, bass, vocals; Hillarie Sidney, drums, vocals; Robert Schneider, guitar, keyboards, vocals.

The Denver-based Elephant 6 record label somewhat defined indie rock steeped in the tradition of the Velvet Underground and the Beach Boys. Along with Elephant 6 labelmates Olivia Tremor Control and Neutral Milk Hotel, the Apples in Stereo set out to preserve pop music as they saw it. The Apples' brand of pop borrows from the Zombies and Sonic Youth, though the latter is more fully represented in their earlier works. Robert Schneider chose pre-adolescence as the topic of many of his songs, from "Green Machines" to tunes about breakfast cereal. Schneider relives his fond memories of growing up in a television decade to anyone that will listen. But it wasn't until the release of 1997's *Tone Soul Evolution* that the Apples approached utter brilliance; the sounds they achieved on that record were more concise and focused. Instead of noise, the Apples delivered catchy pop songs with brilliant harmonies, making this their best record to date. With the newfound success of fellow Elephant 6 labelmates and a return to favor of pop music in general, the Apples in Stereo will have an easy time making the world a better place to listen to music.

what to buy: As far as classic pop records go, *Tone Soul Evolution* ♫♫♫♫ (Spin Art, 1997, prod. Robert Schneider) is just that—a bona fide classic. The songs are layered in bright acoustics, with arrangements rivaling those of Brian Wilson. In a perfect world, "We'll Come to Be" and "Seems So" would be instant hits, and after one listen you'll be humming half of these songs in your sleep.

what to buy next: *Science Faire* ♫♫♫ (Spin Art, 1996, prod. Robert Schneider) is a compilation of rarities and early vinyl releases that shows the growth of Apples in Stereo. *Science Faire* also contains some early versions of songs from their first record, *Fun Trick Noisemaker* ♫♫♫ (Spin Art, 1995, prod. Robert Schneider).

influences:

◄◄ The Beach Boys, the Beatles, Sonic Youth

►► Olivia Tremor Control, Neutral Milk Hotel, Sloan

Chris Richards

Aqua

Formed 1993, in Denmark.

Lene Grawford Nystrom, vocals; Rene Dif, vocals; Soren Rasted, keyboards; Claus Norreen, keyboards.

Popular dance DJ Rene Dif put together this band with his pals Claus Norreen and Soren Rasted, who had recently won a national songwriting contest. The duo, who had been working at a gas station at the time, won the opportunity to write the soundtrack for a children's film. On one of his road trips as a DJ, Dif met Lene Grawford Nystrom and figured he'd found a frontperson for the group. The success of three group-written singles in Denmark turned into intercontinental acclaim when the third single, a piece of ear candy called "Barbie Girl," drew the attention of U.S. radio and the toymaker Mattel, which unsuc-

Fiona Apple (© Ken Settle)

cessfully sought an injunction against the song it felt did not show enough reverence towards its prize product. With the advent of Aqua, all three Scandinavian countries (Denmark, Sweden, and Norway) have had a breakout pop group with a two-syllable name bookended by the letter a. The open question is which career path Aqua is headed down—ABBA's or a-ha's?

what's available: *Aquarium* ♫♫♫ (MCA, 1997, prod. Soren Rasted, Claus Norreen, Rene Dif, others) pits Nystrom's Madonna-like vocals against Rif's deep-voiced cartoon histrionics, a perfect formula for big, bright pop. "Barbie Girl," the big hit, depends on a goofy "social comment" about undressing Barbie, and the best efforts here profit from similar lightheartedness. The "serious" ballads, such as "Be a Man," are standard-issue adult-contemporary fodder that suggest a long, irritating career is in the offing.

influences:

◀◀ Madonna, Ace of Base, ABBA, Missing Persons, the Chipmunks

Salvatore Caputo

The Aqua Velvets

Formed 1990, in San Francisco, CA.

Miles Corbin, guitar, piano, vocals; Michael Linder, bass, keyboards; Hank Maninger, guitar; Señor Jalapeño, percussion; Donn Spindt, drums; Steve Cameron, drums.

Shooting the curl of the surf-music revival is San Francisco's Aqua Velvets. Drawing inspiration from the glory days of guitar instrumentals—surfers like the Ventures, Dick Dale, and the Chantays, and the inland melodies of England's Hank Marvin & the Shadows—the Aqua Velvets have plunged forward to form their own distinctive reverb-happy sound sure to please the beach party crowd of the '90s. From the signature twang of a ripping surf guitar romp to a Link Wray–influenced spaghetti Western theme to a relaxing, feet-buried-in-the-sand lounge number, the band manages to separate itself from many neo-surf cohorts by blending a variety of genres into an inspiring, ultra cool, sun-soaked original.

what to buy: *Surfamania* ♫♫♫♫ (Mesa, 1995, prod. Michael Linder) is a 12-song collection of signature surf guitar romps, Henry Mancini–inspired spy anthems, and laid-back interstellar lounge numbers that give birth to thoughts of white sand and tropical breezes. *Guitar Noir* ♫♫♫♫ (Milan, 1997, prod. Michael Linder) is one of the best collections of modern surf guitar culture, offering a special mixture of exotic Middle Eastern sounds, instrumental surf serenades, and homages to the film noir soundtracks of the '40s, '50s, and early '60s.

what to buy next: The band's debut album, *The Aqua Velvets* ♫♫♫ (Heyday, 1992, prod. Michael Linder), was recorded in a mechanic's workshop, an atmosphere that apparently added zest to this distinguished assortment of garage rock–inspired surf originals.

the rest:

Nomad ♫♫♫ (Milan, 1996)

worth searching for: The soundtrack to the documentary film *Surfer Girl* (Mesa, 1995) features the Aqua Velvets along with an array of contemporaries.

influences:

◀◀ The Ventures, Link Wray, Hank Marvin & the Shadows, Dick Dale, the Sandals

▶▶ The Mermen, Jon & the Nightriders, the Malibooz

William Harmer

The Aquabats

Formed 1996, in Huntington Beach, CA.

Christian Jacobs (The Bat Commander), vocals; James Briggs (Jaime the Robot), saxes, clarinet, piano, vocals; Courtney Pollack (Chainsaw the Prince of Karate), guitars, vocals, samples; Adam Diebert (Prince Adam), trumpet, vocals; Chad Larson (Crash McLarson), bass guitar, organ, vocals; Boyd Terry (Catboy), trumpet, vocals; Travis Barker (The Baron Von Tito), drums, percussion; Charles Grey (Ultra Kyu), guitar, piano, banjo.

Headed by the "Bat Commander," Christian Jacobs, the Aquabats are equal parts madcapped (or -caped) adventure fantasists and ska-rock heroes. Chaos and a cartoonish theatricality characterize the band's live shows, where "aquacadets" (card-carrying fan club members) gather to "skank" with ska's only Super Friends. While it fits in musically with '90s bands such as the Mighty Mighty Bosstones, No Doubt, and Sublime, the Aquabats' intentionally oddball image makes them an acquired taste—especially when you're exposed to the Spandex, masks, and funny stage names.

what's available: *The Fury of the Aquabats* ♫♫♫ (Goldenvoice/Time Bomb, 1997 prod. Jim Goodwin) is a danceable Saturday morning cartoon-style riot that features "Captain Hampton and the Midget Pirates" and "Cat with 2 Heads."

influences:

◀◀ The Specials, Mighty Mighty Bosstones, No Doubt, Sublime, Spinal Tap

Norene Cashen

Arc Angels
/Storyville
/Doyle Bramhall II

Formed 1992, in Austin, TX.

Charlie Sexton, vocals, guitar; Doyle Bramhall II, guitar, vocals; Tommy Shannon, bass; Chris Layton, drums.

Following the tragic death of Stevie Ray Vaughan, Arc Angels came together for one album. Tommy Shannon and Chris Layton were the rhythm section for Vaughan's band Double Trouble, Doyle Bramhall II was a longtime Vaughan collaborator (and son of another well-known Austin blues singer, Doyle Bramhall), and Charlie Sexton was a teen rock prodigy burned out on the hype and looking for a situation in which he could grow. It wasn't to be, however, as the band split quickly and moved on to other projects—Bramhall and Sexton did solo albums, while Shannon and Layton went on to form Storyville with guitarist David Grissom and vocalist Malford Milligan.

what to buy: *Arc Angels* 🎵🎵🎵 (DGC, 1992, prod. Little Steven) reflects the band's Texas blues-rock background and is obviously meant as a tribute and final farewell to Stevie Ray; you can almost hear his voice on the track that laments his death, "See What Tomorrow Brings." Storyville's *Dog Years* 🎵🎵🎵 (Atlantic, 1998, prod. Stephen Bruton) is the best of this crew's offerings; it's a sharp, soulful set with laudable songcraft pumped by passionate musical performances.

solo outings:
Doyle Bramhall II:
Doyle Bramhall II 🎵🎵🎵 (Geffen, 1996)

Storyville:
Bluest Eyes 🎵🎵🎵 (November, 1994)
A Piece of Your Soul 🎵🎵🎵 (Atlantic, 1996)

influences:
◀◀ Stevie Ray Vaughan, Doyle Bramhall, the Fabulous Thunderbirds

see also: *Stevie Ray Vaughan, Charlie Sexton*

Jim Craddock and Gary Graff

Arcadia

See: Duran Duran

Tasmin Archer

Born in Bradford, Yorkshire, England.

With her silky voice and acoustic/synth-pop soul, British vocalist/songwriter Tasmin Archer evokes the intimate spirit common to Joan Armatrading and Seal. Far from merely imitating their efforts, Archer manages to make distinctive and only mildly derivative music on themes that are both confessional and inspirational.

what's available: *Great Expectations* 🎵🎵 (Capitol, 1993, prod. Steve Fitzmaurice, John Hughes, Peter Kaye, Julian Mendelsohn, Paul "Wix" Wickens) is promising, but despite the optimistic title it is certainly not the ground-breaking debut that would place Archer in the pantheon of British soul artists. The compelling opener, "Sleeping Satellite" (a hit in much of Europe), roots into the brain with a melody that grows organically from Archer's rich voice. It's a hard act to follow, as the rest of the album proves, although the sparely arranged "In Your Care" and the soul-bearing "Ripped Inside" are nicely done. Archer fares a little better with *Shipbuilding* 🎵🎵🎵 (Capitol EP, 1994, prod. Julian Mendelsohn), an album on which she hones her interpretative skills with capable covers of Elvis Costello songs ("Shipbuilding," "Deep Dark Truthful Mirror," "All Grown Up," "New Amsterdam") in addition to three live cuts and an acoustic version of "Sleeping Satellite."

worth searching for: Voted one of the top 40 albums of 1996 by Britain's *Mojo* magazine, *Bloom* (EMI, 1996, prod. Mitchell Froom), with its strong songwriting and Froom's sensuous production, is arguably Archer's strongest work to date. It's currently available only as a German import.

influences:
◀◀ Joan Artmatrading, Seal, Paul Weller
▶▶ Des'ree, R. Kelly

Christopher Scapelliti

Archers of Loaf
/Eric Bachmann

Formed 1991, in Chapel Hill, NC.

Eric Bachmann, guitar, vocals; Eric Johnson, guitar; Mark Price, drums; Matt Gentling, bass.

Along with the Grifters and Pavement, the Archers of Loaf are frequently cited as one of '90s indie rock's Great Hopes. Like those bands, the Archers go heavy on the open-tuned guitar drones, jagged hooks, and obtuse lyrics. Moreover, they're not above using the rock underground itself as subject matter—which may or may not insure that they age poorly. There's something very 1994 about a song such as "Greatest of All Time," in which "the frontman of the world's worst rock 'n' roll band" is chased and drowned by an angry mob. On the plus side, the Archers are extremely prolific, and principle songwriter Eric Bachmann's artier leanings always have room for bubblegum hooks. Even at his skronkiest, Bachmann is a hook machine.

what to buy: Their full-length debut, *Icky Mettle* 🎵🎵🎵 (Alias, 1993, prod. Caleb Southern), captures the Archers at their catchiest and most accessible. The single "Web in Front" (featuring the immortal chorus tagline, "All I ever wanted was to be your spine") carved the group's niche with college radio and made a prediction the Archers subsequently lived up to: "There's a chance that things will get weird." Bachmann's solo albums show a marked influence from Tom Waits; in fact, *Barry Black* 🎵🎵🎵 (Alias, 1995, prod. Caleb Southern) may be the best Waits album this side of *Rain Dogs*, with a cinematic vibe perfect for dark rainy nights. Equally quirky is *Tragic Animal Stories* 🎵🎵🎵 (Alias, 1997, prod. Eric Bachmann), which sounds as if Bachmann is bucking for a job as soundtrack director for Mutual of Omaha's *Wild Kingdom*. It's perfect background music for watching animals devour each other.

what to buy next: While the Archers have yet to make a bad record, those whose indie-rock credentials aren't in order may find the rest of the band's catalog a shade too tribal. That said, both *Vee Vee* 🎵🎵🎵 (Alias, 1995, prod. Archers of Loaf, Bob Weston) and *All the Nation's Airports* 🎵🎵🎵 (Alias/Elektra, 1996, prod. Brian Paulson, Archers of Loaf) have many fine moments. The latter album also betrays signs of an intriguing Brian Eno drone fetish that should prove interesting to watch develop.

the rest:
Archers of Loaf vs. the Greatest of All Time 🎵🎵🎵 (Alias, 1994)
The Speed of Cattle 🎵🎵🎵 (Alias, 1996)

worth searching for: The limited-edition live EP *Vitus Tinnitus* (Alias, 1997, prod. Brian Paulson) catches the Archers on a good night, with six live cuts, and adds worthwhile radio remixes of two tracks from the *Airports* album. Also worth tracking down is the EP *Cakes* (Pond Scum/Rockville, 1993, prod. Jerry Kee) by Bachmann's former band Small, which is solid in a Buffalo Tom/Dinosaur Jr. mold.

influences:
⏪ Pavement, Flaming Lips, Superchunk, Polvo, Rocket from the Crypt

⏩ Pipe

David Menconi

The Archies

Formed 1968, in Riverdale, NY.

Ron "Archie" Dante, vocals; Andy Kim, vocals; Ellie Greenwich, vocals; Toni Wine, vocals; Tony Passalacqua, vocals.

The Archies, who with the bubblegum classic "Sugar Sugar" were responsible for the top-selling American single of 1969, were often referred to within the music industry as "Kirshner's Revenge"—Kirshner being music mogul Don Kirshner, the self-proclaimed Man with the Golden Ears who was the musical director behind the Monkees' phenomenally successful television series. Frequent creative clashes with Michael Nesmith in

particular brought a rude end to Kirshner's Monkee business by early 1967, but within a year he'd confidently bounced back with his own label and a new band of TV popsters upon whom to work his charms. Only this time he made sure there would be no chance of "artistic differences" soiling his master plan. His new band would never, ever be able to question his decisions, musical or otherwise, for the Archies were merely comic book characters and soon-to-be-stars of their own Saturday morning cartoon series. When it came time to create hit records for this inanimate band, Kirshner, as he had with the Monkees, assembled a crack team of songwriters (Jeff Barry, Andy Kim) and session players (Dave Appell, Hugh McCracken) who, with Ron Dante's lead vocals, quickly scored a #1 hit with the Barry-Kim composition "Sugar Sugar" (originally planned as a vehicle for Monkee Davy Jones and later covered by Wilson Pickett). Other frothy Barry-produced (and Kirshner-published) hits followed before the Archies inevitably gave way to such real-life radio confections as the Osmonds and Bobby Sherman. Dante went on to create many successful records for Cher, Barry Manilow, and Pat Benatar as well as being the voice behind McDonald's "You Deserve a Break Today" jingle. Kim enjoyed a string of hits such as "Rock Me Gently" and a fine cover of Phil Spector's "Baby I Love You." And as for the Man with the Golden Ears, he arranged his greatest-ever marriage between television and rock in the mid-'70s as creator and host of *Don Kirshner's Rock Concert*, which in some quarters earns him the dubious title of "Father of MTV."

what's available: The only album even the most discerning student of cartoon rock need own is *The Archies Greatest Hits* 🎵🎵🎵 (Prime Cuts, 1997, prod. various), which includes each and every sugar-frosted hit and then some.

worth searching for: The original vinyl albums *Everything's Archie* (Calendar, 1969) and *Sunshine* (Kirshner, 1970) sport those big cereal box-size graphics which is an essential part of the Archies experience.

influences:
⏪ Bob Montana, Dante & the Evergreens, the Royal Guardsmen

⏩ The Cuff Links, the Banana Splits, the Wombles, Matthew Sweet

Gary Pig Gold

Jann Arden

Born Jann Arden Richards, March 27, 1962, in Calgary, Alberta, Canada.

Jann Arden's story is one of which rock 'n' roll books are made. As soon as she turned of age, Arden left the Calgary farming community in which she grew up to pursue a music career. Her first stages were street corners; these proved to be unhealthy venues, however, for she was "punched out" and "robbed" during such busking gigs. But the sidewalk soon led to safer ground in lounges where she covered a variety of artists including Olivia Newton-John, Mahalia Jackson, and Ray Charles.

what to buy: A collection of beautifully structured, full-throated pop songs, Arden's second album, *Living under June* ♪♪♪♪ (A&M, 1994, prod. Ed Cherney), made her a minor force in the burgeoning AAA radio format. Her songwriting, as in the delicate but spiteful ode to an ex-love, "Insensitive" ("I'm out of vogue/I'm out of touch/I fell too fast/I feel too much/I hope that you might have some advice to give/on how to be insensitive"), show a gem that's been shining from the beginning. Even on *Happy?* ♪♪♪♪ (A&M, 1998, prod. Ed Cherney, Jann Arden) Arden seems leery to accept happiness. On this album, however, she seems to have begun healing. The musically upbeat "I Know You" shows Arden's support for a friend she calls "a loser." The first single, "Wishing That," showcases Arden's wide-ranging vocal abilities, but once again she wishes for someone to love her the way she loves that person. With its music cascading like a waterfall, the most striking cut on the album is her cover of Lulu's "To Sir, with Love."

what to buy next: Her debut album, *Time for Mercy* ♪♪♪ (A&M, 1993, prod. Ed Cherney), boosted her into the spotlight in Canada and earned her two Juno Awards (the Canadian equivalent of the Grammys) for Most Promising Solo Performer and Best Video for "I Would Die for You." Required listening for anyone depressed over a lover.

influences:
◄◄ Sarah McLachlan, Joni Mitchell
►► Jewel, Chantal Kreviazuk

Christina Fuoco

Argent

Formed 1969, in London, England. Disbanded 1976.

Rod Argent, keyboards, vocals; Russ Ballard, guitar, vocals (1969–74); Jim Rodford, bass, vocals; Bob Henrit, drums; John Grimaldi, guitar, strings (1974–76); John Verity, guitar, bass, vocals (1974–76).

Arising from the ashes of the Zombies, Argent took the former's ethereal, minor-key approach a step further by adopting a more "progressive" approach, balancing Rod Argent's tasteful keyboards with Russ Ballard's guitar. All of its first album (*Argent*) and most of its second (*Ring of Hands*) are wondrous, harmony-laden delights, with songs such as "Like Honey," the original "Liar," "Bring You Joy," "Celebration," and "Pleasure" particular standouts; unfortunately, you can only get them

these days via the import route. By the time of its third album, Argent began sacrificing its vocal and songwriting strengths in favor of a slide down the Emerson, Lake & Palmer chute of wretched keyboard excess—though not before scoring a defining hit with "Hold Your Head Up."

what to buy: *All Together Now* ♪♪♪ (Epic, 1972/Koch International, 1997, prod. Chris White) features "Hold Your Head Up." The 1997 reissue contains seven bonus B-sides that weren't on the original album.

what to avoid: Regrettably, *The Argent Anthology: A Collection of Greatest Hits* ♪♪ (Epic, 1978/1987) gives short shrift to the band's first two albums in favor of its later output, which from the fourth album on is virtually unlistenable.

influences:
◄◄ The Zombies, the Beatles, Yes, Genesis
►► Starcastle, Kansas, James Taylor Quartet

see also: *The Zombies*

Mike Greenfield

Arkarna

Formed 1996, in London, England.

James Barnett, vocals, guitar, bass, keyboards; Ollie Jacobs, vocals, programming, keyboards; Lalo Creme, guitar, bass; Sebastian Beresford, drums.

In the midst of electronic music's late '90s resurgence rose the somewhat opportunistic rock-dance hybrid of England's Arkarna. Noted for its celebrity lineage (Lalo's dad is famed video director and former 10cc member Lol Creme) as much as for its predictable techno-fed apocalyptic angst, the band failed to really turn heads on either side of the Atlantic with its major label debut. Previous session work with Leftfield on the acclaimed *Leftism* record didn't really carry over into any noticeable industry credibility. Arkarna was, however, featured less-than-prominently on the mulitmillion dollar industry tool named *Batman & Robin: The Soundtrack*—a testimony to its importance, to be sure.

what's available: *Fresh Meat* ♪ (Reprise, 1991, prod. Arkarna) does less to defend its existence than it does to distract and eventually anger its listener. Insipid breakbeats and gratuitous guitar solos announce some vague revolution amenable to well-fed suburban 17-year-olds. "Future's Overrated," "House on Fire," and "Born Yesterday" (presented here in two movements) are clunky pretenders to the Prodigy throne, although perhaps with their older sister's EMF and Jesus Jones cutouts stuffed neatly in pocket.

influences:

◀◀ Jesus Jones, EMF, Prodigy, Leftfield, Carter the Unstoppable Sex Machine

Billy Manes

Joan Armatrading

Born December 9, 1950, in Basseterre, St. Kitts, West Indies.

Joan Armatrading's loyal cult following has kept her touring and recording for more than 25 years. Her revealing, emotionally charged lyrics and excellent though underrated guitar playing reveal a solid, consistent talent. Raised in England, Armatrading's first public notice came in 1970 when she appeared in *Hair* and began a folk collaboration with songwriter Pam Nestor. After one duo album, Armatrading went solo with a sound that blended jazz, Caribbean, and rock influences into a folk format; she was also among the first to bring synthesizers into an essentially acoustic setting. Her later work featuring electric guitars is less satisfying, but her steady songwriting skills have maintained the integrity of the music. The coordination and interplay between her vocals and her guitar playing lends distinction to much of her work.

what to buy: *Joan Armatrading* 𝄞𝄞𝄞𝄞 (A&M, 1976, prod. Glyn Johns) is full of pining lyrics and sparse arrangements that color and enhance her pleasing, husky voice. The anthemic gospel ending to "Love and Affection" tops off one of the most joyous and revealing ever looks at the effects of love. Some of her electric stuff does hit, and *The Key* 𝄞𝄞𝄞𝄞 (A&M, 1983, prod. Steve Lillywhite, Val Garay) is one of Armatrading's least introspective forays. There's a taste of the old Joan on "Drop the Pilot," "(I Love It When You) Call Me Names," and the title song, but she also casts an eye on the social ravages of drugs and violence. *Greatest Hits* 𝄞𝄞𝄞𝄞 (A&M, 1996, prod. various) is exactly that, and generous at 19 tracks.

what to buy next: Much of what fans like most about Armatrading is on *Back to the Night* 𝄞𝄞𝄞𝄞𝄞 (A&M, 1975, prod. Pete Gage), a spare, folkish work with great songs such as "Dry Land," "Cool Blue Stole My Heart," and "Body to Dust."

what to avoid: Armatrading's ability to produce a hook or memorable line largely evaded her on *Hearts and Flowers* 𝄞𝄞 (A&M, 1990 prod. Joan Armatrading), although the title tune is a keeper.

the rest:

Whatever's for Us 𝄞𝄞𝄞 (A&M, 1972)
Show Some Emotion 𝄞𝄞𝄞 (A&M, 1977)
To the Limit 𝄞𝄞𝄞𝄞 (A&M, 1978)
Me, Myself and I 𝄞𝄞𝄞𝄞 (A&M, 1980)
Walk under Ladders 𝄞𝄞𝄞 (A&M, 1981)
Track Record 𝄞𝄞𝄞𝄞 (A&M, 1983)

Sleight of Hand 𝄞𝄞𝄞𝄞 (A&M, 1986)
Classics, Vol. 21 𝄞𝄞𝄞𝄞 (A&M, 1986)
The Shouting Stage 𝄞𝄞𝄞 (A&M, 1988)
Square the Circle 𝄞𝄞𝄞 (A&M, 1992)
What's Inside 𝄞𝄞𝄞𝄞 (A&M, 1995)

worth searching for: The hard-to-find *Secret Secrets* (A&M, 1985, prod. Mike Howlett) contains some of Armatrading's most densely produced music, including horns, but the change does her good. There's a pervasive joy here so that even a bluesy lyric such as "Friends Not Lovers" gets delivered with a bouncy, infectious beat.

influences:

◀◀ Odetta, Joni Mitchell

▶▶ Tracy Chapman, Dionne Farris

Lawrence Gabriel

Army of Lovers

Formed 1990, in Sweden.

Alexander Bard, vocals, sitar, programming; Jean-Pierre Barda, vocals, drums; La Camilla, vocals (1990–92, 1995–present); De La Cour, vocals (1992–95).

Although they were billed as an international collective of diverse rhythms and sounds, Army of Lovers quickly grew into the audacious campfest they spent the bulk of their career revelling in. Blame it on the tiaras and tutus, if you'd like, but if nothing else, the unexpected bravado of this revolving trio on such gems as "Love Me Like a Loaded Gun" and the ubiquitous club anthem "Crucified" insured that it was all good fun. Add to that the wanton detachment of unexpected Euro-balladry in "Obsession" and "I Am," both fairly successful European singles, and you've got a winning combination more embarrassing than ABBA ever dreamed of being. The swapping of female leads at mid-career did little to change the sounds; the guys wrote the songs after all, and were arguably more effeminate, anyway. Army of Lovers has continued to record for its European audiences, releasing two more garish LPs and a well-received *Greatest Hits* (original vocalist, La Camilla, returned for all three after an acrimonious departure). A single, "Israelism," sparked international controversy for joking about Jewish stereotypes (despite the Jewish origins of two members) and consequently topped the Israeli pop charts. While Army is currently on hiatus, Alexander Bard fronts dance act Vacuum, and La Camilla is trying her luck as a solo act.

what to buy: The band hit its sequined apex with *Maximum Luxury Overdose* 𝄞𝄞𝄞 (Giant, 1992, prod. Alexander Bard, Anders Wollbeck, Per Adebradt), a variety show of dance pop with shaved legs and a hairy chest. Alternately cloying and endearing, Bard and company keep the kitsch at full volume throughout, crafting some truly classic pop moments in the process. Most of the record is a hands-in-the-air, anthemic blizzard (see the highly irreverent "Crucified"), but the rich texturing and vibrato shamelessness of it all sustain interest well enough to avoid promised overdose. Glam never bounced so hard.

what to buy next: *Army of Lovers* ♫♫♡ (Giant, 1991, prod. Alexander Bard) is a splendid affair of garish means. "Ride the Bullet" and "Baby's Got a Neutron Bomb" and their likes infuse an obvious high-energy dance routine with a costumed eccentrism. For the most part, it's a success, although many of its ideas seem undeveloped by comparison with later productions.

worth searching for: *Greatest Hits* (WEA Import, 1995) compiles the bands singles and a few remixes along with some other missed hits of later origin, specifically the charming "I Am" (which includes the confession, "I am . . . a Liberace fan.")

influences:
◀◀ Abba, B-52s, Pet Shop Boys, Ofrah Haza, Dead or Alive
▶▶ Aqua, Spice Girls

Billy Manes

Arrested Development /Speech /Dionne Farris

Formed 1988, in Atlanta, GA. Disbanded 1996.

Speech (born Todd Thomas), vocals; Headliner, DJ; Rasa Don, vocals, drums; Aerle Taree, vocals, dancer, stylist (1988–94); Montsho Eshe, dancer, choreographer; Baba Oje, spiritual adviser; Dionne Farris, vocals (1992–94); Ajile, vocals, dancer (1994–96); Kwesi, DJ, vocals (1994–96); Nadirah, vocals (1994–96).

Billed as the "positive" rap band that would counter all the "negative" gangstas and braggarts, Arrested Development borrowed liberally from Sly and the Family Stone and built on De La Soul to make one of the best albums in 1992 pop. Led by the upbeat young rapper Speech, the band eschewed violence, hatred, and misogyny and played up African American self-esteem and even Christianity. Drawing a connecting line through the history of 20th-century black music, AD built its songs out of blues samples and '70s funk riffs. Spike Lee was so impressed with the band's sense of history that he gave AD the leadoff track, "Revolution," to his jazz- and R&B-dominated *Malcolm X* soundtrack. Unfortunately, the band had little staying power, breaking up after its tedious sophomore album. Dionne Farris, a part-time singer in the band, surprisingly outshone Speech when her solo album was better received and became a bigger hit than his.

what to buy: Packed with sunny chants and Dionne Farris's strong singing, the hit single, "Tennessee," was just one of the many highlights on the band's terrific debut, *3 Years, 5 Months & 2 Days in the Life of . . .* ♫♫♫♫ (Chrysalis/EMI, 1992, prod. Speech). Among the others: the decidedly anti-gangsta "People Everyday," which slyly reworks "Everyday People."

what to buy next: Farris's solid solo debut, *Wild Seed—Wild Flower* ♫♫♫ (Columbia, 1995, prod. Dionne Farris, others), led off with the year's funkiest hit, "I Know."

what to avoid: *Unplugged* ♫♫ (Chrysalis, 1993, prod. Alvin Speights, Speech) doles out inferior alternate versions of the debut's fresh songs.

the rest:
Zingalamaduni ♫♫ (Chrysalis, 1994)

worth searching for: The soundtrack to *Malcolm X* (Reprise/Warner Bros., 1992, prod. Spike Lee, Quincy Jones) brilliantly lines up AD's "Revolution" (also released on an extended EP), with classics by bluesmen Joe Turner and Junior Walker, jazz legends Billie Holiday, John Coltrane, and Duke Ellington, and R&B stars Ray Charles, Louis Jordan, and Aretha Franklin.

solo outings:
Speech:
Speech ♫♫♡ (Chrysalis, 1996)

influences:
◀◀ Public Enemy, De La Soul, Sly & the Family Stone, Gang Starr, Jungle Brothers, Dream Warriors, Last Poets, Boogie Down Productions
▶▶ Fugees, Digable Planets, Basehead, Spearhead

Steve Knopper

The Art of Noise

Formed 1983, in London, England. Disbanded 1990. Re-formed 1997.

Anne Dudley, keyboards, string arrangements (1983–90, 1997–present); J.J. Jeczalik, Fairlight, keyboards (1983–90); Gary Langan, engineer (1983–86); Lol Creme (1997–present).

Hailed by hip-hop and techno musicians for its pioneering use of samplers as song construction tools rather than random noise boxes, the Art of Noise was formed in 1983 as a side project of studio wizards J.J. Jeczalik, Gary Langan, and Anne Dudley, who had been brought together by Trevor Horn for the production of Yes's *90125* album and Frankie Goes to Hollywood's *Welcome to the Pleasuredome* sessions. With guidance from Horn and conceptual packaging by Paul Morley, the group's first experiments, captured on *Into Battle* and *Who's Afraid*, were catchy, arty instrumentals assembled almost entirely from pre-recorded sound snippets via Horn's newly-purchased Fairlight sampling keyboard—one of the first such devices ever made. After scoring dance chart success with "Beat Box" and its drastically remixed counterpart, "Close (to the Edit)," the Art of Noise split from the ZTT camp in 1985 over creative differences. Its subsequent releases through China Records, although generally well-received, included syrupy orchestral arrangements, dodgy novelty collaborations (a dance track featuring manufactured media personality Max Headroom, a cover of Prince's "Kiss" featuring Tom Jones, and the Grammy award-winning "Peter Gunn" remake with twang legend Duane Eddy), and an uninteresting string of remixes, compilations, and reissues. An amicable parting in 1990 allowed Dudley and Jeczalik to pursue solo projects; Dudley continued her orchestral work for film soundtracks, and Jeczalik released a sample CD, then emerged as progressive house act Art of Silence in late 1995. After losing Seal, Horn and Morley re-formed Art of Noise on Horn's faltering ZTT label in 1997, this time with Dudley and 10cc vet Lol Creme as the principal members, hoping to "marry Debussy with drum 'n' bass." The album *The Seduction of Claude Debussy* is due on ZTT in late 1998.

what to buy: An electronic music classic, the concept album *Who's Afraid Of? (The Art of Noise!)* ♫♫♫♫ (ZTT/Island, 1984, prod. Trevor Horn, Paul Morley, the Art of Noise) has itself been sampled by scores of musicians in tribute. *In Visible Silence* ♫♫♫♫ (China/Chrysalis/Off Beat, 1986, prod. the Art of Noise) is more accessible and equally competent, although it is markedly different from—in fact, almost a parody of—the band's ZTT-era sound. Although bombastic at times, *In No Sense? Nonsense!* ♫♫♫♫ (China/Chrysalis, 1987, prod. Anne Dudley, J.J. Jeczalik) is an engaging stereophonic tour de force, seamlessly gliding from string interludes to boys choirs to dance tracks and beyond; worlds away from "Beat Box," it is the cream of the post-ZTT Art of Noise.

what to buy next: Dismissed as "pretentious" by some critics, *Below the Waste* ♫♫♫ (China/Polydor, 1989, prod. Anne Dudley, J.J. Jeczalik) is the least challenging of the band's output but makes a good follow-up to *In No Sense? Nonsense!* The African-influenced tracks—"Dan Dare", "Chain Gang," and "Yebo!"—are well worth the price.

what to avoid: Steer clear of all the post-ZTT cash-in compilations, including all variations of *The Best of the Art of Noise* ♫♫ (China/Polydor/Discovery, 1988); the lackluster and dated remix albums *The Ambient Collection* ♫♫ (China/Polydor/Discovery, 1990), *The FON Mixes* ♫♫ (China/Discovery, 1991), and *The Drum and Bass Collection* ♫♫ (China/Discovery, 1996); and the *State of the Art* (China/Discovery, 1997) compilation of the three remix albums.

the rest:
Re-Works of Art of Noise ♫ (China/Chrysalis, 1986)
The Best of the Art of Noise (second edition) ♫♫ (China/Discovery, 1992)

worth searching for: The import-only compilation *Daft* (ZTT/Warner, 1986) contains all of *Who's Afraid . . .* plus remixes of "Moments in Love" and a long version of "Snapshot." The band's vinyl debut, *Into Battle with the Art of Noise* (ZTT/Island, 1983), contains the original hit versions of "Beat Box" and "Moments in Love," neither of which has yet seen a re-release.

solo outings:
Anne Dudley:
(With Jaz Coleman) *Songs from the Victorious City* ♫♫♫♫ (China/Polydor/TVT, 1991)
Alice in Wonderland: Symphonic Variations ♫♫♫ (Sound Stage, 1994)
Ancient and Modern ♫♫♫ (The Echo Label, 1995)

J.J. Jeczalik:
The Art of Sampling ♫♫♫ (AMG, 1994)
(As Art of Silence) *artofsilence.co.uk* ♫♫♫♫ (Permanent, 1996)

influences:
◀◀ Kraftwerk, Claude Debussy, Tangerine Dream, Mike Oldfield, John Cage

▶▶ Future Sound of London, the Orb, 808 State, William Orbit, Yello, Shinjuku Thief, Global Communication, Severed Heads, Goldie, Roni Size & Reprezant

Mike Brown

Artful Dodger
Formed as Brat, c. 1973, in Fairfax, VA. Disbanded c. 1981.

Steve Brigida, drums, percussion; Steve Cooper, bass, vocals; Gary Cox, guitar, vocals (1975–79); Gary Herrewig, guitar, backing vocals; Billy Paliselli, lead vocals; Peter Bonta, piano (1980).

What if Badfinger and the Faces merged into one band? Artful Dodger combined the best qualities of those acts into a powerful pop approach that should have ruled the AM and FM airwaves by divine right. The group was an incredible live act, and it cut some terrific tracks. But, although big in Cleveland, the group's records never even charted, and Artful Dodger never got its due. The group split at the dawn of the MTV era but left behind a legacy of prime power pop that is overdue for rediscovery and reappraisal.

what to buy: *Artful Dodger* ♫♫♫♫ (Columbia, 1975/Pendulum, 1997, prod. Jack Douglas) is one of the great forgotten pop classics of the '70s, an essential album nearly on a par with the best of Big Star, the Raspberries, and the Flamin' Groovies. "Wayside," "You Know It's Alright," "Think Think," "Things I'd Like to Do Again," the transcendent "It's Over," and the unbelievable "Follow Me" are the sort of sparkling, radio-ready gems that no self-respecting pop fan can ignore; the fact that such a superb album remains relatively obscure and unknown is nothing short of maddening.

what to buy next: *Honor among Thieves* ♫♫♫ (Columbia, 1976/Pendulum, 1997, prod. Edward Leonetti, Jack Douglas) isn't as consistent as the debut but still succeeds on the strength of infectious Beatlisms like "Not Enough" and "Hey Boys."

worth searching for: Artful Dodger's third and fourth albums have yet to be reissued, so completists will need to hunt through the used LP bins. *Babes on Broadway* (Columbia, 1977, prod. Eddie Leonetti) is the group's least-essential work, done in by too much plodding material; only the album-opening "Can't Stop Pretending" and a closing rave-up of Eddie Cochran's "C'mon Everybody" redeem matters. *Rave On* (Ariola, 1980, prod. Artful Dodger, Bob Dawson) is a welcome return to form and a far more fitting farewell from this great band.

influences:

◄◄ The Beatles, the Rolling Stones, the Faces, the Dave Clark Five, Badfinger, the Raspberries

►► The Romantics, the Babys, the Flashcubes, Off Broadway USA, Del Amitri

Carl Cafarelli

Artificial Joy Club

Formed 1995, in Ottawa, Canada.

Sal, vocals; Leslie Howe, guitar, keyboards; Michael Goyette, guitar; Tim Dupont, bass; Andrew Lamarche, drums.

The mid-'90s will most likely be remembered in the volumes of music history as a time of disposable guitar pop about disposable lifestyles—clumsy prose of uncultivated defiance splattered about heady guitar whine and electronic sample beats to the delight of those under the age of 17. Alanis Morissette's now legendary felatio invective spawned a whole slew of similarly explosive, ready-to-rant she-rockers who preferred to eschew the process and shoot straight to the point. Whether or not this is a good thing is irrelevant, as the marketability of said abrasive behavior has already, by most accounts, outlasted its welcome. Artificial Joy Club is a collaboration of several Canadian scenesters—including early Morissette mentor Leslie Howe—that grew out of Sal's Birdland and is probably one of the movements casualties. Sal, the uni-monikered frontwoman, stands as a compromise between the crowd-pleasing bounce of Gwen Stefani and the stumbling pop-culture thesaurus of Morissette. But this spectacle lacks the actual song structures that save the others from their own caricatured silliness.

what's available: *Melt* ♫ (Crunchy, 1997, prod. Leslie Howe, Serge Cote) is about as obvious as alt-pop gets; the band holed up in an L.A. studio for a rigorous month of sweatlodged pop-thought, and all we got was this lousy T-shirt. Mining the internet for nearly every insincere reference imaginable (including dated unsavories Jack Kevorkian and *Forrest Gump*), the record is a clumsy grocery list of insincerities. Taken as a study in Gen-X apathy, that would be fine, but as an album it is almost as devoid of interest as its smug perpetrators seem to be. A jagged little pill, indeed.

worth searching for: For additional punishment, Artificial Joy Club can be found on the soundtrack to the 1998 Jon Bon Jovi film *Homegrown*.

influences:

◄◄ Blondie, Scandal (featuring Patti Smythe), T'Pau, Alanis Morissette, No Doubt

Billy Manes

Daniel Ash

See: Love & Rockets

Asia

Formed 1981, in Los Angeles, CA.

Carl Palmer, drums; Geoff Downes, keyboards; John Wetton, bass, vocals (1981–83, 1985–92); Steve Howe, guitar (1981–85, 1992); Greg Lake, bass, vocals (1983–85); Mandy Meyer, guitar (1985–86); Pat Thrall, guitar (1990–92); John Payne, bass, vocals (1992); Al Pitrelli, guitar (1992).

Formed from alumni of '70s art-rock bands such as Emerson, Lake & Palmer, Yes, and King Crimson, Asia became the last true supergroup of that era, cranking out albums that vacillated between arty instrumental pretension and intermittent stabs at pop success. Though its debut record launched two huge hits, each subsequent album seemed less and less focused, probably because of the revolving door of members that saw both John Wetton and Steve Howe leave and rejoin the group twice each. By the mid-'90s, the band was intermittently active and propped up by various studio musicians and road hacks—a brand name good for nostalgia tours and anthology records only.

what to buy: With two hit singles and a few listenable instrumental excursions, *Asia* ♫♫♫ (Geffen, 1982, prod. Mike Stone) is the best example of the group's formula, a precarious balance between arty rock ambition and bombastic pop appeal. Sure, it's crass and pretentious, but "Heat of the Moment" and "Only Time Will Tell" are the most appealing tunes this band has ever produced.

what to buy next: To save endless plodding through pointless collections of instrumental noodling and directionless art-pop compositions, the compilation-of-sorts *Then and Now* ♫♫ (Geffen, 1990, prod. various) collects Asia's six most successful tunes with four new ones. Of course, this means you'll have to wade through the new stuff, co-written by the likes of former teen idol David Cassidy and Sex Pistol Steve Jones and about as brainless as art rock gets.

what to avoid: *Aqua* **woof!** (JRS, 1992, prod. Geoff Downes) is the worst of a bad lot, a pointless excursion that misses Wetton's vocals and suffers for ex–Alice Cooper guitarist Al Pitrelli's hamhanded noodling.

the rest:
Alpha ♫♫♫ (Geffen, 1983)
Astra ♫♫ (Geffen, 1985)
Live in Moscow ♫♫ (Rhino, 1990)
Aria ♫♫ (JRS, 1994)
Archiva, Vol. 1 ♫♫♫ (Resurgent, 1996)
Archiva, Vol. 2 ♫♫♫ (Resurgent, 1996)
Archives, Vol. 1 ♫♫♫ (Pavement, 1997)
Archives ♫♫ (CAS, 1997)
Now Nottingham Live ♫♫ (Resurgent, 1997)
Live in Osaka ♫♫♫ (Resurgent, 1997)
Live in Köln ♫♫ (Resurgent, 1997)
Live in Philadelphia ♫♫ (Resurgent, 1997)

worth searching for: Without exception, Asia bandmembers did their best work elsewhere. Check out the catalogs of Yes (Howe, Downes), U.K. and King Crimson (Wetton), Emerson, Lake & Palmer (Palmer), and the Buggles (Downes) to hear these musicians in their primes.

influences:
◄◄ Yes, King Crimson, Emerson, Lake & Palmer, Kansas, Styx
►► Zebra, Marillion, Saga, Dream Theater

see also: *Yes, King Crimson, the Buggles, Roxy Music, Uriah Heep, Emerson, Lake & Palmer*

Eric Deggans

Ass Ponys

Formed 1989, in Cincinnati, OH.

Randy Cheek, bass, vocals; Chuck Cleaver, vocals, guitar; John Erhardt, guitar, vocals (1989–95); Don Kleingers, drums, percussion, vocals (1989–91; David Morrison, drums, percussion, organ (1991–present); Bill Alletzhauser, guitar (1996–present).

The Ass Ponys may have formed in Cincinnati, amidst sagging urban industry and Victorian houses, but their music remains inescapably rooted in the small Ohio town that gave birth to Chuck Cleaver and where he has lived for some years. Cleaver has a high, uncertain voice reminiscent of Pere Ubu's David Thomas, writes short song-portraits reminiscent of Sherwood Anderson, and outfits them with a jangle vaguely reminiscent of every band that once influenced R.E.M. After two indie releases and perhaps on the strength of producer John Curley, whose full-time gig is with the Afghan Whigs, the Ass Ponys were swept onto a major label during the mid-'90s alt-rock frenzy, and they did nothing right except make fine music. Too old, unexceptional when photographed, and, well, how were you going to get that name back-announced on radio? (And never mind that the Butthole Surfers finally had a hit; the Ass Ponys had already been dropped by then.) Of course they got dropped, but not before recording portaits of small town life far more authentic than anything Bruce Springsteen (or even Steve Earle) has managed in years.

what to buy: A&M picked up the $2,500 (or so the myth goes) *Electric Rock Music* ♫♫♫♫ (A&M, 1994, prod. John Curley, Ass Ponys) for good reason. Created in the creatively freeing vacuum of indifference, *Electric Rock Music* is a gentle masterpiece, full of the oddments of small town life (including grandma's craftworks, which adorn the album cover), told with the winsome bent of a whiskey-sipping crackerbarrel philosopher.

what to buy next: Reflecting the trauma caused by the departure of John Erhardt, and probably an attempt to please the label, *The Known Universe* ♫♫♫ (A&M, 1996, prod. John Curley, Ass Ponys) is a more careful creation. In any kind of just universe, however, the glorious dry pop of "It's Summertime Here" should have become an annual radio ritual.

what to avoid: Despite the usual stunning vignettes, *Mr. Superlove* ♫♫♫ (Okra, 1990, prod. John Curley) suffers a bit from Curley's then-primitive recording facilities (Cleaver recalls cutting a guitar solo while jumping on the bed).

the rest:
Grim ♫♫♫ (Safe House, 1993)

worth searching for: Back in 1994 or so, the Ass Ponys recorded "Not Happy" for the *Pere Ubu Tribute Thing* which may or may not have come out on a label called Datapanik. If it can be found, please forward a copy to the author, for it's an inspired linking of two of Ohio's most engaging eccentrics.

influences:
◄◄ Pere Ubu, R.E.M., Afghan Whigs
►► They're kind of in a class by themselves now.

Grant Alden

The Associates /Associates

Formed 1976, in Dundee, Scotland. Disbanded 1982.

Billy Mackenzie, vocals, various instruments; Alan Rankine, various instruments except drums.

The early-'80s music of the Associates would sound just fine at any rave today. At the earliest part of the group's career, lyricist Billy Mackenzie and composer Alan Rankine produced some impressive dance music, distinguished by Rankine's tuneful arrangements and Mackenzie's theatrical voice, which was only somewhat less high and shrill than that of the Cure's Robert Smith. As the Associates, they wrote gloomy, nihilistic music about rejection and doomed relationships. Uncharacteristic of many bands from this period, the group shied away from synthesizers, concentrating arrangements on solid dance rhythms driven by percussion and bass. The music could be harsh and stark ("Tell Me Easter's on Friday," "It's Better This Way"), but the duo also was capable of producing well-textured dance pop devoid of the usual techno-synth excesses, as it did on the excellent single "Party Fears Two." But by the group's first American release, 1982's *Sulk*, Rankine had succumbed to the lure of synthesizers, and Mackenzie had subverted his intellectual perspective on relationships to shallow, self-conscious posturing. The duo split on the eve of its first major British tour in 1982. Rankine moved to Brussels, where he has worked extensively with ex–Josef K member Paul Haig on a number of solo recordings. Mackenzie continued recording and performing solo under the name Associates and later the Associates, teaming up with guitarist Steve Reid and producers Martin Rushent and Julian Mendelsohn. While Mackenzie's musical output has at times been surprisingly strong (as on the 1985 flop *Take Me to the Girl*), his better instincts have been undone repeatedly by his Eurodisco fascination.

worth searching for: *Popera: The Singles Collection* (Sire/ Warner Bros., 1990, prod. various) compiles the essential material from the Associates' unsteady career, including "Party Fears Two." The omission of "It's Better This Way" is unforgivable, however. Now out of print, you'll have to dig around to find this one.

influences:

◀◀ David Bowie, Kraftwerk, Joy Division

▶▶ The Cure, New Order, nine inch nails, Goldie

Christopher Scapelliti

The Association

Formed 1965, in Los Angeles, CA. Disbanded mid-'70s. Re-formed 1981.

Russ Giguere, guitar (1965–68, 1981–present); Brian Cole, bass (1965–72); Terry Kirkman, woodwinds; Gary Alexander, guitar (1965–68); Jim Yester, guitar, sax; Ted Bluechel, drums; Terry Ramos, guitar (1968–present); Richard Thompson, guitar (1970–73).

The Association is remembered today as wimp-rock specialists, but the group made its early reputation as progressive folk-rockers with a counterculture message, albeit a rumored one: "Along Comes Mary," the group's peppy first hit in 1966, was supposedly about marijuana, and some radio stations refused to play it. The group made a more overt statement with the funereal anti–Vietnam War ode "Requiem for the Masses" in 1967. But its biggest hits were memorable for their keen melodies and airy, chorale-like harmonies, though the songs that have lasted are indeed sappy puffs of pop—"Cherish," "Windy," "Never My Love." The Association can be found these days on the oldies circuit.

what to buy: *Greatest Hits* ✠✠✠✠ (Warner Bros./Seven Arts, 1968, prod. various) has all the chart-climbers plus the lofty-minded but ponderous "Requiem for the Masses" and the generational anthem "Enter the Young."

what to buy next: History buffs can enjoy rocking versions of "Along Comes Mary" and "Windy" on Rhino's box set *Monterey International Pop Festival* ✠✠✠✠ (Rhino, 1992, prod. Stephen K. Peeples, Geoff Gans, executive prod. Lou Adler). The Association played the first day of the festival, but the collection is more notable for other artists.

what to avoid: The group in one form or another continues to release albums. Don't bother with *Association 1995: A Little Bit More* **woof!** (On Track, 1995, prod. Stan Vincent, John Allen), a vile album of mostly Vegas-style oldies covers that only serves to stain the original group's accomplishments with a greasy veneer of cheap nostalgia.

influences:

◀◀ The Weavers, the Kingston Trio, Peter, Paul & Mary, Simon & Garfunkel, the Mamas & the Papas, the Byrds

▶▶ The Carpenters, Bread, Up with People

Gil Asakawa

Rick Astley

Born February 6, 1966, in Newton-le-Willows, England.

Discovered by the production team of Stock, Aitken, and Waterman, Rick Astley sent many teenage girls' hearts aflutter with his soulful voice and patented dance songs, but it never got deeper than that, and he was eventually discarded as a temporary flavor that had lost its appeal.

what to buy: His debut, *Whenever You Need Somebody* ✠✠✠ (RCA, 1987, prod. Phil Harding, Ian Curnow, Daize Washbourn), made him a certified teeny-bop star with the hits "Never Gonna

Give You Up," "Together Forever," "It Would Take a Strong, Strong Man," and the oft-covered "When I Fall in Love."

what to avoid: Astley's fans got older and his crack production team got weaker—all of which dampened his sophomore effort, *Hold Me in Your Arms* &&& (RCA, 1988, prod. Matt Aitken, Rick Astley, Ian Curnow, Phil Harding, Daize Washbourn). "She Wants to Dance with Me" inundated the airwaves, but the album's success ended there.

the rest:
Free &&& (RCA, 1991)

influences:
◄◄ Marvin Gaye, Smokey Robinson, Bobby Sherman, George Michael

►► Lisa Stansfield, Jimmy Ray

Christina Fuoco

The Astronauts

Formed 1961, in Boulder, CO. Disbanded 1966.

Rich Fifield, guitar; Jim Gallagher, drums; Bob Demmon, guitar; Dennis Lindsey, guitar; Jon "Stormy" Patterson, bass.

A surf band from Boulder, Colorado? The lack of water didn't deter the Astronauts, who during the early '60s were legitimate rivals of the Beach Boys. Rich Fifield's echoey, staccato plucking—part of the band's three-guitar attack—drew heavily from the king of surf guitar, Dick Dale. The young, primly dressed band quickly strung together a big Colorado following before RCA decided to make the musicians stars. The Astronauts briefly tasted national fame when their 1963 version of Lee Hazelwood's "Baja" hit #64. When the surf craze gave way to the British Invasion, however, the Astronauts found themselves without music careers. Only Fifield continues to play in bands, mostly around Boulder, and Lindsey, who apparently never fully re-adjusted after military service in Vietnam, died in 1992.

what to buy: The Astronauts' original albums have finally been reissued on CD: *Surfin' with the Astronauts* &&& (RCA Victor, 1963/Collectables, 1997, prod. Al Schmitt), which contains fun surf songs such as "Baja," Dale's "Miserlou," the "Batman" theme, and others, was at the time an attempt to simply package an entire LP around a popular single. But the album, now a two-in-one CD paired with *Everything Is A O-K* &&& (RCA Victor/Collectables, 1997)—which, evidenced by the version of "If I Had a Hammer," isn't quite as worthwhile—stays surprisingly fresh for its short duration. The two-LP collection *Competition Coupe/Orbit Campus* &&& (RCA Victor, 1964/Collectables, 1997) is worth the price for the great *Competition Coupe*, which shifts the focus from surf boards to hot rods ("'55 Bird," "650 Scram-

bler," "Devil Driver's Theme," and, go figure, "The Hearse"). *Orbit Campus* doesn't have quite the same oomph, however.

what to buy next: Notable Astronauts songs continue to hit prominent CD compilations: *Legends of Guitar—Rock: The '60s, Vol. 1* &&&& (Rhino, 1990, prod. various) showcases Fifield's echoey surf style on "Hot-Doggin'" among tracks featuring Ry Cooder, Chet Atkins, Jeff Beck, Steve Cropper, and Dick Dale. The superb four-disc *Cowabunga! The Surf Box* &&&& (Rhino, 1996, compilation prod. John Blair, James Austin) does a great job of recalling the forgotten early-'60s surf bands, including the 'nauts with "Baja."

what to avoid: The band's early LPs, after *Surfin' with the Astronauts* and *Competition Coupe*, are valuable only for collectors and diehard surf-music fans. The two-in-one collections *Down the Line/Travelin' Man* && (RCA Victor/Collectables, 1997) and *Go Go Go/For You from Us* && (RCA Victor/Collectables, 1997) are the sad sounds of an uninspired band that had lost its trend.

worth searching for: The only way to find the Astronauts' two best albums, *Competition Coupe* and *Surfin' with the Astronauts* packaged together is on a German import label, the Bear Family, which also put out the *Live* and *Rarities* collections during 1992.

influences:
◄◄ Dick Dale, the Ventures, the Beach Boys, Chuck Berry, the Rolling Stones

►► Man or Astro-Man?, Laika & the Cosmonauts

Steve Knopper

Aswad

Formed 1975, in Ladbroke Grove, England.

Brinsley Forde, vocal, guitar; Courtney Hemmings, vocal, keyboard (1975–78); Donald Benjamin, vocal, guitar (1975–83); Ras George Levi, bass (1975–80); Angus "Drummie" Zeb, vocal, drums; Tony Gad Robinson, vocal, keyboards, bass (1979–present).

Aswad ranks among the best and most long-lived of British reggae bands. The group first hit the scene with a militant brand of reggae, though later it proved itself adept at rock, too. It was the first U.K. reggae group to sign with a major recording company, Island, in 1976. Although a hit among reggae enthusiasts, Aswad aspired to larger audiences. During the '80s, the group began adding pop influences to the music. The results were uneven, crossover stardom never came, and reggae purists charged that the group had lost its roots. A trio since 1986, Aswad's recent return to more rootsy music has gained some critical attention, but the outside influences remain. As Forde says: "We're driving a reggae vehicle, but we're carrying a lot of passengers."

what to buy: The group has been through a lot of changes, but *Aswad* 🎵🎵🎵🎵 (Island, 1976, prod. Tony Platt, Aswad) captures the uncompromising stance of mid-'70s reggae. "I a Rebel Soul," "Can't Stand the Pressure," and "Back to Africa" are all classics, and the band showed some dub ability on "Ethiopian Rhapsody" and "Red Up." *Crucial Tracks—The Best of Aswad* 🎵🎵🎵🎵 (Mango, 1989, prod. various) culls the best from the '80s work and pulls out some pearls. "Gimme the Dub," a U.K.-only single included here, is a dance-club slammer. Fans with deeper pockets and greater interest may want to spring for the two-disc set *Roots Rocking: The Island Anthology* 🎵🎵🎵🎵.

what to buy next: *Rise and Shine Again!* 🎵🎵🎵🎵 (Mesa, 1995, prod. various) is full of uplifting messages and upbeat dance grooves. "Shine," "Warriors," and "Pickin' Up" move the militant attitude into a self-improvement mode.

what to avoid: *Distant Thunder* 🎵🎵 (Mango, 1988, prod. Aswad) aimed at an elusive crossover audience it never reached.

the rest:

Hulet 🎵🎵🎵 (Mango, 1979)
A New Chapter of Dub 🎵🎵🎵 (Mango, 1982)
Live and Direct 🎵🎵🎵🎵 (Mango, 1983)
Rebel Souls 🎵🎵🎵🎵 (Mango, 1984)
Going to the Top 🎵🎵 (Simba, 1986)
To the Top 🎵🎵 (Mango, 1989)
Too Wicked 🎵🎵🎵 (Mango, 1990)
Showcase 🎵🎵🎵🎵 (Mango, 1990)
Rise and Shine 🎵🎵🎵🎵 (Mesa, 1994)
Dub: The Next Frontier 🎵🎵🎵🎵 (Mesa, 1995)
Big Up 🎵🎵🎵🎵 (Mesa, 1997)

influences:

◀◀ Toots & the Maytals, Freddie McGregor

▶▶ Patra, Big Mountain

Lawrence Gabriel

Atari Teenage Riot

Formed 1992, in Berlin, Germany.

Alec Empire, programming, shouts; Hanin Elias, vocals; Carl Crack, MC.

Atari Teenage Riot is interested in things coming together—be it the processed textures of electronica and the spontaneous fury of punk in its self-coined genre of "digital hardcore," or the divided communities and music world of post–Cold War Germany. Based in a troubled Berlin and drawing its lineup from that city, Syria, and Swaziland, ATR makes a stand against both escalating racism and the stylistically sectarian club scene with which it is coming to have all too much in common. Defiantly individualistic, the trio records in Germany on its own label and pack squatter-occupied alternative venues for concerts of their music and that of other artists they judge unjustly deprived of mainstream exposure. Its stance and sound are extreme to some ears, but not inappropriate to its home situation. ATR is as much mission as music: In the words of founder Empire, "Riot sounds produce riots!"

what's available: ATR's one U.S. release so far, the compilation *Burn, Berlin, Burn!* 🎵🎵🎵 (Grand Royal, 1997, prod. Alec Empire), neatly summarizes its parallel tendencies toward artful subversion and artless harangue. "Atari Teenage Riot," "Delete Yourself," "Into the Death," "Death Star," and "Speed" comprise the truly unique stuff; they all combine bleepy minimal melodies and insinuating vocals to sound like a video-game or computer screen suddenly reprogrammed by pirate satellite or poltergeist to play hypnotic tunes and issue cryptic provocations. This would make a good EP, but the other nine tracks are full of infantile slogan-screaming, ultra-derivative hardcore, and humorlessly elementary electronica that make ATR sound like some major-label CEO's crack at an aggro Spice Girls.

influences:

◀◀ Public Enemy, Rage Against the Machine, Emergency Broadcast Network, Dead Kennedys

Adam McGovern

A3
/Alabama 3

Formed 1995, in Brixton, South London, England.

Larry Love, vocals; the Very Reverend Dr. D. Wayne Love, vocals; the Mountain of Love, harmonica, analog terrorism; Sir Real "Congaman" Love, percussion, acoustic guitar; Mississippi Guitar Love, guitar; L.B. Dope, drums; the Spirit, keyboards; the Book of Love, security; I.V. Lenin, socialism in the Mainline; Lady Love and Little Eye Tie, D. Wayne's ladies.

Arising from the Coldharbour Lane scene in Brixton along with fellow technotronic raconteurs the Headrillaz, A3 mixes joyous electronic dance music with twisted bits of Southern gospel and an almost divine reverence toward Elvis Presley. Imagine Dexy's Midnight Runners tossed into the retro-blown future and you begin to understand the full blown, country time neon cowboy/back woods ecclesiastical jamboree that is A3. The group was originally called Alabama 3 but the country group Alabama brought a lawsuit against the Brits, causing them to shorten the name to A3. The group made waves by releasing two singles, "Ain't Goin' to Goa" and "Woke up This Morning" on Elemental Records in the U.K. prior to its debut album.

what's available: *Exile on Coldharbour Lane* 🎜🎜🎜🎝 (Geffen, 1997, prod. Matthew "Boss Hog" Vaughan & the Ministers at Work) launched successful tracks such as the title cut and the rousing "Ain't Goin' to Goa," which flips some weird gospel of the electronic meditation vibes, dusted country joe two-step breakbeats, and supercharged harmonica blasts into a catchy rhythm shaker. The rest of the album is firmly packed with a tasty aural potpourri ranging from the burbling bass and mouth harp jammy "Speed of Loneliness," which sounds like ultra·hip Billy Joel crossed with electric cowboy aesthetics, to the twang infested barroom boogie of "The Night We Nearly Got Busted." Never willing to succumb to categorization, the group also dishes out some acoustic Lonesome Dove–inflected DJ tricknology on "Peace in the Valley" as well as some revelatory synth-riddled dance grooves on the "Bourgeoisie Blues."

influences:
◀◀ Dexy's Midnight Runners, Stereo MC's, Headrillaz, Elvis Presley, Happy Mondays, Super Lager (Scottish brewed lager), Timothy Leary, acid house & techno

Spence D.

Juan Atkins
/Model 500
/Infiniti
/Cybotron

Born December 9, 1962, in Detroit, MI.

When it comes to electronic subgenres, definition is a matter of fierce debate. But if fans and artists can agree on anything these days, it would be with regard to the man who coined—and continues to characterize—the term "techno." In this respect, Juan Atkins is to the futuristic music scene what DJ Kool Herc is to old school hip-hop—a technological forefather, visionary, and icon. Atkins, alongside friends Derrick May and Kevin Saunderson, pioneered the postmodern Detroit sound during the early '80s, watching as it caught fire in Europe years before he and other American artists would get recognized in the U.S. Curiously, Atkins is said to have adopted the word "techno" from a book he read in a high school Future Studies class. The music's definition never has been academic, or even well-defined, but at techno's core are elements of funk and soul fused with the synth-pop sensibilities of disco and European new wave. From its embryonic stage, techno paralleled the development of equally electro-keen hip-hop, with Atkins's first group, Cybotron, serving up funky futurisms in the spirit of Afrika Bambaataa's Soulsonic Force. Today, both music forms

have branched into separate, often mutually exclusive, scenes that find identity through club or street culture, respectively. Atkins, who simply describes his aesthetic as "music that sounds like technology," has always maintained a vision for industry. He founded Metroplex Records in 1985, and its thriving underground output stands in contrast to the surroundings that inspire his music—the forgotten Motor City. When the auto industry hit hard times during the '80s, Atkins's techno was the rarest of exports, sought in faraway lands such as Bristol, England, and Belgium. It is a cursed blessing that this overseas interest leaves the American listener with precious little to pick from; in short, finding Atkins's full-length albums—all imports at this juncture—can be as hard as defining his style.

what to buy: *Magic Tracks: Deep Detroit, Vol. II* 🎜🎜🎜🎜 (Pow Wow, New York, 1993) is a domestic compilation that is as good an introduction as any to the Detroit school of techno. Under the moniker Infiniti, Atkins constructs the sonic throbbing of "Hardrive" and the brilliantly cosmic eight-minute "Flash Flood." Techno's granddaddy is joined on the disc by other keepers of the Detroit tradition, including Eddie Fowlkes and Ron Cook. Atkins's contributions on this album show the textured sophistication that make his songs at once soundtracks for deindustrialization and all-night dance parties.

what to buy next: *Sonic Sunset* 🎜🎜🎜🎝 (R&S, Belgium/Sony, 1994) is Atkins's most critically acclaimed work to date. This mini-LP features rich composition and trance subtleties with an aura slightly less house-influenced than previous works.

the rest:
Mind and Body (R&S, Belgium/Sony, 1998)
The Godfather Mix (TVT/Wax Trax, New York, 1998)

worth searching for: Any of these imports are well worth the hunt to get a greater taste of Atkins's pioneering work: *Model 500 Classics* (R&S, Belgium/Sony, 1993); *Deep Space* (R&S, Belgium/Sony, 1995); *The Infiniti Collection* (Metroplex, Detroit/Tresor, Germany, 1996)

influences:
◀◀ Kraftwerk, Parliament-Funkadelic

▶▶ Scan 7, Ron Cook, Eddie Fowlkes, Alan Oldham, Carl Craig, Richie Hawtin, John Acquaviva

Corey Takahashi

The Atlanta Rhythm Section
/ARS

Formed 1971, in Doraville, GA. Disbanded 1981. Re-formed as ARS in 1989.

Barry Bailey, guitar; Rodney Justo, vocals (1971–72); Paul Goddard, bass; Robert Nix, drums (1971–77); James R. Cobb, guitar; Dean

Daughtry, keyboards; Ronnie Hammond, vocals (1972–present); Roy Yeager, drums (1978–81). ARS (1989): Barry Bailey, guitar; Ronnie Hammond, vocals; Dean Daughtry, keyboards; Steve Stone, guitar; Sean Burke, drums; Justin Senker, bass.

Former studio cats with a flair for slippery southern boogie, the Atlanta Rhythm Section managed to make a name for itself during the late '70s with buttered up, fluid guitar lines and a proficient yet restrained musical tone. Although Hammond is an unremarkable frontman and the band never really forged revealing identity traits, it did garner several hit singles as well as gold and platinum albums. It may not be Fleetwood Mac, but ARS is currently another reunion machine, slogging away at faded hits.

what to buy: *A Rock and Roll Alternative* 🎵🎵🎵🎵 (Polydor, 1976, prod. Buddy Buie) is the group's most fully realized blend of harder jams and ballads. It contains its biggest hit, the smoky "So Into You." *Champagne Jam* 🎵🎵🎵🎵 (Polydor, 1978, prod. Buddy Buie) is the platinum selling follow-up and has the "So Into You" rewrite "Imaginary Lover" as well as the near-recklessness of "I'm Not Gonna Let It Bother Me Tonight."

what to buy next: *The Best of Atlanta Rhythm Section* 🎵🎵🎵🎵 (Polydor, 1991, prod. Buddy Buie) tracks the band's less distinguished early material through its peak years and shortly thereafter in an ample, hour-plus sampler.

what to avoid: Little did MTV know when it unleashed its Unplugged series that nearly every sagging rocker within earshot would be dusting off his acoustic and joining in—like ARS does on *Partly Plugged* 🎵🎵 (River North, 1997, prod. Buddy Buie). Enough already.

the rest:
Quinella 🎵🎵 (Columbia, 1981)
Atlanta Rhythm Section '96 🎵🎵 (CMC International, 1996)

influences:
◄◄ Lynyrd Skynyrd, Little Feat
►► Toto, the Fabulous Thunderbirds

Allan Orski

Murray Attaway
See: Guadalcanal Diary

The Au Pairs
Formed 1978, in Birmingham, England. Disbanded 1981.

Leslie Woods, vocals, guitar; Jane Munro, bass, vocals; Paul Foad, guitar, vocals; Pete Hammond, drums.

This band featured the female vocals and feminist perspective of Leslie Woods, with her dissections of male-female relations and women's place in society, role-playing her way through situations rather than delivering screeds. Though she was accused of being humorless, her lyrics were often quite funny in the blackest, most sardonic way, delivered in a grating voice that demands attention. Rhythmically similar to the herky-jerky avant-funk of Gang of Four, the Au Pairs' music was generally sparer, and the politics less radical and strident, though just as left-leaning. Besides placing singles in the indie charts, the group was censored by the BBC and toured as the opener for Gang of Four and later UB40.

worth searching for: *Playing with a Different Sex* (Human U.K., 1981/RPM U.K., 1992, prod. Au Pairs, Ken Thomas) offers thoughtful yet danceable punk fun—fleshed out to a full 72 minutes on the CD reissue by the addition of eight single tracks from 1979 through 1981. Neither that nor the group's second album, *Sense and Sensuality* (Kamera U.K., 1982/RPM U.K., 1993), were ever released in the U.S. A third studio album was made but never issued; fans can find some compensation in *Live in Berlin* and *Equal but Different: BBC Sessions 1979–1981* (RPM, U.K., 1994).

influences:
◄◄ Funkadelic, Patti Smith, Gang of Four, Raincoats, Talking Heads
►► Delta 5, Minutemen

Steve Holtje

Audio Adrenaline
Formed 1992, in KY.

Mark Stuart, lead vocals; Bob Herdman, keyboards, guitar; Will McGinniss, bass; Ben Cissell, drums; Tyler Burkum, guitar (1997–present); Barry Blair, guitar (1992–97).

Formed at Kentucky Christian College, where Will McGinniss and Mark Stuart were students, Audio Adrenaline successfully followed the lead of progressive contemporary Christian music peers D.C. Talk and constructed a searing musical amalgamation of rock, rap, and funk. Also similar to its contemporaries, AA deftly combines forthright religious messages with edgy tunefulness, often mirroring the intensity of meat-and-potatoes rock 'n' rollers like Aerosmith or Van Halen. The band's later recordings also incorporate more loops, samples, strings, and synthesizers, which enhance its sound rather than pop-ify it. In 1997, shortly after AA achieved its greatest success with its Grammy nominated *Bloom* album, original guitarist (and active songwriter) Barry Blair departed to pursue a career in production, replaced by Tyler Burkum. Also in 1997, the band released a book, *Some Kind of Journey: On the Road with Audio Adrenaline,* which documents a week on tour with AA, from the viewpoints of seven fans who were invited to accompany the group.

what to buy: With *Bloom* 🎵🎵🎵🎵 (Chordant, 1996, prod. the Goatee Brothers, John Hampton), AA not only nabbed its first Grammy nomination (Best Rock Gospel Album) but veered slightly from the mellifluous sounds of its earlier work in favor of distorted guitars ("Secret") and crashing drumbeats ("I'm Not the King").

what to buy next: *Some Kind of Zombie* 🎵🎵🎵🎵 (Capitol, 1997, prod. John Hampton) presents AA's most challenging lyrics to date, particularly on the title track, which stemmed from singer Stuart's time spent with his parents on Haiti where he witnessed real-life zombies. The theme of being dead, then reborn, is also revisited on the guitar-crunching "New Body." But the band also explores its quieter side, turning on the acoustic magic for "Lighthouse" and "Flicker."

the rest:
Don't Censor Me 🎵🎵🎵 (ForeFront, 1993)
Audio Adrenaline 🎵🎵🎵 (ForeFront, 1994)
Live Bootleg 🎵🎵🎵 (Chordant, 1995)

worth searching for: The band's glorious "Man of God" makes an appearance on *Wow 1998: The Year's 30 Top Christian Artists and Songs* (EMI Christian Music Group/Word Entertainment, 1997, prod. various).

influences:
◀◀ D.C. Talk, Geoff Moore & the Distance, DeGarmo & Key

▶▶ Rebecca St. James, Jars of Clay

Melissa Ruggieri

Brian Auger /Oblivion Express

Born July 18, 1939, in London, England.

During the mid-'60s, Brian Auger teamed up with vocalist Julie Driscoll in England and created music that brought together elements of progressive rock, blues, and R&B-laced jazz. When he formed Oblivion Express in 1970, Auger—along with artists such as Herbie Hancock, Chick Corea, and Stanley Clarke—helped usher in and popularize the jazz-rock fusion era of the early '70s. Over the years, the band featured the talents of super session drummer Steve Ferrone, future Santana vocalist Alex Ligertwood, and future Average White Band drummer Robbie McIntosh. After a number of albums but precious little U.S. success, the group splintered. Auger continued to tour and record as a solo act; these days he occasionally teams up with formal Animals singer Eric Burdon and tours with a band that includes his son and daughter.

what to buy: Oblivion Express' finest album, *Closer to It* 🎵🎵🎵🎵 (RCA, 1974/One Way, 1995), features the propulsive opening

track "Whenever You're Ready," displaying a supple, mainstream-leaning sound. There's also "Happiness Is Just Around the Bend," which landed the group on more than a few progressive American rock stations. Auger's Oblivion Express days are captured on *The Best of Brian Auger's Oblivion Express* 🎵🎵🎵 (Chronicles, 1996, prod. various), a smart two-disc set.

the rest:
(With Julie Tippetts, a.k.a. Julie Driscoll) *Encore* 🎵🎵 (RCA, 1978/One Way, 1996)
Here and Now 🎵🎵 (Grudge, 1987/One Way, 1996)

Oblivion Express:
Brian Auger's Oblivion Express 🎵🎵 (RCA, 1971/One Way, 1995)
A Better Land 🎵🎵🎵 (RCA, 1971/One Way, 1996)
Second Wind 🎵🎵 (RCA, 1972/One Way, 1995)
Straight Ahead 🎵🎵🎵 (RCA, 1975/One Way, 1995)
Reinforcements 🎵🎵🎵 (RCA, 1975/One Way, 1995)
The Complete Live Oblivion 🎵🎵 (One Way, 1995)

The Trinity:
Definitely What! 🎵🎵 (Marmalade, 1968/One Way, 1994)
Befour 🎵🎵 (RCA, 1970/One Way, 1995)

influences:
◀◀ John Mayall, Miles Davis, Bob Dylan

▶▶ Return to Forever, Herbie Hancock

Michael Isabella and Daniel Durchholz

Autechre /Gescom

Formed 1987, in Manchester, England.

Sean Brown, programming, drum machines, synths, samplers; Rob Brown, programming, drum machines, synths, samplers.

Autechre is among the forefront of musicians creating intelligent dance music—in fact, music that's more suited to headphone listening with the lights down low than the dance floor. Appropriately enough, the group was introduced to the outside world via Warp Records's seminal 1993 *Artificial Intelligence* compilation along with kindred spirits such as Richie Hawtin and the Aphex Twin. Autechre excels at developing rhythms that evolve from engaging funky grooves to complex polyrhythmic nightmares that can shift time signatures in the blink of an eye while at the same time keeping the listener grounded with emotive synthesizer melodies and ambient textures. While its early music bears the influence of electro and hip-hop's sharp angular rhythms, Sean Booth and Rob Brown have gradually developed Autechre's sound over the course of four albums into a more complex and alien beast, much in the same way that Hendrix and Led Zeppelin transformed the blues into an exciting new music that explored previously uncharted territories. With its fifth album expected from Trent Reznor's nothing Records in 1998, Autechre is in a position to expose its adventurous sounds to a much larger audience.

what to buy: *Tri Repetae++* 𝄞𝄞𝄞𝄞 (TVT/Wax Trax/Warp, 1996, prod. Autechre) is Autechre's masterpiece and is a must-have that includes two of the group's U.K. EPs on a single bonus disc.

what to buy next: While the music on *Tri Repetae++* is more complex than the group's previous efforts, *Amber* 𝄞𝄞𝄞𝄞 (TVT/Wax Trax/Warp, 1994, prod. Autechre) and *Incunabula* 𝄞𝄞𝄞𝄞 (TVT/Wax Trax/Warp, 1993, prod. Autechre), it's the otherworldly sounds that Booth and Brown manage to sculpt that really draw you in. *Amber* is a more laid-back affair, as reflected by the album's beautiful photography of a beachhead and is arguably its most ambient work. *Incunabula* is especially recommend for those looking for evidence of hip-hop's influence on techno.

worth searching for: Autechre's fourth album, *Chiastic Slide* (Warp U.K., 1997, prod. Autechre), sees the group continuing along the lines of *Tri Repetae++* 's rhythmic complexity while exploring harsher, noisier textures. The group's various U.K. EPs are also worth searching out, especially the *Anti EP* (Warp U.K., 1994, prod. Autechre), which features "Flutter," an amazing track that doesn't repeat the same rhythm twice and was composed in reaction to the U.K.'s draconian anti-rave legislation, the Criminal Justice Bill, which bans music that contains repetitive beats. However, before diving into the rather pricey realm of imports, you should check out *Skampler* (Silent/Skam, 1997, prod. various), a domestic compilation of tracks from the underground U.K. techno label Skam with whom Autechre is closely tied. The album features Autechre working under its Gescom alias in addition to excellent tracks by other experimental techno artists who've been influenced by the band.

influences:

◄◄ Afrika Bambaata, Mantronix, Meat Beat Manifesto, Renegade Soundwave, Kraftwerk

►► Push Button Objects, Freeform, Funkstorung, Phoenecia

Howard Shih

The Auteurs

Formed 1992, in London, England.

Luke Haines, vocals, piano, guitar; Alice Readman, bass; Glenn Collins, drums (1992–94); Barney Crockford, drums (1994–present); James Banbury, cello, organ (1993–present).

After a stint as guitarist with the '80s band the Servants, Luke Haines formed the Auteurs with girlfriend Alice Readman and Glenn Collins. Named after the French word for "author" (and the theory that some film directors, the best ones, are the "au-

thors" of their works just as novelists, poets, etc. are of theirs), the Auteurs were quickly touted as intelligent English pop by the music press. Now considered a Britpop pioneer, the Auteurs remain true to their essence by blending offbeat, sometimes cynical lyrics with aching pop melodies.

what to buy: The band's stunning first release, *New Wave* 𝄞𝄞𝄞𝄞𝄞 (Hut, 1993, prod. Phil Vinall, Luke Haines) introduces the band's strong songwriting skills. The combination of noise merchant Steve Albini's production and Luke Haines's sarcasm on *After Murder Park* 𝄞𝄞𝄞𝄞 (Hut, 1996, prod. Steve Albini) creates tense, unforgettable songs. From the atmospheric "Dead Sea Navigators" to the Beatles-influenced "Unsolved Child Murder," Haines sings his private obsessions with a sneer in his voice and a melody in his heart.

what to buy next: *Now I'm a Cowboy* 𝄞𝄞𝄞𝄞 (Hut, 1994, prod. Phil Vinall, Luke Haines) offers a scorching set filled with social commentary.

the rest:
Kid's Issue 𝄞𝄞𝄞 (Hut EP, 1996)

worth searching for: *μ-Ziq vs. the Auteurs* (Astralwerks, 1995, prod. Michael Paradinas) is an album of Auteurs songs covered and reconstructed by electronic musician Michael Paradinas, a.k.a. μ-Ziq.

influences:

◄◄ The Beatles, David Bowie

Anna Glen

Frankie Avalon

Born Francis Thomas Avallone, September 18, 1939, in Philadelphia, PA.

The first and probably most accomplished of all the teen idols who attempted to fill Elvis Presley's army boots while he was stationed overseas during the late '50s, Avalon actually had some musical talent and experience to back up his good looks and soft-rocking style. Taking a cue from Kirk Douglas in *Young Man with a Horn*, Avalon became a local celebrity while still in school, playing trumpet on Paul Whiteman's *TV Teen Club* show before joining his first band, Rocco & the Saints, in 1957 (which also featured future pop heartthrob Bobby Rydell on drums). When hometown impresarios Bob Marcucci and Peter de Angelis caught the act, it was Avalon they singled out to sign to their new Chancellor label, writing his first hit, "Dede Dinah," and guiding his career steadily upwards for the next several years. A constant presence on both Dick Clark's *American Bandstand* and the bigger package tours of the day (e.g., filling in for the late Buddy Holly on the ill-fated Winter Dance Party tour during 1959), Avalon had little trouble placing seven songs high into the Top 10—including the #1 classic "Venus"—before turning his attention towards motion pictures during the '60s. Although this facet of his career began promisingly enough with a featured role in John Wayne's *The Alamo*, Avalon rode out the remainder of the decade in a slew of beach and hot rod B-films for American International Pictures. He has spent most of the 30 years since revisiting past glories (a disco remake of "Venus," a cameo appearance in *Grease*, and several high-profile reunions with his beach movie paramour Annette Funicello)—when not hawking pain relievers and tanning solutions on late-night television, that is. Still, he remains to this day an engaging performer, and many of his hits have proven durable enough to keep him in work while most of his *Bandstand*-manufactured contemporaries have long ago vanished into the mists of time.

what's available: One listen to the expertly assembled *Venus: The Best of Frankie Avalon* 𝄞𝄞𝄞 (Varese Vintage, 1995, compilation prod. Cary E. Mansfield) should demonstrate to even the most cynical skeptic just how well-crafted for their time most of these 18 songs are, and that Avalon's voice was worthy enough to give even Elvis a run for the money—at least until he got home from the army.

influences:

◀◀ Pat Boone, Paul Anka, Ricky Nelson

▶▶ Fabian, Donny Osmond, Edan

Gary Pig Gold

The Avengers

Formed 1977, in San Francisco, CA. Disbanded 1979.

Penelope Houston, vocals; Greg Westermark, guitar (1977–78); James Calvin Wilsey, bass; Danny Furious, drums; Brad Kent, guitar (1979).

While most of the world in 1977 focused on New York and London as the centers of punk rock, Los Angeles and San Francisco also produced vital scenes and a small handful of records that remain the most sought-after artifacts and sounds of that incredible era. The unquestioned leaders of the red-hot San Francisco explosion were the Avengers, led by sensationally gorgeous Penelope Houston. In keeping with punk's progressive and radical-social stances, Houston used her cutting intelligence, biting social criticism, and teeth-sharpened attitude to define the group instead of her looks (plus a gutsy, edgy voice), blazing a trail for women in indie rock that was revolutionary in its refusal to play the star-making sex-role gender game. Meanwhile, her three band mates were blazing their own crunch-and-pummel trails, with a punishing sound and ashen playing every bit the equal (and largely surpassing) their more famous (outside of California) contemporaries. It is perhaps impossible

now in these punk-infested days to accurately express how shocking the group was in comparison to the popular rock music of its time, breaking and spitting on every ridiculous rule handed down in glorious, but also remarkable fashion. Sadly, with limited money and no recording contract, the quartet left behind only two paltry indie records, a blistering three-song single 7-inch, plus a four-song 12-inch EP produced by the Sex Pistols' Steve Jones that was released just as they were calling it quits. (They'd met Jones opening for the final ever Pistols show at San Francisco's Winterland in January 1978.)

worth searching for: Fortunately, the Avengers were the first of that scene to rate a retrospective album, four years after their demise. *The Avengers* (Go! Records, 1983, prod. the Avengers, David Fergusson) compiles their seven released songs along with six unreleased tunes from demos to form the LP. Complete with photos that capture the excitement, it is now universally regarded as the finest U.S. punk LP the West Coast produced, pre-hardcore, and it rates among any American punk LP period. Caution, though: Those seeking it of late have reported that both the CD and the vinyl versions are proving tough finds. But the album remains one of the quintessential documents of perhaps the last time that punk had the ability to truly shake up the foundations of rock like an earthquake.

influences:

◀◀ The Rolling Stones, the Stooges, the Sex Pistols

▶▶ Dead Kennedys, Bikini Kill, Jawbox, Cold Cold Heart

see also: *Penelope Houston*

Jack Rabid

Average White Band

Formed 1972, in Glasgow, Scotland. Disbanded 1981. Re-formed 1989 and 1995.

Alan Gorrie, bass, vocals; Onnie McIntyre, guitar, vocals; Roger Ball, keyboards, saxes; Malcom Duncan, tenor saxophone (1972–80); Robbie McIntosh, drums (1972–74); Hamish Stuart, guitar, vocals (1972–80); Steve Ferrone, drums (1974–80); Alex Ligertwood, vocals (1989–92); Elliot Lewis, keyboards, bass, guitar, lead vocals (1995–present); Pete Abbott, drums, percussion (1995–present).

Heralded as a bunch of Scottish guys who played funk like they were born in one of America's Chocolate Cities (with a name supposedly bestowed by Bonnie Bramlett of Delaney and Bonnie), the Average White Band came together with members from several Scottish soul tribute groups. Though a 1973 debut failed to catch fire, AWB soon struck gold with Atlantic in 1974, concocting a mix of James Brown–style funk and old-school R&B that captivated the then-emerging disco movement. Unfortunately, success took its toll, as drummer Robbie McIntosh died at a Hollywood party, snorting a fatal mix of heroin and morphine (Gorrie reportedly inhaled the same mixture but was kept awake by Cher and survived). Friend and Bloodstone member Steve Ferrone replaced McIntosh, helping the band sharpen its focus on authentic funk sounds. But as disco waned, AWB's material became curiously focused on that dying genre—until fans of its original funk flavor stopped buying records. Disbanded in 1980, AWB was revived by Alan Gorrie, Roger Ball, and Onnie McIntyre in 1989, with former Santana vocalist Alex Ligertwood as lead singer, though the relative failure of its comeback album doomed the band to the nostalgia circuit. Reviving the group again in 1995, Gorrie, McIntyre, and Ball drafted two new members to craft a sound much like Tower of Power's high-octane funk.

what to buy: Fans of '70s funk *must* own the group's first two Atlantic albums, *Average White Band* 𝄐𝄐𝄐𝄐 (Atlantic, 1974, prod. Arif Mardin) and *Cut the Cake* 𝄐𝄐𝄐𝄐 (Atlantic, 1975, prod. Arif Mardin). Both helped set the tone for '70s funk, ranging from horn-fueled workouts such as the instrumental hit "Pick up the Pieces" to silky slow jams like "Schoolboy Crush," "If I Ever Lose This Heaven," and "Person to Person." Unlike many Europeans trying to do funk, AWB sounded as authentic as every other act on R&B radio—a feat as impressive as it was surprising.

what to buy next: Greatest hits packages, when done well, are the best way to get the good stuff from an artist's career without the clinkers. And few collections do this job better than *Pickin' up the Pieces: The Best of the Average White Band, 1974–1980* 𝄐𝄐𝄐𝄐 (Rhino, 1992, prod. various). Here, fans can check out the group's biggest successes and album cuts on one 18-track excursion.

what to avoid: The band's first reunion effort, *Aftershock* **woof!** (Track Record, 1989, prod. John Robie) reached new depths of disappointment. Featuring just three original members and a formulaic sound, the album reminds everybody why the group broke up in the first place.

the rest:
Show Your Hand 𝄐𝄐𝄐 (MCA, 1973)
Put It Where You Want It 𝄐𝄐𝄐 (MCA, 1975)
Soul Searching 𝄐𝄐𝄐 (Atlantic, 1976)
Person to Person 𝄐𝄐𝄐𝄐 (Atlantic, 1977)
Benny and Us 𝄐𝄐 (Atlantic, 1977)
Warmer Communications 𝄐𝄐 (Atlantic, 1978)
Feel No Fret 𝄐𝄐 (RCA, 1979)
Average White Band, Vol. 8 𝄐𝄐𝄐 (Atlantic, 1980)
Shine 𝄐𝄐 (Arista, 1980)
Volume VIII 𝄐𝄐𝄐 (Atlantic, 1980)
Cupids in Fashion 𝄐𝄐 (RCA, 1982)
Best of the Average White Band 𝄐𝄐𝄐 (RCA, 1984)

Warmer Communications—and More 𝄐𝄐𝄐𝄐 (WEA/Atlantic/Rhino, 1994)
Live on the Test 𝄐𝄐 (Windsong, 1995)
Old Grey Whistle Test Series 𝄐𝄐𝄐 (Alex, 1995)
Soul Tattoo 𝄐𝄐𝄐 (Artful, 1997)
The Very Best of the Average White Band 𝄐𝄐𝄐 (Crimson, 1998)

worth searching for: Members of AWB have lent their talents as session musicians to works by several artists, including Chaka Khan, Paul McCartney, Eric Clapton, Duran Duran, and Tom Petty—often making better contributions there than on their own records. Particularly worthwhile is *Benny and Us* (Atlantic, 1977), with R&B great Ben E. King.

influences:

◀◀ James Brown, Tower of Power, Brian Auger, Ben E. King

▶▶ Prince, K.C. & the Sunshine Band, Little Steven & the Disciples of Soul, Red Hot Chili Peppers

Eric Deggans

Hoyt Axton

Born March 25, 1938, in Duncan, OK.

From a songwriting family (his mother, Mae Axton, co-wrote "Heartbreak Hotel"), the bearish, gruff-voiced Hoyt Axton has been a prolific songwriter and actor (*Heart Like a Wheel*, *Gremlins*) and sometime performer/recording artist. His songs have been covered by the Kingston Trio, Waylon Jennings, Glen Campbell, Tanya Tucker, John Denver, and Commander Cody, although his biggest hits came from Three Dog Night ("Joy to the World," "Never Been to Spain") and Steppenwolf ("Snowblind Friend," "The Pusher"). Axton's albums were more modest, but he had a minor country hit with 1974's "When the Morning Comes."

what's available: *Snowblind Friend* 𝄐𝄐𝄐 (Demon, 1995), recorded in 1977, includes guests Jeff Baxter, Jim Messina, and Byron Berline and includes "Never Been to Spain" and the title track. One stateside disc, *American Originals* 𝄐𝄐𝄐𝄐 (Capitol, 1992, prod. Todd Everett), is hard to find but includes downhome sessions with the cream of L.A. folk/country musicians and offers a good selection of Axton's early 1970s Capitol recordings. The Edsel label has re-released *Free Sailin'* 𝄐𝄐𝄐 (MCA, 1978/Edsel, 1996) and *My Griffin Is Gone* 𝄐𝄐 (Columbia, 1969/Edsel, 1998).

worth searching for: They're long out of print, but two of his A&M albums, *Life Machine* (A&M, 1974), which includes "When the Morning Comes," and *Road Songs* (A&M, 1977), a best-of, include some of his best writing and typically professional musicianship.

influences:

◀◀ Bobby Bare, Elvis Presley, Waylon Jennings

▶▶ Three Dog Night, Uncle Tupelo, Son Volt

Leland Rucker

Kevin Ayers

Born August 16, 1945, in Herne Bay, Kent, England.

Although Kevin Ayers was born in England, he spent much of his youth in Malaya. Returning to Britain while in his teens, Ayers ended up at Kent University, where he joined the Wilde Flowers (along with Robert Wyatt) in 1963. Initiating a pattern that would continue throughout much of his rather haphazard career, Ayers took leave of the group in 1965 for a hedonistic holiday in Majorca that reportedly featured plenty of drugs and alcohol. When he came back in 1966, Ayers and Wyatt (along with Daevid Allen—an Australian that Ayers met in Majorca—Mike Ratledge, and Larry Nolan) formed the first edition of Soft Machine, a group that blended psychedelic proclivities with free jazz influences while serving as a model for many of the "Canterbury" groups that came later, such as Caravan, Egg, and Hatfield & the North. Ayers, who was the chief songwriter and bassist, left the group in 1968 for another sabbatical in the Mediterranean, where he wrote much of the material that made up his solo debut, *Joy of a Toy*. He still used some of his former Soft Machine bandmates for the project, but Ayers was already looking forward to future undertakings. His next group, the Whole World, featured prospective progressive rock luminaries Lol Coxhill, Mike Oldfield, and David Bedford but managed to eke out only one album, *Shooting at the Moon*, and some sporadic touring before breaking up. Oldfield and Bedford stayed with Ayers long enough to work on his next solo release, *Whatevershebringswesing*. By the time *Bananamour* came out, Ayers had pared his basic touring group down to a trio with bassist Archie Legget and drummer Eddie Sparrow, with a free floating arsenal of guest musicians. Adopting more of a mainstream rock attitude (especially apparent in 1974 when guitarist Ollie Halsall joined the aggregation), the mid-'70s version of Ayers's band was called the Soporifics and served as the backing group for a theoretically memorable concert that Ayers took part in with John Cale, Nico, and Brian Eno. The resultant album, *June 1, 1974*, was at the front end of a prolonged period of mediocrity, a turn of events that, despite releasing occasional musical gems, would continue for nearly two decades until he whipped off the relatively stunning *Still Life with Guitar*. The quirky originality that was the foundation of Ayers's work didn't really mature until the very tail end of the '80s. Despite sporadic flashes of brilliance much of his music prior to then—while charming in an anglicized Jimmy Buffett–meets–Pink Floyd sort of way—

sounds dated to ears honed on the cusp of the millennium. All of his albums are out of print domestically, but the imports listed can be readily found.

what to buy: *Whatevershebringswesing* 𝄢𝄢𝄢𝄢 (Harvest/BGO, 1972, prod. Kevin Ayers, Andrew King), Ayers's third album, is the most consistent of his earlier releases and features some of his finest tunes—including a loopy psychedelic/neo-rockabilly hybrid called "Stranger in Blue Suede Shoes" and the blissed out title track with Robert Wyatt contributing vocal harmonies.

what to buy next: The clever and whimsical *Joy of a Toy* 𝄢𝄢𝄢𝄢 (Harvest, 1969/BGO, 1990, prod. Pete Jenner) was Ayers's solo debut and introduced many of the themes that would show up in tunes throughout his career. Loved more than listened to, *Joy of a Toy* was the initial site of one of his most popular songs, "Lady Rachel," and the ditty that unveiled Ayers's most frequently cited lyric (" . . . so let's drink some wine and have a good time"), "All This Crazy Gift of Time."

the rest:
Shooting at the Moon 𝄢𝄢𝄢 (Harvest, 1970/BGO, 1990)
BBC Live 𝄢𝄢𝄢 (Windsong, 1972)
Confessions of Dr. Dream 𝄢𝄢𝄢 (Island/BGO, 1974)
Rainbow Takeaway 𝄢𝄢𝄢 (EMI, 1978/BGO,1995)

worth searching for: *Yes We Have No Mañanas* (Harvest, 1976, prod. Kevin Ayers) provided Ayers with the closest thing to commercial success he ever received on this side of the pond. It was also a beacon of hope in the morass of mediocrity that Ayers had fallen into. Guitarist Ollie Halsall had some hip guitar licks going throughout this project—especially on "Blue"—but Ayers provided the goofy, if surprisingly focused, vision for this release making it his most consistently satisfying album since *Whatevershebringswesing*. It is hard to imagine Ayers as a mature individual, but aural proof is in the listening for *Still Life with Guitar* (Permanent, 1992, prod. Kevin Ayers, Dave Vatch), as wonderful, sardonic songs such as "M 16" and "There Goes Johnny" are nestled alongside a disturbing take on Leadbelly's "Goodnight Irene."

influences:

◀◀ Chuck Berry, the Beatles, Terry Riley, Ornette Coleman

▶▶ Michael Oldfield

see also: *Soft Machine*

Garaud MacTaggart

Aztec Camera

Formed 1980, Glasgow, Scotland.

Roddy Frame, guitar, vocals; Alan Welsh, bass (1980); Dave Mulholland, drums (1980–81); Campbell Owens, bass (1980–86); Craig Gan-

non, guitar (1981–83); David Ruffy, drums (1982–86); Malcolm Ross, guitar (1983–86).

Emerging from Scotland's fledgling new wave movement, Aztec Camera demonstrated a level of compositional excellence and performance virtuosity lacking in much of this period's pop music. Built around Roddy Frame's ample songwriting and guitar-playing talents, the band—its members still in their teens—showed an ability to turn out sophisticated, jazzy, acoustic-oriented guitar pop without falling on its face. Frame's fragile, enchanting voice engaged in clever word play that made him sound like the optimistic kid brother of Elvis Costello (who, notably, gave the band a plug in 1983 when he dubbed Frame the most promising songwriter of the day). Although well received in Britain, the group had less success in the U.S., where Frame's ambitious mix of genres made the group difficult to pigeonhole. By 1987, with his ever-increasing musical interests spread to house and rap music, Frame jettisoned the band, making Aztec Camera essentially a recurring front for his occasional solo efforts.

what to buy: Aztec Camera's debut effort, *High Land, Hard Rain* ♫♫♫♫ (Sire, 1983, prod. John Brand, Bernie Clark), bubbles over with jangly pop and jazz-guitar riffing. "Oblivious" and "Pillar to Post" are particularly lovely and memorable, evoking the naivete of early new wave while rising above the preciousness typical of the genre.

what to avoid: Recorded in the U.S. with studio musicians and a half-dozen different producers, *Love* ♫ (Sire, 1987, prod. various) is a misguided trip down Philly-soul lane, its heavy production obscuring Frame's earnest, boyish voice. On the other hand, U.K. record buyers made this Frame's biggest commercial hit to date.

the rest:
Knife ♫♫ (Sire, 1984)
Stray ♫♫♫♫ (Sire, 1990)
Dreamland ♫♫♫ (Sire, 1993)
Frestonia ♫♫♫ (Reprise, 1995)

worth searching for: Two promotional-only compilations—Japan's *The Best of Aztec Camera* (WEA, 1993, prod. various) and its U.S. counterpart, *Retrospect* (Sire/Reprise, 1993, prod. various)—both deliver worthy overviews of the group's catalog and include Frame's humorously deadpan take on Van Halen's "Jump."

influences:
◀◀ The Byrds, Elvis Costello, Dire Straits

▶▶ 10,000 Maniacs, Nick Heyward, the Style Council, the Housemartins

Christopher Scapelliti

B

Howie B
Born Howard Bernstein, 1963, in Glasgow, Scotland.

Howie B was studying psychology at Manchester University when he started working in a local studio as a tea boy. His keen sense of psychoanalysis translated well into his musical work, which could be described as a clinical dissection of popular club styles. After three years as assistant to soundtrack composer Stanley Myers and some time with a band called Nomad Soul, Howie got his break producing and remixing high profile artists such as Soul II Soul, Robbie Robertson, and Björk. But it was his work with stadium rock adventurers U2 that brought him global attention. Unfortunately, the mega-group's fans soon learned what electronic music purists knew all along—Howie's musical leanings are often criminally bland. Howie also runs his own label in England called Pussyfoot Records, on which he releases solo albums under pseudonyms such as Daddylonglegs and Olde Scottish.

what to buy: Released shortly after Howie worked on U2's techno-slanted *Pop* album, *Turn the Dark Off* ♫♫ (Island, 1997, prod. Howie B) contains the producer's most mature work. Robbie Robertson makes a chilly vocal appearance on "Take Your Partner by the Hand," while "Angels Go Bald" served as the appropriate theme music for U2's doomed Pop-Mart tour.

the rest:
Music for Babies ♫♫ (Island, 1996)

influences:
◀◀ Massive Attack, New Order, Soul II Soul

Aidin Vaziri

The B-52's /Fred Schneider
Formed 1976, in Athens, GA.

Fred Schneider, vocals; Cindy Wilson, vocals (1976–90, 1994–present); Kate Pierson, vocals, keyboards; Keith Strickland, drums, guitar; Ricky Wilson, guitar (1976–85).

The B-52's, the second most popular band to come out of Athens, Georgia, had its roots in parties, so the best of the band's sounds—particularly the oddball hits "Rock Lobster," "Private Idaho," and "Planet Claire"—go after an off-beat, whacky kind of fun. It's also one of the first rock bands to be affected directly by AIDS; guitarist Ricky Wilson died of the disease in 1985. The rest of the group, including his sister Cindy, decided to go on without replacing him (drummer Keith Strickland learned to play guitar) and wound up with the biggest album of the group's career, 1989's *Cosmic Thing*, and the smash hits "Love Shack" and "Roam." The B-52's haven't reached that pinnacle since, but it can still be counted on to get a crowd to "dance this mess around."

what to buy: *The B-52's* 𝄞𝄞𝄞𝄞 (Warner Bros., 1979, prod. Chris Blackwell, Robert Ash) is *the* indispensable new wave party record. Its stripped-down, surf-twang retro makes it sound ever-modern, and its party chants still rule the floor.

what to buy next: *Time Capsule: Songs for a Future Generation* 𝄞𝄞𝄞𝄞 (Reprise, 1998, prod. various) covers the most popular ground from the early days to the "Love Shack" comeback, just in time for a reunion tour. *Cosmic Thing* 𝄞𝄞𝄞𝄞 (Reprise, 1989, prod. Don Was, Nile Rogers) is the sprightly comeback with "Love Shack," "Roam," and "Deadbeat Club."

what to avoid: *Good Stuff* 𝄞𝄞 (Reprise, 1992, prod. Don Was, Nile Rogers) found the band down to just three B-52's, and the lackluster songs made its title misleading at best.

the rest:
Wild Planet 𝄞𝄞𝄞 (Warner Bros., 1980)
Whammy! 𝄞𝄞𝄞𝄞 (Warner Bros., 1983)
Bouncing off the Satellites 𝄞𝄞𝄞 (Warner Bros., 1986)
Party Mix/Mesopotamia 𝄞𝄞𝄞𝄞 (Warner Bros., 1991)

worth searching for: The British import *Dance This Mess Around* (Island, 1990, prod. various) offers a superlative collection from the pre-*Cosmic Thing* albums that should keep the party out of bounds for its duration.

solo outings:
Fred Schneider:
Fred Schneider 𝄞𝄞𝄞 (Reprise, 1991)
. . . Just Fred 𝄞𝄞𝄞 (Reprise, 1996)

influences:
◀◀ Yoko Ono, Dick Dale, the Shangri-La's, Ricky Ricardo
▶▶ Deee-Lite, Cibo Matto, Technotronic

Roger Catlin

Babble
See: Thompson Twins

Babe the Blue Ox
Formed 1989, in Brooklyn, NY.

Rose Thomson, vocals, bass; Tim Thomas, vocals, guitar; Hanna Fox, vocals, drums.

This bass-heavy alternative power trio with a high skronk factor and a wry sense of humor incorporates a broad range of disparate sounds into a seamless, distinctive style. The members trade off vocals in the same casual yet energetic way they blast through their loose-limbed grooves, with Rose Thomson's high vocals recalling Juliana Hatfield. Tim Thomas and Hanna Fox had to deal with carpal tunnel syndrome, a result not of musical endeavors but of heavy typing at their full-time day jobs (Fox had to quit drumming for four months).

what to buy: *Color Me Babe* 𝄞𝄞𝄞𝄞 (Homestead, 1994, prod. Bruce Hathaway, Babe the Blue Ox) shows the band's highest development of its indie sound.

what to buy next: *BOX* 𝄞𝄞𝄞 (Homestead, 1993, prod. Bruce Hathaway, Garris Shipon, Babe the Blue Ox) was the band's first non-single release and has a winningly raw sound.

the rest:
Je m'Appelle Babe 𝄞𝄞𝄞 (Homestead EP, 1993)
People 𝄞𝄞𝄞 (RCA, 1996)
The Way We Were 𝄞𝄞𝄞 (RCA, 1998)

influences:
◀◀ Pixies, fIREHOSE, Tar Babies, Blake Babies

Steve Holtje

Babes in Toyland
Formed 1987, in Minneapolis, MN.

Katherine "Kat" Bjelland, vocals, guitar; Lori Barbero, drums; Michelle Leon, bass (1987–92); Maureen Herman, bass (1992–present).

Babes in Toyland make a racket. First among the riot grrrl groups (Bjelland wore baby doll dresses *before* Courtney Love, thank you), the trio rages against the machine and everything else, including mates, parents, rivals, and Barbie dolls. It's primal scream therapy with electric guitars, with emphasis on the primal—often it sounds like Chrissie Hynde singing in front of the (old) Sex Pistols. Bjelland came to Minneapolis from San Francisco, where she was in the band Sugar Baby Doll with Courtney Love of Hole and Jennifer Finch of L7. Babes earned its indie credibility quickly, winning a powerful patron in Sonic Youth—and, in 1993, a spot on the Lollapalooza tour.

what to buy: On its major label debut, *Fontanelle* 𝄞𝄞𝄞𝄞 (Reprise, 1992, prod. Lee Ranaldo, Kate Bjelland), the group towns down the rage just a bit and makes the most of strong songs and production help from Sonic Youth's Lee Ranaldo.

what to buy next: *Spanking Machine* 𝄞𝄞𝄞 (Twin/Tone, 1990, prod. Jack Endino) is an assured debut, all spite and bile in anticipation of the big grunge breakthrough the following year. *Painkillers* 𝄞𝄞𝄞 (Reprise EP, 1993), released to coincide with the Lollapalooza tour, features five standard songs and a sneaky sixth track that's actually a 35-minute live set.

what to avoid: *To Mother* ✍✍ (Twin/Tone EP, 1991, prod. John Loder) has the sound and feel of an exercise in treading water.

the rest:
Nemesisters ✍✍✍ (Reprise, 1995)

worth searching for: *Live at the Academy* (Reprise, 1992) is a promotion-only live collection featuring the *Fontanelle* single "Won't Tell."

influences:
◄◄ The Stooges, the Pretenders, Sonic Youth, the Pixies
►► Hole, 7 Year Bitch, Veruca Salt

Gary Graff

Baby Bird
Born Stephen Jones, September 16, 1962, in Telford, England.

A true believer in the D.I.Y aesthetic, and an even truer eccentric, Baby Bird has broken through in the music business in the most unorthodox way imaginable: without any help whatsoever. After he met with failure at all the major labels in the U.K. and British pop radio wouldn't touch him as an independent, Jones decided to forgo due process and issue his own music. He established the Baby Bird label in 1995 and, over the course of a year, released four separate discs of original material in runs of 1,000. Each sold out quickly and Jones became something of a media darling, a maverick one-man band, winning a sizable cult following by thumbing his nose at the music industry. (As a "sarky" gesture, Jones inserted ballots in all of his CDs encouraging fans to vote for the songs they would like to hear on his fifth disc, a so-called "greatest hits" package.) A self-anointed "young man in the bedroom with beautiful ideas for the future," Jones's musical style—lo-fi, low budget, with almost childlike instrumentation—draws on lugubrious and melodramatic influences like Pulp's Jarvis Cocker, Leonard Cohen, and Scott Walker, but without their high ideals. Lovelorn and despondent one moment, arch and bitter the next, Jones's wild mood swings make for refreshing, unpredictable listening. Following his "hits" collection, Jones signed to a major label, though with many clauses built in to suit his independent ethic. For his first commercial project, *Ugly Beautiful* he assembled a real band. The album met with mediocre reviews, but radio and the public were ready for a bigger dose of Baby Bird. Jones is fast becoming a pop icon in the U.K.

what to buy: Jones's slapdash songs—he's said he's written over 500 in six years—proffer legitimate hooks, his own cracked vocals, and unusually sordid lyrics. *Greatest Hits* ✍✍✍ (Atlantic, 1997, prod. Stephen Jones) offers the best cross section of his individualistic early work.

what to buy next: Though his first major label effort may be a bit of a departure with slightly slicker production values and a real studio band, *Ugly Beautiful* ✍✍✍ (Atlantic Baby Bird, 1997, prod. Stephen Jones) is a nice introduction to a very eccentric pop talent.

worth searching for: Having sampled Jones's quirky oeuvre on his major-label efforts, true believers will want to search for his independent releases, all of which are worth a listen. They include: *Bad Shave* (Baby Bird, 1995), *I Was Born a Man* (Baby Bird, 1995), *Fatherhood* (Baby Bird, 1995), *The Happiest Man Alive* (Baby Bird, 1995), and *Dying Happy* (Baby Bird, 1996).

influences:
◄◄ Leonard Cohen, the Walker Brothers, Scott Walker

Bob Gulla

The Babys
See: John Waite

Burt Bacharach
Born May 12, 1928, in Kansas City, MO.

Nearly three decades after the golden era of his work, and years after his last significant chart hit, Burt Bacharach has become a cultural signifier of the mostly lost art of pop songwriting. And no wonder: His hits, many of which were written with lyricist Hal David, are complex mini-dramas, filled with odd time signatures, unconventional orchestrations, and innovative melodies. The pair wrote dozens of timeless tracks for a wide array of performers, including Marty Robbins, "The Story of My Life"; Gene Pitney, "24 Hours from Tulsa"; Tom Jones, "What's New Pussycat?"; Dusty Springfield, "The Look of Love"; Jerry Butler, "Make It Easy on Yourself"; the Carpenters, "(They Long to Be) Close to You"; and B.J. Thomas, "Raindrops Keep Fallin' on My Head." Then there was Dionne Warwick, in whom the duo's muse came to full flower: "You'll Never Get to Heaven (If You Break My Heart)," "Alfie," "A House Is Not a Home," "Do You Know the Way to San Jose?," "Don't Make Me Over," "I Just Don't Know What to Do with Myself," "This Girl's in Love with You," and "I Say a Little Prayer" are some of the many hits they wrote for her. Bacharach and David split in the early '70s after their score for *Lost Horizon* sank like the embarrassing film it accompanied. Bacharach hit only sparsely after that, writing "On My Own" for Patti LaBelle with his third wife, Carole Bayer Sager, and "Arthur's Theme (The Best That You Can Do)" with Sager, Peter Allen, and Christopher Cross, who sang it. Bacharach and Sager also wrote "That's What Friends Are For," which was originally sung by Rod Stewart over the credits of the film *Night Shift*, but was resurrected several years later by Dionne and Friends to benefit and American Foundation for

AIDS Research. Inexplicably, a decade later, Bacharach is suddenly everywhere: on the soundtracks of *Austin Powers*, *My Best Friend's Wedding*, and *Grace of My Heart*; on the turntables of "bachelor-pad music" aficionados; and once again in the minds of record executives—at press time Rhino was preparing what promises to be the definitive Bacharach box set. Few pop resurrections have been so long in coming or so well deserved.

what to buy: It's reportedly only the first wave of a flood of Bacharach reissues, but *Burt Bacharach Plays His Hits* 𝄢𝄢𝄢𝄽 (MCA, 1997, compilation prod. Jim Pierson) is an interesting place to start your reassessment of his work. Many of the famous Bacharach/David hits are here, but mostly in instrumental versions augmented only by the occasional lead vocal and a female chorus. The effect is kind of cheesy, but Bacharach's orchestrations are especially lively, making for some enjoyable listening. *Plays His Hits* is a newer and lengthier version of an album released in the '60s under the same title, which, as a mark of added kitsch value, was featured in the movie *Austin Powers* as the album in the secret agent's possession when he was cryogenically frozen.

what to buy next: Though one of the great pop composers, Bacharach is not much of a singer, and it's best to seek out his songs in versions by other artists. One such collection is *The Burt Bacharach Songbook* 𝄢𝄢𝄢𝄽 (Varese Sarabande, 1998, prod. various), which offers some of the hits sung by Jackie De-Shannon, Gene Pitney, Dusty Springfield, Jerry Butler, and others. *Greatest Hits* 𝄢𝄢𝄢 (A&M, 1973, prod. various) is a prime selection of Bacharach's own recordings of his easy-listening classics. *Classics, Vol. 23* 𝄢𝄢𝄢 (A&M, 1991, prod. various) fulfills the same function with a greater song selection.

what to avoid: The sappy Bacharach/David score to *Lost Horizon* **woof!** (Bell, 1973/Razor & Tie, 1997) was so dispiriting, it caused one of pop's most successful duos to acrimoniously split.

the rest:
Reach Out 𝄢𝄢𝄢 (A&M, 1967/Rebound, 1995)
(With Elvis Costello) *Painted from Memory* 𝄢𝄢𝄢𝄢 (Mercury, 1998)
The Look of Love: The Burt Bacharach Collection 𝄢𝄢𝄢𝄢 (Rhino, 1998)

worth searching for: Proof positive of Bacharach's resurgent popularity and influence can be found on *Great Jewish Music: Burt Bacharach* (Tzadik, 1997, prod. various), a two-disc set of Bacharach compositions deconstructed by avant-gardist executive producer John Zorn and a number of today's more adventurous musicians, including Marc Ribot, Robin Holcomb, Wayne Horvitz, Fred Frith, Bill Frisell, Kramer, and Elliott Sharp. Some of the tracks are pointlessly vexing—easy listening made difficult, if you will—but the set definitely achieves its goal of re-

vealing Bacharach's genius in completely unexpected ways. McCoy Tyner's *What the World Needs Now: The Music of Burt Bacharach* (Impulse!, 1997, prod. Tommi LiPuma) offers straight-jazz versions of Bacharach's hits with symphonic accompaniment. *What the World Needs Now: Big Deal Recording Artists Perform the Songs of Burt Bacharach* (Big Deal, 1998, prod. various) is an earnest tribute to Bacharach by rock artists, but not the high-profile treatment he deserves.

influences:
◀◀ Irving Berlin, George Gershwin, Johnny Mercer

▶▶ Dionne Warwick, Elvis Costello, Noel Gallagher, John Zorn, Pizzicato Five

Daniel Durchholz

Bachman-Turner Overdrive

Formed 1972, in Winnipeg, Manitoba, Canada. Disbanded 1980. Periodic reunions.

Randy Bachman, guitar, vocals (1972–77); Tim Bachman, guitar, vocals (1972–73); Robbie Bachman, drums, vocals; C.F. (Fred) Turner, bass, vocals; Blair Thornton, guitar, vocals (1974–80); Jim Clench, bass, vocals (1977–80).

The prairie city of Winnipeg spawned two of the most successful rock bands of the '70s: the Guess Who and Bachman-Turner Overdrive. Guitar legend Randy Bachman had a large hand in both. By 1970, Guess Who co-founders Randy Bachman and singer Chad Allan had quit the band they started in 1962. They reunited, and in 1971 formed Brave Belt with Bachman's brother Robbie on drums. After two records, another Bachman brother, Tim, and C. F. Turner replaced Allan, and the new band became Bachman-Turner Overdrive. (Legend has it that the band drew inspiration for its name after it visited a truck stop in Windsor, Ontario, and noticed a copy of Overdrive magazine, a trucking industry trade journal.) As he had done in the Guess Who, Bachman was able to craft great rock songs on simple guitar riffs; by 1977 that skill had netted the band sales of seven million records in the U.S. BTO disbanded in 1980 but has regrouped for tours in various configurations ever since. Randy Bachman also records as a solo artist—often with fellow countryman Neil Young as a guest—and occasionally tours with various versions of the Guess Who.

what to buy: Every teenager in America was aware of *Bachman-Turner Overdrive II* 𝄢𝄢𝄢𝄢 (Mercury, 1973, prod. Randy Bachman) after its release, and the five opening guitar notes on "Takin' Care of Business" can still make heads bob today. It also contains the hits "Welcome Home," a jazzy homage to the rock life, and the Doobie Brothers–influenced "Let It Ride." The band followed with another strong record, *Not Fragile* 𝄢𝄢𝄢𝄢 (Mercury, 1974, prod. Randy Bachman), which features the still-popular hits "You Ain't Seen Nothing Yet" and "Roll on Down the Highway."

what to buy next: *Bachman-Turner Overdrive: The Anthology* ♫♫♫♫ (Mercury, 1993, prod. Randy Bachman, BTO, Jim Vallance) is a whopping two-disc set with a nicely chosen chunk of material from the group's heyday and afterwards. *Best of B.T.O. (Remastered Hits)* ♫♫♫♫ (Mercury/Chronicles, 1998, prod. Randy Bachman) is a more compact overview, with 12 bona fide radio smashes.

what to avoid: *All Time Greatest Hits—Live* ♫ (Curb, 1990) is not exactly the band's all-time greatest performance.

the rest:
Bachman-Turner Overdrive ♫♫ (Mercury, 1973)
Four Wheel Drive ♫♫♫ (Mercury, 1975)
BTO's Greatest ♫♫♫ (Mercury, 1981)
You Ain't Seen Nothing Yet ♫♫ (PolyGram, 1993)
Best of—Live ♫♫♫ (Curb, 1994)

worth searching for: Bachman's *Plugged In—The Garage Tapes* (Ranbach EP, 1993, prod. Randy Bachman), a Canadian import of a relaxed sounding Bachman solo performance in Seattle, features "You Ain't Seen Nothin' Yet," "Takin' Care of Business," and three Guess Who favorites.

solo outings:
Randy Bachman:
Any Road ♫♫♫ (Guitar Recordings, 1994)

influences:
◄◄ The Box Tops, Free, the Who

►► The Smithereens, Soundgarden, Stone Temple Pilots

see also: *The Guess Who*

William Hanson

Eric Bachmann
See: Archers of Loaf

Backstreet Boys
Formed mid-1990s, in Orlando, FL.

Brian Littrell, vocals; A.J. McLean, vocals; Nick Carter, vocals; Kevin Richardson, vocals; Howie Dorough, vocals.

If at first you don't succeed. . . . Well, Backstreet Boys *did* succeed, just not in its home country at first. The quintet, which grew up in the shadow of Walt Disney World, brought out its eponymous debut album of frilly, R&B-laced pop in 1995. U.S. audiences, caught up in modern rock, yawned, but the rest of the world lapped up nearly 5.5 million copies. So the Boys tried again at home in 1997, and this time it clicked. The teenybopper market, stoked by the Spice Girls and Hanson, made smash hits out of "Quit Playing Games (With My Heart)," "As Long As You Love

Me," and "Everybody (Backstreet's Back)." They also bought up lots of makeup kits that included Backstreet Boys cassette samplers. Not *only* in America, but still. . . .

what's available: Though they could be the male counterpart to the Spice Girls—this is pretty sugary stuff—the boys at least show some good taste and melodic sensibility on *Backstreet Boys* ♫♫♫ (Jive, 1997, prod. various). Producers include Full Force and PM Dawn, and the songs demonstrate that the five singers are not groove impaired. Definitely one to keep an eye on.

influences:
◄◄ Bobby Brown, New Kids on the Block, All-4-One

Gary Graff

Bad Brains
Formed 1979, in Washington, DC.

H.R. (a.k.a. Joseph I), vocals (1979–83, 1986–87, 1988–89, 1994–95); Dr. Know, guitar (1979–95); Darryl Aaron Jenifer, bass (1979–95); Earl Hudson, drums (1979–83, 1986–87, 1989, 1994–95); Israel Joseph-I, vocals (1992–94); Mackie Jayson, drums (1983–86, 1988–89, 1992–93).

Bad Brains are the most influential band in hardcore, often overlooked due to an all-black lineup that's out of synch with the punk stereotype. But the band's pioneering mix of punk with reggae also makes it an unusual giant of world music and a founder of the barrier-breaking aesthetic now spreading through all forms of art. Their explosive sound has the creative tension of cultures actually facing each other for the first time—call it Hard World. The Brains' sensibility stems from an upbringing in the ghettos around the capital of the free world; it embodies the past shame and future promise of American multiculturalism—bassist Darryl Jenifer even traces his lineage to a slave-owning signer of the constitution. Reversing rock's usual trend, Bad Brains were not amateurs who gradually built up their sound, but fusion-jazz types who learned the value of simplicity from the late '70s punk revolution. When they discovered the beliefs and music of Rastafarianism, the Brains set their cultural blender on high and threw away the knob. The creative energies involved make for a volatile brew, and since 1983 the band has literally made albums between breakups, with vocalist H.R. and his brother Earl Hudson departing regularly to pursue more straightforward reggae recordings. Narrowly marketed to the punk audience, portrayed more as historical figures than contemporary players, and eclipsed by violent incidents involving an unbalanced H.R., the Brains have been in limbo since their last album in 1995. Meanwhile, vital unreleased sessions regularly surface to keep the future open and the legend alive.

what to buy: The debut, *Bad Brains* ♫♫♫♫ (ROIR, 1982/1996, prod. Jay Dublee) is not only the definitive hardcore album, but the standard by which all nonconformist music can be measured. With oddly melodic power chords and vocal wails, polyphonic noise guitar, unpredictable acrobatics of rhythm and tempo, and precociously expert reggae, the Brains transcended a genre even as they defined it. On *I against I* &&&& (SST, 1986, prod. Ron St. Germain) the band grounds metal-leaning rock with the syncopation of funk, takes pop to blistering extremes, and keeps its playing tight while ambitiously stretching out its song-structure. H.R. turns in his best lyrics and inflects his singing with a rich soul texture (after a drug bust, the vocals for "Sacred Love" were resourcefully recorded by phone from prison). The stunning *Quickness* &&&& (Caroline, 1989, prod. Ron St. Germain) shifts genres within individual songs. The prodigal H.R. returned to create the lyrics and vocal melodies in one night; some remnants of his *a capella* demos contrast the otherwise fat production sound with a fabulous rawness. His sometimes overly macho lyrics, and a few repeated musical ideas from *I Against I*, are the only things that qualify the album's success. Released after 17 years as *Black Dots* &&&& (Caroline, 1996, prod. Bad Brains), the Brains' first-ever live-in-the-studio recording session instantly took its place among the definitive documents of rock essence.

what to buy next: *God of Love* &&&& (Maverick, 1995, prod. Ric Ocasek) slows the pace of experimentation a bit and may seem to lack the other albums' visionary sweep. But it marks the band's most decisive same-song synthesis of hard rock and reggae yet, and features the must-have ambient reggae odyssey "How I Love Thee" and the metal-gospel-country-western prayer call (believe it!) of "Thank JAH." The Brains' first multi-track recording session, laid down in 1980 but released much later as the EP *Omega Sessions* &&&& (Victory, 1997), is an intriguing artifact of a studio polish the band would sand off before its debut album. *Live* &&&& (SST, 1988, prod. Phil Burnett) is a sterling example of the Brains on stage.

what to avoid: Even a bad album for the Brains would be a good one for many others. But *Rock for Light* &&& (PVC, 1983/Caroline, 1991, prod. Ric Ocasek) is packed with inferior versions of songs from the (then-rare) first album.

the rest:
Bad Brains &&& (Alternative Tentacles EP, 1982)
I and I Survive/Destroy Babylon && (Important EP, 1982)
Attitude: The ROIR Session && (ROIR/Important, 1989)
The Youth Are Getting Restless: Live in Amsterdam &&&& (Caroline, 1990)
Spirit Electricity &&&& (SST EP, 1991)
Rise &&& (Epic, 1993)

worth searching for: The soundtrack for *Pump up the Volume* (MCA, 1990, prod. various) features the band's cover of the MC5's "Kick Out the Jams" with Henry Rollins on vocals.

solo outings:
Darryl Jenifer:
Sacred Love Meets Black Vova Under the Irish Moss N/A (Rawkus, 1998)

influences:
◀◀ Bob Marley, Parliament-Funkadelic, the Sex Pistols, the Clash, the Damned, the Ramones, Mahavishnu Orchestra, Return to Forever

▶▶ Living Colour, Beastie Boys, Consolidated, Bad Religion, Cornershop, Goldfinger, Sting, Babe the Blue Ox, Spearhead, Skunk Anansie, the Urge

Adam McGovern

Bad Company

Formed 1973, in London, England. Disbanded 1983. Re-formed 1986.

Mick Ralphs, guitar; Simon Kirke, drums; Paul Rodgers, vocals, guitar, keyboards (1973–82); Boz Burrell, bass (1973–82); Brian Howe, vocals (1986–92); Rick Wills, bass (1992–present); Robert Hart, vocals (1992–present); Dave "Bucket" Colwell, guitar (1992–present).

Like Led Zeppelin (with whom it shared a record label and manager), Bad Company was the culmination of the British blues-rock scene, a "supergroup" formed with a conscious eye toward the sales charts and an ear for radio-ready songwriting. The group was formed by two members of Free, throaty vocalist Paul Rodgers and drummer Simon Kirke, after that quirkier hard rock group broke up. They lured Mick Ralphs from Mott the Hoople, who was disgruntled with his group's turn toward glam-rock with their hit version of David Bowie's "All the Young Dudes." Bassist Boz Burrell of King Crimson rounded out the lineup. Bad Company's first album was a machismo-dripping blueprint for post-blooz FM rock. Subsequent records continued the hits and made the group one of the biggest concert attractions of the '70s, but the mega-touring took its toll. The original group called it quits after the 1982 album *Rough Diamonds*. Rodgers has gone his own way since, but Kirke and Ralphs reconvened Bad Company in 1986. The group is still trotting out the macho moves and pounding away with hard-rock riffs, though the albums have been nothing if not predictable.

what to buy: The biggest hit on *Bad Company* &&&& (Swan Song, 1974, prod. Bad Company) was the lusty "Can't Get Enough," but several others—the slow-grinding "Rock Steady," the pretty Mott the Hoople remake "Ready for Love," the brooding "Bad Company," and the gleeful "Movin' On"—remain part of the foundation of the classic-rock canon. It never got any better.

what to buy next: *Straight Shooter* && (Swan Song, 1975, prod. Bad Company) and *Run with the Pack* && (Swan Song, 1976, prod. Bad Company) both have strong songs to recom-

Paul Rodgers of Bad Company (© **Ken Settle**)

mend them: If nothing else, Bad Company knew how to build an entire song instead of just jamming on a riff. A hit from *Straight Shooter*, "Feel Like Makin' Love," rose to #10 on the *Billboard* charts, making it the group's biggest hit after "Can't Get Enough," which made it to #5.

what to avoid: *What You Hear Is What You Get: The Best of Bad Company Live* **woof!** (Atlantic, 1993, prod. Simon Kirke) is a poor live set featuring shrill vocalist Brian Howe. It's so clichéd it's almost a parody of arena rock. Except Spinal Tap did that better.

the rest:
Burnin' Sky 🎵🎵 (Swan Song, 1977)
Desolation Angels 🎵🎵 (Swan Song, 1979)
Rough Diamonds 🎵🎵 (Swan Song, 1982)
10 from 6 🎵🎵🎵🎵 (Atlantic 1985)
Fame and Fortune 🎵🎵 (Atlantic, 1986)
Dangerous Age 🎵🎵 (Atlantic, 1988)
Holy Water 🎵 (Atco, 1990)
Here Comes Trouble 🎵 (Atco, 1992)
Company of Strangers **woof!** (EastWest, 1995)
Stories Told and Untold 🎵 (EastWest, 1996)

worth searching for: *Can't Get Enough of That Stuff* (Oh Boy), a bootleg from a 1974 concert in Boston, finds Bad Company at its tough, rocking best.

solo outings:
Paul Rodgers:
Cut Loose 🎵🎵🎵 (Atlantic, 1983)
(With the Firm) *The Firm* 🎵🎵 (Atlantic, 1985),
(With the Firm) *Mean Business* 🎵🎵 (Atlantic, 1986)
(With the Law): *The Law* 🎵 (Atlantic, 1991)
Muddy Waters Blues 🎵🎵 (Victory, 1993)
The Hendrix Set 🎵🎵 (Victory, 1993)
Now & Live 🎵🎵🎵 (Velvel, 1997)

influences:
◀◀ Alexis Korner, the Yardbirds, Fleetwood Mac, Free, Led Zeppelin

▶▶ Bon Jovi, Def Leppard, the Black Crowes

Gil Asakawa

Bad English
See: John Waite

Bad Livers
Formed 1990, in Austin, TX.

Danny Barnes, banjo, guitar, mandolin, vocals; Ralph White, fiddle, accordion; Mark Rubin, bass, tuba, vocals; Bob Grant, mandolin, guitar (1997–present).

Call it thrash-grass or bluegrass-punk, call it pickin'-and-grimacin', but don't call the Bad Livers late to dinner. This genre-

busting trio plays a postmodern form of bluegrass that is informed as much by the Butthole Surfers and Motörhead as it is by Bill Monroe and Ralph Stanley. *Delusions of Banjer*, after all, was produced by Butthole Surfer Paul Leary, and the Livers have been known to reel off a high-stepping version of rock icon Iggy Pop's "Lust for Life" that inspires fits of furious tater-diggin'. It would be easy to dismiss the group as a novelty—Mark Rubin's occasional tuba playing sticks out and takes things a little over the top—but they've got the chops to back up their nontraditional take on a traditional music.

what to buy: *Horses in the Mines* 🎵🎵🎵🎵 (Quarterstick, 1994, prod. Danny Barnes) contains plenty of attitude, but, for the most part, de-emphasizes the novelty elements that crop up on *Delusions of Banjer*. Anyone doubting the Livers' ability to play pure bluegrass should check out their lightning-fast take on the old-time breakdown "Blue Ridge Express." White's "Chainsaw Therapy" is a fine fiddle tune, and the group's punk influences get a nod on "Puke Grub."

what to buy next: *Delusions of Banjer* 🎵🎵🎵🎵 (Quarterstick, 1992, prod. Paul Leary) is a little schticky but a fine effort, nonetheless. Hard-bitten banjo tunes such as "Git Them Pretty Girls," "I Know You're Married," and "Crow Black Chicken" lead the way, but they're undercut by the bathroom humor of "Shit Creek" and "The Adventures of Pee Pee the Sailor," which are less about rock 'n' roll attitude than the band would wish.

the rest:
Dust on the Bible 🎵🎵🎵 (self-released, 1991/Quarterstick, 1994)
Hogs on the Highway 🎵🎵🎵🎵 (Sugar Hill, 1997)
Industry and Thrift 🎵🎵🎵🎵 (Sugar Hill, 1998)

worth searching for: Mark Rubin served as music director and Danny Barnes wrote the score for the Richard Linklater film *The Newton Boys* (Epic, 1998, prod. Mark Rubin, Dave McNair), a brilliant rendering of string-band and hot-jazz music from the early part of the century. *The Golden Years* (Southern Studios, 1992, prod. Bad Livers), an import-only gold-vinyl EP, collects early radio transcriptions of covers and a medley of fiddle tunes.

influences:
◀◀ Bill Monroe, Ralph Stanley, Killbilly, Motörhead

▶▶ Southern Culture on the Skids, Asylum Street Spankers

Daniel Durchholz

Bad Manners
Formed 1978, in London, England.

Buster Bloodvessel, vocals; Louis Cook, guitar; Davis Farren, bass; Martin Stewart, keyboards; Brian Tuitti, drums; Gus Herman, trumpet; Chris Kane, saxophone; Andrew Marson, saxophone.

The two-ton girth of cue-ball Buster Bloodvessel and his goofy onstage antics helped make Bad Manners one of the leading post-Specials ska bands of the '80s. Sporting a hyper novelty sound that resulted in a string of U.K. hits, Bad Manners continued the ska revival throughout most of the '80s and remained a touring band into the '90s, despite recent years of commercial indifference that's left most of its albums out of print on these shores. Thanks to the recent ska craze, the times seem to have finally caught up with the band.

what to buy: *The Collection* 𝄢𝄢𝄢 (Cleopatra, 1998, prod. various) serves as a de facto greatest hits, collecting the band's best tunes and showing off their occasional novelty bent with a ska version of the *Bonanza* theme and their remake of the (retitled) classic hit "My Girl Lollipop."

the rest:
Skinhead 𝄢𝄢 (Lagoon Reggae, 1994)
Heavy Petting 𝄢𝄢𝄢 (Moon Ska, 1997)

worth searching for: Among the band's individual albums that are now out of print, look for *Return of the Ugly* (Blue Beat-Relativity, 1989/Lagoon Reggae, 1995); *Forging Ahead* (Portrait, 1982/Magnet, 1995); and the compilation *Lip up Fatty* (Dojo, 1996), which collects their work for the Bluebeat label and adds some live tracks.

influences:
◀◀ Madness, the Specials

▶▶ Mighty Mighty Bosstones

Allan Orski

Bad Religion
Formed 1980, in Los Angeles, CA.

Greg Graffin, lead vocals; Brett Gurewitz, guitar, vocals (1980–94); Greg Hetson, guitar, vocals (1984–present); Brian Baker, guitar (1994–present); Jay Bentley, bass; Jay Ziskrout, drums (1980–81); Peter Finestone, drums (1981–91); Bobby Schayer, drums (1992–present).

From its first album, *How Could Hell Be Any Worse?,* in 1982, through 1993's *Recipe for Hate*, Bad Religion issued its records on its own label, Epitaph, which became a huge indie success story, also putting out albums by the Offspring, Rancid, Down by Law, L7, Dag Nasty, and others. Along with Fugazi, Bad Religion stood as the epitome of indie-ness, so its signing by Atlantic Records in 1993 came as a shock. The most intellectual punk band since Gang of Four, Bad Religion features a lead singer (Graffin) who interrupted the band's career to get a graduate degree in sociology and who subsequently structured the band's tours around his teaching schedule. Graffin offers penetrating analyses of socio-political issues, frequently sending listeners to their dictionaries with polysyllabic words never

used before or since in popular music. The group is hardly a bunch of eggheads, however, producing some of the most intense, hard-rocking punk ever made (1988's *Suffer* had just one song longer than 2:02). But then came a gradual progression to increased stylistic versatility, with harmony vocals and more varied tempos added to the fury—which neatly folded into the group's decision to go with a major label. Eventually the success of Epitaph led guitarist Brett Gurewitz to leave the group in favor of running the business.

what to buy: *Generator* 𝄢𝄢𝄢𝄢 (Epitaph, 1992, prod. Bad Religion) is one of the most majestic punk albums ever made, with "Atomic Garden" dissecting the infantilism of doomsday diplomacy and "Fertile Crescent" putting the Persian Gulf War in historical perspective. Bobby Schayer proves himself one of the greatest punk drummers throughout. *80–85* 𝄢𝄢𝄢𝄢 (Epitaph, 1991, prod. Jim Mankey, Bad Religion) collects the debut album, *How Could Hell Be Any Worse?*, plus EPs and compilation tracks of the first phases of the group's career.

what to buy next: *Recipe for Hate* 𝄢𝄢𝄢𝄢 (Epitaph/Atlantic, 1993, prod. Bad Religion) shows how Bad Religion has changed in 10 years, though with 14 hard 'n' fast songs clocking in at 37:42, it's still securely punk. The band manages to add intricacy, however, with simple ingredients such as trademark harmony vocals, solid guitar riffs, and lyrics that are simpler and more direct and as dead-on analytical as always. For something completely different, there's the eponymous album by Graffin's solo acoustic project *American Lesion* 𝄢𝄢𝄢 (Atlantic, 1997, prod. Greg Graffin). Musically it's a bit closer to mainstream pop, with tracks alternately suggesting country or, when he adds piano, early Steely Dan. But the lyrics are still hard-hitting.

what to avoid: *All Ages* 𝄢𝄢 (Epitaph, 1995, prod. Bad Religion) is compiled from the five in-print Epitaph albums and baited with a mere two otherwise unavailable live tracks. At just 50 minutes, it's not a good value despite a well-chosen program.

the rest:
Suffer 𝄢𝄢𝄢 (Epitaph, 1988)
No Control 𝄢𝄢𝄢 (Epitaph, 1989)
Against the Grain 𝄢𝄢𝄢𝄢 (Epitaph, 1990)
Stranger than Fiction 𝄢𝄢𝄢 (Atlantic, 1994)
The Gray Race 𝄢𝄢 (Atlantic, 1995)
No Substance 𝄢𝄢𝄢𝄢 (Atlantic, 1998)

worth searching for: *Into the Unknown* (Epitaph, 1983), the band-disowned second album, is long out of print. Occasionally there's talk of reissuing it in a remixed form, presumably with the prog-rock keyboards buried or erased, since there's nothing else about this album that the group could be ashamed of. It's a mystery why Atlantic didn't want to release *Tested* (Dragnet/Sony Germany, 1996, prod. Bad Religion, Ronnie Kimball), which sprinkles three new studio tracks and 24 favorites recorded live, making it a much better overview of the group than *All Ages*.

influences:

◀◀ The Clash, Crass, the Buzzcocks, Bad Brains

▶▶ Offspring, Pennywise, NOFX

Steve Holtje

Badfinger /Joey Molland

Formed 1968, in London, England. Disbanded 1975. Re-formed 1978.

Pete Ham, vocals, guitar, piano (1968–75); Tom Evans, vocals, guitar, bass (1968–83); Mike Gibbins, drums (1968–75); Ron Griffiths, bass (1968); Joey Molland, vocals, guitar, keyboards (1968–74, 1978–81); Bob Jackson, keyboards (1974–75); Joe Tanzin, guitar (1978); Kenny Harck, drums (1978); Tony Kaye, keyboards (1981); Glenn Sherba, guitar (1981); Richard Bryans, drums (1981).

Originally called the Iveys, Badfinger signed with the Beatles' Apple Records in 1968 after Paul McCartney discovered the band's demo. With a power-pop sound derivative of its famous mentors, Badfinger produced some wonderful songs during the early '70s, including "Come and Get It," "No Matter What," "Day After Day," and "Baby Blue," but suffered a tragic and short-lived existence. The Badfinger song "Without You" was covered by Harry Nilsson on his *Nilsson Schmilsson* album and hit #1 in 1972. The group backed ex-Beatles on tours and albums, and it performed at George Harrison's landmark benefit concert for Bangladesh in 1971. Clouds appeared on the horizon in 1974 when Joey Molland, upset over bungled management at Warner Bros., quit the band. The deluge came soon after, when bandleader and chief songwriter Pete Ham hanged himself in his London home in 1975. Molland and Tom Evans revived the band in 1978, but business problems continued, and Evans took his own life in 1983, also by hanging. Molland and Mike Gibbins now live in the U.S. and tour periodically under the Badfinger moniker.

what to buy: *No Dice* 🎵🎵🎵🎵🎵 (Apple, 1970/Gold Rush, 1992, prod. Geoff Emerick, Mal Evans), Badfinger's glorious second album, contains beautifully layered pop songs and established Ham as a versatile rock vocalist and imaginative songwriter. It spawned the classic hit "No Matter What" and the original version of "Without You." The band's third album, *Straight Up* 🎵🎵🎵🎵🎵 (Apple, 1971/Gold Rush, 1996, prod. Todd Rundgren, George Harrison, Geoff Emerick), assured it a spot in pop history. It features guest artists Leon Russell on piano and Harrison on slide guitar, as well as the unforgettable tunes "Baby Blue" and "Day After Day."

what to buy next: *Come and Get It: The Best of Badfinger* 🎵🎵🎵🎵 (Capitol, 1995, prod. various) is a comprehensive collection with all the big hits.

what to avoid: The band's debut album, *Magic Christian Music* 🎵🎵 (Apple, 1970/Gold Rush, 1991, prod. Paul McCartney), was also the soundtrack for the Peter Sellers–Ringo Starr film *The Magic Christian*. Although the songs aren't horrible, just inconsistent, the album produced the group's first hit, the McCartney-penned "Come and Get It."

the rest:
The Best of Badfinger, Volume 2 🎵🎵🎵🎵 (Rhino, 1989)
Day After Day 🎵🎵🎵 (Rykodisc, 1990)

solo outings:
Joey Molland:
The Pilgrim 🎵🎵 (Rykodisc, 1992)

Pete Ham:
7 Park Avenue 🎵🎵🎵 (Rykodisc, 1997)

influences:

◀◀ The Beatles, Manfred Mann, Herman's Hermits

▶▶ Teenage Fanclub, Suede, Del Amitri, Oasis

William Hanson

Badlands

Formed 1988, Los Angeles, CA. Disbanded 1991.

Jake E. Lee, guitars; Ray Gillen, vocals; Greg Chaisson, bass; Eric Singer, drums (1989–90); Jeff Martin, drums (1990–91).

A throwback to bombastic arena supergroups of the '70s, Badlands—along with bands such as Cinderella and Mr. Big—attempted to lead a blues-rock resurgence during the late '80s and early '90s, a movement that quickly fizzled out. Former Ozzy Osbourne guitarist Jake E. Lee recruited former Black Sabbath fill-in vocalist Ray Gillen for a blues-based group that would be a rootsy alternative to the frilly pop of then-big sellers like Whitesnake and Bon Jovi. Former Racer X singer Jeff Martin replaced Eric Singer after the group's first album, and soon after Badlands died a quiet death. Singer replaced the late Eric Carr in Kiss but was on the sidelines for the 1996 makeup-and-all reunion tour and was eventually dismissed. Singer and Chaisson are now in smaller metal bands, while Lee is working on his own.

what to buy: With Singer and Greg Chaisson, *Badlands* 𝄞𝄞𝄞 (Atlantic, 1989, prod. Paul O'Neill, Badlands) featured plenty of acoustic balladry and electric crotch rock that was supposedly Free-influenced but had Led Zeppelin stamped all over it.

the rest:
Voodoo Highway 𝄞𝄞 (Atlantic, 1991)

influences:
◀◀ Led Zeppelin, Free

▶▶ Seven Mary Three

Todd Wicks

Joan Baez

Born January 9, 1941, in Staten Island, NY.

The acknowledged diva of the folk-music world, Joan Baez has recorded albums in five different decades and remains an influence to a whole new generation of female song interpreters today. Baez peaked commercially some 35 years ago with an array of studio and live albums that celebrated the protest movement and helped give credentials to the writings of Bob Dylan and Phil Ochs. Though that movement faded, Baez remains a politically committed artist, and she has delved into a variety of music forms, including Celtic, Latin, and country. During the early 1970s, Baez brought Robbie Robertson's "The Night They Drove Old Dixie Down" within a whisker of the top of the charts, and a few years later went gold again with her collection *Diamonds and Rust* before reuniting with Dylan in the Rolling Thunder Review. Recently, Baez has toured and recorded with such folk and country voices as Mary Chapin Carpenter, Tish Hinojosa, and Dar Williams. Williams, in addition to country songsmith Sharon Rice, offers songwriting assistance on Baez's most recent effort, *Gone from Danger*.

what to buy: Baez's most influential work comes from her early 1960s period, a good chunk of which is included on *The First Ten Years* 𝄞𝄞𝄞 (Vanguard, 1970/1987, prod. Maynard Solomon). To

catch a glimpse of the singer as she moved into the "modern" folk era, check the enduring work *Joan Baez 5* 𝄞𝄞𝄞 (Vanguard, 1964, prod. Maynard Solomon), in which Baez helped raise the profile of Dylan, Ochs, and other important songwriters.

what to buy next: More than 20 years since its release, *Diamonds and Rust* 𝄞𝄞𝄞 (A&M, 1975, prod. David Kershenbaum) remains a remarkable "comeback" album in which Baez demonstrated to the world that she wasn't about to be retired as an old-fogie folkie. Besides the memorable title track (her own), she covers Jackson Browne, John Prine, and the Allman Brothers with real flair. Baez's most recent effort, *Gone from Danger* 𝄞𝄞𝄞 (Guardian, 1997, prod. Wally Wilson, Kenny Greenberg), finds her doing what she's often done so well in the past—unearthing excellent material from promising young songwriters, in this case Dar Williams and Richard Shindell.

the rest:
Joan Baez in Concert, Volume 1 𝄞𝄞𝄞𝄞 (Vanguard, 1962/1990)
Joan Baez in Concert, Volume 2 𝄞𝄞𝄞𝄞 (Vanguard, 1963/1990)
Farewell Angelina 𝄞𝄞𝄞 (Vanguard, 1965)
Noel 𝄞𝄞𝄞 (Vanguard, 1966/1997)
Joan 𝄞𝄞𝄞 (Vanguard, 1967)
Any Day Now 𝄞𝄞𝄞 (Vanguard, 1968)
Baptism 𝄞𝄞𝄞 (Vanguard, 1968)
One Day at a Time 𝄞𝄞 (Vanguard, 1969)
David's Album 𝄞𝄞 (Vanguard, 1969)
Carry It On 𝄞𝄞𝄞 (Vanguard, 1972)
Ballad Book 𝄞𝄞𝄞𝄞 (Vanguard, 1972)
Blessed Are . . . 𝄞𝄞𝄞 (Vanguard, 1972)
Hits/Greatest and Others 𝄞𝄞𝄞 (Vanguard, 1973)
Lovesong Album 𝄞𝄞𝄞 (Vanguard, 1975)
From Every Stage 𝄞𝄞 (A&M, 1976)
Best Of 𝄞𝄞𝄞 (A&M, 1977)
Blowin' Away 𝄞𝄞𝄞 (Epic Legacy, 1977/1990)
Honest Lullaby 𝄞𝄞𝄞 (Vanguard 1979/1990)
The Night They Drove Old Dixie Down 𝄞𝄞𝄞 (Vanguard, 1979)
The Joan Baez Country Music Album 𝄞𝄞𝄞 (Vanguard, 1979)
Very Early Joan 𝄞𝄞𝄞𝄞 (Vanguard, 1983)
The Contemporary Ballad Book 𝄞𝄞𝄞 (Vanguard, 1987)
Ballad Book, Volume 2 𝄞𝄞𝄞 (Vanguard, 1990)
Play Me Backwards 𝄞𝄞𝄞 (Virgin, 1992)
Rare Live and Classic 𝄞𝄞𝄞 (Vanguard, 1993)
Joan Baez Ballad Book 𝄞𝄞𝄞𝄞 (Vanguard, 1994)
Ring Them Bells 𝄞𝄞𝄞 (Guardian, 1995)
Live at Newport 𝄞𝄞𝄞 (Vanguard, 1996)
Recently 𝄞𝄞𝄞𝄞 (Capitol, 1996)
Vanguard Sessions: Baez Sings Dylan 𝄞𝄞𝄞𝄞 (Vanguard, 1998)

influences:
◀◀ Mother Maybelle Carter, Bob Dylan, Pete Seeger

▶▶ Dar Williams, Mary Chapin Carpenter, Indigo Girls, Jewel

David Simons

Chris Bailey
See: The Saints

Bailter Space
Formed 1987, in New Zealand.

John Halvorsen, guitar, bass, vocals; Alister Parker, guitar, bass, vocals; Hamish Kilgour, drums, samples (1987–89); Brent McLachlan, drums (1990–present).

Growing out of the seminal guitar-noise band the Gordons, and eventually replicating the Gordons lineup, Bailter Space has soldiered on, gradually building up an alternative following in the U.S. (the trio eventually based itself in New York). The Gordons did clangorous, non-chordal guitar sound-sculptures before Sonic Youth saw the inside of a studio, and the comparison is obvious. But Bailter Space is more consistently excellent and less annoyingly self-conscious, though a Bailter Space track such as *Vortura*'s "Voices" suggests the influence eventually went both ways. The music is dark and guitar-oriented, often with bass-heavy, minor-key riffs and hauntingly minimal melodies. Oblique song titles and buried vocals emphasize the tone of angst and confusion.

what to buy: *Wammo* 𝄢𝄢𝄢𝄢 (Matador, 1995, prod. Rod Hui, Bailter Space) has the group's most radio-friendly song, "Splat," and its most abrasively forbidding, "Voltage," thus offering a good cross-section of the band's styles and virtues. *Vortura* 𝄢𝄢𝄢𝄢 (Matador, 1994, prod. Bailter Space, Paul Berry) is just as good in its subtle sonic variations.

what to buy next: *Thermos* 𝄢𝄢𝄢 (Flying Nun, 1990/Matador, 1991, prod. Bailter Space, Nick Roughan) witnesses the early development of the above albums' virtues and marked the reversion to the Gordons lineup.

the rest:
Aim 𝄢𝄢𝄢 (Matador EP, 1992)
Robot World 𝄢𝄢𝄢 (Matador, 1993)
Nelsh/Tanker 𝄢𝄢𝄢 (Matador, 1995)

worth searching for: The most recent Bailter Space CD is on a small NY label. *Capsul* (Turnbuckle, 1997, prod. Bailter Space) continues in the trio's grungy guitar-focused rock vein, but with more variety. There are quieter moments than before, balanced by punkier, more driven tracks than on recent albums.

influences:
◀◀ The Velvet Underground, the Stooges, Television
▶▶ Sonic Youth, Band of Susans, Come, Nirvana

Steve Holtje

WHAT ALBUM CHANGED YOUR LIFE?

The first time I heard Pete Seeger sing 'The Bells of Rhymney,' that was it for me. That's the one that turned me around, at least in terms of my musical life. His character is just so powerful.

Joan Baez

Merrill Bainbridge
Born June 2, 1968, in Melbourne, Australia.

Shy, angelic-voiced Merrill Bainbridge began her musical career singing in cover bands as a teenager. Unable to afford the high costs of studio time, Bainbridge sang back-up for several Australian bands and accepted studio time as her payment, with which she worked up the songs for her debut album.

what to avoid: The plucky debut *The Garden* 𝄢𝄢 (Universal Records, 1996, prod. Siew) proved Bainbridge an adept singer. But the music is boring. With its sparse piano, "Song for Neen" sounds like a '90s version of the Carpenters' "Close to You." The flute lead-in to the angressive pop song "Sleeping Dogs" is painful. The quirky "Mouth" is a catchy little number, but its novelty quickly wears off. Hopefully, Bainbridge found some new collaborators to make an improved second effort.

the rest:
Between the Days N/A (Universal, 1998)

influences:
◀◀ The Carpenters, the Go-Go's, Donna Lewis

Christina Fuoco

Dan Baird
See: The Georgia Satellites

LaVern Baker
Born Delores Williams, November 11, 1929, in Chicago, IL. Died March 10, 1997, in New York, NY.

LaVern Baker's sassy, gospel-drenched vocals made her novelty hits exhilarating to teenagers of the '50s and helped pave the way for '60s soul music. Baker got her professional start in Chicago nightclubs under the name Little Miss Sharecropper; she would dress in raggedy clothes and amuse spectators by outshouting the great Joe Williams. Billed variously under other names as well (Bea Baker, LaVern in LaVern and Maurice King & His Wolverines), she recorded unsuccessfully with National, RCA, and Columbia/OKeh before joining the Todd Rhodes Orchestra and settling on the name LaVern Baker for her lone outing on King Records. She signed with Atlantic in 1953, and her first chart offerings ("Soul on Fire," "Tomorrow Night") were soulful ballads. "Tweedlee Dee," a Latin-tempoed novelty with nursery rhyme lyrics, was Baker's breakthrough hit. Teens loved it—when they could hear it, that is. It was common practice at the time for white singers to cover black R&B hits, and pop singer Georgia Gibbs's version of "Tweedlee Dee" (recorded with the same musicians and arrangements) garnered far more airplay and greater sales. (Gibbs also covered Baker's "Tra-la-la.") Baker unsuccessfully mounted a lawsuit over the theft of her sound. Eventually, disc jockeys such as Alan Freed boycotted competing white versions of R&B hits, and Baker's career took off in earnest. The torchy "Play It Fair" and "I Can't Love You Enough" were solid hits on the R&B charts, but during 1956 another teen-oriented shouter, "Jim Dandy" (the flipside of "Tra-la-la"), was a crossover smash. A sequel record, "Jim Dandy Got Married," did not fare as well. Baker appeared in two of Alan Freed's teen flicks, *Rock, Rock, Rock* (1956) and *Mister Rock 'n' Roll* (1957); in the latter she lip-synched "Humpty Dumpty Heart," a trite ditty sung to the tune of "A Froggy Went-a-Courtin'." It was her last nursery rhyme-type success, as 1958 saw the release of Baker's biggest hit and best ballad, "I Cried a Tear," which featured King Curtis on sax. At a career crossroads, Baker wanted her music to take a more adult direction. Her 1958 LP *LaVern Baker Sings Bessie Smith* was critically well-received, but sales were disappointing. Baker returned to alternating teen novelties with heartache ballads, but her chart clout had diminished; 1960's "Bumble Bee" was a small hit, though a stylistic anachronism. Baker's career was briefly revived when producers Jerry Leiber and Mike Stoller had her cut a rough 'n' ready version of Chuck Willis's "C.C. Rider" ("See See Rider") and the raving gospel classic "Saved." Vocally, Baker was at her peak, but no more hits were forthcoming. In 1964 she left Atlantic, and five years later, after contracting pneumonia following a troop entertainment tour of Vietnam, Baker moved to the Philippines for her health. During the next 20 years she operated a serviceman's club in Subic Bay, where she periodically sang. In 1990 she returned to America to replace her friend and former lablemate, Ruth Brown, in the critically acclaimed Broadway revue *Black & Blue*. That year Baker was voted into the Rock and Roll Hall of Fame and received a career achievement award from the Rhythm & Blues Foundation. Baker also resumed recording, doing an LP for the DRG label, a live LP for Rhino Records, duets with Ben E. King, and a memorable sexy blues cut on the *Dick Tracy* soundtrack. Diabetes eventually forced the amputation of her legs, but she sang until her death from a wheelchair, with all the gusto and verve at her command.

what to buy: *Soul on Fire: The Best of LaVern Baker* 𝄫𝄫𝄫𝄫𝄫 (Rhino/Atlantic, 1991, prod. Ahmet Ertegun, Jerry Wexler) 𝄫𝄫𝄫𝄫𝄫 contains 20 of her best-known recordings ("Tweedlee Dee," "Jim Dandy") but is skewed more towards her adult titles such as "Saved," "I Cried a Tear," and "Tomorrow Night."

what to buy next: *LaVern Baker Sings Bessie Smith* 𝄫𝄫𝄫𝄫 (WEA/Atlantic, 1958, prod. Nesuhi Ertegun) is an excellent tribute/compilation of Smith's songs ("Gimme a Pigfoot" is a real standout), and Baker does not compromise her own sound one iota.

what to avoid: It's not really a bad disc, but *Woke up This Mornin'* 𝄫𝄫 (DRG, 1992, prod. Hugh Fordin) contains some unlikely covers (James Taylor's "You've Got a Friend," the Bee Gees' "To Love Somebody") clumsily mixed with updated blues standards.

the rest:
Live in Hollywood 1991 𝄫𝄫𝄫 (Rhino, 1991)

worth searching for: A top-notch, 26-song import, *Blues Side of Rock 'n' Roll* (Star Club, 1993, prod. Ahmet Ertegun, Jerry Wexler) boasts several of Baker's lesser teen-oriented hits ("Bumble Bee," "Tra-la-La," "Humpty Dumpty") as well as much of the material on the Rhino disc. The soundtrack *Dick Tracy* (Sire Records, 1990, prod. Andy Paley) has one track by Baker, the wonderfully lewd "Slow Rollin' Mama." *The Sullivan Years—The Rhythm & Blues Revue* (TVT, 1993, prod. Steve Gottlieb) is hampered by dull sound, but Baker is terrific on her live version of "Tweedlee Dee." Also, on the Jackie Wilson anthology *Mr. Excitement* (Rhino, 1992), Baker and Wilson duet on their minor hit "Don't Think Twice."

influences:
◀◀ Bessie Smith, Esther Phillips
▶▶ Linda Hopkins, Aretha Franklin

Ken Burke

Ginger Baker's Air Force
See: Cream

The Balancing Act
Formed 1983, in Los Angeles, CA. Disbanded 1989.

Jeff Davis, acoustic guitar, vocals; **Steve Wagner**, bass, acoustic guitar, vocals; **Willie Aron**, acoustic and electric guitars, keyboards, melodica, drums, bass, kitchen sinks; Robert Blackmon, drums, percussion, vocals.

At a time when most L.A. bands were either trying to out-metal Poison and Mötley Crüe, follow the Dream Syndicate and Green on Red into rootsy psychedelia, or create the Stateside version of British gothdom, the Balancing Act bravely and quietly carved out their own path. Although they never sold albums in large quantities, they provided an important link between folk-rock groups of the 1960s and 1970s and the eclectic urban folk-influenced artists of the '90s. In the late '80s, a rebirth of acoustic-based music (briefly called Nu Folk) began flowering in Los Angeles, ultimately leading to the thriving coffeehouse scene of today. Whether they know it or not, current-day practitioners of the genre are following in the Balancing Act's footsteps. Just as the band's funky folkiness had earned them a bit of modern-rock airplay (with their version of George Clinton's "Can You Get to That?"), internal pressures and the differing ambitions of the group's four members led to an early breakup. Since then, each of them has been involved in other musical projects (Aron toured with Syd Straw; Blackmon played with an early version of Box the Walls; Davis has recently resurfaced in San Francisco as leader of electronic folkies Niagara), but the Balancing Act never rode the high wire together again. Pity.

what to buy: It's unfortunate that *Curtains* ꗏꗏꗏꗏ (I.R.S., 1988, prod. Andy Gill) turned out to be the foursome's final release, because it shows that they were starting to move in more interesting directions, adding electric guitars to several cuts, and generally spicing up their backing grooves. Former Gang of Four member Gill brings some of his jangly post-punk expertise to the mix, and the band's odd, folky cover of George Clinton's "Can You Get to That?" actually became a left-field alterna-hit. Also noteworthy are the group's lyrics, which examine relationships, often from a unique perspective.

what to buy next: More inventive than the debut EP, and more quintessentially Balancing Act than *Curtains*, *Three Squares and a Roof* ꗏꗏꗏ (Primitive Man/I.R.S., 1987, prod. Vic Abascal, the Balancing Act) exemplifies the group's quirky indie folk-rock sound.

what to avoid: Less accomplished than their later work, *New Campfire Songs* ꗏꗏ (Primitive Man EP, 1986, prod. Peter Case) can just as well be skipped, especially if you can find the CD of *Three Squares*, which includes these six early songs.

influences:
◀◀ Simon & Garfunkel, Crosby, Stills & Nash, the dB's, Jonathan Richman

▶▶ Semisonic, Barenaked Ladies, 10,000 Maniacs, Downy Mildew, Trip Shakespeare, Syd Straw, Box the Walls

Bob Remstein

Long John Baldry

Born January 12, 1941, in East Maddon, England.

A bona fide giant of a man, both in height (6 feet, 7 inches) *and* in stature, Baldry's background in folk, blues, and jazz, and his uncanny blending of all three, paralleled the very birth of the entire British rock scene, and history rightfully records the man as a key player in its subsequent development. Touring his homeland during the late '50s accompanying such visiting U.S. stars as Memphis Slim and Ramblin' Jack Elliott, Baldry inspired keen onlookers Eric Clapton and Spencer Davis, to name but two, to pick up their first guitars. In 1962 he helped launch Britain's first electric blues band, Alexis Korner's Blues Incorporated, providing an all-important training ground for people like Mick Jagger, Charlie Watts, Paul Jones, and Jack Bruce in the process. Ever-restless, Baldry spent the mid-'60s forming and dissolving bands with everyone from Cyril Davies to Julie Driscoll, but it wasn't until he recorded a series of lush beat-ballads in 1967 that he enjoyed his first successes on record—success that, despite assistance from protégés such as Rod Stewart and Elton John (who were quickly becoming enormous international stars in their own right), remained confined to the British Isles. After recording a pair of deplorable "white suit" albums for Casablanca at the height of the disco craze, he sought refuge in the comparative calm of Canada, where he happily resides today. When not recording and touring the globe (his fan base, particularly in Germany, has remained strong for over thirty years), he enjoys a lucrative side-career as a commercial voice-over artist, and with typical self-effacing style sums up his landmark career thusly: "Legend? Of course, dear boy. So when does the next set start?"

what to buy: Tough, vital, smoky, but with the man's inimitable air of class, *On Stage Tonight: Baldry's Out!* ꗏꗏꗏꗏ (Stony Plain, 1993, prod. Holger Petersen) captures Long John and a crack back-up combo blasting it out on the stage of Hamburg's Fabrik Club to a suitably ribald crowd. Equally thrilling, and essential, is the historic *R&B from the Marquee* ꗏꗏꗏꗏ (Mobile Fidelity Sound Lab, 1996, prod. Jack Good). Here are vintage 1962 recordings by Blues Incorporated in which the very foundation of '60s British rock can be heard.

what to buy next: Both *Let the Heartaches Begin/Wait for Me* ꗏꗏꗏ (Beat Goes On, 1995, prod. Tony Macauley) and *A Thrill's a Thrill: The Canadian Years* ꗏꗏꗏꗏ (EMI Music Canada, 1995, prod. various) provide fine retrospectives of the man's late '60s and early-'80s work, respectively.

the rest:
It Still Ain't Easy ꗏꗏꗏ (Stony Plain, 1991)
Right to Sing the Blues ꗏꗏꗏ (Stony Plain, 1996)

worth searching for: Another BGO import, *Long John's Blues/Looking at Long John* (Beat Goes On, 1995, prod. various) combines the man's sizzling 1964 and 1966 Pye albums on one disc. File alongside John Mayall's Bluesbreakers as prime examples of the British blues revival at its best. *It Ain't Easy* (Warner Bros., 1971, prod. Elton John, Rod Stewart) was supposed to lay the groundwork for Long John's conquering of America, only its rollicking "Don't Try to Lay No Boogie Woogie on the King of Rock and Roll" became an early FM radio staple instead.

influences:

◄◄ Sonny Terry, Big Bill Broonzy, Leadbelly, Willie Dixon, Lonnie Johnson, Muddy Waters

►► Eric Clapton, Mick Jagger, Rod Stewart, Reginald Kenneth Dwight (Elton John)

Gary Pig Gold

Hank Ballard
/Hank Ballard
& the Midnighters

Born November 18, 1936, in Detroit, MI.

Radio may have banned his biggest '50s hits, and Chubby Checker cashed the big paycheck for "The Twist," but Rock and Roll Hall of Famer Hank Ballard towered over the R&B landscape of the day. His 1954 record "Work with Me Annie" proved too hot for the timid times, but the song inspired many sanitized rewrites and answer records. Censorship didn't slow down Ballard, who followed that record with the infamous "Annie Had a Baby" and the even more incendiary "Sexy Ways." While Ballard & the Midnighters served as a fixture on the R&B charts through the '50s, the group didn't hit home on the pop Top 10 until 1960 with "Finger Popping Time" and "Let's Go, Let's Go, Let's Go." Ballard joined doo-woppers the Royals in time to cut the group's first R&B chart entry, "Get It," in 1953 and set the stage for the historic recordings they made together. The group finally disbanded in '65, and Ballard went on to tour and record with James Brown before reviving the Midnighters during the '80s and recreating his classic '50s stage show. By bucking the sexual mores of the times, he may have been denied his just due on the charts, but Ballard's records serve to demonstrate an important point—rock 'n' roll never got any better than this, only different.

what to buy: *Sexy Ways: The Best of Hank Ballard and the Midnighters* 🎵🎵🎵🎵 (Rhino, 1993, prod. various) is the only Midnighters collection necessary. The 20 tracks cover all the highlights of his original King sessions.

what to buy next: An English import, *Live at the Palais* 🎵🎵🎵 (Charly, 1987, prod. John White) captures Ballard's current stage show, merrily mixing his classic rhythm and blues with more contemporary soul.

the rest:
Their Greatest Jukebox Hits 🎵🎵🎵🎵 (King, 1956/1990)
Spotlight on Hank Ballard 🎵🎵🎵 (King, 1960/1994)
Hank Ballard and the Midnighters 🎵🎵🎵 (King, 1961)
What You Get When the Gettin' Gets Good 🎵🎵🎵🎵 (Charly U.K., 1986)
Singin' and Swingin' the Twist 🎵🎵🎵🎵 (King, 1990)
And His Midnighters 🎵🎵🎵 (King, 1990)
Naked in the Rain 🎵🎵 (After Hours, 1993)
Let 'em Roll 🎵🎵🎵 (Charly, 1993)
Sings 24 Hit Tunes 🎵🎵🎵 (King, 1994)
The One and Only 🎵🎵🎵 (King, 1994)
Dance Along 🎵🎵🎵 (King, 1994)
All 20 of Their Chart Hits (1953–1962) 🎵🎵🎵🎵 (King/Federal, 1995)
Greatest Hits 🎵🎵🎵 (King, 1996)

worth searching for: One of the prime collectors' items of '50s R&B, the Midnighters' 1954 10-inch album *Their Greatest Jukebox Hits* invariably brings more than $1,000 for a copy in reasonable condition.

influences:

◄◄ Gene Autry, Jimmy Rushing, the Five Royales

►► James Brown, Swamp Dogg, John Fogerty, Lou Ann Barton

Joel Selvin and Ken Burke

Bananarama
/Shakespear's Sister

Formed 1981, in London, England.

Bananarama: Sarah Dallin, vocals; Karen Woodward, vocals; Siobhan Fahey, vocals (1981–87); Jacqui Sullivan, vocals (1988–91). **Shakespear's Sister:** Siobhan Fahey, vocals; Marcella Detroit, vocals, guitar.

The advent of MTV surely lent an upper hand to acts with charm and visual appeal, and the ladies of Bananarama had that in abundance. They also had songs with plenty of hooks and danceable accessibility—sweet cotton candy for the ears. Bananarama enjoyed a handful of hits before splintering, with Fahey starting the artsier Shakespear's Sister with former Bob Seger/Eric Clapton backup singer Marcy Levy (a.k.a. Marcella Detroit); self-conscious where Bananarama was light and airy, the duo had far less commercial action before splitting up.

what to buy: Bananarama's *Greatest Hits Collection* 🎵🎵🎵 (London, 1988, prod. various) isn't quite comprehensive, but it has the major hits and offers a painless listen.

what to buy next: Shakespear's *Hormonally Yours* ⟡⟡⟡ (London, 1991, prod. Alan Moulder, Chris Thomas, Shakespear's Sister) features a more grown-up kind of pop that produced the polished "Stay" and "I Don't Care." *True Confessions* ⟡⟡⟡ (London, 1986/Razor & Tie, 1995, prod. Stock/Aitken/Waterman), Bananarama's last real success in the marketplace, contains its hit rendition of Shocking Blue's "Venus."

what to avoid: *Pop Life* ⟡⟡ (London, 1991, prod. Youth) can be very cruel indeed when you're out of fashion.

the rest:
Ultraviolet ⟡⟡ (Curb, 1996)

worth searching for: Bananarama's U.S. debut, *Deep Sea Skiving* (London, 1983) is really a collection of its early singles: "He Was Really Sayin' Somethin" (with Fun Boy Three), "Shy Boy," and "Na Na Hey Hey (Kiss Him Goodbye)" are all gushing group vocal confections.

solo outings:
Marcella Detroit:
Jewel ⟡⟡⟡ (London, 1994)

influences:
◀◀ The Mamas & the Papas, the Chiffons, the Shangri-La's

▶▶ Wilson Phillips, Milli Vanilli, the Tuesdays, Spice Girls, All Saints

Allan Orski

Banco de Gaia

Formed 1991, in London, England.

Toby Marks, various instruments.

Multifaceted English electronic music pioneer Toby Marks (born in 1964 in England) is Banco de Gaia. Marks has been making music since 1991 when he issued a batch of cassette-only releases that explored mostly ambient musical textures. The environmentally-conscious and politically-aware musician is involved with a Tibetan support group in the U.K., and his social and political convictions inform the themes of his music. The name Banco de Gaia ostensibly comes from a bank in a small Portuguese town.

what to buy: Most of Marks's albums delve into the realm of ambient music. His second full-length album, *Last Train to Lhasa* ⟡⟡⟡⟡ (Planet Dog/Mammoth Records, 1995, prod. Toby Marks), is perhaps his best, infused with trance-like beats and tribal chants.

what to buy next: According to Marks, the music of *Live at Glastonbury* ⟡⟡⟡ (Planet Dog/Mammoth Records, 1996, prod. Toby Marks) captures one of his best live performances ever. The

music is far more upbeat and groove-oriented than his previous albums, with big, bending bass rhythms and energetic crowd noise to boot. *Big Men Cry* ⟡⟡⟡ (Planet Dog/Mammoth Records, 1997, prod. Toby Marks), on the other hand, is a lot more mellow. It features sharp songwriting and the inclusion of live instruments coupled with his sample-heavy production skills.

the rest:
Maya ⟡⟡⟡ (Planet Dog/Mammoth Records, 1994)

worth searching for: Real fans will want to track down bootlegs of the cassette-only releases (now out of print): *Medium* (1991), *Freeform Flutes & Fading Tibetans* (1992), and *Deep Live* (1993).

influences:
◀◀ Brian Eno
▶▶ EAT-STATIC

Joseph Patel

The Band

Formed 1967, in Woodstock, NY.

Robbie Robertson, vocals, guitar (1967–76); Levon Helm, vocals, drums; Rick Danko, vocals, bass, guitar; Richard Manuel (died March 4, 1986), vocals, piano (1967–86); Garth Hudson, keyboards, saxophone; Jim Weider, guitar (1983–present); Randy Ciarlante, vocals, percussion (1983–present); Richard Bell, vocals, piano (1986–present).

By the time they became known simply as the Band, the four cocky, young Canadians with the drummer from Arkansas had played together for almost seven years. As part of Ronnie Hawkins's backup group and later on their own as the Hawks, they had became the baddest of the bad-ass bands that roamed the lounge-lizard circuit from Ontario and Quebec in Canada through the Rust Belt and the American South during the early 1960s. But they worked as hard as they played, and by the time Bob Dylan tapped them as his electric backing band for a world tour in the summer of 1965, the Hawks had become a sophisticated, seasoned quintet with several secret weapons: three equally individualistic lead singers, including Richard Manuel's seductive soul pipes; Garth Hudson's multi-instrumental mastery; Robbie Robertson's pin-point guitar and increasingly incisive song lyrics; and the well-lubricated rhythm section of Levon Helm and Rick Danko. After working with Dylan on what later became known as *The Basement Tapes*, the group released *Music from Big Pink* in 1967, their first collection of distinctly American short stories told in a musical language that bridged the growing generation gap. (Is there anybody under 55 who doesn't know what it feels like to "(pull) into Nazareth feelin' 'bout half past dead"?) With the release of its second album, the Band emerged as a live unit, but the high expectations created by those two albums were never met again. The group

Rick Danko of the Band (© **Ken Settle**)

toured sporadically and sputtered and coughed through a series of less interesting albums; the best of the later work would
be reworkings of their bedrock material. They ended it all in
1976 by throwing a huge farewell party dubbed, fittingly, *The
Last Waltz*; the film of the event, which features an all-star array
of acts, was directed by Martin Scorsese, and it more or less
hides the acrimony that had developed among the members,
especially between Helm and Robertson. It would be the last
time the five of them would appear on stage together, although
Danko, Helm, and Hudson still perform and record as the Band,
and Robertson has carved out a low-profile solo career that includes four albums, some acting, and an impressive portfolio of
film and soundtrack work.

what to buy: Fortunately, the Band's music is plentiful and
readily available. You still can't beat *Music from Big Pink*
🎵🎵🎵🎵🎵 (Capitol, 1968, prod. John Simon) and *The Band* 🎵🎵🎵🎵🎵
(Capitol, 1969, prod. John Simon), two of rock's most original,
imaginative, enduring, and enigmatic albums. *Moondog Matinee* 🎵🎵🎵🎵🎵 (Capitol, 1973, prod. the Band) is a rousing return
to their roadhouse days, a set of old favorites that evokes their

youthful charisma by showing off their mature sophistication.
Rock of Ages 🎵🎵🎵🎵 (Capitol, 1972, prod. the Band) is a superb
live recording with Allen Toussaint's soulful horn charts sprinkling heavy gris-gris all over their rock 'n' roll grit.

what to buy next: *Stage Fright* 🎵🎵🎵🎵 (Capitol, 1970, prod. the
Band), their third album, includes several classics, including
"The Shape I'm In," "W.S. Wolcott Medicine Show," and the autobiographical title track. *Across the Great Divide* 🎵🎵🎵🎵 (Capitol, 1995, prod. various) includes most of the best songs with
more than a third devoted to rarities and early Hawks' material
found nowhere else; it's a must-have for true-blue fans.

what to avoid: *Islands* **woof!** (Capitol, 1977, prod. the Band) is an
uneven plate of leftovers that, as the title suggests, demonstrates the huge divisions that had isolated the group members.

the rest:
Cahoots 🎵🎵🎵 (Capitol, 1971)
Northern Lights—Southern Cross 🎵🎵🎵🎵 (Capitol, 1975)
The Best of the Band 🎵🎵 (Capitol, 1976)
The Last Waltz 🎵🎵🎵🎵 (Capitol, 1978)
Jericho 🎵🎵🎵 (Pyramid/Rhino, 1993)

The Night They Drove Old Dixie Down 🎵🎵🎵 (Capitol Special Products, 1994)

The Band Live at Watkins Glen 🎵🎵🎵 (Capitol, 1995)

High on the Hog 🎵🎵 (Pyramid/Rhino, 1996)

Jubilation N/A (River North, 1998)

worth searching for: *The Band* (Rhino, 1997) is a riveting retrospective film about the making of the first two records, with home movie clips, impromptu performances, and in-the-studio commentary by all members about making the group's best music—and it beats *The Last Waltz* for insight. Now only available as an import, *To Kingdom Come* (Capitol, 1991/1996) is a two-disc overview. The wrongly titled *Concert at Royal Albert Hall* bootleg of the Manchester, England, concert Dylan and the Hawks played in 1965 captures them at their most musically audacious at a time when hostile audiences were booing them (because Dylan had "gone electric").

solo outings:

Robbie Robertson:

Robbie Robertson 🎵🎵🎵 (Geffen, 1987)

Storyville 🎵🎵 (Geffen, 1991)

Music for the Native Americans 🎵🎵🎵 (Capitol, 1995)

Contact from the Underground of Redboy 🎵🎵🎵 (Capitol, 1998)

Rick Danko:

Rick Danko 🎵🎵🎵 (Arista, 1977)

Danko Fjeld Anderson:

Rick Danko/Eric Anderson/Jonas Fjeld 🎵🎵🎵 (Ryko, 1991)

Ridin' on the Blinds 🎵🎵🎵🎵 (Ryko, 1997)

Levon Helm:

Levon Helm and the RCO All-Stars 🎵🎵🎵 (ABC, 1977/Edsel, 1996)

American Son 🎵🎵🎵 (MCA, 1980/Edsel, 1997)

Levon Helm 🎵🎵 (Capitol, 1982/Edsel, 1998)

influences:

◀◀ Ronnie Hawkins, Clarence "Frogman" Henry, Bobby "Blue" Bland, the Impressions, Chuck Berry, the Miracles, Marvin Gaye, Booker T. & the MG's, Curtis Mayfield, the Staple Singers

▶▶ Graham Parker & the Rumour, Eric Clapton, McGuinness-Flint, the Long Ryders, Uncle Tupelo, Wilco, Son Volt, subdudes

see also: *Bob Dylan, Ronnie Hawkins*

Leland Rucker

Band of Susans
/Robert Poss

Formed 1986, in New York, NY. Disbanded 1995.

Robert Poss, guitar, vocals; Susan Stenger, bass, vocals; Ron Spitzer, drums; Susan Lyall, guitar, vocals (1986–87); Susan Tallman, guitar, vocals (1986–87); Alva Rogers, vocals (1986–87); Page Hamilton, guitar, vocals (1988–89); Karen Haglof, guitar, (1988–89); Mark Lonergan, guitar, (1989–95); Anne Husic, guitar, (1989–95).

This downtown Manhattan band went the Sonic Youth–Live Skull distortion-feedback-drone crowd one better. Not only did Band of Susans have *three* guitarists (and, for a while in its early days, three Susans), it also featured monolithic songs based on intertwining or alternating riff patterns rather than standard rock song progressions. Leaders Susan Stenger (who has an alternate career as a flutist) and Robert Poss (who worked with Rhys Chatham) had strong backgrounds in the avant-garde. Still, no BOS stuff is beyond open-minded rock listeners, though the heavy, dense sound is hardly easy listening. Poss's fascination with guitar sound produces the aural equivalent of an Ad Reinhardt painting, in which different shades of black are subtly contrasted. Stenger stepped increasingly to the fore—vocally, instrumentally, and compositionally—during the band's latter days, but he has since moved to England. There, she and Poss have collaborated with former Wire ideaman Bruce Gilbert, among others. Meanwhile, Poss has gotten into producing other bands.

what to buy: The powerful *Veil* 🎵🎵🎵🎵 (Restless, 1993, prod. Robert Poss) has the most memorable riffs and patterns in the group's catalog, including "Mood Swing," "The Red and the Black" (*not* the Blue Öyster Cult song), the implacably spooky "Following My Heart," and the anthemic, oddly uplifting

---

WHAT ALBUM CHANGED YOUR LIFE?

One that I thought had an influence on myself and a lot of other people was this record called *The Best of Muddy Waters*. It was before there was such a thing as best-ofs. I've had discussions with everybody from Miles Davis to Gil Evans to Eric Clapton about what a tremendous impact this record had on the music world. It's just so powerful in so many ways.

Robbie Robertson (of the Band)

"Blind." This is the most perfect, consistent, and original expression of the sound at the core of the BOS sonic juggernaut.

what to buy next: *The Word and the Flesh* 🎸🎸🎸 (Restless, 1991, prod. Robert Poss) has a greater sense of space, spreading out rather than compacting the guitar assault. The minimal melodies are more memorable than before, especially on "Now Is Now." *Here Comes Success* 🎸🎸🎸 (Restless, 1995, prod. Robert Poss) stretches out the structures, injects different rhythms (the proto-funk riff of "Hell Bent," the Bo Diddley beat of "Stone Like a Heart"), tries out a few new ideas—as represented in "Elizabeth Stride (1843–1888)," a descriptive, menacing tribute to a victim of Jack the Ripper—and indulges in a short study of feedback ("As Luck Would Have It"). The final BOS album, it's a worthy valedictory.

what to avoid: Poss's second solo album, *Inverse Guitar* 🎸🎸 (Trace Elements 1988), is less grounded in rock than BOS, more for lovers of feedback, distortion, and sampling.

the rest:
Love Agenda 🎸🎸🎸 (Blast First, 1989)
The Peel Sessions 🎸🎸🎸 (Strange Fruit, 1992)
Now 🎸🎸🎸 (Restless EP, 1992)

worth searching for: All four songs on the EP *Blessing and Curse* (Trace Elements, 1987, prod. Robert Poss) are included on *Hope against Hope* (Blast First, 1988, prod. Robert Poss), offering the early manifestations of the group's dark sound (the actual *B&C* versions of two are here; the other two are on *Love Agenda*). The import compilation *Wired for Sound* (Blast First, 1995, prod. Robert Poss) may be the easiest way to hear material from the out-of-U.S.-print first two releases.

solo outings:
Robert Poss:
Sometimes 🎸🎸🎸 (Trace Elements, 1986)

influences:
◀◀ The Rolling Stones, Wire, Rhys Chatham, the Psychedelic Furs, Joy Division, Live Skull

▶▶ aMiniature, Sculpey

see also: *Helmet*

Steve Holtje

The Bangles
/Susanna Hoffs

Formed 1981, in Los Angeles, CA. Disbanded 1988.

Susanna Hoffs, guitar; Vicki Peterson, lead guitar; Debbi Peterson, drums; Michael Steele, bass (1984–88); Annette Zilinskas, bass (1981–82).

If the Go-Go's were new wave's giddy girl group, the Bangles were their leather-jacketed, street-smart cousins. Originally known as the Bangs, the all-female band charged onto the indie scene as a Beatlesque pop group with psychedelic overtones. Signing with Columbia Records in 1984, they added former Runaways member Michael Steele and scored a radio hit in 1986 with "Manic Monday," written specially for them by the Artist Then Known As Prince Who Cleverly Credited Himself As Christopher. With guitarist-singer Susanna Hoffs emerging as the star in a band that shared everything from lead vocals and songwriting duties to interviews, the Bangles imploded from the internal friction and split up in 1988. Band members have been keeping low profiles since then, with Hoffs pursuing a bumpy solo career that finally hit its stride in 1996 with her self-titled sophomore effort. Vicki Peterson became a charter member of the Continental Drifters with Peter Holsapple and Susan Cowsill and, in an ironic twist, substituted for Charlotte Caffey on the Go-Go's' 1994 reunion tour.

what to buy: *All Over the Place* 🎸🎸🎸 (Columbia, 1984, prod. David Kahne), their major-label debut, blends *Revolver* -era guitars with luscious Mamas & the Papas harmonies on such jangly gems as "James," "Hero Takes a Fall," and a charming cover of Katrina and the Waves's "Going Down to Liverpool." Their swan song, *Everything* 🎸🎸🎸 (Columbia, 1988, prod. Davitt Sigerson), gets dismissed as the source of their sappiest single, "Eternal Flame," but it also houses their darkest, hardest-rocking material, "Watching the Sky," "Glitter Years."

what to buy next: Hoffs's second solo effort, the criminally ignored *Susanna Hoffs* 🎸🎸🎸 (London, 1996, prod. Susanna Hoffs, David Baerwald, David Kitay, Jack Joseph Puig), is a cunning collaboration with many of the same musicians who helped Sheryl Crow create *Tuesday Night Music Club*. Acoustic guitars abound, but such hard-driving songs as "King of Tragedy," the Bowie-like "Beekeeper's Blues," and the glorious "All I Want" rank with the Bangles's best songs. It includes hidden-track covers of Lulu's "To Sir with Love" and Stealers Wheel's "Stuck in the Middle with You."

what to avoid: *When You're a Boy* **woof!** (Columbia, 1991, prod. David Kahne), Hoffs's 1991 solo debut, plays to her sexpot image ("My Side of the Bed") and penchant for oddball covers (David Bowie's "Boys Keep Swinging"), and it buries her charm under glossy, keyboard-driven production. A sellout that didn't sell.

the rest:
The Bangles 🎸🎸🎸 (Faulty Products EP, 1983)
Different Light 🎸🎸🎸 (Columbia, 1986)
Greatest Hits 🎸🎸🎸 (Columbia 1990)

worth searching for: *Rainy Day* (Rough Trade, 1983, prod. various) is a compilation of psychedelic folk covers by L.A.'s "Paisley Underground" scene (including members of the Three O'-Clock and Rain Parade) that features Hoffs singing a gorgeous version of Bob Dylan's "I'll Keep It with Mine."

solo outings:

Debbie Peterson:

(With Kindred Spirit) *Kindred Spirit* ♪♪ (Gai Saber, 1995)

influences:

◀◀ The Beatles, the Mamas & the Papas, Big Star, the Go-Go's

▶▶ Gin Blossoms, L7, Veruca Salt, Sheryl Crow

see also: *Continental Drifters*

David Okamoto

Banyan

See: fIREHOSE

The Barbarians

Formed 1965, in Providence, RI.

Bruce Benson, guitar; Jeff Morris, guitar; Jerry Causi, bass; Victor "Moulty" Moulton, drums.

In an era that sported a bevy of garage-rock heroes such as the Seeds and the Remains, the Barbarians hit the airwaves full of amateurish vocalizing, dumb-ass playing, and lots of heart and soul. "Are You a Boy or Are You a Girl" made it all the way to up #55 on *Billboard*'s Hot 100, but it was the follow-up, "Moulty," that singlehandedly (if you don't know that's a nasty pun, read on) cemented the group's reputation in the punk-garage pantheon. "Moulty," you see, is drummer Victor Moulton, who lost his hand in a pipe-bomb accident at age 14 and learned to play drums with a hook; in the song he tells the world of his triumph over adversity, which includes getting a band, making a record and, in the end, scoring the perfect chick—all the while a chorus sings "don't turn away" for just the right dramatic flourish. As a historical aside, bandmembers later revealed that Levon & the Hawks (a.k.a. the Band) performed on "Moulty."

what's available: Unfortunately, "Moulty" was only released as a single, so the balance of the Barbarians' original album, *Are You a Boy or Are You a Girl* ♪♪♪ (Laurie, 1966/One Way, 1994, prod. Joe Early) is top-heavy with covers of songs like "Mr. Tambourine Man" and "Memphis." However, the One-Way CD reissue includes "Moulty" as a bonus track.

worth searching for: *Boston Rock and Roll Anthology #20* (Varulven, 1998, prod. Joe Viglione) includes a pair of previously unreleased Barbarians tracks.

influences:

◀◀ The Beatles, Chuck Berry, Buddy Holly

▶▶ Jonathan Richman, the Ramones

David Simons

Barenaked Ladies

Formed 1990, in Toronto, Ontario, Canada.

Steven Page, vocals, guitar; Ed Robertson, guitar, vocals; Jim Creeggan, bass; Tyler Stewart, drums; Andrew Creeggan, keyboards (1990–94); Kevin Hearn, keyboards (1994–present).

Perhaps the most talented group of musicians to come out of Toronto since Rush, Barenaked Ladies (BNL for short) has attracted a rabidly loyal group of fans and amassed a slew of Canadian music awards. Founding members Steven Page and Ed Robertson, who grew up together in suburban Toronto, began playing together as a musical comedy duo, opening for minor acts in Toronto clubs. With the additions of the Creeggan brothers and drummer Tyler Stewart, the band began writing music that blended pop, rock, jazz, rap, and just about every other musical style in various configurations. Based upon the success of their five-song independent cassette and a cover of Bruce Cockburn's "Lovers in a Dangerous Time" (featured on a tribute album), BNL won funding from Toronto radio station CFNY's "Discovery-to-Disc" program to record its debut album, *Gordon*. The ensuing tour established a record for most sellouts in Canadian music history, chiefly due to the group's highly energetic and entertaining performances—typified by Page and Robertson's humorous banter and the band's penchant for launching seamlessly into a host of ad-libbed songs, not to mention the audiences' habit of hurling macaroni and cheese at the stage during the popular "If I Had $1,000,000," which prominently mentions the Kraft dining delicacy. Unfortunately, the silliness of some of the band's first singles—"Be My Yoko Ono" and "$1,000,000"—hung it with a novelty act tag, unfair since even a casual listen to their albums reveals the group's copious, if quirky, songwriting talents. In 1994, keyboardist Andrew Creeggan left to continue his academic studies; he was replaced later that year by Kevin Hearn.

what to buy: It is best to begin at the beginning, with *Gordon* ♪♪♪♪ (Sire/Reprise, 1992, prod. Michael-Philip Wojewoda). Though a bit lighter in spots than its later recordings, BNL's debut captures the group's wide-ranging mix of the earnest ("What a Good Boy," "Enid," "Blame It on Me"), the musically-referential ("Brian Wilson," "New Kid on the Block," "Box Set"), and the humorous ("This Is Me in Grade 9," "King of Bedside Manner").

what to buy next: *Born on a Pirate Ship* ♪♪♪♪ (Sire, 1996, prod. Michael-Philip Wojewoda) is more serious and more assured than BNL's previous recordings, featuring ambitious writing, experimentation with nontraditional instruments, and some of Page's most impressive singing. *Stunt* ♪♪♪ (Reprise, 1998, prod. Susan Rogers, David Leonard, Barenaked Ladies) found the BNL, coinciding with its stint on the 1998 HORDE tour, em-

Steven Page of Barenaked Ladies (© **Ken Settle**)

bracing more "serious" popcraft, though it still took time out for fun with the tricky lyricism of "I'll Be That Girl," "One Week," and "Who Needs Sleep."

the rest:

Maybe You Should Drive ♪♪♪ (Sire, 1994)
Shoe Box ♪♪♪ (Sire EP, 1996)
Rock Spectacle ♪♪♪♪ (Sire, 1996)

worth searching for: The soundtrack to the film *Coneheads* (Warner Bros., 1993) features the band doing a cool—and surprisingly faithful—rendition of Public Enemy's "Fight the Power."

influences:

◄◄ The Beach Boys, the B-52's, Bruce Cockburn, the Beatles

Brandon Trenz and Gary Graff

Barnes & Barnes

Formed 1970, in Los Angeles, CA.

Bill Mumy, various instruments; Robert Haimer, various instruments.

Friends since grammar school, Bill Mumy (Will Robinson of *Lost in Space* fame) and Robert Haimer decided to channel their shared fondness of science fiction, DC comics, and warped humor into music. They took on the identities of Art and Artie Barnes, brothers from the planet Lumania. Novelty songs such as "Boogie Woogie Amputee", "Swallow My Love," and "Party in My Pants" made them a big favorite on Dr. Demento's syndicated radio show, and the video for their 1979 hit "Fish Heads" still gets play on MTV and VH1.

what to buy: *Voobaha* ♪♪♪ (Oglio, 1996, prod. Carl Caprioglio, Michael Byer) gathers 23 B&B classics, including "Fish Heads," "Boogie Woogie Amputee," and "Cruising through Westwood." The laughs don't necessarily increase over repeated listenings, but the duo's craft and outright zaniness is always easy to appreciate.

the rest:

Spazchow ♪♪♪ (Oglio, 1997)

worth searching for: A companion video is available for *Voobaha*, showing that B&B didn't only think in aural terms.

influences:

◄◄ Frank Zappa, Ray Bradbury, Harlan Ellison, the Marx Brothers, Captain Beefheart

▶▶ Barenaked Ladies, Moxy Früvous

Gary Graff and Gary Plochinski

The Barracudas

Formed 1979, in London, England.

Jeremy Gluck, vocals; Robin Wills, guitar, vocals; David Buckley, bass, vocals (1979–82); Nicky Turner, drums, vocals (1979–82); Jim Dickson, bass, vocals (1982–84); Graeme Potter, drums (1982); Chris Wilson, guitar, vocals (1983–84); Terry Smith, drums (1983–84); Jay Posner, drums, vocals (1989–present); Steve Robinson, bass, vocals (1989–present).

The Barracudas scored exactly one British hit—the Kenny Laguna–produced "Summer Fun" in 1980—before bidding farewell to the charts and getting on with the business of being an underappreciated cult act. The group never made any impression at all in the U.S.

what to buy: What a debut that was, though. *Drop Out with the Barracudas* ♪♪♪♪♪ (Voxx, 1981/1984, prod. various) is a nonstop barrage of punk-pop energy, surf 'n' sun hooks, and an overriding death wish that would be frightening if it weren't so damn catchy.

the rest:

A Plane View of the Barracudas ♪♪♪ (Collectables, 1968/1995)

worth searching for: Those hooked by the debut can look for: *Mean Time* (Closer, 1983, prod. Peter Gage), the French import of the group's second album. There's also *Endeavour to Perse-*

vere (Closer, 1984, prod. John David), another French import, and the British title *Wait for Everything* (Shake, 1991), which, while not in the same league as *Drop Out*, is still pretty good.

influences:

Roky Erickson, the Byrds, Creedence Clearwater Revival

see also: *Flamin' Groovies, Lords of the New Church*

Carl Cafarelli

Syd Barrett

Born January 6, 1946, in Cambridge, England.

Listening to Syd Barrett is like watching a condemned house fall to pieces. His flaming disintegration led to the former Pink Floyd leader's dismissal after the group's first album. Propped up by his bandmates, he managed two fleeting albums before completely submerging into the LSD netherworld. All of his albums are currently out of print; they're worth seeking out mainly for the glimpses of cracked genius they offer, however sad it all is to look back on.

worth searching for: *Crazy Diamond—The Complete Syd Barrett* (Capitol, 1994, prod. various) is your one-stop source of Barrett material, collecting practically every snippet he recorded onto three CDs, mostly in the form of alternate takes, along with a detailed booklet. Also look for *The Madcap Laughs* (Harvest, 1970, prod. David Gilmour, Roger Waters), a harrowing set of rough sonic quality, full of false starts and half-finished compositions that harshly illuminate the demise of a bright talent.

influences:

Pink Anderson, Floyd Council, the Beatles

Roky Erikson, Ozric Tentacles, the Orb, Radiohead

see also: *Pink Floyd*

Allan Orski

John Barry

Born November 3, 1933, in York, England.

The spooky, orchestral spy music that follows 007 around in *Goldfinger* and *Dr. No,* among other famous James Bond flicks, usually came from John Barry's lively and dramatic imagination. He's amazing at arranging horns to give a scene the right kind of personality, be it playful or frightening. Although he earned an Oscar nomination for his *Chaplin* soundtrack, and did famous scores for *Body Heat* and *Out of Africa,* most moviegoers know his music as another Bond prop, as crucial to the mythology as the shaken, not stirred martini or the ubiquitous Miss Moneypenny. Barry, the son of a classical pianist and a movie

theater owner, developed a love for both symphonies and film as a teenager. After a stint in the U.S. Army, he formed a rock 'n' roll band—John Barry & the Seven—then signed an EMI record deal for tinkly instrumental music. (The Seven frequently backed British pre-rock singing star Adam Faith.) His spare, playful first score, for the 1959 movie *Beat Girl,* barely sounds like the big orchestral sound that made him famous. But that led to several other movies, in addition to pop singles, until his career-defining break, *Dr. No,* in 1962. Since then, he has remained incredibly prolific, but the shadow of Bond continues to hang over his career.

what to buy: Both *Moviola* &&& (Sony, 1992, prod. John Barry) and *Moviola II: Action and Adventure* &&&& (Sony, 1995, prod. John Barry) make for excellent samplings of Barry's soundtrack history, including the familiar suites from *Body Heat, Chaplin, Out of Africa, Dances with Wolves,* and *Born Free.* The second volume packs the most punch, however, opening with eight straight Bond songs, including the Jaws-jumping-out-of-the-plane "007." Most are performed by the Royal Philharmonic Orchestra, with liner notes by Barry himself.

what to buy next: *John Barry: The EMI Years, Vol. 3: 1962–64* &&& (Scamp, 1996, prod. various) is a funny glimpse of the composer's pop and rock oriented side. His versions of Fats Domino's "Blueberry Hill" and Perez Prado's signature mambo, "Cherry Pink and Apple Blossom White," are tinkly and bouncy, unintentionally fitting the space-age bachelor pad feel pioneered by Enoch Light and Juan Garcia Esquivel. The soundtrack *Octopussy* &&& (1983/Rykodisc, 1997, prod. John Barry) had been so rare that collectors were known to pay $250 for the original album. Luckily, Rykodisc recently reissued it.

what to avoid: *Film Music of John Barry* &&& (Sony, 1988, prod. various) essentially collects the same handful of James Bond themes you can find on the better packages, like *Moviola II* or even the various-artist *The Best of James Bond: 30th Anniversary Collection* &&&& (EMI, 1992, compilation prod. Ron Furmanek), which also includes familiar Bond themes (many written by Barry) from Paul McCartney, Tom Jones, Dionne Warwick, Duran Duran, and Shirley Bassey.

best of the rest:

Until September/Car Crash &&& (Silva Screen, 1992)
Chaplin &&&& (Epic Soundtrax, 1992)
Film Scores &&& (Silva America, 1994)
Across the Sea of Time && (Epic Soundtrax, 1995)
John Barry: The EMI Years, Vol. 1 &&& (Scamp, 1996)
John Barry: The EMI Years, Vol. 2 &&&& (Scamp, 1996)

worth searching for: Barry's original soundtracks, especially the older ones, are tough to find—despite the glut of excellent packages and reissues on the market. In fact, Barry's original LPs, not to mention out-of-print James Bond soundtracks in general, are frequently high-priced collectors' items. *Beat Girl* (Columbia, 1959) is his first soundtrack, and while it sounds nothing like the Bond spy-drama to come, it's an interesting transitional piece between Barry's early pop product and his more substantial soundtracks.

influences:

◀◀ Ennio Morricone, Benny Goodman, Glenn Miller, Louis Armstrong, Duke Ellington, Rodgers & Hammerstein

▶▶ Lalo Schifrin, Phil Spector, Phil Ramone, Bruce Springsteen

Steve Knopper

Barry & the Remains

Formed 1964, in Boston, MA. Disbanded 1966.

Barry Tashian, guitar, vocals; Bill Briggs, keyboards, vocals; Vern Miller, bass, vocals; Chip Damiani, drums (1964–66); N.D. Smart II, drums (1966).

Bostonian Barry Tashian took a shine to British rock during a trip across the pond, and he formed the Remains soon after he returned. The band earned a reputation for a strong live show, but recordings of those don't seem to hold up. More interesting are the band's fine original songs, group harmonies, and identifiable (if derivative) group sound. Clearly, this was a band that should have gone farther. Although its singles made a splash in the Northeast, Barry & the Remains couldn't seem to cross the line to national acceptance. Even TV appearances and a slot on the Beatles' last U.S. tour in 1966 didn't help. Disappointed by the lack of commercial success, original drummer Chip Damiani left the band before the Beatles tour. His former bandmates gave up afterward. Tashian remained in the music biz and today is a folk-country-bluegrass singer working with his wife, Holly.

what to buy: *Remains* ♪♪♪♪♪ (Epic/Legacy, 1991, prod. Ted Cooper, Robin McBride, Bob Morgan, Billy Sherrill) is a 21-song retrospective that makes a strong case that the group should have been bigger. Non-album singles and unreleased songs are added to the group's lone album, and the group's tight, tuneful songs echoed the British Invasion but added an earthier, American twist.

what to avoid: *Session with the Remains* ♪♪♪ (Sundazed, 1996) is the demo of the Remains's audition for Capitol Records after its commercially unsuccessful run at Epic. Any one of these cuts would be a perfectly acceptable addition to the Remains's debut album, but together they don't add up to an inspired audition or an album that will hold much interest after the first playing. For diehard collectors only.

influences:

◀◀ The Beatles, the Zombies

▶▶ The Amboy Dukes, the Troggs

Salvatore Caputo

Dave Bartholomew

Born December 24, 1940, in Edgard, LA.

One of the true unsung heroes of rock 'n' roll, bandleader Dave Bartholomew laid one of the music's cornerstones with the records he made with Fats Domino starting in 1949. But as the New Orleans–based artist and repertoire director for Imperial Records, the trumpeter and songwriter conducted a series of rich, vibrant recordings with dozens of lesser known artists throughout the '50s that never traveled far beyond jukeboxes in the deep South. Although the Domino million-sellers were Bartholomew's only taste of nationwide success as a producer, he made equally satisfying records, steeped in the traditional sounds of New Orleans, with the same studio musicians backing himself, Smiley Lewis, Tommy Ridgely, the Spiders, and Earl King, as well as visiting R&B dignitaries such as Big Joe Turner, Roy Brown, T-Bone Walker, and Charles Brown. His solo records have been covered by a scattered but select few such as the Fabulous Thunderbirds—who did a marvelous job with "The Monkey"—Elvis Costello, and Buster Poindexter. He went into semi-retirement during the early '60s, though he continued to play music around New Orleans and occasionally joined Fats Domino's band on tour. But his work as one of the prime designers of the New Orleans R&B sound echoes throughout the rock world to this day.

what to buy: A double-disc set, *The Spirit of New Orleans: The Genius of Dave Bartholomew* ♪♪♪♪ (EMI, 1992, prod. Dave Bartholomew) blends his solo recordings with his productions of other artists, providing a detailed panoramic look at his landmark work.

what to buy next: Bartholomew's spirit presides over the four-disc box set *Crescent City Soul: The Sound of New Orleans 1947–1974* ♪♪♪ (EMI, 1996, prod. various). The set samples not only his work with artists such as Fats Domino, Smiley Lewis, and many lesser-knowns, but also key Bartholomew productions such as "Lawdy Miss Clawdy" by Lloyd Price. Unfortunately, the set duplicates many of the selections from *The Spirit of New Orleans* and ranges far beyond Bartholomew's work.

the rest:

Dave Bartholomew and the Maryland Jazz Band ♪♪♪ (GHB, 1995)
New Orleans Big Beat ♪♪♪ (Landslide, 1998)

worth searching for: His early solo recordings for the DeLuxe and King labels were collected on the British CD *In the Alley* (Charly, 1991, prod. various).

influences:

◄◄ Louis Armstrong, Fats Pinchon, Louis Jordan

►► Allen Toussaint, Paul McCartney, Dirty Dozen Brass Band

Joel Selvin and Ken Burke

Bash & Pop

See: The Replacements

Basia

Born Basia Trzetrzelewska, September 30, 1956, in Jaworzno, Poland.

If there is such a thing as a truly international brand of music, it should sound something like the work of Basia. Born in Poland, where she performed with the female trio Alibabki, Basia toured the Soviet Union and later lived in Chicago, where she soaked up American R&B and blues, and in London, where she joined the band Matt Bianco, whose album *Whose Side Are You On?* (now out of print) was a hit in England and Europe. She went solo in 1985, continuing to collaborate with Matt Bianco keyboardist Danny White. On her own albums, Basia surveys an intriguing mix of pop-jazz and especially Latin styles such as samba and bossa nova.

what to buy: Recorded during a 1994 stint at New York City's Neil Simon Theater, *Basia on Broadway* ✒✒✒✒ (Epic, 1995, prod. Danny White, Basia) is a de facto greatest hits package, featuring Basia's best-known numbers ("Copernicus," "Cruising for Bruising," "Baby You're Mine," "New Day for You," "Time and Tide") and several new songs. In concert, Basia's classy sound comes through loud and clear. Spyro Gyra saxophonist Jay Beckenstein sits in on "Yearning."

what to buy next: *London Warsaw New York* ✒✒✒✒ (Epic, 1989, prod. Basia, Danny White) is the album on which Basia's music truly came of age, kicking off with the slick pop-jazz of "Cruising for Bruising," a bittersweet lover's kiss-off. "Best Friends" apes ebullient Gloria Estefan–style pop, but the soaring self-actualization "Brave New Hope," the Aretha Franklin cover "Until You Come Back to Me," and the rhythmic hands-across-the-water wish "Copernicus" make this a fine effort. *The Sweetest Illusion* ✒✒✒✓ (Epic, 1994, prod. Danny White, Basia) is nearly as fine, thanks to the optimistic "Third Time Lucky," the grooving "Drunk on Love," and the elegant "Yearning."

the rest:

Time and Tide ✒✒✒ (Epic, 1987)

Brave New Hope ✒✒✒ (Epic EP, 1991)

worth searching for: The now-deleted Matt Bianco album *Whose Side Are You On?* (Atlantic, 1984, prod. Mark Reilly) offers a nice dose of Basia.

influences:

◄◄ Astrud Gilberto, Gloria Estefan, Sade

►► Swing Out Sister, Lisa Stansfield

Daniel Durchholz

Fontella Bass

Born July 3, 1949, in St. Louis, MO.

Born into a gospel singing family, Fontella Bass turned her back on that music to play piano in a series of blues bands during the early 1960s. She stumbled into singing after filling in one night for a drunk Little Milton and later became a featured vocalist in the Oliver Sain Revue. Bass brought a brassy gospel voice to her blues and R&B singing; her biggest hit came in 1965 when "Rescue Me" hit the top of the R&B charts and garnered a Grammy nomination. Her marriage to avant garde trumpeter Lester Bowie led to life in Paris from 1968 to 1971 and a largely unrecognized body of jazz work—although the powerful "Theme De Yoyo" on the Art Ensemble of Chicago's *Les Stances a Sophie* album shows her in top form. After divorcing Bowie, Bass was off the scene during most of the 1970s and 1980s raising her family, and when she returned, she slipped back into gospel.

what to buy: Her 1960s work is compiled on *Rescued—The Best of Fontella Bass* ✒✒✒✒✒ (MCA, 1992, prod. various), a good accounting of gospel-influenced 1960s soul with "Don't Mess up a Good Thing", "Joy of Love", and, of course, "Rescue Me".

what to buy next: Her recent gospel work still touches the jazz world. *No Ways Tired* ✒✒✒✒ (Nonesuch, 1995, prod. Wayne Horvitz) features jazzmen Bowie, David Sanborn, and Hamiett Blueitt.

the rest:

Everlasting Arms ✒✒✒✒ (Silver Spring, 1991)

Now That I Found a Good Thing ✒✒✒✓ (Jewel, 1996)

worth searching for: Bass injects some soul into a couple of songs on the World Saxophone Quartet's 1994 release *Breath of Life* (Nonesuch, 1994).

influences:

◄◄ Bessie Smith, Dinah Washington, Mahalia Jackson, Clara Ward

►► Ann Peebles, Chaka Khan, Mariah Carey

Lawrence Gabriel

Bassomatic

See: William Orbit

The Bats

Formed 1983, in Christchurch, New Zealand.

Robert Scott, vocals, guitar, keyboards; Paul Kean, bass, vocals, keyboards; Kaye Woodward, guitar, vocals, keyboards; Malcolm Grant, drums.

One of the premier '80s bands to emerge from New Zealand and to make an impact in the States, the Bats' melodic jangle has become inextricably entwined with the charming indie pop to come out of the Kiwi nation. Founded in 1983 by gifted songwriter and former Clean member Robert Scott along with Paul Kean, the Bats quickly became synonymous with a refreshingly acoustic, endearingly harmonized sound. Though Scott sang frequently of dark subject matter, his exhilarating acoustic strums and crisp arrangements became the band's trademark. With Scott's sweet, high-register vocals the top layer of a joyous pop confection, the Bats became one of acoustic pop's best formula-fired bands. Despite generous receptions in its native land and Australia, which allowed them to record at will at home, the band chose to follow other pursuits, including parenthood, rather than aspire to success in America. After being together almost six years the band finally signed a domestic recording contract with Mammoth in 1990, and began establishing higher visibility with American audiences. But as expected, commercial success would be hard to come by. Despite a couple of stellar recordings, including the terrific *Fear of God*, the Bats disbanded for 18 months in the mid-'90s, when Scott rejoined the Clean for a reunion tour and album. But, undaunted by the hiatus, they reformed in 1995 to release the dark and aggressive *Couchmaster*. As of mid-'98, the future of the band, still signed to Mammoth, remains uncertain.

what to buy: The first records to see release here from their New Zealand catalog include *Daddy's Highway* ✍✍✍✍ (Flying Nun, 1988/Flying Nun/Mammoth, 1994, prod. John Milton, the Bats), *Compiletely Bats* ✍✍✍✍ (Flying Nun, 1987/Communion, 1991, prod. various), and *The Law of Things* ✍✍✍✍ (Flying Nun/Mammoth, 1990, prod. the Bats, Brent McLachlan), and all are worth searching out. Though the band rarely strays too far from their formula, it's a really good formula.

what to buy next: The best of the releases to originate in the U.S. is *Fear of God* ✍✍✍✍ (Flying Nun/Mammoth, 1992, prod. Nicholas Sansano), a recording that distills the Bats' material down to its gorgeous essence: great hooks, beautiful rhythm guitar tracks, and singalong choruses.

the rest:
Silverbeet ✍✍✍ (Flying Nun/Mammoth, 1993)
Spill the Beans ✍✍✍ (Flying Nun/Mammoth EP, 1994)
Couchmaster ✍✍✍ (Flying Nun/Mammoth, 1995)

worth searching for: Unfortunately, much of the earliest Bats material—its defining records—remains available only as expensive imports. These include *By Night* (Flying Nun EP, 1984), *"And Here Is 'Music for the Fireside'!"* (Flying Nun, 1985), and *Made up in Blue* (Flying Nun, 1986). Fortunately, portions of these records are reprised on *Compiletely Bats*.

influences:
◀◀ Early R.E.M., the Feelies, the Byrds, the Beatles

see also: *The Clean*

Bob Gulla

Bauhaus

Formed 1979, in Northampton, England. Disbanded 1983.

Peter Murphy, vocals; Daniel Ash, guitar, vocals; David J(ay), bass; Kevin Haskins, drums.

Bauhaus led and begat what would come to be called gothic rock, a genre that's been slammed as gloom or death rock but actually has intellect, theatrics, and an ethereal, brooding emotion. Bauhaus was not without a sense of humor; when detractors accused it being too Bowie-esque, it responded by covering T-Rex's "Telegram Sam." Due to Peter Murphy's bout with pneumonia during the recording of the final album, *Burning from the Inside*, David J and Daniel Ash took over vocal responsibilities, which, with Ash's desire for creative control stoked, precipitated the breakup of the band and the pursuit of new careers by all parties. The group reunited for two special shows during July 1998 in Los Angeles, which were taped for an intended live album.

what to buy: *Mask* ✍✍✍✍ (Beggars Banquet, 1981/1995, prod. Bauhaus) is Bauhaus's finest, showing a variety of styles and extremes in both musicianship and verse. *In the Flat Field* ✍✍✍✍ (4AD, 1980, prod. Bauhaus) burrowed into the human mind to uncover the density and raw force that was to become a signature of Bauhaus.

what to buy next: *Burning from the Inside* ✍✍✍ (Beggars Banquet/A&M, 1983/1989, prod. Bauhaus) is more the work of a collective than a band, with Ash and J singing on various tracks and a new, acoustic bent to some of the material. A definite stepping stone toward Love and Rockets.

what to avoid: *The Sky's Gone Out* ✍✍ (Beggars Banquet/A&M, 1982, prod. Bauhaus) lacks the pensive and tongue-in-cheek lyrics that define so much of Bauhaus' best work.

the rest:
Press the Eject and Give Me the Tape ✍✍✍ (Beggars Banquet, 1982)
Kick in the Eye (Searching for Satori) ✍✍✍ (Beggars Banquet 1982)
Ziggy Stardust ✍✍✍ (Beggars Banquet EP, 1982)

Lagartija Nick ♫♫♫♩ (Beggars Banquet EP, 1982)

4AD ♫♫♫♩ (4AD EP, 1983)

The Singles 1981–1983 ♫♫♫♩♩ (Beggars Banquet, 1983)

1979–1983 ♫♫♫♩♩ (Beggars Banquet, 1985)

1979–1983, Vol. 1 and Vol. 2 ♫♫♫♩ (Beggars Banquet, 1986)

Swing the Heartache: The BBC Sessions ♫♫♫ (BBC/Beggars Banquet, 1989)

Rest in Peace: The Final Concert ♫♫♫♩ (Nemo/Beggars Banquet, 1992)

Crackle ♫♫♫♩ (Beggars Banquet, 1998)

worth searching for: *Bela Lugosi's Dead* (Small Wonder, 1979), a 12" single that also includes "Boys" and "Dark Entries," was produced on six colors of vinyl—black, clear, red, green, blue and glow-in-the-dark (our favorite).

influences:

◀◀ David Bowie, Pere Ubu, John Cale

▶▶ Christian Death, Alien Sex Fiend, Sisters of Mercy, Marilyn Manson

see also: *Love & Rockets, Peter Murphy*

J.D. Cantarella

The Bay City Rollers

Formed 1970, in Edinburgh, Scotland. Disbanded 1982. Re-formed 1993.

Leslie McKeown, vocals (1970–78); Stuart Wood, guitar; Ian Mitchell, bass (1976–78); Eric Faulkner, guitar; Derek Longmuir, drums (1970–78); Alan Longmuir, bass (1970–76, 1993–present); Nobby Clarke, vocals (1971–73); John Devine (1971–73); Pat McGlynn, bass (1977–78); Duncan Faure, vocals (1978); Kass, drums, vocals (1993–present).

The name Bay City Rollers was chosen by the group's manager, who arbitrarily stuck a pin in a map of the United States and wound up hitting Bay City, Michigan. Known for their tartan outfits touting their Scottish heritage, the Rollers' music was pure bubblegum. Rollermania took over the U.K. for a time, but never really caught fire in the U.S. beyond their #1 single, "Saturday Night."

what's available: *Greatest Hits* ♫♫♫ (Arista, 1977, prod. various) may not get you to dig that tartan scarf out of the closet, but it's the one to have nonetheless. A true artifact of a more innocent—if infinitely more stupid—time.

influences:

◀◀ The Beatles

▶▶ "If it's not Scottish, it's crap."

Anna Glen and Daniel Durchholz

Be Bop Deluxe

Formed 1972, in Wakefield, England. Disbanded 1979.

Bill Nelson, guitar, vocals, keyboards; Ian Parkin, guitar (1972–74); Rob Bryan, bass (1972–74); Nicholas Catterton-Drew, drums (1972–74); Richard Brown, keyboards (1972–74); Milton Reame-James, keyboards (1974); Paul Jeffreys, bass (1974); Simon Fox, drums (1974–79); Andrew Clark, keyboards (1975–79); Charles Tumahai, bass, vocals (1974–79).

When he chose to play it, Be Bop Deluxe founder Bill Nelson produced some stunning music with an electric guitar. Unfortunately, Nelson's tendency toward overwrought production, quirky arrangements, and lyrical visions of the future obscured some of the fiercest guitar licks in mid-'70s rock. After releasing *Axe Victim* (1974) and *Futurama* (1975) in the band's native England, Be Bop Deluxe issued its first U.S. release, *Sunburst Finish* (1976), which produced a minor hit with "Ships in the Night." But the band never quite connected with the average suburban Jimmy Page fan, even though Be Bop Deluxe toured the United States widely during 1976, opening for bands as diverse as Patti Smith, Golden Earring, and the Electric Light Orchestra. *Modern Music* was released that same year and stands as the band's best effort and one of the lost treasures of mid-'70s rock. The final studio album, *Drastic Plastic*, was released in 1978. Nelson has produced and recorded prolifically over the years and while many of his albums are now keyboard-based, you can sometimes hear a glimpse of his guitar mastery.

what to buy: With the vast majority of the Be Bop Deluxe catalog tragically out of print, fans have to be content with some concert recordings. *Be Bop Deluxe Radioland—BBC Radio One Live in Concert* ♫♫♫ (Griffin, 1995) comes from excellent shows recorded during 1976 and 1978, featuring a generous sampling of songs from the seminal *Modern Music* album.

what to buy next: *Live! in the Air Age* ♫♫♫ (Harvest, 1977/One Way, 1994) is another fine live concert performance, though at this point we're really crying for some of the studio material to be made available.

what to avoid: *Axe Victim* ♫♫ (Harvest, 1974) is available via import CD. Save your money.

worth searching for: Too much belongs in this section, unfortunately. But *Sunburst Finish* (Harvest, 1976) is available as an import and is essential for fans of melodic guitar rock, though the even better *Modern Music* (Harvest, 1976) remains inexplicably out of print. *Singles A's and B's* (See for Miles, 1994) is one collection that's still in print, though only available as an import. There's also a good Nelson solo album, *On a Blue Wing* (Portrait, 1986), that has yet to be issued on CD.

Bill Nelson:

Red Noise 🎵🎵 (Cocteau, 1979)

Vistamix 🎵🎵🎵 (Epic, 1982)

The Love that Whirls (Diary of a Thinking Heart) 🎵🎵🎵🎵 (Cocteau, 1989)

Blue Moons & Laughing Guitars 🎵🎵🎵 (Virgin, 1992)

Practically Wired 🎵🎵🎵 (Gyroscope, 1995)

After the Satellite Sings 🎵🎵🎵 (Caroline, 1996)

influences:

◀◀ Jimi Hendrix, Jeff Beck, David Bowie, Roxy Music

▶▶ A Flock of Seagulls, the Fixx, Joe Satriani

Michael Isabella

The Beach Boys

Formed 1961, in Hawthorne, CA.

Brian Wilson, piano, guitar, bass, vocals; Carl Wilson (died February 6, 1998), guitar, vocals; Dennis Wilson (died December 28, 1983), drums, vocals; Mike Love, vocals; Alan Jardine, guitar, vocals (1961–62, 1963–present); David Marks, guitar (1962–63); Bruce Johnston, keyboards, vocals (1965–72, 1978–present); Blondie Chaplin, guitar, vocals (1971–74); Ricky Fataar, drums, vocals (1972–74).

The Beach Boys were America's first major and longest-running rock 'n' roll band/soap opera. Led by reclusive, unstable prodigy Brian Wilson, the group peaked early but has managed to sustain a substantial career that, at least as a live act, continues long after its members became Beach Men. Rising from the sun-and-convertible culture of post-war southern California, and swirling together Chuck Berry's small-combo rock 'n' roll, pristine Four Freshman harmonies, and the surf craze of the period, the Beach Boys' early hits—"Surfin' U.S.A.," "Be True to Your School," "Fun, Fun, Fun," "Help Me, Rhonda," "I Get Around," "California Girls"—were and remain colorful aural slices of teenage life form 1962 and 1963, before the J.F.K. assassination and before the war in Vietnam became widely debated and protested. Brian Wilson was an auteur, a sensitive, intelligent kid whose fun-and-sun themes were a smokescreen for a darker side (his father, Murry Wilson, a violent, abusive musician-wannabe, was particularly jealous of his oldest son's gifts), a perceptible hue in songs like "In My Room." Though deaf in one ear, Wilson grew in confidence and his writing, arranging, and production skills developed with each album and hit single. Inspired by the equally groundbreaking work of the Beatles and Phil Spector, Wilson found himself locked in musical competition with them. He responded with *The Beach Boys Today* and *Summer Days and Summer Nights* in 1965 and the magnificent *Pet Sounds* in 1966, which also became the Boys' first commercial failure. The pressures of producing a sequel, the never-officially-released *Smile*, left Wilson in a state of se-

vere emotional duress from which he seems still to be recuperating. With Brian in well-publicized seclusion—he's only been an occasional member since 1966—the group tried to carry on as a recording unit, with less than convincing results, increasing friction among the members, and distressingly fallow albums. They haven't had a hit in years, but the Beach Boys' music ranks among the '60s finest.

what to buy: Beware of duplicate titles and much overlapping of material on so-called best-ofs when shopping for this band. (Hint: Stay with the official releases.) *Pet Sounds* 🎵🎵🎵🎵 (Capitol, 1966, prod. Brian Wilson), recorded in pure monaural, still sounds fresh and young and irresistibly romantic. Fanatics will enjoy the bloated *The Pet Sounds Sessions* 🎵🎵🎵🎵 (Capitol, 1996, prod. Brian Wilson) with outtakes, noodling, studio chatter, and even a stereo version of the album for comparison—though it's still much better in mono. *Smiley Smile* 🎵🎵🎵🎵 (Capitol, 1967/1996, prod. Brian Wilson) picks up some of the remnants of the aborted *Smile*, while the ragged soul of *Wild Honey* 🎵🎵🎵🎵 (Capitol, 1967, prod. Brian Wilson) is considered by some fans to be the band's best recorded moments. *Surf's Up* 🎵🎵🎵🎵 (Caribou/Epic, 1971, prod. the Beach Boys) is the group's most collaborative album and a fascinating puzzle, with contributions from all members as well as two of Brian's all-time best tunes, "Until I Die" and "Surf's Up," written with Van Dyke Parks and originally slated for *Smile*.

what to buy next: *Good Vibrations* 🎵🎵🎵🎵 (Capitol, 1993, prod. Brian Wilson) is a cluttered, eccentric box set that's a blast, with a fascinating collage of hits, remixes, studio talk, interviews, and other arcane material—beginning with a young Brian pounding out "Surfin' U.S.A." on the piano and including a "version" of *Smile* with yet more tidbits of that ghost. Some aficionados prefer *The Beach Boys Today* 🎵🎵🎵🎵 (Capitol, 1965/1990, prod. Brian Wilson) and *Summer Days and Summer Nights* 🎵🎵🎵🎵 (Capitol, 1965/1990, prod. Brian Wilson), the two albums that led up to *Pet Sounds*, over their more-hyped successor; either way, don't pass up "I'm Bugged at My Old Man" on the latter. *The Beach Boys Love You* 🎵🎵🎵🎵 (Caribou/Epic, 1977, prod. Brian Wilson) is a congenial, low-key, partial return-to-earth from Brian isolated in the general dreck of the other albums that surround it.

what to avoid: Take your pick of those surroundings: the woefully mistitled *15 Big Ones* **woof!** (Caribou/Epic, 1976, prod. the Beach Boys); *M.I.U.* **woof!** (Caribou/Epic, 1978, prod. the Beach Boys); or *L.A. (Light Album)* **woof!** (Caribou/Epic, 1979, prod. the Beach Boys), which finds the group hard in the grip of Love's meditation obsession.

best of the rest:

All Summer Long 🎵🎵🎵 (Capitol, 1964, 1994)

Friends 20/20 🎵🎵🎵 (Capitol, 1968/1969, 1990)

20-20 ♫♫♫ (Capitol, 1969, 1994)
Sunflower ♫♫♫♩ (Caribou/Epic, 1970)
Carl and the Passions—So Tough ♫♫♫ (Caribou/Epic, 1972)
Beach Boys in Concert ♫♫♫ (Caribou/Epic, 1973)
Holland ♫♫♫ (Caribou/Epic, 1973)
Endless Summer ♫♫♫♫ (Capitol, 1974)
Spirit of America ♫♫♫ (Capitol, 1975)
Ten Years of Harmony ♫♫♫ (Caribou/Epic, 1979)
Keepin' the Summer Alive ♫♫ (Caribou/Epic, 1980)
Rarities ♫♫♫♩ (Capitol, 1983)
Lost and Found: 1961–62 ♫♫♫♩ (DCC, 1991)
20 Good Vibrations ♫♫♫♩ (Capitol, 1995)
Perfect Harmony—Limited Edition ♫♫♫ (Capitol, 1997)
All-Time Greatest Hits ♫♫♫ (Capitol, 1997)
Best of Beach Boys on TV ♫♫♫ (Capitol, 1997)

worth searching for: In 1990 Capitol released all its Beach Boys albums in budget, two-fer packages that included original album art, extensive liner notes by Brian Wilson and outtakes and other rare tracks. All are now out of print, replaced by more expensive single album releases, but they remain the best Beach Boys bargains, especially the above-mentioned *Today/Summer Days and Summer Nights* (Capitol, 1990, prod. Brian Wilson), and *Smiley Smile/Wild Honey* (Capitol, 1990, prod. Brian Wilson). Among the strangest Beach Boys recordings is *Stars and Stripes, Vol. 1* (River North, 1996, prod. Brian Wilson, Joe Thomas), a wild affair with country artists interpreting Beach Boys songs with the Boys themselves adding their trademark harmonies. You haven't lived until you've heard Junior Brown's solo on "409" or Timothy B. Schmitt warbling "Caroline No."

solo outings:
Dennis Wilson:
Pacific Ocean Blue ♫♫♫ (Caribou, 1977)

Mike Love:
Looking Back with Love **woof!** (Boardwalk, 1981)

influences:
◀◀ The Four Freshmen, Chuck Berry, the Lettermen, the Everly Brothers, Phil Spector
▶▶ The Beatles, the Byrds, Jan & Dean, the Eagles, Porno for Pyros, New Kids on the Block, Backstreet Boys, Hanson

see also: *Brian Wilson*

Leland Rucker

Beastie Boys

Formed 1981, in New York, NY.

Adam Yauch (a.k.a. MCA), vocals, bass; Michael Diamond (a.k.a. Mike D.), vocals, drums; Adam Horovitz (a.k.a. King Ad-Rock), vocals, guitar (1982–present); John Berry, guitar (1981–82); Kate Schellenbach, drums (1981–82).

Formed as a punk outfit, the Beastie Boys turned to rap after meeting Def Jam Records co-owner Rick Rubin during the mid-'80s. All sons of affluent New Yorkers, the core trio developed a uniquely in-your-face style that mixed suburban references such as Led Zeppelin and Budweiser with hip-hop vernacular and attitude. Accordingly, the group's first album drew a sharp line between hip-hop fans attracted by the trio's outlaw style and outspoken critics who felt these three white guys' exaggerated style was an insult to the rap genre. Thanks to a couple of MTV-fed hits, the Beasties' debut became one of the best-selling rap albums, but the trio proved with their next record—an in-depth exploration of '70s influences—that they weren't just dilettantes, weaving their obnoxious image into a funky sound pastiche. By the third record, the band had picked up its instruments again, adding punk sounds and trippy instrumentals into their arsenal and showing that, despite attempts to write them off as an untalented publicity stunt, the Beastie Boys were a group deserving of serious props.

what to buy: *Licensed to Ill* ♫♫♫♫ (Def Jam, 1986, prod. Rick Rubin) caught pop audiences flatfooted with the Beastie's baldfaced rhymes about drugs, drinking, and crimes, along with dope beats and an engaging lyrical style. Forget about the frat rock anthem "(You Gotta) Fight for Your Right (to Party)"; instead, check out high-octane jams such as "She's Crafty" (fueled by a spot-on Led Zeppelin sample) and the hip-hop outlaw tale "Paul Revere" (backward drum machine parts make the groove here). The inspired follow-up, *Paul's Boutique* ♫♫♫♫♩ (Capitol, 1989, prod. the Beastie Boys, the Dust Brothers), is even better, mixing a '70s vibe with a flood of pop culture references and a psychedelic-style wash of sonics. DJs and rappers of today are still trying to catch up with the densely layered beats and broad stylistic sweep captured on this record.

what to buy next: With instruments in hand, the Beasties hopscotch from raps to '70s jazz/soul shadings to full-out punk abandon on *Ill Communication* ♫♫♫♫ (Grand Royal/Capitol, 1994, prod. the Beastie Boys, Mario Caldato Jr.), cranking out groundbreaking jams such as the rocked-out "Sabotage" and the funkified "Root Down."

what to avoid: The EP featuring the early hardcore punk singles, *Some Old Bullshit* **woof!** (Capitol, 1994, prod. the Beastie Boys, Scott Jarvis, Dug Pomeroy) is aptly named, with tunes that barely hint at the ambitions that lay ahead.

the rest:
Check Your Head ♫♫♫♩ (Capitol, 1992)
Root Down ♫♫♩ (Grand Royal/Capitol EP, 1995)
Hello Nasty ♫♫♫♫ (Grand Royal/Capitol, 1998)

worth searching for: For a different take on the Beasties, check out *The In Sound from Way Out* (Grand Royal/Capitol, 1996, prod. the Beastie Boys, Mario Caldato Jr.), a collection of instrumentals from *Check Your Head* and *Ill Communication*, featuring a loose, urbane sound that proves a welcome departure from their vocal cuts.

influences:

◀◀ Led Zeppelin, Run-D.M.C., Public Enemy, Kurtis Blow

▶▶ G. Love & Special Sauce, Disposable Heroes of Hiphoprisy, Consolidated

Eric Deggans

The Beasts of Bourbon

See: The Cruel Sea

The Beat /Paul Collins

Formed 1979, in Los Angeles, CA.

Paul Collins, lead vocals, guitar; Steven Huff, bass, vocals; Larry Whitman, guitar, vocals, (1979–82); Jimmy Ripp, guitar (1983); Michael Ruiz, drums (1979–82); Jay Dee Daugherty, drums (1983).

Power popster Paul Collins formed the Beat after the Nerves (for whom he drummed) broke up in 1978. Collins's new group struck it big in San Francisco, with Bill Graham agreeing to manage the band after it opened for Eddie Money at Graham's Kabuki Theater. Collins and Money co-wrote "Let Me Into Your Life," which made it onto the debut album, as did "Rock 'n' Roll Girl," which has since been covered by the Muffs. The second album was credited to Paul Collins's Beat to differentiate it from the group known on this side of the Atlantic as the English Beat. Columbia dropped the group soon after issuing its sophomore effort. After personnel changes, the group's final U.S. release came out, but no offers were forthcoming. A number of Collins's solo albums released in Europe may eventually be released in the United States by Wagon Wheel.

what to buy: *The Beat* ♫♫♫ (Columbia, 1979/Wagon Wheel, 1994, prod. Bruce Botnick) sounds a bit thin but has plenty of energy. The reissue adds "There She Goes" from the *Caddyshack* soundtrack.

what to buy next: *The Kids Are the Same* ♫♫♫ (Columbia, 1982, prod. Bruce Botnick) improves on the sound but slips a bit in the songwriting.

the rest:
The Beat:
To Beat or Not to Beat ♫♫♫ (Passport EP, 1983)

The Paul Collins Band:
From Town to Town ♫♫♫ (Wagon Wheel, 1993)

influences:

◀◀ The Beatles, the Hollies, the Byrds, the Shoes, Dwight Twilley

▶▶ The Rubinoos, the Romantics, the Plimsouls, Material Issue

Steve Holtje

The Beat Farmers

Formed 1983, in San Diego, CA. Disbanded 1995.

Jerry Raney, vocals, guitar; Rolle Dexter, bass; Country Dick Montana, drums, vocals; Buddy Blue, guitar, vocals (1983–86); Joey Harris, vocals, guitar (1986–95).

Pre–Dwight Yoakam, country music spent the first half of the '80s choking on its own schlock. About the only place you heard honest twang back then was from underground rock bands such as X, Jason & the Scorchers, and this crack country-rock crew from Mojo Nixon's hometown. The Beat Farmers were the last word in beer-soaked good times, especially drummer/ringleader Country Dick Montana's basso profundo tales of debauchery. Unfortunately, its live appeal never quite translated to records. And as time wore on, the band's onstage alcoholic excesses began to approach George Jones–ian proportions. Years of self-abuse finally caught up with Montana in 1995, when he died onstage in Canada of heart failure at age 40. He left behind a partially finished solo album that his bandmates helped complete for posthumous release.

what to buy: For pure, unpretentious charm, it's tough to top the Beat Farmers' debut, *Tales of the New West* ♫♫♫ (Rhino, 1985, prod. Steve Berlin, Mark Linett). Montana's two vocal cameos set the tone, especially on the epochal "California Kid" (imagine Johnny Cash covering "Big Bad John"). Elsewhere, every note rings perfectly true on ace originals as well as covers of everybody from John Stewart to the Velvet Underground.

what to buy next: Although one hesitates to encourage the Beat Farmers' boozy mythology, *Loud and Plowed and . . . LIVE!!* ♫♫♫ (Curb, 1990, prod. Denny Bruce) does make for a representative sampler. Recorded before a well-oiled New Year's Eve hometown crowd, it captures the band in prime form on a career-spanning selection of material. The group's swan song, *Manifold* ♫♫♫ (Sector 2, 1995, prod. the Beat Farmers), contains "Texas Heat," a fare-thee-well song written by Joey Harris and sung by Montana in a manner that qualifies as both eerie and sad.

what to avoid: By any standard, *Best of the Beat Farmers* ♫ (Curb, 1995, prod. various) is appallingly shoddy. Ten tracks (none from their best album), and just 35 minutes. Awful. If you want a compilation, stick with the live album.

the rest:
Glad 'n' Greasy ♫♫♫ (Demon EP, 1986/Rhino, 1991)
Van Go ♫♫♫ (Curb/MCA, 1986)
The Pursuit of Happiness ♫♫♫ (Curb/MCA, 1987)
Poor & Famous ♫♫ (Curb/MCA, 1989)
Viking Lullabys ♫♫♥ (Sector 2, 1994)

worth searching for: Look for *Live in Las Vegas* (HighTone, 1993, prod. Mark Linett, Country Dick Montana), a relaxed and friendly outing by the Pleasure Barons, an ad hoc 13-piece outfit featuring Montana and Harris with Mojo Nixon, Rosie Flores, Katy Moffatt, Dave Alvin, John Doe, and others.

solo outings:
Joey Harris:
Joey Harris and the Speedsters ♫♫ (MCA, 1983)

Buddy Blue:
(With the Jacks) *Jacks Are Wild* ♫♫♫ (Rounder, 1988)
Guttersnipes 'n' Zealots ♫♫♥ (Rhino, 1991)

Country Dick Montana:
The Devil Lied to Me ♫♫♫ (Bar None, 1996)

influences:
◀◀ The Flying Burrito Brothers, Neil Young, the Rolling Stones, Johnny Cash

▶▶ Go to Blazes, Old 97's, Backsliders, Uncle Tupelo

David Menconi

Beat Happening

Formed 1984, in Olympia, WA.

Calvin Johnson, vocals, guitar, drums; Heather Lewis, vocals, guitar, drums; Bret Lunsford, vocals, guitar, drums.

Besides heavily influencing Nirvana and spawning the independent K Records label, Beat Happening is most notable for being perhaps the only band whose members regularly swap all vocal and instrumental duties. Deep-voiced Johnson (kind of a modern rock Barry White) used to walk around Olympia in "Hello Kitty" accessories and was the de facto leader of the Calvinists, a mini-movement of adults who aspired to be childlike. He took the same approach with Beat Happening's music: using simple tom-tom drumbeats and rudimentary guitar, all very low-fi, with the musicians droning or awkwardly crooning over the music. The results range from hypnotic to simply boring. Johnson's K Records was also a groundbreaking label, pre-dating the more celebrated Sub Pop and releasing early music by Nirvana, Screaming Trees, and Beck. Beat Happening was last heard from (on record) in 1992, with each of its members now working on other projects—most notably Johnson with Dub Narcotic Sound System and Halo Benders. The group has not formally disbanded.

what to buy: *Dreamy* ♫♫♫ (K/Sub Pop, 1991, prod. Steve Fisk) is a short and sweet example of the band's whimsical charm. Songs such as "Hot Chocolate Boy" and "Redhead Walking" could be radio hits in an alternate—not just alternative—universe.

what to buy next: The anthology *1983–85* ♫♫♫ (K, 1990, prod. various) collects the best of the rest, the sound of the beginning of grunge.

what to avoid: *You Turn Me On* ♫♫ (K/Sub Pop, 1992) comes off like an old joke repeated once too often.

the rest:
Beat Happening ♫♫ (K, 1985)
Jamboree ♫♫ (K/Rough Trade, 1988)
Black Candy ♫♫♥ (K, 1989)

worth searching for: *Beat Happening/Screaming Trees* (K-Homestead EP, 1988) is a lumbering but fun four-song joint project by two of Olympia's chief exports. *Fortune Cookie Prize* (Simple Machines USA, 1992) is a tribute album with the usual mixed results; it features several bands with mixed-gendered lineups: Superchunk, Velocity Girl, Scrawl, and so on.

influences:
◀◀ The Doors, the Stooges

▶▶ Beck, Nirvana, the Spinanes

Todd Wicks

The Beatles

Formed 1960, in Liverpool, England. Disbanded 1970.

John Lennon, guitar, vocals; Stuart Sutcliffe, bass (1960–61); Paul McCartney, bass, guitar, keyboards, vocals; George Harrison, guitar, vocals; Pete Best, drums (1960–62); Ringo Starr, drums, vocals (1962–1970).

At a time when rock music and its creators could be described as one-dimensional, the Beatles were intelligent, innovative, and perceptive interpreters of their generation. During the 40-year history of rock, no one has matched the group's far-reaching impact and enduring influence. From infectious three-minute pop songs to sophisticated studio production and trend-setting fashions and album art, the Beatles revolutionized popular music by liberating rock 'n' roll from its once-narrow definitions.

John Lennon met fellow Liverpool teens Paul McCartney and George Harrison in 1957 while seeking members for his skiffle group, the Quarrymen. Sharing a fondness for black R&B, the

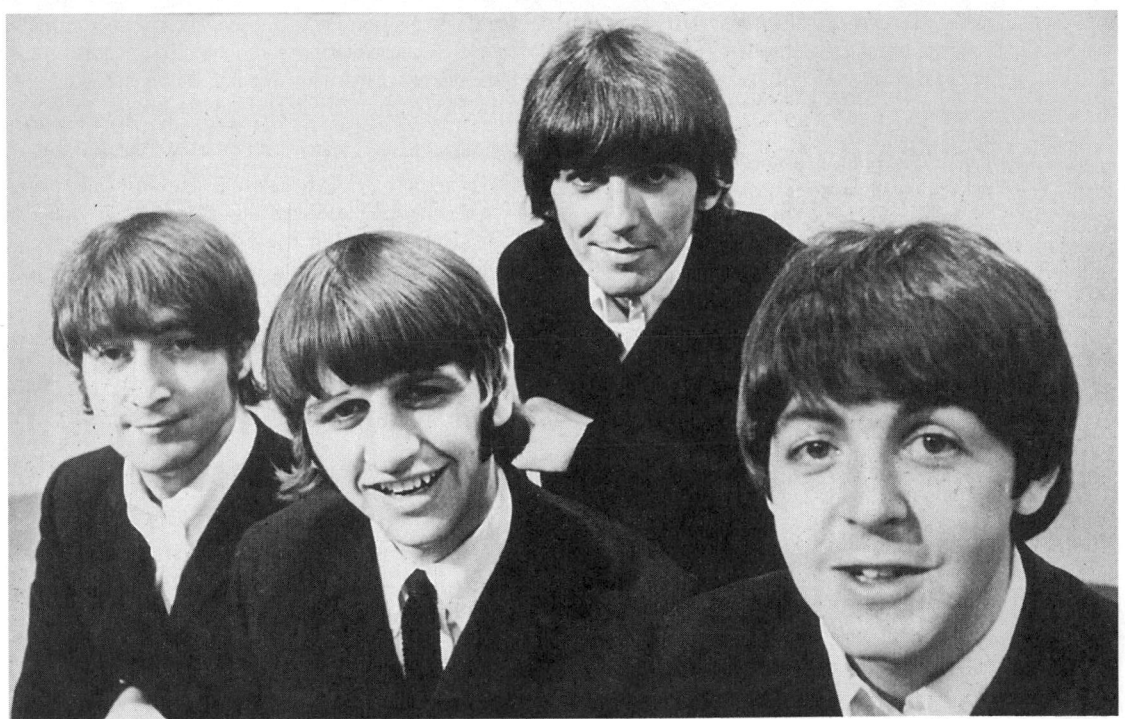

The Beatles (from left): John Lennon, Ringo Starr, George Harrison, and Paul McCartney **(Archive Photos)**

trio weathered personnel changes and initially lackluster critical response to forge a uniquely aggressive sound based on driving guitars, a solid backbeat, and high vocal harmonies. The group honed its skills by playing constantly in clubs in Liverpool and Hamburg, Germany, becoming a solidly professional and enormously popular live act. When the independently popular Ringo Starr was hired to replace Pete Best on drums, the newly dubbed Fab Four took Britain by storm with its debut LP. With skillful management and marketing, the Beatles became the first rock group to gain international fame, as Beatlemania swept Europe, Asia, and America.

As composers, Lennon and McCartney eventually blew away rock's artless image, giving the genre credibility with sophisticated chord structures, innovative lyrics, and intricate three-part harmonies. By 1966, fed up with the pressures of touring, the Beatles committed themselves to studio work, ushering in a revolutionary era in audio recording. With producer George Martin, the group advanced the concept of "recording studio as laboratory," furthering the art of audio production with multi-track recording and tape-loop effects. As founders of Apple

Records in 1968, the Beatles were the first group to create their own label, with acts that included Liverpool's Badfinger and U.S. folk singer James Taylor.

Solo projects, clashing egos, and family life began dividing the group in 1968, and by early 1970 the end was official. Solo careers followed—Lennon's and McCartney's being the most consistently noteworthy. All hopes of a Beatles reunion ended with Lennon's 1980 assassination in New York City, although a "reunion" of sorts was devised in the studio when the three remaining members added their voices and instruments to two Lennon demos to create new songs for the enormously successful *The Beatles Anthology* multimedia documentary project.

what to buy: As milestones go, there is little to compare with *Sgt. Pepper's Lonely Hearts Club Band* 𝄢𝄢𝄢𝄢 (Parlophone, 1967, prod. George Martin). Rock 'n' roll's first concept album, *Sgt. Pepper's* simmers with confidently adventurous songwriting and production while it marks a major step in the group's development. A fascinating listen even by today's standards. *Abbey Road* 𝄢𝄢𝄢𝄢 (Apple, 1969, prod. George Martin)— dubbed "Sgt. Pepper mark two" by Martin—can hardly be beat for sheer songwriting excellence and audio sophistication. Amidst internal animosity and feuds, the Beatles shone one last time as a group, showing mastery of their craft most notably on Lennon's "Come Together," McCartney's "Oh! Darling," and Harrison's "Here Comes the Sun" and "Something." *Revolver* 𝄞𝄞𝄞𝄞 (Parlophone, 1966, prod. George Martin), while musically uneven, shows an emerging sophistication in the group's songwriting ("Eleanor Rigby," "I'm Only Sleeping") and recording techniques ("Tomorrow Never Knows") without the self-consciousness that marred later efforts. For a look at the group's early years, *A Hard Day's Night* 𝄞𝄞𝄞𝄞 (Parlophone, 1964, prod. George Martin) shows the band at the peak of its Beatlemania-era productivity and talents. More than 30 years on, it holds its own as a solid and satisfying rock artifact.

what to buy next: While self-indulgent and at moments unlistenable, the double CD *The Beatles* 𝄞𝄞𝄞𝄞 (Apple, 1968, prod. George Martin) (a.k.a. *The White Album*) is a necessary taproot to the freeform nihilism echoed ever since in the punk and alternative music genres. Among the 30 songs, a few fascinating standouts—"While My Guitar Gently Weeps," "Happiness Is a Warm Gun," and "Helter Skelter"—make this worth owning. *Past Masters: Volume Two* 𝄞𝄞𝄞𝄞 (Parlophone, 1988, prod. George Martin)—a compilation of non-LP singles from 1966 to 1970—provides crucial creative links between this period's albums while demonstrating the group's giddy mastery of the 45 rpm pop song format (most notably "Lady Madonna" and "Revolution").

what to avoid: *Let It Be* 𝄞 (Apple, 1970, prod. Phil Spector) is a grim reminder that there is nothing so depressing as the sound of breaking up. A salvage effort by Spector renders the LP's few worthy tunes unlistenable with lush strings and choirs.

the rest:
Please Please Me 𝄞𝄞𝄞 (Parlophone, 1963)
With the Beatles 𝄞𝄞𝄞 (Parlophone, 1963)
Beatles for Sale 𝄞𝄞 (Parlophone, 1964)
Help! 𝄞𝄞𝄞𝄞 (Parlophone, 1965)
Rubber Soul 𝄞𝄞𝄞𝄞 (Parlophone, 1965)
Magical Mystery Tour 𝄞𝄞𝄞 (Parlophone, 1968)
Yellow Submarine (Soundtrack) 𝄞 (Apple, 1969)
The Beatles: 1962–1966 𝄞𝄞𝄞𝄞 (Apple, 1973)
The Beatles: 1967–1970 𝄞𝄞𝄞𝄞 (Apple, 1973)
The Beatles in the Beginning: Early Tapes (Circa 1960) 𝄞 (PolyGram, 1984)
Past Masters: Volume One 𝄞𝄞𝄞 (Apple, 1988)
Live at the BBC 𝄞𝄞𝄞 (Apple, 1994)
Anthology I 𝄞𝄞 (Apple, 1995)
Anthology II 𝄞𝄞𝄞 (Apple, 1996)
Anthology III 𝄞𝄞𝄞 (Apple, 1996)

worth searching for: The bootleg *Posters, Incense, and Strobe Candles* (Vigotone, 1993) offers a 1969 radio broadcast of "Get Back," the album that many overdubs later would become *Let It Be*. A fascinating relic from rock's psychedelic era.

influences:

◀◀ Lonnie Donegan, Elvis Presley, Buddy Holly, Carl Perkins, Chuck Berry, Little Richard, the Coasters, the Everly Brothers, Roy Orbison, Arthur Alexander

▶▶ Badfinger, Big Star, Utopia, the Jam, Squeeze, XTC, the dB's, Crowded House, Oasis

see also: *George Harrison, John Lennon, Paul McCartney, Ringo Starr*

Christopher Scapelliti

The Beau Brummels

Formed 1964, in San Francisco, CA. Disbanded 1968. Re-formed 1974.

Sal Valentino, vocals; Ron Elliott, guitar, vocals; Declan Mulligan, guitar, bass, vocals (1964–65, 1974–75); Ron Meagher, bass (1964–67); John Petersen, drums (1964–66, 1974–75).

The first San Francisco band, well before the Summer of Love gang, the Beau Brummels were also one of the very first self-contained groups from America to respond to the British onslaught (with "Laugh, Laugh" in the fall of 1964); their initial image and sound tricked many into thinking they were British, too. The Brummels were among the few to successfully make the transition (artistically, at least) from Top 40 popsters to respected "serious" rock musicians. The group boasted one of rock's most distinctive vocalists in Sal Valentino and one of its finest guitarists and songwriters in Ron Elliott. And, finally, you can listen to Beau Brummels music from any era—from its earliest pop forays to the later folk and country experiments—and come away satisfied that it was among the best at what it was doing.

what to buy: For a sampling of prime Brummels Mark I, *The Best of the Beau Brummels, 1964–1968* 𝄞𝄞𝄞𝄞 (Rhino, 1987, prod. Sly Stone) will do nicely. The Top 40 hits "Laugh Laugh" and "Just a Little" are here, along with "Don't Talk to Strangers," a song that defines folk-rock perhaps even better than the Byrds' "Turn, Turn, Turn."

what to buy next: *Autumn of Their Years* 𝄞𝄞𝄞𝄞 (Big Beat, 1994, prod. Sly Stone) collects unreleased songs and alternate takes from the group's early period on the Autumn label. *San Francisco Sessions* 𝄞𝄞𝄞𝄞 (Sundazed, 1996, prod. Sly Stone) has even more of the same, including demos that are as good as most contemporary groups' released output.

the rest:

Introducing the Beau Brummels ♫♫♫ (Autumn, 1965/Sundazed, 1994)

You Tell Me Why/Don't Talk to Strangers ♫♫♫ (Autumn, 1965/Sundazed, 1994, prod. Sly Stone)

worth searching for: During the late '60s, a pared-down Beau Brummels released two highly-regarded albums that sold zilch but enhanced the band's cachet among the lucky few who knew of them. *Triangle* (Warner Bros., 1967, prod. Lenny Waronker) has a mystic slant to much of it, while *Bradley's Barn* (Warner Bros., 1968/Epic U.K., 1997, prod. Lenny Waronker) was recorded at that very locale in Nashville and is more country-oriented. Both have recently been reissued on CD in Great Britain.

influences:

◄◄ The Beatles, the Searchers

►► Toad the Wet Sprocket, Del Amitri

Mike Greenfield

The Beautiful South

See: The Housemartins

Beck

Born Beck Hansen, July 8, 1970, in Los Angeles, CA.

As alternative music's golden child for the '90s, Beck made a name for himself with an rich, intoxicating blend of folk, rap, and indie rock that might find a beatbox behind a pedal steel guitar one minute, followed by a white-noise thrashfest the next. The son of hip, punk-rock parents, he first gained recognition as an eccentric songwriter/performer in Los Angeles. Finding his niche mixing creaky acoustic guitar with oddball, stream-of-consciousness lyrics, Beck recorded several hard-to-find singles and independently-released albums before the intentionally goofy "Loser"—with Beck rapping badly over a hip-hop beat—set off a bidding war between labels and made him a star overnight. A prolific artist, Beck's deal with DGC allows him to continue recording for small labels, even if these stripped-down experiments do go mostly ignored. Live, Beck is almost as impressive as he is on record: After the sloppy scissor kicks and splits of his manic Lollapalooza sets in 1995, he honed his act to incorporate James Brown–like stage moves and choreographed dance numbers with his backing musicians. With his game now complete, Beck is the closest thing around to a Bob Dylan for the '90s—with the favor of critics and the public alike, it seems he can do no wrong.

what to buy: *Mellow Gold* ♫♫♫ (DGC, 1994, prod. various) begins with the brilliant rock/folk/hip-hop marriage "Loser" and takes off through a style-hopping cornucopia of sounds that establishes Beck as much more than a one-hit wonder.

what to buy next: *Odelay* ♫♫♫ (DGC, 1996, prod. Dust Brothers) isn't as surprising as its predecessor, but it is a more mature, fully formed album, again featuring audacious experiments, "Jack-Ass," "The New Pollution"; and cheesy but fun rap-based numbers, "Where It's At," "High 5 (Rock the Catskills)."

the rest:

One Foot in the Grave ♫♫ (K Records, 1994)

Steropathetic Soul Manure ♫♫♫ (Flipside, 1994)

Mutations N/A (DGC, 1998)

influences:

◄◄ Robert Johnson, Bob Dylan, the Beastie Boys, Public Enemy, Miles Davis, Chet Baker, Pavement, Guided by Voices

►► 2 Skinnee J's

Todd Wicks

Jeff Beck

Born June 24, 1944, in Surrey, England.

Beck might be the least-known of the three guitar heroes who populated the Yardbirds, but as a sonic innovator he eclipses Jimmy Page and Eric Clapton—and most others—with his explosive, avant-noise style. Beck's post-Yardbirds career has been an erratic one filled with tempestuous behavior, long gaps between albums, and lead vocalists who never quite mesh with his playing (though Rod Stewart came pretty close). As a result, many of Beck's best albums are instrumental, though he's also veered off into soundtracks (*Twins, Frankie's House*) and salutes to his influences (*Crazy Legs*).

what to buy: *Truth* ♫♫♫♫ (Epic, 1968, prod. Mickie Most) is the first Jeff Beck Group album and features the vocals of a young Rod Stewart. It has been been dubbed the first true heavy metal album, and while that's misleading, this blues-rock workout certainly reset the limits on just how guttural and raunchy a guitar could sound. The jazz- and funk-oriented *Blow by Blow* ♫♫♫♫ (Epic, 1975, prod. George Martin) is Beck's all-instrumental masterpiece and features the crowd favorite "Freeway Jam."

what to buy next: *Rough and Ready* ♫♫♫ (Epic, 1971, prod. Jeff Beck), featuring singer Bobby Tench, chronicles Beck's first foray into soulful jazz-metal, and *There and Back* ♫♫♫ (Epic, 1980, prod. Jeff Beck, Ken Scott) is a collection of Beck's potent instrumentals, with backing from the sympathetic rhythm section of drummer Simon Phillips and keyboardist Tony Hymas.

what to avoid: *Jeff Beck with the Jan Hammer Group Live* ♫♫ (Epic, 1977, prod. Jan Hammer) provides several strong arguments for banning synthesizer solos.

Beck (© Ken Settle)

the rest:
Beck-Ola ♫♫♫ (Epic, 1969)
Jeff Beck Group ♫♫♫ (Epic, 1972)
Beck, Bogert and Appice ♫♫♫ (Epic, 1973)
Wired ♫♫♫ (Epic, 1976)
Flash ♫♫♫ (Epic, 1985)
Jeff Beck's Guitar Shop ♫♫♫♫ (1989)
Beckology ♫♫♫♫ (Epic, 1991)
Frankie's House ♫♫♫ (soundtrack) (Epic, 1992)
Crazy Legs ♫♫♫♫ (Epic, 1993)
Best of Beck ♫♫♫♫ (Epic, 1995)

worth searching for: *Rock 'n' Roll Spirit, Vol. II: Jeff Beck Session Works* (Epic, 1994, prod. various) is a Japanese import that studies his contributions to various works by Malcolm McLaren, Donovan, Stanley Clarke, and others.

influences:

◀◀ Cliff Gallup, James Burton, Les Paul, Buddy Guy

▶▶ Eddie Van Halen, Joe Satriani, Stevie Ray Vaughan, Vernon Reid

Thor Christensen

Walter Becker

See: Steely Dan

The Bee Gees

Formed 1958, in Brisbane, Australia.

Barry Gibb, vocals, guitar; Robin Gibb, vocals (1958–69, 1970–present); Maurice Gibb, vocals, bass, keyboards, guitar, percussion.

Before John Travolta strode down the sidewalk swinging a paint can to the disco sway of "Stayin' Alive," the Bee Gees were regarded as a pop vocal group of estimable talent that could take a good song and make it sound great. The trio had a few of those early on—"New York Mining Disaster 1941," "To Love Somebody," "Run to Me"—but it wasn't until the group recorded a few songs for the *Saturday Night Fever* soundtrack that it became a phenomenon, making hits not just for itself but also for singer Yvonne Elliman and late younger brother Andy Gibb. The brothers Gibb are, first and foremost, pop craftsmen with an intuitive knack for harmonies and decent melodic sensibilities. Were it not for the film—and the subsequent co-starring role in the disastrous *Sgt. Pepper's Lonely Hearts Club Band*—the Bee Gees likely would have remained modest also-rans in the pop pantheon, neither celebrated nor scorned. Now they have a lot of money, but also an artistic albatross that they haven't been able to shake since 1977. There was a sense of new embrace, however, from pop's hip elite when the trio was inducted into the Rock and Roll Hall of Fame in 1997.

WHAT ALBUM CHANGED YOUR LIFE?

Sgt. Pepper, without a doubt—not our version, the original. It was just so unique. Every time you knew the Beatles were going to have a new album out, it was an excitement build like you wouldn't believe in London. And a whole period started with *Sgt. Pepper,* like all of London changed when it came out. It's just an amazing album, beautifully crafted. It made us feel like, 'We've got to be better. We've got to be good.' There are not many people around today like that, influencing younger groups the way the Beatles did.

Maurice Gibb (of the Bee Gees)

what to buy: *Main Course* ♫♫♫♫ (RSO, 1975/Polydor, 1994, prod. Arif Mardin) is a transitional album, pop with R&B touches that would turn into a full-fledged disco movement for *Saturday Night Fever*. On *Main Course*, however, it's a welcome switch from the bland pop path the Bee Gees were on before, yielding tuneful hits such as "Jive Talkin' " and "Nights on Broadway." *Bee Gees Gold* ♫♫♫♫ (Polydor, 1976, prod. various) is a solid gathering of pre-"Fever" favorites.

what to buy next: Worth considering—but carefully—is the box set *Tales from the Brothers Gibb* ♫♫♫ (Polydor, 1990, prod. various). It covers everything you'd want, but its four discs also have plenty that you don't.

what to avoid: *Spirits Having Flown* ♫ (RSO, 1979/Polydor, 1994, prod. the Bee Gees, Karl Richardson, Albhy Galuten), the slick, calculated, and vapid follow-up to the *Fever* success.

the rest:
Bee Gees 1st ♫♫♫ (Atco, 1967/Rebound, 1994)
Odessa ♫♫ (Atco, 1969/Polydor, 1988)
Best of the Bee Gees, Vol. 1 (Atco/Polydor, 1969)
To Whom It May Concern ♫♫ (Atco, 1972/Polydor, 1992)

Best of the Bee Gees, Vol. 2 (Atco/Polydor, 1973)
Mr. Natural ♫♫ (RSO, 1974/Polydor, 1992)
Children of the World ♫♫♫ (RSO, 1976/Polydor, 1994)
Here at Last . . . Live ♫♫♫ (RSO, 1977/Polydor, 1990)
Size Isn't Everything ♫♫ (Polydor, 1993)
Still Waters ♫♫♫♪ (Polydor, 1997)
One Night Only N/A (Warner Bros., 1998)

worth searching for: The *veddy* late '60s *Cucumber Castle* (Atco, 1970, prod. Robert Stigwood, the Bee Gees), recorded by Barry and Maurice during Robin's brief hiatus from the band, has hysterical medieval cover art that guests will get a kick out of.

influences:

◄◄ The Four Freshmen, the Kingston Trio, the Beatles, the Beach Boys

►► Yvonne Elliman, Andy Gibb, Air Supply, Bread, Mr. Mister

Gary Graff

Bel Canto

Formed 1985, in Tromsoe, Norway.

Anneli M. Drecker, vocals, keyboards; Nils Johansen, guitar, violin, mandolin, programming; Andreas Eriksen, percussion; Kirsti Nyutstumo, bass; Geir Jenssen (1985–90).

Formed in the remote east coast port city of Tromsoe, Bel Canto mixes slices of classical music with ambient tones and dance-oriented grooves. The group released three independent albums in Europe—*White-Out Conditions* in 1986, *Birds of Passage* in 1989, and *Shimmering, Warm and Bright* in 1992—prior to its American debut in 1996.

what's available: *Magic Box* ♫♫♫ (Lava/Atlantic, 1996, prod. Ulf Holand, Bel Canto, Jah Wobble) treads the line between delicate folk trappings and lightly ambient atmospheria. Hypnotic female vocals and exotic musicality are the modus operandi here. Drecker's whispy vocals whirl with an airy magnitude that is purely hypnotic and fits perfectly with the band's eclectic traditional folk-meets-the-dancefloor groove theory. The title track is a lilting almost *a capella* number that flits and flutters as a sparce musical backdrop of plinking keyboards coats Drecker's delicate voice. From there the ablum slips seamlessly into the upbeat rhythm surge of "In Zenith," the loping groove of "Freelunch in the Jungle," the snappy soul of "Rumour," and the slinky Middle Eastern swirl of the Jah Wobble–produced "Bombay." The CD contains a bonus "Abstract Hip-hop Mix" of "Rumour" that is a multi-layered, serpentine slice of ambient mysticism.

worth searching for: The 12-inch single of "Rumour" contains a serious house-oriented dancefloor remix courtesy of Masters at Work, in addition to the album edit and the CD bonus "Abstract" edit.

influences:

◄◄ Kate Bush, Jah Wobble, Gavin Friday, late period Siouxie & the Banshees

►► Mono, Brigid Boden

Spence D.

Adrian Belew /The Bears

Born Robert Steven Belew, December 23, 1949, in Covington, KY.

The Bears: Adrian Belew, guitar, vocals; Rob Fetters, guitar, vocals; Bob Nyswonger, bass; Chris Arduser, drums.

A journeyman guitar virtuoso, Adrian Belew has always been at his best supporting other players—beginning with his first step into the big leagues, a spot in Frank Zappa's mid-'70s band. Launched into that gig when the rock orchestrator saw him performing in a Cincinnati club band, Belew became a sideman extraordinaire, lending his amazing arsenal of sounds to David Bowie, Talking Heads, and the Tom Tom Club before helping to reinvent King Crimson for the '80s. As a solo artist, his material has usually emphasized instrumental craft and creative abstraction over accessible melodies, hampering any commercial success. Getting together with pals from an old Cincinnati band called the Raisins, Belew developed a commercial venue for arty rock/pop tunes—kind of a new wave Beatles—dubbed the Bears in 1986. But the concept didn't catch on, so after two appealing yet underpromoted records, Belew returned to his own erratic recording projects, most recently using guitar synthesizers to perform original orchestral works and reuniting with King Crimson in 1994.

what to buy: His first solo album, *Lone Rhino* ♫♫♫♫ (Island, 1983, prod. Adrian Belew), is an engaging showcase for Belew's astounding guitar abilities, showing off arty rock and funk tunes written and produced by the guitarist himself. From the haunting title track—complete with guitar-produced rhinoceros bellows—to the rocking "Big Electric Cat," Belew served notice that he was an artist to be watched. Unfortunately, it took another 10 years before the guitarist would live up to his solo debut. *Inner Revolution* ♫♫♫♫♪ (Atlantic, 1992, prod. Adrian Belew) is a Beatles pastiche record that allows him to stretch his compositional skills and instrumental capabilities (he plays every instrument and produces).

what to buy next: The two Bears albums, *The Bears* ♫♫♫♫ (Primitive Man/I.R.S., 1987, prod Adrian Belew) and *Rise and Shine* ♫♫♫♫ (Primitive Man/I.R.S., 1988, prod. Adrian Belew), are the next-best examples of Belew in pop mode, whipping out intelligent, accessible tunes with a Beatle-esque flair, spiced with some burning chops. His backing musicians are no slouches either, offering spot-on support throughout these guitar-fueled rock tunes—material that failed only because it was probably 10 years ahead of its time.

what to avoid: Belew's biggest mistakes come when he allows his own virtuosity and musical smarts to get ahead of good songwriting. As a solo artist, those missteps are most glaring on *Young Lions* **woof!** (Atlantic, 1990, prod. Adrian Belew) and *Twang Bar King* **woof!** (Island, 1983, prod. Adrian Belew). On both records he lets his own complex ideas and innovative playing get away from him—surrounding mediocre compositions with top-notch playing and production.

the rest:
Desire Caught by the Tail ♪♪♪ (Island, 1986)
Mr. Music Head ♪♪♪♪ (Atlantic, 1989)
Desire of the Rhino King ♪♪♪ (Island, 1991)
Here ♪♪♪ (Plan 9/Caroline, 1994)
Acoustic Adrian Belew ♪♪♪ (Discipline, 1995)
Experimental Guitar Series, Vol. 1 ♪♪♪ (ABP, 1995)
The Guitar as Orchestra ♪♪♪♪ (Adrian Belew Presents, 1995)
Op Zop Too Wah N/A (Passenger, 1998)

worth searching for: Belew's guitar trickery lights up the classic but hard to find live album *The Name of This Band Is Talking Heads* (Sire, 1992, prod. Talking Heads), particularly on the funky world music cut "I Zimbra." In a more recent example, Belew adds guitar fireworks to nine inch nails's *The Downward Spiral* (Nothing, 1994, prod. Flood, Trent Reznor).

influences:
◀◀ Frank Zappa, King Crimson, the Beatles

▶▶ John Frusciante, Joe Satriani, Beck

see also: *King Crimson*

Eric Deggans

Chris Bell
See: Big Star

Joey Belladonna
See: Anthrax

Belle & Sebastian
Formed 1995, in Glasgow, Scotland.

Isobel Campbell, cello; Richard Colburn, drums; Stuart David, bass; Chris Geddes, keyboards; Stevie Jackson, guitar; Sarah Martin, violin; Stuart Murdoch, guitar, lead vocals.

If a band named after a French children's cartoon strikes you as a bit too clever, you're not alone. Even so, what some might see as a liability, others delight in. Belle & Sebastian have made a career out of wrapping syrupy-sweet melodies around the powder-dry wit of guitarist/vocalist Stuart Murdoch. The Glasweigian septet specializes in gorgeous chamber pop bearing the marks of folk-rock and '60s/'70s pop à la Donovan and Nick Drake. With breathtaking lo-fi melodies created by a host of instruments—cello, violin, piano, guitar, and recorder, among others, Belle & Sebastian seamlessly blend kitsch and pop chic. The group met and formed while in art school, so it's no surprise that its rise has been somewhat idiosyncratic. Following the release of its 1996 debut, *Tigermilk*, the band rode a swell of word-of-mouth support and—despite the demise of its first U.S. label, the Enclave—continued to churn out EPs to satiate growing demand for its music. Much of its state-side success can be attributed to fervent critical acclaim, which whipped up a considerable wave of interest and eventually led to a deal with Matador Records at the beginning of 1998.

what to buy: *If You're Feeling Sinister* ♪♪♪♪♪ (Enclave/Capitol, 1996) is the group's most satisfying album. Brimming with infectious arrangements built around charming stories, the album tends to get a bit sugary. But for those looking for a fresh and witty take on folk-pop from a bygone era, this one's for you.

what to buy next: Initially pressed in a quantity of 1,000 by its own label, *Tigermilk* ♪♪♪♪ (Electric Honey Recordings, 1996) is a bold debut for Belle & Sebastian, showcasing its trademark sound and putting cheese in the trap for the tempted.

the rest:
Dog on Wheels ♪♪♪♪ (Jeepster EP, 1997)
Lazy Line Painter Jane ♪♪♪ (Jeepster EP, 1997)
3..6..9 Seconds of Light ♪♪♪♪ (Jeepster EP, 1997)

influences:
◀◀ Nick Drake, Felt, Love, Donovan, the Velvet Underground, Richard Davies

Brandon Barber

Belly
/Tanya Donelly
Formed 1991, in Providence, RI. Disbanded 1996.

Tanya Donelly (Born July 16, 1966, in Newport, RI.), vocals, guitar; Thomas Gorman, guitar, organ, piano; Fred Abong, bass (1991–93); Leslie Langston, bass (1992); Gail Greenwood, bass (1993–96); Chris Gorman, drums.

After years of seeing only a few of her standout songs appear on each Throwing Muses album (and then on Breeders releases), Tanya Donelly put Belly together with the Gorman brothers, borrowing Muses bassist Fred Abong (earlier Muses bassist Leslie Langston filled in for a while but has not recorded with the group). With vocals nearly as distinctively quirky as the Muses' Kristin Hersh, but with a brighter and more pop-oriented sound, Donelly and her band appeared just as alternative rock became a recognized radio category and parlayed play on suddenly influential college radio into broader success with their debut album, *Star*. But the follow-up, *King*, didn't do nearly as well, and Donelly chose to dissolve the group and start a solo career.

what to buy: *Star* ♫♫♫♫ (Sire/Reprise, 1993, prod. various) contains the hits "Feed the Tree" and "Gepetto," with lots of fine, elliptical lyrics set to billowy alternative rock. Donelly's solo debut, *Lovesongs for Underdogs* ♫♫♫♫ (Reprise, 1997, prod. Tanya Donelly, Wally Gagel, Gary Smith), is full of ethereal songs, sometimes built around acoustic guitar, with a few throwbacks to *Star* for variety. In particular, Donelly's lyrics are more coherent than ever.

what to buy next: *King* ♫♫♫ (Sire/Reprise, 1995, prod. Glyn Johns) partly continues the familiar sound of *Star*, though the production is more varied and sometimes harder. But nothing is as immediately catchy as the debut's highlights. The Belly EP *Moon* ♫♫♫ (Sire/Reprise, 1993, prod. various) is noteworthy for covers of "Are You Experienced" (done for a Hendrix tribute album) and the Tom Jones hit "It's Not Unusual."

what to avoid: Donelly's EPs and CD singles have often contained non-album tracks that make paying their relatively exorbitant prices worthwhile, but on *Slow Dust* ♫ (Sire/Reprise, 1992, prod. Belly, Tracy Chisholm) "Dancing Gold" isn't worth the investment.

the rest:
Geppeto ♫♫♫ (Sire/Reprise EP, 1992)
Feed the Tree ♫♫♫ (Sire/Reprise EP, 1992)
Now They'll Sleep ♫♫ (Sire/Reprise EP, 1995)
Judas My Heart ♫♫♫ (Sire/Reprise EP, 1995)

worth searching for: Among the artists captured in live radio performances on *KCRW Rare on Air, Vol. 2* (Mammoth, 1995, prod. Chris Douridas, Bob Carlson) is Donelly singing the non-album "Sweet Ride" with just one acoustic guitar for that trendy unplugged feel—but it works well with her inimitable voice.

solo outings:
Tanya Donelly:
Sliding and Diving ♫♫♫ (Sire/Reprise EP, 1996)

influences:
◄◄ Lena Lovich, R.E.M.

see also: *Throwing Muses, the Breeders*

Steve Holtje

Pat Benatar

Born Pat Andrzejewski, January 10, 1953, in Brooklyn, NY.

The daughter of an opera singer and herself a classically trained singer in her teens, Pat Benatar was headed for the Juilliard School of Music until her rock 'n' roll attitude got in the way. Instead, she married army recruit Dennis Benatar and followed him to Virginia, only to move back to her native New York a few years later. Eventually divorcing Dennis (but keeping his surname), Benatar caught the eye of Catch a Rising Star owner Rick Newman, who became her manager. Though a few record labels turned down her tough-girl rocker material, Chrysalis Records signed the diminutive vocalist in 1978. Debuting as a sexpot singer more likely to sing up-tempo rock tunes about beating up men than loving them, Benatar exploded onto the charts with energetic tunes powered by her impressive vocals. Her reign as the queen of hard-headed rock 'n' roll continued through most of the '80s, even as she and producer Neil Geraldo (who eventually became her second husband) added more keyboards and pop elements to her arena rock sound. By the early '90s, as the grunge revolution made such pop-rockers passe, Benatar released a blues record that drove off the few fans who were left, putting the brakes on a career that had already been slowed by time off to raise children—though she came back to active duty during the late '90s.

what to buy: Benatar's first two albums—*In the Heat of the Night* ♫♫♫♫ (Chrysalis, 1979, prod. Mike Chapman, Peter Coleman) and *Crimes of Passion* ♫♫♫♫ (Chrysalis, 1980, prod. Keith Olsen)—are her most consistent. Arena rock classics such as "Heartbreaker," "Hit Me With Your Best Shot," and John Cougar's "I Need a Lover" cemented her reputation as a toughie with pipes of solid brass—an antidote to the coy and antiseptic female pop stars of the time.

what to buy next: Since Benatar's records grew increasingly more inconsistent during the '80s, her first hits collection, *Best Shots* ♫♫♫♫ (Chrysalis, 1989, prod. various), remains the best way to sample everything. Featuring many significant hits from her career, including a live version of "Hell Is for Children" and the *Legend of Billie Jean* soundtrack hit "Invincible," it's a cheap and easy way to skim the cream of Benatar's mid-to-late '80s work without wading through every album.

what to avoid: It's pretty obvious that Benatar's ill-fated blues record *True Love* **woof!** (Chrysalis, 1991, prod. Neil Geraldo) was the biggest nail in her career's coffin. Filled with awkward, clueless versions of B.B. King and Albert King tunes, this is that most horrible of rock star indulgences—a blues album by players who never bothered learning how to play the blues.

the rest:
Precious Time ♫♫♫ (Chrysalis, 1981)

Get Nervous ♫♫♫ (Chrysalis, 1982)
Live from Earth ♫♫♫ (Chrysalis, 1983)
Tropico ♫♫ (Chrysalis, 1984)
Seven the Hard Way ♫♫♫ (Chrysalis, 1985)
Wide Awake in Dreamland ♫♫ (Chrysalis, 1988)
Gravity's Rainbow ♫♫ (Chrysalis, 1993)
Very Best Of: All Fired Up ♫♫♫♫ (Chrysalis, 1994)
16 Classic Performances ♫♫♫ (EMI, 1996)
Innamorata ♫♫ (CMC International, 1997)

worth searching for: Benatar was a regular guest of such '80s-era television music series as *In Concert* and *Don Kirshner's Rock Concert*. Catching her on reruns of either is a guaranteed hoot, if only to see her macho posturing and drummer Myron Grombacher's new wave Keith Moon impersonation.

influences:

◄◄ Janis Joplin, Grace Slick, Patti Smith

►► Scandal, 4 Non Blondes, Melissa Etheridge

Eric Deggans

Brook Benton

Born Benjamin Franklin Peay, September 19, 1931, in Camden, SC. Died April 9, 1988, in New York, NY.

With his satin-smooth baritone and easygoing delivery, Brook Benton became one of the few black crooners of the '50s to successfully cross over into the pop-rock realm. Benton cut his teeth first on the gospel circuit and later with writer/producer Clyde Otis, singing and co-writing demos for hundreds of other musicians (including Nat King Cole and Clyde McPhatter). By the late '50s, Benton was signed by Otis to Mercury, where he put his deep, rich voice to work on lushly orchestrated R&B songs. The arrangements were the perfect showcase for Benton's intimate vocal style, and he scored an impressive 21 gold records in five years. In a move typical of record labels of this period, Mercury teamed Benton with a popular female singer—his labelmate Dinah Washington, whose easygoing voice meshed delightfully with Benton's. Together they scored a number of hits on the R&B charts—"Baby (You've Got What It Takes)," "A Rockin' Good Way"—until Washington's untimely death in 1963. Benton's encore was the 1970 hit "A Rainy Night in Georgia," an emotionally powerful deep-blues ballad that is the finest recording of his career. Although he never charted again, he remained a popular tour attraction into the early '80s.

what to buy: *Anthology* ♫♫♫ (Rhino, 1986, prod. various) is a fine 24-track retrospective of Benton's long and varied career, but it loses points for excluding Benton's mid-'60s stint at RCA, where he made a number of excellent recordings of pop standards. But it does serve up the early hits, "It's Just a Matter of Time," "Kiddio," "Fools Rush In"; the duets with Washington,

"Baby (You've Got What It Takes)," "A Rockin' Good Way"; and his later classic recordings for Atlantic's Cotillion label, including the hit "Rainy Night in Georgia."

what to buy next: *This Is Brook Benton* ♫♫♫ (BMG/RCA, 1989, prod. various) fills the gaps in Rhino's *Anthology*. This 20-track compilation of his 1965 to 1966 recordings for RCA features Benton backed by a full orchestra on a wide number of pop standards of the day, including "Call Me Irresponsible," "A Nightingale Sang in Berkeley Square," and Nat King Cole's signature tune, "Unforgettable." A pleasant reminder that Benton could croon as well as he could swing.

what to avoid: It is, in all likelihood, impossible to put out a bad album of Benton hits. So while *Greatest Hits* ♫♫ (WEA/Atlantic/Curb, 1991, prod. various) isn't necessarily poor, it's a lackluster sampling of Benton's catalog. Any of the other compilations listed here would make a stronger choice.

the rest:
Best of Brook Benton ♫♫♫♫ (PolyGram, 1987)
All His Best ♫♫♫ (Charly Budget, 1992)
Greatest Songs ♫♫♫ (WEA/Atlantic/Curb,1995)

worth searching for: *40 Greatest Hits* (Mercury, 1989, prod. Clyde Otis) is the best retrospective of Benton's Mercury years ever assembled. Although the album is out of print, sharp shoppers can usually locate unpurchased or used copies.

influences:

◄◄ Arthur Prysock, Frank Sinatra, Nat King Cole

►► Etta James, Ray Charles, Clyde McPhatter, Joe South

Christopher Scapelliti

Berlin

Formed 1979, in Venice, CA.

Terri Nunn, vocals (1979–88, 1996–present); John Crawford, bass (1979–88); David Diamond, synthesizer, guitar, vocals (1981–84); Rob Brill, drums, vocals (1983–88); Ric Olsen, guitar (1981–85); Matt Reid, synthesizer (1982–85).

Few careers better describe the state of musical affairs during the '80s than that of Berlin. Auspicious beginnings in the late '70s saw extensive turnovers in the band, leaving it at the turn of the decade with none of its original members (Toni Childs is said to have at one time been involved). But no worry. Struggling actress Terri Nunn simply dyed the ends of her white bob black and proceeded with the post-punk aplomb of a new wave seductress. "Sex . . . (I'm A)," from Berlin's debut, *Pleasure Victim*, brought the band national acclaim for its perverse slant on feminism, including the inimitable squawks, "I'm a Geisha!" and the then-controversial remark "I'm a slut!" But these are not the things careers are built on, so Berlin forayed into the Benatar-isms of the moment, saturating MTV with the schlocky concept/story videos that so epitomized the times. "No More Words" wasn't at all about political revolution, but the video was. The second album, *Love Life*, raised the drama a bit with its takes on romantic disillusionment and glitter's eminent fade. But it was the soundtrack hit, "Take My Breath Away"— lifted from the Tom Cruise vehicle *Top Gun*—that would seal Berlin's place in pop history, and, to some degree, erase all that happened before it. The song, not a Berlin composition, was a bloated affair of typically polished means—meaning it was nothing like Berlin at all. Still, it managed to rise to #1 during 1987 and become one of the biggest songs of the year. Unfortunately, the public did not succumb to melodrama, and so went Berlin. Rob Brill and John Crawford immediately formed an unsuccessful metal/grunge outfit named the Big F, while Nunn released an equally dismal solo effort, *Moment of Truth*, that found her trying to reclaim the glory of her tuneless squealing days. Both spinoffs are now out of print, and Nunn has recently reformed a new Berlin (featuring session musicians) for touring purposes and promises future recordings. Good luck.

what to buy: *The Best of Berlin, 1979–88* ♪♪♪ (Geffen, 1989, prod. various) chronicles the band's less-than-meteoric rise and fall, stumbling occasionally on the gems that made them matter in the first place.

what to buy next: *Love Life* ♪♪♪ (Geffen, 1983, prod. Georgio Moroder, Mike Howlett) stands as Berlin's only truly cohesive record. It's still listenable today, even, if you can forgive the frigid synth loops. Meanwhile, *Pleasure Victim* ♪♪♪ (Geffen, 1982, prod. Maomen, Daniel Van Patten) is their most randomly entertaining release. Unfettered by the pressures of industry packaging, Nunn has an almost frightening sense of humor.

what to avoid: *Count Three and Pray* ♪ (Geffen, 1987, prod. Bob Ezrin) is glass-shattering bombast when it's not swoony calculation. Late '80s excess prevails, and if there ever was a heart, it certainly isn't here.

influences:

◀◀ Suzi Quatro, Nina Hagen, Pat Benatar, Blondie

▶▶ No Doubt, Celine Dion

Billy Manes

Dan Bern

Born in IA.

What can we say about folk-punk singer-songwriter Dan Bern that he hasn't already said himself? On "Jerusalem," the first cut on his first album, he claims to be the Messiah. On "Tiger Woods," the leadoff track on his second album, he tells us he's

got "big balls." Reacting to the obvious New Dylan hype, Bern has said he considers Dylan "the Dan Bern of the '60s." Big balls indeed.

what to buy: His first album, *Dan Bern* ♪♪♪♪♪ (Work, 1997, prod. Chuck Plotkin), proved that Bern was worthy of his own high opinion of himself. Backed for the most part by just bass, drums, an occasional keyboard, and his own acoustic guitar, he delivered a set of beat-style rants that were often hilarious and occasionally surprisingly touching. "Wasteland" in particular mines a deep vein of pathos, perfectly capturing the nihilism of Generation X in a few quick and startling images ("I saw the best of my generation playing pinball"), while the seven-and-a-half minute stream-of-consciousness "Estelle" has a thin, wild mercury sound that could have held its own on Dylan's *Blonde on Blonde*.

what to buy next: *Fifty Eggs* ♪♪♪♪ (Work, 1998, prod. Ani DiFranco) is another gem. "Tiger Woods" is the kind of razor-sharp character-driven satire we rarely hear (it has almost nothing to do, however, with the golfer), and "Oh Sister" is one of the loveliest sibling tributes ever recorded; it hints that, if Bern is willing to look inside a bit more often, he may one day find himself on a par with the best of his influences.

what to avoid: Bern followed the critical success of his major-label debut by re-releasing his independently produced EP *Dog Boy Van* ♪♪♪ (Work, 1997), which, aside from rehashing "Jerusalem," is either a bit too cute ("Talking Alien Abduction Blues") or a bit too topical ("Kurt," about Cobain; the seven minute "Oklahoma," about the bombing).

worth searching for: The charity album *Diamond Cuts* (Hungry for Music, 1997, prod. various) features Bern's heartfelt baseball ballad "This Side of the White Line" alongside baseball songs by Bob Dylan ("Catfish"), Bruce Springsteen ("Glory Days"), and others. (Available by phone or mail order from Hungry for Music, 1-888-843-0933, 2020 Pennsylvania Ave. NW, Washington, D.C. 20006.)

influences:

◀◀ Bob Dylan, Loudon Wainwright III, Elvis Costello, John Wesley Harding, Ani DiFranco

Jeff Schwager

Chuck Berry

Born Charles Edward Anderson Berry, October 18, 1926, in St. Louis, MO.

Next to Elvis Presley, Chuck Berry is rock 'n' roll's most influential performer. In terms of innovation, though, he stands second to no one. Berry's ringing guitar gave the nascent genre its most identifiable sound, and his wide-ranging, poetic lyrics

Chuck Berry (© Jack Vartoogian)

gave it a vision. A black man with a taste for country music as well as the blues, Berry's souped-up anthems to teendom were irresistible because of his well-enunciated, theoretically raceless vocals, acceptable for airplay on radio stations that refused to broadcast R&B. But how the mighty have fallen; beyond these staggering accomplishments, Berry's contributions to rock 'n' roll include sexual deviancy (he was jailed for transporting a teenage prostitute across state lines during the early '60s and fined for videotaping the bathroom activities at his Wentzville, Missouri, restaurant in the early '90s) and tax evasion, for which he was sent to prison during the late '70s. Embittered, perhaps justifiably so, at the treatment he has received in exchange for his music, Berry for years has toured in a mercenary fashion, insisting on payment in cash, not rehearsing the pickup bands that back him, and phoning in his performances. He was the father of rock 'n' roll, but somehow he's turned into its deadbeat dad.

what to buy: Featuring 71 cuts over a span of three discs, *The Chess Box* 🎵🎵🎵🎵 (Chess/MCA, 1988, prod. Leonard Chess, Phil Chess) is an essential purchase for any serious fan of rock 'n'

roll. It covers all his essential hits—too numerous to mention here—and delves into other areas, such as his blues playing, and it includes some of the instrumental jams that the Chess brothers would record surreptitiously in the studio and use to flesh out Berry's albums. The set may be long for the novice listener, but remember: Berry's accomplishments are such that this book—not to mention rock 'n' roll itself—would not have existed without him. Those on a tighter budget are directed to *The Great Twenty-Eight* 🎵🎵🎵🎵 (Chess/MCA, 1982, prod. Leonard Chess, Phil Chess), which contains the essentials, but nothing else.

what to buy next: Berry wasn't really an album-oriented artist, so deciding on which of his individual albums to buy largely depends on the hits contained therein, and what happens to be in print at any given moment *St. Louis to Liverpool* 🎵🎵🎵🎵 (Chess, 1964, prod. Leonard Chess, Phil Chess) is probably his best single album, featuring "Promised Land," "Little Marie," "No Particular Place to Go," and "You Never Can Tell," plus a couple of good covers and a slow blues tune. For someone who owns the box set, it's worth checking out the rarities series—*Rock 'n'*

Roll Rarities 🎵🎵🎵 (Chess/MCA, 1986, prod. Leonard Chess, Phil Chess), *More Rock 'n' Roll Rarities* 🎵🎵🎵 (Chess/MCA, 1986, prod. Leonard Chess, Phil Chess), and *Missing Berries: Rarities, Vol. 3* 🎵🎵🎵 (Chess/MCA, 1990, prod. Leonard Chess, Phil Chess). After that, the early albums *After School Session* 🎵🎵🎵 (Chess, 1957/MCA Special Products, 1995, prod. Leonard Chess, Phil Chess), *One Dozen Berrys* 🎵🎵🎵 (Chess, 1958, prod. Leonard Chess, Phil Chess), and *Chuck Berry Is on Top* 🎵🎵🎵 (Chess, 1959/Chess/MCA, 1987, prod. Leonard Chess) are all worthwhile.

what to avoid: Berry left Chess during the mid-'60s to record for Mercury, and most of the undistinguished work he turned in there is justifiably out of print. Still available, though, are *Golden Hits* **woof!** (Mercury, 1967, 1989, prod. Chuck Berry), which features needless re-recordings of his seminal hits, and *Live at the Fillmore Auditorium* 🎵🎵 (Mercury, 1967/Rebound, 1994, prod. Abe Kesh), an unimpressive concert recording. Also avoid *Chuck Berry on Stage* **woof!** (Chess, 1963, prod. Leonard Chess, Phil Chess), which is not what its title advertises but rather studio recordings with a dubbed-in audience. *The London Chuck Berry Sessions* 🎵🎵 (Chess, 1972/Chess/MCA, 1989 prod. Esmond Edwards) yielded one of Berry's biggest hits, the novelty song "My Ding-a-Ling," but the album is a marginal effort nonetheless. Finally, Berry's work has been repackaged many times on many labels. Unless you know enough about what you're looking at, don't buy it.

the rest:
Rockin' at the Hops 🎵🎵🎵 (Chess, 1960/Chess/MCA, 1987)
New Juke Box Hits 🎵🎵🎵 (Chess, 1961/Chess/MCA, 1989)
Twist 🎵🎵🎵 (a.k.a. *More Chuck Berry*) (Chess, 1962)
Chuck Berry's Greatest Hits 🎵🎵🎵 (Chess, 1963)
(With Bo Diddley) *Two Great Guitars* (a.k.a. *Guitar Legends* 🎵🎵 (Checker, 1964/MCA Special Products, 1997)
Chuck Berry in London 🎵🎵🎵 (Chess, 1965)
Fresh Berrys 🎵🎵🎵 (Chess, 1966)
Chuck Berry's Golden Decade 🎵🎵🎵🎵🎵 (Chess, 1967)
Back Home 🎵🎵🎵 (Chess, 1970)
San Francisco Dues 🎵🎵 (Chess, 1971)
Bio 🎵🎵🎵 (Chess, 1973)
Chuck Berry's Golden Decade, Vol. 2 🎵🎵🎵🎵🎵 (Chess, 1973)
Chuck Berry's Golden Decade, Vol. 3 🎵🎵🎵 (Chess, 1974)
Chuck Berry 🎵🎵 (Chess, 1975)
Rockit 🎵🎵 (Atco, 1979)
Hail! Hail! Rock 'n' Roll 🎵🎵🎵🎵 (MCA, 1987)
His Best, Volume 1 🎵🎵🎵🎵🎵 (MCA/Chess, 1997)
His Best, Volume 2 🎵🎵🎵🎵🎵 (MCA/Chess, 1997)

worth searching for: *Chuck Berry Is on Top* (Chess, 1959) and *Rockin' at the Hops* (Chess, 1960), two of Berry's best albums, are available, in original mono, via French imports.

influences:

◄◄ Muddy Waters, Louis Jordan, T-Bone Walker, Hank Williams

►► The Beatles, the Rolling Stones, the Beach Boys, Bob Dylan, and everyone else who has ever played rock 'n' roll

Daniel Durchholz

Dave Berry
/Dave Berry & the Cruisers

Born David Holgate Grundy, February 6, 1941, in Beighton, Sheffield, Yorkshire, England.

A would-be R&B belter who ultimately found more success as a beat balladeer, Dave Berry started his career as one half of an Everly Brothers–style duo in northern England. Upon rechristening himself in honor of Chuck Berry and commandeering a local group called the Cruisers, he came to the attention of producer Mickie Most in 1963, and a cover of Chuck's "Memphis, Tennessee" became the group's first entry in the U.K. Top 20 that autumn. Unfortunately, on the remainder of his records the Cruisers (who were an able if unspectacular group) were replaced by session musicians (though future Led Zeppeliners Jimmy Page and John Paul Jones were among them), and the choice of material was suspect, veering aimlessly from American rock and rhythm chestnuts to soppy weepers from the Bobby Goldsboro and B. J. Thomas songbooks. Consequently, Berry failed to establish a musical identity for himself and is remembered today mainly as the original voice behind "The Crying Game" theme song from the hit 1992 movie.

what's available: Both *The Very Best of Dave Berry* 🎵🎵🎵 (Spectrum, 1997, compilation prod. John Tracy) and *The Best of Dave Berry* 🎵🎵🎵 (See for Miles, 1993, prod. various) cover the man's career more than adequately, and the latter is of particular note as it includes the early Ray Davies composition "This Strange Effect" (Holland's biggest-selling single ever) as well as "Don't Gimme No Lip, Child," purportedly a big favorite of the Sex Pistols.

influences:

◄◄ Chuck Berry, Long John Baldry, Eric Burdon, Mick Jagger

►► Ian & the Zodiacs, Alan Clayson & the Argonauts, Boy George, John Lydon

Gary Pig Gold

Heidi Berry

Born in Boston, MA.

Tied more to the timeless marriage of melody and lament than to the commercial aspirations of the Lilith revolution, Heidi Berry's astute pop indeed rings timeless among its peers. Her career precedes the meteoric rises of Tori and Sarah, after all, and she has yet but to nibble the fruits of even moderate retail success. Despite American birth, Berry was raised in England and found most of her musical origins in the Celtic folklore and urban ecclecticism of the surrounding region. Her initial recordings, released only in England on the fledgling Creation label, were buoyed by the guitar jangle and sonic texturing of the late '80s British mope. *Below the Waves* was eventually released stateside, introducing the moodier, more pristine Berry. Slight classical instrumentation and nimble string pickery by her brother, Christopher Berry, saw her adopting a more enigmatic, 4AD style. Fortunately, 4AD saw the same thing, and signed her for her next three recordings—two of which were released in America, including her self-titled masterpiece in 1993.

what's available: Unfortunately, all of Berry's releases are unavailable save *Miracle* ⨪⨪⨪ (4AD, 1996, prod. Hugh Jones), a subdued, folky affair that's not her brightest moment.

worth searching for: Her debut, *Heidi Berry* (4AD, 1993, Hugh Jones) is essential. Dig through those cut-out bins!

influences:

◄◄ This Mortal Coil, Joni Mitchell, Bel Canto

►► Sarah McLachlan, Katell Keineg

Billy Manes

Richard Berry

Born April 11, 1935, in Extension, LA. Died January 23, 1997, in Los Angeles, CA.

Richard Berry died a happy man. For most of his life, he was a forgotten doo-wopper, a practitioner of a musical style that dated as fast as unrefrigerated milk. But a song he scribbled on a napkin between sets in an Los Angeles nightclub in 1957 became the quintessential, mindless rock 'n' roll song, a Latin-tinged blues number by the name of "Louie Louie." Berry's own version sank without a trace, and even after the Seattle-based Kingsmen drove FBI agents goofy trying to decipher their gargled cover, he received little recognition and no residuals. It took radio, "Louie Louie" marathons, and the support of lawyers, music critics, and thousands of lovers of garage rock to win Berry the royalties and honor he deserved. Stricken with polio not long after his family moved to Los Angeles during his childhood, Berry was on crutches until he was six. By high school, he was playing the ukulele and had met a pack of future doo-wop stars, among them crooner Jesse Belvin and future Coaster Cornell Gunter. The high school friends soon joined in a rotating roster of R&B groups—the Flairs, the Dreamers, the Pharaohs—and recorded for Dolphin, Modern, and Flip. Berry was a natural songwriter, able to spin double entendres in "Jelly Roll" and satirize the mañana mentality in

"Next Time." But it was his menacing, sex-dripping voice that became his stock-in-trade. Leiber and Stoller used him, uncredited, as the lead singer on the Robins' classic "Riot in Cellblock #9," and he was the nasty Henry voice in "The Wallflower," Etta James's answer to Hank Ballard's "Work with Me, Annie." Session work kept him in clover for awhile, but by the late 1950s, Berry's star was fading. He kept churning out records, among them "Louie Louie." The song is a takeoff on Chuck Berry's "Havana Moon" and the calypso craze, but it was basically overlooked by Flip Records and released as the B-side to a fluffy version of "You Are My Sunshine." Berry had already relinquished his rights when scuffling bands in Seattle found old copies of the song in the early 1960s. Soon, every Seattle band had "Louie Louie" in its repertoire; the Kingsmen and Paul Revere & the Raiders were the first to record it. It was the Kingsmen's noise-congested version, shouted up at a high-hung microphone, that sent dozens of FBI agents hunting around the country—and eventually interviewing a bewildered Berry—in a vain attempt to identify obscene lyrics. The song did nothing for Richard Berry until the 1980s, when new versions began to litter the landscape like forest toadstools—ranging from truly pornographic live Iggy Pop performances to kazoo-band marches. Berry won back some royalties, and when the song rights were sold again in 1992, he won a substantial settlement. In recent years, he had begun to perform again, mostly in the Los Angeles area—a promising development cut short by his death from a heart attack.

what to buy: *Get out of the Car* ⨪⨪⨪ (Flair, 1994, prod. Joe Bihari) is funky, uptempo L.A. doo-wop and dreamy ballads, almost all written by Berry. It includes "Jelly Roll" and "The Big Break"—the sequel to "Riot in Cellblock #9"—but no "Louie Louie."

what to avoid: *Best of Louie Louie, Vol. 1* ⨪⨪ (Rhino, 1988) is only for "Louie" fanatics. Berry's version is here, and so is the Kingsmen's, but can you really stand a second listen to the Sandpipers or the Rice University Marching Owl Band?

worth searching for: *The Best of Flip Records, Vols. 1–3* (Titanic, 1997, prod. Max Freitag) documents Berry's Pharaoh recordings, mixed in among tough doo-wop by Arthur Lee Maye (who went on to a career as a Baltimore Orioles slugger) and some cloying girl group ditties. "Louie Louie" is on Vol. 3, and on Vol. 1 is "Have Love Will Travel," covered by the Sonics in the 1960s and 20 years later in a riotous version by Bruce Springsteen on his *Tunnel of Love* tour. The sound is spectacular, but these are Italian imports, so you'll have to dig.

influences:

◄◄ Jesse Belvin, Big Jay McNeely, Chuck Berry, Harry Belafonte

►► The Kingsmen, the Kinks, Paul Revere & the Raiders, the

Sonics, the Beach Boys, Iggy Pop, Toots & the Maytals, Bruce Springsteen, Dave Barry

Steve Braun

Cindy Lee Berryhill

Born in Los Angeles, CA.

Originally running with the post-punk folk crowd that included Kirk Kelly and Roger Manning, San Diego–based Cindy Lee Berryhill was one of the first new acts signed to reissue kingpin Rhino Records during the late '80s. A precocious teenager, Berryhill grew up with an affection for performing music (she once played in a punk band called the Stoopuds) and documenting her deepest thoughts and strongest opinions in her journal. As a result, her first two albums were suitably driven by attitude and backhanded feminist statements ("Damn, I Wish I Was a Man," "Baby, Should I Have the Baby?") but they also were overloaded with yippie-skippy, Beat-poetry earmarks. In 1990, frustrated with the commercial indifference to her work, Berryhill temporarily relocated to Taos, New Mexico. There, she cleared her mind, delved back into her journal and reinvented herself with a broader sound and outlook that was more playful than ponderous: she followed Alejandro Escovedo's chamber-rock lead, enhancing her swooping soprano with a swirling mix of cellos, tympanis, violins, vibraphones, and offbeat percussion. The economics of touring still force her to perform solo, but she continues to find ways to make it more fun: In 1997, she and fellow San Diego songwriter Elizabeth Hummel traveled to the homes of several fans and played in their living rooms, charging admission only to cover their travel expenses.

what to buy: *Garage Orchestra* ✍✍✍ (Cargo, 1994, prod. Cindy Lee Berryhill, Michael Harris), boasting such engaging numbers as "I Wonder Why," "Song for Brian" (a love letter to Brian Wilson), and "UFO Suite," dabbles in avant-garde dissonance but mostly demonstrates the tasteful, textural range that strings can bring to pop music.

what to buy next: *Straight Outta Marysville* ✍✍✍ (Cargo, 1996, prod. Cindy Lee Berryhill, Michael Harris) finds her striking the perfect balance between the daring textures of *Garage Orchestra* and her earlier folk sound on quirky tracks such as "Just Like Me," "High Jump," and a funky cover of Donovan's "Season of the Witch."

the rest:
Who's Gonna Save the World? ✍✍ (Rhino, 1987)
Naked Movie Star ✍✍✍ (Rhino, 1989)

influences:
◀◀ Jack Kerouac, Patti Smith, Jonathan Richman

▶▶ Brenda Kahn, Jane Gillman, Dar Williams

David Okamoto

Best Kissers in the World
See: Gerald Collier

Better Than Ezra
Formed 1988, in New Orleans, LA.

Kevin Griffin, vocals, guitars; Cary Bonnecaze, drums, vocals (1988–96); Travis Aaron McNabb, drums (1996–present); Tom Drummond, bass.

Tragedy has followed Better Than Ezra since its early days as a Dinosaur Jr.–influenced combo. Former drummer Cary Bonnecaze was shot in the back as a teen, though he fully recovered. And its original lead singer, Joel Rundell, died accidentally. The remaining trio forayed into modern rock, picking up early support from college radio stations.

what to buy: *Deluxe* ✍✍✍ (Elektra, 1995, prod. Dan Rothchild) elevated the band to the pop mainstream thanks to the infectious wuh-huh choruses of "Good."

the rest:
Friction, Baby ✍✍ (Elektra, 1996)
How Does Your Garden Grow ✍✍✍ (Elektra, 1998)

influences:
◀◀ Dinosaur Jr., Cracker
▶▶ Matchbox 20, Dishwalla

Christina Fuoco

Bettie Serveert
Formed 1990, in Amsterdam, Holland.

Carol van Dijk, vocals, guitar; Peter Visser, guitar; Herman Bunskoeke, bass; Berend Dubbe, drums.

Ah, art school students. Who else could have have come up with a name like Bettie Serveert, culled from a random passage—"serve to Betty"—in a tennis instructional book by Dutch tennis star Betty Stove? The quartet's sound was founded on classic influences, notably the guitar flailing of Crazy Horse, the chiming pop of the Byrds, and the ballads of the Velvet Underground, with Carol Van Dijk's dusky vocals and schoolgirlish folk musings serving as a focal point. With the 1992 college-rock hit "Tom Boy," Bettie Serveert became the biggest thing out of Holland since—hold on to your nose rings!—Golden Earring. The band has been unable to expand on that commercial success, but has continued to release atmospheric folk-rock albums and cut back on the wanky guitar solos that marred early live shows.

what to buy: *Palomine* ♪♪♪♪ (Matador/Atlantic, 1992, prod. Edwin "Hank" Heath, Frans Hagenaars, Bettie Serveert) has three highly addictive tracks: "Tom Boy," "Kid's Allright," and the title song. Van Dijk's conversational, girl-next-door delivery is framed by the band's understated mood swings between brooding and buoyant. The Betties exude an innocence lacking in many other bands' more mannered attempts to traverse the same well-trod landscape between Neil Young's "Zuma" and the Velvet Underground's "Loaded."

what to buy next: *Dust Bunnies* ♪♪♪ (Matador/Capitol, 1997, prod. Bryce Goggin) didn't get the same notices as *Palomine*, but it's an engaging collection of folk-pop, with Visser's more concise guitar building delicate spider webs around Van Dijk's vocal incense.

the rest:
Lamprey ♪♪♪ (Matador/Atlantic, 1995)

worth searching for: *Tomboy* (Matador CD-5, 1992) contains a handful of outtakes and a cover shot of Van Dijk as the tomboy of every college kid's dreams.

influences:
◄◄ Neil Young & Crazy Horse, the Byrds, the Velvet Underground

Greg Kot

Betty Boo

Born Alison Moira Clarkson, 1970, in Kensington, London, England.

British soul/rap singer Betty Boo is one part hooky hip-hop artist and one part kooky novelty tune writer. Mostly her music is about dancing, and Boo whips up plenty of exuberant booty-shaking rhythms. Originally performing under the name of cartoon character Betty Boop (legalities forced her to drop the "p"), Boo established herself with inventive hooks and comic-style videos that showed off her exotic Scottish-Malaysian beauty. Her career began to flounder when, while lip-synching on live British TV, she dropped her microphone, revealing a canned vocal track. No great crime, but the public was still shaking its head over the Milli Vanilli scandal. Boo disappeared after her poorly received sophomore release, and despite signing to Madonna's Maverick label in early 1996, no new material has been forthcoming.

what to buy: *Boomania* ♪♪♪♪ (Rhythm King, 1990, prod. various) simmers with layers of guitar licks, keyboard riffs, and bass lines, the whole of which conspire to blow the roof off your sugar shack—from the Top 10 raps "Doin' the Do" and "Where Are You Baby?" to the ace instrumental "Boo's Boogie," plus the straightforward dance number "24 Hours," on which she sounds uncannily like Paula Abdul.

WHAT ALBUM CHANGED YOUR LIFE?

I'm from the era when singles happened. Top 40 meant you'd hear 40 different songs. But I guess *The Beatles,* the white album; it was just so avant garde and out there. It was just, All right! This is different, really sonically intense.

Fred Schneider (of the B-52's)

what to buy next: *Grrr! It's Betty Boo* ♪♪♪♪ (Sire, 1992, prod. Betty Boo) continues in the vein of *Boomania* but offers mellower tunes such as "Close the Door" and "Let Me Take You There." Boo shows especially good form on "I'm on My Way"; instead of sampling the brass on the Beatles' "Lady Madonna," she brings in the original sax players (including Ronnie Scott) to reprise their parts. That's class.

influences:
◄◄ Madonna, Paula Abdul, Milli Vanilli
►► Deee-Lite, Aqua

Christopher Scapelliti

Bewitched
See: Sonic Youth

Jello Biafra
See: Dead Kennedys

Big Ass Truck
Formed 1993, in Memphis, TN.

Steve Selvidge, vocals, guitar; Robert Barnett, drums; Robby Grant, vocals, guitar; Colin Butler, turntables, percussion, trumpet; Dros Liposcak, bass (1997–present); Al Greene, keyboards (1993–94); Chris Parker, keyboards (1994–96); Joe Boone, bass (1993–96); John Stubblefield, bass (1996–97).

Giving its hometown Stax/Volt sound a decidedly '90s twist, Big Ass Truck combines turntable acrobatics, clever samples

(Slick Rick, Wolfman Jack, Bill Withers, TV commercials), and occasional punk and reggae flurries with greasy organ vamps, burbling rhythms, and a funkdafied double-guitar attack to make genre-bastardizing music that would make both Beck and Uncle Jam proud. Uncle John's Band would also approve, as BAT occasionally rides spacey, wide-open grooves as if it's the Grateful Dead or something. Then again, the Dead would never give their songs titles such as "Heavy Petting Zoo," "Sharin' the Sherbert," "Sparkle Inner Eye," and "Dog Chases an Iguana up a Tree and Barks at It All Night (Parts I & II)." The Dead also wouldn't dare to cover Isaac Hayes's funk opus, "Hyperbolicsyl-labicsesquedalymystic," as BAT did on its 1997 EP, *Sack Lunch.*

what to buy: *Kent* ♫♫♫ (Upstart, 1996, prod. Ross Rice, Eric Fettrich, Big Ass Truck) is a greasy, funk-rockin' post-hip-hop album that sounds like a Jon Spencer experiment gone great—either that or the Bar-Kays gone modern. Though this is just its sophomore album, BAT plays together as if they've been doing it since, say, before Elvis left the building. Selvidge's lazy-boy chicken-shack vocals, meanwhile, often sound like a cross between the Spin Doctors' Chris Barron and Beck (that's a good thing).

the rest:
Big Ass Truck ♫♫♫ (Inbred/Upstart, 1994/1995)
Sack Lunch EP (Yep Roc, 1997) ♫♫♫

solo outings:
Robert Grant:
Unleavened Bread ♫♫♫ (Yep Roc, 1997)

influences:
◄◄ Stax/Volt, Hi Records, Parliament-Funkadelic, Jon Spencer Blues Explosion, Beck, Sublime, Big Star, the Grateful Dead, James Brown

►► Mac Swanky Trio

Josh Freedom du Lac

Big Audio Dynamite
/B.A.D. II
/Big Audio

Formed 1984, in London, England.

Mick Jones, vocals, guitars; Don Letts, keyboards (1984–90); Leo Williams, bass (1984–90); Greg Roberts, drums (1984–90); Dan Donovan, keyboards (1984–90); Gary Tonadge, bass (1991–present).

Unceremoniously booted from the Clash, Mick Jones—who was responsible for some of that band's more adventurous music—put together this multimedia, multi-genre ensemble that's become one of the longest-running parties of the post-Clash bunch. Jones blended his rock instincts with his growing interests in hip-hop, rave, and dance fads of the day. And while Big

Audio Dynamite has changed personnel almost as often as it changed band names, it has been a dependable source for a good single every couple of years, even as Jones slowly returned to the ragged guitar sound of his roots.

what to buy: *Planet B.A.D.: Greatest Hits* ♫♫♫♫ (Columbia, 1995, prod. various) goes above and beyond such collections by including not only the crucial cuts from every Columbia album, but also leasing one from the label he defected to, "I Was a Punk," to bring the chronicle full circle.

what to buy next: *This Is Big Audio Dynamite* ♫♫♫♫ (Columbia, 1985, prod. Mick Jones) seemed a little bareboned at the time; its atmosphere is as stark as the spaghetti Western milieu it reflected in its tracks—not so far from Jones's work in Clash, but a definite jump to something new, a mix of rock and dance that sounded natural and still sounds fresh many years later.

what to avoid: *F-Punk* ♫♫ (Radioactive, 1995, prod. Mick Jones, Andre Shapps) is a rote return to the more guitar-oriented music of Jones's Clash past.

the rest:
No. 10 Upping Street ♫♫♫ (Columbia, 1986)
Tighten Up, Volume '88 ♫♫♫ (Columbia, 1988)
Megatop Phoenix ♫♫♫ (Columbia 1989)
B.A.D. II ♫♫♫ (Columbia, 1991)

worth searching for: *Looking for a Song 2 CD Set* (Columbia, 1994) is a promotion-only set with three versions of the band's last single for Columbia; it also includes a succinct greatest hits collection.

influences:
◄◄ The Clash, the Who, Chicago house music, Detroit techno

►► Soup Dragons, the Chemical Brothers, Black Grape, Chumbawamba, Propellerheads

see also: *The Clash*

Roger Catlin

Big Bad Voodoo Daddy
/BBVD

Formed 1989, in Los Angeles, CA.

Scotty Morris, vocals, guitar; Kurt Sodergren, drums; Dirk Shumaker, bass (1992–present); Andy Rowley, saxophone; Glen "The Kid" Marhevka, trumpet (1995–present); Jeff Harris, trombone (1995–present); Karl Hunter, saxophone, clarinet (1995–present); Josh Levy, piano (1995–present).

In 1989, fed up with the L.A. music scene, session guitarist Scotty Morris formed a three-piece swing combo. Gigs led to more gigs, and soon Morris realized that there was more than just a market for old-time swing music; there was, in fact, a thriving subculture based upon it. Zoot suits and fedoras were the order of the day, and soon BBVD was at the top of its game, playing classic swing tinged with Morris's punk rock roots. More musicians were added to the mix, and, in 1992, the band was officially dubbed Big Bad Voodoo Daddy. It quickly released an independent self-titled album and by 1995 had become the house band at the Derby, an L.A. club. A year later, an appearance in the film *Swingers* gave the group national exposure, and its blistering live show got it gigs all over the country. During early 1998, it landed a major league contract and released a different self-titled album. Unfortunately, its label, E-Prop, a division of EMI, folded shortly after the record hit shelves.

what to buy: The band's second self-titled album, *Big Bad Voodoo Daddy* 𝄞𝄞𝄞𝄞 (EMI-Capitol, 1998, prod. Brad Benedict, Michael Frondelli, Scotty Morris), is a perfect example of the nouveau swing movement. Big band swing, slower ballads (the one cover on the record is "Minnie the Moocher"), and even a hint of mambo can be found here. Some of the tunes, such as "You & Me & the Bottles Makes 3 Tonight" and "The Boogie Bumper," clip right along with a sense of pacing that originated better than 50 years ago.

what to buy next: *Whatchu' Want for Christmas* 𝄞𝄞𝄞 (Hepcat, 1995) includes the three BBVD songs that appeared on the *Swingers* soundtrack, along with some swingin' holiday hits.

worth searching for: The original *Big Bad Voodoo Daddy* (Hepcat, 1992) is out of print but features another great set of original '90s swing.

influences:

◀◀ Cab Calloway, Louis Prima, Chet Baker, Tom Waits

Anders Wright

Big Black

Formed 1982, in Chicago, IL. Disbanded 1987.

Steve Albini, vocals, guitar; Santiago Durango, guitar; David Riley, bass; Roland, percussion.

About as pleasant as an acetone lollipop, Big Black is an incredible listening experience for those who like to suffer. Predating Trent Reznor's fake pain and Ministry's "evil" stage, the Big Black (which included "drummer" Roland, a rhythm machine) were brutal and callous before it was a hip and stylish trend. Led by recording studio magnate and vehement fanzine contributor Steve Albini, Big Black released records that not only dared you to like them, but hated you if you did. That being said, it's, er, nirvana for folks who enjoy a trebly mix of post–Gang of Four guitar, screechy vocals, and throbbing (but not dancey) beats.

what to buy: *Songs about Fucking* 𝄞𝄞𝄞𝄞 (Touch & Go, 1987/1992, prod. Steve Albini) is as subtle as a drop kick. With covers of Kraftwerk's "The Model" and Cheap Trick's "He's a Whore," this is Big Black at its most, er, fun. As dense as always, *Songs . . .* combines the brittle attack with a more discernable sense of humor than previously evidenced by the band. This slight maturation was followed by the news of the band's demise, reputedly due to Durango's decision to attend law school.

what to buy next: *Rich Man's Eight Track* 𝄞𝄞𝄞 (Touch & Go, 1987/1892, prod. Steve Albini) is not a true album but a combination of some previous releases. No matter, the track "Kerosene," which contains lyrics that could get Beavis and Butthead off the hook with fire enforcement authorities, is included here and is likely the most essential Big Black song. Angry and remorseless, the entire collection could easily be used to clear a cocktail party in seconds. The liner notes, damning digital audio technology, are nearly worth the price of admission alone.

the rest:

The Hammer Party 𝄞𝄞𝄞 (Touch & Go, 1986/1992)
Atomizer 𝄞𝄞𝄞𝄞 (Touch & Go, 1986/1992)
Headache 𝄞𝄞𝄞 (Touch & Go EP, 1987/1992)
Pigpile 𝄞𝄞𝄞 (Touch & Go, 1992)

worth searching for: *Sound of Impact* (Walls Have Ears, 1987) is an impossible-to-find, vinyl-only import that culls live tracks from a few early concerts. Cryptic and different, this record resembles a bootleg in more ways than one. Happy hunting.

influences:

◀◀ PiL, Gang of Four, Kraftwerk, Wall of Voodoo, construction sites

▶▶ nine inch nails, Ministry, Arsenal, Breaking Circus, Marilyn Manson

Barry M. Prickett

The Big Bopper

Born Jiles Perry "J.P." Richardson, October 24, 1930, in Sabine Pass, TX. Died February 3, 1959, near Clear Lake, IA.

Was he for real or a joke? We never got the answer to that question, because the Big Bopper died in the same plane crash that took the lives of Buddy Holly and Ritchie Valens, less than a year after J.P. Richardson from KTRM radio in Beaumont, Texas, came to international prominence with his hit "Chantilly Lace." The truth is, Richardson—who began writing songs during a stint in the army—was an entertainer. His other songs were novelties—"The Purple People Eater Meets the Witch-Doctor," "The Big Bopper's Wedding," "Little Red Riding

Hood." His stage show played on his radio persona, a big man with a big voice and that famous come-hither call of "Hel-looooo baby!"

what's available: *Hellooo Baby! The Best of Big Bopper* ♪♪♪ (Rhino, 1989) has 'em all—and probably more than you ever wanted. The original but skimpier *Chantilly Lace* ♪♪ (Mercury, 1958/1994) is also available.

influences:

◀◀ Cab Calloway, Dean Martin

▶▶ Buster Poindexter, Perry Farrell, the Mighty Mighty Bosstones

Gary Graff

Big Chief

Formed 1989, in Ann Arbor, MI.

Barry Henssler, vocals; Mark Dancey, guitar; Matt O'Brien, bass; Phil Durr, guitar; Mike Danner, drums.

Paying tribute to its geographical roots, Big Chief took the hard edge of Ann Arbor legends the Stooges and the MC5 and combined it with the Motor City funk sounds of George Clinton's Parliament-Funkadelic projects. The result was an aggressive, powerful mix as much hardcore funk as funky hardcore. Big Chief tempered its big sounds with liberal doses of humor (the members also worked on the popular underground humor/culture mag Motorbooty). The album *Platinum Jive*, for example, was a mock greatest hits collection with booklet pictures of the members' purported solo outings—such as Henssler's *The Sexual Intellectual*. But due to low record sales, Big Chief was dropped by Capitol Records in 1995, and it seems likely that the band is finished.

what to buy: *Mack Avenue Skullgame* ♪♪♪♪ (Sub Pop, 1993, prod. Big Chief, Al Sutton) is the funky "original soundtrack" to the nonexistent movie of the same name. Judging by the music, the movie would have been a gritty, violent '70s flick with plenty of females, flares, and 'fros.

what to buy next: *Face* ♪♪♪ (Sub Pop, 1992, prod. Al Sutton, Big Chief) came out on a Seattle label in the prime days of grunge, but Big Chief rises above the fray with more of an in-your-face, heavy metal/soul melange.

what to avoid: Big Chief choked on its major label debut. The lightheartedness of the concept of *Platinum Jive* ♪♪♪ (Capitol, 1994, prod. Phil Nicolo, Big Chief) didn't translate to the generally heavy-handed music.

the rest:
Drive It Off ♪♪♪ (Get Hip, 1991)

worth searching for: Big Chief was a big supporter of vinyl and put out several limited edition singles, most of them on colored vinyl. The most coveted of these is the band's first, the "Brake Torque"/"Superstupid" (Big Kiss, 1989, prod. Big Chief) 7-inch on mauve and green vinyl.

influences:

◀◀ Parliament-Funkadelic, James Brown, MC5, the Stooges

see also: *Thornetta Davis*

Jill Hamilton

Big Country

Formed 1981, in Dunfermline, Scotland.

Stuart Adamson, vocals, guitars; Bruce Watson, guitars, vocals; Tony Butler, bass; Mark Brzezicki, drums.

When former Skids member Stuart Adamson and Bruce Watson formed Big Country, they essentially redefined the roles of the then-typical dual guitar band. The sounds they created were like nothing heard before, meshing traditional guitar tones with E-bow effects (a magnetic device that vibrates individual guitar strings without actually touching them) that resulted in a sound that couldn't be easily described. The rhythm section they recruited—the team of Tony Butler and Mark Brzezicki—had honed their chops playing in Who leader Pete Townshend's late '70s solo band. Their first record was the extremely successful *The Crossing*, which contained the colossal hit "In a Big Country." But the follow-up records—*Wonderland* (an EP) and *Steeltown*—turned out to be their swan songs. The songs were perfect, and Steve Lillywhite's production caught the band at its finest moment, but radio abandoned the group. Unfortunately, subsequent albums suffered from confusing production and poorly written songs, which sealed the group's fate in the U.S. It's rather unfortunate that Big Country's success has now been diminished to the inclusion of "In a Big Country" on every cheesey '80s compilation available.

what to buy: Best-of albums, in most cases, are efficient representations of a band, and in this case *The Best of Big Country* ♪♪♪♪ (Mercury, 1994, prod. various) takes you all over this bands career. Starting off with familiar hits like "Fields of Fire," "In a Big Country," "Wonderland," and "East of Eden," the good outweighs the mediocre on this collection—which is for-tunate since most of Big Country's classic records are out of print in the U.S.

what to buy next: Big Country's second album, *Steeltown* ♪♪♪♪ (Mercury, 1984, prod. Steve Lillywhite), is quite an amazing record and contains some fine songs that were inadvertently left of the *Best of* record—"Where the Rose Is Sown" and "Flame of the West." The import version adds some tracks, making the playing time over 70 minutes. The group's debut, *The Crossing* 🎵🎵🎵 (Mercury 1983, prod. Steve Lillywhite), contains the hits ("In a Big Country" and "Fields of Fire") that put this band on the map.

what to avoid: During 1988 Big Country signed with Warner Bros. and delivered the worst record of its career. On first listen, *Peace in Our Time* 🎵 (Reprise 1988, prod. Peter Wolf) sounds as though Adamson was no longer in the group. But he's there, even though he sounds more lightweight than the lead singer from a-ha. And, clearly, he and his mates had forgetten how to write good songs.

the rest:
The Buffalo Skinners 🎵 (Fox 1993)
Why the Long Face 🎵🎵 (Transatlantic, 1995)

worth searching for: The expanded import versions of *The Crossing* and *Steeltown* are recommended if you come across them. Also try to check out *Sweet Suburbia* (Caroline, 1995) from the Skids, Adamson's first band.

influences:
◀◀ The Buzzcocks, the Beatles
▶▶ U2, Hothouse Flowers

Chris Richards

Big Head Todd & the Monsters

Formed 1987, in Boulder, CO.

Todd Park Mohr, guitar, vocals; Brian Nevin, drums; Rob Squires, bass.

Dominated by "Big Head" Todd Park Mohr—a fan of old blues, soul, and funk records—the Monsters developed a wide-ranging rock style. In concert, Mohr's guitar solos go off on neverending tangents, sounding like Stevie Ray Vaughan or Dire Straits' Mark Knopfler, and Brian Nevin and Rob Squires fall in behind him, improvising like the Grateful Dead when necessary. On record, they're much tighter: Mohr writes strong songs with good detail and sings them with a booming, friendly voice, while the versatile rhythm section knows when to be dominant and when to back off.

what to buy: *Sister Sweetly* 🎵🎵🎵 (Giant, 1993, prod. David Z) is a straightforward, finely polished rock album with catchy, bluesy singles such as "Broken Hearted Savior" and "Bittersweet." It's still in heavy rotation in hippie bars throughout the Rocky Mountains.

what to buy next: The self-produced albums *Another Mayberry* 🎵🎵🎵 (Big Records, 1989/Giant, 1994, prod. Big Head Todd & the Monsters) and *Midnight Radio* 🎵🎵🎵 (Big Records, 1990/Giant, 1994, prod. Big Head Todd & the Monsters), with the original,

jazzier version of "Bittersweet" and interesting non-hits such as "Flander's Fields," helped the band attract loyal followings in Colorado and Chicago.

what to avoid: *Sister Sweetly* 🎵 (Giant EP, 1993) contains bland live versions of Monsters songs and a cover of Sly Stone's "Everyday People."

the rest:
Strategem 🎵🎵🎵 (Giant, 1994)
Beautiful World 🎵🎵🎵 (Revolution, 1997)

influences:
◀◀ Buddy Guy, Albert Collins, Sly & the Family Stone, Stevie Ray Vaughan, Blues Traveler
▶▶ Dave Matthews Band, Rusted Root, Widespread Panic

Steve Knopper

Big Rude Jake

Formed mid-1990s, in Toronto, Ontario, Canada.

Jake Rude (born Jake Hiebert), vocals, acoustic guitars; "Buddha" Jerry Willems, guitars (1997–present); "Mean" Jordan McLean, trumpet (1997–present); "Spike" Arenella, trombone (1997–present); "Doghouse" Jay Brunka, double bass (1996–present); Dylan "the Rifleman" Fusillo, drums (1996–present); Michael "Stonewall" Johnson, trumpet (1997); Cheong Liu, bass (1997); Jesse Barksdale, guitar (1997); Marks Lockhart, drums (1997); "Gentleman" Hal Greer, bass (1997); Mark "the Falcon" Caruana, guitar (1997); "Sluggo" James Stager, trombone, keyboards (1996); Dr. Tom Hamilton, drums, violin (1996); James "Mugshot" Munroe, trombone (1996).

Bored with the folk music scene in suburban Toronto, Jake Hiebert swung the musical pendulum back to the '20s as he founded Big Rude Jake & his Gentlemen Players. He earned his Big Rude Jake nickname with his arrogant pose and sexually graphic lyrics that attracted and repelled fans. But as the '90s swing revival hit, Big Rude Jake was in the right place, winning converts everywhere from martini bars to modern rock concert stages.

what to buy: If you can imagine Andrew "Dice" Clay singing *a capella,* you have a sense of what the songs on *Blue Pariah* 🎵 (Spanky/Outside, 1997) are like. The song "The Girl in the Pink Canoe" offers Hiebert's graphic description of oral sex with a woman, displaying a characteristic lack of subtlety that misses the sly, winking nature of original swing music.

the rest:
Butane Fumes and Bad Cologne 🎵🎵 (Spanky, 1993)
23/12/94 **woof!** (Spanky, 1995)

influences:
◀◀ Cab Calloway, Louis Jordan, Brian Setzer Orchestra

Christina Fuoco

Big Star
/Chris Bell

Formed 1971, in Memphis, TN. Disbanded 1975.

Chris Bell, guitar, vocals (1971–73); Alex Chilton, guitar, vocals; Andy Hummell, bass (1971–74); Jody Stephens, drums, vocals.

Big Star has long since outgrown its original cult status, though it was indeed one of the lost pop wonders of the early '70s. How such dismal commercial impact has grown into a revered power pop influence amongst later generations of guitar janglers is surely as much underdog romanticism as it is the staying power of its actual music. Frontman Alex Chilton, a perfect antihero for the rock star jet set, steeped his songs in '60s Britpop sensibility. Melancholy threads skewered through the songs, lending some actual barbs to the hooks. As the first rock act on the Stax subsidiary, Ardent, Big Star fell victim to poor distribution and promotion in addition to its own frequently sloppy live shows. After years of fitful solo work, Chilton and Stephens reformed Big Star with disciples Jon Auer and Ken Stringfellow of the Posies in 1992 for a one-off gig at Missouri University. With no promotion, Big Star was brought back after nearly 20 years with a simple phone call from Missouri students asking if the band would play at their college. The four have since performed as Big Star sporadically and planned a new release for 1998 or 1999.

what to buy: Now available as a twofer, *#1 Record/Radio City* ♫♫♫♫♫ (Stax, 1992, prod. John Fry) is fairly loaded with sadly beautiful three-minute pop songs. Now seen as a seminal influence among power popsters everywhere, the band's real strength was in its slow tempo tales of lost innocence and resignation. Lines such as "I loved you/ Well, never mind" from the chiming "September Gurls" would inspire a whole generation of slouchers like Paul Westerberg and Kurt Cobain.

what to buy next: The alternatively titled *Third/Sister Lovers* ♫♫♫♫ (Rykodisc, 1992, prod. Jim Dickinson) has been released under both titles in various forms, but Ryko's 1992 version appears to be the final and closest version of the original idea Chilton had. By this point, only he and Stephens remained and the disintegration had reached levels of pure desperation and often perverse destruction, all of which is duly recorded for your listening pleasure. Bell's posthumous release, *I Am the Cosmos* ♫♫♫♪ (Rykodisc, 1992, prod Chris Bell) points to the fact that while he may have not been as inherently tuneful as Chilton, he knew his way around misery and despair well enough to record his emotionally fragile state with surprisingly sturdy results.

what to avoid: Big Star had trouble recreating its sound outside the studio as *Big Star Live* ♫♫ (Rykodisc, 1992, prod. Big Star) indicates. Chilton sounds uncomfortable, if not bored, and the performance is a bit sluggish. The reunion gig in 1992 is far better.

the rest:
Columbia: Live at Missouri University ♫♫♫ (Zoo, 1993)

worth searching for: *Big Star's Biggest* (Line, 1988, prod. various) is a German import compilation that has all the right selections.

influences:

◀◀ The Beatles, the Kinks, the Who, the Rolling Stones, the Hollies, Moby Grape, Otis Redding, Booker T. & the MG's, Badfinger, the Beach Boys, the Move

▶▶ The Replacements, R.E.M, the dB's, Teenage Fanclub, the Posies, the Raspberries, Elvis Costello, Marshall Crenshaw, Tommy Keene, Matthew Sweet, Game Theory, the Loud Family, Jelly Fish, Aimee Mann, Letters to Cleo

see also: *Alex Chilton*

Allan Orski

Big Wreck

Formed 1992, in Boston, MA.

Ian Thornley, lead guitar, vocals; David Henning, bass; Forrest Williams, drums; Brian Doherty, guitars.

It's sad when a bright child forgoes his education to play around. The same could be said for Big Wreck. The quartet gave up studies at Berklee College of Music to create Big Wreck—a hard-hitting modern rock band that seems to be little more than a big accident.

what's available: *In Loving Memory Of* ♫ (Atlantic,1997, prod. Matt DeMatteo, Big Wreck) is a melodic but not necessarily interesting record. Awash with unoriginal guitar riffs, moody lyrics, and a taste of blues, *In Loving Memory Of* is easily lost in the sea of mediocre rock bands inundating radio airwaves. Even the songtitles imply forgetability—"Overemphasizing," "By the Way," and "Fall through the Cracks."

influences:
◀◀ Tonic, Matchbox 20

Christina Fuoco

Bikini Kill

Formed 1990, in Olympia, WA.

Kathleen Hanna, vocals; Kathi Wilcox, bass; Tobi Vail, drums; Billy Karren, guitar.

The house band for the riot grrrrl movement of the early '90s, Bikini Kill served notice on its first EP that not only can women rock, they can rock with a vengeance. Hanna's outrageous Johnny Rotten vocal stylings, combined with her band's Iggy Pop-meets-X-Ray Spex rock assault, leave no doubt that women in punk rock have arrived.

what to buy: *The CD Version of the First Two Records* 𝄢𝄢𝄢𝄢 (Kill Rock Stars, 1992/1994 prod. Bikini Kill) combines the first two EPs for an instant punk classic, a melody-infused treatise that's instantly memorable and features the fist-flinging manifesto "Double Dare Ya" and the incestuous "Suck My Left One."

what to buy next: *Pussy Whipped* 𝄢𝄢𝄢 (Kill Rock Stars, 1992, prod. Stuart Hallerman) keeps the rage intact but adds a bit of studio polish. *Reject All American* 𝄢𝄢𝄢 (Kill Rock Stars, 1996, prod. John Goodmanson) features greater songwriting contributions from all the band members, though Hanna's remain the standouts.

influences:

◀◀ The Runaways, the Sex Pistols, X-Ray Spex, the Pandoras

▶▶ Hole, Tracy Bonham, Babe the Blue Ox

Jim Cummer

Birddog

Born Bill Santen, 1974, in Lexington, KY.

Although he left Lexington "in search of" California at age 18, Bill Santen's musical journey really didn't begin in earnest until he landed in Portland, Oregon, and came under the influence of Elliott Smith. The plaintive folk rock maestro produced a handful of Santen's songs, two of which (oddly enough, they sound like B-sides from Smith's self-titled second release) found their way onto his debut album.

what's available: *The Trackhouse, the Valley, the Liquor Store Drive Thru* 𝄢𝄢𝄢 (Sugar Free, 1997, prod. Dave Way, Elliott Smith, Paul K.) is a folk/country work with intermittent steps toward rock. Its strength lies in Santen's ability—with flowing, hypnotic vocals and non-linear narratives—to craft delicate and highly emotive imagery. Instrumentation is sparse; acoustic guitar, drums, and upright bass form the nucleus, with occasional cello, harmonica, and lap steel woven in for effect.

worth searching for: Santen released a pair of singles—"Ten Later" and "Broken Lady Blues"—on Casting Couch Records.

influences:

◀◀ Elliott Smith, Freedy Johnston, Merle Haggard, Son Volt

Isaac Josephson

The Birthday Party

Formed 1980, in Melbourne, Australia. Disbanded 1983.

Nick Cave, vocals; Mick Harvey, guitar, drums, keyboard; Rowland S. Howard, guitar; Tracey Pew, bass (1980–81); Phil Calvert, drums (1980–82); Barry Adamson, bass (1982–83).

The Birthday Party was born out of Nick Cave and Mick Har-

vey's Boys Next Door, which was formed by the two while at a Melbourne boarding school in the late '70s. That band released a single and an EP before moving to London and changing their name to the Birthday Party. Under this deceivingly tame name, the band created some of the darkest, most violent, and raucous music of the time. Cave's poetic yet disturbing lyrics often dealt with love, death, and religion, themes that would continue throughout his career. Their reputation and live shows matched their abrasive, perverse sound and garnered a cult following of British punks. Their first album, *Prayers on Fire*, received critical and popular acclaim. The band's legendary excesses led to personnel changes (bassist Pew was imprisoned for drug and alcohol charges) and they moved to Berlin after recording their second album, *Junkyard*. There, they experimented with post-punk acts like Lydia Lunch and Einstürzende Neubauten and recorded an EP, *The Bad Seed*. However, continued drug and personal problems led to the band's demise while recording their final album, *Mutiny!* All of the band members went on to other projects, with Nick Cave & the Bad Seeds faring the best.

what to buy: Although purists might disagree, *Hits* 𝄢𝄢𝄢𝄢 (4AD, 1992, prod. Tony Cohen, Nick Launey, the Birthday Party), a best-of compilation from a band that had no actual hits, provides an excellent representation of their blistering punk/blues/noise assault.

what to buy next: *Prayers on Fire* 𝄢𝄢𝄢 (4AD, 1981/2.13.61, 1997) features Cave's spooky, howling vocals supported by Pew's throbbing bass and Richardson's fire and brimstone guitar fury; it burst onto the post-punk scene with a reckless abandon not seen since the Stooges.

the rest:

Hee Haw 𝄢𝄢𝄢 (4AD, 1980/1989/2.13.61, 1997)
Junkyard 𝄢𝄢𝄢 (4AD, 1982/2.13.61, 1997)
Drunk on the Pope's Blood EP 𝄢𝄢 (4AD, 1982)
Mutiny! EP 𝄢𝄢𝄢 (4AD, 1983)
It's Still Living 𝄢𝄢𝄢 (Missing Link, 1985)
A Collection 𝄢𝄢𝄢 (Missing Link, 1985)
The Birthday Party: The Peel Sessions 𝄢𝄢 (Strange Fruit, 1987)

worth searching for: Of their many EPs, *The Bad Seed* (4AD, 1983) is the best, showcasing the band at its peak shortly before its demise.

solo outings:

Mick Harvey:
Alta Maria & Waterland 𝄢𝄢𝄢 (Ionic, 1993)
Intoxicated Man 𝄢𝄢 (Mute, 1995)
Pink Elephants 𝄢𝄢 (Mute, 1997)

influences:

◀◀ The Stooges, the Doors

▶▶ The Sex Pistols

see also: *Nick Cave & the Bad Seeds*

Christopher Scanlon

Elvin Bishop

Born October 21, 1942, in Tulsa, OK.

When singer-guitarist Elvin Bishop stomps clumsily onto the stage with his electrified frizzy hair, clunky boots, and a pair of overalls, he looks like a psycho-hillbilly. But he quickly establishes his skill, first as a flashy, bombastic guitar player, then as a serious bluesman reverential and determined to honor his heroes, including Jimmy Reed and Jimi Hendrix. A voracious record collector and radio listener who grew up in the South, Bishop earned a University of Chicago scholarship in the late 1960s, hooked up with harpist Paul Butterfield, and managed to score guest appearances with Buddy Guy and Muddy Waters. With Butterfield and guitarist Michael Bloomfield, Bishop cofounded the Paul Butterfield Blues Band, which helped introduce traditional blues to young white audiences and pioneered the spacey, stretched-out two-guitar jam that influenced both the Allman Brothers and the Grateful Dead. Jumping on the southern blues bandwagon, Bishop's post-Butterfield solo career yielded his first hit, "Fooled Around and Fell in Love," in 1976. Since then, he's worked the blues circuit and frequently plays package shows with artists such as John Lee Hooker, Lonnie Brooks, and Luther Allison.

what to buy: Though Bishop's first solo album came out in 1969, he didn't catch commercial fire until *Struttin' My Stuff* 𝄢𝄢𝄢𝄢 (Capricorn, 1976, prod. Allan Blazek, Bill Szymczyk), an explosive collection containing "Fooled Around and Fell in Love." *Don't Let the Bossman Get You Down!* 𝄢𝄢𝄢 (Alligator, 1991, prod. Elvin Bishop) is the refreshing highlight of his pure-blues comeback phase after almost 10 years away from the studio.

what to buy next: A terrific document of Bishop's Marin County, California, phase—when he was represented by promoter Bill Graham and played frequently at San Francisco's Fillmore theaters—is *Best of Elvin Bishop: Tulsa Shuffle* 𝄢𝄢𝄢𝄢 (Epic/Legacy, 1994, prod. various), which samples his first four years, including the instrumental jam "Hogbottom" and other songs with Carlos Santana's Latin-dominated rhythm section.

what to avoid: During Bishop's long career, he has never been above coasting or releasing an album because it seemed like the right business move at the time. We recommend any best-of collection (even the mediocre *The Best of Elvin Bishop: Crabshaw Rising* 𝄢𝄢 (Epic, 1972, prod. various)) above *Hometown Boy Makes Good!* 𝄢𝄢 (Capricorn, 1977), *Raisin' Hell* 𝄢𝄢 (Capricorn, 1977), and the over-soloed *Ace in the Hole* 𝄢𝄢 (Alligator, 1995, prod. Elvin Bishop, Bill Thompson).

the rest:
The Elvin Bishop Group 𝄢𝄢𝄢 (Fillmore, 1969)
Feel It! 𝄢𝄢𝄢 (Epic, 1970)
Applejack 𝄢𝄢𝄢 (Epic, 1971)
Rock My Soul 𝄢𝄢 (Epic, 1971)
Let It Flow 𝄢𝄢𝄢 (Capricorn, 1974)
Juke Joint Jump 𝄢𝄢𝄢 (Capricorn, 1975)
Hog Heaven 𝄢𝄢𝄢 (Capricorn, 1978)
Big Fun 𝄢𝄢𝄢 (Alligator, 1988)
Sure Feels Good: The Best of Elvin Bishop 𝄢𝄢𝄢𝄢 (PolyGram, 1992)
The Skin I'm In N/A (Alligator, 1998)

worth searching for: Bishop's work on all three classic Butterfield albums, *Paul Butterfield Blues Band* (Elektra, 1965, prod. Paul Rothchild), *East-West* (Elektra, 1966, prod. Paul Rothchild, Mark Abramson, Barry Friedman), and *The Resurrection of Pigboy Crabshaw* (Elektra, 1968, prod. John Court), sounds overly psychedelic and slightly dated today, but they're essential links between traditional Chicago blues and the late 1960s San Francisco rock scene and inspirations for contemporary bands such as Blues Traveler and Phish.

influences:
◀◀ Muddy Waters, Buddy Guy, Jimi Hendrix, B.B. King, John Lee Hooker, Elmore James, Michael Bloomfield, Rev. Gary Davis

▶▶ The Allman Brothers Band, the Grateful Dead, Blues Traveler, Phish

see also: *The Paul Butterfield Blues Band*

Steve Knopper

Bitch Magnet

Formed 1987, in OH. Disbanded c. 1991.

David Grubbs, guitar; Sooyoung Park, bass, vocals; Orestes Martin, drums.

One of several precursors to what is now referred to as "math-rock," this quartet left a cryptic, if not worthy, legacy. Guitar player David Grubbs (now of Gastr del Sol) had another band, Bastro, at the same time, while Sooyoung Park would go on to form Seam and Orestes Martin would later beat skins for Walt Mink. That said, Bitch Magnet's records are certainly worth hearing, with angular riffs, melodic, driving bass lines, scratchy vocals, and complex drumming, all of which made for a heady sonic mix.

what to buy: Don't search for epiphany in the lyrics on *Ben Hur* 𝄢𝄢𝄢𝄢 (Communion, 1990, prod. Arden Geist, Howie Gano, M. McMackin), as lines such as "Shut up you in the lousy hot gray spare . . ." from "Lookin' at the Devil" will attest. But you can find great solace in the grooves. Almost unethically powerful, *Ben Hur* is a keeper.

what to buy next: *Star Booty/Umber* 🐾🐾🐾 (Communion 1988/1989, prod. Mike McMakin, Bitch Magnet), originally two separate records, is now available on one CD. Its complex song structures, largely incomprehensible vocals, and engaging playing make this dense disc the sonic equivalent of a mugging.

influences:

◀◀ Big Black, Scratch Acid, Breaking Circus, Nice Strong Arm, Fugazi

▶▶ Don Caballero, June of 44, Jesus Lizard

see also: *Seam, Squirrel Bait, Gastr del Sol*

Barry M. Prickett

Björk /Sugarcubes

Born Björk Gudmundsdottir, November 21, 1965, in Reykjavík, Iceland. Sugarcubes formed 1987, in Reykjavík, Iceland. Disbanded 1992.

The Sugarcubes: Björk, vocals, keyboards; Einar Orn, vocals, trumpet; Bragi Olafsson, bass; Thor Eldon, guitar; Margaret (Magga) Ornolfsdottir, keyboards; Sigtryggur (Siggi) Baldursson, drums.

Sugarcubes promoted the primal anarchy embraced by U.S. groups such as the Pixies; that they hailed from Iceland only made the music that much more exotic to American ears. Punctuated by a meandering, atonal trumpet and stellar Neanderthal drumming, the 'cubes produced a feisty mix of dance-oriented rhythms and glowering Teutonic moodiness. Holding it all together was lead singer Björk, an imp of a young woman whose intoxicating vocal range extends from cooing child to growling animal and everything in between. A promising debut album gave way to bland self-imitation, although the group's third and, to date, final album showed evidence that it had learned how to harness its erratic talent. The Sugarcubes' breakup in 1992 seems to have done well by Björk, whose solo career has shown moments of buoyant and inspired strokes of genius. The group reformed without Björk in 1995.

what to buy: *Stick Around for Joy* 🐾🐾🐾🐾 (Elektra, 1992, prod. Paul Fox) is the Sugarcubes' most accessible and, true to its name, happiest sounding album, packed end to end with lively and tuneful dance pop. Producer Fox lightens up the group's sound, revealing inspired rhythmic grooves ("Hit," "Lucky Night," and "Walkabout") while providing a perfect showcase for Björk's amazing wail of a voice. Björk's appropriately titled solo premiere, *Debut* 🐾🐾🐾🐾 (Elektra, 1993, prod. Björk, Nellee Hooper), is a sonically beautiful work that finds the young

singer stretching artfully into jazz-funk stylings ("Big Time Sensuality") and haunting torch songs ("Venus As a Boy"). Björk scored a minor hit here with the whimsical "Human Behavior."

what to buy next: The Sugarcubes' debut, *Life's Too Good*, (Elektra, 1988, prod. R. Shulman, Derek Birkett) 🐾🐾🐾🐾, is a satisfying bite of everything that made the group so exciting: punchy rhythms, inspired singing, and a compelling sense of the surreal. "Motorcrash" and "Blue Eyed Pop" are fun and funky, while "Birthday" is simply the most gorgeous piece of debauchery ever wrought in the name of rock music.

what to avoid: The Sugarcubes' unenthusiastic sophomore effort, *Here Today, Tomorrow, Next Week!* 🐾 (Elektra, 1989, prod. Derek Birkett), has none of its predecessor's charm and far too much of Einar Orn's affected, "Velcome to Shprockets"–style utterances—though two of the songs, "Regina" and "Planet," are gems.

the rest:
Björk:
Post 🐾🐾 (Elektra, 1995)
Telegram 🐾🐾🐾 (Elektra, 1997)
Homogenic 🐾🐾🐾🐾 (Elektra, 1997)

The Sugarcubes:
It's-It 🐾🐾🐾 (Elektra, 1992)
Great Crossover Potential 🐾🐾🐾🐾 (Elektra, 1998)

worth searching for: *Illur Arfur!* (One Little Indian, 1989) offers the same tracks as the group's second album but sung in Icelandic. A fascinating listen. Issued abroad under the group's native name, Sykurmolarnir.

influences:

◀◀ Cocteau Twins, Dead Can Dance, Joy Division, Siouxsie & the Banshees

▶▶ Deee-Lite, Pizzicato Five, Shelleyan Orphan

Christopher Scapelliti

Cilla Black

Born Priscilla Maria Veronica White, May 27, 1943, in Liverpool, England.

At best, the early British rock 'n' roll stars were, with few exceptions, wholly whitewashed retreads of their American counterparts. All that changed forever when Brian Epstein began bringing his stable of Liverpool talent to the London record companies in 1962. Among the acts he launched the following year was "Swinging Cilla," a former hat-check girl from the Cavern Club who, with access to the songwriting talents of her pals J. Lennon and P. McCartney, had no trouble sending her first few releases high into the British charts. With her everygirl looks and saucy, boisterous personality, Black was quite unlike anything Britain had ever seen or heard before from their previously demure, well-mannered female pop stars. Although she never did crack the all-important U.S. market, Black was slowly but surely being groomed by Epstein for bigger and better things at home, with successful roles on the stage and screen leading in 1968 to the first of several popular, long-running U.K. television series. Although she spent most of the '80s raising a family, she is still an unavoidable, well-loved presence on the British entertainment scene, as flippant and outspoken as ever, and highly regarded for the groundbreaking work she did to help forever demystify and liberate female performers in her homeland.

what's available: The superb 26-track *Best of the EMI Years* ✍✍✍ (EMI, 1994, prod. George Martin) contains not only several obscure Paul McCartney compositions but surprisingly rambunctious versions of songs by Phil Spector, Burt Bacharach, and Randy Newman, all of which were highly influential best-sellers in England. *The Abbey Road Decade, 1963–1973* ✍✍✍✍ (EMI Zonophone, 1997, prod. George Martin), an exhaustive three-disc compilation of practically everything she recorded in the fabled London studio, goes even further to demonstrate how assuredly Black matured from the untrained Cavern Club belter to the suave, sweetly sexy ingenue of British TV screens.

influences:

◀◀ Susan Maughan, Helen Shapiro, Dionne Warwick, Shirley Bassey

▶▶ Lulu, Sandie Shaw, Tracey Ullman, Dolores O'Riordan

Gary Pig Gold

Frank Black

Born Charles Michael Kitteridge Thompson IV, 1965, in Los Angeles, CA.

Black Francis, the former frontman for the Pixies, went solo in 1993, inverting his pseudonym along the way to become Frank Black. In this latest guise, Black emphasizes the innovative melodicism that was always lurking in the dark background of the Pixies' music. While his lyrics continue to draw from such murky references as spies, outer space, UFOs, and (as always) Los Angeles, he's more focused musically, playing up his finely tuned pop sensibilities on his first two solo efforts. As if to contradict all expectations, Black returned to the post-punk fray with his 1995 release *The Cult of Ray*. One can't even begin to guess where he'll go next.

what to buy: Black put all of his pop music references into one basket on his eponymous debut, *Frank Black* ✍✍✍ (4AD/Elektra, 1993, prod. Eric Drew Feldman, Frank Black). A few songs ("Los Angeles" and "Ten Percenter") harken back to the full-

throttle rage of the Pixies, but most of the tunes show a surprising range of 1960s influences, including David Bowie, John Lennon, and Brian Wilson.

what to buy next: Clocking in at more than an hour, *Teenager of the Year* ✍✍✍ (4AD/Elektra, 1994, prod. Eric Drew Feldman, Frank Black, Al Clay) is an ambitious and frequently restrained follow-up. Black keeps his erratic tendencies in check and delivers back-to-back beauties with "(I Want to Live on An) Abstract Plain," "Calistan," "Speedy Marie," and "Headache."

what to avoid: *The Cult of Ray* ✍✍ (American Recordings, 1995, prod. Frank Black) is a fairly dull, heard-it-all-before affair that isn't nearly as clever or tuneful as Black's previous solo efforts. Black avails himself with "I Don't Want to Hurt You (Every Single Time)"—easily his loveliest melody and most passionate lyric—but there's little else here to get worked up over.

the rest:

The Black Sessions/Live in Paris ✍✍✍ (Anoise Annoys, 1995)
Frank Black & the Catholics N/A (spinART, 1998)

worth searching for: Black is joined by members of Teenage Fanclub for *The John Peel Sessions* (Strange Fruit, 1995, prod. Ted de Bono), a terrific four-song EP featuring punked-out versions of Del Shannon's "Sister Isabel" and the Otis Blackwell chestnut "Handyman."

influences:

◀◀ Dick Dale & His Del-Tones, the Ventures, Brian Wilson, the Beatles, the Velvet Underground, David Bowie, Iggy Pop, the Ramones, Jonathan Richman

▶▶ Dinosaur Jr., the Feelies, the Flaming Lips, Nirvana, Sonic Youth, Throwing Muses, Belly, Weezer, the Lemonheads, the Sugarcubes, Hüsker Dü, the Pixies, Jonny Polonsky

see also: *The Pixies*

Christopher Scapelliti

The Black Crowes

Formed 1988, in Atlanta, GA.

Chris Robinson, vocals; Rich Robinson, guitar; Jeff Cease, guitar (1988–91); Johnny Colt, bass (1988–97); Steve Gorman, drums; Marc Ford, guitar (1991–97); Eddie Harsch, keyboards (1991–present); Sven Pipien, bass (1998–present).

The Black Crowes made a stunningly confident debut with 1990's *Shake Your Money Maker*. Despite the fact that the group didn't seem to have an original idea in its collective head, it was great to see a young band with the good taste to rip off the right bands (the underrated Faces and Humble Pie, along with the Rolling Stones) and enough moxie to credibly take Otis Redding's "Hard to Handle" to the top of the charts

Chris Robinson of the Black Crowes (© **Ken Settle**)

during an era dominated by soulless corporate rock. Since then, the band has gone its own way, briefly veering into hard rock before delving whole hog into trippy, flowing jams. Ironically, as the Black Crowes have become more original, they haven't necessarily become more memorable: the songwriting has been spotty, there just aren't enough tunes that are as vibrant as *Moneymaker* gems like "Twice As Hard," "Seeing Things," and "She Talks to Angels." The Crowes seem to be in it for the long haul, however, and there is every reason to believe that the band has plenty of good music left in it. After some major membership changes following its headlining spot on the 1997 Furthur Festival, the Crowes were preparing to drop its next album during the fall of 1998.

what to buy: *Shake Your Money Maker* 🎵🎵🎵🎵 (American, 1990, prod. George Drakoulias) won't win any points for originality, but who needs 'em when you've got this much swagger, energy, and soul? *Three Snakes and One Charm* 🎵🎵🎵🎵 (American, 1996, prod. Jack Joseph Puig, the Black Crowes) finds the band getting ever more psychedelic, stretching out into straight funk, loping country, and searing Southern rock. An ambitious success.

what to buy next: *Amorica* 🎵🎵🎵 (American, 1994, prod. Jack Joseph Puig, the Black Crowes) sounds great, with malleable song structures and a smooth, flowing sound that includes mandolin and pedal steel, but there are few songs here that stick in the cranium. An in-your-face, bone-dry production makes *The Southern Harmony and Musical Companion* 🎵🎵🎵 (American, 1992, prod. George Drakoulias, the Black Crowes) a challenge to listen to all the way through, but it has plenty of high points, including "Remedy" and "Hotel Illness."

the rest:
By Your Side N/A (American, 1998)

worth searching for: If you're so inclined, look around for a copy of *Amorica* with the original, semi-pornographic cover—a close-up of a woman's genitals covered by an American flag bikini.

influences:

◀◀ The Allman Brothers Band, the Faces, Humble Pie, Led Zeppelin, Little Feat, the Rolling Stones, Rod Stewart, War, Aerosmith

▶▶ Blues Traveler, Widespread Panic, Primal Scream, the Quireboys

Alan Paul

Black Flag
/Greg Ginn

Formed 1977, in Hermosa Beach, CA. Disbanded 1986.

Greg Ginn, guitar; Charles (Chuck) Dukowski, bass (1977–84); Kira Roessler, bass (1983–86); C'el, bass (1986); Dez Cadena, guitar (1981–83); Robo, drums (1978–83); Keith Morris, vocals (1977–78); Chavo Pederast, vocals (1978–81); Henry Rollins, vocals (1981–86); Brian Migdol, drums (1977–78); Bill Stevenson, drums (1981, 1983–85); Emil, drums (1982); Chuck Biscuits, drums (1982); Anthony Martinez, drums (1985–86).

The original purveyors of the DIY work ethic, Black Flag was formed in 1977 by Greg Ginn, who founded the SST label as a vehicle to release his band's material. The group's loud, testosterone-laced attack made Black Flag the country's premier hardcore punk band during the early '80s. The band went through a series of vocalists, including Keith Morris, who went on to form the Circle Jerks, before Washington, D.C., punker Henry Rollins jumped on board—literally, by leaping on stage during a show. His would be the career that took off after Black Flag called it quits.

what to buy: After wandering into jazz and other styles, Black Flag returned to its abrasive punk roots for *In My Head* 🎵🎵🎵🎵 (SST, 1985, prod. Dave Tarling, Greg Ginn, Bill Stevenson). The music and lyrics express the unyielding rage of an animal ready to pounce on its prey. This is Black Flag at its finest.

what to buy next: The live album *Who's Got the 10.5?* 🎵🎵🎵 (SST, 1986, prod. Greg Ginn) captures the concert spirit of Black Flag, including Rollins's vein-popping intensity and angst-ridden lyrics and Ginn's crafty guitar work.

what to avoid: *Family Man* 🎵🎵 (SST, 1984, prod. Spot) is an oddity, half group instrumentals and half Rollins reading poetry—before he became a proficient spoken word performer.

the rest:
Damaged I 🎵🎵🎵 (SST, 1981)
Everything Went Black 🎵🎵 (SST, 1983)
The First Four Years 🎵🎵 (SST, 1984)
Live '84 🎵🎵 (SST 1984)
My War 🎵🎵 (SST, 1984)
Slip It In 🎵🎵 (SST, 1984)
Loose Nut 🎵🎵🎵 (SST, 1985)
Wasted . . . Again 🎵🎵🎵 (SST, 1987)

worth searching for: Want to know what it was like to be a member of Black Flag? Read the journals Rollins kept while he was in the band. They were published and released as a book-on-tape entitled *Get in the Van* (2.13.61, 1994).

solo outings:
Greg Ginn:
My War 🎵🎵🎵 (SST, 1984)
In My Head 🎵 (SST, 1985)
Let's Get Real, Real Gone for a Change 🎵🎵 (SST, 1986)
Gone II, But Never Too Gone! 🎵🎵 (SST)
Getting Even 🎵🎵🎵 (Cruz, 1993)
Dick 🎵🎵 (Cruz, 1993)

Let It Burn (Because I Don't Live) 𝄢𝄢 (Cruz, 1994)
Belly to the Ground 𝄢𝄢 (Cruz, 1994)
Red Dog 𝄢𝄢 (New Alliance, 1994)
All the Dirt That's Fit to Print 𝄢𝄢 (SST, 1994)
Just Do It 𝄢𝄢𝄢 (SST EP, 1995)
House 𝄢𝄢 (SST, 1995)

influences:

◄◄ The Ramones, the Sex Pistol, MC5, the Stooges

►► Circle Jerks, Green Day, the Offspring, NOFX, Pennywise, Wayne Kramer

see also: *Henry Rollins, Circle Jerks*

Christina Fuoco

Black 47

Formed 1989, in New York, NY.

Larry Kirwan, guitar, keyboards, percussion, lead vocals; Chris Byrne, uilleann pipes, tin whistle, bodhran, vocals; Fred Parcells, trombone, tin whistle, vocals; Geoffrey Blythe, saxophone, clarinet; Thomas Hamlin, drums, percussion; Andrew Goodsight, bass (1995–present); Kevin Jenkins, bass, (1993–95); David Conrad, bass (1985–93).

Black 47 is an Irish-American band combining the attitude of the Big Apple with the pride of the Emeral Isle. Essentially an extremely rowdy bar band in the best sense, Black 47 is so named for the peak year of the Irish famine in the 19th century. Larry Kirwan—an erstwhile playwright hailing from the old sod—and Chris Byrne—an ex–New York City cop with a passion for Irish traditional music, rap, and punk—shared several pints one night at the hole-in-the-wall called Paddy Reilly's while complaining about the dismal state of modern music. At some point that evening, Black 47 was born, and soon thereafter, Paddy Reilly's became the band's home. Kirwin and company's reputation for original music and a confrontational attitude soon attracted a loyal following in the city. Kirwin's songs, crowded with lyrics and ecstatic horn arrangements, tended toward the rousing anthem as the band wailed like a Memphis soul revue trapped in the body of an Irish folk singer. The group received high-profile production help from Cars auteur Ric Ocasek and ex-Talking Head Jerry Harrison on its first two albums, but has mostly failed to catch fire commercially.

what to buy: The first release is the essential Black 47 album. *Fire of Freedom* 𝄢𝄢𝄢 (SBK Records, 1992, prod. Ric Ocasek, Larry Kirwan) is Celtic to its core, while still strongly suggesting the band's American roots. Songs range from the swing of "Funky Ceili" to the rabble-rousing pint raising of "James Connelly." While the production seems a bit crowded and thin, the band's exuberant personality is well captured. The independent label version of this album, eponymously titled, contains

a slightly different song list. An EP version of the SBK album also is available, with a selection of songs from both versions of the first release.

what to buy next: *Green Suede Shoes* 𝄢𝄢𝄢 (SBK Records, 1996, prod. Larry Kirwin) returns the band to its pub roots, supplying a sweaty, passionate sound supporting the usual free-the-Irish-or-we'll-really-bang-on-the-bodhran anthems ("Bobby Sands MP").

the rest:
Home of the Brave 𝄢𝄢 (SBK Records, 1994)

influences:

◄◄ The Pogues, Enemy Orchard, Them, Bruce Springsteen, Booker T. & the MG's

►► Goats Don't Shave, Young Dubliners

Martin Connors

WHAT ALBUM CHANGED YOUR LIFE?

The Psychedelic Furs' *Talk Talk Talk* changed my life because there was a time in high school when the only thing I would listen to was punk rock, specifically American hardcore—mostly Minor Threat and Aggression was what we listened to and skated to. I think I was becoming a bit obnoxious in my punkness. So my older brother, who had a much more broad catalog of music he listened to, said, 'Dude, you need to listen to this.' He gave me the Psychedelic Furs, and it was the first time I ever heard pop music that was angry and substantial, that wasn't about just making something pretty. It showed me you could make melodies and still be cool.

Paul Durham (of Black Lab)

Black Grape

See: Happy Mondays

Black Lab

Formed 1995, in Berkeley, CA.

Paul Durham, vocals, guitar; Michael Belfer, guitar; Geoff Stanfield, bass; Bryan Head, drums.

Paul Durham, a native of Twin Falls, Idaho, has been searching for redemption, happiness, and meaning. He had his sights set on becoming a philosophy professor until he wrote his honors thesis on Nietzsche. Taking a cue from his subject's exaltation of the Dionysian, Durham left Oberlin College after earning his degree because "the university was about studying life, not living life." Durham moved to Oakland, California, and worked as a substitute teacher while struggling to make it as a folk singer. Fed up with the music business, he traveled to Israel with a girlfriend and found himself "pummeled with lyrics." Upon returning, he fired his band and formed Black Lab.

what's available: Black Lab's debut, *Your Body Above Me* ♫♫♫ (DGC, 1997, prod. David Bianco, Black Lab), could be a stellar release if singer-songwriter Paul Durham got over his obsession with water metaphors and subtle '80s rock guitar influences. "Thin White Lie" has that Rick Springfield–ish driving-rock guitar that conjures up those clichéd visions of bad videos in which the band is seen playing passionatley in the rain. On the other hand, even though it falls into the "water" category, "Wash It Away," with Durham's yearning vocals and addictive chorus, is a must-listen.

influences:

◀◀ Radiohead, PJ Harvey, Echo & the Bunnymen, Rick Springfield, Matchbox 20

▶▶ Athenaeum, Stegosaurus

Christina Fuoco

Black Oak Arkansas

Formed 1969, in Black Oak, AR. Disbanded 1980.

Jim (Dandy) Mangrum, vocals; Harvey Jett, guitar (1969–74); James Henderson, guitar (1974–80); Stanley Knight, guitar, fiddle, saxophone (1969–76); Jack Holder, guitar (1976–80); Rickie Reynolds, guitar (1969–76); Greg Reding, guitar (1976–80); Pat Daugherty, bass (1969–76); Andy Tanas, bass (1976–80); Wayne Evans, drums (1969–75); Thomas Aldrich, drums (1975–76); Joel Williams, drums (1976–80); Ruby Starr, vocals (1973–80).

Before Lynyrd Skynyrd or .38 Special began making their cases on the radio, Black Oak Arkansas offered the purest distillation of 100-proof boogie ever produced south of the Mason-Dixon line. Lead singer Jim Dandy Mangrum was a David Lee Roth–Ted Nugent wildman whose rough, good ol' boy holler paved every three-guitar monster riff with tar and gravel. The group's rough-and-ready attitude resulted in some good-and-greasy party music, although the occasional dip into the murky pools of southern mysticism suggests the group was probably hoping for greater credibility. The band's music gained considerable breadth when Mangrum brought in Ruby Starr, a gutsy vocalist whose saucy come-ons made a good foil for his sexed-up persona. With Starr in tow, the group solidified its name with a hit remake of LaVern Baker's "Jim Dandy." Extensive touring (50 weeks per year) took its toll on the members, resulting in numerous personnel changes through the late '70s. BOA called it quits in 1980 after Mangrum suffered a heart attack; after recovering, he continued with solo work but never reestablished his presence after BOA.

what to buy: *Hot & Nasty: The Best of Black Oak Arkansas* ♫♫♫♫ (WEA/Atlantic/Rhino, 1992, prod. various) picks the plums from BOA's erratic catalog, from the hits ("Hot & Nasty," "Jim Dandy," "Strong Enough to Be Gentle") to a fascinating selection of bizarre covers such as the Byrds' "(So You Want to Be a) Rock & Roll Star" and the Beatles' "Taxman."

what to buy next: *Jim Dandy* ♫♫♫ (WEA/Atlantic/Rhino, 1996, prod. various) pares things down to 10 essential tracks, while *High on the Hog* ♫♫♫♫ (WEA/Atlantic/Rhino, 1973, prod. Ed Barton, Ron Albert, Howie Albert), the album that put BOA on the map, remains in print to demonstrate the high-livin', hard-drinkin', good-lovin' hellraising at the heart of BOA.

influences:

◀◀ Muddy Waters, LaVern Baker, the Rolling Stones, the Allman Brothers Band, Led Zeppelin

▶▶ Lynyrd Skynyrd, .38 Special, Molly Hatchet, Ted Nugent, David Lee Roth, Guns N' Roses, Georgia Satellites, the Black Crowes, Nashville Pussy, Swamp Boogie Queen

Christopher Scapelliti

Black Sabbath

Formed 1967, in Birmingham, England.

Ozzy Osbourne, vocals (1967–79, 1997–present); Ronnie James Dio, vocals (1979–82, 1991–92); Tony Iommi, guitar; Bill Ward, drums (1967–81, 1982–85, 1997–present); Terry "Geezer" Butler, bass (1967–85, 1991–95, 1997–present); Vinnie Appice, drums (1981–82, 1991–93); Dave Donato, vocals (1982–83); Ian Gillan, vocals (1983–84); Glenn Hughes, vocals (1985–87); Geoff Nichols, keyboards, (1985–89, 1990); Dave Spitz, bass (1985–87, 1989); Eric Singer, drums (1985–87); Tony Martin, vocals (1987–91, 1993–96); Bev Bevan, drums (1987); Bob Daisley, bass (1987); Cozy Powell (died

April 5, 1998), drums (1989–91); Lawrence Cottle, bass (1989); Neil Murray, bass (1990); Bob Rondinelli, drums (1993–96).

Ominous, menacing, and deafeningly loud, Black Sabbath was in many ways the prototypical heavy metal band. While much of the band's infamy centered on Osbourne's pseudo-Satanic howlings (he insisted the band's lyrics were anti-Lucifer), it was Iommi's narcotic guitar work the made up the backbone of the Sabbath sound: if not for his dark, fuzz-toned riffs and solos, speed, thrash, and death metal would never exist, and grunge would still be a synonym for grime. Sabbath created some truly devastating metal with Osbourne, but the singer left in the late '70s to launch a successful solo career. The band stayed afloat for awhile by recruiting ex-Rainbow singer Dio, but after he quit Sabbath became a self-parody with a revolving-door lineup. At least four vocalists (including ex–Deep Purple wailer Ian Gillan) tried to replace the Great Oz, and a battalion of drummers and bassists came and went. The only constant has been Iommi, who seems more than willing to slog away under the Sabbath mantle as long as the headbangers will take it. Osbourne, Iommi, and Butler reunited to play as Black Sabbath on Osbourne's 1997 Ozzfest tour, then brought Ward back into the fold later that year. The reunited group released a live album, with two new studio tracks, in late 1998.

what to buy: Metal doesn't get more frightening than *Paranoid* 𝄞𝄞𝄞𝄞 (Warner Bros., 1971, prod. Roger Bain), which features the title track and "Iron Man." *Master of Reality* 𝄞𝄞𝄞𝄞 (Warner Bros., 1971, prod. Roger Bain) was another brilliant skull-crusher, featuring the timeless "Children of the Grave" and "Sweet Leaf." The 16-song best-of, *We Sold Our Soul for Rock and Roll* 𝄞𝄞𝄞𝄞 (Warner Bros., 1976, prod. various) is a thorough introduction to early Sabbath.

what to buy next: *Black Sabbath* 𝄞𝄞𝄞𝄞 (Warner Bros., 1970, prod. Roger Bain), the band's opening salvo, includes the wicked psycho-blooze instrumental "The Wizard." On *Sabbath Bloody Sabbath* 𝄞𝄞𝄞𝄞 (Warner Bros., 1973, prod. Black Sabbath) the band successfully mixed its stun-gun guitars with synthesizers. If Dio's faux operatic wailing doesn't turn you off, *Heaven and Hell* 𝄞𝄞𝄞𝄞 (Warner Bros., 1980, prod. Martin Birch) made it seem as if there was indeed life after Ozzy. Briefly.

what to avoid: *Seventh Star* **woof!** (Warner Bros., 1986, prod. Jeff Glixman) and *Headless Cross* **woof!** (I.R.S., 1989, prod. Tony Iommi, Cozy Powell) were Black Sabbath albums in name only, as Iommi and his faceless cohorts sank lower then Hades itself.

the rest:
Black Sabbath, Vol. 4 𝄞𝄞𝄞 (Warner Bros., 1972)
Sabotage 𝄞𝄞𝄞 (Warner Bros., 1975)
Technical Ecstasy 𝄞𝄞𝄞 (Warner Bros., 1976)
Never Say Die! 𝄞𝄞𝄞 (Warner Bros., 1978)
The Mob Rules 𝄞𝄞 (Warner Bros., 1981)

Live Evil 𝄞𝄞 (Warner Bros., 1982)
The Eternal Idol 𝄞𝄞 (Warner Bros., 1987)
T Y R 𝄞𝄞 (I.R.S., 1990)
Dehumanizer 𝄞𝄞 (Reprise, 1992)
Cross Purposes 𝄞 (I.R.S., 1994)
Reunion 𝄞𝄞𝄞 (Epic, 1998)

worth searching for: *Between Heaven and Hell* (Castle, 1995, prod. various), a British collection compiled by Osbourne and Butler, culls the cream of the Osbourne-Dio years. The four-CD box *Under Wheels of Confusion* (Castle, 1996, prod. various) goes even deeper.

influences:

◀◀ Cream, Muddy Waters, Bela Lugosi

▶▶ Soundgarden, Nirvana, Metallica, Megadeth, Anthrax

Thor Christensen

Black Swan Network
See: Olivia Tremor Control

Black Tie
See: T-Bone Burnett

Black Uhuru
Formed 1974, in Kingston, Jamaica.

Don Carlos, vocals, (1974–77, 1987–present); Rudolph "Garth" Dennis, vocals (1974–77, 1987–present); Derrick "Duckie" Simpson, vocals; Errol Nelson, vocals (1977); Michael Rose, vocals (1977–85); Sandra "Puma" Jones, vocals (1978–87); Delroy "Junior" Reid, vocals (1985–90); Olafunke, vocals (1987–90).

With incisive vocal harmonies, contributions from reggae's finest riddim section, and excellent songwriting, Black Uhuru—reggae's first Grammy winner—was one of the biggest post–Bob Marley acts of the '80s. The only constant through several incarnations of the vocal trio has been harmony singer Derrick "Duckie" Simpson. Black Uhuru peaked with lead singer and songwriter Rose and harmonist "Puma" Jones; Sly Dunbar and Robbie Shakespeare—known best as producers and session players—were equal members of the group during the Rose years, and their skills helped Black Uhuru become a dub pioneer. Still, the essential vocal drive of the group is often lost in that highly instrumental reggae offshoot. The original lineup of Carlos, Dennis, and Simpson re-formed in 1987.

what to buy: *Red* 𝄞𝄞𝄞𝄞 (Mango, 1981, prod. Sly Dunbar, Robbie Shakespeare) is the group's slam-dunk best. All the songs are written or co-written by Rose, and the high harmony singing on "Youth of Eglington" shows what made the group great. There's more of the same on the superbly produced *Chill*

Out (Island, 1982, prod. Sly Dunbar, Robbie Shakespeare), ♪♪♪♪ with a slicker sound and a higher profile for the rhythm section.

what to buy next: *The Dub Factor* ♪♪♪♪ (Mango, 1983, prod. Sly Dunbar, Robbie Shakespeare) reworks past material with tricky dub effects, but it keeps you dancing.

what to avoid: The title gives you a hint: *Brutal* ♪♪ (Ras, 1986, prod. various) was the only outing by short-lived lead singer Reid. The dub version of this was better.

the rest:
Sensimilla ♪♪♪♪ (Mango, 1980)
Tear It Up—Live ♪♪♪♪ (Mango, 1982)
Brutal Dub ♪♪♪ (Ras, 1986)
Guess Who's Coming to Dinner ♪♪♪♪ (Heartbeat, 1987)
Black Uhuru ♪♪♪♪ (Mango, 1989)
Now ♪♪♪ (Mesa, 1990)
Now Dub ♪♪♪ (Rhino, 1990)
Black Sounds of Freedom ♪♪♪♪ (Shanachie, 1990)
Iron Storm Dub ♪♪♪♪ (Mesa, 1992)
Mystical Truth Dub ♪♪♪♪ (Mesa, 1993)
Liberation—The Island Anthology ♪♪♪♪♪ (Mango, 1993)

influences:
◀◀ Burning Spear, the Wailers

▶▶ Fugees, UB40

Lawrence Gabriel

The Blackeyed Susans
See: The Triffids

blackgirls /Dish
blackgirls formed 1986, in Raleigh, NC. Disbanded 1991. Dish formed 1992, in Raleigh, NC. Disbanded 1997.

blackgirls: Dana Kletter, piano, vocals; Eugenia Lee, guitar, vocals; Hillis Brown, violin, backup vocals. Dish: Dana Kletter, piano, vocals; Bo Taylor, guitar, vocals; Sara Bell, bass, mandolin, vocals; Jerry Kee, drums.

The common thread of these two groups is Dana Kletter, a spectacularly gifted singer who remains virtually unknown to the public at large. To date, her biggest claim to fame was singing backup vocals on Hole's *Live through This*. Kletter makes difficult music, no question about that, with an old-world vibe that the attention span–impaired will find challenging. But her work is plenty rewarding, if only because of that drop-dead gorgeous voice. Kletter initially emerged in blackgirls, a group that was truly years ahead of its time. Where the trio's gothic, women-on-the-verge-of-nervous-breakdowns chamber pop once seemed

uncomfortably weird and atonal, in retrospect blackgirls sounds like it was just waiting for Tori Amos to catch up. After blackgirls ran its course, Kletter formed the band Dish, building on blackgirls' more accessible side with better hooks and rocked-up guitar, courtesy of Motocaster guitarist Bo Taylor. Tragically, Dish didn't last beyond one full-length album, after which Kletter began performing acoustically with a revolving cast of players, including her twin sister Karen.

what to buy: Proceeding in the order of accessibility, the record to get is Dish's *Boneyard Beach* ♪♪♪♪ (Interscope, 1995, prod. John Agnello), a supremely elegant collection of 13 biting essays on the nuances of betrayal, highlighted by a blazing cover of "Tears of Rage" that stands tall alongside the original by Bob Dylan and the Band. Dana and Karen Kletter's *Dear Enemy* ♪♪♪♪ (Rykodisc, 1998, prod. Joe Boyd) sharpens things even further by positing that betrayal invariably begins at home. Both sonically lovely and lyrically harrowing, *Dear Enemy* rages against family dysfunctionality ("Meteor Mom," a scarifying cover of Scrawl's "Your Mother Wants to Know"). Poi Dog Pondering's Susan Voelz adds evocative violin throughout.

what to buy next: The definitive blackgirls album is *Procedure* ♪♪♪♪ (Mammoth, 1989, prod. Joe Boyd), which registers as a series of wild mood swings. Eugenia Lee sounds almost unhinged ("I am a loser" and "I am waiting for you to realize that I'm alive" are just two of her declarations), while Kletter comes across as calm in the face of rising panic.

the rest:
blackgirls:
Speechless ♪♪♪ (Black Park/Tom Tom EP, 1987)

Dish:
Mabel Sagitarius ♪♪♪ (Engine EP, 1994)

worth searching for: Dish guitarist Bo Taylor's power trio Motocaster sounds not a thing like Dish, specializing instead in go-to-11 excess. Motocaster shows genuine affection for both punk verities and '70s bonehead rock on the hard-to-find *Acid Rock* (Fistpuppet/Cargo EP, 1994, prod. Mitch Easter), with a furious overdrive cover of the Who's "Dogs Part Two" that will have you reaching for the air guitar. Motocaster's full-length follow-up, *Stay Loaded* (Interscope, 1994, prod. Mitch Easter), suffers from a shade too much white noise.

influences:
◀◀ Richard Thompson/Fairport Convention, Marianne Faithfull, Kurt Weill

▶▶ Tori Amos, Suddenly Tammy

David Menconi

BlackHawk
See: The Outlaws

Otis Blackwell

Born 1931, in Brooklyn, NY.

A songwriter in the same league with Leiber & Stoller and Chuck Berry, Otis Blackwell crafted sexy, clever, hook-filled songs that young white stars such as Elvis Presley and Jerry Lee Lewis turned into memorable anthems of the early rock 'n' roll movement. During the early 1950s, Blackwell was an artist in his own right, and had a minor R&B hit with "Daddy Rollin' Stone" for the Jay-Dee label. A better writer than vocalist, he soon began pitching his songs to other artists. Both Little Willie John and Peggy Lee scored hits with versions of "Fever," a song Blackwell wrote under the name John Davenport. (For various legal and financial reasons, Blackwell has written under different pen names throughout his career.) When Col. Tom Parker insisted he share a writer's credit with Elvis Presley before the King would record "Don't Be Cruel" and "All Shook Up," Blackwell (figuring 50% of something was better than 100% of nothing) reluctantly agreed. Presley studied Blackwell's demo recordings closely, imitating many of the writer's vocal fillips and idiosyncrasies, and in the process racked up two of his biggest hits. Blackwell eventually penned such Presley classics as "Return to Sender," "One Broken Heart for Sale," and the controversial (for its time) "Paralyzed." While writing songs for the 1957 teen flick *Jamboree*, Blackwell was approached by Jack Hammer with a song titled "Great Balls of Fire." Blackwell discarded Hammer's song but kept the title. The rest is history. Jerry Lee Lewis, who initially rejected the song as blasphemy, turned in one of the greatest rock 'n' roll performances ever, and sold five million copies of the song. Blackwell also wrote "Breathless," "Let's Talk about Us," "Livin' Lovin' Wreck," and "It Won't Happen with Me" for Lewis, who felt the writer understood his style better than any other tunesmith. Blackwell recorded several singles for Atlantic, MGM, Epic, and smaller labels, but it was the big hits he wrote for others, such as "Just Keep It Up" and "Hey Little Girl" for Dee Clark, "Handy Man" for Jimmy Jones (which James Taylor later revived MOR-style), and "Nine Times Out of Ten" for Cliff Richard that provided the bulk of his living. After writing hundreds of songs for nearly every major act of the '50s through early '60s, Blackwell's services were rendered obsolete by emerging British Invasion groups who wrote their own material. He continued to work as a producer, session man, and artist—he recorded a belated LP for Inner City, and played small clubs until a stroke paralyzed him in 1991. However, 35 years of near obscurity doesn't diminish his importance one iota; the songs of Otis Blackwell—many of which are still being performed—are the lifeblood of rock 'n' roll.

what's available: Many of Blackwell's most famous songs are given the all-star treatment on *Brace Yourself: A Tribute to Otis Blackwell* ��� (Shanachie, 1993, prod. Dave Edmunds), which features such luminaries as Graham Parker, Kris Kristofferson, Ronnie Spector, Deborah Harry, the Smithereens, Chrissie Hynde, and others. Fifty percent of the royalties are earmarked for Blackwell to defray his medical expenses. To hear Blackwell's classic songs by some of the artists who made them famous, check out the following LPs: Elvis Presley's *The Number One Hits* ���� (RCA, 1987, compilation prod. Greg Geller), which includes "Don't Be Cruel" and "All Shook Up"; Jerry Lee Lewis's *Original Sun Greatest Hits* ���� (Rhino, 1984, compilation prod. Art Fein), which features "Great Balls of Fire" and "Breathless"; and Dee Clark's *Raindrops* ���� (Vee-Jay, 1993, prod. Calvin Carter, Bob Fisher), which has "Just Keep It Up" and "Hey Little Girl" among its many fine moments. All these discs are still available and well worth owning.

worth searching for: You'll have to hit the import racks and specialty shops for *Otis Blackwell: 1953–55* (Flyright, 1997), a smart collection of Blackwell's own sides for the Jay-Dee label that includes his only hit, "Daddy Rollin' Stone," and 16 other historically important pre-rock sides. The out-of-print *All Shook Up* (Inner City, 1977/Shanachie, 1995, prod. Otis Blackwell, Herb Abramson) features recordings Blackwell made of his most famous songs with the rock band Grande Union. The original Inner City LP was meant to cash in on the wave of publicity (and enormous sales) spurred by the death of Elvis Presley. (There was a crude painting of Presley in the background of the original cover). The raspy-voiced Blackwell seems to be having a good time, and he tries hard to sound like Elvis and Jerry Lee on some tunes but is undermined by unimaginative bar-band backing and dull sound. Shanachie's reissue might hold some interest for collectors as it features four previously unreleased demos, including "One Broken Heart for Sale," which was a hit for Presley in 1963.

influences:

◄◄ Doc Pomus, Jessie Stone, Leiber & Stoller, Chuck Willis

►► Elvis Presley, Jerry Lee Lewis, Dee Clark, Mack Vickery

Ken Burke

Ruben Blades

Born July 16, 1948, in Panama City, Panama.

A Harvard-trained lawyer and movie star, the singing Ruben Blades emerged with the mid-'70s Fania label that popularized much of the New York salsa scene. After a stint with trombonist Willie Colon, Blades eschewed the jazz influence in salsa for a more pop-oriented sound incorporating synthesizers and working with the band Son/Seis Del Solar. Blades's music is hugely popular among Latin Americans due to his lyrical examination of some of the sadder realities of life in that community; he's closer to the Nuevo Cancion (New Song) movement of Latino leftists than to the exuberant party salsa of New York. For non-Spanish speakers Blades always provides translations of his songs with the albums. Major movie roles—in *Crossover Dreams, The Milagro Beanfield War,* and others—as well as a turn on stage in Paul Simon's failed musical *The Capeman,* have given him a public profile well beyond the parameters of music. And his social concerns have taken him into politics; Blades came in second in the 1994 elections for Panama's presidency (which is better than Joe Walsh ever did in his periodic campaigns to run the U.S.).

what to buy: Blades took a piercing look at hard lives on *Buscando America (Searching for America)* ♫♫♫♫ (Elektra, 1984, prod. Ruben Blades). "Decisions" spotlights a pregnant teenage girl and a philandering husband. "Disappearances" depicts loved ones searching for disappeared family members, and the title song despairs that the promise of America has been kidnapped by dictators. Throughout, Blades avoids preachiness by letting his characters tell their own stories. The Colon-Blades collaboration *Siembra* ♫♫♫♫ (Fania, 1978, prod. Willie Colon) is a more traditional salsa scorcher, with the Fania Crew providing grooves and Colon's trombone adding a jazzy touch. This disc is legendary among salsa fans. *Greatest Hits* ♫♫♫ (WEA Latina, 1996, prod. various) is as good a place as any for Blades novices to begin, though it's skimpy at only 10 tracks.

what to buy next: *Nothing but the Truth* ♫♫♫ (Elektra, 1988, prod. various) is Blades's first all-English outing, with songs written by Sting, Lou Reed, and Elvis Costello. Not one for the salsa fans, but it merits listening.

what to avoid: *Agua de Luna (Moon Water)* ♫♫ (Elektra, 1987, prod. Ruben Blades) features less-than-memorable arrangements and conceptual lyrics that seldom feel lived in by the songs' characters.

the rest:
Escenas ♫♫ (Elektra, 1985)
Crossover Dreams (Soundtrack) ♫♫♫ (Elektra, 1986)
Antecedente ♫♫♫ (Elektra, 1988)
Amor y Control ♫♫♫ (Sony Discos, 1992)
La Rosa de Los Vientos ♫♫♫ (Sony Tropical, 1996)
Fabulosos Calavera ♫♫♫ (BMG U.S. Latin, 1997)

worth searching for: *Ruben Blades and Son de Solar . . . Live* (Elektra, 1990, prod. Ruben Blades) features a smoking dance set driven by the salsa ethos of his earlier work. Blades performs one of the lead character roles in Paul Simon's *The Capeman* (Warner Bros., 1997, prod. Paul Simon), which is filled with Latin music and street-corner doo-wop. Happily, the album makes much more sense than the short-lived production ever did.

influences:

◄◄ Celia Cruz, Fania All Stars

►► Victor Manuel, Jon Secada, Robbie Robertson

Lawrence Gabriel

Blake Babies

Formed 1986, in Boston, MA. Disbanded 1991.

Juliana Hatfield, vocals, bass, guitar, piano (1986–90); John Strohm, guitar, vocals; Freda (Boner) Love, drums; Andrew Mayer, bass (1986); Seth White, bass (1987); Evan Dando, bass, (1988); Mike Leahy, guitar (1990–91).

Juliana Hatfield was studying voice at Berklee College of Music when she co-founded Blake Babies, a band whose sound, ironically, was largely defined by her seemingly erratic, untrained singing (which was even more strained on stage than on record). Her other co-founders were Indiana natives Freda Boner and John Strohm, who has had two stints as a Lemonhead, first on drums and later on guitar, as well as time with Evan Dando in the Hatin' Spores, a Black Sabbath cover band. Although Hatfield frequently swerved out of tune, she conveyed utter sincerity and a newly emerging female toughness, which were epitomized by the bitter, spit-out lyrics of *Sunburn*'s "I'm Not Your Mother" and the "Sanctify" line, "kick a boy and teach him how to cry." Hatfield's departure in 1990 effectively ended the group; she went on to a more celebrated solo career, while Boner and Strohm went on to other bands—Antenna, Velo-Deluxe, and Mysteries of Life.

what to buy: The album that broke the group to a sizable audience, *Sunburn* ♫♫♫♫ (Mammoth, 1990, prod. Gary Smith) is full of great songs, including "Out There," "Star," "Look Away," and "Train." Strohm's guitar sound—mixing electric sinew and acoustic jangle—is at its apex here.

what to buy next: *Earwig* ♫♫♫♫ (Mammoth, 1989, prod. Gary Smith) incorporates the vinyl album of that name plus the *Slow Learners* EP recorded the previous year. *Earwig* has the same merits as *Sunburn* but is slightly less consistent. A rowdy cover of the Stooges' "Loose" fits Hatfield's persona well. *Rosy Jack World* ♫♫♫♫ (Mammoth, 1991, prod. Gary Smith, Paul Mahern, Blake Babies), a five-song EP, was a worthy swan song highlighted by Hatfield's "Nirvana" (a tribute to Cobain and company before most of the world had heard of them) and a brilliant cover of the Grass Roots' "Temptation Eyes."

the rest:
Nicely, Nicely ♫♫ (Chew-bud, 1987/Mammoth, 1994)
Innocence and Experience ♫♫♫ (Mammoth, 1993)

influences:

◀◀ R.E.M., Keith Richards, Buffalo Tom, the Velvet Underground, the Feelies

▶▶ Jill Sobule, Lemonheads

see also: *Juliana Hatfield, Antenna/Velo-Deluxe/Mysteries of Life*

Steve Holtje

The Blasters

Formed 1979, in Los Angeles, CA. Disbanded 1986. Re-formed 1996.

1979–85: Phil Alvin, vocals, guitar; Dave Alvin, guitar; John Bazz, bass; Bill Bateman, drums; Gene Taylor, piano. 1996–present: Phil Alvin, vocals, guitar, harmonica; James Intveld, guitar; John Bazz, bass; Jerry Angel, drums.

The Blasters may have been at the forefront of the late '70s, early-'80s rockabilly revival, but that's not the whole story. It's instructive to remember that the Blasters were contemporaries of X and Dwight Yoakam, and they were equally conversant with both styles. The group combined the energy of the burgeoning L.A. punk scene with a solid base in rock 'n' roll history and a taste for R&B and country. Theirs was not a simple revivalism, but a genuine expression of a shared musical sensibility that drew on, but didn't ape, Jerry Lee Lewis, Big Joe Turner, and many others. After a too-brief run that included some critical if not commercial triumph, the group split, with Dave Alvin going on to pursue a successful solo career. Phil Alvin released a couple of solo albums, too, but mainly concentrated on graduate school, where he studied advanced mathematics. Eventually he reformed the band, but without brother Dave's vision, it just doesn't work.

what to buy: Unfortunately only two albums from the group's original incarnation are in print today. A definitive overview, *The Blasters Collection* 𝄢𝄢𝄢𝄢 (Slash/Warner Bros., 1990, prod. the Blasters, Jeff Eyrich) is the place to start. The much-anticipated rerelease of the group's independent debut, *American Music* 𝄢𝄢𝄢𝄢 (Rollin' Rock, 1980/HighTone, 1997, prod. the Blasters), takes the group back to its raw, raucous beginnings, and features six bonus tracks from the same sessions.

the rest:
At Home 𝄢𝄢 (Private, 1997)

worth searching for: The group's major-label debut, *The Blasters* (Slash/Warner Bros., 1981, prod. the Blasters), is its best single effort, thanks to such memorable songs as "Marie Marie," "So Long Baby Goodbye," and the genre-defining "American Music."

solo outings:
Phil Alvin:
Un "Sung Stories" 𝄢𝄢𝄢 (Slash, 1986)
County Fair 2000 𝄢𝄢𝄢 (HighTone, 1994)
see also: *Dave Alvin*

Daniel Durchholz

The Blazers

Formed 1990, in Los Angeles, CA.

Manuel Gonzales, vocals, guitars; Ruben Guarderrama, vocals, guitars; Lee Stuart, bass, vocals; Ruben C. Gonzalez, drums.

Originally guided through the music-industry swamp pit by East Los Angeles neighborhood pal Cesar Rosas of Los Lobos, the Blazers had no trouble establishing themselves on a national scale. Ruben Guarderrama and Manuel Gonzales, pals since they met in high school around 1971, are the kind of musical partners who know instinctively what the other is thinking. They shift quickly from traditional Mexican music (such as the catchy "El Año Veijo," from *Short Fuse*) to sweaty rockabilly ("Yeah, Yeah, Yeah!") without acknowledging any possible cultural difference between the two. In their mix of Billy Zoom–inspired guitar leads and a drop-dead rhythm section, it all comes out as rock 'n' roll. On record, the Blazers are still not as distinctive as Los Lobos, but they improve steadily with each album, even if the more recent *Just for You* lacks the explosive spontaneity of the debut.

what to buy: *Short Fuse* 𝄢𝄢𝄢𝄢 (Rounder, 1994, prod. Cesar Rosas) finds the rich intersection between Buddy Holly's American country-western and Richie Valens's hopped-up Mexican balladry. At first, it's a little jarring to hear the Blazers lurch from English-language rockabilly ("I'll Be Gone, Gone") to Spanish-language norteño music ("Tiburon, Tiburon") then to a slow song mixing both ("How You Make Me Feel"). But it all seems natural after a few listens.

what to buy next: *East Side Soul* 𝄢𝄢𝄢 (Rounder, 1995, prod. Cesar Rosas) was the one Rosas-produced album too many; the guitarist is totally supportive of his pals' original sounds, but he can't help making them seem like Los Lobos part two. It's a good album, but not as revolutionary as the debut.

the rest:
Just for You 𝄢𝄢𝄢 (Rounder, 1997)

influences:

◀◀ Richie Valens, Buddy Holly, Elvis Presley, Los Lobos, Texas Tornados, the Blasters, X, Joe Ely

▶▶ The Mavericks, Wayne Hancock, Big Sandy & His Fly-Rite Boys

Steve Knopper

Blessid Union of Souls

Formed 1993, in Cincinnati, OH.

Eliot Sloan, vocals; Jeff Pence, guitars; Eddie Hedges, percussion; Tony Clark, bass (1996–present); C.P. (Charly) Roth, keyboard, drums, bass.

Dubbed "rural soul," Blessid Union of Soul's music is based on gospel, folk, classic R&B, and pop. Eliot Sloan and Eddie Hedges began building the base of Blessid Union of Souls in the mid-'80s band Movies, which toured with Bell Biv Devoe. For about a second, the Cincinnati R&B band found a home on Columbia Records. In 1993 Hedges and Sloan reworked the band as Blessid Union of Souls, scoring a hit with "I Believe." Later, however, they were victimized by a record company re-organization that paralyzed the progress of the group's sophomore album.

what to buy: The feel good album *Blessid Union of Soul* ♪♪♪ (Capitol, 1997, prod. Emosia) shows the band at its best so far, with the charming, acoustic-driven "I Wanna Be There" and "Light in Your Eyes." Most compelling is "I Believe," about Sloan's struggle in an inter-racial relationship (it has a happy ending on the album, though in real life the father of his girlfriend forced her to dump him).

the rest:
Home ♪♪♪ (EMI, 1995)

influences:
◀◀ Collective Soul, Arrested Development, Hootie & the Blowfish

Christina Fuoco

Blind Faith

Formed and disbanded in 1969, in London, England.

Eric Clapton, guitar, vocals; Steve Winwood, keyboards, vocals; Rick Grech, bass, violin; Ginger Baker, drums.

In the heady world of late '60s rock, when both musicians and fans began taking everything just a wee bit seriously, the word "supergroup" was being thrown around far too indiscriminately. Nevertheless, when two-thirds of the freshly disbanded Cream began holding informal jam sessions with members of Family and Traffic, the British music press in particular—before even a single note had been heard—was already proclaiming this new quartet as nothing less than the Second Coming. Wryly noting as much, the band named itself Blind Faith and debuted in front 120,000 people in London's Hyde Park on June 7, 1969. It was to be its *only* U.K. appearance as, after the release of a single LP and a sold-out American tour the following month, Clapton fled for the comparative calm of the Delaney &

Bonnie group, Winwood briefly reformed Traffic before launching, like Clapton, a successful solo career, and Grech joined Baker in the totally ludicrous Air Force band.

what's available: Hindsight reveals *Blind Faith* ♪♪♪ (Atco, 1969/Polydor, 1986, prod. Jimmy Miller) to be a surprisingly cohesive, relatively ego-free exercise in musical woodshedding in the spirit of the Band's early work. Both Winwood's "Can't Find My Way Home" and especially Clapton's "Presence of the Lord" are candid, uplifting compositions that remain in each of their repertoires to this day, while the version of Buddy Holly's "Well All Right" is as playful as it is reverent to the original. Only the 15-minute "Do What You Like" hints at the pointless over-indulgence that ultimately destroyed Cream (and unfortunately inspired a generation of hard rock noodling to come).

influences:
◀◀ Cream, Traffic, Al Kooper's Super Session, the Dirty Mac

▶▶ Derek & the Dominos, Ginger Baker's Air Force, KGB, Band Aid

see also: *Eric Clapton, Cream, Traffic, Steve Winwood*

Gary Pig Gold

Blind Melon

Formed 1990, in Los Angeles, CA.

Shannon Hoon (died October 21, 1995), vocals; Rogers Stevens, guitar; Christopher Thorn, guitar; Brad Smith, bass; Glen Graham, drums.

Blind Melon's mix of hippie style and moderately hard rock didn't seem to have much of a future until the video for its sprightly single "No Rain," with its indelible image of a bespectacled little girl in a bee costume, took MTV by storm and made the group's debut album, *Blind Melon*, a hit. The first release also includes some heavy jams and the piercing vocals of Shannon Hoon, a friend of Guns N' Roses frontman Axl Rose (to whom he was often compared as both singer and prima donna). Their second album tanked commercially, though, and Hoon was found dead on the band's tour bus, another victim of a drug overdose.

what to buy: *Blind Melon* ♪♪♪ (Capitol, 1992, prod. Rick Parasher) is only fair, since "No Rain" loses much of its charm without the visual presence of the Bee Girl.

the rest:
Soup ♪♪♪ (Capitol, 1995)
Nico ♪♪ (Capitol, 1996)

influences:
◀◀ Led Zeppelin, the Grateful Dead, Guns N' Roses

Simon Glickman

Shannon Hoon of Blind Melon (© Ken Settle)

Blink 182

Formed 1993, in San Diego, CA.

Mark Hoppus, bass, vocals; Tom Delonge, guitar, vocals; Scott Raynor, drums.

Tuneful, snotty, and barely legal, Blink 182 continue the tradition of fast and amusing punk *rawk* à la NOFX. This SoCal trio has a penchant for galloping beats, demi-metal guitars, and hummable choruses. An energetic and talented live act, Blink tends to lose a bit in the translation to disk, however.

what's available: With potty jokes and four-letter words in tow, *Dude Ranch* 𝄢𝄢𝄢𝄢 (Cargo/MCA, 1997, prod. Mark Trombino) will rock you if you're younger than 20, a snowboarder or skater, and buy everything on Epitaph. If not, then it is an unessential but catchy collection of alterna-punk tunes, including the adolescent hit "Dammit."

the rest:
Cheshire Cat 𝄢𝄢𝄢 (Grilled Cheese, 1995)

influences:
⏮ Agent Orange, Bad Religion, NOFX, Green Day

Barry M. Prickett

Blondie
/Deborah Harry
/Jimmy Destri

Formed 1975, in New York, NY. Disbanded 1983. Reunited 1997.

Deborah Harry, vocals; Chris Stein, guitar, vocals; Clem Burke, drums; Jimmy Destri, keyboards; Gary Valentine, bass (1975–76); Frank Infante, bass, guitar (1975–83); Nigel Harrison, bass (1978–83).

Blondie's emergence paralleled the rise of punk rock and new wave, but even though the group drew on the energy and attitude of these scenes, it had a more eclectic sensibility, charm galore, and pronounced pop songwriting chops. Drawing on British Invasion melodicism, the teenage devotional tunes of Brian Wilson and Phil Spector, horror-movie kitsch, and punk's defiant posturing, Blondie crafted a commercially appealing hybrid that rarely lost its subversive edge. After releasing a spiky debut on an indie label, the band signed with Chrysalis Records; its second album for the major, *Parallel Lines*, achieved widespread success on the strength of the disco-pop crossover smash "Heart of Glass." More hits followed—"Dreaming," "Sunday Girl," the Eurodisco "Call Me," the protorap gem "Rapture," and the calypso cover "The Tide Is High"—and Blondie rode the new wave to megastardom until Chris Stein was struck by a debilitating illness, forcing a breakup. Harry nursed her husband-bandmate back to health and pursued careers as a solo musician and film actor. Blondie's pow-

erful influence on a new generation of bands, notably such Britpop outfits as Elastica and Sleeper, has been chronicled via a handful of compilations in the '90s. In 1997, the members of Blondie began working together again and were creating new material in earnest the following year.

what to buy: *Parallel Lines* 𝄢𝄢𝄢𝄢 (Chrysalis, 1978, prod. Mike Chapman) encompasses everything that made the band great: winsome pop, exhilarating guitar rock, danceable grooves, some arty touches, and Harry's tough, droll, infinitely appealing persona. *Lines* includes the dance floor standard "Heart of Glass," the rocking "Hangin' on the Telephone," and the luminous pop ditty "Picture This" among its outstanding tracks.

what to buy next: For a collection of the band's hits—which in Blondie's case means some of their finest work—pick up *The Best of Blondie* 𝄢𝄢𝄢𝄢 (Chrysalis, 1981, prod. various), which tracks the group's hits through its peak years, including "Call Me" from the *American Gigolo* soundtrack. The more curious should check out the double-CD *The Platinum Collection* 𝄢𝄢𝄢𝄢 (EMI, 1994, prod. various). *Eat to the Beat* 𝄢𝄢𝄢𝄢 (Chrysalis, 1979, prod. Mike Chapman) has fewer highlights but is a solid effort and features the engaging pop songs "Dreaming" and "Atomic." *Plastic Letters* 𝄢𝄢𝄢𝄢 (Chrysalis, 1977, prod. Richard Gottehrer) is hit-and-miss and marred occasionally by intrusive synthesizers, but it contains several intimations of greatness, notably "(I'm Always Touched by Your) Presence, Dear," "Fan Mail," and "I Didn't Have the Nerve to Say No."

what to avoid: *The Hunter* 𝄢𝄢 (Chrysalis, 1982, prod. Mike Chapman) chronicles the band's rapid dissolution amid commercial and other pressures—a sign that not only Blondie but the whole new wave was moribund. It's redeemed solely by "Island of Lost Souls," which is available on a few compilations. Steer clear also of Harry's solo efforts *KooKoo* 𝄢𝄢 (Chrysalis, 1981, prod. Mike Chapman) and *Def, Dumb, and Blonde* 𝄢𝄢 (Sire, 1989, prod. Mike Chapman), both of which are rife with gimmickry and lack all of Blondie's finesse.

the rest:
Blondie 𝄢𝄢𝄢 (Chrysalis, 1976)
Autoamerican 𝄢𝄢𝄢 (Chrysalis, 1980)
Once More Into the Bleach 𝄢𝄢𝄢 (Chrysalis, 1988)
Blonde and Beyond 𝄢𝄢𝄢𝄢 (Chrysalis 1993)
The Remix Project 𝄢𝄢𝄢 (Chrysalis, 1995)
Picture This Live 𝄢𝄢𝄢 (EMI-Capitol, 1998)

worth searching for: *The Complete Picture: The Very Best of Deborah Harry and Blondie* (Chrysalis, 1991, prod. various) is a British compilation that, while not as complete as *The Platinum Collection*, is still the best single-CD collection.

solo outings:
Deborah Harry:

Rockbird ♪♪✓ (Chrysalis, 1986)
Debravation ♪♪✓ (Sire/Reprise, 1993)

Jimmy Destri:
Heart on a Wall ♪♪♪ (Chrysalis, 1982)

Checquered Past (Burke and Harrison):
Checquered Past ♪ (EMI, 1984)

influences:

◄◄ Phil Spector, Brian Wilson, the Beatles, Motown, James Brown, Toots & the Maytals, David Bowie, T. Rex, Television, the Ramones, Iggy Pop, Grandmaster Flash & the Furious Five, Marilyn Monroe

►► The Bangles, Elastica, Sleeper, Echobelly, Letters to Cleo

Simon Glickman

Blood Oranges

See: Cheri Knight

Blood, Sweat & Tears

Formed 1967, in New York, NY.

Al Kooper, keyboards, vocals (1967–68); Steve Katz, guitar, vocals (1967–72); Fred Lipsius, saxophone, piano (1967–72); Jim Fielder, bass (1967–73); Bobby Colomby, drums (1967–76); Dick Halligan, keyboards, trombone, flute (1967–72); Randy Brecker, trumpet, flugelhorn (1967–68); Jerry Weiss, trumpet, flugelhorn (1967–68); David Clayton-Thomas, vocals (1968–72, 1974–present); Chuck Winfield, trumpet, flugelhorn (1968–72); Lew Soloff, trumpet, flugelhorn (1968–73); Jerry Hyman, trombone (1968–70); Dave Bargero, trumpet, trombone, tuba (1970–76); Bobby Dole, vocals (1972); Lou Marini Jr., reeds (1972–73); Georg Wadenius, guitar (1972–75); Jerry Fisher, vocals (1972–74); Tom Malone, trumpet, flugelhorn, trombone, saxophone (1972–73); Ron McClure, bass (1973–75); Jerry LaCroix, vocals, reeds, harmonica (1973–74); Joe Giorgianni, trumpet, flugelhorn (1974–75); and many others over the years.

Horns were not strangers to pop music in 1967, but horn sections weren't commonplace in rock 'n' roll bands; there was something Vegas-y and adult about the concept. But Blood, Sweat & Tears sought to change that by bringing its particular big band idea into play as a way to effectively merge styles—in this case rock, jazz, and blues. Formed by Blues Project refugees Al Kooper and Steve Katz, BS&T did succeed in making one landmark album—*Child Is Father to the Man*—and in assembling a volatile bunch of artistic personalities that wouldn't be able to stay together much longer than one album. Kooper was one of the first out, bristling over group demands that he step aside from or at least share the vocal spot. This became a trend; over the years BS&T would shift personnel with almost every album, becoming something of a musical lab for hot young players. That is, in fact, how front-man David Clayton-Thomas—the voice behind hits such as "Spinning Wheel," "You've Made Me So Very Happy," and "Hi-De-Ho"—runs the band these days. Ironically, the once-provocative BS&T has in fact become what it set out not to be—a family oriented show band playing big, brassy hits in casinos, nightclub, and parks.

what to buy: *Child Is Father to the Man* ♪♪♪♪♪ (Columbia, 1968, prod. John Simon) is indeed a landmark synthesis of styles and musical sensibilities, winding jazzy horn charts, lush string sections, and a soulful rock 'n' roll rhythm section into the same song. It still sounds fresh today—though, to be honest, Kooper's thin vocals keep the album just a wee bit earthbound. *The Best of Blood, Sweat & Tears: What Goes Up!* ♪♪♪♪ (Columbia/Legacy, 1995, prod. various) is a strong two-CD set that tracks the group's recordings up to 1976, when drummer Colomby was the final original member to leave the band.

what to buy next: The bands that recorded *Live & Improvised* ♪♪♪♪ (Columbia/Legacy, 1991, prod. Bobby Colomby) in 1975 may not resemble the first two or three BS&T lineups at all, but they're still hot ensembles (including Clayton-Thomas and guitarists Mike Stern and Steve Kahn) that wail away on long, jammy versions of some of BS&T's best-known songs.

what to avoid: Things get a little bit out there on *Blood, Sweat & Tears 3* ♪♪ (Columbia, 1970, prod. Bobby Colomby, Roy Halee), especially on the ill-advised "Symphony for the Devil/Sympathy for the Devil" suite. Mick Jagger at least got a good laugh out of it.

the rest:
Blood, Sweat & Tears ♪♪♪♪ (Columbia, 1969/1988)
BS&T 4 ♪♪♪ (Columbia, 1971/Legacy, 1996)
Greatest Hits ♪♪♪♪ (Columbia, 1972)
Found Treasures ♪♪♪ (Columbia Special Products, 1972)
Live ♪♪♪ (Avenue, 1980/1994)
Nuclear Blues ♪♪ (Avenue, 1980/1995)

worth searching for: The out-of-print *Mirror Image* (Columbia, 1974) features an interesting version of the band fronted by full-throated singer Jerry LaCroix, a musician who brings more of a player's sensibility to the group.

influences:

◄◄ The Blues Project, the Electric Flag, Duke Ellington, Count Basie, the Beatles, Ike Turner's Kings of Rhythm

►► Chicago, Tower of Power, Michael Bolton, the Brecker Brothers, Stevie Wonder, Liquid Soul

see also: *Al Kooper, the Blues Project*

Gary Graff

The Bloodhound Gang

Formed 1994, in King of Prussia, PA.

Jimmy Pop Ali, vocals, samples; Lupus, guitar, vocals; Evil Jared, bass, vocals (1996–present); D.J. Q-Ball, turntables, vocals (1996–present); Spanky G, drums, vocals (1996–present).

The Bloodhound Gang is a ragtag Philadelphia-area outfit that combines the childish sexual innuendo of Howard Stern, the raucous white-boy rap of the early Beastie Boys, and the faux-metal posturing of Anthrax into an oddly coherent, yet loopy, musical potion. Riding the success of an accidental MTV hit, the droning "Fire Water Burn" (a takeoff on the standard hip-hop callout, "The roof is on fire!"), and the magnetically repulsive personality of frontman Jimmy Pop Ali, the Bloodhound Gang has managed to extend its allotted 15 minutes of fame. What originally began as a sample-driven collaboration between Jimmy Pop and pal Lupus has since expanded into a touring ensemble that includes guitars, drums, and a live DJ.

what to buy: On *One Fierce Beer Coaster* ✒✒✓ (Geffen, 1996, prod. Ave, Jimmy Pop Ali), the Bloodhound Gang unleashes a dozen childish joke-songs ("I Wish I Was Queer So I Could Get Chicks," "Kiss Me Where It Smells Funny") that will make you laugh and feel ashamed at the same time. If Howard Stern is your kind of funny, this record's for you.

the rest:
Dingleberry Haze EP ✒✒ (Cheese Factory, 1994)
Use Your Fingers ✒✒ (Columbia, 1996)

influences:
◀◀ The Beastie Boys, Anthrax, Primus, Howard Stern

Scott Hess

Luka Bloom

Born Barry Moore, May 23, 1955, in Newbridge, County Kildare, Ireland.

The brother of Irish minstrel Christy Moore, Barry Moore began his career in the pubs of Dublin before moving to Washington, DC., in 1987. There he changed his name to Luka Bloom—derived incongruously from the boy in Suzanne Vega's song "Luka" and a character in James Joyce's *Ulysses*—and became a favorite on the Eastern Seaboard club circuit, perfecting an intense, explosive rhythmic guitar attack and a mix of introspective and socially aware folk-rock. His style owes as much to the romanticism and mysticism of his Irish roots as it does to traditional folk balladeers like Woody Guthrie and modern folksters such as Joan Armatrading and Joni Mitchell. A charismatic, riveting live performer, Bloom's recordings have increasingly emphasized somber melodies and reflective lyrics that only suggest the power he brings on stage.

what to buy: Although Bloom's debut album is stirring, his second, *The Acoustic Motorbike* ✒✒✒ (Reprise, 1992, prod. Paul Barrett) is more immediately engaging. Recorded in Ireland with musical assists from brother Christy and Hothouse Flowers, the album peaks with the passionate Celtic rap of L.L. Cool J's "I Need Love," and the strumming charm of the title song.

what to buy next: Bloom came to national note with *Riverside* ✒✒✒✒ (Reprise, 1990, prod. Jeffrey Wood) for good reason: it's a striking first album, notable for its earnestness, melodies, and Irish soul.

the rest:
Turf (Reprise, 1994) ✒✒✒

influences:
▶▶ The Boomtown Rats, Cowboy Junkies, Joan Armatrading, Suzanne Vega, Michelle Shocked, Joni Mitchell

Martin Connors

Michael Bloomfield

Born July 28, 1944, in Chicago, IL. Died February 15, 1981, in San Francisco, CA.

Born into an enormously wealthy Chicago family, Michael Bloomfield chose to make his mark in the world in his own way, and by doing so helped push the electric guitar into the forefront of the rock and blues revolution of the 1960s. Bloomfield immersed himself in Chicago's blues scene as a teenager, and he endeared himself to the older players with his sincere and passionate support of the music and by being a quick study when they taught him how to play. His charisma, powerful attack, and lyrical style, which he learned from players like Albert King and Muddy Waters, while not commercially successful, was highly influential. He backed James Cotton and joined Paul Butterfield's hard-nosed blues unit in time for the group's seminal appearance at the Newport Folk Festival in 1965. That same year, his explosive guitar work kicked Bob Dylan's *Highway 61 Revisited* into the stratosphere. Bloomfield's contributions to the Butterfield Band were immense, especially in the modal-scaled songs on *East-West*, but he left in 1967 to form the horn-oriented Electric Flag. He lasted for one album before making *Super Session* with Stephen Stills and Al Kooper and *The Live Adventures of Michael Bloomfield and Al Kooper*, which raised his profile immensely. After the much-admired Flag, Bloomfield's career settled into a quieter mode. He toured the country as a solo act, often dividing his shows between acoustic guitar and piano songs; these concerts were both musically satisfying and educational, as he would comment on the songs and share his encyclopedic knowledge of the blues and American traditional music. At home in San Francisco he performed electric blues with a band that often included friend Mark Naftalin on keyboards. He recorded a number of albums, wrote soundtrack music for low-budget films (including *The Trip, You Are What You Eat, Steelyard Blues*), and wrote a nonfiction book called *Me and Big Joe* (Re/Search Productions, 1980), which chronicled his relationship with bluesman Joe Lee "Big Joe" Williams. Bloomfield was a lifelong insomniac and had an open-ended prescription for sleeping pills. He also struggled at times with alcohol abuse. His apparently accidental death in 1981 is attributed to these factors.

what to buy: In general, Bloomfield was only as good as his surroundings dictated, so it's not a surprise his best work is in ensemble situations. Start with *The Lost Sessions* ⵣⵣⵣⵣ (Elektra, 1964/Rhino, 1995, prod. Paul Rothchild) and *East-West* ⵣⵣⵣⵣ (Elektra, 1966, prod. Paul Rothchild, Mark Abramson, Barry Friedman), his early recordings with the Paul Butterfield Band. Follow that with *Super Session* ⵣⵣⵣⵣ (Columbia, 1968, prod. Al Kooper) and *The Live Adventures of Michael Bloomfield and Al Kooper* ⵣⵣⵣⵣ (Columbia, 1969/Legacy, 1997, prod. Al Kooper). The Electric Flag, with its hard-bitten horn section, provided a nice backdrop for Bloomfield's charms. Check out *Old Glory: The Best of Electric Flag* ⵣⵣⵣⵣ (Columbia/Legacy, 1995) and *A Long Time Coming* ⵣⵣⵣⵦ (Columbia, 1968/1988, prod. John Court).

what to buy next: Dylan's *Highway 61 Revisited* ⵣⵣⵣⵣⵣ (Columbia, 1965, prod. Bob Johnston) is an excellent example of his sideman abilities, especially on the blues numbers. While none are great, *Don't Say That I Ain't Your Man! Essential Blues 1964–69* ⵣⵣⵣⵦ (Columbia/Legacy, 1994, prod. various), *It's Not Killing Me* ⵣⵣⵣⵦ (Columbia, 1969), and *Living in the Fast Lane* ⵣⵣⵣⵦ (Waterhouse, 1981, prod. Norman Dayron) offer sometime flashes of brilliance after his glory days.

what to avoid: *Triumvirate* ⵣⵣ (Columbia, 1973/1989) is a jam with Dr. John and John Hammond that just doesn't catch the fire it should have.

the rest:
Try It before You Buy It ⵣⵣⵦ (CBS, 1975)
Between the Hard Place & the Ground ⵣⵣⵣⵣ (Takoma, 1979)
The Best of Michael Bloomfield ⵣⵣⵣ (Takoma, 1987)
I'm with You Always ⵣⵣⵣ (Demon, 1987)
Blues, Gospel and Ragtime Guitar Instrumentals ⵣⵣⵣ (Shanachie, 1993)
The Gospel of Blues ⵣⵣⵣ (Laserlight, 1994)
Rx for the Blues ⵣⵣⵦ (Eclipse, 1996)
At the Old Waldorf ('76–'77) N/A (Legacy, 1998)

worth searching for: Never miss a chance to see *Festival,* an obscure, long-out-of-print film on the Newport fest in the early 1960s. It includes part of the infamous 1965 Butterfield Band workshop, an interview with a bushy-tailed Bloomfield about

his love for the blues, and plenty of other worthwhile performances by famous bluesers of that era.

influences:
⏪ B.B. King, Albert King, Muddy Waters, Elmore James, Son House, T-Bone Walker

⏩ Peter Green, Bob Dylan, the Band, Blood, Sweat & Tears, Chicago, the Black Crowes, Buddy Miles

Leland Rucker

Blotto
Formed 1979, in Albany, NY. Disbanded 1986.

Blanche Blotto, vocals, keyboards (1979–80); Bowtie Blotto, vocals, guitar; Broadway Blotto, vocals, guitar; Cheese Blotto, vocals, bass; Lee Harvey Blotto, vocals, drums; Sergeant Blotto, vocals, percussion; Chevrolet Blotto, vocals, keyboards (1980–81).

Blotto was the flat-out funniest rock 'n' roll band of all time, with a hilarious live act and sufficient musical prowess to back up the laughs with rockin' pop panache—evidenced by the surf 'n' swim put-on "I Wanna Be a Lifeguard" and the spy thriller knockoff "Goodbye, Mr. Bond."

what's available: *Collected Works* ⵣⵣⵣ (One Way, 1994, prod. various) gives you the whole story, reprising in their entirety the group's two EPs and one album, along with a B-side ("The B-Side"), a live track, a non-album cover of Lou Christie's "Lightning Strikes," and a karaoke version of "I Wanna Be a Lifeguard." Often silly, frequently downright goofy, Blotto steamrolls through its material with a wink and a smirk, but also with unerring style and elan.

influences:
⏪ The Bonzo Dog Band

⏩ Spinal Tap, Weird Al Yankovic

Carl Cafarelli

Bobby Blue
See: Beat Farmers

The Blue Aeroplanes
Formed 1981, in Bristol, England.

Gerard Langley, vocals; Ian Kearey, guitar, banjimer, harmonium; Nick Jacobs, guitar, vocals; Dave Chapman, guitar, bass, harmonica, mandolin, vocals; Angelo Bruschini, guitar, accordion, vocals; John Langley, drums, keyboards, vocals; Wojtek Dmochowski, dancer; John Stapleton, records, tapes.

A musical consortium with few fixed members, the Blue Aeroplanes are among the least definable and most tenacious pop groups to come along. With vocalist Gerard Langley as the only constant, the Aeroplanes have somehow managed to sound consistent through some 10 albums and more than a dozen changes in personnel. While guitars are the dominant instruments, the group generously blends in hurdy-gurdy, melodeon, bagpipes, and other old-world instrumentation, creating a rustic rock-pop that is both fresh and nostalgic. There is little to compare it with. Langley, the main songwriter, alternately snaps out his lyrics in a scouse snarl (scouse is a dialect of English spoken in Liverpool) or sings them in a voice pleasantly chafed with whiskey and wind. His themes tend toward love on the brink, but he can just as easily create a somber and romantic mood of reverie, using fractured phrases a drunk might spout as the last bar closes. Heady and moving stuff.

what to buy: *Spitting Out Miracles* ♬♬♬ (Fire, 1987, prod. Gerard Langley, Charlie Llewellin) is a friendly place to check out the Aeroplanes' stuff. Langley's singing-talking vocals work to great effect across many styles here, including laidback folk ("Cowardice and Caprice"), cajun-rock ("Spitting Out Miracles"), and lovely waltz-time reveries ("Ceiling Roses"). It's an amazingly well-paced record, given its alphabet-soup eclecticism, with fast and happy rockers like "Winter Sun" and "Bury Your Love Like Treasure" punctuating the calmer moments.

what to buy next: Following a three-year period during which it released no new material, the band returned in full force on *Swagger* ♬♬♬♬ (Chrysalis, 1990, prod. Gil Norton), a 12-song extravaganza driven by pure pop power. Layers of guitars create a lovely chiming wash for Langley's introspections on relationships. The usual cavalcade of Aeroplane friends—including R.E.M.'s Michael Stipe and ex-Belle Stars saxophonist Clair Hirst—lends a bit of star power to the enterprise.

what to avoid: Not bad so much as unnecessary, *World View Blue* ♬♬ (Ensign, 1990) is a lackluster collection of live tracks, leftovers, and covers, including the Velvet Underground's "Sweet Jane" and a live version of Bob Dylan's "I Wanna Be Your Lover."

the rest:
Tolerance ♬♬ (Fire, 1986)
Friendloverplane ♬♬♬♬ (Fire, 1988)
Beatsongs ♬♬♬♬ (Ensign-Chrysalis, 1991)
Friendloverplane 2 (Up in a Down World) ♬♬♬ (Ensign-Chrysalis, 1992)
Life Model ♬♬ (Beggars Banquet, 1994)
Rough Music ♬♬♬ (Beggars Banquet, 1995)

worth searching for: Long out of print, the Aeroplanes' first album, *Bop Art* (Regeneration, 1984, prod. Blue Aeroplanes), has been re-released as a mail-order CD via its Blue Aeroplanes Information service in Bristol, England. Filled with the trademark sounds that would define the group's later work, *Bop Art* is a highly accessible record that's every bit as good as *Spitting Out Miracles*.

influences:

◄◄ The Velvet Underground, Leonard Cohen, Paul Winter Consort, Fairport Convention

►► Nick Cave & the Bad Seeds, Poi Dog Pondering

Christopher Scapelliti

Blue Cheer

Formed 1967, in Boston, MA. Disbanded 1971. Re-formed 1985.

Dickie Petersen, bass, vocals; Leigh Stephens, guitar (1967–68); Paul Whaley, drums (1968–69, 1985–89); Randy Holden, guitar (1968–69); Norman Mayell, drums (1969–71); Bruce Stephens, guitar, vocals (1969–70); Ralph Burns Kellogg, keyboards (1969–71); Gary Yoder, guitar (1970–71); Tony Rainier, guitar (1985–present).

Blue Cheer epitomized acid rock, the forerunner to heavy metal. The power trio, which took its name from a potent form of LSD, played hard, loud, and fast. Its remake of Eddie Cochran's "Summertime Blues" in 1968 is considered one of the first heavy metal songs ever recorded. The group moved to San Francisco shortly thereafter, but after six average-selling albums, it broke up in 1971. Blue Cheer has regrouped on occasion, and its latest incarnation has produced three new albums, though only one was released in the U.S.

what to buy: Most of Blue Cheer's albums are long out of print, but *The Good Times Are So Hard to Find: The History of Blue Cheer* ♬♬♬ (Mercury, 1988, prod. various) pulls together largely overlooked originals and choice covers—and, of course, "Summertime Blues"—on one budget-priced CD.

the rest:
Vincebus Eruptum ♬♬♬ (Mercury, 1968)
Outsideinside ♬♬ (Mercury, 1968)

influences:

◄◄ Eddie Cochran, Chuck Berry, the Rolling Stones, the Kinks, the Yardbirds

►► Steppenwolf, Led Zeppelin, Blue Öyster Cult, Bachman-Turner Overdrive

Doug Pullen

Blue Meanies

Formed 1991, in Chicago, IL.

Billy Spunke, vocals; Jimmy Flame, trumpet; John Paul Camp III, saxophones; Chaz Linde, organ; Rev. Jim Cooley, guitar (1991–95); Jason Vance, bass (1991–95); Tony Aimone, drums (1991–95); Dave Lump, bass (1996–present); Mike Pearson, guitar (1996–present); Robert Trondson, drums (1996–present).

Graduates of the Southern Illinois University frat-party circuit in Carbondale, the charismatic, pint-sized vocalist Billy Spunke and the rest of the founding members of the Blue Meanies were already seasoned live performers by the time they arrived in Chicago. They set up a mock record label, No Record Company, with a dozen other no-name bands across the country in order to grease the wheels for live bookings, mostly on the ska-punk circuit. The ploy worked. The band now tours the world and performs 200 shows a year. Its indie records, most of which are out of print, remain word-of-mouth hits in the underground ska community, even as the band has outgrown the blue-beat sound and become something a good deal more complex and ferocious—a Midwestern equivalent of Japan's avant-punkers the Boredoms.

what to buy: *Full Throttle* ♫♫♫♪ (Thick, 1997, prod. Mark Haines) is the album that distinguishes the Meanies from the dime-a-dozen party bands that emerged during the mid-'90s ska revival. It's a nearly chaotic swirl of punk, polka, klezmer, metal, avant-garde, and ska, topped by Spunke's unusually introspective and thoughtful lyrics about everything from family relationships ("Smash the Magnavox") to urban violence ("The Great Peacemaker").

worth searching for: *Peace Love Groove* (No Record Company, 1992, prod. Blue Meanies) is the debut live EP, with bratty anthems such as "Grandma Shampoo" and "Aquarium Bong." It's notable primarily for its artwork: a terrific re-creation of the banned butcher cover for the Beatles' *Yesterday . . . and Today* album, which suggests the Meanies took its name from the villains in the animated Beatles movie *Yellow Submarine*.

influences:
◄◄ Bad Brains, the Boredoms, John Zorn, Frank Zappa

►► Insane Clown Posse, Apocalypse Hoboken

Greg Kot

Blue Mountain

Formed 1991, in Los Angeles, CA.

Cary Hudson, guitar, vocals, mandolin; Laurie Stirratt, bass, vocals; Frank Coutch, drums.

After the breakup of the Hilltops—a slightly punkier alt.country band that included Cary Hudson, Laurie Stirratt, and Stirratt's brother John, currently of Wilco—the members of Blue Mountain repaired to both their former Mississippi home their musical roots. Drawing on country, Southern rock, and Neil Young–style acoustic guitar and harmonica balladry, the husband-and-wife team of Hudson and Stirratt went through a succession of drummers before settling on Frank Coutch. For a trio, Blue Mountain is extraordinarily versatile, turning in raging rockers that, even at their edgiest, are shot through with an ap-

pealing melodicism, and folkish country tunes, many of which recount the simple, bucolic pleasures of the South.

what to buy: *Dog Days* ♫♫♫♪ (Roadrunner, 1995, prod. Eric "Roscoe" Ambel) is a memorable effort from start to finish. The band's ensemble playing is tight and Ambel's production is nearly perfect. More important, though, these songs are actually about something: "Mountain Girl" is a gorgeous mandolin-driven remembrance of good times past; "A Band Called Bud" reports the hapless history of Memphis' Grifters, a band that never really made it but refuses to quit; "ZZQ" celebrates a now-defunct Mississippi radio station whose playlist was laced with punk rock; and "Jimmy Carter" is a surprising two-stepper that posits the oft-denounced ex-president as a great man, if not a great politician. Hudson's vocals are soulful, if unspectacular, but that's in keeping with the band's m.o. Their music is never flashy, but it's as easy to get into as a favorite old pair of shoes.

the rest:
Homegrown ♫♫♪ (Roadrunner, 1997)

worth searching for: The group's self-released debut, *Blue Mountain* (4 Barrel, 1993, prod. Blue Mountain), contains a handful of songs that eventually wound up on *Dog Days*, but it sounds like the $1,000 it cost to make it. Also, *The Hilltops* (Fishtone, 1992/Black Dog 1996, prod. Hilltops), which saw its initial release only after that band had already split, was reissued after Blue Mountain gained some notoriety.

influences:
◄◄ Creedence Clearwater Revival, Uncle Tupelo, Blue Rodeo

Daniel Durchholz

The Blue Nile

Formed 1982, in Glasgow, Scotland.

Paul Buchanan, vocals, guitar; Robert Bell, bass; Paul Joseph, keyboards.

The Blue Nile started out playing nearly entirely sampled and synthesized music. Paul Buchanan's whispery vocals—over the layered textures of synthesized strings and horns, programmed drums, and turned-down electric guitars—evoke that moment when the late of the night changes to the early morning. Not a prolific group, the trio let five years lapse between its first two albums, and seven years went by between its second and third.

what to buy: The group's middle album, *Hats* ♫♫♫♫ (Linn/Virgin, 1989, prod. the Blue Nile), is the best of the lot. It relies heavily on synthesized instruments and Buchanan's restrained singing, but the melodies are well-defined and accessible, with major chord arrangements at least providing a bit—and only a bit—more oomph to the proceedings.

the rest:
A Walk across the Rooftops 🎵🎵🎵 (Linn/Virgin, 1983)
Peace at Last 🎵🎵 (Warner Bros., 1996)

influences:
◀◀ John Cale, Joni Mitchell

Joshua Zarov

Blue Öyster Cult

Formed 1970, in Stony Brook, NY.

Eric Bloom, vocals, "stun" guitar, keyboards, bass; Donald Roeser (a.k.a. Buck Dharma), guitar, keyboards, vocals, bass; Allen Lanier, guitar, keyboards (1970–84, 1987–present); Tommy Zvonchek, keyboards (1984–86); Joe Bouchard, bass, vocals (1970–86); Jon Rogers, bass, vocals (1992–97); Danny Miranda, bass, vocals (1997–present); Albert Bouchard, drums, synthesizer, vocals (1970–81, 1986–88); Rick Downey, drums (1981–84); Thommy Price, drums (1984–85); Jimmy Wilcox, drums (1985–86); Ron Riddle, drums (1989–92); Chuck Burgi, drums, vocals (1992–present).

This was the '70s heavy metal band that critics could respect. In fact, seminal rock critic Richard Meltzer co-wrote songs with the band, as did British fantasy author Michael Moorcock and Patti Smith, during her relationship with guitarist Allen Lanier. Initially featuring a three-guitar attack and black-humored satire, BOC—which grew out of the Long Island college-town band Soft White Underbelly—explored the supernatural, pondered mortality, and mocked the gullible in an odd combination of progressive rock, hippie concerns, camp, and down-and-dirty club rock. Incessant touring and its sinister, sardonic live presentation cemented BOC's reputation. Their increased musical sophistication paid off on the fifth album, *Agents of Fortune*, which went platinum partly on the strength of Buck Dharma's surprise hit, "Don't Fear the Reaper." Later, Lanier's "In Thee" (from *Mirrors*) became BOC's first ballad single; *Fire of Unknown Origin*'s similarly poppy "Burning for You" was a Top 40 single during 1981. The band's focus moved from heavy metal to progressive pop (with every member but Joe Bouchard dabbling with synthesizers), and after years of a steady lineup, declining commercial success (and perhaps tour burnout) led to an ongoing series of personnel shifts, with the Eric Bloom/Dharma frontline a constant and the other core members moving in and out. The long-promised concept album *Imaginos*, recorded over a six-year period, was finally realized but proved to be the band's final new Columbia album. The band existed fitfully during the early '90s, but publicity from the use of BOC hits in the Stephen King TV movie *The Stand* (see *Cult Classic*—the vocal-less "TV mix" tracks of "Don't Fear the Reaper" and "Godzilla" will delight the karaoke-inclined) and a revival of the "Black & Blue" tour with Black Sabbath

(the first one was in 1980) put BOC back on the radar screens of pop culture. In 1998 the group released its first album of new material in a decade.

what to buy: *Agents of Fortune* 🎵🎵🎵🎵 (Columbia, 1976, prod. Murray Krugman, Sandy Pearlman, David Lucas) is perhaps the most sophisticated metal album ever. "Don't Fear the Reaper" and "E.T.I." are the favorites, but every cut is good. This is also where Patti Smith's presence is strongest. *Spectres* 🎵🎵🎵🎵 (Columbia, 1976, prod. Murray Krugman, Sandy Pearlman, David Lucas, Blue Öyster Cult) is nearly as good musically and funnier lyrically, with the riotous one-two punch of "Godzilla" and "Golden Age of Leather" and the anthemic "R.U. Ready 2 Rock." *Workshop of the Telescopes* 🎵🎵🎵🎵 (Legacy, 1996, prod. various) is an exemplary two-CD compilation that supplements the obvious choices with rare items and cherry-picks the post-*Spectres* albums for their only worthwhile cuts.

what to buy next: The first three albums—*Blue Öyster Cult* 🎵🎵🎵 (Columbia, 1973, prod. Murray Krugman, Sandy Pearlman), *Tyranny & Mutation* 🎵🎵🎵 (Columbia, 1974, prod. Murray Krugman, Sandy Pearlman), and *Secret Treaties* 🎵🎵🎵 (Columbia, 1974, prod. Murray Krugman, Sandy Pearlman)—can be bought together in a slipcase for $25, a bargain for the group's hardest-rocking work. *Heaven Forbid* 🎵🎵🎵 (CMC International, 1998, prod. Buck Dharma) is a heartening comeback that shows the group's melodic knack and dark humor remain intact, with nods to speed metal working well.

what to avoid: *Career of Evil: The Metal Years* 🎵 (Columbia, 1990, prod. various) fails as a compilation because it picks and chooses from the wrong sources: each album that is represented you'll want to own in its entirety, and it ignores the later releases that, although you don't need all of any of them, nonetheless contain some gems. *Club Ninja* **woof!** (Columbia, 1986, prod. Sandy Pearlman) is uninspired by-the-numbers rock by a lineup that includes neither Albert Bouchard nor Allen Lanier and depends heavily on mediocre outside songwriting.

the rest:
On Your Feet or on Your Knees 🎵🎵 (Columbia, 1975)
Some Enchanted Evening 🎵🎵🎵 (Columbia, 1978)
Mirrors 🎵🎵 (Columbia, 1979)
Cultosaurus Erectus 🎵🎵 (Columbia, 1980)
Fire of Unknown Origin 🎵🎵🎵 (Columbia, 1981)
Extraterrestrial Live 🎵🎵 (Columbia, 1982)
Revolution by Night 🎵🎵🎵 (Columbia, 1983)
Imaginos 🎵🎵🎵 (Columbia, 1988)
Cult Classic 🎵🎵 (Herald, 1994)

worth searching for: Buck Dharma's out-of-print solo LP *Flat Out* (Portrait/Sony, 1982, prod. Donald Roeser) is predictably and welcomely guitar-oriented. Roeser/Dharma wrote himself a bunch of good songs too and closes with a surprising cover of the Fleetwoods' "Come Softly to Me."

influences:

◀◀ Led Zeppelin, Steppenwolf

▶▶ Judas Priest, Metallica, MInutemen/fIREHOSE, Def Leppard

Steve Holtje

Blue Rodeo

Formed 1984, in Toronto, Ontario, Canada.

Greg Keelor, vocals, guitar; Jim Cuddy, vocals, guitar; Bazil Donovan, bass; Kim Deschamps, pedal and lap steel (1991–present); Bob Wiseman, keyboards (1984–92); James Gray, keyboards (1992–present); Mark French, drums (1984–91); Glenn Milchem, drums (1991–present).

One of Canada's most successful bands, Blue Rodeo continues to develop its sound over the course of each new song. With its ragged rock 'n' roll sound that combines country, R&B, and '60s-inflected elements, Blue Rodeo has established a large and loyal following across Canada and in border cities in the U.S.

what to buy: The group's gritty, guitar-based debut album, *Outskirts* ♪♪♪♪ (Atlantic, 1987/Discovery, 1995, prod. Terry Brown) is a good place to start, with Beatles/Byrds–style harmonies and songs—"Try" and "Heart Like Mine"—that still sound fresh.

what to buy next: With *Casino* ♪♪♪♪ (Atlantic, 1991/Discovery, 1995, prod. Pete Anderson), the band's sound takes on more country touches, while *Five Days in July* ♪♪♪♪ (Discovery, 1993, prod. Blue Rodeo) marks the addition of Deschamps and a more acoustic approach.

the rest:

Diamond Mine ♪♪♪ (Atlantic, 1989/Discovery, 1995)
Lost Together ♪♪♪ (Atlantic, 1992/Discovery, 1995)
Nowhere to Here ♪♪♪ (Discovery, 1995)

influences:

◀◀ Tom Petty & the Heartbreakers, Neil Young

▶▶ Uncle Tupelo, the Jayhawks, Wilco, Son Volt, the Volebeats

Matthew Merta

The Blue Shadows

Formed 1990, in Vancouver, British Columbia, Canada. Disbanded 1995.

Billy Cowsill, vocals, rhythm guitar; Jeffrey Hatcher, vocals, lead guitar; Barry Muir, vocals, bass; J. B. Johnson, drums.

After a decade spent recovering from his stint as leader of

WHAT ALBUM CHANGED YOUR LIFE?

The Doors' first record was a huge influence on us, just because as good as the songs were, it was style. It was their style that was such a move. Very impressive.

Donald "Buck Dharma" Roeser (of Blue Öyster Cult)

America's self-proclaimed "First Family of Song," the Cowsills, big brother Bill found himself in Vancouver where, during 1979, he formed Canada's legendary Blue Northern band. Unfortunately, Blue Northern was so ahead of its time (the New Country genre had not yet come to be) that its only record slipped through the cracks without a trace. The experience dispirited Cowsill so deeply that he was about to seek refuge in Nashville's Songwriters Row. What stopped him was Jeffrey Hatcher, a native of Winnipeg, Manitoba, and a veteran of several renowned Canadian bands (Fuse, Jeffrey Hatcher & the Big Beat); he was highly regarded as a "walking pop and country songbook." Providing the perfect foil to Cowsill's somewhat gruffer world-weariness, the duo immediately began writing and performing together, forming the Blue Shadows soon afterward. As raucous and exuberant on stage as they were defiantly radio-ready on record, the band was poised to tackle the U.S. market head-on when, falling victim to the deadly Canadian Curse (too much roadwork/too little industry support), the group disbanded on Christmas Day, 1995. Cowsill, however, continues to be active with behind-the-scenes work in his adopted country, most recently recording with Canadian folk hero Murray McLaughlin.

what's available: Nominated for a Juno Award (the Canadian Grammy), the Blue Shadows' debut, *On the Floor of Heaven* ♪♪♪♪ (Sony Music Canada, 1993, prod. Jeffrey Hatcher, Billy Cowsill), has been perfectly described as "Hank Williams goes to the Cavern Club"; and the follow-up, *Lucky to Me* ♪♪♪♡ (Sony Music Canada, 1995, prod. Jeffrey Hatcher, Billy Cowsill), soundly expands on this innovative yet hummable Beatles-invade-Bradley's-Barn ethos.

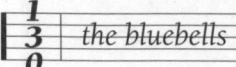
influences:

◀◀ The Everly Brothers, the Beatles, Foster & Lloyd

▶▶ Roy Furness, the Waltons, Ghost Rockets

see also: *The Cowsills*

Gary Pig Gold

The Bluebells

Formed 1982, in Glasgow, Scotland. Disbanded 1984.

Kenneth McCluskey, vocals, harmonica; Robert Hodgens, guitar, vocals; Russell Irvin, guitar (1982–83); Craig Gannon, guitar (1983–84); Lawrence Donegan, bass (1982–83); Neil Baldwin, bass (1983–84); David McCluskey, drums, vocals, guitar.

While much of the music world was revelling in new wave electronica, a small movement was quietly afoot in Scotland to move pop away from synthesizers and back to its guitar-driven roots. Like its Glaswegian compatriots Aztec Camera, the Bluebells crafted rustic, jangly music awash with tempting hooks and utterly wonderful melodies. Formed by songwriter and exfanzine publisher Robert Hodgens, the Bluebells made marvelous music and earned an impressive amount of support from the industry in a short time. (Among the group's producers and fans were Colin Fairley and Elvis Costello.) Although the Bluebells managed to place two singles ("I'm Falling" and "Young at Heart") in the U.K. Top 10 during 1984, the group disbanded soon afterward, leaving everyone to wonder what might have been.

what to buy: *Bluebells* ♫♫♫ (Sire, 1983, prod. various) is the masterful five-song EP that put the group on the map. Standouts among the pack are the lovely Scottish folk-rocker "Cath," the up-tempo "Everybody's Somebody's Fool," and the anthemic "Sugar Bridge." *Sisters* ♫♫♫ (London, 1984, prod. various) is the group's first full-length album. In addition to including three tracks from *Bluebells*, the album features seven new tracks, among the best of which is "I'm Falling (Down Again)." The songs interweave seamlessly in an appealing wash of chiming guitars, fiddles, and mandolin, spilling over with memorable hooks and infectious choruses.

what to buy next: *Second* ♫♫♫ (London, 1992, prod. various) gathers previously unreleased recordings for a convincingly cohesive "second" album.

influences:

◀◀ The Sutherland Brothers, Aztec Camera, Big Country

▶▶ The Pogues, the Drovers

Christopher Scapelliti

The Blues Brothers

Formed 1977, in New York, NY..

Jake Blues (a.k.a. John Belushi), vocals (1977–82); Elwood Blues (a.k.a. Dan Aykroyd), harmonica, vocals.

During *Saturday Night Live*'s heyday, pals and blues enthusiasts John Belushi and Dan Aykroyd came up with a revue-style act to perform on the show. Backed by authentic soul veterans (including Booker T. & the MG's alums Steve Cropper and Donald "Duck" Dunn), the two adopted dark-suited, sunglassed personas and performed enthusiastic (if not always accomplished) renditions of R&B classics. The Blues Brothers became a popular recurring segment of SNL and even toured behind its million-selling albums; during 1980, director John Landis turned the concept into a hit film. Belushi's death from a drug overdose in 1982 cemented the Blues Brothers as cult legends. During the '90s, Aykroyd resurrected his Elwood persona to promote his House of Blues nightclub chain, which spun off into a radio show and vanity record label. The film sequel, *Blues Brothers 2000*, with actors John Goodman and Joe Morton replacing Belushi on vocal duties, brought Aykroyd's genuine love of roots music into the spotlight once again.

what to buy: *The Definitive Collection* ♫♫♫♫ (Atlantic, 1992, prod. various) contains all the favorites, including their popular versions of Sam and Dave's "Soul Man," the Spencer Davis Group's "Gimme Some Lovin'," and the quirkier numbers sung by Aykroyd.

what to buy next: The soundtrack to the original film, *The Blues Brothers* ♫♫♫♫ (Atlantic, 1980, prod. Bob Tischler), is almost as much fun as the movie itself, featuring priceless numbers from James Brown, Ray Charles, and Aretha Franklin.

what to avoid: *Red, White & Blues* ♫♫ (Turnstyle, 1992, prod. various) features most of the grizzled veterans from Jake and Elwood's backing band, but the proceedings aren't much fun without the principals around.

the rest:
Briefcase Full of Blues ♫♫♫ (Atlantic, 1978)
Made in America ♫♫♫♫ (Atlantic, 1980)
The Best of the Blues Brothers ♫♫♫♫ (Atlantic, 1980)
Live from the House of Blues ♫♫♫ (House of Blues, 1997)
Blues Brothers 2000 (Soundtrack) ♫♫ (Atlantic, 1998)

influences:

◀◀ Ray Charles, James Brown, Sonny Boy Williamson, the Blues Project, Stax

▶▶ Blues Traveler, Treat Her Right

Todd Wicks

The Blues Magoos

Formed as the Trenchcoats, 1964, in Bronx, NY. Disbanded c. 1970.

Ralph Scala, vocals, keyboards; Ronnie Gilbert, bass; Emil "Peppy Castro" Theilhelm, guitar; John Finnegan, drums (1964–66); Dennis Lapore, guitar (1964–66); Mike Esposito, guitar (1966–69); Geoff Daking, drums (1966–69).

A group called the Blues Magoos that played while wearing electric suits that lit up? It *had* to be the '60s. But the Blues Magoos transcended its perceived gimmickery with a snarling spunk that made it a prevailing touchstone for fans of '60s garage punk. A one-hit wonder with the classic and furious "(We Ain't Got) Nothin' Yet," the Blues Magoos cut several worthy tracks of similar surly charm over the course of three LPs for Mercury from 1966 to 1968. A different lineup of Blues Magoos (including only Peppy Castro from the original group) did two subsequent albums for ABC before pulling the plug on the electric suits for good in 1970.

what to buy: The best of the Blues Magoos' Mercury output is collected on *Kaleidescopic Compendium: The Best of the Blues Magoos* 𝄞𝄞𝄞 (Mercury, 1992, prod. Bob Wyld, Art Polhemus, Rick Shorter). "(We Ain't Got) Nothin' Yet" is the obvious high point, but its original B-side, "Gotta Get Away," is nearly its equal in catchy, cantankerous rebelliousness. Meanwhile, "Love Seems Doomed" fulfills the essential hidden drug reference requirement, while the pre-Mercury track "So I'm Wrong and You Are Right" is a winner in the New Colony Six mold. And if some of the album tracks succumb to the self-conscious excesses of post-*Sgt. Pepper* giddy psychedelia, the wonderfully pop "One by One" and a cover of the Move's "I Can Hear the Grass Grow" balance things out agreeably.

influences:

◀◀ The Beatles, the Rolling Stones, the Lovin' Spoonful, the Pretty Things

▶▶ The Vanilla Fudge, the Chesterfield Kings, the Lyres

Carl Cafarelli

Blues Project

Formed 1965, in New York. Disbanded 1972.

Danny Kalb, guitar; Roy Blumenfeld, drums; Andy Kulberg, bass, flute (1965–67); Steve Katz, guitar, harmonica (1965–67); Tommy Flanders, vocals (1965–66, 1972); Al Kooper, keyboards, vocals (1965–67); Don Kretmar, bass, saxophone (1971–72); David Cohen, piano (1972); Bill Lussenden, guitar (1972).

"The Jewish Beatles," as this mid-'60s New York–based band was once dubbed by member Al Kooper, were more important and influential than its lack of sales success might first indicate. The Project was a transitional phase for many of its mem-

bers: Kooper and Katz went on to found Blood, Sweat & Tears, and Kooper became even more successful as a producer and solo artist; Kulberg and Blumenfeld headed for Seatrain. The members, individualists all, came up with a potent, sophisticated, East Coast blast of blues, folk, and rock with slightly jazzy overtones that fit the times. Flanders left early on; the rest toiled together for little more than two years and the project was over. Still, after Paul Butterfield and along with English bands like Cream, the group was instrumental in educating rock audiences back to blues—at the same time they were learning it themselves.

what to buy: For a single-disc retrospective, you can't beat *The Best of the Blues Project* 𝄞𝄞𝄞𝄞 (Rhino, 1989, prod. various), a 16-track overview that includes all the essentials—even "Flute Thing" in both its studio and live incarnations. For a more detailed look, try *Anthology* 𝄞𝄞𝄞𝄞 (Polydor, 1997, prod. various), which includes 36 tracks, including some rarities and outtakes from their albums.

what to buy next: *Projections* 𝄞𝄞𝄞 (Verve-Forecast, 1967, prod. Tom Wilson), the Blues Project's only real studio album, is still the best indication of the breadth of its eclectic talent, from the lilting jazz melody of "Flute Thing" (sampled by the Beastie Boys on *Ill Communications*) to their intense, 10-minute-plus kidnapping of Muddy Waters's "Two Trains Running."

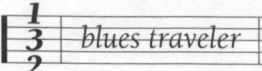
what to avoid: *Lazarus* **woof!** (Capitol, 1971, prod. Shel Talmy) was an uninspired attempt by Kalb, Blumenfeld, and Flanders to bring back the magic.

the rest:
Live at Town Hall 🎵🎵 (Verve Forecast, 1967/One Way, 1994)
Planned Obsolescence 🎵 (Verve Forecast, 1968/One Way, 1996)
Reunion in Central Park 🎵🎵🎵 (MCA, 1973/One Way, 1996)

worth searching for: *Live at the Cafe Au Go Go* (Verve Forecast, 1966), with Flanders on vocals, is a gritty document of their early blues/folk synthesis. Who else would have chosen "Catch the Wind" and "Violets of Dawn" in the same set as "Spoonful" and "Who Do You Love?"

influences:
◀◀ Muddy Waters, Willie Dixon, Chuck Berry, Bob Dylan, the Rolling Stones, the Beatles

▶▶ Blood, Sweat & Tears, Seatrain, Beastie Boys

see also: *The Paul Butterfield Blues Band, Blood, Sweat & Tears*

Leland Rucker

Blues Traveler

Formed 1985, in Princeton, N.J.

John Popper, vocals, harmonica, guitar; Chan Kinchla, guitar; Bobby Sheehan, bass; Brendan Hill, drums, percussion.

In a lesson learned from the Grateful Dead, Blues Traveler found that it was possible to sustain a musical career without the benefit of hit singles or huge album sales. Instead, they built an often fanatical following by touring relentlessly—their H.O.R.D.E. tour concept became one of the more successful Lollapalooza knockoffs—and stressing musicianship over songsmithery. Of the so-called "jam" bands that emerged in the early to mid-'90s, Blues Traveler led the pack in large part due to frontman John Popper, whose harmonica playing is distinctive and dexterous. Vocally, Popper makes up with moxie what he lacks in range, though his lyrics are often ponderous. Bassist Bobby Sheehan and drummer Brendan Hill provide a solid groove, while guitarist Chan Kinchla's lightning-fast runs complement Popper's harp nicely. The group eventually did hit the airwaves in 1995 with "Run-Around" from *Four*, but popular success altered their style not a whit.

what to buy: *Four* 🎵🎵🎵 (A&M, 1994, prod. Steve Thompson, Michael Barbiero) contains "Run-Around," which is easily the band's most memorable song, though it comes off like a bastard son of the Grateful Dead's "Uncle John's Band" and Bruce Springsteen's "Rosalita." The album also includes the punchy "Stand" and the self-effacing "Hook." *Blues Traveler*

🎵🎵🎵 (A&M, 1990, prod. Justin Niebank) includes the band's other signature song, "But Anyway," plus "Gina," "100 Years," and "Sweet Talking Hippie," which are among the band's live staples.

what to buy next: *Live from the Fall* 🎵🎵🎵 (A&M, 1996, prod. Dave Swanson, Rich Vink, Blues Traveler) is a two-disc concert recording that captures Blues Traveler in its element, stretching out their arrangements—several beyond the 15-minute mark—and showing off their often impressive chops. The set does act as a serviceable retrospective, even if, as with most live albums, you probably had to be there. Fans will cherish this; detractors will find it pointless.

the rest:
Travelers & Thieves 🎵🎵🎵 (A&M, 1991)
Save His Soul 🎵🎵🎵 (A&M, 1993)
Straight on Till Morning 🎵🎵🎵 (A&M, 1997)

influences:
◀◀ The Grateful Dead, David Peel, the Blues Brothers, the Allman Brothers Band

▶▶ Spin Doctors, Joan Osborne, Dave Matthews Band

Daniel Durchholz

The Bluetones

Formed 1994, in Hounslow, England.

Mark Morriss, vocals; Scott Morriss, bass; Adam Devlin, guitar; Eds Chesters, drums.

Lumped in with the Britpop wave that crested with Oasis, the Bluetones are a good deal more subtle and intimate than its more famous countrymen. Perhaps too subtle. The group's debut album went to #1 in the U.K., then was released in America in 1996, where it proceeded to tank commercially. The band has been unable to find a domestic deal for the follow-up, *Return to the Last Chance Saloon*.

what to buy: *Expecting to Fly* 🎵🎵🎵 (A&M, 1996, prod. Hugh Jones) is a terrific little slice of Rickenbacker-powered pop. Whereas Oasis swaggers and stomps, the Bluetones prefer to sway and soar. No attitude here—just glorious, chiming '60s-style pop that picks up where the Stone Roses left off.

influences:
◀◀ The Byrds, the Beatles, the Stone Roses

Greg Kot

Colin Blunstone

See: The Zombies

Blur

Formed 1989, in Colchester, England.

Damon Albarn, vocals; Graham Coxon, guitar; Alex James, bass; Dave Rowntree, drums.

Blur didn't make much of a mark when it first hit the London music scene. Trading under the name Seymour, the group of dropout art students played several small club dates before EMI picked them up on the strength of a demo. With an aesthetic name change came a push to cash in on the trendy dance-rock hybrid of the day. The group managed to turn out a few methodical hit singles but was largely written off as a pale imitator of the Stone Roses' and Happy Mondays' baggy sound. It took Blur two more albums and some serious soul-searching to find its own groove, and by the time it released its third disc, *Parklife*, the group won the hearts of the public and critics alike. Conjuring up the brash attitude and enthusiastic brevity of its childhood mod heroes, the group finally hit on a formula that suited it perfectly. Not only was the musicianship impressive, but lyricist Albarn revealed a remarkable knack for writing about the lives of the British middle class. Blur rapidly earned its place as one of England's top bands. As a testament to the group's looming celebrity, a full-on chart rivalry with Oasis erupted around the time of its fourth album, *The Great Escape*, and Blur sadly came out on the losing end. The public debacle was enough to make the band lose much of its momentum and reconsider its direction once again. For its self-titled fifth album, Blur tried its hand at American indie pop with disappointing results. The band, however, remains a potent force on the British music scene.

what to buy: It took Blur two albums before it hit its stride with *Parklife* 𝄞𝄞𝄞𝄞 (Food/SBK, 1994, prod. Stephen Street). Blending tight punk rhythms with catchy melodies and lyrics that championed London life, the group finally found its niche in songs such as "Girls & Boys," "End of the Century," and "London Loves."

what to buy next: Its follow-up, *The Great Escape* 𝄞𝄞𝄞 (Food/Virgin, 1995, prod. Stephen Street), held the stylistic ground of the previous disc, but ushered in more refined songwriting on exquisite tracks such "Country House" and "The Universal."

what to avoid: Although it features some pivotal songs from the Blur catalog ("Chemical World," "Oily Water"), the spiritless *Modern Life Is Rubbish* 𝄞 (Food/SBK, 1993, prod. Stephen Street) tracks the group's difficult transitional period between its baggy and mod phases.

the rest:
Leisure, (Food/SBK, 1991) 𝄞𝄞
Blur 𝄞𝄞 (Food/Virgin, 1997)

worth searching for: *Blur-ti-go* (Food/SBK, 1992) is a raucous live promotional EP that signals the group's move away from its dance-pop origins. It also includes the rare punk-fueled "Popscene" single. For further live antics, seek out the import-only *Live at the Budokan* (Food, 1995), an album recorded while the band was still flowing with confidence.

influences:
◀◀ Buzzcocks, the Kinks, XTC, the Stone Roses
▶▶ Elastica, Sleeper, Supergrass

Aidin Vaziri

The BMX Bandits

Formed 1985, in Scotland.

Duglas Stewart, vocals, guitar; Sean Dickson, bass (1985–89); Jim McCulloch, guitar (1985–89); Willie McArdle, drums (1985–87); Joe McAlinden, bass (1988–90); Francis McDonald, drums (1988–90); Norman Blake, guitar (1988–90); Gordon Keen, guitar (1989–92); Eugene Kelly, guitar (1990–92).

The BMX Bandits may not be a household name, but that shouldn't diminish the sheer historical impact of this Scottish pop troop. Think of the BMX Bandits (led by Duglas Stewart), as a glorified pop farm club where future stars learned the ways of pop from the Beach Boys to Big Star. The bands that have splintered off from the BMX Bandits include a literal who's who of Scottish pop—Teenage Fanclub, the Soup Dragons, Eugenius, and Superstar. In the beginning, this band was intended to be a one-off live act. What blossomed, however, was a long-lived pop band with a liberal membership criteria. At times, its records can be a rough listen: One second you're gliding through soft, textured pop tapestries, then suddenly you're dropped from that blissful cloud into a clammer of sound that is as frightening as it is intriguing. One large problem facing the BMX Bandits is the availability of its records in the U.S.—it wasn't until mid-1997 that Big Deal Records issued the 1996 Creation Records release *Theme Park*.

what's available: *Theme Park* 𝄞𝄞𝄞 (Big Deal, 1997, prod. Kim Fowley) is a departure from previous BMX Bandits records, more so for the production and arrangement of Kim Fowley than the actual songs. The simple pop-sounding songs are gone, as is the low-fi production. Sadly, the trade is not quite even: *Theme Park* sounds like Stewart handed over full control to Fowley, who in turn churned out a very happy sounding pop record unlike the previous—and better—BMX Bandits records.

worth searching for: During late 1997, the Elefant Records label in Spain released the BMX Bandits classic *C-86* (Elefant, 1997) with a bunch of great bonus tracks. Most of these recordings feature the talents of Teenage Fanclub's Norman Blake and

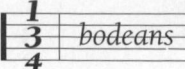
Francis McDonald. Effortless pop at its finest, raw but just enough sugar to make it pop.

influences:

◀◀ Alex Chilton, the Beach Boys, the Beatles

▶▶ Teenage Fanclub, Soup Dragons, the Cardigans

see also: *Teenage Fanclub*

Chris Richards

BoDeans

Formed 1985, in Waukesha, WI.

Kurt Neuman, guitar, vocals; Sam Llanas, guitar, vocals; Bob Griffin, bass; Guy Hoffman, drums (1985–89); Michael Ramos, keyboards (1989–95); Rafael "Danny" Gayol, drums (1991–93).

Hailing from the American heartland, BoDeans offered a fresh, straightforward, and slightly twangy brand of rock that was missing from the pop scene at the time. The combination of songcraft and beautiful harmonies led to instant critical acclaim for the debut album, *Love & Hope & Sex & Dreams*, but not an instant audience. Rather, BoDeans have slogged it out for a decade—trying various lineups, stylistic tweakings, and top-shelf producers—before the mass audience embraced "Closer to Free," a 1993 song that became a hit two years later as the theme for the Fox TV show *Party of Five*. Meanwhile, BoDeans could console themselves with the knowledge that they were a catalyst of the '90s explosion of American roots rock, an inspiration for bands like the Jayhawks, Uncle Tupelo, Wilco, Son Volt, and the Bottle Rockets.

what to buy: *Love & Hope & Sex & Dreams* 🎸🎸🎸 (Slash/Warner Bros., 1986, prod. T-Bone Burnett) starts off with a one-two-three punch of "She's a Runaway," "Fadeaway," and "Still the Night"—earthy, guitar-driven rockers that feel decidedly and distinctively American Midwestern. BoDeans' second album, *Outside Looking In* 🎸🎸🎸🎸 (Slash/Reprise, 1987, prod. Jerry Harrison), was even better, a lively sophomore effort with strong, vivid songs about hard-working characters and their high hopes for life ("Dreams") and romance ("Say about Love"). *Joe Dirt Car* 🎸🎸🎸🎸 (Slash/Reprise, 1995, prod. various) is a double-disc live retrospective that features most of the band's key tracks in performances that are mostly better than their studio counterparts.

what to buy next: *Go Slow Down* 🎸🎸🎸 (Slash/Reprise 1993, prod. T-Bone Burnett) takes a slightly more acoustic path. It has "Closer to Free," but the album's real highlight is the harmony laden "Idaho."

the rest:

Home 🎸🎸🎸 (Slash/Reprise, 1989)

Black and White 🎸🎸🎸 (Slash/Reprise, 1991)

Blend 🎸🎸🎸🎸 (Slash/Reprise, 1996)

worth searching for: *Live @ Tower 10/11/93* (Slash/Reprise, 1994, prod. Mark McGraw) is a promotion-only live recording that was a nice stop-gap until *Joe Dirt Car* came along. It still holds up as a strong representation of BoDeans in concert.

influences:

◀◀ The Band, the Byrds, the Everly Brothers, the Buffalo Springfield

▶▶ Big Head Todd & the Monsters, Freddy Jones Band, the Jayhawks, Uncle Tupelo, Wilco, Son Volt, the Bottle Rockets

John Nieman

Brigid Boden

Born in Dublin, Ireland.

Irish chanteuse Brigid Boden expertly merges two disparate sonic cultures—the traditional Irish folk aesthetic and the cyber intensity of the electronic age—into a cohesive and enrapturing new mileau. By mixing Celtic jigs and ballads with heavy doses of intoxicating electronic rhythm surge, she created with her first album a set of songs teeming with rhythmic swirls of mesmerizing sonic enchantment. Her bend of traditional Irish instruments such as fiddle, tin whistle, and uillean pipes with sweltering hip-hop beats, samples, and funk-laden dance grooves is simply brilliant and captivating.

what to buy: On *Brigid Boden* 🎸🎸🎸🎸 (A&M, 1996, prod. Kevin Armstrong) Boden's vocal mysticism wraps itself around you like a lilting sonic will-o-the-wisp the moment the needle drops on the futuro Irish folksong "Must Go On." "I'll Always Stay," a mournful lost love lament, is lyrically epic, the modern sonic coating making it a transcendental love song for all eternity. "Child on a Cloud" features hypnotic echo lilts that swim over symphonic strings and ethereal ambiance like a morning fog dancing above the oceanic waves. And "Paddy's Call" is a brilliant update of a traditional arrangement.

worth searching for: The 12-inch single "Must Go On" (A&M, 1996) features energetic remixes by William Orbit, D.J. Spen, and Kevin Armstrong, while the "Oh How I Cry" (A&M, 1996) 12-inch features remixes by Todd Terry and the Dust Brothers.

influences:

◀◀ Sinéad O'Connor, U2, Stereo MC's, the Chieftans

Spence D.

Body Count

Formed 1991, in Los Angeles, CA.

Ice-T, vocals; Ernie-C, guitars; Mooseman, bass; D-Roc, rhythm guitar; Beatmaster "V," drums.

Rapper and free-speech advocate Ice-T had what seemed like a brilliant idea: on his last good rap album, *O.G. (Original Gangster)*, he introduced a heavy-metal band on one raw but potentially cool song. Then he unveiled the band during the first Lollapalooza tour and quickly won over amphitheater crowds across the country. Body Count's self-titled debut is a terrific metal album because it's the sound of raucous, untrained enthusiasm instead of slick speed-metal or bland pop-metal. The quality of the music wasn't what sold records, however; shortly after its release, police groups began protesting the uncompromising attack on inner-city police brutality, "Cop Killer," saying it encouraged violence against officers. Ice-T spoke out against their protests, even landing on the cover of *Rolling Stone* in a police uniform. But he couldn't stop the massive backlash. A cornered Warner Bros. eventually re-released the album without the song and dropped Ice-T, who continues to record, act, and perform.

what to buy: The heavy metal on *Body Count* ♫♫♫ (Sire/Warner Bros., 1991, prod. Ice-T, Ernie C) is hardly as polished or intense as, say, Slayer or Pantera, with plodding drums and unimpressive guitar parts. But Ice-T is as flamboyant a frontman as any band could ever want, and he singlehandedly pushes the music from forgettable to attention-getting. Even now, when the Los Angeles riots are a distant memory, "Cop Killer"—included only on the original version of the CD—sounds both scary and exhilarating. Also notable are "Evil Dick" and a few songs that, much to the chagrin of those who defended Ice-T's right to speak out, disparage Tipper Gore and her family in a rather untoward way. Nobody can exaggerate to make a humorous point like Ice-T.

what to avoid: *Born Dead* ♫♫ (Virgin, 1994, prod. Ice-T, Ernie-C) is a flimsy album of bad metal and boring social commentary despite a slightly interesting version of "Hey Joe."

the rest:

Violent Demise: The Last Days ♫♫ (Virgin, 1997)

worth searching for: Though Ice-T gets only one cut, "Disorder," his collaboration with Slayer on the soundtrack to *Judgment Night* (Epic Soundtrax, 1993, prod. Happy Walters, Glen Brunman, Amanda Scheer), is the kind of thrash-metal Body Count strove to achieve. Other solid collaborations of rappers and metal/alternative bands include Pearl Jam and Cypress Hill doing "Real Thing," and Helmet and House of Pain with the memorably catchy "Just Another Victim."

influences:

◄◄ Slayer, Run-D.M.C., Public Enemy, Anthrax, Beastie Boys

►► Rage Against the Machine, Onyx, Bloodhound Gang, Pantera

Steve Knopper

The Body Lovers

See: Swans

The Bogmen

Formed 1990, in Huntington, Long Island, NY.

Billy Campion, vocals, guitar; Bill Ryan, guitar; Brendan Ryan, keyboards; PJ O'Connor, percussion; Mark Wike, bass; Clive Tucker, drums.

Had there been a boom box handy, Nero surely would've blasted the Bogmen while Rome burned. Certainly the band's gleeful perversity and skewered optimism would've made the Titanic a better boat ride. While the band has been gallantly forging a studio path from percussive giddiness to near-baroque ornateness, it is the live arena where the Bogmen dominate. Leading the crashing charge is Billy Campion, twitching, lurching, and nearly breaking his own neck thanks to an influence trinity of the Tasmanian Devil, Ethel Merman, and Keith Moon. Balanced by Bill Ryan's Charlie Watts–like detachment on the guitar, Campion is as captivating a frontman as you're likely to find.

what to buy: The price for fiddling while Rome burns is wandering around the debris afterwards, as the dark *Closed Caption Radio* ♫♫♫ (Arista, 1998, prod. the Bogmen, Bill Laswell, Godfrey Diamond) indicates. Dissonant verses give way to sonorous choruses before snapping, but the feelings of aftershock have permeated by that point. The core of the album—"Highway of Shame," "Mad Larry," and "Extended Family"—wails and croons, delivering stirring results.

what to buy next: The party before the apocalypse is in full swing on *Life Begins at 40 Million* ♫♫♫ (Arista, 1995, prod. Jerry Harrison), a galloping debut of hedonistic cowards, sex-crazed shrinks, and ulcerous drunks. Harrison's airtight production is a bit too tidy for the proceedings, however.

worth searching for: Though it only hints at the band's live power, the limited release *Bogmen Live* (Arista, 1997, prod. Jeff Young) offers some interesting non-album material, notably the Spanish-English "Salvation."

influences:

◄◄ Frank Zappa, the Replacements, Echo & the Bunnymen

Allan Orski

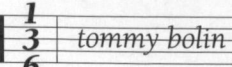

Tommy Bolin

Born Thomas Richard Bolin, August 1, 1951, in Sioux City, IA. Died December 4, 1976, in Miami, FL.

Tommy Bolin was a self-taught guitar hero whose crying, slashing signature slide sound didn't fit any of the stylistic molds of his day (or even the present day, for that matter). Throughout his career, Bolin managed to bounce between bluesy hard-rock riffing and intense jazz fusion à la John McLaughlin and Larry Coryell. A teenaged rebel who quit high school when ordered to cut his hair, he migrated to Colorado in 1968 and began his career with Zephyr. The group never caught on commercially despite several albums for ABC/Probe, but Bolin caught the attention of sometime-Boulder resident Joe Walsh, who recommended him to replace Domenic Troiano in Walsh's old group, the James Gang. Bolin gave the James Gang a second commercial life during 1973 and 1974 with the albums *Bang* and *Miami*; at the same time he played on jazz drummer Billy Cobham's ground-breaking 1973 album *Spectrum*. Though Bolin was frustrated as a backup player, he accepted another replacement job in 1975, when Ritchie Blackmore left Deep Purple. He wrote the majority of the songs on Deep Purple's 1975 album *Come Taste the Band* at the same time he was recording his solo debut, *Teaser*, a remarkably commercial funk-rock collection that showcased his sensual vocals, slinky, soul-based songwriting, and that ever-present, instantly identifiable guitar style. He juggled his two careers until Deep Purple broke up (for the first time), allowing Bolin to pursue his own music. Bolin released *Private Eye* in 1976, but he died of a drug overdose in a Miami hotel room after the first concert of what should have been a breakout tour, opening for Jeff Beck.

what to buy: *Teaser* 𝄢𝄢𝄢𝄢 (Nemperor, 1975, prod. Tommy Bolin, Lee Kiefer) and *Private Eyes* 𝄢𝄢𝄢𝄢 (Columbia, 1976, prod. Tommy Bolin, Dennis McKay) display Bolin's songwriting skill and instrumental chops at their peak.

what to buy next: Billy Cobham's *Spectrum* 𝄢𝄢𝄢 (Atlantic, 1973, prod. William E. Cobham Jr.) shows Bolin's dexterity at music more complex than hard rock. A box set, *The Ultimate . . .* 𝄢𝄢𝄢𝄢 (Geffen, 1989, prod. various) is a scattershot but ultimately fascinating overview of Bolin's music that includes wistful demos, rare tracks from Energy, and long out-of-print material by Zephyr. *Tommy Bolin: From the Archives, Volume 1* 𝄢𝄢𝄢 (Rhino, 1995, prod. Mike Drumm, Bob Ferbrache) gathers together more demos and alternate takes. It doesn't work as an album, but it's welcome manna for Bolin's cult of devotees.

the rest:
(With Zephyr) *Zephyr* 𝄢𝄢𝄢 (ABC/Probe 1970)
(With Zephyr) *Going Back to Colorado* 𝄢𝄢𝄢 (Warner Bros., 1971)

worth searching for: *Live*, a bootleg, has varying sound quality but includes two tracks recorded during a May 1976 concert that's still talked about in both Colorado music circles and among Bolin fans.

influences:

◀◀ Elvis Presley, Jimi Hendrix, Eric Clapton, Jeff Beck, David Bowie

▶▶ Eddie Van Halen, Stevie Ray Vaughan, Randy Rhodes, Mötley Crüe

see also: *Joe Walsh, Deep Purple*

Gil Asakawa

The Bolshoi

Formed 1984, in London, England. Disbanded 1988.

Trevor Tanner, vocals, guitar; Nick Chown, bass; Jan Kalicki, drums; Paul Clark, keyboards.

While not technically a one-hit wonder (it had two, "Away" and "Please"), the Bolshoi pounced on the British music scene with an interesting cover of Jimi Hendrix's "Crosstown Traffic" and a passel of dark, danceable new wave. Sadly, the group broke up in a hurry, and none of its members have resurfaced elsewhere.

what to buy: *Friends* 𝄢𝄢𝄢𝄢 (I.R.S./Beggars Banquet, 1986, prod. Mick Glossip, Andy Warwick) made a modest commercial impact thanks to the brooding dance hit "Away," which, sounding like a cross between vintage Cure and *Love* -era Cult, received airplay on college radio and MTV.

what to avoid: *Lindy's Party* 𝄢𝄢 (I.R.S./Beggars Banquet, 1987, prod. the Bolshoi) is an odd mix of even darker rock (listen to "Barrowlands") with a smattering of comical, novelty songs ("TV Man") that confused its fans.

influences:

◀◀ The Cure, the Cult, Bauhaus

▶▶ Stone Roses, Nirvana, Marilyn Manson

Tim Davis

Michael Bolton

Born Michael Bolotin, February 26, 1953, in New Haven, CT.

A screamer on the New England hard rock circuit for years, Michael Bolton split for Los Angeles to concentrate on songwriting and was churning out emotional hits for others before someone noticed he had a pretty stirring voice himself on those demo tapes. With long hair flowing and a strong chin, he became a middle-of-the-road matinee idol, a Fabio for former Barry Manilow fans. His over-the-top style (and penchant for remaking classic soul songs) earned him sneers from critics and swoons from his fans. He got kudos from Ray Charles and Otis

Redding's widow for his soul remakes, but the Isley Brothers successfully sued over the similarities between Bolton's 1991 hit "Love Is a Wonderful Thing" and one of their 1966 songs. In recent years, Bolton charted a hit from a Disney film, recorded an album of arias, and cut his hair. And even his charity came under press scrutiny in 1998 for allegedly not getting enough funds to the children it was designed to help.

what to buy: The essence of Bolton is almost too strong to take for a whole album, but *The Greatest Hits, 1985–1995* ♪♪♪ (Columbia, 1995, prod. various) covers the highlights, though the five new cuts don't compare to the proven hits.

what to buy next: *Soul Provider* ♪♪♪ (Columbia, 1989, prod. Peter Bunetta) finds Bolton at the height of his powers, before the arrogance and bombast became a problem. This includes his cover of "Georgia on My Mind" and his own "How Am I Supposed to Live without You?"

what to avoid: Accused of ripping off the past, Bolton decided to rub his critics' noses in an entire album of inferior cover tunes, *Timeless: The Classics* ♪ (Columbia, 1992, prod. David Foster). He even misspells the name of Four Tops frontman Levi Stubbs in the credits. Ouch.

the rest:
The Hunger ♪♪♪ (Columbia, 1987)
Time, Love and Tenderness ♪♪ (Columbia, 1991)
The One Thing ♪♪ (Columbia, 1993)
This Is the Time: The Christmas Album ♪♪ (Columbia, 1996)
All That Matters ♪♪♪ (Columbia, 1997)
My Secret Passion—The Arias ♪♪ (Sony Classical, 1998)

worth searching for: If you're a fan and want a taste of Bolton with more hair and less ego, try *Michael Bolton* (Columbia, 1983), his first, and worst-selling, album on the label.

influences:
◀◀ Percy Sledge, Otis Redding, Patti LaBelle, Al Jolson, Luciano Pavarotti

▶▶ Mariah Carey, Celine Dion

Roger Catlin

Bomb Bassetts
See: The Mr. T Experience

Bomb the Bass
Born Tim Simenon, 1968, in London, England.

In Britain's seething reaction to the late '80s death of the pop song came a certain wit and ambition not seen on the scene since the heydays of punk. Alas, those who knew more of the street spirits than of the industry loopholes were gaining some

chartworthy renegade promise, and without knowing it they provided a whole new outlook for expression to a generation tired of the chorus. Tim Simenon released "Beat Dis" in 1987, and with it came a certain ambient refinement to the brewing U.S. hip-hop influence. Broader strokes and deeper beats pilfered the best moments of dub, reggae, and rap, and combined them with atmospheric sampling to make music expressly meant for its time and, perhaps, for the future. It was a darker answer to the happy (acid) house of Britain's ecstatic club scene, and it spawned what was later to become the as yet undead trip-hop scene.

what to buy: The third BTB effort, *Clear* ♪♪♪♪ (Island, 1995, prod. Tim Simenon), marked Simenon's ascension into production genius (and industry wizard, as he launched his own imprint, Stoned Heights). The stark tone carried throughout is matched by a celebrity variety show of spoken word and vocal ruminations featuring, among others, Justin Warfield, Sinéad O'Connor, and famously miserable British author Will Self. Simenon went on to produce some of Depeche Mode's darker, later recordings.

the rest:
Into the Dragon ♪♪♪ (Island, 1988)
Unknown Territory ♪♪♪ (Island, 1991)

influences:

◀◀ M/A/R/R/S, Run-D.M.C., Al Green

▶▶ Massive Attack, Neneh Cherry, Portishead, Björk

Billy Manes

Bon Jovi
/Jon Bon Jovi

Formed 1983, in Sayreville, NJ.

Jon Bon Jovi (born John Francis Bongiovi Jr., March 2, 1962, in Sayreville, NJ), vocals, guitar; Richie Sambora, guitar, vocals; David Bryan, keyboards, vocals; Alec John Such, bass (1983–94); Tico Torres, drums; Dave Sabo, guitar, vocals (1983).

Formed in the rough-and-tumble heyday of New Jersey's bar band scene—in the same dives that gave us Bruce Springsteen and Southside Johnny & the Asbury Dukes—Bon Jovi won its record deal with PolyGram on the strength of a song called "Runaway," which turned into a regional hit after its inclusion on a radio station sampler of local music. Though the band enjoyed some initial success with its first two albums, the group really took off after Jon Bon Jovi—who picked up his pop smarts while sweeping floors at his cousin's New York recording studio, the legendary Power Station—enlisted gun-for-hire Desmond Child as a co-writer to help craft a hitmaking formula. Breaking big in 1986 on the strength of videogenic good looks and hit singles that perfectly captured the pop/metal market that ruled MTV then, Bon Jovi reached heights it would rarely scale again. By the late '80s, both Bon Jovi and Richie Sambora were itching to try solo projects, though the group survived and came back back together during the early and late '90s, creatively weaker but still a commercial force to be reckoned with around the world.

what to buy: Bon Jovi's triumphant, multi-million selling *Slippery When Wet* 🎵🎵🎵🎵 (Mercury, 1986, prod. Bruce Fairbairn) totally focuses the band's appeal into concise, innovative pop/metal nuggets that don't lose the palooka joyousness of a good "Joisey" Shore bar band. Hit singles such as "Wanted: Dead or Alive," "You Give Love a Bad Name," and "Livin' on a Prayer" defined the spirit of mid-'80s commercial metal.

what to buy next: The hits collection *Cross Road: 14 Classic Grooves* 🎵🎵🎵 (Mercury, 1994, prod. various) offers all of the best singles in one volume, skipping the pointless filler weighing down many of the original albums.

what to avoid: *7800 Fahrenheit* **woof!** (Mercury, 1985, prod. Lance Quinn) is simply lousy. Forgettable and formulaic, it gave little hint of the success that would shortly follow.

the rest:
Bon Jovi 🎵🎵🎵 (Mercury, 1984)
New Jersey 🎵🎵🎵 (Mercury, 1988)
Keep the Faith 🎵🎵🎵 (Jambco/Mercury, 1992)
These Days 🎵🎵🎵 (Jambco/Mercury, 1995)

worth searching for: *Most Requested* (Jambco/Mercury, prod. various) is a promotional sampler that rivals the publicly released hits set *Cross Road*.

solo outings:
Jon Bon Jovi:
Young Guns II: Blaze of Glory 🎵🎵🎵 (Mercury, 1990)
Destination Anywhere 🎵🎵🎵 (PolyGram, 1997)

Richie Sambora:
Stranger in This Town 🎵🎵🎵 (Jambco/Mercury, 1991)
Undiscovered Soul 🎵🎵 (Mercury, 1998)

David Bryan:
Netherworld 🎵🎵 (Moonstone, 1992)
On a Full Moon 🎵🎵 (Ignition, 1995)

influences:

◀◀ Aerosmith, Cheap Trick, Kiss, Bruce Springsteen, the Asbury Jukes, Alice Cooper

▶▶ Ratt, Poison, Winger, Warrant

Eric Deggans

Gary U.S. Bonds

Born Gary Anderson, June 6, 1939, in Jacksonville, FL.

Regardless of what Bruce Springsteen may think, it just may be that Gary U.S. Bonds is little more than a cipher, a singer with a gritty and soulful but ultimately unexceptional voice who happened to be in the right place at the right time—twice. Bonds's first 15 minutes of fame came thanks to producer Frank Guida, who put Anderson in front of a mic, multitracked his voice, and added a party ambience to songs such as "New Orleans," "Quarter to Three," and "School Is Out." His fame slipped away almost as fast as it came, and Bonds hit the oldies circuit, where Springsteen—who frequently performed "Quarter to Three" in concert—found him, got him a record deal, and co-produced a pair of albums for him. Except for brief appearances on albums by Springsteen cohort Steven Van Zandt, Bonds slipped into relative obscurity once again.

what to buy: *The Best of Gary U.S. Bonds* 🎵🎵🎵 (Rhino, 1990, prod. various) collects the hits from Bonds's early days. If you and your friends are mindful of rock 'n' roll's past, you couldn't ask for a better party tape. Confusing as it may be, another album called *The Best of Gary U.S. Bonds* 🎵🎵🎵 (EMI, 1996, prod. Bruce Springsteen, Miami Steve Van Zandt) completes

Jon Bon Jovi (© **Ken Settle**)

the story, collecting the cream from his latter-day period, including "Rendezvous," "This Little Girl," and "Out of Work," and padding it out with live versions of "Quarter to Three" and "New Orleans."

the rest:
Dedication ♫♫♫ (EMI America, 1981/Razor & Tie 1991)
On the Line ♫♫♫ (EMI America, 1982/Razor & Tie, 1992)
The Very Best Of ♫♫♫♪ (Varese Vintage, 1998)

influences:
◀◀ Fats Domino, Little Richard

▶▶ Bruce Springsteen, Southside Johnny, Peter Wolf

Daniel Durchholz

Bongwater

Formed 1985, in New York, NY. Disbanded 1992.

Mark Kramer, all instruments, vocals; Ann Magnuson, vocals; Dave Rick, guitar (1986–91); Randolph A. Hudson (1991–92); David Licht, drums.

When New York actress/celebutante Ann Magnuson stumbled upon ex–Butthole Surfer/record label guy Mark Kramer, it was to be an odd relationship indeed. Not only were the two immersed in the popular culture in their own rights—she starred with Richard Lewis on television's *Anything but Love* and carried Susan Siedelman's *Making Mr. Right,* he played with King Missile and Galaxie 500 in addition to running his label Shimmy Disc—they were also great interpreters of the rhythm and fodder of the fame-obsessed New York that surrounded them. Magnuson's after-the-fact summations of a world going by(e) bounced unwittingly over the cracked musical landscapes of Kramer's bumpy manifesto—all painfully quirky, but all sharp as a knife.

what to buy: *The Power of Pussy* ♫♫♫♫ (Shimmy Disc, 1991, prod. Kramer) pulled the real strengths of Magnuson as a lyricist. Here a notion of hope for the world through the cascades of laughter and tears seems to resound anew in the clunky, garagey noise of the band's grand collage. A very womanly album, *Pussy* dares to set its protagonist (Magnuson) equally against sincerity and kitsch in the search for true self, resulting in what must be the most fully realized 10 minutes of karmic speculation on records—with a Richard Gere reference, even—in "Folk Song."

what to buy next: Bongwater's debut, *Double Bummer* ♫♫♫♫ (Shimmy Disc, 1988, prod. Kramer), is an ambitious double disc, ripe with lucid rambling and a DIY rock slump. But it's clearly not as simple as that; Magnuson is a wizard of cultural therapy whose ground is composed of the talking heads of the glitter world. Like a long post-modern road trip, Kramer and

company run up, down, and off the FM dial with songs such as "David Bowie Wants Ideas" and the riveting "Dazed & Chinese" (yes, Led Zeppelin sung Chinese!). It's all delivered with a rabid lo-fi dissonance that would surely be annoying were it not so rich in its moment. *Too Much Sleep* ♫♫♫♫ (Shimmy Disc, 1990, prod. Kramer) surfaced with a similarly skewed bit of perspective-shifting, only with some sense of song structure rising in the place of the spin-haze mania of *Bummer.*

the rest:
The Big Sellout ♫♫♫ (Shimmy Disc, 1991)

solo outings:
Ann Magnuson:
The Luv Show ♫♫♫ (Geffen, 1996)

influences:
◀◀ Patti Smith, Iggy Pop, Parliament, the Carpenters, the B-52's

▶▶ Babe the Blue Ox, Ani DiFranco

Billy Manes

Bonham /Jason Bonham Band /Motherland

Formed 1988, in Los Angeles, CA.

Jason Bonham (born 1967 in England), drums, vocals; John Smithson, keyboards, bass; Ian Hatton, guitar (1989–94); Daniel MacMaster, vocals (1989–92); Marti Frederiksen, vocals (1994); Tony Catania, guitar (1995–present); Charles West, vocals (1995–present).

From the age of five, Jason Bonham was impressing audiences as a drummer. As the son of legendary Led Zeppelin sticksman John Bonham, little Jason was often awakened by his father to show off during late-night, post-gig parties and performed on a scaled-down kit in the Led Zeppelin movie *The Song Remains the Same.* By age 17, he had his own band, Air Race, and a major-label record deal. But Air Race and the early '80s metal band Virginia Wolf would just be learning experiences for Bonham, who spent time backing Zep guitarist Jimmy Page on his *Outrider* album and subsequent tour in 1988 before joining the three remaining members of Led Zeppelin for a show at Atlantic Records' 40th aniversary party (his dad, John, died in 1980, and the band called it quits soon after). By 1989, the drummer had a new, self-named band, Bonham, which released a gold record that year. Formed at the tail end of the '80s metal boom, Bonham hit on hard times following its early success, prompting the drummer to join Bad Company vocalist Paul Rodgers for a blues tribute record in 1993 before assembling Motherland with two ex-Bonham members a year later. By 1995, Jason had convened the Jason Bonham Band with Bonham bassist/keyboardist John Smithson and two new players, cashing in on his father's legacy first with a live record of Zeppelin cover tunes and then a 1997 album boasting samples of his dad's best-known drum grooves.

what to buy: Buoyed by some interesting playing from Bonham and the hit single "Wait for You," Bonham's debut album, *The Disregard of Timekeping* 𝄢𝄢𝄢 (WTG, 1989, prod. Bob Ezrin), surprises with its inventiveness and power. But the group's Achilles' heel—an undeniable tendency to sound way too much like Led Zeppelin—is already painfully evident.

what to buy next: Though the Led Zeppelin influences shine through from the first track, the Jason Bonham Band's *When You See the Sun* 𝄢𝄢𝄢 (MJJ Music/Sony/Work, 1997, prod. Marti Frederiksen) offers some appealing tunes and expert musicianship.

what to avoid: It probably sounded like a good idea at the time, but offering a collection of live Led Zeppelin covers on *In the Name of My Father* **woof!** (Sony/Work, 1997, prod. Jason Bonham) only serves to remind us what a cool album the soundtrack to Zeppelin's own concert film, *The Song Remains the Same*, actually was.

the rest:
(With Air Race) *Shaft of Light* 𝄢𝄢 (Atlantic, 1984)
(With Virginia Wolf) *Virginia Wolf* 𝄢𝄢 (Atlantic, 1986)
(With Virginia Wolf) *Push* 𝄢𝄢 (Atlantic, 1987)
(With Bonham) *Mad Hatter* 𝄢𝄢 (WTG, 1992)
(With Motherland) *Peace for Me* 𝄢𝄢 (Epic, 1994)

worth searching for: Some of Bonham's best playing has come on other people's records, including Page's *Outrider* (Geffen, 1988, prod. Jimmy Page) and Rodgers's *Muddy Water Blues: A Tribute to Muddy Waters* (Victory, 1993, prod. Billy Sherwood).

influences:
◄◄ Led Zeppelin, Jeff Beck Group, Def Leppard
►► Dream Theater, Soundgarden

Eric Deggans

Tracy Bonham

Born 1968, in Eugene, OR.

After Alanis Morissette turned modern-rock radio stations into playgrounds for angry young women, Tracy Bonham's catchy, introspective, and, indeed, angry song "Mother Mother" was the perfect beginning for a next wave. Surrounding her sharp voice with buzzing punk guitars, the Boston-based singer-songwriter writes more straightforward, catchy melodies than Morissette and does a better job of starting soft and cranking suddenly to a climax. Her lyrics are a little creepy—"That's the sound of your

brain cracking," goes one chorus, and she writes images about blood, man-eating sharks, death, and crooked necks—but she's convincing, even when she doesn't make any sense. A violinist by training (at the prestigious Berklee College of Music), Bonham played in the string section on the Robert Plant–Jimmy Page reunion tour before record company scouts discovered her performing at a nightclub. On her major-label debut, *The Burdens of Being Upright*, Bonham lampoons fly-by-night rockers in "One Hit Wonder"—but the criticism cuts a little close to home for an artist who has yet to prove her staying power.

what to buy: The highlight of *The Burdens of Being Upright* 𝄢𝄢𝄢 (Island, 1996, prod. Paul Kolderie, Sean Slade) is clearly "Mother Mother," a forceful, disturbingly honest punk-rock letter to mom ("I'm hungry, I'm dirty, I'm losing my mind. Everything's fine!"). A few songs, such as "Tell It to the Sky," have the same guitar-rock intensity and strong melodies, but Bonham's self-obsession and Nirvana-style soft-to-loud formula get old after a few songs.

the rest:
Trail of a Dust Devil N/A (Island, 1998)

worth searching for: Almost impossible to find, Bonham's pre-record deal EP, *Liverpool Sessions* (CherryDisc, 1995), hints at her upcoming style with the Boston-area hit "Dandelion," but it also includes bizarre ephemera such as "Big Foot," on which her grandfather warbles lyrics he made up on the spot.

influences:
◄◄ Led Zeppelin, Nirvana, Alanis Morissette, Jen Trynin, Janis Joplin

Steve Knopper

Karla Bonoff
/Bryndle

Born December 27, 1951, in Los Angeles, CA.

A singer-songwriter who came to prominence when Linda Ronstadt chose three of her songs to perform on the album *Hasten Down the Wind*, Karla Bonoff has had a solo career marked by consistently good material but precious little public acclaim. As a performer, Bonoff—who first hit the stage with the singer-songwriter collective Bryndle (which also included Kenny Edwards, Andrew Gold, and Wendy Waldman)—displays considerable charm and intellect, if not overpowering expressiveness. In other words, it's clear why her chief success has been as a songwriter. Still, her albums have their moments, and looking back on them now—particularly the first three—they recall a time during the late '70s when and an "El Lay" singer-songwriter was something to be. Songs from that first trio of albums were covered by Nicolette Larson, Bonnie Raitt, Maria Muldaur,

Kim Carnes, and Judy Collins, among others. In recent years, Bonoff has turned her eye toward Nashville; Wynonna scored a country smash with "Tell Me Why," and Bonoff has written for and performed on albums by Reba McEntire, Kathy Mattea, and Wynonna, among others. That makes perfect sense, given that Bonoff's brand of West Coast pop is what passes for Nashville country these days. What goes around comes around.

what to buy: *Karla Bonoff* ♫♫♫♫ (Columbia, 1977, prod. Kenny Edwards) reprises versions of the Ronstadt-covered "Someone to Lay Down Beside Me," "Lose Again," and "If He's Ever Near." But the surprise here is that, in taking those three, Ronstadt didn't exhaust Bonoff's supply of good songs; the album also features the lovely waltz "Home," the lightly rocking "I Can't Hold On," and "Isn't It Always Love," and the yearning "Falling Star."

what to buy next: *New World* ♫♫♫♫ (Gold Castle, 1988/Music-Masters, 1995, prod. Mark Goldenberg) predated the adult-contemporary format by enough to keep it from getting the attention it deserves. Goldenberg's too-rich production aside, the album contains Bonoff's best batch of songs since her debut, including "All My Life"—which Ronstadt and Aaron Neville turned into a Grammy-winning hit. Bryndle, which re-formed for some gigs in 1993, finally released an album, *Bryndle* ♫♫♫♫ (MusicMasters, 1995, prod. Josh Leo, Bryndle). Written in almost total collaboration, it sounds like the result of an old-fashioned guitar pull. All four members trade lead vocals and contribute honeyed harmonies.

what to avoid: *Restless Nights* ♫♫♫ (Columbia, 1979, prod. Kenny Edwards) is pleasant, but it's carried more by its two covers—the Searchers' "When You Walk in the Room" and the traditional "The Water Is Wide"—than by Bonoff's originals.

the rest:
Wild Heart of the Young ♫♫♫ (Columbia, 1982)

worth searching for: Bonoff performs "The Water Is Wide" on the soundtrack for the TV series *Thirtysomething* (Geffen, 1991, prod. various).

influences:
◀◀ Stone Poneys, Laura Nyro, Wendy Waldman

▶▶ Kathy Mattea, Wynonna, Trisha Yearwood

Daniel Durchholz

The Bonzo Dog Band

Formed 1965, in London, England. Disbanded 1971.

Vivian Stanshall, vocals, trumpet, ukelele; Neil Innes, vocals, guitar, keyboards; Roger Ruskin Spear, kazoos, Jew's harp (1965–70); Rodney Slater, saxophone (1965–70); Vernon Dudley Bohay-Nowell,

guitar (1965–68); "Legs" Larry Smith, drums (1965–70); Sam Spoons, percussion (1965–70); Dennis Cowan, bass (1968–71); Bubs White, guitar (1971); Andy Roberts, guitar, fiddle (1971); Dave Richards, bass (1971); Dick Parry, flute (1971); Hughie Flint, drums (1971).

The only other band to appear in a movie by the Beatles (they were in the nightclub scene in *Magical Mystery Tour*), the Bonzo Dog Band—originally the Bonzo Dog Doo Dah Band—mined a rare vein of humor in rock with a series of albums generally ignored beyond the British borders. The group, born out of art college, was about the size of an orchestra before it was honed to creative forces Vivian Stanshall, Neil Innes, and a band that included Roger Ruskin Spear and "Legs" Larry Smith. Originally formed to re-create big band, jazz, vaudeville, and '50s rock touches, the group eventually used conventional rock sounds in pursuit of its always amusing songs. Some were just one gag (an intro to "I Left My Heart in San Francisco," a cacophony of "A Sound of Music"), but there was also some extraordinary pop ("Ready Mades"). The band's humor had a direct influence on Monty Python, especially since Innes was called on for music (and eventually came up with the brilliant Beatle knockoffs for the Rutles). Stanshall's voice became best known as the narrator on Mike Oldfield's "Tubular Bells."

what to buy: *Urban Spaceman* ♫♫♫♫♫ (Liberty, 1968/One Way, 1993, prod. Apollo C. Vermouth—a.k.a. Paul McCartney) is the U.S. version, more or less, of the album known as *The Doughnut in Granny's Greenhouse*. It the group's funniest, most assured album, with a Top 5 U.K. single in the title track.

what to buy next: *Keynsham* (Liberty, 1970/One Way, 1993, prod. Neil Innes, Vivian Stanshall) is a concept album, sort of. It includes "Noises for the Leg."

what to avoid: *Let's Make up and Be Friendly* (Liberty, 1972/One Way, 1994) is a half-hearted attempt at a reunion, with just Stanshall and Innes returning from the original lineup.

the rest:
Gorilla ♫♫♫♫ (Liberty, 1967/One Way, 1993)
Tadpoles ♫♫♫♫ (Liberty, 1969/One Way, 1993)

worth searching for: *Best of the Bonzo Dog Band* (Rhino, 1990, prod. various) is a decent enough career overview, with a couple of examples of solo work.

influences:
◀◀ Spike Jones, the Beatles

▶▶ Monty Python, the Rutles, Weird Al Yankovic

see also: *The Rutles*

Roger Catlin

The Boo Radleys

Formed 1988, in Liverpool, England.

Martin Carr, guitar; Sice, vocals, guitar; Tim Brown, bass; Steve Hewitt, drums (1988–90); Rob Ceika, drums (1990–present).

The Boo Radleys debuted from the land of the Beatles with the totally obscure *Ichabod and I*, which was merely baby steps away from the brilliance the group would show on subsequent works. Led by rapidly developing writer Martin Carr, the Boos were not content to be kingpins on a scene that was sadly destined to lose favor in trend-conscious England; after signing to the more popular indie label Creation in the U.K., and a U.S. major, the group embraced a trancey dreampop that soon evolved into a more straightforward pop approach—the results were often brilliant records. Its 1995 release *Wake Up!* was its commercial breakthrough at home, though its newfound commercial success failed to translate into any kind of profile in the U.S.

what to buy: On the often brilliant and varied *Giant Steps* 🎵🎵🎵🎵 (Columbia, 1993, prod. Martin Carr, Tim Brown, Andy Wilkinson), the song "Lazarus" is the Boo Radleys at its lush and visionary best, with regal, blaring trumpets that have stopped listeners dead in their tracks ever since it was first released as a stand-alone single. Still challenging itself, the group went even more streamlined and helter-skelter with *Wake Up!* 🎵🎵🎵🎵 (Creation, 1995, prod. Boo Radleys) just in time to herald the forthcoming Britpop explosion with the smash U.K. hit "Wake up, Boo!"

what to buy next: Two of the group's three EPs on Rough Trade Records provide absolutely brilliant examples of the emerging "shoegaze" or "dreampop" scene. These EPs were compiled much later onto one CD (along with unreleased 1991 Peel session covers of New Order and Love) as *Learning to Walk* 🎵🎵🎵🎵 (Rough Trade U.K., 1995), and anyone who wants to hear this British post–My Bloody Valentine pop scene at its true zenith (even bettering the earliest works of Lush, Ride, Pale Saints, and Moose), must take in the blissful yet mesmerizing and powerful cascades of "The Finest Kiss," "Sometime Soon She Said," and the greatest track of the band's career, "Everybird." Wow.

the rest:
Everything's Alright Forever 🎵🎵🎵 (Creation/Columbia, 1992)
C'mon Kids 🎵🎵🎵 (Mercury, 1996)

worth searching for: The prescient *Ichabod and I* (Action U.K., 1990) boasts a lo-fi yet frantic sound and is now an expensive collector's item.

influences:
◀◀ The Beatles, My Bloody Valentine, Lush

Anna Glen and Jack Rabid

James Booker

Born December 17, 1939, in New Orleans, LA. Died November 8, 1983, in New Orleans, LA.

James Booker stood in for Huey "Piano" Smith on tour and Fats Domino in the studio, and the Clash covered his theme song, "Junco Partner," on *Sandinista!* There are many authorities who gladly testify to his amazing abilities, from Dr. John to Harry Connick Jr. In a city noted for great piano players, Booker was the greatest—if judged on sheer technique, not on hits or personal stability. Born into a musical family, Booker had an amazing musical memory and excelled at classical piano (giving recitals at age six), but he was seduced by boogie woogie. By the age of 11 he was playing regularly on a local radio station, and at 14 he cut his first single, "Doing the Hambone/Thinkin' about My Baby," for Imperial Records; it was produced by Rock and Roll Hall of Famer Dave Bartholomew, who gave Booker session work based on his ability to copy anybody's style instantly. But though he had a hit with his 1960 record "Gonzo," made singles for a variety of labels during the '50s and '60s (often under aliases), and was a sideman on records by everyone from Joe Tex, Bobby Bland, and Lloyd Price to Maria Muldaur, the Doobie Brothers, and Ringo Starr, Booker didn't record an album of his own until 1976, partly because he spent the mid-'60s in prison. He went through periods of drug abuse, though New Orleans guitarist Earl King backs up Booker's contention that he wasn't an addict; his metabolism allowed him to quit with no ill effects. After his prison stint, Booker did a little session work and then more or less retired. He reappeared in 1975 for a European package tour that garnered him recording offers. He played regularly in New Orleans thereafter, until his death.

what to buy: Every Booker album is great and precious and full of awe-inspiring keyboard feats, but *New Orleans Piano Wizard: Live!* 🎵🎵🎵🎵 (Rounder, 1981, prod. Bernard Henrion) wins top recommendation for the crucial repertoire it includes— "Come Rain or Come Shine," "Please Send Me Someone to Love," and especially his diametrically opposed favorites, "On the Sunny Side of the Street" and the heartfelt "Black Night." His vocals have a narrow stylistic range but are utterly appropriate. *Spiders on the Keys* 🎵🎵🎵🎵 (Rounder, 1993, prod. Scott Billington, John Parsons) draws on hours and hours of recordings at the Maple Leaf Bar to present a fascinating picture of Booker as strictly a pianist. His left hand is so strong that he makes even the Beatles' "Eleanor Rigby" totally *fonky*.

what to buy next: *Junco Partner* 🎵🎵🎵🎵 (Hannibal, 1976, prod. Joe Boyd, John Wood) was Booker's first released album and one of only three proper studio albums under his own name. It's crucial not only for "Black Minute Waltz" (showing his classical side), and a great "Junco Partner," but also for George Winston's liner notes, analyzing the pianistic and compositional particulars of each performance. *Classified* ✍✍✍ (Rounder, 1982, prod. Scott Billington, John Parsons) is the only album available in the U.S. on which Booker recorded with a band (which included saxophonist Alvin "Red" Tyler, long Booker's bandleader). The album's highlight is his tune "Classified," which Dr. John covered. For the feeling of an all-stops-out club date, *Resurrection of the Bayou Maharajah* ✍✍✍ (Rounder, 1993, prod. Scott Billington, John Parsons) can't be beat. The rowdy, rollicking set of Maple Leaf Bar performances (at 76+ minutes, it's the most generous in his catalog) has lots of vocal tunes, everything from "St. James Infirmary" to "Bony Maronie," and a total lack of inhibition or playing it safe.

worth searching for: A couple of albums on small indie labels fill in our picture of Booker prior to the Hannibal and Rounder albums. *The Lost Paramount Tapes* (DJM, 1995, prod. Daniel Moore, David Johnson) was recorded in 1973 and would have been Booker's first album if the tapes hadn't been lost. It's the only full-length album where Booker (on tack piano and adding organ overdubs) plays with a New Orleans band throughout, with such Crescent City luminaries as John Boudreaux, Richard "Didimus" Washington, Alvin "Shine" Robinson, Jessie Hill, and David Lastie. The rhythmic feel these players achieve is reason enough to track this CD down (reach DJM at 1-888-356-2583). *Gonzo: More Than All the 45's* (Night Train, 1996, prod. various) offers the only CD look at his early work, including his classic singles.

influences:

◀◀ Huey "Piano" Smith, Tuts Washington, Professor Longhair, Jelly Roll Morton, Frederic Chopin, Louis Moreau Gottschalk, Meade Lux Lewis

▶▶ Little Richard, Dr. John, Allen Toussaint, Henry Butler, George Winston

Steve Holtje

Booker T. & the MG's

Formed 1961, in Memphis, TN. Disbanded 1973. Reunited 1990.

Booker T. Jones, organ; Steve Cropper, guitar; Al Jackson Jr., drums; Lewis Steinberg, bass (1961–63); Donald "Duck" Dunn (1963–present); Willie Hall, drums (1975–77); James Gadson, drums (1994); Steve Potts, drums (1994).

This racially integrated quartet mapped out the instrumental blueprint of '60s Southern soul not only on deceptively simple ensemble instrumental sides, but as the house band at Stax/Volt recording studios. The four original musicians appear to interact instinctually, stitching together tight, intricate musical lines with evident ease. The band's 1962 Top 10 hit "Green Onions" put the small regional soul label on the nationwide map, setting the stage for a soul music uprising that echoes ever more resonantly through the years. At the core of this signature sound was the collaborative backbone of Booker T. & the MG's, whose members often ended up as part-writers of the many classics they created in the studio with giants such as Otis Redding ("Dock of the Bay") or Albert King ("Born Under a Bad Sign"). On their own, the band members sculpted a trademark sound—a churning, throbbing tidy knot of sound topped by Booker T. Jones's mellifluous organ and tacked together by Al Jackson Jr.'s left foot—a style they became comfortable and conversant enough with to stretch out considerably on later albums. In the wake of Stax's dissolution during the early '70s, the band also disintegrated. Jones moved to the West Coast and produced hit Willie Nelson albums. Steve Cropper and Duck Dunn joined the Blues Brothers. Al Jackson Jr., who carried on the tradition playing on Al Green recordings, was murdered in his home in 1975. The other three members began performing together again in 1990 and have appeared most notably as the house band at the Bob Dylan tribute at Madison Square Garden in 1992, backing Neil Young on a 1994 summer tour, and performing at the 1995 Rock and Roll Hall of Fame concert in Cleveland. But none of the MG's many latter-era accomplishments match the towering contributions of the Memphis recordings.

what to buy: The band's fourth album, *Hip Hug-Her* ✍✍✍✍ (Stax, 1967/Rhino, 1992 prod. Jim Stewart), brims with confidence and seamless instrumentals—from succulent originals such as the haunting title track, the rousing "Double or Nothing," and the cool "Slim Jenkins' Joint" to radically transformed covers like "Groovin'" and "Sunny."

what to buy next: The jazzy *Melting Pot* ✍✍✍ (Stax, 1983, prod. Booker T. & the MG's) and the tour-de-force instrumental rendering of the Beatles' *Abbey Road*, titled *McLemore Avenue* ✍✍✍ (Stax, 1971, prod. Booker T. & the MG's) (named after the street where the Stax studios were located in Memphis), capture the mature, confident band stretching its sound into new, rich realms.

what to avoid: The reincarnation's major label outing, *The Way It Should Be* ✍ (Columbia, 1994, prod. Booker T. Jones), suffers from over-directing by the Columbia A&R department and a palpable lack of spirit.

the rest:
Green Onions ✍✍✍ (Atlantic, 1962)
Soul Dressing ✍✍✍ (Atlantic, 1965)
And Now ✍✍✍ (Atlantic, 1966)
In the Christmas Spirit ✍✍✍ (Atlantic, 1966)
The Mar-Keys and Booker T. & the MG's: Back to Back ✍✍✍ (Atlantic, 1967)
Doin' Our Thing ✍✍✍ (Atlantic, 1968)

Soul Limbo 🎵🎵🎵 (Stax, 1968/1991)
The Best of Booker T. & the MG's 🎵🎵🎵 (Atlantic,1968/Rhino, 1989)
Booker T. Set 🎵🎵🎵 (Stax, 1969/1987)
The Best of Booker T. & the MG's 🎵🎵🎵🎵 (Stax, 1986)
Uptight 🎵🎵🎵 (Stax, 1991)

worth searching for: While the two volumes of the 1967 European tour by the Stax/Volt entourage—*The Stax/Volt Revue: Volume One—Live in London* (Atlantic, 1967, prod. Jim Stewart) and *The Stax/Volt Revue: Volume 2—Live in Paris* (Atlantic, 1967, prod. Jim Stewart)—capture Booker T. & the MG's serving as the protean house band for the Memphis soul caravan, *The Complete Stax/Volt Singles 1959–1968* (Atlantic, 1991, prod. various) is really nothing more than a nine-disc tribute to the greatest soul accompanists of all time.

influences:

◀◀ The Mar-Keys, Cannonball Adderley

▶▶ Creedence Clearwater Revival, Elvis Costello & the Attractions

see also: *The Blues Brothers*

Joel Selvin

Boom Crash Opera

Formed 1985, in Melbourne, Australia.

Peter Farnan, guitar, vocals; Dale Ryder, lead vocals, harmonica; Peter Maslen, drums, vocals; Greg O'Connor, keyboards; Richard Pleasance, guitar, bass, vocals (1985–92); Ian Tilley, bass (1992–present).

Formed at the peak of Northern Hemisphere interest in Australian rock, Boom Crash Opera embodied all the strengths of the antipodean sound: an artful accessibility that was equal parts British new wave quirkiness and American rock muscle. Like many fellow Aussies of the same generation—Midnight Oil, INXS, the Models, Spy vs. Spy, and Hunters & Collectors among them—BCO coupled a commanding lead singer with a propulsive, tight-as-cling-wrap rhythm section, snaky guitar, and a sharp sense of heads-down, no-nonsense pop. It was the sweaty sound of the Australian pubs, hard and loud enough to keep 2,000 beer-addled brains awake, yet it was all hooky enough to sing along with. The group's chanted war-cry choruses—best heard on its 1987 album *Boom Crash Opera* and 1989's *These Here Are Crazy Times*—and poster-boy alt-rock good looks made it an immediate hit in Australia. Such tracks as "Great Wall," "Hands up in the Air," "Onion Skin," "Get Out of the House," "Best Thing," and "Dancing in the Storm" were all Top 20 at home, though success in the U.S. and U.K. didn't follow. After co-writer Richard Pleasance was forced to quit due to severe tinnitus, BCO jumped on the industrial bandwagon in

1995, which only hastened the decline of its already waning popularity.

worth searching for: A remix disc of early hits, *Look! Listen!* (Ariola Australia, 1994, prod. various) distills everything that made BCO fun—Dale Ryder's snarl, the rhythm section's pummeling beat, and the group's bright, shiny, stainless-steel choruses—into one indispensable package. The first two albums, *Boom Crash Opera* (Warner Bros., 1987, prod. Alex Sadkin) and *These Here Are Crazy Times* (Giant, 1989, prod. Pete Smith, Richard Pleasance), now out of print, are less consistent but certainly have their moments.

influences:

◀◀ David Bowie, INXS, the Models

Cary Darling

The Boomtown Rats /Bob Geldof

Formed 1975, in Dun Laoghaire, Ireland. Disbanded 1986.

Bob Geldof (born October 5, 1954 in Dublin, Ireland) vocals; Johnny Fingers, keyboards; Pete Briquette, bass; Simon Crowe, drums; Gerry Cott, guitar (1975–81); Garry Roberts, guitar.

Bob Geldof made his name more for his humanitarian efforts—organizing the Live Aid concerts and the all-star "Do They Know It's Christmas" single—than for his nasal delivery and outspoken lyrics. With a Nobel Peace Prize nomination in the late '80s, Geldof seemed light years from "I Don't Like Mondays," the Rats' biggest U.S. hit. A spare, piano-based single concerning a murder spree, even that song was uncharacteristic of the Rats' sound, which drew on more conventional sources than punk and new wave. Much of their music rose and fell on the weight of Geldof's charisma as a frontman. At their best—on songs like "Rat Trap," "Looking After Number One," and yes, "I Don't Like Mondays"—they were terrific. Unfortunately, those moments came too few and far-between for the Rats to parlay their U.K. success into stardom in America. Geldof's solo career has been similarly disappointing.

what to buy: *Great Songs of Indifference* 🎵🎵🎵🎵 (Legacy, 1997, prod. various) compiles the best of the Rats' material, including the abovementioned songs plus the engaging "Mary of the Fourth Form" and "She's So Modern," as well as some of Geldof's solo work, including the anthemic "This Is the World Calling."

worth searching for: All of the band's individual albums, as well as Geldof's solo albums, are out of print. The best of the lot is *A Tonic for the Troops* (Columbia, 1978). As for Geldof's solo work, check out *Deep in the Heart of Nowhere* (Atlantic, 1986).

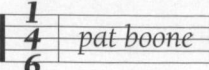
influences:

◀◀ Van Morrison, Bruce Springsteen, Mott the Hoople, Dr. Feelgood

▶▶ USA for Africa

Allan Orski and Daniel Durchholz

Pat Boone

Born Charles Eugene Boone, June 1, 1934, in Jacksonville, FL.

Though he's now known best for his gospel albums and for supporting conservative politicians, Pat Boone was once nearly crowned the king of rock 'n' roll—with more pop hits during the late '50s and early '60s than any artist save Elvis Presley. Raised in rural Tennessee, Boone parlayed an appearance on the *Ted Mack Amateur Hour* television show into a year-long stint on Arthur Godfrey's amateur show and a recording contract. Boone enjoyed a few pop hits with songs such as "Two Hearts, Two Kisses" in 1955, but it wasn't until he began recording sanitized, de-ethnicized versions of R&B and rock hits—including Little Richard's "Tutti Frutti" and "Long Tall Sally"—that Boone's place in history was assured. With his crewcut and white buckskin shoes, Boone was the bridge between early rock 'n' roll "race records" and the white pop mainstream, covering tunes by Fats Domino, Ivory Joe Hunter, and others. Beatlemania eventually made his efforts irrelevant, but not before Boone had moved on to his own television show and movie soundtrack work. In all, Boone enjoyed 38 chart topping hits. In 1996, however, he began preparing an ill-advised album of heavy metal covers, *In a Metal Mood*, while also working the infomercial circuit, proving himself an opportunist of the highest caliber.

what to buy: Most of what's available are retrospectives, holiday collections, and Christian recordings. Many—though not all—of the hits are on *Pat Boone's Greatest Hits* 𝄢𝄢𝄢 (MCA, 1993, prod. various). With another compilation, *Greatest Hits* 𝄢𝄢𝄢 (Curb, 1990, prod. various), you'll have a fairly representative set of Boone's music. If you want it.

what to buy next: For a unique perspective on Boone's rock career, check out the readily available import *Jivin' Pat* 𝄢𝄢𝄢 (Bear Family, 1986, prod. various), a collection of his early rock cover tunes.

what to avoid: An ill-conceived joke that nearly cost him his Christian music career, *In a Metal Mood: No More Mr. Nice Guy* **woof!** (Hip-O, 1997) features lame-o big band versions of well-known metal tunes such as "Smoke on the Water" and "Panama."

the rest:
Pat Boone 𝄢𝄢 (Dot, 1956)
Best of Pat Boone: April Love 𝄢𝄢 (Dot, 1957)

White Christmas 𝄢𝄢𝄢 (MCA, 1959)
Best of Pat Boone: Love Letters in the Sand 𝄢𝄢 (Laserlight, 1974)
Merry Christmas 𝄢 (Delta, 1992)
Family Christmas 𝄢𝄢𝄢 (Laserlight, 1995)
Greatest Hymns 𝄢𝄢 (Curb, 1995)
Pat Boone 𝄢𝄢 (Eclipse, 1996)

worth searching for: If the thought of watching Boone in his white buckskins while awkwardly warbling through cuts such as "Tutti Frutti" seems like a hoot, there's always the video anthology of his chart successes, *40 Years of Hits* (Rhino, 1995).

influences:

◀◀ Fats Domino, Frank Sinatra, Red Foley

▶▶ Harry Connick Jr., Debby Boone, Barry Manilow

Eric Deggans

Boss Hog

Formed 1989, in New York, NY.

Jon Spencer, guitar; Christina Martinez, vocals; Jens Jurgensen, bass (1991–present); Hollis Queens, drums (1991–present); Kurt Wolf, bass (1989–91); Jerry Teel, guitars (1989–91); Charlie Ondras, guitars (1989–91).

After the demise of his other band, Pussy Galore, Jon Spencer formed Boss Hog in 1989 on the spur of the moment to fill a vacant slot at iconoclastic punk venue CBGB's in New York. Boss Hog captured the same sort of loose energy that characterized Pussy Galore, not surprising since Spencer and wife-to-be Christina Martinez played together in that band. During that first show, the beautiful lead vocalist Martinez performed the entire set in the nude and, subsequently, the band's next two album covers featured her in the buff as well. Boss Hog—which took its name not from the sheriff on *The Dukes of Hazard* but from an underground biker magazine—continues to be a side band indulgence for Spencer when he's not fronting his three-man Jon Spencer Blues Explosion.

what to buy: Initially released as a cassette and vinyl-only EP, *Drinkin', Lechin' & Lyin'* 𝄢𝄢𝄢 (Amphetamine Reptile Records, 1989, prod. Steve Albini) features a raucous sound by the "Boss Hog All-Stars" that isn't unlike Pussy Galore. But it was on the group's full-length album, *Girl +* 𝄢𝄢𝄢𝄢 (Amphetamine Reptile Records, 1993, prod. Boss Hog), that the group nailed its own identity. A borderline glam-band, Boss Hog forged the R&B and funk-influenced aesthetic that Spencer fully realized with his own band.

what to avoid: *Boss Hog* 𝄢𝄢 (DGC, 1995, prod. Jonathan Spencer, Steve Fisk) was the group's major label debut and, for whatever reason, the band just didn't sound like a cohesive unit, playing noisy and rambunctious songs that carried little weight.

the rest:
Cold Hands ♫♫ (Amphetamine Reptile Records, 1990)

influences:
◀◀ Pussy Galore, Honeymoon Killers

▶▶ Jon Spencer Blues Explosion

see also: *Jon Spencer Blues Explosion*

Joseph Patel

Boston

Formed 1971, in Boston, MA.

Tom Scholz, guitars, keyboards; Brad Delp, vocals, guitar; Barry Goudreau, guitar (1975–early '80s); Fran Sheehan, bass (1975–early '80s); John "Sib" Hashian, drums (1975–early '80s); Gary Pihl, guitar (1985–present); David Sykes, vocals, guitar (1992–present).

While critics and fans have poked fun at Boston leader Tom Scholz's legendary finicky behavior—some called the eight-year delay between the group's second and third records "the other Boston Marathon"—there's no doubt it gets results. A graduate of Massachusetts Institute of Technology who worked by day as an engineer for Polaroid, Scholz spent years cobbling together a series of demos on his basement 12-track recorder that eventually snagged a deal with Epic Records. With a few additional parts added here and there, those demos became the group's multi-platinum debut album, recently certified as one of the best-selling rock records of all time. Based on the twin towers of Brad Delp's high, powerful vocals and Scholz's wall of guitars and harmonized lead passages, Boston's signature sound struck a chord with fans. All its records have featured this formula, and nearly all have sold in multi-platinum numbers. The only problem, it seems, is Scholz's perfectionism, which has made it hard to keep a regular group of musicians together (not that they contribute significantly to the albums, anyway). Sony Music, Epic's parent company, sued Scholz for breach of contract; Scholz won the suit and continues to put out albums—for another label, mind you—whenever he's satisfied he has something good enough to release. Meanwhile, he concentrates on social action projects and on developing musical equipment; his Rockman personal amplifier is one of the best-selling rock toys of all time. More recently he began taking figure skating lessons, though the U.S. Olympic Committee hasn't sent out any feelers.

what to buy: The Scholz formula sounds freshest on the debut, *Boston* ♫♫♫ (Epic, 1976, prod. John Boylan, Tom Scholz). Bouncy, slick tracks such as "More than a Feeling" and "Peace of Mind" defined new parameters for rock radio during the '70s, with soaring vocals, searing guitars, and trite lyrics.

what to buy next: *Greatest Hits* ♫♫♫ (Epic, 1997, prod. Tom Scholz) is a good way to pick up the best of the rest, along with the unintenionally hilarious version of "The Star Spangled Banner."

what to avoid: *Walk On* ♫ (MCA, 1994, prod. Tom Scholz), the first Boston album devoid of Delp's bionic yelping, sounds like absolutely irrelevant '90s post-punk.

the rest:
Don't Look Back ♫♫ (Epic, 1978)
Third Stage ♫♫ (MCA, 1986)

worth searching for: *We Found It in the Trashcan, Honest!* (Ruthless Rhymes, 1977), a bootleg of some of Scholz's demos, with slightly different lyrics and a rawer sound than the Teflon perfection of the *Boston* album.

solo outings:
Barry Goudreau:
Barry Gourdreau ♫♫ (Razor & Tie, 1980)

Orion the Hunter (Goudreau and Delp):
Orion the Hunter ♫♫♫ (Portrait, 1984)

RTZ (Delp and Goudreau):
Return to Zero ♫♫♫ (Giant, 1991)

influences:
◀◀ Led Zeppelin, the Beatles, Yes

▶▶ Foreigner, Survivor, Night Ranger

Eric Deggans

The Bottle Rockets

Formed 1993, in Festus, MO.

Brian Henneman, guitar, vocals; Tom Parr, guitar, vocals; Mark Ortmann, drums; Tom Ray, bass (1993–97).

Like Ronnie Van Zandt and Lynyrd Skynyrd before them, guitarist/vocalist Brian Henneman and the Bottle Rockets are not the unreconstructed hawbucks they seem at first glance. Henneman's songs, which are populated with hot-to-trot trailer mamas and Confederate-flag-waving idiots, convey a deeply conflicted sense of small town values, offering alternate celebrations and condemnations of redneck culture. After a stint as guitar tech and occasional second guitarist with alt.country compadres Uncle Tupelo, Henneman scored a solo deal with independent label East Side Digital. Instead of going solo, he decided he'd prefer to do a band album and signed up guitarist Tom Parr, drummer Mark Ortmann, and bassist Tom Ray (the former two from Henneman's previous outfit, Chicken Truck). In a rare instance of a rock 'n' roll band being too smart for its own good, the Bottle Rockets' versatility and insight have been at odds with their image and demeanor, and the disparity may

Tom Scholz of Boston (© Ken Settle)

have hurt them in terms of winning over the large audience they deserve. On the one hand, some of their songs are wise and incisive, likely alienating the bar-band fans who just want to hoist a few without having to think too much. On the other, the band members are unkempt and rowdy—imagine Hank Williams Jr. if he weren't an asshole—which is too far over the top for the alt.country fans who'll take their tunes sad 'n' mournful, and hold that can of whup-ass, please. Then too there have been label problems. ESD went belly-up; they signed with Tag/Atlantic, a division that shut down just as their second album, *The Brooklyn Side*, was being issued. And Atlantic proper has since failed to get behind their third record. Hopefully they'll soldier on until they get a proper hearing.

what to buy: The band's vision of America via its blue highways and backroads comes fully formed on its debut, *The Bottle Rockets* ♫♫♫ (East Side Digital, 1993, prod. John Keane), which ranges from lusty low humor ("Gas Girl," "Every Kinda Everything") to high drama ("Kerosene," in which a family dies in a senseless trailer fire). There's also the smart, mournful "Got What I Wanted" and "Wave That Flag," which takes the piss out of four-wheelin' faux rebels. Altogether enough material for a season's worth of Jerry Springer shows.

what to buy next: *The Brooklyn Side* ♫♫♫ (East Side Digital, 1994/Tag Atlantic, 1995 prod. Eric "Roscoe" Ambel) continues in the same vein, imparting social justice ("Welfare Music"), folk wisdom ("1000 Dollar Car"), and genuine desperation ("Sunday Sports"), but adding a radio ready pop sheen to songs such as "I'll Be Comin' Around" and "Gravity Fails." *24 Hours a Day* ♫♫♫ (Atlantic, 1997, prod. Eric "Roscoe" Ambel) is another fine set, sporting the uproarious road tale "Indianapolis" and the pensive "Smokin' 100's Alone."

influences:
◀◀ Lynyrd Skynyrd, ZZ Top, John Anderson, Neil Young, Aerosmith

Daniel Durchholz

The Bouncing Souls

Formed 1988, in New Brunswick, NJ.

Greg Attonito, vocals; Pete Steinkopf, guitar; Bryan "Papillon" Kienlen, bass; Shal Khichi, drums.

The New Jersey punk quartet the Bouncing Souls rose to national fame in the punk underground during the mid-'90s by playing more than 200 all-ages shows a year all over North America, becoming the unofficial "most touring band in punk rock." The Souls first met while students at Ridge High School in New Brunswick, New Jersey, during the late '80s. After graduation they moved in together at 174 Commercial Ave., where they hosted numerous house parties, honing their live show. Through their own Chunksaah Records label, the Souls released several limited-edition 7-inches during the late '80s and early '90s, prompting attention from Nevada's BYO Records (7 Seconds, Hepcat). Following the release of their BYO debut, *The Good, the Bad, and the Argyle*, the Bouncing Souls began touring constantly, playing houses, rented halls, and small clubs up and down the East Coast, and later, throughout the U.S. and Canada. Vaguely Anglophilic, often juvenile and obsessed with '80s teen movies, forgotten new wave hits, BMX biking, argyle patterns, and hatred of MTV, the Bouncing Souls became one of the top punk bands of the '90s with the release of 1996's acclaimed *Maniacal Laughter*, also on BYO. A deal with West Coast punk giant Epitaph Records followed.

what to buy: *Maniacal Laughter* ♫♫♫ (BYO, 1996, prod. Thom Wilson) clocks in at less than two minutes per song but rocks hard from start to finish. Highlights include the skinhead singalongs "Lamar Vannoy" and "Here We Go," the punk rock love song "Quick Check Girl," and the passionate "Ballad of Johnny X." One of the classics of the '90s East Coast punk scene.

what to buy next: *The Good, the Bad, and the Argyle* ♫♫♫ (BYO, 1994, prod. Bouncing Souls) is more uneven than *Maniacal Laughter*, but contains a few classic Souls tunes such as "Neurotic," "Joe Lies," "These Are the Quotes from Our Favorite '80s Movies," and the immortal "I Like Your Mom" ("I like your mom and it's no fad/I wanna marry her and be your dad").

what to avoid: The Souls' latest album, *Bouncing Souls* ♫♫ (Epitaph, 1997, prod. Thom Wilson), is a let-down to long-time fans, but its often chaotic, near-hardcore approach might appeal to aficionados of bands such as Pennywise.

influences:
◀◀ The Clash

Seth Hindin

Jean-Paul Bourelly

Born November 23, 1960, in Chicago, IL.

Jazz fans know guitarist Jean-Paul Bourelly for his work on albums by Miles Davis, McCoy Tyner, Elvin Jones, Muhal Richard Abrams, and Cassandra Wilson, while R&B/hip-hop fans have heard him on records by Jody Watley, DJ Jazzy Jeff & the Fresh Prince, Bel Biv DeVoe, and Charles & Eddie. He has combined the influences of a number of greats, including rockers Jimmy Page, Jimi Hendrix, and Frank Zappa, to invent his own distinctive, uniquely rich guitar sound. Mixing jazz, blues, and rock playing and his gruffly soulful vocals with funk and hip-hop rhythms, often with his group Blue Wave Bandits, he builds dense, complex music he calls "New Breed Funk Jazz." Bassists

Melvin Gibbs (Rollins Band), Darryl Jones (Rolling Stones), and Me'shell N'degéocello all passed through his groups prior to their more famous gigs, and "Kundalini" Mark Batson of the hip-hop group Get Set VOP plays Sly Stone–esque keyboards and sometimes raps for Bourelly's Blue Wave Bandits.

what to buy: *Saints & Sinners* &&&& (DIW, 1993, prod. Jean-Paul Bourelly, Kazunori Sugiyama) distills the core of his stylistic fusion on "Got to Be Able to Know" and "Rumble in the Jungle," while "Muddy Waters (Blues for Muddy)" is a slow, simmering update of the blues. Many tracks, especially "Skin I'm In," show his matter-of-fact socio-political/racial consciousness without being preachy.

what to buy next: *Trippin'* &&&& (Enemy, 1991, prod. Jean-Paul Bourelly) features some of Bourelly's best guitar playing, focusing on his integration of lead and rhythm, and some of his tighter material. The lush, intensely lovely instrumental rave-up "Love Crime" is especially memorable.

the rest:
Blackadelic-Blu &&& (DIW, 1994)
Tribute to Jimi &&& (DIW, 1995)
Fade to Cacophony: Live! &&&& (DIW, 1995/Evidence, 1997)

worth searching for: Bourelly's debut as a leader, *Jungle Cowboy* (JMT, 1987, prod. Stefan Winter, Jean-Paul Bourelly), is his best album and definitely the easiest way in for the uninitiated. It predates Bourelly's incorporation of hip-hop beats, and it features a guest appearance by late jazz sax great Julius Hemphill.

influences:

◄◄ Muddy Waters, Jimi Hendrix, Wes Montgomery, Jimmy Page, John McLaughlin, Sly & the Family Stone, Frank Zappa, Miles Davis

►► Milo Z

Steve Holtje

Bow Wow Wow

Formed 1979, in London, England. Disbanded 1983. Re-formed 1997.

Annabella Lwin, vocals; Matthew Ashman, guitar (1979–83); Leigh Gorman, bass; David Barbarossa, drums (1979–83); Dave Calhoun, guitar (1997–present); Eshan K., drums (1997–98).

The pet project of Sex Pistols manager Malcolm McLaren, Bow Wow Wow was comprised of singer Annabella Lwin (a 14-year-old Burmese immigrant that McLaren found waiting on tables) and the Ants from Adam & the Ants. The band's incorporation of Burundi "Afrobeat" drumming into its pissed-off punk tunes, coupled with McLaren's publicity-hound instincts, won instant attention. When McLaren vacated the producer's chair to be replaced by Kenny Laguna and, later, Mike Chapman of Blondie fame, the

novelty of Bow Wow Wow began to wear thin. The band dissolved in 1983, though Lwin and Leigh Gorman put it back together in 1997 to cash in on the new wave of '80s nostalgia.

what to buy: Bow Wow Wow was best at its inception, when the group was still, um, safely under McLaren's wing. Its debut, *Your Cassette Pet* &&&& (EMI, 1980, prod. Malcolm McLaren), provides the most consistently palatable collection of Afrobeat pop. To further churn the publicity mill, McLaren released the album—with its pro-taping single "C-30, C-60, C-90, Go!"—during the midst of the British recording industry's accusations that home recording was killing sales. Most of *Your Cassette Pet* was later released on *12 Original Recordings* &&& (Capitol, 1982, prod. Malcom McLaren) along will a few B-sides.

what to buy next: The unmarketably-titled *See Jungle! See Jungle! Go Join Your Gang, Yeah! City All Over! Go Ape Crazy!* &&& (RCA, 1981, prod. Malcolm McLaren) comes the closest to the successful formula originated on *Your Cassette Pet*.

what to avoid: Though its title song, a thumping cover of the Strangeloves' beach-pop hit, has become a retro favorite and a fixture at sporting events, *I Want Candy* && (RCA, 1982, prod. various) is a tired re-release of *Last of the Mohicans* && (RCA EP, 1982) with a handful of sub-par B-sides tacked on.

the rest:
When the Going Gets Tough (the Tough Get Going) && (RCA, 1983)
Best of Bow Wow Wow &&& (Receiver, 1989)
Live in Japan && (Receiver, 1989)
Girl Bites Dog &&& (Alliance, 1993)

solo outings:
Annabella Lwin:
Fever & (RCA, 1986)

influences:

◄◄ Adam & the Ants, the Sex Pistols, Bo Diddley

►► Oingo Boingo, Siouxsie & the Banshees, Belly

Brandon Trenz

David Bowie

Born David Robert Jones, January 8, 1947, in London, England.

After several failed attempts throughout England's mod and hippie eras, Bowie molded himself into the consummate rock star in the '70s. He brought androgyny and glamour to the mainstream, while pursuing a rare compositional and emotional balance in his music. Throughout the decade, he adopted a variety of guises and pushed his sound into several different arenas. His experiments rarely faltered. From the folksy "Space Oddity" to the funky "Fame," few artists displayed as much vision and dexterity as Bowie. His best material even rivaled the work of Lennon and McCartney in its verve. By the time the '80s hit, however, Bowie had adopted a more straightforward pop approach with less satisfying results—though his work with a caterwauling side band called Tin Machine explored a more avant noise tip. While the experimentation continues with Bowie's most recent releases, the results rarely capture the same spirit as his prime material. Still, you have to admire him for his persistence.

what to buy: *The Rise and Fall of Ziggy Stardust and the Spiders from Mars* 𝄞𝄞𝄞𝄞 (RCA, 1972, prod. David Bowie, Ken Scott) is Bowie's crowning achievement, his finest fusion of concept and songs ("Moonage Daydream," "Suffragette City," "Starman"). Driven by exquisite melodies, stellar playing, and the songwriter's singular vision, it is one of the finest albums of the '70s. Its follow-up, *Aladdin Sane* 𝄞𝄞𝄞𝄞 (RCA, 1973, prod. David Bowie, Ken Scott), pushes the boundaries of pop music by prominently incorporating jazzy pianos in the rock 'n' roll mix. Written during Bowie's *Ziggy Stardust* tour, the album focuses on the singer's peculiar view of life in America, as captured in songs such as "Drive-in Saturday" and "Panic in Detroit." To get a better taste of Bowie's experimental side, *Station to Station* 𝄞𝄞𝄞𝄞 (RCA, 1976, prod. David Bowie, Harry Maslin) is a good start, marking Bowie's first real attempts at deconstructionism—which, in turn, led to the Bowie/Brian Eno collaborative trilogy of *Low*, *Heroes*, and *Lodger* (see below), though it also included ace pop tunes like "Golden Years" and "Wild Is the Wind." Bowie also released several greatest hits packages throughout his career, which serve as excellent primers to the dynamic span of his work. *The Singles 1969–1993* 𝄞𝄞𝄞𝄞 (Rykodisc, 1993, compilation prod. Jeff Rougvie) is the best, a double-album set that touches on every crucial move forward.

what to buy next: On *Young Americans* 𝄞𝄞𝄞𝄞 (RCA, 1975, prod. Tony Visconti) Bowie delves into soul grooves, with dazzling results. It includes such sensuous groovers as the title track and "Fame." *Hunky Dory* 𝄞𝄞𝄞𝄞 (RCA, 1971, prod. Ken Scott) was a similarly moving affair, with meditative melodies and lush string arrangements for "Changes," "Oh, You Pretty Things," and "Life on Mars?" As for the Bowie/Eno collaborations, *Heroes* 𝄞𝄞𝄞𝄞 (RCA, 1977, prod. David Bowie, Tony Visconti) is the highlight, incorporating some of Bowie's finest melodies into the atmospheric soundscapes. The title track is stellar, as are "Beauty and the Beast" and "Joe the Lion." Bowie's debut, *Space Oddity* 𝄞𝄞𝄞𝄞 (RCA, 1969, prod. Tony Visconti, Gus Dudgeon), which was originally released as *Man of Words, Man of Music*, still stands as a psychedelic masterpiece. Innocent and suggestive, it captures just the right balance of wide-eyed wondering and young man coming of age, particularly on such stirring songs as "Letter to Hermione" and "An Occasional Dream."

WHAT ALBUM CHANGED YOUR LIFE?

When I heard the Sex Pistols, that changed my life. Up to that point I'd been into muso and fusion, all that stuff, Return to Forever's *Romantic Warrior* or *Made in Japan* by Deep Purple. Then I heard the Sex Pistols and I thought, 'Fuck me.' that was just another level completely.

Leigh Gorman (of Bow Wow Wow)

what to avoid: Most of Bowie's mid-'80s recordings are criminally bland, the biggest culprit of the lot being the insipid *Never Let Me Down* **woof!** (EMI, 1987, prod. David Bowie, David Richards), with its listless single "Day In Day Out." The vulgar "Glass Spider" tour that promoted it wasn't much better.

the rest:
The Man Who Sold the World 𝄞𝄞𝄞𝄞 (RCA, 1970)
Pin Ups 𝄞𝄞𝄞 (RCA, 1973)
Diamond Dogs 𝄞𝄞𝄞𝄞 (RCA, 1974)
David Live 𝄞𝄞𝄞 (RCA, 1974)
Low 𝄞𝄞𝄞𝄞 (RCA, 1977)
Stage 𝄞𝄞𝄞 (RCA, 1977)
Lodger 𝄞𝄞𝄞 (RCA, 1979)
Scary Monsters 𝄞𝄞𝄞𝄞 (RCA, 1980)
Ziggy Stardust: The Motion Picture 𝄞𝄞𝄞 (RCA, 1983)
Let's Dance 𝄞𝄞 (EMI, 1983)
Tonight 𝄞 (EMI, 1984)
Sound + Vision 𝄞𝄞𝄞 (Rykodisc, 1989/1994)
(With Tin Machine) *Tin Machine* **woof!** (EMI, 1989)
(With Tin Machine) *Tin Machine II* **woof!** (Victory, 1991)
(With Tin Machine) *Tin Machine Live: Oy Vey, Baby* **woof!** (Victory, 1992)
Black Tie White Noise **woof!** (Savage, 1993)
The Buddha of Suburbia **woof!** (Virgin, 1993/1995)
Santa Monica '72 𝄞𝄞𝄞 (Griffin, 1995)
Outside **woof!** (Virgin, 1995)
Earthling 𝄞𝄞𝄞𝄞 (Virgin, 1997)

worth searching for: The deluxe edition of *The Rise and Fall of Ziggy Stardust and the Spiders from Mars* (Rykodisc, 1990, prod.

David Bowie (© Ken Settle)

David Bowie, Ken Scott) gives this wondrous album a royal treatment with superior sound quality, bonus tracks, and a lavish booklet to enhance an already marvelous listening experience.

influences:

◀◀ The Beatles, Pink Floyd, Funkadelic, the Rolling Stones

▶▶ Smashing Pumpkins, U2, Duran Duran, Nirvana, the Smiths

Aidin Vaziri

The Box Tops

See: Alex Chilton

Boy George

See: Culture Club

Boymerang

Formed 1994, in London, England.

Graham Sutton, programming.

Graham Sutton started his first band, Bark Psychosis, while he was still a teenager. Steeped in the sound collage aesthetic, the group worked primarily with a guitar and drum machine in shaping its abstract compositions. By the early '90s, Sutton had moved on to sampler and synthesizer technology and started listening to British pirate radio stations that specialized in new forms of club music. After Bark Psychosis split following an appearance at the Phoenix Festival in 1994, Sutton dove headfirst into London's burgeoning drum 'n' bass scene. He released several early singles to much acclaim from his older peers; Goldie even took him in as a member of his elite circle of jungle talent.

what's available: Named after an installment in the forthcoming Star Wars trilogy, *Balance of the Force* ✍✍✍♥ (Astralwerks, 1997, prod. Graham Sutton) stands above other standard issue drum 'n' bass discs in that it sounds like a fully realized musical mission. Every song offers a new twist on the staid formula, with great grooves and inventive production techniques at the forefront.

influences:

◀◀ Grooverider, Fabio, Goldie

Aidin Vaziri

Brad
/Satchel

Formed 1992, in Seattle, WA.

Shawn Smith, vocals, organ, keyboards; Stone Gossard, guitar; Regan Hagar, drums; Jeremy Toback, bass (1992–97); Mike Berg, bass (1997–present).

Brad's problem is that it will always be thought of as Stone Gossard's side project. In 1992, when Pearl Jam was in full

swing, Gossard hooked up with Seattle musicians Smith, Hagar, and Toback to play music without the giant hype surrounding a Pearl Jam record. A year later they released *Shame*, and then Gossard went back to focussing on his bigger band, Jeremy Toback worked on his solo career, and Smith and Hagar formed another Seattle mainstay, Satchel. In 1997, between Pearl Jam projects, Brad came back together and released *Interiors*. The band, which had essentially become a side project for *all* involved, found it had a hit on their hands with the single, "The Day Brings." A supporting tour saw Satchel bassist Mike Berg fill in for Toback, who was out promoting his own record, *Perfect Flux Thing*.

what to buy: *Interiors* ✍✍✍♥ (Epic, 1997, prod. Brad) made many people think that perhaps Brad should become more than a once-in-a-while project. Smith is one of the best Seattle musicians to ever not make it big, and the best song on the album, "The Day Brings," showcased his talents to a mainstream radio audience. Satchel's *EDC* ✍✍✍ (Epic, 1994, prod. Satchel, Dennis Herring, Bruce Calder) deserved the same kind of forum. It's a smart, wonderfully crafted album that further displayed Smith's talents as a singer and songwriter.

what to buy next: There's only one other album, *Shame* ✍✍✍ (Epic, 1993, prod. Bashiri Johnson, Brad). While not as solid as *Interiors*, *Shame* has a nice mellow groove that hardcore Pearl Jam fans might find tough to adapt to.

the rest:
Satchel:
Family (Epic, 1996 ✍✍✍

influences:

◀◀ The Beatles, the Beach Boys, Van Dyke Parks, Randy Newman

▶▶ Ben Folds Five

see also: *Pearl Jam, Jeremy Toback*

Anders Wright

Robert Bradley's Blackwater Surprise

Formed 1995, in Detroit, MI.

Robert Bradley, vocals; Michael Nehra, guitar; Andrew Nehra, bass; Jeff Fowlkes, drums; Tim Diaz, keyboard (1997–present).

The story of Robert Bradley's Blackwater Surprise sounds like, but is not, a tall tale or legend. Bradley, who is blind, is perhaps one of Detroit's best-known street performers in the city's downtrodden downtown. After police kicked him out of a populous open-market area, Bradley started performing on the sidewalk beneath the White Room studios, where the Nehra brothers, former members of the band Second Self, heard his soulful, bluesy vocals through the window and invited him to jam with them. After a long period of woodshedding, the group released its first album, touring tirelessly until the song "Trouble Man," used in the film *The Devil's Own,* prompted MTV to begin playing its video, which generated a bit of heat behind the fledgling but seasoned operation.

what's available: *Robert Bradley's Blackwater Surprise* 🎵🎵 (1996, RCA, prod. Michael Nehra, Andrew Nehra) successfully melds Bradley's love of Motown and gospel with the rest of the band's rock sensibilities. In the style of legendary singers such as Marvin Gaye and Van Morrison, Bradley brings a sense of honesty and romance to his rock 'n' roll, pledging devotion in "After Your Love" and poignantly recalling the pain of being dirt poor in the soulful "Governor." "Trouble Man" is pure, funky fun, while T. Rex–style guitar licks and hand claps accompany Bradley on the hook-laden "Burn."

influences:
◀◀ Van Morrison, Marvin Gaye, Ted Hawkins

Christina Fuoco

Billy Bragg
Born December 20, 1957, in Essex, England.

The sight of this brash Brit busking with an electric guitar and speakers mounted on his backpack was an irresistible image in 1983, as was his fiery mixture of the Clash's energy and Woody Guthrie's political fervor. Since he often performs solo, Billy Bragg could be dismissed as just another angry folk singer, but underneath the sometimes laborious left-wing rhetoric is a startling command of pop music that made his better albums a fascinating tug-of-war between message and melody. Other songwriters have certainly noticed: His best known song, "A New England," was turned into a British radio hit by Kirsty Mac-Coll; and Mary Lou Lord ("Ontario, Quebec and Me") and Sara Hickman ("Valentine's Day Is Over") have made his songs a staple of their live shows. But the ultimate tribute came from Woody Guthrie's daughter, Nora, who asked Bragg to write music to accompany some of her father's unused lyrics—which he did in collaboration with the group Wilco for 1998's landmark *Mermaid Avenue.*

what to buy: *Talking with the Taxman about Poetry* 🎵🎵🎵 (Elektra, 1986, prod. Kenny Jones, John Porter) reflects a marked jump in maturity as a songwriter ("Levi Stubbs' Tears," "Greetings to the New Brunette") and the start of a warmer, more-fleshed out sound that reaches fruition on *Don't Try This at Home* 🎵🎵🎵 (Elektra, 1991, prod. Grant Showbiz). The latter includes his prettiest, most reflective material and backing from members of R.E.M. on "You Woke up My Neighborhood." The

success of pairing Woody Guthrie's lyrics with new music composed by Bragg and members of Wilco on *Mermaid Avenue* 🎵🎵🎵 (Elektra, 1998, prod. Billy Bragg, Wilco, Grant Showbiz) owes as much to the folksinger's legacy as it does to Wilco's Jeff Tweedy and his bandmates—their solid and sympathetic backing ventures beyond dustbowl duskiness: "Hoodoo Voodoo" erupts into a Farfisa-fueled rave-up, while "She Came Along to Me" and "I Guess I Planted" sound like great lost *Sgt. Pepper's* outtakes. *Mermaid Avenue* is a reverent yet rollicking tribute that avoids even the slightest whiff of nostalgic pandering by taking risks with Guthrie's ideas rather than being intimidated by them.

what to buy next: *Back to Basics* 🎵🎵🎵 (Elektra, 1987, prod. Kenny Jones) compiles his first three British releases—*Life's a Riot with Spy vs. Spy*, *Brewing Up*, and *Between the Wars*—and offers the most cohesive look at Bragg's earlier, gruff appeal. *Workers Playtime* 🎵🎵🎵 (Elektra, 1988, prod. Joe Boyd) is Bragg's first attempt to integrate a band sound. Such infectious tunes as "Life with the Lions," "She's Got a New Spell," and "Waiting for the Great Leap Forwards" foreshadow what he will achieve on *Don't Try This at Home.*

what to avoid: *The Internationale* 🎵 (Elektra, 1990, prod. Wiggy, Grant Showbiz) is a turgid EP which finds Bragg on his socialist soapbox offering heavy-handed adaptations of protest anthems dating back to the Industrial Revolution of the 19th century.

the rest:
Help Save the Youth of America EP (Elektra, 1988) 🎵🎵🎵
William Bloke 🎵🎵🎵 (Elektra, 1996)

worth searching for: The CD single "You Woke up My Neighborhood" (Elektra, 1991, prod. Grant Showbiz) is a treasure trove of non-LP material, including the lovely "Ontario, Quebec and Me," "Bread and Circuses" (a duet with Natalie Merchant), and a cover of the McGarrigle sisters' "Heart Like a Wheel."

influences:
◀◀ The Clash, Woody Guthrie, Elvis Costello
▶▶ Hammell on Trial, John Wesley Harding

David Okamoto

Brainiac
Formed 1992, in Dayton, OH. Disbanded 1997.

Tim Taylor (died May 23, 1997), keyboards, vocals; Juan Monasterio, bass; Tyler Trent, drums; John Schmersal, guitar (1993–97); Michelle Bodine, guitar (1992–93).

Dayton's Brainiac, quite simply, is the latest in that somehow logical progression of bands—Pere Ubu, the Cramps, Dead

Boys, Guided by Voices, the Breeders, Devo—from Ohio's aesthetically-challenged open spaces and industry-ravaged landscape. In 1992, while the rest of the world was waiting for Nirvana to explode, Brainiac was formulating its dark, electonic science rock that seemed to revel in the notion of a post-apocalyptic, de- then re-constructed new wave mechanical dance party. Tim Taylor laid the groundwork for the Brainiac sound with the ever-futuristic-yet-retro Moog synthesiser and his desperate, wracked and distorted vocals and lyrics, with Michelle Bodine (and later John Schmersal) laying discordant, attention-challenged guitar lines over Trent and Juan Monasterio's punchy rhythm combo. The sum effect was striking in its vision of rock's out-there possibilities within the pop song structure. The band's first full-length record, the relatively frolicking *Smack Bunny Baby*, was released on Grass Records in 1993 with the added cachet of an indie-world-established producer, Girls Against Boys' keyboardist Eli Janney—a partnership that lasted for the band's entire existence. Bodine, however, would not be long for the band: her exit and Schmersal's entrance were coincidental to the band really finding its voice on 1994's *Bonsai Superstar*. Constant touring brought Brainiac to Chicago, among other locales, and consequently to the attention of Touch & Go Records, which signed the band and helped it secure a spot on the second stage of Lollapalooza 1995, alongside acts such as Coolio and Yo La Tengo. Brainiac's manic music was matched only by the band's utterly spastic, masterfully entertaining live show. So it's no surprise that by the time of 1997's *Electro-Shock for President*, the band's reputation and popularity were only beginning to gather supersonic momentum. This makes Taylor's death on May 23, 1997, in a single-car crash, even more tragic. It ended a band that was really just getting started.

what to buy: Brainiac hit its stride with *Hissing Prigs in Static Couture* ♫♫♫♫ (Touch & Go, 1996, prod. Eli Janney). Science fiction met with visceral reality to create a discomforting record to shake your butt while simultaneously scratching your head. *Bonsai Superstar* ♫♫♫♫ (Grass, 1994, prod. Eli Janney) is the record on which Brainiac's songwriting really starts to fire on all microchips.

what to buy next: Brainiac's final recording, *Electro-Shock for President* ♫♫♫♫ (Touch & Go, 1997, prod. Jim O'Rourke), shows a starker, less muscular, more sinewy side to the band on songs such as the desperate, electro-noir of "Fresh New Eyes" and "Mr. Fingers." *Smack Bunny Baby* ♫♫♫ (Grass, 1993, prod. Eli Janney) is a more straightforward, fun indie-rock record very much of its time, but in its grooves you can hear the Brainiac sound coming together.

what to avoid: The one dud in the Brainiac catalog is the EP *Internationale* ♫♫ (Touch & Go, 1995, prod. Kim Deal). Deal

seems to just let the "Record" button do the work and, consequently, the dense impact of the music is lost amidst shabby, DIY production.

worth searching for: In September of 1992, Brainiac recorded a live show in Dayton with Olympia, Washington, riot grrrls Bratmobile. A hard-to-find split live single was released on Dayton's 12X12 Records. As a raw document of the times and for superfans, it's worth the effort to find.

influences:
◀◀ Devo, Kraftwerk, the Pixies

Chris Handyside

Bram Tchaikovsky
See: The Motors

Doyle Bramhall II
See: Arc Angels

Bran Van 3000
Formed 1996, in Montreal, Quebec, Canada.

James "Bran Man" Di Silvio, songwriter, rapper, various instruments; "Electronic-Pierre" Bergen, DJ, keyboards; Jayne Hill, vocals; Sara Johnston, vocals; Stephane Moraille, vocals; Steve "Liquid" Hawley, rapper; Gary McKenzie, bass; Nick Hynes, guitar; Rob Joanisse, drums.

A filmmaker and music video director since he was a teenager, James "Bran Man" Di Silvio had no experience writing or producing music before 1996. His career path changed, however, when he took a DJ job in New York, where he was directing a video for jazz artist Branford Marsalis. Having been bitten by the musical bug, Di Silvio called on friend "Electronic-Pierre" Bergen to form Bran Van 3000, a collective of nine Montreal musicians.

what's available: *Glee* ♫♫♫ (Capitol, 1998, prod. James Di Salvio, "Electronic Pierre" Bergen, Haig Vartzbedian) is an unfocused combination of hip-hop, jazz, metal, lo-fi rock, reggae, acoustic, and country music—which isn't necessarily a bad thing, just a lot like a pre-made mix tape. The smooth-flowing first single, "Drinking in L.A.," is the stand-out track, incorporating hip-hop drum loops, piano, and distorted raps with R&B-style vocals. The flip side of "Drinking in L.A." is the acoustic-cum-lo-fi cover of Slade's "Cum on Feel the Noize," on which the women of the group sing.

influences:
◀◀ Beck, Snoop Doggy Dogg, Gary Numan

Christina Fuoco

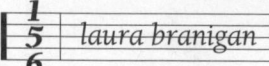
Laura Branigan

Born July 3, 1957, in Brewster, NY.

Laura Branigan blurted out overly dramatic, studio-pumped pop hits during the early to mid-'80s with enough ebullience to guarantee at least a few hit singles before fading away. Whether her healthy set of pipes could have been used to better effect is a moot question now that her decade-plus career has yet to produce anything even remotely organic.

what to buy: *The Best of Branigan* ♫♫♪ (Atlantic, 1995, prod. various) offers the radio dramas all in a row, including her first hit, "Gloria" (not the Them stomper), the quicky follow-up "Solitaire," and "Self Control."

what to buy next: *Branigan* ♫♫ (Atlantic, 1982, prod. Jack White), her debut album, contains "Gloria," which showcases her flair for bluster and willingness to be submerged in glossy production.

what to avoid: *Branigan 2* ♫ (Atlantic, 1983, prod. Jack White) begs listeners to indulge the notion that covering the Who's "Squeeze Box" is an imaginative idea. Right. And maybe Joni Mitchell should try "Me So Horny."

the rest:
Self Control ♫♪ (Atlantic, 1984)
Touch ♫ (Atlantic, 1987)
Laura Branigan ♫ (Atlantic, 1990)
Over My Heart ♫ (Atlantic, 1994)

influences:
◀◀ Tina Turner, Donna Summer, Hall & Oates, Irene Cara
▶▶ Alanis Morrisette, Mariah Carey, Celine Dion

Allan Orski

Brave Combo

Formed 1979, in Denton, TX.

Carl Finch, vocals, accordion, guitar; Bubba Hernandez, bass, vocals; Jeffrey Barnes, saxophone, clarinet, percussion.

A self-described "nuclear polka" band, Brave Combo is often shortchanged as a novelty act since its frenetic live shows zigzag from stampede-inducing romps through "Who Stole the Kishka" and "The Happy Wanderer" all the way to a surf version of "Oh, What a Beautiful Morning" and a swinging take on Wayne Newton's "Danke Schoen." But over the years, the Combo—a revolving six-piece band built around the nucleus of Finch, Hernandez, and Barnes—has evolved into a versatile outfit capable of being both faithful and funky as they parade through polkas, rancheras, sambas, and cumbias and expose the hidden melodic link between Lou Reed's "Walk on the Wild Side" and Van McCoy's "The Hustle" (oh yes there is). Still a fa-

vorite at weddings, bar mitzvahs, Oktoberfests, and alt-rock clubs, Brave Combo was once a band to simply get wrecked to; now, it's a group to be reckoned with.

what to buy: *No, No, No, Cha Cha Cha* ♫♫♫ (Rounder, 1993, prod. Brave Combo) focuses on the group's Latin influences and boasts a seamless medley of the Rolling Stones' "Satisfaction" and Ringo Starr's "No No Song," a festive salsa version of Cher's "The Way of Love," and a boss bossa nova rendition of "Fly Me to the Moon." *Polkas for a Gloomy World* ♫♫♫ (Rounder, 1995, prod. Brave Combo) is its Grammy-nominated return to straight-ahead polka, mixing infectious originals like "Flying Saucer" with traditional Mexican, Russian, and German polkas. *Group Dance Epidemic* ♫♫♪ (Rounder, 1997, prod. Brave Combo) collects studio versions of live favorites such as "The Chicken Dance," their Devo-like demolition of "The Hokey Pokey," and other vintage tunes designed for conga lines and bunny-hop parades. It also includes their politically correct update of Reed's "Walk on the Wild Side" ("And the African-American girls sing . . ."), inventively medleyed with "The Hustle."

what to buy next: A surprisingly listenable collaboration with the late Tiny Tim, *Girl* ♫♫♫ (Rounder, 1996, prod. Brave Combo, Bucks Burnett) demonstrates the depth of Brave Combo's musical vocabulary and its astounding ability to make anyone sound good. Check out the hepcat-jazz version of "Stairway to Heaven" and the "Wooly Bully"–like reworking of "Bye Bye Blackbird."

what to avoid: *Musical Varieties* ♫♫ (Rounder, 1988, prod. Brave Combo) is a compilation of pre-Rounder tracks from the early '80s. Although hardly horrid, they lean toward predictable gimmickry ("People Are Strange" and "Sixteen Tons" as polkas), sideswiping genres the band would eventually tackle head-on.

the rest:
Polkatharsis ♫♫♫ (Rounder, 1987)
Humansville ♫♫♫ (Rounder, 1989)
A Night on Earth ♫♫♫♪ (Rounder, 1990)
It's Christmas, Man! ♫♫♫♪ (Rounder, 1992)
The Hokey Pokey ♫♫♫ (denTone, 1994)
Mood Swing Music ♫♫♫ (Rounder, 1996)
Polka Party with Brave Combo ♫♫♫ (Easydisc/Rounder, 1998)

worth searching for: *Kiss of Fire* (Watermelon, 1996, prod. Brave Combo) is a sublime collaboration with Lauren Agnelli, formerly of folk trio the Washington Squares, on torch songs ranging from the French chansons of Edith Piaf and Francoise Hardy to the fiery tangos of Carlos Gardel.

influences:
◀◀ You name it
▶▶ The New Orleans Klezmer All Stars

David Okamoto

Bread

Formed 1969, in Los Angeles, CA. Disbanded 1973. Reunited 1976.

David Gates, vocals, guitar, bass, keyboards, violin; James Griffin, vocals, guitar, keyboards; Robb Royer, guitar, bass, keyboards, flute (1969–71); Larry Knechtel, keyboards, bass, guitar, harmonica (1972–77); Jim Gordon, drums (1969); Mike Botts, drums (1970–77).

Bread was put together by three veteran session musicians and songwriters (whose credits include Lesley Gore, the Monkees, Bobby Darin, and Connie Stevens) to take advantage of music trends they saw coming. Their foresight was accurate, as the group scored 11 Top 40 hits. But the hit singles, all penned by David Gates, caused critics to reject them with the label "soft rock," and the group is thought of mostly for ballads perceived as saccharine, insincere odes written solely to achieve commercial success. Though there's some truth to the accusation, since a few of Gates's biggest hits are almost unbearably sappy, other Gates tunes and some James Griffin efforts are pop masterpieces. Bread started its hit parade on its second album, when the single "Make It with You" hit #1 on the strength of Gates's casual declaration of love; intended as a change of pace on a relatively intense album that belies the perceived image of the quartet, it ended up defining Bread's sound. The string continued with "Baby I'm-a Want You," "Everything I Own," and "It Don't Matter to Me," though before long tension arose between Gates and Griffin, who wanted to pursue more rock-oriented directions. (It also must have hurt that none of the 10 singles Griffin had a hand in writing made the Top 40.) In 1973, the group broke up after an incredibly productive run. A 1976 reunion suffered from the same tensions and produced one hit. Gates, not surprisingly, had the most successful post-Bread solo career (his big hit was the title song for the film *The Goodbye Girl* in 1978), though it hardly matched Bread's accomplishments. Griffin began concentrating on country work during the '80s and spent time in an all-star band called Black Tie that featured alumni of Poco, the Eagles, and the Beach Boys.

what to buy: *On the Waters* ♫♫♫♫ (Elektra, 1970, prod. David Gates, James Griffin, Robb Royer) has many of Gates's best ballads ("Been Too Long on the Road," "Make It with You," "In the Afterglow," "The Other Side of Life") and the peaks of the Griffin/Robb Royer collaboration ("Why Do You Keep Me Waiting," "Look What You've Done," "I Am That I Am," "Coming Apart," "Call on Me"). It's a superb mix of mellow tracks and more intense numbers, with nobody pigeonholed into a role yet and no cloying songs. *Guitar Man* ♫♫♫♫ (Elektra, 1972, prod. David Gates) stands out thanks to the title track, "Make It by Yourself," "Fancy Dancer," "Let Me Go," and Knechtel's "Picture in Your Mind."

what to buy next: The two-CD *Retrospective* ♫♫♫♫ (Elektra/Rhino, 1996, prod. Bread, David McLees, Bill Inglot) is a model set, with all the Bread hits plus samples of the solo work by Gates and Griffin (including the demo of "For All We Know").

what to avoid: The reunion album *Lost without Your Love* ♫ (Elektra, 1977, prod. David Gates) was tepid and uninspired.

the rest:
Bread ♫♫♫♫ (Elektra, 1969)
Manna ♫♫♫ (Elektra, 1971)
Baby I'm-a Want You ♫♫♫♫ (Elektra, 1972)

worth searching for: Gates's *Goodbye Girl* (Elektra, 1979, prod. David Gates) skims tracks from his first two solo albums (like this one, long out of print) and adds the hit title track and a few new songs of similar vintage. Griffin's *Breakin' up Is Easy* (Polydor, 1973, prod. James Griffin, Robb Royer) suffers from dated production but has some good material, and Griffin sings well. Two tracks here with Gates and Knechtel were left over from an aborted Bread album.

solo outings:
David Gates:
First ♫♫ (Elektra, 1973)
Never Let Her Go ♫♫ (Elektra, 1975)
Love Is Always Seventeen ♫♫♫ (Discovery, 1994)

influences:
◀◀ Chet Atkins, the Association, the Beatles

▶▶ America, Air Supply, Chris von Sneidern, Matthew Sweet

Steve Holtje

The Breeders /The Amps

The Breeders, 1990–present: Kim Deal, vocals, guitar; Tanya Donelly, vocals, guitar (1990–93); Josephine Wiggs, bass; Shannon Doughton, drums (1990–93); Kelley Deal, guitar, vocals (1992–present); James Macpherson, drums (1993–present). The Amps, 1995-present: Kim Deal, vocals, guitar; Nathan Farley, vocals, guitars, bass; Luis Lerma, bass; James Macpherson, drums.

Once a side project for Kim Deal to escape from Black Francis's dominance in the Pixies—and for Tanya Donelly, who eventually moved on to Belly, to find a respite from similar circumstances in Throwing Muses—the Breeders quickly transcended their previous groups' commercial success with the transfixing rock 'n' roll single "Cannonball," which earned the band a spot on the 1994 Lollapalooza tour. Shortly after that, however, Deal's guitarist sister Kelley encountered drug problems and dropped out of the band, forcing Deal to start over yet again with the Amps, whose music is more spacey but still rocking. But with Kelley's subsequent treatment—she also formed a side band, the countryish Kelley Deal 6000—the siblings have openly discussed the possibility of more Breeders work.

what to buy: The Breeders' *Last Splash* ♫♫♫♫ (4AD/Elektra, 1993, prod. Kim Deal, Mark Freegard) finds Deal wriggling away from Black Francis and proving her love of twisted pop melodies was a key driving force behind the Pixies; the dripping strawberry heart on the album cover somehow perfectly captures the juicy hooks in "Cannonball," "Drivin' on 9," "I Just Wanna Get Along," and "No Aloha."

what to avoid: The Amps' *Pacer* ♫♫ (4AD/Elektra, 1995, prod. various) sounds like a transitional album before the talented Deal figures out a more creatively lucrative direction.

the rest:
The Breeders:
Pod ♫♫♫ (4AD/Elektra, 1990)

worth searching for: The Breeders' four-song EP *Safari* (4AD/Elektra, 1992, prod. the Breeders) is the sound of a new band getting its act together. "Don't Call Home" is the spookiest thing Deal ever wrote, and an explosive cover of the Who's "So Sad about Us" sheds new light on that song's greatness.

solo outings:
Kelley Deal 6000:
Go to the Sugar Altar ♫♫ (Nice, 1996)
Boom! Boom! Boom! ♫♫♫ (New West, 1997)

influences:
◄◄ The Ramones, the Beach Boys, the Jesus and Mary Chain, the Who, Hüsker Dü, Throwing Muses, Raincoats, the Replacements

►► Juliana Hatfield, Belly

see also: *Belly, the Pixies, Throwing Muses*

Steve Knopper

Brice Glace
See: Jim O'Rourke

Edie Brickell & New Bohemians
Formed 1985, in Dallas, TX. Disbanded 1991.

Edie Brickell (born March 10, 1966), vocals, guitar; Kenny Withrow, guitar, vocals; Brad Houser, bass; Wes Burt-Martin, guitar, vocals; Matt Chamberlain, drums; John Bush, percussion.

Meet the new boho, same as the old boho. Like the eternal hipoisie from whom they take their name, Edie Brickell & New Bohemians were merely unconventional as opposed to revolutionary, and merely clever as opposed to smart. Brickell's shy-

girl personality comes through in her vocals, which are low-key and charmingly unassuming, and in her lyrics, which read like pages of a schoolgirl's journal. And while the group displayed undeniable instrumental chops in its laid-back mix of rock, folk, and jazz, it was a pretty faceless bunch, which led to discord when Brickell—who, after all, first sat in with the band on a dare—became its unmistakable star and, ultimately a solo artist. After New Bohemians split, and Brickell married Paul Simon, her writing picked up his habits of detailing the intricacies of quotidian ups and downs, but with much less success and style.

what to buy: *Shooting Rubberbands at the Stars* ♫♫♫ (Geffen, 1988, prod. Pat Moran) contains the hit "What I Am," a loping bit of anti-intellectualism driven by Withrow's neo-Garcia guitar noodlings, and "Little Miss S.," a tribute to bohemian shooting star Edie Sedgewick.

what to buy next: *Ghost of a Dog* ♫♫♫ (Geffen, 1990, prod. Tony Berg) produced no hits, but it's a less-studied outing than the debut, with the nursery-rhyme rocker "Black & Blue" and accordionist Jo-el Sonnier sitting in on "Carmelito."

solo outings:
Edie Brickell:
Picture Perfect Morning ♫♫♫ (Geffen, 1994)

influences:
◄◄ Rickie Lee Jones, Joni Mitchell, the Grateful Dead

Daniel Durchholz

Brinsley Schwarz
Formed 1970, in London, England. Disbanded 1975.

Brinsley Schwarz, guitar, vocals; Nick Lowe, bass, vocals; Billy Rankin, drums; Bob Andrews, keyboards, vocals; Ian Gomm, guitar (1970–74).

Historically speaking, Brinsley Schwarz is a known entity in the U.S. mainly because of some band members' later successes—and, indirectly, because it originated the future Elvis Costello hit "(What's So Funny 'Bout) Peace, Love and Understanding." Brinsley Schwarz and Bob Andrews were part of Graham Parker's Rumour, while Nick Lowe built a respectable solo career; he and Ian Gomm co-wrote Lowe's biggest hit, "Cruel to Be Kind." Eschewing the post-Woodstock acid hangovers in favor of a basic, roots-oriented pub-rock, Schwarz was out of step with most early '70s rock trends. Although its country-tinged party-rock won a solid fan base in England, the band never broke in the U.S.

worth searching for: Any fan of late '70s and early '80s new wave would do well to hunt down the British imports *Please*

Don't Ever Change (Edsel, 1993), *Silver Pistol* (Edsel, 1993), or the compilation *Surrender to the Rhythm* (EMI, 1991).

influences:

◀◀ The Who, the Beatles, Graham Parker and the Rumour

▶▶ Rockpile, Elvis Costello, Robyn Hitchcock

see also: *Nick Lowe, Graham Parker*

Allan Orski

David Bromberg

Born September 19, 1945, in Philadelphia, PA.

Known as the consummate "musician's musician," multi-instrumentalist David Bromberg is a virtual jukebox of American roots music. Equally at home in folk, blues, rock, jazz, country, bluegrass, Texas swing, and Irish traditional, a Bromberg album is like a musical stew. Drawn to the Greenwich Village folk scene of the mid-'60s, Bromberg—who was studying to be a musicologist—dropped out of Columbia University to work full time as a performer. His proficiency as a guitarist combined with his eclectic range of styles led to a substantial career as a session musician, appearing on close to 80 albums for the likes of Bob Dylan, Jerry Jeff Walker, Ringo Starr, Phoebe Snow, and others. Following a stunning last-minute performance at the 1970 Isle of Wight Festival, Bromberg was offered his own recording contract with Columbia. In 1976 he moved to the Fantasy label and formed the David Bromberg Band, which featured, on any given tune, a bluesy assault of electric guitars or a blend of fiddles, mandolin, clarinet, trombone, and acoustic guitar. An electrifying performer, it's no accident that many of Bromberg's albums include live performances, both solo and with his tight-knit band. Currently semi-retired (his last album was in 1989, and he rarely performs), Bromberg lives in Chicago where he buys, sells, and builds violins.

what to buy: His debut, *David Bromberg* 𝄞𝄞𝄞𝄞 (Columbia, 1971, prod. David Bromberg), showcases all of his influences with a mostly acoustic album of blues, folk, rock, and a tune co-written with George Harrison ("The Holdup"). "The Holdup" surfaces again on *Wanted Dead or Alive* 𝄞𝄞𝄞𝄞 (Columbia, 1974, prod. David Bromberg), along with a Bob Dylan tune ("Wallflower"), a Blind Willie McTell classic ("Statesboro Blues"), and Bromberg's own blend of acoustic folk/blues ("The New Lee Highway Blues"). *How Late'll Ya Play Til?* 𝄞𝄞𝄞𝄞 (Fantasy, 1976, prod. David Bromberg, Steve Burgh) is available as a two-disc set or individually. One disc is a studio recording, the other live, and both show Bromberg and his band in top form.

what to buy next: *Out of the Blues: The Best of David Bromberg* 𝄞𝄞𝄞𝄞 (Columbia, 1977, prod. David Bromberg) provides a good introduction, but unfortunately it relies too much

on novelty tunes such as "Sharon" and "The Holdup," and not enough on the rootsier side of Bromberg's music. It's still worth it for a great rendition of "Mr. Bojangles."

what to avoid: *Bandit in a Bathing Suit* 𝄞 (Fantasy, 1978, prod. David Bromberg, Hugh McDonald). Perhaps it was an attempt to sound more commercial, but the unemotional pop songs included on this album don't even approach the capabilities of this band.

the rest:

Demon in Disguise 𝄞𝄞𝄞𝄞 (Columbia, 1972)
Midnight on the Water 𝄞𝄞𝄞 (Columbia, 1975)
Reckless Abandon 𝄞𝄞𝄞 (Fantasy, 1977)
My Own House 𝄞𝄞𝄞 (Fantasy, 1978)
You Should See the Rest of the Band 𝄞𝄞𝄞 (Fantasy, 1980)
Long Way from Here 𝄞𝄞𝄞 (Fantasy, 1986)
Sideman Serenade 𝄞𝄞𝄞 (Rounder, 1989)
The Player: A Retrospective 𝄞𝄞𝄞𝄞 (Legacy, 1998)

worth searching for: Fiddler Vassar Clements's *Hillbilly Jazz* (Flying Fish, 1974, prod. Michael Medford) features Bromberg on a nice western swing recording.

influences:

◀◀ The Beatles, Rev. Gary Davis, Bob Dylan, Jerry Jeff Walker

▶▶ David Grisman, Chris Whitley

Brian Escamilla

Bronski Beat

See: Jimmy Somerville

WHAT ALBUM CHANGED YOUR LIFE?

Jeff Buckley's album *Grace* has really moved me. I just think he's a tremendous singer and there's so much passion on that record. The arrangements are great and the songs are weird and intense, not really paying attention to harmonic rules. And I love that.

Jonatha Brooke

Jonatha Brooke
/Jonatha Brooke & the Story

Formed 1990, in Boston, MA.

Jonatha Brooke, vocals, guitar, piano; Jennifer Kimball, harmony vocals (1990–94).

If Jonatha Brooke & the Story's music was easier to classify, perhaps she'd be a household name by now. Deftly combining elements of pop, folk, and jazz, her songs can be thoughtful or humorous, and they often sport unusual harmonic and melodic twists. She and Jennifer Kimball began the Story as a Boston-area coffeehouse duo, working bits of theatricality into their performances. By 1994, when Elektra dropped them due to sub-superstar sales of their excellent sophomore release, *The Angel in the House*, Kimball left to sing with fellow Boston singer-songwriter Patti Larkin. Brooke kept the band name going for her jazzy solo debut, produced by her keyboardist (and now husband) Alain Mallet. With her following album, though, she went solo in name as well as in deed, churning out a fine pop effort that rivals the recent work of Suzanne Vega, Jill Sobule, and Sam Phillips. Brooke remains an underappreciated artist.

what to buy: Start with the Story's most accomplished effort, *The Angel in the House* ♪♪♪♪ (Green Linnet/Elektra, 1993, prod. Alain Mallet, Ben Wittman), which features their best-known song, the poignant and striking "So Much Mine." Not only are Brooke and Kimball's vocals terrific throughout, but they merge pop, folk, jazz, and Brazilian and Latin styles without batting an eye.

what to buy next: Possibly aiming for a better commercial response, Brooke and husband/keyboardist Alain Mallet tightened the arrangements and gussied up the sound on *10¢ wings* ♪♪♪♥ (MCA, 1997, prod. Alain Mallet), giving it a greater immediacy than previous Brooke albums. The production gets fussy in spots, but the melodic and harmonic writing on "Blood from a Stone," "Secrets and Lies," and the aching "Shame on Us" is hard to beat.

the rest:
Grace in Gravity ♪♪♪ (Green Linnet/Elektra, 1991)
Plumb ♪♪♪♥ (Blue Thumb/GRP, 1995)

influences:
◄◄ Joni Mitchell, Jane Siberry, Shawn Colvin

►► Jill Sobule, Dar Williams, Milla

Bob Remstein

Gary Brooker

See: Procol Harum

Meredith Brooks

Born near Portland, OR.

Music became Meredith Brooks's main interest early in her life. By the time she was a teenager, she was playing guitar and writing songs. After years of pursuing music as a career—including a stint in the Graces with former Go-Go Charlotte Caffey—she emerged with the hit single "Bitch" in 1997. One hit does not a career make, and she took some critical potshots as another Alanis-come-lately. (Or is that a Liz Phair-come-lately?) The marketing of "Bitch" (indeed, its selection as a single) certainly was influenced by the whole angry-young-grrrl thing, especially its most commercial manifestation—Morissette. However, Brooks seems just to be taking advantage of the door opened by Alanis-hungry record companies. Brooks's songwriting is not out on the edges where Phair and P.J. Harvey tread, but it's sturdy and could build into a long career. Or she can be sunk by being unjustly labeled an Alanis clone.

what's available: On *Blurring the Edges* ♪♪♪ (Capitol, 1997, prod. David Ricketts), "Bitch" may be the hit, but it's almost a one-off pastiche of Morissette. The rest of the album finds Brooks in a more standard pop-rock vein. She's just one of the grrrls, if the grrrls include the likes of Carole King and Sheryl Crow.

influences:
◄◄ Carole King, Sheryl Crow

Salvatore Caputo

Brotherhood of Lizards

See: Martin Newell

Arthur Brown

Born June 24, 1942, in Whitby, England.

One of the first truly theatrical rockers, Arthur Brown was using fire in his act before either Jimi Hendrix or Kiss did. His first band, the Crazy World of Arthur Brown, was also his most successful, scoring a Top 10 hit with the novel "Fire" and its ominous intro: "I am the god of hell fire!!" That band included drummer Carl Palmer, later of Emerson, Lake & Palmer. Brown never did much after that. He put together an electronic band, Kingdom Come, during the early '70s and all but disappeared until the '80s, when he relocated to Austin, Texas, and hooked up with former Mothers of Invention drummer Jimmy Carl Black.

what to buy: *The Crazy World of Arthur Brown* ♪♪ (Atlantic, 1968/Touchwood, 1994, prod. Kit Lambert) includes the immortal hit "Fire," which is the only essential Brown track. But it's a doozy. In a quizzical move, the reissue features bonus tracks: the first half of the album repeated in mono.

the rest:

(With Jimmy Carl Black) *Brown, Black and Blue* ♪♪ (BlueWave)

influences:

◀◀ Little Richard, London's West End theaters

▶▶ Alice Cooper, David Bowie, Sensational Alex Harvey Band

Doug Pullen

Greg Brown

Born in IA.

Iowa singer-songwriter Greg Brown possesses a quirky sensibility, a gift for wordplay, a wry, ironic stage presence, and a rumbling, phlegmatic baritone voice that has found much favor with festival-goers and folk club fans over the past 15 years. Probably the Brown song most familiar to traditional country music fans is "The Train Carrying Jimmie Rodgers Home," which was recorded by the Nashville Bluegrass Band. It also appears on his first Red House album.

what to buy: *Down in There* ♪♪♪♪ (Red House, 1990, prod. Bo Ramsey) contains 10 of Brown's most endearing, quirky originals. *The Live One* ♪♪♪♪ (Red House, 1995) captures Brown in the venue best suited for full appreciation of his sense of humor and wordplay.

what to buy next: On *Songs of Innocence and Experience* ♪♪♪♪ (Red House, 1986, prod. Bob Feldman, Greg Brown), Brown sets to music and sings the poems of William Blake, while Michael Doucet accompanies on fiddle. Greg Brown and Bill Morrissey team up on *Friend of Mine* ♪♪♪♪ (Philo, 1993, prod. Ellen Karas), a batch of songs they've sung together at parties, backstage, and in green rooms. The album has a loose, amiable feel to it, and the repertoire is eclectic enough—everything from "Little Red Rooster" and "You Can't Always Get What You Want" to Hank Williams's "I'll Never Get Out of this World Alive."

the rest:

44 & 66 ♪♪♪ (Red House, 1980)
In the Dark with You ♪♪♪ (Red House, 1986)
One More Goodnight Kiss ♪♪♪ (Red House, 1987)
One Big Town ♪♪♪ (Red House, 1989)
Dream Cafe ♪♪♪♪ (Red House, 1992)
Bathtub Blues ♪♪♪ (Red House, 1993)
The Poet Game ♪♪♪ (Red House, 1994)
Further In ♪♪♪ (Red House, 1996)
Slant 6 Mind ♪♪♪♪ (Red House, 1997)

influences:

◀◀ John Prine, Tom Waits

▶▶ Bill Morrissey, John Gorka

Randy Pitts

James Brown

Born May 3, 1933, in Barnwell, SC.

In terms of soul music, nobody save perhaps Ray Charles can top the contributions or the pervasive influence of James Brown. He is a living link between the R&B swing bands of Louis Jordan and today's rap minimalists. The great soul singers of the middle and late '60s—and more than a few rockers—took lessons from his early records and that animalistic scream he called a voice and those incredible onstage moves. Brown literally invented funk, still the dominant influence on black music—especially on disco and rap over the last two decades. Like Charles, Brown faced off the spiritual passion and cadences of black gospel preachers with the supercharged sexual beat and rhythms of R&B. "Please, Please, Please," "Try Me," and "Think" introduced Brown's considerable skills to a generation of budding soul stars that would explode in the mid-'60s. His stage show, from the corny-yet-effective cape routines to the rigorously rehearsed, ultra-professional, dapper Famous Flames revue, set a sweaty standard. Nobody worked harder than the self-dubbed Hardest Working Man in Show Business (a.k.a. Mr. Dynamite, the Godfather of Soul). Beginning in 1965, he began treating the recording studio with the same precision and exuberance of an Apollo midnight performance, and his incredibly high standards for band membership paid off with "Papa's Got a Brand New Bag" (1965) and "It's a Man's, Man's, Man's World" (1966), music as revolutionary and innovative as any from the better-known and higher-praised Beatles, Rolling Stones, or Bob Dylan. As the '60s wore on, Brown's lyrics became more strident and often focused on civil rights issues. As the lyrics eschewed sex and romance to stress black individualism ("Say It Loud, I'm Black and I'm Proud"), the music turned in on itself in ever more primal ways. Brown's band became an incubator of soul, home to innovative, talented musicians—Maceo Parker, Bobby Byrd, Fred Wesley, and Bootsy Collins—as stubborn, professional, moody, and self-determined as their boss. Solos and verse-chorus patterns were dumped in favor of extended, repetitive grooves pushed to fever pitch by Brown's call-and-response vocal chants ("Take me to the bridge!" "Give the drummer some!"). Before long, every instrument was playing some sort of percussion role—an approach that evolved into the dance music that became known as funk, then disco, and then the even more fragmented hip-hop styles. Brown has achieved enormous wealth and success, but he's also been dogged by addictions and personal problems that landed him in prison during the late '80s. But there's no denying Brown's importance, the proof of which is found in 40 years of solid, ground-breaking grooves.

what to buy: Brown's recorded output is as fragmented as the funk he created. He was really a singles artist, and whether you're at all interested in his importance or just want to shake your booty 'til it drops off, nothing can possibly top *Star Time* 𝄞𝄞𝄞𝄞𝄞 (Polydor, 1991, prod. various), a solid, comprehensive, chronological, and funkifying four discs of his very best and most important works, with many of the singles expanded back to their original lengths and liner notes that detail his accomplishments. If you're a bit more cautious, you shouldn't be without *Solid Gold: 30 Golden Hits* 𝄞𝄞𝄞𝄞𝄞 (Polydor, 1986, prod. various), which boasts about half of those incredibly visionary, exhausting, and shake-your-booty singles. *Live at the Apollo* 𝄞𝄞𝄞𝄞𝄞 (King, 1963/Polydor, 1990, prod. James Brown) captures the midnight show of August 24, 1962, that put Brown on the national map, an electrifying documentation of pure showtime; the compact disc adds some tracks to the original.

what to buy next: When Sid Nathan of King Records wouldn't release an instrumental called "(Do the) Mash Potatoes," Brown put it out on another label under a pseudonym (Nat Kendrick & the Swans). Not surprisingly, it was a hit. His limitless proficiency on instrumental tracks matches (or at least augments) the creativity of the vocal hits, and many of his bands' finest performances are featured on *Soul Pride: The Instrumentals, 1960–1969* 𝄞𝄞𝄞𝄞 (Polydor, 1993, prod. James Brown). The insights are many; Brown, for instance, stands out as an intuitive organ player whose fluid style is perfectly suited to the music. *Roots of a Revolution* 𝄞𝄞𝄞𝄞 (Polydor, 1983/1992, prod. James Brown, Tim Rogers) is a producer's choice of recordings from 1956 to 1964 that show how Brown and his Famous Flames went from imitative to innovative in the years leading up to "Papa's Got a Brand New Bag." His blues side gets a rare spotlight on *Messing with the Blues* 𝄞𝄞𝄞𝄞 (Polydor, 1990, prod. James Brown), which illuminates his individualistic

approach toward cover material and proves him as impressive a stylist as Ray Charles.

what to avoid: *Black Caesar* **woof!** (Polydor, 1973/1992, prod. James Brown) and *Slaughter's Big Rip-Off* **woof!** (Polydor, 1973/1992, prod. James Brown), two Brown-penned blaxploitation scores, prove him mortal.

best of the rest:
Try Me 𝄞𝄞𝄞 (King, 1959/A&M, 1996)
Think 𝄞𝄞𝄞 (King, 1960/A&M, 1996)
Please, Please, Please 𝄞𝄞𝄞𝄞 (King, 1962/Polydor, 1996)
Out of Sight 𝄞𝄞𝄞 (Polydor, 1968/A&M, 1996)
Say It Loud: I'm Black and I'm Proud 𝄞𝄞𝄞𝄞 (King, 1968/A&M, 1996)
The Payback 𝄞𝄞𝄞𝄞 (Polydor, 1974/1992)
Sex Machine 𝄞𝄞𝄞𝄞 (Polydor, 1975/1993)
In the Jungle Groove 𝄞𝄞 (PolyGram, 1987)
Soul Jubilee 𝄞𝄞 (Blue Moon, 1991)
Soul Syndrome 𝄞𝄞𝄞 (Rhino, 1991)
20 All-Time Greatest Hits 𝄞𝄞𝄞𝄞 (Polydor, 1991)
The Greatest Hits of the Fourth Decade 𝄞𝄞 (Scotti Brothers, 1992)
Love Power Peace: Live at the Olympia, Paris, 1971 𝄞𝄞𝄞 (PolyGram, 1992)
Hot Pants 𝄞𝄞𝄞𝄞 (PolyGram, 1993)
Live at the Apollo (Gold Disc) 𝄞𝄞𝄞𝄞𝄞 (Ultradisc, 1993)
Revolution of the Mind: Live at the Apollo, Vol. III 𝄞𝄞𝄞 (PolyGram, 1993)
Is Back 𝄞𝄞 (Hollywood, 1994)
Turn It Loose 𝄞𝄞 (Drive Archive, 1994)
Hell 𝄞𝄞𝄞 (PolyGram, 1995)
Living in America 𝄞𝄞𝄞 (Scotti Brothers, 1995)
Live at the Apollo 1995 𝄞𝄞 (Scotti Brothers, 1995)
Get on the Good Foot 𝄞𝄞𝄞 (PolyGram, 1995)
'70s Funk Classics 𝄞𝄞𝄞 (PolyGram, 1995)
Funky Christmas 𝄞𝄞𝄞𝄞 (Polydor, 1995)
40th Anniversary Collection 𝄞𝄞𝄞𝄞 (Polydor, 1996)
Foundations of Funk, 1964–69 𝄞𝄞𝄞𝄞 (A&M, 1996)
Funk Power 1970: A Brand New Thang 𝄞𝄞𝄞𝄞 (A&M, 1996)
Golden Hits 𝄞𝄞𝄞 (Masters, 1996)
Greatest Hits 𝄞𝄞 (PolyGram, 1996)
Hooked on Brown 𝄞𝄞 (Scotti Brothers, 1996)
James Brown Sings Raw Soul 𝄞𝄞𝄞𝄞 (A&M, 1996)
Make It Funky: The Big Payback, 1971–75 𝄞𝄞𝄞 (A&M, 1996)
Dead on the Heavy Funk, 1975–83 𝄞𝄞𝄞𝄞 (Polydor/Chronicles, 1998)
Say It Live and Loud 𝄞𝄞𝄞𝄞 (Polydor/Chronicles, 1998)
The Very Best Of 𝄞𝄞𝄞𝄞 (Polydor/Chronicles, 1998)

worth searching for: If you're interested in Brown's early recordings, the out-of-print collection *The Federal Years: Parts One and Two* (Solid Smoke, 1984) offers nascent versions of Brown's early vision and the growing pangs of the Famous Flames that you won't find anywhere else. Also look for his collaboration with hip-hop pioneer Afrika Bambaataa, *Unity* (Tommy Boy, 1984, prod. Tom Silverman, Afrika Bambaataa), just in case you were wondering about Brown's connection to rap. (The track "Unity Pt. 1" can be found on *Star Time*.)

influences:

◄◄ Hank Ballard & the Midnighters, Ray Charles, Louis Jordan, Bo Diddley, Wynonie Harris, Roy Brown, the Dominos, the "5" Royales

►► Michael Jackson, Otis Redding, Sly & the Family Stone, Jimi Hendrix, Mick Jagger, Parliament-Funkadelic, George Clinton, Bootsy Collins, Peter Wolf, Isaac Hayes, Chic, Afrika Bambaataa, Prince, Eric B. & Rakim, Hammer, Rod Stewart, Alison Moyet, Ashford & Simpson, Average White Band, Bobby Byrd, Bohannon, Earth, Wind & Fire, Full Force, Maze, Public Enemy, Slave, Steve Winwood, Beastie Boys, the Brothers Johnson, the JBs, the Ohio Players, War

Leland Rucker

Ruth Brown

Born Ruth Alston Weston, January 30, 1928, in Portsmouth, VA.

Modern audiences probably know Ruth Brown best as Motormouth Mabel in the 1988 film *Hairspray,* as the Tony Award-winning actress from the Broadway revue *Black & Blue,* or as the host of NPR's "Blues Stage." Brown's more resonant legacy is her string of hits for Atlantic Records during the '50s, which not only helped establish that label but also R&B's crossover appeal in the early rock era. Brown's first hits ("So Long," "Teardrops from My Eyes," "I'll Wait for You") were torchy jazz à la Billie Holiday and Dinah Washington, but as the age of rock 'n' roll dawned, she developed her own rough and ready style. Tunes such as "(Mama) He Treats Your Daughter Mean," "Wild Wild Young Men," "Mambo Baby," and "As Long As I'm Moving" were squealing, rocking paeans to youthful expectations, sexuality, and groove. Brown mixed her bawdy rockin' with sensual, romantic songs such as "Oh What a Dream" (written for her by Chuck Willis), "Love Has Joined Us Together" (with Clyde McPhatter), and "It's Love Baby." Her biggest hits were 1957's "Lucky Lips," a mainstream pop record that seems beneath her today, and the 1958 teen romper "This Little Girl's Gone Rockin'" (written by Bobby Darin), which eventually inspired a popular video on the Disney Channel. By the end of the '50s, hits for Brown were not coming as easily, and she was lost in the shuffle on Atlantic's crowded roster of stars. Signing with Phillips/Mercury, Brown recorded two solid LPs and had a minor hit single with her version of Faye Adams's "Shake a Hand" in 1962. Brown's career tailspinned badly after that; she was forced to join the Head Start program, and she trained to be a beautician while working as a maid, nurse's aide, cashier, and babysitter. During the mid-'70s, comedian Redd Foxx helped revive Brown's career by bringing her to Los Angeles

and casting her in bit parts on his hit sitcom *Sanford & Son.* Brown also had recurring roles on the ill-fated sitcoms *Hello, Larry* and *Checking In,* but her experiences in live theater would ultimately prove more rewarding. Roles in *Amen Corner* and *StaggerLee* won her critical praise and led to her Tony Award–winning role in 1989's *Black & Blue.* Brown signed with Fantasy Records in 1988 and has recorded four well-regarded discs featuring fresh interpretations of jazz and blues standards as well as occasional rip-it-up R&B. Other successes just as important followed. Her decade-old legal battle with Atlantic over unpaid royalties was finally resolved in her favor, and her old label helped set up the Rhythm & Blues Foundation as part of the settlement. Brown was elected to the Rock and Roll Hall of Fame in 1991. These days, Ruth Brown still records and plays live dates whenever time and health permit (often with protégé Bonnie Raitt), and 1996 saw the release of her autobiography, *Miss Rhythm.*

what to buy: The great string of records that resulted in Atlantic being nicknamed "The House That Ruth Built" are on the excellent *Rockin' in Rhythm: The Best of Ruth Brown* 🎵🎵🎵🎵 (Rhino, 1996, prod. Ahmet Ertegun, Jerry Wexler, Herb Abramson, Jerry Leiber, Mike Stoller), a 23-track compilation featuring her biggest hits as well as previously unreleased live versions of "(Mama) He Treats Your Daughter Mean" and "Oh What a Dream" from 1959. For a smart introduction to Brown's resurrection as a purveyor of soulful jazz, check out *Blues on Broadway* 🎵🎵🎵 (Fantasy, 1989, prod. Ralph Jungheim), which earned her a Grammy Award for Best Jazz Female Vocal Performance and mixes torch songs with such ribald sass as "If I Can't Sell It, I'll Keep Sittin' on It" and "Tain't Nobody's Biz-ness if I Do."

what to buy next: Many additional facets of Brown's salad days are revealed on *Miss Rhythm: Greatest Hits and More* 🎵🎵🎵🎵 (Atlantic, 1989, prod. Ahmet Ertegun, reissue prod. Bob Porter), a 40-song, two-CD set that not only includes all her Atlantic hits but also several pleasing LP tracks and four fine previously unreleased songs. Also, Brown proves she's lost none of her vocal chops or dramatic verve on *R+B = Ruth Brown* 🎵🎵🎵 (Bullseye Blues/Rounder, 1997, prod. Scott Billington), a potent grab bag of blues, R&B, and jazz featuring highly entertaining guest spots by Johnny Adams, Clarence "Gatemouth" Brown, and Bonnie Raitt.

what to avoid: For completists only, *Fine Brown Frame* 🎵🎵 (EMI/Capitol, 1993, prod. Sonny Lester) is not so much a bad LP as it is a disappointing one. Brown is in fine voice, but the Thad Jones/Mel Lewis Orchestra distracts from her performance with its brassy, jazz effrontery.

the rest:

Black Is Brown and Brown Is Beautiful 🎵🎵🎵 (DCC Records, 1981)
The Soul Survives 🎵🎵🎵 (DCC, 1982)

Takin Care of Business ♪♪♪ (Mr. R&B/Stockholm, 1984)
Have a Good Time ♪♪♪ (Fantasy, 1988)
Gospel Time ♪♪♪ (Lection Records, 1989)
Black and Blue ♪♪♪♪ (original cast recording) (DRG, 1989)
Help a Good Girl Go Bad ♪♪♪ (DCC Records, 1990)
Fine and Mellow ♪♪♪ (Fantasy 1991)
Sweet Baby of Mine ♪♪♥ (Route 66, 1992)
The Songs of My Life ♪♪♪ (Fantasy, 1993)
Live in London ♪♪♪♥ (Jazz House Records, 1995)

worth searching for: Hit the import racks for *Late Date with Ruth Brown* (Atlantic, 1956, prod. Ahmet Ertegun, Jerry Wexler), a reissue of Brown's best early LP, with romantic standards gorgeously framed by arranger/conductor Richard Wess. Also, Brown makes guest appearances on Charles Brown's *All My Life* (Bullseye Blues/Rounder, 1990, prod. Ron Levy) and B.B. King's *How Blue Can You Get: Classic Live, 1964–1996* (MCA, 1996, prod. various), which are still in print.

influences:

◄◄ Bessie Smith, Billie Holiday, Dinah Washington

►► Irma Thomas, Little Richard, Koko Taylor, Bonnie Raitt

Ken Burke

Jackson Browne

Born October 9, 1948, in Heidelberg, West Germany.

Jackson Browne was the right artist for his times—during a decade in which rock fans were growing up and dealing with real-life problems for the first time, Browne's thoughtful personal reflections seemed, well, thoughtful. When he titled his second LP *For Everyman*, a generation of fans took it for granted that they were the "everyman" Browne was writing about. At his best, he's a powerful songwriter because he writes personal truths and sings realistically about love from a post-collegiate point of view (Joni Mitchell was the female equivalent emotionally, though musically she was much more complex and experimental). His early songs, such as "Ready or Not" and "Take It Easy," may have been sexist drivel, but guys were like that then. And over the course of his albums you could watch Browne grow up; his best work—songs such as "Fountain of Sorrow" or "For a Dancer"—weren't macho manifestoes, but thoughtful (there's that word again) ruminations of lost love that went well beyond the simple romanticism of Top 40 radio. But on *Late for the Sky*—the same album that yielded "For a Dancer"—Browne planted the seeds of his ultimate downfall as an artist. His socio-political conscience, revealed on the anti-nuke song "Before the Deluge," which was powerful and moving as an album closer, was the beginning of Browne's immersion in issues of the day. By the 1980s, Browne's somewhat one-dimensional sound sounded strident because of his insistence in using his position as a pop star to issue political harangues, albeit important ones, about Central America, the environment, and modern America in general. Most of his recent output makes him sound as tedious and preachy as Bruce Cockburn, even though he's tried to reach back to earlier styles and musical values.

what to buy: *Late for the Sky* ♪♪♪♪ (Asylum, 1974, prod. Jackson Browne, Al Schmitt) is a bit mopey, but it hangs together as Browne's strongest and most melodious album, with a couple of rockers thrown in to perk up the listeners. The best song, the fondly reflective "Fountain of Sorrow," is typical of Browne's ability to make personal experience seem universal.

what to buy next: *The Pretender* ♪♪♪♪ (Asylum, 1976, prod. Jon Landau) gets a little ponderous on songs such as "Sleep's Dark and Silent Gate" and the title track, Browne's first rant at middle America, but it also was emotionally powerful, with songs of regret ("Your Bright Baby Blues," "Here Come Those Tears Again") and hope for the future ("The Only Child," "Daddy's Tune") in the face of tragedy (his first wife's 1976 suicide). It also solidified his commercial cachet and was his first platinum LP.

what to avoid: *Running on Empty* ♪ (Asylum, 1977, prod. Jackson Browne) was hailed at the time as a brilliant concept album about life on the road, but it hasn't held its luster. It now sounds like an indulgent pastiche thrown together with second-rate, emotionally uncompelling material, and a couple of curio-like cover songs (Rev. Gary Davis's "Cocaine" and the Zodiacs' "Stay," with a cameo vocal by guitarist David Lindley).

the rest:
Jackson Browne ♪♪ (Asylum, 1972);
For Everyman ♪♪♥ (Asylum, 1973)
Hold Out ♪♪♥ (Asylum, 1980)
Lawyers in Love ♪♪ (Asylum, 1983)
Lives in the Balance ♪♪ (Asylum, 1986)
World in Motion ♪♪ (Elektra, 1989)
I'm Alive ♪♪♥ (Elektra, 1993)
Looking East ♪♪ (Elektra, 1996)
The Next Voice You Hear: The Best of Jackson Browne ♪♪♪♪ (Elektra, 1997)

worth searching for: The promotional CD for Browne's 1993 single "I'm Alive" was accompanied by a well-chosen 12-song retrospective that was digitally remastered and sounds better than Browne's regular CDs.

influences:

◄◄ Leonard Cohen, Eric Andersen, Phil Ochs

►► David Wilcox, Garth Brooks, Natalie Merchant, Alanis Morissette, Indigo Girls, Bruce Cockburn

Gil Asakawa

Jackson Browne (© Ken Settle)

Brownsville Station /Cub Koda

Formed 1969, in Ann Arbor, MI. Disbanded 1979.

Cub Koda, guitar, vocals; Michael Lutz, guitar, bass, vocals; T.J. Cronley, drums (1969–72); Tony Driggins, bass (1969–73); Henry (H-Bomb) Weck, drums (1972–79); Bruce Nazarian, guitar, bass, vocals (1975–79).

Following the lead of fellow Ann Arborites Iggy Pop & the Stooges, Brownsville Station was a punk-rock pioneer, serving up raw-edged guitar tunes that featured the quirky snarl of lead singer Cub Koda. The band hit its commercial apex with the 1974 smash "Smokin' in the Boys' Room," the snot-nosed anthem for a generation of teens and pre-teens that reached #3 on the charts.

what to buy: Besides the essential title track, *Smokin' in the Boys' Room: The Best of Brownsville Station ♪♪♪♪* (Rhino, 1993, prod. various) includes the wonderful "Let Your Yeah Be Yeah," the wacky "Martian Boogie," and "I'm the Leader of the Gang," a punk-rock prototype from the band's 1974 LP *School Punks*.

what to buy next: On his own, Koda has released the well-received *Welcome to My Job: The Cub Koda Collection, 1963–1993 ♪♪♪* (Blue Wave, 1993) and *Abba Dabba Dabba: A Bananza of Hits ♪♪♪* (Schoolkids, 1994).

worth searching for: Coda's *Live at B.L.U.E.S. 1982* (Wolf, 1991) is available as an import.

influences:
◀◀ MC5, the Bob Seger System, the Stooges

▶▶ Mötley Crüe, Joan Jett

William Hanson

Jack Bruce

Born May 14, 1943, in Glasgow, Scotland.

Awarded a scholarship for cello and composition, Jack Bruce dropped out of the Royal Scottish Academy of Music to play jazz bass, then moved to London and hooked up with some of the key players of the '60s British blues boom—Alexis Korner, John Mayall, and Graham Bond. He also was with Manfred Mann before teaming up with Eric Clapton and Ginger Baker to form the influential blues-rock power trio Cream in 1966. It was Bruce's clear tenor voice, pop sensibilities, and improvisational jazz spirit that set a solid foundation for Clapton's aggressive guitar explorations. After the supergroup split up in 1968, Bruce went on to create a powerful mix of blues, pop, rock, and jazz. He's also worked with premier guitarists such as John McLaughlin, Larry Coryell, Gary Moore, and Robin Trower. But

he's never come close to the synthesis of power, art, and public acclaim he enjoyed with Clapton and Cream.

what to buy: *A Question of Time ♪♪♪♪* (Epic, 1989, prod. Joe Blaney, Jack Bruce) features subtly compelling melodies, superb vocals, a balance of scorching rock and soothing acoustic guitars, and a challenging mix of styles. In other words, it is a microcosm of Bruce's diverse post-Cream solo career.

what to buy next: The two-disc set *Willpower ♪♪♪♪* (Polydor, 1989, prod. various) is a solid retrospective of 17 songs that cover Bruce's broad spectrum of styles. Eric Clapton guests on two songs. *Cities of the Heart ♪♪♪♪* (CMP, 1994, prod. Jack Bruce) was recorded live in Cologne, Germany, in 1993, and features some tasty Cream morsels including, "Spoonful," "Sunshine of Your Love," and "Politician."

what to avoid: *How's Tricks ♪* (Polydor, 1977, prod. Bill Halverson), an uninspired set of 10 lackluster tunes performed by a thankfully short-lived version of the Jack Bruce Band.

the rest:
Songs for a Tailor ♪♪♪ (Polydor, 1969)
Things We Like ♪♪♪ (Polydor, 1970)
Harmony Row ♪♪ (Polydor, 1971)
Out of the Storm ♪♪♪ (Polydor, 1974)
Somethinels ♪♪♪♪ (CMP, 1993)

influences:
◀◀ Willie Dixon, John Mayall, Charlie Parker, Dizzy Gillespie

▶▶ Ozzy Osbourne, Robert Plant, Geddy Lee, Stanley Clarke, Rob Wasserman, Jaco Pastorius, Jack Casady

see also: *Cream*

David Yonke

David Bryan

See: Bon Jovi

Bryndle

See: Karla Bonoff

bt

Born Brian Transeau, in Washington, DC.

A bit pretentious in his presentation but entirely listenable, bt blends dance music with headphone trippiness in his recorded output. Attending (but not graduating from) the prestigious Berklee College of Music, Brian Transeau was a classically trained pianist and otherwise accomplished musician from his early teens on. After branching out into DJ-driven dance tracks with various collaborators, bt began to record on his own. The result was the lush instrumentation that pervades both of his full-length releases.

what's available: *IMA* ♫♫♫♫ (Perfecto/Kinetic/Reprise, 1995/1996, prod. Brian Transeau) is a varied introduction to his wide array of stylistic approaches. Packaged as a double CD and containing early singles "Loving You More" and "Deeper Sunshine" as well as "Blue Skies," his collaboration with Tori Amos, *IMA* is an impressive debut. *ESCM (Electric Sky Church-Music)* ♫♫♫♫ (Perfecto/Kinetic/Reprise, 1997, prod. Brian Transeau) is a bit more derivative, with the New Orderesque bassline on "Lullaby for Gaia" and the nine inch nails–like "Solar Plexus," but equally enjoyable. With guest assistance from former Morrissey cohort (and ex-Durutti Column member) Vinnie Reilly and the Pyschedelic Furs' Richard Butler, *ESCM* actually sounds a tad more accomplished than *IMA*.

influences:

◄◄ Kraftwerk, nine inch nails, New Order, Depeche Mode, Pink Floyd, Moby, Aphex Twin, Andreas Vollenvider, Kitaro, Mike Oldfield, George Winston, Transglobal Underground, Dead Can Dance, DJ Shadow

Barry M. Prickett

Roy Buchanan

Born September 23, 1939, in Ozark, TN. Died August 14, 1988, in Fairfax, VA.

Roy Buchanan was a virtuoso of the Fender Telecaster. His expressive use of harmonics and controlled feedback, among many other techniques, set a high standard for all the guitarists who came after him. Among his admirers are jazz legend Stanley Jordan, Jeff Beck, the Band's Robbie Robertson, Stax/Volt's Steve Cropper, and the Rolling Stones, who considered Buchanan as a replacement for Mick Taylor during the mid-'70s. A teenaged guitar prodigy, Buchanan first made a name for himself playing behind Checker Records' rockabilly star Dale Hawkins on his minor hits "My Babe" and "Grandma's House." Stints with Canadian rocker Ronnie Hawkins & the Hawks (he preceded Robertson), Bob Luman, and Freddy Cannon led to his own unsuccessful recordings for various small labels. During the early '60s, he settled into a long, steady nightclub gig in Maryland with his band, the Snakestretchers, and dazzled the faithful with his ever-growing instrumental prowess. Buchanan's national discovery came in 1971 via a PBS documentary titled *The Best Unknown Guitarist in the World*, which led to a multi-album deal with Polydor. Benefiting from FM-radio's we'll-play-anything start-up, Buchanan's extended jams (he seldom sang or used singers) found great favor among college students and blues enthusiasts. His switch to Atlantic Records in 1976 resulted in a more polished overall

sound and fresh musical explorations, but FM's instrumental rock phase had ended, and sales fell off. Buchanan resurfaced during the mid-'80s, cutting a few brisk-selling blues LPs for the Chicago-based Alligator label. However, he enjoyed little of his renewed success: A shy and reticent man who had trouble accepting his lot as a guitar god, Buchanan let insecurities drive him to drink. In 1988 he was jailed for public drunkenness, and, according to police reports, committed suicide (though many dispute these findings). Despite his tragic death, Buchanan's recorded legacy lives on, inspiring (and frustrating) new generations of would-be guitar heroes.

what to buy: Buchanan tackles an impressive array of styles (jazz, blues, hard rock, funk, rockabilly) on *Guitar on Fire: The Atlantic Sessions* ♫♫♫♫ (Rhino, 1993, compilation prod. Jean-Charles Costa), a superior 16-track collection culled from his three LPs for Atlantic. Contributions from the likes of Steve Cropper, Donald "Duck" Dunn, Stanley Clarke, and Luther Vandross help make this a perfect introduction to a master guitarist.

what to buy next: Far more extensive, *Sweet Dreams: The Anthology* ♫♫♫♫ (Polydor, 1992, prod. various) covers two CDs and 26 tracks containing Buchanan's best start-to-finish LP, nine previously unreleased tracks, and in-depth liner notes from Colin Escott. Lengthy rock jams and blues galore are dominant here, but occasional nods to soul and country attest to the depth and versatility of his technique. Blues aficionados will especially appreciate *Dancing on the Edge* ♫♫♫♫ (Alligator, 1986, prod. Roy Buchanan), which boasts some fine versions of "You Can't Judge a Book by the Cover" and "Beer Drinkin' Woman," as well as inspired vocal contributions from Delbert McClinton.

what to avoid: Poor sound quality greatly hampers *Malagueña: The Collector's Edition* ♫♫ (Annecillo, 1997), an eccentric grab bag of live shows, radio appearances, and rehearsal jams. For completists only.

the rest:
Butch and the Snake Stretchers ♫♫♫ (Bioya, 1971/Adelphi, 1992)
First Album ♫♫♫♫ (Polydor, 1972/1986)
Second Album ♫♫♫ (Polydor, 1973)
That's What I'm Here For ♫♫♫ (Polydor, 1974)
Livestock ♫♫♫♫ (Polydor, 1975)
My Babe ♫♫♫ (Era, 1980)
When a Guitar Plays the Blues ♫♫♫ (Alligator, 1985)
Hot Wires ♫♫♫ (Alligator, 1987/1993)

worth searching for: For some good old-time rock 'n' roll, check out *The Early Years* (Krazy Kat, 1989), a collection of tracks Buchanan cut during the early '60s. Those who wish to hear Buchanan backing up Dale Hawkins should pick up a copy of *Oh Susie Q: The Best of Dale Hawkins* (Chess, 1995), a historically important collection that also features contributions from James Burton, Scotty Moore, Willie Dixon, and the Moonglows.

influences:

◄◄ Scotty Moore, Johnny "Guitar" Watson, Roy Nichols, James Burton, Kenny Paulsen

►► Steve Cropper, Robbie Robertson, Jeff Beck, Jimi Hendrix, Stanley Jordan, Stevie Ray Vaughan, Danny Gatton

Ken Burke

Lindsey Buckingham

Born October 3, 1947, in Palo Alto, CA.

Although it's hard to separate Lindsey Buckingham from his years with Fleetwood Mac, it's the only way to fully appreciate his impact on that band as well as his achievements as a solo artist. By the time that he and girlfriend Stevie Nicks joined Fleetwood Mac in 1974, the two had already spent time together in the acid rock band Fritz and recorded a mostly folk-rock collection under the billing Buckingham Nicks. It was this album that brought them to the attention of Mick Fleetwood; Nicks gave Fleetwood Mac its first sex symbol, but it was Buckingham's brilliant musicianship, luscious arrangements, and studio acumen that influenced the sound of the band and led Fleetwood Mac to the top of the charts. Inspired by the punk rock movement and given the role as musical director for the band, Buckingham began to push the group's music into more adventurous directions, which met with some resistance from the rest of the group after the *Tusk* album failed to reach the same commercial heights as its record-setting predecessor, *Rumours*. Buckingham released his first two solo albums while still part of Fleetwood Mac, but in 1987 the longing to spend more time in the studio crafting his own sound got the best of him and Buckingham formally left the band—though he was an enthusiastic participant in the group's 1997 reunion tour.

what to buy: *Out of the Cradle* 🎵🎵🎵🎵 (Reprise, 1992, prod. Linsdey Buckingham, Richard Dashut) is Buckingham's finest moment, full of sophisticated arrangements, lush harmonies and vocal treatments, classic finger-picked guitar work, and smart pop craftsmanship.

what to buy next: *Law and Order* 🎵🎵🎵 (Asylum, 1981, prod. Lindsey Buckingham, Richard Dashut), his first solo outing, is fun, quirky, and quick. The singles "Trouble" and "Bawana" and his re-make of "A Satisfied Mind" insure a winner on their own.

the rest:
Go Insane 🎵🎵🎵 (Elektra, 1984)

worth searching for: The soundtrack to *National Lampoon's Vacation* (Warner Bros., 1983) includes the Buckingham songs "Dancing across the U.S.A." and "Holiday Road," which could have fit perfectly on *Law and Order* or Fleetwood Mac's *Tusk*. Also, *Buckingham Nicks* (Polydor, 1973) has yet to be released on CD.

influences:

◄◄ Brian Wilson, the Kingston Trio, the Sex Pistols, the Clash

►► John Stewart, Matthew Sweet, Marshall Crenshaw

see also: *Fleetwood Mac*

Mike Joiner

The Buckinghams

Formed mid-1965, in Chicago, IL. Disbanded 1970. Re-formed 1980.

Dennis Tufano, vocals; Carl Giannarese, lead guitar; Nick Fortune, bass; Dennis Miccolis, keyboards (1965–67); Marty Grebb, organ (1967–69); Jon-Jon Poulos, drums; John Turner, keyboards (1969–70).

Although the group changed its name from the Pulsations to the Buckinghams to glom onto the British Invasion, this quintet from northwest Chicago sounded more like the West Coast acts emerging at the time, most notably Paul Revere & the Raiders and Gary Puckett & the Union Gap. Denny Tufano's pleasantly engaging voice and the group's punchy combination of guitar, organ, and brass made for some stirring white-boy soul stylings, but much of the group's success was owed to outside forces: songwriter Jim Holvay had a talent for crafting hooky melodies, resulting in a string of highly durable hit singles for the group; and ex–Mother of Invention James William Guercio acted as something of a sixth member, producing, arranging, conducting, and even composing for the band.

what's available: Although its 18 songs are a bit indulgent, *Mercy, Mercy, Mercy (A Collection)* 🎵🎵🎵 (Legacy, 1991, prod. various) features all of the Buckinghams' bona fide hits—"Kind of a Drag," "Don't You Care," "Hey Baby (They're Playing Our Song)," and "Susan." A pleasant reminder of a fun and wistful period in rock's history.

influences:

◄◄ The Rascals, Paul Revere & the Raiders, Gary Puckett & the Union Gap, the Nazz

►► Neil Diamond, Barry Manilow

Christopher Scapelliti

Jeff Buckley

Born Jeffery Scott Moorhead Buckley, November 17, 1966, in Anaheim, CA. Died May 29, 1997, in Memphis, TN.

Like his estranged father Tim Buckley, this young and extravagantly gifted songwriter lived a troubled life. Leaving behind just one exquisite full-length album, *Grace*, Jeff Buckley's career was cut short during a moonlight swim in the Mississippi River a day prior to commencing work on a proper follow-up at Memphis' Easley Studio. By the time of his death, Buckley had won a loyal following across the world on the strength of his insightful musical flights—a flamboyant mix of glitter and angst, bared emotion and entrancing sensuality. There was more to the singer than his expressive voice and articulate guitar playing let on, though. The impenetrable soul that ran through his songs and live shows informed a rare gravity in a performer, as if he always knew his time on earth would expire prematurely.

what to buy: Lush and compelling, Buckley's debut, *Grace* 𝄞𝄞𝄞𝄞 (Columbia, 1994, prod. Andy Wallace, Jeff Buckley), demonstrates the ethereal singer's staggering range, from falsetto heights to startling growls. "Last Goodbye" and "So Real" showcase his instinct for inventive arrangements and warm sentimentality; while covers of Leonard Cohen ("Hallelujah") and Nina Simone ("Lilac Wine") threaten to outshine the originals.

what to buy next: Compiled posthumously by his mother, Mary Guibert, and Buckley's surviving associates, *Sketches (For My Sweetheart, the Drunk)* 𝄞𝄞𝄞 (Columbia, 1998, prod. Tom Verlaine, Andy Wallace, Jeff Buckley) is a double album full of material never intended to be heard by a mass audience. Now it serves as the last testament of the singer's touched existence. The first half includes songs recorded with producer Tom Verlaine. Sprinkled with vibrant images of love, lust, and, most hauntingly, death, the music gorgeously coalesces Buckley's fondness of soul, jazz, and classic rock into a trembling, poetic noise. The second half of the album consists of raw home demos and radio recordings. It takes a few listens to get past the rough edges, but soon enough the chilling melodies begin to emerge, particularly on the soaring "Haven't You Heard" and the longing "Your Flesh Is So Nice."

the rest:
Live at Sin-E 𝄞𝄞𝄞 (Columbia 1993)

worth searching for: Because of his international popularity, much of Buckley's pivotal material wound up on import-only EPs. *Live from the Bataclan* (Columbia, 1993), recorded in Paris, is a small concert document that provides a fine example of the singer's acrobatic vocal capabilities. There is a supreme version of "Dream Brother" and a moving take on Van Morrison's "The Way Young Lovers Do."

influences:

◄◄ Nusrat Fateh Ali Khan, Led Zeppelin, Van Morrison

►► Radiohead, Mark Eitzel, Shudder to Think

Aidin Vaziri

Tim Buckley

Born February 14, 1947, in Washington, DC. Died June 29, 1975, in Santa Monica, CA.

One of numerous folk singer-songwriters to surface in Bob Dylan's mid-60's wake, Tim Buckley soon parted company with his peers to chart a path very much his own. Though his earliest records seem innocently romantic today (he was just 19 when his first album appeared), his turn towards a more freeform, jazz-influenced sound pushed his introspective and always impassioned vocals right off the map. For it was Buckley's voice, above all, that distinguished him—a stunning, four-octave wonder that ranged from angelic tenderness to blistering passion. Recording for Frank Zappa's Straight label from 1970 to 1973, his folk/jazz experimentation—and angst-ridden, sexually direct material (e.g., "Get on Top of Me Woman")—was critically admired but found little commercial acceptance. By 1975, Buckley was dead of a heroin overdose. Ironically, his underappreciated legacy was to a degree rediscovered two decades later through the popularity of his son Jeff Buckley, who sounded uncannily like his father, and came to an equally premature death.

what to buy: Oddly, for a singer of Buckley's improvisational talents, no live recordings appeared during his lifetime. Two recent releases have remedied that—and they are a perfect place for the uninitiated to start. *Dream Letter: Live in London, 1968* 𝄞𝄞𝄞 (Manifesto, 1990, prod. Bill Inglot, Lee Hammond) is a two-CD set recorded by the BBC. It captures the passion of Buckley's early performances, with jazz-textured guitar, bass, and vibraphone backing. *Honeyman* 𝄞𝄞𝄞 (Manifesto Records, 1995) is from a 1973 New York radio show—and an altogether edgier, more incendiary affair from a man who had now left his '60s innocence far behind.

what to buy next: Adventurous listeners should proceed directly to *Starsailor* 𝄞𝄞𝄞 (Rhino, 1970, prod. Tim Buckley), Buckley's most uncompromising work—by a long shot. Consciously experimental, its raw passion still outweighs its avant-garde pretensions. The more accessible, languidly melancholy *Blue Afternoon* 𝄞𝄞𝄞 (Straight, 1969) is the best of the '60s discs. *Greetings from LA* 𝄞𝄞𝄞 (Straight, 1972, prod. Jerry Goldstein) is gloriously decadent late-era Buckley, with the singer in full carnal heat.

what to avoid: Near the end, the inspiration was sadly lacking. *Look at the Fool* 𝄞 (Planet 3 Records, 1974, prod. Joe Falsia) provides the evidence.

the rest:
Tim Buckley 𝄞𝄞𝄞 (Elektra, 1966, 1992)
Goodbye and Hello 𝄞𝄞𝄞 (Elektra, 1967, 1989)
Happy/Sad 𝄞𝄞𝄞 (Elektra, 1969, 1989)
Lorca 𝄞𝄞 (Elektra, 1970, 1992)
Sefronia 𝄞𝄞 (Discreet, 1974/Planet 3 Records, 1994)
The Peel Sessions 𝄞𝄞𝄞 (Dutch East India, 1991)
Live at the Troubadour, 1969 𝄞𝄞𝄞 (Rhino, 1994)

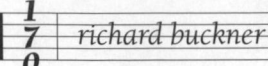

worth searching for: If you can find it, Buckley's soundtrack for the 1969 Hall Bartlett film *Changes* is worth hearing.

influences:

◄◄ Bob Dylan, Leadbelly, Miles Davis, John Coltrane

►► This Mortal Coil, Bono, Patti Smith, Jeff Buckley

Doug Pippin

Richard Buckner

Born 1964, in Chico, CA.

Richard Buckner's music is a lot like West Texas—flat and seemingly featureless, it nevertheless yields charms if you know what to look for—especially at night. Buckner makes late-night records that perfectly capture that moment when night lurches toward dawn and one's thoughts turn toward why one is still awake and alone. He writes intensely autobiographical songs that make him out to be a modern-day Manfred (a doer of good as well as evil, and extremes in both), and he seems like the sort of guy who goes looking for dysfunctional relationships to provide song fodder. But he is also the rare singer-songwriter who makes his own self-absorption interesting, which he does with his voice as well as his pen. "I shot my insides out with grief" is not a line you can go halfway with; Buckner's saving grace is that he never holds back.

what to buy: Buckner made his debut with *Bloomed* ����� (Dejadisc, 1995, prod. Lloyd Maines), laying out a basic formula—quiet country-rock arrangements, impressionistic lyrics, and his nakedly emotional voice. It all coheres into music as spare, dry, and evocative as a Georgia O'Keefe painting. The standout track is "22," a haunting first-person account of suicide so convincing that it's miraculous Buckner lived through writing and singing it. Even better is the follow-up, *Devotion + Doubt* ����� (MCA, 1997, prod. J.D. Foster), which is as Dustbowl-stark as the shadowy picture of the moon on the cover. Buckner is in love with the loss of love, and spends this entire album in pursuit of ghosts. Difficult, but also magnificent.

the rest:

Since ����� (MCA, 1998)

influences:

◄◄ Townes Van Zant, Guy Clark, Butch Hancock, Rosanne Cash, Nick Drake

►► Whiskeytown

David Menconi

Buffalo Springfield

Formed 1966, in Los Angeles, CA. Disbanded 1968.

Stephen Stills, guitar, vocals; Neil Young, guitar, vocals; Richie Furay, guitar, vocals; Dewey Martin, drums, vocals; Bruce Palmer, bass, vocals (1966); Jim Fielder, bass, vocals (1967), Ken Koblun, bass (1967); Jim Messina, bass, vocals (1968).

This was a transitional group that could be considered more important for what its members did after they left this seemingly jinxed band—especially Stephen Stills (Crosby, Stills & Nash), Richie Furay (Poco), and Neil Young. Short-time bassist Jim Fielder went on to Blood, Sweat & Tears, and Jim Messina, after a stint with Poco, hooked up with Kenny Loggins for a successful run. Young, of course, became Neil Young. Still, its traumatic and short career doesn't take away from the immense charm of Buffalo Springfield's music. "There's something happening here/What it is ain't exactly clear," from the band's first hit single, "For What It's Worth," became a catchphrase for the growing counterculture and introduced Stills as a songwriter (it recently found another life as the chief sample for rap group Public Enemy's title song for the Spike Lee film *He Got Game*). Young's contributions, from "I Am a Child" to "Broken Arrow" and "Mr. Soul," are early blueprints of his formidable talent. There are kernels of CSN, Poco, the Eagles, and every other West Coast rock group in the Springfield's mostly pleasant soft folk and country-flavored rock.

what to buy: *Buffalo Springfield Again* ����� (Atco, 1967/1987) is the group's strongest effort song-wise, with Young's durable "Mr. Soul," fragmented "Broken Arrow," and hopeful "Expecting to Fly"; and Stills's kicking "Rock and Roll Woman" and lyrical "Bluebird." If you see Young as the key to the Springfield, the 23 tracks of *Buffalo Springfield/Neil Young* ����� (Atlantic, 1986) will do wonders for your argument.

what to buy next: *Retrospective* ����� (Atco, 1969/1986, prod. various), released soon after the group broke up and, at 12 tracks, thin by contemporary standards, will have to do until the overdue box set comes out. In its new CD version, *Buffalo Springfield* ����� (Atco, 1966/Elektra Entertainment, 1997, prod. Charles Greene, Brian Stone) is more than a surprising debut, with "For What It's Worth," "Go and Say Goodbye," "Sit Down I Think I Love You," "Nowadays Clancy Can't Even Sing," and "Burned"; it's a historical document as well, with a total of 41 tracks that represent the two versions in which the album was released.

the rest:

Last Time Around ���� (Atco, 1968)

worth searching for: Bootlegs of *Stampede*, the group's aborted final album, boast a few keepers such as "Neighbor Don't Worry" and "Down to the Wire."

influences:

◄◄ The Everly Brothers, the Beatles, the Byrds

►► Crosby, Stills & Nash, Poco, the Flying Burrito Brothers, Linda Ronstadt, the Eagles, Loggins & Messina, Warren Zevon, Blue Rodeo, Crazy Horse, the Long Ryders, the Band, Uncle Tupelo, Michael Nesmith, Fairport Convention, Moby Grape

see also: *Crosby, Stills & Nash, Neil Young, Poco, Loggins & Messina, Moby Grape*

Leland Rucker

Buffalo Tom

Formed 1986, in Boston, MA.

Bill Janovitz, vocals, guitar; Chris Colbourn, bass; Tom Maginnis, drums.

Dinosaur Jr. frontman J Mascis co-produced Buffalo Tom's first two albums; that and sonic similarities at first led critics to tag the trio Dinosaur Jr. Jr. Minimal melodies carried by Bill Janovitz's everyman vocals generally rise out of an inexorable wash of sound rather than a messy din, though the debut's single, "Reason Why," gets kind of rowdy; contrarily, there are periodic acoustic forays later on. These ordinary Joes have cultivated an unpretentious, song-driven, jangle-crunch guitar band destined by its unprepossessing attitude to be perpetually underrated.

what to buy: On the group's third album, *Let Me Come Over* ✐✐✐✐ (Beggars Banquet, 1992, prod. Paul Kolderie, Sean Slade, Buffalo Tom), the distinctive musical personality first heard on *Birdbrain* blossoms fully, typified by a jangly acoustic/electric blend—"Taillights Fade" has a Neil Young–ish guitar solo, "Mountains of Your Head" is as catchy as the Lemonheads, and "Larry" is positively anthemic—with variety coming from the changing proportions. The emphasis on songs increases with the higher profile of the vocals.

what to buy next: *Birdbrain* ✐✐✐✐ (Beggars Banquet, 1990, prod. Buffalo Tom, J Mascis, Sean Slade) mixes in more acoustic guitar and ups the hummability quotient several notches over the debut while maintaining its power. Of note are two bonus tracks—a quieter "Reason Why" and a totally acoustic cover of Psychedelic Furs' "Heaven" (with cello). *big red letter day* ✐✐✐✐ (Beggars Banquet, 1993, prod. the Robb Brothers, Buffalo Tom) picks up where *Let Me Come Over* left off, if somewhat less distinctively.

what to avoid: The debut, *Buffalo Tom* (SST, 1989/Beggars Banquet, 1992, prod. J Mascis, Buffalo Tom) ✐✐, isn't bad, but the band still sounds too much like an aspiring Dinosaur Jr. at this point.

the rest:

Sleepy Eyed ✐✐✐✐ (EastWest, 1995)
Smitten N/A (Polydor, 1998)

solo outings:

Bill Janovitz:

Lonesome Billy ✐✐✐ (Beggars Banquet, 1996)

influences:

◄◄ Dinosaur Jr., Mission of Burma, Hüsker Dü

►► Grant Lee Buffalo

Steve Holtje

Jimmy Buffett

Born December 25, 1946, in Pascagoula, MS.

Jimmy Buffett's tropical tunes and seafaring tales offer a temporary escape for every office-bound baby boomer with a mortgage, a two-car garage, and a surly boss. Few can resist the singer-songwriter's balmy fantasyland filled with palm trees, sandy beaches, cold beer, fast boats, cheeseburgers, margaritas, and romance. Sure, there are sharks to reckon with and volcanoes to flee and broken hearts to mend. But, as Buffett's message dictates, they can be dealt with. Buffett majored in journalism at Auburn University and the University of Southern Mississippi, working briefly at *Billboard* magazine before launching his career as a folk and country singer-songwriter. A failed marriage and a move from Nashville to Key West, Florida, triggered a new appreciation for the healing powers of the tropical sun. Buffett started writing earnest, positive songs with humor and wit, and his audiences grew slowly but steadily. He scored his first hit in 1974 with the wonderfully wistful ballad "Come Monday," but it was the booze-in-the-blender philosophical shrug of "Margaritaville" that put the wind in Buffett's sails. With little radio play and a glaring shortage of hit singles—but with a loyal and large group of Parrothead fans—Buffett has become one of the wealthiest beach bums in history—as well as a best-selling author, a playwright (a stage adapation of Herman Wouk's *Don't Stop the Carnival*), and a filmmaker.

what to buy: *Songs You Know by Heart: Jimmy Buffett's Greatest Hit(s)* ✐✐✐✐ (MCA, 1985, prod. Jimmy Buffett) is an essential first step for anyone curious about the Parrothead phenomenon. The album includes the hit(s)—"Margaritaville," "Cheeseburger in Paradise"–and the concert favorites—"Fins," "Volcano," "Pencil Thin Mustache." Buffett's breakthrough album, *Changes in Latitudes, Changes in Attitudes* ✐✐✐✐ (MCA, 1977, prod. Norbert Putnam), is a perfect sampler of feel-good folk-rockers (the title track, "Margaritaville") and pensive ballads ("Biloxi," "Wonder Why We Ever Go Home"). Another good overview is *Feeding Frenzy* ✐✐✐ (MCA, 1990, prod. Michael

Utley, Elliot Scheiner), a live recording featuring 72 minutes of classic concert craziness.

what to buy next: If Buffett has cast his spell on you, you won't mind indulging in the four-disc box set *Boats Beaches Bars & Ballads* 🎵🎵🎵🎵 (Margaritaville/MCA, 1992, prod. various), an extensive retrospective dividing the 72 songs by the categories listed in the title. *Living and Dying in 3/4 Time* 🎵🎵🎵 (MCA, 1974, prod. Don Gant) captures the lyrical charm of early Buffett ("Come Monday," "The Wino and I Know"), while *Banana Wind* 🎵🎵🎵 (MCA, 1996, prod. Russ Kunkel) shows some justifiable crankiness ("Jamaica Mistaica," "Cultural Infidel") along with the steel-drum calypso instrumental title track, a first for Buffett.

what to avoid: *Last Mango in Paris* **woof!** (MCA, 1985, prod. Jimmy Bowen) and *Off to See the Lizard* 🎵 (MCA, 1989, prod. Elliot Scheiner) wander around in a sea of overly slick production losing sight of Buffett's laid-back charm.

the rest:
A White Sport Coat and a Pink Crustacean 🎵🎵🎵 (MCA, 1973)
A-1-A 🎵🎵🎵🎵 (MCA, 1974)
Havana Daydreamin' 🎵🎵🎵 (MCA, 1976)
Son of a Son of a Sailor 🎵🎵🎵 (MCA, 1978)
You Had to Be There 🎵🎵🎵 (MCA, 1978)
Volcano 🎵🎵🎵 (MCA, 1979)
Coconut Telegraph 🎵🎵🎵 (MCA, 1981)
Somewhere over China 🎵🎵 (MCA, 1981)
One Particular Harbor 🎵🎵 (MCA, 1983)
Riddles in the Sand 🎵🎵 (MCA, 1985)
Floridays 🎵🎵 (MCA, 1986)
Hot Water 🎵🎵 (MCA, 1988)
Before the Beach 🎵🎵🎵 (Margaritaville/MCA, 1993)
Fruitcakes 🎵🎵🎵 (Margaritaville/MCA, 1994)
Barometer Soup 🎵🎵🎵 (Margaritaville/MCA, 1995)
Christmas Island 🎵🎵🎵 (Margaritaville/MCA, 1996)
Don't Stop the Carnival 🎵🎵🎵 (Margaritaville/MCA, 1998)

worth searching for: *All the Great Hits* (Prism Leisure, 1994, prod. various) is a British hits collection that's a bit more generous than *Songs You Know by Heart*.

influences:
◄◄ Gamble Rogers, Irma Thomas, Benny Spellman, Jerry Jeff Walker

►► The Iguanas, subdudes, Blues Traveler

David Yonke

The Buggles
Formed 1979, in London, England. Disbanded 1981.

Trevor Horn, vocals, keyboards; Geoffrey Downes, vocals, keyboards.

The Buggles earned a footnote in rock history by having the du-

bious honor of being the first act whose video was played on MTV—the aptly titled "Video Killed the Radio Star." It's a catchy enough tune, although much of the credit goes to its then high-tech production—an ominous prelude to the hollow electronic pop that was to ensue throughout the first half of the '80s. Horn and Downes shockingly agreed to join prog-rock stalwarts Yes in 1980, an experiment that ended a year later. Downes went on to the band Asia, while Horn has become an in-demand producer who, among other things, has helped guide Seal to stardom.

what to buy: *The Age of Plastic* 🎵🎵 (Island, 1979, prod. the Buggles) has about the same texture of its title, but it does contain "Video Killed the Radio Star," as prescient a hit as you're likely to find circa 1979.

influences:
◄◄ Devo, Kraftwerk

►► Flash & the Pan, Soft Cell

see also: *Asia, Yes*

Allan Orski

Buick MacKane
See: Alejandro Escovedo

Built to Spill
Formed 1993, in Boise, ID.

Doug Martsch, vocals, guitar; Ralf Youtz, drums (1993); Andy Capps, drums (1994–present); Scott Plouf, drums (1997); Brett Netson, guitar (1993, 1997); Brett Nelson, bass (1994, 1997).

Essentially the studio-focused recording project of former Treepeople frontman Doug Martsch and a rotating cast of Idaho (and occasionally Pacific Northwest) sidemen, Built to Spill has gone through four distinct incarnations since its 1993 inception. And though the group's sound has ranged from Crazy Horse–style guitar workouts to more intimate, fractured indie-rock, the one thing that has remained consistent is Martsch's talent for both smart songwriting and elaborate, twisted arrangements. Built to Spill may have its roots in punk, but Martsch's songs almost always go beyond the genre's verse-chorus-verse conventions. Tired of touring and sick of Seattle, Martsch left the Treepeople to return to his native Idaho in 1992 and founded the first version of Built to Spill the following year. Aided by Caustic Resin's Brett Netson (not to be confused with occasional sideman Brett Nelson), he set the blueprint for his expressive, formally complex songs with *Ultimate Alternative Wavers*. With a completely different lineup, he turned down his guitar heroics a little to record *There's Nothing Wrong with Love*, then made a more sonically convoluted EP with the Boise band Caustic Resin. A major label recording contract only brought out his experimental side even more—*Perfect from Now On* is filled with mind-blowing time signatures, prog-rock touches, and feedback-heavy jams.

what to buy: Martsch the songwriter comes through strongest on *There's Nothing Wrong with Love* ♫♫♫♫ (Up, 1994, prod. Built to Spill), an album that deephasizes feedback and borrows from the fractured pop of Pavement.

what to buy next: The initial blast of *Ultimate Alternative Wavers* ♫♫♫♫ (C/Z, 1993, prod. Built to Spill) is still a strong one, all the more striking because no band had ever before combined punk rock angst with prog-rock instrumental virtuosity. By *Perfect from Now On* ♫♫♫♫ (Warner Bros., 1997, prod. Built to Spill), virtuosity gained the upper hand, but Martsch had become a more evocative player, conjuring emotions with guitar lines as surely as he does with his voice. A compilation of singles and outtakes from every Built to Spill lineup, *The Normal Years* ♫♫♫♫ (K, 1996, prod. Built to Spill) is a mixed bag but an enjoyable one; some of the group's singles are among its best work.

what to avoid: Martsch's tendency to bury tuneful songs beneath walls of guitar feedback spirals out of control on the EP *Built to Spill/Caustic Resin* ♫♫♫ (Up, 1995, prod. Built to Spill).

influences:

◀◀ Neil Young, Pavement

▶▶ Archers of Loaf

Robert Levine

LTJ Bukem

Born Danny Bukem, in England.

LTJ Bukem is one of the initial architects of the jungle/drum & bass dance movement. Trained on piano and classical music as a child, this British DJ grew up listening to the wide-ranging radio shows of hip-hop DJ Tim Westwood and jazz-head Gilles Peterson. As Bukem describes it, "If you want to get ahead, get eclectic." The burgeoning rave scene in Great Britain during the early '90s made its impact on Bukem, and he began to create lush tapestries of dance music rich with beautiful melodies and soothing bass lines. His style of drum & bass was in complete contrast to the harder, dancehall-influenced music of the earlier times, a soulful, almost gentle style that, in essence, has been dubbed "quiet storm." Many new drum & bass artists—including Peshay and Alex Reece—are indebted to Bukem and his own label, Good Looking Records.

what's available: Bukem was one of the first artists to release drum & bass in the United States with his two-CD compilation *LTJ Bukem Presents Logical Progression* ♫♫♫ (Good Looking/

WHAT ALBUM CHANGED YOUR LIFE?

Probably [the Beatles'] *Sgl. Pepper*. It changed my life musically. I thought that was the most incredible album, 'cause it happened at a time when I was in a copy band on Bourbon Street. It was the most incredible music to play. We went out and learned the entire album. That's the first time and, I think, the last time we ever went and we sat down and learned the entire record and played it good. We were known for playing *Sgt. Pepper* better than anybody on Bourbon Street in 1969.

Jimmy Buffett

ffrr Records, 1996, prod. various). Featuring many artists in the Good Looking family, the songs paint a panoramic picture of jazzy dance music. It includes the single "Demon's Theme," considered a classic.

worth searching for: Bukem has released many singles and albums in the U.K., but two in particular are worth the hunt: *LTJ Bukem Presents Earth, Vol. 1* (Good Looking, 1996) and *LTJ Bukem Presents Earth, Vol. 2* (Good Looking, 1997).

influences:

◀◀ Roy Ayers, Chick Corea, Brian Eno, Juan Atkins, Inner City

▶▶ Peshay, Alex Reece, Photek

Joseph Patel

Bulletboys

Formed mid-1980s, in Los Angeles, CA.

Marq Torien, vocals; Mick Sweda, guitar (1988–94; 1997–present); Lonnie Vencent, bass; Jimmy D'Anda, drums (1988–94; 1997–present); Tommy Pittam, guitar (1994–97); Rob Karras, drums (1994–97).

Bulletboys, like most of its late '80s metal peers, shone brightest with its debut album. With Marq Torien's David Lee

Roth–like vocals, Ted Templeman's producing, and a contract with Warner Bros., all (somewhat accurately) pointed to a neo–Van Halen image. But the band was more than capable of mindlessly entertaining, raunchy fun, as evidenced on *Bulletboys*, a harder, grittier proposition than most efforts by the band's hair-metal counterparts. Bulletboys soon splintered but eventually joined those hard-rock leftovers on the club circuit, endlessly touring once its original lineup had reformed.

what to buy: *Bulletboys* 🎵🎵🎵 (Warner Bros., 1988, prod. Ted Templeman) delivers the raunchy goods, and features the hits "Smooth up in Ya" and a cover of the O'Jays' "For the Love of Money."

what to avoid: *Za-Za* 🎵 (Warner Bros., 1993) and *Acid Monkey* 🎵 (Perris, 1995) prove that Bulletboys had one good album in them, and after that it was a quick ride downhill.

the rest:
Freakshow 🎵🎵 (Warner Bros., 1991)

influences:
◀◀ Van Halen, Judas Priest, Led Zeppelin, Aerosmith
▶▶ Jackyl

Todd Wicks

Sonny Burgess

Born Albert Burgess, May 28, 1931, Newport, AR.

With his flaming red suit, red shoes, red guitar, and dyed red hair, Sonny Burgess probably looked like the devil incarnate to audiences in Arkansas and Tennessee circa 1956. And he pretty much sounded like him on the records he made for Sun between 1956 and 1958. Songs such as "We Wanna Boogie," "Red Headed Woman," and "Ain't Got a Thing" featured shouted, nearly unintelligible vocals, slapback bass, thundering drums, pounding piano, machine-gun bursts of guitar, and a blurting, out-of-context trumpet. Burgess's records were wild even by Sun standards—perhaps too wild, for his intense mix of rockabilly boogie and white-boy rhythm & blues never made him more than a regional hit. After Sun, Burgess retreated to playing in Conway Twitty's band and eventually took a day job until he was coaxed out of rock 'n' roll retirement in 1986 to play with the Sun Rhythm Section. In the early '90s, roots rocker Dave Alvin produced his fine comeback effort, *Tennessee Border*, returning him to recording after a too-long absence.

what to buy: The best of his Sun sides can be found on *Hittin' that Jug! The Best of Sonny Burgess* 🎵🎵🎵🎵 (AVI, 1995, prod. Sam Phillips, Jack Clement), more than a hour's worth of glorious chaos in two-and-a-half minute bursts. The better of his two recent comeback efforts, *Sonny Burgess* 🎵🎵🎵 (Rounder,

1996, prod. Garry Tallent) contains spirited performances of songs by Bruce Springsteen, Steve Forbert, Radney Foster, Dave Alvin, and Chris Gaffney, among others. As a special treat, the Jordanaires and Scotty Moore sit in on "Bigger than Elvis."

the rest:
We Wanna Boogie 🎵🎵🎵 (Rounder, 1990)
Tennessee Border 🎵🎵🎵 (HighTone, 1992)

influences:
◀◀ Elvis Presley, early R&B, the Grand Ole Opry
▶▶ The Blasters, Robert Gordon, Big Sandy & His Fly-Rite Boys

Daniel Durchholz

Paul Burlison

Born February 4, 1929, in Brownsville, TN.

As a member of the Johnny Burnette & His Rock 'n' Roll Trio, Paul Burlison let fly with some of the most distinctive lead guitar riffs of the late '50s. Whether playing shrill and speedy on "Tear It Up" or chugging rhythmically on "Lonesome Train on a Lonesome Track," Burlison's guitar brought support and musical nuance to the group's manic recordings. His simultaneous use of fuzz-tone and harmonics on the 1956 classic "Train Kept A-Rollin'" was a bold innovation. One of the few Memphis acts to not record for the legendary Sun label, the group's Coral recordings accentuated rockabilly's punk edge and its commitment to raw, youthful energy. Though the Trio made a slew of great records and appeared in the Alan Freed flick *Rock, Rock, Rock*, it never achieved more than regional success. In 1959, after brothers Johnny and Dorsey disbanded the group to forge solo careers, Burlison returned to the Memphis area (where he once worked at Crown Electric alongside Elvis Presley) and started his own contracting business. During the '60s, British groups such as Johnny Kidd & the Pirates and the Yardbirds rediscovered Burlison's work with the Trio and recorded faithful versions of their songs. Despite his acknowledged influence on other famous groups (Aerosmith included), Burlison didn't resurface until Presley's death revitalized interest in original rock 'n' roll and its makers. He appeared with an early '80s version of the Trio, featuring Johnny's son Rocky with Johnny Black and Tony Austen in England. (Both Johnny and Dorsey had died by this time.) In 1983, Burlison joined with Marcus Van Story, Jimmy Lee "Smoochy" Smith, Stan Kessler, Sonny Burgess, and J.M. Van Eaton to form the Sun Rhythm Section. (The fact that Burlison had never recorded at Sun didn't seem to matter.) The group played rockabilly standards for the dwindling faithful in the U.S. and the larger, more receptive crowds in Europe. After years of touring and one LP for Rounder, Burlison left the group in 1994. Semi-retired, he cut his first solo LP in 1997, showing much of the fire he brought to his '50s recordings and a far more fluid technique.

what's available: The only disc issued under Burlison's own name, *Train Kept A-Rollin'* ♫♫♫ (Sweetfish, 1997, prod. Jim Weider) is an all-star tribute to Johnny Burnette & His Rock 'n' Roll Trio and features Billy Burnette, Rocky Burnette, Kim Wilson, Rick Danko, Levon Helm, Garry Tallent, and others. Burlison proves he can still cut rock 'n' roll with the youngsters, and his flashy leads are the heart and soul of this fine LP.

worth searching for: Burlison's work with the Sun Rhythm Section can be found on the cassette-only *Old Time Rock 'n' Roll* (Rounder, 1987, prod. Stan Kessler). However, Burlison's claim to fame is his groundbreaking recordings with Johnny Burnette & His Rock 'n' Roll Trio, which are compiled on *Rockabilly Boogie* (Bear Family, 1989, prod. Richard Weize), an essential 28-track collection featuring some of the wildest early rock 'n' roll, country, and blues ever heard.

influences:

◀◀ Luther Perkins, Scotty Moore, Merle Travis, Chet Atkins, Joe Maphis

▶▶ James Burton, Link Wray, Johnny Kidd & the Pirates, the Yardbirds, Aerosmith

Ken Burke

T-Bone Burnett

Born John Henry Burnett, January 14, 1948, in St. Louis, MO.

Spiritual yet sharp-tongued, witty but sometimes preachy and oblique, T-Bone Burnett has all the qualities of a down-to-earth Episcopalian preacher. Burnett first came to public attention through Bob Dylan's Rolling Thunder Revue in the '70s and has created a distinctive body of work coming from a folk-country base. Though he's managed only a cult audience as a performer, Burnett has found considerable success as a producer, working with such acts as Bruce Cockburn, Los Lobos, Elvis Costello, Counting Crows, and Marshall Crenshaw.

what to buy: Always adept at exposing moral charlatans, Burnett turns his gaze inward on *The Criminal Under My Own Hat* ♫♫♫♫ (Columbia, 1992, prod. T-Bone Burnett), and in the process he creates an album that utilizes his most creative musical and lyrical tendencies.

what to buy next: Burnett's first solo album, *Truth Decay* ♫♫♫ (Demon, 1980, prod. Reggie Fisher), goes for a post-Sun-era rockabilly sound with a four-piece band and features some of Burnett's simplest and most pointed songs, like "Madison Avenue," "Talk Talk Talk," and "Boomerang." *Trap Door* ♫♫♫♫ (Warner Bros., 1984, prod. Reggie Fisher, T-Bone Burnett), the

six-song EP that followed, is even better—especially a sarcastic, spoken rendition of "Diamonds Are a Girl's Best Friend."

what to avoid: Burnett is sometimes criticized for preachiness, but he's even worse when he gets obtuse, as he did on the currently out-of-print *The Talking Animals* ♫♫♫ (Columbia, 1988, prod. T-Bone Burnett).

the rest:

(As J. Henry Burnett) *The B-52 Band & the Fabulous Skylarks* ♫♫♫ (UNI, 1972/One Way, 1994)
Proof through the Night ♫♫♫ (Demon, 1983)
Behind the Trap Door ♫♫♫ (Demon, 1984)
T-Bone Burnett ♫♫♫♫ (Dot/MCA Special Products, 1986)

worth searching for: *Spark in the Dark* (Arista, 1977, prod. Larry Hirsch) is the best of Burnett's three albums with the Alpha Band, his post–Rolling Thunder trio with Steve Soles and David Mansfield. *When the Night Falls* (Bench, 1990, prod. Reggie Fisher) by Black Tie is a quasi–Rolling Thunder reunion featuring Burnett and many longtime cronies, including Billy Swan and his Alpha Bandmates Steven Soles and David Mansfield. There's also the 1995 Rykodisc reissue of Elvis Costello's 1986 Burnett-produced masterpiece *King of America* (Rykodisc, 1995, prod. T-Bone Burnett). Among the reissue's bonus tracks are two songs Costello recorded with Burnett under the name the Coward Brothers—Leon Payne's "They'll Never Take Her Love from Me" and the brilliant proto-twangcore "The People's Limousine."

influences:

◀◀ Bob Dylan, Kris Kristofferson, Roger McGuinn, Buddy Holly, Randy Newman, Van Dyke Parks, John Prine

▶▶ Peter Case, Tonio K., Joe Henry, Alejandro Escovedo, Sam Phillips, Counting Crows

Brian Mansfield and David Menconi

Dorsey Burnette

Born December 28, 1932, in Memphis, TN. Died August 19, 1979.

Like a number of faded rock 'n' roll mavericks, Dorsey Burnette slid securely into the country field after his career in pop came to a close when "Tall Oak Tree" and "Hey Little One" faded off the charts in 1960. Recording for more than a dozen labels up to his death, and even notching a few mid-chart country hits, he never left any lasting work in the field behind him, and his career in country is largely a forgotten footnote to his earlier work. Burnette will more likely be best remembered for his service with his brother, Johnny Burnette, and guitarist Paul Burlison in the Rock 'n' Roll Trio, a pioneer Memphis rockabilly band. After cutting two searing albums during the band's brief and stormy career, the brothers moved to Hollywood and wrote hits for Ricky Nelson ("Waitin' in School," "It's Late") before Johnny hit the Top 40 on his own, followed shortly thereafter by brother Dorsey.

what's available: Burnette's hits on the ERA label are collected on *The Best of Dorsey Burnette* 𝄞𝄞 (K-Tel, 1994, prod. various), a disc that contains more country and country pop than good old rock 'n' roll, but should please you archivists and historians out there.

worth searching for: Burnette's best moments as a solo rocker can be found on *Great Shakin' Fever* (Bear Family, 1992, compilation prod. Richard Weize), a 25-song collection brilliantly annotated by Colin Escott. Also, you should know that copies of the Rock 'n' Roll Trio album *Johnny Burnette and the Rock and Roll Trio* (Coral, 1956) routinely fetch four-figure prices among collectors, although the music has been reissued and bootlegged over the years in less collectible editions.

influences:

◀◀ Elvis Presley, Roy Hamilton

▶▶ Johnny Black, Glen Campbell, Rocky Burnette

Joel Selvin and Ken Burke

Johnny Burnette

Born March 24, 1934, in Memphis, TN. Died August 1, 1964, in Clear Lake, CA.

Johnny Burnette went to the same high school in Memphis as Elvis Presley. He and his brother Dorsey Burnette were troubled boys, sent to Catholic schools for discipline, not religion. But these two hard-scrabble sometime-prizefighters led—with guitarist Paul Burlison—the Rock 'n' Roll Trio, one of Memphis's first rockabilly outfits to emerge from the local hillbilly roadhouses. Although the trio cut one of the great rock 'n' roll albums of the '50s, the Burnettes had very little to show for it. None of the singles for Coral Records even nicked the charts, and the band spent the better part of '56, a crucial year, touring with the *Ted Mack Amateur Hour* traveling show after winning three consecutive weeks on the televised talent contest. When the band broke up shortly thereafter—during an onstage fist fight between the two brothers—the Burnettes moved their families to Los Angeles, where they showed up on Ricky Nelson's door one day offering to write songs for the burgeoning teen idol. Burnette compositions such as "Waitin' in School," "It's Late," and "Believe What You Say" became landmarks in the Nelson repertoire. But Johnny Burnette was destined to become best known for the sappy teen pop that he recorded—but did not write—under the supervision of producer Snuff Garrett, particularly the two Top 10 hits "You're Sixteen" and "Dreamin'." When he died in a boating accident in '64, his career was in decline. But Burnette was one of rock 'n' roll's great

originals—a burly, feisty hard-luck loser who never got credit for his most genuine accomplishments.

what's available: Burnette's years at Liberty Records have been scrupulously covered with *You're Sixteen: The Best of Johnny Burnette* 𝄞𝄞 (EMI, 1992, prod. Snuff Garrett), 25 songs and a 13-minute interview (huh?), although his best known material is not necessarily his best.

worth searching for: The first two LPs by Johnny Burnette & the Rock 'n' Roll Trio have been included on the excellent *Rock 'n' Roll Trio/Tear It Up* (Beat Goes On, 1996, prod. Bob Thiele, Paul Cohen). However, you can get all of its 1956 through 1957 sessions on one CD, *Rockabilly Boogie* (Bear Family, 1989, prod. Bob Thiele, Paul Cohen), which leaves little doubt how masterful Burnette's early recordings were.

influences:

◀◀ Elvis Presley, Gene Vincent

▶▶ Billy Burnette, Rocky Burnette, the Cramps

Joel Selvin

The Burns Sisters

Formed late 1970s, in Binghamton, NY.

Marie Burns, vocals; Jeannie Burns, vocals; Annie Burns, vocals; Terry Burns, vocals (late 1970s–93); Sheila Burns, vocals (late 1970s–93).

An accomplished vocal group from upstate New York, the Burns Sisters survived a brief affiliation with the cookie-cutter record biz during the '80s to re-emerge as an independent and confident act with proud roots in country, folk, bluegrass, blues, world music, and Cajun. Two of the sisters dropped out of the act to pursue their own interests, but the remaining trio has remained strong and vibrant. The group's stunningly sharp harmonies are to die for, and its choice of material—both self-penned tunes and judiciously-chosen covers—reflects a mature blend of commercial accessibility and roots authenticity. And did we mention the harmonies? Oh, those *harmonies. . . !*

what to buy: *In This World* 𝄞𝄞𝄞 (Philo, 1997, prod. Gary Talent) offers a fine batch of appealing songs, performed with grace and gusto. A few of the tracks ("Dance upon This Earth," "My Father's Blue Eyes," and "No More Silence") are re-recordings of songs that appeared on previous Burns Sisters records, but the versions here are more fully-realized, more commercial without sacrificing a smidgen of credibility. Country fans should delight in "Dance upon This Earth" and "Heavenly Blue." Pop fans should dig "I Won't Turn My Back" (co-written by Annie Burns and pop icon Bill Lloyd), while "My Father's Blue Eyes" won't leave a dry eye in the house.

what to buy next: *Close to Home* 𝄞𝄞𝄞 (Philo, 1995, prod. Rich DePaolo) lacks the essential sheen of *In This World*, but it does contain the sprightly "We Never Said Goodbye" and the wonderful "Into the Wild," a tune Annie Burns also recorded for her own 1994 album. A cover of Little Steven & the Disciples of Soul's "I Am a Patriot" earns slight demerits for not living up to the gooseflesh-inducing thrill of the Burns Sisters' own early live renditions of the song; whoever's responsible for convincing the group to rein in its formerly-transcendent, superbly emotional version is most emphatically *not* a patriot.

the rest:
Songs of the Heart 𝄢𝄢𝄦 (1993)
Tradition 𝄢𝄢𝄦 (Philo, 1996)

worth searching for: The two out-of-print LPs that the Burns Sisters made for Columbia during the '80s are interesting curios, though neither is all that great. *The Burns Sisters Band* (Columbia, 1986, prod. Richard Gottehrer, Ron Riddle) is a very poppy debut, but its synthesizers, goofy dance beats, and meatball guitar detract from its appeal; "I Wonder Who's Out Tonight" almost survives this overproduction and cries out for a remixed release (or, preferably, the same vocal tracks with a totally different instrumental backing). *Endangered Species* (Columbia, 1989, prod. Bob Marlette, David Kershenbaum) is an ill-advised bid for rock radio airplay, replete with a Pat Benatar–like cover of "My Boyfriend's Back."

solo outings:
Annie Burns & the Rain:
Into the Wild 𝄢𝄢𝄦 (1994)

influences:
◄◄ Sweet Honey in the Rock, Holly Near, Ann Peebles, Van Morrison, Rosanne Cash

Carl Cafarelli

William S. Burroughs

Born February 5, 1914, in St. Louis, MO. Died August 2, 1997, in Lawrence, KS.

Like fellow Beat writers Jack Kerouac and Allen Ginsberg, William S. Burroughs influenced rock 'n' roll in purely peripheral ways. Many artists, from Lou Reed and Patti Smith to Nirvana and the Disposable Heroes of Hiphoprisy, cited the author's groundbreaking 1959 novel *Naked Lunch* as divine inspiration. (It was banned for years as pornographic.) Burroughs's fascination with drugs and the enslavement of addiction—he was addicted off and on for decades to various opiate narcotics, which he initially sought in the spirit of literary experimentation that produced his first novel, *Junky*—as well as his sophisticated political and intellectual irreverence proved highly attractive to several generations of disenfranchised (and drug-using) rock stars. After beginning his career as a St. Louis newspaper reporter, Burroughs hooked up early on with the younger Ginsberg and Kerouac, who encouraged their mentor to piece together his written rants, literary "routines," and clear-eyed commentary into *Naked Lunch*; his inspiration inaugurated the Beat Generation. In his later years, he jumped in and out of pop culture, enlivening the movie *Drugstore Cowboy* with a cameo role and collaborating with Nirvana's Kurt Cobain and the Disposable Heroes. He died of a heart attack just a few months after Ginsberg's death.

what to buy: *Dead City Radio* 𝄢𝄢𝄢𝄦 (PolyGram, 1990, prod. Hal Willner, Nelson Lyon) is mostly Burroughs's spoken-word material intermingling with moody, bizarre backing music by Sonic Youth, former Velvet Underground member John Cale, and others. Burroughs speaks with sarcastic humor, as on the monotone "A Thanksgiving Prayer," which gives thanks for horrible things we'd clearly be better off without. On some of the *Naked Lunch* excerpts he sounds like the bogeyman, ominously stretching sentences like "he never got the needle out of his arm" into devastating madness.

what to buy next: *Spare Ass Annie and Other Tales* 𝄢𝄢𝄢𝄦 (Island, 1993, prod. Hal Willner, Michael Franti, Rono Tse) initially sounds like a marriage made in hell—Burroughs's spoken-word voice rambling about dying brains and unfeeling eyes above the hip-hop beats of Michael Franti's political group Disposable Heroes of Hiphoprisy. But gradually, as Burroughs moves through the riveting "The Last Words of Dutch Schultz" and the hilarious "Did I Ever Tell You about the Man That Taught His Asshole to Talk?," words and music come together with the same purpose. Franti and his partner, Rono Tse, connect perfectly with the material, adding acoustic guitar and reggae-style chants to the transitional one-minute piece "Last Words with Ras I. Zulu" and occasional snippets of maniacal laughter.

best of the rest:
Call Me Burroughs 𝄢𝄢𝄢 (Rhino, 1995)

worth searching for: The most comprehensive Burroughs set, *10%: File Under Burroughs* (Sub Rosa, 1996, prod. various), is only available on an import label, but the two-disc spoken-word collection, with a 36-page booklet, is a Beat-and-music treasure. Highlights include "William Burroughs Don't Play Guitar," with a hip-hop groove; "Dying on the Vine," with John Cale on vocals and piano; "I Travelled Mostly on the Road," a Pink Floyd–style piece of psychedelic rock; and "My Only Friend," a weird, irritating flute song.

influences:
◄◄ Jonathan Swift, Franz Kafka, James Joyce

►► Allen Ginsberg, Jack Kerouac, Bob Dylan, Patti Smith, the Clash, David Bowie, Nirvana, Disposable Heroes of Hiphoprisy, Thomas Ligotti

Steve Knopper

Tony Burrows

Born c. 1942, in Great Britain.

The only artist to be considered a one-hit wonder five times, Tony Burrows was the anonymous lead singer for Edison Lighthouse, "Love Grows (Where My Rosemary Goes)"; White Plains, "My Baby Loves Lovin'"; and First Class, the incomparable Beach Boys pastiche "Beach Baby"; and he shared lead vocals on "United We Stand" by the Brotherhood of Man and "Gimme Dat Ding" by the Pipkins. A session vocalist in England, Burrows was a member of the Ivy League, a group he joined well after its own 1965 chart success with "Tossing and Turning." The Ivy League evolved into the Flowerpot Men, which in turn became White Plains. Burrows continued to serve as a valued voice-for-hire and even had one low-charting (#87) single under his own name, 1970's "Melanie Makes Me Smile." Otherwise, Burrows's voice is far better-known than his name, and one of his hits is probably playing on an oldies station near you this very minute.

what's available: Credited to "the Voice of Tony Burrows," *Love Grows (Where My Rosemary Goes)* ♫♫♫ (Varese Sarabande, 1996, compilation prod. Cary E. Mansfield, Gordon Pogoda) collects all of the above-mentioned Burrows-sung tracks and bolsters them with several other worthies, including Edison Lighthouse's "Take Me in Your Arms," Burrows's "Every Little Move She Makes" and "In the Bad Bad Old Days," Touch's "Better Fly, Butterfly," and First Class's "Dreams Are Ten a Penny" and "Too Many Golden Oldies." Not everything here is a hit or even a shoulda-been hit, but this is still an unexpectedly consistent set of AM pop/bubblegum circa 1969–77; though a 1985 track, "Summertlme," by West End Boys, is forgettable. And if anyone out there wants to support an act of Congress that would make "In the Bad Bad Old Days" a retroactive hit and mandate its airplay on oldies airwaves, you'll get no argument from these quarters.

influences:

◀◀ The Beach Boys, the Foundations, the Archies, Spanky & Our Gang

▶▶ Bo Donaldson & the Heywoods, Paper Lace, Material Issue

Carl Cafarelli

Bush

Formèd 1992, in London, England.

Gavin Rossdale, vocals, guitar; Nigel Pulsford, guitar; Dave Parsons, bass; Robin Goodridge, drums.

Despite being labeled a Nirvana/Pearl Jam rip-off, Bush has managed to sugarcoat what the Americans gave them and sell it back with tremendous success. The band was originally conceived by Gavin Rossdale and Nigel Pulsford, who met, hit it off, and formed a band called Future Primitive. Rossdale then recruited Parsons, who was part of the '80s band Transvision Vamp. After seeing them play, drummer Robin Goodridge told the trio that their drummer "sucked" and told them he could play much better. Rossdale called his bluff and the rest is history. They were signed by Trauma toward the end of the grunge movement in the early '90s. The band has gone on to sell a ton of records, and even distanced themselves from their American predecessors somewhat. A critical washout, Bush has earned countless "fan friendly" awards, such as the MTV Viewer's Choice Award. Rossdale remains the band's focal point, and he plays his celebrity role to the hilt, even engaging in a high-profile relationship with No Doubt's Gwen Stefani. The band tried to gain some measure of credibility in 1997 by releasing a remix album featuring techno-based remixes by Tricky, Goldie, and Jack Dangers of Meat Beat Manifesto. But you still have to call a spade a spade.

what to buy: When Bush's debut album, *Sixteen Stone* ♫♫♫♫ (Trauma/Interscope, 1994, prod. Clive Langer, Alan Winstanley), was released, it was seen as a direct Nirvana rip-off based on their first single, "Everything Zen." As their popularity grew, songs like "Comedown," "Machinehead," and "Glycerine" gave the band a more firm identity as a rock band.

what to buy next: *Razorblade Suitcase* ♫♫♫ (Trauma/Interscope, 1996, prod. Steve Albini) sounds a little rushed, but it's still a solid album, thanks in part to the hits "Swallowed," "Greedy Fly," and "Mouth."

the rest:

Deconstructed ♫♫♪ (Trauma, 1997)

influences:

◀◀ The Pixies, Joy Division, Nirvana, the Replacements

▶▶ Creed, Days of the New

Darren Davis

Kate Bush

Born July 30, 1958, in Surrey, England.

Depending on your temperament for eclectic art rock, Kate Bush either comes across like an angel or like that weird drama teacher from your high school; she is an individualist who wears her creativity without shame. Despite obvious eccentricities, however, she is a unique and frequently compelling artist. Discovered by Pink Floyd guitarist David Gilmour, Bush's material has drawn heavily from Elizabethan stage dramas and medieval fantasy, as well as British art rock and traditional Celtic music. Where her male contemporaries often sully the art-rock banner with flatulent instrumental excess, however, she is

Gavin Rossdale of Bush (© Ken Settle)

more concerned with narrative flow, character motivation, and the emotional depth of romantic relationships. Her work achieves this with a keen talent for musical hybridization and an understanding of theatrical pacing and tension. In many of her songs, Bush assumes multiple roles, playing out mini-dramas against ambitious sonic backdrops. Essential in Bush's delivery is her multifarious voice, an instrument that can, by turns, evoke childlike wonder, irresistible seduction, heartrending sadness, and chilling malevolence. To her many fans, it is this unique voice that defines the Bush experience; for others, it is her flair for the dramatic (an accomplished scenarist, Bush designed and staged a landmark tour in 1979—her only one to date—and wrote, directed, and starred in the 1993 film *The Line, the Cross, the Curve*, a companion piece to her 1993 album *The Red Shoes*). Bush's rise to mainstream success guaranteed a host of imitators swimming in her wake (most notably Tori Amos), but their work pales in comparison to the originality and style of Bush's best music.

what to buy: *Hounds of Love* 🎵🎵🎵🎵 (EMI America, 1985, prod. Kate Bush) rode to the #1 spot on the British album charts in 1985, and the singles "Running up That Hill" and "Cloudbusting" propelled Bush to her greatest U.S. success since "Wuthering Heights" in 1978. The hoopla was justified; with *Hounds*, Bush finally struck the perfect balance, leavening the melodrama with canny Celtic touches and sensual polyrhythms, and tempering her penchant for fantasy with more corporeal concerns—from the lulling warmth of "Mother Stands for Comfort" to the eerie beauty of "And Dream of Sheep" to the propulsive fury of "Jig of Life."

what to buy next: While sonically similar to *Hounds of Love*, *The Sensual World* 🎵🎵🎵🎵 (Columbia, 1989, prod. Kate Bush) finds Bush dealing with much more mature subject matter. Still preoccupied with romance, the relationships depicted in *The Sensual World* are decidedly more earthbound than those in Bush's past recordings. But she still infuses songs such as "The Fog" and the title track with enough mystery and foreboding to recall her chimerical work. And in "Love and Anger" she delivers a dynamic anthem for the complications and compensations of modern romance. Also of interest is the greatest-hits package *The Whole Story* 🎵🎵🎵🎵 (EMI, 1986, prod. various), which provides an excellent overview of Bush's first five albums. While each song is a standout, the album as a whole lacks the thematic unity that Bush's individual albums boast.

what to avoid: *Lionheart* 🎵🎵 (EMI America, 1978, prod. Andrew Powell) is a hastily put together album that attempted to quickly cash in on Bush's success with the single "Wuthering Heights" (off of her debut album, *The Kick Inside*, and later covered by Pat Benatar) and a clear example of her indulgence to excess. While the album does boast the outstanding cut

"Wow," to reach it you must first brave the over-the-top sentimentality of "Symphony in Blue" and "In Search of Peter Pan."

the rest:
The Kick Inside 🎵🎵🎵 (EMI America, 1978)
Kate Bush on Stage 🎵🎵🎵 (EMI America, 1979)
Never for Ever 🎵🎵🎵 (EMI America, 1980)
The Dreaming 🎵🎵🎵🎵 (EMI America, 1982)
This Woman's Work 🎵🎵🎵🎵 (Columbia, 1990)
The Red Shoes 🎵🎵🎵 (Columbia, 1993)

worth searching for: *Aspects of the Sensual World* (Columbia EP, 1990, prod. Kate Bush) is a collection of unreleased material that coincided with the release of *The Sensual World*. In addition to two versions of the title song, the EP contains the previously unavailable cuts "Be Kind to My Mistakes" (from the 1987 Nicolas Roeg film *Castaways*), "I'm Still Waiting," and "Ken."

influences:

◀◀ Pink Floyd, the Moody Blues, Fairport Convention, Sandy Denny, Genesis, Peter Gabriel, Celtic folk music

▶▶ Sinéad O'Connor, Tori Amos, Dolores O'Riordian (the Cranberries), Siouxsie Sioux (Siouxsie & the Banshees)

David Galens

Bush Tetras

Formed 1980, in New York, NY.

Cynthia Sley, vocals; Pat Place, guitar; Laura Kennedy, bass; Dee Pop, drums.

New York's early '80s "No Wave" movement spawned a handful of pioneering indie bands, among them Sonic Youth and the Bush Tetras. The latter combined gritty, garage-y, Stooges-like rock 'n' roll energy with primal, tribal, African-inspired rhythms—an excellent pairing of punk guitar and dancefloor-friendly grooves.

what to buy: *Better Late than Never* 🎵🎵🎵🎵 (ROIR, 1983) compiles the whole of Bush Tetras studio work from 1980 to 1983, including the group's debut *Rituals* EP, various singles, and demos.

what to buy next: *Beauty Lies* 🎵🎵🎵 (Tim Kerr/PolyGram, 1996, prod. Nona Hendryx) offers evidence of the band's continuing vitality beyond its '80s heyday.

the rest:
Wild Things (Live) 🎵🎵🎵 (ROIR, 1983)
Boom in the Night 🎵🎵 (ROIR, 1995)
Tetrafied 🎵🎵🎵 (2.13.61, 1997)

influences:

influences:

◄◄ The Stooges, the Sex Pistols, Nona Hendryx, Chic, Fela Kuti, Talking Heads

►► Talking Heads, Laurie Anderson

Mike Bieber

Jon Butcher Axis

Formed 1980, in Boston, MA. Disbanded 1985.

Jon Butcher, guitar, vocals; Derek Blevins, drums; Chris Martin, bass (1980–84); Jimmy Johnson, bass (1984–85).

Because he was a black guitarist leading a trio with the word Axis in its name, Jon Butcher got pushed as a "New Hendrix." But he's actually closer to a cross between Jeff Beck, Eric Johnson, and Pat Metheny, with a better feel for textured ambient pop than high-voltage riffing. As a consequence, almost every Butcher album has a handful of decent tracks, but they're all unfocused and not fully realized. If ever a proper best-of compilation emerges (and *Butcher Block* ain't it, because it draws too heavily from his later Capitol period), it would probably stand head and shoulders above anything else in Butcher's catalog. Butcher dumped the Axis in 1985 and continued on under his own name.

what to buy: Between them, *Jon Butcher Axis* 𝄢𝄢𝄢 (Polydor, 1983, prod. Pat Moran) and the follow-up, *Stare at the Sun* 𝄢𝄢𝄢 (Polydor, 1984, prod. Pat Moran), add up to one really good record. They haven't aged particularly well, but the synth-pop atmospherics of "Life Takes a Life" and "Walk on the Moon" show promise and would have been a direction worthy of further pursuit.

what to avoid: Coming late in the game, *Pictures from the Front* 𝄢𝄢 (Capitol, 1989, prod. Glen Ballard, Jon Butcher, Spencer Proffer) is a desperate-sounding grab bag. Also forgettable is the eponymous debut of Butcher's most recent band, *Barefoot Servants* 𝄢𝄢 (Columbia, 1994, prod. Michael Frondelli), a misguided super-session with assorted studio hacks.

the rest:
Along the Axis 𝄢𝄢 (Capitol, 1985)
Wishes 𝄢𝄢𝄢 (Capitol, 1987)
Butcher Block: The Best of Jon Butcher 𝄢𝄢𝄢 (Razor & Tie, 1998)

influences:

◄◄ Jeff Beck, Pat Metheny, Thin Lizzy

►► Eric Johnson

David Menconi

Bernard Butler

See: Suede

Jerry Butler

Born December 8, 1939, in Sunflower, MS.

The Ice Man, Jerry Butler, is doo-wop's living link to soul music. Butler's early style was formed by singing with the Northern Jubilee Gospel Singers in Chicago. After meeting Curtis Mayfield at the Traveling Souls Spiritualistic Church, the two began singing in doo-wop groups such as the Quails and the Alphatones before joining the Roosters, an early version of the Impressions. Recording for the Vee-Jay subsidiary Falcon Records in 1958, Jerry Butler & the Impressions recorded "For Your Precious Love," a romantic doo-wop ballad, which became a smash hit on both the pop and R&B charts. Butler's billing as soloist caused much dissension within the group, but after their two follow-up records failed to chart, billing became a moot point: Vee-Jay kept Butler and dropped the Impressions. (They would resurface during the '60s with Mayfield as lead singer.) Butler's first solo records met with limited success, but when Mayfield rejoined him in the studio, their collaborations resulted in big hits such as "He Will Break Your Heart," "Find Another Girl," and "I'm A-Telling You." Butler broadened his appeal further with his hit interpretation of Henry Mancini's "Moon River," which beat the *Breakfast at Tiffany's* soundtrack version onto the charts by two weeks. The Burt Bacharach/Hal David penned "Make It Easy on Yourself" was a dual-market smash as well. Butler's cool mixing of gospel soul with supper club MOR kept him on the charts at a time when British acts had chased most American artists off pop playlists. Indeed, at the peak of Beatlemania, his duet with Betty ("The Shoop Shoop Song") Everett, "Let It Be Me," was a Top 5 pop hit. He has recorded for several labels over the years, including the R&B titans Motown and Philadelphia International. Since 1980, however, music has become something of a lucrative part-time job for Butler, as he began serving the first of four terms as Cook County Commissioner in Illinois. Butler was inducted into the Rock and Roll Hall of Fame in 1991 and into the Rhythm & Blues Foundation in 1994. He still records sporadically for his own labels, has been featured in a CLIO Award-winning McDonald's commercial with Aretha Franklin, and plays live gigs whenever he has the time.

what to buy: A great starting point, *Best of Jerry Butler* 𝄢𝄢𝄢𝄢𝄢 (Rhino, 1987, compilation prod. Bill Inglot) contains Butler's biggest hits with Vee-Jay and Mercury, as a solo artist, with Betty Everett, and with the Impressions.

what to buy next: The cream of Butler's work during his years as a major solo hit maker with Mercury is on *Iceman— Mercury Years Anthology* 𝄢𝄢𝄢𝄢 (PolyGram, 1992, prod. Kenny Gamble, Leon Huff), a comprehensive two-disc, 44-track helping. Also, dig into *The Ice Man—Jerry Butler* 𝄢𝄢𝄢𝄢 (Vee-Jay, 1992, prod.

Calvin Carter), which has 25 tracks of Butler's best from his Vee-Jay years, with and without the Impressions.

what to avoid: Though it features some unusual source material, *Greatest Hits* 𝄞𝄞 (Pilz, 1993, prod. various) is a budget disc with terribly muddy sound. For completists only.

the rest:
Love's on the Menu 𝄞𝄞 (Motown, 1990)
Suite for the Single Girl 𝄞𝄞 (Motown, 1990)
Greatest Hits 𝄞𝄞𝄞𝄞 (Curb, 1991)
Time & Faith 𝄞𝄞 (Ichiban, 1992)
For Your Precious Love 𝄞𝄞𝄞 (Classic, 1994)
Simply Beautiful 𝄞𝄞𝄞 (Valley Vue/Navarre, 1994)
Best Love 𝄞𝄞𝄞 (Capitol Special Products, 1994)
Essential Jerry Butler 𝄞𝄞𝄞 (PolyGram Special Products, 1996)

worth searching for: The cool stage presence and smooth, evocative style that caused a Philly DJ to admiringly dub him the Ice Man is smartly showcased on *Jerry Butler's Golden Hits Live* (Mercury, 1968, prod. various), which features live versions of material from his Vee-Jay years.

influences:
◀◀ Joe Williams, Curtis Mayfield

▶▶ Chuck Jackson, Donny Hathaway

see also: *Curtis Mayfield*

Ken Burke

Paul Butterfield Blues Band

Formed 1963, in Chicago, IL. Disbanded 1972.

Paul Butterfield (born December 17, 1941 in Chicago, IL; died May 4, 1987 in North Hollywood, CA), vocals, harmonica; Smokey Smothers, guitar (1963–64); Elvin Bishop, guitar, vocals (1963–69); Jerome Arnold, bass (1963–67); Sam Lay, drums, vocals (1963–65); Michael Bloomfield, guitar, vocals (1965–67); Mark Naftalin, piano/keyboards (1964–69); Billy Davenport, drums/percussion (1965–67); Gene Dinwiddie, tenor saxophone, mandolin, flute, vocals (1967–71); David Sanborn, tenor/alto/soprano saxophones (1967–71); Keith Johnson, trumpet, keyboards (1967–69); Philip Wilson, drums/percussion, vocals (1967–69); Bugsy Maugh, bass, vocals (1967–69); Buzzy Feiten, guitar (1968–69); Steve Madaio, trumpet (1968–71); Rod Hicks, bass, vocals (1969–71); Trevor Lawrence, baritone saxophone (1969–71); Ted Harris, keyboards (1968–69); Ralph Wash, guitar, vocals (1970–71); George Davidson, drums (1970–71); Dennis Whitted, drums (1971).

It would be difficult to overstate the importance the Butterfield Blues Band had on the course of blues, pop, and rock 'n' roll when it burst on the scene in the mid-1960s. Initially introduced on a 1965 sampler LP of Elektra artists by what became its signature tune—"Born in Chicago"—the Butterfield Band was no group of rank amateurs or folkies attempting to make the jump to amplification; these were already seasoned musicians, trained playing six sets a night in the South Side's legendary blues clubs. Paul Butterfield, a child prodigy on flute, had left his middle-class home in Chicago's Hyde Park and moved into the South Side in his late teens. He immersed himself in the blues, studying with Little Walter and James Cotton, and becoming a respected member of the scene and an adopted son of Muddy Waters and Smokey Smothers. Elvin Bishop had taken a similar route from his home in Tulsa, as had Mike Bloomfield, as much a blues musicologist as guitarist at first. The rhythm section of Jerome Arnold and Sam Lay had served years with Howlin' Wolf. This fully integrated group floored the audience at the 1965 Newport Folk Festival, and the appearance there firmly established it as a leader in the new movement of amplified American bands on the East Coast. The band had a similar impact on the West Coast scene, especially in San Francisco and Los Angeles, where the level of its musicianship and professionalism placed it in a class high above any of the groups working there. The 1965 West Coast tour not only introduced the band's highly respectful, energetic take on the blues, but also showcased its growing interest in jazz and Indian music, especially in the long, improvisational approach to Cannonball Adderley's "Work Song" and Bloomfield's raga/rock "East-West." The latter, based on Eastern scales and motifs, would set the tone for the entire San Francisco sound, exemplified by the Grateful Dead, Jefferson Airplane, Quicksilver Messenger Service, et al. The band's impact on club owners like the Fillmore's Bill Graham was also immense and would lead to his reliance on its recommendations to book Muddy, B.B. King, Wolf, and others, which would open a new white audience to these masters.

By 1966 almost everyone in blues and rock—from coast to coast—was watching and aping the Butterfield Blues Band. Bloomfield left in 1967, claiming fatigue from the road, but his creative energies were clearly heading in other directions. Butterfield, always hearing a new and different type of blues in his head, elevated Bishop to the lead guitarist role, gave Mark Naftalin more room as both pianist and arranger, and added bassist/vocalist Bugsy Maugh, as well as a group of young jazz players—Gene Dinwiddie, Keith Johnson, and David Sanborn—heavily influenced by both the blues and avant-jazz. This first big band reached its zenith with *In My Own Dream*, an assemblage of songs evocative of the blues but entirely unique to the genre, an album of democratic input and superb soloing by Sanborn and Bishop, whose squawking style would predate the similar efforts of New York's East Side jazz guitarists of the 1980s. Bishop would leave in 1969 to pursue solo fame but was followed by a stellar array of guitarists, including Buzz Feiten and Ralph Wash. By 1970 the band was as much a jazz outfit as a blues group, and Butterfield's harp playing was on another level from that of his Chicago predecessors—swinging, exploratory, and highly emotional. The big band opened musical doors for its many progeny, including Blood, Sweat & Tears and Chicago. However, by 1971 musical trends were changing, and the band was suffering from a plague of drugs and recording inertia. Although still famous for its live shows and highly profitable on the road, the band disbanded after its final album, *Sometimes I Feel Like Smilin'*, stiffed.

what to buy: Invaluable for the long out-of-print tracks from the last four LPs, *The Anthology: The Elektra Years* ♬♬♬♬ (Elektra, 1997, compilation prod. Bruce Harris) finally collects the great examples of each evolution of the Butterfield Band, from its unreleased (until 1995) first studio effort through to the end. Taken as a tour-de-force representation of Butterfield's leadership abilities, proof of his harmonica genius and artistry, and of his bands' incredible blowing power, there's nary a wasted moment. The album that made Bloomfield and Butterfield legends, *The Paul Butterfield Blues Band* ♬♬♬♬♬ (Elektra, 1965, prod. Paul Rothchild) is the group's episodic debut, wherein a variety of blues styles are respectfully altered to the Butterfield sound—loud, aggressive, and incredibly musical. *The Lost Sessions* ♬♬♬♬ (Elektra, 1964/Rhino, 1995, prod. Paul Rothchild) marks Bloomfield's initial days with the band but really showcases the tough unit of Lay, Arnold, and Bishop that wowed Chicago audiences. *East-West* ♬♬♬♬ (Elektra, 1966, prod. Paul Rothchild, Mark Abramson, Barry Friedman) is Bloomfield's swan song, and although not representative of the band's live prowess, it sets the stage for all rock experimentation to follow and marked Bloomfield as a guitar deity.

what to buy next: The three versions of the title tune (at 12, 15, and 28 minutes) on *East-West Live* ♬♬♬♬ (Winner, 1997, prod. Mark Naftalin), a low-fi masterpiece mastered from live tapes, freeze-frame the brilliance of a band whose playing seems modern and progressive even today; this album is a timeless recording of ferocious artistry and proof this was possibly the greatest blues and rock band of its time. The final version of the song (from 1967) is pure musical genius, with all players firing off one another. Expect greatness from Bloomfield, but the real discovery is Davenport, and Butterfield's remarkable explorations on harp. Rushed out not long after the big band had been formed, there are a lot of covers on *The Resurrection of Pigboy Crabshaw* ♬♬♬ (Elektra, 1968, prod. John Court), but it's a harbinger of what would develop with the horn players.

what to avoid: Half of *An Offer You Can't Refuse* ♬♬ (Red Lightnin', 1997) features Butterfield with mentor Smokey Smothers, Lay, and Arnold from a mediocre 1963 live date at Chicago's Big John's.

worth searching for: Five cuts from the Butterfield Band's live set at the Monterey Pop Festival in 1967 can be found on *The Monterey International Pop Festival* (Rhino, 1992) alongside dozens of other influential musicians of the time. And watch for used copies of *In My Own Dream* (Elektra, 1968, prod. John Court), *Sometimes I Feel Like Smilin'* (Elektra, 1972, prod. Paul Rothchild), and *Keep on Movin'* (Elektra, 1969, prod. Jerry Ragovoy). Tracks from each are included on *The Anthology*, but all are now out of print, as are *The Butterfield Blues Band Live* (Elektra, 1974) and *Golden Butter: The Best of the Butterfield Blues Band* (Elektra, 1972).

influences:

◄◄ Little Walter, Sonny Boy Williamson II, James Cotton, Muddy Waters, Howlin' Wolf, Otis Rush, Bobby "Blue" Bland

►► Eric Clapton, Cream, Electric Flag, Bob Dylan, the Band, Blood, Sweat & Tears, Chicago, Stephen Stills, Quicksilver Messenger Service, the Grateful Dead, Robben Ford, Janis Joplin, Maria Muldaur, Bonnie Raitt, Charlie Musselwhite, Rod Piazza, J. Geils Band, Canned Heat, John Mayall, Blues Traveler

see also: *Elvin Bishop, Mike Bloomfield*

Tom Ellis III

Butthole Surfers

Formed 1981, in San Antonio, TX.

Gibby Haynes, vocals; Paul Leary, guitar; King Coffey (King Coffee), drums (1983–present); Theresa Nervosa, drums (1983–89); Jeff "Tooter" Pinkus, bass (1986–96).

This Texas group—whose name can only be broadcast on brave radio stations—staked its reputation by flouting a lack of polite taste and an embrace of anything remotely vulgar. College students Gibby Haynes and Paul Leary joined forces in 1977, and by the early '80s they were known as Ashtray Baby Heads and Nine Foot Worm Makes Home Food before an announcer bestowed the band's permanent name after mistaking a song title for the group's moniker. Originally signed to free speech advocate and Dead Kennedys frontman Jello Biafra's Alternative Tentacles label, the group developed a reputation for bizarre live shows featuring films of medical operations and lots of fire. The songs featured a mishmash of rockabilly, '70s art rock and post-punk, trashy lyrics about drug abuse and the decline of suburban America, and some unclassifiable avant-garde noise—all at once. Featuring stiff, repetitive percussion, jagged, colliding and twangy guitars, and often nasal, abrasive singing (but with a certain melody and infectious quality nonetheless), the group often grates on conventional pop/rock tastes. Longtime fans got a double shock during the early '90s, when—after more than 10 years on various independent labels—the band scored a major-label deal with Capitol Records in 1992 and then a major hit with the hip-hop flavored tune "Pepper" in 1996. Despite success, these musicians are never killjoys; they make music to amuse themselves, and at their best, they give us enough berth to get a sense of the joke, too.

what to buy: *Locust Abortion Technician* 🎵🎵🎵 (Touch & Go, 1987, prod. Butthole Surfers) is the Surfers' most direct and concentrated album; all of the songs make a point without dragging on or becoming dull experiments in sound manipulation (as many Surfers' records do). The lyrics often contain a fascinating, albeit grotesque, appeal, while others are truly disturbing. Musical influences still swing from one side of the pendulum to the other, but always come back to a fixed center. *The Hole Truth and Nothing Butt* 🎵🎵🎵 (Trance Syndicate, 1995, prod. Butthole Surfers) compiles many of the Surfers' best singles along with some live performances and B-sides. Despite that, it's more cohesive than most of the other albums, with a few more catchy tracks than the average Surfers album. *Hairway to Steven* 🎵🎵🎵 (Touch & Go, 1988, prod. Butthole Surfers) features a messed up, distorted '70s feel and includes some of Leary's best guitar work.

what to buy next: *Independent Worm Saloon* 🎵🎵🎵 (Capitol, 1993, prod. John Paul Jones) is one of the Surfers' hardest-rocking albums, and the band finally gets around to playing a few songs that actually sound like punk music. *Electriclarryland* 🎵🎵🎵 (Capitol, 1996, prod. Paul Leary, Steve Thompson) grows the fan base with even more accessible songs and a modern rock radio hit, "Pepper."

what to avoid: On *Pioughd* 🎵🎵 (Rough Trade, 1991, prod. Butthole Surfers) (it's pronounced P.O.'d), the band sounds like it's just going through the motions, despite the college radio hit version of "Hurdy Gurdy Man." Not much better is *After the Astronaut* 🎵🎵 (Capitol, 1998, prod. Paul Leary, the Butthole Surfers), which is a Buttholes record without the humor or inspired, jarring musical experiments. In a word: boring.

the rest:
PCPPEP Live 🎵🎵🎵 (Alternative Tentacles, 1984)
Rembrandt Pussyhorse/Cream Corn from the Socket of Davis 🎵🎵🎵 (Touch & Go, 1985/1986)
Psychic . . . Powerless . . . Another Man's Sac 🎵🎵🎵 (Touch & Go, 1985)
Double Live 🎵🎵 (Latino Buggerveil, 1989)

worth searching for: The out-of-print debut, *Butthole Surfers* (Alternative Tentacles, 1983, prod. Butthole Surfers), is one of the band's finest, rawest recordings.

solo outings:
Paul Leary:
History of Dogs 🎵🎵🎵 (Rough Trade, 1990)

Gibby Haynes & Jeff Pinkus:
Jack Officers 🎵🎵🎵 (Rough Trade, 1990)

Gibby Haynes & Johnny Depp:
P 🎵🎵🎵 (Capitol, 1995)

influences:

◀◀ 10cc, Hawkwind, Fall, Flipper

▶▶ Ween, NoMeansNo, Killdozer, Reverend Horton Heat, Cherubs, Alice Donut

Bryan Lassner and Eric Deggans

Buzz Hungry
See: Bob Mould/Sugar

Buzzcocks

Formed 1976, in Manchester, England. Disbanded 1981. Re-formed 1993.

Steve Diggle, guitar, vocals; John Maher, drums (1976–81); Pete Shelley, guitar, vocals; Howard Devoto, vocals (1976–77); Garth Smith, bass (1976–77); Steve Garvey, bass (1977–81); Tony Barber, bass (1993–present); Phil Barker, drums (1993–present).

Created after its members saw the Sex Pistols perform in February 1976, the Buzzcocks became the harmonic side of punk minimalism, blending buzz-saw guitars with sweet vocals, like the Kinks at warp speed. The first of a succession of punk groups from Manchester, the Buzzcocks became one of the most successful singles bands in one of the great ages of English singles, right up there alongside the Jam, the Clash, and the Pistols. Pete Shelley's brash love songs and deadpan delivery were kick-started by Steve Diggle's erratic, brawny guitar and a rhythm section in permanent overdrive. Like many first-era punk bands, the Buzzcocks put a premium on attire and the art and design of their singles and albums. After undistinguished solo work, the band reformed under Diggle in the early '90s and continues to tour and make records.

what to buy: Since the Buzzcocks were a singles band first and foremost, its first American album, *Singles Going Steady* 🎵🎵🎵🎵 (IRS, 1979/1992, prod. Martin Rushent) is the most appropriate choice, collecting eight singles, both A and B sides. It's one of punk's best documents.

what to buy next: *A Different Kind of Tension* 🎵🎵🎵 (IRS, 1980, prod. Martin Rushent) is a lofty attempt to get away from the group's pop origins. *Trade Test Transmission* 🎵🎵🎵 (Caroline, 1993) is the strongest of its recent efforts. *Another Music in Another Kitchen* 🎵🎵🎵 (IRS, 1980/1994, prod. Martin Rushent), its first album without original member Howard Devoto, catches Shelley at his best and is now packaged with *Love Bites* on one

CD. *Lest We Forget* ✍✍✍ (ROIR, 1980) is a live set from the 1979–80 tour.

what to avoid: *French* ✍✍ (IRS, 1995) is a 23-song live album that doesn't speak well of the band's decision to reunite.

the rest:
Live at the Roxy Club: April '77 ✍✍✍ (Trojan, 1989)
Operator's Manual: Buzzcocks Best ✍✍✍✍ (IRS, 1991)
The Peel Sessions Album ✍✍✍✍ (Strange Fruit/Dutch East India, 1991)
Entertaining Friends ✍✍✍ (IRS, 1992)
All Set ✍✍✍ (IRS, 1996)

worth searching for: Now out of print, *Product* (Restless Retro, 1989, prod. Martin Rushent) offers three discs of most of the group's classic material dressed up in artsy, somewhat confusing packaging. Many consider the raw power EP *Spiral Scratch* (New Hormones, 1977, prod. Martin Rushent), with original member Devoto, to be the group's best moment.

solo outings:
Pete Shelley:
Homosapien ✍✍✍✍ (Genetic/Arista, 1982)
XL1 ✍✍✍ (Genetic/Arista, 1983)

Steve Diggle & John Maher:
(With Flag of Convenience) *Life on the Telephone* ✍✍✍ (PVC/Sire, 1982)

influences:
◀◀ The Sex Pistols, the Ramones, the Stooges, Television
▶▶ Magazine, Hüsker Dü, the Knack, Green Day

Leland Rucker

The Byrds

Formed 1964, in Los Angeles, CA. Disbanded 1973.

Roger McGuinn (born James Joseph McGuinn III), guitars, vocals; Chris Hillman, bass, vocals (1964–68); Gene Clark, vocals, tambourine (1964–66); David Crosby, guitar, vocals (1964–67); Michael Clarke, drums, vocals (1964–67); Kevin Kelley, drums (1967–68); Gram Parsons, guitar, vocals (1967–68); Gene Parsons, drums, vocals (1968–72); Skip Battin, bass, vocals (1968–73); John York, bass (1968); Clarence White, guitar, vocals (1968–73); John Guerin, drums (1972–73).

The Byrds were, in terms of guitar sound, among the most important American rock 'n' roll groups of the '60s. Inspired by the Beatles in the film *A Hard Day's Night*—especially the Rickenbacker 12-string guitar George Harrison occasionally shouldered—Roger McGuinn and company jump-started a hazy Bob Dylan lyric called "Mr. Tambourine Man,'" initiating a challenge that would ring back and forth across the Atlantic for several years. It's not that someone wouldn't have stumbled onto playing folk songs on an electric guitar; it's that it was done by Jim McGuinn, David Crosby, Chris Hillman, Gene Clark, and Michael Clarke in Los Angeles—especially McGuinn, whose eclectic tastes and proficiency on the 12-string were far beyond most pop practitioners of the time. The essence of the original sound and appeal was simple: folk songs played on jangling electric guitars, accompanied by bass and drums, and choirboy harmonies soaring above it all. They exposed the beauty and textures of the electric guitar; McGuinn's 12-string work on "Mr. Tambourine Man," "Turn, Turn, Turn," and "Eight Miles High" became blueprints for folk-rock, one of the longest-running rock music subgenres. The Byrds became a jumping-off place for Clark, Hillman, Crosby, and Clarke, but McGuinn and company added jazz, Moog synthesizers, and psychedelia before stripping it all away back to country music with *Sweetheart of the Rodeo*. It's not hard to hear echoes of their music everywhere today.

what to buy: The Byrds catalog is still pretty intact, and be aware when buying that Sony has repackaged the first eight original studio albums with alternate tracks and well-researched historical data—avoid the older packaging whenever possible. *Mr. Tambourine Man* ✍✍✍✍✍ (Columbia, 1965/Sony, 1997, prod. Terry Melcher) is still filled with mystery, harmonies, intrigue, wry humor, and electrified Dylan songs. One of rock's all-time great debuts. Though flawed, *Sweetheart of the Rodeo* ✍✍✍✍✍ (Columbia, 1968/Sony, 1997, prod. Gary Usher) is still the album that turned rock back to country, and the enhanced reissue is a good argument that the original could even have been better. *The Byrds* ✍✍✍✍ (Columbia/Sony, 1990, prod. Don DeVito, Bob Irwin, Roger McGuinn) is a box set actually worth its price, with four discs that pretty much cover the band's rise and fall. And except for the reunion tracks at the end, there's little fluff.

what to buy next: "So You Want to Be a Rock 'n' Roll Star" still rings true today, as does most of the rest of the moody, countryish *Younger Than Yesterday* ✍✍✍✍ (Columbia, 1967/Sony, 1996, prod. Gary Usher), and now you can program out David Crosby's mind-numbing "Mind Gardens." *The Notorious Byrd Brothers* ✍✍✍✍ (Columbia, 1968/Sony, 1997, prod. Gary Usher) is the lesser-known prequel to *Sweetheart of the Rodeo*, between Crosby's departure and Gram Parsons's arrival. If you don't want to spring for the box set, *20 Essential Tracks from the Boxed Set: 1965–1990* ✍✍✍✍ (Columbia/Sony, 1992, prod. Don DeVito, Bob Irwin, Roger McGuinn) is a fulfilling, one-disc start-up kit. *The Byrds (Untitled)* ✍✍✍✍ (Columbia/Sony, 1970/Mobile Fidelity, 1998, prod. Terry Melcher, Jim Dickson) includes McGuinn's ethereal equine meditation, "Chestnut Mare," and a live set that features the Clarence White version of the band.

what to avoid: Like the pictures of the individual members on the front cover, *Byrds* **woof!** (Asylum, 1973) was stitched together to *look* like a reunion—but it wasn't!

the rest:

Turn! Turn! Turn! 𝄢𝄢𝄢 (Columbia/Sony 1966)

Fifth Dimension 𝄢𝄢𝄢 (Columbia/Sony 1966)

Byrds Greatest Hits 𝄢𝄢𝄢𝄢 (Columbia/Sony, 1967)

Dr. Byrds and Mr. Hyde 𝄢𝄢𝄢 (Columbia/Sony, 1969)

Preflyte 𝄢𝄢𝄢 (Together, 1969, Columbia/Sony, 1973)

The Ballad of Easy Rider 𝄢𝄢𝄢 (Columbia/Sony, 1970)

Farther Along 𝄢𝄢 (Columbia/Sony, 1971)

Byrdmaniax 𝄢𝄢 (Columbia/Sony, 1971)

The Best of the Byrds (Greatest Hits, Vol. 2) 𝄢𝄢𝄢 (Columbia/Sony, 1972)

The Byrds Play Dylan 𝄢𝄢𝄢 (Columbia/Sony, 1980)

The Original Singles (1965–1967) 𝄢𝄢𝄢 (Columbia/Sony, 1981)

The Very Best of the Byrds 𝄢𝄢𝄢 (Pair, 1986)

worth searching for: *Never Before* (Re-flyte, 1988, prod. Bob Hyde) includes, on good vinyl if you want it, the "other" version of "Eight Miles High." And if you want other Byrds information, check the Byrds official web site, http://cavern.uark.edu/~kadler/rmcguinn/, mastered by Byrdman McGuinn himself, who will even answer e-mail. But read the Byrds FAQ page before asking him how they came up with the name of the group or why Crosby got kicked out.

solo outings:

Roger McGuinn:

Roger McGuinn 𝄢𝄢𝄢𝄢 (Columbia, 1973)

Peace on You 𝄢𝄢 (Columbia, 1974)

Roger McGuinn and Band 𝄢𝄢 (Columbia, 1975)

Cardiff Rose 𝄢𝄢 (Columbia, 1976)

Thunderbyrd 𝄢𝄢 (Columbia, 1977)

Back from Rio 𝄢𝄢 (Arista, 1991)

Born to Rock and Roll 𝄢𝄢𝄢𝄢 (Columbia Legacy, 1991)

Live from Mars 𝄢𝄢𝄢𝄢 (Hollywood, 1996)

McGuinn, Clark & Hillman:

McGuinn, Clark and Hillman 𝄢𝄢𝄢 (Capitol, 1979)

McGuinn & Hillman:

City 𝄢𝄢 (Capitol, 1980)

Gene Clark:

With the Gosdin Brothers 𝄢𝄢𝄢𝄾 (Columbia, 1966/Edsel, 1997)

Two Sides to Every Story 𝄢𝄢𝄢𝄾 (Polydor, 1977)

Echoes 𝄢𝄢𝄢𝄢 (Legacy, 1991)

Roadmaster 𝄢𝄢𝄢𝄢 (Edsel, 1992)

American Dreamer (1964–74) (Raven (DNA), 1994) 𝄢𝄢𝄢𝄾

Firebyrd 𝄢𝄢𝄢 (Multimedia, 1997)

This Byrd Has Flown 𝄢𝄢𝄢 (Monster, 1997)

influences:

◀◀ New Christy Minstrels, the Beatles, Bob Dylan, John Coltrane, Ravi Shankar, Merle Haggard, the Limeliters, Chad Mitchell Trio, Bobby Darin, Judy Collins, Les Baxter's Balladeers, the Hillmen

▶▶ Bob Dylan, the Flying Burrito Brothers, Desert Rose Band, the Beatles, R.E.M., Buffalo Springfield, Crosby, Stills & Nash, Poco, the Eagles, Blue Öyster Cult, the Searchers, Gin Blossoms, Tom Petty & the Heartbreakers, Elvis Costello & the Attractions, Soul Asylum, the Church, Big Star, Flamin' Groovies, the Bangles, the Animals, the Band, John Mellencamp, T-Bone Burnett, Robin Lane & the Chartbusters

see also: *Crosby, Stills & Nash, the Flying Burrito Brothers, Gram Parsons*

Leland Rucker

David Byrne

Born May 14, 1952, in Dumbarton, Scotland.

As the main man of the Talking Heads, brainy David Byrne's solo work hasn't been nearly as successful, although a lot of the music from the performer *Time* magazine called "Rock's Renaissance Man" has been easily as good. A voracious student of all cultures, Byrne was sometimes criticized for adapting it for his own purposes—though rarely did he get complaints from the Brazilians whose rhythms he borrowed or from the Cubans whose music he reintroduced, via his Luaka Bop label, to U.S. audiences following a more than 20-year ban. More recently, his four-piece rock approach has come closer to the Heads than anything he's done previously.

what to buy: *Feelings* 𝄢𝄢𝄢𝄢𝄾 (Luaka Bop, 1997, prod. David Byrne, Morcheeba, Joe Galdo) seems to combine many of Byrne's various interests—trip-hop, twang, and retro '70s (with Devo members chipping in). The result ends up sounding more like a solid Talking Heads record than any of his other solo work.

what to buy next: *My Life in the Bush of Ghosts* 𝄢𝄢𝄢𝄢𝄾 (Sire, 1981, prod. David Byrne, Brian Eno), a collaboration with Brian Eno while Byrne was still in the Talking Heads, began the groundbreaking work incorporating found rhythms, odd radio transmissions, and a dance beat a decade before such practices became commonplace in pop.

what to avoid: Byrne's artsy works for the avant-garde theater can be deadly listening, none moreso than the score for Robert Wilson's *The Forest* 𝄢𝄾 (Luaka Bop/Sire, 1991).

the rest:

The Complete Score from the Broadway Production of "The Catherine Wheel" 𝄢𝄾 (Sire, 1981)

Rei Momo 𝄢𝄢𝄢𝄢 (Luaka Bop/Sire, 1989)

Uh-Oh 𝄢𝄢𝄢𝄢 (Luaka Bop/Sire, 1992)

David Byrne 𝄢𝄢𝄢𝄢 (Luaka Bop/Sire, 1994)

worth searching for: *Hanging Upside Down* (Sire, 1992, prod. Nick Launay) is an import CD single that includes Byrne's first stab at an old Talking Heads song, "(Nothing But) Flowers," while on his *Uh-Oh* tour.

influences:

◀◀ Terry Allen, Robert Wilson, Desi Arnaz

▶▶ Primitive Radio Gods, Beck, Hayden

see also: *Talking Heads, Brian Eno*

Roger Catlin

Cabaret Voltaire

Formed 1974, in Sheffield, England.

Richard H. Kirk, guitar, synthesizer, horns; Stephen Mallinder, bass, vocals; Christopher Watkins, organ, tapes (1974–83); Bill Nelson, guitar (1987).

Coming from the bleak industrial landscape of Sheffield, England, it's not hard to see where the so called "industrial" sounds so regularly attributed to the Cabs come from. Cabaret Voltaire was one of the earliest pioneers of found sounds, sampling, tape manipulations, and the bleak, over-processed vocal style now so familar to fans of the commercially successful post-industrial movement of the early to mid-'90s. Although hard to pin down stylistically, the band's material ranges in sounds from the almost funk (*Code*) to more stripped-down techno sounds à la nine inch nails (which only came more than a decade after the Cabs had been putting out material). One could argue the unifying principal in almost all of Cabaret Voltaire's body of work is that you can dance to it, and the group has blazed major trails for many who would come later; even Joy Division's bleak psuedo-industrial sounds were influenced by this band that even pre-dates punk. The do-it-yourself mentality really holds sway with the Cabs; while earlier efforts did break sonic boundries never before considered, the band's earliest material actually sounds primitive, underproduced, and, well, old, in comparison to the techonlogical innovations in synthesizers, electronics, and sampling present in today's music. The word industrial is often bandied about with regard to bands like Ministry, nine inch nails, and Skinny Puppy, but this is the real deal. With dozens of releases, from live albums to solo efforts from the band's primary duo (Richard Kirk and Stephen Mallinder), it's hard to pin down what exactly makes the band tick—they've changed from almost an Eastern style at the beginning to an all too familiar psudeo-industrial style (like Ministry's *Twitch* album) to danceable funk (inspired by the On-U Sound label's founder Adrian Sherwood), a foray into the House music styles, and then into the ambiant/techno realm— all the while true to its dark, atmospheric, industrial roots. The Cabs have made inroads into the mainstream from time to time, primarily as a dance club standard; there were points during the mid-to-late '80's that you couldn't hit an alternative dance club and not hear "James Brown" or "Sensoria." It's been quite some time since any new material was released by the band, but the official word, depsite many solo projects, is that Kirk and Mallinder are still planning more releases as Cabaret Voltaire. The hardest part of collecting the Cabs is the fact that a huge portion of the band's material has been released as imports only, and on small independant labels to boot. Much of the library is out of print, but well worth searching out in the used record stores.

what to buy: *Technology: Western Re-Works 1992* 𝄞𝄞𝄞𝄞 (Caroline, 1992, prod. various) is, to date, the only legit Cabaret Voltaire greatest hits collection. This lengthy collection covers most of the band's more notable tracks, providing the perfect introduction to one of the most influential electronic acts.

what to buy next: *Code* 𝄞𝄞𝄞 (EMI, 1987, prod. Adrian Sherwood) was the band's first, and only, major label release. It marked a venture into the mainstream but still stood true to the original roots of found-sounds, raspy vocals, and electronic atmospherics—all the while making you tap your toes. *Extended Play* 𝄞𝄞𝄞 (Rough Trade, 1978, prod. Cabaret Voltaire) was the band's first official release, although there is material from earlier days available. This show's the beginings of the electronic movement, and while, truthfully, it's not that great of an album, it warrants inclusion for historical and influential merit alone.

what to avoid: *The Living Legends* 𝄞𝄞 (Mute-Restless, 1990, prod. various) presents itself as a greatest hits collection but is actually a B-sides/alternate takes compilation. If you're a huge Cabs fan, you may want this. Otherwise, it's rather weak.

best of the rest:
Three Mantras 𝄞𝄞𝄞 (Rough Trade, 1980/Mute-Restless, 1990)
The Voice of America 𝄞𝄞𝄞𝄞 (Rough Trade, 1980/Mute-Restless, 1990)
Red Mecca 𝄞𝄞𝄞 (Rough Trade, 1981/Mute-Restless, 1990)
Drinking Gasoline 𝄞𝄞𝄞 (Caroline, 1985)
Once upon a Time 𝄞𝄞𝄞𝄞 (A&M, 1985)
Arm of the Lord 𝄞𝄞𝄞𝄞 (A&M, 1985)
The Drain Train 𝄞𝄞𝄞 (Caroline, 1986/Mute-Restless, 1990)
Eight Crepuscule Tracks 𝄞𝄞𝄞 (Giant, 1987)
Colours 𝄞𝄞𝄞 (Mute, 1991)
International Language 𝄞𝄞𝄞 (Instinct, 1993)
Plasticity 𝄞𝄞𝄞 (Insinct, 1993)

The Conversation ♫♫♫ (Instinct, 1994)

worth searching for: *Micro-Phonies* (Some Bizzare-Virgin, 1984, prod. Cabaret Voltaire) is one of the strongest releases in the band's catalog. It features many tracks that, if you frequented the club scene of the '80s, would make you say "Oh, *that's* who did that song. . . ." This one is out of print and import only.

influences:

◄◄ Phillip Glass, Brian Eno, King Crimson, Genesis

►► Ministy, nine inch nails, Depeche Mode, Filter

Tim Davis

Chris Cacavas & Junkyard Love

See: Green on Red

Cactus

See: Vanilla Fudge

John Cafferty

Born in Narrangansett, RI.

New Jersey band leader John Cafferty took his Bruce Springsteen obsession out for a quick drag race on the highway of fame before disappearing with his Beaver Brown Band back into the welcoming hands of Asbury Park obscurity. Sure, his engine stalled, but not before his streamlined Jersey rock and retooled oldies took over the soundtrack for the film *Eddie and the Cruisers*. The film's success was a mixed blessing, however, as Cafferty remained behind the scenes while actor Michael Paré mouthed the words. It did get him more recognition than he would've on his own, however. After *Eddie* faded, so did Cafferty. He can be spotted nowadays in VH1 "Whatever Happened To . . ." specials, ruminating about life on the dark side.

what to buy: The soundtrack for *Eddie & the Cruisers* ♫♫♫ (Scotti Bros., 1983, prod. Kenny Vance) is Cafferty's moment in the sun. His Bruce-lite anthem, "On the Dark Side" gave *Eddie* a radio-ready hit, with an album full of catchy but shortsighted roots rock and covers of oldies but goodies.

what to avoid: The rest of his output is an exercise in redundancy. Skip it all.

the rest:
Tough All Over ♫ (Scotti Bros., 1985)
Roadhouse ♫ (Scotti Bros., 1988)
Eddie & the Cruisers II: Eddie Lives ♫♫ (Scotti Bros., 1989)
Eddie & the Cruisers: The Unreleased Tapes ♫ (Scotti Bros., 1991)

influences:

◄◄ Bruce Springsteen, Southside Johnny & the Asbury Jukes, Dion Dimucci

►► Joe Grushecky, Jon Bon Jovi

Allan Orski

Cake

Formed 1991, in Sacramento, CA.

John McCrea, vocals, guitar; Greg Brown, guitar (1991–98); Todd Roper, drums; Vince DiFiore, trumpet, keyboards; Gabe Nelson, bass (1991–92; 1997–present); Victor Damiani, bass (1992–97).

Cake is proof that songwriters' songwriters can make festive music, too. While bandleader John McCrea's economical, off-kilter musings on basic human dynamics have caught the attention of Rosanne Cash, Jonathan Richman, Captain Beefheart, and Counting Crow Adam Duritz, it has been the rhythmic, genre-bastardizing groove behind those droll, deadpan vocals that has driven the band to platinum success. In other words, it's got a funky beat and you can dance to it—McCrea's abundant cynicism and pessimism be damned. On record and, especially, on stage, this dynamic has resulted in compelling artistic tension, with McCrea almost working against the country-funkin' alternarock band to create a precarious sound that always seems as if it's about to implode. But that tension hasn't been limited to recordings and live performances: in 1995, guitarist Greg Brown momentarily quit the band over a long-simmering dispute with McCrea. He was soon back in the fold, though, working on Cake's sophomore breakthrough, *Fashion Nugget*. Ironically, it was Brown's sole songwriting contribution to that album, "The Distance," that brought the band its biggest success. Brown celebrated by quitting Cake once again—this time, apparently, for good (to form a new band called Misty)—just as the group was preparing to record its third album in January 1998. Cake soldiered on, with several Sacramento musicians playing guitar on the album that was tentatively scheduled for a fall 1998 release.

what to buy: On *Fashion Nugget* ♫♫♫♫ (Capricorn, 1996, prod. Cake), McCrea sings 13 sad songs and one country waltz (a cover of Willie Nelson's middle-finger-to-the-industry, "Sad Songs and Waltzes") that are predominantly about dysfunctional relationships and, even in their most superficially positive moments, largely devoid of any hint of actual optimism (see the strangely downbeat cover of the disco classic "I Will Survive"). All rhythmic, melodic, and stylistic variance, the album plays sonically like the diary of a mad band of musical gypsies.

what to buy next: The acerbic, alt-rock novelty hit "Rock 'n' Roll Lifestyle" got the most attention, but the true highlights of the idiosyncratic debut album, *Motorcade of Generosity* ♫♫♫ (Stamen, 1994/Capricorn, 1995, prod. Cake), are the wickedly witty honky-tonk get-up "Jesus Wrote a Blank Check" and the sprawling concert favorite "Jolene."

the rest:
Prolonging The Magic N/A (Capricorn, 1998)

influences:

◀◀ Camper Van Beethoven, Sly & the Family Stone, Jimmy Buffet, Lou Reed, Hank Williams Sr., George Jones, Willie Nelson, Dr. John

▶▶ Soul Coughing, Mac Swanky Trio

Josh Freedom du Lac

Cake Like

Formed 1992, in New York, NY.

Kerri Kenney, vocals, bass; Nina Hellman, guitars, vocals; Jody Seifert, drums.

The ingredients of Cake Like were mixed at New York University's Experimental Theatre Wing, where Kerri Kenney and Nina Hellman longed for something more creative. Hellman fell in love instantly with the guitar, while Kenney took on the bass— which she had never played before. Legend has it that Cake Like's first drummer left its first practice close to tears, so the duo called on Hellman's roommate Jody Seifert to ice the cake. The band members' side projects are almost as interesting as the music: Hellman is an off-Broadway actress; Seifert works for designer Donna Karan; and Kenney is a two-time Cable ACE award-nominee for Comedy Central's *Viva Variety*.

what's available: With vocals that sound like cats in heat, Cake Like's sophomore effort, *Bruiser Queen* 🎸🎸🎸 (Vapor Records, 1997, prod. Carl Glanville, Craig Wedren), requires more than one listen. Framed by stop-and-start guitars, *Bruiser Queen* covers cool in "Groovy," a *con leche* in the droll "Latin Lover," and the admiration of a blonde in "The American Woman," which is sung entirely in French. The standout track is "Mr. Fireman," a smartly written 911 call begging him to come right now because "I want you I need you! . . . Bring your God damn truck and some water!"

worth searching for: Available only on import, the over-produced debut, *Delicious* (Avant, 1994, prod. Eli Janney, Craig Wedren), is fun to listen to not only for its great song titles and subjects ("Bum Leg," "Fruitcake," "Suck," "Homewrecker," and "Abraham Lincoln") but to see the springboard from which *Bruiser Queen* came.

influences:

◀◀ L7, Babes in Toyland, Hole

▶▶ Pee Shy, the Donnas

Christina Fuoco

J.J. Cale

Born Jean Jacques Cale, December 5, 1938, in Oklahoma City, OK.

J.J. Cale is a low-fi roots rocker and songwriter who, besides having more success when other artists cover his songs, can whip up some brilliant guitar playing when he so desires. He's also one of the first artists to utilize drum machines and other new technology without losing the organic sensibilities of his songs about honky-tonk livin' and wonder. A limited vocalist but an overachiever as a tunesmith, Cale can lull you into an ambient splendor. His best known covers include: Eric Clapton's interpretations of "Cocaine" and "After Midnight"; "Call Me the Breeze" as done by both Lynyrd Skynyrd and the Mavericks; the versions of "Same Old Blues" by Bryan Ferry and Captain Beefheart; the Band's crackling "Crazy Mama"; and Randy Crawford's jazzed-up version of "Cajun Moon." Not bad company for this unassuming Okie.

what to buy: *Naturally . . . J.J. Cale* 🎸🎸🎸🎸 (Mercury, 1972, prod. Audie Ashworth) is a cornucopia of roots rockin' tunes that features the hit song "Crazy Mama" (one of the first songs to utilize a drum machine) and stellar backing from Tim Drummond and Carl Radle on bass and David Briggs on piano and organ. *Anyway the Wind Blows: The Anthology* 🎸🎸🎸🎸 (Mercury, 1997, prod. various) is a two-disc compilation boasting the well-covered hits plus some live and previously unreleased tracks. *The Very Best of J.J. Cale* 🎸🎸🎸🎸 (Mercury, 1998, prod. various) whittles that down to an even more concise single disc. *Closer to You* 🎸🎸🎸🎸 (Virgin, 1994, prod. J.J. Cale) is Cale's first album for Virgin and his 11th overall, another display of top-notch guitar playing and songwriting.

what to buy next: *Number 10* 🎸🎸🎸🎸 (Silvertone, 1992, prod. J.J. Cale) may be a just a notch below *Naturally* in the song department but more than makes up for it with Cale's guitar heroics throughout.

what to avoid: There's nothing terribly wrong with *Five* 🎸🎸🎸 (Mercury, 1979, prod. Audie Ashworth, J.J. Cale), but there's a sense of interchangeability about the albums Cale recorded around this time.

the rest:
Really, J.J. Cale 🎸🎸🎸 (Mercury, 1972)
Okie 🎸🎸🎸 (Mercury, 1974)
Troubadour 🎸🎸🎸 (Mercury, 1976)
Shades 🎸🎸🎸 (Mercury, 1980)
Grasshopper 🎸🎸🎸 (Mercury, 1982)
Fight 🎸🎸🎸 (Mercury, 1983)
Special Edition 🎸🎸🎸🎸 (Mercury, 1984)
Travel-Log 🎸🎸🎸 (Silvertone, 1990)
Guitar Man 🎸🎸🎸 (Virgin, 1996)

John Cale (© Jack Vartoogian)

influences:

◀◀ Chet Atkins, the Grand Ole Opry

▶▶ Dire Straits, Eric Clapton, Wilco, Uncle Tupelo, John Campbell

Mark J. Petracca

John Cale

Born March 9, 1942, in Garnant, South Wales.

Few figures in rock history have had the wide-reaching influence and broad background of musician/composer/producer John Cale. A classically trained pianist and violist, the Welsh-born Cale has been a vital player in American music's avant garde, first as a student and cohort of jazz artist/minimalist La-Monte Young and later as a founding member of the seminal pre-punk group the Velvet Underground. As producer for artists such as Iggy Pop, Patti Smith, and Jonathan Richman, Cale defined the raw, sonic excesses that would shape punk music. Throughout the '70s, his associations with the likes of Brian Eno and Roxy Music guitarist Phil Manzanera put him at the center of rock music's most bizarre and experimental period. His own solo work has been eccentric and unpredictable, marked by flashes of brilliance and artistic malaise. Cale's post-Velvet albums saw him venturing into British folk of the haunted, Nick Drake variety, but by the early '70s (his most productive period) he seemed to have found his niche writing morbidly fascinating rock songs about murder and debauchery that consolidated his tastes for rock, folk, classical, and electronic music. His post-punk work is erratic and uninspired, although recent collaborations with former musical partners Lou Reed and Eno, as well as his own return to his classical roots, have resulted in some fine recordings.

what to buy: There's no better place to start than with *The Island Years* 🐾🐾🐾🐾 (Island, 1996, prod. various), a masterstroke of repackaging that combines Cale's three albums for Island (*Fear*, *Slow Dazzle* and *Helen of Troy*) in one two-CD package. The music here is from Cale's artistically (and rather commercially) successful rock-dementia period, and includes classic gems like "Fear Is a Man's Best Friend," "Gun," and his doomy cover of Elvis Presley's "Heartbreak Hotel."

what to buy next: Cale's second solo album, *The Academy in Peril* ♫♫♫ (Edsel, 1972, prod. John Cale), is a lovely and well-humored exploration of his classical and avant-garde musical training. An imaginative and ambitious record (Cale commissioned the Royal Philharmonic Orchstra for two cuts), it's still among the freshest items in his extensive catalog. For a look at Cale's lighter work, check out *Paris 1919* ♫♫♫ (Reprise, 1973, prod. Chris Thomas). Recorded in California with members of Little Feat, the album is an enigmatic and breathtaking work, beautifully orchestrated and featuring lovely songs throughout—most notably "Hanky Panky Nohow," "The Endless Plain of Fortune," and "Andalucia."

what to avoid: Like several of the albums from Cale's post-punk period, *Caribbean Sunset* ♫ (ZE-Island, 1984, prod. John Cale) is too erratic and unfocused to hold much interest. Aside from the strong title track, the rest of the album plods along without much aim or enthusiasm.

the rest:
Vintage Violence ♫♫ (Columbia, 1969)
Church of Anthrax ♫♫ (Columbia, 1971)
Fear ♫♫♫ (Island, 1974)
(With Kevin Ayers, Eno, and Nico) *June 1, 1974* ♫♫♫ (Island, 1974)
Slow Dazzle ♫♫♫ (Island, 1975)
Helen of Troy ♫♫♫ (Island, 1975)
Honi Soitx ♫♫♫ (A&M, 1981)
Music for a New Society ♫♫♫ (ZE-Passport, 1982)
Artificial Intelligence ♫♫♫ (Beggars Banquet-PVC, 1985)
Words for the Dying ♫♫♫ (Opal/Warner Bros., 1989)
(With Lou Reed) *Songs for Drella* ♫♫♫ (Sire-Warner Bros., 1990)
Even Cowgirls Get the Blues ♫♫ (ROIR, 1991)
Fragments of a Rainy Season ♫♫♫ (Hannibal/Carthage, 1992)
Seducing Down the Door: A Collection, 1970–1990 ♫♫♫ (Rhino, 1994)
Nico N/A (Detour, 1998)

worth searching for: After years of assisting with each other's albums, Cale and Eno finally collaborated on the brilliant but out of print *Wrong Way Up* (Opal-Warner Bros., 1990, prod. Brian Eno), resulting in one of the best albums either artist has ever made.

influences:
◀◀ John Cage, LaMonte Young, the Beach Boys, the Beatles, the Velvet Underground

▶▶ Nick Drake, King Crimson, Robert Fripp, Pink Floyd, Roxy Music, Brian Eno, Patti Smith, Tom Waits, Television, Tom Verlaine, Robert Wyatt

see also: *The Velvet Underground*

Christopher Scapelliti

Randy California

See: Spirit

The Call

Formed 1980, in Los Angeles, CA.

Michael Been, vocals, guitar; Scott Musick, drums, vocals; Tom Ferrier, guitar, vocals; Greg Freeman, bass; Jim Goodwin, keyboards.

The Call made its mark with a steely aggressiveness and apocalyptic post-punk sound, propelled in large part by chief songwriter Michael Been. A limited but passionate singer, he attracted the likes of the Band's Garth Hudson, who lent his hand to a number of songs. Standing apart from the early '80s new wave scene, the Call has much more in common, ideologically, with '70s punk in its uncompromising drive and railings against the status quo.

what to buy: *The Walls Came Down: Best of the Mercury Years* ♫♫♫ (Mercury, 1991, prod. various) is Been's own compilation from the Call's first three albums, providing an excellent intro to the band's work—especially the scathing title track and the floor-shaking indictments of "Turn a Blind Eye." Another compilation, *The Best of the Call* ♫♫♫ (Warner Resound, 1997, prod. various) repeats the best tracks and adds those that came later.

what to buy next: *Reconciled* ♫♫♫ (Elektra, 1986, prod. Michael Been, the Call) features guest shots from Robbie Robertson, Peter Gabriel, and Simple Minds' Jim Kerr, which can't help but tip the scales in the right direction.

what to avoid: *The Call* ♫♫ (Mercury, 1982, prod. Hugh Padgham) is tentative, with the band just finding its style and sound—completists, though, won't be too disappointed.

the rest:
Modern Romans ♫♫♫ (Mercury, 1983)
Scene beyond Dreams ♫♫♫ (Mercury, 1984)
Into the Woods ♫♫♫ (Elektra, 1987)
Red Moon ♫♫♫ (MCA, 1990)
To Heaven and Back ♫♫♫ (Fingerprint/Sky, 1997)

worth searching for: *Let the Day Begin* (MCA, 1989) didn't get much recognition, but it's full of hard-hitters in addition to the title track.

influences:
◀◀ The Clash, Joy Division

▶▶ The Alarm, nine inch nails

Allan Orski

Camel

Formed 1971, in London, England.

Andrew Latimer, guitar, synthesizer, vocals; Doug Ferguson, bass (1971–76); Peter Bardens, keyboards (1971–79); Andy Ward, drums, percussion; Richard Sinclair, bass, vocals (1976–84); Jan Schelhaas,

keyboards (1982–84); Mel Collins, saxophone (1976–84); Colin Bass, bass, vocals (1979–84).

One of the more ethereal of Britain's progressive-rock bands of the 1970s, Camel created ambitious, conceptual pieces that never quite found an audience in the U.S. Lacking a strong visionary, such as Pink Floyd's Roger Waters or Genesis's Peter Gabriel, the group simply never got much attention. But its keyboard washes, layered guitars, and breezy vocals made for some of the most pleasant, entrancing music of the prog-rock era and prefaced the new age movement. Pete Bardens went on to acclaim as the keyboardist on Van Morrison's *Wavelength* album, while Mel Collins's feverish, high-pitched tenor sax solo was a highlight of the Rolling Stones hit "Miss You."

what to buy: The two-CD set *Echoes: The Retrospective* 🎵🎵🎵 (Deram/Chronicles, 1993, prod. various) is a far-ranging collection that manages to string together some of its best mid-'70s work with hard-to-find songs from its '80s and early '90s incarnations.

the rest:

A Compact Compilation 🎵🎵🎵 (Rhino, 1985)

worth searching for: Most of Camel's records are out of print now, including its best album, the Brian Eno collaboration *Rain Dances* (Deram, 1977). *I Can See Your House from Here* (Deram/One Way, 1979, prod. Rupert Hine) is worth seeking out for its controversial cover alone.

influences:

◄◄ Pink Floyd (with Syd Barrett), Genesis (with Peter Gabriel), King Crimson, Procol Harum

►► Cocteau Twins, Dead Can Dance, Enya

Doug Pullen

Ali Campbell

See: UB40

Glen Campbell

Born April 22, 1936, outside Billstown, AR.

Although unjustly remembered as a somewhat ingratiating, over-the-top cornball (the memory of his hugely successful CBS television series *The Glen Campbell Goodtime Hour* can still strike terror into the faint-of-heart), Glen Campbell's long and successful career as an entertainer is testament to the obvious drive and abundant talent behind the rhinestones. First leaving home as a teen to tour with his uncle's Western swing combo, the Dick Bills Band, Campbell landed in Los Angeles in 1960 at the perfect time to make use of his growing prowess on the guitar. Over the next five years he was one of the city's most sought-after studio musicians, performing be-

hind everyone from Spector to Sinatra. He was even a bonafide Beach Boy for a while. Signed to Capitol Records in 1962, he first appeared in the Top 50 three years later with a version of Donovan's "Universal Soldier," and in 1967 his signature tune, John Hartford's "Gentle on My Mind," placed respectably on both the country and pop charts. But it wasn't until Campbell began recording the brilliant songs of Jimmy Webb that he became a regular visitor to the Top 10; "By the Time I Get to Phoenix," "Wichita Lineman," and "Galveston" remain classics of their genre. After several years spent entertaining on both the small and big screens (joking that his role in *True Grit* helped co-star John Wayne win an Academy Award), he returned to the top of the charts in 1975 with "Rhinestone Cowboy" and again in '77 with "Southern Nights" before hitting the scandal sheets with Tanya Tucker and letting years of pharmaceutical dabbling get the better of him. The following decade was spent bouncing somewhat aimlessly from label to label and from style to style, culminating with a self-confessed "work-horse" stint in the career graveyard of Branson, Missouri. The '90s, however, found Campbell both physically and spiritually cleansed and refreshed, and he remains a popular performer—and red-hot guitarist. And he can still sing Jimmy Webb like nobody else.

what to buy: The *Essential Glen Campbell* 🎵🎵🎵🎵 (Capitol Nashville, 1995, prod. various) gathers, in three volumes (with upgraded sonics), all the hits as well as just enough rarities, instrumentals, and live recordings to demonstrate both the depth and scope of this decidedly all-around entertainer. *The Glen Campbell Collection (1962–1989)* 🎵🎵🎵 (Razor And Tie, 1997, prod. various) provides a more compact and concise overview.

what to buy next: Capitol has begun a long-overdue reissue of Campbell's earliest albums, starting with his very first from '62, *Big Bluegrass Special* 🎵🎵🎵 (Capitol Nashville, 1996, prod. Nick Venet), originally released under the name the Green River Boys. Also newly available are his three fine breakthrough albums from '67 and '68: *Gentle on My Mind* 🎵🎵🎵 (Capitol, 1967/Capitol Nashville, 1996, prod. Al DeLory), *By the Time I Get to Phoenix* 🎵🎵🎵🎵 (Capitol, 1967/Capitol Nashville, 1996, prod. Al DeLory, Nick Venet), and *Wichita Lineman* 🎵🎵🎵🎵 (Capitol, 1967/Capitol Nashville, 1996, prod. Al DeLory).

what to avoid: Beware the myriad greatest-hits and in-concert recordings, all of which have been rendered superfluous by the *Essential* series.

best of the rest:

Favorite Hymns 🎵🎵🎵 (Word/Epic, 1992)
Christmas with Glen Campbell 🎵🎵 (Laserlight, 1995)
Wings of Victory 🎵🎵🎵 (Intersound International, 1996)
Jesus and Me: The Collection 🎵🎵🎵 (New Haven, 1997)

worth searching for: Campbell's oft-overlooked gift as an instrumentalist is readily apparent on any of the budget reissues of his early Folkswingers recordings, particularly the *12-String Guitar* albums on World Pacific. Also fascinating is his just-before-fame work with the baroque Beach Boy band Sagittarius alongside Gary Usher, Terry Melcher, Bruce Johnston, and Curt Boettcher.

influences:

◄◄ Django Reinhardt, Barney Kessel, Roger Miller, Jimmy Dickens

►► Jim Stafford, Ricky Skaggs, Garth Brooks

Gary Pig Gold

Camper Van Beethoven

See: Cracker

Candlebox

Formed 1991, in Seattle, WA.

Kevin Martin, vocals, guitar; Peter Klett, guitar; Scott Mercado, drums (1991–97); Bardi Martin, bass; Dave Krusen (1997–present).

Candlebox may have started in Seattle, but it wasn't part of the city's exploding angst-fuzz-and-flannel grunge scene. The quartet plays straightforward, muscular arena rock with a wisp of the blues. Named after a Midnight Oil lyric, Candlebox was the first rock band Madonna signed to her Maverick label after the quartet built a grass-roots following among hard-rock fans with its dynamic live shows. Candlebox has flickered, however, failing to fully deliver on the early potential shown by Peter Klett's strategically sharp guitar attacks and Kevin (no relation to Bardi) Martin's emotionally intense, tempered vocal screams.

what to buy: The debut, *Candlebox* &&& (Maverick, 1993, prod. Kelly Gray, Jon Plum, Candlebox), is a solid mix of guitar energy and power ballads, highlighted by pensive lyrics ("Mother's Dream," "Far Behind") and well-crafted melodies ("You," "Rain").

what to avoid: Except for the steady rise of "Understanding," there's less restraint or melodic wit on *Lucy* && (Maverick, 1995, prod. Kelly Gray, Jon Plum, Candlebox), as Candlebox cranks out high-voltage guitars and screeching vocals, hitting peak form on the patient thumper, "Bothered."

the rest:

Happy Pills &&& (Maverick, 1998)

worth searching for: The single "Far Behind" (Maverick, 1994) features a live cover of Jimi Hendrix's "Voodoo Chile."

influences:

◄◄ Midnight Oil, Jimi Hendrix, Guns N' Roses

David Yonke

Canned Heat

Formed 1966, in Los Angeles, CA.

Bob "Bear" Hite, vocals, harmonica (1966–81); Al "Blind Owl" Wilson, guitar, vocals, harmonica (1966–70); Henry "The Sunflower" Vestine, guitar (1966–69, 1970); Frank Cook, drums (1966–68); Larry Taylor, bass (1966–70, 1994–present); Adolpho "Fito" de la Parra, drums (1968–present); Harvey Mandel, guitar (1969–70); Antonio de la Barreda, bass (1970–72); Richard Hite, bass (1972–91); James Thornbury, guitar, hamonica, vocals (1984–present); Junior Watson, guitar, vocals (1994–present); Ron Shumake, bass, vocals (1994–present).

The boogie, ever since John Lee Hooker created it in the late '40s in Detroit, has been a timeless thing. So it is that this bunch of players from southern California plugged in their jug band and started playing the rolling, loose-limbed blues they loved so much on their John Lee Hooker records. If Canned Heat were a new band today, it would be part of the H.O.R.D.E. festival. As it is, the group continues—though without its original frontmen, Bob Hite and Al Wilson—but with an increasing number of original and prime-time members each year, as if they're coming back to the mothership for a bit of boogie nourishment.

what to buy: *Uncanned! The Best of Canned Heat* &&&& (Liberty/EMI, 1994, prod. various) is an expansive two-disc, 41-song set that has the hits ("On the Road Again," "Going up the Country," "Fannie Mae") and a disarming number of highly listenable jams. How quickly we forget.

what to avoid: *The King Biscuit Flower Hour Presents Canned Heat* && (KBFH, 1996) is a radio concert taken from a flat and forgettable 1979 show.

the rest:

The Best of Canned Heat &&& (EMI America, 1987)
Internal Combustion &&& (River Road, 1994)
Gamblin' Woman && (Mausoleum, 1996)
The Ties That Bind: 1975 Studio Sessions &&& (Archive, 1997)

worth searching for: One of the group's most consistent albums, *Future Blues* (Liberty, 1970/See For Miles, 1993, prod. Skip Taylor, Canned Heat) is available as an import.

influences:

◄◄ John Lee Hooker, Howlin' Wolf, Sonny Boy Williamson

►► The Grateful Dead, the Fabulous Thunderbirds, Blues Traveler

Gary Graff

Freddy Cannon

Born Frederick Martin Picariello, December 4, 1939, in Lynn, MA.

Freddy Cannon's exuberant sides for Swan and Warner Bros. forged the link between early rock's golden age and the teen idol/*American Bandstand* era. His upper-register raving (in a voice some have likened to Jerry Lewis's) brought a playful, ragtime feel to a series of doo-wop inspired novelties, a few of which are genuine pop classics. In 1955, 15-year-old Cannon got in on rock's ground floor, playing electric rhythm guitar behind the G-Clefs as well as fronting his own group, Freddy Karmon & the Hurricanes. His first taste of national success came as the lead singer for the doo-wop group the Spindrifts, who had a Top 50 hit with "Cha Cha Doo" in 1958. As a solo act, Cannon's career really took off under the guidance of producers Frank Slay and Bob Crewe, who added choruses, hand claps, and a stomping beat to a rockabilly grinder co-written by Cannon's mother. The resultant "Tallahassee Lassie" featured the glittering guitar work of Kenny Paulsen and Cannon's trademark "woo's," clearly anticipating both the surf and go-go music trends. Cannon's string of hits led to a record 110 appearances on Dick Clark's *American Bandstand* (it also helped that Clark was part owner of Swan Records), as well as roles in such teen-oriented flicks as *Village of the Giants* and *Disk-O-Tek Holiday*. His finest moment on record came with 1962's "Palisades Park," a lighthearted, effects-laden production (written by future *Gong Show* host Chuck Barris) that epitomized the youth-driven spirit of the era of "The Twist." Cannon's star faded during the late '60s, though in 1981 he briefly teamed with the Belmonts (sans Dion) to record "Let's Put the Fun Back in Rock 'n' Roll," which skirted the bottom of the charts. Since then, Cannon has become a staple of oldies revues, reunion concerts, and auto shows, where his enthusiasm and zeal personify what his brand of rock is all about.

what's available: There are two hits collections to choose from. *His Latest & His Greatest* 𝄞𝄞𝄞 (Critique Records, 1991, prod. Bob Crewe, Frank Slay, Dick Glasser, Harry King, Fred Lewis, Michael Jonzun) is an 18-track compilation featuring Cannon's biggest hits ("Palisades Park," "Way Down Yonder in New Orleans," "Tallahassee Lassie") mixed with the seldom-heard goodies such as "Everybody Monkey," "The Boom-Boom Man," "Opportunity," and his previously unreleased version of "Hanky Panky." If it's just the big hits you want, the 20-track *Big Blast from Boston: The Best of Freddy "Boom Boom" Cannon* 𝄞𝄞𝄞𝄞 (Rhino, 1995, compilation prod. Freddy Cannon, James Austen) has 'em all.

worth searching for: Those who want to check out Cannon's contributions to the G-Clefs are well-advised to track down *Ka-Ding-Dong* (Relic, 1995, prod. various), a solid doo-wop collection featuring the group's hits "I Understand (Just How You Feel)," "'Cause You're Mine," "A Girl Has to Know," and the title track. Fine material from an underrated doo-wop group.

influences:

◀◀ The G-Clefs, Dale Hawkins, Little Richard, Lloyd Price

▶▶ Frankie Valli, Len Barry, Gary Lewis

Ken Burke

Cappadonna
See: Wu-Tang Clan

The Captain & Tennille
Formed 1974, in Los Angeles, CA.

Toni Tennille (born Catheryn Antoinette Tennille, May 8, 1943, in Montgomery, AL), vocals; Daryl Dragon (born August 27, 1942, in Los Angeles, CA), piano.

A partnership often better known for its industry savvy and knack for making the most of career opportunities, the Captain & Tennille made their name by scoring a series of pop hits during the mid- and late '70s. The duo pushed an inoffensive brand of pop-rock built on catchy melodies and Tennille's expert if generic vocal abilities. Both students of classical piano for nearly a decade each, Dragon and Tennille met when the singer developed a musical, *Mother Earth,* for which her husband-to-be played keyboards. When the show closed days after opening, Dragon took Tennille along as a backing vocalist on his new gig, as keyboardist for the Beach Boys. By 1974, the two had recorded a single together, "The Way I Want to Touch You." But it was a year later that their recording of Neil Sedaka's "Love Will Keep Us Together" exploded onto the pop charts. By the year's end, both songs would be Top 10 hits. The next year, a version of Smokey Robinson's "Shop Around" became another big hit, allowing the duo to land an ABC television series that lasted two years. The couple also had great success with a remake of America's "Muskrat Love," but its 15 minutes ran out after the 1979 smash "Do That to Me One More Time." Tennille releases occasional albums of big band tunes, while Dragon helms the pair's Nevada studio, producing albums and writing film soundtracks.

what to buy: Never an album-oriented act, it's no surprise that the best example of their work is *Captain and Tennille's Greatest Hits* 𝄞𝄞𝄞 (A&M, 1977, prod. Daryl Dragon), a collection that came out too early to include "Do That to Me..." Aw, shucks.

what to buy next: As a near-perfect example of the pop-rock that ruled the airwaves back then, *Love Will Keep Us Together* 𝄞𝄞𝄞 (A&M, 1975, prod. Daryl Dragon, Morgan Cavett) holds the breakthrough title track hit and the ballad "The Way That I Want to Touch You."

what to avoid: Vapid and cloying, *20 Years of Romance* **woof!** (Nouveau, 1988) presents all the reasons why this duo never survived the '70s.

the rest:
Por Amor Viviremos 𝄞𝄞 (A&M, 1976)
Song of Joy 𝄞𝄞 (A&M, 1976)
Come in from the Rain 𝄞𝄞 (A&M, 1977)
Make Your Move 𝄞𝄞 (Casablanca, 1979)

Keeping Our Love Warm 🎵🎵 (Casablanca, 1980)
Dream 🎵🎵 (A&M, 1988)

solo outings:
Toni Tennille:
Never Let Me Go 🎵🎵 (Bay Cities, 1991)
Things Are Swingin' 🎵 (Purebred, 1994)
Toni Tennille Sings Big Band 🎵🎵 (Honest, 1998)

influences:
◀◀ The Beatles, Sonny & Cher
▶▶ Celine Dion

Eric Deggans

Captain Beefheart & His Magic Band

Formed 1964, in Lancaster, CA.

Captain Beefheart (born Don Van Vliet, January 15, 1941, in Glendale, CA), vocals, harmonica, tenor and soprano sax, bass clarinet. Notable Magic Band alumni include: Zoot Horn Rollo (born Bill Harkleroad), guitar (1969–73); Winged Eel Fingerling (born Eliot Ingber), guitar (1968–73); Antennae Jimmy Semens (born Jeff Cotton), guitar (1966–70); Alex St. Claire, guitar (1966–70); Ry Cooder, guitar (1966); Gary Lucas, guitar (1978–80); Jeff Morris Tepper, guitar (1978–82); Rockette Morton (born Mark Boston), bass (1969–72); Orejon (born Roy Estrada), bass (1972); Eric Drew Feldman, keyboards (1978–82); Bruce Lambourne Fowler, trombone (1978–82); Drumbo (born John French), drums (1966–82); Ed Marimba (born Art Tripp), drums (1972); Robert Arthur Williams, drums (1978–82).

The profoundly playful godfathers of all things alternative in rock, Captain Beefheart & His Magic Band stripped songs down to their bare bones and let them run free. Though clearly rooted in the most primitive blues, Beefheart's music is full of angles and cross rhythms, stuttering, snaky guitar lines, and free jazz dissonance—a fitting backdrop for the holy terror of the Captain's Howlin' Wolf-on-acid vocals and dadaist lyrics. While his early recordings were marred by record company-induced compromise, in 1969 he was given carte blanche by longtime friend Frank Zappa on his Bizarre label. The result was the enormously influential *Trout Mask Replica*, a still-crucial art-rock reference point. Despite some mid-'70s stumbles, Beefheart returned with a new Magic Band in 1978 to make music as challenging as ever—though its point was somewhat blunted by the advent of punk. The Captain, who last recorded in 1983, has moved to the northern California coast, where he paints full-time. With gallery representation in New York City and Europe, his canvases command five figures and have brought him financial rewards he never found with his music. Rumors of failing health have been floating about for most of the '90s, and present-day footage of him in a 1997 BBC documentary bear this out.

what to buy: Fractured, ferocious, and full of Delta Blues–meets–Sun Ra surprises—along with Beefheart's wondrously surreal lyrics—*Trout Mask Replica* 🎵🎵🎵🎵 (Reprise, 1969, prod. Frank Zappa) remains the indisputable benchmark for what lurks under, over, and beyond rock. Thirty years later, the music still sounds as if it was made tomorrow.

what to buy next: Beefheart followed *Trout Mask Replica* with the self-produced and only marginally less turbulent *Lick My Decals Off Baby* 🎵🎵🎵🎵 (Bizarre, 1970, prod. Don Van Vliet). His next two albums, *The Spotlight Kid/Clear Spot* 🎵🎵🎵🎵 (Reprise, 1972, prod. Ted Templeman), now available on one CD, found the Captain and his band rocking a little harder and in a more recognizable rock song format—which is why these records are the more accessible favorites of many fans. Of Beefheart's recordings with the reincarnated Magic Band, *Doc at the Radar Station* 🎵🎵🎵🎵 (Blue Plate, 1980, prod. Don Van Vliet) marked the most powerful return of his "fast and bulbous" sound.

what to avoid: *Bluejeans & Moonbeams* 🎵 (Blue Plate, 1974, prod. Don Van Vliet) was Beefheart's overt and truly dubious attempt to make a "pop" record.

the rest:
Safe As Milk 🎵🎵🎵 (One Way Records, 1967)
Mirror Man 🎵🎵🎵🎵 (One Way Records, 1973)
Unconditionally Guaranteed 🎵🎵 (Blue Plate, 1974)
Shiny Beast (Bat Chain Puller) 🎵🎵🎵🎵 (Bizarre, 1978)
Ice Cream for Crow 🎵🎵🎵 (Blue Plate, 1982)
The Legendary A&M Sessions 🎵🎵🎵 (A&M, 1984)

worth searching for: A seminal early Beefheart recording, *Strictly Personal* (Blue Thumb, 1968), is available as a British import on Liberty Records. Outtakes from those sessions can be heard on a French import, *I May Be Hungry, but I Sure Ain't Weird* (Sequel, 1993).

solo outings:
Mallard (Bill Harkleroad, Mark Boston, Art Tripp):
Mallard/In a Different Climate 🎵🎵🎵 (Virgin, 1994)

John French:
Waiting on the Flame 🎵🎵🎵 (Demon, 1994)

influences:
◀◀ Howlin' Wolf, Bo Diddley, Ornette Coleman, Eric Dolphy, Sun Ra, Karlheinz Stockhausen
▶▶ Sonic Youth, the Residents, Nick Cave, Tom Waits, Eugene Chadbourne, PJ Harvey, Henry Kaiser

see also: *Frank Zappa*

Doug Pippin and David Greenberger

Caravan

Formed 1968, in England.

Pye Hastings, guitar, vocals; David Sinclair, keyboards; Richard Sinclair, bass, vocals; Richard Coughlan, drums.

This was the freshest-sounding, least self-absorbed of the progressive rock bands from England during the late '60s. Using English folk and renaissance music styles along with superior musicianship, Caravan was adept at performing tight song structures and creating exciting vamps in suite-like arrangements.

what to buy: *Canterbury Tales: The Best of Caravan ♪♪♪♪* (Deram/Chronicles, 1994) is a fine two-disc sampling of Caravan's first seven albums.

worth searching for: It's worth a little digging to find the deleted *For Girls Who Grow Plump in the Night* (London, 1973), the band's smartest, most powerful album.

influences:

◄◄ Gil Evans, the Beach Boys, Pink Floyd

►► The Soft Machine, Genesis

Patrick McCarty

Carbon

See: Elliott Sharp

The Cardigans

Formed 1992, in Jonkoping, Sweden.

Bengt Lagerberg, drums, flutes; Lasse Johansson, guitar, keyboards; Magnus Sveningsson, bass; Nina Persson, vocals; Peter Svensson, guitar.

If nothing else, the Cardigans are one of the most stylistically restless bands in Scandinavian pop. In the span of just three albums, the quintet already has undergone two major overhauls, moving first from the jazzy-cool, Smiths- and Sundays-inspired pop of the introverted debut, *Emmerdale*, to the thoroughly giddy easy-listening feel of *Life*—and, most recently, to the sprightly pop-rock of the less-infectious U.S. breakthrough, *First Band on the Moon*. The band itself takes its latest effort most seriously and even considers the sweet, '60s-lounge flashback *Life* to be (and we quote) "a joke." But the latter recording will live the longest in space-age bachelor pad-ville, with its lush, cocktail-jazz arrangements and instrumentation and, of course, Nina Persson's dreamy vocals.

what to buy: *Life ♪♪♪♪* (Minty Fresh, 1996, prod. Tore Johansson) is a kitschy but loveable compilation of the group's first two European albums. Loaded with '60s motifs, the almost cinematic recording goes heavy on the vibraphones, woodwinds, synthesizers, strings, finger snaps, and even awkward guitar licks. The band has a knack for crafting delectable pop hooks ("Daddy's Car," "Rise & Shine"), but it can also go the ambient route, as evidenced by the trip-hop of "Our Space." And you'll never be able to look Ozzy Osbourne straight in the eyes again after hearing the cooing cover of Black Sabbath's heavy-metal classic, "Sabbath Bloody Sabbath."

what to buy next: *First Band on the Moon ♪♪♪* (Mercury, 1996, prod. Tore Johansson) features the band's infectious U.S. breakthrough, "Lovefool," and is highlighted by a perversely sweet cover of yet another erstwhile heavy metal classic, Black Sabbath's "Iron Man." But the band takes the rock thing a bit far, including too many power-pop chords for its own good.

the rest:

Gran Turismo N/A (Mercury, 1998)

worth searching for: Much of the material from the group's uneven debut, *Emmerdale* (Trampolene, 1994, prod. Tore Johansson), is duplicated on the U.S. version of *Life*, but it shows just how much more serious the band was when it first arrived.

influences:

◄◄ Peggy Lee, Burt Bacharach, Ennio Morricone, Astrud Gilberto, Francoise Hardy, Abba, Black Sabbath, Nick Drake, the Sundays, Pizzicato Five, St. Etienne, Stereolab, the Smiths

►► The Rentals, Dubstar

Josh Freedom du Lac

Cardinal

See: Richard Davies

Mariah Carey

Born March 27, 1970, on Long Island, NY.

A product of a black Venezuelan father and Irish-American mother, Mariah Carey seemed born to be a pop star—wielding a soulfully astonishing seven-octave voice while offering a supermodel look that barely hints at her ethnic origins. Working as a backup singer for various R&B sessions around Manhattan during her late teens—while supporting herself as the self-described "world's worst waitress"—the singer honed her songwriting talents with keyboardist Ben Margulies. On one such gig, backing R&B one-hit wonder Brenda K. Starr at a party, Carey got her big break; Starr presented a demo tape of hers to Columbia Records chief Tommy Mottola, who was so taken with the material while driving home, he headed back to the party to meet Carey. Before long, with Mottola guiding her career—eventually he was named Sony Music president and married Carey in 1993—the singer released a single, "Visions of Love," that shot to #1 on the pop charts in 1990. Carey would eventually earn five consecutive #1 pop singles over two albums, along with two Grammy Awards. From that point, Carey—most often compared

Mariah Carey (© Jack Vartoogian)

to fellow hitmaking diva Whitney Houston—could do no wrong, offering an appealing pop sound leavened with touches of soul. An EP version of her *MTV Unplugged* performance soared to the top of the charts in 1992, along with her third record a year later. Though her first-ever concert tour in 1993 met with mixed reviews, a chart-topping duet with Boyz II Men in 1995 proved she still retained her golden touch. Divorced from Mottola in 1997, Carey added a dash of hip-hop flavor to her release that year as a sign of her growing independence.

what to buy: For anyone looking at Carey's catalog, the choice of what to buy next depends on what the collector wants. Fans of her treacly pop sound—a generically accessible approach that nearly suffocates her amazing vocal abilities—will want *Mariah Carey* 𝄢𝄢𝄢𝄢 (Columbia, 1990, prod. Mariah Carey, Walter Afanasieff, Rhett Lawrence, Narada Michael Walden, Ben Margulies, Ric Wake). Featuring the hits "Vision of Love" and "Love Takes Time," it's the most vibrant of her studio discs.

what to buy next: For those who yearn to hear Carey break free of her commercial prison, the closest she comes is *MTV Unplugged* 𝄢𝄢𝄢𝄢 (Columbia EP, 1992, prod. Mariah Carey, Walter Afanasieff). Though the 26-plus people performing on this disc seem to belie the unplugged ethic, Carey's vibrant live delivery is nearly worth the heresy. As schmaltzy as it might seem, her take on the Jackson 5's "I'll Be There" really does impress—at least on the first hundred listens.

what to avoid: For fans of truly expressive soul music, everything in Carey's catalog goes down like a sawdust sandwich. But *Merry Christmas* 𝄢𝄢 (Columbia, 1994, prod. Walter Afanasieff), which mixes standards such as "Silent Night" with originals like "All I Want for Christmas Is You," is enough to make anyone reach for a few stiff shots of eggnog.

the rest:
Emotions 𝄢𝄢𝄢 (Columbia, 1991)
Music Box 𝄢𝄢𝄢 (Columbia, 1993)
Daydream 𝄢𝄢𝄢 (Columbia, 1995)
Butterfly 𝄢𝄢𝄢 (Columbia, 1997)
Ones N/A (Columbia, 1998)

worth searching for: Look for a videotape of the 1995 Grammy Awards telecast, if only to see the consternation on Carey's face as she is consistently edged out (and eventually shut out, despite four nominations) by Alanis Morissette and Annie Lennox.

influences:
◀◀ Whitney Houston, Minnie Ripperton, Irene Cara

▶▶ Toni Braxton, Celine Dion

Eric Deggans

Belinda Carlisle

See: The Go-Go's

Kim Carnes
Born July 20, 1945, in Los Angeles, CA.

Though her singing voice more closely recalls another leading lady of Hollywood's past—Marlene Dietrich—Kim Carnes is most famous for her rendition of "Bette Davis Eyes," the Donna Weiss–Jackie DeShannon composition that reigned at #1 for nine weeks in 1981 and won Carnes a Grammy for Record of the Year. With her readily recognizable raspy vocals—the result of too many smoke-filled venues and one-night engagements in her long career—Carnes got her start in the late 1960s working the Los Angeles nightclub scene. She later became a member of the New Christy Minstrels alongside Kenny Rogers and her future husband and songwriting partner, Dave Ellington. In 1971 Carnes and Ellington left the Minstrels, Carnes embarking on a solo career with Ellington a member of her backup band. Though her solo work brought her critical acclaim, she garnered even greater success as a songwriter, with Frank Sinatra, Barbra Streisand, Anne Murray, and Rita Coolidge all covering her material. Her biggest break came in 1980 when Rogers reunited with Carnes and Ellington to record their songs for his album, *Gideon*. Carnes also lent her vocals to the project, and her duet with Rogers, "Don't Fall in Love with a Dreamer," peaked at #4. The advent of MTV also helped to propel her career as the video for "Bette Davis Eyes" catapulted her album *Mistaken Identity* to platinum status and opened the door to other projects. Soon to follow: "I'll Be Here Where the Heart Is" from the Grammy-winning *Flashdance* soundtrack, the Top 20 hit "What about Me?" with Kenny Rogers and James Ingram, participation in USA for Africa's "We Are the World," and a string of solo albums and outside collaborations.

what to buy: There's enough gravel to cover a country driveway on *Gypsy Honeymoon: The Best of Kim Carnes* 𝄢𝄢𝄢 (Alliance, 1997, prod. various), a 15-song compilation that focuses on her trademark "Bette Davis Eyes" as well as her duets with Rogers, Barbra Streisand ("Make No Mistake He's Mine"), and Gene Cotton ("You're a Part of Me"). Sadly, the best studio balancing act can't mask the deterioration of Carnes's already brittle voice in latter-day 1990s tracks like "Don't Cry Now" and the title cut.

the rest:
Crazy in the Night 𝄢𝄢 (Capitol Special Products, 1994)
King Biscuit Flower Hour Presents: Kim Carnes 𝄢𝄢𝄢 (King Biscuit Entertainment, 1998)

influences:
◀◀ Janis Joplin, New Christy Minstrels, Jackie DeShannon, Kenny Rogers, Rod Stewart, Robert Plant, Tina Turner

▶▶ Laura Branigan, John Waite, Sheena Easton, Michael Bolton, Victoria Williams

Jeff Hatch

Mary Chapin Carpenter

Born February 21, 1958, in Princeton, NJ.

Though signed to Columbia's Nashville division, Mary Chapin Carpenter is no more country than Nick Lowe—another power-pop specialist whose lyrics seem perfectly suited for short, fast rock 'n' roll songs. Though her voice has a hint of a southern twang and her lyrics occasionally focus on honky-tonks and highways, Carpenter studies the Beatles and Joni Mitchell much more than Merle Haggard or Johnny Cash. She has managed to build a substantial crossover audience of mainstream country fans and neo-folkies clinging to albums by Carpenter's friends, Shawn Colvin and Rosanne Cash. Her best songs, including "I Feel Lucky" and a polished version of Lucinda Williams's wonderful "Passionate Kisses," have hit the top of the country charts, and she consistently racks up Grammys and Country Music Awards.

what to buy: *Come On Come On* 🎸🎸🎸🎸 (Columbia, 1992, prod. John Jennings, Mary Chapin Carpenter) produced seven country hits (which also received substantial pop airplay), including "Passionate Kisses" and "I Feel Lucky," which drops the names of Lyle Lovett and Dwight Yoakam.

what to buy next: *Shootin' Straight in the Dark* 🎸🎸🎸 (Columbia, 1990, prod. John Jennings, Mary Chapin Carpenter) began Carpenter's commercial breakthrough with the romping "Down at the Twist and Shout." *Stones in the Road* 🎸🎸🎸🎸 (Columbia, 1994, prod. John Jennings, Mary Chapin Carpenter) has songs that are generally quieter and more introspective, but still engaging.

the rest:
Hometown Girl 🎸🎸🎸 (Columbia, 1988)
State of the Heart 🎸🎸🎸 (Columbia, 1989)
Place in the World 🎸🎸🎸 (Sony, 1996)

worth searching for: *On Location: Conversation and Music by Mary Chapin Carpenter* is a 1992 one-hour radio special on CD that features Carpenter performing and talking about the songs from her first four albums.

influences:
◀◀ Carlene Carter, the Beatles, Joni Mitchell, Bob Dylan, Rosanne Cash

▶▶ Shawn Colvin, Trisha Yearwood, Patty Loveless, Suzy Bogguss, Dar Williams

Tracey Birkenhauer and Steve Knopper

The Carpenters

Formed 1969, in Downey, CA.

Richard Carpenter (born October 15, 1946, in New Haven, CT), vocals, keyboards; Karen Carpenter (born March 2, 1950, New Haven, CT; died February 4, 1983, in Los Angeles, CA), vocals, drums.

The best Carpenters songs weren't the sappy, perky mega-hits the duo specialized in during the mid-'70s—such as "Top of the World," "Can't Smile without You," "Sing," or "Touch Me When We're Dancing." Rather, they were the sad numbers on which Karen's pure voice conveyed restrained yet heart-wrenching agony or wistful nostalgia. Only Richard's slick arrangements could get such downbeat lyrics on the radio. In fact, the juxtaposition of Karen's melancholy sound with Richard's lush settings lends many tracks an oddly menacing irony in view of Karen's 1983 death from cardiac arrest connected to anorexia. The Carpenters' rise from child prodigies to superstardom and the duo's subsequent fall has been well-chronicled, in the 1988 TV movie *The Karen Carpenter Story* and in a biography by Ray Coleman. Although much was made of Karen being a drummer (a genuine oddity back then), most of the best drum parts on the first half-decade's albums are by studio great Hal Blaine; in fact, they redefined the art and sound of studio drumming. Karen nonetheless assumed iconic significance for feminists. In 1996 A&M finally released her 1979 solo album, shelved for years because the lyrics didn't fit the duo's goody-two-shoes image, and because its then-current production sound (courtesy of Phil Ramone) was a big departure from the Carpenters' mellower sound.

what to buy: *Carpenters* 🎸🎸🎸🎸 (A&M, 1971, prod. Jack Daugherty) is by far the group's pinnacle, with "Rainy Days and Mondays," "Let Me Be the One," "For All We Know," "Superstar," "One Love," and "Sometimes." The production may sound dated, but it still has a fresh innocence only slightly tainted by Richard's whiny anti-groupie screed "Druscilla Penny." Full of pop classics, *Yesterday Once More* 🎸🎸🎸🎸 (A&M, 1985, prod. various) is a two-CD compilation that, though it includes some of the more cloying hits, largely avoids the out-and-out dross.

what to buy next: *Close to You* 🎸🎸🎸🎸 (A&M, 1970, prod. Jack Daugherty), with "We've Only Just Begun" and "I'll Never Fall in Love Again," and *A Song for You* 🎸🎸🎸 (A&M, 1972, prod. Jack Daugherty), with "Hurting Each Other" and the great "Goodbye to Love" (with its brilliant outro of fuzz guitar solo over massed oohs-n-aahs), have the same dewy freshness as *Carpenters*, though with less consistent material. A large proportion of the Carpenters' pop prowess was based on Richard's ear for great songs by other writers, as documented on *Interpretations* 🎸🎸🎸🎸 (A&M, 1995, prod. various). It's interesting to hear Karen's pure voice on music identified more with other performers: "This Masquerade," "When I Fall in Love," "Tryin' to Get the Feeling Again."

what to avoid: *Now and Then: The Singles, 1969–1973* 🎸 (A&M, 1973, prod. various) is from the group's most listenable period, but it overlaps the songs in a no-gap flow and has been superseded by *Yesterday Once More*. *Once from the Top: The Ultimate Retrospective* 🎸🎸 (A&M, 1991, prod. various) is a four-CD set with some merit for the die-hard fans (most people will find it overkill), but Richard overdubbed parts in a decades-late, obsessive attempt to improve some songs. Richard's *Pianist-Arranger-Composer-Conductor* 𝄞 (A&M, 1998, prod. Richard Carpenter) is only for fans of lounge music (the airport variety), full of easy-listening versions of Carpenters classics (and some not-so-classics) that usually feature piano or harmonica playing the melody over string arrangements.

the rest:
Ticket to Ride 𝄞𝄞𝄞 (A&M, 1969)
Horizon 𝄞𝄞𝄞 (A&M, 1975)
A Kind of Hush 𝄞𝄞 (A&M, 1976)
Passage 𝄞𝄞 (A&M, 1977)
Made in America 𝄞𝄞 (A&M, 1981)
Voice of the Heart 𝄞𝄞𝄞 (A&M, 1983)
Lovelines 𝄞𝄞 (A&M, 1989)

worth searching for: *If I Were a Carpenter* (A&M, 1994, executive prod. Matt Wallace, David Konjoyan) is an all-star tribute album that helps '90s ears appreciate the Carpenters' material. The stellar lineup—including Sonic Youth ("Superstar"), the Cranberries ("Close to You"), and Matthew Sweet (a sweet, pedal steel–drenched "Let Me Be the One")—makes this rank way above the average tribute album.

solo outings:
Karen Carpenter:
Karen Carpenter 𝄞𝄞𝄞 (A&M, 1996)

influences:
◄◄ The Beatles, Burt Bacharach, Mantovani, the Association
►► Air Supply, Sheryl Crow

Steve Holtje

Carpetbaggers

Formed 1990, in Minneapolis, MN.

Rich Copley, bass, vocals; Mike Crabtree, guitar, lap steel guitar, vocals; John Magnuson, guitar, vocals; Dewey Roy Hucklenut, fiddle.

Criticized by some observers for jumping on the alterna-country bandwagon, Minneapolis's Carpetbaggers have managed to stake out a sound that is more traditional than alternative. How is all that possible in the city that gave the world flannel-shirt-wearing Midwesterners the Replacements, Soul Asylum, and Hüsker Dü, you ask? The band members did start their musical meanderings in various punk bands before listening to that very first Ernest Tubbs record, if that helps any. Despite the backlash from critics, the Carpetbaggers offer some countrified and spirited foot-stomping tunes, dimly-lit break-up ballads, and an occasional humorous parody of a country music standard—"Suburban Boy" to the tune of John Denver's "Thank

God I'm a Country Boy." The band was given a boost after opening several gigs for Son Volt during 1995—it even played at Son Volt frontman Jay Farrar's wedding reception.

what to buy: The 16 tracks contained on *Nowhere to Go but Down* 𝄞𝄞𝄞 (Clean/Twin-Tone, 1993, prod. Brian Paulsen) visit a variety of '50s musical forms, ranging from rockabilly ("Sober Again") to honky-tonk, as well as an occassional ode to drinking ("Drink for Free"). The lyrics are a little too clever in their wordplay but often very humorous and full of "white trash" references.

what to buy next: After being dropped by Twin-Tone, the band signed with HighTone Records and released the more purist country leaning *Sin Now . . . Pray Later* 𝄞𝄞𝄞 (HighTone, 1996, prod. Ed Ackerson). Fans of BR5-49 may take a liking to this release, which harkens back to the classic era of Nashville. Of particular charm is the band's amusing cover of Marvin Rainwater's "Last Time."

the rest:
Country Miles Apart 𝄞𝄞𝄞 (Clean/Twin-Tone, 1992)

influences:
◄◄ Johnny Cash, Little Feat, Gram Parsons, Louvin Brothers

William Harmer

Paul Carrack
/Ace

Born April 22, 1951, in Sheffield, Yorkshire, England.

Gifted with a spine-tingling, blue-eyed soul voice and an unassuming, workmanlike approach to music, Paul Carrack has assembled an impressive musical resume—despite his knack for making the least of any commercial success. He first came to national attention via the pub rock group Ace, bringing his emotive, soulful vocals to bear on its monster 1974 hit "How Long." When the band failed to match that success in subsequent work, Carrack briefly joined Frankie Miller's band before signing up for two albums with Roxy Music. Though he next released his first solo album, it wasn't long before Carrack was back in a band—this time with Squeeze, contributing to its landmark album *East Side Story* and singing lead vocals on its biggest hit, the R&B-influenced ballad "Tempted." Carrack's subsequent work included stints with Eric Clapton and a permanent spot with Genesis guitarist Mike Rutherford's Mike & the Mechanics, as well as an intermittently successful solo career and guest spots on albums by the Pretenders, Roger Waters, Elton John, and the Smiths.

what to buy: His impressive *One Good Reason* 𝄞𝄞𝄞𝄞 (Chrysalis, 1987, prod. Christopher Neal) is the Carrack album every fan hoped for—good songs, impressive performances, and lots of gritty, blue-eyed soul shouting from the man himself. The cry-in-your-beer single "Don't Shed a Tear" is worth the price of admission alone.

what to buy next: The only thing better than a good Carrack album is a collection of all the cool work he's done with other people. *Collection: Twenty-One Good Reasons* &&&& (Chrysalis, 1994, prod. various) features his solo best plus the hits he sang with with Ace, Squeeze, Mike & the Mechanics, and a couple songs from his brief stint in Carlene Carter's band.

what to avoid: Nothing stinks worse than a halfhearted greatest hits package, and *The Carrack Collection* **woof!** (Chrysalis, 1988, prod. various) reeks. This skimpy assemblage feels like a dress rehearsal for the more complete 1994 collection.

the rest:
Nightbird && (Vertigo, 1980)
Suburban Voodoo &&& (Epic, 1982)
When You Walk in the Room && (Chrysalis, 1987)
Ace Mechanic &&& (Demon, 1987)
(With Ace) *Best of Ace: How Long* &&&& (See For Miles, 1988/1994)
Groove Approved &&& (Chrysalis, 1989)
Carrackter Reference &&& (Demon, 1995)
Blue Views &&& (IRS/EMI, 1996)
Beautiful World && (Ark, 1997)

worth searching for: Get the original Ace albums—the best being *Five-a-Side* (Anchor, 1974)—for a taste not only of Carrack's early days but also of the roots from which he and a good chunk of what became known as new wave sprang from.

influences:
◀◀ Jackie Wilson, Otis Redding, Ray Charles
▶▶ Michael Bolton, Little River Band

see also: *Squeeze, Genesis*

Eric Deggans

Joe "King" Carrasco

Born Joseph Teutsch, 1954, in Dumas, Texas.

With various incarnations of his band the Crowns (or Las Coronas), Carrasco has steadfastly sustained a career playing a rockified version of Tex-Mex, the rhythmic music he heard growing up. Like Doug Sahm a generation before him, Carrasco soaked up the Spanish influence of his native Texas, applied it to rock 'n' roll, and revived it with the accordion metamorphosing into cheeseball Farfisa organ bleats during punk's heyday, later replacing the organ once again with the more traditional (and cooler) accordion. Early in his career, the irrepressible Carrasco was famous for crazy antics like leaping from the stage (this was a long time before stage-diving was adopted by

thrashers) or running through a club or concert hall with an incredibly long guitar chord so he could play from a balcony, a bathroom, or outside the lobby. In recent years, Carrasco has also added more reggae influence to his music, a reflection of the time he spends hanging out in the Caribbean and in Central America. But no matter how he filters his energy, Carrasco's trademark enthusiasm and yelping vocals remain undiluted. The Crowns' MCA albums from the '80s are out of print but worth searching for on vinyl.

what to buy: *Tales from the Crypt* &&&&& (ROIR Cassette, 1984, prod. Joe Gracey) was the long-awaited release of the demo tapes that got Carrasco his original notoriety and, ultimately, his record deal. It was recorded in bits and pieces during the late '70s (whenever Carrasco could afford time in a basement studio in Austin) and passed around to New York rock critics in 1979, when the Crowns made their first attack on the Manhattan clubs. It's a distillation of Carrasco's lifelong immersion in both Tex-Mex and roots rock 'n' roll, featuring covers such as "Sweet Little Rock 'n' Roller" alongside wild-eyed originals like "Caca de Vaca." Writer John Morthland hit it on the head in the liner notes when he called this cassette release "garage-band heaven."

what to buy next: *Joe "King" Carrasco and the Crowns* &&&& (Hannibal, 1981, prod. Billy Altman), the first official U.S. release by the band, is cleaner than the cassette demos. And almost as fun.

what to avoid: *Party Weekend* && (MCA, 1983) is a passable but flat album—particularly compared to Carrasco's other efforts.

the rest:
Party Safari && (Hannibal, 1981)
Joe "King" Carrasco and El Molino &&& (ROIR, 1984)
Border Town &&& (New Rose/Big Beat, 1985)
Bandito Rock &&& (Rounder, 1987)
Royal, Loyal & Live && (Royal Texicali Records, 1990)
Dia de las Muertos && (Royal Texicali Records, 1994)
Anthology &&& (One Way, 1995)

worth searching for: The British import version of *Joe "King" Carrasco and the Crowns* (Stiff, 1980, prod. Billy Altman) is pressed on lavender vinyl so repugnant it's desirable.

influences:
◀◀ Sir Douglas Quintet, ? & the Mysterians, Sam the Sham & the Pharaohs, Flaco Jimenez
▶▶ Doug Sahm, Flaco Jimenez, Texas Tornados

Gil Asakawa

Jim Carroll

Born 1950, in New York, NY.

After squandering a promising future in basketball, surviving addiction and incarceration, and enjoying literary fame from age 16, poet and novelist Jim Carroll still had time for a career in rock 'n' roll from 1979 to 1985. A fine writer who now thinks his poetic rhythm had to recover from rock song–structure, his three albums' significance is more stylistic and historical than literary. A makeshift but powerful kind of punk plainsong made the Jim Carroll Band one of the first (and still only) acts to widen the form's audience and not sell it out. Carroll influenced the do-it-yourself grunge generation, who paid him homage on the soundtrack to the 1995 film version of his memoir, *The Basketball Diaries,* though few among them have matched his ambition. Other than a remake (performed with Pearl Jam) of his song "Catholic Boy" on that soundtrack, Carroll has concentrated since 1985 on his truest love, the word, publishing books and releasing an album of readings, *Praying Mantis,* in 1991. He remains an inspiration to the sadder and wiser alike, a rare rebel icon less fascinating for his tragedy than for his survival.

what to buy: Carroll's best albums are the first and last. *Catholic Boy* 🎵🎵🎵🎵 (Atco, 1980, prod. Earl McGrath, Bob Clearmountain) features his one hit, "People Who Died," a cathartic bon voyage to lost young friends that has only gained resonance in the age of AIDS and juvenile gunplay. After a slight decline, *I Write Your Name* 🎵🎵🎵🎵 (Atlantic, 1984, prod. Earl McGrath) regained the spontaneity and coiled energy of the first album and headed off in other directions, most of them fruitful. "Voices" is excessively Devo-derivative, and his rendition of "Sweet Jane" joins a whole sub-genre of unnecessary Velvet Underground covers. But the title track is an improbable masterwork of gutsy new wave, and the ghostly choral vocal arrangement blowing through "Hold Back the Dream" marks a complete breakaway from Carroll's punky precedent. As good an album song-for-song as *Catholic Boy* is for overall atmosphere.

what to buy next: While only one of the songs demoed for *Catholic Boy* made it to that album, *Dry Dreams* 🎵🎵🎵 (Atco, 1982, prod. Earl McGrath) found Carroll doing his exploring in public, with mixed results. Side one shows some growth, but the second half suffers for his standardized, yelpy vocals, drawn-out Jersey Shore–style arrangements, and often diluted production.

what to avoid: *A World without Gravity: The Best of the Jim Carroll Band* 🎵🎵🎵 (Rhino, 1993, prod. Larry Lieberman, David McLees) misses many of the highs and keeps many of the lows, including two non-essential unreleased studio tracks. You're better off hunting down the original albums.

the rest:
Praying Mantis 🎵🎵🎵 (Giant, 1991)
The Basketball Diaries (Soundtrack) 🎵🎵 (Island, 1995)

influences:
◀◀ The Sex Pistols, Leonard Cohen, Jim Morrison, Graham Parker, Bruce Springsteen, Lou Reed

▶▶ Pearl Jam, Soundgarden, Alice in Chains

Adam McGovern

Johnny Carroll

Born John Lewis Carrell, October 23, 1937, in Cleburne, TX. Died February 18, 1995, in Dallas, TX.

Johnny Carroll threw himself into his music with a playful, sexy intensity matched by few of his '50s contemporaries. His intense, yelping vocal style epitomized the short-lived rockabilly movement, and his great Decca recordings are highly prized by the genre's aficionados. "Wild, Wild Women," "Crazy Crazy Lovin'," and "Hot Rock" all one-upped Elvis Presley on the King's own turf (though none of them sold well outside of Texas), and Carroll's onstage antics caused riots among teenage girls. Management disputes and rip-offs stalled Carroll's career just as it was taking off, and Decca dropped him after only a few potent singles. While playing the *Louisiana Hayride* with Scotty Moore and Bill Black (who had temporarily quit Elvis Presley's band), Moore urged Carroll to develop his abilities as a lead guitarist and set up a meeting with Sun Records owner Sam Phillips. Carroll's self-produced recordings for Sun ("Rock Baby Rock It," "That's the Way I Love") were peak performances augmented by Jordanaire-type choruses, and they might've been hits on a less crowded or better run label. The move to Warner Bros. seemed to be his artistic undoing, for while Carroll's humor remained intact ("Ragmop," "Little Otis") and his idolizing of Gene Vincent was ably expressed ("The Swing," "Sugar"), slicker pop choices ("Bandstand Doll," "Run Come See," "The Sally Ann") and changing times reduced Carroll's work from that of an inspired rockabilly chanter to mere Elvis wannabe. During the '60s, Carroll concentrated on booking other bands, running a recording studio, and managing a bar; the latter nearly cost him his life when he was shot by a hot-tempered patron. Though he recovered, Carroll's health was permanently affected, and erroneous rumors of his death spread. As a tribute, fellow Texan Mac Curtis cut "Johnny Carroll Rock" for Ronny Weiser's Rollin' Rock label, which led to Carroll's reemergence in 1977. Cutting the LP *Texabilly* in one 28-hour session, Carroll revealed a gruffer, more country-leaning sound along with the sharp lead guitar playing taught to him by Scotty Moore. Encouraged by his girlfriend-protégé Judy Lindsey (the Dodge poster girl), Carroll toured Europe extensively and recorded for small Texas-based labels until his death during a liver transplant.

what to buy: Carroll's entire mid-'70s output for the Rollin' Rock label is collected on *Texabilly* ♫♫♫ (HMG/HighTone, 1997, prod. Rockin' Ronny Weiser). Though his voice is gravelly and deeper, and much of the music is country, Carroll, assisted by fellow legend Ray Campi, is in fine rockin' form for tunes such as "Teenage Sweetie," "Her Throbbing Lips," and "Bowlegged Woman." Also included is Carroll's brilliant imitation of Gene Vincent on "Gene Vincent Rock" (a.k.a. "Black Leather Rebel"), and Mac Curtis's tribute "Johnny Carroll Rock." These were his last shining moments as a recording artist.

what to avoid: Late in his career Carroll cut *Screamin' Demon Heatwave* ♫♫ (Seville, 1983, prod. Dave Travis) with the Dave Travis Band. Carroll seems worn out (though willing), and the shrill, off-key vocals of his girlfriend Judy Lindsey destroy everything she sings. For collectors only.

worth searching for: Carroll's powerful Decca sides, early demos, and stints at Sun and Warner Bros. are chronicled on the import *Rock Baby Rock It (1955–1960)* (Bear Family, 1996, compilation prod. Bob Jones, Richard Weize), a 33-song set that encompasses everything he did during the '50s—some of the best early rock 'n' roll music you probably never heard. Also, the cheapest looking movie ever made—the 1957 drive-in feature *Rock Baby Rock It* (Rhino Home Video, 1989)—contains the only known footage of Johnny Carroll in his greasy, cater-wauling rockabilly prime.

influences:

◀◀ Gene Vincent, Elvis Presley, Mac Curtis

▶▶ Ronnie Dawson, Jimmie Lee Maslon, Flat Duo Jets

Ken Burke

The Cars

Formed 1976, in Boston, MA. Disbanded 1988.

Ric Ocasek, vocals, guitar; Ben Orr, bass, vocals; Elliot Easton, guitar; Greg Hawkes, keyboards; David Robinson, drums.

Combining smart, artful, and accessible pop songs with a clickety new wave sound, the Cars quickly became one of America's top bands during the late '70s and early '80s. With its debut album, the band single-handedly crafted some of the genre's best sounding and best-selling songs. Peppered with lite keyboards, drum machines, and airy background vocals, the Cars' sound had an almost aloof, detached feel that made the songs instantly recognizable. After a short venture into an even more synthesized sound with 1980's *Panorama*, the Cars quickly bounced back to their pop sensibilities and became more popular than ever with its 1984 release *Heartbeat City*. By 1988,

however, the band was ready to call it quits; machines had all but replaced Robinson and Easton, and personal conflicts made the recording of its final album, *Door to Door*, a difficult process. Of the individual members, Ocasek has had the greatest success, producing albums for Weezer, Bad Brains, and other modern rock groups.

what to buy: *The Cars* ♫♫♫♫ (Elektra, 1978, prod. Roy Thomas Baker) remains the group's finest album. Kicking off with "Let the Good Times Roll," "My Best Friend's Girl," and "Just What I Needed," the album sounds more like a greatest hits collection than a debut. Before long, its Teflon production became state-of-the-art for sonic wannabes. *The Cars Anthology: Just What I Needed* ♫♫♫♫♫ (Elektra Traditions/Rhino, 1995, prod. various) is a splendid collection of all the right tracks and even non-album gems such as "Breakaway."

what to buy next: *Heartbeat City* ♫♫♫♫♫ (Elektra 1984, prod. Robert John "Mutt" Lange, the Cars) rivals *The Cars* for freshness and churned out four hits, each with its own trendsetting video.

what to avoid: *Panorama* ♫♫ (Elektra, 1980, prod. Roy Thomas Baker) isn't different enough to sound experimental, though that seems to be the intent. Mostly it sounds like a collection of half-finished ideas.

the rest:

Candy O ♫♫♫ (Elektra, 1979)
Shake It Up ♫♫♫♫ (Elektra, 1981)
Greatest Hits ♫♫♫♫♫ (Elektra, 1985)
Door to Door ♫♫♫ (Elektra, 1987)

solo outings:

Ric Ocasek:
Beatitude ♫♫♫ (Geffen, 1983)
This Side of Paradise ♫ (Geffen, 1986)
Fireball Zone ♫♫♫ (Geffen, 1991)
Quick Change World ♫♫♫ (Reprise, 1993)
Troublizing ♫♫♫ (Columbia, 1997)

Ben Orr:
The Lace ♫♫♫ (Elektra, 1986)

Greg Hawkes:
Niagra Falls ♫ (Passport, 1983)

Elliot Easton:
Change No Change ♫♫ (Elektra, 1985)

influences:

◀◀ Blondie, Talking Heads, Modern Lovers, Kraftwerk, the Velvet Underground

▶▶ Weezer, Matthew Sweet, Lloyd Cole, Bad Religion, Afghan Whigs

Mike Joiner

Lori Carson

Born on Long Island, NY.

While a solo artist in her own right, Carson didn't come to prominence until she became the lead vocalist for Anto Fier's sonic carnival the Golden Palominos. Carson debuted her lilting alto on the Golden Palominos' 1993 album *This Is How It Feels* and continued her tenure with the band with 1994's *Pure*. But Carson soon returned to her solo roots following the 1995 release of *The Pure Remix* EP.

what to buy: *Everything I Touch Runs Wild* ♫♫♫♫ (Restless, 1996, prod. Lori Carson, Anton Fier) is a brilliant mix of acoustic folk trappings and groove-oriented beatology. The two-CD set, which features a bonus disc of remixes, starts off with the infectious "Something's Got Me," a lilting hip-hop/jazz/folk concoction that highlights Carson's hypnotic vocal serenity. The rest of the album treads along more traditional folk singer-songwriter terrain, with Carson playing piano and strumming her guitar, albeit with added misty ambience floating in the sonic backdrop. The album also includes Carson's bobbing rendition of Todd Rundgren's "I Saw the Light," while the remix disc contains three reworkings of "Something's Got Me" and an additional mix of "I Saw the Light."

what to buy next: The 10 songs on *Where It Goes* ♫♫♫ (Restless, 1995, prod. Anton Fier) find Carson affecting an understated singer-songwriter pose, somewhat reminiscent of Cindy Lee Berryhill and early Michelle Shocked. Carson's voice possesses a light, airy quality, but it also has a certain degree of strength and forcefulness. Accompanied largely by piano, Carson sings about dreams, love, faith, and life. Her music is instilled with a fleeting romantic quality—a delicate warm simplicity that was commonplace years ago but has become unique in this day and age. "Down Here" sets the tone of the album, as the calming musical sparseness allows Carson's powerful wisp of a voice to dominate the track as she sings about "real love" and "peace of mind."

worth searching for: Carson's solo debut, *Shelter* (Geffen, 1990), is now out of print.

influences:

◄◄ The Golden Palominos, Joni Mitchell, Suzanne Vega, Michelle Shocked, Cindy Lee Berryhill

see also: *The Golden Palominos*

Spence D.

Clarence Carter

Born January 14, 1936, in Montgomery, AL.

For a blind guy, Clarence Carter sure did a lot of cheatin' and homewreckin'. Bad for the monogamous, good for us, as his leacherous ways produced a bona fide classic, "Slip Away." A back-door proposition with Carter woefully copping to the tawdriness of it all as he slides his foot in the door, the song is a close second to "Dark End of the Street" as the greatest stolen-love soul song ever. The rest of his body of work follows the seamy tracks that "Slip Away" laid down, with no less lascivious results, as his trademark "heh-heh-heh" growl can still make the dudes pull their girlfriends a little closer.

what to buy: *Snatching It Back: The Best of Clarence Carter* ♫♫♫♫ (Rhino, 1992, prod. Rick Hall) is a solid 21-track compilation that contains "Slip Away" and "Patches," as well as other important tracks, such as his absurdly profound reworking of "Dark End of the Street." Preaching over the song's subtle groove, Carter fuses the sexual and the spiritual into a dizzying stir of desire.

what to buy next: *Dr. C.C.* ♫♫♫ (Ichiban, 1987, prod. C. Carter) is highlighted by the gloriously lewd "Strokin'."

what to avoid: *The Dr.'s Greatest Prescriptions* ♫♫♫ (Ichiban, 1992, prod. Clarence Carter) isn't a bad compilation, but the Rhino package renders it obsolete.

the rest:

Touch of Blues ♫♫♫♫ (Ichiban, 1988)
Hooked on Love ♫♫♫ (Ichiban, 1988),
Messin' with My Mind ♫♫♫ (Ichiban, 1988)
Between a Rock and a Hard Place ♫♫♫ (Ichiban, 1990)
Have You Met Clarence Carter ♫♫♫ (Ichiban, 1992)
Legendary ♫♫♫ (MCA Special Products, 1995)
I Couldn't Refuse ♫♫ (Ronn, 1995)

worth searching for: *Sixty Minutes with Clarence Carter* (Fame, 1973, prod. Rick Hall) chronicles Carter's out-of-print final session with the Muscle Shoals gang, which brought some new and more modern elements into his mix.

influences:

◄◄ Lightnin' Hopkins, Otis Redding, Solomon Burke

►► Rick James, Aerosmith, Keith Sweat, R. Kelly

Allan Orski

Carter the Unstoppable Sex Machine

Formed 1987, in Streatham, South London, England. Disbanded 1997.

James "Jimbob" Morrison, lead vocals, guitar; Les "Fruitbat" Carter, lead guitar, backing vocals; Wesley "Wez" Boynton, drums (1994–96); Salvatore "Salv" Alessi, bass (1997); Simon Painter, key-

boards (1997); Steve Boynton, guitar (1997); Ben Lambert, keyboards (1997).

Like two horsemen of the apocalypse, Carter's Jimbob and Fruit-bat consistently managed to find every festering sore on the thin skin of society and rub salt in it—with catchy samples and power-punk guitar strumming to pound home their message of general hopelessness in the face of the world's absurdities. Their brand of clever sarcasm and aggressive playing was lifted straight from the pages of the punk rock instruction manual, but they also snuck in infectious underground dance beats, theatrical sensibilities, and a keen awareness of pop culture and world events. But the duo, which later expanded into a full band, was never able to earn widespread popularity in the U.S., and its once-large U.K. fan base began to decline midway through its career. Eventually, Carter USM decided it wasn't fun anymore and called it a day in 1997. Its official breakup was followed by the release of *I Blame the Government*, and the duo also planned to release a posthumous live album.

what to buy: *101 Damnations* 🎧🎧🎧 (Big Cat/Chrysalis, 1991, prod. Sex Machine, Simon Painter) is a wickedly brilliant opus of human depravity, a world in which two characters feed a homeless man, then come back and set him on fire; in which Sheriff Fatman the drug-pushing slumlord gets away with bleeding the downtrodden; in which a line from *It's a Wonderful Life* closes a song about suicide. The music is good, but the lyrics—which refer to other songs, films, and cultural icons so slyly you might miss some the first time around—are wonderfully venomous. *Post Historic Monsters* 🎧🎧🎧 (Chrysalis/I.R.S., 1993, prod. Sex Machine, Simon Painter) is yet another conceptual album filled with Carter's dismal world visions—and great lyrics throughout. "Stuff the Jubilee" is a clever rip on royalty, "Being Here" is a delightful Brechtian track, and "Sing Fat Lady Sing" takes a jibe at the Rolling Stones, who sued Carter USM early on for copyright infringement ("Should I call the mortician, you're a bag of bones/You should audition for the Rolling Stones"). A U.S.-only bonus track, "Commercial Fucking Suicide Part 1," insists, "Bono ain't the new messiah/Michael Jackson is a liar," proving these guys sure love sticking pins in any self-inflated hot air balloon they can find.

what to buy next: *30 Something* 🎧🎧🎧 (Chrysalis, 1991, prod. Sex Machine, Simon Painter) drips venom with nearly every word, in the finest punk tradition, but with more chops (and such uncredited samples as the "Wham bam thank-you ma'am" line from David Bowie's "Suffragette City"). *1992—The Love Album* 🎧🎧🎧 (Chrysalis, 1992, prod. Sex Machine, Simon Painter) is more nihilism from the kings of hate, with a dramatic rendering of "The Impossible Dream" by guest Ian Dury to finish the whole thing off. *Bloodsport for All* 🎧🎧 (Chrysalis, 1991,

prod. Sex Machine, Simon Painter) is an EP worth hearing particularly for the downright scary "2001: A Clockwork Orange," with its spoken samples of kids discussing their ambitions.

the rest:
World without Dave 🎧🎧 (Cooking Vinyl, 1997)
I Blame the Government 🎧🎧 (Cooking Vinyl, 1998)

influences:

◄◄ The Sex Pistols, the Beatles, the Who, Ian Dury, the Monkees, Grandmaster Flash, Bertolt Brecht

►► Space, Sneaker Pimps

Lynne Margolis

Peter Case /The Plimsouls

Case born April 5, 1954, in Buffalo, NY. The Plimsouls formed 1978, in Los Angeles, CA.

Peter Case, vocals, guitar; Eddie Muñoz, guitar, vocals; Dave Pahoa, bass; Lou Ramirez, drums (1978–84); Clem Burke, drums (1995–present).

Starting out as the bassist for San Francisco punk-pop band the Nerves during the mid-'70s and later fronting influential

Los Angeles underground group the Plimsouls, Peter Case gradually evolved into an acoustic troubadour, though he never really abandoned his rockin' roots (indeed, a reunited Plimsouls surfaced in 1995, though Case's solo career is the priority). The Plimsouls were one of the great early-'80s little trains that couldn't: Its two major-label albums floundered amidst the arena-rock climate of the era. During the mid-'80s, Case married Victoria Williams (they divorced at the end of the decade), became a born-again Christian and went out on his own musically, establishing himself as one of the most powerful solo acoustic acts on the club circuit. He released three albums for Geffen, never quite making a commercial impact; in the mid-'90s he signed with folk-oriented independent label Vanguard.

what to buy: *Blue Guitar* ♫♫♫♫ (Geffen, 1989, prod. J. Steven Soles, Larry Hirsch, Peter Case) is a folk-rock classic, an impassioned 10-song portrait of down-and-out losers and star-crossed lovers seeking redemption. *Peter Case* ♫♫♫♫ (Geffen, 1986, prod. T Bone Burnett, Mitchell Froom) is slightly less focused but loaded with first-rate songwriting. The Plimsouls' *Everywhere at Once* ♫♫♫♫ (Geffen, 1983, prod. Jeff Eyrich) includes the group's two best-known songs, "A Million Miles Away" and "Oldest Story in the World" (both of which were also featured in the movie *Valley Girl*).

what to buy next: *Torn Again* ♫♫♫♫ (Vanguard, 1995, prod. Larry Hirsch, J. Steven Soles) was a fine return to form for Case, featuring some of the best songs he'd written in years. *Sings Like Hell* ♫♫♫ (Vanguard, 1994, prod. Marvin Etzioni) was recorded live in a living-room studio and features mostly traditional tunes performed solo acoustic; it's hit-and-miss but worth seeking out for the inclusion of the longtime concert favorite "Lakes of Ponchartrain."

what to avoid: *Six-Pack of Love* ♫♫ (Geffen, 1992, prod. Mitchell Froom, Peter Case) seems in retrospect like an attempt to save the major-label deal with a more commercially viable effort, but the beefed-up arrangements didn't help a set of songs that was sub par by Case's standards.

the rest:
Peter Case:
Full Service No Waiting ♫♫♫ (Vanguard, 1998)

The Plimsouls:
Zero Hour ♫♫♫ (Beat EP, 1980)
The Plimsouls ♫♫♫ (Planet, 1981)
The Plimsouls . . . Plus ♫♫♫ (Rhino, 1992)

influences:
◀◀ Woody Guthrie, Blind Lemon Jefferson

▶▶ The Replacements, Alejandro Escovedo

Peter Blackstock

Johnny Cash
Born February 26, 1932, in Kingsland, AR.

A larger-than-life figure who looms over the history of both rock 'n' roll and country music, Johnny Cash scarcely needs an introduction to anyone whose ears have been open during the past 40 years. Yet for someone who is as recognizable as the faces on Mount Rushmore, Cash has always been a surprisingly mercurial artist; he was the most country-leaning of the Sun rockabilly crowd, yet his pill-popping, hell-raising lifestyle would likely make any of today's alternarockers blanch. Soon after he embraced country he deserted Nashville and moved to California, where, for better and worse, he remained his own man. He later moved back, but he was always considered an outsider in Music City. Amid the politically conservative world of country music, Cash has always been a firebrand, championing minority rights, especially for Native Americans, and condemning the war in Vietnam. And he traded songs with the rock world, notably with Bob Dylan, and in later years, with Bruce Springsteen and U2. Yet for all that, he is a passionately evangelical Christian whose best friends are the Rev. Billy Graham on the one hand, and fellow hell-raiser Waylon Jennings on the other. Not for nothing did Kris Kristofferson celebrate him as "a walking contradiction." A member of the Country Music Hall of Fame, the Rock and Roll Hall of Fame, and Nashville's Songwriter's Hall of Fame—the only person to be so honored—Cash casts as long a shadow as anyone over almost the whole of American popular music.

what to buy: Might as well begin at the beginning. Cash started out with the rest of the rockabillies at Sun Records, where he developed his trademark boom-chicka-boom sound on such classics as "Folsom Prison Blues," "Hey Porter," "Get Rhythm," and "I Walk the Line." *The Sun Years* ♫♫♫♫♫ (Sun/Rhino, 1990, prod. Jack Clement) collects all of those tunes plus many more. The fruits of Cash's labors at his second label are amply covered on *The Essential Johnny Cash, 1955–1983* ♫♫♫♫ (Columbia/Legacy, 1992, prod. various), a three-disc set that belongs in every serious collection of rock and country. For the budget-minded, there's *Columbia Records, 1958–1986* ♫♫♫♫ (Columbia, 1987, prod. various), a single-disc collection that will suffice but also whet your appetite for the larger set. Cash's roots are in folk music as much as in country, and *American Recordings* ♫♫♫♫ (American, 1994, prod. Rick Rubin) returns him to the form he had not explored extensively since the early part of his Columbia era. Featuring songs by younger rockers, the album and its attendant hoopla introduced Cash to a new generation of fans who likely had never heard him before. Its follow-up, *Unchained* ♫♫♫♫ (American Recordings, 1996, prod. Rick Rubin), is a fiery rock 'n' country set with Cash backed up by Tom Petty &

the Heartbreakers. The standout track is a remarkable, if unlikely, version of Soundgarden's "Rusty Cage."

what to buy next: *At Folsom Prison/At San Quentin* ♪♪♪♪♡ (Columbia, 1975, prod. Bob Johnston) compiles Cash's two legendary prison recordings from the late 1960s on one disc, and it constitutes some of the bravest recordings ever made. Before the very definition of a captive audience, Cash's "Folsom Prison Blues," "Wanted Man," "Cocaine Blues," and "San Quentin" tell it like it is to such a degree that you expect a riot to bust out any minute. *Classic Cash* ♪♪♪♪ (Mercury, 1988, prod. Johnny Cash) is one of those rare occasions when an album featuring re-recordings doesn't merely avert disaster; it actually offers a few new insights into such well-known favorites as "Get Rhythm" and "Sunday Morning Coming Down." Another exception to the rule, *Water from the Wells of Home* ♪♪♪♪ (Mercury, 1988, prod. Jack Clement) transcends the usual empty hype that attends most duet albums—this one includes vocalists Emmylou Harris, Tom T. Hall, Hank Williams Jr., the Everly Brothers, and Paul McCartney, among others.

what to avoid: Most of Cash's unworthy albums have fallen out of print. In assessing those that remain, take as a general rule of thumb the old saw that you get what you pay for. Steer clear of the many budget releases of Cash's work that exist, such as *Super Hits* ♪♪♡ (Columbia Special Products, 1994), *The Ultimate Johnny Cash* ♪♪♡ (Bransounds, 1994), and *The Many Sides of Johnny Cash* ♪♪♡ (Columbia Special Products, 1993). They may contain several hits apiece, but for the most part they have too few tracks to make them truly worthwhile.

the rest:

Now There Was a Song! Memories from the Past ♪♪♪ (Columbia, 1960)
Ring of Fire: The Best of Johnny Cash ♪♪♪ (Columbia, 1963)
Blood, Sweat and Tears ♪♪♪ (Columbia, 1963)
Bitter Tears: Ballads of the American Indian ♪♪♪ (Columbia, 1964)
Greatest Hits, Volume 1 ♪♪♪♪ (Columbia, 1967)
Greatest Hits, Volume 2 ♪♪♪♪ (Columbia, 1971)
Biggest Hits ♪♪♪ (Columbia, 1982)
(With Jerry Lee Lewis and Carl Perkins) *The Survivors* ♪♪♡ (Columbia, 1982/Razor & Tie, 1995)
(With the Highwaymen) *Highwayman* ♪♪ (Columbia, 1985)
(With Waylon Jennings) *Heroes* ♪♪♪ (Columbia, 1986/Razor & Tie, 1995)
Boom Chicka Boom ♪♪♡ (Mercury, 1990)
Patriot ♪♪ (Columbia, 1990)
(With the Highwaymen) *Highwayman 2* ♪ (Columbia, 1990)
The Mystery of Life ♪♪♡ (Mercury, 1991)
Best Of ♪♪♪♡ (Curb, 1991)
The Gospel Collection ♪♪♡ (Columbia/Legacy, 1992)
Ride This Train ♪♪♡ (Collector's Series, 1993)
Wanted Man ♪♪♪ (Mercury, 1994)
Hello I'm Johnny Cash ♪♪ (Sony Music Special Products, 1995)
Ring of Fire: Best of Johnny Cash ♪♪♡ (Columbia, 1995)
Gospel Glory ♪ (Sony Music Special Products, 1995)
Giant Hits ♪ (Sony Music Special Products, 1995)
Christmas Spirit ♪ (Sony Music Special Products, 1995)
Sings His 20 Best ♪ (TeeVee, 1995)
(With the Highwaymen) *The Road Goes on Forever* ♪♪♪ (Liberty, 1995)
The Hits ♪♪♪ (Mercury, 1997)
Country Christmas ♪ (Laserlight, 1997)
Personal Christmas Collection ♪♪♡ (Columbia, 1997)
(With Willie Nelson) *VH1 Storytellers* ♪♪♪ (American Recordings, 1998)

worth searching for: Hardcore Cash fans with truly deep pockets will want the comprehensive multi-disc sets released in Europe by the Bear Family label. They include *The Man in Black (1951–58)* (Bear Family, 1990); *The Man in Black (1959–62)* (Bear Family); *The Man in Black (1963–69)* (Bear Family, 1995); and *Come Along and Ride This Train* (Bear Family). They're great, but be prepared to mortgage the house. Also, the definitive Cash cameo appearance is on U2's *Zooropa* (Island, 1993, prod. Flood, Brian Eno, the Edge), where he sings "The Wanderer," a song Bono wrote for him. It finds the Man in Black in a futuristic setting of synthesizer bleeps and burbles, yet the song fits his legend to a tee, and his performance is perfect.

influences:

◄◄ Louvin Brothers, the Carter Family, Jimmie Rodgers

►► Bob Dylan, Waylon Jennings, Kris Kristofferson, Marty Stuart, Bruce Springsteen, Rosanne Cash, Carlene Carter, Nick Lowe, Uncle Tupelo, Waco Brothers

Daniel Durchholz

Rosanne Cash

Born May 24, 1956, in Memphis, TN.

Rosanne Cash survived her royal Nashville pedigree (her dad is Johnny Cash) to carve out an identity in the '80s as an innovative and remarkably successful country artist. On a string of records starting in 1979, Cash and producer/husband Rodney Crowell progressively expanded the boundaries of what a female performer could accomplish in Music City and eventually transcended it altogether. Her emphatic fusion of hard-hitting rock and classic country, maverick for that time, still scored big on the hidebound country radio charts. But Cash's critically acclaimed balancing act crashed in 1990. With her marriage to Crowell dissolving and her affinity for the country establishment plummeting, Cash released the somber, commercially disastrous *Interiors* and packed it in for life in a Greenwich Village brownstone. She has concentrated since on raising her three daughters, writing fiction (her first collection, *Bodies of Water*, appeared in 1996), and recording spare, ironic songs with a lyric confessionalism that's about as far from conventional Nashville tunesmithery as you can get. It's also awfully good.

what to buy: *King's Record Shop* ♪♪♪♪ (Columbia, 1988, prod. Rodney Crowell) is unquestionably the summation of Cash's Nashville work. It arcs smoothly from wistful pop ("If You Change Your Mind") to playful nostalgia ("Tennessee Flat Top Box") to edgy social balladry ("Rosie Strike Back," a call to arms for battered wives). Cash authoritatively demonstrates that she could take everything Nashville threw at her and throw it right back. Her first major effort, 1979's *Right or Wrong* ♪♪♪♪ (Columbia, 1979, prod. Rodney Crowell) still sounds surprisingly fresh, with the title tune's ironic exploration of adultery and the first of Cash's sassy take-that-guys anthems, "Man Smart, Woman Smarter." Cash's current incarnation is best represented by *Ten Song Demo* ♪♪♪♪ (Capitol, 1996, prod. John Leventhal, Rosanne Cash), a stripped-down collection redolent of her frank, biting wit. After listening to "Take This Body," just try looking at a cosmetic-surgery ad without wincing.

what to buy next: *Seven Year Ache* ♪♪♪♪ (Columbia, 1981, prod. Rodney Crowell) features some of the trenchant songwriting (the title track and "Blue Moon with Heartache") that would blossom more fully for Cash once she began leaving the country-heartbreak constraints behind. She also has genderbending fun with "My Baby Thinks He's a Train" and "What Kinda Girl?"

what to avoid: As the analysts say, Cash had some issues to work through, and by God, she did on *Interiors* ♪ (Columbia, 1990, prod. Rosanne Cash)—with a frankness that teeters into the maudlin. Significant in that it marks Cash's definitive break with Nashville, but not a pretty sight. Or sound.

the rest:
Somewhere in the Stars ♪♪♪ (Columbia, 1982)
Rhythm and Romance ♪♪♪ (Columbia, 1985)
The Wheel ♪♪♪♪ (Columbia, 1993)

worth searching for: *Live at the Bottom Line* (RSM) is a cleansounding bootleg of a hot 1988 performance in New York. Also, on 1997's *Time and Love: The Music of Laura Nyro* (Astor Place, 1997, prod. various) Cash delivers a smoldering take on "Save the Country."

influences:
◀◀ Roy Orbison, the Everly Brothers, Emmylou Harris, Joni Mitchell. Oh yeah, and the Man in Black—what was his name again?

▶▶ Mary Chapin Carpenter, Shawn Colvin

Elizabeth Lynch

David Cassidy
/The Partridge Family
Born April 12, 1950, in New York, NY.

If ever there was a textbook case of the joys and heartbreak, fears and frustrations, and all around ups and downs of life as a teen idol, it would be the story of David Cassidy. Born into a showbiz family and raised in Hollywood, Cassidy as a youngster was already a veteran of the stage and screen, but it was when he was cast, alongside stepmother Shirley Jones, as lead singer of the sitcom rockers the Partridge Family that his career was truly launched. The television band's first record, "I Think I Love You," sold more than a million copies in 1970, and when Cassidy embarked on a simultaneous solo career with a cover of the Association's classic "Cherish," he became the idol of countless schoolgirls the world over. Almost immediately, however, Cassidy began playing a foolhardy game of Risk with his newfound fame (e.g.: posing nude for *Rolling Stone*), and when a 14-year-old fan was crushed to death at a 1974 show in London, Cassidy resolutely turned his back on weenybopdom and released the shockingly bitter *The Higher They Climb, the Harder They Fall* the following year. Despite continued success outside of the U.S., a decade of career missteps and tabloid headlines at home followed until, in the late '80s, Cassidy seemed finally ready to not only confront his past, but make an uneasy peace with it. Today he gladly sings his old Partridge hits, occasionally can even be found chumming around with his old television nemesis Danny Bonaduce (himself no stranger to the perils of child stardom), and remains active pursuing his pre-Partridge love of acting on the legitimate stage, having apparently taken his own advice at last to just "Come on, Get Happy!"

what to buy: The best of Cassidy's solo career is available on *When I'm a Rock 'n' Roll Star: The David Cassidy Collection* ♪♪♪♪ (Razor & Tie, 1996, compilation prod. Mike Ragogna). It's full of surprisingly solid singing and playing by an all-star cast including Mick Ronson, Bruce Johnston, and Richie Furay. Meanwhile, "Keith Partridge" is best represented, along with all of his make-believe siblings, on *The Partridge Family's Greatest Hits* ♪♪♪ (Arista, 1989, prod. Wes Farrell), a terrifyingly complete and authentic collection—right down to the vintage Partridge lunch box on the cover.

the rest:
The Partridge Family:
The Partridge Family Album ♪♪♪ (Bell, 1970/Razor & Tie, 1993)
Up to Date ♪♪ (Bell, 1971/Razor & Tie, 1993)
The Partridge Family Sound Magazine ♪♪ (Bell, 1971/Razor & Tie, 1993)
A Partridge Family Christmas Card ♪♪♪ (Bell, 1971/Razor & Tie, 1995)

The Partridge Family Shopping Bag ♪♪ (Bell, 1972/Razor & Tie, 1993)

David Cassidy:
Didn't You Used to Be? ♪♪♪ (Scotti Brothers, 1992)
Classic Songs ♪♪ (Curb, 1998)
Old Trick New Dog ♪♪♪ (Slamajama, 1998)

influences:

◀◀ Ricky Nelson, the Cowsills, the Monkees, Bobby Sherman

▶▶ The Brady Kids, the Bay City Rollers, Shaun Cassidy, Hanson

Gary Pig Gold

Shaun Cassidy

Born September 27, 1959, in Los Angeles, CA.

Oh, quit your damn snickering. His teenybopper status notwithstanding, Keith Partridge's younger half-brother was actually a pretty good singer, and he had good taste in material as well. Pop fans cherish Shaun Cassidy for his capable covers of two Eric Carmen songs, "That's Rock 'n' Roll" and "Hey Deanie," each of which Cassidy took to the Top 40. Such assured pop recordings illustrated how Cassidy was capable of being a breed apart from most contemporary teen idols; as Cassidy himself remarked to *Newsweek* at the time, "I'm not teeny-bop, I'm power pop . . . melodic." Cassidy's pop career was relatively brief, and he subsequently concentrated exclusively on his acting career.

what's available: *Greatest Hits* ♪♪♪ (Curb, 1992, prod. Michael Lloyd, Shaun Cassidy, Todd Rundgren) is a perfunctory but satisfying retrospective, including all the hits ("Da Doo Ron Ron," "That's Rock 'n' Roll," "Hey Deanie," "Do You Believe in Magic") and the key album tracks (Cassidy's own autobiographical "Teen Dream," and ace covers of Brian Wilson's "It's Like Heaven" and the Who's "So Sad about Us"). Unfortunately, it also includes Cassidy's horrid take on Ian Hunter's "Once Bitten Twice Shy."

worth searching for: *Wasp* (Warner Bros., 1980, prod. Todd Rundgren), perceived as Cassidy's bid for post-teen respectability, is interesting primarily for the incongruous mix of Cassidy and producer Rundgren.

influences:

◀◀ Eric Carmen, the Beach Boys, Phil Spector, the Lovin' Spoonful, the Partridge Family, the Bay City Rollers

▶▶ Leif Garrett, Hanson, Candy, the Flashcubes, Ken Sharp, the Nicoteens

Carl Cafarelli

Cast
/The La's

The La's formed 1985, in Liverpool, England. Disbanded 1992. Cast formed 1992, in Liverpool, England.

The La's: Lee Mavers, vocals, guitar; Paul Hemmings, guitar (1985–89); Cammie, guitar (1989–92); John Power, bass, vocals; John Timson, drums (1985–89); Neil Mavers, drums (1989–92). **Cast:** John Power, vocals, guitar; Liam Tyson, guitar; Peter Wilkinson, bass; Keith O'Neill, drums.

Rarely has a band so completely despised its own great album. The Liverpool four the La's—who nicely integrated lovely and innocent hints of classic Merseybeat, rockabilly, R&B, soul, and pop so pure it was like fresh snow—spent four years recording the same LP over and over. Half a dozen big-name producers took a crack at capturing the same songs, only to find themselves in a dogfight (on the side of the label, London Records) against the band members, who universally loathed each attempt. Finally, the exasperated label put together their own version of the debut LP, *The La's*, which the band so wholly disapproved of that the members refused to have their individual names listed on the credits. The La's should have been big stars. Instead, the fighting with the label dragged on until the band disintegrated around 1992, and wearied bassist John Powers left to lead his own band, Cast, making the switch to guitar in the process.

what to buy: *The La's* ♪♪♪♪ (Go! Discs/London, 1991, prod. Steve Lillywhite) was wholly seductive, with irresistible material that was gorgeous and cute without being sappy or maudlin, and a golden-voiced singer in wide-eyed, good looking Lee Mavers. The pop treasure single "There She Goes" was later the centerpiece of the movie *So I Married an Axe Murderer*, which featured both the La's version and a cover by Boo Radleys.

what to buy next: Cast's debut album, *Allchange* ♪♪♪ (A&M, 1995, prod. John Leckie) contains many of the same elements that made La's fans swoon, and Power proves himself a capable singer. However, he lacks the highs found in Mavers's crystal voice, and the songs, though hooky, also can't quite match Mavers's either. Finally, the lyrics are sometimes too ho-hum and clichéd. All in all it's a promising, if lightweight, debut.

influences:

◀◀ The Beatles, Gerry & the Pacemakers, Cilla Black, Freddie & the Dreamers, the Hollies

Jack Rabid

Cat Power

Formed 1994, in New York, NY.

Chan Marshall, vocals, guitar; Steve Shelley, drums; Tim Foljahn, guitar.

Cat Power and singer-songwriter Chan Marshall are an enigma

that encompasses a series of apparent contradictions: an indie-rock project that serves up the long-gone ghosts of country; a southern-bred songwriter who found her voice recording for a hip New York independent label; a voice that seems to scream without ever rising much above a whisper. Reared throughout the South—Georgia, Tennessee, North Carolina—singer-songwriter Marshall moved to New York City and wrote songs that blended the down-home desperation of Patsy Cline with the lo-fi approach of roots revisionists such as the Palace Brothers and what seems to be the lyrical influence of short story writer Flannery O'Connor. In 1994, she hooked up with Sonic Youth drummer Steve Shelley and guitarist Tim Foljahn to record *Myra Lee* and the EP *Dear Sir*; the former was released on Shelley's independent Smells Like label. Unguarded and striking in their emotional intimacy, they won the band—really Marshall and her sidemen—enough of a following that it released its next record, *What Would the Community Think*, on Matador.

what's available: Emotionally raw and profoundly unsettling, *Myra Lee* ◊◊◊◊ (Smells Like, 1994, prod. Cat Power) is a must for anyone who doubts an indie-rocker can really channel Hank Williams. On *What Would the Community Think* ◊◊◊◊◊ (Matador, 1996, prod. Cat Power), Marshall seems to gain confidence without obscuring any of her feeling; "Nude As the News" is particularly breathtaking.

worth searching for: Recorded the same day as *Myra Lee*, the Italian label EP *Dear Sir* (Runt, 1994, prod. Cat Power) is just as affecting as her first album.

influences:

◀◀ Hank Williams, Patsy Cline, the Palace Brothers

Robert Levine

Catatonia

Formed 1993, in Cardiff, Wales.

Cerys Matthews, vocals; Mark Roberts, guitar; Paul Jones, bass; Owen Powell, guitar; Aled Richards, drums.

Revered by many as the Janis Joplin of Wales, or even the second coming of Björk, Cerys Matthews is at the very least one of the more engaging voices in British pop today. In effect, Catatonia is about as far away from its name's implication as possible. Matthews's infectious swings that bleat into the nethers of rasp and wit make a strong case for superlatives, and the kinetic accompaniment—sometimes starlit folk, sometimes street-trash swagger—set to life a feeling of, well, bliss. But it's the sweetest pills that bring the hardest realities, and Catatonia is distinctly broken folk in the Welsh tradition.

what to buy: It's that tempering of sweet with a slyly confrontational glare that makes *International Velvet* ◊◊◊◊ (Vapor, 1998, prod. Tommy D, Catatonia), the group's sole U.S. release, so impressive. Playful in tone, *Velvet* carries the throwaway pop metaphor of a first single, "Mulder and Scully" (as in "a case for . . ."), to an unexpected imperative of sterling proportions. The album improves throughout, closing with a stumbling regret that's as much of spite as it is sadness: "My selfish gene/It fills my spleen with bile/And all the while I thought you gave a damn."

worth searching for: Still awaiting release in the U.S., *Way Beyond Blue* (Blanco Y Negro, 1996) is the band's fine major-label debut.

influences:

◀◀ The Sugarcubes, Curve, Wendy O. Williams, the Pretenders

Billy Manes

Catherine Wheel

Formed 1990, in Yarmouth, England.

Rob Dickinson, vocals, guitar; Brian Futter, guitar; Dave Hawes, bass; Neil Sims, drums.

Hailing from a small seaside town in England, Catherine Wheel was able to develop its unique sound in large part by being so removed from London. Attempts to classify its four astonishingly strong albums have met roadblocks at every turn, thanks to the mix of styles and approaches.

what to buy: *Ferment* ◊◊◊◊◊ (Mercury, 1992, prod. Tim Friese-Greene), the group's debut, certainly hinted at the then-current U.K. "shoegaze" or "dreampop" sound, but there was more of a House of Love guitar feel (and other more shimmering, subconscious, pastoral influences) than the hazy, blurred My Bloody Valentine style. Furthermore, the vocals and words of singer Rob Dickinson—ironically, a first cousin of ex–Iron Maiden leader Bruce Dickinson—are both out front and discernible. Thus, two memorable singles—"I Want to Touch You" and the hypnotic, repetitive epic "Black Metallic"—helped establish the quartet in America at a time when British acts were mostly unwelcome. *Adam and Eve* ◊◊◊◊◊ (Mercury, 1998, prod. GGGarth, Bob Erzin, Rob Dickinson) is considered by many the band's masterpiece, the culmination of so much sterling work. Backing away from the proto-Alterna blasts to indulge even further in a contemplative mood, somewhere between early Pink Floyd and the best atmospheric groups of the '90s, Catherine Wheel stretches out the sonic spaces masterfully on such brooding works as "Here Comes the Fat Controller" and "Ma Solituda," revs up the engine for "Broken Nose" and "Delicious," and, best of all, crawls and screams through two alternatively quiet and full-throttle tantalizers that end the affair, "Goodbye" and "For Dreaming." Truly challenging material.

what to buy next: The sophomore release, *Chrome* ♫♫♫♪ (Mercury, 1993, prod. Gil Norton), toughened up the sound and even adds minor metal touches the elder Dickinson might favor, without diluting the group's overall immediacy or strengths. Such mighty, steely bombs as "I Confess" and "Broken Head" are offset by the straight-ahead drive of "Strange Fruit" and "Chrome," while the more ponderous side two dabbles in bits of Pink Floyd and later (more ambient) Talk Talk, babbling mood setters they carry off convincingly. *Happy Days* ♫♫♫♫ (Mercury, 1995, prod. Gil Norton, Rob Dickinson) proves no letup. Not so much a departure from *Chrome* as an even harder version, several tracks—"Little Muscle," "Kill My Soul," "Receive," and the scary single "Way Down"—push the envelope on the group's odd ability to make harsh hard rock and post-punk seem so compatible in one blasting number after another. Yet it still shows a more tender side on the melancholic "Heal" and a sparkling anti-heroin single "Judy Staring at the Sun" that pairs Dickinson in a duet with Belly's Tanya Donelly.

the rest:
Like Cats & Dogs ♫♫♫♪ (Mercury, 1996)

influences:
⏪ House of Love, Comsat Angels, Pink Floyd, Talk Talk, Hüsker Dü

Jack Rabid

The Caulfields

Formed 1992, in Newark, DE.

John Faye, lead vocals, guitar; Sam Musumeci, bass, trumpet, guitar, keyboards, background vocals; Ritchie Rubini, drums, piano, percussion, guitar, background vocals; Mike Simpson, lead guitar, background vocals.

This Pennsylvania-based band was a melodic aberration in the waning days of grunge and angst rock. Basing its sound on tight-as-a-drum songwriting and passionate Elvis Costello–influenced vocals, the Caulfields were barely noticed by pierced-nosed twentysomethings. Still, songwriter John Faye remains a talent to watch.

what to buy: Giving a Jellyfish melody a splash of reggae, "Devil's Diary," from the Caulfields' debut, *Whirligig* ♫♫♫♪ (A&M, 1995, prod. Kevin Moloney, the Caulfields), also plays off the Beatles' bigger-than-Jesus fiasco. Really, though, it's a divine song about a human relationship.

what to buy next: *The Caulfields* ♫♫♫ (A&M, 1997, prod. David Bianco) has songs that are nearly as good as the debut's, but

the dirtier production and squealier guitar tones are a slight surrender to the musical climate.

influences:
⏪ Joe Jackson, the Smithereens, Jellyfish
⏩ Ben Folds Five

Jordan Oakes

Nick Cave & the Bad Seeds

Formed 1984, in London, England.

Nick Cave (born Nicholas Edward Cave, September 22, 1957, in Warracknabeal, Australia), vocals, piano, organ; Mick Harvey, drums, keyboard, guitar, bass; Blixa Bargeld, guitar, vocals; Barry Adamson, guitar, piano (1984–86); Hugo Race, guitar (1984); Thomas Wydler, drums (1985–present); Kid Congo Powers, guitar (1986–90); Martyn P. Casey, bass (1992–present); Conway Savage, piano (1990–present); Jim Sclavunos, drums, percussion (1994–present).

Since the mid-'80s, Nick Cave and his rotating band of collaborators, the Bad Seeds, have specialized in turning Cave's dark obsessions with love, murder, and Old Testament religion into sometimes clanging, sometimes hushed, but always extremely intense music. Cave and Harvey met in their native Melbourne, Australia, high school and formed their first band, the Boys Next Door, during the late '70s. In 1980, that band dissolved into the Birthday Party and moved to London, where it released three albums in three years and influenced the burgeoning

Nick Cave (© Ken Settle)

British new wave scene. In 1983, the group moved to West Berlin, where the musicians' notorious indulgences in alcohol and drugs brought an end to the Party. Cave, Harvey, and Barry Adamson persevered, adding Blixa Bargeld of Einstürzende Neubauten and Hugo Race to form the Bad Seeds. The group's masterfully understated musical style proved the perfect backing for Cave's poetic lyrics and alternately raging/sorrowful vocals. This combination won it a small but faithful following in the U.S.; however, after a disastrous stint performing to indifferent audiences on the Lollapalooza main stage during 1994, Cave reportedly swore never to tour the U.S. again. He has since kept his word and concentrated on Europe, where he is both a critical and popular favorite. The lineup of the Bad Seeds has changed considerably since 1984, but Cave—who's also dabbled in writing, acting, and filmmaking—Harvey, and Bargeld remain the unflappable core.

what to buy: *Kicking against the Pricks* ♫♫♫♫ (Homestead, 1986, prod. Nick Cave, the Bad Seeds) is an all-covers album featuring Cave's dark, theatrical renditions of songs ranging from blues standards ("Muddy Water") to gospel to rock classics ("Hey Joe"). *The Best of Nick Cave and the Bad Seeds* ♫♫♫♫ (Mute/Reprise, 1998, prod. various) focuses on the singles and best tracks from the group's '90s output, plus earlier essentials such as "The Mercy Seat" and "From Her to Eternity."

what to buy next: The Bad Seeds' debut, *From Her to Eternity* ♫♫♫♫ (Mute, 1984, prod. Nick Cave, the Bad Seeds), establishes a strong foundation of themes (i.e., murder, religion, and a fascination with Americana, particularly Elvis Presley) that every subsequent album would build upon. Of the band's later albums, *The Boatman's Call* ♫♫♫♫ (Mute/Reprise, 1997, prod. Nick Cave, the Bad Seeds, Flood) is the real gem, a stark, piano-based collection of somber ruminations on love.

what to avoid: *Murder Ballads* ♫♫ (Mute/Elektra, 1996, prod. the Bad Seeds, Victor Van Vugt, Tony Cohen) gained lots of press for its "100% murder songs" content, but this guest-studded (Kylie Minogue, PJ Harvey, Shane MacGowan, etc.) affair is also one of Cave's laziest, with most songs seemingly written on autopilot.

the rest:
The Firstborn Is Dead ♫♫♫♫ (Mute/Homestead, 1985)
Your Funeral . . . My Trial ♫♫♫♫ (Mute/Homestead, 1986)
Tender Prey ♫♫♫ (Mute/Enigma, 1988)
The Good Son ♫♫♫ (Mute/Elektra, 1990)
Henry's Dream ♫♫♫ (Mute/Elektra, 1992)
Live Seeds ♫♫♫♫ (Mute/Elektra, 1993)
Let Love In ♫♫♫ (Mute/Elektra, 1994)

worth searching for: *Tupelo* (Homestead EP, 1985) features the opening number from *The Firstborn Is Dead* and adds some non-album tracks, including a remake of the Birthday Party fa-

vorite "The Six Strings That Drew Blood." The three-song single *What a Wonderful World* (Mute/Elektra, 1992) finds Cave and equally wounded collaborator MacGowan duetting on an oddly touching version of that chestnut, with each singer also covering one of the other's songs.

solo outings:
Nick Cave, Mick Harvey & Blixa Bargeld:
Ghosts . . . of the Civil Dead ♫♫♫ (Mute, 1989)

Barry Adamson:
Mass Side Story ♫♫♫ (Mute/Restless, 1989)
Delusion (Soundtrack) ♫♫ (Mute, 1991)
Oedipus Schmoedipus ♫♫♫ (Mute, 1996)

influences:
◀◀ The Doors, Leonard Cohen, Nick Drake
▶▶ PJ Harvey, Dirty Three

see also: *The Birthday Party, Einstürzende Neubauten*

Christopher Scanlon and Todd Wicks

Paul Cebar

Born in Milwaukee, WI.

Were it not for Paul Cebar's wonderfully soulful voice, which recalls Van Morrison and Eric Clapton (on his better days), the singer and his backup band, the Milwaukeeans, might be just another great bar band, like Joe Grushecky's Iron City Houserockers or the Skeletons. But Cebar, who occasionally experiments with ska and samba styles in an American soul context, can flat-out sing. Plus, he's a part-time DJ who indulges his obsessions with off-the-subject musical forms and does an excellent job of incorporating the knowledge into his music. The only lingering problem is Cebar's inability to stretch his reach beyond samey sounding classic rock. Instead of innovating, the Milwaukeeans too often seem like they're reproducing the music of their collective childhoods.

what to buy: *The Get-Go* ♫♫♫ (Don't, 1997, prod. Jeff Hamilton, Paul Cebar, the Milwaukeeans) opens with the Morrison-like "She Found a Fool" and stays its soulful course despite detours into reggae ("Trying") and horn-heavy R&B ("Clap for the Couple"). He's a clever songwriter, too, coming up with titles such as "Spacelab Girls from Hutsville." Overall, though, Cebar sounds destined to be a reliable nightclub/concert draw rather than a groundbreaking genius.

what to buy next: Less experimental than *The Get-Go*, *Upstroke for the Downfolk* ♫♫♫ (Don't, 1995, prod. Paul Cebar, Jeff Hamilton, the Milwaukeeans) is full of fun touches, such as the stomping, chanting "Bright Night Train," the melancholy title track, and the upbeat "Love Don't Have a Clue." No surprises, though.

the rest:
That Unhinged Thing ♪♪♪ (Shanachie, 1993)

influences:
◄◄ Van Morrison, Parliament, Bob Marley, Steve Winwood, Joe Grushecky, the Skeletons, Bruce Springsteen

Steve Knopper

Exene Cervenka
See: X

Chad & Jeremy
Formed 1963, in London, England.

Chad Stuart (born December 10, 1941, in Windermere, Durham, England), vocals, guitar, piano; Jeremy Clyde (born March 22, 1941, in Buckinghamshire, England), vocals, guitar.

Chad & Jeremy were second only to fellow London folk-rockers Peter & Gordon in the quest to be the most popular Everly Brothers knock-offs of the original British Invasion. Although probably more talented and certainly more qualified to reinterpret the Odetta songbook in the Merseybeat-style than their rivals, the duo had an undeniable disadvantage in their hunt for new material: they didn't have, as Peter Asher of Peter & Gordon did, a sister who was dating Paul McCartney. So immediately following Chad & Jeremy's first appearance on the American charts with "Yesterday's Gone" in 1964, the two relocated to the U.S. where they quickly became fixtures on the small screen (*Hullabaloo*, *Shindig*, even *The Dick Van Dyke Show*). Their biggest hit, "A Summer Song," came soon afterwards, before Jeremy returned to England to take a role in a London musical. That left Chad to form a duet with his wife until his partner returned in '67. What followed were their two heavy-handed but well-meaning stabs at the post–*Sgt. Pepper's* sweepstakes, *Of Cabbages and Kings* and *The Ark*, after which Jeremy again returned to the world of musical comedy. Chad briefly served as musical director on the Smothers Brothers' first TV series and, like Jeremy, began dabbling in the theater. The two still reunite occasionally on stage and on record, and they can still sing the Everlys better than Peter & Gordon ever could.

what to buy: The 20-track *Best of Chad & Jeremy* ♪♪♪ (One Way, 1996, compilation prod. Terry Wachsmuth) features among its sampling of early hits the delightful "My How the Time Goes By" that, as the Redcoats, they once used to serenade Rob and Laura Petrie. Likewise, the cream of their Columbia Records crop is colorfully compiled on *Painted Dayglow Smile* ♪♪♪♪ (Sony Legacy, 1992, compilation prod. Bob Irwin),

on which the pair bravely begin applying their Simon & Garfunkel–lite approach to the material of Van McCoy and Rogers and Hammerstein.

what to avoid: *Chad Stuart and Jeremy Clyde* ♪♪ (Rocshire, 1983, prod. Chad Stuart) is yet another misguided reunion album that proves, as so many such projects do, that you simply cannot reheat a souffle.

the rest:
Yesterday's Gone: A Golden Classics Collection ♪♪ (Collectables, 1993)
Yesterday's Gone ♪♪ (Drive Archive, 1994)
Summer Song ♪♪ (K-Tel, 1995)
Best of Chad & Jeremy ♪♪♪ (Quicksilver, 1997)

worth searching for: Fans of the dreaded concept album must have *Of Cabbages and Kings* (Columbia, 1967, prod. Gary Usher) if only for the 17-minute-plus "Progress Suite," which bravely mixes nuclear explosions with the first-ever appearance on record of the Firesign Theatre. Cudos are also given for this record's ultra-cheesy, sub-*Satanic Majesties Request* cover shot, which brings all new meanings to the question "Why do you think they call it dope?"

influences:
◄◄ Peter, Paul & Mary, the Everly Brothers, Flanders & Swann, the Jerks

►► Boyce & Hart, Wham!, the Proclaimers, the Keller Brothers

Gary Pig Gold

Eugene Chadbourne
Born January 4, 1954, in Mount Vernon, NY.

Meet the creator of such unique instruments as the electric rake, the electric plunger, and the skull harmonica. Flitting between the worlds of absurdist rock and free jazz, Eugene Chadbourne is a talented guitarist whose uncompromising vision is a whacked-out and uncommercial approach to the vagaries of the recording industry that virtually defines niche marketing. His impatience with the standard distribution arrangements demanded by most companies hasn't really hindered his ability and desire to churn out material that avoids the mainstream. Not only does the man occasionally make albums for a batch of small, specialist labels but he also trods the aural guerrilla trail by recording his concerts and then selling the tapes to fans, sometimes including artwork and sometimes not. According to Chadbourne, "I don't have a catalog, it doesn't exist. I'm sure there have been hundreds of tapes and on some of them there may have only been one of them made. Nobody knows. There are other ways of releasing music than what has been accepted by the public as THE WAY." He has recorded so prolifically that no discography could ever do him justice, especially since so much of it is either out of print or only on the tapes he sells at concerts and through the mail.

As a teenager growing up in Boulder, Colorado, Chadbourne's listening habits progressed rapidly from the Beatles, Jimi Hendrix, and Frank Zappa to John Coltrane, Eric Dolphy, and Ornette Coleman (with occasional stops for Hank Williams, Roger Miller, and other country stars), an audio path that was to culminate in his discovery of Derek Bailey, the idiosyncratic guitar improvisor from Britain. The early '70s found Chadbourne taking up residency in Calgary, Alberta, Canada, as a substitute for doing what the American Selective Service wanted him to do. When President Jimmy Carter declared an amnesty for draft evaders, Chadbourne came back to the States, ending up in North Carolina with his family. During 1982, Chadbourne joined up with bassist Kramer and drummer Dave Licht to form Shockabilly, a band whose claim to fame was the twisted cover versions they did, turning songs like the Count 5's "Psychotic Reaction" and "19th Nervous Breakdown" by the Rolling Stones into recognizable shreds. After the demise of Shockabilly in 1985, Chadbourne took up his solo career again. On the rock side of things Chadbourne has recorded projects with members of the Violent Femmes, Camper Van Beethoven, and Evan Johns & the H-Bombs, while the jazz and avant garde aspects of his playing have found kindred souls in John Zorn, Tom Cora, Frank Lowe, and the aforementioned Bailey. Chadbourne's most recent project is a large scale concert piece he calls "Insect and Western for Symphony Orchestra, Balinese Gamelan Orchestra and Jazz Band" that had yet to be recorded in 1998.

what to buy: *Jesse Helms Busted with Pornography* ♫♫♫♫ (Fire Ant, 1996, prod. Eugene Chadbourne) pushes Chadbourne's leftist political agenda, beating his targets over the head—but with a sense of humor. For his version of a C&W opera, Chadbourne takes on Jesse Helms, his state's powerful conservative senator, slashing out rapid-fire guitar licks and cornpone savvy with Eugene's distinctive vocals (akin, at times, to a barely post-pubescent teenager) propelling a batch of savage, heretical themes such as "Sex with the Sheriff."

what to buy next: *Chadbourne Barber Shop* ♫♫♫ (Airline 61, 1997, prod. Eugene Chadbourne, Karl Straub, Jason Stelluto) features a weird lineup with Brian Ritchie of the Violent Femmes alongside the former drummer for the Mothers of Invention Jimmy Carl Black, avant garde saxophonist Charles Tyler, and, to top it all off, the great contemporary bluegrass band the Red Clay Ramblers. Still, the album follows the usual pattern for Chadbourne's more pop-oriented stuff, with plenty of political asides—including a reprise of "Sword and Shield" that appeared on the now out of print *The Eddie Chaterbox Double Trio Love Album.* Chadbourne's loving yet anarchic version of the old Ernest Tubb standard "Waltz Across Texas" is

buried in a medley along with "The Shah Sleeps in Lee Harvey's Grave."

the rest:
(With Jimmy Carl Black) *Pachuco Cadaver: The Jack and Jim Show Present the Music of Don Van Vliet, Captain Beefheart* ♫♫♫♫ (Fire Ant, 1995)
End to Slavery ♫♫♫ (Intakt, 1997)
(With Paul Lovens) *Patrizio* ♫♫♫♫ (Victo, 1997)

worth searching for: The most accessible Chadbourne albums from a rock standpoint are the titles he recorded for Fundamental Records that, unfortunately, are out of print. Of those, the titles he did as part of Camper Van Chadbourne with various members of Camper Van Beethoven are pretty solid, especially *The Eddie Chatterbox Double Trio Love Album* (Fundamental, 1988, prod. Eugene Chadbourne). Half of the songs on the album were authored by the late, great Tim Buckley, and the other half of the set consisted of Chadbourne-penned tunes, some of which ("Sword and Shield" and "Life X 2" in particular) have become concert favorites.

influences:

◀◀ Frank Zappa, Ornette Coleman, Hank Williams, Anthony Braxton, Derek Bailey

▶▶ Camper Van Beethoven, the Violent Femmes, Molly Chadbourne

Garaud MacTaggart

Chalk FarM

Formed 1994, in Los Angeles, CA.

Michael Duff, guitar, vocals; Trace Ritter, guitar (1995–present); Toby Scarbrough, drums; Orlando Sims, bass.

Chalk FarM formed as a three-piece in Los Angeles when Michael Duff, an East Coast native, moved west to pursue his musical dream, and Orlando Sims, Los Angeles native and session player, began writing and recording together. Performing as an acoustic trio with Toby Scarbrough, the band decided to fill out its sound and brought Ritter on board in January 1995. Porno for Pyros and Holy Barbarians producer Matt Hyde heard the band's demo and helped Chalk FarM rework its sound. In December of 1995, the band signed with Columbia Records.

what's available: No stone—politics, relationships, drugs— goes unturned on Chalk FarM's debut, *Notwithstanding* ♫♫ (Columbia, 1996, prod. Matt Hyde). The jangley single "Lie on Lie" is a frank look at the sad state of government according to Riter, Duff, and Sims, while in "Lose You Now" Duff tries to convince a girlfriend that his ex means nothing to him. Unfortunately, the mediocre, middle-of-the-road rock of *Notwithstanding* renders it all rather flaccid.

influences:

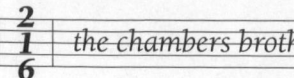 Dishwalla, Collective Soul

Christina Fuoco

The Chambers Brothers

Formed 1961, in Los Angeles, CA.

George Chambers, bass; Willie Chambers, guitar; Lester Chambers, harmonica; Joe Chambers, guitar; Brian Keenan, drums (1965–72).

With their roots in gospel, the Chambers Brothers would seem unlikely psychedelic-funk crossover pioneers, but they provided a reference point for other groups beginning to hit their stride at the same time, including Parliament/Funkadelic and Sly & the Family Stone. The acoustic gospel band made its first amplified appearance at the 1965 Newport Folk Festival to great acclaim. White drummer Brian Keenan joined in 1965, and the band hit the rock club circuit, where a typical set would include any number of lengthy jams that would have made another young southern brother act, the Allmans, proud. In 1968, the Brothers had a hit single with "Time Has Come Today," an edited version of the powerful 12-minute psychedelic epic on their Columbia debut. The band pulled from equal parts Otis Redding, Wilson Pickett, and Haight Ashbury, always with a nod back to their beginning at the Mount Calvary Baptist Church near Carthage in Lee County, Mississippi.

what to buy: A terrific sampling of the band is available on *Time Has Come: The Best of the Chambers Brothers* 𝄢𝄢𝄢𝄢 (Columbia, 1996, prod. various), which contains two versions of "Time Has Come Today" plus the blistering "I Can't Turn You Loose" and the more traditional gospel crooning of "People Get Ready."

the rest:
People Get Ready 𝄢𝄢𝄢𝄢 (Vault, 1965)
Chambers Brothers Now 𝄢𝄢𝄢 (Vault, 1966)
Time Has Come 𝄢𝄢𝄢𝄢 (Columbia, 1967)
Shout! 𝄢𝄢𝄢 (Vault, 1968)
Love, Peace and Happiness 𝄢𝄢𝄢 (Columbia, 1969)
Feelin' the Blues 𝄢𝄢𝄢𝄢 (Vault, 1970)
Chambers Brothers Live at Fillmore East 𝄢𝄢𝄢𝄢 (Columbia, 1970)
Greatest Hits 𝄢𝄢𝄢𝄢 (Columbia, 1971)
Unbonded 𝄢𝄢𝄢 (Avco, 1974)
Right Move 𝄢𝄢𝄢 (Avco, 1975)

influences:

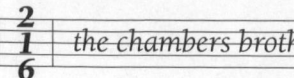 Wilson Pickett, Otis Redding, James Brown, the Animals

▶▶ George Clinton, Sly & the Family Stone, Run-D.M.C, War

Martin Connors

The Chameleons

Formed 1980, in Manchester, England. Disbanded 1986.

Mark Burgess, vocals, bass; Dave Fielding, guitars, keyboards; Reg Smithies, guitar; John Lever, drums.

This is one of those bands with the distinction of having more records released after it broke up than while it was together. The group has three official studio albums, but almost a dozen after-the-fact titles are available. During the band's heyday in the mid-to late '80s, the British music press frequently called the Chameleons "sonic architects," which is an apt description; the quartet created sounds and atmospheres that were unparalleled, while Mark Burgess's lyrics and vocals were remarkably expressive. As a whole, the band easily ranks as one of the best—if also one of the most under-appreciated—of its decade. The downfall tragically centers around Burgess's excessive drinking; his binges, along with wild mood swings and abusive behavior toward his bandmates, finally created a rift so great that a lifetime friendship with guitarist Reg Smithies ended along with the band shortly after the release of 1986's *Strange Times*. While drawing on the bleak industrial landscapes that surrounded it, the Chameleons did not become weighted down by the environment, but attempted to overcome it; despite the dark sound, Burgess kept his lyrics generally bright and hopeful.

what to buy: *Script of the Bridge* 𝄢𝄢𝄢𝄢 (Statik/MCA, 1983, prod. the Chameleons, Colin Richardson) is a brilliant album. From classic songs such as "Second Skin" to the inspired "As High As You Can Go," this takes the brooding sounds of Joy Division and the Smiths to the next level. *Live Shreds* 𝄢𝄢𝄢𝄢 (Cleopatra, 1996) offers a solid lead into the band's raw power on stage at a reasonable price, with very good sound quality.

what to buy next: *Strange Times* 𝄢𝄢𝄢𝄢 (Geffen, 1986, prod. David Allen), the band's first proper release in the U.S., was a college radio sensation with the epic "Swamp Thing," an inspired cover of David Bowie's "John, I'm Only Dancing," and an alternate version of the beautiful "Tears." The band's debut, *What Does Anything Mean? Basically* 𝄢𝄢𝄢𝄢 (Statik/MCA, 1981, prod. the Chameleons, Colin Richardson), isn't quite as phenomenal as the other two, but is still a strong set.

what to avoid: Generally approach posthumously released live albums and radio shows with caution, as they vary widely in quality. Smithies's label Imaginary is usually the most reliable source for these recordings. Additionally, while a nice treat for die-hard fans, there are a number of videos of live shows out there that are of mediocre quality at best.

the rest:
The Peel Sessions 𝄢𝄢𝄢𝄢 (Strange Fruit, 1990)
Here Today . . . Gone Tomorrow (Live) 𝄢𝄢𝄢𝄢 (Imaginary, 1992)

Live in Toronto ♪♪♪♪ (Imaginary, 1992)

Dali's Picture/Live in Berlin ♪♪♪♪ (Imaginary, 1993)

worth searching for: The import *Return of the Roughnecks: Best Of* (Dead Dead Good, 1996, prod. various) covers it all from beginning to end. *The Fan and the Bellows* (Hybrid/Caroline, 1986), billed as "a collection of classic early recordings," gathers out-of-print early singles and demos (later versions appear on *What Does Anything Mean? Basically*) into one volume. With a more raw, less produced sound, these songs paint a picture closer to what the band is like live.

solo outings:

The Reegs (Smithies):

Return of the Seamonkeys ♪♪♪♪ (Imaginary, 1988)

influences:

◀◀ Joy Division, Peter Gabriel/Genesis, King Crimson

▶▶ Bush, the Smiths, the Afghan Whigs, James, Green Day

Tim Davis

The Champs

Formed 1957, in Los Angeles, CA. Disbanded 1965.

Dave Burgess, guitar (1957–60); Danny Flores (a.k.a. Chuck Rio), saxophone (1957–58); Cliff Hils, bass (1957–58); Buddy Bruce, guitar (1957–58); Gene Alden, drums (1957–58); Dale Norris, guitar (1958–62); Joe Burness, bass (1958); Van Norman, bass (1958–60); Dean Beard, piano (1958–60); Jimmy Seals, saxophone (1958–64); Dash Crofts, drums (1958–65); Bobby Morris, bass (1960–61); Glen Campbell, guitar (1960); John Trombatore, bass (1961–62); Keith MacKendrick, guitar (1961–65); Maurice "Mo" Marshall, guitar (1963–65); Curtis Paul, bass (1963–65).

"Being on the road with the Champs was like being in the army," said long-time drummer Dash Crofts—albeit from the perspective of his mid-'70s soft-rock stardom with fellow ex-Champ Jimmy Seals. "Someone told you when to get up, how to dress, where to go, what to play, and how to play it." Perhaps it was exactly this strict, stick-to-the-formula regimentation that helped the Champs milk a long and lucrative career from little more than two novelty instrumental hits (the first of which, the Grammy Award–winning "Tequila," was tossed off as a mere B-side during a few minutes of spare studio time). With an ever-revolving membership roster, which at times included guitarists Glen Campbell, Delaney Bramlett, and former Gene Vincent Blue Cap Johnny Meeks, the band followed the million-selling "Tequila" with "Too Much Tequila" and bristled when Chubby Checker hit #2 on the charts by adding lyrics to their song "Limbo Rock," causing the Champs to respond with "Limbo Dance," "Latin Limbo," and then "Tequila Twist"—well, you get the picture. But what this band may have lacked in the

creative thinking department it more than made up for with a tight, entertaining stage act and always professional sounding recordings. And though this discipline may have been military-like in its execution, it certainly provided a much-sought-after proving ground for musicians on the burgeoning West Coast rock scene. For that alone, the Champs deserve a place as an important—if minor—part of rock history.

what to buy: The 18 selections on *Tequila: The Very Best of the Champs* ♪♪♪♪ (Music Club, 1997, prod. various) contain each and every variation upon the "Tequila" and "Limbo" themes humanly possible, while *The Challenge Album Collection* ♪♪♪♪ (One Way, 1997, compilation prod. Terry Wachsmuth), with its 48 tracks culled from the band's four original albums, delves even deeper.

the rest:

Tequila: Golden Classics ♪♪♪ (Collectables, 1993)

Greatest Hits: Tequila ♪♪ (Curb, 1994)

The Best of the Champs ♪♪♪ (Laserlight, 1995)

worth searching for: There seems to be an immense Champs cult operating within the ranks of Ace Records in Britain, which has released five discs the discriminating student of instrumental rock should seek out: *Tequila* (Ace, 1987/1992, compilation prod. Ted Carroll) remains the definitive Champs collection, whereas *The Early Singles: 30 Great "A" & "B" Sides* (Ace, 1996, compilation prod. John Broven) and *The Later Singles* (Ace, 1997, compilation prod. John Broven) collect both sides of *every* 45 the band originally recorded for the Challenge label.

influences:

◀◀ Bill Doggett, Bill Justis, Bill Haley & His Comets, Gene Autry

▶▶ Johnny & the Hurricanes, the Shindogs, Art Garfunkel, Pee-wee Herman, Rock en Español

Gary Pig Gold

James Chance /James White

Born James Siegfried, April 20, 1953, in Milwaukee, WI.

Bullshit artist or inspired genre mutator? Supreme ironist or self-deluding "White Negro?" Probably all four. James Chance, a pompadoured, multiply-monikered saxophonist-keyboardist-vocalist comes off as utterly self-indulgent and personal, yet possibly the most intense vocalist on the New York punk scene, epitomized by the tortured screams on his frequently recorded anthem, "Contort Yourself." He started out sitting in on the jazz loft scene and was in an early version of Lydia Lunch's Teenage Jesus & the Jerks, and her use of slide guitar was a major influence of the sound he pursued with his band, the Contortions. Harshly dissonant, jerky organ chords (whether by White or, at first, Adele Bertai), White's squealing alto sax, clanging guitar riffs, and slippery, atonal slide guitar combined in frenzied abandon held together by rock-solid bass and drums. White's obvious self-loathing and obsession with James Brown's "King Heroin" (which appears on all four of his live albums) suggest reasons for the constant turnover in his groups (one guitarist who passed through his band dubbed him a "major league asshole"). His stylistic range on sax and organ were severely limited, and after awhile he slipped into an overly ironic parody of himself—though he *was* great at what he did. In 1995, he resumed regular performance in New York. (His first three albums—*Buy the Contortions*, *Off White*, and *Sax Maniac*—have been reissued, with bonus tracks, by the Henry Rollins–Rick Rubin label Infinite Zero.)

what to buy: The Contortions' *Buy the Contortions* 𝅘𝅥𝅘𝅥𝅘𝅥𝅘𝅥𝅘𝅥 (Ze, 1979, prod. James White) is the single greatest studio product of No Wave, a groundbreaking shotgun wedding of New York post-punk with sped-up funk and disco rhythms topped off with abrasive, unsettling NYC sullenness. White never again matched the overwhelming intensity and jagged nastiness of his debut, though he would come close on some live albums. James Chance & the Contortions' *Soul Exorcism* 𝅘𝅥𝅘𝅥𝅘𝅥𝅘𝅥 (ROIR, 1991, prod. James White) has fairly good sound (the best of the domestically available live albums) and a must-hear cover of Michael Jackson's "Don't Stop Till You Get Enough."

what to buy next: Instead of the hard rhythms of *Buy*, James White & the Blacks' *Off White* 𝅘𝅥𝅘𝅥𝅘𝅥𝅘𝅥 (Ze, 1979, prod. James White) mostly uses a simple, campy disco beat, accenting the increasingly sleazy White persona heard on "Stained Sheets" and other tracks. Pat Place's slippery slide guitar riffs are conceptually more subversive given this musical context. James White & the Blacks' *Sax Maniac* (Animal/Chrysalis, 1982, prod. James White) is a compromise between *Buy* and *Off White*, and was White's only flirtation with a major label.

what to avoid: *Live in New York* 𝅘𝅥𝅘𝅥 (ROIR, 1981, prod. James Chance, John Hanti) has the worst sound of any of the live albums and can safely be bought last. But on two tracks it does document a particularly interesting 1980 band with guitarist Bern Nix (Ornette Coleman's Prime Time) and trombonist/vocalist Joseph Bowie (Defunkt), as well as an otherwise unavailable song, "Sophisticated Cancer."

the rest:
James Chance & the Contortions:
Lost Chance 𝅘𝅥𝅘𝅥𝅘𝅥 (ROIR, 1995)

worth searching for: The Contortions' four tracks on *No New York* (Antilles, 1978, prod. Brian Eno) show the early group at its confrontational, raggedy best.

influences:

◄◄ James Brown, Albert Ayler, Teenage Jesus & the Jerks

►► Defunkt, the Raybeats, Bush Tetras, Living Colour, Tar Babies, the Minutemen

Steve Holtje

The Chantays

Formed 1962, in Santa Ana, CA.

Bob Spickard, guitar; Brian Carman, guitar; Bob Welch, drums; Rob Marshall, keyboards (1962–66); Warren Waters, bass (1962–64, 1966); John Longstreth, guitar (1965); Mark Howlett, bass (1965); Steve Khan, drums (1964–65); Tommy Hannigan, drums (1965); Brian Nussie; Ricky Lewis.

While its members were still in their teens, this unassuming little California quintet wrote and recorded one of the most innovative and consistently popular songs of the entire instrumental rock genre. Although Bob Spickard and Brian Carman first picked up guitars in order to perform Freddy King and Jimmy Reed favorites on the local dance club scene, one viewing of a surf film in high school inspired them to rename a popular song of theirs ("Liberty's Whip") after the giant Hawaiian wave funnels they saw on the screen: Turning the reverb knob on their amps all the way up, "Pipeline" was born. Recorded and released on the tiny Downey label, it soared to #4 after being leased to Dot Records, and suddenly the band found itself performing on labelmate Lawrence Welk's television show to a nationwide audience. But classroom commitments, not to mention financial squabbles between Downey and Dot, prevented the band from touring extensively or following up the hit quickly enough, and before long the Beatles arrived and changed all of the rules (forcing even the Chantays to try *singing*—Buddy Holly and Sinatra songs no less!—on its second album). A tour of Japan—where, thanks to the Ventures' lead, guitar-oriented instrumentals were becoming all the rage—kept the band alive a bit longer, and several singles were released under other names—such as the Ill Winds and the Leaping Ferns—before the Chantays finally unplugged in 1966. Over two decades later however, with surf music again becoming popular in its homeland, the band duly reunited and was honored, alongside Jan & Dean, the Surfaris, and the Ventures, on the Hollywood Rock Walk in recognition of its considerable achievements. Remarkably, after all these years—and over a *hundred* cover versions—it is the Chantays' original "Pipeline" that still sounds best. (And although Dick Dale may have called it "Sewerline" back in '63, that didn't stop him from recording a Grammy-nominated version alongside Stevie Ray Vaughan for the 1987 cinematic milestone *Back to the Beach*.)

what to buy: The debut album, *Pipeline* 🎵🎵🎵 (Dot, 1963/Varese Vintage, 1994, prod. Art Wenzel), with renditions of "Sleep Walk" and Del Shannon's "Runaway," shows the Chantays to be far more versatile in its approach than many of its contemporaries. Keyboardist Rob Marshall, for instance, took many of the solos that, in traditional surf music, would be reserved solely for the guitar or saxophone—and damned if these kids weren't confident enough to tackle even the Mar-Keys' "Last Night" without wiping out!

the rest:

Two Sides of the Chantays/Pipeline 🎵🎵🎵 (Dot, 1963, 1966/Repertoire, 1994)

Next Set 🎵🎵🎵 (Chantay Productions, 1994)

Waiting for the Tide 🎵🎵 (Vesper Alley/Rocktopia, 1997)

influences:

◄◄ The Rhythm Rockers, Duane Eddy, Bruce Brown

►► The Challengers, The Pyramids, Bruce Johnston, El Caminos, the Aqua Velvets, the Mermen

Gary Pig Gold

Harry Chapin

Born December 7, 1942, in New York, NY. Died July 16, 1981.

U2, Bruce Springsteen, and Sting may be championed as stars with high ideals and big hearts, but singer-songwriter Harry Chapin valiantly carried the flag for compassion during the pre-Live Aid era—when it wasn't cool to care. He invested much of his time and energy into raising awareness of world hunger: More than half of his annual concerts were benefits for the cause, and in 1978, prodded by Chapin's relentless badgering on Capitol Hill, President Jimmy Carter appointed him to the Presidential Commission on World Hunger. His humanitarian passions mixed with his irreverent sense of humor to transform his underrated live shows into intimate, captivating experiences that were rarely duplicated on his uneven studio albums. Chapin scored Top 40 hits with "Taxi," the parentally challenged father-son tale "Cat's in the Cradle," and "W.O.L.D.," despite a penchant for lengthy narratives that unfolded more like musical short stories than songs. Such tenacious but taxing melodramas as "Sniper," "What Made America Famous," and "The Mayor of Candor Lied" became his trademarks, but they also branded him a heavy-handed overachiever. Indeed, Chapin was at his most affecting when he scaled back his dramatic ambitions and simply tapped into the everyday doubts and dreams that fuel such heartfelt ballads as "Any Old Kind of Day," "If My Mary Were Here," "I Wonder What Happened to Him," "Last Stand," and his stirring ode to '60s idealism, "Remember When the Music." In one of rock's cruelest ironies,

Chapin died in 1981 in a car crash—rushing to get to a benefit performance.

what to buy: Although its ragged sound quality confirms it originally was recorded for archival purposes, *The Bottom Line Encore Collection* 🎵🎵🎵 (Bottom Line, 1998, prod. Peter Fornatale, Hank Medress) stands as the most affecting testament to Chapin's appeal. Marking his 2,000th-concert milestone, this January 1981 show captures the manic energy, raucous humor, and unapologetic passion that were barely hinted at on 1976's best-selling but heavily overdubbed *Greatest Stories Live*. His spirited performances of "A Better Place to Be," "W.O.L.D.," "Mr. Tanner," and "I Miss America" are so loose they almost wobble. But then, Chapin never tried to be perfect: He was too busy being human.

what to buy next: Chapin's fascination with the saga of the Titanic was the backdrop for the politically and emotionally charged concept album *Dance Band on the Titanic* 🎵🎵🎵 (Elektra, 1977, prod. Stephen Chapin). Using the doomed ship as a metaphor for an ambivalent society blind to the dangers lurking ahead, the rollicking title track raises a convincing ruckus while the gospel-flavored "One Light in a Dark Valley" and the achingly vulnerable "I Wonder What Happened to Him" rival his most touching performances. The 14-minute "There Only Was One Choice"—an autobiographical art-rock collage—eerily foreshadows the car crash that killed him.

what to avoid: Commemorating his posthumous awarding of the Congressional Gold Medal, the two-CD *Gold Medal Collection* 🎵🎵 (Elektra, 1988, prod. various) slaps together singles, album tracks, live performances, and interview/speech snippets with no regard for context or content. Chapin's legacy deserves better preservation.

the rest:

Heads and Tales 🎵🎵🎵 (Elektra, 1972)

Sniper and Other Love Songs 🎵🎵 (Elektra, 1972)

Short Stories 🎵🎵 (Elektra, 1973)

Verities and Balderdash 🎵🎵🎵 (Elektra, 1974)

Portrait Gallery 🎵🎵 (Elektra, 1975)

Greatest Stories Live 🎵🎵🎵 (Elektra, 1976)

On the Road to Kingdom Come 🎵🎵🎵 (Elektra, 1976)

Living Room Suite 🎵🎵🎵 (Elektra, 1978)

Legends of the Lost and Found 🎵🎵🎵 (Elektra, 1979)

Sequel 🎵🎵🎵 (Boardwalk, 1980)

Anthology of Harry Chapin 🎵🎵🎵 (Elektra, 1985)

Remember When the Music 🎵🎵🎵 (DCC, 1987)

The Last Protest Singer 🎵🎵🎵 (DCC, 1988)

worth searching for: Pat Benatar, the Hooters, Judy Collins, Richie Havens, and others perform Chapin's tunes on *Harry Chapin Tribute* (Relativity, 1990, prod. Stephen Chapin), recorded live at Carnegie Hall. But the most inspired match is

Bruce Springsteen's touching rendition of "Remember When the Music," complete with a monologue about Chapin's commitment to keeping "a good clear eye on the dirty ways of the world" that stands as his finest epitaph.

influences:

◀◀ Phil Ochs, Pete Seeger

▶▶ Mary Chapin Carpenter, James McMurtry, John Mellencamp, Sheryl Crow

David Okamoto

Beth Nielsen Chapman

Born in Harlington, TX.

Forever edging the line of pop into country, Beth Nielsen Chapman has made a respectable name for herself during the past two decades as a top-quality purveyor of melodic sentiment. She's historically maintained a low profile, content to just write the songs while country folk such as Alabama, Tanya Tucker, and Willie Nelson wear their faces. But the early '90s saw Chapman come into the fore as an Adult Contemporary staple, with her eponymous 1990 major label debut (she released an indie record, *Hearing It First*, in 1980) charting four Top 10 singles, including "Walk My Way" and "All I Have" (the latter of which remains a favorite wedding weepie today). In 1993, Chapman returned with a well received second record and a few more AC hits, including a duet with Paul Carrack ("In the Time It Takes") and "You Say You Will." But it was the prolonged illness and 1995 death of her husband, Ernest Chapman, and the subsequent rallying of friends like Bonnie Raitt, Michael McDonald, and new age guru Deepak Chopra that brought to life Chapman's most redeeming record, 1997's *Sand and Water*.

what to buy: *Sand and Water* 🎵🎵🎵🎵 (Reprise, 1997, prod. Rodney Crowell, Beth Nielsen Chapman, Michael McDonald, Bonnie Raitt, Jelly Roll Johnson) brings much of the heartful yearning of Chapman's career to a mortal climax, and does so without reaching for Kleenex or sympathy.

what to buy next: *Beth Nielsen Chapman* 🎵🎵🎵 (Reprise, 1990, prod. Beth Nielsen Chapman) introduces a savvy hybrid of Carole King and Bonnie Raitt to the piano-heavy AC radio wash of the decade's turn. Sure it's sappy, but it does the trick with a good deal less flashy pain than, say, Bette Midler. Also, *You Hold the Key* 🎵🎵🎵 (Reprise, 1993, prod. Beth Nielsen Chapman) offers a rich texture of similarly inoffensive paens to love, including one, "In the Time It Takes," that features the duet with Carrack.

influences:

◀◀ Bonnie Raitt, Joan Baez, Carole King

▶▶ Lauren Christy, Sheryl Crow, Patty Loveless

Billy Manes

Tracy Chapman

Born March 20, 1964, in Cleveland, OH.

On the heels of Suzanne Vega's breakthrough with "Luka," Boston coffeehouse singer Tracy Chapman snared the attention of Elektra Records in 1988 and scored an unlikely Top 10 hit with "Fast Car," a gently rendered treatise on soured dreams driven by a captivating depth rarely heard on radio. The momentum of that shortlived pre–Alanis Morissette women's movement, coupled with Chapman's skills at examining such emotionally charged topics as domestic violence and racial injustice without preaching, made her an instant star: the alternative band Thelonious Monster covered her "For My Lover," Neil Diamond recorded "Baby Can I Hold You," and she joined a high-profile Amnesty International tour with Sting, Peter Gabriel, and Bruce Springsteen. Despite her lyrical strengths and good intentions, Chapman still hasn't made another album as riveting as her self-titled 1988 debut. But then, few artists have.

what to buy: *Tracy Chapman* 🎵🎵🎵🎵 (Elektra, 1988, prod. David Kershenbaum) is an impressive calling card, detailing the frustrations of inner-city life while championing inner strength. There's a quiet, compelling sense of dignity bubbling under the fear and futility of "Fast Car," "Behind the Wall," and "Across the Lines."

what to buy next: *New Beginning* 🎵🎵🎵 (Elektra, 1996, prod. Don Gehman) finds Chapman on the artistic rebound thanks to Gehman's mostly acoustic production and the singer's ability to rally attention for her causes without railing.

what to avoid: *Matters of the Heart* 🎵🎵 (Elektra, 1992, prod. Tracy Chapman, Jimmy Iovine) settles for easy targets like yuppie materialism and grumpy sketches instead of her usually thoughtful portraits.

the rest:

Crossroads 🎵🎵🎵 (Elektra, 1989)

worth searching for: On *Rubaiyat* (Elektra, 1990, prod. various), a double-CD commemorating Elektra's legacy, Chapman performs an upbeat "Fever"-like cover of "House of the Rising Sun" with help from E Street Band pianist Roy Bittan.

influences:

◀◀ Joan Armatrading, Joan Baez, Joni Mitchell

▶▶ Jewel, Ani DiFranco, Poe, Patty Griffin, Dionne Farris

David Okamoto

Craig Chaquico

See: Jefferson Starship

Tracy Chapman (© Ken Settle)

The Charlatans

Formed 1966, in San Francisco, CA. Disbanded 1970.

The official recording lineup consisted of: Hank Bradley, violin; Lynne Hughes, guitar, vocals; Patrick Gogerty, piano; Dan Hicks, guitar, vocals.

The story of '60s Haight-Ashbury counterculture band the Charlatans can easily be likened to that of Mersey Beat rockers Rory Storm & the Hurricanes: Both were big fishes in small ponds who pioneered a style and sound but were among the last bands in their respective regions to be signed to a record label. Subsequently, discs by both groups hit the market after interest in their genres had waned. Though never as commercially successful as other San Francisco–based bands such as the Grateful Dead and Jefferson Airplane, the Charlatans were a highly influential act. Its penchant for antiauthoritarian satire, street theater, and outrageous attire challenged other Bay Area groups to weigh in with more of the same. Also, its musical blend of electric folk, jugband blues, and psychedelia was daring for its time, and much imitated by later acts. The band's existence was chaotic, resulting in many lineup changes. One constant was Dan Hicks, whose group Dan Hicks & His Hot Licks eventually refined the puckish antics of the Charlatans and brought them to a much wider audience. The Charlatans recorded only two LPs during their brief recording career, but they left behind a treasure trove of demos and unreleased tapes to be savored by future generations.

what's available: The reissue of the group's first official album, *The Charlatans* 𝄞𝄞 (Eva, 1969/One Way, 1995, prod. Dan Healy), doesn't quite capture its wiseass hippie spirit, and the instrumentation is a bit staid. But it does contain some nice moments.

worth searching for: Better by far is the import *The Amazing Charlatans* (Big Beat, 1996, compilation prod. Alec Palao), a collection of 23 demo tapes and unreleased studio gems that run the gamut from psychedelia to washboard jugband blues. In-depth liner notes and pristine sound really make this the one to get. Also, the group's two LPs have been reissued on *First Album/Alabama Bound* (Roir, 1996, prod. various), which features superior sound and generous track selections.

influences:

◀◀ The Great Society, the Jefferson Airplane

▶▶ Country Joe & the Fish, Dan Hicks & His Hot Licks, the Flamin' Groovies, the Grateful Dead

see also: *Dan Hicks*

Ken Burke

The Charlatans UK

Formed 1988, in Northwich, England.

Tim Burgess, vocals; Martin Blunt, bass; Jon Brookes, drums; Mark Collins, guitar (1991–present); Tony Rogers, keyboards (1996–present); Rob Collins, keyboards (1988–96); Jon Baker, guitar (1988–91); Baz Kettley, vocals (1988–89).

Few bands on the contemporary British scene have suffered as much misfortune as the Charlatans UK. After initially hitting the charts with its promising wah-wah-drenched debut album *Some Friendly*, the band suffered its first piece of bad luck. Bassist Martin Blunt was hospitalized for nervous exhaustion, while guitarist Jon Baker felt so overwhelmed by the impending success that he bailed on the group the day after it played London's Royal Albert Hall. The Charlatans resumed pumping out Farfisa-fueled grooves with replacement guitarist Mark Collins, helping define the Manchester sound during the early '90s. Shortly after touring in support of their second record, *Between 10th and 11th*, however, keyboardist Rob Collins got snagged in a bungled armed robbery attempt and was incarcerated for nearly a year. In that time, the Charlatans completely lost direction, barely managing to write and release a dismal third record (*Up to Our Hips*) using prerecorded keyboard parts. A fourth, self-titled disc foreshadowed further tragedy, as it cast the band in a darker, considerably more serious vibe. Touring America became harder as a result of Collins's brush with the law and the album's sales reflected it. The ultimate blow came to the Charlatans while recording their fifth album, *Tellin' Stories*. After a late-night session, an intoxicated Rob Collins swerved his car off the road near Rockfield studio and died from the resultant injuries. The band quickly decided to carry on in the name of the deceased band member and, in an ironic twist, received some of its best critical praise for the tragic record.

what to buy: The Charlatans' debut, *Some Friendly* 𝄢𝄢𝄢𝄢 (Beggar's Banquet/RCA, 1990, prod. the Charlatans), is packed with youthful energy and unforgettable melodies. It also merges house rhythms, psychedelic keyboards, and jangly guitars, creating the perfect soundtrack for England's Summer of Love revival in 1990. Songs like "The Only One I Know" and "Then" are considered modern British pop classics. The group moved further into dance music territory with *Between 10th and 11th* 𝄢𝄢𝄢

(Beggar's Banquet/RCA, 1992, prod. Flood), which remains the group's most polished record to date, as well as its most infectious. Songs like "Weirdo" and "Tremolo Song" showcase a jazzier edge to the Charlatans' sound.

what to buy next: The Charlatans' fifth album, *Tellin' Stories* 𝄢𝄢𝄢 (Beggar's Banquet/Atlantic, 1997, prod. the Charlatans, Dave Charles), was considered a return to form for the group after Collins's death. Its straight-ahead rock sound on songs like "North Country Boy" and "One to Another" court comparisons to rock greats such as Bob Dylan and the Rolling Stones.

what to avoid: The Charlatans momentarily lost direction on *Up to Our Hips* 𝄢 (Beggar's Banquet/Atlantic, 1994, prod. Steve Hillage). Recorded mostly while Collins was serving time, it features the group's most lethargic grooves and half-hearted attempts at songwriting. "Patrol" blatantly borrows its chorus from De La Soul's "Eye Patch," released only a year earlier.

the rest:
The Charlatans 𝄢𝄢𝄢 (Beggar's Banquet/Atlantic, 1995)
Melting Pot 𝄢𝄢𝄢𝄢 (Beggar's Banquet/Atlantic, 1998)

worth searching for: *Isolation 21.2.91* (Live Live Good, 1992) was recorded live at the Chicago Metro during the Charlatans' first tour of the States and features energetic reinterpretations of songs from the debut album as well as rare tracks like "Indian Rope" and "10th and 11th."

influences:

◀◀ The Stone Roses, Bob Dylan, Deep Purple, Stevie Wonder, the Rolling Stones

▶▶ The Chemical Brothers, Blur, Oasis

Aidin Vaziri

Ray Charles

Born Ray Charles Robinson, September 23, 1930, in Albany, GA.

Not for nothing is Ray Charles known as "The Genius." In his extraordinary recording career he has done more than almost any other artist to obliterate the lines between genres of nearly every stripe, from R&B and gospel to country and pop to blues and rock. Beginning as an imitator of the smooth stylings of Nat "King" Cole and Charles Brown, Charles eventually forged his own style, combining gospel music and harmonies with decidedly earthier lyrics reflecting love, lust, heartbreak, and hard times. He was also passionate about jazz, recording Count Basie–style big band arrangements on the one hand, and stripped-down bluesy bop with Milt Jackson on the other. A bigger leap still were his two albums of country & western music that Charles infused with righteous soul. A man of Herculean determination, few opponents have faced him down. Not all of his decisions have been right ones, but he stands behind them all. And why not? His voice is one of the most recognizable in all of music, thanks to such timeless hits as "I Got a Woman," "What'd I Say," "The Night Time Is the Right Time," "Hit the Road Jack," "Georgia on My Mind," "Unchain My Heart," "You Don't Know Me," "Busted," and countless others, to say nothing of his famous Diet Pepsi commercials. Over the years, many of his albums have gone out of print, but plenty of quality box sets, anthologies, and samplers exist. Meanwhile, Rhino records is currently embarked on an ambitious reissue campaign, offering a number of the original works configured as two-fers. Most of these are worth seeking out, though the place to start with Charles is one of the best-of sets.

what to buy: It's big and expensive, but you won't find many box sets that are the equal of the five-CD set *Genius & Soul: The 50th Anniversary Collection* ♪♪♪♪ (Rhino, 1997, prod. various), the first collection that successfully represents every phase of Charles's career, with material from every label. The music is unparalleled, the sound is terrific, the notes are scholarly, and the back of the booklet is even in Braille. This set belongs in every serious collection of 20th-century American music. The merely curious or the more budget minded, on the other hand, might want to sample the two main periods of Charles's early career with *Anthology* ♪♪♪♪ (Rhino, 1988, prod. various) and *The Best of Ray Charles: The Atlantic Years* ♪♪♪♪ (Rhino, 1994, prod. Jerry Wexler, Zenas Sears, Neshui Ertegun, Ahmet Ertegun). The 20-track *Anthology* contains some of the ABC material, including "Georgia on My Mind," "Let's Go Get Stoned," "Eleanor Rigby," "Hit the Road Jack," and "Unchain My Heart." *The Atlantic Years*, which also contains 20 tracks, features "I Got a Woman," "What'd I Say," "The Night Time Is the Right Time," and "Drown in My Own Tears."

what to buy next: For those wanting to delve a little deeper into the Atlantic material, you can't go wrong with *The Birth of Soul: The Complete Atlantic Rhythm & Blues Recordings, 1952–1959* ♪♪♪♪ (Rhino, 1991, prod. various), a three-CD chronicle tracking Charles's development from his years as a Cole imitator to his breakout as a talent of almost unparalleled intuition and ability. Charles was and remains an explosive live performer, and two of his best in-concert albums, 1958's *Ray Charles at Newport* and 1960's *Ray Charles in Person*, are now configured as *Ray Charles Live* ♪♪♪♪ (Atlantic, 1973, 1987, prod. Neshui Ertegun, Zenas Sears). The experiments Charles was carrying out in the studio are extended to the stage, and his feverish versions of "The Right Time," "What'd I Say," and "Drown in My Own Tears," among others, shout, plead, testify, and rock.

what to avoid: Some of Charles's albums are ill-conceived or poorly executed, but none are truly wretched. Beware of numerous, cheap repackagings of his hits; if it's not on Atlantic, ABC, Columbia, Warner Bros., or Rhino, proceed with caution.

the rest:
The Great Ray Charles/The Genius After Hours ♪♪♪ (Atlantic, 1957, 1961/Rhino, 1987)
(With Milt Jackson) *Soul Brothers/Soul Meeting* ♪♪♪ (Atlantic, 1958, 1961/Rhino, 1989)
The Genius of Ray Charles ♪♪♪♪ (Atlantic, 1959/Rhino 1990)
The Genius Hits the Road ♪♪♪ (ABC/Paramount, 1960/ Rhino, 1997)
Genius + Soul = Jazz/My Kind of Jazz ♪♪♪♪ (Impulse!, 1961/Tangerine, 1970/Rhino, 1997)
Modern Sounds in Country and Western Music ♪♪♪♪♪ (ABC/Paramount, 1962/Rhino, 1988)
Ingredients in a Recipe for Soul/Have a Smile with Me ♪♪♪♪ (ABC/Paramount, 1963/1964/Rhino 1997)
Sweet & Sour Tears ♪♪♪ (ABC/Paramount, 1964/Rhino, 1997)
Super Hits (a.k.a. Friendship) ♪♪♪ (Columbia, 1984, 1998)
The Spirit of Christmas ♪♪♪ (Columbia, 1985)
Greatest Hits, Vol. 1 ♪♪♪♪ (Rhino, 1988)
Greatest Hits, Vol. 2 ♪♪♪♪ (Rhino, 1988)
Would You Believe? ♪♪ (Warner Bros., 1990)
My World ♪♪♪ (Warner Bros., 1993)
Ain't That Fine ♪♪♪ (Drive Archive, 1994)
Blues + Jazz ♪♪♪♪ (Rhino, 1994)
The Early Years ♪♪♪ (Tomato, 1994)
Classics ♪♪♪♪ (Rhino, 1995)
Strong Love Affair ♪♪♪ (Qwest, 1996)
Berlin, 1962 ♪♪♪♪ (Pablo, 1996)
Standards ♪♪♪♪♪ (Rhino, 1998)
The Complete Country & Western Recordings, 1959–86 ♪♪♪ (Rhino, 1998)

worth searching for: On the soundtrack to *The Blues Brothers* (Atlantic, 1980, prod. Bob Tischler), Brother Ray kicks in with a houserockin' version of "Shake Your Tailfeather." No big deal, perhaps, but the film and soundtrack offered a vehicle for high profile comebacks for a number of R&B stars, not least of whom was Charles.

influences:

◄◄ Nat "King" Cole, Charles Brown, Count Basie, the Grand Ole Opry, Louis Jordan, Claude Jeter

►► Van Morrison, Billy Joel, Joe Cocker

Daniel Durchholz

Charm Farm

Formed 1991, in Grosse Pointe Woods, MI.

Dennis White, vocals, guitar, keyboards, drums; Steve Zuccaro, guitars; Dean "Dino" Zoyes, bass; Eric Meyer, drums; Tom Onyx, keyboards (1991–93); Ken Roberts, keyboards (1994–present); Taj Bell, backing vocals (1994–present).

Formed by ex–Inner City music directors Dennis White and Tom Onyx, Charm Farm won over hometown fans in Detroit through its blend of techno-pop and guitar-driven modern rock. The group had a minor club hit with the disco-pop song "Superstar," but its parent album didn't sell well, and the group eventually parted ways with Mercury Records. It was working on a new album during 1998.

what's available: The group's major-label debut, *Pervert* 𝄞𝄞𝄞 (Mercury, 1996, prod. Dennis White), offers hypnotic ear candy, from the sensual slow groove of the title track, the guitar-heavy "Sick," and the hooky "Superstar," which pokes fun at New York's Studio 54 scene of the '70s.

influences:

◄◄ Jesus Jones, INXS, Juan Atkins

Christina Fuoco

Chavez

Formed 1993, in New York, NY.

Matt Sweeney, vocals, guitar; Clay Tarver, guitar; James Lo, drums; David Hoskins, bass (1993–94); Scott Masciarelli, bass (1994–present).

Commercial appeal is not a phrase in the Chavez vocabulary. This band uses tightly woven washes of guitars wrapped around complex rhythms to create music that is challenging, brilliant, and never too far from dissonant. Fellow New York noisemeisters Sonic Youth would be proud. Founding Chavez members Matt Sweeney (formerly with Skunk and Wider) and Clay Tarver (axeman par excellence for the seminal Boston band, Bullet LaVolta) hooked up with drummer James Lo (formerly in Live Skull) and bassist David Hoskins to produce the first Chavez single, "Repeat the Ending." This took college radio by storm when it was first released in 1994, and intermittent live shows in the band's hometown of New York City had the musical cognoscenti gushing. Chavez's two follow-up albums, with new bassist Scott Masciarelli, created similar ripples of adoration, but commercial radio largely ignored the band. However, the members of Chavez have no pretensions of arena-rock stardom (a tongue-in-cheek video for "Unreal Is Here," from *Ride the Fader*, notwithstanding); they prefer instead to cultivate their unique brand of passionate bombast on their terms.

what to buy: *Pentagram Ring* 𝄞𝄞𝄞𝄞 (Matador, 1995, prod. Chavez) contains the anthemic single "Repeat the Ending," which started all the fuss in the first place. Ringing guitars fuse with intelligent song structure to keep listeners on their toes. To top it off, the insistent chorus is unshakeable. *Gone Glimmering* 𝄞𝄞𝄞𝄞 (Matador, 1995, prod. Bryce Goggin), the first full-length Chavez album, just gets better the louder and more often it's played. The last track, "Relaxed Fit," brings it all together, a superb follow-up to the glorious wail and cathartic chorus of "Repeat the Ending."

what to buy next: *Ride the Fader* 𝄞𝄞𝄞 (Matador, 1996, prod. John Agnello, Bryce Goggin) is the second album from Chavez, and it continues where *Glimmering* left off, spewing out waves of tension and taut, focused arrangements. Sweeney's reedy, slightly sneering vocals get you in a headlock with "Top Pocket Man" and never let go. This is powerful stuff.

worth searching for: Chavez helped produce and appeared on "Little Twelvetoes" on the compilation *Schoolhouse Rock! Rocks* (WEA/Atlantic/Lava, 1996, prod. various).

influences:

◄◄ Volcano Suns, Bullet LaVolta, Moving Targets, Rapeman, Hüsker Dü, Sonic Youth, Band of Susans, Rhys Chatham

►► Sleater-Kinney, Bardo Pond

Lisa M. Moore

Cheap Trick

Formed 1974, in Rockford, IL.

Rick Nielsen, guitar, vocals; Robin Zander, vocals, guitar; Tom Petersson, bass, vocals (1974–80, 1986–present); Pete Comita, bass (1980–81); Jon Brant, bass (1981–86); Bun E. Carlos, drums.

The new wave movement gets credit for puncturing the stuffy, humorless corporate-rock mentality that ruled the airwaves during the late '70s, and Cheap Trick fired the first salvo. While many bands had lead singers you couldn't tell apart from the roadies, Cheap Trick—pretty boys Robin Zander and Tom Petersson flanked by the nerdy Rick Nielsen, who looked like a demonic paper boy, and Bun E. Carlos, who could pass for a chain-smoking CPA—offered a goofy respite that made its merger of Beatle-esque pop and heavy metal thunder even more endearing. Japanese audiences caught on first, prompting the group to put out *Live at Budokan* overseas in 1978. Epic released the album stateside a year later, and its platinum success has made it the band's signature work. Since then, Cheap Trick has floundered from producer to producer (Todd Rundgren, George Martin, Roy Thomas Baker, Ted Templeman) in search of the magical combination that will recapture the success of its early albums. Save for the occasional killer tune ("She's Tight," "If You Want My Love," "Let Go"), they still haven't found what they're looking for.

what to buy: Aerosmith producer Jack Douglas brought a crunchy credibility to *Cheap Trick* 𝄞𝄞𝄞 (Epic, 1977, prod. Jack Douglas), which introduced the group as a metal act. But *In Color* 𝄞𝄞𝄞𝄞 (Epic, 1977, prod. Tom Werman) brings out the band's pop instincts via "Southern Girls," "So Good to See You," and "I Want You to Want Me." That album just beats out *Heaven Tonight* 𝄞𝄞𝄞 (Epic, 1978, prod. Tom Werman), whose overbearing rockers ("Stiff Competition," "Auf Wiedersehen") are overshadowed by such power-pop anthems as "Surrender" and a blistering cover of the Move's "California Man."

what to buy next: The remastered two-CD *Cheap Trick at Budokan: The Complete Concert* 🎵🎵🎵 (Epic/Legacy, 1998, prod. Bruce Dickinson) recreates the group's legendary April 28, 1978 setlist in Tokyo by combining *Live at Budokan* with nine leftover tracks released 15 years later on *Budokan II*, in chronological order. The band is in its roaring prime, and the squealing audience makes the Beatles' *Live at the Hollywood Bowl* sound like a James Taylor concert.

what to avoid: Despite the dream pairing with Beatles producer George Martin, *All Shook Up* 🎵🎵 (Epic, 1980, prod. George Martin) falls flat as the band chokes under the pressure of meeting its spiritual mentor.

the rest:
Live at Budokan 🎵🎵🎵 (Epic, 1978)
Dream Police 🎵🎵🎵 (Epic, 1979)
Found All the Parts 🎵🎵 (Epic EP, 1980)
One on One 🎵🎵 (Epic, 1982)
Next Position Please 🎵🎵🎵 (Epic, 1983)
Standing on the Edge 🎵🎵 (Epic, 1985)
The Doctor 🎵🎵 (Epic, 1986)
Lap of Luxury 🎵🎵🎵 (Epic, 1988)
Busted 🎵🎵 (Epic, 1990)
The Greatest Hits 🎵🎵🎵 (Epic, 1991)
Budokan II 🎵🎵🎵 (Epic, 1993)
Woke Up with a Monster 🎵🎵 (Warner Bros., 1994)
Sex, America, Cheap Trick 🎵🎵🎵 (four-CD box set) (Epic Legacy, 1996)
Cheap Trick 🎵🎵 (Red Ant, 1997)

worth searching for: To hype its 1997 self-titled comeback and reestablish some street cred, Cheap Trick teamed with producer Steve Albini for a one-off single on Seattle's SubPop label, "Baby Talk"/"Brontosaurus" (SubPop, 1997, prod. Steve Albini); the B side is a cover of the Move song.

solo outings:
Robin Zander:
Robin Zander 🎵🎵 (Interscope, 1993)

influences:
◀◀ The Move, the Beatles, the Who
▶▶ Enuff Z'Nuff, Material Issue, Johnny Bravo

David Okamoto

Chubby Checker

Born Ernest Evans, October 3, 1941, in Andrews, SC.

Chubby Checker is a fair-to-middling singer who got extremely lucky when his version of Hank Ballard's "The Twist" hit #1 (in both 1960 and in 1962) and spawned an unparalleled dance craze whose presence can still be felt in films such as *Pulp Fiction* and at any wedding or Bar Mitzvah reception. Unfortunately, Checker had little to say after "The Twist." Not that it mattered; the song has been a consistent meal ticket, and he even turned it into a hit *again* in 1988, this time as a duet with rappers the Fat Boys.

what to buy: *Chubby Checker's Dance Party* 🎵🎵 (K-tel, prod. various) is the most extensive compilation, with the innocent insistence of "The Twist" and its follow-up, "Let's Twist Again."

the rest:
All Time Greats 🎵🎵 (Special Music)
Mr. Twister 🎵🎵 (Charly, 1992)

influences:
◀◀ Chuck Berry, Hank Ballard, Fats Domino
▶▶ The Fat Boys, Heavy D

Allan Orski

The Cheepskates

Formed 1982, in New York, NY. Disbanded 1993.

Shane Faubert, guitar, keyboards, vocals; Tony Low, bass, guitar, vocals; David Herrera, guitar, harmonica, vocals (1982–85); Van Keith, drums (1982–85); Jeremy Lee, drums, vocals (1985–93); Larry Lozier, guitar, vocals (1986); Rich Punzi, guitar, mandolin, harmonica, vocals (1989–93).

In the rich New York garage-rock scene, which flourished briefly after punk burned itself inside out, the Cheepskates emerged as the most unfailingly melodic yet musically adventurous band of the bunch. Building upon the sturdy foundation of Shane Faubert's songwriting, the band slowly but steadily matured from its Farfisa organ-driven, bash 'n' pop beginnings to a rich and textured combo that produced several albums of rare merit—while never forgetting, as did so many of its contemporaries, to have lots of fun in the process. Although always popular in Europe, the band eventually fell victim to a lack of support in its homeland and splintered into two distinct factions: the rhythm section, Tony Low and Jeremy Lee, to form the harder-rocking Static 13; and Faubert, continuing his baroque 'n' roll experimentations on a series of critically acclaimed solo releases. Still, the Cheepskates as a whole have proven to be an undeniable influence on the power pop movements that followed in its wake.

what to buy: Recorded in less than two days for under $300, and newly available on CD in all its ragged splendor, *Run Better Run* 🎵🎵🎵 (Midnight, 1984/Music Maniac, 1997, prod. J. D. Martignon) is a rambunctious, rollicking debut in the grand tradition of the first Beach Boys, Kinks, and Ramones records. Conversely, *It Wings Above* 🎵🎵🎵🎵 (Music Maniac, 1988, prod. Lane

Hollend) shows the band at the very peak of its creative powers, with songwriting and vocal work particularly pure and shimmering throughout.

what to buy next: Live albums really are supposed to sound just like *Waiting for Unta* ♫♫♫ (Music Maniac, 1989, prod. Lane Hollend), which captures the 'Skates during a typically ribald European jaunt through rooms full of hardcore fans. The version of Peggy Lee's "Fever" herein only hints at the crazed sense of genius behind *Songs, Volume One: Perry Como* ♫♫♫ (Music Maniac, 1989, prod. the Cheepskates) and *Songs, Volume Two: The Residents* ♫♫♫ (Music Maniac, 1992, prod. the Cheepskates), surprisingly reverent tributes to two of Faubert's most beloved musical icons.

the rest:
Second and Last ♫♫♫ (Midnight, 1986)
Remember ♫♫♫ (Music Maniac, 1987)
Confessional ♫♫♫♫ (Music Maniac, 1990)

solo outings:
Shane Faubert:
Kalkara ♫♫♫♫ (Music Maniac, 1990)
San Blass ♫♫♫♫♫ (Music Maniac, 1993)
Squirrelboy Blue ♫♫♫♫ (Music Maniac, 1997)

David Herrera:
A Handout from a Cheepskate ♫♫♫ (Midnight, 1989)

Static 13:
eye won't fool i ♫♫ (Call Back in an Hour, 1997)

influences:
◄◄ The Everly Brothers, Brian Wilson, Phillip K. Dick, Neil Young, the Millennium

►► Died Pretty, R.E.M., Bob Mould, Bill Lloyd, Michael Mazzarella

Gary Pig Gold

The Chemical Brothers

Formed 1994, in Manchester, England.

Tom Rowlands, programming; Ed Simons, programming.

Tom Rowlands and Ed Simons met while studying history at Manchester University during the early '90s and bonded over their passion for the electronic-flavored dance music that flowed across the Atlantic to nourish the U.K. rave scene: Chicago house, Detroit techno, Bronx hip-hop. The duo initially called themselves the Dust Brothers, in homage to the West Coast hip-hop producers, and released a handful of big-beat independent records in England, which won them remix work for high-profile artists such as the Prodigy, Manic Street Preachers, and Charlatans. They have since become one of the corner-

stone acts of the commercial genre known as "electronica," in part because they're not electronic purists: They have a fondness for heavy beats and sampled guitars, and they've collaborated frequently with rock performers.

what to buy: Techno snobs consider it a sellout, but *Dig Your Own Hole* ♫♫♫♫ (Astralwerks, 1997, prod. Chemical Brothers) cut through the morass of sample-heavy digital discs to reach American audiences because it rocked as hard as any guitar band this side of Rage Against the Machine. It featured collaborations with Oasis's Noel Gallagher ("Setting Sun") and psychedelic folkie Beth Orton ("Where Do I Begin?") even as it paid tribute to old-school hip-hop with samples of Schooly D and Keith Murray, and pumped out the hardest break beats since the heyday of Public Enemy's Bomb Squad.

what to buy next: The Chems' stateside debut, *Exit Planet Dust* ♫♫♫ (Astralwerks, 1995, prod. Chemical Brothers), is a blueprint for what followed with its huge beats and monster-movie sampling.

the rest:
Loops of Fury ♫♫♫ (Astralwerks, 1996)
Brothers Gonna Work It Out (remix album) N/A (Freestyle Dust/Astralwerks, 1998)

influences:
◄◄ Public Enemy, Schooly D, the Dust Brothers, Ultramagnetic MC's

►► Propellerheads, Oasis

Greg Kot

Cher

See: Sonny & Cher

Neneh Cherry

Born Neneh Mariann Karlsson, March 10, 1964, in Stockholm, Sweden.

"You never seen a girl like this before/Because she's so sassy and completely secure" rapper Guru comments in the lead track of Neneh Cherry's sophomore album, perhaps as accurate and concise a summation of the singer/rapper's appeal as is possible. The daughter of Swedish artist Moki Cherry and West African percussionist Amadu Jah, Neneh is also the stepdaughter of avant-garde jazz trumpeter Don Cherry, and all of their work seems to have made an impact on her innovative, rhythmic, and jazz-inflected hip-hop/pop. Cherry performed with the ska band the Nails and the punk act the Slits before recording several albums as a percussionist with the irreverent jazz-fusion outfit Rip Rig + Panic, which in turn evolved into Float Up C.P. (The albums of both the latter two acts are out of print.) Cherry has enjoyed some popularity, but compared to the success of many lesser talents, she remains a tragically over-looked artist. Her mix of sung/spoken vocals presaged so-called "alternative" rap, and her sampledelic grooves paved the way for trip-hop. Her influence has been somewhat acknowledged by artists such as Tricky, with whom she's recorded, but mostly she is a queen without a kingdom.

what to buy: Cherry's debut, *Raw Like Sushi* 🎜🎜🎜 (Virgin, 1989, executive prod. Cameron "Booga Bear" McVey), leads off with the irrepressible and street-smart "Buffalo Stance," a single that blazed several hip-hop trials by incorporating jazz riffs, a sung chorus, and a strong, self-assured female perspective. The rest of the album doesn't quite rise to that standard, but it has many fine moments, including the conscious "Inna City Momma" and "The Next Generation" as well as the breezy follow-up single "Kisses on the Wind," and the unabashedly sensualist "Outré Risqué Locomotive."

the rest:
Homebrew 🎜🎜🎜 (Virgin, 1992)

worth searching for: For unknown reasons, Cherry's third album, *Man* (Circa/Virgin, 1996), has never been released in the U.S. It contains her version of Marvin Gaye's "Trouble Man" and "7 Seconds," a duet with Youssou N'Dour.

influences:
◀◀ Don Cherry, the Sex Pistols, Madonna
▶▶ Fugees, Tricky, Björk

Daniel Durchholz

Cherry Poppin' Daddies

Formed 1988, in Eugene, OR.

Steve Perry, vocals, guitar; Jason Moss, guitar; Dana Heitman, trumpet, trombone; Dan Schmid, bass; Sean Flannery, saxophone; Ian Early, saxophone; Dustin Lanker, keyboards; Tim Donahue, drums.

Call them swing, call them ska, call them punk rock. The Cherry Poppin' Daddies are all of the above. Coming out of Eugene, Oregon, at the tail end of the '80s, the band has made a living playing an amalgamation of all three genres. Its first album, 1990's *Ferociously Stoned*, was very swing oriented, but in subsequent albums, the group let its ska and punk influences hang out. In 1997, the Daddies signed with Universal's Mojo label, releasing a compilation album, *Zoot Suit Riot*, which spawned their first radio-friendly single of the same name.

what to buy: *Zoot Suit Riot* 🎜🎜🎜 (Mojo/Universal, 1997, prod. Steve Perry) may be a best-of, but it gives listeners a great impression of the Daddies's blistering swing. The album also features four new songs, including the title track, which ended up being their first radio hit and forever cemented them under the

label of swing, a marketing-friendly catagorization the band has always tried to avoid.

what to buy next: *Ferociously Stoned* 🎜🎜🎜 (Sub Par, 1990, prod. Steve Perry) is the band's first foray into swing and perhaps its most interesting. While many of the songs appear on *Zoot Suit Riot*, the rest of them are a little more raw and experimental, the results of a young band just trying to have fun.

the rest:
Rapid City Motor Car 🎜🎜🎜 (Sub Par, 1994)
Kids on the Street 🎜🎜🎜 (Caroline, 1996)

influences:
◀◀ The Specials, Louis Prima, Count Basie
▶▶ Big Bad Voodoo Daddy

Anders Wright

Vic Chesnutt

Born November 12, 1964, in Jacksonville, FL.

With his raw, acoustic music and heart-tugging songs, Athens, Georgia, resident Vic Chesnutt has become a cult figure. Half court jester and half tragic hero, the wheelchair-bound Chesnutt (he was paralyzed in a 1983 drunk driving accident) is a brilliant and eccentric singer-songwriter who combines beautiful melodies and lyrics that lay truths uncomfortably bare. His eloquent songs tell stories about fellow eccentrics and document his drunken screwups and hopes for transcendence. It was R.E.M.'s Michael Stipe who prodded Chesnutt into recording, dragging him out of Athens' 40 Watt Club and into the studio for his 1988 debut album. In 1996, Chesnutt's songs were covered by various admirers, including Madonna and the Smashing Pumpkins, on a tribute album. The same year also brought his major label debut and an appearance in the film *Sling Blade*.

what to buy: The stripped-down yet rich sound of *West of Rome* 🎜🎜🎜🎜 (Texas Hotel, 1992, prod. Michael Stipe) is Chesnutt at his best—sad, funny, and poignant. Chesnutt's stark, raw debut, *Little* 🎜🎜🎜🎜 (Texas Hotel, 1990, prod. Michael Stipe), proves him to be a capable interpreter of his own profound little songs.

what to buy next: *About to Choke* 🎜🎜🎜 (Capitol, 1996, prod. John Keane, Vic Chesnutt, John deVries, Mark LaFaice), Chesnutt's major label debut, is not his masterpiece, but it should have garnered him more attention than it did. *Drunk* 🎜🎜🎜 (Texas Hotel, 1994, prod. Vic Chesnutt) was the result of a few drunken weekend recording sessions. Like many inebriated experiences, it's a mix of highlights (the haunting "Supernatural") and the embarrassing (the repetitive title track).

what to avoid: Chesnutt's collaboration with the group Widespread Panic on *Nine High a Pallet* 🎵🎵🎵 (Capricorn, 1995, prod. Scott Stuckey) ends up sounding like Vic Lite.

the rest:

Is the Actor Happy? 🎵🎵🎵🎵 (Texas Hotel, 1995)

worth searching for: Chesnutt does a low-key tune with friend Michael Stipe on the well put-together soundtrack *The End of Violence* (Outpost, 1997, prod. various). The benefit album *Sweet Relief II: Gravity of the Situation, The Songs of Vic Chesnutt* (Columbia, 1996, prod. various) is filled with intriguing renditions of Chesnutt's works.

influences:

◀◀ Bob Dylan, Leonard Cohen

▶▶ Victoria Williams, Joe Henry, Gillian Welch

Jill Hamilton

Chicago
/Peter Cetera

Formed 1967, in Chicago, IL.

Terry Kath, guitar, vocals (1967–78); Peter Cetera, bass, vocals (1967–84); Robert Lamm, piano, vocals; Walter Parazaider, reeds; Danny Seraphine, drums (1967–89); James Pankow, trombone; Lee Loughnane, trumpet; Lauder De Oliveira, percussion (1974–80); Donnie Dacus, guitar, vocals (1978–79); Chris Pinnick, guitar (1979–81); Bill Champlin, vocals, guitar, keyboards (1981–present); Jason Scheff, bass, vocals (1984–present; DaWayne Bailey, guitar (1988–present); Tris Imboden, drums (1990–present); Keith Howland, guitar (1995–present).

Rock bands with horn sections were not commonplace when Chicago came along, though Blood, Sweat & Tears and the Electric Flag had already begun using them. Christened first the Big Thing and then Chicago Transit Authority, Chicago played a more down-the-middle brand of brass-fueled rock than its predecessors, using the horns for additional rhythmic pump as well as for solos and melodic accents. Its lyrics were counterculture friendly, but the tunes were as palatable to an adult audience as they were to the kids, giving Chicago a wide commercial appeal and a string of hit singles throughout the '70s—as well as remarkably good album sales considering its first three albums (all with numbered titles) were double-record sets and the fourth was a four-record live set. But Terry Kath died after accidentally shooting himself in the head in 1978, and the group was never quite the same after that. Chicago's commercial success has come in fits and starts, but much of its music during the past decade and a half has been adult-contemporary pabulum, a far cry from the bolder sonic adventures of its earlier releases.

what to buy: *Chicago IX: Chicago's Greatest Hits* 🎵🎵🎵🎵 (Columbia, 1975/Chicago Records, 1995, prod. James William Guercio) is the essential singles collection, a testament to the commercial force Chicago was during the late '60s and early 70s. *Chicago II* 🎵🎵🎵🎵 (Columbia, 1970/Chicago Records, 1995, prod. James William Guercio) provides the best exhibition of the group's early ambitions via Kath's epic guitar solo in "25 or 6 to 4" and the pop suite "Ballet for a Girl in Buchannon."

what to buy next: *Chicago V* 🎵🎵🎵 (Columbia, 1972/Chicago Records, 1995, prod. James William Guercio) is a more modest affair but still has plenty of melodic clout with "Saturday in the Park" and the charmingly dated "Dialogue, Parts I and II." The box set *Group Portrait* 🎵🎵🎵 (Columbia/Legacy, 1991, prod. various) is comprehensive but gets a little weak on the later discs. *Live in Japan* 🎵🎵🎵 (Chicago Records, 1981, prod. James William Guercio) is a solid live document of the group at peak strength, much better than the bloated *Chicago at Carnegie Hall* recording from the '70s.

what to avoid: There's lots, really, that could be listed here, but *Night & Day (Big Band)* **woof!** (Giant, 1995, prod. Bruce Fairbairn) is a wretched and ill-conceived collection of swing era covers, with little of the grace or subtlety that marked the original recordings.

the rest:

Chicago Transit Authority 🎵🎵🎵 (Columbia, 1969/Chicago Records, 1995)

Chicago III 🎵🎵🎵 (Columbia, 1971/Chicago Records, 1995)

Chicago at Carnegie Hall 🎵🎵🎵 (Columbia, 1971/Chicago Records, 1995)

Chicago VI 🎵🎵🎵 (Columbia, 1973/Chicago Records, 1995)

Chicago VII 🎵🎵🎵 (Columbia, 1974)

Chicago VIII 🎵🎵 (Columbia, 1975)

Chicago X 🎵🎵🎵 (Columbia, 1976/Chicago Records, 1995)

Chicago XI 🎵🎵 (Columbia, 1977/Chicago Records, 1995)

Hot Streets 🎵 (Columbia, 1978/Chicago Records, 1995)

Chicago 13 **woof!** (Columbia, 1979/Chicago Records, 1995)

Chicago XIV 🎵 (Columbia, 1980/Chicago Records, 1995)

Greatest Hits, Vol. II 🎵🎵🎵 (Columbia, 1981/Chicago Records, 1995)

Chicago 16 🎵🎵 (Full Moon/Warner Bros., 1982)

If You Leave Me Now 🎵🎵 (Columbia, 1983)

Chicago 17 🎵 (Full Moon/Warner Bros., 1984)

Chicago 18 🎵 (Full Moon/Warner Bros., 1986)

Chicago 19 🎵 (Full Moon/Warner Bros., 1988)

Greatest Hits 1982–1989 🎵🎵 (Full Moon/Warner Bros., 1989)

Twenty 1 **woof!** (Full Moon/Warner Bros., 1991)

Chicago Presents the Innovative Guitar of Terry Kath 🎵🎵🎵 (Chicago Records, 1996)

The Heart of Chicago 1967–1997 🎵🎵🎵 (Reprise, 1997)

The Heart of Chicago 1967–1998, Volume II 🎵🎵🎵 (Reprise, 1998)

worth searching for: The slightly bizarre *Chicago/Blood, Sweat & Tears Live Toronto '69/Live Frankfurt 80* (K-Tel, 1986) is, if nothing else, a brief look at Chicago in its fledgling state.

solo outings:

Peter Cetera:

Peter Cetera ⅃⅃ (Full Moon/Warner Bros., 1981)

Solitude/Solitaire ⅃⅃⅃ (Warner Bros., 1986)

One More Story ⅃ (Warner Bros., 1988)

World Falling Down ⅃⅃ (Warner Bros., 1992) (River North, 1995)

influences:

◄◄ Maynard Ferguson, Herb Alpert & the Tijuana Brass, Blood, Sweat & Tears, the Electric Flag

►► Grass Roots, American Breed, Uptown Horns, UB40

Gary Graff

The Chiffons

Formed 1960, in the Bronx, NY. Disbanded 1995.

Patricia Bennett, vocals; Barbara Lee, vocals; Judy Craig, vocals (1960–69); Sylvia Peterson, vocals (1962–95).

With infectious chants of "doo-lang, doo-lang" and a sugary sweet demeanor, the Chiffons epitomized all the most innocent qualities of the girl-group sound, yet strong material and never less-than-assured performances helped them create several absolute classics that remain among the best of their genre. Patricia Bennett, Barbara Lee, and Judy Craig had already met and begun singing together in high school when a local writer named Ronnie Mack hired them in 1960 to record simple demo tapes of his songs. Impressed with their abilities, he cut a version of the Shirelles' "Tonight's the Night" with the trio and sold it to the small Big Deal label shortly thereafter, resulting in a minor national hit. The following year, Mack began working with the Tokens, hot off their chart-topper, "The Lion Sleeps Tonight"; together they helped record Mack's song "He's So Fine" with the Chiffons, which hit #1 in March of 1963. The follow-up, "One Fine Day," was originally written for the Tokens by Gerry Goffin and Carole King; their demo recording, featuring Little Eva of "Locomotion" fame on lead vocals and King's own distinctive piano accompaniment, was given to the Chiffons instead, who recorded their vocals over Eva's and sent it to #5 by July. That same year, two other Chiffons/Tokens collaborations were released under the pseudonym the Four Pennies, but the next Chiffons release—their third of 1963 (and the third to use the word "fine" in its title)—stalled at a disappointing #40. Then the British Invasion banished practically every girl group not on Motown from the charts, and despite a slot opening for the Rolling Stones on their first-ever American tour, the Chiffons failed to place another record in the Top 10 until "Sweet Talkin' Guy" in 1966. It was their last U.S. best-seller, yet even

after the departure of lead vocalist Craig in 1969 and bitter legal disputes with the Tokens' Bright Tunes company, the group continued touring and occasionally recording (including a 1976 release of George Harrison's "My Sweet Lord," a song which Harrison had just been found guilty of "subconsciously plagiarizing" from "He's So Fine"). The Chiffons, in one form or another, persevered well into the 1990s, until Lee's death from a heart attack at the age of 48.

what's available: The sorrowfully skimpy *Chiffons' Greatest Hits* ⅃⅃⅃ (Capitol/The Right Stuff, 1996, compilation prod. Tom Cartwright) is the easiest to find, and although it contains all of their most popular recordings, at a mere 10 tracks it's really too brief to offer the group the overview it deserves. *One Fine Day* ⅃⅃⅃ (Laurie, 1963/Remember Records, 1996), a reissue of the Chiffons' third album, provides a picture-perfect glance at pre-Beatle pop and R&B in its original form.

worth searching for: Two British imports, *The Fabulous Chiffons* (Ace, 1992, prod. various) and *Greatest Recordings* (Ace, 1994, prod. various), are fairly readily available, and the latter contains many B-sides and album tracks that show there was much more than mere "doo-lang"-ing going on within the ranks.

influences:

◄◄ The Chantels, the Shirelles, Phil Spector

►► The Angels, the Go-Go's, George Harrison

Gary Pig Gold

Toni Childs

Born 1958, in Orange, California.

Singer-songwriter Toni Childs grew up in small towns all over the U.S.; her parents, missionaries for the Assemblies of God, moved the family on a regular basis, preaching their beliefs to as many as possible—and not letting much popular culture into the household. It's no wonder she became a bit rebellious. After spending three months in prison on a drug charge, Childs first moved to London, then to Los Angeles where she met David Ricketts of David + David. *Union* chronicles their broken romance, with songs that examine the different aspects of love and relationships. After a slight letdown on the follow-up, *House of Hope*, Childs offered *The Woman's Boat*, a concept album that takes the listener through a spiritual journey of life, from a woman's point of view, all done in Childs's unique style of rock and world music. The album features guest appearances by Peter Gabriel, Karl Wallinger (World Party), Robert Fripp, and Nusrat Fateh Ali Khan.

what to buy: Childs's seamless fusion of blues, folk, pop, and world music on *Union* ⅃⅃⅃⅃ (A&M, 1988, prod. David Tickle,

David Ricketts) is an amazing achievement, featuring memorable tunes such as "Don't Walk Away," "Hush," and "Let the Rain Come Down."

the rest:
House of Hope 𝄞𝄞𝄞 (A&M, 1991)
The Woman's Boat 𝄞𝄞𝄞𝄞 (DGC, 1994)

influences:
◀◀ Peter Gabriel, Joni Mitchell, David + David

Joshua Zarov

The Chills
Formed 1981, in Dunedin, New Zealand. Disbanded 1992.

Martin Phillips, guitar, vocals; Justin Harwood, bass; Andrew Todd, keyboards; Caroline Easther, drums (1987–90); Jimmy Stephenson, drums (1990–92).

Like its Dunedin compatriots—the Verlaines and the Clean—the Chills made pretty, hook-laden pop awash with chiming guitars and interwoven harmonies. In character with its frigid name, the group embraced topics of death and broken hearts, setting them in rain and frost on New Zealand's remote Otago Peninsula and dressing them up with cool, pastel production. But while the themes tended toward hurt and loss, Martin Phillips kept his lyrics a good 12 steps away from cloying sentiment and pathos, writing straightforward lyrics devoid of pretension. Although *Submarine Bells* (the Chills's first American release) garnered praise from critics and play on college radio, it failed to solidify an American audience. The group's next effort, *Soft Bomb*, bombed softly, and in 1993, Phillips iced the Chills.

what to buy: *Kaleidoscope World* 𝄞𝄞𝄞𝄞 (Homestead, 1986, prod. various) is a worthy and valued collection of singles the group cut for Flying Nun, New Zealand's influential independent record label; it also includes songs from the group's EP *Lost* 𝄞𝄞𝄞 (Homestead, 1988), including "Pink Frost," a chilling song about death and one of the band's best pieces of music. On *Submarine Bells* 𝄞𝄞𝄞𝄞 (Slash/Warner Bros., 1990, prod. Gary Smith), the Chills for once establish a full and cohesive sound over the expanse of an entire album, with individual gems such as "Heavenly Pop Hit," the title track, and the punky change-of-pace tracks "The Oncoming Day" and "Familiarity Breeds Contempt."

what to buy next: *Brave Words* 𝄞𝄞𝄞 (Homestead, 1987, prod. Mayo Thompson) is the group's first real album, with 13 insidious little pop songs that work their way slowly through your skin.

what to avoid: With its unfortunately prescient title, *Soft Bomb* 𝄞𝄞𝄞 (Warner Bros., 1992, prod. Gavin MacKillop) found the Chills abandoning its diamond-edged pop for something lighter

and quieter. But certainly nothing among these 17 tracks suggests that the Chills should have called it a day.

influences:
◀◀ Split Enz, Cocteau Twins, the Easybeats
▶▶ The Sundays, the Posies, the Cranberries

Christopher Scapelliti

Alex Chilton /The Box Tops
Born December 28, 1950, in Memphis, TN.

With the possible exception of Rod Stewart, no artist has betrayed his talent so completely as Alex Chilton. After the quiet demise of the commercially ignored Big Star, he set out on a course of perverse self-destruction, with a flagrant disregard for record making. The bittersweet pop gems he previously penned mutated into trashy toss-offs, and he reverted to touring sets filled with standards and oldies. As legions began to discover the brilliance of Big Star, they were often greeted with insolent indifference and sporadic, off-the-cuff record releases. One needs only to hear seconds of the Box Tops material to catch the full sweep of his demise. A gruff-voiced, teenage Chilton belting out blue-eyed soul took to the charts a number of times in the band's brief career. Bristling under the heavy production of Dan Penn and Chips Moman, Chilton soon departed for more autonomous pastures, his path perhaps already set.

what to buy: The most recent compilation, *The Best of the Box Tops* 𝄞𝄞𝄞𝄞 (Arista, 1996, prod. various) is the most well-rounded and has the best liner notes. It may have been more Penn and Moman's show, but Chilton's over-the-top emotion is gripping. The classics he helped create—"The Letter," "Cry Like a Baby," and "Soul Deep"—are all here, standing among the best of '60s white soul. Chilton's *19 Years: A Collection* 𝄞𝄞𝄞 (Rhino, 1991, prod. various) presents a tellingly scattershot picture of his slipshod solo career. Some late period Big Star material (which was essentially a solo project by then) is included, and occasionally his exuberance pops up, like sparks from a burning building.

what to buy next: *High Priest/Black List* 𝄞𝄞𝄞 (Razor & Tie, 1994, prod. Alex Chilton) is a two-fer reissue of his 1987 comeback (of sorts) and the 1990 follow-up. The set finds Chilton rocking in good humor all over the map from his Memphis soul beginnings to garage thumpers. Unexpected takes of "Volare" and Charlie Rich's "Lonely Weekends" are pleasant surprises.

what to avoid: *Like Flies on Sherbet* 𝄞 (Aura, 1979, prod. Jim Dickinson) is the best showcase of Chilton's disintegration, a drunken spree that tramples potentially good material.

the rest:

Bach's Bottom 🎵🎵🎵 (Razor & Tie, 1981)

The Ultimate Box Tops 🎵🎵🎵 (Warner Special Products, 1987)

Feudalist Tarts/No Sex 🎵🎵 (Razor & Tie, 1994)

Cliché 🎵🎵🎵🎵 (Ardent, 1994)

A Man Called Destruction 🎵🎵 (Ardent, 1995)

1971 🎵🎵🎵 (Ardent, 1996)

worth searching for: *Alex Chilton's Lost Decade*, a sprawling French fan club release that features obscurites and tracks Chilton produced for other singers.

influences:

◀◀ Otis Redding, the Beatles, the Who, Dan Penn

▶▶ The Replacements, R.E.M., the dB's, the Posies

Allan Orski

China Crisis

Formed 1979, in Liverpool, England.

Garry Daly, vocals, keyboards; Eddie Lundon, guitar, vocals; Gary "Gazza" Johnson, bass, programming; Kevin Wilkinson, drums, percussion.

Quiet philosophers with a yen for lightly funky dance-pop, China Crisis found it difficult to compete commercially with its early '80s Brit-pop brethren. As a result, its earlier semi-hits—e.g., 1983's "Working with Fire and Steel," from the album of the same name—tended towards annoying over-the-top New Romanticism. But with 1985's *Flaunt the Imperfection*, it achieved a subtler, more muted sound, aided immeasurably by the then-former Steely Dan member Walter Becker. With the follow-up, *What Price Paradise*, the group opted for a more straightforward approach that removed most of what little personality it once had to offer. Alas, those albums have all fallen out of print, leaving only an import to account for the band's legacy.

worth searching for: Those listeners beguiled by *Imperfection* may want to search for the U.K.-only *The China Crisis Collection* (Virgin, 1990, prod. various).

influences:

◀◀ Steely Dan, Level 42, Toto

Bob Remstein

The Chipmunks
/Alvin & the Chipmunks

Formed 1958, in Hollywood, CA, by David Seville (born Ross Bagdasarian, 1919, in Fresno, CA; died 1972, in Beverly Hills, CA).

Oddly enough, this is where many adults got their initiation to contemporary music. The Chipmunks are an anonymous vocal trio whose Munchkin-like voices (the result of recording at half speed and playing back at full speed) graced a slew of hit records from 1958 to the present. The group is the handiwork of Ross Bagdasarian, a composer, author, actor, and cousin of playwright William Saroyan who, under the pseudonym David Seville, wrote a number of novelty records during the early '50s, including Rosemary Clooney's 1951 hit "Come On-A My House." By and large a children's sing-along act, the Chipmunks—individually named Alvin, Simon, and Theodore—jumped on the Beatlemania bandwagon in 1964 with *The Chipmunks Sing the Beatles' Hits*. More recently, Bagdasarian's son revived the group for a million-selling series of albums covering punk and country & western classics. The hits just keep on coming.

what to buy: *Sing-Alongs* 🎵🎵🎵🎵 (Chipmunk Records, 1993, prod. various) is a tempting collection of classic children's songs. *Here's Looking at Me* 🎵🎵🎵 (Sony Wonder, 1994, prod. various) is a 35-year retrospective that includes '80s rock ("Uptown Girl," "Girls Just Wanna Have Fun"), country & western ("On the Road Again"), and the song that started it all, Bagdasarian's 1958 hit "Witch Doctor."

what to buy next: What holiday season would be complete without *A Very Merry Chipmunk* 🎵🎵🎵 (Sony Wonder, 1994, prod. Ross Bagdasarian, Janice Karman, Steve Lindsey), on which the trio's cute performances even cover the adult-contemporary blather of Celine Dion, Patty Loveless, and Kenny G? The versatile rodents' country side is showcased best on *Urban Chipmunk* 🎵🎵🎵 (Epic, 1981, prod. Ross Bagdasarian), which makes good fun of the early '80s cowboy craze with redneck tunes such as "The Gambler" and "On the Road Again."

what to avoid: And break all the kids' hearts? Forget it!

the rest:

Christmas with the Chipmunks 🎵🎵 (EMI America, 1962)

Christmas with the Chipmunks, Vol. 2 🎵🎵 (EMI America, 1963)

A Chipmunk Christmas 🎵🎵🎵 (Sony Kids, 1981)

Chipmunks in Low Places 🎵🎵🎵 (Sony Kids, 1992)

worth searching for: *The Chipmunks Sing the Beatles' Hits* (Liberty, 1964, prod. Ross Bagdasarian) is such a novel treat that it's worth searching flea markets and garage sales to find a copy. If you thought the Beatles' harmonies were tight, wait till you hear these little varmints put their voices together on "Love Me Do" and "Please Please Me."

influences:

◀◀ *The Wizard of Oz* and all of your favorite singers, from every generation

▶▶ Geddy Lee (Rush)

Christopher "Il Rodento" Scapelliti

Chixdiggit!

Formed 1990, in Calgary, Alberta, Canada.

K.J. Jansen, vocals, guitar; Mark O'Flaherty, guitar, vocals; Mike Eggermont, bass, vocals; Jason Hirsch, drums (1990–95); Dave Alcock, drums (1995–present).

If the Mr. T Experience and the Ramones are *Saturday Night Live*—pioneering, highly original ensembles that underwent too many lineup changes and overstayed their welcome—then Chixdiggit! is *Kids in the Hall*—a group of young, upstart Canadian imitators that borrow heavily from the originals but successfully recapture their long-lost verve and irreverence. Though usually lumped in with the indie rock scene due to its frequent 21-and-over shows and affiliation with Sub Pop, Chixdiggit! is still very much a straight-up pop-punk band, setting itself apart from the pack with energetic live shows and goofy lyrics that are actually funny. Perhaps not surprisingly, Chixdiggit! actually began as a joke—frontman K.J. Jansen and pals sold fake band t-shirts that said "Chixdiggit!" as a prank on local scenesters before actually starting a group of the same name.

what to buy: *Chixdiggit!* ✍✍✍ (Sub Pop, 1996, prod. Brent Cooper) is the best work so far by this humorous Canadian punk quartet. With song titles such as "Henry Rollins Is No Fun," how can you go wrong? Production by Brent Cooper of Huevos Rancheros gives the album a vaguely garagey feel.

what to buy next: *Born on the First of July* ✍✍ (Honest Don's, 1998, prod. Ryan Greene) is Chixdiggit!'s first release on Honest Don's, a subsidiary label of Fat Wreck Chords. Like all Fat Wreck Chords debuts, it features more conservative songwriting and production than the group's earlier work. Still, not a bad sophomore effort.

influences:

◀◀ The Ramones, Mr. T Experience, Descendents, Fastbacks, the Goo Goo Dolls

Seth Hindin

The Chocolate Watch Band

Formed 1965, in Los Altos, CA. Disbanded 1968.

Dave Aguilar, vocals (1965–66); Chris Flinders, vocals (1967); Danny Phay, vocals (1968); Mark Loomis, lead guitar (1965–66, 1968); Tim Abbot, lead guitar (1967); Phil Scoma, lead guitar (1968); Sean Tolby, guitar; Bill Flores, bass; Gary Andrijasevich, drums (1965–66, 1968); Mark Whittaker, drums (1967).

The quintessential '60s psychedelic group, the Chocolate Watch Band was not that genre's best-known band (that would be the Standells), but its legacy has survived longer and stronger than most. Sounding like a punkier version of the Rolling Stones, the Watch Band combined English-style R&B with quasi-mysticism, rendering it in a blaze of fuzz guitar, sitar, and hallucinogenic lyrics. While most of the group's releases were cover versions, its excellent ensemble musicianship and distinctively upstart sound earned it a spot in the 1966 cult film *Riot on Sunset Strip* and a contract with Tower Records that same year. The group was already breaking up by the time it released its full-length debut, *No Way Out*.

what to buy: Perhaps the finest major-label example of garage-punk, *No Way Out* ✍✍✍✍ (Sundazed Records, 1967, prod. Ed Cobb) is a trippy little time capsule album that dips deeply into the underbelly of the American dream on such tracks as "Dark Side of the Mushroom," "Are You Gonna Be There (At the Love-In)," and the now-classic "Let's Talk about Girls."

what to buy next: Producer/manager Cobb reassembled Flores, Tolby, Andrijasevich, Loomis (later replaced by Scoma), and the group's original vocalist, Danny Phay, for *The Inner Mystique* ✍✍✍ (Sundazed Records, 1968, prod. Ed Cobb). While not as focused as *No Way Out*, it still satisfies with a raucous collection of cover tunes (the Kinks' "I'm Not Like Everybody Else," Dylan's "It's All Over Now, Baby Blue," and the Standell's "Medication") and hip-to-the-bone acid-trip noodling, most successfully on the neat little gem, "In the Past." Cobb also had one last shot at milking money from the group's name with *One Step Beyond* ✍✍✍ (Sundazed Records, 1969, prod. Ed Cobb) which, despite some bottom-of-the-barrel tunes, is rescued by Aguilar's punchy "Don't Need Your Lovin'," killer bonus tracks ("Sitting There Standing"), and comprehensive liner notes that put a tidy close to the Watch Band trilogy.

influences:

◀◀ The Rolling Stones, the Thirteenth Floor Elevators

▶▶ The Electric Prunes, the Standells, the Dukes of Stratosphear

Christopher Scapelliti

The Choir

Formed as the Mods, 1964, in Mentor, OH. Disbanded 1970.

Dann Klawon, drums, guitar, harmonica, bass (1964–67, 1968, 1969); Dave Smalley, guitar, vocals (1964–68); Dan Heckel, guitar (1964); Tom Boles, vocals (1964); Wally Bryson, guitar (1965–68); Dave Burke, bass (1965–67); Dave Smalley, guitar, vocals (1965–68); Jim Bonfanti, drums, vocals, tambourine (1965–70); Jim "Snake" Skeen, bass (1967–68); Kenny Margolis, keyboards (1967–70); Jim Anderson, guitar (1968); Phil Giallombardo, organ (1968–70); Randy Klawon, guitar (1968); Denny Carleton, bass (1968); Rick Caon, guitar (1969–70); Bob McBride, bass (1969–70).

The roots of power pop started growing right here. The Choir is best remembered as an embryonic version of the Raspberries; its

1967 lineup included Wally Bryson, Dave Smalley, and Jim Bonfanti, the trio that would, with the addition of Eric Carmen, eventually comprise the 'Berries. Carmen himself is even said to have made an unsuccessful attempt to join the Choir in 1967. The group scored a #68 near-hit with "It's Cold Outside," but otherwise never really broke outside of Cleveland. *That* task would be left up to the Choir's successors, who did indeed go all the way.

what to buy: *Choir Practice* ♫♫♫♫ (Sundazed, 1994, prod. Bob Irwin, Jeff Jarema) is an essential pure pop primer, opening with the heart-stopping 1-2-3 punch of "I'd Rather You Leave Me," "It's Cold Outside," and the gorgeous, Beach Boys–influenced "When You Were with Me" (heard here in a previously-unissued alternate version). Some of the rest is uneven, and the sorry state of some of the source material means that sound quality on some tracks is considerably less than pristine. It doesn't matter; many of the songs are simply wonderful, and they're worth hearing in whatever ragged form they can be preserved.

worth searching for: Three Choir tracks not included on *Choir Practice* appear on the sampler album *My Rainbow Life—Psychedelic Microdots, Vol. 3* (Sundazed, 1992, compilation prod. Bob Irwin). This sampler also includes the single version of "When You Were with Me" (replete with orchestral backing) and, of course, "It's Cold Outside."

influences:

◀◀ The Beatles, the Who, the Beach Boys, the Kinks, the Small Faces, the Byrds, the Zombles

▶▶ The Raspberries, Stiv Bators, the Flashcubes, Pezband, Off Broadway usa, Blue Ash, Candy

see also: *The Raspberries*

Carl Cafarelli

Chopper

Formed c. 1989, in Milford, CT. Disbanded 1997.

Steven Deal, vocals, guitar; Robert Dietrich, vocals, guitar.

Although a very fine pop act, Chopper never really seemed to receive its just due even among pop fans. Its debut album was released only in Australia, with a belated American release five years later. Its 1993 American debut contained some perfectly swell bubblepop moments but was mercilessly overshadowed by the release that same year of the first *Yellow Pills* collection *and* Chris von Sneidern's landmark debut. Chopper's underrated final album was largely ignored by the pop cognoscenti, and the group soon quietly ceased to exist. Following Chopper's demise, Steven Deal upped the adrenalin level a notch to form the Absolute Zeros with Chopper associate Nick Appleby; one hopes that group will achieve the notoriety that eluded Chopper.

what to buy: *Slogans and Jingles* ♫♫♫ (Big Deal, 1993, prod. Steven Deal, Robert Dietrich), Chopper's second album and first American release, is driven primarily by Robert Dietrich's vibrant bubblepop tunes such as "Tripping on You," "Swirling Girl," and the simply gorgeous "If You Knew Susie." Deal's songs are generally lower-key affairs, but his "Edie (Will You Marry Me?)" is catchy as can be, and "But It Doesn't Make a Difference" offers a luxurious pop texture. A cover of the Records' fab "The Same Mistakes" pays tribute to roots and adds a perfectly appropriate complement to the group's originals.

what to buy next: Originally released in Australia in 1991, the debut album *Chopper* ♫♫♫ (Big Deal, 1996, prod. Chopper) is slightly punkier than its successor but still filled to the brim with buoyant hooks and irresistible pop sparkle.

the rest:
Supersmile EP ♫♫♫ (Big Deal, 1994)
Madhouse on Castle Street ♫♫♫ (Big Deal, 1995)

solo outings:
The Absolute Zeros:
Dreams Gone Sour ♫♫♫♫ (Big Deal, 1998)

influences:

◀◀ Squire, the Plimsouls, the Scruffs, the Buzzcocks, DM3

▶▶ The Phenomenal Cats

Carl Cafarelli

The Chordettes

Formed 1946, in Sheboygan, WI. Disbanded 1962. Re-formed 1988.

Janet Ertel, bass vocals (1946–62); Carol Buschman, baritone vocals (1946–62); Dorothy Schwartz, lead vocals (1946–52); Jinny Lockard, tenor vocals (1946–53); Lynn Evans, lead vocals (1953–62, 1988–present); Margie Needham, tenor vocals (1953–62); Nancy Overton, bass vocals (1954–60, 1988–present); Joyce Weston, bass vocals (1960–62); Jean Swain, vocals (1988–present); Doris Alberti, vocals (1988–present).

Demonstrating a rare ability to transcend genres and remain appealing to listeners of many persuasions, the Chordettes were one of the few post-war vocal groups who managed to not only withstand but even thrive under the tumultuous new regime of mid-'50s rock 'n' roll. While initially intent on recreating the vocal blend of more traditional, folk-oriented groups, under Jinny Osborn's influence the quartet began to tackle the more complex harmonies and stylings involved in barbershop and even jazz singing on their early Columbia recordings. Successful appearances on the highly-rated *Arthur Godfrey's Talent Scouts* show led to a contract with a new, artist-oriented label Godfrey's musical director, Archie Bleyer, formed in 1952. Under Bleyer's direction, the Chordettes soon hit #1 with the utterly charming "Mr. Sandman," one of the biggest—and final—hits of the pre-rock era. The group's next Top 20 entry was a surprisingly facile take on the Teen Queens' R&B hit "Eddie My Love," helping the group remain relevant and, consequently, a much-requested presence on the first rock 'n' roll package tours and television broadcasts. The Chordettes continued hitting with everything from teen pop ("Lollipop") to Disney themes ("Zorro") and even show tunes ("Never on Sunday") before disbanding during the early '60s—ironically, just as its deceptively simple vocal style was becoming a staple of the early girl group sound. However, a late '80s reunion, kicking off with a wildly successful appearance on the Royal New York Doo-Wop Show, proved the Chordettes' unique approach to vocalizing remains as popular—if as hard to categorize—as ever.

what to buy: The 18 selections comprising *The Best of the Chordettes* &&& (Rhino, 1989, compilation prod. Bill Inglot) offer a flawless overview of the group's multifaceted career, and Archie Bleyer's equally unique arrangements and productions survive the transfer to the digital domain in shining form.

the rest:
The Chordettes' Greatest Hits && (Curb, 1996)
Golden Classics &&& (Collectables, 1997)

worth searching for: The keen listener is also advised to seek out further examples of Bleyer's studio magic for a wide variety of acts on *The History of Cadence Records, Volumes One and Two* (Varese Vintage, 1996, compilation prod. Cary E. Mansfield, Steve Massie).

influences:
◄◄ The Weavers, the Andrews Sisters, the Hi-Lo's, Ronald & Ruby
►► The Angels, the Honeys, Dave Edmunds, Manhattan Transfer

Gary Pig Gold

Lou Christie

Born Lugee Alfredo Giovanni Sacco, February 19, 1943, in Glen Willard, PA.

In the spirit of the great falsettos Del Shannon and Frankie Valli, '60s heartthrob Lou Christie wailed his way to stardom with a string of distinctive hit songs. From his early start as Roulette Records' first breakthrough artist in 1962, Christie cut a figure as a tough-but-sensitive crooner, infusing his repertoire of "boy meets girl" tunes with just a blush of sexual urgency via his distinctive falsetto. By the late '60s, he was part of the stable at bubblegum label Buddah Records, where he enjoyed one last hit ("I'm Gonna Make You Mine") before becoming a fixture in traveling revues.

what's available: Christie's best songs ("The Gypsy Cried," "Two Faces Have I," "Rhapsody in the Rain," and his ambitious million-seller "Lightnin' Strikes") are dutifully collected in *Enlightenment: The Best of Lou Christie* &&& (Rhino, 1991, prod. various).

influences:
◄◄ Frank Sinatra, Roy Orbison, Del Shannon, Frankie Valli
►► Hanson

Christopher Scapelliti

Lauren Christy

Born 1970, in London, England.

What if Kate Bush had never made a deal with God? Would there still be an endless turnaround of wispy-voiced fallen angels tampering with the world's sensitivities? Would *The Feminine Mystique* still be alive and well in the guarded gazes of pretense, or better, self-control? Don't ask Lauren Christy, who has in the course of two albums decided that schizophrenia isn't really that bad at all, at least not when there's a market for it. In her vocal chords, fey whispers give way to primal screams atop percussive explosions in what can best be described as a notable attempt—notable just for being so different.

what to buy: On *Lauren Christy* &&& (Mercury, 1995, prod. Tony Peluso), Christy seems like the nicer sister of Tori Amos: all of the tears, but with cleaner knees. AC hits like "You Read Me Wrong" and "Steep" saw her reaching such lofty heights as an American Music Award nomination. And a strange song, "Vanessa's Father," assured some darker corners (although not so dark as would arise later) by dealing with a story line about a teenage sleepover that results in an actual relationship (one that ends in marriage, even) between the singer and her best friend's (Vanessa's) father. Tawdry.

what to avoid: *Breed* & (Mercury, 1997, prod. Lauren Christy, Andy Scott) is a transparent reach for Alanis-ized declaration. But the vanity of tracks such as "Letterbomb" and "You Make Me Laugh" do little to make a case for Christy as a worthwhile torch bearer of high emotions.

influences:
◄◄ Kate Bush, Tori Amos, Alanis Morissette

Billy Manes

Chumbawamba

Formed mid-1980s, in Leeds, England.

Lou Watts, vocals, keyboards; Danbert Nobacon, vocals, keyboards; Boff, guitar, vocals; Dunstan Bruce, vocals, percussion; Harry Hamer,

drums; Alice Nutter, vocals, percussion; Paul Greco, bass; Jude Abbott, trumpet, vocals.

Chumbawamba is by no means an overnight, tubthumping success. The eight-piece collective spewed its anarchist thoughts for 15 years before hitting big with the bar anthem "Tubthumping." Each of its albums, released on its own Agit-Prop label, displays one of Chumbawamba's schizophrenic music personalities. For example, the group's debut, *Pictures of Starving Children Sell Records*, is a pop diatribe against Live Aid. The band quickly followed that up with the punk-rocking *Never Mind the Ballots!*, a response to the conservative turn of the U.K. general election in 1987. *A capella* harmonies laced "English Rebel Songs" while 1990's *Slap!* tackled dance music. Unfortunately, all of those albums are unreleased in the U.S. but have become increasingly visible in import bins in light of the group's success.

what's available: *Tubthumper* 🐾🐾🐾 (Republic/Universal, 1997, prod. Chumbawamba) put the group's music and its beliefs on the map in the U.S. thanks to the single "Tubthumping." The rousing, irresistible chorus of "I get knocked down/but I get up again/You're never gonna keep me down" makes drinking and defiancy sound like a kegful of fun. Unfortunately, on the rest of *Tubthumper*, Chumbawamba's talent doesn't reach further than a trumpet-led concoction of guitars and keyboards. More striking, however, are the antics that garnered press for the self-proclaimed anarchists. Alice Nutter was accused of encouraging people to steal Chumbawamba's album during an appearance on the TV show *Politically Incorrect*; she retorted in a press release that shoplifting is fine because it is the decision of the person taking that risk. Danbert Nobacon was arrested for cross-dressing in Europe, and the band allowed its Pontiac, Michigan, show to be used as a podium for striking Detroit newspaper workers.

worth searching for: Like *Tubthumper*, Chumbawamba's other albums have their charms and pitfalls. If you want a sample of the group's pre-*Tubthumper* fare, check out the debut, *Pictures of Starving Children Sell Records* (Agit-Prop, 1986), if only for its wonderfully irreverent title.

influences:

◀◀ Sinéad O'Connor, Fugazi, the MC5

▶▶ Rage Against the Machine

Christina Fuoco

The Church

Formed 1980, in Sydney, Australia.

Steven Kilbey, bass, vocals, keyboards; Marty Willson-Piper, guitar, vocals; Peter Koppes, guitar, vocals (1980–92); Richard Ploog, per-

WHAT ALBUM CHANGED YOUR LIFE?

The Clash's first album, because up to that point I was probably listening to a lot of dross, a lot of '70s prog-rock, probably still having arguments about whether Jimmy Page is a better guitarist than Ritchie Blackmore—which he was, of course. It reached a low point where I had *Kiss Alive!* in my record collection. So when punk came along, it was just amazing. There was obviously stuff that came out before that first Clash album, but that was the one where I thought the music was absolutely brilliant

Dunstan Bruce (of Chumbawamba)

cussion, drums, vocals (1981–90); Jay Dee Daugherty, drums (1990–92).

Almost as catchy as the Beatles and almost as lush and dense as the Cocteau Twins, the Church dragged a bunch of guitars from Australia and have churned out more than a dozen albums. Founders Koppes and Willson-Piper sometimes focus on sprightly pop and other times make music so gloomy and dark it would embarrass the Sisters of Mercy. The Church has been popular in its homeland since it began recording, but U.S. audiences didn't catch on until 1988, when "Under the Milky Way" courted some radio attention. That was hardly a permanent breakthrough; despite sporadic subsequent radio play and a wide array of solo releases, the Church remains a cult-level band at best on these shores.

what to buy: *Starfish* 🐾🐾🐾 (Arista, 1988, prod. Waddy Wachtel, Danny Kortchmar), the Church's international breakthrough, is a soothing, ethereal album with the cleanly produced, radio-friendly hits "Under the Milky Way" and "Destination."

what to buy next: *Heyday* 🐾🐾🐾 (Warner Bros., 1986/Arista, 1988, prod. Peter Walsh) is one of the group's most straightforward and hard-hitting albums. *Priest=Aura* 🎵🎵🎵 (Arista, 1992, prod. Gavin MacKillop) is appealingly woozy and ambient.

what to avoid: *Remote Luxury* 🎵🎵 (Warner Bros., 1984/Arista, 1988, prod. Ken Perry) compiles two inconsequential Australian EPs.

the rest:
Of Skins and Heart 🎵🎵 (Parlophone, 1981/Arista, 1988)
The Blurred Crusade 🎵 (Carrere, 1982/Arista, 1988)
Seance 🎵🎵 (Carrere, 1983/Arista, 1988)
Gold Afternoon Fix 🎵🎵🎵 (Arista, 1990)
Sometime Anywhere 🎵🎵 (Arista, 1994)
Hologram of Baal N/A (Thirsty Ear, 1998)

worth searching for: *Almost Yesterday, 1981–1990* (Raven, 1991, prod. various), an Australian best-of collection, contains all the key tracks through *Gold Afternoon Fix.*

solo outings:
Steve Kilbey:
Unearthed 🎵🎵 (Enigma, 1987)
Earthed 🎵🎵 (Rykodisc, 1988)
The Slow Crack 🎵🎵🎵 (Rough Trade, 1989)
Transaction 🎵🎵 (Red Eye-Polydor EP, 1989)
Remindlessness 🎵🎵🎵 (Red Eye-Polydor, 1990)

Jack Frost (Kiley and Grant McLennan):
Jack Frost 🎵🎵🎵 (Arista, 1991)
Snow Job 🎵🎵🎵 (Beggars Banquet, 1996)

Peter Koppes:
Manchild & Myth 🎵 (Rykodisc, 1988)
From the Well 🎵🎵 (TVT, 1989)

Marty Willson-Piper:
In Reflection 🎵 (Chase, 1987)
Art Attack 🎵🎵 (Rykodisc, 1988)
Rhyme 🎵🎵 (Rykodisc, 1989)
Spirit Level 🎵🎵 (Rykodisc, 1992)

influences:
◀◀ The Byrds, the Beatles, David Bowie, Cocteau Twins, the Fall, Leonard Cohen

▶▶ The Stone Roses, Galaxie 500, Luna, Lush, Ride, Slowdive

see also: *Grant McLennan*

Tracey Birkenhauer and Steve Knopper

Cibo Matto

Formed 1994, in New York, NY.

Miho Hatori, lead vocals; Yuka Honda, keyboards, sampler.

What do you get when the cultures and cuisine of Japan and New York's Lower East Side have a head-on collision? Cibo

Matto! The name is Italian for "food madness," and it aptly represents the cross-cultural stew served up by these two innovative young women. Keyboardist Yuka Honda (Sean Lennon's girlfriend) cut her teeth playing with a diversified collection of groups, ranging from free-form jazz/noise artist John Zorn to Brazilian popster Caetano Veloso to the Brooklyn Funk Essentials. Through a mutual friend, she and singer Miho Hatori briefly joined the punkish Leitoh Lychee in 1994, but when the two discovered their mutual passion for the foods of the world, they began developing the wild hybrid that became Cibo Matto. With the release of their major-label debut, *Viva! La Woman*, in 1996, they quickly won a devoted following on the fringes of radio, aided by the weird but ultra-catchy "Know Your Chicken." A second album was planned for fall 1998, among the most anticipated releases of the season. Once you've tasted Cibo Matto, nothing else will satisfy your hunger.

what to buy: Part tease, part tantrum, *Viva! La Woman* 🎵🎵🎵🎵 (Warner Bros., 1996, prod. Mitchell Froom, Tchad Blake, Cibo Matto) mixes hip-hop, jazz, and even bits of impressionistic classical music to form one of the most dazzling and unpredictable albums of recent years. Sure, "Know Your Chicken" has an infectious hook, but it only hints at the invention and entertainment hidden within these tracks.

the rest:
Cibo Matto 🎵🎵🎵 (El Diablo EP, 1995)
Super Relax 🎵🎵🎵🎵 (Warner Bros. EP, 1997)

influences:
◀◀ Ryuichi Sakamoto, Pizzicato Five, Material, Latin Playboys, Boredoms

▶▶ Sean Lennon

Bob Remstein

Ciccone Youth

See: Sonic Youth

Cinderella

Formed 1983, in Philadelphia, PA.

Tom Keifer, guitar, keyboards, vocals; Eric Brittingham, bass; Jeff LeBar, guitar; Tony Destra, drums (1983–86); Jody Cortez, drums (1986); Fred Coury, drums, vocals (1986–90).

Cinderella was a big-haired heavy metal band that immediately clicked thanks to Tom Keifer's banshee wail and a searing guitar attack that must have seemed particularly heavy to the pop-metal Bon Jovi/Def Leppard crowd that lapped it up.

what to buy: *Once upon A . . .* 🎵🎵🎵 (Mercury, 1997, prod. various) is a well-chosen hits collection that tracks the group's growth from anonymous, screaming hard rock to more sophisticated stylings that included touches of acoustic and roots music.

what to buy next: Cinderella proved its mettle with its third album, *Heartbreak Station* 🎵🎵🎵🎵 (Mercury, 1990, prod. John Jansen, Tom Keifer), an impressively varied set that mixed rootsy touches, strings, horns, and gospel choruses with the pro-forma crunch of previous albums.

what to avoid: *Night Songs* 🎵🎵 (Mercury, 1986, prod. Andy Johns), Cinderella's first album, sounded like a dozen other guitar-weilding bands at the time, though it did receive a boost from MTV.

the rest:
Long Cold Winter 🎵🎵🎵 (Mercury, 1988)
Still Climbing 🎵🎵 (Mercury, 1994)

worth searching for: It's worth hunting for the Japanese import *Live Train to Heartbreak Station* (Mercury EP, 1991), an exuberant, if brief, look at the band in concert.

influences:
◀◀ Led Zeppelin, Deep Purple, Willie Dixon, the Rolling Stones

▶▶ D Generation

Gary Graff

Cinnamon
Formed 1994, in Stockholm, Sweden.

Frida Diesen, vocals, guitar, keyboard; Jiri Novak, guitar, programming.

Cinnamon broke through the superficial shell surrounding popular Swedish music (ABBA, Aqua, et al). Hearing the scholarly Jiri Novak and the helium-voiced Frida Diesen—a couple inspired in equal parts by Motown, mod films, and classic liteature—bang out the songs on their group's debut album was a revelation. While they have yet to entice worldwide audiences beyond Japan, Cinnamon's charisma arrived fully formed.

what to buy: *The Courier* 🎵🎵🎵🎵 (Soap Records/Island, 1997, prod. Jiri Novak) is a near perfect debut, filled with gorgeous pop songs like "Backwards" and "Me As Helen of Troy."

influences:
◀◀ Scott Walker, Momus, Orange Juice

Aidin Vaziri

The Circle Jerks
Formed 1980, in Hollywood, CA.

Keith Morris, vocals; Greg Heston, guitar; Zander Schloss, bass, baritone guitar; Keith Clark, drums, background vocals.

Formed by ex–Black Flag headman Keith Morris and former Redd Kross guitarist Greg Heston, the Circle Jerks became one of the most respected hardcore bands from the first wave of American punk. The band's brutal style helped to define the melodic music that became known as California surf punk. The group takes the standard "screw the establishment" punk message and puts on its own special twist, infusing the lyrics with a wise-guy ethos filled with bad jokes, often done in bad taste. The music is fast, hard-hitting, and unpolished, but the band's best offers quick, melodic riffing incorporating a variety of stylings while still maintaining a consistent—and heavy—feel.

what to buy: *Golden Shower of Hits* 🎵🎵🎵🎵 (Rhino, 1983, prod. Gary Hirstius, David Anderle, Circle Jerks) contains a huge selection of the Jerks' best material—a whirlwind of vulgar thrash rock, with a little social commentary thrown in to balance things out.

what to buy next: *Group Sex/Wild in the Streets* 🎵🎵🎵🎵 (Frontier, 1986, prod. Cavy Markoff) combines and remixes the group's first two albums for a 30-track feast—though the *Group Sex* material is clearly weaker. *VI* 🎵🎵🎵🎵 (Relativity, 1987, prod. Circle Jerks) takes the band back to its punk roots, raging full-on for the Jerks' finest post-*Golden Shower* release.

what to avoid: *Wonderful* 🎵 (Relativity, 1985, prod. Circle Jerks) is anything but. The band sounds timid and unassuming, and the guitarists play unimaginative, standard punk chord progressions.

the rest:
Group Sex 🎵🎵🎵 (Frontier, 1980)
Wild in the Streets 🎵🎵🎵🎵 (Frontier, 1982)
Oddities, Abnormalities, and Curiosities 🎵🎵🎵 (Mercury, 1985)
Gig 🎵🎵🎵 (Relativity, 1992)

influences:
◀◀ XTC, the Jefferson Airplane, the Kinks, the Cramps, the Rolling Stones, the Dictators, the Sex Pistols

▶▶ Bad Religion, the Dead Kennedys, Hüsker Dü, Agent Orange

see also: *Black Flag, Redd Kross*

Bryan Lassner

CIV
Formed 1993, in Brooklyn, NY.

Anthony "Civ" Civorelli, vocals; Charlie Garriga, guitar; Arthur Smilios, bass (1993–98); Cache Tolman, bass (1998–present); Guyora Katz, organ, vocals (1998–present); Sammy Siegler, drums.

CIV is the latest project from legendary hardcore vocalist Anthony "Civ" Civorelli, who first established his underground reputation during his years fronting the seminal New York straightedge act Gorilla Biscuits. Civorelli originally included fellow ex–Gorilla Biscuits Arthur Smilios (bass) and Sammy Siegler (drums), as well as ex-Outface/Quicksand guitarist Charlie Garriga, and built upon the lyrically upbeat, crunchy-sounding hardcore that made Gorilla Biscuits underground heroes—but with a distinctly poppy, commercial sheen. After recording 1998's *Thirteen Day Getaway*, Smilios was replaced by bassist Cache Tolman of the artsy Salt Lake City–based jazz/punk group Iceburn Collective, and renowned New York City–based keyboardist Guyora Katz joined the group, signaling that CIV would be taking a "new direction" musically—with coded messages and slowed down songs.

what to buy: CIV's debut album, *Set Your Goals* 𝄞𝄞🎵 (Lava/Atlantic, 1995, prod. Walter Schreifels, Don Fury), picks up where the Gorilla Biscuits left off—metalish guitar with ultra-positive lyrics and plenty of macho attitude—but it's decidedly more radio-friendly. Lou from Sick of It All makes a cameo appearance on the bouncy MTV single "Wait One Minute More."

what to avoid: *Thirteen Day Getaway* 𝄞 (Lava/Atlantic, 1998, prod. Steve Thompson) attempts to explore new, more commercial directions with alternative-ish pop songs ("Secondhand Superstar"), but manages only to camouflage CIV's strengths.

influences:

◀◀ Gorilla Biscuits, Youth of Today, Sick of It All, Minor Threat

Seth Hindin

Eric Clapton

Born Eric Patrick Clapp, March 30, 1945, in Surrey, England.

Eric Clapton's reputation as a guitarist and his stature in popular music have made it very difficult to assess his work dispassionately. This may help explain why Clapton has remained consistantly revered for the last 20 years, even though his output has been exceptionally mediocre—with occassional forays into outright wretchedness. Clapton's work with Cream and Blind Faith is truly brilliant and groundbreaking, and his sole studio album with Derek & the Dominos, *Layla and Other Assorted Love Songs*, is a certifiable masterpiece. And his first few solo albums range from very good to pretty good, as he seemed to be settling into a laid-back singer-songwriter groove, something which he did pretty well even if it displeased old fans waiting to hear fiery, innovative guitar soloing. In retrospect, these early and mid-'70s albums, most of which were largely dismissed at the time, sound like high points. Since then, he has made some truly despicable albums. In 1989 he seemed content with the comfortable plateau he had reached, actually titling an album *Journeyman*. But his next release, *Unplugged*, catapulted him to international stardom greater than any he had previously known. Clapton *can* still play, and he continues to sparkle sporadically—largely on guest appearances like Chuck Berry's *Hail, Hail Rock and Roll* and Jimmie Vaughan's *Tribute to Stevie Ray Vaughan*, but he seems to have long since stalled creatively.

what to buy: On *Layla and Other Assorted Love Songs* 𝄞𝄞𝄞𝄞🎵 (Polydor, 1970, prod. Tom Dowd) Clapton was spurred to perhaps the greatest playing of his career by the presence of Duane Allman. The results speak for themselves. A rock classic. *461 Ocean Boulevard* 𝄞𝄞𝄞🎵 (Polydor, 1974, prod. Tom Dowd) and *Slowhand* 𝄞𝄞𝄞🎵 (Polydor, 1977, prod. Glyn Johns) are the best of Clapton's mellow-period albums. *Crossroads* 𝄞𝄞𝄞𝄞 (Polydor, 1988, prod. various) is pretty much a model box set, though the fourth CD is filled with padding, illustrating Clapton's decline.

what to buy next: *Eric Clapton* 𝄞𝄞𝄞🎵 (Polydor, 1970, prod. Delaney Bramlett), his solo debut, is loose and filled with great playing, though it in many ways sounds more like a Delaney Bramlett (producer/arranger/bandleader) album than a Clapton recording. *The Rainbow Concert* 𝄞𝄞𝄞 (Polydor, 1973/1995, prod. Glyn Johns, John Astley, Andy Macpherson), featuring Pete Townshend, Ron Wood, Steve Winwood, and others, sounds much better today than its reputation would lead you to believe.

what to avoid: *Behind the Sun* 𝄞 (Duck/Warner Bros., 1985) and *August* 𝄞 (Duck/Warner Bros., 1986), both produced by Phil Collins, are vile albums: soulless, pandering, overdone, and inexcusable. *From the Cradle* 𝄞𝄞🎵 (Warner Bros., 1994, prod. Eric Clapton, Russ Titelman) was hailed as Clapton's return to his blues roots and indeed it includes lots of great guitar playing. Unfortunately, his all-English backing band wouldn't know a groove if it it fell into one, and Clapton's singing is overemotive, patronizing blues belting at its worst. For lessons on how to effectively cover blues classics, he should listen to his own versions of Robert Johnson's "Steady Rollin' Man" (*461 Ocean Blvd.*), Elmore James's "The Sky Is Crying" (*There's One in Every Crowd*), or Arthur Crudup's "Mean Old Frisco" (*Slowhand*), where he took them at his own speed and made them his own, rather than slavishly—and pointlessly—mimicking the originals.

the rest:

There's One in Every Crowd 𝄞𝄞𝄞🎵 (Polydor, 1974)
E.C. Was Here 𝄞𝄞𝄞 (Polydor, 1975)
No Reason to Cry 𝄞𝄞𝄞🎵 (Polydor, 1976)
Backless 𝄞𝄞𝄞 (Polydor, 1978)
Just One Night 𝄞𝄞𝄞 (Polydor, 1980)
Another Ticket 𝄞𝄞🎵 (Polydor, 1981)
Timepieces (The Best of Eric Clapton) 𝄞𝄞𝄞𝄞 (Polydor, 1982)
Timepieces, Vol. II (Live in the Seventies) 𝄞𝄞𝄞 (Polydor, 1983)
Money and Cigarettes 𝄞𝄞 (Duck/Warner Bros., 1983)
Journeyman 𝄞𝄞𝄞 (Reprise, 1989)

Eric Clapton (© Ken Settle)

(With Derek & the Dominos) *The Layla Sessions—20th Anniversary*
𝄞𝄞𝄞𝄞 (Polydor 1990)
24 Nights 𝄞𝄞𝄞 (Reprise, 1991)
Rush 𝄞𝄞𝄞 (Reprise, 1992)
Unplugged 𝄞𝄞𝄞 (Reprise, 1992)
(With Derek & the Dominos) *Live at the Fillmore* 𝄞𝄞𝄞 (Polydor/Chronicles, 1994)
Crossroads 2 (Live in the Seventies) 𝄞𝄞𝄞 (Polydor, 1996)
Pilgrim 𝄞𝄞 (Reprise, 1998)

influences:

◀◀ Albert King, Freddie King, Jimi Hendrix, the Band, J.J. Cale

▶▶ Stevie Ray Vaughan, the Allman Brothers Band

see also: *Blind Faith, Cream, John Mayall, the Yardbirds*

Alan Paul

Gene Clark
See: The Byrds

Petula Clark
Born November 15, 1932, in Epsom, Surrey, England.

Riding in on the last wave of the '60s British Invasion, film actress–singer Petula Clark confided a sense of homespun reassurance during one of rock's most turbulent periods. A precursor to the Carpenters and Olivia Newton-John, Clark was blessed with a clear, precise voice and wholesome good looks that gave her instant access to the adult pop market. With producer-arranger-composer Tony Hatch she spun out a string of chirpy hits—"Downtown," "My Love," "This Is My Song," all #1 hits in the U.S.—whose melding of strings and brass with basic pop rhythm sections recalled the sprightly music of a '60s Broadway musical. (Not surprisingly, it was in a hit Broadway musical, *Blood Brothers,* that Clark revived her career during the mid-'90s.)

what to buy: *The Pye Years, Vol. 1/Don't Sleep in the Subway* 𝄞𝄞𝄞𝄞 (RPM, 1996, prod. various) is an excellent reissue that combines two of Clark's albums (*The International Hits* and *These Are My Songs*) with extra singles. In addition to numerous standards of the day, the CD contains two of Clark's biggest hits, "Don't Sleep in the Subway" and "This Is My Song." The hits continue with *The Pye Years, Vol. 2/Wind of Change* 𝄞𝄞𝄞 (RPM, 1996, prod. various), which features Clark's final Pye album, *Pet '71,* all relevant singles from this period, and several alternate takes made for a never-issued American version of the LP. All of the RPM reissues feature extensive liner notes, original LP art, rare singles sleeves, and lavish photo spreads. A first-class job all the way.

what to buy next: If the above-mentioned albums whet your appetite, then jump for *Greatest Hits* 𝄞𝄞𝄞𝄞 (GNP/Crescendo,

1986, prod. various), a first-rate retrospective of her early years featuring all the essential Clark classics ("Don't Sleep in the Subway," "Downtown," "A Sign of the Times," "My Love").

what to avoid: Given the plethora of Clark reissues, don't bother wasting your money on *Treasures, Vol. 1* 𝄞 (WEA/Scotti Bros., 1992, prod. various). The record skimps on essential cuts and, despite the suggestive title, there is no Vol. 2 to round out the collection. Stick with the recommended picks.

the rest:
I Know a Place 𝄞𝄞𝄞 (Sequel, 1965)
My Love 𝄞𝄞𝄞 (Sequel, 1966)
Other Man's Grass Is Always Greener 𝄞𝄞 (See for Miles Records, 1968)
Portrait of Petula 𝄞𝄞 (Sequel, 1969)
Live at the Royal Albert Hall 𝄞𝄞 (GNP/Crescendo, 1972)
The Polygon Years, Vol. 1 𝄞𝄞 (RPM, 1996)
The Polygon Years, Vol. 2 𝄞𝄞 (RPM, 1996)
The Nixa Years, Vol. 1/Another Door Opens 𝄞𝄞𝄞 (RPM, 1996)
The Nixa Years, Vol. 2/Gonna Find Me a Bluebird 𝄞𝄞𝄞 (RPM, 1996)

worth searching for: The three-CD package *I Love to Sing* (Sequel, 1995, prod. various) is a comprehensive retrospective that includes the hits, the misses, and the rare. For diehards only.

influences:
◀◀ Lulu

▶▶ The Carpenters, Olivia Newton-John, Anne Murray, Linda Ronstadt

Christopher Scapelliti

The Dave Clark Five
Formed 1961, in Tottenham, England. Disbanded 1970.

Dave Clark, vocals, drums, percussion; Mike Smith, vocals, piano, organ; Lenny Davidson, guitars, vocals; Dennis Payton, saxophone, harmonica, acoustic guitar, vocals; Rick Huxley, bass, acoustic guitar, vocals.

While the Dave Clark Five has been roundly dismissed as a pale imitation of the Beatles, you have to give drummer Clark credit for being a talented songwriter and a savvy businessman. In addition to writing much of the group's hit material, Clark (a former movie stuntman with more than 40 film credits) managed and produced the band himself. He was smart enough to set his sights on the U.S. after the Beatles' 1964 concert tour, making the DCF the first British group to break into the American charts after the Beatles. With 17 Top 40 hits between 1964 and 1967 (including "Do You Love Me," "Bits and Pieces," "Glad All Over," and "Catch Us If You Can"), the band was considered the only true contender to the Beatles' throne. And while its music was never as sophisticated as the Fab Four's,

DCF had a good sense of melody and a well-tuned ear for harmony that was supported by Smith's raucous vocals and Clark's solid, heavy backbeat. The group had a rather successful foray into film (*Catch Us If You Can*, an imitation of the Beatles' *A Hard Day's Night*) and television (the British TV sensation *Hold On, It's the Dave Clark 5* and more appearances on the *Ed Sullivan Show* than any other rock act). With perhaps fitting timing, the group disbanded in 1970, the same year the Beatles broke up. Clark has continued to be a successful producer in TV and music, while his legacy as a marketer of prefab pop remains in evidence in such groups as Menudo, New Kids on the Block, and Milli Vanilli—to name but a few.

what to buy: *The History of the Dave Clark Five* 𝄽𝄽𝄽𝄽 (Hollywood, 1993, prod. Dave Clark) offers a whopping 50 tracks, including all the hits, plus a 32-page booklet featuring rare photos, interviews, and a history of the band. Enough bits and pieces to make you glad all over.

influences:

◄◄ The Beatles, Gary Lewis & the Playboys

►► Ringo Starr, Phil Collins

Christopher Scapelliti

Gilby Clarke

See also *Guns N' Roses*

The Clarks

Formed 1986, in Indiana, PA.

Scott Blasey, vocals, guitars; Robert James (a.k.a. Robert James Hertweck), guitars, vocals, harmonica; Greg Joseph, bass, mandolin, acoustic guitar, vocals; Dave Minarik, drums, vocals.

The Clarks, a favorite of the Pittsburgh music scene, are one of those refreshing rarities: a talented band with strong songwriting and performing skills, yet no obnoxious airs or attitudes. Four friends who met at Indiana University of Pennsylvania and turned their affinity for music into a healthy career, the Clarks played to Pittsburgh and regional audiences for 10 years and recorded on their own King Mouse label before finally signing a major-label deal with Way Cool Records, an MCA subsidiary, in 1997. Flaunting strong harmonies, tight instrumental interplay, and a playful presence in lead singer Scott Blasey, the Clarks were influenced early on by the Rave-Ups (featuring another Pittsburgh native, Jimmer Podrasky), Tom Petty, and similar pop-tinged rock artists. But over the course of their years together, they musicians developed a strong identity, rooted in musicianship and well-crafted tunes.

what to buy: *Someday Maybe* 𝄽𝄽𝄽𝄽 (King Mouse, 1996/ Way Cool/MCA, 1997, prod. Tim Bomba) is a disc of well-honed rock

songs with melodic pop sensibilities and just a little bit of edge. The national release is slightly different than the band's indie version; it includes "Cigarette," the song that, thanks to its inclusion in the Winona Ryder film *Boys*, made Pennsylvania's Fayette County Fair famous (and turned it into an indelible American image by rhyming it with "big hair"). It also includes a Rave-Ups tune, "These Wishes," and the flawless "Fatal."

what to buy next: *The Clarks* 𝄽𝄽𝄽𝄽 (King Mouse, 1991, prod. Nason Gieg, Mike Michalski, the Clarks) features "Penny on the Floor," an early glimmer of Blasey's lyrical talent, and a fine cover of the Beatles' "Dear Prudence." *Love Gone Sour, Suspicion and Bad Debt* 𝄽𝄽𝄽𝄽 (King Mouse, 1994, prod. Barney Lee, the Clarks) takes its title from the lyric of "Cigarette," which made its first appearance on this disc. Further evidence of this band's progress from a really good bar band to one worthy of greater recognition, the album also includes particularly evocative lyrics in "Sun Don't Shine."

the rest:

The Clarks 𝄽𝄽𝄽 (King Mouse, 1988/1997)

influences:

◄◄ The Beatles, the Rave-Ups, Tom Petty, Elvis Costello, the Replacements, the Rainmakers

Lynne Margolis

The Clash

Formed 1976, in London, England. Disbanded 1985.

Joe Strummer, vocals, guitar; Mick Jones, guitar (1976–84); Paul Simonon, bass; Tory Crimes, drums (1976–77, 1982–85); Nicky "Topper" Headon, drums (1976–82); Pete Howard, drums (1984–85); Vince White, guitar (1984–85); Nick Sheppard, guitar (1984–85).

Along with the Ramones and Sex Pistols, the Clash were one of the three touchstones of punk rock. From the start, the group played a similar sort of buzzsaw, power-chord-driven distorted rock. But it also had a genuine political sense—with Joe Strummer railing against commercial culture, American imperialism, and the abuses of capitalism—as well as an open, non-doctrinaire musical philosophy that shot everything from reggae to rap and disco to rockabilly into the band's sound. These same traits that helped separate the Clash from the pack eventually turned around and bit it on the ass; its open-minded ambition led to overblown, maddeningly inconsistent efforts like the three-album set *Sandanista!* The band's relentless political awareness made some songs just so much sloganeering and eventually even led Strummer to fire founding guitarist Jones for some sort of political incorrectness. The Clash only lasted one album after that split, however, and, unlike the Pistols, has so far resisted big money reunion pitches from Lollapalooza and other concert promoters. On the other hand, they have let their music be used in a Levi's commercial.

what to buy: *London Calling* ♪♪♪♪♪ (Epic, 1979, prod. Guy Stevens) is the band's masterpiece, balancing high-energy punk efficiency with forays into roots rock, blues, and reggae. Less intense than the band's debut, but also more accessible, this is simply a great collection of songs. *The Clash* ♪♪♪♪ (CBS U.K., 1977/Epic, 1979, prod. M. Foote, L. Perry, the Clash, B. Price) is pure punk heaven—overdriven fury, tuneful reggae, snarled vocals, great guitar riffs. *The Story of the Clash, Volume One* ♪♪♪♪♪ (Epic, 1988, prod. various) is a first-rate, double-length compilation.

what to buy next: The band's U.S. debut, *Give 'Em Enough Rope* ♪♪♪♪ (Epic, 1978, prod. Sandy Pearlman), borders on the overproduced, but the results work surprisingly well; call it arena punk. *Combat Rock* ♪♪♪♪ (Epic, 1982, prod. Glyn Johns) was the band's commercial breakthrough—including "Should I Stay or Should I Go?" and "Rock the Casbah"—as well as its last worthwhile creative grasp.

what to avoid: Cut after Strummer and Simonon fired Jones, *Cut the Crap* ♪♪ (Epic, 1985, prod. Jose Unidos) is a hollow echo of a once-great band.

the rest:
Sandanista! ♪♪ (Epic, 1980)
Super Black Market Clash ♪♪♪♪ (Epic, 1980/1994)
Return to Brixton ♪♪♪♪ (Epic EP, 1990)
The Clash on Broadway ♪♪♪♪ (Epic/Legacy, 1991)

worth searching for: The vinyl only promotional sampler *Sandanista Now!* (Epic, 1980, prod. the Clash) is the magnificent 12-song single album *Sandanista* could have been.

solo outings:
Topper Headon:
Waking Up ♪♪♪ (Mercury, 1986)

Havana 3 A.M. (Paul Simonon):
Havana 3 A.M. ♪♪♪ (I.R.S., 1991)

Joe Strummer:
Walker ♪♪♪ (Virgin, 1987)
Earthquake Weather ♪♪ (Epic, 1987)
Gangsterville ♪♪ (Epic, 1989)
Island Hopping ♪♪ (Epic, 1989)

influences:
◀◀ The Sex Pistols, the Ramones, Bo Diddley, Eddie Cochran, Junior Marvin, David Bowie, the Who

▶▶ Rancid, Nada Surf, Green Day, the Pogues

see also: *Big Audio Dynamite*

Alan Paul

Classics IV
Formed 1965, in Jacksonville, FL. Disbanded early 1970s.

Dennis Yost, vocals; James R. Cobb, guitar; Wally Eaton, guitar; Joe Wilson, bass; Kim Venable, drums.

Long before he helped put southern boogie on the map with the Atlanta Rhythm Section, James Cobb was playing guitar and co-writing for Classics IV. Noted for its smooth jazz-rock style and Dennis Yost's warm, sandpapery voice, Classics IV would have easily fit into the adult-contemporary niche, if it had existed during the '60s. The band had U.S. hits with "Spooky," "Stormy," and "Traces" (its last million-seller) before breaking up. Cobb and producer Buddy Buie revived "Spooky" in 1979 with ARS.

what's available: Both *Greatest Hits* ♪♪♪ (Capitol Special Products, 1992, prod. Buddy Buie) and *Very Best of the Classics IV* ♪♪♪ (EMI America, 1988, prod. Buddy Buie) are solid compilations that comprise both the group's big hits and lower chart entries ("Soul Train," "Every Day with You, Girl," and "Change of Heart"). Oddly, neither album offers "What Am I Crying For?," the group's final Top 40 entry and a fine example of this group's distinctive, easygoing sound.

influences:
◀◀ Stax-Volt, the Rascals

▶▶ Southern rock, the Doobie Brothers, Steely Dan

see also: *Atlanta Rhythm Section*

Christopher Scapelliti

The Clean
Formed 1978, in Dunedin, New Zealand.

Hamish Kilgour, drums; David Kilgour, guitar; Peter Gutteridge, guitar; Robert Scott, bass; Ross Humphries, bass.

The roots of influential New Zealand label Flying Nun Records all run through one band—the original lo-fi popsters known as the Clean. (In fact, frothy Clean fan Roger Shepherd was partly inspired to form the label as a platform for dispersing the group's jagged pop songs.) Although the band's founding incarnation persevered for less than two years, the ever-evolving group's core members—brothers Hamish and David Kilgour, Peter Gutteridge, and occasional bassist Robert Scott—have regrouped and reunited several times during the past two decades for live and recorded sessions, all the while founding and/or contributing to many of the most influential Auckie acts of the past decade, including the Chills, the Bats, and Bailter Space. The band most recently released 1996's *Unknown Country*, a typically quirky, uneven collection of punk-tinged pop experiments.

what to buy: *Compilation* ♪♪♪♪ (Homestead, 1986, prod. various) compiles all the early classics, plus six live bonus tracks.

what to buy next: Proving that advancing age, layoffs, and lineup changes have not dispersed its songwriting prowess, *Modern Rock* ♫♫♫ (Summershine, 1995, prod. the Clean, Tex Houston, Stephen Kilroy) is a smarmy collection of delicate almost-pop gems.

the rest:
Unknown Country, (Flying Nun, 1996)

influences:
◀◀ The Ramones

▶▶ Pavement, Apples in Stereo

see also: *Bailter Space, the Bats, the Chills*

Scott Hess

Cleaners from Venus
See: Martin Newell

Johnny Clegg & Savuka /Juluka

Johnny Clegg born June 7, 1953, in Rochdale, England.

Johnny Clegg & Savuka (1986–95): Johnny Clegg, vocals, guitar, mouth bow; Steve Mavuso, keyboards; Keith Hutchinson, keyboards, saxophone, flute; Derek De Beer, drums, percussion; Solly Letwaba, bass; Dudu Zulu, percussion. Juluka (1979–85, 1996): Johnny Clegg, vocals, guitar, mouth bow; Derek De Beer, drums, percussion; Sipho Mchunu, vocals, guitar, concertina; Gary Van Zyl, bass, percussion (1981–85); Scorpion Madondo, flute, saxophone (1982–85); Cyril Mnculwana, keyboards (1983–85); Glenda Millar, keyboards (1982–85).

Born in England but raised in Zimbabwe and South Africa, Johnny Clegg learned Zulu dancing at an early age and, depending on which version of the story you believe, he met Sipho Mchunu either when Mchunu heard about this white boy who could dance like a Zulu, or when Clegg, already a lecturer in anthropology, was sought out by Mchunu because of Clegg's reputation as a hotshot guitarist. The first story maintains that the two met as teenagers around 1970 and worked together for nine years before hooking up with producer/impresario Hilton Rosenthal. The second one likely would indicate that they had only worked together for a little while before they started making records in 1979. Either way, the idea of a white man and a black man co-leading a South African band was a political statement in itself, and in some ways became more important than their novel melding of South African mbaqanga or "township" music, Western pop/rock, and Zulu chants. By 1981, the duo put together a backup band, and before long Juluka's colorful and energetic performances made it a hot concert draw—and brought them into direct conflict with the racist practices of South Africa's apartheid government. By 1982, it was wowing

audiences in Britain, and soon after, Juluka was signed to an American major label. Commercial success never came, and after the group broke up, Clegg returned as sole leader of a new ensemble, Savuka. Blander and more formulaic than Juluka, Clegg and Savuka became a serious concert draw across the world, but its albums never really rose above the level of stylish professionalism, and the group was dropped by Capitol after 1993's *Heat, Dust, and Dreams*. Meanwhile, Clegg and Mchunu have reunited for some concerts and are reportedly planning a new Juluka album.

what to buy: Both groups are the subject of greatest-hits collections. *A Johnny Clegg & Juluka Collection* ♫♫♫ (Putumayo, 1996, compilation prod. Dan Storper) provides a nice initiation to Clegg's international pop style. *In My African Dream: The Best of Johnny Clegg & Savuka* ♫♫♫ (Priority, 1994, prod. various) contains 16 tracks, several of them previously unreleased. More energetic and a bit more focused than Clegg and Savuka's earlier work, *Cruel, Crazy, Beautiful World* ♫♫♫ (Capitol, 1989, prod. Hilton Rosenthal, Bobby Summerfield) in some ways parallels the rising tide of optimism that was about to overtake South Africa when the album was released.

what to buy next: Highlighted by Juluka's South African breakthrough hit, "Impi," *African Litany* ♫♫♫ (Rhythm Safari, 1982/1991, prod. Hilton Rosenthal) offers a view of the earlier band just as it was about to make the jump from national to international status.

what to avoid: Tame and somewhat disappointing coming after the breakup of Juluka, Savuka's debut, *Third World Child* ♫♫ (Capitol, 1987/Gold Rush 1996, prod. Hilton Rosenthal) is fairly pleasant but unremarkable stuff.

the rest:
Juluka:
Ubuhle Bemvelo ♫♫ (Rhythm Safari, 1982/1991)
Scatterlings ♫♫♫ (Warner Bros., 1983)
Stand Your Ground ♫♫♫ (Warner Bros., 1984)

Johnny Clegg & Savuka:
Shadow Man ♫♫♫ (Capitol, 1988)
Heat, Dust, and Dreams ♫♫♫ (Capitol, 1993)

influences:
◀◀ Mahlathini & the Mahotella Queens, Ladysmith Black Mambazo, the Police, Men at Work, Aswad

▶▶ Paul Simon (circa *Graceland*), Dave Matthews Band, Rusted Root

Bob Remstein

Clarence Clemons
See: Bruce Springsteen

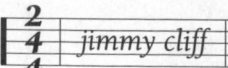
Jimmy Cliff

Born April 1, 1948, in St. James, Jamaica.

Jimmy Cliff shot to international stardom in 1971 with his lead role in the movie *The Harder They Come* and his contributions to its all-star soundtrack, which still stands as one of the primary textbooks of Reggae 101. However, he had been recording since the early 1960s, making some of reggae's first sounds heard outside of Jamaica. Working with famed producer Leslie Kong, Cliff had a handful of hits on the island, leading to more far-reaching success with "Wonderful World, Beautiful People" in 1969. After the success of *The Harder They Come,* Cliff was os-tracized by the Jamaican community, perhaps jealous over his newfound stardom, or merely insulted by his conversion from Rastafarianism to Islam. The sad truth is that for all the liberat-ing forces at play during Cliff's moment in the sun, he's never been able to translate them into consistent music or attain that level of success again. Instead, he opted for a light MOR pop-soul approach that culminated in a two-album collaboration, *The Power and the Glory* and *Cliff Hanger*, with Kool & the Gang during the first half of the 1980s. Besides nabbing a Grammy for *Cliff Hanger* (so keyboard-laden it could be the *Footloose* soundtrack), Cliff appeared in *Club Paradise* with Robin Williams and added seven songs to its soundtrack in 1986, although nei-ther generated a wider audience for the singer.

what to buy: Perhaps the best quick indoctrination into 1970s reggae, *The Harder They Come* 𝄞𝄞𝄞𝄞 (Island, 1972, prod. vari-ous) is Cliff's crowning glory. A taut and yearning soundtrack filled with top-notch performances from all artists involved. Cliff's efforts on the title track, "Sitting in Limbo," "You Can Get It If You Really Want," and, most of all, "Many Rivers to Cross" remain timeless and moving as all classics do.

what to buy next: One of his more consistent studio albums, *Wonderful World, Beautiful People* 𝄞𝄞𝄞 (A&M, 1970, prod. Larry Fallon, Leslie Kong) paved the way to superstardom with its title track, the protest of "Vietnam" (which drew high praise from Bob Dylan), and the foreboding "Time Will Tell."

what to avoid: Cliff's records of late have a disturbing light-ness, and although *Hanging Fire* 𝄞𝄞 (Columbia, 1988, prod. Khalis Bayyan, I.B.M.C., Jimmy Cliff) is really not much better or worse than the bulk of his more recent releases, there's a sink-ing feeling that he may break into "Let's Hear It for the Boy" at any moment. Mediocrity from Cliff may not be so unsettling had he not once reached greatness.

the rest:
In Concert: The Best of Jimmy Cliff 𝄞𝄞𝄞 (Reprise, 1976)
Special 𝄞𝄞 (Columbia, 1982)
The Power and the Glory 𝄞𝄞𝄞 (Columbia, 1983)
Reggae Greats 𝄞𝄞𝄞 (Mango, 1985)

Cliff Hanger 𝄞𝄞 (Columbia, 1985)
Images 𝄞𝄞𝄞 (Cliff, 1991)
Struggling Man 𝄞𝄞𝄞 (Mango, 1993)
Live 1993 𝄞𝄞𝄞 (Lagoon Reggae, 1993)
Samba Reggae 𝄞𝄞 (Lagoon Reggae, 1995)
Super Hits 𝄞𝄞𝄞 (Columbia Legacy, 1997)

worth searching for: Although it's a hit and miss soundtrack, *Marked for Death* (Delicious Vinyl, 1990) contains some stirring Cliff numbers. The ominous "John Crow" is stronger than any-thing he's done during the past 10 years.

influences:

◀◀ Toots & the Maytals, Desmond Dekker, Bob Marley

▶▶ UB40, Third World, General Public, Pinchers

Allan Orski

George Clinton /Parliament-Funkadelic

Born July 22, 1940, in Kannapolis, NC.

MusicHound, meet the Atomic Dog. It's not like there weren't other funk bands around, but George Clinton and his primary vehicles, Parliament and Funkadelic, distilled the funk to its purest elements and gave it metaphysical properties. No other group has mastered the intricacy of layering rhythms, grooves, and vocals into a sophisticated whole the way Clinton and his P-Funk mob have done. And no other group has influenced black pop music as strongly over the last 20 years. After mi-grating to Detroit from New Jersey and flunking out at Motown during the mid-1960s, Clinton and his Parliament pals (at that time a vocal group formed during the mid-1950s in Plainfield, New Jersey) decided to loosen up their music and take on a wild street image. In the process they revolutionized popular music and added multiple new agendas to black music. Clin-ton's raw, rock-tinged music and irreverent black conscious-ness were like breaths of fresh air to the slick and suited ve-neer of most R&B acts. While P-Funk's antics spawned a grow-ing underground buzz and occasional pop airplay, it wasn't until 1975's *The Clones of Dr. Funkenstein* that its heavy bass, chanted lyrics, wriggling guitars, and phat horn lines went over the top. From 1975 to 1980, the P-Funk mob churned out hit after hit with the added spinoff groups, Bootsy's Rubber Band and the Brides of Funkenstein. In 1976, the group—a collective that rivals James Brown's assorted bands, with celebrated tenures by bassist Bootsy Collins, keyboardists Bernie Worrell and Walter "Junie" Morrison, guitarist Eddie Hazel, saxophonist Maceo Parker, and percussionist Larry Fratangelo—released five albums under four names for three different labels. Com-mon belief is that Clinton used the name Parliament for his

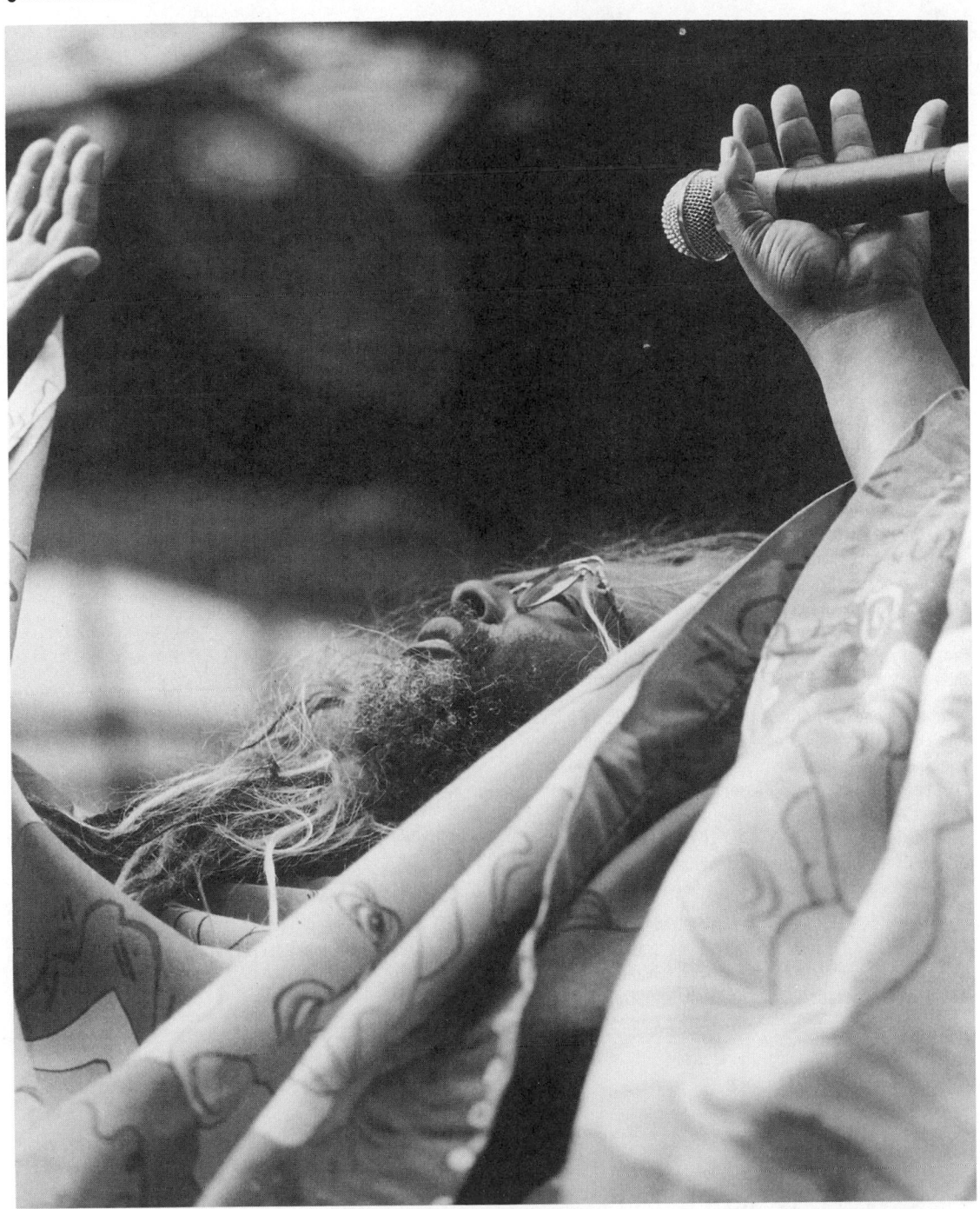

George Clinton (© Jack Vartoogian)

more R&B, dance club-oriented records and Funkadelic for his rock side. That may be, but the original intention behind the Funkadelic name was for Clinton & Co. to continue on after temporarily losing legal rights to the Parliament name. When he lost legal rights to both names in the 1980s, Clinton started recording under his own name. Regardless of the title, it's basically the same band; even after the group splintered in 1981, Clinton's records have featured many of the same musicians. Legal hassles dogged Clinton and other funkateers through much of the 1980s—though theirs was a peaceable induction into the Rock and Roll Hall of Fame in 1997. Clinton has produced hit records for Thomas Dolby, the Red Hot Chili Peppers, and others, and has become an elder statesman for the hip-hop nation as rapper after rapper samples his work, most notably "Atomic Dog." Not content to be just a figure for nostalgia, 1993's *Hey, Man . . . Smell My Finger* showed he could still throw down, while "If Anybody Gets Funked Up (It's Gonna Be You)" from *T.A.P.O.A.F.O.M.* signaled a full-scale return to form.

what to buy: Almost anything from the '70s is a good choice, but Parliament's *Mothership Connection* ♪♪♪♪ (Casablanca, 1975, prod. George Clinton) lays out the P-Funk philosophy in a capsule with relentless grooves and happy horns. "Give up the Funk (Tear the Roof Off the Sucker)" is the big hit, but the title tune is like losing yourself in a bumping cartoon. Funkadelic gets on the good foot, too, with *One Nation under a Groove* ♪♪♪♪♪ (Warner Bros., 1987/Priority, 1993, prod. George Clinton). If you don't like this record, you weren't dancing when you heard it.

what to buy next: For the early years, *Funkadelic's Greatest Hits* ♪♪♪♪♪ (Westbound, 1975, prod. George Clinton) covers things pretty well with "Can You Get to That," "I'll Bet You," and "I Got a Thing. . . ." The only essential early hit missing is Parliament's "I Wanna Testify." The 10-minute title track of Funkadelic's *Maggot Brain* ♪♪♪♪♪ (Westbound, 1971, prod. George Clinton) proves that Jimi Hendrix wasn't the only black freaky rock guitarist.

what to avoid: Things looked bad for Funkadelic with *The Electric Spanking of War Babies* ♪ (Warner Bros., 1980, prod. George Clinton), which is burdened by no substantial jams and by Sly Stone's pathetic bleating on "Funk Gets Stronger."

the rest:
George Clinton:
Computer Games ♪♪♪♪ (Capitol, 1982)
U Shouldn't—Nuf Bit Fish ♪♪♪♪ (Capitol, 1983)
Some of My Best Jokes Are Friends ♪♪♪ (Capitol, 1985)
R&B Skeletons from the Closet ♪♪ (Capitol, 1986)
The Best of George Clinton ♪♪♪♪ (Capitol, 1986)
The Cinderella Theory ♪♪♪ (Paisley Park, 1989)
P. Funk All-Stars Live ♪♪♪ (Westbound, 1990)
George Clinton Family Series, Vols. 1–5 ♪♪♪♥ (AEM, 1992/1994)

George Clinton's Sample Some of Disc, Sample Some of D.A.T. Series, Vols. 1–6 ♪♪♪ (AEM, 1992/1994)
Hey, Man . . . Smell My Finger ♪♪♪ (Paisley Park, 1993)
Live Greatest Hits, 1972–1993 ♪♪♪♪ (AEM, 1993)
T.A.P.O.A.F.O.M. (The Awesome Power of a Fully Operational Mothership) ♪♪♪♪ (Sony 550, 1996)
Greatest Funkin' Hits ♪♪♪♥ (Capitol/EMI, 1996)
Lie and Kickin' ♪♪♪ (Intersound, 1997)

Parliament:
Up for the Down Stroke ♪♪♪♪ (Casablanca, 1974)
Chocolate City ♪♪♪♥ (Casablanca, 1975)
Clones of Dr. Funkenstein ♪♪♪♪♥ (Casablanca, 1976)
Funkentelechy vs. the Placebo Syndrome ♪♪♪♪ (PolyGram, 1977)
P-Funk Earth Tour ♪♪♪♪♥ (Warner Bros., 1977)
Motor Booty Affair ♪♪♪ (Casablanca, 1978)
Gloryhallastupid ♪♪♪♥ (Casablanca, 1979)
Tear the Roof Off 1974–1980 ♪♪♪♪ (Casablanca/Chronicles, 1993)
The Best of Parlet featuring Parliament ♪♪♪♪ (Casablanca/Chronicles, 1994)
The Best of Parliament: Give up the Funk ♪♪♪♪ (Casablanca/Chronicles, 1995)

Funkadelic:
Free Your Mind and Your Ass Will Follow ♪♪♪ (Westbound, 1970)
Funkadelic ♪♪♪♪♪ (Westbound, 1971)
America Eats Its Young ♪♪♪ (Westbound, 1972)
Cosmic Slop ♪♪♪♪ (Westbound, 1973)
Standing on the Verge of Gettin' It On ♪♪♪ (Westbound, 1974)
Let's Take It to the Stage ♪♪ (Westbound, 1975)
Hardcore Jollies ♪♪♪ (Warner Bros., 1976)
Uncle Jam Wants You ♪♪♪♪ (Warner Bros., 1979)

worth searching for: The out-of-print *Music for Your Mother* (Ace/Westbound, 1992, prod. various) is a collection of Funkadelic singles offering an interesting and valid perspective on what is, nevertheless, a definitely album-oriented band.

influences:

◀◀ James Brown, Screamin' Jay Hawkins, Ike Turner, Sun Ra

▶▶ Dr. Dre, Prince, Groove Collective, Eric B. & Rakim, Digital Underground, Red Hot Chili Peppers

see also: *Bootsy Collins*

Lawrence Gabriel

The Clovers

Formed 1946, in Washington, DC. Disbanded 1961.

John "Buddy" Bailey, vocals (1946–53); Charlie White, vocals (1953–54); Billy Mitchell, vocals (1954–61); Harold Winley, vocals; Matthew McQuater, vocals; Harold Lucas Jr., vocals; Bill Harris, guitar.

One of the groups that popularized rock 'n' roll before it even had a name, the Clovers set a high early standard for '50s R&B.

Whether crooning cool and romantic or panting sexy blues, the Clovers pioneered a style that would be copied and refined by all the early R&B groups that followed. Initially smoothies in the Ink Spots tradition, the group cut its first single for the Rainbow label in 1950. At Atlantic Records the following year, producer Ahmet Ertegun and songwriter Jesse Stone sought to toughen its style by supplying a leering saxophone and blusier material—a style that spawned classic R&B hits such as "Don't You Know I Love You," "Fool, Fool, Fool," "One Mint Julep," "Good Lovin'," "Lovey Dovey," and "Your Cash Ain't Nothin' But Trash." The group made an impact on white artists as well: Elvis Presley, a frustrated R&B singer at heart, included "Fool, Fool, Fool" in his early repertoire and later recorded a faithful version of "Down in the Alley," while Bobby Vee scored with his version of "Devil or Angel." The 1956 hit "Love, Love, Love" was a major crossover success, but the Clovers were eventually eclipsed by other, less earthy R&B groups later in the decade. After leaving Atlantic, the Clovers put together a final volley of hits for United Artists, including "Pennies from Heaven," "Lovey," and its best-remembered number, "Love Potion #9." The group eventually dissolved, then re-formed and recorded for a variety of smaller labels into the early '60s. Since then, many different lineups of the Clovers (usually featuring only one original member) have toured the world as part of oldies revivals, though none have come close to matching the soulful style or winking bravado of the original cast.

what to buy: The group's biggest hits from both the Atlantic and United Artists labels are on *The Very Best of the Clovers* ♪♪♪♪♪ (Rhino, 1998, compilation prod. James Austen, Billy Vera), 16 tracks of pure R&B and doo-wop that no digger of early rock 'n' roll should be without.

what to buy next: Those wanting more should seek out *Down in the Alley: The Best of the Clovers* ♪♪♪♪½ (Atlantic, 1991, prod. Ahmet Ertegun, Jerry Wexler, Herb Abramson), a 21-track collection of the group's finest moments at Atlantic, along with goodies such as "Nip Sip" and "Love Bug" in addition to its big run of early '50s hits.

worth searching for: For even more of the seminal sounds of the Clovers, hit the import racks and catalog services for *The Clovers* (Atlantic, 1956/Sequel, 1997, prod. Ahmet Ertegun, Jerry Wexler, Herb Abramson) and *Dance Party* (Atlantic, 1959, prod. Ahmet Ertegun, Jerry Wexler), two strong reproductions of classic LPs from the '50s. Also, those not easily shocked should check out the group's profane *a capella* version of "Darktown Strutter's Ball" on *Copulatin' Blues, Vol. 2* (Stash Records, 1984, compilation prod. Will Friedwald), an adults-only collection of racy blues and R&B tunes.

influences:

◄◄ The Mills Brothers, the Ink Spots, the Orioles, the Charioteers

►► The Flamingos, the Moonglows, Frankie Lymon & the Teenagers, the Coasters

Ken Burke

Clutch

Formed 1991, in Germantown, MD.

Neil Fallon, vocals, guitars; Tim Sult, guitars; Dan Maines, bass; Jean Paul Gaster, drums.

Neil Fallon created Clutch as a way to set his prose to music—albeit some of the heaviest music imagainable. The band quickly earned a cult following in nearby Baltimore and soon won a recording deal that elevated it to the heavy rock stage shared by kindred spirits such as Marilyn Manson, Pantera, Bad Religion, and Prong. But what sets Clutch apart is its ability to flawlessly switch gears from serious issues to humorous one-liners while maintaining the collision of machine-gun drums, rock-solid bass, and driving guitars. "Little bunny foo-foo" and "bebopaloobopa wam shamboo domo arigoto if I got to" are two of the lines that the dimunitive Fallon frequently growls when things get a bit too serious.

what to buy: Clutch's debut, *Transnational Speedway League: Anthems, Anecdotes and Undeniable Truths* ♪♪♪♪ (EastWest, 1993, prod. Jonathan Burnside, Steven Haigler) is still its best, with the strobing guitars of "A Shogun Named Marcus" and the cool groove of "El Jefe Speaks" standing out in particular.

what to buy next: *Clutch* ♪♪♪½ (Elektra, 1995/Atlantic, 1996, prod. Clutch, Larry Packer) is a close second to *Transnational Speedway League* but falls short due to musical redundancy. "Big News I" and "Big News II" pay homage to the ferocity of pirates, and Clutch maintains its ferocious guitar work—particularly Tim Sult's sultry groove through the memorable "Escape from the Prison Planet."

the rest:

The Elephant Riders ♪♪½ (Columbia, 1998)

influences:

◄◄ Pantera, Prong, Sepultura

►► Sevendust, Limp Bizkit

Christina Fuoco

The Coasters

Formed 1955, in Los Angeles, CA. Disbanded 1976.

Carl Gardner, tenor vocals; Billy Guy, baritone vocals (1955–65); Bobby Nunn, bass vocals (1955); Leon Hughes, tenor vocals (1955); Will "Dub" Jones, bass vocals (1956–65); Cornell Gunter, tenor vocals

(1956–60); Earl "Speedo" Carroll, tenor vocals (1961–76); Ronnie Bright, tenor vocals (1965–76); Jimmy Norman, baritone (1965–76).

At the end of the white-bread '50s, America's mainstream chose the comical Coasters as their most beloved black entertainers. Under the watchful eye of writer-producers Jerry Leiber and Mike Stoller, the Coasters issued a number of playful singles, which kept the group at the top of the charts well into the early '60s. Although the contributions of Leiber and Stoller can't be overstated, the group's sound was largely characterized by Nunn's low bottoms and Gardner's wolf-in-sheep's-clothing tenor.

what to buy: *50 Coastin' Classics: Anthology* 🎸🎸🎸🎸 (Rhino, 1992, prod. various), by far the best Coasters compilation on the market, is nearly overwhelming; going back to the pre-Coasters group, the Robins, the album has a wealth of obscurities and ample liner notes, with comments by Leiber and Stoller. *The Very Best of the Coasters* 🎸🎸🎸🎸 (Rhino, 1993, prod. various) offers a compact version of the above that focuses on such chart-toppers as "Yakety-Yak," "Charlie Brown," and "Poison Ivy," as well as "What about Us," a track that shows the band had more to offer than just yuks.

the rest:
The Coasters featuring Cornell Gunter 🎸🎸🎸 (1969/New Rose, 1993)
Golden Hits 🎸🎸 (ITC Masters, 1997)

influences:
◄◄ The Robins, Ray Charles, the Mills Brothers
►► Elvis Presley, Leon Russell

Allan Orski

Eddie Cochran

Born October 3, 1938, in Oklahoma City, OK. Died April 17, 1960, in Bristol, England.

Eddie Cochran is probably the most overrated member of the early rock 'n' roll pantheon. He is remembered more for his suave, Elvis-like style than the enduring quality of his songs, although a handful—"Summertime Blues," "20 Flight Rock," "Somethin' Else," "Teenage Heaven," "C'mon Everybody"—are certified classics. His influence was felt more in England, where he died in the same car crash that crippled Gene Vincent. British rock stars such as Rod Stewart, the Rolling Stones, the Who, and even the Sex Pistols have kept his songs in the book. By the time British reissue labels finished sorting through his work, the entire body looked rather less than impressive; Ricky Nelson records held up better. Some of his recordings stand up against any from his time, but just don't dig too deep.

what to buy: The 20-song collection *Somethin' Else—The Fine Looking Hits of Eddie Cochran* 🎸🎸🎸🎸 (Razor & Tie, 1998, compi-

lation prod. David Richman) focuses on his signature driving rock sound and includes a bare minimum of schlocky ballads. It is virtually interchangeable with *Eddie Cochran: The Legendary Masters Series, Vol. One* 🎸🎸🎸🎸 (EMI, 1990, compilation prod. Ron Furmanek), which boasts the cult favorite "Pink Pegged Slacks" in addition to the hits.

what to avoid: *The Early Years* 🎸🎸 (Ace, 1988, prod. various) is a slapdash collection of his experiments in country music mixed with some rock. The coupling of *Singin' to My Baby* and *Never to Be Forgotten* 🎸🎸 (EMI, 1993, prod. various) sticks a dreadful teen pop album with a posthumous collection of worthy lesser-known rockers.

the rest:
Greatest Hits 🎸🎸 (Curb, 1990)

worth searching for: Airchecks from 1960 British television programs collected for one side of a major label album, *Eddie Cochran: On the Air* (EMI, 1987) gets across some of Cochran's personality that often got stifled on recordings. Who let this one out? Take a bow.

influences:
◄◄ Elvis Presley, Hank Cochran, Carl Perkins
►► Ricky Nelson, Paul McCartney, Glen Campbell, Brian Setzer

Joel Selvin

Jackie Lee Cochran

Born February 5, 1941, in Dalton, GA. Died March 15, 1998, in Burbank, CA.

One of rockabilly's "great unknowns," singer-songwriter Jackie Lee Cochran made music every bit as good as some of the genre's breakout stars without ever really hitting the big time. Nicknamed "Jack the Cat," his '50s trademark was a laminated black cat face with illuminated eyes that hung onstage while he indulged in the rock histrionics that drove girls crazy. While still a teenager, Cochran turned pro for the Sims label, laying down two of his ballsiest sides, "Hip Shakin' Mama" and "Riverside Jump." His surprisingly mature ability to blend blues with a driving country beat led to successful appearances on *The Big D Jamboree* and *The Louisiana Hayride*. In 1957, Cochran cut "Ruby Pearl" and "Mama Don't You Think I Know" (with a key-rattling piano solo by Jimmy Pruett) for Decca, which sold quite well regionally. But contractual disputes between record labels stalled the underaged singer's career, and he lost his shot at being the "next Elvis Presley." Once free of legal problems, Cochran tried unsuccessfully to reestablish career momentum with singles on the Viv, ABC-Paramount, Spry, and Jaguar labels. Bit parts in films such as Disney's *Sancho* and the Marilyn Monroe vehicle *Let's Make Love* (in which he played a Presley-styled singer) did little for his career. But after years of steady work in small-time country bars, Cochran's star began to rise anew with rockabilly collectors and fellow musicians. During the mid-'70s, after neorockabillies the Cramps cut a sizzling (though neurotic) remake of Cochran's ode to a gin-guzzling prostitute, "Georgia Lee Brown," he was rediscovered by legendary rockabilly fanatic Ron Weiser. Cochran's sides for Weiser's Rollin' Rock label featured top musicianship by Ray Campi, Steve Clark, Jimmie Lee Maslon, and Rip Masters, as well as Cochran's own subtle yet expressive guitar work. These hard-hitting rock, country, and blues tracks not only fulfilled the promise of Cochran's early sides, but are the strongest of the label's brief history as well. Though Rollin' Rock shut down during the early' 80s, Cochran went on to record for Hydra Records and toured Europe to great acclaim. At home, he kept up a steady gig at the Gaslite club in Santa Monica, California, until his death in 1998.

what's available: Twenty of Cochran's best Rollin' Rock sides are on *Rockabilly Music* 𝄞𝄞𝄞 (HMG/HighTone, 1997, prod. Rockin' Ronny Weiser). This strong compilation mixes such convincing country tunes as "I Musta Drove My Mules Too Hard" and "They Oughta Call You Miss Heartbreak" with the bluesy ramble "Swamp Fox," the driving anthems of "Rockabilly Legend" and "That Gal's Wicked," and tough remakes of "Hip-Shakin' Mama" and "Mama Don't You Think I Know." Roots music doesn't get much better than this.

worth searching for: You can find Cochran's original versions of "Mama Don't You Think I Know" and "Ruby Pearl" on *That'll Flat Git It!, Vol. 2: Rockabilly from the Decca Vaults* (Bear Family, 1992, prod. Richard Wieze), a strong anthology of rockabilly and country boogie from the likes of Johnny Carroll, Roy Hall, and Terry Noland. Also, *Rockabilly Legend* (Rollin' Rock, 1977, prod. Rockin' Ronny Weiser) is Cochran's best start-to-finish LP and features several self-penned boppers not yet released on CD.

influences:

◀◀ Elvis Presley, John Lee Hooker, Hank Snow, Muddy Waters

▶▶ Tony Conn, Hank Mizell, Johnny Legend, the Cramps

Ken Burke

Bruce Cockburn

Born May 27, 1945, in Ottawa, Ontario, Canada.

Bruce Cockburn has had a fascinating musical development, starting as a folk singer during the early '70s but eventually incorporating rock and world music elements to create a more complex style. His maturation came on 1979's *Dancing in the Dragon's Jaws*, when he was being influenced by reggae, jazz,

and African pop while also discovering world politics (the album also featured his only American Top 40 hit, "Wondering Where the Lions Are"). He fully realized that sound with 1984's *Stealing Fire* and would eventually turn his music inward again to American folk and blues. Cockburn is limited as a vocalist, but his spiritual convictions shine through his music, making him an incredibly emotional singer at times.

what to buy: *Stealing Fire* 𝄞𝄞𝄞𝄞 (Columbia, 1984, prod. Jon Goldsmith, Kerry Crawford), which came out of Cockburn's visits to Central American refugee camps, is one of the most moving works of politically motivated rock ever created. Instead of launching into polemics, Cockburn personalizes the songs, singing about love during wartime in "Lovers in a Dangerous Time" and dreaming visions of vengeance in the shattering "If I Had a Rocket Launcher." Incorporating worldbeat rhythms into his own folk experience, Cockburn makes powerfully emotional melodies, even turning the line "Who put the bullet hole in Peggy's kitchen wall?" into an unforgettable hook.

what to buy next: Working with a band that included Booker T. Jones and Nashville fiddle virtuoso Mark O'Connor, Cockburn did for inner spiritual turmoil what he had done for Latin American politics in *Nothing but a Burning Light* 𝄞𝄞𝄞𝄞 (Columbia, 1991, prod. T-Bone Burnett), weaving original songs and old gospel blues into a phosphorescent statement of faith.

what to avoid: Though the albums aren't bad, Cockburn's two earliest releases—*Bruce Cockburn* 𝄞𝄞 (True North, 1970, prod. Eugene Martynec) and *High Winds, White Sky* 𝄞𝄞 (Columbia, 1971)—are folk singer-songwriter albums that exhibit little of the eclecticism that would make some of Cockburn's later work so involving.

the rest:
Sunwheel Dance 𝄞𝄞𝄞 (Columbia, 1972)
Night Vision 𝄞𝄞𝄞 (Columbia, 1973)
Salt, Sun & Time 𝄞𝄞𝄞 (True North, 1974)
Joy Will Find a Way 𝄞𝄞𝄞𝄞 (True North, 1975)
In the Falling Dark 𝄞𝄞𝄞 (True North, 1977)
Circles in the Stream 𝄞𝄞𝄞 (True North, 1977)
Further Adventures Of 𝄞𝄞𝄞 (True North, 1978)
Dancing in the Dragon's Jaws 𝄞𝄞𝄞𝄞 (Columbia, 1979)
Humans 𝄞𝄞𝄞𝄞 (Columbia, 1980)
Inner City Front 𝄞𝄞𝄞 (Columbia, 1981)
The Trouble with Normal 𝄞𝄞𝄞 (Columbia, 1983)
World of Wonders 𝄞𝄞𝄞𝄞 (Columbia, 1986)
Big Circumstance 𝄞𝄞𝄞 (Columbia, 1989)
Bruce Cockburn Live 𝄞𝄞𝄞 (True North, 1990)
Christmas 𝄞𝄞𝄞 (Columbia, 1993)
Dart to the Heart 𝄞𝄞𝄞 (Columbia, 1994)
The Charity of Night 𝄞𝄞𝄞 (Rykodisc, 1997)
You Pay Your Money and You Take Your Chance: Live 𝄞𝄞𝄞 (True North/Rykodisc, 1997)

worth searching for: *Mummy Dust* (True North, 1981) and *Waiting for a Miracle* (True North, 1987), two best-ofs from Cockburn's Canadian label, collect the singer's most popular works from different periods in his career.

influences:

◀◀ Gordon Lightfoot, Bob Dylan, the Weavers

▶▶ Mark Heard, Tragically Hip, Ian Tamblyn

Brian Mansfield

Joe Cocker

Born John Robert Cocker, May 20, 1944, in Sheffield, England.

With his gruff voice and passion-fueled delivery, Joe Cocker is one of rock's great stylists—which can be as much a curse as a blessing. Because he seldom writes his own material, Cocker is usually at its mercy and dependent on the producers who help him choose it. With sympathetic cohorts—Denny Cordell and Leon Russell at the start of his career, for instance—Cocker's brilliance, schooled in the classic blues and R&B of Ray Charles and Big Joe Turner, shines through; it takes *cajones* and rare talent to not only cover but also reinvent hits such as the Beatles' "With a Little Help from My Friends" and Traffic's "Feelin' Alright." But Cocker has also laid his estimable pipes on some real schmaltz, even though sometimes it's brought him tremendous success ("Up Where We Belong" from the film *An Officer and a Gentleman*). In his fifties now, Cocker still has the voice—and his distinctive spastic air guitar performing style—that he began with in 1969. But each new venture is a crap-shoot, and we can only hope that he again finds the right combination of songs and collaborators to fulfill his potential.

what to buy: With a signature tune, "Delta Lady," as well as another hot Beatles cover ("She Came in through the Bathroom Window"), *Joe Cocker!* 𝄞𝄞𝄞𝄞 (A&M, 1969, prod. Denny Cordell, Leon Russell) built on Cocker's triumphant Woodstock appearance and marked the arrival of a tremendous new talent. Though the band Russell assembled for the live *Mad Dogs and Englishmen* 𝄞𝄞𝄞𝄞 (A&M, 1970, prod. Denny Cordell, Leon Russell) at times seems loose and intrusive, Cocker really shows his mettle by never letting it overwhelm him. *Classics, Volume 4* 𝄞𝄞𝄞𝄞𝄞 (A&M, 1987, prod. various) offers the best of his early period.

what to buy next: *The Best of Joe Cocker* 𝄞𝄞𝄞𝄞 (Capitol, 1993, prod. various) captures the best of his spotty later work, though every collection should have his rendition of "Unchain My Heart" and "You Can Leave Your Hat On." At four CDs, *The Long Voyage Home: The Silver Anniversary Collection* 𝄞𝄞𝄞

(A&M, 1995, prod. various) is flabby in spots, but there are more than enough electrifying moments to compensate.

what to avoid: Tepid originals and vapid cover choices dog Cocker's last two albums, *Night Calls* 𝄞 (Capitol, 1992, prod. various) and *Have a Little Faith* **woof!** (Sony 550, 1994, prod. Chris Lord-Alge, Roger Davies).

the rest:
With a Little Help from My Friends 𝄞𝄞𝄞𝄞 (A&M, 1969)
Joe Cocker 𝄞𝄞𝄞 (A&M, 1972)
I Can Stand a Little Rain 𝄞𝄞𝄞 (A&M, 1974)
Jamaica Say You Will 𝄞𝄞𝄞 (A&M, 1975)
Sting Ray 𝄞𝄞 (A&M, 1976)
Live in L.A. 𝄞𝄞𝄞 (A&M, 1976)
Greatest Hits 𝄞𝄞𝄞𝄞 (A&M, 1977)
Luxury You Can Afford 𝄞𝄞 (A&M, 1978)
Sheffield Steel 𝄞𝄞𝄞 (Island, 1982)
Civilized Man 𝄞𝄞𝄞 (Capitol, 1984)
Cocker 𝄞𝄞𝄞𝄞 (Capitol, 1986)
Unchain My Heart 𝄞𝄞𝄞 (Capitol, 1987)
One Night of Sin 𝄞𝄞 (Capitol, 1989)
Joe Cocker Live 𝄞𝄞𝄞𝄞 (Capitol, 1990)
Across from Midnight 𝄞𝄞 (CMC International, 1998)

worth searching for: *Woodstock Twenty-Fifth Anniversary Collection* (Atlantic, 1994, prod. Eric Blackstead) features portions of the performance that launched Cocker's career in the U.S.

influences:

◀◀ Ray Charles, Big Joe Turner, James Brown, the Beatles, B.B. King

▶▶ Kim Wilson (the Fabulous Thunderbirds), Roger Daltrey (the Who), Robert Palmer, Bryan Adams

Gary Graff

Cockeyed Ghost

Formed 1994, in Los Angeles, CA.

Adam Marsland, guitar, vocals; Rob Cassell, bass, vocals (1994–97); Kurt Medlin, drums (1994–95); Paul "Wally" Presson, drums (1995); James Hazley, drums, vocals (1996–present); Robbie Rist, bass, vocals (1997–present).

One of the most visible and hardest-working acts on L.A.'s burgeoning pop scene, Cockeyed Ghost is one power pop act that pays considerable attention to the *power* part of that moniker. With amps set at 11 and the car radio set to whatever station plays both Green Day *and* the Hollies, Cockeyed Ghost charges full-throttle through a batch of original tunes that are loaded with deadly hooks and fueled by an apparent diet of white sugar, coffee, beer, and Lucky Charms cereal. Singer-guitarist Adam Marsland has been a tireless promoter of both his own band and the L.A. pop scene in general; his zeal is infectious and readily evident in everything Cockeyed Ghost does. Bassist Rob Cassell's sweet harmonies provide the necessary balance to Marsland's rough-hewn vocals and to drummer James Hazley's thunderous drumming. Since Cassell's departure, that role has been filled (temporarily?) by Robbie Rist, known to pop fans as the *wunderkind* fronting L.A.'s Wonderboy, and to pop culture fans as the actor that played Cousin Oliver in the latter days of TV's *The Brady Bunch* series.

what to buy: *Keep Yourself Amused* ✽✽✽✾ (Big Deal, 1996, prod. Earle Mankey, Cockeyed Ghost) is an aggressive pop tour de force, a power pop assault with intent to really, really mess you up. "About Jill," "Disappear," "Dirty Bastard," "Keep the Sun," and "Banished" all slam guitar-first into the very good and the very brave. The more delicate "At the Bookstore" leaves you some room to breathe before the attack is renewed. If playing this loud doesn't get you evicted, then nothing short of a nuclear detonation will.

what to buy next: *Neverest* ✽✽✽ (Big Deal, 1997, prod. Earle Mankey, Cockeyed Ghost, Steve Refling) starts off promisingly, with the ace "Buzz" and "Binghamton," a delicious kiss-off to the upstate New York city of Marsland's formative years. The rest of the album can't quite maintain the momentum of the debut, but it does include superior tracks "Special" and "Asian Hero Worship."

worth searching for: Cockeyed Ghost contributed a cover of "Name of the Game" to *Come and Get It—A Tribute to Badfinger* (Copper, 1996, prod. Darrell M. Clingman).

influences:

⏪ The Beach Boys, the Jam, the Buzzcocks, Cheap Trick, the Raspberries, Kiss

Carl Cafarelli

Cocteau Twins

Formed 1980, in Grangemouth, Scotland.

Elizabeth Fraser, vocals; Robin Gutherie, guitars; Will Heggie, bass (1980–83); Simon Raymonde, bass (1984–present).

For the better part of a decade, the Cocteau Twins represented not only 4AD Records as the label's anchor act, but also the British commercial avant-garde. Laying the groundwork for virtually every female-fronted band that used atmospheric guitars and moody synthesizers was tough work—so tough, in fact, that virtually no Cocteau Twins song has proper lyrics. Elizabeth Fraser sings from a stream of consciousness in most cases, and her verbal repertoire consists almost exclusively of made-up sounds she finds pleasing to her ears. While there are moments when proper English comes into play, they tend to be

infrequent. Along with contemporary Kate Bush, Fraser also laid the groundwork for a more classical approach to modern music—not symphonic à la Yes or the Moody Blues, but in a more daring attempt to convey emotions and ideas. In the beginning, the Cocteaus were a stripped-down unit creating dark and sinister music using a keyboard, drum machine, some guitar effects and Fraser's voice. When bassist Will Heggie left to start his own band, Lowlife, it was obvious he had been holding the group back; once Simon Raymonde joined the band, Fraser and Gutherie both cut loose. The songs began to shimmer, which had a positive effect; during the mid-'80s, the group began to sell hundreds of thousands of records in the U.S. as imports. Ironically, the Twins' deal with Capitol Records marked the beginning of the end, qualitatively. Perhaps the Twins have succumbed to the pressures of a major label. Or perhaps the group ran out of new ideas. But the next three releases were syrupy-pop records, and with the number of female chanteuses on the rise, the originals need to stay a step ahead—and the Cocteau Twins just aren't doing it. The Twins have since been dropped by Capitol and been rebuffed by 4AD when they asked to return. With no label support of merit, the band is waiting in the wings for new opportunities, while fans await a return to the more adventurous stylings of the earlier albums. Frasier did turn up on the Massive Attack single "Teardrop" from the CD *Mezzanine* (Virgin, 1998).

what to buy: *Treasure* ✽✽✽✽ (Capitol, 1984, prod. Ivo Watts Russell) set the sonic standard for the "shoegazer" movement of the late '80s. But the bulk of the band's best material appeared on the EPs it released in Britain through the '80s; they've been compiled for the U.S. on *The CD Single Box Set* ✽✽✽✽ (4AD/Capitol, 1991, prod. various).

what to buy next: *Garlands* ✽✽✽✽✾ (Capitol, 1980, prod. Ivo Watts Russell, the Cocteau Twins) sounds like the soundtrack to a nightmare; Fraser's vocals are raspy and harsh, and the music is scary and cold. *The Pink Opaque* ✽✽✽✽ (4AD/Relativity, 1986), technically the band's first U.S. release, collects tracks from each previous album as well as several EPs. To date it stands as the Cocteau's only official compilation.

what to avoid: *The Moon and the Melodies* ✾ (4AD/Relativity, 1986) was not recorded under the name the Cocteau Twins, but rather as Harold Budd, Elizabeth Fraser, Robin Gutherie, and Simon Raymonde. Whether it was an attempt to blossom as artists or just to make a buck hooking up with new age pianist and Brian Eno pal Budd, the project is uninspired and features Fraser's singing on only three songs.

the rest:

Head over Heels ✽✽✽✽ (Capitol/4AD, 1983)
Victorialand ✽✽✽ (Capitol/4AD, 1987)
Blue Bell Knoll ✽✽✽✽ (Capitol/4AD, 1988)

Heaven or Las Vegas 𝄞𝄞𝄞 (Capitol/4AD, 1990)
Four Calendar Cafe 𝄞𝄞𝄞 (Capitol, 1993)
Milk and Kisses 𝄞𝄞𝄞 (Capitol, 1996)

worth searching for: *Cocteau Twins* (4AD/Capitol, 1994, prod. various) is a self-titled promotional-only release recapping the band's history that came out in conjunction with *The CD Single Box Set*.

influences:

◄◄ Kate Bush, Simple Minds, Joy Division, Siouxsie & the Banshees

►► Curve, Tori Amos, Dead Can Dance, Sarah McLachlan, This Mortal Coil, the Cranes

see also: *This Mortal Coil*

Tim Davis

Phil Cody

Born October 18, 1968, in Cleveland, OH.

Calling Phil Cody a folk singer is tempting, but the term is too limiting; he's more a ragtag patchwork of folk, punk, and rock 'n' roll, all balled up under his wool cap.

what's available: *The Sons of Intemperance Offering* 𝄞𝄞𝄞 (Interscope Records, 1996, prod. Thom Wilson) is a hiccuping, no-frills debut recorded live in the studio. The whizzing-by details of the opening jig "House of Lust" nearly trip over themselves under Cody's rushed delivery. With a vivid eye for detail, Cody writes pungent story-songs that are the mark of many a folk singer, minus the sanctimony. Any further doubters are referred to his acoustic cover of the Clash's "Straight to Hell," which retains its martial atmosphere while also giving license to Cody's freewheeling bursts of singing.

influences:

◄◄ Phil Ochs, Billy Bragg, the Clash

Allan Orski

Leonard Cohen

Born September 21, 1934, in Montreal, Quebec, Canada.

Leonard Cohen was a published poet and novelist in his native Canada well before Judy Collins first recorded his songs in 1966. He was 34 years old when his debut album appeared in 1968, and though he was often grouped with such songwriters as Joni Mitchell, he seemed wiser, like a far worldlier uncle. His most popular early songs—"Suzanne" and "Bird on the Wire"—stamped him as the ultimate long-suffering romantic and erotic victim of countless beautiful women. But as his lyrics grew darker and more obsessive through the '70s, his

fans dwindled; he was simply too depressing, many complained. Yet Cohen continues to be rediscovered by younger listeners who are drawn to his poetic artistry as much as his romanticized gloom. And, in fact, his work over the past decade is some of his strongest. Two tribute albums—1991's *I'm Your Fan* and 1995's *Tower of Song* (with Cohen tunes done by R.E.M., Nick Cave, and the Pixies, among others)—revealed his influences on a new generation of songwriters.

what to buy: The best place to start is with two albums that span nearly 30 years of Cohen's output. His debut, *Songs of Leonard Cohen* 𝄞𝄞𝄞𝄞 (Columbia, 1968, prod. John Simon) immediately established his credentials as an utterly original lyricist, while producer Simon's arrangements gave a romantic shimmer (which Cohen, at the time, detested) to the music's deep melancholia. On *The Future* 𝄞𝄞𝄞𝄞 (Columbia, 1992, prod. various) Cohen casts an unsparing eye on the state of the world and the hopeless politicians, priests, and lovers who inhabit it. Musically, it's his most adventurous album ever—and it shows his wit is definitely improving in middle age. *Best of Leonard Cohen* 𝄞𝄞𝄞𝄞 (Columbia, 1975, prod. various) is a fine introduction to his work, though it only covers his first five albums (put Cohen high on the list of artists deserving of a box set).

what to buy next: *Songs from a Room* 𝄞𝄞𝄞𝄞 (Columbia, 1969, prod. Bob Johnston) is perhaps Cohen's most haunting record, with very spare, sympathetic production ("Bird on the Wire" debuted here). Cohen released little in the U.S. during the '80s, but reemerged with the stunning *I'm Your Man* 𝄞𝄞𝄞𝄞 (Columbia, 1988, prod. Leonard Cohen) featuring an entirely new palette of sounds in his musical backing—and an uncharacteristically bold sense of humor. Taking up where the last best-of compilation left off, *More Best of Leonard Cohen* 𝄞𝄞𝄞𝄞 (Columbia, 1997, prod. various) offers quality tracks from *I'm Your Man* and *The Future*, along with two live cuts and two unpublished gems.

what to avoid: One of the oddest collaborations in pop music annals, *Death of a Ladies' Man* 𝄞𝄞 (Columbia, 1977, prod. Phil Spector) paired Cohen with producer Spector. Truly bizarre.

the rest:

Songs of Love and Hate 𝄞𝄞𝄞 (Columbia, 1971/1995)
New Skin for the Old Ceremony 𝄞𝄞𝄞 (Columbia, 1975/1995)
Recent Songs 𝄞𝄞𝄞 (Columbia, 1979/1990)
Various Positions 𝄞𝄞 (Columbia, 1985/1995)
Cohen Live 𝄞𝄞𝄞 (Columbia, 1994)

worth searching for: On the all-star tribute *Weird Nightmare: Meditations on Mingus* (Columbia, 1992, prod. Hal Wilner), Cohen teams with performance artist Diamanda Galas for a compellingly oddball version of "Eclipse."

influences:

◄◄ Hank Williams, Leadbelly, Jacques Brel, Bob Dylan

▶▶ Nick Cave, the Sisters of Mercy, Morrissey

see also: *Jennifer Warnes*

Doug Pippin and Eric Deggans

Marc Cohn

Born July 5, 1959, in Cleveland, OH.

Pop singer-songwriter Marc Cohn has been plagued by the seemingly eternal success of his breakthrough 1991 single, "Walking in Memphis," which still stands as his most deserving achievement. Three albums and many struggling years later, although Cohn has been mildly charmed with adult-contemporary radio success, his path has been less than spectacular by industry standards. Cohn began as a cover-band singer in junior high and gradually grew into a coffeehouse-circuit performer around Oberlin College, his alma mater. He relocated to New York and put together a 14-piece outfit called the Supreme Court, which played Caroline Kennedy's wedding. His singer-songwriter vein was popping through, though, so he left to pursue that course. A fabled 50-song demo won the attention of Atlantic Records, and Cohn quickly got to work on his debut. Quickly, a Billy Joel–James Taylor (who appears on the debut record) light was hung over his career, and Cohn was marketed towards a bankable graying demographic—all of which suited his casual, storytelling, piano-man style. When he won the Grammy for Best New Artist in 1991, it looked as if Cohn was unstoppable. But bittersweet clouds covered his second release, which attempted the impossible feat of making everyday bourgeois boredom (wife, children, yardwork) look tragic, or even interesting. Minus the hooks, Cohn seemed a drip, so he reenlisted his first album's guitarist, John Leventhal, to resurrect his poignancy via a third record that, not surprisingly, walks similar lines with divorce and parenthood at the center.

what to buy: *Marc Cohn* 𝄞𝄞𝄞𝄞 (Atlantic, 1990, prod. Ben Wisch, Marc Cohn) is about as good as maple syrup gets. Recalling the confessional tone of Chris Rea and smoothing it over with the charismatic style of Billy Joel, Cohn constructs an often compelling collection of blues and pop tunes, including the smash "Walking in Memphis."

the rest:
The Rainy Season 𝄞𝄞𝄞 (Atlantic, 1993)
Burning the Daze 𝄞𝄞𝄞 (Atlantic, 1998)

influences:
◀◀ Billy Joel, Chris Rea, Leonard Cohen, Phil Collins

▶▶ Counting Crows, Matchbox 20, Shawn Colvin

Billy Manes

WHAT ALBUM CHANGED YOUR LIFE?

Hejira by Joni Mitchell. I remember sitting down, listening to that record, and I realized there was a whole other realm of accomplishment. It's a beautiful turning point in her writing and storytelling and language, definitely in a way never heard in the pop world. I remember I was in college when that record came out, trying to convince my creative writing teacher to let me write lyrics as part of fulfilling my creative requirements for the course.

Marc Cohn

Coldcut

Formed 1986, in London, England.

Matt Black, programming, sampling, sequencing; Jonathan More, programming, sampling, sequencing.

Along with hip-hop production innovators Double D and Steinski, the British duo Coldcut can be cited as helping propel the sampling aesthetic in modern music. After scoring a hit with its first single, "Say Kids, What Time Is It?"—a catchy, sample-heavy dance tune—the duo made one of the all-time classic remixes when it reworked Eric B. & Rakim's "Paid in Full" into a dance-floor classic. Matt Black and Jonathan More, who started out as DJs in the U.K. party scene, went on to influence a number of producers ranging from Prince Paul to DJ Shadow. Nowadays Coldcut runs its own independent label, Ninjatune, which in just a few short years has come to be known as a premier source for independent hip-hop and electronic dance music. Its roster includes artists such as Kid Koala, junglist Amon Tobin, Herbaliser, and DJ Food.

what to buy: Though Coldcut's early work is no longer in print in the U.S., the new stuff captures the same sort of vibe. *Let Us Play* 𝄞𝄞𝄞𝄞 (Ninjatune, 1997, prod. Coldcut) cribs everything from children's sing-a-long records to old pop records taking the listener on a funky, beat-filled audio trip.

what to avoid: Seemingly affected by its pop work with Yaz and Lisa Stansfield, the group's *Philosophy* 𝄞𝄞 (Arista, 1994, prod. Coldcut) noticeably lacks the edge of its most ambitious work.

worth searching for: "More Beats & Pieces" was the single sequel to the early classic "Beats & Pieces," and it features remixes of the track from Tortoise's John McIntyre, Kid Koala, and scratch wizard DJ Q-Bert. A quick check of some used record stores might help you track down the group's first album, *What's That Noise* (Big Life, 1988).

influences:

◄◄ Kraftwerk, Afrika Bambaataa, Eric B. & Rakim

►► Herbaliser, DJ Food, DJ Shadow

Joseph Patel

Holly Cole

Born 1963, in Halifax, Nova Scotia, Canada.

One of the most exciting pop/jazz/lounge singers to come along in the past 10 years, Holly Cole is inventive, seductive, and fearless. She hit it big in 1993 with *Don't Smoke in Bed*—a collection of jazz standards performed with her drummer-less trio. Aaron Davis, her pianist, is a gentle, impressionistic player who never gets in the way of Cole's big vocals. Acoustic bassist David Piltch provides the foundation for the music—plucking strings and slapping the hell out of the instrument for percussion. In her more recent works, the creatively restless Cole has strayed from her lounge/jazz roots to do an album of Tom Waits songs, which featured a more avant-garde sound. With a big, physical presence, her stage shows continue to be riveting no matter what type of music is striking her fancy.

what to buy: *Don't Smoke in Bed* 𝄞𝄞𝄞𝄞 (Manhattan/Capitol, 1993, prod. David Was), her can't-miss breakthrough album, contains a selection of cheesy showtunes turned cool: "Tennessee Waltz," "Que Sera Sera," and "I Can See Clearly Now."

what to buy next: *Temptation* 𝄞𝄞𝄞 (Capitol, 1995, prod. Craig Street) and *Dark Dear Heart* 𝄞𝄞𝄞 (Warner Bros., 1997, prod. Larry Klein), two of Cole's later, darker albums, are effective avenues for her considerable pipes, but not exactly relaxing. For devoted Cole fans. *It Happened One Night* 𝄞𝄞𝄞 (Metro Blue, 1996) is a collection of Cole's greatest hits—plus a very nice offering of interviews and music videos via a CD-ROM included in the set.

the rest:

Blame It on My Youth 𝄞𝄞𝄞 (Blue Note, 1992)

influences:

◄◄ Marlene Dietrich, Doris Day, Billie Holiday, Tom Waits

Carl Quintanilla

Jude Cole

See: The Records

Lloyd Cole

Born January 31, 1961, in Buxton, England.

"She's got cheekbones like geometry/And eyes like sin/And she's sexually enlightened by/*Cosmopolitan*." There aren't many singer-songwriters who could make a stanza like that sound matter-of-fact, and fewer still who could conceive it. Such is the genius of Lloyd Cole, a literate hip-flask hipster with a mordant wit and a tongue sharpened for repartee. In many respects, Cole is Scotland's answer to (depending on the song) Leonard Cohen or Morrissey, though he's more tuneful than the former and less lugubrious than the latter. During the early '80s, while still a philosophy student at the University of Glasgow, Cole assembled the Commotions—Neil Clark (guitar), Blair Cowan (keyboards), Lawrence Donegan (bass), and Stephen Irvine (drums)—the crack band with whom he recorded his first three albums. The debut, *Rattlesnakes*, charted at #13 in the U.K., and *Mainstream* fared even better there (#9 in 1987). The Commotions garnered a substantial college following on both sides of the Atlantic; unfortunately, in the States, nobody else paid much attention. Cole split the band in 1988, moved to New York City (with Cowan in tow) and pursued a solo career, which led to 1990's eponymous effort.

what to buy: The question of what to do with Cole's wonderfully arch, occasionally ungainly prose would pose a considerable challenge for any backup band, but on *Rattlesnakes* 𝄞𝄞𝄞𝄞 (Capitol, 1984, prod. Paul Hardiman) the Commotions make it look easy. Anchored by a rhythm section schooled in crisp backbeats and spacious grooves, guitarist Neil Clark's chiseled jangle and Cowan's bleeding organ perfectly silhouette Cole's cool nods, winks, and name-checks (Truman Capote, Eve Marie Saint, Norman Mailer, Simone de Beauvoir, et al.).

what to buy next: The Commotions were at their best when playing it close to Cole's hip. Ironically, the new recruits—bassist Matthew Sweet, ex-Voidoid guitarist Robert Quine, and Lou Reed drummer Fred Maher—on *Lloyd Cole* 𝄞𝄞𝄞 (Capitol, 1990, prod. Lloyd Cole, Fred Maher, Paul Hardiman) shine brightest when playing it hard and loose, as on "What Do You Know about Love?," "Sweetheart," and "I Hate to See You Baby Doing That Stuff." With T. Rex and the Rolling Stones as obvious musical touchstones, *Lloyd Cole* is easily the Scottish singer's hardest rocking effort. The album's party riffing seems even to have rubbed off on the otherwise melancholic Cole: "I'm not even drinking and I feel fine," he reluctantly admits in "Undressed."

what to avoid: The record company sold it as Cole getting back to his roots, and the press bought it hook, line, and sinker. In

Paula Cole (© Ken Settle)

reality, *Love Story* 🎵🎵 (Rykodisc, 1995, prod. Lloyd Cole, others) barely tells half the story: the ballad half. And guess what? *Yaaaawn*. It's the weaker half.

the rest:

Lloyd Cole:
Don't Get Weird on Me, Babe 🎵🎵🎵♪ (Capitol, 1991)
Bad Vibes 🎵🎵🎵 (Rykodisc, 1993)

The Commotions:
Easy Pieces 🎵🎵🎵♪ (Capitol, 1985)
Mainstream 🎵🎵🎵🎵 (Capitol, 1987)
1984–1989 🎵🎵🎵♪ (Capitol, 1989)

worth searching for: The European versions of *Rattlesnakes* and *Easy Pieces* each contain three bonus tracks. The former adds "Sweetness," "Andy's Babies," "The Sea and the Sand," and "You Will Never Be No Good." The latter includes "Her Last Fling," "Big World," and "Nevers End."

influences:

◀◀ The Beatles, Bob Dylan, the Byrds, Leonard Cohen, Velvet Underground, the Smiths, Television, Big Star, T. Rex

▶▶ Michael Penn, American Music Club, Ivy, John Wesley Harding, Gene, the Verve

Greg Siegel

Paula Cole

Born 1969, in Rockport, MA.

Trained in jazz vocal technique at the Berklee College of Music in Boston, Paula Cole moved to New York, where she was spotted by Imago Records chief Terry Ellis. But before Cole's debut CD hit the marketplace, Peter Gabriel heard the disc and asked Cole to join his 1993 "Secret World Tour" to portray "a Jungian vision of womanhood," as she says. A year later, her entrancing brand of art-pop was released. Hampered by Imago's 1995 bankruptcy, Cole toured with Sarah McLachlan and Melissa Etheridge before negotiating a new record deal with Warner Bros., which thankfully rereleased her debut. But it was Cole's sophomore release, *This Fire*, powered by the catchy single "Where Have All the Cowboys Gone?" and years of hardcore touring, that proved the charm, bringing a bit of fame that exploded during her participation in singer-songwriter Sarah McLachlan's all-female Lillith Tour.

what to buy: *Harbinger* 🎵🎵🎵 (Imago, 1994/Warner Bros, 1995, prod. Kevin Killen) is artistically the better of Cole's two records, but bears no hits. It'll make a deeper impact than the album that made her famous.

what to buy next: As her breakthrough album, *This Fire* 🎵🎵🎵 (Warner Bros, 1996, prod. Paula Cole, Kevin Killen) welds Cole's arty compositions to more commercial melodies, bringing a platinum album, a heap of Grammy nominations and lots of critical praise. All that and a duet with Peter Gabriel, too.

worth searching for: Cole's backing vocals add an electric energy to art-rock king Peter Gabriel's show on the live concert recording *Secret World Live* (Geffen, 1994, prod. Peter Gabriel, Peter Walsh).

influences:
◀◀ Tori Amos, Peter Gabriel, Natalie Merchant
▶▶ Jewel

Eric Deggans

Jaz Coleman
See: Killing Joke

Collective Soul
Formed c. 1990–93, in Stockbridge, GA.

Ed Roland, vocals, guitar; Dean Roland, guitar; Will Turpin, bass; Shane Evans, drums; Ross Childress, guitar.

For Collective Soul, the big break came after it had broken up, prompting Ed Roland to get back together with his younger brother, Dean, and resurrect the band. A college radio station in Atlanta acquired a demo tape Roland put together in hopes of landing a songwriting contract, and the song "Shine," with its vocal warmth and chugging, stutter-step guitars, became an instant sensation. That twist of fate led to a major-label contract and demands for a tour, spurring the rebirth of Collective Soul. The group, named after a phrase from Ayn Rand's novel *Atlas Shrugged,* rocks with restraint, alternating fluid rhythms with timely bursts of guitar power. Roland structures the songs on solid melodies and delivers his deftly phrased lyrics with vocal charm.

what to buy: The sophomore effort, *Collective Soul* 🎵🎵🎵 (Atlantic, 1995, prod. Ed Roland, Matt Serletec), is actually the first album written and performed as a band. More focused than the debut, *Hints Allegations and Things Left Unsaid*, it features the band's melodic surge-rock ("Gel," "December") along with crunching rockers ("Untitled," "Where the River Flows") and dreamy power ballads ("The World I Know," "She Gathers Rain").

what to buy next: Fans who like more of the same will appreciate *Disciplined Breakdown* 🎵🎵🎵 (Atlantic, 1997, prod. Ed Roland), featuring the group's distinctive guitar stutters, emotional vocals, and cinematic arrangements with a bit more polish ("Precious Declaration," "Listen").

the rest:
Hints Allegations and Things Left Unsaid 🎵🎵🎵 (Atlantic, 1993)

influences:
◀◀ Dire Straits, the Doors, R.E.M., the Allman Brothers Band

David Yonke

Gerald Collier
Born 1963, in Oakland, CA.

Gerald Collier wears his Beatles influence on his sleeve. Well, almost; he sports allegiance to Elton John via a "Don't Let the Sun Go Down on Me" tattoo on his left arm. Collier's penchant for humorous, wryly sarcastic lyrics are found throughout his work, which is also laden with catchy hooks. The one-time resident of Arizona and Michigan began his music career in 1989 when he co-founded the underrated pop band Best Kissers in the World with Danny Bland, formerly of the Dwarves and the current manager of the Supersuckers. Best Kissers' brilliant albums sadly went unnoticed, but they contained some of his best lines, such as "she won't get under me 'til I get over you." The lack of success has left the disbanded group's material tragically out of print while Collier pursues greater success on his own.

what to buy: Collier's major-label solo debut, *Gerald Collier* 🎵🎵🎵 (Revolution Records, 1998, prod. Paul Q. Kolderie, Sean Slade), is an almost painfully intimate album. Collier tells of a lover's bad temper and drunken nights in the twangy "Hittin' the Wall": "And when you don't remember/when you don't recall/I start losin' my temper/and hittin' the wall." "Whored Out Again" is a disturbing tale of betrayal told to fuzzy guitars, and he even throws in a dreamy, acoustic cover of Pink Floyd's "Fearless."

the rest:
I Had to Laugh Like Hell 🎵🎵🎵 (C/Z Records, 1996)

worth searching for: Although most of Best Kissers' albums are worth searching for, all of them are out of print. *Puddin'* (MCA Records, 1993, prod. Chris Shaw) is an incredible alternapop release, featuring the revved-up, saracastic love song, "Pickin' Flowers For."

influences:
◀◀ Flop, the Replacements, Cheap Trick
▶▶ Everclear

Christina Fuoco

Bootsy Collins

Born William Collins, October 26, 1951, in Cincinnati, OH.

First known as a session musician in Cincinnati, Bootsy Collins came to the national spotlight when James Brown recruited him for his backing band in 1969. After fueling Brown's band for two years, the bassist left to join George Clinton's Parliament-Funkadelic menagerie. Within a few years, the colorful bassist—taken to wearing glitzy, sequined clothes with stars all over and playing a bass shaped like a huge star—became one of P-Funk's most popular ingredients, leading to a solo deal with his Bootsy's Rubber Band in 1976. Featuring fellow P-Funkers such as Bernie Worrell and past Brown sidemen Fred Wesley and Maceo Parker, the Rubber Band presented a boatload of cartoon-like space-based tunes grounded in seriously psychedelic funk grooves. After six solo records filled with the same science-fiction funk, Bootsy turned to session work with artists such as Malcolm McLaren and Dee-Lite. But the funk returned again during the late '80s, with Collins presenting a series of records even trippier than before, courtesy of his collaborations with avant-garde producer Bill Laswell.

what to buy: Collins's solo debut, *Stretching Out in Bootsy's Rubber Band* ♪♪♪♪ (Warner Bros., 1976, prod. George Clinton, Bootsy Collins), is one of the bassist's most consistent records, showcasing both his nimble, effects-filled bass work and out-of-this-world sense of humor. You have to fast-forward 12 years to get to his next-best effort, the aptly titled *What's Bootsy Doin'?* ♪♪♪♪ (Columbia, 1988, prod. Bootsy Collins, Bill Laswell). Recorded after a six-year layoff, it features some of the bassist's tightest, most powerful funk grooves, including the expansive workout "Party on Plastic."

what to buy next: As a convenient way to get the real funk without time-consuming detours, Collins's greatest-hits record, *Back in the Day: The Best of Bootsy* ♪♪♪♪ (Warner Bros., 1994, prod. various), offers plenty of bang for the buck, collecting near-legendary singles such as "Bootzilla," "The Pinocchio Theory," and "Hollywood Squares" in the same package.

what to avoid: As an artist, consistent focus has never been one of Collins's strong points. Still, the all-over-the-place *Ultra Wave* ♪ (Warner Bros., 1980/1996, prod. Bootsy Collins, George Clinton) sets new lows for lack of direction and less-than-distinctive material. Collins's live album, *Keepin' Dah Funk Alive 4 1995* **woof!** (Rykodisc, 1995, prod. At'c Inoue) presents a mediocre band trying its best to re-create the bassist's legendary grooves.

the rest:
Ahh . . . the Name Is Bootsy Baby ♪♪♪♡ (Warner Bros., 1977/1996)
Bootsy? Player of the Year ♪♪♪♡ (Warner Bros., 1978)
This Boot Is Made for Fonk-N ♪♪♪ (Warner Bros., 1979)
The One Giveth, the Count Taketh Away ♪♪♪ (Warner Bros., 1982)
Jungle Bass ♪♪♪ (4th and Broadway, 1990)
Save What's Mine for Me ♪♪ (CBS, 1991)
Blasters of the Universe ♪♪ (Rykodisc, 1994)
Zillatron, Lord of the Harvest ♪♪♪ (Rykodisc, 1994)
Fresh Outta "P" University ♪♪ (WEA, 1997)

worth searching for: *Funk Power 1970: A Brand New Day* (Polydor/Chronicles, 1996) chronicles Collins's term as a JB, showing the roots of the "space bass" style that would drive P-Funk and the Rubber Band in later years.

influences:
◄◄ James Brown, George Clinton, Larry Graham

►► T.M. Stevens, Rick James, Flea (Red Hot Chili Peppers)

see also: *James Brown, George Clinton*

Eric Deggans

Edwyn Collins

Born August 23, 1959, in Glasgow, Scotland.

From 1979 to 1985, Edwyn Collins was a member of the seminal band Orange Juice, which led the Scottish pop-punk revolution with singles such as "Rip It Up," "Felicity," and "Louise Louise," songs that featured ragged yet sunny pop fronted by Collins's dark crooning. After eventually caving in due to the lack of commercial success, Orange Juice split, and Collins embarked on a solo career that finally brought him before the public at large with the wonderful single "A Girl Like You" in 1995.

what to buy: His most fully realized album to date, *Gorgeous George* ♪♪♪♪ (Bar/None, 1995, prod. Edwyn Collins) is Collins at his best—cynical, honest, ironic, and funny. From the memorable hit "A Girl Like You" to the social commentary of "The Campaign for Real Rock" and "Low Expectations," the album mixes '60s soul with Euro-pop and balladry.

the rest:
I'm Not Following You ♪♪♪ (Epic, 1997)

worth searching for: Collins's first two post–Orange Juice solo albums, *Hope and Despair* (Demon, 1989, prod. Edwyn Collins) and *Hellbent on Compromise* (Demon, 1990, prod. Edwyn Collins), are available as imports.

influences:
◄◄ Philadelphia International, David Bowie

Anna Glen

Judy Collins

Born May 1, 1939, in Seattle, WA.

Judy Collins seemed to be the great earth mother of folk—yet her roots were in classical music. Collins grew up in Denver and studied piano with the pianist and conductor Antonia Brico. At age 13, Collins gave her debut piano performance with the Denver Businessmen's Symphony. However, at age 16, she gave up classical for folk music. She married Peter Taylor in 1957, and they had a son, Clark. (They divorced in 1962, and Clark Taylor died in 1992.) Soon afterward, she began performing professionally in Boulder. By 1960 the family had moved to Chicago where she broke into the big time. Later, after she moved to New York and became a part of the Greenwich Village scene, she was signed by Elektra when it was still the house that Jac Holzman built. Collins always had a good ear for tunes, picking traditional folk songs that she could make her own. By her third album, she was more politically involved and recording protest tunes by the likes of Bob Dylan and Tom Paxton. She quickly became even more stylistically adventurous, opening up her repertoire with theater music and art songs. She championed such then-unknown songwriters as Leonard Cohen and Joni Mitchell. She made charming albums with classically oriented arrangements, and eventually tried electric back-ups as well. In 1972, she took a year off her musical career to produce and co-direct a documentary on Brico called *Antonia: A Portrait of a Woman,* which was nominated for an Academy Award in 1975. Collins's voice has suffered a bit as the years have gone by, but she continues to exhibit a good ear for songs.

what to buy: *Forever . . . The Judy Collins Anthology* ♫♫♫♫ (Elektra, 1997, prod. Judy Collins, others), a two-CD set, sums up Collins's move from folk chanteuse to art-song diva. It's not in chronological order, so there are stylistic shifts from piece to piece, but the song sequences make sense. Although it includes many of Collins's hits and signature tunes, it's not a greatest-hits anthology—"Amazing Grace" and "Hard Times for Lovers" are among the conspicuously absent titles. *Wildflowers* ♫♫♫♫♫ (Elektra, 1967, prod. Mark Abramson) boasts the most interesting song sequence of any Collins album—including "Both Sides Now," "Michael from Mountains," and "La Chanson des Vieux Amants"—bolstered by Joshua Rifkin's rich, baroque-influenced arrangements, which set off Collins's soprano well. *In My Life* ♫♫♫♫ (Elektra, 1966, prod. Jac Holzman, Mark Abramson) is the album on which Collins first experimented with bigger arrangements and theater music ("Marat/Sade"). The shift from acoustic folk proved perfectly suited to her voice.

what to buy next: With such tasty numbers as Richard Fariña's "Pack up Your Sorrows," Eric Andersen's "Thirsty Boots," and Gordon Lightfoot's "Early Morning Rain" (as well as a slew of Dylan), *Fifth Album* ♫♫♫♫ (Elektra, 1965, prod. Jac Holzman, Mark Abramson) stands among Collins's best. *Who Knows Where the Time Goes* ♫♫♫♫ (Elektra, 1968, prod. David Anderle)

is another great collection that includes Cohen's "Bird on the Wire" and Ian Tyson's "Someday Soon." *Whales & Nightingales* ♫♫♫♫ (Elektra, 1970, prod. Mark Abramson) is a bit startling in its diversity, containing her hit version of "Amazing Grace" and "Farewell to Tarwathie," a Scottish whaling song that is "backed up" by humpback whale "singing."

what to avoid: On *Hard Times for Lovers* ♫ (Elektra, 1979, prod. Gary Klein) the arrangement for the title song just follows the late '70s crowd, the album reeks of the smug "El Lay" atmosphere, Collins isn't singing well, and the collection seems phoned in.

the rest:
Recollections ♫♫♫♪ (Elektra, 1969)
Living ♫♫♫ (Elektra, 1971)
Colors of the Day: The Best of Judy Collins ♫♫♫♪ (Elektra, 1972)
True Stories and Other Dreams ♫♫♫ (Elektra, 1973)
Judith ♫♫♫ (Elektra, 1975)
Times of Our Lives ♫♫♫ (Elektra, 1982)
Home Again ♫♫♪ (Elektra, 1984)
So Early in the Spring: The First 15 Years ♫♫♫♫ (Elektra, 1987)
Sanity and Grace ♫♫♫ (Delta, 1989)
Fires of Eden ♫♫♫♪ (Columbia, 1990)
Wind beneath My Wings ♫♫♪ (Laserlight, 1992)
Judy Sings Dylan . . . Just Like a Woman ♫♫♫♪ (Geffen, 1994)
Shameless ♫♫♫ (Mesa/Bluemoon, 1994)
Come Rejoice! Judy Collins Christmas ♫♫♫ (Mesa/Bluemoon, 1994)
Live at Newport ♫♫♫♪ (Vanguard, 1995)
Christmas at Biltmore Estate ♫♫♫ (Elektra, 1997)

worth searching for: *Maid of Constant Sorrow* (Elektra, 1961, prod. Jac Holzman), *Golden Apples of the Sun* (Elektra, 1962, prod. Jac Holzman), and *Judy Collins #3* (Elektra, 1963, prod. Jac Holzman, Mark Abramson) are out of print and available only on vinyl. The first two are Collins's first albums. The third features arrangements by Jim McGuinn (who became Roger and the master of the Byrds) and begins Collins's experimentation with more contemporary material.

influences:
◄◄ Mimi & Richard Fariña, Joan Baez
►► Joni Mitchell

Salvatore Caputo

Paul Collins
See: The Beat

Phil Collins
Born January 31, 1951, in London, England.

The only thing more surprising than Phil Collins's seamless shift from drummer to lead vocalist after Genesis frontman

Phil Collins (© Ken Settle)

Peter Gabriel's 1974 departure was the folically challenged percussionist's transformation into a solo artist more successful than the band. Crafting a stark sound filled with powerhouse drums—Collins was among the first to develop the wide open, reverb-drenched drum sounds that dominated '80s-era records—scratchy guitars, moody keyboards, and his own reedy yet muscular wail, Collins exploded onto the rock charts with a debut effort that veered from R&B/funk to atmospheric art rock. Injecting his work with increasing amounts of pop songcraft, Collins was rewarded with a succession of 13 straight Top 10 hits and records that rode a fine line between commercial appeal and creative vision. Eventually, his distinctive sound seeped into Genesis's work, giving the group's albums at least a flavor of his solo efforts. In 1996, his place among the biggest names in rock assured, Collins announced he was leaving the band he'd performed with for more than two decades in order to concentrate on his solo career—which at that point also included periodic excursions with a big band.

what to buy: As a near-perfect combination of Collins's emerging songwriting and production chops, *Face Value* 𝄢𝄢𝄢𝄢 (Atlantic, 1981, prod. Phil Collins, Hugh Padgham) details the disintegration of Collins's first marriage through innovative tunes that range from the atmospheric bombast of "In the Air Tonight" to the greasy, horn-drenched funk of "I Missed Again/Behind the Lines." Nearly as impressive is Collins's third solo outing, *No Jacket Required* 𝄢𝄢𝄢𝄢 (Atlantic, 1985, prod. Phil Collins, Hugh Padgham), which presents the singer's aggressively commercial formula in full bloom—as evidenced by hits such as the danceable "Sussudio" and the heartbreak ballad "One More Night."

what to buy next: As the next step in Collins's seemingly unshakeable domination of '80s-era pop radio, . . . *But Seriously* 𝄢𝄢𝄢𝄢 (Atlantic, 1989, prod. Phil Collins, Hugh Padgham) featured his take on somber subjects, ruefully addressing homelessness in the smash hit "Another Day in Paradise."

what to avoid: Generally, Collins's attempts to step outside the traditional album format have brought terrible results. Several of his efforts—the collection of 12-inch dance remixes *12"ers* **woof!** (Atlantic, 1988, prod. Phil Collins, Hugh Padgham), the soundtrack to the film *Buster* **woof!** (Atlantic, 1988, prod. various), and a live record, *Serious Hits . . . Live!* **woof!** (Atlantic, 1990, prod. Phil Collins, Robert Colby)—are serious wastes of recording tape.

the rest:
Hello, I Must Be Going 𝄢𝄢𝄢 (Atlantic, 1982)
Both Sides 𝄢𝄢𝄢 (Atlantic, 1993)
Dance into the Light 𝄢𝄢 (Atlantic, 1996)
Hits 𝄢𝄢𝄢 (Atlantic, 1998)

worth searching for: To get an idea of just how good a drummer Collins is, check out his work with the '70s-era British jazz-

fusion band Brand X, conveniently collected on the compilation *Xtrax* (Passport, 1986, prod. Brand X).

influences:
◀◀ Peter Gabriel, Earth, Wind & Fire, Motown
▶▶ Seal, Howard Jones, Mike & the Mechanics

see also: *Genesis*

Eric Deggans

Christine Collister
See: Clive Gregson & Christine Collister

Colony
Formed 1994, in Columbia, MO.

Ted Bruner, lead vocal, guitar; Matt Hickenbotham, drums, background vocals; Jon Armstrong, lead guitar; John Stuller, bass.

Uniting the dusky folk-rock of early R.E.M. with the brisk pop of Crowded House, Colony combines melody and mysticism in just the right portions. The band began at the University of Missouri at Columbia, then relocated to St. Louis. In addition to its strength as a live act, the group exploits the sharp songwriting skills of Ted Bruner.

what's available: *Siren* 𝄢𝄢𝄢 (MCA, 1997, prod. Ben Mink) is a loud-and-clear assertion of Colony's collegiate pop smarts. Songs like "Breathe" pump new blood into a genre that died when R.E.M. began writing lyrics instead of transcribing vocal sounds.

worth searching for: Colony released some early examples of its burgeoning pop-folk, among them the self-released disc *Colony* (1995, prod. Jack Petracek), which contained early versions of some *Siren* songs, and a self-released EP, also called *Colony* (1995, prod. Jack Petracek). Those who find *Siren* seductive should buy these if they can find them, as they were distributed regionally before the band colonized other areas.

influences:
◀◀ R.E.M., Crowded House, Richard Barone

Jordan Oakes

The Colourfield
Formed 1983, in Manchester, England. Disbanded 1987.

Terry Hall, lead vocals; Toby Lyons, vocals; Karl Shale, vocals.

Largely a vehicle for British hipster/vocalist Terry Hall (ex-member of the Specials and Fun Boy Three), the Colourfield spent a few shining years as purveyors of lush, melodic pop songs, colored by kitschy psychedelic playfulness.

what's available: Its stunning album-length debut, *Virgins and Phillistines* (Chrysalis, 1985, prod. Jeremy Green, Hugh Jones), yielded a minor U.K. hit with "Thinking of You," but it was the track-to-track consistency that made this record so remarkable. Combining Donovanesque shimmer with Hall's trademark vocal swagger, *Virgins and Phillistines* is one of the overlooked classics of mid-'80s alternapop.

influences:

◀◀ Donovan

▶▶ The Legendary Jim Ruiz Group

see also: *Fun Boy Three, the Specials*

Scott Hess

Shawn Colvin

Born Shanna Colvin, January 10, 1958, in Vermillion, SD.

Shawn Colvin picked up her first guitar when she was 10, and after high school she chose to pursue music full-time. During the '70s, she moved to Texas to join a swing band, the Dixie Diesels, then spent a few years in San Francisco before settling in New York. There she played in the Buddy Miller Band, a pop group, before deciding to start working on her own. Influenced by Joni Mitchell, and later, Suzanne Vega—a patron of sorts who used Colvin for backup vocals on the hit "Luka" and as an opening act on tour—Colvin's poetic lyrics, flawless finger-picking, and use of alternate guitar tunings gave her songs a distinctive character, while her voice, breathy and gentle, is capable of swelling with strength and emotion when necessary. An independently released live album in 1988 attracted attention from the record industry, as did thorough gigging on the East Coast club circuit. Though she tends to take her time between albums, Colvin remains a writer and performer of rare and special abilities who was justly recognized for two major Grammy Awards—Song of the Year and Record of the Year for "Sunny Came Home"—in 1998.

what to buy: Colvin's debut, *Steady On* (Columbia 1989, prod. Shawn Colvin, John Leventhal, Steve Addabbo), offers an excellent balance of her crystal clear vocals, poetic lyrics, and folk influences, along with the accompaniment and contributions of a full band—plus guests David Sanborn, Bruce Hornsby, and Vega. Nearly every song's a gem, though the album closes on a yawn with the string-laden "The Dead of Night"—which was, unfortunately, a sign of things to come.

what to buy next: *A Few Small Repairs* (Columbia, 1996, prod. John Leventhal) catapulted Colvin to commercial radio saturation and more success than she had ever seen. *A Few Small Repairs* combines great pop sensibilities with Colvin's folk roots, abandoning the bubble gum sounds of lush string and keyboard arrangements from *Cover Girl* and parts of *Fat City* for a more roots-rock instrumentation of guitars, drums, and Hammond organ. These ingredients, mixed with her honest and moving lyrics, make for an unsweetened, more serious mood than her previous two works.

what to avoid: *Cover Girl* (Columbia 1994, prod. Shawn Colvin, Stewart Smith, David Kahne) seemed promising on paper, with Colvin covering songs by others—including personal favorites from Bob Dylan, the Police, Talking Heads, and Tom Waits. But she doesn't deliver. The same over-production that burdened "The Dead of Night" hampers Colvin's renditions on this album, including "Every Little Thing (He) Does Is Magic," in which lush strings divert the ears from her beautiful guitar picking.

the rest:

Fat City (Columbia, 1992)
Holiday Songs and Lullabies N/A (Sony, 1998)

worth searching for: *Live '88* (Plump Records, 1988/1995, prod. Carol Young) is Colvin's live independent album, which has been reissued on CD. Many of the songs wound up on *Steady On*, and while we miss some of the arrangements from that album, Colvin still carries the songs with the purity of her guitar and vocal performances.

WHAT ALBUM CHANGED YOUR LIFE?

I discovered Buddy Rich just when he came out of big band retirement in 1966. Prior to that he'd been playing in little groups, smaller groups, 'cause of the financial side of taking a big band out. But he managed to get financed for a big band, and he made this record live in Vegas called *Swingin' New Big Band*. And he had the *West Side Story* medley on it, which really turned me around 'cause I loved that music. I thought, 'This is what I want to do when I grow up.'

Phil Collins

influences:

◀◀ Tom Waits, Joni Mitchell, Suzanne Vega, Mary Chapin Carpenter

▶▶ Jewel, Amanda Marshall, Natalie Merchant

Joshua Zarov

Combustible Edison

Formed 1991, in Boston, MA.

Michael "the Millionaire" Cudahy, guitars; Liz "Miss Lily Banquette" Cox, drums, vocals; Peter Dixon, organ; Aaron Oppenheimer, vibes.

Think of it as the Buddy Love of lounge music, a twisted but ultra-suave Frankenstein born out of a nerdy past. When an unnoticed underground group called Christmas got its first dose of stereophonic wizard Juan Garcia Esquivel's groovy tunes, that band's jangle-pop proliferators Michael Cudahy and Liz Cox became, respectively, the Millionaire and Miss Lily Banquette, while the ailing Christmas picked up some Moog keyboards, a theremin, and a harpsichord, some exotic instrumentation like marimba and gamales . . . and a new name, Combustible Edison. In 1991, Cudahy wrote and premiered a two-hour performance-art piece called *The Tiki Wonder Hour* that featured a 14-piece outfit called the Combustible Edison Heliotropic Oriental Mambo and Foxtrot Orchestra. A few more shows, a demo, and a record label later, and the group was pitted as the Sherpas of Snazzy, the heads of honorable hip, the chiefs of the Cocktail Nation—to the point that equally "now" movie directors such as Quentin Tarantino and Robert Rodriguez hit the band up to score their episodic film *Four Rooms*. (Which, despite some choice Edison cuts, was an artistic disaster for all involved.) A better application of Edison's influence has come via an attempted resuscitation of Esquivel's career, though the pioneer is now 80 and fairly infirm. Still, Combustible Edison is the deserved keeper of his flame, keeping one foot steeped firmly in an experimental (though melodic) tradition, the other skipping lightly along a camp surface.

what to buy: The band's debut, *I, Swinger* ♫♫♫♫ (Sub Pop, 1994, prod. Carl Plaster), was partly responsible for the lounge revival that swept through major cities in the mid-'90s and sent hordes of easy-listening collectors to trample through used-record stores before new fans devoured every last Three Suns and Enoch Light platter they could find. As devoted to its sources as to further progression—though equally in love with the culture as much as the sound (the cover sports a highball on the rocks)—it's no surprise that after a few years *I, Swinger* holds up remarkably well, ironically because it already sounds aged; songs such as "The Millionaire's Holiday" and "Breakfast at Denny's" seem stolen from another era.

what to buy next: Though not as successful a project as the debut, *Schizophonic! The Progressive Sound of Combustible Edison* ♫♫♫ (Sub Pop, 1996, prod. Combustible Edison, Brian Capouch) is still worth hearing. The mood is decidedly darker, which isn't always beneficial, but it's a sign that Edison is taking its sound seriously enough to expand it beyond kitsch boundaries. (Though that could also lead to its downfall; fun with a laid-back twist, after all, is the point.) And though the soundtrack to *Four Rooms* ♫♫♫ (Elektra, 1995, prod. various) is long on atmospheric fluff, it does contain the irresistible "Vertigogo," a sassy, nonsensical gem that deserved to be a modern-rock hit when it was released, as well as some classic Esquivel moments and the theme from *Bewitched*.

worth searching for: The CD-single version of *Blue Light* (Domino, 1993, prod. various) features early tracks "Satan Says" and "Intermission"; *Spy S.O.U.N.D.S.* (Mai Tai Records, 1995, prod. various) is a collection of spy and crime-noir tunes with Henry Mancini's "A Shot in the Dark"; *Short Double Latte* (Bungalo Records, 1996, prod. various) is a Europe-only single release with "Hellraiser"; and *Get Easy! Vol. 2: The Future Collection* (Motor Music, 1996, prod. various) is one-half of a two-volume German set of past and present easy-listening favorites, including "Intermission."

influences:

◀◀ Juan Garcia Esquivel, Martin Denny, Enoch Light, the Three Suns, Les Baxter

▶▶ Love Jones, Friends of Dean Martinez, the Lounge Lizards

Ben Wener

Come

Formed 1990, in Boston, MA.

Thalia Zedek, guitar, vocals, clarinet; Chris Brokaw, guitar, vocals, keyboards, percussion; Sean O'Brien, bass (1990–95); Winston Bramen, bass (1997–present); Arthur Johnson, drums (1990–95); Daniel Coughlin, drums (1997–present).

Lesbian and recovering junkie Thalia Zedek, formerly of Live Skull, Uzi, Via, and Dangerous Birds, joined with Chris Brokaw (ex-Codeine drummer), and musicians Sean O'Brien (Kilkenny Cats) and Arthur Johnson (Bar-B-Q Killers) from Athens, Georgia; after one Sub Pop 7-inch single, "Cars," the buzz was awesome, but despite rumors of intense major label interest, Zedek's experience with Matador owner Gerard Cosley when he was at Homestead and she was in Live Skull made the decision easy. The band's darkly menacing sound was not constructed from grunge influences but is emotionally akin, with Zedek apparently drawing from her own tortured past life, snarling and spitting the resulting lyrics over gnarled guitar Sonic Youth could envy. After O'Brien and Johnson quit in the summer of '95, Zedek and Brokaw soldiered on with a variety of Chicago rhythm sections on *Near Life Experience*.

what to buy: *Eleven:Eleven* &&&& (Matador, 1992, prod. Come, Tim O'Heir, Carl Plaster) delivers Come's sonic bludgeoning in its purest, most compelling form. A cover of the Rolling Stones' "I Got the Blues" pays tribute to one of the band's strongest conceptual sources. *Gently, Down the Stream* &&& (Matador, 1998) suggests that time off and performances in different formats have led Zedek and Brokaw to explore some new sounds. Their bludgeoning, locked-together guitar riffs remain, but now there's more variety and space for the music to breath. Brokaw sings two tunes, and there's even a quiet instrumental ("The Former Model") that uses a couple of clarinets and a cheap electric piano, achieving a wistful mood unlike anything ever before heard on a Come album.

what to buy next: *Don't Ask Don't Tell* &&&& (Matador, 1994, prod. Carl Plaster, Mike McMackin, Bryce Goggin, Come) is slightly more aggressive and less drone-oriented than the debut. *Near Life Experience* &&&& (Matador, 1996) gains stylistic and textural flexibility from the rotating rhythm sections (borrowed from indie stalwarts including Jesus Lizard, Gastr del Sol, and Rachel's). For the first time, Brokaw's vocals supplement Zedek's exquisitely ravaged singing.

the rest:
The Come EP &&& (Matador, 1994)

worth searching for: The non-album track "Cimmaron" is one of the better items on the benefit compilation *Ain't Nothing But a Girl Thing* (London, 1995, prod. various). The original lineup of Come backs Steve Wynn on the former Dream Syndicate frontman's *Melting in the Dark* (Zero Hour, 1996, prod. Steve Wynn); its dark, bluesy, compressed energy provides the heft Wynn's tunes require, while his strong songwriting gives the group more structured material and draws the players into a slightly different sound.

influences:
◄◄ The Rolling Stones, Neil Young, Live Skull, the Swans, the Velvet Underground

►► Steve Wynn

Steve Holtje

Commander Cody & His Lost Planet Airmen

Formed 1967, in Ann Arbor, MI.

Commander Cody (born George Frayne, July 19, 1944, in Ann Arbor, MI), piano, vocals; John Tichy, guitar; West Virginia Creeper, steel gui- tar (1967–70); Billy C. Farlow, harmonica, vocals (1968–76); Bill Kirchen, guitar (1968–76); Bruce Barlow, bass (1968–76); Lance Dickerson, drums (1968–76); Andy Stein, fiddle, saxophone (1968–76); Bobby Black, steel guitar (1970–76); plus others over the years.

A band before its time, Commander Cody & the Lost Planet Airmen can be seen as a precursor to the Austin music scene of the '8os. In fact, Austin kingpins Asleep at the Wheel first moved to San Francisco under the influence of the Cody outfit and worked clubs there as a kind of satellite of the pioneering rockabilly/western swing revivalists. The band's first four classic albums laid the groundwork for a whole wing of retro-revisionists in country-rock, as far as possible from the slick Los Angeles hybrid practiced by the Byrds, Poco, and others. Cody's crew practiced a loose-jointed, rollicking brand of barroom boogie that sounded like it had been steeped in beer fumes in front of rowdy crowds as ready to fight as dance. Despite scoring a Top 10 hit ("Hot Rod Lincoln") off its debut album, Cody's band was never accorded appropriate acclaim, and the original players splintered in disarray in 1976—though the Commander continues to record and tour with an always changing squadron of Airmen.

what to buy: The first three albums have been cannibalized for an inconsistent collection, *Too Much Fun: The Best Of Commander Cody and his Lost Planet Airmen* &&&& (MCA, 1990, compilation prod. Andy McKaie).

what to buy next: The fourth album, a jaunty concert recording originally titled *Live from Deep in the Heart of Texas*, has been reissued as *Sleazy Roadside Stories* &&& (Relix, 1995, prod. Tom Anderson), hard evidence of the original lineup's swinging blend of country and rock 'n' roll.

what to avoid: Without the balance of the Last Airmen personalities, Cody's solo albums have suffered from contrivance and the unmitigated dominance of his personality—none more so than *Let's Rock* && (Blind Pig, 1987, prod. Bill Kirchen, Mike Rennick), despite the presence of veteran Airmen Kirchen and Barlow.

the rest:
We Got a Live One Here && (Warner Bros., 1976/1996)
Lost in Space && (Relix, 1993)
Bar Room Classics && (1973/Aim, 1993)
Thirst Case Scenario &&& (Aim, 1994)
Relix's Best of Commander Cody &&& (Relix, 1995)
The Tour from Hell—1973 &&& (Aim, 1996)

worth searching for: The first two, long-deleted albums—*Lost in the Ozone* (Paramount, 1971) and *Hot Licks, Cold Steel and Trucker's Favorites* (Paramount, 1972)—qualify as certified classics in the field. During that period, the band cut a spectacular Christmas song, "Daddy's Drinking up Our Christmas," which has been rescued from obscurity by *Hillbilly Holiday* (Rhino, 1988, prod. various).

solo outings:
Commander Cody:
Ace's High ♬♬♪ (Relix, 1990)

Bill Kirchen:
Tombstone Every Mile ♬♬♬ (Black Top, 1994)
Have Love Will Travel ♬♬♬ (Black Top, 1996)

influences:
◄◄ Bob Wills, Moon Mullican, Dave Dudley
►► Asleep at the Wheel, Nick Lowe

Joel Selvin

Communards
See: Jimmy Somerville

Concrete Blonde
Formed 1981, in Los Angeles, CA. Disbanded 1994.

Johnette Napolitano, vocals, bass; Jim Mankey, guitar; Harry Rushakoff, drums (1981–89, 1992); Paul Thompson, drums (1989–92, 1993–94); Alan Bloch, bass (1989–90).

Concrete Blonde was built on Johnette Napolitano's spooky, quavering voice, which sounds like Chrissie Hynde if she were a practicing witch—a sound that connected seamlessly with Halfnelson/Sparks progressive-rock guitarist Jim Mankey's dramatic plucking. Though the band had one Top 20 hit—the yearning "Joey"—it never fully overcame its complex financial problems. As a result, the trio put out several almost-great albums, sometimes with two or three incredible, distinctively gloomy pop songs, but never fulfilled its potential. The group split up in 1994, with Napolitano forming a new band called Pretty & Twisted and collaborating briefly with Holly Vincent of Holly & the Italians in the interestingly named band Vowel Movement. She also replaced David Byrne for a 1996 Talking Heads (renamed the Heads) reunion tour; it made for some fun concerts, but Napolitano's shrieking gloom was a strange fit with the band's whimsical funk.

what to buy: Though overproduced and too polished, *Bloodletting* ♬♬♬♪ (I.R.S., 1990, prod. Concrete Blonde, Chris Tsangarides) showcases Napolitano's invitingly dark songwriting. "Tomorrow, Wendy" is a chilling hymn about a woman dying from AIDS, and the stomp of "Days and Days" complements the more measured hit "Joey."

what to buy next: *Walking in London* ♬♬♬ (I.R.S., 1992, prod. Concrete Blonde, Chris Tsangarides), which features a downright weird version of James Brown's "It's a Man's Man's Man's World," could have been a successful album, but the band's unfocused label, I.R.S., didn't know what to do with it.

what to avoid: While *Mexican Moon* ♬♬ (Capitol, 1993, prod. Concrete Blonde, Sean Freehill) has some nice ideas, including a snippet of actual conversation by infamous cult leader Jim Jones, it's clearly the band's last gasp.

the rest:
Free ♬♬♪ (I.R.S., 1989)
Still in Hollywood ♬♬ (Capitol, 1994)
Concrete Blonde y Los Illegals ♬♬ (Ark 21, 1997)

worth searching for: Unfortunately, the band never put its soaring version of Leonard Cohen's "Everybody Knows," on one of its own records, though it was used to great effect in the film and on the sountrack to *Pump up the Volume* (MCA, 1990, prod. various). Napolitano was also featured on a couple tracks of the Heads' David Byrne–less reunion album, *No Talking Just Head* (MCA, 1996, prod. the Heads), which was bland and clunky despite Napolitano's best efforts

solo outings:
Johnette Napolitano:
(With Holly Vincent) *Vowel Movement* ♬♬♬ (Atlantic, 1995)
(With Pretty & Twisted) *Pretty & Twisted* ♪ (Warner Bros., 1995)

influences:
◄◄ Patti Smith, the Pretenders, James Brown, Leonard Cohen
►► 4 Non Blondes, Alanis Morissette

Steve Knopper

Congo Norvell
Formed 1991, in Los Angeles, CA.

Kid Congo Powers, guitars; Sally Norvell, vocals.

After playing with such seminal alternative acts as Nick Cave & the Bad Seeds, the Gun Club, and the Cramps, guitarist Kid Congo Powers made a move more to the forefront when he teamed with a little-known vocalist out of Texas named Sally Norvell. The pair seemingly had little in common, other than the odd coincidence of both having appeared in films by Wim Wenders: Norvell played a prostitute in *Paris, Texas*, while Powers was an angel in the critically acclaimed *Wings of Desire*. From the beginning they tapped into a dark, primitive, alluring, cinematic sound that intrigued critics and excited the fans lurking in the depths of the underground. Powers says that directors like John Cassavetes and Roman Polanski have been a big influence on the group's sound. After living in L.A. for years and establishing a strong fan base there, Powers and Norvell relocated to New York in 1996, fulfilling a longtime goal. The impetus for moving was the band they had used on a European tour, which, in Norvell's words, "gave us a new sound that we had been searching for."

what to buy: A conceptual look at family life from the black sheep's perspective, *Abnormals Anonymous* ♫♫♫♪ (Jetset, 1997, prod. Sally Norvell, Kid Congo, Jim Sclavunos) features guest vocalist Mark Eitzel on four tracks, including the evocative "She's like Heroin to Me" and the melancholy "Blue Sky." While Congo Norvell's lyrics are always thought-provoking, the band's strength continues to be Norvell's husky, torch-song vocal delivery. A cross between Concrete Blonde's Johnette Napolitano and Billie Holiday, Norvell has the kind of voice that can seduce vampires. The proof is in the intoxicating "Warm Tonight," with which you can feel your temperature rise and your knees start to buckle on the first listen. Or the 50th.

the rest:
Lullabies ♫♫♪ (Fiasco EP, 1992)
Music to Remember Him By ♫♫♫ (Basura/Priority, 1994)

worth searching for: *The Dope, the Lies, the Vaseline* (Basura/Priority, 1995, prod. Joe Chicarelli), one of the band's best CDs, unfortunately never saw the light of day. However, several promo copies did make their way to journalists and other members of the music industry, meaning that there are bound to be copies out there to be had in the used bins of your local record store. Another project worth seeking out is the 7-inch EP *Live at the Mission* (Triple X Records, 1995), if only for collector's sake.

influences:
◀◀ The Cramps, Nick Cave & the Bad Seeds, the Gun Club

Steve Baltin

The Connells

Formed 1984, in Raleigh, NC.

Mike Connell, guitar, vocals; Doug MacMillan, vocals, guitar; George Huntley, guitar, vocals; David Connell, bass; Peele Wimberley, drums; Steve Potak, keyboards, organ (1991–present).

Started by two brothers, the Connells quickly struck a responsive chord with the college crowd thanks to its irresistible melodies and jangly guitars. With a solid foundation of songwriting, the Connells had excellent timing as a rush of indie and major label signings swept through the region fueled by R.E.M.'s growing reputation, though the group would never enjoy the same success as many caught in the same wake. The Connells' rootsy brand of power pop rode the wave of the college charts as "alternative" music went through its changes. With a strong cult audience and a continuous touring schedule, the group enjoyed some regional success and even had some modest commercial success with the 1993 album *Ring* and the singles "Slackjawed" and "74-75." If nothing else, the Connells

are survivors, continuing to make viable music both on record and on stage.

what to buy: The Connells' sophomore outing, *Boylan Heights* ♫♫♫♫ (TVT, 1987, prod. Mitch Easter), is a lively record with catchy songs and exciting harmonies, making for one of the most distinctive college rock albums of the '80s. Highlights include "Scotty's Lament," "Over There," and "Pawns." The follow-up, *Fun & Games* ♫♫♫ (TVT, 1989 prod. Gary Smith) continues down the same path, with greater group contributions—in particular more vocals by Huntley.

what to buy next: *One Simple Word* ♫♫♫♪ (TVT, 1990, prod. Hugh Jones) has a more commercial feel and really shows off the skilled guitar work of Mike Connell. *Still Life* ♫♫♫♪ (TVT, 1998, prod. Jim Scott) is a strong effort with a return to the earlier straightforward, melodic style of the band. All members contributed to this work, with a rejuvinated passion. Standout songs include the title track, "Gonna Take a Lie" and a great instrumental called "Pedro Says."

what to avoid: Compared to later releases, *Darker Days* ♫♫ (Black Park, 1986/TVT, 1987, prod. Dave Adams, Steve Gronback, Ron Dash, Don Dixon), the group's debut, sounds like the skeletal outline for what would become a more compelling sound.

the rest:
Ring ♫♫♫ (TVT, 1993)
Weird Food and Devastation ♫♫♫ (TVT, 1996)

worth searching for: The 12-inch single "Hats Off" (Black Park, 1986, prod. Steve Gronback, Ron Dash, Don Dixon, Joe Harvard), which features remixes of the title track, "Darker Days," and an early version of "If It Crumbles."

influences:
◀◀ R.E.M., the dB's, Wire Train

▶▶ Gin Blossoms, Freddy Jones Band, Wilco, Son Volt, the Jayhawks, the Wallflowers

John Nieman

Chris Connelly /The Bells

Born 1964, in Edinburgh, Scotland.

Chris Connelly was a key component in a variety of industrial bands during the '80s and early '90s, first as a member of Scotland's Fini Tribe, then with the Revolting Cocks, Ministry, and Pigface in Chicago. During the '90s he began making a series of solo records that explored a more lyrical and contemplative side of his personality. Cocks fans were not amused, and some of his solo concerts were greeted with boos. Nonetheless, the singer—blessed with a crooning tenor deeply indebted to "Hunky Dory"–era David Bowie—persevered, and in 1997 created the Bells, a Chicago-based touring group that marked a complete break with his past.

what to buy: *Shipwreck* 🎵🎵🎵🎵 (Wax Trax!/TVT, 1994, prod. the New Pain) by itself would justify Connelly's decision to abandon the industrial-noise camp; it's one of the great, overlooked albums of the decade. Its folkish melodies have a dark, sweeping grandeur that suggest the early solo records of Scott Walker.

what to buy next: *The Ultimate Seaside Companion* 🎵🎵🎵 (Hit It!, 1997, prod. Camelo Pardalis) marked Connelly's debut as the Bells. It's sparser and more intimate than *Shipwreck*, its atmospheric folk-pop tunes recorded as a series of low-fi duets with three collaborators—former Ministry pal William Rieflin, Jim O'Rourke, and Seal guitarist Chris Bruce.

what to avoid: Even Connelly would prefer to disown *Phenobarb Bambalam* 🎵 (Wax Trax!, 1992), which sounds like the train wreck the singer's personal life had become at the point.

the rest:
Whiplash Boychild 🎵🎵🎵 (Wax Trax!, 1991)

influences:
◄◄ David Bowie, Scott Walker, Nick Drake, Lou Reed, Leonard Cohen

see also: *Ministry*

Greg Kot

Consolidated

Formed 1988, in Portland, OR.

Adam Sherburne, vocals, guitar; Mark Pistel, keyboards, programming; James Dickson, programming (1989–90); Philip Steir, drums (1988–94); Michael Dunne, bass (1997–present); Todd Bryerton, drums (1997–present).

Consolidated is unique in being as much a political organization as it is a band—and refreshing in having musical chops as strong as its messages. Not only does it give over much CD-insert and tour-lobby space to activist groups (a not-uncommon practice nowadays), but the group concludes each concert with an open-mic issues forum. Its passion about feminism, animal rights, racial unity, anti-militarism, and other causes is matched with an uncanny proficiency in rap, heavy rock, electronica, funk, jazz, blues, and other forms. Consolidated also has a sense of humor and lyrics that don't overpower with rhetoric but impress with cleverness. Consolidated considers it very important to address a spectrum of audiences in their own preferred musical languages, but the band's occasional adoption

of black dialect has unintended echoes of minstrelsy, which is perhaps the one issue the musicians haven't dealt with. Nonetheless, Consolidated's sharp ear for infectious compositions in a gamut of genres makes their relative obscurity something of a mystery; could each album's scathing record-industry parodies have something to do with it?

what to buy: The band's debut, *The Myth of Rock* 🎵🎵🎵🎵 (Nettwerk, 1990, prod. Michael Ahearn), is impassioned but fun, a sonic odyssey of precision grooves, wry slogan collages, and communist reeducation-style lecture-raps delivered in the style of a commercial voice-over. The EP that preceded it, *Consolidated* 🎵🎵🎵🎵 (Nettwerk, 1989, prod. Consolidated, Michael D. Ahearn), is in the same vein but even better, with few overlapping tracks. *Play More Music* 🎵🎵🎵🎵 (Nettwerk, 1992, prod. Consolidated, others) perfects the mature Consolidated sound, with uncompromising but moving rhymes, a stylistic horizon stretching from industrial jazz to metal-improv to Santana-ism, and the Consolidated catalog's only featured raps from actual women (the Yeastie Girls) and people of color (Paris, Crack M.C.). The band's recorded arguments with audience Q&A-ers defeat the purpose of an open mic, and some of the groove-backed speeches would work better as liner notes, but it's still a stunner. *Business of Punishment* 🎵🎵🎵🎵 (London/PolyGram, 1994, prod. Consolidated) is the band's most consistently impressive album, a prime balance between hard music and humanistic lyrics, with worldbeat textures and anthemic structures.

what to buy next: On *Friendly Fa$cism* 🎵🎵🎵 (Nettwerk, 1991, prod. Consolidated) the band starts its transition from master sound-assemblers to master rhyme-composers, though often indulging a persecution complex not so different from your basic "angry white male" whimperings. *Dropped* 🎵🎵🎵 (Sol 3, 1997, prod. Adam Sherburne, Mark Pistel) credibly extends the band's musical vocabulary to blues and a strategic, substantive kind of power pop. Adam Sherburne's lyrics are brilliant, though sometimes burdened with melodramatic delivery.

the rest:
Dysfunctional Relationship EP (Capitol, 1990) 🎵🎵🎵🎵
Unity of Oppression EP (Capitol, 1990) 🎵🎵🎵🎵
This Is a Collective EP (Capitol, 1991) 🎵🎵🎵🎵
This Is Fa$cism EP (Capitol, 1991) 🎵🎵🎵
Tool & Die EP (Capitol, 1992) 🎵🎵🎵🎵🎵
Warning: Explicit Lyrics EP (Nettwerk, 1993) 🎵🎵🎵🎵
Butyric Acid single (London/PolyGram, 1994) 🎵🎵🎵

influences:
◄◄ Public Enemy, Negativland, Dead Kennedys, Parliament-Funkadelic, John Stoltenberg

►► Emergency Broadcast Network, Rage Against the Machine

Adam McGovern

The Continental Drifters

Formed 1990, in Los Angeles, CA.

Peter Holsapple, guitar, keyboards, vocals; Susan Cowsill, vocals, guitar, mandolin; Vicki Peterson, vocals, guitar; Mark Walton, bass; Robert Mache, guitar; Rob Ladd, drums; Carlo Nuccio, drums (1990–95); Gary Eaton, vocals, guitar (1990–94); Ray Ganucheau, guitar (1990–94).

On the strength of a 1992 single and a 1994 indie album, the Continental Drifters were named one of *Rolling Stone* magazine's "Best Unsigned Bands" of 1994. That's a lot of hype to live up to, but between them, the members have lived through several lifetimes of hype as members of other bands. Holsapple was a founder of the celebrated early '80s power-pop band the dB's; Cowsill was the ingenue in the '60s family band the Cowsills; Peterson was the underrated lead guitarist in the Bangles; and Nuccio used to play in a New Orleans bar band called the Continental Drifters that eventually evolved into the subdudes. Despite its power-pop pedigree, these Drifters play a rambling survey of American music that recalls nothing short of the Band and includes folk, rock, pop, country, and soul in its stylistically mixed bag.

what to buy: *Continental Drifters* ↗↗↗↗ (Monkey Hill/Ichiban, 1994, prod. Continental Drifters) features catchy originals like "Mixed Messages" but also covers Michael Nesmith's nearly forgotten chestnut "Some of Shelly's Blues" and even the Box Tops' "Soul Deep."

worth searching for: The original lineup worked the LA club scene and created a buzz at the start of the '90s, and released one single, "The Mississippi" b/w "Johnny Oops" (Singles Only Label, 1992).

solo outings:

Peter Holsapple & Chris Stamey:

Mavericks ↗↗↗ (Rhino New Artists, 1991)

influences:

⏪ The Byrds, the Band, Gram Parsons, the Nitty Gritty Dirt Band

⏩ Son Volt, Wilco, the Jayhawks, the subdudes

see also: *The dB's, the Bangles, the Cowsills*

Gil Asakawa

Ry Cooder

Born Ryland Peter Cooder, March 15, 1947, in Los Angeles, CA.

Like so many of his guitar-playing contemporaries—Jimmy Page, Jeff Beck, and Eric Clapton among them—Cooder started his career playing blues and folk songs in the early '60s. Instead of becoming a rock 'n' roll superstar, though,

he slowly developed his skills and built his reputation as a thorough musicologist and reputable session musician. He was in a few bands early in his career, including one with soul singer Jackie DeShannon, another—the short-lived-but-influential Rising Sons—with fellow blues fanatic Taj Mahal and one with the musically complex lunatic Captain Beefheart (around 1967). Cooder's many solo albums, particularly 1976's *Chicken Skin Music* and 1974's *Paradise and Lunch*, have a raw, refreshing sense of humor, and they're almost always rooted in '50s rockabilly and harder-than-they-sound guitar licks. Cooder has never been willing to stick to one style for very long, even his beloved blues and rockabilly, and he has stretched out considerably on the movie soundtracks he has written. Master of slide guitar, mandolin, banjo, and plenty of other more exotic instruments, Cooder's interests lurched from American rockabilly to Tex-Mex to Hawaiian slack-key guitar music, and he expanded his breadth with each new style. Beginning with the Rolling Stones's landmark *Let It Bleed* album—Cooder claims to have come up with the "Honky Tonk Women" riff—he became a prolific sideman, working on albums by Little Feat, Randy Newman, John Hiatt, Arlo Guthrie, and Van Dyke Parks. He delved into soundtrack albums, most notably *Paris, Texas*, *The Long Riders*, and *Trespass* (in which he plays behind Ice Cube and Ice-T in what could be the first example of rap-blues fusion). He served dutifully in Little Village, a quick-lived supergroup featuring fellow session musician extraordinaire Jim Keltner, bassist Nick Lowe, and Hiatt, and he collaborated with Indian musician V.M. Bhatt on 1993's superb *A Meeting by the River*. The Rising Sons never led to superstardom like the Yardbirds and Led Zeppelin did for Jimmy Page and the Rolling Stones did for Keith Richards, but Cooder nevertheless has managed to build a long career with great respect from his peers.

what to buy: *Paradise and Lunch* ↗↗↗↗ (Reprise, 1974, prod. Lenny Waronker, Russ Titelman) includes the heartwarming "Mexican Divorce" and a fun, definitive version of "Ditty Wa Ditty." *Chicken Skin Music* ↗↗↗↗ (Reprise, 1976, prod. Ry Cooder) predated Paul Simon's *Graceland* by incorporating Tex-Mex accordion hero Flaco Jiminez (who helps with a killer "Stand by Me") and Hawaiian slack-key guitarist Gabby Pahlnui into Cooder's more American-sounding rock 'n' roll. Both *Into the Purple Valley* ↗↗↗ (Reprise, 1972, prod. Lenny Waronker, Jim Dickinson), with its Johnny Cash, Woody Guthrie, and Jackie Wilson songs, and *Bop Till You Drop* ↗↗↗ (Warner Bros., 1979, prod. Ry Cooder), with "Down in Hollywood," showcase Cooder's fun-loving history-of-rock side. Finally, his collaborations with world-music heavies V.M. Bhatt, on *A Meeting by the River* ↗↗↗↗ (Water Lily Acoustics, 1993, prod. Kavichandran Alexander), and Ali Farka Toure, on *Talking Tim-*

buktu ✍✍✍ (Hannibal, 1994, prod. Ry Cooder), round out any full Cooder collection.

what to buy next: The two-disc *Music by Ry Cooder* ✍✍✍ (Warner Bros., 1995, prod. Ry Cooder, Joachim Cooder) is such a thorough collection of Cooder's movie music it saves you the trouble of combing through his uneven soundtrack albums. Individually, his better soundtracks are *Paris, Texas* ✍✍✍ (Warner Bros., 1984, prod. Ry Cooder), *Johnny Handsome* ✍✍✍ (Warner Bros., 1989, prod. Ry Cooder), *The Long Riders* ✍✍✍ (Warner Bros., 1980, prod. Ry Cooder), *The Border* ✍✍✍ (Backstreet, 1981) (which features interesting collaborations with Hiatt, Freddie Fender, and the long-lost Sam Samudio), and the much-maligned *Crossroads* ✍✍✍ (Warner Bros., 1986, prod. Ry Cooder), a terrible movie that features great Cooder pure-blues slide work with fellow string enthusiast David Lindley.

what to avoid: Cooder's experiments and ambitions occasionally backfire, especially on the tedious *Jazz* ✍✍ (Warner Bros., 1978, prod. Ry Cooder, Joseph Byrd), which has interesting ideas—such as a cover of the 1880 folk song "The Dream"—but nothing else to recommend it. He sounds plain bored on *Get Rhythm* ✍✍ (Warner Bros., 1987, prod. Ry Cooder), despite the presence of old friend Jiminez and the always-unusual Van Dyke Parks. Also not up to snuff is his solo debut, *Ry Cooder* ✍ (Reprise, 1970, prod. Van Dyke Parks, Ry Cooder).

the rest:
Boomer's Story ✍✍✍ (Reprise, 1972)
Show Time ✍✍✍ (Warner Bros., 1977)
Borderline ✍✍ (Warner Bros., 1980)
The Slide Area ✍✍ (Warner Bros., 1982)
Alamo Bay ✍✍ (Slash, 1985)
Blue City ✍✍ (Warner Bros., 1986)
Geronimo: An American Legend ✍✍✍ (Warner Bros., 1993)
Trespass ✍✍✍ (Sire, 1994)
Buena Vista Social Club ✍✍✍✍ (Elektra/Nonesuch, 1997)

worth searching for: The long-collected rarity, *Rising Sons* (Columbia/Legacy, 1992, prod. Terry Melcher), puts Cooder's legendary band with Taj Mahal in a nice historical light, with some great blues-rock cuts like "Statesboro Blues." But there's also a lot of unfocused, messy stuff.

influences:

◀◀ Elmore James, Charlie Christian, Mississippi Fred McDowell, Tampa Red, the Rolling Stones, Jimi Hendrix, Buddy Guy, Taj Mahal

▶▶ Sonny Landreth, Bonnie Raitt, Rory Block, Daniel Lanois, Robbie Robertson

see also: *Little Village*

Steve Knopper

Sam Cooke

Born January 22, 1931, in Clarksdale, MS. Died December 11, 1964.

Producer Jerry Wexler always thought Sam Cooke had the greatest voice of his generation. Considering Wexler made all those great records with Ray Charles and Aretha Franklin, among others, that says something. Cooke's life story is practically a parable for the story of soul music itself—from the innocence of shouting gospel to a sordid death outside a hooker's seedy hotel room. He became one of the first major black artists to establish his creative self-determination with a major label. He laid the cornerstones of the music called soul. As the lead vocalist (and sex symbol) of a top sanctified gospel group, the Soul Stirrers, Cooke had to hold his first pop sessions in secret, releasing the results under a pseudonym to relative indifference. But his next single, "You Send Me," went #1 in 1957, and Cooke never looked back. He not only expertly explored a vast cross-section of music on his own recordings—blues, supper club pop, epic ballads, Top 40 jive—but he wrote and produced brilliantly for other artists. His extraordinary impact cannot be overestimated. The pure sound in his throbbing, sensual voice intoxicated so many other vocalists—as well as listeners—that his style continues to echo throughout the pop scene long after his death. His many and momentous accomplishments live, well preserved in a number of different collections of his work.

what to buy: You can bask in the aural glow of Cooke's finest pop achievements with *Greatest Hits* ✍✍✍✍ (RCA, 1998, compilation prod. Paul Williams), an essential 22-song collection with tracks mixed in original mono and stereo. However, no picture of Sam Cooke can be complete without *One Night Stand: Live at the Harlem Square Club, 1963* ✍✍✍✍ (RCA Victor, 1985, prod. Hugo & Luigi). Here is sweaty, smokey, persuasive evidence of his mesmerizing powers over an audience from the scene of the crime.

what to buy next: His expressions covered so many different areas, and there are at least three albums immediately worth investigating. *Night Beat* ✍✍✍✍ (RCA, 1963/Abkco, 1995, prod. Al Schmitt), his 1963 small combo late-night blues album, was one of soul's lost masterpieces until its digital release. *Sam Cooke with the Soul Stirrers* ✍✍✍✍ (Specialty, 1991, prod. various) contains some of the most sublime gospel vocals ever put to record. *Sam Cooke's SAR Story* ✍✍✍✍ (Abkco, 1994, prod. Sam Cooke) is a two-disc box that commemorates his skills as a writer and producer on one disc of rare gospel and another disc of obscure pop songs that originally appeared on his own record label.

the rest:
The Best of Sam Cooke ✍✍✍✍ (RCA Victor, 1963)
The Gospel Soul of Sam Cooke with the Soul Stirrers ✍✍✍ (Specialty, 1970/1989)

Alice Cooper (© Ken Settle)

That's Heaven to Me 🎵🎵🎵🎵 (Specialty, 1972/1991)
At the Copa 🎵🎵🎵 (Abkco, 1987)
Forever 🎵🎵🎵 (Specialty, 1992)
Jesus Gave Me Water 🎵🎵🎵🎵 (Specialty, 1992)
The Rhythm and the Blues 🎵🎵🎵🎵 (RCA Victor, 1995)

worth searching for: The recently deleted *The Man and His Music* (RCA Victor, 1986, compilation prod. Greg Geller) documents his commercial successes, from the early Soul Stirrers records to the towering final ballad, "A Change Is Gonna Come," over the chronological course of 28 selections. A number of rewarding selections that did not find their way onto CD remain resting in the original vinyl version of his album *Shake* (RCA Victor, 1965), a collector's item that draws large bounties in record stores these days.

influences:

◀◀ R.H. Harris, Kylo Turner, Charles Brown

▶▶ Otis Redding, Rod Stewart, Marvin Gaye, Steve Perry, Maxwell, D'Angelo, Tony Rich

Joel Selvin and Ken Burke

Alice Cooper

Born Vincent Furnier, February 4, 1948, in Detroit, MI.

Alice Cooper wasn't the world's first shock rocker; Screamin' Jay Hawkins and Arthur Brown and his Crazy World were direct forebears. But Cooper was the first to take it to theatrical extremes with the snakes, hacked-up baby dolls, guillotines, and gallows that populate his stage shows. With Cooper, the show was the thing—particularly during his early '70s heyday—and that usually obscured some good rock 'n' roll he and his band were cranking out at the time. Though raised in Phoenix, Cooper brought his band to Detroit during the late '60s, and the group schooled itself on the burgeoning Motor City rock of the MC5 and Stooges. Guitarist Michael Bruce, Cooper's main foil in the early days, churned out Stones-ish guitar hooks and taut rock melodies, over which the singer laid out his macabre tales of "Dead Babies" and "Sick Things." But with "I'm Eighteen," Cooper created a "Smells Like Teen Spirit" for the post-hippie generation, and his well-orchestrated shock spectacle took things from there, generating controversy over issues that seem comparatively tame today. Over the years, Cooper's music has been as good as his collaborators; guitarists Dick Wagner and Steve Hunter filled in after Cooper dropped his original band, and gun-for-hire Desmond Child helped craft some '80s hits. But while he continues to record, Cooper will always be the guy with the girl's name who wore mascara, played with snakes, and alternately entertained and freaked out audiences of a quarter century ago.

what to buy: Absent a good box set—which has been in the making for several years now—*Alice Cooper's Greatest Hits* 🎵🎵🎵🎵 (Warner Bros., 1974, prod. various) is the essential singles collection and proof that there's more to Cooper than a cheap-thrills horror show. Of the individual albums, *Love It to Death* 🎵🎵🎵 (Warner Bros., 1971, prod. Bob Ezrin) still holds its own as an early angst rock touchstone, with "I'm Eighteen" and "Black JuJu" among the standout tracks.

what to buy next: *Killer* 🎵🎵🎵 (Warner Bros., 1971, prod. Bob Ezrin), *School's Out* 🎵🎵🎵 (Warner Bros., 1972, prod. Bob Ezrin), and *Billion Dollar Babies* 🎵🎵🎵 (Warner Bros., 1973, prod. Bob Ezrin) are all entertaining efforts with songs to serve both radio listeners and concert attendees. *Classicks* 🎵🎵🎵 (Epic, 1995, prod. various) highlights Cooper's brief '80s resurgence ("Poison," "Hey Stoopid"), though nothing holds up to the six older songs that are represented via live renditions.

what to avoid: Both of Cooper's mid-'80s "comeback" albums—*Constrictor* 🎵 (MCA, 1986, prod. Beau Hill, Michael Wagener) and *Raise Your Fist and Yell* **woof!** (MCA, 1987, prod. Michael Wagener)—mistakenly tried to maneuver him into the heavy metal camp.

the rest:
Pretties for You 🎵🎵 (Straight, 1969/Enigma Retro, 1989)
Easy Action 🎵🎵🎵 (Straight, 1970/Enigma Retro, 1989)
Muscle of Love 🎵🎵🎵 (Warner Bros., 1974)
Welcome to My Nightmare 🎵🎵🎵 (Warner Bros., 1975)
Alice Cooper Goes to Hell 🎵🎵🎵 (Warner Bros., 1976)
Lace and Whiskey 🎵🎵 (Warner Bros., 1977)
The Alice Cooper Show 🎵🎵🎵 (Warner Bros., 1977)
From the Inside 🎵🎵 (Warner Bros., 1978)
Flush the Fashion 🎵🎵 (Warner Bros., 1980)
Special Forces 🎵🎵 (Warner Bros., 1981)
Zipper Catches Skin **woof!** (Warner Bros., 1982)
DaDa **woof!** (Warner Bros., 1983)
Prince of Darkness 🎵🎵 (MCA, 1989)
Trash 🎵🎵🎵 (Epic, 1989)
Hey Stoopid 🎵🎵 (Epic, 1991)
Live at the Whiskey A-Go-Go 1969 🎵🎵 (Rhino EP, 1992)
The Last Temptation 🎵🎵 (Epic/Sony, 1994)
A Fistful of Alice 🎵🎵🎵 (Guardian, 1997)

worth searching for: *The Beast of Alice Cooper* (Warner Bros., 1989, prod. various) is an import collection that's slightly more thorough than *Greatest Hits*. But, please, bring on that box set already!

influences:

◄◄ Little Richard, the Crazy World of Arthur Brown, the Stooges, the MC5, Boris Karloff, Bela Lugosi

►► Ozzy Osbourne, Kiss, Mötley Crüe, GWAR, Guns N' Roses

Gary Graff

Cop Shoot Cop /Firewater

Cop Shoot Cop formed 1987, in New York, NY. Disbanded 1996. Firewater formed 1996, in New York, NY.

Cop Shoot Cop: Tod A., vocals, guitar, high-end bass, drums, percussion, sampling; Natz, low-end bass, drums, yelling; Phil Puleo, drums, percussion; Filer, sampling, piano; Jim Colarusso, trumpet; Joe Ben Plummer, saxophone; Dave Ouimet, trombone, sampling; James Coleman, sampling. Firewater: Tod A., guitars, vocals; Duane Denison, guitar; Yuval Gabay, drums, percussion; Kurt Hoffman, saxophone, accordion; Jim Kimball, drums; Dave Ouimet, piano; Hahn Rowe, violin.

Rarely has an artist's personal evolution been so transparently cataloged in a group setting as in the case of New York's Tod A. First, as the diabolical leader of Big Apple noise rockers Cop Shoot Cop, Tod and his mates melded their no-wave musical sensibilities (think dissonant, experimental, and dark) into edgy, impressionistic noise anthems. Their oddball lineup (two bass players, keyboards, samplers, and a drum kit), jumpy rhythms, and raw-voiced delivery suggested the kind of ugly bastard marriage that only happens in New York—part Joe Strummer, part John Zorn, smelling of filterless cigarettes and dressed in black. Six records later, internal clashes busted up the band, and Tod A. went off to forge Firewater (known briefly as the Organ Grinders), an indie-rock supergroup that includes members of Jesus Lizard and Soul Coughing. Combining the noise of CSC with a booze-soaked ethnic flavor (polkas, klezmer, tango, etc.), Firewater is a more coherent, more musical realization of Tod A.'s dark visions, coalesced around his Shane MacGowanesque snarl.

what to buy: *Ask Questions Later* 🎵🎵🎵 (Interscope, 1993, prod. Martin Bisi) is as essential a CSC document as there is, an experimental yet accessible record that blusters and wails through anti-anthems like "Everbody Loves You When You're Dead." Firewater's equally cathartic *Get Off the Cross, We Need the Wood for the Fire* 🎵🎵🎵 (Jetset, 1996) is a must for fans of CSC and the Pogues alike, crafting an invitingly dark songscape dotted by ethnic themes and apocalyptic visions.

what to buy next: Firewater's sophomore effort, *The Ponzi Scheme* ✲✲✲ (Jetset, 1998) is a perfect extension of the first record's seamy brilliance.

the rest:
Cop Shoot Cop:
Consumer Revolt ✲✲ (Big Cat, 1990)
White Noise ✲✲✲ (Big Cat, 1991)
Suck City ✲✲✲ (Interscope, 1992)
Suck City/Nowhere/Days ✲✲✲ (Atlantic, 1994)
Release ✲✲✲ (Interscope, 1994)

influences:
◄◄ DNA, Mars, the Fall, Sonic Youth, the Pogues

see also: *Jesus Lizard, Soul Coughing*

Scott Hess

Julian Cope
/The Teardrop Explodes

Born October 21, 1957, in Deri, Mid Glamorgan, Wales. Teardrop Explodes formed 1979, in Liverpool, England. Disbanded 1983.

Julian Cope, vocals, bass, synthesizers; David Balfe, organ, piano, marimba; Gary Dwyer, drums; Michael Finkler, guitar (1979–81); Troy Tate, guitar (1981–82).

If high aspirations and good intentions were everything, Julian Cope would be one of the world's greatest popular musical figures. An iconoclast with a spaced-out head and a heart of gold, the one-time frontman for Liverpudlian psychedelic pop/rockers the Teardrop Explodes has neither an interesting enough singing voice nor the musical smarts to bring his wild-eyed concepts to complete fruition. And yet, for music fans seeking edgy guitar pop placed in the service of global concerns, Cope offers occasional bursts of genius within an oeuvre that is never uninteresting. Along with Echo & the Bunnymen, and to some extent the Psychedelic Furs, the Teardrop Explodes helped usher in the spacier side of post-punk. Unlike the other groups, though, its music was bright and straightforward; only its lyrics were fuzzy and complex. The band quickly built a large following in Britain, and Cope, artiste that he is, became uneasy and broke up the group. He soon surfaced with two very strange and decidedly uncommercial albums, *World Shut Your Mouth* (which does not include the hit song of the same name) and *Fried*. Apparently having changed his mind about being a smug, self-indulgent auteur, Cope rebounded with his two most accessible efforts, 1987's *Saint Julian* (which does include the driving, sassy "World Shut Your Mouth") and the more laid-back, '60s-ish *My Nation Underground*, which is probably the best Cope album for non-Cope fans. Since then, he's entered a period of utter conceptual weirdness, beginning with two "offi-cial" bootlegs, *Skellington* and *Droolian*, both of which are better left to die-hard collectors. Next up was a massive trilogy dedicated to the planet's environmental and spiritual problems, followed most recently by the more upbeat *20 Mothers* and the import-only *Interpreter*. At least *20 Mothers* offers the bouncy "Try, Try, Try," evidence that Saint Julian still has a few infectious numbers left in him.

what to buy: After a period of drug-induced haziness, *Saint Julian* ✲✲✲✲ (Island, 1987, prod. Ed Stasium, Warne Livesey) marked Cope's return to form. "World Shut Your Mouth," one of his best singles, is the best-known track, but "Trampolene" heads a list of several other memorable cuts.

what to buy next: *Floored Genius: The Best of Julian Cope and the Teardrop Explodes, 1979–91* ✲✲✲ (Island, 1992, prod. various) provides a good overview, although it stops short of his four most recent albums. Also, the concepts that have been so important to his recent work are lost in a compilation format. Of the four releases since, *Jehovahkill* ✲✲✲ (Island, 1992, prod. Julian Cope, Donald Ross Skinner) is the best—more listenable than the extravagant *Peggy Suicide*, yet more ambitious and varied than *Autogeddon*. The entire three-phase magnum opus features strong material and savvy production. Of the Teardrop Explodes' two original releases, the debut, *Kilimanjaro* ✲✲✲✲ (Mercury, 1980, prod. Bill Drummond, David Balfe, Clive Langer, Alan Winstanley), is more consistent. Once somewhat groundbreaking, this album now seems moderate in its power-pop approach, especially in light of Cope's '90s work.

what to avoid: Wildly self-indulgent and uncompromising in its weirdness, the double-LP *Peggy Suicide* ✲✲ (Island, 1991, prod. Julian Cope, Donald Ross Skinner) generally goes too far off the deep end, although the guitars snarl ferociously and there are a few strong tunes (the Caribbean-influenced "Beautiful Love," for instance).

the rest:
(With the Teardrop Explodes) *Wilder* ✲✲✲ (Mercury, 1981)
World Shut Your Mouth ✲✲✲ (Mercury, 1984)
Fried ✲✲✲ (Mercury, 1985)
My Nation Underground ✲✲✲✲ (Island, 1988)
Floored Genius II ✲✲✲ (Dutch East India, 1993)
Autogeddon ✲✲✲ (American, 1994)
20 Mothers ✲✲✲ (American, 1995)
Interpreter ✲✲✲ (Echo Label Limited import, 1997)

influences:
◄◄ The Jam, Syd Barrett, the Kinks, the Doors, Todd Rundgren
►► Icicle Works, Inspiral Carpets, Psychedelic Furs, the Outfield

Bob Remstein

Stewart Copeland
/Klark Kent
/Animal Logic

Born July 16, 1952, in Alexandria, Egypt.

Interviewed for a technical magazine, Stewart Copeland once said his compositional technique consisted of playing rhythms into a computer and assigning pitches later—an approach that makes a strange kind of sense, considering the drummer's bent toward creating herky-jerky, eccentric sounds. The son of a CIA official, Copeland moved during the mid-'70s to England, where he joined progressive rockers Curved Air. Once that band dissolved in 1986, he assembled the Police with a former schoolteacher on bass (Sting) and an ex-Animals member on guitar (Andy Summers). Continually frustrated by Sting's exercise of control, Copeland turned to solo projects early on to satisfy his songwriting muse. Working as Klark Kent, he released a punky, off-kilter album in 1982 before composing the score for Francis Ford Coppola's film *Rumble Fish*. In 1985, the same year Sting announced a sabbatical that would turn into a full-fledged departure, Copeland offered another solo record—this time under his own name—documenting his collaborations with various African musicians. Soundtracks for the films *Wall Street* and *Talk Radio* expanded his film credentials just before the drummer formed another rock band, Animal Logic, with bassist Stanley Clarke and vocalist-songwriter Deborah Holland. But the group collapsed after two albums, unable to reconcile Copeland's and Clarke's unique instrumental approaches into songs radio-friendly enough to make a difference. Instead, Copeland found success composing *King Lear* for the San Francisco Ballet and writing two operas—*Holy Blood and Crescent Moon* and *Horse Opera*.

what to buy: Certainly Copeland's most listenable post-Police work came with Animal Logic, the only thing approaching a pop project he's tackled since his first band's demise. Animal Logic's second record, *Animal Logic II* 🎵🎵🎵 (I.R.S., 1991, prod. Animal Logic, Tony Berg, Frankie Blue), finds the band getting over the initial shock of playing together and digging into the compositions more, adding subtle textures to moody laments such as "Through a Window" and "Rose-Colored Glasses."

what to buy next: As the perfect extension of his white-guy reggae grooving with the Police, Copeland's *The Rhythmatist* 🎵🎵🎵 (A&M, 1985, prod. Stuart Copeland, Jeff Seitz) neatly presages future pop stars' preoccupation with Third World flavors. Be warned, though, that this is heady and adventurous stuff, channeling mind-blowing African influences through Copeland's own twisted vision of rhythm and melody.

what to avoid: Copeland's early punk work as Klark Kent was particularly stinky—immortalized on the collection *Kollected Works* **woof!** (I.R.S., 1995, prod. Stewart Copeland), as tuneless and nonsensical as the Police were melodic and well-crafted.

the rest:
Klark Kent 🎵🎵 (I.R.S., 1980)
Rumble Fish 🎵🎵🎵 (A&M, 1983)
The Equalizer and Other Cliff Hangers 🎵🎵🎵 (I.R.S., 1988)
(With Animal Logic) *Animal Logic* 🎵🎵🎵 (I.R.S., 1989)
Noah's Ark 🎵 (Lightyear, 1990)
Leopard Son 🎵🎵 (Capitol, 1996)
Four Days in September 🎵🎵🎵 (Milan, 1998)

worth searching for: Check out the Police's video *Synchronicity Concert* (A&M, 1983) for a look at the drummer in his most effective element—behind a drum kit driving one of the greatest rock bands ever.

influences:
◄◄ Edgar Varese, Frank Zappa

►► Manu Katche, Carter Beauford (Dave Matthews Band)

see also: *The Police*

Eric Deggans

Cornershop

Formed 1992, in London, England.

Tjinder Singh, vocals, guitar; Ben Ayres, guitar; Avtar Singh, guitar; Anthony Saffery, sitar, keyboards; Nick Simms, drums; Pete Hall, percussion.

Musical innovation these days is all about pastiche, and which styles a band chooses to blend are sometimes more critically important than how well they blend them. Illustrating this phenomena nicely is Cornershop, whose attempted fusion of Indian music (sitars, wind instruments, and lyrical chants) and contemporary pop has legions of rock writers all in a tizzy. In truth, "Brimful of Asha," the band's only hit single to date, is bereft of those highly touted subcontinential soundscapes. Cornershop does two things well: writing solid pop songs and spacing out on sitar drones. Though it's getting better at both, the group has yet to fully integrate the two ideas. Initially known more for its strong anti-racist politics than its music, Cornershop enjoyed a rise that was, at the start, a sign of the times. British popular culture was entering into a minor infatuation with Eastern culture (the screen adaptation of *The Buddha of Suburbia* aired on the BBC during the fall of 1993), creating a somewhat sympathetic ear and nurturing atmosphere. The band eventually improved enough to catch the ear of the patron saint of polyethnic music, David Byrne, who signed it to his Luaka Bop label in 1995. But in the wake of "Brimful's" success, band leader Tjinder Singh spoke about concentrating more on a dance-music side project called Clinton than on Cornershop. Go figure.

what to buy: *When I Was Born for the 7th Time* ✂✂✂✝ (Luaka Bop, 1997, prod. Tjinder Singh) was a critical darling of 1997 largely due to the unbelievable leap in tightness and tonality it took from its predecessor. The album moves nimbly between mid-fi jangle pop and polyrythmic sitar drones, all laced with DJ scratches, synthesizer swells, and electronic dubs to mark the times. "Sleep on the Left Side" and "Brimful of Asha" are irresistible singles, and "When the Light Appears Boy" features the poetry and the voice of Allen Ginsberg. But Singh's cover of "Norwegian Wood," sung in Punjabi, is more of a novelty than a visceral experience.

what to avoid: *Woman's Gotta Have It* ✂✝ (Luaka Bop, 1996, prod. Tjinder Singh) veers abruptly between sitar drones with Punjabi rants laid over funky rhythmic tracks, and angry, lo-fi guitar rock. "Wog" gets the best of both worlds, combining great percussion with muted guitar jangles. "Looking for a Way Out" comes off like a simple, solid indie-pop song with stripped down melodies. Most of the vocals on the record are not in English.

worth searching for: *Hold on It Hurts* (Merge, 1995, prod. Tjinder Singh), an out-of-print album put out by the independent label Merge that shows early signs of what Cornershop became.

influences:

⏮ George Harrison, David Byrne, the Velvet Underground

Isaac Josephson

Corrosion of Conformity

Formed 1982, in Raleigh, NC.

Woody Weatherman, guitar; Reed Mullin, drums, vocals; Mike Dean, bass, vocals (1982–90, 1994–present); Phil Swisher, bass (1990–94); Eric Eycke, vocals (1982–86); Simon Bob, vocals (1986–90); Karl Agell, vocals (1990–94); Pepper Keenan, vocals, guitar (1990–present).

Corrosion of Conformity merits respect simply for not sitting still, for not finding one metal groove and comfort zone and staying there. When it started, C.O.C. played a blazing blend of punk and metal—one of the first to do so. But when others followed, C.O.C. slowed the tempos and mined a more dark and ominous vein; pre-grunge, if you will. But when everyone and their flannel shirt followed that route, C.O.C. switched again, broadening its sonic palette just in time for its major label debut, *Deliverance*. Without question one of the most ambitious and inventive hard rock bands in the land, C.O.C. has in-

fluenced many of those who have leaped beyond it in the sales column. Its day will come, too.

what to buy: *Deliverance* ✂✂✂✂ (Columbia, 1994, prod. John Custer) steps away from grunge mode and finds C.O.C. adding more subtle sounds to its attack, such as the weepy pedal steel of "Shelter," though the thundering "Heaven's Not Overflowing" and "Pearls Before Swine" prove C.O.C. hasn't gone soft on us.

what to buy next: *Deliverance*'s predecessor, *Blind* ✂✂✂✂ (Relativity, 1991/Columbia, 1995, prod. John Custer, C.O.C.) thrashes a bit more, though "Dance of the Dead" and "Vote with a Bullet" won over traditional metal audiences and even the harder edge of the metal crowd.

what to avoid: With 21 songs, *Eye for an Eye* ✂✂ (Caroline, 1983/1995, prod. C.O.C.) is an impressively prolific debut, but it's also a lot of songs played pretty much the same way.

the rest:
Animosity ✂✂✂ (Metal Blade, 1985)
Technocracy ✂✂✂✝ (Metal Blade, 1987)
Wise Blood ✂✂✂ (Columbia, 1996)

worth searching for: *Nola* (Elektra, 1995) is from a surprisingly cohesive side project called Down formed by Pepper Keenan, Pantera singer Phil Anselmo, and members of Crowbar and Eye Hate God.

influences:

⏮ MC5, Black Sabbath, ZZ Top, Lynyrd Skynyrd, Black Flag, Samhain

⏭ Pantera, Soundgarden, Alice in Chains

Gary Graff

The Corrs

Formed at birth, in Dundalk, Ireland.

Jim Corr, keyboards, guitars, vocals; Andrea Corr, lead vocals, tin whistle; Caroline Corr, drums, bodhran, vocals; Sharon Corr, violin, vocals.

Three sisters and a brother, the Corrs began playing music together in the tiny of village of Dundalk, serving up a stew of traditional Irish and straightforward pop music. With their movie-star good looks and unmistakable musical talent, it didn't take long for the quartet to win attention from the record industry—in the Corrs' case from producer David Foster, who was the group's patron and co-producer of its debut album. In between albums, Andrea Corr stepped into movies by serving as the singing voice of the heroine in the animated film *The Quest for Camelot* and as Juan Peron's mistress in *Evita*.

what to buy: The siblings' sophomore album, *Talk on Corners* ♪♪♪ (143/Lava/Atlantic, 1998, prod. Oliver Lieber, Glen Ballard, Billy Steinberg, Rick Nowells, Jim Corr), takes the Corrs' successful sound a step further. Backward drum loops appear in the middle of "When He's Not Around," while the previously "nice" Corrs take on a bitter tone in "I Never Loved You Anyway." The title track sounds like a Spice Girls' B-side, but don't let that discount the lush harmonies.

the rest:
Forgiven Not Forgotten ♪♪♥ (Lava/Atlantic, 1995)

influences:
◄◄ Wilson Phillips, the Cranberries

Christina Fuoco

Elvis Costello /Elvis Costello & the Attractions

Born Declan Patrick McManus, August 25, 1954, in London, England.

Elvis Costello, vocals, guitar; Steve Nieve, keyboards; Bruce Thomas, bass; Pete Thomas, drums.

Elvis Costello and his band the Attractions were among the chief proponents of the British new wave. Emerging during the height of the punk era, Costello combined that form's anger with an astonishing sense of songcraft that combined beautiful melody with a smart and biting lyricism; despite their difference in age and attitude, it's no accident that Paul McCartney invited Costello to collaborate with him during the late '80s and into the '90s. Costello's two decades of recording, with and without the Attractions, has generated as impressive a body of pop music as any of his contemporaries. His first three albums—*My Aim Is True*, *This Year's Model*, and *Armed Forces*, all produced by fellow new waver and erstwhile pub-rocker Nick Lowe—form one of the most impressive pop trilogies ever. Since then, Costello has remained an intriguing, important, and changing artist, unafraid to cover country songs (*Almost Blue*) or to record with a string quartet (*The Juliet Letters*). Of late, he's become rock's ambassador to easy-listening music, dueting with Tony Bennett on *MTV Unplugged* and writing and recording with Burt Bacharach. (Note: Costello's Columbia catalog was reissued by Rykodisc during 1993 and 1994, with appropriate bonus tracks for each album.) A recent label change to PolyGram includes an innovative proviso that allows Costello to release albums on whichever of the conglomerate's labels best fit the style of music he's recorded.

what to buy: Costello's second album and first with the Attractions, *This Year's Model* ♪♪♪♪ (Columbia, 1978, prod. Nick Lowe) is his first great work, showcasing spectacular hooks, a delightfully venomous tone, and ace songs such as "Pump it Up," "Radio Radio," and "The Beat." *Armed Forces* ♪♪♪♪ (Columbia, 1979, prod. Nick Lowe) brilliantly continues along the same vein, with instant classics such as "Oliver's Army," "Accidents Will Happen," and the Lowe-penned "What's So (Funny 'bout Peace Love and Understanding)." *Imperial Bedroom* ♪♪♪♪♪ (Columbia, 1982, prod. Geoff Emerick) is as impassioned and varied an album as you'll find in his oeuvre, a collection of lushly produced pop songs, aching ballads, and film noir-influenced narratives. *King of America* ♪♪♪♪♪ (Columbia, 1986, prod. J. Henry "T-Bone" Burnett, Declan Patrick Aloysius MacManus) is an exceptional album, notable for Costello's decision to record with T-Bone Burnett and use three members of the other Elvis's (Presley's) T.C.B. band. The ventures into rockabilly territory, along with biting commentaries on American culture, are worth the price of admission.

what to buy next: *My Aim Is True* ♪♪♪♪ (Columbia, 1977, prod. Nick Lowe) is a phenomenal debut album notable for the Costello classics "(The Angels Wanna Wear My) Red Shoes," "Alison," and "Watching the Detectives." As is typical for the best Costello albums, it sounds as good today as it did when it was originally released. *Get Happy!!* ♪♪♪♪ (Columbia, 1980, prod. Nick Lowe) is a purely fun Costello outing, remarkably consistent over its whopping 21 songs—including excellent covers (Sam & Dave's "I Can't Stand up for Falling Down," the Merseybeats' "I Stand Accused") and fine Costello originals such as "High Fidelity" and "Riot Act." *Blood and Chocolate* ♪♪♪♪ (Columbia, 1986, prod. Nick Lowe, Colin Fairley) marks something of the end of an era; it was Costello's final album for Columbia, and his last with the Attractions for eight years. But with Lowe back in the producer's chair, it contained all the elements that had won Costello attention in the first place.

what to avoid: *Goodbye Cruel World* ♪♥ (Columbia, 1984, prod. Clive Langer, Alan Winstanley) is the one Costello album that should never have been made. It's listless and uninspired and one even he acknowledges is his worst album with the Attractions.

the rest:
Taking Liberties ♪♪♪♪ (Columbia, 1980)
Almost Blue ♪♥ (Columbia, 1981)
Trust ♪♪♪♪ (Columbia, 1981)
Punch the Clock ♪♪♪ (Columbia, 1983)
The Best of Elvis Costello and the Attractions ♪♪♪♪♥ (Columbia, 1985)
Out of Our Idiot ♪♪♪ (Demon U.K., 1987)
Girls, Girls, Girls ♪♪♪♪ (Columbia, 1989)
Spike ♪♪♪ (Warner Bros., 1989)
Mighty Like a Rose ♪♥ (Warner Bros, 1991)
The Juliet Letters ♪♥ (Warner Bros., 1993)
2 1/2 Years ♪♪♪♪ (Rykodisc, 1993)

Elvis Costello (© Jack Vartoogian)

Brutal Youth ☼☼☼ (Warner Bros., 1994)

The Very Best of Elvis Costello and the Attractions, 1977–86 ☼☼☼☼ (Rykodisc, 1994)

Kojak Variety ☼☼☼ (Warner Bros., 1995)

All This Useless Beauty ☼☼☼☼ (Warner Bros., 1996)

Extreme Honey: The Very Best of the Warner Bros. Years ☼☼☼☼ (Warner Bros., 1997)

(With Burt Bacharach) *Painted from Memory* ☼☼☼☼ (Mercury, 1998)

worth searching for: The bootleg *Our Aim Is True* (Slipped Disc) contains the demos Costello did with his first band, Flip City. Highlights include his rendition of "Knockin' on Heaven's Door" and early versions of "Radio, Radio" ("Radio Soul") and "Living in Paradise." The out-of-print box set *Costello & Nieve* (Warner Bros., 1996) finds Costello reassessing some of his catalog and covering some of his favorite tunes in various live settings and with the sparest accompaniment.

influences:

◀◀ Hank Williams, the Beatles, the Rolling Stones, the Byrds, Stax, Motown Booker T. & the MG's, George Jones, Johnny Cash, Bob Dylan, the Band, Randy Newman, Gram Parsons, Brinsley Schwarz, Van Morrison, Bruce Springsteen

▶▶ The Clash, the Jam, Richard Thompson, Joe Jackson, Nick Lowe, Rockpile, Dave Edmunds, Graham Parker, Madness, the Specials, the English Beat, Squeeze, the Pogues, Kirsty MacColl, Any Trouble, Ian Dury, Wreckless Eric, Billy Bragg, Paul McCartney, T-Bone Burnett, John Hiatt, Crowded House, Peter Case, John Wesley Harding, Roger McGuinn, Aimee Mann

Marc Fenton

Cotton Mather

Formed 1994, in Austin, TX.

Whit Williams, guitar, vocals; Robert Harrison, vocals, guitar, piano; Greg Thibeaux, drums, vocals, guitar; Matt Hovis, bass (1994–96).

Pop music since the Beatles has taken on various styles, all very unique but unified with the understanding of how incredible the Beatles influence has been on the world of pop. Intentionally or unintentionally, most pop bands end up paying homage to the Fab Four. Cotton Mather is no exception, as it craftily manipulates sonic tones and fuses them with simple melodies generating songs that, with some creative production techniques, wouldn't sound out of place on the *White Album*. What Cotton Mather brings to the pop table are tight harmonies, overtly intellectual lyrics, and at times groundbreaking production. The group's two records are like night and day, ranging from the tightly produced, standard-issue Big Star-influenced debut, which somehow makes the Gin Blossoms sound second rate, to the sophomore effort *Kontiki*, which embraces low-fi recording techniques to transform this happy-go-

lucky pop band into to an all-out experimental sonic assault team. On *Kontiki*, Cotton Mather teamed up with producer and pop wonderboy Brad Jones (Jill Sobule, Steve Forbert), a combination that proves to the disenchanted that pop music is alive and well. Cotton Mather has given the pop world two records, both incredibly unique and both pop classics.

what to buy: *Kontiki* ☼☼☼☼ (Copper Records, 1997, prod. Robert Harrison, Whit Williams, Brad Jones) is the record you've dreamed about. The stark and haunting melodies fill the room while the very sparse instrumentation takes you on a trip back to the '60s. From the opening bar chord crash of "Camp Hill Rail Operator," the group takes the listener from trippy ballads like "Spin My Wheels" to the all-out power pop rocker "My Before and After."

what to buy next: The equally brilliant *Cotton Is King* ☼☼☼ (Elm Records, 1994, Prod. Bryan Martin) might suffer a bit from Robert Harrison's thesaurus style of writing wordy songs. That said, it's the melodies that build the foundation for this record and the masterful *Kontiki* to follow.

worth searching for: Cotton Mather has appeared on a few power pop compilations and tribute album, the most interesting unreleased tracks being "Innocent Street" on the Spanish release *The Bam Balam Explosion, Vol 4* (Bam Balam Records, 1996) and its take on Badfinger's "Flying" on *Come and Get It—A Tribute to Badfinger* (Copper Records, 1997).

influences:

◀◀ The Beatles, Big Star, Badfinger

Chris Richards

Neal Coty

Born May 5, 1969.

A native—by adoption—of rural Maryland, singer-songwriter Neal Coty wound up with a record deal out of Nashville after kicking around in Baltimore and Los Angeles. There might have been some consideration of making him a country singer (he'd had tunes cut by Kim Richey and Sawyer Brown, and his voice possesses a twang deeper than most country artists), but Coty was too wild-eyed a writer to work in such a tightly defined format. Instead, he made a sprawling debut that received raves from people who knew what to make of it. A compelling live act as well, Coty's a promising talent with an uncertain future.

what's available: *Chance and Circumstance* ☼☼☼ (Mercury, 1997, prod. Keith Stegall) is an impressive debut that drew immediate comparisons to Steve Earle and Bruce Springsteen both for Coty's earnest rasp and for his ability to fit dark family secrets into four-minute songs. *Chance and Circumstance* contains its share of country-rock anthems ("Ghost Town," "I Just

Can't Slow Down"), but the really good stuff comes when he goes for the heart in "She's the Girl for Me" or sings about the kinship he feels towards an unknown father in "Heaven in the Dark." It's the kind of country-blues-soul fusion that the Band once did so well, and which now falls into the loose categorization of Americana.

influences:

◀◀ Todd Snider, Steve Earle, Randy Newman

Brian Mansfield

Mary Coughlan

Born 1956, in Galway, Ireland.

Few singers possess the emotional power of Galway's Mary Coughlan. Fewer have the actual pain of real life history to temper their vocalized indulgences. The sound of Coughlan's voice indicates a life of abuse and alcohol, neglect and insanity, the lives of five children, and all of the grit of a life-realization in rebound. An appearance on Irish television brought the turnabout she needed and pushed her debut record, the aptly titled *Tired and Emotional*, to sales of 100,000 units in her home country alone. Hers is an affected alto, akin to such emotional talents as Marianne Faithfull and Tracey Thorn, but touched as well by the rich Celtic influences of her heritage. She is an interpreter of rare means, able to deliver the tunes of her songwriters and even some of her own to the peaks of emotional release, and then knock them down to the blues of learned humility. Coughlan's public bouts with alcohol and her well-worn personality have made her a favorite in the U.K. as well. But no sympathy is necessary for her success stateside: her talent will get that job done.

what to buy: Seven records later, Coughlan finally began her career in America with an introductory live album, *Live in Galway* ♫♫♫♫ (Big Cat, 1996, prod. Erik Visser), and her strongest studio record to date, *After the Fall* ♫♫♫♫ (V2, 1997, prod. Erik Visser).

influences:

◀◀ Marianne Faithfull, Melanie, Van Morrison

▶▶ Everything but the Girl, Toni Childs

Billy Manes

Count Five

Formed 1965, in San Jose, CA.

Ken Ellner, vocals; John Michalski, guitar; Sean Byrne, guitar; Roy Chaney, bass; Craig Atkinson, drums.

If you've got to be a one-hit wonder, you couldn't do better than Count Five's "Psychotic Reaction" in 1966. Like some

twisted Yardbirds cover band sprinting on high octane, the harp, thump, and wail of this single still packs a wallop.

worth searching for: The out-of-print *Psychotic Reaction: The Complete Psychotic Reaction* (Performance, 1994) gives you the hit plus 17 other songs—which may be about 17 more than you want from this band. If all you want is "Psychotic Reaction," you'd be better off with the various-artists collection *Nuggets: Classics from the Psychedelic '60s* (Rhino, 1986, compilation prod. Bill Inglot) instead.

influences:

◀◀ The Yardbirds

▶▶ 13th Floor Elevators, Amboy Dukes, Tom Petty

Patrick McCarty

Counting Crows

Formed August 1991, in San Francisco, CA.

Adam Duritz, lead vocals, piano; David Bryson, guitar, vocals; Dan Vickrey, guitar, vocals (1993–present); Charles Grilling, keyboards, vocals; Matt Malley, bass, vocals; Ben Mize, drums, vocals.

Few debut albums have matched the impact of Counting Crows' *August and Everything After*. The multi-platinum masterpiece set the standard for rootsy, literate rock during the early '90s and established leader/vocalist Adam Duritz, at least temporarily, as the voice of his generation. Duritz met guitarist David Bryson in 1989, and the pair soon began writing songs together and playing as an acoustic duo in coffeehouses. Eventually, they recruited enough members to round out their band, wowed the industry at a showcase performance, and were signed by DGC Records. From the start, Counting Crows seemed bound for glory, opening for Bob Dylan in L.A. and subbing for Van Morrison at the Rock and Roll Hall of Fame induction ceremony before releasing its first album. Even so, no one could have predicted the enormous success of *August*, which is sure to go down as one of the great albums of the decade.

what to buy: From the jangling opening strains of "Round Here," singer-lyricist Duritz's haunting exploration of Generation X disillusionment, to the sensual-but-desperate groove of "Mr. Jones" to the driving finale, "A Murder of One," there's not a bum cut on *August and Everything After* ♫♫♫♫ (DGC, 1993, prod. T-Bone Burnett). While some critics harped that the influences of Dylan, Morrison, and Bruce Springsteen were all-too-evident, they missed the point: everyone has influences, but not everyone can filter them through an original sensibility—and it's unimaginable that anyone but Duritz could have written the words that laid the foundation for these songs. Not that Counting Crows are a one-man show: Duritz's bandmates and producer T-Bone Burnett managed to find just the right sound-

Adam Duritz of Counting Crows (© **Ken Settle**)

track for each of the frontman's monologues; it's rare to find lyrics this raw and literate in songs that actually rock.

what to buy next: *Recovering the Satellites* 🎜🎜🎜 (DGC, 1996, prod. Gil Norton), the long-awaited follow-up to *August*, isn't quite as consistent as its predecessor, but it still has its share of spellbinding moments. The lead single, "Angels of the Silences," Is a blazing rocker, while "Daylight Fading" fits the country rock tradition of the Band and the Eagles without sounding derivative. Even better are the title track, an edgy, transcendent homecoming song, and "A Long December," a heartbroken ballad that may be the most beautiful song of the '90s. Complain all you want that Duritz sounds like Morrison, but Van hasn't turned out anything this potent since the '70s.

the rest:
Across a Wire: Live in New York 🎜🎜🎜 (DGC, 1998)

worth searching for: Counting Crows have yet to release a CD single in the U.S., but a variety of imports have featured some terrific bonus cuts. The overseas single of "Mr. Jones" (DGC, 1994) features an alternate, acoustic version of that song, as well as an acoustic rendition of "Rain King," while the "Omaha" single features a stunning live performance of "Round Here." Hardcore fans can also find a selection of live bootlegs, including *Flying Demos*, which collects the band's original demos for *August and Everything After* and includes a couple of songs that weren't released.

influences:
◀◀ Bob Dylan, Van Morrison, the Band, Bruce Springsteen

▶▶ The Wallflowers, Dog's Eye View

Jeff Schwager

Country Joe & the Fish

Formed 1966, in Berkeley, CA. Disbanded 1970. Re-formed 1977.

Country Joe McDonald, vocals, guitar; Barry Melton, guitar; David Cohen, keyboards, guitar (1965–69); Bruce Barthol, bass (1965–68); John Francis Gunning, drums (1965–66); Paul Armstrong, washboard (1965–66); Chicken Hirsh, drums (1965–69); Mark Ryan, bass (1968-69).

A largely forgotten giant of psychedelic rock, Country Joe & the Fish towered over their contemporaries and left behind one masterpiece album, their first—*Electric Music for the Mind and Body*—one of the definitive albums of American acid rock. Like the psychedelic scene itself, the album mixed the trippy and bizarre with the jocular and whimsical, and crafted folk-pop with adventuresome experimentation, electric blues with political satire. Both Joe McDonald and Barry Melton, who grew up next door to Woody Guthrie in Brooklyn, brought decidedly folk backgrounds with them to the free-wheeling band they

founded. The Berkeley-based group qualified as one of the original five Fillmore headliners, although these days the Fish are not regarded in the same breath as the Grateful Dead and Jefferson Airplane. The original, high-spirited group of hippies began to dissolve after its third album; by the time the group made its famous appearance at the 1969 Woodstock Festival, only McDonald and Melton remained. The group disappeared altogether the following year, although McDonald continued a fruitful and active musical career.

what to buy: Even the official greatest hits collection includes seven of the 11 tracks from the band's 1967 debut, *Electric Music for the Mind and Body* 🎜🎜🎜🎜 (Vanguard, 1967, prod. Sam Charters), one of the first albums to carry the sound of the San Francisco ballrooms across the country.

what to buy next: The band's second album was recorded so quickly after the debut that the group made do with less potent pieces from its existing repertoire. At least it saved the Vietnam era's #1 anthem, "I-Feel-Like-I'm-Fixin'-to-Die Rag," for this album. Coupled with McDonald's elegant elegy to his romance with the girl singer from Big Brother & the Holding Company, "Janis," the two side-openers lifted *I-Feel-Like-I'm-Fixin'-to-Die Rag* 🎜🎜🎜 (Vanguard, 1967, prod. Sam Charters) above the ordinary.

what to avoid: By the time the original group started to fall apart, the band had recorded three albums, and nothing on the subsequent two albums, *Here We Are Again* 🎜🎜 (Vanguard, 1968) and *C.J. Fish* 🎜 (Vanguard, 1970, prod. Tom Wilson), added anything to the band's repertoire.

the rest:
Together 🎜🎜🎜 (Vanguard, 1968)
The Life and Times of Country Joe and the Fish 🎜🎜🎜🎜 (Vanguard, 1971)
The Collected Country Joe and the Fish 🎜🎜🎜 (Vanguard, 1987)

worth searching for: Two authentic Country Joe & the Fish psychedelic artifacts have been brought into the digital domain. *Collectors Items: The First Three EPs* (One Way, 1994) captures the early Berkeley records that launched the band in the Bay Area, while *Live! At the Fillmore West 1969* (Vanguard, 1996, prod. Bill Belmont) may want for superb sonics but contains the rare sound of a genuine ballroom jam—a free-for-all celebrating the original group's final performance with guests that include Steve Miller, Jerry Garcia, Jorma Kaukonen, Jack Casady, and Mickey Hart.

solo outings:
Country Joe McDonald:
Thinking of Woody Guthrie 🎜🎜🎜 (Vanguard, 1970)
Tonight I'm Singing Just for You 🎜🎜 (Vanguard, 1970/One Way, 1995)
Hold On: It's Coming 🎜🎜🎜 (Vanguard, 1971/One Way, 1995)
War War War 🎜🎜 (Vanguard, 1971/One Way, 1995)

Paris Sessions ♫♫♫ (Vanguard, 1972/One Way, 1996)
Incredible! Live! ♫♫ (Vanguard, 1972/One Way, 1995)
Country Joe ♫♫♫ (Vanguard, 1974/One Way, 1996)
Paradise with an Ocean View ♫♫♫ (Fantasy, 1975)
On My Own ♫♫ (Rag Baby, 1980/One Way, 1997)
Into the Fray ♫♫♫ (Rag Baby, 1981)
Child's Play ♫♫ (One Way, 1983)
Peace on Earth: The Vietnam Experience ♫♫♫ (Rag Baby 1985/One Way 1995)
Country Joe Classics ♫♫♫ (Fantasy, 1989)
The Best of Country Joe ♫♫ (Vanguard, 1990)
Superstitious Blues ♫♫♫ (Rykodisc, 1991)
Carry On ♫♫♫ (Line, 1994/Shanachie, 1996)
Something Borrowed, Something New ♫♫ (Big Beat, 1998)

influences:

◀◀ Woody Guthrie, Reverend Gary Davis, Big Brother & the Holding Company

▶▶ The B-52's, the Boomtown Rats, Tom Robinson Band

Joel Selvin and Ken Burke

Dave Cousins

See: The Strawbs

Don Covay

Born March 24, 1938, in Orangeburg, SC.

Skilled and influential as both a singer and a songwriter, Don Covay has enjoyed a 40-plus-year career, in various facets of the business, that is a testament not only to the man's great talent, but to his undeniable love of the music and of the people who make it. The son of a Baptist minister, Covay was a member from an early age of his family's gospel quartet, the Cherry-Keys. He spent his teen years parking cars at Washington, D.C.'s renowned Howard Theatre, which exposed him to the more secular sounds of Clyde McPhatter and the Dominoes. Soon afterwards, as a member of the Rainbows (in which the young Billy Stewart and Marvin Gaye also apprenticed), Covay enjoyed a minor local hit with "Mary Lee" in 1955, and followed this with a brief stint in the Moonglows. Two years later, opening a show for Little Richard, Covay so impressed the headliner that he was quickly asked to join his legendary back-up band, the Upsetters, and, under the name Pretty Boy, was duly signed to Atlantic Records. He found more success in subsequent years as a songwriter, however, penning hits for both Chubby Checker ("Pony Time") and Gladys Knight ("Letter Full of Tears"), while his own releases on a variety of labels made little impact. Finally in 1964, he hit with his own recording of "Mercy Mercy" (which immediately made its way into the Rolling Stones' repertoire), followed by "See Saw" a year later. Re-signed with Atlantic and working as both an artist and pro-

ducer alongside the likes of Wilson Pickett, Joe Tex, Ben E. King, Solomon Burke, Otis Redding, and Arthur Conley, Covay won widespread acclaim and success in 1968 when Aretha Franklin scored huge hits with covers of "See Saw" and the Grammy-nominated "Chain of Fools". Covay then spent the 1970s working in a variety of capacities for both Mercury and Philadelphia International, and he toured with old pals Pickett and Burke as the Soul Clan during the early 1980s. Covay has been forced to slow his activities somewhat in recent years due to health problems. Nevertheless, his songs and style not only remain an important part of R&B's golden age, they continue to inspire writers and singers of all genres.

what's available: One can't go wrong with *Mercy Mercy: The Definitive Don Covay* ♫♫♫♫♫ (Razor & Tie, 1994, compilation prod. Billy Vera), which collects all of the key tracks, from Pretty Boy's first record, "Bip Bop Bip," onward.

worth searching for: *Checkin' in with Don Covay* (Mercury, 1992, prod. Don Covay) is a fine overview of the man's '70s work, wherein he displays a vocal style that's more mature but with a passion and fire undimmed since his Howard Theatre days. Also of note is the multi-artist *Back to the Streets: Celebrating the Music of Don Covay* (Shanachie, 1993, prod. Jon Tiven, Joe Ferry). Tribute albums are usually anything but, yet the dozens of fans and friends, from Jimmy Witherspoon to Iggy Pop, who pay respectful, entertaining homage to the man and his music herein make this collection a marvelous exception to the rule.

influences:

◀◀ The Soul Stirrers, the Dells, Little Richard

▶▶ Mick Jagger, Peter Wolf, Bad Acoustics

Gary Pig Gold

Cowboy Junkies

Formed 1979, in Toronto, Ontario, Canada.

Margo Timmins, vocals; Michael Timmins, guitar; Peter Timmins, drums; Alan Anton, drums.

Teetering between hypnotic and narcoleptic, ambient and ambivalent, the Cowboy Junkies snared attention during the late '80s by reducing such hallowed country and rock staples as Neil Young's "Powderfinger," the Velvet Underground's "Sweet Jane," Patsy Cline's "Walking after Midnight," and Hank Williams's "I'm So Lonesome I Could Cry" to moody shadows of their former selves. After two failed rock bands, guitarist Michael Timmins drafted siblings Margo and Peter to join him and drummer Alan Anton in the Cowboy Junkies, which debuted on Canada's Latent Records in 1986 with *Whites off Earth Now*, consisting mostly of covers of blues classics and Bruce Springsteen's "State Trooper." The group's major-label debut,

1988's *The Trinity Session*, was recorded direct to DAT in an abandoned church for $250 and spotlighted Margo Timmins's trance-like murmuring against a gloomy backdrop of fiddles, mandolins, and pedal steel guitars. When it explores the thin line between regret and anguish, pain and suffering, the Cowboy Junkies offer an ethereal catharis. But when the group starts fumbling around in its self-created darkness, it sometimes forgets the difference between chilling and merely cold.

what to buy: Listeners who prefer Bruce Springsteen's *Ghost of Tom Joad* to *Born to Run* no doubt worship *The Trinity Session* ♫♫♫♫ (RCA, 1988, prod. Peter Moore), which established the Junkies as minimalist visionaries. But *Black Eyed Man* ♫♫♫ (RCA, 1992, prod. Michael Timmins) remains the group's masterpiece, swinging rather than lurching and tweaking its atmospheric sound by adding two missing ingredients—melody and hope. Highlights include "If You Were the Woman and I Was the Man," a duet with John Prine, and "A Horse in the Country," a stirring lament about marital restlessness.

what to buy next: Switching to a new label and new producer, the Junkies experiment with strings and a more traditional rock approach on *Lay It Down* ♫♫♫ (Geffen, 1996, prod. Michael Timmins, John Keane). "A Common Disaster" rocks without sacrificing the group's trademarks, "Angel Mine" is sweetly melodic and "Speaking Confidentially" borders on funk. At last, a Junkies album you can listen to while operating heavy machinery.

what to avoid: Subtitled "Selected Studio Recordings 1986–1995," *Studio* ♫♫ (RCA, 1996, prod. Peter Moore, Michael Timmins, John Keane) is the contract-fulfilling counterpart to the live *200 More Miles* that unearths a previously unreleased 1993 outtake called "Lost My Driving Wheel." The piecemeal approach captures the group's best-known songs, but not its essence.

the rest:
Whites off Earth Now ♫♫ (RCA, 1990)
Caution Horses ♫♫♫ (RCA, 1990)
Pale Sun, Crescent Moon ♫♫♫ (RCA, 1993)
200 More Miles: Live Performances 1985–1994 ♫♫ (RCA, 1995)
Miles from Our Home ♫♫♫ (Geffen, 1998)

worth searching for: A haunting treatment of another sacred country-rock cow, the Rolling Stones's "Dead Flowers" turns up on the 12-inch promotional single for "'Cause Cheap Is How I Feel" (RCA, 1990).

influences:
◀◀ Hank Williams, the Velvet Underground, Patsy Cline
▶▶ Lisa Germano, Dead Can Dance

David Okamoto

Cowboy Mouth

Formed early 1990s, in New Orleans, LA.

Fred LeBlanc, drums, vocals, percussion, guitar; Paul Sanchez, rhythm guitar, vocals, acoustic guitar; John Thomas Griffith, lead guitar, vocals; Rob Savoy, bass, vocals.

"The Mouth," as it is affectionately known by fans, is an amalgam of a former punk hitmaker (John Thomas Griffith, who scored the hit "China" with the Red Rockers), a southern pop star (Fred LeBlanc from in Dash Rip Rock), and solo artists. After releasing two independent efforts successful enough that the band courted attention in its hometown of New Orleans, Cowboy Mouth signed on with MCA Records and began building a grass roots following through constant touring.

what to buy: *Are You with Me* ♫♫ (MCA, 1996, prod. Michael Wanchic) fuses the individual influences of the band members, offering a shot of pop, roots rock, country, and honky tonk ("How Can You Tell Someone?"). Unfortunately for longtime Cowboy Mouth fans, many of these songs have been heard before. Six of *Are You with Me*'s 12 tracks were taken from the band's three previous efforts, and Dash Rip Rock did a version of the XTC-flavored rousing single "Jenny Says."

the rest:
Word of Mouth ♫♫ (Domino, 1996)
Mercyland N/A (MCA, 1998)

worth searching for: Those smitten with *Are You with Me* might want to look for the two harder-to-find Mouth offerings, *Mouthing Off* (Viceroy Records, 1993) and the five-song EP *It Means Escape* (Monkey Hill, 1995, prod. Gene Holder).

influences:
◀◀ XTC, Jerry Lee Lewis, Dash Rip Rock

Christina Fuoco

Cows

Formed 1987, in Minneapolis, MN.

Shannon Selberg, vocals, bugle, trombone; Kevin Rutmanis, bass; Thor Eisenstrager, guitar; Norm Rogers, drums (1987–1997); Freddy Votel, drums (1997–present).

Somewhere between early period Sonic Youth and equally early period Butthole Surfers graze Minneapolis's Cows, a bunch of guys who you'd just as likely find pissing on your front lawn as playing at your local saloon. Led by the verbal assault of singer/ranter/social commentator Shannon Selberg, Cows played an important role in the underground post-punk, pre-grunge noise-rock era of the late '80s and early '90s, which also included bands like Big Black, Sonic Youth, and Killdozer. Selberg, known for such live antics as wearing a fur-covered football uniform, covering his otherwise naked body with shaving cream, and drawing lewd pictures on himself with a marker, has always been intent on making his listeners feel uneasy, but at the same time hitting them with a visceral and very distorted rock guitar attack. His awkward menace and perverted sense of humor, combined with his band's bristling and dissonant psycho-roar, has made Cows one of the period's most notorious and enduring noise-rock bands.

what to buy: Over the course of their decade together, Cows have rarely made the kind of records their live shows promised, but through nine albums and a compilation, two have stood horns and flanks above the rest. *Cunning Stunts* ♫♫♫♫ (Amphetamine Reptile, 1992, prod. Cows) is a noise-rock masterpiece, spearheaded by Thor Eisenstrager's crisp metallic guitar lines and Selberg's brutally explicit social comments. *Sorry in Pig Minor* ♫♫♫♫ (Amphetamine Reptile, 1998, prod. King Buzzo) is another noise opus, this time broadening the band's suffocating sound to include mangled merengue and vintage pop.

what to buy next: *Peacetika* ♫♫♫♫ (Amphetamine Reptile, 1991, prod. Cows) bridges the gap between the band's muddled early sets and their later, more sonically defined affairs, though it still makes hardcore punk easy listening by comparison.

what to avoid: Cows' earliest releases, *Taint Pluribus Taint Unum* **woof!** (Treehouse, 1987, prod. Tim Mac) and *Daddy Has a Tail!* **woof!** (Amphetamine Reptile, 1989, prod. Tim Mac) sound like Selberg and company are recording in a wood chipper. A good thing, too: It disguises their amateurish, though energetic, earliest ramblings.

the rest:
Effete and Impudent Snobs ♫♫♫ (Amphetamine Reptile, 1990)
Sexy Pee Story ♫♫♫ (Amphetamine Reptile, 1993)
Orphan's Tragedy ♫♫ (Amphetamine Reptile, 1995)
Whorn ♫♫♫♫ (Amphetamine Reptile, 1996)
Old Gold, 1989–1991 ♫♫♫ (Amphetamine Reptile, 1996)

influences:
◄◄ The Sex Pistols, Flipper, Sonic Youth, Butthole Surfers

►► Pavement, Kyuss, Hole

Bob Gulla

The Cowsills

Formed 1964, in Newport, RI.

Barbara Cowsill (died January 21, 1985), vocals (1967–72); Bill Cowsill, guitar, vocals (1964–70); Bob Cowsill, guitar, vocals; Paul Cowsill, keyboards, vocals (1968–present); Barry Cowsill, bass, vocals (1965–72); John Cowsill, drums (1965–present); Susan Cowsill, vocals, guitar (1967–present).

They proudly called themselves America's First Family of Song, and though some Jacksons might take issue with that, there's no

denying that for two brief years in the late 1960s, these all-singing, all-playing Rhode Islanders made musical history (they were MGM Records' top-selling act in 1968) along with some undeniably sunshine-sweet music. Formed by father William "Bud" Cowsill as a way to supplement his navy pension checks, the Cowsills became a familiar fixture at local dances and clubs before releasing their first record on Johnny Nash's Joda label in late 1965. Within a year they had come to the attention of writer/producer Artie Kornfeld, and with his assistance they relocated to New York City, signed to MGM, and produced two innovative, harmony-drenched Top 10 hits of distinction, "Indian Lake" and the classic "The Rain, the Park and Other Things." Sporting the same genetic vocal blend that has always been the trademark of the best musical households from the Beach Boys to the Bee Gees and beyond, the clan had in Bill and Bob two writers and arrangers of sufficient merit to make even their albums' filler tracks surprisingly solid (note, for example, the Brian Wilson–esque complexities of "Poor Baby"). Unfortunately, after one last hit in 1969 (the theme from the musical *Hair*), the Cowsills' fresh-scrubbed, milk-boosting image began to work against them, unfairly tossing the group into the unhip heap long before their time—but not before they'd been Xeroxed and made into a weekly television series (yes, those Partridges were but a poor Hollywood imitation Cowsill family). Bill was first to fly the coop, entering into the world of record production and then downright debauchery (of the soul-searching kind) before surfacing in Canada to form the legendary Blue Shadows band. Paul became one of Helen Reddy's sound engineers, John began working on stage and in the studio with Jan & Dean, and Barry continues to perform solo under such aliases as Elvis Franklin. Susan recorded with husbands Dwight Twilley and Peter Holsapple, formed the alternative-pop supergroup the Continental Drifters with Holsapple and ex-Bangle Vicki Peterson, and with brothers Bob, Paul, and John proudly in tow recorded again under the Cowsills moniker in the early 1990s; only one track from those sessions ever surfaced on disc, however—the brilliant "Is It Any Wonder" on the first *Yellow Pills* compilation. Ironically, an unlabeled demo tape from these sessions generated interest from several major labels, only to be soundly rejected after it was revealed to be the work of the Cowsills. Nevertheless, this re-formed First Family continues to perform and record, never failing to impress listeners both old and new with their sharper-than-ever instrumental and vocal skills.

what to buy: *The Best of the Cowsills* ♫♫♫♫ (Rebound, 1994, prod. various) is just what it says: the songwriting and choice of cover material is strong throughout, the playing joyful and spirited, the singing is truly breathtaking—and li'l Susie sure could beat a mean tambourine, couldn't she?

what to buy next: *The Cowsills in Concert* ♫♫♫♫ (MGM, 1969/Razor & Tie, 1994, prod. Bill Cowsill, Bob Cowsill) captures all the action of a typical shriek-drenched public appearance by the clan: twice the thrills of *Cheap Trick at Budokan*, with some Beatles songs (and, as a bonus track, their "Milk Song" jingle) thrown in for good measure. The vinyl debut, *The Cowsills* 🎵🎵🎵 (MGM, 1967/Razor & Tie, 1994, prod. Artie Kornfeld), has been made even more irresistible on CD with the addition of their "Love American Style" theme.

influences:

◀◀ The Beatles, the Mamas & the Papas, the Von Trapp Family

▶▶ The Partridge Family, Lauren Ardor, Hanson

see also: *Blue Shadows, the Continental Drifters*

Gary Pig Gold

Peter Cox

See: Go West

Cracker
/Camper Van Beethoven

Camper Van Beetheoven formed 1984, in Santa Cruz, CA. Disbanded in 1989. Cracker formed 1992.

Camper Van Beethoven: David Lowery, vocals, guitar; Chris Molla, vocals, guitar, drums (1984–86); Victor Krummenacher, bass, vocals; Jonathan Segel, violin, keyboards, mandolin (1984–89); Greg Lisher, guitar; Chris Pederson, drums (1986–90); Morgan Fichter, violin (1989). Cracker (1992–present): David Lowery, vocals, guitar; Johnny Hickman, guitar, vocals; Davey Faragher, vocals, bass; Michael Urbano, drums (1992–93); Charlie Quintana, drums (1993–95); Johnny Hott, drums (1996–present).

With David Lowery's nerdy voice and sarcastic sense of humor, plus an enthusiasm for Middle Eastern rhythms and unusual rock instruments, Camper Van Beethoven staked its spot as the "funny band" to R.E.M.'s "serious band" in the independent underground. The group's early albums were the sounds of surfing ska fans trying to crack each other up, and sometimes they did it in a hilariously lazy way. "Take the Skinheads Bowling," a dumb joke that lampooned racist punk concertgoers, became Camper's college-radio hit. Gradually, the members began incorporating more complex songwriting and relying more on the violins and mandolins that were only novelties on early albums. The band became very good, but also very serious; eventually tension about their musical direction led to a breakup. Members went in all directions. The first post-Camper band was the Monks of Doom, featuring Greg Lisher, Victor Krummenacher, Chris Pedersen, and sort-of Camper member David Immerglick; that band rocked but had trouble writing good, tight songs. Lowery's band, Cracker, didn't have that problem. Drawing from punk persona non grata Tom Petty, Lowery cut out the fat and put together Cracker's three albums of snappy, bluesy pop songs, including the MTV-driven hits "Teen Angst (What the World Needs Now)," "Low," and "Euro-Trash Girl."

what to buy: Camper's *Telephone Free Landslide Victory* 🎵🎵🎵 (Independent Project/Rough Trade, 1985/I.R.S., 1993) is a refreshing blast of humor given the angst-ridden drunkenness that characterized so much '80s postpunk, and it has both "Where the Hell Is Bill" and "Take the Skinheads Bowling." The group's swan song, *Key Lime Pie* 🎵🎵🎵 (Virgin, 1989, prod. Dennis Herring), features a brilliant, stomping cover of Status Quo's "PIctures of Matchstick Men" and a new Lowery political edge in "Jack Ruby," "When I Win the Lottery," and "(I Was Born in a) Laundromat." Cracker's debut, *Cracker* 🎵🎵🎵🎵 (Virgin, 1992, prod. Don Smith), contains several songs that sound great on the radio, including the propulsive "Teen Angst (What the World Needs Now)" and the new birthday classic, "Happy Birthday to Me."

what to buy next: Cracker's *Kerosene Hat* 🎵🎵🎵 (Virgin, 1993, prod. Don Smith) adds "Low," "Get off This," and "Movie Star," which finally gave the underappreciated Lowery a presence on MTV and in national music magazines. Camper's major-label debut, *Our Beloved Revolutionary Sweetheart* 🎵🎵🎵 (Virgin, 1988, prod. Dennis Herring), continued to mix all sorts of psychedelic, Indian, and traditional rock sounds that sometimes went together and sometimes didn't.

what to avoid: The EP *Vampire Can Mating Oven* 🎵🎵 (Pitch-A-Tent/Rough Trade, 1987/I.R.S., 1993) clears the closet before Camper moved to a major label, sounding sometimes like that last box of found junk you toss together and know you might never open in the new place.

the rest:

Camper Van Beethoven:

Camper Van Beethoven II & III 🎵🎵🎵 (Pitch-A-Tent/Rough Trade, 1986/I.R.S.,1993)

Camper Van Beethoven 🎵🎵🎵 (Pitch-A-Tent/Rough Trade, 1986/I.R.S., 1993)

Cracker:

The Golden Age 🎵🎵🎵 (Virgin, 1996)

Gentleman's Blues 🎵🎵🎵 (Virgin, 1998)

worth searching for: *Camper Van Chadbourne* (Fundamental, 1987), a collaboration with equally twisted guitarist Eugene Chadborne. *Camper Vantiquities* (I.R.S., 1993), a rarities collection put out when I.R.S. rereleased all the group's old Rough Trade albums, is worth a few extra bucks for its version of the Animals' "I'm Not Like Everybody Else."

solo outings:

Jonathan Segel:

Storytelling 🎵🎵 (Pitch-A-Tent/Rough Trade, 1989)

Dolores O'Riordan of the Cranberries (© Ken Settle)

Monks of Doom:

Breakfast on the Beach of Deception (Soundtrack) 𝄞𝄞 (Pitch-A-Tent/Rough Trade, 1988; IRS, 1993)

The Cosmodemonic Telegraph Company 𝄞𝄞𝄞 (Pitch-A-Tent/Rough Trade, 1989; IRS, 1993)

The Insect God EP (C/Z, 1992) 𝄞𝄞𝄞

Forgery 𝄞𝄞𝄞 (I.R.S., 1992)

influences:

◄◄ Tom Petty, the Grateful Dead, Indian raga music, Bob Marley, the Specials, R.E.M., Jan & Dean

►► The Dead Milkmen, the Presidents of the United States of America, Sublime, the Mighty Mighty Bosstones

Steve Knopper

The Cramps

Formed 1975, in New York, NY.

Lux Interior (born Erick Lee Purkiser), vocals; Poison Ivy Rorschach (born Christine Marlana Wallace), guitar; Pam Gregory, drums (1975); Miriam Linna, drums (1975–77); Nick Knox (born Nicholas Stephanoff), **drums (1977–80); Kid Congo Powers (born Brian Tristan), guitar (1980–82); Candy Del Mar, bass (1989–1990); Slim Chance, bass (1991–present); Jim Scalavunos, drums (1991); Harry Drumdini, drums (1994–present).**

In the explosion of punk, this neo-rockabilly band seemed to emerge from some sort of primeval ooze, its members as scary as the swampy music they played. First under the control of the mysterious Brian Gregory (who left one day and was never seen again), the band charges along during the '90s under the unerring leadership of junk culture mavens Lux Interior and Poison Ivy Rorschach (who moved from second guitar to lead guitar, writer, producer, and cover model). Few other couples have been further steeped in the arcane world of trash culture, and their music is all the better for it, virtually creating the spicy subgenre of psychobilly.

what to buy: *Bad Music for Bad People* 𝄞𝄞𝄞𝄞 (I.R.S., 1984, prod. the Cramps, Alex Chilton) is an early compilation from the Cramps' first few recordings, not a bad place to start exploring the swampy, murky early stuff. After years of legal wrangling and a virtual disappearance from U.S. releases, *Stay Sick!*

ЛЛЛ (Restless, 1990, prod. the Cramps) brings the band's power and edge back stronger than ever on funny, uncompromising rockers.

what to buy next: *Songs the Lord Taught Us* *ЛЛЛ* (I.R.S., 1981/1989, prod. Alex Chilton) is an album as important for its historical significance—it's the Cramps' full-length debut—as well as for its throbbing versions of "Tear It Up" and "T.V. Set."

what to avoid: *Big Beat from Badsville* *ЛЛ* (Epitaph, 1997, prod. Poison Ivy, Lux Interior) was the first time in which the band seems to sound tired and somewhat trapped within its own confines.

the rest:
Gravest Hits EP (I.R.S., 1979/1989) *ЛЛЛ*
Psychedelic Jungle *ЛЛЛ* (I.R.S., 1981/1989)
Smell of Female *ЛЛЛ* (Enigma EP, 1983)
A Date with Elvis *ЛЛЛ* (Big Beat, 1986)
Look Mom, No Head! *ЛЛЛ* (Restless, 1991)
Flame Job *ЛЛЛ* (Medicine, 1994)

worth searching for: *Rockin' 'n' Reelin' in Auckland, New Zealand* (Vengeance, 1987), an authorized bootleg from one night on the *A Date with Elvis* tour, with two otherwise unavailable Presley covers—"Do the Clam" and "Heartbreak Hotel."

influences:
◀◀ Hasil Adkins, Ed Wood, Ed Gein

▶▶ The Rev. Horton Heat, Jason & the Scorchers, the Amazing Royal Crowns, the Bomboras, White Zombie

Roger Catlin

The Cranberries

Formed 1990, in Limerick, Ireland.

Dolores O'Riordan, vocals, guitar; Noel Hogan, guitar; Mike Hogan, bass; Feargal Lawler, drums.

When former church choir member Dolores O'Riordan joined with brothers Mike and Noel Hogan and Feargal Lawler, the band's name was the Cranberry Saw Us (say it fast). They gave her a tape of guitar chords, and O'Riordan came up with "Linger," one of the hits from the group's debut, *Everybody Else Is Doing It, So Why Can't We*. That album introduced the band's lush folk-pop style to the world, and the world bought it—making the Cranberries one of the most popular newcomers of the decade. It remains the essential purchase, though the group's two succeeding albums are also worthwhile. *No Need to Argue* is a continuation of the group's gentle, Celtic-influenced music, though the hit "Zombie" hits hard, both sonically and politically. *To the Faithful Departed* goes even further in that direction, with a rawer sound that reflects producer Fairbairn's hard rock touch.

what to buy: *Everybody Else Is Doing It, So Why Can't We* *ЛЛЛ* (Island, 1993, prod. Stephen Street) is an impressive mix of lilting Celtic melodies and pop-rock led by O'Riordan's fetching delivery and the scintillating "Linger." Other impressive tracks include "Pretty," "I Still Do" and "Dream."

the rest:
No Need to Argue *ЛЛЛ* (Island, 1994)
To the Faithful Departed *ЛЛЛ* (Island, 1996)

influences:
◀◀ U2, Sinéad O'Connor

Anna Glen

Cranes

Formed 1986, in Portsmouth, England.

Alison Shaw, vocals, bass; Jim Shaw, drums, piano, guitar; Mark Francome, guitar (1989–present); Matt Cope, guitar (1989–present).

The Shaw siblings bought an eight-track recorder during the late '80s and made private cassettes before their 1989 vinyl release *Self Non Self* was played by taste-making BBC deejay John Peel, who did a session with the Shaws. They made the cover of *Melody Maker* and Dedicated Records signed them, after which Mark Francombe and Matt Cope were drafted into the group. Alison Shaw's breathy, shy vocals are easily overwhelmed, so much of the instrumentation is subdued, with lots of acoustic guitar strumming, harpsichord-style keyboards, and string arrangements, with screaming shards of electric guitar usually entering only between verses.

what to buy: *Wings of Joy* *ЛЛЛ* (Dedicated/Arista, 1991, prod. Cranes) is delicate, at times almost frightened, but includes some impressive guitar maelstroms. Considering that the songs on the sturdier *Forever* *ЛЛЛ* (Dedicated/Arista, 1993, prod. Cranes) have titles such as "Cloudless," "Jewel," and "Far Away," the textures (and the matching stasis-evoking chord progressions) seem appropriate. If Shaw's hyper-girlish singing makes it nearly impossible to understand what everything's about, this is so masterfully constructed that it's highly evocative even if you can't really tell of what.

what to buy next: The many EPs the group has done add up to a fine overview of its career on the two-CD set *EP Collections vols. 1+2* *ЛЛЛ* (Dedicated, 1997, prod. Cranes, Ray Shulman, Mark Freegard). The Joy Division–ish 1990 EPs *Inescapable* and *Espero* are especially impressive on tracks where Alison Shaw's vocals cut through loud guitar on the verses, proving she's not all wispy shyness. Some of the tracks were also on albums, and a few non-EP album tracks (including two from the unavailable *Orestes & Electre*) are included for a fuller story of the group's growth. *Loved* *ЛЛЛ* (Dedicated/Arista, 1994, prod. Cranes) is a confident and more instrumentally competent album, though in a way that sacrifices a bit of the uniqueness that gives this band its charm.

the rest:
Self Non Self ♫♫♫ (Biteback! U.K., 1989/Dedicated/Arista, 1992)
Population Four ♫♫♫♫ (Dedicated, 1997)

worth searching for: *Orestes & Electre* (Dedicated, 1996, prod. Cranes) was recorded by the Shaws during the sessions for the third album. It's based on Jean-Paul Sartre's play *The Flies* and consists of Alison singing entirely in French over a kind of "film score" composed by Jim Shaw. It was available in the U.S. only in a now out-of-print limited edition, but fans will definitely enjoy it.

influences:
◀◀ Cocteau Twins, Joy Division, Foetus, Lydia Lunch
▶▶ Mazzy Star

Steve Holtje

Crash Test Dummies

Formed mid-1980s, in Winnipeg, Manitoba, Canada.

Brad Roberts, vocals, guitar, piano; Benjamin Darvill, mandolin, harmonica; Ellen Reid, piano, keyboards, accordion, vocals; Dan Roberts, bass; Michel Dorge, drums.

Comprised of friends from the University of Winnipeg in Manitoba, Canada, Crash Test Dummies started as the house band for an after-hours club, passing up names such as Skin Graft to choose its current moniker. Passing around a demo tape to get work outside of Winnipeg, the band ended up with a record deal instead. Although the band hails from Winnipeg, which spawned the Guess Who and BTO, it's more stylistically akin to XTC, Leonard Cohen, and Talking Heads, with arrangements that show off songwriter-leader-singer Brad Roberts's lush baritone, which shows traces of influence from Bauhaus vocalist Peter Murphy. More equally divided between folk and rock influences early on, the Dummies have ratcheted up the alternative and rock flavors with each subsequent release, enlisting Talking Heads keyboardist Jerry Harrison to produce its second album after the debut disc sold three million copies—mostly in Canada. Buoyed by the nonsensical hit single, "Mmm Mmm, Mmm Mmm," the band became an unlikely MTV staple and again sold millions of records. Alas, the winning streak didn't continue with its third record, which wound up sounding a little too oddball for rock radio or the video channels.

what to buy: With the release of the second album, *God Shuffled His Feet* ♫♫♫♫ (Arista, 1993, prod. Jerry Harrison, Crash Test Dummies), the group scored a pair of international hits— "Mmm Mmm Mmm Mmm" and "Afternoons & Coffee Spoons"—that boosted its stature beyond its homeland.

what to buy next: The Dummies took Canada by storm in 1991 with its debut album, *The Ghosts That Haunt Me* ♫♫♫ (Arista, 1991, prod. Steve Berlin), which featured the Canadian smash "Superman's Song."

what to avoid: Thumbing its nose at stardom, the band next offered *A Worm's Life* ♫♫♫ (Arista, 1996, prod. Brad Roberts, Dan Roberts, Mitch Dorge), an eclectic work that combined a harder sound with Brad Roberts's traditionally impenetrable lyrics.

worth searching for: The band pays tribute to XTC by covering the band's songs on two interesting projects. *Testimonial Dinner: The Songs of XTC* (Thirsty Ear, 1995, prod. various) includes the Dummies' cover of "All You Pretty Girls," while its version of "The Ballad of Peter Pumpkinhead" on *Dumb and Dumber (Soundtrack)* (RCA, 1994, prod. various) features a rare lead vocal from keyboardist Ellen Reid.

influences:
◀◀ XTC, They Might Be Giants, 10,000 Maniacs, Talking Heads
▶▶ Barenaked Ladies, the Rembrandts

William Hanson and Eric Deggans

Robert Cray

Born August 1, 1953, in Columbus, GA.

From the minute Robert Cray arrived on the national scene, with 1983's *Bad Influence*, he was marked as the blues' best chance to come up from the underground and into suburban living rooms. He was, after all, a handsome young man with a soulful, pleasing voice, a stinging, true blues guitar attack, and an ear for a nifty pop hook. Indeed, Cray became the blues' first modern pop star three years later, with *Strong Persuader*, his Mercury debut. Since then, his music became ever more R&B-based and, unfortunately, largely less interesting. While his guitar playing and singing have only improved over the years, he has sadly lost some of the sense of fun and buoyancy that made his early music so special. The strength of his most recent effort, *Some Rainy Morning*, however, provides hopeful indications that Cray may have turned the corner on creative stagnation. His success with classic covers on early albums—and on 1996's *Tribute to Stevie Ray Vaughan*—suggests that one way he may enliven his work in the future is to occasionally turn to the past for material.

what to buy: *Bad Influence* ♫♫♫♫ (HighTone, 1983, prod. Bruce Bromberg, Dennis Walker) is illuminated by that special spark that separates great music from good. Some of the performances may be a tad sloppy, but the album swings with a robust energy while spotlighting Cray's songwriting, sense of humor ("So Many Women, So Little Time"), and ability to seamlessly incorporate soul, rock, and pop touches into his blues.

Strong Persuader ♪♪♪ (Mercury, 1986, prod. Bruce Bromberg) contains most of the same traits as well as better production values and a more pristine sound. Cray proved his true blues mettle with *Showdown!* ♪♪♪ (Alligator, 1985, prod. Bruce Iglauer, Dick Shurman), his sparkling collaboration with Albert Collins and Johnny Copeland.

what to buy next: On *Some Rainy Morning* ♪♪♪ (Mercury, 1995, prod. Robert Cray), Cray rebounds nicely after several mediocre albums, ditching the horns and producing a taut, excellent album.

what to avoid: Cray followed up the success of *Strong Persuader* by trying to force out pop songs on *Don't Be Afraid of the Dark* ♪♪ (HighTone/Mercury, 1988), a bad move for a guy who is basically a natural pop tunesmith anyhow.

the rest:
Who's Been Talkin' ♪♪♪ (Tomato, 1980/Atlantic, 1986)
False Accusations ♪♪♪ (HighTone, 1985)
Midnight Stroll ♪♪♪♪ (Mercury, 1990)
I Was Warned ♪♪♪ (Mercury, 1992)
Shame + a Sin ♪♪♪ (Mercury, 1993)
Sweet Potato Pie ♪♪♪ (Mercury, 1997)

worth searching for: *Black Heart White Hand* (Buccaneer, 1991), a solid bootleg from a 1987 show in Philadelphia, offers a good indication of Cray's live skills as well as an encore version of "The Crawl" with the Fabulous Thunderbirds.

influences:
◀◀ Albert Collins, Eric Clapton, Magic Sam, O.V. Wright, Johnny "Guitar" Watson, Howlin' Wolf, Hubert Sumlin

▶▶ Joe Louis Walker, Sherman Robertson, Eric Clapton

Alan Paul

Crazy Horse
Formed 1969, in Northern CA.

Ralph Molina, drums; Billy Talbott, bass; Frank "Pancho" Sampedro, guitar (1975–present); Danny Whitten, vocals, guitar (1969–72).

Called the "greatest garage band of all-time," Crazy Horse is best know as the powerful backing band on many of Neil Young's most memorable albums. Billy Talbott, Ralph Molina, and Danny Whitten first came together in 1962 as Danny & the Memories and were briefly known as the Rockets before hooking up with Young on the seminal album *Everybody Knows This Is Nowhere*. Powerful three-chord guitar work, feedback, and just plain noise (in the best sense of the word) are the band's sonic trademarks. While Crazy Horse released several albums of its own (none since 1981's *Left for Dead*), its best work definitely has been done when backing Young, with whom the band has recorded 14 albums, including several live sets. Origi-

nal member Whitten died of a drug overdose in 1972, a death that was eulogized on vinyl in Young's "The Needle and the Damage Done" from his album *Harvest*.

what to buy: *Crazy Horse* ♪♪♪ (Reprise, 1971, 1994, prod. Bruce Botnick) is the band's first outing without Young as a frontman. The presence of Jack Nitzsche and Nils Lofgren make this the only consistently strong Crazy Horse solo album.

what to avoid: *At Crooked Lake* ♪ (Epic, 1973) is unfocused, rambling, and plagued by unusually sloppy guitar work.

the rest:
Loose ♪♪ (Reprise, 1971)
Crazy Moon ♪♪ (RCA, 1978/One Way, 1998)
Left for Dead ♪♪ (Curb, 1981)

influences:
◀◀ The Rolling Stones, the Yardbirds, Buffalo Springfield

▶▶ The Black Crowes, Pearl Jam

see also: *Neil Young*

Brad Morgan

The Crazy World of Arthur Brown
See: Arthur Brown

Cream
Formed 1966, in London, England. Disbanded 1968.

Eric Clapton, guitar, vocals; Jack Bruce, bass, harmonica, vocals; Ginger Baker, drums, vocals.

During its relatively short lifespan, Cream revolutionized rock 'n' roll. For the first time, three established rock stars left three separate groups and joined forces—Clapton from the Yardbirds and John Mayall's Bluesbreakers, Baker from the Graham Bond Organization, and Bruce from Graham Bond and the Manfred Mann band. They opted for the demanding trio format instead of the standard four-or five-piece band. In the span of just two years and four albums (more were released afterward), Cream blazed a trail for power trios, supergroups, and wide-ranging, adventuresome music making. The group created crisp pop songs—perfect for radio—as well as fierce, rambling jams that combined the brute force of rock with the technical demands of jazz improvisation and the soul of the blues. The trio's excessive volume and exceptional talent set new standards for rock, and its music remains a major influence even 30 years later. Superstar egos, as well as Clapton's ravenous demand for new challenges, prompted Cream to split up in November 1968. The band's entire catalog was digitally remastered from the original tapes and reissued with a superb sonic quality in 1998 on the Polydor label.

what to buy: Cream's dual identities—disciplined singles band and full-tilt concert jammers—merge magnificently on *Wheels of Fire* 𝄢𝄢𝄢𝄢 (Polydor, 1968, prod. Felix Pappalardi). The first disc is a solid studio session ("White Room," "Born Under a Bad Sign," "Sitting on Top of the World"), but it's the four-song second disc that captures the trio at maximum power, swooping and diving like jet fighters in an aerial display. Clapton's explosive lead halfway through "Crossroads," lightning fast with startling tone, is one of the greatest rock-guitar solos ever recorded.

what to buy next: A four-disc box set, *Those Were the Days* 𝄢𝄢𝄢𝄢 (Polydor, 1997, prod. Bill Levenson) is a thorough document of Cream's bright and brief glory days. The first two discs contain nearly all of the trio's studio recordings, and the second two are all live. It includes rarities and demos, including a commercial for Falstaff Beer. Although trapped in '60s psychedelia, *Disraeli Gears* 𝄢𝄢𝄢𝄢𝄢 (Polydor, 1967, prod. Felix Pappalardi) displays Cream's pop sensibility ("Strange Brew," "Tales of Braves Ulysses") without any loss of its blues-rock power ("Sunshine of Your Love," "Outside Woman Blues"). The band's debut, *Fresh Cream* 𝄢𝄢𝄢𝄢 (Polydor, 1966, prod. Robert Stigwood) offers melodic, blues-based rock with what would prove to be uncharacteristic restraint. *Strange Brew: The Very Best of Cream* 𝄢𝄢𝄢𝄢 (Polydor, 1983, prod. Felix Pappalardi, Robert Stigwood) is a fine compilation focusing on the singles.

what to avoid: The spirit was gone when Cream bade farewell in concert at Royal Albert Hall on November, 26, 1968, and it shows in the four self-indulgent live tunes on *Goodbye* 𝄢𝄢 (Polydor, 1969, prod. Felix Pappalardi).

the rest:
Live 𝄢𝄢 (Polydor, 1970)
Live, Volume 2 𝄢𝄢 (Polydor, 1972);
The Very Best of Cream 𝄢𝄢𝄢𝄢 (Polydor, 1995)

worth searching for: *Secret History*, a two-disc bootleg of studio outtakes and BBC radio performances that's an illuminating complement to Cream's legitimate releases.

solo outings:
Ginger Baker's Air Force:
Anthology 𝄢𝄢𝄢 (Chronicles, 1998)

influences:
◄◄ Robert Johnson, Muddy Waters, Willie Dixon, Alexis Korner, Charlie Parker

►► The Jimi Hendrix Experience, Mountain, ZZ Top, Van Halen

see also: *Eric Clapton, Jack Bruce, Blind Faith*

David Yonke

The Creatures
See: Siouxsie & the Banshees

Creed
Formed 1995, in Tallahassee, FL.

Scott Stapp, vocals; Brian Marshall, bass; Scott Phillips, drums; Mark Tremonti, guitars, vocals.

Creed is proof positive that although Seattle may be gone, its market lives on. And though the press alternately ignored and scorned the Florida grunge outfit for its likeness to Alice in Chains, Pearl Jam, and Stone Temple Pilots, it doesn't matter, because at last check its independently financed debut, *My Own Prison*, had steamed past the platinum mark. As in so many cases, the public is having its say.

what's available: To Creed's credit, *My Own Prison* 𝄢𝄢𝄢 (Wind Up, 1997, prod. John Kurzweg) shows the musicians can certainly play their instruments, shifting smoothly from made-for-radio melodies ("My Own Prison," "One") to bass-heavy hard rockers such as "Illusion" and "Torn." On the down side, Mark Tremonti and Scott Stapp's lyrics fall slightly on the preachy side of passionate; "What's This Life For" rails self-righteously against teenage suicide, and "In America" sports lyrical nuggets like, "Only in America we kill the unborn/to make ends meet."

influences:
◄◄ Black Sabbath, Alice in Chains, Pearl Jam, Stone Temple Pilots, Live

Isaac Josephson

Creedence Clearwater Revival
Formed 1959, in El Cerrito, CA. Disbanded 1972.

John Fogerty, guitar, vocals; Tom Fogerty, guitar (1959–71); Stu Cook, bass; Doug Clifford, drums.

Widely dismissed as a mere Top 40 band at the time, the work of Creedence Clearwater Revival has endured to become recognized as classic American rock. At the height of the group's career, Creedence outsold the Beatles, and auteur rocker John Fogerty crafted a dozen or more records that became known as rock standards. When the band first began, it was as the Blue Velvets, an after-school enterprise conducted in one of their parents' garages. But when John's older brother joined, the band turned more professional; Tommy Fogerty & the Blue Velvets notched a modest 1961 hit on local radio before returning to the realm of high school dances and frat parties as the Golliwogs. But when John Fogerty cut an eight-and-a-half-minute version of the Dale Hawkins oldie "Suzie Q" and the tape landed on the legendary San Francisco underground radio station KMPX, the newly named Creedence Clearwater Revival vaulted from playing tiny unknown clubs to the marquee of the Fillmore Auditorium almost overnight. An edited version became the group's first nationwide hit, but in 1969, "Proud Mary" exploded Creedence into the top ranks of rock bands of the day. Nine consecutive Top 10 hits later, the band began to disintegrate when Tom Fogerty left the group and the other three members agreed to equally share songwriting responsibilities. One album after that, the band was finished, and mastermind John Fogerty entered the studio by himself to record an album of country and western staples. But Creedence left behind a luminous body of work that has only grown more lustrous over the years—one of the great American rock 'n' roll originals. Fogerty continues to perform as a solo act, irked that Stu Cook and Doug Clifford continue on as Creedence Clearwater Revisited, a glorified cover band.

what to buy: Author Stephen King thinks *Cosmo's Factory* 𝄞𝄞𝄞𝄞𝄞 (Fantasy, 1970, prod. John Fogerty) is the best rock album ever. He may be right. The group's sixth album finds the band at the peak of its powers on an album crowded with five hit singles, reworkings of first-generation rock gems, and an epic eleven-minute workout on "I Heard It through the Grapevine."

what to buy next: Although *Chronicle* 𝄞𝄞𝄞𝄞 (Fantasy, 1976, prod. John Fogerty) offers a fairly comprehensive overview on the band's hits, the prime Creedence albums—*Bayou Country* 𝄞𝄞𝄞𝄞 (Fantasy, 1969, prod. John Fogerty), *Green River* 𝄞𝄞𝄞𝄞 (Fantasy, 1969, prod. John Fogerty), and *Willy and the Poor Boys* 𝄞𝄞𝄞𝄞 (Fantasy, 1969, prod. John Fogerty)—provide a deeper, richer look at the band with album tracks every bit as persuasive as the hit singles.

what to avoid: The last album, *Mardi Gras* **woof!** (Fantasy, 1971, prod. John Fogerty), featured only the three Blue Velvets and may have been one of the worst albums ever released by a major band. Also, there are several budget items such as *Travelin' Band* 𝄞𝄞𝄞 (Fantasy, 1992, prod. John Fogerty) and *Have You Ever Seen the Rain* 𝄞𝄞 (Fantasy, 1993, prod. John Fogerty), which feature a famous title track and disgracefully short running times. You don't need these when, for a few extra dollars, you can have a full masterwork by one of rock's greatest bands ever.

the rest:
Creedence Clearwater Revival 𝄞𝄞𝄞 (Fantasy, 1968)
Pendulum 𝄞𝄞𝄞 (Fantasy, 1970)
Creedence Gold 𝄞𝄞𝄞𝄞 (Fantasy, 1973/1991)
More Creedence Gold 𝄞𝄞𝄞 (Fantasy, 1973/1991)
Creedence Clearwater Revival: 1969 𝄞𝄞𝄞𝄞 (Fantasy, 1978)
The Concert 𝄞 (Fantasy, 1980)
Creedence Country 𝄞𝄞𝄞 (Fantasy, 1981)
Chronicle, Volume Two 𝄞𝄞𝄞 (Fantasy, 1986)
Live in Europe **woof!** (Fantasy, 1987)

worth searching for: The bootleg *Fantasy Session '70* (Main Street) features nearly 70 minutes of CCR jamming with hero Booker T. Jones on a combination of Fogerty originals and soul covers.

solo outings:
Creedence Clearwater Revisited (Cook, Clifford):
Recollection 𝄞𝄞𝄞 (Fuel 2000, 1998)

influences:
◀◀ Booker T. & the MG's, Elvis Presley, Little Richard, Dale Hawkins

▶▶ The Hollies, Bob Seger, Bruce Springsteen

see also: *John Fogerty*

Joel Selvin and Ken Burke

Marshall Crenshaw

Born November 11, 1953, in Detroit, MI.

Since he wears glasses, writes and sings mostly his own material, and plays guitar, Marshall Crenshaw was likened to Buddy Holly when his debut album was released in 1982. And while artists have every reason to resent being called "the next" anybody, in this case the reference did legitimately point to Crenshaw's musical roots; for further proof, check out the hard-to-find promotional single for "Cynical Girl," which features a live and very evocative performance of Holly's "Rave On." And let's not forget that he portrayed Holly in the Ritchie Valens bio-flick, *La Bamba*. But Crenshaw's roots include all great pop music that preceded him, including the Beatles; he played John Lennon in one production of Beatlemania. The *Marshall Crenshaw* album instantly established him as a comer, but it was also Crenshaw's commercial peak; never an MTV favorite, he explored various nuances of sophisticated pop music-making to (mostly) critical raves and little more than cult-level notoriety. Crenshaw has soldiered on nonetheless, continuing to record as well as writing a book about the evolution of rock music in film (*Hollywood Rock*).

what to buy: *Marshall Crenshaw* 𝄞𝄞𝄞𝄞𝄞 (Warner Bros., 1982, prod. Richard Gottherer, Marshall Crenshaw) is filled with catchy, up-tempo pop songs that sound as vibrant today as they did in 1982. An essential album for any rock collection.

what to buy next: For some reason, *Field Day* 𝄞𝄞𝄞𝄞 (Warner Bros., 1983, prod. Steve Lillywhite) was attacked by many of the same people who championed Crenshaw's first album—a bunch of hooey, since the album, while not as polished as the debut, is another collection of excellent songs. After a bit of stylistic drifting in the interim, *Life's Too Short* 𝄞𝄞𝄞𝄞 (Paradox/MCA, 1991, prod. Ed Stasium) marks a return to form that should please longtime fans and newcomers alike. Ditto *Miracle of Science* ♫♫♫ (Razor & Tie, 1996, prod. Marshall Crenshaw), which boasts many of Crenshaw's most celebrated attributes and enjoys a tighter focus as his first self-produced album.

what to avoid: *Good Evening* ♫♫ (Warner Bros., 1989, prod. David Kershenbaum, Paul McKenna) is the weakest of the lot, with the best songs coming from other writers.

the rest:
Downtown ♫♫♫ (Warner Bros., 1985)
Mary Jean & 9 Others ♫♫♫ (Warner Bros., 1987)
Live . . . My Truck Is My Home ♫♫♫ (Razor & Tie, 1994)
The Nine Volt Years: Battery Powered Home Demos & Curios (1979–198?) ♫♫♫ (Razor & Tie, 1998)

worth searching for: Prior to the release of *Life's Too Short*, MCA released the excellent—but promotional only—career retrospective *Marshall Crenshaw: A Collection* (Paradox/MCA, 1991, prod. various).

influences:
◀◀ The Beatles, Buddy Holly, the Everly Brothers, Arthur Alexander, Motown

▶▶ Matthew Sweet, BoDeans, Hootie & the Blowfish, Toad the Wet Sprocket

Michael Isabella

The Crew Cuts

Formed 1952, in Toronto, Ontario, Canada. Disbanded 1963.

John Perkins, lead vocals; Pat Barrett, tenor vocals; Rudi Maugeri, baritone vocals; Ray Perkins, bass vocals.

Assessing the dubious practice of record labels seeking out white acts to cover black R&B hits for white radio—it was all too common in the earliest days of rock 'n' roll—is tricky. For while victims of the practice like Bo Diddley bemoan the fact that it prevented the best R&B stars from crossing over onto the pop charts, and kept them from the recognition—not to mention the royalties—they so obviously deserved, others have expressed thanks that the songs got circulated. The Crew Cuts, a seemingly unassuming vocal quartet from Toronto, were among the earliest and most successful practitioners of this wily game, launching a career off the very backs of the doo-wop and R&B masters of the day. Although the group's first Mercury Records release in 1954 was self-penned, its follow-up—a version of the Chords' "Sh-Boom"—became the #1 song in the nation, and the race was quickly on to find more obscure R&B hits to subjugate. For the next several years the Crew Cuts, among many others, regularly shot into the Top 20 with whitewashed, clean-cut renditions of non-pop hits, while the original artists and the tiny, cash-strapped labels they recorded for languished in near total obscurity. By 1958 however, this game had—for a time, at least—come to an abrupt end, with Chuck Berry for one having defiantly bucked the trend by consistently hitting the pop Top 10 with his *own* recordings. The Crew Cuts were subsequently bounced from label to label and from style to style (check out the unfortunate *Crew Cuts Go Folk* album) before finally dissolving altogether in 1963, claiming somewhat weakly in their own defense, "If we came out with a cover that was hot, it would certainly squelch the smaller distributor. But that was (Mercury's) doing and we really didn't even think about it at all."

what's available: The 22 tracks on *The Best of the Crew Cuts: The Mercury Years* ♫♫♫ (Mercury, 1996, compilation prod. Ron Furmanek, Steve Kolanijan) may well include over a dozen slickly sanitized, mainstreamed hits; still, the quartet's voices—if not necessarily its hearts—always seemed to be in the right place. Discriminating students of early rock are, of course, urged to seek out the *real*—meaning original—versions of "Earth Angel," "A Story Untold," "Seven Days," and the rest, all of which are thankfully much more readily available to listeners today than they would have been four decades ago.

influences:
◀◀ The Four Lads, the Four Aces, the Charms, the Penguins

▶▶ The Diamonds, Pat Boone, the Nylons, the Haircuts

Gary Pig Gold

The Crickets

See: Buddy Holly

A.J. Croce

Born Adrian James Croce, September 28, 1971, in Bryn Mawr, PA.

Anybody who picked up the eponymous 1993 debut album from Jim Croce's kid A.J. expecting to hear more plaintive folk fare was in for a shock. Instead they got a barrelhouse piano player, a saloon tunesmith who pre-dated the late '90s swing affectation by several years. A.J. Croce was nearly two years old when his father died in a plane crash, and his mother, Ingrid, relocated the family to Costa Rica for a year, then to San Diego. When Croce was four, he developed a brain tumor that left him completely blind, though after several operations sight was restored to his left eye. Meanwhile, he started playing piano at age six, listening to Stevie Wonder and Ray Charles and then to 78s (which he began collecting), tapping into much of the older music that influenced his father as well. Croce played rock with a band, the Hottentots, but at the same time he was developing his own blend of pop, jazz, swing, and soul, often via solo performances in southern California piano bars. His music has grown and varied considerably since the debut, and while he hasn't had his "Time in a Bottle" yet, Croce has certainly established himself as a songwriter and performer worthy of greater attention.

what to buy: Croce's third release, *Fit to Serve* 🎧🎧🎧 (RUF/Platinum/PolyGram, 1998, prod. Jim Gaines), is his best so far, an expansive, stylistically challenging outing that takes the areas he explored on his first two albums, stirs them together and adds even more to the mix—mostly by incorporating more fully drawn band arrangements. Croce sings with authority over the bigger sound, with a convincing gospel flavor in the songs "So in Love" and "Judgment Day."

what to buy next: His debut, *A.J. Croce* 🎧🎧🎧 (Private Music, 1993, prod. John Simon, T-Bone Burnett), was shocking at the time, as everyone expected another troubadour of his father's stripe. But Croce sat down at the piano and rambled through "I Found Faith," "Smokin' Good Time," and "Which Way My Steinway" like a seasoned piano bar veteran (which he was) who could sing you a song, keep the piano pumping, *and* light your cigar—all at the same time.

the rest:
That's Me in the Bar 🎧🎧 (Private Music, 1995)

influences:
⏪ Ray Charles, Stevie Wonder, Cab Calloway, Stax

Gary Graff

Jim Croce

Born January 19, 1943, in Philadelphia, PA. Died September 20, 1973, in Natchitoches, LA.

By the end of the '60s, folk music had, at the hands of artists such as Joni Mitchell and Gordon Lightfoot, evolved from themes of social relevance to issues of personal introspection. Enter Jim Croce, a singer-songwriter from the East who captured everyman themes in his easygoing folk-pop music. Croce's warm, reassuring voice gave his songs a universal appeal, and he enjoyed tremendous success during the early '70s with humorous uptempo hits—"Bad, Bad Leroy Brown," "Workin' at the Car Wash Blues"—and heartfelt ballads—"Operator (That's Not the Way It Feels)," "Time in a Bottle." His career was cut painfully short in 1973 when a plane carrying Croce and his lead guitarist Maury Muehleisen crashed. His death was a major loss to music, a fact that is proven by the enduring quality and timeless appeal of his songs.

what to buy: *50th Anniversary Collection* 🎧🎧🎧 (WEA/Atlantic, 1992, prod. Terry Cashman, Tommy West) is a comprehensive two-CD set covering Croce's career from 1969 to 1973. In addition to the hits, the collection features many lesser-known LP tracks, including "Rapid Roy (The Stock Car Boy)" and a cover

of the Red Ingles novelty hit "Cigarettes, Whiskey and Wild, Wild Women." All tracks have been digitally remastered from the original master tapes, and the set includes vital liner notes from Croce's wife, Ingrid.

what to avoid: *Down the Highway* 🎧 (WEA/Atlantic, 1975, prod. Terry Cashman, Tommy West) is a slick compilation that offers too few hits and too many lesser-known songs that offer little insight to Croce's mastery.

the rest:
I Got a Name 🎧🎧 (Capitol, 1973)
Photographs & Memories: His Greatest Hits 🎧🎧🎧 (WEA/Atlantic, 1974)
Time in a Bottle 🎧🎧🎧 (Atlantic, 1976)
24 Carat Gold in a Bottle 🎧🎧🎧 (Digital Compact Classics, 1994)
The Definitive Jim Croce Collection 🎧🎧🎧 (Reader's Digest/EMI-Capitol, 1996)
Ultimate Collection 🎧🎧🎧 (Recall, 1998)

worth searching for: Recorded during Croce's last tour in the summer of 1973, *Live: the Final Tour* (Saja, 1973, prod. Terry Cashman, Tommy West) is an intimate look at the singer-songwriter's ability to hold an audience and turn a tale. While it's light on the hits, many of the other tunes (including "New York's Not My Home" and "Hard Time Losin' Man") receive nice turns.

influences:
⏪ Paul Simon, Gordon Lightfoot, Joni Mitchell, James Taylor

⏩ Don McLean, Cat Stevens, Jackson Browne, Harry Chapin, Jesse Winchester, Dan Fogelberg, Lyle Lovett

Christopher Scapelliti

David Crosby

Born August 14, 1941, in Los Angeles, CA.

A supporting player to Roger McGuinn in the Byrds and one-third of the supergroup Crosby, Stills & Nash, David Crosby has seen his solo career overshadowed by his other associations. Of course, there's also the fact that Crosby has received more headlines than any of his bandmates for nonmusical reasons, including being in trouble with the law, usually stemming from substance abuse, which he happily kicked during the late '80s after a stint in prison. Like many of his peers from the '60s, Crosby's best work came in that decade and during the early '70s. By and large, Crosby, like a lot of people who are better known for group involvement than solo projects, thrives in the band situation. Crosby's much like George Harrison, who always contributed one or two brilliant songs to each Beatles album, but also never more than that to his own albums. But Crosby—who underwent a liver transplant in 1994—seems re-energized in the late '90s by a new band (CPR) that he has formed with his long-lost son, James Raymond, and guitarist Jeff Pevar, who has worked on Crosby's solo projects. Of course, he still plays with CSN, as well as occasionally working as a duo with Graham Nash.

what to buy: Crosby's best solo album is easily *If I Could Only Remember My Name* ♪♪♪ (Atlantic, 1971, prod. David Crosby). It's actually more like a supergroup project, with Crosby as the ringmaster leading Graham Nash, Neil Young, Joni Mitchell, and members of the Grateful Dead, Jefferson Airplane, and Santana.

what to buy next: The in-concert *It's All Coming Back to Me Now* ♪♪♪ (Atlantic, 1994, prod. Chris "Hoover" Rankin) combines solo tunes with some of Crosby's CSN tracks and edges out his other live album due to appearances by Graham Nash and Chris Robinson of the Black Crowes on "Almost Cut My Hair."

the rest:
Oh Yes I Can ♪♪ (A&M, 1989)
Thousand Roads ♪♪ (Atlantic, 1993)
The King Biscuit Flower Hour Presents David Crosby ♪♪♪ (KBFH, 1996)

worth searching for: There are two albums by Crosby's new band, CPR—"C" for Crosby, "P" for Pevar, "R" for Raymond. Both of them, *CPR* (Samson Music, 1998) and the two-CD live set *Live at Cuesta College* (Samson Music), are available from the independent label Samson Music.

influences:

◄◄ Bob Dylan, Pete Seeger, Joan Baez, the Byrds

►► Hootie & the Blowfish, the Black Crowes, Melissa Etheridge, Phil Collins

see also: *The Byrds, Crosby, Stills & Nash*

Brian Ives

Crosby, Stills & Nash /Crosby, Stills, Nash & Young /The Stills-Young Band

Formed 1968, in Los Angeles, CA.

David Crosby (born August 14, 1941, in Los Angeles, CA), guitar, vocals; Stephen Stills (born January 3, 1945, in Dallas, TX), guitar, bass, keyboards, vocals; Graham Nash (born February 2, 1942, in Blackpool, England), guitar, keyboards, vocals; Neil Young (born November 12, 1945, in Toronto, Ontario, Canada), guitar, vocals.

One of the most celebrated and enduring of the late '60s supergroups, Crosby, Stills & Nash—with and without Neil Young—continued and built on musical foundations initiated with their previous bands. David Crosby was in the Byrds, Stephen Stills and Neil Young had fronted Buffalo Springfield, and Graham Nash was a signature voice in the Hollies. The decision to use

their last names for their moniker stemmed from the desire not to be thought of as just another band but as a group of individuals who worked together when it felt right. CSN formed as a trio to record their first album, and the blend of their voices combined with the songwriting skills of each—as well as Stills's instrumental prowess—became a cornerstone of the southern California folk-rock movement. With the addition of Young and his darker, more contemplative songs, CSNY became a powerful collective voice of the times, infusing desperate love songs and political theory with the same emotional harmonies. Though dogged by personality conflicts and assorted substance abuse addictions (which necessitated Crosby's liver transplant in 1994), the original trio seems inextricably drawn together, though its last work with Young was in 1988. In 1997, feeling neglected by its record company, the group broke off their long-time relationship with Atlantic Records and began searching for a new home for future recordings.

what to buy: *Crosby, Stills & Nash* ♪♪♪♪ (Atlantic, 1969, prod. Crosby, Stills & Nash) is an impressive blend of voice and guitar, beginning with Stills's complex and timeless "Suite: Judy Blue Eyes" and continuing through Nash's bouncy "Marrakesh Express," Crosby's paean to Robert Kennedy, "Long Time Gone," and the apocalyptic fairy tale, "Wooden Ships." The first album with Young, *Deja Vu* ♪♪♪♪ (Atlantic, 1970, prod. Crosby, Stills, Nash & Young), solidified the quartet's status as *the* superstar American band of the Woodstock generation. With a hippie anthem by Crosby ("Almost Cut My Hair"), Stills's guitar heroics ("Carry On"), Nash's sing-along tunes ("Our House," "Teach Your Children"), and Young's introspective "Helpless," they still found room for another songwriter's work (Joni Mitchell's "Woodstock"). *So Far* ♪♪♪♪ (Atlantic, 1974, prod. Bill Halverson, Crosby, Stills, Nash & Young), a greatest hits package after only two albums, contains the high points of those releases as well as the scathing single that came out in the wake of the Kent State shootings, "Ohio/Find the Cost of Freedom."

what to buy next: The four-CD box set *CSN* ♪♪♪♪ (Atlantic, 1991, prod. Graham Nash, Gerry Tolman) is filled with strong material from all of the musicians' catalogs—together and apart—but it may be for serious fans only. The first two discs are essential; it's the final one, comprised of latter-day solo and CSN recordings, that's hard to listen to all the way through. The live *4 Way Street* ♪♪♪ (Atlantic, 1971/1992, prod. Crosby, Stills, Nash & Young) became more attractive after it was expanded with four more songs on the 1992 CD reissue, but it may put off casual listeners who prefer the polish of the group's studio work.

what to avoid: *Live It Up* ♪ (Atlantic, 1990, prod. Crosby, Stills & Nash, Joe Vitale, Stanley Johnston) is a phone-in effort in which the voices sound as synthetic as the layered keyboards backing them up. The exception: Stills's "Haven't We Lost Enough?"

the rest:
Crosby, Stills & Nash:
CSN ♫♫♫♪ (Atlantic, 1977)
Replay ♫♫♪ (Atlantic, 1980)
Daylight Again ♫♫♪ (Atlantic, 1982)
Allies ♫♫♪ (Atlantic, 1983)
After the Storm ♫♫♪ (Atlantic, 1994)

Crosby, Stills, Nash & Young:
American Dream ♫♫♪ (Atlantic, 1988)

The Stills-Young Band:
Long May You Run ♫♫♪ (Reprise, 1976/1988)

worth searching for: The promotional CD single for *Chippin' Away* (Atlantic, 1989, prod. Crosby, Stills & Nash, Stanley Johnston, Craig Doerge), a song the trio—with guest James Taylor—recorded as a reaction to the fall of the Berlin Wall, was rush-released to radio but never made it on a CSN album.

influences:
◀◀ The Beatles, Bob Dylan, the Everly Brothers, Fred Neil
▶▶ America, the Eagles, Poco, Michael Hedges

see also: *David Crosby, Stephen Stills, Graham Nash, Neil Young*

Brian Escamilla

Christopher Cross
Born Christopher Geppert, 1951, in San Antonio, TX.

Once considered a promising pop/rock artist, Christopher Cross eventually became the quintessential three-hit wonder, capturing five Grammy awards and millions of record sales with his debut album, an effort buoyed by the hits "Ride Like the Wind" and "Sailing," along with guest appearances by Nicolette Larson and Michael McDonald. Signed to Warner Bros. after an apprenticeship in a popular Austin, Texas, cover band, Cross proved his pop smarts again with the 1981 hit "Arthur's Theme (The Best That You Can Do)," from the film *Arthur*. But the new wave revolution made Cross's easygoing pop sound quite irrelevant, though he continues to record.

what to buy: With all the hits, *Christopher Cross* ♫♫♫♪ (Warner Bros., 1980, prod. Michael Omartian) is a no-brainer-type purchase.

what to buy next: A German compilation, *Ride Like the Wind* (Warner Bros., 1992, prod. various) puts the few hits that aren't on his debut together with the classic Cross material in one place. Also, pick up ex–Van Halen lead singer David Lee Roth's

first solo disc *Crazy from the Heat* (Warner Bros., 1985) and see if you can pick out Cross's vocals in the background.

what to avoid: *Back of My Mind* **woof!** (Warner Bros., 1988, prod. Michael Omartian), an uninspired effort that doesn't seem to realize that the '70s are long gone.

the rest:
Another Page ♫♫ (Warner Bros., 1983)
Every Turn of the World ♫♫ (Warner Bros., 1985)
Rendezvous ♫♫ (BMG, 1993)
Window ♫ (Rhythm Safari, 1995)
Walking In Avalon ♫♫ (CMC International, 1998)

influences:
◀◀ Stephen Bishop, Dan Fogelberg, Loggins & Messina
▶▶ Peter Cetera, Bob Carlisle

Eric Deggans

David Cross
See: King Crimson

Sheryl Crow
Born February 2, 1962, in Kennett, MO.

During the early '90s, when the term "girls with guitars" implied either glowering punkettes or retiring folkies, Sheryl Crow emerged as something else entirely. A former grade school teacher whose big break came through singing on dozens of sessions and touring with the likes of Michael Jackson and Don Henley, Crow's success was one instance where a record label's unusually high degree of patience paid off. Initially slated to be a slick, down-the-middle pop singer whose debut album was being produced by Hugh Padgham (Genesis, Sting), Crow had that album shelved and started all over. This time the record grew organically from a loose-knit group of musicians she'd fallen in with that included David Baerwald, Kevin Gilbert, Bill Bottrell, and others. The group jammed, wrote music and created in a fertile, free-form fashion. The resulting album, *Tuesday Night Music Club*, started slowly saleswise, but thanks to relentless touring it eventually became a blockbuster hit, spawning the smash singles "All I Wanna Do," "Leaving Las Vegas," and several others. Recriminations and backbiting from her side musicians in the wake of the bizarre death of Crow's former beau, Kevin Gilbert (he died as a result of auto-erotic asphyxiation), soured Crow's triumph; but it didn't stop her momentum. Her second album found her collaborating with others but producing the record herself. It sold many fewer copies than the debut, but it solidified her base and expanded her sound, making clear that she's an artist to be reckoned with for some time to come.

what to buy: The songs on *Tuesday Night Music Club* ♫♫♫♪ (A&M, 1993, prod. Bill Bottrell) are emotionally raw, literate,

Sheryl Crow (© Ken Settle)

and stylistically various. "All I Wanna Do"—essentially Wyn Cooper's poem "Fun" set to a Stealer's Wheel groove—got the nation's attention and won a Grammy as 1994's Record of the Year. The rest of the album is just as impressive, though, especially "What I Can Do for You," which capitalized on the country's growing awareness of sexual harassment, and "Leaving Las Vegas," which captures in three lines—"Such a muddy line between/The things you want/And the things you have to do"—the essence of John O'Brien's self-excoriating novel of the same name, which it is based on.

what to buy next: The self-produced *Sheryl Crow* 🎜🎜🎜🎜 (A&M, 1996, prod. Sheryl Crow) proved that her initial success was no fluke and that she wasn't dependent on her former Tuesday night friends for fresh ideas. Low-key hits "A Change" and a pair of Stones-derived songs "If It Makes You Happy" and "It's Hard to Make a Stand" are among the highlights.

the rest:
The Globe Sessions 🎜🎜🎜🎜 (A&M, 1998)

worth searching for: Good luck finding a copy, but a few advance tapes of the Hugh Padgham–produced debut-that-wasn't, *Sheryl Crow* (A&M, unissued), slipped out to reviewers who somehow hung onto them. The album mostly sounds like another artist entirely (it contains the original version of "Father Sun," later covered by Wynonna) but hardcore fans will enjoy contemplating what might have happened had this music been issued.

influences:
◀◀ The Rolling Stones, Rod Stewart (ca. *Gasoline Alley*), Stevie Nicks, Don Henley, David + David

Daniel Durchholz

Crowded House

Formed 1985, in Melbourne, Australia. Disbanded 1996.

Neil Finn, vocals, guitar, keyboards; Paul Hester, drums, vocals, keyboards (1985–94); Nick Seymour, bass, vocals; Tim Finn: piano, guitar, vocals (1991–93); Mark Hart, keyboards, guitar (1993–96).

Crowded House sprang from the ashes of Split Enz, which Neil Finn joined as second fiddle to his brother Tim, though Neil eventually became chief songwriter. The new band took its name from the cramped Hollywood bungalow where it rehearsed its 1985 debut. Those quarters may have been a creative asset because Crowded House went on to produce some of the most melodically stunning pop this side of John Lennon and Paul McCartney. Airplay and attention built slowly for the first release, but eventually the singles "Don't Dream It's Over" and "Something So Strong" won an audience. Crowded House would never be so commercially successful again, though its

music continued to evolve and become more sophisticated. The group finally fizzled in 1996, though it was over for all practical purposes a couple of years before. Still, lovers of well constructed and intensely melodic post-Beatles pop should find every Crowded House album a treasure. The Finn brothers went their separate ways, reuniting for a duo album in 1996.

what to buy: On *Woodface* 🎜🎜🎜🎜 (Capitol, 1991, prod. Mitchell Froom, Neil Finn) Tim Finn joins brother Neil for a blend of up-tempo, quirky numbers ("Chocolate Cake," "Italian Plastic") with gorgeous ballads such as "Four Seasons in One Day," "Fall at Your Feet," and "Weather with You." This is not only Crowded House's finest, but also one of the very best of the post-Beatles anglo-pop releases, period.

what to buy next: *Crowded House* 🎜🎜🎜🎜 (Capitol, 1985, prod. Mitchell Froom) is a fine debut and has the big hits ("Something So Strong," "Don't Dream Its Over"). *Together Alone* 🎜🎜🎜🎜 (Capitol, 1993, prod. Youth) is very nearly on par with *Woodface* and features the outstanding Finn ballads "In My Command," "Fingers of Love," "Private Universe," and "Distant Sun." *Recurring Dream: The Very Best of Crowded House* 🎜🎜🎜🎜 (Capitol, 1996, prod. various) is a generous (19 songs) collection that lives up to its subtitle.

the rest:
Temple of Low Men 🎜🎜🎜🎜 (Capitol, 1988)

worth searching for: The CD single for "I Feel Possessed" (Capitol, 1989) includes three Byrds classics recorded in concert with Roger McGuinn.

solo outings:
Tim Finn:
Tim Finn 🎜🎜🎜 (Capitol, 1989)
Before & After 🎜🎜 (Capitol, 1993)
(With Alt) *Altitude* 🎜🎜🎜 (Cooking Vinyl, 1995)

Neil Finn:
Try Whistling This 🎜🎜🎜🎜 (Work, 1998)

Finn Brothers:
Finn Brothers 🎜🎜🎜 (Discovery, 1996)

influences:
◀◀ The Beatles, the Everly Brothers, the Byrds, Procol Harum, Split Enz

▶▶ The Rembrandts, Oasis

see also: *Split Enz*

Michael Isabella

Kacy Crowley

Born Kimberly Christine Crowley, July 3, 1968, in Northampton, MA.

Music is in Kacy Crowley's blood. The daughter of a piano

teacher, Crowley was five when she saw her first concert—John Denver at the Hartford, Connecticut, Civic Center—and began playing the guitar soon thereafter. She ditched the guitar, though, and in an ultimate act of preteen rebellion, Crowley took piano lessons from someone other than her mother. At age 14 she picked up the guitar once again and began writing songs. Dropping out of the University of Massachusetts after one semester, Crowley honed her folk music skills following the Grateful Dead. She wound up in Los Angeles, where she soaked up the coffeehouse folk scene and the wild life. After losing her apartment, she packed up and went home. Clean and sober, she headed to New York City and then Austin, Texas, where she graduated from busking on Sixth Street to the Dallas-based Carpe Diem label before moving to Atlantic Records, where she's established herself as a noteworthy voice amidst the post-Lilith cadre of female singer-songwriters.

what's available: Crowley took her experiences with addiction, Deadheads, and broken relationships and turned them into the clever lyrics and addictive melodies of *Anchorless* 🎵🎵🎵 (Atlantic Records, 1997, prod. Dave McNair). In "Rebellious," she confronts her mom after following the Grateful Dead and not shaving her legs for "at least two years"; "My mother said, 'What happened? You used to be beautiful.'/I dyed my hair and I got tattooed/And I let my body be recklessly used." And in the lush, rollicking "Singers Are Ugly," she pays tribute to Mick Jagger.

influences:

⏮ Sheryl Crow, Jude Cole

Christina Fuoco

The Cruel Sea

Formed 1988, in Melbourne, Australia.

Tex Perkins, vocals, harmonica, guitar; Dan Rumour, guitars, clavinet; James Cruickshank, guitars, keyboards, vocals; Ken Gormly, bass; Jim Elliott, drums.

What happens when basic blues-rock is shot through with blasts of reggae, Afro-pop, swamp boogie, and California surf guitar? That's something the Cruel Sea has been toying with since charging to the top of the Aussie pub scene during the early '90s. In fact, the band began as an all-instrumental quartet but added a member after fervent fan Tex Perkins, the manic leader of the Beasts of Bourbon, was asked to join as singer and co-lyricist. The band's first album, the bluesy, country *Down Below*, came in 1990, but the band really didn't hit its stride until the 1992 release of *This Is Not the Way Home*, which included the sunny, surf-flecked instrumental "4," a track popularized in Australia by its use in director Bill Bennett's road movie, *Spider and Rose*. Yet the album was counterbalanced by drifts into twilight and dark-

ness, much of it propelled by Dan Rumour and James Cruickshank's Link Wray–style guitar and Perkins's back-alley bad boy demeanor. Even stronger was the 1993 follow-up, *The Honeymoon Is Over*, released in the U.S. in 1995. Infectious Afro-Caribbean surf instrumentals such as "Orleans Stomp," "The Right Time," "Sly Din," and "X-N-Pop" sat cheek-by-jowl with blues-rockers such as the brutish "Delivery Man" and the darkly romantic "Blame It on the Moon." The album went double platinum in Australia, and the Cruel Sea bested such favorites as Midnight Oil, INXS, and Crowded House at that year's ARIA Awards, Australia's equivalent of the Grammys. Two years later, *Three Legged Dog* mined a similar musical mixture but was less effective. An album of early and unreleased tracks, *Rock'n Roll Duds*, was released in Australia during 1994. After a three-year layoff, the Cruel Sea returned in 1998 with *Over Easy*.

worth searching for: Though none of the Cruel Sea's albums is currently in print in the U.S., *The Honeymoon Is Over* (A&M, 1995, prod. Tony Cohen, the Cruel Sea, Mick Harvey) is by far the group's best. Also worth the hunt are the all-instrumental four-track *4* (Polydor/Red Eye EP, 1992, prod. various) and *This Is Not the Way Home* (Polydor/Red Eye, 1992, prod. Tony Cohen, the Cruel Sea), the album in which the group's sound began to come together.

solo outings:

The Beasts of Bourbon (Perkins):
The Axeman's Jazz 🎵🎵🎵 (Green Australia, 1984/Big Time, 1985)
Sour Mash 🎵🎵🎵 (Red Eye, 1988)
Black Mil 🎵🎵🎵 (Red Eye, 1990)

influences:

⏮ Link Wray, Nick Cave, Dick Dale, King Sunny Ade

⏭ The Dirty Three

Cary Darling

Julee Cruise

Born December 1, 1956, in Creston, IA.

Julee Cruise was a French-horn prodigy growing up in Iowa and apprenticed to the Chicago Symphony Orchestra. But she was drawn to acting and musical theater, performing off-Broadway and in radio and TV commercials before film director David Lynch discovered her and used her wispy vocals on the *Blue Velvet* soundtrack. Lynch called upon her again when making the unconventional TV series *Twin Peaks*, and he found more avenues for her ethereal vocals, teaming with composer Angelo Badalamenti to write an entire album for her, *Floating*, in 1989. They strung her up, literally, for "Industrial Symphony #1," staged later that year at the Brooklyn Academy of Music, and Cruise subbed for Cindy Wilson during the B-52's 1992 tour.

what to buy: *Floating* 𝄞𝄞𝄞 (Warner Bros., 1989, prod. David Lynch, Angelo Badalamenti), released at the height of the *Twin Peaks* hype in 1989, perfectly captured the eerie, haunting nature of the show, especially on the sadly narcotic "Falling." The coolly detached, retro lounge lizard jazz quality of the record presaged today's cocktail scene.

what to avoid: The Lynch-Badalamenti partnership reunited for a second Cruise album, *The Voice of Love* 𝄞 (Warner Bros, 1993, prod. David Lynch, Angelo Badalamenti), which unfortunately didn't measure up to *Floating*'s standard.

influences:

◀◀ Cocteau Twins, Dead Can Dance, Marianne Faithfull

▶▶ Tori Amos, the Cardigans

Doug Pullen

Cry of Love

Formed 1990, in Raleigh, NC. Disbanded 1997.

Audley Freed, guitar; Jason Patterson, drums; Robert Kearns, bass; Kelly Holland, vocals (1990–94); Robert Mason, vocals (1997).

You can glean Cry of Love's classic-rock intentions from its moniker, which is a nod to the 1971 Jimi Hendrix album of the same name. Drawing members from veteran Tarheel bands such as Nantucket and Sidewinder, Cry of Love played highly accomplished blues-rock tailor-made for traditional album-rock radio. The group had considerable rock radio success with its 1993 debut album, which yielded a couple of substantial radio hits. But Cry of Love's incessant touring proved too much for vocalist Kelly Holland, who bowed out in late 1994 because of health problems. The band dabbled with numerous potential replacements, including Canadian singer Sass Jordan, before finally settling on former Ozzy Osbourne backup vocalist Robert Mason. While Mason filled in capably enough, Cry of Love's enforced three-year hiatus proved to be too much to overcome and the band broke up not long after its second album was released. Bassist Robert Kearns subsequently joined the Bottle Rockets.

what to buy: Released into the teeth of alternative rock's early-'90s onslaught, Cry of Love's first album, *Brother* 𝄞𝄞𝄞 (Columbia, 1993, prod. John Custer), sounds strangely out of time—decidedly unfashionable guitar rock of a piece with Bad Company or Humble Pie. But it's flawlessly rendered, especially Audley Freed's cutting lead guitar. "Peace Pipe" and "Bad Thing" were the big hits.

what to avoid: *Diamonds & Debris* 𝄞𝄞 (Columbia, 1997, prod. John Custer) is fine as far as it goes, which is the problem—it doesn't go any further than *Brother*, meaning it sounds like a

dead end. Coming after a four-year gap, that wasn't good enough.

worth searching for: Cry of Love was always a fine live band. For evidence, there's *August 25, 1993* (Columbia, 1993, prod. Mitch Maketansky), a promo-only four-track EP. It has live versions of three *Brother* tracks, plus a nifty cover of the Willie Dixon chestnut "I Ain't Superstitious."

influences:

◀◀ Humble Pie, Bad Company, Black Crowes

▶▶ Brother Cane

David Menconi

Cryan' Shames

Formed as the Travelers, 1966. Became the Cryan' Shames later that year. Disbanded 1969. Re-formed 1970, 1975, and 1990.

Tom Doody, vocals; Jim Fairs, bass, flute, lead guitar; Dennis Conroy Born, drums (1968–69); Al Dawson, drums (1969); Gerry Stone, bass, guitar, keyboards (1966–67); Isaac Guillory, bass, guitar, keyboards (1967–69); J.C. Hooke, percussion; Dave Purple, bass, guitar, organ, harpsichord (1966–67); Lenny Kerley, bass, guitar, organ, harpsichord (1967–69).

The Cryan' Shames were a Chicago-based band whose run of hits were scarcely heard outside the Midwest. Its sound blended quasi–Beach Boys harmonies with glittering Yardbirds/Byrds–style guitars, which resulted in a sort of folk-rock MOR. At a time when local radio could make or break careers, the Shames received constant airplay on both WLS (a 50,000-watt clear channel station) and the trendsetting WCFL. After their lone national Top 40 entry, 1966's "Sugar & Spice" (a sped-up version of the Searchers' earlier hit), the Shames scored such Chicago-area smashes as "I Wanna Meet You," "Mr. Unreliable," "It Could Be We're in Love," "Up on the Roof," and "Greenburg, Glickstein, Charles, David Smith & Jones." (The latter was performed on Lloyd Thaxton's NBC summer replacement series *Showcase '68*.) The Shames boasted two fine songwriters in Jim Fairs and Lenny Kerley, both of whom tried to move the group into progressive, country-rock balladry. However, when the regional radio phenomenon ended in the late '60s, so did the band's chart clout. They had talent, drive, musicianship, and a gimmick (J.C. Hooke's exuberant display of the hook in place of his left hand), but the Cryan' Shames never realized their artistic or commercial potential.

what's available: The best moments from the three original LPs, the big Chicago-area hits, and some fine B-sides are on *Cryan' Shames—Sugar & Spice (A Collection)* 𝄞𝄞𝄞𝄞 (Columbia/Legacy, 1992, prod. Jim Golden), a strong 18-track compilation that boasts great remastered sound and a detailed, informative booklet. The group's evolution from British Invasion wannabes to country-rock troubadours is neatly chronicled on this eye-opening disc.

worth searching for: The last of its three LPs, *Synthesis* (Columbia, 1969, prod. Jim Golden), shows a transition in musical identity, which is startling if not engaging.

influences:

◀◀ The Beach Boys, the Searchers, the Yardbirds, the Byrds

▶▶ New Colony Six, the Buckinghams, the Stone Canyon Band

Ken Burke

The Crystal Method

Formed 1993, in Las Vegas, NV.

Ken Jordan, programming, samples; Scott Kirkland, programming, samples.

Initially formed in Las Vegas, Crystal Method didn't really happen until Ken Jordan and Scott Kirkland relocated to Los Angeles. The duo's music is reminiscent of England's Chemical Brothers, combining breakbeat grooveology with electronic dance theory to create massive big beat orientation. It hit the scene with a bang in 1994 with the release of the "Now Is the Time" single on City of Angels Records. Its place in the post-'80s American electronic movement was further cemented when the duo opened up for the Chemical Brothers in L.A. during January of 1995.

what's available: *Vegas* ✍✍✍ (Outpost, 1997, prod. the Crystal Method) is a megablast romp through breakbeat and electronic aural mayhem. The album is a non-stop, thunderous groove, from the synergistic "Trip Like I Do"—which judiciously mixes shifting electro-rhythm surge with breathy sound bites, sirens, and ominous backbeats—to the blurry rhythm shift and burbling electronic tweakage of "Busy Child" and the ethereal Pink Floydian ambiance-cum-phaser stun digital theatrics of "Keep Hope Alive."

worth searching for: *Spawn: The Album* (Immortal, 1997, prod. various) includes a reworking of "Trip Like I Do" that features industrial fusion rockers Filter. "Keep Hope Alive" has been remixed several times; look for the 12-inch "Keep Hope Alive" (City of Angels, 1995), which features the "There Is Hope Mix," the "Trip Hope Mix," and "More," and the CD-5 *Keep Hope Alive* (City of Angels, 1996), which features additional mixes.

influences:

◀◀ The Chemical Brothers, Kraftwerk, Aphex Twin

Spence D.

The Crystals

Formed 1961, in Brooklyn, NY. Disbanded 1967. Re-formed 1971.

Dee Dee Kennibrew, vocals (1961–67, 1971–present); Barbara Alston, vocals (1961–67); Dolores "La La" Brooks, vocals (1961–67); Mary Thomas, vocals (1961–64); Patricia Wright, vocals (1961–64); Frances Collins, vocals (1964–67); Marilyn Byers, vocals (1986–present); Gretchen Gale, vocals (1986–present).

A crucial yet oft-overlooked element in producer Phil Spector's Wall of Sound, the Crystals were the first—and most malleable—act he signed when he launched his own record company. And in many ways the group laid the foundation upon which he, and many other artists and producers to follow, bridged the gap between R&B and the pop Top 10. Kennibrew, Alston, Brooks, Thomas, and Wright, who were all friends in high school, first came together musically to help songwriter Leroy Bates cut demo recordings of his material for Hill and Range Music (in fact, they named themselves after Leroy's daughter, Crystal). Shortly after forming, they auditioned for Spector's new Philles label, and with one of Bates's tunes, "There's No Other (Like My Baby)," gave the company its first hit in 1962. The surprisingly (yet subliminally) topical "Uptown," written by Barry Mann and Cynthia Weil, provided the group with its second Top 20 entry only four months later, but a controversy surrounding the lyrics of "He Hit Me (It Felt Like a Kiss)" kept this third release from cracking the Hot 100. Rather than battle on behalf of this record, Spector decided to release instead a brand new Gene Pitney composition, "He's a Rebel," which he overheard while visiting friends at Liberty Records. Rushing to scoop Liberty's release of the song (planned for Vikki Carr), Spector tore across country to Los Angeles to surreptitiously record his own version utilizing the vocals of that city's hot new session trio the Blossoms (Darlene Love, Fanita James, Gracia Nitzsche). Released in the fall of 1962 under the name the Crystals—though not one member of the group was involved in its recording—"Rebel" soared to #1 in November and became a Top 20 hit in England as well. The *real* Crystals, with Brooks handling the majority of the lead vocals, scored twice more the following year with "Then He Kissed Me" and the classic "Da Doo Ron Ron." But by 1964 they were already tiring of Spector's increasingly tyrannical methods, not to mention the possible disgrace involved in promoting and touring behind records they did not actually perform on. Following a final pair of unsuccessful releases on Philles, they bought out their contract and signed with United Artists in 1965, where they cut several records in a Motown vein before being dropped the following year, after which they unceremoniously disbanded. However, unable to resist the lure of the oldies revival of the late 1960s, they re-formed five years later and continue touring to this day, though now Kennibrew is the only original member.

what's available: The Wall of Sound was built with 45-RPM singles, and *The Best of the Crystals* 𝄞𝄞𝄞𝄞 (Abkco, 1992, prod. Phil Spector) contains no less than seven indisputable evergreens of the genre, along with enough intriguing B-sides and inexplicable flops ("All Grown Up") to constitute a virtual 19-track '60s girl-group primer.

influences:

◀◀ The Chantels, the Shirelles, Rosie & the Originals

▶▶ The Shangri-Las, Brian Wilson, the Motels, Sit 'n Spin

see also: *Darlene Love, Phil Spector*

Gary Pig Gold

Rick Cua
See: The Outlaws

Warren Cuccurullo
See: Missing Persons

The Cult
/The Holy Barbarians
Formed 1983, in Brixton (London), England. Disbanded 1995.

Ian Astbury, vocals, tambourine; Billy Duffy, guitar; Jamie Stewart, bass (1983–89); Les Warner, drums (1983–87); Matt Sorum, drums (1989–90); Craig Adams, bass (1991–95); Scot Garrett, drums (1991–95).

Out of the ashes of Ian Astbury's Southern Death Cult and Billy Duffy's Nosebleeds came the Cult, a hard rocking quartet that at times flirted with great commercial success but never quite achieved it. Combining Astbury's love of Native American imagery (fire, phoenixes, etc.) with Duffy's penchant for blockbuster riffs, the Cult's early albums were subversive before alternative rock became a marketing category. Ironically, its later efforts were more forthright at a time when mainstream ears finally opened to what the Cult was doing early on. Its popularity peaked in 1989 with heavy MTV and rock radio play for the anthem "Fire Woman" and a well-timed tour opening for the about-to-be-huge Metallica. But Astbury and Duffy publicly feuded, and there were several lineup changes and far too many fallouts and reunions between its principals for the Cult to remain healthy for long. The band formally disintegrated in 1995, with Astbury moving on to the Holy Barbarians and eventually a solo career.

what to buy: *Sonic Temple* 𝄞𝄞𝄞 (Sire, 1989, prod. Bob Rock) is an excellent introduction to the band's irresistible brand of mystic, stomping hard rock, containing not only "Fire Woman" but also "Sweet Soul Sister" and "Edie (Ciao Baby)."

what to buy next: On *Electric* 𝄞𝄞𝄞𝄞 (Sire, 1987, prod. Rick Rubin) producer Rubin helps the Cult pare away the dense psychedelia that marked its albums to that point and comes up with perhaps the best AC/DC album that band never made.

what to avoid: *Ceremony* 𝄞𝄞 (Sire, 1991, prod. Richie Zito) is occasionally stirring but too often a yawn.

the rest:
Dreamtime 𝄞𝄞𝄞 (Beggars Banquet, 1984)
Love 𝄞𝄞𝄞 (Sire, 1985)
The Cult 𝄞𝄞𝄞 (Sire, 1994)
High Octane Cult 𝄞𝄞𝄞𝄞 (Reprise, 1996)

worth searching for: *Pure Cult* (Beggars Banquet, 1992, prod. various) is an import collection that compiles the singles and best material up through the early '90s. The first copies came with a limited-edition live CD.

solo outings:
The Holy Barbarians (Astbury):
Cream 𝄞𝄞𝄞𝄞 (Reprise, 1996)

influences:

◀◀ Led Zeppelin, AC/DC, the Doors, the Sex Pistols, Killing Joke

▶▶ Bush, Candlebox, Alice in Chains, Guns N' Roses

Todd Wicks

Culture Club
/Boy George
Formed 1981, in London, England. Disbanded 1987. Re-formed 1998.

Boy George (born George O'Dowd), vocals; Roy Hay, guitar, keyboards; Mikey Craig, bass; Jon Moss, drums.

Culture Club frontman Boy George brought pure ear candy with a healthy dose of androgyny to the top of the U.S. charts. Part of a long line of androgynous rock singers, Boy George took it to the extreme, primping himself with makeup, braided hair, and tunics. The fad wore off after the group's first two albums, which launched a string of hit singles and earned the group a Grammy for Best New Artist in 1983. Personal dissension—particularly the end of George's relationship with drummer Jon Moss—and drug addictions eventually brought the group to an end. After a dry spell, Boy George's career was temporarily revived when his cover of Dave Berry's 1964 British hit "The Crying Game" was featured in the 1992 movie of the same name. Meanwhile, Culture Club regrouped for a tour during the summer of 1998.

what to buy: Pop music doesn't get much better than *Colour by Numbers* 𝄞𝄞𝄞𝄞 (Virgin, 1983, prod. Steve Levine) and its danceable singles "Karma Chameleon," "Church of the Poison Mind," and "Miss Me Blind."

what to buy next: Culture Club's debut album, *Kissing to Be Clever* 𝄞𝄞𝄞 (Virgin, 1982, prod. Steve Levine), disarmed the masses with George's appearance and the plucky hits "Do You Really Want to Hurt Me?," "Time (Clock of the Heart)," and "I'll Tumble 4 Ya."

what to avoid: On *From Luxury to Heartache* 𝄞𝄞 (Virgin, 1986, Virgin, prod. Arif Mardin, Lew Hahn), you can smell the end of the band coming.

the rest:
Waking up with the House on Fire 𝄞𝄞𝄞 (Virgin, 1984)
This Time: The First Four Years 𝄞𝄞𝄞 (Virgin, 1987)
At Worst . . . The Best of Boy George and Culture Club 𝄞𝄞𝄞𝄞 (SBK, 1993)
VH1 Storytellers: Greatest Moments 𝄞𝄞𝄞𝄞 (Virgin, 1998)

solo outings:
Boy George:
Sold 𝄞𝄞𝄞 (Virgin, 1987)
High Hat 𝄞𝄞𝄞 (Virgin, 1989)
The Martyr Mantras 𝄞𝄞 (Virgin, 1991)
Cheapness and Beauty 𝄞𝄞𝄞 (Virgin, 1995)

influences:
◄◄ Smokey Robinson, Queen, David Bowie, Bow Wow Wow, the Village People

►► Right Said Fred, Pulp, RuPaul, Madonna

Christina Fuoco

Burton Cummings

See: The Guess Who

The Cure

Formed 1976, in Crawley, England.

Robert Smith, vocals, guitar; Michael Dempsey, bass (1976–80); Laurence "Lol" Tolhurst, drums, keyboards (1976–91); Porl Thompson, guitar (1984–94); Simon Gallup, bass (1980–present); Mathieu Hartley, keyboards (1980); Boris Williams, drums (1984–93); Roger O'Donnell, keyboards (1988–91); Perry Bamonte, guitar, keyboards (1991–present).

While nowhere near as heady or neo-apocalyptic as early '80s bands such as Bauhaus, Sisters of Mercy, or Joy Division, the Cure has managed to get rich, which makes the band different. Having established a fan base early on with the winsome British hit "Boys Don't Cry," not to mention bandleader Robert Smith's connection to another British favorite, Siouxsie & the Banshees, with whom he had toured, the Cure took the small independent label Fiction Records and catapulted it into a mul-

timillion-dollar enterprise almost overnight. With a unique brand of gloomy, overly romanticized music dealing with love, loss, and sex in almost every song, the Cure managed to capture the heart of every angst-filled British teenager possible. Once the band members determined the British Isles were too small to confine them, they set their eyes on the U.S., where they quickly gained cult status and eventually superstardom despite little radio airplay during the earliest days of the assault. Despite a chaotic—at best—personnel situation, Smith maintained the integrity of the band's musical style across a dozen albums with at least as many different members. While not necessarily redundant or derivative, virtually every LP has a consistent style and quality that does not disappoint. Smith's lyrics sometimes make Morrissey seem chipper and positive in comparison, but he's never veered into the self-pitying school of songwriting. Despite the gloom and angst that dominate the work, Smith frequently sneaked in a playful and more upbeat song that invariably was a hit ("Love Cats," "Why Can't I Be You," "Let's Go to Bed," "Friday I'm in Love"). Despite lackluster sales and airplay from more recent efforts, the band still packs 'em in for concerts—although Smith regularly opines that each tour may be the Cure's last, which surely puts a few folks in the seats. Smith appeared as himself in an episode of the animated sensation *South Park*, fueling requests for "that band with the guy from *South Park*." While still continuing to produce new material and no end for the band in sight, you can rest assured that ambition, and talent, will prevail.

what to buy: *Staring at the Sea* 𝄞𝄞𝄞𝄞 (Elektra, 1986, prod. various) is a singles package collecting U.K. hits up to the mid-'80s, a good way to introduce the band to U.S. audiences.

what to buy next: Smith's doom and gloom is nowhere more apparent than in the frighteningly somber *Faith* 𝄞𝄞𝄞 (Elektra, 1981, prod. Mike Hedges, the Cure), a great Halloween soundtrack or mood music for a seance. It doesn't get loud or fast, but rather provides a deluge of gray sound. *Kiss Me, Kiss Me, Kiss Me* 𝄞𝄞𝄞 (Elektra, 1987, prod. Allen Smith) is a little lighter, with a higher bop quotient in "Hot, Hot, Hot" and "Just Like Heaven." *Galore: The Singles 1987-1997* 𝄞𝄞𝄞 (Elektra, 1997, prod. various) shows how prominent the band was commercially. Though not as good as the earlier material, the songs here are all very familiar to most and show the band's departure from the moody atmospherics of yesterday and its progression into the group it is today. The album features the new track "Wrong Number," which proved moderately successful in its own right.

what to avoid: *Paris* 𝄞 (Elektra, 1993, prod. Robert Smith, Bryan New), taken from a Paris live show during 1992, has only average sound quality and a middling selection of tracks.

the rest:
Boys Don't Cry 𝄞𝄞𝄞 (Elektra, 1980)

Seventeen Seconds ♫♫♫ (Elektra, 1980)
Pornography ♫♫♫ (Fiction/A&M, 1982)
Head on the Door ♫♫♫♫ (Elektra, 1985)
Disintegration ♫♫♫♫ (Elektra, 1989)
Mixed Up ♫♫♫ (Elektra, 1990)
Wish ♫♫♫ (Elektra, 1992)
Japanese Whispers ♫♫♫ (Fiction/Sire, 1993)
Wild Mood Swings ♫♫♫ (Elektra, 1996)

worth searching for: The cassette version of *Staring at the Sea* adds a full dozen extra B-sides.

solo outings:
Presence (Lol Tolhurst):
Inside ♫♫♫ (Smash, 1993)

The Glove (Robert Smith):
The Glove ♫♫♫ (Rough Trade, 1990)

influences:

◀◀ Genesis, Joy Division, the Sex Pistols

▶▶ The Essence, Siouxsie & the Banshees, Jesus & Mary Chain

Tim Davis

Mac Curtis

Born Wesley Erwin Curtis Jr., January 16, 1939, in Fort Worth, TX.

One of the original Texas rockabillies, Mac Curtis started his first boppin' band before he had even heard of Elvis Presley. A ducktailed, hep-cat teenager, Curtis dug transforming the boogie-woogie of Piano Red and Big Joe Turner into country music with a stomping beat. With his band the Country Cats, he signed with King Records at the age of 17 and recorded "If I Had a Woman," "Grandaddy's Rockin'," and "You Ain't Treatin' Me Right." These definitive rockabilly performances didn't sell particularly well outside the Dallas–Ft. Worth area, though they became highly prized cult items. At his early peak, Curtis played the *Big D Jamboree* with Elvis Presley and appeared on *Alan Freed's 1956 Christmas Rock 'n' Roll Revue*, holding his own against such stiff competition as Shirley & Lee, Screamin' Jay Hawkins, Jessie Belvin & the Cadillacs. Curtis's career momentum was stopped short after he was drafted into the U.S. Army. Though he kept his musical ambitions alive in various GI country bands, Curtis worked primarily as a disc jockey and music director for American Forces Radio in Korea. He has made the bulk of his living as a disc jockey ever since, though his stint in Los Angeles allowed him to record for labels big and small. With GRT and Epic, Curtis placed six singles in the lower regions of the country charts, the best of which was a cover of Carl Perkins's "Honey Don't." In 1971, he met up with the now-legendary early rock champion Ron Weiser, who convinced Curtis to return to recording rockabilly for his tiny Rollin' Rock

label. In Weiser's crude living room studio, Curtis was aided heavily by another Texas great, Ray Campi, and they recorded and overdubbed most of the backing tracks themselves. The resulting discs, while sometimes lacking in tonal fidelity, were first-class American rockabilly replete with slappin' bass, Merle Travis–inspired guitar fills, hiccupping vocals, and a driving, enthusiastic feel. Curtis recorded extensively for Rollin' Rock until the label went dormant during the early '80s. These days, Mac Curtis continues to work in radio but tours overseas occasionally, where he is a major draw and regarded as a true hero of "real" rock 'n' roll music.

what's available: The cream of Curtis's work during the '70s is on *Rockabilly Uprising: The Best of Mac Curtis* ♫♫♫ (HMG/HighTone, 1997, prod. Rockin' Ronny Weiser), 19 tracks of bass-slappin' rockabilly, country, and flat-out rock 'n' roll. Billy Zoom plays sax on one track, and fellow Rollin' Rocker Ray Campi provides heavy support. Curtis is especially hot on such numbers as "Good Rockin' Tomorrow," "Wild, Wild Women," and commanding remakes of "If I Had a Woman" and "Grandaddy's Rockin'." A fine introduction.

worth searching for: Curtis's great sides for King are compiled on the import *Blue Jean Heart* (Charly, 1991, prod. various), including the original versions of "If I Had a Woman," "Grandaddy's Rockin'," and many other hot tunes for cool cats. Also, check out Johnny Carroll's *Texabilly* (HMG/HighTone, 1997, prod. Rockin' Ronny Weiser) to hear Curtis belt out his tribute "Johnny Carroll Rock."

influences:

◀◀ Piano Red, Sonny Fisher, Carl Perkins, Marty Robbins, Elvis Presley

▶▶ Johnny Carroll, Ray Campi, Billy Zoom, the Blasters

Ken Burke

Curve

Formed 1990, in London, England.

Toni Halliday, vocals; Dean Garcia, bass, guitars, keyboards, programming.

Toni Halliday and Dean Garcia were introduced by Dave Stewart of the Eurythmics and played together in a band called State of Play, which released one album and a couple of singles during the late '80s before dissolving. After that foray into semi-dance music, the duo reunited a few years later to form Curve. Like Alanis Morissette, they got a complete musical makeover, from goofy dance tunes to credible indy-press darlings. Halliday and Garcia fared considerably better this time out, making the cover of all the British music mags (due in part to the incredibly photogenic Halliday) and even getting some airplay in the U.S. Curve's recipe of fuzzy guitar, moody vocals, and danceable electronic drums was hardly original—it has quite a bit in common with "Darklands"-era Jesus & Mary Chain and even My Bloody Valentine. The band was one of the few "wall-of-sound" groups fronted by a female vocalist. Later releases show a definite progression away from its reliance on harsh noise toward stronger pop sensibilities and better songwriting.

what to buy: *Doppleganger* 𝄞𝄞𝄞 (Charisma, 1992, prod. Curve, Flood) hit #1 in the U.K. and produced a semi-hit single, "Fait Accompli." *Pubic Fruit* 𝄞𝄞𝄞 (Charisma, 1992, prod. Curve) collects tracks from some early EPs that where available as imports only.

the rest:
Cuckoo 𝄞𝄞𝄞 (Charisma, 1993)
Chinese Burn 𝄞𝄞𝄞 (Universal EP, 1997)
Come Clean 𝄞𝄞𝄞 (Universal, 1998)

influences:
◀◀ Cocteau Twins, Jesus & Mary Chain, My Bloody Valentine, Siouxsie & the Banshees

▶▶ Garbage, Veruca Salt, Breeders, Sneaker Pimps, Alanis Morissette

Tim Davis and Christopher Scanlon

Cybotron

See: Juan Atkins

Cypress Hill

Formed 1988, in Los Angeles, CA.

B-Real (born Louis Freese), vocals; Sen Dog (born Senen Reyes), vocals (1988–1996); DJ Muggs (born Lawrence Muggerud), deejay.

Lawrence Muggerud was an East Coast transplant to the hard streets of L.A.'s Southgate area who fell in with a number of rappers before finally hooking up with ex-local gang members Louis Freese and Senen Reyes. Although he'd previously produced an excellent crew called 7A3, it was with B-Real and Sen Dog that Muggs would find his greatest success. B-Real's nasal voice recalled the Beastie Boys' King Ad-Rock, but he had the sort of street creed the Beasties would never even dream of, carrying a slug in his body from a previous shooting. Sen Dog's own street life led him in and out of trouble before he completed the circle by becoming the group's hype man.

what to buy: When it was first released, *Cypress Hill* 𝄞𝄞𝄞𝄞 (Ruffhouse/Columbia, 1991, prod. DJ Muggs) felt to some West Coast true believers like another irrefutable answer to the Boogie Down Productions album *Criminal Minded*—the first, of course, being N.W.A.'s *Straight Outta Compton*. The record

eventually went double platinum because of East Coast support and, especially, because of the use of the chilly "How I Could Just Kill a Man" in the climax of Ernest Dickerson's film *Juice*; also important was the crossover legitimacy that the group's Lollapalooza stint brought. Still, everything about this record spoke West Coast: its murky, dusted samples; its hazy, ultraviolent, seedy midnight-on-Santa Monica Boulevard imagescape; its Spanglish accent; its earthy obsession with pot. Muggs is at his peak, deploying samples in odd structures that complement B-Real's blunt-distorted storytelling and Sen Dog's punctuation marks. "Pigs," "Stoned Is the Way of the Walk," "How I Could Just Kill a Man," and "Hand on the Pump" redefine L.A. noir for the hip-hop generation, shot through with cop brutality, lowrider oldies, concentrated THC, and snarling driveby menace. That they again made marijuana (especially smoked in blunt form) the drug of choice for a generation was beside the point.

what to buy next: When Reyes left to work on other projects (including the Latino group Delinquent Habits), B-Real and Muggs released *The Soul Assassins* 𝄞𝄞𝄞 (Columbia, 1997, prod. Muggs), a compilation of excellent new tracks, over which a stellar cast (KRS-One, Goodie Mob, RZA and GZA, MC Eiht, and, especially, Wyclef) gives solid performances.

the rest:
Black Sunday 𝄞𝄞𝄞 (Ruffhouse/Columbia, 1993)
Cypress Hill III—Temples of Boom 𝄞𝄞𝄞 (Ruffhouse/Columbia, 1995)
Unreleased & Revamped 𝄞𝄞𝄞 (Ruffhouse/Columbia, 1996)

influences:
◀◀ Public Enemy, the Bomb Squad, N.W.A., Ice Cube, 7A3, the Beastie Boys, Rammellzee & K-Rob

▶▶ Wu-Tang Clan, Call O' Da Wild, Mista Grimm, Total Devastation, House of Pain, Funkdoobiest

Jeff "DJ Zen" Chang

The Cyrkle

Formed 1961, in Easton, PA. Disbanded 1969.

Don Dannemann, guitar, vocals; Tom Dawes, bass, guitar, sitar, harmonica, vocals; Marty Fried, drums (1965–69); Earl Pickens, keyboards (1961–66); Michael Losekamp, keyboards, bass (1967–69); Jim Maiella, drums (1961–64).

Despite some impressive music-biz connections (Brian Epstein, Paul Simon) and a more-than-sufficient modicum of ability, this New York–based trio spent barely a year in the spotlight before plunging back into obscurity faster than one could say "Where are they now?" It all began on the coffeehouse/frat circuit in the early 1960s where, as the Rhondells, the group honed its close-knit vocal and instrumental style before hitting the eastern club circuit seriously in 1963. Like so many others, they learned from the British Invasion to electrify their act, and by 1965 they'd become an accomplished, if not necessarily original, unit. The group caught Beatles manager Epstein's ear (and eye) the following year and, having been rechristened the Cyrkle by none other than John Lennon himself, was signed to Columbia Records and given a Simon & Garfunkel reject, "Red Rubber Ball," to record. Although Paul Simon to this day claims it's the worst song he's ever written, it quickly hit #2 on the charts. By the time the Cyrkle was warming up for the Fab Four on their final American tour, they'd placed still another song into the Top 20 (the splendid "Turn Down Day"). It was their second—and last—hit. They continued touring throughout 1967, did a bit of soundtrack work in '68, and had disbanded by the turn of the decade. Dawes went into record production (working with such groups as Foghat) and Dannemann built a life in jingle work, taking time out in 1981 to remember his slain mentor with a John Lennon tribute most appropriately titled "Full Circle."

what's available: The never less than bouncy *Red Rubber Ball: A Collection* ♫♫♫ (Columbia Legacy, 1991, prod. John Simon) is as good an overview as any two-hit wonder deserves. You even get a United Way radio spot outtake thrown in, just for good measure.

influences:

◄◄ The Kingston Trio, the Beatles, Simon & Garfunkel

►► The Loved Ones, Heyday, the Diodes

Gary Pig Gold

D

Chuck D.

See: Public Enemy

D Generation

Formed 1991, in New York, NY.

Jesse Malin, vocals; Danny Sage, lead guitar; Richard Baccus, rhythm guitar (1991–97); Howie Pyro, bass; Michael Wildwood, drums; Todd Youth, rhythm guitar (1998–present).

The undeniable heroes (and darlings) of the East Village's early-'90s post-punk scene, D Generation emerged in 1991 with a noble (if somewhat pretentious) mission: reinvigorate New York with a rock 'n' roll energy not seen since the punk heyday of the late '70s. D Gen's slightly glammed-up image, combined with big guitars and better-than-average songs (which typically ad-dressed "corporate" rock, as well as a preponderance of local bands that, according to D Generation, were killing rock and roll), earned a rabid following among veteran and neophyte punks alike. Comparisons to the New York Dolls abounded but, really, they are much more like the Dead Boys. Unfortunately, D Generation's success as a "hot" live band wouldn't translate into much of a recording career. D Gen miscalculated by signing to Chrysalis in 1994, and the label quickly lost interest. They switched to Columbia, where they were produced by former Cars auteur Ric Ocasek, but that album flopped as well.

what's available: *No Lunch* ♫♫♫ (Columbia, 1995, prod. Ric Ocasek) combines remakes of several songs from the disappointing and out-of-print debut album, *D Generation* ♫♫♫ (Chrysalis, 1994, prod. Michael Barbiero), with a batch of newcomers. Like *D Generation*, it doesn't quite capture the energy of the band's live shows.

worth searching for: A white vinyl 7-inch single, "No Way Out" b/w "Guitar Mafia" (Gasatanka, prod. Daniel Rey, Andy Shernoff), was released on Jello Biafra's label and captures the D Gen vibe better than either of the band's CDs.

influences:

◄◄ The Dead Boys, the New York Dolls, Cheap Trick, the Ramones

Mike Bieber

dada

Formed 1990, in Los Angeles, CA.

Joie Calio, vocals, bass; Michael Gurley, vocals, guitars; Phil Leavitt, drums.

This California trio prides itself on smartly written lyrics and music overflowing with hooks. The group brings together any number of sprightly '80s pop influences, from XTC to the Police. If there's a failing in what seems to be dada's formula for pop stardom, it's that their music is somewhat same-sounding, resulting in a pleasant enough listen for the duration of a CD, but not much that is memorable beyond that. The exception, of course, is the group's irrepressible hit, "Dizz Knee Land."

what to buy: The wiseass pop gem "Dizz Knee Land" is the draw for dada's debut album, *Puzzle* ♫♫♫ (I.R.S., 1992, prod. Ken Scott), making it the one dada album to own.

what to buy next: *El Subliminoso* ♫♫♫ (I.R.S., 1996, prod. dada) failed to make the same impact as the debut, which is a shame. It explores western funk in "Bob the Drummer," acoustic lushness in "Star You Are," and raw pop in "I Get High," which should have been a mainstream smash.

the rest:

American Highway Flower ♫♫♫ (I.R.S., 1994)

influences:

◀◀ Crowded House, INXS, XTC

Christina Fuoco and Daniel Durchholz

Daft Punk

Formed 1993, in Paris, France.

Thomas Bangalter, keyboards, programming; Guy-Manuel de Homem-Christo, keyboards, programming.

Thomas Bangalter and Guy-Manuel de Homem-Christo met at school in 1987, and by 1992 they were members of the group Darlin, which released a single on Stereolab's Duophonic label. After a *Melody Maker* reviewer characterized the tune as "a bunch of daft punk," the pair quit the group. Using the critical barb as their new name, the still-teenage duo began recording simple, punchy, invigorated singles that quickly won them a devoted following in the French dance-club scene. With the release of "Da Funk" in April 1995, their popularity leapt the Channel into Britain. They spent much of 1996 devising the crafty *Homework*, and in early 1997 it earned them a pair of Stateside hits—"Da Funk" and the teasingly repetitive "Around the World." Although their music can certainly be engaging and even joyful, Daft Punk may wind up mired in novelty status unless their follow-up releases expand upon their cleverly pinpoint style.

what to buy: Highlighted by the scratchy, irresistible all-instrumental hit "Da Funk," *Homework* 𝄞𝄞𝄞♩ (Virgin, 1997, prod. Daft Punk) is a veritable model of economy and wit. A little more wit and a little less economy might have perked up the less interesting cuts, but when you're in the realm of Dadaist minimalism, colorful embellishments are hard to come by.

influences:

◀◀ Kraftwerk, Brian Eno, Grandmaster Flash, Dr. Dre

Bob Remstein

Dick Dale

Born Richard Anthony Monsour, May 4, 1937, in Boston, MA.

Until 1994, when Quentin Tarantino's smash film *Pulp Fiction* stuck the 1962 surf instrumental "MIsIrlou" in the opening credits, Dick Dale was a tremendously overlooked rock 'n' roll trailblazer. The surfer-guitarist's early hits, including "Let's Go Trippin'" and "Misirlou," not only invented the entire genre of surf music, but also influenced such younger legends as Jimi Hendrix and Brian Wilson. Dale's style, which he said was an approximation of the sound a wave makes when it's next to your ear, has a natural rumble and sometimes sounds like a person screaming. As "King of the Surf Guitar" in the early '60s, Dale was one of

the few rock celebrities to gain fame between Buddy Holly's death and the birth of the Beatles—*Life* magazine ran a huge spread of Dale at home, surrounded by his pet lions. Eventually, the Beach Boys and the rest of the '60s eclipsed Dale, who survived a major bout with cancer in his intestines, and he faded into obscurity. He continued to tour with the Del-Tones, recorded with Stevie Ray Vaughan, and in 1986 released a comeback record that went nowhere. But Dale's second comeback, *Tribal Thunder*, got people listening again and recast him as a forebear of heavy-metal guitar. Then came *Pulp Fiction,* and the smiling, pony-tailed Dale, last seen touring in nightclubs around the country, had a meal ticket once again.

what to buy: *King of the Surf Guitar: The Best of Dick Dale and His Del-Tones* 𝄞𝄞𝄞𝄞 (Rhino, 1989, prod. various) has all the early hits, including "Let's Go Trippin'," "Riders in the Sky," "Mr. Eliminator," and, of course, "Misirlou." They all have a snap that sounds fresh today and must have seemed positively out of this world in 1961. Dale's comeback, *Tribal Thunder* 𝄞𝄞𝄞 (HighTone, 1993, prod. Scott Mathews, Joel Selvin), shows he has been paying attention to his protégés all these years, and without sacrificing his style he pays homage to heavy metal and the British Invasion.

what to buy next: It's unclear why Rhino decided to eclipse its previous Dale collection, but the two-disc *Better Shred Than Dead: The Dick Dale Anthology* (Rhino, 1997, prod. various) is souped-up with rare tracks (including Dale's non-surf stabs at pop and rock) and more comprehensive liner notes.

the rest:
Unknown Territory 𝄞𝄞𝄞 (HighTone, 1994)
Calling up Spirits 𝄞𝄞𝄞 (Beggars Banquet, 1996)

worth searching for: Dale's early albums are difficult to find, but snap them up—particularly if you come across *Surfer's Choice* (Deltone, 1962) or *King of the Surf Guitar* (Capitol, 1963).

influences:

◀◀ Link Wray, Duane Eddy, Chuck Berry, Chet Atkins, Merle Travis

▶▶ The Beach Boys, the Chantays, the Ventures, Jimi Hendrix, Van Halen, Metallica, Man or Astro-Man?, the Aqua Velvets

Steve Knopper

Roger Daltrey

See: The Who

The Dambuilders

Formed 1989, in Honolulu, HI.

Dave Derby, vocals, bass; Eric Masunaga, vocals, guitar; Kevin March, drums (1992–present); Joan Wasser, vocals, violin, keyboards

(1991–present); Tryan George, guitar (1989–90); Debbie Fox, violin (1990–91); Stuart Wright, drums (1991); Keoki Van Orden, drums (1989); Daniel Glass, drums (1990).

Formed out of a new wave group called the Exactones, the Dambuilders managed to make innovative music without sacrificing the genre's infectious sense of fun. Even after its violin-spiked pop grew smoother and more expertly produced, the group still pursued its "50 songs for 50 states" project—an oddball effort to chronicle America in song. The Dambuilders formed in the 50th state, only moving to the mainland after releasing *A Young Person's Guide*. Its move to Boston brought personnel changes—the second guitarist was out, violinist Joan Wasser was in—and a decreasing dependence on its new wave influences, replaced by a willingness to experiment with both Velvets-style distortion and rock songs that were almost anthemic. Drummer Kevin March joined for the *Tough Guy Problem* EP, completing the band's longest-running lineup and pushing it further toward a bigger, stronger sound. Though *Islington Porn Tapes* was dark, punchy, and purposeful, *Encendedor* comes off as something of a holding action, if only because much of the material was from previous releases. *Ruby Red* wasn't as angular as previous releases—the band's sound got a little too big for its songs—but *Against the Stars* found a compelling middle ground between smoothly produced rock and the off-kilter inventiveness that has marked the band's best work. Soon after, the Dambuilders parted ways with Elektra and went on what bandmembers are calling an "extended hiatus."

what to buy: After shaking free of its almost slavish devotion to new wave roots, the Dambuilders combined tack-sharp power-pop with experimental touches on *Islington Porn Tapes* 𝄞𝄞𝄞𝄞 (Cuacha!, 1993, prod. Eric Masunaga). By its last album, *Against the Stars* 𝄞𝄞𝄞𝄞 (EastWest, 1997, prod. Eric Masunaga), that combination sounds seamless, effortless, and completely masterful.

what to buy next: Firmly rooted in the accessibly spastic sound of the Exactones, *A Young Person's Guide* 𝄞𝄞𝄞𝄞 (Cuacha!, 1989, prod. Eric Masunaga) is pure pop for new wave people—enough of a blast to succeed on its own terms but too derivative to offer more than a few hints that the Dambuilders are an innovative band with lasting power. As much a best-of as a new effort, *Encendedor* 𝄞𝄞𝄞𝄞 (EastWest, 1994, prod. Eric Masunaga, the Dambuilders) is both an essential primer on the band's middle years and an indication of where it would go later.

the rest:
Geek Lust 𝄞𝄞𝄞𝄞 (Cuacha!, 1991)
Tough Guy Problem 𝄞𝄞𝄞 (SpinArt EP, 1992)
Ruby Red 𝄞𝄞𝄞 (EastWest, 1995)

worth searching for: Released only in Australia, *God Dambuilders Bless America* (Shock, 1996, prod. Eric Masunaga) collects some of the band's state-oriented songs, offering an engaging glimpse at their quirkier side.

influences:
◀◀ Talking Heads, Devo, Violent Femmes
▶▶ Gin Blossoms, the Rentals

Robert Levine

Damn Yankees
See: Night Ranger

The Damned
Formed 1976, in London, England. Disbanded 1989.

Dave Vanian, vocals; Brian James, guitar (1977–79); Captain Sensible, bass, guitar (1976–84); Rat Scabies, drums (1976–77, 1979–89): Lu, guitar (1977–79); Jon Moss, drums (1977–78); Alistair Ward, bass (1979–80); Paul Grey, bass (1980–82); Roman Jugg, keyboards, guitar (1981–89); Bryan Merrick, bass (1984–85).

Never mind the Sex Pistols; here's the Damned. By one month, the Damned was the first punk band to put out an album, and the first to tour the U.S. The Damned was certainly a colorful bunch—Dave Vanian in his vampire get-up, Captain Sensible in his tutu, Rat Scabies diving into the audience for punchups. The music, though, was prototypical—hard and fast, with a fourth chord allowed only after arduous decision making. What the Damned didn't do is flame out quickly; despite significant personnel changes the group soldiered on, and, in fact, put out some of its biggest hits (and best material) during the mid-'70s with "Smash It Up" and "Love Song." The Damned outlived the Pistols, the Clash, and its other punk peers, finally breaking up in 1989 (with a brief reunion tour during 1997). But the band left behind a fairly inspiring collection of music.

what to buy: *Damned, Damned, Damned* 𝄞𝄞𝄞𝄞 (Stiff U.K., 1977/Frontier, 1993, prod. Nick Lowe) is the Damned's blazing debut and the only studio recording by the original quartet. Like the early Stooges and MC5 albums, it retains its power and freshness two decades after the fact. After several personnel changes, *Machine Gun Etiquette* 𝄞𝄞𝄞𝄞 (Chiswick/Roadrunner, 1979) came as a surprise. It's as loud and proud as *Damned, Damned, Damned*, but there's just a touch more sophistication and, dare we say, songcraft on tracks such as "Smash It Up," "Love Song," and "I Just Can't Be Happy Today."

what to buy next: *The Light at the End of the Tunnel* 𝄞𝄞𝄞𝄞 (MCA, 1987, prod. various) is a well-selected retrospective that also includes B-sides and other rarities. *The Final Damnation*

𝄢𝄢𝄢𝄢 (Restless, 1989) is a worthy representation of the Damned's adrenaline-rush live show—though by the time it was recorded in 1988, the group had even slowed the tempos a bit to reveal the lean, tightly written virtues of its songs.

what to avoid: Vanian's Dracula fixation takes over on *Phantasmagoria* 𝄢𝄢 (MCA, 1985/Off Beat, 1994, prod. Jon Kelly), the aural equivalent of a late-night horror flick that comes off as intolerably silly.

the rest:
The Best of the Damned 𝄢𝄢𝄢 (Roadrunner, 1980/1993)
Live at the Lyceum 𝄢𝄢𝄢 (Restless, 1981/1990)
Strawberries 𝄢𝄢 (Bronze, 1982/Cleopatra, 1993)
Damned but Not Forgotten 𝄢𝄢𝄢 (Dojo, 1985/One Way, 1994)
Anything 𝄢 (MCA, 1986)
The Peel Sessions 𝄢𝄢𝄢𝄢 (Dutch East India, 1991)
Sessions of the Damned 𝄢𝄢𝄢𝄢 (Dutch East India, 1993)
Tales from the Damned 𝄢𝄢𝄢𝄢 (Cleopatra, 1993)
Collection 𝄢𝄢𝄢𝄢 (Griffin, 1995)

worth searching for: The British issue *The Black Album* (I.R.S., 1980) pairs one of the group's most musically sophisticated albums with a concert recording.

influences:
◀◀ The Stooges, the Ramones, the Sensational Alex Harvey Band

▶▶ The Germs, the Offspring, NOFX, Marilyn Manson

Gary Graff

Dance Hall Crashers

Formed 1989, in Orange County, CA.

Tim Armstrong, guitar, vocals (1989); Matt Freeman, bass, vocals (1989); Elyse Rodgers, vocals (1989–90, 1992–present); Jason Hammon, guitar (1990, 1992–present); Karina Denike, vocals (1990, 1992); Scott Goodell, guitar (1992); Mikey Weiss, bass (1992–present); Gavin Hammon, drums (1992–present).

Dance Hall Crashers started as a side band of Operation Ivy's Tim Armstrong and Matt Freeman. Vocalist Elyse Rodgers met them after catching some Operation Ivy shows in San Francisco. However, Armstrong and Freeman left quickly and went on to form Rancid. Elyse's early version of the band lasted only a year. After fans wrote to the band saying they were irked by their disappearance, the band re-formed in 1992. Eventually the Crashers caught the attention of management; they were the first band signed to the 510/MCA label and were among the first of the current wave of bands exploring a potent mix of ska, punk, and pop.

what to buy: *Lockjaw* 𝄢𝄢 (510/MCA Records, 1994, prod. Stoker) is the Dance Hall Crashers' hardest album from a rock point of view, and it spawned the hit "Enough." Armstrong even contributed a song, "Pictures," to the album. It's a perfect punk/ska hybrid.

what to buy next: The wonderfully titled *Honey I'm Homely* 𝄢𝄢 (510/MCA Records, 1997, prod. Stoker) finds Dance Hall Crashers getting back to their early ska roots.

the rest:
Dance Hall Crashers 1989–1992 𝄢𝄢 (Moon Records, 1992)

influences:
◀◀ The Go-Go's, the Specials, the Jam, the Clash

▶▶ No Doubt, Save Ferris, Reel Big Fish

Darren Davis

Dandy Warhols

Formed 1993, in Portland, OR.

Courtney Taylor, singer, songwriter, guitars, keyboards; Peter Holmstrom, guitars; Zia McCabe, bass, keyboards, percussion; Eric Hedford, drums, harmonies, keyboards (1993–98).

Shoegazing is one of those musical trends that never should have gone away. Following in the footsteps of Lush, Galaxie 500, and My Bloody Valentine, this Oregon-based quartet resurrects the sound with its swirl of psychedelic guitars, keyboards, and drugged-up vocals. The group's independent single "TV Theme Song," caught the attention of critics and record companies alike, spurring a bidding war that was eventually won by Capitol Records.

what to buy: On *The Dandy Warhols Come Down* 𝄢𝄢𝄢𝄢 (Tim/Kerr/ Capitol, 1997, prod. Tony Lash, Courtney Taylor), Courtney Taylor's sense of humor comes through the fuzzy guitars and low-fi sound. In "Minnesoter," he rhymes the word "doctor" with "Minnesoter," which is almost as good as Jakob Dylan matching "Cindereller" and "all together." A wave of Beach Boys influence overwhelms "Not If You Were the Last Junkie on Earth," while former Pixies member and Breeders leader Kim Deal is the object of Taylor's affection in the '60s-flavored "Cool As Kim Deal."

the rest:
Dandy's Rule OK 𝄢𝄢𝄢 (Tim/Kerr, 1995)

influences:
◀◀ The Velvet Underground, the Jesus & Mary Chain, the Stone Roses, Ginger

Christina Fuoco

Charlie Daniels Band

Formed 1970, in Nashville, TN.

Charlie Daniels (born 1937, in Wilmington, NC), vocals, fiddle, guitar; Joel "Taz" DiGregorio, keyboards, vocals; Jack Gavin, drums; Bruce Ray Brown, guitar, vocals; Chris Wormer, guitar, saxophone, vocals; Charlie Haywood, bass; and numerous others over the years.

A North Carolina native who became a popular session fiddler in Nashville, Daniels is best known for his 1979 hit "The Devil Went Down to Georgia," which country music fans and detractors alike cite to support their cases. Daniels, along with Lynyrd Skynyrd, was one of the early southern rockers, building his Charlie Daniels Band in the Allman Brothers Band's image but keeping a little more twang in his guitars and a bit more weep in his fiddle. Hard touring during the '70s led to radio play for "Uneasy Rider" and "The Legend of Wooly Swamp," as well as a moving Vietnam vets' tribute, "Still in Saigon." Unfortunately, his stay-out-of-my-backyard myopia and lunkheaded jingoism (the anti-drug diatribes of his later born-again Christian years are at odds with his earlier "Long Haired Country Boy" pronouncements, and are simplistic enough to embarrass even Nancy Reagan) have helped undercut his earlier accomplishments. Daniels has been off the charts for well more than a decade, though he has made strides within the contemporary Christian market and still can make a living touring the country's most yee-hawlering country bars.

what to buy: The three-disc set *Roots Remain* 🎵🎵🎵🎵 (Sony, 1996, prod. various) is a nice way to own Daniels's best stuff without poring through endless feet of record store bins. More cost-effective but less comprehensive is *A Decade of Hits* 🎵🎵🎵🎵 (Epic, 1983, prod. various), which contains many of the intermittent gems Daniels fiddled onto the radio. The consistent *Million Mile Reflections* 🎵🎵🎵 (Epic, 1979, prod. John Boylan) has "The Devil Went Down to Georgia."

what to buy next: *Full Moon* 🎵🎵🎵 (Epic, 1980, prod. John Boylan) is Daniels's most successful album, featuring "In America" and "The Legend of Wooly Swamp."

what to avoid: *Super Hits* 🎵 (Epic, 1994, prod. various) is a skimpy best-of. For all his flaws, Daniels deserves better.

the rest:
Te John, Grease and Wolfman 🎵 (Kama Sutra, 1970)
Honey in the Rock a.k.a. *Uneasy Rider* 🎵🎵🎵 (Buddah-Kama Sutra, 1973/Epic, 1977)
Fire on the Mountain a.k.a. *Simple Man* 🎵🎵🎵 (Buddah-Kama Sutra, 1974/Epic, 1989)
Way Down Yonder a.k.a. *Whiskey* 🎵 (Buddah-Kama Sutra, 1974/Epic, 1977)
Night Rider 🎵🎵🎵 (Buddah-Kama Sutra, 1975)
Saddle Tramp 🎵🎵 (Epic, 1976)

High Lonesome 🎵🎵 (Epic, 1977)
Midnight Wind 🎵🎵 (Epic, 1977)
Volunteer Jam III and IV 🎵🎵 (Epic, 1978)
Volunteer Jam VI 🎵🎵 (Epic, 1980)
Windows 🎵🎵 (Epic, 1982)
Me and the Boys 🎵🎵 (Epic, 1985)
Powder Keg 🎵🎵 (Epic, 1987)
Homesick Heroes 🎵🎵🎵 (Epic, 1988)
Christmas Time Down South 🎵🎵 (Epic, 1990)
Fiddle Fire: 25 Years of the Best of the Charlie Daniels Band 🎵🎵 (Blue Hat, 1998)

worth searching for: *Volunteer Jam* (Capricorn, 1976), which chronicles the first of Daniels's long-running all-star festivals, was an idea that worked here, though it sounded tapped out on subsequent editions.

solo outings:
Charlie Daniels:
Charlie Daniels 🎵🎵 (Capitol, 1971)
Renegade 🎵🎵 (Epic, 1991)
America, I Believe in You 🎵🎵 (Liberty, 1993)
The Door 🎵🎵 (Sparrow, 1994)
Same Ol' Me 🎵🎵 (Capitol, 1995)
Steel Witness 🎵🎵🎵 (Chordant, 1996)
Blue Hat (Blue Hat, 1997) 🎵🎵🎵
By the Light of the Moon: Campfire Songs and Cowboy Tunes 🎵🎵🎵 (Sony, 1997)

influences:

◄◄ The Allman Brothers Band, Waylon Jennings, Hank Williams Jr., Merle Haggard

►► Marshall Tucker Band, Lynyrd Skynyrd, Alabama, Oak Ridge Boys, Little Texas, Brooks & Dunn

Steve Knopper and Gary Graff

Rick Danko
See: The Band

Danny & the Juniors /Danny & the Juniors Featuring Joe Terry

Formed 1955, in Philadelphia, PA. Disbanded 1964. Re-formed 1970.

Danny Rapp (born May 10, 1941, in Philadelphia, PA; died April 5, 1983, in Parker, AZ), lead vocals; Joe Terranova, baritone vocals; Frank Maffei, second tenor vocals; David White, first tenor vocals (1955–60); Bill Carlucci, first tenor vocals (1960–63).

This nondescript vocal quartet, which originally formed as the Juvenaires in high school, created a bona fide rock 'n' roll classic with "At the Hop"—a song that, decades after its initial release, remains one of the most popular and beloved Top 40 hits of all time. It began life as "Do the Bop" until hometown entrepreneur Dick Clark suggested a change to "At the Hop," promising an appearance on his then-new television show, *American Bandstand*. Pressed locally on a small label, the record sold an astounding 7,000 copies before ABC-Paramount released it nationally. "Hop" spent the first two months of 1958 at the top of the international charts, quickly followed by another defining song of the era, "Rock and Roll Is Here to Stay," before the quartet began to falter under misguided musical direction. Although they remained popular as a concert attraction, Danny & the Juniors floundered on a variety of small labels after chief songwriter David White left, and they finally disbanded a decade later. White later used his "At the Hop" and ". . . Here to Stay" royalties to create the Spokesmen's 1965 anti-protest cult classic "The Dawn of Correction," as well as Len Barry's hit "1, 2, 3"; one of the Juniors' original back-up musicians formed Sha Na Na in 1968, a band whose cartoon approach to '50s rock added a much-needed touch of levity at the Woodstock festival. Ironically, it was this very fondness for rock's fun-loving early days that led the Juniors to reform and join many of their contemporaries on the Rock 'n' Roll Revival tours of the early '70s. Danny himself committed suicide a decade later, but various bands of Juniors, usually under the direction of Joe Terranova, continue to perform and even sometimes record to this day, proving that the kind of music they did so much to help popularize the world over really *is* here to stay.

what's available: Both *Rockin' with Danny and the Juniors* ♫♫♫ (MCA, 1983, prod. various) and *A Golden Classics Edition* ♫♫♫ (Collectables, 1997, prod. various) contain the band's two big hits and all the additional material one really needs to hear.

worth searching for: Completists will want to check out the 27 tracks from the group's post-hit period collected on *Back to the Hop* (Swan/Rollercoaster, 1992, compilation prod. Joe Terry, Krazy Greg), which includes several rare and unreleased tunes stunningly reproduced from the original masters tapes.

influences:

◀◀ The Ravens, the Orioles, the Crows, the Spaniels

▶▶ The Del-Vikings, Dion & the Belmonts, Sha Na Na

Gary Pig Gold

Danzig /Samhain

Formed 1986, in Los Angeles, CA.

Glenn Danzig, vocals; John Christ, guitar; Eerie Von, bass; Chuck Biscuits, drums (1986–93); Joey Castillo, drums (1994–present).

From the burnt offerings of the Misfits came the short-lived full-metal racket of Samhain, which evolved into the more varied but no less threatening Danzig. Oh, how the PMRC must get its undies in a bunch over the evil obscenities bellowing from the muscle-bound, tattooed frontman and namesake Glenn Danzig. The open-throttled demonic aura of the band, tempered with a forked tongue-in-cheek bravado, captured the hearts (if not the souls) of critics—and Beavis and Butt-Head, thanks to heavy MTV rotation of a live version of the song "Mother." Fire is cool, heh-heh.

what to buy: The richly textured *4* ♫♫♫♫ (American, 1994, prod. Glenn Danzig, Rick Rubin) is the band's most ambitious album. *Danzig* ♫♫♫♫ (Def American, 1988, prod. Glenn Danzig) has enough five-pointed imagery to make Aleister Crowley cringe; it also has the original take on "Mother."

what to buy next: *Danzig III: How the Gods Kill* ♫♫♫ (Def American, 1992, prod. Glenn Danzig) pushes the mainstream envelope with tighter songs and more polished production.

what to avoid: *Black Aria* ♫♫ (Plan 9/Caroline, 1993, prod. Glenn Danzig) is an operatic experimentation the artiness of which would have Beavis shriek in real horror.

the rest:

Danzig II: Lucifuge ♫♫♫ (Def American, 1990)
Thrall: Demonsweatlive ♫♫♫ (Def American, 1993)

Samhain:

November-Coming-Fire ♫♫♫ (Plan 9/Caroline, 1986)
Final Descent ♫♫♫ (Plan 9/Caroline, 1990)

worth searching for: The first Samhain release, *Initium* (Plan 9/Caroline, 1984/1986, prod. Glenn Danzig), is a punkier effort than either the latter-day Misfits or Danzig would offer.

influences:

◀◀ Black Sabbath, Led Zeppelin, AC/DC

▶▶ Metallica, Slayer

see also: *The Misfits*

Allan Orski

Vanessa Daou

Born October 4, 1967, in the U.S. Virgin Islands.

Unlike many female artists of the mid-'90s, Vanessa Daou maintains a strong sense of control throughout all of her recorded work. Her songs are not attacks but rather invitations, even flirtations, to sensual involvement. A publicized marriage to manager, collaborator, and label executive Peter Daou inspired some controversy in the beginning, but the results have been a fairly ingenious blend of jazz, pop, and poetry. The duo originated as simply The Daou and released one album, *Head Music*, on Columbia in 1992. Relative failure inspired a new direction into sultry, poetic pop, and a new name. *Zipless* was a unique album in that it relied completely on the love poems of sex-laureate Erica Jong for its lyrics and a well-worn ambience for complimentary ornamentation. One other album followed on MCA until, in 1997, the duo put out *Plutonium Glow* on its own label, Daou Music.

what to buy: *Slow to Burn* 𝄞𝄞𝄞𝄞 (MCA, 1996, prod. Peter Daou) stands as the greatest mix of the Daou's components, those being sex and jazz. "Two to Tango" brought some jazz airplay, and the rest of the record soars with a cinematic wit and immaculate production. Sexy, but with a cool distance.

what to buy next: *Zipless* 𝄞𝄞𝄞 (MCA, 1995, prod. Peter Daou) provides slightly pretentious interpretations of fad-sexuality auteur Erica Jong, laced around percolations of the ambient studio variety. *Plutonium Glow* 𝄞𝄞𝄞 (Daou Music, 1997, prod. Peter Daou) advances the duo into even more esoterica, flipping through such fancy as "Cherries in the Snow" and "Flowers of My Fear."

influences:

◀◀ Ingrid Chavez, Madonna, Billie Holiday

▶▶ Me'Shell Ndegéocello, Lori Carson

Billy Manes

Terence Trent D'Arby

Born March 15, 1962, in New York, NY.

Known for bringing the original grit of soul and funk back to popular music during the mid-1980s, Terence Trent D'Arby—an American and former journalist who moved to England around that time—scored quickly with his first album, *Introducing the Hardline According to Terence Trent D'Arby*, but then encountered difficulties. Fans and reviewers were put off by his overwhelming arrogance and, later, by his misguided musical experiments. Still—following the spirit of headstrong R&B greats Prince and Marvin Gaye—D'Arby continues to do things his own way despite the continual lack of commercial triumphs.

what to buy: *Introducing the Hardline According to Terence Trent D'Arby* 𝄞𝄞𝄞𝄞 (Columbia, 1987, prod. Martyn Ware, Terence Trent D'Arby) is a remarkable document of D'Arby's expansive range and sonic breadth. Highlights include the urgent "If You Let Me Stay," the cool "Wishing Well," and the mournful "Let's Go Forward."

what to buy next: Despite the critical and commercial disregard, D'Arby continued to put out solid, interesting material after his popular debut. *Neither Fish nor Flesh* 𝄞𝄞𝄞 (Columbia, 1989, prod. Terence Trent D'Arby) contains several moving and innovative tracks, including "This Side of Love" and "To Know

Someone Deeply Is to Know Someone Softly." Likewise, *Symphony or Damn* 𝄞𝄞𝄞𝄞 (Columbia, 1993, prod. Terence Trent D'Arby) features many fiery soul cuts, including the immaculate "Do You Love Me Like You Say?" and "Wet Your Lips."

what to avoid: While still bolstered by Terence Trent D'Arby's vast creative vision, *Vibrator* 𝄞𝄞 (Work, 1995, prod. Terence Trent D'Arby) suffers a distinct lack of focus. Songs such as "Supermodel Sandwich" and "Surrender" simply don't pack the same appeal as past works.

worth searching for: The Bruce Springsteen bootleg *New York City Night* (Crystal Cat, 1993) features D'Arby—who was rudely booed by the crowd at this 1993 benefit concert—joining the Boss for some inspired duets.

influences:

◀◀ Stevie Wonder, Marvin Gaye, Prince, the Rolling Stones, the Jackson 5

▶▶ Lenny Kravitz, Seal, Living Colour, Maxwell

Aidin Vaziri

Bobby Darin

Born Walden Robert Cassotto, May 14, 1936, in Bronx, NY. Died December 20, 1973, in Los Angeles, CA.

Although he never reached his lofty goal of being "bigger than Sinatra," Bobby Darin influenced a generation of American pop singers—Dion, Fabian, and Frankie Avalon to name a few. He's remembered primarily as a teen idol of the 1950s, but Darin was also an accomplished musician, a bridge between the older, Vegas-leaning saloon singers and the rock 'n' roll generation, and a fine writer who penned more than 75 songs, including his first hit, "Splish Splash," which reached #3 in 1958. Several more gold singles followed: "Queen of the Hop," his own "Dream Lover," and "Mack the Knife," which sold more than two million copies in 1959. The hits continued during the early '60s with "Beyond the Sea," "Bill Bailey," "Things," and "Artificial Flowers," on which he never sounded better. Darin had a folk-rock hit in 1966 with Tim Hardin's "If I Were a Carpenter"; he also had stints as an actor and worked for Robert Kennedy's presidential campaign in 1968. Darin died much too early, in 1973, from complications during surgery to repair a faulty heart valve. In 1990 he was inducted into the Rock and Roll Hall of Fame.

what to buy: *As Long As I'm Singing: The Bobby Darin Collection* 𝄞𝄞𝄞𝄞 (Rhino, 1995, prod. various) is a four-disc box set well worth the money for serious fans. It features an all-star cast of musicians and some great liner notes. *That's All* 𝄞𝄞𝄞𝄞 (Atco, 1959/Atlantic, 1994, prod. Ahmet Ertegun, Nesuhi Ertegun, Jerry Wexler) is Darin's first album and features the classics "Beyond the Sea" and "Mack the Knife."

what to buy next: *Two of a Kind: Bobby Darin with Johnny Mercer* ℣℣℣ (Atco, 1961/Atlantic, 1990, prod. Ahmet Ertegun) is an arresting collaboration, and *The Bobby Darin Story* ℣℣℣℣ (Atco, 1961/Atlantic, 1989, prod. various) is a concise but rewarding disc loaded with big hits.

what to avoid: *Best of Bobby Darin* ℣ (Curb, 1990, prod. various) is a skimpy discount offering. There are plenty of better choices.

the rest:
This Is Darin ℣℣ (Atlantic, 1960, 1994)
25th Day of December ℣℣ (Atco, 1961, 1991)
Darin, 1936–1973 ℣℣℣ (Motown, 1974, 1989)
The Ultimate Bobby Darin ℣℣℣℣ (Warner Special Products, 1986)
Capitol Collector's Series ℣℣℣ (Capitol, 1989, 1996)
Splish Splash: The Best of Bobby Darin, vol. 1 ℣℣℣℣ (Atco, 1991)
Mack the Knife: The Best of Bobby Darin, vol. 2 ℣℣℣℣ (Atco, 1991)
Spotlight on Bobby Darin ℣℣ (Capitol, 1995)

worth searching for: *Darin at the Copa* (Atco, 1960, prod. Ahmet Ertegun, Nesuhi Ertegun) is a fine live recording that includes Darin signature songs "Mack the Knife" and "Bill Bailey."

influences:
◀◀ Frank Sinatra, Ella Fitzgerald, Bing Crosby

▶▶ Harry Connick Jr., Burton Cummings, Brian Setzer, Billy Joel

William Hanson

The Darling Buds

Formed 1986, in Cardiff, Wales. Disbanded 1993.

Andrea Lewis, vocals; Harley Farr, guitar; Chris McDonogh, bass; Bloss, drums (1986–90); Jimmy Hughes, drums (1990–93).

Exponents of the short-lived "Blonde" vogue in late '80s Great Britain, the Buds started out with a frothy but irresistible blend of '60s girl group and '70s new wave. The first album's songs are straight-ahead pop ditties, filled with hooks, high spirits, ringing guitars, and an alluring blend of youthful innocence and sass from singer Andrea Lewls—who also supplies most of the harmonies that made the band favorites of power pop aficionados. Regrettably, that magic was never recaptured, as each succeeding album became more "alternative" (and therefore a lot less fun). After lukewarm response to its final LP, the band broke up in 1993.

what to buy: The Darling Buds' debut, *Pop Said* ℣℣℣℣ (Epic, 1989, prod. Pat Collier), is a high-energy burst of sugar and spice; it includes the hit single "Hit the Ground" and standout

tracks "Let's Go Round There" and "She's Not Crying." The best track of all, "The Other Night," features a chiming 12-string and glorious, harmony-laden chorus.

what to buy next: Though the rot had already begun to set in, the Buds' second album, *Crawdaddy* ℣℣℣ (Epic, 1990, prod. Pat Collier), did contain two good tracks, "Crystal Clear" and "Do You Have to Break My Heart," that successfully updated their original style without compromising it.

the rest:
Erotica ℣℣ (Epic, 1992)

influences:
◀◀ The Shangri-las, Blondie

▶▶ The Cardigans

Mike Greenfield

Dash Rip Rock

Formed 1986, in Baton Rouge, LA.

Bill Davis, guitar, vocals; Ned Rathbone Hickel Jr., bass; Fred LeBlanc, drums, vocals (1986–90); Chris Luckette, drums (1990–present).

While critical tastes continue their pendulous drift from the raw to the synthetic and back again, there remains the simple utility of the party band. The members of Dash Rip Rock have never purported to be anything more, really, than products of their own collective good mood set to the celebratory swing of a good night out. Which makes it all the more pleasing that they can actually do what they do quite well—good-time blues-rock with a knowing wink and beer on their breath.

what to buy: *Boiled Alive* ℣℣℣℣ (Mammoth, 1991, prod. the Homer Noodlemen, Keith Keller) compiles the spiced riches of the first three albums into a live album. But in the case of Dash Rip Rock, live is exactly where it's at. Recorded during three performances in New Orleans and Texas, this is Dash at its meatiest.

what to buy next: *Tiger Town* ℣℣℣ (Dr. Dream, 1993, prod. Michael E. Hutchinson) offers more drunk love songs of swamp and liquor, and finds the band coming into its own with new drummer Chris Luckette. "Loosen up Your Wig" fits nicely in the trailer with "True Drunk Love" and, once again, little is left to the idle imagination.

the rest:
Dash Rip Rock ℣℣℣ (Mammoth, 1987)
Ace of Clubs ℣℣℣ (Mammoth, 1989)
Not of This World ℣℣℣ (Mammoth, 1990)
Get You Some of Me ℣℣℣℣ (Sector 2, 1995)
Pay Dirt N/A (Ichiban, 1998)

influences:

◀◀ The Georgia Satellites, the Radiators, the Fabulous Thunderbirds

▶▶ Southern Culture on the Skids

Billy Manes

David + David
/David Baerwald

Formed c. mid-1980s, in Los Angeles, CA.

David Baerwald, guitar, vocals; David Ricketts, guitar, vocals.

A short-lived duo that recorded one remarkable album and then disappeared, David Baerwald and David Ricketts scored with the remarkable *Boomtown*, a virtual concept album about Los Angeles and the underside of the American Dream in the 1980s, the decade of unbridled greed. Strangely, they never recorded anything else as a duo—Baerwald went on to a critically acclaimed but commercially failed solo career, and Ricketts took up with singer Toni Childs and did production work. Both were part of the loose aggregation of musicians that met weekly in Los Angeles to write and record the material for Sheryl Crow's *Tuesday Night Music Club*.

what's available: *Boomtown* (A&M, 1986, prod. Davitt Sigerson) 𝄞𝄞𝄞𝄞 presents a desolate picture of life during the Reagan years. Beneath the smooth production and winning melodies lie horror stories, replete with drug dealers and spousal abuse. The sharp display of moral bankruptcy won the duo a Top 40 hit with "Welcome to the Boomtown."

worth searching for: Largely ignored by the buying public (one bitter pill is enough, thank you), both of Baerwald's out-of-print albums, *Bedtime Stories* (A&M, 1990, prod. Larry Klein) and the wildly paranoiac *Triage* (A&M, 1992, prod. Bill Bottrell, David Baerwald, Dan Schwartz), are compelling enough to root around for.

influences:

◀◀ The Eagles, Steely Dan

▶▶ Sheryl Crow, Toni Childs, the Wallflowers

Allan Orski

Richard Davies
/Cardinal
/The Moles

Born March 9, 1964, in Sydney, Australia.

Artists like Brian Wilson may have invented orchestral pop, but Australian multi-talent Richard Davies helped make it relevant

in—if not always commercially safe for—the post-grunge era. First with the Moles, then with Cardinal, and then on his own, Davies marched bravely into pop music's past to the jazzy beat of his own drummer, crafting catchy, complex pop at a time when the zeitgeist smelled more like teen spirit. His first record with the Moles, *Untune the Sky*, only hints at the grandeur of his later work, but it made enough of a splash in England that the band moved to London from its home city of Sydney, Australia, in 1992. Unfortunately, commercial success proved elusive, and the original quartet broke up. After moving to Boston and recording an album (*Instinct*) with another edition of the Moles, Davies met transplanted Oregonian Eric Matthews, who shared his interest in making pop that combined the studio sophistication of late-period Beatles with the orchestral instrumentation of Burt Bacharach. With Davies handling the lion's share of the singing and songwriting, and Matthews adding elaborate arrangements, they made one album together as Cardinal before splitting up. Recording on his own, Davies toned down the arrangements to make understated, personal records that combine the swinging grace of the Moles with the moody introspection of singer-songwriters like Nick Drake.

what to buy: It's hard to go wrong with Davies, but *Cardinal* 𝄞𝄞𝄞𝄞 (Flydaddy, 1994, prod. Cardinal, Thee Slayer Hippy, Tony Lash) is the culmination of Davies's more orchestral visions. *Telegraph* 𝄞𝄞𝄞𝄞 (Flydaddy, 1998, prod. Richard Davies, Ronald Jones) is the more artful and more fully realized of his two solo releases.

what to buy next: *There's Never Been a Crowd Like This* 𝄞𝄞𝄞𝄞 (Flydaddy, 1996, prod. Richard Davies) is an affecting bridge between Davies's more orchestral work and his more emotionaly direct second record. The Moles records *Untune the Sky* 𝄞𝄞𝄞 (Waterfront/Seaside, 1992, prod. the Moles) and *Instinct* 𝄞𝄞𝄞𝄞 (Flydaddy, 1994, prod. Richard Davies, Greg Talenfeld) not only show where Davies came from aesthetically but also make for engaging listening when taken on their own terms.

influences:

◀◀ The Beatles, Brian Wilson, Nick Drake

Robert Levine

Alana Davis

Born May 6, 1976, in New York, NY.

Even in an era suffuse with young, sassy female singer-songwriters, Alana Davis stands out. Splitting the difference between the attitude-laden jazz/pop of Fiona Apple and the more political funkiness of a Me'Shell Ndegéocello, Davis comes off as a worldly R&B-ish folk-rocker, wise beyond her years. Although her 1997 debut, *Blame It on Me*, didn't rocket up the charts immediately, within a few months Davis was making it clear that she would not be denied her place in the public eye. Bigger and better things are in store for her in years to come.

what's available: Both earthy and sophisticated, and helmed by Davis's warm, sensuous voice, *Blame It on Me* ⚬⚬⚬⚬⚬ (Elektra, 1997, prod. Ed Tuton) is a wondrous debut, all the more so for a 21-year-old. Her cover of Ani DiFranco's "32 Flavors" made an obvious choice for leadoff single, but "Turtle," the slightly funky "Love & Pride," and the dreamy "Weight of the World" are even better. Be the first on your block to own one.

influences:

◀◀ Me'Shell Ndegéocello, Joni Mitchell, Phoebe Snow, Stevie Wonder, Tracy Chapman, Maria Muldaur

Bob Remstein

Spencer Davis /The Spencer Davis Group

Born July 17, 1937, in Swansea, West Glamorgan, Wales.

Like his closest musical cousin, John Mayall, Spencer Davis is today remembered more for the astounding string of future notables he recruited for his bands than for the wealth of good-rocking, always jumping British R&B he produced during a long and industrious career. Starting in 1963, when he first set aside his folk and blues aspirations to begin performing with ex-trad jazz players Muff and Stevie Winwood, Davis consistently demonstrated a rare knack for combining musical styles and, as a result, always kept one step ahead of rock's fickle trends. The early Spencer Davis Group recordings, particularly "Keep on Running" and "Gimme Some Lovin'," were deserving worldwide hits that remain classics of their genre, but later incarnations of the band (through whose ranks passed, among many others, Nigel Olsson, Dee Murray, Zoot Money, and Chris Farlowe) produced several notable albums as well, each as creatively adventurous as they were strong and true to their bluesy roots. Upon relocating to California in 1970, Davis performed acoustically alongside Peter Jameson, enlisted luminaries Booker T. Jones and Dusty Springfield to help record his magnificent *Crossfire* album, and still found time to work behind the scenes in A&R for Island Records and with Linda Ronstadt on several video projects. His Classic Rock All Stars band, featuring former members of Rare Earth, Iron Butterfly, and Sugarloaf, toured the world in 1993, and the latest incarnation of the Spencer Davis Group has just completed its new album. Still involved in television work and occasionally even lecturing on his long and winding ride through the music business, Davis resolutely has no plans whatsoever to slow down. Why? Because, in the man's own words, "I'm having more fun now than I ever did!"

what to buy: His earliest and most recognizable work is fully collected on *The Best of the Spencer Davis Group* ⚬⚬⚬⚬ (EMI America, 1985/Gold Rush, 1996, prod. Chris Blackwell, Jimmy Miller). This is hard, soul-tinged pop at its very finest, featuring absolutely stellar vocal work from the teenaged Steve Winwood. These songs echoed through the British pub and punk scenes of the '70s, and to this day they remain a staple of discriminating bar bands everywhere.

what to buy next: The immediate post-Winwood years are best showcased on *Funky* ⚬⚬⚬ (Date, 1969/One Way, 1997, compilation prod. Lewis Merenstein), which adds several wonderful demos and live tracks to the original LP release.

the rest:

With Their New Face On ⚬⚬⚬⚬ (United Artists, 1968/Repertoire, 1997)
Gluggo ⚬⚬⚬ (Vertigo, 1973/Repertoire, 1997)
Living in a Back Street ⚬⚬⚬ (Vertigo, 1974/Repertoire, 1997)
Keep on Running ⚬⚬⚬ (Riviere International, 1997)

worth searching for: The excellent British compilation *Eight Gigs a Week: The Steve Winwood Years* (Island, 1996, prod. various) contains every single note that "Little Stevie" sang for Davis, and, better than any prior release, this album traces the group's evolution from undisciplined R&B belters to proto-psychedelic dabblers (work Winwood would soon expand upon in Traffic).

influences:

◀◀ Muddy Waters, John Lee Hooker, Ray Charles, Long John Baldry, Jackie Edwards

▶▶ The Small Faces, Grant Smith & the Power, Brian Auger, Ducks Deluxe, Downchild Blues Band

see also: *Steve Winwood*

Gary Pig Gold

Thornetta Davis

Born in Detroit, MI.

Perennial Detroit Music Awards nominee Thornetta Davis is an entertainer for all occasions, but she almost didn't become one at all. She began her singing career after being coerced by some friends to enter a high school talent show; although reluctant, she soon felt at home on the stage and joined the all-female group Chanteuse, which performed covers of songs by the Pointer Sisters and the Emotions. Davis found her niche in blues and R&B with the band Lamonte Zodiac & the Love Signs, which recruited her as a background vocalist in 1986. Two years later, when the group changed its name to the Chisel Bros., she moved to the forefront. Her break came in 1991 when the Ann Arbor, Michigan–based funk-rock band Big Chief urged Davis to add vocals to the songs "Fresh Vines" and "Reduced to Tears" on its Sub Pop debut, *Face*. When the quartet returned to the studio in 1992 to record the soundtrack *Mack Avenue Skull Game*, Davis made the single "One Born Every Minute" the highlight of the album.

what's available: The Seattle rock label Sub Pop recognized her talent to twist together gospel, R&B, rock, soul, and blues, and brought Davis onboard to record *Sunday Morning Music* ♪♪♪ (Sub Pop, 1996, prod. Al Sutton, Mike Danner, Phil Durr, Matt O'Brien). With Big Chief alumni Matt O'Brien, Phil Durr, and Mike Danner serving as the band, *Sunday Morning Music* sounds like a mix tape tracing the history of Detroit music. The bluesy ballad "Cry" opens the album, followed by the funky "Helpless," the Motown-flavored "Come Go with Me," and the gospel feel of the standout title track.

influences:
◀◀ Etta James, Koko Taylor

Christina Fuoco

Ronnie Dawson
Born Ronald Monroe Dawson, August 12, 1939, in Dallas, TX.

Ronnie Dawson owes his career resurgence almost entirely to obsessive rockabilly record collectors. Dawson was the youngest of the '50s rockabillies, and like Jerry Lee Lewis (they both attended the Southern Bible Institute), he eschewed a career in religion to make music with a beat. His first band, Ronnie Dee & the D Men, played R&B and rockabilly to enthusiastic crowds in Waxahachie, Texas, where it won the Big D Jamboree talent contest 10 weeks in a row. In 1957 Dawson signed with Gene Vincent's manager, Jack Rhodes, who wrote his first two singles, "Rockin' Bones" and "Action Packed." These two remarkably hot singles should've made Dawson a star; he was talented, fresh-faced, and energetic, and his peroxide blonde crew cut provided a distinct and recognizable image. Yet these records sold poorly outside of his hometown. After an unsuccessful stint at Dick Clark's Swan label, Dawson played Western swing with the Light Crust Doughboys, recorded under different names and did session work for eccentric Texas producer Major Bill Smith (Dawson played drums on Bruce Channel's "Hey Baby" and Paul & Paula's "Hey Paula"). During the mid-'60s, Dawson stopped playing full-time and started a career in radio & TV advertising. But more than a decade later, his early sides began to fetch high prices at auctions, while the Cramps and other neorockabillies covered his hits. Rhino Records stirred interest by including "Action Packed" on its *Rock This Town* anthology. During the late '80s, Dawson reemerged, touring overseas to enthusiastic audiences and recording again. More than just a well-preserved legend from rock's golden era, Dawson, like Sleepy LaBeef, has actually improved with age.

His voice is more powerful than ever, he's become an exciting lead guitarist, and he displays honest joy and intensity on stage. Though he's nearly 60, Dawson is just now reaching the peak of his powers.

what to buy: *Rockin' Bones: The Legendary Masters 1957 1962* ♪♪♪ (No Hit, 1993/Crystal Clear, 1996, prod. David Dennard), a 2-CD set featuring an informative booklet with some great photos, captures all of Dawson's '50s work—including 20 previously unreleased tracks, demos, and outtakes—with a few icky early '60s pop and country sides.

what to buy next: For proof positive that Dawson is indeed the real deal, check out *Rockinitis* ♪♪♪ (No Hit, 1993/Crystal Clear, 1996, prod. Boz Boorer, Barney Koumis), which was recorded in 1989 with backing provided by various members of the Planet Rockers and the Playboys. Also, on *Just Rockin' & Rollin'* ♪♪♪ (Upstart, 1996, prod. Ronnie Dawson, Liam Watson, Bernie Koumis), the guitars snarl almost as much as Dawson does on a series of guitar-based R&B, Tex-Mex, and flat-out rockers that are more entertaining and danceable than 90% of the stuff you'll hear on radio these days.

the rest:
Monkey Beat ♪♪♪ (No Hit/Crystal Clear, 1994)

worth searching for: Dawson's guest appearance is the best thing about *Cheap Women, Cheap Booze, Cheaper Thrills* (Pravda, 1997, prod. Andy Babiuk, Greg Prevost), on which he sings his own composition, "Boy Next Door," and shows the Russian rockers what it's really all about.

influences:
◀◀ Gene Vincent, Johnny Carroll, Mac Curtis

▶▶ The Cramps, High Noon, Big Sandy & His Fly-Rite Boys, Marc Bristol

Ken Burke

Taylor Dayne
Born Leslie Wunderman, March 7, 1963, in Baldwin, NY.

Wielding a powerful voice molded in the spirit of the R&B and soul records she idolized as a child, Taylor Dayne offered the perfect package for crossover success from the dance world to the pop charts. A performer since age six, she kicked around in rock and pop bands after graduating from high school, eventually changing her name on the advice of friend Dee Snider of Twisted Sister. Paying her dues singing in Russian-American nightclubs throughout Brighton Beach, Dayne joined forces with producer Ric Wake to create a percolating dance version of a ballad called "Tell It to My Heart." That single became Dayne's first Top 10 hit, paving the way for an album that fused her powerhouse blue-eyed soul vocal licks to full-throttle '80s-style disco grooves. The result was a string of seven Top 10 singles through the end of the '80s. But the fickle marketplace that dampened many a dance diva's career during the early '90s crippled Dayne's, too—a problem that wasn't helped by her participation in the soundtrack for the ill-fated film *The Shadow.*

what to buy: Like that of all great dance divas, the appeal of Dayne's work lies mostly in her singles, making her career ripe for a good greatest-hits record. And there is one—*Taylor Dayne: Greatest Hits* ♫♫♫ (Arista, 1995, prod. various), which sandwiches classic Dayne cuts such as "Tell It to My Heart" and the frenetic "Don't Rush Me" with her remake of Barry White's "Can't Get Enough of Your Love."

what to avoid: For *Soul Dancing* **woof!** (Arista, 1993, prod. various), she hired every hitmaker in sight to save her career from the ash heap of pop music that had already claimed peers such as Tiffany, Debbie Gibson, and Shanice Wilson. Alas, all they could do was prolong the inevitable with a bunch of pop tunes no one cared to hear.

the rest:
Tell It to My Heart ♫♫♡ (Arista, 1987)
Can't Fight Fate ♫♫♡ (Arista, 1989)

worth searching for: Dayne collectors take note—Arista made two different versions of the singer's debut, redesigning the cover layout when the first pressing sold out.

influences:
◄◄ Madonna, Janet Jackson, Donna Summer

►► Celine Dion, Mariah Carey

Eric Deggans

Days of the New
Formed 1996, in Louisville, KY.

Travis Meeks, vocals, guitar; Todd Whitener, guitar; Jesse Vest, bass; Matt Taul, drums.

Travis Meeks was only 19 years old when Days of the New released its debut album, but he'd already gone through a treatment center and special education classes, become a father at 14, and roughed up a cop. To escape the "rednecks" and the troubles of Charlestown, Indiana, Meeks moved with his father to Louisville, Kentucky, and took out his angst on paper. Jesse Vest and Matt Taul soon followed Meeks to Louisville, where they met up with Todd Whitener. After only a handful of shows, Days of the New inked a deal with R.E.M. producer Scott Litt, making the band the first signing to his Outpost label.

what's available: The dark, heavy *Days of the New* ♫♫♫ (Outpost/Geffen, 1997, prod. Scott Litt) traces Meeks's struggle

with adolescence. He tells stories of isolation, abuse, and hopelessness over beautiful acoustic melodies played with the ferocity of electric guitars. The lyrics are worthy of songwriters twice his age. In the successful single "Touch, Peel, and Stand," Meeks sings, "Yes I've finally found a reason/I don't need an excuse/I've got this time on my hands/You are the one to abuse." "Face of the Earth" includes the lyrics "I'm the one receiving the pain from you/You would make these lies/I would take them true/You're self existing." According to reports, Days of the New is considering adding a female vocalist for its second album, tentatively titled *Phobics of Tragedy.*

influences:
◄◄ Alice in Chains, Metallica

►► Creed

Christina Fuoco

The dB's
/Peter Holsapple
/Will Rigby
Formed 1978, in New York, NY. Disbanded 1987.

Chris Stamey, vocals, guitar, organ (1978–83); Peter Holsapple, vocals, guitar, organ, drums; Gene Holder, bass, guitar (1978–87); Rick Wagner, bass (1984); Jeff Beninato, bass (1984–87); Will Rigby, drums, vocals.

After working together in various North Carolina bands, Peter Holsapple, Chris Stamey, and Will Rigby reunited after they each had separately moved to New York. Their referential rock, constructed from allusions to British Invasion bands, roots rock, and various '60s styles, made the dB's critical favorites, but the group remained obscure; the first two albums originally were issued only in England. The band experienced some bad luck when the video of the sophomore release's catchy "Amplifier" was rejected by MTV for its depiction of a hanging suicide. Stamey then left for an equally off-the-radar-screen solo career, and Holsapple soldiered on, again encountering bad luck after releasing the group's third album on Bearsville—label boss Albert Grossman died and operations were halted. The band more or less broke up after 10 years, though there have been fitful reunions. Holsapple has rented his instrumental abilities out to everyone from R.E.M. to Hootie & the Blowfish, and in his free time leads the mini-supergroup Continental Drifters with wife Susan Cowsill. Rigby has played with Matthew Sweet, while Holder joined the Individuals and became a producer.

what to buy: *Repercussion* ♫♫♫♫ (Albion, U.K., 1982/I.R.S., 1989, prod. Scott Litt) contains the original, notorious "Amplifier" and features sturdy production. *Like This* ♫♫♫♫

(Bearsville, 1984/Rhino, 1988, prod. Chris Butler, the dB's), with Stamey gone, is much more American-sounding, proving Holsapple's songwriting is strong enough to stand alone.

what to buy next: *Stands for deciBels* 🎵🎵🎵 (Albion, U.K., 1981/I.R.S., 1989, prod. Alan Betrock, the dB's) is a great debut full of sing-along melodies. *Ride the Wild TomTom* 🎵🎵🎵 (Rhino, 1993, prod. Chris Stamey, Wes Lychot) gathers 26 recordings and demos from the band's early peak, most of which didn't make it onto the albums.

what to avoid: *Paris Avenue* 🎵🎵 (Monkey Hill, 1994, prod. Peter Holsapple) has a somewhat hollow sound, and Holsapple's voice is ragged. There are some good songs such as "Girlfriend," though, so fans will want it anyway.

the rest:
The Sound of Music 🎵🎵🎵 (I.R.S., 1987)

solo outings:
Peter Holsapple and Chris Stamey:
Mavericks 🎵🎵🎵 (Rhino, 1991)

Peter Holsapple:
Out of My Way 🎵🎵 (Monkey Hill, 1997)

Will Rigby:
Sidekick Phenomenon 🎵🎵 (Egon, 1985)

Chris Stamey:
Wonderful Life 🎵🎵🎵 (ESD, 1982/1992)
Christmas Time 🎵🎵 (ESD EP, 1986)
It's Alright 🎵🎵🎵🎵 (A&M, 1987)
(With Kirk Ross) *Fireworks* 🎵🎵🎵 (Rhino, 1991)
The Robust Beauty of Improper Linear Models in Decision Making 🎵🎵🎵 (ESD, 1995)

influences:
◀◀ Big Star/Alex Chilton, the Beatles, the Nazz, Elvis Costello, Grass Roots

▶▶ R.E.M., Continental Drifters, Individuals, Wygals, Schramms

see also: *Continental Drifters*

Steve Holtje

DC Talk

Formed 1987, in Washington DC.

Toby McKeehan, rapper; Michael Tait, rapper; Kevin Smith, rapper.

Religion has long been a part of hip-hop (Five Percenters surely accounted for more than five percent of the late '80s rap world), but hip-hop hasn't necessarily been a big part of religion—particularly not Christianity. DC Talk tried to change that: with 1988's *DC Talk*, the group introduced hip-hop to the Christian music ranks, fusing it with traditional pop and rock—and,

of course, messages of faith. In the process, DC Talk was anointed as the leader of Christian music's new guard. Formed by Toby McKeehan and Michael Tait, DC Talk was named originally as a nod to the pair's hometown; but its record label, ForeFront, suggested that it stand for "decent Christian talk." Whatever the meaning of the moniker, DC Talk's message has always remained constant: you've got to have faith. Even so, the group has recently (and unsuccessfully) tried to rid itself of the "Christian" label, making a controversial video that featured burning crosses and repeatedly telling interviewers: "Courtney Love and Tina Turner are Buddhists, but you wouldn't call them 'Buddhist rock.'" So?

what to buy: Hip-hop, fuzzy guitars, and synthesizers fill *Jesus Freak* 🎵🎵🎵 (ForeFront/Virgin, 1995, prod. Toby McKeehan, John Painter), upping DC Talk's mainstream potential. With the group tackling the stereotype of Christian bands by mixing hard-driving guitars with pop-styled raps, the album sold more than 85,000 copies during its first week and had the highest-ever debut for a Christian act on *Billboard's* pop album charts. Although more subtle than previous DC Talk releases, *Jesus Freak* still shows the musicians placing a premium on message; the lyrics tell you why you need Jesus in your life ("Like it, Love it, Need it"), why you need to confess ("Between You and Me"), and why racism needs to end ("What Have We Become," "Colored People").

the rest:
DC Talk 🎵🎵 (ForeFront, 1988)
Nu Thang 🎵🎵 (Heartwarm, 1991)
Free at Last 🎵🎵🎵 (Forefront, 1992)
Welcome to the Freak Show: DC Talk Live in Concert 🎵🎵🎵 (The Forefront Communications Group, 1997)

influences:
◀◀ PM Dawn, Vanilla Ice, Seal, Beck, Nirvana

▶▶ All-Star United, Jars of Clay

Christina Fuoco and Josh Freedom du Lac

Chris de Burgh

Born October 15, 1948, in Buenos Aires, Argentina.

A storyteller of depth and detail, Chris de Burgh brings an old-world sensibility to much of his work, a solidly crafted oeuvre that blends folk, pop, and rock styles. He's long had enthusiastic followings abroad, and with his hit "Lady in Red," from the 1986 album *Into the Light*, he finally achieved recognition in the U.S.—briefly. Ballads set in the worlds of legend or in the future are his hallmark; he's written about everything from a mysterious maiden "with April in her eyes" to the last broadcast from planet Earth. An incurable romantic who nevertheless recognizes and wrestles intelligently and sensitively with the darker sides of life, de Burgh has a strong interest in spiritual-

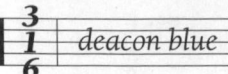

ity and in the personal and religious aspects of war. Born to British parents and now living in Ireland, he might appeal to those who enjoy the Moody Blues or Gordon Lightfoot, but like those artists he creates a body of work very much his own.

what to buy: On *The Getaway* 🎵🎵🎵 (A&M, 1982, prod. Rupert Hine) de Burgh grabs the ears with the rousing rock folktale "Don't Pay the Ferryman," a strong opening to an album that shows off his range of power and sensitivity. Focusing largely on spiritual and personal concerns, *Crusader* 🎵🎵🎵 (A&M, 1979, prod. Andrew Powell) is anchored by an emotional and thoughtful three-part epic on the Third Crusade.

what to buy next: *Into the Light* 🎵🎵🎵 (A&M, 1986, prod. Paul Hardiman) is another solid set of mostly rock tunes; it contains "Lady in Red," though that song is not representative of the album.

the rest:
Man on the Line 🎵🎵 (A&M, 1984)
Flying Colours 🎵🎵 (A&M, 1988)
Spark to a Flame: The Very Best of Chris de Burgh 🎵🎵 (A&M, 1989)
High on Emotion: Live from Dublin 🎵🎵 (Avalanche, 1990)
The Power of Ten (A&M, 1992)
This Way Up 🎵🎵🎵 (A&M, 1994)
Beautiful Dreams (A&M, 1995)
The Love Songs (A&M, 1997)

worth searching for: *Spanish Train and Other Stories* (A&M, 1976, prod. Robin Geoffrey Cable) is available as a German import. It contains some of de Burgh's best early storytelling and an interesting mix of subjects and styles.

influences:
◀◀ The Beatles, the Bee Gees, the Moody Blues, Donovan, Dixieland jazz

▶▶ Martin Simpson, Bryan Adams, Chris Rea, Paul Brady

Polly Vedder

Deacon Blue

Formed 1986, in Glasgow, Scotland.

Ricky Ross, lead vocals; James Prime, keyboards; Graeme Kelling, guitars; Lorraine McIntosh, vocals; Ewen Vernal, bass; Douglas (Dougie) Vipond, drums, percussion.

Although this sextet is named after a well-known Steely Dan hit, the group is in no way influenced by the sophisticated jazz/rock or the wry lyrics of Becker and Fagen. Instead they go for a typically northern heart-on-sleeve approach, which works as long as they don't try to show how soulful they are. With its hint of gravel, Ricky Ross's voice is a dead ringer for Grant McLennan's (formerly of the Go-Betweens), but unlike McLennan, he doesn't indicate much emotional connection to the melodies he sings.

Lyrically, Ross attempts to be both poetic and socially conscious, but too often winds up writing lines like "Let freedom unfurl" (from 1993's "All Over the World"). After a flurry of rave reviews in London following a show there in late 1986, the group scored a hit in the U.K. with the leaden "Dignity" from its debut album, *Raintown*, and soon its albums were debuting on the British charts at #1. Yet even with the more commercially viable material on its fourth album, *Whatever You Say, Say Nothing*, the group has never managed to make a name for itself in the U.S.

what to buy: On *Fellow Hoodlums* 🎵🎵🎵 (Columbia, 1991, prod. Jon Kelly) Deacon Blue achieved whatever artistic heights it's ever likely to hit. "The Wildness" comes close to reaching Van Morrison–like charm, and "Your Swaying Arms" is another strong yet romantic track. Finally, Ross and McIntosh create a distinctive vocal sound here, moving away from the Prefab Sprout/Go-Betweens approach that made their earlier work seem derivative.

what to buy next: If you like the looseness of *Hoodlums*, you may want to check out the band's debut, *Raintown* 🎵🎵 (Columbia, 1988, prod. Jon Kelly). For something more exciting and more pop/dance oriented (although it has slightly slimy, near-INXS overtones), try *Whatever You Say, Say Nothing* 🎵🎵🎵 (Chaos/Columbia, 1993, prod. Steve Osborne, Paul Oakenfold). The percolating opening track "Your Town" is the band's best single, and both "Only Tender Love" and "Last Night I Dreamed of Henry Thomas" are compelling.

what to avoid: *When the World Knows Your Name* 🎵🎵 (Columbia, 1989, prod. Warne Livesey, David Kane, Deacon Blue) may have been the band's big-time breakthrough in England, but the album sounds stiff and dated, with only the perky "Real Gone Kid" to recommend it.

worth searching for: *Our Town: The Greatest Hits* (Columbia, 1994, prod. various) is a generous (19 tracks) British import that nicely surveys the group's four albums.

influences:
◀◀ Simple Minds, the Go-Betweens, Prefab Sprout, Jackson Browne

▶▶ Goodbye Mr. Mackenzie, Oasis

Bob Remstein

Dead Boys
/Stiv Bators
/Lords of the New Church

Formed 1976, in Cleveland, OH. Disbanded 1979. Re-formed 1987.

Dead Boys: Stiv Bators (born Stivin Bator; died June 4, 1990, in Paris, France) vocals; Cheetah Chrome, guitar; Jimmy Zero, guitar; Jeff Mag-

nus, bass; Johnny Blitz, drums. Lords of the New Church (1981–85): Stiv Bators, vocals; Brian James, guitar; Dave Tregunna, bass; Nick Turner, drums.

Having been birthed by such trailblazers as the New York Dolls, the Ramones, the Sex Pistols, and the Damned, punk rock achieved the embodiment of its most extreme tenets of nihilism and violence thanks to the New York-via-Cleveland outfit the Dead Boys. Led by Stiv Bators, whose sneering whine outdid that of even Johnny Rotten, the Boys cranked it up for two extreme studio albums and one live set before calling it a day. Bators recorded a solo album, then went on to form Lords of the New Church. The Dead Boys reunited in the late '80s, but that effort came to an end when Bators died, following complications after being hit by a car in 1990.

what to buy: Shot like a big gob in punk's infancy, the Dead Boys' *Young Loud and Snotty* 𝄞𝄞𝄞𝄞 (Sire, 1977, prod. Genya Ravan) is actually more vulgar than anything by the Sex Pistols. The gnashing artlessness of the band's attack and Bators's guttural roar remains pungent, like urine on a radiator. It's the only one of their albums that remains in print.

the rest:
Lords of the New Church:
Killer Lords 𝄞𝄞 (I.R.S., 1985)
Lords of the New Church 𝄞𝄞𝄞 (I.R.S., 1982)

influences:
◄◄ The Stooges, the New York Dolls, the Sex Pistols, the Damned

Allan Orski

Dead Can Dance

Formed 1983, in London, England.

Brendan Perry, vocals, various instruments; Lisa Gerrard, vocals, various instruments; Peter Ulrich, percussion.

Easily one of the most influential and recognizable bands of the modern gothic scene, Dead Can Dance (DCD) has built a significant career by incorporating into its music French depressive poetry (Charles Baudelaire) and Eastern European field chants, along with baroque instrumentation and religious symbolism. Listeners who coddled artists such as Enya and Enigma might find DCD a bit challenging, but if those artists leave you flat or longing for something along the same lines with a little more substance, DCD would likely fill the bill. As one of the earliest members of the elite 4AD record label, the band served to bolster the company's image of releasing arty, if pretentious, material. DCD's following is small but fervent, and it wasn't until 1994 that the group's catalog was available domestically in the U.S. While no official state-

ment has been made to the effect that the band is splitting, look for fewer and fewer Dead Can Dance releases, as both Brendan Perry and Lisa Gerrard have publicly indicated their desires for more solo efforts and collaborations with other musicians.

what to buy: The Baudelaire-inspired *Spleen and Ideal* 𝄞𝄞𝄞𝄞 (4AD, 1985, prod. Dead Can Dance, John Rivers) is the touchstone of the band's style—brooding music in a minor key with beautifully atmospheric male and female vocals. While more stylized, almost pop-Gregorian music, *Dead Can Dance* 𝄞𝄞𝄞𝄞 (4AD, 1984, prod. Dead Can Dance, John Rivers) is less lush and more synthesizer-driven than later efforts, but it's still a brilliant piece of work. The CD includes the band's first EP, *In the Garden of Arcane Delights,* as a bonus—the only way to get these songs domestically.

what to buy next: The band's progression from the early goth/baroque influences into a fully cohesive two-piece of Perry and Gerrard is realized on *Aion* 𝄞𝄞𝄞𝄞𝄞 (4AD, 1990, prod. Dead Can Dance). This album shows the full pursuit of organic instrumentation and strong medieval ties, along with field chants, may pole dances, flutes, and stunning vocal arrangements.

what to avoid: *The Serpent's Egg* 𝄞𝄞 (4AD, 1988, prod. Dead Can Dance, John Rivers) finds the band at a turning point; the album is an incoherent muddle.

the rest:
Within the Realm of a Dying Sun 𝄞𝄞𝄞𝄞 (4AD, 1987)
Into the Labyrinth 𝄞𝄞𝄞 (4AD, 1993)
A Passage in Time 𝄞𝄞𝄞 (Rykodisc, 1994)
Toward the Within 𝄞𝄞𝄞𝄞 (4AD, 1994)
Spiritchaser 𝄞𝄞𝄞𝄞 (4AD, 1996)

worth searching for: *Dead Can Dance* (4AD, 1994) is a promotional-only 13-track sampler recapping the band's history up to 1994; it was issued to introduce the previously import-only material to radio programmers upon the release of *Into the Labyrinth.*

solo outings:
Peter Ulrich:
"Talaquaha's Leaving" (12-inch single) (Corner Stone, 1990) 𝄞𝄞𝄞𝄞

influences:
◄◄ Gregorian chants, Bauhaus, medieval minstrels, chamber orchestras, Sisters of Mercy, Johan Sebastian Bach

►► Enigma, Enya, Deep Forest, Cocteau Twins, This Mortal Coil, SPK, Cindytalk, Le Mystere De Voix Bulgare, Adiemus

see also: *This Mortal Coil, Lisa Gerrard*

Tim Davis

Dead Kennedys

Formed 1978, in San Francisco, CA. Disbanded 1991.

Jello Biafra, vocals; East Bay Ray, guitar; Klaus Fluoride, bass; J.H. Pelligro, drums.

Jello Biafra, a rabble-rouser from hippie-happy Boulder, Colorado, connected early with punk rock's angry young men and political possibilities. Armed with a sarcastic sense of humor and a belief that all politicians were stupid (especially Republicans), he moved to San Francisco to form a band and possibly run for office. He did both. The Dead Kennedys, purposely provocative with their name, album covers, and titles such as "In God We Trust, Inc.," were more influential for what they did than how they sounded. Biafra's nasal whines didn't so much sing as lecture, and his lyrics didn't so much rhyme as proselytize, but his points were usually effective and necessary. Sonically, the hardcore punk is so dense and intense on some Kennedys' albums you can barely listen to them today. But when Biafra makes his mark—on the minute-long "Nazi Punks Fuck Off" or the essay "Chickenshit Conformist," for example—he's tough to ignore. Biafra also sustained an interesting public-activism career, running unsuccessfully for mayor of San Francisco. Later, his influential and fiercely independent underground label, Alternative Tentacles, was charged with distributing pornography for reproducing H.R. Giger's "Landscape #XX" (nicknamed "penis landscape") on an album cover. The charges were eventually dropped, but the Kennedys broke up shortly thereafter. Biafra then struck out on the lecture circuit, relentlessly trashing the Persian Gulf War and, of course, conservative political and social agendas. Pathetically, after befriending Ice-T and speaking to the first Lollapalooza crowds, he was beaten up and had his leg broken by some San Francisco punks just after Nirvana-punk hit the mainstream.

what to buy: The best expression of Biafra's bizarre yodel and the Kennedy's faster-than-anything rhythm section came on the debut, *Fresh Fruit for Rotting Vegetables* ♫♫♫ (I.R.S., 1980/Alternative Tentacles, 1993, prod. Norm), which contains such sarcastic titles as "Kill the Poor" and "California Uber Alles."

what to buy next: You only need one or two of the Kennedys' albums, which are hilarious, powerful, and unlistenable. The EP *In God We Trust, Inc.* ♫♫♫ (Alternative Tentacles, 1981, prod. Thom Wilson, Dead Kennedys) and *Plastic Surgery Disasters* ♫♫♫ (Alternative Tentacles, 1982, prod. Thom Wilson, Dead Kennedys) are the best.

what to avoid: Don't bother with too many of Biafra's spoken-word discs; though his rambling speeches make deserved mincemeat of George Bush and the Persian Gulf War, and occasionally come up with pretty good band name suggestions, one of these mouthfests ought to be plenty. Draw the line at *High*

Priest of Harmful Matter/Tales from the Trial ♫♫ (Alternative Tentacles, 1989). Overdoing it would be *Beyond the Valley of the Gift Police* ♫♫ (Alternative Tentacles, 1994), a three-disc spoken-word retrospective.

the rest:
Frankenchrist ♫♫♫ (Alternative Tentacles, 1985)
Bedtime for Democracy ♫♫♫ (Alternative Tentacles, 1986)
Give Me Convenience or Give Me Death ♫♫♫ (Alternative Tentacles, 1987)

worth searching for: *Virus 100* (Alternative Tentacles, 1992, prod. Greg Werckman, John Yates, Jason Traeger) is a top-notch tribute album, with NoMeansNo doing an *a capella* version of "Forward to Death" and the Disposable Heroes of Hiphoprisy rapping on "California Uber Alles."

solo outings:
Jello Biafra:
No More Cocoons ♫♫ (Alternative Tentacles, 1987)
I Blow Minds for a Living ♫♫ (Alternative Tentacles, 1991)
(With D.O.A.) *Last Scream of the Missing Neighbors* EP (Alternative Tentacles, 1989) ♫♫
(With NoMeansNo) *The Sky Is Falling and I Want My Mommy* ♫♫♫ (Alternative Tentacles, 1991)
(With Mojo Nixon and the Toadliquors) *Will the Fetus Be Aborted?* EP (Alternative Tentacles, 1993) ♫♫
Prairie Home Invasion ♫♫ (Alternative Tentacles, 1994)

influences:
◀◀ MC5, Iggy Pop, the Sex Pistols, the Avengers, the Dickies, the Germs, X

▶▶ Rage Against the Machine, Ice-T, Disposable Heroes of Hiphoprisy, Bikini Kill, Black Flag

Steve Knopper

The Dead Milkmen

Formed 1983, in Philadelphia, PA. Disbanded 1995.

Dean Clean, drums, vocals; Joe Jack Talcum, vocals, guitar; Dave Blood, bass, vocals; Rodney Anonymous, vocals.

Punk rock cleared the way for forceful social leaders whose voices screamed and fingers bled. It also gave smartass teenagers with warped senses of humor an equal chance for stardom. The Dead Milkmen, whose wit runs from cheap butt jokes to incisive parodies of mindless punk-rock kids, almost became stars. Instead, like so many other bands that rely on the one-liner instead of the right note, they grew up, became unfunny, petered out, and broke up. Before that, though, the group's college-radio hit "Bitchin' Camaro" lampooned underground apathetic slacker culture even before it officially arrived. The song was so stupid it was hilarious. After that came a career of great titles—"Methodist Coloring Book" (chorus: "But if you color outside the lines/Then God will send you to Hell"), "(Theme from) Blood Orgy of the Atomic Fern," "Let's Get the Baby High." In the end, the Milkmen weren't as musically creative as contemporaries such as They Might Be Giants, Camper Van Beethoven, or even Too Much Joy, so their demise was inevitable. Their concerts were fun, though.

what to buy: *Big Lizard in My Back Yard* ♫♫♫ (Fever/Restless, 1985, prod. the Dead Milkmen, John Wicks) establishes the sound—sloppy experiments with rambling rap, reggae, and loungey jazz, along with a hint of hardcore. In terms of songs, there's "Bitchin' Camaro" and lots of good offensive jokes such as "Takin' Retards to the Zoo." *Eat Your Paisley!* ♫♫♫ (Fever/Restless, 1986, prod. John Wicks, Dead Milkmen, Dave Reckner) and *Bucky Fellini* ♫♫♫ (Fever/Enigma, 1987, prod. Brian "Mud Lounge" Beattie) are more of the same, with slightly more interesting humor ("The Thing That Only Eats Hippies").

what to buy next: *Beelzebubba* ♫♫♫ (Fever/Enigma, 1988, prod. Brian "Orchid Breath" Beattie, Mike Stewart) contains the band's second "hit," "Punk Rock Girl" (later ripped accurately on *Beavis and Butt-head*), and a hilarious "Ringo Buys a Rifle," with the lines "Hey Paul! You asshole!" *Metaphysical Graffiti* ♫♫♫ (Enigma, 1990, prod. Brian "Bongwizard" Beattie), the cover of which is a spoof of the similarly named Led Zeppelin album that preceded it, takes on Yes, Sha Na Na, brown-nosers, political correctness, and Methodists. The individual albums are more fun and cohesive, but nostalgic Milkmen fanatics will appreciate *Death Rides a Pale Cow: The Ultimate Collection* ♫♫♫ (Restless, 1997, prod. various), although it may make them a little sad.

what to avoid: The Milkmen probably should have quit after, oh, *Bucky Fellini*—but the creative well was really dry by the release of *Not Richard, But Dick* ♫ (Hollywood, 1993, prod. Dead Milkmen, Jon Lupfer).

the rest:
Instant Club Hit (You'll Dance to Anything) ♫♫ (Fever/Enigma EP, 1987)
Chaos Rules: Live at the Trocadero ♫♫ (Restless, 1994)
Stoney's Extra Stout (Pig) ♫ (Restless, 1995)

influences:
◄◄ The Minutemen, They Might Be Giants, the Dead Kennedys, Run-D.M.C.

►► The Presidents of the United States of America, King Missile, Too Much Joy, Beastie Boys

Steve Knopper

Kelley Deal 6000

See: The Breeders

Paul Dean

See: Loverboy

Death Metal

Thrash plus hardcore plus growling unintelligible vocals combined with a healthy dose of satanic imagery sums up the typical death metal song. The genre's roots can be traced back to the '70s, when Black Sabbath introduced a new kind of rock music—heavy metal with a gloomy core and references to the occult. It was a great posture, but it was almost another decade before death metal took its next embryonic step. In 1979, black metal was born from the lips and guitar strings of its first practitioner, Venom. Venom moved the genre forward by creating faster songs with high-pitched screaming for vocals and lyrics that dealt more openly with Satan and mythology. After Venom's demise, dark metal went underground—more specifically, to Scandinavia, where Norwegian bands such as Bathory and Hellhammer sang about death and dismemberment in the long, dark Norse nights. The latest revival began during the late '80s, after speed and thrash metal took on more mainstream forms in the hands of bands such as Metallica and Megadeth. Concurrently, Florida became a hotbed for up-and-coming death bands, including groups such as Morbid Angel, Death, and Deicide. Already accustomed to the gothic stylings of Danzig and the speed metal of Slayer and Motörhead, death metal didn't *sound* appreciably different to the metal crowd, and it was certainly more subversive than going to see Metallica in a giant stadium with Guns N' Roses, but as bands started to grow beyond local phenomena they quickly became targets for censorship by Christian and parental-advocacy groups. Cannibal Corpse in particular came to national awareness when their albums were banned in many areas. As U.S. death metal started to wear thin, attention was soon placed on foreign groups; Brazil's Sepultura gained a U.S. following after touring with Pantera, and the prolific Scandinavian death metal scene became the focus of many collectors. For the most part, however, death metal remains a cult-level phenomenon; most metal fans dismiss the music as too rudimentary and repetitive, while the mainstream audience simply has no appetite for songs about cannibalism and ritual slaughter. Death metal is now being written off by its own insiders as uninspiring and unemotional, but the music seems to be taking a turn for the better as the more melodic and innovative black metal and its varieties come back into vogue.

what to buy: *Black Metal* ♫♫♫♫ (Combat, 1982) is Venom's genre-defining record, although like many pioneering efforts it sounds different from more contemporary releases. Cannibal Corpse's *Butchered at Birth* ♫♫♫ (Metal Blade, 1991) is death metal's most infamous album; banned in many parts of the U.S. and Europe, it drew attention and followers to the genre and served as a template for a host of imitators. It's a brutal record; titles such as "Meat Hook Sodomy" and "Covered with Sores" pretty much sum it up. Morbid Angel's *Covenant* &&&& (Giant, 1994, prod. Morbid Angel, Flemming, Rasmussen) is that band's finest release—not very innovative, but definitely a ferocious rocker. Bathory's *Under the Sign of a Black Mark* &&&&& (New Renaissance, 1986) is one of the first releases from the new wave of black metal; raw evil oozes from these songs, and the album is already a classic in the genre. *Nordic Metal—A Tribute to Euronymous* &&&& (Necropolis, 1996) is a comprehensive sampling of the new school of Norse black/death metal; it contains a variety of progressive acts that invoke the Viking spirit through battle hymns and tales of the cold north. Artists featured include Marduk, Emperor, and Mortiis.

what to buy next: My Dying Bride's *Turn Loose the Swans* &&&& (Futurist, 1994) and Emperor's *In the Nightside Eclipse* &&&& (Century Black, 1994) are two far-reaching and innovative albums. Both have set new trends in motion. The liberal use of violins on *Turn Loose the Swans* adds a sad, funereal ambience to the music, while *In the Nightside Eclipse* creates a hauntingly evil, yet paradoxically beautiful and rich musical landscape via keyboards. Both approaches have been heavily copied, but few match up to the originals. Hellhammer's *Apocalyptic Raids 1990 AD* (Noise, 1990), another defining album for the genre, is somewhat slow and simple, but the music hits hard. Sepultura's *Beneath the Remains* &&&& (Roadrunner, 1989) brings a consciousness to death metal, albeit a morbid one; it manages to speak out against political conditions in Brazil while maintaining death metal's distinctive musical signature. Cradle of Filth's *Vempire or Dark Faerytales in Phallustein* &&&& (Cacophonous, 1996) offers surprisingly interesting black metal from England (which doesn't have much of a death/black metal scene). But this album's songs range from speed 'n' grind to gothic orchestral pieces, generously overlayed with a female choir that gives a full and haunting atmosphere to the album.

worth searching for: If you aren't above having a few laughs with your death metal, check out Lawnmower Deth's *Ooh Crikey It's . . . Kids in America* (Combat, 1991) for a hilarious thrash/death metal parody. Or even better yet, try anything from GWAR; the music is at times barely listenable but the liner notes and comics included with the CDs are hysterical. But GWAR's real forte is live shows, in which the group—the members of which are unrecognizable in their elaborate comic-book costumes and make-up—stages epic battles between space aliens, pimps, demons, and O.J. Simpson for the right to copulate and destroy the earth. GWAR was one of Beavis & Butthead's favorite bands.

Bryan Lassner

Deconstruction
See: Jane's Addiction

Joey Dee
/Joey Dee & the Starliters
/Joey Dee & Hawk
Born Joseph DiNicola, June 11, 1940, in Pasaaic, NJ.

Remember the Macarena, that insidious dance craze from the mid-'90s? Well, there was an even larger, more all-encompassing forefather to it—in fact, the undisputed, worldwide Mother of All Dance Crazes. That would be the Twist, which for about a year had people both old and new, rich and poor, with-it and inescapably square, wriggling on dance floors from Harlem to the House of Windsor. Joey Dee's Starliters, after having toiled in obscurity up and down the East Coast for years, found itself the house band at New York's Peppermint Lounge when, in 1960, Chubby Checker's recording of "The Twist" made the first of several stays at #1. Cannily sensing a way to not only latch onto this new fad but promote its gig at the same time, Dee and Roulette Records producer Henry Glover composed and released a wonderful piece of ear candy they called "The Peppermint Twist." When it, too, quickly hit the top spot in the nation, Joey and the Starliters embarked on a lightning fast shot of stardom, complete with television and movie appearances (most notably in the 1961 jukebox classic *Hey, Let's Twist*) and a clutch of additional Top 20 hits. By the time Beatlemania had duly swept the Twist clear off the floor, Dee was running his very own Manhattan nightspot, and the new groups of Starliters he installed there included three-quarters of the soon-to-be Young Rascals and a hotshot new guitarist whose last name was Hendrix. However, unlike those unfortunate souls, Dee continues performing to this day, recently alongside his old nemesis Checker in the excellent documentary film *Twist*. More importantly, perhaps, he has established the Starlite Starbrite Foundation for the Love of Rock and Roll, which, despite its unruly moniker, does remarkable work helping support older casualties of the music wars with health care, housing, and of course legal work—to help track down all those royalties that mysteriously never made it into the pockets of many of Dee's contemporaries.

what to buy: Dance craze or not, *Hey Let's Twist: The Best of Joey Dee and the Starliters* &&&& (Rhino, 1990, compilation prod. Steve Kolanijan) is full of good, old-fashioned, pre-Beatles rock 'n' roll. Call it hardcore lounge music if you will, but get set for an hour's worth of greasy, all-American fun nonetheless.

worth searching for: For a fuller glimpse of the whole Starliter experience, *Doin' the Twist at the Peppermint Lounge/Back at* *the Peppermint Lounge* (Roulette, 1961, 1962/Sequel, 1994, prod. Henry Glover) contains the first two Joey Dee albums in all of their original smoky, twistin' splendor. Also recommended as your anthropological studies continue is the home video of Ron Mann's film *Twist* (Columbia Tristar/Image Entertainment, 1993).

influences:

◀◀ The Hi-Fives, Hank Ballard & the Midnighters, Teddy Randazzo, the Isley Brothers

▶▶ The Ronettes, Wayne Cochran & the C.C. Riders, KC & the Sunshine Band

Gary Pig Gold

Dave Dee, Dozy, Beaky, Mick & Tich
/Dozy, Beaky, Mick & Tich

Formed 1960, in Salisbury, Wiltshire, England. Disbanded 1975. Reformed 1978.

Dave Dee (born David Harman), vocals (1960–69, 1974, 1983–85); Dozy (born Trevor Davies), bass, vocals; Beaky (born John Dymond), guitar, accordion, drums, vocals (1960–89); Mick (born Michael Wilson), drums, vocals (1960–75); Tich (born Ian Amey), guitar, mandolin, vocals; Peter Lucas, guitar, vocals (1978–82); John Hatchman, drums, vocals (1982–present); Paul Bennett, guitar, vocals (1989–93); Tony Carpenter, guitar, vocals (1993–present).

Although it hardly made a dent on the American charts, this wildly theatrical British quintet enjoyed a long and influential run of European hits, and in retrospect it can be seen as an important link between traditional English Music Hall entertainment and the garish glitter-rock outfits of the early '70s. Originally formed by a group of police cadets (Dee, for example, officiated at the 1960 car crash that killed Eddie Cochran), the band spent its early career honing its craft and becoming extremely popular in the nightclubs of Hamburg's notorious Reeperbahn district. Upon returning to its homeland in 1964 and securing a choice gig on the Butlin's holiday camp circuit, the act—now a highly polished blend of vocally-dense, carefully choreographed R&B and old-time rock—came to the attention of impresarios Ken Howard and Alan Blaikley, who signed the group to Fontana Records and began writing new material for it. The string of U.K. Top 10's which followed was a highly imaginative blend of American surf-rock stomps, *Zorba*-styled bazouki whirls, and mock-Caribbean chants, all set to a wickedly infectious pop beat and performed in stage shows awash with props and outlandish costuming. Easy to dismiss as mere lightweight musical fluff, DDDBM&T's records and never less than flamboyant presentation made it a sort of harder-rocking Monkees for the indiscriminate ear, yet its influence was an unmistakable one once rock as a whole turned increasingly theatrical during the David Bowie era—not to mention the MTV age of a decade hence.

what to buy: Although certain key tracks are absent, *Hold Tight! The Best of the Fontana Years* 🎵🎵🎵 (Collectables, 1995, prod. various) contains not only the infectious title song (a clever reworking of the Routers' "Let's Go") but the ingenious pseudo-Greek smut of "Bend It," the psychedelic bubblegummer "Touch Me Touch Me," and 11 other slices of rude Britannia, all of which may appear unfamiliar at first but certainly deserve a listen—provided your tongue is planted firmly in cheek beforehand.

worth searching for: A better compilation by far is the British double-disc *Complete Collection* (Mercury, 1997, prod. various), which contains nearly 50 lyrically light but unfailingly bass and drum-heavy masterpieces of profoundly bent, vaudevillian rock.

influences:

◀◀ Joe Meek, Herman's Hermits, the Troggs

▶▶ The Move, Slade, Roxy Music, the Bay City Rollers, Adam & the Ants

Gary Pig Gold

Deee-Lite

Formed 1988, in New York, NY.

Lady Miss Kier Kirby, vocals; Super DJ Dmitry, programming, various instruments; DJ Towa Tei, turntables (1988–92); DJ On-e, turntables (1992–present).

Deee-Lite was the perfect antidote to the dreary music of the late 1980s. Rising out of New York's club scene, the multicultural trio not only made music that combined influences like house, hip-hop, and disco, but topped off its image with a good dose of 1960s idealism, style, and positivity. Singer Lady Miss Kier Kirby, Soviet emigre DJ Dmitry, and Japanese mixmaster Jungle DJ Towa Towa (later renamed Towa Tei) quickly became icons for the new decade, with their platform heels and the impossibly catchy grooves of their debut single, "Groove Is in the Heart," and its accompanying album, *World Clique*. The spell didn't last, however, as the group's focus shifted toward politics and club kid credibility on later albums—with disastrous results. Tei set out for a solo career midway through the completion of Deee-Lite's third album, *Dewdrops in the Garden*, and the group has since filled its time by making solo cameo appearances at various raves.

what to buy: The creative success of Deee-Lite's debut album, *World Clique* 🎵🎵🎵 (Elektra, 1990, prod. Deee-Lite), may have been a fluke, but it changed the landscape of popular music indefinitely. Its funky grooves and rosy sentiments perfectly captured the optimism of the new decade, while its mix of club, jazz, and hip-hop influences reflected the ever-expanding regression of stylistic barriers.

what to buy next: *Dancefloor Oddities & Sampladelic Relics—Deee Remixes* ♫♫♫ (Elektra, 1996, prod. Deee-Lite) presents the group with the opportunity to redeem itself and breathe new life into its predominantly irrelevant newer material. Even though the hits—"Groove Is in the Heart," "Runaway"—only get minor rewrites, a majority of Deee-Lite's more limber material benefits from potent junglist meltdowns and breakbeat deconstructions, particularly "Call Me" and "I Had a Dream I Was Falling Thru a Hole in the Ozone Layer."

what to avoid: Deee-Lite's initial burst of creative energy didn't last long. The group's positive vibes were crushed by the cynicism ushered into popular music by the big angst explosion of 1992. Instead of embracing the dark side with further wicked grooves and pointed insanity, like they should have, Deee-Lite disintegrated into a generic club act and released a pair of utterly forgettable follow-up albums, the politically bogged-down *Infinity Within* ♫♫ (Elektra, 1992, prod. Deee-Lite) and the bloodless *Dewdrops in the Garden* ♫ (Elektra, 1994, prod. Super DJ Dmitry).

solo outings:
DJ Towa Tei:
Future Listening ♫♫♫ (Elektra, 1995)
Sound Museum ♫♫♫♪ (Elektra, 1998)

influences:
◀◀ Sly & the Family Stone, Parliament-Funkadelic, Larry Heard, Donna Summer

▶▶ Björk, Arrested Development, Betty Boo, Brand New Heavies

Aidin Vaziri

Deep Forest
Formed 1992, in Paris, France.

Eric Mouquet, keyboards, programming; Michel Sanchez, keyboards, programming.

Not a band, per se, Deep Forest is the work of two French musicians who sample ethnic music and then combine these exotic sounds into world-music/dance hybrids. At times their CDs can be fascinating to hear, but they carry with them a stigma that no politically responsible listener can, or should, ignore. Just because these two western Europeans bought the rights to the vocal samples they manipulate doesn't make their cut-and-paste modernizations any less odious. And just because their own press materials acknowledge that Deep Forest albums aren't intended to be "ethically correct" doesn't make their in-

herent disrespect toward the cultures they sonically plunder any more forgivable. In defense of Deep Forest, it must be noted that some of the vocal parts they employ were recorded specifically for their CDs. Still, where Deep Forest is concerned, it's up to the listener to decide what's most important.

what to buy: Although the group's debut is not as consistent or varied as its third album, *Deep Forest* ♫♫♫ (Epic, 1992, prod. Dan Lacksman) is the one to buy first, largely because it includes two "hits," the Peter Gabriel–influenced title track and the alluring "Sweet Lullaby."

what to buy next: The group's most accomplished musical collage, *Comparsa* ♫♫♫ (550 Music/Sony, 1998, prod. Deep Forest), uses more Latin American vocal samples than African ones. As always with Deep Forest, however, let your conscience be your guide.

what to avoid: Despite the vocal contributions of Hungarian folk star Marta Sebestyen, *Boheme* ♫♫ (550 Music/Sony, 1995, prod. Eric Mouquet, Michel Sanchez) embodies the worst aspects of designer world music. It won a Grammy, but that says more about the Grammys than it does about the album.

influences:
◀◀ Enigma, Peter Gabriel, African Pygmy folk melodies

Bob Remstein

Deep Purple
Formed 1968, Hertford, England.

Ritchie Blackmore, guitar (1968–75, 1984–94); Jon Lord, keyboards (1968–present); Ian Paice, drums (1968–present); Rod Evans, vocals (1968–69); Nick Simper, bass (1968–69); Ian Gillan, vocals (1969–73, 1984–89, 1993–present); Roger Glover, bass (1969–73, 1984–present); David Coverdale, vocals (1973–76); Glenn Hughes, bass, vocals (1973–76); Tommy Bolin, guitar (1975–76); Joe Lynn Turner, vocals (1989–93); Steve Morse, guitar (1994–present).

Scoring first with the lava-lamp special "Hush," Deep Purple quickly evolved into one of rock's heaviest bands, churning out dense, crushing slabs of metallic fury (the loudest band in the world, according to the *Guinness Book of World Records*) with great drama and an endless array of solos from Blackmore, whose mercurial temper harnessed him to the second strata of guitar heroedom. Purple's heyday came during the early '70s—when "Smoke on the Water" entered the pantheon of hard rock classics—but frequent personnel changes always seemed to hamper the group's forward progress. Purple disbanded in 1976 but enjoyed a much ballyhooed reunion of its "Smoke on the Water" lineup six years later. The more recent addition of former Dixie Dregs guitarist Steve Morse has breathed some life back into the band, and it continues to lumber along, more popular in Japan and Europe than in North America.

what to buy: *Machine Head* 🎵🎵🎵🎵 (Warner Bros., 1972, prod. Deep Purple) is Purple's definitive moment, a powerful and seamless document of a band at its peak with all-time power tracks such as "Smoke on the Water," "Space Truckin'," and "Highway Star." Those tracks are highlights of *Made in Japan* 🎵🎵🎵🎵 (Warner Bros., 1972, prod. Deep Purple), a molten live album that also features Gillan's piercing, tortured screams on "Child in Time." Considering the circumstances—namely the departure of Gillan and Glover—*Burn* 🎵🎵🎵🎵 (Warner Bros., 1974, prod. Deep Purple) is a remarkable feat, bringing Coverdale and Hughes into the group without losing stride.

what to buy next: *Fireball* 🎵🎵🎵 (Warner Bros., 1971, prod. Deep Purple) is the "Machine Head" sound in evolution; Purple still plays with an appealingly raw abandon. *Come Taste the Band* 🎵🎵🎵 (Warner Bros., 1975, prod. Martin Birch, Deep Purple), Bolin's only studio album with the band, brings an interesting R&B flavor to the Purple attack. *When We Rock, We Rock and When We Roll, We Roll* (Warner Bros., 1978, prod. Deep Purple) is incomplete as a retrospective but is still the most palatable way to get "Hush" and Purple's rendition of Neil Diamond's "Kentucky Woman" into the collection.

what to avoid: *Concerto for Group and Orchestra* **woof!** (Warner Bros., 1970, prod. Deep Purple) is a misbegotten exercise in highbrow pretension. Emerson, Lake & Palmer they weren't.

the rest:
Shades of Deep Purple 🎵🎵 (Tetragrammaton, 1968)
Book of Taliesyn 🎵🎵 (Tetragrammaton, 1968)
Deep Purple 🎵 (Tetragrammaton, 1969)
Deep Purple in Rock 🎵🎵 (Warner Bros., 1970)
Purple Passages 🎵🎵🎵 (Warner Bros., 1972)
Who Do We Think We Are! 🎵🎵 (Warner Bros., 1973)
Stormbringer 🎵🎵 (Warner Bros., 1974)
24 Carat Purple 🎵🎵🎵 (Warner Bros., 1975)
Made in Europe 🎵🎵 (Warner Bros., 1976)
Deepest Purple 🎵🎵🎵 (Warner Bros., 1980)
In Concert 🎵🎵 (Portrait, 1982)
Perfect Strangers 🎵🎵 (Mercury, 1984)
The House of Blue Light 🎵 (Mercury, 1987)
Nobody's Perfect 🎵🎵🎵 (Mercury, 1988)
Slaves and Masters 🎵 (RCA, 1990)
Purple Rainbows 🎵🎵🎵🎵 (EMI, 1991)
Knocking on Your Back Door: The Best of Deep Purple in the '80s 🎵🎵🎵 (Mercury, 1992)
The Deep Purple Family Album 🎵🎵🎵 (Connoisseur, 1993)
The Battle Rages On 🎵 (Giant, 1993)
Come Hell or High Water 🎵🎵🎵 (RCA, 1994)

King Biscuit Flower Hour Presents Deep Purple 🎵🎵 (KBFH Records, 1995)
Purpendicular 🎵🎵🎵 (CMC International, 1996)
Live at the California Jam 🎵🎵🎵🎵 (Mausoleum Classix, 1996)
Abandon 🎵🎵🎵 (CMC International, 1998)

worth searching for: *Purple Chronicle* (Purple/Warner Bros., 1994, prod. various) is a lovingly compiled three-volume Japanese box set that collects all the key tracks plus alternate versions and rare songs ("Painted Horse," "Cry Free"). A definitive Purple chronicle—even if the accompanying booklet is in Japanese.

solo outings:
Ian Gillan:
Jesus Christ Superstar 🎵🎵🎵 (MCA, 1972)
Ian Gillan Band: Child in Time 🎵 (Oyster, 1976)
Clear Air Turbulence (EMI, 1977)
Scarabus 🎵🎵 (Island, 1978)
Live at Budokan 🎵🎵 (Virgin, 1979)
Glory Road 🎵🎵🎵 (Virgin, 1980)
Future Shock 🎵🎵 (Virgin, 1981)
Double Trouble 🎵🎵🎵 (Virgin, 1981)
Magic 🎵🎵 (Virgin, 1982)
Naked Thunder 🎵 (EastWest, 1990/Resurgent, 1997)
Tool Box 🎵🎵 (EastWest, 1991)
Dreamcatcher 🎵🎵 (Ark 21 U.K., 1997)

Roger Glover:
Roger Glover 🎵 (Oyster)
The Butterfly Ball and the Grasshopper's Feast 🎵 (Oyster, 1974)
Elements 🎵🎵 (Oyster, 1978)
The Mask 🎵🎵 (PolyGram, 1984)

Ian Gillan & Roger Glover:
Accidentally on Purpose 🎵🎵 (Virgin, 1988)

influences:
⏪ Johnny Kidd & the Pirates, the Yardbirds, Screaming Lord Sutch & the Savages, the Animals, Gustav Mahler

⏩ Metallica, Iron Maiden, Rainbow, Dio, Guns N' Roses, Dokken, UFO, Whitesnake

see also: *Rainbow, Tommy Bolin, Whitesnake, Black Sabbath*

Gary Graff

Def Leppard
Formed 1977, in Sheffield, England.

Joe Elliot, vocals; Steve Clark, guitar, vocals (1977–91); Rick Allen, drums; Rick Savage, bass; Pete Willis, guitar, vocals (1977–81); Phil Cohen, guitar, vocals (1981–present), Vivian Campbell, guitar (1992–present).

In addition to being the most successful pop-metal act of the

Joe Elliot of Def Leppard (© **Ken Settle**)

'80s, Def Leppard has also weathered more setbacks than Job—notably drummer Rick Allen losing his arm in a New Year's Eve 1985 auto accident, and founding guitarist Steve Clark's fatal substance abuse. Instead of the usual guitar flash and mudraking rhythm section of most metal bands, Leppard's main assets have been studio craft and songwriting skills, first evidenced on *High 'n' Dry* 's "Bringin' on the Heartbreak." Much of the credit goes to producer Robert John "Mutt" Lange, an instrumental force in developing the band's trademark crystalline, bubblegum flavor, which helped bring the girls into the metal party—thereby doubling the group's audience. The group's meticulous work habits often result in long spells between albums, which sometimes works to its disadvantage, but Def Leppard soldiers on, increasing its radio-friendly studio layering with each subsequent release.

what to buy: The compilation *Vault 1980–1995* 𝄞𝄞𝄞𝄞 (Mercury, 1995, prod. various) delivers a potent hookfest, eschewing the faceless tracks that subtract from even the band's better albums. *Hysteria* 𝄞𝄞𝄞𝄞 (Mercury, 1987, prod. Robert John "Mutt" Lange) hits the high water mark as studio prowess and songcraft blend into a tuneful froth with "Pour Some Sugar on Me" and "Armageddon It."

what to buy next: *Pyromania* 𝄞𝄞𝄞𝄞 (Mercury, 1983, prod. Robert John "Mutt" Lange) marked the real break from other heavy metal acts, with its clean production tempered with just enough crunch to make "Photograph" a powerfully efficient and, for metal, technically complex single.

what to avoid: The first two releases, *On through the Night* 𝄞𝄞 (Mercury, 1980, prod. Tom Allom) and *High 'n' Dry* 𝄞𝄞 (Mercury, 1981, prod. Robert John "Mutt" Lange), contain neither the melodies nor the polished riffs to hold anybody's attention, except perhaps air guitarists lurking below the "Wayne's World" level.

the rest:
Adrenalize 𝄞𝄞𝄞𝄞 (Mercury, 1992)
Retro Active 𝄞𝄞𝄞 (Mercury, 1993)
Slang 𝄞𝄞𝄞 (Mercury, 1996)

worth searching for: Import versions of *Vault* are considerably different and have more to offer than the U.S. release. Our favorite is the Japanese edition, with its nine-track bonus live CD and excellent booklet.

influences:
◀◀ Kiss, Boston, Sweet, Slade, AC/DC, the Beatles
▶▶ Bon Jovi, Poison, Ratt, Candlebox, Shania Twain

Allan Orski

deftones
Formed 1988, in Sacramento, CA.

Chino Moreno, vocals; Stephen Carpenter, guitar; Chi Cheng, bass, vocals; Abe Cunningham, drums.

A club stalwart in Sacramento for many years, deftones got their break when their demo tape found the ears of KoЯn's producer and then Madonna, who signed the group to her Maverick label. These thoughtful moshers make music that has the sonic impact of a spinning roundkick, with probing lyrics and a knack for melody. Even when a track is bludgeoning you like a mallet, you can still hum along. The band's name is likely derived from either the deafening tones of their music or the subtle hip-hop influence that occasionally surfaces in their work.

what to buy: deftones' second album, *Around the Fur* 𝄞𝄞𝄞𝄞 (Maverick, 1997, prod. Terry Date, deftones), raises the bar a bit. Instead of preaching to the choir, the 'tones branch out, employing more space and creatively odd touches to their songs. Aided by former Sepultura (and current Soulfly) singer-guitarist Max Cavalera on one track and "audio" specialist Frank Delgado on five others, *Around the Fur* further expands deftones' oeuvre, transcending the often limited heavy rock genre. Note that the CD includes an unlisted bonus track.

what to buy next: The first album, *adrenaline* 𝄞𝄞𝄞 (Maverick, 1995, prod. Terry Date, deftones), is about as subtle as a band saw and deceptively varied. Singer Chino Moreno's vocals range from a quiet purr to a brutal shriek, usually within the same song. "Lifter" and the expletive-laden "7 Words" are perfect examples of deftones' powerful vehemence.

influences:
◀◀ Rage Against the Machine, KoЯn, Quicksand, Bad Brains, Helmet, Sepultura, Slayer, Burn
▶▶ Orange 9mm, Limp Bizkit, Headcrash, Downset

Barry M. Prickett

Del Amitri
Formed 1982, in Glasgow, Scotland.

Justin Currie, vocals, bass; Iain Harvie, guitar; Paul Tyagi, drums (1982–91); Bryan Tolland, guitar (1982–88); Michael Slaven, guitar (1989–91); David Cummings, guitar (1992–96); Brian McDermott, drums (1992–94); Andy Alston, keyboards, accordion (1992–present); Ashley Soan, drums (1995–97); Jon McLoughlin, guitar (1996–97); Kris Dollimore, guitar (1997–present); Mark Price, drums (1997–present).

Few bands can survive the indignity of being dropped by their label after only one album. It's a testament to both the talent and tenacity of Del Amitri principals Justin Currie and Iain Harvie that, four fruitless years after their break with Chrysalis, they were able to reinvent themselves so effectively on A&M's *Waking Hours*. Gone were the hyperactive folk songs with their breathlessly phrased bon mots and percolating acoustic guitars. Instead, with songs like "Kiss This Thing Goodbye" and "Hatful of Rain," *Waking Hours* established Del Amitri's mature sound: no-nonsense blues- and country-tinged rock married to smart, introspective lyrics that owed much to the '70s singer-songwriter tradition. For better and for worse, it's a formula Del Amitri continues to ply to this day.

what to buy: Despite its title, *Change Everything* 𝄞𝄞𝄞𝄞 (A&M, 1992, prod. Gil Norton) is no wholesale overhaul of Del Amitri's sound, but rather an inspired refinement of it. Whether he's reeling from love's heady brew ("Be My Downfall," "Sometimes I Just Have to Say Your Name") or bitterly lamenting its all-too-fleeting effects ("The First Rule of Love," "The Ones That You Love Lead You Nowhere"), Currie chronicles the ups and downs of human relationships with extraordinary wit and candor. And more so than any Del Amitri album before or since, *Change Everything* strikes the right balance between the band's polar proclivity for low-key folk and out-and-out roots rockers.

what to buy next: On *Twisted* 𝄞𝄞𝄞 (A&M, 1995, prod. Al Clay), Del Amitri brings the noise, if only on a few songs. Opening with a clenched-fist diatribe set to an onslaught of plangent guitars, megaphone vocals, and thunder-rumble drums, "Food for Songs" is three minutes and 38 seconds of pure rock 'n' roll catharsis. Likewise, "Being Somebody Else" shares that song's distorted-guitar saturation and loose-limbed raucousness—two qualities in short supply on most Del Amitri albums. Ironic for an album in which Currie and company were trying out a harder edge, "Roll to Me," a breezy, Beatlesque confection reminiscent of the band's debut album, became their biggest U.S. hit.

what to avoid: With nary a stand-out song, albeit many serviceable ones, *Some Other Sucker's Parade* 𝄞𝄞 (A&M, 1997, prod. Mark Freegard) has little to recommend it. Undistinguished from start to finish, the album emits the well-oiled hum of a band gliding on automatic pilot.

the rest:
Del Amitri 𝄞𝄞𝄞 (Chrysalis, 1985)
Waking Hours 𝄞𝄞𝄞𝄞 (A&M, 1989)
Hatful of Rain: The Best Of 𝄞𝄞𝄞𝄞 (A&M, 1998)

worth searching for: The three-part U.K. CD-single for "Some Other Sucker's Parade" contains otherwise unavailable live tracks recorded at Leeds Town and Country Club on July 13, 1997, including "Driving with the Brakes On," "Move Away Jimmy Blue," "Hatful of Rain," "Stone Cold Sober," and others.

influences:
◀◀ The Beatles, the Byrds, Buddy Holly, the Smiths, the Fall, the Rolling Stones, Jackson Browne

▶▶ Toad the Wet Sprocket, Counting Crows, Gin Blossoms, Better Than Ezra, the Devlins, Hootie & the Blowfish

Greg Siegel

Del Fuegos
/Dan Zanes

Formed 1980, in Oberlin, OH. Disbanded 1989.

Dan Zanes, guitar, vocals; Tom Lloyd, bass, vocals; Warren Zanes, guitar; Brent "Woody" Giessmann, drums.

Mere children when they began appearing in Boston clubs at the turn of the 1980s (Warren Zanes was recruited the day he graduated from high school), the Del Fuegos formed as a white garage band that thought it was an R&B outfit. The young quartet made its reputation by covering Elvis Presley and Sam & Dave songs; Zanes often snarled rather than sang, and his original lyrics were matched by wrenching guitars and a crazy rhythm section. Simplicity was the key to the group's success, epitomized by the raucous, twitching "Nervous and Shakey," "Longest Day," and "Don't Run Wild." Known for its anything-goes lifestyle, the band came quickly, burned brightly, and flamed out.

what to buy: Until a good best-of comes along, it's a toss-up between the first two albums. Both *Boston, Massachusetts* 𝄞𝄞𝄞𝄞 (Warner Bros., 1985, prod. Mitchell Froom) and *The Longest Day* 𝄞𝄞𝄞𝄞 (Warner Bros., 1984, prod. Mitchell Froom) offer the above-mentioned songs and best capture the group's charismatic, explosive strength. Dan Zanes's solo album, *Cool Down Time* 𝄞𝄞𝄞𝄞 (Private, 1995, prod. Mitchell Froom), is a stripped-down, wryly humorous album that sounds like a soul band in love with Jamaican dub.

what to buy next: Though the production values on *Stand Up* 𝄞𝄞𝄞 (Warner Bros., 1987, prod. Mitchell Froom) often will draw chuckles (check the background voices that wind down "A Town Called Love"), songs such as "Wear It Like a Cape" and the harrowing, prescient "He's Had a Lot to Drink Today" are among Zanes's best efforts.

what to avoid: *Smoking in the Fields* 𝄞 (RCA, 1989) was recorded after Warren Zanes and Giessmann left the group. Even Dan Zanes considers this one forgettable.

influences:
◀◀ Bo Diddley, Chuck Berry, Stax, Tom Petty & the Heartbreakers

▶▶ The Jayhawks, Afghan Whigs

Leland Rucker

The Del Lords
/Eric Ambel
/Scott Kempner

Formed 1982, in New York, NY. Disbanded 1991.

Eric Ambel, guitar, vocals; Scott Kempner, guitar, vocals; Manny Caiati, bass, vocals; Frank Funaro, drums, vocals.

Not quite anarchic enough to be considered punk, and slightly too urban to be lumped in with the countrified roots movement, the Del Lords slipped between the cracks during the absurdly fickle '80s. That's too bad, because former Dictator Scott Kempner's songs of love and determination set against a backdrop of hard times were far more relevant than anything that made it onto MTV back then. The group came to an end after Eric Ambel left, but our loss is also our gain, since he and Kempner have both started ambitious solo careers.

what to buy: The group's debut, *Frontier Days* &&&& (Enigma/ EMI America, 1984, prod. Lou Whitney, the Del Lords), contains its best material, including "Get Tough," "Burning in the Flame of Love," and a smoking cover of Alfred Reed's "How Can a Poor Man Stand Such Times and Live." Ambel's aptly titled *Loud & Lonesome* &&&& (East Side Digital, 1995, prod. Eric Ambel) cranks the volume a few notches and partners Ambel with ace songwriters Kevin Salem, Terry Anderson, Dan Baird, and Dan Zanes. Ambel's whinny of a singing voice is further left of center than Neil Young's, but his guitar work will blister your wallpaper.

what to buy next: Hiring Pat Benatar's husband Neil Geraldo to produce two of its albums—including *Based on a True Story* &&&' (Enigma, 1988, prod. Neil Geraldo), brought a metallic sheen to the Del Lords's sound. Likely a stab at gaining radio play, it ultimately failed, albeit without significant damage to the band's down-the-middle sound. The wistful "Cheyenne" and the hard-rocking "Judas Kiss" are especially fine. Kempner's sole solo effort (so far), *Tenement Angels* &&&' (Razor & Tie, 1992, prod. Lou Whitney, Manny Caiati, Scott Kempner), hearkens back to the classic sound of the Del Lords' debut album, thanks in large part to producer Whitney and his band, the Skeletons, who perform bar-band magic on Kempner's three-chord rockers.

what to avoid: The live mini-album *Howlin' at the Halloween Moon* &&' (Restless, 1989) is a disappointment, offering a relatively bland selection of originals and covers.

the rest:
Johnny Comes Marching Home &&& (Enigma/EMI America, 1986)
Lovers Who Wander &&& (Enigma, 1990)

solo outings:
Eric Ambel:
Roscoe's Gang &&&& (Enigma, 1988)

influences:
◄◄ Bruce Springsteen, Dion, Link Wray, Woody Guthrie
►► The Skeletons, Syd Straw

see also: *The Dictators*

Daniel Durchholz

Delaney & Bonnie

Formed 1967, in Los Angeles, CA.

Delaney Bramlett (born July 1, 1939, in Pontotoc County, MS), vocals, guitar; Bonnie Bramlett (born November 8, 1944, in Acton, IL), vocals.

This husband-and-wife team divorced after a recording career that lasted from the late '60s to the early '70s. Something of an offshoot of traveling bands like those fronted by Leon Russell as well as Joe Cocker's Mad Dogs and Englishmen, they relied on the same stable of musicians—including Russell, Carl Radle (bass), Rita Coolidge (vocals), Jim Gordon (drums), and Bobby Keys (saxophone)—to create their powerhouse and grit-stained rocking blues with a southern-fried edge.

what to buy: *Delaney & Bonnie & Friends on Tour with Eric Clapton* &&&&' (Atco, 1970, prod. Jimmy Miller, Delaney Bramlett) is a joyous live romp tinged with soul-satisfying gospel. Clapton is loose and plays at his searing best, while Delaney's forceful vocal delivery and Bonnie's lead and harmony vocals sway between over-the-top dynamics and reflective balladry.

what to buy next: *The Best of Delaney & Bonnie* &&&& (Rhino, 1990, prod. various) is a terrific compilation of memorable songs and high-stepping performances.

influences:
◄◄ Ike & Tina Turner, Aretha Franklin, Leon Russell, Joe Cocker
►► Bonnie Raitt, Eric Clapton, Bekka Bramlett

Patrick McCarty

Victor DeLorenzo

See: Violent Femmes

Iris DeMent

Born 1961, in Paragould, AR.

A singer with a distinctive voice that seems to embody the entire tradition of American folk music, and a songwriter with an unerring ability to tell moving and believable stories, Iris DeMent is an anomaly in the music business. She was the youngest of eight children born in Arkansas and raised in California in a strict Pentecostal family, and she had never thought of being a musician until she was in her late twenties. She now colors the influence of singer-songwriters like Joni Mitchell with her lifelong love of artists like Kitty Wells, and she delivers her story-songs with a charmingly down-home voice that never sounds affected. DeMent also has some eminent fans, including Emmylou Harris and Nanci Griffith. John Prine wrote the liner notes for her debut album, and Merle Haggard, who collaborated on a song for her third album, sang her praises to anyone who'd listen; he also asked her to tour with him, which she did.

what to buy: DeMent's songs on her debut, *Infamous Angel* ✍✍✍✍ (Philo/Warner Bros., 1992, prod. Jim Rooney), include "Let the Mystery Be" and "Our Town" (later used over the credits for the final episode of the TV show *Northern Exposure*) and already sound like Smokey Mountain traditionals. Warner Bros. re-released that album and its follow-up, *My Life* ✍✍✍✍ (Warner Bros., 1994, prod. Jim Rooney), a thoughtful though implacably sad and deeply moving collection of autobiographical songs and fictional sketches.

what to buy next: Her third album, *The Way I Should* ✍✍✍✍ (Warner Bros., 1996, prod. Randy Scruggs), finds the vocalist broadening her stylistic base and adding frank political broadsides to her repertoire of autobiographical tunes and narrative vignettes. The sound is more commercial, but some of the songs are much less so.

influences:

◄◄ Kitty Wells, Joni Mitchell, Emmylou Harris, Nanci Griffith, Bruce Springsteen

►► Kate Campbell

Gil Asakawa

Cathy Dennis

Born 1969, in Norwich, England.

Getting her start as Dancin Danny D's diva in the one-off house band D-Mob ("Come on and Get My Love," "We Call It Acieed"), Cathy Dennis found success during the early '90s as a brisk bubblegum popster in a diva pose. Besides Danny D, she worked with a vareity of production luminaries, including Nile Rogers and Shep Pettibone, who polished her less-than-dynamic vocal stylings to a more lustrous matte finish. Two albums and a pair of moderately successful house numbers, "You Lied to Me" and "Falling," failed to rally much support, and the result was an almost immediate disappearance with all but one of her albums out of print.

what's available: *Move to This* ✍✍✍ (Polydor, 1990, prod. Danny D, Nile Rogers, Shep Pettibone) finds Dennis twirling through the ingratiating "All Night Long (Touch Me)" and almost-viable power ballad, "Too Many Walls."

worth searching for: *Into the Skyline* (Polydor, 1992, prod. Danny D, Shep Pettibone, Cathy Dennis) was more ambitious but ultimately failed to convince the masses. Two of Dennis's tracks can be found on compilations—"Too Many Walls" is on the benefit album *Women for Women* and "All Night Long (Touch Me)" is on *Dance Mix USA*.

influences:

◄◄ Samantha Fox, Rick Astley, Kylie Minogue, Madonna

►► Celine Dion, Robyn, the Cardigans

Billy Manes

Sandy Denny

See: Fairport Convention

John Denver

Born Henry John Deutschendorf, December 31, 1943, in Roswell, NM. Died October 12, 1997, in Monterey Bay, CA.

Rock 'n' roll hipsters always had a football-field day making fun of John Denver for writing sunny, heartfelt songs about his unconditional love for trees, flowers, mountains, and his wife. His early albums veered toward cheesy, middle-of-the-road balladry—we can even remember tuning into a Top 40 station in 1974 and hearing "Annie's Song" playing while the DJ imitated a cow mooing in the background. But Denver also built a sturdy career out of three impressive country-folk albums—1971's *Poems, Prayers and Promises* (which featured his career-making hit, "Take Me Home, Country Roads"), 1972's *Rocky Mountain High*, and 1974's *Back Home Again*—that deftly captured the aw-shucks charm and jaded innocence that eventually elevated him to superstardom. Odd obsessions such as his desire to fly in space and to star in TV specials with the Muppets aside, Denver possessed an unwavering commitment to humanitarian causes: he stood up for what he believed in, no matter how "far-out" or square it made him look. In 1985, he bravely stood beside Frank Zappa and Dee Snider of Twisted Sister at a Senate hearing to argue against mandatory labeling of sexually explicit rock albums. Active in the Windstar Foundation, an environmental education and research center that he co-founded, and a reforestation project called Plant-It 2000, Denver was even regaining some of his artistic stature when the single-engine airplane he was piloting crashed into Monterey Bay, California, on October 12, 1997. The enjoyable *Wildlife Concert*, a 1995 two-CD set benefitting the Wildlife Conservation Society, marked one of the rare perfect marriages of his social consciousness and his art. And a 1997 one-disc distillation of that work called *The Best of John Denver Live* put his name back on the country charts for the first time in a decade.

what to buy: Of his early works still in print in the U.S., *Rocky Mountain High* 🎵🎵🎵 (RCA, 1972, prod. Milton Okun) sounds the least dated, with fine musicianship, genuinely gorgeous ballads in "For Baby (For Bobbie)" and "Goodbye Again," and cool covers of John Prine ("Paradise") and the Beatles ("Mother Nature's Son"). *An Evening with John Denver* 🎵🎵🎵🎵 (RCA, 1975, prod. Milton Okun) captures him at the height of his fame, when all he had to do was utter "far out" to get applause. The between-song patter and notorious cover of New Christy Minstrels leader Randy Sparks's "Saturday Night in Toledo, Ohio" complement the faithful renderings of the hits. Even before his death, RCA shoehorned his hits into a plethora of oddly conceived compilations. If you're not one of the 10 million who already owns 1973's *Greatest Hits*, then the two-disc *Rocky Mountain Collection* 🎵🎵🎵 (RCA, 1996, prod. various) is the best primer, with 39 tracks spanning his career and his three greatest-hits collections. It's a better bargain than the sprawling four-CD *Country Roads Collection* and makes more chronological sense than *Reader's Digest*'s *His Greatest Hits and Finest Performances*.

what to buy next: The songs are familiar, but the rustic feel, acoustic band instrumentation, and laid-back, western-flavored arrangements on *The Wildlife Concert* 🎵🎵🎵 (Sony/Legacy, 1995, prod. Bob Irwin) lend an infectious vitality to this two-disc set. We could do without the flutes, but former Elvis Presley guitarist James Burton adds some tasteful fuel to "Wild Montana Skies," "Back Home Again," and an Appalachian-style "Take Me Home, Country Roads." A one-CD version, inexplicably titled *The Best of John Denver Live* 🎵🎵🎵 (Sony, 1997, prod. Bob Irwin), takes 15 of the original 28 performances and adds previously unreleased live versions of "I Think I'd Rather Be a Cowboy" and "I'm Sorry."

what to avoid: In a weak attempt at a concept album about the environment, *Earth Songs* 🎵 (Windstar, 1990, prod. Lee Holdridge) gathers lackluster re-recordings of such '70s favorites as "Rocky Mountain Suite," "Rocky Mountain High," "Sunshine on My Shoulders," "Eagle and the Hawk," and "Calypso" around new compositions such as "Earth Day, Every Day."

the rest:
Poems, Prayers and Promises 🎵🎵🎵 (RCA, 1971)
Farewell Andromeda 🎵🎵 (RCA, 1973)
Greatest Hits 🎵🎵🎵 (RCA, 1973)
Back Home Again 🎵🎵🎵 (RCA, 1974)
Rocky Mountain Christmas 🎵🎵 (RCA, 1975)
Spirit 🎵🎵🎵 (RCA, 1976)
Windsong 🎵🎵 (RCA, 1976)
I Want to Live 🎵🎵 (RCA, 1977)
Greatest Hits, Vol. 2 🎵🎵🎵 (RCA, 1977)
Some Days Are Diamonds 🎵🎵 (RCA, 1981)
Seasons of the Heart 🎵🎵 (RCA, 1982)

It's about Time 🎵🎵 (RCA, 1983)
Greatest Hits, Vol. 3 🎵🎵 (RCA, 1984)
Dreamland Express 🎵🎵 (RCA, 1985)
One World 🎵🎵 (RCA, 1986)
The Flower That Shattered the Stone 🎵🎵 (Windstar, 1990)
Christmas Like a Lullaby 🎵🎵 (Windstar, 1990)
Different Directions 🎵🎵 (Windstar, 1991)
Higher Ground 🎵🎵 (Windstar, 1991)
Take Me Home 🎵 (Laserlight/Delta Music, 1995)
Reflections: Songs of Love and Life 🎵🎵 (RCA, 1996)
Country Roads Collection 🎵🎵🎵 (RCA, 1997)
His Greatest Hits and Finest Performances 🎵🎵 (Reader's Digest Music, 1997)
Annie's Song 🎵 (Laserlight/Delta Music, 1997)
Calypso 🎵 (Laserlight/Delta Music, 1997)
Sunshine on My Shoulder 🎵 (Laserlight/Delta Music, 1997)
Take Me Home, Country Roads 🎵 (Laserlight/Delta Music, 1997)
John Denver: 1943–1997 Live 🎵 (Rivier're International, 1997)
All Aboard 🎵🎵 (Sony, 1997)
A Celebration of Life (1943–1997) 🎵🎵 (River North, 1997)

worth searching for: *Minneapolis Does Denver* (October Records, 1995, prod. John Strawberry Fields) features such Minneapolis rock acts as the Honeydogs, Steeplejack, Tina & the B-Side Movement, and the Delilahs paying surprisingly faithful tribute to Denver's '70s material. If there's any doubt that he always knew how to write a memorable melody, check out Marlee McLeod and Kristin Mooney's duet on a jangly, up-tempo rendition of "Follow Me."

influences:
◀◀ The New Christy Minstrels, Tom Paxton, James Taylor, Bread

▶▶ Dan Fogelberg, Michael Martin Murphey

David Okamoto

Depeche Mode

Formed 1980, in Basildon, England.

Martin Gore, keyboards, vocals; David Gahan, vocals, guitar; Andy Fletcher, percussion; Vince Clark, keyboards (1980–81); Alan Wilder, drums, keyboards, vocals (1982–95).

One could make a convincing case that Depeche Mode was the biggest new wave band of the '80s; the sheer influence and weight the band enjoyed within the music industry was on par with any of the more mainstream superstar acts of the era. This once-obscure artsy-synth band brought electronic music to the mainstream through catchy hooks, instantly danceable rythms, and obtuse, world-weary lyrics that, while simple in retrospect, were groundbreaking for the time. Born of England's New Romantic movement, Depeche was the cornerstone of Mute Records, one of a number of independent British labels that would control the music scene there for years. Depeche has gone through many many phases since its inception—from the esoteric electro-pop of its first few releases to the more industrial, rock-with-a-conscience leanings during the latter part of the decade. During the '90s, when guitars reclaimed dominance over the modern rock scene, Depeche's style seemed stale and predictable, but the group proved up to the challenge with *Songs of Faith and Devotion*, which is marked by the prominent use of guitar and walls of feedback noise. Still, Depeche is trying to assess its spot in the new world musical order. Making this mission more difficult was the departure of Alan Wilder, plus singer David Gahan's suicide attempt and subsequent drug bust in 1996. Even in light of these trials and tribulations, or perhaps because of them, Depeche Mode is still vying, vigorously, for a place in contemporary music and trying to keep up with the times. You only have to go as far as the band's two singles collections to realize just how important and influential Depeche has been over the decades.

what to buy: *Catching up with Depeche Mode* 🎵🎵🎵🎵🎵 (Mute/Sire, 1985, prod. various) is a safe singles collection designed to introduce the group to the U.S. audience.

what to buy next: For a taste of early '80s electro-pop heaven, don't miss *Speak and Spell* 🎵🎵🎵 (Mute/Sire, 1981, prod. Daniel Miller), the band's first full release; it features Vince Clark, who would soon leave the band to form Yaz and then Erasure. Fluffy from start to finish despite attempts at Cabaret Voltaire–style found sounds and apocalyptic subtleties, this is pure ear candy. The band's midpoint is found on *People Are People* 🎵🎵🎵🎵 (Mute/Sire, 1984, prod. Depeche Mode, Daniel Miller), featuring the breakthrough U.S. single of the same name. This release finds the band farming in more industrial territory but still maintaining its pop sensibilities. If you're looking for that record to listen to when you think your life is as bad as it can get, *Black Celebration* 🎵🎵🎵🎵 (Mute/Sire, 1986, prod. Depeche Mode, Daniel Miller) may be just the thing. Somber and brooding from start to finish, this record shows a bleak side of the band that had only been hinted at before.

what to avoid: *Violator* 🎵 (Mute/Sire, 1990, prod. Daniel Miller) is nothing but pure pop. It lacks the distinct stylization of the band's earlier releases that, while light, were not formulaic. That said, it was also the band's biggest commercial success in the U.S.

the rest:
A Broken Frame 🎵🎵🎵 (Mute/Sire, 1982)
Construction Time Again 🎵🎵🎵🎵 (Mute/Sire, 1983)
Some Great Reward 🎵🎵🎵🎵 (Sire Mute, 1984)
101 Live 🎵🎵🎵🎵 (Mute/Sire, 1989)
Box Set of Singles 1–3 🎵🎵🎵🎵 (Mute/Sire, 1991)
Songs of Faith and Devotion 🎵🎵🎵 (Sire/Mute, 1993)
Music for the Masses 🎵🎵🎵 (Mute/Sire 1994)

Songs of Faith and Devotion: Live 🎵🎵 (Mute/Sire, 1994)
Ultra 🎵🎵🎵 (Mute/Sire, 1997)
The Singles 83–98 🎵🎵🎵🎵 (Reprise, 1998)

worth searching for: A limited-edition pairing of *Songs of Faith and Devotion* and its live follow-up was issued for a spring 1994 tour of Australia.

solo outings:
Martin Gore:
Counterfeit 🎵🎵🎵🎵 (Mute/Sire EP, 1989)

Recoil (Andy Fletcher):
Hydrology 1 + 2 🎵🎵🎵 (Mute/Enigma, 1989)
Bloodline 🎵🎵🎵🎵 (Mute/Reprise, 1992)
Unsound Methods 🎵🎵🎵🎵 (Mute/Reprise, 1997)

influences:
◀◀ Kraftwerk, Throbbing Gristle, Silicon Teens, Cabaret Voltaire
▶▶ Soft Cell, Erasure, Yaz, Recoil, the Orb, Orbital

Tim Davis

Derek & the Dominos
See: Eric Clapton

Rick Derringer /The McCoys
Born Rick Zehringer, August 5, 1947, in Union City, IN.

The McCoys: Rick Zehringer (later Derringer), guitar, vocals, keyboards (1960–70); Randy Jo Hobbs, bass; Robert Peterson, keyboards; Randy Zehringer, drums.

Typical of '60s garage-rock groups, the McCoys made simple, straightforward pop-rock in the vein of "Louie Louie" and "La Bamba." While still in high school, the quartet was pegged by the Strangeloves production team of Feldman-Goldstein-Gottehrer to record for Bang Records; the group's first single, "Hang on Sloopy," was a #1 smash built around a monotonous three-chord riff and a nonsense sing-along chorus. Unfortunately, the group's producers confined the McCoys's output to vapid clones of this prototype; the group's most original material, the folk-driven "Sorrow," ended up being a hit for the English group the Merseys. The group broke with Bang Records during the '60s, finding its voice as a psychedelic progressive-rock group. Most of the band members joined up with guitarist Johnny Winter during the early '70s. Zehringer, now known as Rick Derringer, left Johnny to join brother Edgar Winter's group as guitarist before embarking on a solo career in 1974. Derringer also continued to produce and play sessions, working with a wide range of acts including Steely Dan, Cyndi Lauper, and Weird Al Yankovic.

what to buy: Derringer's *All American Boy* 𝄞𝄞𝄞𝄞 (Blue Sky, 1973, prod. Rick Derringer, Bill Szymczyk) is a classic power-rock album that shows inspired genius over 12 tracks, beginning with the hit "Rock and Roll Hootchie Koo" and continuing through pop dramas ("The Airport Giveth," "Teenage Queen"), dark ballads ("Jump, Jump, Jump" and "Hold," cowritten with Patti Smith), and gloriously hooky rock ("Slide on Over, Slinky," "Teenage Love Affair"). He even manages to sneak in two of the most infectious Latin rhythm instrumentals ever committed to tape—"Joy Ride" and "Time Warp."

what to buy next: *The Best of the McCoys* 𝄞𝄞𝄞 (Legacy Rock Artifacts, 1995, prod. Feldman-Goldstein-Gottehrer) is a comprehensive collection of the group's Bang Records catalog, with 22 tracks that include all the group's significant A- and B-sides (including "Hang on Sloopy" and "Sorrow," of course) as well as two previously unreleased cuts ("Gaitor Tails and Monkey Ribs" and "Bald Headed Lena").

the rest:
Rick Derringer:
Back to the Blues 𝄞𝄞 (Blues Bureau International, 1994)
Electra Blues 𝄞𝄞 (Blues Bureau International, 1994)
Rock & Roll Hoochie Koo: Best of Rick Derringer 𝄞𝄞𝄞𝄞 (Sony, 1996)
King Biscuit Flower Hour Presents Rick Derringer & Friends 𝄞𝄞𝄞 (KBFH, 1998)
Guitars and Women 𝄞𝄞𝄞 (Razor & Tie, 1998)

The McCoys:
The Psychedelic Years 𝄞𝄞𝄞 (One Way, 1994)

worth searching for: Derringer's self-named band of the mid-'70s was a solid rock outfit given to invigorating performances. Both *Derringer* (Blue Sky, 1976) and *Live* (Blue Sky, 1977) are well worth the hunt.

influences:
◀◀ Chuck Berry, Jerry Lee Lewis, Carl Perkins, the Kingsmen Johnny Winter, Edgar Winter

▶▶ Cyndi Lauper, Slash (Guns N' Roses), Bryan Adams, Billy Squier

see also: *Johnny Winter, Edgar Winter*

Christopher Scapelliti

Descendents
Formed 1978, in Los Angeles, CA.

Bill Stevenson, drums (1978–present); Milo Aukerman, vocals (1979–89, 1996–present); Stephen Egerton, guitar (1987–present); Karl Alvarez, bass (1987–present); Frank Navetta, guitar (1978–85); Tony Lombardo, bass (1978–86); Ray Cooper, guitar (1983–86).

In keeping with punk rock's embrace of misfits (no pun intended), Descendents invited the nerds to partake in Los Angeles's early-'80s punk explosion. The group began inauspiciously enough as a power trio with the surf-inflected "Ride the Wild" single. But it wasn't long before Bill Stevenson, Frank Navetta, and Tony Lombardo found Milo Aukerman, the tall, bespectacled future biochemist who became the icon and singer for their caffeinated brand of music and messages of teenage angst, alienation from the female of the species, and the wonders of being social outcasts. Although that lyrical content may seem common rock fare, Descendents couched it all in the all-encompassing and completely vague philosophy they called ALL. An ongoing quest for extreme experiences, ALL manifested itself in the band's shortest (10 seconds) and, ironically, best-known songs ("Weiner-schnitzel," for example, is a brief, explosive exchange between the band and a fast food drive through employee). The original lineup has remained basically intact, though Stevenson divided his time from 1982 to 1985 between the Descendents and fellow Los Angeles punks Black Flag; Aukerman took a seven-year break from 1989 to 1996 to enter the world of science (the Descendents, appropriately, commemorated the break by releasing *Milo Goes to College*). During that time the remaining members of Descendents formed the band ALL with singer Dave Smalley. ALL has a charm all its own: the band has succeeded in slaking, through constant touring, Descendents fans' thirst for the hyperactive foursome; ALL has also, in its decade of existence, made the Descendents' raw punk-era energy more polished, melodic, and grown up. When Aukerman returned in 1996, it was clear that while still young at heart, Descendents—the band that penned "I Don't Want to Grow Up" and "My Dad Sucks"—have grown up. But alienated punk rock teens still have the records to keep them comfortable in their parents' suburban homes.

what to buy: The perfect introduction to the breadth of the Descendents' bent sense of humor and poppy, melodic punk is the compilation *Somery* 𝄞𝄞𝄞𝄞 (SST Records, 1991, prod. Bill Stevenson). It's a double album and samples the band's entire output to that point. All of the signature songs are included, and though it's a lot of snottiness to take in one sitting, it's worth the effort and should suffice for all but the converted. The other crucial Descendents release is the live document *Liveage* 𝄞𝄞𝄞𝄞 (SST, 1987, prod. Bill Stevenson). There's a real sense of Aukerman preaching to the throngs and the band is spot-on tight. *Liveage* also gives a good cross-section of the band's material, be that funny, moronic, or poignant.

what to buy next: The next records to seek out are both included on *Two Things at Once* 𝄞𝄞𝄞𝄞 (SST, 1987, prod. Bill Stevenson). Here we have *Bonus Fat* 𝄞𝄞𝄞𝄞 (SST, 1987, prod. Bill Stevenson) and *Milo Goes to College* 𝄞𝄞𝄞𝄞 (SST, 1982, prod. Bill Stevenson). *Bonus Fat* is a re-release of the 1981 EP *Fat* with bonus tracks, and it gives a good sense of the early band.

what to avoid: *Everything Sux* ♫♫♫ (Epitaph, 1996, prod. Bill Stevenson) isn't bad, and it's surely nice to have Descendents back in action. But it's not nearly as engaging as the albums mentioned above, which were made before the group "grew up."

the rest:
I Don't Want to Grow Up ♫♫♫ (SST, 1985)
Enjoy ♫♫♫ (SST, 1986)
ALL ♫♫♫ (SST, 1987)
Hallraker ♫♫♫♫ (SST, 1988)

worth searching for: The self-released early single, 1979's "Ride the Wild," sounds totally different than what Descendents became when Aukerman joined.

influences:
◄◄ Black Flag

►► Green Day, Mr. T Experience, Blink 182, Operation Ivy

Chris Handyside

The Desert Rose Band

See: Flying Burrito Brothers

Jackie DeShannon

Born August 21, 1944, in Hazel, KY.

A talented, pioneering singer and one of the best female songwriters of the early rock era, Jackie DeShannon never achieved the fame of some of her contemporaries, though she did score two Top 10 hits with 1965's "What the World Needs Now is Love" (the Burt Bacharach–Hal David theme from the movie *Bob and Carol and Ted and Alice*) and her own "Put a Little Love in Your Heart" in 1969. She began writing at an early age, and her songs have been recorded by artists such as Kim Carnes ("Bette Davis Eyes"), Brenda Lee ("Dum-Dum"), the Byrds ("Don't Doubt Yourself Babe"), Marianne Faithful ("Come Stay with Me"), the Searchers ("When You Walk into the Room"), the Carpenters ("Boat to Sail"), and the dream pairing of Annie Lennox and Al Green ("Put a Little Love in Your Heart"). Though often uncredited, she has produced her own material, worked with Jimmy Page, Van Morrison, and Ry Cooder, wrote themes for films (*Splendor in the Grass* and more) and was an opening act on the Beatles's first American tour.

what to buy: Two CD compilations tell the DeShannon story: *What the World Needs Now Is—Jackie DeShannon: The Definitive Collection* ♫♫♫♫ (EMI, 1994, compilation prod. Bruce Harris) covers her Liberty/Imperial years (1958–69), while *The Best of Jackie DeShannon* ♫♫♫♫ (Rhino, 1991, prod. various) is more expansive and includes her version of "Bette Davis Eyes."

what to avoid: *The Very Best of Jackie DeShannon* **woof!** (Collectables, 1988/1996) is less than a half hour long—it's one of those knock-off collections by a company known for its shoddy product and packaging.

worth searching for: *You're the Only One/Quick Touches* (Edsel, 1995) is a British import that pairs two of her better albums.

influences:
◄◄ Bob Dylan, the Beatles, Burt Bacharach, Hal David

►► Marianne Faithful, Kim Carnes, the Searchers, the Byrds, Annie Lennox, Karen Carpenter

Leland Rucker

Jimmy Destri

See: Blondie

Marcella Detroit

See: Bananarama

Willy DeVille /Mink DeVille

Born August 27, 1953, in New York, NY.

Numerous label changes coupled with an industry blackball due to previous drug problems (and, to be fair, poor sales) have left Willy DeVille's catalog woefully depleted despite its solid foundations. Mink DeVille began in the midst of the late '70s punk scene, an inauspicious spot for a street-inflected R&B group with a Latino flair. The fusion of those styles, matched with DeVille's romantic songwriting and the grit-grease of his impassioned vocals, brought a credible grandeur to the well-mined soul trove. Eventually, DeVille dropped the "Mink" and used his own name on future releases, though his solo career seems equally star-crossed.

what's available: Of DeVille's solo work, which remains rooted in R&B, only his last two releases are in print—which is unfortunate, as they do not demonstrate the full depth of his work. *Backstreets of Desire* ♫♫♫♫ (Forward, 1992, prod. various) is a fairly rigorous comeback but lacks the leanness of his best work. *Loup Garou* ♫♫♫ (EastWest, 1995/Discovery, 1996, prod. John Phillip Shenale, Willy DeVille) finds the singer returning to New Orleans (where he's recorded and lived), and although "When You're Away from Me" shines, a number of the ballads seem overwrought and rehashed.

worth searching for: Although it costs a bit more, the import-only *Spanish Stroll 1977–1987* (Raven, 1993, prod. various) is worth tracking down as it recaps the singer's early years on a generous 21-song disc. The slinky title track, the easy roll of "'A' Train Lady," and all his majestic early ballads demand attention.

influences:

◄◄ Allen Toussaint, Dr. John, Dave Bartholomew, Motown

Allan Orski

The Devlins

Formed 1989, in Dublin, Ireland.

Colin Devlin, vocals, guitar, keyboards; Peter Devlin, bass, guitar, mandolin, vocals; Sean Devitt, drums, percussion, vocals; Niall Macken, keyboards (1989–96).

This fresh, dreamy folk-rock troupe from Dublin has been blessed with generally favorable reviews and cursed by generally indifferent promotion from its record labels. Brothers Colin and Peter Devlin lead the group, which has garnered its following via word of mouth, compensating for its lack of label support by persistent touring with the likes of Sheryl Crow and Sarah McLachlan. That's allowed it to build a small following in North America, although a true breakthrough has so far proven elusive.

what to buy: For its sophomore album, *Waiting* 🐾🐾🐾 (Universal, 1997, prod. Pierre Marchand), the group pared down to a trio, dabbled with sampling, signed on with McLachlan's managers, and teamed up with her producer for an edgier folk-pop album—another impressive turn that, like its debut, *Drift*, received little promotional support.

the rest:
Drift 🐾🐾🐾 (Capitol, 1993)

influences:

◄◄ Fairport Convention, U2, Van Morrison, Sarah McLachlan

Doug Pullen

Devo

Formed 1972, in Akron, OH.

Mark Mothersbaugh, vocals, guitar, keyboards; Gerald V. Casale, vocals, bass, keyboards; Bob Mothersbaugh, guitar, vocals; Bob Casale, keyboards, guitar; Alan Myers, drums (1972–88); David Kendrick, drums (1988–present).

Possibly the most unlikely success story in pop, Devo's music, wardrobe, stage show, interviews, and mini-movies all preached a vague philosophy of "de-evolution," the dehumanization of mankind by technology, industry, and apathy—an idea Devo alternately praised and derided. Formed on the campus of Kent State University (shortly after the shooting of four students by the National Guard), Devo gained underground popularity during the mid-'70s due to its bizarre stage shows, in which the musicians would dress in identical yellow jumpsuits, plastic masks, and fake hair, sometimes accompanied by the helmeted

---

WHAT ALBUM CHANGED YOUR LIFE?

If you want to go back early, for me it was the Beatles. Before that, I was convinced that music was just a methodology of torturing me and making my life unpleasant. While other kids were out playing, I was inside rehearsing, playing songs like 'Ebb Tide' and 'Autumn Leaves' that my parents liked, and they wanted me to play organ in their church, so I was learning religious hymns and stuff. It was just a depressing experience. Then the Beatles came on *Ed Sullivan,* and I went, 'Oh, that's why people have music.' I got really excited and went out and bought the sheet music book for *A Hard Day's Night* . . . and after about a week we had this sinking, horrible realization that we spent all our lives learning the wrong instruments.

Mark Mothersbaugh (of Devo)

"General Boy" (actually the Mothersbaughs' father). Playing an early form of synth-pop, the group won a contract with Warner Bros. in 1978, bowing before a quizzical public with *Q: Are We Not Men? A: We Are Devo* and its kinetic cover of the Rolling Stones' "(I Can't Get No) Satisfaction." Devo was a curiosity until it won over the masses with its 1980 single, "Whip It," but the spotlight faded fast. Though never officially disbanded—Devo performed at the 1996 Sundance Film Festival and on the 1996 and 1997 Lollapalooza festivals—the musicians have, since 1990, concentrated on film, TV, and multimedia projects, including the animated children's series *Rugrats*.

what to buy: Nowhere is Devo more Devo than on its first album, *Q: Are We Not Men? A: We Are Devo* 🐾🐾🐾 (Warner Bros.,

1978, prod. Brian Eno). Containing songs both curious—"Mongoloid," "Space Junk," "(I Can't Get No) Satisfaction"—and perverse—"Uncontrollable Urge," "Sloppy (I Saw My Baby Gettin')"—it is a much better rebellion against the stagnant music of the '70s than many of the most celebrated punk albums.

what to buy next: *Oh, No! It's Devo* 🎜🎜🎜 (Warner Bros., 1983, prod. Roy Thomas Baker) displays the band's ability to create catchy tunes without watering down its trademark philosophy.

what to avoid: *Total Devo* 🎜🎜 (Virgin, 1988, prod. Devo), while featuring some strong songs, is burdened by poor production that renders the songs flat and lifeless. (Fortunately, many of them appear in better form on the live recording *Now It Can Be Told*.)

the rest:
Duty Now for the Future 🎜🎜 (Warner Bros., 1979)
Freedom of Choice 🎜🎜🎜 (Warner Bros., 1980)
Live 🎜🎜🎜 (Warner Bros. EP, 1981)
New Traditionalists 🎜🎜🎜 (Warner Bros., 1981)
Shout 🎜🎜 (Warner Bros., 1984)
Now It Can Be Told 🎜🎜🎜 (Enigma, 1989)
Smooth Noodle Maps 🎜🎜🎜 (Enigma, 1990)
Hardcore Devo, Volume 1: 1974–1977 🎜🎜🎜 (Rykodisc, 1990)
Devo's Greatest Hits 🎜🎜🎜 (Warner Bros., 1990)
Devo's Greatest Misses 🎜🎜🎜 (Warner Bros., 1990)
Hardcore Devo, Volume 2: 1974–1977 🎜🎜🎜 (Rykodisc, 1991)
Devo Live: The Mongoloid Years 🎜🎜🎜 (Rykodisc, 1992)
Adventures of the Smart Patrol 🎜🎜 (Warner Bros./Sire/Discovery, 1996)

worth searching for: The satiric *Devo E-Z Listening Disk* (Rykodisc, 1987, prod. Devo) features the band performing elevator music versions of its songs, muzaking its own work before Muzak can get it.

influences:
◀◀ Kratfwerk, Can, Brian Eno, Robert Fripp, the Rolling Stones

▶▶ They Might Be Giants, the Residents, Tony Basil, Nirvana, Foo Fighters

Brandon Trenz

Howard DeVoto

See: Magazine

Dexy's Midnight Runners /Kevin Rowland & Dexy's Midnight Runners

Formed 1979, in Birmingham, England.

Kevin Rowland (born August 17, 1953, in Wolverhampton, England), vocals; Billy Adams, banjo, guitar; Giorgio Kilkenny, bass; Micky Billingham, accordion, piano, organ; Seb Shelton, drums; Big Jimmy Patterson, trombone; Paul Speare, flute, tin whistle, saxophone; Brian Maurice, saxophone.

When new wave raised its ugly commercial voice in 1980, punk singer Kevin Rowland answered back with Dexy's Midnight Runners, a high-octane mix of traditional Irish music, soul, and rock. Although Rowland's vision was inevitably short-sighted (he burned bridges with his first label and abused journalists and band members), he managed to find success producing honest, hard-working soul music at a time when it was anything but the fashion. For the group's 1982 hit album *Too-Rye-Ay* and its hit "Come on Eileen," Rowland reconfigured Dexy's as a dungaree-clad Celtic rock group, featuring a two-piece fiddle section, vocal trio, and the occasional horn backup. After a poor 1988 solo showing, Rowland has remained out of sight and ear shot. There's no word yet on his next move.

what to buy: Sadly, Dexy's catalog is out of print in the U.S., but many of the band's albums are still available in England. Of them, *Searching for the Young Soul Rebels* 🎜🎜🎜 (EMI UK, 1980, prod. Kevin Rowland) is a foot-stomping raveup of earnest soul tributes, while *Too-Rye-Ay* 🎜🎜🎜 (Mercury UK, 1982, prod. Kevin Rowland) isn't as focused but has some great moments shifting between rustic folk-rock ("The Celtic Soul Brothers") to blazing soul (a cover of Van Morrison's "Jackie Wilson Said") and rollicking pop (the international hit "Come on Eileen").

what to buy next: *It Was Like This* 🎜🎜🎜 (Premier, prod. various) is essentially a repackaging of *Geno* (EMI UK, 1983), a compilation of early singles, and shows the band at its youthful and gritty best.

what to avoid: Rowland revamped Dexy's for the band's last outing, *Don't Stand Me Down* 🎜🎜 (Creation, 1985). While "Listen to This" shows the singer could still turn out a solid soul-infused tune, the record sinks under its own pretentiousness, which includes long spoken-word passages.

the rest:
Because of You 🎜🎜🎜 (Spectrum Germany, 1993)
BBC Radio One Live in Concert 🎜🎜🎜 (Griffin, 1997)

worth searching for: If Rowland is your guy, get busy searching for his full-length solo effort, *The Wanderer* (Mercury, 1988, prod. Deodato). MOR jazz-fusion maestro Deodato gives Rowland the lounge-pop treatment, placing the angry young Brit some 10 years ahead of the late 1990s lounge revival. Maybe Rowland knew what he was doing after all.

influences:
◀◀ Sam & Dave, Geno Washington, Van Morrison, the English Beat

▶▶ The Commitments, the Style Council

Christopher Scapelliti

Dennis DeYoung

See: Styx

Dharma Bums

Formed 1988, in Portland, OR.

Jeremy Wilson, vocals; Eric Lovre, guitar; Jim Talstra, bass; John Moen, drums.

The name comes from the classic Jack Kerouac novel, and despite the fact that the band members appear to be drawling hillbillies one minute, post-punkers the next, and R.E.M. wannabes the one after that, the Dharma Bums' music tends to dissipate into a droning blend of mediocre modern rock and poorly executed country. Some of the songs do have initial appeal and are catchy (which may help explain the amount of college-radio airplay they receive), but after just a few listenings you can no longer get past the simple chords and uninspired lyrics.

what to buy: *Bliss* 𝄃𝄃𝄃 (Frontier, 1990, prod. Dharma Bums) is their strongest and most varied album; a few tracks like "Pumpkinhead" manage to hold their own, and while there's certainly nothing innovative going on, they mix things up enough to maintain a good flow.

the rest:
Haywire: Out through the Indoor 𝄃𝄃⅞ (Frontier, 1989)
Welcome 𝄃𝄃𝄃 (1991, Frontier)

influences:
◄◄ R.E.M., the Replacements

Bryan Lassner

Neil Diamond

Born January 24, 1941, in Brooklyn, NY.

Neil Diamond has been so entrenched in pop's middle-of-the-road mainstream for so long that it's easy to forget he was—for a lime—a decent rock songwriter and something of a maverick whose material was more personalized than most of what came out of the Brill Building song factory where Diamond began his career. A former premed student (he attended New York University on a fencing scholarship), Diamond can lay claim to one of pop's great three-chord wonders, 1966's "Cherry, Cherry," as well as to a string of songs covered by a wide array of performers, including the Monkees ("I'm a Believer"), Deep Purple ("Kentucky Woman"), UB40 ("Red Red Wine"), Chris Isaak ("Solitary Man"), and Urge Overkill ("Girl, You'll Be a Woman Soon"). These days he's more defined by the schmaltzier portion of his oeuvre ("You Don't Bring Me Flowers," "Heartlight"), but his 30 years of recording—and worldwide record sales of nearly 100 million—merit respect.

what to buy: *Classics: The Early Years* 𝄃𝄃𝄃𝄃 (Columbia, 1983, prod. various) contains all of his wonderful late '60s hits, songs that stake a claim for Diamond as one of the finest pop craftsmen of the era.

what to buy next: *His Twelve Greatest Hits* 𝄃𝄃𝄃 (MCA, 1974, prod. Tom Catalano) captures the next evolution of Diamond's career, a commercial peak even though the sing-along slickness of "Sweet Caroline" and "Song Sung Blue" is a dramatic come-down from the *Classics* selection. *Beautiful Noise* 𝄃𝄃𝄃 (Columbia, 1976, prod. Robbie Robertson) is a concept album about the Brill Building/Tin Pan Alley scene, an ambitious and listenable venture that stands apart from the lackluster albums that preceded and followed it.

what to avoid: *Heartlight* **woof!** (Columbia, 1982, prod. Burt Bacharach, Carole Bayer Sager, Neil Diamond) is emblematic of how slight and lightweight the bulk of Diamond's albums have been.

the rest:
Velvet Gloves and Spit 𝄃𝄃 (Uni, 1968)
Brother Love's Traveling Salvation Show 𝄃𝄃⅞ (Uni, 1969)
Touching You, Touching Me 𝄃𝄃 (Uni, 1969)
Neil Diamond Gold 𝄃𝄃𝄃 (Uni, 1970)
Tap Root Manuscript 𝄃𝄃𝄃 (Uni, 1970)
Stones 𝄃𝄃𝄃 (MCA, 1971)
Moods 𝄃⅞ (MCA, 1972)
Hot August Night 𝄃𝄃𝄃 (MCA, 1972)
Rainbow 𝄃𝄃 (MCA, 1973)
Jonathan Livingston Seagull **woof!** (Columbia, 1973)
Serenade 𝄃𝄃 (Columbia, 1974)
And the Singer Sings His Songs 𝄃⅞ (MCA, 1976)
Love at the Greek 𝄃𝄃⅞ (Columbia, 1977)
I'm Glad You're Here with Me Tonight 𝄃 (Columbia, 1977)
You Don't Bring Me Flowers 𝄃 (Columbia, 1978)
September Morn **woof!** (Columbia, 1979)
The Jazz Singer 𝄃𝄃⅞ (Capitol, 1980)
On the Way to the Sky 𝄃 (Columbia, 1981)
12 Greatest Hits, Volume 2 𝄃𝄃 (Columbia, 1982)
Primitive **woof!** (Columbia, 1984)
Love Songs 𝄃𝄃⅞ (MCA, 1985)
Headed for the Future 𝄃 (Columbia, 1986)
Hot August Night II 𝄃𝄃 (Columbia, 1987)
The Best Years of Our Lives **woof!** (Columbia, 1988)
Lovescape **woof!** (Columbia, 1991)
The Greatest Hits 1966–1992 𝄃𝄃𝄃 (Columbia, 1992)
Glory Road—1968 to 1972 𝄃𝄃𝄃 (MCA, 1992)
The Christmas Album 𝄃𝄃 (Columbia, 1992)
Up on the Roof: Songs from the Brill Building 𝄃𝄃 (Columbia, 1993)
Live in America 𝄃𝄃⅞ (Columbia, 1994)
The Christmas Album, Volume II 𝄃⅞ (Columbia, 1994)
In My Lifetime 𝄃𝄃𝄃⅞ (Columbia, 1995)
Tennessee Moon 𝄃𝄃⅞ (Columbia, 1996)

As Time Goes By N/A (Columbia, 1998)

worth searching for: Diamond's earliest albums—*The Feel of Neil Diamond* (Bang, 1966) and *Just for You* (Bang, 1967) have collector's value as well as their share of those early hits.

influences:

◀◀ Bob Dylan, Hank Williams, George & Ira Gershwin, Elvis Presley, Barbra Streisand

▶▶ Barry Manilow, Mary's Danish, Michael Bolton

Gary Graff

The Diamonds

Formed 1954, in Toronto, Ontario, Canada. Disbanded 1961. Reformed 1973.

Stan Fisher, lead vocals (1954); Phil Leavitt, baritone vocals (1954); Ted Kowalski, tenor vocals (1954–56); Bill Reed, bass vocals (1954–56); Dave Somerville, lead vocals (1954–61); Mike Douglas, baritone vocals (1955–61); Evan Fisher, tenor vocals (1956–61); John Felton, bass vocals (1956–61).

Like hometown heroes the Crew Cuts, the Diamonds were a Toronto vocal quartet shrewd enough to adapt their jazz and minstrel chops to the exciting new doo-wop and R&B sounds emanating from south of the border. The group's first recordings for Coral Records in New York were fairly nondescript, but an *a capella* rehearsal in Cleveland shortly afterwards lead to a long and fruitful association with Mercury, which in 1956 released a Diamonds rendition of Frankie Lymon's "Why Do Fools Fall in Love." It was not until a year later, however, that the remarkable (if borderline bizarre) version of the Gladiolas' "Little Darlin'" made the Diamonds worldwide stars—if only fleetingly. Awash in castanets and making full use of the group's magnificent vocal range, this song, and its Top 5 follow-up, "The Stroll," earned the group frequent guest spots on all the choice television shows and package tours of the day. But as the '50s drew to a close, so did the Diamonds' appeal as mere interpreters of other artists' material. Nevertheless, the original quartet briefly reunited during the mid-'70s, and various groups of Diamonds continue to haunt the lounge circuit, where, despite nary an original member on stage, they can still bring down the house with their unique trademark, a thoroughly unglued rendition of the classic "Little Darlin'."

what's available: Although the group's earliest recordings are not included, *The Best of the Diamonds: The Mercury Years* ♪♪♪ (Mercury, 1996, compilation prod. Ron Furmanek, Steve Kolanijan) contains all of the hits along with a respectful reading of Buddy Holly's "Words of Love," an early Bill Medley composition, and even a trio of rarities. Sure, the Diamonds' repertoire was entirely derivative; but at least the execution was

never less than colorful, and it was always humorous enough to separate the group from totally crass, personality-devoid R&B plunderers like Pat Boone.

influences:

◀◀ The Crew Cuts, the Penguins, the Rays, the Coasters

▶▶ Barry Gibb, Ruben & the Jets, the Four Preps, Kokomo Beach Band

Gary Pig Gold

Dick & Dee Dee

Formed 1961, in Santa Monica, CA.

Dick St. John, vocals; Mary Sperling, vocals.

Arguably the most talented of the '60s boy-girl duos, Dick & Dee Dee used the miracle of overdubbing to sound like a much bigger group. Their style heartily embraced '50s doo-wop while adding undercurrents of folk and gospel, unique for their time. A prolific songwriter, Dick St. John had recorded two regionally successful singles for the Rona and Pom Pom labels before he teamed up with Mary Sperling, an old high school chum. Experimenting in a garage studio, the duo had a distinctive style as a result of dubbing different harmonies on top of one another, with the final touch being St. John's freakish (yet tuneful) falsetto. After signing with Lama Records, Dick & Mary changed their billing to the more alliteratively pleasing Dick & Dee Dee. Their recording of "The Mountain's High" proved so popular in San Francisco that Liberty Records picked it up for national distribution, and it rose to #2 on the pop charts. After a Top 20 follow-up with the romance-oriented "Tell Me," Dick & Dee Dee became lost in the shuffle at Liberty and demanded their release (which took some guts). Their producers found them a new home at Warner Bros., where they hit the charts with such lush teen-pop/MOR as "Young and in Love," "Turn Around," and "All My Trials" (which Elvis Presley later cobbled into his "American Trilogy"). St. John wrote most of the duo's hits, but John D. Loudermilk penned one of their most memorable doo-wop hybrids, "Thou Shall Not Steal." At their peak, Dick & Dee Dee appeared regularly on TV's *Shindig* and recorded two songs ("Blue Turns to Grey," "Some Things Stick in Your Mind") in England with the Rolling Stones as their backing group. Tastes changed and the duo's final hurrah was singing "Heartbeats" in the 1966 teen-flick *Wild Wild Winter*. Sperling left the act shortly thereafter. St. John's solo career stalled, but he went on to write "Yellow Balloon" for the band of the same name and "Sweet Country Woman," which became a #1 hit for country singer Johnny Duncan. With his wife Sandy in the role of Dee Dee, St. John keeps the act alive on the oldies circuit, and the new duo has collected recipes for *The Rock & Roll Cookbook* (with Pamela Des Barres) in order to raise funds for the National Music Foundation. (St. John's favorite dish? Bo Diddley's custard.)

what to buy: All of Dick & Dee Dee's chart singles from "The Mountain's High" to "Be My Baby" are on *The Best of Dick & Dee Dee* ♪♪♪♪ (Varese Vintage, 1995, compilation prod. Cary E. Mansfield). This superior 12-song compilation also includes the ultra-rare Rolling Stones–backed "Blue Turns to Grey," a top-flight booklet, vintage photos, and better sound than was available way back when.

worth searching for: You'll have to scan the tiny print of auction lists to find *Songs We've Sung on Shindig* (Warner Bros., 1965, prod. Don Ralke, the Wilder Brothers), but St. John's favorite LP is well worth the eyestrain.

influences:

◄◄ Frankie Lymon & the Teenagers, the Nutmegs, Shirley & Lee, Mickey & Sylvia

►► Lou Christie, the Newbeats, Jackie & Gayle, Paul & Paula, Yellow Balloon, Donny & Marie Osmond

Ken Burke

The Dickies

Formed 1977, in Los Angeles, CA.

Leonard Graves Phillips, vocals; Stan Lee, guitar; Billy Club, bass; Chuck Wagon, keyboards; Karlos Kaballero, drums.

West Coast punk rock of the '80s had it all—tight, upbeat melodies and an incredibly off-kilter sense of humor. The Dickies blazed a trail for bands that had tomfoolery as a main focus rather than the standard dream of hit records. Beyond their downright clown-like theatrics, the Dickies were a credible pop-punk band, ignoring the political anthems in favor of songs about zombies and circus performers. And they could sing like the Beach Boys, something they did better than any punk band before them. Although the humor in the songs the Dickies penned themselves might only reach the heights attained by Ruth Buzzi, their real comedic brilliance lay in their choice (and execution) of classic rock songs such as "Paranoid" by Black Sabbath, "Sounds of Silence" by Simon and Garfunkel, and their hyper take on the Moody Blues's "Nights in White Satin," which is so Dickies-like that you forget it's a cover. Unfortunately the bulk of the Dickies' classic A&M material is out of print, leaving fans with only average '80s and '90s Dickies material.

what to buy: After their fruitful tenure with A&M, the Dickies re-emerged with the West Coast indie Restless Records. *Stukas over Disneyland* ♪♪ (Restless, 1983) finds the Dickies starting out right where they left off with a hyped-up cover of Led Zeppelin's "Communication Breakdown" and soon-to-be classics such as "She's a Hunchback" and "Pretty Please Me." *Stukas over Disney-*

land also found the Dickies trading their patented pop-punk production for a more accessible and in-vogue power pop sound.

the rest:
We Aren't the World ♪♪ (Roir, 1986)
Killer Klowns from Outer Space ♪♪ (Enigma, 1988)
Second Coming ♪♪ (Enigma, 1989)
Live in London, Locked 'n' Loaded ♪♪ (Taang!, 1991)

worth searching for: In 1989 A&M released a great collection by the Dickies, *Great Dictations*, which was cut out within two years of its initial release. But out of print doesn't mean inaccessible, so scour those used bins because this CD is well worth the hunt. And who knows—you might end up finding one of the other wondrous A&M CDs, *The Incredible Shrinking Dickies* or *Dawn of the Dickies*.

influences:

◄◄ The Ramones, the Beatles, the Chipmunks

►► Green Day, the Offspring, NOFX, Devo

Chris Richards

Bruce Dickinson

See: Iron Maiden

The Dictators

Formed 1974, in the Bronx, NY. Disbanded 1980.

Handsome Dick Manitoba, vocals; Andy Shernoff, vocals, bass, keyboards; Ross "The Boss" Funichello, guitar; TopTen, guitar; Mark "The Animal" Mendoza, bass (1975–77); Stu Boy King, drums (1974–75); Richie Teeter, drums, vocals (1975–80).

It has been argued (most strongly by critic/booster Richard Meltzer) that this was the first punk group. If it's admitted that Television was too arty and musically adept, and that the New York Dolls were really glam, then the argument stands up. Of course, some would say there was too much heavy metal in the Dictators' music—especially Ross "The Boss" Funichello's frenetic "quantity is quality" solos—for the group to be considered punk. But, punk was as much attitude as anything else, and the 'tators had attitude out the wazoo. Handsome Dick Manitoba, who certainly doesn't sound like a singer, started as the band's roadie, but, with his parodistic wrestling image, he made a perfect "secret weapon" comic-macho frontman (his "machismo" got him into trouble one night at CBGB when he heckled transvestite Wayne County; County whacked his head with the microphone stand, sending Manitoba to the hospital). The group was put together by fanzine (*Teenage Wasteland Gazette*) editors Andy Shernoff, Scott Kempner, and Funichello, and it quickly became a mainstay of the early CBGB scene. Shernoff's songs (he wrote all the originals, often in collaboration) were irreverently referential to the history and iconography of rock, as on the

$\begin{array}{c}3\\3\\8\end{array}$ *bo diddley*

debut album's "(I Live for) Cars and Girls" (as well as their covers of Sonny & Cher's "I Got You Babe" and "California Sun"). *Go Girl Crazy!*, like all the group's studio efforts, was produced by the same team (Murray Krugman and Sandy Pearlman) that made Blue Öyster Cult stars; the Dictators had to settle for being commercially unsuccessful critic's faves. Since breaking up in 1980, the Dictators have sporadically and temporarily reunited, using any handy excuse (the 10th anniversary of punk, the 20th anniversary of CBGB) or for no reason at all. Later, Manitoba, Shernoff, and Funichello combined their talents again in the short-lived group Manitoba's Wild Kingdom.

what to buy: The perfect blend of '60s pop takeoffs and aggressive punk humor on *Go Girl Crazy!* 𝄢𝄢𝄢 (Epic, 1975, prod. Murray Krugman, Sandy Pearlman) shows the group at its crudest and funniest, often skirting the limits of taste but doing so in such a goofy way ("Master Race Rock") that it undermined any attempt to mold the jokes into ideology.

what to buy next: *Fuck 'em If They Can't Take a Joke* 𝄢𝄢𝄢 (ROIR, 1981) comes from a 1981 reunion show. The early tunes are less punk and more metal at this juncture, and highlights include "Loyola," covers of Mott the Hoople's "Moon Upstairs" and the Velvet Underground's "What Goes On," and a funny, lounge-style verse to open "Search and Destroy."

worth searching for: *Manifest Destiny* (Asylum, 1977, prod. Murray Krugman, Sandy Pearlman) features slightly better songwriting than the debut but isn't quite as hilarious. Ditto *Bloodbrothers* (Asylum, 1978, prod. Murray Krugman, Sandy Pearlman), which boasts another great cover (the Flamin' Groovies' "Slow Death") and the anthem of purpose "Faster & Louder." Neither of these long-out-of-print Asylum albums has ever been digitized.

solo outings:
Manitoba's Wild Kingdom:
. . . And You? 𝄢𝄢𝄢𝄢 (MCA, 1990)

influences:
⏪ The Stooges, the Flamin' Groovies, the Kinks, the Who, the Seeds, Mott the Hoople, Blue Öyster Cult

⏩ The Ramones, the Surf Punks, Circle Jerks, Twisted Sister, Mötley Crüe

see also: *The Del-Lords, Twisted Sister*

Steve Holtje

Bo Diddley
Born Elias Bates, December 30, 1928, in McComb, MS.

One of the most influential musicians in rock 'n' roll, Bo Diddley patented the distinctive "chunka, chunka" rhythm guitar riff that is the very substance of rock's foundation. Born near the Mississippi Delta, Diddley was raised by sharecroppers and earned his nickname in school. The family that adopted him—and changed his last name to McDaniel—moved to Chicago, where Diddley began making his guitars and playing them on the street and in small clubs. He signed with Checker Records during the mid-'50s and released a string of albums and singles through the mid-'60s that would influence countless rockers, from Elvis Presley and Buddy Holly to the Rolling Stones and Jimi Hendrix. Diddley's recorded output since then has been erratic, and most of what he has released has been either uninspired, ill-advised, or both—though the star-studded 1996 album *A Man Amongst Men*, his first for a major label in 25 years, showed there's life in the old man yet. Diddley, a member of the Rock and Roll Hall of Fame, has stayed active on the concert trail, his rectangular guitars and Coke-bottle glasses as familiar to generations of admirers as that gritty voice and gutbucket guitar sound.

what to buy: *Bo Diddley/Go Bo Diddley* 𝄢𝄢𝄢𝄢 (Chess, 1958, 1959/1987) captures the primal "Bo Diddley Beat" in all its fever. Some of Diddley's greatest songs appeared on the records paired here, including "Bo Diddley," "I'm a Man," "Who Do You Love," and "Crackin' Up."

what to buy next: If you're willing to shell out a few more bucks, check out *The Chess Box* 𝄢𝄢𝄢𝄢 (Chess, 1990, compilation prod. Andy McKaie), an exhaustive warehouse of Diddley's early and influential work for the famous Chicago label. All of his most popular and important work is here, as well as worthwhile obscurities and previously unreleased material. *His Best* 𝄢𝄢𝄢 (MCA/Chess, 1997, prod. various) also serves up digitally remastered versions of classic Bo in a more affordable set, with extensive liner notes and credits.

what to avoid: Just about everything Diddley did for the small, well-meaning Triple X Records label were poorly executed attempts to make Diddley relevant. Among them: *Breakin' through the B.S.* 𝄢 (Triple X, 1989, prod. Scott Free), *The Mighty Bo Diddley* 𝄢𝄢 (Bokay Productions, 1985), and *This Should Not Be* 𝄢 (Triple X, 1993, prod. Scott Free).

the rest:
Bo Diddley 𝄢𝄢𝄢𝄢 (Chess, 1958)
Bo Diddley Is a Gunslinger 𝄢𝄢𝄢 (Chess, 1960)
In the Spotlight 𝄢𝄢𝄢 (Chess, 1960)
(With Chuck Berry) *Two Great Guitars* 𝄢𝄢𝄢 (Chess, 1964)
(With Muddy Waters and Little Walter) *Superblues* 𝄢𝄢𝄢 (Chess, 1967)
(With Muddy Waters and Howlin' Wolf) *The Super Super Blues Records* 𝄢𝄢𝄢𝄢 (Chess, 1968)
The London Bo Diddley Sessions 𝄢𝄢𝄢 (Chess, 1973)
His Greatest Sides, Vol. 1 𝄢𝄢𝄢 (Chess, 1986) cassette only

Rare and Well Done 🎵🎵🎵 (Chess, 1991)
A Man Amongst Men 🎵🎵 (Code Blue/Atlantic, 1996)

worth searching for: Completists just have to track down one of Diddley's most opportunistic albums, *Surfin' with Bo Diddley* (Chess, 1963), a record that proved that Bo knows trends, but doesn't always know when to avoid them.

influences:

◀◀ Louis Jordan, Muddy Waters, John Lee Hooker

▶▶ The Rolling Stones, Eric Burdon, Jimi Hendrix, Buddy Holly, Elvis Presley, Bow Wow Wow, U2

Doug Pullen

Ani DiFranco

Born September 23, 1970, in Buffalo, NY.

In an industry ruled by pigeonholes and demographics, Ani DiFranco has built a rabid cult following out of old folkies and young punks, men and women, gays and straights by recording fiercely personal music on her own label, Righteous Babe, at a staggering rate of two albums per year. In between tackling abortion, sexuality, stereotypes, and decaying relationships in striking, stream-of-consciousness detail, DiFranco has also emerged as an underground heroine with such savage salvos at the corporate music industry as "Egos Like Hairdos," "The Next Big Thing," and "The Million You Never Made," which baits the major record companies still sniffing at her backstage door. Since appearing on the covers of *Ms.* and *Spin* and having her business savvy championed by *Forbes* and the *New York Times*, DiFranco has certainly raised her profile beyond most "underground" icons. But she clearly has her own unflappable agenda, showing a remarkable knack for bucking expectations while clinging to her ideals. "People talk about my image like I come in two dimensions," she sings on the sneering title track of 1998's *Little Plastic Castle*, ". . . Like what I happen to be wearing the day that someone takes a picture is my new statement for all of womankind." She is well aware of her role as rock's nose-thumbing, nose ring-wearing indie queen, but she's not going to reject opportunities (opening for Bob Dylan, incorporating elements of hip-hop and ska, moving her enthralling live shows to larger venues) just because they might make her appear to be selling out. Many acts struggle to maintain artistic integrity—but to DiFranco, it just comes naturally.

what to buy: DiFranco has been fleshing out her aggressive solo acoustic sound with other instruments since her third album. But *Out of Range* 🎵🎵🎵🎵 (Righteous Babe, 1994, prod. Ani DiFranco, Ed Stone) marks a pivotal move toward a band feel without overwhelming the bite of her voice, especially on the electric version of the title track. *Not a Pretty Girl* 🎵🎵🎵🎵

(Righteous Babe, 1995, prod. Ani DiFranco) is a hard-nosed hybrid of jagged confessionals, poetic imagery, and punkish diatribes ranging from sexual aggressiveness ("Shy") to social inadequacy ("This Bouquet") to capital punishment ("Crime for Crime"). *Dilate* 🎵🎵🎵🎵 (Righteous Babe, 1996, prod. Ani DiFranco) is both her noisiest and most challenging album, fueled by the relentlessly funky "Shameless," a trip-hop arrangement of "Amazing Grace," and the brutal "Napoleon," her most pointed diatribe against rock stardom to date.

what to buy next: The two-CD *Living in Clip* 🎵🎵🎵🎵 (Righteous Babe, 1997, prod. Ani DiFranco) is marred slightly by choppy editing but boasts ferocious live versions of her most popular tunes, including "Letter to a John," "Untouchable Face," "Anticipate," and "Shameless."

what to avoid: *Like I Said* 🎵🎵🎵 (Righteous Babe, 1993, prod. Ani DiFranco, Ed Stone) is a compilation of re-recorded versions of songs from her first two albums. These are faster, but not necessarily better, than the originals.

the rest:
Ani DiFranco 🎵🎵🎵🎵 (Righteous Babe, 1990)
Not So Soft 🎵🎵🎵 (Righteous Babe, 1991)
Imperfectly 🎵🎵🎵 (Righteous Babe, 1992)
Puddle Dive 🎵🎵🎵 (Righteous Babe, 1993)
More Joy, Less Shame EP (Righteous Babe, 1996) 🎵🎵🎵
(With Utah Phillips) *The Past Didn't Go Anywhere* 🎵🎵🎵 (Righteous Babe, 1996)
Little Plastic Castle 🎵🎵🎵🎵 (Righteous Babe, 1998)

worth searching for: *Women in (E)motion* (T&M, 1997, prod. Ani DiFranco) is a German radio broadcast from the 1994 *Out of Range* tour available only as a European import.

influences:

◀◀ Joni Mitchell, Rickie Lee Jones, Tracy Chapman, Fugazi

▶▶ Dar Williams, Alanis Morissette, Lisa Loeb, Alana Davis

David Okamoto

Steve Diggle
See: Buzzcocks

Pat DiNizio
See: Smithereens

Dino, Desi & Billy
Formed 1964, in Beverly Hills, CA. Disbanded 1970.

Dean Paul "Dino" Martin Jr. (died March 20, 1987), bass, guitar, vocals; Desiderio Alberto Arnaz y Ball (a.k.a. Desi Arnaz Jr.) drums, vocals; William Ernest Joseph "Billy" Hinsche, guitar, keyboards, vocals.

The age-old showbiz axiom "it's not what you know, it's *who*

3/4/0 dinosaur jr.

you know" was never truer than in the case of '60s pop group Dino, Desi & Billy. While still attending classes at Good Shepherd Catholic School in Beverly Hills, this trio of would-be Beatles had no difficulty whatsoever in arranging for a recording contract: all they had to do was ask a pal of Dino's dad to drop by for an "audition." Over drinks it was arranged to have the kids sign with Frank Sinatra's Reprise label, and six months later their "Louie Louie"/"Hang on Sloopy" pastiche "I'm a Fool" was the #17 record in the land. Several other singles and four entire albums followed, along with appearances in their parents' various television shows and movies, before the boys graduated from high school and embarked on solo careers (Billy, to this day, is an auxiliary member of the Beach Boys, for whom DD&B first opened during the summer of 1965). Nevertheless, don't for a minute think every shrewd young music and TV producer in Los Angeles wasn't paying strict attention, and making notes for the future, as this make-believe group of child stars became an instant, overnight teen sensation.

what's available: You might dismiss *The Rebel Kind: The Best of Dino, Desi and Billy* &&&& (Sundazed, 1996, compilation prod. Bob Irwin) as a cute but trite study in proto-bubblegum. Of course, there is a goodly amount of fun if flippant filler herein ("If You're Thinkin' What I'm Thinkin'," however, was cool enough to get into a Matt Helm movie), but in their later days, the boys were getting seriously "progressive," in a Romper Room kinda way (e.g., "The Inside Outside Caspar Milquetoast Eskimo Flash"). Why, they even corralled Brian Wilson to co-write one of their final releases!

worth searching for: Young Dino's solemn reading of "Spanish Harlem Incident" on *Memories Are Made of This* (Reprise, 1966, prod. Lee Hazlewood) will more than make the hunt for this period piece worthwhile—that is, until someone gets around to issuing an entire *Dino Sings Dylan* collection.

influences:

◄◄ The Beatles, the Beach Boys, Gary Lewis & the Playboys

►► The Monkees, the Ohio Express, the Partridge Family, Wilson Phillips, the Beverly Hills Blues Band, Hanson

Gary Pig Gold

Dinosaur Jr.
/J Mascis

Formed 1984, in Amherst, MA. Disbanded 1997.

J Mascis (born Joseph D. Mascis), guitar, vocals; **Lou Barlow,** bass, ukelele, tapes, vocals (1984–88); **Donna Biddell,** bass (1989); **Van Conner,** bass (1991); **Mike Johnson,** bass (1992–97); **Murph,** drums (1984–94).

Dinosaur Jr. (the Jr. was appended after a similarly named

bunch of veteran San Francisco musicians objected) is directly or indirectly one of the most influential bands of the late '80s, inspiring sounds in both the U.S. and Great Britain. The enigmatic, untalkative Mascis—often deemed the ultimate slacker as much for his lazy vocals as for his diffidence—is a powerful guitarist whose Neil Young (c. *Zuma*)–inspired feedback fests and high-volume distortion assaults resulted in some of the most intense underground rock of the mid-'80s. Long before grunge was an acknowledged genre, the term was frequently used to describe the thick, messy, guitar-heavy sound of this trio, which through it all still managed to maintain a modicum of pop catchiness. During the '90s Mascis began using more acoustic guitar, an approach culminating in his 1996 solo album. Mascis has also demonstrated some acumen as a drummer, playing on Dinosaur Jr. albums as well as with Deep Wound (with Lou Barlow), Gobblehoof (with Deep Wound's Charles Nakajima), Upside Down Cross, and others. Original bassist Barlow, frustrated by Mascis's unrelenting control, eventually bolted to form Sebadoh. A succession of bassists followed before Johnson nailed down the role.

what to buy: *Bug* &&&& (SST, 1988) features the college radio hit "Freak Scene" and the thickest guitar sound of Mascis's career—"No Bones" is a firestorm of distortion and Neil Young–esque reverb splashes—as well as primal hooks on nearly every chorus and quite a few verses, too. Only the shapeless closer "Don't" keeps this from five-bone perfection. Mascis's solo album, *Martin + Me* &&&& (Reprise, 1996), is a live solo acoustic set (with guitarist Kurt Fedora joining on the last two tracks), a logical progression that works superbly, thanks to the sturdiness of Mascis's originals as well as an inspired assortment of covers that includes Greg Sage's "On the Run," Carly Simon's "Anticipation," Lynyrd Skynyrd's "Every Mother's Son," and the especially apt Smiths' selection "The Boy with the Thorn in His Side."

what to buy next: *Green Mind* &&& (Sire/Warner Bros., 1991, prod. J Mascis), the first post-Barlow album after a three-year gap, is practically a Mascis solo album, with Murph drumming on only three songs and guests Don Fleming and Jay Spiegel (both from Velvet Monkeys, which Mascis played with on *Rake*) filling in some textures. The electric/acoustic mix is a startling but effective change. The eight-song singles collection *Fossils* &&& (SST, 1991) is worth having for covers of "Show Me the Way" (Peter Frampton), "Just like Heaven" (the Cure), and "Chunks" (seminal Boston hardcore punkers Last Rights).

what to avoid: The two best tracks from *You're Living All over Me* && (SST, 1987)—"Little Fury Things" and "In a Jar"—are also on *Fossils*, the two Barlow tracks are utter crap, and some of the other Mascis songs sound suspiciously like second-rate heavy metal riffing (especially the end of "SludgeFest").

the rest:
Dinosaur ♫♫ (Homestead, 1985)
The Wagon ♫♫♫ (Blanco y Negro France/Warner Bros. EP, 1991)
Whatever's Cool with Me ♫ (Blanco y Negro France/Warner Bros. EP, 1991) ♫
Where You Been ♫♫ (Sire/Warner Bros., 1993)
Without a Sound ♫♫♫ (Sire/Reprise, 1994)
Hand It Over ♫♫♫ (Sire/Reprise, 1997)

worth searching for: *Keeblin': Australasian Tour Edition 1995* (Warner Music Australia, 1995, prod. J Mascis, Paul Nickson) consists of *Without a Sound* and a 32-minute bonus CD with five long, furious live tracks recorded in Brixton by the BBC. Two of them, "What Else Is New" and "Sludge," can also be found on the three-song European EP *I Don't Think So* (Warner Bros., 1994, prod. J Mascis, Paul Nickson), which is easier to find.

influences:
◀◀ Neil Young, Velvet Underground, Black Flag, the Cure, R.E.M.

▶▶ My Bloody Valentine, Buffalo Tom, Afghan Whigs

see also: *Mike Johnson, Sebadoh*

Steve Holtje

Ronnie James Dio /Dio

Born Ronald Padavona, July 10, 1949, in Portsomouth, NH.

Dio is a band but mostly a man—singer Ronnie James Dio, who was discovered when Deep Purple guitarist Ritchie Blackmore snared Dio from the band Elf to front Blackmore's solo project, Rainbow. With his gutsy, melodramatic delivery, Dio fit the role perfectly and stayed with the irascible Blackmore until 1978, when he replaced Ozzy Osbourne in Black Sabbath. By 1982, Dio was done with that and had moved on to his solo career, sounding more like the big, Mahler-esque epic rock of Rainbow than the leaner high-speed model he pursued with Sabbath. Dio has gone through its share of members—even a hiatus when Dio returned to Sabbath from 1991 to 1993—and was for a while the home of future Whitesnake and Def Leppard guitarist Vivian Campbell. The latest version of the band includes former Sabbath drummer Vinny Appice and ex-Dokken bassist Jeff Pilson.

what to buy: Dio's albums are largely interchangeable, so stick with the first, *Holy Diver* ♫♫♫ (Warner Bros., 1983), which benefits from the sound of a charged-up Dio and his band lighting out on a new adventure.

what to avoid: The live *Intermission* ♫ (Warner Bros., 1986) is a disappointment—there are far better recordings of Dio in concert with Rainbow and Sabbath.

the rest:
Seeds of Change ♫♫♫ (Rennaissance, 1980/1986)
Last in Line ♫♫♫ (Warner Bros., 1984)
Sacred Heart ♫♫ (Warner Bros., 1985)
Dream Evil ♫♫♫ (Reprise/Warner Bros., 1987)
Lock up the Wolves ♫♫ (Reprise, 1990)
Strange Highways ♫♫ (Reprise, 1994)
Angry Machines ♫♫♫ (Mayhem, 1996)
Inferno: Live in Line ♫♫♫ (Mayhem, 1998)

worth searching for: *Hear 'n Aid* (Mercury, 1986, prod. various) is the hard rock all-star project for famine relief—"We Are the World" in leather—that features "Stars," the communal song that Dio co-wrote and produced.

influences:
◀◀ Led Zeppelin, Deep Purple, Rainbow, Arthur Brown, King Crimson

▶▶ Metallica, Y&T, Queensryche, Soundgarden, Pearl Jam

see also: *Rainbow, Black Sabbath*

Gary Graff

Dion

Born Dion DiMucci, July 18, 1939, in the Bronx, NY.

Pulling themselves up from the street corners, Dion DiMucci and his band the Belmonts won national acclaim with the hit "I Wonder Why" in 1959; the group was also the fourth-billed act for the tour on which Buddy Holly died. But unlike the innumerable stars of the era that came and went in a flash, Dion showed staying power by forging a solo career that didn't rely on his doo-wop past, but evolved to fit the era of the singer-songwriter. Effectively beginning in 1960 with the #1 hit "Runaround Sue," he continued into various styles of rock 'n' roll and R&B. Maintaining a streetwise soulfulness, he has remained a figure in the fickle music industry for more than 30 years.

what to buy: *Runaround Sue* ♫♫♫♫ (Laurie, 1961/The Right Stuff, 1993, reissue prod. Eli Okun), his early '60s solo break, is highlighted by the title track, "The Wanderer," "The Majestic," and "Little Star." Classic stuff.

what to buy next: From 1962 to 1965, Dion branched out to sing blues, gospel, and country, and the best songs of that period are found in sterling sound quality and accompanied by informative liner notes on *Bronx Blues: The Columbia Recordings* ♫♫♫♫ (Columbia/Legacy, 1991, compilation prod. Greg Geller).

what to avoid: *When You Wish upon a Star* ♫♫ (1960/Collectables, 1983) has absolutely crappy sound.

the rest:
Lovers Who Wander ♫♫♫♫ (Laurie, 1962/The Right Stuff, 1993)

Dion 🎝🎝🎝 (Columbia, 1968/The Right Stuff, 1994)
The Return of the Wanderer 🎝🎝🎝🎝 (Lifesong, 1978/DCC, 1990)
Velvet and Steel 🎝🎝🎝 (Columbia, 1986/1991)
Yo, Frankie 🎝🎝🎝 (Arista, 1989)
Reunion: Live at the Madison Square Garden 1972 🎝🎝🎝 (Rhino, 1993)
The Road I'm On 🎝🎝🎝 (Legacy, 1997)

worth searching for: *The Fabulous Dion* (Ace) is a solid import greatest-hits collection with "Runaround Sue" and "The Wanderer."

influences:

◀◀ The Orioles, the Cadillacs, the Del-Vikings

▶▶ Lou Reed, Billy Joel, Paul Simon

Allan Orski

Celine Dion

Born March 30, 1968, in Charlemagne, Quebec, Canada.

Although American audiences only became aware of Celine Dion's five-octave vocal power in 1991 (she sang mostly in French until that point), she had been winning accolades as a singer since her teenage years in her native Canada. The child of working-class parents in a small town east of Montreal, Dion was introduced to current manager/husband Rene Angelil via a demo tape sent by her brother Michel. According to legend, Angelil was so taken by her ability that he mortgaged his home to pay for her first recording session. Through the '80s she built a strong following in Canada, but it wasn't until she sang the theme for Disney's hit animated film *Beauty and the Beast* in 1991 that Dion won over the masses. Her next English-language record, released in 1992, pushed her success further, but it was her 1993 album that truly made her a stateside star—featuring the schmaltzy duet "When I Fall in Love" from the film *Sleepless in Seattle* and the hit single "Power of Love." While fans fell for her VH1-style pop sound, critics disparaged her overtly commercial focus, penchant for cover tunes, and a soulless vocal dexterity that brought little passion to her work. Poised for a big splash with a 1996 English-language record, Dion's reputation was sullied slightly by a conflict with legendary producer Phil Spector, who dropped out of work on the album after tussling with her management over the record's focus. Still, the album remained among the country's 10 best-selling records more than 18 weeks after its release. In 1997, Dion's emotional delivery turned a song on the soundtrack of a movie about one of history's worst seafaring disasters—"My Heart Will Go On" from the movie *Titanic*—into a chart-topping hit of almost unimaginable proportions.

what to buy: As a true pop diva, Dion's best work is the one that has the most hit singles—*Celine Dion* 🎝🎝🎝 (Epic, 1992,

prod. Ric Wake, Humberto Gatica, Walter Afanasieff, Guy Roche). Produced by many of the same people who made Mariah Carey a household name, this record did the same for Dion, powered by singles such as "Beauty and the Beast" and "Love Can Move Mountains."

what to buy next: After that you'd need, of course, the next-biggest collection of hits. For Dion, that would be *The Colour of My Love* 🎝🎝🎝 (550 Music/Epic, 1993, prod. various), featuring the smash hit "Power of Love" along with her maudlin duet with singer Clive Griffin, "When I Fall in Love," from the film *Sleepless in Seattle*.

what to avoid: Dion's weakness is the same shared by many producer-created, hit-driven divas; in the search for ever-broader appeal, true emotion, passion, and creativity can get lost. Nowhere is that more apparent than on *Falling into You* **woof!** (Epic, 1996, prod. various), a soulless collection of pop pap aimed at baby boomers' wallets with more movie treacle like "Because You Loved Me" from the film *Up Close and Personal*.

the rest:
Incognito 🎝🎝🎝 (Sony Music Canada, 1988/1995)
Unison 🎝🎝🎝 (Epic, 1990)
Dion Chante Plamondon 🎝🎝🎝 (Sony Music Canada, 1991/1994)
Celine Dion a L'Olympia 🎝🎝🎝 (Sony Music Canada, 1994)
Premieres Anees 🎝🎝 (Tristar, 1994)
Des Mots Qui Sonnet 🎝🎝🎝 (Tristar, 1994)
French Album 🎝🎝🎝 (Epic, 1995)
D'eux 🎝🎝🎝 (Sony Music Canada, 1995)
Live a Paris 🎝🎝🎝 (Columbia, 1996)
Let's Talk about Love 🎝🎝🎝 (550 Music, 1997)
These Are Special Times N/A (550 Music, 1998)

worth searching for: Phil Spector claims to have masters from his *Falling into You* sessions with Dion—some recorded with a 60-piece orchestra. After his falling out with the singer, he threatened to mix them himself and release them on his own label.

influences:

◀◀ Mariah Carey, Barbra Streisand, Carly Simon

▶▶ Donna Lewis

Eric Deggans

Dire Straits

Formed 1977, in London, England.

Mark Knopfler, guitar, vocals; John Illsley, bass, vocals; David Knopfler, guitar (1977–80); Pick Withers, drums (1977–82); Hal Lindes, guitar (1980–85); Alan Clark, keyboards (1981–present); Terry Williams, drums (1982–86); Guy Fletcher, keyboards, vocals (1983–present).

During the late '70s, most new bands out of England fit into the

Mark Knopfler of Dire Straits (© Ken Settle)

punk/new wave category. Against the grain, Dire Straits released a self-titled LP that introduced the world to the double-fingered guitar picking of Mark Knopfler, a former school teacher whose skillful work showed country and blues influences with a rock and roll sensibility. Knopfler, with his brother David, a social worker, and friend and sociology student John Illsley began rehearsing Mark's compositions during late 1977 with drummer Withers, a session man from Dave Edmund's studios. The group's brand of rock—loaded with extended pieces considered passe at the time—took the U.K. and U.S. by storm, with its first single, "Sultans of Swing," charting extremely well in both countries. It wasn't until 1985, however, that Dire Straits would become a supergroup, thanks to its *Brothers in Arms* album—20 million copies sold worldwide—and the massive hit single, "Money for Nothing." Since then, however, the group's output has been spare, with Mark Knopfler seemingly more interested in his solo career and soundtrack work than in the band.

what to buy: *Making Movies* 𝄞𝄞𝄞𝄞 (Warner Bros., 1980, prod. Jimmy Iovine, Mark Knopfler) is one of rock's great records. The

songwriting and expert musicianship, combined with Knopfler's gruff vocals, display an impressive range, from the thematic "Tunnel of Love" and "Romeo and Juliet" to the irreverent "Skateaway" and the aptly named "Solid Rock." The band's debut, *Dire Straits* 𝄞𝄞𝄞𝄞 (Warner Bros., 1978, prod. Muff Winwood), hinted at what the band could do with solid tracks such as "Sultans of Swing" and "Water of Love," and Knopfler's guitar work instantly put him in a league with rock's masters. *Brothers in Arms* 𝄞𝄞𝄞𝄞 (Warner Bros., 1985, prod. Mark Knopfler, Neil Dorfsman) was the watershed point for the band, a shimmering, full-digital production—one of rock's first—that made Knopfler's evocative guitar parts seem like lyrics themselves. The songs were as strong as the sound, though, offering searing commentary in the anti-rock star anthem "Money for Nothing" (with guest vocalist Sting) and on power and politics in "The Man's Too Strong."

what to buy next: *Love over Gold* 𝄞𝄞𝄞 (Warner Bros., 1982, prod. Jerry Wexler, Barry Beckett) contains some solid tracks—including the epic "Telegraph Road" and "Private Investigations"—even if it isn't quite in the same league as the above

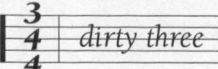

picks. *Money for Nothing* 🎵🎵🎵 (Warner Bros., 1988, prod. various) is a retrospective with loads of good numbers, although it lacks the cohesion of their finer studio records.

what to avoid: The band's most recent studio release, *On Every Street* 🎵 (Warner Bros., 1991), was six years in the making, and perhaps that was the problem for a prolific songwriter and producer like Knopfler. To follow up *Brothers in Arms* was a daunting task, and Knopfler choked.

the rest:
Communique 🎵🎵🎵 (Warner Bros., 1980)
Alchemy 🎵🎵🎵 (Warner Bros., 1984)
On the Night 🎵🎵 (Warner Bros., 1993)
Live at the BBC 🎵🎵🎵 (Warner Bros., 1995)
Sultans of Swing: The Very Best of Dire Straits N/A (Warner Bros., 1998)

worth searching for: *Twisting by the Pool* (Warner Bros., 1983, prod. Mark Knopfler) is a four-song EP that hints at the more pop-infused direction that was coming with *Brothers in Arms*.

solo outings:
Mark Knopfler:
Screenplaying 🎵🎵🎵 (Warner Bros., 1993)
(With the Notting Hillbillies) *Golden Heart* 🎵🎵🎵 (Warner Bros., 1996)
Missing . . . Presumed Having a Good Time 🎵🎵🎵 (Warner Bros., 1990)
(With Chet Atkins) *Neck and Neck* 🎵🎵 (Columbia, 1990)
Golden Heart 🎵🎵🎵🎵 (Warner Bros., 1996)
Wag the Dog 🎵🎵🎵🎵 (Mercury, 1998)

David Knopfler:
The Giver 🎵🎵🎵 (Mesa/Bluemoon, 1994)
Small Mercies 🎵🎵🎵 (Mesa/Bluemoon, 1995)

influences:

◀◀ Chet Atkins, Ry Cooder, Bob Dylan, Van Morrison

▶▶ Aztec Camera, John Hiatt, Mary Chapin Carpenter, the Mavericks

David Goldberg

Dirty Three

Formed 1993, in Melbourne, Australia.

Warren Ellis, violin, viola, piano; Mick Turner, guitar, organ, melodica; Jim White, drums, percussion.

Rarely has music ever been as melancholy as that performed by Australia's Dirty Three. It's entirely instrumental, with the odd combination of violin, guitar, and drums providing more depth than most vocal ensembles achieve. Often sounding improvisational, as if a jazz trio, Dirty Three records beautifully sad music that will never merit a Weird Al Yankovic cover but richly rewards repeated listenings. Warren Ellis's violin takes the role of lead instrument, cutting and flying across the songs, frantically searching for the perfect sound. Mick Turner's guitar sets the jagged backdrop for their truly arty sound, while Jim White's drums are alternately brushed and struck in a more musical than purely percussive manner. Not rock per se, Dirty Three is one of very few modern acts performing truly alternative music.

what to buy: Released as a double album—or, if you prefer, a single hour-plus CD, *Ocean Songs* 🎵🎵🎵🎵 (Touch & Go, 1998, prod. Steve Albini, Dirty Three) is a masterpiece. Thematically linked to the water, *Ocean Songs* sounds like the soul searchings of a doomed sailor. Bitterly introspective yet not vindictive, this epiphany of a record is nearly perfect, with songs that drift and shimmer, lulling you at one moment and jarring you the next. Listen in a darkened room with only a single candle for illumination. If you dare.

what to buy next: *Horse Stories* 🎵🎵🎵 (Touch & Go, 1996) is nearly as good as *Ocean Songs*; it displays a subtle variety of tones that's surprising from what should be a limited trio. No one-trick pony, Dirty Three succeeds in its own right, as a cleverly twisted band that speaks volumes without the use of a single vocal phrase. Songs such as "Hope" give them away as the sentimental lads they try not to be, but within this record's pained approach lies a feeling of hope.

the rest:
Sad & Dangerous 🎵🎵🎵 (Poon Village, 1994/Forced Exposure, 1995)
Dirty Three 🎵🎵🎵 (Touch & Go, 1995)

influences:

◀◀ Gastr Del Sol, Can, Captain Beefheart, Tortoise, the Velvet Underground

Barry M. Prickett

Dishwalla

Formed 1993, in Santa Barbara, CA.

Scot Alexander, bass, tabla, bells, synthesizer, vocals; Rodney Browning, guitar, vocals; George Pendergast, drums, percussion, vocals; J.R. Richards, vocals, Hammond organ, piano, synthesizer.

Just like its music, Dishwalla has blasé beginnings. Singer J.R. Richards met drummer George Pendergast in a music store when they were in their early teens. Pendergast's bandmate, bassist Scot Alexander, followed. The duo came across guitarist Rodney Browning literally in Richards's backyard, which doubles as his recording studio. Dishwalla performed around the Santa Barbara, California, area for years before getting recognition through its participation in the Carpenters tribute album.

what to buy: Dishwalla's debut, *Pet Your Friends* 🎵🎵 (A&M, 1995, prod. Phil Nicolo, Dishwalla), falls into the same generic rock category as Matchbox 20 and Tonic. With his exaggerated "look at me, I'm a rock star" vocals, Richards suggests that God may be a woman in the hit single "Counting Blue Cars." Unexpectedly, the song ends with a jazzy organ solo quite similar to that found in Ambrosia's hit "You're the Biggest Part of Me." "Haze" has potential to be a striking song, but the rest is not very interesting. Two songs on the album earn points for clever titles and subjects—"Charlie Brown's Parents" and "Miss Emma Peel," a nod to the character from television's *The Avengers*.

the rest:
And You Think You Know What Life's About 🎵🎵♩ (A&M, 1998)

influences:
◀◀ Ambrosia, dada, Supertramp

▶▶ Matchbox 20

Christina Fuoco

Divine Comedy

Formed 1991, in Ireland.

Neil Hannon, vocals, piano.

Divine Comedy is Neil Hannon—that's it. There was a band in the conventional sense on the early releases, but on the masterpieces, *Cassanova* and *A Short Album about Love*, it's just one man. One man who thinks he's great. Just ask him, he'll tell you. Lucky for him he truly is great, albeit a maestro of the kind of over-orchestrated, over-emotional, and over-dramatic poetry that went out of style when Scott Walker went off the deep end in the mid-'70s. Hannon, a bishop's son, lived a shy, waifish, and almost friendless childhood. Thank God he had a grand piano that his father never tired of listening to him hammer on. Divine Comedy's early efforts featured a tantalizing mix of electropop, new wave, and overly abundant literary references. Hannon came to England's attention when he shed his bandmates in 1996 and released *Cassanova*. The track "Something for the Weekend" became a minor hit, but Hannon himself, using words like "genuinely inspired" to describe his own work, became a star—on British soil, at least.

what to buy: On *A Short Album about Love* 🎵🎵🎵🎵♩ (Setanta, 1997, prod. Jon Jacobs, Neil Hannon)—especially in the chain-smoking, lovelorn masterpieces "Everyone Knows (I Love You)" and "If"—Hannon's tendency for simpy, syrupy arrangements and poetic lyrical indulgences peaks with his commandeering of a 32-piece orchestra.

what to buy next: *Cassanova* 🎵🎵🎵🎵♩ (Setanta, 1996, prod. Darren Allison, Neil Hannon), despite even more musicians than *A Short Album about Love*, is less orchestral and atmospheric. Highlights include the minor hit "Something for the Weekend,"

the unintentional Burt Bacharach tribute "Becoming More Like Alfie," and "The Frog Princess."

what to avoid: *Fanfare for the Comic Muse* 🎵 (Setanta, 1990) is an unfocused, jangly mess.

the rest:
Liberation 🎵🎵 (Setanta, 1993)
Promenade 🎵🎵🎵 (Setanta, 1994)

influences:
◀◀ Burt Bacharach, Scott Walker, Neil Diamond

▶▶ Tindersticks

Sam Wick

Divinyls

Formed 1980, in Sydney, Australia.

Christina Amphlett, vocals; Mark McEntee, guitar; Bjarre Ohlin, guitar, keyboards (1980–91); Rick Grossman, bass (1980–91); Richard Harvey, drums (1980–91).

The widespread audience that discovered Divinyls through its 1991 hit "I Touch Myself" likely knew little about the Australian band's long past or four previous albums. Songwriters and on-stage foils Christina Amphlett and Mark McEntee quickly became the most visible members of the group—she as a female Angus Young in a sexy schoolgirl getup, he as the stoic blond guitarist. Their music—a sometimes sweet, sometimes sleazy brand of Stones-ish rock—was much hyped during the '80s Australian mini-invasion spearheaded by INXS and Men at Work. Unfortunately, Divinyls had its one hit, placed a song on the 1994 *Melrose Place* soundtrack and hasn't been heard from since in the U.S. A subsequent album was available only in Australia, and Amphlett has begun applying her talents to musical theater.

what to buy: *Divinyls* 🎵🎵🎵🎵 (Virgin, 1990, prod. Divinyls, David Tickle) not only has the novelty value of "I Touch Myself" but also a consistent batch of lean rockers and cool ballads.

what to buy next: *Essential Divinyls* 🎵🎵🎵 (Chrysalis, 1991, prod. various) doesn't have the same level of easy melodicism as *Divinyls* but still gleans the cream from the group's releases prior to that breakthrough.

what to avoid: *What a Life!* 🎵 (Chrysalis, 1985, prod. Mark Opitz, Mike Chapman, Gary Langan) is a distressingly anonymous album that sounds more like the work of the production team than the band.

the rest:
Monkey Grip 🎵🎵🎵 (WEA, 1982)
Desperate 🎵🎵 (Chrysalis, 1983)
Temperamental 🎵🎵🎵🎵 (Chrysalis, 1988)

worth searching for: *Divinyls Live* is an official but unmarked 1991 promo release that features concert renditions of "I Touch Myself," "Temperamental," and "Guillotine."

influences:

◀◀ AC/DC, the Rolling Stones, Pat Benatar

▶▶ Hole, Magnapop

Todd Wicks

The Dixie Cups

Formed 1963, in New Orleans, LA.

Barbara Ann Hawkins, vocals; Rosa Lee Hawkins, vocals; Joan Marie Johnson, vocals (1963–66); Dale Mickle, vocals (1987–present).

The story of this New Orleans trio is inextricably linked to its career at Red Bird Records, an upstart New York City label founded in 1964 by rock 'n' roll veterans Jerry Leiber and Mike Stoller. Auditioning there a year after forming, the Dixie Cups were signed and immediately given "Chapel of Love," a song written by Phil Spector and Red Bird's in-house writers, Jeff Barry and Ellie Greenwich. Though the song had already been recorded twice with no commercial success, the Dixie Cups' version was a hit and spent three weeks at #1. The group followed it up with "People Say" and "Iko Iko"; the latter, recorded during an after-session jam, was adapted from a traditional New Orleans chant. Unfortunately, the Dixie Cups were soon beckoned to record for bigger labels. Without a team of established writers and sympathetic producers, however, the group floundered and eventually returned to Louisiana. Red Bird itself didn't survive the increasingly corporate environment of the record business, dissolving in the late '60s; it did provide, though, a blueprint for later, more successful artist-oriented labels such as Apple and Stiff. The Dixie Cups began touring extensively again after "Iko Iko" became a hit song from the 1988 film *Rain Man*.

worth searching for: The best way to sample "Chapel of Love" et al. is on *The Red Bird Sound, Volume One* (Diamond Recordings, 1997, compilation prod. Barry Lazell), the first in a U.K. series collecting material by the Dixie Cups alongside such labelmates as the Jelly Beans and the Butterflys. An important but often overlooked element of the Girl Group sound, these Red Bird productions were brilliant amalgamations of the Spector and Motown styles, and as such profoundly influenced late 1960s British pop and soul in particular.

influences:

◀◀ Joe Jones, the Marvelettes, the Chiffons, the Raindrops

▶▶ Wild Magnolias, the Belle Stars, the Pfister Sisters, Stormy Weather

Gary Pig Gold

The Dixie Dregs /The Dregs

Formed 1973, in FL. Disbanded 1982. Re-formed 1992.

Steve Morse, guitar (1973–82, 1992–94); Andy West, bass (1973–82); Rod Morgenstein, drums (1973–82, 1992–present); Steve Davidowski, keyboards (1973–77); T Lavitz, keyboards (1978–82, 1992–present); Allen Sloan, electric violin (1973–80, 1992); Mark Parrish, keyboards (1977–82); Mark O'Connor, violin (1980–82); David LaRue, bass (1992–present); Jerry Goodman, violin (1992–present).

With a wild inventive streak, brilliant musicians, serious (sometimes serio-comic) arrangements, and flawless execution, the Dixie Dregs showered listeners with an explosion of notes on their dynamic 1977 debut, *Free Fall*. Frontman and lead guitarist Steve Morse assembled the heart of the band while studying at University of Miami's School of Music. What separates the Dregs (which dropped the "Dixie" in 1981) from a host of other fusion bands is their sense of humor; complex, cosmic jazz-inflected boogie performed at warp-speed envelops popular music melodies and careens into percussive, highly textured jazz, rock, and country romps. It's heady music, steered with a firm hand by Morse. There is plenty of subtlety to be detected, too—though that detection must be made at a frenetic pace. Simply put, Morse is a guitar guru whose mantra does not include the word restraint, though, thankfully, it does include melody. Proof of the Dregs' artistry is found in their live recordings; with fast tempo, rhythm, melody, and key changes, the group members' potent musicianship rings clear without a lot of processing or chicanery. An odd career excursion took Morse into the fold of the middleweight rock group Kansas for two ignored albums during the mid-'80s. More recently, he's gone on to take the guitar chair in Deep Purple.

what to buy: *Divided We Stand: Best of the Dixie Dregs* ♪♪♪♪ (Arista, 1989, prod. Steve Morse) offers a solid sampling of the Dregs' formative work on Capricorn during the late '70s and early '80s. Included are such well-structured and -executed songs as "Cruise Control," "Take It off the Top," and "Twiggs Approved." But at 44 minutes, it's a little sparse.

what to buy next: The Dregs flex an impressive amount of creative muscle on *What If* ♪♪♪ (Polydor, 1978, prod. Ken Scott), with its funky, shifting tempos on "Ice Cakes"; a country, funk grin on "Gina Lola Breakdown"; the sweeping "Night Meets Light"; and one of the most beautiful guitar solos ever recorded in the melancholy "What If." Morse's *Structural Damage* ♪♪♪♪ (High Street, 1995, prod. Steve Morse, Dave LaRue) finds him working in a trio format, soaring on his guitar with the encumbrance of keyboards.

the rest:

Night of the Living Dregs ♪♪♪ (Polydor, 1979)

Bring 'Em Back Alive ♪♪♪ (Capricorn, 1992)
Full Circle ♪♪♪♪ (Capricorn, 1994)
King Biscuit Flower Hour Presents: The Dixie Dregs ♪♪♪ (King Biscuit Entertainment, 1997)

solo outings:

Steve Morse:

The Introduction ♪♪♥ (Elektra Musician, 1984)
High Tension Wires ♪♪ (MCA, 1989)
Southern Steel ♪♪ (MCA 1991)
Coast to Coast ♪♪♪♥ (MCA, 1992)
Stress Fest ♪♪♪♥ (High Street, 1996)

influences:

◀◀ The Flock, Frank Zappa, Mahavishnu Orchestra, Weather Report

▶▶ Col. Bruce Hampton & the Aquarium Rescue Unit, Michael Hedges

see also: *Deep Purple, Kansas*

Patrick McCarty

Don Dixon

Born December 13, 1950, in Lancaster, SC.

Don Dixon's name appears in fine print on some of the finest pop albums of the '80s, from his engineering stint with Mitch Easter on R.E.M.'s *Reckoning* to production credits on the Smithereens' *Especially for You*, Marshall Crenshaw's *Mary Jean and 9 Others*, Guadalcanal Diary's *Flip Flop*, and wife Marti Jones's *Used Guitars*. But the former lead singer for the North Carolina rock band Arrogance has made his best music on the other side of the mixing board, where his affection for British Invasion pop, Memphis soul, and new wave quirkiness has resulted in a small but smartly crafted catalog of solo albums that proudly rank with the best work of fellow pop purists Crenshaw and Nick Lowe. Recently, Dixon and Jones became the first pop acts signed to country-bluegrass label Sugar Hill Records, and he has been winning rave reviews for his role in a musical called *King Mackerel and the Blues Are Running*, which also stars Bland Simpson of the Red Clay Ramblers and *Pump Boys and Dinettes* composer Jim Wann.

what to buy: *Most of the Girls Like to Dance but Only Some of the Boys Like To* ♪♪♪♥ (Enigma, 1985, prod. Don Dixon) is mostly demos and live tracks. But the ragged charms of "Praying Mantis," "You're a Big Girl Now," "Southside Girl," and the marvelous title track make this sound more like the product of a playground than a studio. *EEE* ♪♪♪♪ (Enigma, 1989, prod. Don Dixon) is the most consistent example of his offbeat production style and musical range, including the Elvis

Costello–like "Oh Cheap Chatter" and soulful covers of James Carr's "Dark End of the Street," Brenton Wood's "Gimme Little Sign," and John Hiatt's "Love Gets Strange."

what to buy next: A fine retrospective, *If I'm a Ham, Well, You're a Sausage* ♪♪♪♪ (Restless, 1992, prod. Don Dixon) gathers 15 of his best songs and adds the previously unreleased "Teenage Suicide (Don't Do It)," which he penned and performed for the dark teen comedy *Heathers*.

what to avoid: *The Chi-Town Budget Show* ♪♪♥ (Enigma, 1989, prod. Don Dixon) is a live radio broadcast replete with muffed lyrics and frenetic pacing that makes it more of a souvenir than a statement.

the rest:

Romeo at Julliard ♪♪♪ (Enigma, 1987)
Romantic Depressive ♪♪♪♥ (Sugar Hill, 1995)

worth searching for: Dixon provides lead vocals on *Hillbilly Fever* (Upstart, 1997, prod. Michael Lipton), the twangy debut by West Virginia guitar phenom Robert Shafer that is built around covers of Carl Perkins, alt-country stalwart Tim Carroll, and even Kitty Wells ("Will Your Lawyer Talk to God").

influences:

◀◀ Percy Sledge, the Searchers, Nick Lowe

▶▶ Marti Jones, Hootie & the Blowfish, John Hiatt

David Okamoto

DJ Krush

Birthdate and birthplace unknown.

While DJ Shadow was making noise stateside with a decidedly progressive brand of abstract hip-hop, his eventual MoWax labelmate DJ Krush was doing likewise in Japan, although Krush's warm soundscapes lean on jazz much harder than Shadow's moody breakbeat collages.

what to buy: Guest appearances by jazz-minded MCs CL Smooth, Guru, and the Roots' Black Thought and Malik B. are a nice touch, but *Meiso* ♪♪♪♪ (MoWax, 1996, prod. DJ Krush) is clearly Krush's show as he concocts a series of soothing, dynamic, ambient soundscapes that rarely meander. Fellow abstract hip-hop heavyweight DJ Shadow emerges from the album's shadows, too, for the stunning "Duality."

what to buy next: Old-school beats and older-school horn lines mark the improvisational *DJ Krush* ♪♪♪♪ (Shadow, 1995, prod. DJ Krush), on which Krush is joined by capable Japanese jazz musicians.

the rest:

MiLight ♪♪♪♪ (MoWax/ffrr/London, 1997)

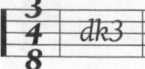

influences:

◄◄ DJ Premier, Ali Shaheed Muhammad

►► DJ Honda

Josh Freedom du Lac

DK3
/Denison/Kimball Trio

Formed 1994, in Chicago, IL.

Duane Denison, guitar; Jim Kimball, drums; Ken Vandermark, saxophones (1997–present).

The DK3 began as a duo. Its namesake members are best known for their "day jobs" in the Midwest noise-rock scene (both are currently members of the Jesus Lizard, and Kimball has also been the drummer in Laughing Hyenas and Mule). But they began moonlighting as an atmospheric, jazz-influenced instrumental combo, first by scoring the soundtrack for an independent film, Jim Sikora's *Walls in the City.* Concerts showed off a quieter, improvisational aspect to their playing, with Jim Kimball using brushes and Duane Denison in Wes Montgomery mode—these guys were "post-rock" long before British journalists caught their first whiff of fellow Chicago scenesters Tortoise. Later, the formidable free-jazz improviser Ken Vandermark (Vandermark 5, NRG Ensemble) joined, and the duo became a true trio.

what to buy: *Neutrons* 𝄢𝄢𝄢𝄢 (Quarterstick, 1997, recorded by Jeff Lane), Vandermark's first outing as a full-fledged band member, touches on jazz improvisation, movie-soundtrack textures, rock aggression, and even some electronic, studio-as-an-instrument experimentation.

what to buy next: *Soul Machine* 𝄢𝄢𝄢𝄢 (Skin Graft, 1995, prod. D/K Trio, Casey Rice) finds Denison and Kimball fleshing out their sound with a handful of guests, including Vandermark, Seam's Reg Schrader, and Jesus Lizard's David Wm. Sims. The highlight is a swinging version of Ornette Coleman's "Lonely Woman," rearranged for guitar and drums.

the rest:
Walls in the City 𝄢𝄢𝄢 (Skin Graft, 1994)

influences:

◄◄ Ennio Morricone, Ornette Coleman, Miles Davis, Chet Baker

Greg Kot

DM3

See: The Someloves

DMZ

Formed 1976, in Boston, MA. Disbanded 1978.

Jeff "Mono Mann" Conolly, vocals, keyboards; J.J. Rassler, guitar; Peter Greenberg, guitar (1976); Mike Lewis, bass (1976); Mike Lewis (a different one), drums (1976); Adam Schwartz, vocals (1976); David Robinson, drums (1976); Rick Coraccio, bass (1976–78); Paul Murphy, drums (1976–78); Preston Wayne, guitar (1978).

DMZ was one of the first bands to make an overt connection with the original punk rock of the '60s—the brash, sloppy party music slurred through by the likes of the Standells, the Seeds, the Raiders, the Sonics, and the 13th Floor Elevators. Fronted by maniacal raver Jeff Conolly, DMZ reveled in trash aesthetic but eschewed any trace of condescension or camp. How could it be otherwise, given Conolly's stated goal "of trying to fuse the Chocolate Watch Band with the Stooges"? Conolly could wail like a man possessed (or like Roky Erickson of the 13th Floor Elevators—same thing, really) while showing off the depth of his cool record collection with dips into the Pretty Things, Troggs, Flamin' Groovies, and Wailers songbooks, and with rampaging original tunes of an identical garage-punk mindset.

what to buy: *When I Get Off* 𝄢𝄢𝄢𝄢 (Voxx, 1993) is the essential DMZ set, collecting 18 primal sides—some previously unreleased—but all crackling with vibrant, grungedelic shake 'n' sweat.

worth searching for: You might want to track down *DMZ* (Sire, 1978, prod. Flo & Eddie), the group's sole official album, but it doesn't even come close to matching the intensity of *When I Get Off.*

influences:

◄◄ The Standells, the Seeds, the Raiders, the Sonics, the 13th Floor Elevators

►► Black Flag, Fugazi, Circle Jerks

see also: *The Lyres*

Carl Cafarelli

DNA

Formed 1977, in New York, NY. Disbanded 1982.

Arto Lindsay, guitar, vocals; Ikue Ile Mori, drums; Robin Crutchfield, keyboards (1977–78); Tim Wright, bass, guitar (1978–82).

Rejecting rock norms, DNA stood in the forefront of the late '70s downtown Manhattan movement dubbed No Wave, which went past punk and new wave into more radical recastings of musical structure while still using rock instrumentation. This trio was the first context for Arto Lindsay's astonishingly nonchordal, self-taught guitar style. Basically linear, albeit knotty, it leaves lots of space for the other musicians, whose parts are intertwined rather than stacked within a hierarchy. Such an approach implies conciseness and equality, which on a piece such as "Calling to Phone" can strip the music down to a collection of discrete rhythmic outbursts. Lindsay's singing often matches this guitar style as he compacts lyrics and blurts them out in a rush, like bursts of electronic information coming across in bunched form rather than smoothly. It's as close as rock has come to the ultra-expressive miniatures of serialist composer Anton Webern, and it's unrelated to the equally short but more conventionally structured mini-song thrashings of hardcore punk. The extreme spareness of DNA's material, in which no sound is casual or superfluous, heightens the impact of every single moment and action. After DNA broke up, Lindsay played with the Lounge Lizards and James Chance before forming a new group, Ambitious Lovers, and working under his own name. Tim Wright played with David Byrne and Brian Eno. Ile Mori played violin, viola, and cello with Mars and recorded a solo album.

what to buy: The four-band compilation *No New York* ♫♫♫ (Antilles, 1978, prod. Brian Eno) shows the early DNA lineup, with keyboardist Robin Crutchfield, playing closer to normal rock structures than on later efforts—but it's still far from the mainstream. *Live at CBGB* ♫♫♫ (Avant, 1993, prod. DNA), documenting the group's 1982 farewell concert, offers concert versions of all six pieces on *A Taste of DNA* as well as another nine tracks, all showing the final evolution of the group's sound.

worth searching for: The single "Little Ants/You and You" (Medical Records/Lust\Unlust Music, 1978, prod. Robert Quine), the group's debut, shows it at its most aggressive and unschooled. *A Taste of DNA* (American Clave, 1980, prod. DNA), with six songs in less than 10 minutes, severely deconstructs rock gestures and then compacts them into a new musical language. It's the pinnacle of DNA's aesthetic, and to this day there's never been anything quite like it.

solo outings:
Ikue Ile Mori:
Painted Desert ♫♫♫ (DIW, 1995)

influences:
◄◄ Derek Bailey, Television, Pere Ubu

►► Lounge Lizards, John Zorn, Marc Ribot, Bill Frisell

see also: *Ambitious Lovers, Arto Lindsay, Peter Scherer*

Steve Holtje

Dr. Buzzard's Original Savannah Band

See: Kid Creole & the Coconuts

Dr. Hook & the Medicine Show /Dr. Hook

Formed 1968, in Union City, NJ. Disbanded 1985. Reunited 1988.

Original members: Ray Sawyer, vocals, guitar, piano; Dennis Locorriere, vocals, guitar, bass, harmonica; William Francis, keyboards, percussion; George Cummings, pedal steel guitar, vocals; John "Jay" David, drums. Other members: Jance Garfat, bass; Rick Elswit, guitar, vocals; John Walters, drums, vocals.

The only group in history to shamelessly campaign for its photo on the cover of Rolling Stone magazine through a hit song—and have its dream come true the following year (after which the members each bought five copies for their mothers, just as the lyrics promised)—Dr. Hook & the Medicine Show got its start as a cover band in New Jersey. Ray Sawyer, the group's founder, christened himself "Dr. Hook" due to the trademark black eye patch he wears. Developing a rock parody style full of eccentric and off-color humor, the band was asked to be backup musicians for new material by quirky songwriter-cartoonist Shel Silverstein. It included a crop of Silverstein songs on its 1971 debut outing, which featured the pseudo-sentimental Top 10 hit "Sylvia's Mother," and recorded for and appeared in the Dustin Hoffman movie *Who Is Harry Kellerman and Why Is He Saying Those Terrible Things about Me?* that same year. The group managed to capture the inspired looniness of its stage show on its next—and generally considered its best—album, *Sloppy Seconds*, also composed by Silverstein. The band had another Top 10 hit with "The Cover of *Rolling Stone*" before venturing out to write its own material for the next release. It was a questionable move: Dr. Hook & the Medicine Show quickly went broke, filing for bankruptcy in 1974 and falling off the Columbia roster. The following year the group shortened its name to Dr. Hook, signed with Capitol (where its first album was titled "Bankrupt") and reemerged as a force in the soft-rock market. It went on to have a string of Top 10 hits, from "When You're in Love with a Beautiful Woman" to its cover of Sam Cooke's "Only Sixteen." A long-simmering internal rivalry between Sawyer and Dennis Locorriere came to a head when Sawyer left in 1984, with the band splintering a year later. Sawyer returned to touring in 1988, reviving the Dr. Hook name with a new lineup, while Locorriere served as a backup singer on Randy Travis's *Always & Forever* LP before emerging as a solo performer in 1991.

what to buy: There are at least four different Dr. Hook greatest hits albums available—which is as it should be, since this is a group most memorable for its lyrical, bawdy singles. However, because the band's catalog is divided among several labels, the quality of the compilations is grossly uneven. *Dr. Hook's*

Greatest Hits (and More) 🎵🎵🎵 (Capitol/EMI, 1980, prod. Ron Haffkine) offers the most comprehensive look at Hook, including all the requisite hits ("The Cover of *Rolling Stone*," "Sylvia's Mother," "Only Sixteen," "When You're in Love with a Beautiful Woman") as well as a representative sampling of solid second-tier tunes ("Sexy Eyes," "Better Love Next Time"). It's absent "Queen of the Silver Dollar," but hey, nothing's perfect.

what to buy next: Possibly no band used double entendre to greater effect than Dr. Hook. The LP that catapulted the group to prominence, *Sloppy Seconds* 🎵🎵🎵 (Columbia, 1972/1989, prod. Ron Haffkine), remains a hallmark of lusty, crusty country rock, highlighted by the Silverstein masterpiece "Freakin' at the Freakers Ball," the hookers' anthem "Queen of the Silver Dollar," and "Get My Rocks Off." The CD reissue includes a bonus track that apparently has to do with the search for a lost kitten: it's called "Looking for Pussy."

what to avoid: *Dr. Hook: At His Best* 🎵 (Queen, 1996). No, he's not.

the rest:
Dr. Hook and the Medicine Show 🎵🎵🎵 (Sony, 1972/1992)
Dr. Hook Revisited 🎵🎵🎵 (Sony, 1977/1987)
Dr. Hook's Greatest Hits 🎵🎵🎵 (CEMA Special Projects, 1992/1994)
Sharing the Night Together 🎵🎵🎵 (CEMA Special Projects, 1992/1994)
Rx Dr. Hook 🎵🎵 (Sony, 1996)

influences:
◄◄ Shel Silverstein, Jerry Lee Lewis, Bobby Bare, Jerry Reed, Delbert McClinton, Nitty Gritty Dirt Band

►► Firefall, Gene Cotton, Amazing Rhythm Aces, Pure Prairie League, Billy Swan

Jeff Hatch and Jim McFarlin

Dr. John

Born Malcolm John "Mac" Rebennack Jr., November 21, 1940, in New Orleans, LA.

With his spooky, voodoo-drenched debut as the Night Tripper in 1967 and his guided tour of New Orleans roots music on *Dr. John's Gumbo* in 1972, Dr. John paved the way for America's discovery of the Crescent City's rich musical heritage. It was Dr. John who led listeners to legendary New Orleans artists such as Professor Longhair and Huey "Piano" Smith. And his 1973 hits "Right Place, Wrong Time" and "Such a Night" helped bring national attention to regional stars such as the Meters and Allen Toussaint. Born and raised in New Orleans, Rebennack already was performing and recording in his teens, mainly as a guitarist. But it was his funky piano and distinctive gravelly drawl that made him a star with the release of the *In the Right Place* album in 1973. Financial and drug problems plagued him well into the '80s, but the growing popularity of New Orleans music helped him regain his stride. Today, he reigns as the acknowledged master of the New Orleans sound; no one has done more to popularize it.

what to buy: *Mos' Scocious* 🎵🎵🎵🎵 (Rhino, 1993, prod. various) is the definitive Dr. John anthology—a two-CD set that begins with rare early sides cut with local bands such as Ronnie & the Delinquents, then marches on through more than 30 years of the doctor's finest. A virtual encyclopedia of the New Orleans sound. *The Very Best of Dr. John* 🎵🎵🎵 (Rhino, 1995, prod. various) is a single-CD collection that skims the cream of *Mos' Scocious*. *Dr. John's Gumbo* 🎵🎵🎵 (Atlantic, 1972, prod. Jerry Wexler, Harold Battiste) is Dr. John's landmark tribute to the Crescent City's R&B roots—while, a year later, *In the Right Place* 🎵🎵🎵 (Atco, 1973, prod. Allen Toussaint) gave him a hit. (Both *Gumbo* and *In the Right Place* are combined on a Mobile Fidelity Sound Lab 24K disc.)

what to buy next: *Goin' Back to New Orleans* 🎵🎵🎵 (Warner Bros., 1992, prod. Stewart Levine) is another fine reflection of his early influences, with lots of stellar guest artists. *In a Sentimental Mood* 🎵🎵🎵 (Warner Bros., 1989, prod. Tommy LiPuma) is Rebennack's career-reviving take on standards such as "Makin' Whoopee" (a Grammy-winning duet with Rickie Lee Jones) and "Accentuate the Positive." And have your mojo hand ready should you fall under the hoodoo spell of the Night Tripper on *Gris Gris* 🎵🎵🎵 (Atco, 1968).

what to avoid: *At His Best* 🎵🎵🎵 (Special Music Co., 1989) is a set that's been rendered redundant by the several more complete best-ofs.

the rest:
The Ultimate Dr. John 🎵🎵🎵 (Warner Bros., 1987)
The Brightest Smile in Town 🎵🎵🎵 (Clean Cuts, 1989)
Afterglow 🎵🎵🎵 (Blue Thumb, 1995)
Trippin' Live 🎵🎵🎵 (Surefire, 1997)
Anutha Zone 🎵🎵🎵 (Virgin/Pointblank, 1998)

worth searching for: An import CD of formative, loose-limbed 1960s sessions, *Cut Me While I'm Hot* (Magnum America) is well worth finding.

influences:
◄◄ Professor Longhair, James Booker, Tuts Washington, Joe Liggins, Huey (Piano) Smith

►► The Neville Brothers, Marcia Ball, the Radiators

Doug Pippin

Dr. Octagon
See: Kool Keith

Dodgy

Formed 1992, in Hounslow, England. Disbanded 1998.

Andy Miller, lead guitar, vocals; Nigel Clark, bass, vocals; Matthew Priest, drums.

While Oasis climbed to the top of the international charts with shameless comparisons to the Beatles, the also British Dodgy unintentionally dodged fame in America, despite having hits in its homeland. In fact, Mercury Records gave up on this trio at the last minute, canceling plans to release its third album, *Free Sweet Peace*, in the States after promos had already been sent out. That's a shame, because Dodgy is responsible for perhaps the best pop albums in England, making use of every inch of sonic space with crevice-filling vocals and far-reaching melodies. As a bonus, the group doesn't emulate, or brag about emulating, past icons; it doesn't even necessarily sound British. Getting by on a simple diet of great songwriting and beguiling harmonies, Dodgy has made albums that are pure nourishment for pop people. A Dodgy compilation is planned for imminent release in Britain.

worth searching for: All three of Dodgy's albums are only available as imports, but they should be easily found or ordered. *The Dodgy Album* (A&M, 1993, prod. Ian Broudie), is the perfect place to start—imagine a cross between the early Who, the Beatles, and the Moody Blues. The follow-up, *Homegrown* (A&M, 1994, prod. Hugh Jones, Ian Broudie), is equally fine. *Free Peace Sweet* (A&M, 1996, prod. Hugh Jones) continues the group's devotion to harmony.

influences:
◄◄ The Beatles, Squeeze, the Who, the Moody Blues

Jordan Oakes

John Doe

See: X

Dogma

Formed 1994, in Brooklyn, NY.

Phil Allocco, guitar, vocals, keyboards; Sean Carmody, bass; Dave Femia, drums; Randy Dzielak, guitar.

Friends since high school, Sean Carmody and Phil Allocco tried for years in a variety of band combinations to enter the music business, encountering frustration and complications at every turn. But while none of their initial efforts panned out, they did end up learning some valuable lessons, the major one being to avoid the business of music and to start having fun. To that end they found bassist Randy Dzielak in a *Village Voice* ad, recruited pal Dave Femia to play the drums, and subsequently began playing the kind of heavy rock 'n' roll they believed in.

Who cared about the big picture? Of course, as soon as they forgot about that big picture, they were awarded the distinction of becoming the first rock band signed to the rap-focused Def Jam label.

what's available: The band's first album, *Feeding the Future* ✧✧ (Def Jam/King Recordings, 1997, prod. Steve Thompson), is an earnest collection of hard-hitting alternative rock, led by Alloco's candid story songs and the band's voracious enthusiasm.

influences:
◄◄ Hüsker Dü, Helmet, Led Zeppelin

Bob Gulla

The Dogmatics

Formed 1981, in Boston, MA. Disbanded 1986.

Pete O'Halloran, guitar, vocals; Paul O'Halloran, bass, vocals; Jerry Lehane, guitar, vocals; Tommy Long, drums.

Mainly a local attraction in Boston's mid-'80s modern rock scene, the Dogmatics was a decidedly less polished bunch of slopmeisters than most of its peers. The band slapped together rudimentary, beer-spittin' rock 'n' roll with a ruckus-making disregard for anything other than a garage band's clanging. Therein lies the charm, for the Dogmatics apparently had no artistic ambitions. Paul O'Halloran was killed in a motorcycle wreck in 1986, which effectively ended the band.

worth searching for: The now out-of-print *The Dogmatics: 1981–86* (Vagrant Records, 1995, prod. Johnny Angel) is a career-spanning, 20-track sampler covering the band's lewd three-chord bursts and proto-punk rockabilly. It presents the band in its proper (dirty basement window) light.

influences:
◄◄ Eddie Cochran, Dion, the Dictators

Allan Orski

Dog's Eye View

Formed 1995, in New York, NY.

Peter Stuart, guitar, vocals; Alan Bezozi, drums, percussion; John Abbey, guitar, bass, cello (1995–96); Marvin Etzioni, mandolin, guitar (1995–96); Oren Bloedow, dobro, guitar, lap steel guitar (1995–96); Tim Bradshaw, guitar, vocals (1996–present); Dermot Lynch, bass (1996–present).

Singer-songwriter Peter Stuart, fueled both by the death of his father when Stuart was eight years old and his passion for the music of Cat Stevens, developed a solo career opening shows for Tori Amos, Cracker, and Counting Crows; his incendiary and good-humored performances often convinced those in the crowd to take a chance on the homemade cassettes he sold at the gigs. But after getting a major label record deal, Stuart decided to build a band around his earnest, heartrending tunes, which were of a piece with the fare of Counting Crows and Hootie & the Blowfish. It worked for one buzz-building album, but when the second failed to match, Stuart shifted gears and is presently working on a new album that will reportedly come out under his own name.

what to buy: The dreamy and evocative *Happy Nowhere* 𝄢𝄢𝄢 (Sony, 1995, prod. James Barton) features the single "Everything Falls Apart," which became a hit thanks to months of touring and promotion. There's more to the album than that, however, and it rightly established Stuart's as one of the few voices worth paying attention to in a crowded field.

the rest:
Daisy 𝄢𝄢𝄢 (Sony, 1997)

influences:
◀◀ XTC, Bob Dylan, Cheap Trick, Elvis Costello, Counting Crows

Eric Deggans

Dogstar

Formed 1990, in Los Angeles, CA.

Keanu Reeves, bass, vocals; Bret Domrose, guitar, vocals; Rob Mailhouse, drums.

Originally formed as a way for movie star Keanu Reeves (*Speed, Bill and Ted's Excellent Adventure*) to blow off steam between projects, Dogstar never stood apart from its bassist's long shadow. Though the group sold out dates across the country during a 1995 tour, one listen to its raggedy, garage-band sound on its only album establishes the fact that those fans were responding more to Reeves's movie-star appeal than any musical quality. Fortunately for the rest of us, the album was only sold at gigs after Dogstar's label, Zoo, shut down before its release.

what to avoid: *Our Little Visionary* 𝄢𝄢 (self-released, 1996). 'Nuf said.

influences:
◀◀ Nirvana, Pearl Jam, Jane's Addiction

Eric Deggans

Dokken

Formed 1979, in Hollywood, CA. Disbanded 1988. Re-formed 1995.

Don Dokken, vocals; George Lynch, guitar (1982–88, 1995–97); Juan Croucier, bass (1979–83); Jeff Pilson, bass; (1983–present); Mick Brown, drums.

Though undeniably a product of the big-hair glam rock scene that exploded in Los Angeles during the early '80s, Dokken dis-

played a little more talent and musicianship than many of its peers—due mostly to Don Dokken's strong, versatile vocals and Lynch's flashy, melodic guitar work. After several years of relative success, including a slot alongside Metallica, Scorpions, and Van Halen in 1988's "Monsters of Rock" tour, friction between Dokken and Lynch peaked, causing the band to split up. Lynch and Brown formed a new band, Lynch Mob, while Dokken recorded a solo album. In 1992 the band reformed, but its once-rabid fans barely noticed.

what to buy: *Tooth and Nail* 𝄢𝄢𝄢𝄢 (Elektra, 1984, prod. Tom Werman), the first album with Pilson (original bassist Croucier left to join Ratt), is probably as good as Dokken is capable of. With radio hits such as "Into the Fire" and "Alone Again (Without You)," Lynch emerged as a standout in the crowded field of speedy Hollywood guitarists.

what to buy next: Though not as consistently satisfying as *Tooth and Nail*, *Under Lock and Key* 𝄢𝄢𝄢 (Elektra, 1985, prod. Neil Kernon, Michael Wagner) features some of the band's best songs, "In My Dreams" and "It's Not Love."

what to avoid: *Back for the Attack* 𝄢 (Electra, 1987, prod. Neil Kernon) appears to be where the band ran out of ideas. It's disjointed, derivative, and dull, dull, dull.

the rest:
Back on the Streets 𝄢𝄢 (Carrere, 1979)
Breaking the Chains 𝄢𝄢𝄢 (Elektra, 1983)
Beast from the East 𝄢𝄢 (Elektra, 1988)
Greatest Hits 𝄢𝄢𝄢 (Warner Bros., 1994)
Dokken 𝄢𝄢 (Victor, 1994)
One Live Night 𝄢𝄢𝄢 (CMC International, 1995)
Dysfunctional 𝄢𝄢 (Columbia, 1995)
Shadowlife 𝄢𝄢 (CMC, 1997)

solo outings:
Lynch Mob:
Wicked Sensation 𝄢𝄢𝄢 (Elektra, 1990)
Lynch Mob 𝄢𝄢 (Elektra, 1992)

George Lynch:
Sacred Groove 𝄢𝄢𝄢 (Elektra, 1993)

Don Dokken:
Up from the Ashes 𝄢𝄢 (Geffen, 1990)

War & Peace:
Time Capsule 𝄢 (Shrapnel, 1991)

influences:
◀◀ AC/DC, Van Halen, Black Sabbath, Ozzy Osbourne, Judas Priest

Brandon Trenz

George Lynch of Dokken (© Ken Settle)

Thomas Dolby

Born Thomas Morgan Robertson, October 14, 1958, in Cairo, Egypt.

The son of a respected British archaeologist, Thomas Dolby made his reputation as a songwriter-producer-backing musician for new wave siren Lena Lovich, mainstream rockers Foreigner, singer-songwriter Joan Armatrading, and even rappers Whodini. Stepping out on his own during the early '80s, Dolby became known as a wirehead extraordinaire, creating witty, extravagant synth-pop singles filled with electronic keyboards, percussion, and his own frantic vocals. His solo efforts benefited from forays into film soundtracks and outside production work, with later efforts integrating more organic sounds and complex sonic textures. By the '90s, Dolby had also branched into computer programs, presenting the soundtrack to a video game as his most recent solo release.

what to buy: Dolby's breakthrough debut, *The Golden Age of Wireless* &&&& (Capitol, 1982, prod. Thomas Dolby, Tim Friese-Green), cements his image as a synth-pop mad scientist, fueled by the success of the whimsical single, "She Blinded Me with Science." Harnessing an impressive array of keyboards to service an inventive and hook-laden collection of songs, the album serves as a perfect introduction to Dolby's twisted sonic world.

what to buy next: His third full-length release, *Aliens Ate My Buick* &&&& (EMI Manhattan, 1988, prod. Thomas Dolby, Bill Bottrell), brings all of Dolby's disparate artistic sides together—the wittily acerbic rock/pop of "Airhead," the complex atmospherics of "Budapest by Blimp," and members of George Clinton's P-Funk All Stars on "May the Cube Be with You."

what to avoid: Generally, Dolby's soundtrack work has been the weak link in his efforts, with the 1986 soundtracks for the movies *Gothic* and *Howard the Duck* filled with pointless atmospherics and pointless pop tunes, respectively.

the rest:
The Flat Earth &&&& (EMI, 1984)
Astronauts and Heretics &&&& (Giant, 1992)
The Gate to the Mind's Eye && (Giant, 1994)
The Best of Thomas Dolby: Retrospectacle &&&& (Capitol, 1995)

worth searching for: *Live Wireless*, an extended video tour document from the early '80s, provides a fascinating look at Dolby's creative process, while *The Gate* (Miramar Productions, 1994) is a full-length video album available on video and laserdisc with breathtaking visuals to accompany the "Mind's Eye" sonics.

influences:
◀◀ Frank Zappa, George Clinton, Gary Wright, Kraftwerk

▶▶ Trent Reznor, Beck, Self

Eric Deggans

Fats Domino

Born Antoine Domino, February 26, 1928, in New Orleans, LA.

Not only is Fats Domino responsible for an astounding 63 charted singles and more than 65 million in record sales, but he did it with nothing more than pure musical charm. A short-statured man of ample girth, Domino possessed none of the titillating antics or wild personality traits of contemporaries such as Little Richard and Chuck Berry. Instead, he smiled and let the rolling triplets of his piano and his warm New Orleans drawl steer his never-ending string of self-penned hits. Nearly everything the man recorded has a rollicking charm and gentleness, and they retain their impact and innocence to this day. He cut his first hit, "The Fat Man," in 1949; it is arguably one of the first rock 'n' roll songs. The rest is music history, and it would be difficult to overstate Domino's influence.

what to buy: The four-disc box set *They Call Me the Fat Man* &&&&& (EMI, 1991, prod. Dave Bartholomew) chronicles his stay at the Imperial label and renders almost every other release redundant. It includes hits such as "Blueberry Hill," "Ain't That a Shame," "Walkin' to New Orleans," "I'm Walkin'," and "Whole Lotta Lovin'." *My Blue Heaven* &&&&& (EMI, 1990, prod. Dave Bartholomew) is a fine introductory single-disc sampler to the warm Creole sound of the Fat Man.

what to buy next: *Antoine "Fats" Domino* &&&&& (Tomato, 1992, prod. Kevin Eggers, Robert G. Vernon) is a vivacious live document, recorded when Domino was 61 and still in full possession of all his friendly energy. Plus, it offers a good version of "Red Sails in the Sunset."

what to avoid: *Christmas Is a Special Day* && (The Right Stuff/EMI, 1993). Yes it is. So buy the box set and leave the caroling to cardigan-clad setsters such as Perry Como.

the rest:
The Best of Fats &&& (Pair, 1990)
All-Time Greatest Hits &&& (Curb, 1991)
Best of Fats Domino Live, Vol. 1 &&& (Curb, 1992)
Best of Fats Domino Live, Vol. 2 &&& (Curb, 1992)
Fats Domino—The Fat Man: 25 Classics &&&&& (EMI, 1996)
That's Fats! A Tribute to Fats Domino &&& (EMI, 1996)

worth searching for: *Out of New Orleans* (Bear Family, 1993) is an eight-disc import that presents the complete Imperial recordings, along with unedited alternate takes and a 72-page book containing extensive liner notes and a complete sessionography.

influences:
◀◀ Big Joe Turner, Louis Jordan, Professor Longhair

▶▶ Van Morrison, Paul Simon, Billy Joel, Bruce Hornsby, the Neville Brothers, Allen Toussaint

Allan Orski

Lonnie Donegan

Born Anthony James Donegan, April 29, 1931, in Glasgow, Scotland.

Scottish guitarist Lonnie Donegan plundered the catalogs of American folk singers (such as Leadbelly and Woody Guthrie) and in turn inspired a generation of British rock heroes such as Cliff Richard and John Lennon. A regular performer on Britain's jazz circuit—he supposedly took his stage name from blues guitarist Lonnie Johnson—Donegan was England's undisputed leader of skiffle, a down-and-dirty brand of uptempo folk played on acoustic guitars, washboards, and tea-chest bass. His version of "Rock Island Line" became an instant U.K. hit in 1955, and skiffle groups appeared practically overnight throughout the country thanks to the music's simplicity and the high availability of common instruments. The craze lasted through 1959, when Donegan was knocked out of the charts by the very rock 'n' roll acts he helped inspire. Following a lengthy absence due to a heart attack, he returned in 1978 with "Putting on the Style," an all-star skiffle record featuring Ringo Starr, Brian May, Elton John, and other musicians inspired by his music.

what to buy: For a solid introduction to Donegan, check out *Collection* 🎵🎵🎵 (Castle Communications, 1989, prod. various), a single-disc sampler of essential Donegan tracks.

worth searching for: If *Collection* whets your appetite—in a big way only—move on up to the import *More than Pie in the Sky* (Bear Family, 1993), a massive eight-CD box set stuffed to the gills with 209 tracks.

influences:
◀◀ Leadbelly, Woody Guthrie, Hank Williams, the Weavers

▶▶ Bob Dylan, the Beatles, the British Invasion

Christopher Scapelliti

Donovan

Born Donovan Leitch, February 10, 1946, in Glasgow, Scotland.

An early British folky-turned-pop-star, Donovan incorporated rock and psychedelic elements into his music during the mid- and late '60s. From such tender ditties as "Catch the Wind" in 1965 to the grinding buzz of 1968's "Hurdy Gurdy Man" (with guitarist Jeff Beck), Donovan was all over the stylistic map. His credibility suffered from an early and much-hyped comparison to Bob Dylan, but producer Mickie Most molded Donovan from a reformed folkie to a pop singer with clever lyrics and wit—which started the "e-lect-ri-cal banana" craze of "Mellow Yellow." From pop star, Donovan changed colors again and turned himself into an early new ager. And all of these transitions took place in a span of only four or five years. From 1965 to 1969 he released 14 albums, making him something of a one-man

British Invasion with hits like "Universal Soldier," "Colours," "Wear Your Love Like Heaven," "Season of the Witch," "Atlantis," and "Barabajagal." But after that his career declined rapidly, as if so much work so soon had sapped Donovan of his creative strength. His work from the late '70s into the '80s was eminently forgettable. In 1996 he plotted a comeback with modern rock and rap producer Rick Rubin and a new album, *Sutras*. It, too, misfired.

what to buy: *Troubadour: The Definitive Collection 1964–1976* 🎵🎵🎵🎵 (Legacy, 1992, prod. various) is the one stop to hear his best. This comprehensive collection—handpicked by Donovan—includes 44 songs and all of his hits.

what to avoid: *The Classics Live* **woof!** (Great Northern Arts Ltd., 1991) is an unfortunate concert recording, best left unheard.

the rest:
Catch the Wind 🎵🎵🎵 (Hickory, 1965/Sequel, 1996)
Fairytale 🎵🎵🎵 (Hickory, 1966/Castle, 1996)
Sunshine Superman 🎵🎵🎵 (Epic, 1966/Legacy 1990)
A Gift from a Flower to a Garden 🎵🎵🎵 (Epic, 1967/Beat Goes On, 1994)
Hurdy Gurdy Man 🎵🎵🎵 (Epic, 1968/1986)
Barabajagal 🎵🎵🎵 (Epic, 1969/1987)
Greatest Hits 🎵🎵🎵 (Epic, 1987)
In Concert 🎵🎵 (Beat Goes On, 1994)
Peace & Love Songs 🎵🎵🎵 (Sony Music Special Products, 1996)
Golden Hits 🎵🎵🎵 (ITC Masters, 1996)
Sunshine Superman: 20 Songs Of 🎵🎵🎵 (Remember, 1996)
Sutras 🎵🎵 (American, 1996)
Performance 🎵🎵🎵 (Beacon, 1997)
Mellow 🎵🎵🎵 (Recall, 1997)

worth searching for: *Mellow Yellow* (Epic, 1967), one of his more consistent '60s albums, has yet to see the laser light of CD reissue. Its title track is a defining piece of '60s pop counterculture.

influences:
◀◀ Bob Dylan, the Beatles

▶▶ David Crosby, XTC/Dukes of Stratosphear, the Housemartins

Patrick McCarty

The Doobie Brothers

Formed 1970, in San Jose, CA. Disbanded 1982. Re-formed 1987.

Tom Johnston, guitar, vocals (1970–77, 1987–present); Patrick Simmons, guitar vocals (1970–82, 1987–present); John Hartman, drums (1970–78, 1987–present); Dave Shogren, bass (1970–71); Tiran Porter, bass, vocals (1971–81, 1987–present); Michael Hossack, drums (1971–73, 1987–present); Keith Knudsen, drums (1973–83); Jeff "Skunk" Baxter, guitar (1974–78); Michael McDonald, keyboards, vocals (1975–82, 1995–present); John McFee, guitar (1979–82); Chet

McCracken, drums, (1979–82); Cornelius Bumpus, sax, keyboards (1979–82); Willie Weeks, bass (1982); Bobby LaKind, percussion, (1987–present).

The Doobie Brothers thought themselves bad boys at the start of their career, flaunting their friendship with the San Jose biker scene and naming themselves—nudge, nudge, wink, wink—after a slang name for a marijuana joint. Like the Allman Brothers, they had a multiple-guitar front flanked by a double-drum foundation. But by the end of the group's first run at the charts, the Doobies were chasing after mainstream acceptance with pop pap, and their musical base was the electric keyboard. The balance switched with the mid-career addition of Michael McDonald, the sultry-voiced singer and keyboardist who joined the group after several years of singing with Steely Dan. McDonald's first album with the group, *Takin' It to the Streets*, steered the Doobies away from their double-guitar country-boogie into an urbane, faux-sophisticated R&B style. Early fans cried sellout; new fans thought early FM hits such as "China Grove" and "Long Train Runnin'" were gauche and trashy. Truth be told, neither version of the group made music for the ages, though their hits—especially those written by Pat Simmons, whose love for folk music led to the prettiest picking and melodies throughout the Doobies' career—are fun to hear again. Once in a while, anyway. Like many '70s groups that broke up in the early '80s, the Doobies (more or less the original version), reunited in 1987 for a couple more albums and money-making tours.

what to buy: *Toulouse Street* 🎵🎵🎵 (Warner Bros., 1972, prod. Ted Templeman) is the strongest effort of the pre-McDonald group. Though it didn't include the biggest hits, it did have a nice balance of hard rock á la "Rockin' Down the Highway" and folksiness in the better-known version of the Byrds' "Jesus Is Just Alright." *Takin' It to the Streets* 🎵🎵🎵 (Warner Bros., 1976, prod. Ted Templeman) is the first and best of the latter-day Doobies, with McDonald bringing his voice to hits like "It Keeps You Running" and the title track, with Johnston still around to add a little rock 'n' roll grit.

what to buy next: You can't lose with hits compilations for a band whose strength was singles. Stick with *Best of the Doobies* 🎵🎵🎵 (Warner Bros., 1976, prod. Ted Templeman) and *The Best of the Doobies, Volume II* 🎵🎵🎵 (Warner Bros., 1981, Ted Templeman).

what to avoid: Tired, retread ideas are all you'll hear on the reunion albums *Cycles* **woof!** (Capitol, 1989, prod. Rodney Mills) and *Brotherhood* **woof!** (Capitol, 1991, prod. Rodney Mills).

the rest:
The Doobie Brothers 🎵🎵 (Warner Bros., 1971)
The Captain and Me 🎵🎵🎵 (Warner Bros., 1973)

What Were Once Vices Are Now Habits 🎵🎵🎵 (Warner Bros., 1974)
Stampede 🎵🎵 (Warner Bros., 1975)
Livin' on the Faultline 🎵🎵🎵 (Warner Bros., 1977)
Minute by Minute 🎵🎵🎵 (Warner Bros., 1978)
One Step Closer 🎵🎵 (Warner Bros., 1980)
The Doobie Brothers Farewell Tour 🎵 (Warner Bros., 1983)
Rockin' Down the Highway: The Wildlife Concert 🎵🎵🎵 (Legacy, 1996)

worth searching for: *Listen to the Music* (Warner Bros., 1993, prod. Ted Templeman) is a British best-of that's fatter and more complete than either of its domestic counterparts.

solo outings:
Tom Johnston:
Everything You've Heard Is True 🎵 (Warner Bros., 1979)
Still Feels Good 🎵 (Warner Bros., 1981)

Patrick Simmons:
Arcade 🎵🎵 (Elektra, 1983)

Michael McDonald:
If That's What It Takes 🎵🎵 (Warner Bros., 1982)
No Lookin' Back 🎵🎵 (Warner Bros., 1985)
Take It to Heart 🎵 (Reprise, 1990)
Blink of an Eye 🎵🎵 (Reprise, 1993)
Blue Obsession 🎵🎵 (Reprise, 1997)

influences:

◄◄ The Allman Brothers Band, Moby Grape, Hot Tuna

►► The Georgia Satellites, the Black Crowes, the Screamin' Cheetah Wheelies

Gil Asakawa

The Doors

Formed 1965, in Los Angeles, CA. Disbanded 1973.

Jim Morrison (died July 3, 1971), vocals, Robby Krieger, guitar; John Densmore, drums; Ray Manzarek, keyboards.

Who but the Doors could have comfortably covered both Weill/Brecht ("Alabama Song") and Howlin' Wolf ("Back Door Man") on the same album? That they did it on their debut, in between their own masterpieces like "Break on Through" and "Light My Fire," only makes it all the more impressive. The Doors were true originals—nobody before or after has ever sounded quite like them. The band's music tended toward the dark even while most of their peers were preaching all-we-need-is-love utopianism, prefiguring the grisly, violent end of the peace-and-love era. They also brought the seamy underside of southern California to light at a time when the nation was California dreamin'. The focus rightly tends to go to Jim Morrison, the hyper-charismatic and super-pretty frontman who was also a commanding, dramatic singer and fine rock poet (the latter should not be confused with *real* poet, by the

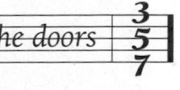

Jim Morrison of the Doors (© Jack Vartoogian)

$\frac{3}{5}$
$\frac{}{8}$ | *lee dorsey* |

way). The minimalist, atmospheric music of Robby Krieger, Ray Manzarek, and John Densmore created the perfect frame for Morrison's lyrics. The band's love for the blues became increasingly clear over the course of their amazingly prolific career—six studio albums in five years. In a strange way, the band's sloppy original take captured the spirit of the blues better than any of their peers' slavish, overly reverential imitations. It's pointless to speculate what the future may have held for the Doors, but the fact that the band's last album before Morrison's death, *L.A. Woman*, was one of its best certainly indicates that there was plenty of good music left.

what to buy: As a starting point, you couldn't do better than to begin at the beginning. All of the Doors' most notable traits are apparent on *The Doors* ♫♫♫♫ (Elektra, 1967, prod. Paul Rothchild)—acid-on-the-beach philosophy ("Break on Through"), palatable avant gardism ("The Crystal Ship"), a unique take on the blues ("Back Door Man"), paisley pop masterpieces ("Light My Fire"), and extended mind trips ("The End"). *Morrison Hotel* (Elektra, 1970, prod. Paul Rothchild) kicks off with "Roadhouse Blues" and never really looks back, as the Doors sound more and more like a hard-hitting rock band. Its swan song, *L.A. Woman* ♫♫♫♫ (Elektra, 1971, prod. Bruce Botnick), is also a masterpiece, all the more poignant for the fact that Morrison sounds distinctly tired throughout—in a good way. It's looser, bluesier, and more bare-bones than anything that preceded it.

what to buy next: *Strange Days* ♫♫♫♫ (Elektra, 1967, prod. Paul Rothchild) lacks some of the debut's swagger, but it's still quite fine. The heavily orchestrated *The Soft Parade* ♫♫♫♫ (Elektra, 1969, prod. Paul Rothchild) is uneven, but tends toward the great and includes some of the band's most ambitious, original material.

what to avoid: *American Prayer* ♫♫ (Elektra, 1978/1995, prod. the Doors), featuring Morrison reading poetry to the Doors' musical accompaniment, is for cult members only.

the rest:
Waiting for the Sun ♫♫♫♫ (Elektra, 1968)
Thirteen ♫♫♫♫ (Elektra, 1970)
Best of the Doors ♫♫♫♫ (Elektra, 1980)
Classics ♫♫ (Elektra, 1985)
In Concert ♫♫♫♫ (Elektra, 1991)
The Doors Box Set ♫♫♫♫ (Elektra, 1997)

worth searching for: The out-of-print compilation *Weird Scenes Inside the Gold Mine* (Elektra, 1972, prod. various) is a perfect overview, though the regular albums are still the way to go.

solo outings:
Robby Krieger:
RKO Live ♫♫♫ (One Way, 1995)

Ray Manzarek:
(With Michael McClure) *Love Lion* ♫♫ (Shanachie, 1993)
The Doors, Myth and Reality: The Spoken Word History ♫♫♫♫ (Monster Sounds, 1996)

influences:
◄◄ Willie Dixon, Howlin' Wolf, Jimmy Reed, Bertolt Brecht
►► Jane's Addiction, Patti Smith, the Cult, INXS, Marilyn Manson, Lords of the New Church

Alan Paul

Lee Dorsey
Born December 24, 1926, in New Orleans, LA. Died December 1, 1986, in New Orleans, LA.

Lee Dorsey's Allen Toussaint–produced sessions sound almost like collaborations between the two—Toussaint fitting his own high, light, almost faint vocals against Dorsey's on monuments such as "Workin' in a Coal Mine" and "Yes We Can." But it is easy to understand the producer's attraction to Dorsey's rough-hewn, chunky vocal style, sharpened considerably on a series of vernacular R&B hits during the early '60s, most notably "Ya Ya." When the hits ran dry for Dorsey, who continued to occasionally make fine records with Toussaint long past his chart life, he simply relied on his prosperous New Orleans auto body shop for a livelihood, banging out dents for all the city's taxi cabs. But Dorsey remained a popular figure, cutting a duet with Southside Johnny & the Asbury Jukes and opening a 1980 U.S. tour for the Clash—not to mention his virtually annual appearances at the New Orleans Jazz and Heritage Festival.

what to buy: The 20-song *Wheelin' and Dealin': The Definitive Collection* ♫♫♫♫ (Arista Masters, 1997, compilation prod. Bob Irwin) is just what it claims to be—all of Dorsey's hit singles, remastered from the original tapes, in the most sparkling sound quality yet available.

what to buy next: *Golden Classics* ♫♫♫ (Collectables, 1993, prod. various) has mid-'60s Toussaint-produced tracks ("Workin' in a Coal Mine," "Holy Cow") along with samples of Dorsey's worthy earlier work from the "Ya Ya" era, when he recorded for Bobby Robinson's Fury label.

the rest:
Great Googa Mooga ♫♫♫ (Charly, 1991)
Ya Ya ♫♫♫♫ (Relic, 1994)

worth searching for: Recently deleted, Dorsey's 1970 masterpiece *Yes We Can*—also a high-water mark for producer-arranger-writer Toussaint—had been released on CD in expanded form as *Yes We Can . . . and Then Some* (Polydor, 1970/1993, prod. Allen Toussaint). Though the work wasn't necessarily improved by adding outtakes and miscellaneous singles, the frequently covered "Freedom for the Stallion" is a welcome, fitting inclusion. Also, the final Dorsey-Toussaint collaboration, *Night People* (ABC, 1978, prod. Allen Toussaint), is one of the great lost R&B albums of the disco era—not that Toussaint's supple funk has anything to do with disco.

influences:

◀◀ Professor Longhair, Ray Charles, Huey Piano Smith

▶▶ The Pointer Sisters, Robert Palmer, Devo

Joel Selvin and Ken Burke

Dos

See: fIREHOSE

Down

See: Pantera

Downy Mildew

Formed c. early 1980s, in Los Angeles, CA.

Charlie Baldonado, vocals, guitar, piano, organ; Jenny Homer, guitar, vocals; Nancy McCoy, bass, cello; Mike Marasse, drums, percussion.

One of the most well-known bands around southern California during the late '80s, Downy Mildew built a reputation that depended as much on the company it kept as its music. One of Downy Mildew's biggest supporters was R.E.M. frontman Michael Stipe, who became friends with the quartet and could often be spotted at its L.A. gigs. Downy Mildew even had the chance to back up Stipe and then–10,000 Maniacs singer Natalie Merchant at a benefit at McCabe's Guitar Shop, adding greatly to the group's So. Cal legacy. Despite support from college radio nationwide, the band was never able to transcend cult status. Ironically, Downy Mildew's greatest asset was its timeless sound, but the success of Mazzy Star and bands of that ilk indicates that Downy Mildew may have just been ahead of its time.

what to buy: The band's second CD, *Broomtree* ⟡⟡⟡ (Texas Hotel, 1997), is a prototypical '80s college rock record, with jangly guitars, enthusiastic vocals, engaging melodies, and a variety of tempos. The record is effective when the group attempts to rock out, like on "Sally Pt. III" and "Burnt Bridges." However, its neo-psychedelic moments, such as the pseudo-swirl of the aptly-named "Good Dream," the influence of Pink Floyd (circa *Wish You Were Here*) on "Hollow Girl," or the lavish orchestration of "Ocean Motorkid" are where the record moves into unique terrain. At its best, listening to Downy Mildew is like walking into a lush, Technicolor dream.

the rest:

Downy Mildew EP ⟡⟡⟠ (Texas Hotel, 1986)

Mincing Steps ⟡⟡⟡ (Texas Hotel, 1988)

influences:

◀◀ The Velvet Underground, R.E.M., Marianne Faithfull

▶▶ Mazzy Star, Tarnation

Steve Baltin

Nick Drake

Born June 19, 1948, in Rangoon, Burma. Died November 25, 1974, in Tanworth-in-Arden, England.

Of all the names to come out of the English folk movement of the late 1960s, only Nick Drake had to wait some 20 years after his death to be recognized for his achievements and impact. During his brief life, Drake released three touching, heartfelt albums that met with critical adulation and public dismissal. This lack of commercial acceptance sent the already melancholy Drake into an even deeper state of depression. Through his pain, or perhaps because of it, Drake was able to write songs that were at times personal, often mystical, sometimes tragic, and always enchanting. Behind the English lilt of his hush-be-quiet voice was Drake's radiant and hypnotic guitar playing, a lyrical triad of alternate tunings, complex chord progressions, and intricate finger picking. But, his chronic shyness and aversion to performing live did little to get his name in front of those who could have appreciated him while he was alive. A few months after beginning to record his fourth album, Drake overdosed on Tryptizol, an antidepressant medication. The coroner declared it a suicide, though friends and family disagreed. Today, interest in Drake is far greater than it ever was while he was alive, with his CDs reaching a new audience and generating talk about tribute albums and a feature film about his life.

what to buy: Even with the lush background of Robert Kirby's string arrangements, the delicate power of Drake's acoustic guitar rings through *Bryter Layter* ⟡⟡⟡⟡ (Island/Hannibal, 1970, prod. Joe Boyd). The jazzy "One of These Things First" and "At the Chime of the City Clock" share space with haunting instrumentals and emotionally intense love songs such as "Northern Sky." Drake reportedly recorded the songs on *Pink Moon* ⟡⟡⟡⟡⟡ (Island/Hannibal, 1972, prod. Nick Drake) in two days, with just his voice and a guitar, then without a word dropped the tape off at the Island Records reception desk and disappeared. After several days someone opened the package and realized they had the new Nick Drake album. After a few listens, this scenario makes perfect sense; he said all he needed to with one voice, six strings, and 11 songs.

what to buy next: Drake's first album, *Five Leaves Left* ⟡⟡⟡⟡ (Island/Hannibal, 1969, prod. Joe Boyd), was recorded when he was just 20 years old. But he belies his youth with skillful playing, and the production blends his guitar, voice, and string arrangements magnificently. "Cello Song" is as close to perfection as it gets. *Time of No Reply* ♫♫♫ (Hannibal, 1986, prod. Joe Boyd, Frank Kornelussen) consists of unreleased songs recorded during the *Five Leaves Left* sessions, as well as home recordings and four songs recorded in 1974 that were to be included on Drake's fourth album. All are solo acoustic performances except for an alternate version of "The Thoughts of Mary Jane," which features Richard Thompson on electric guitar. Once you're hooked, splurge for *Fruit Tree* ♫♫♫ (Hannibal, 1986, prod. Joe Boyd), a four-CD box set that contains all three original releases and *Time of No Reply*, along with a 16-page booklet.

the rest:

Way to Blue: An Introduction to Nick Drake ♫♫♫ (Hannibal, 1994)

worth searching for: *Tanworth-in-Arden 1967/68* is an Italian bootleg that features 18 tracks, mostly cover songs, from a homemade tape. *The Complete Home Recordings* (Boyds Music) is a German bootleg featuring 24 tracks.

influences:

◀◀ The Beatles, Tim Buckley, Bob Dylan, Tim Hardin, John Renbourn, Joni Mitchell

▶▶ Jeff Buckley, the Cure, Mark Eitzel, J Mascis, R.E.M., the Smiths, Paul Weller

Brian Escamilla

Dramarama

Formed 1982, in Wayne, NJ. Disbanded 1994.

John Easdale, vocals, acoustic guitar; Chris Carter, bass; Mark "Mr. E. Boy" Englert, guitar, e-bow, mandolin; Peter Wood, guitar; Theothorous Athanasious Ellenis, keyboards (1982–87); Jesse Farbam, drums (1982–90); Tim Edmondson, drums (1990); Brian MacLeod, drums (1990); Clem Burke, drums (1993–94).

Full of pop culture references and the sounds of '60s and '70s mainstream rock, this group's trademark mixture of Beatles melodicism, Rolling Stones energy, and New York Dolls glampunk never quite earned it the attention it deserved, though Los Angeles DJ Rodney Bingenheimer's enthusiasm and support made the first album's "Anything, Anything (I'll Give You)" a local hit (in 1994 the listeners of KROQ, where Bingenheimer deejays, voted it the #1 modern rock song of all time). But the group's first two albums had to be made for French labels, and when it did get signed in America, it was by a label (Chameleon) that led an intermittent existence. Drummer Jesse Farbam (who was always credited as simply Jesse) quit just before the *Vinyl* sessions to join an eastern religious sect and was replaced by Wire Train's Brian Macleod (for the recording) and by Tim Edmondson (on tour); ex-Blondie skinsman Clem Burke

joined for the group's swan song. Chameleon went under for the last time in 1993, though the albums remain available, and the group dissolved the following year. After taking time off, which included working as a writer and editor, frontman John Easdale made his solo debut in 1998.

what to buy: The six-song *Live at the China Club* ♫♫♫♫ (Chameleon EP, 1990, prod. Val Garay) is the perfect introduction to the band, with frenetic, barely controlled energy harnessed to the band's most memorable tunes ("Last Cigarette" is the highlight) plus a cover of the New York Dolls' "Private World." *Vinyl* ♫♫♫ (Chameleon, 1991, prod. Don Smith, Chris Carter, John Easdale) is Dramarama's most consistent full-length album, a fuller embodiment of the band's belief in the rock verities.

what to buy next: Besides "Anything, Anything," the best tunes on the low-budget debut, *Cinema Verite . . . Plus* ♫♫♫ (New Rose, France, 1985/Rhino, 1995, prod. Chris Carter, John Easdale), are "Scenario," "Some Crazy Dame," and "All I Want." The Rhino reissue adds eight bonus tracks, mostly demos. *18 Big Ones* ♫♫♫ (Rhino, 1996, prod. various) is a useful if not ideal compilation baited with some rarities.

the rest:

Box Office Bomb . . . Plus ♫♫♫ (Questionmark, France, 1987/Rhino, 1995)
Stuck in Wonderamaland ♫♫♫♫ (Chameleon, 1989)
Hi-Fi Sci-Fi ♫♫♫ (Chameleon, 1993)

worth searching for: For some reason *Looking Through . . .* (Eggbert, 1994, prod. Chris Carter, John Easdale) is credited to the Bent Backed Tulips (it's a Beatles reference). It collects 1988 outtakes from *Stuck in Wonderamaland*, some of which came out in France on a shorter 1992 album of the same name. The grab-bag aspects make it uneven, but there are some good tunes, with more acoustic-based songs than usual.

solo outings:

John Easdale:
Bright Side ♫♫♫ (Harvey/Eggbert, 1998)

influences:

◀◀ The Rolling Stones, the New York Dolls, Neil Young, Mott the Hoople, Blondie, dB's

▶▶ The Gin Blossoms, Tragically Hip, Velvet Crush

Steve Holtje

Dread Zeppelin

Formed 1989, in Los Angeles, CA.

Fresh Cheese & Cheese, drums (1989–91); Butt Boy (a.k.a. Gary B.I.B.B.), "porn bass," lead vocals (as B.I.B.B. in 1992), guitar; Jah

Paul Jo, guitar (1989–95); Carl Jah, guitar (1989–94); Tortelvis, vocals, tacos (1989–91, 1993–present); Ed Zeppelin, congas, reggae love vibes (1989–91, 1993–94); Spice, drums (1992–94); Rasta Li-Mon, keyboards (1992–present); Fernandez (Ed Zeppelin's "twin brother"), congas (1994–present); Derf Nasna-Haj, bass (1995–present); SilverShower Raven, drums (1995–present).

WARNING! If you're religiously in love with the music of Led Zeppelin, then you may want to avert your eyes from this entry. This is the story of Dread Zeppelin, a band of fellas who thought it would be a good idea to re-record some of Led Zeppelin's material . . . as reggae songs, featuring the singing of an overweight, jumpsuit-era Elvis impersonator. Guess what? It *was* a good idea. The Wagnerian pomposity of Led Zeppelin was ripe for satire, and Dread Zeppelin's irreverent wit (its 1995 album is titled *No Quarter Pounder*) was just the ticket. With the corpulent talents of vocalist Tortelvis out front, this merry band of genre-confused lads offers some of the most creative and hilarious rock parody this side of Spinal Tap. Not content with the mere gimmick of their delivery, Dread Zeppelin also took the pains to create an entire faux history for the band, replete with seamy pasts, illegitimate offspring, and overripe indulgences (band lore also states that the band played their first live gig on Elvis's birthday, January 8th, which, using the transatlantic time difference to fudge the numbers, is also Led Zeppelin founder Jimmy Page's birthday). Tortelvis briefly left the building in 1991—to return two years later—and the general Dread Zeppelin sound stayed consistent. Or, if you will, the song remained the same.

what to buy: Of its available catalog, Dread Zeppelin's major-label debut—the prophetically titled *Un-Led-Ed* ♫♫♫♫ (I.R.S., 1990, prod. Rasta Li-Mon, Jah Paul Jo)—is easily its most inspired and enjoyable recording. The wacko hybrid of Zeppelin stompers and reggae rhythms is deliciously effective and, at times, induces an epiphanous delirium—you listen to this stuff enough and you may start to believe that nature intended "Heartbreaker" to segue into Elvis Presley's "Heartbreak Hotel." Irie!

what to buy next: *5,000,000* ♫♫♫ (IRS, 1991, prod. Jah Paul Jo, Rasta Li-Mon) is more of the same from the calypso-crazed hammer of the gods. This release finds the band still mining (and having its rasta way with) the classic Led Zeppelin catalog—including a typically goofball mauling of "Stairway to Heaven"—along with some non-Zeppelin tunes such as the Yardbirds' "Train Kept a Rollin'." By the end of this album, however, the joke is beginning to repeat itself.

what to avoid: *It's Not Unusual* **woof!** (I.R.S., 1992, prod. Jah Paul Jo, Rasta Li-Mon) is a misguided attempt to apply the band's schtick to disco hits of the 1970s, with Butt Boy (transformed to Gary B.I.B.B.) vainly attempting to fill the considerable girth of Tortelvis's jumpsuit.

the rest:
Hot and Spicy Beanburger ♫♫♫ (Birdcage, 1993)
The First No-Elvis ♫♫♫ (Birdcage, 1994)
No Quarter Pounder ♫♫♫ (Birdcage, 1995)
The Fun Sessions ♫♫ (Cash Cow, 1995)

worth searching for: *Live on Blueberry Cheesecake* (Cash Cow, 1996) is a live set that offers a neat snapshot of the spectacle that is a Dread Zeppelin concert—though Tortelvis really must be *seen* to be truly believed.

influences:

◄◄ Vegas-era Elvis Presley, Led Zeppelin, Bob Marley, Weird Al Yankovic, Spinal Tap

►► Are you kidding? Nobody sounds like these guys.

David Galens

The Dream Academy

Formed 1983, in London, England.

Gilbert Gabriel, keyboards; Nick Laird-Clowes, vocals, guitar; Kate St. John, vocals, oboe, saxophone.

Adhering to a '60s psychedelic-pop aesthetic (Pink Floyd's David Gilmour was a patron), the nostalgic "Life in a Northern Town," with its dreamlike chanting "Hey-ah ma-ma-ma" chorus, got this trio a lucky break in 1985. The employment of a timpani and cellos almost cover up Laird-Clowes's bland singing, which typifies the group's sophisticated but pointless and backward-looking meanderings. Out of this, though, reed player Kate St. John has carved a solo niche, guesting on a number of albums, including those by Van Morrison, Blur, and Everything but the Girl, doing soundtrack work, and releasing albums of her own.

worth searching for: As all of the Dream Academy's material is out of print, you're left to search for *Remembrance Days* (Reprise, 1987), which contains "Life in a Northern Town" (the title of which was supposedly suggested by Paul Simon to save fans the embarrassment of walking up to the record counter and just chanting).

solo outings:
Kate St. John:
Indescribable Night ♫♫♫♫ (Gyroscope, 1995)
Second Sight ♫♫♫♫ (Thirsty Ear, 1997)

influences:

◄◄ The Beatles, the Association, the Moody Blues

Allan Orski and Daniel Durchholz

The Dream Syndicate
/Steve Wynn
/Opal
/Guild of Temporal Adventurers
/Kendra Smith

Formed 1981, in Los Angeles, CA. Disbanded 1989.

Steve Wynn, guitar, vocals; Karl Precoda, guitar (1981–84); Paul Cutler, guitar (1985–89); Kendra Smith, bass, vocals (1981–83); Dave Provost, bass (1983–84); Mark Walton, bass (1985–89); Dennis Duck, drums.

The name came from Faust-member Tony Conrad's album *Outside the Dream Syndicate*, which ironically was a reference (apparently unknown to Steve Wynn) to a '60s band that featured Conrad, minimalist composer LaMonte Young, and John Cale, who went on to join the Velvet Underground—a group that Wynn's Dream Syndicate continually was compared to, though he brazenly denied any influence. Lumped in with the so-called Paisley Underground of the early '80s West Coast despite a less psychedelic sound, the band basically did what Wynn felt like doing (which led Kendra Smith and then Karl Precoda to quit), with Wynn's muse eventually taking him into more of a country-rock sound. It might have worked if the quality of his writing hadn't faded. After Dream Syndicate broke up, Wynn went on to an intermittent solo career, sometimes guesting during the mid-'90s with Mark Walton's Continental Drifters. Smith went on, for a time, to the somnolent Opal.

what to buy: The original quartet's debut, *The Days of Wine and Roses* ♫♫♫♫ (Slash/Ruby, 1982, prod. Chris Desjardins), remains the group's finest moment, thanks to Wynn's haunting songs ("Tell Me When It's Over," "When You Smile") and the perfect VU-style reproduction.

what to buy next: In the absence of most of the catalog, *Tell Me When It's Over: The Best of Dream Syndicate* ♫♫♫♫ (Rhino, 1992, prod. various) will have to do. *The Day before Wine and Roses* ♫♫♫♫ (Atavistic, 1995) is from a 1982 radio gig; all three of the live tracks on the EP *Tell Me When It's Over* ♫♫♫ (Rough Trade, 1983) were from this concert and are on the CD. Smith's *Five Ways of Disappearing* ♫♫♫♫ (4AD, 1995, prod. Kendra Smith, A. Phillip Uberman) radiates the expected VU-like drones, but with a stronger love of melody and instrumental variety than in her Dream Syndicate and Opal incarnations. The frequent use of pump organ embodies the brooding twilight tone of the album, and her pure, gorgeous voice lends a cool grace to all tracks.

what to avoid: The overrated *Out of the Grey* ♫♫ (Big Time, 1986, 1987/Atavistic, 1997, prod. Paul Cutler) delivers tepid, amorphous country rock of no distinction.

the rest:
Medicine Show/This Is Not the New Dream Syndicate Album . . . Live! ♫♫♫ (A&M, 1984/1985)
Ghost Stories ♫♫ (Enigma, 1988)
Live at Raji's ♫♫♫ (Restless, 1989)
3-1/2: The Lost Tapes 1983–1988 ♫♫♫ (Atavistic, 1996)

worth searching for: The raw and very VU-ish four-song EP *Dream Syndicate* (Down There, 1982) has a jagged, conceptual integrity that equals that of the first album. *Rainy Day* (Llama/Enigma, 1983, prod. David Roback) was a tribute album (before tributes were a tired trend) on which Smith, Precoda, and Duck joined members of the Bangles, Rain Parade, and 3 O'Clock to record covers of songs by artists who inspired the Paisley Underground scene—from the Byrds, Jimi Hendrix, the Beach Boys, and the Who to Buffalo Springfield, Alex Chilton, and the Velvet Underground. Opal's out-of-print compilation *Early Recordings* (Rough Trade, 1989, prod. various) includes the two non-album tracks from the EP *Northern Line* (One Big Guitar, 1985) and all four songs from the precursor group's EP *Fell from the Sun* (Serpent-Enigma, 1984). Smith's *Kendra Smith Presents the Guild of Temporal Adventurers* (Fiasco, 1992, prod. Kendra Smith) is a low-key but subtly brilliant amalgam that at one turn anticipates the neo-lounge sound and at another recalls early Eno.

solo outings:
Steve Wynn:
Kerosene Man ♫♫ (Rhino, 1990)
Dazzling Display ♫♫ (Rhino, 1991)
Fluorescent ♫♫♫ (Mute, 1994)
Melting in the Dark ♫♫♫♫ (Zero Hour, 1996)
Sweetness & Light ♫♫♫ (Zero Hour, 1997)

Opal:
Happy Nightmare Baby ♫♫♫ (SST, 1987)

influences:

◀◀ The Velvet Underground, Neil Young, the Rolling Stones, Brian Eno

▶▶ R.E.M., American Music Club, Red House Painters, the Continental Drifters

see also: *The Continental Drifters*

Steve Holtje

Dream Theater

Formed as Majesty, 1985. Became Dream Theater in 1988.

John Petrucci, guitar; John Myung, bass; Mike Portnoy, percussion; Kevin Moore, keyboards (1985–94); Derick Sherinian, keyboards

(1994–present); Charlie Dominici, vocals (1987–89); James LaBrie, vocals (1991–present).

Few bands blend chord-crunching heavy metal with art-rock aesthetics as imaginatively as Dream Theater. Comprised of re-markably accomplished musicians, this group can conjure at-mospheric macabre tones, execute subtle, jazz-like key changes, and scatter-gun the hell out of a fast tune whenever it feels like it. As composers, the musicians have a solid knack for transforming modern-day emotional complexities into poignant parables of rock mythology. The group called itself Majesty until it discovered a band in Las Vegas had taken the name first. It was Mike Portnoy's father who suggested adopting the name of a California movie house, Dream Theater—a name that labeled the musical style as well. After the band's first LP stiffed, lead singer Charlie Dominici quit the band to be replaced by James LaBrie. With LaBrie's powerful, opera-trained voice, the band's sound finally jelled. When video versions of "Pull Me Under" and "Take the Time" actually made it into MTV's rotation, radio also began adding these tunes to their playlists. Since then, the band's albums have gotten more intricately planned, becoming challenging affairs for both the group and its fans. Though the music (and musicianship) has grown by leaps and bounds, its sales have not; Dream Theater is more popular in Japan and Germany than at home, but it continues to wail away for its chance at becoming an icon of American progressive rock.

what to buy: *Images and Words* ♫♫♫♫ (EastWest, 1992, prod. David Prater), Dream Theater's first album with LaBrie on vo-cals, remains its most accessible offering, featuring such thought-provoking tunes as "Learning to Live," "Pull Me Under," and the ambitious "Metropolis Part I."

what to buy next: Some powerful and dark thirsts are quenched on *Awake* ♫♫♫ (EastWest, 1994, prod. John Purdell, Duane Baron), the group's complexly arranged yet effortlessly executed paranoiac tour de force. Also, the intensely dramatic *A Change of Seasons* ♫♫♫ (EastWest, 1995, prod. David Prater, Dream Theater) takes its instrumental prowess up a notch. After an arty seven-part song-novella, "A Change of Seasons," the band lashes out with a live 10-minute tribute to Kansas, Queen, the Dixie Dregs, and others in "The Big Medley." Heady stuff, indeed.

what to avoid: Substandard sound quality and pointless re-hashes of superior studio material make *Live at the Marquee* ♫♫ (WEA International, 1993) a fans-only item.

the rest:
When Dream and Day Unite ♫♫ (Mechanic, 1989/One Day, 1996)
Falling into Infinity ♫♫♫ (EastWest, 1997)

worth searching for: There are lots of previously unreleased goodies for fans on *Hollow Years* (EastWest, 1997, prod. Dream

Theater), a German collection of deeply expressionistic work boasting superior sound. Less pricey is another import, *The Silent Man* (EastWest, 1994, prod. Dream Theater), a five-song set featuring previously uncollected LP cuts and demos.

influences:

◄◄ Emerson, Lake & Palmer, Iron Maiden, Metallica, Queen, Rush, Deep Purple, Kansas

►► Prong, Kyuss, Ethyl Mertz

Ken Burke

The Drifters

Formed 1953, in New York, NY.

Key lead vocalists: Clyde McPhatter (1953–54); David Baughan (1954–55); Johnny Moore (1955–57, 1964–65); Bobby Hendricks (1957–58); Ben E. King (1959–60); Rudy Lewis (1961–64).

The Drifters are to doo-wop what Elvis Presley is to rock 'n' roll; it could have existed without them, but a big ol' chunk would be missing. The Drifters were actually two different groups of two dif-ferent eras—the classic doo-wop of the McPhatter-Moore group of 1953 to 1958, and the more pop-oriented lineups led by Ben E. King, Rudy Lewis, and Johnny Moore from 1959 to 1964. Both in-carnations were giants of their time; few groups, after all, could have survived the departure of a talent such as McPhatter, who sang lead on hits such as "Money Honey," "Honey Love," and "White Christmas." But the harmony lineup of the group proved they could go on, backing Moore on "Adorable," "Ruby Baby," and "You Promise to Be Mine." Manager George Treadwell dis-banded the group in 1958 and signed the Five Crowns to perform as the Drifters. First King led the group on "There Goes My Baby," "This Magic Moment," and "Save the Last Dance for Me." Then Lewis took the lead for "Sweets for My Sweet," "Under the Board-walk," and "On Broadway." Finally, Moore returned to the group in time for "Up on the Roof." Since about 1967, the Drifters have been more a name than a group, with makeshift lineups pack-aged to play the supper club and hotel circuit. At times there have been two so-called Drifters groups touring simultaneously, a sad way to carry on a truly legendary legacy.

what to buy: The Drifters that most will remember are in evi-dence on *1959–1965 All-Time Greatest Hits and More* ♫♫♫♫♫ (Atlantic, 1988, prod. Bob Porter, Kim Cook), a compilation that has been re-engineered to put a new sheen on the group's im-maculate harmonies. The other side of the coin gets its due on *Let the Boogie Woogie Roll* ♫♫♫♫ (Atlantic, 1988, prod. vari-ous), which covers the harmony heavy doo-wop of the 1950s.

what to buy next: There are lots of crummy collections of the same rehashed songs available, but the three-disc set *Rockin' and Driftin': The Drifters Box* ♫♫♫♫ (Atlantic & Atco Remasters,

1996, prod. various) is excellent, rightly emphasizing the McPhatter years (and his solo work) and featuring a booklet full of great photos.

what to avoid: *Up on the Roof, Under the Boardwalk, and On Broadway* 𝄢𝄢𝄢 (Rhino, 1993, prod. various) trades on the title tunes, but after those three there's not a lot to recommend.

the rest:
16 Greatest Hits 𝄢𝄢𝄢𝄢 (Deluxe, 1987)
Greatest Hits 𝄢𝄢𝄢 (Hollywood/Rounder, 1987)
Live at Harvard University 𝄢𝄢 (New Rose, 1993)
Save the Last Dance for Me 𝄢𝄢𝄢 (Avid, 1995)

worth searching for: *The Very Best of the Drifters* (Rhino, 1993, prod. Mike Stoller) compiles the hits and only the hits for those who just want to dance and not delve into the intricacies of doo-wop.

influences:
◄◄ The Ink Spots, the Orioles, the Ravens

►► The Temptations, the Four Tops, the Parliaments, Boyz II Men

see also: *Ben E. King*

Lawrence Gabriel

Drivin' N' Cryin' /Kevn Kinney /Kathleen Turner Overdrive /Toenut

Formed 1985, in Atlanta, GA.

Kevn Kinney, guitar, vocals; Tim Nielsen, bass, mandolin; Jeff Sullivan, drums; Buren Fowler, guitar (1989–94); Joey Huffman, keyboards (1994–present).

Formed in the midst of Georgia's fertile Atlanta/Athens scene of the mid-'80s, Drivin' N' Cryin' broke the region's jangle-pop prototype with an unlikely blend of country-folk that emphasized acoustic instrumentation and hard-rock that bordered on heavy metal. DNC started out on independent label 688 Records but quickly jumped to the major-label ranks in 1988 for a deal with Island that lasted until the mid-'90s, when the group moved to Geffen. An opening slot for pals R.E.M. on a 1989 arena tour helped expose the band to wider audiences; its records have sold reasonably well, though it continues to be primarily a club-level draw. Frontman Kevn Kinney also has released a couple of solo albums that veer specifically toward his more acoustic inclinations, while bassist Tim Nielsen and drummer Jeff Sullivan work in the outside groups Kathleen Turner Overdrive and Toenut, respectively.

what to buy: *Mystery Road* 𝄢𝄢𝄢 (Island, 1989, prod. Scott MacPherson, Kevn Kinney, Tim Nielsen) is the band's best overall collection of songs and the one that suffers least from its often-jarring juxtaposition of soft and hard styles. It includes the concert-favorite anthem "Straight to Hell." *Wrapped in Sky* 𝄢𝄢𝄢 (Geffen, 1995, prod. John Porter) marks a welcome return to form after a noticeable slide during its latter years with Island. Ironically, both of Kinney's solo releases—*MacDougal Blues* 𝄢𝄢𝄢𝄢 (Island, 1990, prod. Peter Buck) and *Down Out Law* 𝄢𝄢𝄢𝄢 (Mammoth, 1994, prod. Kevn Kinney)—are head-and-shoulders above anything he's ever done with his band. *MacDougal Blues*, which features acoustic accompaniment by all of his bandmates (plus Buck, John Keane, and other Georgia scene standbys), has the wonderfully comfortable feel of a late-night hootenanny, while *Down Out Law* is a deeply affecting and personal recording of Kinney playing by himself on most songs.

what to buy next: *Scarred but Smarter* 𝄢𝄢𝄢 (688 Records, 1986/Island, 1989, prod. George Pappas) is a fine first record: it's rawer and gutsier than subsequent efforts, but it's also a little less refined. *Whisper Tames the Lion* 𝄢𝄢𝄢 (Island, 1988, prod. Anton Fier) offers a clear representation of what the band is all about by sequencing the hellfire screamer "Powerhouse" directly after the sprightly, countryish ditty "Catch the Wind."

what to avoid: *Smoke* 𝄢 (Island, 1993, prod. Geoff Workman, Drivin' N' Cryin') is a glaring low point, with hardly a single memorable song and an unhealthy turn toward a harder-edged sound that ultimately sold short the band's more significant melodic talents.

the rest:
Fly Me Courageous 𝄢𝄢𝄢 (Island, 1990)
Live on Fire 𝄢𝄢 (Island EP, 1991)
Drivin' N' Cryin' 𝄢𝄢𝄢 (Ichiban, 1997)

solo outings:
Kevn Kinney:
(With Frank French) *Everything Looks Better in the Dark* 𝄢𝄢𝄢 (Twilight, 1987)

Tim Nielsen:
(With Kathleen Turner Overdrive) *Kathleen Turner Overdrive* 𝄢𝄢𝄢 (Booger's Banquet, 1994)

Jeff Sullivan:
(With Toenut) *Information* 𝄢𝄢𝄢𝄢 (Mute, 1994)
Two in the Piñata 𝄢𝄢𝄢 (Mute, 1997)

influences:
◄◄ Hank Williams, Bob Dylan, the Ramones, John Denver

►► Indigo Girls, Black Crowes

Peter Blackstock

Pete Droge

Born March 11, 1969, in Eugene, OR.

With a lyrical gift that says "folkie" and a band that answers "rock 'n' roll," Pete Droge can have it both ways. But he mostly plays it down the middle, creating solid, acoustic-based rockers that are literate, soulful, and earnest to a fault. Considering he began his career in Seattle (he later moved to Portland), it's surprising that he chose not to hide his lyrics in a sea of sonic sludge (though he's cranked the volume knob a bit of late). But Droge has the air of an iconoclast about him, and, backed by his simple guitar-bass-drums-keyboard arrangements, his laconic delivery makes him sound like Tom Petty backed by the Band.

what to buy: *Find a Door* ♫♫♫♫ (American, 1996, prod. Brendan O'Brien) has his backing outfit solidifying into a band he calls the Sinners, but the sound is no less than heavenly, particularly on the rocking single "Wolfgang," which coasts along on a George Harrison–style slide guitar. The horn-augmented "Mr. Jade" rants at a clueless yuppie, and it's perhaps Droge's own "Ballad of a Thin Man." And on "Dear Diane," Droge regresses to the wise-ass moroseness of his debut, instructing, "Dear Diane/Today was worse/Call the Reverend and a hearse."

what to buy next: On *Necktie Second* ♫♫♫♫ (American, 1994, prod. Brendan O'Brien) Droge indulges in a fair amount of self-pity, but at least some of the time—as on the rocking opening cut, "If You Don't Love Me (I'll Kill Myself)"—he plays it for yuks. Elsewhere, he engages in a bit of Dylanesque wordplay ("Sunspot Stopwatch") and proves himself a capable storyteller ("Fourth of July"). The album is suffused with regret and longing, yet there is just enough humor to keep things moving.

the rest:
Spacey and Shakin ♫♫♫♫ (57 Records, 1998)

influences:
◄◄ Bob Dylan, Tom Petty, Neil Young
►► Elaine Summers

Daniel Durchholz

Drugstore

Formed 1990, in London, England.

Isobel Montero, vocals, bass; Mike Chylinski, drums; Dave Hunter (1992–93); Daron Robinson, guitar, piano (1993–present); Ian Burge, cello (1996–present).

Isobel Montero could hardly have predicted that her move from Sao Paulo, Brazil, to London in 1989 would result in international superstardom; she was, after all, just looking for a new life. Similarly, Mike Chylinski's stints as the L.A. drummer in various London rock bands didn't seem promising in the age of

WHAT ALBUM CHANGED YOUR LIFE?

Recently, the Beach Boys' *Good Vibrations* box set. There's a track on there, only the music from 'I Get Around,' no vocals. It's mind-blowing how cool, original, and complex it is. It sounds remarkably simple, yet it has some really interesting, cool things that Brian Wilson was trying and pulling off; just the way he put melody and chords together. The guy was amazing.

Pete Droge

incidental electronic percussion. But, as luck would have it, promise came in the form of their meeting. After tooling around a bit, the band stumbled upon Daron Robinson and quickly formed Drugstore. Their first single, "Alive," a self-distributed introduction, caught the attention of Go Records, which signed them in 1994. A Glastonbury festival appearance in 1995 sent the press home wagging, and the band recently collaborated with the hottest possible property, Radiohead frontman Thom Yorke, on the song "El President," from its as-yet British-only release, *White Magic for Lovers*.

what's available: On *Drugstore* ♫♫♫♫ (London, 1995, prod. Keith Cleversly, Drugstore), the group's peculiar blend of vocally driven dirge-rock saw the Curve generation through to its prog-rock apex.

influences:
◄◄ Curve, Cocteau Twins, My Bloody Valentine

Billy Manes

Chris Duarte Group

Formed 1991, in Austin, TX.

Chris Duarte, guitar, vocals; John Jordan, bass; Jeff Hodges, drums (1991–93); Brannen Temple, drums (1993–96); Eric Tatuaka, drums 1996–present).

Two things separate an acclaimed bluesman from a low-impact, adult alternative artist these days—scorching solos and resonant vocals. And while Chris Duarte's axework is steadily growing more hard-charging, even blues whiz kid Jonny Lang—barely into adolescence—has a more powerful howl. Duarte grew up in the Austin music scene, gaining valuable experience as a sideman in local blues, jazz, and funk bands throughout the '80s. In 1988, his jazz outfit Justus won the *Austin Chronicle* Music Award for Best Jazz Band. Duarte held a deep affinity for the music of John Coltrane, John McLaughlin, and their peers. Unfortunately, he was also hooked on one of their worst vices—heroin. By 1990, Duarte's addiction had wreaked havoc on his personal and professional life, and he escaped to New Hampshire to shake the drug. Friends and fans flew a clean Duarte back to Austin a year later, and the Chris Duarte Group was born.

what to buy: *Tailspin Headwhack* ♪♪♪ (Silvertone, 1997, prod. David Z.) attacks the uncertainty of Duarte's previous album, partially through more heated guitar work and hook-laden intros, and partially through stepping out of the blues box altogether on rock numbers such as "Walls." As an added bonus, Duarte's aptitude for jazz surfaces, with non-standard chordings and scalings occasionally percolating up out of nowhere.

what to buy next: Although Duarte doesn't usually genuflect before the altar of big Austin blues, he does pay homage to it in the nine-minute instrumental "Shiloh" from *Texas Sugar Strat Magik* ♪♪ (Silvertone, 1994, prod. Dennis Herring). Dedicated in the liner notes to the Vaughan brothers, the song is a fluid series of guitar roars, whispers, peaks, and valleys. Other than that, *Texas Sugar* lacks a few dozen degrees of vitality.

influences:

◄◄ Stevie Ray Vaughan, Albert King, John McLaughlin

►► Kenny Wayne Shepherd

Isaac Josephson

Dubstar

Formed 1993, in Gateshead, England.

Sarah Blackwood, vocals; Steve Hiller, keyboards; Chris Wilkie, guitar.

Dubstar was originally a duo named Joan's consisting of Steve Hiller on vocals and keyboards and Chris Wilkie on guitars. The pair soon started looking for a female singer, hiring Sarah Blackwood after Hiller heard one of her demo tapes. The band was subsequently signed to Food Records in London and changed its name to Dubstar, which it lifted from a Porno for Pyros lyric. After two U.K. albums—*Goodbye* in 1994 and the gold-selling *Disgraceful* in 1995—the fledgling group signed a deal with Polydor that brought its brand of electronic dance-pop to the U.S.

what's available: *Cathedral Park* ♪♪♪ (Polydor, 1997, prod. Stephen Hague, Graeme Robinson) is a captivating blend of '80s-styled electronic orchestration, programmed beats, darkly lit washes of dub, energetic bursts of house, and bubbly (borderline bubble gum) Anglo-pop—all fronted by Blackwood's alternately mournful and jubilant tenor. The album prominently features three versions of "Stars," which was the group's big U.K. hit. The rest of the album covers a wide range of sonic terrain, from the rousing, horn-filled title track to the subdued, shimmering ambience of "Just a Girl She Said," the jangly pop of "It's Clear," and the piano-based house tinge of "I Will Be Your Girlfriend."

worth searching for: Dubstar contributed a cover of "Everyday I Die" to the Gary Numan tribute album *Random* (Beggars Banquet, 1997, prod. various).

influences:

◄◄ William Orbit, Cocteau Twins, Durutti Column, Colourbox, St. Etienne, New Order

Spence D.

Slim Dunlap

See: The Replacements

Francis Dunnery

Born December 25, 1962, in Egremont, England.

Guitar whiz Francis Dunnery has lent a hand to various projects (a stint in English band It Happens and touring with Robert Plant) before starting on the kinder and gentler road of singer-songwriter fare. Foregoing the axe pyrotechnics for introspection and self-discovery, he now fills the gap for flavored coffee drinkers too keyed up for Cat Stevens and too old for Led Zeppelin. Dunnery's a nimble guitar player capable of writing clever folk-pop vignettes with a strong melodic sense, but his tendency towards an "I'm OK, you're OK" worldview threatens to turn his powers of positive thinking into glib self-absorption.

what to buy: *Let's Go Do What Happens* ♪♪♪♪ (Razor & Tie, 1998, prod. Francis Dunnery) is a much fuller affair than the stripped-down *Tall Blonde Helicopter* from a few years prior. The sharper sound is a plus, as the pop surroundings serve to cover some of Dunnery's "let me tell you all about me" themes.

what to buy next: Dunnery may be a *Tall Blonde Helicopter* ♪♪♪ (Atlantic, 1995, prod. Richard Dodd), but he's a sensitive one. To his credit, he's not afraid to poke fun at himself. Then again, he isn't afraid to reveal how handy he is with the ladies either.

the rest:
Fearless ♪♪♪ (Atlantic, 1994)

worth searching for: Dunnery's short stint with Plant can be found on the track "Promised Land" from the ex-Zep singer's album *Fate of Nations* (Atlantic, 1993, prod. Chris Hughes, Robert Plant).

influences:

◄◄ Cat Stevens, Paul Simon, David Gray

Allan Orski

Duran Duran
/Arcadia
/The Power Station
/John Taylor
/Andy Taylor

Formed 1979, in Birmingham, England.

Simon LeBon, vocals; Nick Rhodes, keyboards; John Taylor, bass, vocals (1979–97); Andy Taylor, guitar, vocals (1979–85); Roger Taylor, drums (1979–85); Warren Cuccurullo, guitar (1987–present); Steve Ferrone, drums (1986–88); Sterling Campbell, drums (1990–92).

The teen hysteria that ushered Duran Duran into the '80s was the very thing that nearly destroyed the band later in its career. Formed while John Taylor and Nick Rhodes were still art students in working-class Birmingham, the group hardly expected the overwhelming international success its first two albums, *Duran Duran* and *Rio*, brought on. Unwittingly, Duran Duran set the pace for the decade with its innovative synthesizer based music, exotic videos, and sexy posturing. A third, less adventurous album, *Seven and the Ragged Tiger*, saw the group's popularity reach epic proportions, even rivaling that of Michael Jackson the same year *Thriller* was released. After an exhaustive world tour, a ramshackle live album and some one-off hit singles, the pressure became too much and the group split off into side projects Arcadia and the Power Station. Neither one proved entirely successful, and founding members Roger Taylor and Andy Taylor pulled out of Duran Duran before it reconvened for its next record, *Notorious*. Things were never the same. The group spent the late '80s and early '90s hitting new sales lows. In 1993, however, Duran Duran scored an unexpected comeback with "Ordinary World" and its accompanying self-titled album. A bizarre covers album, however, killed the momentum again. This time John Taylor bailed. The group, however, continues to press on. Duran Duran's most recent album, *Medazzaland*, marked a return to the synthesizer pop of its early days. However, it has yet to yield the same successful results.

what to buy: *Rio* ♫♫♫♫♫ (Capitol, 1982, prod. Colin Thurston) blends tropical themes, savvy synthesizer work, and catchy

WHAT ALBUM CHANGED YOUR LIFE?

The soundtrack to *A Clockwork Orange* was the most incredible musical experience that I'd ever had. I'd been aware of Beethoven and classical music; I'd grown up, sung in church choir, my mother had been a pianist. To hear that music, and I read the book as well, to have those imaginative visuals going on with this music, it gave me something which was completely mine. Nobody I knew was into it at all. I was in a club of one with that record. I'd lie in-between the speakers on the floor and listen to it, at least twice a day. It was so incredibly beautiful.

Simon LeBon (of Duran Duran)

melodies to become one of the defining records of the early '80s. Songs such as "Hungry Like the Wolf" and "Save a Prayer" showcase the dynamic powers at work behind this band and prove there is much more to Duran than pretty faces and fancy videos. However, Duran was primarily a singles band, and *Decade* ♫♫♫♫ (Capitol, 1991, prod. various) collects some of its most stellar recordings, including "Is There Something I Should Know," "A View to a Kill," and "Skin Trade."

what to buy next: The debut, *Duran Duran* ♫♫♫♫ (Capitol, 1981, prod. Colin Thurston), made it clear from the start that this was a band that was serious about its music. Songs such as "Girls on Film" and "Planet Earth" are still staples on modern rock radio. Even though they were both commercial bombs, *Big Thing* ♫♫♫ (Capitol, 1988, prod. Duran Duran, Jonathan Elias, Daniel Abraham) and *Medazzaland* ♫♫♫ (Capitol, 1997, prod. Duran Duran) represented new levels of maturity for a band that is constantly reinventing itself.

what to avoid: *Thank You* **woof!** (Capitol, 1995, prod. Duran Duran), the group's covers album, is its most unnecessary exercise in self-mutilation. Hearing the former teen idols take on songs as bewildering as Public Enemy's "911 Is a Joke," the Doors' "Crystal Ship," and Elvis Costello's "Watching the Detectives," proves nothing more than laughable.

the rest:
Seven and the Ragged Tiger ♪♪ (Capitol, 1983)
Arena **woof!** (Capitol, 1984)
Notorious **woof!** (Capitol, 1986)
Liberty ♪♪ (Capitol, 1990)
Duran Duran ♪♪♪ (Capitol, 1993).
Essential Duran Duran (Night Versions) ♪♪♪♪ (EMI-Capitol Entertainment Properties, 1998)

worth searching for: *Carnival* (Capitol, 1982), a vinyl EP of extended remixes of four songs from Duran Duran's first two albums, captures the excitement the group brought to dance clubs during the early '80s.

solo outings:
Arcadia:
So Red the Rose ♪♪♪ (Capitol, 1985)

The Power Station:
The Power Station ♪ (Capitol, 1985)
Living in Fear **woof!** (Guardian, 1997)

Warren Cuccurullo:
Requim for the Americas ♪ (Enigma, 1989)
Thanks to Frank **woof!** (Imago, 1996)
Machine Language **woof!** (Imago, 1996)

John Taylor:
Feelings Are Good and Other Lies **woof!** (B5, 1996)

Andy Taylor:
American Anthem O.S.T. **woof!** (Atlantic, 1986)
Thunder **woof!** (MCA, 1986)
(With Michael Des Barres) *Somebody up There Likes Me* **woof!** (MCA, 1986)
(With Rod Stewart) *Out of Order* ♪ (Warner Bros., 1988)
Dangerous **woof!** (A&M, 1990)

influences:
◀◀ David Bowie, Roxy Music, Chic, the Sex Pistols
▶▶ Smashing Pumpkins, Live, Blur, Hole

Aidin Vaziri

Ian Dury
/Ian Dury & the Blockheads

Formed 1977, in London, England. Disbanded 1982.

Ian Dury (born May 12, 1942, in Upminster, Essex, England), vocals; Chas Jankel, keyboards, guitar (1977–79, 1981–82); John Turnbull, guitar; **Mickey Gallagher, keyboards; Norman Watt Roy, bass; Charley Charles, drums; Wilco Johnson, guitar (1980–81).**

The bawdiest and most unpredictable chip off the British pub-rock block, Ian Dury parlayed a warped sense of humor, charismatic stage presence, and a laundry list of physical limitations to become one of the most memorable cult music figures of the '70s. Despite the ravages of a childhood bout with polio and a Cockney accent thick enough to cut with a machete, Dury emerged as the unlikeliest of pop stars through a string of arresting singles like "What a Waste," "Hit Me with Your Rhythm Stick," "Sex & Drugs & Rock & Roll," and "Reasons to be Cheerful (Part 3)," each becoming a Top 10 U.K. hit with a weird mix of music hall raunchiness, punk rock intensity, and disco sensibility. Forced to spend two years in a hospital and attend a school for the handicapped after being stricken at the age of seven, Dury eventually graduated from the Royal College of Art and taught painting at Canterbury Art College. During 1970—at the relatively ripe rock 'n' roll age of 28—he formed his first band, Kilburn & the High Roads, whose eccentric blend of '50s rock and be-bop jazz proved so successful on the British pub circuit that Dury was able to quit his teaching job. Kilburn landed a label deal but couldn't get the group's first album released, and it disbanded within five years. Dury, however, continued to work with High Roads pianist Chas Jankel and in 1977 signed as a solo act with now-legendary indie label Stiff Records. He and Jankel assembled a band of pub-rock veterans to record Dury's debut album, *New Boots & Panties!!*; when Stiff asked him to be part of its "Live Stiffs" package tour to support the LP, Dury formed the Blockheads. The tour made Dury an extremely popular live act, propelling *New Boots & Panties!!* onto the U.K. charts, where it would stay for almost two years and eventually sell more than a million copies worldwide. "Hit Me with Your Rhythm Stick," the subsequent single, shot all the way to #1. Dury was suddenly a superstar, and U.S. labels were falling over themselves to capitalize. Arista won the bidding war to distribute Stiff's product in America, but for whatever reason—the strange Cockney brogue, the decidedly British wit, the music hall roots—*New Boots & Panties!!* stiffed in the States, and Arista dropped him immediately. Nevertheless, he remained a star attraction at home, releasing albums in the U.K. into the '90s. Between recordings, Dury turned his attention to acting, landing movie roles in Roman Polanski's *Pirates* and Peter Greenaway's *The Cook, The Thief, His Wife, and Her Lover*. He has also written jingles for British commercials, hosted a late-night U.K. television show, and penned a musical called *Apples* with Mickey Gallagher. In May 1998, Dury announced that he had been diagnosed with colon cancer and that the disease had spread to his liver, going public with the news on his 56th birthday in hopes of providing encouragement to other cancer patients.

what to buy: Most of Dury's albums will force fans to go scrambling through the import racks, since he never exactly took America by storm—a shame, since "Hit Me with Your Rhythm Stick" is the most memorable, unappreciated pure romp to survive the '70s. But the outstanding Rhino compilation *Sex & Drugs & Rock & Roll: The Best of Ian Dury & the Blockheads* ♪♪♪♪ (WEA/Atlantic/Rhino, 1992, compilation prod. Bill Inglot) is basically all the curious listener needs to know about Dury's quirky genius. In addition to the sardonic title track, the 15-song package includes his breakout U.K. hit "What a Waste" and a progression of tracks—"Sweet Gene Vincent," "Inbetweenies," "Common As Muck," and the seriously silly "Razzle in My Pocket"—that distill Dury's Cockney disco-funk formula into a danceable, enduring testament. Once you get used to the accent, pay close attention to Dury's always engaging lyrics.

what to avoid: The 12-cut Dutch import *Best of Ian Dury* ♪♪♪ (Disky, 1996) pales in comparison to the Rhino anthology.

the rest:
Warts 'n' Audience ♪♪ (Damon, 1991)
Do It Yourself ♪♪♪ (Disky, 1996)
Jukebox Dury ♪♪ (Mush, 1996)
Laughter ♪♪♪ (Disky, 1997)
Reasons to Be Cheerful ♪♪♪♪ (Repertoire, 1997)

worth searching for: The Australian import reissue of Dury's first LP, *New Boots & Panties!!* (Repertoire, 1996), is remastered and includes five bonus Dury singles that practically make the release another greatest hits disc. To hear the progression (or regression, depending on your view) of his musical skills, you might also consider Dury's last recorded work, *The Bus Driver's Prayer and Other Stories* (Damon, 1992). For the true Dury devotee, his first and only album for Polydor, *Lord Upminster* (Polydor, 1981, prod. Sly Dunbar, Robbie Shakespeare) is out of print but memorable on two fronts: it was recorded in the Bahamas with the renowned reggae duo of Sly and Robbie; and it featured the outrageous single "Spasticus Autisticus," a song about the United Nations Year of the Disabled that even a disabled artist like Dury should have thought twice about releasing. To the surprise of no one, the U.N. rejected the theme song.

influences:
◀◀ Rockpile, John Cale, Dr. Feelgood, Ian Hunter, Nick Lowe, the Damned, Sly & Robbie, Eddie & the Hot Rods, Gary Glitter

▶▶ The Specials, Box of Frogs, Blondie, UB40, Green Day

Jim McFarlin

Bob Dylan
Born Robert Allen Zimmerman, May 24, 1941, in Duluth, MN.

Decades from now, when all the dust has settled and the rock music revolution is viewed with historical hindsight, Bob Dylan will stand out as one of the three most important people to ever pick up a guitar. George Harrison feels even more strongly; he's been quoted as saying that 500 years from now, Dylan will be the most remembered and revered name from this era, eclipsing even the Beatles. Unlike the Fab Four and Elvis Presley, Dylan's profound influence on the music world—and on society in general—was never matched by his sales. Nonetheless, his key material truly serves as the soundtrack for a generation and is deeply ingrained in our daily lives. Phrases like "The Times They Are A-Changin'" have worked their way into everyday journalistic vernacular; his song "Like a Rolling Stone" even helped give a moniker to our biggest music magazine. Dylan's most important contribution was giving the voice of social consciousness to contemporary music lyrics, starting with folk music and then evolving into rock. When girl groups and teenage idols were topping the charts in 1962 and 1963, Dylan woke up a sleeping public with songs about racial injustice and the ravages of war. All of this has earned Dylan a continuing level of respect that is on a par with greats like Duke Ellington, Leonard Bernstein, and Miles Davis. His influence may be best illustrated by the fact that one scholarly study concluded that he was the one person, from all walks of life, most responsible for stopping the Vietnam war. Musically, his career has been up and down through the '80s and '90s; it is most recently on the upswing again despite a life-threatening bout with the rare affliction histoplasmosis in 1997.

what to buy: To this day, Dylan's legacy is still very much that of a folk artist, and his key work in that genre is *The Freewheelin' Bob Dylan* ♪♪♪♪ (Columbia, 1963, prod. John Hammond). This album single-handedly launched the mid-'60s protest movement with such venerable songs as "Blowin' in the Wind" and "A Hard Rain's A-Gonna Fall." Once Dylan started rocking full-time, he made *Highway 61 Revisited* ♪♪♪♪ (Columbia, 1965, prod. Bob Johnston, Tom Wilson), which many pundits feel is one of the greatest albums ever released, right up there with the Beatles' *Sgt. Pepper's Lonely Hearts Club Band*. It is hard to overpraise an album that opens with "Like a Rolling Stone" and closes with "Desolation Row" and doesn't have an ounce of fat in between. Directly following that was *Blonde on Blonde* ♪♪♪♪ (Columbia, 1966, prod. Bob Johnston), another highly regarded album that always winds up in the top 10 of any greatest-albums-of-all-time poll. Probably Dylan's most popular record among his legions of hard-core fans, the album is a folk-rock masterpiece featuring "Rainy Day Women #12 & 35," "I Want You," and "Just Like a Woman." Although Dylan's creative output peaked with that record, nine years later he shocked everyone with the brilliance of *Blood on the Tracks* ♪♪♪♪ (Columbia, 1975, prod. Bob Dylan). As his marriage started to crumble, Dylan wrote and sang songs like "Tangled up in Blue" and

Bob Dylan (© Ken Settle)

"Idiot Wind" from the soul, causing critics everywhere to pull out and dust off the "masterpiece" moniker once again.

what to buy next: *Bringing It All Back Home* 🎵🎵🎵🎵 (Columbia, 1965, prod. Tom Wilson) is many fans' favorite Dylan album, and it kick-started the folk-rock movement with "Mr. Tambourine Man" and "It's Alright, Ma (I'm Only Bleeding)." Before that, however, *The Times They Are A-Changin'* 🎵🎵🎵🎵 (Columbia, 1964, prod. Tom Wilson) set the music world on fire with its title song and "With God on Our Side," and *Another Side of Bob Dylan* 🎵🎵🎵🎵 (Columbia, 1964, prod. Tom Wilson) showed his softer—though no less ingenious—side with "It Ain't Me Babe" and "Chimes of Freedom." The double-disc *The Basement Tapes* 🎵🎵🎵🎵 (Columbia, 1975, prod. Bob Dylan, the Band) was recorded in 1967 with the Band and has achieved legendary status with off-the-wall yet compelling songs like "Please, Mrs. Henry" and "Nothing Was Delivered" (plus the brilliant "Tears of Rage"). If it's an overview of Dylan's career that you need, however, nothing beats the box set *Biograph* 🎵🎵🎵🎵 (Columbia, 1985, prod. various), featuring three CDs full of his most compelling material, spanning all of his most important phases.

what to avoid: Without Dylan's consent, his former record label released the unfortunately titled *Dylan* **woof!** (Columbia, 1973, prod. Bob Johnston) after he had jumped ship to David Geffen's Asylum label. It was a dirty trick that now stands alone as a black eye in Dylan's canon. The album is so insignificant that, to this day, Columbia still hasn't reissued it on CD in America.

the rest:
Bob Dylan 🎵🎵 (Columbia, 1962)
Bob Dylan's Greatest Hits 🎵🎵🎵 (Columbia, 1967)
John Wesley Harding 🎵🎵🎵🎵 (Columbia, 1968)
Nashville Skyline 🎵🎵🎵🎵 (Columbia, 1969)
Self Portrait 🎵🎵 (Columbia, 1970)
New Morning 🎵🎵🎵 (Columbia, 1970)
Greatest Hits, Vol. II 🎵🎵🎵 (Columbia, 1971)
Pat Garrett & Billy the Kid (Soundtrack) 🎵 (Columbia, 1973)
Planet Waves 🎵🎵🎵🎵 (Asylum, 1974)
Before the Flood 🎵🎵 (Asylum, 1974)
Desire 🎵🎵🎵🎵 (Columbia, 1976)
Hard Rain 🎵 (Columbia, 1976)
Street Legal 🎵🎵 (Columbia, 1978)
Bob Dylan at Budokan 🎵🎵 (Columbia, 1979)
Slow Train Coming 🎵🎵🎵🎵 (Columbia, 1979)
Saved 🎵 (Columbia, 1980)
Shot of Love 🎵🎵🎵 (Columbia, 1981)
Infidels 🎵🎵🎵 (Columbia, 1983)
Real Live 🎵 (Columbia, 1985)
Empire Burlesque 🎵🎵 (Columbia, 1985)
Knocked Out Loaded 🎵🎵 (Columbia, 1986)
Down in the Groove 🎵🎵 (Columbia, 1988)
Dylan & the Dead 🎵🎵 (Columbia, 1989)

Oh Mercy 🎵🎵🎵 (Columbia, 1989)
Under the Red Sky 🎵 (Columbia, 1990)
The Bootleg Series: Vols. 1–3, 1961–1991 🎵🎵🎵🎵 N/A (Columbia, 1991)
Good As I Been to You 🎵🎵 (Columbia, 1992)
World Gone Wrong 🎵🎵 (Columbia, 1993)
Greatest Hits, Vol. 3 🎵🎵🎵🎵 (Columbia, 1994)
MTV Unplugged 🎵🎵 (Columbia, 1995)
Time Out of Mind 🎵🎵🎵🎵 (Columbia, 1997)
The Bootleg Series, Vol. 4: Live—The "Royal Albert Hall" Concert 🎵🎵🎵🎵🎵 (Columbia/Legacy, 1998)

worth searching for: DCC Compact Classics' gold-disc version of *Highway 61 Revisited*, remastered in the early '90s with sparkling sound, is well worth its $25–$30 price tag. *The Concert for Bangladesh* (Apple/Capitol, 1971) contains a highly charged five-song acoustic set by Dylan, including his greatest-ever live version of "Just Like a Woman."

influences:

◄◄ Woody Guthrie, Hank Williams, Leadbelly, Little Richard, Elvis Presley, the Weavers, Joan Baez

►► The Byrds, Sonny & Cher, Joan Baez, Tom Petty & the Heartbreakers, Bruce Springsteen, John Mellencamp, Garth Brooks, Joe Henry, Bob Seger, Beck

see also: *The Traveling Wilburys*

Pete Howard

E
See: eels

The Eagles
Formed 1971, in Los Angeles, CA. Disbanded 1981. Reunited 1994.

Don Felder, guitar, vocals (1974–present); **Glenn Frey,** vocals, guitar, keyboards; **Don Henley,** vocals, drums; **Bernie Leadon,** guitar, banjo, mandolin, vocals (1971–76); **Randy Meisner,** bass, vocals (1971–77); **Timothy B. Schmit,** bass, vocals (1977–present); **Joe Walsh,** guitar, vocals (1976–present).

Bred in Los Angeles' fertile country-rock community, the Eagles came together first as the backing band for Linda Ronstadt's *Silk Purse* album in 1970; individually, the musicians had already played with the Flying Burrito Brothers, Poco, Rick Nelson's Stone Canyon Band, and Bob Seger. But it was the Eagles' sound—smooth harmonies and polished, twangy arrangements—that defined southern California rock during the '70s. By the time they rolled out the seminal *Hotel California* album, Don Henley and Glenn Frey had become astute social commentators—despite a bit of cynicism that lent a nasty edge to some of their songs. Always too serious, the Eagles succumbed to the pressures of success and called it quits in 1981. But after 13 years of solo recordings they reunited for an MTV concert that yielded the top-selling *Hell Freezes Over* album and a phenomenally successful world tour (with $100+ tickets). It's unclear whether they'll record another full album of new music again, however.

what to buy: A little inconsistent during their early years, the Eagles are best served by *Their Greatest Hits, 1971–75* 🎵🎵🎵🎵🎵 (Asylum, 1975, prod. Glyn Johns, Bill Szymczyk), an awesome collection of singles—from "Take It Easy" to "One of These Nights"—that established the Eagles as one of rock's top groups of the time. *Hotel California* 🎵🎵🎵🎵 (Asylum, 1976, prod. Bill Szymczyk) made the most of that momentum. Bolstered by the addition of Joe Walsh's stinging guitar solos and a collection of poignant, pointed songs, it's as much a cultural barometer as a great rock 'n' roll album.

what to buy next: *The Long Run* 🎵🎵🎵🎵 (Asylum, 1979, prod. Bill Szymczyk) is another sharp, skillful work marked by the title track and Timothy B. Schmit's aching love song *I Can't Tell You Why*. *One of These Nights* 🎵🎵🎵 (Asylum, 1975, prod. Bill Szymczyk) is the apex of the Eagles's twang time with some truly gorgeous moments in "Lyin' Eyes" and "Take It to the Limit."

what to avoid: *Desperado* 🎵🎵 (Asylum, 1973, prod. Glyn Johns) is a misbegotten concept album and its best songs can be found on *Their Greatest Hits*.

the rest:
Eagles 🎵🎵🎵 (Asylum, 1972)
On the Border 🎵🎵🎵 (Asylum, 1974)
Live 🎵🎵🎵 (Asylum, 1980)
Greatest Hits, Vol. 2 🎵🎵🎵🎵 (Asylum, 1982)
Hell Freezes Over 🎵🎵🎵 (Geffen, 1994)

worth searching for: *Peaceful Easy Feeling* (Cuttlefish bootleg) is one of many recordings of a landmark 1974 show at New York's Bottom Line, at which Rondstadt and Jackson Browne joined the Eagles for a rendition of "Take it Easy."

solo outings:
Don Felder:
Airborne 🎵🎵 (Elektra, 1983)

Glenn Frey:
No Fun Aloud 🎵🎵🎵 (Asylum, 1982)
The Allnighter 🎵🎵 (MCA, 1984)
Soul Searchin' 🎵🎵🎵 (MCA, 1988)
Strange Weather 🎵🎵 (MCA, 1992)
Live 🎵🎵🎵 (MCA, 1993)
Best of 🎵🎵🎵 (MCA, 1995)

Randy Meisner:
One More Song 🎵🎵 (Epic, 1980)
Randy Meisner 🎵🎵🎵 (Epic, 1982)

Timothy B. Schmit:
Playin' It Cool 🎵🎵 (Asylum, 1984)
Timothy B 🎵🎵 (MCA, 1987)
Tell the Truth 🎵🎵 (MCA, 1990)

influences:

◀◀ The Byrds, Gram Parsons, the Beatles, the Everly Brothers, Hank Williams

▶▶ Travis Tritt, Garth Brooks, the Mavericks, the Gin Blossoms, Uncle Tupelo, the Jayhawks, Vince Gill

see also: *Don Henley, Joe Walsh*

Gary Graff

Fred Eaglesmith

Born July 9, in Hamilton, Ontario, Canada.

This Canadian writes about real life—a wife who drinks too much, a sweet old Pontiac that may have been a murderer's get-away car, a troubling decision to buy a gun—and sings with a solemn, completely believable twang that belies his north-of-the-border roots. His simple turns of phrase are perfect for country music: in "Time to Get a Gun," he says, "I could afford one, if I did a little less drinking," a line that's simultaneously humorous and frightening. Eaglesmith, who decided to be a songwriter at age 18 and wrote 65 songs in roughly six weeks, nurtured a reputation at Canadian coffeehouses and clubs. To support himself, he took odd jobs as a carpenter and farm worker, among other things. Eventually word got out, and artists such as the Cowboy Junkies and Jimmie Dale Gilmore invited him to open their tours. In interviews, Eaglesmith links his music to that of Wilco, Son Volt, and the rest of the alternative-country crowd. But really, he should set his sights even higher; some of his songs, such as the explosive "Seven Shells" and "Pontiac," perhaps the ultimate driving song, are as universal and eloquent as early Bruce Springsteen or Steve Earle.

what's available: *Lipstick Lies & Gasoline* 🎵🎵🎵🎵 (Razor & Tie, 1997, prod. Scott Merritt) is a near-classic rock 'n' roll album. It opens with "Seven Shells," a frightening song about a troubled, insecure character who equates bravery with owning a shotgun, and closes with an even more boisterous version of the same song. "Pontiac" begins as a typical car-loving rocker—"It's a '63 stratochief with a three on the tree"—then builds into a dramatic murder story. Eaglesmith's only missteps are when he gets too solemn, listing Hank Williams, Elvis Presley, Janis Joplin, Gram Parsons, and Jimi Hendrix as if they were tragic figures nobody had ever heard of. But he more than makes up for it on "Drinking Too Much," required listening for anybody who has ever loved an alcoholic.

worth searching for: Eaglesmith's debut, *Drive-In Movie* (Vertical, 1996, prod. Scott Merritt, Fred Eaglesmith), is currently out of print.

influences:

◀◀ Hank Williams, Elvis Presley, Woody Guthrie, Bruce Springsteen, Steve Earle, Tammy Wynette, George Jones, Cowboy Junkies, John Prine

Steve Knopper

Steve Earle

Born January 17, 1955, in Fort Monroe, VA.

Rebounding from a heroin haze to take control of his life and his music, Steve Earle is living proof that sometimes you can start all over again. The son of an air traffic controller, Earle infiltrated Nashville in 1986 with a twangy, hardcore-hillbilly sound filtered through the heartland rock 'n' roll of John Mellencamp and *Nebraska*-era Bruce Springsteen. Although signed to mainstream MCA Records, he quickly established himself as a rebel without a pause by worshiping Townes Van Zandt, opening shows for the Replacements, and eventually battling cocaine and heroin addictions. Despite Earle's string of powerful albums—capped by 1990's underrated *The Hard Way*—radio resisted the big, bad good ol' boy, and the back-to-back releases of a live album and a greatest-hits collection confirmed that even MCA had lost patience with him. But Earle has confronted and conquered his demons: now clean and sober, he released a 1996 comeback album called *I Feel Alright* that confirms the title with a hearty, hard-rocking relish. He is now recording for his own E-Squared label, which is developing into an exalted outpost for young, like-minded acts such as Cheri Knight, the V-Roys, and Six String Drag, who recognize that country music is an essential ingredient of, not an alternative to, great rock 'n' roll.

what to buy: *Guitar Town* 🎸🎸🎸🎸 (MCA, 1986, prod. Emory Gordy Jr., Tony Brown) is an auspicious debut of small-town frustration ("Someday") and romantic yearning ("Fearless Heart"). *I Feel Alright* 🎸🎸🎸🎸 (E-Squared/Warner Bros., 1996, prod. Richard Dodd, Ray Kennedy, Richard Bennett) finds him defiantly addressing his past in "Cocaine Can't Kill My Pain" and "The Unrepentant." But the brightest signs are the brash but breezy twang-pop confections "Hard-Core Troubador," "More Than I Can Do," and "You're Still Standin' There" (a duet with Lucinda Williams). The equally hard-nosed follow-up, *El Corazon* 🎸🎸🎸🎸 (E-Squared/Warner Bros., 1997, prod. Steve Earle, Ray Kennedy), finds him spitting, spewing, and sparkling against backdrops ranging from the Crazy Horse–like caterwaul

of "Taneytown" to the Beatlesque bounce of "Somewhere Out There" to the protest-folk of "Christmas in Washington." The highlight is "Here I Am," a pummeling declaration of independence that sounds like a garage-band throwaway but resonates like a manifesto.

what to buy next: For new fans who just discovered him, the two-CD *Ain't Ever Satisfied: The Steve Earle Collection* 🎸🎸🎸🎸 (Hip-O/MCA, 1996, prod. various) renders 1993's *The Essential Steve Earle* obsolete by adding such album tracks as "Fearless Heart" and "Nothing but a Child," as well as his promo-only live version of Bruce Springsteen's "State Trooper."

what to avoid: *Early Tracks* 🎸 (Koch, 1987, prod. Roy Dea, Pat Carter) is a CD reissue of Epic's hurriedly assembled vault-raiding compilation originally designed to cash-in on his *Guitar Town* accolades. The Koch disc adds four previously unreleased tracks, including a cover of John Hiatt's "The Crush," but the performances are still tentative, if not tepid.

the rest:
Exit O 🎸🎸🎸🎸 (MCA, 1987)
Copperhead Road 🎸🎸🎸 (MCA, 1988)
BBC Live 🎸🎸🎸 (Windsong, 1988)
The Hard Way 🎸🎸🎸🎸 (MCA, 1990)
Shut up and Die Like an Aviator 🎸🎸🎸 (MCA, 1991)
Essential Steve Earle 🎸🎸🎸🎸 (MCA, 1993)
Train a Comin' 🎸🎸🎸 (Winter Harvest, 1995)
Fearless Heart 🎸🎸🎸 (MCA, 1995)

worth searching for: Earle teams up with the V-Roys for a deliciously rowdy cover of "In the Jailhouse Now" on *The Songs of Jimmie Rogers: A Tribute* (Egyptian/Columbia, 1997, prod. various).

influences:

◄◄ Townes Van Zandt, Waylon Jennings, Bruce Springsteen, Bob Dylan

►► Travis Tritt, Todd Snider, Jack Ingram, Chris Knight

David Okamoto

John Easdale

See: Dramarama

The Easybeats

Formed 1963, in Australia. Disbanded 1969.

Stevie Wright, vocals; George Young, guitar, vocals; Harry Vanda, guitar, vocals; Dick Diamonde, bass; Gordon (Snowy) Fleet, drums (1963–66); Tony Cahill, drums (1966–69).

While the Beatles were taking the world by storm, the Easybeats were having a heyday in Australia. Comprised of friends who met in a youth hostel, the group became the most successful Australian band of the '60s, scoring a string of seven Top 10 Down Under singles that fused the Merseybeat pop of the Beatles with the amphetamine drive of the Who and the Kinks. The group came to London in 1966, where, under the guiding hand of producer Shel Talmy, it cracked the international pop market with the herky-jerky rave-up "Friday on My Mind" in 1967. The songwriting/production team of George Young and Harry Vanda came up with fine, adventurous music that was right in step with the ambitious musical trends of the period. But while the group earned raves from contemporaries such as Paul McCartney and Lou Reed, listeners' ears were tuned elsewhere. Oddly, the group's best support came from cover versions of its songs performed by the Lemon Pipers, the Buckinghams, the Music Explosion, and Los Bravos. Vanda and Young continued working together after the breakup, masterminding the new wave group Flash & the Pan and assisting Young's brothers Angus and Malcolm in starting Australia's most successful group, AC/DC. The Easybeats' influence remained in evidence throughout the '80s in groups such as the Three O'Clock, the Plimsouls, Divinyls, and INXS, all of which have covered their songs.

what to buy: *Absolute Anthology* ♫♫♫♫ (EMI, 1980, prod. various) is a two-CD set that offers everything you could ever want (and more); those with less prodigious appetites will prefer the more compact *The Best of the Easybeats* ♫♫♫♫ (Rhino, 1985, prod. various), which includes all of the group's essential cuts.

influences:

◄◄ The Beatles, the Kinks, the Who

►► David Bowie, Three O'Clock, the Plimsouls, INXS

Christopher Scapelliti

Echo & the Bunnymen /Electrafixion

Formed 1978, in Liverpool, England. Disbanded 1991. Reunited 1997.

Ian McCulloch, vocals, (1978–89, 1997–present); Pete De Freitas, drums (1978–89); Will Sergeant, guitar; Les Pattinson, bass; Noel Burke, vocals (1989–91); Damon Reece, drums (1989–91).

Musicians can't grow up in Liverpool without feeling some influence from you-know-who, so it's no surprise that there's more than a little tunefulness in the music of Echo & the Bunnymen. But there's a dark melancholia, too; lest we forget, this was the punk era, and group leaders Ian McCulloch and Will Sergeant also shared a fondness for the Doors' moody tone poems. McCulloch set Echo in motion after getting the boot from an early incarnation of Teardrop Explodes, and the group's original lineup included a drum machine named Echo until De Freitas joined in. With the textured, ambient wash of hits such as "The Killing Moon," "Silver," and "Bring on the Dancing Horses," Echo joined Depeche Mode and the Cure in defining a particularly strong wave of British rock during the early '80s. McCulloch left for a solo career in 1989, and the group unravelled shortly thereafter. But in 1994, McCulloch and Sergeant were back together again in a new, very Echo-ish band Electrafixion, which led to a full-fledged Echo reunion three years later with bassist Les Pattinson.

what to buy: *Ocean Rain* ♫♫♫♫ (Sire, 1984, prod. David Lord, Echo & the Bunnymen) is the pinnacle of the group's gorgeously moody approach. Sergeant blends his guitar with a full string section to create enduring gems such as "Seven Seas," "Silver," and "The Killing Moon." *Songs to Learn & Sing* ♫♫♫♫♫ (Sire, 1985, prod. various) has those and eight others in a stunning best-of that more than validates the title.

what to buy next: Few debut albums have the potent flavor of a major new talent arriving as does *Crocodiles* ♫♫♫♫ (Sire, 1980, prod. David Balfe, Bill Drummond). McCulloch voices his angst before it became a cliché, while Sergeant's guitar playing has an appealing roughness to it. Electrafixion's *Burned* ♫♫♫ (Sire, 1995, prod. Ian McCulloch, Will Sergeant) is, despite the duo's denial, a de facto Bunnymen album, with many of the same melodic virtues, though it tends to rock a little harder.

what to avoid: *Reverberation* ♫♫ (Sire, 1990), the album after McCulloch left the group, has its good points, but the group ultimately sounds like a diluted version of its former self.

the rest:
Heaven up Here ♫♫♫♫ (Sire, 1981/1988)
Echo & the Bunnymen ♫♫♫♫ (Sire, 1987)
BBC Live ♫♫♫ (Windsong, 1993)
Evergreen ♫♫♫ (London, 1997)

worth searching for: McCulloch's solo catalog is out of print, but his first effort, *Candleland* (Sire, 1989, prod. Ray Shulman), is a fine, Echo-ish album with a somewhat more personal touch to the lyrics.

influences:

◀◀ The Beatles, the Doors

▶▶ Suede, Oasis, Happy Mondays, Stone Roses

Gary Graff

Echobelly

Formed 1992, in London, England.

Sonya Aurora Madan, vocals; Glenn Johansson, guitar, mandolin, vocals; Debbie Smith, guitar (1993–97); Alex Keyser, bass, piano, whistle (1992–95); Andy Henderson, drums; James Harris, bass (1995–present); Julian Cooper, guitar (1995–present).

Introduced, oddly enough, in Sweden while Sonya Aurora Madan was away from her English home attending school, Madan and Swede Glenn Johansson relocated to London, where they eventually formed a band that inclued Alex Keyser and Andy Henderson. The resulting quartet played around London and garnered the attention of fledgling label Rhythm King. While recording their debut, the band received the pop hook they needed in recruiting outspoken black lesbian Debbie Smith (formerly of Curve) to cover for Johansson while his arm was broken. They got on well, so Smith became a (semi-)permanent fixture.

what to buy: The band's second release, *On* ✽✽✽✽ (550 Music, 1995, prod. Sean Slade, Paul Kolderie), displays ripping confidence of both music and voice. Gone are the mopey Smiths resplendances of Echobelly's debut. In their place are a tough-girl biker-bar mentality and spitfire wit embodied by the fiesty hit "King of the Kerb."

what to buy next: The debut album, *Everyone's Got One* ✽✽✽✽ (Rhythm King, 1994, prod. Simon Vinestock, Clive Martin), Is a mix of Blondie swagger and X-Ray Spex drive. Jangley to the point of shimmer, it made Echobelly a press darling overnight, ranking with other revivalists Elastica, Oasis, and Blur.

what to avoid: Previously available only as an import, *Lustra* ✽✽ (Epic, 1997/1998, prod. Gil Norton) failed to captivate hearts in the group's homeland, which prompted Smith to leave the band acrimoniously, replaced by Julian Cooper.

influences:

◀◀ Blondie, X-Ray Spex, Voice of the Beehive, Wire

▶▶ Sleeper

Billy Manes

Eddie & the Hot Rods

Formed 1975, in Southend, Essex, England. Disbanded 1981.

Barrie Masters, vocals; Dave Higgs, guitar, vocals, piano; Graeme Douglas, guitar (1977–80); Paul Gray, bass, vocals (1975–80); Tony Cranney, bass (1980–81); Steve Nicholl, drums, vocals; Lew Lewis, harmonica (1975–76).

One of the main links between pub rock and punk, Eddie & the Hot Rods were formed by ex-amateur boxer Barrie Masters and quickly found success playing the London pub circuit, showcasing a mix of rock and soul covers and originals. There was no Eddie in the group, though manager/producer Ed Hollis was practically a member; onstage a life-size dummy named Eddie was regularly beaten up as part of the group's high-energy show. Island signed them, and by 1976 the group scored British hits with a cover of "Wooly Bully" and Higgs's "Teenage Depression." The Island album of the same name was issued in England that year, though it wouldn't come out in the U.S. until 1977. Ex–Kursaal Flyer Graeme Douglas came on board in '76 and became an instant factor, co-writing most of the best songs on the group's second album. But by the late '70s, the group was splintering, and in 1981 Masters split up what remained of the group and joined the Inmates. There have been intermittent partial Hot Rods reunions.

what to buy: With the band's best album unavailable, *Curse of the Hot Rods/Ties That Bind* ✽✽✽✽ (Dojo, 1996, prod. various) becomes valuable despite being a coupling of two albums of previously unreleased material. *Curse of the Hot Rods* consists of post-Island 1979 sessions (produced by Graeme Douglas) for an album that wasn't issued. It's raw and rocking stuff, including a rousing cover of Bruce Springsteen's "Ties That Bind." That song isn't on *Ties That Bind*, which collects five pre-Island demos (two Higgs originals and three covers), a B-side cover of Creedence Clearwater Revival's "Hey Tonight," and half of the live 1985 EP *One Story Town*, including the *Life on the Line* classics "Quit This Town" and "Do Anything You Wanna Do," by a partially reunited group.

what to buy next: *BBC Radio One Live in Concert* ✽✽✽ (Windsong, 1994, prod. Jeff Griffin) contains appearances recorded in 1977 and 1978 for British radio. The boisterous energy invigorates some of the Higgs tunes (though they blur together). It's particularly good to have his "I Might Be Lying," a fine non-album single, in two versions here.

what to avoid: The Hot Rods' final studio album, *Fish 'n' Chips* woof! (EMI, 1980, prod. Al Kooper), was made without Douglas and Gray. Nobody has ever had a good word to say about this pallid, misguided (and now out-of-print) effort.

the rest:

Teenage Depression ✽✽✽ (Island, 1977)

Thriller ✽✽ (Island, 1979)

worth searching for: *Life on the Line* (Island, 1977, prod. Ed Hollis) is an absolutely crucial document of its time and still stands up musically and lyrically. Hollis and Douglas form an ace songwriting team, and songs such as "Do Anything You Wanna Do," "Quit This Town," "Ignore Them (Still Life)," the title track, and "And Don't Believe Your Eyes" are enduring standouts. It's a travesty that this album is out of print. Also seek out *One Story Town* (Waterfront EP, 1985), a six-song British import documenting a spirited reunion gig led by Masters and Nicholl.

influences:

◄◄ Bob Seger, the Rolling Stones, the Who, Dr. Feelgood

►► Rockpile, the Buzzcocks, Graham Parker & the Rumour

Steve Holtje

Duane Eddy

Born April 26, 1938, in Corning, NY.

"The Twangiest Guitar of Them All" was a red Gretsch 6120 wielded by Duane Eddy. Not well-remembered today, Eddy ruled the guitar scene of the late '50s with his tremolo-heavy instrumentals. His shadow fell especially long in England, where a generation of young guitar players—from Hank Marvin of the Shadows to George Harrison of the Beatles—came under his spell. His records essentially came down to duets between Eddy, who scrupulously and carefully stated the melodic themes drenched in ringing, "twangy" tones, and saxophonist Steve Douglas, who replied in squawking, screeching blasts that came to define the sound of rock 'n' roll saxophone. Douglas went on to record all the solos on the famous Phil Spector records and, with King Curtis, supplied one of the two fountainheads of the instrument's rock vocabulary. The man behind the hits, producer Lee Hazlewood, parlayed his Eddy success into a career as one of Hollywood's masterful pop visionaries on records with Nancy Sinatra—work that is as fully realized and imaginative in scope as anything by his contemporaries, such well-recognized *auteurs* as Spector and Brian Wilson. Eddy drifted into an uncomfortable obscurity, settling in Lake Tahoe, touring as guitarist for Italianate pop vocalist Al Martino and shunning the spotlight. Sporadic efforts to revive his career have been made, including a 1976 single with then-hot Willie Nelson and Waylon Jennings providing lead vocals; a short-lived 1983 reformation of his vintage studio band with the addition of Ry Cooder on second guitar; a remake of "Peter Gunn" in 1986 by the British dance band the Art of Noise; and a 1987 album featuring help from Paul McCartney, John Fogerty, George Harrison, Steve Cropper, and others. But, despite his seminal work in the foundations of rock and country guitar, Eddy's contributions seem to be drifting further beyond the horizon.

what to buy: The double-disc retrospective *Twang Thing: The Duane Eddy Anthology* 𝄞𝄞𝄞𝄞 (Rhino, 1993, compilation prod. Duane Eddy) covers the full breadth of his career—from the earliest hits and album sides to '80s recordings with McCartney, Harrison, and Cooder.

what to avoid: Beware abbreviated, cut-price collections such as *Rebel Rouser* 𝄞𝄞 (Sony Music Special, 1996, prod. various) and *Rebel Rouser: Roots of Rock 'n' Roll* 𝄞𝄞 (Columbia River, 1998), which don't even scratch the surface of Eddy's remarkable body of work.

the rest:

The Twang's the Thang/Songs of Our Heritage 𝄞𝄞𝄞𝄞 (Jamie, 1959, 1960/Bear Family, 1995)
Especially for You/Girls, Girls, Girls 𝄞𝄞𝄞 (Jamie, 1959, 1961/Bear Family, 1995)
Dance with the Guitar Man/Twistin' & Twangin' 𝄞𝄞𝄞 (RCA, 1962, 1963/One Way, 1998)
Twangin': Golden Hits/Twang a Country Song 𝄞𝄞 (RCA, 1963/One Way, 1998)
Best Of/Lonely Guitar 𝄞𝄞𝄞 (RCA, 1964/One Way, 1998)
His Twangy Guitar and the Rebels 𝄞𝄞 (See for Miles, 1994)
That Classic Twang 𝄞𝄞𝄞𝄞 (Bear Family, 1995)
Great Guitar Hits 𝄞𝄞 (Curb, 1996)

worth searching for: His debut album, *Have Twangy Guitar Will Travel* (Jamie, 1958, prod. Lee Hazlewood), is one of the keystones of modern rock guitar. Also, his comeback effort, *Duane Eddy* (EMI, 1987, prod. various), is not one to pass up in a cutout bin. Still want more? *Twangin' from Phoenix to Los Angeles* (Bear Family, 1994, prod. Richard Weize) is a five-disc box from Europe that collects virtually the complete Jamie Records sessions and more.

influences:

◄◄ Chet Atkins, Les Paul, Jerry Byrd, Al Casey

►► George Harrison, John Entwistle, John Fogerty, George Thorogood

Joel Selvin and Ken Burke

Dave Edmunds /Rockpile

Dave Edmunds, born April 15, 1943, in Cardiff, Wales. Rockpile formed 1976, in London, England. Disbanded 1981.

Rockpile: Dave Edmunds, vocals, guitar; Nick Lowe, bass, vocals; Terry Williams, drums, vocals; Billy Bremner, guitar, vocals.

Dave Edmunds is the quintessential musician's musician—a producer, performer, lead guitarist, sideman, frontman. He's done them all, and all of them well—even if he's still a cult item to the masses. You'd never believe it from his early efforts in the band Love Sculpture, but his surprise first (and biggest) hit single, 1971's "I Hear You Knocking," contained the core of every track he recorded afterwards, a modern sound based in the rhythms of rockabilly that he took for his own. Edmund's name will always be associated with Rockpile—the second-tier supergroup that included Nick Lowe on bass, drummer Terry Williams, and Billy Bremner on guitar. The band kick-started the sound of the '50s, equal parts Chuck Berry and the Everly Brothers, but added a '70s pub-rock sensibility. Rockpile only released one album under its own name, but (due to contractual difficulties and solo career conflicts) the band enjoyed a fruitful period between 1977 and 1980, recording on a total of six Edmunds and Lowe solo albums that still sound as fresh as the day they were recorded—before a rancorous breakup in 1981. Edmunds's myriad production credits include the Stray Cats's first two (British) albums, the Everly Brothers' comeback effort *EB '84*, and Lowe's *Party of One*.

what to buy: Edmunds's Swan Song albums are uniformly excellent. *Get It* 𝄞𝄞𝄞𝄞 (Swan Song, 1977, prod. Dave Edmunds) is the first actual Rockpile collaboration and includes "I Knew the Bride (When She Used to Rock 'n' Roll)," "Get Out of Denver," and "JuJu Man." *Tracks on Wax 4* 𝄞𝄞𝄞𝄞 (Swan Song, 1978/Atlantic, 1990, prod. Dave Edmunds) is Rockpile's hardest rocking collection, while *Repeat When Necessary* 𝄞𝄞𝄞 (Swan Song, 1979/Atlantic, 1991, prod. Dave Edmunds) is amazingly sharp considering the band was working on Lowe's strong *Labour of Lust* at the same time.

what to buy next: *The Dave Edmunds Anthology (1968–90)* 𝄞𝄞𝄞 (Rhino, 1993, prod. various) is a 41-track overview that includes too much Love Sculpture among its many gems. *D-E7* 𝄞𝄞𝄞 (Columbia, 1982/Sony, 1991, prod. Dave Edmunds) includes the Bruce Springsteen–composed "From Small Things, Big Things Come." *Best of Dave Edmunds* 𝄞𝄞𝄞𝄞 (Swan Song, 1982/Atlantic, 1991, prod. Dave Edmunds) features all the right tracks from his classic period.

what to avoid: Anything by Love Sculpture, Edmunds's first real band, most of which approaches headache-inducing guitar music.

the rest:
Rockpile 𝄞𝄞 (MAM, 1972)
Subtle as a Flying Mallet 𝄞𝄞 (RCA, 1975/One Way, 1998)
Twangin' 𝄞𝄞 (Swan Song, 1981)
Information 𝄞𝄞 (Columbia, 1983/Sony, 1991)
Riff Raff 𝄞𝄞 (Columbia, 1984)
I Hear You Rockin' 𝄞𝄞 (Sony, 1988)
Closer to the Flame 𝄞𝄞 (Capitol, 1990)
Plugged In 𝄞𝄞𝄞 (Pyramid, 1994)

Rockpile:
Seconds of Pleasure 𝄞𝄞𝄞 (Columbia, 1980)

worth searching for: Rockpile bootlegs—in particular *I Hear You Rocking* (GLR, 1991) and *Provoked Beyond Endurance* (Oh Boy)—capture the Rockpile experience better than *Seconds of Pleasure*. *Rocking* features guest appearances by Robert Plant and the Rolling Stones's Keith Richards.

influences:

◄◄ Les Paul & Mary Ford, Chet Atkins, Elvis Presley, Gene Vincent, Ricky Nelson, Smiley Lewis, Jerry Lee Lewis, Chuck Berry, the Everly Brothers, Bo Diddley, Del Shannon

►► The Stray Cats, the Blasters, the Bottle Rockets, Bob Seger, Brian Setzer, Brinsley Schwarz, Bruce Springsteen, Dr. Feelgood, Ducks Deluxe, Eggs over Easy, Elvis Costello, Graham Parker, Mickey Jupp, NRBQ, the Flamin' Groovies

see also: *Nick Lowe*

Leland Rucker

eels

Formed 1994, in Los Angeles, CA.

E, vocals, guitars, keyboards; Tommy, bass, vocals (1994–97); Butch, drums, vocals.

Isolation and sadness are two feelings common in the work of eels' frontman E (Mike Edwards). The Virginia native began his career as a solo artist, releasing two keyboard-heavy albums—*A Man Called (E)* and *Broken Toy Shop*, both of which are out of print. Tired of being pigeonholed as a singer-songwriter, E sought out a band. It was at an open mic night at the Mint in Los Angeles that he met Tommy and Butch, with whom he created a loopy, trippy kind of modern pop that took off thanks to the single "Novocaine for the Soul."

what to buy: eels' debut, *Beautiful Freak* 𝄞𝄞𝄞 (DreamWorks, 1996, prod. E, Michael Simpson), is a collage of stories about dysfunctional relationships, violence, and isolation told to hip-hop, jazz, and pop accompaniment. With its simple drum loop, "Susan's House," the highlight of the album, is a stunning narrative of violence and teenage pregnancy ("That must be her sister, right?") in his home base of Los Angeles's Echo Park. E slithers between rambling and strong vocals on "Novocaine for the Soul," in which the main character begs for painkiller: "Novocaine for the soul/You better give me something to fill the hole/before I sputter out." Pop noir at its best, *Beautiful Freak* is a cleverly written album that simply did not get the attention it deserved.

the rest:
Electro-Shock Blues N/A (DreamWorks, 1998)

worth searching for: E's *A Man Called (E)* (Polydor, 1992, prod. Parthenon Huxley, E) is a flawed but ambitious pop album with

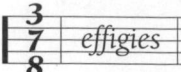

enough good moments ("Hello Cruel World," "Fitting in with the Misfits," "Nowheresville") to merit a listen.

influences:

Beck, INXS

Forest for the Trees

Christina Fuoco

Effigies

Formed 1980, in Chicago, IL.

John Kezdy, vocals; Earl Letiecq, guitar (1980–84); Robert O'Connor, guitar, keyboards (1985–86); Paul Zamost, bass; Steve Economou, drums.

Though lacking the notoriety of its Chicago brethren Big Black and Naked Raygun, the Effigies were among the first great postpunk bands to emerge in the Midwest. The group exuded a no-nonsense, no-frills attitude that reflected its hardy Rustbelt environs; the band wore regular-guy street clothes onstage, and John Kezdy delivered his vocals in short, sharp sing-speak bursts. It wrote pithy anthems with a melodic verve that drew on the best of British punk and paved the way for the better-known do-it-yourself bands to follow. Though the band dissolved during the late '80s, the original lineup reunited occasionally for club shows in the '90s with no decline.

what's available: Only one record from the band's brief history survives, but it's a doozy: *Remains Nonviewable* ♪♪♪♪♪ (Touch & Go, 1995, prod. Effigies, Scott Stienmman) ranks in the top tier of early '80s postpunk. It includes 15 shots of sociopolitical bile, including "Body Bag," the ska-tinged "Security," and a snide tribute to Mayor Richard Daley's legacy, "We're Da Machine."

worth searching for: The band's final albums, *Fly on a Wire* (Fever/Enigma, 1985, prod. John Kezdy, Iain Burgess) and *Ink* (Fever/Enigma, 1986, prod. Effigies), are long out of print but worth seeking out for the art-punk ambition they add to the band's arsenal.

influences:

The Ruts, the Stranglers, the Jam, Killing Joke, Joy Division

Naked Raygun, Big Black, Hüsker Dü, Bloodsport, Breaking Circus

Greg Kot

The Egg

Formed 1994, in Oxford, England.

Mark Revell, guitar; Dave Gaydon, bass; Maff Scott, drums; Ned Scott, keyboards.

This is the Egg. This is the Egg on your CD player: a little bit ambient, a little bit psychedelic, a little bit funky, and very much

trance-inducing, sort of like George Clinton leading Pink Floyd in some instrumental space-jazz excursions, with BT sitting in just for fun. Any questions? Oh, and the Egg is also one of electronica's only actual bands and, therefore, doesn't crack under pressure on stage, where it appears in matching white jumpsuits á la Devo and plays its dynamic music with incredible intensity in front of a quick-cut film pastiche.

what's available: On *Albumen* ♪♪♪♪ (China/Discovery, 1997, prod. Joe Gibb) the Egg avoids the sort of static repetition that makes much electronic dance music dull, topping its hard-boiled grooves and spacey psychedelic flavors with dramatic chord changes that give the cinematic, mostly wordless album even stronger personality and character. It doesn't hurt, either, that *Albumen* has a funky beat that you can definitely bug out to.

influences:

Pink Floyd, Parliament-Funkadelic, Sun Ra, the Bomb Squad, BT, Massive Attack, Moby, James Taylor Quartet, Orbital

Josh Freedom du Lac

808 State

Formed 1988, in Manchester, England.

Martin Price (1988–92); Graham Massey; Gerald Simpson (1988–89); Andrew Barker (1989–present); Darren Partington (1989–present).

Taking its name from the Roland 808 drum machine, 808 State was the driving force behind the late '80s rave/acid house scene in Manchester, England. Founded by techno-whizzes Graham Massey, Martin Price, and Gerald Simpson, the group eschewed conventional rock in favor of electronic loops and beats. Under 808's control, this technologically complex music had both critics and clubbers on both sides of the Atlantic raving, literally and figuratively. 808 State took its cues from the hip-hop beats of the Detroit house scene, as well as from the relentless industrial pulsations created by bands such as Kraftwerk. The band's albums are deep, layered affairs that offer new sounds with each successive listen, a fact that's helped the band transition smoothly from the dance floor onto fans' CD players. 808 State was not afraid to experiment, and the band often used a technique called "silhouetting" that involved building a track around a sample that was then removed, leaving only a musical ghost image. Simpson left the band after only one EP, *Newbuild*, to form A Guy Called Gerald. Barker and Partington came on board, and they helped craft *Quadrastate*, the EP that yielded the massive dance hit (and a slew of remixes) "Pacific State." 808 State's first album, *Utd. State 90* helped put the house/techno/rave scene on the map and almost single-handedly proved that electronic music was as commercially viable as anything with a guitar and bass. Although primarily known for their trademark atmospheric instrumentals, 808 State occasionally enlists the help of vocal collaborators, notably Björk, Ian McCulloch from Echo & the Bunnymen, and Bernard Sumner from New Order. 808 State's unique approach to sound manipulation also puts them in great demand as producers and remixers, and the list of bands that the group has worked with reads like a who's who of the '90s rock and dance scenes in the U.S. and Europe. Following the release of another critical fave, *ex:el*, founding member Price left the band in 1992. 808 State has remained a trio, releasing two more albums during the mid-'90s. The band's members continue to work as remixers and club DJs, spinning nights around the U.K. and in Europe. Capitalizing on the explosive popularity of electronic music during the late '90s—a movement built on their pioneering sound—808 State released a 10-year retrospective, *808:88:98*, during mid-1998 and announced plans for new material.

what to buy: *Utd. State 90* ♪♪♪♪ (Tommy Boy, 1990, prod. 808 State) is the definitive album from 808 State. It features the club classics "Pacific 202," "Cubik," and "808080808," tracks that lose nothing in the translation from late-night rave to CD player. The intricate layers of samples and beats help each track flow seamlessly from one to the next, a technique that adroitly re-creates the live club DJ experience.

what to buy next: *ex:el* ♪♪♪♪ (Tommy Boy, 1991, prod. 808 State) takes a slightly mellower approach than earlier 808 State material, although "In Yer Face" ranks up there with the band's signature hard instrumental dance music. Vocals from New Order's Bernard Sumner transform the sumptuous "Spanish Heart" into the closest thing to a ballad that 808 would create, and "Ooops" and "Qmart" feature Björk's trademark chirpings. A slightly revamped version of "Cubik" shows up on this CD as well.

the rest:
Gorgeous ♪♪♪♪ (Tommy Boy, 1993)
Don Solaris ♪♪♪♪ (ZTT/Hypnotic/Cleopatra, 1997)

worth searching for: *Statetostate* (State to State, 1994) is a worthwhile, fan club-only promo album.

influences:
◄◄ Juan Atkins, the Art of Noise, Can, Cabaret Voltaire, Kraftwerk, Derrick May, New Order, Gary Numan, Kevin Saunderson, Yello

►► Aphex Twin, the Chemical Brothers, Faithless, Future Sound of London, Moby, the Orb, Orbital, Underworld

Lisa M. Moore

Einstürzende Neubauten

Formed 1980, in Berlin, Germany.

Blixa Bargeld, vocals, guitar; N.U. Unruh, vocals, guitar, percussion, industrial percussion; Mark Chung, bass; Alexander Hacke, guitar, electronics; F.M. Einheit, industrial percussion. Additional personnel: Anita Lane, vocals; Mathis Fischer, violin; Reinhard Allenberg, viola; Jan Tilman Schade, cello; Roland Wolf, organ.

It doesn't get much harsher than Einstürzende Neubauten. Combine some of the most truly industrial music of the past two decades with glass-gargling vocals and add the fact that most lyrics are sung only in German and you have the makings of a migraine waiting to happen. Add instruments as diverse as drills, saws, and other power tools, as well as Tibetan thighbone trumpets, and you have Einstürzende Neubauten, a band that has never sold out—but has managed to sell quite a few records. This is a band for the adventurous and open-minded. You say you like Ministry? Well, that's a start—but this is light years ahead of Al Jourgenson's twisted ravings. This is dyed-in-the-wool industrial music, with a German minimalist slant to boot. Very little in the band's catalog is danceable, it's certainly not comfortable listening, and at loud volumes it probably injures small animals. All of this is not to say they band isn't good; on the contrary, Neubauten is prolific, creative, and influential. How many other bands can you name that can make music with hammers, pipes, and aluminum siding? (Stomp doesn't count.) If you like the electro-beat of the '80s and the post-industrial sounds of the '90s, then you may be a candidate for a Neubauten record or two. But unless you have an open mind and appreciate noise, this may be a bit challenging. An example of this band's ferocity: when Blixa Bargeld wants to mellow out, he "relaxes" as one of Nick Cave's Bad Seeds. Neubauten's style has remained fairly consistant, but time has softened it a bit; the releases from the '90s are a bit more in the ambient/techno vein, but they're still not suggested for the faint of heart. Happily, many of the band's previously out-of-print efforts were reissued domestically via Thirsty Ear Records, making them available to an unsuspecting American audience for the first time. But Neubauten is yet another incredibly influential band that has seen much of its catalog lapse into vapor, and the reissues only scratch the surface of the band's long and interesting history.

what to buy: *Volume 1: Strategies against Architecture* ♪♪♪♪ (Mute, 1984/Homestead, 1986/Mute-Restless, 1991, prod. various) and *Volume 2: Strategies against Architecture* (Mute-Restless, 1991, prod. various) ♪♪♪♪ collect the band's work from 1980 to 1983 (*Volume 1*) and 1984 to 1990 (*Volume 2*). Giving some insight into the band's influence and value, *Volume 1* has been released by three different labels during the last decade and a half. These releases provide an exceptional overview of

Neubauten, containing some hard to find tracks as well as what could hesitantly be called greatest hits. While never charting on any list of singles, the band has had some magical moments in sound. If you're curious, these are nice starting points.

what to buy next: *Haus Der Luege* 𝄢𝄢𝄢𝄢 (Some Bizzare/Rough Trade, 1989/Thirsty Ear, 1995) shows the band at one of its most accessible moments. This CD is not far removed from where Ministry would be four or five years later. *Tabula Rasa* 𝄢𝄢𝄢𝄢 (Mute, 1993) is another shining moment in Neubauten's history. Not as harsh as past efforts, it shows a band more comfortable with traditional instruments, song structure, and even melody. Though not ballroom music by any stretch, it's actually listenable for long periods—without the headache normally associated with a Neubauten record.

what to avoid: *2X4* 𝄢 (Roir, 1984/1993) is not full of bad songs—it's just poorly recorded. Originally released as a cassette only, it has since been reissued on CD, with barely tolerable sound quality that muddies many of the more interesting sounds, effects, and screams.

the rest:

Drawings of Patient O.T. 𝄢𝄢𝄢 (Some Bizzare, 1983/PVC, 1985/Thirsty Ear, 1995)

1/2 Mensch 𝄢𝄢𝄢𝄢 (Some Bizarre/Rough Trade, 1985/Thirsty Ear, 1995)

Feunf auf der Nach Oben Offen Richterskala 𝄢𝄢𝄢𝄢 (a.k.a. *Five on the Open-Ended Richter Scale*) (Some Bizarre/Rough Trade, 1985/ Thirsty Ear, 1995)

Faustmusik 𝄢𝄢𝄢 (Mute, 1996)

worth searching for: *Kollaps* (Zick-Zak, 1981) is incredibly difficult to find, but if noise is your thing, this is a masterpiece. Disturbing would be an understatement. Don't listen to it with the lights off. Only released in Germany, this little gem of the industrial music world would be a crown in any collection

influences:

◀◀ White noise experiments of the '60's, Cabaret Voltaire, Throbbing Gristle, the Sex Pistols

▶▶ Crime & the City Solution, Ministry, nine inch nails, Diamanda Gallas, Depeche Mode, filter

see also: *Nick Cave & the Bad Seeds, the Birthday Party*

Tim Davis

Mark Eitzel
/American Music Club

Born January 30, 1959, in Walnut Creek, CA. American Music Club formed 1983, in San Francisco, CA. Disbanded 1995.

Mark Eitzel, acoustic guitar, keyboards, vocals; Bruce Kaphan, pedal steel, keyboards, guitars, vocals; Mark "Vudi" Pankler, guitars, vocals; Danny Pearson, bass, guitars, mandolin, vocals; Tim Mallon, bass, drums (1985–88); Mike Simms, drums (1989–92); Tim Mooney, drums (1993–95).

With Mark Eitzel at its helm, AMC was a brooding, thought-provoking quintet that created dazzling emotional landscapes drawn by the Eitzel's evocative singing and obtuse songwriting. The former punk rocker from Columbus, Ohio, found the perfect marriage with guitarist Vudi Pankler and multi-instrumentalist Bruce Kaphan for his tortured musings on life and love. Drawing its musical form from folk, country, and rock with a pinch of psychedelic texture, AMC has never fit comfortably into any clichéd radio programmer's format. Sadly, Eitzel's departure in 1995 for a solo career marked the end of an era—and the band—as he embarked on a challenging path that included an evocative collaboration with R.E.M.'s Peter Buck.

what to buy: AMC's *Everclear* 𝄢𝄢𝄢𝄢 (Alias, 1991, prod. Bruce Kaphan) is a tour de force that perfectly captures the dynamics of Eitzel's songs with the band's playing, from the raucously punky "Crabwalk" to the poignant ballad "Ex-Girlfriend" to "What the Pillar of Salt Held Up," a stripped-down voice-and-guitar piece that's one of Eitzel's best ballads. *San Francisco* 𝄢𝄢𝄢𝄢 (Reprise, 1994, prod. Joe Chiccarelli, AMC) is the band's last album before Eitzel split. A return to form reuniting the band with *Everclear* engineer Joe Chiccarelli, it features more moody, dark acoustic tunes ("Fearless," "Cape Canaveral"), twisted mid-tempo songs with cool titles ("How Many Six Packs Does It Take to Screw in a Light"), and plenty of spirited rockers ("It's Your Birthday," "Wish the World Away," and "Hello Amsterdam"). On his solo debut, *60 Watt Silver Lining* 𝄢𝄢𝄢𝄢 (Warner/Reprise, 1996, prod. Mark Eitzel), Eitzel explores the aching ruminations of Chet Baker with spare, melancholy arrangements that highlight the prominent trumpet solos. *West* 𝄢𝄢𝄢𝄢 (Warner Bros., 1997, prod. Peter Buck, Mark Eitzel) takes a turn into sunnier weather with a set of songs written jointly by Eitzel and Buck.

what to buy next: AMC's *Engine* 𝄢𝄢𝄢𝄢 (Frontier, 1987, prod. Tom Mallon) is on a par with *Everclear* and includes concert favorites "Big Night" and "Nightwatchman." Eitzel's *Caught in a Trap and I Can't Back out 'Cause I Love You Too Much, Baby* 𝄢𝄢𝄢 (Matador, 1998) was a one-off project with Matador and features only the most minimal accompaniment (from Steve Shelley, James McNew, and Kid Congo Powers) on just a third of the otherwise completely solo recordings.

the rest:

Engine 𝄢𝄢𝄢𝄢 (Frontier, 1987)

California 𝄢𝄢𝄢𝄢 (Frontier, 1988)

Mercury 𝄢𝄢𝄢𝄢 (Reprise, 1993)

worth searching for: *California/United Kingdom* (Demon, 1989), a British import combo, and the vinyl-only *The Restless Stranger* (Grifter, 1985), which, according to some, may get a CD release in the near future, are both worth the effort to find.

influences:

◀◀ Nick Drake, Tim Buckley, Love, Big Star

▶▶ Red House Painters, Swell, Idaho

Mark J. Petracca and David Greenberger

El Chicano

Formed 1970, in East Los Angeles, CA.

Ersi Arviszu, tambourine, scratch, maraca; Andrew Baeza, congas; John DeLuna, drums; Bobby Espinosa, organ; Mickey Lespron, guitar; Freddie Sanchez, vocals, electric bass; Max Garduno, conga, flute; Rudy Regalado, timbales; Rudy Salas, vocals; Steve Salas, vocals; Jerry Salas, guitar; Joseph Perreira, bass, synthesizer, vocals.

El Chicano emerged among the vanguard of the Eastside Sound—a community of Mexican American musicians from Los Angeles' east end during the '60s. Originally starting life as the V.I.P.'s, El Chicano took its name from the nascent Chicano Power Movement of the era, tranlating its political perspectives into musical expression. The group came to national recogniton with a remake of jazzist Gerald Wilson's "Viva Tirado," which later became the title of its debut album on Kapp Records. The early records on Kapp and the last record, on Shadybrook, were raucous affairs of Latin-infused funk, rock, and soul, filled with energetic organ vamps by Bobby Espinosa and fiery guitar play from Mickey Lespron. In the middle were four years with MCA that largely failed to turn the group into national stars and led to some of its lesser work. At its worst the group indulged in some milquetoast songs that reeked of '70s rock and pop conventionality. At its best, El Chicano carved out a distinctive sonic space that proclaimed them as "Brown and Proud" and certainly helped pave the way for the new rock en Español movement.

what to buy: *Viva! Their Very Best* ♫♫♫ (MCA, 1988, prod. various) is a good overview of the band's seven-year history. Its bigger pop hits, such as "Brown Eyed Girl" and "Tell Her She's Lovely," find their way on here, but the compilation wisely leaves off its blander efforts. Best of all, it includes a fine selection of some earlier works: "Viva Tirado," the seminal hit, is a smoky Latin jazz groove, as is the group's cover of Herbie Hancock's "Cantaloupe Island."

what to buy next: *Chicano Chant* ♫♫♫ (MCA, 1997, prod. various) is themed to focus on the Chicano pride songs. This compilation, while featuring Brown Power anthems such as "Sabor a Mi" and "Gringo en Mexico," doesn't quite capture the musical beauty of El Chicano, though jams such as "Cubano Chant" and "Juntos" are fierce in their own right.

what to avoid: *The Best of Everything* ♫♫ (MCA, 1975, prod. Lenny Roberts) is the ill-named final album El Chicano recorded with MCA. By this point, the group had hit a dreadfully conventional rut, sounding like any number of mid-'70s rockers.

worth searching for: Unfortunately, all of El Chicano's original releases were on vinyl, and none of them are in current release. For vinyl junkies (and fans of the group), El Chicano's first two albums, *Viva Tirado* (Kapp, 1970, prod. Billy Watson, Eddie Davis) and *Revolución* (Kapp, 1971, prod. Tom Catalano) are must-haves, capturing its fine Latin jazz/soul/funk and Chicano consciousness years. A more difficult album to locate, but worth the effort, is *This Is El Chicano* (Shadybrook, 1976, prod. El Chicano), where freedom from MCA meant a much more progressive fusion sound, including an absolutely funky rendition of Mongo Santamaria's "Para Ti."

influences:

◀◀ The Midniters, the Village Callers, Cannibal & the Headhunters, Tierra

▶▶ Los Illegals, Ruben & the Jets, Los Lobos, Ozomatli

Oliver Wang

El Vez

Born Robert Lopez, 1961, in Chula Vista, CA.

On first glance, one might mistakenly assume that El Vez, the "Mexican Elvis," is yet another variation in the tired Elvis-impersonator circuit. As Ed McMahon may have said, "You are incorrect, sir!" During the late '80s, more than a decade after a high school stint in the semi-legendary punk band the Zeros, Robert Lopez adopted the El Vez moniker. From the outset he was bringing more and different agendas to the table than anyone would have expected; socialist and Hispanic issues have been present all along, but by the time of his fourth album, *Graciasland*, he succeeded in creating a work that, though chock full of wide-ranging musical reference points, is completely his own. The basis and original inspiration for El Vez is Presley; not just Elvis the icon but also Elvis as the headlight on the front of a train speeding through decades of the American cultural landscape.

what to buy: *Graciasland* ♫♫♫♫ (Sympathy for the Record Industry, 1994, prod. El Vez) is his crowning achievement. It draws liberally from the past 30 years of music (everyone from Santana to the Beatles, T. Rex, and Traffic are quoted), but those references are played neither for parody nor nostalgia, but as legitimate touchstones from our popular history.

the rest:

How Great Thou Art ♫♫♫ (Sympathy for the Record Industry, 1993)
Fun in Español ♫♫♫ (Sympathy for the Record Industry, 1993)
Merry MeX-mas ♫♫♫ (Sympathy for the Record Industry, 1994)

influences:

◄◄ Elvis Presley, the Fugs, the Rutles, Buster Poindexter

David Greenberger

Elastica

Formed 1992, in London, England.

Justine Frischmann, vocals, guitar; Donna Mathews, guitar,vocals; Annie Holland, bass (1994–95); Abby Travis, bass (1995–96); Sheila Chipperfield, bass (1996–present); Justin Welch, drums.

Cooler than your older sister when she thought she was Debbie Harry, derivative of Wire when they were worth a damn, Elastica from 1993 to 1995 was *it!* Good-looking, with good songs, the group was a smash, with irresistible hooks that, while unoriginal—they led to successful copyright infringement suits from the Stranglers and Wire—were nonetheless captivating. In former Suede member Justine Frischmann the group has a bona fide star, though the lengthy wait for its second full-length album puts the group at risk of being a temporary flavor rather than a lasting proposition.

what's available: *Elastica* 𝄞𝄞𝄞 (DGC, 1995, prod. Marc Waterman, Elastica) makes for good, sit-around-and-pick-out-the-influences kind of fun. On this good, nearly great record, "Line Up" and "Stutter" practically send you storming to the bathroom to put on some black eye makeup and fishnet stockings.

influences:

◄◄ Blondie, Wire, the Stranglers, Romeo Void

▶▶ Garbage

see also: *Suede*

Barry M. Prickett

Electrafixion

See: Echo & the Bunnymen

Electric Hellfire Club

See: My Life with the Thrill Kill Kult

Electric Light Orchestra /Jeff Lynne /ELO II

Formed 1971, in Birmingham, England. Disbanded 1990. Re-formed as ELO II in 1991.

Jeff Lynne, guitar, vocals, synthesizers (1971–90); Bev Bevan, drums; Rick Price, bass (1971–72); Roy Wood, guitar, vocals (1971–72); Richard Tandy, guitar, keyboards (1972–90); Michael D'Albuquerque, bass (1972–74); Mike Edwards, cello (1972–74); Colin Walker, cello (1972–73); Wilf Gibson, violin (1972–73); Hugh McDowell, cello (1973–77); Mik Kaminsky, violin (1973–77, 1991–present); Kelly Groucutt, bass, vocals (1974, 1991–present); Melvyn Gale, bass, vocals (1974–77); Eric Troyer, keyboards, vocals (1991–present); Phil Bates, guitar, vocals (1991–present).

Formed out of the ashes of successful '60s British rock band the Move, ELO began as an idea by Roy Wood to carry the orchestral ideas of *Sgt. Pepper's* –era Beatles further. But Wood was gone before the group bagged its first big single, a heavily orchestrated version of Chuck Berry's "Roll Over Beethoven." With Wood gone, Jeff Lynne became the group's sole producer and creative leader, refining the band's blend of classical string sounds and Beatle-esque rock/pop tunes. As one of the only rock bands that experimented with strings and actually tried to tour, ELO met with horrible results in early concerts, eventually resorting to taped backing tracks as '70s-era sound technology lagged behind the group's vision. After hitting a creative stride during the '70s—17 Top 40 hits between 1975 and 1981—ELO became the victim of changing tastes and watched its slick, seamless pop sound sell fewer and fewer records until the notoriously stage-shy Lynne abandoned the band in favor of a growing career as a producer. A short, misguided attempt to continue without him as ELO II has produced two stiff albums and some lame live performances.

what to buy: The band's formula first jelled into a sleek hit-making machine with *Face the Music* 𝄞𝄞𝄞 (Jet, 1975, prod. Jeff Lynne), an album on which Lynne's producing chops finally match his songwriting prowess, fueling songs such as the radio staple "Evil Woman" and dreamy ballad "Strange Magic." The precision of that record was quickly surpassed by *A New World Record* 𝄞𝄞𝄞𝄞 (Jet, 1976, prod. Jeff Lynne), which ranges from the operatic rock of "Rockaria" to the mournful "Telephone Line" and a remake of an early Move hit, "Do Ya."

what to buy next: To avoid the moribund filler that often hampers even the best ELO records, seek out its second greatest hits compilation, *ELO's Greatest Hits* 𝄞𝄞𝄞 (Jet, 1979, prod. Jeff Lynne), which collects favorites such as "Telephone Line," "Rockaria," and "Evil Woman" on a single album. For more, the two-CD *Strange Magic: The Best of Electric Light Orchestra* 𝄞𝄞𝄞 (Legacy/Epic, 1995, prod. Jeff Lynne) cobbles together every interesting cut the band ever released, excluding only the ELO II efforts.

what to avoid: Forget any ELO album released after 1980. All of them—*Time* woof! (Jet, 1981, prod. Jeff Lynne), *Secret Messages* woof! (Jet, 1983, prod. Jeff Lynne), and *Balance of Power* woof! (Epic, 1986, prod. Jeff Lynne)—represent the drawn-out decline and death of Lynne's slicked-up ultra-pop vision, made impossibly obsolete by newer, more vibrant rock flavors. The only thing worse is Lynne's former bandmates' baldfaced attempt to cash in on the group's 20-year legacy with *Part 2* **woof!** (Scotti Bros., 1991, prod. Jeff Glixman), featuring a new lineup without the one guy who made it all happen. Predictably, it falls flat in the worst way.

the rest:
No Answer 🎝🎝🎝 (Jet, 1972)
Masters of Rock 🎝🎝 (Harvest, 1973)
ELO II 🎝🎝🎝 (Jet, 1973)
On the Third Day 🎝🎝🎝 (Jet, 1973)
Showdown 🎝🎝🎝 (Harvest, 1974)
The Night the Lights Went On in Long Beach 🎝🎝 (United Artists, 1974)
Eldorado 🎝🎝🎝 (Jet, 1974)
Light Shines On 🎝🎝 (Harvest, 1976)
Ole' ELO 🎝🎝🎝 (Jet, 1976)
Out of the Blue 🎝🎝🎝 (Jet, 1977)
Discovery 🎝🎝🎝 (Jet, 1979)
Afterglow 🎝🎝🎝 (Epic, 1990)
ELO Classics 🎝🎝🎝 (Sony, 1990)
Burning Bright 🎝🎝 (Columbia Special Products, 1992)
Moment of Truth 🎝🎝 (Edsel, 1995)
(ELO II) One Night—Live 🎝🎝 (CMC International, 1997)

worth searching for: Check out Lynne's excruciatingly overproduced contributions to the soundtrack for Olivia Newton-John's film *Xanadu* (MCA, 1980), if only to laugh at the outdated fashions on the album cover and in the grooves.

solo outings:
Jeff Lynne:
Armchair Theater 🎝🎝🎝 (Reprise, 1989)

influences:
◀◀ The Beatles, the Move, Roy Orbison
▶▶ The Traveling Wilburys, Enya, Eurythmics

see also: *The Move, the Traveling Wilburys*

Eric Deggans

The Electric Prunes

Formed 1965, in Woodland Hills, CA. Disbanded 1969.

Jim Lowe, vocals, guitar, autoharp (1965–68); Ken Williams, guitar (1965–68); James "Weasel" Spagnola, guitar, vocals (1965–67); Mark Tulin, bass, keyboards (1965–68); Preston Ritter, drums (1965–67); Michael "Quint" Weakley, drums (1967–68); Mike Gannon, guitar (1967); John Herren, keyboards (1968); Mark Kincaid, guitar, vocals (1968–69); Ron Morgan, guitar (1968–69); Brett Wade, bass, flute, vocals (1968–69); Richard Whetstone, drums, guitar, vocals (1968–69).

Here is a group with prairie bluegrass roots that draws to its ranks one Hawaiian and one Canadian; becomes the garage-rock toast of pre-Doors L.A.; suddenly morphs into a dark,

brooding psychedelic-choir; then bows out playing good ol' '50s rock 'n' roll before disbanding altogether—just as it's about to be rediscovered on the soundtrack of the era's most highly acclaimed road movie. The Electric Prunes, in four short years, achieved all of this, and they even had a Top 20 hit to boot; their story is a microcosm of all the good, the bad, and the ugly that could befall an unsuspecting rock band during the '60s. In their initial incarnation, under the direction of early Rolling Stones engineer Dave Hassinger, the Prunes produced two magnificent proto-punk albums along with one timeless fuzz-box classic, "I Had Too Much to Dream (Last Night)." Left to their own devices, they probably would have been more than happy to follow the same paisley path towards underground immortality as their hometown pals Love & the Seeds. Instead, they fell under the evil spell of writer/arranger David Axelrod and recorded two laughably noble exercises in pseudo-religious pomposity, *Mass in F Minor* and *Release of an Oath: The Kol Nidre*, before finally sinking to the depths of a second-rate boogie band on their swan-song, *Just Good Old Rock 'n' Roll*. Proving, however, that you can't keep a good joke quiet for long, "Kyrie Eleison," a typically moronic slice of mock-Hebraic litany from the *Mass* album, was used to accompany Peter Fonda and Dennis Hopper's long strange trip through a graveyard in *Easy Rider*. By then, however, the real Prunes had, um, dried up and were nowhere to be found, but they still have fans eagerly awaiting the *next* chapter in their fascinatingly sordid tale of music and madness. Howzabout it, guys: time for a reunion?

what's available: Although they're becoming increasingly hard to track down, both *Long Day's Flight* 🎝🎝🎝 (Edsel, 1986, prod. Dave Hassinger) and the magnificent *Stockholm '67* 🎝🎝🎝 (Heartbeat, 1997, prod. Simon Edwards) showcase the band in all of its earliest, fuzziest glory. The latter, recorded live for a Swedish radio broadcast, brutally demonstrates just how much more exciting and proficient a band the Prunes were in its prime compared to their much over-hyped contemporaries from up San Francisco way.

worth searching for: Of dubious legality, *I Had Too Much to Dream Last Night/Underground* (Reprise, 1967/Head, 1997, prod. Dave Hassinger) reissues the band's first two—and best—albums on a single disc. Essential listening for all students of genuine *Nuggets*-rock.

influences:
◀◀ The Yardbirds, Count Five, Gypsy Trips, Chocolate Watchband, 13th Floor Elevators
▶▶ Strawberry Alarm Clock, H. P. Lovecraft, Marshmallow Overcoat, Ant Bee, Spinal Tap

Gary Pig Gold

Electronic

Formed 1989, in Manchester, England.

Johnny Marr, guitar, keyboards, programming; Bernard Sumner, vocals, keyboard, programming.

Influenced by new Manchester bands such as the Stone Roses and Happy Mondays, Electronic was formed in 1989 as an interim project by two members of Britain's most innovative bands of the '80s—guitarist Johnny Marr from the Smiths and vocalist Bernard Sumner of New Order. But the experiment quickly turned into a legitimate gig for the pair after topping the U.K. charts and hitting the American Top 40 with their debut single, "Getting Away with It."

what to buy: *Electronic* 🎵🎵 (Warner Bros., 1990, prod. Bernard Sumner, Johnny Marr) was released at the height of England's acid house obsession and captured the moment perfectly with Marr's innovative guitar playing and Sumner's bright vocals on singles like "Get the Message" and "Feel Every Beat." Pet Shop Boys singer Neil Tennant guested on several tracks.

what to avoid: Six years later, on the duo's follow-up disc, *Raise the Pressure* 🎵 (Warner Bros., 1996, prod. Electronic), the formula just didn't click. Working with former Kraftwerk member Karl Bartos and sounding hooked on Prozac, the British pop veterans turned out a lackluster set of generic dance floor anthems.

influences:
◀◀ 808 State, Happy Mondays, Pet Shop Boys

see also: *The Smiths, New Order, Joy Division*

Aidin Vaziri

The Elevator Drops

Formed in the mid-1990s, in Boston, MA.

GoolKasian, vocals, bass; Garvey J., guitar, vocals; Fitts, drums, vocals.

This Boston band prefers to hide behind strange pseudonyms and an obscure history. It's a gimmick that has its ups and downs. Brandishing a new wave sound a decade and a half after the fact, the group sounds pleasantly nostalgic, but in a knowing way. Only time will tell if the Elevator Drops rise to success or hit rock bottom.

what's available: The Sub Pop inversion of *Pop Bus* 🎵🎵🎵 (Time Bomb, 1996, prod. the Elevator Drops) will take you back to the early '80s, when bands remained emotionally distant. The equally transporting *People Mover* 🎵🎵🎵 (Time Bomb, 1997, prod. the Elevator Drops, Tim O'Heir) offers driving parcels of new wave pop that are as hard to define as they are not to hum along with.

influences:
◀◀ David Bowie, T. Rex, the Cars, Devo

Jordan Oakes

Eleventh Dream Day

Formed 1983, in Chicago, IL.

Janet Beveridge Bean, drums, vocals; Rick Rizzo, guitar, vocals; Shu Shubat, bass (1983–85); Douglas McCombs, bass (1985–present); Baird Figi, guitar (1985–91); Matthew "Wink" O'Bannon, guitar (1991–94).

Long before alternative rock became a marketing catch phrase and the Chicago underground scene became nationally renowned, Eleventh Dream Day was at the leading edge of both. The guitar front line of primary songwriter Rick Rizzo and Baird Figi fused the twisted, spiraling interplay of Television to the barbed-wire stomp of Crazy Horse and became the focal point of a scorching live act that attained legendary status in Chicago. On record, the quartet prefigured grunge—Nirvana once opened for it in Chicago—and then, as grunge became popular, outgrew it. The band, now reduced to its core of husband-and-wife Rizzo and Janet Bean, plus Doug McCombs, continues to make accomplished music, though it records infrequently and tours even less. Side projects have brought further acclaim—McCombs with the avant-garde instrumental group Tortoise and Bean with the roots-country band Freakwater.

what to buy: *Prairie School Freakout* 🎵🎵🎵🎵 (Amoeba, 1988, prod. Eleventh Dream Day, Matthew "Wink" O'Bannon) was recorded in one beer-soaked session with a buzzing amplifier, and it comes the closest to capturing the guitar-fired frenzy of the quartet in its concert prime. The darkly beautiful *Ursa Major* 🎵🎵🎵🎵 (Atavistic, 1994, prod. John McEntire) is a major departure from the band's country- and Neil Young–tinged earlier output, with producer McEntire and the band exploring more atmospheric terrain.

what to buy next: *Beet* 🎵🎵🎵🎵 (Atlantic, 1989, prod. Gary Waleik) finds the band reining in the guitars slightly to emphasize Rizzo's turbulent song narratives.

the rest:
Eleventh Dream Day 🎵🎵🎵 (Amoeba EP, 1987)
Lived to Tell 🎵🎵🎵 (Atlantic, 1991)
El Moodio 🎵🎵🎵🎵 (Atlantic, 1993)
Eighth 🎵🎵🎵🎵 (Thrill Jockey, 1997)

worth searching for: The hard-to-find *Wayne* (Amoeba EP, 1989, prod. Eleventh Dream Day) contains the 10-minute guitar burner "Tenth Leaving Train," a cover of Neil Young's "Southern Pacific," and a ripping punk-Young homage, "Go."

influences:

◀◀ Neil Young, Television

▶▶ Grunge

see also: *Freakwater*

Greg Kot

Danny Elfman

See: Oingo Boingo

The Elvis Brothers

Formed 1981, in Champaign, IL. Disbanded 1985. Re-formed 1990.

Graham Elvis, bass; Rob Elvis, guitar; Brad Elvis, drums (1981–96); Marty Winer, drums (1996–97).

A merry blend of Nick Lowe, the Beatles, and the Three Stooges, the Elvis Brothers were a rockin' novelty during the lean days of synth-pop. With a chemistry you couldn't find in science class, the guys also had a Monkees-like appeal that drove audiences bananas. In fact, they were invited to star in the ill-fated *New Monkees* TV series (the accompanying album covered one of their songs)—but, with an integrity befitting the King, they turned it down. It would have meant changing their moniker, anyway, and three Elvises for three Monkees just didn't seem like a fair trade. In the tradition of some "brother" bands (the Walkers, the Righteous, even the Ramones), Rob, Brad, and Graham had no parents in common—but they were kindred spirits in writing and performing styles, and they dressed alike. Not long after their second album, *Adventure Time*, the Brothers lived out their namesake's "Separate Ways" by breaking up. Always a big live draw in the Chicago-area circuit, though, they re-formed a few years later.

what to buy: *Movin' Up* 𝄞𝄞𝄞 (Portrait, 1983, prod. Lennie Petze, Tony Bongliovi, Lance Quinn) is the perfect display of their loosened-up power-pop, combining roots and Beatle boots in a perfect synthesis.

what to buy next: *Adventure Time* 𝄞𝄞𝄞 (Portrait, 1985, prod. Adrian Belew) is more of the same, but not as fresh and lively.

the rest:

Now Dig This 𝄞𝄞𝄞 (Recession, 1991)

worth searching for: The two-fer *Movin' Up/Adventure Time* (Recession, 1995) combines the first two Elvis Brothers albums on one CD.

influences:

◀◀ Nick Lowe, the Stray Cats, Cheap Trick, Elvis Presley

▶▶ Walter Clevenger

Jordan Oakes

Joe Ely

Born February 9, 1947, in Amarillo, TX.

Too rock for country, too country for rock, Texan Joe Ely has managed to exist somewhere in the middle, touring with both Merle Haggard and the Clash. He's never turned all of his critical acclaim into record sales, but he's managed to make a living. Ely blew out of the hot, windy south plains of Lubbock—Buddy Holly's home town—during the late '70s. A prolific writer who had wandered the wilds of the Southwest as a teenager, Ely had the gritty voice and raucous mix of honky-tonk country, blues-rock, and Tex-Mex to turn those experiences into vivid songs. The earlier, new wave honky-tonk sound gave way to a harder edge by the time he moved from MCA to HighTone. Ely returned to MCA in 1990, releasing a second live album before he returned to the more contemplative side first heard on *Down on the Drag*. Ely surrounds himself with resourceful musicians (band members have included guitarists David Grissom and Charlie Sexton, accordionist Ponty Bone, and steel guitarist Lloyd Maines).

what to buy: *Love and Danger* 𝄞𝄞𝄞 (MCA, 1992, prod. Joe Ely, Tony Brown) was a return to form for Ely after he'd ventured away from his honky tonk roots to a rootsy blues-rock sound during his stretch with HighTone. Ely's at his best when he's writing compelling narratives or interpreting songs by wonderful but overlooked Texas writers—Robert Earl Keen, in this case. *Twistin' in the Wind* 𝄞𝄞𝄞 (MCA, 1998, prod. Joe Ely) is quintessential Ely—the humor, heartbreak, and hurtin'. He wrote all but one of its dozen songs himself. Bringing together recent find Teye on flamenco guitar with Ely vets such as guitarists Jesse Taylor and David Grissom and steel man extraordinaire Lloyd Maines was a stroke of genius.

what to buy next: The smoky, sweaty bars, hot summer nights, and desperate characters are all there on *Honky Tonk Masquerade* 𝄞𝄞𝄞 (MCA, 1978, prod. Chip Young), the product of Ely's restless spirit and his tenure as the king of West Texas honky tonks. Ely classics "West Texas Waltz" and "Fingernails" ("I keep my fingernails long so they click when I play the piano," goes the song's opening line) are among the album's most colorful inclusions.

what to avoid: The raucous rockabilly of *Must Notta Gotta Lotta* 𝄞𝄞 (MCA/Southcoast, 1981, prod. Joe Ely, Michael Brovsky) is fun but not as memorable as his best work.

the rest:

Joe Ely 𝄞𝄞𝄞 (MCA, 1977)

Down on the Drag 𝄞𝄞𝄞 (MCA, 1979)

Live Shots 𝄞𝄞𝄞 (MCA/Southcoast, 1980)

Lord of the Highway 𝄞𝄞𝄞 (HighTone, 1987)

Dig All Night 𝄞𝄞 (HighTone, 1988)

Live at Liberty Lunch 𝄞𝄞𝄞 (MCA, 1990)

Letter to Laredo 𝄞𝄞𝄞 (MCA, 1995)

worth searching for: All but one of Ely's albums are available on CD. The exception is the experimental *Hi-Res* (MCA, 1984), which marked Ely's one and only plunge into the world of computers and synthesizers. It's pretty clunky, but there are some superb songs under the layers of electronics, including "Cool Rockin' Loretta," which appears on his *Live at Liberty Lunch*, and "Letter to Laredo," which was recast to be the title song of his Mexican-flavored 1995 album of that name.

influences:

◄◄ Buddy Holly, Hank Williams

►► Son Volt, Uncle Tupelo, Alejandro Escovedo

see also: *The Flatlanders*

Doug Pullen

Elysian Fields

Formed 1995, in New York, NY.

Jennifer Charles, vocals; Oren Bloedow, guitar, bass; Ed Pastorini, piano, guitars, vocals; James Genus, bass; Ben Perowsky, drums.

Elysian Fields' presence and personality revolves around frontwoman and chanteuse Jennifer Charles. A poetess and on-again/off-again young theater actress, Charles's haunting vocals give the group the spooky but alluring sexiness that is its charm. The backing band, including aspiring producers Oren Bloedow and Ed Pastorini, create lush, dark, and melodic soundscapes to set the appropriate mood.

what to buy: Some critics might find the group's torch-lit sound a bit contrived, but the songs on its debut EP, *Elysian Fields* 𝄞𝄞𝄞 (Radioactive, 1996, prod. Elysian Fields), are engaging nonetheless. The seductive songwriting, intoxicating instrumental tracks, and Charles's subverted sexiness lend a cool disposition to the work.

what to buy next: Though Elysian Fields' first full-length album, *Bleed Your Cedar* 𝄞𝄞𝄞 (Radioactive Records, 1996, prod. Elysian Fields), reveals some of the band's shortcomings, if you've bought into its sound, you will be pleased.

influences:

◄◄ Portishead, Lounge Lizards

Joseph Patel

The Embarrassment

Formed 1979, in Wichita, KS. Disbanded 1983.

Bill Goffrier, guitar, vocals; Brent Giessmann, drums, vocals; Ron Klaus, bass; John Nichols, vocals, guitar, keyboards.

Back in the early '80s, when the term "alternative" was truly needed, indie rock was born, and it lived up to its proper definition as a polar opposite to what was then considered mainstream rock. The main aspects of indie releases generally meant limited distribution and an independent source of financial backing. The Embarrassment was one of indie rock's first offerings; the group focused its musical attention on monotonus rhythms and low-fi guitars creating a sound all its own, one filled with anger and intellect that made it impossible to categorize. What made the Embarrassment that much more intriguing was that it did not come from New York or Los Angeles, but from, of all places, Wichita, Kansas. Still, its music was immersed in overtones from some of New York's greatest and most influential avante-garde rock bands, including the Velvet Underground and Television, and was topped off with its brand of simple pop. The Embarrassment released a slew of music between the years 1979 and 1983. All of these releases were compiled on one CD that was re-released in 1995. After the demise of the Embarrassment, guitarist Bill Goffrier formed the extraordinary Big Dipper.

what's available: Every worthwhile and embarrassing track that the Embarrassment recorded during the '80s has been compiled on *Heyday 1979–83* 𝄞𝄞𝄞 (Bar None, 1995, prod. various). *Heyday* has it all and more—live tracks, demos, and original album tracks, all packed on two CDs. *Heyday* contains all the Embarrassment's cult hits, including "Sex Drive" and "Patio Set," and more obscure material, such as a great live version of Michael Jackson's "Don't Stop 'Till You Get Enough." The overall demand for this one might be minimal, and chances are we'll never see a wing dedicated to the Embarrassment in the Rock 'n' Roll Hall of Fame, but as far as the indie rock community is concerned, the release of *Heyday* insures that this legendary influence shall prevail in digital eternity.

worth searching for: Although all of Bill Goffrier's Big Dipper records are long out of print, they're well worth searching for. Big Dipper released a couple of classic records for Homestead—*Craps* and *Heavens*—and one for Epic called *Slam*.

influences:

◄◄ The Velvet Underground, Iggy & the Stooges

►► Freedy Johnston, Throwing Muses, the Pixies

Chris Richards

Emergency Broadcast Network

Formed 1991, in Brookline, MA.

Joshua Pearson, audio/video production, sequence programming, voiceovers; Gardner Post, audio/video production, display systems development; Ron O'Donnell, audio/video production, turntable operation.

Emergency Broadcast Network is a multimedia troupe that first came to prominence through its nightmare-sitcom opener for

U2's American ZOO TV tour—a manipulated video clip of then-President George Bush announcing the Persian Gulf War twisted into a rendition of "We Will Rock You." EBN reshuffles mass-media images to create works that expose and ridicule the leaders soliciting our trust, and the group re-orchestrates the gunplay and gratuitous sex of the airwaves into infectious grooves that retain the sources' seductiveness while spotlighting their silliness. Pioneers of electronica for the eyes, EBN have supplied visuals to MTV's groundbreaking show *Amp* and produced episodes of U2's poetic but wry non-linear "magazine" series, *ZOO TV—The Television Program.* But the group is most in its element as media saboteur, going to the video tape to give an instant replay of the lies you may have just missed—all to an irresistible backbeat. In short, the Emergency Broadcast Network would like to pre-empt your regular programming.

what to buy: For a band like this, it's appropriate to start with video. *The Commercial Entertainment Product* (TVT, 1992) is a dystopian channel-surfing free-for-all that somehow makes our authority figures both scarier and funnier than ever before. Pop EBN's debut disc, *Telecommunication Breakdown* 𝄢𝄢𝄢𝄢 (TVT, 1995, prod. Jack Dangers, EBN, AVX Design), into your CD player and hear a disco inferno of syncopated sound-bites. Pop it into your CD-ROM drive and juggle both the track sequence and a personal vid-wall of images for a fascinating are-you-manipulating-it-or-is-it-manipulating-you experience.

what to buy next: Two remix EPs, *Behavior Modification/We Will Rock You* 𝄢𝄢𝄢𝄢 (TVT, 1992, prod. EBN) and *3:7:8* 𝄢𝄢𝄢𝄢 (TVT, 1995, prod. Jack Dangers), offer more of the same—which, when it comes to EBN, is never *quite* the same.

influences:

◄◄ Devo, Psychic TV, Negativland, Consolidated

►► Atari Teenage Riot, U2, nine inch nails

Adam McGovern

Emerson, Lake & Palmer /Emerson, Lake & Powell

Formed 1970, in London, England. Disbanded 1979. Re-formed 1986.

Keith Emerson, keyboards; Greg Lake, bass, guitar, vocals; Carl Palmer, drums, percussion (1972–79, 1987, 1992–present; Cozy Powell (died April 5, 1998), drums (1986).

Few bands can match ELP's ability to elicit an equal amount of thrills and yawns with its version of progressive rock. Keith Emerson, who was in the Nice, and Greg Lake, who left King Crimson, auditioned drummers and chose the powerhouse style of Carl Palmer, who had played with the Crazy World of Arthur Brown and Atomic Rooster. The trio of veterans had all the musical skills, dynamic range, and practiced showmanship

to ignite a crowd; what they lacked was a modicum of restraint, which often led to marathon pomp-rock displays of shallow flash, especially in their pseudo-rock interpretations of classical music. The trio was at its best on majestic ballads ("Lucky Man") or when turning with controlled aggression to vaguely ominous rockers framed with classical structure ("The Endless Enigma"). Palmer's industrial-strength drums provided the foundation as Emerson opened the floodgates on his synthesizers and Lake floated through the mix with his velvety vocals and deft bass lines. ELP's stage shows were legendary for their theatrics, including Palmer and his drums twirling in mid-air and Emerson throwing knives at his fire-breathing keyboards. Eventually ELP's musical strengths lost out to circus-like concerts and misguided classical ambitions. The rise of punk rock was largely a revolt against the bloated, scripted, stilted rock the punkers saw in ELP and Pink Floyd. The trio disbanded in 1978. In 1986, Emerson and Lake briefly tried to resurrect ELP with veteran drummer Cozy Powell. The three original members met for a soundtrack project in 1991 and decided to give ELP another shot.

what to buy: *Trilogy* 𝄢𝄢𝄢 (Atlantic, 1972, prod. Greg Lake) is bold without getting boorish, featuring one of ELP's finest ballads ("From the Beginning"), a convincing fusion of rock and classical ("The Endless Enigma"), plus one of Emerson's zippiest synthesizer discourses on Aaron Copland's "Hoedown." *Emerson, Lake and Palmer* 𝄢𝄢𝄢 (Atlantic, 1971, prod. Greg Lake) offers the signature song "Lucky Man" and the dynamic tension of "Knife Edge." *The Best of ELP* 𝄢𝄢𝄢 (Atlantic, 1980, prod. Greg Lake) offers a concise review of ELP's first incarnation.

what to buy next: *The Return of the Manticore* 𝄢𝄢𝄢 (Victory, 1993/Rhino, 1995, prod. various) is a four-disc box set that differs from the usual retrospective because it not only covers ELP's heyday from 1970 to 1978 but adds some worthwhile new material from the band's second incarnation, including the hefty "Black Moon" and fresh covers of older songs: "Fire" from Palmer's days with the Crazy World of Arthur Brown; "21st Century Schizoid Man," which Lake wrote with King Crimson; and "Touch and Go."

what to avoid: *Pictures at an Exhibition* 𝄢 (Atlantic, 1971, prod. Greg Lake) is a contrived concept album recorded live that puts a stale rock spin on Russian composer Mussorgsky's great classical work. It has neither the majesty of the original nor the earthy power of rock 'n' roll.

the rest:

Tarkus 𝄢𝄢 (Atlantic, 1971/Rhino, 1996)
Brain Salad Surgery 𝄢𝄢𝄢 (Atlantic, 1973/Rhino, 1996)
Welcome Back My Friends to the Show that Never Ends 𝄢𝄢 (Atlantic, 1974/Rhino, 1996)

Works, Volume I ♫♫ (Atlantic, 1977/Rhino, 1996)
Works, Volume II ♫♫ (Atlantic, 1977/Rhino, 1996)
Love Beach ♫♫ (Atlantic, 1979/Rhino, 1996)
Works Live ♫♫ (Atlantic, 1979/Rhino, 1996)
Black Moon ♫♫♫ (Victory, 1992)
Live at the Royal Albert Hall ♫♫ (Victory, 1994/Rhino, 1996)
The Best of Emerson, Lake and Palmer ♫♫♫ (Rhino, 1996)
The King Biscuit Flower Hour Presents Emerson, Lake and Palmer ♫♫♫ (KBFH Records, 1998)

worth searching for: The deluxe edition of *Brain Salad Surgery* (Victory, 1992/Rhino, 1996) re-creates the original album's slick, fold-out graphics in the CD format.

solo outings:

Greg Lake:
From the Beginning: The Greg Lake Retrospective ♫♫♫ (Rhino, 1997)
The King Biscuit Flower Hour Presents Greg Lake ♫♫ (KBFH Records, 1997)

influences:

◄◄ Charlie Parker, Sergey Prokofiev, King Crimson, the Nice, Jerry Lee Lewis

►► Yes, Asia, David Bowie, U2, Kansas, Mission UK, Depeche Mode

see also: *King Crimson, Asia*

David Yonke

EMF

Formed 1989, in Forest of Dean, England. Disbanded 1997.

James Atkin, vocals; Ian Dench, guitar; Derry Brownson, keyboards; Zac Foley, bass; Mark Decloedt, drums.

Before Oasis and Blur returned British rock to the Beatles, the U.K. was obsessed with a heavily hyped but short-lived form of boisterous, rocking dance music. Its pioneers were the Happy Mondays, but, with the possible exception of Jesus Jones, no single band rode it more successfully up the pop charts than EMF. The quintet's 1991 song "Unbelievable" was such a huge international smash it effectively destroyed EMF's subsequent career, no matter how hard guitarist and bandleader Ian Dench struggled to stay relevant. Though the band wrote excellent songs and went from grossly overhyped to sadly underrated, its members tried far too hard to stay hip. They insisted EMF was a provocatively profane acronym, and caused a minor media controversy by releasing the voice of Mark David Chapman, John Lennon's killer, in the background of a song. (Bowing to pressure from Yoko Ono's lawyers, the band released a new version of its big-selling debut, *Schubert Dip*, without the clip.) EMF rode the British dance-rock wave to the very bottom, putting out a decent but desperate version of the Stooges'

punk classic "Search and Destroy." Ultimately, they disbanded, never truly able to shake their one-hit-wonder status.

what to buy: It earned good reviews at the time, but almost nobody can remember songs from *Schubert Dip* ♫♫♫ (EMI, 1991/Alliance, 1996, prod. Pascal Gabriel, Ralph Jezzard) other than "Unbelievable." There's a nice tension within the group, as Derry Brownson pounds his keyboards against Dench's aggressive guitars, and James Atkin sings prettily above the din. The album is worth revisiting, although it already sounds dated, for the follow-up hits "I Believe" and "Children."

what to avoid: Neither the EP *Unexplained* ♫♫ (EMI, 1992), rushed into print to take advantage of the brief EMF frenzy (and which includes the trying-too-hard version of "Search and Destroy"), nor the gloomy, wholly unfun *Stigma* ♫♫ (EMI, 1992/Alliance, 1996, prod. Ian Dench, James Atkin, Ralph Jezzard) managed to extend EMF's popularity. Besides, by then the dance-rock craze had run its course.

worth searching for: A final burst of desperation, the British release *Cha Cha Cha* (EMI, 1995) includes some interesting thrash-punk experiments and strange noise. It was a commercial dud, though, and never came out in the U.S.

influences:

◄◄ Happy Mondays, Madonna, Iggy Pop & the Stooges, Jesus Jones, the Stone Roses

►► Smash Mouth, the Chemical Brothers, Junkie XL, Fatboy Slim

Steve Knopper

The English Beat /General Public

Formed 1978, in Birmingham, England. Disbanded 1983.

The English Beat (1978–83): Andy Cox, guitar; Everett Morton, drums; David Steele, bass; Dave Wakeling, guitar, vocals; Ranking Roger, vocals, percussion (1979–83); Saxa, saxophone (1979–82). General Public (1984–87, 1994–present): Dave Wakeling; Ranking Roger; Micky Billingham, keyboards, vocals (1984–87); Horace Panter, bass (1984–87); Kevin White, guitar (1984–85); Stoker, drums (1984–85); Gianni Minardi, guitar (1986–87); Mario Minardi, drums (1986–87); Michael Railton, keyboards, programming, vocals (1994–present); Wayne Lothian, bass (1994–present); Dan Chase, drums (1994–present); Norman Jones, percussion, vocals (1994–present).

One good thing to come out of the racial strife that engulfed England during the late '70s and early '80s was the two-tone movement, a cluster of racially mixed bands dedicated to uniting British youth through song and dance. Followers of the music, which was a hybrid of punk rock and Jamaican ska, sported black-and-white clothing and short hair, as did the musicians. Among the best and most important of these bands was the English Beat, known simply as the Beat everywhere but in America due to trademark concerns. The Beat, which formed in 1978, released its first single in 1979, Smokey Robinson's "Tears of a Clown," on the 2-tone record label owned by another key band in the movement, the Specials. The single went to #6 on the British charts and featured the frenetic saxophone work of veteran Jamaican musician Saxa, who had played with the Beatles and the ska stars Desmond Dekker and Prince Buster. Saxa later joined the band full time, as did Ranking Roger, a young Birmingham percussionist whose specialty was toasting (melodic chanting). The Beat generated a string of U.K. hits, including "Hands Off . . . She's Mine," "Mirror in the Bathroom," "Best Friend," and the politically charged "Stand Down Margaret," which pleaded for "peace, love, and unity" as well as the departure of the British prime minister. The Beat enjoyed a loyal following in the U.S., too, scoring its biggest hits with 1982's "I Confess" and "Save It for Later." The band broke up in 1983, resulting in two new outfits. Cox and Steele formed Fine Young Cannibals, while Wakeling and Ranking Roger became General Public. Wakeling and Roger split up in 1988 after a falling out but have since reformed General Public, enjoying a hit remake of the Staple Singers' "I'll Take You There" in 1994, when it was featured in the film *Threesome*.

what to buy: *I Just Can't Stop It* ✒✒✒✒✒ (Sire, 1980, prod. Bob Sargeant) is the English Beat's debut album and one of the best records of the '80s. Mixing Chuck Berry–like guitar sounds, Beach Boyish harmonies, sizzling sax lines, and Caribbean rhythms, this spellbinding record sounds as good today as it did 16 years ago. *Special Beat Service* ✒✒✒✒ (I.R.S., 1982, prod. Bob Sargeant) is the English Beat's third record and features the band's best-known singles in the U.S., "Save It for Later" and "I Confess," as well as the verbal acrobatics of Ranking Roger and guest Pato Banton in the delightful "Pato and Roger Ago Talk."

what to buy next: Wakeling and Roger's first effort as General Public, . . . *All the Rage* ✒✒✒ (I.R.S., 1984, prod. General Public, Gavin MacKillop, Colin Fairley), has harder edges than anything the Beat did. The two excellent singles from the record, "Tenderness" and "Never You Done That," have a distinctly Motown feel.

what to avoid: The English Beat compilation *What Is Beat?* ✒✒✒ (I.R.S., 1983, prod. Bob Sargeant, the English Beat, Mike Hedges, David Peters) provides some answers to that question, but earlier records offer a clearer picture.

the rest:
The English Beat:
Wha'ppen ✒✒✒ (I.R.S., 1981)

General Public:
Hand to Mouth ✒✒✒ (I.R.S., 1986)
Rub It Better ✒✒✒ (Epic, 1995)

The International Beat:
The Hitting Line ✒✒✒ (Triple X, 1986)

worth searching for: *The Beat Goes On* (I.R.S., 1991) features some of the English Beat's biggest hits as well songs by Fine Young Cannibals, Wakeling, Ranking Roger, and the International Beat.

solo outings:
Ranking Roger:
Radical Departure ✒✒✒ (I.R.S., 1988)

Dave Wakeling:
No Warning ✒✒✒ (I.R.S., 1991)

influences:
◀◀ Prince Buster, Desmond Dekker, Smokey Robinson, Sly & the Family Stone

▶▶ Barenaked Ladies, Dave Matthews Band, Rancid, Sublime, Save Ferris, No Doubt

see also: *Fine Young Cannibals*

William Hanson

Jeremy Enigk

Born 1974, in Everett, WA.

Not yet in his mid-twenties, Jeremy Enigk has already established himself as an ambitious, spiritually minded alternative-rock singer and recording artist with a taste for anguished drama and a willingness to experiment. Starting out as frontman for Seattle's Sunny Day Real Estate, he provided the Bono-ish wail for which the band supplied the U2-goes-grunge support. Its 1994 debut, *Diary*, proved to be the high point of its first incarnation, though the band splintered shortly afterwards, due in part to Enigk's much-publicized conversion to born-again Christianity. While one half of SDRE went on to become the rhythm section for the Foo Fighters, Enigk took a strange and wonderful sidestep, resulting in his haunting, lyrical solo debut, *Return of the Frog Queen*. Interestingly, SDRE has now re-formed (with ex-Mommyheads member Jeff Palmer taking over for Nate Mendel on bass). One can only guess whether it will incorporate any of Enigk's orchestral leanings into the band's established sound.

what's available: Though it's flawed in spots and less than half an hour in length, *Return of the Frog Queen* ✒✒✒ (Sub Pop, 1996, prod. Greg Williamson) serves notice that Enigk doesn't need the electric punch of Sunny Day Real Estate behind him in order to make enticing, evocative music. With the backing of a

21-piece orchestra, Enigk and his keening, crackly tenor forge an intriguing recording reminiscent of early '70s British psychedelic pop.

influences:

⏮ John Lennon, Nick Drake, U2, Rod Stewart, Cardinal

⏭ Our Lady Peace, Glitterbox

see also: *Sunny Day Real Estate*

Bob Remstein

Enigma

Formed 1990, in Ibiza, Spain.

Curly M.C. (Michael Cretu), programming, guitars, keyboards, percussion; F. Gregorian (Frank Peterson), songwriting (1990); Sandra Lauer, vocals; David Fairstein, songwriting; Angel (Andy Hard), vocals (1993); Jens Glad, guitar (1993); Louisa Stanley, vocals (1996); Peter Cornelius, guitar.

Michael Cretu, a classically trained pianist and respected European producer and engineer, created Enigma in order to experiment combining diverse types of musical styles and influences. With a revolving cast of musicians credited anonymously, Cretu's goal was to record a project that forced listeners to respond only to the music, not the performers. A canny mix of styles that picked up on the rise of techno music and the Gregorian-chant craze of the early '90s, Enigma hit with "Sadeness" a bit of campy yet seductive fluff that they never equalled for audaciousness or catchiness.

what to buy: With the single "Sadeness" already a hit, Enigma's debut album *MCMXC A.D.* 𝄞𝄞𝄞𝄞 (Charisma, 1990, prod. Michael Cretu) combines layered keyboards, hip-hop beats, and tape loops, while phrases spoken in French and Gregorian chants bring a warm, organic feel to what could otherwise be cold, synthetic-sounding music. The album plays like one extended song as tracks merge together.

what to buy next: *Enigma2: The Cross of Changes* 𝄞𝄞𝄞 (Charisma, 1993, prod. Michael Cretu) uses various indigenous sounds, most notably the Indian lapp chant, in place of the Gregorian chants. It doesn't have quite the same richness or flow as *MCMXC A.D.*, though the engrossing "Return to Innocence" is an exception.

the rest:

Enigma3: Le Roi Est Mort, Vive Le Roi! 𝄞𝄞𝄞 (Virgin, 1996)

influences:

⏮ Pink Floyd, the Alan Parsons Project, Benedictine Monks of Santo Domingo de Silos

Bryan Lassner

Brian Eno

Born Brian Peter George St. John le Baptiste Eno, May 15, 1948, in Suffolk, England.

Brian Eno began his professional music life with the rock group Roxy Music but has gone on to become an innovator of enormous influence in pop, progressive electronic, and new age music circles. Eno became enamored of synthesizers during the late '60s and entered Roxy as a technical aide, though his role grew throughout his involvement with the band. He left in 1973 to produce his own quirky music, which became more and more experimental with ambient sounds and minimalist techniques. Rather than songs, Eno produced soundscapes meant to be experienced as much as heard, to serve as part of the background texture of a room. Eno is also a visual artist and has created ambient music to be played at his art installations. Even though his own muse leads along more esoteric line, Eno has also produced highly popular recordings for the likes of Talking Heads, U2, David Bowie, and Devo, and he's engaged in critically acclaimed collaborations with Robert Fripp, David Byrne, and John Cale, among others.

what to buy: Before he took a sharp turn to ambience, Eno did some incisive experimental rock work. His ear for melody and musical hooks shows through on *Another Green World* 𝄞𝄞𝄞𝄞𝄞 (Island, 1975/E.G. 1982) prod. Brian Eno, Rhett Davies) with its thick mixes and otherworldly atmosphere. The hook on "Sky Saw" seems capable of ripping the heavens apart, and "I'll Come Running" shows how he can turn out a banal pop lyric, then twist it into a comment on the whole genre. The David Byrne collaboration *My Life in the Bush of Ghosts* 𝄞𝄞𝄞𝄞 (Sire, 1981, prod. Brian Eno, David Byrne) mixes Byrne's world music fascination with Eno's bag of ambient tricks. It contains dense, African-like rhythms mixed in a danceable format with the authors' cache of found sounds, prepared instruments, and synthesized riffs.

what to buy next: Airy and spare, *Ambient 1: Music for Airports* 𝄞𝄞𝄞𝄞 (PVC, 1979/E.G., 1982, prod. Brian Eno) shows the side of Eno that eventually influenced new age sounds—incidental music that is not meant to be listened to closely, yet sets an overall calming mood. Eno's first record out of the gate, *Here Come the Warm Jets* 𝄞𝄞𝄞𝄞 (Island, 1973/E.G., 1982, prod. Brian Eno), is a pastiche of quirky rock tunes with cunning lyrics. "Baby's on Fire," "Cindy Tells Me," and "On Some Faraway Beach" show a pop sensibility but always with a twist that pokes a stick in the eye of tradition.

the rest:

(With Robert Fripp) *No Pussyfooting* 𝄞𝄞𝄞 (Antilles,1973/E.G., 1981)
Taking Tiger Mountain (By Strategy) 𝄞𝄞𝄞𝄞 (Island, 1974/E.G, 1982)
Discreet Music 𝄞𝄞𝄞 (Antilles, 1975/E.G. 1982)
(With Robert Fripp) *Evening Star* 𝄞𝄞𝄞 (Antilles, 1975/E.G. 1981)

Before and After Science 🦴🦴🦴⁷ (Island, 1978/E.G., 1982)
Music for Films 🦴🦴🦴🦴 (Antilles, 1978/E.G. 1982)
(With John Hassell) *Fourth World, Vol. 1: Possible Musics* 🦴🦴🦴
    (1980/E.G., 1993)
(With Harold Budd) *Ambient 2: Plateaux of Mirrors* 🦴🦴🦴 (E.G., 1980)
Ambient 4: On Land 🦴🦴🦴🦴 (Caroline, 1982/E.G., 1986)
(With Daniel Lanois and Roger Eno) *Apollo: Atmospheres & Sound-
    tracks* 🦴🦴🦴 (E.G., 1983)
(With Harold Budd) *The Pearl* 🦴🦴🦴 (E.G, 1984)
Thursday Afternoon 🦴🦴 (E.G., 1985)
More Blank than Frank 🦴🦴🦴 (E.G., 1986)
Desert Island Selection 🦴🦴🦴 (E.G., 1989)
(With John Cale) *Wrong Way Up* 🦴🦴🦴🦴 (Warner Bros., 1990)
The Shutov Assembly 🦴🦴🦴⁷ (Opal/Warner Bros., 1992)
Nerve Net 🦴🦴🦴🦴 (Opal, 1992)
Neroli 🦴🦴⁷ (All Saints/Gyroscope, 1993)
Brian Eno II: Vocal 🦴🦴🦴🦴 (Virgin, 1994)
(With Robert Fripp) *The Essential Fripp and Eno* 🦴🦴🦴🦴 (Venture, 1994)
(With Jah Wobble) *Spinner* 🦴🦴🦴 (Gyroscope, 1995)
(With Dieter Moebius and Hans-Joachim Roedelius) *After the Heat* 🦴🦴🦴
    (Gyroscope, 1996)
(With Dieter Moebius and Hans-Joachim Roedelius) *Begegnungen* 🦴🦴🦴
    (Gyroscope, 1996)
(With Dieter Moebius and Hans-Joachim Roedelius) *Begegnungen II*
    🦴🦴🦴 (Gyroscope, 1996)
The Drop 🦴🦴🦴 (Thirsty Ear, 1997)

worth searching for: The box set *Brian Eno I: Instrumental* (Virgin, 1994, prod. Brian Eno) contains some of his most compelling works, including selections from David Bowie's Berlin
trilogy of albums that launched a thousand keyboard bands.

influences:

◀◀ Soft Machine, King Crimson, John Cage

▶▶ Talking Heads, David Arkenstone, Michael Brook, U2

see also: *Roxy Music, Robert Fripp, U2*

Lawrence Gabriel and Daniel Durchholz

John Entwistle

Born October 9, 1944, in Chiswick, London, England.

Within the flash 'n' trash world of the Who, John Entwistle perhaps played his role as the stolid, quiet bassist a bit too well, for
he is still the one member of the legendary band who could
probably ride a crowded elevator without being noticed. However, being noticed is precisely the reason behind Entwistle's ultimately frustrating quarter-century-plus solo career. For a man
of such large talent and stature, it must be difficult to be relegated to touring America, between Who reunions, in an Econo-
van playing 200-seat sports bars. Much like Ringo Starr's, his
own identity seems destined to be hidden by the part he played

in a larger-than-life showbiz entity. John Entwistle deserves better. He did as much as James Jamerson and, yes, Beatle Paul to
redefine the way rock bass was played, and his sick 'n' funny
songs were easily the highlights of many a Who record. He possesses a remarkable singing voice as well—one minute rumbling from the depths of hell ("Boris the Spider"), the next
minute soaring magnificently into the nose-bleed heights of the
harmonies ("A Quick One While He's Away"). Still, his career
outside of the Who failed to carve a much-deserved niche in the
grand scheme of rock things, despite an abundance of fine
songs, fine performances, and hilarious cover art.

what to buy: The aptly-named *Thunderfingers: The Best of
John Entwistle* 🦴🦴🦴🦴 (Rhino, 1996, compilation prod. Gary
Stewart) deftly spans a decade of Ox rock, from 1971 through
1981, though it leans heavily, as it should, toward selections
from his first two albums.

what to buy next: Entwistle's entire catalog is finally getting
the deluxe reissue treatment, so if you missed them first time
around, there's no excuse now not to pick up *Smash Your Head
against the Wall* 🦴🦴🦴🦴 (Decca, 1971/Sundazed, 1997, prod.
John Entwistle) and *Whistle Rymes* 🦴🦴🦴🦴 (Decca, 1972/Sun-
dazed, 1997, prod. John Entwistle, John Alcock), both wry, hard-
hitting collections of bottom-heavy rock with the odd—in more
ways than one—ballad thrown in, just to throw you off. Peter
Frampton actually plays his guitar tastefully throughout the latter. *John Entwistle's Rigor Mortis Sets In* 🦴🦴🦴🦴 (MCA, 1973/Sun-
dazed, 1998, prod. John Entwistle, John Alcock) closes the cof-
fin-lid, literally, on all the rock 'n' roll revival nonsense that was
still festering in the pre-glitter era. Entwistle's takes on such
classics as "Hound Dog" and "Lucille" are as devastatingly
wicked as the Sex Pistols' Monkees covers, and every bit as
loud. Also guaranteed to blow your system's woofers in no time
flat is *King Biscuit Flower Hour Presents John Entwistle* 🦴🦴🦴
(KBFH Records, 1997, prod. Jon Astley, Andy Macpherson), a
delicious 1975 recording of Entwistle and his Ox band attacking
both Who ("My Wife") and solo ("My Size") material in front of
an uproarious Philadelphia audience.

what to avoid: *Too Late the Hero* **woof!** (Atco, 1981/Sundazed,
1998, prod. Cy Langston, John Entwistle) is a misguided, overblown collaboration with the severely unwitty Joe Walsh. The
sound of two old rockers creaking on the front porch.

the rest:

Mad Dog 🦴🦴🦴 (MCA, 1975/Sundazed, 1998)
John Entwistle: The Rock 🦴🦴 (Griffin Music, 1996)
The John Entwistle Band Soundtrack from "Van-pires" 🦴🦴🦴 (MSH
    Records, 1998)

influences:

◀◀ Duane Eddy, Bob Bogle, Boris Karloff

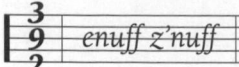

▶▶ Jack Bruce, Geddy Lee, Bruce Foxton

see also: *The Who*

Gary Pig Gold

Enuff Z'Nuff
Formed mid-1980s, in Chicago, IL.

Donnie Vie, guitar, vocals; Derek Frigo, guitar; Chip Z'Nuff, bass, guitar, vocals; Vikki Foxx, drums.

What initially gave Enuff Z'Nuff a commercial identity came back to haunt the band later, when heavy metal—so big (like its singers' hair) during the mid-'80s—corroded during the '90s. Enuff Z'Nuff was never a metal band anyway; it was a Beatles-influenced power-pop combo that often watered down its potent songs with generic, grating guitar solos. By contrast, fellow Illinois rockers Cheap Trick also had thundering, metal-influenced riffs but wove them into the fabric of the band's sound. In the case of Enuff Z'Nuff, the riffing was often painfully extraneous—the band could have fired its guitarist and been a better band. Still, the sparkling songs shone through the rusty metal, and there are enough of them to make the band one of the bright lights of recent power-pop.

what to buy: *1985* 𝄢𝄢𝄢𝄢 (Big Deal, 1994) gathers some of the group's first recordings in a cohesive package of pure pop, catching the group before it grasped the metal mantle. Down to a two-piece—founders Donnie Vie and Chip Z'Nuff—the band's *Tweaked* 𝄢𝄢𝄢𝄢 (Mayhem, 1995, prod. Enuff Z'Nuff) shows what the group can do without the riffing that filled its major label releases. The songs are melodic confessions that evoke the dreaminess of classic ELO ("My Dear Dream") and the horrors of substance abuse (the appropriately bluesy "My Heroin"). *Seven* 𝄢𝄢𝄢𝄢 (Mayhem, 1997, prod. Chip Z'Nuff, Donnie Vie) is basically a domestic release of the Japanese-only *Chip & Donnie*, with the addition of two bonus tracks. The metal days remain a thing of the past—if anything, *Seven* is like a Bon Jovi album lifted by memories of John Lennon instead of Springteen. The haunting melodies are a consistent foil, without going metal, to the occasional ambiguity and craftlessness of the lyrics. One gets the feeling Vie and Z'Enuff are trying to relate real feelings and occurrences, but they have a much better ear for music than words.

what to buy next: *Enuff Z'Nuff* 𝄢𝄢𝄢𝄢 (Atco, 1989, prod. Enuff Z'Nuff, Ron Fajerstein) contains the melodically euphoric "New Thing," the group's best song and one of the best pop songs in recent memory. *Strength* 𝄢𝄢𝄢𝄢 (Atco, 1991, prod. Enuff Z'Nuff, Paul Lani) has nothing as stunning as "New Thing" but is a more consistent record, beautifully haunted by the ghost of John Lennon.

the rest:
Peach Fuzz 𝄢𝄢𝄢𝄢 (Big Deal, 1986/1990)
Animals with Human Intelligence 𝄢𝄢𝄢 (Arista, 1992)

influences:
◀◀ The Beatles, Mott the Hoople, Badfinger, Off Broadway
▶▶ Jellyfish

Jordan Oakes

Epic Soundtracks
See: Soundtracks, Epic

Erasure
Formed 1985, in London, England.

Vince Clarke, synthesizer; Andy Bell, vocals.

After splitting from Yaz (a.k.a. Yazoo), songwriter and keyboard wizard Vince Clarke paired up with the flamboyant vocalist Andy Bell to form another synthesizer duo—this one characterized by bouncy synth-pop and Bell's distinctive flair for melodrama. Riding one approach—more or less—since its inception, the group has successfully wooed the jilted club kids with lovelorn pop confections and catchy dance piffle.

what to buy: *Pop! The First 20 Hits* 𝄢𝄢𝄢 (Mute/Sire/Reprise, 1992, prod. various) offers a Nutrasweet collection of the band's singles, including "Chains of Love," "Victim of Love," and "Oh L'Amour." Its U.S. breakthrough, *The Innocents* 𝄢𝄢𝄢 (Mute/Sire/Reprise, 1988, prod. Stephen Hague), is the pseudo-soul dance peak of the band, containing "A Little Respect" and "Ship of Fools" in addition to "Chains of Love."

what to buy next: *Wonderland* 𝄢𝄢𝄢 (Mute/Sire, 1986, prod. Flood), the band's debut, comes off like Yaz part two, more as an extension of Clarke's electronic inventions than a mere rehashing of his former work.

what to avoid: On *Circus* 𝄢𝄢 (Mute/Sire, 1987, prod Flood) Clarke's synth work is frothy as ever but Bell's woe-is-me delivery is too self-indulgent for even the heaviest dose of ecstasy.

the rest:
The Two Ring Circus 𝄢𝄢𝄢 (Mute/Sire, 1987)
Wild! 𝄢𝄢 (Mute/Sire/Reprise, 1989)
Crackers International 𝄢𝄢𝄢 (Mute/Sire/Reprise EP, 1989)
Chorus 𝄢𝄢 (Mute/Sire/Reprise, 1991)
Abba-esque 𝄢𝄢𝄢 (Elektra EP, 1992)
I Say, I Say, I Say 𝄢𝄢 (Mute/Elektra, 1994)
Erasure 𝄢𝄢 (Mute/Elektra, 1995)
Cowboy 𝄢𝄢𝄢 (Maverick, 1997)

influences:
◀◀ Depeche Mode, ABBA

▶▶ New Order, Simply Red, Electronic

see also: *Alison Moyet/Yaz/Yazoo*

Allan Orski

Roky Erickson

Born July 15, 1947, in Dallas, TX.

An extremely disturbed singer who makes Daniel Johnston seem like a pillar of stability, Roky Erickson is a songwriter whose work represents not so much the gurgling of an idiot savant as the few salvaged remains of a mind wiped out by acid and mental institutions. From the wellsprings of his formative band, the truly psychedelic 13th Floor Elevators, came a piddly pot charge to which he inexplicably pleaded insanity and was thus institutionalized. Upon release, Erickson's erratic solo career began with horrifying rock 'n' roll; the demonic dementia that inhabits much of his material is heightened by his belief that he and Satan are in cahoots. Amidst the true-life tribulations that make up his daily existence, he has penned an arresting number of staggering rockers and disarmingly sweet acoustic ballads that have influenced a couple generations of rockers. Numerous unauthorized releases have been in circulation since the early '80s, making his catalog as difficult to define as his songs are, sometimes, to comprehend.

what to buy: *You're Gonna Miss Me: The Best of Roky Erickson* 🎵🎵🎵♪ (Restless, 1991, prod. various) makes the publicity-seeking Satanism of most metal bands seem like a childproof lighter compared to this searing document of rock 'n' roll damage. Underneath B-movie titles such as "Two Headed Dog" and "I Walked with a Zombie" is shuddering conviction matched with crack delivery. It's a bracing representation of his '80s output.

what to buy next: *All That May Do My Rhyme* 🎵🎵🎵 (Trance Syndicate, 1995, prod. Casey Monahan, Speedy Sparks, Stuart Sullivan) is a surprisingly cohesive, acoustically based effort comprised of new material and some decade-old recordings. His childlike tenor gives the melodic tunes a ringing note of sincere frailty that most folk singers would trade their tea bags for.

the rest:
Holiday Inn Tapes 🎵🎵🎵 (Fan Club, 1987)
Beauty and the Beast 🎵🎵 (Sympathy for the Record Industry, 1993)
The Evil One 🎵🎵🎵 (Restless, 1993)

worth searching for: One of the finest tribute albums ever, *Where the Pyramid Meets the Eye: A Tribute to Roky Erickson* (Sire, 1990, prod. various) features high-profile groups such as R.E.M. and ZZ Top paying homage to their warped hero, and drawing deserved attention toward some truly fine songs. Erickson's own *Gremlins Have Pictures* (Pink Dust, 1986) is an im-

port of live recordings that reveal his fragile emotional state more than anything else.

influences:
◀◀ The 13th Floor Elevators, Black Sabbath
▶▶ R.E.M., Daniel Johnston, Katy McCarty

Allan Orski

Eric's Trip
/Elevator to Hell

Formed 1990, in Moncton, New Brunswick, Canada. Disbanded 1996.

Rick White, vocals, guitar; Jane Doiron, bass, vocals; Tara White, bass, vocals; Chris Thompson, guitar; Mark Gaudet, drums.

The first dissonant incarnation of the band Eric's Trip was named after a Sonic Youth song—let that be your guide in trying to understand the enigma that it is. Eric's Trip was the first of a string of Canadian bands to sign with the Seattle-based Sub Pop label, releasing a series of albums built around sad, fuzzy pop and unrelenting melancholy. The group broke up during 1996, with Rick White, his wife Tara, and Mark Gaudet continuing on as Elevator to Hell, while Jane Doiron went on to run her own 7-inch label, Sappy, and sign a solo deal with Sub Pop.

what to buy: The group's debut, *Tara* 🎵🎵🎵🎵 (Sub Pop, 1993, prod. Rick White), is its best, a style-setter that they built on but never really bettered. Elevator to Hell's *Parts 1–3* 🎵🎵🎵🎵 (Sub Pop, 1996, prod. Rick White) is nearly *Tara's* equal, a powerful opening line for these musicians' next chapter.

the rest:
Eric's Trip:
Forever Again 🎵🎵🎵 (Sub Pop, 1994)
Purple Blue 🎵🎵🎵♪ (Sub Pop, 1996)

Elevator to Hell:
Eerieconsiliation 🎵🎵🎵♪ (Sub Pop, 1997)

influences:
◀◀ Sonic Youth, Bill Laswell, Neil Young

Norene Cashen

Alejandro Escovedo

Born January 10, 1951, San Antonio, TX.

In concert, the nattily-attired Alejandro Escovedo at first sounds like any country-tinged singer-songwriter—the songs are a bit downbeat attitudinally, a bit rocking musically. By the time he reaches his droning version of Iggy Pop's "I Wanna Be Your Dog," though, he gives himself away. Despite three moody, pristinely written solo albums, Escovedo hangs tightly to his roots as a Texas punk rocker. Escovedo, who comes from a musical family—his brothers are Santana band members Pete and Coke Escovedo, and his niece is former Prince protégé Sheila E.—played in the Nuns, Rank & File, and the True Believers (with his brother, Javier) throughout the '80s. Despite critical acclaim, he has never tasted any significant commercial success, and while his record label, Rykodisc, kept his punk side project, Buick MacKane, it dumped him as a solo artist after the underrated *With These Hands*.

what to buy: *Gravity* 𝄞𝄞𝄞𝄞 (Watermelon, 1992, prod. Turner Stephen Bruton), a hushed, moody album written after Escovedo's first wife committed suicide, contains the explosive rocker "One More Time" and the chanting tear-jerker "Bury Me."

what to buy next: Both of the catchy, rocking, self-titled True Believers' albums (the first was out-of-print, the second never released) came out as *Hard Road* 𝄞𝄞𝄞𝄞 (Rykodisc, 1994, prod. Jim Dickinson, Jeff Glixman). Escovedo's second solo album, *Thirteen Years* 𝄞𝄞𝄞 (Watermelon, 1993, prod. Turner Stephen Bruton), is overly repetitive and harder to listen to than *Gravity*, but "Ballad of the Sun and the Moon" is one of many well-written highlights.

the rest:
With These Hands 𝄞𝄞𝄞 (Rykodisc, 1996)
(With Buick MacKane) *The Pawn Shop Years* 𝄞𝄞𝄞 (Rykodisc, 1997)
More Miles Than Money—Live 1994–96 𝄞𝄞𝄞 (Bloodshot, 1998)

influences:
◀◀ The Blasters, Jimmie Dale Gilmore, Buddy Holly, Richie Valens, Iggy Pop, X

▶▶ Uncle Tupelo, Jason & the Scorchers, Wilco, the Bottle Rockets

see also: *Rank & File*

Steve Knopper

ESP Summer

See: Pale Saints

David Essex

Born David Albert Cook, July 23, 1947, in Plaistow, London, England.

Seemingly a relic from a long-gone era, David Essex epitomized the Teen Idol genre of the early '60s—even though it was 1973 when he hit the international Top 10 with a simple little exercise in rhythm called "Rock On." Sure, he'd studied and worked hard to get to this career plateau, toiling in near obscurity for years on the British stage, but he seemed no more sincere in his approach—and remained in the limelight no longer—than did the rock star he so eloquently portrayed in his excellent *That'll Be the Day* and *Stardust* movies.

what to buy: A thoroughly adequate period piece, nothing more and nothing less, *Rock On* 𝄞𝄞𝄞 (Columbia, 1973/Sony, 1989, prod. Jeff Wayne) contains not only the big hit, but a curious clutch of covers including Simon and Garfunkel's "For Emily, Whenever I May Find Her" and—in an ill-advised nod to his pin-up predecessor—a bizarre reading of Fabian's "Turn Me Loose."

what to avoid: This game of musical chairs continues on the more recent *Living in England* 𝄞𝄞𝄞 (Lambo/Cleveland International, 1995, prod. various), during which Essex not only attempts to re-invent "Paint It, Black" and "Everlasting Love," but even *himself*, with a superfluous up-date of "Rock On."

worth searching for: Rock columnist Ray Connolly's story of fictitious singing sensation Jim MacLaine, interpreted brilliantly on film by Essex alongside Ringo Starr, Keith Moon, and others, tells a two-part story of the rise and fall of British pop music far better than *The Beatles Anthology* ever did. The soundtrack to the second installment, *Stardust* (Arista, 1974, prod. various), contains not only three LP sides of immaculately chosen oldies from the '60s, but several original songs created for MacLaine's movie band the Stray Cats by none other than Dave Edmunds. Quite possibly Essex's greatest recordings, these also show Edmunds at the absolute peak of his retro-productive powers.

influences:
◀◀ Buddy Guy, Buddy Holly, Tommy Steele, Marc Bolan

▶▶ David Cassidy, Michael Damian

Gary Pig Gold

Gloria Estefan /Miami Sound Machine

Born Gloria Fajardo, September 1, 1957, in Havana, Cuba.

Simply put, Gloria Estefan has terrific pipes that were co-opted—willingly—away from Miami's Cuban dance scene into the blander but phenomenally successful realm of middle-of-the-road pop. The Cuban native, who fled that country's revolution with her family and moved to the U.S. when she was two, started out fronting the Miami Sound Machine, a former wedding band led by husband Emilio Estefan Jr., whose South of the Equator polyrythms provided an interesting mainstream pop alternative during the mid-'80s. It didn't last long; as Estefan's voice grew from chirpy to assured, the Miami Sound Machine moniker gradually disappeared from the album covers in order to showcase the singer. During 1990, Estefan's tour bus was hit by a tractor-trailer, fracturing one of her vertebrae; but a year later, she was back in action, singing "Coming Out of the Dark," a song inspired by the accident, to #1. Give Estefan this much; she's no producer's tool, writing many of her own lyrics and checking off on the creative decisions. If only one of those decisions would be a return to the those irresistible club grooves. . . .

what to buy: *Eyes of Innocence* ♫♫♫♪ (Epic, 1984/1989, prod. Emilio & the Jerks) had only the minor hit "Dr. Beat," but the Miami Sound Machine's debut is an intoxicating blend of Caribbean rhythms. You won't find anything from that album on *Greatest Hits* ♫♫♫ (Epic, 1992, prod. Emilio Estefan) but you do get her best, a largely upbeat collection that includes "Conga," "Rhythm Is Gonna Get You," and "Get on Your Feet."

what to buy next: *Gloria!* ♫♫♫ (Epic, 1996, prod. various) brings back some of the percolating spirit of the early Miami Sound Machine, blending Caribbean rhythms with South Beach disco beats, though with nary a hint of industrial or techno styles. But "Don't Release Me," her collaboration with Wyclef Jean of the Fugees, shows she's not ignorant of current musical affairs.

what to avoid: There are lots of songs Estefan can probably sing very well. Why'd she pick the ones on *Hold Me, Thrill Me, Kiss Me* ♫♪ (Epic, 1994, prod. various) ?

the rest:
Into the Light ♫♫ (Epic, 1981)
Primitive Love ♫♫♫ (Epic, 1985)
Let It Loose ♫♫♫ (Epic, 1987)
Cuts Both Ways ♫♫♪ (Epic, 1989)
Mi Tierra ♫♫♫ (Epic, 1993)
Christmas through Your Eyes ♫♫♪ (Epic, 1993)
Abriendo Puertas ♫♫♪ (Epic, 1995)
Destiny ♫♫ (Epic, 1996)

worth searching for: Estefan's guest vocal on the song "Africa" from Arturo Sandoval's *Dayon* (GRP, 1994, prod. Arturo Sandoval, Richard Eddy) is terrific.

influences:
◀◀ Carmen Miranda, Tito Puente, Herb Alpert & the Tijuana Brass, Aretha Franklin, Donna Summer

▶▶ Debbie Gibson, Celine Dion

Gary Graff

Maggie Estep
Born March 20, 1963, in Summit, NJ.

After a childhood in which Maggie Estep's family moved frequently, she settled in New York, intent on being a writer. Reading poetry in downtown clubs, she covered her nervousness with a thrashing, visceral presentation that was just one step removed from rock 'n' roll. The East Village's unusual rock/spoken-word hybrid scene (which also produced John S. Hall's King Missile and several collaborators with the Golden Palominos) soon had another band when Estep formed I Love Everybody

and branched out from poetry readings to performances at the Mecca of punk, CBGB. During spoken word's mid-'90s moment in the pop-culture spotlight, Estep gained exposure on MTV with her aggressive, humorous readings, which led to a recording contract. Estep has also published a novel, *Diary of an Emotional Idiot* (Harmony/Crown, 1997), which is well worth picking up.

what to buy: On *No More Mr. Nice Girl* ♫♫♫♫ (NuYo/Imago, 1994, prod. Steve Boyer), Estep speaks her verses (except on the nearly pop "Rip Trip Strip"), sings her choruses (though not all the tracks have one), and slips in a few solo readings, all the while wittily deconstructing various aspects of everyday life (well, maybe not *your* everyday life). You'll laugh, you'll cry, you'll never think of non-dairy creamer in the same way again. The accompanying band of downtown NYC punks/post-punks includes guitarist Pat Place (Contortions, Bush Tetras), and this album best reflects Estep's concert performances.

what to buy next: *Love Is a Dog from Hell* ♫♫♫♫ (Mouth Almighty/Mercury, 1997, prod. Steve Lyon, Knox Chandler, Maggie Estep) is a collaboration with Knox Chandler, who plays all the instruments (except for drums on two tracks), and is much more a studio construction. The styles range from the near-metal "Master of Lunacy" and catchy alterna-rock ("I Want Mangoes," "Welcome to the Monkeyhouse") to the murky acoustic/electric "Fireater," which, like several tracks, suggests a sort of folkie trip-hop, or ambient dub with words. There's a low-key rearrangement of Lou Reed's "Vicious," quotes from Russian poet Vladimir Mayakowsky's "A Cloud in Trousers" and from Patti Smith's spoken bit at the beginning of Blue Öyster Cult's "The Revenge of Vera Gemini," all suggesting possible influences. But though the album title is taken from poet Charles Bukowski, there's no track quoting him.

worth searching for: *Grand Slam! Best of the National Poetry Slam, Volume 1* (NuYo/Imago, 1994, prod. Gary Glazner) has Estep reciting her spoken-word circuit hit, "Sex Goddess of the Western Hemisphere," sans musical backup.

influences:
◀◀ King Missile, Bob Holman, Bush Tetras, Lou Reed, Patti Smith

Steve Holtje

Melissa Etheridge
Born May 29, 1961, in Leavenworth, KS.

Raised on heartland rock, Melissa Etheridge delivers the sort of music that sounds perfect from the vantage point of a bar stool after a couple of cold ones on a hot summer night. But like a few too many brews, Etheridge's songs can leave a bad taste in your mouth and make you wonder what all the fuss was about the night before. Her best attribute is her powerful, gritty voice that's part Janis Joplin, part Rod Stewart. But her writing often bogs down in arena-rock clichés, and her specialty—odes to lost love rendered carefully in gender-neutral terms—is ultimately too limiting. Still, when Etheridge calms down and realizes she doesn't always have to play to the back rows, she can be an insightful and affecting artist. Not surprisingly, since coming out as a lesbian, she has attracted a great deal of attention, and her music has almost become a side issue. She appeared on the cover of a major newsweekly, not because of her art, but because she and her partner, filmmaker Julie Cypher, decided to have a baby (they now have two children). It's interesting, however, and more relevant here, that her most recent albums are among her best and most intimate, indicating that she's finally learning how to write from the heart, not merely ape her '70s AOR influences. It'll be interesting to see which direction her next album takes her in.

what to buy: The title of *Yes I Am* ✧✧✧ (Island, 1993, prod. Hugh Padgham, Melissa Etheridge) is an obvious reference to her declaration of sexual orientation, which she addresses in various asides throughout the album. "I'm the Only One" is in the too-familiar vein of Etheridge's songs of unrequited lust; so is "Come to My Window," but at least that has a rich melody and memorable chorus that makes it Etheridge's best composition. What makes the album her most listenable, though, is Padgham's measured production, which reins in Etheridge's tendencies to rock out aimlessly. Her debut, *Melissa Etheridge* ✧✧✧ (Island, 1988, prod. Craig Krampf, Kevin McCormick, Melissa Etheridge, Niko Bolas), alternates between earnest ballads and acoustic-based rockers, but it's the trio of pissed-off anthems—"Similar Features," "Like the Way I Do," and "Bring Me Some Water"—that made some rock radio inroads.

what to buy next: The material on *Your Little Secret* ✧✧✧ (Island, 1995, prod. Hugh Padgham, Melissa Etheridge) is nearly the equal of that on *Yes I Am*, especially "Nowhere to Go" and "I Want to Come Over." But the album has the feeling of a sequel, making it a less-than-essential purchase.

what to avoid: *Never Enough* ✧✧ (Island, 1992, prod. Kevin McCormick, Melissa Etheridge) earned Etheridge a Grammy for the song "Ain't It Heavy," but the album finds her overreaching, overemoting, and writing nary a memorable tune. And the neo–*Born in the U.S.A.* shot on the cover (Springsteen is a hero and buddy) is just too much.

the rest:
Brave and Crazy ✧✧ (Island, 1989)

worth searching for: Good luck finding them, but both of her live, promotion-only CDs—*Melissa Etheridge Live* (Island, 1988, prod.

Kevin McCormick, Melissa Etheridge) and *Melissa Etheridge Live* (Island, 1989, prod. Kevin McCormick, Melissa Etheridge)—give a sense of her gutsy and robust concert performances.

influences:

◄◄ Bruce Springsteen, John Mellencamp, Janis Joplin, Joan Jett

►► Sass Jordan, Sheryl Crow, Joan Osborne, Alannah Myles

Daniel Durchholz

The E-Types

Formed 1965, in Salinas, CA. Disbanded 1967.

Bob Wence, vocals, guitar; Dan Shephard, guitar, vocals; Reggie Shaffer, drums; Jody Wence, keyboards, vocals; Danny Monigold, bass.

When the British Invasion hit the States during the mid-'60s, it sent the somewhat sedate music scenes of both coasts into a Mersey Beat frenzy. Most record labels tried to capitalize by releasing records by bands with that distinctive European sound, and the E-Types certainly fit that bill. The E stood for English, and that British influence was quite evident in the sound of these long-haired lads from sunny California. The E-Types released only a few singles during their short-lived career, but these singles, from the incredibly Zombies-like "I Can't Do It" to an unreleased Beatles gem, "Love of the Loved," would leave an indelible mark on the equally short-lived American Mersey Beat scene. After a brief and disappointing period of courting major label interests, the E-Types called it quits in the summer of '67.

what's available: The E-Types' recording output is relatively marginal, consisting of a handful of singles, a few crudely recorded live tracks, and a couple demos. The first and only piece to chronicle the group's career is *Introducing the E-Types* ✧✧✧ (Sundazed, 1995, compilation prod. Judy Cost), a CD filled with released and unissued demo tracks and live recordings. Like most pop bands of the early '60s, the E-Types depended on covers, from the Merry Go Round's "Live" to the Yardbirds "Shape of Things." But the true gems here are some unreleased demos, one of which, "I Can't Do It," sounds more inspired than the released single version.

influences:

◄◄ The Beatles, Herman's Hermits, the Dave Clark Five, Billy J. Kramer & the Dakotas

►► R.E.M., the Three O'Clock, Klaatu

Chris Richards

Eugenius

See: The Vaselines

Euro Boys

Formed 1996, in Oslo, Norway.

Kare Joao Pedersen, drums; Knut Schreiner, guitar; Dag F. Gravem, bass; Anders Moller, percussion.

Started by four childhood friends who grew up playing in various bands together, the Euro Boys were momentarily the most coveted unsigned band in Norway. They settled for a deal with Virgin Records in Europe and proceeded to make heads turn with their over-the-top live shows and thunderous, if slightly kitschy, instrumental rock. So far, the group—which could visually pass for a Moby Grape cover band—has only recorded one album, but word about the phenomenon is already spreading across the globe.

what's available: Not only does *Jet Age* ♫♫♫♫ (Sympathy for the Record Industry, 1997, prod. Euro Boys) offer brilliant new interpretations of "(Theme from) Enter the Dragon" and the Jewish traditional "Hava Negilah," but it also boasts more than its fair share of Earth-trembling originals, including "Girlfriend in Tacoma" and "Hong Kong Cockfight." A classic.

influences:

◀◀ Lalo Schifrin, Ennio Morricone, Burt Bacharach

Aidin Vaziri

Eurythmics
/Annie Lennox
/Dave Stewart

Formed 1980, in London, England. Disbanded 1990.

Dave Stewart, guitar, keyboards; Annie Lennox, vocals, flute, keyboards.

Emerging from the ashes of British folk/psychedelic/new wave rock band the Tourists, Annie Lennox and Dave Stewart became the oddest of couples—breaking up as lovers before forming Eurythmics together. Melding new wave synth-pop sounds with Lennox's '60s soul vocal influences, the pair scored big once Stewart took full control of their sound as producer, recording their breakthrough record on an eight-track machine with arrangements emphasizing his partner's amazing vocals. Tired of the baby doll blonde image she'd fostered in the Tourists, Lennox appeared in men's suits and dressed as Elvis during the group's early years. As synth-pop began to take a back seat on the charts, Stewart leavened the group's sound with garage rock and earthier soul touches, only to try a return to techno form just before the duo went on indefinite hiatus in 1990.

what to buy: The pair's breakthrough album, *Sweet Dreams (Are Made of This)* ♫♫♫♫ (RCA, 1983, prod. Dave Stewart) provides a neat summation of the group's appeal. Stewart's eerily emotionless, synthesizer-bred arrangements stand in stark contrast to Lennox's expressive vocals, making the hit title track and the driving dance cut "Love Is a Stranger" sizzle with the friction. With full band backing, *Be Yourself Tonight* ♫♫♫♫ (RCA, 1985, prod. Dave Stewart) enjoys an energetic, live group flavor with the charging "Would I Lie to You?," the midtempo hit "It's Alright (Baby's Coming Back)," and Lennox's muscular duet with Aretha Franklin, "Sisters Are Doin' It for Themselves."

what to buy next: For an overview of the duo's biggest commercial triumphs, it's hard to beat *Greatest Hits* ♫♫♫ (RCA, 1991, prod. various), a collection of the group's top cuts. The best '90s-era representation of the Eurythmics' sound is on Lennox' first solo album, *Diva* ♫♫♫♫ (Arista, 1992, prod. Stephen Lipson), a record that blends the updated synth-pop of "Legend in My Living Room" with the pop-rock of "Walking on Broken Glass"—a potent reminder why we liked the group so much in the first place.

what to avoid: As a film soundtrack that even the director denounced publicly, *1984* **woof!** (RCA, 1984, prod. Dave Stewart) upsets Eurythmics' delicate stylistic balance, drowning Lennox's evocative vocals in an oppressive flood of downbeat techno-pop.

the rest:
In the Garden ♫♫ (RCA UK, 1981)
Touch ♫♫♫ (RCA, 1983)
Touch Dance ♫♫ (RCA, 1984)
Revenge ♫♫ (RCA, 1986)
Savage ♫♫ (RCA, 1987)
We Too Are One ♫♫ (Arista, 1989)
Remix Collection ♫♫ (Alex, 1992)
Live 1983–1989 ♫♫ (Arista, 1993)

worth searching for: *Rough & Tough at the Roxy* (RCA, 1986) is a promotional EP sporting four live cuts recorded with Eurythmics best-ever touring band. Or check the bargain bins for the soundtrack to the movie *Scrooged* (A&M, 1998, prod. Dave Stewart), which features Lennox's powerful duet with soul star Al Green on "Put a Little Love in Your Heart."

solo outings:
Annie Lennox:
Medusa ♫♫♫ (Arista, 1995)

Dave Stewart:
Lily Was Here (Soundtrack) ♫♫ (Anxious, 1989)
Dave Stewart and the Spiritual Cowboys ♫♫♫ (Arista, 1990)
Honest ♫♫ (Arista, 1991)
Greetings from the Gutter ♫♫ (EastWest, 1995)
Sly Fi N/A (N2K, 1998)

influences:

◀◀ Lene Lovich, Aretha Franklin, Kraftwerk, Can

▶▶ Garbage, Roxette

Eric Deggans

The Eurythmics: Dave Stewart (l) and Annie Lennox (© Ken Settle)

Eva Trout

Formed 1995, in Sydney, Australia.

Matt Galvin, guitars; Steph Miller, accordian, mandolin, organ, tin whistle, bouzouki, vocals; Grant Shanahan, bass, vocals; Bek-Jean Stewart, vocals, guitars; Bert Thompson, percussion; Blue Dalton, harmonica (1995–97).

With crisp, folksy instrumentation, warm vocals, and a confident and earthy frontwoman, this Australian quintet crafts a charmingly rural, timeless sound. Named for an Elizabeth Bowen novel the band members never read, Eva Trout bounced around down under for two years before a copy of the single "Beautiful South" found its way into the hands of an Atlanta DJ, who slid it into high rotation, which led to a recording contract.

what's available: *Eva Trout* ♫♫♫ (Trauma, 1997, prod. Rob Taylor, Eva Trout) is an engaging, mostly acoustic collection of single-worthy, effervescent pop. Blue Dalton's harmonica and Steph Miller's occasional forays into accordion, Hammond organ, and the tin whistle give the album a slight roots-rock sensibility. Bek-Jean Stewart and Grant Shanahan, whose lyrics dabble heavily in parochial imagery, add a layer of depth to the music.

influences:

◄◄ 10,000 Maniacs, the Sundays

Isaac Josephson

Everclear

Formed 1991, in Portland, OR.

Art Alexakis, vocals, guitar; Craig Montoya, bass; Scott Cuthbert, drums, vocals (1991–94); Greg Eklund, drums (1994–present).

The center of this group, Art Alexakis, was 34 when it finally broke through in 1996 after MTV picked up the video to the casually apocalyptic "Santa Monica." He'd grown up in the housing projects of Culver City, California, in a broken family; his older brother was involved in dealing heroin and ODed. Alexakis soon was doing and dealing a multiplicity of drugs himself, and after a girlfriend ODed, he tried to commit suicide. At age 22, he survived his own overdose and then went cold turkey on everything. He traveled the West Coast, leading a band (Colorfinger) and an indie label (Shindig), both of which failed. During 1991 he followed his wife-to-be to Portland and soon formed Everclear with Craig Montoya (formerly of Soul Hammer) and Scott Cuthbert. Alexakis's material draws heavily on his background without necessarily being autobiographical. The Everclear sensibility and sound (especially Alexakis's vocals) owe a debt to Nirvana, but they stop just short of being derivative—it's a power trio that learned some lessons and uses them toward distinctive ends. One of its most effective

WHAT ALBUM CHANGED YOUR LIFE?

Pet Sounds. I always really liked the Beach Boys and have a huge respect for the talent of Brian Wilson—but also for someone who's gone through a lot of drugs. I have some damage from it, too, and when I see someone who had 10 times more damage than me, it's sad. I get mad at him and other people allowing it to happen. He didn't do it all on his own. But I love the Beach Boys.

Art Alexakis (of Everclear)

tactics is to contrast the verses and choruses not with the now-clichéd quiet/loud dichotomy, but instead with spareness shifting into density. Tight, tuneful songwriting and ferociously powerful guitar riffs and drumming complete the picture.

what to buy: The breakthrough *Sparkle and Fade* ♫♫♫♫ (Capitol, 1995, prod. Art Alexakis) contains the hit "Santa Monica." Neither the melodies nor the riffs seem memorable, but the way they fit together works well and sounds familiar, accented by plainspoken lyrics that pop out freshly. *So Much for the Afterglow* ♫♫♫♫ (Capitol, 1997, prod. A.P. Alexakis) transcends Nirvana comparisons by expanding the group's sound, complete with an instrumental, horns, and Beach Boys–like harmonies at various points. Alexakis's emotional openness produces songs about Prozac, the son's perspective of his father's abandonment of the family, growing up poor and trying to compensate later, and even a number about a "One Hit Wonder"— all of the songs are simple and unpretentious, yet eloquent.

what to buy next: The debut album, *World of Noise* ♫♫♫♫ (Tim/Kerr, 1993/Capitol, 1994, prod. Art Alexakis), is less polished than *Sparkle and Fade* and lives up to its name with recordings ranging from endearingly scruffy to uncompromisingly ferocious.

the rest:

Nervous & Weird ♫♫♫♫ (Tim/Kerr EP, 1993)
Fire Maple Song ♫♫♫♫ (Capitol EP, 1994)

worth searching for: The stylistically diverse soundtrack of *William Shakespeare's Romeo + Juliet* (Capitol, 1996, prod. various) contains lots of crappy music, but among its three or four excellent tracks is Everclear's hilarious "Local God"; since it's not on any of the band's albums, fans will want to pick this up. A more traditional import CD single, *Heartspark Dollarsign* (EMI Australia, 1995, prod. Art Alexakis), supplements the single edit of the title track (from *Sparkle and Fade*) with three radio session live recordings of *World of Noise* tunes.

influences:

◄◄ Nirvana, Hüsker Dü

Steve Holtje

Everlast

See: House of Pain

The Everly Brothers

Formed 1954, in Brownie, KY.

Don Everly (born February 1, 1937 in Brownie, KY), vocals, guitar; Phil Everly (born January 19, 1939, in Chicago, IL), vocals, guitar.

Having begun their singing careers as children on their parents' radio program in 1949, brothers Don and Phil Everly qualified as country music veterans by the time their first rock 'n' roll records hit the charts eight years later, their deeply entwined high-mountain harmonies practically instinctual. The blood harmonies of the Everly Brothers may be the main tributary feeding all rock vocal styles; the Beatles, among many others, styled their harmony sound after the Everlys'. But the Everly Brothers were not only the children of long-standing members of the country music community, they were also an officially sanctioned Nashville project. Guitarist Chet Atkins conducted the sessions and Acuff-Rose frontliners Boudleaux and Felice Bryant supplied the material. Though they may have slipped off the charts during the 1960s, the brothers never stopped making heart-stoppingly beautiful records. When matched with the right piece of material and sympathetic production, the Everlys cut records that matched the finest work of their early years, right up to the modest 1984 comeback with Paul McCartney's "On the Wings of a Nightingale" (produced by Dave Edmunds) and beyond. And the Everlys never strayed far from the country field; one of their best-loved albums of their wilderness years was, in fact, the country-oriented *Roots*, not unlike the *Songs Our Daddy Taught Us* album of many years earlier. The duo split—bitterly—in 1973, breaking up literally in front of a Knott's Berry Farm audience when Don splintered a guitar across his brother's back and walked offstage. It turned out that nobody wanted to hear one Everly brother singing alone. They reunited for a sentimental 1983 Royal Albert Hall concert that was recorded and filmed. Apparently they found an uneasy truce that allowed them to continue to perform and record together, and interest in the duo—mainly as an oldies act—is still strong.

what to buy: *Cadence Classics: Their 20 Greatest Hits* 𝄞𝄞𝄞𝄞 (Rhino, 1985, prod. Archie Bleyer) contains the basic fundamentals of the Everlys' repertoire, from the acoustic guitar-accented rockabilly of "Wake Up Little Susie" and "Claudette" to almost ethereal ballads such as "Let It Be Me."

what to buy next: *Walk Right Back: The Everly Brothers on Warner Bros. 1960–1969* 𝄞𝄞𝄞 (Warner Archives, 1993, compilation prod. Greg Geller) is a 50-song survey that begins where the Cadence era left off and takes the Everlys through the flowering of the Los Angeles country-rock that their early work did so much to inspire. The four-disc box set *Heartaches and Harmonies* 𝄞𝄞𝄞𝄞 (Rhino, 1994, compilation prod. Andrew Sandoval, Bill Inglot, Gary Stewart) offers a detailed retrospective that smoothly covers nearly 40 years of Everlys recordings.

what to avoid: During the mid-'60s, the brothers re-recorded a set of their Cadence hits for Warners. Released as *The Very Best of the Everly Brothers* 𝄞𝄞 (Warner Bros., 1964, prod. Wesley Rose), the songs here pale vastly in comparison to the original versions.

the rest:
The Everly Brothers 𝄞𝄞𝄞𝄞 (Cadence, 1958/Rhino, 1988)
Songs Our Daddy Taught Us 𝄞𝄞𝄞𝄞 (Cadence, 1958/Rhino, 1988)
The Fabulous Style of the Everly Brothers 𝄞𝄞𝄞𝄞 (Cadence, 1960/Rhino, 1988)
Golden Hits 𝄞𝄞𝄞 (Warner Bros., 1962/1988)
Roots 𝄞𝄞𝄞 (Warner Bros., 1968)
Stories We Could Tell 𝄞𝄞𝄞 (RCA, 1972/One Way, 1997)
Pass the Chicken and Listen 𝄞𝄞𝄞 (RCA, 1973/One Way, 1997)
Reunion Concert 𝄞𝄞 (Mercury, 1984)
EB 84 𝄞𝄞𝄞𝄞 (Mercury, 1984/Razor & Tie, 1994)
All-Time Greatest Hits 𝄞𝄞 (Curb, 1990)
Rare Solo Classics 𝄞𝄞𝄞 (Curb, 1991)
The Mercury Years 𝄞𝄞𝄞 (Mercury, 1993)
The Everly Brothers/The Fabulous Style of the Everly Brothers 𝄞𝄞𝄞𝄞 (Ace, 1994)
16 of Their Greatest Recordings 𝄞𝄞𝄞𝄞 (Music Club, 1997)

worth searching for: In assembling the reissues of the Everlys' Cadence material, Rhino Records researchers unearthed a set of unreleased demo tapes—*All They Had to Do Was Dream* (Rhino, 1985, prod. Archie Bleyer)—that showcase the pure vocal sound of the brothers; these are perhaps some of rock's first "unplugged" sessions, and they glisten with a maturity and depth that artists this young rarely possess. If you want everything from their stint at Cadence all at once, check out the German import *Classic Everly Brothers* (Bear Family, 1992, compilation prod. Richard Weize), a powerful multi-disc set that includes early demos, radio transcriptions, and their ground-breaking hits from 1955 to 1960.

influences:

◀◀ The Stanley Brothers, the Louvin Brothers, Bo Diddley

▶▶ The Belew Twins, the Beatles, Simon & Garfunkel, Foster & Lloyd

Joel Selvin and Ken Burke

Everything but the Girl

Formed 1983, in London, England.

Tracey Thorn, vocals; Ben Watt, guitar, vocals.

Naming themselves after a London boutique that claims to sell everything but the girl behind the counter, former Marine Girls singer Tracey Thorn and Ben Watt joined Sade and Matt Bianco as the most visible proponents of London's early '80s jazz-pop movement. Although their engaging sound—a sensitive, savvy blend of Stan Getz–inspired Brazilian jazz and acoustic guitar-driven pop—won over U.K. audiences, Americans enamored by the chanteuse-like Sade weren't as quick to embrace Everything but the Girl's dour outlook and moody, often mopey image. So it was black-clad teens with Bauhaus T-shirts and Smiths albums who first recognized the alternately soothing and aching beauty of Thorn's cool but emotive alto. However, after 10 years of vainly cramming everything from orchestras to dance rhythms onto their subtle sound, EBTG scaled the *Billboard* charts with the groove-enhanced remix of "Missing," a late-blooming single from 1994's *Amplified Heart* that made them one of pop's oldest overnight success stories. Thorn has become an in-demand guest vocalist for acts ranging from Massive Attack to Adam F, while Watt received accolades for his 1996 autobiography, *Patient: The True Story of a Rare Illness* (Grove Press/Atlantic), which chronicled in bone-chilling detail his life-threatening battle with a rare autoimmune disorder that left him emaciated and with only three feet of his intestines.

what to buy: *Amplified Heart* ♫♫♫♫ (Atlantic, 1994, prod. Ben Watt, Tracey Thorn) deftly blends every style that the duo has experimented with into a cool, cohesive whole—it's beautiful music in every sense of the phrase. The beat-heavy follow-up, *Walking Wounded* ♫♫♫ (Atlantic, 1996, prod. Ben Watt, Spring Heel Jack), builds upon the house remixes of "Missing" and Thorn's collaborations with trip-hop group Massive Attack for a seductive, sonically captivating work. *Love Not Money* ♫♫♫ (Sire, 1985, prod. Robin Millar) forsakes the heavy jazz leanings of their debut album for jangling pop with a social conscience that includes a lovely cover of the Pretenders' "Kid."

what to buy next: Thorn's interpretive skills are spotlighted on *Acoustic* ♫♫♫ (Atlantic, 1992, prod. Tracey Thorn, Ben Watt),

which includes covers of Elvis Costello's "Alison," Cyndi Lauper's "Time After Time," and Bruce Springsteen's "Tougher than the Rest."

what to avoid: *Language of Life* ♫♫ (Atlantic, 1990, prod. Tracey Thorn, Ben Watt, Tommy Lipuma) teams them with Tommy LiPuma, the late Stan Getz, and several American jazz session players—but the result is all surface and little substance.

the rest:
Everything but the Girl ♫♫♫♫ (Sire, 1984)
Baby, the Stars Shine Bright ♫♫♫ (Sire, 1986)
Idlewild ♫♫♫ (Sire, 1988)
Worldwide ♫♫ (Atlantic, 1991)

worth searching for: Thorn's pre-EBTG solo album, *Distant Shore* (Cherry Red, 1982), offers a gorgeous reading of the Velvet Underground's "Femme Fatale" that shames all other covers.

solo outings:
Ben Watt:
North Marine Drive ♫♫♫ (Cherry Red, 1983)

influences:

◀◀ Astrud Gilberto, Stan Getz, Massive Attack

▶▶ Eddi Reader, Tanita Tikaram

David Okamoto

Extreme

Formed 1987, in Boston, MA. Disbanded 1996.

Nuno Bettencourt, guitar; Gary Cherone, vocals; Pat Badger, bass; Paul Geary, drums.

Distinguished from the hard-rock pack by arty ambitions, choirboy harmonies, and the ferociously inventive fretwork of guitarist Nuno Bettencourt, Extreme enjoyed both chart success and critical plaudits during the early '90s. The quartet came together when singer Gary Cherone met Portuguese-born Bettencourt while the two were in separate bands; their immediate chemistry led to a large early catalog of material, some of which appeared on Extreme's eponymous 1989 A&M debut. But it was the sophomore effort, *Pornograffitti*, that caught the ears of reviewers and discriminating rock fans: it's hard-hitting yet thoughtful rock, a mix of prog-rock virtuosity, feel-good funk-rock, and power-pop sweetness. Ironically, it was the yearning acoustic ballad "More than Words" that brought Extreme mass success. Subsequent records saw the band moving into even more stylistically adventuresome territory, and becoming increasingly preachy in lyrical content. But the advent of "alternative" rock soon dampened its appeal, though its well-crafted albums retained an enthusiastic core following. In

1996, Cherone was tapped to replace Sammy Hagar as the lead vocalist in Van Halen, and Bettencourt embarked on a solo career using only his first name.

what to buy: *Extreme II: Pornograffitti* ♫♫♫ (A&M, 1990, prod. Michael Wagener) is chock full of radio-friendly hooks and shows Bettencourt in full feather. "Get the Funk Out" is a party anthem that would make the Red Hot Chili Peppers proud.

what to buy next: *III Sides to Every Story* ♫♫♫ (A&M, 1992, prod. Nuno Bettencourt) errs on the side of self-indulgence but shows an admirable eagerness to experiment—cranking out more power ballads would've been easy.

what to avoid: *Waiting for the Punchline* ♫♫ (A&M, 1995, prod. Nuno Bettencourt) misses the songwriting and thematic unity of its predecessors.

the rest:
Extreme ♫♫♫ (A&M, 1989)

worth searching for: The Japanese import *Extragraffitti* (A&M, 1990, prod. Extreme, Michael Wagener) gathers some interesting and hard-to-find B-sides.

solo outings:
Nuno:
Schizophonic ♫♫♫ (A&M, 1997)

influences:
◀◀ Queen, the Beatles, Van Halen, ELO, the Red Hot Chili Peppers

▶▶ Dream Theater, Spacehog, the Deftones, Jars of Clay

see also: *Van Halen*

Simon Glickman

Fabian
Born Fabiano Forte Bonaparte, February 6, 1943, in Philadelphia, PA.

Although Fabian was not a powerful or especially skillful vocalist, his records have been unjustly maligned. Crafted by sturdy studio professionals and frequently written by the respected team of Mort Shuman and Doc Pomus, his Chancellor Records singles, fodder for '50s teenyboppers, hold up remarkably well more than 30 years after their release. Discovered as a teenager by a pair of music business entrepreneurs, Fabian came to epitomize the cultivated teen idol whose pinup-boy looks were more important to his success than talent. After

several years of Top 40 hits, *American Bandstand* appearances, and grueling national tours on package shows, he eased into a motion picture career in which he appeared as the youthful foil to such older stars as John Wayne, Jimmy Stewart, and Bing Crosby. During the '80s, much to his own amazement, he experienced a singular comeback as part of "The Golden Boys of Bandstand" with Frankie Avalon and Bobby Rydell, an act that would headline Atlantic City and Las Vegas casinos. No lesser a contemporary than Dion transformed Fabian's "Turn Me Loose" into a minor gem for the 1995 Doc Pomus tribute album.

what to buy: The most thorough examination of Fabian's work is on the British import *This Is Fabian!* ♫♫♫ (Ace, 1991, prod. Bob Marcucci), a 26-track compilation that includes the cream of his faux-rock recordings.

worth searching for: There are still some copies around of *The Best of Fabian* (Varese Vintage, 1995, compilation prod. Cary E. Mansfield), which makes up for its skimpy 10-song line-up (all hits) with an extremely informative and interesting booklet.

influences:
◀◀ Elvis Presley, Frankie Avalon, Ricky Nelson

▶▶ Bobby Sherman, Bobby Rydell, Milli Vanilli, Hanson

Joel Selvin

The Fabulous Thunderbirds
Formed 1974, in Austin, TX.

Kim Wilson, vocals, harmonica; Jimmie Vaughan, guitar, vocals (1974–90); Michael "Duke" Robillard, guitar (1990–93); Doug "the Kid" Bangham (1990–93); Kid Ramos, guitar (1994–present); Keith Ferguson, bass (1974–86); Preston Hubbard, bass (1986–93); Harvey Brooks, bass (1994–95); Willie J. Campbell, bass (1996–present); Mike Buck, drums (1974–80); Fran Christina, drums (1980–95); Jimmy Bott, drums (1995–present); Gene Taylor, keyboards (1994–present).

Bringing hard rock muscle to Chicago blues, the Fabulous Thunderbirds were the hottest band on Texas' spicy rock 'n' blues bar circuit during the '70s, when disco was king and nobody in Texas thought they had a snowball's chance in, well, Texas to make it big. But word spread, the band got a deal with the independent label Takoma Records (home to John Fahey and Leo Kottke), then signed with the major label Chrysalis a year later. Its 1986 hit "Tuff Enuff" brought the group mainstream success and helped spur a surge of interest in the blues, but all the years of hard work that founders Kim Wilson and Jimmie Vaughan (Stevie Ray Vaughan's older brother) had put into it began to unravel. The group started repeating itself, Vaughan left to pursue a solo career, and personnel changes persisted. Wilson, an expert harmonica player, put the band on hold to cut a couple of overlooked solo albums, then put together a new version of the band, which signed to Private Music and released the Danny Kortchmar-produced *Roll of the Dice* in 1995. More personnel changes followed, with long-time drummer Fran Christina departing, but the new lineup planned to remain active as a touring and recording unit.

what to buy: *The Essential Fabulous Thunderbirds Collection* ♫♫♫ (Chrysalis, 1991, prod. Denny Bruce, Nick Lowe) is prime stuff from the band's early days, when it still played smokey bars and didn't even think about writing a hit song. The collection is drawn from its first four albums, including the debut on Takoma, all of which are now out of print.

what to buy next: *Tuff Enuff* ♫♫♥ (Columbia, 1986, prod. Dave Edmunds) is slick, but not so much so that it hides the T-Birds' usual virtues. The title track and a remake of Sam & Dave's "Wrap It Up" sound terrific on the radio, too.

what to avoid: *Powerful Stuff* ♫♫ (Epic, 1989, prod. Terry Manning), Vaughan's last date with the band, is quite the opposite of its title.

the rest:
Hot Number ♫♫ (Epic/Associated, 1987)
Walk That Walk, Talk That Talk ♫♫ (Epic, 1991)
Hot Stuff: The Greatest Hits ♫♫ (Epic, 1992)
Roll of the Dice ♫♫♥ (Private Music, 1995)
High Water ♫♫♥ (High Street, 1997)

worth searching for: *Butt Rockin'/T-Bird Rhythm* (Beat Goes On, 1993, prod. Denny Bruce, Nick Lowe) and *The Fabulous Thunderbirds/What's the Word* (Beat Goes On, 1993, prod. Denny Bruce) are import double-CD repackagings of the band's first four albums, released originally on Chrysalis and now out of print.

solo outings:
Kim Wilson:
Tigerman ♫♫ (Antone's, 1993)
That's Life ♫♫ (Antone's, 1994)
My Blues N/A (Blue Collar Music, 1998)

influences:
◀◀ Muddy Waters, Bo Diddley, Slim Harpo, Freddie King

▶▶ Stevie Ray Vaughan & Double Trouble, the Red Devils

Doug Pullen

Face to Face

Formed 1990, in Victorville, CA.

Trever Keith, vocals, guitar; Chad Yaro, guitar, vocals (1994–present); Matt Riddle, bass, vocals (1990–96); Scott Shiflett, bass, vocals (1996–present); Rob Kurth, drums, vocals.

Face to Face is a power punk band from suburban Los Angeles

that rose from obscurity to major label fame (well, sorta) during the mid-'90s thanks to a melodic, catchy NOFX-style sound and positive, upbeat lyrics that made the group a skate video mainstay. Face to Face has participated in several Vans Warped Tours, as well as outings with NOFX, Bouncing Souls, and the Rev. Horton Heat, cementing its status as one of the more popular West Coast punk groups of the decade by being able to turn in an energetic live set night after night while maintaining its trademark good-natured attitude. By the way, there is absolutely no connection between Face to Face and two '80s groups with the same name (one was an obscure hair metal band, the other a Boston-based hip-hop/rock fusion act that received minor MTV airplay).

what to buy: *Big Choice* ♫♫♫ (Victory, 1995, prod. Thom Wilson, Face to Face) is one of the better Epitaph/Fat Wreck Chords–style punk albums of recent years. Bonus tracks include a solid version of the group's best-known song, "Disconnected," plus a cover of Descendents' "Bikage."

what to buy next: *Face to Face* ♫♫♥ (A&M, 1996, prod. Trever Keith, Jim Goodwin) finds the band straying toward Green Day–style pop-punk on several cuts, making this album more accessible and radio-friendly than its earlier releases. The broken-mirror cover art is a nice tribute to Black Flag's *Damaged*.

the rest:
Don't Turn Away ♫♫ (Dr. Strange, 1993/Fat, 1994)
Over It ♫♫ (Victory, 1994)
Live ♫♫ (Vagrant, 1998)

influences:
◀◀ NOFX, the Descendents, Vandals, Agent Orange, Youth Brigade, Black Flag

▶▶ Pulley, 22 Jacks

Seth Hindin

The Faces /The Small Faces

Formed 1965, in London, England. Disbanded 1976. Small Faces reformed 1976-79.

Steve Marriott (died April 20, 1991), guitar, vocals (1965–69, 1976–79); Jimmy Winston, keyboards (1965); Ian McLagan, keyboards; Ronnie Lane (died June 4, 1997), bass, (1965–73); Kenny Jones, drums; Rod Stewart, vocals (1969–74); Ron Wood, guitar (1969–75); Tetsu Yamauchi, bass (1973–76); Rick Wills, bass (1976–79); Joe Brown, guitar (1976–78); Jimmy McCulloch (died September 27, 1979), guitar (1978–79).

The Small Faces became popular in England as much for their natty Mod outfits and short stature as for their raw, R&B-based rockers. The group recorded its first hit single ("Whatcha Gonna

Do about It?") just weeks after forming, though it never made much of a dent in the United States. When Steve Marriott left in 1969 to form Humble Pie, he was replaced by the taller duo of Rod Stewart and Ronnie Wood, and the new band shortened its name to the Faces. The group had fun onstage and off, crafting a loose, boozy, occasionally sloppy kind of rock that was marked by Stewart's scratchy voice, Wood's sinewy guitar riffs, and Ian McLaglan's rock-boogie piano. Stewart eventually launched a dual career as a solo artist, but when his solo projects began eclipsing the band's popularity it put a strain on the Faces that ultimately pulled the group apart. Wood went on to join the Rolling Stones, Jones hooked up with the Who, and Lane began suffering from multiple sclerosis and became an activist fighting against the disease. The Small Faces were considering yet another reunion when Marriott died in a 1991 house fire.

what to buy: *A Nod Is as Good as a Wink . . . to a Blind Horse* 𝄞𝄞𝄞𝄞 (Warner Bros., 1971, prod. Glyn Johns, Faces) offers all of the Faces' best sides, from Wood's slashing slide guitar on "That's All You Need" to Lane's sensitive ballad "Debris" to Stewart's macho boasts on "Stay with Me."

what to buy next: *Long Player* 𝄞𝄞𝄞 (Warner Bros., 1971, prod. Faces) captures the party-hearty sound of the Faces, highlighted by boisterous live versions of Paul McCartney's "Maybe I'm Amazed" and Big Bill Broonzy's "I Feel So Good."

what to avoid: Growing tensions in the band stifled *Ooh-La-La* 𝄞𝄞 (Warner Bros., 1973, prod. Glyn Johns), whose 10 tracks sound flat despite the opening track's title, "Silicone Grown."

the rest:
Small Faces:
There Are but Four Small Faces 𝄞𝄞𝄞 (Immediate, 1967/Sony Music Special Products, 1991)
Ogden's Nut Gone Flake 𝄞𝄞𝄞 (Immediate, 1968/Sony Music Special Products, 1991)
All or Nothing 𝄞𝄞𝄞 (Sony Music Special Products, 1992)

Faces:
First Step 𝄞𝄞𝄞 (Warner Bros., 1970)
Coast to Coast: Overtures and Beginnings 𝄞𝄞 (Warner Bros., 1974)
Snakes and Ladders: The Best of the Faces 𝄞𝄞𝄞 (Warner Bros., 1978)

worth searching for: *Singles A's and B's* (See for Miles, 1990, prod. various) is a solid and relatively comprehensive import collection of the Small Faces' hits that will have to do until a decent domestic compilation comes out.

solo outings:
Ronnie Lane:
Anymore for Anymore 𝄞𝄞 (GM, 1974)
Ronnie Lane's Slim Chance 𝄞𝄞𝄞 (A&M, 1975)
(With Ron Wood) *Mahoney's Last Stand* 𝄞𝄞𝄞 (Atco, 1976)
(With Pete Townshend) *Rough Mix* 𝄞𝄞𝄞𝄞 (MCA, 1977)

Ian McLaglan:
Troublemaker 𝄞𝄞 (Mercury, 1979)
Bump in the Night 𝄞𝄞 (Mercury, 1981)

influences:

◄◄ Muddy Waters, Sam Cooke, Otis Redding, Elvis Presley, Jerry Lee Lewis

►► The Black Crowes, the London Quireboys

see also: *Rod Stewart, Humble Pie, Ron Wood*

David Yonke

Donald Fagen
See: Steely Dan

John Fahey
Born February 28, 1939, in Takoma Park, MD.

Guitarist John Fahey is more than just a filter for American roots music. While seminal stylists such as Jimmie Rodgers and Blind Willie Johnson were undeniable influences, Fahey's compositions and performance technique are quite distinct, forming a unique style he has called "American Primitive Guitar." This deceptively simple-sounding term was created by the guitarist/composer as a blanket label for an ever evolving and complex artistry that combined folkloric techniques with unusual tunings and (later in his career) taped sounds of trains, gamelan orchestras, and other atmospherics. Many new age–oriented artists have mentioned Fahey as an influence, including guitarist Will Ackerman and pianist George Winston, but Fahey has actively disavowed any association with this style of music. What most of the new age guitarists seemed to have picked up on was Fahey's use of space as an element of composition; what they've missed is the spark of genius that blends blues, gospel, classical, and '50s-era rock with a unique vision. The fact that Sonic Youth guitarist Thurston Moore has claimed Fahey as a "secret influence" seems to have pleased him however since the two of them combined for a brief tour of the northeastern United States in 1996. While the past 30 years have seen Fahey's reputation and influence grow, his concerts and albums had become rare events. Some of this can be attributed to a series of rough experiences, including three failed marriages, bouts with Epstein-Barr Syndrome, diabetes, and alcoholism, and living for a period in a homeless shelter. The latter half of the '90s found Fahey on an upswing, apparently able to hold his demons in check long enough to record three albums worth of material that included samples from Stereolab and other industrial-oriented sounds as well as some of his trademark sublime acoustic guitar playing.

what to buy: *The Return of the Repressed: The John Fahey Anthology* ♫♫♫♫ (Rhino, 1994, compilation prod. Barry Hansen, James Austin) is a well-chosen double CD that covers more than 30 years of Fahey's career in a variety of settings. It is a good introductory sampler that works well as a career retrospective for long-time fans as well with rare material included in the mix alongside classic riffs such as "In Christ There Is No East or West," "On the Sunny Side of the Ocean," and "Steamboat Gwine 'round de Bend." Some of Fahey's finest moments on his own Takoma label have been reissued on CD with extra tracks, the most welcome of which is *America* ♫♫♫♫♫ (Takoma, 1969/1997, prod. John Fahey), on which nine cuts added onto the four found on the original release restore this album to the double-set state it was intended to be in the first place. Despite the hubris inherent in the title, *The Essential John Fahey* ♫♫♫♫ (Vanguard, 1974, prod. John Fahey) is a pretty solid release, including all of *The Yellow Princess* ♫♫♫♫ (Vanguard, 1967, prod. John Fahey) and most of *Requia and Other Compositions for Guitar Solo* ♫♫♫♫♫ (Vanguard, 1968, prod. John Fahey). If not as legendary as Fahey's first album, *The Transfiguration of Blind Joe Death* ♫♫♫♫ (Riverboat, 1969/Takoma, 1997, prod. John Fahey) is still a substantial part of his history, including, as it does, one of his finest creative moments, "Brenda's Blues," which clocks out at a minuscule yet mighty 1:45.

what to buy next: *The Epiphany of Glenn Jones* ♫♫♫♫ (Thirsty Ear, 1997, prod. John Williams), on which Fahey works with avant rock group Cul de Sac, will certainly disturb many fans of his older work. But it is not a rejection of what has gone before so much as it is an amplification of Fahey's direction now. The Glenn Jones of the title is a member of Cul de Sac and his erudite liner notes reveal that Fahey can be a difficult hero to work with when trying to fit him into a pattern he was using 30 years ago. At the other extreme is *The Legend of Blind Joe Death* ♫♫♫♫ (Takoma, 1959/1964/1967/1996, prod. John Fahey), Fahey's first album. Simple-sounding guitar playing combines with sophisticated guitar concepts in a release that was years ahead of its time. *The Legend of Blind Joe Death* also has a history of revisionism, with its lineup changing every year that it is reissued. Fahey's series of Christmas albums have always been the biggest sellers in his voluminous catalog; it's too bad that most of them are out of print, but you can get a taste of why they were so popular on *The John Fahey Christmas Album* ♫♫♫♫ (Burnside, 1991, prod. Terry Robb, Don MacLeod).

what to avoid: *City of Refuge* ♫♫♫ (Tim/Kerr, 1997, prod. Scott Colburn) is one weird album. Fahey has either gone around the bend with his experimentalism or he has created a subtle masterpiece that blends Stereolab samples, noise generators, and acoustic guitar noises. The title tune and "Hope Slumbers Eternal" have a halfway familiar Fahey imprint to them, but they are surrounded by material guaranteed to fry the wigs of 99 percent of his old fans. Problematical as this sounds, it is still worth hearing at least once, even if you end up tossing it in the garbage.

best of the rest:
The Voice of the Turtle ♫♫♫♫ (Takoma, 1968)
I Remember Blind Joe Death ♫♫♫♫ (Varrick, 1987)
God, Time, and Causality ♫♫♫♫ (Shanachie, 1990)
Old Girlfriends and Other Horrible Memories ♫♫♫ (Varrick, 1992)
Womblife ♫♫♫♫ (Table of Elements, 1997)

worth searching for: *Of Rivers and Religion* (Reprise, 1972, prod. John Fahey, Denny Bruce) remains the most important album in the Fahey canon to grace the cut-out lists—a dubious award for such an awesome achievement. If you can't find it, you can at least taste the leadoff tune, "Steamboat Gwine 'round de Bend," on *The Return of the Repressed: The John Fahey Anthology.*

influences:

◀◀ Blind Willie Johnson, Bill Monroe, Charlie Patton, Charles Ives

▶▶ Leo Kottke, Peter Lang, Terry Robb, Glenn Jones, Woody Mann, Will Ackerman, Thurston Moore

Garaud MacTaggart

Fairground Attraction /Eddi Reader

Formed 1985, in London, England. Disbanded 1989.

Eddi Reader, vocals; Mark E. Nevin, guitar; Simon Edwards; Will Hasley.

This short-lived British skiffle-swing quartet lasted for one album, but *First of a Million Kisses* happens to be one of the most gorgeous, unabashedly romantic works to ever drift across the Atlantic. Blending the finger-snapping cool of early Rickie Lee Jones with the hushed, elegant folk-pop of Everything but the Girl, Fairground Attraction relied on acoustic instrumentation ranging from mandolins and guitarrons to vibraphones and clarinets. The giddy "Perfect" was a minor MTV hit, but the band's main virtues were songwriter Mark E. Nevin's gift for imagery ("A Smile in a Whisper," "Moon on the Rain") and Glasgow-born Eddi Reader's sensual, soaring voice. Since the band broke up, Nevin has collaborated with Kirsty MacColl, while Reader has launched a solo career that has established her as a devilishly eccentric diva in Europe but relegated her to cult-favorite status in the United States.

what to buy: *First of a Million Kisses* ♫♫♫♫ (RCA, 1988, prod. Kevin Moloney, Fairground Attraction) is a delightful mix of giddy pop and street-corner primitivism that showcases Reader's range. Uptempo tracks such as "Perfect" and "Falling Backwards" are balanced by such jazzy torch songs as "Moon on the Rain" and the frantic "Clare," which uses a shrieking clarinet as a metaphor for sexual betrayal.

what to buy next: *Eddi Reader* 🎵🎵🎵 (Reprise, 1994, prod. Greg Penny) is a soothing, soulful pop triumph whose strongest songs come from the pens of Nevin ("The Exception," "Dear John") and the prolific Boo Hewerdine ("Joke," "Patience of Angels").

what to avoid: The import-only *Ay Fond Kiss* 🎵🎵 (RCA, 1990, prod. Fairground Attraction, Kevin Moloney) looks like a sophomore album but is a haphazard collection of singles, B-sides, and outtakes, including an unusually jaunty interpretation of Patsy Cline's "Walking after Midnight."

worth searching for: The British version of *Candyfloss and Medicine* (Blanco y Negro, 1996, prod. Eddi Reader, Teddy Borowiecki) has fewer tracks than its stateside counterpart, but it boasts a lighthearted reading of Gene Pitney's "Town without Pity."

solo outings:
Eddi Reader:
Mirmama 🎵🎵🎵 (Compass, 1992)
Candyfloss and Medicine 🎵🎵🎵 (Reprise, 1997)

influences:
◀◀ Everything but the Girl, the Smiths, Ella Fitzgerald
▶▶ Jane Siberry, Sara Hickman, k.d. lang

David Okamoto

Fairport Convention /Fairport /Sandy Denny /Fotheringay

Formed 1967, in London, England. Disbanded 1976. Re-formed 1985.

Richard Thompson, guitar, vocals (1967–71); **Simon Nicol**, guitar, banjo, bass, vocals (1967–71); **Judy Dyble**, piano, vocals (1967–68); **Ashley "Tyger" Hutchings**, bass, guitar, vocals (1967–69); **Martin Lamble**, drums (1967–69); **Iain Matthews** (born Ian MacDonald), vocals, percussion, guitar (1967–68); **Sandy Denny** (died April 21, 1978), vocals, guitar, keyboards (1968–69, 1974–76); **Dave Swarbrick**, violin, mandolin, vocals (1969–present); **Dave Mattacks**, drums, keyboards, vocals (1969–74, 1985–present); **Dave Pegg**, guitar, viola, vocals (1969–present); **Roger Hill**, guitar, mandolin (1971–72); **Tom Farnell**, drums (1972); **David Rea**, guitar (1972); **Trevor Lucas**, guitar (1972–76); **Jerry Donahue**, guitar, vocals (1972–76); **Paul Warren**, drums (1974); **Bruce Rowland**, drums (1974–76); **Martin Allcock**, bass,

guitar, bouzouki (1985–96); **Ric Sanders**, violin (1985–present); **Chris Leslie**, bouzouki, mandolin, violin, vocals (1997–present).

Bringing Celtic folk traditions to the forefront, Fairport Convention made its mark with the evanescent vocals of Sandy Denny and Richard Thompson's brave, soulful songwriting and guitar work. Though Denny and Thompson departed after a handful of releases, the group soldiered on through the next decade with a huge, rotating cast of players. Initially called Tim Turner's Narration, the group was named for the "convention" of musicians at founder Ashley Hutchings's house in Muswell Hill, a London suburb. It was Denny's entrance—replacing Judy Dyble—that helped change the group from American folk acolytes to English folk-rock pioneers. The collective became simply Fairport in 1976, split in 1979—overwhelmed briefly by the lack of commercial success that has always been its lot—but reformed in 1985 and has released records periodically ever since. Because of Denny's powerful presence, the group chose never to install another female lead singer, letting the musicians take over vocal chores themselves. The group reunited briefly with Denny during the '70s. Members of Fairport have also been part of Jethro Tull, Soft Machine, and Richard & Linda Thompson's band, and several have done extensive session work. Thompson continues to win fans for his solo work, and Fairport stages its annual Cropredy Festival weekend which brings many of its old members back into the fold for the event.

what to buy: Recorded with Fairport's best lineup—including Thompson, Denny, and fiddler Dave Swarbrick—*Liege and Leaf* 🎵🎵🎵🎵 (A&M, 1969, prod. Joe Boyd) is a fully realized fusion of folk and rock sensibilities best heard on songs such as "Tam Lin" and "Crazy Man Michael." During its 30 years this album has never been out of print. *Unhalfbricking* 🎵🎵🎵 (Hannibal, 1969, prod. Joe Boyd, Simon Nicol, Fairport Convention) is a stunning mix of Thompson and Denny originals, traditional songs, and several renditions of Bob Dylan tunes—notably a French version of "If You Gotta Go." Denny's solo debut, *What We Did on Our Holidays* 🎵🎵🎵🎵 (Hannibal, 1969, prod. Joe Boyd), is a standout that mixes great songs both old ("She Moves through the Fair") and new ("Fotheringay," "Meet on the Ledge"). *Full House* 🎵🎵🎵 (Hannibal, 1970, prod. Joe Boyd) features the powerful but short-lived line-up featuring Swarbrick and Thompson. Their jointly written "Walk Awhile" and "Sloth" both appear here for the first time. *Meet on the Ledge—The Classic Years (1967–1975)* 🎵🎵🎵 (Chronicles, 1998, prod. various) is a solid compilation of the group's glory years—not as cohesive as its best individual albums, but a good introduction nonetheless.

what to buy next: *House Full* 🎵🎵🎵 (Hannibal, 1986, prod. Joe Boyd, Frank Kornelussen) revises a 1977 live album that showcases another of Fairport's formidable units. *Five Seasons*

𝄢𝄢𝄢𝄢 (Rough Trade, 1990, prod. Fairport Convention) and *Jewel in the Crown* 𝄢𝄢𝄢𝄢 (Green Linnet, 1995, prod. Fairport Convention) are latter-day Fairport releases—*Jewel* with a pronounced political edge—that show the group hasn't lost much.

what to avoid: *In Real Time: Live '87* 𝄢𝄢 (Island, 1989, prod. Dave Mattacks) is a pleasant enough reunion album, but hardly shows the fire and invention of the group's best work.

the rest:
Fairport Convention 𝄢𝄢𝄢𝄢 (Polydor, 1968)
Angel Delight 𝄢𝄢𝄢 (A&M, 1971)
Babbacombe Lee 𝄢𝄢𝄢 (A&M, 1971)
Rosie 𝄢𝄢𝄢 (A&M, 1973)
Nine 𝄢𝄢 (A&M, 1973)
A Fairport Live Convention 𝄢𝄢𝄢 (Island, 1974)
Rising for the Moon 𝄢𝄢𝄢 (Island, 1975)
Fairport Chronicles 𝄢𝄢𝄢𝄢 (A&M, 1976)
Gottle o' Geer 𝄢𝄢 (Island, 1976)
Bonny Bunch of Roses 𝄢𝄢 (Vertigo, 1977)
Live at L.A. Troubadour 𝄢𝄢 (Island, 1977)
Tipplers Tales 𝄢𝄢𝄢 (Vertigo, 1978)
Farewell, Farewell 𝄢𝄢𝄢 (Simon's, 1979)
Moat on the Ledge 𝄢𝄢𝄢 (Stony Plain, 1982)
Glady's Leap 𝄢𝄢𝄢 (Varrick, 1985)
Expletive Delighted! 𝄢𝄢𝄢 (Varrick, 1986)
Heyday 𝄢𝄢𝄢𝄢 (Hannibal, 1987)
In Real Time: Live '87 𝄢𝄢 (Island, 1987)
Red & Gold 𝄢𝄢 (Rough Trade, 1989)
Old.New.Borrowed.Blue 𝄢𝄢𝄢𝄢 (Woodworm, 1996)
Encore, Encore 𝄢𝄢𝄢 (Folkprint, 1997)
Who Knows Where The Time Goes? 𝄢𝄢𝄢𝄢 (Woodworm, 1997)
The Cropredy Box 𝄢𝄢𝄢 (Woodworm, 1998)

worth searching for: *25th Anniversary Concert* (Woodworm, 1993, prod. Dave Pegg) is the import document of the jovial 1992 celebration that brought back a good chunk of the band's past—including Thompson and Swarbrick—as well as admirers such as Robert Plant.

solo outings:
Fotheringay (Denny & Donahue):
Fotheringay 𝄢𝄢𝄢𝄢 (Hannibal, 1970)

Sandy Denny:
All Our Own Work 𝄢𝄢𝄢 (Pickwick, 1968)
Sandy Denny 𝄢𝄢𝄢 (Saga, 1970)
North Star Grassman and the Ravens 𝄢𝄢𝄢 (Hannibal, 1971)
The Bunch 𝄢𝄢𝄢 (A&M, 1972)
Sandy 𝄢𝄢𝄢𝄢 (A&M, 1972)
Like an Old Fashioned Waltz 𝄢𝄢𝄢 (Hannibal, 1973)
Rendezvous 𝄢𝄢𝄢 (Hannibal, 1977)
Sandy Denny & the Strawbs 𝄢𝄢𝄢 (Hannibal, 1985)
Who Knows Where the Time Goes? 𝄢𝄢𝄢𝄢 (Hannibal, 1986)
The Best of Sandy Denny 𝄢𝄢𝄢𝄢 (Hannibal, 1989)

Original Sandy Denny 𝄢𝄢𝄢 (Trojan, 1991)
Sandy Denny, Trevor Lucas & Friends: The Attic Tapes 𝄢𝄢𝄢 (Raven, 1994)
The BBC Sessions, 1971–73 𝄢𝄢𝄢 (Strange Fruit, 1996)
Gold Dust 𝄢𝄢𝄢𝄢 (Island, 1998)

Dave Pegg and Friends:
Birthday Party 𝄢𝄢𝄢 (Woodworm, 1998)

influences:

◀◀ Martin Carthy, Bob Dylan, Joni Mitchell, the Byrds, Pentangle, the Everly Brothers

▶▶ The Albion Band, Steeleye Span, the Continental Drifters, Nick Drake, Dire Straits

Sarah Weber, Simon Glickman, and David Greenberger

Adam Faith

Born Terence Nelhams, June 23, 1940, in Acton, West London, England.

British rock 'n' roll before the Beatles consisted of, with few exceptions, a pale parade of pretty boys and girls doing their damnedest to emulate—and emasculate—the sounds and styles of Elvis, the Everlys and Buddy Holly's Crickets. Adam Faith typified this safely derivative state of affairs, hitting the U.K. Top 10 with alarming regularity between 1959 and 1963 before resorting to a decade of television and film work. He's spent the years since in record production (Roger Daltrey) and artist management (Leo Sayer) before succumbing totally to the world of high finance (with a stake in, among many other properties, London's Savoy Hotel). Still, with his magnificent back-up combo the Roulettes (which included future Argent member and hit songwriter Russ Ballard), Faith produced some moments of surprisingly ferocious rock before being swept under by the Liverpool Sound he, in some small way, helped inspire.

what's available: His recently reissued debut album *Adam* 𝄢𝄢𝄢 (Parlophone, 1960/EMI, 1997, prod. John Burgess) is the kind of wholesome pop to be expected from a British rock record of the time, though John Barry's arrangements portended his James Bond scores of future years with their wit and economy.

worth searching for: Recorded live in the Abbey Road Studios before a boisterous crowd of more than 100 Adam Faith Fan Club members, *Faith Alive* (Parlophone, 1965) is an uncharacteristically tough and rugged racketfest, with the ever-able Roulettes helping wallop home "High Heel Sneakers," "Little Queenie," and even "Heartbreak Hotel" with boundless enthusiasm. Faith's fine "comeback" effort, *I Survive* (Warner Bros. 1974, prod. Adam Faith, David Courtney) features contributions from his old chart rival Paul McCartney, among many others.

influences:

◄◄ Lonnie Donegan, Cliff Richard, Billy Fury

►► Frank Ifield, Billy J. Kramer, David Essex, the Viletones

Gary Pig Gold

Th' Faith Healers

Formed 1990, in Hampstead, England. Disbanded 1994.

Roxanne Stephen, vocals; Tom Cullinan, guitar/vocals; Ben Hopkin, bass; Joe Dilworth, drums.

Th' Faith Healers prove the theory that to make engaging, inspiring guitar rock, you don't need to understand theory and learn finger-tangling tunings; all you gotta do is find an interesting groove, examine it over and over again and then freak out the guitar as the rhythm carries on single-mindedly. As the first signing to the influential Too Pure imprint in England, which would go on to release debut records from PJ Harvey, Stereolab, and Pram, th' Faith Healers' focus on guitar mantras created a world of repetitive fascination, and foreshadowed the collision of linear based electronic music with rock and roll. While at times these grooves resulted in overworked tautologies, mostly they were engaging successes. After the band's breakup, guitarist Tom Cullinan formed Quickspace, which treads similar terrain but has a more synthetic feel.

what to buy: *Lido* 𝄞𝄞𝄞 (Too Pure/Elektra, 1992, prod. Ott & Robs) is a rhythmically steady marathon that moves from quiet, intricate patterns to flat-out explosions that come in waves and fluctuate while they steadily meander; *Imaginary Friend* 𝄞𝄞𝄞 (Too Pure/Elektra, 1993) contains a few more hooks and tons more space. Songs stretch to their limits, and the overwhelming tension that the band is able to eke out of such a seemingly simplistic approach is a fascinating achievement.

what to buy next: *L'* 𝄞𝄞𝄞 (Too Pure/American, 1995) is comprised of all the band's early singles and extant recordings, and illustrates a band just hitting its stride.

worth searching for: Th' Faith Healers' inspired cover of Abba's "S.O.S." (Clawfist, 1994) was offered as a limited edition 45. It's worth tracking down to witness two extremely opposing styles clashing to great effect.

influences:

◄◄ Can, My Bloody Valentine, Kraftwerk, Neu!

►► Breeders, Seefeel, Bowery Electric

see also: *Quickspace*

Randall Roberts

Faith No More
/Mr. Bungle
/Imperial Teen

Formed 1982, in Los Angeles, CA. Disbanded 1998.

Faith No More: Mike Bordin, drums; Roddy Bottum, keyboards; Billy Gould, bass; Chuck Mosely, vocals (1983–88); Jim Martin, guitar (1984–94); Mike Patton, vocals (1989–present); Dean Menta, guitar (1994–present). Mr. Bungle: Mike Patton, vocals; Trey Spruance, guitar; Trevor Dunn, bass; Clinton McKinnon, tenor sax, clarinets; I Quit, percussion; Theo, reeds. Imperial Teen: Roddy Bottum, vocals, guitar; Will, vocals, guitar; Lynn, vocals, drums; Jone, vocals, bass.

Faith No More rose out of the early '80s post-punk scene in Los Angeles. The initial lineup, with original singer/shouter Chuck Mosely, yielded two albums that were notable only for their funk-tinged hard rock grooves. Mosely was sent packing in 1988 (he subsequently went on to a brief stint fronting seminal punkers Bad Brains) and the band, sans singer, began work on the album *The Real Thing*. Vocalist Mike Patton was brought aboard in 1989 with the daunting task of quickly composing the lyrics for the near-finished album; he did so with considerable flourish, and the recording yielded the smash single "Epic." Patton's wild antics, broad vocal abilities, and conceptual facility took the band to a new level that successfully combined such disparate elements as funk, metal, rap, jazz, art rock, and theater of the absurd. Using his newfound clout, Patton secured a deal for his side project, Mr. Bungle, a band whose no-rules approach was highly influenced by the scatter-jazz aesthetics of saxophonist John Zorn (who produced its debut). The line between Faith No More and Mr. Bungle blurred somewhat during 1994 when Faith's guitarist Jim Martin was fired and Mr. Bungle guitarist Trey Spruance filled in on the group's latest album. By the early '90s, both bands—while still exhibiting the considerable might of the musicians—had primarily become arenas for the prolific imagination of Patton. Part of the reason Faith No More opted to call it quits in 1998 was so the musicians—particularly Patton and Roddy Bottum—could devote more time to what had become their primary interests.

what to buy: Faith No More's *Angel Dust* 𝄞𝄞𝄞𝄞 (Slash/Reprise, 1992, prod. Matt Wallace, Faith No More) took the concepts that were hinted at on *The Real Thing* and exploded them to gargantuan proportions. This album finds the band at the height of its powers, playing material that is caustically aggressive, psychically violent, and compulsively listenable. Songs such as "Midlife Crisis," "Caffeine," "Smaller and Smaller," and "Everything's Ruined" are both harrowing and irresistible. Martin's guitar is loud and chunky, Mike Bordin and Billy Gould's rhythm section is solid and insistent, and keyboardist Bottum supplies eclectic subtleties. Best of all is Patton, who displays

Mike Patton of Faith No More (© Ken Settle)

frightening growth in his lyrical vision and vocal delivery; his *The Real Thing* persona of a schizophrenic imp is wiped away and replaced with that of a ghoulish cynic lurking in the shadows of a dark subculture. *Mr. Bungle* ♫♫♫ (Warner Bros., 1991, prod. John Zorn, Mr. Bungle) takes the darker fringe elements of Faith No More's sound and brings them to the fore; the result is something very close to stream-of-consciousness music, with ideas and musical genres zooming in and out at a relentless pace. Much like producer Zorn's work (particularly with his band Naked City), the music careens deliriously from fast to slow, jackhammer loud to lullaby soft. To say that the material is restless is a gross understatement; the myriad styles crowding the songs conjure images of a psychotic calliope while the lyrics examine society's slimy underbelly with darkly comic effects. Granted this is not music for the faint of heart, but it *is* musically challenging, rewarding, and, like fear, never boring. Finally, Bottum's group, Imperial Teen, stripped away Faith No More's heavy production sound and focused on the basics: guitars, bass, drums, harmonies and catchy melodies. The quartet's debut, *Seasick* ♫♫♫ (Slash/London, 1996, prod. Steve McDonald, Imperial Teen), contains one bona fide rock classic, the irresistible "You're One," which recalls the Breeders in layering the four band members' vocals and instruments in such a complex way it sounds simple. That song hit alternative-rock radio stations' playlists briefly during 1996 and 1997, but the album is full of undiscovered gems, such as the slow, hypnotic "Imperial Teen" (with its "2, 3, 4, 1" chorus) and the Kurt Vonnegut-name-dropping "Pig Latin."

what to buy next: *King for a Day . . . Fool for a Lifetime* ♫♫♫ (Slash/Reprise, 1995, prod. Andy Wallace, Faith No More) and *Disco Volante* ♫♫♫ (Warner Bros., 1995, prod. Mr. Bungle), the follow-up albums from Faith No More and Mr. Bungle, respectively, both deliver pleasures similar to their predecessors. Unfortunately, these albums bear the cross of following brilliant outings, and the results are neither as fresh nor as diverse. Both, however, come highly recommended to anyone who enjoyed *Angel Dust* and *Mr. Bungle*.

what to avoid: Faith No More's *Introduce Yourself* ♫♫ (Slash/Reprise, 1987, prod. Steve Berlin, Matt Wallace, Faith No More) is a frustrating album that just evades being listenable. The musicianship is solid and inventive, although the band is clearly still searching for its own turf. The problem lies with Mosely's vocals, which veer from whiny to wailing without much musicality in between.

the rest:
Faith No More:
We Care a Lot ♫♫ (Mordam, 1985)
The Real Thing ♫♫♫ (Slash/Reprise, 1989)
Album of the Year ♫♫♫ (Warner Bros., 1997)

Imperial Teen:
What Is Not to Love N/A (Slash, 1998)

worth searching for: In 1993 Faith No More recorded a cover version of the Commodores hit "Easy" for a limited EP release; it also appeared on later import copies of the *Angel Dust* album. Like the version of the theme from *Midnight Cowboy* that closes *Angel Dust*, this is a fairly straightforward rendering of the song that still manages a good dose of ironic humor.

influences:
◀◀ Black Sabbath, Public Enemy, Parliament, Frank Zappa, Black Flag, John Zorn/Naked City, Roky Erikson, William S. Burroughs, Tom Waits

▶▶ White Zombie, Tool, Therapy?, Primus

David Galens and Steve Knopper

Marianne Faithfull

Born December 29, 1946, in London, England.

The daughter of a British college lecturer and an Austrian baroness, Marianne Faithfull was a beautiful young model with no real singing aspirations until she fell in love with Mick Jagger. He wrote her first hit, 1964's "As Tears Go By," with fellow Rolling Stone Keith Richards. She helped write their "Sister Morphine," but went uncredited until a few years ago. Faithfull's various descents into drug addiction hell are now legendary, including a nearly fatal bout with heroin at the time she broke up with Jagger. But she's always managed to land on her feet, and her ragged, haggard, Dietrich-like voice powerfully reflects her painful experiences. The infamous lady in the rug—Faithfull was found clad in nothing but a floor covering during a drug bust at Richards's home—became a singer in her own right during the late '70s but succumbed to chemical temptations several times during the '80s. She emerged clean, clear-headed, and candid in her 1994 autobiography, which was accompanied by a greatest hits album. Faithfull followed it a year later with her most ambitious and conceptual album, *A Secret Life*, on which she collaborated with director David Lynch's musical collaborator, Angelo Badalamenti (*Twin Peaks, Blue Velvet*).

what to buy: *Faithfull: A Collection of Her Best* ♫♫♫ (Island, 1994, prod. various) is a surprisingly cohesive 11-song collection that draws from the various and varied aspects of Faithfull's 32-year recording career. Selections range from that first innocent blush of "As Tears Go By" to the bitterly vulgar "Why'd Ya Do It" (from *Broken English*), the moody "Trouble in Mind" theme song, torch numbers from the Hal Willner–produced "Strange Weather," and a sample from the then-upcoming album *A Secret Life*.

what to buy next: *Broken English* ♫♫♫ (Island, 1979, prod. Mark Miller Mundy) couldn't possibly have the dramatic impact today that it did when it was released 17 years ago. There was no way then to be prepared for the stark deterioration of Faithfull's formerly breathy voice, a withered but powerful emotive tool ravaged by drugs and a beautiful life turned hard. Producer Mundy and guitarist Barry Reynolds showcased that voice without obstructing it. *Blazing Away* ♫♫♫ (Island, 1990, prod. Hal Wilner) is a powerful live album that showcases Faithfull at her dramatic best, backed by people such as Dr. John, former Tom Waits and Elvis Costello guitarist Mark Ribot, and the Band's Garth Hudson. Powerful stuff.

what to avoid: Faithfull's collaboration with composer Badalamenti, *A Secret Life* ♫♫ (Island, 1995) is an interesting idea that doesn't work. Both make haunting music on their own, but this is just a little too dull.

the rest:
Marianne Faithfull's Greatest Hits ♫ (Abkco, 1969)
Dangerous Acquaintances ♫♫♫ (Island, 1981)
A Child's Adventure ♫♫♫ (Island, 1983)
Strange Weather ♫♫ (Island, 1987)
20th-Century Blues ♫♫♫ (RCA, 1997)

worth searching for: High-quality sound (at a high price) is the lure of Mobile Fidelity's Ultradisc combination of *Broken English* and *Strange Weather* (1995). Real collectors might have a tough time hunting down three rarities—the import-only *Faithless* (Sony, 1978) which broke an 11-year recording gap, and her long out-of-print '60s albums *Come My Way* (Decca, 1965) and *Faithfull Forever* (London, 1966). And then there's Faithfull's truly spooky guest vocal on "The Memory Remains" from the Metallica album *Re-Load*.

influences:
◀◀ Joan Baez, Buddy Holly, Everly Brothers, Charlie Parker

▶▶ Björk, Rickie Lee Jones

Doug Pullen

Jason Falkner

Born June 2, 1968, in Los Angeles, CA.

California scenester Jason Falkner became the guitarist for the late Three O'Clock on *Vermillion*, which was far from its finest hour. Next he joined Jellyfish for its debut, once again taking a back seat to the songwriters who fronted the band. Finally given a chance to cut loose on his own, Falkner skims influences from the top of the pops, such as Todd Rundgren, XTC, and even Seals & Crofts and Bread, but he turns the cream of that crop into his very own butter. No hindrance to his tasty ideas, Falkner's oddly soothing voice mingles the breathiness of the Zombies' Colin Blunstone with the sweet shrillness of Peter Holsapple. Precise craftsmanship and flawless, inventive playing make Falkner a pop necessity, but what elevates him to the rank of innovator is his fresh, wide-eyed sense of wonder and excitement; he's like a child who just discovered pop underneath his Christmas tree. The fact that he wants to open it up to show to the world is a sign of his unique gift. It's playful, all right—Falkner shakes up power-pop like an Etch-a-Sketch—but his music is something more durable, unflinching, and permanent. It actually stays with you.

what to buy: *Presents Author Unknown* ♫♫♫♫ (Elektra, 1996, prod. Jason Falkner) is one of the best pop albums of the '90s. With his unique voice, Falkner creates a gorgeous foray into the limitless possibilities of pop music. Not one song fails in the melody department, though some of the lyrics are ambiguous-sounding, others ungrammatical. Still, most of the words fit the organic, whimsical lilt of the tunes.

what to buy next: *Amazing the Survivors* ♫♫♫♫ (Elektra, 1998, prod. Jason Falkner, Nigel Godrich) starts out with a muted, dreamy snippet that's evocative of both the Beatles' "Honey Pie" and the mock-vinyl beginning of XTC's "Respectable Street." It then slips into "Author Unknown," which could have been the title track of his first album, but Falkner's too cryptic and slippery for that.

worth searching for: Falkner was part of the Grays, a three-writer, one-off band whose out-of-print album *The Grays* (Epic, 1994, prod. Jack Joseph Puig) is a gloom-darkened pop masterpiece that offers shades of itself. Two of Falkner's best songs, "Friend of Mine" and "Both Belong," are on this album, which also features the stellar songs and accomplished instrumentation of Jon Brion and Buddy Judge.

influences:
◀◀ Todd Rundgren, Tommy Keene

see also: *Jellyfish*

Jordan Oakes

The Fall

Formed 1976, in Manchester, England.

Mark E. Smith, vocals, guitar, keyboards, tapes; Una Balnes, keyboards (1976–78), keyboards; Yvonne Pawlett, electric piano (1978–79); Marcia Schofield, keyboards, vocals (1987–90); David Bush, keyboards (1991–present); Martin Bramah, guitar, vocals (1976–78, 1989–90); Craig Scanlan, guitar (1979–present); Brix Smith, guitar, keyboard, vocals (1983–89, 1994); Tony Friel, bass (1976–78); Marc Riley, keyboards, guitar, bass (1978–83); Steve Hanley, bass, guitar (1979–present); Simon Rogers, bass, keyboards, guitar (1984–87); Karl Burns, drums, bass (1976–79, 1981–86, 1993–present); Mark Leigh, drums (1979–80); Paul Hanley, drums, keyboards

(1980–84); John Simon Wolstencroft, drums (1986–present); Kenny Brady (a.k.a. Nigel Kennedy), violin (1990).

Mark E. Smith was working on the docks when punk hit. Reacting against some of the mundane examples of the genre, he formed his own group, simultaneously informed by his love of German experimentalists such as Can and of American rockabilly. He's reputedly tone deaf and has said his sing-songy spoken vocal style is inspired by reggae toasters—in other words, he's a rapper, with an extra "uh" added to the ends of words being his trademark. It's a gloriously confrontational style that conveys his cranky spirit even when American listeners haven't the slightest idea what he's talking about—and when the odd one-liner cracks you up, so much the better. Debuting with one of the finest albums to come out of punk, the Fall has lasted longer than all but a few bands, and has been more productive (more than 30 albums if compilations are counted) and consistent than any of them. The group's name came from the existential Albert Camus work of the same title, and Smith makes no effort to hide his high opinion of himself and low opinion of most music fans. There's a socio-political edge to many of his lyrics, refracted so eccentrically as to avoid preachiness. Thus, after an initial progression into more forbiddingly dissonant and ragged sound, it was a shock when the group developed a cleaner style that was occasionally even catchy. An appreciation for guitar hooks and something approximating a steady rhythm remain, and there's even a bit of synthesizer, all making Smith's rants a little more accessible. The Fall is an acquired taste, to be sure (especially for Americans), but one worth the effort.

what to buy: The stunning debut *Live at the Witch Trials* 𝄐𝄐𝄐𝄐𝄐 (Step Forward, 1978/I.R.S., 1979, prod. Bob Sargeant) should be in the collection of anyone who cares about punk even slightly. With a new sound and a new attitude, it was the beginning of a great run but never quite equalled thereafter in impact or purity of vision.

what to buy next: *The Legendary Chaos Tape* 𝄐𝄐𝄐𝄐 (Feel Good All Over, 1995) contains a 1980 London concert with a classic early lineup, with fairly good sound compared to some other live Fall albums. *The Infotainment Scan* 𝄐𝄐𝄐𝄐 (Matador/Atlantic, 1993, prod. Rex Sargeant, Mark E. Smith, Simon Rogers) contains some recent Fall standards. "Paranoia Man in Cheap Sh*t Room" is a classic semi-intelligible Smith rant. "Glam-Racket No. 3" wittily rips the contemporary British music trend, and the cover of Sister Sledge's disco anthem "Lost in Music" shows a sense of humor.

what to avoid: *The Frenz Experiment* 𝄐 (Beggars Banquet/RCA, 1988, prod. Simon Rogers) matches rants that are incoherent with music so bare there's nothing to hold onto. Most of the songs on *Middle Class Revolt* 𝄐𝄐 (Matador, 1994, prod. Rex Sargeant) leave no impression.

the rest:
Dragnet 𝄐𝄐𝄐 (Step Forward, 1979)
Grotesque (after the Gramme) 𝄐𝄐𝄐𝄐 (Rough Trade, 1980)
Totale's Turns 𝄐𝄐𝄐 (Rough Trade, 1980)
Room to Live 𝄐𝄐𝄐 (Kamera, 1982)
Hex Enduction Hour 𝄐𝄐𝄐 (Line, 1982)
A Part of America Therein, 1981 𝄐𝄐𝄐𝄐 (Cottage/Rough Trade, 1982)
Perverted by Language 𝄐𝄐𝄐 (Rough Trade, 1983)
Palace of Swords Reversed 𝄐𝄐𝄐𝄐 (Cog-Sinister/Rough Trade, 1987)
Hip Priests and Kamerads 𝄐𝄐𝄐 (Situation 2, 1985)
The Wonderful and Frightening World of the Fall 𝄐𝄐𝄐𝄐 (Beggars Banquet/WEA, 1984)
This Nation's Saving Grace 𝄐𝄐𝄐 (Beggars Banquet/PVC, 1985)
The Fall 𝄐𝄐 (PVC EP, 1986)
The Domesday Payoff 𝄐𝄐𝄐 (Big Time/RCA, 1987)
I Am Kurious Oranj 𝄐𝄐𝄐 (Beggars Banquet/RCA, 1988)
Seminal Live 𝄐𝄐 (Beggars Banquet/RCA, 1989)
458489 A Sides 𝄐𝄐𝄐𝄐 (Beggars Banquet/RCA, 1990)
458489 B Sides 𝄐𝄐𝄐𝄐 (Beggars Banquet/RCA, 1990)
Extricate 𝄐𝄐𝄐𝄐 (Cog-Sinister/Fontana, 1990)
Shift-Work 𝄐𝄐 (Cog-Sinister/Fontana, 1991)
Code: Selfish 𝄐𝄐𝄐 (Cog-Sinister/Fontana, 1992)
Kimble (Peel Sessions EP) 𝄐𝄐 (BBC/Dutch East India, 1993)
27 Points 𝄐𝄐𝄐 (Permanent/BMG, 1995)
Cerebral Caustic 𝄐𝄐𝄐 (Permanent/Caroline, 1995)
BBC Radio 1 Live in Concert 𝄐𝄐 (Windsong U.K., 1993/Griffin, 1995)
Sinister Waltz 𝄐𝄐𝄐 (Receiver, 1996)
Light User Syndrome 𝄐𝄐𝄐 (Jet, 1996)
Fiend with a Violin 𝄐𝄐 (Receiver, 1996)
Oswald Defence Lawyer 𝄐𝄐𝄐 (Receiver, 1996)
Fall in a Hole 𝄐𝄐𝄐 (Cog-Sinister, 1997)
The Less You Look the More You Find 𝄐𝄐𝄐 (Recall/Snapper, 1997)
Levitate 𝄐𝄐𝄐 (Artful, 1998)

worth searching for: Not normally noted as tribute-album contributors, the Fall redo the Beatles' "A Day in the Life" on the British charity collection *Sgt. Pepper Knew My Father* (NME, 1988, prod. various).

influences:

◀◀ Sex Pistols, Can, Faust, the Velvet Underground, Gene Vincent, the Kinks

▶▶ Joy Division, Public Image Ltd., Sugarcubes, Sonic Youth, Swans, Pavement, Trumans Water

Steve Holtje

Georgie Fame

Born Clive Powell, June 26, 1943, in Leigh, Lancashire, England.

Having served his apprenticeship touring behind Gene Vincent, Eddie Cochran, and British proto-rocker Billy Fury, Georgie Fame settled in London in 1962 where, equipped with one of the first Hammond B3 organs in the land, his Blue Flames combo quickly came to rival Alexis Korner's Blues Incorporated and John Mayall's Bluesbreakers as the most influential musical training ground in the land (guitarist John McLaughlin and future Hendrix drummer Mitch Mitchell were but two to pass through Fame's ranks at this time). Signed to EMI Columbia Records in 1963, the band cut its classic debut LP live at the Flamingo Club and had a U.K. chart-topper with the infectious Afro-Cuban "Yeh Yeh." But success on stage and on record seemed sadly restricted to England: U.S. promoters, although starving at the time for anything British, were reluctant to book a racially integrated act like Fame's. In 1966, following a second U.K. #1 with the self-composed "Get Away," Fame inexplicably disbanded the Blue Flames in order to pursue a more "flexible" career, squandering what many believed to be a fine future in R&B and jazz with a vain quest for all-round entertainer status. Despite the occasional class move (for example, a Royal Albert Hall gig accompanied by the Count Basie Orchestra), he spent the next two decades puttering around on English television and cabaret stages with fellow MOR victim (and ex-Animal) Alan Price, producing such fluff as "The Ballad of Bonnie and Clyde" and eventually even Esso Oil and Maxwell House Coffee jingles. Thankfully the '90s found Fame's profile—to say nothing of his musical credibility—restored as he began touring and recording with the inimitable Van Morrison when not doing occasional soundtrack work (*Glengarry Glen Ross*). Recently spotted performing alongside Albert Lee and Peter Frampton in Bill Wyman's Rhythm Kings, the artist proudly sits once again behind his trusty B3, weaving the same bluesy, jazzy mix that rightfully gave his name Fame in the first place.

what's available: Other than his work with Van the Man, the most highly recommended of which is *How Long Has This Been Going On* ♪♪♪♪ (Verve, 1996, prod. Van Morrison, Georgie Fame), recorded live at Ronnie Scott's in London, all that is readily available on Fame in the States is *Cool Cat Blues* ♪♪♪ (Bean Bag, 1996, prod. Ben Sidran) and *The Blues and Me* ♪♪♪ (Bean Bag, 1996, prod. Ben Sidran), two pleasing if unspectacular returns-to-form for the former Blue Flame guiding light. Fame also appears on *The Go Jazz All-Stars* ♪♪♬ (Bean Bag, 1996, prod. Ben Sidran) and *Hoagy Carmichael, Fame & Ross: In Hoagland* ♪♪♬ (DRG, 1998).

worth searching for: The best of several (unfortunately import-only) career retrospectives is the wonderful *20 Beat Classics* (Polydor U.K., 1997, prod. various), which contains just enough hits and key album tracks to demonstrate what a remarkably trail-blazing and trend-setting outfit the Blue Flames were in their pre-"Bonnie & Clyde" prime. And of course, if you can find

it, don't let the legendary *Rhythm & Blues at the Flamingo* (EMI Columbia, 1963, prod. Ian Samwell) slip through your fingers.

influences:

◀◀ Mose Allison, Fats Domino, Jerry Lee Lewis, Ray Charles, Booker T. & the MG's

▶▶ Eric Burdon & the Animals, Brian Auger, the Specials

see also: *Van Morrison*

Gary Pig Gold

Mary Ann Farley

Born in Newark, NJ.

Known as the "Queen of Anti-Folk" in her homebase of Hoboken, New Jersey (and to a growing nationwide following), Mary Ann Farley is one of the most adventurous and accomplished artists currently moving up through the indie-music ranks. Restlessly (but not recklessly) creative, Farley graduated from an intriguing, synthed-up Motown gothic sound on her 1993 debut EP, *First Few Words*, to a stylistically expansive folk, by turns reflective and tenacious, on her first full-length album, *Daddy's Little Girl*, in 1996. Her idiosyncratic approach—and her attraction of substantial national attention while sticking to independent labels—bears the legacy of Ani DiFranco, but Farley will one day be recognized as just as much of an original. With an uncommon ambition and an even rarer ability to pull it off, Farley will never do the same album twice, giving ample reason to anticipate her next evolution.

what to buy: *Daddy's Little Girl* ♪♪♪♪ (Deko, 1996, prod. Alan Douches, Mary Ann Farley) is the album that got everyone noticing. Its highlights include: the dreamy, bittersweet "If I Were Younger," whose ambient/acoustic arrangement ranks with the best of Suzanne Vega in widening the sonic definition of folk; the audacious "My Bare Hands," which sets a declaration of forthright but refreshingly uncompliant female sexuality to a drunken *Prairie Home Companion*–style arrangement; and the title track, which solidifies Farley's coffeehouse credentials with stark solo guitar and an incisive sketch of dysfunctional family values.

worth searching for: The dance-oriented debut EP *First Few Words* (River Records, 1993, prod. Mary Ann Farley) was precociously sophisticated and assured, giving insight into Farley's ability to assume a range of musical personae no less convincing for their variety.

influences:

◀◀ Ani DiFranco, Suzanne Vega, Buffy Sainte-Marie

Adam McGovern

Chris Farlowe
/Chris Farlowe
& the Thunderbirds
/The Hill

Born John Henry Deighton, October 13, 1940, in Berkhamstead, England.

Never a particularly unique singer or even notable interpreter of others' material, Chris Farlowe's true talent seemed to be in positioning himself in the right place—with the right people—at all the right times. After first making a name for himself as winner of the 1957 All-England Skiffle Championships, he aligned himself with the burgeoning British R&B movement alongside his first electric band, the Thunderbirds—which included, at various times, drummer Carl Palmer and the brilliant guitarist Albert Lee. Soon he was recording Rolling Stones rejects for Andrew Loog Oldham's Immediate label, later attempted to mine Manfred Mann's jazz leanings with the band Colosseum, recast himself during the early '70s as a poor man's Rod Stewart in Atomic Rooster and a decade later sang on some of Jimmy Page's early solo recordings. Through all of these incarnations, Farlowe gamely lent his smoke-coated vocals and try-as-he-might stage persona, but in attempting to be all things to all audiences ended up never quite establishing an audience—or lasting career—for himself.

what's available: The 20 mid-'60s recordings comprising *The Soulful Chris Farlowe: The Immediate Collection* ♫♫♫ (Sony Special Products, 1991, prod. various) are, in retrospect, of most use only to Stones completists; they include Jagger-produced versions of "Paint It Black," "Out of Time," and "Think," providing often histrionic but always interesting contrasts to their more familiar versions.

worth searching for: Difficult to find but well worth the hunt, *Chris Farlowe & the Thunderbirds featuring Albert Lee* (Charly, 1977, compilation prod. Mike Collier) provides a generous, well-annotated sampling of Farlowe's early recordings. The choice of material will be of no surprise to students of early British R&B, and Lee's guitar-playing throughout is nothing short of amazing.

influences:

◄◄ Long John Baldry, Eric Burdon, Paul Jones, Nanker Phelge

►► Rod Stewart, Paul Rodgers, Little Joe Cook

Gary Pig Gold

The Farm

Formed 1984, in Liverpool, England. Disbanded 1994.

Peter Hooton, vocals; Steve Grimes, guitar; Phil Strongman, bass (1984–90); Andy McVann (died 1986), drums (1984–86); Roy Boulter, drums (1986–94); Carl Hunter, bass (1990–94); Benjamin Leach, keyboards; Keith Mullen, guitar; Anthony Evans; horns; Steve Levy, horns; George Maher, horns; John Melvin, horns.

After Peter Hooton and Steve Grimes founded the Excitements in 1983, the duo fleshed out the lineup and became the Farm, delivering a string of synth pop-oriented U.K. hits, including a cover of the Monkees' *Stepping Stone* and a song based on Pachelbel's Canon in D, *All Together Now* (both in 1990). Drummer Andy McVann died in 1986 while trying to elude police; he was replaced by Roy Boulter in the first of several lineup changes that left Hooten and Grimes the only constant factors in the band. Not until 1991 did the group release its first album, *Spartacus*, which entered the British charts at #1 and provided a career peak that would never be duplicated—partly because the band's sound remained firmly based in the '80s while releasing records during the '90s.

what to buy: *Spartacus* ♫♫♫ (Sire, 1991, prod. Graham McPherson, Paul Heaton, Stan Cullimore) is the best of the band's three releases. Its detached, ennui-filled '80s sound is charming in places, but not outstanding anywhere. A bit of emotion might have helped.

what to avoid: *Love See No Color* ♫♫ (Sire, 1992, prod. Mark Saunders, Graham McPherson) is '80s synth-pop, more Smiths-like (i.e., whiney) than *Spartacus*, and full of lifeless, disco-y touches, including drum machines. It's got a cover of the Human League's *Don't You Want Me* that hit the U.K. Top 20, but isn't distinguishable enough from the original to merit significant attention. *Hullabaloo* ♫♫ (Sire, 1994, prod. Gary Wilkinson) offers more chimey synth pop, with lots of repetitive beats that sound fine blaring mindlessly out of disco sound systems but boring anywhere else.

worth searching for: *Groovy Train* (Warner Bros., 1991) is a maxi-single containing three mixes (single, club, and alternative) of the song, plus "All Together Now" and a 12-inch mix of "Stepping Stone."

influences:

◄◄ Human League, the Smiths, Happy Mondays, Madness, Frankie Goes to Hollywood

Lynne Margolis

Farm Dogs

Formed 1995, in Los Angeles, CA.

Bernie Taupin, vocals; Dennis Tufano, vocals, harmonica (1995–96); Jim Cregan, guitar, vocals; Robin LeMesurier, guitar, Dobro; Tony Brock, drums; Tad Wadhams, bass, vocals (1997–present).

You'd think that with the millions he rakes in from royalties to Elton John songs, lyricist Bernie Taupin would be satisfied. Not quite; a performer at heart, with a taste for the country flavored rock of John's *Tumbleweed Connection*, Taupin decided to get back into the performing game with Farm Dogs, an outfit he put together with other musical vets—including former Rod Stewart guitarist Jim Cregan. Farm Dogs plays a gentle, rootsy, swinging brand of country rock, not quite as laid back as Poco but hardly close to the more hell-bent edges of the alt-country crowd. This is no side project, however; Taupin swears he's as committed to Farm Dogs as he is to John, and the group even hit the road during 1998 to play small halls in support of its second album, *Immigrant Sons*.

what's available: Neither of Farm Dogs' albums make a substantial impression, mostly because Taupin is not a particularly strong singer, and his cohorts don't have Elton John's melodic sensibilities. *Last Stand in Open Country* ♫♫ (Discovery, 1996, prod. David Cole, Farm Dogs) is particularly wispy, despite the pleasant "Cinderella '67" and a guest shot by Sheryl Crow. *Immigrant Sons* ♫♫♪ (Sire, 1998, prod. David Cole, Farm Dogs) is more substantial and instrumentally meatier, but the vocals still leave something to be desired, and there's nothing here that sticks the way you'd expect from a group with this kind of talent.

influences:
◄◄ Hank Williams, Sonny Terry, Muddy Waters, the Highwaymen

Gary Graff

Farmer Not So John

Formed 1995, in Nashville, TN.

Mack Linebaugh, vocals, guitar; Brian Ray, bass, vocals; Richard McLaurin, guitar, lap steel, vocals; Sean Keith, drums, vocals; Sean Ray, pedal steel guitar.

Everything but country!? These were the classic words of suburban Gen-Xers everywhere during the early '80s when asked what kind of music they preferred. Today's insurgent country explosion has made believers out of many former detractors; in the same manner that punk rock reacted against the stadium acts of the '70s, the alterna-country movement can be seen as a backlash against the glossy, predictable star manufacturing machine of the Nashville sound. Now that it has become a movement with a convenient marketing tag to boot, the danger becomes the temptation for groups and industry folk to produce cookie-cutter sounds rather than sincere and earnest roots music in order to sell discs. One band that appears bent on destroying the matrix is, ironically enough, Nashville's own Farmer Not So John, a quartet that owes more to Neil Young than the Grand Ole Opry and has the right mix of public appeal and keen musicianship on which to build a prospective body of work.

WHAT ALBUM CHANGED YOUR LIFE?

It would have to be the Band albums, *Music from Big Pink* and the second album [*The Band*]. They were the kinds of albums you wish you'd made: 'Oh God, somebody's saying everything I want to say and doing it so much better!' After I heard the Band was when I wrote [the lyrics for Elton John's] *Tumbleweed Connection*. It was a blatant rip-off, but I wanted to make a record like that.

Bernie Taupin (of Farm Dogs)

what to buy: *Farmer Not So John* ♫♫♫ (Compass, 1998, prod. Richard McLaurin) offers up a unique blend of Southern country rock along with the astute grass root songwriting talents of Mack Linebaugh and Brian Ray. Particularly impressive is the opening track, "Fire in the Valley," a brooding philosophical reflection on contemporary American values gone askew. Equally convincing is the band's prowess with their instruments, ranging from lap steel to mandolin, as well as acoustic and electric guitars.

solo outings:
Sean Ray:
Travelogue ♫♫♪ (self-released, 1997)

influences:
◄◄ Neil Young, the Jayhawks, Uncle Tupelo

William Harmer

Dionne Farris

See: Arrested Development

Farside

Formed 1989, in Orange County, CA.

Michael "Popeye" Vogelsang, vocals, guitar; Rob Haworth, guitar (1989–92); Kevin Murphy, guitar, vocals (1992–present); Zack de la

Rocha, guitar (1990–91); Josh Stanton, bass (1989–90); Bryan Chu, bass (1990–present); Bob "Violence" Beshear, drums.

Farside is a melodic punk quartet from suburban Los Angeles. Outside of the underground punk scene, it's probably best known as the band that Zach de la Rocha performed in before starting his own hardcore group, Inside Out, and, later, the political rap-core outfit Rage Against the Machine; the only Farside "album" on which he appears is the odds-and-ends collection *Scrap*. Farside has also released two full-length albums and one EP on the Huntington Beach, California-based hardcore label Revelation Records. After its 1998 LP, the band planned to break up for good.

what to buy: *Rigged* 𝄢𝄢𝄢 (1995, Revelation, prod. Jim Monroe, Farside) is a strong collection of highly melodic yet not overtly poppy '90s punk rock, easily the group's most accessible album.

the rest:
Rochambeau 𝄢𝄢 (Revelation, 1992)
Farside 𝄢𝄢 (Revelation EP, 1996)
The Monroe Doctrine N/A (Revelation, 1998)

influences:
◀◀ Rage Against the Machine

Seth Hindin

Fastbacks

Formed 1979, in Seattle, WA.

Kim Warnick, bass, vocals; Lulu Gargiulo, guitar; Kurt Bloch, guitar, drums.

Predating its more famous Seattle brethren isn't what this group should be known for; out-rocking them is. Dripping energy and always sounding like they're having the time of their lives, Fastbacks are powered by songwriter and future Young Fresh Fellow Kurt Bloch's punkish pop gems, which then-Sub Pop staffer Kim Warnick tackles with vigor. Lulu Gargiulo adds occasional guitar and vocal support, while the list of former Fastbacks drummers—which includes a pre-Guns N' Roses Duff McKagen—rivals that of Spinal Tap.

what to buy: The place to start is the Sub Pop collection *The Question Is No* 𝄢𝄢𝄢𝄢 (Sub Pop, 1992, prod. various), which gathers some of the group's best songs and loose ends from 1980–92 and is guaranteed to get you out of your seat. "Lose" is a pop punk classic, and "Everything That I Don't Need" just plain rocks.

what to buy next: *Fastbacks . . . & His Orchestra* 𝄢𝄢𝄢 (Pop Llama, 1987, prod. various) adds nine more songs to the original . . . *& His Orchestra* LP and features such Fastback classics

as "Seven Days" and the super catchy "In America." *New Mansions in Sound* 𝄢𝄢𝄢𝄢 (Sub Pop, 1996) shows the group is still in good form, sliding slightly more towards a power pop direction.

the rest:
Very Very Powerful 𝄢𝄢𝄢𝄢 (Popllama, 1992)
Zucker 𝄢𝄢𝄢 (Sub Pop, 1993)
Answer the Phone, Dummy 𝄢𝄢𝄢 (Sub Pop, 1994)
Win, Lose, or Both 𝄢𝄢𝄢 (Popllama, 1998)

influences:
◀◀ Patti Smith, Joan Jett
▶▶ Hole, the Donnas, Everclear

see also: *Young Fresh Fellows, Flop*

Keith Klingensmith

Fastball

Formed as Magneto USA, 1994, in Austin, TX.

Miles Zuniga, guitar, vocals; Tony Scalzo, bass, vocals; Joey Shuffield, drums.

One day during 1997, Fastball bassist Tony Scalzo read a newspaper article about an elderly couple who had gone for a drive and were missing. Before he learned the outcome of the story (the couple was killed when their car drove off the road), Scalzo had penned "The Way," which during 1998 was this Austin trio's ticket from obscurity into radio hitdom. The good news is that anybody who picked up the group's second album, *All the Pain Money Can Buy*, for "The Way" found a treasure chest of well-crafted, rock-edged pop tunes with sturdy, sinuous melodies and marvelous vocal harmonies that spoke to the acknowledged Beatles influence—particularly on guitarist Miles Zuniga. This marked an evolution from Fastball's debut, *Make Your Mama Proud*, but it was a welcome change that bodes well for the trio's future.

what to buy: *All the Pain Money Can Buy* 𝄢𝄢𝄢𝄢 (Hollywood, 1998, prod. Julian Raymond) is a treat, an album loaded with some of the catchiest, radio-ready melodies you could hope to find in the post-modern rock revolution. "The Way" is the hook in, but once there you'll find tracks such as "Which Way to the Top?," "Warm Fuzzy Feeling," "Damaged Goods," and "Charlie the Methadone Man" and never want to leave.

the rest:
Make Your Mama Proud 𝄢𝄢𝄢 (Hollywood, 1996)

influences:
◀◀ The Beatles, the Minutemen, Alejandro Escovedo

Gary Graff

Faust

Formed 1971, in Hamburg, Germany. Disbanded 1973. Re-formed early '90s.

Uwe Nettlebeck, producer, multi-instrumentalist; Werner "Zappi" Diermaier, drums, vocals; Hans Joachim Irmler, organ; Jean-Herve Peron, guitar; Rudolf Sosna; Kurt Graupner; Gunther Wusthoff.

With an obsessive flair for audio experiments and improvisation, Faust found its place among '70's "Krautrock" outfits such as Kraftwerk and Can. Founder and producer Uwe Nettlebeck formed the band after getting an advance from Polydor Germany; its 1971 debut LP *Faust* was a landmark in sonic and lyrical experimentation blending jazz, rock, and noise into a sound that was derivative of no other. An elaborately packaged LP that featured the artwork of German-born Edda Kochl titled *Faust So Far* followed in 1972. Even though the band had a cult following in Europe, the world wasn't ready to admit electronic meddling and tape experiments into the mainstream just yet. Faust got little recognition during its first life span, a brief four years. But it lasted long enough to leave something behind for a plethora of experimental, noise, and electronic bands that followed. Making its exit in 1973 with *The Faust Tapes* on Virgin Records, the band reappeared in the early '90s—with a slighlty altered line-up—and played some of its most radical shows ever, smashing TV sets and wielding chain saws. It returned to the studio in 1995 with producer Jim O'Rourke, adding a new album to a growing catalog of live recordings and reissues of its early work. Many are imports manufactured by Faust's own German-based label, Klangbad.

what to buy: *71 Minutes of Faust* ♫♫♫ (ReR Recommended, 1990) includes two early LPs *Munich and Elsewhere* and *The Last LP*, plus two extra tracks. *You Know Faust* ♫♫♫ (ReR Recommended, 1997, prod. Hans Joachim Irmler) recalls the raucous sounds of early years. *Faust Tapes* ♫♫♫ (ReR Recommended, 1996) reissues a first-phase favorite from 1973.

what to buy next: *Rien* ♫♫♫ (Table of the Elements, 1995, prod. Jim O'Rourke) marks Faust's first studio effort after nearly two decades of silence. The CD features pieces of the band's 1994 U.S. tour with guest artists Michael Morley and Keiji Haino.

what to avoid: *Faust Concerts, Vol. 1 & 2* ♫♫ (Table of the Elements, 1994) document Faust's 1990 U.S. tour. They are very noisy and difficult to listen to without feeling as if you had to be there to appreciate what went on at these concerts.

the rest:
Wakes Nosferatu ♫♫♫ (Klangbad, 1996/Ufa/Caroline, 1998)
Faust IV ♫♫♫ (Blue Plate/Caroline, 1993)

worth searching for: *Outside the Dream Syndicate* (Table of the Elements, 1993) features Faust with minimalist Tony Conrad. A reissue of the debut, *Faust* (Polydor, 1996, prod. Uwe Nettlebeck), is available as a Japanese import.

influences:

◄◄ Mothers of Invention, the Velvet Underground, Soft Machine

►► Jim O'Rourke, Gastr del Sol, Einstürzende Neubauten, Tortoise, Stereolab, Flying Saucer Attack, Julian Cope

Norene Cashen

Fear

Formed 1979, in Los Angeles, CA. Disbanded 1987. Re-formed 1995.

Lee Ving (born Jude Lee James), lead vocals, guitar; Philo Cramer, guitar, vocals (1979–92); Derf Scratch (born Frederick Charles Millner III), bass, saxophone, vocals (1978–81); Spit Stix (born Tim Leitch), drums (1979–92); Flea (born Michael Balzary), bass, (1981–83); Scott Thunes, bass (1995–96); Andrew Jaimez, drums (1995–present), Sean Cruse, guitars (1995–96).

Like its contemporaries the Circle Jerks, Black Flag, and the Dead Kennedys, Fear proved that punk rock could be musically inventive and aggressive at the same time. Led by the deliberately controversial Lee Ving, the band created taut, genre-defining hardcore punk that walked a fine line between irony and insurrection. Fear formed during the late '70s heyday of the Los Angeles punk movement. Its debut album, *The Record*, introduced a band that wasn't afraid of a little sonic experimentation (the jazz-inflected "New York's Alright If You Like Saxophones") or even dark humor ("Let's have a war—we could use the space"). Fear was noted for its explosive live shows, the most famous being a 1981 appearance on *Saturday Night Live*. (In fact, Fear is said to have been the late John Belushi's favorite band.) Ving and Co. drove the *SNL* audience into a slam-dancing frenzy and, in a single stroke, created the stereotype that most Americans would come to associate with the word "punk." Following the release of *The Record*, the band underwent several line-up changes, and in 1987 Ving decided to throw in the proverbial towel. He embarked on a successful acting career, offering up memorable bad-guy turns in *Flashdance* and *Streets of Fire*, among other films. However, Fear wasn't ready to die that easily, and in 1995, riding the crest of the neo-punk revival, Ving reformed the band. Some were happier than others about that; Fear has always espoused sentiments that were decidedly less than politically correct (anti-women, anti-gay, etc.). However, given Ving's flare for the darkly ironic, it is possible that Fear's lyrics were all part of one big joke. Unfortunately, this humor was usually lost on many Fear fans (predominantly young, white males), who took Ving's rantings at face value. Regardless, Fear left an indelible mark on the early American punk scene, and the band's musical influence, if not its philosophical leanings, can be clearly heard in '90s punk-pop outfits such as Green Day and the Offspring.

what to buy: *The Record* ♪♪♪♪ (Slash, 1981, prod. Gary Lubow, Fear) showed what punk music could sound like in the hands of talented musicians who weren't afraid to go out on a limb and musically acknowledge their jazz and blues influences. Like all good punk, though, everything was short and bitter. Slashing guitars and breakneck rhythms provided the musical foundation for Ving's bellicose roar, and the lyrical content of the songs (namely, beer and anarchy) was tinged by a dark wit that, while often offensive, made Fear the thinking punk's band of choice. Ving collaborated with Megadeth leader Dave Mustaine on MD .45's *The Craving*.

what to buy next: On *Have Another Beer with Fear* ♪♪♪ (Sector II, 1995/I'll Be Dead in Hell, 1997, prod. Lee Ving, Ron Goudie), the band didn't exactly break new musical or thematic ground. Sure, Fear's members proved they could still generate the nihilistic hardcore buzz of old, but the beer joke ("Beerfight," "Free Beer," etc.) was starting to wear thin. Of course, true Fear fans probably didn't care, and new fans were probably too young to remember the first batch of beer odes, anyway.

the rest:
More Beer ♪♪ (Restless, 1985)
Live—For the Record ♪♪♪ (Restless, 1991)

worth searching for: Renowned for tumultuous live performances, Fear revels in being part of the mayhem it incites. This crowd-baiting is immortalized on the epic *The Decline of Western Civilization* (Slash, 1980, prod. Alan Kutner, Gary Hirstius), taken from the Penelope Spheeris classic "punkumentary" of the same name. Many fans consider the tracks on this album— "I Don't Care about You," "I Love Livin' in the City," and "Fear Anthem"—the best Fear on record. Fear also contributed "Let's Have a War" to the soundtrack for *Repo Man* (MCA, 1984, prod. Glen E. Friedman, Jerry Goldstein).

solo outings:
MD.45:
The Craving ♪♪♪ (Slab/Capitol, 1996)

influences:
◄◄ The Dickies, the Dictators, the Germs, Black Flag, the Clash, the Sex Pistols, Social Distortion, the Dead Kennedys

►► The Offspring, Rancid, H2O, Green Day, Sick of it All, Samiam, NOFX, the Didjits

Lisa M. Moore

Charlie Feathers

Born Charles Arthur Feathers, June 12, 1932, in Myrtle, MS. Died August 29, 1998, in Memphis, TN.

Charlie Feathers was never much of a commercial force, yet he is revered by his legion of fans as the father of rockabilly. Vocally he combined the keening wail of bluegrass with a feel for down and out blues, which he accented with playful hiccups, shrieks, and growls. A functional illiterate, Feathers wrote or "made up" a great many of his tunes, the best of which brim over with self-mocking irony. During the mid-'50s, Feathers recorded for the legendary Sam Phillips, who teamed him with honky tonk veterans Quinton Claunch and Bill Cantrell for a pair of unsuccessful hillbilly singles. Feathers claimed he had been doing "bluegrass rock" as early as the late '40s, but that Phillips was only interested in him as a country singer. While at Sun, he also co-wrote "I Forgot to Remember to Forget" for Elvis Presley. In subsequent years, Feathers would enlarge his role in Presley's success, claiming to have arranged "Good Rockin' Tonight" and produced hot, unreleased sessions. More believably, he has also charged that his best material was erased by the penny-pinching Phillips, who often reused (rather than stored) demo tapes. Feathers moved on to Meteor Records, where he established his reputation with the vocal gymnastics of "Tongue Tied Jill" backed with "Get with It"—the latter another tune he claimed to have written for Presley. However, his true classics were recorded for King Records with string bass player Jody Chastain and lead guitarist Jerry Huffman; together they wrote and recorded the defiant masturbatory ode "One Hand Loose," the hiccuping masterpiece "Everybody's Lovin' My Baby," and the tauntingly slow "Can't Hardly Stand It." Appearances on the *Big D Jamboree* spread Feathers's popularity throughout the middle South, but when rockabilly died during the late '50s, so did his career. Admirably, he never gave up or abandoned his faith in the music he helped pioneer. When not working day jobs, Feathers continued to record for small labels such as Kay, Walmay, Philwood, Holiday Inn, Redneck, Rollin' Rock, Barrelhouse, and his own Feathers' Records. Many of these recordings mix gut-wrenching country and blues remakes with refurbished rockabilly and feature Feathers's son, the underrated Bubba Feathers, on lead guitar. By the '70s, European enthusiasts had rediscovered Feathers and demanded the re-release of his early music, but bouts with cancer and diabetes made it difficult for him to capitalize on this fresh momentum. His 1991 LP for Elektra/Nonesuch (his lone major label outing) garnered fine reviews, though Feathers himself was critical of the finished product. And just when critics and fans had written him off due to declining health, he recorded an LP whose title speaks to both his stubbornness and musical devotion, *I Ain't Done Yet*. Several years later, he died of complications following a stroke.

what to buy: Though it contains no recordings from his eras with Sun, King, or Meteor, *Uh Huh Honey* ♪♪♪♪ (Norton, 1992, compilation prod. Billy Miller) is Feathers's most compelling start-to-finish LP. Besides containing all of his 1973 release *That Rock-a-Billy Cat!*, this powerful compilation includes his lone single for Rollin' Rock, sharp remakes of "Tongue Tied Jill" and

"Tear It Up," and five remarkable live tracks from his appearance on TV's *The Little Ole Show*. If you're a fan of bass-slappin' rockabilly or bone-chillin' country music, this is a must-have.

what to buy next: Backed by fellow Sun alumni Roland Janes, Stan Kesler, and J.M. Van Eaton on *Charlie Feathers* ♫♫♫ (Elektra/Nonesuch, 1991, prod. Ben Vaughn), the sometimes erratic Feathers delivers some first-rate rockabilly pyrotechnics and heartfelt country music in a modern recording environment. Longtime fans interested in Feathers's home demos of his many songs (which are often substantially different than the subsequent records) should check out *Tip Top Daddy: Unissued Acoustic Demos 1958–73* ♫♫♫ (Norton, 1995, compilation prod. Billy Miller), a nifty piece of music archaeology that reveals the underlying depths of his passion and artistry.

what to avoid: Sidestep *Rockabilly Shakeout* ♫♫ (Ace, 1992, prod. various) unless you want tracks by Sleepy LaBeef and Link Davis mixed in with those by Charlie Feathers.

the rest:

Good Rockin' Tonight/Live In Memphis ♫♫♫ (Barrelhouse, 1976/Edsel, 1993)

That Rock-a-Billy Cat! ♫♫♫ (Edsel, 1979/1994)

Wild Wild Party ♫♫♫ (Rockstar, 1987)

I Ain't Done Yet ♫♫♥ (Sunjay, 1993)

Honky Tonk Man ♫♫♥ (New Rose, 1994)

Rock-a-Billy ♫♫♫ (Zu-Zazz, 1994)

Get with It: Essential Recordings ♫♫♫♫♥ (Revenent, 1998)

worth searching for: All of Feathers's best King and Sun sides have been collected on *Gone Gone Gone* (Charly, 1991, prod. various), an essential British import which is really the best place to start. In the United States, flip through the vinyl bins for *King Federal Rockabillies* (King, 1978, prod. various), a powerful compilation boasting Feathers's "One Hand Loose," "Bottle to the Baby," "Nobody's Woman," and "Everybody's Lovin' My Baby," along with other amazing rockabilly tracks from Mac Curtis, Hank Mizell, and Bob & Lucille.

influences:

◀◀ Junior Kimbrough, Hank Williams, Bill Monroe, Elvis Presley

▶▶ Johnny Burnette & the Rock 'n' Roll Trio, Hasil Adkins, Bubba Feathers, Marcus Van Story, High Noon

Ken Burke

Danny Federici

See: Bruce Springsteen

The Feelies

Formed 1976, in Haledon, NJ. Disbanded 1991.

Bill Million (born William Clayton), guitar, vocals; Glenn Mercer, guitar, vocals; John J., bass (1976–77); Dave Weckerman, drums, percus-sion (1976–77, 1986–91); **Keith Clayton (born Keith DeNunzio), bass (1977–86); Vinny D (born Vincent DeNunzio), drums (1977–78); Anton Fier, drums (1978–86); Stanley Demeski, drums (1986–91); Brenda Sauter, bass, violin (1986–91).**

Using the sound of the Velvet Underground's rapidly strummed, trancy guitars on "What Goes On" as a blueprint, the Feelies became the stuff of cult legend in the New Jersey–New York area with the members' numerous side projects (the Trypes, Yung Wu, Speed the Plough), rare live performances, and even less frequent recordings. The debut album, *Crazy Rhythms*, remains a landmark of jittery American post-punk guitar rock, even if the shy monotone vocals were all but an afterthought. But it was six years before the Feelies would record again, returning in 1986 with a new lineup and more pastoral sound on *The Good Earth*, co-produced by kindred spirit Peter Buck of R.E.M. During this period, the Feelies appeared in Jonathan Demme's movie *Something Wild* as a cover band at a high school reunion, performing deadpan covers of the Monkees' "I'm a Believer" and David Bowie's "Fame." Subsequent albums failed to capitalize on this glimmer of mainstream attention, and the group disbanded after the 1991 release, *Time for a Witness*, with Glenn Mercer and Dave Weckerman forming Wake OoLoo, Brenda Sauter reemerging as the lead vocalist of Wild Carnation, and Stanley Demeski joining Luna.

what to buy: The debut, *Crazy Rhythms* ♫♫♫♫♥ (A&M, 1980, prod. Bill Million, Glenn Mercer), opens with a song called "The Boy with Perpetual Nervousness," and the band did indeed project a nerdy, caffeinated energy that echoed punk but also looked back to embrace the Velvets, the Stones, Neil Young, and the Beatles (whose "Everybody's Got Something to Hide" is covered). The guitars of Million and Mercer trace twisted, giddy spirals around the—you guessed it—crazy rhythms of future Golden Palominos founder Anton Fier.

what to buy next: On *The Good Earth* ♫♫♫♫♥ (Coyote-Twin/Tone, 1986, prod. Bill Million, Glenn Mercer, Peter Buck) Buck's early R.E.M. production eases the band into an electro-folk groove, and with the steady Demeski replacing the more free-form Fier on drums the pulse gets downright trancy at times. The group's pinnacle is "Slipping (Into Something)," which surges from chamber pop into a transcendent, Eastern-tinged guitar workout.

the rest:

No One Knows ♫♫♥ (Coyote-Twin/Tone EP, 1986)

Only Life ♫♫♫♥ (Coyote-A&M, 1988)

Time for a Witness ♫♫♫ (Coyote-A&M, 1991)

worth searching for: *Four Free Feelies Songs* (A&M, 1989, prod. various) is a promotional disc that includes covers of the Patti Smith Group's "Dancing Barefoot" and live renditions of

the Beatles' "Everybody's Got Something to Hide" and Jonathan Richman's "Egyptian Reggae."

influences:

◀◀ The Velvet Underground, Wire, Neil Young, Rolling Stones, the Monkees, Brian Eno, Patti Smith Group, the Beatles, R.E.M.

▶▶ Wild Carnation, Luna, Wake OoLoo, Yo La Tengo

see also: *Luna*

Greg Kot

Lee Feldman

Born 1959, in Seattle, WA.

Having lived there since the age of three, Lee Feldman can call himself a native New Yorker. This piano-playing, singing songwriter is following the career trajectory of someone in it for the duration—his debut release appeared when he was 38. With a trio fleshed out by a rhythm section, his songs have their roots in Broadway, the Brill Building, and Tin Pan Alley. If he has any forebears from the past several decades, they're limited to those who eschew confessionalism for third-person songcraft. Classically trained, pop and jazz elements intermingle freely in both his writing and playing. Comparisons to Randy Newman have been plentiful but a tad misleading in that Feldman presents a much softer vocal approach and, as a pianist, is much less orchestral in his arrangements, sticking closer to the interplay of a compact trio.

what's available: *Living It All Wrong* ♪♪♪♪ (Mercury, 1997, prod. Roger Peltzman) succeeds admirably and bodes well for the future. There's variety (string quartet, accordion, and clarinet are each sparingly and judiciously employed), and the production rewards repeated listenings with all manner of discoveries; the deceptively simple mix is actually quite painstakingly assembled.

influences:

◀◀ John Simon, Andy Pratt, Randy Newman

David Greenberger

Jay Ferguson

See: Spirit

Melissa Ferrick

Birthdate and birthplace unknown.

Among the flurry of women-in-rock stories that dominated the music media in the '90s, one name that was, in most cases, overlooked was Melissa Ferrick's. Too bad, because her powerful, dramatic voice and talent for writing memorable melodies

and incisive lyrics are worthy of attention. A violin prodigy who later attended the Berklee School of Music on a trumpet scholarship, Ferrick played guitar during her college years, garnering attention from mope-rock maven Morrissey, for whom she opened a show in Boston. Morrissey took her along for the rest of his tour, including a stop at Madison Square Garden, which landed Ferrick a recording contract of her own. Both of her major label albums stiffed, and she was released from her contract, though she resurfaced with the independent live album, *Melissa Ferrick + 1* in 1997.

what to buy: *Massive Blur* ♪♪♪♪ (Atlantic, 1993, prod. Gavin MacKillop) shows Ferrick's considerable range, rocking it up on "Happy Song" and tugging at heartstrings with "Hello Daddy," about an unloving, alcoholic father.

the rest:

Willing to Wait ♪♪♪♪ (Atlantic, 1995)
Melissa Ferrick + 1 ♪♪♪ (What Are Records?, 1997)

worth searching for: The promo-only single "The Juliana Hatfield Song" (Atlantic) humorously compares her success, or the lack thereof, to then-labelmate Hatfield.

influences:

◀◀ Joan Baez, Melissa Etheridge, Joni Mitchell, Tracy Chapman

▶▶ Tori Amos, Tracy Bonham, Ani DiFranco

Daniel Durchholz

Bryan Ferry

Born September 26, 1945, in Washington, England.

Bryan Ferry's slick, doomed, romantic persona doesn't jibe with his upbringing as a British coal miner's son. His artsy ways were cultivated at the University of Newcastle, where he studied art and played in his first bands. Ferry formed the influential British avant-pop band Roxy Music in 1970, and guided it through several personnel changes (producer Brian Eno was a member) and musical incarnations. Ferry started making solo records early into Roxy's run, at first to do something decidedly different from the group's edgy, sometimes tongue-in-cheek rock. But the lines began to blur late in Roxy's life, and by the early '80s there wasn't much difference between what he was doing under the group's name or his own.

what to buy: *Boys and Girls* ♪♪♪♪ (Warner Bros., 1985, prod. Rhett Davies, Bryan Ferry) took the lush, layered sound Ferry had begun perfecting on Roxy's *Flesh + Blood* and *Avalon* albums and tweaked it a notch, piling gently plucky guitars on shifting rhythms and washes of keyboards, topped by Ferry's pained tenor. There are no big hits on this, but there's not a weak link in the bunch. *Bete Noire* ♪♪♪♪ (Reprise, 1988, prod. Patrick Leonard, Bryan Ferry) updated the sleek, silky sound of its predecessor with a slightly darker, more detached edge. The title cut, which closes the album, has a tasty gypsy violin part that just bores into your brain.

what to avoid: There's hardly a weak link in Ferry's post-Roxy solo work, but the one exception, *Taxi* 🎵🎵 (Reprise, 1993, prod. Bryan Ferry, Robin Trower), is a real let-down. Ferry had reached an impasse on a project (which eventually evolved into the recent *Mamouna* album), so he resorted to his old trick of interpreting other people's songs. But what worked on occasion doesn't work over the course of an entire album.

the rest:

These Foolish Things 🎵🎵 (Atlantic, 1973)
Another Time, Another Place 🎵🎵🎵 (Atlantic, 1974)
Let's Stick Together 🎵🎵 (Atlantic, 1976)
In Your Mind 🎵🎵🎵 (Atlantic, 1977)
The Bride Stripped Bare 🎵🎵🎵 (Atlantic, 1978)
Mamouna 🎵🎵🎵 (Virgin, 1994)

worth searching for: The Japanese "single" for his cover of "Girl of My Best Friend" from *Taxi* is actually a 13-song disc (Virgin, 1993, prod. various) that mixes *Taxi* tracks and B-sides with live recordings form a 1988 show in Glasgow, Scotland.

influences:

◀◀ Frank Sinatra, Tony Bennett, David Bowie

▶▶ ABC, A-ha, Duran Duran, Edwyn Collins

see also: *Roxy Music*

Doug Pullen

54.40

Formed 1980, in Vancouver, British Columbia, Canada.

Neil Osborne, vocals, guitar; Brad Merritt, bass guitar; Phil Comparelli, trumpet, guitar; Ian Franey, drums (1980–83); Daryl Neudorf, drums (1983–84); Matt Johnson, drums (1984–present).

Born out of the Vancouver underground scene during the era of the Sex Pistols and the Clash, 54.40 has been one of Canada's most influential bands since the early '80s. Early years saw the band honing a gritty and sometimes confrontational guitar-driven sound that drew heavily from R.E.M. and other guitar-pop bands. Major-label success in the 1980s led to a slicker, synthesizer-backed sound that turned off some early fans but gained success on college radio in the United States. The 1990s has seen the band reinvent itself more than once, first opting for a rawer, more bluesy sound, and then returning to its roots for its most recent releases. Frontman and lyricist Neil Osborne is well-known throughout Canada for leading the battle to maintain Canadian content standards on Canadian radio and television stations. Who says self-interest isn't a rock 'n' roll sentiment?

what to buy: *54.40* 🎵🎵🎵🎵 (Warner/Reprise, 1986, prod. 54.40, Dave Ogilvie), also known as *The Green Album*, is the band's major-label debut and it's the one most representative of its early sound. It features the song "I Go Blind," later covered by Hootie & the Blowfish. *Smilin' Buddha Cabaret* 🎵🎵🎵🎵 (Sony Canada, 1994, prod. Don Smith) is called the band's "K-Tel album" by drummer Johnson because no two songs are alike. Written largely while on a European tour, the album is a return to the band's early Vancouver roots and is considered by many to be its best work.

what to buy next: *Show Me* 🎵🎵🎵 (Warner Bros., 1987, prod. Dave Jerden) is the band's first album made entirely after signing with Warner Bros. Far slicker than its independent releases and featuring synthesizers and heavily processed guitar and drum sounds, the album's highlight is the anthemic "One Gun."

what to avoid: *Fight for Love* 🎵🎵 (Reprise, 1989, prod. Neil Osborne, Dave Ogilvie) failed to capitalize on the success of *Show Me* and alienated some fans with its acoustic focus and long guitar solos.

the rest:

Things Are Still Coming Ashore 🎵🎵🎵 (MO=DA=MU, 1981)
Selection 🎵🎵🎵 (MO=DA=MU, 1982)
Set the Fire 🎵🎵🎵 (MO=DA=MU, 1984)
Sweeter Things—A Compilation 🎵🎵🎵 (Warner Music Canada, 1991)
Trusted by Millions 🎵🎵🎵 (Sony Canada, 1996)

worth searching for: *Dear, Dear* (Sony Canada, 1992, prod. Don Smith) was released in Canada only, where it yielded a slew of radio hits featuring a more stripped down sound. The hits included "She La," "Nice to Luv You," "Music Man," and "You Don't Get Away (That Easy)."

influences:

◀◀ R.E.M.

▶▶ Hunters & Collectors, the Tragically Hip

Brad Morgan

Fig Dish

Formed 1991, in Glenview, IL.

Blake Smith, vocals, guitar; Rick Ness, vocals, guitar; Mike Willison, bass; Andy Hamilton, drums (1992–95); Bill Swartz, drums (1996–present).

Future Fig Dish songwriters Blake Smith and Rick Ness stoked up a friendship after running into each other at a concert by a Cheap Trick cover band. True or not, the story fits: this power pop quartet is yet another in a long line of Midwestern guitar bands that sounds like, tastes like, and practically smells like the real thing. Alas, Fig Dish is to Cheap Trick as Andrew "Dice"

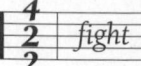

Clay is to Richard Pryor; their boozy way with a hook—redolent of another Midwestern powerhouse, the Replacements—and their self-deprecating live shtick (including a roadie dressed as the Easter bunny) contrast with disciplined records short on originality but long on short, sharp pop tunes.

what to buy: *When Push Comes to Shove* ♫♫♫ (Polydor, 1997, prod. Phil Nicolo) manages to be aggressive and tuneful while saying almost nothing. The group's shaggy-dog pop is loaded with hooks and the lyrical equivalent of a what-me-worry? shoulder shrug, right down to the pick-up lines: "It's just a single night/It's not gonna change your life."

what to buy next: *That's What Love Songs Often Do* ♫♫♫ (Atlas/A&M, 1995, prod. Lou Giordano) is a thoroughly respectable blast of tuneful noise. Giordano's production tightens up the band's sloppy live dynamics into taut, sing-along bursts.

influences:
◀◀ Cheap Trick, the Replacements, Material Issue, Nirvana

▶▶ triplefastaction, Local H

Greg Kot

Fight
See: Judas Priest

The Figgs
Formed late 1980s, in Saratoga Springs, NY.

Mike Gent, guitar, vocals, keyboards; Guy Lyons, guitar, vocals, keyboards; Pete Hayes, drums, keyboards, vocals; Pete Donnelly, bass, keyboards, vocals.

Starting out as a bunch of punks in upstate New York, the Figgs have always had more exuberance than finesse. But then, so did bands like the Kinks and the Rumour, ensembles from which the Figgs take considerable cues. Early on, before signing a record deal, the band did the "punk thing" and chose to release a couple of self-produced cassettes on their own. Those projects, *Ginger* and *Ready, Steady, Stoned*, offer a playful perspective on the nascent days of the band, when its sound benefitted as much from a lack of maturity as from its budding ability. The band's first official recording, *Low-Fi at Society High*, also proved creatively successful, though this time the commercial exposure from a legitimate release proved valuable for the band. The non-stop touring that followed helped them acquire a sizable audience, and though radio was reluctant to jump at the band's brand of vintage pop, the reception overall was excellent. When their label dissolved, the Figgs moved to Capitol, where they released the follow-up *Banda Macho*, a slightly more tentative album that casts off the retro image in favor of a more original sound. As a lark, the band

chose to hit the road following the album not as the Figgs but as the backing band to longtime hero Graham Parker on his *Acid Bubblegum* tour.

what to buy: *Low-Fi at Society High* ♫♫♫♫ (Imago, 1994, prod. Don Gehman) is the best example of the Figgs' manic, yet drum-tight noise. Writer Mike Gent knows how to move a song from beginning to end, but he also enjoys a good, sloppy, rock 'n' roll fracas.

the rest:
Hi-Fi Drop-Outs ♫♫♫♫ (Imago, 1994)
Banda Macho ♫♫♫ (Capitol, 1996)

worth searching for: Good luck finding the band's early self-released cassettes, *Ginger* and *Ready, Steady, Stoned*.

influences:
◀◀ The Kinks, Graham Parker, the Knack, U.K. pub rock

Bob Gulla

Fiji Mariners
See: Col. Bruce Hampton

Filter
Formed 1993, in Cleveland, OH.

Richard Patrick, vocals, guitars, bass, programming, drums; Brian Liesegang (1993–98), programming, keyboards, guitar, drums.

Everything comes full circle. Filter began as a one-man operation with Richard Patrick laying its foundation on an eight-track in his parents' basement in Cleveland. He temporarily put the project on hold when he joined nine inch nails. The stint proved to be beneficial to Patrick as it was Trent Reznor who introduced Patrick to his future collaborator, Brian Liesegang. During a visit to the Grand Canyon, the two decided to work together. Filter became a nom de plum for Patrick when Liesegang split from his partner in spring 1998. Before working on the next Filter album, Patrick toured with Smashing Pumpkins during 1996.

what's available: Patrick stressed that he did not intend on insulting handicapped children when he named Filter's debut album *Short Bus* ♫♫ (Reprise, 1996, prod. Richard Patrick, Brian Liesegang). In the Filter bio issued by Reprise Records, Patrick said he believes that "there is much to be learned from the special and the different." Although *Short Bus* is an enjoyable album, there isn't much that separates Filter from its industrial brethren. "Hey Man Nice Shot" was a logical single, showing Patrick's ability to write hook-laden songs and waver between monotone vocals and primal screams.

influences:
◀◀ nine inch nails, Ministry

Christina Fuoco

Fine Young Cannibals

Formed 1984, in London, England.

Andy Cox, guitar; David Steele, bass, keyboards; Roland Gift, vocals.

Following the break-up of the English Beat, Andy Cox and David Steele lit out on their own and teamed up with singer/actor Roland Gift. The combination proved a winner, if a somewhat short-lived one, as the group has recorded only a pair of albums while Gift attempted to parlay his video-friendly image into a film career.

what to buy: FYC's second album, *The Raw & the Cooked* ♫♫♫♫ (I.R.S., 1989, prod. Fine Young Cannibals), provided their breakthrough thanks to the massive hits "She Drives Me Crazy" and "Good Thing."

what to buy next: The debut, *Fine Young Cannibals* ♫♫♫♫ (I.R.S., 1985, prod. Robin Millar, Pela, Fine Young Cannibals), is a stylish demonstration of the group's brand of dance pop fused with Motown-style R&B. Gift's richly emotional vocals shine on "Johnny Come Home," "Don't Ask Me to Choose," and a cover of Elvis Presley's "Suspicious Minds."

the rest:
The Raw & the Remix ♫♫ (I.R.S., 1990)
The Finest ♫♫♫♪ (MCA, 1996)

influences:
◀◀ Motown, Elvis Presley, the Buzzcocks

▶▶ Neneh Cherry, Soul II Soul, Lisa Stansfield, Rebekah

see also: *The English Beat*

Anna Glen

Fingerprintz

Formed 1978, in Scotland.

Jimme O'Neill, lead vocals, guitar; Cha Burnz, lead guitar, vocals; Kenny Alton, bass, vocals; Bogdan Wiczling (a.k.a. Bob Shilling), drums; Step Lang, vocals (1978–79).

Scottish guitarist and songwriter Jimme O'Neill formed Fingerprintz during 1978, adding lead singer to his duties the following year after the departure of Step Lang (who appears on the *Dancing with Myself* EP, which was never released in the United States). *The Very Dab* showed Fingerprintz to have the smarts of XTC and the spunk of the Undertones. It also began a trio of sadly overlooked albums. Never receiving their due, each of the releases was marked by increasing efforts to crack the marketplace. *Distinguishing Marks* had the label behind it even to the point of packaging the album in a costlier perforated cover which could be broken up into a dozen postcards. By the time of the swansong, *Beat Noir*,

Fingerprintz had been dropped by Virgin and picked up by Stiff, which set up shop in America for a brief time, with little success.

worth searching for: None of the Fingerprintz albums are currently in print, nor ever released on CD. All of them are worthy of attention and full of rewards: *The Very Dab* (Virgin, 1979, prod. Fingerprintz) includes "Wet Job," which may be the penultimate O'Neill song; it captures paranoia and intrigue in words and sound, as well as foretelling the rhythmic concerns that would take over two years later. *Distinguishing Marks* (Virgin, 1980, prod. Nick Garvey) added just enough gloss to have taken its recipe to the banquet, but nobody came. Perhaps in an effort to break out of the stall, *Beat Noir* (Stiff, 1981, prod. Chris Kimsey, Jimme O'Neill, Chris Porter) brought in an overwhelming focus on funky rhythms, both urban and island, but lost something along on the way. It's not without merit, but get to this one last.

influences:
◀◀ The Kinks, XTC, the Buzzcocks

David Greenberger

Neil Finn

See: Crowded House

Tim Finn

See: Crowded House, Split Enz

Finn Brothers

See: Crowded House

Firefall

Formed 1974, in Boulder, CO.

Rick Roberts, guitar, vocals (1974–83); Jock Bartley, guitar, vocals (1974–present); Larry Burnett, guitar, vocals (1974–83); Mark Andes, bass (1974–80); Michael Clarke, drums (1974–83); David Muse, sax, flute, (1977–83); Steven Weinmeister, vocals, guitars (1983–present); Sandy Ficca, drums (1983–present); Bil Hopkins, bass, vocals (1983–present); Stephen Thomas Manshel, vocals, guitars (1983–present); Dan Clawson, saxophone, flute, harmonica, keyboards (1983–present).

Firefall is perhaps the nadir of the folk- and country-rock evolution sparked by the Byrds. The formula was perfect; bring together veteran country-rockers from the Byrds (Michael Clarke), Flying Burrito Brothers (Rick Roberts, who took over that band after Gram Parsons went solo), Gram Parsons's Fallen Angels Band (Jock Bartley, who had been jamming with Tommy Bolin before joining Parsons in mid-tour), and even the psychedelic band Spirit (Mark Andes), and give it a flawlessly glossy commercial surface for the hits to skate on. The formula was too good: skate is exactly what they did, with Top 40 hits from the harmless "You Are the Woman" and the amazingly misogynistic "Cinderella" to the wimpy "Just Remember I Love You" and the weird "Strange Way." The music was catchy but insincere, and it doesn't come close to matching the quality of any of these guys' original bands. At best, Firefall helped perpetuate a breezy, beautiful Boulder, Colorado ethos by capturing something of the town's freewheeling spirit. Andes left the band to join Heart full-time in 1980; Roberts was last heard writing children's music; and Bartley still leads a harder-rocking version of Firefall in the Boulder area.

what to buy: *Greatest Hits* 𝄞𝄞 (Rhino, 1992 prod. various) gathers together the hits, which dribbled on into the early '80s ("Always," from 1983, was the last), and is mostly listenable.

what to buy next: *Firefall* 𝄞𝄞 (Atlantic, 1976/Rhino, 1992, prod. Jim Mason) is the best of the rest, although it's nearly fatally flawed by some really dumb songs such as "Cinderella," "No Way Out," and "Sad Ol' Love Song" (all written by the machismo-stricken Larry Burnett).

what to avoid: *Messenger* **woof!** (Redstone, 1994, prod. Jim Mason, Jock Bartley) is a completely lame collection under Bartley's leadership. Though it has all the right stylistic elements, the songs are empty-headed—including one wretched, unsubtle ode against child abuse.

the rest:
Luna Sea 𝄞 (Atlantic, 1977/Rhino, 1995)
Elan 𝄞 (Atlantic, 1978/Rhino, 1995)
Undertow 𝄞 (Atlantic, 1980/Rhino, 1995)
Clouds across the Sun 𝄞 (Atlantic, 1981)
Break of Dawn 𝄞 (Atlantic, 1983)
You Are the Woman 𝄞𝄞 (Rhino, 1993)

solo outings:
Rick Roberts:
Windmills 𝄞𝄞 (A&M, 1972)
She Is a Song 𝄞𝄞 (A&M, 1973)

influences:
◀◀ The Byrds, the Flying Burrito Brothers, Poco
▶▶ Brooks & Dunn, Shenandoah

see also: *The Byrds, the Flying Burrito Brothers, Gram Parsons, Heart, Spirit*

Gil Asakawa

fIREHOSE
/Mike Watt
/Banyan
/Dos

Formed 1986, in San Pedro, CA. Disbanded 1994.

Mike Watt, bass, vocals; Ed fROMOHIO (born Ed Crawford), guitar, vocals; George Hurley, drums.

fIREHOSE came form the ashes of the Minutemen, perhaps the greatest band to come out of the California hardcore punk scene. Following singer guitarist D. Boon's death in a 1985 car crash, Ed Crawford, a Minutemen fan from Ohio, persuaded surviving members Mike Watt and George Hurley to continue with him. Crawford had his merits but was no match for Boon, and Watt's fIREHOSE material tends to sit comfortably at a respectable plateau rather than scale the heights. The band broke up in 1994, and Watt re-surfaced in 1995 with an alternative all-star project called *Ball-hog or Tugboat?*. He toured with a band that included Pearl Jam's Eddie Vedder and Dave Grohl from Nirvana and Foo Fighters, and the following year Watt joined Perry Farrell's band Porno for Pyros. Other side projects include Dos, an off-and-on two-bass duo with Watt's wife, Kira Roessler (Black Flag), and Banyan, a quartet led by drummer Stephen Perkins (Jane's Addiction, Porno for Pyros) that includes guitarist Nels Cline (Geraldine Fibbers) and somebody billed as The Freeway Keyboardist that plays moody instrumentals.

what to buy: The Watt-led alternative all-stars on his *Ball-hog or Tugboat?* 𝄞𝄞𝄞𝄞 (Columbia, 1995, prod. Mike Watt) get better material to work with than he'd written in years, with "Against the '70s" and "Piss-Bottle Man" highlights, plus some excellent cover choices ("Big Train," "Tuff Gnarl," "Maggot Brain"). Among the more than 50 guests are Eddie Vedder (Pearl Jam), Evan Dando (Lemonheads), Frank Black (Pixies), Flea (Red Hot Chili Peppers), Mark Lanegan (Screaming Trees), members of the Beastie Boys and Meat Puppets, Kathleen Hanna (Bikini Kill), J Mascis (Dinosaur Jr.), 3/4 of Sonic Youth, the surviving members of Nirvana, Dave Pirner (Soul Asylum), Bernie Worrell (Parliament-Funkadelic), Pat Smear (Germs), Henry Rollins (Black Flag), and John Strohm (Blake Babies). This context gave Watt the freedom to indulge all his musical impulses, and the overall effect is both stimulating and surprisingly coherent.

what to buy next: fIREHOSE's *if'n* 𝄞𝄞𝄞𝄞 (SST, 1987, prod. Mike Watt, Ethan James) is the group's most varied and inspired album by a wide margin, including everything from Watt's dead-on parody of R.E.M. to Crawford's acoustic finger-picking folk tribute "In Memory of Elizabeth Cotton." The *Sometimes* EP 𝄞𝄞𝄞 (SST, 1988, prod. Mike Watt, Ethan James) has two outtakes from the same sessions that should've been added to the 40-minute album.

what to avoid: fIREHOSE's *Mr. Machinery Operator* ♪♪ (Columbia, 1993, prod. J. Mascis) has some (if not enough) decent material but subjects it to sludgy production.

the rest:
fIREHOSE:
Ragin' Full-on ♪♪♪ (SST, 1986)
fROMOHIO ♪♪♪ (SST, 1989)
Flyin' the Flannel ♪♪♪ (Columbia, 1991)
Live Totem Pole ♪♪♪♪ (Columbia EP, 1992)

Mike Watt:
Contemplating the Engine Room ♪♪ (Columbia, 1997)

Banyan:
Banyan ♪♪♪ (CyberOctave, 1997)

Dos:
Dos ♪♪ (New Alliance, 1986)
Numero Dos ♪♪♪ (New Alliance EP, 1989)
Uno Con Dos ♪♪♪ (New Alliance, 1991)
Justamente Tres ♪♪ (Kill Rock Stars, 1996)

worth searching for: Get the double LP of Minutemen's *Double Nickels on the Dime* (SST, 1985, prod. Ethan James), since the single CD didn't have room for everything, and you don't want to miss the menacing "Little Man with a Gun in His Hand." In terms of stylistic coherence, this is the greatest punk album ever made.

influences:
◀◀ Wire, the Clash, Effigies, Dils, Blue Öyster Cult, Bob Dylan, Richard Hell & the Voidoids, Ornette Coleman

▶▶ Victim's Family, Tar Babies, Jane's Addiction, UYA, Universal Congress of . . .

Steve Holtje

The Firm
See: Bad Company

Fish
See: Marillion

Fishbone
Formed 1980, in Los Angeles, CA.

John (Norwood) Fisher, bass, vocals; Phillip Dwight (Fish) Fisher, drums; Kendall Rey Jones (1994–present), guitar, vocals; Angelo Christopher Moore, vocals, saxophone; Christopher Gordon Dowd, trombone, keyboards; Walter Adam Kibby, trumpet; John Bigham, guitar, keyboards (1990–present).

Without benefit of mainstream radio play, Fishbone has built its fan base on the strength of blistering live performances. Were the band able to bring some focus to its hyper blend of punk, ska, hardcore and funk long enough to sufficiently focus, Fishbone might achieve the transcendence it's been threatening for quite some time. Instead, the music is most often a supercharged hodgepodge of styles and social messages, which creates an air of rootlessness covered up by fiery chops.

what to buy: As the 'bone had difficulty controlling its firepower throughout entire albums, *Fishbone 101: Nuttasurursmeg Fossil Fuelin' the Fonkay* ♪♪♪ (Columbia Legacy, 1996, prod. various) traces singles and key album tracks in a manner that's eminently more listenable than the rest of the band's catalog. Rarities and unreleased recordings are included as well. The band's most consistent studio effort, *Truth and Soul* ♪♪♪ (Columbia, 1988, prod. David Kahne), is still a mixed bag, featuring a steroid take on Curtis Mayfield's "Freddie's Dead" and scorchers such as "Bonin' in the Boneyard" mixed in with some forgettable riff-o-ramas.

what to buy next: *In Your Face* ♪♪♪ (Columbia, 1886, prod. David Kahne) is a slicked-up bid for commercial play, but it *is* Fishbone at its most accessible as the band keeps (more or less) a ska-inflected backbeat to "A Selection" and "Cholly."

what to avoid: *Give a Monkey a Brain and He'll Swear He's the Center of the Universe* ♪♪ (Columbia, 1993, prod Terry Date, Fishbone) is as obtuse as the title—overreaching, schizophrenic, and frustrating.

the rest:
Fishbone ♪♪♪ (Columbia EP, 1985)
It's a Wonderful Life (Gonna Have a Good Time) ♪♪♪ (Columbia EP, 1987)
Bonin' in the Boneyard ♪♪♪ (Columbia EP, 1990)
The Reality of My Surroundings ♪♪♪ (Columbia, 1991)
Chim Chim's Badass Revenge ♪♪♪ (Rowdy, 1996)

worth searching for: *Singles* (Sony, 1993, prod. various), a Japanese collection of some of Fishbone's best tracks, is highlighted by a handful of fiery live performances.

influences:
◀◀ Curtis Mayfield, Rush, James Brown, Sly Stone

▶▶ Living Colour, Weapon of Choice

Allan Orski

Matthew Fisher
See: Procol Harum

The Five Americans

Formed as the Mutineers, 1963, in Durant, OK. Disbanded 1969.

Michael Rabon, guitar, vocals; Norman Ezell, guitar, vocals (1963–68); Johnnny Coble, drums (1963–64); John Durrill, keyboards, vocals (1963–68); Jim Grant, bass, vocals; Jimmy Wright, drums (1964–69).

Best remembered for one big hit single, the sublime "Western Union," and one classic garage-punk raver (the freakin' *incredible* "I See the Light"), the Five Americans were yet another mid-'60s grass-roots rock 'n' roll juggernaut to enjoy but a brief moment in the spotlight before marching off into obscurity. Their all-American name notwithstanding, the Five Americans were most definitely a band smitten with the Brits; a prevailing affection for British Invasion rock 'n' roll pervades the group's best efforts, most of which were self-penned. (One imagines it must have been most gratifying for the Five Americans when the Searchers—an obvious influence on the group—actually turned around and covered "Western Union.") The Five cut a few other worthy sides, but were unable to sustain themselves at the top of the pops and split by decade's end.

what to buy: *Western Union ✍✍✍* (Sundazed, 1989, prod. Bob Irwin) is a fairly sturdy best-of, with a few duff tracks redeemed by the presence of "Western Union," "I See the Light," the DC5ish "Good Times," "Zip Code" (an obvious clone of "Western Union"), the percolating "The Train," and the lovely "Evol-Not Love," a minor (#52) hit that should have gone Top 10. Some weak material indicates that we shouldn't rush to proclaim the Five Americans as an unsung pop savant, but there's enough of interest here that the guys in the group should be proud to have been Americans.

what to buy next: *I See the Light ✍✍✍* (HBR, 1966/Sundazed, 1994) is an expanded reissue of the group's first album, with only four tracks overlapping the best-of set. It's a low-key but perfectly agreeable exercise in garage pop.

influences:

◀◀ The Beatles, the Yardbirds, the Dave Clark Five, the Searchers, the Beau Brummels, the Knickerbockers

▶▶ The Music Machine, the Searchers, the Cowsills, the Three O'Clock, Jellyfish

Carl Cafarelli

The "5" Royales

Formed 1952, in Winston-Salem, NC. Disbanded 1965.

Lowman Pauling (died 1974), guitar, vocals; John Tanner, vocals; Jimmy Moore, vocals; Obadiah Carter (died 1993), vocals; Otto Jeffries, vocals; Eugene Tanner (died 1993), vocals.

If the Rock and Roll Hall of Fame was worth the dirt it stands on, the "5" Royales would've been the first group inducted. Instead, it's the greatest R&B vocal group nobody's ever heard of—nobody, that is, except the folks who have copped from them over the years. Everybody from the Temptations to James Brown borrowed onstage moves and choreography from the Royales' live show, while Steve Cropper learned most everything he knows about playing guitar from Lowman Pauling. Like many of their peers, the Royales started out as a gospel group—the Royal Sons Quintet, which formed in the early '40s. Upon discovering that love songs addressed to "you" paid much better than the ones to "You," they changed their name to the "5" Royales (with quotation marks because there were actually six members) and their style to secular R&B in the early '50s. An amazing string of hits followed, including "Think" (later a hit for James Brown), "Dedicated to the One I Love" (also a hit for the Shirelles as well as the Mamas & the Papas), and "Tell the Truth" (profitably covered by Ray Charles and Ike & Tina Turner). The group's greatest asset was guitarist/songwriter Pauling, the only Royale who played as well as sang (Charlie "Little Jazz" Ferguson & His Orchestra handled the rest of the backing music). Pauling essentially invented the role of call-and-response rhythm guitar in a vocal group context. He also frequently handled the vocal answer part with his deep bass voice, a humorous touch later used to great effect by the Coasters on novelty hits like "Yakety Yak." Pauling could be hilariously raunchy on goofy knockoffs such as "Baby Don't Do It," with the immortal chorus, "If you leave me pretty baby/I'll have bread without no meat." But the Royales' best songs were the ones that sounded like they weren't too far removed from church—"Come On and Save Me" and, of course, the epochal "Dedicated to the One I Love." Since they've never truly received due credit, the "5" Royales seem destined to remain a secret treasure for the few people fortunate enough to stumble across them.

what to buy: A record no home should be without is *Monkey Hips and Rice: The "5" Royales Anthology ✍✍✍✍* (Rhino, 1994, prod. Gary Stewart, James Austin), with 41 tracks on two discs. It includes all the songs mentioned above, impeccable credits, and very fine liner notes by critic Ed Ward (who wrote about the Royales in the 1978 collection of desert-island discs essays *Stranded*).

worth searching for: The Royales were truly without peer when it came to raunchy double entendres. Their "Laundromat Blues" is a standout on the various artists compilation *Risque Rhythm: Nasty '50s R&B* (Rhino, 1991, prod. James Austin), which includes equally delightful odes to lasciviousness from Wynonie Harris, Dinah Washington, Roy Brown, and others. As the Royales put it, "Don't rush folks, just take your time/Give my baby 20 minutes, and she'll make you lose your mind."

influences:

◄◄ Cab Calloway, the Soul Stirrers

►► James Brown, Steve Cropper, the Coasters, the Drifters, Ray Charles, Otis Redding, Jackie Wilson, the Temptations

David Menconi

The Fixx

Formed 1980, in London, England.

Cy Curnin, vocals; Jaime West-Oram, guitars; Adam Woods, drums; Rupert Greenall, keyboards; Charlie Barrett, bass (1980–83); Dan K. Brown, bass (1983–91).

Initiated by a college friendship between Cy Curnin and Adam Woods, the remaining members joined the Fixx in answer to a newspaper advertisement. After a short stint under a different name, the quintet recorded a demo of its first single, "Lost Planes," and snagged a record deal. For a brief moment during the early '80s, the group's calculated brand of synth-pop found an audience, back in the days when A Flock of Seagulls seemed like the wave of the future. But as that cold brand of keyboard-dominated rock began to fall off the charts, so did the Fixx. A belated attempt to change sounds by casting off longtime producer Rupert Hine (now closely involved with Rush) didn't help, and by the early '90s, the Fixx had faded into pop music oblivion.

what to buy: It isn't often that a band's most commercial record is its best, but in the Fixx's case, the million-selling *Reach the Beach* ♪♪♪♪ (MCA, 1983, prod. Rupert Hine) turned out to be the band's most consistent, engaging work, led by the singles "One Thing Leads to Another" and "Saved by Zero." Here, the formula of cascading guitars, spacey keyboards, and urgent vocals reached its peak. Best of all, the band's hits album—*One Thing Leads to Another: Greatest Hits* ♪♪♪♪ (MCA, 1989, prod. Rupert Hine, Hugh Padgham)—highlights its best work without the album filler.

what to buy next: Some dismiss it as a collection of synth-pop curiosities, but the moody, keyboard-drenched tunes on *Phantoms* ♪♪♪♪ (MCA, 1984, prod. Rupert Hine) strike a creative, complex chord on '80s hits such as "Are We Ourselves?" and "Sunshine in the Shade."

what to avoid: The band always had trouble reproducing its lush, complex recorded sound in concert, so it's no surprise that its live album, *React* **woof!** (MCA, 1987, prod. Hugh Padgham), falls flat.

the rest:

Shuttered Room ♪♪♪ (MCA, 1982)
Walkabout ♪♪♪ (MCA, 1986)
Calm Animals ♪♪ (MCA, 1988)
Ink ♪♪ (Impact, 1991)

WHAT ALBUM CHANGED YOUR LIFE?

Walls and Bridges by John Lennon, just because when I was going through puberty, middle puberty, becoming a complicated human, and women were starting to really chew at my wood and childhood arrogance disappeared, it just took me off. ['#9 Dream'], that song blew me away.

Cy Curnin (of the Fixx)

The King Biscuit Flower Hour Presents the Fixx ♪♪ (KBFH, 1996)
Real Time Stood Still ♪♪♪ (Varese, 1997)
Elemental ♪♪♪♪ (CMC International, 1998)
1011 Woodland N/A (CMC International, 1998)

worth searching for: For a taste of a Fixx concert that wasn't quite so bad, check out *Live in the U.S.A.* (MCA, 1991), a live video that, while heavy on material from *Phantoms*, is a sympathetic rendering of the group's concert skills.

influences:

◄◄ Gary Numan, Ultravox, David Bowie

►► Erasure, Howard Jones

Eric Deggans

The Flamin' Groovies

Formed 1966, in San Francisco, CA. Disbanded 1992.

George Alexander, bass, vocals; Cyril Jordan, guitar, vocals; Roy Loney, vocals, guitar (1966–71); Tim Lynch, guitar, vocals (1966–71); Danny Mihm, drums (1966–73, 1982); James Farrell, guitar (1971–76); Chris Wilson, vocals, guitar (1971–81); Terry Rae, drums (1973–75); David Wright, drums (1975–80); Mike Wilhelm, guitar (1976–82); Mark Dunwoody, keyboards, vocals (1980–82); Paul Zahl, drums (1983–92); Jack Johnson, guitar, vocals (1984–92); Ron Ronco, vocals (1989).

It could be argued that no rock 'n' roll act was ever so good and simultaneously so commercially ignored as San Francisco's legendary Flamin' Groovies. Throughout its long history and many personnel changes, the group (which added the apostrophe to Flamin' during the mid-'70s) was consistently out of step with the times. While its contemporaries were properly freaking out and endlessly jamming in a tedious soundtrack to an emerging counterculture, the Groovies drew on its unfashionable rock 'n' roll roots, alternately purveying good-time jug band music à la the Lovin' Spoonful and rockin' the mother-lovin' house down with a ferocity to rival the Rolling Stones and the Stooges. By the time reduced-frills rock started making a comeback in the '70s, a new incarnation of the Groovies was dressed up in Mod clothing and playing polished power pop as if it were 1965 and the band was some mythic combination of the Beatles, Byrds, Beach Boys, and Rolling Stones heading into the studio for a session with Phil Spector. And by the time "jangly pop" became a buzz phrase, the Groovies were so far underground that no amount of excavating could bring it to the surface, let alone to the pop stardom that should have been its divine right. As it is, the Groovies produced some unforgettable work, including three oft-covered classics—"Slow Death," "Teenage Head," and the incomparable, booming "Shake Some Action," which sounded like the eleventh-hour announcement of pop-rock Armageddon. Groovies fans are generally divided into two camps: those who favor the manic-rockin' original Groovies fronted by Roy Loney, and those who prefer the pop perfection of the Sire years (1976–79) with Chir Wilson. In each incarnation, Cyril Jordan and George Alexander kept the flame burning brightly. While the world at large remains criminally unaware of the group's virtues, an ever-faithful block of fans retains its affection for all things red-hot and groovy.

what to buy: *Groovies' Greatest Grooves* 𝄞𝄞𝄞𝄞𝄞 (Sire, 1989, prod. various) does a fine job of anthologizing the Sire years, with the Loney-sung "Teenage Head" and scattered non-LP singles (including "Slow Death") thrown in as bonuses. *Teenage Head* 𝄞𝄞𝄞𝄞 (Kama Sutra/One Way, 1971, prod. Richard Robinson) is the Loney-era Groovies' crowning achievement, a triumphant Stonesy swagger that Keith Richards is said to have preferred to *Sticky Fingers*.

what to buy next: *Rock Juice* 𝄞𝄞𝄞𝄞 (National, 1992, prod. Cyril Jordan, Karl Derfler) offers a swell swan song for the Groovies, with a batch of fine Jordan originals (bolstered by the prerequisite covers) serving notice that the Flamin' Groovies were gonna go out in style. *California Born and Bred* 𝄞𝄞𝄞𝄞 (Norton, 1995, prod. various) lives up to its billing as "a rock 'em-sock 'em set of 23 revved-up teenage blasts from the vaults," chronicling the original Groovies via a collection of hard-to-find and previously-unreleased Loney-era goodies.

what to avoid: *A Collection of Rare Demos & Live Recordings* 𝄞𝄞 (Marilyn, 1993) is licensed by Chris Wilson, but it is muddy-sounding bootleg material just the same.

the rest:
Supersnazz 𝄞𝄞𝄞 (Epic, 1969/CBS Special Products, 1990)
Rockin' at the Roundhouse 𝄞𝄞𝄞𝄞 (Mystery, 1993)
Supersneakers 𝄞𝄞 (Sundazed, 1996)
In Person!!! 𝄞𝄞𝄞 (Norton, 1997)

worth searching for: There are lots of import-only Groovies discs, chief among them *Shake Some Action* (Sire, 1976/Aim 1987, prod. Dave Edmunds), the quintessential Flamin' Groovies pop record and a vital part of any respectable power pop fan's permanent record library.

solo outings:
Roy Loney & the Phantom Movers:
The Scientific Bombs Away!!! 𝄞𝄞𝄞 (Norton, 1989)
Action Shots! 𝄞𝄞𝄞 (Marilyn, 1993)

Roy Loney & the Longshots:
Full Grown Head 𝄞𝄞𝄞 (Shake, 1994)

Chris Wilson:
Random Creatures 𝄞𝄞 (Marilyn, 1993)

Chris Wilson & the Sneetches:
Pop! 𝄞𝄞𝄞 (Marilyn, 1993)

Chris Wilson & Friends:
Back on the Barbary Coast 𝄞𝄞𝄞 (Marilyn, 1993)

influences:
◀◀ The Rolling Stones, the Lovin' Spoonful, the Beatles, the Byrds, Phil Spector, the Beach Boys, Eddie Cochran

▶▶ The Hoodoo Gurus, R.E.M., Tommy Keene, the Long Ryders, the Sneetches, the Plimsouls, the Flashcubes, the Barracudas

see also: *The Barracudas*

Carl Cafarelli

The Flaming Lips

Formed 1984, in Oklahoma City, OK.

Wayne Coyne, vocals, guitar; Mark Coyne, vocals (1984–86); Michael Ivins, bass; Richard English, drums (1984–89); John "Dingus" Donahue, guitar (1989–90); Nathan Roberts, drums (1989–90); Ronald Jones, guitar (1990–96); Steven Drozd, drums (1990–present).

Isolation such as that imposed on bands who choose to live and record in Oklahoma City can be an incubator for originality, genius, or just plain weirdness. In the case of the Flaming Lips, it's a little of all three. The group genially shares the crackpot wing of rock's psychedelic fringe with founding father Syd Barrett and elder statesmen such as Julian Cope, Robyn Hitchcock, and the Meat Puppets. With its blend of acid-rock and bubblegum, spaced-out jams that run for 20 minutes or more (check out

"Hell's Angel's Cracker Factory" from *Telepathic Surgery*), and relatively concise folk ballads, the Lips' albums can be bewildering to neophytes. But spend a little time with the best records and the group becomes rock's version of a Fellini movie, in which the most mundane details—a trip to the grocery store, a postal carrier making his rounds, a cloud pattern—are made wondrous, strange, and awesome. With the addition of guitar-effects maestro Ronald Jones and the Bonham-like Steven Drozd on drums in 1990, the group's sometimes fragmented ideas coalesced into consistently evocative songs, and its live shows attained a power few rock bands have approached in recent years. Wayne Coyne balanced his more accessible pop moments by staging avant-garde listener-participation events, such as a homemade symphony for 40 synchronized cassette tapes designed to be played on boom boxes or car stereos arranged in a circle.

what to buy: *Transmissions from the Satellite Heart* 𝄞𝄞𝄞𝄞𝄞 (Warner Bros., 1993, prod. Flaming Lips, Keith Cleversly) is one of the decade's finest rock records. It includes the band's fluke hit, "She Don't Use Jelly," hardly the disc's best, or even catchiest, song. Amid a dazzling funhouse of 3-D sound ideally suited for headphone listening but also rocking enough to blast at a beach party, Coyne's oblique lyrical imagery and wobbly voice resonate almost in spite of themselves. The Lips' strangely optimistic songs suggest that to survive the world, sometimes you have to imagine a more fantastic one.

what to buy next: *In a Priest-Driven Ambulance* 𝄞𝄞𝄞𝄞 (Restless, 1990, prod. Flaming Lips, Dave Fridmann) is the band's first great leap forward in songwriting. The sleeve (misleadingly) lists the running times for all 10 tracks as 3:26, but the disc is among the group's most successful stabs at writing more concise (albeit enticingly odd) pop songs and concludes with the Lips' unoffical anthem, a relatively straight reading of the standard "What a Wonderful World."

what to avoid: *Telepathic Surgery* 𝄞𝄞𝄞 (Restless, 1989, prod. Flaming Lips) isn't a total disaster, but for a group that thrives on wild stylistic and sonic experimentation, this is surprisingly tame, one-dimensional rock.

the rest:
The Flaming Lips 𝄞𝄞𝄞 (Restless, 1985)
Hear It Is 𝄞𝄞𝄞 (Restless, 1986)
Oh My Gawd!!!... the Flaming Lips 𝄞𝄞𝄞𝄞 (Restless, 1987)
Unconsciously Screamin' 𝄞𝄞𝄞 (Atavistic EP, 1990)
Hit to Death in the Future Head 𝄞𝄞𝄞𝄞 (Warner Bros., 1991)
Providing Needles for Your Balloons 𝄞𝄞𝄞 (Warner Bros. EP, 1994)
Clouds Taste Metallic 𝄞𝄞𝄞𝄞𝄞 (Warner Bros., 1995)
A Collection of Songs Representing an Enthusiasm for Recording... By Amateurs: 1984–1990 N/A (Restells, 1998)

worth searching for: *Zaireeka* (Warner Bros., 1997) is a 45-minute version of Coyne's cassette symphony; it contains four CDs designed to be played simultaneously on four stereos. The perfect psychedelic soundtrack for your next bong party.

influences:
◄◄ Syd Barrett, Plastic Ono Band, Echo & the Bunnymen, Hawkwind

►► Pavement, Presidents of the United States of America

Greg Kot

The Flamingos

Formed as the Swallows, 1951, in Chicago, IL. Disbanded 1956. Reformed 1957.

Earl Lewis, lead vocals (1951); Zeke Carey, second tenor vocals; Jake Carey, bass vocals; Johnny Carter, second tenor vocals; Tommy Hunt, lead vocals (1957–61); Sollie McElroy (died January 15, 1995), lead vocals (1951–54); Paul Wilson, baritone vocals (died May 1988); Nate Nelson (died April 10, 1984), lead vocals (1954–57); Terry Johnson, tenor vocals; Isaiah "Buzzy" Terry, vocals, guitar.

It's impossible to gauge just how many car windows were steamed up by young couples necking while listening to the Flamingos. Of all the great doo-wop groups, they were the most romantic and sensual, imbuing supper club standards with a sense of intimacy both tender and pure. However, the group could also rock gospel-style, and its inventive precision choreography earned it a well-deserved reputation as a top visual act. Recording first for the Chance and Parrot labels, the group's constant search for superior producers and studio sounds led to label-hopping from Decca (where they hit with "The Ladder of Love") to End Records, where owner George Goldner encouraged the group to rework standards into its own style and accentuated their jazzy background vocals. With this new approach, the Flamingos created its ethereal masterpiece "I Only Have Eyes for You" along with a string of dual-market hits such as "Love Walks In," "Nobody Loves Me Like You," and "Time Was." After Goldner sold off End Records' assets to pay gambling debts, the Flamingos were without a label or a sympathetic producer, and the hits stopped coming. A radically changed version of the group made minor noise on the Soul charts with "Boogaloo Party" during 1966, but this and subsequent hits featured little of its trademark elegance. Interest in the group was revived in 1975 when Art Garfunkel recorded a note-for-note remake of "I Only Have Eyes for You"; since then, various incarnations of the Flamingos have toured the world, reminding the faithful about the subtle, rhythmic magic of young love.

what to buy: All of the group's great hits from its stints with the Chance, Parrot, End, Decca, and Checker labels are on *The Best of the Flamingos* 𝄞𝄞𝄞𝄞 (Rhino, 1990, compilation prod. James Austen, Bob Hyde), a remarkably romantic 18-track collection.

4
3
0

flash cadillac

Whether you're reminiscing about the good old days of doo-wop or looking for music to dance slow and dreamy by, this is the one to get.

what to buy next: Those who want much more of the Flamingos' run at End Records should check out *For Collector's Only* 𝄞𝄞𝄞𝄞 (Collectables, 1993, prod. various), a two-CD, 38-song set containing doo-wop versions of many great standards in addition to some of the biggest hits of the late '50s and early '60s.

the rest:
Flamingo Serenade 𝄞𝄞𝄞 (End, 1959/Collectables, 1991)
Requestfully Yours 𝄞𝄞 (End, 1960/Collectables, 1991)
The Sound of the Flamingos 𝄞𝄞𝄞 (End, 1962/Collectables, 1991)
Flamingo Favorites 𝄞𝄞𝄞 (End, 1960/Collectables, 1992)
The Fabulous Flamingos 𝄞𝄞𝄬 (Collectables, 1992)
I Only Have Eyes for You 𝄞𝄞𝄬 (Remember, 1996)
The Complete Chess Masters—Plus 𝄞𝄞𝄞𝄞 (Chess, 1997)
Greatest Hits 𝄞𝄞𝄬 (DJT, 1997)
I Only Have Eyes for You 𝄞𝄞𝄬 (Sequel, 1997)

worth searching for: If you dig detailed liner notes and generous track selections, check the catalog services and import racks for *Requestfully Yours/The Sound of the Flamingos* (Westside, 1998, prod. various) and *Flamingo Serenade/Flamingo Favorites* (Westside, 1998, prod. various). These compilations both contain reissues of two original LPs by the group as well as previously unreleased alternate takes.

influences:
◀◀ The Clovers, the Five Keys, the "5" Royales, the Crows, the Orioles

▶▶ The Moonglows, the Dells, the Five Satins, the Temptations, the Spinners, the Chi-Lites, Harold Melvin & the Blue-Notes

Ken Burke

Flash Cadillac /Flash Cadillac & the Continental Kids

Formed 1969, in Boulder, CO.

Harold "Marty" Fielden, drums (1969–71); Warren "Butch" Knight, bass, vocals (1969–present); Mick "Flash" Manresa, guitar, vocals (1969–71); Kris "Angelo" Moe, keyboards, vocals (1969–present); Linn "Spike" Phillips III, guitar (1969–93); John "Ricco" Masino, drums (1971–74), Sam "Flash" McFadin, guitar, vocals (1971–present); George "Eddie" Robinson, sax (1972); Dwight "Spider" Bement, sax, keyboards (1973–present); Jeff "Wally" Stewart, drums (1974–76); Paul Wheatbread, drums (1976–78); Ken "King Kenny" Gingrich, drums (1978–94); Dave "Thumper" Henry, drums (1994–present).

What began as a lark—playing good old rock 'n' roll to beered-up college rowdies during the hippie era—has led to a long career for Flash Cadillac as "America's favorite party band." In addition to recording two great LPs for Epic and one for Private Stock during the '70s, the Kids have appeared on *American Bandstand, Happy Days,* and in the movies *Apocalypse Now* and *American Graffiti*. The boys went Hollywood for a time and produced a few chart hits—notably "Did You Boogie (With Your Baby)," featuring Wolfman Jack in 1976 and "Good Times, Rock & Roll" in 1974—while going through more drummers than Spinal Tap. Starting in 1977, the group retreated to its studio ranch near Colorado Springs and have continued to release a string of solid independent albums (via Flash Marketing, P.O. Box 783, Woodland Park, CO 80866) while touring the United States to play with symphonies or for corporate functions. The death of Linn Phillips and the retirement of Kris Moe to the studio may have removed some of the band's crazed energy, but in concert and on CD it still has a good time playing stripped-down mountain rock 'n' roll in an oldies vein.

what to buy: *Twenty-Five Years* 𝄞𝄞𝄞𝄞 (Flash Cadillac, 1996, prod. Sam McFadin, Flash Cadillac), is probably the best place to start as it summarizes the group's entire career, with time-outs for total weirdness and studio mayhem (see "Spike's Psycho Corner"). The disc begins with the Phil Spectoresque production of "See My Baby Jive" and also offers "At the Hop" and "Louie Louie" from *American Graffiti*.

what to buy next: Its most recent release, *Rock & Roll Rules* 𝄞𝄞𝄞𝄞 (Flash Cadillac, 1997, prod. Flash Cadillac), is also among its best, offering remakes of "She's So Fine," "Nothin' for Me," and "Betty Lou" from the self-titled 1972 Epic LP. *Souvenirs* 𝄞𝄞𝄞𝄞 (Flash Cadillac, 1994, prod. Sam McFadin, Flash Cadillac) feature some of the group's best originals, notably "Feel's So Good" and "Hearts."

what to avoid: *Later than Midnight* 𝄞𝄞 (Great American Music Hall, 1987, prod. Sam McFadin, Flash Cadillac) is redundant, as all tracks are on other CDs.

the rest:
A Night at the Symphony 𝄞𝄞 (Flash Cadillac, 1994)
Drivetime 𝄞𝄞 (Flash Cadillac, 1994)
Ghost of Christmas Past 𝄞𝄞𝄬 (Flash Cadillac, 1996)

worth searching for: If you still own a turntable (hint—it has a needle and spins at various speeds), check out the killer debut *Flash Cadillac & the Continental Kids* (Epic, 1972, prod. Kim Fowley). Its third LP, *Sons of the Beaches* (Private Stock, 1975, prod. Toxey French), comes in two versions, with the one to seek adding "Did You Boogie (With Your Baby)" to an already stocked record. And while not a band release per se, the top CD Flash Cadillac has appeared on is the soundtrack for *American Graffiti* (MCA, 1973, prod. various), which features two Flash tracks: "She's So Fine" and "At the Hop."

influences:

◀◀ The Beatles, the Beach Boys, Danny & the Juniors, Sha Na Na

▶▶ The Stray Cats, the Blasters

George W. Krieger

The Flashcats

Formed 1979, in Pittsburgh, PA.

"Miss Cindy" Sotak, lead vocals, guitar; "Skinny Dave" Kent, guitar, vocals; "Sweet Pete" Loria, trumpet, vocals; "Jim Jr." Fanning, bass, vocals; Brian "Crusher" Anater, tenor saxophone, vocals; Carl M. Grefenstette, drums; Phil "Harmonic" Brontz, tenor sax, vocals.

An irreverent bar band with a love of R&B and silly stage antics, the Pittsburgh-based Flashcats—guided by zany, Beatles-worshipping drummer-manager Carl M. Grefenstette—made its mark in rock history by resuscitating the career of legendary R&B crooner Bull Moose Jackson. Performing his "Big Ten Inch Record" and "Nosey Joe" (the only cover tune the band had ever recorded) nightly for years, the Flashcats learned in 1984 that Jackson was, indeed, alive and well and working in a cafeteria at Howard University in Washington, D.C. The group invited Jackson to Pittsburgh to perform, and the collaboration continued until Jackson's death in 1989. The Flashcats took Bull Moose into the studio to make his first recording in 30 years, the single "Get Off the Table Mable (The Two Dollars Is for the Beer)," followed by the album *Moosemania!*, which earned positive reviews around the world. On its own, the Flashcats are never afraid to stoop to new lows for laughs—including stage props (tea bags for the "Red Rose Tea" jingle) and audience participation. It was also among the first bands to cover TV theme songs with *Bonanza*. Though its brand of funk-flavored, harmony-filled rock hasn't been what radio has been looking for during the '80s and '90s, the Flashcats endure through annual reunion shows and stunts such as Grefenstette's 1995 compilation CD release *Yesterday . . . and a Week from Friday*, featuring the band's recreation of the Beatles' famous *Yesterday . . . and Today* butcher cover—complete with peel-off top layer. In 1991 Grefenstette's Bogus label released a tribute album, *Bonograph . . . Sonny Gets His Share*, which earned international TV and press coverage that was rekindled when Bono died in 1997.

what to buy: *Bull Moose Jackson & the Flashcats: The Final Recordings* 𝄢𝄢𝄢 (Bogus, 1992, prod. Carl M. Grefenstette) is a fine chronicle of Jackson's talent—and the band's. A re-release of *Moosemania!* with two new songs, it also contains the only known live recording of "Big Ten Inch Record" by the man who first made it a hit. The two new songs come from an album the band and Bull Moose were in the process of recording when he died.

what to buy next: *Yesterday . . . and a Week from Friday* 𝄢𝄢𝄢 (Bogus, 1995, prod. Carl M. Grefenstette) showcases the band's pop songwriting talent and its performing chops on four covers recorded live (plus a fifth, as a hidden final track). As an audio scrapbook (with liner notes serving a similar function), it's a must for Flashcats fans—and not a bad investment for fans of pre- and post-Motown-influenced R&B-rock.

the rest:

Ten Years of Flashcats Christmas Records 𝄢𝄢𝄢 (Bogus, 1990)

influences:

◀◀ Wynonie Harris, Bull Moose Jackson, Aretha Franklin, Sam & Dave, the Temptations, the Beatles

Lynne Margolis

The Flashcubes
/Gary Frenay

Formed 1977, in Syracuse, NY. Disbanded 1980. Re-formed 1993.

Tommy Allen, drums; Paul Armstrong, guitar, vocals (1977–79, 1993–present); Gary Frenay, bass, vocals; Arty Lenin, guitar, vocals; Mick Walker, guitar, vocals (1979–80).

The Flashcubes were the great lost power pop band of the late '70s; if you can imagine an act that sounded like a supergroup summit of, say, Eric Carmen, Alex Chilton, Keith Moon, and the Sex Pistols' Steve Jones, and if you can further imagine such an act failing to even snag a friggin' record deal, then you can understand both the appeal of the Flashcubes and the frustration of its fans as the group burned out and faded away in total obscurity. Paul Armstrong went on to form the Richards; Tommy Allen toured with Paul Young, co-produced the Sighs and helped develop Kara's Flowers; Arty Lenin joined the Paul Collins Band for that group's 1993 *From Town to Town* album; and Gary Frenay has continued to hone his skills as a singer-songwriter. Rhino exhumed the Flashcubes' 1978 indie single "Christi Girl" for the power-pop sampler *DIY: Come Out and Play*, and the original foursome reunited in 1993 for occasional recording and live shows.

what to buy: *Bright Lights* 𝄢𝄢𝄢𝄢 (Northside, 1997, prod. Ducky Carlisle, Bill Murphy, Barry Rowe) is both a career overview and the Flashcubes' belated debut album, a 21-track explosion of pure pop, punk pop, and power pop that includes "No Promise," the greatest evocation of the Raspberries this side of Cleveland. Most of the album consists of unreleased recordings from the group's original run, bolstered by four '90s tracks and a blistering live track from '78.

what to buy next: Frenay's solo work frequently seems a world apart from the barbusting pop of prime Flashcubes, but is nonetheless characterized by style, hooks, and an understated sense of the music's own power. Frenay chose an all-acoustic approach for his solo debut, *Armory Square* ♫♫♫ (Northside, 1993/Tangible Music, 1995, prod. Gary Frenay, Ducky Carlisle, Mike Jaffarian, Tim Harrington), a beguiling collection of quiet pop gems. A fuller production approach fleshes out Frenay's second album, *Jigsaw People* ♫♫♫ (Tangible Music, 1996, prod. Mark Doyle, Ducky Carlisle, Gary Frenay), a mature and accomplished work that encompasses the full spectrum of Frenay's musical environment; it includes an otherwise-unavailable track by the Flashcubes, the sparkling, radio-ready "You Only Get One Life."

worth searching for: The Flashcubes also contributed tracks to a couple of tribute albums: "All Over the World" appeared on the Paul Collins tribute *The Beat or Not the Beat* (Pop Attack, 1994) and "Don't Want to Say Goodbye" appeared on *Raspberries Preserved* (Ginger, 1996, prod. various). The Richards' best track, "Five Personalities," appeared on *Pop under the Surface* (Yesterday Girl, 1997, prod. various), a superb pop sampler album isued in Sweden.

solo outings:
The Richards:
Over the Top ♫♫♫ (Northside, 1995)

influences:
◄◄ The Beatles, the Who, the Raspberries, the Kinks, Big Star, Eddie & the Hot Rods, the Sex Pistols, the Jam, Eddie Cochran, the New York Dolls, the Knickerbockers

►► Chris von Sneidern, the Poptarts, the Kennedys, the Sighs, Kara's Flowers, the Brambles

see also: *The Beat/Paul Collins*

Carl Cafarelli

Flat Duo Jets

Formed 1984, in Chapel Hill, NC.

Dexter Romweber, vocals, guitar, piano; Crow, drums, vocals.

The Flat Duo Jets emerged from the North Carolina music scene in the early '80s with a love of blues and rockabilly and a disdain for anything remotely resembling production values. Using only guitars and drums, with the occasional bass line or piano thrown in for good measure, the duo of Dexter Romweber and Crow (friends since elementary school) churned out thrashy, emotive rave-ups that could make teetotalers reach for a shot of whisky and a cigarette. Staying true to the recording sessions that produced many of the classics they so revered, Romweber (whose sister, Sara, was a onetime member of Let's Active) and Crow never spent much time in the studio. As a result, many Jets' albums retained

the raw, smoldering energy that characterized their performances. Thanks to incessant touring, the Jets developed a rabid cult following, and the resurgent popularity of everything '50s finally helped them snag a major label deal in 1998.

what to buy: *Introducing—Flat Duo Jets* ♫♫♫♫ (Norton, 1995, prod. Billy Miller) opens at a breakneck pace that rarely lets up. Except for their live recordings (or better yet, their live shows), this album is the epitome of the Jets' modus operandi: loving interpretations of roots rock classics ("So Long I'm Gone," "I've Been Loving You Too Long") blended with surf-inflected originals ("Crow's Feet," "Torpedo"). Speaking of live recordings, *Wild Blue Yonder* ♫♫♫ (Norton, 1998) captures the Jets at their hepped-up, propulsive best.

what to buy next: *Go Go Harlem Baby* ♫♫♫ (Sky, 1991, prod. Jim Dickinson) represents a major step up in terms of production quality, but the band's live energy doesn't always translate. However, covers of tracks from Lee Hazlewood and Duane Eddy ("Stalkin'"), Earl Hagan ("Harlem Nocturne"), and Lou Willie Turner ("TV Mama") reaffirm the Jets' commitment to chronicling their roots.

what to avoid: *In Stereo* ♫ (Sky, 1992, prod. Josh Grier) includes five covers and an instrumental original from the band's first foray into a recording studio in 1984, and although completists might disagree, the EP is rough, even by the Jets' no-tech standards.

the rest:
Flat Duo Jets ♫♫♫ (Dog Gone, 1990)
Safari ♫♫♫ (Norton, 1993)
White Trees ♫♫♫ (Sky, 1993)
Red Tango ♫♫♫ (Norton, 1996)

solo outings:
Dexter Romweber:
Folk Songs ♫♫♫ (Permanent, 1996)

influences:
◄◄ The Cramps, Elvis Presley, Evan Johns, Gene Vincent, Stray Cats, Eddie Cochran, Screamin' Jay Hawkins, Duane Eddy, Carl Perkins, the Ventures, Link Wray

►► Reverend Horton Heat, Southern Culture on the Skids, Mojo Nixon, House of Freaks

Lisa M. Moore

The Flatlanders

Formed 1970, in Lubbock, TX.

Jimmie Dale Gilmore, vocals, guitar; Joe Ely, vocals, harmonica, Dobro, guitar; Butch Hancock, vocals, guitar; Tommy Hancock, fid-

dle; Syl Rice, string bass; Tony Pearson, mandolin; Steve Wesson, musical saw.

Spawned during roughly the same era as the *Sweetheart of the Rodeo* Byrds and the Flying Burrito Brothers, the Flatlanders represented that period's clash between traditional and radical values: the attempt to build on the legacies of Jimmie Rodgers and Hank Williams while gaining a higher consciousness and rejecting the outdated symbols of a bygone era. Perhaps the group's fatal error was to attempt this in Nashville, which didn't want to hear about such nonsense, rather than L.A., which likely would have taken to the band's lonesome West Texas warblings like it took to the Eagles and the Nitty Gritty Dirt Band. Through the years Jimmie Dale Gilmore, Joe Ely, and Butch Hancock have frequently sung each other's songs, and reunited occasionally, though they've never all gotten back together on record until the 1998 soundtrack for *The Horse Whisperer*, to which they contributed one song.

what's available: *More a Legend than a Band* 𝄢𝄢𝄢𝄢 (Rounder, 1990, prod. Royce Clark) is a reissue of the Flatlanders' original album, which, in 1972, only saw the light of day on 8-track tape. It's one of the great lost albums and contains the seeds of a generation of West Texas talent that has since gone on to fame, if not fortune. Gilmore's tremulous voice hovers above the proceedings on most of the tracks, which include two of his finest songs, "Dallas" and "Tonight I'm Gonna' Go Downtown." Wesson's musical saw may as well be a sitar amidst these country & Eastern musings. Hancock contributes a handful of tunes, including the mournful "She Had Everything," while Ely settles mostly for being the session's hot-shot guitarist. Prompted by the growing reputation of these three as solo artists, Charly reissued the album in 1980, and Rounder a decade later in a slightly different configuration. Shelby S. Singleton Jr., who owned the original sessions, got into the act in 1995, re-releasing the album under the moniker Jimmie Dale Gilmore & the Flatlanders, with the then-trendy title *Unplugged* 𝄢𝄢𝄢 (Sun, 1995, compilation prod. Jim Wilson, Shelby S. Singleton Jr.). It includes two fewer tracks than the Rounder and substitutes for two others. The Rounder disc is the better reissue.

worth searching for: The soundtrack to the Robert Redford film *The Horse Whisperer* (MCA, 1998, prod. various) is a compendium of left-of-center country music circa 1998, a slot in which the Flatlanders fit perfectly. They contribute the gorgeous "South Wind of Summer," on which they all share vocal chores.

influences:

◄◄ Jimmie Rodgers, Hank Williams, Eastern Religion 101

►► Joe Ely, Butch Hancock, Jimmie Dale Gilmore

see also: *Joe Ely, Jimmie Dale Gilmore*

Daniel Durchholz

WHAT ALBUM CHANGED YOUR LIFE?

Aja by Steely Dan. I'd always liked Steely Dan. That particular album, when we first achieved quite a lot of success with Fleetwood Mac and I'd moved from rather a humble little house in Hollywood to this rather large place in Beverly Hills, I can distinctly remember bringing that record. This house used to belong to Anthony Newley, and he had this huge speaker system, rather archaic, great old foghorn speakers out by the pool. The first thing I did was go through all the crates of furniture and everything, take out a bottle of champagne and sit by the pool, cranking up *Aja* really loud.

Christine McVie (of Fleetwood Mac)

Mick Fleetwood /Mick Fleetwood's Zoo

See: Fleetwood Mac

Fleetwood Mac

Formed 1967, in London, England.

Mick Fleetwood, drums; John McVie, bass; Peter Green, guitar, vocals (1967–69); Jeremy Spencer, guitar, vocals, piano (1967–70); Danny Kirwan, guitar, vocals (1968–72); Christine McVie, piano, vocals (1970–93, 1997–present); Bob Welch, guitar, vocals (1971–74); Dave Walker, guitar, vocals, harmonica (1972–73); Bob Weston, guitar, banjo, harmonica (1972–73); Lindsay Buckingham, guitar, vocals (1975–87, 1997–present); Stevie Nicks, vocals (1975–90, 1997–present); Billy Burnette, guitar, vocal (1987–96); Rick Vito, guitar (1987–91); Bekka Bramlett, vocals (1993–96); Dave Mason, guitar, vocals (1994–96).

From 1975 to 1982, a band that started out playing pure blues had 12 consecutive Top 20 singles and over their whole career has totaled 18 Top 40 hits, despite personnel turmoil and turnover that make Spinal Tap seem stable by comparison. Fleetwood Mac went from being the Peter Green-founded blues group—which was very popular in the British blues scene—to a bland, West Coast pop outfit under the lead of guitarist Bob Welch. The crucial evolution came when Welch was replaced in 1975 by two fellow Californians—Lindsey Buckingham and Stevie Nicks—who had recently recorded the fine album *Buckingham Nicks* (which inexplicably remains un-reissued). Buckingham was capable of incendiary guitar work and in concert proved himself worthy of Green's legacy on older material. But he would ultimately contribute much more with his disarmingly accessible pop stylings, which made Fleetwood Mac one of pop's hottest groups during the '70s. *Fleetwood Mac* in 1975 launched three hit singles and broke the band in America. The follow-up, *Rumours*—inspired by the break-ups in the various intra-band couples (Buckingham and Nicks, the McVies)—remains one of the highest-selling albums ever. Ultimately, the magic of this incarnation slowly fizzled when subsequent albums didn't equal *Rumours'* once-in-a-lifetime standard. Becoming more interested in their solo careers, Buckingham and Nicks eventually quit the group—though the lineup reunited to perform the hit "Don't Stop" during one of President Bill Clinton's 1993 inaugural galas—and were replaced by journeyman rocker Dave Mason and Bekka Bramlett, the daughter of the rock duo Delaney & Bonnie. That lineup (which included Christine McVie for recording only) recorded one album, which didn't sell quite like *Rumours* either. In 1997 the *Rumours* lineup reunited for an MTV concert special, a new live album, *The Dance*, and a sold-out reunion tour. Plans for new music are up in the air, however.

what to buy: *Rumours* 𝄞𝄞𝄞𝄞𝄞 (Warner Bros., 1977, prod. Fleetwood Mac, Richard Dashut, Ken Caillat, Cris Morris), with 11 great songs and no duds, is as good as mainstream pop gets. *Fleetwood Mac* 𝄞𝄞𝄞𝄞 (Reprise, 1975, prod. Fleetwood Mac, Keith Olsen), with "Landslide," "Rhiannon," "Over My Head," and "I'm So Afraid," nearly matches that standard. *Tusk* 𝄞𝄞𝄞𝄞 (Warner Bros., 1979, prod. Fleetwood Mac, Richard Dashut, Ken Caillat) is more an eccentric masterpiece than a pop masterpiece, with Buckingham running wild and reinventing lo-fi on his pieces, while Nicks ("Sara") and Christine McVie ("Think about Me") keep the group in the mainstream.

what to buy next: Fleetwood Mac's blues period can be comfortably sampled on *English Rose* 𝄞𝄞𝄞𝄞 (Blue Horizon, 1969, prod. Mike Vernon), known in the U.K. in somewhat different form as *Mr. Wonderful*. If Green and Jeremy Spencer weren't always convincing blues singers, they were gifted guitarists. The double album *Fleetwood Mac in Chicago 1969* 𝄞𝄞𝄞 (Blue Horizon/Sire, 1975, prod. Mike Vernon, Marshall Chess), with

guests Otis Spann, Willie Dixon, Shakey Horton, Honeyboy Edwards, Buddy Guy, and other bluesmen, is also a good context in which to hear the Brits' six-string blues expertise with more competent singers to the fore. *Future Games* 𝄞𝄞𝄞𝄞 (Reprise, 1971, prod. Fleetwood Mac), with both Welch and Danny Kirwan, has an appealingly spacy sound, plus Christine McVie's pretty "Show Me a Smile."

what to avoid: *Kiln House* 𝄞𝄞 (Reprise, 1970, prod. Fleetwood Mac) is a rudderless album drifting aimlessly in search of a tunesmith. *Penguin* 𝄞 (Reprise, 1973, prod. Fleetwood Mac, Martin Birch) is the sort of nondescript album on which the only moments that stand out are howlingly obvious lapses in taste and judgment. *Tango in the Night* 𝄞𝄞 (Warner Bros., 1987, prod. Lindsay Buckingham, Richard Dashut) is so enervated it's downright annoying once the first three tracks, which at least are familiar, are done.

the rest:
Fleetwood Mac 𝄞𝄞 (Blue Horizon, 1968)
Then Play On 𝄞𝄞𝄞 (Reprise, 1969)
Bare Trees 𝄞𝄞𝄞 (Reprise, 1972)
Mystery to Me 𝄞𝄞𝄞 (Reprise, 1973)
Heroes Are Hard to Find 𝄞𝄞𝄞 (Reprise, 1974)
Live 𝄞𝄞𝄞 (Warner Bros., 1980)
Mirage 𝄞𝄞 (Warner Bros., 1982)
Behind the Mask 𝄞𝄞 (Warner Bros., 1990)
25 Years—The Chain 𝄞𝄞𝄞 (Warner Bros., 1992)
Time 𝄞𝄞 (Warner Bros., 1995)
Peter Green's Fleetwood Mac Live at the BBC 𝄞𝄞𝄞 (Castle, 1995)
The Dance 𝄞𝄞𝄞 (Warner Bros., 1997)

worth searching for: *The Chain Sampler* (Warner Bros., 1992, prod. various) is an 18-song promotional sampler from the box set that's a fine retrospective unto itself.

solo outings:
Mick Fleetwood:
The Visitor 𝄞𝄞 (RCA, 1981)
Mick Fleetwood's Zoo: Shakin' the Cage 𝄞𝄞 (Warner Bros., 1992)

Christine McVie:
The Legendary Christine Perfect Album 𝄞𝄞𝄞 (Blue Horizon, 1969/Sire, 1976)
Christine McVie 𝄞𝄞 (Warner Bros., 1984)

influences:
◄◄ Elmore James, Etta James, John Mayall, the Beach Boys
►► Matthew Sweet, Tori Amos

see also: *Lindsey Buckingham, Stevie Nicks, Bob Welch*

Steve Holtje

The Fleshtones

Formed 1976, in Queens, NY.

Peter Zaremba, vocals, harmonica, organ; Keith Streng, guitar; Danny Gilbert, guitar (1976); Jimmy Bosco, drums (1976); Jan Marek Pakulski, bass (1976–87); Lenny Calderone, drums (1976–79); Bill Milhizer, drums (1979–present); Brian Spaeth, horns (1978–79); Gordon Spaeth, alto sax, organ, harmonica (1978–90); Kenny Fox, bass (1990–present).

The Fleshtones rose from New York's punk/new wave movement during the late '70s and have since been touring almost non-stop, preaching the gospel of fun '60s garage rock. The band's experience hasn't translated into commercial success, but the members have learned how to put on quite a show; a typical Fleshtones performance includes go-go dance moves, silly Farfis, organ jams, and a relentless party atmosphere. Its campy, hedonistic music never quite made it with the early '80s MTV crowd and was an absolute anomaly in the grunge era. Despite various hopeful signs—such as singer Peter Zaremba's stint hosting MTV's '80s new wave show "The Cutting Edge"—the Fleshtones seem destined to remain an under-appreciated bar band.

what to buy: The Fleshtones have a reputation for being a band that can't replicate its onstage fire in the studio. An exception is *Powerstance* 🎵🎵🎵 (Ichiban, 1991, prod. Dave Faulkner), which sounds like it was recorded in the middle of sweaty concert ecstasy. On *Beautiful Light* 🎵🎵🎵 (Naked Language, 1993, prod. Peter Buck), the Fleshtones shed its cocktail shaker image and put out a pure pop record.

what to buy next: *Laboratory of Sound* 🎵🎵🎵 (Ichiban, 1995, prod. Steve Albini) also rises above typical Fleshtones fare with the band's most mature songwriting efforts to date.

what to avoid: *Blast Off* 🎵🎵 (RIOR/Danceteria, 1982, prod. various) is a collection of early material, much of it taken from low-quality audio cassettes. For fans only.

the rest:
More than Skin Deep 🎵🎵🎵 (Ichiban, 1998)
Angry Years '84-'86 🎵🎵🎵 (Impossible Records, 1993)

worth searching for: The out-of-print *Fleshtones vs. Reality* (Emergo, 1987, prod. James Ball, Fleshtones) is arguably the band's finest recorded moment.

solo outings:

Keith Streng (with Full Time Men):
Your Face My Fist 🎵🎵🎵 (Coyote/ Twin/Tone, 1988)

Peter Zaremba (with Love Delegation):
Spread the Word 🎵🎵🎵 (Celluloid/Moving Target, 1986)
Delegation Time 🎵🎵 (Accord, 1988)

influences:
◀◀ The Zombies, the Monks, Dick Dale, the Dictators

▶▶ Green Day, the Mighty Mighty Bosstones, the Dead Milkmen

Jill Hamilton

Flipper

Formed c. 1980, in San Francisco, CA. Disbanded 1987. Re-formed 1992.

Bruce Lose, vocals, bass; Will Shatter, vocals, bass; Ted Falconi, guitar; Steve DePace, drums.

Flipper was post-punk's most inspired and likable dadist. Despite its turgid tempos and monosyllabic rants, stupid it was not. Indeed, few of its contemporaries betrayed such warmth and intelligence. After Will Shatter overdosed in 1987, the band called it quits, only to reform five years later to record *American Grafishy*, a great-sounding album that lacked the band's calling card—a sense of humor.

what to buy: *Album—Generic Flipper* 🎵🎵🎵🎵 (Subterranean, 1982/Warner Bros., 1992, prod. Flipper, Garry Creiman) is the band's classic debut. Here, much as Iggy and the Stooges did a decade or so prior, Flipper embodies the idiocy and monotony of its surroundings, in the process gaining mastery over them—not to mention finding a shred of humanity in them, too. As Shatter sings in "Life:" "I, too, have sung death's praises/But I'm not gonna sing that song anymore/'Cause I found out what living is all about/It's Life! It's Life!/ Life is the only thing worth living for!"

what to buy next: *Sex Bomb Baby!* 🎵🎵🎵🎵 (Subterranean 1987/Warner Bros., 1995, prod. Flipper, Garry Creiman, Bob McCarthy, Michael Fox) collects singles and other ephemera from the group's early years, functioning more or less like a greatest "hits" package.

the rest:
Blow 'N' Chunks 🎵🎵🎵 (ROIR, 1984/1987)
American Grafishy 🎵🎵 (Def American, 1993)

influences:
◀◀ The Stooges, Pere Ubu

▶▶ Violent Femmes, the Presidents of the United States of America, Faith No More, Primus

Bill Friskics-Warren

A Flock of Seagulls

Formed 1980, in Liverpool, England.

Mike Score, vocals, keyboards; Ali (Alistair) Score, drums; Paul Reynolds, guitar (1980–84); Frank Maudsley, bass; Gary Steadin, guitar (1984–87); Chris Chryssaphis, keyboards (1984–87).

With sculpted hair and lite synthesizer pluckiness, a Flock of

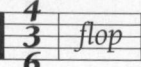

Seagulls typified the lightweight side of the new wave craze of the early '80s. England's punk scene dissolved into congenial pop and parents all breathed a sigh of relief when the kids started singing "I Ran" instead of "White Riot." The former was a big smash, as was the band's self-titled debut. Although you can actually hear the guitar lines, keyboards and a half-assed sci-fi imagery are at the heart of the English pop stars' songs ("Telecommunication," "Space-Age Love Song"). The band scored minor hits with "Wishing" and "Nightmares" (melodic, but not too scary) from *Listen* before disbanding in 1986. It's since gotten back together for nostalgia package tours and one new album, but has had little, if any, artistic impact.

what to buy: An essential item for any '80s nostalgia party (but not much else), *The Best of a Flock of Seagulls* 𝄢𝄢𝄢 (Jive, 1987) contains as much of the band's spacey dance-pop music as you'll require, including "I Ran," "Telecommunication," and 10 other tracks.

the rest:
A Flock of Seagulls 𝄢𝄢 (Jive, 1982)
Listen 𝄢𝄢 (Jive, 1983)
The Story of a Young Heart 𝄢 (Jive, 1984)
Dream Come True 𝄢 (Jive, 1986)
Magic 𝄢𝄢 (GNP/Crescendo, 1989)
Light at the End of the World 𝄢 (Big Shot, 1995)

influences:
◀◀ David Bowie, Marc Bolan, Kraftwerk
▶▶ The Rentals, Electronic, Pet Shop Boys

Allan Orski

Flop

Formed 1989, in Seattle, WA.

Rusty Willoughby, guitar, vocals; Bill Campbell, guitar; Paul Schurr, bass; Nate Johnson, drums.

Flop's spiky power-pop emerged in the shadow of Seattle's grunge-rock scene; while Nirvana meshed similar influences with a noisier attack and angst-ridden worldview and other Seattleites looked to '70s arena rock for inspiration, the Flop-sters paired a sly, sarcastic outlook with a punk-pop that owes much to English bands from the Kinks to the Buzzcocks. The quartet, which came together with refugees from bands such as the Fastbacks and Pure Joy, is anything but grunge-by-the-numbers as you might expect from yet another Seattle band. Their debut earned them a substantial cult following—and the presence of Seattle rock superstars at their shows—but the group has failed to gain a larger audience since. Nonetheless, Flop's infectious attack and cheeky absurdism deserve a listen.

what to buy: Flop's debut album, *Flop & the Fall of the Mopsqueezer* 𝄢𝄢𝄢 (Frontier, 1992, prod. Karl Bloch), is still the best showcase of the band's perverse but irresistible pop-punk.

the rest:
Whenever You're Ready 𝄢𝄢𝄢 (Frontier/550/Epic, 1993)
World of Today 𝄢𝄢𝄢 (Frontier, 1995)

influences:
◀◀ Nirvana, the Buzzcocks, the Beatles, the Kinks

Simon Glickman

Flotsam & Jetsam

Formed 1982, in Phoenix, AZ.

Eric AK (born Eric A. Knutson), vocals; Jason Newsted, bass (1982–86); Edward Carlson, guitar; Michael Gilbert, guitar; Kelly David Smith, drums; Troy Gregory, bass (1988–91); Jason B. Ward, bass (1991–present).

By the time Flotsam & Jetsam formed, "thrash" and "speed metal" were well-defined, and the original members were big fans of the style. They met up during their high school days while playing in other bands in north Phoenix and Scottsdale, Arizona. The common-denominator influence, though, wasn't Metallica or Megadeth, but AC/DC. But unlike AC/DC, Flotsam & Jetsam didn't represent unrepentant lust; instead, the band wrote dark, sexless tunes full of anger's explosive energy and comic-book horror. Eric AK's voice is "operatic" compared with the growl-and-shout meisters more common to the genre, while the twin guitars of Michael Gilbert and Eric Carlson are the links to heaviness before the new wave of British heavy metal. Unfortunately for Flotsam & Jetsam, the band may always be known as a hard-luck case, or worse, "Jason New-sted's old band." Although Newsted left with the other members' blessing (Hey! They were fans, after all!) to replace Cliff Burton in Metallica after Burton's death in a tour-bus crash, it was a blow. Newsted played a pivotal role in the band's well-received debut, *Doomsday for the Deceiver*, and contributed to the band's major-label debut *No Place for Disgrace*. Elektra bounced the band unceremoniously, but MCA picked it up for the 1990 release *When the Storm Comes Down*. Finding a permanent bass player in Jason B. Ward with the 1992 release of *Cuatro*, which appears influenced by the *Metallica* album, did not lift the band out of cult status. After *Drift*, an underrated album that seemed to anticipate Metallica's *Load* as the next frontier for metalheads, the band left MCA for the specialty Metal Blade label.

what to buy: *Doomsday for the Deceiver* 𝄢𝄢𝄢𝄢 (Roadrunner, 1986/Metal Blade, 1991, prod. Brian Slagle), with crucial tracks such as "She Took an Axe," "Hammerhead," and "Desecrator," gives the full flavor of early Flotsam work. Despite Newsted's departure, *No Place for Disgrace* ♫♫♫ (Elektra, 1988, prod. Bill Metoyer) shows this is still a young and hungry band that can cut a very heavy groove. Check out "I Live You Die."

what to buy next: In *Drift* ♫♫♫ (MCA, 1995, prod. Neil Kernon), Flotsam begins to engage real emotions rather than comicbook style darkness. *Drift* offers a surprising diversity of styles and a retreat from technical complexity for complexity's sake. It's a mature work—which may be the kiss of death in the metal realm. *Cuatro* ♫♫♫ (MCA, 1992, prod. Neil Kernon) started Jason Ward's association with the band. Also on board for the first time was Neil Kernon, who seemed to urge the band to experiment and think outside the speed-metal box. The album began the band's move toward the stylistic diversity of *Drift*.

what to avoid: Flotsam thrashes again on *High* ♫♫ (Metal Blade, 1997, prod. Bill Metoyer), but it's still a disappointment after the unrealized promise of *Drift*.

worth searching for: The out-of-print *When the Storm Comes Down* (MCA, 1990, prod. Alex Perialas) is just a step below the first two albums, refining the band's attack and throwing complex meters and rhythmic left turns into the head-banging mix.

influences:

◄◄ AC/DC, Iron Maiden, Metallica, Megadeth

►► Metallica, Sacred Reich

see also: *Metallica*

Salvatore Caputo

The Fluid

Formed 1985, in Denver, CO. Disbanded 1994.

John Robinson, vocals; James Clower, guitar, vocals; Richard Kulwicki, vocals, guitar; Matt Bischoff, vocals, bass; Garrett Shavlik, drums.

Plagued with bad luck and worse business advisors, the Fluid narrowly missed being the right grungey punk band at the right time. They recorded several terrific early singles for Sub Pop Records—the Seattle label that launched Nirvana and Soundgarden—but never gained enough momentum for success outside Denver or Seattle. Their live shows were spectacular, with John Robinson wearing lacy undergarments and commanding center stage like Iggy Pop, while the rest of the band skated through its loud-guitar punk music with charisma and confidence. They recorded one album for Hollywood Records that went nowhere, and broke up shortly after that.

what to buy: *Glue/Roadmouth* ♫♫♫♫ (Sub Pop, 1990, prod. various) collects two raw, wonderful albums of sloppy guitar music and great melodies that, when it peaks—on "Girl Bomb"

and the Troggs' "Our Love Will Still Be There"—sounds like the bastard child of the Monkees and Slayer.

what to buy next: *Purplemetalflakemusic* ♫♫♫ (Hollywood, 1993, prod. Mike Bosley, Fluid) is uneven, but has "Mister Blameshifter," "On My Feet," and "My Kind," which are almost at the level of the Fluid's early rivals and friends, Nirvana.

what to avoid: The debut, *Punch 'n' Judy* ♫ (Rayon, 1986), is boring, derivative, and, fortunately, hard to find.

the rest:

Clear Black Paper ♫♫ (Sub Pop, 1988)

worth searching for: *The Grunge Years* (Sub Pop, 1991, prod. various) stacks the Fluid's "Tomorrow" with early songs by Babes in Toyland, Afghan Whigs, Screaming Trees, L7, Love Battery, and, of course, Nirvana.

solo outings:

Garrett Shavlik:

(With Spell) *Mississippi* ♫♫♫ (Island, 1994)

influences:

◄◄ Iggy Pop, MC5, the Troggs, David Bowie, the Sex Pistols

►► Nirvana, L7, Baldo Rex

Steve Knopper

Flying Burrito Brothers

Formed 1968, in Los Angeles, CA.

Gram Parsons (died September 19, 1973), vocals, guitar (1968–70); Chris Hillman, vocals, guitar, bass (1968–72); Chris Etheridge, bass (1968–75); "Sneaky" Pete Kleinow, steel guitar (1968–71, 1974–present); Michael Clarke, drums, harmonica (1969–72); Bernie Leadon, guitar, banjo, Dobro, vocals (1969–71); Rick Roberts, guitar, vocals (1970–73); Al Perkins, pedal steel (1971–72); Byron Berline, fiddle (1971–73); Roger Bush, bass (1971–73); Kenny Wertz, guitar (1971–73); Al Munde, banjo, guitar (1972–73); Don Beck, pedal steel (1972–73); Erik Dalton, drums (1972–73); John Beland, guitar (1981—present); Joe Scott Hill, bass, vocals (1974–present); Floyd "Gib" Gilbeau, fiddle, guitar, vocals (1974–present); Gene Parsons, drums, (1974–present); Skip Battin, bass, (1976–present); Ed Ponder, drums; Jim Goodall (1985–88).

Formed by ex-Byrds Chris Hillman and Gram Parsons, the Flying Burrito Brothers are generally considered a transition period for Parsons between the Byrds and his solo work. But the group, arguably first to play what's now considered country/rock, still performs despite the absence of its two founders. During the early '80s, a version of the group relocated to Nashville and released a series of moderately successful country singles as both the Flying Burrito Brothers and simply the Burrito Brothers (the biggest of which, "She Belongs to

Everyone but Me," reached #16 in 1981). A group including Sneaky Pete, Skip Battin, Greg Harris, and Jim Goodall also recorded as the Flying Brothers.

what to buy: *The Gilded Palace of Sin* ✍✍✍✍ (A&M, 1969/Edsel, 1991, prod. Flying Burrito Brothers, Larry Marks, Henry Lewy) was a grand experiment that fused notions of country music, California hippie rock, and Southern soul. Parsons and Hillman were writing some of their best songs—among them "Sin City" (later cut by Dwight Yoakam) and "Hot Burrito No. 1" (covered by Elvis Costello)—and also covered the Muscle Shoals classics "Do Right Woman" and "Dark End of the Street." For a thorough overview, *Farther Along: The Best of the Flying Burrito Brothers* ✍✍✍✍ (A&M, 1988, prod. various) contains 21 cuts, including nine from *The Gilded Palace of Sin* and some rare outtakes.

what to buy next: Not quite the groundbreaker that *The Gilded Palace of Sin* was, *Burrito Deluxe* ✍✍✍ (A&M/Edsel, 1970, prod. Jim Dickson, Henry Lewy) nevertheless offered some fine moments in the same vein. It also contains the Burritos' version of "Wild Horses," which Mick Jagger and Keith Richards allegedly wrote for Parsons (according to the same legend, he rearranged "Honky Tonk Woman" as "Country Honk" for the Rolling Stones).

what to avoid: The quality of the band's recordings took a sharp drop after Parsons left, so all but the most die-hard fans could live without anything recorded after the group left A&M. Be especially wary of the live *Cabin Fever* ✍✍ (Relix, 1985) and *Eye of a Hurricane* ✍✍ (One Way, 1994).

the rest:
The Flying Burrito Bros. ✍✍✍ (A&M/Mobile Fidelity Sound Lab, 1971)
Airborne ✍✍ (Columbia, 1976)
Flying Again ✍✍ (Columbia, 1975)
Close Up the Honky Tonks ✍✍✍ (A&M, 1974)
Last of the Red Hot Burritos ✍✍✍ (A&M, 1972/Rebound, 1994)
Sleepless Nights ✍✍✍ (A&M, 1976)
From Another Time ✍✍ (Shiloh, 1976/Sundown, 1991)
Live from Europe ✍✍ (Relix, 1986)
Back to the Sweethearts of the Rodeo ✍✍ (Sundown/Appaloosa, 1990)
Close Encounters to the West Coast ✍✍ (Relix, 1991)
Hollywood Nights 1979–'82 ✍✍ (Sundown, 1991)
Sin City ✍✍ (Relix, 1992)
Best of the Flying Burrito Brothers ✍✍✍ (Relix, 1995)
Live in Amsterdam ✍✍ (Relix, 1997)
California Jukebox ✍✍ (American Harvest, 1997)

worth searching for: Parsons fans will want *Dim Lights, Thick Smoke, and Loud, Loud Music* (Edsel, 1993), which contains outtakes and rarities from around the time of the group's first two albums.

solo outings:
Chris Hillman:
Morning Sky ✍✍ (Sugar Hill, 1982)

Desert Rose ✍✍ (Sugar Hill, 1984)
Like a Hurricane ✍✍✍ (Sugar Hill, 1998)

The Desert Rose Band (Hillman):
The Desert Rose Band ✍✍✍✍ (Curb, 1987)
Pages of Life ✍✍✍ (Curb, 1990)
A Dozen Roses: Greatest Hits ✍✍✍✍ (Curb, 1991)
Traditional ✍✍✍ (Curb, 1993)

Alan Munde:
(With Country Gazette) *Keep on Pushing* ✍✍✍ (Flying Fish, 1991)
Festival Favorites Revisited ✍✍✍ (Rounder, 1993)
Blue Ridge Express ✍✍✍ (Rounder, 1994)

influences:

◀◀ The Byrds, Hank Williams, Memphis/Muscle Shoals soul

▶▶ The Eagles, Gram Parsons, the Desert Rose Band, the Jayhawks, Uncle Tupelo, Wilco, Son Volt

see also: *The Byrds, Gram Parsons*

Brian Mansfield

Focus

Formed 1969, in Amsterdam, Netherlands. Disbanded 1978. Briefly reformed 1990.

Thijs Van Leer, organ, flute, vocals; Martin Dresden, bass (1969–70); Cyrill Havermanns, bass (1970); Bert Reuter, bass (1970–78); Hans Cleuver, drums (1969–71); Pierre Van der Linden, drums (1970–73, 1976–78); Colin Allen, drums (1973–75); Jan Akkerman, guitar, lute (1970–76); Phillip Catherine, guitar (1976–78); Eef Albers, guitar (1976–78); Steve Smith, drums (1976).

Progressive rock's classical roots are strongly evident in the work of Focus. Its ability to arrange improvisational jazz and classical themes for the rock era (with more than a hint of cerebral musical parody) won the group worldwide acclaim during the '70s. Initially a trio, Focus lured guitar virtuoso Jan Akkerman from another Dutch group, Brainbox, which gave its mostly instrumental music a harder thematic edge. Though always more successful in Europe than in the United States, Focus managed to hit #9 on the U.S. pop charts with the catchy "Hocus Pocus" during 1973. Its follow-up, "Sylvia," also charted, but after that Focus was primarily an album-oriented group. Eccentrically yin-yanging between electric-flavored classical concertos and modern pop songs, Focus never failed to impress listeners with its overwhelming technical mastery. After Akkerman left to pursue his solo career, he took many of his fans with him, and the band foundered. Focus cut a final, unsatisfying disc with '60s pop star P.J. Proby before splintering off into various solo projects, none of which had the impact of its work as a group.

what to buy: Largely collected from its first three albums, *Best of Focus: Hocus Focus* ♫♫♫◊ (IRS, 1994, prod. Mike Vernon, Focus) is a 16-track sampler featuring the big hits—"Hocus Focus," "Sylvia," and "House of the King"—along with many zany yet atmospheric B-sides and LP cuts.

what to buy next: The free-flowing jams and creative sidesteps on *Focus III* ♫♫♫ (IRS, 1973/1990, prod. Mike Vernon) showcase the group at the peak of its instrumental powers.

the rest:

In and Out of Focus ♫♫◊ (IRS, 1970/1990)
Pass Me Not ♫♫◊ (Pure, 1994)

worth searching for: Arguably the group's finest start-to-finish LP, *Moving Waves* (IRS, 1971/1990, prod. Mike Vernon) is the one that introduced the group to worldwide audiences and contains the hit "Hocus Focus," as well as exceptional tracks such as "Janis" and "Focus II."

influences:

◄◄ Brainbox, Genesis, Jethro Tull, Yes

►► Jan Akkerman, PFM

Ken Burke

Dan Fogelberg

Born August 13, 1951, in Peoria, IL.

Dan Fogelberg was raised in the Midwest, rose to prominence on the West Coast amidst Southern California's burgeoning folk-rock singer-songwriter scene of the early '70s, and ended up in Boulder, Colorado—a fitting final destination for a "quiet man of music," to borrow one of his better-known lyrics. He dropped out of art school at the University of Illinois in 1971 and moved to L.A. to try his hand at a music career; he earned a deal with Columbia (eventually settling on the CBS subsidiary Full Moon/Epic). As Fogelberg's career progressed, his music veered away from the West Coast's country-pop stylings and more toward an unlikely mix of sentimental ballads and atmospheric prog-rock. The ballads are what eventually made him famous, likely on the strength of Fogelberg's distinctive high-tenor voice. He became a staple of adult-contemporary radio stations during the late '70s and early '80s with such hits as "Longer" and "Leader of the Band." Since the mid-'80s, Fogelberg has shown an increasing and generally healthy willingness to experiment with other styles—sometimes with refreshing results, as on 1985's bluegrass-oriented *High Country Snows*, other times less successfully (1993's world-music-influenced *River of Souls*).

what to buy: Even after more than a quarter century and a dozen albums, Fogelberg's debut, *Home Free* ♫♫♫◊ (Columbia, 1972, prod. Norbert Putnam), still stands as his best work, simply because it's so unaffected by the more commercial considerations of his subsequent efforts. Such songs as "To the Morning" and "Hickory Grove" capture the innocence of his Illinois youth at an early enough stage in his career that he could still feel it pulling on him.

what to buy next: *High Country Snows* ♫♫♫ (Full Moon/Epic, 1985, prod. Dan Fogelberg, Marty Lewis) was a welcome venture into bluegrass, with guest appearances by the likes of Doc Watson, David Grisman, Chris Hillman, and Herb Pedersen. For a straightforward collection of chart successes, *Greatest Hits* ♫♫♫ (Full Moon/Epic, 1982, prod. various) is a serviceable document, despite its revealingly yuppified cover photo. *Portrait: The Music of Dan Fogelberg* ♫♫◊ (Full Moon/Epic, 1997, prod. various) covers more of Fogelberg's career and spreads the results over four discs. It's more than most will want, but it's not a bad investment for someone switching their collection from vinyl to CD.

what to avoid: *Windows and Walls* ◊ (Full Moon/Epic, 1984, prod. Dan Fogelberg) represents the depths of Fogelberg's shallowness; hardly a song on here is even worth hearing. *Love Songs* ◊◊ (Full Moon/Epic, 1995, prod. various) isn't so much bad as it is unnecessary, an apparent attempt by the label to rehash Fogelberg's hits one more time after he'd moved on to a different record company. *Super Hits* ♫♫◊ (Epic, 1998, prod. various) contains quality material, but only enough of it to justify the budget price. There are better ways to acquire these songs.

the rest:

Souvenirs ♫♫♫ (Full Moon/Epic, 1974)
Captured Angel ♫♫◊ (Full Moon/Epic, 1975)
Nether Lands ♫♫♫ (Full Moon/Epic, 1977)
(With Tim Weisberg) *Twin Sons of Different Mothers* ♫♫ (Full Moon/Epic, 1978)
Phoenix ♫♫ (Full Moon/Epic, 1979)
The Innocent Age ♫♫♫◊ (Full Moon/Epic, 1981)
Exiles ♫◊ (Full Moon/Epic, 1987)
The Wild Places ♫♫◊ (Full Moon/Epic, 1990)
Greetings from the West ♫♫♫◊ (Full Moon/Epic, 1991)
River of Souls ♫♫ (Full Moon/Epic, 1993)
(With Tim Weisberg) *No Resemblance Whatsoever* ♫♫ (Giant, 1995)

worth searching for: Sony packaged three of Fogelberg's '70s albums, *Souvenirs/Captured Angel/Netherlands* (Full Moon/Epic, 1997, prod. various) together as a budget-line box set. *Home Free* and *Captured Angel* were paired together on a 1987 cassette that can still be purchased from some retail outlets.

influences:

◄◄ Cascades, Jackson Browne, James Taylor, Bruce Cockburn

►► Garth Brooks, David Wilcox, James McMurtry

Peter Blackstock and Brian Mansfield

John Fogerty

Born May 28, 1945, in Berkeley, CA.

Since Creedence Clearwater Revival's 1972 breakup, John Fogerty has led a frustrating solo career, plagued by crippling writer's block and labyrinthine lawsuits. His 1985 #1 comeback album, *Centerfield*, was nothing less than a personal triumph over haunting demons. But his first solo outing was a recreation of classic country and western standards, with Fogerty playing all the instruments himself under the pseudonym Blue Ridge Rangers. His first authentic solo album returned to the Creedence sound, but with only modest success. A second "proper" solo album was delayed for nine years, until *Centerfield* came, seemingly out of nowhere, with the hit, "Old Man down the Road." That was a success Fogerty's subsequent solo album did not duplicate. He remains a fussy, intense craftsman with an unparalleled flair for treating classic themes in a timeless way—which is just what he did with 1997's *Blue Moon Swamp*, which came after another long wait (11 years) but brought Fogerty back to sound and stage, tearing it up in concert like a guy who'd never been away.

what to buy: *Centerfield* 𝄢𝄢𝄢 (Warner Bros., 1985, prod. John Fogerty) is a jaunty celebration of Americana, shaded lightly by some dark undertones.

what to buy next: Although he didn't write a single song on *Blue Ridge Rangers* 𝄢𝄢𝄢 (Fantasy, 1972, prod. John Fogerty), Fogerty gives a glistening pop sound to country numbers from the songbooks of Merle Haggard, George Jones, and others. *Blue Moon Swamp* 𝄢𝄢𝄢𝄢 (Warner Bros., 1997, prod. John Fogerty) is a startling and welcome return to form, while the live *Premonition* 𝄢𝄢𝄢𝄢 (Reprise, 1998, prod. John Fogerty, Elliot Scheiner) captures the fire of Fogerty's concerts in support of that album, with an ample supply of Creedence tunes to boot.

what to avoid: His *Centerfield* follow-up, *Eye of the Zombie* 𝄢𝄢 (Warner Bros., 1986, prod. John Fogerty), despite a couple of high spots, didn't really do his talents justice.

the rest:
John Fogerty 𝄢𝄢𝄥 (Asylum 1975)

worth searching for: A couple of his Warner Bros. singles contain highly worthy non-LP B-sides, especially his rollicking take on the zydeco hit "My Toot Toot" on the flip of "Change in the Weather" (Warner Bros., 1985, prod. John Fogerty).

influences:

◀◀ Buddy Holly, Ronnie Hawkins, Screamin' Jay Hawkins, Chuck Berry, Elvis Presley, Jerry Lee Lewis, Bill Monroe, Creedence Clearwater Revival, Dave Edmunds

▶▶ Dave Edmunds, Southern Culture on the Skids

see also: *Creedence Clearwater Revival*

Joel Selvin and Gary Graff

Foghat

Formed 1971, in London, England. Disbanded 1984. Re-formed 1993.

"Lonesome" Dave Peverett, vocals, guitar (1971–84, 1993–present); Rod Price, guitar (1971–80, 1993–present); Tony Stevens, bass (1971–73, 1993–present); Roger Earl, drums (1971–84, 1993–present); Nick Jameson, bass, keyboards (1973–75); Craig MacGregor, bass (1975–84); Erik Cartwright, guitar (1980–84).

Formed by Savoy Brown refugees Dave Peverett, Tony Stevens, and Roger Earl, Foghat dished up a basic, straightforward brand of blues-oriented boogie, both in its own crunchy originals and in revved-up covers of oldies such as "Maybelline," "Sweet Home Chicago," and its first big hit, Willie Dixon's "I Just Want to Make Love to You." Foghat was blessed with good producers (Dave Edmunds, Dan Hartman), and Earl's slide guitar work helped raise the group's music above the pedestrian. Foghat's zenith—artistic and commercial—was the 1975 album *Fool for the City*, which contained the hit "Slow Ride." But this kind of stuff gets old fast, and by the late '70s Foghat had become an also-ran. It broke up during the early '80s, but the original foursome regrouped in 1993 to mine the classic rock oldies circuit.

what to buy: *The Best of Foghat* 𝄢𝄢𝄢𝄥 (Bearsville/Rhino, 1989, prod. various) and *The Best of Foghat, Volume 2* 𝄢𝄢𝄢 (Bearsville/Rhino, 1992, prod. various) are fine samplers of Foghat's output. The former has all the hits, while the latter dishes up worthwhile album tracks such as "Step Outside."

what to buy next: *Fool for the City* 𝄢𝄢𝄢 (Bearsville, 1975, prod. Nick Jameson) is Foghat's best album and houses hits in the funk-rocker "Slow Ride" and the driving title track. Its successor, *Night Shift* 𝄢𝄢𝄢 (Bearsville, 1976, prod. Dan Hartman), doesn't have hits but is a consistent serving of meat-and-potatoes hard rock.

what to avoid: *Zig-Zag Walk* **woof!** (Bearsville, 1983, prod. Nick Jameson) proved beyond a doubt that Foghat had overstayed its welcome on the scene.

the rest:
Foghat 𝄢𝄢 (Bearsville, 1972)
Rock and Roll 𝄢𝄢 (Bearsville, 1973)
Energized 𝄢𝄢𝄥 (Bearsville, 1974)
Rock & Roll Outlaws 𝄢𝄢 (Bearsville, 1974)
Live 𝄢𝄢 (Bearsville, 1977)
Stone Blue 𝄢𝄢𝄥 (Bearsville, 1978)
Boogie Motel 𝄢𝄥 (Bearsville, 1979)
Tight Shoes 𝄢 (Bearsville, 1980)
Girls to Chat and Boys to Bounce 𝄢 (Bearsville, 1981)
In the Mood for Something Rude 𝄢𝄥 (Bearsville, 1982)
Road Cases 𝄢𝄢𝄢 (Plum/Oxygen, 1998)

influences:

◀◀ Savoy Brown, Fleetwood Mac, the Rolling Stones, John

John Fogerty (© Ken Settle)

Mayall's Bluesbreakers, Chuck Berry, Howlin' Wolf, Willie Dixon, John Lee Hooker

▶▶ Georgia Satellites, Brother Cane, Badlands, Black Crowes, Lenny Kravitz, Pearl Jam

see also: *Savoy Brown*

Gary Graff

Ben Folds Five

Formed 1994, in Chapel Hill, NC.

Ben Folds, piano, vocals; Robert Sledge, bass, vocals; Darren Jessee, drums, vocals.

Irony abounds in the world of Ben Folds Five. The group is actually a trio, not a quintet, and its lead instrument is a piano, not a guitar—which is no small feat, considering it hails from Chapel Hill, North Carolina, considered in many circles to be jangle-pop's ground zero. In its often irreverent interviews, the group carries its schtick even further, making up elaborate lies about the Five's relatively bland genesis, expounding on the relative merits of such '70s juggernauts as Journey and Styx, and blithely tagging its piano/drums/fuzz bass sound as "punk rock for sissies." Then there are the songs, which on its debut album range from "Underground," a brutal piss-take on the studied dourness of the alt-rock scene, to "Julianne," a flailing relationship post-mortem that includes a brief tryst with "a girl who looks like Axl Rose," to "Boxing," an imagined conversation between an aging Muhammad Ali and Howard Cosell. More recent offerings include "Song for the Dumped," in which the wronged lover demands, "Gimme my money back, you bitch," and "One Angry Dwarf and 200 Solemn Faces," the title of which by itself tells you a lot about this band's attitude (or rather, the lack thereof). But there's nothing funny about "Brick," the group's breakthrough hit, which is uncharacteristic musically—it has a hushed, meditative quality—and lyrically—the subject is never mentioned by name, but the song is about a young couple who goes to get an abortion, which ultimately has devastating consequences for their relationship. In the ironic world of Ben Folds Five, it figures that *this* would be the song that would turn the group into a household name.

what to buy: Thanks to the brilliant "Brick," perhaps the most thoughtful piece of popcraft to hit the airwaves in years, *Whatever and Ever Amen* ♪♪♪ (550 Music, 1997, prod. Caleb Southern, Ben Folds) is the first place to go to check out Ben Folds Five. On the rest of the album, they're up to their usual wackiness, with delightful odes to broken relationships such as "Song for the Dumped" and "Battle of Who Could Care Less," and the only-somewhat-mean-spirited "Steve's Last Night in

Town." If you like the Five's sensibility on *Whatever*, chances are you'll also dig the debut, *Ben Folds Five* ♪♪♪♪ (Caroline, 1995, prod. Caleb Southern). The sounds recall everything from vintage Todd Rundgren to early Squeeze and Joe Jackson, with hints of Brian Wilson and Queen thrown in—quite a mix. And the songs, including "Underground," "Julianne," and "Philosophy," couldn't be more entertaining.

what to avoid: To satisfy its contractual obligations to Caroline, the Five released *Naked Baby Photos* ♪♪ (Caroline, 1998), an odds 'n' sods package of live cuts and previously unreleased material. It's for Five fanatics only.

influences:

◀◀ Todd Rundgren, Elton John, Queen, Joe Jackson, Billy Joel, Squeeze

Daniel Durchholz

The Folk Implosion

See: Sebadoh

Wayne Fontana & the Mindbenders

Formed 1963, in Manchester, England. Disbanded 1969.

Wayne Fontana (born Glynn Geoffrey Ellis, October 28, 1945, in Manchester, England), vocals (1963–65); Eric Stewart, guitar, vocals; Bob Lang, bass, vocals (1963–68); Ric Rothwell, drums (1963–68); Jimmy O'Neill, keyboards (1968–69); Graham Gouldman, bass (1968–69); Paul Hancox, drums (1968–69).

For solid, straightforward, meat 'n' potatoes British Beat, one need look no further than Wayne Fontana & the Mindbenders, for what these guys may have lacked in originality they more than made up for with loads of good, old-fashioned panache and exuberance. It was at a 1963 audition in Manchester's Oasis club that Glynn Ellis's band the Jets was discovered by producer Jack Baverstock (with Eric Stewart and Ric Rothwell standing in for A.W.O.L. Jets at the very last minute). Brought to London to record in the wake of the Merseybeat gold rush, the newly formed quartet first entered the U.K. Top 10 in 1964 with a cover of Major Lance's "Um, Um, Um, Um, Um, Um," and within a year had hit the world over with the infectious "Game of Love." Soon afterwards Ellis/Fontana left to pursue a solo career (his only minor hit being "Pamela, Pamela") while the Mindbenders, as a three-piece, scored another transatlantic smash with "A Groovy Kind of Love," a song so durable it even withstood a 1988 cover by Phil Collins. After appearing with Lulu in the film *To Sir with Love*, the Mindbenders recruited songwriter-extraordinaire ("For Your Love," "Bus Stop") Graham Gouldman, who remained with the group for two years until he and Eric Stewart left to form the incredible Hotlegs

("Neanderthal Man") and then 10cc. However, to this day Wayne Fontana can still be found circling the European cabaret circuit with various pickup groups of "Mindbenders" in tow.

what's available: The superb 20-track *Best of Wayne Fontana & the Mindbenders* 🐾🐾🐾 (Fontana, 1994, prod. various) features all the hits, all the should'a-been's ("It's Just a Little Bit Too Late" and the wistful "Ashes to Ashes"), and even the song Sidney Poitier valiantly tried to frug to in *To Sir with Love*.

worth searching for: Their debut album *Wayne Fontana & the Mindbenders: The Game of Love* (Fontana, 1965, prod. Jack Baverstock) may well be one of those "Okay boys: run through your set" quickies, but, like the first Beatles and Stones albums, it provides a perfect, rock-hard snapshot of a group of kids with brand new guitars and electricity to burn.

influences:

◄◄ Brook Benton, Bo Diddley, Major Lance

►► Racing Cars, Martin & the E-Chords, De La Soul

see also: *10cc*

                                        Gary Pig Gold

Foo Fighters
See: Nirvana

For Against
Formed 1984, in Lincoln, NE.

Jeffrey Runnings, bass, guitar, vocals; Harry Dingman, guitar (1984–89); Steven "Mave" Hinrichs, guitar (1990–present); Jeff Gaskins, bass (1989–91); Greg Hill, drums (1984–89); Steve Schultz, drums (1989–91); Paul Engelhard, drums (1991–present).

For Against has long suffered in relative obscurity despite releasing five fine, very different albums—records well appreciated by those who've heard them–but sadly, too few have. Part of the problem is geography; it's hard to get noticed when you hail from Nebraska. The rest has been bad luck, lack of resources, poor timing, and the crime of making independent-minded, atmospheric, aggressive pop when the U.S. market craved punk and grunge. After an early self-released single "Autocrat" drew the attention of Independent Projects Records, For Against released two albums, 1987's *Echelons* and 1988's *December*, with its original lineup before the personnel changes began. The results since have been even more impressive, with some of the most inwardly affecting music made during the '90s, as the group presses on through its second decade undeterred so far by its lack of commercial success. In particular, few write more soul-searching lyrics without a trace of self-indulgence than the melancholic-voiced Jeffrey Runnings, who's been

known to reduce some of the fans the band has managed to garner to actual tears with his more recent work.

what to buy: *Mason's California Lunchroom* 🐾🐾🐾🐾 (Rainbow Quartz, 1994, prod. For Against, Tom Ware) may mark the arrival at the place Runnings always envisioned in his head. This is one of those rare albums that combines an attack-oriented, post-punk rhythm section on half the songs (gassed burners such as the standout "Tagalong," plus "Seesick," "Crossed," "Coursing," and "Reinventing the Wheel") with some surprisingly beautiful guitar playing. Steven Hinrichs spits out a variety of tones, alternately biting, shimmering, ringing, distorting, and flanging; a one-man tour de force. And on the slower stuff, such as "Blow," "Vacuum," and especially the moving, vulnerable "Hindsight," the overall mood is gentle, poignantly fragile, evocative, and spellbinding.

what to buy next: *Shelf Life* 🐾🐾🐾 (Independent Projects/World Domination, 1998, prod. For Against) turns out to be worth the two-year wait between recording and actual release, as two pretty covers (first-ever for this band) of East River Pipe and Tracy Thorn end another spine-tingling, roller-coaster affair. No departure from previous works, but a harder, thicker expression of the band's sound/ethic, the LP's explosive rumblers such as "Shadow," "Forever," and "Harbor" maintain their ethereal background waft, while the slower, moody, and reflective work such as "Wintersong" and "Lilacs" retains enough bite to keep the band from floating away. *Aperture* ♫♫♫♫ (Rainbow Quartz, 1992, prod. For Against, Randy Watson) is more patchwork but still convincing. "Today Today" is as startling as "Hindsight" in its harrowing melancholy, and there are plenty more insidious melodies and sonorous bangers such as "Mindframed" and the single "Don't Do Me any Favors." For those who want a more dense and complicated thrill ride, *December* ♫♫♫♫ (Independent Projects, 1988, prod. For Against, Randy Watson) is a claustrophobic but enveloping guitar record with occasional, curious neo-reggae rhythms undercutting the solid punch of post-punk pop in "Stranded in Greenland," "Clandestine High Holy," and "The Last Laugh," alongside the moody title track, and the introspective "The Effect."

what to avoid: A 10-inch, vinyl-only mini-LP of the group's pre-first album days called *In the Marshes* ♫♫♫♫ (Independent Projects, 1990, prod. For Against) is the least of its works, though if one has already procured and dug all five albums, this early 4AD side of the group as a studio project of sorts—complete with drum machine—is occasionally fascinating, particularly the relentless, hypnotic "Purgatory Salesman" and "Amnesia."

the rest:
Echelons ♫♫♫ (Independent Projects, 1987)

influences:
◀◀ Comsat Angels, Lowlife, Joy Division

▶▶ Springhouse, Half String, Scenic

Jack Rabid

For Squirrels /Subrosa

Formed 1993, in Gainesville, FL.

For Squirrels: John Francis Vigliatura IV (died September 8, 1995), vocals; Travis Michael Tooke, guitar; William Richard White (died September 8, 1995), bass; Thomas Jacob Griego Jr., drums. Subrosa: Travis Michael Tooke, vocals, guitar; Andy Jim Lord, bass; Jack Griego, drums.

Few things are sadder in music than a promising career that is cut short before it is allowed to really begin. That is the sorrowful legacy of For Squirrels, a promising Gainesville, Florida, band that was about to release its major label debut when its tour van blew a tire, causing vocalist Jack Vigliatura, who was driving, to lose control of the vehicle. It flipped over, killing Vigliatura, bassist Bill White, and tour manager Tim Bender. After recovering from their own injuries, guitarist Travis Michael Tooke and drummer Jack Griego carried on, first as For Squirrels and then, with bassist Andy Jim Lord, as the hard rocking Subrosa.

what to buy: For Squirrels' *Example* ♫♫♫♫ (550/Epic, 1995, prod. Nick Launay) proved that the group was on the verge of transcending its influences (including obvious reference points such as Live's dramatic tension and release, and Soul Asylum's punky garage pop) and truly coming into its own. "8.02 PM" and "Long Live the King," for example, thrash about impressively. "Superstar" is a triumphant anthem, and "Under Smithville" and "Mighty K.C." are ringing, melodic, power pop.

the rest:
For Squirrels:
Bay Path Road ♫♫♫ (self-released, 1994)
Plymouth ♫♫♫ (Y&T EP, 1994)

Subrosa:
Never Bet the Devil Your Head ♫♫♫ (550 Music, 1997)

influences:
◀◀ R.E.M., Live, Soul Asylum

▶▶ Creed, Matchbox 20

Daniel Durchholz

Steve Forbert

Born 1955, in Meridian, MS.

Already saddled with the "New Dylan" tag because of his raspy voice and guitar-harmonica accompaniment, Steve Forbert debuted in 1978 with *Alive on Arrival*, a charming concept album celebrating his country-boy-moves-to-the-Big-Apple dreams. His proclamations of peach-fuzzed optimism were so earnest and life-affirming that the scores of critics who adopted him as their folk-rock Peter Pan didn't want him to ever grow up. Forbert managed to score one hit single, 1980's "Romeo's Tune," and send a not-so-subtle declaration of maturity via the snide title of his 1980 album, *Little Stevie Orbit*, before a six-year feud with Columbia Records kept him out of the record stores. Forbert re-emerged on Geffen Records in 1988—older, wiser and, no surprise, much more cynical. As a singer, Forbert has learned to get the most out of his gruff tenor, frequently sinking into a compelling whisper that intensifies the hushed intimacy of his lyrics. Like John Hiatt's recent work, such albums as *Rocking Horse Head* and *The American in Me* are short on dreams but still full of hope, the work of a battle-scarred veteran who is learning to adapt his idealistic beliefs to the daunting pressures of adulthood.

what to buy: *Alive on Arrival* ♫♫♫♫ (Nemperor, 1978, prod. Steve Burgh) remains a joyful testament to youthful idealism, thanks to such timeless songs as "Goin' down to Laurel," "Steve Forbert's Midsummer Night's Toast," and "What Kinda Guy?" *The American in Me* ♫♫♫♫ (Geffen, 1992, prod. Pete Anderson) is the grown-up bookend to *Alive on Arrival*, using the reflection and self-doubt of "You Cannot Win 'em All" and "Responsibility" as tools for resilience, not resignation. The more-rustic instrumentation on *Rocking Horse Head* ♫♫♫ (Paladin, 1996, prod. Brad Jones), recorded with members of Wilco, inspires some of Forbert's most quiet singing as well as some of his most bubbly ("Moon Man," with its irresistible "Call, fax, e-mail soon" chorus) and wistful ("Some Will Rake the Coals") songs.

what to buy next: Forbert's 1982 tour with his road band, the Flying Squirrels (anchored by future Shawn Colvin/Rosanne Cash producer John Leventhal), produced his most memorable rock 'n' roll-driven shows. *King Biscuit Flower Hour Presents* ♫♫♫ (KBFH/BMG, 1996) captures a fiery set at My Father's Place on Long Island, mixing his best-known material with convincing romps through Chuck Berry's "Too Much Monkey Business," the Searchers' "When You Walk in the Room," and a lovely reading of the Troggs' "Love Is All Around."

what to avoid: *Jackrabbit Slim* ♫♫ (Nemperor, 1979, prod. John Simon) spawned his hit, "Romeo's Tune," but compared to the rest of his catalog, the horn-driven, strings-drenched production now sounds more syrupy than soulful.

the rest:
Little Stevie Orbit ♫♫♫ (Nemperor, 1980)
Streets of This Town ♫♫♫ (Geffen, 1988)
What Kinda Guy: The Best of Steve Forbert ♫♫♫ (Epic/Legacy, 1993)
Mission of the Crossroad Palms ♫♫♫ (Giant, 1995)
Here's Your Pizza ♫♫ (Paladin, 1997)

worth searching for: *Steve Forbert* (Nemperor, 1982, prod. Steve Burgh) is an unjustly forgotten album still unavailable on CD that features the rousing "Ya Ya (Next to Me)," a heartfelt cover of "Everytime You Walk in the Room," and his funniest song, "He's Gotta Live up to His Shoes." *Be Here Now* (Rolling Tide, 1994, prod. Marrow Demerle) is a solo acoustic live recording from his 1994 tour available only at shows and through his fan club newsletter, *Squirrelmad*.

influences:
◀◀ Jimmie Rodgers, Bob Dylan, Chuck Berry, John Prine

▶▶ Michael McDermott, Joe Henry, Will T. Massey

David Okamoto

Frankie Ford

Born Frank Guzzo, August 4, 1940, in Gretna, LA.

Few white teenagers assimilated the sounds of New Orleans R&B as well as Frankie Ford. Backed by Huey "Piano" Smith & the Clowns and many of the same musicians who played on sessions for Little Richard, Ford's swinging jump tunes and emotive ballads were as credible in their way as those by his heroes, Fats Domino and Professor Longhair. A stage performer since age five, Ford sang and played piano in a high school group called the Syncopators before he signed with Ace Records in 1958. Under the guidance of producer Johnny Vincent, Ford cut "Cheatin' Woman," a tough, sax-drenched rocker and solid regional hit. For a follow-up, Vincent wiped Bobby Marchan's vocals off a Huey "Piano" Smith song which featured a fog-horn and Navy bells, and brought Ford in to redo the vocals in Marchan's style. The result was the monster hit "Sea Cruise," which landed Ford on *American Bandstand* and on tours with some of the biggest stars of the era. He also found the time to form a group with Huey Smith and Mac Rebbenack (the future Dr. John) called Morgus & the Three Ghouls; their one and only release, "Morgus the Magnificent," a musical tribute to the host of a local TV horror movie program, became a solid favorite in New Orleans. Subsequent releases such as the jumpin' "Alimony," "I Want to Be Your Man," the pop ballad "Time after Time," and the inevitable remake of "Danny Boy" hit the bottom third of the national charts—though they were much bigger hits in New Orleans. After a royalty dispute, Ford left Ace and began recording with Dave Bartholomew (Fats Domino's producer) at Imperial Records, scoring a couple of minor hits before he was drafted into the U.S. Army. During the late '60s and '70s, Ford recorded without much success for the Doubloon, Paula, Cinnamon, and ABC labels. Though always a star in New Orleans, Ford's cameo in the 1978 Alan Freed biopic *American Hot Wax* led to many successful tours overseas, where they still appreciate the original rockers. Ford resumed recording with Johnny Vincent at Ace Records in 1995, his voice deeper but still demonstrating the same authentic feel for R&B.

what to buy: Some copies of *Let's Take a Sea Cruise* ♫♫♫ (Ace, 1959/1991, prod. Johnny Vincent), which contains Ford's hits "Sea Cruise," "Roberta," "Alimony," and "Time after Time," are still in stores. However, the best collection of Ford's hits, B-sides, and previously unreleased tracks is on the readily available British import *Oowee-Baby! The Best of Frankie Ford* ♫♫♫♫ (Westside, 1998, prod. Johnny Vincent), a 27-track disc boasting crisp digital sound and an informative booklet written by the editor of *Now Dig This*, Tony Cajiano. In addition to such jumpin' New Orleans rockers as "I Want to Be Your Man," "Cheatin' Woman," "What's Going On," and even "Morgus the Magnificent," this disc includes Ford's underrated R&B ballads "The Last One to Cry" and "Can't I Tell My Heart What to Do."

what to buy next: A less-complete but more readily available collection is *Sea Cruise: The Very Best of Frankie Ford* ♫♫♫ (Music Club, 1998, prod. various), which has 18 tracks, although with just 43 minutes of disc space taken up, it sacrifices potential quality (i.e., more songs) for cost.

what to avoid: Know what you're getting with the deceptively titled, 10-song Canadian compilation *The All-Time Greatest Hits of*

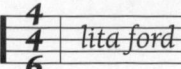

lita ford

Frankie Ford ♫♫♫ (Stardust, 1996, prod. various). Though it does contain Ford's big hits for Ace, four tracks recorded anew during the '80s cheapen the idea of this being a true hits package.

the rest:
Frankie Ford—A New Orleans Tradition ♫♫♫ (Avanti, 1997)

worth searching for: The out-of-print *Hot & Lonely* (Ace, 1995, prod. Johnny Vincent) is Ford's somewhat successful return to the label and the producer who made him famous. Also, the vinyl-only *New Orleans Dynamo* (Brand New, 1984, prod. Mike Vernon) is Ford's comeback LP, recorded in England. His cover versions of Fats Domino's "Whiskey Heaven," "I Wanna Walk You Home," and other R&B standards sound absolutely authentic. This disc was never issued in the United States, but Ford's fans will definitely want to track it down.

influences:
◀◀ Fats Domino, Johnnie Ray, Huey "Piano" Smith, Professor Longhair, Bobby Marchan, Clarence "Frogman" Henry

▶▶ Jimmy Clanton, Johnny Rivers, Freddy Cannon, Joe Jones, Dr. John

Ken Burke

Lita Ford

Born Rosanna Ford, September 23, 1959, in London, England.

Without the inherent pop sense of her Runaways mate Joan Jett, Lita Ford has languished as something of a token metal pin-up, as much a precursor to the riot grrrl groups as Jett but not quite as durable. She does enjoy the distinctions of being the first woman to appear on the cover of *Hit Parader* and the first woman inducted into *Circus* magazine's Hall of Fame in 20 years—as well as a member of the house band for comedian Howie Mandel's *Howie* on CBS. That can probably carry you through a lot of world's great hard rock dive clubs.

what to buy: *Lita* ♫♫♫ (RCA, 1988, prod. Mike Chapman) has everything Ford has to offer—including her hits "Kiss Me Deadly" and "Close My Eyes" (with Ozzy Osbourne), as well as a songwriting collaboration with Motörhead's Lemmy Kilmister on "Can't Catch Me."

what to buy next: *Greatest Hits* ♫♫♫ (RCA, 1993, prod. various) and *The Best of Lita Ford* ♫♫♫ (RCA, 1992, prod. various) each do an adequate job of winnowing the best of Ford's output.

what to avoid: Ford's first couple of solo albums—*Out for Blood* ♫ (Mercury, 1983/1990, prod. Neil Merryweather) and *Dancin' on the Edge* **woof!** (Mercury, 1983/1990, prod. Lance Quinn)—make the Runaways sound like the Beatles.

the rest:
Stiletto ♫♫ (RCA, 1990)

Dangerous Curves ♫♫ (RCA, 1991)
Black ♫♫ (ZYX, 1995)

influences:
◀◀ Jimi Hendrix, Suzi Quatro, Black Sabbath, Motörhead, Slade

▶▶ L7, 7 Year Bitch, Hole

Gary Graff

Julia Fordham

Born August 10, 1962, in Portsmouth, Hampshire, England.

Is Julia Fordham a jazz, pop, or folk singer? In truth, she's all three, which makes her one of those artists with considerable talent who fall between the cracks of regimented radio formats. Possessed of a rich contralto voice that at times is reminiscent of jazz diva Nina Simone, Fordham rose through the ranks singing backup for Mari Wilson and Kim Wilde. She's been a songwriter since her teens, and her experience is plainly in evidence on her four albums; for though her songs tend to focus mostly on lost love, the situations never repeat themselves, and Fordham injects surprising insights and pathos into each of them. Still, it's understandable that some listeners find her a bit of a cold fish, mostly due to the studied, every-hair-in-place production of her first three albums.

what to buy: *Porcelain* ♫♫♫♫ (Virgin, 1989, prod. Grant Mitchell, Hugh Padgham) was an adult-contemporary and VH1 favorite thanks to the exquisite title track, the gentle Latin rhythms of "Genius," and the lyrically compelling "Girlfriend."

what to buy next: *Falling Forward* ♫♫♫ (Virgin, 1994, prod. Larry Klein, Julia Fordham) benefits from slightly less restrained performances that show off the extraordinary range and expressiveness of Fordham's voice.

the rest:
Julia Fordham ♫♫♫ (Virgin, 1988)
Swept ♫♫♫ (Virgin, 1991)
East West ♫♫♫♫ (Virgin, 1997)
Best Of N/A (Virgin, 1998)

influences:
◀◀ Nina Simone, Mari Wilson, Lisa Stansfield, Joni Mitchell
▶▶ Jewel, Sarah McLachlan

Daniel Durchholz

Foreigner

Formed 1976, in New York, NY.

Mick Jones, guitar, vocals; Lou Gramm (born Louis Grammatico), vocals (1976–90, 1992–present); Ian McDonald, flute, keyboards, reeds,

guitar, vocals (1976–80); Al Greenwood, keyboards, synthesizers (1976–80); Ed Gagliardi, bass (1976–79); Dennis Elliot, drums (1976–92); Rick Wills, bass (1979–92); Johnny Edwards, vocals (1990–92); Mark Schulman, drums (1994–present); Jeff Jacobs, keyboards (1994–present); Bruce Turgon, bass (1994–present).

One of the most successful purveyors of album-oriented rock during the '70s and '80s, Foreigner started as a project organized by ex–Spooky Tooth and Leslie West guitarist Mick Jones. Stumbling on ex–King Crimson saxophonist/keyboardist Ian McDonald, Jones handpicked the other members for his group—including a little-known singer named Lou Grammatico, then fronting a New York band called Black Sheep. Foreigner's 1977 debut sold more than four million copies on the strength of Jones's power pop arrangements and Gramm's incendiary pop-metal vocals. The hits kept coming through the '80s—from the keyboard-drenched "Cold as Ice" to the rocker "Dirty White Boys" to the majestic ballad "I Want to Know What Love Is." Jones streamlined the band as time went on, including a two-year split with Gramm, who tried his hand at a solo career. Foreigner continues to release albums, but its greatest success these days is on the summer oldies circuit.

what to buy: A band like Foreigner is all about hits, so it makes sense that its best album would be *The Very Best . . . and Beyond* 🎵🎵🎵🎵 (Atlantic, 1992, prod. various). From '70s rock hits like "Hot Blooded" and "Head Games" to the band's mellower '80s smashes such as "Waiting for a Girl like You" and "I Want to Know What Love Is," this offers the most complete chronicle of the group's prolonged classic rock dominance—though a few flaccid new tunes don't make much of a case for its future.

what to buy next: For a taste of the band's status as sorta' metal, sorta' classic rockers, try the sophomore album *Double Vision* 🎵🎵🎵 (Atlantic, 1978, prod. Mick Jones, Ian McDonald, Keith Olsen). Fortified with hits such as "Blue Morning, Blue Day" and the title track, it's a prototypical '70s arena rock album. If the group's crafted, pop-oriented material is more your style, then *4* 🎵🎵🎵 (Atlantic, 1981, prod. Mick Jones, John "Mutt" Lange) dishes up slick hits such as "Waiting for a Girl like You" and the anthemic "Jukebox Hero."

what to avoid: The worn-out performances filling its only live record, *Classic Hits Live* **woofl** (Atlantic, 1993, prod. Bud Prager), serve as ample evidence that Foreigner is but a hair's breadth away from opening for the Beach Boys or Chicago on the VH1 nostalgia circuit.

the rest:
Foreigner 🎵🎵🎵 (Atlantic, 1977)
Head Games 🎵🎵🎵 (Atlantic, 1979)
Records 🎵🎵🎵🎵 (Atlantic, 1982)
Best of Foreigner 🎵🎵🎵 (Atlantic, 1982)

Agent Provocateur 🎵🎵🎵 (Atlantic, 1984)
Inside Information 🎵🎵🎵 (Atlantic, 1987)
Unusual Heat 🎵🎵 (Atlantic, 1991)
Mr. Moonlight 🎵🎵 (Rhythm Safari, 1994)

worth searching for: *Foreigner Profiled!* (Atlantic, 1991) is a promotion-only interview disc that's amusing in hindsight for its declarations that short-time singer Johnny Edwards was the future of Foreigner.

solo outings:
Lou Gramm:
Ready or Not 🎵🎵🎵 (Atlantic, 1987)
Foreigner in a Strange Land 🎵🎵🎵 (Collectables, 1988)
Long Hard Look 🎵🎵 (Atlantic, 1989)
Best of the Early Years 🎵🎵🎵 (Collectables, 1993)

Mick Jones:
Mick Jones 🎵🎵 (Atlantic, 1989)
Jones Alone 🎵🎵 (Atlantic, 1989)

influences:
◄◄ The Shadows, Elton John, Spooky Tooth, Mountain, Jefferson Airplane

►► Cutting Crew, Survivor, Loverboy, Matchbox 20

Eric Deggans

Forest for the Trees

Carl Stephenson (born June 9, 1967 in Olympia, WA); others.

Like Pink Floyd's Syd Barrett, Carl Stephenson is a troubled genius. Raised in Olympia, Washington, Stephenson began playing the violin at age seven and went on to master the guitar, sitar, drums, keyboards, and the didgeridoo. At age 20 he made the trek to Houston to produce songs for Rap-a-Lot Records and the Geto Boys. Four years later he moved to L.A. where he met Beck, with whom he co-wrote the smash "Loser" before signing his own deal with Geffen Records. But mental illness—including paranoia and anxiety attacks—sidelined Stephenson and put his work on hiatus, and it took five years for him to finish his debut. Even as he finished it, Stephenson suffered more mood swings and had to be hospitalized. Once he was released, he set to work on more music, as well as a series of seven children's stories titled *The Adventures of Bitsy Eddie and Paisley Bean,* about a jumping bean who turns into a worm and befriends a squirrel.

what to buy: *Forest for the Trees* 🎵🎵🎵 (DreamWorks, 1997, prod. Carl Stephenson) is a clever amalgamation of Celtic folk music, synth pop, hip-hop, samples, and Stephenson's imaginative lyrics. In the bagpipe-laced first single "Dream," Stephenson sings "When I get up/I don't know if I'm truly awake/or if I'm still dreaming." In contrast, "Thoughts in My

Mind" is a moody exploration of Stephenson's illness, while flamenco guitar adds a dash of Spanish flavoring to the dance number "Planet Unknown."

influences:

◄◄ Devo, Beck, eels

Christina Fuoco

Robert Forster

See: Grant McLennan

The Fortunes

Formed 1963, in Birmingham, England.

Rod Allen, bass, vocals; Andy Brown, drums; Barry Pritchard, guitar, vocals (1963–95); Glen Dale, guitar, vocals (1963–66, 1969); David Carr, keyboards (1963–68); Shel MacRae, (a.k.a. Andrew Semple), guitar, vocals; Rodney Bainbridge, guitar, vocals; Bob Jackson, guitar, vocals (1995–present); George McAllister.

Primarily a vocal group (which caused a big stir during the '60s for actually *admitting* session musicians played on most of its records), the Fortunes owe a great deal of its success to the golden age of British "Light" radio. One of its earliest releases became the signature tune of the popular pirate station Radio Caroline, and between the biggest hits "You've Got Your Troubles" (an international smash in 1965) and "Here Comes That Rainy Day Feeling Again" (a belated U.S. Top 20 in 1971), the group kept itself busy recording slews of radio ads, primarily for soft drink companies. As any good advertising agency will tell you, the less personality in a jingle singer's voice, the better. Perhaps this faceless, unadventurous approach helped prevent the Fortunes from establishing a musical identity and, as a result, build a solid career on record. Still, the group remains active on the European nostalgia circuit, apparently unashamed to bill itself with the dubious footnote, "From 1965 through 1972, the Fortunes were the voice for Coca-Cola."

what's available: Of the dozen tracks on *The Very Best of the Fortunes* ♬♬♬ (Taragon, 1995, compilation prod. Eliot Goshman, Steve Kolanijan), equal credit is due to the *real* talent at work here: the songwriters behind the hits—most notably the team of Roger Greenaway and Roger Cook. Also interesting to hear are the Fortunes' takes on "Gasoline Alley Bred" and especially "Fire Brigade," which should have fans of the Move especially raising an eyebrow or two.

worth searching for: Two of the band's last album releases, *Storm in a Teacup/Here Comes That Rainy Day Feeling Again* (Capitol, 1972 and 1973/Beat Goes On, 1996, prod. Roger Cook, Roger Greenaway), are rife with the group's trademark lush, vocal-heavy balladry—though at the time the Hollies, for one, were having a much better go working this sap-filled trough.

influences:

◄◄ The Cliftones, the Bachelors, David & Jonathan, the Birmingham Chants

►► The Walker Brothers, the Foundations, the Spiral Staircase, the New Seekers

Gary Pig Gold

Foster & Lloyd
/Bill Lloyd

Formed 1987, in Nashville, TN. Disbanded 1992.

Radney Foster (born July 20, 1959 in Del Rio, TX), vocals, guitar; Bill Lloyd (born December 6, 1955, in Bowling Green, KY), vocals, guitar.

Foster & Lloyd's run was short lived but of high quality. They specialized in country-tinged romantic angst cut with a healthy dose of wry detachment. Listening to the three albums they made together summons up wistful memories of one of those heady five-minute timeouts in Nashville (in this case, post-Barbara Mandrell, pre-Garth Brooks) when it seemed as if off-center artists might possibly find a niche. Lyle Lovett, Dwight Yoakam, and Steve Earle were shaking things up, and Rosanne Cash hadn't yet fled to New York. Out of this interesting atmosphere came Radney Foster and Bill Lloyd, along with the O'Kanes—sharp-eyed songwriting teams who turned to performing with the blessing—and creative license—of major recording labels. Foster, a lawyer's son, and Lloyd, an army brat and communications major, didn't fit the traditional country-act mold, coveting greater pop and rock influences than Nashville tolerated at the time. They were, however, writers of hit songs for the likes of the Sweethearts of the Rodeo and Holly Dunn, which gave them strong potential as a recording act. After they split in 1992, Foster followed a more traditional country path, while Lloyd recorded a couple of albums that were pure pop pleasures.

what to buy: *Foster & Lloyd* ♬♬♬♬ (RCA, 1987, prod. Radney Foster, Bill Lloyd) is a charmer—deft songwriting, tight arrangements, enough rockabilly backbeat to keep things hopping, and enough engaging harmony to keep things down-home. The pleading "Don't Go Out with Him," for instance, almost sounds like something the Ronettes could have sung.

what to buy next: The duo's other releases—*Faster and Llouder* ♬♬♬♬ (RCA, 1989, prod. Radney Foster, Bill Lloyd, Rick Will) and *Version of the Truth* ♬♬♬♬ (RCA, 1990, prod. Radney Foster, Bill Lloyd, Rick Will)—weren't quite as good but were still compelling.

solo outings:
Radney Foster:
See What You Want to See N/A (Arista Austin, 1998)

Bill Lloyd:
Set to Pop 🎵🎵🎵 (ESD, 1994)
Feeling the Elephant 🎵🎵🎵 (Bar/None, 1997)

influences:

◀◀ The Beatles, the Eagles, Alabama, Big Star

▶▶ Uncle Tupelo, Whiskeytown

Elizabeth Lynch

Fotheringay

See: Fairport Convention

The Foundations

Formed 1967, in London, England. Disbanded 1970.

Clem Curtis, vocals (1967–68); Colin Young, vocals (1969–70); Allan Warner, guitar, vocals; Peter MacBeth, bass; Tim Harris, drums; Tony Gomez, organ; Pat Burke, tenor sax; Mike Elliott, tenor sax; Eric Allandale, trombone.

Predating such racially integrated British groups as the Specials and the English Beat, the Foundations combined three white Londoners, two Jamaicans, a Trinidadian, a Dominican, and a Ceylonese for a brief but successful foray into R&B-pop. Britain had been importing soul acts for years, but the Foundations marked one of the first home-grown outfits. The group was signed to Pye Records by Tony Macauley, who basically ordered it to sing and play his songs. With Clem Curtis on vocals, the Foundations enjoyed a string of U.K. hits beginning with the Motown-influenced "Baby, Now That I've Found You," a #1 record in England. Colin Young sang the group's U.S. smash, "Build Me Up, Buttercup," a feisty soul-pop record that demonstrated an excellent balance of organ, brass, and call-and-response vocals.

what's available: *The Very Best of the Foundations* 🎵🎵🎵 (Taragon, prod. various) is a worthy compilation of the group's upbeat and uptempo tunes that should appeal to fans of such later British acts as the English Beat, Fine Young Cannibals, and General Public.

influences:

◀◀ Ska, Motown, the Skatalites, Desmond Dekker

▶▶ The Specials, the English Beat, Joboxers, General Public, Fine Young Cannibals

Christopher Scapelliti

Fountains of Wayne

Formed 1995, in New York, NY.

Chris Collingwood, vocals, guitar, keyboards; Adam Schlesinger, drums, guitar, keyboards, vocals; Danny Weinkauf, bass.

When Atlantic Records prepared to release the self-titled record by Fountains of Wayne in 1996, it was faced with the same old problem—how to break an extremely catchy and excessively intelligent pop band to the somewhat homogenized record buyer. Despite the modest successes of Matthew Sweet and the Posies, this barrier has proven hard to break down. But a Grammy nomination for "That Thing You Do," the title song for the film produced by Tom Hanks that was written by Fountains' Adam Schlesinger, brought the group tons of national press and subsequent radio play. From the opening guitar crash of "Radiation Vibe," all pop lovers knew they were in for something special, a unique blend of witty lyrics and vocal harmonies which, coupled with its various production styles, makes the Fountains' debut sound like a collection of unique pop bands. The songs are what matter the most, and chances are you will be humming them for weeks to come. On a similar note, Schlesinger is also the brains behind the more art-synth-mood pop outfit, Ivey.

what to buy: *Fountains of Wayne* 🎵🎵🎵🎵 (Atlantic, 1996, prod. Adam Schlesinger) was easily one of the best records of 1996. The record is a pop rollercoaster of sounds, ranging through various styles of pop, from the moody ballad "Everything's Ruined" to the all-out-pop of "Survival Car" and the Brian Wilson-inspired "Sick Day." Any way you like your pop, it's here.

worth searching for: Like most American pop bands, Fountains of Wayne enjoys significant sales overseas. To capitalize on both the American and European markets, it released several CD singles that contain an array of unreleased material, from demos to live recordings. One of the best is "Sink to the Bottom," whose extra tracks include a live rendition of Electric Light Orchestra's "Can't Get It out of My Head."

influences:

◀◀ Matthew Sweet, the Lemonheads, the Beatles

Chris Richards

The Four Seasons
/Frankie Valli

Formed as the Four Lovers, 1956, in Newark, NJ. Disbanded 1974. Reformed 1980.

Frankie Valli, vocals; Tommy Devito, guitar (1956–70); Nick Devito, guitar (1956–60); Hank Majewski, bass, (1956–60); Bob Gaudio, keyboards (1960–74); Nick Massi, bass (1960–65); others.

Spanning 40 years and boasting more than 100 million records sold, the Four Seasons are the longest surviving and most successful doo-wop group ever. The main focus has always been on Frankie Valli and his soaring three-octave tenor, which shifts with frightening ease. Hopping constantly over the years from frontman to solo performer, Valli has nearly always struck commercial gold, whether it be with the street-corner harmonies of "Sherry" or the unbearable disco dreck of "Grease." The Four Seasons have re-formed countless times (usually for the worse), but by 1976 it was still capable of something as engaging as "December 1963 (Oh What a Night)," which hit #1 and has re-charted with an inhuman regularity ever since—most recently as part of the soundtrack for *Forrest Gump.*

what to buy: Since the band's catalog is a virtually endless stream of repackaged collections of their greatest hits, only the most noteworthy are listed. Pinning down what to buy is maddening as every album has a gem like "Big Girls Don't Cry" and something execrable like "Grease." *25th Anniversary* ♪♪♪♪ (Rhino, 1987, prod. various), a three-disc set, is by far the most comprehensive document of the band's output (including Valli's solo excursions) and contains virtually everything you do and don't want to hear. *Anthology* ♪♪♪♪ (Rhino, 1988, prod. Bill Inglot) is a more streamlined, 26-track single disc that doesn't wallow too long in the disco years.

what to buy next: *Greatest Hits, Vol. 1* ♪♪♪♪ (Rhino, 1991, prod. Bob Crewe) compacts most of the early hits like "Walk like a Man" and "Sherry." *Greatest Hits, Vol. 2* ♪♪♪ (Rhino, 1991, prod. various) focuses more on the later material. If you must own "Swearin' to God" and "Who Loves You," this is probably the most painless of the later-era compilations on the market.

what to avoid: Steer clear of *Dance Album* ♪ (Curb, 1993). We could dance to the originals just fine, thank you.

the rest:
Christmas Album ♪♪ (Rhino, 1967)
Working My Way Back to You and More ♪♪♪♫ (Rhino, 1966)
Rarities, Vol. 1 ♪♪♪ (Rhino, 1990)
Rarities, Vol. 2 ♪♪♪ (Rhino, 1990)
Gold Vault of Hits ♪ (Curb, 1997)
2nd Vault of Hits ♪♪♪ (Curb, 1997)

influences:
◀◀ The Drifters, the Platters, the Penguins
▶▶ The Beach Boys, the Beatles, Billy Joel

Allan Orski

The Four Tops

Formed 1971, in Detroit, MI.

Levi Stubbs; Abdul "Duke" Fakir; Renaldo "Obie" Benson; Lawrence Payton (died 1997).

One of Motown's two mightiest male vocal groups, the Four Tops held its power by remaining intact, while the Temptations, by contrast, came and went. The gruff authority of Levi Stubbs's voice has been a wondrous thing, celebrated in songs by other artists

years later. As a group, few in Motown exemplified the real powerhouse of the label—the songwriting of Holland-Dozier-Holland and the power of the in-house band—as the Tops did. Amid a flurry of mid-'60s hits, the highlight may have been "Reach Out I'll Be There," which kicked off with its heralding flutes and military drumbeats; few songs of support and solidarity have been so grippingly recorded. The group relied on its strong vocals and less on dancing, à la the Tempts, with whom the Tops staged a friendly rivalry at various song "showdowns." But the Tops didn't enjoy a second run of psychedelic hits as did its Motown rivals; in fact, when Holland-Dozier-Holland left the label, so did Stubbs and company. The Tops scored a couple of quick hits in "Keeper of the Castle" and "Ain't No Woman (Like the One I've Got)" in 1972 but had little else on the pop charts afterwards. The 1990 Rock and Roll Hall of Fame inductees continue to tour—even after the death in 1997 of Lawrence Payton from liver cancer at the age of 59—with longtime conductor George Roundtree taking the harmony parts on stage. In all, it shows a remarkable determination for a group consigned to the oldies circuit.

what to buy: The double-length *Anthology* ♪♪♪♪♪ (Motown, 1974/1989, prod. various) spans the Tops' Motown songs, showcasing the group's awesome run of hits.

what to buy next: For a more intense rush of the group's heyday, the silver-covered *Greatest Hits* ♪♪♪♪♪ (Motown, 1967/1987, prod. Holland-Dozier-Holland) is relentless. *Until You Love Someone: More of the Best* ♪♪♪♪ (Rhino, 1993, prod. various) is worthwhile for those who want to delve deeper than the hits.

what to avoid: The group's latest, and last with the original lineup, *Four Tops Christmas* ♪ (Motown, 1995, prod. Four Tops) is a sagging holiday effort in which each of the members produces his own selection and nothing but a visit from Aretha Franklin helps them.

the rest:
Live ♪♪♪ (Motown, 1965/1991)
Four Tops Reach Out ♪♪♪♪ (Motown, 1967/1983)
Still Waters Run Deep ♪♪ (Motown, 1970/1982)
Greatest Hits (1972–76) ♪♪♪ (MCA, 1982/1987)
Great Songs & Performances that Inspired the Motown 25th Anniversary Television Special ♪♪♪♫ (Motown, 1983/1989)
Ain't No Woman . . . ♪♪♪♫ (MCA, 1987/1994)
When She Was My Girl ♪♪ (Mercury, 1992)
Motown Legends: It's the Same Old Song ♪♪♪ (Motown, 1994)
Live and in Concert ♪♪♪ (MCA, 1995)
Keepers of the Castle/Their Best 1972–1978 ♪♪♪ (MCA, 1997)
The Ultimate Collection ♪♪♪♪ (Motown, 1997)

worth searching for: The soundtrack for the film version of *Little Shop of Horrors* (Geffen, 1986, prod. Bob Gaudio) features Stubbs as the wickedly soulful voice of the man-eating plant.

influences:

◄◄ The Orioles, the Drifters, the Moonglows

▶▶ The Temptations, Darius Rucker (Hootie & the Blowfish), Boyz II Men

Roger Catlin

The Fourmost /The Four Jays /The Four Mosts /Format

Formed 1958, in Liverpool, England.

Brian O'Hara, guitar, vocals; Billy Hatton, bass, vocals; Joey Bowers, guitar, vocals (1958–61, 1969–95); Brian Redmen, drums (1958–62); Mike Millward, guitar, vocals (1961–65); Dave Lovelady, drums (1962–1995); Freddie Self, guitar (1965); Bill Parkinson, guitar, vocals (1966); George Peckham, guitar, vocals (1966–68).

Although they actually performed rock 'n' roll at Liverpool's legendary Cavern Club *before* the Beatles were ever deemed worthy enough to, the Fourmost's subsequent career was inextricably linked to the Fab Four's—no doubt due to the fact it shared the same manager (Brian Epstein) and producer (George Martin) and, as a result, was given Lennon/McCartney songs to record on a regular basis. Ironically, what ultimately doomed this more-than-competent beat combo was its taking the sort of career advice from Epstein that John Lennon, for one, would certainly have had nothing to do with. For example, when the group should have been out on the road promoting its first records, "Eppy" had the Fourmost bound to the stage of the London Palladium for *eight* straight months, performing alongside Frankie Vaughan and Cilla Black in an antiquated variety show called *Startime*. At least the wholesome on-stage banter and knock-about humor the band was forced to develop while trapped there came in handy when, after a string of flop 45s, the Fourmost found itself exiled to the cabaret-and-supper-club circuit, where it gallantly remains to this day.

what's available: The group's one and only original album, *First and Fourmost* ♫♫♫♪ (Parlophone, 1965/EMI, 1997, prod. George Martin), is an exuberant if extremely rote collection of American pop-rock material, with the band's infamous sense of zaniness—no doubt encouraged by *Goon Show* enthusiast Martin—allowed to creep through every so often.

influences:

◄◄ The Beatles, the Coasters, the Four Tops, George Formby

▶▶ The Barron Knights, the Rockin' Berries, the Turtles, Bonzo Dog Doo-Dah Band

Gary Pig Gold

Kim Fox

Born November 18, 1969, in New York, NY.

Although she signed with DreamWorks during 1996, "The Year of the Woman in Rock," Kim Fox's talents do not quite fit the mold of her Lilith Fair counterparts. A product of the Vassar College opera program, the diminutive urbanite switched to pop in 1994, but has yet to sever the tendrils of her classical training.

what's available: On *Moon Hut* ♫♫ (Dreamworks SKG, 1997, prod. Clyde Lieberman), Fox's classical remnants are both refreshing and hindering. Still unsure of herself in the role of the pop singer, her vocals come off as stilted and unsure. At times this works to her advantage, as on a cover of Bruce Springsteen's pained and desolate "Atlantic City," or in "Flowers Have O's," a haunting ode to Helium's Mary Timony. Mostly, though, it's hard to be engaged by someone who sounds like she'd rather be hiding behind the music. On the upside, Fox's compositional chops are a force to be reckoned with, and the album showcases her amazing command of the piano.

influences:

◄◄ Tori Amos, Jill Sobule, Helium

Isaac Josephson

Samantha Fox

Born April 15, 1966, in London, England.

Discovered by photographers for the *Daily Sun* newspaper at the tender age of 16, Samantha Fox posed topless for the British publication's notorious Page Two pinup portrait enough times to become the most popular model ever featured there. From that point, it was a short hop to a career as a producer-developed dance diva. Her debut single in 1986, "Touch Me," traded on the same trend that made sexy dance sirens such as Madonna and Taylor Dayne worldwide hits—solid grooves, sexually charged lyrics, and barely there melodies. Although that record did well, it wasn't until her second album that the former model hit big, welding her sultry image to a perfectly suitable song, "Naughty Girls (Need Love Too)." Continuing her production-by-committee approach to assembling albums (15 different producers), Fox offered two more albums of new music. When the bottom fell out of dance pop during the early '90s, Fox's singing career went with it, though she gamely tried her hand at acting. There're always newspapers to be sold. . . .

what to buy: Since all that really matters is the singles, a fan's best bet is her *Greatest Hits* ♫♫♫ (Jive, 1992, prod. various), a fine assembly of her best-known cuts without the filler.

the rest:

Touch Me ♫♫♫ (Jive, 1986)

Peter Frampton (© Ken Settle)

Samantha Fox 🎵🎵🎵 (Jive, 1987)
Rocking with My Radio 🎵🎵 (Genie, 1987)
I Wanna Have Some Fun 🎵🎵 (Jive, 1989)
Remix Collection 🎵🎵 (Alex, 1990)
Just One Night 🎵 (Jive, 1991)
Best Is Yet to Come 🎵🎵 (Alex, 1993)
Collection 🎵🎵 (Alex, 1995)

worth searching for: If you can find it, an interview-only picture disc from 1991 features one of Fox's old topless photos, providing a glimpse of her, um, revealing past.

influences:

◀◀ Madonna, Donna Summer

▶▶ Mariah Carey, Adina Howard

Eric Deggans

Peter Frampton
Born April 22, 1950, in Beckenham, England.

It would have taken a certain prescience to peg Peter Frampton

as pop music's biggest superstar of the pre-*Thriller* era. Before 1976, when *Frampton Comes Alive* made him a mass market phenomenon, Frampton enjoyed a reputation as an estimable guitarist, singer, and songwriter, logging moderately successful tenures with the Herd and Humble Pie. After leaving the latter in 1971, Frampton embarked on a solo career that was only modestly successful—but building—until the live album heard 'round the world. Some bad decisions followed that breakthrough, however, including the fallow follow-up ballad "I'm in You" and an ill-advised starring role in the wretched *Sgt. Pepper's Lonely Hearts Club Band* movie. Those undermined whatever cache Frampton had built for himself, and through the '80s and '90s he's mostly been the answer to a "What ever happened to. . .?" question. None of his periodic comebacks—including a spot in David Bowie's band during 1987 and a *Frampton Comes Alive II* release in 1995—have taken flight, and a reunion with Humble Pie mate Steve Marriott tragically crashed when Marriott died in a 1991 house fire.

what to buy: *Shine On: A Collection* 🎵🎵🎵🎵 (A&M, 1992, prod. various) offers a solid overview of Frampton's career, making a case for the strong—if not overwhelming—solo albums that preceded *Frampton Comes Alive*. It also includes two songs he recorded with Marriott during early 1991.

what to buy next: Go ahead; everybody else owns *Frampton Comes Alive* 𝄢𝄢𝄢 (A&M, 1976, prod. Peter Frampton), and you should, too. Its energetic performances are still infectious, even if the "spontaneous" crowd outbursts do get tired.

what to avoid: Sidestep just about anything after *Frampton Comes Alive*.

the rest:
Wind of Change 𝄢𝄢 (A&M, 1972)
Frampton's Camel 𝄢𝄢𝄢 (A&M, 1973)
Something's Happening 𝄢𝄢 (A&M, 1974)
Frampton 𝄢𝄢𝄢 (A&M, 1975)
I'm in You 𝄢𝄢 (A&M, 1977)
Where I Should Be 𝄢 (A&M, 1979)
Breaking All the Rules 𝄢𝄢 (A&M, 1981)
The Art of Control 𝄢 (A&M, 1982)
Premonition 𝄢𝄢 (Atlantic, 1986)
When All the Pieces Fit 𝄢 (Atlantic, 1989)
Peter Frampton 𝄢𝄢 (Relativity, 1994)
Frampton Comes Alive II 𝄢𝄢 (Relativity, 1995)

worth searching for: Frampton guests on a couple of songs on the Grand Funk Railroad live album *Bosnia* (EMI-Capitol, 1997, prod. Ron Nevison).

influences:
◀◀ The Shadows, the Beatles, the Searchers

▶▶ Bryan Adams, Tom Cochrane

Gary Graff

Connie Francis

Born Concetta Rosa Maria Franconero, December 12, 1938, in Newark, NJ.

Along with Brenda Lee, Connie Francis was the most popular female rock singer between the rise of Elvis Presley and the arrival of the Beatles. She had 35 Top 40 hits between 1958 and 1964, including three #1s: "Everybody's Somebody's Fool," "My Heart Has a Mind of Its Own," and "Don't Break the Heart That Loves You." But Francis more closely resembled a pop singer of the classic mold than she did a rock 'n' roller. An Italian-American from New Jersey, young Connie showed her musical precociousness at age three when she learned to play accordion; by age 10 she was performing on local television. When she began recording, Francis's popularity crossed from pop into country, R&B, and film markets as well. Francis's material ranged from new songs from the likes of Jeff Barry, Ellie Greenwich, and John Loudermilk to the tunes of such classic

pop writers as Sammy Cahn, Jule Styne, and Jimmy Van Heusen, making her popular with both teens and their parents. She starred in four films: *Where the Boys Are* (which included one of her biggest hits), *Follow the Boys, Looking for Love,* and *When the Boys Meet the Girls*. She frequently recorded new vocal tracks for her hit singles in Italian, Spanish, and other languages; by the time her hits stopped coming in the mid-'60s, Francis had developed a substantial international market. Francis's status as a teen idol decreased dramatically as rock grew more rebellious in the late '60s, and medical problems and a traumatic rape and robbery kept her from performing for much of the '70s and '80s. But lately, nostalgic listeners have grown to appreciate the talent that made her the best-selling female singer of her time.

what to buy: *The Very Best of Connie Francis* 𝄢𝄢𝄢 (Polydor, 1986, compilation prod. Tim Rogers) contains most of Francis's biggest pop singles, including the chart-topping "My Heart Has a Mind of Its Own" and "Don't Break the Heart That Loves You." Also, "Everybody's Somebody's Fool," from 1962, was a cross-format smash, and "Second-Hand Love" is a Phil Spector tune recorded in Nashville.

what to buy next: *Souvenirs* 𝄢𝄢𝄢 (Polydor, 1996, compilation prod. Don Charles, Bill Levenson, Patrick Niglio) provides a wide-ranging overview of Francis's recordings during her heyday, from her first single, 1958's "Who's Sorry Now," to 1969's "Zingara (Gypsy)," her final single for MGM. In between, there are all her major hits; pop, country, and R&B songs; plus tunes in Italian, Spanish, and Hebrew.

what to avoid: Too many of Francis's original recordings remain in print to settle for the remakes on *Greatest Hits* 𝄢𝄢 (Dominion, 1994).

the rest:
Greatest Hits 𝄢𝄢𝄢 (Polydor)
Greatest Italian Hits 𝄢𝄢𝄢 (Polydor)
The Very Best of Connie Francis, Vol. II 𝄢𝄢 (Polydor, 1988)
Where the Hits Are 𝄢𝄢 (Malaco, 1990)
Hits Of 𝄢𝄢 (Sound Choice, 1992)
Best of Connie Francis 𝄢𝄢𝄢 (PolyGram Special Markets, 1996)
Christmas in My Heart 𝄢𝄢𝄢 (Polydor, 1996)
The Return Concert: Live at Trump's Castle 𝄢𝄢 (Sony, 1996)
Swinging Connie Francis 𝄢𝄢𝄢 (Audiophile, 1996)
Where the Boys Are: Connie Francis in Hollywood 𝄢𝄢𝄢 (Rhino, 1997)
On Guard 𝄢𝄢𝄢 (Jazz Band, 1997)
Christmas Cheer 𝄢𝄢 (PolyGram Special Markets, 1997)
Italian Collection, Vol. 1 𝄢𝄢𝄢 (PGD, 1997)
Italian Collection, Vol. 2 𝄢𝄢𝄢 (PGD, 1997)

worth searching for: The German label Bear Family has issued the duets Francis recorded in 1964 with Hank Williams Jr. on *Sing Great Country Favourites* (Bear Family), which are worth hearing mainly for the sheer strangeness of the concept. Bear Family has also released two five-CD box sets of Francis's recordings: *White Sox, Pink Lipstick . . . and Stupid Cupid* (Bear Family, 1994) and *Kissin' Twistin' Goin' Where the Boys Are* (Bear Family, 1996). *De Colección* (Polydor, 1995) is a collection of Spanish-language tunes, including "Besame Mucho" and "Vaya Con Dios."

influences:

◀◀ Kay Starr, Jo Stafford, Patti Page

▶▶ Brenda Lee, Petula Clark

Brian Mansfield

The Frank & Walters

Formed 1990, in Cork, Ireland.

Paul Linehan, vocals, bass; Ashley Keating, drums; Niall Linehan, guitars.

Though the Frank & Walters has yet to develop its own identity—the trio's sound is a little bit Smiths, a little bit Kinks, a little bit Wonder Stuff—it plays the kind of tight, sprightly rock 'n' roll that stays afloat no matter what's in vogue. Excellent songwriters, the Franks worked day jobs in Ireland (Paul Linehan was an antique furniture restorer, while Ashley Keating served in the Irish Navy for four years) before moving to Brooklyn to make music their full-time career. After four albums (just one, plus an EP, released in the United States), the eight-year-old trio is just getting started; there's definitely talent here, but it still hasn't jelled completely.

what to buy: The band's U.S. debut, *Grand Parade* 🎵🎵🎵 (Red Ink/Setanta, 1998, prod. David Couse, Frank & Walters), would have fit right in with the jangly early-'80s rock movement led by R.E.M. and Let's Active—Niall Linehan's guitars are strong and sharp, and his brother Paul sings with personable melancholy. "How Can I Exist" is a conventional can't-live-without-you song, but the fresher "Mrs. Xavier" is about a romance with a widow who has "worked for so long you don't know anymore."

what to buy next: The EP *Indian Ocean* 🎵🎵🎵 (Red Ink/Setanta, 1997, prod. David Couse, Frank & Walters, Cenzo Townshend, Liz Roberts) came out in the United States just before *Grand Parade*. With a live acoustic version of the well-written "Little Dolls" and non-CD songs such as "Fast Anthony," it's a nice complement to the debut. But unless you're fascinated with the Franks, *Grand Parade* is sufficient.

influences:

◀◀ The Smiths, the Wonder Stuff, the Beatles, Edwyn Collins

Steve Knopper

Frankie Goes to Hollywood

Formed 1982, in Liverpool, England. Disbanded 1988.

William "Holly" Johnson, vocals; Mark O'Toole, bass; Paul Rutherford, vocals, dancing; Brian Nash, guitar; Peter Gill, drums.

Frankie Goes to Hollywood changed the landscape of British pop music when it released the double-length debut, *Welcome to the Pleasuredome*, in 1984. Mixing bombastic attitude, overtly hedonistic themes, and unorthodox covers (Bruce Springsteen's "Born to Run") with irresistible originals, the record was nothing short of a revelation at a time when England was overflowing with tame synthesizer bands. Frankiemania lived, including a series of T-shirts and badges bearing legends such as "Frankie Say War! Arm Yourself." What started out with a bang, however, ultimately ended in a bust. Due to its massive exposure with the first LP and growing dissension within the group, FGTH's second and final disc, *Liverpool*, died quietly shortly after its release in 1986. While various members of the group tried to carry on with solo careers, none ever came close to repeating the success of FGTH's debut.

what to buy: *Welcome to the Pleasure Dome* 🎵🎵🎵 (ZTT/Island, 1984, prod. Trevor Horn) was very much a product of producer and ZTT head Horn's studio adventures. A majority of the songs on the double-album surfaced in the British charts following the album's release, and for good reason. Singles such as "Relax," "Two Tribes," and "The Power of Love" were immaculate slices of pop, mixing a gritty disco bite with charming melodies and smart sonic finesse.

what to avoid: *Liverpool* 🎵 (ZTT/Island, 1986, prod. Stephen Lipson, Trevor Horn) captured the band at an obvious creative void. Containing only eight tracks and offering a pair of insignificant singles ("Watching the Wildlife" and "Rage Hard"), it served as a pathetic finale to the group's fleeting career.

worth searching for: *Bang!. . .The Greatest Hits of Frankie Goes to Hollywood* (ZTT, 1993, prod. various) is a European collection that presents an agreeably tight winnowing of the group's flash 'n' bang success.

solo outings:

Holly Johnson:
Blast **woof!** (Uni, 1989)
Hollelujah **woof!** (MCA EP, 1990)
Dreams That Money Can't Buy **woof!** (MCA, 1991)

Paul Rutherford:
Oh World **woof!** (ZTT/Island, 1989)

influences:

◀◀ Village People, Duran Duran, the Sex Pistols, Burt Bacharach

Aretha Franklin (© Ken Settle)

▶▶ Sigue Sigue Sputnik, Pet Shop Boys, Seal

Aidin Vaziri

Aretha Franklin

Born March 25, 1942, in Memphis, TN.

For the daughter of famous Detroit preacher C.L. Franklin, gospel was second nature. Having achieved young stardom in the gospel world, Aretha Franklin's first venture to the secular world was an uneasy one at Columbia Records. But Atlantic's Jerry Wexler pursued her after her contract ran out. Together they made an astounding string of classics during the late '60s that not only defined soul music but also crowned her "Queen of Soul" for life. Besides being a joy to hear, Franklin's work was also culturally significant, helping to define black self-awareness at a time when a little bit of R-E-S-P-E-C-T was much needed. Her continued success seems tied to her various recording companies; none could match Atlantic, but she enjoyed odd bouts of success once more on Arista during the early '80s and a major comeback in 1998, with a hit, "A Rose Is

a Rose," written and produced by Lauryn Hill of the Fugees. Her study of classical music was a help when she pitched in at the last minute for an ill Luciano Pavarotti during the 1998 Grammys to sing "Nessun Dorma."

what to buy: *I Never Loved a Man (The Way I Loved You)* 🎵🎵🎵🎵 (Atlantic, 1967, prod. Jerry Wexler) is a startling achievement. There's no way her Atlantic debut could have been more electrifying. With the Muscle Shoals backing and Wexler production, it includes her searing "Respect" as well as the enduring "Do Right Woman, Do Right Man" and "Dr. Feelgood."

what to buy next: If your billfold is thick enough, the opulently packaged box set *The Queen of Soul* 🎵🎵🎵🎵 (Rhino/Atlantic, 1992, prod. various) has it all—the hits, the surprises, the achievements of her career. In an economic pinch, *30 Greatest Hits* 🎵🎵🎵🎵 (Atlantic, 1968, prod. various) distills the hit period. *Amazing Grace* 🎵🎵🎵🎵 (Atlantic, 1972, prod. Jerry Wexler, Arif Mardin, Aretha Franklin) is her triumphant return to gospel. *Aretha's Greatest Hits (1980–1994)* 🎵🎵🎵🎵 (Arista, 1994, prod. various) shows she's still able to sing with soul even when the material is uneven.

what to avoid: On *La Diva* 𝄞 (Atlantic, 1979), Lady Soul gets stuck in the disco period.

best of the rest:

Lady Soul 𝄞𝄞𝄞𝄞 (Atlantic, 1968)
Aretha Sings the Blues 𝄞𝄞𝄞 (Columbia, 1980/1985)
Jump to It 𝄞𝄞𝄞 (Arista, 1982/1998)
Who's Zoomin' Who? 𝄞𝄞𝄞 (Arista, 1985)
From Jazz to Soul 𝄞𝄞𝄞𝄞 (Columbia Legacy, 1992)
The Very Best of Aretha Franklin, Vol. 1 𝄞𝄞𝄞𝄞 (Rhino, 1994)
The Very Best of Aretha Franklin, Vol. 2 𝄞𝄞𝄞𝄞 (Rhino, 1994)
Love Songs 𝄞𝄞𝄞𝄞 (Rhino, 1997)
The Early Years 𝄞𝄞𝄞 (Columbia, 1997)
The Delta Meets Detroit 𝄞𝄞𝄞𝄞 (Rhino, 1998)
A Rose Is Still a Rose 𝄞𝄞𝄞𝄞 (Arista, 1998)

worth searching for: *The Gospel Soul of Aretha Franklin* (Checker, 1956/Chess, 1991) captures Franklin tearin' it up in church at age 14; likewise, *One Lord, One Faith, One Baptism* (Arista, 1987), one of many out-of-print Aretha albums, finds her back in church, electrifying as ever.

influences:

◀◀ Celia Ward, Ruth Brown, the Rev. C.L. Franklin, Sam Cooke, Mahalia Jackson

▶▶ Whitney Houston, Anita Baker, Chaka Khan

Roger Catlin

Freakwater

Formed 1983, in Louisville, KY.

Catherine Irwin, vocals, guitar; Janet Bean, vocals, guitar; David Gay, bass (1989–present); Bob Egan, pedal steel, mandolin (1994–95); Max Johnston, mandolin, pedal steel (1996–present).

Friends from childhood, Catherine Irwin and Janet Bean began blending their voices to old Carter Family and Loretta Lynn songs in Bean's parents' basement and continued to collaborate when Bean moved to Chicago to join her future husband, Rick Rizzo, in the rock band Eleventh Dream Day, for which she plays drums and sings backing vocals. Freakwater anticipated the rise of the insurgent-country movement—a reaction to Nashville-bred commercialism led by the underground rock community during the '90s.

what to buy: On *Old Paint* 𝄞𝄞𝄞𝄞 (Thrill Jockey, 1995, prod. Brad Wood, Freakwater) and the even more accomplished *Springtime* 𝄞𝄞𝄞𝄞 (Thrill Jockey, 1998, prod. Brendan Burke, Freakwater), Irwin's songs dominate and with good reason: their spiritual resolve in the face of sometimes tragic circumstances is timeless.

what to buy next: With *Dancing under Water* 𝄞𝄞𝄞 (Amoeba, 1991, prod. Brad Wood) and *Feels like the Third Time* 𝄞𝄞𝄞 (Thrill Jockey, 1993, prod. Brad Wood, Freakwater), the duo's

splendid high-and-lonesome harmonies and string band instrumentation are split between a batch of well-chosen covers and a handful of Irwin originals, most notably "Drunk Friend" from the latter. (The debut album, *Freakwater,* and *Dancing under Water* were later repackaged together on a single CD.)

the rest:

Freakwater 𝄞𝄞𝄞 (Amoeba, 1989)

worth searching for: *June 6, 1994* (Glitterhouse, 1994) presents a terse career overview from a German concert, with between-songs banter adding an element of humor not always evident in the songs.

influences:

◀◀ The Carter Family, Loretta Lynn, Gram Parsons, Emmylou Harris, Sweethearts of the Rodeo

▶▶ Uncle Tupelo, Wilco, Son Volt

see also: *Eleventh Dream Day*

Greg Kot

Freddie & the Dreamers

Formed 1959, in Manchester, England. Disbanded 1970.

Freddie Garrity (born November 14, 1936, in Manchester, England), vocals; Derek Quinn, guitar, harmonica; Roy Crewsdon, guitar, keyboards; Pete Birrell, bass, accordion; Bernie Dwyer, drums.

Freddie Garrity and his band the Dreamers seemed content to be the clown princes of the British Invasion, leap-frogging into the hearts of the least musically discriminating during the mid-1960s with a string of cotton-candy hits and dozens of film and television appearances. Today, such an outfit would undoubtedly tour alongside Weird Al Yankovic—between guest spots on the Cartoon Network, that is—but back in their glory days the Dreamers racked up impressive sales both overseas and in the United States. It all began when, tiring of life as a milkman, Garrity used his Buddy Holly resemblance to front various bands in the north of England before forming what eventually became the Dreamers. Producer/composer John Barry discovered the band in 1963 and quickly arranged a recording test; duly contracted to the Columbia label, the group's very first release shot to #3 on the U.K. charts. Beatles manager Brian Epstein then stepped in to help the group score its first U.S. hit, "I'm Telling You Now," whereupon a savvy record company executive decided to fashion Garrity's gyrations into a new dance craze: the resulting ditty, "Do the Freddie," was quickly recorded (with nary a Dreamer in sight) and sent into the American Top 20. Success was short-lived however, and by 1970 the band was no more. Garrity, nevertheless, continues to leap through Merseybeat reunions and similar nostalgia-fests, seemingly as energetically as he did in his long-lost youth.

what's available: The suspiciously titled *Best of Freddie & the Dreamers: The Definitive Collection* ♬♬♬ (EMI Tower, 1992, compilation prod. Ron Furmanek) is an adequate, if slightly padded, sampling of the band's work.

worth searching for: Tucked away on the soundtrack for the band's 1965 cinematic milestone *Seaside Swingers* (Mercury, 1965, prod. John Burgess) is a bizarre, possibly-ahead-of-its-time six-minute track titled "What's Cookin'" which, even without the accompanying images of the band dressed in egg-splattered chef uniforms, easily makes the soft-boiled psychedelia of "I Am the Walrus" seem downright quaint by comparison. Garrity's act always was as much visual as it was musical, so the various *Hullabaloo* and *Shindig* video compilations might also help the curious understand, and perhaps even appreciate, the Dreamers' own particular brand of acrobatic pop.

influences:

◀◀ Al Jolson, James Ray, the Shadows

▶▶ The Monkees, Madness, *Sweatin' to the Oldies*

Gary Pig Gold

Freddy Jones Band

Formed 1991, in South Bend, IN.

Marty Lloyd, vocals, acoustic and electric guitar; Wayne Healy, vocals, guitars, talk box; Jim Bonaccorsi, bass (1990–98); Rob Bonaccorsi, vocals, lead electrics, slide guitar, mandolin (1990–98); Simon Horrocks, drums, percussion, acoustic guitar, mandolin; Mark Murphy, bass (1998).

Rockers in a Southern-comfort vein, the Freddy Jones Band evokes comparisons to the Allman Brothers, a funky Hootie & the Blowfish, a little bit of Little Feat, and even some Dave Matthews Band. The boys in this band have been known to deliver more than a little blues, and vocalize at times like the BoDeans. But when it's all packaged up, the best description is good ol' roots rock. Formed as a duo by Marty Lloyd and Wayne Healy, who allegedly named the band after a guy who helped them fix a flat tire on the way to a gig, they moved back to their native Chicago and expanded the lineup. Eventually, they started double-dating with Southern rockers Sister Hazel, gaining fans and a higher profile. In late March of '98, however, the Bonaccorsi brothers were out of the band, the inevitable "musical differences" was cited as the reason, and Mark Murphy joined the remaining members as they honored tour commitments for their latest release, *Lucid*.

what to buy: *Freddy Jones Band* ♬♬♬♩ (self-released, 1992/Capricorn, 1994, prod. Freddy Jones Band, Craig Williams,

Justin Niebank) is a wonderful example of tuneful, eloquent roots rock. Smooth, immaculate harmonies and instrumentation abound. *Lucid* ♬♬♬♬ (Capricorn, 1997, prod. David Z.) is a more fully realized, cohesive album than this band's earlier Capricorn efforts. "Wonder" and "Mystic Buzz" were well received by radio.

what to buy next: *Waiting for the Night* ♬♬♬♩ (Capricorn, 1993, prod. Justin Niebank) shows the band's musical versatility and blues edge, and "Crosscut Saw" has got some really swingin' Hammond action.

the rest:

North Avenue Wake up Call ♬♬♬ (Capricorn, 1995)

influences:

◀◀ Allman Brothers Band, the BoDeans, Little Feat, Crowded House, the Eagles

Lynne Margolis

Free

Formed 1968, in London, England. Disbanded 1971. Re-formed 1972. Disbanded 1973.

Paul Rodgers, vocals; Paul Kossoff (died March 19, 1976, in New York, NY), guitar (1968–72); Andy Fraser, bass, (1968–71); Simon Kirke, drums; Tetsu Yamauchi, bass (1972–73); John "Rabbit" Bundrick, keyboards (1972–73).

Along with Cream, Free's tough, spartan brand of hard rock provided a prototype for '70s arena rock—a model its own members would follow in groups such as Bad Company and Backstreet Crawler. Formed in the blues-drenched London pubs—and named by British music icon Alexis Korner—the quartet's assets were the envy of its colleagues: Paul Rodgers was one of the scene's richest, most passionate singers; Simon Kirke was as solid a drummer as you'd find; Paul Kossoff was an estimable guitar player; and Andy Fraser crafted inventive, lyrical bass parts. It all coalesces on Free's enduring hit, "All Right Now," in which Rodgers wails over a taut groove provided by Kossoff and Kirke, while Fraser's bass swoops in on the choruses to drive the song into another dimension. Free split up briefly in 1971, and when it got back together the following year, Kossoff and Fraser had moved on to Backstreet Crawler and the Sharks, respectively. Rodgers and Kirke kept Free alive until 1973, when they became part of the burgeoning Bad Company.

what to buy: The two-disc *Molten Gold: The Anthology* ♬♬♬♬ (A&M/Chronicles, 1993, prod. various) is a well-chosen overview of Free favorites, its only mistake being the inclusion of a live rendition of "Fire and Water" rather than the more economical studio version.

what to buy next: *Fire and Water* ♫♫♫♪ (A&M, 1970, prod. Free) is as good an album as Free produced, featuring the title track and the seminal "All Right Now."

what to avoid: *Heartbreaker* ♫♫ (Island, 1973, prod. Free, Andy Johns) has an ace in "Wishing Well" but mostly makes you wonder why the group got back together to make this diminished work.

the rest:
Best of Free ♫♫♫ (A&M, 1975)

worth searching for: *Message to Love: The Isle of Wight Festival 1970* (Essential/Castle, 1995, prod. Jon Astley, Andy Macpherson) opens with Free performing a hot rendition of "All Right Now."

influences:

◄◄ John Mayall's Bluesbreakers, the Yardbirds, the Rolling Stones, Sonny Boy Williamson, John Lee Hooker

►► Bad Company, Backstreet Crawler, Foreigner, Kiss

see also: *Bad Company*

Gary Graff

Gary Frenay
See: The Flashcubes

John French
See: Captain Beefheart

French, Frith, Kaiser & Thompson
See: Richard Thompson

Frente!
Formed 1989, in Melbourne, Australia.

Angie Hart, vocals; Simon Austin, guitars, piano, vocals; Alastair Barden, drums; Tim O'Connor, bass (1989–95); Bill McDonald, bass, guitar (1995–present).

With Angie Hart's sweet, angelic vocals and Simon Austin's shimmering guitar tones, Frente! is a breath of fresh air in the primarily stagnant alternative rock scene. Named after the Spanish word for "front," the Australian group plays easy-on-the-ears pop that's melodic and nicely framed, if not exactly earth-shakingly original. It was good enough to put a single, a cover of New Order's "Bizarre Love Triangle," in the Top 40, though Frente!'s sophomore effort did not fair as well commercially.

what to buy: Frente!'s debut, *Marvin: The Album* ♫♫♫ (Mammoth/Atlantic, 1994, prod. Michael Koppelman, Frente!) spawned the group's two best-known songs—"Labour of Love"

and the acoustic cover of New Order's "Bizarre Love Triangle." A refreshing listen.

the rest:
Shape ♫♫♫♪ (Mammoth/Atlantic, 1996)

influences:

◄◄ Spanky & Our Gang, the Mamas & the Papas, the Cranberries, the Sundays

►► Getaway Cruiser, Sneaker Pimps

Christina Fuoco

Gavin Friday
Born Fionan Hanvey, October 8, 1959, in Dublin, Ireland.

Friends with U2's Bono Hewson since the two were teenagers, Gavin Friday has built a fascinating career ranging from artsy punk rock to flamboyant yet sensitive and thought-provoking post-cabaret pop. Beginning in the late '70s, he served as co-frontman for the Virgin Prunes, an undeniably weird, androgynous goth-punk band. Dadaist and decidedly anti-commercial, the Prunes split up in 1986, feeling that they had lost their sense of spontaneity. After taking some time off from music to concentrate on painting, Friday returned in 1989 with the darkly romantic *Each Man Kills the Thing He Loves*, his first collaboration with keyboardist and "musical director" Maurice Seezer. While with the Prunes, Friday's vocals already leaned towards the style of pre-WWII German cabaret music. In his solo career, he has plunged himself more fully into that milieu, incorporating whimsical arrangements with dissonant organ riffs, evocative clarinet lines, and near-comical beats. Like the work of Kurt Weill and Bertolt Brecht, Friday's songs unearth the seamier side of human nature. He examines the lives of everyone from suburban homemakers to saucy transvestites, and somehow manages to find both humor and pathos in all of them. As a live performer, he combines punkish intensity with loungy theatricality in a way that suggests a Bowie/Bono composite. It remains to be seen whether Friday will someday progress from cult status to full-scale stardom, but he has already established himself as a unique and dynamic musical figure whose every move deserves attention.

what to buy: A remarkably original album that veers from deep emotion to loopy humor, *Adam 'n' Eve* ♫♫♫♪ (Island, 1992, prod. Hal Willner, Flood, Dave Bascombe) marks the height of Friday's still-developing style. Maria McKee adds affecting vocal parts on two songs, particularly the strange and wondrous "Falling off the Edge of the World." The Marc Bolan-influenced "King of Trash" was a minor modern-rock hit.

what to buy next: Although *Shag Tobacco* ♫♫♫♪ (Island, 1995, prod. Tim Simenon) benefits sonically from Tim Simenon's (Bomb the Bass) full, glossy production, some of the feeling gets lost in the overly synthetic sound. Still, "Angel" is a gloriously dreamy piece of dance-pop, and "Kitchen Sink Drama" paints a subtly heartbreaking tale of a housewife sinking all too willingly into depression.

the rest:

The Boxer Soundtrack 🐾🐾🐾♥ (MCA, 1998, prod. Gavin Friday, Maurice Seezer)

worth searching for: Darker than *Adam 'n' Eve* and more directly influenced by '30s German cabaret songs, Friday and the Man Seezer's *Each Man Kills the Thing He Loves* (Island, 1989, prod. Hal Willner) is out of print in the United States and not easy to track down, but it's definitely worth the search. Easier to find, but only offering a couple of Friday/Bono duets, the soundtrack to *In the Name of the Father* (Island, 1994, prod. various) is still worth picking up, especially for "You Made Me the Thief of Your Heart," a brilliant hip-hop/Irish orchestral folk hybrid that Friday, Seezer, and Bono wrote for Sinéad O'Connor.

influences:

◀◀ Jacques Brel, Kurt Weill, T. Rex, Serge Gainsbourg, Tom Waits, Pet Shop Boys, Marc Almond

▶▶ U2, Björk

Bob Remstein

Friends of Dean Martinez

Formed 1995, in Tucson, AZ.

Bill Elm, steel guitar; Joey Burns, guitar, bass; Van Christian, drums; Tom Larkins, percussion; John Convertino, percussion.

Somewhere between alt-country and New Lounge lies this group from Tucson, Arizona. The name is not, in fact, mocking the classic crooner—after releasing its first single as Friends of Dean Martin, the group changed its moniker after word came down from Deano's legal department. Its sound is all instrumental, taken from the surf rock 'n' roll of the late '50s but infused with both a country twang and a Rat Pack sensibility. Led by Bill Elm's steel guitar, the band members are all members, current or former, of Giant Sand and Naked Prey. The Friends would like you to know that it is *still* available for parties, weddings, and soundtracks.

what to buy: *Retrograde* 🐾🐾🐾 (Sub Pop, 1997, prod. Bill Elm, Craig Schumacher) pushes the limits of what the group accomplished in the past. Tracks such as "Rattler" and the cover of Henry Mancini's "Lonesome" languidly slide off of Elm's guitar, evoking an image of the Southwest through beatnick glasses.

what to buy next: Just prior to releasing *The Shadow of Your Smile* 🐾🐾🐾 (Sub Pop, 1995, prod. Friends of Dean Martinez), the band changed its name to pacify the legal forces of Dean

Martin. More surf and less experimental than *Retrograde*, this album is nonetheless a great place to begin your friendship with this band. Giant Sand leader Howe Gelb guests.

influences:

◀◀ Santo & Johnny, Dick Dale, Henry Mancini, Dean Martin

Anders Wright

Robert Fripp
/League of Crafty Guitarists
/Fripp & Eno
/Sylvian & Fripp
/Fripp & Summers

Born May 16, 1946, in Dorset, England.

Primarily known and revered as the leader of King Crimson, Robert Fripp is a tireless musician/producer/collaborator whose love of playing and of challenging new situations (not to mention the demand for his distinctive guitar styles) has led to a bulging solo catalog and a vast array of collaborations. He's teamed with musical conceptualist Brian Eno of Roxy Music, former Japan frontman David Sylvian, and guitarist Andy Summers of the Police. He started a New Wave-ish dance rock quartet, the League of Gentlemen, with ex-XTC keyboardist Barry Andrews, Gang of Four bassist-to-be Sara Lee, and drummer Jonny Toobad, and also formed the League of Crafty Guitarists, an outgrowth of his Guitar Craft school. Fripp has also remixed his catalogs, including all of King Crimson's output, for release on CD, finally starting his own label, Discipline. Even as King Crimson continues to release albums, however sporadically, on a major label (currently Virgin), Discipline has enabled Fripp to issue more from his various projects.

what to buy: *The Essential Fripp and Eno* 🐾🐾🐾🐾 (Caroline, 1994, prod. Robert Fripp, Brian Eno) collects both side-long tracks from 1973's *(No Pussyfooting)*, half of 1975's *Evening Star*, and four linked tracks from an unissued third album. The '73 album is the most essential; towering edifices of sound are constructed by putting Fripp's soaring guitar lines through Eno's processing. Fripp's first solo album, *Exposure* 🐾🐾🐾🐾 (EG, 1979, prod. Robert Fripp), features Peter Gabriel (the best version of his "Here Comes the Flood"), Eno, Phil Collins, Peter Hammill, and Terre Roche, among others. Running the gamut from nearly mainstream to just plain weird, it's a brooding album of great intensity. *The League of Gentlemen* 🐾🐾🐾🐾 (EG, 1981, prod. Robert Fripp) anticipates future dance trends on a conceptual level while at the same time creating Frippertronic-sounding pieces in real time.

what to buy next: The first part of of Fripp's *God Save the Queen/Under Heavy Manners* 🎸🎸🎸♪ (EG, 1979, prod. Robert Fripp) is solo Frippertronics loops; the second half is Discotronics, Fripp's repetitively structured dance music, featuring a hilariously alienated recitation by the Talking Heads' David Byrne. Sylvian & Fripp's *The First Day* 🎸🎸🎸🎸 (Virgin, 1993, prod. David Sylvian, David Botrill) mixes Frippertronics with ambient and new age production on a beautiful, tuneful, and emotional triumph.

what to avoid: The League of Gentlemen bootleg *The Bunch of Women* 🎸🎸🎸🎸 (Editions EF, 1981) supposedly captures the group's 22nd gig. It's good, but Fripp despises bootlegs, and if anything gets enough attention, he'll issue something comparable with better sound.

the rest:
Robert Fripp:
Let the Power Fall 🎸🎸 (EG, 1981)
Live in Argentina 🎸🎸🎸 (Discipline, 1994)
Radiophonics 🎸🎸🎸 (Discipline, 1996)
Blessing of Tears 🎸🎸🎸 (Discipline, 1996)
The Gates of Paradise 🎸🎸♪ (Discipline, 1996/DGM, 1998)

Fripp & Brian Eno:
Evening Star 🎸🎸♪ (Island, 1975)

Sunday All over the World:
Kneeling at the Shrine 🎸🎸♪ (EG, 1991)

Fripp & Andy Summers:
I Advance Masked 🎸🎸🎸♪ (A&M, 1982)
Bewitched 🎸🎸♪ (A&M, 1984)

The League of Gentlemen:
THRANG THRANG GOZINBULX 🎸🎸🎸 (Discipline, 1996)

The League of Crafty Guitarists:
Live! 🎸🎸🎸 (EG/Caroline, 1986)
Show of Hands 🎸🎸🎸♪ (EG/Caroline, 1991)
Intergalactic Boogie Express 🎸🎸♪ (Discipline, 1995)

Toyah & Fripp:
The Lady or the Tiger 🎸♪ (EG, 1986)

Robert Fripp String Quartet:
The Bridge Between 🎸🎸♪ (Discipline, 1994)

worth searching for: Sylvian and Fripp's limited-edition *Damage: Live* (Virgin, 1994) mixes five tracks from *The First Day* with three from Sylvian's *Gone to Earth* and four others (including Rain Tree Crow's "Every Colour You Are"). The live setting lends new urgency, and Fripp seldom repeats himself.

influences:
◄◄ Jimi Hendrix, the Beatles, John McLaughlin, Phillip Glass

►► Iceburn, His Name Is Alive, the Orb, Living Colour

see also: *King Crimson*

Steve Holtje

Bill Frisell

Born March 18, 1951, in Baltimore, MD.

A remarkable guitarist whose distinctive and sometimes quirky playing is capable of producing ethereal voices and atonal skronking, Bill Frisell is probably the only musician, let alone guitarist, who sounds equally at home playing mellow ECM-style jazz, thrash jazz/metal compositions with John Zorn's Naked City, or instrumental country music with veteran Nashville session musicians. As a child, Frisell was an adept clarinet player before he switched to electric guitar after hearing the Byrds' "Eight Miles High." While in high school he played covers of R&B tunes and songs by the Beatles and the Stones with his friends and later went on to study with legendary jazz guitarist Jim Hall after attending the University of Colorado and receiving a degree in arrangement and composition from Boston's Berklee School of Music. After recording numerous albums (including three as a bandleader) with musicians such as Paul Motian, Jan Garabek, and other ECM artists, Frisell departed for uncharted territory during the late '80s and hooked up with the likes of John Zorn, Arto Lindsay, Wayne Horvitz, and others as part of New York City's downtown avant-jazz scene. During the early- to mid-'90s, Frisell recorded some of his most impressive work with a trio consisting of himself, bassist Kermit Driscoll, and the remarkable drummer Joey Baron, which was often augmented with horns, accordion, and the inventive clarinet playing of Don Byron. The group explored distinctly American themes (blues, Aaron Copland, country & western, Buster Keaton, Madonna) within a swinging avant-jazz context. Since disbanding the group during 1995, Frisell has recorded music for Gary Larson's *The Far Side* TV special in addition to recording a popular album of country/bluegrass music, *Nashville*.

what to buy: A cover album of American composers including Sonny Rollins, John Philip Sousa, Bob Dylan, and Charles Ives, *Have a Little Faith* 🎸🎸🎸🎸🎸 (Nonesuch, 1993, prod. Wayne Horvitz) is Frisell's masterpiece. Frisell and his band manage to make the material entirely their own while swinging their butts off in the process (especially on a song such as "I Can't Be Satisfied"). Frisell displays his ability to mix sensitive playing with a ripping solo on Madonna's "Live to Tell" that would do Hendrix proud, while his interpretation of Copland's classical work "Billy the Kid" paints a perfect sonic portait of the American praire. Almost as good are *This Land* 🎸🎸🎸🎸 (Nonesuch, 1994 prod. Lee Townsend) and *Where in the World* 🎸🎸🎸🎸 (Nonesuch, 1991 prod. Wayne Horvitz), both of which feature Baron and Driscoll. ("Spell," off of *Where in the World*, features Frisell in particularly fiery form.)

what to buy next: *Bill Frisell/Kermit Driscoll/Joey Baron: Live* 🎸🎸🎸🎸 (Grammavision, 1995, prod. Hans Wendl) is taken from a 1991 concert of Frisell's trio and perfectly documents the group's ability to paint beautiful aural landscapes and abstract fury. Those of you who are intimidated by the avant-jazz tag are directed to two of Frisell's more recent works, *Nashville* ♫♫♫♫ (Nonesuch, 1997, prod. Wayne Horvitz) and *Gone like a Train* ♫♫♫♫ (Nonesuch, 1998, prod. Lee Townsend). Whereas Frisell's previous work has often alluded to country and bluegrass themes, *Nashville* fully explores his affinity for the material by teaming him up with veteran players such as Victor Krauss of Lyle Lovett's band and Dobro virtuoso Jerry Douglas. Robin Holcolmb contributes vocals to three songs, including a countrified version of Neil Young's "One of These Days." *Gone like a Train* teams Frisell with Krauss and legendary session drummer Jim Keltner (Traveling Wilburys, Eric Clapton, etc.) and features Frisell's playing in a more straight-forward "groove" session than his work with Baron and Driscoll.

the rest:
In Line ♫♫♫ (ECM, 1983)
(With Vernon Reid) *Smash & Scatteration* ♫♫♫ (Minor Music/Ryko, 1984)
Rambler ♫♫♫ (ECM, 1985)
Lookout for Hope ♫♫♫♫ (ECM, 1988)
Before We Were Born ♫♫♫ (Nonesuch, 1989)
Is That You? ♫♫♫ (Nonesuch, 1990)
Music for the Films of Buster Keaton: Go West ♫♫♫♫ (Nonesuch, 1995)
Music for the Films of Buster Keaton: The High Sign and One Week ♫♫♫♫ (Nonesuch, 1995)
Bill Frisell Quartet ♫♫♫♫ (Nonesuch, 1996)

worth searching for: If you're of the mind that jazzbos can't rock, track down a copy of Power Tools' *Strange Meeting* (Antilles, 1987 prod. David Breskin), a rather intense outing with Melvin Gibbs, currently with Henry Rollins's band, on bass, free-jazz veteran Ronald Shannon Jackson on drums, and Frisell skronking up a storm.

influences:
◄◄ Wes Montgomery, Jim Hall, Jimi Hendrix

Howard Shih

Front 242

Formed 1981, in Brussels, Belgium.

Jean-Luc De Meyer, vocals, guitar, samples; Richard 23 (a.k.a. Richard JK) Joncknee, vocals, keyboards (1983–present); Daniel "B." Bressanutti, various instruments; Patrick Codenys, various instruments.

If you want to get to the root of bands such as Ministry, nine inch nails, Filter, Gravity Kills, White Zombie, and others, Front 242 is the common ancestor. Born of the electronic movement that spawned bands such as Cabaret Voltaire, Kraftwerk, and

even Depeche Mode, Front 242 has always taken its own path. While not nearly as harsh as Einstürzende Neubauten, 242's contemporaries from Germany, nor as eclectic as Cabaret Voltaire, and certainly not as focused on the pop side as Depeche Mode, Front 242 has managed to combine elements from all of the electronic/dance/industrial influences so abundant throughout the '80s. Probably one of the most well known, and certainly the most successful, of the original industrial bands, Front 242 has managed to have several songs enter the *Billboard* charts. While diversity of sound has never been the band's strong suit—and many critics have argued they've been putting out essentially the same LPs for almost two decades—242 has managed to chronicle the industrial to post-industrial landscapes through its various releases. During the early days listeners were greeted with sparse, bleak pulsating beats and angry vocals—all very stripped down and basic. As the decade rolled by, the band started producing fuller sounding efforts (mostly due to technology moving forward), and by the '90s they'd even added a screaming guitar that almost buries the unintelligable vocals. It's hard to believe that songs such as "Headhunter," "Welcome to Paradise," and "Master Blaster" were once considered pinnacles of harsh, dark, industrial rock; listening to them today, they are almost pop-like in their simplicity and infectious dance grooves. As times have changed, so has the band—somewhat. Having been a Wax Trax! Records staple during the late 80's (most of the band's material was release between 1987–88), 242 signed to Epic Records for its 1991 release, *Tyranny for You*. While many assumed this would relegate the band to a softer, less controversial position (242 made no bones about its political and ideological stance, which lay far outside the mainstream), this was hardly the case. This album marked the band's entrance to the '90s, with style. The beats came faster, the noises more intense and the anger more fully expressed. In addition to the new release, Epic picked up rights to the entire catalog and released it on CD for the first time.

what to buy: *Official Version* ♫♫♫♫♫ (Wax Trax!, 1987/Epic, 1992, prod. Front 242) is a pinnacle release in the electro-industrial sound of the '80s. This album was chock full of music that is guaranteed to make your heart race and your toes tap. It's not harsh—just dark and cold. The songs are instantly catchy and made for extra loud playback in the hippest of Eurodance/new wave clubs. Several tunes from this disc actually made it on to MTV.

what to buy next: *Front by Front* ♫♫♫♫ (Wax Trax!, 1988/Epic, 1992, prod. Front 242) is the release that made Front 242 famous. With songs such as "Headhunter" not only exploding in clubs, but also getting commercial radio airplay, the band even embarked on a U.S. tour to support this LP. While not that far from earlier and later releases, the album alternates between the esoteric and the blatantly pop, not that there's anything wrong with that. *Backcatologue* 🎵🎵🎵 (Epic, 1991, prod. Front 242) serves as a great introduction to the band's earlier, more minimalist work. It features early singles, album cuts, live tracks, and some previously unreleased material. While not of consistent quality throughout, it covers a great deal of material released as singles and EPs only during the first half of the 1980s and is otherwise difficult to find.

what to avoid: *05:22:09:12 Off* 🎵🎵 (Epic, 1993, prod. Front 242) is just a rehashing of the band's previous release, *06:21:03:11 Up Evil.* Just to clarify, the numbers correspond to letters of the alphabet; in this album's case, it's advice well taken. If you pick up one, the other is just not needed.

the rest:
Geography 🎵🎵🎵 (RRE, 1982/Wax Trax!, 1987/Epic, 1992)
No Comment 🎵🎵🎵🎵 (Wax Trax!, 1987/Epic, 1992)
Tyranny (For You) 🎵🎵🎵 (Epic, 1991)
06:21:03:11 Up Evil 🎵🎵🎵 (Epic, 1991)
Mutage Mixage 🎵🎵🎵 (Play It Again Sam, 1997)

worth searching for: *Headhunter Video-CD* (Wax Trax!, 1988) was one of the first video CDs released. It contains the video to "Headhunter" as well as remixes of the song and "Welcome to Paradise."

influences:

◀◀ Cabaret Voltaire, Throbbing Gristle, Kraftwerk, Joy Division

▶▶ Ministry, nine inch nails, Depeche Mode, Filter, KMFDM, Skinny Puppy

see also: *Ministry*

Tim Davis

Jack Frost
See: The Church, Grant McLennan

John Frusciante
See: Red Hot Chili Peppers

Fugazi
Formed 1987, in Arlington, VA.

Ian MacKaye, vocals, guitar; Guy Picciotto, vocals, guitar; Joe Lally, bass; Brendan Canty, drums.

Ian MacKaye, former leader of Washington hardcore legend Minor Threat—not to mention the lesser-known Teen Idols, Egg Hunt, and Embrace—set out with Fugazi to create the ultimate independent punk-rock band. Fugazi has never once compromised—its songs are harsh and raw, its melodies are sometimes catchy but often dense, and it has never considered signing with

a major record label. MacKaye, to the delight of his loyal fans, has refused to let concert tickets rise above $5. This has resulted in less money for the band-owned record label, Dischord, but at least nobody has ever accused Fugazi of selling out.

what to buy: *13 Songs* 🎵🎵🎵🎵 (Dischord, 1989, prod. various) combines the debut album *Fugazi* 🎵🎵🎵🎵 (Dischord, 1988, prod. Ted Nicely, Fugazi) and the follow-up EP *Margin Walker* 🎵🎵🎵🎵 (Dischord, 1989, prod. John Loder). It opens with Fugazi's best songs, the catchy "Waiting Room" and "Bulldog Front," which sound like hardcore-and-uncheesy variations on Queen.

what to buy next: *Repeater* 🎵🎵🎵 (Dischord, 1990, prod. Ted Niceley), which includes the "Three Songs" seven-inch single, is the sound of a great band aiming all its weapons in the same direction—the bass and drums create a glorious cacophony, and MacKaye's forceful, slightly whiny vocals slip nicely on top.

the rest:
Steady Diet of Nothing 🎵🎵🎵 (Dischord, 1991)
In on the Kill Taker 🎵🎵 (Dischord, 1993)
Red Medicine 🎵🎵🎵 (Dischord, 1995)

worth searching for: The Guy Picciotto–led band Rites of Spring lacks punch and noodles a bit too much, but its only album, *Rites of Spring* (Dischord, 1985, prod. Ian MacKaye, Michael Hampton), is a decent addition to a Fugazi/Minor Threat collection.

influences:

◀◀ Queen, Motörhead, the Dead Kennedys, the Minutemen, Descendents, the Sex Pistols

▶▶ The Offspring, Nirvana, Soundgarden, Guns N' Roses, Pearl Jam, Nada Surf

see also: *Minor Threat*

Steve Knopper

Fugees /Wyclef Jean
Formed 1989, in South Orange, NJ.

Nel Wyclef Jean, vocals, guitar, keyboards, bass; Lauryn Hill, vocals; Prakazrel Michael, vocals, keyboards.

The group's name is short for refugees, a reminder of the Haitian heritage of cousins Nel Wyclef Jean and Prakazrel Michael. While their brand of hip-hop is musical and conscious, the Fugees are no sucker MCs; in their struggle to keep it both positive and real, their music falls squarely between the hardcore jeep beats of gangsta rap and the trippier alternarap of Arrested Development and De La Soul. With two of their three principals being instrumentalists, the group emphasizes musicality as well as grooves. On the mic, they earn extra points for according Lauryn Hill as much—and perhaps even more—time out front as 'Clef and Pras, a rare act of equality in the rap game. Even better, she's up to the task, turning in smoothly sung vocals and a cool measured rap flow. More than almost any other hip-hop act, the Fugees set their goals high and then took well-measured steps toward achieving them.

what to buy: Alternarap's long-awaited breakthrough, *The Score* ♫♫♫♪ (Ruffhouse/Columbia, 1996, prod. Fugees, Diamond D, others) moves hip-hop forward even as it looks back to pay tribute to seminal influences such as Bob Marley and Roberta Flack. The covers of Marley's "No Woman, No Cry" and Flack's "Killing Me Softly" are less than revelatory, but the original tracks "Fu-Gee-La," "Ready or Not," and "Family Business" prove that the Fugees are worthy successors to their heroes. Equally impressive is the album's almost cinematic quality, combining occasionally noirish grooves, compelling and sometimes uplifting tales from the 'hood, and the only funny skit to grace a rap album in recent memory. The multiplatinum disc deservedly won the 1997 Grammy Award for Best Rap Album.

what to buy next: Distinguishing himself as the group's true visionary, Wyclef Jean followed *The Score* with *Wyclef Jean Presents the Carnival* ♫♫♫♪ (Ruffhouse/Columbia, 1997, prod. Wyclef Jean, others), an astonishingly adventurous and wide-reaching solo album on which he receives more than a little help from his musically gifted friends (i.e., Celia Cruz, the 62-piece New York Philharmonic Orchestra, the Neville Brothers, and, of course, Pras and Hill). Although it features the same sort of righteous undertones and thoughtful, albeit paranoid, lyrics that highlighted *The Score*, musically, the album is in a different world, throwing in a Bee Gees sample or sweet soprano vocalist here, remaking a Cuban folk tune there. On four newly composed songs, 'Clef even dares to use French patois as he sings about Haitian pride and politics. If the hip-hop headz only knew.

the rest:
Blunted on Reality ♫♫♫♪ (Ruffhouse/Columbia, 1994)
Bootleg Versions ♫♫♫♪ (Ruffhouse/Columbia EP, 1996)

solo outings:
Lauryn Hill:
The Miseducation of Lauryn Hill ♫♫♫♪ (Ruffhouse/Columbia, 1998)

influences:
◀◀ Bob Marley, Roberta Flack, De La Soul, Neneh Cherry, Arrested Development

Daniel Durchholz and Josh Freedom du Lac

The Fugs

Formed 1965, in New York, NY. Disbanded 1969. Re-formed 1984.

Tuli Kupferberg, vocals, percussion (1965–69, 1984–present); Ed Sanders, guitar, vocals (1965–69, 1984–present); Ken Weaver, drums, vocals (1965–66); John Anderson, bass (1965–67); Vinnie Leary, guitar (1965–67); Pete Stampfel, guitar, fiddle (1965–66); Steve Weber, guitar (1965–66); Lee Crabtree, keyboards (1966–67); Pete Kearney, guitar (1966–67); Charles Larkey, bass (1967–68); Dan Kootch, guitar (1967); Ken Pine, guitar (1967–68); Bill Wolf, bass (1968); Bob Mason, drums (1968); Richard Lee, organ (1968); Howard Johnson, tuba, saxophone (1968); Julius Watkins, French horn (1968).

The Fugs were quite possibly the first punk band. Hardly able to play instruments, the Fugs traded on a raw folk-rock sound that backed neo-beat poets Ed Sanders and Tuli Kupferberg, who wrote most of the band's material. The songs went beyond drugs, sex, and anti-war paeans to deliberate filth ("Coca-Cola Douche") that was calculated to shock. Still, there was a method to its madness, grounded in the '50s beat scene. Poet Allen Ginsberg contributed to the Fugs' lyrics, and one of the few songs that received radio play, "How Sweet I Roamed from Field to Field," was an adaptation of a work by romantic poet William Blake.

what's available: *The Fugs' First Album* ♫♫♫♪ (ESP, 1965/Fantasy, 1994 prod. Harry Smith) has plenty of antisocial sentiments via "Slum Goddess," "I Couldn't Get High," and more. Buy the reissue, since it contains the entire album plus 11 bonus tracks. *The Fugs' Second Album* ♫♫♫♪ (Fantasy, 1994, prod. Harry Smith) continues in the same vein, with "Kill for Peace" and "Morning, Morning," their most popular ballad.

worth searching for: Two of the group's later albums, *No More Slavery* (PVC, 1986/Big Beat, 1996) and *Songs for a Portable Forest* (Gazell, 1991) are available as imports. Also recommended for fans is Ed Sanders's collection of poetry, *Thirsting for Peace in a Raging Century*, which won an American Book Award in 1988.

solo outings:
Tuli Kupferberg:
No Deposit, No Return ♫♫ (Shimmy-Disc)

influences:
◀◀ Bob Dylan, Allen Ginsberg
▶▶ Beck

Lawrence Gabriel

Full Time Men

See: The Fleshtones

The Bobby Fuller Four

Formed 1963, in El Paso, TX.

Bobby Fuller (died July 18, 1966), guitar, vocals; Randy Fuller, bass, vocals; Jim Reese, guitar; Dalton Powell, drums (1963–64); DeWayne Querico, drums (1964–66).

The Bobby Fuller story reads like a treatment for a major motion picture. Fade in: Young man growing up in a Texas town falls in love with rock 'n' roll, particularly that of fellow Texan Buddy Holly. In time, the young man—a musical prodigy—forms his own band and starts attracting attention. He and his band tour, make records and television appearances, and even have a smash hit across the country. But with fame come the pleasures and perils of fame, and a young man is unlikely to resist the charms of the many women now enamored of his new pop stardom. The young man runs into trouble with one such woman, a woman linked to a reputed mobster. One morning, the young man is found dead in his parked car, his body bruised, beaten, and covered with gasoline. Though the young man obviously was murdered, the police officially list the death as accidental and privately call it a suicide. With justice not served, the questions linger for decades, never to be answered. The music, meanwhile, lives on as well, never to be forgotten. Fade out. The tabloid aspects of Fuller's demise may yet draw Hollywood's interest (and, lest this be written off as another crackpot conspiracy theory, let there be no mistake about our position: Paul ain't dead, Elvis ain't alive, but Bobby Fuller was murdered), but it is Fuller's music that continues to entertain and fascinate fans 30 years after his death. The unforgettable "I Fought the Law," itself a cover of a song by the Crickets, was the Bobby Fuller Four's only Top 40 entry, though there were scattered regional hits—notably the sublime "Let Her Dance." Fuller's recorded legacy is an essential set of American mid-'60s rock 'n' roll surviving and thriving in the wake of the British Invasion.

what to buy: The three-disc *Never to Be Forgotten* 𝄞𝄞𝄞𝄞𝄞 (Del-Fi, 1998, prod. Bob Keane) collects all of Fuller & Company's superlative recordings for the Mustang label, including all the hits and album cuts, unreleased tracks, alternate versions, two tracks by the Randy Fuller Four, a commercial for Gallencamp Shoes, and the live, heretofore-unreleased *Celebrity Night at PJ's* album in its entirety. Far from the odds-and-sods exercise you might expect, this set is compelling listening from start to finish, and an absolutely essential purchase.

what to buy next: *Shakedown! The Texas Tapes Revisited* 𝄞𝄞𝄞𝄞 (Del-Fi, 1996, prod. Gary Tanenbaum, Randy Fuller) is a two-disc collection of Fuller's pre-fame Texas recordings, including two earlier versions of "I Fought the Law." The same era is also covered on *El Paso Rock Early Recordings, Vol. 1* 𝄞𝄞𝄞 (Norton, 1996) and *El Paso Rock, Vol. 2* 𝄞𝄞𝄞 (Norton, 1997), each of

which bolsters its selection of Texas tapes with otherwise-unavailable live tracks. A third volume is promised at this writing.

the rest:
The Best of the Bobby Fuller Four 𝄞𝄞𝄞 (Rhino, 1990)

influences:
◀◀ Buddy Holly, Eddie Cochran, Ritchie Valens

▶▶ Tom Petty & the Heartbreakers, John Mellencamp, Phil Seymour, Marshall Crenshaw

Carl Cafarelli

Fun Boy Three

Formed 1981, in Coventry, England. Disbanded 1983.

Lynval Golding, vocals; Terry Hall, vocals; Neville Staples, guitar, vocals.

Formed by three ex-members of the Specials, Fun Boy Three retained the ska sound of that band, but showed more of an African-based influence. The group disbanded in 1983, and Hall went on to form the Colour Field.

what to buy: *Waiting* 𝄞𝄞𝄞𝄞 (Chrysalis, 1983, prod. David Byrne) is their strongest album, marked by the slowed-down version of the Go-Go's "Our Lips Are Sealed"—which Terry Hall co-wrote.

the rest:
Fun Boy Three 𝄞𝄞𝄞 (Chrysalis, 1982)
The Best of Fun Boy Three 𝄞𝄞𝄞𝄞 (Chrysalis, 1984)

solo outings:
Terry Hall:
The Collection 𝄞𝄞𝄞 (Chrysalis, 1993)

influences:
◀◀ Bob Marley, the Specials, the Selecter

▶▶ The Go-Go's, Bananarama

see also: *The Specials*

Anna Glen

Fun Lovin' Criminals

Formed 1993, in New York, NY.

Huey, vocals, guitar; Fast, bass, trumpet, harmonica, vocals; Steve, drums.

Try as they might to come off as hoodlums, New York City's Fun Lovin' Criminals' tough, streetwise image is belied by its warm, blues-based hip-hop sound. After a series of unsuccessful electronic music projects, longtime friends Huey, Fast, and Steve began experimenting with Beastie Boys-type grooves, with Huey rapping over heavy doses of his hollow-body blues guitar.

The lean, muscular mix proved potent, and EMI was reportedly interested in the group after it had played only a handful of dates. The hardworking trio also toured hard, opening for everyone from Social Distortion in small theaters to U2 in stadiums.

what to buy: The group's major-label debut, *Come Find Yourself* ♫♫♫ (EMI, 1996, prod. Fun Lovin' Criminals), is a wonderful party record, filled with warm, soulful grooves and some nonthreatening gangsta boasting. Song subjects are typical—New York, drugs, and bank heists, plus an unabashed mobster tribute with the refrain "La-di-da-di/Free John Gotti" ("King of New York"). The jangly single "Scooby Snacks" sampled choice dialogue from Quentin Tarantino films and made the album a hit.

the rest:
Fun Lovin' Criminals ♫♫♫ (Silver Spotlight EP, 1995)

influences:
◄◄ Beastie Boys, House of Pain

Todd Wicks

Funkadelic
See: George Clinton

Richie Furay /Richie Furay Band
See: Poco

Billy Fury
Born Ronald Wycherley, April, 17, 1941, in Liverpool, England. Died January 28, 1983.

Billy Fury was the best of Britain's Elvis Presley wannabes and its first rock singer-songwriter. During the late '50s through the mid-'60s, Fury racked up nearly two dozen hit singles, none of which were heard in America. Initially a struggling songwriter, the teenaged Ronald Wycherley talked his way backstage at a Marty Wilde show and made a song pitch so impressive that Wilde's manager instantly signed him up. Rechristened Billy Fury (the coolest name in early British rock), he quickly hit the charts with such self-written Presleyesque tunes as "Maybe Tomorrow," "Margo (Don't Go)," "That's Love," and "Wondrous Place." Continuous touring and appearances on the BBC TV shows *Oh Boy!*, *Boy Meets Girls,* and *Wham!* helped make him one of the biggest stars of the era. His 1960 LP *The Sound of Billy Fury* was closer than any pre-Beatles artist had come to the sounds of American rockabilly. However, Fury's record label insisted that subsequent recordings mix in more ballads, lightweight pop, and carefully chosen cover versions of American hits, though he continued to rock onstage with the Tornados of "Telstar" fame. With this formula, Fury scored a series of pop hits such as "Halfway to Paradise," "I'd Never Find Another You," "When Will You Say I Love You," and "In Summer." Appearances in the films *Play It Cool* (with Cliff Richard) and *I've Got a Horse* didn't establish a hoped-for acting career, and his own poor health (he suffered from chronic heart disease) cut short several important engagements. Though still quite popular, the emergence of the Beatles and other Mersey Beat groups quickly rendered his pop style irrelevant. By 1967 the hit records had dried up and Fury retired until the 1975 film *That'll Be the Day* reintroduced him to nostalgic British audiences. At the time of his death, Fury was back to recording in his original rock 'n' roll style and experiencing a modest career revival.

worth searching for: In the United States there are no Billy Fury compilations available. So hit the import bins for *The Billy Fury Hit Parade* (Decca, 1988, prod. various), the two-LPs-on-one disc reissue *We Want Billy/Billy* (BGO, 1995, prod. various), or, best of all, *Sounds of Billy Fury Plus 10* (Decca, 1988/1998, prod. Jack Good), the first true rockabilly LP written and sung by a British artist.

influences:
◄◄ Elvis Presley, Marty Wilde, Cliff Richard, Adam Faith, Johnny Kidd & the Pirates
►► Joe Brown, the Tornados, the Beatles, Shakin' Stevens

Ken Burke

Future Sound of London /Amorphous Androgynous
Formed 1988, in Manchester, England.

Gary Cobain, keyboards; Brian Dougan, keyboards.

Gary Cobain and Brian Dougan have recorded under numerous aliases in their explorations of electronic music (Stakker Humanoid, Semi Real, Yage, Metropolis, Art Science Technology, Mental Cube, Candese, Intelligent Communication, Smart Systems, Far Out Son of Lung, Amorphous Androgynous, and other "secret projects"). Each has had varying degrees of underground success, but it is their primary project, Future Sound of London, that has attracted the most worldwide attention. In 1988 their early anthem "Humanoid" (as Stakker Humanoid) hit just as the acid house movement exploded in the U.K. From there, FSOL was born, and alongside it the single "Papua New Guinea," considered by many rave historians to be one of the defining songs of the phenomenon. That was enough to place FSOL at the forefront of techno, and its position hasn't wavered.

what to buy: *Accelerator* ♫♫♫♫ (Virgin U.K., 1992/Cleopatra, 1996, prod. Gary Cobain, Brian Dougan) is worth any price based solely on the singular, orgasmic beauty of "Papua New

Guinea," with its heavenly vocals (borrowed from Dead Can Dance) and sinful bass line (borrowed from Meat Beat Manifesto). Oh yeah, it's also got great songs such as "Moscow," "Central Industrial," and "It's Not My Problem," but you'll be too stuck on "Papua New Guinea" to care. As Amorphous Androgynous, Cobain and Dougan recorded *Tales of Ephidrena* ♪♪♪♪ (Virgin U.K., 1993, prod. Gary Cobain, Brian Dougan), an album of ambient techno that gracefully covered the spectrum between beatless soothers and dance floor movers.

what to buy next: *Lifeforms* (Astralwerks, 1994, prod. Gary Cobain, Brian Dougan), the follow-up to *Accelerator*, features the ethereal vocal talents of the Cocteau Twins' Liz Fraser, manipulated in ways you'd never thought they could go.

what to avoid: The duo's lackluster house full-length release *Humanoid* **woof!** (Jumpin' and Pumpin' U.K., 1989, prod. Gary Cobain, Brian Dougan) is anything but. Fortunately, it's extremely hard to find.

the rest:
(With Various Artists) *Earthbeat* ♪♪♪♪ (Jumpin' and Pumpin' U.K., 1992)
Art Futura ♪♪♪✩ (Astralwerks, 1996)

worth searching for: *ISDN* (Astralwerks, 1995, prod. Gary Cobain, Brian Dougan) is a limited edition release of their live ISDN transmission events.

influences:
◀◀ Brian Eno, Tangerine Dream, Master Musicians of Jajouka
▶▶ Small Fish with Spine

Tamara Palmer

Reeves Gabrels

Born June 4, 1956, in Staten Island, NY.

Reeves Gabrels will go down as one of the true originals in the guitar-hero pantheon, even as his fusion of fretwork and computer processing questions and redefines that instrument's very place in the rock canon. A furious cut-and-paster in the studio and an evil genius of atonal improvisation on stage, Gabrels explores sonic extremes with a great, adaptive intuition for what each song needs most. Among those who know him at all, he is either loved or hated but never ignored; this alone guarantees his staying power. After an apprenticeship in several Boston-area indie bands, Gabrels was put in the spotlight—and hot seat—as head axeman for David Bowie's controversial Tin Ma-

chine project. He has resurfaced as the musical director for Bowie's late '90s electronica-derived comeback. In between, he released one of the most engaging—and overlooked—alterna-pop albums of the decade, *The Sacred Squall of Now*. Behind the scenes but influential, you'll be hearing a lot more from him—whether or not you know it's him you're hearing.

what to buy: With everyone from Frank Black to Gary Oldman (!) on guest vocals, hairpin detours into symphonic ambience and Eastern European roots, and a base of tuneful crunch that finds the golden mean between catchiness and quirkiness, *The Sacred Squall of Now* ♪♪♪♪ (Upstart, 1995, prod. Reeves Gabrels) is that rare pop album that has something for everyone while pandering to none.

what to buy next: On *Night in Amnesia* ♪♪♪♪ (Upstart, 1995, prod. Tom Dubé, David Tronzo, Reeves Gabrels), Gabrels teams with slide-guitar god David Tronzo for an hour of post-Zappa improv psycho-jazz. Though inventive and economical, this studious affair is actually less avant garde than Gabrels's genre-colliding, unpredictable pop. *Hard Row to Hoe* ♪♪♪ (Monolyth, 1994, prod. Tom Dubé, Modern Farmer), the debut from one of Gabrels's band projects, Modern Farmer, is an album of inoffensive but uninspired meat 'n' potatoes rock.

influences:
◀◀ Robert Fripp, Adrian Belew, Jimi Hendrix, Living Colour
see also: *David Bowie*

Adam McGovern

Peter Gabriel

Born February 13, 1950, in London, England.

Made a star as the first lead singer for British art-rockers Genesis, Peter Gabriel gained attention as much for his outlandish stage outfits (including a way-early mohawk haircut and a flower suit) as his forward-thinking songwriting ideas. Feeling stifled by the group's growing commercial success, Gabriel struck out on his own in 1975, eschewing the theatrics to focus on a style that melded his art-rock and folk roots with a strong social conscience and desire to push creative boundaries. Building critical and commercial success with each release, Gabriel (who named his first four solo records *Peter Gabriel*, like issues in a magazine) refined his style into an amazingly creative blend of rock, soul and worldbeat styles—mixing Euro-centric rock touches with tribal music conventions and commercial rock tunes with viewpoints on apartheid, Native American issues, and his own divorce. Eventually, he channeled his own success into a world music label, Real World, along with an annual world music festival called WOMAD and multimedia projects. One of rock's great visionaries, each subsequent re-

Peter Gabriel (© Ken Settle)

lease opens new creative doors that others seem to follow a couple of years after Gabriel walks through them.

what to buy: Though his first two solo releases set the stage, it wasn't until his third self-titled album, *Peter Gabriel* ♪♪♪♪ (Geffen, 1980, prod. Steve Lillywhite), that the singer fully stepped away from his art-rock roots to craft pop music unlike anything made before. Forbidding drummers Phil Collins and Jerry Marotta to use cymbals, Gabriel combined unorthodox percussion parts, brittle guitar textures, and outlandish synthesizer sounds to create edgy, arty classics such as the hit "Games without Frontiers" and the majestic tribute to slain anti-apartheid activist Steven Biko, "Biko."

what to buy next: Gabriel's commercial breakthrough, *So* ♪♪♪♪♪ (Geffen, 1986, prod. Daniel Lanois, Peter Gabriel), melds the singer's arresting creative vision with actual hit songs, from the soulful celebration "Sledgehammer" to the percolating, ironic take on rock star ego, "Big Time." Add the mesmerizing, worldbeat flavored ballad "In Your Eyes," a tender duet with Kate Bush on "Don't Give Up," and the powerful, passionate groove "Red Rain," and you have the makings of an instant classic. As a showcase for Gabriel's growing sonic palette, the fourth *Peter Gabriel* ♪♪♪♪ (aka *Security*) (Geffen, 1982, prod. Peter Gabriel, David Lord) bounds from an epic Native American tale ("San Jacinto") to the buoyant "Kiss of Life" and the kinetic single "Shock the Monkey."

what to avoid: The singer's two stabs at film scoring, *Music from the Film Birdy* ♪♪♥ (Geffen, 1984, prod. Peter Gabriel) and *Passion: Music for The Last Temptation of Christ* ♪♪♥ (Geffen, 1989, prod. Peter Gabriel), do little more than cobble together reworked versions of songs from whatever album preceded them. You'd be better off buying the records that inspired them.

the rest:
Peter Gabriel ♪♪♪ (Atco, 1977)
Peter Gabriel ♪♪♪ (Atlantic, 1978)
Plays Live ♪♪♪ (Geffen, 1983)
Shaking the Tree: 16 Golden Greats ♪♪♪♪ (Geffen, 1990)
Revisited ♪♪♪♥ (Atlantic, 1992)
Us ♪♪♪♪ (Geffen, 1992)
Secret World Live ♪♪♪♪ (Geffen, 1994)

worth searching for: The mind-bending CD-ROM *Xplora* (Real-World/Virgin, 1994) not only features stereo sound videos of many tunes from *Us*, but also allows the user to mix a few of Gabriel's tunes on their computer as if they were engineering the record.

influences:
◀◀ Sam Cooke, Otis Redding, King Crimson, David Bowie, Brian Eno

▶▶ George Michael, Paula Cole, Daniel Lanois, Youssou N'Dour

see also: *Genesis*

Eric Deggans

Galaxie 500

Formed 1986, in Boston, MA. Disbanded 1991.

Dean Wareham, vocals, guitar; Naoimi Yang, bass; Damon Krukowski, drums.

Galaxie 500 was comprised of Harvard grads, yet they played lo-fi slacker dirges like they didn't have the energy to sit up, much less complete their secondary education. Based on simple repetitions of gaining intensity and spare jazzy rhythms, Galaxie drew immediate comparisons to the Velvet Underground. In its more inspired dirges, the band did weave a seductive and tuneful morass. After Galaxie split up, Dean Wareham went on to found Luna. Rykodisc has recently reissued the band's catalog in addition to a box set that includes its three studio releases and a rarities disc. True believers were rewarded in 1997 with a live token recorded in Copenhagen, Denmark, during 1990.

what to buy: The mopey charm of "Tugboat Captain" from the debut album, *Today* ♪♪♪ (Rough Trade, 1987/Rykodisc 1997), will shrug its way into your heart, although the less melodic groans leave you feeling like you've been drinking too much cough syrup.

the rest:
On Fire ♪♪♪ (Rough Trade, 1989/Rykodisc 1997)
Blue Thunder ♪♪♪ (Rough Trade, 1989)
This is Our Music ♪♪♪ (Rough Trade, 1990/Rykodisc 1997)
Galaxie 500 ♪♪♪♥ (box set) (Rykodisc, 1996)
Copenhagen ♪♪♪ (Rykodisc, 1997)

worth searching for: Glance through the used bins for Ryko's sampler *Selected Galaxie 500* (Rykodisc, 1996), a quickie way to get a smattering of Galaxie on disc without buying the box.

influences:
◀◀ Velvet Underground, Modern Lovers, Big Star, Roky Erickson

▶▶ Luna, Luna 2, Morphine, My Bloody Valentine

see also: *Luna*

Allan Orski

Rory Gallagher

Born March 2, 1949, in Ballyshannon, Ireland. Died June 14, 1995, in London, England.

A blues-rock guitarist and singer, Rory Gallagher had a lengthy career beginning with his trio Taste, something of an Irish response to the success of England's Cream. After that outfit disbanded, Gallagher became a solo artist. One of the most aggressive guitarists in the blues-rock genre, his style wasn't diluted by changing musical tastes and attitudes. Given some of the experimentation he had done with Taste, it's a pity that Gallagher didn't spread his creative wings further; while his recordings were accomplished, there is a strong similarity to them. He penned most of the blues songs, which tended to be lengthy with increasingly dynamic improvisations. Unlike contemporaries such as Eric Clapton, Jeff Beck, Jimmy Page, and Jimi Hendrix, Gallagher never strayed far from his blues roots. If nothing else, with Gallagher you always knew what to expect.

what to buy: *The Best of Taste Featuring Rory Gallagher* ♪♪♪♪ (Polydor, 1994) is a solid sampling of Gallagher's early, raw-boned blues guitar and vocal attack. These recordings were long out of print; they are a welcome return and the linchpin to Gallagher's career.

what to buy next: *Tattoo* ♪♪♪♪ (Polydor/Griffin, 1973), Gallagher's fifth solo album, contains a number of strong songs, including "Cat Cradle," "Living like a Trucker," and "They Don't Make It like That Anymore."

what to avoid: *Blueprint* ♪♪ (Polydor/Griffin, 1973) is one of those moribund, same-sounding collections.

the rest:
Irish Tour '74 ♪♪♪ (Polydor/I.R.S., 1974)
Against the Grain ♪♪♪♪ (Chrysalis/Griffin, 1975)
Calling Card ♪♪♪ (Chrysalis/I.R.S., 1976)
Top Priority ♪♪♪ (Chrysalis/I.R.S., 1979)
Defender ♪♪♪ (I.R.S., 1987)
Fresh Evidence ♪♪♪ (I.R.S., 1991)
Live in Europe/Stage Struck ♪♪♪ (I.R.S., 1991)

influences:
◀◀ Albert King, Freddie King, Muddy Waters, Bo Diddley

▶▶ Gary Moore, George Thorogood & the Destroyers

Patrick McCarty

Gallon Drunk

Formed 1990, in London, England.

James Johnston, vocals, guitar, organ; Mike Delanian, bass; Max Decharne, drums; Joe Byfield, maracas; Terry Edward, horns (1993–present).

Since its beginning, Gallon Drunk's musical style has stayed the same: dark, boozy rock 'n' roll soundtracks for a lounge generation. Rising, appropriately from the London pub scene, the group, led by charismatic frontman James Johnson, is highly theatrical and sonically chaotic, like a train wreck that you can't help but look at.

what to buy: The band's debut album, *Tonite . . . the Singles Bar* ♪♪♪♪ (Rykodisc, 1992, prod. Gallon Drunk), remains the best introduction to its primal sound. The album collects the songs from the group's early U.K. singles, which made its reputation.

what to buy next: *You, the Night . . . & the Music* ♪♪♪ (Rykodisc, 1992, prod. Gallon Drunk, Tony Harris) is nearly as fine as the debut, but adds traces of Memphis soul and rockabilly to the mix.

the rest:
From the Heart of Town ♪♪♪ (Sire, 1993)

influences:
◀◀ Nick Cave, the Cramps, Tom Waits

Anna Glen

Game Theory
/The Loud Family
/Scott Miller

Scott Miller (born April 4, in Sacramento, CA).

Does Scott Miller—the one-man force behind Game Theory and the Loud Family since 1982—use power pop as a tool for conveying his emotions, or are his emotional lyrics an excuse for great power-pop? Whatever the case, Miller is one of the few in the genre who has a sound all his own; whatever influences he has are sublimated within his originality. His melodies are the musical equivalent of intricate math problems, and his vocals—often compared to Chris Stamey's and Alex Chilton's—launch into emotional falsettos at the drop of a hat (or, considering Miller's allusiveness, the drop of a reference). Repeat plays are essential to understanding his songs; Miller asks the listener to do half the work, but over the course of several listens you'll get to the top (or the bottom) of this artistic peak. The songs pour Miller's stream-of-consciousness into distinct bottles of varying tones, and before long you'll be humming to the chorus of a shampoo ingredient ("Sodium Laureth Sulfate") or the closer-to-the-skull intellectual tearjerker "Where They Walk over Sainte Therese." The songs in between will test your skills as a Scott Miller champion.

what to buy: Game Theory's *Real Nighttime* ♪♪♪♪ (Enigma, 1984, prod. Mitch Easter) is full of Big Starrish melodies and lyrics reflecting rejection, dejection, and young adult confusion. *Lolita Nation* ♪♪♪♪ (Enigma, 1987, prod. Mitch Easter) is a self-indulgent but gorgeous double-length album. The Loud Family's *Plants & Birds & Rocks & Things* ♪♪♪♪ (Alias, 1993, prod. Mitch Easter) is a richly textured pop masterpiece; it contains some of Miller's best songs, and the arrangements are chilling. *Distortion of Glory* ♪♪♪♪ (Alias, 1993, prod. Michael

Quercio, Scott Miller) combines Game Theory's first album (though many songs were clinically re-recorded) with two subsequent (and excellent) EPs and bonus tracks.

what to buy next: *Tinkers to Evers to Chance* 𝄞𝄞𝄞 (Enigma, 1990, prod. various) is a Game Theory compilation with fairly well-chosen tracks—including a couple of new recordings of pre-Game Theory songs—but you'd do better with one of the regular albums. The Loud Family's *Tape of Only Linda* 𝄞𝄞𝄞 (Alias, 1994, prod. Mitch Easter) is denser than *Plants & Birds* . . . but almost as good; ultimately, the other musician's contributions only blur Miller's vision. *Days for Days* 𝄞𝄞𝄞 (Alias, 1998, prod. Scott Miller) at first sounds like the usual mess of melodic scraps and lyrical conundrums. Subsequent listens put everything in the (hy)perspective that Miller intended. The sound hearkens back to the helium melodies of *Big Shot Chronicles*, punctured by jagged mood swings. "Deee-Pression" has the hit-record chorus that Miller can write in his sleep (or dreams), but its connective track comes on like a Vietnam flashback.

what to avoid: Though perfectly respectable, *Two Steps from the Middle Ages* 𝄞𝄞𝄞 (Rational/Enigma, 1988, prod. Mitch Easter) has some of Miller's best songs, but also some that don't quite connect.

the rest:
Game Theory:
Big Shot Chronicles 𝄞𝄞𝄞 (Rational/Enigma, 1985)

The Loud Family:
Tape of Only Linda 𝄞𝄞𝄞 (Alias, 1994)
Interbabe Concern 𝄞𝄞𝄞 (Alias, 1996)

worth searching for: A vinyl import called *Dead Center* (Lolita, 1994) combines the EP tracks with an otherwise-unavailable Game Theorized cover of the Box Tops' "The Letter."

influences:

◄◄ Big Star, the dB's, Roxy Music

►► Ultra Vivid Scene, the Posies, Veruca Salt

Jordan Oakes

Gang of Four /Shriekback

Gang of Four formed 1977, in Leeds, England. Disbanded 1984. Reformed 1990. Shriekback formed 1981, in London, England. Disbanded 1989. Re-formed 1992.

Gang of Four: Jon King, vocals, melodica; Andy Gill, guitar, vocals; Dave Allen, bass (1977–81); Hugo Burnham, drums, (1977–82); Busta "Cherry" Jones, bass, (1981–82); Sara Lee, bass, vocals (1982–84). Shriekback: Dave Allen, bass (1981–86, 1992–94); Carl Marsh, guitar, vocals (1981–85); Barry Andrews, vocals, keyboards; Martyn Barker,

drums; Mike Cozzi, guitar (1985–89, 1992–present); Doug Wimbush, bass (1986–89).

Gang of Four numbers among the most important post-punk bands to emerge from England, departing from the thrashing nihilism of punk and pursuing a stark sound influenced by funk and avant-garde music, with lyrics from an analytical, leftist point of view. The band was formed by art students Jon King, Andy Gill, and Hugo Burnham, who came into focus with the arrival of experienced pro Dave Allen. Gill's minimalist guitar work rebelled against rock's traditional chordal barrage, scattering dissonant shards over the uptight grooves of Burnham and Allen while King punctuated his chanted critiques with ghostly bursts of melodica. The space opened up by Gill's crafty restraint ratcheted up the tension level of the music immeasurably. The group's 1979 debut album, *Entertainment!*, has since earned classic status among alternative music fans. Allen departed after Gang of Four's second album, citing the liberal drift of King's thinking, and formed the dance-oriented Shriekback. With Talking Heads veteran Busta Jones, the Gang continued touring until bassist-singer Sara Lee was brought in to add an appealing pop presence to the more melodic *Songs of the Free* and its mini-hit, "I Love a Man in Uniform." The group took an ill-fated turn toward processed alterna-soul with 1984's *Hard*, however, and after the firing of Burnham (who became an A&R executive) and the release of a live album recorded in Los Angeles, the Gang disbanded. Gill pursued a career in film scoring and record producing. During the intervening years, the group's contribution to modern rock and to the stripped-down grooves of rap was recognized, and a Gill-King reunion in 1991 yielded a Gang of Four reunion.

Shriekback, meanwhile, enjoyed its own bit of radio success, particularly with the nightmarish anthem "Nemesis." Mixing funk and soul grooves with post-punk songcraft and industrial soundscapes, the group enjoyed moderate success throughout the 1990s—as well as a brief breakup and subsequent reunion. Allen also founded the modern rock label World Domination, which released Shriekback's 1992 effort *Sacred City*.

what to buy: Gang of Four's *Entertainment!* 𝄞𝄞𝄞𝄞 (Warner Bros., 1979, prod. Andy Gill, Jon King, Rob Warr, Rick Walton) is a spellbinding collection of politicized, funky post-punk. Because the lyrics are fragmented and opaque, they largely avoid the truisms that befall preachier songwriters. Shriekback's *Oil & Gold* 𝄞𝄞𝄞 (Island, 1985, prod. Barry Andrews) catches the band at its noisy but pop-savvy peak and features the unstoppable "Nemesis."

what to buy next: Gang of Four's *Solid Gold* 𝄞𝄞𝄞 (Warner Bros., 1981, prod. Jimmy Douglass, Gang of Four) continues in the debut's uncompromising vein, while *Songs of the Free* 𝄞𝄞𝄞 (Warner Bros, 1982, prod. Mike Howlett, Andy Gill, Jon King) moves in a somewhat more melodic direction and shows greater stylistic breadth. Those wanting to dabble first should obtain *A Brief History of the Twentieth Century* ♫♫♫♫ (Warner Bros., 1990, prod. various), a compilation that gathers the band's finest moments. Shriekback's *Dancing Years* ♫♫♫ (Island, 1990, prod. Barry Andrews) is a diverse anthology featuring remixes, unreleased material, and live tracks.

what to avoid: Gang of Four's initial reunion effort *Mall* ♫♫ (Polydor, 1991, prod. Andy Gill) lacked the chemistry of the early releases, leaning on programmed and sampled drums and sound collages.

the rest:
Gang of Four:
Gang of Four ♫♫♫ (Warner Bros., 1980)
Hard ♫♫♫ (Warner Bros., 1984)
At the Palace ♫♫♫ (Mercury, 1984)
Shrinkwrapped ♫♫♫ (Castle, 1995)

Shriekback:
Care ♫♫♫ (Warner Bros., 1983)
Jam Science ♫♫♫ (Arista, 1984)
Big Night Music ♫♫♫ (Island, 1986)
Go Bang! ♫♫♫ (Island, 1988)
Sacred City ♫♫ (World Domination, 1992)

worth searching for: Worth hunting down is *The Peel Sessions* (Strange Fruit, 1990), which contains interesting alternate versions of some of the key early songs.

influences:
◀◀ James Brown, Funkadelic, Jimi Hendrix, Marxism-Leninism, Sex Pistols, the Mekons, Pere Ubu

▶▶ The Red Hot Chili Peppers, Rage Against the Machine, the Disposable Heroes of Hiphoprisy, nine inch nails, Ministry

Simon Glickman

Gordon Gano

See: Violent Femmes

Garbage

Formed 1994, in Madison, WI.

Shirley Manson, vocals, guitar; Steve Markes, guitar, bass, samples, loops; Duke Erikson, guitar, keyboards, bass; Butch Vig, drums, programming.

Talk about good timing: Butch Vig, best known as the guy who helped grunge music to graduate from being indie rock to arenas by producing key works for Nirvana, Smashing Pumpkins, L7, Sonic Youth, and Soul Asylum, switched his sights to electronic-based pop music two years before the record industry began putting its eggs in the so-called "electronica" basket. He

also has an eye for talent; after seeing a video by a band called Angelfish (the only time it was ever shown on MTV, as it happens), Vig decided to go after that band's singer, Shirley Manson, for an upcoming project he was putting together with a couple of hometown pals. Three years and a few million records later, the public thinks of Garbage as Manson's, not Vig's band, although it is in reality a collaborative effort between all four members. Manson is a sex symbol, however, and she's appeared on countless magazine covers—which certainly doesn't hurt sales.

what to buy: The band's debut, *Garbage* ♫♫♫♫ (Almo Sounds/Geffen, 1995, prod. Garbage), combined rock with dance music before such a combination was in vogue, and in a way that rock and dance acts are still trying to achieve—mostly without success. But it's the sturdy songcraft of the hits "Vow," "Only Happy When It Rains," "Queer," and "Stupid Girl," plus the great "Supervixen" and "Mil," that ensures the album will still sound good long after the trends that it predated peter out.

what to buy next: *Version 2.0* ♫♫♫ (Almo Sounds/Interscope, 1998, prod. Garbage) finds Garbage staying one step ahead of the pack, with more tracks—"Temptation Waits," "Push It," "The Trick Is to Keep Breathing," and "You Look So Fine"—that show Garbage knows how to write good songs and then dress them up for the dance club.

worth searching for: The "Vow" CD single (Almo Sounds/Geffen, 1995), which came out a few weeks before the band's debut album, contains a bonus remix of the song, showing that the band could have gone the full industrial route had it wished to do so. Meanwhile, Garbage's "#1 Crush" was one of the main reasons why *William Shakespeare's Romeo & Juliet: Music for a Motion Picture* (Capitol, 1996) was a huge hit.

solo outings:
Shirley Manson:
Angelfish ♫♫♫ (Radioactive/MCA, 1993)

influences:
◀◀ The Clash, James Brown, Nirvana, nine inch nails

▶▶ Sneaker Pimps, Transistor

Brian Ives

Art Garfunkel

Born November 5, 1941, in New York, NY.

The masterful harmony singer with Paul Simon in Simon & Garfunkel through the '60s, Art Garfunkel's solo albums concentrate on his main asset—that choirboy voice. That worked up to a point; without Simon as an artistic foil and songwriter, Garfunkel's work reached an artistic dead-end during the '80s, although the late 1990s found him once again active and recording.

what to buy: *Garfunkel* 𝄢𝄢𝄢 (Columbia, 1990, prod. various) is a best-of that covers the bases and includes all his Top 40 hits save 1974's "I Shall Sing."

what to buy next: *Angel Clare* 𝄢𝄢𝄢 (Columbia, 1973, prod. Roy Halee, Art Garfunkel) is his most effective solo recording, with nice versions of Van Morrison's "I Shall Sing" and Randy Newman's "Old Man." *Watermark* 𝄢𝄢𝄢 (Columbia, 1977, prod. Phil Ramone) is a an intriguing collaboration with writer Jimmy Webb.

what to avoid: Steer clear of *Lefty* **woof!** (Columbia, 1988, prod. various), if for no other reason than Garfunkel's treacly version of "When a Man Loves a Woman."

the rest:
Breakaway 𝄢𝄢 (Columbia, 1975)
Fate for Breakfast 𝄢𝄢 (Columbia, 1979)
Scissors Cut 𝄢𝄢 (Columbia, 1981)
Up 'til Now 𝄢𝄢 (Sony, 1993)
Across America 𝄢𝄢𝄢 (Discovery, 1997)
Songs from a Parent to a Child 𝄢𝄢𝄢 (Sony, 1997)

influences:
◀◀ Sam Cooke, Judy Garland, the Beach Boys

▶▶ Stephen Bishop, Babyface, Jackson Browne, Bobby Kimball

see also: *Simon & Garfunkel*

Leland Rucker

Greg Garing

Born 1966, in Erie, PA.

While his junior high classmates were listening to Kiss and AC/DC, Greg Garing was scouring his family's attic for whatever other kinds of music he could find: Celtic tunes, Scott Joplin rags, '40s big band, anything that would enlighten him to the broader possibilities of music. With his affinity for guitar, piano, and any other instrument that he encountered, it didn't take long for Garing to embrace these various idioms, and he developed a wide panorama of musical expression. After witnessing a Bill Monroe performance, Garing fell in love with bluegrass. When he turned 18, he headed South, a beat-up motor home his mode of transport. In 1993 Garing formed a hard rockin' honky-tonk band based in Nashville that made it to the brink of stardom. Folks started seeing this flourishing talent as a Hank Williams for the '90s. But just before signing on as a honky-tonker, Garing pulled back, nagged by doubts about what he wanted from his career. As he reflected on his future, he came across the band Garbage, which featured drum loops, overt

sensuality, and intrigue. The encounter was opportune. Now, rather than see the tried and true idiom of honky-tonk through, he instead merged his roots rock with the same kind of loopy electronica. His *Alone* would find Garing straddling the two approaches with a graceful elan.

what's available: A bizarre unification of roots and loops, Garing's debut, *Alone* 𝄢𝄢𝄢 (Revolution, 1997, prod. David Kahne), is a daring attempt at merging two seemingly disparate musical entities. And it works.

influences:
◀◀ Hank Williams, Garbage, Bill Monroe, Chris Isaak

Bob Gulla

Nick Garvey

See: The Motors

Gastr del Sol

Formed 1993, in Chicago, IL.

David Grubbs, guitar, piano, vocals; Jim O'Rourke, guitar, keyboards, programming, tape editing (1994–98); Bundy Brown, bass, keyboards (1993).

Gastr del Sol is less a band than a hothouse for the experiments of former Squirrel Bait punk rocker David Grubbs and avant-garde improviser Jim O'Rourke. The band's records and live performances have featured the cream of Chicago's rock, jazz, and avant-garde communities, including drummer John McEntire, table-top guitarist Kevin Drumm, and clarinetist Gene Coleman, as well as internationally renowned figures such as violinist Tony Conrad and saxophonist Mats Gustafsson. In the studio, experiments with collage, tape editing, and pure sound are balanced by a quirky pop sensibility. O'Rourke quit the group after the release of *Camoufleur* in 1998, leaving its future in doubt.

what to buy: *Camoufleur* 𝄢𝄢𝄢𝄢 (Drag City, 1998, prod. Jim O'Rourke) is Gastr's final album from the O'Rourke years and also its most accessible. Drones, austere lyricism, unconventional song forms, and odd noises remain a part of the vocabulary, but they are blended with melodies and orchestrations that suggest an avant-garde Van Dyke Parks.

what to buy next: *Upgrade & Afterlife* 𝄢𝄢𝄢𝄢 (Drag City, 1996, prod. Jim O'Rourke) may puzzle fans of straight-ahead rock with its abstract—though alluring—song forms. But it provides a fascinating glimpse into Gastr's world, notably a mesmerizing, 14-minute trance version of John Fahey's "Dry Bones in the Valley," with violinist Tony Conrad (whose '60s work influenced the Velvet Underground).

the rest:
The Serpentine Similar 𝄢𝄢𝄢 (Teen Beat, 1993/Dexter's Cigar, 1997)

Crookt, Crackt, or Fly 🎸🎸🎸🎸 (Drag City, 1994)
Mirror Repair 🎸🎸🎸 (Drag City, 1994)
The Harp Factory on Lake Street 🎸🎸🎸 (Table of the Elements, 1995)

influences:

◀◀ Derek Bailey, John Fahey, John Cage, Brian Wilson, Scott Walker

▶▶ Tortoise, the Sea & Cake, Stereolab

Greg Kot

David Gates

See: Bread

The Gathering Field

Formed 1994, in Pittsburgh, PA.

Bill Deasy, guitars, vocals; Dave Brown, guitars; Ray DeFade, drums; Eric Riebling, bass; John Burgh, Hammond organ.

A heartland rock band whose frontman, Bill Deasy, is considered an outstanding songwriter, the Gathering Field delivers earnest tales of longing and deliverance with a soulful style and folk-blues-rock grounding. Deasy's expressive voice, while occasionally lapsing toward whininess on disc, can be quite powerful when wrapped around his vivid, often literary lyrics (Jack Kerouac is a favorite reference; Dylan Thomas made it into a song title). Guitarist/producer Dave Brown (Rusted Root), a former jazz player who's sided with Herbie Hancock and Larry Coryell, shows flashes of brilliance on guitar; together, the pair made a demo, "Lost in America," that became such a big hit on local radio, they had to record an album around it. That disc, their second, led to a deal with Atlantic Records, which rereleased *Lost in America* in 1996. By then the duo had gathered a permanent lineup, tapping former Affordable Floors bassist Eric Riebling (brother of Letters to Cleo's Scott Riebling) and drummer Ray DeFade, a former Nashville session player, along with nontouring member John Burgh on Hammond organ. In 1997 Deasy was invited to Miles Copeland's castle in the south of France for his special songwriting "camp," where writers of varying disciplines are put together to see what creative collaborations evolve. Deasy wound up working with Jane Wiedlin, Stewart Copeland, and Howard Jones, among others, and could easily have a terrific writing career even if the band never brings him stardom.

what to buy: *Lost in America* 🎸🎸🎸 (Mudpuppy, 1995/Atlantic 1996, prod. Dave Brown) has a couple of cuts that deserved to be hits—and were in Deasy's hometown of Pittsburgh. "Rhapsody in Blue," "Love Me Good," "Are You an Angel?," and "Lost in America" are well above average songs; sooner or later, one of them will become a hit for someone.

what to buy next: *The Gathering Field* 🎸🎸🎸 (Mudpuppy, 1994, prod. Dave Brown) is an album that shows real promise, particularly in such tunes as "Bordertown," "Lost It in the Sun," and "I Believe! I Believe!" Guests include the Clarks' Scott Blasey and Rusted Root's Liz Berlin and Jim DiSpirito.

influences:

◀◀ Van Morrison, the BoDeans, Bruce Springsteen, James Taylor, Neil Young, Elvis Presley

Lynne Margolis

Danny Gatton

Born 1945, in Washington, DC. Died October 20, 1994.

One of the most talented instrumentalists ever to pick up a guitar, Danny Gatton combined lightning-fast chops with an encyclopedic knowledge of jazz, blues, country, rockabilly, and swing. Anything that could be done on the guitar, Gatton could do it better, faster, and cooler. Something of a child prodigy, Gatton played in several bands during the late '50s, '60s and '70s, including the Offbeats, Redneck Jazz Explosion, and the American Music Company. But his fame never extended far beyond his home territory of Washington, D.C., even though in 1989 he was deemed "The World's Greatest Unknown Guitarist" in *Guitar World* magazine ("but what famous guitarist could outplay him?," the mag pointed out), an accolade that led to a two-record deal with Elektra, his first major label contract, at the age of 44. Though the resulting albums, *88 Elmira St.* and *Cruisin' Deuces*, earned Gatton critical praise and a somewhat larger audience, both financial success and fame continued to elude him. He committed suicide at his home in October 1994.

what to buy: First-timers should begin with *88 Elmira St.* 🎸🎸🎸🎸 (Elektra, 1990, prod. Danny Gatton), a well-produced collection that features Gatton's best band (Bill Holloman, horns and keyboards; John Previti, bass; Shannon Ford, drums). Gatton's mile-wide range is well represented here, from the Eddie-Cochran-on-speed licks of "Elmira St. Boogie" to the gorgeous cover of the Beach Boys' "In My Room." If you don't like this, you don't like guitar, period.

what to buy next: Gatton's second record for Elektra, *Cruisin' Deuces* 🎸🎸🎸🎸 (Elektra, 1994, prod. Danny Gatton, Billy Windsor), continues where *Elmira St.* left off, using Gatton's masterful guitar playing to weave a tapestry of various musical styles. *In Concert 9/9/94* 🎸🎸🎸🎸 (Big Mo, 1997, prod. Timm Biery, John Previti), recorded just weeks before Gatton's death, is a jazz-tinged free-for-all that shows just how amazing Gatton was when in his element: playing before his hometown crowd in Alexandria, Virginia.

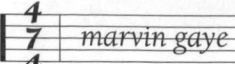
what to avoid: The American Music Co.'s *American Music* 𝄞𝄞𝄞 (Aladdin, 1975) has moments, but it's the work of a fledgling player who's a few steps away from the mature talent Gatton would become.

the rest:
(With Danny & the Fat Boys) *Vintage Masters, 1976–78* 𝄞𝄞𝄞 (Hippo, 1989)
Redneck Jazz 𝄞𝄞𝄞 (NRG, 1978)
Unfinished Business 𝄞𝄞𝄞𝄞 (NRG, 1987)
(With Tom Principato) *Blazing Telecasters* 𝄞𝄞𝄞𝄞 (POW, 1990)
New York Stories 𝄞𝄞𝄞𝄞 (Blue Note, 1992)
(With Joey DeFrancesco) *Relentless* 𝄞𝄞𝄞 (Big Mo, 1994)
Redneck Jazz Explosion 𝄞𝄞𝄞𝄞 (NRG, 1996)
(With Robert Gordon) *The Humbler* 𝄞𝄞𝄞𝄞 (NRG, 1997)

worth searching for: Guitarists would be wise to look for Gatton's two "Hot Licks" instructional video tapes, "Licks & Tricks" and "Strictly Rhythm Guitar."

influences:

◄◄ Les Paul, Carl Perkins, Chet Atkins, Roy Clark, Roy Buchanan, Dave Brubeck, Thelonious Monk, Charlie Christian, Albert Lee, Duane Eddy, Gene Vincent

►► Vince Gill, Brian Setzer, Junior Brown, Radney Foster, Steve Earle

Brandon Trenz

Marvin Gaye

Born Marvin Pentz Gay Jr., April 2, 1939, in Washington, DC. Died April 1, 1984, in Los Angeles, CA.

A moody, mercurial soul who always seemed to be searching for some elusive happiness but reveled in—and sometimes seemed to invent—his own personal miseries, Marvin Gaye was Motown's most ambivalent pop star. His real desire, so he said, was to be a crooner along the lines of Frank Sinatra and Nat King Cole. But his fame—and, indeed, his best music—came from his early pop hits and his socially conscious spiritual journeys, culminating in the 1971 masterpiece *What's Going On*. Gaye came to Motown via the Marquees (a group that enjoyed the patronage of Bo Diddley) and the Moonglows; it was during one of the latter's performances in Detroit that Berry Gordy Jr. heard Gaye and signed him to his burgeoning label. Starting as a session drummer and marrying Gordy's sister Anna (their breakup would be the focus of his harrowing 1978 album *Here, My Dear*), Gaye began his string of hits in 1962 with "Stubborn Kind of Fellow," a run that would last into the mid-'70s. Gaye also established himself as a generous duet partner, scoring hits with Mary Wells, Kim Weston, Tammi Terell, and Diana Ross. Gaye's biggest solo hit, "I Heard It through the Grapevine" in 1968, signaled a shift into deeper

material—and darker subject matter; he fought hard to get Motown to release *What's Going On*, an epic song cycle on which Gaye took total control and weaved his observations about inner city youth, the ecology, and race relations. He followed that with *Let's Get It On*, an immersion in eroticism that remained a focus through his last big hit, 1982's "Sexual Healing." Addled by drugs and depression, Gaye was in the midst of a career comeback when his father fatally shot him after an argument. His has been one of the most lamented of the Motown passings, commemorated every year in Detroit with a special ceremony or concert.

what to buy: You have to ask? *What's Going On* 𝄞𝄞𝄞𝄞𝄞 (Motown, 1971, prod. Marvin Gaye) is not just a great Gaye album, but one of the great pop albums of all time. Splurge and get the deluxe edition. *The Master, 1961–1984* 𝄞𝄞𝄞𝄞𝄞 (Motown, 1995, prod. various) is one of those rare box sets that sustains its quality over the course of four discs. *Superhits* 𝄞𝄞𝄞𝄞 (Motown, 1970/1991, prod. various) isn't the most comprehensive of Gaye's collections, but it was *the* Gaye album to own at the time and is still worth having for its cheesy superhero caricature on the cover.

what to buy next: *Let's Get It On* 𝄞𝄞𝄞𝄞 (Motown, 1973, prod. Marvin Gaye) offers the visceral desire of a man in serious heat. *Midnight Love* 𝄞𝄞𝄞𝄞 (Columbia, 1992, prod. Marvin Gaye) is much the same, though it's a little softer and just a touch more subtle. *Marvin Gaye & His Girls* 𝄞𝄞𝄞𝄞 (Motown, 1969/1990, prod. various) is a nice collection of his duets with Wells, Weston, and Terrell, missing only Diana Ross to make it a complete overview.

what to avoid: *Dream of a Lifetime* 𝄞 (Columbia, 1985, prod. Marvin Gaye, Gordon Banks, Harvey Fuqua), a posthumous release of material Gaye was working on at the time of his death, is as bald a violation of his artistry as the releases that came out after Jimi Hendrix's death.

the rest:
Together with Mary Wells 𝄞𝄞𝄞𝄞 (Motown, 1964/1991)
A Tribute to the Great Nat King Cole 𝄞𝄞𝄞𝄞 (Motown, 1965/1989)
The Soulful Moods of Marvin Gaye 𝄞𝄞𝄞 (Motown, 1966/1994)
I Heard It through the Grapevine 𝄞𝄞𝄞 (Motown, 1968/1989)
Trouble Man 𝄞𝄞𝄞𝄞 (Motown, 1972/1989)
Live 𝄞𝄞𝄞 (Motown, 1974)
I Want You 𝄞𝄞𝄞 (Motown, 1976)
Greatest Hits 𝄞𝄞𝄞𝄞 (Motown, 1976/1989)
Live at the London Palladium 𝄞𝄞𝄞 (Motown, 1977)
Here, My Dear 𝄞𝄞𝄞𝄞 (Motown, 1978/1994)
In Our Lifetime: The Final Motown Sessions 𝄞𝄞 (Motown, 1981/1994)
Every Great Motown Hit 𝄞𝄞𝄞𝄞 (Motown, 1983)
Great Songs & Performances That Inspired Motown 25 𝄞𝄞𝄞 (Motown, 1983)

J. Geils (© Jack Vartoogian)

Romantically Yours ♫♫ (Columbia, 1985/1989)
A Musical Testament ♫♫♫ (Motown, 1988)
The Marvin Gaye Collection ♫♫♫♫ (Motown, 1990)
The Last Concert Tour ♫♫♫ (Giant, 1991)
Adults ♫♫ (Hollywood/Rounder, 1992)
Seek and You Shall Find: More of the Best ♫♫♫ (Rhino, 1993)
The Norman Whitfield Sessions ♫♫♫♫ (Motown, 1994)
Motown Legends ♫♫♫♫ (ESX, 1994)
Classics Collection ♫♫♫♫ (Motown, 1994)
When I'm Alone I Cry ♫♫♫ (Motown, 1994)
Anthology ♫♫♫♫♫ (Motown, 1995)
Vulnerable ♫♫ (Motown, 1997)

worth searching for: In 1986, Motown put both *What's Going On* and *Let's Get It On* on a single CD. The fidelity isn't quite up to the standards of later CD releases, but it's still a wonderful trip to slap it on and hear two of Gaye's finest albums flow back-to-back.

influences:

◀◀ Nat King Cole, Frank Sinatra, Billie Holiday, Ray Charles, Clyde McPhatter, Little Willie John, Rudy West, the Orioles, the Capris

▶▶ Stevie Wonder, Frankie Beverly, Rick James, Terence Trent D'Arby, Barry White, Al B. Sure!, Keith Sweat, El DeBarge

Gary Graff

Gear Daddies
See: Martin Zellar

J. Geils Band /Bluestime

Formed 1967, in Boston, MA. Disbanded 1985.

J. (Jerome) Geils, guitar; Peter Wolf (born Peter Blankfield), vocals (1967–83); Seth Justman, keyboards, vocals (1968–85); Magic Dick (Salwitz), harmonica; Danny Klein, bass; Stephen Jo Bladd, drums.

Part barroom blues ensemble, part soul revue, part arena rabble rousers, the J. Geils Band was a quintessentially American rock 'n' roll band, drawing from sources that stretched from

Mississippi Delta blues to Motown to the Rolling Stones. During its 18 years together, the Geils gang was always painfully inconsistent, and for a minute—with 1981's multi-million-selling *Freeze-Frame*—it was the hottest band in the land. The inconsistency was always frustrating for fans, because Geils had a loaded arsenal of talent—the motor-mouthed histrionics of former disc jockey Peter Wolf, the sharp melodic sense of Seth Justman, the truly enchanting harp skills of Magic Dick. When it clicked, few could beat Geils, and its concerts were usually 'til-we-all-drop marathons. The bottom fell out when the group was at the top, and Wolf left in 1983. The Geils chemistry was never the same without him, and a break-up was inevitable. Wolf has had a middling solo career, while J. Geils and Magic Dick went on to form the rootsier group Bluestime. There's periodic talk of a Geils reunion, but it has yet to transpire.

what to buy: The two-CD *Houseparty: The J. Geils Band Anthology* ♫♫♫ (Atlantic & Atco Remasters/Rhino, 1993, prod. various) nails it, housing all the truly great Geils moments (though we'd rather have the full-length version of the 70s hit "Give It to Me"); it's essential either on its own or as a guide for future purchases. *Monkey Island* ♫♫♫♫ (Atlantic, 1977, prod. J. Geils Band) and *Love Stinks* ♫♫♫♫ (EMI, 1980, prod. Seth Justman) are the best of the studio sets, both of them marked by adventurous sonic forays that don't abandon the group's melodic roots.

what to buy next: *Freeze-Frame* ♫♫♫♫ (EMI, 1981, prod. Seth Justman) was Geils' smash and remains entertaining, if not as consistently fresh as *Love Stinks*. No Geils collection is complete without a live recording, and *Blow Your Face Out* ♫♫♫♫ (Atlantic, 1976/Rhino, 1993, prod. Allen Blazek, Bill Szymczk, J. Geils Band) is the choice there: a rowdy representation of the group's onstage charisma, including Wolf's stream-of-consciousness raps.

what to avoid: *Hotline* ♫ (Atlantic, 1975/1990, prod. Bill Szymczk, Allen Blazek) is typical of the ineffectual studio work Geils was capable of during the early and mid-70s.

the rest:
The J. Geils Band ♫♫♫ (Atlantic, 1970)
The Morning After ♫♫♫ (Atlantic, 1971)
Full House ♫♫♫ (Atlantic, 1972)
Bloodshot ♫♫♫ (Atlantic, 1973)
Ladies Invited ♫♫ (Atlantic, 1973)
Nightmares. . .and Other Tales from the Vinyl Jungle ♫♫ (Atlantic, 1974)
Sanctuary ♫♫♫ (EMI, 1978)
The Best of the J. Geils Band ♫♫♫ (Atlantic, 1979)
You're Getting Even While I'm Getting Odd ♫♫ (EMI, 1984)
Flashback: The Best of the J. Geils Band ♫♫♫♫ (EMI, 1985)

worth searching for: Available only as an import, the live *Showtime!* (EMI, 1982/BGO, 1995, prod. Seth Justman) isn't quite as definitive as *Blow Your Face Out*, but it catches an exuberant Geils stand at the end of its triumphant *Freeze-Frame* tour.

solo outings:
Bluestime (J. Geils and Magic Dick):
Bluestime ♫♫♫ (Rounder, 1994)
Little Care of Blues ♫♫♫♫ (Rounder, 1996)

influences:

◄◄ James Brown, Jackie Wilson, the Yardbirds, John Mayall, the Rolling Stones, John Lee Hooker, Motown, Stax, Bill Haley & the Comets

►► Aerosmith, Bruce Springsteen & the E Street Band, Michael Stanley Band, the Iron City Houserockers, Blues Traveler

see also: *Peter Wolf*

Gary Graff

Howe Gelb
See: Giant Sand

Bob Geldof
See: The Boomtown Rats

Gene
Formed 1993, in London, England.

Martin Rossiter, vocals; Steve Mason, guitar; Kevin Miles, bass; Matt James, drums.

While some quarters have attempted to write off this British quartet as mere Smiths copyists, there have been as many championing Gene as one of the few acts to convey sweeping emotion with intelligence, wit, charm (like the Smiths before them), and guts. The latter of these contrasting views is in fact more the case.

what to buy: Gene's debut album, *Olympian* ♫♫♫♫ (A&M, 1995, prod. Phil Vinall), actually encompasses many great influences in pop history, from mod to punk, soul, rockabilly, and glam, all with effortless dexterity. Best of all, Martin Rossiter turns out to be a singular human-relationship lyricist, with as much humor and eye for detail as empathy. Behind him, Steve Mason is a wonderkind, mixing delicate and pounding riffs with brilliantly understated runs and a knack for moodsetting, while the rhythm section handles hush as well as harsh with equal effectiveness. The versatility thus encompasses the bounce of the opening "Haunted by You" through the more epic feel of "London, Can You Wait" and the title track.

what to buy next: *Drawn to the Deep End* ✍✍✍✌ (A&M, 1997) builds on all the above strengths and by toughing the sound, largely leaves all Smiths comparisons in the dust.

worth searching for: Also worth picking up is an import-only collection of British B-sides and live/demo/BBC session versions of "Olympian" material called *To See the Lights* (Costermonger Records U.K., 1996), which even betters the first LP for consistent highs.

influences:

◀◀ The Smiths, Echo & the Bunnymen, T. Rex, Carl Perkins, the Who

Jack Rabid

General Public

See: The English Beat

Generation X

See: Billy Idol

Genesis

Formed 1966, in Godalming, England.

Tony Banks, keyboards; Mike Rutherford, guitar, bass, vocals; Peter Gabriel, vocals (1966–75); Anthony Phillips, guitar (1966–70); Chris Stewart, drums (1966–68); John Silver, drums (1968–69); John Mayhew, drums (1969–70); Phil Collins, drums, vocals (1970–96); Steve Hackett, guitar (1970–77); Ray Wilson, vocals (1996–present).

Formed at England's private Charterhouse secondary school, Genesis has been the most enduring group of the art rock movement, having not only survived but become more popular with each significant personnel change. The group's early touchstone was Jonathan King's hit "Everyone's Gone to the Moon," and its earliest recordings ape that song's pastoral psychedelia. But a later influence, King Crimson's *In the Court of the Crimson King*, was more profound; Genesis began crafting longer, more intricate pieces, combining together individual "bits" and ideas into suite-like compositions that featured Tony Banks's layered keyboards and the ambient guitars of Steve Hackett and Mike Rutherford. This reached a peak on the 23-minute opus "Supper's Ready" and the 1974 concept album *The Lamb Lies Down on Broadway*, after which original singer Peter Gabriel—whose elaborate costumes and theatrical sense resulted in captivating concerts—left for a celebrated solo career. With Phil Collins in front, Genesis never abandoned its longer compositions, but made room for more pop fare and became a consistent resident of the Top 40 with hits such as "Follow You, Follow Me," "Invisible Touch," and "Land of Confusion." As Collins's solo career reached phenomenon peaks (Rutherford had a more modest success with his side band,

Mike & the Mechanics, while Banks concentrated on film soundtracks), Genesis albums came further and further apart. Collins's inevitable departure in 1996 could have been the band's death blow, but Rutherford and Banks found new singer Ray Wilson from the band Stiltskin and decided to soldier on. Genesis has shown nothing if not a track record for resilience, particularly in the face of adversity. (Note: During 1994–95, Atlantic re-released most of Genesis' catalog in a Definitive Edition Remaster series. The titles are clearly marked, and all others should be avoided.)

what to buy: Genesis' sound truly gels on *Foxtrot* ✍✍✍✍ (Atlantic, 1972, prod. David Hitchcock). Gabriel's array of voicings give depth to the characters in "Get 'em out by Friday" and the massive "Supper's Ready," while "Watcher of the Skies" is one of the majestic classics of art rock. Because its narrative is fairly oblique, *The Lamb Lies Down on Broadway* ✍✍✍✌ (Atlantic, 1974, prod. John Burns, Genesis) works as a flowing, almost formless concept piece, a musical journey rather than a dogmatic treatise. *A Trick of the Tail* ✍✍✍✍ (Atco, 1976, prod. David Hentschel, Genesis) quickly establishes that the group could survive Gabriel's departure, and the comparative brevity of songs such as "Squonk" and the title track is actually a welcome change of pace after the sprawl of *The Lamb*. *Abacab* ✍✍✍✍ (Atlantic, 1981, prod. Genesis) is the sonic pinnacle of the Collins years, a smart pop album that flows from the taut title track to the muscular swell of "Dodo/Lurker" to straightforward hit fare such as the horn-laden "No Reply at All" and the spare "Man on the Corner."

what to buy next: The politically pointed *Selling England by the Pound* ✍✍✍✍ (Atlantic, 1973, prod. John Burns, Genesis) refines many of *Foxtrot*'s virtues but without the same sense of drama. *Wind & Wuthering* (Atco, 1977, prod. David Hentschel, Genesis) is, in hindsight, the final work of Genesis as a full-scale "progressive" rock band. *Seconds Out* ✍✍✍✍ (Atco, 1977, prod. David Hentschel, Genesis) is the best of Genesis' several live albums. At four CDs, *Genesis Archives, Volume 1: 1967–1975* ✍✍✍✍ (Atlantic, 1998, prod. various) is a big drink of water, but it's well worth it for the live tracks—including a full rendition of *The Lamb Lies Down on Broadway*—as well as for a set of demos from 1967–69 that offer a glimpse at the band's creative, er, genesis.

what to avoid: The problem with *Calling All Stations* ✍ (Atlantic, 1997, prod. Nick Davis, Tony Banks, Mike Rutherford) isn't so much new singer Wilson as it is the transitional nature of the album. Banks and Rutherford had written the material prior to hiring Wilson, which makes the whole affair sound stiff and tentative.

the rest:

From Genesis to Revelation/In the Beginning ✍ (PolyGram, 1968)

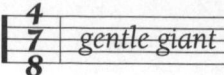

Trespass ♪♪♪ (Charisma/MCA, 1970)
Nursery Cryme ♪♪♪ (Atlantic, 1971)
...And Then There Were Three... ♪♪ (Atlantic, 1978)
Duke ♪♪♪♪ (Atlantic, 1980)
Three Sides Live ♪♪♪♪ (Atlantic, 1982)
Genesis ♪♪♪ (Atlantic, 1983)
Invisible Touch ♪♪♪ (Atlantic, 1986)
We Can't Dance ♪♪♪♪ (Atlantic, 1991)
Live/The Way We Walk, Vol. 1: The Shorts ♪♪♪ (Atlantic, 1992)
Live/The Way We Walk, Vol. 2: The Longs ♪♪♪ (Atlantic, 1993)

worth searching for: The import collection *Turn It on Again: Best of '81–'83* (Vertigo, 1991, prod. Genesis, Hugh Padgham) takes a nice snapshot of this three-year period, fleshing it out with some non-album singles ("Paperlate") and live tracks, including the entertaining "Turn It on Again" medley.

solo outings:
Tony Banks:

A Curious Feeling ♪♪ (Charisma, 1979)
The Fugitive ♪♪♪ (Charisma, 1983)
The Wicked Lady ♪♪ (Atlantic, 1983)
Quicksilver ♪♪♪ (Atlantic, 1986)
Bankstatement ♪♪ (Atlantic, 1989)

Steve Hackett:

Voyage of the Acolyte ♪♪♪ (Chrysalis, 1976/Blue Plate, 1991)
Please Don't Touch ♪♪♪ (Chrysalis, 1978/Caroline, 1991)
Spectral Mornings ♪♪♪ (Chrysalis, 1979/Blue Plate, 1991)
Defector ♪♪ (Charisma, 1980/Blue Plate, 1991)
Cured ♪♪♪ (Epic, 1981/Caroline, 1991)
Highly Strung ♪♪♪ (Charisma, 1983/1991)
Bay of Kings ♪♪ (Chrysalis, 1983/Caroline, 1994/Camino, 1997)
Till We Have Faces ♪♪♪ (Chrysalis, 1984/Herald/Caroline, 1994)
(With GTR) *GTR* ♪ (Arista, 1986)
Momentum ♪♪ (Chrysalis, 1988/Herald/Caroline, 1994/Camino, 1997)
Time Lapse ♪♪ (Blue Plate, 1992/Camino, 1997)
Guitar Noir ♪♪ (Viceroy, 1993/Camino, 1997)
Blues with a Feeling ♪ (Caroline, 1995/Camino, 1997)

Mike Rutherford (with Mike & the Mechanics):

Mike + the Mechanics ♪♪♪♪ (Atlantic, 1985)
The Living Years ♪♪♪ (Atlantic, 1988)
Word of Mouth ♪♪ (Atlantic, 1991)
Beggar on a Beach of Gold ♪♪ (Atlantic, 1995)

influences:

◀◀ Jonathan King, King Crimson, Procol Harum, the Beatles

▶▶ Marillion, Styx, Kansas, Saga

see also: *Phil Collins, Peter Gabriel*

Gary Graff

Gentle Giant

Formed 1969, in England. Disbanded 1980.

Derek Shulman, guitar, bass, vocals; Ray Shulman, bass, violin, vocals; Phil Shulman, saxophone; Kerry Minnear, keyboards; Gary Green, guitar; Martin Smith, drums; John Weathers, drums.

Gentle Giant was something of a working man's progressive rock group. It wasn't as flashy as Yes or Emerson, Lake & Palmer, as literary as Genesis, as pop-oriented as the Move or 10cc, as psychedelic as Pink Floyd, or as AM-friendly as Styx or Kansas. However, Gentle Giant brought a light-hearted twist to even the most complex material, deftly avoiding the artistic pretensions that dogged its contemporaries. The band was also intensely prolific and creatively diverse, able to meld many variants of hard rock into its distinctive, almost personal style. Initially a psychedelic, R&B-based band called Simon Dupree & Big Sound, the group changed both name and styles just as the progressive rock movement began to take hold in Great Britain. Though immensely popular in Europe, Gentle Giant had a difficult time building career momentum in the United States. Some LPs—particularly *Acquiring the Taste*, *Three Friends*, and *In a Glass House*—were deemed by the record label as "too uncommercial" for release. This gave the group's harder-to-find works the cache of "forbidden goods," earning it the undying loyalty of a generation of college students. Gentle Giant was beginning a move towards the mainstream when the rise of punk rendered it irrelevant, and the musicians disbanded. During the '90s, a series of CD reissues have finally earned the group the appreciation of discerning U.S. audiences.

what to buy: The band's finest start-to-finish LP, *Octopus* ♪♪♪♪♪ (Columbia, 1973/Legacy, 1990, prod. Gentle Giant), with its otherworldly vocals and thematic intensity, still holds up 25 years after its initial release. However, *Edge of Twilight* ♪♪♪♪ (Vertigo, 1997, prod. Gentle Giant), might be the best introduction to this band. The two-disc, 31-song set features highlights from its first five LPs as well as a smart job of digital remastering.

what to buy next: Gentle Giant rocks a little harder than usual on *Free Hand* ♪♪♪♪ (Capitol, 1975/One Way, 1993), a satisfying set of peak-level performances. Also, of all the live discs out right now, *The Official Live Gentle Giant: Playing the Fool* ♪♪♪♪ (Capitol, 1977/One Way, 1996, prod. Paul Northfield) boasts the largest track selection, best sound, and several pieces from the Europe-only set *In a Glass House*.

what to avoid: Possibly its weakest album, *The Power & the Glory* ♪♪ (Capitol, 1974/One Way, 1996, prod. Gentle Giant) suffers from indulgent keyboard playing and some irritating sonic dissonance.

the rest:
Gentle Giant ♪♪♪ (Mercury, 1970/1990)

Acquiring the Taste ♫♫♫♪ (Mercury, 1971/1990)
Three Friends ♫♫♫♪ (Columbia, 1972/1989)
Interview ♫♫♪ (Capitol, 1976/One Way, 1995)
The Missing Piece ♫♫ (Capitol, 1977/One Way, 1995)
Giant for a Day ♫♫♪ (Capitol, 1978/One Way, 1995)
Civilian ♫♫ (Capitol, 1980/One Way, 1997)
King Biscuit Flower Hour Presents Gentle Giant ♫♫♫♪ (KBFH, 1997)

worth searching for: Devoted fans will definitely want to hunt through the import racks for *Out of the Woods: The BBC Sessions* (Band of Joy, 1996, prod. Gentle Giant), a 14-song set recorded live between 1970 and 1975 that boasts exceptional sound quality.

influences:

◀◀ Simon Dupree & Big Sound, Jethro Tull, Genesis, the Nice

▶▶ Big Elf, Camel, Art of Noise, the Sugarcubes

Ken Burke

Boy George
See: Culture Club

Georgia Satellites /Dan Baird

Formed 1983, in Atlanta, GA. Disbanded 1991. Re-formed 1993.

Dan Baird, vocals, guitar (1979–91); Rick Richards, guitar; Mauro Megellan, drums (1983–91); Rick Price, bass; Joey Huffman, keyboards (1993); Billy Pitts, drums (1993).

Unfairly written off as a one-hit wonder ("Keep Your Hands to Yourself"), the Georgia Satellites did have more to say than their ode to unrequited love implied. A no-nonsense bar band in the middle of the video-crazed hair-band '80s, the Satellites' rough-and-tumble approach cut a brief swath through Top 40 radio. Their albums seldom failed to provide solid, if unspectacular entertainment. After the band split, singer Dan Baird went solo and enjoyed a modicum of success without changing his musical approach a whit. Nothing wrong with that, either.

what to buy: *Let It Rock: The Best of the Georgia Satellites* ♫♫♫♪ (Elektra, 1993, prod. various) offers a generous 20-track retrospective that covers the smash "Keep Your Hands to Yourself" as well as "Battleship Chains" and the Satellites' version of "Hippy Hippy Shake." Baird's solo debut hit with "I Love You Period," a grammar lesson laid on top of a brilliant, crunching pop tune. The album, *Love Songs for the Hearing Impaired* ♫♫♫♪ (American, 1992, prod. Brendan O'Brien) provided plenty of howling good fun.

the rest:
Georgia Satellites ♫♫♫♪ (Elektra, 1986)
In the Land of Salvation and Sin ♫♫♫♪ (Elektra, 1989)

solo outings:
Dan Baird:
Buffalo Nickel ♫♫♪ (American, 1996)

influences:

◀◀ The Rolling Stones, Little Feat, Wet Willie

Allan Orski and Daniel Durchholz

Geraldine Fibbers

Formed 1993, in Los Angeles, CA.

Karla Bozulich, vocals; Daniel Keenan, guitar (1993–95); William Tutton, bass; Jessy Greene, violin; Kevin Fitzgerald, drums; Nels Cline, guitar.

The Geraldine Fibbers started as a rootsy respite for southern California punk scene vet Carla Bozulich during the early '90s, after she fronted such caustic projects as Ethyl Meatplow. The Fibbers have become so adept at joining the two disparate genres that they've inspired writers to create such lexicon-bending tags as cowpunk, waltzfusion, and cattleprog in order to describe the group's sound. And all, of course, fall just short. Driven by Bozulich's painfully introspective writing and dusky vocal phrasing, the Fibbers' "sound" is something that is best defined track by track. Despite the lack of a neat little box to put it in, critics embraced the group's first high and lonesome release, *Lost Somewhere between the Earth and My Home*. The praise increased as did the tempo—thanks in part to the punk sensibilities of new guitarist Nels Cline—on its 1997 follow-up, *Butch*.

what to buy: *Butch* ♫♫♫♪ (Virgin, 1997, prod. Geraldine Fibbers) is full of powerful, wrenching songs that get away from the twangy stuff found on *Lost Somewhere between the Earth and My Home* in favor of a more guitar-driven post-grunge sound. Psycho blasts such as "Toy Box" are voyeuristic enough to give you that not-so-fresh feeling, but in the end it's the burning honesty of the songs that breaks through.

the rest:
Lost Somewhere between the Earth and My Home ♫♫♫♪ (Virgin, 1995)
What Part of "Get Thee Gone" Don't You Understand ♫♫♫♪ (Sympathy for the Record Industry, 1997)

influences:

◀◀ X, Uncle Tupelo, L7, John Doe, Patti Smith, John Hiatt

Brandon Barber

Lisa Germano

Born 1958, in Mishawaka, IN.

The daughter of classical musicians, Lisa Germano and her five siblings were all expected to learn an instrument, so the shy brunette studied the violin from age seven through high

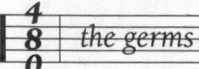
school. Though she started playing classical music, her efforts eventually turned to country, culminating in a gig at the Little Nashville Opry in Indiana. In these circles, she eventually befriended John Cougar Mellencamp's drummer, Kenny Aronoff, who brought Germano to Mellencamp's attention when the Indiana rocker needed violin sounds for 1987's *The Lonesome Jubilee*. Germano spent the next few years touring and recording with Mellencamp, as well as squeezing in work with acts like Simple Minds, Bob Seger, and Billy Joel before releasing her first solo record in 1991. By now a multi-instrumentalist who had expanded her repertoire to include piano, mandolin, guitar, accordion, and harmonica, she performed every track on the recording herself—a feat she would repeat on subsequent releases. Crafting an intense, introspective style, Germano's own music offers an oddball mix of traditional instruments used in non-traditional ways. Signed to Capitol Records for her second solo record, the singer-songwriter grew frustrated with the label and eventually moved to 4AD Records, which rereleased her second album before offering her third solo disc several months later. In 1998 she was to join Smashing Pumpkins as a touring musician, but a falling out with the band left her free to pursue her solo career again.

what to buy: Though she clashed repeatedly with her label while making it, *Happiness* 𝄢𝄢𝄢 (Columbia, 1993, prod. Lisa Germano, Malcolm Burn) remains the best combination of Germano's quirky vision and oddball, accessible appeal. Veering from a stark cover of Nancy Sinatra's "These Boots Are Made for Walkin'" to the percolating sound collage "Sycophant," Germano makes dissonance and dark thoughts an appealing prospect.

what to buy next: As the sonic tale of a young woman's coming of age, *Geek the Girl* 𝄢𝄢𝄢 (4AD, 1994, prod. Lisa Germano, Malcolm Burn) stands as a rich, darkly textured sonic journey. Blending a sample of a terrifying 911 call into the herky-jerky tune "A Psychopath"—inspired by her own longtime problems with a stalker—and enlisting a pennywhistle to kick off the dark brooding of "My Secret Reason," Germano makes disparate sounds serve a single purpose. At once earthy folk and dreamy performance art–style atmospherics, this record stands out as an intense, complex work.

what to avoid: Despite its delicate, darkly disturbing beauty, *On the Way down from the Moon Palace* 𝄢𝄢𝄢 (Major Bill, 1991, prod. Lisa Germano) is by far the slightest of her solo efforts.

the rest:
Excerpts from a Love Circus 𝄢𝄢𝄢 (4AD, 1996)
Slide 𝄢𝄢𝄢 (4AD, 1998)

worth searching for: Germano's many contributions to other's records, including Mellencamp's *The Lonesome Jubilee* and *Big*

Daddy albums, the Indigo Girls' *Swamp Ophelia*, and Bob Seger's *The Fire Inside*.

influences:
◀◀ Indigo Girls, Aimee Mann, Patti Smith
▶▶ Michelle Malone, Mae Moore

Eric Deggans

The Germs
Formed 1977, in Los Angeles, CA. Disbanded 1980.

Darby Crash (born Paul Beahm; died December 6, 1980), vocals; Pat Smear, guitar; Lorna Doom, bass; Donna Rhia, drums (1977); Don Bolles, drums (1977–79); Nickey Beat, drums (1979–80).

The Germs were America's punk rockers. Let the Sex Pistols put safety pins in their clothes; the Germs—particularly frontman Darby Crash—staged food fights and wore leopard fur jock straps. The Germs' story is almost prototypical punk legend: kindred spirits get together, can't really play or sing, but do so anyway. A cult scene sprouts up around the group, which records one album and flames out, with one member (in this case Crash) winding up dead from a drug overdose. The Germs didn't quite get their due while together, but the group finally received some recognition during the mid-'90s thanks to Pat Smear's involvement in Nirvana and Foo Fighters and the 1996 tribute album *The Germs (Tribute): A Small Circle of Friends*.

what to buy: The music the Germs left behind is prototypical—brutal, driving punk songs that blaze for a couple of minutes (or less) before a martial count launches the next one. It's captured in all its noisy and low-fi glory on *Germs (MIA): The Complete Anthology* 𝄢𝄢𝄢𝄢 (Slash, 1993, prod. various), a 30-track wonder that contains the group's legendary 1979 album *(GI)* and an assortment of other tracks, including the "Forming/Sex Boy" single and a so-sloppy-it's-fun rendition of Chuck Berry's "Round and Round" that features X D.J. Bonebrake on drums.

the rest:
Media Blitz 𝄢𝄢𝄢 (Cleopatra, 1993)
Germicide—Live at the Whisky 1977 𝄢𝄢 (ROIR, 1982)

worth searching for: *The Germs (Tribute): A Small Circle of Friends* (Grass, 1996, prod. various) features performances by L7, Matthew Sweet, the Meat Puppets, the Posies, Thurston Moore, Kim Gordon, J. Mascis, and other modern rockers who have felt the Germs' touch.

influences:
◀◀ The Stooges, MC5, the Troggs, New York Dolls, the Ramones
▶▶ Nirvana, Sonic Youth, L7, Meat Puppets, Soundgarden, Dinosaur Jr.

Gary Graff

Lisa Gerrard

Born in Melbourne, Australia.

In many ways, Australian band Dead Can Dance typified the goth scene of the '80s, with its cemetery soundscapes and keening vocal theatrics, but unlike its brethren, the band not only outgrew the gloom movement, but developed into a far-reaching experiment in eclecticism. By the time DCD ran aground, the band was making music that was heavily inflected with world music—particularly with exotic Far Eastern and lonely Eastern European traditional arrangements. Lisa Gerrard's supple voice was getting a rigorous workout with DCD, and when this Australian musician released her first solo album, *The Mirror Pool*, she demonstrated a talent for imbuing richly textured arrangements with both extreme reverence and extreme wackiness. Her voice swept from the ethereal to the operatic, an instrument that didn't need the too-heavy production it has sometimes been paired with.

what to buy: The self-produced *The Mirror Pool* 🎵🎵🎵 (4AD, 1995) is built on a foundation of wild and wooly outtakes from DCD projects. As a solo effort, it proves that Gerrard is more than just a voice. Her ability to arrange and adapt complex material is aurally astonishing.

what to buy next: On *Duality* 🎵🎵🎵 (4AD, 1998) Gerrard teams up with Soma's Pieter Bourke, who also worked on her solo debut. These songs are more in the mood of DCD than those on *The Mirror Pool*: elegant and exotic background music that pleases without asking too terribly much of the listener.

influences:

◀◀ Cocteau Twins, This Mortal Coil

▶▶ The Dirty Three, Deep Forest

see also: *Dead Can Dance*

Amy Weivoda

Gerry & the Pacemakers

Formed 1959, in Liverpool, England. Disbanded 1966.

Gerry Marsden, vocals; Les Maguire, piano; Les Chadwick, bass; Freddie Marsden, drums.

Like their fellow Liverpudlians, the Beatles, Gerry & the Pacemakers found roots in Britain's late '50s skiffle craze. The band cut its teeth in the same Hamburg clubs where the Beatles played, and it was the first group signed by Brian Epstein after he secured the Beatles. But that's where the two groups parted ways. The music of Gerry & the Pacemakers was softer; Marsden's gentle vocals were sunny and reassuring, and only rarely did he cut loose into raunchier styles. Ironically, the group had its first hit with a number recorded but rejected by the Beat-les—the 1963 U.K. hit "How Do You Do It?" The band made music history as the first rock group to have its first three records reach #1: "How Do You Do It?" and "I Like It," both written by Mitch Murray, and the unlikely Rodgers & Hammerstein ballad "You'll Never Walk Alone." Marsden went solo in 1967 and enjoyed success in stage work (*Charlie Girl*) and children's TV. He has occasionally re-formed the group for revival shows.

what to buy: *Gerry Cross the Mersey: All the Hits of Gerry & the Pacemakers* 🎵🎵🎵 (Razor & Tie, 1995, prod. George Martin, Ron Richards) is a worthy compilation filled with the sun-behind-the-clouds hopefulness that permeates the band's catalog. The 16 tracks include the group's U.K. and U.S. hits ("How Do You Do It?," "You'll Never Walk Alone," "Don't Let the Sun Catch You Cryin'") plus some excellent B-sides, including the wistful and lovely "Ferry Cross the Mersey."

influences:

◀◀ Lonnie Donegan, Elvis Presley, Roy Orbison, the Beatles

▶▶ Cilla Black, Petula Clark, Lulu, the Monkees

Christopher Scapelliti

Getaway Cruiser

Formed 1995, in Ann Arbor, MI.

Dina Harrison, vocals; Chris Peters, guitar, harmonica, turntables, mellotron, synths, talkbox; Drew Peters, guitar, backing vocals, Tascam 488, accordion, mellotron, piano; Dan Carroll, drums; Mark Dundon, bass.

Growing up in well-heeled West Bloomfield, Michigan, the Peters brothers were inspired early on by the diversity of Detroit radio as well as the music played in their home—including the Cuban rhythms of their grandfather as well as the urban sounds of Run-D.M.C. mixed with the white-boy rock of Aerosmith and Skid Row. Meanwhile, the diminutive Dina Harrison found jazz and showtunes to be her cup of tea. The duo and Harrison, along with Dan Carroll and Mark Dundon, came together at the University of Michigan after the Peters brothers' former band, Whirling Road, fell apart. Getaway Cruiser was somewhat of a savior for Harrison, who was unhappily studying opera at U-M and craved the sound of pop.

what's available: It sounds like an odd pairing, but rap, hip-hop, rock, and the intense sentiments of love found in show tunes were melded to form *Getaway Cruiser* 🎵🎵 (Sony, 1998, prod. Butcher Brothers, Getaway Cruiser). The music on the band's debut album is remarkable, but Harrison's vocals fall flat, resting within the comfortable confines of a monotone soprano. Songs such as "Wasting Away," which tells about the hopeless feeling that drives young adults to suicide, and "I'm Fine (I Find)" are bolstered by the help of Kool Keith (Ultramagnetic MCs, Dr. Octagon) and Pras of the Fugees, respectively. Led by Chris Peters's sultry guitar, "Something about You" is topped off with a bluesy harmonica solo. "Come to Stay" reflects early 1980s synth-pop tunes, while a cover of Tony! Toni! Tone's "Let's Get Down" is covered with drum loops, turntable scratching, and an accordion.

the rest:
Getaway Cruiser 𝄢𝄢 (Sony, 1998)

influences:
◀◀ Beastie Boys, Run-D.M.C., Sneaker Pimps, Wu-Tang Clan

Christina Fuoco

Giant Sand

Formed 1985, in Tuscon, AZ.

Howe Gelb, guitars, lead vocals; Scott Garber, bass (1985–87); Tom Larkins, drums (1985–87); Paula Jean Brown, guitars, bass (1986–94); Neil Harry, pedal steel (1987–88); Chris Cacavas, organ, accordion (1988–92); John Convertino, drums (1988–present); Joey Burns, bass (1991–present); Pappy Allen, guitars, background vocals (1992–95); Victoria Williams, guitars, vocals (1992–95); Rainer Ptacek, guitar (1993–94).

Keeping tabs on the storm that is Giant Sand is rough; eye-of-the-hurricane Howe Gelb works his musical mind in mysterious ways, acting as the conductor, songwriter, and agitator of a cast of dozens, some of whom are official members, and others who appear on a record or two and then disappear over the horizon. The band's twang-infused rock—part Neil Young stutter-guitar, part Captain Beefheart desert confusion—is chaotic, yet always settles in a similar place, even if that place moves around from time to time. Since Giant Sand's inception, they've gone through countless record labels, seemingly unconcerned with thoughts of "marketability" or "career." Instead, Gelb and company chase the tumbleweed wherever it leads them, and often these journeys result in extraordinary, dream-like music.

what to buy: Point of departure for Giant Sand would be the glorious *The Love Songs* 𝄢𝄢𝄢 (Homestead, 1988, prod. Eric Westfall, Howe Gelb), which combines the more traditional country rock of its earlier releases with a sprawling, inventive looseness that begins to offer a glimpse into Gelb's restless curiosity. On "One Man's Woman/No Man's Land," Gelb finds a great melody, stretches it to its breaking point, then proceeds to destroy it and reconstruct it, all in a matter of minutes. *Swerve* 𝄢𝄢𝄢 (Amazing Black Sand/Restless, 1993, prod. Howe Gelb) is a sturdier rock album with harder guitar chords and a more cohesive vision that examines huge existential issues, personal history, and complicated love. From there jump to Giant Sand's most complete album, *Center of the Universe*

𝄢𝄢𝄢𝄢 (Restless, 1992, prod. Howe Gelb, Michael Dumas, John Convertino), a record that combines the best of it all—utilitarian restraint, hard desert anthems ("Center of the Universe" is one of most glorious shout-out love songs of the '90s), and moaning regret. It's one of the great overlooked rock records of the decade.

what to buy next: Break-up records can be dangerous, but Gelb's separation from his wife/bassist Paula Jean Brown led to the raw, stripped down *Long Stem Rant* 𝄢𝄢𝄢 (Homestead, 1989, prod. Howe Gelb), which featured only guitar and percussion—supplied by a snare, file cabinet, and water cooler—to create its sorrowful, desperate tone. *Ramp* 𝄢𝄢𝄢 (Amazing Black Sand/Restless, 1994, prod. Howe Gelb) is a more erratic record, one that jumps from chaos to construction and back and forth throughout its length; it's a rollercoaster, it's a blast, but not every time.

what to avoid: Occasionally Gelb's roaming, experimental curiosity gets the best of him; *Purge and Slouch* 𝄢𝄢 (Restless, 1994) is a mess, and while it opens up after repeated listenings, it's mostly unbearable.

the rest:
Valley of Rain/Ballad of a Thin Line Man 𝄢𝄢𝄢 (1986)
Storm 𝄢𝄢𝄢 (Zippo, 1988)
Giant Sandwich 𝄢𝄢𝄢 (Homestead, 1989)
Giant Songs: The Best of Giant Sand 𝄢𝄢𝄢𝄢 (Demon U.K., 1989)
Giant Songs, Vol. 2: The Best of Giant Sand 𝄢𝄢𝄢𝄢 (Demon U.K., 1995)
Backyard Barbecue Broadcast 𝄢𝄢𝄢 (Koch, 1995)

worth searching for: Predictably, Giant Sand's only major-label effort, *Glum* (Imago, 1994), failed to make any impact on the public at large, and within a year the label itself was gone. Which is a shame, because, despite its dreary title, *Glum* is a sprawling ride, highlighted by Victoria Williams's—according to the liner notes—"ending lip flip" and "lush timbre."

solo outings:
Howe Gelb:
Dreaded Brown Recluse 𝄢𝄢𝄢 (Restless, 1993)

Band of Blacky Ranchette:
Heartland 𝄢𝄢𝄢 (Zippo U.K., 1986)
Sage Advice 𝄢𝄢𝄢 (Restless, 1990)

influences:
◀◀ Neil Young, mid-period Bob Dylan, Green on Red, Captain Beefheart

▶▶ Poi Dog Pondering, the Jayhawks, Uncle Tupelo

see also: *Victoria Williams, Friends of Dean Martinez*

Randall Roberts

Debbie Gibson
/Deborah Gibson

Born August 31, 1970, in Brooklyn, NY.

A precocious if not entirely original talent, Debbie Gibson was barely out of kindergarten when she'd composed her first song ("Make Sure You Know Your Classroom") and begun piano classes with Billy Joel's tutor. She won a $1,000 songwriting contest at age 12 with "I Come from America," then successfully auditioned for the lead role in *Les Miserables*—and would have gotten it too, had the director not discovered she was only 15. By then, under the guidance of manager Doug Breithart (who'd given her a crash course in arranging, engineering, and production), Gibson had already demo'd more than 100 songs and was duly awarded a contract with Atlantic Records in time to celebrate her Sweet Sixteen. What followed was a string of effortlessly charming if candy-coated international hits, each written and performed by Gibson so as to provide the ideal soundtrack for mid-'80s, John Hughes–directed teendom. By the turn of the decade however, her perky sweetness ran afoul of the Nirvana generation, and after a brave attempt at collaborating with the Circle Jerks—we kid you not—she sought refuge back on the Broadway stage, where today she works as hard as ever in the casts of *Funny Girl, Grease, Beauty and the Beast,* and—finally—*Les Miserables.*

what to buy: Only the most cynical listener won't ultimately be won over by Gibson's *Greatest Hits* 𝄢𝄢𝄢𝄢 (Atlantic, 1995, prod. various). Taking a cue from the self-assuredness of Madonna but crossing it with a never-failing Brady Bunch–like wholesomeness, this album really is as fine a cross-section of '80s all-American dance-pop as you're likely to find anywhere under one cover.

what to buy next: Freshman efforts don't come much more strong and true—not to mention absolutely hit-laden—as *Out of the Blue* 𝄢𝄢𝄢 (Atlantic, 1987, prod. Deborah Gibson, Fred Zarr, Lewis A. Martinee, John Morales, Sergio Munzibai), while the recent *Only in My Dreams 1998* 𝄢𝄢𝄢 (Espiritu/Jellybean Recordings, 1998, prod. Junior Vasquez) shows Gibson is more than ready, willing, and able to recast herself for a comparatively adult market (under the more mature first name of "Deborah," that is) with this collection of fun-but-tough remixes of her 1987 breakthrough hit.

what to avoid: Of course it's always painful when little girls grow up, but *Anything Is Possible* 𝄢𝄢 (Atlantic, 1990, prod. Deborah Gibson, Lamont Dozier, Jellybean, Fred Zarr), despite an all-star roster of helping hands, remains one of the most disconcerting lunges at so-called maturity ever captured on tape.

the rest:
Electric Youth 𝄢𝄢𝄢 (Atlantic, 1989)

Body Mind Soul 𝄢𝄢𝄢 (Atlantic, 1993)
Think with Your Heart 𝄢𝄢 (SBK, 1995)
Deborah 𝄢𝄢𝄢 (Espiritu, 1997)

worth searching for: In one of the most inspired or insipid (take your choice) duets ever attempted, the Circle Jerks compilation *Oddities, Abnormalities, and Curiosities* (Mercury, 1995, prod. Niko Bolas) features Ms. Gibson getting semi-jiggy with her hardcore pals on the Soft Boys' "I Wanna Destroy You." Robyn Hitchcock could not be reached for comment.

influences:

◀◀ Lesley Gore, Carole King, Olivia Newton-John

▶▶ The Party, Candi & the Backbeat, Mitsou, Chris Breetveld

Gary Pig Gold

Gigolo Aunts

Formed 1987, in Potsdam, NY.

Dave Gibbs, rhythm guitar, vocals; Phil Hurley, lead guitar, vocals (1987–96); Steve Hurley, bass, vocals; Paul Brouwer, drums, vocals (1987–96); Fred Eltringham, drum, vocals (1996–present); Jon Skibic, lead guitar, vocals (1996–present).

It took awhile for the small-town band Gigolo Aunts to grow into its big sound. Beginning as unsure purveyors of so-called guitar-pop—a catch-all genre that briefly flourished in the wake of R.E.M.'s initial success—the most interesting thing about the Aunts was that they took their name from a Syd Barrett song. Soon, however, the group found a niche by appropriating the melodic "oomph" of Big Star, the Raspberries, and Badfinger, and laying it over their own raw gusto. They parlayed that approach, bolstered by notoriously kickin' live shows, into a moderate success that culminated with their musical contribution to the soundtrack of the Tom Hanks film *That Thing You Do.*

what to buy: First released on vinyl in England with a bonus seven-inch single, *Flippin' Out* 𝄢𝄢𝄢𝄢 (RCA, 1994, prod. Mike Deneen) is an aural swirl of Dave Gibbs's raspy, emotional lead vocals and the more boyish pop tones of brothers Phil and Steve Hurley. The end result filters the band's influences—everything from Big Star to Big Dipper—through its own vortex of harmony-smoothed grittiness. More alt-rock than art-rock, *Flippin' Out* is a lost masterpiece that cleverly hammers power-pop guitars to a modern wall of sound. While the songwriting is suitably consistent, the best song is the haunting title track, ironically authored not by the band but one V. Casey, of the mysterious, super-obscure Wizards.

what to buy next: The EP *Full-On Bloom* 𝄢𝄢𝄢 (Alias, 1993, prod. Mike Deneen, Paul Q. Kolderie, John Wood) gave one of the subsequent album's best songs a wonderful introduction, rounded out with four other non-LP originals and a definitive cover of BMX

Bandits' "Serious Drugs." By this point fully bloomed, Gigolo Aunts were just what power-pop fans were looking for, years before the music style came back in vogue in an underground capacity. *Learn to Play Guitar* ♪♪♪♪ (Wicked Disc, 1997, prod. Gigolo Aunts, Brian Charles, Charlton Pettus) is, as the title implies, a back-to-the-drawing-board sort of affair. With its original lead guitarist and drummer gone, the revamped group rocks its way through six powerful new songs (one co-written with Jules Shear). Though the EP is generally excellent, something is missing; it's probably that the homemade indie production and garage-rocking arrangements are a comedown from the major-label glory of *Flippin' Out*. Also, the distinctively beautiful overdrive of Phil Hurley's guitars is sorely missed.

what to avoid: *Everybody's Happy* ♪♪ (Coyote, 1988, prod. Rob Norris) is a boring, R.E.M.-influenced jingle-jangle.

worth searching for: A Spanish import, *Tales from the Vinegar Side* (Impossible, 1990, prod. Paul Q. Koldrie), features a fine, if oddly upbeat, cover of Big Star member Chris Bell's "I Am the Cosmos."

influences:
◀◀ Big Star, R.E.M., Badfinger

Jordan Oakes

Jimmie Dale Gilmore

Born May 6, 1945, in Amarillo, TX.

Blessed with a voice of extraordinary range and expressiveness—think Roy Orbison if he'd wanted to be Jimmie Rodgers instead of Mario Lanza—and a lyrical vision that is equal parts West Texas lonesome and the sound of one hand clapping, Jimmie Dale Gilmore is a unique presence in contemporary music. Silent for nearly two decades after his abortive debut with the supergroup-in-retrospect Flatlanders, Gilmore's solo career began in fairly conventional country territory and moved further left-of-center with each release. His interpretive skills have led him to become the definitive performer of songs by fellow Texas visionary (and former Flatlander) Butch Hancock, while Gilmore's own songs have been covered by Natalie Merchant and David Byrne.

what to buy: *After Awhile* ♪♪♪♪ (Elektra, 1991, prod. Stephen Bruton) is a stunning showcase for Gilmore's original artistry, notably the elliptical, Zenlike "Tonight I Think I'm Gonna Go Downtown" and "Treat Me like a Saturday Night." But the album's otherworldly feel is nicely undercut by the gentle humor of Gilmore's own "Go to Sleep Alone" and the not-so-gentle humor of Butch Hancock's "My Mind's Got a Mind of Its Own." To complete the package, the blazing "Midnight Train" proves Gilmore can play with intensity. Just try keeping your

jaw from dropping repeatedly while listening to this one. *Spinning around the Sun* ♪♪♪♪ (Elektra, 1993, prod. Emory Gordy Jr.) relies more heavily on covers than its predecessor, and it would rate as a superior work if only for Gilmore's near-definitive take on Hank Williams's "I'm So Lonesome I Could Cry." But there's also a loping cover of the Elvis B-side "I Was the One" and Hancock's devastating lover's putdown, "Just a Wave." If anything proves Gilmore's mettle, it's his cover of his ex-wife Jo Carol Pierce's "Reunion," which imagines a couple sundered on earth to be joined again in the hereafter.

what to buy next: If *Magical Mystery Tour* had been recorded in Austin, Texas, it might sound something like *Braver Newer World* ♪♪♪♪ (Elektra, 1996, prod. T-Bone Burnett). Producer Burnette removes Gilmore almost entirely from a country context, surrounding him instead with saxophones, echo-laden drums, and stinging, sitar-like guitar leads, making explicit Gilmore's country & Eastern leanings. It's a radical experiment, but it works.

the rest:
Fair & Square ♪♪♪ (HighTone, 1988)
Jimmie Dale Gilmore ♪♪♪ (HighTone, 1989)

worth searching for: *Mudhoney/Jimmie Dale Gilmore* (Sub Pop EP, 1994, prod. various) is a peculiar artifact on which Gilmore and the Seattle grunge pioneers cover each others' songs and team up for the late Townes Van Zandt's "Buckskin Stallion Blues." Also, Gilmore and Hancock's *Two Roads: Live in Australia* (Virgin Records Australia, 1990/Caroline 1993, prod. Keith Glass, Jimmie Dale Gilmore, Butch Hancock), which finds the two performing solo and in tandem, is an immensely satisfying live album from way, way south of the border.

influences:
◀◀ Hank Williams, Roy Orbison, Buddy Holly, Jimmie Rodgers, Willie Nelson, Alan Watts

▶▶ Jim Lauderdale, Kevin Welch, Iris DeMent, Gillian Welch

see also: *Flatlanders*

Daniel Durchholz

David Gilmour

See: Pink Floyd

Gin Blossoms

Formed 1987, in Tempe, AZ. Disbanded 1997.

Robin Wilson, vocals (1988–97); Doug Hopkins (died December 5, 1993), guitar (1987–91); Scott Johnson, guitar, vocals (1991–97); Jesse Valenzuela, guitar, vocals; Bill Leen, bass, vocals; Phillip Rhodes, drums, vocals (1988–97).

Friends Douglas Hopkins and Bill Leen had played together in Tempe bands for years when, on a Christmas night, they debuted the Gin Blossoms with Jesse Valenzuela on vocals. Within months, Robin Wilson had joined and gradually took over lead vocals, his plaintive high voice becoming the group's sonic trademark. But Hopkins's drinking, chronicled perhaps too much on the first album's songs, increasingly made him unreliable, and he was replaced between the first EP and the debut album, *New Miserable Experience*; he received all due songwriting credits, but there were no playing credits—just a band roster listing his replacement, Scott Johnson. It took over a year for the band's singles to become hits, but A&M stuck with it. Ultimately the material's jangling guitars and tight harmonies benefited from changing formats and spearheaded the return of a sound once again considered commercial—the friendly side of the modern rock/alternative coin. Hopkins, despite the success of his songs, committed suicide shortly before Christmas 1993. The Gin Blossoms recorded a second album but disbanded after its disappointing commercial showing.

what to buy: *New Miserable Experience* 𝄢𝄢𝄢 (A&M, 1992, prod. John Hampton, Gin Blossoms) has the hits "Jealousy" and "Found Out about You," which made the Gin Blossoms a flavor of the season during 1993–94.

the rest:
Up and Crumbling 𝄢𝄢𝄢 (A&M, 1991)
Congratulations I'm Sorry 𝄢𝄢𝄢 (A&M, 1996)

worth searching for: "Found Out about You" is a single worth hunting down the import CD-5 (A&M, 1994) for; added bonuses are live versions of "Hands Are Tied," "29," and Johnny Cash's "Folsom Prison Blues."

influences:
◀◀ The Byrds, the Beatles, Tom Petty

Steve Holtje

Greg Ginn
See: Black Flag

Girls Against Boys
Formed 1990, in Washington, DC.

Scott McCloud, vocals, guitar; Eli Janney, bass, organ, vibraphone; Brendan Canty, drums (1990–92); Johnny Temple, bass, keyboards, samples (1992–present); Alexis Fleisig, drums (1992–present).

The members of Girls Against Boys (GvsB) all have hardcore backgrounds—Scott McCloud, Johnny Temple, and Alexis Fleisig were in Soulside, while Brendan Canty is Fugazi's drummer—and while GvsB incorporate hardcore elements, their slower, darker, and groovier basslines set them far apart from their more traditional roots. Although the group never intended to maintain a full-time band, GvsB has recently been taking metal to new extremes. Their self-proclaimed "ultra-rock"—electronic music combined with a heavy but melodic rhythm section—is a hard yet surprisingly sensual sound. Their secret lies in dual bass players and being able to maintain the delicate balance of using tape loops and synthesizers while keeping enough power and human element to still rock a live show. After a fierce bidding war, the band signed to Geffen but stuck to its indie roots by reminding the new label that it still owed Touch & Go another record; and the suits must have winced when the band released its finest record to date, *House of GvsB*, on an indie label. But they shouldn't worry; even as the record industry is so "over" the indie rock thing, GvsB bring back the electronic effects for the equally compelling *Freak*on*Ica*, both staking their claim in the sounds of electronica and poking fun at the record industry's over-hyping of it.

what to buy: *House of GvsB* 𝄢𝄢𝄢𝄢 (Touch & Go, 1996, prod. Ted Nicely) polishes the "ultra-rock" approach to a smooth, sexy finish. But *House* takes the band beyond its normal boundaries to effortlessly incorporate elements of techno, jazz, and art-rock into its impressive range of musical styles.

what to buy next: *Cruise Yourself* 𝄢𝄢𝄢 (Touch & Go, 1994, prod. Ted Nicely) is all about dark lyrics and industrial-strength rhythm; the beat is hard and slow, but so intense that if it were any faster, it would be causing nose bleeds. On *Venus Luxure No. 1 Baby* 𝄢𝄢𝄢 (Touch & Go, 1994, prod. Ted Nicely), the beats are kept bold and the humor dark, but a lack of variety forces the record to lose too much steam. The most recent effort, *Freak*on*Ica* 𝄢𝄢𝄢 (Geffen, 1998, prod. Nick Launay), bypasses the middleman that gets many records into the dance clubs; instead of getting remixed by a DJ, the band put its own beats on the record.

the rest:
Nineties vs. Eighties 𝄢𝄢 (Adult Swim, 1991, prod. Scott McCloud, Eli Janney)

influences:
◀◀ Fugazi, Ministry, Einstürzende Neubauten, Skinny Puppy, Soulside

see also: *Fugazi*

Brian Ives

Gladhands
Formed 1993, in Omaha, NE.

Jeff Carlson, guitar, vocals, keyboards, bass, percussion; Doug Edmunds, drums, vocals, percussion; Pat McGraw, bass, vocals (1993–96).

If *Summer Days (and Summer Nights!!)* –era Brian Wilson and *Something/Anything?* –era Todd Rundgren were somehow able to come together within a single recording project, the result might sound sort of like a Gladhands record. Not that the Gladhands are in the same league as Wilson or Rundgren, but the group does manage to hit many of the same appealing pop buttons as the masters, and it throws in a healthy dose of caffeine-charged "oomph" to keep the blood circulating properly. Nebraska sons relocated to the more familiar indie-pop Mecca of Chapel Hill, North Carolina, the Gladhands are an unabashed pop band making records in a classic style without seeming the least bit retro. The group is relatively unheralded, even among the pop cognoscenti, but is unassailably one of the best around.

what to buy: Pure pop rarely gets purer or more inviting than *From Here to Obscurity* ♪♪♪ (Big Deal, 1995, prod. Jim Homan, Gladhands), an ace collection of catchy verses and catchier choruses that evokes the memory of Jellyfish without that band's drippier moments. "Reckless" is a fist-in-the-air call-to-arms for soldiers of love everywhere, and the '70s-style AM-pop guitar on "Sisters" conjures a welcome memory of Rundgren's "I Saw the Light." *La Di Da* ♪♪♪ (Big Deal, 1997, prod. Wes Lachot, Gladhands) is basically more of the same, and the drop-dead gorgeous chorus of "Forget All about It" would be blasting out of transistor radios nationwide in the perfect pop world of our imagination. More!

influences:
◀◀ The Beatles, Jellyfish, the Posies, Todd Rundgren, the Beach Boys

Carl Cafarelli

Glass Eye
See: Kathy McCarty

Gary Glitter
Born Paul Francis Gadd, May 8, 1940, in Banbury, England.

An important figure in the era of glam rock—though not nearly as influential as David Bowie or T. Rex—Gary Glitter was the third incarnation of aspiring pop star Paul Gadd. After years of toiling in a ballad-heavy teen pop-star mode, Gadd reinvented himself as Glitter and charted 11 consecutive Top 10 singles in the U.K. His trademarks were cheesy handclap effects, sleazy guitar riffs and massive, singalong choruses—basically rock 'n' roll sports cheers. Glitter's legacy is mostly wrapped up in one song—"Rock and Roll Part II"—whose rousing "Hey!" chorus is played at virtually every sporting event. Appearing onstage in tacky, sparkling outfits that often showcased his growing girth, Glitter nevertheless seemed in on the joke and could be a hilarious, rousing stage performer. While critics and other musicians sniggered, he inspired a manic following that inevitably departed as his fame fleeted. He declared bankruptcy in 1980, but soon came out of retirement to begin touring again to cash

in on "Rock and Roll"'s burgeoning popularity. A mini-resurgence in the late '90s as part of the Who's "Quadrophenia" tour in 1996 and on his own 25th anniversary tour was effectively cut short when he was hit with child pornography allegations back home in England.

what to buy: *Greatest Hits* ♪♪♪♪ (Rhino, 1991, prod. Michael Leander) not only showcases Glitter's chart-topping run of great singles, but is as infectious a singalong record as any you'll encounter.

the rest:
Gary Glitter Gangshow: The Gang, the Band, the Leader ♪♪ (Castle Communications, 1989)

influences:
◀◀ David Bowie, T. Rex
▶▶ Kiss, Joan Jett, Def Leppard, Oasis

Todd Wicks

Glitterbox
Formed 1993, in London, England.

Johnny Green, lead vocals, guitar; Miles Heseltine, guitar, vocals; Tony Holland, bass; Mark Servaes, drums.

A little out of place in the late '90s British rock scene, Glitterbox seems an update on early U2's thoughtful but agitated post-punk style. The band members met at a London art school in 1990, and by 1993 the group—called She at that point—was knocking out club audiences with its adrenaline-drenched but sloppy shows. Deciding to woodshed before making their assault on the big time, they honed their arrangements for a year and a half and became an impressive band. A prior legal claim on the name She forced them to choose Glitterbox, a scatological Cockney slang term, instead. Their 1997 debut, *Tied & Tangled*, struck nerves on both sides of the Atlantic, generating a love/hate reaction among critics, largely due to Johnny Green's over-the-top vocal style and lyrics. If he can develop a bit of restraint, the group may ultimately fulfill its potential, which is considerable. Fans of the Verve's *Urban Hymns* may especially want to check these guys out.

what to buy: Singer-guitarist Green writes his lyrics in what he calls "first person spectacular," but it is his first-person hysterical vocal style that dominates *Tied & Tangled* ♪♪♪♪ (Atlantic, 1997, prod. Dave Eringa). Behind his emotive outpourings, Miles Heseltine tears off fiery guitar licks and Mark Servaes provides dynamic, varied drumming in a U2-influenced style. Nearly every song is ear-catching; some are both beautiful and aggressive. But some will no doubt judge this to have too many sonic exclamation points.

influences:

◀◀ U2, the Waterboys, Verve, James

Bob Remstein

The Glove

See: The Cure

Corey Glover

See: Living Colour

The Go-Betweens

See: Grant McLennan

The Go-Go's

Formed 1978, in Hollywood, CA. Disbanded 1984. Reunited 1990 and 1994.

Belinda Carlisle, vocals; Charlotte Caffey, guitar; Jane Wiedlin, guitar (1978–84, 1990–94); Margot Olaverra, bass (1978–80); Elissa Bello, drums (1978–79); Gina Schock, drums (1979–present); Kathy Valentine, bass (1980–present).

Not the first all-female rock band, but certainly the most popular, the Go-Go's began in the late '70s Los Angeles punk scene and honed its act in clubs and on tour in England. Its debut album went to #1 and produced two enduring anthems, "We Got the Beat" and "Our Lips Are Sealed," providing inspiration for untold numbers of future female rockers. The group's subsequent two albums were considered relative failures but managed to produce some solid singles as well. Each member has dabbled in music since the 1984 breakup, including a serious solo career for lead singer Belinda Carlisle. The group reunited for a tour in 1990 and again in 1994, when they recorded a few new songs to accompany a compilation.

what to buy: The group's buoyant, giddy fun is captured perfectly on the delicious first album, *Beauty and the Beat* 🐾🐾🐾🐾🐾 (I.R.S., 1981, prod. Richard Gottehrer, Rob Freeman), and not just in the hit singles; check out "This Town," "Lust to Love," "Skidmarks on My Heart," "Tonight," and "Fading Fast."

what to buy next: *Greatest Hits* 🐾🐾🐾🐾 (I.R.S., 1990, prod. various) covers the high points, with lots from the first album and essentials from the next two (now out of print), including "Turn to You," "Head over Heels," and "Vacation."

what to avoid: *Return to the Valley of the Go-Go's* 🐾🐾🐾 (I.R.S., 1994, prod. various) is recommended for firm fans only. It goes beyond the greatest hits to present revealing early punk incarnations of the group and decent but unexceptional reunion recordings.

worth searching for: An acoustic solo performance of "We Got the Beat" climaxes guitarist Wiedlin's best-of compilation *The Very Best of Jane Wiedlin: From Cool Places to Worlds on Fire* (EMI, 1993, prod. various).

solo outings:

Belinda Carlisle:

Belinda 🐾🐾🐾 (I.R.S., 1986)

Heaven on Earth 🐾🐾🐾🐾 (MCA, 1987)

Runaway Horses 🐾🐾🐾 (MCA, 1989)

Her Greatest Hits 🐾🐾🐾🐾 (MCA, 1992)

Real 🐾🐾 (Virgin, 1993)

A Woman & a Man 🐾🐾🐾 (Ark 21, 1997)

Jane Wiedlin:

(With froSTed) *Cold* 🐾🐾🐾🐾 (DGC, 1996)

influences:

◀◀ The Chordettes, the Shangri-La's, the Germs

▶▶ The Bangles, Bikini Kill, Tiger Trap, the Donnas, the Tuesdays

Roger Catlin

Go West

Formed 1980, in Twickenham, England. Disbanded 1993.

Peter Cox, lead vocals, keyboards, guitar, programming; Richard Drummie, guitar, keyboards, backing vocals, programming.

Friends since discovering an early, shared interest in the rock band Free, Peter Cox and Richard Drummie made their partnership official in 1980, scored a publishing deal in 1982, and released their first record two years later. Blending Cox's powerhouse vocals with a blend of highly produced, synthesizer-heavy dance-pop, the duo made a minor U.S. splash with its well-crafted debut. Fearing its teen-idol good looks and seamless pop sound would get them tagged as the next Wham!, the duo turned in a sophomore record that was more arty and adventurous—and watched as its minor U.S. following evaporated in its wake. Its career got a second boost with 1990's "King of Wishful Thinking," mostly due to its prominence in the hit film *Pretty Woman*. The duo's last release surrounded that single with similarly crafted, horn-drenched soul/pop—kind of like Phil Collins with earthier singing—but its relatively modest success didn't keep Cox from ditching Drummie to go it alone for a 1997 release.

what to buy: For those who enjoy the duo's agonizingly crafted sound—and it's definitely an acquired taste—the debut *Go West* 🐾🐾🐾🐾 (Chrysalis, 1984, prod. Gary Stevenson) offers an impressive sample of its strengths: namely, interesting grooves, spot-on playing, and Cox's amazingly soulful and skillful belting. Hearing his impassioned performance on the ballad

"Goodbye Girl," perhaps the best blue-eyed soul workout in recent memory, is worth owning the album alone.

what to buy next: The retrospective *Aces and Kings: The Best of Go West* 𝄢𝄢𝄢𝄢 (ERG, 1993, prod. Gary Stevenson) gathers the group's many sterling film soundtrack contributions—including hip-shaking songs from *Rocky IV, White Men Can't Jump,* and *Pretty Woman*—in one package.

what to avoid: Though Go West was consistent in its mediocrity, its second album, *Dancing on the Couch* 𝄢𝄢𝄢 (Chrysalis, 1987, prod. Gary Stevenson), suffers for its artsy and insincere efforts to get away from the group's commercial sound.

the rest:
Bangs and Crashes 𝄢𝄢𝄢 (Chrysalis, 1985)
Indian Summer 𝄢𝄢𝄢 (EMI, 1992)

worth searching for: Cox's unmistakable backing vocals make the hip-hop-tinged "Come the Revolution" the coolest cut on former Tears for Fears bassist Curt Smith's solo album *Soul on Board* (Mercury, 1993).

solo outings:
Peter Cox:
Peter Cox 𝄢𝄢𝄢𝄢 (Chrysalis, 1997)

influences:
◄◄ Smokey Robinson, Earth, Wind & Fire, Gary Numan
►► Seal, the Rembrandts

Eric Deggans

God Street Wine

Formed 1990, in New York, NY.

Lo Faber, vocals, guitar; Aaron Maxwell, vocals, guitar; Dan Pifer, bass, vocals; Jon Bevo, keyboards, vocals; Tomo, drums, vocals.

One of the many '90s bands chasing the jam-happy ideals (and the audience) of the Grateful Dead, God Street Wine plays a loose-limbed kind of rock, but goes a step or two further than some of its peers by embracing a variety of styles—though it also falls victim to concentrating too much on tones and not enough on tunes. But GSW is certainly on a learning curve, and each subsequent album shows progress; not necessarily polish, but a better sense of how to combine tunefulness with the group's prediliction towards jamming.

what to buy: *Red* 𝄢𝄢𝄢 (Mercury, 1996, prod. God Street Wine) finds the songs getting mildly tighter and more focused ("RU4 Real" borders on power pop), while its stylistic reach is broader than ever, moving from blues shuffles to percolating reggae. *God Street Wine* 𝄢𝄢𝄢 (Mercury, 1997, prod. Bill Wray) offers more of the same, with guest shots by Blues Traveler John Popper and Little Feat's Bill Payne spicing the proceedings.

what to buy next: Always better live (so far), *Who's Driving* 𝄢𝄢𝄢 (Ripe & Ready/Performance, 1993, prod. Dean Mulla) captures GSW at its indulgent best, though its earnest spirit compensates for some of the more interminable jams.

the rest:
Bag 𝄢𝄢 (Ripe & Ready, 1992)
$1.99 Romances 𝄢𝄢 (Geffen, 1994)

influences:
◄◄ Grateful Dead

Gary Graff

The Godfathers

Formed 1986, in London, England.

Peter Coyne, vocals; Chris Coyne, bass, vocals; Kris Dollimore, guitar (1986–90); Mike Gibson, guitar (1986–93); George Mazur, drums (1986–93); Chris Burrows, guitar (1990–present); Ali Byworth, drums (1993–present).

The very British, working-class bluster of the Godfathers is a reflection of the social and political climate of the group's heyday. Formed from the remains of the notorious Sid Presley Experience, the band is led by the brothers Coyne, who fused their love of '60s maximum R&B with their frustrations with life in Margaret Thatcher's England during the mid-'80s. Paired with veteran producer Vic Maile (who worked with the band's beloved Kinks, Small Faces, and the Who), the result was a raw, hard-rocking sound that was usually more impressive than the band's songwriting skills. Dressed smartly in suits and coiffed à la Spandau Ballet, the Godfathers were popular for a time in England and scored a U.S. hit in the early days of alternative rock with "Birth, School, Work, Death," a stinging account of the fatalistic English worldview that remains their best song.

what's available: The title track is featured twice on *Birth, School, Work Death: The Best of the Godfathers* 𝄢𝄢𝄢 (Epic/Legacy, 1996, prod. Vic Maile, Steve Brown), which compiles an excessive 18 tracks from the group's three out-of-print Epic albums and its early self-released singles. Maile's death at the dawn of the '90s coincided with the Godfathers' sharp drop in popularity, but the group continues to release albums independently, albeit with a consistently fluctuating lineup.

influences:
◄◄ The Kinks, the Who, Eddie & the Hot Rods
►► Tin Machine, Oasis

Todd Wicks

Golden Earring

Formed 1961, in The Hague, Netherlands.

George Kooymans, lead guitar, vocals; Rinus Gerritsen, bass, harmonica; Barry Hay, lead vocals, guitar, flute (1967–present); Cesar Zuiderwijk, drums, percussion (1969–present); Hans van Herwerden, guitar (1961–63); Fred van der Hilst, drums (1961–64); Frans Krassenburg, vocals (1963–66); Peter de Ronde, guitar (1963–67); Jaap Eggermont, drums (1963–67); Sieb Warner, drums (1967–69); Rober-Jan Stips, keyboards (1975); Eelco Gelling, guitar (1976).

The most enduring and successful Dutch import since windmills, Golden Earring has tallied more than 20 hit singles in the Netherlands spanning three decades, yet remains best known worldwide for its two perennial album-rock radio classics, "Radar Love" from 1974 and 1982's "Twilight Zone." Formed by Rinus Gerritsen and George Kooymans as a quartet called the Tornados, the band initially was the Dutch version of ABBA: its first hit, "Please Go" in 1964, was blatant bubblegum; its first #1 record in the Netherlands was titled "Dong-Dong-Di-Ki-Di-Gi-Dong;" and the group experimented with various musical styles, names, and personnel before settling on a straight-edge, hard-rock approach. The move paid off as the band, by then known as Golden Earring, was courted by the Who to open its 1972 European tour. The Who subsequently signed the group to its Track Records label, where Golden Earring prospered and soon after released "Radar Love." Curiously, the band was unable to achieve follow-up success in the United States until "Twilight Zone" returned Golden Earring to the U.S. charts during the early '80s. But once again the group failed to sustain momentum in the States. Golden Earring releases became sporadic during the late '80s as each member of the band recorded as a solo artist, but they continue to make frequent performances, primarily in Europe. "Radar Love" enjoyed a resurgence in 1989 when the band White Lion covered the tune, and again during 1997 as the musical bed in ads for a new car stereo system.

what to buy: Almost all of Golden Earring's more than 40 album releases are Dutch or German imports, and it seems like almost all of them include "Radar Love." Of the LPs available in the U.S., *The Continuing Story of Radar Love* ����� (UNI/MCA, 1989, prod. various) is as much Dutch as any casual fan could want. In addition to the "Radar Love" and "Twilight Zone," the collection centers on many of the group's big European hit singles of the mid-'70s and mid-'80s, including "She Flies on Strange Wings," "Quiet Eyes," "Ce Soir," and "The Devil Made Me Do It."

the rest:
Moontan �� (UNI/MCA, 1974)

worth searching for: The Dutch import CD of the group's 1965 debut album, *Just Earrings* (Polydor, 1994), while a relatively lightweight confection, offers interesting insight into the group's origins. Known then as the Golden Earrings, the band was a continental pop outfit that took its cues from the Beatles and other emerging British rock acts. "Please Go," its first hit, is contained here, as are airy bits of ear candy such as "Lonely Everyday," "Holy Witness," and "Nobody but You."

influences:

⏮ The Beatles, the Kinks, Cream, the Who, the Zombies, the Yardbirds

⏭ Led Zeppelin, Deep Purple, Bad Company, Montrose, Shocking Blue

Jeff Hatch and Jim McFarlin

The Golden Palominos

Formed 1981, in New York, NY.

Anton Fier, drummer; Bill Laswell, bass; Micky Skopelitis, guitar; others.

"These records are totally self-indulgent projects for me. I don't make my living off of them and I never have. They're just ways to explore different processes and ways for me to learn about different elements of music, ways to learn about different elements of process," says Palominos ringleader, percussionist Anton Fier, whose drumming and producing gigs would keep two ordinary men busy. Furthermore, he leads a "group" of himself and whomever he feels like working with; the other near-constants are fellow eclectics Bill Laswell on bass and Nicky Skopelitis on guitar. Not surprisingly, the Palominos sound changes from album to album, from the downtown New York City avant-gardisms of the group's 1983 debut through four albums that were more song-oriented yet still stylistically varied, and then dreamy ambient-influenced work. Fier's most recent album, *Dead Inside*, features the poetry of Nicole Blackman.

what to buy: *A History (1982–1985)* ����� (Metrotone/Restless, 1992, prod. various) contains all but one track ("Clean Plate," worth seeking out) off the debut album, *The Golden Palominos* ����� (Celluloid, 1981, prod. Anton Fier, Bill Laswell), and the entire sophomore effort, *Visions of Excess* ����� (Celluloid, 1985, prod. Anton Fier)—both masterpieces in entirely different ways. The former features the avant-garde shenanigans of guitarist/vocalist Arto Lindsay and John Zorn, who toots not only alto sax and clarinet but also game calls. Bassist Jamaaladeen Tacuma (Ornette Coleman's Prime Time) and guitarist Fred Frith show up on a few tracks too. It's structured improvisation in which any sound may happen. *Visions of Excess* tackles mainstream rock from the periphery and makes more explicit the rotating-cast concept, with vocalists alone including Michael Stipe (R.E.M.), John Lydon (Sex Pistols/Public

Image Ltd.), Jack Bruce (Cream), Syd Straw, and Lindsay. The largely collaborative songwriting is strong enough that every tune is memorable.

what to buy next: On the spacey *This Is How It Feels* 𝄞𝄞𝄞𝄞 (Restless, 1993, prod. Anton Fier), Laswell's dub-like bass lines, Fier's super-steady rhythms, Bernie Worrell's swirling Hammond organ licks, and the breathy vocals of Lori Carson (who recorded a 1990 singer-songwriter album, *Shelter*, for Geffen) and Lydia Kavanagh (of She Never Blinks) combine to flirt with a sort of real-time ambient/trip-hop feel. The lyrics are based on Graham Greene's 1951 novel *The End of the Affair*, except for a striking cover of Jackson Browne's "These Days."

what to avoid: *A Dead Horse* 𝄞 (Celluloid, 1989, prod. Anton Fier) is as tired and uninspired as its title suggests.

the rest:
Blast of Silence 𝄞𝄞𝄞 (Celluloid, 1986)
Drunk with Passion 𝄞𝄞𝄞 (Charisma, 1991)
A History (1986–1989) 𝄞𝄞 (Metrotone/Restless, 1992)
Prison of the Rhythm—The Remixes 𝄞𝄞𝄞 (Restless, 1993)
Pure 𝄞𝄞𝄞𝄞 (Restless, 1994)
No Thought, No Breath, No Eyes, No Heart 𝄞𝄞𝄞 (Restless, 1995)
Dead Inside 𝄞𝄞𝄞𝄞 (Restless, 1996)

worth searching for: The "Omaha" 12-inch (Celluloid, 1985) is notable for a non-album B-side cover of Ennio Morricone's movie theme "For a Few Dollars More," produced by Material/OAO. The flip side of the 12-inch "The Animal Speaks" (Celluloid, 1985) includes a version with vocals by Bruce instead of Lydon.

influences:
◀◀ Steely Dan, DNA, Bill Laswell, David Sylvian, Cocteau Twins

▶▶ Hector Zazou, Jeff Buckley, Matthew Sweet

see also: *Bill Laswell*

Steve Holtje

Golden Smog

Formed 1992, in Minneapolis, MN.

Gary Louris, guitar, vocals; Dan Murphy, guitar, vocals; Kraig Johnson, guitar, vocals; Marc Perlman, bass, vocals; Chris Mars, drums (1992); Jeff Tweedy, guitar, vocals (1994–present); Noah Levy, drums (1994–present).

Initially an inter-band collective from Minneapolis groups such as Soul Asylum (Dan Murphy), the Jayhawks (Gary Louris, Marc Perlman), the Replacements (Chris Mars), and Run Westy Run (Kraig Johnson), Golden Smog was formed for the sole purpose of hanging out and goofing on tunes like Bad Company's "Shooting Star" and Thin Lizzy's "Cowboy Song" (both of which are on the debut EP). In the band's second incarnation, though,

which includes Wilco's Jeff Tweedy & the Honeydogs' Noah Levy, the Smog became alternative country's first supergroup (though the record sales of the various bands in question may be too modest to make that appellation stick). The group conveys spontaneity and a charming, homespun feel—attributes considered manna from heaven by the alt-country crowd, even if it lacks consistency. Due to contractual obligations, or mere perverseness, the group members go not by their own names, but by monikers consisting of their middle name in place of their first name, and the street they grew up on in place of their last name. For example, Jeff Tweedy is Scott Summit. Cute, no? A second full-length Smog album is reported to be on the way.

what to buy: A batch of fine songs thrown together with almost no rehearsal, *Down by the Old Mainstream* 𝄞𝄞𝄞 (Rykodisc, 1995, prod. James Bunchberry Lane, Golden Smog) is a potentially great album that wound up being just an average one. The vocals are particularly ragged, and while that may be considered the album's general aesthetic, you only have to listen to records by the group's forbears, the Byrds and the Flying Burrito Brothers, to see what was possible here. Some songs come off better than others—Louris's "V" and "Won't Be Coming Home" would fit well on any Jayhawks album, Murphy's contributions capture the energy and drama of his work with Soul Asylum, and Tweedy's "Pecan Pie" is completely charming. But Johnson's vocals are woefully amelodic. The best advice on this group is to catch them live, where they rarely disappoint, or wait for the next album.

the rest:
On Golden Smog EP (Crackpot, 1992/Rykodisc, 1995) 𝄞𝄞
Weird Tales N/A (Rykodisc, 1998)

worth searching for: Hardcore fans will no doubt want the promo-only version of *Mainstream* (Rykodisc, 1994) made up to look like a three-disc box set, containing two phony discs and a booklet that, in a convoluted and occasionally hilarious manner, explains the fake history of the band.

influences:
◀◀ The Byrds, the Flying Burrito Brothers, Buffalo Springfield

Daniel Durchholz

Goldfinger

Formed 1993, in Los Angeles, CA.

John Feldmann, guitar, vocals; Simon Williams, bass; Charlie Paulson, guitar; Darrin Pfeiffer, drums.

Combining old-school punk with a '90s pop sensibility, Goldfinger is the biggest thing to emerge from a shoe store since Al Bundy. The group formed when John Feldmann met Simon Williams while selling footwear at NANA, a store in Los Angeles. He also sold shoes to Mojo Records–exec Patrick McDow-ell, who signed the band. For the most part, Goldfinger's live show outdoes its recorded work—though it's likely neither compares to Feldmann's way with a shoehorn.

what to buy: The band's debut, *Goldfinger* ♫♫♫ (Mojo, 1996, prod. John Feldmann), garnered a huge buzz, thanks to the super-catchy "Here in Your Bedroom," which alt-rock stations gobbled up. The album also spawned the tracks "Mable" and "King for a Day." Suburban pop/punk fans and skateboarders will dig this, but don't expect to find any heavy messages or political leanings in their songs.

what to avoid: *Hang-Ups* ♫♫ (Mojo, 1997, prod. John Feldmann, Jay Rifkin) is a multi-textured effort, but a bit scattered. And fans didn't take to the emphasis track, "This Lonely Place," like they did to "Here in Your Bedroom."

worth searching for: The group's introduction to the world came via the EP *Richter* (self-released), which college radio jumped on, giving it more than 1,000 spins per week across the United States. Good luck finding it today, though; there were only 2,000 pressed, and Charlie Paulson doesn't even own a copy.

influences:

◀◀ Bad Brains, Bad Religion, Kiss, Elvis Costello, the Replacements, the Specials

▶▶ Blink 182

Darren Davis

Goldie

Born 1965, in Wolverhampton, England.

Goldie, the biracial son of a Scot and a Jamaican, was at the forefront of the new dance music in England at the outset of the '90s. Previously, British club music had been heavily influenced by imported trends: shantytown reggae, hip-hop, Detroit techno, and Chicago house. Goldie and other electronic whiz kids created the first homegrown response with drum 'n' bass (originally dubbed "jungle," a term that was quickly discredited because of its unsavory ethnic connotations). Drum 'n' bass layers frantic snare beats across fat bass lines. Though dance music is traditionally obsessed with linear motion, Goldie and his fellow drum 'n' bass pioneers made "time-stretching" records that suggested lateral movement, free-floating above the dance floor into a head space once occupied by dub reggae and experimental electronic music. While this music swept England and Europe and made Goldie a superstar, it remained a fringe movement in the United States, where Goldie alternated DJ stints at clubs with live performances opening for acts such as Björk and Jane's Addiction. But his innovations have proven to be a major influence on U.K. rock acts

from David Bowie to Stereolab, and have also filtered into the American underground.

what to buy: *Timeless* ♫♫♫♫ (Metalheadz/ffrr, 1995, prod. Goldie) is one of the landmark dance albums of the '90s. It was the first drum 'n' bass collection released by a solo artist in the States, and its 21-minute title track is among the genre's masterpieces. The 103-minute opus blends lush female vocals, strings, and synthetic effects with slippery rhythm tracks. Rather than suggesting the ebullient vibe of a rave, Goldie's brand of dance music is inward looking, as dark and evocative of the ghetto landscape as hardcore hip-hop, yet also oddly tranquil, suggestive, and frequently beautiful.

what to avoid: On the double-disc *Saturnz Return* ♫♫♫ (London/ffrr, 1998, prod. Goldie), Goldie's ambitions get the best of him. The most egregious failure is the heavily orchestrated "Mother," which never develops its meager five-note melody into anything that would justify its 60-minute length. The second disc presents a series of shotgun marriages, with Goldie collaborating with rapper KRS-One, Oasis rocker Noel Gallagher, and Bowie, but he succeeds only when left on his own to create strange, lovely worlds that orbit between despair and transcendence on "Dragonfly" and "Letter of Fate."

influences:

◀◀ Juan Atkins, Lee "Scratch" Perry, King Tubby, Public Enemy, Massive Attack

▶▶ Roni Size, David Bowie, Tortoise, Stereolab

Greg Kot

Goo Goo Dolls

Formed 1986, in Buffalo, NY.

Johnny Rzeznik, guitar, vocals; Robby Takac, bass; George Tutuska, drums (1986–95); Mike Malinin, drums (1995–present).

Diehard Replacements fans (are there any other kind?) write this trio off as Paul Westerberg wannabes, but they're not listening closely. Pulling themselves out of the speed-metal/thrash heap with 1990's *Hold Me Up*, the Goos have emerged as a brash but bracing power pop outfit that is far more tuneful and optimistic than the 'Ments ever wanted to be. Beneath the crunching guitars, frat-pack stage antics, and lunkheaded garage-band charm lie guitarist Johnny Rzeznik's simple but heartfelt proclamations of romantic and youthful desire. When you call yourselves the Goo Goo Dolls and frequently encore with Tommy Tutone's "867-5309," you can't expect people to take you seriously. But the unlikely success of a ballad called "Name," from 1995's *A Boy Named Goo*, brought the trio much-deserved MTV and radio exposure and even some controversy when Wal-Mart threatened to pull the album off its shelves because some customers thought its innocuous cover of a child covered with jam depicted child abuse. The Dolls have been taking their time recording the follow-up album, but they've been sprinkling new tunes onto sound-tracks for *Batman and Robin* ("Lazy Eye") and *City of Angels* ("Iris") that suggest the wait will be worth it.

what to buy: *Superstar Car Wash* 𝄞𝄞𝄞𝄞 (Warner Bros., 1993, prod. Gavin MacKillop) sustains the guitar-driven assault tactics of earlier albums but tightens the arrangements, brightens the choruses, and dares to invite even more Replacements comparisons by co-writing one tune ("We Are the Normal") with Paul Westerberg. The band teams with noted producer Lou Giordano for its platinum breakthrough, *A Boy Named Goo* 𝄞𝄞𝄞𝄞 (Warner Bros., 1995, prod. Lou Giordano), which contains the hit "Name" and a ragged cover of the obscure "Slave Girl" by the Australian band Lime Spiders.

what to buy next: The fascinating sound of a young band in transition is captured on *Hold Me Up* 𝄞𝄞𝄞𝄞 (Warner Bros., 1990, prod. Armand John Petri), which combines tough-rocking originals such as "Just the Way You Are" and "There You Are" with covers of the Plimsouls' "A Million Miles Away" and Prince's "I Could Never Take the Place of Your Man" (with guest vocals by Buffalo lounge lizard Lance Diamond).

what to avoid: Recorded before Rzeznik matured as the band's visionary, the thrashy *Goo Goo Dolls* 𝄞𝄞 (Celluloid/Metal Blade, 1987, prod. Goo Goo Dolls) has little in common with the Dolls you know now, save for a penchant for cool covers (in this case, Blue Öyster Cult's "Don't Fear the Reaper" and Cream's "Sunshine of Your Love").

the rest:
Jed 𝄞𝄞𝄞 (Metal Blade, 1989)
Dizzy up the Girl 𝄞𝄞𝄞 (Warner Bros., 1998)

worth searching for: A Japan-only EP titled *Bang!* (Warner Bros., 1996) features live unplugged versions of "Name," "Girl Right Next to Me," "Another Second Time Around," and a cover of INXS' "Don't Change." A raging studio version of "Don't Change" can be found on, of all things, the soundtrack for *Ace Ventura: When Nature Calls* (MCA, 1995, prod. various).

influences:
◀◀ The Replacements, Cheap Trick
▶▶ The Lemonheads, Soul Asylum, Gin Blossoms

David Okamoto

Steve Goodman

Born July 25, 1948, in Chicago, IL. Died September 20, 1984, in Seattle, WA.

Steve Goodman was a folk singer from Chicago and a good friend of John Prine who emerged in the early '70s with a gift for blues guitar playing, an infectious, impish onstage charm and, like Prine, compassionate, often humorous songwriting skills. His compositions have been recorded often—by Jimmy Buffett, Prine, David Allen Coe, and the Clancy Brothers, among others. His classic, "The City of New Orleans" has been done by Arlo Guthrie, John Denver, and Willie Nelson. After a bout with major labels, Goodman settled into a groove with his own Red Pajamas imprint until he died in 1984 of leukemia at age 36. His grave is among the most-visited in the world; his ashes are buried beneath home plate in his home town's Wrigley Field.

what to buy: *No Big Surprise* 𝄞𝄞𝄞𝄞 (Red Pajamas, 1994, prod. various) is a worthy anthology, with a disc each of Goodman in the studio and onstage. *Santa Ana Winds* 𝄞𝄞𝄞𝄞 (Red Pajamas, 1980, prod. Steve Goodman) is his best collection, produced just the way his music ought to be. The loosey-goosey *The Easter Tapes* 𝄞𝄞𝄞𝄞 (Red Pajamas, 1996, prod. Al Bunetta) are taken from radio shows recorded with Vin Scelsea that showcase Goodman's off-the-wall humor, charm, and command of his instrument. Who else could pull off Marty Robbins's "Big Iron" and a letter-perfect version of "Splish Splash" on the same program?

what to buy next: *Affordable Art* 𝄞𝄞𝄞𝄞 (Red Pajamas, 1983, prod. Steve Goodman, Dan Einstein) includes "Talk Backwards," "Watching Joey Glow," and "A Dying Cub Fan's Last Request," perhaps the most poignant of all baseball tales.

what to avoid: Like many good songwriters, Goodman had problems with major labels who had no easily marketable niches for him. *High and Outside* 𝄞 (Asylum, 1979, prod. Steve Goodman) is a prophetic title; though the songs aren't bad, this stab at slick arrangements (the soul wanna-be "Just Lucky I Guess," for instance) strangles them in a death grip.

best of the rest:
Artistic Hair 𝄞𝄞𝄞𝄞 (Red Pajamas, 1983)
Unfinished Business 𝄞𝄞𝄞𝄞 (Red Pajamas, 1987)
The Best of the Asylum Years, Vol. 1 𝄞𝄞𝄞𝄞 (Red Pajamas, 1988)
The Best of the Asylum Years, Vol. 2 𝄞𝄞𝄞 (Red Pajamas, 1989)
Gathering at the Earl of Old Town 𝄞𝄞𝄞𝄞 (Drive Archives, 1998)

worth searching for: *Somebody Else's Troubles* (Buddah, 1972, prod. Arif Mardin) is a hard-to-find early collection that includes "The Dutchman," "The Loving of the Game," and the powerful "The Ballad of Penny Evans," but watch for *The Essential—Steve Goodman* (Buddah, 1972, 1976), which includes *Somebody Else's Troubles* and other Buddah tracks. *Tribute to Steve Goodman* (Red Pajamas, 1985, prod. Al Bunetta) is a loving salute with lots of special guests, among them Prine, Arlo Guthrie, John Hartford, Bonnie Raitt, and David Bromberg performing some of Goodman's best tunes.

influences:

◀◀ Bob Gibson, Josh White, Woody Guthrie, Bob Wills, Hank Williams, Big Bill Broonzy, Jethro Burns, Bob Dylan

▶▶ James McMurtry, Michael Penn, Steve Forbert

Leland Rucker

Robert Gordon

Born in 1947, in Washington, DC.

Robert Gordon was the lead singer of New York's Tuff Darts, but left the microphone before their first album was recorded. He then resurfaced with petrified hair and swiveling hips, just rarin' to carry on the rockabilly torch. It was up for grabs, anyhow, and Gordon came along before anyone else when it came to appropriating '50s rock for the new wave era. He had reverence for bygone heroes, but wasn't the man who would be King. With just enough abandon, Gordon embodied the classic cockiness of rockabilly without becoming a one-man oldies act. By the same token, despite the arty-punky New York scene he found himself a part of, he wasn't some Warholian freak show that held up the greaser-rocker as an ironic buffoon of American culture. Think honest pompadours standing the test of time, not revivalist pomposity rockin' around some old clock. More Elvis and Gene Vincent than Buddy Holly, more "Hound Dog" than Stray Cats, Gordon's rock 'n' roll was as hot as a classic-Chevy engine, and just as revved up. By the early '80s, he was dousing his rockabilly with a poppy new wave energy without losing a bit of the old spark.

what to buy: Although the One Way label has reissued Gordon's individual RCA albums, *Red Hot: 1977–1981* ♪♪♪♪ (Razor & Tie, 1995, prod. Richard Gotterher, Robert Gordon) is a good place to start. It's an ideal overview of the bulk of Gordon's career, including definitive renditions of Bruce Springsteen's "Fire," Roy Orbison and Carl Perkins covers, and two Marshall Crenshaw songs. Or you can go with *The Robert Gordon Story* ♪♪♪♪ (One Way, 1997), a 12-song compendium representing the exciting chapters of the rocker's career, with many songs in common with *Red Hot* and three previously unreleased live tracks.

what to buy next: When all is said and done, Gordon in his element may be best represented by *King Biscuit Flower Hour Presents* ♪♪♪♪ (King Biscuit Entertainment, 1996), which finds him caught in the down 'n' dirty act in a Philadelphia performance circa 1979. Chris Spedding gives the rockabilly licks a hyperspeed push, edging the music just far enough away from revivalism to give it context in the punk arena. He even has a chance to show off solo on the instrumental "Gunfight." Equally accessible to those who wear safety pins and pom-

padours, this live album rests coolly in between the Cramps and Gordon's classic influences.

the rest:

Robert Gordon with Link Wray ♪♪♪♪ (Private Stock, 1977/One Way 1998)

Rock Billy Boogie ♪♪♪♪ (RCA, 1979/One Way, 1997)

Bad Boy ♪♪♪ (RCA, 1980/One Way, 1997)

Are You Gonna Be the One ♪♪♪♪ (RCA, 1981/One Way, 1997)

Too Fast to Live, Too Young to Die ♪♪♪♪ (RCA, 1982/One Way, 1998)

All for the Love of Rock 'n' Roll ♪♪♪ (Viceroy, 1994)

(With Danny Gatton) *The Humbler* ♪♪♪♪ (NRG, 1996)

worth searching for: The import reissue two-fer of Gordon with Link Wray/Fresh Fish Special (Raven, 1996) contains both albums plus nine bonus tracks. *Greetings from New York City* (New Rose, 1996) is also worth tracking down.

influences:

◀◀ Gene Vincent, Elvis Presley

▶▶ Monte Warden, Jimmy Ray

Jordan Oakes

Lesley Gore

Born May 2, 1946, in New York, NY.

The music of Lesley Gore provided the soundtrack for the lives of countless suburban teenage girls during the mid-'60s. Her hit "It's My Party (And I'll Cry If I Want To)" and its sequel, "Judy's Turn to Cry," brilliantly tapped into the soap opera mentality of early high school romance. "Sunshine, Lollipops, and Rainbows" (co-written by Marvin Hamlisch) expressed the manic-depressive joy of going steady with just the right guy, while "She's a Fool" mined the critical thoughts of a jealous (rejected?) rival. With "You Don't Own Me," a less boy-crazy Gore demanded to be treated as an individual, not chattel, and struck an early commercial blow for feminism in the process. Then she backslid a bit with the doormat posturing of "Maybe I Know," which was entirely in character with the times. Gore's biggest hits were produced by Quincy Jones, who brought in punchy horn arrangements and double-tracked the singer's voice, in effect making her a one-artist girl group. (Trivia note: The crying "oh-oh's" at the end of "It's My Party" were the result of Gore singing out-of-synch with the primary track—but the effect was so dramatic Jones left it in.) At her peak, Gore lip-synched in teen films such as *Ski Party* and *Girls on the Beach*, and showed she really could sing live when she headlined in *The T.A.M.I. Show*. During late 1965 Bob Crewe took over the production chores and, with Gore's help (she began writing her own B-sides and LP cuts), pursued a more mature sound. Their most successful collaboration, "California Nights," should've signaled the beginning of a fine career in MOR, but pop tastes had changed, and soon her run of 19 chart singles was over. Gore kept at it, playing cabaret dates and recording unsuccessful sides with the Crewe, MoWest, and A&M labels well into the '70s. She achieved a comeback of sorts when she and her brother Michael wrote the hit "Out Here on My Own" for the 1980 movie *Fame*. Since then she's been a popular fixture on the oldies circuit, and a version of "You Don't Own Me," featured in the hit 1996 film *The First Wives Club*, has revived interest in this important but often overlooked artist.

what to buy: The best domestic overview of Gore's talents and career can be found on *It's My Party: The Mercury Anthology* ♫♫♫♫ (Mercury, 1996, compilation prod. Bas Hartong, Bill Levenson), a two-disc, 52-song set that brilliantly chronicles Gore's transformation from Queen of Teen Angst to Adult Balladeer. All her chart singles are included, along with many important self-penned B-sides and an informative, detailed booklet with cool photos. If you have this one, you won't need any others.

what to buy next: If it's just the hits you want, *The Golden Hits of Lesley Gore* ♫♫♫♫ (Mercury, 1987, compilation prod. Tim Rogers) has 'em all in one very satisfying 18-track budget disc. Equally good, *The Best of Lesley Gore* ♫♫♫♫ (Rhino, 1998,

prod. Quincy Jones, Bob Crewe) has the benefit of more current remastering technology in addition to an impressive collection of Gore's hits. You can get all the hits plus several choice LP tracks and B-sides on both *The Lesley Gore Anthology* ♫♫♫♫ (Rhino, 1986, prod. Quincy Jones, Bob Crewe) and the import *Start the Party Again* ♫♫♫♫ (Raven, 1994, prod. Quincy Jones, Bob Crewe).

worth searching for: Everything Gore recorded during her salad days for Mercury has been collected on the import *It's My Party* (Bear Family, 1994, compilation prod. Richard Weize), a five-disc set that may seem like overkill to some, the fulfillment of a lifelong dream to others. Those interested in seeing Gore at her performing peak should track down the video *Born to Rock* (Music Media, 1988), an expurgated version of both *The T.A.M.I. Show* and the *The T.N.T. Show*.

influences:

◄◄ Connie Francis, the Shirelles, Eydie Gorme, Brenda Lee

►► Helen Reddy, Cyndi Lauper, Debbie Gibson

Ken Burke

Martin Gore

See: Depeche Mode

John Gorka

Born July 27, 1958, in Edison, NJ.

With dark good looks, subtle humor, and a rich, sensitive baritone, John Gorka has become one of the best-known names in the American folk scene of the '80s and '90s. A native of New Jersey who works out of steel country in Pennsylvania, his most touching songs often personalize those displaced by changing times. He first gained attention by winning the New Folk Award at the Kerrville Folk Festival in 1984 and has since released a number of albums that showcase his voice as well as his songs. Gorka's characters typically feel out of place or out of step with the world around them. In his songs, this can make for some harrowing or sometimes just plain funny stories. He's carved a niche for himself as a writer and vocalist who sings about the process of living, and the quietly emotional nature of his songs has won him fans outside the usual folk circles.

what to buy: *Jack's Crows* ♫♫♫ (High Street, 1991, prod. Dawn Atkinson, Will Akerman) is perhaps the most intimate of Gorka's albums, highlighted by "Houses in the Fields," a heart-wrenching take on the development of America's farmland that extended Gorka's popularity well beyond the New England folk circuit.

what to buy next: *Out of the Valley* ♫♫♫ (High Street, 1994, prod. John Jennings) is Gorka's first album with a full band, a host of Nashville musicians who help provide a different slant to his songs.

the rest:
I Know 𝄞𝄞𝄞 (Red House, 1987)
Land of the Bottom Line 𝄞𝄞𝄞 (Windham Hill, 1990)
Temporary Road 𝄞𝄞𝄞 (High Street, 1992)
Between Five and Seven 𝄞𝄞𝄞 (High Street, 1996)

worth searching for: *Motor Folkin'* (High Street, 1994) is a promotional CD containing a live version of "Furniture" recorded at a Seattle radio station.

influences:
◀◀ Stan Rogers, Woody Guthrie, Nanci Griffith
▶▶ Shawn Colvin, Dar Williams, Bill Morrissey

Brian Mansfield and Doug Pullen

Gorky's Zygotic Mynci

Formed mid-1990s, in Camarthen, Wales.

Euros Childs, vocals, keyboards; Richard James, bass; John Lawrence, guitar; Euros Rowlands, drums; Megan Childs, violin.

The members of the quixotically named Gorky's Zygotic Mynci, who originally sang in their native Welsh language, create their music with a mixture of influences from the art-rock palette. That would seem to include the early Soft Machine, Pink Floyd, the Incredible String Band, the Beach Boys, Brian Eno—even some Mothers of Invention, Renaissance, and Kinks. The result is music that sounds willfully uncommercial, but that occasionally overlaps with the late '90s spate of British pop.

what to buy: *Introducing* 𝄞𝄞𝄞𝄞 (Mercury, 1996, prod. Alan Holmes, Gorky's Zygotic Mynci) collects songs from two albums, an EP, and three singles that were released overseas. As the title suggests, it makes a fine introduction to this anomalous combo. Gorky's music will make you hum one minute, hypnotize you the next, with a bottomless supply of quirkiness and invention. A song called "Kevin Ayers" sings the praises of one of their influences, much in the way Paul Westerberg said thanks in "Alex Chilton."

what to buy next: Its first real album released in the States—and which contains a bonus track only available on the domestic version—is *Barafundle* 𝄞𝄞𝄞𝄞 (1997, Mercury, prod. Gorwell Owen, Gorky's Zygotic Mynci), an even weirder foray into Gorky's almost mystical folk-pop. If you're already spaced out, listening to this band may smear your mind across the universe.

influences:
◀◀ Soft Machine, the Beach Boys, Syd Barrett

Jordan Oakes

Barry Goudreau
See: Boston

Gov't Mule
Formed 1995, in New York, NY.

Warren Haynes, guitar, vocals; Allen Woody, bass; Matt Abts, drums.

Formed as a side project by Warren Haynes and Allen Woody while they were members of the '90s comeback version of the Allman Brothers Band, Gov't Mule soon became bigger than most side projects, and the duo decided to quit their "day job" in 1997 and dedicate themselves to the Mule as a full-time endeavor. The band does sound influenced by the Allmans—drummer Matt Abts even played in Allman guitarist Dickey Betts's solo band while the Allmans were broken up—and it also shares some of the Allmans' influences, particularly a taste for lengthy blues and jazz improvisations. But being a few years younger than its old bosses, the Mule's sound has an added kick from having been influenced by some of the other great bands of the '60s and '70s, most notably Led Zeppelin, Cream, and the Jimi Hendrix Experience.

what's available: *Gov't Mule* 𝄞𝄞𝄞 (Relativity, 1995, prod. Michael Barbiero) may have been recorded while the band was

Mel Schacher (l), Don Brewer, and Mark Farner of Grand Funk Railroad (© Ken Settle)

a side project, but the Mule kicks like lives depend on it. The album reflects the trio's wide influences in the choice of covers (Son House's "Grinnin' in Your Face," Free's "Mr. Big"), as well as in "Trane," which is dedicated to jazz saxophone great John Coltrane, and "Left Coast Groovies (For FZ)," which is dedicated to the late Frank Zappa. *Live at Roseland Ballroom ♫♫♫* (Foundation, 1996) is brief (six songs), but captures the Mule in a concert setting, where it comes across a bit better than in the recording studio. *Dose ♫♫♫* (Capricorn, 1998, prod. Michael Barbiero) shows the band sticking to the formula of the first album, with a country blues cover (the traditional "John the Revelator") and a trippy '60s cover (the Beatles' "She Said, She Said"), along with tributes to Thelonious Monk and Jeff Beck ("Thelonious Beck") and Miles Davis ("Birth of the Mule," a reference to Davis's "Birth of the Cool"). Most importantly, the album finds the group carving its own niche as a classic-styled rock band for the '90s.

worth searching for: Gov't Mule's cover of Steppenwolf's "Don't Step on the Grass, Sam" appears on the pro-pot compilation *Hempilation* (Capricorn, 1995, prod. various). Haynes's

pre-Mule solo album, *Tales of Ordinary Madness* (Megaforce, 1993, prod. Chuck Leavell), is out of print but has lots of tasty playing and some interesting guests (including keyboardist Bernie Worrell).

influences:

⏪ The Allman Brothers Band, Cream, Led Zeppelin, Jeff Beck, John Coltrane

Brian Ives

Lawrence Gowan /Gowan

Born in Scotland.

Canadian artist (by way of Scotland) Lawrence Gowan has sell-out concerts and triple-platinum albums at home, but his polished pop-rock tunes get precious little airplay stateside. A founding member of Rheingold before going solo with an unsuccessful self-titled debut, he broke into the Canadian charts in 1985 with the album *Strange Animal* and two of his most enduring songs: the quirky and amusing title tune and an atmospheric ode about an unrepentant convict, "Criminal Mind." Almost from the beginning Gowan has worked with top-notch backing musicians, including several from Yes, Rush, and Peter Gabriel and Stevie Nicks's bands. His early synth-pop sound and a fairly theatrical arena-rocker image gave way in the '90s to basics as he toured alone, holding the stage with just his piano and guitar. Classically trained, Gowan is comfortable with both rolling over Beethoven and telling Tchaikovsky the news, and his dramatic and passionate songs cover a range of subjects and styles, sung in a throaty tenor that rocks and croons.

what to buy: *Best of . . . ♪♪♪♪* (Columbia, 1997, prod. various) is an excellent chronological overview—all the hits plus bonus tracks including a heartfelt tribute to Lady Diana, "Healing Waters," originally written some years earlier but revised after the princess's death. . . . *But You Can Call Me Larry ♪♪♪♪* (Anthem/Columbia, 1993, prod. Jerry Marotta, Eddie Schwartz) is an assured studio set demonstrating notable maturity in sound and songwriting while losing none of Gowan's energy and individuality.

the rest:

Strange Animal ♪♪♪ (Columbia, 1985)
Great Dirty World ♪♪♪♪ (Columbia, 1987)
Lost Brotherhood ♪♪♪ (Atlantic, 1990)
The Good Catches Up ♪♪♪ (Gowan Productions, 1995)
Sololive: No Kilt Tonight ♪♪♪ (Algae, 1997)

influences:

⏪ The Beatles, the Guess Who, Tchaikovsky, ragtime

Polly Vedder

Lou Gramm

See: Foreigner

Grand Funk Railroad

Formed March 1969, in Flint, MI. Disbanded 1976. Re-formed 1980. Disbanded 1983. Re-formed 1996.

Mark Farner, guitar, vocals, keyboards, harmonica; Don Brewer, drums, vocals; Mel Schacher, bass (1969–76, 1996–present); Craig Frost, keyboards (1972–76); Dennis Bellinger, bass (1980–83).

Grand Funk Railroad was one of the loudest, rawest and most successful rock bands to ever rumble out of Michigan. Formed in the blue collar town of Flint—home to General Motors and the United Auto Workers—Grand Funk was rooted in the aggressive guitar rock of then-dominant power trios such as Cream and the Jimi Hendrix Experience, as well as nearby Motown. Mark, Don and Mel—as fans often referred to them—were one of the first groups to be known as a "people's band," meaning critics hated it. The group made a reported $5 million

in 1971 alone, the same year it broke the Beatles' gross ticket sales mark at New York's Shea Stadium—a show that sold out faster than the Fab Four's 1965 appearance there. GFR's first 11 albums went either platinum or gold, with more than 20 million sold by the time the band broke up after the Frank Zappa-produced *Good Singin' Good Playin'* in 1976. A brief early '80s reunion, with former band tech Dennis Bellinger taking a reluctant Mel Schacher's place, fell flat, but the original trio reunited in 1996 with plans to record again—including new songs for a planned box set—while Capitol Records is in the process of re-mastering and re-releasing nine of the group's classic titles.

what to buy: Because only a handful of the group's titles are available domestically on CD, there aren't many to choose from. The compilation *Capitol Collector's Series ♪♪♪♪* (Capitol, 1991, prod. various) is an effective time capsule of its '70s heyday, collecting singles from 1969's quasi-psychedelic "Time Machine" to 1974's sweet "Bad Time" and chronicling the band's transition from underground heroes ("Inside Looking Out," "Heartbreaker") to Top 40 sell-outs ("Some Kind of Wonderful," "The Loco-Motion").

what to buy next: Capitol, the band's label home from 1969 to 1975, is re-mastering and re-issuing 11 Grand Funk titles as part of a budget CD line, but it's been a slow process. *Closer to Home ♪♪♪* (Capitol, 1970, prod. Terry Knight) is the best of what's out, a solid studio effort notable for its inspirational centerpiece, "Closer to Home/I'm Your Captain."

what to avoid: Either of the band's now-out-of-print reunion albums—*Grand Funk Lives ♪* (Full Moon/Warner Bros., 1981, prod. Grand Funk Railroad, Andrew Cavaliere) and *What's Funk* ♪ (Full Moon/Warner Bros., 1983, prod. various)—which, like the last couple of albums before the 1976 breakup, found the group searching for direction. Its rendition of "Queen Bee," however, did get some notice, thanks to its appearance on the *Heavy Metal* soundtrack.

the rest:

E Pluribus Funk ♪♪ (Capitol, 1971/1995)
We're an American Band ♪♪♪ (Capitol, 1973/1996)
Caught in the Act ♪♪ (Capitol, 1975/1995)
Bosnia ♪♪ (Capitol/EMI Properties, 1997)

worth searching for: *Grand Funk Railroad* (Capitol, 1970), also known as the "Red Album" because of its bright red cover, is the group's best studio effort and will be part of the reissue series. Those who can't wait might want to hunt down a Canadian edition on the Collector's Pipeline label, though the art reproduction is horrid. Many of Grand Funk's original albums are also available via Japanese import, but beware of the inferior sound quality.

solo outings:

Mark Farner:

Just Another Injustice ♪♪ (Frontline, 1988)
Some Kind of Wonderful ♪♪ (Frontline, 1991)

influences:

◀◀ Motown, Cream, Jimi Hendrix

▶▶ Kiss, Bon Jovi, Foreigner, Boston, Soul Asylum

Doug Pullen

Amy Grant

Born November 25, 1960, in Augusta, GA.

The first contemporary Christian artist to cross fully into mainstream pop, Amy Grant remains the undisputed queen of the genre. Raised in Nashville, Grant released her self-titled debut at 17 and quickly culled the image of an innocuous songstress—the sweet, innocent girl-next-door who sang about God, love, and friendship. Her early material reflected the acoustic folkiness of idols such as Carole King and Joni Mitchell, but as she moved into the '80s, her sound shifted to glossy, synthesized pop. Grant is also responsible for launching the pop career of fellow contemporary Christian artist Michael W. Smith, whose melodic keyboards became the cornerstone of Grant's 1985 album, *Unguarded*. But it wasn't until 1991's landmark *Heart in Motion* that Grant became a household name and spurred the gradual convergence of Christian and secular music. Chastised by staunch religious activists for seemingly deserting God to sing about frothy romance on Top 40 hits such as "Baby Baby" and "Every Heartbeat," Grant nonetheless sold more than five

million copies of *Heart* and became an early VH1 poster girl. The follow-up to *Heart, House of Love,* fared decently on the charts, thanks to the title track duet with country star Vince Gill. As the '90s progressed, so did Grant's lyrical maturity. Her 1997 release, *Behind the Eyes,* was a commercial dud, but it marked Grant's return to rootsy, introspective material. Despite rumors of marital upheaval, Grant remains settled in Franklin, Tennessee, with husband and fellow performer Gary Chapman and their children, Matthew, Millie, and Sarah. Grant and Chapman were married in 1982 after Grant recorded the Chapman-penned "My Father's Eyes." The pair wrote, recorded, and toured together until Chapman became host of the Nashville Network's *Primetime Country* in 1996.

what to buy: *Lead Me On* ♪♪♪♪ (A&M, 1988, prod. David Anderle, Michael Blanton, Gary Chapman) showcases Grant at her insightful best. From the sweeping title track dealing with the Holocaust, to her stark tender cover of Jimmy Webb's "If These Walls Could Speak," the album is gut-tugging, yet never maudlin. Peppered with Mark O'Connor's mandolin and Benmont Tench's ethereal organ, the songs are wise, accessible affirmations of hope and spirituality. For the playful side of Grant, check out *Unguarded* ♪♪♪♪ (A&M, 1985, prod. Brown Bannister), the prelude to her impressive pop breakthrough during the '90s. The infectiously melodic "Find a Way" proves the magical pairing of Grant's lyrics and Michael W. Smith's swirling synthesizers, while the lite-funk backbeat and street-smart words of "Wise Up" are a must-hear for any troubled teen. The closing ballad, "The Prodigal (I'll Be Waiting)," co-written by Grant and husband Chapman, is a stunning yet subtle tale of redemption that merits repeated listens.

what to buy next: *The Collection* ♪♪♪ (A&M, 1986, prod. Brown Bannister) is a comprehensive compilation of Grant's early work, including her signature concert hit "El Shaddai," country-tinged live tracks such as "I'm Gonna Fly," "I Have Decided," and "Too Late," and two new tracks. *Heart in Motion* ♪♪♪ (A&M, 1991, prod. Amy Grant, Michael Blanton) is notable for expanding Grant's name beyond the contemporary Christian niche, but it hardly embodies her skills as a songwriter and unfairly paints her as a non-descript Top 40 chirper. "Good for Me," "Every Heartbeat," and the ubiquitous "Baby Baby," which spent two weeks at the top of the charts, are sprightly, keyboard-laden ditties, but the real meat comes with the haunting "Ask Me" and "How Can We See That Far?" The oft-endour *Behind the Eyes* ♪♪♪ (A&M, 1997, prod. David Anderle, Michael Blanton, Amy Grant) is nonetheless gripping as "Like I Love You," "Turn This World Around," and "Leave It All Behind" intimately portray a woman at a crossroads.

what to avoid: Grant's debut, *Amy Grant* ♪♪ (Myrrh, 1977, prod. Chris Christian), is clearly the work of a teenager with promise, but her early self-penned songs are trite and cringe-inducing. When Grant tackles a live performance, as in *Amy Grant: In Concert* ♫♫ (Reunion, 1981, prod. Brown Bannister), her inexperience is blatant. Save for the charming "Mimi's House" and the uplifting "Walking away with You," these songs—many from her debut—fare no better live. Tinny production combined with textbook tunes do not a joyful noise make.

the rest:
My Father's Eyes ♫♫♪ (A&M, 1979)
Never Alone ♫♫♪ (A&M, 1980)
In Concert, Vol. 2 ♫♫♪ (A&M, 1981)
Age to Age ♫♫♫ (A&M, 1982)
A Christmas Album ♫♫♫♫ (A&M, 1983)
Straight Ahead ♫♫♫ (A&M, 1984)
Home for Christmas ♫♫♫♪ (A&M, 1992)
House of Love ♫♫♫♪ (A&M, 1994)

worth searching for: Grant's personal church project *Songs from the Loft* (Reunion, 1993) finds her joined by husband Chapman, Smith, and a slew of other top Christian artists for a compilation album highlighted by Grant's "Hey Now" and "We Believe in God." Her duet on "Somewhere, Somehow" from Smith's *Change Your World* (Reunion, 1992) album is a glorious love piffle, and Grant even boldly covers the King on the soundtrack to *Honeymoon in Vegas* (Epic Soundtrax, 1992), where she delivers a shivery "Love Me Tender."

influences:
◀◀ Carole King, Joni Mitchell, Bonnie Raitt

▶▶ Beth Nielsen Chapman, Sheryl Crow, Amanda Marshall, Kathy Troccoli

Melissa Ruggieri

Grant Lee Buffalo

Formed 1991, in Los Angeles, CA.

Grant Lee Phillips, guitar, vocals; Paul Kimble, bass, keyboards (1991–97); Joey Peters, drums; others.

Grant Lee Buffalo emerged from the L.A. club scene in 1993 with the release of its first album, *Fuzzy*. The band's style, though rootsy, boasts modern influences such as David Bowie and R.E.M. While songwriter Grant Lee Phillips isn't afraid to tackle social and political views, he presents them with the flavor of an intimate discussion rather than a stirring oratory. The trio grew considerably over its first three albums, from the rip-roaring, outspoken rock band of *Fuzzy* to the more thoughtful and reflective ensemble reflected in *Copperopolis* and, even more so, on the masterful *Jubilee*, which was recorded after the departure of Paul Kimble left Phillips and drummer Joey Peters—along with a number of guests—to find a new course for the band.

WHAT ALBUM CHANGED YOUR LIFE?

Early on, Johnny Cash's *At San Quentin* and *At Folsom Prison.* He was probably the greatest icon that I can remember as a child, this dark, mysterious figure singing these tales drenched in reverb and performing for a crowd of prisoners. That's pretty enticing.

Grant Lee Phillips (of Grant Lee Buffalo)

what to buy: *Jubilee* ♫♫♫♫ (Slash/Warner Bros., 1998, prod. Paul Fox) is a richer, bigger-sounding album than anything GLB has produced to date. There's a ringing, cinematic quality to the arrangements, and songs such as "Seconds," "Super Slo Motion," "Everybody Needs a Little Sanctuary," and the title track convey an almost spiritual release—thanks in part to the fuller sound achieved with the help of guests such as the Wallflowers' Rami Jaffee and R.E.M.'s Michael Stipe.

what to buy next: *Copperopolis* ♫♫♫♫ (Slash/Reprise, 1996, prod. Paul Kimble) is a more layered and multi-dimensional sonic experience, the result of more relaxed, off-tour time spent constructing and arranging the songs.

the rest:
Fuzzy, (Slash, 1993) ♫♫♫
Mighty Joe Moon ♫♫♫♪ (Slash/Reprise, 1994)

influences:
◀◀ R.E.M., the Band, Counting Crows, David Bowie

Kim Forster and Gary Graff

The Grapes of Wrath /Ginger

Formed 1983, in Kelowna, British Columbia, Canada. Disbanded 1992. Re-formed 1998.

Tom Hooper, vocals, bass, marimba; Chris Hooper, drums (1983–92); Kevin Kane, vocals, piano, guitar; Vincent Jones, keyboards (1989–92); Adam Drake, drums (1992–present).

The Hooper brothers, Tom and Chris, along with childhood

friend Kevin Kane, spent time playing—separately and together—with a series of art, punk, and hardcore bands before forming the Grapes of Wrath. The musicians raised money to record their four-song demo through yard and flea-market sales, and what was supposed to be an independent EP went national (in Canada) when it was swept up by Terry McBride for his then-fledgling label Nettwerk records. After a number of releases, the group produced its definitive work, *These Days*, but broke up the following year. The Hoopers and Jones carried on as Ginger, while Kane worked as a producer and solo act. In April 1998, Kane and Tom Hooper put aside their differences and reformed the band with former Holly McNarland drummer Adam Drake.

what to buy: *These Days* ✍✍✍ (Capitol, 1991, prod. John Leckie) showcases the Grapes' finest traits—picturesque storytelling, gorgeous harmonies, and lush arrangements, especially in the songs "You May Be Right," "I Am Here," and "Travelin.'"

what to buy next: *Now and Again* ✍✍✍ (Capitol, 1989, prod. Anton Fier) has some nice moments, notably "All the Things I Wasn't," but at some points the band is nearly overwhelmed by outside musicians, including pedal-steel player Sneaky Pete Kleinow, keyboardist Chuck Leavell, and producer Anton Fier.

the rest:
The Grapes of Wrath EP (Nettwerk, 1984) ✍✍
September Bowl of Green ✍✍ (Nettwerk, 1985/Capitol, 1986)
Treehouse ✍✍✍ (Capitol, 1987)
Seems like Fate 1984–1992 ✍✍ (Nettwerk/EMI, 1994)

worth searching for: Kane's solo album *Neighborhood Watch* (Cargo) is out of print but still available online through his own label, OnOff Records.

solo outings:
Ginger:
Ginger EP ✍✍✍ (Nettwerk, 1994)
Far Out ✍✍✍ (Nettwerk, 1995)

influences:
◀◀ the Beatles, Railway Children
▶▶ Ginger, Collective Soul

Christina Fuoco

The Grass Roots

Formed 1966, in Los Angeles, CA.

Warren Entner, guitar, vocals, keyboards; Creed Bratton, guitar, banjo, sitar (1966–69); Ricky Coonce, drums (1966–72); Rob Grill, bass, vocals (1966–75); Dennis Provisor, organ (1969–72); others over the years.

The Grass Roots was the brainchild of songwriters and producers P.F. Sloan and Steve Barri. Needing a band to front their material, the members were assembled after the 1966 hit "Where Were You When I Needed You." The band's style shifted from a folk-rock beginning to a nearly power-pop/soul sound by its end. From socially aware tunes to dewy-eyed ballads and romantic pop, the Roots hit with "Let's Live for Today," "Midnight Confessions," "I'd Wait a Million Years," and "Sooner or Later."

what to buy: The best collection so far of the band's mid-'60s to early '70s work is the two-disc, 36-track *Anthology: (1966–1975)* ✍✍✍ (Rhino, 1991, prod. P.F. Sloan), which contains "Let's Live for Today," "Midnight Confessions," and the breezy "Sooner or Later," among many other hits.

the rest:
Where Were You When I Needed You ✍✍✍ (Dunhill, 1966/Varese Vintage, 1994)
Greatest Hits, Vol. 1 ✍✍ (MCA, 1988)
Greatest Hits, Vol. 2 ✍✍ (MCA, 1988)

influences:
◀◀ The Beatles, Blood, Sweat & Tears, Neil Diamond, the Brill Building
▶▶ Chicago, the Raspberries, Dwight Twilley

Patrick McCarty

The Grassy Knoll /Bob Green

Formed early 1990s, in San Francisco, CA.

The Grassy Knoll is the musical *nom de plume* of Bob Green, a San Francisco-based multimedia artist (formerly a documentary photographer) whose idiosyncratic musical exploits are predominately a trancey combination of ambient, dub-like samples and loops, repetitious bass and drum patterns, and miscellaneous instrumentation with sound effects and turntable scratching—all of which jams along, structureless, without any kind of discernable melody or head. Not that there's anything wrong with that.

what to buy: It's debut album, *The Grassy Knoll* ✍✍✍ (Nettwork/Antilles, 1995), combines muted trumpet noodling and bass clarinet (reminiscent of *Bitches Brew* –era Miles Davis) and twangy, tremolo-driven guitar with loops and patterns in what is a diverse and unusual musical collage, merging everything from avant-jazz elements to industrial noise.

the rest:
Positive ✍✍✍ (Nettwork/Antilles, 1997)
The Grassy Knoll III ✍✍ (Nettwork/Antilles, 1998)

influences:
◀◀ Miles Davis, the Art of Noise, Ennio Morricone, Einstürzende Neubauten

Mike Bieber

The Grateful Dead

Formed 1965, in San Francisco, CA. Disbanded 1995.

Jerry Garcia (died August 9, 1995), guitar, vocals; Bob Weir, guitar, vocals; Phil Lesh, bass, vocals; Bill Kreutzmann, drums; Mickey Hart, drums (1967–69, 1974–95); Ron (Pig Pen) McKernan (died March 8, 1973), vocals, keyboards (1965–72); Tom Constanten, keyboards (1968–70); Keith Godchaux (died July 23, 1980), keyboards (1972–79); Donna Godchaux, vocals (1972–79); Brent Mydland (died July 26, 1990), keyboards, vocals (1979–90); Vince Welnick, keyboards, vocals (1990–95).

Separating the sociological phenomenon from the musical force has always been difficult with the Grateful Dead. In a single performance, few groups could span an equivalent breadth of 20th century music, as the Dead merrily careened from the delta blues of Robert Johnson through the pure sonics of Karlheinz Stockhausen, from the giddy Gypsy jazz of Django Reinhardt to the cheery rock 'n' roll of Chuck Berry. The musicians' commitment to the art of ensemble improvisation produced some extraordinary bursts of imagination, but the delicate chemistry of the Dead never translated well to the recorded medium. That they came to represent a quickly bygone era of San Francisco '60s utopianism never less than bewildered band members, who unceremoniously followed their own path in blissful indifference to the commercial conventions of the music business until the death of the group's central figure, guitarist Jerry Garcia, finally spelled an end to their adventures in 1995. After Garcia's death, Bob Weir and Mickey Hart—as part of their annual summer Furthur Festival extravaganza—coaxed Phil Lesh back onto the road during 1998 for a Dead mini-reunion.

what to buy: A live recording using the finest modern technology to wring fine-point detail out of relatively ancient source tape, *Two from the Vault* 🎵🎵🎵🎵 (Grateful Dead Records, 1992, prod. Dan Healy) is Grateful Dead 101: a two-disc set that covers the band's basic 1968 repertoire and abundantly displays the band's occasionally extravagant gifts. Of course, *Workingman's Dead* 🎵🎵🎵🎵 (Warner Bros., 1970, prod. Grateful Dead) remains the crucial studio work, inspired by the clapboard honesty of "Music from Big Pink" by the Band.

what to buy next: The follow-up to *Workingman's Dead*, *American Beauty* 🎵🎵🎵🎵 (Warner Bros. 1970, prod. Grateful Dead) also manages to convey the band's fluid lyricism with somewhat darker undertones. *The History of the Grateful Dead, Vol. 1 (Bear's Choice)* 🎵🎵🎵🎵 (Warner Bros., 1973, prod. Owsley Stanley) is a selection of live recordings taken from an epic series of shows at the Fillmore East during 1970, fully released on a three-disc set from the band's mail order label.

what to avoid: *Steal Your Face* 🎵 (Grateful Dead, 1976, prod. Grateful Dead), the live record from the band's 1974 Winterland

engagement that was also filmed for a concert movie, has long been a source of embarrassment to the band because of the badly botched sound quality. But the hackneyed attempts at commercial relevance in which the band indulged in the late '70s—*Terrapin Station* 🎵🎵 (Arista, 1977, prod. Keith Olsen); *Shakedown Street* 🎵 (Arista, 1978, prod. Lowell George, Dan Healy); and *Go to Heaven* **woof!** (Arista, 1980, prod. Gary Lyons)—have even less to do with what the band is really about.

the rest:
Grateful Dead 🎵🎵🎵🎵 (Warner Bros., 1967)
Anthem of the Sun 🎵🎵🎵🎵 (Warner Bros., 1968)
Aoxomoxoa 🎵🎵🎵 (Warner Bros., 1969)
Live Dead 🎵🎵🎵🎵 (Warner Bros., 1970)
Grateful Dead 🎵🎵🎵 (aka Skull & Roses) (Warner Bros., 1971)
Europe '72 🎵🎵🎵 (Warner Bros., 1972)
Wake of the Flood 🎵🎵 (Grateful Dead, 1973)
From the Mars Hotel 🎵🎵🎵 (Grateful Dead, 1974)
Blues for Allah 🎵🎵 (Grateful Dead, 1975)
Reckoning 🎵🎵🎵 (Arista, 1981)
Dead Set 🎵🎵 (Arista 1981)
In the Dark 🎵🎵🎵 (Arista, 1987)
Dylan and the Dead 🎵 (Columbia, 1989)
Built to Last **woof!** (Arista, 1989)
Without a Net 🎵 (Arista, 1990)
One from the Vault 🎵🎵🎵 (Grateful Dead, 1991)
Dick's Picks, Vol. 1 🎵🎵🎵 (Grateful Dead, 1993)
Infrared Roses 🎵🎵🎵 (Grateful Dead, 1994)
Dick's Picks, Vol. 2 🎵🎵🎵 (Grateful Dead, 1995)
Dick's Picks, Vol. 3 🎵🎵🎵 (Grateful Dead, 1995)

Jerry Garcia of the Grateful Dead (© Ken Settle)

Hundred Year Hall 🎵🎵🎵 (Grateful Dead, 1995)
Grayfolded 🎵🎵 (Plunderphonics, 1995)
Dick's Picks, Vol. 5 🎵🎵🎵 (Grateful Dead, 1996)
Best of the Grateful Dead 🎵🎵🎵 (Arista, 1996)
Dozin' at the Knick 🎵🎵🎵 (Grateful Dead, 1996)
The Phil Zone 🎵🎵🎵 (Grateful Dead, 1997)
Fillmore East 2-11-69 🎵🎵🎵 (Grateful Dead, 1997)
Dick's Picks, Vol. 7 🎵🎵🎵🎵 (Grateful Dead, 1997)
Dick's Picks, Vol. 8 🎵🎵🎵 (Grateful Dead, 1997)
Dick's Picks, Vol. 9 🎵🎵🎵 (Grateful Dead, 1997)
Dick's Picks, Vol. 10 🎵🎵🎵 (Grateful Dead, 1998)

worth searching for: In 1965 the Dead and author Ken Kesey and his band of Merry Pranksters dropped acid and entered a recording studio for several hours of noodling and assorted craziness, editing the mass of tapes down to a strange album, *The Acid Test* (A Sound City Production, 1965). Although virtually impossible to find, the album is a priceless relic of the mishigass out of which the Dead was born.

solo outings:
Jerry Garcia:
Garcia 🎵🎵🎵 (Warner Bros. 1970)
(With Howard Wales) *Hooteroll* 🎵🎵🎵 (Douglas, 1970)
(With Merl Saunders and Tom Fogerty) *Fire Up* 🎵🎵 (Fantasy, 1973)
(With Merl Saunders and Tom Fogerty) *Live at Keystone Berkeley* 🎵🎵🎵 (Fantasy, 1973)
Compliments of Garcia 🎵🎵🎵 (Grateful Dead, 1974)
(With Old & in the Way) *Old and in the Way* 🎵🎵🎵 (Grateful Dead, 1975)
Reflections 🎵🎵🎵 (Grateful Dead, 1976)
Cats under the Stars 🎵🎵 (Arista, 1976)
Run for the Roses 🎵🎵 (Arista, 1982)
Jerry Garcia Band 🎵 (Arista 1991)
(With David Grisman) *Jerry Garcia/David Grisman* 🎵🎵🎵🎵 (Acoustic Disc, 1991)
(With David Grisman) *Not for Kids Only* 🎵🎵🎵 (Acoustic Disc, 1993)
(With David Grisman) *Shady Grove* 🎵🎵🎵🎵 (Acoustic Disc, 1996)
(With Old & in the Way) *That High Lonesome Sound* 🎵🎵🎵 (Acoustic Disc, 1996)
How Sweet It Is 🎵🎵🎵 (Grateful Dead/Arista, 1997)
A Talk with Jerry Garcia 🎵🎵🎵 (Beserkley/Mercury, 1998)

Bob Weir:
Ace 🎵🎵🎵 (Warner Bros., 1970)
Heaven Help the Fool 🎵 (Arista, 1978)
(With Kingfish) *Kingfish* 🎵🎵 (Grateful Dead, 1976)
(With Kingfish) *Live 'n' Kickin'* 🎵 (United Artists, 1977)
Bobby & the Midnites 🎵 (Arista 1981)
(With Kingfish) *King Biscuit Flower Hour Presents Kingfish* 🎵🎵 (KBR, 1995)

Mickey Hart:
Rolling Thunder 🎵🎵 (Warner Bros., 1972)
Dafos 🎵🎵 (Reference, 1983)

WHAT ALBUM CHANGED YOUR LIFE?

An Otis Redding album; *Live in Europe* was the name of it. It was him at his peak. I had seen him at the Fillmore, and I knew he was big and playing powerful music. On this live record, he really connected that night. What it did was reinforce my feelings for live music and being able to capture that one, special, miraculous moment. He never sounded that good again. It was a great record.

Mickey Hart (of the Grateful Dead)

Rhythm Devils Play River Music: The Apocalypse Now Sessions 🎵🎵🎵 (Passport, 1980)
Music to Be Born By 🎵 (Rykodisc, 1989)
At the Edge 🎵🎵🎵 (Rykodisc, 1990)
Planet Drum 🎵🎵🎵🎵 (Rykodisc, 1991)
Mickey Hart's Mystery Box 🎵🎵🎵🎵 (Rykodisc, 1996)
Supralingua 🎵🎵🎵🎵 (Rykodisc, 1998)

Vince Welnick & Missing Man Formation:
Vince Welnick & Missing Man Formation 🎵🎵🎵 (Grateful Dead, 1998)

influences:
◀◀ Cannon's Jug Stompers, Le Hot Club de France, Jimmy Reed, Rolling Stones, Bob Dylan

▶▶ Allman Brothers, Los Lobos, Spin Doctors, Phish, Blues Traveler

Joel Selvin

Gravity Kills
Formed 1995, in St. Louis, MO.

Jeff Scheel, vocals, guitars; Kurt Kerns, bass, drums; Matt Dudenhoeffer, guitars; Douglas Firley, keyboards.

It wasn't long after it began performing that the industrial rock band Gravity Kills soon found success. On a whim, the band submitted a demo of the song "Guilty" to radio station KPNT for a compilation album it was releasing. "Guilty" was not only accepted for the CD but became the station's top-requested song—all before Gravity Kills played its first gig.

what to buy: TVT Records swept up the band, put it in the studio, and released *Gravity Kills* 🎵🎵🎵 (TVT, 1996, prod. Gravity Kills). Purging radio with its inferno of pounding drum loops, Jeff Scheel's acerbic vocals, and guitars, Gravity Kills seemed to use every sound available in recording its debut. Computer-generated music clashes with classic metal guitar riffs and drum beats. Although the lyrics are brooding, they don't delve into the hell that is suicide attempts and death, putting it a step above Marilyn Manson and nine inch nails.

what to buy next: For its next proper album, Gravity Kills took an organic approach—as organic as a band can get in the industrial field, at least—and relied more on guitars and less on programming. *Perversion* 🎵🎵 (TVT, 1998, prod. Gravity Kills, Roli Mosimann) also shies away from downtrodden lyrics. To the tune of raging guitars and keyboards, Scheel describes life on the road as frustrating and pleasing. The spooky "Always" relates the loss he felt being separated from friends and family. "Belief" tells the story of Gravity Kills' upward rise.

the rest:
Manipulated 🎵🎵 (TVT, 1997)

influences:
⏪ nine inch nails, Stabbing Westward

⏩ Sevendust

Christina Fuoco

David Gray

Born early 1970s, in Manchester, England.

We may like to think that every Welsh-bred singer-songwriter can spew fire and brimstone like David Gray, but the facts don't bear that out. He is one of a kind: a committed, tuneful songwriter with a serrated voice and an aching heart. Moving to Wales with his family at age eight, he clearly absorbed some of that rural land's rocky beauty. After attending college in Liverpool, Gray headed down to London to make it big. His 1993 debut helped get him signed to Virgin, and 1994's more electric *Flesh* led to a U.S. club tour in support of the Dave Matthews Band. But *Flesh* failed to win him a large following in America, and he shifted to EMI for his third album, which was a somewhat weaker effort—although it did win him an opening slot on Radiohead's U.S. tour. With the dismantling of EMI, he suddenly found himself without a label. Reportedly, he's now developing new material; one hopes that Gray's wild, willing spirit won't allow his career to go the way of all flesh.

what to buy: As visceral as folk/rock generally gets, *Flesh* 🎵🎵🎵 (Vernon Yard/Virgin, 1994, prod. Jim Abiss, Jock Loveband) shoots off into the stratosphere, fueled by the twin rockets of "What Are You?" and "Made up My Mind." But Gray doesn't forget his sensitive side here, as he shows on "Falling Free" and "Lullaby."

what to buy next: Not as consistently strong as *Flesh*, *A Century Ends* 🎵🎵🎵 (Caroline, 1993, prod. Dave Anderson) was an impressive debut nonetheless. The title track is an especially thoughtful but still quite cynical view of modern times.

what to avoid: Gray's lack of sales success apparently had an adverse affect on *Sell, Sell, Sell* 🎵🎵 (EMI, 1996, prod. Dave Nolte). Although the title track sports plenty of righteous indignation, much of the songwriting either seems unfocused or overly self-conscious.

influences:
⏪ The Waterboys, Ewan MacColl, Christy Moore, Van Morrison

⏩ Glitterbox

Bob Remstein

Great White

Formed 1981, in Los Angeles, CA.

Jack Russell, vocals; Mark Kendall, guitars; Michael Lardie, keyboards; Audie Desbrow, drums; Teddy Cook, bass.

One of the many faceless, dismissable hair bands that emerged from Los Angeles during the late '80s, Great White combined titillation with a straightforward blues-influenced hard rock. Its first EP was produced by then-hot Don Dokken; it went nowhere but helped the band land a deal with Capitol Records, where it built a following that culminated in the platinum sales of its *Once Bitten*, *Twice Shy* (out of print), and *Hooked* albums.

what's available: *Hooked* 🎵🎵 (Capitol, 1991, prod. Alan Niven, Michael Lardie) caught the band at its most cocky and confident, bolstered by the mounting buzz created by the two albums that preceded it and seasoned by extensive touring and the groupiedom that goes with it.

the rest:
Once Bitten 🎵🎵 (Capitol, 1987)
Recovery: Alive 🎵🎵 (Enigma, 1988)
Best of Great White 🎵🎵 (Capitol, 1993)
Sail Away **woof!** (Zoo, 1994)
Stage 🎵 (Zoo, 1996)
Let It Rock 🎵 (Imago, 1996)

influences:
⏪ Mott the Hoople, Scorpions, Brownsville Station

Doug Pullen

Billie Joe Armstrong of Green Day (© **Ken Settle**)

Green Day

Formed 1989, in Berkeley, CA.

Billie Joe Armstrong, guitar, vocals; Mike Dirnt (born Mike Pritchard), bass, vocals; Al Sobrante, drums (1989–90): John Kiftmeyer, drums (1990); Tré Cool, (born Frank Edwin Wright III), drums, vocals (1990–present).

With a booger on their middle fingers, the band Green Day burst on to the national scene with the huge success of its album *Dookie* in 1994. From the humble confines of Berkeley's famed punk palace 924 Gilman Street to sports arenas (and Woodstock '94, even), the band forged a sound suitable for both extremes. Billie Joe Armstrong's distinctive whine and charismatic stage presence made him the perfect front man; Cuddly cute in an unwashed way, it was still his strong song writing skills that took the band farther than most of its compatriots. Bass player Mike Dirnt made for a strong sidekick, and with the addition of talented drummer Trè Cool in 1990, Green Day was ready for the big time. Success didn't exactly fall out of the sky, however; Armstrong and Dirnt recorded with two drummers prior to Cool and released one full-length album and several EPs and singles before *Dookie* hit. Perhaps it was the video for the first single, "Longview," that did it. Or maybe it was the trio's energetic live shows (often including short covers of junk rock such as Scorpions' "Rock You like a Hurricane" or Survivor's "Eye of the Tiger"). Possibly, the time was simply right for a punky Kinks/Ramones hybrid that even girls liked to hit the airwaves. No matter what the reason, Green Day's records each have their own merits, and. hell, most of the guitar parts are easy. What's not to like?

what to buy: The unfortunately titled (and colored) *Dookie* 𝄞𝄞𝄞𝄞 (Reprise, 1994, prod. Rob Cavallo, Green Day) is probably the best starting point for the uninitiated. With more hits than a free porn web site, *Dookie* is nearly the punk version of Fleetwood Mac's *Rumours*. At least five singles gained massive airplay, including the remake of their own paean to the punk lifestyle in Berkeley, "Welcome to Paradise."

what to buy next: *Dookie's* follow-up, *Insomniac* 𝄞𝄞𝄞 (Reprise, 1995, prod. Rob Cavallo, Green Day), didn't deserve the backlash slagging it took. But the nature of trends is that *Dookie* paved the road that many lesser bands soon followed, which now made Green Day just another punk band. And punk rock has about the same shelf-life as hip-hop. Regardless, Green Day returned with the equally catchy and listenable *Insomniac*. Slightly more metallic than its predecessor (check out the hesher riffs on "Brain Stew") and with fewer hits than *Dookie, Insomniac* is a still an excellent record. With *Nimrod* 𝄞𝄞𝄞𝄞 (Reprise, 1997, prod. Rob Cavallo) the boys deserve some credit. A little maturity was bound to creep in to their

sound, and it works here. A string section finds its way into a couple tracks, one of which—"Good Riddance (Time of Your Life)"—is drum-free and utterly gorgeous. Harmonica, horns and acoustic guitar also can be found here.

the rest:
1,039/Smoothed Out Slappy Hours 𝄞𝄞𝄞 (Lookout, 1990)
Kerplunk 𝄞𝄞𝄞𝄞 (Lookout, 1992)

worth searching for: Green Day's unthrottled live performance is captured on the 10-track Japanese import *Foot in Mouth* (Reprise, 1996, prod. Rob Cavallo, Green Day).

influences:

◀◀ The Kinks, the Ramones, Dickies, the Buzzcocks, the Jam, Clash, Vibrators, UK Subs, Cheap Trick, Bad Religion, Dag Nasty, Descendents, Seven Seconds

▶▶ Blink 182, Alcohol Funnycar, Playground

Barry M. Prickett

Green Jellÿ

Formed as Green Jellö, 1981, in Kenmore, NY.

Developed more as a practical joke than a band, Green Jellö was named after a flavor the whole band hated, a reflection of the work they expected to produce. The group prided itself on being the world's worst band during a mid-'80s appearance on *The Gong Show,* but it wasn't until it began making its own on-stage props that it began to join the realm of such shtick rockers as GWAR and the Impotent Sea Snakes. Building an entire album around a heavy metal version of the "Three Little Pigs" story, the group crafted a clever Claymation video for the song that went into heavy rotation on MTV and made them modern rock's most unlikely stars. Forced by legal concerns to change the name to Green Jellÿ, the group produced a highly entertaining debut album, then released a much more forgettable album in 1994. Only time will tell if it will live down to *Rolling Stone* magazine's 1993 designation of the group as "this year's musical lowpoint."

what to buy: It's sometimes hard to believe anyone would want to buy one of this group's albums, but for the adventurous, there's *Cereal Killer Soundtrack* 𝄞𝄞𝄞 (Zoo, 1993, prod. Sylvia Massy, C.J. Buscaglia), a lovable mess fortified by a cover of the Sex Pistols' "Anarchy in the U.K."

what to avoid: By the group's second record, *333* 𝄞𝄞𝄞 (Pavement, 1994, prod. Matt Hyde, Richard Mouser, Bill Pfordresher), the joke had worn a little thin.

worth searching for: *Green Jellÿ Suxx* (Zoo, 1995) is an EP that lives up/down to its title.

Green on Red

Formed 1980, in Tucson, AZ. Disbanded 1992.

Dan Stuart, lead vocals, guitar (1980–92); Chuck Prophet IV, guitar, vocals (1985–92); Chris Cacavas, piano, organ, harmonica, vocals (1980–88); Jack Waterson, bass, vocals (1980–88); Van Christian, drums (1980–81); Alex MacNicol, drums (1981–86); Keith Mitchell, percussion (1987–88).

Starting out as an Arizona punk group called the Serfers, the band had already become Green on Red by the time it hit Los Angeles in 1981. Within a few years, it was lumped in with the area's burgeoning psychedelic rock scene—the so-called Paisley Underground that also included Dream Syndicate, the Three O'Clock, the Rain Parade, and the Long Ryders. And yet, by 1985, it had—with the help of guitarist Chuck Prophet—eliminated most of its psychedelic trappings in favor of a hard-hitting country-rock sound that recalled Neil Young, Bob Dylan, and even the Velvet Underground. Finally, whiny-voiced and somewhat contrived lead singer Dan Stuart had a strong foil to play off of, although Chris Cacavas's organ and piano work remained the band's most colorful ingredient. A pair of releases for major label Mercury Records followed, and though they include some strong moments, those albums proved to most that the band was out of its league. Stuart and Prophet apparently thought so too, firing the rest of the band but continuing to make records without garnering much attention. They eventually called it quits in 1992. Since then, Prophet has released a few solo records, Stuart just one. Cacavas and Alex MacNicol each put out records on their own during the late '80s. Although Green on Red never quite achieved modern rock iconhood, it did prefigure the mid-'90s movement back to country-rock.

what to buy: In retrospect, *Gas Food Lodging* 🎵🎵🎵🎵 (Enigma, 1985, prod. Paul Cutler) seems to have been the album where Green on Red found its rough-and-ready country-rock sound. On it, "Hair of the Dog" cranks along in rip-roaring fashion, while "That's What Dreams" is surprisingly touching in a proto-New Sincerity style. *Here Come the Snakes* 🎵🎵🎵 (Restless, 1989, prod. Jim Dickenson, Joe Hardy) represents Stuart and Prophet's best effort after they fired the rest of the band.

what to buy next: *The Best of Green on Red* 🎵🎵🎵 (Off Beat, 1994, prod. various) provides a decent overview, although it's weighted heavily towards material from 1989 on and includes no tracks from either of the Mercury releases. The band's major label debut, the mini-LP *No Free Lunch* 🎵🎵🎵 (Mercury, 1985,

prod. Dan Stuart), has enough twangy character that is sometimes over the top, as on a version of Willie Nelson's "Funny How Time Slips Away" that borders on parody but which somehow works.

what to avoid: *The Killer Inside Me* 🎵🎵 (Mercury, 1987, prod. Jim Dickenson) suffers equally from forgettable songwriting and heavyhanded production. The gloriously soulful gospel backup singers only served to emphasize how ludicrous Stuart's lead vocals could sometimes be.

the rest:
Green on Red 🎵🎵 (Green on Red, 1981)
Green on Red 🎵🎵 (Down There/Enigma, 1982)
Gravity Talks 🎵🎵🎵 (Slash, 1983)
Live at the Town and Country Club 🎵🎵🎵 (China/Polydor, 1989)
This Time Around 🎵🎵🎵 (Off Beat, 1989)
Scapegoats 🎵🎵🎵 (Off Beat, 1991)

worth searching for: Danny and Dusty's *The Lost Weekend* (A&M, 1985, prod. Paul Cutler) is the great urban twang-rock album that Green on Red never quite made on its own. Featuring the alternating lead vocals of Stuart and Dream Syndicate's Steve Wynn, plus instrumental contributions by members of both of their bands and the Long Ryders, the disc is loose and fun, but it's got some anger and heart too.

solo outings:
Dan Stuart:
Can o' Worms 🎵🎵🎵 (Monkey Hill, 1995)

Chuck Prophet IV:
Brother Aldo 🎵🎵🎵 (Fire, 1990)
Balinese Dancer 🎵🎵🎵 (China/Dutch East India Trading)

Feast of Hearts 𝄢𝄢𝄢 (China, 1995)
Homemade Blood 𝄢𝄢𝄢 (Cooking Vinyl, 1997)

Chris Cacavas and Junkyard Love:
Chris Cacavas and Junkyard Love 𝄢𝄢𝄢 (Heyday, 1989)

Jack Waterson:
Whose Dog? 𝄢𝄢 (Heyday, 1988)

influences:

◀◀ Neil Young, the Violent Femmes, the Faces

▶▶ Uncle Tupelo, Son Volt, Blue Mountain

Bob Remstein

Green River

See: Pearl Jam

Greenberry Woods /Splitsville

Greenberry Woods: formed 1993, in Baltimore, MD. Disbanded 1983.
Splitsville: formed 1995, in Baltimore, MD.

Greenberry Woods: Brandt Huseman, vocals, bass; Matt Huseman, vocals, lead guitar; Ira Katz, vocals, rhythm guitar; Miles Rosen, drums, percussion. Splitsville: Messiah Kari (Matt Huseman), guitar, vocals; Captain Dusty (Paul Krysiak), bass, vocals; Johnny Immaculate (Brandt Huseman), drums, vocals.

Baltimore's Greenberry Woods wore matching shirts that had Monkees written all over them—figuratively speaking. The group was a herald of the pop rainbow after the grunge thunderstorm. After Greenberry Woods broke up, the band's nucleus, the Huseman twins, joined with bassist Paul Krysiak to form the pseudo-cartoon-character-comprised Splitsville.

what to buy: The Greenberry Woods' second album, *Big Money Item* 𝄢𝄢𝄢𝄢 (Sire, 1995, prod. Andy Paley), is a fine pop collection that makes full use of CD technology's spaciousness by stuffing it with 18 songs. The presumed cynicism of the release's title (is it any coincidence that its abbreviation is BMI?) belies the warmth and sincerity of its contents. With the songwriters passing the pen around (though they're all credited as collaborators), the album sustains its enthusiasm and momentum. A counterpart to the debut's strongest song, the high-bounding "Trampoline" and "Parachute" from *Big Money Item* are no letdown. The highlight, though, is the vaguely Beach Boys-ish "Smash-Up," which may be the world's second-best anti-hot rod song (after "Dead Man's Curve"). "Go without You" also has a Brian Wilson feel, which may be no fluke since producer Andy Paley produced Wilson's first solo album.

what to buy next: *Rapple Dapple* 𝄢𝄢𝄢 (Sire, 1994, prod. Andy Paley), the Greenberry Woods' promising debut, has fewer songs and less consistency. Still, two of the band's best tracks,

"Trampoline" and "Sentimental Role," make it a must-have for pop fans. Splitsville's *Pet Soul* 𝄢𝄢𝄢𝄢 (Big Deal, 1998, prod. Dave Nachodsky) is a limited-edition EP evoking the ocean of emotion that flowed from the late '60s Beach Boys, a predictable direction considering its title. Each of the four songs dip themselves in the sea of homage without drowning in it. In a modern context, it sounds like a lost Jellyfish release.

the rest:
Splitsville:
Splitsville USA 𝄢𝄢 (Big Deal, 1996)
Ultrasound 𝄢𝄢 (Big Deal, 1996)

worth searching for: Fans of the Greenberry Woods can find more nuggets by the band by digging through various releases. A promo-only EP called *Shorty* (Sire, 1995) contains "Super Geek," two non-LP originals and a sweetened version of the Velvet Underground's "Candy Says." The power-pop compilation *Yellow Pills: Vol. 3* (Big Deal, 1995) has the non-LP, Lemon Pipers-ish "You Know the Real." The soundtrack of *Naked in New York* (Sire, 1994) features the band's cover of "Too Good to Be True," a country-pop tune that originally appeared on producer Andy Paley's *Paley Brothers* album.

influences:

◀◀ The Byrds, Grapes of Wrath, the Sneetches, Redd Kross, Guided by Voices

▶▶ Elliot Smith, the Diggers

Jordan Oakes

Clive Gregson & Christine Collister /Clive Gregson /Christine Collister

Formed 1985, in Manchester, England. Clive Gregson born January 4, 1955, in Manchester, England. Christine Collister born on the Isle of Man, U.K.

Between 1980 and 1984, Clive Gregson led an offbeat pub-rock band called Any Trouble. Clever and attractive, but neither groundbreaking nor commercial, the band eventually broke up without leaving Gregson in any position to carve out a hitmaking solo career. Sizing up his options, he happened to hear Christine Collister performing in a small bar and was immediately taken with her smoky alto voice and impassioned delivery. He agreed to produce some tracks for her, and the pair began performing in clubs. Soon, both were on tour as members of Richard Thompson's backup band, and with that extra experience behind them, they launched what would be a seven-year period of smart, poignant folk/rock. Because they were romantically linked during that time, the story of their musical career parallels that of their affair, shifting from tentative (*Mischief*, highlighted by the lovely, but cutting "I Specialise") to self-assured and powerful (1989's classic *A Change in the Weather*) to sniping and bitter (1992's *The Last Word*). Like Thompson, Gregson is a terrific guitarist, and he's not a bad singer, but his real skill lies in his ability to pen canny and insightful country/rock and pop/rock tunes. He has gone on to record several rather impressive solo albums, but he'll probably never again have as potent an instrument to write for as Collister's voice. She recently put out a live album that, sadly, shows what can happen when someone with great pipes loses direction. The sound is there, but the feeling and intent are not.

what to buy: Varied and peppy, but often melancholy and/or dramatically moving, *A Change in the Weather* ♫♫♫♪ (Rhino, 1989, prod. Clive Gregson) features two absolutely heartstopping vocal performances by Collister, plus a host of other strong numbers, particularly "This Is the Deal," a touching tale of domestic abuse. Either "A Blessing in Disguise" or "How Weak I Am" would be worth the price of admission for any disc; together, they beautifully demonstrate the magic of Gregson's songwriting and Collister's singing.

what to buy next: Stranger than *Weather*, *The Last Word* ♫♫♫♫ (RNA/Rhino, 1992, prod. Clive Gregson) was the album Gregson and Collister made after their relationship had come to an end. Although some cuts provide a dose of levity, much of this disc deals with darker subjects. The best of Gregson's solo releases, *People & Places* ♫♫♫♫ (Compass, 1995, prod. Clive Gregson) shows him to be a thoughtful and witty singer-songwriter when everything clicks.

what to avoid: An album of cover tunes by Jackson Browne, Bruce Springsteen, Aztec Camera, Merle Haggard, and others, *Love Is a Strange Hotel* ♫♫♫ (RNA, 1990, prod. Clive Gregson, Christine Collister) should have been brilliant. But both Gregson's arrangements and Collister's vocals are too tame, too reverent, and other than Browne's "For a Dancer," the album floats along without making much of an impression.

the rest:
Home and Away ♫♫♫ (Cooking Vinyl, 1987)
Mischief ♫♫♫♪ (Rhino, 1988)

solo outings:
Clive Gregson:
Strange Persuasions (Demon/Compass, 1985/1995)
Welcome to the Workhouse (Special Delivery, 1990)
Carousel of Noise (Compass, 1994)
I Love This Town ♫♫♪ (Compass, 1996)

Christine Collister:
Live ♫♫ (Green Linnet, 1995)
The Dark Gift of Time N/A (Koch, 1998)

influences:
◄◄ Richard & Linda Thompson, Hank Williams, Sandy Denny, Nick Drake

►► John Wesley Harding, Eleanor McEvoy, Mary Coughlan

see also: *Any Trouble*

Bob Remstein

James Griffin
See: Bread

Patty Griffin
Born March 16, 1964, in Old Town, ME.

It wasn't until she was in her late twenties that waitress Patty Griffin mustered the courage to expose her bedroom compositions to audiences in Boston's coffeehouses and clubs. Backed by only an acoustic guitar, these early solo performances showcased both Griffin's beguiling voice—part Bonnie Raitt's homespun twang, part Rickie Lee Jones's urbane slur—and her starkly rendered vignettes of loss, rage, suffering, and, ultimately, hard-won redemption. She signed with A&M in 1993.

what to buy: Released amid the major labels' mad rush to exploit every female singer-songwriter with a cute face and a weepy guitar, Griffin's *Living with Ghosts* ♫♫♫♫ (A&M, 1996, prod. Steve Barry) threatened to be just another forgettable debut by just another forgettable folk-rock "artist." In fact, it's anything but, thanks largely to Griffin and producer Steve Barry's gutsy decision to scrap the label's hired guns (i.e., backing musicians) and do it demo-style: just one singer, one acoustic guitar, and one digital recorder. A spartan *tour de force*.

what to avoid: On *Flaming Red* ♫♫♪ (A&M, 1998, prod. Jay Joyce, Angelo), Griffin sounds hell-bent on sloughing off the acoustic-folkie typecast; unfortunately, she ends up sounding mostly confused. (To wit: the overcompensatory album opener, "Flaming Red," with its bronco-kick backbeat and its Nirvana-gone-cowpoke guitar assault.) Buttressed by a seasoned studio band and burnished to waxy luster by producer Jay Joyce, Griffin's sophomore effort can claim its share of worthwhile songs—"One Big Love" and "Wiggley Fingers" chief among them. Ultimately, though, *Flaming Red* lacks the very qualities that made *Living with Ghosts* such a triumph: intimacy, simplicity, coherence, restraint, passion, and consistency.

worth searching for: Issued to promote *Living with Ghosts*, *Let Him Fly* (A&M, 1997, prod. various) is a three-song promo-only CD featuring alternate versions of "Let Him Fly" and "Every Little Bit," in which instrumental tracks (keyboards, electric guitar, bass, drums) are superimposed on Griffin's vocals and acoustic guitar.

influences:

◀◀ Rickie Lee Jones, Bonnie Raitt, Steve Earle, Rosanne Cash, Bruce Springsteen, Emmylou Harris, Maria McKee

Greg Siegel

Nanci Griffith

Born July 16, 1954, in Seguin, TX.

Nanci Griffith has spent a career bridging the uneasy gap between country and folk, earning critical praise, devoted fans and minimal mass market success. Emerging from the Austin folk scene during the mid-'70s, she recorded two albums for tiny labels and crisscrossed the country performing at festivals. By the time she cut her first Nashville album in 1984, she had a reputation as a writer of tight, insightful songs. Griffith released her first work for MCA in 1987, but big-label backing did not translate into chart success for her idiosyncratic style (in the United States, anyway; Griffith has consistently topped charts in Ireland and Britain). Her songs, meanwhile, became Top 10 country hits for other singers (Kathy Mattea, Suzy Bogguss). A move to MCA's pop division in 1989 pointed Griffith toward a mass audience emphasis that better suited both her distinctive voice and the burgeoning adult-contemporary format. Griffith held this course while changing labels to Elektra and remains in demand as a session mate for everyone from the Chieftains to R.E.M. She broadened her reach further in 1997 by collaborating with the Nashville Ballet on "This Heart," an evening of dances set to a suite of her songs. Still, she's best known as a musical storyteller whose slice-of-life vignettes like "Trouble in the Fields," "Love at the Five and Dime," and "It's a Hard Life" only gain impact with repeated handlings by other singers.

what to buy: Merely mentioning *Last of the True Believers* ⚑⚑⚑⚑ (Rounder/Philo, 1986, prod. Jim Rooney, Nanci Griffith) reduces many Griffith fans to mindless mush. It is a beauty, with a sup-

porting cast of musicians' musicians (Bela Fleck, Roy Huskey Jr., Maura O'Connell, Lyle Lovett) and a fistful of classic Griffith songs ("Love at the Five and Dime," "More than a Whisper," "Lookin' for the Time"). Another fine introduction to the Griffith songbook is the live *One Fair Summer Evening* ⚑⚑⚑⚑ (MCA, 1988, prod. Nanci Griffith, Tony Brown), with moving versions of much of her best material and an understated reading of Julie Gold's "From a Distance" that eclipses Bette Midler's mawkish rendition.

what to buy next: *Other Voices, Other Rooms* ⚑⚑⚑⚑ (Elektra, 1993, prod. Jim Rooney) is a study of Griffith's interpretative abilities, featuring 17 songs by everyone from Woody Guthrie to John Prine to Janis Ian. On *Late Night Grande Hotel* ⚑⚑⚑⚑ (MCA, 1992, prod. Peter Van-Hooke, Rod Argent), the most successful to date of Griffith's VH1-style albums, Phil Everly duets on the nervous, driving "It's Just Another Morning Here," and Griffith continues her tradition of incisive political commentary with "One Blade Shy of a Sharp Edge."

what to avoid: The problem with *Lone Star State of Mind* ⚑⚑ (MCA, 1987, prod. Tony Brown, Nanci Griffith) isn't material; nor is it collaborators (Fleck, Huskey et al.). It's the production, which attempts to jam Griffith's music into a pair of pink sequined cowboy boots. Lots of twangin' that's plenty annoyin'.

the rest:

Poet in My Window ⚑⚑⚑ (Philo/Rounder, 1982)
Once in a Very Blue Moon ⚑⚑⚑⚑ (Philo/Rounder 1984)
Little Love Affairs ⚑⚑⚑⚐ (MCA, 1988)
Storms ⚑⚑⚑ (MCA, 1989)
The MCA Years: A Retrospective ⚑⚑⚑ (MCA, 1993)
Flyer ⚑⚑⚑ (Elektra, 1995)
Blue Roses from the Moon ⚑⚑⚑ (Elektra, 1997)
Other Voices, Too (A Trip Back to Bountiful) ⚑⚑⚑⚐ (Elektra, 1998)

worth searching for: *There's a Light beyond These Woods* (MCA U.K., 1982, prod. Mike Williams, Nanci Griffith) is a British reissue of Griffith's first album, recorded live in an Austin studio and originally released in 1978.

influences:

◀◀ Carolyn Hester, Bill Staines, the Weavers, Judy Collins, Tom Paxton

▶▶ Lucinda Williams, Iris DeMent, Gillian Welch

Elizabeth Lynch

The Grifters

Formed 1989, in Memphis, TN.

David Shouse, guitar, keyboards, harmonica, vocals; Scott Taylor, guitar, vocals; Tripp Lamkins, bass; Stan Gallimore, drums.

Beginning as a three-piece outfit called Bud in 1989, the Grifters released an independent cassette and two EP's before putting out its first full-length album. The group first established a lo-fi identity, letting its music wander from blues to rock, with a thick layer of distortion covering the proceedings. But it would eventually grow and expand its sound, with a clearer, less cluttered pop approach that's certainly more engaging.

what to buy: The Grifters' third release, *Ain't My Lookout* 𝄢𝄢𝄢𝄢 (Sub Pop, 1996, prod. Doug Easley), brought the group to Sub Pop with a cleaner, more pop-oriented sound. Still, songs such as "Return to Cinder" and "Boho/Alt" show that the band is determined to maintain a sarcastic tone in its lyrics and at least a slightly subversive edge to its music.

the rest:
So Happy Together 𝄢𝄢𝄢 (Sonic Noise, 1992)
One Sock Missing 𝄢𝄢𝄢 (Shangri-La, 1993)
Full Blown Possession 𝄢𝄢𝄢 (Sub Pop, 1997)

influences:
◀◀ Sonic Youth, Antenna, Bailter Space, Blake Babies

Kim Forster

Solomon Grundy
See: Screaming Trees

Joe Grushecky
/Iron City Houserockers
Born May 6, 1948, in Pittsburgh, PA.

Like Michael Stanley and early Bob Seger, Joe Grushecky exudes a kind of everyman quality, even when he's on an arena stage. With the Iron City Houserockers, the band he formed in Pittsburgh in 1976, Grushecky played tough, workmanlike barroom rock, steeped in R&B and early rock 'n' roll roots (Chuck Berry meets Sam & Dave). On his own, Grushecky—who has worked as a special education teacher during down times in his music career—is a somewhat more reflective troubadour; he still rocks, mind you, but songs cut a bit deeper, with more observations about the vagaries of life and the *American Babylon* he sings about on his latest album.

what to buy: The aptly titled *Pumping Iron & Sweating Steel: The Best of the Iron City Houserockers* 𝄢𝄢𝄢𝄢 (Rhino, 1992, prod. various) is filled with high-energy performances that convey an it's-the-weekend exuberance. Every city might have a band (or three) like this, but the Houserockers blow with a steel mill toughness that separates it from that pack. His own *Coming Home* 𝄢𝄢𝄢𝄢 (Viceroy, 1998, prod. Joe Grushecky, Rick Witknowski) is a soulful, mature, and, at times, sentimental pondering over the varied paths life takes, reaching unapolo-

getically simple yet truthful conclusions such as "It's a Hell of a Life" and "Innocence Is Beautiful."

what to buy next: Grushecky's *End of the Century* 𝄢𝄢𝄢 (Razor & Tie, 1992, prod. Joe Grushecky, Rick Witkowski) is a thoughtful work whose best songs ("No Man's Land," "Talking to the King," the title track) make sharp observations about the human spirit.

what to avoid: Sad to say, *American Babylon* 𝄢𝄢 (Razor & Tie, 1995, prod. Bruce Springsteen, Joe Grushecky, Rick Witkowski) too often sounds like a Springsteen wannabe—a criticism Grushecky's heard before.

the rest:
Rock & Real 𝄢𝄢𝄢 (Rounder, 1987)
Swimming with the Sharks 𝄢𝄢𝄢 (Rounder, 1988)

worth searching for: The Houserocker's second album, *Have a Good But . . . Get Out Alive!* (MCA, 1980), is another tough-spirited album that's the most consistent of the group's individual titles.

influences:
◀◀ Stax-Volt, Bruce Springsteen, Mitch Ryder & the Detroit Wheels, the Rockets

▶▶ Hootie & the Blowfish

Gary Graff

Guadalcanal Diary
/Murray Attaway
Formed 1981, in GA. Disbanded 1989.

Murray Attaway, vocals, guitar; Rhett Crowe, bass; John Poe, drums, vocals; Jeff Walls, guitars, keyboards, vocals.

Southern rock, in generic terms, reached national acclaim due to the massive success of the Allman Bros, Lynyrd Skynyrd, and .38 Special. It was not until the incredible success of R.E.M. and the B-52's during the early '80s that the world would take notice of the new sounds coming from the South. Guadalcanal Diary took the same road as R.E.M., fusing a Byrds-influenced sound with lyrics about southern living to craft a style that was its own. Frontman Murray Attaway took the role as America's beloved storyteller; he wove songs of love, lost love, ghosts, and religious icons—without sounding at all pretentious. Guadalcanal Diary recorded four albums for Elektra, all sadly long out of print. Like most of the successful southern pop bands of the time, it had one major proponent in common: producer Don Dixon. Dixon always captured the band at its rawest, using minimal overdubs and ringing guitars—a production style that bands and producers tried to emulate for years to come. But each subsequent Diary record sounded somewhat tired and indistinguishable, which led to the band's ultimate demise. In 1993 Geffen released Attaway's first solo record, *In Thrall*; unfortunately, Geffen tried some unusual marketing techniques—including giving the record to retail at no cost!!—which ultimately sealed the fate of this landmark album.

what to buy: Attaway's first, and so far only, solo record, *In Thrall* 𝄢𝄢𝄢𝄢 (Geffen, 1993, prod. Tony Berg), is absolutely his finest moment. *In Thrall* enlisted some of pop music's best, including Jackson Browne, Jon Brion, Aimee Mann, Nicky Hopkins, and producer Tony Berg (Michael Penn, Ted Hawkins). In terms of music, the songs rarely visit Guadalcanal territory, but lyrically, Attaway returned to his wordy style of songwriting, with titles like "Allegory" and "The Evensong." Due to the fact this record was literally given away, Attaway never received the proper funds to work the project and was subsequently dropped from the Geffen roster. On a very sad note, due to that debacle, he has not released anything solo or as part of a band since 1993, a true loss to all pop fans.

worth searching for: Unfortunately there are no Guadalcanal Diary albums in print, domestic or import. But don't stop trying to find its first, and finest, record *Walking in the Shadow of the Big Man* (Elektra, 1984) and *2 x 4* (Elektra, 1987), both of which are rare but well worth the effort.

influences:

◀◀ R.E.M., Jackson Browne

▶▶ Gin Blossoms, Freedy Johnston

Chris Richards

The Guess Who

Formed as Chad Allen & the Expressions (later the Reflections), 1962, in Winnipeg, Manitoba, Canada. Renamed the Guess Who in 1965. Disbanded 1975. Re-formed 1979, 1983.

Chad Allen (born Allan Kobel), vocals, guitar (1962–66); Bob Ashley, piano (1962–65); Randy Bachman, guitar, vocals (1962–70); Garry Peterson, drums; Jim Kale, bass (1962–72, 1979–present); Burton Cummings, vocals, keyboards, flute (1965–75); Bruce Dekker, vocals (1966); Greg Leskiw, guitar, vocals (1970–72); Kurt Winter, guitar, vocals (1970–74); Don McDougall, guitar, vocals (1972–74, 1979–present); Bill Wallace, bass, vocals (1972–75); Dominic Troiano, guitar, vocals (1974–75).

In 1968, convinced that the Guess Who was destined for stardom, record producer Jack Richardson mortgaged his house to finance a New York recording session for the band. The fruits of that trip were realized the next year when the group enjoyed a string of gold hits south of the border with "These Eyes," "Laughing," and "Undun," and Richardson hasn't worried about house payments since. Guitarist and co-founder Randy Bachman and lead singer/keyboardist Burton Cummings (who replaced co-founder Chad Allen) formed one of the most successful songwriting duos of the era and put Canada on the pop music map for good. In 1970 the band scored a #1 hit with the politically charged "American Woman" and charted at Number Five with "No Time." But both men were immensely talented musicians and were often at odds over band matters. Bachman quit the Guess Who in 1970, later forming Bachman-Turner Overdrive. Cummings replaced Bachman with two guitarists, Kurt Winter and Greg Leskiw, and answered Bachman's departure with a string of hits that included "Share the Land," "Hand Me Down World," and "Clap for the Wolfman." Bassist Jim Kale, who owns the Guess Who name, re-formed the band in 1979 with Don McDougall; there have been several different configurations since then.

what to buy: *The Best of the Guess Who* 𝄢𝄢𝄢𝄢 (RCA, 1971, prod. Jack Richardson) is a compact collection of some of the best AM radio rock hits of all time. The guitar-hook-rich *Share the Land* 𝄢𝄢𝄢𝄢 (RCA, 1970, prod. Jack Richardson) is significant because it was the band's first album without Bachman. But new guitarists Winter and Leskiw deliver big-time on such gems as "Hand Me Down World," "Bus Rider," and the title track.

what to buy next: *Track Record* 𝄢𝄢𝄢𝄢 (RCA, 1988, prod. Jack Richardson) is a two-disc set with all the hits and some interesting liner notes from Cummings and Richardson. Those seeking the full box-set treatment will savor *The Ultimate Collection* 𝄢𝄢𝄢𝄢 (RCA, 1997, prod. various), a 56-song set boasting crisp sound and a mix of live songs and rehearsal tracks in addition to all the hits and important LP tracks. *Canned Wheat* 𝄢𝄢𝄢 (RCA, 1969, prod. Jack Richardson) and *Wheatfield Soul* 𝄢𝄢𝄢 (RCA, 1969, prod. Jack Richardson) are two strong early outings.

what to avoid: *Lonely One* **woof!** (Intersound, 1995) features original members Kale and Peterson, who had little to do with shaping the Guess Who sound.

the rest:

All This for a Song 𝄢 (Valley Vue, 1979)
The Greatest of the Guess Who 𝄢𝄢𝄢 (RCA, 1988)
American Woman, These Eyes & Other Hits 𝄢𝄢 (RCA, 1990)
At Their Best 𝄢𝄢𝄢 (RCA, 1993)
It's Time 𝄢𝄢𝄢 (Legend, 1997)
The Spirit Lives On: Greatest Hits Live 𝄢𝄢 (J-Bird, 1998)

worth searching for: Canadian CD imports of the original albums—*So Long, Bannatyne* (RCA, 1971), *Rockin'* (RCA, 1972), *#10* (RCA, 1973), and *Road Food* (RCA, 1974)—are worth tracking down.

solo outings:

Burton Cummings:

The Burton Cummings Collection 𝄢𝄢𝄢 (Rhino, 1994)
Up Close and Alone 𝄢𝄢𝄢 (Hip-o, 1997)

influences:

◄◄ Big Joe Turner, Buddy Holly, Johnny Kidd & the Pirates, Gerry & the Pacemakers, the Beatles, the Deverons, Jim Morrison

►► Neil Young & the Squires, the Shakers, the Northern Pikes, the Evaporators, Queen, Pearl Jam, Blues Traveler, Del Amitri

see also: *Bachman-Turner Overdrive*

William Hanson and Ken Burke

Guided by Voices

Formed 1983, in Dayton, OH.

Robert Pollard, vocals; Jim Pollard, guitar, bass; Tobin Sprout, guitar, vocals, bass, drums, piano (1983–96); Mitch Mitchell, guitar (1983–96); Kevin Fennell, drums (1983–96); Don Thrasher, drums (1983–94); Dan Toohey, bass (1983–94); Greg Demos, bass (1994, 1996–present); Jim Greer, bass (1994–95); Doug Gillard, guitar (1997); John Petkovic, guitar (1997); Don Depew, bass (1997); Dave Swanson, drums (1997).

Less a band than a hobby for a loose aggregation of drinking buddies, Guided by Voices is the obsession of prolific songwriter Robert Pollard. While teaching elementary school in Dayton, Pollard wrote and recorded with his accomplices on four-track tape a private history of rock 'n' roll that mashed together three decades of influences culled from his massive record collection. It wasn't until they were in their mid- to late 30s and had released a half-dozen albums over 10 years that the members of GBV attracted notice with their first nationally distributed release, *Vampire on Titus*. Even as the critical acclaim started to roll in and a deal with Matador Records was clinched, GBV continued to make engaging if eccentric low-fi records characterized by insidious melodies, ripping guitars, terse arrangements (many under two minutes in length), tape hiss, and Pollard's elliptical, fairy-tale lyrics, sung in a fake British accent. During the mid-'90s, GBV stood as perhaps the most celebrated cult band in North America.

what to buy: The two-albums-on-one-CD *Vampire on Titus/Propeller* ✍✍✍ (Scat, 1993, prod. Guided by Voices) is the breakthrough, with Pollard's prog-rock and British Invasion flourishes—evoking early Genesis, the Syd Barrett-led Pink Floyd, and the mid-'60s Who—delivered with punkish brevity and a thrilling sense of spontaneity. Rather than detracting from the allure, the dim, tinny sound gives the discs an otherworldly cohesiveness. *Bee Thousand* ✍✍✍✍ (Scat/Matador, 1994, prod. Guided by Voices) answered the critical hype with what is arguably the band's most consistent batch of pop songs, including the Indie-rock classic "I Am a Scientist." *Under the Bushes under the Stars* ✍✍✍✍ (Matador, 1996, prod. Kim Deal, Steve

Albini) moves subtly toward a richer sound and longer, more fully realized songs with help from the group's first pair of outside producers.

what to buy next: *Alien Lanes* ✍✍✍✍ (Matador, 1995, prod. Guided by Voices) is a more hit-and-miss affair, with several brilliant tunes: "My Valuable Hunting Knife," "Striped White Jets," "Closer You Are," and "Motor Away." *Box* ✍✍✍ (Scat/Matador, 1995, prod. Guided by Voices) is a five-CD collection that gathers the band's early, highly uneven albums and some unreleased songs. *Mag Earwhig!* ✍✍✍ (Matador, 1997, prod. Guided by Voices) finds Pollard ditching his Dayton-based band and replacing it with would-be arena rockers Cobra Verde from Cleveland. It's a more overtly mainstream effort, with the usual quota of terrific pop and a spectacular space-rock voyage ("Portable Men's Society"), but it's marred by obvious filler.

worth searching for: *Crying Your Knife Away* (Lo-Fi, 1994, prod. Guided by Voices) is a reckless, beer-soaked live document, with Pollard's humorous banter an added bonus.

solo outings:
Robert Pollard:
Not in My Airforce ✍✍✍ (Matador, 1996)

Tobin Sprout:
Carnival Boy ✍✍✍✍ (Matador, 1996)
Moonflower Plastic ✍✍✍✍ (Matador, 1997)

influences:

◄◄ Pink Floyd, the Who, Genesis, Sex Pistols, the Jam, the Damned

►► Presidents of the United States of America

Greg Kot

Guild of Temporal Adventures
See: Dream Syndicate

Gun Club

Formed 1980, in Los Angeles, CA.

Jeffrey Lee Pierce (died 1996), vocals; Ward Dotson, guitar; Jim Duckworth, guitar; Kid Congo Powers, guitar; Rob Ritter, bass; Patricia Morrison, bass; Romi Mori, bass; Terry Graham, drums; Dee Pop, drums; Nick Sanderson, drums.

L.A. native Jeffrey Lee Pierce may have expressed his love for music by volunteering as president of Blondie's fanclub in the late '70s, but he sure didn't stay fey for too long. Pierce ended up fronting one of the mid-'80s' most explosive bands to hit the post punk scene. From the opening salvos of the near classic psychobilly of Gun Club's debut *Fire of Love*, it was clear Pierce had a precisely defined creative ethic, one involving abundant and often violent energy, lots of drugs and alcohol, and a real attempt to conjure the ghostly, murderous blues of early troubadors like Robert Johnson and Leadbelly. Pierce's reputation as an unreliable wildman took root when the band moved from L.A. to Manhattan's Lower East Side. Though his well-publicized bouts with alcoholism and drugs kept the band's career from truly taking off in the States, he did become a highly anticipated act, due largely to Pierce's unpredictability. In 1981 the Gun Club debuted with *Fire of Love*, a wild-eyed punk/blues hybrid fueled by Pierce's radically unschooled delivery and Ward Dotson's unorthodox slide guitar. On 1982's *Miami* Pierce finally got his wish, being joined by Blondie's Chris Stein as producer and Debbie Harry on vocals, though the results of the album and its follow-up, *Las Vegas Story*, were mixed. In 1984 Pierce's inability to move forward with the band forced him to hang it up for awhile. During the next three years he attempted to launch a solo career with the EP *Flamingo* and the longplayer *Wildweed*, in which Pierce does his best to imitate the dusty old bluesmen he so reveres. In 1987 Pierce patched up the Gun Club again with a remarkably revitalized album, *Mother Juno*, this time rejoining forces with guitarist extraordinaire Kid Congo Powers, formerly of the Cramps. The band finally signed to a stable U.S. independent, Triple X, in 1992 and released three proper albums without much commercial success. In 1996, after drying-out and seemingly steering his topsy turvy life back on course, Lee died of a cerebral blood clot in Utah, leaving an exceptional, decidedly rock 'n' roll legacy behind.

what to buy: Of all Pierce's Gun Club recordings, the first, *Fire of Love* 𝄞𝄞𝄞𝄞 (Ruby, 1981/Slash, 1993, prod. Chris D., Tito Larriva), is still the best. His incendiary hellhound attack and possessed blues growl is by turns frightening and exhilarating, haunting and visceral. The second most salient entry in Pierce's discography is quite different by comparison. Produced by the Cocteau Twins' Robin Guthrie, *Mother Juno* 𝄞𝄞𝄞𝄞 (Fundamental, 1987; 2.13.61/Thirsty Ear, 1996, prod. Robin Guthrie) frames Pierce's angst in a much more accessible way, despite the appearance of Bad Seeds' guitarist Blixa Bargeld on the warped "Yellow Eyes."

what to buy next: *Pastoral Hide & Seek* 𝄞𝄞𝄞 (New Rose, 1990; 2.13.61, 1997, prod. Jeffrey Lee Pierce) is worthwhile, not for Pierce's gut-punching rock, which had abated to a great degree by this point, but for his newfound aesthetics, his attention to craft, and pop hooks. The reissue CD contains the 1991 EP *Divinity*.

the rest:
Miami 𝄞𝄞𝄞 (Animal, 1982; IRS, 1990)
The Las Vegas Story 𝄞𝄞𝄞 (Animal, 1984; Animal/IRS, 1990)
Danse Kalinda Boom 𝄞𝄞𝄞 (UK Dojo, 1985; Triple X 1994)
In Exile 𝄞𝄞𝄞 (Triple X, 1992)

Live in Europe 𝄞𝄞𝄞 (Triple X, 1992)
Lucky Jim 𝄞𝄞𝄞𝄞 (Triple X, 1993)

worth searching for: Hardcore fans will want to search for some of the band's live recordings, including *Sex Beat 81* (Lolita, 1984) and *The Birth of the Death of the Ghost* (ABC UK, 1984; Revolver, 1990).

solo outings:
Jeffrey Lee Pierce:
Wildweed 𝄞𝄞𝄞 (Triple X, 1985/1994)
Ramblin' Jeffrey Lee & Cypress Grove with Willie Love 𝄞𝄞𝄞 (Triple X, 1992)

influences:
◄◄ Robert Johnson, Blondie, Led Zeppelin, the Velvet Underground, X

►► Sixteen Horsepower, Whiskeytown

Bob Gulla

Jo Jo Gunne
See: Spirit

Guns N' Roses
Formed 1985, in Los Angeles, CA.

Axl Rose (born William Bailey), vocals; Slash (born Saul Hudson), guitar (1985–97); Izzy Stradlin (born Jeff Isabelle), guitar, vocals (1985–92); Gilby Clarke, guitar, vocals (1992–94); Duff "Rose" McKagan (born Michael McKagan), bass, vocals (1985–97); Dizzy Reed, keyboards (1991–present); Steven Adler, drums, (1985–89); Matt Sorum, drums, (1989–97).

The rise of Guns N' Roses during the late '80s signalled the demise of the big hair glam-metal bands—the Warrants, the Cinderellas, the Bon Jovis—that had dominated the hard rock scene for the previous few years. Formed by Axl Rose and Izzy Stradlin, who had grown up together in Indiana, and joined by Slash and Duff McKagan, Guns sought to distance itself from the pop-metal scene, eschewing slick ballads in favor of songs about the seamy, destructive underbelly of cities such as Hollywood. Its first full-length album, *Appetite for Destruction*, offered a ferocious litany of indulgence, corruption, and abuse—and sold several million copies. Guns was in a position to take over the world—to, in effect, be the Led Zeppelin for a new generation. Instead it fumbled the opportunity with feuds, overindulgence (the two separate *Use Your Illusion* albums), and concerts that started hours late and always risked the temperamental Rose walking off at any given time. As the lineup shifted, the cohesion that was so vital to the group disappeared, and during the early '90s Guns began an extended hiatus. Most recently, Slash and McKagan have left the group, while Rose was rumored to be bringing a new group of players

Axl Rose of Guns N' Roses (© Ken Settle)

into the studio for a release that may or may not be heard before the millenium.

what to buy: Truly a landmark album, *Appetite for Destruction* ♫♫♫♫ (Geffen, 1987, prod. Mike Clink) offers the Gunners at their best, before ego and eccentricity caused them to come unglued. Many of the band's seminal tunes ("Welcome to the Jungle," "Sweet Child o' Mine," "Paradise City") can be found in a package that is solid from start to finish.

what to buy next: Though often self-indulgent, much of the material on the expansive *Use Your Illusion I* and *Use Your Illusion II* ♫♫♫♫ (Geffen, 1991, prod. Mike Clink, Guns N' Roses) is of high enough quality to compensate. Slicker and more tempered than *Appetite*, the *Illusion* set is also darker and more mature. Start with the first volume if you can only buy one at a time, but be sure to get both.

what to avoid: McKagan's guest-saturated solo album *Believe in Me* ♫♫ (Geffen, 1994, prod. Jim Mitchell, Duff McKagan) is a dull, pedestrian affair that misses the collaboration of his bandmates.

the rest:
G'n'R Lies ♫♫♫♫ (Geffen, 1988)
The Spaghetti Incident? ♫♫♫ (Geffen, 1993)

worth searching for: To date, the most recent recording by Guns N' Roses is a cool cover of the Rolling Stones' "Sympathy for the Devil," included on the soundtrack to the film *Interview with the Vampire* (Geffen, 1994).

solo outings:
Slash's Snakepit (Slash, Sorum, Clarke):
It's Five o'clock Somewhere ♫♫♫ (Geffen, 1995)

Gilby Clarke:
Pawn Shop Guitars ♫♫♫♫ (Virgin, 1995)
Rubber N/A (Pavement, 1998)

Izzy Stradlin:
Izzy Stradlin & the JuJu Hounds ♫♫♫ (Geffen, 1992)
117° ♫♫♫ (Geffen, 1998)

Neurotic Outsiders (McKagan, Sorum):
Neurotic Outsiders ♫♫♫ (Maverick, 1996)

influences:
◄◄ AC/DC, Aerosmith, Rolling Stones, Nazareth, Frank Zappa, David Bowie, Brian Eno

►► L.A. Guns

Brandon Trenz

Arlo Guthrie

Born July 10, 1947, in Coney Island, NY.

Think being called the next Bob Dylan is tough? How about the next Woody Guthrie? To his credit, Arlo Guthrie never traded on his father's legend; humble and grateful for the man, the younger Guthrie stayed close to his father's peers (particularly Pete Seeger) and developed his own relaxed style of folk-rock. The 18-minute "Alice's Restaurant Massacree" was a fine introduction, a winding, humorous narrative that encapsulated the generational struggles and draft paranoia that were so prevalent during the mid-'60s. Guthrie scored a couple of other hits with the Woodstock nation—"Coming into Los Angeles," Steve Goodman's "The City of New Orleans"—before settling into a niche. When Warner Bros. dropped him from its roster, Guthrie formed his own label, Rising Son, bought up his old recordings, and continues to make music and do charitable works based out of Upstate New York.

what to buy: *Alice's Restaurant* ♫♫♫♫ (Reprise, 1967/1988, prod. Fred Hellerman) isn't the kind of thing you listen to every day, but it's always an entertaining listen when you get the hankering. *The Best of Arlo Guthrie* ♫♫♫♫ (Warner Bros., 1977/1989, prod. various) has the other important hits. On *Woody's 20 Grow Big Songs* ♫♫♫♫ (Rising Son, 1992) Arlo and the extended Guthrie clan pay homage to his father with a conceptually inspired children's album that works for adults, too.

what to buy next: *Amigo* ♫♫♫ (Warner Bros., 1976/Rising Son, 1990) is Guthrie's hardest rocking and most focused collection, with a killer cover of the Rolling Stones' "Connection." *Mystic Journey* ♫♫♫ (Rising Son, 1996, prod. Arlo Guthrie, Abe Guthrie) is a richly crafted and introspective record that shows he's hardly played out.

what to avoid: *Alice's Restaurant: The Massacree Revisited* ♫♫ (Rising Son, 1995) updates the sonics of the original but can't quite capture its same moment-in-time quality. *Power of Love* ♫♫ (Warner Bros., 1981/Rising Son, 1990) isn't bad so much as it is anonymous, without the warm character of Guthrie's better albums.

the rest:
Arlo ♫♫♫ (Reprise, 1968/Rising Son, 1991)
Running down the Road ♫♫♫ (Reprise, 1969/Rising Son, 1991)
Washington County ♫♫♫ (Reprise, 1970/Rising Son, 1991)
Hobo's Lullabye ♫♫♫ (Reprise, 1972/Rising Son, 1990)
Last of the Brooklyn Cowboys ♫♫♫♫ (Reprise, 1973/Risng Son, 1991)
Arlo Guthrie ♫♫♫ (Reprise, 1974/Rising Son, 1991)
One Night ♫♫ (Reprise, 1978/Rising Son, 1991)
Outlasting the Blues ♫♫♫♫ (Reprise, 1979/Rising Son, 1991)
(With Pete Seeger) *Power of Love* ♫♫♫ (Reprise, 1981/Rising Son, 1990)
Precious Friend ♫♫♫ (Warner Bros., 1982/1988)
Someday ♫♫♫ (Reprise, 1986/Rising Son, 1990)
Baby's Storytime ♫♫♫ (Lightyear, 1990/1993)
All over the World ♫♫♫ (Rising Son, 1991/1993)
Son of the Wind ♫♫♫ (Rising Son, 1992)

(With Pete Seeger) *More Together Again in Concert* ♫♫♫ (Rising Son, 1994)

worth searching for: Arlo duets with Nanci Griffith on Townes Van Zandt's "Tecumseh Valley" for her album *Other Songs, Other Rooms* (Elektra, 1993, prod. Jim Rooney).

influences:

◀◀ Woody Guthrie, Pete Seeger, Leadbelly, Bob Dylan

▶▶ Tom Petty, John Mellencamp, Jackson Browne, the Eagles

Gary Graff

GWAR

Formed 1985, in Richmond, VA.

Odorus Urungus (David Brockie), vocals; Balsac the Jaws of Death (Michael Derks), guitar; Flattus Maximus (Peter Lee), guitar; Beefcake the Mighty (Michael Bishop), bass; Jizmak the Gusha (Brad Roberts), drums; Slymenstra Hymen (Danyelle Stampe), whips; Sexicutioner (Charles Varga), chains; Sampler Sound-EFX (David Musel), electronic devices; Techno-Destructo (Hunter Jackson), vocals; Sleazy P. Martini (Don Drakulich), manager.

With shows that resemble performance art more than heavy-metal concerts, this group of creatively twisted Richmond college students declared itself the most disgusting band of all time and set out to prove it—or, more accurately, they declared themselves aliens from Venus, clothed themselves in futuristic caveman outfits with giant phalluses and bizarre weapons, and put on outrageous, terrific shows. GWAR changes themes with every tour, but generally the musicians lop off the heads of costumed nemeses on stage (sometimes the Pope, sometimes the President) and send quarts of fake blood spurting into the audience. The first thing you notice at a GWAR show is everything, from the speakers to the overhead lights, is covered in plastic; later, when the fluids start gushing from the stage, you understand why. Many critics rip the band's music, but occasionally, as on the hilarious "Slaughterama" and *Beavis and Butt-head* favorite "Jack the World," they're as tight and destructive, not to mention imaginative, as any good metal band.

what to buy: The definitive GWAR album is *Scumdogs of the Universe* ♫♫♫ (Metal Blade, 1990, prod. Ron Goudie), which contains "Maggots," "Vlad the Impaler," "Sexecutioner," and the anti-hippie game-show parody "Slaughterama."

what to buy next: *This Toilet Earth* ♫♫ (Metal Blade, 1994, prod. Scott Wolfe) has a few good songs, including "Jack the World," a rip against the band's laughable Grammy video nomination, but it is incredibly sick and enthusiastically makes fun of rape and pedophilia.

what to avoid: *Hell-o* **woof!** (Shimmy Disc, 1988, prod. Kramer), GWAR's debut, is absolutely unlistenable.

the rest:
America Must Be Destroyed ♫♫ (Metal Blade, 1992)
The Road Behind ♫♪ (Metal Blade, 1993)
Raq Na Rock ♫♫♫ (Priority, 1995)
Carnival of Chaos ♫♫♫ (Metal Blade, 1997)

influences:

◀◀ The Tubes, Motörhead, Alice Cooper, Kiss, the Dead Kennedys

▶▶ My Life with the Thrill Kill Kult, Marilyn Manson, nine inch nails, *Beavis and Butt-head*

Steve Knopper

Sammy Hagar

Born October 13, 1947, in Monterey, CA.

Before joining the Van Halen party in 1985, Sammy Hagar was a member of Montrose, a band he left to begin cultivating a middling solo career opening for acts like Boston, Kiss, and Foghat during the late '70s. "The Red Rocker" (nicknamed for his penchant for wearing all things red: spandex, headbands, socks) has decent metal-lite vocal chops (like Journey with chest hair), but his right-wing politics and complete lack of panache and subtlety make for some tedious expressions of "hard" rock. He and Van Halen split unexpectedly in 1996, making Hagar a free agent again. So far he's responded with a retaliatory solo album in 1997—it features a perplexing guest list that includes Roy Rogers, Huey Lewis, Bootsy Collins, Mickey Hart, Slash, and yes, a full Montrose reunion on one track. Whoopee.

what to buy: *Standing Hampton* ♫♫♫ (Geffen, 1982, prod. Keith Olsen) is easily the most consistent album of his career. It features Hagar's strongest set of songs put to radio-friendly pop production. "I'll Fall in Love Again" is his best song and as good as anything he and Van Halen did together. It also includes the under-appreciated "Heavy Metal," which rocks harder than Eddie Van Halen's recent smiley-faced fingerflash.

what to buy next: *Unboxed* ♫♫♫ (Geffen, 1994, prod. Mike Clink) is a fair summation of his Geffen years, with "I'll Fall in Love Again," "Heavy Metal," and the rigid "There's Only One Way to Rock." Strangely, it omits the pop hit "Your Love is Driving Me Crazy" from *Three Lock Box*.

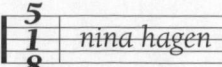
what to avoid: Originally titled *Sammy Hagar, I Never Said Goodbye* ♫♫ (Geffen, 1987/1992, prod. Sammy Hagar, Eddie Van Halen) finds Hagar obviously fullfilling contractual obligations with uninspired, slick pop and overwrought power ballads.

the rest:
Nine on a Ten Scale ♫♫ (Greenlight, 1976/One Way, 1993)
Sammy Hagar ♫♫ (Capitol, 1977/One Way, 1997)
Musical Chairs ♫ (Capitol, 1977/One Way, 1997)
Street Machine ♫♫ (Capitol, 1979/One Way, 1997)
All Night Long ♫♫ (Capitol, 1979/One Way, 1997)
Danger Zone ♫♫ (Capitol, 1979/One Way, 1997)
Three Lock Box ♫♫ (Geffen, 1983)
VOA ♫♫ (Geffen, 1984)
Sammy Hagar/Neal Schon/Kenny Aaronson: Through the Fire ♫♫ (Geffen, 1984/1997)
The Best of Sammy Hagar ♫♫ (Capitol, 1992)
Red Hot ♫♫ (CEMA Special Products, 1994)
Marching to Mars ♫♫ (Track Factory, 1997)
Live 1980 ♫♫ (One Way, 1997)

worth searching for: *The Anthology (1973–84)* (Connoisseur Collection, 1994, prod. various) is an import retrospective that's a notch better than its domestic counterparts thanks to the inclusion of some Montrose tracks.

influences:
◀◀ Montrose, Foghat, Kiss
▶▶ Van Halen, Journey, Loverboy

see also: *Van Halen, Montrose*

Allan Orski

Nina Hagen

Born March 11, 1955, in East Berlin, Germany.

Nina Hagen's eccentric wailing may not be the stuff you'd normally associate with the Eastern bloc, but her German-sung version of the Tubes' "White Punks on Dope" will dispel any illusions of alternate citizenship. Musically, her daredevil experiments embraced themes of religion and space saucers, and she recorded with the disparate likes of Paul Shaffer, Chris Spedding, and Giorgio Moroder. Uncompromising and over-the-top, Hagen is one of those artists who has to be heard to be believed.

what to buy: *14 Friendly Abductions: The Best of Nina Hagen* ♫♫♫ (Legacy, 1996, prod. various) is a career-spanning disc capturing the caterwauling Hagen in all her hyper-intensity. The diversity of her takes on the club scene ("New York, New York") and other cover-version deconstructions ("My Way," "Spirit in the Sky") careen over the line of sacrilege with glee.

the rest:
Nunsexmonkrock ♫♫♫ (Legacy, 1991/1982)

worth searching for: Most of Hagen's albums are out of print, but a couple are worth digging up, including the edgy *Unbehagen* (CBS, 1980) and the dance-oriented *Fearless* (Columbia, 1983).

influences:
◀◀ The Sex Pistols, Lene Lovich, the Tubes
▶▶ Babes in Toyland, Hole

Allan Orski

Haircut 100
See: Nick Heyward

Bill Haley
Born July 6, 1925, in Highland Park, MI. Died February 9, 1981, in Harlingen, TX.

It's kind of cute how the history books depict Haley's "Rock Around the Clock" as inciting teenagers to riot, rip up theater seats, flash knife blades, you name it. Try imagining the chunky singer, with his goofy ever-present grin and greased curly-Q hair, putting fear in the hearts of the religious right today. On the contrary, he'd be lauded as wholesome family entertainment. But in 1954, the former country & western singer's lumpen tunes were at the helm of rock 'n' roll's birth and thus brought with them the air of revolution. His songs were plodding, his arrangements barely existent, he was fat, and he was already 30. Yet he still managed to drive the kids nuts. Why? Because there was no one else on the playing field. When the sex-drenched Elvis Presley and the lunatic Little Richard burst upon the American public, Haley was revealed as the square he always was and lost his teenage cachet as quickly as he found it. As a country singer with a fondness for cutting R&B songs, Haley first dabbled in cultural miscegenation with a 1951 recording of the Jackie Brenston R&B hit "Rocket 88"; he was Bill Haley & the Saddlemen then. The first record by the renamed Bill Haley & the Comets, "Crazy Man Crazy," on the independent Essex Records label became the first rock 'n' roll record to make the nationwide Top 20. After signing to Decca Records in 1954, he recorded the epochal "Rock Around the Clock," which failed on its initial release but scorched up the charts after a film, *The Blackboard Jungle,* used the song as a theme the following year. Haley's records tended toward the cutesie ("Skinny Minnie") and novelty ("Mambo Rock"), but Decca producer Milt Gabler, a savvy veteran, sagaciously styled Haley's sound after another one of his charges, the rollicking Louis Jordan, and came up with some stunning, underrated pieces. Haley's "Rip It Up," for instance, may actually out-rock the Little Richard original. Ultimately, however, his career amounted to little more than "Rock Around the Clock," and he spent many years living in Mexican exile before settling in Texas, where a bitter, deranged Haley would show strangers his driver's license to prove who he was.

what to buy: All compilations on the market have nearly identical song listings, but *From the Original Master Tapes* ♫♫♫ (MCA, 1985, original prod. Milt Gabler, compilation prod. Steve Hoffman) is the most thorough and provides adequate detail for most libraries. A good boost in sound quality finds the congenial Haley remastered for the modern age.

what to buy next: Haley's evolution from a country singer to the first rock 'n' roll star is examined in fine-point detail on *Rock the Joint! The Original Essex Recordings, 1951–1954* ♫♫♫ (Schoolkids, 1994), a historic 24-song collection that hews closely to Haley's developing rock and roll style.

what to avoid: An unilluminating late '60s interview with Haley, interspersed with snatches of music, *The Haley Tapes* **woof!** (Jerden, 1995, prod. Red Robinson) does not make an interesting or rewarding CD.

the rest:
Rock & Roll ♫ (Orfeon)
Greatest Hits ♫♫♫ (MCA, 1968/1991)
Shake, Rattle and Roll ♫♫♫ (Drive Archive, 1994)
Rock 'n' Roll Scrapbook ♫♫ (Sequel, 1994)
Later Alligator ♫♫ (Chicago, 1995)
Los Grandes Hits De Haley ♫ (Orfeon, 1996)
Vol. 20—American Legends ♫♫♫ (Laserlight, 1996)
Rock Around the Clock ♫♫ (ITC Masters, 1997)

worth searching for: The German reissue specialists, Bear Family, produced a five-disc box set called *The Decca Years & More* (Bear Family, 1990, compilation prod. Richard Weize), although that may be overkill in this case.

influences:
◀◀ Big Joe Turner, Bob Wills, Louis Jordan

▶▶ Pat Boone, Bruce Springsteen, the Ramones

Joel Selvin and Allan Orski

Kristen Hall
Birthdate and birthplace unknown.

Kristen Hall is blessed with a smoky voice and a penchant for confessional-but-catchy songwriting. She emerged from the same Atlanta singer-songwriter scene that spawned the Indigo Girls and Michelle Malone, developing a following at Atlanta clubs such as the Point, Trackside Tavern, and, later, Eddie's Attic. She recorded for the local Daemon label before signing

with High Street Records, a member of the Windham Hill/BMG group. No longer affiliated with either label, Hall recently relocated to Los Angeles.

what to buy: *Fact & Fiction* ♫♫♫ (Daemon, 1991, prod. Don Mc-Collister, Kristen Hall) succeeds at first listen and improves with repeated plays. Its lyricism and simplicity are its principal virtues; another is subtle support on two cuts from Emily Saliers.

what to buy next: *Be Careful What You Wish For . . .* ♫♫♫ (High Street, 1994, prod. Jerry Marotta) is so relentlessly dark and heavy as to risk drowning under its own weight, despite guest spots from Saliers, John Sebastian, Jules Shear, Kristian Bush, Larry Gowan, and Matthew Sweet. Still, it's fuel enough for those who want to commiserate over a failed relationship ("I was kind enough to love you, you were cruel enough to leave," etc.), but tough going otherwise.

worth searching for: *Real Life Stuff* (Daemon, 1994, prod. Kristen Hall, Kay Busbey), now out of print, shares *Fact & Fiction* 's clean, straightforward production. Hall may also have self-produced material available at live shows.

influences:
◀◀ Indigo Girls

Bryan Powell

Terry Hall
See: Fun Boy Three

Hall & Oates
Formed 1972, in Philadelphia, PA.

Daryl Hall (born Daryl Franklin Hohl, October 11, 1948, in Pottstown, PA), vocals, keyboards, guitar; John Oates (born April 7, 1949, in New York, NY), vocals, guitar.

The most commercially successful duo in rock history, Hall & Oates have had 29 Top 40 hits, six of them #1, and have come to epitomize the term "blue-eyed soul" (in other words, they're white guys who sound black, or at least soulful). The two singers met at Temple University after growing up in the Philadelphia suburbs, and Oates joined Hall's failed group Gulliver in 1969, just before it fell apart. They then went their separate ways but reunited and signed with Atlantic, which never quite knew what to do with the duo as it bounced from near-folk to soul to rock. Their sole Atlantic hit, "She's Gone," charted only after they'd switched to RCA, riding the coattails of "Sara Smile," the hit from their first RCA album. For several years after that, though they charted, their occasionally experimental tack dampened their commercial success; in fact, RCA long refused to issue Hall's first solo album, an adventurous effort produced by Robert Fripp. Hall & Oates recovered from their commercial slump not by going along with the record company, but by producing their 1980 album *Voices* themselves. Inventing a perky pop style particularly distinctive for its bouncy electric keyboard parts, but with plenty of room for Hall's virtuosic vocal fillips and melismata, it yielded four Top 40 hits, including the #1 "Kiss on My List." That launched a four-year string during which Hall & Oates dominated radio playlists, pop charts, and even MTV. But by the late 1980s, the duo was, if not over, at least spent. These days they work together intermittently, and their music—together and apart—no longer causes the stir it once did.

what to buy: *Voices* 𝄞𝄞𝄞 (RCA, 1980, prod. Daryl Hall, John Oates) and *Private Eyes* 𝄞𝄞𝄞𝄞 (RCA, 1981, prod. Daryl Hall, John Oates) have far more good tunes than could go on any compilation, and the production style has held up well over the years. Hall's *Sacred Songs* 𝄞𝄞𝄞𝄞 (RCA, 1980, prod. Robert Fripp) in a way proved RCA right; it isn't even slightly commercial, or even pop. But its chilly contrast to his passionate vocal style makes it great, and it's not an offputting listen.

what to buy next: How convenient that practically all the duo's good tracks for Atlantic were all on one album. *Abandoned Luncheonette* 𝄞𝄞𝄞 (Atlantic, 1973, prod. Arif Mardin) is most notable for "She's Gone" but is tuneful throughout. *Along the Red Ledge* 𝄞𝄞𝄞 (RCA, 1978, prod. David Foster) exhibited the first fruits of Hall's adventurous recasting of the group's sound, and while the (slight) hit was "It's a Laugh," the highlights are the haunting "Melody for a Memory" and "I Don't Wanna Lose You."

what to avoid: The debut *Whole Oats* **woof!** (Atlantic, 1972, prod. Arif Mardin) is lame singer-songwriter mellowness having nothing to do with the duo's later strengths. On Daryl Hall's bloated *Three Hearts in the Happy Ending Machine* 𝄞 (RCA, 1986, prod. Daryl Hall, David A. Stewart, Tom "T-Bone" Wolk) he just never knows when to stop—all the songs go on forever, with the overdubs piled on way past the point of overkill.

the rest:
Hall & Oates:
War Babies 𝄞𝄞𝄞 (Atlantic, 1974)
Daryl Hall & John Oates 𝄞𝄞𝄞 (RCA, 1975)
Bigger than Both of Us 𝄞𝄞𝄞 (RCA, 1976)
Beauty on a Back Street 𝄞𝄞 (RCA, 1977)
Livetime 𝄞𝄞𝄞 (RCA, 1978)
X-Static 𝄞𝄞𝄞 (RCA, 1979)
H2O 𝄞𝄞𝄞 (RCA, 1982)
Rock 'n Soul Part 1 𝄞𝄞𝄞𝄞 (RCA, 1983)
Bigbamboom 𝄞𝄞𝄞 (RCA, 1984)
Live at the Apollo 𝄞𝄞𝄞 (RCA, 1985)
Ooh Yeah! 𝄞𝄞 (Arista, 1988)
Change of Season 𝄞𝄞 (Arista, 1990)
Marigold Sky 𝄞𝄞𝄞 (Push, 1997)

Daryl Hall:
Soul Alone 𝄞𝄞 (Epic, 1993)

worth searching for: The ultimate H&O best-of is no longer the 12-song *Rock 'n Soul Part 1*, though completists will still want its live version of "Wait for Me." The new king is the two-CD, 32-track *Greatest Hits* (Razor & Tie/BMG Direct Marketing, 1997, prod. various), which can be found via mail-order only at 1-800-633-9577. It only covers the RCA years but does so with admirable thoroughness, containing every RCA Top 40 hit except the live Motown medley from the Apollo concert album and throwing in such key albums tracks as "Every Time You Go Away" and "I Don't Wanna Lose You." Fanatics will want to look for an import of dubious legitimacy, *Really Smokin'* (Magnum, 1993), which contains not only 1970 through '71 Hall demos but also some 1970 Gulliver material.

influences:
⏮ The O'Jays, Gamble & Huff, Sam & Dave, the Temptations
⏭ Charles & Eddie, Boyz II Men, Go West

Steve Holtje

Pete Ham
See: Badfinger

Hamell on Trial
Born Edward Hamell, Syracuse, NY.

Rant 'n' roll singer/performance artist Ed Hamell adopted the Hamell on Trial moniker to illustrate his philosophy that a performer is always on trial when he's onstage, thereby inviting the audience to judge him. It's a confusing name for a bald, acoustic guitar-wielding storyteller, but considering the overwhelming conviction and maniacal energy that powers his concerts, it's far more accurate than "folk singer." "I'm rocking like the Clash/it's acoustic kind of meanery," he sings in "The Meeting," his signature anthem. "I'm as bad as nine inch nails/except I don't need machinery." No kidding: Hamell's songs don't just tug at heartstrings—they challenge preconceptions, rail against prejudices, and flail away at complacency in an adrenaline-rush of staccato strumming, narrative angst, and stiletto-sharp, machine-gun-fast wordplay. In 1993, that intense yet entertaining combination snared the struggling Hamell a weekly residence at the famed Electric Lounge in Austin, Texas. He eventually befriended fellow Velvet Underground fanatic Alejandro Escovedo, who helped produce demos for his 1994 album, *Big as Life*. Local buzz drew a slew of salivating record-company execs to his South by Southwest showcase in 1995; he moved back to New York after signing with Mercury Records, which introduced him by reissuing *Big as Life* in 1996, with a new sleeve.

what to buy: Originally released by Austin's Doolittle Records in 1994, the raw *Big as Life* 🎵🎵🎵 (Mercury, 1996, prod. Jeff Cole) finds Hamell attacking rock-star wannabes in "Z-RoXX" ("Get a buck and try and buy a clue/You ain't Hüsker Dü/You ain't even Mötley Crüe") and recounting the tale of a crazed childhood friend who robs a Kentucky Fried Chicken outlet with a fork in "Blood of the Wolf." But his most passionate song is also his tenderest: "Open Up the Gates," in which he demands, not requests, that God accept his mother into heaven.

what to buy next: Making him more radio-friendly with hard-rocking band arrangements, *The Chord Is Mightier than the Sword* 🎵🎵🎵 (Mercury, 1997, prod. Phil Nicolo) brings out his melodic side ("No Delays," "New World"). But none of the band tracks match the urgency of such blistering solo numbers as "John Lennon" (about a chance childhood run-in with the ex-Beatle at an art exhibit) and "The Meeting."

the rest:
Conviction 🎵🎵🎵 (Blue Wave, 1989)

influences:
◀◀ The Velvet Underground, Bob Dylan, the Clash

▶▶ Dan Bern

David Okamoto

Col. Bruce Hampton /Aquarium Rescue Unit /Fiji Mariners

Born Bruce Hampton, in Atlanta, GA.

It's hard to believe that Col. Bruce Hampton ever heard a musical style he didn't like. His work is a melting pot of eccentric takes on familiar genres—a unique brew of rock, R&B, country, soul, swing, bluegrass, psychedelic, and jazz influences stirred for a seamless shower of musical exuberance. In a lesser artist the result could be rampant pandemonium; in Hampton's skewed vision, it is a magical, vibrant listening experience. A cult figure on the Southern music scene, he fronted the Hampton Grease Band, which released *Music to Eat* in 1969 (re-released in 1996). His involvement with such projects as New Ice Age and Late Bronze Age during the '70s and early '80s paved the way for Hampton's Aquarium Rescue Unit, a quirky if instrumentally solid outfit that recorded one album before he abruptly left the band (it continued on without him). Hampton went on to a new band, Fiji Mariners, but with somewhat less success (if that were possible). Hampton is an interesting footnote in the history of Southern rock.

what to buy: *Col. Bruce Hampton & the Aquarium Rescue Unit* 🎵🎵🎵🎵 (Capricorn, 1992, prod. Johnny Sandlin), recorded live at the Georgia Theatre in Athens, finds Hampton conjuring up sonic memories of everything from the early Allman Brothers, Weather Report, and Les McCann to latter day Dregs.

what to buy next: *Mirrors of Embarrassment* 🎵🎵🎵 (Capricorn, 1993) is solid, but lacks the live, whirling dervish effect of the debut.

the rest:
(With the Fiji Mariners) *Fiji* 🎵🎵🎵 (Capricorn, 1996)

influences:
◀◀ Captain Beefheart, Root Boy Slim, Frank Zappa

▶▶ Blues Traveler, Screaming Cheetah Wheelies, Dave Matthews Band

see also: *Hampton Grease Band*

Patrick McCarty

Hampton Grease Band

Formed 1967, in Atlanta, GA.

Bruce Hampton, vocals, trumpet; Harold Kelling, guitar, vocals; Glenn Phillips, guitar, saxophone; Mike Holbrook, bass; Jerry Fields, percussion, vocals.

Born out of blues and dance band backgrounds, the Hampton Grease Band incorporated the Dadaist spirit of the times to become a wailingly absurdist outfit that was as apt and able to embark on tantalizing 20-minute improvs as it was to revel in staged happenings. Its sole release was 1971's *Music to Eat*, which bowed not an inch to any pressures of the marketplace. It was a seven-song double album of friendly inscrutability that holds the distinction of being Columbia Record's worst selling album by any band, ever. The group broke up two years later when Bruce Hampton quit and headed to California, where he unsuccessfully auditioned as a vocalist for Frank Zappa. Back in Atlanta he has fronted a series of assorted combos, all bearing his unmistakable stamp. His greatest commercial success came with the Aquarium Rescue Unit, an outfit he soon grew tired of and left. Guitarist Glenn Phillips, also based in Atlanta, formed his own instrumental group, which has released 10 albums.

what's available: With his own custom label funded by CBS, one of the first things producer Brendan O'Brien (Pearl Jam, Stone Temple Pilots, etc.) did in 1996 was to reissue *Music to Eat* 🎵🎵🎵🎵 (Shotput/Columbia, 1971, prod. Hampton Grease Band, David Baker, Tom McNamee). This album, nearly three decades after it was first released, is a document of its times; it offers a glimpse of a unique world with no apologies or explanations needed.

influences:

◀◀ Captain Beefheart, the Mothers of Invention, Bonzo Dog Band

▶▶ The Swimming Pool Qs, the Aquarium Rescue Unit, Fiji Mariners

see also: *Col. Bruce Hampton*

David Greenberger

Handsome

Formed 1993, in New York, NY.

Jeremy Chatelain, vocals; Tom Capone, guitar; Pete Hines, drums; Peter Mengede, guitar; Eddie Nappi, bass.

The roots of Handsome run deep into the underground of the New York City metal and avant-guitar scenes. Guitarist Peter Mengede was a founding member of Helmet, Tom Capone played guitar with the acclaimed post-hardcore outfit Quicksand, and drummer Hines came via two other reputable hardcore bands, Murphy's Law and the Cro-Mags. Together they found Utah transplant Jeremy Chatelain from Iceburn and Insight to man the vocal duties, and scenester guitar player Eddie Nappi to handle the bass. Handsome rehearsed just four days before playing its first gig, at New York's CBGB's with Girls vs. Boys. The chemistry between these very post-hardcore musicians showed up immediately, with guitarists Mengede and Capone leading an adventurous attack that is as heavy as it is melodic, and as emblematic of the part of the city from which it stems as crime-infested streets and dirty yellow cabs.

what to buy: *Handsome* ♫♫♫♫ (Epic, 1997, prod. Terry Date, Handsome) is by all counts an auspicious debut, combining impact and melody, innovation and ability, with the vision to back it up on tracks like "Needles" and "Left of Heaven."

influences:

◀◀ Band of Susans, the Velvet Underground, Sonic Youth, Black Flag, Helmet

Bob Gulla

The Hang Ups

Formed 1988, in Minneapolis, MN.

Brian Tighe, guitar, vocals, sax, keyboards; Jeffrey Kearns, bass, vocals, guitar; Stephen Ittner, drums, vocals, guitar, bass; John Crozier, guitar, harmonica, organ (1992–present).

The core of this band met at Minneapolis College of Art and Design, and Brian Tighe's senior project was the Hang Ups' first real demo tape. The inclusion of Muskellunge guitarist John Crozier added density and complexity. The group's sound is classic American jangle-pop augmented with inventiveness and imagination, insuring that this won't sound like just another Minneapolis raw power band; the Hang Ups' twilight moodiness suggests more the influence of the English shoe-gazer scene.

what to buy: *He's After Me* ♫♫♫♫ (Clean/ Twin/Tone, 1993, prod. Ed Ackerson) is catchy in a casual way, the songs hanging in the air like vapour until suddenly condensing into fluid choruses.

what to buy next: The EP *Comin' Through* ♫♫♫ (Clean/Restless, 1993, prod. various) was released prior to *He's After Me* and includes a cover of "Eight Miles High" from a Hüsker Dü tribute and three non-album songs. *So We Go* ♫♫♫ (Clean/Restless, 1996, prod. Bryan Hanna, John Fields, the Hang Ups) is chock-full of winsome vocals—often with nice harmonies—on lovely melodies. Even though it's an uptempo number, the title track is one of the most beautiful songs of the decade.

influences:

◀◀ The Byrds, the Hollies, Kitchens of Distinction, Mega City 4

Steve Holtje

The Hangdogs

Formed 1993, in New York, NY.

Matthew Grimm, vocals, rhythm guitar; Automatic Slim, guitar; Kevin Baier, drums; J.C. Chmiel, bass.

If the prevailing theme of modern country music is city dwellers yearning for their rural roots, then the Hangdogs, not Garth Brooks, are the perfect country band for New York City. Consisting of a transplanted Iowan (Matt "Banger" Grimm) and three locals, the Hangdogs write songs of urban angst and small-town desolation with a macho swagger that belies a romantic heart. Grimm is among alt.country's best songwriters, and the Hangdogs may be the scene's only band able to play a live medley of George Jones and AC/DC that shows a firm grasp of both acts. Its DIY approach has probably cost them some renown, but renown doesn't pay rent.

what to buy: *East of Yesterday* ♫♫♫ (Crazyhead, 1997, prod. Bruce Henderson) is a considerable improvement over their self-released debut, with highlights that include a guy who sells his record collection to buy a wedding ring ("The Ring") and a biting ode of love to actress Janeane Garofalo ("Hey Janeane").

the rest:

The Same Old Story ♫♫♫ (Crazyhead, 1995)

influences:

◀◀ Dwight Yoakam, Bruce Springsteen, Steve Earle, the Gear Daddies

▶▶ Tim Carroll, Paul Thorn

Brian Mansfield

Hanoi Rocks /Michael Monroe

Formed 1980, in Finland. Disbanded 1985.

Michael Monroe, vocals, sax, piano, harmonica; Andy McCoy, guitar, backing vocals; Nasty Suicide, guitar, backing vocals; Sam Yaffa, bass; Gyp Casino, drums (1980–82); Razzle (born Nicholas Dingley), drums (1982–84).

Hanoi Rocks may have hopped on the glam bandwagon after the fact and far from the scene, but the band still managed to rekindle the fire of drugged decadence and tragic pop for fans around the world. The group moved from Scandinavia to the U.K. during 1982, where the appropriately titled "Love's an Injection" was already in the charts. That same year the group released its second album, *Oriental Beat,* and replaced Casino. But the band's new drummer Razzle was killed in a car accident (the vehicle was driven by Mötley Crüe singer Vince Neil) the same year its most celebrated album, *Two Steps from the Move,* was released. Hanoi Rocks broke up in 1985, and the members scattered: Nasty Suicide and Andy McCoy started the Cherry Bombz; and pouty blonde frontman Monroe made a few solo records. Geffen started releasing the entire Hanoi Rocks catalog during late '80s.

what to buy: *Two Steps from the Move* ♪♪♪♪ (Epic, 1984/1989) shows Hanoi Rocks closest to its potential, with lyrics by Ian Hunter of Mott the Hoople and a cover of Creedence Clearwater Revival's "Up around the Bend."

what to buy next: *All Those Wasted Years* ♪♪♪♡ (Geffen, 1986/1996, prod. Overland Watts) is a live album that's raucous and exuberant, if a bit sloppy.

the rest:
Bangkok Shocks, Saigon Shakes, Hanoi Rocks ♪♪♪♡ (Geffen, 1981/1996)
Self Destruction Blues ♪♪♡ (Geffen, 1982/1996)
Oriental Beat ♪♪♡ (Geffen, 1982/1996)
Back to Mystery City ♪♡ (Geffen, 1983/1996)

worth searching for: The Japanese collection *All Those Glamourous Years . . . Best of Hanoi Rocks & Michael Monroe* (Mercury, 1996) is a first-rate compilation that provides most everything you need to know about the group.

solo outings:
Michael Monroe:
Not Fakin' It ♪♪♡ (Mercury, 1989)

influences:
◄◄ Lou Reed, Led Zeppelin, T. Rex, the New York Dolls, the Stooges, the Sex Pistols

►► D Generation

Norene Cashen and Gary Graff

Hanson

Formed 1992, in Tulsa, OK.

Isaac Hanson (born Clark Isaac Hanson), guitars, vocals; Taylor Hanson, keyboards, vocals; Zachary Hanson, drums, vocals.

Marilyn Manson, faceless generic rock, and blasé pop inundated the airwaves of the late '90s until a little song came out of nowhere to rid us of pain. Hanson has been eagerly working toward a pop career since about the time the three brothers were able to mumble "MmmBop." Isaac wrote his first song at age eight and began harmonizing with Taylor soon thereafter. Honing their skills singing *a capella* around their Tulsa home, the brothers headed out to state fairs and neighbors' homes to show off their musical talents. A trip to the influential South by Southwest music conference proved to be uneventful, but a Mercury Records rep gave Hanson another chance and saw them perform at the state fair in Kansas in 1996. Soon thereafter, Hanson—and their parents—inked a six-album deal.

what to buy: *Middle of Nowhere* ♪♪♪♪ (Mercury, 1997, prod. Steve Lironi, the Dust Brothers) captures the boys' love of jubilant pop, rock, '70s soul, and gospel. Most modern rock fans would probably dismiss the threesome as pre-fab romper rock, but what sets Hanson apart from kiddie groups like New Kids on the Block is that the angelic-looking brothers write their own material and play their own instruments. It also doesn't hurt that *Middle of Nowhere* is a classic pop album. The first single, "MmmBop," spiced up with turntable scratching, may be cute, but it's also contagious—one of those songs that, if you're past 16, you tell your friends you hate but secretly you hum it in your car, around the house, and at school. Same goes for the rest of the album. Blending pop and rock vocals, "Where's the Love?" is an irrestible break from the deluge of angst-ridden rock and gangsta rap. The ballad "Yearbook" is a sweet tale of high school—make that middle school—love. If history has a way of repeating itself, Hanson will vanish from pop music in short order, but we should cherish this infectious power pop as long as we can.

what to buy next: *Three Car Garage* ♪♪♪♡ (Mercury, 1998) features demos and B-sides from Hanson's pre-major label days, including a formative version of "MmmBop" that proves that the studio trickery on *Middle of Nowhere* just enhanced the talent the boys already have.

the rest:
Snowed In ♪♪♡ (Mercury, 1997)

influences:
◄◄ The Jackson 5, New Kids on the Block, Another Bad Creation

Christina Fuoco

Zac Hanson of Hanson (© Ken Settle)

Happy Mondays /Black Grape

Formed 1985, in Manchester, England. Disbanded 1993.

Shaun Ryder, lead vocals; Paul Ryder, bass; Paul Davis, keyboards; Gary Whelan, drums; Mark Day, guitar; Mark "Bez" Berisford, percussion, dancing.

Riding on the euphoric wave of good vibes that swept Britain at the outset of the '90s, the Happy Mondays provided a perfectly suited soundtrack for loose-limbed kids who embraced Ecstasy culture and 26-inch flares. But there was much more to the group than its frivolous music suggested. Mainly, it exhibited an unyielding knack for turning out songs of substantial caliber. That, in combination with exaggerated tales of rock 'n' roll excess, made the band members natural candidates for stardom. Success came at the group with blinding intensity, and the working-class Manchester natives of which the band consisted espoused its evils with not one second thought. Soon enough, the strain of overnight success started to unravel the Happy Mondays at the core. "We all hated each other," singer Shaun Ryder said after the group's split in 1993. "I just started speaking to me brother again." After rehab, Ryder and Mark "Bez" Berisford attempted to keep the band's spirit alive with a new group called Black Grape, which also included Kermit from the Ruthless Rap Assassins. The personal turmoil, however, has yet to cease.

what to buy: While Happy Mondays had its fair share of decent album tracks, the group's strength was primarily in its remarkable string of singles. *Double Easy: The U.S. Singles* ΔΔΔΔ (Elektra, 1993, prod. various) is the perfect showcase for the Manchester group's chaotic chemistry, collecting impeccable groove-oriented guitar numbers such as "Hallelujah," "Kinky Afro," and "Loose Fit" on one exhaustive package. *Pills 'N' Thrills and Bellyaches* ΔΔΔ (Elektra, 1990, prod. Paul Oakenfeld, Steve Osborne) caught the group at the height of its creative apex, mixing funk rhythms, soulful backing vocals, and classic melodies. "Bob's Yer Uncle" and "Step On" fulfilled the Happy Mondays' sonic objective.

what to buy next: For those who were tuned into Happy Mondays for rave appeal, there is no better document of the band's dance leanings than *Hallelujah* ΔΔΔ (Elektra, 1989, prod. Martin Hannett), a seven song disc comprised of remixes by club gurus Andrew Weatherall, Steve Lillywhite, and Paul Oakenfeld ("Hallelujah," "Rave On" and "W.F.L."), along with trance-inducing B-sides ("Clap Your Hands," "Holy Ghost").

what to avoid: By the time Happy Mondays got around to making its final album, *Yes, Please* Δ (Elektra, 1992, prod. Chris Frantz, Tina Weymouth), the members of the group had fallen victim to drug abuse and general disinterest in music. While a few noteworthy songs ("Sunshine and Love," "Cut 'em Loose Bruce") did rise out of the wreckage, the record was a mostly staid affair.

the rest:
Squirrel and G-Man Twenty-Four Party People Plastic Face Carnt Smile (White Out) Δ (Factory, 1987)
Bummed ΔΔ (Elektra, 1988)
Live **woof!** (Elektra, 1991)

worth searching for: *The Peel Sessions* (Strange Fruit/Dutch East India Trading, 1991, prod. Dale Griffin), recorded during 1986, captures the ramshackle glory of Happy Mondays right before the group fell into the habit of making production-heavy records.

solo outings:
Black Grape (Ryder and Berisford):
It's Great When You're Straight ΔΔ (Radioactive, 1995)
Stupid Stupid Stupid Δ (Radioactive, 1998)

influences:
◄◄ New Order, the Beatles, Curtis Mayfield, Public Enemy
►► Oasis, the Charlatans, Primal Scream, Chemical Brothers

Aidin Vaziri

Tim Hardin

Born December 23, 1941, in Eugene, OR. Died December 29, 1980, in Los Angeles, CA.

Tim Hardin was a dark-hued and often mournful singer-songwriter whose place in the late '60s folksinger movement was ensured not so much by his own commercial success but by later versions of his songs covered by other artists. Hardin's originals were marked by spare performances—nearly outlines, really—and brief running times (most clock in at under two minutes). But the undeniable strength inherent in his sketchy yet potent style earned the singer substantial critical acclaim, if relatively little else. By the early 1970s, Hardin's career had been effectively wiped out by a nasty drug addiction that eventually killed him at age 39.

what to buy: *Hang On to a Dream: The Verve Recordings* ΔΔΔΔ (Polydor, 1994, prod. Erik Jacobsen) is a far-reaching and comprehensive document, collecting every Verve recording plus 17 unreleased tracks of pure melancholy. His most notable tracks, including "Reason to Believe," "Misty Roses," "If I Were a Carpenter," and "Black Sheep Boy," are all included.

the rest:
Tim Hardin Live in Concert ΔΔ (PolyGram Special Products, 1968/1995)
Reason to Believe (Best of) ΔΔΔ (Polydor, 1987)
Simple Songs of Freedom: The Tim Hardin Collection ΔΔΔ (Legacy, 1996)

influences:
◀◀ Bob Dylan, Phil Ochs
▶▶ Paul Siebel, Neil Young

Allan Orski

John Wesley Harding
Born October 22, 1965, in Hastings, England.

Although he started his stateside career as a pop songsmith with Brian Wilson dreams and Elvis Costello pretensions, John Wesley Harding has reverted to his politically charged folk roots since parting ways with Sire Records in 1992. This isn't a shock to most fans; the brash singer-songwriter—who took his name from the classic Bob Dylan album—has always laced his shows with biting commentaries in the form of rambling monologues as well as tersely but cleverly worded numbers such as "Scared of Guns," "Hitler's Tears," "The Triumph of Trash," and "July 13th 1985" (about how Live Aid was really more about bloated egos than starving children). Over the years, the Costello comparisons have passed and Wes's up-beat, often frantic stage show has developed into a more thoughtful, though still pointed platform that even caught the attention of Bruce Springsteen, who hired him as an opening act in 1995. Now a resident of San Francisco, Harding has found an unexpected artistic home with New York indie label Zero Hour, joining a noisy roster that includes Varnaline and Swervedriver.

what to buy: *Here Comes the Groom* ♫♫♫♫ (Sire, 1989, prod. Andy Paley) bubbles with the youthful fervor and manic word-play of Costello's *My Aim Is True* (no surprise since the backing band includes Pete Thomas and Bruce Thomas of the Attractions) and the heel-clicking splendor of the Lovin' Spoonful. *Awake* ♫♫♫ (Zero Hour, 1998, prod. John Wesley Harding, Chris Von Sneidern) finds Harding experimenting with drum loops, samples, and other daring textures. But ragged rockers such as "Your Ghost (Don't Scare Me No More)," "Burn," and the defiant "I'm Staying Here (And I'm Not Buying a Gun)" are still fueled by his acrid wit and fierce dedication to melody.

what to buy next: Harding's straight-faced acoustic cover of Madonna's "Like a Prayer" is one of three non-LP oddities on *God Made Me Do It: The Christmas EP* ♫♫♫ (Sire, 1989, prod. John Wesley Harding). *Pett Levels: The Summer EP* ♫♫♫ (Sire, 1992, prod. Andy Paley, Steve Berlin, Scott Matthews) boasts five previously unreleased tracks highlighted by the glorious "Summer Single," his final flirtation with wall-of-sound pop, and the hardnosed live favorite "One Shot."

what to avoid: *It Happened One Night* ♫♫ (Rhino, 1991, prod. Wes Stace a.k.a. John Wesley Harding), a live solo acoustic album originally released in England in 1988, is driven more by adrenalin than vision.

the rest:
The Name Above the Title ♫♫♫ (Sire, 1991)
Why We Fight ♫♫♫ (Sire, 1992)
John Wesley Harding's New Deal ♫♫♫♫ (Forward/Rhino, 1996)

worth searching for: *Dynablob* (Mod Lang, 1996, prod. John Wesley Harding) is a collection of studio outtakes and radio performances sold via his fan club and Mod Lang Records (P.O. Box 10111, Berkeley, CA 94709). It includes the original country version of "The Devil in Me" and his much-requested "Talking Return of the Great Folk Scare Blues."

influences:
◀◀ Phil Ochs, Bob Dylan, Elvis Costello, Billy Bragg
▶▶ Dan Bern

David Okamoto

Françoise Hardy
Born January 17, 1944, in Paris, France.

Françoise Hardy emerged from France's pop music scene in the mid-'60s singing lovesick ballads and baroque pop songs in a voice that was as inscrutably waifish and delicate as her movie-star good looks. As a Parisian teen, Hardy was weaned on American rock 'n' roll and the sultry stylings of the immensely popular French singer Sylvie Vartan. By the time she was 15, Hardy had already taught herself how to play guitar and write her own songs. At 17, she was singing professionally in local clubs, which eventually led to her signing a recording contract with French label Vogue Records in 1961. Her recording of the song "Tous les Garçons et les Filles" became a massive hit throughout Europe in 1962, and it reached the U.K. Top 40. Hardy, who wrote most of her own material, recorded steadily throughout the decade, tackling everything from over-the-top pop to the blues and cabaret music. Hardy also made appearances in films as diverse as Jean-Luc Godard's *Masculin-Feminin* and *What's New Pussycat?*, both of which were released in 1966. In recent years, Hardy's coolly detached style has been discovered by a new generation of artists—she has appeared on recent recordings by the British pop band Blur and dance-music impresario Malcolm McClaren.

what's available: The mediocre *Danger* ♫♫ (Virgin, 1996) is Hardy's only domestic release available on CD. But *Ma Jeunesse Fout le Camp* ♫♫♫ (Virgin, 1967) best captures Hardy's florid pop style. Her writing and singing had matured considerably by the time she recorded *Le Question* ♫♫♫♫ (Virgin, 1971), an all-acoustic album of smoldering, moody torch-pop songs. *Françoise Hardy en Anglais* ♫♫ (Sonopress, 1969) finds Hardy attempting to capture the English-speaking market, but her vocals come off sounding stilted and stiff.

influences:

⏮ Sylvie Vartan, Elvis Presley, Ann-Margret

⏭ Blur, Madeleine Peyroux

Marc Weingarten

Ben Harper

Born October 28, 1969, in Pomona, CA.

Ben Harper made quite an initial critical splash, partly because it's still unusual nowadays for a young black man to sing reflective, acoustic folk-rock rather than hip-hop or straight-up R&B. Given the political bent of some of Harper's lyrics, it would be easy to tag him as a male version of Tracy Chapman, but his voice is less distinctive and his sound more so, making particular use of the Weissenborn, a rare Hawaiian guitar with a thin but singular tone. With a small but avid international following, Harper would seem to have a solid, and lengthy, career ahead of him, especially given his reputation as a dynamic, committed live performer. Interestingly, his records are getting louder as time goes by, including more electric guitar and more soloing.

what to buy: Harper's debut album, *Welcome to the Cruel World* 𝄞𝄞𝄞 (Virgin, 1994, prod. Ben Harper, J.P. Plunier), remains his best. Highlights range from the funny, reggae-ish "Mama's Got a Girlfriend Now," to the surprisingly upbeat "How Many Miles Must We March?," to the dreamy "I'll Rise." He and his main collaborator/producer J.P. Plunier keep the instrumental arrangements simple but cleverly nuanced throughout, often adding choir-like backing vocals.

what to buy next: *Fight for Your Mind* 𝄞𝄞𝄞 (Virgin, 1995, prod. Ben Harper,, J.P. Plunier) gets more electric on a few numbers, but mostly it sticks to the same Bob Marley– and Neil Young–influenced folk-rock. Occasionally he gets too ambitious for his own good, adding a string quartet to the already dark "Power of the Gospel" and winding up with something tedious instead of stirring. Still, "Ground on Down" is powerful, damning stuff. *The Will to Live* 𝄞𝄞𝄞 (Virgin, 1997, prod. J.P. Plunier) was promoted as a sudden shift from acoustic to electric, and a special edition of the disc includes a live EP that gives some indication of Harper's in-concert persona. The Sly Stone–like "Mama's Trippin'" and the stinging blues shuffle "Homeless Child" are potent tracks, but the haunting "Widow of a Living Man," in which Harper's voice speaks for a beaten, but not defeated, woman, is the real standout. The lyrics get clichéd in spots, but he remains an artist with integrity, and these days, that's something special.

WHAT ALBUM CHANGED YOUR LIFE?

It would have to be Mississippi John Hurt. There are so many amazing John Hurt records and compilations. I think the one for me was the *John Hurt Sessions* album, recorded in a five-year period in the '60s, or something like that. His finger picking and styling really changed my life in a big way.

Ben Harper

influences:

⏮ Richie Havens, Taj Mahal, Curtis Mayfield

Bob Remstein

Harpers Bizarre

Formed 1963, in Santa Cruz, CA. Disbanded 1970.

Ted Templeman, guitar, drums, trumpet, vocals; Dickie Scoppettone, guitar, bass, vocals; Dick Yount, bass, guitar, drums, vocals; Eddie James, guitar, vocals (1963–68); John Petersen, drums, vocals (1966–70).

Into the anything-goes kaleidoscope that was pop music circa 1966, Harpers Bizarre rose from the remnants of San Francisco–based surf band the Tikis, signed with Warner Bros. Records under the supervision of producer Lenny Waronker, and became basically an in-studio playpen for several of the West Coast's brightest young composing and arranging talents. After scoring big with its version of Paul Simon's "59th Street Bridge Song"—which helped the Summer of Love feel even groovier with its tooty, carefree sing-song sound—the band set about similarly recasting in baubles and bangles a gigantic hodgepodge of material, stretching all the way back to Cole Porter's big band standards. While far from being a strict novelty act such as Britain's make-believe New Vaudeville Band, Harpers Bizarre, with its reliance on cleverness as opposed to originality, nevertheless cast itself as a faux-*Pepper* flavor of the era, and consequently is looked back upon today as a quaint, cushy curiosity at best.

what's available: Compiled from its four original albums, *Feelin' Groovy: The Best of Harpers Bizarre* ♫♫♫♪ (Warner Archives, 1997, compilation prod. Gregg Geller, Ted Templeman, Lenny Waronker) gathers together a fine collection of flawlessly sung, meticulously arranged, and sparklingly produced numbers from the pens of Randy Newman, Harry Nilsson, Van Dyke Parks, and even Sammy Cahn. If you've ever wondered what the Beatles would have sounded like playing "Chattanooga Choo Choo," this disc is for you.

influences:

◄◄ Brian Wilson, the Beau Brummels, George Martin, George Washington Brown

►► The Association, the West Coast Pop Art Experimental Band, Brave Combo

Gary Pig Gold

Emmylou Harris

Born April 2, 1947, in Birmingham, AL.

Her musical trademark is a pure, aching soprano, but Emmylou Harris's defining musical characteristic is curiosity. It has led her to traditional country, new songwriters, and maverick producers. Practically every hotshot on the country scene today, from Garth Brooks on down, claims Harris as an inspiration, but few can match her creative daring. Harris began as a '60s-style folkie, working clubs around Washington, D.C. Through ex-Byrd Chris Hillman she met Gram Parsons. Their duets on Parsons's *Grievous Angel* are pioneering moments in country-rock and brought a well-deserved spotlight to Harris's voice. Parsons's death in 1973 left Harris fiercely committed to continuing his vision in her solo work. With her 1975 major-label debut, *Pieces of the Sky*, she unveiled the sound that would become an influential trademark—classic country touches like galloping rhythm guitar and heartfelt vocals, cut with a driving rock backbeat. Early on, Harris demonstrated both her interest in country's past (e.g., the Louvin Brothers) and her commitment to new or unconventional material (e.g., the Beatles' "Here, There and Everywhere," or "Easy from Now On" by the young Carlene Carter). Harris's Hot Band, which toured with her through the '80s, was an incubator of top talent; alumni include Ricky Skaggs, Vince Gill, and Rodney Crowell, as well as producers Emory Gordy Jr. and Tony Brown. Opting for a bare-bones traditional sound during the '90s, Harris formed the Nash Ramblers and released the acclaimed *At the Ryman* in 1992. Her fan base is solid enough to offset country radio's indifference, and her most recent work reflects both a stronger rock flavor and a continued willingness to stretch the boundaries.

what to buy: For a warp-speed trip through Harris's early career, start with *Profile: The Best of Emmylou Harris*, ♫♫♫♪ (Warner Bros., 1978, prod. various), which offers the cream of her early studio work. High points include covers of Dolly Parton's "To Daddy" and the Louvins' "If I Could Only Win Your Love." Fast forward to the daring *Wrecking Ball* ♫♫♫♫ (Asylum, 1995, prod. Daniel Lanois) to hear a Harris now completely confident in her musical impulses. Within rock producer Lanois's otherwordly arrangements, she pushes her voice to a raw, urgent edge and continues to dig up great material by underappreciated writers such as Lucinda Williams and Gillian Welch. Two live albums provide excellent introductions to important phases of Harris's music: *Last Date* ♫♫♫♫ (Warner Bros., 1982, prod. Brian Ahern), an exuberant country-rock manifesto, summarizes why Harris's Hot Band work had such impact; and *At the Ryman* ♫♫♫♫ (Reprise, 1992, prod. Allen Reynolds, Richard Bennett) offers Harris as acoustic purist, achieving an unplugged sound that is firmly traditional and astoundingly flexible, encompassing everything from Steve Earle to Stephen Foster.

what to buy next: Any would-be country traditionalist should own *Roses in the Snow* ♫♫♫♫ (Warner Bros., 1980, prod. Brian Ahern), Harris's valentine to old-timey music (with assists from the likes of Parton, Skaggs, Linda Ronstadt, and Johnny Cash). The ambitious concept album *The Ballad of Sally Rose* ♫♫♫♪ (Warner Bros., 1985, prod. Emmylou Harris, Paul Kennerley) doesn't meld into a convincing dramatic whole, but it features wonderful songwriting by Harris and Kennerley—"Woman Walk the Line" in particular has become a country standard. Two very different albums with spirituality as a theme are *Angel Band* ♫♫♫♪ (Warner Bros., 1987, prod. Emmylou Harris, Emory Gordy Jr.), a spare collection of country gospel hymns, and the introspective *Cowgirl's Prayer* ♫♫♫♪ (Asylum, 1993, prod. Allen Reynolds, Richard Bennett), which features an eerie, ethereal version of Leonard Cohen's "Ballad of a Runaway Horse." Those who can't resist box sets will find *Portraits* ♫♫♫♪ (Warner, 1996, prod. various) a respectable and massive effort, but it misses many gems from Harris's essential albums (*Last Date*, in particular).

what to avoid: *Cimarron* ♫♫ (Warner, 1981, prod. Brian Ahern) is mostly listless Nashville-by-the-book—and Harris is infinitely better when she chucks the rulebook.

the rest:
Pieces of the Sky ♫♫♫♪ (Reprise, 1975)
Elite Hotel ♫♫♪ (Reprise, 1976)
Luxury Liner ♫♫♫ (Warner Bros., 1977)
Quarter Moon in a Ten Cent Town ♫♫♪ (Warner Bros., 1978)
Blue Kentucky Girl ♫♫♫ (Warner Bros., 1979)
Light of the Stable ♫♫♫♪ (Warner Bros., 1980)
Evangeline ♫♫♫♪ (Warner Bros., 1981)
White Shoes ♫♫♫ (Warner Bros., 1983)
Profile II: The Best of Emmylou Harris ♫♫♫♪ (Warner Bros., 1984)
Thirteen ♫♫♫ (Warner Bros., 1986)

Bluebird ♫♫♫ (Reprise, 1989)
Brand New Dance ♫♫♫ (Reprise, 1990)
Duets ♫♫♫ (Reprise, 1990)
Songs of the West ♫♫♫ (Warner, 1994)
Portraits ♫♫♫ (Warner, 1995)

worth searching for: *Gliding Bird* (Jubilee, 1969), Harris's very first album, reportedly turns up from time to time in the record collections of Harris junkies. See if they'll let you tape it.

influences:

◀◀ The Carter Family, Buck Owens, the Louvin Brothers, Hazel & Alice, Tom Rush, Gram Parsons

▶▶ Alison Krauss, the Mavericks, Cowboy Junkies

see also: *Gram Parsons*

Elizabeth Lynch

Joey Harris

See: Beat Farmers

George Harrison

Born February 25, 1943, in Liverpool, England.

The Quiet Beatle was actually the first of the fabs to go solo, with one album of *Electronic Sounds* and an obscure soundtrack, *Wonderwall Music*, whose title was later borrowed for an Oasis hit. Creatively stymied by his former group, which only allowed one or two contributions per album, George Harrison seemed the happiest to see the group break up—though he did bring Ringo Starr and Paul McCartney together again for his 1981 tribute to John Lennon, "All Those Years Ago." His pent-up creativity fairly burst upon release, though, with the epic and audacious triple-album set *All Things Will Pass*. It made way for his planning of rock's first huge benefit spectacle, the Concert for Bangladesh. But Harrison's output sputtered surprisingly quickly during the '70s and early '80s; his albums tend to have a couple of worthy tunes, but each is successively worse than its predecessor. Unlike Starr, Harrison never suffered the indignity of an album turned down for release, but it might have been close around the time of *Extra Texture* or *Gone Troppo*. His five-year hiatus from music, when he became a movie producer, helped clear Harrison's head and helped make the 1987 comeback, *Cloud Nine*, a delight that produced the last #1 hit single for an ex-Beatle. Perhaps superstitious, he has yet to follow it up in the intervening decade, although a 1991 tour with Eric Clapton, which lasted only for a few dates in Japan, was captured on a worthy live album. Harrison was also responsible for starting the chain of events that led to the formation of the Traveling Wilburys—him, Bob Dylan, Roy Orbison, Tom Petty, and Jeff Lynne—in 1988.

what to buy: *All Things Must Pass* ♫♫♫♫ (Apple, 1970, prod. Phil Spector) remains one of the greatest recordings from an ex-Beatle. The dense production and rich songs topped off by the extra album of jamming (something that doesn't work quite as well on the double CD set. Among the key tracks are "If Not for You," co-written with Dylan, and "My Sweet Lord," for which Harrison was found guilty of having "unknowingly" plagiarized the Shirelles' "He's So Fine."

what to buy next: *Cloud Nine* ♫♫♫♫ (Warner Bros., 1987, prod. Jeff Lynne) is a remarkable comeback album that spoke to several generations and had a few radio hits to boot in "Got My Mind Set on You" and "When We Was Fab." *Live in Japan* (Warner Bros., 1992, prod. George Harrison, Eric Clapton) is a remarkable live set, featuring Harrison backed by Clapton and his band and playing a repertoire that blends the best of his Beatles writing with his solo material.

what to avoid: *Electronic Sounds* ♫ (Zapple, 1969) may interest students of early synthesizer experiments, but nobody else.

the rest:
Wonderwall Music ♫♫ (Apple, 1968)
Concert for Bangladesh ♫♫♫♫ (Apple, 1972)
Living in the Material World ♫♫♫ (Apple, 1973)
Dark Horse ♫♫♫♫ (Apple, 1974)
Extra Texture (Read All about It) ♫♫ (Apple, 1975)
33 1/3 ♫♫ (Dark Horse, 1976)
The Best of George Harrison ♫♫♫ (Capitol, 1976)
George Harrison ♫♫ (Dark Horse, 1979)
Somewhere in England ♫♫ (Dark Horse, 1981)
Gone Troppo ♫♫ (Dark Horse, 1982)
The Best of Dark Horse 1976–1989 ♫♫♫ (Capitol, 1989)

worth searching for: *Fourth Night Live* (Platypus, 1992) is a bootleg from the '91 Japanese tour; it features Clapton's set—which was excluded from the legitimate album—and a reproduction of the tour program.

influences:

◀◀ Chet Atkins, the Beatles, Carl Perkins, Ravi Shankar

▶▶ Jeff Lynne, Paul Simon, Grant McLennan, Crowded House, Oasis

see also: *The Beatles, the Traveling Wilburys*

Roger Catlin

Deborah Harry

See: Blondie

Grant Hart

See: Hüsker Dü

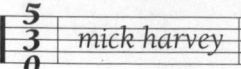
Mick Harvey

See: The Birthday Party

PJ Harvey

Born Polly Jean Harvey, October 9, 1969, in Yeovil, England.

One of the most intriguing post-punk artists to emerge in years, Polly Jean Harvey makes blues-based rock that's raw, angry, and challenging. But unlike her angst-merchant peers, she has the voice and the hooks to make her rage matter. Her band—also called PJ Harvey—included bassist Stephen Vaughan and drummer Rob Ellis until 1993, when both were replaced by studio musicians when Harvey veered into a more ambient, sonically experimental sound. Seething with punk energy, female rage, and emotional turbulence, Harvey's first couple of records contain some of the most vital music music of the '90s.

what to buy: *To Bring You My Love* 𝄢𝄢𝄢𝄢 (Island, 1995, prod. Flood, PJ Harvey, John Parish) was voted the best album of 1995 in the *Village Voice* Pazz & Jop Critics' Poll, and for good reason: even including a few duds, this strange collection of blues-punk is one of the most harrowing rock records ever made. Her debut, *Dry* 𝄢𝄢𝄢𝄢 (Mango, 1992, prod. Robert Ellis, PJ Harvey, Head), was recorded on a shoestring budget and didn't sell squat, but songs such as "Sheela-Na-Gig" and "Oh My Lover" come on with the force of a Mack truck.

what to buy next: *Rid of Me* 𝄢𝄢𝄢 (Island, 1993, prod. Steve Albini) is more abrasive than its predecessor, but "50 Ft. Queenie" and Harvey's deconstruction of Bob Dylan's "Highway 61 Revisited" rank with her best performances. *4-Track Demos* 𝄢𝄢𝄢 (Island, 1993) is an insightful collection of demos from *Rid of Me*, plus several previously unheard tracks.

the rest:
(With John Parish) *Dance Hall at Louse Point* 𝄢𝄢𝄢 (Island, 1996)
Is This Desire? N/A (Island, 1998)

influences:
◀◀ Patti Smith, Howlin' Wolf, Pere Ubu, Tom Waits
▶▶ Hole, the Verve

Thor Christensen

Harvey Danger

Formed 1993, in Seattle, WA.

Sean Nelson, vocals; Jeff J. Lin, guitar, organ, violin, backing vocals; Aaron Huffman, bass; Evan Sult, drums.

Not your older brother's Seattle band, Harvey Danger annexes the unclaimed niche between the goofy escapism of a Presidents of the United States of America and the self-indulgent gloom of a Nirvana. Its rapier-witted sketches of debilitating ob-

session and unearned self-righteousness ring just true enough to strike a chord with the outcast demographic and keep just enough distance to allow that same audience to laugh at itself. With rich folky vocals ringing out over punk pyrotechnics and 5th Dimension–style harmonies struggling strangely up through the guitar anguish, Danger is the kind of stylistic moving target whose forward momentum revitalizes rock.

what's available: The band's avenging-nerd stage persona completes the picture, but its first recorded work, *Where Have All the Merrymakers Gone?* 𝄢𝄢𝄢 (The Arena Rock Recording Company, 1997/ Slash/London, 1998, prod. John Goodmanson, Harvey Danger) conveys the immediacy and impact of its live performances with an accuracy uncommon to debut albums. It's one of the most promising releases of the late '90s.

influences:
◀◀ R.E.M., Morrissey, Pavement, Pearl Jam, Noel Coward

Adam McGovern

Hater

See: Soundgarden

Juliana Hatfield

Born July 27, 1967, in Wiscasset, ME.

With her pixie voice, buzzed-out guitar, and brash, sometimes brutal honesty, Juliana Hatfield presents a compelling clash of contradictions. She sounds like a fragile waif, plays guitar like a headbanger, and writes songs with plenty of pop appeal and lyrical weight. The daughter of a *Boston Globe* reporter, Hatfield earned a degree in composition and writing at the prestigious Berklee College of Music. That's where she hooked up with two fellow students in 1987 to form the alternative rock trio the Blake Babies, in which she played bass and sang. Hatfield went solo in 1990 and has steadily gained confidence as a singer, songwriter, and guitarist. She sent some shockwaves through the media—and asserted her independent spirit— when she told an interviewer in 1992 that she was a virgin at age 25. An update on her sexual status was unavailable at press time.

what to buy: *Only Everything* 𝄢𝄢𝄢 (Atlantic/Mammoth, 1995, prod. Sean Slade, Paul Q. Kolderie, Juliana Hatfield) churns with metallic pop power as waves of guitars crash behind Hatfield's airy vocals. Her heart is broken on "My Darling" and "Universal Heart-Beat," but she bounces back, bruised but wiser ("What a trip/I'm better for it"). She also quiets down for a few relatively mellow ballads ("You Blues," "Live on Tomorrow").

what to buy next: *Become What You Are* 𝄢𝄢𝄢 (Atlantic/Mammoth, 1993, prod. Scott Litt) is more cryptic and less forceful than *Only Everything*, but Hatfield still puts her righteous indignation to good work in protesting women's vulnerability ("A Dame with a Rod") and superficiality ("Supermodel").

the rest:
Hey Babe ♪♪ (Mammoth, 1992)
Bed ♪♪♪ (Zoe, 1998)

worth searching for: A limited edition of *Only Everything* featured fake fur on the cover's buffalo image.

influences:
◄◄ R.E.M., X, the Replacements, Patti Smith, 'til Tuesday

►► Alanis Morissette, Magnapop

see also: *The Blake Babies*

David Yonke

Havana 3 A.M.

See: The Clash

Richie Havens

Born January 21, 1941, in Brooklyn, NY.

Though he first established himself as a folk singer on the New York coffee house circuit, Richie Havens's rich, craggy voice and prowess as an interpreter of others' material gained him national recognition during the late 1960s. His first couple of albums stiffed, but subsequent releases for MGM/Verve—notably *Mixed Bag*—encapsulated the humanistic, progressive mood of the time. Almost distinctive as his clarion vocals was Havens's powerful guitar playing, which involved hooking his thumb over the open-tuned strings and strumming furiously. His moment of greatest visibility came with his extended improvisation on the old spiritual "Motherless Child" at the Woodstock festival in 1969. He scored several hit singles during the next few years, recording memorable renditions of songs by Bob Dylan and the Beatles, as well as his own material. After a decade-long hiatus from recording, he began turning out albums again in 1987 and has appeared frequently with other '60s pop veterans at nostalgic reunion concerts. Aside from his musical endeavors, Havens has long worked as an environmental activist and done commercial voice-over work (he's best known in this regard as the singer of the Amtrak train jingle), as well as some film acting.

what to buy: *Resume: The Best of Richie Havens* ♪♪♪♪ (Rhino, 1993, compilation prod. Johanan Vigoda) is a generous anthology that draws from his best original songs and covers.

what to buy next: *Mixed Bag* ♪♪♪♪ (Verve, 1967, prod. Johanan Vigoda) is an early peak, boasting the anti-war classic "Handsome Johnny" and his versions of Dylan's "Just like a Woman" and the Beatles' "Eleanor Rigby."

what to avoid: *Mixed Bag II* ♪♪ (Verve, 1974, prod. Johanan Vigoda) is, like so many sequels, inferior to the original.

the rest:
A Richie Havens Record ♪♪ (Douglas, 1965)
Electric Havens ♪♪ (Douglas, 1966)
Something Else Again ♪♪♪ (Verve, 1968)
Richard P. Havens ♪♪ (Verve, 1969/1983)
Stonehenge ♪♪♪ (Stormy Forest, 1970)
State of Mind ♪♪♪ (Verve, 1971)
Alarm Clock ♪♪♪ (Verve, 1971)
Great Blind Degree ♪♪♪♪ (Verve, 1971)
Richie Havens on Stage ♪♪♪ (Verve, 1972)
Portfolio ♪♪♪ (Verve, 1973)
Richie Havens ♪♪ (Polydor, 1975)
The End of the Beginning ♪♪ (A&M, 1976)
Mirage ♪♪ (A&M, 1977)
Connections ♪♪ (Elektra, 1980)
Common Ground ♪♪♪ (EMI, 1984)
Simple Things ♪♪♪ (RBI, 1987)
Collection ♪♪♪ (Rykodisc, 1987)
Now ♪♪♪ (Solar/Epic, 1991)
Live at the Cellar Door ♪♪♪ (Five Star, 1991)
Cuts to the Chase ♪♪♪ (Forward, 1994)
Classics ♪♪♪ (Rebound, 1995)

worth searching for: *Richie Havens Sings the Beatles and Bob Dylan* (Rykodisc, 1986, prod. Douglas Yeager, Richie Havens) is an album full of covers from Havens's favorite songwriters.

influences:
◄◄ Bob Dylan, the Beatles, Sam Cooke, Leadbelly, Robert Johnson, Muddy Waters

►► Tracy Chapman, Ben Harper, Hootie & the Blowfish

Simon Glickman

Dale Hawkins

Born on August 22, 1938, in Goldmine, LA.

The guitar licks that anchored "Suzie Q," Dale Hawkins's piece of rock 'n' roll immortality, were played by James Burton, who left Louisiana for Hollywood—where he backed Ricky Nelson for the next 10 years and ultimately joined Elvis Presley's band. But Hawkins, a first cousin of another wild Louisiana rocker, Ronnie Hawkins, replaced Burton with Roy Buchanan. Before his recording career at Chicago's Chess label ended, Hawkins would also have Elvis's original guitarist, Scotty Moore, backing him up, not to mention the great blues sidemen that peopled most of the Chess sessions in Chicago. "Suzie Q" resonated through rock annals; from the Rolling Stones' version to the first hit single by Creedence Clearwater Revival. Hawkins gave up performing in favor of producing during the early '60s, ensuring his place as one of the many unsung greats of early rock 'n' roll.

what to buy: An 18-song collection, *Oh! Suzie Q: The Best of Dale Hawkins* ✍✍✍ (MCA Chess, 1995, prod. various) has the cream of his two-year association (1956–58) with Chess. Legendary guitarslingers James Burton, Roy Buchanan, and Scotty Moore add distinctive, hot licks to Hawkins's big hits, "Susie Q" and "My Babe," as well as the rockabilly-blues of "Ain't That Lovin' You Baby," "Tornado," and "Liza Jane."

what to buy next: A nice bit of rock archaeology, *Daredevil* ✍✍✍ (Norton, 1997, compilation prod. Billy Miller) unearths his early demos and previously unreleased alternate takes for a raw set Hawkins's fans have waited too long to hear.

worth searching for: Completists may want to check the import racks for *Let's All Twist: At the Miami Beach Peppermint Lounge* (Roulette, 1962/Edsel, 1995), positive proof that Hawkins was competing in the "Twist" era with style and vigor.

influences:

◄◄ Bill Haley, Howlin' Wolf, Jimmy Reed

►► Bobby Charles, Frankie Ford, Creedence Clearwater Revival

Joel Selvin and Ken Burke

Ronnie Hawkins

Born January 10, 1935, in Huntsville, AR.

There was once one brief shining moment, circa 1960, when Rompin' Ronnie Hawkins was poised to take over the world. All the crucial elements were in place: he and drummer Levon Helm were slowly assembling one of the greatest bands of all time (someday to become legendary in their own right as the Band); the head of Hawkins's label, Roulette, was spreading the word that his boy "moved better than Elvis, looked better than Elvis, and sang better than Elvis" (and you know, he wasn't that far off the mark); and most important of all, the stagnating state of rock simply begged for a talent like Hawkins's to grab it by the horns and shake it back to life. Unfortunately, Rompin' Ronnie chose to remain in his adopted home of Toronto, Canada, where he spent the 1960s buying up nightclubs and making money as opposed to making history. Oh sure, he made great music and even had a few hits ("Mary Lou," "Forty Days"), but unless you happened to be spending your Saturday nights on Toronto's Yonge Street strip, you would never know that the kind of rumble the Beatles were busy producing in Liverpool and the Stones were starting outside London was already well under way wherever Ronnie & the Hawks were performing. Sadly, as one by one his musicians left to seek their deserved fortunes outside of Toronto (guitarists Robbie Robertson and Roy Buchanan among them),

Hawkins stubbornly remained in Canada, only occasionally committing to tape his very special brand of Razorback rock. Still, when Toronto threw him a 60th birthday bash a few years back, Carl Perkins and even Jerry Lee Lewis felt they owed it to the Hawk to make an appearance, and that night the rafters shook as much as they had back in 1960. Still not convinced Hawkins is one of the greatest talents ever to sing rock 'n' roll? Well, name one other singer Jerry Lee would fly 1,000 miles to play piano for.

what to buy: *The Best of Ronnie Hawkins and the Hawks* ✍✍✍✍ (Rhino, 1990, prod. various) contains a decade's worth of the sounds Ronnie said "took us from the hills and the stills and on to the pills," culminating with his 1970 comeback hit "Down in the Alley," produced in Muscle Shoals with Duane Allman. And speaking of ferocious guitar solos, Robbie Robertson's on "Who Do You Love" sounds no less awe-inspiring now as it must have back in '63.

what to buy next: *Ronnie Hawkins: The Roulette Years* ✍✍✍✍ (Sequel, 1994, prod. various) fleshes out the years 1959 to 1963, and it's of particular interest in that it demonstrates just how fully the Band's unique approach to music was in evidence long before Mr. Dylan high-jacked them.

the rest:

Rock 'n' Roll Resurrection/Giant of Rock 'n' Roll ✍✍✍ (Monument, 1972, 1974/One Way, 1996)

influences:

◄◄ Muddy Waters, Jimmie Rodgers, Leadbelly, Bo Diddley, Hank Williams

►► David Clayton-Thomas, Creedence Clearwater Revival, Redneck Greece Delux

see also: *The Band*

Gary Pig Gold

Screamin' Jay Hawkins

Born Jalacy Hawkins, July 18, 1929, in Cleveland, OH.

Primarily known as one of early rock's great showmen, Hawkins found fame promoting himself as a rock 'n' roll lunatic—appropriate for both Wolfman Jack and Dr. Demento. A former Golden Gloves boxing champion, he embarked on a musical career working small clubs with an energetic R&B revue show that often found him carried onstage in a flaming coffin, using flash powder or waving spears with skulls on them at the audience. His work was attacked by the usual authorities; early singles, particularly the classic "I Put a Spell on You" (reportedly cut by a dead-drunk Hawkins), featured so much of his wild moaning and vocal thrashing that they were banned from some radio stations and, therefore, sold little. He continues to record for various independent labels, still singing about things like sex and cannibalism. A surprising cameo in Jim Jarmusch's 1989 cult film *Mystery Train,* as well as a song for *The X-Files* album project *Songs in the Key of X,* were enthusiastically received and led to a minor resurgence of interest in his career.

what to buy: *Portrait of a Man* 🎵🎵🎵 (Demon Records, 1995, prod. various) compiles his crucial tracks, with all the great histrionics of near-misses and should've-beens such as "The Whammy" and "Little Demon."

the rest:

Voodoo Jive: The Best of Screamin' Jay Hawkins 🎵🎵🎵 (Rhino, 1990)
Cow Fingers and Mosquito Pie 🎵🎵🎵 (Epic/Legacy, 1991)

influences:

◄◄ Howlin' Wolf, Muddy Waters

►► Bobby "Boris" Pickett, Marilyn Manson

Todd Wicks

Sophie B. Hawkins

Born Sophie Ballantine Hawkins, c. 1967, in New York, NY.

An accomplished musician who studied ethnic percussion and jazz, Sophie Hawkins prefers to call herself a songwriter—though she also has a bit of performance-artist exhibitionism in her, attested to by the nude photo of herself inside her debut album and by her declarations that she's "omnisexual," an intriguing term she never really took the next step to define. Nevertheless, Hawkins took her musical pursuits seriously, studying with Nigerian percussion master Babatunde Olatuni and doing a stint in Bryan Ferry's band before emerging as a solo artist during the early '90s.

what to buy: Hawkins emerged as a fully formed artist on her debut *Tongues and Tails* 🎵🎵🎵 (Columbia, 1992, prod. Rick Chertoff, Ralph Schuckett), which spawned the dance-floor hit "Damn, I Wish I Was Your Lover" that proudly hinted at homosexuality. Dig farther than that and you'll experience her abilities to seamlessly weave in and out of jazz, folk, and dance with a driving kind of tribal percussion sensibility. You'll also find an original, if not necessarily seminal, cover of Bob Dylan's "I Want You."

what to buy next: *Whaler* 🎵🎵🎵 (Columbia, 1994, prod. Stephen Lipson) displays Hawkins's quieter side with "As I Lay Me Down" and "The Ballad of Sleeping Beauty."

the rest:

Timbre N/A (Columbia, 1998)

influences:

◄◄ Sarah McLachlan, Belinda Carlisle

►► Jewel, Paula Cole

Christina Fuoco

Ted Hawkins

Born 1936, in Biloxi, MS. Died January 1, 1995, in Los Angeles, CA.

Singer-songwriter Ted Hawkins was one of the rawest and most unschooled musicians to ever record, yet he was able to convey deep emotions through his rudimentary vocal and guitar skills. Unknown for most of his life—though he recorded as early as 1971—Hawkins attracted attention as a street singer in the Venice Beach area near Los Angeles during the early '80s. His style is that of a country bluesman with a little city soul thrown in. He was on the verge of breaking big, with a new major label deal, when he died in 1995.

what to buy: Two posthumous releases capture Hawkins's essence, a nicely coordinated tandem that displays his mastery in both the studio and on stage. *The Ted Hawkins Story: Suffer No More* 🎵🎵🎵🎵 (Rhino, 1998, prod. various) is a well-chosen career summary, with all of the crucial songs represented. Even better is *The Final Tour* 🎵🎵🎵🎵 (Evidence, 1998, prod. Jerry Gordon), which features Hawkins where he's best—in front of a crowd, telling a few stories but mostly playing, singing, and conveying emotions from the depth of his soul.

what to buy next: Some of Hawkins's best work is on *Happy Hour* 🎵🎵🎵🎵 (Rounder, 1986/1993, Rounder, prod. Bruce Bromberg, Dennis Walker), where his vocals and guitar work wonders on such original tunes as "Bad Dog," "Revenge of Scorpio," and the title song. The tune "Happy Hour" should be a country-western standard with its barroom-worthy heart-break lyrics. Hawkins also kicks it out pretty good on *Songs from Venice Beach* 🎵🎵🎵🎵 (Evidence, 1995, prod. H. Thorp Minister III), a spare solo outing where he puts the country soul touch on such Motown classics as "Too Busy Thinking" and "Just My Imagination," and shows the Sam Cooke side of his heart on other songs.

the rest:

Watch Your Step 🎵🎵🎵 (Rounder, 1982/1993)
The Next Hundred Years 🎵🎵🎵 (DGC, 1994)

influences:

◄◄ Woody Guthrie, Leadbelly, Muddy Waters, Robert Johnson, Otis Redding, Sam Cooke, Curtis Mayfield

►► Beck, Robert Cray, Chris Isaac

Lawrence Gabriel and Gary Graff

Hayden

Born Hayden Desser, February 12, 1971, in Toronto, Ontario, Canada.

"Just a guy with a guitar" is how '90s troubadour Hayden frequently describes himself in interviews. A rising star in his native Canada, the fiercely private singer-songwriter specializes in dark acoustic numbers with droning, multi-tracked vocals and lyrics detailing the everyday boredom and romantic frustration of suburbia. Between part-time jobs (including one as a videomaker for Toronto bands), Hayden honed his act with acoustic sets in local clubs, often as the opener for nationally known acts. A collection of four-track recordings done in his bedroom in his parents' house interested the independent Canadian label Hardwood Records, which released them as his debut album. This record was subsequently picked up by Outpost, a subsidiary of Geffen Records, which made it a minor hit in the U.S.

what's available: *Everything I Long For* ♪♪ (Outpost Recordings, 1995, prod. Hayden) is somber, brooding, and inconsistent, ranging from the genuinely affecting ("Hardly") to the bombastic and overwrought ("Skates"). His follow-up, *The Closer I Get* ♪♪ (Outpost Recordings, 1998, prod. Hayden), suffers from Second-Album Syndrome, using kooky instrumentation (Hayden is credited with playing 16 instruments) in an attempt to make a familiar formula sound new.

worth searching for: Hayden contributed his best song to date to *Trees Lounge* (MCA Soundtracks, 1996, prod. various). His world-weary title track fits in brilliantly with a soundtrack of boozy, retro lounge tunes.

influences:

◀◀ Neil Young, Mark Eitzel

▶▶ Elliot Smith

Todd Wicks

Lili Haydn

Born 1971, in Los Angeles, CA.

Lili Haydn is the daughter of performer Lotus Weinstock, who at one time was romantically linked with Lenny Bruce and Jim Morrison. As a child, Haydn lived in an L.A. commune with her mother; she was allowed not only to follow the arts but to choose her name, which was Cherub until the age of 12. Haydn was a child actor and was in a handful of TV series, including *Kate Columbo* at the age of 7. She also played Rodney Dangerfield's daughter in the movie *Easy Money*. Haydn used her acting money to enter Brown University, where she graduated with a BA in political science. By the time she arrived there she was a talented violinist, eventually playing with the L.A. Philharmonic, the Rolling Stones, Jimmy Page and Robert Plant, Tony! Toni! Tone!, Porno for Pyros, B.B. King, No Doubt, Hootie & the Blowfish, Chaka Khan, Nusrat Fateh Ali Khan, Bush, Tracy Chapman, Tom Petty, and Me'Shell Ndegéocello. Haydn then decided to go it alone, doing her residency, so to speak, at the Viper Room in L.A. Backed by two cellos, bass, guitar, drums,

percussion, and keyboard, she's revealed herself to be part Nusrat Fateh Ali Khan and part Soundgarden.

what's available: Her debut album, *Lili* ♪♪♪ (Atlantic, 1997, prod. Lili Haydn), is a catharsis. Lili Haydn's mother had been suffering from a brain tumor, and her hospitalization and battle with the condition took its toll on her daughter. Haydn kicks off the album by blending funk, pop, and classical in "Stranger." The rest of the album features an eclectic mix of styles—including the spirituality of "Real" and the poignant "Mama" and "Daddy"—though her diversity is bound to confuse those looking for a simple, guitar-driven pop tune.

influences:

◀◀ Poe, Nusrat Fateh Ali Khan, Tori Amos

Darren Davis

Justin Hayward & John Lodge
See: The Moody Blues

Hazard
See: The Samples

Hazel

Formed 1991, in Portland OR.

Pete Krebs, vocals, guitar; Jody Bleyle, vocals, drums, guitar, organ; Brady Smith, bass; Fred Nemo, dancing.

Possibly the coolest band out of Portland, Hazel churns up a highly listenable batch of vaguely new-waveish songs in its own unique style. Despite being on Sub Pop, nary a trace of grunge is evident in the group's sound. Pete Krebs and Jody Bleyle alternate and combine their vocals in a dizzy flourish that infuses nearly all of their songs with an introspective urgency. And yes, Fred Nemo does indeed dance. Drummer Bleyle, though, is a lethal weapon with her distinctive stick work (on what appears to be a junior-sized drum kit) and atypically cutting vocals. Krebs's lead guitar and vocals are nearly as catchy, while Brady Smith's nimble basslines keep the often barely controlled (albeit beautiful) chaos grounded. Infectiously tuneful, Hazel should be huge stars.

what to buy: Originally titled *Lucky Dog*, *Toreador of Love* ♪♪♪♪ (Sub Pop, 1993/1995, prod. Jack Endino) is a beaut. With songs about baseball slugger Boog Powell, a cosmic chick, and boxer Joe Louis, this record has more hooks than a tackle box. Bleyle breathlessly sings each of her parts as if they will be her last, which Krebs's slightly understated vocals offset nicely. When the two sing in tandem, it seems like a race—where the listener is the winner.

what to buy next: *Airiana* ♫♫♫ (Candy Ass EP, 1997, prod. John Goodmanson, Tony Lash) is an excellent yet altogether too-short EP. "Mr. Magazine Man" is sung as a disconnected duet where both Bleyle's and Krebs's lyrics are printed separately on the sleeve. Hazel shows growth in both skill and dynamics on this record, which was released on the label co-owned by Bleyle. *Airiana* is an important record by a somewhat underappreciated yet fantastic band.

the rest:
Are You Going to Eat That? ♫♫♫ (Sub Pop, 1995)

worth searching for: *Jilted* (Sub Pop EP, 1993, prod, Kurt Bloch) is a rare, four-song CD single that features production from Fastback Kurt Bloch and assistance from Spinnane Rebecca Gates. Featuring two tracks ("Jilted," "Gilly's Legs") that are unavailable elsewhere and two ("Truly," "Constipation") that appear in slightly different form on *Toreador of Love*, this EP is well worth seeking out.

influences:

◀◀ The Velvet Underground, X, the Breeders, Game Theory, Ultra Vivid Scene

Barry M. Prickett

Roy Head

Born January 9, 1943, in Three Rivers, TX.

Roy Head is a top-notch blue-eyed country/soul singer whose 1965 hit "Treat Her Right" is still being played on oldies radio. Besides being a convincing soul vocalist, Head's good looks and dynamic sense of showmanship made him a popular club attraction. (Once Head participated in an eight-hour show where he more than held his own with the great Jerry Lee Lewis.) Head's first recordings with his band the Traits raved and rocked, but they sold poorly outside of Texas. After he signed with Back Beat Records, Head wrote and recorded "Treat Her Right," as convincing a soul record as anything on Stax-Volt. The single hit #2 on both the pop and soul charts, and he performed the number on ABC-TV's *Shindig*; the network's censors commanded him to substitute the word "kissin'" for "lovin'." Yeeesh! Head followed up with a strong interpretation of Roscoe Gordon's "Just a Little Bit" and his own "Apple of My Eye." Both registered in the lower regions of the pop Top 40, but none of his subsequent singles did as well. Head kept recording and made LPs for Dot, Dunhill, ABC, T.M.T., and Elektra. In 1977, Head shifted his focus from soul to country music, where he hit the Top 20 with "Come to Me" and "Now You See 'em, Now You Don't." His biggest country hits were duets with Janie Fricke on a remake of Rod Stewart's "Tonight's the Night" and "In Our Room." Though Head's country career dried up during the early '80s and none of his LPs

from that period remain in print, interest in his early hits remains strong.

what to buy: Head's greatest rock and soul hits are deftly compiled on *Treat Her Right: The Best of Roy Head* ♫♫♫ (Varese Vintage, 1995, compilation prod. Cary E. Mansfield) and includes "Treat Her Right," "Just a Little Bit," "Apple of My Eye," and "Teenage Letter" from the Backbeat Records era, plus three fine tracks that were previously unreleased. This stuff throbs with excitement.

what to buy next: Though short on hits, liner notes, and other collector information, *Slip Away—His Best Recordings* ♫♫♫ (Collectables Records, 1993) contains worthwhile blue-eyed soul versions of "Before You Accuse Me," "Bring It to Jerome," and "Money."

worth searching for: The vinyl-only import *Treat Me Right* (Bear Family, 1988) features no hits, but Head and his group the Traits rip-it-up and rave, bar-band style, on 10 pre-"Treat Her Right" recordings. Also, Head can be seen doing a dynamic version of his biggest hit on *Shindig Presents: Frat Party* (Rhino Home Video, 1991), which also features vintage TV performances by the Kingsmen, the Sir Douglas Quintet, the Righteous Brothers, and Jerry Lee Lewis on America's best-ever rock TV show.

influences:

◀◀ James Brown, Billy Lee Riley, the Righteous Brothers

▶▶ Tony Joe White, Delbert McClinton

Ken Burke

Topper Headon
See: The Clash

The Jeff Healey Band

Formed 1985, in Toronto, Ontario, Canada.

Jeff Healey (born March 25, 1966), vocals, guitar; Joe Rockman, bass; Tom Stephen, drums.

America's first glimpse of Jeff Healey's talent was in the Patrick Swayze movie *Road House*, where the blind guitarist demonstrated his five-fingered (he uses his thumb for effects) lap-top guitar work. The widespread exposure has been a mixed blessing, as his unusual technique has received more attention than his legitimately exciting playing. His path to guitar wizardry is further hampered by his penchant for playing generally unchallenging album-rock songs which don't make the most of his talents; Healey often opens up more when he's jamming with others.

what to buy: *See the Light* ♫♫♫ (Arista, 1988, prod. Greg Ladanyi, Jimmy Iovine, Thom Panunzio) is a strong debut, with the sweet balladry of "Angel Eyes" and bar band rave-ups such as "Confidence Man."

what to buy next: *Hell to Pay* ♫♫♫♪ (Arista, 1990, prod. Ed Stasium) tightens up the sound with better straightforward rockers, although mawkish cameos by George Harrison (on "While My Guitar Gently Weeps") and others knock it back a bit.

what to avoid: *Cover to Cover* ♫♫ (Arista, 1995, prod. Thom Panunzio, the Jeff Healey Band) is an unremarkable, pedestrian album of—as advertised—other peoples' songs.

the rest:
Feel This ♫♫♫ (Arista, 1992)

worth searching for: The deleted soundtrack *Road House* (Arista 1987, prod. various) finds Healey cutting loose with some of his best playing on covers of the Doors' "Roadhouse Blues," "Hootchie Cootchie Man," and Bob Dylan's "When the Night Comes Falling from the Sky." But beware of the two Swayze songs lurking amidst other contributions from Bob Seger, Otis Redding, and Little Feat.

influences:

◄◄ Eric Clapton, Willie Dixon, John Lee Hooker, Jeff Beck, Stevie Ray Vaughan

Allan Orski

The Health & Happiness Show

Formed 1990, in New York, NY.

James Mastro, lead vocals, guitar, bouzouki, harmonica; Vincent DeNunzio, drums, vocals; Dave de Castro, bass, vocals (1995–present); Graham Maby, bass, vocals (1990–91); Tony Shanahan, bass, vocals, keyboards (1992–94); Sean Grissom, cello (1990–91); Todd Reynolds, fiddle (1992–94); Kerryn Tolhurst, mandolin, lap steel, Dobro, guitar (1992–94); Richard Lloyd, guitar; Ivan Julian, guitar; Erik Della Penna, guitar; Kevin Salem, guitar.

Finding himself in dire need of some honest, simple music-making after the sour break-ups of the Bongos and Strange Cave, songwriter James Mastro initiated a series of kitchen-table hoots alongside old pal St. Vincent DeNunzio (ex-Feelies, the Richard Hell Band), and the modern-day jug music that resulted as additional friends joined in led to the formation of a bona fide band several months later. Naming itself after the Hank Williams radio show sponsored by half alcohol/half laxative elixir Hadacol ("the music was the laxative and beer was the alcohol," Mastro recalls), the Health & Happiness Show wasted no time committing to tape its uniquely countrified brand of pop, and the two resulting albums are cited today as the alt.country movement's opening salvos.

what's available: The group's splendid debut, *Tonic* ♫♫♫ (Bar/None, 1993, prod. James Mastro, Tony Shanahan), mixed the Gram-Parsons-plays-*Revolver*-sound H&H was already becoming known for with refreshing hints of Fairport Convention–styled neo-folk. On *Instant Living* ♫♫♫ (Bar/None, 1995, prod. James Mastro, Tony Shanahan), a louder, leaner, almost Crazy Horse approach became readily apparent, thanks in no small part to the guitar interplay between Mastro and new recruit Richard Lloyd.

influences:

◄◄ Hank Williams, Howlin' Wolf, Television

►► The Delevantes, Demolition String Band, Agnelli & Rave

Gary Pig Gold

Heart /Lovemongers

Formed 1970, in Seattle, WA.

Ann Wilson, vocals, guitar, flute; Nancy Wilson, guitar, mandolin, vocals; Howard Leese, guitar, keyboards; Roger Fisher, guitar (1970–80); Michael Derosier, drums (1970–82); Steve Fossen, bass (1970–82); Mark Andes, bass (1982–93); Denny Carmassi, drums (1982–93).

Considering Heart's status as one of the rare female-fronted rock groups during the '70s, it's ironic that the band's history didn't begin until Ann Wilson decided to move to Vancouver, Canada, to live with her then-boyfriend, Roger Fisher. Before long, they had sent for Ann's kid sister Nancy and formed Heart with some friends from Seattle. The group's debut album, combining the Wilsons' singer-songwriter material with harder-edged rock, sold slowly at first but eventually scored three hit singles and sold more than three million copies. Through the '70s and early '80s the band recorded several classic rock anthems, only to find its audience waning in the wake of heavy metal's new popularity during the '80s. Drafting a new rhythm section, the group turned to metalized power ballads and videos featuring Nancy's impressive good looks for a mid-'80s career resurgence that lasted until grunge turned '90s radio upside down. With yet another rhythm section—bassist Fernando Saunders and drummer Denny Fongheiser—Howard Leese and the Wilson sisters developed a stripped-down, unplugged presentation before cutting an album with longtime pals and collaborators Sue Ennis and Frank Cox under the name the Lovemongers.

what to buy: From the complex, synthesizer-drenched classic rock mysticism of "Magic Man" to the straight-up rock of "Crazy on You" and the dreamy title track, *Dreamboat Annie*

♫♫♫♫ (Capitol, 1976, prod. Mike Flicker) expertly melds a singer-songwriter's imagination with a rocker's muscle.

what to buy next: Although less focused than the debut, *Little Queen* ♫♫♫ (Portrait, 1977, prod. Mike Flicker) brings more of what made Heart a groundbreaking arena rock band, with legendary workouts such as "Barracuda" and the title track powering the airwaves for years to come. Similarly, the first live record, *Heart Greatest Hits/Live* ♫♫♫ (Epic, 1980, prod. various), brings together all the classic tracks from the group's first five albums along with a shot of moderately interesting live tracks that let you avoid the sometimes-embarrassing filler on past records.

what to avoid: Stung by reaction among the rock crowd to its mid-'80s ballads, Heart tried to present a harder edge on *Brigade* **woof!** (Capitol, 1990, prod. Ritchie Zito), a record that only wound up demonstrating how badly the group's songwriting skills had deteriorated. And since *Rock the House Live!* **woof!** (Capitol, 1991, prod. Heart, Richard Erwin) compounds the mistake by featuring six cuts from *Brigade*, its pathetic results are predictable.

the rest:
Magazine ♫♫♫ (Mushroom, 1978)
Dog and Butterfly ♫♫♫ (Portrait, 1978)
Bebe Le Strange ♫♫♫ (Epic, 1980)
Private Audition ♫♫ (Epic, 1982)
Passionworks ♫♫♫ (Epic, 1983)
Heart ♫♫♫ (Capitol, 1985)
Bad Animals ♫♫♫ (Capitol, 1987)
With Love From ♫♫♫ (Capitol, 1988)
Desire Walks On ♫♫ (Capitol, 1993)
Road Back Home ♫♫♫♫ (Capitol, 1995)
Definitive Collection ♫♫♫ (Feedback, 1995)
Greatest Hits ♫♫♫ (Capitol, 1997)
Greatest Hits ♫♫♫♫ (Legacy, 1998)

worth searching for: Heart is one of the first bands to issue a multimedia CD-ROM of its history, called *Heart: 20 Years of Rock N' Roll*. It's a great way for novices to familiarize themselves with the group's exhaustive history.

solo outings:
Lovemongers:
Battle of Evermore ♫♫♫ (Capitol, 1993)
Whirlygig ♫♫♫ (Will, 1997)

influences:
◀◀ Led Zeppelin, Joni Mitchell, Janis Joplin

▶▶ Veruca Salt, Alannah Myles, 4 Non Blondes, Hole, Meredith Brooks

Eric Deggans

WHAT ALBUM CHANGED YOUR LIFE?

The [Beatles'] white album, I think. It's just got every single different type of song on there that the Beatles ever produced. It was so diverse; it just spun my head around. It got me thinking what a band could be, that a band didn't have to just be like Gary Puckett & the Union Gap, and have one little schtick and stick to it. You could be a complete chameleon.

Ann Wilson (of Heart)

The Reverend Horton Heat
Formed 1990.

Jim Heath (a.k.a. the Reverend Horton Heat), guitar, vocals; Jim Wallace (a.k.a. Jimbo), upright bass; Patrick Bentley (a.k.a. Taz), drums (1990–94); Scott Churilla, drums (1994–present).

Rockabilly seemed to be a forgotten art during the early and mid-'90s; after the demise of '80s revivalists the Stray Cats, no one seemed to pick up the twang torch—that is until the Reverend Horton Heat took the podium. But unlike the Cats, the Rev—the man and the trio—started out on an indie label and were able to play as rough as they wanted to, without worrying about hits, or (importantly) political correctness. The result is that RHH is the best rockabilly act since they heyday of Carl Perkins and Eddie Cochran. While some critics have regarded the band as something of a novelty—an accusation that the Reverend has combated by no longer doing "sermons" during the band's shows—they are no more so than blues bands or ska groups. Like those traditionalists, they go with what they know.

what to buy: *The Full-Custom Gospel Sounds of the Reverend Horton Heat* ♫♫♫♫ (Sub Pop, 1993, prod. Gibby Haynes) is one of the few records that may appeal to fans of vintage rockabilly, the Ramones, *and* AC/DC. Plus, the group eschews the political correctness of many other bands of the era, making the album all the more entertaining.

what to buy next: *Smoke 'em If You Got 'Em* ♫♫♫ (Sub Pop, 1990, prod. the Reverend Horton Heat), the band's debut, shows RHH before it grew out of its kitchy phase. But, camp or not, the group rocked from the get-go.

what to avoid: *Liquor in the Front* ♫♫ (Interscope, 1994, prod. Al Jourgensen) was an experiment that probably looked good on paper. Having Ministry's Al Jourgensen produce RHH probably seemed like a good idea at the time, but it resulted in the band's least memorable album.

the rest:
It's Martini Time ♫♫♫ (Interscope, 1996)

worth searching for: The Rev and the Supersuckers did a great split CD single during 1995 for Sub Pop, with the Rev covering the Suckers' "Caliente" and the Suckers doing the Rev's "400 Bucks" (it also includes the original versions). Also worth checking out: the Rev's cover of "Hello Walls" from the Willie Nelson tribute album *Twisted Willie* (Justice Records, 1996), on which Willie even sings a verse (!), and a medley of the cartoon themes for *Johnny Quest* and *Stop that Pigeon* from the *Saturday Morning Cartoon's Greatest Hits* (MCA, 1995) compilation.

influences:
◀◀ Carl Perkins, Eddie Cochran, the Stray Cats, AC/DC, the Ramones

Brian Ives

Heatmiser
See: Elliott Smith

Heaven 17
Formed 1979, in Sheffield, England. Disbanded 1988.

Martyn Ware, synthesizers; Ian Craig Marsh, synthesizers; Glenn Gregory, vocals.

A spinoff from the Human League, Heaven 17 was a synthesizer driven techno-trio with a bit more to it than the average slick-boy outfit plucking single notes from their racks of keyboards. The trio sought a more interesting, albeit less accessible and commercially rewarding, route of innovative electro-funk. And in Glenn Gregory it had a singer who could actually express himself, which is more than most of his electronic peers can warble in their one-note defense. Of course, this kind of thing can't go on forever and the band called it quits in 1988, after failing to make sufficient forays into radio gaga.

what to buy: *Penthouse and Pavement* ♫♫♫ (Virgin, 1987/Caroline, 1997) and *Luxury Gap* ♫♫♫ (Virgin, 1987/Caroline, 1997) establish an innovative sophistication level that's higher than the group was given credit for.

what to buy next: *Teddy Bear, Duke, and Psycho* ♫♫♫♫ (Caroline/Virgin, 1988) is a solid last effort, full of highly crafted atmospheric soundscapes and out-and-out funk.

worth searching for: The recently deleted *The Best of Heaven 17: Higher and Higher* (Virgin, 1993, prod. various) is a solid compilation of key tracks and remixes.

influences:
◀◀ Human League, Kraftwerk
▶▶ Orbital, the Orb, the Egg

Allan Orski

Michael Hedges
Born December 31, 1953, in Enid, OK. Died November 30, 1997, near Boonville, CA.

Michael Hedges's radical approach to the acoustic guitar effectively transformed it into a different instrument, creating sounds no one else has attempted with six strings. He changed the tunings, hammered and pulled the chords, tapped the frets, tossed off lightning leads, and chose unusual chord progressions. Hedges studied classical guitar, earned a degree in composition from the Peabody Conservatory, and then attended Stanford University's electronic music department. At first, Hedge's meditative instrumentals were tagged new age, but he soon added his own vocals and his playing became too bold and quirky for that, or any, label. His own descriptions, although told in jest, were the most accurate, including "violent acoustic," "heavy mental," and "wacka-wacka." Hedges's virtuoso technique led *Guitar Player* magazine to elect him to their "Gallery of the Greats," but he used the instrument as a tool for artistic expression, not just to thrill guitar fans. In 1997, Hedges was found dead in his car at the bottom of a ravine, having driven off the side of the road in a late-night accident near his California home.

what to buy: *Oracle* ♫♫♫♫ (Windham Hill, 1996, prod. Michael Hedges) is a magnificent display of Hedges's broad-ranging guitar forays, from the flashy fun of "Jitterboogie" and "Jitterboogie (family version)" to the weighty sadness of "Dirge," made more poignant by Hedges's untimely death. *Live on the Double Planet* ♫♫♫♫ (Windham Hill, 1987, prod. Michael Hedges) is a safe introduction to Hedges's unorthodox guitar style and compositional talents. His covers of rock classics ("All Along the Watchtower," "Come Together") show his ability to reinvent the obvious. The instrumental majesty of *Aerial Boundaries* (Windham Hill, 1984, prod. William Ackerman, Michael Hedges, Steven Miller) marks Hedges's emergence as a guitar rebel but is relatively tame and much more accessible than his later efforts.

what to buy next: *Taproot* ♫♫♫ (Windham Hill, 1990, prod. Michael Hedges) is a concept album in which Hedges's instrumental prowess explores "classic mythic archetypes" with themes centering on planting, growth, and harvesting. The concept is obscure but Hedges's guitar brilliance is not.

what to avoid: *Breakfast in the Field* ♫ (Windham Hill, 1981, prod. William Ackerman), his recording debut, is tepid new age fare.

the rest:
Watching My Life Go By ♫♫♫ (Windham Hill, 1985)
The Road to Return ♫♫♫ (Windham Hill, 1994)
Best Of N/A (Windham Hill, 1998)

worth searching for: Hedges's playing is a highlight on the David Crosby solo album *Oh Yes I Can* (Atlantic, 1989, prod. various). Also, *Sounds of Wood & Steel: A Windham Hill Collection* (Windham Hill, 1998, prod. T.J. Baden, Larry Hamby) is a guitar compilation featuring one of Hedges's last tunes, "Java Man."

influences:
◀◀ Leo Kottke, Martin Carthy, John Martyn, Edgar Varese

▶▶ Chris Whitley, Ben Harper, Craig Chaquico

David Yonke

Helium

Formed 1992, in Boston, MA.

Mary Timony, guitar, vocals; Brian Dunton, bass (1992–95); Ash Bowie, bass (1995–present); Shawn King Devlin, drums.

Mary Timony, of the infamous D.C. band Autoclave, was asked to come in on a new project headed by Jason Hatfield (Julianna's brother) and backed by the former Dumptruck rhythm section of Brian Dunton and Shawn King Devlin. Soon after, Hatfield was arrested for carjacking, so Timony took over as leader, renamed the band, and Helium was born. Wallowing in distortion-heavy punk, melancholy lyrics, and Timony's paradoxically waifish yet powerful voice, the band produces an interesting, if not particularly unusual, sound.

what to buy: *Dirt of Luck* ♫♫♫ (Matador, 1995, prod. Adam Laus) deals with many of the same themes as its precedessor, *Pirate Prude*, but this time out Helium introduces a sound with lush, interweaving hooks and notably improved musical prowess.

what to buy next: *Pirate Prude* ♫♫♫ (Matador EP, 1994, prod. Adam Laus) offers a rich musical experience complete with dissonant, moody guitar and sad, apocalyptic vocals that tell the tragic tale of lost innocence and femininity.

influences:
◀◀ My Bloody Valentine, Sonic Youth

Bryan Lassner

Richard Hell & the Voidoids

Formed 1976, in New York, NY.

Richard Hell (born Richard Meyers, October 2, 1949 in Lexington, KY), vocals, bass; Robert Quine, guitar (1976–82); Ivan Julian, guitar (1976–79); Naux, guitar, (1980–82); Mike Paumgardhen, guitar (1983); Jeff Freeman, guitar (1983); Jody Harris, guitar (1985); Jerry Antonius, bass, keyboards (1978–79); John (or Jahn) Xavier (a.k.a. Xcessive), bass (1979); Ted Horowitz, bass (1985); Marc Bell, drums (1976–78); Frank Mauro, drums (1978–79); James Morrison, drums (1979); Fred Maher, drums (1980–82); Chuck Wood, drums (1983); Anton Fier, drums (1985).

Poet/writer Richard Hell formed his own group after being a founding member of the Neon Boys (in 1971), a band which by 1973 had split into Television and the Heartbreakers. The Neon Boys are heard on a posthumous 1980 EP on Shake Records, now out of print; Hell appears on Television's "Little Johnny Jewel" single and the bootleg album *Double Exposure*, consisting of demos produced by Brian Eno and live recordings. Famously, it was Hell's fashion sense—ripped clothes, slogans scrawled on T-shirts, safety pins—that influenced Malcolm McLaren's construction of the Sex Pistols' look. Even more influentially, Hell blurted out nihilistic, decadent lyrics ("Love Comes in Spurts") in a tuneless voice, epitomizing the attitude and sound of punk, with the band's rhythms matching his lurching cadences. A major collaborator in the Voidoids sound was guitarist Robert Quine, who combined the choppy chording of Lou Reed in the Velvet Underground with the dissonant polytonal jagged lines of Miles Davis's '70s guitarists. Myriad personnel changes found Hell the only constant (drummer Bell became Marky Ramone), though Quine figures in all the important lineups—which is to say all the lineups before the original group split up in 1982. (Dare we say that fitful appearances of later Voidoids lineups were financially motivated? Hell's bad habits, which he has chronicled freely, required some cash flow.) After eventually retiring (more or less) from playing, Hell concentrated on writing and also got a few acting gigs, including a cameo in *Desperately Seeking Susan*. A one-shot band, Dim Stars, was built around him by admirers from the next generation of downtown New York rockers—Sonic Youth's Thurston Moore and Steve Shelley and producer/Gumball leader Don Fleming.

what to buy: *Blank Generation* ♫♫♫♫ (Sire, 1977, prod. Richard Gottehrer, Richard Hell) is a seminal punk album showcasing Quine's guitar imagination. Though Hell has insisted that the title track speaks of the open possibilities of an unlabeled generation, it has inevitably been interpreted more cynically, which in hindsight doesn't seem like a mistake. The CD varies from the original LP by adding two bonus tracks; but it also substitutes an inferior version of "Down at the Rock and Roll Club" when, at less than 41 minutes, there's room for both.

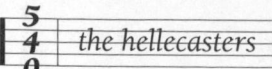
what to buy next: *Destiny Street* ♪♪♪ (Red Star, 1982/Razor & Tie, 1994, prod. Alan Betrock) is less reckless than *Blank Generation*, though "polished" would be an overstatement. Mostly it's more reflective, especially on "Time" and the funky title track, and the songwriting seems more thorough and less reliant on shock effects.

the rest:
R.I.P. ♪♪♪ (ROIR, 1986)
Funhunt ♪♪♪ (ROIR, 1990)

worth searching for: If you ever find the Voidoids' debut 7" (Ork, 1976), be prepared to shell out a lot. Besides early versions of "Blank Generation" and "Another World," it includes the non-album "You Gotta Lose."

solo outings:
Richard Hell:
Go Now ♪♪♥ (Tim Kerr, 1995)

Dim Stars (Hell, Quine) :
Dim Stars ♪♪ (Caroline, 1992)

influences:

◀◀ The Velvet Underground, Lou Reed, the Stooges, Captain Beefheart, Arthur Rimbaud, Charles Baudelaire

▶▶ The Sex Pistols, DNA, Arto Lindsay, the Contortions, the Minutemen, Sonic Youth, Matthew Sweet

see also: *Robert Quine*

Steve Holtje

The Hellecasters

Formed 1990, in Los Angeles, CA.

Will Ray, guitars, sitar, bull horn; John Jorgenson, guitars, keyboards, bass, mandocaster; Jerry Donahue, guitars.

What happens when three of the nation's most acclaimed guitarists get together for a one-off gig in a Hollywood nightclub armed with, in their own words, "three screaming Telecasters on a mission to spread the Gospel According to Leo Fender"? Well, for one thing, a contract with "thinking Monkee" Michael Nesmith's Pacific Arts label, and eight years later this one-off is still going strong. Comprising a trio of already-established talents—John Jorgenson was a founding member of the Desert Rose Band, Will Ray has recorded alongside everyone from Steve Earle to Tom Jones, and Jerry Donahue was no less than Richard Thompson's replacement in Fairport Convention—the Hellecasters set out to construct a surprisingly ego-free musical playground in which to weave their own particular brand of madness, unencumbered by such things as lead singers or producers shouting "Turn it down!" Applying both sounds and material from past masters and attacking them anew with their

own unique approach and, in Ray's case particularly, technique, the Hellecasters are confidently, and with humor always intact, dragging the fine art of instrumental rock kicking and screaming towards the next millennium.

what's available: One listen to "Orange Blossom Special" from *The Return of the Hellecasters* ♪♪♪ (Pacific Arts, 1993/Pharaoh, 1997, prod. Hellecasters, Dan Fredman) demonstrates perfectly how each guitarist's style complements, rather than battles, the others'. This unholy trinity is even more evident on the equally ambitious *Escape from Hollywood* ♪♪♪ (Rio, 1994/Pharaoh, 1997, prod. Hellecasters) and the brand new *Hell III: New Axes to Grind* ♪♪♪♪ (Pharaoh, 1997, prod. Hellecasters), albums which are showing an influence already on musicians battling within the rock, alternative country, and even jazz idioms.

solo outings:
Jerry Donahue:
Telecasting ♪♪♪ (Spindrift, 1986)
Neck of the Wood ♪♪♪ (Cross Three, 1992)

John Jorgenson:
After You've Gone ♪♪♪♥ (Curb, 1988)

Will Ray:
Invisible Birds ♪♪♪♪ (Country Town Music, 1996)

influences:

◀◀ James Burton, Duane Eddy, Danny Gatton, the Ventures

▶▶ Eddie Shaver, Human Tornados, Phil Emmanuel

see also: *Fairport Convention*

Gary Pig Gold

Levon Helm

See: The Band

Helmet

Formed 1989, in New York, NY.

Page Hamilton, vocals, guitar; Peter Mengede, guitar (1989–94); Rob Echeverria, guitar (1994–present); Henry Bogdan, bass; John Stamier, drums.

Helmet burst onto the rock scene quite literally—with a barrage of volume, riffs, rage, and power. Led by ex–Band of Susans guitarist Page Hamilton, Helmet cranked out some of the heaviest, thickest power chord rock around. Dubbed the next Nirvana, Helmet was the subject of an intense major label bidding war and was saddled with astronomical expectations which it never lived up to in the commercial sense. What separated the group from the grunge scene was its short-haired, straight-edge appearance (à la Fugazi), and the fact that its members were university-educated musicians whose formal training made Helmet a tighter, more efficient unit—which in turn, only enhanced the power of its start-stop monster riffs and locomotive rhythms.

what to buy: *Meantime* ✯✯✯✯ (Interscope, 1992, prod. Steve Albini) is really all the Helmet one needs. Punctuated by short but beyond-powerful blasts of guitar fury, this album gets in and gets out quickly, leveling everything in its path with its molten, bare-bones attack.

the rest:

Born Annoying ✯✯ (Amphetamine Reptile EP, 1989)
Strap It On ✯✯✯ (Amphetamine Reptile, 1990/Interscope, 1992)
Betty ✯✯✯✯ (Interscope, 1994)
Born Annoying ✯✯ (Amphetamine Reptile, 1996)
Aftertaste ✯✯✯✯ (Interscope, 1997)

influences:

◀◀ Black Sabbath, Black Flag, Glenn Branca

see also: *Handsome*

Christopher Scanlon

Mike Henderson

Born July 7, 1951, in Yazoo City, MS.

Mississippi-born and Missouri-raised, Mike Henderson makes music that is a high-octane mix of country, blues, and rock 'n' roll. A former member of the Missouri blues-rock outfit the Bel-Airs, Henderson kicked around Nashville doing session work for artists such as Kevin Welch and Tracy Nelson and writing songs (including the Fabulous Thunderbirds' "Powerful Stuff"). After an abortive run with RCA's Nashville branch, Henderson signed with Dead Reckoning, an artist-run label where he's clearly more at home.

what to buy: The bluesiest of Henderson's albums, *First Blood* ✯✯✯✯ (Dead Reckoning, 1996, prod. Peter Coleman) (with the Bluebloods), is a scorcher, but it shares a roadhouse mentality with the best honky-tonk country music. And besides, a song titled "When I Get Drunk" can surely fit in either genre..

the rest:

Edge of Night ✯✯✯✯ (Dead Reckoning, 1996)

worth searching for: The unjustifiably deleted *Country Music Made Me Do It* (RCA, 1994) confounded Henderson's label, who didn't know how to market his renegade sound.

influences:

◀◀ Jerry Lee Lewis, Merle Haggard, Dave Alvin

Daniel Durchholz

Jimi Hendrix
/The Jimi Hendrix Experience
/Band of Gypsys

Born James Marshall Hendrix, November 27, 1943, in Seattle, WA. Died September 18, 1970, in London, England.

The Experience, 1966–69: Jimi Hendrix, guitar, vocals; Noel Redding, bass, vocals; Mitch Mitchell, drums. Band of Gypsys, 1969-70: Jimi Hendrix, guitar, vocals; Billy Cox, bass; Buddy Miles, drums, vocals.

Rock 'n' roll would not be what it is today without Jimi Hendrix's influence. He defined the electric guitar as the quintessential rock instrument in ways that no player before him did. As Charlie Parker's name is synonymous with the jazz saxophone, so is Hendrix's name with the rock electric guitar. While many guitarists deserve credit for various innovations during rock's infancy, it was Hendrix who assimilated the instrument's known vocabulary, exploded its preconceptions, and, through his genius for color and sound, created for it a new sonic form. Hendrix's singular style evolved from a heady brew of musical and cultural sources; his playing was influenced by both the blues and jazz, and his early professional outings—most notably as a member of the Isley Brothers' band—bore these influences out in a competent but unremarkable fashion. Increasingly, however, Hendrix was drawn to the evolving rock scene of the mid-'60s; influenced by the flowering psychedelic scene and the social conscience of musicians such as Bob Dylan, he developed a philosophy of personal freedom and unfettered expression, a mission of universal emancipation through music. Armed with this world view and his technical skills, Hendrix approached the guitar as an extension of his own personality and beliefs, making it an instrument of emotional expression without boundaries. While he was undeniably a virtuoso on the instrument, it was not just his guitar playing that made Hendrix a rock legend. Perhaps just as important was his commitment to song structure and ideology; his songs served a purpose beyond being a forum for guitar histrionics. He did not see his guitar as an end unto itself but as just one part of a unified musical vision. In addition, he believed that his music should speak to people, challenge presentiments, and provoke change; he was committed to the hippie ideal of making the world a better place through music. Also important to the Hendrix legend was the mythic gypsy persona he chose for himself and his bands (the Experience and Band of Gypsys), one that had great influence on fashion in the '60s and '70s. This canny incarnation—that of a colorful, fantastic character—helped him straddle the color line and reach a vast white audience without compromising his musical roots. His ability to make a wide variety of musical styles widely accessible (notably his later forays into jazz) also made him an ideal musical ambassador and teacher. Hendrix's career as a solo artist lasted only three years; that he exercised such a tremendous influence on modern music—both sonically and visually—in that short period is just further evidence of his brilliance. Hendrix fans were thrilled in 1996 when his father Al gained control of his recordings and—with daughter Janie Hendrix at the helm—established Experience Hendrix, a record label and magazine enterprise that began making Hendrix's original recordings as well as music from his vaults available in its best-ever sound quality—even setting up a side label, Dagger Records, to release authorized "bootlegs" of great audience and soundboard tapes and therefore undercut some of the pirate market that had grown around Hendrix's work.

what to buy: The foundation of the Hendrix collection is his three studio albums with the Experience. *Electric Ladyland* ♫♫♫♫ (Reprise, 1968/Experience Hendrix/MCA, 1997, prod. Jimi Hendrix) is Hendrix's masterpiece with the Experience (bassist Noel Redding and drummer Mitch Mitchell), the album that provided a breathtaking glimpse into the guitarist's future potential and ambitions. Just as the Beatles' *Sgt. Pepper's Lonely Hearts Club Band* raised the bar on what could be called pop, so did *Electric Ladyland* change the perception of what a rock record could be; sonically, the album is light-years ahead of any of its contemporaries, with Hendrix making copious use of then-new multi-track recording technology. *Axis: Bold As Love* ♫♫♫♫ (Reprise, 1968/Experience Hendrix/MCA, 1997, prod. Chas Chandler) preceded *Electric Ladyland* by less than a year, and it is an excellent illustration of the rate at which Hendrix and the Experience matured, sonically and thematically, between the two releases. This is not to say that *Axis* is any less of an album than its follow-up—many songs rival those found on *Electric Ladyland*. For those fond of Hendrix's gentle side, the album offers a bounty of beauty in the delicate chording and melodies of "Little Wing," "Castles Made of Sand," and the title song. There are also plentiful examples of the master's molten way with blues-rock, particularly "If 6 Was 9" and the warped "Up from the Skies." *Are You Experienced?* ♫♫♫♫ (Reprise, 1967/Experience Hendrix/MCA, 1997, prod. Chas Chandler) is the first blast, an awesome recording that had nearly the impact that *Sgt. Pepper* had earlier that same year. "Purple Haze," "Manic Depression," and "Hey Joe" comprise as formidable an opening salvo as any album, before or since, and with later tracks such as "The Wind Cries Mary," "Fire," "Foxey Lady," and the title track, it's a wonder every other guitarist didn't simply lay down his or her instrument in surrender.

what to buy next: Hendrix's Experience era is also well-served by *BBC Sessions* ♫♫♫♫ (Experience Hendrix/MCA, 1998, prod. Janie Hendrix, Eddie Kramer, John McDermott), a stellar collection of broadcast recordings that tracks the growth in Hendrix's playing between 1967 and 1969; it also features some brief but illuminating interview snippets. *Band of Gypsys* ♫♫♫♫ (Capitol, 1970/1997, prod. Heaven Research), capturing an amazing and amazingly funky New Year's Eve 1970 live performance at the Filmore East in New York City, is Hendrix's uncertain but still arresting transition toward a new direction, one that would incorporate more of his soul and jazz influences, as well as a new fluidity to his playing that's best displayed in the sublime (all 12-plus minutes of it) "Machine Gun." (For the record, Hendrix's spelling of "Gypsys" is wrong, it should be "Gypsies"; but it isn't worth correcting, just noting.) *First Rays of the New Rising Sun* ♫♫♫♫ (Experience Hendrix/MCA, 1997, prod. Jimi Hendrix, Eddie Kramer, Mitch Mitchell, John Jansen) is the most legitimate representation of what Hendrix was after following the Experience, with exceptional performances on tracks such as "Freedom," "Angel," "Room Full of Mirrors," and "Hey Baby (New Rising Sun)." Much of this material was issued soon after his death as *Cry of Love*; that album, however, was poorly mixed by people unfamiliar with the project and included overdubs by other musicians—*First Rays*, lovingly produced by Hendrix's studio collaborators, is a far better representation of the man's intentions.

what to avoid: *Voodoo Soup* ♫♫ (MCA, 1994, prod. Alan Douglas), which repeats the same mistakes that were made on *Cry of Love*, claims to be the unfinished masterpiece that Hendrix was working on before his untimely death. Unfinished is what the material sounds like, despite the best efforts of studio swamis to conjure the spirit of Hendrix in completing these tracks. Again, much of the same material is better served by *First Rays*.

the rest:
Blues ♫♫♫♫ (MCA, 1994)
Live at Winterland ♫♫♫♫ (Rykodisc, 1987)
Radio One ♫♫♫♫ (Rykodisc, 1988)
Woodstock ♫♫♫♫ (MCA, 1994)
The Ultimate Experience ♫♫♫♫ (MCA, 1993)
South Saturn Delta ♫♫♫♫ (Experience Hendrix/MCA, 1997)
Live at the Oakland Coliseum ♫♫♫ (Dagger, 1998)

worth searching for: If your mission is to search out Hendrix's out-of-print classics, you've got your work cut out for you. A morass of legal wranglings over ownership and MCA's purchase of his Reprise catalog have left many of his recordings in limbo. Of special note is the album he recorded with the Band of Gypsys lineup (and others), *Cry of Love*. Noting the caveats mentioned above, this is still an interesting introduction to the steps Hendrix was taking after the demise of the Experience.

influences:

◀◀ Buddy Guy, Freddie King, the Beatles, Chuck Berry, Bob Dylan, the Yardbirds, Howlin' Wolf, Robert Johnson

▶▶ Stevie Ray Vaughn, Robin Trower, Van Halen, Ernie Isley,

Jimi Hendrix **(Archive Photos)**

Don Henley (© Ken Settle)

Lenny Kravitz, Prince, Miles Davis, Carlos Santana, Eric Clapton, Sly Stone, Eric Johnson

David Galens and Gary Graff

Don Henley

Born July 22, 1947, in Gilmer, TX.

Don Henley has had the greatest solo success of all the Eagles, both commercially and artistically. Not only has he scored substantial hits—"The Boys of Summer," "The End of the Innocence"—but he's also advanced a thoughtful, populist viewpoint that, unlike the cynical disdain of late-period Eagles, is filled with hope and a desire to affect change. Henley's solo career was slowed by a contractual battle with his label (he switched from Geffen to Warner Bros. in 1996) and by the Eagles' 1994 reunion; but "The Garden of Allah"—a new track on his 1995 best-of set, shows that his virtues remained intact.

what to buy: *Building the Perfect Beast* ♪♪♪♪ (Geffen, 1984, prod. Don Henley, Danny Kortchmar, Greg Ladanyi) mixes the high-tech sheen of its rockers ("The Boys of Summer," "All She Wants to Do Is Dance") with aching, gentle ballads. Painstakingly crafted, *Beast* propelled Henley from the shadow of the Eagles.

what to buy next: Any of the rest of his output will do. *I Can't Stand Still* ♪♪♪ (Asylum, 1982, prod. Don Henley, Danny Kortchmar, Greg Ladanyi) is an estimable solo debut. *The End of the Innocence* ♪♪♪♪ (Geffen, 1989, prod. Don Henley, Danny Kortchmar) suffered a bit for following *Building the Perfect Beast* but was still solid; the title track and "The Heart of the Matter" are perhaps his finest ballads. *Actual Miles: Henley's Greatest Hits* ♪♪♪♪ (Geffen, 1995, prod. various) is a creditable, if incomplete, sampler, with new songs that are worth having.

worth searching for: *An Eagle Out East* (KTS, 1993) is a strong bootleg from a 1990 performance in Tokyo, a mini-greatest hits set that also includes Eagles favorites such as "Hotel California," "Life in the Fast Lane," and "Desperado."

influences:

◄◄ Henry David Thoreau, Leonard Cohen, Bob Dylan, Gram Parsons, the Byrds

>> Tom Petty, Bryan Adams, Sheryl Crow, Mojo Nixon

see also: *The Eagles, Bruce Hornsby, Joe Walsh, Sheryl Crow*

Gary Graff

Joe Henry

Born December 2, 1960, in Charlotte, NC.

That Joe Henry remains best known to the public at large as Madonna's brother-in-law is nothing short of criminal. He's a fine singer and drop-dead brilliant songwriter, responsible for some of the finest country-rock of the 1990s. Plus he has never shied away from pushing himself in unexpected or even difficult directions, as his body of work shows.

what to buy: While it's not fair to say it came out of nowhere, *Short Man's Room* 𝄞𝄞𝄞𝄞 (Mammoth, 1992, prod. Joe Henry) is still a startling record that makes absolute mincemeat of Henry's preceding three albums. Originally recorded as demos (with the Jayhawks as his backup band), the album has an offhanded freshness Henry has never duplicated, plus a timelessly airy sound that should ensure that it will age well. *Short Man's Room* also comes with Henry's best-ever set of songs, from the title track (a waltz!) to the doom-laden "A Friend to You." Magnificent, and a landmark.

what to buy next: *Kindness of the World* 𝄞𝄞𝄞𝄞 (Mammoth, 1993, prod. Joe Henry) tries to duplicate its predecessor's formula, with the Jayhawks again on board. Its only real flaw is that it's a shade too predictable, with material not quite as start-to-finish strong as *Short Man's Room*. But it's still intermittently stunning, especially "Third Reel" and the "Fireman's Wedding" single. Henry bounced back strong with *Trampoline* 𝄞𝄞𝄞𝄞 (Mammoth, 1996, prod. Patrick McCarthy, Joe Henry), the bravest album in his catalog. Just when alternative country was catching on, Henry chose to make his Tom Waits move, ditching the Jayhawks and enlisting Helmet guitarist Page Hamilton. While the results are strange and clattery (an opera sample adorns one track), *Trampoline* is also mesmerizing.

what to avoid: Henry's amateurish debut, *Talk of Heaven* 𝄞𝄞 (Profile, 1986, prod. Joe Henry), is most notable as proof of how far he's come—and that what he does ain't near as easy as he makes it look. It is the only black mark on an otherwise honorable career.

the rest:
Murder of Crows 𝄞𝄞𝄞 (Coyote/A&M, 1989)
Shuffletown 𝄞𝄞𝄞 (Coyote/A&M, 1990)

worth searching for: Henry appears on the Vic Chesnutt tribute album *Sweet Relief II: Gravity of the Situation* (Columbia, 1996, prod. various). A predictable enough place for him to be, right?

The punchline is his duet partner—sister-in-law Madonna—on a cover of "Guilty by Association," a song Chesnutt originally wrote about Michael Stipe. It has a terrifyingly high irony quotient.

influences:
◀◀ Steve Forbert, John Prine, Bob Dylan, Tom Waits, Van Morrison, the Band, Charlie Rich, T-Bone Burnett

>> Uncle Tupelo, Son Volt, Wilco

David Menconi

Herman's Hermits

Formed 1963, in Manchester, England. Disbanded 1971.

Peter Noone, vocals, piano, guitar; Karl Green, guitar, harmonica; Keith Hopwood, guitar; Derek Leckenby, guitar; Barry Whitwam, drums.

Twenty years later it would be the home of modern rock favorites such as Stone Roses and Happy Mondays, but in 1963, Manchester gave the world Herman's Hermits—smiling, happy people playing pop songs that practically commanded listeners to bop. Fronted by Peter Noone and produced by Britain's reigning hitmaker Mickie Most, the Hermits reeled out a string of hits during the mid-'60s that included "I'm Into Something Good," "Mrs. Brown You've Got a Lovely Daughter," and the Dr. Demento favorite "I'm Henry the Eighth, I Am." The Hermits lived something of a charmed life; besides Most, the group had future Led Zeppelin members Jimmy Page and John Paul Jones play on its records; and the Kinks' Ray Davies penned one of its Top 5 hits, "Dandy." Since the group split, Noone has had the most high-profile post-Hermits career, recording some solo albums (his big hit was David Bowie's "Oh! You Pretty Thing"), appearing in a Broadway production of *The Pirates of Penzance*, and hosting the *My Generation* program on VH1. He's recently started a "Teen Idols" tour package with former Monkees frontman Davy Jones and Bobby Sherman.

what's available: *Their Greatest Hits* 𝄞𝄞𝄞 (ABCKO, prod. Mickie Most) does the trick with 16 songs from the era.

influences:
◀◀ The Beatles, Rory Storm, Lonnie Donnegan

>> The Monkees, the Archies, R.E.M.

Gary Graff

Kristin Hersh

See: Throwing Muses

Richard X. Heyman

Born in Plainfield, NJ.

Fans of the Smithereens, World Party, or Matthew Sweet ought to love Richard X. Heyman, whose one-man-band records of acid-tongued pop songs are both wonderful and undeservedly obscure. And if you think you don't like jingle-jangle pop records because they don't groove, Heyman is the rare exception: His records DO groove, in part because he's a drummer who has played with everyone from Link Wray to Brian Wilson.

what to buy: The hooks are simply to die for on Heyman's tremendous debut *Living Room!!* 𝅘𝅥𝅘𝅥𝅘𝅥𝅘𝅥 (N.R. World Records Unlimited, 1988/Cypress, 1990, prod. Richard X. Heyman). The album shows impressive range and texture, especially given the fact that it was recorded in, yes, a living room. In a virtuoso performance, Heyman plays virtually everything on *Living Room!!* himself, even keeping time on the closing track "Local Paper" on a clacking typewriter.

what to buy next: *Hey Man!* 𝅘𝅥𝅘𝅥𝅘𝅥𝅘𝅥 (Sire, 1991, prod. R.X. Heyman, Andy Paley) is almost as strong, continuing Heyman's odd fondness for exclamatory titles as well as military metaphors ("Back to You," "Private Army," "Civil War Buff"). An ensuing period of prolonged record company blues apparently did nothing to dim Heyman's fire, because *Cornerstone* 𝅘𝅥𝅘𝅥𝅘𝅥 (Permanent Press, 1998, prod. Richard X. Heyman) offers up more of the same—which in this case is a very fine thing. Love songs just don't get much colder than "From This Day Forever": "There's an old saying that goes love is blind, but we can see each other most of the time."

influences:

◀◀ Matthew Sweet, Todd Rundgren, the Smithereens, World Party, Warren Zevon, John Hiatt, the Beatles

▶▶ High Llamas, Eric Matthews

David Menconi

Nick Heyward /Haircut 100

Haircut 100 formed late 1970s, in England. Disbanded 1984.

Nick Heyward (born May 20, 1961 in Beckenham, England), guitar, vocals; Graham Jones, guitar; Les Nemes, bass; Memphis Blair Cunningham, drums; Phil Smith, saxophone; Mark Fox, percussion.

Perhaps the cleanest-cut group of the new wave era, Haircut 100 made a pretty-boy fusion of light funk with jazz and pop. Heyward had a touchingly youthful voice with an ear-catching marbles-in-the-mouth inflection. Although not as gutsy as either the Style Council or the English Beat, Haircut 100 would in all likelihood appeal to fans of those groups. The band was hot in Britain for a brief time during 1982 with the hit song "Love Plus One." When Heyward left to pursue a solo career in 1983, the group carried on without him, but broke up after its second album, *Paint on Paint*.

what to buy: After years of silence, Heyward re-surfaced with the back-to-basics *From Monday to Sunday* 𝅘𝅥𝅘𝅥𝅘𝅥𝅘𝅥 (Epic, 1993, prod. Nick Heyward), which features chiming Merseybeat guitars and flourishes of brass and string, ear candy that any popster would be proud to call his own. Heyward turns in a varied collection of straightforward pop songs on *The Apple Bed* 𝅘𝅥𝅘𝅥𝅘𝅥𝅘𝅥 (Big Deal, 1998, prod. various), and the result is easily his most fun and accessible effort to date. Highlights include the beat-box driven "Stars in Her Eyes," a Beatlesque romp called "My Heavy Head," and the hooky "Today." As an added bonus, the U.S. release adds three tracks culled from Heyward's British singles.

what to buy next: Although Heyward's *North of a Miracle* 𝅘𝅥𝅘𝅥𝅘𝅥 (Arista, 1983, prod. Geoff Emerick, Nick Heyward) did little to remove him from the light funk-jazz-pop fusion of his former group, it did establish him as a talented and sophisticated songwriter on the order of Aztec Camera's Roddy Frame.

the rest:
(With Haircut 100) *Pelican West* 𝅘𝅥𝅘𝅥 (Arista, 1982)

influences:

◀◀ Herb Alpert, Sergio Mendez

▶▶ Aztec Camera, Dexy's Midnight Runners, Culture Club, Rick Astley, the Housemartins

Christopher Scapelliti

John Hiatt

Born August 20, 1952, in Indianapolis, IN.

Few of rock's angstful young men have matured with the grace and dignity of John Hiatt. While other middle-aged rockers fret about their mortality and receding hairlines, this resilient singer-songwriter takes pride in his domestic bliss: *Bring the Family* and *Slow Turning* are filled with delightfully skewered observations of adulthood and passionate paeans to shaping up ("These days the only bar I ever see/has got lettuce and tomatoes") and settling down. A respected songwriter who has penned hits for everyone from Three Dog Night ("Sure As I'm Sittin' Here") to Rosanne Cash ("The Way We Make a Broken Heart"), and Bonnie Raitt ("Thing Called Love"), Hiatt jumped on the new-wave bandwagon during the early '80s with such strained, strident efforts as *Slug Line* and *All of a Sudden*. His teaming with former mentor Ry Cooder, as well as Jim Keltner, and Nick Lowe, in 1987 for *Bring the Family* stirred up some volatile creative chemistry (the four would later form the group Little Village) and reunited him with his country/blues roots. But he's found his most inspiring compatriots in Cracker bassist Davey Faragher and the younger musicians who have been backing him since 1993's *Perfectly Good Guitar*, resulting in some of his wildest and most youthful-sounding music. If you doubt it, check out the funky title track to 1997's *Little Head*, which is about exactly what you think it's about.

what to buy: *Bring the Family* ♪♪♪♪ (A&M, 1987, prod. John Chelew) and *Slow Turning* ♪♪♪♪ (A&M, 1988, prod. Glyn Johns) trace Hiatt's development as a family man and a much-improved singer. Johns's crisp production lends the latter a tough-rocking edge on "Drive South," "Trudy and Dave," "Tennessee Plates," and the title track. On *Perfectly Good Guitar* ♪♪♪♪ (A&M, 1993, prod. Matt Wallace), Hiatt gets a hall pass from his parental duties and paints the town with Wallace, who beefs up Hiatt's country-tinged melodies with a barrage of fuzzy, feedback-drenched guitars that echo the reckless abandon of Neil Young's *Ragged Glory*. *Walk On* ♪♪♪♪ (Capitol, 1995, prod. Don Smith) strikes a keen balance between his primitive and paternal sides with the barnstorming country-rock of "Good As She Could Be," the elegant "You Must Go," and the shimmering pop of "Shredding the Document."

what to buy next: *Riding with the King* ♪♪♪♪ (Geffen, 1983, prod. Ron Nagel, Scott Matthews, Nick Lowe) is the most listenable remnant from his "new wave" period, with backing on half the disc from Nick Lowe and his Paul Carrack–led Cowboy Outfit.

what to avoid: On *Slug Line* ♪♪ (MCA, 1979, prod. Denny Bruce) promising songs are drowned in cliché-ridden production that leaves him sounding more nerdy than nervy. At best, Elvis Costello Lite.

the rest:
Hanging Around the Observatory ♪♪ (Epic, 1974)
Overcoats ♪♪ (Epic, 1975)
Two Bit Monsters ♪♪♪ (Geffen, 1980)
Warming up to the Ice Age ♪♪♪ (Geffen, 1985)
Y'All Caught? The Ones That Got Away, 1979–1985 ♪♪♪ (Geffen, 1989)
Stolen Moments ♪♪♪♪ (A&M, 1990)
Hiatt Comes Alive at Budokan ♪♪♪♪ (A&M, 1994)
Living a Little, Laughing a Little: 1974–85 ♪♪♪♪ (Raven, 1996)
Little Head ♪♪♪♪ (Capitol, 1997)
The Best of John Hiatt ♪♪♪♪ (Capitol, 1998)

worth searching for: *Love Gets Strange: The Songs of John Hiatt* (Rhino, 1993, prod. various) is a various-artists collection of diverse treatments by the Neville Brothers ("Washable Ink"), Rosanne Cash ("Pink Bedroom"), Jeff Healey ("Angel Eyes"), and Marshall Crenshaw ("Someplace Where Love Can't Find Me").

influences:
◀◀ Ry Cooder, Elvis Costello, Bob Seger, Bob Dylan
▶▶ Joe Henry, Syd Straw, Bob Seger

see also: *Little Village*

David Okamoto

Dan Hicks

Born December 9, 1941, in Little Rock, AR.

Dan Hicks polished the old-timey style of the Charlatans, a little-known but influential San Francisco band in which he served as drummer, into a campy, acoustic-flavored cabaret act, Dan Hicks & His Hot Licks. The group would presage such full-blown period pieces as Bette Midler, the Pointer Sisters, and the Manhattan Transfer by several years. Hicks's sarcastic persona and well-developed sense of irony gave him a determined deadpan attitude and helped obscure the fact that his songwriting was really first-rate. With his jazzy mien and caustic air, he made a modest splash with his Blue Thumb albums of the early 1970s, which had the zippy nonchalance of an R. Crumb cartoon come to life. Hicks continues an active performing career, although his recordings have been few and far between since the heyday of the Hot Licks.

what to buy: *Where's the Money* ♪♪♪♪ (MCA, 1971/1989, prod. Tommy LiPuma) probably best reflects the zany intransigence of Hicks and company.

what to buy next: *Striking It Rich* ♪♪♪ (MCA, 1972, prod. Tommy LiPuma) captures the live ambiance of the band's appearances.

the rest:
Last Train to Hicksville ♪♪ (MCA, 1973)
Shootin' Straight ♪♪♪ (Private Music, 1994)
Return to Hicksville: The Blue Thumb Years 1971-1973 ♪♪♪♪ (Hip-O, 1997)

worth searching for: His debut album, *Dan Hicks & His Hot Licks* (Epic, 1969/Collectors,1995, prod. Bob Johnston), is his best, with such signature songs as "How Can I Miss You When You Won't Go Away," "Canned Music," and "I Scare Myself" (later covered by Thomas Dolby).

influences:
◀◀ Le Hot Club de France, the Andrews Sisters, the Charlatans
▶▶ The Pointer Sisters, Thomas Dolby

Joel Selvin

High Llamas

Formed 1992, in London, England.

Sean O'Hagan, vocals, guitar, keyboards; Marcus Holdaway, keyboards, vocals; John Fell, bass; Rob Allum, drums; John Bennett, guitars.

Dedicating oneself to recreating the sound of the Beach Boys is one thing; but painstakingly recreating the sound of Brian Wilson's unfinished demos represents another order of obsessiveness altogether. That is the course Sean O'Hagan has taken since his former group, Microdisney, disbanded during the late '80s. There is an oddly liturgical feel to the High Llamas, in both the mood and stately pacing of its music (the tempos are the most deliberate this side of the Cowboy Junkies). While *Pet Sounds* and *Smile* are the Beach Boys albums most frequently cited as reference points for High Llamas, a more precise one is *Stack-O-Tracks*, the 1968 karaoke collection of Beach Boys backing tracks, without vocals. In recent years, O'Hagan has also been an unofficial member of Stereolab, contributing invaluable studio and arranging smarts.

what to buy: *Gideon Gaye* ✍✍✍ (Alpaca Park/Epic, 1995, prod. Sean O'Hagan, Charlie Francis) is a high point O'Hagan is unlikely to surpass anytime soon. The album has beautifully tuneful and detailed arrangements, copping from the Beatles as well as the Beach Boys. After this album's 1994 European release, O'Hagan and the Llamas toured as backup band for former Love singer-guitarist Arthur Lee, the '60s psychedelic pop equivalent of Bob Dylan's 1986 tour with Tom Petty & the Heartbreakers.

what to buy next: *Hawaii* ✍✍✍ (Alpaca Park/V2, 1997, prod. Sean O'Hagan, Charlie Francis) is not unlike Utopia's 1980 Beatles parody/tribute *Deface the Music*. Most of the 29 tracks sound more like sketches than complete songs, evoking Brian Wilson's mid-'60s California dreams. As O'Hagan himself puts it in the oft-quoted manifesto "The Hot Revivalist," "Let's rebuild the past/'Cause the future won't last." (Note that the U.S. version of *Hawaii* includes a six-song bonus disc with a lovely cover of Nick Drake's "Chime of a City Clock.") Though hardly any less derivative than *Hawaii*, *Cold and Bouncy* ✍✍✍ (Alpaca Park/V2, 1998, prod. Sean O'Hagan) nevertheless shows encouraging forward movement, transposing more overt electronic flourishes onto the Beach Boys formula. Somehow both spacier and better-focused than its predecessor, *Cold and Bouncy* sounds like the record *Hawaii* should've been—and like the best Stereolab record of recent years.

the rest:
Lolla Rosso N/A (V2, 1998)

worth searching for: Before the High Llamas became a formal group, O'Hagan made an extremely whimsical solo album titled *High Llamas* (Demon, 1990, prod. Sean O'Hagan), which is less fussily detailed than his subsequent work and could almost pass for the Steely Dan–influenced lounge-pop of China Crisis. Turn on, O'Hagan's side band with Stereolab's Tim Gane and Andy Ramsay, released *Turn On* (Drag City, 1997, prod. Sean O'Hagan), an intriguing midpoint between the High Llamas' ornate pop and Stereolab's space-age fuzak.

influences:
◄◄ The Beach Boys, the Beach Boys, the Beach Boys; the Beatles, Love, Stereolab

►► Eric Matthews

see also: *Stereolab*

David Menconi

Chris Hillman
See: Flying Burrito Brothers

Peter Himmelman
Born November 23, 1959, in Minneapolis, MN.

A former Elvis Costello disciple in a Minneapolis power-pop band called Sussman Lawrence, Peter Himmelman changed his life and his sound after his father's death. He became an Orthodox Jew, married Bob Dylan's daughter, Maria, and started writing thoughtful examinations of emotional and spiritual strife and the resilience of the human spirit that have established him as one of rock's most passionate songwriters. He's also an intriguing paradox: despite the brooding tone of his songs, his acclaimed live shows are part performance art and part "Let's Make a Deal" as he invites audience members onstage, makes up songs on the spot, hands out Play-Doh, and exudes a hilarious, brink-of-disaster spontaneity so sadly lacking in the modern-day concert experience. Since leaving Epic/Sony 550 after the commercial failure of a daring concept album called *Skin*—about the death and rebirth of a hedonistic egomaniac named Ted—Himmelman has been concentrating on solo tours (documented on 1996's *Stage Diving*) and his family. In 1997, he released a playful children's album called *My Best Friend Is a Salamander* and signed with Six Degrees Records, which released the bracing full-band effort *Love Thinketh No Evil* in 1998.

what to buy: The intimate *From Strength to Strength* ✍✍✍ (Epic, 1991, prod. Peter Himmelman) includes his near-hit, "Woman with the Strength of 10,000 Men" and such concert staples as "Only Innocent" and "Mission of My Soul." *Flown This Acid World* ✍✍✍ (Epic, 1992, prod. Don Smith, Peter Himmelman) is the hard-rocking follow-up, boasting blistering renditions of "Beneath the Damage and the Dust" and "Untitled," a harrowing story song about the night he rode in a taxi driven by a neo-Nazi.

what to buy next: *This Father's Day* ✍✍✍ (Island, 1986/Razor & Tie, 1995, prod. Peter Himmelman) is his first post–Sussman Lawrence album and traces his evolution from sneering punk to soulful singer-songwriter. The title track is a heartfelt, gutsspilling demo written on Father's Day 1983 that captures him breaking down toward the end of the song.

what to avoid: The keyboard-laden *Synesthesia* ✍✍ (Island, 1989, prod. Peter Himmelman) tries too hard for rock credibility and sounds distant, strained, and overproduced—everything his other albums are not.

the rest:
(With Sussman Lawrence) *Hail to the Modern Hero* ✍✍ (Regency 1980)
(With Sussman Lawrence) *Pop City* ✍✍✍ (Orange, 1984)
Gematria ✍✍✍ (Island, 1987)

Skin 🎵🎵🎵 (Sony 550, 1994)
Stage Diving 🎵🎵🎵 (Plump, 1996)
My Best Friend Is a Salamander 🎵🎵🎵 (Baby Boom Music, 1997)
Love Thinketh No Evil 🎵🎵🎵 (Six Degrees, 1998)

worth searching for: *The Musings of Someone* (Epic, 1991, prod. Peter Himmelman) is a promotional interview disc showcasing Himmelman's offbeat sense of humor interspersed with acoustic performances and the bane of his existence, a two-minute ditty about an independent dachshund called "Dixie the Tiny Dog" that still gets requested more than "Free Bird" at a Lynyrd Skynyrd concert.

influences:

◀◀ Bob Dylan, Elvis Costello, Randy Newman

▶▶ Hayden, Beck, David Gray

David Okamoto

His Name Is Alive /Liquorice

Formed 1989, in Livonia, MI.

Karen Oliver, vocals, cello; Angie Carozzo, vocals (1990); Warren Defever, guitar, bass, samples; Trey Many, drums (1993–present).

The eerie, foreboding sparseness of this band evokes existential angst as originally as anything out there, bringing post-punk principles to bear on progressive rock ideas, mixing acoustic and electric instruments in alternately cool and powerful sounds. Think of His Name Is Alive as a sort of new age college radio version of King Crimson. Similarities include: rousing, guitar-powered rock alternating with quiet, sometimes drum-less chamber music; clearly articulated but deliberately obscure lyrics; and seemingly pointless filler to wade through on the way to the good parts. Dissimilar and frustrating is the brevity of many of those good parts on the first two albums. Warren Defever played in his older brother's totally different band, Elvis Hitler, from which he borrowed the first album's guest drummer. He has put together a number of permutations of HNIA and produced guitarist Melissa Elliott's much louder HNIA offshoot, the Dirt Eaters; tracks Defever did with them were used on *Mouth by Mouth*, lending it more variety than other HNIA efforts. Current HNIA drummer Trey Many was drafted into the indie super group Liquorice, with Jenny Toomey (Tsunami) and Dan Littleton (Hated). A new NHIA album, *Fort Lake*, is supposed to be released in the U.S. by the end of 1998.

what to buy: On *Mouth by Mouth* 🎵🎵🎵🎵 (4AD, 1993, prod. His Name is Alive) some tunes are marginally more traditional than earlier efforts thanks to more prominent use of bass and drums, but surreal lyrics and juxtapositions place the results on a different plane from rock. On, for example, "Drink, Dress and Ink" and "Can't Go Wrong without You," the placid pulse and nearly new age mellowness are countered by barbed bursts of electric guitar fuzz and disjunctive structure, resulting in compelling eeriness. A cover of Big Star's "Blue Moon" stands out.

what to buy next: *Stars on ESP* 🎵🎵🎵🎵 (4AD, 1996, prod. Warren Defever) isn't as singular a work of art, but it is more accessible. Several of the songs draw heavily on recognizable styles—the Beach Boys ("Good Vibrations" is reworked as the basis of "Universal Frequencies"), surf guitar, Big Star desolation—and a high percentage of the material is fully developed into nearly normal song forms.

what to avoid: *Livonia* 🎵🎵 (4AD, 1990) is so fragmentary that it requires putting more into listening than anyone but fanatics should be willing to do.

the rest:
Home Is in Your Head 🎵🎵🎵 (4AD, 1991)
Universal Frequencies 🎵🎵🎵 (4AD EP, 1996)
Nice Day 🎵🎵 (4AD EP, 1998)

worth searching for: *King of Sweet* (Perdition Plastics, 1993), available in a limited pressing of 2,000, collects outtakes of an obviously unfinished nature, but it will appeal to fans.

solo outings:
Liquorice (Trey Many):
Listening Cap 🎵🎵🎵 (4AD, 1995)

influences:

◀◀ King Crimson, Led Zeppelin, Karlheinz Stockhausen, Brian Eno, Phillip Glass, Cocteau Twins, This Mortal Coil, Colin Newman, Guided by Voices, Brian Wilson, Big Star, King Tubby

Steve Holtje

Robyn Hitchcock /Robyn Hitchcock & the Egyptians

Robyn Hitchcock born 1953, in West London, England. The Egyptians formed 1985, in Cambridge, England.

Robyn Hitchcock, vocals, guitar; Andy Metcalfe, bass, vocals; Morris Windsor, drums, vocals; Roger Jackson, keyboards (1985–86).

Robyn Hitchcock more or less retired from music after the Soft Boys dissolved. He painted, wrote songs for Captain Sensible, and licked his wounds. Eventually the pull of songwriting and performing was too strong, and he began to return regularly to the studio, alone and with the Egyptians—who, for their part, were the Soft Boys minus lead guitarist Kimberly Rew. Regardless of the setting, Hitchcock writes songs that make inescapable the connection between West Coast psychedelia and folk music. They're sweet, idiosyncratic, sometimes dada, frequently surrealistic, and often tainted with the odor of love (past, present or future). Always a critic's favorite, at least in the United States (and rarely any kind of commercial success), Hitchcock has bounced from label to label. Throughout, his body of work (with one notable exception) has been first-rate. In live performance, his sets are festooned with a stream-of-unconsciousness patter that is almost as fascinating as the songs are beautiful.

what to buy: Where to begin? *I Often Dream of Trains* ⎜⎜⎜⎜ (Midnight Music, 1984/Rhino 1995, prod. Robyn Hitchcock) is an exquisite album, relaxed and focused and studded with kind, wry, sad songs like "Sometimes I Wish I Was a Pretty Girl," the music hall-ish "Uncorrected Personality Traits," and the stunning title track. It is a simple, winsome record, and quite fetching. The Egyptians' college radio hit, "Balloon Man," from *Globe of Frogs* ⎜⎜⎜ (A&M, 1988, prod. the Egyptians), marked the group's ascension to a major label in the States. It is as quirky, eccentric, and ebullient a record as the band would make. That *Perspex Island* ⎜⎜⎜ (A&M, 1991, prod. Paul Fox) didn't produce a breakthrough hit—what with the likes of "So You Think You're in Love" and "She Doesn't Exist"—is a testimony only to the unfairness of things.

what to buy next: The first Egyptians opus *Fegmania!* ⎜⎜⎜ (Midnight Music, 1985/Rhino 1995, prod. Pat Collier) includes the haunting (pun intended) "My Wife and My Dead Wife" and "The Man with the Lightbulb Head." *Element of Light* ⎜⎜⎜ (Relativity/Glass Fish, 1986/Rhino, 1995, prod. Robyn Hitchcock, Andy Metcalfe) features the most linear storytelling of the Hitchcock canon, including "Raymond Chandler Evening" and "Ted, Woody and Junior." Not to mention the laughably misunderstood "Tell Me About Your Drugs." *Moss Elixir* ⎜⎜⎜ (Warner Bros., 1996, prod. Robyn Hitchcock) is striking for its calm, almost adult tone, if murky pop gems like "The Devil's Radio" can ever be construed as the work of a full-fledged adult.

what to avoid: No question here. The sessions for *Groovy Decay* (Albion, 1982), most recently issued as *Gravy Deco* ⎜ (Rhino, 1995, prod. Matthew Seligman, Steve Hillage), were so wretched Hitchcock reissued an alternate version titled *Groovy Decay* (Midnight Music, 1985)—and retired from music for three years, again. All right, so "Grooving on a Inner Plane" and "America" are worth hearing, but this is an assortment of bad ideas in which Hitchcock was a disinterested participant. Not a pretty picture, that.

the rest:
Black Snake Diamond Role ⎜⎜⎜ (Armageddon, 1981/Rhino, 1995)
Gotta Let This Hen Out! ⎜⎜⎜ (Midnight Music, 1985/Rhino, 1995)
Eye ⎜⎜⎜ (Twin/Tone, 1989/Rhino, 1995)

Queen Elvis ⎜⎜⎜ (A&M, 1989)
Respect ⎜⎜⎜ (A&M, 1993)
Invisible Hitchcock ⎜⎜⎜ (Rhino, 1995)
You and Oblivion ⎜⎜ (Rhino, 1995)
Greatest Hits ⎜⎜⎜ (A&M, 1996)
Storefront Hitchcock N/A (Warner Bros., 1998)

worth searching for: Rhino produced a promotional sampler, creatively titled *Catalog Sampler*, in 1995 on the occasion of its reissue of Hitchcock and/or the Egyptians, back catalog in 1995, and it's a smashing greatest hits summation. A&M produced the promo-only seven-song *Live Death* in an edition of 1,000 or something equally ridiculous; it includes some Hitchcock standards as well as Richard Thompson's "Withered and Died" and the Lennon/McCartney "A Day in the Life." A vinyl-only fully alternate edition titled *Mossy Liquor* (Warner Bros., 1996) is more fun than the formal release, including a Swedish take on "Alright, Yeah," and much other glorious mischief.

influences:
◀◀ John Lennon, Syd Barrett, Bob Dylan
▶▶ Crowded House, 16 Horsepower, Pete Droge

see also: *The Soft Boys*

Grant Alden

Hoarse

Formed 1993, in Detroit, MI. Disbanded 1998.

John Speck (born John Liccardello), vocals, guitars; Jimmy Paluzzi, drums, vocals; Robby Graham, bass, vocals.

This volatile trio isn't one to talk about its equally volatile past for fear that history may repeat itself. John Speck was fired from the rock band Paw without receiving credit for his work. In 1995, drummer Jimmy Paluzzi was let go from Sponge. The two incidents seemed to be for the best. Childhood friends Robby Graham and Speck formed the blue-collar rock band Hoarse in 1993 and brought Paluzzi on board two years later. Speck wrote the band's first single, "Diamond," about Graham's bad break-up with his ex-fiancee. Again, things happen for a reason. The single found its way onto Detroit radio although Hoarse had no music available for purchase. A bidding war ensued and RCA proposed a record deal. Unfortunately, Hoarse split up shortly after the release of its debut album.

what's available: The band's first and only full length release, *Happens Twice* ⎜⎜ (RCA, 1997, prod. Tim Patalan), showed promise for what could have been. Musically and vocally, "Diamond" shares the fury that Graham experienced. Speck's too-many-cigarettes vocals and a guitar assault similar to Social Distortion's is at its best on the title track.

worth searching for: Prior to *Happens Twice*'s release, RCA put out a three-song sampler recorded live at a hometown show, which is a nice souvenir of Hoarse's muscular live attack.

influences:

⏪ Social Distortion, Cheap Trick, the Clash

Christina Fuoco

Roger Hodgson

See: Supertramp

Kristian Hoffman

See: The Mumps

Hole

Formed 1990, in Los Angeles, CA.

Courtney Love, vocals, guitar; Eric Erlandson, guitar; Jill Emery, bass (1990–91); Caroline Rue, drums (1990–91); Patty Scheme, drums (1992–present); Kristen Pfaff, bass (1992–94); Melissa Auf Der Maur, bass (1994–present).

With two lines from the song "Miss World"—"I want to be the girl with the most cake" and "I fake it so real I am beyond fake"—Courtney Love exhibits two self-defining personal traits: an extraordinary degree of self-knowledge, and absolutely no shame. The most successful rock 'n' roll social climber in recent memory, Love, to her credit, was at least able to deliver the goods when it counted most. But it wasn't always that way. When she formed Hole after brief stints in an early incarnation of Faith No More and Sugar Baby Doll (the latter with Kat Bjelland, later of Babes in Toyland, and L7's Jennifer Finch), the angry punk stance was there, but the songs and the performance were not. That changed dramatically when Love teamed up romantically with Nirvana frontman Kurt Cobain; she became both the princess of grunge and a surprisingly credible artist in her own right. Debate still rages about how much help Cobain supplied in turning *Live through This* into a well-crafted commercial juggernaut. And until the much-anticipated follow-up album (now four years in the making) is released, no answer is readily available. Tellingly, though, Love hasn't been frittering away her time in the studio. Instead she's been working on achieving all-around celebrityhood, earning raves for her portrayal of a junk-addicted strumpet in *The People vs. Larry Flynt*—her harsher critics called it type casting—having semi-frequent dustups with journalists she dislikes, and trading in the love-me-I'm-a-mess Courtney we've come to know for a surgically enhanced, designer-wearing babe-o-rama. What does all of this have to do with music? Not much.

what to buy: *Live through This* 🎵🎵🎵🎵 (DGC, 1994, prod. Paul Q. Kolderie, Sean Slade) benefits from her husband's undeniable influence in terms of song structure and dynamics. Love's voice, though still limited, is nuanced here, and her scream is used judiciously. Interestingly, her writing also took a quantum leap, and songs such as "Softer Softest," "Plump," "Asking for It," and "Miss World" deal with a variety of feminist issues in a gut-wrenchingly personal fashion. Cobain's suicide a week before the album's release added resonance to every line, making the ironically titled disc a '90s punk classic.

what to avoid: The EP *Ask for It* **woof!** (Caroline, 1995, prod. Mike Robinson) is a brief, non-essential, and occasionally excruciating collection of leftovers, covers, and live shots.

the rest:
Pretty on the Inside 🎵🎵🎵 (Caroline, 1991)
Celebrity Skin 🎵🎵🎵🎵 (DGG, 1998)

influences:

⏪ Joan Jett, the Slits, Babes in Toyland, Nirvana

Daniel Durchholz

The Hollies

Formed 1962, in Manchester, England.

Graham Nash, vocals, guitar (1962–68, 1983); Allan Clarke, vocals, harmonica (1962–71, 1973–81, 1983); Anthony Hicks, guitar; Donald Rathbone, drums (1962–63); Eric Haydock, bass (1962–66); Robert Elliott, drums (1963–81, 1983); Bernard Calvert, bass (1966–81); Terry Sylvester, vocals, guitar (1968–81); Mikal Rikfors, vocals (1971–73).

Although the Hollies are often dismissed as a lightweight singles band, their world-wide legion of fans knows better. The group's remarkable career spans many different phases, but the key through it all has been those glorious three-part harmonies that instantly distinguish a Hollies song. And while vocals are the trademark, the Hollies also deserve credit for the tightness of its instrumental attack and for its well-crafted songwriting. Fueled by vastly underrated guitarist Anthony Hicks and propulsive drummer Robert Elliott—universally acclaimed by his peers as a top stick man of the British beat era—Hollies music has always had a thoroughly professional sheen to it, leavened by a great deal of infectious energy. Though the band's very early period, when it was covering well-worn American R&B songs, has little to recommend it, once the Hollies started generating original material and getting top songs from other writers, the group never looked back. The pure pop songs are a delight; the experimentation with more open forms in the psychedelic era was usually interesting, and the band continued to create finely-crafted music with emotional resonance well into the '70s.

what to buy: *The Hollies 30th Anniversary Anthology* 🎵🎵🎵🎵 (EMI, 1993, prod. various) gathers material from all phases of the

Courtney Love of Hole (© Ken Settle)

group's career and is the only official collection of pre-1967 output available in the U.S. It's hard to dislike a compilation with such a rich array of great tracks; on the other hand, the compilers chose to re-mix the pre-'67 material into stereo, and despite their good intentions, it's a major mistake. The early tracks lose all sense of power and cohesiveness when they're broken apart into separate elements. Also, the emphasis is almost entirely on hit singles, while strong album tracks are ignored. *The Hollies Anthology* ♫♫♫♫ (Epic, 1990, prod. various) is a nicely done package that covers the 1967 to 1975 era with better mixes and a marvelous acoustic take of "Magic Woman Touch."

what to buy next: Virtually all the original Hollies albums have been re-released on CD in Great Britain in their original form, and while they're technically imports, many are available via a label (Beat Goes On) that's widely distributed to North American retailers. Of special note is the second album, *In the Hollies Style* ♫♫♫♪ (Beat Goes On, 1964), with material never released in the U.S. The *Sgt. Pepper's* -influenced *Butterfly* ♫♫♫ (Beat Goes On, 1967) marks the high point of their experimental phase.

what to avoid: *All Time Greatest Hits* ♫♫♫ (Curb, 1990) has the biggies but lacks the depth and the packaging of the ♫♫♫♫♫ collections.

the rest:
A Distant Light ♫♫♪ (Epic, 1971/Columbia, 1991)
The Hollies ♫♫♫ (Epic, 1974/Columbia, 1974)
The Best of ♫♫♫♪ (Capitol)
Greatest Hits ♫♫♫♪ (Columbia, 1987)
Looking Back ♫♫♪ (CEMA Special Products, 1995)

worth searching for: For proof that the Hollies could cut it live just as surely as in the studio, an LP called *Hollies Live*, originally released during 1976 in Canada, is the one to look for.

influences:
◀◀ Buddy Holly, the Everly Brothers

▶▶ Crosby, Stills & Nash, the Posies, Material Issue, Barenaked Ladies

see also: *Crosby, Stills & Nash*

Mike Greenfield

Buddy Holly

Born Charles Hardin Holley, September 7, 1936, in Lubbock, TX. Died February 3, 1959, near Clear Lake, IA.

In the mere 22 months that Buddy Holly spent on the pop charts, he etched his name indelibly into the music's history with easy charm and tuneful mastery of rock's basics. Guileless but not naive, Holly captured the essential angst of young love with wit and an underlying aggressive edge that gave his sim-

ple songs a durability none of his contemporaries could match. As a young country singer, Holly fell under the sway of Presley when Elvis made one of his early concert stops in Holly's native Lubbock, Texas; a home movie caught the suddenly transformed Holly and his pals backstage at this crucial turning point in his life. His initial 1956 recording sessions with Nashville stalwart Owen Bradley survived the steely hand of the producer, unsympathetic to the emerging new music. Isolated numbers such as "Rock with Ollie Vee" display the exuberant joy Holly could bring to rock 'n' roll. Under the less restraining influence of Norman Petty in his Clovis, New Mexico, studios, Holly found the free rein he needed to write his page in rock 'n' roll history. The re-recorded version of "That'll Be the Day," literally remade in its second incarnation, launched the chart career of the Crickets, as Holly and his associates were called by the record label. With "Peggy Sue" three months later, producer Petty used the same group of musicians to establish Holly as a solo artist. The Holly single was rising on the charts as the Crickets' single was slipping down. Although a plane crash ended his career at a time when Holly appeared to be turning a rewarding artistic corner—experimenting with saxophonist King Curtis and cutting ballads with New York session musicians—he had already left behind a legacy that would prove to be one of rock's most enduring treasures.

what to buy: Although at least three different box sets were released during the '70s covering, to different degrees, the complete works of Holly, the existing two-disc set, *The Buddy Holly Collection* ♫♫♫♫ (MCA, 1993, compilation prod. Andy McKaie), distills the essence into an admirable 50-song collection.

what to buy next: Holly's first two post-Nashville albums, *The Chirping Crickets* ♫♫♫♫ (MCA, 1958, prod. Norman Petty) and *Buddy Holly* ♫♫♫♫ (MCA, 1958, prod. Norman Petty) have been made available as compact discs and are well worth picking up.

what to avoid: The over-produced tribute album *Not Fade Away: Remembering Buddy Holly* ♫♪ (Decca, 1996, executive prod. Mark Wright) may boast some big names, but the Holly spirit just doesn't survive these mostly ham-fisted covers.

the rest:
For the First Time Anywhere ♫♫♫ (MCA, 1983)
Buddy Holly—From the Original Master Tapes ♫♫♫♫ (MCA, 1985)
Oh Boy ♫♫ (MCA, 1987)
The Great Buddy Holly ♫♫ (MCA, 1988)
The Buddy Holly Tapes ♪ (Jerden, 1995)
Greatest Hits ♫♫♫♫ (MCA, 1996)

worth searching for: During a brief 1995 dalliance with audiophile vinyl pressings, MCA put out an absolutely gorgeous edition of *Buddy Holly* (MCA, 1995) on its so-called "heavy vinyl" series—a breathtaking audio experience, like listening to the playbacks in the studio control room. Also, there are still sets available of *The Complete Buddy Holly* (MCA, 1981, compilation prod. John Beecher, Malcolm Jones), a powerful multi-tape collection with a stunning booklet and nearly everything he cut in his remarkably prolific career. Apartment tapes, Buddy & Bob sessions, home jams, and interviews are all included in this archivist's dream set.

solo outings:

The Crickets:

The Liberty Years ♫♫ (EMI, 1991)

Still in Style ♫♫♫ (Bear Family, 1992)

Collection: California Sun/She Loves You ♫♫ (Beat Goes On, 1995)

influences:

◄◄ Hank Williams, Hank Ballard, the Clovers, Elvis Presley, Carl Perkins

►► Bobby Vee, Tommy Roe, Waylon Jennings, the Beatles, the Rolling Stones

Joel Selvin and Ken Burke

Holly & the Italians

See: Holly Vincent

Peter Holsapple

See: The dB's

Holy Barbarians

See: The Cult

The Honeycombs /The New Honeycombs

Formed 1963, in Hackney, London, England. Disbanded 1967.

John Lantree, bass; Ann "Honey" Lantree, drums; Denis d'Ell (born Denis Dalziel), vocals, harmonica (1963–66); Alan Ward, guitar, keyboards (1963–66); Martin Murray, guitar (1963–64); Peter Pye, guitar (1964–66); Rod Butler, guitar (1966–67); Colin Boyd, vocals (1966–67); Eddie Spence, keyboards (1966–67).

Of all the dozens upon dozens of colorful characters within legendary producer Joe Meek's stable of acts, the Honeycombs alone succeeded at taking on the joyous thud of the early Liverpool Sound, stomp for high-heel-booted stomp. After de rigueur skiffle and Shadows apprenticeships, the band was spotted by songwriters Ken Howard and Alan Blaikley, who brought it to the attention of Meek and Pye Records as well as supplying its first—and biggest—hit, the epochal "Have I the Right." Quickly soaring into Top Fives the world over, it seemed the ideal launch for this charismatic bunch (with the media's attention invariably focused upon female drummer Honey), but

no sooner had "Have I the Right" hit than tragedy and misfortune did as well: leader Martin Murray's fall from a ballroom stage quickly incapacitated their key musical member; a long Australiasian tour kept the band contracted Down Under when it should have been solidifying their success via, for example, *The Ed Sullivan Show*; and subsequent attempts at follow-up hits—including an interesting remake of Pye labelmate Ray Davies's "Something Better Beginning"—fell upon unanimously deaf ears. Meek's suicide in 1967 was the final blow to the Honeycombs, who'd already attempted to reorganize both their sound and their line-up in the face of ever-changing musical trends, but their glorious moment in the sun seemed to have already passed. However, "Have I the Right" remains as powerful and unique a recording now as it was in 1964, and as a result keeps various versions of ersatz Honeycombs merrily thumping around the European nostalgia circuit to this day.

what to buy: Both of the group's original albums, *The Honeycombs* ♫♫♫♫ (Pye, 1964/Repertoire, 1991, prod. Joe Meek) and *All Systems Go* ♫♫♫ (Pye, 1965/Repertoire, 1991, prod. Joe Meek), remain perfect pop-rock artifacts from the golden age of English Beat. Captured in all of its thunderous, tape-compressed glory by the Ed Wood Meets Phil Spector production aesthetic of Meek, tracks such as "I Can't Stop" and, of course, "Have I the Right" are absolutely without equal within the ranks of British Invasion classics.

what to buy next: Originally issued in Japan as a souvenir of the group's 1965 tour there, the newly available *Live in Tokyo* ♫♫♫♫ (Repertoire, 1991) rightfully deserves to now take its place alongside *Beach Boys Concert*, *The Live Kinks*, and the Stones' *Got LIVE If You Want It* as time-capsule-worthy documents of pre-Monterey Pop rock concerts. Of course, the brave Honeycombs deserve bonus bones for even *attempting* to recreate the incomparable Meek Sound on stage.

influences:

◄◄ The Ravens, Gene Pitney, the Dave Clark Five, Joe Meek

►► Dave Dee, Dozy, Beaky, Mick & Tich, Zarabanda, the Revillos, Too Much Trouble

Gary Pig Gold

The Honeydogs

Formed 1994, in Minneapolis, MN.

Adam Levy, guitar, vocals; Noah Levy, drums, vocals; Trent Norton, bass, vocals; Tommy Borschied, guitar (1995–present).

Falling more on the rock side of the roots-rock equation, the Honeydogs' sound is informed as much by the high-energy antics of their Twin Cities forebears the Replacements as by the high-harmonies of their other Twin Cities forebears, the Jayhawks. Songwriter Adam Levy has a knack for memorable melodies and simple but affecting lyrics, and the band falls in behind him with a memorable brand of bash, twang, and pop. Drummer Noah Levy is also a member of the low-key alt.country supergroup Golden Smog.

what to buy: The group's debut, *The Honeydogs* ✻✻✻✻ (October, 1995/TRG, 1997, prod. John Strawberry Fields, the Honeydogs) attests to its versatility, scoring on the one hand with the rockers "What I Want" and "That's Me," both of them supercharged pleas of naked need, and on the other with "Lost Again" and "Can I Change Your Mind," country flavored plaints that purposely pour salt into old wounds. The sharply-rendered "Those Things Are Hers" is the highlight, detailing through a catalog of left-behind artifacts—a dress, a leather coat—how one relationship is haunted by a previous one that splintered, but won't quite disappear. Levy is a songwriting talent to watch.

the rest:
Everything I Bet You ✻✻✻✻ (October, 1996/TRG, 1997)
Seen a Ghost ✻✻✻ (Mercury, 1997)

influences:
◀◀ The Replacements, the Jayhawks, the Gear Daddies

see also: *Golden Smog*

Daniel Durchholz

The Hoodoo Gurus

Formed 1981, in Sydney, Australia. Disbanded 1997.

Dave Faulkner, vocals, guitar; Brad Shepherd, guitar, vocals; Clyde Bramley, bass (1981–88); James Baker, drums (1981–85); Mark Kingsmill, drums (1985–97); Rick Grossman, bass (1988–97).

A contemporary of INXS and Midnight Oil, the Hoodoo Gurus emerged from Australia's notoriously difficult club scene with a passel of wonderfully crafted songs, jangly guitars, an entertaining (and sometimes humorous) pop sensibility, splendid vocal harmonies, hooks that could grab any living creature out of the sea, and an energetic performance style. The group never quite cracked the U.S. mainstream, though the college radio audience has been receptive. It's our loss.

what to buy: The band's second album, *Mars Needs Guitars* ✻✻✻✻ (Elektra, 1985, prod. Charles Fisher), is a must-have thanks to irresistible pop/rock confections such as "Bittersweet," "Poison Pen," "Show Me Some Emotion," and "The Other Side of Paradise." But it goes further, with humorous stories in "Hayride to Hell," "Like Wow-Wipeout," and the celestial solution offered in the title track. With help from the Bangles and other friends, *Blow Your Cool* ✻✻✻✻ (Elektra, 1987, prod. Mark Opitz, Hoodoo Gurus) turns the guitars up a notch with even more pop hooks. "What's My Scene" is the standout track.

what to buy next: The debut, *Stoneage Romeos* ✻✻✻✻ (Big Time/A&M, 1983, prod. Alan Thorne), is the zaniest of the Hoodoo Gurus' output, with off-beat classics such as "I Was a Kamikaze Pilot," "Zanzibar," and "I Want You Back." *Magnum Cum Louder* ✻✻✻✻ (RCA, 1989, prod. Hoodoo Gurus) launches out of the box with "Come Any Time" and continues to roar with "Another World," "Shadow Me," and "All The Way," as well as the baseball ode "Where's That Hit?"—not bad for a band from Down Under. *Electric Soup* ✻✻✻✻ (RCA, 1992, prod. various) is a shortcut to a Hoodoo Gurus experience, a singles collection that comprises most of the band's top tunes.

the rest:
Kinky ✻✻✻✻ (RCA, 1991)
Gloria Biscuit B-Sides and Rarities ✻✻✻ (RCA, 1993)
Crank ✻✻✻ (Zoo, 1994)
In Blue Cave ✻✻✻✻ (Mushroom/Zoo, 1996)

worth searching for: The import *Electric Chair* (Mushroom, 1997) is a comprehensive two-CD overview that should sate fans and neophytes alike.

influences:
◀◀ The Cramps, the Kinks, the Turtles, Skyhooks

▶▶ The Smithereens, Jellyfish

John Nieman

John Lee Hooker

Born, depending on your source, either a) August 22, 1920 in Clarksdale, MS., b) August 22, 1917 in Clarksdale, MS., or c) before God.

John Lee Hooker is a giant of the blues and one of its most distinctive voices; he's also the father of the boogie, which makes him one of rock 'n' roll's great antecedents. Hooker's deep, primitive rhythms and his dark, growly, hypnotic vocals have inspired innumerable performers over his 50-plus year career. A semi-transient street musician from the age of 15, Hooker moved to Detroit in 1943. His recording career began in 1948 with "Boogie Chillun," a blues classic that topped the R&B charts in 1949. He was a raw, undisciplined musician who seldom played a song the same way twice, yet he managed to record prolifically through the '50s on a number of labels. His output—under such names as Johnny Lee, John Lee Booker, John Lee Chance, Birmingham Sam, Delta John, Texas Slim, Boogie Man, and John Williams—is second only to that of Lightnin' Hopkins. His songs "Dimples" and "Boom Boom" made waves on the '60s British blues scene, and he went acoustic during the blues revival and played the hippest clubs in the U.S. and Europe. During the '70s, Hooker went electric again and did records with Canned Heat, Elvin Bishop, Van Morrison, and other rockers. The aging Hooker faded into semi-retirement during the '80s, but 1989's *The Healer*, featuring Bonnie Raitt, Carlos Santana, Robert Cray, and George Thorogood, won a Grammy and put Hooker back at center stage. He has managed to remain there with several more solid albums since then. Although Hooker tends to recycle tunes, such classics as "Crawlin' King Snake," "I'm in the Mood," "One Bourbon, One Scotch, One Beer," "Little Wheel," "Boogie with the Hook," and "I'm Bad Like Jesse James" all bear retelling. A true legend in his own time, Hooker's spots in the Rhythm and Blues Foundation's Hall of Fame and in the Rock and Roll Hall of Fame—among other honors—are well deserved.

what to buy: *The Ultimate Collection, 1948–1990* 𝄢𝄢𝄢𝄢 (Rhino, 1991, compilation prod. James Austin) lives up to its title, with 31 of Hooker's best-known cuts and a bevy of guests such as Jimmy Reed, Willie Dixon, and Raitt. The septuagenarian Hooker seems to boogie effortlessly on *Chill Out* 𝄢𝄢𝄢𝄢 (Pointblank, 1995, prod. Roy Rogers), and with Santana adds a Latin edge to his mantra-like boogie on "Chill Out (Things Gonna Change)." *The Real Folk Blues* 𝄢𝄢𝄢𝄢 (MCA, 1987) finds Hooker catching up with the folk blues revival, but not having to compromise to do it. The album features the perennial classic "One Bourbon, One Scotch, One Beer."

what to buy next: Hooker is clearly having fun on *The Healer* 𝄢𝄢𝄢𝄢 (Chameleon, 1989, prod. Roy Rogers), the record that sprang him back into the limelight with friends like Raitt and Cray helping out.

what to avoid: Hooker may have presaged the funk, but the slick '70s edge on *Free Beer and Chicken* 𝄢𝄢 (ABC, 1974, prod. Ed Michel) just didn't fit, regardless of the rock and roll heavies in tow.

best of the rest:
Endless Boogie 𝄢𝄢𝄢𝄢 (MCA, 1971)
Never Get Out of These Blues Alive 𝄢𝄢𝄢𝄢 (Pickwick, 1978)
Simply the Truth 𝄢𝄢𝄢 (One Way, 1988)
Mr. Lucky 𝄢𝄢𝄢𝄢 (Charisma, 1991)
I Feel Good 𝄢𝄢𝄢𝄢 (Jewel, 1995)
Boom Boom 𝄢𝄢𝄢𝄢 (Capitol, 1995)
Alone 𝄢𝄢𝄢𝄢 (Blues Alliance, 1996)
Don't Look Back 𝄢𝄢𝄢𝄢 (Pointblank, 1997)
His Best Chess Sides 𝄢𝄢𝄢𝄢 (Chess/MCA, 1997)
Best of Friends 𝄢𝄢𝄢𝄢 (Pointblank/Virgin, 1998)
The Complete '50s Chess Recordings 𝄢𝄢𝄢𝄢 (Chess/MCA 1998)

worth searching for: *Hooker 'N' Heat* (Liberty, 1971/EMI, 1991, prod. Skip Taylor, Robert Hite Jr.) was the equivalent of *The Healer* 20 years earlier. Though it's a rougher-edged affair, Hooker's collaboration with Canned Heat made the rock crowd take notice.

influences:
◀◀ Robert Johnson, Charley Patton

▶▶ James Brown, George Clinton, Bonnie Raitt, John Mayall, Savoy Brown, Canned Heat, Robert Cray, George Thorogood

Lawrence Gabriel

The Hooters
/Largo

Formed 1978, in Philadelphia, PA.

Rob Hyman, vocals, keyboards; Eric Bazilian, vocals, guitar; John Lilley, guitar; Rob Miller, bass (1978–87); David Uosikkinen, drums; Fran Smith Jr., bass, vocals (1987–present).

Supposedly named after the nickname for the melodica—the musical instrument used on the hit "And We Danced"—the Hooters spent nearly a decade building a following in Philadelphia (it was reportedly considered a rite of passage for young area bands to open for them). With a wholesome image and radio-ready sound, the band sold 100,000 copies of a self-released album (1983's *Amore*), which caught the attention of major labels and eventually netted the group a deal with Columbia. Though its debut, *Nervous Night*, scored some hits and made the band a momentary Next Big Thing, it didn't quite hold onto its commercial cachet. Meanwhile, Rob Hyman and Eric Bazilian built a legacy away from the band, writing more enduring hits for artists such as Cyndi Lauper ("Time After Time") and Joan Osborne ("One of Us"). In 1998, Hyman and producer Rick Chertoff put together the rootsy all-star Largo project that also featured Bazilian.

what to buy: The group's debut, *Nervous Night* 𝄢𝄢𝄢 (Columbia, 1985, prod. Rick Chertoff), was a breakthrough that launched the hits "And We Danced," "Day By Day," and "Where Do the Children Go." The album *Largo* 𝄢𝄢𝄢𝄢 (Blue Gorilla/Mercury, 1998, prod. Rob Hyman, Rick Chertoff) is a gem of earnest, rootsy songcraft that features a blow-you-away guest list including Joan Osborne, Cyndi Lauper, Taj Mahal, the Band's Levon Helm, the Chieftains, Willie Nile, and others.

what to buy next: *Zig Zag* 𝄢𝄢𝄢 (Columbia, 1989, prod. Rick Chertoff) is a more mature, complex effort that was unjustly ignored by the masses.

what to avoid: None of the performances on *Greatest Hits II: The Hooters Live* 𝄢 (Sony International, 1994) are as interesting as their studio counterparts.

the rest:
Amore 𝄢𝄢𝄢 (Antenna, 1983)
Out of Body 𝄢𝄢 (MCA, 1993)
Greatest Hits I 𝄢𝄢𝄢𝄢 (Sony International, 1994)
Hooterization: A Retrospective 𝄢𝄢𝄢 (Columbia/Legacy, 1996)

worth searching for: The Japanese hits collection *Star Box* (Sony, 1993, prod. various) features a generous (18 tracks) set that samples all of the Hooters' albums.

influences:

◄◄ Bruce Springsteen, the Band

►► The Levellers, Hothouse Flowers, Whiskeytown, Agents of Good Roots

Todd Wicks

Hootie & the Blowfish

Formed 1986, in Columbia, SC.

Darius Rucker, vocals, guitar; Mark Bryan, guitar, keyboards, vocals; Dean Felber, bass, vocals; Brantley Smith, drums (1986–89); Jim "Soni" Sonefeld, drums, vocals (1989–present).

Hootie & the Blowfish's blend of bouncy folk-rock and hummable melodies seemed to leap out of nowhere to win America's hearts—and wallets—during 1995 as its major-label debut, *Cracked Rear View*, racked up sales of 14 million and counting. In reality, the group had been polishing its sound for years, graduating from a cover band at frat parties to a huge folk-rock favorite throughout the Carolinas and Mid-Atlantic states. Hootie is a group in the truest sense of the word, with all the pieces coming together to create a sound greater than the sum of its individual parts. Darius Rucker's soulful baritone vocals are elevated by his colleagues' soaring background harmonies. Mark Bryan's tactful, mild-thing guitars are gracefully supported by Dean Felber's understated bass lines and Jim Sonefeld's steady rhythmic kick. With roots spread across the spectrum—from Nanci Griffith and John Hiatt to R.E.M. and the Allman Brothers, Hootie & the Blowfish has forged a distinctive southern folk rock sound that strikes a chord with the masses.

what to buy: After three independent releases, *Cracked Rear View* ♫♫♫♫ (Atlantic 1994, prod. Don Gehman) makes people feel good with the upbeat rhythms and stirring melodies of "Hold My Hand," "Hannah Jane," and "Only Wanna Be with You," while two ballads—"I'm Goin' Home" and "Not Even the Trees"—touch the heart as Rucker grieves his mother's death.

what to buy next: The group's sophomore effort, *Fairweather Johnson* ♫♫♫ (Atlantic, 1996, prod. Don Gehman), is lyrically darker than its predecessor but is brightened by the same brisk musical mix. Rucker tends to get sloppily emotional as he wails about lost love and emptiness ("When I'm Lonely," "Let It Breathe") but the jaunty "Old Man & Me" echoes the catchy southern spunk of the Allman Brothers, while "Tucker's Town" exemplifies Hootie at its best with its melodic hook, sweet harmonies, and balanced musicianship.

WHAT ALBUM CHANGED YOUR LIFE?

Definitely Al Green, *Call Me.* I heard that album so much as a kid. Anytime I'd go too far to the rock 'n' roll side at the house, it was *Call Me* that I was to listen to to really hear what music's supposed to sound like.

Darius Rucker

(of Hootie & the Blowfish)

the rest:

Musical Chairs ♫♫♫ (Atlantic, 1998)

worth searching for: The band's self-produced cassette *Time* was sold only at its concerts and at Carolina-area record stores during the early '90s. The six-song CD *Kootchypop* was released independently in 1993.

influences:

◄◄ Led Zeppelin, R.E.M., John Hiatt

David Yonke

Jamie Hoover

See: The Spongetones

Hooverphonic

Formed c. 1995, in Belgium.

Liesje Sadonius, vocals; Raymond Geerts, guitar, breaths; Frank Duchéne, engineering, keyboards; Alex Callier, programming, keyboards.

With a heavy debt to Portishead, Hooverphonic washed up on our shores with a richly rendered, mostly danceable sound. Liesje Sadonius's vocals are the key as her sultry coo lends itself grandly to the ear-candy that Hooverphonic so adeptly produces. Synthetic beats and occasional acoustic drumming (by guest Eric Bosteels) blend with shimmering orchestration to provide a dense backdrop for songs more about sound and feel than what the lyrics attempt to convey.

what's available: *A New Stereophonic Sound Spectacular* ♫♫♫♫ (Epic, 1997, prod. Hooverphonic) is a sample-heavy foray into what has become the "new style"; electronica mixed with guitar and female, diva-type vocals are the ticket here. It's not as morose as the aforementioned Portishead, but a heavy debt is owed here. Burt Bacharach's "Walk on By" (as performed by Chef Isaac Hayes) provides the hook for the single "2Wicky," which appeared on the soundtrack of *Stealing Beauty*. Highly enjoyable—if you don't think too much.

influences:

◀◀ Portishead, Morcheeba, Sade, Everything but the Girl

Barry M. Prickett

Mary Hopkin

Born 1950, in Pontardawe, Wales.

Paul McCartney was seeking talent for the fledgling Apple Records label in 1968 when he struck gold with waif folksinger Mary Hopkin. Blessed with a sweet country-lass voice and a face of apple-pie purity, Hopkin (under McCartney's guidance) spun out a short but hit-studded career of precious Olde Worlde ballads and lilting folk-pop. Following their work together on her 1971 album *Earth Song/Ocean Song*, Hopkin married record producer Tony Visconti and retired from music, returning to active duty as a backup singer on David Bowie's *Low* and as a member of the short-lived trio Oasis (with Julian Lloyd Webber, brother of Andrew) in 1984.

what's available: *Post Card* ✍✍✍ (Capitol, 1969, prod. Paul McCartney) is a pretty album of twee but romantic confections that includes her hit "Those Were the Days," a terrific cover of Donovan's "Lord of the Reedy River," and a few odd novelty numbers ("Puppy Song," "Inchworm")—music the whole family can enjoy. Hopkin shed her woman-child image for *Earth Song/Ocean Song* ✍✍✍ (Capitol, 1971, prod. Tony Visconti), a fine collection of lovely folk-rock tunes that are capably rendered.

influences:

◀◀ Bing Crosby, the Weavers, Bob Dylan, the Beatles, Julie Andrews

▶▶ Melanie, Suzanne Vega, Juliana Hatfield, Joan Osborne

Christopher Scapelliti

Bruce Hornsby

Born November 23, 1954, in Richmond, VA.

Bruce Hornsby's deep, wide musical roots and professionalism have made him a studio favorite, guesting on more than 50 albums by artists ranging from Willie Nelson and Bob Dylan to Liquid Jesus and Squeeze. He co-wrote the Huey Lewis & the News hit "Jacob's Ladder" and assisted Don Henley with "The End of the Innocence," a track that defines Hornsby's writing style and piano playing. Hornsby's three albums with his band, the Range, featured laid-back, slickly crafted tunes that smoothly blended rock, blues, jazz, and folk. For 18 months starting in September, 1990, Hornsby performed more than 100 concerts with the Grateful Dead, filling in after the death of Brent Mydland. (He also performs on and owns a piece of the annual Dead-inspired Furthur Festival.) Hornsby broke up the Range in 1993, finding inspiration for his solo albums with a stellar supporting cast that included Bonnie Raitt, Branford Marsalis, Jerry Garcia, Phil Collins, and Pat Metheny.

what to buy: *Hot House* ✍✍✍ (RCA, 1995, prod. Bruce Hornsby) is an infectiously upbeat collection of dreamy melodies set against precise jazz-rock twists and turns reminiscent of Steely Dan. Hornsby's laid-back vocals and breezy keyboards also shine on *Harbor Lights* ✍✍✍ (RCA, 1993, prod. Bruce Hornsby), offering the steamy rhythmic bop of "Talk of the Town," about an interracial couple, to sprawling, picturesque ballads such as the title track and "Fields of Gray."

what to buy next: Hornsby's debut, *The Way It Is* ✍✍✍ (RCA, 1986, prod. Bruce Hornsby, Elliot Scheiner, Huey Lewis), established his talents early with a Grammy Award and three Top 10 singles in the title track, "Mandolin Rain" and "Every Little Kiss."

what to avoid: Polished production renders *Scenes from the Southside* ✍✍ (RCA, 1988, prod. Bruce Hornsby, Neil Dorfsman) slick and nondescript, lacking grit and personality.

the rest:

A Night on the Town ✍✍ (RCA, 1990)
Spirit Trail ✍✍✍ (RCA, 1998)

worth searching for: *Bruce Hornsby and the Range Live: The Way It Is Tour 1986–87*, (RCA, 1987) is a promotion-only concert recording from the first tour that features a strong performance as well as Hornsby's dazzling piano solo that leads into "The Way It Is."

influences:

◀◀ Bob Dylan, the Grateful Dead, Steely Dan, Keith Jarrett

▶▶ Bonnie Raitt, Ben Folds Five

David Yonke

Hot Tuna

Formed 1969, in San Francisco, CA.

Jorma Kaukonen, guitar, vocals; Jack Casady, bass; Will Scarlet, harmonica (1970–71); Papa John Creach, violin (1971–72); Sammy Piazza, drums (1971–74); Bob Steeler, drums (1974–77); Michael Falzarano, guitar, mandolin, harmonica, vocals (1990–present).

Formed in hotel rooms across the country after Jefferson Airplane concerts, when guitarist Jorma Kaukonen and bassist

Jack Casady couldn't stop playing, Hot Tuna slowly emerged into the public, first as an acoustic duo and then as an electric quartet appearing often as a support act for the Airplane mothership. Essentially a vehicle for Kaukonen's remarkable skills as a country blues guitarist, Tuna specializes in lengthy improvisations, in which Casady's fluid, inventive bass figures wrap around Kaukonen's delta blues lines almost endlessly. The band, on one occasion at least, performed for eight hours straight. Friends since childhood, Kaukonen and Casady split in the late '70s and reformed about 10 years later. The original unplugged band, Tuna remains the sole surviving unit of the San Francisco psychedelic scene's heyday.

what to buy: Either *First Pull Up—Then Pull Down* ♫♫♫ (RCA, 1971, prod. Jorma Kaukonen) or *Burgers* ♫♫♫ (RCA, 1972, prod. Jorma Kaukonen) will provide the quintessential Tuna experience, mixing the Rev. Gary Davis/Mississippi John Hurt fingerpicking nobody does any better than Kaukonen with Casady's imaginative bass playing.

what to buy next: The duo's quiet acoustic debut, *Hot Tuna* ♫♫♫♪ (RCA, 1970, prod. Al Schmitt), captured the lads fresh out of the hotel rooms, in a small Berkeley nightclub playing relatively straight-ahead elaborations on traditional country blues, unplugged before its time.

what to avoid: The sound quality on *Classic Hot Tuna Acoustic* ♫♫ (Relix, 1996, prod. Michael Falzarano), taken from a radio broadcast, leaves much to be desired, although the companion piece, *Classic Hot Tuna Electric* ♫♫♫ (Relix, 1996, prod. Michael Falzarano), fared better since it was taken from multi-track recordings made during the 1971 final week at the Fillmore West.

the rest:
The Phosphorescent Rat ♫♫ (RCA, 1973)
America's Choice ♫♫ (RCA, 1975)
Yellow Fever ♫♫ (RCA, 1975)
Hoppkorv ♫♫ (RCA, 1976)
Double Dose ♫♫♪ (RCA, 1977)
Pair a Dice Found ♫♫♫ (Epic, 1991)
Live at Sweetwater ♫♫♫♪ (Relix, 1992)
Live at Sweetwater Two ♫♫ (Relix, 1993)
The Best of Hot Tuna N/A (RCA, 1998)

worth searching for: The first five definitive albums, arguably all the Hot Tuna anybody might ever need, have been collected on *Hot Tuna in a Can* (RCA Victor, 1996), a clever limited edition package.

solo outings:
Jorma Kaukonen:
Quah ♫♫♫ (Relix, 1974)
Magic ♫♫♫ (Relix, 1985)
Too Hot to Handle ♫♫♫ (Relix, 1986)
Land of Heroes ♫♫♫♪ (American Heritage, 1995)

influences:
◄◄ Rev. Gary Davis, Mississippi John Hurt, Scott LeFaro
►► Keb' Mo', Jeff Buckley, Chris Whitley, Jeff Healey

Joel Selvin

Hothouse Flowers
Formed 1986, in Dublin, Ireland.

Liam O'Maonlai, vocals, keyboards, harmonica; Fiachna O'Braonain, guitar, bouzouki, vocals; Peter O'Toole, bass, bouzouki, vocals; Leo Barnes, saxophone, keyboards, vocals; Jerry Fehily, drums, percussion.

Hothouse Flowers blends Celtic mysticism with R&B and gospel. The result is clearly Irish in its quest for the transcendental, though the band displays its spirituality more boldly than most. When the group gained critical acclaim for its debut, *People*, many of the reviews cited the band's apparent disdain for U2's more mainstream heroic vision. With Hothouse Flowers, the embrace of American soul and traditional Celtic sounds as the road to God is more consistent, and for that matter, much more Irish. Liam 'O Maonlai's impassioned vocals and the musicianship of guitarists Fiachna O'Braonain and Peter O'-Toole frequently reach glorified heights, though occasionally 'O

Maonlai has a tendency to over testify. Unfortunately, the group has been less than prolific over the years.

what to buy: *People* 🎸🎸🎸🎸 (London, 1988, prod. Clive Langer, Alan Winstanley) is a beautiful merging of original vision and mainstream influences and became the best-selling debut in Irish pop history. Standout cuts include "The Older We Get," which speaks of hard-earned wisdom and the rollicking single "Don't Go."

what to buy next: With an effective reworking of Johnny Nash's chestnut "I Can See Clearly Now" and the gorgeous "Christchurch Bells," *Home* 🎸🎸🎸🎸 (London, 1990, prod. various) is a strong follow-up to the debut. Fiddler Steve Wickham, late of the Waterboys, guests on the live "Dance to the Storm."

the rest:
Songs from the Rain 🎸🎸🎸 (London, 1993)

influences:
◀◀ U2, the Waterboys, Van Morrison

▶▶ 54.40, the Young Dubliners

see also: *Split Enz*

Martin Connors

The House of Love

Formed 1986, in London, England. Disbanded 1993.

Guy Chadwick, vocals, guitar; Chris Groothuizen, bass guitar; Pete Evans, drums; Terry Bickers, guitar (1986–90); Simon Walker, guitar (1990–92); Andrea Heukamp, backing vocals (1986–88, 1993).

Although he never achieved widespread acclaim, Guy Chadwick was one of the great songwriters of the late '80s and early '90s. With the House of Love (HOL), he helped usher in a new awareness of guitar rock in England and was partially responsible for launching the big Velvet Underground revival in his homeland. Even though HOL gained moderate alternative radio play with its remarkable single "I Don't Know Why I Love You," Chadwick struggled with the group's lack of all-out success and ended up dissolving the band in 1993 after years of internal conflict and self-doubt. It took him nearly five years to return to making music. He launched a low-key solo career in 1998.

what to buy: The House of Love's American major label debut, *The House of Love (Butterfly)* 🎸🎸🎸🎸 (Fontana/PolyGram, 1990, prod. Stephen Hague, Tim Palmer, Paul Staveley O'Duffy), captured the group's vision perfectly. It included such immaculate guitar rocks songs as "I Don't Know Why I Love You," "Beatles and the Stones," and "Shake and Crawl." Its studio follow-up, *Babe Rainbow* 🎸🎸🎸🎸 (Fontana/Mercury, 1992, prod. Wayne Livesey), held the most promise of a commercial breakthrough for the group with exquisite tracks such as "You Don't Under-

stand" and "Feel." But its moody thunder did not fit in well with pop radio's prevailing grunge fetish.

what to buy next: The House of Love's early albums were raw, but the songwriting was consistently excellent, particularly on *The House of Love (Faces)* 🎸🎸🎸🎸 (Creation/Relativity, 1988, prod. the House of Love), which included an early version of "Shine On" and the monumental single "Christine."

what to avoid: As a reaction to the House of Love's inability to break through to American ears, the group recorded an uncharacteristically dreary disc on the verge of its break-up. *Audience with the Mind* 🎸 (Fontana/Mercury, 1993, prod. the House of Love) is a tough listen, but it does contain occasional sparks ("Hollow," "You've Got to Feel").

the rest:
The House of Love (Group) 🎸🎸🎸 (Creation, 1987)
A Spy in the House of Love 🎸🎸🎸 (Fontana/Mercury, 1990)

worth searching for: *The House of Love Live* (Fontana/PolyGram, 1990, prod. Timothy Powell) was a promotional-only disc, recorded for radio off a live broadcast on WXRT-FM in Chicago. It includes blistering renditions of "Christine" and "Never."

solo outings:
Guy Chadwick:
Lazy Soft and Slow 🎸🎸🎸 (Setanta, 1998)

influences:
◀◀ The Velvet Underground, the Beatles, Echo & the Bunnymen

▶▶ Radiohead, the Stone Roses, the Verve

Aidin Vaziri

House of Pain

Formed 1990, in Los Angeles, CA.

Everlast (born Eric Schrody), vocals; Danny Boy (born Daniel O'Connor), vocals; D.J. Lethal (born Lear DiMant), deejay.

Unlike many white acts performing rap, House of Pain is no mere novelty. Their old-school rhymes, combined with a dense soundscape littered with heavy jeep beats and shrill effects (thanks in part to producer DJ Muggs from Cypress Hill) makes for a heady brew. And if you're buying, make theirs a Guinness Stout. The L.A. rappers wear their Irish heritage proudly, singing a snippet of "Danny Boy" here, and claiming "I never eat pig, but I can f—up a potato" there. The group flirted with going pop on its debut, but since then have turned toward a more hardcore posture, albeit with mixed results.

what to buy: It's tough to recommend *House of Pain* 🎸🎸🎸 (Tommy Boy, 1992, prod. DJ Muggs, DJ Lethal), if only because of the ease with which it gives in to hip-hop culture's worst tendencies: Its lyrics are laced with homophobia, misogyny, racism, and pointless posturing. Which is too bad, because the irrepressible romps "Jump Around" and "Top o' the Morning to Ya" are terrific.

the rest:
Same As It Ever Was ♪♪♪ (Tommy Boy, 1994)
Truth Crushed to Earth Shall Rise Again ♪♪♪ (Tommy Boy, 1996)

solo outings:
Everlast:
Forever Everlasting ♪♪ (Warner Bros., 1990)

influences:
◄◄ Beastie Boys, Black Flag, Ice-T

Daniel Durchholz

The Housemartins /The Beautiful South /Beats International

The Housemartins formed 1984, in Hull, England. Disbanded 1988.

The Housemartins (1984–88): Paul Heaton, vocals, guitar; Stan Cullimore, bass; Ted Key, guitar (1984–85); Hugh Whitaker, drums (1984–86); Norman Cook, bass, guitar, vocals (1985–88); Dave Hemingway, drums (1986–88). The Beautiful South (1988–present): Paul Heaton, vocals; Dave Hemingway, vocals; David Rotheray, guitar; Sean Welch, bass; Briana Corrigan, vocals; David Stead, drums; Jacqueline Abbott, vocals; Damon Butcher, keyboards. Beats International: Norman Cook, bass; Lindy Layton, vocals; Lester Noel, vocals; Andy Boucher, keyboards; MC Wildski, vocals.

Named for the swallow known in this country as the purple martin, the Housemartins were a group of angry young fellows from Hull, England, proud of their Northern working-class roots and eager to chip at the excesses of booming Thatcherite England to the south. Singer-songwriter Paul Heaton, whose voice lies somewhere between Morrissey and George Michael, crafted sweet-sounding songs with sarcastic and often bitter lyrics. His clever, socially conscious material met with mixed reviews in the English press, but the band enjoyed a fair amount of commercial success in Britain, scoring hits such as "Caravan of Love" and "Happy Hour"; the video of the latter was seen frequently on MTV in America. In 1988 the band split up. Heaton and drummer Dave Hemingway formed the Beautiful South (the name is a sarcastic jab at London), and guitarist Norman Cook created Beats International (not to be confused with the English Beat or the International Beat; see separate entries). Heaton has maintained his sharp pencil lyrically, but now points it more at the politics of love and relationships. Musically, the Beautiful South's songs combine strong melodies with lush orchestrations that recall late '60s American pop in

the style of Jimmy Webb or Harry Nilsson. The band recorded a version of the 1969 Nilsson hit "Everybody's Talkin'" in an obvious tip of the cap to that period. The formula has worked well, and has earned the band a slew of hits in Britain. Cook's efforts with Beats International are decidedly more modern; the former DJ has experimented with samples, overdubbing, and multiple vocalists to shape the band's techno-dance sound, which earned a British chart-topper with '90s "Dub Be Good to Me." Neither group has made much impact in the U.S.; the silver lining is that because there's so little product available, it's all of a high quality, without anything to be avoided.

what to buy: *Carry on up the Charts: The Best of the Beautiful South* ♪♪♪♪ (Mercury, 1995, prod. various) is a sterling collection of perfect pop tunes, establishing Heaton and Rotheray in the big league of British tunesmiths. (Note: The limited-edition Go! Discs import of *Charts* offers a second disc of material, including a stripped-down and effective reworking of the Bee Gees' "I Started a Joke.") Beats International's *Let Them Eat Bingo* ♪♪♪♪ (Elektra, 1990, prod. Norman Cook) is a rhythmic rave of a record with samples galore and guests Billy Bragg and the Damned's Captain Sensible.

what to buy next: The Beautiful South's *0898* ♪♪♪♪ (Elektra, 1992, prod. Jon Kelly) features the British hits "Old Red Eyes Is Back," "We Are Each Other," and "Bell Bottomed Tear." The Housemartins' debut, *London 0 Hull 4* ♪♪♪♪ (Elektra, 1986, prod. John Williams), features edgy, guitar-driven pop with the spry but tart anti-yuppie anthem "Happy Hour," and the Kinks-like "Anxious."

the rest:
The Housemartins:
The People Who Grinned Themselves to Death ♪♪♪ (Elektra, 1987)

The Beautiful South:
Welcome to the Beautiful South 🎵🎵🎵🎵 (Elektra, 1989)
Choke 🎵🎵🎵🎵 (Elektra, 1990)

Beats International:
Excursion on the Version 🎵🎵🎵 (PolyGram, 1991)

worth searching for: The generous Housemartins' retrospective *Now That's What I Call Quite Good!* (Go! Discs, 1988, prod. various) is only stocked as an import.

influences:
◀◀ The Kinks, the Clash, the Specials, the English Beat

▶▶ Green Day, Supergrass, Oasis, Blur

William Hanson

Penelope Houston

Birthdate and birthplace unknown.

After the break-up of her incredible 1977 to 1979 San Francisco punk group the Avengers, well-admired singer Penelope Houston disappeared from the recording/performing world for seven years, a long sabbatical broken only by a brief stint in England during 1982 as a backing vocalist for ex-Magazine star (and Buzzcocks founder) Howard Devoto. But thereafter she began a long and respectable solo career playing a much different music that nevertheless allowed her fine voice to flourish, namely folk-rock (with some Latin influences). Her new career began 12 years ago with a 7-inch single released under a short-lived band called -30- (pronounced "Dash-30-Dash," formerly known as Treehouse); thereafter she released records under her own name. The bulk of her work, particularly between 1993 and 1995, came out in Europe, but her most recent release was on Warner Bros. in 1996. That no follow-up has appeared since (as of this writing, at least) is cause for concern, however, as that LP was well-received but failed to light the charts on fire, leading to speculation that her deal with the major label giant was short-lived.

what to buy: Intelligent as ever, Houston used her Warner Bros. debut as an opportunity to take stock of her entire solo career, re-recording the best of her previous output for *Cut You* 🎵🎵🎵 (Reprise, 1996, prod. Jeffrey Wood, Penelope Houston). Since it was unlikely that many had heard any of her previous five releases, this updated "best of" forms a well-produced (if unfortunately, and predictably, more polished sounding) "debut" that showcases her singing and strumming strengths better than ever. It also allowed her to take side excursions, such as the bossanova hints richly sprinkled in.

what to buy next: With the earnest solo debut *Birdboys* 🎵🎵🎵 (Subterranean, 1987, prod. Snakefinger), Houston she established her more winsome but still impassioned style with a

light-hearted backing band of acoustic, piano, string bass, mandolin, and accordion. Interestingly enough, her old Avengers mate, guitarist Greg Ingraham, resurfaced to co-write two songs, and the bright, sunny, light-and-airy folk production was one of the last works of Snakefinger before his untimely death (the LP is dedicated to him). But in Houston's two-decade catalog, this is probably her weakest outing, as the songwriting overall is inconsistent. It took another six years for a follow-up, but *The Whole World* 🎵🎵🎵 (Heyday, 1993) is an across-the-board improvement. The acoustic band seems to gel more and the sound approaches a lovely chamber folk, while Houston herself stretches out on melodica and autoharp. And just to prove her Avengers' sense of topical matter remains within her, check out "Glad I'm a Girl."

worth searching for: Her music was better noticed in Europe than in her homeland, so three of Houston's LPs were released solely in Germany: *Silk Purse (From a Sow's Ear)* (Return to Sender/Normal Germany, 1994), *Crazy Baby* (Return to Sender/Normal Germany, 1994), and *Karmal Apple* (Normal Germany, 1995). Also, *Words + Music* (Reprise, 1994), a promotional interview and music disc that preceded *Cut You*, offers not only a fine interview with Houston but also several selections for her previous albums.

influences:
◀◀ Pentangle, Fairport Convention, Incredible String Band, Joni Mitchell

▶▶ Elliott Smith

see also: *The Avengers*

Jack Rabid

Whitney Houston

Born August 9, 1963, in Newark, NJ.

The daughter of soul and gospel singer Cissy Houston and cousin to pop vocalist Dionne Warwick, Whitney Houston's talent may be genetic. But you don't have to call cousin Didi's Psychic Friends Network to know that, in strong contrast to Houston's voice—one of the most powerful, yet supple, instruments in all of pop music—her albums have been less than spectacular thanks to middling material and cheesy '80s synth-pop production that has not aged as gracefully as Houston herself. Like Michael Jackson, Houston is more interesting as a phenomenon than as an artist; her albums have sold in the tens of millions worldwide, and, along with Jackson, Houston helped break the racial barriers that once kept black artists off of MTV. Unlike the gloved one, however, Houston's success has spilled over onto the silver screen, and she has starred in several high-profile films including *The Bodyguard, Waiting to Ex-*

hale, and *The Preacher's Wife.* She also has enjoyed massive non-album hits with "One Moment in Time," the theme to the 1988 Summer Olympics, and her Super Bowl rendition of "The Star Spangled Banner," which rode a wave of Desert Storm patriotism all the way to the bank. As impressive as her past has been, Houston's future remains a question mark. It's been eons since she made a non-soundtrack pop album, and her career has been waylaid by the birth of two children, several miscarriages, and her marriage to pop singer/miscreant Bobby Brown.

what to buy: *Whitney Houston* ✍✍✍ (Arista, 1985, prod. L.A. Reid) rocketed the young singer to superstardom almost instantly, and not without reason. Houston demonstrates her astonishing talent as a balladeer on "Saving All My Love for You" and "You Give Good Love." "The Greatest Love of All" may be a little over the top in its vapid self-help message, but Houston delivers it sincerely. And while it's but a bit of fluff, "How Will I Know" is Houston's most infectious single ever. After its release, copies of the soundtrack to *The Bodyguard* ✍✍✍ (Arista, 1992, prod. various) were issued upon entrance to a shopping mall, or so it seemed at the time. Still, much of the attention was deserved; the album contains Houston's best vocal performance ever, a triumphant take on Dolly Parton's "I Will Always Love You" that you probably still haven't dislodged from your memory banks, even if you want to. The album also contains five other Houston performances, as well as contributions by Kenny G and Aaron Neville, Lisa Stansfield and Joe Cocker, among others.

what to buy next: The soundtrack to Houston's second film, *Waiting to Exhale* ✍✍✍ (Arista, 1995, prod. Babyface) is a tour de force for producer/songwriter 'Face, but it contains only three Houston tracks—one of them the too-slight "Exhale (Shoop Shoop)" and one of them a duet with CeCe Winans. A fine return to Houston's gospel roots, the soundtrack to *The Preacher's Wife* ✍✍✍ (Arista, 1996, prod. Mervyn Warren, Whitney Houston, Stephen Lipson, Rickey Minor, Babyface, David Foster) finds her collaborating with stars from the worlds of music both sacred (The Georgia Mass Choir, Cissy Houston, Shirley Caesar) and secular (Bobby Brown, Ralph Tresvant, Johnny Gill, Monica, Faith Evans).

what to avoid: *I'm Your Baby Tonight* ✍✍ (Arista, 1990, prod. various) is a mess, thanks to its crazy quilt of producers and the fact that, for a star of Houston's magnitude, the material is extraordinarily weak. The sole standout is the bombastic "He's All the Man I Need"—which refers to God, in case you were wondering.

the rest:
Whitney ✍✍✍ (Arista, 1987)

influences:

◂◂ Aretha Franklin, Cissy Houston, Dionne Warwick, Chaka Khan, Diana Ross

▸▸ Toni Braxton, Mariah Carey, Brandy

Daniel Durchholz

Howlin' Maggie
See: Royal Crescent Mob

Howlin' Wolf
Born Chester Arthur Burnett, June 10, 1910, in Aberdeen, MS. Died January 10, 1976, in Hines, IL.

Bow at the very mention of his name. Howlin' Wolf was the volcanic core of the blues, a singer/persona whose ferocity has never been equalled and rarely even approached. He, Muddy Waters, Little Walter, and Sonny Boy Williamson were the Big Four of Chess Records, but his story starts long before he cut for the Chicago label. Wolf was schooled down South by Charley Patton, and by 1949 he fronted a band that included pagan-toned guitarist Willie Johnson and a pianist called Destruction. In 1949 he started broadcasting on KWEM in West Memphis, alternating between musical performances and pitches for farm goods. Soon he started recording. Even the baldest summary of this is complicated. He cut for Sam Phillips's Memphis Recording Service (Phillips had yet to form Sun Records); tapes were sent to the Biharis (of Modern in Los Angeles) and to Chess in Chicago. The Biharis were PO'ed that tapes were being sent to their rivals; they were all the more so when Chess released Phillips's recording of Wolf's "How Many More Years" on a 78 in August 1951. So the Biharis got Ike Turner to cut Wolf for their RPM imprint, with the result that Wolf material started coming out on both RPM and Chess. To court went the record men, their legal slugfest colorful enough for *Billboard* magazine to give intermittent coverage. All the while Wolf played—in a band called the House Rockers with Johnson and prison-bound Pat Hare on guitar. The Chess/Bihari feud ceased when Modern swapped its claim on Wolf for Chess's Rosco Gordon, and Wolf moved to Chicago. Discussion of Wolf's Chess output could fill volumes. His old henchman Johnson was on some of his sessions, as were a raft of the hottest sidemen around, including Hubert Sumlin (Wolf's great main guitar player at Chess), Jody Williams, Lee Cooper, Jimmy Rogers, Sam Lay, and the ubiquitous Otis Spann. The drubbing mantra of "Smokestack Lightning," the blast-off dynamics of "Killing Floor," the evil of "Evil," and much more represent the zenith of power in recorded blues. Wolf was possessed of divine/demonic presence in live performance, as well. He stopped making truly great recordings around 1965, but tales abound of his magnificent showmanship until only months before his death a decade later. Loremakers who tell of

Wolf must strain their vocabularies to even hint at how his music could thrill and chill. Better to recount the famous profundity of Sam Phillips, who said of Wolf: "This is where the soul of man never dies."

what to buy: Though Wolf's best-known material was on Chess, the sides on *Howlin' Wolf Rides Again* ♪♪♪♪ (Flair/Virgin, 1991, prod. Ike Turner) have a rawness and ferocity that must be heard to be believed. The disc opens fittingly with "House Rockin' Boogie," four minutes of hell-bent mania taken at breakneck pace, with Turner moshing a gloriously out-of-tune piano. As for Willie Johnson—mall rockers spend fortunes on special FX devices for their guitars and still can't get tones as leprous and depraved as his! For proof that Wolf was a naturally prescient proto-rocker, consult this cut and the comparably frenzied "Keep What You Got." Scarcely less essential is *Howlin' Wolf: His Best* ♪♪♪♪ (MCA/Chess, 1997, prod. Leonard Chess, Phil Chess, Sam Phillips, Willie Dixon), a 20-cut anthology that presents most of his prime work for Chess. "Little Red Rooster," "Spoonful," and "Back Door Man" became staples for rock bands. The sound quality's good, and an informative booklet is enclosed.

what to buy next: Wolf was an artist of such high merit even his second-string stuff rewards attention. Some of the material on the two-disc *Ain't Gonna Be Your Dog* ♪♪♪♪ (MCA/Chess, 1994, prod. Leonard Chess, Phil Chess, Sam Phillips, Willie Dixon) saw release, as did 1952's rousing "Oh Red" and the snake-hipped "Come to Me Baby," from 1955. Rounding out the set are unreleased gems, arguably not of commercial quality in their day but revealing treasures to students of Wolf's body of work.

what to avoid: Know how irretrievably bad movies have a perverse appeal to them? Same story with *Super Super Blues* ♪♪ (MCA/Chess, 1991, prod. Marshall Chess). Wolf, Mud, and Bo were grouped in a studio for the purpose of achieving competitive and hopefully comedic badinage on jivey versions of their standards, awash in wah-wah guitar and trillings from a remarkably tasteless trio of chick singers. Also, *Howlin' Wolf: The Chess Box* ♪♪ (MCA/Chess, 1992) has great material and a very informative booklet, but the CDs in my copy are tonally so harsh and toppy that they're a good argument for searching out the rare, five-LP set. Bypass this unless you see it used for a greatly reduced price. Likely, you will. Also avoid the Brit-infested *London Sessions* **woof!** (MCA/Chess, 1971/1989).

best of the rest:
The Real Folk Blues ♪♪♪♪ (MCA/Chess, 1966/1987)
More Real Folk Blues ♪♪♪ (MCA/Chess, 1967/1988)
Cadillac Daddy ♪♪♪♪ (Rounder, 1989)
Moaning at Midnight ♪♪♪♪♪ (MCA/Chess, 1989)
Change My Way ♪♪♪♪ (MCA/Chess, 1990)

worth searching for: Aficionados might want to seek out *Memphis Days: Definitive Edition* (Bear Family, 1989, prod. Sam Phillips), presenting two volumes of Wolf's Sun recordings.

influences:
◄◄ Charley Patton, Tommy Johnson, Mississippi Sheiks, Sonny Boy Williamson II, Jimmy Rogers

►► Tail Dragger, Smokey Wilson, Captain Beefheart, Jimmy Morello

Tim Schuller

H2O

Formed 1994, in New York, NY.

Toby Morse, vocals; Rusty Pistachio, guitars; Adam Blake, bass; Todd Morse, guitars (1995–present); Max Capshaw, drums (1994–95); Todd Friend, drums (1995–present).

A longtime roadie for the New York hardcore band Sick of It All, Toby Morse jumped on stage during an encore as a joke and sang his song "My Love Is Real." The crowd reaction was so strong that Morse formed his own band, which enjoyed the support of hardcore punk fans and fanzine writers who held up H2O as a penultimate example of the DIY ethic.

what's available: Both *H2O* ♪♪ (Blackout 30, 1996) and *Thicker than Water* ♪♪ (Epitaph Records, 1997) raise a ruckus, cranking out super-charged songs that, unfortunately, have minimal lasting power.

influences:
◄◄ Dag Nasty, Minor Threat, Sick of It All

Christina Fuoco

The Hudson Brothers

Formed 1964, in Portland, OR.

Bill Hudson, guitar, vocals; Brett Hudson, bass, vocals; Mark Hudson, drums, guitar, piano, vocals.

The Hudson Brothers come off like the class clowns who are hard to take seriously, despite the fact that they're as smart as the geek with the glasses (which also presumes that the geek made music like the Beach Boys or Paul McCartney). Although the Hudsons' output may not scale the heights of their heroes—mainly because they borrow so much from them—the Northwest brethren made some of the best, most fluent, studio pop of the 1970s. The trio formed in the mid-'60s, calling itself the New Yorkers, soon changing the name to Hudson (which they briefly went back to in the late '70s/early '80s), eventually appending "Brothers" to the moniker. (It was one of the few so-called brother bands whose members really were related.) A 1974 Saturday-morning television show didn't help their credibility, and the Hudsons remain largely a '70s pop obscurity—less remembered than the Raspberries and Big Star, and far less appreciated. It's an undeserved fate, since their best recordings flow with more grace and sparkle than the river that shares their name.

what's available: *So You Are a Star: The Best of the Hudson Brothers* 𝄢𝄢𝄢𝄢 (Varese Sarabande, 1995, prod. various) saves you the trouble of searching out the band's terrific but hard-to-find vinyl albums. Any fan of pop, power-pop, or good-ol'-fashioned melodic rock 'n' roll will need this to complete his or her collection. If the tremendously talented Hudsons have any flaw, it's their incessant borrowing from Badfinger, solo McCartney, and the Beach Boys. Does "So You Are a Star" ring a bell? That's because it's a near-rewrite of Badfinger's "Midnight Caller." But don't knock it—when the song revisits the melodic idea, it brings a new gift. Likewise "Rendezvous," which makes a Beach Boys splash without the Hudsons wading too close to those other brothers, the Wilsons. As good as a career-spanning compilation can possibly be, *So You Are a Star* even has previously unreleased material, making it as solid as brotherly love.

worth searching for: It's not an album, but a movie. 1983's *Hysterical* is just that, and though it's out of print, it's about the only example of the Hudson Brothers' wacky humor you'll be able to find, even if it is closer to *Airplane* than *Duck Soup*. Seeing their comedic talents in action will give you the full picture of the Hudsons—and further appreciation of all facets of their artistry, including their music. Badfinger, after all, wasn't very funny.

influences:

◄◄ Paul McCartney, the Beach Boys

►► Jellyfish, Squeeze

Jordan Oakes

Huevos Rancheros

Formed 1990, Calgary, Alberta, Canada.

Brent J. Cooper, guitar; Richie Ranchero (Lazarowich), drums; Graham Evan, bass (1990–95); Tom Kennedy, bass (1996–present).

Calgary's best surf band, Huevos Rancheros takes a slightly metallic turn to the familiar instrumental surf punk sound. Named for a delicious Mexican egg dish, the boys Rancheros benefit from a *Kerrang* magazine–influenced style of twang. Infused with humor and punch, each record is a worthy addition to your surf collection. They also get extra special praise for covering two Evan Johns & His H-Bombs cuts!

what to buy: Get—and do so quickly—the EP *Get Outta Dodge* 𝄢𝄢𝄢𝄢 (Mint, 1996, prod. Huevos Rancheros). Too short to be trying (18:57) and entirely listenable, *Get Outta Dodge* gets

votes for being the most likely surf recording to start a mosh pit in your living room. Look for the brief cover of AC/DC's "Sin City," used as song intro.

what to buy next: *Endsville* 𝄢𝄢𝄢 (C/Z, 1993, prod. "Sonic" Skip McElfresh) is the most metal of the group's records, as drummer Richie Ranchero can even be heard doing triplets. It's probably best heard blasting from somebody's crappy car stereo in the parking lot of a 7-11.

the rest:

Trouble's A-Brewin' 𝄢𝄢𝄢 (Louie EP, 1997)

worth searching for: While reasonably prolific with singles, split-side recordings, and CDs, Huevos Rancheros isn't likely stocked at your local mall store. Too bad. So order *Dig In* (Mint, 1995, prod. Jeff Burns, Huevos Rancheros) while there's still time. Included is a recording of the drive-in intermission concessions classic—the one with the swingin' food.

influences:

◄◄ The Ventures, the Surfaris, the Raybeats, Jon & the Nightriders, Link Wray, Duane Eddy, Dick Dale, Evan Johns & His H-Bombs, Motörhead, Judas Priest, AC/DC

▶▶ Jackie & the Cedrics, the Volcanos, Galaxy Trio

Barry M. Prickett

Huffamoose

Formed 1992, in Philadelphia, PA.

Craig Elkins, vocals, guitar; Kevin Hanson, lead guitar; Jim Stager, bass; Erik Johnson, drums.

Although barely apparent in its music, Huffamoose was born of jazz musicians. Craig Elkins was performing around Philadelphia as a singer-songwriter when he called Kevin Hanson to fill in for a gig. It lasted several evenings, and eventually Hanson's bandmates in the Philly jazz quintet—Jim Stager and Erik Johnson—joined as well and gave themselves over to the modern rock realm.

what to buy: *We've Been Had Again* 𝄢𝄢𝄢♩ (Interscope Records, 1997, prod. Huffamoose, Erik Horvitz) shows off Elkins's ability to mold his thoughts into crafty pop songs. "Wait," the opening track, is entrancing and sways just like the hips of the girlfriend about whom he sings. A lyrical flipping of the bird to the music industry, "We've Been Had Again" hints at Huffamoose's jazz background and Dinosaur Jr. influence. Elkins sounds like Jerry Seinfeld in the pop ballad "Buy You a Ring" when he sings "What a sorry song/What a stupid idea/I write the songs that make the whole world think/about absolutely nothing." But just like *Seinfeld,* Huffamoose makes everyday happenings entertaining.

influences:

◀◀ Todd Rundgren, Dinosaur Jr., Cowboy Junkies

Christina Fuoco

Hum

Formed 1990, in Champaign, IL.

Matt Talbot, guitar, vocals, Jeff Dimpsey, bass, vocals; Tim Lash, guitar, vocals; Bryan St. Pere, drums, vocals.

About what you'd expect from a big-league Illinois band, Hum offers no great departures from the '90s Midwest rock scene. That said, the quartet is generally quite listenable. Culling its guitar-based sound from a combination of British shoe-gazers and alterna-arena rockers—think My Bloody Valentine meets Smashing Pumpkins—Hum offers a largely half-time rock-out that is occasionally as delightful as the combination of cotton candy and beer (a good thing).

what to buy: *You'd Prefer an Astronaut* 𝄢𝄢𝄢♩ (RCA, 1995, prod. Hum, Keith Cleversley) contains the hit "Stars" but should be remembered for the subtle and somber "Suicide Machine."

the rest:
Downward Heavenward 𝄢𝄢𝄢 (RCA, 1997)
Electra 2000 𝄢𝄢♩ (12 Inch/Cargo, 1993)

influences:

◀◀ Poster Children, My Bloody Valentine, Jesus & Mary Chain, Smashing Pumpkins, Ride, Swervedriver, Catherine Wheel, Seam, Bitch Magnet

▶▶ Tonic

Barry M. Prickett

Human League

Formed 1977, in Sheffield, England.

Phil Oakey, vocals, synthesizer; Martyn Ware, synthesizer (1977–80); Ian Craig Marsh, synthesizer (1977–80); Ian Burden, bass, synthesizer (1980–present); Suzanne Sulley, vocals (1980–present); Joanne Catherall, vocals (1980–present); Jo Callis, synthesizer (1981–present).

The Human League reigned supreme over British new wave pop groups of the early '80s with its slick, synth-driven radio hits. Although it began as a rather dour Kraftwerk-influenced group, its pop machine was in full gear by the time of its first U.S. release in 1982. By bringing various soul-inflected tunes to its programmed pop aesthetic, the band showed considerably more staying power and commercial viability than many of its foppish counterparts. However, the hollow emotional core inhabiting virtually all of '80s synth-pop eventually took over. Most of Human League's studio albums—1982's *Dare* being the most consistent—are out of print.

what to buy: *Greatest Hits* 𝄢𝄢𝄢 (A&M, 1988, prod. various) is a fair reminder of a band that started out with great singles, only to descend into ill-conceived political stabs and empty funk. Some of the better tracks—"Fascination," "Mirror Man," and the group's first smash, "Don't You Want Me"—are included.

the rest:
Octopus 𝄢𝄢 (EastWest America, 1995)
The Very Best Of 𝄢𝄢𝄢 (Ark 21, 1998)

influences:

◀◀ Kraftwerk, David Bowie, Giorgio Moroder

▶▶ Pet Shop Boys, Erasure, Heaven 17, Depeche Mode

see also: *Heaven 17*

Allan Orski

Humble Pie

Formed 1969, in Essex, England. Disbanded 1975. Re-formed c. 1980–81.

Steve Marriott, vocals, guitar, keyboards; Peter Frampton, vocals, guitar (1969–71); Greg Ridley, bass, vocals; Jerry Shirley, drums; David

"Clem" Clempson, guitar, vocals; Bobby Tench, vocals, guitar (1980–81); Anthony Jones, bass (1980–81).

When British pop stars Steve Marriott and Peter Frampton—from the Small Faces and the Herd, respectively—hooked up during the late '70s, few could have guess that they were creating a prototypical boogie 'n' blues-based hard rock outfit. The first few albums hinted at that direction, but it was the ferocious, molten jams of *Performance—Rockin' the Fillmore* that really staked Humble Pie's claim. Things got a bit too heavy for Frampton, who split for his own momentarily successful solo career, while Marriott guided Humble Pie into the realm of non-stop touring and workmanlike albums—though "30 Days in the Hole" endures. By the mid-'70s, Humble Pie was pretty well spent (its role having been taken over by the likes of Foghat and REO Speedwagon), and the turn-of-the-decade attempt to revive it was inconsequential. Sadly, Marriott and Frampton had begun working together again when the former died in a house fire in 1991.

what to buy: *Performance—Rockin' the Fillmore* 𝄢𝄢𝄢𝄢 (A&M, 1971/1988, prod. Humble Pie) is Humble Pie's shining, triumphant moment, rocking up a fury with extended versions of "I Don't Need No Doctor," "I'm Ready," and nearly a half-hour of "I Walk on Gilded Splinters." You'll never believe that Frampton played like this. *Hot 'n' Nasty: The Anthology* 𝄢𝄢𝄢𝄢 (A&M/Chronicles, 1994, prod. various) shows that Humble Pie was more than a boogie band, generously sampling from each of the group's albums for a consistently compelling overview.

what to buy next: *Rock On* 𝄢𝄢𝄢 (A&M, 1971/Rebound, 1994, prod. Glyn Johns, Humble Pie) and *Smokin'* 𝄢𝄢𝄢 (A&M, 1972, prod. the Pie), which bookended *Performance*, are as consistent as Humble Pie ever got on its studio albums. The latter has "30 Days in the Hole."

what to avoid: The first comeback album, *On to Victory* 𝄢 (Atco, 1980/1991, prod. Johnny Wright, Humble Pie), was a defeat. Lord knows why the group tried another one.

the rest:
Town and Country 𝄢𝄢𝄢 (A&M, 1969/Griffin, 1994)
Humble Pie 𝄢𝄢 (A&M, 1970/Griffin, 1994)
Go for the Throat 𝄢 (Atco, 1981/1991)
The Best of Humble Pie 𝄢𝄢𝄢 (A&M, 1982)
Classics, Vol. 14 𝄢𝄢𝄢 (A&M, 1987)
Early Years 𝄢𝄢𝄢 (Griffin, 1994)
Rock On 𝄢𝄢𝄢 (Rebound, 1994)
King Biscuit Flower Hour Presents Humble Pie 𝄢𝄢𝄢𝄢 (KBFH Records, 1995)
The Scrubbers Sessions 𝄢𝄢𝄢 (Archive, 1997)

worth searching for: Humble Pie's first album, *As Safe As Yesterday* (Columbia, 1969/Line, 1987, prod. Humble Pie), currently available as an import, is an intriguing and sometimes trippy record that serves Frampton's more melodic sensibilities particularly well.

solo outings:
Steve Marriott:
30 Seconds to Midnite 𝄢𝄢𝄢 (Griffin, 1989/1994)

influences:
◀◀ John Lee Hooker, Willie Dixon, the Beatles, Spooky Tooth

▶▶ Foghat, REO Speedwagon, Ted Nugent, the Black Crowes, Cry of Love

see also: *Peter Frampton, the Faces*

Gary Graff

Ian Hunter

Born June 3, 1946, in Shrewsbury, England.

When he left Mott the Hoople in 1974—after being hospitalized for exhaustion—Ian Hunter moved to New York and continued along a similar musical path, basically a mix of rowdy, pub-style rockers and dramatic ballads, often dressed with literate and wry lyrics. In the years just before punk, Hunter's collaborations with former Bowie/Mott sidekick Mick Ronson were ill-timed for mass attention but unquestionably made an impact on what came later (the Clash's Mick Jones returned the favor by producing Hunter's *Short Back and Sides* in 1981). Since the early '80s, Hunter has surfaced infrequently, though he has popped up on albums by Def Leppard and on the late Ronson's final effort, *Heaven and Hull*, while his song "Cleveland Rocks" was resurrected for the TV sitcom *The Drew Carey Show*. A good chunk of his recorded output is out of print, which truly is our loss.

what to buy: On his solo debut, *Ian Hunter* 𝄢𝄢𝄢𝄢 (Columbia, 1975/Legacy, 1990, prod. Ian Hunter, Mick Ronson), Hunter sounds like a man with something to prove and comes out gangbusters with "Once Bitten, Twice Shy," "Who Do You Love," and the expansive tone poem "Boy." On *Short Back and Sides* 𝄢𝄢𝄢𝄢 (Chrysalis, 1981/Griffin, 1995, prod. Mick Jones), producer Jones's influence is clearly heard on the funk of "Noises," the reggae touches on "Gun Control," and the bop of "Lisa Likes to Rock 'n' Roll."

what to buy next: *You're Never Alone with a Schizophrenic* 𝄢𝄢𝄢𝄢 (Chrysalis, 1979/Razor & Tie, 1994, prod. Ian Hunter, Mick Ronson) is a smart, snappy set of rockers ("Just Another Night," "Cleveland Rocks"), though it also includes "Ships"—a song so sappy that Barry Manilow covered it.

what to avoid: *Ian Hunter's Dirty Laundry* 𝄢𝄢 (Cleveland International, 1995) came after a period of inactivity and sounds as rusty as you'd imagine.

worth searching for: *Welcome to the Club* (Chrysalis, 1980/1994, prod. Mick Ronson, Ian Hunter), sadly available only via import, is a spirited live album that features solo material, Mott favorites, and even Ronson's "Slaughter on Tenth Avenue." *The Artful Dodger* (Polydor U.K., 1996, prod. Bjorn Nessjo) isn't all that exciting, but it at least lets us know the old boy is still kicking around.

influences:

◀◀ Bob Dylan, David Bowie, Little Richard

▶▶ Graham Parker, Elvis Costello, Great White, Smashing Pumpkins, Def Leppard

see also: *Mott the Hoople, Mick Ronson*

Gary Graff

Hunters & Collectors

Formed 1980, in Melbourne, Australia.

Mark Seymour, vocals, guitar; Jack Howard, trumpet; Michael Waters, trombone, keyboards; Jeremy Smith, French horn, keyboards; John Archer, bass; Doug Falconer, drums; Greg Perano, percussion (1980–84); Martin Lubran, guitar (1980–84).

Starting out as an experimental blend of rugged Australian post-punk rock, tribal percussion jams, and blaring horns, Hunters & Collectors quickly became a popular live act Down Under. But although 1982's fairly alluring single, "Talking to a Stranger," aired on MTV for a brief time, the band didn't really hit its mark until 1986's *Human Frailty* employed tighter song structures that merged the guitars, horns, and rhythm more evenly behind Mark Seymour's wailing, over-the-top vocals. An even better effort, *Fate*, followed, and around the same time the horn section made a significant contribution to Midnight Oil's best album, *Diesel and Dust*. But the creative spark seemingly departed soon after, and although the group remains a sizable draw in Australia, it never really did crack the U.S. market, nor has it released anything here for several years. Seymour's vocals can be too much at times; his feverish approach often sounds as though someone should be hunting for, and collecting, some oxygen for the poor guy. But at its best, the band combines stirring fervor with graceful elements. Plus, there's always that wild horn section and, most important of all, John Archer's wiry, slamming bass parts grooving with Doug Falconer's tom-heavy, tribal drums. It's a combo that's hard to beat.

what to buy: With its '60s-style blend of surf-influenced guitars and TV detective-show horn figures, *Fate* ୪୪୪୪ (IRS, 1988, prod. Greg Howard, Hunters & Collectors) is solid and energetic throughout. The almost Stonesy "Faraway Man" and the rather dark and oddly powerful "Wishing Well" are the standout tracks, but there are few weak cuts here, period.

what to buy next: Although it's less consistent than *Fate*, *Human Frailty* ୪୪୪ (IRS, 1986, prod. Gavin MacKillop, Hunters & Collectors) opens up with three of the band's best, most crackling numbers—"Say Goodbye," "Is There Anybody in There?," and the elegant "Throw Your Arms Around Me." For those who want an overview, *Collected Works* ୪୪୪୪ (IRS, 1990, prod. various) offers five tracks each from *Fate* and *Human Frailty* along with hit and miss selections from other albums.

what to avoid: Despite backing vocals from Crowded House's Neil Finn, *Ghost Nation* ୪୪ (Atlantic, 1990) is a surprisingly lackluster effort, a strange and disappointing development following the band's two best albums.

the rest:

Demon Flower ୪୪୪ (Shake the Record, 1994)

worth searching for: Those seeking something rawer and more industrial/percussion-driven may want to check out *Hunters & Collectors* (Oz/A&M, 1983) or its Australian counterpart, a double album with almost entirely different material.

influences:

◀◀ Gang of Four, Midnight Oil, Bad Manners, Lords of the New Church, the Kinks

▶▶ Hoodoo Gurus, Nick Cave

Bob Remstein

Hurricane #1

See: Ride

Lida Husik /Husikesque

Born c. 1963, in Washington, DC.

Lida Husik was part of the D.C. punk scene of the early '80s before discovering the joys of one-woman band and four-track recording. Her atmospheric folk-pop albums with Shimmy-Disc label founder Kramer presaged the rise of similar, dusky-voiced singers such as Liz Phair. At the same time, she drew attention in Europe's ambient-techno community, resulting in a pair of collaborations with British deejay-mixer Beaumont Hannant.

what to buy: *Joyride* ୪୪୪୪ (Caroline, 1995, prod. Geoff Turner, others) drifts from a pop-solid foundation into psychedelia with Husik's dreamy, Johnny Marr–like guitar strumming and layered voices. Husik's fabulist imagery, reminiscent of author Gabriel Garcia Marquez, merges with a profound spiritualism that is enigmatic and moving. One of the lost mini-masterpieces of the '90s.

what to buy next: Husik, recording as Husikesque in collaboration with British ambient whiz kid Hannant and Richard Brown (a.k.a. Outcast Productions), delves deeper into her mystical side on the lovely, lost-in-space tone poems that comprise the EP *Green Blue Fire* 🎵🎵🎵🎵 (Astralwerks, 1996, prod. Beaumont Hannant, Richard Brown).

the rest:
Bozo 🎵🎵🎵 (Shimmy-Disc, 1991)
Your Bag 🎵🎵 (Shimmy-Disc, 1992)
The Return of Red Emma 🎵🎵 (Shimmy-Disc, 1993)
Fly Stereophonic 🎵🎵🎵🎵 (Alias, 1997)

solo outings:
Lida Husik/Beaumont Hannant:
Evening at the Grange EP 🎵🎵🎵 (Astralwerks, 1994)

influences:
◄◄ Barbara Manning, Mazzy Star, Dead Can Dance, Dentists
►► Liz Phair, Sarah McLachlan, Beth Orton

Greg Kot

Hüsker Dü

Formed 1979, in St. Paul, MN. Disbanded 1988.

Bob Mould, vocals, guitar; Grant Hart, vocals, drums; Greg Norton, bass, vocals.

Hüsker Dü was simply one of the great rock bands of the 1980s, truly communal in terms of band dynamics (at least in the beginning), blazingly intense, and wildly prolific. Under a hail of scathing guitars and a battering rhythm section, the trio combined brute force with carefully constructed and often sweetly melodic songs. Although most punk bands spew their anger outward, Hüsker Dü's themes were painfully personal, displaying an often-unflinching self-awareness. While most critics would have you believe Hüsker Dü and the Replacements invented alternative rock (they didn't), the Hüskers' influence can't be overstated in both musical and commercial terms. One of the first alterna-bands to sign on to a major record label (Warner Bros.) without compromise, Hüsker Dü seemed poised for major recognition. But personal problems, power struggles, and eventual label disagreements (Warner Bros. wanted to nix Grant Hart in favor of programmed drums) led to its ultimate dissolution. Bob Mould has gone on to release his own albums as well as a few with the band Sugar. Hart also went solo before forming Nova Mob; his post-Hüsker work has been less celebrated than Mould's but is no less visceral. Greg Norton, meanwhile, quit the business and went on to become a chef.

what to buy: *Zen Arcade* 🎵🎵🎵🎵🎵 (SST, 1984, prod. Spot, Hüsker Dü), a double-length concept album, was the zenith of the band's collaborative powers. It's an arresting roller coaster ride of epic proportions that reaches its peaks on the wild instrumental "Dream Reoccurring" and the drug lament "Pink Turns to Blue."

New Day Rising 🎵🎵🎵🎵 (SST, 1984, prod. Spot, Hüsker Dü) focuses the band's sound with a set of songs of ferocious momentum. Inherently tuneful and blaring, "I Apologize," "Terms of Psychic Warfare," and "59 Times the Pain" all explode on impact. *Flip Your Wig* 🎵🎵🎵🎵 (SST, 1985, prod. Bob Mould, Grant Hart) is even more concise, played with screamingly tight precision, as if it had been recorded while the group went over a cliff. The airtight pop melodics of "Makes No Sense at All," "Green Eyes," and "Hate Paper Doll" only add to the supercharged atmosphere.

what to buy next: Moving to the majors with typical feral grace results in, if anything, a more emotionally intense map of bitterness and pounding rockers on *Candy Apple Grey* 🎵🎵🎵🎵 (Warner Bros. 1986, prod. Bob Mould, Grant Hart). Two fine acoustic songs mix quite well with the bristling vitriol. *Warehouse: Songs and Stories* 🎵🎵🎵🎵 (Warner Bros., 1987), another double release, was compared to Derek & the Dominoes' *Layla* but it's more like the Beatles' *White Album*. The struggles within the band reached the breaking point with the two creative forces, Mould and Hart, operating as separate entities. The tension is palpable, the implosion inevitable, and the band goes down like titans clashing—a pretty exciting sound, actually.

what to avoid: *Land Speed Record* 🎵🎵 (SST, 1981, prod. Hüsker Dü) is by no means worthless, but the cheap recording of its live shows only hints at the band's power. Check out *The Living End* for a better idea.

the rest:
Everything Falls Apart and More 🎵🎵🎵 (Reflex, 1982/Rhino, 1995)
Metal Circus 🎵🎵🎵 (SST, 1983)
The Living End 🎵🎵🎵🎵 (Warner Bros., 1994)

worth searching for: Grant Hart's *2541* (SST EP, 1988) was a first solo stab, with a touching acoustic title track.

solo outings:
Grant Hart:
Intolerance 🎵🎵🎵 (SST, 1989)
(With Nova Mob) *The Last Days of Pompeii* 🎵🎵 (Rough Trade, 1991)
(With Nova Mob) *Nova Mob* 🎵🎵🎵 (Restless, 1994)

influences:
◄◄ Black Flag
►► Soul Asylum, Nirvana, the Pixies

see also: *Bob Mould*

Allan Orski

Brian Hyland

Born November 12, 1943, in Woodhaven, NY.

Scoring his first and biggest hit at the age of 16 with that immortal piece of beach fluff, "Itsy Bitsy Teenie Weenie Yellow

Polka Dot Bikini," things could not have looked entirely promising for this ambitious young entertainer. While still in high school, Brian Hyland followed that novelty hit with several others in a similar vein ("Lop-Sided, Overloaded and It Wiggled When I Rode It") before apparently taking stock and getting down to some less frivolous music-making. The result? An exquisite 1962 tear-jerker called "Sealed with a Kiss," which established Hyland—briefly—as one of the last of the pre-Beatle teen idols. He returned to the charts in 1966 with "The Joker Went Wild" and again in 1970 with a fine reading of Curtis Mayfield's "Gypsy Woman" (co-produced with old friend Del Shannon) before vanishing into the netherworld of low-budget country albums and summertime nostalgia fairs. Still, he *has* left his mark, although perhaps not as he would have liked to; "Itsy Bitsy Teenie Weenie" remains his best-selling, best-remembered, and most-requested tune to this day.

what's available: Listening closely to *Brian Hyland's Greatest Hits* 𝄢𝄢𝄢 (MCA, 1994, compilation prod. Brian Hyland, Cary E. Mansfield), one can't help but sense that age-old artistic battle between the Silly and the Serious being waged throughout. Naturally, his light-hearted novelty numbers remain the most instantly accessible, but tracks such as "Ginny Come Lately" and "Warmed Over Kisses (Left Over Love)" reveal a brooding, possibly even troublesome spirit behind each lovesick lyric, helping these songs stand the ravages of time as few others from that Brylcreemed Bobby period do.

influences:

◀◀ Del Shannon, Bobby Vee, Neil Sedaka, Sheb Wooley

▶▶ Tommy Roe, Billy Joe Royal, Jason Donovan, Steve O'Brien

Gary Pig Gold

Janis Ian

Born Janis Eddy Fink, May 7, 1951, in New York, NY.

Janis Ian was the Tiffany and Debbie Gibson of her time, with a crucial difference; her music was good, and serious. Ian was just 15 when she courted controversy with "Society's Child," her searing observation about interracial romance that was banned by some radio stations but finally won respect when Leonard Bernstein invited her to perform it on a 1967 TV special he hosted about rock. But the rest of Ian's career has been somewhat fitful, marked as much by commercial slumps and prolonged absences as by hits. She did return to the charts in 1975 with her hit "At Seventeen," but not long after that she

began a 12-year break from recording. When she returned, Ian came out as a lesbian, and though her subsequent albums have not launched hits, they have been among the most moving and resonant of her career.

what to buy: On *Between the Lines* 𝄢𝄢𝄢𝄢 (Columbia, 1975), "At Seventeen" is only one of an album full of luminous, well-crafted songs. *Breaking Silence* 𝄢𝄢𝄢𝄢 (Morgan Creek, 1993, prod. Janis Ian, Jeff Balding) is a bold return to recording on which Ian, never one to scrimp on her emotions, is even more frank and pointed.

what to buy next: Seek out *Society's Child: The Verve Recordings* 𝄢𝄢𝄢 (Polydor/Chronicles, 1995, prod. various) because you have to have "Society's Child," although this two-disc set would have been better as a more judiciously selected single.

what to avoid: *Present Company* 𝄢𝄢 (Capitol, 1971/One Way, 1994) is a transitional effort between Ian's earnest teenage recordings and her more deeply rooted work of the mid-'70s, an awkward phase in anybody's life, much less a recording artist.

the rest:
Revenge 𝄢𝄢𝄢𝄡 (Beacon, 1995)
Hunger 𝄢𝄢𝄢𝄡 (Windham Hill, 1997)

worth searching for: *Between the Lines*' predecessor, *Stars* (Columbia, 1974), marked a new maturity in Ian's music. It also includes "Jesse," which was a hit for Roberta Flack.

influences:

◀◀ Joan Baez, Rev. Gary Davis, Ronnie Gilbert

▶▶ Suzanne Vega, Tracy Chapman, Shawn Colvin

Gary Graff

Jimmy Ibbotson

See: Nitty Gritty Dirt Band

Icehouse

Formed 1980, in Sydney, Australia.

Iva Davies, vocals, guitars, keyboards, oboe, English horn; Robert Kretschmer, guitars (1982–present); Anthony Smith, keyboards (1981–82); Keith Welsh, bass (1981–82); Andy Qunta, keyboards (1982–87); Simon Lloyd, saxophone, trumpet, keyboards (1984–present); Guy Pratt, bass (1982–86); Stephen Morgan, bass (1987–89); John Lloyd, drums, percussion (1981–84); Paul Wheeler, drums (1987–present).

For a while during the mid-'80s, it seemed that Icehouse lead singer and head songwriter Iva Davies was little more than a poor man's Bryan Ferry. He had the soaring tenor voice, and like many other New Romantic groups of that era, Icehouse was influenced equally by the seductive, layered pop/rock of later Roxy Music and the sassier, glam-inflected rock 'n' roll of David Bowie. But Davies has never exhibited much personality, either on stage or on disc, and his albums have rarely featured more than two noteworthy songs apiece. Starting out as Flowers, Davies and his original cohorts received little attention until the band's debut was re-released under the name Icehouse. New wavey and pointedly electronic, the album mixed elements of Ultravox and the Cars to good effect. On the follow-up, *Primitive Man*, the Ferry influence kicked in, with "Hey Little Girl" (a hit in Europe) and "Street Cafe." It wasn't until 1986, though, that the band found its mark with *No Promises*, a dazzling bit of mid-'80s pop—moody, rangy, and a terrific showcase for Davies's vocals. In 1987 the group scored two Top 10 U.S. hits, "Crazy" and "Electric Blue," one overwrought and the other (co-written with John Oates of Hall & Oates) forgettable. Legal problems with Chrysalis Records ensued, and the group never again regained its commercial momentum. After a break of a few years, the band apparently has returned to active duty and recently released (in Australia and Germany, at least) an album of covers titled *The Berlin Tapes*, featuring songs made famous by Bowie, Lou Reed, and the late Frank Sinatra. Be afraid. Be very afraid.

what to buy: Until a decent singles package is released domestically (and don't hold your breath), *Measure for Measure* ♪♪♪ (Chrysalis, 1986, prod. David Lord, Rhett Davies) is probably your best bet, largely because it features the band's best single, the gloriously extravagant "No Promises." Brian Eno lends his sonic talents on a few cuts, but most of the songs just don't hold up.

what to buy next: *Icehouse* ♪♪ (Chrysalis, 1981, prod. Cameron Allan, Iva Davies) offers the band in its early, pre-Roxy Music-influenced version. With its coldly electronic approach, the album sounds like an Icehouse record (for once), and though Davies's vocals have that Midge Ure–like sheen, songs such as "I Can't Help Myself" and the title track are dark and rather interesting.

what to avoid: Wracked by fake Bowie-isms and short on compelling songs, *Sidewalk* **woof!** (Chrysalis, 1984, prod. Iva Davies) is better left in the gutter. And don't get suckered into picking up *Great Southern Land* ♪ (Chrysalis, 1989, prod. various). Although it was marketed as a greatest-hits package, the album leaves out "No Promises," includes cheesily re-recorded versions of first-album tunes, and omits everything from *Man of Colours*, the band's biggest-seller in the United States.

the rest:
Primitive Man ♪♪ (Chrysalis, 1982)
Man of Colours ♪♪♪ (Chrysalis, 1987)

worth searching for: The five-song EP *Fresco* (Chrysalis, 1983, prod. Iva Davies, Keith Forsey) is a less painful way of experiencing Icehouse, as only one real dud is included along with the two best (and most Roxy Music-influenced) songs from *Primitive Man* : "Hey Little Girl" and "Street Cafe."

influences:

◄◄ Roxy Music, David Bowie, the Cars, Alan Parsons Project, Ultravox

►► Cutting Crew, Talk Talk, Tears for Fears

Bob Remstein

The Icicle Works

Formed 1980, in Liverpool, England. Disbanded 1990.

Ian McNabb, vocals, guitar, keyboards; Chris Layhe, bass, vocals, keyboards (1980–88); Chris Sharrock, drums (1980–88); Zak Starkey, drums (1988–89); Dave Green, keyboards (1988–89); Roy Corkhill, bass (1988–90); Dave Baldwin, keyboards (1989–90); Mark Revell, guitar, vocals (1989–90); Paul Burgess, drums (1989–90).

The Icicle Works sprang from the same Liverpool scene that launched Echo & the Bunnymen, Big in Japan, and the Teardrop Explodes. Taking its name from a '60s sci-fi short story, "The Day the Icicle Works Closed" by Frederik Pohl, the Icicle Works was at heart a rock band: guitars and keyboards blended seamlessly and Chris Sharrock's percussive flourishes were always high in the mix. That's not to say the band didn't have its art-rock pretensions—the lyrics often dealt with grand themes like spirituality, love, and sociological ills, and it's highly likely that such heavy subject matter limited the band's commercial appeal. The band released its first single, "Ascending," in 1981. However, the group's first album, the self-titled *Icicle Works*, wasn't released until 1984, and contained what was to become the one song most associated with the group, "Whisper to a Scream (Birds Fly)" (the title was reversed in the U.K. for reasons unknown). No '80s "best of" compilation is complete without it. The band went on to release several other impressive singles and albums, but in the end, personnel changes and musical inconsistency took their toll. Icicle Works disbanded in 1990; however, 1992 saw the release of a compilation and in 1994 the BBC released a live recording from a 1987 concert. Following the break-up, Ian McNabb pursued a solo career and released three critically acclaimed albums. In 1998 he was still touring in support of his own music and as the bass player for former Waterboy Mike Scott's band. Original drummer Sharrock was briefly a member of Ian Broudie's re-formed Lightning Seeds during 1994; he has also played with Del Amitri, Spiritualized, and World Party.

what to buy: *The Best of the Icicle Works* ♪♪♪♪ (Beggars Banquet, 1992, prod. various) is exactly what it says. The band's big hit is here, as are other singles such as "Love Is a Wonderful

Colour," "Understanding Jane," and "Evangeline." *If You Want to Defeat Your Enemy, Sing His Song* 𝄞𝄞𝄞𝄞 (Beggars Banquet/RCA, 1987, prod. Ian Broudie) finds the band in full flower, completely at ease with McNabb's often anthemic songwriting. Widely regarded as the group's best album, it features the stellar track "Understanding Jane," which failed to garner much attention, despite being as catchy and melodious as "Birds Fly."

what to buy next: The band's first full-length album, *Icicle Works* 𝄞𝄞𝄞𝄞 (Beggars Banquet/Arista, 1984, prod. Hugh Jones) contains the band's signature song, "Whisper to a Scream (Birds Fly)," and other standout tracks such as the sweeping "Nirvana" and "Love Is a Wonderful Colour." *The Small Price of a Bicycle* 𝄞𝄞𝄞 (Beggars Banquet/Chrysalis, 1985) explores a more soulful sound, although it still shows flashes of the band's clean, sharp guitar work and smooth vocal harmonies, notably on the track "Hollow Horse."

what to avoid: Both *Blind* **woof!** (Beggars Banquet, 1988) and *Permanent Damage* **woof!** (Epic, 1990) tend to be uninspired and samey. The band was undergoing a series of line-up changes during the two or three years surrounding the release of these albums, and the turmoil is obvious. Even Ringo Starr's son Zak Starkey (on drums, of course) fails to leave much of an impression on *Blind*.

the rest:
Seven Singles Deep 𝄞𝄞 (Beggars Banquet, 1986)
BBC Live in Concert 𝄞𝄞𝄞 (Windsong/BBC, 1994)

worth searching for: The initial release of *The Best of the Icicle Works* contained two CDs, one featuring the band's more recognizable singles, the other featuring a collection of B-sides and live tracks.

solo outings:
Ian McNabb:
Truth and Beauty 𝄞𝄞𝄞𝄞 (This Way Up, 1993)
Head like a Rock 𝄞𝄞𝄞𝄞 (This Way Up, 1994)
Merseybeast 𝄞𝄞𝄞𝄞 (This Way Up, 1996)

influences:
◄◄ The Beatles, the Byrds, the Velvet Underground, the Buzzcocks, Big in Japan, the Teardrop Explodes, Simple Minds, Neil Young

►► A House, Prefab Sprout, the Lucy Show, the Woodentops, World Party

Lisa M. Moore

Idaho

Formed 1992, in Los Angeles, CA.

John Berry, guitar, drums (1992–93); Jeff Martin, bass, vocals, four-string guitar, drums, keyboards; Mark Lewis, drums, trumpet (1995–96); Dan Seta, guitars (1995–present); Terrence Borden, bass, acoustic guitar (1995–96).

Founding members John Berry and Jeff Martin knew each other for years on the L.A. punk scene before they started recording together around 1987. The duo often played all the instruments on its songs but occasionally used various temporary drummers. Berry, the son of TV actor Ken Berry (*Mayberry R.F.D., F Troop*), was an off-and-on heroin junkie who had served time in jail; after his problems forced him out of the band, Martin went on without him, eventually making some of the musicians he used full-time band members. Always he produces a shimmering sound with guitar effects and occasional outbursts set to slow but inexorable rhythms, topped off with his angst-laden vocals. This is an original and unique band, though its dark-hued songs can be hard on weaker psyches.

what to buy: *Year after Year* 𝄞𝄞𝄞𝄞 (Caroline, 1993, prod. Idaho, Martin Brumbach) is an intense, gorgeously moody album from the original duo. Martin's low vocal range, which he uses a lot, sounds at its darkest like Joy Division's Ian Curtis (his bass playing also recalls Joy Division's fat, round sound), while his upper range is a dead ringer for American Music Club's Mark Eitzel. The music, in fact, suggests a snarling, less-mellow AMC.

what to buy next: *This Way Out* 𝄞𝄞𝄞𝄞 (Caroline, 1994, prod. Jeff Martin, Martin Brumbach) opens up the sound a bit while continuing to explore angst and dolor. Martin's voice fits well with his tingling, shuddering guitar riffs and almost poppy melodies, like the Lemonheads on Quaaludes.

the rest:
The Palms 𝄞𝄞𝄞 (Caroline, 1993)
Three Sheets to the Wind 𝄞𝄞𝄞 (Caroline, 1996)
The Forbidden EP 𝄞𝄞𝄞 (Buzz, 1997)

worth searching for: A new album, titled *Alas*, is promised by the end of 1998.

influences:
◄◄ Joy Division, American Music Club, Dinosaur Jr.

►► Red House Painters

Steve Holtje

Billy Idol
/Generation X

Formed 1976, in London, England. Disbanded 1981.

Billy Idol (born William Michael Albert Broad, November 30, 1955, in Stanmore, Middlesex, England), vocals; Tony James, bass, vocals; Bob Andrews, guitar, vocals; John Towe, drums (1976–77); Mark Laff, drums (1977–81).

The first punk to enthusiastically court the mainstream pop audi-

Billy Idol (© Ken Settle)

ence, Billy Idol first used his decent band Generation X, then catchy songs, spikey hair, and a good sneer to sell lots of records. During the mid-'70s, avid trend-follower Idol shifted allegiances from the Beatles to the Sex Pistols, hung out constantly at Malcolm McLaren's famous Sex Shop, and formed Generation X. Though many purists turned up their noses at the band of unashamed punks-for-profit, the group put out some excellent singles, including "Your Generation" and "Ready, Steady, Go," not to mention indirectly inspiring the name of a Douglas Coupland book and a marketing term for an actual generation. Idol's solo career began with a dance retread of the band's popular "Dancing with Myself," which became a huge hit—one of many in his lucrative '80s career. Punks, revolted by Idol's dominant presence on MTV, turned their backs on him, but the masses embraced him wholeheartedly. By the '90s, however, Idol was desperately searching for an audience and unsuccessfully tried to ride the cyberpunk movement's coattails, putting out a computer news release and an abysmal album called *Cyberpunk* before hopping on the Who's *Quadrophenia* tour in the role of the Bell Boy and making a cameo appearance in the '80s nostalgia flick *The Wedding Singer*.

what to buy: Generation X's *Perfect Hits: 1975–1981* 𝄞𝄞𝄞 (Chrysalis, 1991, prod. various) collects the band's best early singles, including "Ready, Steady, Go," "One Hundred Punks," and the original "Dancing with Myself."

what to buy next: Many punk fans still consider Idol verboten for shifting gears into bland pop hits in order to be a big star. Still, *Rebel Yell* 𝄞𝄞𝄞 (Chrysalis, 1983, prod. Michael Frondelli)—bolstered by the slash 'n' burn guitar attack of Steve Stevens—is a formidable commercial accomplishment, featuring a year's worth of smash hits in the title track, "Eyes without a Face" and "Flesh for Fantasy."

what to avoid: Idol's *Cyberpunk* 𝄞 (Chrysalis, 1993, prod. Robin Hancock) unashamedly tries to cash in on a trend, but he forgot to bring the songs.

the rest:
Billy Idol:
Don't Stop 𝄞𝄞 (Chrysalis, 1981)
Billy Idol 𝄞𝄞 (Chrysalis, 1982)
Whiplash Smile 𝄞𝄞 (Chrysalis, 1986)
Vital Idol 𝄞𝄞 (Chrysalis, 1987)
Charmed Life 𝄞𝄞𝄞 (Chrysalis, 1990)

Generation X:
Valley of the Dolls 𝄞𝄞 (Chrysalis, 1979)
The Best of Generation X 𝄞𝄞𝄞 (Chrysalis, 1985)

worth searching for: *Idol Songs* (Chrysalis, 1988, prod. various), a British collection of Idol's hits, is a better compilation than the *Vital Idol* remix collection. Also, *Generation X* (Chrysalis, 1978) is

among the best albums of the punk era, with a cover of John Lennon's "Gimme Some Truth" and the classic Generation X singles "Wild Youth" and "Your Generation."

influences:
◀◀ The Sex Pistols, Siouxsie & the Banshees, the Beatles, the Buzzcocks, the Clash

▶▶ The Offspring, Sigue Sigue Sputnik, Sisters of Mercy, Green Day

Tracey Birkenhauer and Steve Knopper

James Iha
See: Smashing Pumpkins

Natalie Imbruglia
Born February 4, 1975, in Sydney, Australia.

Natalie Imbruglia came from seemingly out of nowhere in late 1997—a stunning Aussie brunette with supermodel features and pouty lips glossed to a video-ready sheen—and made a swift impact with the sleek dance-pop number "Torn." A yearning, sexy meditation on emotional ambivalence that broke records for radio airplay in the U.K., "Torn" garnered heavy duty rotation on both VH1 and MTV, thereby making Imbruglia an instant cross-over diva. Imbruglia originally made a name for herself as an actress on the wildly popular Australian soap opera *Neighbors*, then left the show to pursue a musical career.

what's available: *Left of the Middle* 𝄞𝄞𝄞 (RCA, 1998 prod. Paul Thornalley, Mark Goldenberg, Andy Wright, Matt Bronleewee) is a pleasant enough exercise in adult contemporary pop. Titles like "Cry," "One More Addiction," and "Torn" tell the whole story—Imbruglia is preoccupied with the fallout of dysfunctional relationships. A promising debut, though the singer remains a "wait and see" proposition.

influences:
◀◀ Joni Mitchell, Alanis Morissette, Kylie Minogue

Marc Weingarten

Imperial Teen
See: Faith No More

Indigo Girls
Formed 1984, in Decatur, GA.

Amy Ray, guitar, vocals; Emily Saliers, guitar, vocals.

Amy Ray and Emily Saliers easily won over sensitive folkies and alternative rockers alike with their 1989 major-label debut by baring their souls where others merely beat on their chests. Fusing Biblical imagery, feminist integrity, and poetic pretensions, the Atlanta duo risked coming across as angstful over-achievers, but their unflagging earnestness and soaring harmonies made an indelible impression. Since then, they have struggled to harness the power of their voices and their convictions: For every shimmering pop triumph like "Hammer and a Nail" or "Power of Two," there's a heavy-handed "The Girl with the Weight of the World in Her Hands" or "You and Me of 10,000 Wars." For every tasteful cover of Bob Dylan's "All along the Watchtower" or Elton John's "Mona Lisas and Mad Hatters," there's an overwrought take on Dire Straits' "Romeo and Juliet" and Buffy Sainte-Marie's "Bury My Heart at Wounded Knee." But 1994's hard-rocking *Swamp Ophelia* and 1997's *Shaming of the Sun* (highlighted by "Shame on You," a rousing revision of Van Morrison's "Brown-Eyed Girl") hit the emotional and artistic mark, proving that with each album, Saliers and Ray are indeed getting closer to fine.

what to buy: *Indigo Girls* 𝄢𝄢𝄢✧ (Epic, 1989, prod. Scott Litt) boasts help from R.E.M. and Hothouse Flowers, who lend an edge to "Closer to Fine," "Kid Fears," and "Tried to Be True." *Swamp Ophelia* 𝄢𝄢𝄢✧ (Epic, 1994, prod. Peter Collins) expands the duo's sound with horns, mandolins, African drums, accordions, and other textures that for once are conducive, not cosmetic.

what to buy next: The range of styles covered in their live shows is documented on the sprawling two-CD *1200 Curfews* 𝄢𝄢𝄢 (Epic, 1995, prod. Indigo Girls, Russell Carter), but the intensity is stronger on the eight-song *Back on the Bus Y'all* 𝄢𝄢𝄢✧ (Epic, 1991, prod. Timothy R. Powell), which also features the Ellen James Society.

what to avoid: *Strange Fire* 𝄢𝄢 (Epic, 1989, prod. John Keane), a reissue of their 1987 indie debut, is burdened by an underdeveloped vision and tentative vocals. Their idea of a statement at the time was covering the Youngbloods' "Get Together."

the rest:
Nomads Indians Saints 𝄢𝄢𝄢✧ (Epic, 1990)
Rites of Passage 𝄢𝄢𝄢 (Epic, 1992)
Shaming of the Sun 𝄢𝄢𝄢 (Epic, 1997)

worth searching for: *Jesus Christ Superstar: A Resurrection* (Daemon/Long Play, 1994, prod. Michael Lorant) is a rocking but uneven update of the Andrew Lloyd Webber–Tim Rice musical provocatively featuring Ray as Jesus Christ and Saliers as Mary Magdalene. Their ducts on "Everything's Alright" and "What's the Buzz" top Saliers's shaky "I Don't Know How to Love Him."

influences:
◀◀ Bob Dylan, R.E.M., Simon & Garfunkel, Laura Nyro

▶▶ The Story, Disappear Fear, Melissa Etheridge

David Okamoto

Infectious Grooves
See: Suicidal Tendencies

The Innocence Mission
Formed 1982, in Lancaster, PA.

Karen Perls, keyboards, acoustic guitar, lead vocals; Don Peris, guitar, organ; Mike Bitts, bass, vocals, vibes; Steve Brown, drums, percussion.

In the pantheon of wispy female alt-pop singers, Karen Peris has to rank right near the top. More expressive than Natalie Merchant, less affected than Tori Amos, and a far more accomplished songwriter than Sarah McLachlan, Peris remains underappreciated, even after three fine albums with the Innocence Mission. Her finely sketched songs are imbued with a dreamy, joyful Catholicism, and she and the band (led by its proficient guitarist, Don Peris, her husband) shade them with carefully chosen instrumental textures. She and her bandmates formed the group just out of high school, and after a few years, they recorded an EP and began traveling out of town to play clubs. For Peris, a shy, demure young woman with a gorgeous, feathery voice, performing in a rock club was like a Christian getting thrown to the lions. Somehow, though, she managed to develop her self-confidence, and the group was signed to A&M. Its self-titled debut, though not a big seller, received a good bit of acclaim, and during early 1990 the Innocence Mission wound up opening arena-sized venues on tour with Don Henley. Huge mistake; Peris wore out her voice, and the group was unable to summon up the power necessary to make a substantial impression on audiences waiting for an evening-ending "Hotel California." After a less-successful sophomore CD, the band took some time before returning with the lovely *Glow* in 1995. "Bright as Yellow" found a spot on the *Empire Records* soundtrack, and the group's star shone radiantly once again. Since then, Don Peris has produced an album for a local singer-songwriter, Karen Peris has done some guest vocal performances, including a duet with Natalie Merchant on her *Ophelia* album, and the entire outfit is apparently at work on a fourth album. Those who know can't wait.

what to buy: Not as consistently strong melodically as the group's debut, *Glow* 𝄢𝄢𝄢𝄢 (A&M, 1995, prod. Dennis Herring) still stands as the one to buy first: the guitars are livelier, Peris's lyrics are more detailed, and the whole disc achieves a striking thematic consistency. In essence, it's an album of childhood reminiscences: tiny vignettes that combine to form a total picture much as the French Impressionist painters used small, indistinct daubs of color as building blocks to create their finished works.

what to buy next: Although the album's muted overall sound already seems dated, *The Innocence Mission* 𝄢𝄢𝄢𝄢✧ (A&M,

1989, prod. Larry Klein) is a near-masterpiece, with wonderfully varied songwriting and an intimate but stunning set of vocal performances from Peris. A decade later it remains inventive, multilayered, and beautifully affecting.

the rest:
Umbrella 🎵🎵🎵 (A&M, 1991)

worth searching for: The independent EP *Tending the Rose Garden* (Llist, 1986) offers a look at the Innocence Mission's early stylings.

influences:
◄◄ Kate Bush, Joni Mitchell, Cowboy Junkies, Jane Siberry, Cocteau Twins, Throwing Muses

►► Sarah McLachlan, Tori Amos, the Sundays, Suddenly Tammy!, Over the Rhine

Bob Remstein

Insane Clown Posse

Formed 1992, in Detroit, MI.

Shaggy 2 Dope (Joey Utsler), vocals; Violent J (Joe Bruce), vocals.

Forget the Bible; Insane Clown Posse knows exactly when the world will end. Each of the group's albums is a joker's card, and by the time the sixth card is drawn, the world will end; "Final judgment will be passed, with all those who were evil in life suffering eternal torment," ICP's press kit says. Where, then, will that leave executives at Disney-owned Hollywood Records, who pulled the horrorcore group's fourth album from stores just hours after its release because of "inappropriate" lyrics? Instead of deeming them evil, perhaps Shaggy 2 Dope and Violent J should thank the executives behind the unprecedented action; by recalling *The Great Milenko*, the duo instantly turned the regionally popular act into a nationally known, which it took advantage of after the album was re-released by Island. What's so scary? ICP favors sexually explicit, occasionally shocking lyrics and demented, demonic clown-on-PCP voices and noises, which the little girls and boys seem to fully understand as they bathe themselves in the non-stop stream of Faygo soda pop that ICP pours forth during its performances. Next up; a line of action figures—perhaps in homage to one of its chief influences, Kiss.

what to buy: Although the album was officially recalled by Hollywood Records, many retailers refused to return their original copies of *The Great Milenko* 🎵🎵🎵 (Hollywood, 1997/Island, 1997, prod. Mike Clark). Not only is the original version a collector's item, it's also ICP's strongest and hardest-hitting album, thanks in part to guest guitarist Slash. The Island version features three additional songs Hollywood had trimmed from its version.

the rest:
Carnival of Carnage 🎵🎵 (Psychopathic, 1994)
Ringmaster 🎵🎵 (Psychopathic, 1994)
Riddle Box 🎵🎵🎵 (Psychopathic/Zomba/Jive, 1995)

influences:
◄◄ Geto Boys, Beastie Boys, Kiss, Alice Cooper

►► Flatlinerz, Gravediggaz

Christina Fuoco

Inspiral Carpets

Formed 1986, in Manchester, England. Disbanded 1993.

Stephen Holt, vocals (1986–88); Tom Hingley, vocals (1988–93); Clint Boon, keyboards, vocals; Graham Lambert, guitar; David Swift, bass (1986–88); Martyn Walsh, bass (1988–93); Craig Gill, drums.

The group Inspiral Carpets will be best remembered for having Oasis songwriter and guitarist Noel Gallagher as its roadie, but when the Manchester scene was at its peak during the late '80s, the band was a sober alternative to the euphoric Stone Roses and Happy Mondays. By fusing bare boned neo-psychedelic rock 'n' roll with themes of urban decay, prostitution, and being downright miserable, the quintet's organ-fueled sound served as a reality check to the whole trippy scene. Despite contributing a few classic singles to the Britpop sweepstakes, the Inspiral Carpets eventually fell out of favor and into obscurity.

what to buy: The Inspiral Carpets' debut album, the colossally downtrodden *Life* 🎵🎵🎵 (Mute/Elektra, 1990, prod. Inspiral Carpets, Nick Garside), shows rare depth and maturity for such a young band. Layered with cascading feedback, whopping drums, haunting, Doors-shaded organs, and looping monotone vocals, the album features standout songs such as "This Is How It Feels" and "She Comes in the Fall."

what to buy next: Despite its short tenure in the British pop charts, the Inspiral Carpets left behind a noteworthy collection, *The Singles* 🎵🎵🎵 (Mute, 1995, prod. various), which compiles all of the group's finest material, including underrated tunes such as "Move," "Bitches Brew," and "Biggest Mountain."

what to avoid: The group lost steam by its fourth album, the directionless *Devil Hopping* 🎵 (Mute/Elektra, 1994, prod. Pascal Gabriel).

the rest:
The Beast Inside 🎵🎵 (Mute/Elektra, 1991)
Revenge of the Goldfish 🎵🎵 (Mute/Elektra, 1992)

worth searching for: The import-only EP *Plane Crash* (Playtime, 1988, prod. Dave Fielding), the group's recording debut, features a crisp cover of "96 Tears" along with four raucous originals.

Michael Hutchence of INXS (© Ken Settle)

influences:
◄◄ The Fall, the Doors, Joy Division
►► Oasis, the Charlatans UK, Blur

Aidin Vaziri

The International Beat

See: The English Beat

The Interpreters

Formed 1996, in Philadelphia, PA.

Herschel Mark Gaer, vocals, bass; Patsy Pasquale Palladino, guitar; Brnako Joseph Jakominich, drums.

The Philadelphia trio the Interpreters modeled itself on the great mod bands of the '60s, particularly the Who; it even brought producer Shel Talmy in to produce some demos. The band's debut album, *Back in the U.S.S.A.,* garnered ridiculously favorable reviews in the mainstream press, but a shaky record company prevented the group from delivering on the promise of the inspired tunes.

what's available: The impressive *Back in the U.S.S.A.* 𝄢𝄢𝄢 (Freeworld, 1997, prod. Ron A. Shaffer, Interpreters) was built on two-minute pop gems and raw attitude. The CD booklet was painstakingly fashioned to look like a passport.

influences:
◄◄ The Who, the Kinks, the Buzzcocks

Aidin Vaziri

INXS

Formed 1977, in Sydney, Australia.

Michael Hutchence (died November 22, 1997), vocals (1977–97); Tim Farriss, guitar; Andrew Farriss, keyboards, guitar; Jon Farriss, drums; Gary Beers, bass; Kirk Pengilly, guitar, saxophone.

A durable group that kept its original lineup—including three brothers—together longer than most, INXS was able to keep an equanimity about it even after singer Michael Hutchence became a sex symbol during the mid-'80s (he once turned down a *Rolling Stone* cover because it wouldn't include his bandmates). After several long years toughening its act in front of surfers in Sydney pubs, the band first received widespread attention as an opening act for (then) more successful countrymen Men at Work. One of alternative music's most commercial bands, INXS' ascension peaked when the 1985 single "What You Need" became an international smash and set up the multi-million-selling triumph of the 1987 album *Kick*. The group's popularity slowly waned after that, though the Hutchence/Andrew Farriss songwriting partnership continued to flourish with strong singles such as "Suicide Blonde," "Beautiful Girl," and the industrial-tinged "The Gift." By the mid-'90s, however, Hutchence had become less famous for his music than for his role as the concubine of Bob Geldof's wife Paula Yates, as steadily documented in tabloid gossip columns. After increasingly erratic behavior, he hanged himself in a hotel room in 1997, on drugs and reportedly upset over child-custody matters involving Geldof. True to character, the rest of INXS vowed to continue on together—but in what form remains to be seen.

what to buy: *Kick* 🎵🎵🎵🎵 (Atlantic, 1987, prod. Chris Thomas), which spawned four huge singles, is as radio-ready as an album can be, one of those wonderful '80s packages (à la Def Leppard's *Hysteria* or U2's *The Joshua Tree*) where each track could have been a legitimate single.

what to buy next: *Elegantly Wasted* 🎵🎵🎵 (Capitol, 1997, prod. Bruce Fairbairn, INXS) was a comeback bid that didn't really succeed, but no matter; excellent tunes such as the Stonesy title track play to the band's strengths, and the introspection of "Searching" and other ballads are especially poignant in the light of Hutchence's suicide.

what to avoid: *Live Baby Live* 🎵🎵 (Atlantic, 1991, prod. Mark Opitz) is a head-scratching affair that reduces a usually rousing live act to stiff and bored, with terrible production to boot.

the rest:
INXS 🎵🎵 (Deluxe, 1980/Atco, 1984)
Underneath the Colours 🎵🎵 (Deluxe, 1981/Atco, 1984)
Shabooh Shoobah 🎵🎵🎵 (Atco, 1983)
Dekadance 🎵🎵 (Atco EP, 1983)
The Swing 🎵🎵🎵 (Atco, 1985)
Listen like Thieves 🎵🎵🎵🎵 (Atlantic, 1986)
X 🎵🎵🎵🎵 (Atlantic, 1990)
Welcome to Wherever You Are 🎵🎵🎵🎵 (Atlantic, 1992)
Full Moon, Dirty Hearts 🎵🎵🎵🎵 (Atlantic, 1993)
Greatest Hits 🎵🎵🎵🎵 (Atlantic, 1994)

worth searching for: The soundtrack *The Lost Boys* (Atlantic, 1988, prod. various) was a predecessor to today's chock-full-of-modern-rock movie soundtracks and features two fine INXS performances with Australian screamer Jimmy Barnes.

influences:
◀◀ Roxy Music, the Rolling Stones
▶▶ Jesus Jones, Charm Farm

Todd Wicks

Iron Butterfly

Formed 1966, in San Diego, CA. Disbanded 1971. Re-formed 1974–75 and 1993–present.

Doug Ingle, keyboards, vocals; Ron Bushy, drums, vocals; Darryl De-Loach, vocals (1967); Jerry Penrod, bass (1967); Danny Weis, guitar (1967); Erik Braunn, guitar, vocals (1968–69, 1974–75); Lee Dorman, bass, guitar, piano (1968, 1993); Mike Pinera, guitar, vocals (1970–71, 1993); Larry "Rhino" Reinhardt (1970–71); Phil Kramer, bass (1974); Howard Reitzes, keyboards, guitar (1974–75); Derek Hilland, keyboards, vocals (1993–present); Eric Barnett, guitar (1996–present); Lee Dorman, bass, vocals (1993–present).

If not for the legendary excess of its 17-minute heavy-metal anthem, the now-comical "In-a-Gadda-Da-Vida," few would remember Iron Butterfly. But with its brash guitars, thudding drums, and stilted vocals, the band helped define the heavy-metal era that followed. Its heyday was brief, but from 1967 to 1969, Iron Butterfly toured with the Doors and the Jefferson Airplane and briefly was Atlantic Records' best-selling band, hitting the seven-million mark in album sales. The group has gone through several ill-advised revivals, unable to face the fact that its appeal was limited to the jam-rock scene of the psychedelic '60s.

what to buy: Iron Butterfly's 17 minutes of fame has been perfectly preserved, in triplicate, via a reissue of *In-a-Gadda-Da-Vida* 🎵🎵🎵 (Atco, 1968/Rhino, 1995, prod. Jim Hilton). The original six tunes have been remastered with two bonus takes of "Vida," including a 19-minute live jam and a 2:52 version (no drum solo?!) edited for radio.

what to buy next: Grudgingly, *Light and Heavy: The Best of Iron Butterfly* 🎵🎵 (Rhino, 1993, prod. various) is a cost-effective way to sample the rest of the group's output—if you really want to.

what to avoid: The rest of Iron Butterfly's sludge-rock adventures (all **woof!**): *Heavy* (Atco, 1968/Rhino, 1993); *Ball* (Atco, 1969/1991); *Metamorphosis* (Atco, 1970/Rhino, 1993); *Live* (Rhino, 1989); and *Scorching Beauty* (MCA, 1993).

worth searching for: If you're gonna own it, go for the deluxe version of *In-a-Gadda-Da-Vida* (Rhino, 1995) with cool, hippie-like graphics and a new set of liner notes.

influences:
◀◀ The Troggs, Blue Cheer, the Animals, the Yardbirds
▶▶ Black Sabbath, Judas Priest, Alice Cooper, Kiss

David Yonke

Iron Maiden
/Bruce Dickinson

Formed 1976, in London, England.

Paul Di'anno, vocals (1976–81); Bruce Dickinson, vocals (1982–92); Steve Harris, bass; Dave Murray, guitar; Clive Burr, drums (1980–82); Adrian Smith, guitar (1980–88); Janick Gers, guitar (1990–present); Blaze Bayley, vocals (1993–present); Nicko McBrain, drums (1983–present).

In an unapologetic nod to '70s metal, Iron Maiden's guitar-driven wailing brought about numerous gold and platinum albums and a loyal headbangin' base without the benefit of radio play or much MTV rotation. Anchored by Steve Harris's somewhat obtrusive thumping, the band's literate approach—incorporating mythological themes and movie inspiration—really took hold with the addition of Bruce Dickinson. One of the more prominent male-posturing screamers in heavy metal—and an Olympic-caliber fencer to boot—Dickinson fronted the band throughout the most successful run of its career, from 1982 to 1990, leaving replacement Blaze Bayley a tough task in filling his slot.

what to buy: *The Number of the Beast* ♪♪♪♪ (Harvest, 1982/Castle, 1995, prod. Martin Birch, Iron Maiden, Doug Hall), with its hellish title track, finds the band at a melodic peak, beginning a seven-album winning streak with a scorching brew of memorable tunes and catchy metalloid axe burners. *Iron Maiden* ♪♪♪ (Harvest, 1980/Castle, 1995, prod. Will Malone) is where it all started. Original singer Paul Di'anno and company pull out all the stops in a frenzied guitar attack that laid the groundwork for all subsequent releases.

what to buy next: *Killers* ♪♪♪ (Harvest, 1981/Castle, 1995, prod. Martin Birch), Di'anno's swan song, is a flat-out screech fest, with only slightly less fiery results than the debut, replete with screaming solos and a cool cover of the rotting corpse mascot, Eddie. *Piece of Mind* ♪♪♪ (Harvest, 1983/Castle, 1995, prod. Martin Birch) is a solid mid-period release that introduces drummer Nicko McBrain. Excellent guitar work highlights "Where Eagles Dare" and "Flight of Icarus." The bonus disc includes a crunching take on Jethro Tull's "Cross-Eyed Mary."

what to avoid: *Somewhere in Time* ♪♪ (Capitol/EMI, 1986, prod. Martin Birch) raises a serious question; namely, who the hell let the keyboards In?

the rest:
Maiden Japan ♪♪♪ (Harvest EP, 1981)
Powerslave ♪♪♪ (Harvest, 1984/Castle, 1995)
Live after Death ♪♪♪♪ (Harvest, 1985/Castle, 1995)
Seventh Son of a Seventh Son ♪♪♪ (Harvest, 1988 Castle, 1995)
No Prayer for the Dying ♪♪ (Epic, 1990, Castle, 1995)
Fear of the Dark ♪♪ (Harvest, 1992, Castle, 1995)

A Real Live One ♪♪♪ (Capitol, 1993, Castle, 1993)
A Real Dead One ♪♪♪ (Capitol, 1993/Castle, 1993)
The X-Factor ♪♪♪ (CMC International, 1995)
Best of the Beast ♪♪♪♪ (Castle, 1996)
Virtual XI ♪♪♪ (CMC International, 1998)

solo outings:
Bruce Dickinson:
Tattooed Millionaire ♪ (Columbia, 1990)
Balls to Picasso ♪ (Mercury, 1994)
Alive in Studio A ♪ (CMC International, 1995)
Skunkworks ♪ (Castle, 1996)
Accident of Birth ♪♪ (CMC International, 1997)
Chemical Wedding N/A (CMC, 1998)

influences:
⏪ Led Zeppelin, Black Sabbath

⏩ Metallica, Megadeth, Slayer

Allan Orski

Chris Isaak

Born June 6, 1956, in Stockton, CA.

Someone has to keep alive the spirit of 1950s rock, and these days singer-songwriter Chris Isaak has the job pretty much to himself. Backed by guitarist James Calvin Wilsey, bassist Rowland Salley, and drummer Kenney Dale Johnson, the Bay-area guitarist churns out stripped-to-the-roots rockers and sullen blues numbers that embody the pathos of Roy Orbison with the brooding of Elvis Presley. Isaak enjoyed commercial success after director David Lynch featured the sultry "Wicked Game" (from *Heart Shaped World*) in his 1990 film *Wild at Heart*. The songwriter has also earned some recognition as an actor with roles in *Married to the Mob, Wild at Heart, The Silence of the Lambs,* and *Little Buddha*.

what to buy: True to its title, *San Francisco Days* ♪♪♪♪ (Reprise, 1993, prod. Erik Jacobsen) is a sunny divergence from the melancholy of Isaak's early albums. The sonic landscape opens up to offer some of his most vital and distinctive songs, including the title track and "Round 'n' Round." On the flip side, "Move Along," "5:15," and the vaguely psychotic "Can't Do a Thing (to Stop Me)" demonstrate Isaak's growing command over the deep-blues style that's at his roots.

what to buy next: *Forever Blue* ♪♪♪ (Reprise, 1995, prod. Erik Jacobsen) expands upon the broader soundscape of *San Francisco Days*. While the album tends toward quieter acoustic numbers, the rockers—"Baby Did a Bad Bad Thing," "Go Walking Down There," and "I Believe"—give compelling reason to get up and dance.

what to avoid: *Silvertone* ♪ (Warner Bros., 1985, prod. Erik Jacobsen) is an unpromising debut that isn't bad as much as it is

Chris Isaak (© **Ken Settle**)

one-dimensional. Isaak hit his stride later on, but the songs here lope along without much direction or, for that matter, variation.

the rest:

Chris Isaak ♬♬ (Warner Bros., 1987)
Heart Shaped World ♬♬♬ (Reprise, 1989)
Baja Sessions ♬♬ (Reprise, 1996)
Speak of the Devil ♬♬♬♬ (Reprise, 1998)

worth searching for: *Wicked Game* (Reprise, 1991, prod. Erik Jacobsen) is a solid, import-only compilation of songs from Isaak's first three albums, put together to cash in on the title track's success.

influences:

◀◀ Elvis Presley, Roy Orbison, Eddie Cochran, Neil Diamond

▶▶ Marshall Crenshaw, Dwight Yoakam

Christopher Scapelliti

The Isley Brothers

Formed 1957, in Cincinnati, OH.

Ronald Isley, vocals; Rudolph Isley, vocals (1957–86, 1990–present); O'Kelly Isley (died March 31, 1986), vocals (1957–86); Ernie Isley, guitar, drums (1969–84, 1996); Marvin Isley, bass (1969–84); Chris Jasper, keyboards (1969–84).

The Isley Brothers started out as a gospel group but didn't enjoy much success until—following the death of brother Vernon, who was killed in a 1955 bicycle accident—they added soul to the mix in the early 1960s (during which time a sideman named Jimi Hendrix played guitar for them).The 1959 single "Shout," featuring their church organist, put the Isleys on the charts and remains one of the most popular party anthems of all time. Sporadic success during the '60s, including a stint at Motown, left them bouncing from label to label until the band revived their own T-Neck label and released the funky "It's Your Thing" in 1969. The brothers added a harder rock edge to their mix in the 1970s, thanks to the influence of younger brothers Ernie and Marvin and cousin Chris Jasper, and enjoyed considerable success. An acrimonious split with the younger trio yielded the moderately successful Isley-Jasper-Isley project, while the older brothers soldiered on as a regular presence on the R&B charts. In the 1990s the group successfully sued pop star Michael Bolton for plagiarizing their song "Love Is a Wonderful Thing" for his hit of the same name. Since O'Kelly's death in 1986, the group has spotlighted Ronald with moderate success.

what to buy: African-American rock music took a step forward with *3 + 3* ♬♬♬♬ (T-Neck, 1973, prod. Isley Brothers), which featured Ernie Isley's screaming electric guitar on "That Lady"

and acoustic, soulful treatments of folk-rock tunes such as "Don't Let Me Be Lonely Tonight" and "Summer Breeze." The Isleys crossed the line into funk with *The Heat Is On* ♬♬♬♬ (T-Neck, 1975, prod. Isley Brothers) and its hit "Fight the Power," though they also turned down the lights and crooned the sensual "For the Love of You."

what to buy next: *The Isley Brothers Story, Vol. 1: Rockin' Soul* ♬♬♬♬ (Rhino, 1991, compilation prod. Bill Inglot) gathers the harmonies of the Isleys' 1960s output on tunes such as "This Ol' Heart of Mine" and "Shout."

what to avoid: *In the Beginning . . .* ♬♬ (T-Neck, 1972, prod. Isley Brothers) is a compilation that tries to capitalize on Jimi Hendrix's short stint with the band during 1964–65. Neither Hendrix nor the Isleys had really broken into their signature styles at this point.

the rest:

Get into Something ♬♬♬ (T-Neck, 1969/Legacy, 1997)
The Brothers: Isley ♬♬♬ (T-Neck, 1969/Legacy, 1997)
Givin' It Back ♬♬♬ (T-Neck, 1971/Legacy, 1997)
Brother, Brother, Brother ♬♬♬ (T-Neck, 1972/Legacy, 1997)
Harvest for the World ♬♬♬♬ (T-Neck, 1976)
Winner Takes All ♬♬♬ (Epic, 1979)
Go All the Way ♬♬♬ (Columbia, 1980)
Between the Sheets ♬♬♬ (Epic, 1983)
Smooth Sailin' ♬♬♬ (Warner Bros., 1987)
Spend the Night ♬♬♬ (Warner Bros., 1989)
The Isley Brothers Story, Vol. 2: The T-Neck Years ♬♬♬♬ (Rhino, 1991)
Greatest Hits and Rare Classics ♬♬♬ (Motown, 1991)
Tracks of Life ♬♬♬ (Warner Bros., 1992)
The Isley Brothers Live ♬♬♬ (Elektra, 1993)
Beautiful Ballads ♬♬♬♬ (Legacy, 1994)
Funky Family ♬♬♬♬ (Legacy, 1995)
Mission to Please ♬♬♬ (Island, 1996)
Shout: The RCA Sessions ♬♬♬ (RCA, 1996)

worth searching for: Get an idea of where the Beatles learned their harmony style on *Twist and Shout* (Sundazed, 1993, compilation prod. Bob Irwin), which also features "Rubber Leg Twist," "Spanish Twist," and "Twistin' with Linda."

solo outings:

Isley-Jasper-Isley:
Caravan of Love ♬♬♬ (Epic Associated, 1985)

Ernie Isley:
High Wire ♬♬♬♬ (Elektra, 1990)

influences:

◀◀ The Drifters, Sam Cooke, James Brown, Jimi Hendrix, Sly & the Family Stone

▶▶ Funkadelic, Bone Maxwell, Boyz II Men, Mother's Finest

Lawrence Gabriel and Gary Graff

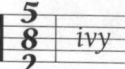

Ivy

Formed 1993, in New York, NY.

Dominique Durand, vocals; Andy Chase, guitar, vocals, various instruments; Adam Schlesinger, bass, drums, keyboards, vocals, various instruments.

Funny what living in New York does to some people. French-born Dominique Durand moved to the Big Apple in 1990 to learn a bit of English. Encouraged by musician/producer Andy Chase, she wound up learning to sing as well. During 1993 the pair, now husband and wife, enlisted future Fountains of Wayne bassist Adam Schlesinger to put the finishing touches on a five-song demo. Those sessions spawned 1994's "Get Enough" single and the *Lately* EP, both released on the now-defunct Seed label.

what to buy: From bossa nova to Britpop, from cocktail jazz to shoegazing psychedelia, from trip-hop ambiance to Brill Building bubblegum, *Apartment Life* ✎✎✎✎ (Atlantic, 1997, prod. Ivy) shimmers with international pop styles. With the resources of a major label behind them (i.e., more time in a better studio), and with the autonomy that attends producing oneself, Chase and Schlesinger are free to follow their fancy, crafting devilishly rich orchestral-pop backdrops for Durand's breathy cooing. It's true that over the course of the 12-song album the chanteuse's cool, French-inflected soprano wears a little thin. No matter; *Apartment Life* is still an iridescent masterpiece.

what to buy next: Candy-kissed by Chase's chiming guitars and awash in Durand's lovelorn daydreams, *Realistic* ✎✎✎✎ (Seed, 1994, prod. Kurt Ralske, Ivy) sets the template for its streamlined successor, although it sometimes gropes for garage rock—a genre for which Durand in particular is ill-suited.

worth searching for: Now out of print, *Lately* (Seed, 1994, prod. Ivy) contains the otherwise unavailable tracks "Wish It All Away," "Twisting," "I Hate December," "Can't Even Fake It," and "I Guess I'm Just a Little Too Sensitive."

influences:

◀◀ Everything but the Girl, Cocteau Twins, Astrud Gilberto, Stereolab, Velvet Underground, Nico, Burt Bacharach, the Smiths, Antonio Carlos Jobim, Lloyd Cole, the Sundays

see also: *Fountains of Wayne*

Greg Siegel

David J

See: Love & Rockets

Janet Jackson

Born Janet Damita Jackson, May 16, 1966, in Gary, IN.

Growing up the youngest daughter in the mega-successful Jackson clan, Janet Jackson stepped into the shadow of a monumental dynasty when she began performing with her brothers during the mid-'70s. Indeed, it seemed at first that Janet's future lay in television, as she found minor success with roles in the sitcoms *Good Times* and *Diff'rent Strokes*. But family patriarch Joe Jackson had other ideas, encouraging Janet to deliver her mostly forgettable self-titled solo debut. A subsequent album produced by Time guitarist Jesse Johnson also stiffed, signaling what seemed the end of a vapid recording career. But then A&M executives got the idea to pair her with former Time members James "Jimmy Jam" Harris III and Terry Lewis, resulting in the singer's first blockbuster success, *Control*. Backed by her producers' cutting-edge dance grooves and a series of hyperkinetic videos choreographed by Paula Abdul, Janet became a major star in her own right. Taking the tone of her breakthrough record to heart, she jettisoned her father as manager and plowed into *Rhythm Nation 1814*, a further distillation of the percolating, Teflon dance-rock formula that also tackled social issues. This record's success shot her into the pop culture stratosphere occupied by stars like Madonna and her brother, Michael—allowing the singer to negotiate a new, multimillion-dollar deal with Virgin Records. The first product of that deal, *janet*, also did massive business, emphasizing the singer's smoldering sexuality while trafficking in the dance pop grooves of the day.

what to buy: No record in her limited catalog matches the impact of *Control* ✎✎✎✎ (A&M, 1986, prod. Janet Jackson, James Harris III, Terry Lewis, Monte Moir), an album that virtually redefined the world of dance-rock and dance-oriented R&B single-handedly. Fresh from work with R&B stalwarts the SOS Band, Harris and Lewis were ready to rewrite the rules for contemporary soul; they just needed a good-looking, videogenic singer to help them do it. From the mechanized funk of the title track to the percolating, sultry grooves of "Nasty" and the sassy hit single "What Have You Done for Me Lately," the trio welds artsy, funky percussion grooves to slashing keyboard sounds and Jackson's breathy, insubstantial voice. The world of hi-tech funk would never be the same.

what to buy next: Jackson's sophomore record, *Rhythm Nation 1814* ✎✎✎✎ (A&M, 1989, prod. Janet Jackson, James Harris III, Terry Lewis, Jellybean Johnson), pushed the team's patented dance formula even further, nicking bits of an old Sly Stone tune for the title track's avalanche of percussive sounds. Forget about the clumsy lyrical references to ill-defined social problems such as homelessness and racism; what matters here are the grooves—from the direct, near-industrial flavor of the hit single "Miss You Much" to the rock-tinged "Black Cat" and frothy pop of "Escapade," every tune here will either make you want to hit the dance floor or the bedroom. And after all, isn't that what good dance jams are all about? The hits collection *Design of a Decade: 1986–1996* ♪♪♪ (A&M, 1996, prod. various) misses the cohesion of the two aforementioned albums but still speaks volumes about Jackson's groundbreaking artistic journey during those 10 years.

what to avoid: Jackson's second pre-Harris/Lewis solo record, *Dream Street* **woof!** (A&M, 1984, prod. Jesse Johnson), reeks of formulaic pandering. Bereft of memorable cuts, it came before the days when a good MTV video could make anyone a star, so even Jackson's talents as a videogenic dance diva couldn't save the day.

the rest:
janet ♪♪♪ (Virgin, 1993)
Janet Remixed ♪♪ (Virgin, 1995)
The Velvet Rope ♪♪♪ (Virgin, 1997)

worth searching for: Jackson's potency as a performer can't really be judged until you see her in action—the complex choreography with a lone chair in the "Pleasure Principle" video, her army of military-style dance recruits in the "Rhythm Nation" clip, her sensuously curvy body moves in the film for "That's the Way Love Goes." That's why she's gathered video clips from every album onto separate anthologies—there are actually two for *Control*—and it's also why any fan worth their weight in 12-inch remix records will buy them.

influences:
◀◀ Michael Jackson, Prince, Madonna, Diana Ross
▶▶ Paula Abdul, Karyn White, Jody Watley

Eric Deggans

Joe Jackson

Born August 11, 1954, in Portsmouth, England.

Touted with Elvis Costello and Graham Parker as the new hopefuls for the angry young man crown, Joe Jackson has been far more experimental (not necessarily more talented) than his contemporaries, making his career a bumpy ride with minimal commercial success but tremendous artistic highs. Classically educated, Jackson evolved from the successful power-pop of his early albums and began his forays into jazz, big band, swing bossanova, ambient instrumental, and reggae. Jackson has never had trouble expressing his disdain for pop music and stardom—nor his resentment over his own lack of commercial success—though at times it has given his music a bile quotient that seems merely snide instead of passionate. Above all, Jackson has rarely been boring, which in this case is a compliment of the highest order.

what to buy: *Look Sharp* ♪♪♪♪ (A&M, 1979, prod. David Kershenbaum) presents hyper and bitter pop with a good beat. Jackson rails intelligence and inspiration against numerous targets, scoring direct hits with the ugly-guy opus "Is She Really Going Out with Him?" and the vituperative white reggae of "Sunday Papers." *I'm the Man* ♪♪♪ (A&M, 1979, prod. David Kershenbaum) continues in the same vein, with a bit less focus but with outstanding songs—the propulsive title track, the biting "On Your Radio," and the pop perfection of "It's Different for Girls"—that more than compensate. *Night and Day* ♪♪♪♪ (A&M, 1982, prod. David Kershenbaum) is a gorgeous, minimalist excursion into jazz-tinged salsa and bossanova stylings, with the hits "Steppin' Out" and "Breaking Us in Two." *Blaze of Glory* ♪♪♪♪ (A&M, 1989, prod. Joe Jackson, Ed Roynesdal) is a sharp autobiographical memoir whose individual songs hold their own outside that conceptual framework.

what to buy next: *Jumpin' Jive* ♪♪♪ (A&M, 1981, prod. Joe Jackson) is the first of Jackson's radical departures from the pop idiom, this time with a swingin' big band that hearkens back 40 or 50 years. Atypically, Jackson seems to be having a great deal of fun.

what to avoid: *Night Music* ♪ (Virgin, 1994, prod. Joe Jackson, Ed Roynesdal) is pretentious and smug synthesizer music for the wine-and-cheese crowd. This is Jackson at his self-important worst.

the rest:
Beat Crazy ♪♪♪ (A&M, 1980)
Body and Soul ♪♪♪ (A&M)
Big World ♪♪ (A&M, 1986)
Will Power ♪ (A&M, 1987)
Live . . . 1980–1986 ♪♪♪ (A&M, 1988)
Laughter and Lust ♪♪♪ (Virgin, 1991)
I'm the Man: Classic Tracks 1979–1989 ♪♪♪ (A&M, 1996)
Greatest Hits ♪♪♪ (A&M, 1996)
Heaven and Hell ♪♪ (Sony Classical, 1997)

worth searching for: The CD-5 for *Stranger than Fiction* (Virgin, 1991, prod. Joe Jackson, Ed Roynesdal) includes a remake of "Different for Girls" that recasts the song as a duet between Jackson and singer Joy Askew.

influences:
◀◀ Bob Dylan, Cole Porter, Louis Jordan
▶▶ Ben Folds Five

Allan Orski and Gary Graff

Michael Jackson

Born August 29, 1958, in Gary, IN.

While others have worked years to win worldwide fame in the

Joe Jackson (© Ken Settle)

music business, for Michael Jackson it seemed like a birthright. A founding member of the Jackson 5, he was bringing his powerful contralto vocals to bear as lead singer for the group at age four. By age 10 he was touring the country, opening for respected Motown acts such as Gladys Knight & the Pips and the Temptations. A year later, he was an international sensation as the Jackson 5 took over the charts with "I Want You Back," "ABC," "I'll Be There," and more. Groomed by Motown mogul Berry Gordy Jr., Jackson was encouraged to go solo in 1972, reportedly as an answer to Donny Osmond's rising popularity. His first solo record, like all of his early and mid-'70s solo efforts, veered between schmaltzy ballads aimed at the pop audience and bits of lightweight fluff aimed at teenyboppers. Though Jackson found some success during these times, his work always seemed guided by older, more domineering hands and overshadowed both by his brother Jermaine's ascent as a teen idol and by the continuing work of the Jacksons (as they were re-christened in 1976). It wasn't until 1979's *Off the Wall*—co-produced by Quincy Jones, whom Michael had met while filming *The Wiz*—that the singer's own creative instincts began to emerge. Fusing an unerring pop sensibility with up-to-date R&B grooves and solid songs, that record set the stage for Jackson's greatest triumph, 1982's *Thriller*. At more than 40 million copies sold, *Thriller* still stands as the most successful album ever, a phenomenon fed by Jackson's creative use of videos—from the dance showcase of the "Billie Jean" clip to the "West Side Story"–style moves of "Beat It" and the horror movie special effects extravaganza, "Thriller." But Jackson's tremendous success was dogged by speculation about his private life; his acquisition of most of the Beatles' song catalog spoke to his business acumen, but reports of severe plastic surgery, his alleged use of hyperbaric oxygen tents, and his reclusive nature portrayed him as eccentric at best, disturbed at worst. His releases since *Thriller* have sold in the multi-millions, but they've been (wrongly) declared failures because they didn't match their predecessor's world-record sales. The shine really came off Jackson's star in 1993, when a 13-year-old boy accused the star of molesting him. The matter was settled out of court, but Jackson lost big: Pepsi-Cola canceled a decade-long endorsement deal, police raided his Los Angeles home, and he admitted to having the skin-lightening disease vitiligo and an addiction to painkillers. Interest in Jackson faded to the point where his two-CD set *HIStory: Past, Present, and Future, Book 1*—which was attacked for anti-Semitic lyrics in one song—fizzled in the amount of time it took to announce both his wedding and subsequent divorce from Elvis Presley's daughter, Lisa Marie. Re-married, he's now the father of two and still trying to figure out the way back to world domination.

what to buy: In this case, it's a no-brainer: the most artistically satisfying record of Jackson's career also happens to be his most successful, *Thriller* ♫♫♫♫ (Epic, 1982, prod. Michael Jackson, Quincy Jones). From the sinewy funk of "Billie Jean" to the rock-tinged "Beat It" (with a guitar solo by Eddie Van Halen) and the epic title track, Jackson and Jones created a perfect fusion of commercial R&B and pop sensibilities—with the good luck to release it at a time when such naked ambition wasn't yet considered uncool.

what to buy next: As the record that first showed Jackson's promise as a solo artist, *Off the Wall* ♫♫♫♫ (Epic, 1979, prod. Michael Jackson, Quincy Jones) lets the singer stretch beyond his teenybopper image. "Rock with You" is a slick, sensual piece of R&B-tinged pop, while "Wanna Be Starting Something" seems tailor-made for the kind of adult-oriented dance clubs that would never go near a Jackson 5 single. Best of all, by welding impressive, inventive production with solid songs, the pair showed hints of what a mature Jackson might be capable of.

what to avoid: In a bald-faced attempt to cash in on Jackson's explosive *Thriller* success, Motown assembled a bunch of lackluster unreleased tracks from 1975 on the album *One Day in Your Life* **woof!** (Motown, 1981, prod. various).

the rest:
Got to Be There ♫♫♫ (Motown, 1972)
Ben ♫♫♫ (Motown, 1972)
Music and Me ♫♫ (Motown, 1973)
The Best of Michael Jackson ♫♫♫ (Motown, 1975)
Anthology ♫♫♫ (Motown, 1976)
Bad ♫♫♫♫ (Epic, 1987)
Dangerous ♫♫♫♫ (Epic, 1991)
12-Inch Mixes ♫♫ (Epic, 1993)
HIStory: Past, Present, and Future, Book I ♫♫♫♫ (Epic, 1995)
Blood on the Dance Floor ♫♫♫ (Epic, 1997)

worth searching for: Two Jackson classics don't appear on any of his solo albums: "Heartbreak Hotel," a moody, complex gem from the Jacksons' *Triumph* (Epic, 1980); and "State of Shock," from the Jacksons' *Victory* (Epic, 1984), a danceable hit charged by his duet with Mick Jagger.

influences:

◀◀ Jackie Wilson, Diana Ross, Gene Kelly, James Brown

▶▶ Janet Jackson, Tevin Campbell, El DeBarge

see also: *The Jackson 5*

Eric Deggans

Jackson 5 /The Jacksons

Formed 1964, in Gary, IN.

Jackie Jackson, vocals; Tito Jackson, guitar, vocals; Marlon Jackson, vocals; Jermaine Jackson, vocals, bass (1964–76, 1984–present);

Michael Jackson, vocals (1964–85); Randy Jackson, vocals (1975–present); Janet Jackson, vocals; Maureen Jackson, vocals; LaToya Jackson, vocals (mid-'70s).

Although the recent years of infighting and controversy have eclipsed this family group's musical output, the Jacksons remain among the most successful vocal soul-pop groups ever. Schooled (some claim brow-beaten—and worse) by father Joe Jackson, the five oldest Jackson boys became a tight, slick performing unit when they were just teenagers, with Michael demonstrating a stylistic maturity unfathomable for his age. Signed to Motown in 1969, the group became a sensation right away—four #1 hits in a row that injected fresh energy into the label, which was suffering from the graying of some of its most popular acts. The Jackson 5 became a Saturday morning cartoon and lunch box caricatures, though the formula was tapped out by the mid-'70s. A move to Epic—after much legal wrangling and Jermaine's departure to stay with Motown and his father-in-law, Berry Gordy Jr.—gave the newly christened Jacksons a chance to modernize, which they did as Michael and Randy in particular exercised more control over the writing and production. But at the beginning of the '80s, Michael's *Off the Wall* gave him a solo career even more successful than that of the group's, irreparably altering the chemistry of the clan and the band. The 1984 "Victory" tour was an arm-twisting last gasp in the wake of Michael's *Thriller* triumph, and the rest of the Jacksons faded into the background as Michael and Janet took off for the pop stratosphere.

what to buy: *The Ultimate Collection* 𝄞𝄞𝄞𝄞𝄞 (Motown, 1995, prod. various) offers a crackling overview of Motown's last great singles group; the sheer exuberance of "ABC," "The Love You Save," and "I Want You Back" is hard to argue with, as is Michael's early solo stuff like "Rockin' Robin." The 82-song box set *Soulsation! The 25th Anniversary Collection* 𝄞𝄞𝄞𝄞 (Motown Records, 1995, prod. various) goes even deeper; it even has one of Jackie's solo cuts!

what to buy next: *Destiny* 𝄞𝄞𝄞𝄞 (Epic, 1978, prod. Jacksons) marks the brothers' first efforts at the production/songwriting helm, and they come up triumphant with ace hits such as "Blame It on the Boogie" and "Shake Your Body (Down to the Ground)." *Triumph* 𝄞𝄞𝄞𝄞 (Epic, 1980, prod. Jacksons) may be even more consistent, with an element of foreboding that would crop up to even better effect on Michael's *Thriller*.

what to avoid: *The Jacksons: An American Dream* 𝄞𝄞𝄞 (Motown, 1992) is an uneven live celebration of the group that adds nothing significant to the Jackson catalog.

the rest:
Diana Ross Presents the Jackson 5 𝄞𝄞𝄞 (Motown, 1969/1989)
ABC 𝄞𝄞𝄞𝄞 (Motown, 1970/1989)

Third Album 𝄞𝄞𝄞𝄞 (Motown, 1970/1989)
Christmas Album 𝄞𝄞 (Motown, 1970/1986)
Maybe Tomorrow 𝄞𝄞𝄞 (Motown, 1971/1989)
Greatest Hits 𝄞𝄞𝄞𝄞 (Motown, 1971/1998)
Skywriter 𝄞𝄞 (Motown, 1973/1990)
Anthology 𝄞𝄞𝄞𝄞 (Motown, 1976)
The Jacksons 𝄞𝄞𝄞 (Epic, 1976)
Goin' Places 𝄞𝄞𝄞 (Epic, 1977)
Victory 𝄞𝄞𝄞 (Epic, 1984)
2300 Jackson Street 𝄞𝄞𝄞 (Epic, 1989)
Great Songs and Performances . . . 𝄞𝄞𝄞 (Motown, 1991)
Pre-History: The Lost Steeltown Recordings 𝄞𝄞𝄞 (Brunswick, 1996)

worth searching for: Led by the disco favorite title track—which approaches the vivaciousness of "ABC"—the now-deleted *Dancing Machine* (Motown, 1974) marks a strong finish to the Jacksons' Motown era.

solo outings:
Jermaine Jackson:
Greatest Hits & Rare Classics 𝄞𝄞𝄞 (Motown, 1991)

LaToya Jackson:
You're Gonna Get Rocked 𝄞 (Private I, 1988)

influences:
◀◀ The Temptations, Smokey Robinson, Frankie Lymon, James Brown, Jackie Wilson

▶▶ Boyz II Men, New Edition, Jodeci

see also: *Michael Jackson, Janet Jackson*

Allan Orski and Gary Graff

Kate Jacobs

Born January 11, 1959, in Alexandria, VA.

Destiny's darling? At first glance, Kate Jacobs may seem like just another eclectic folkie, set to sing her earnest songs about relationships, Siberia, revolutionaries, faith, and impending death. And then you *hear* those songs, with her waifish voice somehow soaring above a potent backing band (which includes guitarist Dave Schramm, who also fronts his own act, the Schramms). Jacobs's best material combines unerring pop hooks and observational lyrics within a straightforward country/folk framework. The result is uplifting, inspirational, and engaging as hell.

what to buy: *The Calm Comes After* 𝄞𝄞𝄞𝄞 (Bar/None, 1993, prod. Kate Jacobs, Dave Schramm, Charlie Shaw, James MacMillan, Jeffrey Wood) is a stunning debut, flawless in conception and execution. "My Siberia" evokes the Kinks' "Waterloo Sunset," not so much in its music or its approach as in the accomplished way it looks at desolation and views it as a wondrous thing of beauty. Every track is of similarly high quality, with "Now They're Here," a heartbreaking tale of a family preparing to deal with the loss of one of its own, stealing the show with grace and aplomb. What a wonderful record.

the rest:
(What about Regret) 🎵🎵🎵 (Bar/None, 1995)
A Sister 🎵🎵🎵 (Bar/None, 1996)
Hydrangea 🎵🎵🎵🎵 (Bar/None, 1998)

worth searching for: Jacobs has also written a children's book, *A Sister's Wish*, based on one of her best songs, "A Sister."

influences:
◀◀ Nanci Griffith, Dolly Parton, Ray Davies, Rosanne Cash

Carl Cafarelli

Mick Jagger

Born July 26, 1943, in Dartford, England.

In the midst of his temporary '80s estrangement from Keith Richards, Rolling Stones frontman Mick Jagger fought to stay current by launching a solo career. As the Stones floundered, Jagger enlisted a load of heavy hitters (Jeff Beck, Pete Townshend, Nile Rogers, Herbie Hancock) to reach more sophisticated heights, even doing sporadic solo dates to further define his independence. None of his albums have done as well as the Stones' own efforts, but they haven't wanted for honest artistic ambition.

what to buy: *Wandering Spirit* 🎵🎵🎵🎵 (Atlantic, 1993, prod. Rick Rubin, Mick Jagger) is by far his best effort. Sporting a much leaner sound, the bass nuances in Jagger's voice flourish throughout the rockers, country ballads, and even the traditional "Handsome Molly." Finally committing to the music rather than trying to keep pace with the young pups, Jagger captures his defiance of time passing in a resoundingly honest album.

what to buy next: *Primitive Cool* 🎵🎵🎵 (Atlantic, 1987, prod. Keith Diamond, David A. Stewart) is interestingly varied, but clunkers such as "Let's Work" and "Shoot off Your Mouth" are flailing, misbegotten attempts to top the charts.

what to avoid: *She's the Boss* 🎵🎵 (Atlantic, 1985, prod. Mick Jagger, Bill Laswell, Nile Rogers) is all punchy sheen and studio gloss, replete with Jagger slinking away from his womanizing image with some sensitive, bloodless blather.

worth searching for: The bootleg *Live at Webster Hall, NY* (Midnight Beat, 1996), made from a radio broadcast, preserves Jagger's hot promotional appearance to support the *Wandering Spirit* album, with a show-closing run-through of seldom-heard Stones favorites such as "Rip This Joint" and "Have You Seen Your Mother, Baby, Standing in the Shadow."

influences:
◀◀ Muddy Waters, Howlin' Wolf, Donna Summer, the Beatles
▶▶ Paul Westerberg, Robert Plant, David Bowie

see also: *The Rolling Stones, Keith Richards*

Allan Orski

Jai

Born Jason Rowe, in England.

Affable young soul singer Jai proudly acknowledges a debt to artists such as Stevie Wonder, Donnie Hathaway, Aretha Franklin, Al Green, and Marvin Gaye, a musical vocabulary he acquired from his parents' rich record collection. After too many late evenings in the pubs of London listening to music he hated, Jai stumbled upon guitarist Joel Bogen, the Johnny Marr to his Morrisey, and the two huddled in Bogen's home studio to create music that melded their love of dance music with their love of past masters.

what's available: On *Heaven* 🎵🎵🎵🎵 (RCA, 1997, prod. Joel Bogen), Jai and Bogen evoke a rare blending of nightclub aesthetics from past to present, cloaking precious crooning in tripnotic dance beats, lush production, and well-tailored suits. By expertly merging modern tricks with timeless melodies, basted in high-gloss production, *Heaven* manages to take us back to the glory days of soul and R&B without playing the retro/gimmick card.

influences:
◀◀ Stevie Wonder, the Smiths, Donnie Hathaway, Aretha Franklin, Al Green, Marvin Gaye

Scott Hess

The Jam /Paul Weller

Formed 1972, in Woking, Surrey, England. Disbanded 1982.

Paul Weller (born John William Weller), guitar, vocals; Bruce Foxton, bass, vocals; Rick Buckler, drums.

Next to the Clash, the Jam was the most enduring group to emerge from England's punk scene. Unlike many of its contemporaries, the group wasn't merely a platform for the social ideals of the dispossessed: the songs were what mattered, ultimately, and Paul Weller, the Jam's main songwriter, wrote terrific numbers drawn from such unlikely and disparate influences as the Small Faces and Curtis Mayfield. Not since the Beatles had a British rock group defined its times so well, and the Jam enjoyed huge success in its homeland. From the group's first release in 1977, its albums showed ever-increasing versatility and promise; thus it was a surprise when Weller broke up the Jam in 1982, at the peak of its popularity. Rick Buckler went on to form Time (UK) with guitarist Danny Kustow (formerly of the Tom Robinson Band) and released a number of singles during the '80s. Bruce Foxton's abortive solo career produced *Touch Sensitive* (out of print) for Arista Records in 1984, and in 1986 he founded the now-defunct band 100 Men. Weller continued to stretch his muse by forming soul-funk-jazz group the Style Council and in 1992 began a successful solo career in the U.K.

what to buy: *Compact Snap!* 🎵🎵🎵🎵 (Polydor, 1983, prod. various) is an excellent sampler that gleans the gems from the band's many LP's, EP's, and singles. Among the highlights are a spirited demo version of "That's Entertainment" as well as "The Bitterest Pill" and "Beat Surrender," both songs from out-of-print EP's. Inspired by the Beatles' *Revolver* album, *Sound Affects* 🎵🎵🎵🎵 (Polydor, 1980, prod. Jam, Vic Coppersmith-Heaven) shows the Jam in a lively, adventurous mood. Known for writing songs with biting social commentary, Weller eases up here to deliver poppy, love-struck tunes such as "Start!," "Boy about Town," and "But I'm Different Now."

what to buy next: The few great songs missing from *Compact Snap!* can be found on *Extras* 🎵🎵🎵 (Polydor, 1992, prod. various), a compilation of EP's, obscure B-sides and unreleased material. The inclusion of tracks from the group's 1982 *Beat Surrender* EP (notably "Shopping" and Curtis Mayfield's "Move on Up") make this a vital addition for fans. The Jam's final studio effort, *The Gift* 🎵🎵🎵 (Polydor, 1982, prod. Peter Wilson, Jam), is a worthy swan song that finds the group merging R&B funk ("Town Called Malice" and "Precious") with terrific soul rockers ("Happy Together").

what to avoid: A live retrospective recorded at various stages of the band's career, *Dig the New Breed!* 🎵 (Polydor, 1982, prod. Vic Coppersmith-Heaven, Peter Wilson) is a neat idea that doesn't work. Never a strong singer while with the Jam, Weller seems to bark out his vocals, and while the songs are performed powerfully, they're better served by their studio counterparts. *Live Jam* 🎵 (Polydor, 1993, prod. Vic Coppersmith-Heaven, Peter Wilson) is a set of entirely different material, suitable only for diehard fans.

the rest:
In the City 🎵🎵 (Polydor, 1977)
This Is the Modern World 🎵🎵 (Polydor, 1977)
All Mod Cons 🎵🎵🎵 (Polydor, 1978)
Setting Sons 🎵🎵🎵 (Polydor, 1979)
Strange Fruit: The Peel Sessions 🎵🎵🎵 (Polydor, 1990)
Greatest Hits 🎵🎵🎵🎵 (Polydor, 1992)
Collection 🎵🎵🎵🎵 (A&M, 1996)

worth searching for: *Direction Reaction Creation* (Polydor U.K., 1997, prod. various) is a British-only, five-disk box set featuring 117 digitally remastered tracks, 22 of which are previously unreleased, plus an 88-page color booklet. It's a magnificent effort, but one that's for serious fans only. *A-Bomb in Oxford Street* (Blue Moon, 1995) is a much-sought-after bootleg of the Jam's scorching 1977 concert at London's infamous punk haven, the 100 Club. Recorded by Polydor U.K. for distribution to a handful of British radio stations, the album shows the band in top form, blasting its way through 19 songs from *In the City* and *This Is the Modern World*. Sound quality is high overall. As an added bonus, the CD tacks on eight studio demos from the same period.

solo outings:
Paul Weller:
Paul Weller 🎵🎵🎵🎵 (Go! Discs/London, 1992)
Wild Wood 🎵🎵🎵🎵 (Go! Discs/London, 1992)
Stanley Road 🎵🎵🎵 (Go! Discs/London, 1995)
Heavy Soul 🎵🎵🎵 (Go! Discs/London, 1997)

influences:
◀◀ The Beatles, the Who, the Kinks, Small Faces, Curtis Mayfield, Motown, Booker T. & the MG's, Traffic, Steve Winwood, Free

▶▶ The Clash, Elvis Costello, Billy Bragg, Sugar, Oasis

see also: *Style Council*

Christopher Scapelliti

James

Formed 1983, in Manchester, England.

Tim Booth, vocals; Larry Gott, guitars, slide guitars (1985–97); Jim Glennie, bass; Gavan Whelan, drums (1983–88); Saul Davies, violins, guitars, cowbells (1988–present); Andy Diagram, trumpet (1988–92); David Bayton Power, drums (1988–present); Mark Hunter, keyboards, accordion (1988–present), Adrian Oxaal, guitars.

One of the chief emigrants from the Manchester music scene, James successfully marries new wave, pop, rock, and folk. Although the group tends to go overboard with what seems like incessant jamming, James is an innovative band that improves with each release. Most of James's albums provide a handful of memorable songs, but Tim Booth's schizophrenic vocals jump from one end of the scale to the other without warning, a characteristic that begins to wear thin by the time the record ends.

what to buy: *James* 🎵🎵🎵 (Fontana, 1990, prod. James) shows the band at its best. For this record, James added a trumpeter and violinist to flesh out its folk-influenced arrangements. It also added a dramatic soundtrack to Booth's socially and politically conscious lyrics, resulting in the band's most consistently satisfying album, with a hit to boot in "Sit Down." Meanwhile, Booth's solo album, *Booth and the Bad Angel* ♫♫♫ (Mercury, 1996, prod. Angelo Badalamenti), a collaboration with composer Angelo Badalamenti, is the singer's most impressive work to date. The album, which features guest appearances by former London Suede guitarist Bernard Butler and Brian Eno, is filled with accessible pop gems.

what to buy next: On *Seven* ♫♫♫ (Fontana, 1992, prod. Youth, Steve Chase, James), James puts aside its alterna-dance influences and concentrates more on the idiosyncrasies of its music. Cascading vocals over lush horns and guitars make "Born of Frustration" one of the best songs the group has ever recorded. *The Best of James* ♫♫♫ (Mercury, 1998, prod. various) is a fine sampler with a generous 18 songs.

what to avoid: A few too many cooks and not enough first-tier songs make *Strip-Mine* ♫♫ (Sire, 1988, prod. Hugh Jones, Steve Power, Steve Lovell) a bit of a stumble on the way to better things.

the rest:
Stutter ♫♫♫ (Sire, 1986)
Laid ♫♫♫ (Mercury, 1993)
Wah Wah ♫♫♫ (Mercury, 1994)
Whiplash ♫♫ (Mercury, 1997)

worth searching for: The import live album *One Man Clapping* (Rough Trade, 1989) captures the soul-freeing spirit of James's live show and includes previously unreleased material.

influences:
◀◀ Neil Young, Patti Smith, Nick Cave

▶▶ The Levellers, Altan

Christina Fuoco

Elmore James

Born Elmore Brooks, January 27, 1918, in Richland, MS. Died May 24, 1963, in Chicago, IL.

In Elmore James's raunchy voice and buzzing electric slide-guitar riffs, you can hear the Chicago blues dissolving into early rock 'n' roll. Best known for "Dust My Broom," which he borrowed from Robert Johnson and souped up, "Shake Your Money Maker," and "Madison Blues," James's licks became as much part of blues and rock standard practice as Bo Diddley's beat and Chuck Berry's school stories. James, who, like Muddy Waters, was born in Mississippi and moved to Chicago to make his name, built his entire career on the electric boogie riff that pulses through his best hits. He also had the Broomdusters, the smokingest band this side of Waters's legendary combo during the early '50s. James influenced generations of bluesmen and rockers, from B.B. King and Jimmy Reed to the Rolling Stones,

Jimi Hendrix, George Thorogood, Stevie Ray Vaughan, and every band that picked up guitars and cranked up the amp volume.

what to buy: James recorded so many sessions with so many different record labels—he put out countless versions of "Dust My Broom," for example—that until 1992 it was tough to compile a definitive collection. *The Sky Is Crying: The History of Elmore James* ♫♫♫♫♫ (Rhino, 1993, compilation prod. Robert Palmer, James Austin) solved that problem, collecting the best versions of "Dust My Broom," "The Sky Is Crying," "Shake Your Money-maker," and the explosive "Rollin' and Tumblin'." More ardent fans will probably want *The Complete Elmore James Story* ♫♫♫♫ (Capricorn/Warner Bros., 1992, prod. various), which has many more songs but drowns you with slide guitar after a while.

what to buy next: The four-part *The Complete Fire and Enjoy Sessions* ♫♫♫♫ (Collectables, 1989, prod. Bobby Robinson) is overwhelming but establishes James as a crucial guitar pioneer whose wailing slide was a powerful force in the blues. *Street Talkin'* ♫♫♫♫ (Muse, 1973/1988, prod. Willie Dixon) also features bluesman Eddie Taylor.

what to avoid: Some of the early compilations—including *Anthology of the Blues: Legend of Elmore James* ♫♫♫ (Kent, 1976, prod. various), *Anthology of the Blues: Resurrection of Elmore James* ♫♫♫ (Kent, 1976, prod. various), *Red Hot Blues* ♫♫ (Quicksilver, 1982, prod. various), *The Classic Early Recordings, 1951–1956* ♫♫♫ (Atomic Beat, 1994, prod. various)—are solid, but have been trumped by the superior Rhino and Capricorn collections.

the rest:
Blues Masters, Vol. 1 ♫♫ (Blues Horizon, 1966)
Tough ♫♫ (Blues Horizon, 1970)
The Sky Is Crying ♫♫ (Sphere Sound, 1971)
I Need You ♫♫ (Sphere Sound, 1971)

worth searching for: *Whose Muddy Shoes* (Chess/MCA, 1969/1991, prod. Phil Chess, Leonard Chess) contains songs by James and the obscure-but-great Chicago bluesman John Brim.

influences:
◀◀ Robert Johnson, Sonny Boy Williamson, Muddy Waters, Robert Nighthawk

▶▶ The Rolling Stones, B.B. King, Jimi Hendrix, Stevie Ray Vaughan, George Thorogood, the Allman Brothers Band, Johnny Winter

Steve Knopper

Etta James

Born Jamesetta Hawkins, January 25, 1938, in Los Angeles, CA.

Is it heresy to suggest that it is Etta James—not schmaltzy, Vegas-ized Aretha Franklin—who rules as Queen of Soul these days? Not only does she come from the lineage—from her days as a '50s R&B teen queen through her time as a '60s soul-shouter—but James has matured into one of the grand dames of R&B. She always sang with a great, intense passion, but the years only seem to have added depth of character and subtle, rich color and emotion. Her first record was a simple answer to a popular Hank Ballard record, "Roll with Me Henry," that landed James on the road in 1954, where she has stayed for the rest of her career. She made one of the great gospel-soul records, "Something's Got a Hold on Me," in 1961; by 1967 she could be found putting the fiery lead vocals on one of the landmarks of Southern soul, "Tell Mama." By 1994 James could assay material some thought indelibly linked with Billie Holiday for *Mystery Lady*, an album that was at once a tribute to her earliest source of inspiration and a personal liberation. Through her own relentless determination and stubborn artistic strength, James steered her own course through the rapid waters of the music's ever-changing path, relying always on instincts and bald-faced honesty. And the years have apparently only strengthened her resolve.

what to buy: A double-disc retrospective of her 1960 to 1974 tenure at Chicago's Chess Records, *The Essential Etta James* 𝄢𝄢𝄢𝄢 (Chess/MCA, 1993, compilation prod. Andy McKaie) collects the backbone of her illustrious career.

what to buy next: *Mystery Lady* 𝄢𝄢𝄢𝄢 (Private, 1994, prod. J. Snyder) is a leap from her vernacular soul and blues into a realm of pure personal expression. With jazz pianist Cedar Walton at the bandstand, the resulting work defies easy categorization and gives James a platform to just be herself in a stunning triumph that finally earned her a Grammy award.

what to avoid: Even her most paltry recent effort, *Stickin' to My Guns* 𝄢𝄢 (Island, 1990), a largely unsuccessful attempt to incorporate rap and hip-hop into a more traditional R&B context, is more of an aberration than an artistic misstep.

the rest:
At Last 𝄢𝄢𝄢𝄢 (Chess, 1961/1989)
The Second Time Around 𝄢𝄢𝄢𝄢 (Chess, 1961)
Tell Mama 𝄢𝄢𝄢𝄢 (Chess, 1968)
Come a Little Closer 𝄢𝄢 (Chess, 1974/1996)
Deep in the Night 𝄢𝄢𝄢 (Bullseye Blues, 1978)
Red Hot 'n' Live (Quicksilver, 1982)
Her Greatest Sides, Vol. 1 𝄢𝄢𝄢 (Chess, 1984)
(With Eddie "Cleanhead" Vinson) *Blues in the Night* 𝄢𝄢 (Fantasy, 1986)
R&B Dynamite 𝄢𝄢𝄢𝄢 (Flair, 1986)
(With Eddie "Cleanhead" Vinson) *The Late Show* 𝄢𝄢 (Fantasy, 1987)
Seven Year Itch 𝄢𝄢𝄢 (Island, 1989)
The Right Time 𝄢𝄢𝄢𝄢 (Elektra, 1992)
How Strong Is a Woman: The Island Sessions 𝄢𝄢𝄢 (Polydor, 1993)
Live from San Francisco 𝄢𝄢𝄢𝄢 (On the Spot, 1994)
Time after Time 𝄢𝄢 (Private, 1994)

These Foolish Things: The Classic Balladry of Etta James 𝄢𝄢𝄢 (MCA, 1995)
Her Best 𝄢𝄢𝄢𝄢 (MCA/Chess 1997)
Love's Been Rough on Me 𝄢𝄢𝄢 (Private, 1997)
Respect Yourself 𝄢𝄢 (ITC, 1997)
Hickory Dickory Dock 𝄢𝄢𝄢𝄢 (Ace, 1998)
Life, Love, & the Blues 𝄢𝄢 (Private, 1998)

worth searching for: *Etta James Rocks the House* (Chess, 1963/1992) is an early album that more than lives up to its title. Also, for a taste of hard-driving mid-'60s soul, check out *The Sweetest Peaches: The Chess Years, Vol. 1* (Chess, 1988), wherein James and her childhood friend Sugar Pie DeSanto raise the roof with two sizzling duets.

influences:

◀◀ Billie Holiday, Hank Ballard, Big Mama Thornton, Bessie Smith

▶▶ Tina Turner, Sugar Pie DeSanto, Janis Joplin, Lou Ann Barton

Joel Selvin and Ken Burke

Tommy James & the Shondells

Formed 1960, in Niles, MI. Disbanded 1970.

Tommy James, vocals, guitar, keyboards; Eddie Gray, guitar, vocals; Ronnie Rosman, keyboards, vocals; Mike Vale, bass, vocals; Pete Lucia, drums, percussion, vocals.

Of the groups dominating the bubblegum music genre during the late '60s, Tommy James & the Shondells were certainly the most sophisticated. Despite such featherweight entries as "Mirage" and "I Think We're Alone Now," the group turned out two of the most inventive pop music gems of the era—the tremolo-heavy "Crimson and Clover," and a wispy, Philly soul-inflected bit of nonsense called "Crystal Blue Persuasion." The group began life in the garage-rock vein, with James's rough-edged vocals seared across the early R&B-flavored hits "Hanky Panky" (cut in 1963 but reissued as a #1 hit in 1966) and "Mony, Mony" (1967). Although both those singles made a significant stir in the United States and Great Britain, the group abandoned R&B, first in favor of lightweight bubblegum hits such as "I Think We're Alone Now" and later to jump on the psychedelic bandwagon. Of this latter period, both "Crimson and Clover" and "Crystal Blue Persuasion" went into the top registers of the charts, displaying what was at the time an impressive use of sound effects and layered instruments and vocals. For all the group's teenybopper appeal, its music remains a delight to hear and has been covered heavily by a number of artists, including Billy Idol ("Mony, Mony"), Joan Jett ("Crimson and Clover"), Tiffany ("I Think We're Alone Now"), and John Wesley Harding ("Crystal Blue Persuasion").

what to buy: *The Very Best of Tommy James and the Shondells* 🎵🎵🎵 (Rhino, 1993, prod. various) is a handy 10-track compilation of the group's best songs, including "Hanky Panky," "I Think We're Alone Now," "Mony, Mony," "Crimson and Clover," and "Crystal Blue Persuasion." True fans will have to have the 27-track *Anthology* 🎵🎵🎵 (Rhino, 1990, prod. various), featuring all the hits and plenty more.

what to buy next: *Crimson & Clover/Cellophane Symphony* 🎵🎵🎵 (Roulette/Rhino, 1969, prod. Tommy James) is a double-package reissue of the group's two 1969 albums that, like all Rhino releases, features completely remastered tracks. Among the gems are "Crimson and Clover" (the longer album version), "Crystal Blue Persuasion," and "Sweet Cherry Wine." A treasure chest of psychedelic bubblegum.

what to avoid: *Night in Big City* 🎵 (Aura, 1995) is an unambitious and completely unnecessary comeback album. In addition to the mediocre material, the band drums up reprised versions of "I Think We're Alone Now" and "Tighter, Tighter." If you hold your memories sacred, stick to the old hits.

the rest:
The Very Best of Tommy James and the Shondells 🎵🎵🎵 (Pair, 1990)
Hanky Panky/Mony Mony 🎵🎵🎵 (Sequel, 1994)

worth searching for: What happened to Tommy James after 1970? Find out with *Discography: Deals & Demos '74–'92: The Complete Post-Roulette Compilation* (Aura, 1993, prod. various), a two-disc set that features James's complete solo recordings, including "Glory Glory," "Tighter, Tighter," and his 1981 Top-20 hit "Three Times in Love."

solo outings:
Tommy James:
Tommy James Solo Years, 1970–1981 🎵🎵 (Rhino, 1991)

influences:
◀◀ Elvis Presley, the Beatles, Motown, Jefferson Airplane

▶▶ The Grass Roots, the Monkees, the Troggs, Paul Revere & the Raiders, Strawberry Alarm Clock, 1910 Fruitgum Company, Tommy Roe, the Five Americans, XTC/the Dukes of Stratosphear

Christopher Scapelliti

Jamiroquai
Formed 1989, in London, England.

Jason Kay, vocals; Stuart Zender, bass; Derrick McKenzie, drums; Simon Katz, guitar; Toby Smith, keyboards; Wallis Buchanan, digeridoo.

Jason Kay, leader of Jamiroquai, does not normally inspire high regard from the music press. He is persistently written off as a white guy playing black music, a hapless Stevie Wonder wannabe, and the walking embodiment of the simple-minded new age hippie. It doesn't help that his outfit's first two albums—1993's *Emergency on Planet Earth* and 1994's *The Return of the Space Cowboy*—are centered around such pedestrian topics as rain forests, romance, and The Man. But the criticism only helped the Brit streamline his craft. Jamiroquai's third disc, *Traveling without Moving*, finally broke the band in America thanks to a slick MTV video for its first single, "Virtual Insanity."

what to buy: Jamiroquai's second album, *The Return of the Space Cowboy* 🎵🎵🎵 (Columbia, 1994, prod. Jason Kay), showcases the band's primary strengths. Funky to the hilt, it maintains the momentum set out by the band's energetic debut while charting a new course with the sweet, soaring chorus of "Stillness in Time," the liquid bassline of "Half the Man," and the assured soul bite of "Light Years." Its predecessor, *Emergency on Planet Earth* 🎵🎵🎵 (Columbia, 1993, prod. Jason Kay), is a lush groove-laden affair packed with strong melodies. Even though critics were quick to chastise the band, it is hard to discredit the sheer disco sunshine of songs like "When You Gonna Learn" and "Too Young to Die."

what to buy next: With *Traveling without Moving* 🎵🎵🎵 (Work, 1996, prod. Jason Kay) Kay abridges the wide-eyed politics, tightens-up the band's nervous musical inertia, and matures with grace. He still upholds the lustrous funk of the '70s, pumping up the album with elaborate and infectious tunes that incorporate elements of straight soul, modern funk, and electro, and with lyrics that deal with more intricate subject matter than previous efforts.

influences:
◀◀ Stevie Wonder, Roy Ayers, Brand New Heavies

▶▶ Maxwell, Jai, A Tribe Called Quest

Aidin Vaziri

Jan & Dean
Formed 1958, in Los Angeles, CA.

William Jan Berry, vocals, piano (born April 3, 1941 in Los Angeles, CA); Dean Ormsby Torrence, vocals, guitar (born March 10, 1940 in Los Angeles, CA).

The incredible California saga of Jan & Dean began inconspicuously enough—under the showers at Emerson Junior High in Los Angeles, where Jan Berry began leading his fellow footballers in after-game doo-wop sessions. Soon these sing-alongs had moved into Berry's garage where, with friends Dean Torrence and Arnie Ginsburg (accompanied by drummer Sandy Nelson and future Beach Boy Bruce Johnston), songs were composed and painstakingly recorded. One of these, a ditty about a local stripper named "Jennie Lee," actually hit the Top 10 in

1958, and over the next several years Jan & Dean placed five songs on the charts before signing with Liberty Records in 1961. The story would probably have ended there if Jan had not soon afterwards befriended Brian Wilson and composed with him the anthemic "Surf City" (Brian's first, and Jan & Dean's only, #1 hit). Shrewdly continuing to record Beach Boy out-takes and sound-alikes, Jan & Dean enjoyed a string of hits through the mid-1960s, each cleverly arranged and produced (by Berry) so as to withstand even the challenge of the British Invaders. But just as music began to change—and the duo seemed ready to pursue non-musical careers (Berry was in pre-med and Torrence was a graphic artist)—Berry, like the hero of his song "Dead Man's Curve," drove his Corvette under a parked truck at 65 m.p.h. and sustained head injuries so severe that they affect him to this day. It wasn't until over a decade later, in the wake of a pop-ular TV movie about the duo, that Jan & Dean began touring and even recording together again, their sense of self-humor amazingly intact and their timeless musical odes to sun, fun, and surf still a powerful elixir.

what to buy: Not only does *All the Hits, from Surf City to Drag City* ♪♪♪♪ (EMI America, 1996, compilation prod. Ron Furmanek) offer an absolutely flawless overview of Jan & Dean's career, its two discs provide no less than a compendium of everything 1960s California stood for and sounded like: that is, before Jan took that "one last ride" and Jimi Hendrix declared "we'd never hear surf music again."

what to buy next: *Teen Suite 1958–1962* ♪♪♪♪ (Varese Vintage, 1995, compilation prod. Cary E. Mansfield, Elliot Kendall) documents Jan & Dean's pre-surf material so thoroughly it even includes a seven-minute session tape from one of their very first garage get-togethers. Until Phil Spector decides to unlock his vaults, this is the closest one can come to eavesdropping on the birth of West Coast rock. Berry's often overlooked talents as both an arranger and producer are best showcased on *Drag City/Jan & Dean's Pop Symphony No. 1 (in 12 Hit Movements)* ♪♪♪♪ (Liberty, 1964, 1965/One Way, 1996, prod. Jan Berry), and for a taste of the duo's decidedly strange, sometimes downright bizarre sense of humor, try *Command Performance: Live in Person/Jan & Dean Meet Batman* ♪♪♪♪ (Liberty, 1965, 1966/One Way, 1996, prod. Jan Berry).

what to avoid: After Jan's crash, Dean gathered together friends (and for the cover shot, Jan's look-alike brother) to produce a positively abysmal "concept album" called *Save for a Rainy Day* **woof!** (Columbia, 1967/Sundazed, 1996, compilation prod. Bob Irwin). Silly enough even during the height of the post–*Sgt. Pepper* follies, its re-release today, containing both full stereo and mono mixes of the original album, makes it doubly hard to sit through. That Jan ever forgave his partner for this travesty is to be forever commended, to say the least.

best of the rest:
Jan & Dean ♪♪♪ (Dore, 1960/Era, 1996)
Golden Hits, Vols. 1, 2, 3 ♪♪♪♪ (Liberty 1962, 1965, 1966/One Way, 1995)
Jan & Dean Take Linda Surfin'/Ride the Wild Surf ♪♪♪ (Liberty, 1963, 1964/One Way, 1996)
Surf City/Folk 'n' Roll ♪♪♪ (Liberty, 1963, 1966/One Way, 1996)
Dead Man's Curve/The New Girl in School ♪♪♪ (Liberty, 1964/One Way, 1996)
The Little Old Lady from Pasadena/Filet of Soul ♪♪♪♪ (Liberty, 1964, 1966/One Way, 1996)
The Jan & Dean Anthology Album ♪♪♪♪ (United Artists, 1971/One Way, 1996)
Gotta Take That One Last Ride ♪♪♪♪ (United Artists, 1974/One Way, 1996)
Golden Summer Days: The Legendary Masked Surfers ♪♪♪ (Varese Sarabande, 1996)

worth searching for: A remarkable series of "fan club-only" CD's featuring acetates of entire unreleased 1960s albums and out-takes stretching back to the garage days are available for the true fan(atic). *The Best of Studio Out-Takes, Vols. 1 and 2, Carnival of Sound*, and especially *Filet of Soul: A "Lost" One* are highly recommended.

solo outings:
Jan Berry:
Second Wave ♪♪♪ (One Way, 1997)

influences:
◄◄ Dion & the Belmonts, Frankie Valli & the Four Seasons, Brian Wilson, Laurel & Hardy

►► Flo & Eddie, Papa Doo Run Run, Endless Summer

Gary Pig Gold

Jandek /The Units
Born Sterling Smith.

He has never performed in public, doesn't grant interviews, his records contain no annotation whatsoever, and, of course, there are no press kits or even photographs of the artist available for perusal. Nevertheless, the remarkable body of work the mysterious man named Jandek has produced—26 albums (at last count) that run the gamut from tortured, naked blues to simple, fun rock 'n' roll to screeching, terrifying experiments in catatonia—can be heard slowly but surely creeping towards the mainstream via such diverse artists as Beck, Courtney Love, and even nine inch nails. Self-issued in extremely limited pressings (but always available direct from Corwood Industries, P.O. Box 15375, Houston, TX 77220), these exercises in often Uneasy Listening defiantly continue to, in the words of critic Byron Coley, "blow around the country like an old dead leaf painted dark purple."

what to buy: It's understandably difficult to know just where to wade into a catalog as vast and cryptic as Jandek's, but his most popular and—if the word can even remotely be applied here—accessible titles remain *Telegraph Melts* 𝄞𝄞𝄞 (Corwood, 1986, prod. Jandek) and *Follow Your Footsteps* 𝄞𝄞𝄞▽ (Corwood, 1986, prod. Jandek). The former contains one of his most truly horrific works, "You Painted Your Teeth." The latter, despite being his most traditionally melodic collection overall, still caused one reviewer to proclaim it "Phil Spector's worst nightmare."

what to buy next: The profoundly disturbing *Six and Six* 𝄞𝄞𝄞𝄞 (Corwood, 1981, prod. Jandek) seems to be a chronicle of the three "lost years" Jandek spent between his debut album and this somnambulant, unsettling sophomore effort. Call it the *ultra* lo-fi *John Lennon/Plastic Ono Band*. The similarly morose yet equally fascinating *Blue Corpse* 𝄞𝄞𝄞 (Corwood, 1987, prod. Jandek) kicks off a seven-album cycle that tackles, wrestles to the ground, and comes close to actually reinventing the very basis of the American rural blues and folk idiom, culminating in the thoroughly rewarding *Lost Cause* 𝄞𝄞𝄞 (Corwood, 1992, prod. Jandek) and *Twelfth Apostle* 𝄞𝄞𝄞𝄞 (Corwood, 1993, prod. Jandek). On the latter, Jandek even dares to take Bob Dylan's "It Alright, Ma. . . ." to task, while *Lost Cause* most adeptly nutshells the man's Janus-faced modus operandi by presenting the positively buoyant "Babe I Love You" alongside a near-20 minute exercise in bashing, whistling, shrieking cacophony.

the rest:
Ready for the House 𝄞𝄞▽ (Corwood, 1978)
Later On 𝄞𝄞𝄞 (Corwood, 1981)
Chair beside a Window 𝄞𝄞𝄞𝄞 (Corwood, 1982)
Living in a Moon So Blue 𝄞𝄞𝄞 (Corwood, 1982)
Staring at the Cellophane 𝄞𝄞▽ (Corwood, 1982)
Your Turn to Fall 𝄞𝄞𝄞 (Corwood, 1983)
The Rocks Crumble 𝄞𝄞𝄞 (Corwood, 1983)
Interstellar Discussion 𝄞𝄞▽ (Corwood, 1984)
Nine-Thirty 𝄞𝄞𝄞 (Corwood, 1985)
Foreign Keys 𝄞𝄞𝄞𝄞 (Corwood, 1985)
Modern Dances 𝄞𝄞▽ (Corwood, 1987)
You Walk Alone 𝄞𝄞𝄞 (Corwood, 1988)
On the Way 𝄞𝄞𝄞 (Corwood, 1988)
The Living End 𝄞𝄞𝄞 (Corwood, 1989)
Somebody in the Snow 𝄞𝄞▽ (Corwood, 1990)
One Foot in the North 𝄞𝄞▽ (Corwood, 1991)
Graven Image 𝄞𝄞𝄞 (Corwood, 1994)
Glad to Get Away 𝄞𝄞𝄞 (Corwood, 1994)
White Box Requiem 𝄞𝄞𝄞𝄞 (Corwood, 1996)
I Woke Up 𝄞𝄞𝄞 (Corwood, 1997)

influences:
◀◀ Harry Partch, Jimmy Reed, the Godz, the Shaggs, Mayo Thompson, Skip Spence, J.D. Salinger

▶▶ Daniel Johnston, Jack Pedler, Girlysound, Ray Carmen

Gary Pig Gold

Jane's Addiction /Deconstruction

Formed 1986, in Los Angeles, CA. Disbanded 1991. Re-formed 1997.

Perry Farrell (born Perry Bernstein), vocals; Eric Avery, bass (1986–91); Dave Navarro, guitars; Stephen Perkins, drums; Flea (born Michael Balzary), bass (1997–present).

Even though Jane's Addiction only had two proper albums before breaking up, the Los Angeles art-rock band made its mark by blending heavy metal, glam, and punk sensibilities with rhythmic funk strains—all under Lollapalooza co-founder Perry Farrell's unique, high-pitched (some might say grating) warble. It was an enormously influential approach, and the band made people pay attention with its provocative album art—including the cover of *Ritual de lo Habitual*, which displayed images of full frontal nudity that prompted some retailers to refuse to stock it; a second cover was created that offers the text of the first amendment. The band split at the end of summer 1991, after inaugurating the Lollapalooza series. Farrell formed Porno for Pyros, which also included Perkins. Navarro and Avery joined drummer Michael Murphy in the band Deconstruction, which recorded one album. Red Hot Chili Peppers bassist Flea came onboard for the 1997 reunion tour and leftovers album *Kettle Whistle*, the four new songs of which don't capture the raw energy of its early releases.

what to buy: On *Ritual de lo Habitual* 𝄞𝄞𝄞 (Warner Bros., 1990, prod. Dave Jerden, Perry Farrell), Jane's Addiction met the mainstream halfway with more accessible melodies and rollicking tunes such as "Stop!" and "Been Caught Stealing." As on all the band's albums, Farrell's voice wears on the listener after a few songs, but *Ritual*'s stronger songs make it a bit more tolerable.

what to avoid: *Jane's Addiction* 𝄞𝄞 (Triple X, 1987, prod. Jane's Addiction), recorded live at the Roxy in Hollywood, introduced Farrell as a flamboyant lead singer and resident eccentric who fancied wearing neon dreadlocks and dark eye-makeup. But it drags. The Deconstruction album, *Deconstruction* 𝄞 (American, 1994, prod. Ron Champagne), is a grating experiment in sound, working with feedback and other dissonance.

the rest:
Nothing's Shocking 𝄞𝄞▽ (Warner Bros., 1988)
Kettle Whistle 𝄞𝄞 (Warner Bros., 1997)

influences:
◀◀ The Stooges, Jimi Hendrix, Parliamet-Funkadelic, Circle Jerks

▶▶ Guns N' Roses, Fishbone, Rage Against the Machine, Red Hot Chili Peppers

see also: *Porno for Pyros, Red Hot Chili Peppers*

Christina Fuoco

Japan
/Rain Tree Crow
/Mick Karn
/Polytown

Formed 1974, in London, England. Disbanded 1982. Re-formed as Rain Tree Crow, 1991. Disbanded 1992.

David Sylvian, vocals, guitar, keyboards; Steve Jansen, drums, percussion; Richard Barbieri, keyboards; Mick Karn, bass, saxophone; Terry Bozzio, drums, percussion, bodhran; David Torn, guitars, loops and processing, Hammond B-3 organ, harmonica.

During four short years as a recording entity, Japan managed one of the most startling transformations in modern rock. Its 1979 debut came as part of the New Romantic movement, which was influenced by artists such as David Bowie and Roxy Music. Being a New Romantic basically boiled down to loud clothes and hair colors, melodramatic vocals, and copious (and unoriginal) use of the synthesizer. By 1979, however, Japan had already moved beyond such superficial accoutrements and was concentrating on more sophisticated forms. Sparked by David Sylvian's interest in Eastern song structure, the band experimented with micro-scales and polyrhythms. Utilizing sophisticated (for the time) synthesizer technology, Sylvian and Richard Barbieri developed a shimmering, detuned keyboard sound. This, coupled with Sylvian's dramatic baritone, Mick Karn's distinctive fretless bass, and the unconventional drumming of Steve Jansen (Sylvian's brother) gave Japan its sonic signature. As the band's music matured, so too did Sylvian's lyrics, which came to deal in dystopian imagery and fractal snapshots of modern culture. In 1982, just as the band reached its fertile peak, it disbanded. Its members pursued solo projects and occasionally worked together in various configurations. In 1991 they formed Rain Tree Crow, which stayed together just long enough to record one album. Polytown consists of Karn along with high-tech guitar wizard David Torn and ex-Zappa and Missing Persons drummer Terry Bozzio.

what to buy: Released a year before the group disbanded, Japan's *Tin Drum* 𝄢𝄢𝄢𝄢 (Caroline, 1991, prod. Japan) bore the full fruit of its evolution from pop band to progressive art-rock outfit. The material here is distinctive and haunting, with Karn's melodic bass counterpointing Sylvian's vocals. Many of the songs, such as "Ghosts," achieve a dark, penetrating beauty, while more kinetic numbers such as "The Art of Parties" and

"Still Life in Mobile Homes" examine the decadence of late 20th-century culture.

what to buy next: *Gentlemen Take Polaroids* 𝄢𝄢𝄢 (Caroline, 1980, prod. John Punter) offers pleasures similar to those found on *Tin Drum*. The material is slightly more upbeat, with Jansen delivering a number of propulsive performances—notably on the title cut and "Methods of Dance." There are also foreshadows of *Tin Drum*'s more contemplative moments in material such as "My New Career" and "Taking Islands in Africa."

what to avoid: *Adolescent Sex* 𝄢𝄢 (Hansa, 1978/Caroline, 1994, prod. Ray Singer) is interesting only as a historical artifact. On its debut album, Japan is little more than a haircut band along the lines of Duran Duran or (gulp!) A Flock of Seagulls. And this record is indistinguishable from the piles of synth-pop belched up in the late 1970s.

the rest:
Obscure Alternatives 𝄢𝄢 (Hansa, 1978/Caroline, 1991)
Quiet Life 𝄢𝄢𝄢𝄢 (Hansa, 1979/Caroline, 1991)
Oil on Canvas 𝄢𝄢𝄢 (Virgin, 1983/Caroline, 1991)

worth searching for: There are a number of Japan recordings—as well as the individual members' solo albums—that are only available as imports. The best of these is the Japan retrospective, *Exorcising Ghosts* (Virgin, 1984). Also of note is the live *Souvenir from Japan* (Hansa, 1989).

solo outings:
Rain Tree Crow:
Rain Tree Crow 𝄢𝄢𝄢𝄢 (Virgin, 1991)

Mick Karn:
Titles 𝄢𝄢𝄢 (Caroline, 1982)
Dreams of Reason Produce Monsters 𝄢𝄢𝄢 (Caroline, 1987)
(With Dali's Car) *The Judgment Is the Mirror* 𝄢𝄢𝄢𝄢 (Beggars Banquet, 1984)
(With Polytown) *Polytown* 𝄢𝄢𝄢 (CMP, 1994)

influences:

◀◀ Roxy Music, David Bowie, Can, Brian Eno, Bebop Deluxe, Lou Reed & the Velvet Underground

▶▶ Depeche Mode, Bill Nelson, Ultravox

see also: *David Sylvian*

David Galens

Jars of Clay

Formed 1994, in Greenville, IL.

Dan Haseltine, vocals; Charlie Lowell, keyboards; Steve Mason, guitar; Matt Bronleewe, guitar (1993–94); Scott Savage, drums; Matt Odmark, guitar (1994–present).

Many secular pop music fans were hooked by Jars of Clay's energetic, texured sound before they realized the group featured a band of dedicated Christians or that their name was taken from a Bible verse. Dan Haseltine, Charlie Lowell, and Matt Bronleewe met while they were students at Greenville College, studying contemporary Christian music at the Methodist university. Before long, Haseltine enlisted Mason, and the four decided to write songs together and later form a band. With Savage along as a drummer for live shows, they played Christian music festivals and churches until winning the Gospel Music Association's Spotlight Competition in April 1994. Record company interest followed, prompting the group to move to Nashville, leaving behind Bronleewe, who wanted to finish school and get married. In 1995, they signed with the smallest record company that had courted them, Essential Records, which proved their luckiest move. Essential employed an intern who was the niece of guitar wizard Adrian Belew, who she convinced to produce two songs on the band's breakthrough record. Powered by the Belew-produced single "Flood," the self-titled record sold two million copies, allowing the band to tour with secular groups such as the Samples, Duncan Sheik, and Matchbox 20. But their tactic of bringing thinly veiled Christian songs to bars and secular music halls nearly lost their audience, as mainstream rock fans grew skeptical of their religious beliefs and Christian fans felt betrayed by the band's tremendous success. Still, its second major-label record debuted at #8, proving the band can still straddle disparate worlds with its earnest, expert music.

what to buy: With a catchy single, earnest lyrics and neo-folksy jangle that fit right in with the alterna-pop sound of the time, it's no wonder *Jars of Clay* ΔΔΔΔ (Essential, 1995, prod. Adrian Belew, Jars of Clay) scored big. Who knew a single about Noah's Ark—the Belew-produced cut, "Flood"—could be so compelling?

what to buy next: While working the same alternative-tinged, radio-friendly pop that made its early name, the group's third album, *Much Afraid* ΔΔΔ (Jive, 1997, prod. Steve Lipson), lacks the kind of catchy single that catapulted its predecessor into pop's stratosphere.

what to avoid: Slight and short, the Christmas EP *Drummer Boy* **woof!** (Essential, 1995, prod. Jars of Clay) is strictly for fans who find songs such as "Flood" too enigmatic.

worth searching for: For a sneak peek at the band's early songwriting efforts, check out its first record, *Frail* (Silvertone, 1994), which finds seminal elements of the band's hitmaking sound already in place.

influences:

◄◄ Sarah McLachlan, Hootie & the Blowfish, Counting Crows, DC Talk

►► Matchbox 20, Duncan Sheik

Eric Deggans

WHAT ALBUM CHANGED YOUR LIFE?

Sarah McLachlan's *Fumbling towards Ecstasy*. I think her lyrics are really honest, really down-to-earth. I think her band is great and the production is really cool. That's a record I've been able to listen to over and over—we even took some ideas from it when we did our album.

Charlie Lowell (of Jars of Clay)

Jason & the Scorchers

Formed 1981, in Nashville, TN. Disbanded 1990. Re-formed 1995.

Jason Ringenberg, vocals, harmonica, guitar; Warner Hodges, guitar, vocals; Jeff Johnson, bass; Perry Baggs, drums, vocals; Andy York, guitar (1989); Ken Fox, bass (1989).

The members of Jason & the Scorchers, along with the Mekons and other punkish '80s bands, decided they understood Hank Williams Sr. better than the Eagles did. So they recreated country/rock in their own sloppy, thrift-store-hat-wearing image. The Scorchers' name was not an exaggeration: Led by Ringenberg's frenzied energy and herky-jerky stage movements, the band cranked up the guitars and turned Williams's music back into the hardcore honky-tonk it used to be. Ringenberg, as legend goes, grew up on his family's hog farm in Sheffield, Illinois, then moved to Nashville to become a star. He hooked up with a few hillbillies who shared his love for Bob Dylan and the Ramones, and they set about crashing punk and country into each other. After opening for Dylan on his 1990 tour, the Scorchers grew fed up with each other and the lack of commercial attention, so they broke up. They re-formed with a 1995 reunion album containing the punkiest version of John Denver's "Take Me Home, Country Roads" you ever heard.

what to buy: *Essential Jason & the Scorchers, Vol. 1: Are You Ready for the Country* ΔΔΔΔ (EMI, 1992, prod. Jeff Daniel, Adam Block) collects two early albums, *Fervor* and *Lost & Found*, along with a bunch of rarities and live tracks. (The double-disc set has since been renamed *Both Sides of the Line*.) The reunion album, *A-Blazing Grace* ΔΔΔΔ (Mammoth, 1995, prod.

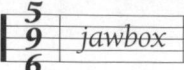

Jason & the Scorchers), is built around an incredible version of John Denver's formerly corny "Take Me Home, Country Roads" and George Jones's "Why Baby Why."

what to buy next: The debut EP, *Reckless Country Soul* 𝄃𝄃𝄃 (Praxis, 1992/Mammoth, 1996, prod. Jack Emerson, Jason & the Scorchers, Jim Dickinson), gets repetitive, but its barnstorming country-punk breathes life into Williams's "I'm So Lonesome (I Could Cry)," plus the consummate Scorchers classic, "Help! There's a Fire."

what to avoid: *Thunder and Fire* 𝄃𝄃 (A&M, 1989) is the sound of thunder and fire slipping away, just before the band broke up.

the rest:
Still Standing 𝄃𝄃𝄃 (EMI, 1986)
Clear Impetuous Morning 𝄃𝄃𝄃 (Mammoth, 1996)
Midnight Roads & Stages Seen 𝄃𝄃𝄃𝄃 (Mammoth, 1998)

worth searching for: *Lost & Found* (EMI, 1985, prod. Terry Manning) and the EP *Fervor* (EMI, 1983, prod. various) are good but hard to find. *Essential* is a better deal.

solo outings:
Jason Ringenberg:
One Foot in the Honky Tonk 𝄃𝄃 (Liberty, 1992)

influences:
◀◀ Hank Williams Sr., Johnny Cash, the Ramones, the Mekons, Gram Parsons

▶▶ Social Distortion, Uncle Tupelo, Golden Smog, the Bottle Rockets

Steve Knopper

Jawbox

Formed 1989, in Washington, DC. Disbanded 1997.

Jay Robbins, vocals, guitar, organ, percussion; Kim Coletta, bass, vocals; W.C. Barbot, guitar, vocals, sax, organ (1991–97); Adam Wade, drums (1989–93); Zachary Barocas, drums (1993–97).

Despite its presence in the D.C. scene, and the fact that Jay Robbins was a former member of Government Issue, Jawbox was not easily pigeonholed. Many post-hardcore elements existed in its sound, yet it was so rigidly bound that it seemed quaint or dated (as many others of its ilk do). The addition of W.C. Barbot was an asset, as he played point guard to Robbins's power-forward; their vocals and guitars intertwine and conflict, all in pursuit of a perfect sound. Kim Coletta was no token chick-bassist; her throbbing style and hyper stage presence was certainly a bonus. Both Adam Wade (who later joined Shudder to Think) and Zachary Barocas were able skin-beaters who drove the songs with precision and ferocity. After doing

the unthinkable—leaving Discord for Atlantic—Jawbox continued with that which brung 'em: great songs with strong lyrics. Sadly, the commercial end of the biz didn't embrace the group, and after being dropped by Atlantic in one of the label's purges, the group disbanded. The void it left has remained empty.

what to buy: *Novelty* 𝄃𝄃𝄃𝄃 (Discord, 1992, prod. Ian Burgess) is timeless. Volatile riffs and catchy melodies blend with Robbins's and Barbot's singing. The two sound almost argumentative, settling disputes with their slicing guitar riffs and their hoarse yet melodic vocals. Coletta's bass is abundantly rhythmic, and Wade plays as if the warranty is about to expire on his gear. The cut "Tongues" is a shoulda-been single, but it probably wouldn't have been proper around easily influenced children.

what to buy next: *For Your Own Special Sweetheart* 𝄃𝄃𝄃𝄃 (Atlantic, 1994, prod. Ted Nicely, Jawbox) showed that Jawbox nearly dared a major label to sign them. "FF=66" is almost atonal, ensuring the group limited exposure. For the uninitiated who don't stop there, however, a treat is in store; the second track, "Savory," combines the best that Jawbox could offer: fat riffs, neat vocals with lyrical hooks, pounding drums, and insistent bass meld for perhaps the group's best moment. Other cuts, such as "Motorist," cruise along to make the record an engaging listen.

the rest:
Grippe 𝄃𝄃𝄃 (Discord, 1991)
Jawbox 𝄃𝄃𝄃𝄃 (Atlantic, 1996)

worth searching for: The single "Airwaves Dream" (Selfless, 1991) is a cool seven-inch split with Jawbreaker that features a solid cover of this Buzzcocks classic.

influences:
◀◀ Rites of Spring, Minor Threat, Fugazi, GI, Edsel

▶▶ Helmet, Quicksand, Pivot

Barry M. Prickett

Jawbreaker

Formed 1988, in New York, NY. Disbanded 1997.

Blake Schwarzenbach, vocals, guitar; Chris Bauermeister, bass; Adam Phaler, drums.

Why must all (or each) great bands whose name begins with "Jaw" break up? Before their demise, Jawbreaker made several must-hear emo-core records during the early '90s. Virtuosos all, and with questionable surnames, the three musicians made music that is necessary listening for those that stray left of the dial. Blake Schwarzenbach sang as if his throat polyps (removed in a mid-tour emergency procedure) were his best asset. Chris Bauermeister played as if he had an additional six fingers on loan, while drummer Adam Phaler probably never gave a clinic but should have with his musically Punk 101 playing. The trio met in New York, moved to the San Francisco Bay Area, signed to a major label, had a small-time hit song ("Fireman"), and broke up. That's a tragedy, for Jawbreaker was one of the most pleasantly diverse and fantastic (pseudo) punk bands of all time—not truly punk because its members were too bright for the genre, but closer to that than any other. Its demise is a regrettable chapter in the history of popular music.

what to buy: The best place to start with is the group's debut, *Unfun* 🎵🎵🎵🎵 (Shredder, 1990/92, prod. Richard Andrews, Michael James, Jawbreaker). The chorus of the first song, "Want" ("Aye, yi, yi, yi, yi, I want you") is enough to melt the best ice sculpture ever made, and the record never falters from there. If you play music, you might quit after hearing this, because you know you'll never equal it, much less top it. The CD also contains the EP *Whack & Blite* (Very Small Records, 1989), which contains the California commuter boredom classic "Eye-5." You really can't own one without the other, so *Dear You* 🎵🎵🎵🎵 (DGC, 1995, prod. Rob Cavallo, Jawbreaker) is only docked half a bone because we knew how good the group was from the start. Each track here has campfire sing-along potential, but it was "Fireman" that finally got the band its much-deserved radio play. Post-surgery Schwarzenbach's vocals are a bit smoother, but it doesn't sound as if he leaves his ashtray empty either. With his English degree in tow, this is one record where the lyrics can be printed to its benefit.

what to buy next: It's a toss up, but *Bivouac* 🎵🎵🎵 (Tupelo/Communion, 1992, prod. Jawbreaker, Billy Anderson, Mike Morasky, Jonathan Burnside) wins out because the band cast aside the shorter, tighter compositions of *Unfun* in favor of longer, passionate epics that never drag. Also important is the inclusion of the 1992 *Chesterfield King* EP. "Tour Song" is an anthem to anyone who has ever played in a small-time band. *24-Hour Revenge Therapy* 🎵🎵🎵 (Tupelo/Communion, 1994, prod. Jawbreaker, Steve Albini) is the stepping stone to a big league signing. The songs are once again shorter and the ideas a bit more concise.

worth searching for: The group's contribution to the R.E.M.-penned compilation *Surprise Your Pig* (Staple Gun) is "Pretty Persuasion." Also of note is the split single with Jawbox and Selfless where Jawbreaker butchers U2's "With or without You."

influences:

◀◀ Sex Pistols, Hüsker Dü, R.E.M.

Barry M. Prickett

Jay & the Americans

Formed as the Harbor-Lites, 1959, in New York, NY. Became Jay & the Americans in 1961.

John "Jay" Traynor, vocals (1959–62); Jay Black (born David Blatt), vocals; Kenny Vance (born Kenny Rosenberg), vocals; Sandy Deane (born Sandy Yaguda), vocals; Howie Kane (born Howard Kerschenbaum), vocals; Marty Saunders, vocals, guitar (1961–70); Donald Fagen, vocals, keyboards (1971); Walter Becker, vocals, guitar (1971).

Jay & the Americans brought dramatic, sometimes operatic kinetic energy to the sounds of '50s doo-wop. Its run of '60s hits embraced modern production techniques and important rising songwriters (Tommy Boyce and Bobby Hart, Neil Diamond, etc.) while straddling the line between pop-rock and MOR. The group was comprised of various members of the Harbor-Lites, the Mystics, and the Empires. After signing with United Artists, where the group spent its entire career, the label suggested the name Binky Jones & the Americans. Blanching at that, the group substituted John Traynor's nickname, Jay, and a classic doo-wop group was born. It was Traynor who sang lead on their first major hit, the haunting "She Cried," a chilling Leiber and Stoller production. When subsequent releases did poorly, Traynor jumped ship and started an unsuccessful solo career. David Blatt (renamed Jay Black for the sake of group continuity), came on board as lead singer. Black's mid-range operatic power, similar in tone to Roy Orbison's, brought a distinctive emotive depth to the group's body of work. The Americans' first hit with Black as lead singer was a hand-me-down from the Drifters, "Only in America." Producers Leiber and Stoller erased the Drifters' vocals from a previously recorded session and recorded the Americans in their place. A string of hits followed, most notably the mariachi-influenced "Come a Little Bit Closer," the Italian-flavored "Cara Mia," and the romantic "Let's Lock the Door." With "Sunday and Me," Jay & the Americans became the first group to record a hit version of a Neil Diamond song, and its version of "Crying" nearly outshone Roy Orbison's original. The group's final volley of hits came during a late '60s doo-wop revival/contemporary rock backlash; its versions of the Drifters' "This Magic Moment" and the Ronettes' "Walkin' in the Rain" actually charted higher than the originals. A slightly altered line-up of Jay & the Americans (with Walter Becker and Donald Fagen, later of Steely Dan fame), continued to record successfully into the early '70s. Since then, Black and various hired hands have played the oldies circuit, where his remarkable vocal range and power still give fans a thrill.

what to buy: The 28-song compilation *Come a Little Bit Closer: The Best of Jay & the Americans* 🎵🎵🎵 (EMI, 1990/Gold Rush, 1996, prod. Jerry Leiber, Mike Stoller) not only features all the hits but has the benefit of digital remixing, rare foreign language versions of "She Cried" and "Come a Little Bit Closer," and, just for fun, a vintage radio ad. If you can find it, this is the one to have.

what to buy next: A solid two-for-one compilation, *Sands of Time/Wax Museum* 𝄞𝄞𝄞 (United Artists, 1969, 1970/Gold Rush, 1996, reissue prod. Ron Furmanek) boasts a sprinkling of hits with many remakes of other doo-wop classics. These two LPs were recorded at the height of a doo-wop revival, and the group's fondness for the material really shines through. Complete liner notes make this an especially strong package.

the rest:
Greatest Hits 𝄞𝄞𝄞 (CEMA Special Products, 1992)
Greatest Hits 𝄞𝄞𝄞 (Curb, 1994)
All-Time Greatest Hits 𝄞𝄞𝄞 (Madacy, 1995)
Jay & the Americans 𝄞𝄞 (ITC, 1997)

worth searching for: If you want the absolute most you can get in one package, track down the Canadian compilation *Jay & the Americans—Masterworks* (United Artists, 1997, prod. various), a three-disc set containing every chart single from all eras of the group's history, as well as many enthralling B-sides and LP tracks.

influences:
◀◀ The Drifters, the Mystics, the Empires, Roy Orbison

▶▶ The Brooklyn Bridge, Steely Dan

Ken Burke

The Jayhawks /The Original Harmony Ridge Creek Dippers

Formed 1985, in Minneapolis, MN.

Gary Louris, guitar, vocals; Mark Olson, guitar, vocals (1985–95); Marc Perlman, bass; Thad Spencer, drums (1985–90); Ken Callahan, drums (1990–95); Karen Grotberg, keyboards; Tim O'Regan, drums (1995–present); Kraig Johnson, guitar (1996–present); Jessy Greene, violin (1996–present).

Hailed as the second coming of the Flying Burrito Brothers, the Jayhawks actually had the goods to hold up to the comparison. Not that the notion was completely off the mark: Mark Olson played Gram Parsons to Gary Louris's Chris Hillman, and the band played sparse, emotion-packed music that tapped into the spirit of country music without ever reflecting Nashville's infatuation with the mainstream. When Olson, the husband of singer-songwriter Victoria Williams, left the band in November 1995, he took band's country influences and harmonies with him. (He later formed the folkish Original Harmony Ridge Creek Dippers with his wife and multi-instrumentalist Mike "Razz"

Russell.) The remaining Jayhawks—Louris, Perlman, Grotberg, and O'Regan—added a guitarist and a violinist and released *Sound of Lies*, which followed an earthy, Midwestern alt-rock path, in 1997.

what to buy: On *Tomorrow the Green Grass* 𝄞𝄞𝄞𝄞 (American, 1995, prod. George Drakoulias), the Jayhawks effectively started shaking off the Flying Burrito Brother comparisons, replacing it with—of all things—'70s power-pop. With songs such as "Blue" and a cover of Grand Funk's "Bad Time," the Jayhawks produced their best hooks without forsaking their country soul.

what to buy next: *Hollywood Town Hall* 𝄞𝄞𝄞𝄞 (American, 1993, prod. George Drakoulias) established the Jayhawks as the premiere country-rock (for lack of a better term) band of its time. The album made best-of lists in the *Village Voice, Entertainment Weekly,* and just about everywhere else.

the rest:
The Jayhawks 𝄞𝄞𝄞 (Bunkhouse, 1986)
Blue Earth 𝄞𝄞𝄞𝄞 (Twin/Tone, 1989)
Sound of Lies 𝄞𝄞𝄞 (American, 1997)

worth searching for: The import CD-5 for *Waiting for the Sun* (American, 1993, prod. George Drakoulias) features four live songs, including a cover of Tim Hardin's "Reason to Believe."

solo outings:
Mark Olson:
The Original Harmony Ridge Creek Dippers 𝄞𝄞𝄞 (self-released, 1997)

influences:
◀◀ Gram Parsons, Neil Young, Flying Burrito Brothers, Big Star, the Byrds

▶▶ Wilco, Son Volt, Victoria Williams, Joe Henry

see also: *Golden Smog*

Brian Mansfield

Jefferson Airplane

Formed 1965, in San Francisco, CA. Disbanded 1972

Marty Balin, vocals (1965–70); Grace Slick, keyboards, vocals; Paul Kantner, guitar, vocals; Jorma Kaukonen, guitar, vocals; Jack Casady, bass; Skip Spence, drums (1965–66); Spencer Dryden, drums (1966–70); Joey Covington, drums (1970–71); Papa John Creach, violin (1971–72); John Barbata, drums (1971–72).

Although the band's reputation has diminished over the years (see Jefferson Starship), the Jefferson Airplane ushered in the Summer of Love with two hits that neatly encapsulated the feeling of the time: "Somebody to Love" and "White Rabbit." An iracsible, contentious group of strong-willed personalities, the Airplane led the San Francisco sound out of the provinces and around the world. Combining the pop sensibilities of founder and vocalist Marty Balin with the folky flavor of Paul Kantner, the peerless delta blues–based guitaristics of Jorma Kaukonen, and the free-wheeling bass of Jack Casady, the band forged a unique signature style best revealed in live performance. Grace Slick may have been the most obvious component of the group, having provided lead vocals to the band's two best-known songs, but the strength of the Airplane was the ensemble collaboration, a tentative creative partnership responsible for some stunning high points in the band's estimable body of work.

what to buy: The pre-Slick debut, *Jefferson Airplane Takes Off* 𝄞𝄞𝄞𝄞 (RCA Victor, 1966, prod. Matthew Katz, Tommy Oliver) has been freshly dusted off for the digital era, complete with one track censored off the initial issue for the inclusion of the word "trips." It's an album few noticed outside the San Francisco Bay Area that nevertheless retains some of the special flavor of the original band. *Surrealistic Pillow* 𝄞𝄞𝄞𝄞𝄞 (RCA Victor, 1967, prod. Rick Jarrard) has been released in a gold disc edition that crystallizes one of the era's great albums in spectacular sonics. *Bless Its Pointed Little Head* 𝄞𝄞𝄞𝄞 (RCA Victor, 1969, prod. Al Schmitt) documents the powerful sweep of the band's epic live performances, including sterling samples of the band's often sprawling improvisations.

what to buy next: The three-disc box set *Jefferson Airplane Loves You* 𝄞𝄞𝄞 (RCA Victor, 1992, prod. various) contains some spectacular previously unreleased 1967 live recordings, a few rewarding outtakes, and early efforts and seemingly hours and hours of less interesting material from the band's later stages. *Early Flight* 𝄞𝄞𝄞 (RCA Victor, 1974, prod. Jefferson Airplane) contains a selection of rather more intriguing outtakes and singles not released on other albums.

what to avoid: By the time the Airplane had recorded its final two albums, *Bark* 𝄞 (Grunt, 1971) and *Long John Silver* **woof!** (Grunt, 1972), the group had dissolved into a fractious battlefield that even founder Balin could no longer endure. *Thirty Seconds over Winterland* **woof!** (RCA Victor, 1973) captures the group in its final moments on one of the worst live albums ever released by a major act.

the rest:
After Bathing at Baxter's 𝄞𝄞 (RCA Victor, 1967/1996)
Crown of Creation 𝄞𝄞𝄞 (RCA Victor, 1986)
Volunteers 𝄞𝄞𝄞 (RCA Victor, 1969)
The Worst of the Jefferson Airplane 𝄞𝄞𝄞 (RCA Victor, 1970)
2400 Fulton Street 𝄞𝄞𝄞 (RCA, 1987)
White Rabbit and Other Hits 𝄞 (RCA Victor 1990)
Live at the Fillmore East 𝄞𝄞𝄞 (RCA Victor, 1998)

worth searching for: The oddball David Crosby solo album, *If I Could Only Remember My Name* (Atlantic, 1971, prod. David Crosby), is an eccentric collaboration between the Airplane, the Grateful Dead, and Santana, with cameos by Neil Young, Graham Nash, and Joni Mitchell.

solo outings:
Paul Kantner:
Blows against the Empire 𝄞𝄞 (RCA Victor, 1970)

Paul Kantner and Grace Slick:
Sunfighter **woof!** (Grunt, 1971)
(With David Freiberg) *Baron Von Tollbooth and the Chrome Nun* **woof!** (Grunt, 1973)

Grace Slick:
Manhole 𝄞 (Grunt, 1974)
Dreams 𝄞 (RCA, 1980)
Welcome to the Wrecking Ball **woof!** (RCA, 1981)
Software 𝄞𝄞 (RCA, 1984)

Marty Balin:
Bodacious DF 𝄞𝄞 (RCA, 1973)
Rock Justice 𝄞𝄞 (EMI, 1980)
Balin 𝄞𝄞𝄞 (EMI, 1981)
Lucky 𝄞 (EMI, 1983)
Balince: A Collection 𝄞𝄞𝄞 (Rhino, 1990)
Better Generation 𝄞𝄞 (GWE, 1991)

KBC Band (Kantner, Balin, Casady) :
KBC Band 𝄞 (Arista, 1986)

influences:
◀◀ The Weavers, Otis Redding, Eric Dolphy, Bob Dylan

▶▶ Jefferson Starship

see also: *Hot Tuna, Jefferson Starship*

Joel Selvin

Jefferson Starship /Starship

Formed 1974, in San Francisco, CA.

Paul Kantner, guitar, vocals (1974–84, 1992–present); Grace Slick, vocals, keyboards (1974–78, 1982–88); Marty Balin, vocals (1975–78, 1994–present), David Freiberg, bass, vocals (1974–84); Craig Chaquico, guitar; John Barbata, drums (1974–78); Papa John Creach (1974–75, 1992–94); Pete Sears, bass, keyboards (1974–86); Aynsley Dunbar (died 1998), drums (1978–83); Mickey Thomas, vocals (1978–90); Donny Baldwin, drums (1983–89); Brett Bloomfield, bass (1990–91); Mark Morgan, keyboards (1990–91); Jack Casady, bass (1992–present); Tim Gorman, keyboards (1992–present); Prairie Prince, drums (1992–present); Darby Gould, vocals (1992–present).

Nobody could have guessed that a wild, untamed band of resolute crazies like the Jefferson Airplane would have degenerated into an MTV coiffure band, churning out useless pre-fab radio fodder like "Find Your Way Back," "Jane," or "We Built This City." Outside of vocalist Marty Balin's three-album stint with this hapless hulk, which included his fairly sublime "Miracles," the Starship left little worth remembering, although the long run on the radio left the once-glowing reputation of the mothership tarnished by association.

what to buy: If you must, *Gold* ♫♫♫ (RCA Victor, 1979/1991 prod. Jefferson Starship, Larry Cox) covers the early part of the Starship era, before the band succumbed to Hollywood session players and hot-rod producers such as Ron Nevison or Narada Michael Walden. That latter period is duly chronicled on *Greatest Hits (Ten Years and Change 1979–1991)* ♫♫ (RCA Victor, 1991, prod. various), for what it's worth. However, *Red Octopus* ♫♫♫ (Grunt, 1977/RCA, 1997, prod. Jefferson Starship, Larry Cox), easily the band's single most cogent album, has been reissued in a gold CD edition.

what to buy next: *Deep Space/Virgin Sky* ♫♫ (Intersound, 1995, prod. Jefferson Starship) is a latter-era, Kantner-led collection that includes Balin and Casady, with a cameo by Grace Slick.

what to avoid: The list here is all-encompassing.

the rest:
Dragon Fly ♫♫♫ (Grunt, 1974/RCA, 1997)
Spitfire ♫♫ (Grunt, 1975/RCA, 1997)
Earth ♫♫ (Grunt, 1978/RCA, 1997)
Freedom at Point Zero ♫♫ (Grunt, 1979/RCA, 1997)
Knee-Deep in the Hoopla ♫♫ (Grunt/RCA, 1985)

worth searching for: Slick's penchant for acerbic wisecracks is well documented on a 1982 radio promotion album that accompanied the album *Winds of Change* (Grunt, 1982).

solo outings:
Paul Kantner:
Planet Earth Rock and Roll Orchestra (RCA Victor, 1983) ♫♫♫

Mickey Thomas:
As Long As You Love Me ♫ (MCA, 1971)
Alive Alone ♫ (Elektra, 1981)

Craig Chaquico:
Acoustic Highway ♫♫ (Higher Octave, 1993)
Acoustic Planet ♫♫ (Higher Octave, 1994)
A Thousand Pictures ♫ (Higher Octave, 1996)
Once in a Blue Universe ♫♫ (Higher Octave, 1997)

influences:
◄◄ Jefferson Airplane

►► Jefferson Starship: The Next Generation

see also: *Jefferson Airplane*

Joel Selvin

Garland Jeffreys
Born mid-1940s, in Brooklyn, NY.

Though critically acclaimed, singer-songwriter Garland Jeffreys never seemed to catch on with the masses except for the single "Wild in the Streets" in 1977. By and large, Jeffreys's low-key rock and thematic tour of life's downside didn't work in the disco and funk-crazed '70s. He first appeared on the New York music scene during the mid-'60s, where he palled around with Lou Reed and the Animals' Eric Burdon. He later assembled the band Grinder's Switch, which recorded a self-titled LP in 1969. Jeffreys went solo in 1970 and recorded several albums through the early '80s, picking up a reggae influence along the way.

what's available: Most of his albums are obscure or out of print, though the few songs that got notice are on *Matador and More* ♫♫♫ (A&M, 1992, prod. David Spinozza). The single "Matador," with its gospel reggae feel, was a hit across Europe. *Escape Artist* ♫♫♫ (Epic, 1981, prod. Garland Jeffreys, Bob Clearmountain) rides on several tales of twisted love and includes one of Jeffreys's rare cover efforts, "96 Tears." Recently reissued under Jeffreys's name, his early band's album *Grinder's Switch* ♫♫ (Vanguard, 1970, prod. Lewis Merenstein) includes well-written songs such as "The Father, the Son and the Holy Ghost" and "Dear Jolly Jack."

influences:
◄◄ Richie Havens, Marvin Gaye, Bob Dylan, Sly & the Family Stone, Bob Marley, Lou Reed

►► Tracy Chapman

Lawrence Gabriel

Jellyfish
Formed 1989, in San Francisco, CA. Disbanded 1994.

Andy Sturmer, vocals, drums, guitars, keyboards; Roger Manning, vocals, keyboards; Jason Falkner, guitar, bass (1989–91); Chris Manning, bass (1989–91); Tim Smith, bass (1991–94); Jon Brion, guitar (1991–94).

Put some Badfinger, Supertramp, Queen, Cheap Trick, and, of course, Beatles into a blender and you get a tasty little pop treat called Jellyfish. The band emerged with a trippy '70s logo, retro clothing, and a hit video for its first single, "The King Is Half Undressed." But make no mistake: Jellyfish was more than cute visuals and a nod and a wink to some rock icons. Sadly, the band dissolved after touring in support of its sophomore release. In Jellyfish's wake, Roger Manning formed the band Imperial Drag, Jon Brion and Jason Falkner released an album as the Grays, and Andy Sturmer is planning a solo career.

what to buy: The first release, *Bellybutton* 🎜🎜🎜🎜 (Charisma, 1990, prod. Albhy Galuten, Jack Joseph Puig), is loaded with strong songs that make reference to the past but also sound wholly fresh and original.

what to buy next: *Spilt Milk* 🎜🎜🎜 (Charisma, 1993, prod. Jack Joseph Puig) comes across slightly forced, bombastic, and brittle, with far more obvious references to forebears, particularly Supertramp and Queen.

worth searching for: *Jellyfish Comes Alive* (Charisma, 1981, prod. Shalom Aberle) is a spectacular five-song, live promotional piece featuring two originals plus covers of Badfinger's "No Matter What" and Wings' "Let 'em In" and "Jet."

influences:

◀◀ The Beatles, the Raspberries, Badfinger, Elton John, Supertramp, Queen

▶▶ Hanson, Ben Folds Five

Michael Isabella

The Jesus & Mary Chain

Formed 1984, in East Kilbride, Scotland.

William Reid, guitar, vocals; Jim Reid, guitar, vocals; Douglas Hart, bass (1984–89); Ben Lurie, bass, guitar (1994–present); Murray Dalglish, drums (1984); Bobby Gillespie, drums (1984–85); John Moore, drums (1985–89); Richard Thomas, drums (1989–95); Steve Monti, drums (1995).

Years before grunge, the Jesus & Mary Chain got maximum mileage out of fuzzy, distorted guitars. They certainly weren't the first to explore guitar feedback and white noise: rock ensembles from the Jimi Hendrix Experience to Sonic Youth had perfected that. But the beauty behind the J&M Chain is its ability to balance the racket and morose lyrics against some of the prettiest melodies this side of the Beach Boys. The band—led by the Reid Brothers—nailed its approach from the get-go, though it didn't evolve much after that. But armed with such beautiful noise, they really didn't need to.

what to buy: The J&M Chain found the perfect link on its very first album, *Psychocandy* 🎜🎜🎜🎜 (Reprise, 1985, prod. Jesus & Mary Chain), a masterful amalgam of pop, punk, and sheer white noise, including the hypnotic hit "Just like Honey."

what to buy next: *Darklands* 🎜🎜🎜🎜 (Warner Bros., 1987, prod. William Reid, Bill Price) was less of a downer than the band's debut, but almost as memorable thanks to gems such as "April Skies." *Stoned and Dethroned* 🎜🎜🎜 (American, 1994, prod. Jim Reid, William Reid) is the group's folkiest effort to date and includes "Sometimes Always," its semi-hit duet with Hope Sandoval of Mazzy Star.

what to avoid: *Automatic* 🎜🎜 (Warner Bros., 1989, prod. Jim Reid, William Reid) has some good songs but is marred by stiff arrangements that find the Reid brothers accompanied mostly by dry, electronic drum patterns.

the rest:
Barbed Wire Kisses 🎜🎜🎜 (Warner Bros., 1988)
Honey's Dead 🎜🎜🎜 (Def American, 1992)
Hate Rock 'n' Roll 🎜🎜🎜 (American, 1995)
Munki 🎜🎜🎜 (Sub Pop, 1998)

worth searching for: The group switched labels with *10 Smash Hits/1985–1992* (Def American, 1992, prod. various), an enjoyable promotion-only retrospective.

influences:

◀◀ Velvet Underground, Jimi Hendrix, the Beach Boys, Phil Spector

▶▶ My Bloody Valentine, Ride, Teenage Fanclub

Thor Christensen

Jesus Jones

Formed 1988, in London, England.

Mike Edwards, vocals, guitars; Jerry De Borg, guitars; Barry D (born Iain Baker), keyboards; Al Jaworski, bass; Gen (born Simon Matthews), drums.

Like fellow Brits EMF, Jesus Jones exposed strongly melodic, hook-filled electronic dance music to a commercial audience. Also like EMF, Jesus Jones was somewhat ahead of its time; it connected with one smash hit, "Right Here, Right Now" in 1991, then faded away as its follow-up album bombed. The group has kept a low profile since—though a new album is said to be in the works.

what to buy: Its sophomore album, *Doubt* 🎜🎜🎜🎜 (SBK, 1991, prod. Mike Edwards), is the most successful—commercially and artistically—with the spritely hits "Right Here, Right Now," a celebration of the end of the Cold War that was briefly Bill Clinton's 1992 campaign theme before he switched to Fleetwood Mac's "Don't Stop." "International Bright Young Thing" and "Real, Real, Real" kept the group on the charts.

the rest:
Liquidizer 🎜🎜🎜 (SBK, 1989)
Perverse 🎜🎜 (SBK, 1993)

influences:

◀◀ Duran Duran, Roxy Music, Depeche Mode

▶▶ EMF, Garbage, Charm Farm

Christina Fuoco

The Jesus Lizard

Formed 1989, in Chicago, IL.

Duane Denison, guitar; Mac McNeilly, drums (1990–96); David Wm. Sims, bass; David Yow, vocals; Jim Kimball, drums (1996–present).

The Jesus Lizard blends the talents of three of the most accomplished instrumentalists in indie rock (whether with original drummer Mac McNeilly or his replacement, Jim Kimball) with the maniacal vocal spew of David Yow, the clown prince of '90s concert showmen. The group is a legendary live act, but its merger of animal fury and angular intellect translates less persuasively on record, primarily because of Yow's unconventional non-singing style and his frequently dour, if not disgusting, subject matter. For those with a taste for uncompromising hard rock, the quartet's albums for Touch & Go, all recorded with Chicago noise-guitar architect Steve Albini, are about as nasty as it gets.

what to buy: *Liar* ♫♫♫♫ (Touch & Go, 1992, prod. Steve Albini) is where the band's songwriting catches up with the hide-and-shriek riffing of David Wm. Sims and Daune Denison. *Blue* ♫♫♫♫ (Capitol, 1998, prod. Andy Gill) captures the group's extraordinarily refined interplay with unsurpassed clarity, throws in some rhythm loops, and beefs up the melodic hooks without stinting on the power—a great place for Jesus Lizard beginners to dive in.

what to buy next: *Down* ♫♫♫♫ (Touch & Go, 1994, prod. Steve Albini) shows the band's instrumentalists flexing their chops without resorting to bombast, and introduces subtle keyboards.

what to avoid: The EP *Pure* ♫♫ (Touch & Go, 1989, prod. Steve Albini) was recorded before the addition of McNeilly, and the group misses his unerring sense of swing.

the rest:
Head ♫♫♪ (Touch & Go, 1990)
Goat ♫♫♫ (Touch & Go, 1991)
Lash ♫♫♫ (Touch & Go, 1993)
Show ♫♫♫ (Collison Arts, 1994)
Shot ♫♫♫♪ (Capitol, 1996)
Jesus Lizard ♫♫♫ (Jetset, 1998)

worth searching for: Scour stores for the group's limited-edition 1993 split single with Nirvana on the Touch & Go label. The Jesus Lizard track, the catchy-in-spite-of-itself "Puss," is from *Liar*, while the Nirvana cut, "Oh, the Guilt," is a previously unreleased heavy metal screed recorded in a Seattle laundry room with producer Barrett Jones.

influences:
◀◀ Birthday Party, Led Zeppelin, Scratch Acid

Greg Kot

Jethro Tull
/Ian Anderson

Formed 1967, in Blackpool, England.

Ian Anderson (born August 10, 1947 in Edinburgh, Scotland), vocals, flute, guitar, keyboards; Mick Abrahams, guitar (1967–68); Martin Barre, guitar (1968–present); Clive Bunker, drums (1967–71); Glen Cornick, bass (1967–71); Barriemore Barlow, drums (1971–76); John Evan, keyboards (1969–79); Jeffrey Hammond-Hammond, bass (1971–76); David Palmer, keyboards (1977–80); John Glascock (died 1979), bass (1976–78); Eddie Jobson, keyboards, violin (1980–81); Dave Pegg, bass (1979–91); Mark Craney, drums (1980–81); Peter-John Vettese, keyboards (1982–87, 1988–91); Jerry Conway, drums (1981–84); Doane Perry (1987–91), drums; Martin Allcock, keyboards (1988–91); Matt Pegg, bass (1991–present); Dave Mattacks, drums (1991–present).

Jethro Tull began as a psychedelic-blues quartet during the late '60s and gained some attention thanks to singer-flautist Ian Anderson's stage antics. Anderson's breathy histrionics on the flute owed much to jazz legend Rahsaan Roland Kirk, and on the band's debut he and original guitarist Mick Abrahams mined a heavily jazz-and-blues-inflected brand of rock. After Abrahams moved on to greater obscurity with Blodwyn Pig, Anderson began taking the band in a new direction, aided by the heavier guitar stylings of Martin Barre. Soon Tull was melding riff-rock, English folk, and the new "progressive" style that hit pay dirt during the early '70s. Its first three albums sold increasingly well, but the fourth, *Aqualung*, made Jethro Tull a superstar attraction. Somewhat perversely, the band followed this with back-to-back album-length songs, but eventually headed back toward AOR material during the mid-'70s, achieving radio hits with "Bungle in the Jungle" and "Too Old to Rock 'n' Roll, Too Young to Die." The late '70s saw them pursuing the Elizabethan strain they'd hinted at earlier, after which time they tried on such diverse styles as space-age prog, mellow folk-rock, and re-tooled metal. A moment of triumph turned into an awkward situation when, in 1988, Tull won a Grammy for Best Hard Rock/Heavy Metal Performance—much to the chagrin of fans of AC/DC and Metallica, groups who were also nominated. Tull remains a major international concert draw, thanks to a well-honed combination of instrumental flash, theatricality, and a willingness to play the old hits without complaint. The "Stonehenge" debacle in the rock film parody *This Is Spinal Tap* seems like a direct spoof of Tull's most grandiose moments. Anderson's solo excursions, *Walk into Light* and *Divinities*, have permitted him to explore his less bombastic side as a songwriter and his more pretentious side as a composer, respectively.

what to buy: *Aqualung* ♫♫♫♫ (Chrysalis, 1971, prod. Terry Ellis, Ian Anderson) remains Tull's crowning achievement, filled with passionate rock and quirky, melodic folk.

what to buy next: *Stand Up* 🎵🎵🎵🎵 (Chrysalis, 1968, prod. Terry Ellis, Ian Anderson) is less pompous—and less ambitious; it does, however, contain several potent rockers and the group's trademark rendition of J.S. Bach's "Bouree." *Living in the Past* 🎵🎵🎵🎵 (Chrysalis, 1972, prod. various) is a generous sampler of the band's early work and contains some bona fide gems. The album-length song *Thick as a Brick* 🎵🎵🎵🎵 (Chrysalis, 1972, prod. Terry Ellis, Ian Anderson) isn't for everyone, but remains one of the more inventive pop creations of the period. *Benefit* 🎵🎵🎵🎵 (Chrysalis, 1970, prod. Ian Anderson) is a leaner, more rock-oriented collection that boasts the hit "Teacher."

what to avoid: *The Broadsword and the Beast* **woof!** (Chrysalis, 1982, prod. Paul Samwell-Smith) shows the band sliding into self-parody. While most of their subsequent work has been mediocre, the campy medievalism and paunchy riffage on display here are woeful.

the rest:
This Was 🎵🎵🎵 (Chrysalis, 1968)
A Passion Play 🎵🎵🎵 (Chrysalis, 1973)
WarChild 🎵🎵🎵 (Chrysalis, 1974)
Minstrel in the Gallery 🎵🎵🎵 (Chrysalis, 1975)
Too Old to Rock 'n' Roll, Too Young to Die 🎵🎵🎵 (Chrysalis, 1976)
M.U.: The Best of Jethro Tull 🎵🎵🎵 (Chrysalis, 1976)
Repeat: The Best of Jethro Tull, Vol. 2 🎵🎵🎵 (Chrysalis, 1977)
Songs from the Wood 🎵🎵🎵 (Chrysalis, 1977)
Heavy Horses 🎵🎵🎵 (Chrysalis, 1978)
Bursting Out 🎵🎵🎵 (Chrysalis, 1978)
Stormwatch 🎵🎵🎵 (Chrysalis, 1979)
A 🎵🎵 (Chrysalis, 1980)
Under Wraps 🎵🎵 (Chrysalis, 1984)
Original Masters 🎵🎵🎵 (Chrysalis, 1985)
A Classic Case 🎵🎵🎵 (RCA, 1985)
Crest of a Knave 🎵🎵 (Chrysalis, 1987)
20 Years of Jethro Tull 🎵🎵🎵 (Chrysalis, 1988)
Rock Island 🎵🎵 (Chrysalis, 1989)
Catfish Rising 🎵🎵 (Chrysalis, 1991)
A Little Light Music 🎵🎵 (Chrysalis, 1992)
25th Anniversary Box Set 🎵🎵🎵 (Chrysalis, 1993)
Best of Jethro Tull: The Anniversary Collection 🎵🎵🎵 (Chrysalis, 1993)
Roots to Branches 🎵🎵🎵 (EMI, 1995)

worth searching for: *Another Christmas Song* (Chrysalis, 1989, prod. Ian Anderson) is a promotional EP that features two versions of the single as well as homey, dressing room recordings of favorites such as "Mother Goose" and "Locomotive Breath."

solo outings:
Ian Anderson:
Walk into Light 🎵🎵 (Chrysalis, 1983)
Divinities: 12 Dances with God 🎵🎵 (EMI, 1995)

influences:

◀◀ The Beatles, Fairport Convention, J.S. Bach, Rahsaan Roland Kirk, Sonny Boy Williamson, the Move

▶▶ Blodwyn Pig, Heart, Spinal Tap

Simon Glickman

Joan Jett

Born September 22, 1960, in Philadelphia, PA.

Ever since her teenage apprenticeship in the all-girl rock band the Runaways, Joan Jett has provided a model for women in rock 'n' roll. Front and center, clad in leather and backed by the all-male Blackhearts, she thrashes away at her electric guitar, sweat and mascara streaming down her face like a river of redemption. Although she writes much of her material, Jett's strongest statements have been her cover songs: With the exception of Lesley Gore's feminist anthem "You Don't Own Me," Jett has doggedly tackled tunes associated strictly with male performers. Even the riot-grrrl acts that she inspired wouldn't have the nerve to cover the Rolling Stones' "Star Star," Jonathan Richman's "Roadrunner," Iggy Pop's "I Wanna Be Your Dog," and ZZ Top's "Tush," let alone pull them off. Although her last chart hit came in 1988 with the Bon Jovi–like "I Hate Myself for Loving You," Jett has survived passing trends. Her resilience was rewarded on 1994's *Pure and Simple*, which featured collaborations with members of Bikini Kill, Babes in Toyland, and L7—bands that are now barreling through the doors that Jett kicked open.

what to buy: Opening with the bouncy, Ramones-like blitzkrieg of the title track, *Bad Reputation* 🎵🎵🎵🎵 (Blackheart, 1980, prod. Kenny Laguna, Ritchie Cordell) found Jett shrugging off her "jailbait-rock" past and asserting her independence via such punk-pop anthems as "You Don't Know What You've Got" and torrid versions of Gary Glitter's "Do You Wanna Touch Me," "Shout," and "Wooly Bully." *I Love Rock 'n' Roll* 🎵🎵🎵🎵 (Blackheart, 1981, prod. Kenny Laguna, Ritchie Cordell) contains the chart-topping title track and "Crimson and Clover," but "Victim of Circumstance"—a fiery kiss-off to her critics—is the linchpin.

what to buy next: Despite a crunching cover of Sly Stone's "Everyday People," *Album* 🎵🎵🎵 (Blackheart, 1983, prod. Kenny Laguna, Ritchie Cordell) paled commercially compared to its predecessor. But rock 'n' roll has produced few commentaries on coattail-riding leeches as pointed as "Fake Friends" and few covers as brave as her take on the Stones' "Star Star."

what to avoid: The lukewarm *Notorious* 🎵🎵 (Epic, 1991, prod. Kenny Laguna, Phil Ramone) pairs Jett with songwriting ringers Desmond Child and Diane Warren. Only "Backlash," a collaboration with Paul Westerberg, raises any semblence of a ruckus.

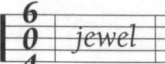
the rest:

Glorious Results of a Misspent Youth 🎸🎸 (Blackheart, 1984)
Good Music 🎸🎸🎸 (Epic, 1986)
Up Your Alley 🎸🎸🎸 (Epic, 1988)
The Hit List 🎸🎸🎸 (Epic, 1990)
Pure and Simple 🎸🎸🎸 (Warner Bros., 1994)
(With members of the Gits) *Evil Stig* 🎸🎸🎸 (Warner Bros., 1995)
Fit to Be Tied: Great Hits 🎸🎸🎸 (Blackheart/Mercury, 1997)

worth searching for: A 22-track collection of B-sides, bonus tracks, and other rarities, *Flashback* (Blackheart, 1994, prod. Kenny Laguna, Ritchie Cordell) rescues such Jett staples as her version of Bruce Springsteen's "Light of Day," the 1910 Fruitgum Co.'s "Indian Giver," David Bowie's "Rebel Rebel," and a 1979 pre-Blackhearts recording of "I Love Rock 'n' Roll" featuring Steve Jones and Paul Cook of the Sex Pistols.

influences:

◀◀ David Bowie, the Rolling Stones, Gary Glitter, Tommy James & the Shondells

▶▶ L7, Babes in Toyland, Bikini Kill

see also: *The Runaways*

David Okamoto

Jewel

Born Jewel Kilcher, May 23, 1974, in Homer, AK.

When it was released in 1994, Jewel's *Pieces of You* introduced a sunny, sensitive folkie with a surfer-chick attitude and a poet's soul. But she immediately started bucking against the singer-songwriter pigeonhole: Compared to the introspective sound of the album, Jewel's live shows were funny, funky, and loose, liberally dosed with cheerful monologues, yodeling exercises, and such sexually charged, unreleased rockers as "Race Car Driver" and the punk-pop "God's Gift to Women." Relentless touring as opening act for everyone from Peter Murphy to Bob Dylan and a provocative video for "Who Will Save Your Soul" helped goose her debut to platinum status during 1996. But by the time she was plastered on the cover of *Time* magazine in 1997 for her role in the Lilith Fair tour, *Pieces of You* had sold an astounding seven million copies. That feat was not a testament to her still-raw talent, but rather to the music industry's desperate need for a mega-platinum superstar in an era of sagging sales: Instead of letting Jewel naturally develop as an artist with successive albums, her record company chose to follow the Hootie Principle and flog *Pieces of You* from a merely promising debut into a "career" record. As result, Jewel was catapulted to an artificially induced level of significance that has prompted a siege of lucrative offers ranging from movie roles to poetry books to a National Anthem spot at the 1998 Super Bowl. If you've seen her live lately, you know songs destined for her long-delayed follow-up—"Under the

Water," "Just Passing Time," "Nikos," and the Dylanesque "Sometimes It Be That Way"—eclipse almost everything on *Pieces of You*, most of which she wrote when she was 19. Let's just hope the industry allows her to mature before she turns 30.

what to buy: Produced by Neil Young collaborator Ben Keith and recorded partly live and acoustic at a San Diego coffee-house, *Pieces of You* 🎸🎸🎸 (Atlantic, 1994, prod. Ben Keith) features "Who Will Save Your Soul" and the original, somewhat anemic versions of "You Were Meant for Me" and "Foolish Games" (both remixed significantly for radio by producer Peter Collins). Her lyrics are sometimes overly earnest, if not clumsy, but her voice—particularly on the majestic "Angel Standing By"—is stunning.

the rest:

Spirit N/A (Atlantic, 1998)

worth searching for: A 1994 Atlantic promo-only EP titled *Save the Linoleum* was designed to push "Who Will Save Your Soul" and "I'm Sensitive," but its non-LP B-sides "God's Gift to Women" and "Race Car Driver" made it an instant collector's item among Jewel fanatics. For those two songs alone, it's worth whatever you have to pay for it.

influences:

◀◀ Tracy Chapman, Sheryl Crow

▶▶ Kacy Crowley, Meredith Brooks, Alana Davis

David Okamoto

Billy Joel

Born May 9, 1949, in the Bronx, NY.

Billy Joel has described himself as "a melody freak," and it's that love of a hummable tune that has made him one of pop music's most enduring, and endearing, stars. From his early days playing in Long Island rock bands to his stretch as a story-telling piano man, to a logical merger of both roles, Joel has consistently penned memorable melodies. He studied classical piano before rocking through the '60s with the Hassles and Attila, then worked briefly as a solo pianist in California, which inspired his first hit, the 1973 ballad "Piano Man." Joel enjoyed moderate success with his next several albums, but when he teamed up with noted producer Phil Ramone, the result was his 1977 pop-rock masterpiece *The Stranger*, Joel's breakthrough album, highlighted by two exquisite odes to the fairer sex— "She's Always a Woman" and "Just the Way You Are." Joel's artistic growth continued as he stretched his lyrical sights to include topical issues ranging from unemployment to the plight of Vietnam veterans. Behind the scenes, Joel has filed several multi-million-dollar lawsuits against his former management over songwriting revenue and other income he was cheated

Jewel (© Ken Settle)

out of, and he has been through two failed marriages, including one to model Christie Brinkley. But whenever he has been knocked down, personally or professionally, the feisty former amateur boxer always manages to bounce back; his 1993 album, *River of Dreams*, was the first of his career to debut at #1 on the *Billboard* chart. In the late 1990s he split his time touring with Elton John and declaring himself through with pop music, planning to write and record only instrumental pieces—a position he's since backed away from.

what to buy: With such a long record of chart success, the two-disc *Greatest Hits, Volumes I & II* ✦✦✦✦ (Columbia, 1985, prod. Phil Ramone) covers the highlights from 1973 to 1985 in fine fashion, with 25 of Joel's most memorable songs. The four-disc box set *The Complete Hits Collection, 1973–1997* ✦✦✦✦ (Columbia, 1997, prod. various) includes 37 songs from Joel's first three greatest-hits packages plus one disc of live performances and his spoken-word lectures on songwriting. This covers the highlights at a moderate price. *River of Dreams* ✦✦✦✦ (Columbia, 1993, prod. Dan Kortchmar) matches soul-baring lyrics to masterful melodies ranging from minor-key blues of "Shades of Grey" to the exotic rhythms of the title track to Beatlesque rock and metaphorical angst of "Great Wall of China." There's more to *The Stranger* ✦✦✦✦ (Columbia, 1977, prod. Phil Ramone) than its four hit singles (the suite "Scenes from an Italian Restaurant," for one), making it a Joel classic.

what to buy next: *The Nylon Curtain* ✦✦✦✦ (Columbia, 1982, prod. Phil Ramone) is one of Joel's most ambitious and satisfying efforts, combining lyrical depth with radio-friendly tunes such as "Allentown" and "Goodnight Saigon." The rhythmic snare of "We Didn't Start the Fire" and the confessional bravado of "Shameless," covered later by Garth Brooks, highlight *Storm Front* ✦✦✦✦ (Columbia, 1989, prod. Billy Joel, Mick Jones). *An Innocent Man* ✦✦✦✦ (Columbia, 1983, prod. Phil Ramone) captures Joel reveling in the start of his relationship with Brinkley, singing feel-good anthems such as "Tell Her about It" and "Uptown Girl."

what to avoid: Joel sounds pretty green on his first album *Cold Spring Harbor* **woof!** (Columbia, 1972, prod. Artie Ripp), which also suffers from recording problems (his voice was mistakenly sped up). *Kohuept (In Concert)* ✦ (Columbia, 1987, prod. Jim Boyer, Brian Ruggles) was recorded live during a tour of the former Soviet Union and released against Joel's objections. They should have listened to him.

the rest:
Piano Man ✦✦✦ (Columbia, 1973)
Streetlife Serenade ✦✦ (Columbia, 1974)
Turnstiles ✦✦✦ (Columbia, 1976)
52nd Street ✦✦✦ (Columbia, 1978)
Glass Houses ✦✦✦ (Columbia, 1980)

Songs in the Attic ✦✦ (Columbia, 1981)
The Bridge ✦✦ (Columbia, 1986)

worth searching for: *Live at the Bottom Line* (Mistral, 1993) is one of many bootlegs of Joel's live radio show on June 10, 1976—a show that was nearly as crucial to his career as Bruce Springsteen's radio broadcast from the same venue was a year earlier.

influences:

◀◀ The Beatles, the Rolling Stones, Ray Charles, Bob Dylan, the Four Seasons, Dion & the Belmonts, George & Ira Gershwin, Elton John

▶▶ Amy Grant, Garth Brooks, Barry Manilow, Richard Marx, Marc Cohn, Ben Folds Five

David Yonke

David Johansen /Buster Poindexter

Born January 9, 1950, in Staten Island, NY.

Known to most listeners as martini-swigging, hip-swiveling loungemeister Buster Poindexter, David Johansen began his career as the flamboyant, Mick Jagger-influenced frontman for the New York Dolls. Late guitarist Johnny Thunders is frequently heralded as the heroin-addicted hero of the short-lived glam-rock band, but Johansen was clearly its hungry heart. Never shy about his commercial aspirations, his subsequent solo career spawned one bona fide rock 'n' roll classic—his staggering 1978 self-titled debut—before he began flirting with disco and reggae on *In Style* and album-rock credibility on *Here Comes the Night*. He toured as Pat Benatar's opening act and became an early fixture on MTV with a cheesy "performance" video of his popular Animals medley before trading Lou Reed for Louis Prima and reinventing himself as Poindexter, the pompadour-wearing pride of Bogalusa, Louisiana, who accomplished with "Hot Hot Hot" what Johansen could never do: a Top 40 hit hit hit. The last laugh may be his, but the loss is ours.

what to buy: *David Johansen* ✦✦✦✦ (Sony/Razor & Tie, 1978, prod. Richard Robinson, David Johansen) combines frantic Dolls leftovers such as "Girls" and "Funky but Chic" with surprisingly soulful ballads and a five-minute tour de force called "Frenchette." The Razor & Tie reissue adds the B-side "The Rope" as a bonus track. Recorded at New York's Bottom Line, *The David Johansen Group Live* ✦✦✦✦ (Epic/Legacy, 1978, prod. David Johansen) was originally released as a radio promo, but its legendary status among fans prompted Epic to reissue it on CD in 1993 with nine bonus tracks. Scorching covers of the Foundations' "Build Me up Buttercup," Wilson Pickett's "I Found a Love," and Bonnie Tyler's "It's a Heartache" combine with a fistful of Dolls favorites to make this one of the fiercest live documents since Warren Zevon's *Stand in the Fire*.

what to buy next: If you must sample Johansen's Poindexter repertoire, stick with the self-titled 1987 debut *Buster Poindexter* 𝄢𝄢𝄢 (RCA, 1987, prod. Hank Medress), which mines such cool R&B obscurities as the Jive Bombers' "Bad Boy," Freddie Scott's "Are You Lonely for Me Baby," and Wynonie Harris's "Good Morning Judge."

what to avoid: *Sweet Revenge* **woof!** (Passport, 1984, prod. Joe Delia, David Johansen) is a last-ditch stab at synth-pop that went directly to cutout bins.

the rest:
David Johansen:
In Style 𝄢𝄢𝄢 (Sony/Razor & Tie, 1979)
Here Comes the Night 𝄢𝄢𝄢 (Sony/Razor & Tie, 1981)
Live It Up 𝄢𝄢𝄢 (Sony/Razor & Tie, 1982)
From Pumps to Pompadours: The David Johansen Story 𝄢𝄢𝄢 (Rhino, 1995)

Buster Poindexter:
Buster Goes Berserk **woof!** (RCA, 1989)
Buster's Happy Hour 𝄢𝄢𝄢 (Forward/Rhino, 1994)
Buster's Spanish Rocket Ship 𝄢𝄢 (PolyGram, 1997)

worth searching for: The 45 rpm release of "Funky but Chic" (Blue Sky, 1978, prod. Richard Robinson, David Johansen) adds female backing vocals to give the song a sassy Stones-like feel.

influences:
◀◀ The Four Tops, the Rolling Stones, Velvet Underground, Louis Prima

▶▶ The modern lounge movement

see also: *The New York Dolls*

David Okamoto

Elton John
Born Reginald Kenneth Dwight, March 25, 1947, in Pinner (London), England.

After establishing himself as a gifted singer-songwriter and pianist during the early '70s, Elton John attained superstar status by the middle of that decade with a non-stop string of hits and top-selling albums. With his mature pop songcraft, campy glam sensibility, and funky virtuosity on the keyboard, John also served as an influence that can be heard all over the musical map, from hard rock rockers Guns N' Roses to underground-cum-mainstream pop groups like Ben Folds Five. During the '80s, John more or less left the rock elements of his early work to reposition himself as a staple of adult-contemporary formats, mostly through impeccably commercial though often

syrupy ballads. By the mid-'90s he was composing hits for family films (Disney's *The Lion King*) and winning Grammys and Oscars for it. In 1994 he was inducted into the Rock and Roll Hall of Fame. John began studying piano when he was four, and by 12 had won a scholarship to the Royal Academy of Music. During his teens he joined a variety of R&B-influenced groups before auditioning for the record label Liberty, where he was paired via mail with lyricist Bernie Taupin. The two only met after collaborating on 20 songs, but their partnership—despite an interruption during the mid-1970s—would span several decades. John's early work showed the influence of master tunesmiths such as George and Ira Gershwin and the Beatles, but it also echoed the sound of Leon Russell and other soul and pop artists. By 1973's *Goodbye Yellow Brick Road* he exhibited greater ambition, both thematically and musically, and metamorphosed from self-effacing piano man to protean stadium rocker, sporting outrageous costumes and glitzy spectacles—both on his face and on stage. His role as the Pinball Wizard in Ken Russell's 1975 film of the Who's rock opera *Tommy* was the apotheosis of this phase. Over the years, John has transformed himself, cleaning up his substance addictions and coming to terms with his homosexuality. He's no longer the phenomenon he was during the '70s, but he's still one of the world's biggest pop stars. When Princess Diana was killed in a Paris car crash in 1997, it was John's rewrite of "Candle in the Wind" that set the tone for the world's mourning. Taupin, meanwhile, has gone on to form the country-tinged group Farm Dogs. (Note: Most of the albums from the first six years of John's career have been reissued on Island/Rocket, many with bonus tracks.)

what to buy: The true marvel of *Goodbye Yellow Brick Road* 𝄢𝄢𝄢𝄢 (Uni, 1973/Island/Rocket, 1975, prod. Gus Dudgeon) is that despite a plethora of hits (the title track, "Saturday Night's Alright for Fighting," "Candle in the Wind"), it still functions as an ambitious and coherent double-length album. *Greatest Hits, Vol. 1* 𝄢𝄢𝄢𝄢 (Uni/MCA, 1974, prod. Gus Dudgeon) is an essential collection of his early hits, from "Daniel" and "Crocodile Rock" to "Your Song" and "Bennie and the Jets."

what to buy next: *Tumbleweed Connection* 𝄢𝄢𝄢 (Uni/MCA, 1971, prod. Gus Dudgeon) is a superb early collection on which John explores blues-rock, soul, and exquisite pop balladry. *Madman across the Water* 𝄢𝄢𝄢 (Uni, 1971/Island/Rocket, 1995, prod. Gus Dudgeon) and *Honky Chateau* 𝄢𝄢𝄢 (Uni, 1972/Island/Rocket, 1995, prod. Gus Dudgeon) are also ambitious, powerful sets, while *Greatest Hits, Vol. II* 𝄢𝄢𝄢 (MCA, 1977) affirms why John ruled the radio during the '70s. *11-17-70* 𝄢𝄢𝄢 (MCA, 1971/Island/Rocket, 1995, prod. Gus Dudgeon) is a scrappy live album that demonstrates his estimable piano

Elton John (© Ken Settle)

chops and a boasts superlative renditions of "Take Me to the Pilot" and "Burn down the Mission."

what to avoid: *The Complete Thom Bell Sessions* ⚡ (MCA, 1989, prod. Thom Bell) is an EP containing six songs from a wisely aborted experiment in R&B-pop with Philadelphia International producer Bell.

the rest:

Empty Sky 🎵🎵🎵 (DJM, 1969/MCA, 1975/Island/Rocket, 1995)
Elton John 🎵🎵🎵 (Uni, 1970)
Friends 🎵🎵 (Paramount, 1971)
Don't Shoot Me I'm Only the Piano Player 🎵🎵🎵 (Uni, 1973/Island/ Rocket, 1995)
Caribou 🎵🎵🎵 (Uni, 1974/Island/Rocket, 1995)
Captain Fantastic and the Brown Dirt Cowboy 🎵🎵🎵 (Uni, 1975 Island/ Rocket, 1995)
Rock of the Westies 🎵🎵 (Uni, 1975/Island/Rocket, 1995)
Blue Moves 🎵🎵 (Rocket/MCA, 1976)
Here & There 🎵🎵 (MCA, 1976)
A Single Man 🎵🎵 (MCA, 1978)
Victim of Love 🎵🎵 (MCA, 1979)
21 at 33 🎵🎵🎵 (MCA, 1980)
The Fox 🎵🎵 (Geffen, 1981)
Jump Up! 🎵🎵🎵 (Geffen, 1982)
Rare Masters 🎵🎵🎵🎵 (Polydor, 1982)
Too Low for Zero 🎵🎵🎵 (Geffen, 1983)
Breaking Hearts 🎵🎵🎵 (Geffen, 1984)
Ice on Fire 🎵🎵 (Geffen, 1985)
Leather Jackets 🎵🎵 (Geffen, 1986)
Greatest Hits, Vol. 3 🎵🎵🎵 (Geffen, 1986)
Live in Australia 🎵🎵 (MCA, 1987)
Reg Strikes Back 🎵🎵 (MCA, 1988)
Sleeping with the Past 🎵🎵 (MCA, 1989)
To Be Continued . . . 🎵🎵🎵 (MCA, 1990)
The One 🎵🎵 (MCA, 1992)
Greatest Hits 1975–86 🎵🎵🎵 (MCA, 1992)
Duets 🎵🎵 (MCA, 1993)
Made in England 🎵🎵🎵 (Rocket/Island, 1995)
The Lion King 🎵🎵🎵 (Disney, 1995)
Love Songs 🎵🎵🎵🎵 (Rocket, 1996)
The Big Picture 🎵🎵🎵 (Rocket, 1997)

worth searching for: *Reg Dwight's Piano Goes Pop* (RPM, 1994) is an oddball import title of pop and R&B covers John recorded for a budget label in England before starting his own career. In the wake of Princess Diana's death, John's tribute, *Candle in the Wind 1997* (Rocket, 1997) became the biggest- and fastest-selling single of all time.

influences:

◄◄ Fats Waller, Duke Ellington, the Beatles, Motown, Stax, the Rolling Stones, Lee Dorsey, Leon Russell

►► Phil Collins, Guns N' Roses, George Michael, Jellyfish, Suddenly Tammy!, Ben Folds Five

see also: *Farm Dogs*

Simon Glickman

John & Mary

See: 10,000 Maniacs

Evan Johns & His H-Bombs

Formed 1979, in Washington, DC.

Evan Johns, guitar, organ, vocals; Mark Korpi, guitar (1979–90); Ivan Brown, bass, vocals (1979–87); Jim Dougherty, drums, vocals (1979–86); Dan McCann, bass, vocals (1988–92); Jim Starboard, drums, vocals (1987–92); Steve Riggs, bass, vocals (1991–92).

As a teen guitar wildcat who sprouted under the wings of D.C. guitar legend Danny Gatton, Evan Johns went on to form the H-Bombs, a group that became known for its lo-fi rockabilly abandon. A move to Austin, Texas, brought with it a tour of duty with the LeRoi Brothers and a surprising, but deserved, Grammy nomination for his participation in the *Big Guitars from Texas* pickers summit. Johns then re-formed the H-Bombs, throwing down the gauntlet with *Rollin' through the Night* and continuing impressively with several more albums into the early '90s. Since then, outside of some work with Eugene Chadbourne, little has been heard from him, with health problems reportedly keeping him relatively localized In Texas.

what to buy: The group achieved its high-water mark early with the frenzied *Rollin' through the Night* 🎵🎵🎵🎵 (Alternative Tentacles, 1986, prod. Evan Johns), the current version of which contains three previously unreleased tracks.

what to buy next: Both *Bombs Away* 🎵🎵🎵 (Rykodisc, 1989, prod. Garry Tallent) and *Rockit Fuel Only* 🎵🎵🎵 (Rykodisc, 1991, prod. Evan Johns) are good frothy fun, full of honest and searing playing (though drummer Jim Starboard's one vocal turn on the latter shows just how flat and pedestrian this stuff would be without Johns's beery-preacher singing). *Please Mr. Santa Claus* 🎵🎵🎵 (Rykodisc, 1990, prod. Evan Johns, Jay Hudson) is one of an elite few holiday albums that sounds good any time of the year.

worth searching for: The group's debut 10-inch EP *Giddy up Girl* (self-released, 1980) should make for an interesting but worthwhile search for latter-day rockabilly fans.

influences:

◄◄ Danny Gatton, Jerry Lee Lewis, Charlie Feathers, NRBQ

►► Liquor Giants, Bottle Rockets

David Greenberger

Eric Johnson

Born August 17, 1954, in Austin, TX.

Like the Beatles, Jimi Hendrix's name is one of the most overused references in rock music. Many guitarists have been touted as "Hendrixian"; in reality, very few players have the talent and vision to merit the comparison. Eric Johnson, just like his Austin contemporary Stevie Ray Vaughan, is one of those players for whom the comparison is apt. What earns Johnson this distinction is not that he sounds or plays like Hendrix (although he can), but that he approaches the guitar with the same reverence, the same attention to detail and song structure. His playing crosses many styles, from country to blues to jazz to fiery rock, yet it always fits perfectly within his material. Like the great Danny Gatton, he seamlessly incorporates myriad references without descending to ostentation. In fact, Johnson's skills with melody and tone create guitar solos that are often more attractive for their melodic beauty and perfect context than for their breathtaking technical mastery. A notorious perfectionist, Johnson is known to work and re-work his albums until they meet his high standards. This time-consuming approach has yielded a remarkably small catalog for an artist who has been recording since the mid-'70s. It has also delivered some of the most stunning guitar playing of the last two decades.

what to buy: Johnson recorded *Ah Via Musicom* ♫♫♫ (Capitol, 1990, prod. Eric Johnson) three times before deeming it suitable for release. It's the best-realized example of the guitarist's musical vision, a recording that unites his virtuosic ability with tightly arranged compositions such as "Cliffs of Dover" and "Steve's Boogie." Smoothly shifting between a broad palette of guitar colors, Johnson creates a dynamic panorama of sound that conveys deep emotion and a unifying theme of music as a life force.

what to buy next: *Tones* ♫♫♫ (Capitol, 1986, prod. Eric Johnson) is the album that told the world what Austin had known for years: that Johnson is one masterful guitarist. Though less ambitious in scope than *Ah Via Musicom*, *Tones* displays Johnson's facility with Chet Atkins–like country picking, James Brown funk, and shimmering psychedelic rock.

what to avoid: Nearly six years in the making, Johnson's third album, *Venus Isle (a.k.a. Travel One Hope)* ♫♫ (Capitol, 1996, prod. Eric Johnson) is an unruly mess—dense, overarranged, and clearly hindered by his perfectionism.

worth searching for: Johnson's initial album, *Seven Worlds* is not available through a label, but the album has been bootlegged fairly extensively. Those interested in his early years may want to seek it out.

influences:

◀◀ Jimi Hendrix, Johnny Winter, Billy Gibbons (ZZ Top), the Yardbirds, Cream, Eric Clapton, Freddie King, Elmore James, Jeff Beck, Nokie Edwards, Merle Travis, Danny Gatton, Chet Atkins, the Beatles, the Rolling Stones, Dixie Dregs

▶▶ Vinnie Moore, Joe Satriani, Steve Vai, Ian Moore, Eric Gale, Steve Morse, Stevie Ray Vaughan, Shawn Lane

David Galens

Johnnie Johnson

Born July 8, 1924, in Fairmont, WV.

Turnabout, as they say, is fair play, and it is sweet irony to note that the career of rock 'n' roll piano legend Johnnie Johnson is flourishing these days, and he is receiving the recognition he so richly deserves, while his former employer, Chuck Berry, can't get arrested (figuratively speaking, that is). For if Berry is the father of rock 'n' roll, then Johnson should be accorded credit as its stepfather. Berry may have been the crucible in which the blues, rhythm & blues, and country gave birth to a new form further shaped by his wit and poetic sense, but it was Johnson who led his band and who contributed, uncredited, the music for some of the songs that are the very cornerstone of the genre. Gracious to a fault, Johnson is willing to let bygones be bygones and his music—more blues-oriented than his work with Berry—to speak for itself. In recent years Johnson has recorded with Eric Clapton, Buddy Guy and Bo Diddley, and Bob Weir. Now entering his mid-70s, Johnson is still going strong.

what to buy: *Johnnie B. Bad* ♫♫♫ (Elektra Nonesuch American Explorer Series, 1991, prod. Terry Adams, Keith Richards) is Johnson's best album overall, thanks in part to an all-star cast that includes Richards, Eric Clapton, and members of NRBQ. "Tanqueray" and "Stepped in What!?" are Johnson's first vocal performances ever, and while far from spectacular, capture perfectly his gentle, self-effacing personality.

what to buy next: *Johnnie Be Back* ♫♫♫ (Musicmasters, 1995, prod. Jimmy Vivino) is another all-star affair, with Phoebe Snow, Buddy Guy, Al Kooper, John Sebastian, and Max Weinberg all lending a hand. There's still plenty of room for Johnson to shine, though. *Rockin' 88's* ♫♫♫ (Modern Blues, 1991, prod. Daniel Jacoubovitch) teams Johnson with two other St. Louis piano greats, Clayton Love, who played with Ike Turner in the 1950s, and Jimmy Vaughn, who played with Albert King, Little Milton Campbell, and Ike Turner, among others. It's an interesting compendium of Midwestern post-war blues styles. Of special note is Johnson's smoking take on "Frances," an instrumental track named for his wife.

the rest:
Blue Hand Johnnie ♫♫♫ (Pulsar, 1988/Evidence, 1993)
(With the Kentucky Headhunters) *That'll Work* ♫♫♫ (Elektra Nonesuch, 1993)

Johnnie B. Live ⚡⚡▽ (self-released, 1997)

influences:

◄◄ Earl "Fatha" Hines, Count Basie, Bud Powell

►► Ian McLagen, Ian Stewart, Long John Baldry

Daniel Durchholz

Mike Johnson

Born Michael Allen Johnson, August 27, 1965.

Mike Johnson's slurred vocal style will elicit comparisons to his Dinosaur Jr. bandmate J Mascis, but his voice is lower and beefier, similar to Mark Eitzel's of American Music Club and exploring the same resigned emotional territory. Before Dinosaur Jr., Johnson was in the legendary Eugene, Oregon, punk band Snakepit with Billy Karin (Bikini Kill), Al Larsen (Some Velvet Sidewalk), Joe Preston (Earth, Melvins), and Robert Christie (Oswald Five-O). Johnson has also worked as co-producer of both solo albums by Screaming Trees singer Mark Lanegan.

what to buy: *Where Am I?* ⚡⚡⚡ (Up/Sub Pop, 1994, prod. Mike Johnson) teams Johnson with Screaming Trees drummer Barrett Martin (on bass, cello, and piano as well as percussion) for a rootsy, sometimes almost unplugged collection that covers Townes Van Zandt, Lee Hazelwood, and Gene Clark—although the song "Atrophy" is a blazing rocker.

what to buy next: Johnson and Martin (who adds vibes to his instrumental duties)—with Mascis on drums—expand their sonic range even further on *Year of Mondays* ⚡⚡⚡ (TAG/Atlantic, 1996, prod. John Agnello, Mike Johnson), with sharper sound.

influences:

◄◄ American Music Club

►► Mark Lanegan

see also: *Dinosaur Jr.*

Steve Holtje

Daniel Johnston

Born 1961, in Sacramento, CA.

Like Roky Erickson and Beach Boy Brian Wilson, Daniel Johnston is a hugely talented rock 'n' roller whose troubled mind takes him farther beyond the cutting edge than most of us would like to go. He sings like a little kid—all wide-eyed, high-pitched, and awestruck—then contradicts the innocence with either weird and biting sarcasm or a determined, fragile intensity. His songs are usually skeleton arrangements, based on a standard blues-rock riff or a bouncy electronic keyboard, and he makes fun of television cartoons ("Casper"), the Beatles (a clunky-but-great piano version of "I Saw Her Standing There"), Elvis Presley (a version of "Heartbreak Hotel"), and Bruce Springsteen ("Funeral Home," a morbid rewrite of "Cadillac Ranch"). Johnston began his career recording lo-fi tapes on a home boombox and distributing them to friends. His work has been wildly uneven, but his moments of brilliance—when we're lucky, they encompass an entire album—vindicate his 16-year recording career. He also shares with Mick Jagger and Alex Chilton the ability to shout "yeah!" in that undefinable purely rocking way.

what to buy: *Yip/Jump Music* ⚡⚡⚡⚡ (Homestead, 1989, prod. Daniel Johnston) is a 1983 recording that contains "Speeding Motorcycle," which, like the best punk rock, creates the ultimate driving song and simultaneously undermines it. Though *Hi, How Are You* ⚡⚡⚡ (Homestead, 1988, prod. Daniel Johnston), another 1983 session, can be unsettling with its nervous spoken introductions, strange noises, and sloppy carnival keyboards, it is incredibly powerful when it hits on "Hey Joe" and the appropriately titled "Desperate Man Blues."

what to buy next: *Fun* ⚡⚡⚡ (Atlantic, 1994, prod. Paul Leary) is Johnston's major-label debut, and it is surreal to comprehend—the singer's simplistic pen-and-ink drawings are on the label next to Atlantic's logo and bar code. The best song is the throbbing rocker "Love Wheel." Recorded with the Austin band Texas Instruments, *Continued Story* ⚡⚡⚡ (Homestead, 1992, prod. Joe Johnson) is particularly paranoid—nobody else would ever record the Beatles' "I Saw Her Standing There" like this.

what to avoid: More than anything else, Johnston's music needs a good editor. His early tapes—*Live at SXSW* ⚡▽ (Stress, 1990, prod. Daniel Johnston) and both *The Lost Recordings, Vol. 1* and *The Lost Recordings, Vol. 2* ⚡▽ (Stress, 1983, prod. Daniel Johnston)—find the songwriter just noodling around, not saying much of anything.

the rest:

Songs of Pain ⚡⚡▽ (Stress, 1980)
More Songs of Pain ⚡⚡▽ (Stress, 1981)
The What of Whom ⚡⚡▽ (Stress, 1982)
Don't Be Scared ⚡⚡▽ (Stress, 1982)
Retired Boxer ⚡⚡▽ (Stress, 1984)
Respect ⚡⚡▽ (Stress, 1985)
Jad Fair and Daniel Johnston ⚡▽ (50 Skadillion Watts, 1989)
1990 ⚡▽ (Shimmydisc, 1990)
Artistic Vice ⚡▽ (Shimmydisc, 1991)

worth searching for: Though Yo La Tengo, Sonic Youth, Pearl Jam (on pirate radio), the Dead Milkmen, and many other good bands have taken a crack at Johnston's oeuvre, the only truly successful tribute came from ex-Glass Eye leader Kathy McCarty, whose *Dead Dog's Eyeball* (Bar/None, 1994, prod. Brian

Beattie, Kathy McCarty) draws out his songs' wonderful weirdness and raunchy rock.

influences:

◄◄ The Beatles, Roky Erickson & the 13th Floor Elevators, the Beach Boys, Bob Dylan, Neil Young, Jerry Lee Lewis

►► Kathy McCarty, Yo La Tengo, Nirvana, Sonic Youth, Pearl Jam, the Dead Milkmen

Steve Knopper

Freedy Johnston

Born March 7, 1961, in Kinsley, KS.

It's sad when a musician peaks too early, but it's easier to stomach when he leaves you with a pop-folk-rock masterpiece as perfect as Freedy Johnston's second album, *Can You Fly*. "Well I sold the dirt to feed the band," he sings on the album's first line, referring to his longtime family farm, which he ditched to become a New York City rock 'n' roll singer. Like the Beatles and Squeeze, Johnston has a knack for squeezing rich poetic images into cleverly rhyming three-minute pop songs; his imaginative world includes a love affair with the mortician's daughter and a town called Hopeless. Since then, though his high-pitched, impossibly clear voice remains a powerful pop tool, Johnston has slowly started trying too hard. After a mass of critical raves earned him enough clout to sign with the major label Elektra Records, Johnston's songs have subtly become more labored and less spontaneous. His Elektra debut, *This Perfect World*, had some excellent moments—including the sublime "Two Lovers Stop," a *Romeo and Juliet*–style fable about a couple jumping to their deaths—but producer Butch Vig imposed a more formulaic rock style on the music. Though Johnston remains an excellent singer and songwriter, recent material like "On the Way Out" is disappointingly competent.

what to buy: The slower songs on *Can You Fly* ♪♪♪♪ (Bar/None, 1992, prod. Graham Maby) tell terrific folk tales, but the rockers, including the opening "Trying to Tell You I Don't Know" and "In the New Sunshine," are what provoke the involuntary dancing around the room. Johnston's lines are consistently sharp and rich; in "The Mortician's Daughter," he observes that "we drew our hearts on the dusty coffin lids" and in "Responsible," he describes the New York City streets as "slick with dew and motor oil." All this in a snappy voice that recalls Paul McCartney, or at least Michael Penn.

what to buy next: Continuing with the dramatic opening lines, the solid-but-disappointing *This Perfect World* ♪♪♪ (Elektra, 1994, prod. Butch Vig) begins with "I know I got a bad reputation, and it isn't just talk, talk, talk." It's gloomier than the opti-

mistic *Can You Fly*, but it's Vig's straightforward production that blunts Johnston's natural wonder and enthusiasm.

what to avoid: There are excellent moments on *Never Home* ♪♪♪ (Elektra, 1997, prod. Danny Kortchmar), mostly because Johnston's talent shines even when he's coasting or loading himself up with bland material. But the catchy "On the Way Out" and the well-written "He Wasn't Murdered" aren't enough to overcome a creeping mediocrity.

the rest:

The Trouble Tree ♪♪♪ (Bar/None, 1990)
Freedy Johnston EP ♪♪♪ (Hello Recording Club, 1995)

worth searching for: *Unlucky* (Bar/None, 1993, prod. Gene Holder) contains one track from *Can You Fly*, but it's most notable for a clear-eyed reading of the country classic "Wichita Lineman."

influences:

◄◄ The Beatles, Squeeze, Jimmy Webb, XTC, Big Star, the Raspberries

►► Jonny Polonsky, Wilco, the Gin Blossoms

Steve Knopper

Tom Johnston

See: The Doobie Brothers

Howard Jones

Born John Howard Jones, February 23, 1955, in Southampton, England.

Combine classical piano training with an interest in technology and a bunch of utopian, hippie ideals, and you get Howard Jones. He emerged in 1984 as a one-man band, singing about love and loving each other amid multiple layers of synthesizer bop while a dancer named Jed gyrated around. *Rolling Stone* magazine called Jones "a synthesized Gilbert O'Sullivan," but he's a bit better than that; his melodies are sturdy, and his arrangements, while relentlessly cheerful ("Things," he reminds us, "can only get better"), were certainly novel at the time. Jones had a run of hits during the mid-'80s, culminating with the 1986 Top Five hit "No One Is to Blame"—on which he shared vocals with Phil Collins. But as the hits dried up, Jones's output became more sporadic, though most recently he's made a comeback with acoustic music.

what to buy: *Human's Lib* ♪♪♪ (Elektra, 1984, prod. Rupert Hine) is a pop confection that's gotten kind of charming with age. The tunes are still of a high quality—even the positively perky "New Song"—and it's nice to remember a time when synthesizers provided a light touch and not just the gloomy ambience of industrial or the bland wash of certain techno acts.

what to buy next: *The Best of Howard Jones* ♪♪♪ (Elektra, 1993, prod. various) culls the highlights of Jones's career, a broader swatch than *Human's Lib*, though it's not quite as cohesive. *Acoustic Live in America* ♪♪♪ (Plump, 1995, prod. Howard Jones) is a shrewd move, stripping his songs down to just his voice, a piano, and a percussionist to reveal that he's not a bad tunesmith at all.

what to avoid: On *In the Running* ♪ (Elektra, 1992, prod. Ross Cullum, Howard Jones) Jones goes for the big, lush pop hit, and his contrivance betrays him.

the rest:
Dream into Action ♪♪♪ (Elektra, 1985)
One to One ♪♪ (Elektra, 1986)
Cross That Line ♪♪ (Elektra, 1989)
People ♪♪♪ (Ark 21, 1998)

worth searching for: *What Is Love?* (EastWest U.K., 1992, prod. various) is an import best-of that collects the better material from Jones's weaker later albums.

influences:
◄◄ Kraftwerk, Joy Division, Depeche Mode, Gary Numan
►► Donnie Iris, Backstreet Boys

Gary Graff

Marti Jones

After making an EP as part of the group Color Me Gone, Marti Jones came out of Ohio and teamed up with North Carolina fixture Don Dixon, producer of R.E.M. and the Smithereens, among others; she eventually married him. The duo delighted critics with savvy cover choices from unlikely sources and their ability to discover unknown talent; for instance, they recorded John Hiatt's songs several years before the rest of the music world discovered him. They also began composing together, eventually lessening their dependence on outside writers. Jones's lack of commercial success stalled her momentum; she was dropped by A&M and didn't last long on RCA, but she's found a low-pressure home on the folk-oriented Sugar Hill label.

what to buy: Fortunately, Jones's only available major-label release is her best. *Used Guitars* ♪♪♪♪ (A&M, 1988, prod. Don Dixon) is the apex of Dixon and Jones's great cover choices, with standouts from Hiatt ("The Real One," "If I Can Love Somebody"), Janis Ian, Jackie DeShannon, and Graham Parker ("You Can't Take Love for Granted"). Dixon and Jones add some original tunes ("Tourist Town," "Twisted Vines"), while Marshall Crenshaw and Sonny Landreth contribute amazing guitar leads.

WHAT ALBUM CHANGED YOUR LIFE?

It seems weird, but I only discovered [the Beach Boys'] *Pet Sounds* and *Surf's Up* [a few] years ago. I'd heard early Beach Boys when I was young, very young—the surfing stuff. I'd heard *Holland* as well. But when I missed those two albums, and when I heard them, I was in tears. I could not believe what I was hearing, things like the track 'Surf's Up' and 'God Only Knows,' just one after another. I wouldn't have thought that at this stage of my life I could be affected so much by music—and music that had been made 20 or more years before I'd heard it.

Howard Jones

what to buy next: *Live at Spirit Square* ♪♪♪ (Sugar Hill, 1996, prod. Don Dixon), recorded during 1990, offers production that will never be dated thanks to the concert/quintet setting. Plus, its whopping 17 tunes act as a fine career summary.

the rest:
My Long-haired Life ♪♪♪ (Sugar Hill, 1996)

worth searching for: With all but one of Jones's major-label releases out of print, several good albums are available only in the used bins—but they're easily found. *Any Kind of Lie* (RCA, 1990, prod. Don Dixon) finds Dixon and Jones carrying an album with almost no covers, and the material (especially the catchy title track) overcomes the overly slick production. Highlights of *Match Game* (A&M, 1986, prod. Don Dixon) include Jones's versions of Elvis Costello's "Just a Memory" and Crenshaw's "Whenever You're on My Mind." *Unsophisticated Time* (A&M, 1985, prod. Don Dixon) has cheesy production, but the two Peter Holsapple tunes ("Lonely Is as Lonely Does," "Neverland") are worth the trouble of tracking it down.

influences:

◄◄ Judy Collins, Dusty Springfield, Jackie DeShannon, Petula Clark

►► Bonnie Raitt, John Doe

Steve Holtje

Mick Jones

See: Foreigner

Rickie Lee Jones

Born November 8, 1954, in Chicago, IL.

A child of restless and volatile parents, Rickie Lee Jones moved across the country with them until she got expelled from high school in Washington state, beginning a journey through the West Coast underclass that would fuel much of her finest work. Eventually spinning a job as a waitress into occasional stage appearances and a career as a singer-songwriter, Jones began hanging out in creative circles that included Tom Waits and Little Feat's Lowell George and scored a record deal of her own during the late '70s. Her first album, fueled by a jazzy R&B and a beat poetry vibe, made her an instant critic's darling and won an audience with the hit "Chuck E's in Love." Subsequent albums ranged from a refinement of the street stories presented on her debut to records filled with jazzy covers of old pop standards. Always, Jones managed to bring a creative, unconventional approach to the material, even when substance abuse problems, a marriage. and the birth of her daughter threatened to distract her.

what to buy: Certainly her debut, *Rickie Lee Jones* 𝄞𝄞𝄞𝄞 (Warner Bros., 1979, prod. Lenny Waronker, Russ Titelman), provides the perfect distillation of Jones's unique approach, fusing her vivid portraits of street characters with supple vocals that can be innocent and knowing, soulful and awkward, breathless and powerful all in the same moment.

what to buy next: The only record that comes close to matching the debut is Jones's sophomore album, *Pirates* 𝄞𝄞𝄞𝄞 (Warner Bros., 1981, prod. Russ Titelman, Lenny Waronker), a complex, open record that grows stronger with repeated listening. Filled with her off-kilter meditations on death and progression, the record offers an amazing peek at a songwriter who isn't afraid to bare her soul on wax.

what to avoid: For any other singer-songwriter, *The Magazine* woof! (Warner Bros., 1984, prod. Rickie Lee Jones, James Newton Howard) might have been a triumph. But with creative expectations of her so high, this mishmash of self-consciously pretentious material goes over like a lead zeppelin, as the saying goes. Not much better is *Traffic from Paradise* woof! (Geffen, 1993, prod. Rickie Lee Jones), a collection of seemingly half-fin-

ished tunes that makes you wonder whether Jones has now resorted to releasing her demo tapes.

the rest:
Girl at Her Volcano 𝄞𝄞𝄞 (Warner Bros., 1983)
Flying Cowboys 𝄞𝄞𝄞𝄞 (Geffen, 1989)
Pop, Pop 𝄞𝄞𝄞 (Geffen, 1991)
Naked Songs: Live and Acoustic 𝄞𝄞𝄞𝄞 (Reprise, 1995)
Ghostyhead 𝄞𝄞𝄞 (Warner Bros., 1997)

worth searching for: Jones turns in an inspired duet with soulful New Orleans pianist-singer Dr. John on the playful groove "Makin' Whoopee" from his *In a Sentimental Mood* (Warner Bros., 1989, prod. Tommy LiPuma).

influences:

◄◄ Laura Nyro, Joni Mitchell, Tom Waits

►► Sheryl Crow, k.d. lang, Suzanne Vega

Eric Deggans

Steve Jones

See: The Sex Pistols

Tom Jones

Born June 7, 1940, in Pontypridd, Wales.

The bumping, the grinding, the bellowing—rarely has a singer been so equally admired and reviled as the hip-swinging Tom Jones. Leering and pandering, he left the '60s pop charts ("What's New Pussycat," "It's Not Unusual," "Delilah") for the cheese of Vegas. Making like Elvis without the fat, Jones led with his crotch in gleeful acts of self-parody. The Welshman made a blindsiding resurgence during the '80s by pairing himself with hip alternative acts, culminating in covers of Prince's "Kiss" and EMF's "Unbelievable" as well as appearances on *The Simpsons*. His totally over-the-top emoting and complete immersion in his own hype have always been his most endearing qualities—and the ones that've kept him amazingly afloat all these years. Approaching 60, the now-grandfather is still fog-horning for his supper in fishnet tank-tops and leather pants, oblivious to the rigors of aging.

what to buy: *The Complete Tom Jones* 𝄞𝄞𝄞𝄞 (Deram, 1993, prod. various) is the best cross-section of his work, containing the standards "It's Not Unusual," "Delilah," and "Green, Green Grass of Home," as well as his pairing with Art of Noise (!) for Prince's "Kiss."

what to buy next: *Things That Matter Most to Me* 𝄞𝄞𝄞 (Mercury, 1988/1993, prod. various) is the best compilation of his country hits such as "Darlin' " and "Green, Green, Grass of Home," which argues that Jones can take his shtick pretty much anywhere for engaging results. *Move Closer* 𝄞𝄞𝄞 (Jive,

1989, prod. various), one of his more consistent studio efforts, is the original home of "Kiss" and a take on the Rolling Stones' "(I Can't Get No) Satisfaction" that makes Mick Jagger seem downright demure.

what to avoid: *Greatest Songs* ♪ (Curb, 1995) doesn't live up to its title.

the rest:
Tom Jones Country ♪♪♫ (Mercury, 1982/1993)
Love Is on the Radio ♪♪ (Mercury, 1984/1993)
Tender Loving Care ♪♪ (Mercury, 1985/1993)
The Lead and How to Swing It ♪♪♪ (Interscope, 1994)
Country Memories ♪♪♫ (Rebound, 1994)

worth searching for: *The Long Black Veil* (RCA Victor, 1995, prod. various), a Chieftains all-star outing, contains a delightful, barrelling-through version of "Tennessee Waltz" by Jones, in his usual powerhouse style.

influences:
◀◀ Elvis Presley

▶▶ Michael Bolton, Buster Poindexter, Wham!

Allan Orski

Janis Joplin
/Big Brother
& the Holding Company

Born January 19, 1943, in Port Arthur, TX. Died October 4, 1970, in Hollywood, CA. Big Brother & the Holding Company formed in San Francisco, CA.

Sam Andrew, vocals; James Gurley, guitar; Peter Albin, bass; David Getz, drums.

The cloudy glass jar filled with dead '60s icons, which pop culture pushes to the front shelf decade after decade, leaves quite an impression—so much so that it's hard to remember that the public life of most of these musicians was a scant few years. And if Janis Joplin's career is the least celebrated of these fallen idols, it's because hers was not only the shortest but the most fitful. It was barely three years between her volcanic career-making performance at the Monterey Pop Festival and the discovery of her needle-tracked body in a Hollywood hotel. And in between? Disastrous relationships, a flood of pharmaceuticals, and a screeching blues mutation whose desperate passion gave her howling a reverberating intensity. When Joplin left the nurturing fold of Big Brother & the Holding Company, she turned into a commodity. Her early recordings with the San Francisco ballroom band capture a raw Joplin enmeshed in the passionate throes of an equally untamed band. Ambition was her true weapon of self-destruction, not the drugs and ill-fated romances. She left behind a frustrating glimpse of something

powerful enough to ignite her enduring legend. Joplin exploded all over the crowd at the historic 1967 Monterey Pop Festival; in a single show she established her reputation. At that very moment, she also sowed the seeds of eventual departure from her helpless communal colleagues in Big Brother. The very week their *Cheap Thrills* album hit #1 she announced her intention to go solo to her unsurprised bandmates. As a solo artist, she was a disaster. She made her debut performance after a mere two days' rehearsal, headlining an authentic soul show to an indifferent audience at an annual Memphis black fundraiser. Her first band never jelled and, although the Full Tilt Boogie Band, which she used by the time she cut her second solo album, represented an improvement, she didn't have time to build up a substantial enough body of work to support her looming posthumous stature. She was dead in 1970 at age 28, before even finishing that final, second solo album. Attempts by producer Paul Rothchild to cast Joplin in the pop-R&B vein then popularized by Chips Moman and his American Group productions of Memphis resulted in her posthumous hit album, *Pearl*, but her insufficiencies as a soul singer undermined even this sleek effort. There are currently two film biographies in the works, one of which is slated to star contemporary Joplin protégé Melissa Etheridge.

what to buy: Even a quarter-century later, *Cheap Thrills* ♪♪♪♪ (Columbia, 1968, prod. John Simon) still sounds nervy, rich, and radical. The album rips along, high-voltage electricity charging every number, until it reaches its climax—"Ball and Chain," which Joplin turns into one of the highpoints of personal expression in rock history.

what to buy next: Although the band's debut album, *Big Brother & the Holding Company* ♪♪♪ (Mainstream, 1967, prod. B. Shad), was a shoddy and hasty affair made in a few days, the record nevertheless captured the warm, sloppy atmosphere of the band and some precious Joplin vocals. Joplin's posthumously released *Pearl* ♪♪♪♪ (Columbia, 1971, prod. Paul Rothchild) is a bloodletting reminder that Joplin was on the rebound. "Me and Bobby McGee" is effortless country while "Cry Baby" is an ear-shredding wail that cements her place as the most exciting white blues singer of her generation. The odd assortment of studio tracks and outtakes doesn't make for a handy introduction, but *18 Essential Songs* ♪♪♪♪ (Columbia, 1995, compilation prod. Bob Irwin) is an interesting toss-up of studio stunners ("Down on Me"), previously unavailable live tracks (a ripping "Ball and Chain" from Monterey), and home tapes ("Trouble in Mind," with Jefferson Airplane's Jorma Kaukonen), all drawn from the *Janis* ♪♪♪♪ (Columbia, 1993) box set.

what to avoid: *I Got Dem Ol' Kozmic Blues Again Mama!* ♪ (Columbia, 1970, prod. Gabriel Meckler) is a sprawling, awful mess of a pseudo-soul album that sounded forced and shrill at the time and that the years have not treated kindly.

Janis Joplin **(Archive Photos)**

the rest:
Joplin in Concert 🎵🎵🎵 (Columbia, 1972)
Farewell Song 🎵🎵🎵 (Columbia, 1982)
Janis Joplin 🎵🎵🎵🎵 (Columbia, 1993)
Live at Winterland '68 🎵🎵🎵 (Columbia Legacy, 1998)

worth searching for: For hard-core collectors, the import-only *Cheaper Thrills* (Made to Last, 1982, prod. David Getz) offers a particularly raw early live performance of the unruly and exciting Big Brother crew.

influences:
◄◄ Memphis Minnie, John Coltrane, Lightnin' Hopkins, Howlin' Wolf

►► Melissa Etheridge, Mariah Carey, Liz Phair, Bette Midler, Courtney Love

Joel Selvin and Allan Orski

Journey

Formed 1973, in San Francisco, CA. Disbanded 1987. Re-formed 1995.

Neal Schon, guitar; Gregg Rolie, vocals, keyboards (1973–81); George Tickner, guitar (1973–75); Ross Valory, bass (1973–85, 1995–present); Aynsley Dunbar, drums (1973–79); Steve Perry, vocals (1978–87, 1995–98); Steve Smith, drums (1979-85, 1995–98); Jonathan Cain, keyboards (1981-87, 1995–present); Steve Augeri, vocals (1998–present); Deen Castronovo, drums (1998–present).

Carefully developing a trademark sound that made it one of the most popular rock groups of the early '80s, Journey evolved from an instrumental fusion ensemble that rose from the ashes of the original Santana into a polished power pop hit machine that eventually reflected some of the worst stylistic tendencies of the genre the band helped create. Journey might have invented the power ballad—a dubious contribution to the literature of pop—but the group's sweeping, pervasive influences on the rock scene of the early '80s may actually have perversely hastened the rise of more visceral, economical brands of rock influenced by the new wave movement. Journey represented the absolute peak of stadium rock. In fact, the band's slow, inexorable rise paralleled the growth of the arena rock business during the '70s. Its gargantuan success was inevitable, given Journey's steady refinements and the bandmembers' utter and complete devotion to shaping their craft to meet the curve of public appeal. Journey's albums reflect that process, zeroing in on popular success with greater accuracy on each subsequent release up to the 1981 supernova, *Escape*, after which the typical diminishing returns led to the acrimonious dissolution of the group. Inescapable reunion talk resulted in an underwhelming reunion during the mid-'90s.

what to buy: While *Greatest Hits* 🎵🎵🎵 (Columbia, 1988, prod. various) will probably spend eternity on the catalog charts, *Es-* *cape* 🎵🎵🎵 (Columbia, 1981, prod. Mike Stone, Kevin Elson) probably shows the group to its best advantage.

what to buy next: The three-CD box set *Time3* 🎵🎵🎵 (Columbia, 1993, prod. various) examines the group's career in fine-point detail, including many illuminating, previously unreleased recordings.

what to avoid: As is so often the case, by the time the group recorded its final album, *Raised on Radio* 🎵 (Columbia, 1986, prod. Steve Perry), ego conflicts and intra-band ambitions made the project more of a Steve Perry solo album than a group effort—although there are those who might argue that would be an improvement.

the rest:
Journey 🎵🎵 (Columbia, 1975)
Into the Future 🎵 (Columbia, 1976)
Next 🎵 (Columbia, 1977)
Infinity 🎵🎵 (Columbia, 1978)
Evolution 🎵🎵 (Columbia, 1979)
Departure 🎵🎵 (Columbia, 1980)
Captured 🎵 (Columbia, 1981)
Frontiers 🎵🎵 (Columbia, 1983)
Trial by Fire 🎵🎵 (Columbia, 1996)
Greatest Hits Live 🎵 (Columbia 1998)

worth searching for: The Japanese-only soundtrack album *Dream after Dream* (Sony, 1980, prod. Kevin Elson, Geoff Workman) captures *Escape*-era Journey in an atmospheric, Floydian mode.

solo outings:
Steve Perry:
Street Talk 🎵🎵 (Columbia, 1984)
For Love of Strange Medicine **woof!** (Columbia, 1994)

Neal Schon:
(With Jan Hammer) *Untold Passion* 🎵🎵 (Columbia, 1981)
(With Jan Hammer) *Made to Stay* (Columbia, 1982)
(With Sammy Hagar) *Through the Fire* 🎵 (Geffen, 1984)
Beyond the Thunder 🎵🎵🎵 (Higher Octave, 1995)

influences:
◄◄ Santana, Queen, Boston, Steve Miller Band

►► Michael Bolton, Survivor, Whitesnake, Bad English

see also: *Santana, John Waite*

Joel Selvin

Joy Division

Formed 1977, in Manchester, England. Disbanded 1980.

Ian Curtis (died May 18, 1980), vocals; Bernard Albrecht (born Bernard Dicken, a.k.a. Bernard Sumner), guitar, vocals; Peter Hook, bass; Stephen Morris, drums.

Sparked into existence by punk, Joy Division was an enormously influential group that connected the original punk revolution and the '80s sounds that came after, including industrial and various post-punk dance forms. Peter Hook and Bernard Sumner, after attending the Sex Pistols' first concert in Manchester on June 4, 1976, were inspired to start bands. Forming first as Warsaw, the quartet changed its name to the term given to the Nazi's involuntary concentration camp brothels. Barely able to play their instruments but immensely compelling nonetheless due to epileptic singer Ian Curtis's dark, morbid lyrics, the group hooked up with local label Factory and producer Martin Hannett. Hannett's contribution to the group's recorded sound cannot be understated; he took a musical concept that could have sounded merely sloppy and incompetent and made it unique with echo, a sense of vast space, and a fattening and highlighting of elements such as Hook's bone-simple bass lines. Just as the second album was coming out, the always-disconsolate Curtis, devastated by the breakup of his marriage, hung himself at the age of 22. The rest of the band regrouped as New Order and, building on the dance elements inherent in Joy Division, once again created a new musical sound.

what to buy: *Unknown Pleasures* 𝆑𝆑𝆑𝆑 (Factory, 1979, prod. Martin Hannett) features "She's Lost Control" and is devastating in its nihilistic vision and raw, jagged sound. *Closer* 𝆑𝆑𝆑𝆑 (Factory, 1980, prod. Martin Hannett) is just as dark but with even better songs and arrangements.

what to buy next: *Substance* 𝆑𝆑𝆑𝆑 (QWest, 1988, prod. Joy Division, Martin Hannett) is a career overview that mostly avoids overlapping the albums, concentrating on singles (including the great "Love Will Tear Us Apart," a response to the Captain & Tennille hit "Love Will Keep Us Together") and rarities. *Still* 𝆑𝆑𝆑𝆑 (Factory, 1981, prod. Martin Hannett) collects live recordings and rarities, including a striking cover of the Velvet Underground's "Sister Ray."

what to avoid: Given the small number of Joy Division releases, *Permanent: Joy Division 1995* **woof!** (QWest, 1995, prod. various) is an unnecessary compilation feebly baited with a 1995 remix of "Love Will Tear Us Apart," tricked up for dance-club play but musically inferior.

the rest:
Peel Sessions 𝆑𝆑𝆑 (Strange Fruit, 1990)

worth searching for: The 80-track, four-CD import set *Heart & Soul* (London, 1997, prod. various) isn't quite complete but is probably close enough for most people. If you can find this, you might as well get everything at once. This concentrated dosage makes their legacy seem all the more stunning. If you need even more, the bootleg LP *Amsterdam* (done up to look like a Factory promo item) preserves an adrenalized live show.

influences:

◀◀ Velvet Underground, Sex Pistols, Kraftwerk, David Bowie

▶▶ The Cure, New Order, Bauhaus, Red Lorry Yellow Lorry, Sisters of Mercy/The Mission U.K., Teardrop Explodes/Julian Cope, nine inch nails, Nirvana, American Music Club/Mark Eitzel, Moby

see also: *New Order, Electronic*

Steve Holtje

Judas Priest

Formed 1969, in Birmingham, England.

Alan Atkins, vocals (1969–72); Rob Halford, vocals (1973–92); K.K. Downing, guitar; Glenn Tipton, guitar; Ian Hill, bass; John Ellis, drums (1969–71); Alan Moore, drums (1971, 1974–77); Chris Campbell, drums (1971–72); John Hinch, drums (1973); Simon Phillips, drums (1977); Les Binks, drums (1978); Dave Holland, drums (1979–90); Scott Travis, drums (1990–92); "Ripper" Owens, vocals (1996–present).

One of heavy rock's pioneers, Judas Priest was metal when metal wasn't cool—in fact, one could argue that the band, along with fellow Brits Deep Purple, Black Sabbath, and Motörhead—*are* the ones that made it cool. Just about every heavy metal band since 1980 has borrowed from Priest's formula of crunching guitars and dark, gothic lyrics, as well as its studded-leather wardrobe. Guitarist K.K. Downing and bassist Ian Hill formed the band in 1969, but they didn't begin recording until vocalist Rob Halford began his long tenure in 1971. It took several years for Judas Priest to find (some might say create) its niche; it didn't really take off in the United States until the early '80s. The group really earned its stripes of credibility due to inane controversies: it was accused by a Christian organization of recording subliminal messages backwards on its albums; it was targeted by the Washington (D.C.) wives' Parents Music Resource Center (PMRC) for its violent and sexually explicit lyrics; and in 1986 supposedly backward lyrics from the album *Stained Class* were said to have induced two boys to attempt suicide (one died); the group was acquitted. In 1992 singer Halford left to form Fight, then Two; the remaining members of Judas Priest vowed to continue with new vocalist "Ripper" Owens, who came from a Priest tribute band in Ohio.

what to buy: By the time Priest recorded *Screaming for Vengeance* 𝆑𝆑𝆑𝆑 (Columbia, 1982, prod. Tom Allom) the band had perfected its sound. The album opens with the thunderous instrumental "The Hellion" and rumbles through hits such as "Electric Eye" and "You've Got Another Thing Coming." Play it loud.

what to buy next: Priest's double-length live package, *Priest . . . Live!* 𝆑𝆑𝆑𝆑 (Columbia, 1986, prod. Tom Allom), may be one of

Rob Halford of Judas Priest (© Ken Settle)

the best live heavy metal albums out there. Glenn Tipton and Downing ably duplicate their two-guitar attack, and Halford's piercing wail is unfailing.

what to avoid: *Painkiller* **woof!** (Columbia, 1990, prod. Chris Tsangarides, Judas Priest) is a dull, strident album that may have been the reason for Halford's departure two years later.

the rest:
Rocka Rolla 🎵🎵 (RCA, 1974)
Sad Wings of Destiny 🎵🎵 (RCA, 1976)
Sin after Sin 🎵🎵🎵 (Columbia, 1977)
Stained Class 🎵🎵🎵 (Columbia, 1978)
Best of Judas Priest 🎵🎵🎵 (RCA, 1978)
Hell Bent for Leather 🎵🎵🎵 (Columbia, 1978)
Unleashed in the East 🎵🎵🎵 (Columbia, 1979)
British Steel 🎵🎵🎵 (Columbia, 1980)
Point of Entry 🎵🎵🎵 (Columbia, 1981)
Defenders of the Faith 🎵🎵🎵🎵 (Columbia, 1984)
Hero, Hero 🎵🎵 (RCA, 1985)
Turbo 🎵🎵🎵🎵 (Columbia, 1986)
Ram It Down 🎵 (Columbia, 1988)
Metalworks '73–'93 🎵🎵🎵 (Columbia, 1993)
Jugulator 🎵🎵 (BMG, 1997)
Best Of: Living after Midnight 🎵🎵🎵 (Sony, 1998)

worth searching for: Not only is the band's 1984 picture disc a neat collectors item, but it contains an excellent selection of its greatest hits (if you dare to actually put it on your turntable).

solo outings:
Rob Halford:
(With Fight) *War of Words* 🎵🎵🎵 (Epic, 1993)
(With Fight) *Mutations* 🎵🎵 (Epic EP, 1994)
(With Fight) *A Small Deadly Space* 🎵🎵 (Epic, 1995)
(With Two) *Voyeurs* 🎵🎵🎵 (nothing, 1998)

Glenn Tipton:
Baptizm of Fire 🎵🎵🎵 (Warner Bros., 1997)

influences:
◀◀ Led Zeppelin, Cream, the Who, Black Sabbath

▶▶ Metallica, Slayer, Anthrax, Accept, Venom, Iron Maiden, Scorpions, Pantera, White Zombie, Tool

Brandon Trenz

Judybats
Formed 1987, in Knoxville, TN. Disbanded 1995.

Jeff Herskell, vocals, minimoog, percussion; Johnny Sighrue, guitar, vocals, piano; Ed Winters, guitar, Dobro, organ; Paul Noe, bass, Dobro, vocals; David Jenkins, drums.

Before the Barenaked Ladies charmed the collective yuppie pants off of North America's smart-pop audience, there were the wry, textured, and oft-unheard musings of Knoxville's Judybats. Building on the informed songcrafting of such Brit-heroes as the Housemartins and Terry Hall, Jeff Herskell's similarly quirky-but-hooky sense of melody took pop a step further on 1991's *Native Son*. The track "Don't Drop the Baby" ("don't touch my soft spot/or I might die"), introduced via the *Just Say . . .* series, remains the best representation of the band's promise, even if it was just its first single. But subsequent albums released each of the three following years were, at times, equally glorious. The band lost the support of its label, Sire, in 1995 and called it quits. But it left a legacy that extends the respectable dynamic of "Being Simple" to "All I Want to Do Is F**k Your Hair"(!).

what to buy: *Native Son* 🎵🎵🎵 (Sire, 1991) bounces with a charm usually reserved for the British. Equal parts Smiths and They Might Be Giants, the Judybats here help to reclaim the relevance of American pop.

what to buy next: *Full Empty* 🎵🎵🎵 (Sire, 1994) closes the band's career with an at times bitter but never unpleasant ode to the pop process. The final single, "Being Simple," is included here, as is "Jive Talkin'," in full po-mo glory.

the rest:
Down in the Shacks (Where the Sattelite Dishes Grow) 🎵🎵🎵 (Sire, 1992)
Pain Makes You Beautiful 🎵🎵🎵 (Sire, 1993)

influences:
◀◀ The Housemartins, Colourfield, They Might Be Giants

▶▶ Barenaked Ladies, Billy Pilgrim, Sister Hazel

Billy Manes

Jules & the Polar Bears
See: Jules Shear

Juluka
See: Johnny Clegg & Savuka

Junk Monkeys
Formed 1986, in Dearborn, MI.

David Bierman, vocals, guitar; Dave Boutette, guitar; Kevin Perri, bass; Dan Allen, drums, vocals (1986–91); Glynn Scanlan, drums, vocals (1992–present).

Building a Detroit-area following by developing the Minneapolis sound exemplified by the Replacements and Soul Asylum, the Junk Monkeys' best album augmented chunky rhythm guitar riffing, hoarsely melodic vocals, and a smidgen of syncopation with simple yet creative use of acoustic piano and organ courtesy of Todd McKinney. Its simple but very effective songs feature sing-along-inducing choruses, while the witty or poignant verses often turn some clichés sideways. The group is considerably less active than it used to be, but can still be found playing the odd Detroit club gig.

worth searching for: An epiphanic focus was attained on the group's moment of glory (and its swan song), *Bliss* (Metal Blade Modern, 1993, prod. Michael Nehra, Al Sutton, David Bierman). It's one of the best guitar-pop releases in a decade rife with great ones. Tracks such as "Idle Up," "And It Caved In," and "Day Away" are as catchy as anything the band's better-known peers have concocted. *Soul Cakes* (Metal Blade, 1989, prod. David Bierman, Michael Nehra) was compiled from locally issued indie releases. The exponantially improved *Five Star Fling* (Metal Blade, 1991, prod. Dave Feeny, Junk Monkeys) has better songwriting, lots of momentum, and much better sound than its predecessor.

influences:

◀◀ The Replacements, Soul Asylum

▶▶ Gin Blossoms

Steve Holtje

Barbara K

See: Timbuk 3

Paul K
/Paul K & the Weathermen
/Paul K & the Prayers

Born Paul Kopasz, 1962, in Detroit, MI.

To some, Paul K is the great lost songwriter of our time. To others, he's the supreme screw-up, a college-educated talent who during the '80s shuttled between New York and Kentucky and took up a life of drugs and petty crime as sort of a twisted tribute to his artistic muses—William Burroughs, Rimbaud, and Lou Reed. There's no denying that in some respects Paul K has made a career (if you could call it that) out of his personal turmoil: heroin addiction, burglary, jail time, divorce. But there's also no denying the power of the music. He cranked out dozens of homemade cassettes—sometimes in a solo acoustic context, more often in full-on electric mode with a rhythm section known as the Weathermen—before his first official domestic release, 1992's *The Blue Sun*. Ever since, he's continued to perfect an approach in which literate verbal imagery is matched by a highly eclectic brand of rock that refuses to acknowledge

there's any distance between the shattering stillness of Townes Van Zandt and the howling wind of Crazy Horse.

what to buy: *Love Is a Gas* ♫♫♫♫ (Alias, 1997, prod. Mo Tucker) is one of the few Paul K discs that actually remains in print, and it's a doozy. He weaves the sharpy observed lyricism of his solo acoustic work into deeply nuanced ensemble performances that suggest blue-eyed soul hymns. A good deal darker and even more ambitious is *A Wilderness of Mirrors* ♫♫♫♫ (Alias, 1998, prod. Chris Allison, Paul K), a series of haunted, despairing love songs based on, of all things, the Book of Job.

the rest:

Achilles Heel ♫♫♫ (Thirsty Ear, 1995)

worth searching for: You can't go wrong in tracking down the countless obscurities floating around in Paul K's many-splintered past, but his solo acoustic records are especially noteworthy, particularly *Blues for Charlie Lucky* (SilenZ, 1993, prod. Paul K), which contains a stark version of one of his best early songs, "Radiant and White."

influences:

◀◀ Townes Van Zandt, Velvet Underground, Bob Dylan, Pete Townshend

▶▶ Afghan Whigs, Wilco, Guided by Voices, Palace

Greg Kot

Brenda Kahn

Born May 3, 1967, in Hartford, CT.

Rising out of the Alphabet City "anti-folk" scene in late '80s Manhattan, singer-songwriter Brenda Kahn took lessons from folk veteran Dave Van Ronk but was equally influenced by punk—especially its DIY ethic and emotional directness. She chose the solo acoustic path because, while growing up in New Jersey, local bands resisted the idea of a female guitarist. She's persevered through horrible record label experiences and continues to put her vividly etched depictions of relationships and occasionally piquant political statements before the public, working solo or with a trio.

what to buy: With minimal bass-and-drums backing, *Goldfish Don't Talk Back* ♫♫♫♫ (Community 3, 1990, prod. Albert Garzon) showcases fantastic songwriting (the elegiac "Winchester Chimes"), powerful politics (the viciously sarcastic "Eggs on Drugs"), and in-your-face romantic plaints. *Epiphany in Brooklyn* ♫♫♫♫ (Chaos/Columbia, 1992, prod. David Kahne) is slightly less consistent, but some of David Kahne's inspired production touches allow Kahn to break out of the acoustic troubadour mold on quiet pieces full of atmosphere and foreboding ("Sleepwalking").

what to buy next: Columbia declined to issue *Destination Anywhere* 𝄞𝄞𝄞 (Through Being Cool/Shanachie, 1996, prod. Tim Patalan), Kahn's rock album, but the catchy "Yellow Sun" deserved to be a hit.

the rest:
Life in the Drug War Trenches 𝄞𝄞 (Crackpot EP, 1992)
Outside the Beauty Salon 𝄞𝄞𝄞 (Shanachie, 1997)

worth searching for: "60-Second Critic" (Chaos/Columbia, 1992, prod. Brenda Kahn, Dave Pirner) is a duet with Soul Asylum's Dave Pirner, a promo-only cassette single bitterly commenting on the choices in the 1992 presidential election campaign.

influences:

◀◀ Bessie Smith, Phil Ochs, Dave Van Ronk, Lou Reed, Elvis Costello, the Clash, X-Ray Spex, the Pretenders, Michelle Shocked, Roger Manning

▶▶ Alanis Morrisette, Ani DiFranco, Karen Ramos

Steve Holtje

Kajagoogoo
/Kaja
/Limahl

Formed 1982, in England. Disbanded 1986. Re-formed 1992.

Limahl, vocals (1982–84); Nick Beggs, bass; others.

According to some, the word Kajagoogoo has now taken on a broader meaning than simply being the name of a foppish British quintet of the early '80s that was known as much for its members' teased-out, bushed-up hairdos as for its thoroughly disposable synth-pop music. Kajagoogoo now refers to anything trendy, false, ephemeral, or faddish, particularly something associated with the New Romantic era in music/fashion/videos. Yes, for one brief, shining moment in early 1983, Kajagoogoo was on top of the pop charts—in the U.K., at least—with "Too Shy," a bubbly concoction of funky dance-lite, the sort of thing that by comparison lent importance to, say, "The Reflex" by Duran Duran.

what's available: Not surprisingly, double-D's keyboard player Nick Rhodes co-produced Kajagoogoo's debut, *White Feathers* **woof!** (EMI, 1982, prod. Nick Rhodes, Colin Thurston, Tim Palmer, Kajagoogoo), a fairly irredeemable dollop of slithery synth-pop goop. The Kajagoogoo album that followed, as well as a final release under the shortened moniker Kaja, were *completely* irredeemable, and are justifiably out of print. By then, though, Limahl (an all-too-clever anagram of his real last name, Hamill) had left to put out a solo album, which featured his giddy, almost Germanic-pop hit theme song to the film *The*

Neverending Story. Both hits, along with a few remixes and a host of unlistenable crap, are included on *Too Shy—The Singles* 𝄞 (EMI, 1993, prod. various).

worth searching for: Smart retro-'80s freaks will pick up the group's hits on either Rhino's *New Wave Hits* series or EMI's *Living in Oblivion* series. At least there the songs are tempered by being placed in context with other better material from the same era.

influences:

◀◀ Duran Duran

▶▶ Culture Club, Nu Shooz, Total Coelo

Bob Remstein

Kansas

Formed 1972, in Topeka, KS.

Kerry Livgren, guitar, keyboards (1972–1983, 1991); Steve Walsh, vocals, keyboards (1972–81, 1986–present); Robby Steinhardt, violin, vocals (1972–83, 1997–present); Richard Williams, guitar; Phil Ehart, drums; Dave Hope, bass (1972–83); John Elefante, vocals, keyboards (1981–83); Steve Morse, guitar (1985–88); Billy Greer, bass (1985–present); David Ragsdale, violin (1990–97).

Fusing the neo-classical sensibilities of progressive rock with an earthy Midwestern rock grind, Kansas enjoyed a brief period of mass popularity during the late '70s with hits such as "Carry on Wayward Son" and "Dust in the Wind." Though often held up as an example of faceless '70s album-rock, there's no faulting the players' chops, nor the creative ambitions that yielded a number of textured, multi-part suites. Ultimately, Steve Walsh's initial departure in 1981 knocked the group off stride, and it's never regained its balance; these days it can be found reliving past glories with '70s kin such as Styx and the Alan Parson Project.

what to buy: Led by the hit "Carry on Wayward Son," *Leftoverture* 𝄞𝄞𝄞𝄞 (Kirshner, 1976, prod. Jeff Glixman) was Kansas's breakthrough album and a thorough representation of its assorted musical sensibilities, from the power ballad "The Wall" to the punchy rock of "What's on My Mind" to the long-winded pomp of "Magnum Opus." Less well-known—but just as good—is *Masque* 𝄞𝄞𝄞𝄞 (Kirshner, 1975, prod. Jeff Glixman), whose lengthier numbers ("Icarus," "The Pinnacle") have a more organic majesty.

what to buy next: The box set *Kansas* 𝄞𝄞𝄞 (Epic Associated/Legacy, 1995, prod. various) captures the crucial tracks and winnows what's interesting from later releases. Those interested in Kansas at its most bombastic are well-served by *Song for America* 𝄞𝄞𝄞 (Kirshner, 1975, prod. Jeff Glixman, Wally Gold), whose title cut is still one of prog-rock's sonic gems.

what to avoid: John Elefante was a thin replacement for Walsh, and *Drastic Measures* **woof!** (CBS Associated, 1983, prod. Kansas) was a bottoming-out that led Kansas to split up for three years.

the rest:
Kansas 🎵🎵 (Kirshner, 1974)
Point of Know Return 🎵🎵🎵 (Kirshner, 1977)
Two for the Show 🎵🎵 (Kirshner, 1978)
Monolith 🎵🎵🎵 (Kirshner, 1979)
Audio-Visions 🎵🎵 (Kirshner, 1980)
Vinyl Confessions 🎵 (Kirshner, 1982)
Power 🎵🎵 (MCA, 1986)
In the Spirit of Things 🎵 (MCA, 1988)
Freaks of Nature 🎵🎵 (Intersound, 1995)
Always Never the Same 🎵🎵🎵 (River North, 1998)

worth searching for: The Japanese *Star Box* (Kirshner/Sony, 1993) is a more compact retrospective that offers a thorough selection of hits and a reasonable assortment of album tracks.

solo outings:
Kerry Livgren:
Seeds of Change 🎵🎵 (Kirshner, 1980)

Steve Walsh:
Schemer-Dreamer 🎵🎵 (Kirshner, 1979)

influences:
◀◀ The Moody Blues, Procol Harum, King Crimson, Humble Pie, B.B. King, Elmore James, Ramsey Lewis, Dave Brubeck

▶▶ The Livgren-Hope Christian Rock Band AD, Shooting Star, the Dave Matthews Band

Gary Graff

Paul Kantner

See: Jefferson Airplane, Jefferson Starship

Kara's Flowers

Formed 1994, in Los Angeles, CA.

Mickey Madden, bass; Jesse Carmichael, guitar, vocals; Ryan Dusick, drums, percussion; Adam Levine, vocals, guitar.

The great pop hope, or just another hype? Kara's Flowers has consciously positioned its avowedly pop approach as the logical successor to the angst of grunge. With a press release proclaiming that "Doom is dead," Kara's Flowers leaves itself open to charges that the band is merely a shill for the record industry's efforts to wrestle control of rock's future away from grunge's "purity." And that is, of course, a pile of piggy poop. Whatever one may make of its motives or goals, Kara's Flowers fills a legitimate niche by providing an alternative to Alterna-

---

WHAT ALBUM CHANGED YOUR LIFE?

Probably *In the Court of the Crimson King* by King Crimson, the very first Emerson, Lake & Palmer album, lots of early Deep Purple, [Genesis'] *The Lamb Lies Down on Broadway,* and *Close to the Edge* by Yes—all British bands. Those are the bands that really influenced this band more than anything. We always looked across the ocean more than at home.

Phil Ehart (of Kansas)

---

tive, offering accomplished, aggressive pop music to those of us who are (to borrow a phrase from the Smithereens) sick of Seattle. We could do much worse than to have Kara's Flowers ruling the radio for a while.

what's available: *The Fourth World* 🎵🎵🎵 (Reprise, 1997, prod. Rob Cavallo) lives up to its hype, with some decent buzz-pop that sounds neither contrived nor retro. The music is punchy, beholden to both punk and power pop, but not at all derivative. "Myself" offers the clearest statement of intent, with its almost-bemused observation, "I can't find anything to be sad about/They say I'm doomed but I feel fine." Very agreeable stuff, and a very impressive debut.

influences:
◀◀ The Monkees, the Buzzcocks, the Knack, Jellyfish, Green Day, the Records, the Flashcubes, the Posies, Material Issue, the Sighs

Carl Cafarelli

Mick Karn

See: Japan

Kathleen Turner Overdrive

See: Drivin' N' Cryin'

Katrina & the Waves

Formed 1981, in London, England.

Katrina Leskanich, guitar, vocals; Kimberley Rew, guitar; Vince De la Cruz, bass; Alex Cooper, drums.

A British-American pop-rock group, Katrina & the Waves formed in 1981 when Air Force brat Katrina Leskanich started playing with former Soft Boys member Kimberly Rew. Four years and some independent recordings later, Capitol released the group's first album in the United States, producing a quick summer hit in "Walking on Sunshine." With Rew's undeniable songwriting skills, the group boasts a body of catchy power pop, though it's never repeated the same commercial impact.

what's available: *Anthology* ♫♫♫ (One Way, 1995, prod. various) is your only choice, but it at least contains the hits—even leads off with "Walking on Sunshine" and "Do You Want Crying"—and offers a 14-track overview that should sate all but the true devotee.

worth searching for: The group's first American album actually contained re-recordings of songs the band already had released in Canada or England. Those recordings included *Shock Horror* (Scoop, 1983, prod. Richard Bishop, Nick Cook, Pat Collier); (as the Waves) *Walking on Sunshine* (Attic, 1983); and *Katrina & the Waves 2* (Attic, 1984, prod. Pat Collier, Katrina & the Waves).

influences:

◄◄ The Soft Boys, Dusty Springfield

►► Ace of Base, the Bangles

see also: *The Soft Boys*

Brian Mansfield

Jorma Kaukonen

See: Hot Tuna

KC & the Sunshine Band

Formed 1973, in Hialeah, FL.

Harry Wayne Casey, vocals, keyboards; Richard Finch, bass; Jerome Smith, guitar; Robert Johnson, drums; Fermin Coytisolo, congas; Ronnie Smith, trumpet; Denvil Liptrot, saxophone; James Weaver, trumpet; Charles Williams, trombone.

KC's funky party strut in many ways typified the feel-good vibe pumping through Miami's dance floors during the polyester-cloaked '70s. After the jittery noises flashing out from Sly Stone, the O'Jays, and Stevie Wonder during the early part of the decade, the Sunshine Band's harmonious horns were, at least in part, an answer to that pervading sense of dread. In place of backstabbers, riots, and superstition, Harry Wayne

Casey rallied like a pre-*Saturday Night Fever* Travolta. His call to arms? Shaking your booty. A low-risk proposition to be sure, and the band's massive crossover appeal in the R&B and pop charts suggested a public thirst for a party with no strings attached; if you doubt that, remember that this was the first group since the Beatles in 1964 to rack up four #1 singles in a year. The songwriting team of Casey and Richard Finch had a way with a catchy phrase, owing more to pop than Parliament, and they kept a stream of instant dance jingles on the lips and hips of boogie children everywhere. The momentum was stopped only by a serious auto wreck Casey suffered during the early '80s. After a lengthy convalescence, he rebounded in 1984 with the pure pop of "Give It Up," but all follow-ups have failed to recapture his former glories. Casey, less mane, more gut, can be found with his latest incarnation of the Sunshine Band shaking its paunchy booties on the oldies circuit.

what to buy: *The Best of KC & the Sunshine Band* ♫♫♫♫ (Rhino, 1989, prod. Harry Casey, Richard Finch) offers all the singles in a row, and it is an infectious bunch—starting with "Sound Your Funky Horn" and "Get down Tonight," leading to the inevitable "(Shake, Shake, Shake) Shake Your Booty," "That's the Way I Like It," and "Keep It Comin' Love." The pull toward the dance floor is still there, even if you leave your white patent leather shoes at home.

what to buy next: *Part 3 . . . and More* ♫♫♫ (TK, 1976/Rhino, 1994, prod. Harry Casey, Richard Finch) is the band's strongest studio album, augmented by eight bonus tracks on CD—many featuring KC sans Sunshine. The Spanish reading of "Please Don't Go" is a dubious treat.

what to avoid: *Get down Live* ♫♫ (Intersound International, 1995) offers inferior treatments of the songs that got you shaking your you-know-what in the first place.

the rest:
Greatest Hits, Vol. 2 ♫♫♫ (Hollywood/Rounder)

influences:

◄◄ The Spinners, the Temptations, Donna Summer

►► C+C Music Factory, Gloria Estefan

Allan Orski

Tommy Keene

Born in Bethesda, MD.

Tommy Keene has such a classic pop voice—high but not squeaky, with enough character to skirt wimpiness but ooze sincere yearning—that even if he didn't write such killer jangle riffs, it would still be a joy to hear his records. The fact that his melodies are memorable and hummable and that he's an excellent finger-style electric guitarist with a distinctive arpeggiated sound just makes his obscurity that much harder to fathom. The title track of his well-received *Places That Are Gone* EP got Keene noticed; it was *Village Voice*'s 1984 Jazz & Pop winner in the EP category. Keene was signed by Geffen and released two fine albums and an EP, but he got nowhere commercially and was dropped. He spent three years recording and shopping demos until some were picked up by Matador and released on a 1992 EP. Alias then put together a collection, including many of the unused demos, and in 1996 and 1998 Matador put out albums of new material, presenting hope that in the more pop-friendly alternative market (and the more alternative-friendly pop market) Keene would finally win the kudos due him.

what to buy: The EP *Sleeping on a Rollercoaster* ✂✂✂✂ (Matador, 1992, prod. Tommy Keene, Steve Carr) has only five songs, but "Love Is a Dangerous Thing" might be the best he's ever done. For a full-length dose of Keene, *Ten Years After* ✂✂✂✂ (Matador, 1996) can't be beat. A dozen power-pop gems (plus the unlisted bonus track, a punkish run-through of a short chunk of the Who's "It's Not True") burst from the speakers with more energy than on earlier outings, with a few good ballads thrown in for variety.

what to buy next: *The Real Underground* ✂✂✂✂ (Alias, 1993, prod. Tommy Keene, Ted Niceley) contains all six songs of the EP *Places That Are Gone* ✂✂✂✂✂ (Dolphin, 1984, prod. Tommy Keene, Ted Niceley) and some unreleased material.

what to avoid: Don't be tempted by *Back Again (Try . . .)* ✂ (Dolphin EP, 1984) just because it has two covers (Bryan Ferry's "All I Want Is You" and the Rolling Stones' "When the Whip Comes Down") left off *The Real Underground*. Neither is a good song to begin with, and they sound worse in these low-fi bar recordings.

the rest:
Strange Alliance ✂✂✂ (Avenue, 1982)
Run Now ✂✂✂ (Geffen, 1986)
Isolation Party ✂✂✂✂ (Matador, 1998)

worth searching for: The mostly out-of-print Geffen material can be found cheaply in used record stores and is must-own stuff for fans of jangly pop. *Based on Happy Times* (Geffen, 1980, prod. Geoff Emerick) includes a new version of "Places That Are Gone" and a hard-rocking cover of Lou Reed's "Kill Your Sons" that shows off Keene's fine guitar style. *Songs from the Film* (Geffen, 1989/1998, prod. Joe Hardy, John Hampton, Tommy Keene) has slightly tougher production and includes guest Peter Buck (R.E.M.) on two tracks, one an obscure Beach Boys tune. The various-artists compilation *Yellow Pills, Vol. 1* (Big Deal, 1993, prod. various) includes Keene's "Disarray."

influences:

◀◀ The Beatles, the Byrds, the Who, Big Star, Shoes, Let's Active

▶▶ Gin Blossoms, Matthew Sweet, Young Fresh Fellows, Teenage Fanclub, Superchunk, Velvet Crush

Steve Holtje

Katell Keineg

Born in Wales.

A modern-age nomad, having moved all around the world in search of cultural influence, Katell Keineg (who now resides in Dublin) has maintained an incredibly sturdy sense of identity throughout her two-album career. Her first break came during 1993 when she recorded her debut single, the potent "Hestia" ("like that proverbial needle/looking for itself"), for Bob Mould's SOL label. Between her two albums she sang lilting backups on Natalie Merchant's solo debut, *Carnival*.

what to buy: "Hestia" opens Keineg's debut album, *O Seasons O Castles* ✂✂✂✂✂ (Elektra, 1994, prod. Katell Keineg, Fred Maher), but nothing prepared us for its complexity, enchantment, or seemingly transcendent wisdom. "Franklin" is a goodbye to a drug-addict lover as well as a moment of self-realization, while the frighteningly beautiful "Gulf of Araby" closes the album with an otherworldly scope of personal plight. *O Seasons* is a piece of rare genius that improves with every listen.

what to buy next: *Jet* ✂✂✂✂ (Elektra, 1997, prod. Eric Drew Feldman, John Holbrook, Katell Keineg) takes a step back from its predecessor's trauma to smooth over a few of the wrinkles. "One Hell of a Life" and "Mother's Map" each further Keineg's more terrestrial wanderings of thought into a more quiet, perhaps more mature, realization.

influences:

◀◀ Joni Mitchell, Janis Joplin, Sinéad O'Connor, Loreena McKennit

▶▶ Jewel, Paula Cole

Billy Manes

Paul Kelly

Born January 13, 1955, in Adelaide, Australia.

Singer-songwriter Paul Kelly pens incisive and mature tales to critical acclaim and weak record sales. Drawing comparisons to Graham Parker and Elvis Costello, Kelly's writing style is, in fact, more minimalist and mournful in its distillation of life's pivotal moments. He's had trouble getting noticed in the United States, resulting in his being dropped from A&M in 1989. Kelly has recently been threatening to gain a wider audience, but his well-thought-out snapshots require too much concentration for the casual radio drone to appreciate.

what to buy: *Words & Music* ♪♪♪♪ (Vanguard, 1998, prod. Mark Opitz, Simon Polinski, Laurence Maddy, Paul Kelly) is perhaps the finest album of his career. Getting back into a band situation after the demise of his old group, the Messengers, *Words & Music* contains some of Kelly's most richly drawn songs and some of the most stirring rock he's ever put on record. And you'll seldom find a song more moving than "How to Make Gravy," an offbeat Christmas tune sung from the perspective of a prison convict.

what to buy next: *Deeper Water* ♪♪♪ (Vanguard, 1995, prod. various) is a splendid return to form that shows Kelly has lost none of his insights during all the label-jumping; his gift for vivid detail seems bottomless in its inspiration.

the rest:
Paul Kelly Live from the Continental and the Esplanade ♪♪♪ (Vanguard, 1996)

worth searching for: The out-of-print *Gossip* (A&M, 1987, prod. Alan Thorn, Paul Kelly) was his the stunning U.S. debut, loaded with dead-on portraits of the damage caused by an alcoholic father. On the lighter side, Kelly shows his gift for ballads ("Randwick Bells") and charming pop ("Don't Ever Harm the Messenger" and "Leaps and Bounds").

influences:
◀◀ Bob Dylan, Raymond Carver
▶▶ John Mellencamp, Steve Earle, Jeff Black

Allan Orski and Gary Graff

Sean Kelly
See: The Samples

Scott Kempner
See: The Del Lords

Eddie Kendricks
See: The Temptations

Kenickie
Formed 1994, in Sunderland, England.

Marie Du Santiago, guitar; Lauren Laverne, vocals, guitars; Emmy-Kate Montrose, bass; Johnny X, drums.

The British media were all over this band of 18-year-old college friends almost from the start—sometimes admittedly because of their looks and not the music. (The three leading Kenickie women, who wear leather pants and fishnets on stage, were compared favorably to the Spice Girls in an *Esquire* photo story not long after their major-label debut, *At the Club*, came out.) The music isn't bad, though, recalling early-'80s new wave such as Holly & the Italians (on the angry "Private Buchowski") and the Go-Go's (on the happy "People We Want"). Although *At the Club* has a thin, tinny sound, as if Du Santiago's guitars actually came from Toys "Я" Us and the vocals were recorded by 11-year-olds, it's consistently catchy and almost as rewarding as a good Muffs album. (More shrieking would help, though.)

what's available: *At the Club* ♪♪♪ (Warner Bros., 1997, prod. Andy Carpenter, John Cornfield, Peter Gofton) is an excellent debut for a young band, and it's possible the only thing preventing Kenickie from widespread pinup superstardom was the simultaneous rise of the Spice Girls. Kenickie has far more musical talent, however, with sharp, short, punk-derived songs and nice interplay between Laverne's vocals and Du Santiago's guitars. Still, they should ditch the bouncy electronic drums. The '80s are over.

influences:
◀◀ The Go-Go's, Holly & the Italians, the Muffs, the Pandoras, Oasis, Bow Wow Wow, Madonna

Steve Knopper

The Kennedys /Pete & Maura Kennedy
Formed as Pete Kennedy & Maura Boudreau, 1993, in Lubbock, TX.

Pete Kennedy (born February 9, 1952, in Arlington, VA), guitar, vocals; Maura Boudreau Kennedy (born October 25, 1963, in Syracuse, NY), guitar, vocals.

Pete Kennedy and Maura Boudreau met as members of Nanci Griffith's touring Blue Moon Orchestra; they soon paired off, both professionally and personally. Kennedy had already released a series of solo albums spotlighting his considerable acoustic guitar prowess, and Boudreau had been recognized as a talented singer and songwriter with her former group, the Delta Rays. Their first date was a visit to Buddy Holly's gravesite, and their first show was an opening slot for Griffith in Liverpool, England. They were married in 1994 and have continued to wow audiences around the world with the stunning vocal and instrumental approach they've dubbed "coffeehouse pop."

what to buy: Credited to Pete and Maura Kennedy, *River of Fallen Stars* ♪♪♪ (Green Linnet, 1995, prod. Pete Kennedy) is a thoroughly engaging collection of acoustic pop, with nearly every song a perfect, polished gem. The audio travelogue "Chelsea Embankment" takes a simple listing of London street names and makes it seem positively profound, just on the strength of the Kennedys' tuneful acumen. "Same Old Way," "Month of Hours," "Winterheart," and "Stephen's Green" likewise inspire a pleasant sense of music's inherent power, whether plugged or unplugged. A cover of Richard Thompson's "Wall of Death" provides a fitting reference point for the source of the Kennedys' considerable inspiration.

what to buy next: *Life Is Large* 𝄢𝄢𝄢 (Green Linnet, 1996, prod. Pete Kennedy) has a few too many guest stars (though it *is* an impressive list that includes Roger McGuinn, Steve Earle, Peter Holsapple, Nils Lofgren, Charlie Sexton, and Susan Cowsill), but it succeeds primarily on the strength of the Kennedys' own singin', playin', and songwritin' virtues. *Angel Fire* 𝄢𝄢𝄢𝄢 (Philo, 1998, prod. Kennedys) represents a return to the uncluttered charm of the duo's debut, with more great songs (particularly "Just like Henry David") and further proof of the enduring vitality of the Kennedys' patented brand of coffeehouse pop.

influences:

◀◀ The Beatles, Buddy Holly, Nanci Griffith, the Byrds, Gram Parsons, Richard Thompson, Gary Frenay

Carl Cafarelli

Nik Kershaw

Born Nicholas David Kershaw, 1958, in Bristol, Somerset, England.

The son of a classical musician and an opera singer, Nik Kershaw must have raised some eyebrows when he taught himself guitar as a teen and began playing in a Deep Purple cover band. Before long he'd moved on to jazz fusion and, later, pop. Following the breakup of a fusion band he'd recorded with, Kershaw signed to MCA Records in England and crafted a wonderful solo debut, showing off his penchant for inventive pop songwriting and production while enlisting such high-powered pals as Level 42 bassist Mark King. Though his first record failed to generate much interest, a 1984 follow-up, featuring a remixed version of the single "Wouldn't It Be Good" hit on both sides of the Atlantic, establishing Kershaw as a pop star. But subsequent albums didn't fare as well, prompting the singer-producer to craft tunes and albums for other artists, most notably Chesney Hawkes and his massive hit, "The One and Only."

what to buy: *Human Racing* 𝄢𝄢𝄢𝄢 (MCA, 1984, prod. Peter Collins) combines Kershaw's soaring vocal talents with ace production and inventive arrangements. Of particular interest is his simmering "Bogart," a tribute to Humphrey, and the percussion-packed "Drum Talk."

WHAT ALBUM CHANGED YOUR LIFE?

[*King of the Delta Blues Singers* by] Robert Johnson. It's just spooky, spiritual, sexual . . . Just something to always refer back to.

Paul Kelly

what to buy next: Gathering together all of the notable work from his too-short career as a solo artist, *Anthology* 𝄢𝄢𝄢 (One Way, 1995, prod. Peter Collins) serves as a great sampling of a quality pop songwriter who never found a steady audience.

what to avoid: As the album on which his muse began to flag, *Radio Musicola* **woof!** (MCA, 1986, prod. Peter Collins) has the unenviable distinction of being the first bit of evidence that Kershaw may have made the right move when he stepped out of the spotlight.

the rest:
The Riddle 𝄢𝄢𝄢𝄢 (MCA, 1984)
The Works 𝄢𝄢𝄢 (MCA, 1990)

worth searching for: Listen to Petula Clark's *Treasures, Vol. 1* (Scotti Bros., 1992, prod. various) and catch Kershaw singing backing vocals.

influences:

◀◀ Elton John, Gary Numan

▶▶ Chesney Hawkes

Eric Deggans

Kid Creole & the Coconuts /Dr. Buzzard's Original Savannah Band

Formed 1974, in New York, NY.

Kid Creole: Thomas August "Kid Creole" Darnell Browder, vocals; Andy "Coati Mundi" Hernandez, vibes, percussion (1980–87); Peter Schott, keyboards; Cheryl Poirier, vocals. Dr. Buzzard's Original Savannah Band: Stoney Browder Jr., guitar, piano (1974–79, 1984); Thomas August "Kid Creole" Darnell Browder, bass (1974–79);

Mickey Sevilla, drums (1974–79, 1984); Sugar Coated Andy Hernandez, vibes, marimba, accordion (1974–79); Corey Daye, vocals (1974–79, 1984); Don Armando Bonilla, percussion (1974–76); Mark Josephsberg, vibes (1984); Michael Almo, horns (1984); Roland Prince, guitars (1984); Michael Boone, bass (1984); Mark Radice, bass (1984).

Decades before swing music became hip again during the late 1990s, Dr. Buzzard's Original Savannah Band brought 1930s big band sounds to the disco era with a witty edge, scoring a hit with "Cherchez La Femme" on 1976's *Dr. Buzzard's Original Savannah Band*, and enjoyed moderate success for a few years. The group broke up in 1980, although it resurfaced in 1984, minus August Darnell and Andy Hernandez, for the badly conceived *Calling All Beatniks*. Kid Creole, on the other hand, based its sound in disco, with Latin and Caribbean rhythms added. That unique mixture was enhanced by Darnell's often tongue-in-cheek lyrics and his Caribbean Cab Calloway image, as well as the party hearty stage show featuring the beautiful Coconuts as backup singers and break dancing by Coati Mundi. With a sound that defies categorization, Kid Creole has more of a cult following than a widespread appeal, although the music itself presaged salsa's popularity in U.S. pop circles. The band enjoyed some greater exposure when it backed Barry Manilow on a cut from his 1987 release *Swing Street*, and it has been featured in the films *Against All Odds, Car 54 Where Are You,* and *The Forbidden Dance.* Darnell has also distinguished himself as a producer.

what to buy: *In Praise of Older Women and Other Crimes* 🎵🎵🎵🎵 (Sire, 1985, prod. August Darnell) finds the band in funky and fun form with "Endicott," a cry of independence from a henpecked husband and the group's best-known tune stateside. The cry becomes the coo of doo-wop on "Particul'y Interested," and soulful on "Name It." The band even takes a break from its usual party mode for musically successful stabs at social concerns on "Caroline Was a Dropout" and "Dowopsalsaboprock (We're Fighting Back)." In an earlier Caribbean party mode, *Wise Guy* 🎵🎵🎵 (Sire, 1982, prod. August Darnell) landed Top 10 hits in the U.K. with "Annie, I'm Not Your Daddy" and "I'm a Wonderful Thing, Baby."

what to buy next: Both of these bands feature strong musicianship and production, and *Dr. Buzzard's Original Savannah Band* 🎵🎵🎵🎵 (RCA, 1976, prod. Sandy Linzer) is a well-played, disco-style delight.

what to avoid: *Calling All Beatniks* **woof!** (Passport, 1984, prod. Sandy Linzer) features bad 1950s-style rock by Dr. Buzzard minus Darnell and Hernandez. It proves the fire in this group really came from Darnell.

the rest:
Kid Creole & the Coconuts:

Fresh Fruit in Foreign Places 🎵🎵🎵 (Sire, 1981)
Doppelganger 🎵🎵🎵🎵 (Sire, 1983)
I, Too, Have Seen the Woods 🎵🎵🎵 (Sire, 1987)
You Should Have Told Me You Were . . . 🎵🎵 (Columbia, 1991)
Kid Creole Redux 🎵🎵🎵🎵 (Sire, 1992)
To Travel Sideways 🎵🎵🎵 (Atoll, 1994)

Dr. Buzzard's Original Savannah Band:
Dr. Buzzard's Original Savannah Band Meets King Penett 🎵🎵🎵 (RCA, 1978)

worth searching for: *Off the Coast of Me* (Antilles, 1980, prod. August Darnell) is the transitional album from Dr. Buzzard to the Coconuts. The Kid steps out front with his humor, but he hasn't dropped the big band feel yet.

solo outings:
The Coconuts:
Don't Steal My Coconuts 🎵🎵🎵 (EMI, 1983)

influences:
◀◀ Machito & His Afro-Cubans, Cab Calloway, Ricky Ricardo
▶▶ Gloria Estefan, Buster Poindexter, Squirrel Nut Zippers

Lawrence Gabriel

Kid Rock

Born Bob Ritchie, January 17, 1971, in Dearborn, MI.

Bob Ritchie began rapping and DJing when he was the same age as most of his fans: in high school. Still, by his debut, the young rapper with the vertical hairdo had clearly already hit puberty, and many of his amusing songs matched Too $hort's in sex-crazed spirit. He eventually brought more of a rock 'n' roll sensibility and instrumentation into the mix, along with a raunchy, scatalogical brand of humor that recalls the early Beastie Boys.

what to buy: The highlight of the underappreciated *Grits Sandwiches for Breakfast* 🎵🎵🎵🎵 (Zomba/Jive/RCA, 1990, prod. Kid Rock, Mike Clark, Too $hort) is "Yo-Da-Lin in the Valley," a wickedly funny (and funky) song in which Rock doesn't really yodel but instead calls oral sex with a woman "a delicious break from potatoes." Elsewhere, the heavy bass and stop-start music of "New York's Not My Home" recalls *Raising Hell* and Run-D.M.C.

what to buy next: Proving why he's called Kid Rock and not Kid Rap, Rock kicks out the metallic jams on *The Polyfuze Method* 🎵🎵🎵 (Continuum, 1993, prod. Kid Rock, Mike Clark), including the hard-hitting single "You Don't Know Me."

the rest:
Fire It Up 🎵🎵 (Continuum, 1994)
Early Morning Stoned Pimp 🎵🎵🎵 (Top Dog, 1996)
Devil without a Cause 🎵🎵🎵🎵 (Lava/Atlantic, 1998)

influences:

◀◀ Beatie Boys, Too $hort

▶▶ Jesse Jaymes, Insane Clown Posse

Christina Fuoco

Greg Kihn

Born 1952, in Baltimore, MD.

A workmanline rock 'n' roller best regarded as a second-tier Bruce Springsteen or Tom Petty, Greg Kihn was part of the Beserkley Records scene after he moved from Baltimore to Berkeley, California, put down his acoustic guitar and troubadouring ambitions, and put together a band that rocked with true crunch and energy (and featured drummer Larry Lynch, brother of Petty's Heartbreakers skin-pounder Stan Lynch). The Greg Kihn Band won fans with its energetic performances, combining strong originals like "The Breakup Song (They Don't Write 'Em)" and "Happy Man" with can't-miss covers of Springsteen's "For You" and the outtake "Rendezvous." But the band hit big with the uncharacteristic "Jeopardy" in 1983, a dance track that was kept out of the Number One spot by Michael Jackson's "Beat It" and gave Kihn's crew its 15 minutes of MTV fame. Ultimately, Kihn's music deserves more recognition—and sales—than it got. He still occasionally performs although his main gig now is as a radio DJ in California.

what to buy: With most of his albums out of print, *Kihnsolidation: The Best of Greg Kihn* 𝄞𝄞𝄞 (Rhino, 1986, prod. various) is a generous 18-track collection with all the right tunes. It'll make you want more.

what to buy next: In that case, pick up the Kihn band's best studio outing, *Rockihnroll* 𝄞𝄞𝄞 (Beserkley/Son of Beserkley, 1981, prod. Matthew King Kaufman), which houses "The Breakup Song" and other crunchy pop gems. *The King Biscuit Flower Hour Presents Greg Kihn* 𝄞𝄞𝄞 (KBFH, 1996) captures the group's live acumen and features a guest appearance by Joe Satriani.

the rest:
Next of Kihn 𝄞𝄞𝄞 (Beserkley/Son of Beserkley, 1978)
Mutiny 𝄞𝄞 (Clean Cuts, 1994)
Horror Show 𝄞𝄞𝄞 (Clean Cuts, 1996)

worth searching for: The out-of-print *Unkihntrollable Live* (Rhino, 1989) offers another look at Kihn and the band in concert, this time with a guest shot by former Creedence Clearwater Revival drummer Doug Clifford.

influences:

◀◀ The Beatles, Tommy Roe, the Kingsmen, Bruce Springsteen, Jonathan Richman

▶▶ John Mellencamp, Social Distortion, Soul Asylum

Gary Graff

Steve Kilbey

See: The Church

Killah Priest

See: Wu-Tang Clan

Killing Joke

Formed 1979, in London, England.

Jaz Coleman, vocals, keyboards; Geordie (Walker), guitar, synthesizers; Youth (born Martin Glover), bass, vocals (1979–82, 1994–present); Guy Pratt, bass (1982); Paul Raven, bass (1983–88, 1990); Andy Rourke, bass (1988); Taff, bass (1988); Paul Ferguson, drums (1979–88); Martin Atkins, drums (1988, 1990).

Sounding like correspondents reporting on the Apocalypse, Killing Joke makes, to quote its debut single "War Dance," "music to march to." From the first notes of its eponymous 1980 debut album—an inexorably pulsing synthesizer tone that practically bored holes in listeners' skulls—this band announced that there was no more business as usual, that the old forms and methods had to be revised for harder times. Rather than using synthesizer as a soothing wash, Killing Joke uses the instrument as a rhythmic tool, combining those sounds with coldly abrasive guitar chords, simple, brutal drum beats, analytical yet passionate lyrics, and Jaz Coleman's rough, urgent vocals. Coming out of punk but aiming to make dance music, this influential band's secret talent is striking a balance between complexity and simplicity. Even when tarted up for the dance crowd, the menacing sound of this industrial originator is classic.

what to buy: *Killing Joke* 𝄞𝄞𝄞𝄞 (EG, 1980, prod. Killing Joke) is one of the purest visions in rock history, a staggering and revolutionary stripping away of all rock ornamentation, revealing the frightening skeleton underneath and then making it slamdance.

what to buy next: The comeback album *Extremities, Dirt, and Various Repressed Emotions* 𝄞𝄞𝄞 (Noise/BMG, 1990, prod. various) takes the heavy guitar inherent in the group's sound and places it in an anthemic rock context devoid of indulgence and flash.

what to avoid: *Outside the Gate* 𝄞 (EG, 1988, prod. Jaz Coleman, Geordie Walker) was ostensibly planned as a Coleman solo album and features just the singer, Geordie, and session drummer Jimmy Copley. It's full of bizarre, incohesive arrangements constructed with numerology.

the rest:
What's This For…! 𝄞𝄞𝄞 (EG, 1981)
Revelations 𝄞𝄞𝄞 (EG, 1982)
Birds of a Feather 𝄞𝄞𝄞 (EG, 1982)

Fire Dances ♪♪♥ (EG, 1983)
Night Time ♪♪♪♪ (EG, 1985)
Brighter Than a Thousand Suns ♪♪♪ (EG, 1987)
An Incomplete Collection 1980–85 ♪♪♪ (EG, 1990)
Laugh? I Nearly Bought One! ♪♪♪♪ (EG, 1992)
Pandemonium ♪♪♥ (Big Life/Zoo, 1994)
Wilful Days ♪♪♥ (Caroline Blue Plate, 1995)
BBC Live in Concert ♪♪♥ (ROIR/Windsong, 1995)
Democracy ♪♪♪♥ (Big Life/Zoo, 1996)

worth searching for: The out-of-print *Ha* (EG EP, 1982, prod. Killing Joke, Konrad Plank) provides a taste of live Killing Joke, including "War Dance." You'll have to go into the classical section to find Coleman's *Fanfare for the Millennium/Symphony No. 1 "Idavoll"* (RCA Victor/BMG Classics, 1996, prod. Chris Kimsey) as performed by the New Zealand Symphony Orchestra conducted by Peter Scholes. Unlike, say, Paul McCartney, Coleman really has the training needed to write classical music (without hiring "assistants" to do the orchestration and such, either). The fanfare is a five-minute piece; the main interest is the 52-minute symphony, which mixes a little modern rhythmic urgency with Romantic harmonic vocabulary, often recalling the serious Hollywood film scores of the '40 and '50s.

solo outings:
Jaz Coleman:
(With Anne Dudley) *Songs from the Victorious City* ♪ (China/TVT, 1991)

influences:

◀◀ Joy Division, Can, Kraftwerk

▶▶ nine inch nails, Nirvana, Ministry, Filter

Steve Holtje

Kindred Spirit
See: The Bangles

Albert King
Born April 25, 1923, in Indianola, MS. Died December 21, 1992, in Memphis, TN.

Never as well known as his like-named contemporary B.B., Albert King was nonetheless almost as big an influence. More rock guitarists—notably Jimi Hendrix, Cream-era Eric Clapton, and Stevie Ray Vaughan—have copped directly from King more than any other bluesman. Standing an imposing six feet five inches and weighing in at 250 pounds, the left-handed former bulldozer driver played with brute force, bending the strings on his upside-down Gibson Flying V with a ferocity that could be downright frightening. King made his first recordings during the early '50s and cut some fantastic sides for the Bobbin and King labels from 1959 to 1963, but he really hit his stride when he signed with Stax in 1966 and began working with Booker T. & the MG's and the Memphis Horns. His collaborations with them worked as well as they did because for all his toughness, King's music swung, a fact well-documented on the excellent live albums, where he re-captures the Stax albums' drive backed by a horn-less quartet. He was also a fantastic, if not particularly flexible, singer.

what to buy: The two-disc compilation *The Ultimate Collection* ♪♪♪♥ (Rhino, 1992, prod. various) offers a fine career overview. Any of the three live albums recorded at San Francisco's Fillmore West Auditorium during 1968 capture the full power of King onstage: *Live Wire/Blues Power* ♪♪♪♪ (Stax, 1968, prod. Al Jackson); *Wednesday Night in San Francisco* ♪♪♪♪ (Stax, 1990, prod. Al Jackson); and *Thursday Night in San Francisco* ♪♪♪♪ (Stax, 1990, prod. Al Jackson).

what to buy next: *I'll Play the Blues for You* ♪♪♪♪ (Stax, 1972, prod. Allen Jones, Henry Bush) includes the killer title track as well as "Little Brother," perhaps King's most tender moment. Soul-blues never got much better than this.

what to avoid: Some people got really excited when they discovered long-missing tapes of King jamming with John Mayall. Then Fantasy released *The Lost Session* ♪♪ (Stax, 1986) and it became painfully clear why the tapes got shoved into the warehouse in the first place.

best of the rest:
Years Gone By ♪♪♪♪ (Stax, 1969)
Lovejoy ♪♪♪♥ (Stax, 1970)
I Wanna Get Funky ♪♪♪ (Stax, 1973)
New Orleans Heat ♪♪♪♥ (Tomato, 1979)
Blues for Elvis ♪♪ (Stax, 1981)
Crosscut Saw: Albert King in San Francisco ♪♪♪♥ (Stax, 1983/1992)
I'm in a Phone Booth Baby ♪♪♥ (Stax, 1984)
Blues at Sunrise ♪♪♪♪ (Stax, 1988)

worth searching for: King's Stax debut, *Born under a Bad Sign* (Atlantic, 1967, prod. Al Jackson), while out of print, is an undisputed classic. Also awaiting CD reissue is *Let's Have a Natural Ball* (Modern Blues, 1989), which collects King's late '50s/early '60s sides backed by a hard-charging horn section.

influences:

◀◀ B.B. King, Jimmy Reed, T-Bone Walker

▶▶ Otis Rush, Eric Clapton, Jimi Hendrix, Stevie Ray Vaughan, Buddy Guy, Billy Gibbons, Joe Louis Walker, Kenny Wayne Shepherd

Alan Paul

B.B. King
Born September 16, 1925, near Itta Benna, MS.

No other blues artist has ever entered mainstream American culture quite like B.B. King. He is the only one to step inside from the commercial cold that has long been the bluesman's fate, to receive presidential citations and honorary degrees and star in commercials for the likes of McDonald's and Northwest Airlines. He has become so omnipresent that it's easy to forget why he's so revered: because he fundamentally changed the way the electric guitar is played. The roots of any blues-based electric guitarist can be traced back to B.B. King, whether they know it or not. King took single-string electric lead guitar playing, pioneered by Charlie Christian and T-Bone Walker, and coated it with Mississippi grit. The result was a highly personalized style—marked by stinging finger vibrato, incredible economy, and uncannily vocal-like phrasing—which had tremendous impact on every electric blues guitarist to follow, including Guy, Albert King, Freddie King, and Otis Rush. These players, in turn, inspired countless rock guitarists, notably Jimi Hendrix, Eric Clapton, and Stevie Ray Vaughan. The rest, as they say, is history.

what to buy: The emergence of King's groundbreaking style can be heard on *The Best of B.B. King, Vol. 1* ♪♪♪♪♪ (Flair/Virgin, 1991, compilation prod. Malcom Jones), an essential collection of '50s recordings that includes his original versions of standard-bearers such as "Three O'Clock Blues," "You Upset Me Baby," and "Five Long Years." King's vocal-like guitar playing is part and parcel of his rare ability to communicate intimately with an audience, a powerful rapport perfectly captured on *Live at the Regal* ♪♪♪♪♪ (MCA, 1971, prod. Johnny Pate), a document of a 1964 performance that is considered by many to be not only his finest recording, but the greatest album in all modern blues. This treasure-trove of sophisticated-yet-downhome music includes such staples as "It's My Own Fault," "Every Day I Have the Blues," and "Sweet Little Angel." *Completely Well* ♪♪♪♪ (MCA, 1969, prod. Bill Szymczyk) contains King's only Top-20 hit, "The Thrill Is Gone," and is solid through and through.

what to buy next: Sooner or later, you'll probably want the four-CD box set *King of the Blues* ♪♪♪♪♪ (MCA, 1992, prod. Andy McKaie), which provides an excellent summary of King's career. *Live at San Quentin* ♪♪♪♪ (MCA, 1990, prod. Trade Martin, Sidney Seidenberg) and *Deuces Wild* ♪♪♪♪ (MCA, 1998, prod. John Porter), which features duets with everyone from Eric Clapton to Maxwell, are King's best recent efforts, both showing that he's still got plenty of both sting in his vibrato and ideas in his head.

what to avoid: *B.B. King in London* ♪♪ (MCA, 1971, prod. Ed Michel, Joe Zagarino) is the usual pointless hook-the-blues-guy-up-with-well-meaning-rockers-who-love-him-but-can't-play-his-stuff-half-as-well-as-his-own-band exercise. Though his '70s and '80s records are often burdened by overproduction, King has not recorded an embarrassing album—and he's released more than fifty.

the rest:
Blues Is King ♪♪♪♪ (MCA, 1967)
Lucille ♪♪♪♪ (MCA, 1968)
The Electric B.B. King—His Best ♪♪♪♪ (MCA, 1968)
Live & Well ♪♪♪♪ (MCA, 1969)
Incredible Soul of B.B. King ♪♪♪♪ (MCA, 1970)
Indianola Mississippi Seeds ♪♪♪♪ (MCA, 1970)
Live in Cook County Jail ♪♪♪♪ (MCA, 1970)
Back in the Alley: The Classic Blues of B.B. King ♪♪♪♪ (MCA, 1973)
The Best of B.B. King ♪♪♪♪ (MCA, 1973)
To Know You Is to Love You ♪♪♪ (MCA, 1973)
Friends ♪♪♪ (MCA, 1974)
B.B. King and Bobby Bland: Together for the First Time Live ♪♪♪♪ (MCA, 1974)
Lucille Talks Back ♪♪♪♪ (MCA, 1975)
B.B. King & Bobby Bland: Together Again . . . Live ♪♪♪ (MCA, 1976)
King Size ♪♪♪♪ (MCA, 1977)
Midnight Believer ♪♪♪ (MCA, 1978)
Take It Home ♪♪ (MCA, 1979)
Live at Ole Miss ♪♪♪♪ (MCA, 1980)
Great Moments with B.B. King ♪♪♪ (MCA, 1981)
There Must Be a Better World Somewhere ♪♪♪♪♪ (MCA, 1981)
Love Me Tender ♪♪♪ (MCA, 1982)
Blues 'n' Jazz ♪♪♪ (MCA, 1983)
Six Silver Strings ♪♪♪ (MCA, 1985)
Do the Boogie: Early '50s Classics ♪♪♪♪♪ (Flair/Virgin, 1988)
King of the Blues 1989 ♪♪♪ (MCA, 1989)
There Is Always One More Time ♪♪♪♪ (MCA, 1991)
The Fabulous B.B. King ♪♪♪♪ (Flair/Virgin, 1991)
Singin' the Blues ♪♪♪♪ (Flair/Virgin, 1991)
Live at the Apollo ♪♪♪ (GRP, 1991)
Sweet Little Angel ♪♪♪♪ (Flair/Virgin, 1992)
Blues Summit ♪♪♪♪ (MCA, 1993)

worth searching for: Somewhere out there is a single CD that combines the seminal *Live at the Regal* with the nearly as good *Live in Cook County Jail* (MCA, 1984) that was taken off the market in favor of the individual CDs. The united volume, while sonically inferior to the later releases, is nothing less than blues bliss.

influences:

◄◄ Blind Lemon Jefferson, T-Bone Walker, Django Reinhardt, Lonnie Johnson, Clarence "Gatemouth" Brown

►► Buddy Guy, Eric Clapton, David Gilmour, Albert King, Otis Rush

Alan Paul

Ben E. King

Born September 23, 1938, in Henderson, NC.

With its reverberating, four-note bass line, "Stand by Me" is a

Hall of Fame song before Ben E. King even starts singing. But when he wraps his smooth tenor around the lyrics, it becomes a hymn for the ages. It's one of the most covered songs on the planet, and it enjoys regular boosts in popularity thanks to TV commercials and movies—most notably Rob Reiner's 1986 film of the same name. It's hardly all King has to offer, though. As one of the many fine lead singers in the Drifters' revolving door of frontmen, he sang lead on "There Goes My Baby," "Save the Last Dance for Me," and "I Count the Tears," and his solo career boasts "Spanish Harlem" and a handful of other pop-R&B gems.

what to buy: *The Ben E. King Anthology* ♪♪♪♪ (Rhino, 1993, prod. various) covers all the aforementioned—plus non-album singles—across a remastered, double-length, and nicely annotated package. *The Very Best of Ben E. King* ♪♪♪♪ (Rhino, 1998, prod. various) is more brief, but equally fine.

what to avoid: *The Best of Ben E. King* ♪ (Curb, 1993) and *The Best of Ben E. King & the Drifters* ♪ (Dominion, 1993) are inferior to the *Anthology* and the *Very Best*.

the rest:
The Ultimate Collection ♪♪♪ (Atlantic, 1987)

influences:
◄◄ The Drifters, Sam Cooke, Chuck Jackson

►► Ted Hawkins, Paul Rodgers, Bruce Springsteen, Terence Trent D'Arby

Allan Orski

Carole King
Born Carole Klein, February 9, 1942, in Brooklyn, NY.

Given pop music's far-flung scope and ever-changing tastes, Carole King's accomplishments are nothing short of extraordinary. As a veteran of the Brill Building song factory, writing with her then-husband Gerry Goffin and on her own, King came up with some of the most memorable hits in pop history. From deft romantic ballads as realistic as they were heartfelt came songs such as "Take Good Care of My Baby," "Up on the Roof," "Crying in the Rain," and "Will You Love Me Tomorrow?" The British Invasion and a generation's mood swing didn't slow the tide. "Don't Bring Me Down," "I'm into Something Good," "I Wasn't Born to Follow," and "Pleasant Valley Sunday" circumnavigated a field of what were career-ending land mines for other songwriters. As an artist in her own right, King recorded the landmark *Tapestry* album, one of the longest-running records on the *Billboard* charts, and deservedly so. Since that album, her career has been more low-key, but she's still regarded as a master songwriter and always-engaging performer.

what to buy: Her third release, *Tapestry* ♪♪♪♪ (Ode, 1971, prod. Lou Adler), is a benchmark recording for King and for pop music. With her earnest yet vulnerable vocals, a fluid backup band, and Adler's sure production, *Tapestry* combined a bit of classic King material ("(You Make Me Feel like) a Natural Woman," "Will You Love Me Tomorrow?") with new, self-assured songs such as "I Feel the Earth Move," "So Far Away," "It's Too Late," and "Home Again." The album was on the charts, deservedly, for more than five years. *A Natural Woman: The Ode Collection 1968–1976* ♪♪♪♪ (Legacy, 1994/1998, prod. Lou Adler) is a two-disc set that surrounds *Tapestry* with King's better solo work and a previously unreleased live duet with James Taylor on "You've Got a Friend."

what to buy next: *City Streets* ♪♪♪ (Capitol, 1989) is an unjustifiably overlooked effort, with King unhesitatingly delivering her most powerful and passionate vocals ever. Eric Clapton guests, and the title track is a killer.

what to avoid: *Fantasy* ♪♪ (Ode, 1973/Legacy, 1991) and *Rhymes and Reason* ♪♪ (Ode, 1972/Legacy 1991) go nowhere in the slow lane.

the rest:
Carole King: Writer ♪♪♪ (Ode, 1970/Legacy, 1991)
Music ♪♪♪ (Ode, 1971/Legacy, 1991)
Wrap around Joy ♪♪ (Ode, 1974/Legacy, 1991)
Really Rosie ♪♪♪ (Ode, 1975/Columbia, 1986)
Thoroughbred (Ode/Legacy, 1976)
Her Greatest Hits (1972–1978) ♪♪♪ (Ode/Columbia, 1978)
In Concert ♪♪♪ (King's X/Rhythm Safari, 1994)
The Carnegie Hall Concert ♪♪♪ (Legacy, 1996)

worth searching for: King's first band, the City, stepped out front and center with her reflective debut *Now That Everything's Been Said* (Ode, 1968). Overlooked but not forgotten, it was as careful as it was an appropriate first recording for King.

influences:
◄◄ Doc Pomus, Mort Shuman

►► Carly Simon, Tori Amos, Bonnie Hayes

Patrick McCarty

Dee Dee King
See: The Ramones

Freddie King
Born September 30, 1934, in Gilmer, TX. Died December 28, 1976, in Dallas, TX.

Not possessing the towering presence on ghetto jukeboxes of his namesake B.B. King or the sweeping influence of his Chicago blues elders Muddy Waters and Howlin' Wolf, Freddie

King nevertheless eventually emerged as one of the great electric bluesmen. His melodic, driving shuffles struck a resonant chord with a younger generation of white blues-rock guitarists who passed around his rare, out-of-print albums like sacred scriptures. His 1961 instrumental hit "Hideaway" provided King with a nationwide reputation, although none of his subsequent singles appeared on even the R&B charts after that year. But the blues boom of the late '60s rescued him from obscurity, and he made a pair of modest albums under the aegis of saxophonist King Curtis and a series of more successful albums produced by Leon Russell. His stinging attack on loping instrumentals laid one of the cornerstones of modern blues guitar vocabulary. Although his reputation rests with his guitar, King also sang with an underrated, powerful style. King's lasting influence has led to his recognition as one of the great post-war blues masters.

what to buy: The best available overview of his long career, *Hideaway: The Best of Freddie King* 𝄢𝄢𝄢 (Rhino, 1993, compilation prod. James Austin) includes three cuts from his later recordings but concentrates on the fruitful abundance of his King Records years (1961–66).

what to buy next: A recently discovered tape, *Live at the Electric Ballroom 1974* 𝄢𝄢𝄢 (Black Top, 1995, executive prod. Hammond Scott) mixes a rare pair of acoustic numbers recorded at a radio show with a blasting, ripping concert appearance.

what to avoid: The two albums King recorded with the customarily savvy King Curtis, *Freddie King Is a Blues Master* 𝄢𝄢 (Cotillion, 1969/Atlantic, 1992) and *My Feeling for the Blues* 𝄢𝄢 (Cotillion, 1970/Atlantic, 1992), both lean heavily on thin accompaniment, little guitar, and reedy vocals.

the rest:
Let's Hideaway and Dance Away 𝄢𝄢𝄢 (King, 1961/1994)
Getting Ready 𝄢𝄢𝄢 (Shelter, 1971/The Right Stuff, 1996)
Texas Cannonball 𝄢𝄢𝄢 (Shelter, 1972/The Right Stuff, 1996)
Woman across the River 𝄢𝄢𝄢 (Shelter, 1973/The Right Stuff, 1996)
1934–1976 𝄢𝄢𝄢 (Polydor, 1977/1993)
17 Hits 𝄢𝄢𝄢 (Federal, 1987)
Texas Sensation 𝄢𝄢𝄢 (Charly, 1988)
Just a Pickin' 𝄢𝄢𝄢 (Modern Blues, 1989)
Live at the Texas Opry House 𝄢𝄢 (Collectables, 1992)
Blues Guitar Hero: The Early Years 𝄢𝄢𝄢 (Ace, 1993)
Live at Liberty Hall 𝄢𝄢𝄢 (Blue Moon, 1993)
Live in Germany 𝄢𝄢𝄢 (King Biscuit, 1993)
Let the Good Times Roll 𝄢𝄢𝄢 (Wolf, 1994)
Key to the Highway 𝄢𝄢𝄢 (Wolf, 1995)
King of the Blues 𝄢𝄢𝄢 (EMI, 1995)
Swamp Boogie 𝄢𝄢 (Orleans, 1995)
Mojo Blues 𝄢𝄢 (Collectables, 1995)
All His Hits 𝄢𝄢𝄢 (King, 1996)

Boogie on Down 𝄢𝄢𝄢 (Ace, 1997)

worth searching for: All of his original King Records albums remain highly prized collector's items, but his especially enduring debut, *Freddy King Sings* (King, 1961), is one of the great modern blues albums and was remixed and released for the first time in stereo on CD by Modern Blues Recordings during 1989.

influences:
◀◀ Otis Rush, Eddie Taylor, Robert Jr. Lockwood
▶▶ Eric Clapton, Jimi Hendrix, Stevie Ray Vaughan

Joel Selvin and Ken Burke

Sid King & the Five Strings
Formed 1952, in Denton, TX. Disbanded 1958.

Sid King (born Sid Erwin, October 15, 1936, in Denton, TX), vocals, guitar; Billy King (born Billy Erwin), lead guitar; Mel Robinson, steel guitar, sax; Ken Massey, bass; Dave White, drums, vocals.

It's all too easy to say rock 'n' roll was invented on Sam Phillips's studio floor the day Elvis crossed Bill Monroe with Arthur Crudup. In truth, during the postwar years the Southland was positively teeming with musical visionaries blindly adapting what they'd hear on late-night "race radio" to their daytime C&W pursuits. As early as 1952, KDNT out of Dallas was sponsoring a show featuring one such combo busy mixing Lefty Frizzell with Fats Domino. Named the Western Melody Makers, the group's brave devotion to R&B—highly unusual for a Texas band at the time—won them a contract with the then-fledgling Starday label in 1953. Their lone release, a bizarre Harry Gibson parody titled "Who Put the Turtle In Myrtle's Girdle?," not surprisingly failed to garner much airplay. But it did bring the band, newly rechristened Sid King & the Five Strings, to the attention of Don Law and Columbia Records. Over the next three years, they cut dozens of sides together, running the gamut from Western Swing to what would soon be called rockabilly, including historic early versions of "Blue Suede Shoes" and "Ooby Dooby" as well as several original compositions of unusual merit. Although their startling originality probably did more to harm than help sales and airplay at the time, to hear this material today is revelatory. Under Law's firm but lenient hand, the Five Strings were free to indulge their every musical whim, from Hank and Elvis to the Drifters, Spike Jones, and beyond, and the body of work they created is without equal in both its polish and its perversity. However, it was most likely this very eccentricity—which caused confusion and ultimately indifference among the record-buying public, to say nothing of Columbia's top brass—that eventually led to the band's unfortunate, inevitable dissolution. The King brothers then spent several years touring with Sonny James and Buddy Knox, and even cut a single for Dot Records (a deal made possible due to the kind-heartedness of Sid's pal, Pat Boone). When not tending to their barber shop in Richardson, Texas, they continue to perform to this day, recently touring the Orient fronting a Japanese rockabilly band called the Rollin' Rocks.

what's available: The exemplary *Gonna Shake This Shack Tonight* 🎵🎵🎵🎵 (Bear Family, 1991, compilation prod. Sid King, Richard Weize) contains literally every note the Five Strings recorded, including the initial Columbia A-side, King's own "I Like It," which sounds as if Frank Zappa had hijacked a Bob Wills session.

worth searching for: *Rockin' on the Radio* (Schoolkids', 1996) presents two live broadcasts from 1954 and 1955 that fully capture the evolution of the Five Strings' sound from accomplished Western cut-ups to trail-blazing proto-rockabillies. *Let's Get Loose* (Rockhouse, 1987, prod. Jim Colegrove) contains an interesting selection of cuts recorded in 1979 and 1980 by the King Brothers & Friends—ironically just as the rockabilly revival was about to rear its immaculately coiffed head.

influences:

◄◄ Milton Brown, Dewey Phillips, Bill Haley

►► Buddy & Bob, Merrill Moore, Commander Cody, Ray Condo & His Ricochets

Gary Pig Gold

King Crimson

Formed 1969, in London, England.

Robert Fripp, guitar, mellotron; Ian McDonald, keyboards, woodwinds (1969); Greg Lake, bass, vocals (1969); Michael Giles, drums; Peter Sinfield, lyricist (1969–72); Mel Collins, woodwinds (1971–72); Boz Burrell, bass, vocals (1971–72); Ian Wallace, drums (1971–72); David Cross, violin, viola, mellotron (1972–74); John Wetton, bass, vocals (1972–74); Bill Bruford, drums (1972–74, 1981–84, 1994–present); Jamie Muir, percussion, (1972–73); Richard Palmer-James, lyricist (1972–74); Adrian Belew, vocals, guitar, lyricist (1981–84, 1994–present); Tony Levin, Chapman Stick, bass, vocals (1981–84, 1994–present); Trey Gunn, guitar, bass (1994–present); Pat Mastelotto, drums (1994–present).

The band that almost gave art rock a good name, King Crimson grew out of a trio that couldn't sell more than 600 copies of its only album in its own country. Brothers Michael and Peter Giles teamed with young guitarist Robert Fripp in Giles Giles & Fripp, whose 1968 album *The Cheerful Insanity of Giles Giles & Fripp* was a legendary flop. Musically more than a historical footnote but less than a revolution, the band's whimsical social commentary sounds too much of its time to be taken seriously.

When Peter Giles chose to work as a computer operator (though he would continue playing sporadically), Greg Lake joined up with Michael Giles, Fripp, and new members Ian McDonald and Peter Sinfield. The new group's debut far surpassed its predecessor's. After one concert, audience member Jimi Hendrix asked Fripp to shake his left hand because it was the one closer to his heart. *In the Court of the Crimson King* showed that progressive rock could be as heavy as Led Zeppelin yet as intricate and full of dynamic contrasts as classical music (the howling, bludgeoning "21st-Century Schizoid Man" was the first of many Crimson classics in unusual time signatures) and sometimes as tuneful as the Beatles. King Crimson has pursued an ideology of musical adventure ever since, through myriad lineup changes and musical personalities. The group works and breaks at Fripp's whim—a formidable calling due to his many other musical projects. Currently, King Crimson is a six-piece "double trio" that performs in various configurations. There certainly are less-than-ideal aspects to the Crimson legacy; for instance, Fripp, by his preference for vocalists who also carry a heavy instrumental load, has consistently burdened the band with unsubtle singers and has seemed content to let the lyrics pursue the writers' fancies no matter how ephemeral or ridiculous. But the instrumental legacy is generally irreproachable, involving a willingness to explore new territory and take risks that most comparably successful bands shun. As part of that quest, near the end of 1997 Fripp and the current six-man lineup began working in smaller groups, which he calls both Fractals and Projekcts. This allows the musicians to explore musical territory beyond the expectations attached to Crimson albums.

what to buy: *In the Court of the Crimson King* 🎵🎵🎵🎵 (Atlantic, 1969/EG, 1989, prod. King Crimson) was immensely influential and stands up well, with "21st-Century Schizoid Man" the best-known highlight. The sonic juggernaut *Red* 🎵🎵🎵🎵 (Atlantic, 1974/EG, 1989, prod. King Crimson) is the definitive studio statement by the most powerful Crimson lineup (Fripp, John Wetton, and Bill Bruford, plus guests). On *Discipline* 🎵🎵🎵🎵 (Warner Bros./EG, 1981, prod. King Crimson, Rhett Davies) the Adrian Belew lineup reinvented the group's principles in lither form. With these albums, the listener has the best of the three most important configurations.

what to buy next: *The Great Deceiver* 🎵🎵🎵🎵 (Caroline, 1992, prod. Robert Fripp) offers a live, four-CD cross-section of the most versatile and wonderfully bombastic band (the 1973–74 lineup) ever to command silence with passages for violin and mellotron and then blow minds with relentless crescendos. An entire 1973 concert in Amsterdam, not included in the above set, makes up the two-CD *The Nightwatch* 🎵🎵🎵🎵 (Discipline Global Mobile, 1997, prod. Robert Fripp), which also includes

CD-ROM material. The best summary of the group's history is *The Essential King Crimson: Frame by Frame* 𝄞𝄞𝄞𝄞 (Caroline, 1991, prod. various), which includes not only a chronological review over three CDs (including previously unreleased or revamped material), but also a fourth CD of live material. The original 1969 lineup—Fripp's personal favorite and in some ways the most innovative—has four concert appearances compiled on the two-CD *Epitaph* 𝄞𝄞𝄞𝄞 (Discipline Global Mobile, 1997, prod. Robert Fripp, David Singleton), with an additional two CDs of two other 1969 gigs available only from DGM's mail order division. Fripp provides detailed liner notes for all four sets.

what to avoid: *The Abbreviated King Crimson* 𝄞 (EG/Caroline, 1991, prod. various), *The Compact King Crimson* 𝄞𝄞 (EG/Caroline, 1987, prod. various), and *The Concise King Crimson* 𝄞𝄞 (Blue Plate/Caroline, 1993, prod. various) are all made superfluous by the vastly better *Frame by Frame*.

the rest:
The Cheerful Insanity of Giles Giles & Fripp 𝄞𝄞 (Deram/London, 1968/1992)
In the Wake of Poseidon 𝄞𝄞𝄞𝄞 (Atlantic, 1970/EG, 1989)
Lizard 𝄞𝄞 (Atlantic, 1971/EG, 1989)
Islands 𝄞𝄞 (Atlantic, 1972/EG, 1989)
Lark's Tongues in Aspic 𝄞𝄞𝄞𝄞 (Atlantic, 1973/EG, 1989)
Starless and Bible Black 𝄞𝄞𝄞 (Atlantic, 1974/EG, 1989)
Beat 𝄞𝄞𝄞 (Warner Bros./EG, 1982)
Three of a Perfect Pair 𝄞𝄞𝄞 (Warner Bros./EG, 1984)
VROOM 𝄞𝄞𝄞 (Discipline EP, 1994)
B'Boom 𝄞𝄞𝄞 (Discipline, 1995)
Thrak 𝄞𝄞𝄞 (Virgin, 1995)
Thrak Attack 𝄞𝄞𝄞𝄞 (Discipline, 1996)
Absent Lovers 𝄞𝄞𝄞𝄞 (DGM, 1998)

worth searching for: The five live 1972 performances on the rare LP *Earthbound* (EG, 1972, prod. Robert Fripp) are sometimes overindulgent and the sound can be clotted, but it documents a somewhat overlooked lineup of Fripp, Mel Collins, Boz Burrell, and Ian Wallace. It's unlikely to appear on CD as Fripp personally fought to have it withdrawn from print. Only one track of the concert in New York City's Central Park captured on *USA* (Atlantic, 1975, prod. King Crimson) made it onto *Frame by Frame*, not nearly enough for a powerful lineup's final live appearance.

solo outings:
David Cross:
Exiles 𝄞𝄞𝄞 (Purple Pyramid, 1997)

Projekct Two (Fripp, Belew, Gunn):
Space Groove 𝄞𝄞𝄞 (Discipline, 1998)

influences:
◄◄ Jimi Hendrix, the Beatles, John McLaughlin

►► Foreigner, U.K., Helmet, Porcupine, No Man, Iceburn, Living Colour, His Name Is Alive

see also: *Robert Fripp, Emerson, Lake & Palmer, Bad Company, Adrian Belew, Yes*

Steve Holtje

King Curtis

Born Curtis Ousley, February 7, 1934, in Ft. Worth, TX. Died August 14, 1971, in New York, NY.

Although he only achieved sporadic fame on his own, King Curtis probably was the most influential rock/R&B saxophone player of his time. He began playing in Texas during the '40s, hooked up with Lionel Hampton in 1952, and later became one of New York's most desired session players. As leader of Atlantic Records' house R&B band, Curtis played some of the most famous sax breaks in pop music, among them the Coasters' "Yakety Yak" and Aretha Franklin's "Respect." He also played for Nat King Cole, Buddy Holly, Sam Cooke, and John Lennon and briefly roomed with Duane Allman. But Curtis, who came from the tradition of hard-blowing Texas blues saxophonists, also had his own hits. Three of his instrumental records reached the Top 40: "Soul Twist" in 1962 and "Memphis Soul Stew" and "Ode to Billie Joe" in 1967. Curtis died when he was only 37, stabbed to death outside his New York City apartment in 1971.

what to buy: *Instant Soul: The Legendary King Curtis* 𝄞𝄞𝄞𝄞 (Razor & Tie, 1994) is an excellent compilation that covers the

years from 1956 to 1970 but concentrates on the recordings he made with the Muscle Shoals Rhythm Section. The 23 tracks include all three of his Top-40 hits.

what to buy next: During the session captured on *King Curtis & Champion Jack Dupree: Blues at Montreux* ♫♫♫♪ (Atlantic, 1973, prod. King Curtis, Joel Dorn), Curtis is at his loosest, with a band that includes Cornell Dupree on guitar and Jerry Jemmott on bass.

what to avoid: *Soul on Soul* ♫♫ (Pickwick, 1972), a cheapie posthumous compilation from Curtis's Capitol period, was issued as part of Pickwick's "Harlem Hitparade" series. *The Best of King Curtis* ♫♫ (Collectables, 1989) doesn't nearly cover the claim of its title.

the rest:
The New Scene of King Curtis ♫♫♫ (Prestige, 1960/New Jazz, 1992)
Soul Meeting ♫♫♫ (Prestige, 1960/1995)
Trouble in Mind ♫♫♫ (Tru-Sound, 1961/Fantasy/OBC, 1988)
Soul Twist & Other Golden Classics ♫♫♫ (Collectables, 1991)
Enjoy . . . the Best of King Curtis ♫♫♪ (Collectables, 1991)
Didn't He Play ♫♫ (Drive, 1995)
Night Train ♫♫♫ (Prestige, 1995)
Old Gold/Doing the Dixie Twist ♫♫♫ (Ace, 1995)
Trouble in Mind/It's Party Time ♫♫♫ (Ace, 1995)
The Best of King Curtis ♫♫♫ (Blue Note, 1996)
Groovin' with the King: Best of King Curtis ♫♫♫ (AIM, 1996)

worth searching for: *Live at the Fillmore West* (Atco, 1971, prod. King Curtis, Arif Mardin) captures a hot set when Curtis opened a Bay Area stand for Franklin, who was recording her own live album of the same name. The three-disc box set *Blow Man, Blow!* (Bear Family, 1992) compiles Curtis's recordings for Capitol from 1962 to 1965 and includes 16 previously unreleased tracks.

influences:

◀◀ Illinois Jacquet, Earl Bostic, Arnett Cobb

▶▶ Junior Walker, Maceo Parker, Clarence Clemons

Brian Mansfield

King Missile

Formed 1986, in New York, NY. Disbanded 1994. Re-formed 1997.

John S. Hall, vocals; Dogbowl, guitar (1987–88); Dave Rick, guitar (1990–94); Chris Xefos, bass, keyboards (1990–94); Roger Murdock, drums (1990–94).

There are often references to rock lyrics being the new poetry, but rarely in the past have poets fronted bands. The viewpoint of poet John S. Hall (the middle initial differentiates him from the mellow-rock guitarist of the '70s), with his skewed yet peculiarly logical method of taking everyday situations or metaphors to extreme conclusions, fits well in front of a band, however, and

for a while he was the most visible point in a trend reversing that situation. The stop-start punkish riff tunes constructed by the musicians should not be underrated merely because Hall is perceived as the focus of the group, since it was actually quite collaborative. Starting out as a duo named King Missile (Dog Fly Religion) with Dogbowl on the local Shimmy Disc label of producer Kramer, King Missile—the name comes from a Japanese comic book character—mutated into a quartet and had a college radio hit with "Jesus Was Way Cool" (from 1990's *Mystical Shit*) that led Atlantic to sign it. King Missile broke up after three more albums when Atlantic dropped it. For a while Hall led a new group, the Body Has a Head, with string players Sasha Forte and Jane Scarpantoni, and Roger Murdock drummed with the ironic country group the Wright Brothers, among others. In 1997 a fourth member was added to the Body Has a Head and the result was called King Missile III.

what to buy: *Happy Hour* ♫♫♫♫ (Atlantic, 1992, prod. Kramer, Steve Watson, King Missile) contains the band's best melding of music and words, including the college radio favorites "Detachable Penis" and "Martin Scorsese."

what to buy next: *The Way to Salvation* ♫♫♫♫ (Atlantic, 1991, prod. King Missile, Lou Giordano) covers a broad topical and attitudinal range, including a cover of Richard Hell & the Voidoids' "Betrayal Takes Two." The best-known tracks are "My Heart Is a Flower" (which demolishes a sappy metaphor by carrying it to its logical extreme) and "Sex with You."

what to avoid: For *Real Men* ♫♫♪ (Shimmy Disc, 1991, prod. Kramer) Kramer took tapes of Hall reading and, without the poet's further participation, played whatever he wanted behind him. It's not a bad album, but the words are a lot more interesting than the sounds.

the rest:
They ♫♫♫ (Shimmy Disc, 1988)
Mystical Shit/Fluting on the Hump ♫♫♫♪ (Shimmy Disc, 1990/1987)
King Missile ♫♫♫ (Atlantic, 1994)
Failure N/A (Shimmy Disc, 1998)

worth searching for: The various-artists compilation *Broome Closet Anti-Folk Sessions* (109, 1989, prod. Roger Manning) contains five Hall poems, some later used by King Missile. The promotional EP *Happy 14 ½* (Atlantic, 1992, prod. Kramer, King Missile) was issued in advance of *Happy Hour* and includes "Detachable Penis," a PG-13 version of the otherwise F-word-filled "Martin Scorsese," and three non-album tracks, including a live version of the notorious "The Bunny Song."

influences:

◀◀ Bob Holman, Allan Ginsberg

▶▶ Maggie Estep

Steve Holtje

King Sunny Ade
/The African Beats

Born Sunday Adeniyi, September 22, 1946, in Ohogbo, Nigeria.

Guitarist-vocalist King Sunny Ade is the most widely acclaimed juju musician outside of Africa and the first to be signed to a major international label. The term "tapestry of sound" was made for his band, with its six guitars, seven vocalists, and eight percussionists, in addition to bass and keyboards. Ade arranges this orchestra into a soothing symphony that rides smooth rhythms and drifting melodies. First appearing in the 1920s, juju is a Yoruban folk music that features interplay between vocals and talking drums. I.K. Cairo is the greatest juju musician to date, with Chief Ebenezer Obey and Ade rivals for second place. Ade's own innovation includes adding pedal steel guitar and synthesizers to the music, making it slightly more listener-friendly to Western pop ears. Beginning with his first band, the Green Spots, in 1966, bandleader Ade was soon known as a guitar virtuoso with a space sound and a "shooting strings" technique of staccato chord strokes. In 1974 he started his own record label, Sunny Alade, renamed his band the African Beats, and put out 40 albums over the next decade. In 1982 the group signed with Island Records, which promoted Ade as a world music star to replace the late Bob Marley; after disappointing record sales he was dropped in 1984. Due to dissension in the ranks, Ade reorganized his band into the New African Beats. He's still a top international draw, and in Nigeria he regularly sells 200,000 of his releases.

what to buy: *Juju Music* 𝄢𝄢𝄢𝄢 (Mango, 1982, prod. Martin Meissonnier) is Ade's first international release and the one that opened the world's ears to juju. The dreamy, mesmerizing groove of "Ja Funmi" sets the tone for this exotic musical journey culled from Ade's past hits. Lightly chiming guitars, bubbling talking drums, ethereal pedal steel, and Ade's soothing voice weave in and out of this delightfully different sound. *Synchro System* 𝄢𝄢𝄢𝄢 (Mango, 1983, prod. Martin Meissonnier) finds the band in the same mode as the previous record, but the guitars are mixed down and the newly added synthesizer provides more sonic tricks.

what to buy next: *Live at the Hollywood Palace* 𝄢𝄢𝄢 (I.R.S., 1994, prod. King Sunny Ade) features the New African Beats at a 1990 show where the group kicked things off with a couple of upbeat Latin-sounding songs before moving into the polyrhythmic space groove. The closer, "Talking Drum," is an absolute clinic on the instrument.

the rest:
Aura 𝄢𝄢𝄢 (Mango, 1984)
The Return of the Juju King 𝄢𝄢𝄢 (Verbe, 1987)
Live Juju Live 𝄢𝄢𝄢 (Rykodisc, 1988)
E Dide (Get Up) 𝄢𝄢𝄢 (Mesa, 1995)
Odu 𝄢𝄢𝄢 (Atlantic, 1998)

worth searching for: *Ajoo* (Makossa International, 1983, prod. King Sunny Ade) was originally released on Ade's own Sunny Alade label for the Nigerian market and displays a less flashy but satisfying side of the band.

influences:
◄◄ I.K. Dairo, Tunde Nightingale

►► Segun Adewale, Kotoja, Johnny Clegg, Peter Gabriel

Lawrence Gabriel

King's X

Formed in 1980, in Springfield, MO.

Doug Pinnick, bass, vocals; Ty Tabor, guitar, vocals; Jerry Gaskill, drums, vocals.

Initially convening as a cover band called the Edge, the trio moved to Houston and eventually hooked up with ZZ Top video producer Sam Taylor, who renamed the group King's X. Its combination of heavy metal instrumentation, Beatle-esque vocal harmonies, and pro-Christian lyrics found little support at major record labels, forcing the band to issue its first record on the New Jersey–based independent Megaforce Records. Before long, the skin-tight musicianship and inventive songs began converting critics and fans alike. But King's X seemed determined to resist any easy route to success; during the metal boom the band resisted that classification, and during the boom in Christian music it avoided that tag as well. In a last-ditch attempt to break the band, Atlantic Records drafted superstar producer Brendan O'Brien (Pearl Jam) to craft its 1995 release, a matchup that produced another great album, but no hits.

what to buy: Among longtime fans, the group's sophomore album, *Gretchen Goes to Nebraska* 𝄢𝄢𝄢𝄢 (Megaforce, 1989, prod. King's X, Sam Taylor) is often cited as its finest, focusing its pop melodicism and hard rock musicality into a potent stew. With a fiery take on Fleetwood Mac's "Over My Head" and the supple ballad "Summertime," this record seemed to forecast a band with significant artistic strides ahead.

what to buy next: Although some will say O'Brien filed off the group's rough edges, *Dogman* 𝄢𝄢𝄢 (Atlantic, 1994, prod. Brendan O'Brien) presents a further refinement of the band's pop/metal sound, with the religious messages sublimated ever further in a refreshing, stripped-down sound. Still, that doesn't keep crackling midtempo cuts such as "Let's Pretend" or "Black the Sky" from rocking hard, along with a live recording of Jimi Hendrix's "Manic Depression."

what to avoid: Some bands take awhile to hit their stride, and King's X first album, *Out of the Silent Planet* **woof!** (Megaforce, 1982, prod. King's X, Sam Taylor), shows it's no different.

the rest:
Faith, Hope, and Love 🎵🎵🎵 (Megaforce, 1990)
King's X 🎵🎵🎵 (Atlantic, 1992)
Ear Candy 🎵🎵🎵 (Atlantic, 1996)
Best of King's X 🎵🎵🎵 (Atlantic, 1997)

worth searching for: One of the few bright spots on the soundtrack to the 1991 film *Bill and Ted's Bogus Journey* (Interscope/EastWest, 1991) is King's X's contribution, "Junior's Gone Wild."

influences:
◀◀ Living Colour, Petra, the Beatles

▶▶ Eye & I, Follow for Now

Eric Deggans

The Kingsmen

Formed 1958, in Portland, OR. Disbanded 1967.

Lynn Eaton, vocals, saxophone; Jack Ely, vocals, guitar (1958–63); Mike Mitchell, guitar; Bob Nordby, bass (1958–63); Don Gallucci, organ (1962); Gary Abbot, drums (1963–67); Norm Sundholm, bass (1963–67).

Think one name two times: "Louie Louie." What the *I Love Lucy* television series is to reruns, the Kingsmen's 1963 smash hit, recorded for just $50, is to oldies radio and shag/frat/beach parties. Both are ubiquitous; written by Richard Berry in 1956 and covered by countless bands, the Kingsmen's rendition remains the one that anyone cares about. That said, the band *did* land other Top 20 hits, such as "Money" in 1964 and "The Jolly Green Giant" in 1965.

what to buy: *The Best of the Kingsmen* 🎵🎵🎵🎵 (Rhino, 1991, prod. various) includes all the hits—yes, even "Louie Louie"—and provides a surprisingly clean sound, with Jack Ely's usually muffled vocals sounding clearer than usual.

what to buy next: Though not as thorough or well-packaged as the Rhino set, other solid Kingsmen collections (almost all containing you-know-what) include *Best of the Kingsmen* 🎵🎵🎵 (Laserlight, 1995, prod. various), *Greatest Hits* 🎵🎵🎵 (K-Tel, 1998, prod. various), *Louie Louie and More Golden Classics* 🎵🎵🎵 (Collectables, 1993, prod. various), and *Very Best of the Kingsmen* 🎵🎵🎵 (Varese Sarabande, 1998, prod. various).

the rest:
On Campus 🎵🎵🎵 (Wand, 1965/Sundazed, 1993)
Live & Unreleased 🎵🎵🎵 (Jerden, 1992)
Up & Away 🎵🎵🎵 (Sundazed, 1993)
Since We've Been Gone 🎵🎵🎵 (Sundazed, 1994)

worth searching for: *The Best of Louie Louie* (Rhino, 1983, prod. various) contains 10 consecutive versions of the classic party song, showing its diverse reach and timelessness. Author

Richard Berry contributes his take, and punk heroes Black Flag and swingmaster Les Dantz and His Orchestra represent the opposite poles. But the tribute album's overall lesson is the Kingsmen's original version, included here, is still clearly the best.

influences:
◀◀ Dick Dale, the Ventures, Elvis Presley, Carl Perkins

▶▶ The Beatles, the Beach Boys, the J. Geils Band, Bruce Springsteen, the Sex Pistols

Patrick McCarty

The Kingston Trio

Formed 1957, in San Francisco, CA. Disbanded 1967.

Bob Shane, guitar, vocals; Nick Reynolds, guitar, vocals; Dave Guard (died March 22, 1991), banjo, vocals (1957–61); John Stewart, banjo, guitar, vocals (1961–67).

The Kingston Trio just made it look too darned easy; it's no wonder the group was reviled by folk-music colleagues who watched it leap to the top of the charts. The Trio—three glib, fun-loving West Coast guys with guitars, banjos, bongos, three-part harmonies, and matching striped shirts and chinos—became big stuff during the late '50s and early '60s, when five of its first six albums went to Number One on the *Billboard* charts, occupying the top spot for a total of 50 weeks. The Trio's basic sound was deceptively simple and its albums—especially the choice of material—much better than its detractors were ready to admit. The group's this-business-is-easy attitude influenced many of its followers to pick up guitars and start groups of their own in country and rock. Dave Guard, the most gifted Trio member, left in 1961 and was replaced by John Stewart, who fit in perfectly before going on to a prolific solo career. Bob Shane has kept a version of the Trio live unit alive into the '90s.

what to buy: The best short collection is *The Kingston Trio* 🎵🎵🎵🎵 (Capitol Collector's Series, 1990, prod. Voyle Gilmore), which includes 20 of the group's best-known tunes and all the Top 10 hit singles. If you're *really* interested, try *The Capitol Years* 🎵🎵🎵🎵 (Capitol, 1995, prod. Voyle Gilmore), an extensive, fascinating four-CD collection that favors outtakes and unreleased tracks and offers a more sympathetic look at the Trio's place in history.

what to buy next: *Live at Newport* 🎵🎵🎵 (Vanguard, 1994, prod. Mary Katherine Aldin) is recorded live at the 1959 Newport Folk Festival before a demanding East Coast audience. And if you still can't get enough, there's *Guard Years* 🎵🎵🎵🎵 (Bear Family, 1997, prod. various), a 10-CD collection of the group's popular early albums.

what to avoid: *Once upon a Time* **woof!** (Tetragrammaton, 1969) was recorded live at Lake Tahoe in 1966; although the singing is fine, the jokes have gone flat, and the song selection is questionable.

the rest:

Stay Awhile ℐℐℐ (Capitol, 1965/Folk Era, 1994)
Children of the Morning ℐℐ (Capitol, 1966/Folk Era, 1997)
Greatest Hits ℐℐ (Curb, 1991)
Tom Dooley ℐℐℐᵛ (Capitol Special Products, 1994)
Greatest Hits ℐℐℐᵛ (Capitol, 1996)
Tom Dooley ℐℐℐᵛ (CEMA Special Products, 1996)
Evening with the Kingston Trio ℐℐℐᵛ (Folk Era, 1997)
Tom Dooley ℐℐℐ (ITC Masters, 1997)

worth searching for: Capitol has released many of the early albums on compact disc, though they don't stay in print very long. You can sometimes find the occasional CD or vinyl LP. Worth the search is *New Frontier* (Capitol, 1962, prod. Voyle Gilmore), which centers around the enthusiasm over John F. Kennedy's presidency; *Live at the Hungry I* (Capitol, 1959, prod. Voyle Gilmore), which captures a hot club show with lots of Dave Guard's deadpan comedy style; *At Large* (Capitol, 1959, prod. Voyle Gilmore), which features Bess Hawes's "M.T.A.," Guard's "Getaway John," "The Long Black Rifle," and Jane Bowers's "Remember the Alamo"; and *String Along* (Capitol, 1960, prod. Voyle Gilmore), which includes Tom Drake's "The Escape of Old John Webb," Cisco Hayes and Lee Hays's "Bad Man's Blunder," and Harlan Howard's "Everglades."

solo outings:

New Kingston Trio:
Lost Masters (1969–1972) ℐℐᵛ (Folk Era, 1996)

influences:

◀◀ The Weavers, Pete Seeger, the Gateway Singers

▶▶ Peter, Paul & Mary, the Brothers Four, the Chad Mitchell Trio, the Limeliters, the Journeymen, the Serendipity Singers, the New Christy Minstrels, Roger McGuinn, Bob Dylan, Simon & Garfunkel, the Rooftop Singers

see also: *John Stewart*

Leland Rucker

The Kinks

Formed 1963, in London, England.

Ray Davies, vocals, guitar; Dave Davies, guitar, vocals; Pete Quaife, bass (1963–83); Mick Avory, drums (1963–77); John Gosling, keyboards (1971–78); Andy Pyle, bass (1977–79); Bob Henrit, drums (1984–present); Ian Gibbons, keyboards (1979–88); Jim Rodford, bass (1979–present).

The Kinks are the oft-forgotten group among the giants of the British Invasion. The young band, interested largely in American blues in the beginning, crashed into the charts and rock history by virtually inventing the distorted power chords of hard rock with "You Really Got Me." Yet the Kinks may have ended up contributing more through the elegiac, literate, sharply observed tunes about British everyday life and traditions gone by. The Kinks were among the first to use Eastern strains on a pop song (months before the Beatles picked up a sitar) and to score a mini-rock opera (*Arthur*, delayed until after *Tommy*). When the original quartet fractured during the late '60s, the band continued as the pair of battling brothers backed by a long line of anonymous rhythm sections. Rediscovered by punks during the first new wave and again during the Britpop movement of the mid-'90s, the Kinks seemed sometimes in peril; but an acoustic retrospective, *To the Bone*, and individual books and solo tours from Dave and Ray Davies proved people loved the band too much for it to quit anytime soon. (Note: the Velvel re-releases listed below all include bonus tracks selected by Ray Davies.)

what to buy: The band's earliest days, and most of its biggest hits, are best compiled on *The Kinks' Greatest Hits* ℐℐℐℐ (Rhino, 1989, prod. Shel Talmy). The buzzsaw of "All Day and All of the Night" makes way for the more insinuating "Set Me Free" and social observation of "A Well Respected Man"—all within the course of three years. A fine introduction to the other side of the Kinks has a decent starting point in *The Kinks Kronicles* ℐℐℐℐ (Reprise, 1972, prod. Shel Talmy, Ray Davies), a double set that introduces Americans to the band's excellent late '60s period in a collection as quirkily anthologized as the music itself.

what to buy next: *Arthur (or the Decline and Fall of the British Empire)* ℐℐℐℐ (Reprise, 1969/Velvel, 1998, prod. Ray Davies) is an album that remains a thrilling song cycle. The Kinks' career, like so many others, was sidetracked by bad business dealings, which are succinctly summarized on *Lola Versus Powerman and the Moneygoround, Part One* ℐℐℐℐᵛ (Reprise, 1971/Velvel, 1998, prod. Ray Davies); this album gave the band one of its biggest hits in the ingeniously sly "Lola."

what to avoid: *Kinky Music: The Larry Page Orchestra Arranged by Ray Davies Plays the Music of the Kinks* **woof!** (Pye, 1966/Rhino, 1983) features early Kinks songs as elevator music!

the rest:

You Really Got Me ℐℐℐ (Reprise, 1965)
Kinda Kinks ℐℐᵛ (Reprise, 1965/Castle U.K., 1998)
Kinks Kontroversey ℐℐℐ (Reprise, 1966/Castle U.K., 1998)
Face to Face ℐℐℐℐ (Reprise, 1966/Castle U.K., 1998)
The Kinks Live at Kelvin Hall ℐℐ (Reprise, 1967/Castle U.K., 1998)
Something Else by the Kinks ℐℐℐℐ (Reprise, 1968/Castle U.K., 1998)
The Kinks Are the Village Preservation Society ℐℐℐℐ (Reprise, 1968/Castle U.K., 1998)
Muswell Hillbillies ℐℐℐ (RCA, 1970/Rhino, 1990/Velvel 1998)

Ace Frehley (l) and Paul Stanley of Kiss (© Ken Settle)

Percy 🎵🎵🎵 (Pye, 1971/Castle U.K., 1998)
Everybody's in Show-Biz 🎵🎵🎵 (RCA, 1972/Velvel 1998)
Preservation Act One 🎵🎵🎵 (RCA, 1973/Velvel, 1998)
Preservation Act Two 🎵🎵🎵 (RCA, 1973/Velvel, 1998)
Preservation: A Play in Two Acts 🎵🎵🎵🎵 (RCA, 1973–74/Rhino, 1991)
A Soap Opera 🎵🎵🎵 (RCA, 1975/Rhino, 1991/Velvel, 1998)
Schoolboys in Disgrace 🎵🎵🎵 (RCA, 1975/Rhino, 1991/Velvel, 1998)
Sleepwalker 🎵🎵🎵🎵 (Arista, 1977/Velvel, 1998)
Misfits 🎵🎵🎵🎵 (Arista, 1978/Velvel, 1998)
Low Budget 🎵🎵🎵 (Arista, 1979/Velvel, 1999)
One for the Road 🎵🎵🎵🎵 (Arista, 1980/Velvel, 1999)
Give the People What They Want 🎵🎵🎵🎵 (Arista, 1981/Velvel, 1999)
State of Confusion 🎵🎵🎵🎵 (Arista, 1983/Velvel, 1999)
Come Dancing with the Kinks 🎵🎵🎵🎵 (Arista, 1986/Velvel, 1999)
Think Visual 🎵🎵 (MCA, 1986)
Phobia 🎵🎵 (Columbia, 1993)
To the Bone 🎵🎵🎵🎵 (Guardian, 1996)

worth searching for: *Kinks on Holiday* (Gold Standard) is a bootleg of BBC broadcasts culled from two impressive 1972 performances.

solo outings:
Ray Davies
Return to Waterloo 🎵🎵🎵 (Arista, 1985)
The Storyteller 🎵🎵🎵🎵 (EMI-Capitol, 1998)

Dave Davies:
ALFI-3603 **woof!** (RCA, 1980)
Glamour 🎵 (RCA, 1981)
Chosen People **woof!** (Warner Bros., 1983)
Unfinished Business 🎵🎵🎵 (Velvel, 1997)

influences:

◀◀ Big Bill Broonzy, the Beatles, Little Richard, Charles Dickens

▶▶ The Who, the Jam, Blur, Pulp

Roger Catlin

Kevn Kinney
See: Drivin' N' Cryin'

Bill Kirchen
See: Commander Cody & His Lost Planet Airmen

Kiss
Formed 1972, in New York, NY.

Gene Simmons, bass, vocals; Paul Stanley, guitar, vocals; Ace Frehley, guitar, vocals (1972–81; 1996–present); Peter Criss, drums, vocals (1972–80; 1996–present); Eric Carr (died November 25, 1991), drums

WHAT ALBUM CHANGED YOUR LIFE?

Meet the Beatles, but it wasn't the album; it was seeing them on TV, on *The Ed Sullivan Show.* It was like a combination of religion and music and I don't know what else. The clock stopped for me; everything stopped. It was like in *2001* when the apes went up to the monolith and touched it— just a quantum leap forward. All of a sudden I understood what my fate was, what I had to do.

Gene Simmons (of Kiss)

(1980–91); Vinnie Vincent, guitar (1982–83); Mark St. John, guitar (1984); Bruce Kulnick, guitar (1985–96); Eric Singer, drums (1991–96).

Kiss fans will forever view 1996 as the year of the second coming. It was the year the four original members reunited to reclaim their glory era, make-up and explosions included. By splattering the greasepaint back on and re-enacting its blood-spittin', fire-breathin' live show, the band cast off recent years of public indifference and was once again selling out arenas in minutes. Without so much as a nod or a wink, the band brought forth the same live spectacle that first earned it worldwide notoriety and sold it all over again. Of course, Kiss has understood the power of show biz since its inception— hence the fantasy personas, devilish images, and elaborate stage shows. Not that all the hoopla overshadowed the fact that most of its albums sounded like stale cat poop rolling around a tin can. This fact, and the base, party thumping lyrics, was never lost on the critics who were quick to lambast the band from day one. Nonetheless, at the height of its popularity there were Kiss dolls (worth a small fortune if you got 'em), a TV movie (with ratings to rival Luke and Laura's wedding), and a comic book. The band even managed to retain a devout faction of its enormous Kiss Army during its post-Frehley/sans make-up bland years. Mercury has re-mastered the Kiss catalog, which has been a blessing in some cases (*Destroyer, Alive*), while in others (*Hotter than Hell, Kiss, Rock and Roll Over*) it merely drives home how thin the sound was in the first place.

what to buy: *Alive!* 🎵🎵🎵 (Casablanca/Mercury, 1975, prod. Eddie Karmer) reveals the power of Kiss in the live arena. Previously lumbering riffs turn thunderous, the bombast catching fire on soon-to-be classics such as "Deuce," "Strutter," "Firehouse," and the party anthem, "Rock 'n' Roll All Night." *Destroyer* 🎵🎵🎵 (Casablanca/Mercury, 1976, prod. Bob Ezrin) is the band's best studio effort by a country mile, as well as its most diverse. Along with greatly improved production, the record has the band's most challenging rocker ("Detroit Rock City"), an orchestra and a choir ("Great Expectations"), fist wavers ("Shout It out Loud" and "Flaming Youth"), and an actual ballad, the Criss-sung "Beth."

what to buy next: *Dressed to Kill* 🎵🎵🎵 (Casablanca/Mercury, 1975, prod. Neil Bogart, Kiss) is the sturdiest of the early albums, nearly matching *Destroyer* in song selection. *Love Gun* 🎵🎵🎵 (Casablanca/Mercury, 1977, prod. Kiss, Eddie Kramer) follows *Destroyer*'s spiffy projection, this time with a decidedly lighter sound. Songs such as "Plaster Caster" and "Christine Sixteen" and a remake of "Then He Kissed Me" tip the scales in the pop direction. Acoustic guitars replace the pyrotechnics on *MTV Unplugged* 🎵🎵🎵 (Mercury, 1996, prod. Alex Coletti). A nod is given to solid but obscure material ("Goin' Blind," "Coming Home") and the spartan setting reminds us that, no matter what the critics say, Kiss knows its way around a pop song or two.

what to avoid: *Creatures of the Night* 🎵 (Casablanca/Mercury, 1982, prod. Paul Stanley, Gene Simmons, Michael James Jackson), the first of the post-Frehley releases, marks a turn toward corporate pop metal that gave fledgling tiger-striped spandex wussies inspiration to buy more mousse. Most subsequent recordings should be approached with caution.

the rest:
Kiss 🎵🎵 (Casablanca/Mercury, 1974)
Hotter than Hell 🎵🎵 (Casablanca/Mercury, 1974)
Rock and Roll Over 🎵🎵🎵 (Casablanca/Mercury, 1976)
Alive 2 🎵🎵🎵 (Casablanca, 1977)
Double Platinum 🎵🎵🎵 (Casablanca/Mercury, 1978)
Dynasty 🎵🎵 (Casablanca/Mercury, 1980)
Kiss Unmasked 🎵 (Casablanca/Mercury, 1980)
Music from the Elder 🎵🎵🎵 (Casablanca/Mercury, 1981)
Lick It Up 🎵🎵🎵 (Mercury, 1983)
Animalize 🎵🎵🎵 (Mercury, 1984)
Asylum 🎵🎵 (Mercury, 1985)
Crazy Nights 🎵🎵 (Mercury, 1987)
Smashes, Trashes & Hits 🎵🎵🎵 (Mercury, 1988)
Hot in the Shade 🎵🎵 (Mercury, 1989)
Revenge 🎵🎵🎵 (Mercury, 1992)
Kiss Alive 3 🎵🎵🎵 (Mercury, 1993)

You Wanted the Best, You Got the Best. . . . 🎵🎵🎵 (Mercury, 1996)
Greatest Kiss 🎵🎵🎵🎵 (Mercury, 1997)
Carnival of Souls: The Final Sessions 🎵🎵 (Mercury, 1997)
Psycho Circus 🎵🎵🎵 (Mercury, 1998)

worth searching for: The Japanese version of *You Wanted the Best. . . .* (Mercury, 1996, prod. various) includes an intriguing, lo-fi version of Frehley's "New York Groove," the best-known track from a Kiss member's solo albums.

solo outings:
Ace Frehley:
Ace Frehley 🎵🎵🎵 (Casablanca/Mercury, 1978)
Frehley's Comet 🎵 (Megaforce, 1987)
Trouble Walkin' 🎵 (Megaforce, 1989)
12 Picks 🎵🎵 (Megaforce, 1997)
Loaded Deck 🎵🎵 (Megaforce, 1998)

Peter Criss:
Peter Criss 🎵 (Casablanca/Mercury, 1978)
Out of Control 🎵🎵 (Casablanca/Mercury, 1980/1998)
Let Me Rock You 🎵 (Casablanca/Mercury, 1982/1998)
Criss Cat No. 1 woof! (Tony Nicole Toney, 1994)

Gene Simmons:
Gene Simmons 🎵🎵🎵 (Casablanca/Mercury, 1978)

Paul Stanley:
Paul Stanley 🎵🎵 (Casablanca/Mercury, 1978)

influences:
◀◀ Lou Reed, Motörhead, the Beatles, Alice Cooper, Led Zeppelin, the Crazy World of Arthur Brown

▶▶ Def Leppard, Poison, the Misfits, Quiet Riot, Ratt, Mötley Crüe

Allan Orski

Kitchens of Distinction

Formed 1987, in Amsterdam, the Netherlands. Disbanded 1995.

Patrick Fitzgerald, vocals, bass; Julian Swales, guitar; Dan Goodwin, drums.

One of the indie-rock world's first overtly gay acts gained its impressive reputation not for its members' sexual orientation but for its vivid, textural music. Kitchens of Distinction made decent headway on the British alternative charts but never broke beyond college radio audiences in America. The group lasted four albums before it was dropped by A&M and eventually split.

what to buy: The breathtaking *Strange Free World* 🎵🎵🎵🎵 (One Little Indian/A&M, 1990, prod. Hugh Jones) marked the group's creative zenith, with dizzying tracks like "Drive That Fast" and the politically ambitious "Gorgeous Love."

what to buy next: The imaginative and expansive *Love Is Hell* 🎵🎵🎵 (One Little Indian/A&M, 1989, prod. Kitchens of Distinction) put kitschy, homoerotic imagery on its cover, but its music was distinctly dark, dramatic, and strong, particularly in songs such as "Prize" and "The Third Time We Opened the Capsule."

the rest:
Death of Cool 🎵🎵 (One Little Indian/A&M, 1992)
Cowboys & Aliens 🎵🎵🎵 (One Little Indian/A&M, 1994)

worth searching for: The EP *Elephantine* (One Little Indian, 1989), later tagged onto the American version of *Love Is Hell*, features the insubordinate "Margaret's Injection" and the dreamy "Anvil Dub."

influences:
◀◀ The Smiths, Cocteau Twins, Burning Spear

Aidin Vaziri

Klaatu

Formed 1973, in Toronto, Ontario, Canada. Disbanded 1981. Reformed 1994.

Terry Draper, drums; Dee Long, guitar; John Woloschuk, bass.

The beneficiaries of one of the most effective music rumors of the 1970s, Klaatu (named for a character in the film *The Day the Earth Stood Still*) achieved fleeting fame when a music critic concluded in print that the group contained one or more of the Beatles working together anonymously. The group's label (Capitol—the home of the Beatles) did nothing to quell the rumors, and the liner notes of the band's debut album didn't contain the musicians' names. When the public discovered the group actually consisted of Canadian session players, sales declined accordingly.

what to buy: *Klaatu* 🎵🎵 (Capitol, 1976, prod. Klaatu) is the album that started the fuss. With baroque-pop arrangements and titles such as "Calling Occupants of Interplanetary Craft" and "Sub Rosa Subway," Klaatu may have shared a sense of whimsy with the Fab Four, but not much else. The album was reissued on Canada's Attic label in 1993 as *3:47 E.S.T.*.

what to avoid: At least *Sir Army Suit* 🎵🎵 (Capitol, 1978, prod. Klaatu) has short, and usually relatively less pretentious, songs than are characteristic of the band. It has since been packaged with the band's follow-up album, *Endangered Species*, as *Double Header* 🎵🎵 (Attic, 1994). The band members started putting their names on the work with *Endangered Species* 🎵 (Capitol, 1980, prod. Christopher Bond). They probably shouldn't have.

the rest:
Hope 🎵🎵 (Capitol, 1976/Attic, 1993)
Magentalane 🎵🎵 (Attic, 1981/Permanent Press, 1995)

WHAT ALBUM CHANGED YOUR LIFE?

The first Led Zeppelin album was such raw, relentless sexuality. It was just staggering—as close to knocking me off my feet as music can come. The first time I heard 'Good Times, Bad Times' I thought someone had unleashed an animal in the speaker. Something was going on there that hit everything primal, sonic, intellectual, visceral.

Paul Stanley (of Kiss)

worth searching for: *Peaks* (Attic, 1993, prod. Klaatu, Christopher Bond) collects the group's best work.

influences:
◀◀ The Beatles
▶▶ Utopia, Jellyfish

Brian Mansfield

Dana & Karen Kletter

See: blackgirls

KMFDM

Formed 1984, in Paris, France.

Sascha Konietzko, vocals, percussion, programming, bass; En Esch, vocals, guitar, percussion; Pig (Nainz Watts/Raymond Watts) vocals, bass (1984–85, 1995); Gunter Schulz (a.k.a. Svet Am/Svetlana Ambrosius), guitar, bass (1990–present); Jennifer Ginsberg, vocals (1989–present); Jr. Blackmale; Mark Durantula (a.k.a. Mark Durante), guitar, steel guitar (1990–92); Christine Siewert, vocals (1990–92); Brute, album art.

The initials KMFDM has been alleged to stand for everything from "Karl Marx Found Dead Masturbating" to the infamous pseudo-acronym, "Kill Mother Fucking Depeche Mode." The official name has always been "Kein Mitleid für die Mehrheit" (No Pity for the Majority). Originally conceived by Sascha Konietzko and his friend Udo Sturm to accompany a Paris art exhibit, the group's first performance consisted of feedback, five bass guitars, and four Polish coal miners banging on the museum's foundations. Since its formation, KMFDM has featured a constantly fluctuating line-up and ever-evolving musical arrangements. While earlier recordings are mainly comprised of a sampled audio-collage laid over heavy, minimalistic drum beats, newer material often sounds closer to heavy metal. In between the two styles lies a vast landscape of fused sounds from disco, techno, hip-hop, and rap. Underlying the recordings is a good ear for a dark, throbbing beat and an off-kilter sense of humor, politics, and sex.

what to buy: *Virus* ♪♪♪♪ (Wax Trax!, 1993, prod. KMFDM) provides a good, low-priced introduction to KMFDM. Easily its strongest EP and one of its better overall releases, *Virus* sports a title track that is an instant classic. If you're not familiar with the hard-edged sound of industrial, this prelude to the band's oeuvre is a necessity. *Money* ♪♪♪♪ (Wax Trax!, 1992, prod. KMFDM) captures KMFDM at their high point between beat-heavy minimalism and guitar-pounding metal in their most traditional industrial album. Although nothing musically new is explored, nobody else does this type of music with the same intensity or precision. They perfectly juxtapose dense guitar riffs with electronic noise, creating a disc that works equally well on the dance floor or in the mosh pit. *UAIOE* ♪♪♪♪ (Wax Trax!, 1989, prod. Paul Barkov, Lee Popa) provides a notion of the range KMFDM is truly capable of; this album presents a fusion of diverse musical styles from reggae to disco to heavy metal, glued together by a strong beat. Although the lyrics are more political than usual, they add a weight that well complements the feeling of the record. *Don't Blow Your Top* ♪♪♪◊ (Wax Trax!, 1988, prod. Adrian Sherwood) is the best of their early work. It features a sparser sound, but crisp production and carefully chosen samples make the album worth owning.

what to buy next: With *XTORT* ♪♪♪◊ (Wax Trax!, 1996, prod. KMFDM) KMFDM returns to the *Naïve* era, with crunchy guitars, tape loops, and female vocal pads. Guest appearances from Chris Connelly, William Rieflin (Ministry, Revolting Cocks), and F.M. Einheit, among others, provide a welcome diversity to the standard KMFDM record.

what to avoid: *What Do You Know Deutschland?* ♪◊ (Wax Trax!, 1986, prod. KMFDM) is an eclectic collection of slow, simple beats and not much else.

the rest:
Angst ♪♪♪◊ (Wax Trax!, 1993)
Naïve/Hell to Go ♪♪◊ (Wax Trax!, 1994)
Nihil ♪♪♪ (Wax Trax!, 1995)
KMFDM ♪♪♪ (TVT, 1997)

worth searching for: The original version of *Naïve* (Wax Trax!, 1990, prod. KMFDM) is one of KMFDM's best releases, unfortunately it is no longer in print due to copyright problems with the samples. There is a remixed/reworked version, but it pales in comparison to the real thing. *Opium* (self-recorded, 1985), a promo tape made before KMFDM had a record deal, is extremely rare. *Retro* (Wax Trax!, 1996, prod. KMFDM, Adrian Sherwood) is a promotional "best of" album and collects the top singles onto one record.

influences:
◄◄ Einstürzende Neubauten, Skinny Puppy, Ministry

►► nine inch nails, My Life with the Thrill Kill Kult, KLF, Pig

Bryan Lassner

The Knack

Formed 1978, in Los Angles, CA. Disbanded 1981. Re-formed 1991.

Doug Fieger, vocals, guitar; Berton Averre, guitar, vocals; Bruce Gary, drums (1978–81); Prescott Niles, bass; Billy Ward, drums (1991–present).

With all the hype the music business could conjure up—basically serving up American Beatles-style mania to the new wave audience—the Knack exploded on the scene in 1979 with one of the most auspicious first albums ever. *Get the Knack* was recorded in 11 days for just $17,000 and sold more than five million copies worldwide, going gold in 13 days and platinum in six weeks. The exuberant hit "My Sharona" sold more than five million copies as a single—making it easily the #1 song of that year. But audience and media reacted to the hype—as well as to the group's inaccessibility—and the descent began. The second album, . . . *But the Little Girls Understand*, fell short of expectations, and the Knack, riddled by inner tensions, split up after its third album. "My Sharona" hit big a second time when it was included in the Generation X film *Reality Bites,* which inspired an unsuccessful Knack reunion during the early '90s—though the group still gets together periodically and is no doubt hoping another generation will one day get the Knack again. Drummer Bruce Gary took some heat during the '90s by grafting drum tracks onto some Jimi Hendrix reissues, while Doug Fieger is almost better known as the brother of Dr. Jack Kevorkian's attorney.

what to buy: *Get the Knack* ♪♪♪♪ (Capitol, 1979, prod. Mike Chapman) is a must in any pop fan's collection—albeit from a decidedly male and teenage perspective. It has "My Sharona" and "Good Girls Don't," but even the ballads—"Your Number or Your Name" and "Maybe Tonight"—are standouts.

what to buy next: . . . *But the Little Girls Understand* ♪♪♪♪ (Capitol, 1980, prod. Mike Chapman) provides more of the same as the group's debut. Fieger wallows in more female disenchantment from the first track, "Baby Talks Dirty," but rebounds for the lusty "I Want Ya" and an energetic cover of the Kinks' "The Hardway." Of the several Knack compilations, *Proof: The Very Best of the Knack* 𝄞𝄞𝄞𝄞 (Rhino, 1998, prod. various) is the most fun thanks to some choice covers—Elvis Costello's "Girls Talk," Nick Lowe's "I Knew the Bride . . .," and the movie theme "That Thing You Do."

what to avoid: *Round Trip* 𝄞𝄞 (Capitol, 1981, prod. Jack Douglas) is the Knack at its weakest, despite a couple of keepers like "Boys Go Crazy" (covered by the Posies in 1996) and "Another Lousy Day in Paradise."

the rest:
Serious Fun 𝄞𝄞𝄞𝄞 (Charisma, 1991)
Retrospective: The Best of the Knack 𝄞𝄞𝄞 (Capitol, 1992)
Zoom 𝄞𝄞𝄞𝄞 (Rhino, 1998)

worth searching for: Fans will want the original 45rpm single with the picture sleeve of "My Sharona" (Capitol, 1979), B-sided by "Let Me Out" and featuring provocative pictures of one of the Knack's female "friends."

influences:
◀◀ The Beatles, the Kinks, the Turtles, Herman's Hermits
▶▶ The Plimsouls, Jellyfish, the Posies, 20-20, the Romantics

John Nieman

Knapsack
See: Samiam

The Knickerbockers
Formed 1964, in Bergenfield, NJ. Disbanded 1967.

Beau Charles, guitar, vocals; John Charles, bass, vocals; Buddy Randell, saxophone, vocals; Jimmy Walker, drums, vocals.

The Knickerbockers were one-hit wonders with the phenomenal "Lies," a sublime rockin' pop powerhouse that almost sounded more like the Beatles than the Beatles did. If the group had never cut another track before or after, it would still deserve recognition for distilling the essence of frenzied Merseybeat as succinctly and triumphantly as they did with "Lies." So it's all the more gratifying to report that the Knickerbockers did, in fact, record several other worthy numbers, including "One Track Mind," "They Ran for Their Lives," "Just One Girl," "I Must Be Doing Something Right," and "She Said Goodbye." None of them were big hits, and none quite ranked in the same league as "Lies," but all were remarkably engaging and crackling with an undeniable pop spark you'd swear was ignited in Liverpool rather than Jersey. (As a matter of fact, Liverpool's Swinging Blue Jeans even

covered the Knickerbockers' "Rumors, Gossip, Words Untrue," though the Knicks' original version is much better.) The Knickerbockers made two middling-to-terrible albums, but their scattered uptempo tracks were nothing short of brilliant. The accomplished mix of deadly hooks and vibrant rock 'n' roll energy in these tracks show the Knicks to have been an ace power pop group years before the term came into vogue. After the group sputtered to a halt, Jimmy Walker went on to be a temporary replacement for Bill Medley in the Righteous Brothers.

what to buy: *Knickerbockerism* 𝄞𝄞𝄞𝄞 (Sundazed, 1997, compilation prod. Bob Irwin) is a two-CD set that does the group proud, with all the crucial tracks and enough rarities to establish that there was more to the band than "Lies."

what to avoid: *Jerk & Twine Time* 𝄞 (Challenge, 1965/Sundazed, 1993, prod. Jerry Fuller, Bob Irwin) is a horrendous coverfest that offers historical interest only.

the rest:
Lies 𝄞𝄞𝄞 (Challenge, 1966/Sundazed, 1993)
The Great Lost Knickerbockers Album 𝄞𝄞𝄞 (Sundazed, 1993)
The Fabulous Knickerbockers 𝄞𝄞𝄞 (Sundazed, 1993)
Lies: Golden Classics 𝄞𝄞𝄞 (Collectables)

worth searching for: You'll be well served if you can find the British import *A Rave up with . . . the Knickerbockers* (Big Beat, 1994, prod. Jerry Fuller, Bob Irwin), a rockin' little compilation that combines the group's two albums.

influences:
◀◀ The Beatles, the Beach Boys, the Righteous Brothers, the Dave Clark Five

▶▶ Dwight Twilley, the Raspberries, the Monkees

Carl Cafarelli

Cheri Knight

Born August 4, 1956, in Albany, NY.

Before embarking on her solo career, Cheri Knight sang and played bass in Boston's Blood Oranges, one of the first and best bands to emerge from the '90s alternative-country boom. Then as now, when Knight isn't touring or recording, she raises flowers on a farm in western Massachusetts. Knight's ties to the land not only explain the organic imagery that pervades her lyrics, they also imbue her mix of country, rock, and Anglo-Celtic folk music with its dark, loamy cast.

what to buy: On the strength of Knight's mordant originals and muscular arrangements, *The Northeast Kingdom* ♪♪♪ (E-Squared, 1998, prod. Twangtrust) surpasses everything in her former band's catalog. Of course, part of this has to do with the contributions that Emmylou Harris, co-producer Steve Earle, and Knight's Blood Oranges Jimmy Ryan and Mark Spencer make to the record.

what to buy next: *The Knitter* ♪♪♪ (East Side Digital, 1996, prod. Eric "Roscoe" Ambel) is Knight's solo debut. A strong record, galvanized by such originals as "Light in the Road" and the title track, it nonetheless doesn't cohere as well as its dark, brooding successor.

solo outings:
Blood Oranges:
Corn River ♪♪♪ (East Side Digital, 1990)
Lone Green Valley ♪♪♪ (East Side Digital EP, 1992)
The Crying Tree ♪♪♪♪ (East Side Digital, 1994)
Wooden Leg ♪♪♪ (East Side Digital, 1996)

influences:
◀◀ Richard & Linda Thompson, Leonard Cohen, the Pixies

Bill Friskics-Warren and Peter Blackstock

The Knitters

See: X

Buddy Knox
/Buddy Knox
& the Rhythm Orchids

Born Wayne Knox, July 20, 1933, in Happy, TX.

A trailblazing musician whose band the Rhythm Orchids helped kick-start the Texas rock scene during the mid-1950s, Buddy Knox led one of the first young combos to bring its uninhibited new sound to Norman Petty's Clovis, New Mexico, recording studio. "Party Doll," written by Knox years earlier but sporting a fresh, uptempo arrangement, became the Number One song in the nation after Petty's original master was leased to the brand new Roulette label in 1957. The Orchids, which also featured singer, bassist, and future country kingpin Jimmy Bowen, quickly became a featured attraction on the biggest package shows of the day, but subsequent attempts to match the success of "Party Doll" on record by and large failed. After releasing the tell-tale "I Think I'm Going to Kill Myself" in 1959, Knox went solo, recording increasingly country-flavored sides for a variety of labels culminating with the 1968 hit "Gypsy Man." Relocating to Canada several years later and opening his own nightclub there, Knox remains a successful, well-invested businessman who to this day can be found touring on the strength of his first, still magical record. Fellow Orchid Bowen, incidentally, went on to become the Rat Pack's producer of choice, recording hits for Frank Sinatra, Dean Martin, and Sammy Davis Jr. during the '60s before eventually settling in Nashville, where he was instrumental in launching the careers of Reba McEntire and Garth Brooks.

what's available: Although there's nothing particularly earth-shattering in his sound or his approach, Knox's *The Best of Buddy Knox* ♪♪♪♭ (Rhino, 1990, compilation prod. Al Kooper, Dave Booth) is a fine collection of tunes concentrating on his trademark rockabilly-lite style. Buddy Holly may have done it better, but Buddy Knox, by a few months at least, did it *first*.

worth searching for: True to its title, *Buddy Knox and Jimmy Bowen: The Complete Roulette Recordings* (Sequel, 1996) contains 60 Rhythm Orchids tracks, including five previously unreleased, from its sessions in Clovis with the remarkable Norman Petty.

influences:
◀◀ Elvis Presley, Roy Orbison, Sonny Fisher, Ray Campi, Sid King, Mac Curtis

▶▶ Waylon Jennings, the Bobby Fuller Four, Chris Isaak, the Bop Cats

Gary Pig Gold

Chris Knox
/Tall Dwarfs

Born September 2, 1952, in Invercargill, New Zealand.

Chris Knox is one of rock's most prolific, eccentric, exciting, and influential figures. He's also virtually unknown. Despite two decades as a major mover in the New Zealand music scene, Knox hasn't quite managed to catch the notice of the rest of the world. Perhaps that has something to do with the fact that his music is so hard to pin down. His start as the lead singer in the early punk groups the Enemy and Toy Love honed his ability to scream and his appreciation for volume. But in 1981 he formed a different kind of band, Tall Dwarfs, with Alec Bathgate. Tall Dwarfs (which continues to make records today) introduced melody, complex song arrangements, outlandish lyrics, and a joyful eclecticism to Knox's palette. His solo work displays these virtues as he leaps from tender, if loopy, love songs to political rants to spacy, experimental dirges. Perhaps Knox's least-lauded talent is his innate grasp of pop hooks. He doesn't seem to like them—too easy?—but they crop up every so often and leave one breathless. Knox produces all of his own work and has recorded albums for other bands on the Flying Nun label, including the Chills and the Clean. Ever the acrobat, he also draws a weekly comic strip and hosts a movie-review television program in Auckland, New Zealand.

what to buy: *Seizure* 𝄞𝄞𝄞 (Flying Nun, 1988, prod. Chris Knox) was mostly underappreciated upon its release but has managed to quietly endure, as its melodic charms and pleasing oddities show Knox to best advantage. Both Marshall Crenshaw and Frente! have covered songs from it. The Tall Dwarfs' *Hello Cruel World* 𝄞𝄞𝄞𝄞 (Flying Nun, 1987/Homestead, 1988) compiles the group's first four EP's and serves as the best available introduction into their unconventional music.

what to buy next: The frenetic, live-wire *Yes!* 𝄞𝄞𝄞𝄞 (Flying Nun, 1997, prod. Chris Knox) boasts the big-ass sound of guitars and . . . bagpipes. A return to Knox's punk roots.

the rest:
(With Tall Dwarfs) *Weeville* 𝄞𝄞𝄞 (Flying Nun, 1990/Homestead, 1991)
Croaker 𝄞𝄞𝄞 (Flying Nun, 1991)
Meat 𝄞𝄞𝄞 (Communion, 1993)
Polyfoto, Duckshaped Pain & Gum 𝄞𝄞𝄞 (Communion, 1993)
Songs of You and Me 𝄞𝄞𝄞 (Flying Nun/Caroline, 1995)
(With International Tall Dwarfs) *Stumpy* (Flying Nun, 1997)

worth searching for: Much of Knox's and the Tall Dwarfs' material is out of print or available only on imports. All is interesting, but the CD *Fork Songs* (Flying Nun, 1992) also includes the fine EP *Dogma* (Flying Nun, 1991).

influences:
◀◀ Iggy Pop, Robyn Hitchcock
▶▶ The Bats, Julian Cope

Amy Weivoda

Cub Koda
See: Brownsville Station

Kool Keith
/Dr. Octagon
Born Keith Thornton.

While LL Cool J is the model of hip-hop longevity, Kool Keith is the genre's version of the Phoenix, showing that hip-hop has developed enough staying power for artists to enjoy second—or, in the case of Keith's ever-expanding roster of alter-egos, third and fourth—lives. One of rap's most accomplished freestylers and arguably its most colorful eccentric, Keith first turned up as a member of the legendary Ultramagnetic MC's. Following that group's breakup, Keith drifted, landing for a spell in the hospital to battle depression before finally resurfacing in 1995 with a series of underground 12-inch sides under the pseudonyms Big Willie Smith, the Cenubites, and, finally, Dr. Octagon. In 1996 Keith hit pay dirt when Bulk Records expanded his Dr. Octagon persona into a self-titled album that proved to be one of the most deliriously inventive and relentlessly bugged hip-hop releases ever. With Dan "the Automator" Nakamura supplying the space-age beats, Keith assumed the guise of a demonic gynecologist, born on Jupiter sometime in the third millennium. The near-epic scope of Keith's impressionistic musings ("Earth People," "Blue Flowers") and loony freestyles turned *Dr. Octagon* into an underground sensation, earning Keith an audience among the growing post-alternative rock crowd. Now calling himself Keith again, his next release, *Sex Style*, ditched Octagon's space talk for an over-the-top sojourn into the world of adult entertainment. Here, Keith plays the leering freak, doing it doggy style with porn starlets while wearing a cape and mask, occasionally dipping into his bag of non-sequiturs ("We pull the drawers off girls/We look out windows and stare" he raps on the delightful "Sly We Fly"). Whatever you say, bro.

what to buy: Keith's bugged-out flow is in full effect on Ultra's seminal *Critical Beatdown* album, but on his own, the best bet is *Dr. Octagon* 𝄞𝄞𝄞𝄞 (Bulk, 1996/Dreamworks, 1997, prod. Automator), which is a feast for fans of lyrical madness.

what to buy next: Keith's *Sex Style* 𝄞𝄞𝄞𝄞 (Funky Ass, 1997, prod. Kutmasta Kurt, T.R. Love) is an expansion of the sex-maddened "Big Willie Smith" persona first who debuted on the "Keep It Real" 12-inch.

worth searching for: Some of Keith's most *out-there* work has come on the 12-inch tip: "So Intelligent" by Sir Menelik, featuring Kool Keith, and the Cenubites' "Fondle 'Em," for instance. Other projects include the *Big Time* LP with Tim Dog (under the Ultra heading; Our Time, 1997) and producer Automator's *Better Tomorrow* EP on Ubiquity, on which Keith appears as Sinister 6000.

influences:
◀◀ Ultramagnetic MC's

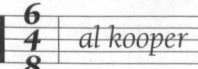
▶▶ Organized Konfusion, Chino XL, Freestyle Fellowship, Ras Kass

Logan Creed

Al Kooper

Born February 5, 1944, in Brooklyn, NY.

Al Kooper is one of those great rock 'n' roll stars many have never heard of. Consider the list of accomplishments: joining the Royal Teens ("Short Shorts") at age 15; co-writing Gary Lewis & the Playboys' #1 hit "This Diamond Ring"; playing the organ hook on Bob Dylan's "Like a Rolling Stone" and the French horn lick for the Rolling Stones' "You Can't Always Get What You Want"; forming the Blues Project and Blood, Sweat & Tears; and producing acts such as Lynyrd Skynyrd, the Tubes, Nils Lofgren, and many others. He loves to play, write and sing, period, and the only thing that's kept Kooper from mass recognition is his own eclecticism and a reedy singing voice that's not quite the stuff of Top 40 hits. Still active today, Kooper remains an estimable talent and a fine rock 'n' roll historian—as anyone who can scare up a copy of his memoir, *Backstage Passes & Backstabbing Bastards* (Billboard Books, 1998), can attest.

what to buy: Much of Kooper's seminal work is out of print. The best buy at the moment is *Super Session* 𝄞𝄞𝄞𝄞 (Columbia, 1968, prod. Al Kooper), a lively project that features guitar whiz Michael Bloomfield on half and Stephen Stills on the other half, subbing after the mercurial Bloomfield disappeared. *The Live Adventures of Mike Bloomfield and Al Kooper* 𝄞𝄞𝄞𝄞 (Columbia, 1969/Legacy, 1997, prod. Al Kooper) puts Elvin Bishop and Carlos Santana in the same role, with all the guitarists sparkling on transcendent versions of "The Weight" and a fresh take on Simon & Garfunkel's "The 59th Street Bridge Song (Feelin' Groovy)."

what to buy next: *Soul of a Man: Al Kooper Live* 𝄞𝄞𝄞𝄞 (Music-Masters, 1995, prod. Al Kooper) captures an electric performance with guest appearances by the Blues Project, John Sebastian, and former BS&T trumpeter Michael Brecker.

the rest:
Rekooperation—A Nonverbal Scenic Selection of Soul Souvenirs 𝄞𝄞𝄞 (MusicMasters, 1994)

worth searching for: The compilation *Al's Big Deal (Unclaimed Freight)* (Columbia, 1989, prod. various) is a solid if scattered retrospective that touches on assorted stages of Kooper's career.

influences:
◀◀ Bob Dylan, Paul Butterfield, the Beatles
▶▶ Todd Rundgren, Talking Heads, Beck

see also: *Blood, Sweat & Tears, Blues Project*

Gary Graff

Peter Koppes
See: The Church

KoЯn

Formed 1992, in Bakersfield, CA.

Jonathan Houseman Davis, vocals, bagpipes; James "Munky" Shaffer, guitars; Brian "Head" Welch, guitars; Reginald "Fieldy Snuts" Arvizu, bass; David Silveria, drums.

KoЯn's background is just as creepy as the dark, brooding, hard rock it produces. Singer Jonathan Davis's pre-KoЯn careers were working as the assistant coroner in Kern County, California, and moonlighting as an undertaker at an area funeral home. The band began as a project with James Shaffer, Brian Welch, Reginald Arvizu, and David Silveria, who released an LP under the collective name LAPD. When the quartet met the bagpipe-playing Davis, then singing in the band Sexart, they invited him to join and renamed the band KoЯn. According to a fan website, Davis initially didn't want to join the band but relented when a psychic told him to do so. After winning over the remnants of the *Beavis and Butt-head* crowd, KoЯn got more publicity than it could have begged for. While in the process of recording its third album, a high school student in Zeeland, Michigan, was suspended for wearing a T-shirt printed with the group's logo. When the school's principal described KoЯn's music as "indecent, vulgar, and obscene," the band issued a cease-and-desist order—in lieu of a thank-you note.

what to buy: The band's debut, *KoЯn* 𝄞𝄞𝄞 (Immortal, 1994, prod. Ross Robinson), is a study in creativity, bringing together the aggressive nature of metal, the melody of pop songs, and the acerbic sound of bagpipes, which Davis learned to play in high school. "Shoots and Ladders" would scare any child off the game board with Davis's psychotic-sounding, sing-songy chorus "ashes, ashes, we all fall down." Nicknamed "HIV," Davis sings about being called a "faget" (sic) in high school in a guitar assault of the same name.

the rest:
Life Is Peachy 𝄞𝄞𝄞 (Immortal, 1996)
Follow the Leader 𝄞𝄞𝄞𝄞 (Immortal, 1998)

influences:
◀◀ nine inch nails, Tool, Clutch
▶▶ Coal Chamber, Limp Bizkit, any Ozzfest artist

Christina Fuoco

Leo Kottke

Born September 11, 1945, in Athens, GA.

Acoustic fingerpickers across the land are perpetually awed by the super-nimble guitar work of Leo Kottke. An eclectic guitar wiz, he has developed a cult following not only for his musicianship but also for his dark humor and deadpan vocal delivery. Labeling him a folkie is too limiting a term, as he prefers to jump all over the map without adhering to any one style. He made an auspicious debut in 1969 as a dazzlingly percussive folk-bluegrass-based instrumentalist. He soon incorporated a rhythm section and gradually softened his whirlwind style. He abandoned the fingerpicks and heavy rhythms altogether near the end of the '70s, when he developed tendonitis. Kottke had to virtually invent another approach to his guitar work—a softer, more muted tone. After concentrating more on live performances during the '80s, Kottke has successfully returned to a regular schedule of album releases.

what to buy: Recorded in three hours, *Six- and 12-String Guitar* 🎸🎸🎸🎸 (Takoma, 1969/Rhino, 1994) is a ripping ride that has Kottke bursting at every seam. It's a must-have album for anyone who takes traditional acoustic music seriously. *Guitar Music* 🎸🎸🎸🎸 (Chrysalis, 1981, prod. Leo Kottke) is his celebrated return to solo acoustic music, with a fine turn on the Everly Brothers' "All I Have to Do Is Dream" and the otherworldly "Sleepwalk."

what to buy next: For a thorough, but not complete, sampler, *The Leo Kottke Anthology* 🎸🎸🎸🎸 (Rhino, 1997, compilation prod. James Austin, Rick Clark) covers Kottke's debut through 1983. Most of his more celebrated material is from this period. They're all here, as well as choice album cuts and self-penned liner notes. His later period work is more diverse. On *Great Big Boy* 🎸🎸🎸 (Private Music, 1991, prod. Steve Berlin), Kottke traipses between funkified folk and Mexican-flavored fare with guests Margo Timmins of the Cowboy Junkies and Lyle Lovett.

what to avoid: *That's What* 🎸🎸 (Private Music, 1990) is too muted to appeal to all but the most devoted listener. It makes for a dull spin that strays too close to new age.

the rest:
Mudlark 🎸🎸🎸🎸 (One Way, 1971/1995)
Greenhouse 🎸🎸🎸🎸 (One Way, 1972/1995)
My Feet Are Smiling 🎸🎸🎸 (One Way, 1973/1995)
Ice Water 🎸🎸🎸 (One Way, 1974/1995)
Time Step 🎸🎸🎸🎸 (255, 1983)
A Shout toward Noon 🎸🎸🎸 (Private Music, 1986)
Regards from Chuck Pink 🎸🎸🎸🎸 (Private Music, 1988)
My Father's Face 🎸🎸🎸 (Private Music, 1989)
Essential (Collection) 🎸🎸🎸🎸 (Alliance, 1991/1996)
Peculiaroso 🎸🎸🎸 (Private Music, 1993)

Live 🎸🎸🎸🎸 (Private Music, 1995)
Dreams and All That Stuff 🎸🎸🎸 (One Way, 1996)
Standing in My Shoes 🎸🎸🎸🎸 (Private, 1997)

worth searching for: *Chewing Pine* (Beat Goes On, 1975/1994) is an apt title for this rootsy import collection.

influences:

◄◄ Igor Stravinsky, Chet Atkins, Carl Perkins, Rev. Gary Davis, Roy Clark

►► Jorma Kaukonen, Edward Wright, Ry Cooder, Chris Whitley

Allan Orski

Kraftwerk

Formed 1970, in Dusseldorf, Germany.

Ralf Hütter, vocals, electronics; Florian Schneider, vocals, electronics; Klaus Roeder, violin, guitar (departed early '70s); Wolfgang Flür, electronic percussion: Karl Bartos, electronic percussion.

What's your idea of sterility? Kraftwerk has provided clean-room synthetics for nearly three decades. Scarce signs of human warmth exist for these German electronic auteurs, though the early, out-of-print stuff that Kluas Roeder had a part in has a bit of hippie aesthetic, but that soon faded for the pleasures of the "Autobahn." Repetition is an instrument for Kraftwerk (which means "power station" in its home language), with records that often contain little more than whirs, clicks, robotic voices, and beats. The neat thing is that it took four guys to make their records. That said, Afrika Bambaata, Buffalo Daughter, Big Black, and many others have used Kraftwerk's spare melodies and songs to further their own work.

what to buy: *Computer World* 🎸🎸🎸🎸 (Warner Bros. 1981/Elektra, 1988, prod. Kraftwerk) is perhaps the best start, although all but the early stuff is good enough for neophytes. "Numbers" is perhaps the second most sampled hip-hop track of all time, with its infectious beat and the "Ich, Nee, San, She" count-off. And "Pocket Calculator" and "Home Computer" bring you closer to your gadgets than you might find comfortable.

what to buy next: *The Mix* 🎸🎸🎸🎸 (Elektra, 1991, prod. Kraftwerk) is a neat update of a range of tracks, going all the way back to 1974's hit "Autobahn" as well as "Trans-Europe Express" and "Music Non Stop." Also, because many of the older records are out-of-print, this collection is the only convenient place to find some of these tracks.

the rest:
Radio Activity 🎸🎸🎸 (Capitol, 1975)
Trans-Europe Express 🎸🎸🎸🎸 (Capitol, 1977)
The Man Machine 🎸🎸🎸🎸 (Capitol, 1978)
Electric Cafe 🎸🎸🎸 (Warner Bros. 1986/Elektra, 1988)

worth searching for: With the label troubles the group has had, Cleopatra, Philips, Warner, Vertigo, Capitol, Elektra, Mercury, EMI, and Germanofon have all held rights to or released product by Kraftwerk. This means there is much to search for. However, one of the cooler and harder-to-find pieces is the 12-inch single "Tour de France" (EMI, 1983, prod. Kraftwerk); replete with bicycle chain noises and the rhythmic "breathing" of a rider, "Tour de France" lists the points along the route taken by the competitors. Utterly essential.

solo outings:

Wolfgang Flür:

(With Yamo) *Time Pie* 🎵🎵 (Hypnotic, 1997)

influences:

◀◀ Philip Glass, John Cage, Perry & Kingsley, Bob Moog, Mozart, Can, early Beach Boys

▶▶ Tangerine Dream, Telex, the Orb, Orbital, Gary Numan, David Bowie, Negativland, Devo, Six Finger Satellite, Neu, Main, Afrika Bambaata, Buffalo Daughter, System 7, Spacemen 3, Spectrum, Air, the Chemical Brothers, Crystal Method

Barry M. Prickett

Billy J. Kramer & the Dakotas

Formed 1963, in Liverpool, England. Disbanded 1968. Re-formed 1989.

Billy J. Kramer (born William Howard Ashton, August 19, 1943, in Bootle, Liverpool, England), vocals; Mike Maxfield, guitar (1963–65, 1989–present); Robin MacDonald, guitar, bass (1963–67); Raymond Jones, bass (1963–64); Mick Green, guitar (1964–68); Tony Mansfield (born Anthony Bookbinder), drums (1963–66, 1989–present); Frank Farley, drums (1966–68); Eddie Mooney, vocals, bass (1989–present); Toni Baker, vocals, keyboards (1989–present).

Producer George Martin had no reason to doubt Beatles manager Brian Epstein when he first brought young Billy J. Kramer and his new back-up group the Dakotas into Abbey Road Studios in 1963. After all, Martin was already scoring British #1 hits with the last two bands Epstein had brought to his attention (Gerry & the Pacemakers and you-know-who). However, soon after putting Kramer on tape, it became apparent they certainly weren't dealing with another John Lennon: not only was Billy's pitch wobbly at best, but his twee crooner's approach, not to mention his hairstyle, seem firmly rooted in another era. Still, given a steady supply of Lennon/McCartney songs (with Martin deceptively ghosting Billy's every vocal track with a matching piano line), the Beatle magic worked its wonders long enough to provide Billy and the Dakotas with two years' worth of hits on both sides of the Atlantic. Perhaps the joyride could have lasted even longer had Kramer, already fearful of his ballad-heavy reputation, not turned down "Yesterday" when Paul Mc-

Cartney offered it to him exclusively in 1964. Four years later the inevitable had taken place: the Dakotas, who often seemed acutely embarrassed performing such numbers as "Little Children," abandoned ship, relegating Kramer to a life of entertaining supper clubs, nostalgia cruises, and Beatle conventions. At least he's finally brushed his hair forward.

what's available: *The Best of Billy J. Kramer* 🎵🎵🎵 (EMI America, 1991, prod. George Martin) is recommended mainly to Beatle completists, for it contains several Lennon/McCartney compositions ("Bad to Me," "From a Window") that went unrecorded elsewhere. And of course Martin's studio wizardry is remarkable throughout.

worth searching for: Alas, the years have not been kind. Recorded in Alaska and released on a tiny label out of Queens, New York, *Kramer versus Kramer* (Attack, 1986, prod. Steve Tatler) presents Kramer bravely tackling five new songs "versus" an equal number of his yester-hits. Meanwhile, the Dakotas' *And the Beat Goes On* (Maxi-Moose, 1990, prod. Toni Baker, Eddie Mooney, Mike Maxfield) presents recent live and studio recordings (without Billy) of Beatles, Badfinger, and even Searchers songs. Never fear though: a new album by Kramer & the Dakotas is due momentarily.

influences:

◀◀ The Phantoms, Ted Knibbs, the Beatles, the Shadows

▶▶ Terry Black, Corduroy, Chrome Omen

Gary Pig Gold

Wayne Kramer

See: MC5

Phil Krauth

See: Unrest

Lenny Kravitz

Born Leonard Albert Kravitz, May 26, 1964, in New York, NY.

As the son of a Jewish television producer and a black actress—Sy Kravitz and the late Roxie Roker of *The Jeffersons*—Lenny Kravitz seemed assured of a career in show business, a fate compounded by high school classmates such as Slash of Guns N' Roses and Lone Justice's Maria McKee. Still, when Kravitz married *Cosby Show* actress Lisa Bonet in 1987 and announced plans to release a record, critics snickered, calling him "Mr. Bonet." But his first album, featuring Kravitz himself on nearly every instrument, silenced many naysayers; even though his sound proved highly derivative of '60s and '70s influences, there was an unmistakable talent emerging. After collaborating with Madonna on her hit "Justify My Love" (Kravitz was later sued by Prince protégé Ingrid Chavez, who claimed to have co-written the tune, while rappers Public Enemy claimed a sample of their work used in the song was not licensed), he recorded an all-star version of the John Lennon hit "Give Peace a Chance" during the Gulf War. His own solo output veers between overt Jimi Hendrix, Curtis Mayfield, and Led Zeppelin influences, selling well enough to keep him in the public eye but never enough to bring blockbuster fame.

what to buy: Although its influences are all too apparent, *Circus* ♪♪♪ (Virgin, 1995, prod. Lenny Kravitz) is Kravitz's most consistent outing yet, mimicking Led Zep in the hit single "Rock and Roll Is Dead" without sacrificing the song's integrity. Elsewhere, he mines '60s and '70s soul and rock with better results than in the past, crafting an engaging, powerful rock/pop record.

what to buy next: As a blueprint for *Circus*, *Are You Gonna Go My Way?* ♪♪♪ (Virgin, 1993, prod. Lenny Kravitz) is an intriguing album, fired up by the Hendrix-inspired titled track and other numbers that trace his fascination with heritage musical styles.

what to avoid: Sabotaged mostly by petulant lyrics detailing the 1991 disintegration of his marriage to Bonet, *Mama Said* ♪♪♪ (Virgin, 1991, prod. Lenny Kravitz) is his most inconsistent work despite the presence of two appealing singles, "It Ain't Over 'til It's Over" and "Always on the Run." And while it's good to see him toss aside his hippie influences for psychedelic rock, here the artistic thievery is so blatant that it's hard to overlook.

the rest:
Let Love Rule ♪♪♪ (Virgin, 1989)
5 ♪♪♪ (Virgin, 1998)

worth searching for: Kravitz's collaboration with Madonna, "Justify My Love" (Warner Bros., 1990, prod. Lenny Kravitz), is worth a listen, if only to marvel that Chavez was dumb enough to claim credit for lyrics this awful.

influences:
◄◄ Led Zeppelin, Jimi Hendrix, Living Colour, Curtis Mayfield, Sly & the Family Stone

►► Self, Maxwell, the Family Stand

Eric Deggans

Chantal Kreviazuk

Born May 18, 1973, in Winnipeg, Manitoba, Canada.

Chantal Kreviazuk was a child prodigy on piano, starting at age five after watching her older brothers practice; Kreviazuk contends she "just knew" how to play when she first sat down at the keyboard. She went on to study classically and was writing commercial jingles as a teenager. At the same time she was hit-

WHAT ALBUM CHANGED YOUR LIFE?

The album that probably changed my life the most was probably *Innervisions* by Stevie Wonder. When I heard that, something happened to me. It just took me to another level. My favorite group was the Jackson 5. I loved Gladys Knight & the Pips, Diana Ross, and so forth. I really loved Motown, through elementary school, big time. I remember hearing *Innervisions,* I sat and listened to it with my mom. It was the first time I really heard everything. It wasn't just hearing the music; I paid attention to the texture of all the instruments and how they were placed. That was the beginning for me of opening my ears.

Lenny Kravitz

ting local lounges and even singing the Canadian national anthem for the NHL's Winnipeg Jets. During 1994 Kreviazuk got into a horrible accident in Italy; she collided head-on with a motorcyclist who didn't have his headlights on. She spent a lengthy hospital stay recovering from a broken jaw and femur, which gave her a chance to do a little soul-searching. Emerging with newfound enthusiasm to write music, she recorded a demo tape and was signed by Columbia. She has quickly become a favorite of Sarah McLachlan and the Lilith Fair set due to the strength of her debut album, *Under These Rocks and Stones*.

what's available: Kreviazuk's debut, *Under These Rocks and Stones* ♪♪♪♪ (Columbia, 1997, prod. Peter Asher, Matt Wallace), was met with enthusiastic response by those who are familiar with the musical exploits of McLachlan and Tori Amos. The album went platinum in Canada, and the somber "Surrounded"—about a boyfriend's suicide—garnered significant airplay and struck a nerve with listeners on both sides of the

Lenny Kravitz (© Ken Settle)

border. But the album is mainly upbeat, with songs such as "God Made Me" and "Grace" more representative of Kreviazuk's overall tone.

influences:

◀◀ Elton John, Alanis Morissette, Tori Amos

Darren Davis

K's Choice

Formed 1991, in Belgium.

Gert Bettens, guitars, vocals; Sarah Bettens, vocals; Jan Van Sichem Jr., guitars; Eric Grossman, bass; Bart Van Der Zeeuw, drums (1995–present).

The brother-sister duo of Gert and Sarah Bettens never really thought about seriously chasing a career in music. While attending school—Sarah for photography and Gert for graphic arts—the duo's music piqued the attention of Double T Records for its quirky alternapop sound. It came as a shock for the Bettens because they never made demos, just pursued music for fun. The siblings teamed up with guitarist Jan Van Sichem Jr., quit school, and recorded their sparkling, harmony-filled debut, *The Great Subconscious Club*, which U.S. listeners ignored. But the group's sophomore effort, *Paradise in Me*, launched the somewhat misunderstood hit "Not an Addict," which vaulted K's Choice to a spot on the modern rock hit parade.

what to buy: *Paradise in Me* 𝄞𝄞𝄞𝄞 (Sony 550, 1996, prod. Jean Blaute) sets K's Choice apart from other alternapop bands, thanks to Sarah Bettens's ability to convey emotion without overdoing it like, say, Dishwalla. The opening track, "Not an Addict," acknowledges the heroin chic fad by illuminating denial: "It's not a habit/it's cool/I feel alive/if you don't have it you're on the other side/I'm not an addict/maybe that's a lie." Sarah's scratchy vocals, harmonies, and sputtering guitars rule on "A Sound That Only You Can Hear." "My Record Company," with guitar parts similar to the Smashing Pumpkins' early works, is a funny take on the music industry: "They like your band/They shake your hand/They smell like food that has gone bad."

the rest:

The Great Subconscious Club 𝄞𝄞𝄞𝄞 (Sony 550, 1994)
Cocoon Crash 𝄞𝄞𝄞 (550 Music, 1998)

influences:

◀◀ Frente!, the Cardigans, Heart

▶▶ Marcy Playground

Christina Fuoco

Ed Kuepper

See: The Saints

Kula Shaker

Formed 1994, in London, England.

Crispian Mills, vocals, guitar; Alonza Bevan, bass; Jay Darlington, keyboards; Paul Winterhart, drums.

Kula Shaker was a key player in the Britpop zeitgeist, pairing whopping English melodies with borrowed Indian mysticism. The group attempted to shroud itself with Eastern religion icons, but at the end of the day it was no different than Blur or Pulp—other than the fact, of course, that the singer was actress Hayley Mills's son. The band's emphasis on heavy guitars insured moderate play on American alternative stations and even landed its version of Deep Purple's "Hush" on the soundtrack for the domestic blockbuster *I Know What You Did Last Summer*.

what to buy: Balancing equal parts spiritual weirdness and good classic rock hooks, *K* 𝄞𝄞𝄞 (Columbia, 1996, prod. John Leckie, Crispian Mills, Alonzo Bevan) is an instantly likeable album, if only because its retro grooves sound already familiar. "Govinda" and "Tattva" provide exceptionally magical moments.

what to buy next: The American-only *Summer Sun* 𝄞𝄞 (Columbia EP, 1997, prod. John Leckie, Crispian Mills, Alonzo Bevan) features several outtakes from *K*, as well as a decent cover of George Harrison's "Gokula."

influences:

◀◀ Deep Purple, the Stone Roses, George Harrison

Aidin Vaziri

Tuli Kupferberg

See: The Fugs

Kyuss

Formed 1989, in Palm Desert, CA. Disbanded 1995.

Josh Homme, guitars; John Garcia, vocals; Scott Reeder, bass (1991–95); Alfredo Hernandez, drums (1994–95); Nick Oliveri, bass (1989–91); Brant Bjork, drums (1989–93).

Kyuss originated as a group of southern Californians who staged infamous, all-night jam sessions in the desert outside their hometown of Palm Desert. Such a venue allowed them to play as long as they wanted, whatever they wanted, and, most important, as loud as they wanted. The group soon gained a loyal following, and after just one independent release, Kyuss was picked up by a major label. Often tagged heavy metal, the group has a much broader sound, incorporating a slower, bluesy edge as well as spacey, psychedelic jams. Multi-layered guitars and heavy grooves elevate Kyuss beyond the incoherent noise of most metal acts, and though the vocals are the weakest link in the band's music, the Herculean fits and starts of Josh Homme's guitar arrangements are the guts of this quartet. Citing creative differences, the group disbanded shortly after its fourth album was released in fall 1995. Homme and drummer Alfredo Hernandez now work with Queens of the Stone Age, while singer John Garcia went on to front Slowburn.

what to buy: Kyuss' major label debut, *Welcome to Sky Valley* 🎵🎵🎵🎵 (Elektra, 1994, prod. Chris Goss, Kyuss) showcases the group's sheer force and spatial, psychedelic capabilities better than its other efforts. The first track, "Gardenia," with its deceivingly soft title, takes raw power to another level. Arranged in three movements, each comprising three songs, this album may seem somewhat pompous for a lesser-known band, but the group claimed it was just a ploy to prevent listeners from skipping tracks.

the rest:
Wretch 🎵🎵🎵 (Dali/Chameleon, 1991)
Blues for the Red Sun 🎵🎵🎵🎵 (Dali, 1992)
And the Circus Leaves Town . . . 🎵🎵🎵🎵 (Elektra, 1995)

solo outings:
Slowburn (Garcia):
Amusing the Amazing 🎵🎵 (Red Ant, 1996)

influences:
⏪ Black Sabbath, the Cult

⏩ KoЯn, Drown

Christopher Scanlon

L.A. Guns

Formed 1987, in Los Angeles, CA.

Tracii Guns, guitar; Phillip Lewis, vocals (1988–95); Mick Cripps, guitar (1988–95); Kelly Nickels, bass (1988–95); Steve Riley, drums (1988–92, 1994–present); Bones, drums (1992–93); Chris Van Dahl, vocals (1995–97); Johnny Crypt, bass (1995–present); Ralph Saenz, vocals (1997–present).

Notable for reportedly requiring its potential members to have black hair, L.A. Guns began after guitarist Tracii Guns opted out of the then-burgeoning Guns N' Roses and recruited former members of Girl (Phillip Lewis) and W.A.S.P. (Steve Riley) for his own band. Toiling in that considerable shadow, the group briefly tasted success with its brand of Mötley Crüe–style guitar raunch and did time as the opening act for countless arena rock tours. As with most bands of its breed, L.A. Guns was inevitably reduced to touring small clubs again after the poor

sales of later albums, and most of the original members left in 1995. Guns remains the only constant member of the group.

what to buy: The group's second album, *Cocked and Loaded* 🎵🎵🎵🎵 (PolyGram, 1989, prod. various), is an excellent primer on late '80s sleaze rock, and gave the group its only hit, "The Ballad of Jayne."

what to buy next: *L.A. Guns* 🎵🎵🎵 (PolyGram, 1988, prod. Jim Faraci) is a sometimes fun but watered-down version of its follow-up.

what to avoid: *American Hardcore* **woof!** (CMC International, 1996) finds the once-proud band at a new low, stripped down to a trio and feebly attempting a hardcore sound.

the rest:
Hollywood Vampires 🎵🎵🎵 (Polydor, 1991)
Cuts 🎵🎵🎵 (Polydor EP, 1993)
Vicious Circle 🎵 (Polydor, 1994)

influences:
⏪ Mötley Crüe, Guns N' Roses

⏩ Faster Pussycat, D Generation, Type O Negative

Todd Wicks

Laika

Formed 1993, in London, England.

Margaret Fiedler, vocals, samples, guitar, keyboards, percussion; Guy Fixsen, vocals, samples, guitar, keyboards, percussion.

Laika plays bittersweet techno-torch from the morning after tomorrow. Heroes to some and villains to others for exploring electronica's fringes while retaining pop personality and song structure, Laika makes humanistic machine music wherein noncommittal vocals are an intentionally transparent camouflage for haunted lyrics. In both its choice of mascot (the First Dog in Space) and a palette of sci-fi-movie synth sonics at once high-tech and nostalgic, the band sifts through abandoned mementos of a future that never quite arrived, with simultaneous melancholy, affection, and wit. Widely hailed by U.S. critics as The Most Important Band You've Never Heard Of, Laika has earned the first part of that title, and deserves to lose the second.

what's available: Laika's debut, *Silver Apples of the Moon* 🎵🎵🎵🎵 (Too Pure/American, 1995, prod. Laika), is a stunning yet subtle audio palimpsest of found sounds, hushed voices, harsh rhythms, and ambient atmospheres that crash and recede like a sonic tide. The band's enigmatic quality is blueprinted here, and it's perfected on *Sounds of the Satellites* 🎵🎵🎵🎵 (Too Pure/Sire, 1997, prod. Laika), a dreamlike soundscape of phantasmal melodies and quiet desperation.

worth searching for: The one full album Fiedler made while in her earlier band Moonshake, *Eva Luna* (Too Pure/Matador/

Atlantic, 1993, prod. Guy Fixsen, Moonshake) gives a valuable look into her and (then-producer) Fixsen's guitar-rock birth pangs.

influences:

◀◀ Peggy Lee, Deborah Harry, Gary Numan, Moonshake

▶▶ Madonna (electronica edition)

Adam McGovern

Greg Lake

See: Emerson, Lake & Palmer

Lamb

Formed 1994, in Manchester, England.

Louise Rhodes, vocals; Andrew Barlow, DJ, producer.

Lamb introduced itself to the music world at the right time: Just as Britain started feeling a resurgence of truly good Britpop (á la Pulp, the Verve, and Oasis), electronic music was going global. It was then that Lamb combined the sultry vocals, hip-hop beats, and R&B that opposed Northern English lad rock with tight ambient rhythms and heavy drum 'n' bass undertones. Singer Louise Rhodes was raised in England on hippie folk music while DJ Andrew Barlow played percussion and listened to early rap music in Philadelphia. Barlow moved to England in 1993 and in 1994 was actively producing music and spinning discs under the moniker Hipoptimist. That same year, something inside Rhodes told her to pick up the phone and call Barlow on a whim. The pair got together and in 1996 released the single "Cotton Wool," which later appeared on its self-titled 1997 debut.

what's available: During Portishead's three-year recording hiatus, *Lamb* ♪♪♪♪ (Mercury/Fontana, 1997, prod. Lamb) carried the torch for experimental techno-infused ambient music. The album displays heavy vocal layering and consistent drum beats for a mix that's anything but dull, thanks in part to the addition of "real" instruments like an upright bass, keyboards, and a vibraphone.

influences:

◀◀ Portishead, Morcheeba, Goldie

Ari Bendersky

Lambchop

Formed 1993, in Nashville, TN.

Kurt Wagner, vocals, guitar; others.

Lambchop, a 10-piece ensemble with horns, steel guitar, and a guy who plays a lacquer-thinner can, is one of the more difficult-to-define outfits making music today. Most of the group's members grew up In Nashville during the '60s, an era in which country, pop, R&B, and soul music mixed freely. A similar liberalism is evident in Lambchop's recordings, all of which contain moments of hushed intimacy and dissonant clang.

what to buy: *Thriller* ♪♪♪♪ (Merge, 1997) is the band's most accomplished record to date, a compelling mix of hillbilly and R&B influences that approaches country as white soul music.

what to buy next: *How I Quit Smoking* ♪♪♪♪ (Merge, 1996, prod. Robb Earls) is an enchanting album that evokes the lush, string-laden records that Owen Bradley and Chet Atkins were producing in Nashville during the late '50s and early '60s.

the rest:

I Hope You're Sitting Down ♪♪♪♪ (Merge, 1994)
Hank ♪♪♪♪ (Merge, 1996)

influences:

◀◀ Jim Reeves, James & Bobby Purify, Yo La Tengo

Bill Friskics-Warren

Sonny Landreth

Born 1951, in Caton, MS.

Sonny Landreth has kept alive the art of slide guitar, which was thought by some to have died with Duane Allman in the early '70s. Most people were first introduced to Landreth as the leader of the Goners, the backup group that helped John Hiatt finally get noticed with the LP *Slow Dancing* and a subsequent barnstorming tour. Landreth, who was born in Elmore James's home town and lives in Lafayette, Louisiana, is steeped in the funky-beat blues music indigenous to that region, though he has his own voice as a player. His sound is distinct in its thick, saturated electricity, and he's a nimble guitarist, creating interesting textures with a flurry of fingers and treating his instrument, in the grand tradition of all bluesy slide masters, as a voice. Landreth's commercial undoing may be that he doesn't have a strong singing voice, but he writes songs that serve his vocal range.

what's available: Both of his albums—*Outward Bound* ♪♪♪♪ (Zoo/Praxis, 1992, prod. R.S. Field, Sonny Landreth) and *South of I-10* ♪♪♪♪ (Zoo/Praxis, 1995, prod. R.S. Field, Sonny Landreth)—are worth owning not just for the six-string pyrotechnics, but for the depth of the material.

influences:

◀◀ Big Bill Broonzy, Elmore James, Eric Clapton, Duane Allman, Bonnie Raitt

▶▶ The Black Crowes, Kenny Wayne Shepherd, Jonny Lang

Gil Asakawa

Ronnie Lane

See: The Faces

Jonny Lang (© Jack Vartoogian)

Mark Lanegan

See: Screaming Trees

Jonny Lang

Born Jon Langseth, January 29, 1981, in Fargo, ND.

Can a boy from the Great White North sing the blues? He can if he's Kid Jonny Lang, who hails from Minneapolis by way of Fargo, but who plays and sings like he was raised on catfish and collard greens, not lutefisk. Lang played saxophone in his middle school band until he took an interest in guitar. A few perfunctory lessons and a year or so of intense practice on his own, and the then-barely teenaged prodigy was leading his guitar teacher's band and hitting the club circuit. Lang's guitar skills are indeed impressive, though he's still copping others' styles at this point—a little Stevie Ray and Eric here, a little Albert and Buddy there. But what makes Lang a well-rounded performer (and a serious contender for long-time stardom) is his equally impressive vocal skill: He convincingly conveys lyrical situations likely out of the bounds of his actual experience. And while that may seem disingenuous, a mere *Star-Search* freak show to some, a little time spent with Lang suggests he will eventually come into his own. After all, how can you live through 17 winters on the northern plains and not come down with a serious case of the blues?

what to buy: You could hardly ask for a sharper contemporary blues debut—regardless of the performers' age—than *Lie to Me* ♪♪♪♪ (A&M, 1996, prod. David Z). Kicking off with the clavinet-driven title track, an honest-to-goodness hit single, the disc starts at a startlingly high level and pretty much stays there for its entire length. There's also a decent song about playing pool, the strutting "Rack 'Em Up," a couple of credible Lang originals, and a nimble take on Sonny Boy Williamson's "Good Morning Little School Girl," perhaps the first version where the singer is not singing about someone else as jailbait, but rather *is himself* jailbait. Disconcerting perhaps, but as with most things concerning Lang, his talent just makes you smile and accept it.

the rest:
Wander This World ♪♪♪♡ (A&M, 1998)

worth searching for: To hear the young guitar hero's not-so-humble beginnings, look for the self-released *Smokin'* (1995, prod. Mike Bullock), which shows his guitar chops already in place, though his vocal skill and blues sensibility were still works in progress. It contains a cover of Robert Johnson's "Malted Milk," apparently as strong a curative for the blues as a teenager can score in these days of enforced temperance.

influences:
◄◄ Stevie Ray Vaughan, Eric Clapton, Luther Allison, Albert Collins

Daniel Durchholz

WHAT ALBUM CHANGED YOUR LIFE?

I think Joni Mitchell's *Miles of Aisles* was probably the turning point where I realized that being a singer was one thing and being a songwriter was another, and that songwriting was very, very important.

k.d. lang

k.d. lang

Born Kathryn Dawn Lang, November 2, 1961, in Consort, Alberta, Canada.

Before venturing into pop turf, k.d. lang was a true revolutionary in country music: claiming to be the reincarnation of Patsy Cline, she dug straight to the roots of country on a series of gutsy records. Nashville barely gave her the time of day—she got a similar cold-shoulder treatment from country radio—and in 1992 lang abandoned her country career and applied her gorgeous vocals to smooth torch songs and other more urbane pop styles. The wildly popular and Grammy award-winning *Ingenue* kicked off this phase of her career, which coincided with lang's coming out and becoming a spokesperson for gay and animal rights.

what to buy: *Absolute Torch and Twang* ♪♪♪♡ (Sire, 1989, prod. Greg Penny, Ben Mink, k.d. lang) is her best country record, ranging from spunky honky-tonk ("Three Days") to Western swing ("Full Moon of Love") to soaring ballads ("Trail of Broken Hearts").

what to buy next: lang's major label debut, *Angel with a Lariat* ♪♪♪♪ (Sire, 1987, prod. Dave Edmunds) mixes pure country with cowpunk. *Ingenue* ♪♪♪♪ (Sire, 1992, prod. Greg Penny, Ben Mink, k.d. lang) lacks the fire of most of her country discs, but her vocals are as stunning as ever on pop ballads such as "Constant Craving" and "Save Me."

what to avoid: Though it took a bit of the edge off following up *Ingenue*, lang's soundtrack for *Even Cowgirls Get the Blues* (Sire, 1994, prod. Ben Mink, k.d. lang) was an unusually disappointing trifle.

the rest:
A Truly Western Experience 🎵🎵🎵 (Bumstead, 1984)
Shadowland 🎵🎵🎵 (Sire, 1988)
All You Can Eat 🎵🎵🎵 (Warner Bros., 1995)
Drag 🎵🎵 (Warner Bros., 1997)

worth searching for: *Blue Sky above Wide Plains* (Flashback, 1993) is a good-sounding bootleg of lang performances in New York (1993) and Chicago (1988).

influences:

◀◀ Minnie Pearl, Patsy Cline, Julie London

▶▶ Melissa Etheridge, Mary Chapin Carpenter, Trisha Yearwood

Thor Christensen

Jon Langford

See: Waco Brothers

Daniel Lanois

Born September 19, 1951, in Gaineau, Quebec, Canada.

Daniel Lanois is an artist of exceptional ambition, musical vision, and lyrical depth. He also produced some of the most important albums of the past two decades. While foremost a musician, he began his professional career as a producer/recording engineer at Grant Avenue Studio, which he owns with his brother. While there, Lanois met ambient rock pioneer Brian Eno, and the two struck up a long friendship and working relationship. Eno brought Lanois to the attention of a number of prominent artists, most notably U2, which hired him to co-produce (with Eno) its landmark 1984 album *The Unforgettable Fire*. From there, Lanois collaborated with Peter Gabriel, the Neville Brothers, and Bob Dylan (including his critically acclaimed *Oh Mercy* and Grammy winning *Time out of Mind*). During the late '80s Lanois turned his attention to an artist of utmost importance: himself. Drawing on his French-Canadian ancestry and his love of blues and rock, he forged a unique sound that is the sum of his knowledge and a hallmark for his prodigious talents.

what to buy: Lanois's second album, *For the Beauty of Wynona* 🎵🎵🎵🎵 (Warner Bros., 1993, prod. Daniel Lanois), is a work of stunning majesty and emotional complexity. Drawing on elements as diverse as Cajun music, guitar-rock, blues, and traditional French-Canadian balladry, Lanois crafts a sound that is greater than the sum of its parts, a style that transcends musical alchemy in its seamless fusion.

what to buy next: Lanois's debut, *Acadie* 🎵🎵🎵 (Opal/Warner Bros., 1989, prod. Daniel Lanois), is a quiet work that showcases his dedication to his French-Canadian roots, with songs populated by characters who seem to have sprung directly from history.

influences:

◀◀ Brian Eno, Nils Lofgren, Lindsey Buckingham, Clifton Chenier

▶▶ U2, Don Was, Peter Gabriel, Morphine

David Galens

Lard

See: Ministry

Largo

See: The Hooters

The La's

See: Cast

Last Exit

Formed February 7, 1986, in Germany and NY.

Sonny Sharrock, guitar; Peter Brotzmann, tenor, alto, bass saxophones, taragato; Bill Laswell, bass; Ronald Shannon Jackson, drums, vocals.

The free improvisation supergroup Last Exit brings together veteran leaders in their own rights: a legendary jazz-noise guitarist who's played with Miles Davis, Pharoah Sanders, and Herbie Mann; a hard-blowing German avant-garde saxophonist; a versatile master conceptualist who happens to be a monster bassist; and a technically and imaginatively awesome jazz drummer who has contributed significantly to records by Ornette Coleman, Albert Ayler, and Cecil Taylor. Reviving the spontaneous spirit of 1960s free jazz, they eschew rehearsals and play with a high level of intensity.

what to buy: *The Noise of Trouble: Live in Tokyo* 🎵🎵🎵🎵🎵 (Enemy, 1987) ranks among the greatest concerts ever documented on tape. Drawing on two nights in October 1986 (with Japanese saxist Akira Sakata joining throughout and Herbie Hancock contributing effectively on acoustic piano on the final track), it balances the free-for-all improvisation with actual songs and a healthy dose of blues from Sharrock and Jackson.

what to buy next: Drawn from two 1989 concerts, the totally improvised *Headfirst into the Flames* 🎵🎵🎵🎵 (MuWorks, 1993, prod. Robert Musso) is Last Exit's best purely free statement, a masterful display of creative empathy nearly as thrilling as *The Noise of Trouble* and a sonic improvement.

what to avoid: The unremitting barrage of *Last Exit* 🎵🎵🎵 (Enemy, 1986), the quartet's first actual release, was awe-inspiring at the time, but its muddy sound makes it no match for subsequent releases.

the rest:
From the Board a.k.a. *Cassette Recordings '87* ⚡⚡⚡ (Celluloid, 1988/ Enemy, 1995)
Köln ⚡⚡⚡⚡ (ITM, 1990)

worth searching for: The out-of-print *Iron Path* (Venture/Virgin, 1988, prod. Last Exit, Bill Laswell) is Last Exit's only studio album. Laswell scripts some nearly ambient moments and, conversely, a few heavy metal–like riffs. Pulsating and throbbing, it never explodes but exudes calm majesty.

influences:
◀◀ Albert Ayler, John Coltrane, Blind Willie Johnson

▶▶ Sonic Youth, William Hooker, Naked City

see also: *Bill Laswell*

Steve Holtje

The Last Roundup
See: Amy Rigby

Bill Laswell /Material
Born February 12, 1955, in Salem, IL.

You can almost tell from his willingness to mix genres and defy stereotypes that Bill Laswell grew up in Detroit, where funk and punk exist side by side. He's one of the busiest producers in music—his credits include Herbie Hancock, Mick Jagger, Motörhead, Iggy Pop, and scores of others—because he's got such an overflow of ideas he wants to enact. He works steadily for a number of labels, several of which he co-owns. The band Material first consisted of Laswell (an exceptional bassist), drummer Fred Maher, and synthesizer/keyboardist/tape processor Michael Beinhorn working on their own or with a small coterie of fellow avant-gardists. The three found success as a production team on modern urban R&B projects, and the breadth of Material's music began increasing. When vast numbers of guest performers were brought in for 1982's *Memory Serves*, the group's future modus operandus was set; an ever-shifting array of performers has kept the group mutating, and Laswell has increased the use of world music artists over the years, particularly from Africa and Asia. Laswell also started experimenting with ambient music long before it was popular and has always pursued his own path in that area, though he's also collaborated with the most interesting members of that genre—from Peter Namlook and Terre Thaemlitz to Jah Wobble & the Orb. His ambient and techno projects incorporate a range of music, often drawing on the bountiful vaults of his labels and completely recontextualizing the performances. He has also nurtured a stable of performers (such as Brain, Bootsy Collins, and the young guitarist Buckethead). He retains a special affection for the funk heroes of his youth, in some cases giving them much-needed work and respect. On the other hand, he always keeps up with trends, and he leaped feet-first into the British drum 'n' bass craze on *Oscillations*, where he worked with Ninj and Transonic.

what to buy: Material's *Memory Serves* ⚡⚡⚡⚡ (Celluloid/Elektra Musician, 1982, prod. Material, Martin Bisi) was the group's first album to take the guest-star approach to the extreme, and it worked fantastically, with the cream of New York's avant/jazz legends—Sonny Sharrock, Billy Bang, Fred Frith, Henry Threadgill, George Lewis, Charles K. Noyes, Olu Dara—concocting music unlike anything ever heard before. But the greatest moment is Laswell's unearthly combination of instrumental virtuosity and timbral imagination on "Silent Land," where he coaxes uncanny harmonics from his bass.

what to buy next: Material's *One Down* ⚡⚡⚡⚡ (Celluloid/Elektra, 1982, prod. Material) is Laswell at his funkiest and most commercial (the CD bonus track "Busting Out" was a club hit). The guests range from jazzers to avant types to R&B players, but the most startling performance is "Memories," with '60s jazz great Archie Shepp playing impassioned solos and a pre-superstar Whitney Houston soaring on a performance she's never equalled on her own. Axiom Ambient's *Lost in the Translation* ⚡⚡⚡⚡ (Axiom, 1994, prod. Bill Laswell) is labeled "Sound Sculptures by Bill Laswell with contributions from Terre Thaemlitz, the Orb, Tetsu Inoue" and represents something of an ambient all-star team. Laswell reshapes performances from Eddie Hazel, Sharrock, Sanders, Nicky Skopelitis, Jah Wobble, Bernie Worrell, Buckethead, Collins, Ginger Baker, Liu Sola, and more into abstract art music with incredible sensitivity to sonic textures. The two-CD, mid-line-priced *Deconstruction: The Celluloid Recordings* ⚡⚡⚡⚡ (Metrotone/Restless, 1993, prod. Bill Laswell) is the fastest way to get an idea of the amazing breadth of Laswell's many 1980s projects. Besides lots of Laswell and Material items, it includes tracks by Timezone, Massacre, Jalal Nuriddin & D.S.T., Manu Dibango, Peter Brotzmann & Laswell, Deadline, the Last Poets, Fela Kuti, Ginger Baker, Mandingo, Fab Five Freddy, Shango, Last Exit, and Toure Kunda, all Laswell-led or -produced acts.

what to avoid: Material's *Live from Soundscape* ⚡ (DIW, 1991, prod. Verna Gillis) is rambling, episodic, free-form improvisation with nothing more to offer than isolated moments of instrumental wizardry. Valis I's *Destruction of Syntax* ⚡⚡ (Subharmonic, prod. Bill Laswell) is a brave but flawed attempt to meld ambient and hip-hop.

the rest:
Bill Laswell:
Baselines 𝄞𝄞𝄞 (Celluloid/Elektra Musician, 1983)
Hear No Evil 𝄞𝄞𝄞𝄞 (Venture/Virgin, 1988)
(With Ryuichi Sakamoto and Yosuke Yamashita) *Asian Games* 𝄞𝄞𝄞𝄞 (Verve, 1994)
(With M.J. Harris) *Somnific Flux* 𝄞𝄞𝄞 (Subharmonic, 1995)
(With Nicholas James Bullen) *Bass Terror* 𝄞𝄞𝄞 (Sub Rosa, 1995)
Silent Recoil: Dub System One 𝄞𝄞𝄞 (Low, 1996)
Oscillations 𝄞𝄞 (Subharmonic, 1996)
Sacred System Chapter One: Book of Entrance 𝄞𝄞𝄞 (ROIR, 1996)
Dark Massive/Disengage: Ambient Compendium 𝄞𝄞𝄞 (M.I.L. Multimedia, 1996)
(With Jonah Sharp) *Visitation* 𝄞𝄞𝄞𝄞 (Subharmonic, 1996)
(With Style Scott) *Dub Meltdown* 𝄞𝄞𝄞𝄞 (WordSound, 1997)
Sacred System Chapter Two 𝄞𝄞𝄞 (ROIR, 1997)
City of Light 𝄞𝄞𝄞 (Sub Rosa, 1997)
Dreams of Freedom: Ambient Translations of Bob Marley in Dub 𝄞𝄞𝄞𝄞 (Axiom, 1997)
(With Terre Thaemlitz) *Web* 𝄞𝄞𝄞𝄞 (Subharmonic)
(With Peter Namlook) *Psychonavigation* 𝄞𝄞𝄞𝄞 (Subharmonic)

Material:
Temporary Music 𝄞𝄞𝄞𝄞 (Celluloid, 1981)
Red Tracks 𝄞𝄞𝄞 (Red, 1985)
Seven Souls 𝄞𝄞 (Virgin, 1989)
The Third Power 𝄞𝄞𝄞 (Axiom, 1991)
Live in Japan 𝄞𝄞𝄞𝄞 (Restless, 1993)
Hallucination Engine 𝄞𝄞𝄞𝄞 (Axiom, 1994)

Massacre:
Killing Time 𝄞𝄞𝄞𝄞 (Celluloid, 1982)

SXL:
Live in Japan 𝄞𝄞𝄞 (CBS/Sony Japan, 1987)
Outlands 𝄞𝄞𝄞𝄞 (Celluloid/Pipeline, 1988)

Deadline:
Down by Law 𝄞𝄞𝄞 (Celluloid, 1985)

Arcana:
The Last Wave 𝄞𝄞𝄞𝄞 (DIW, 1996)

Praxis:
Transmutation (Mutatis Mutandis) 𝄞𝄞𝄞𝄞 (Axiom, 1992)
Sacrifist 𝄞𝄞𝄞𝄞 (Subharmonic, 1993)
Metatron 𝄞𝄞𝄞 (Subharmonic, 1994)

Shango:
Shango Funk Theology 𝄞𝄞𝄞𝄞 (Celluloid, 1984)

Divination:
Distill 𝄞𝄞𝄞𝄞 (Submeta, 1996)

Chaos Face:
Doom Ride 𝄞𝄞𝄞𝄞 (Subharmonic)
Outland 𝄞𝄞𝄞 (PW, 1996)

Somma:
Hooked Light Rays 𝄞𝄞𝄞𝄞 (Low, 1996)

Equations of Eternity:
Equations of Eternity 𝄞𝄞𝄞𝄞 (Word Sound, 1996)

influences:

◀◀ John Coltrane, Sonny Sharrock, Jimi Hendrix, Mad Professor, Parliament-Funkadelic/George Clinton

▶▶ The Orb, Ben Neill, Mitchell Froom, DJ Spooky, Nona Hendryx, Arthur Baker, Golden Palominos

see also: *Last Exit*

Steve Holtje

Latin Playboys
See: Los Lobos

Laughing Hyenas
Formed 1986, in Ann Arbor, MI.

John Brannon, vocals; Larissa Strickland, guitar; Kevin Strickland, bass; Ron Sakowski, bass; Jim Kimball, drums; Todd A. Swalla, drums.

During the late '80s few post-hardcore bands could convey the sound of musical Armageddon the way Laughing Hyenas could. Led by Satanic wailer John Brannon (ex-Negative Approach) and guitarist Larissa Strickland (ex-L7), the band specialized in gnashing out hellish Midwestern hardcore noise instilled with a full-on sense of dread. Rooted in blues rock, the band's sound was a crystallization of bad vibes attempting to depict the same violence and frustration bands like the Birthday Party and the Stooges so expertly communicated. In concert, their message was clear: Audiences beware. To the best of their ability, the band tried to capture that doom on disc, and on the first few tries—which embodied the what-you-don't-know-can't-hurt-you ethic—they succeeded. *Come down to the Merry Go Round* and *You Can't Pray a Lie* were desperate salvos of aggressive post-punk-rock, with Brannon screaming like a man consumed by flames. Unfortunately, the very tough-nosed rhythm section of Jim Kimball and Kevin Strickland left to form the roots-punk outfit Mule, leaving Brannon and Larissa Strickland to move on as the Hyenas. But the band was never really able to replicate that same peril, the same fright-wig frenzy for which they had established their reputation. Subsequent projects became passable but unexceptional works of hard blues rock.

what to buy: Few recordings done during this time conveyed the kind of pale-faced dread supplied by *You Can't Pray a Lie* 𝄞𝄞𝄞𝄞 (Touch & Go, 1989, prod. Butch Vig). It's a perfect coalescing of the violence of punk and the guitar stomp of the coming grunge sound. The album is paired on CD with the 1990 album *Life of Crime*.

what to buy next: *Come down to the Merry Go Round* 🎵🎵🎵🎵 (Touch & Go, 1987, prod. Butch Vig) features the Hyenas at their early best on tracks like the crude "Stain" and the lurching "Hell's Kitchen." Extra tracks on the 1995 CD reissue, including a cover of Alice Cooper's "Public Enemy #9" (originally issued as a Sub Pop single), make this worth tracking down.

the rest:
Crawl 🎵🎵🎵 (Touch & Go, 1992)
Hard Times 🎵🎵🎵 (Touch & Go, 1995)

worth searching for: The group's self-released tape *Stain* came out in 1986.

influences:
◀◀ The Stooges, the Birthday Party
▶▶ Nirvana, Mudpuppy, Alice in Chains

Bob Gulla

Cyndi Lauper
Born June 20, 1953, in Queens, NY.

Armed with a voice that sounded like a Bronx Betty Boop and a wardrobe that looked like a thrift-store explosion, Cyndi Lauper was one of the first artists to benefit from the then-untapped power of MTV. Loopy and loveable, she possessed a sharp sense of humor and a powerful voice that could caress tender ballads ("Time after Time," "True Colors") and tear into raucous rockers ("Money Changes Everything") with a cunning combination of girlish glee and feminist gusto. Her charms were so irresistible that radio programmers didn't even notice that her 1984 hit "She-Bop" was an ode to female masturbation ("They say I'd better get a chaperone/cuz I can't stop messin' with the danger zone"). But Lauper wielded her stardom in strange ways, throwing her celebrity clout behind a rock 'n' roll revitalization of professional wrestling and choosing the ill-conceived *Vibes* as her first starring film role. Despite an impressive comeback in 1993 with *Hat Full of Stars* and a convincing attempt to reinvent herself as a dance diva with 1996's *Sisters of Avalon*, she remains known as the girl who just wants to have fun.

what to buy: Produced by Rick Chertoff (who later discovered Joan Osborne) and backed by members of the Hooters, *She's So Unusual* 🎵🎵🎵🎵 (Portrait, 1983) is a pop treasure chest of well-chosen covers such as Jules Shear's "All through the Night," the Brains' "Money Changes Everything," Prince's "When You Were Mine," and Robert Hazard's "Girls Just Want to Have Fun." Lauper's own "Time after Time," co-written with

Hooter Rob Hyman, was certified a standard when Miles Davis covered it in 1985.

what to buy next: On *Hat Full of Stars* 🎵🎵🎵 (Portrait, 1993, prod. Cyndi Lauper, Junior Vasquez), Lauper grafts hip-hop rhythms, woodwinds, and keyboards onto songs about child abuse ("Lies"), domestic violence ("Broken Glass"), abortion ("Sally's Pigeons," co-written with Mary Chapin Carpenter), and racial strife ("A Part Hate"), revealing a surprising maturity in insight and sound. The infectious "That's What I Think" is her best song to never reach radio.

what to avoid: The melodramatic *A Night to Remember* 🎵 (Portrait, 1989, prod. Cyndi Lauper, Lennie Petze, Phil Ramone, E.T. Thorngren) should have been titled *An Album to Forget*.

the rest:
True Colors 🎵🎵 (Portrait, 1986)
Twelve Deadly Cyns . . . and Then Some 🎵🎵🎵 (Epic, 1994)
Sisters of Avalon 🎵🎵🎵 (Epic, 1996)

worth searching for: Before MTV, Lauper fronted a Blondie-inspired new-wave band called Blue Angel, whose self-titled debut (Polydor, 1980, prod. Roy Halee) hinted at the glass-shattering prowess to come.

influences:
◀◀ Shelley Fabares, Marlene Dietrich, Bette Midler
▶▶ Björk

David Okamoto

The Law
See: Bad Company

Lawson Square Infirmary
See: The Triffids

The League of Crafty Guitarists
See: Robert Fripp

Paul Leary
See: Butthole Surfers

The Leaves
Formed 1966, in Los Angeles, CA. Disbanded 1968.

Jim Pons, bass, vocals; John Beck, guitar, vocals; Bobby Arlin, guitar, vocals; Robert Reiner, drums.

One of the first L.A. folk-rock bands, the Leaves drew inspiration as much from the British Invasion as from the burgeoning West Coast rock scene. The band's strength was its harmony vocals and an alternating jangling and minor-key tone. Not remembered for penning memorable original material, the group was good at emulating others' styles, culling material from the Beatles, Byrds, Rolling Stones, and Bob Dylan.

what to buy: The Leaves' rendition of "Hey Joe" (taken to greater heights by Jimi Hendrix a year later) hit the Top 40 in 1966. The resulting album, *Hey Joe* ✐✐ (MIRA, 1966/One Way, 1993 prod. Norm Ratner), was typically weak.

the rest:
All the Good That's Happening ✐✐ (Capitol, 1967/One Way, 1994)

influences:
◀◀ The Beatles, the Byrds, Bob Dylan

▶▶ Jimi Hendrix, Buffalo Springfield

Patrick McCarty

Led Zeppelin

Formed 1968, in London, England. Disbanded 1980.

Jimmy Page, guitar; Robert Plant, vocals; John Paul Jones, bass, keyboards; John Bonham (died September 25, 1980), drums.

Almost from the start, Led Zeppelin defined rock 'n' roll power and glory. During its prime, the quartet was rock's hottest, heaviest, highest-living player. But there was music to back it up; debatably the progenitors of heavy metal, Led Zeppelin emerged from the ashes of the Yardbirds and set sail with an unholy marriage of bloozy hard rock set to lumbering rhythms and defined by Jimmy Page's state-of-the-craft guitar heroics. Robert Plant's vocals became a rock prototype, influencing generations of singers, while John Bonham's impossibly authoritative drumming was equally revered; in 1984, the British band Frankie Goes to Hollywood—whose flavor-of-the-month dance-pop was a far cry from Led Zep—sampled his trademark whomp for its hit "Relax." Knitting it all together was John Paul Jones, who proved to be one of rock's most valuable utility players. What distinguished Led Zeppelin most was its ability to be eclectic without losing its identity; you always know a Zep song right off the bat, whether it's the primal attack of "Whole Lotta Love" or the acoustic chime of "Going to California." Throughout its 12 years together, the group used blues and rock as its base but incorporated touches of folk, funk, and world music, particularly from the Middle East. Though derivative early on—Willie Dixon successfully sued the band for copyright infringement for "Whole Lotta Love"—Led Zeppelin quickly matured into a unique and distinctive outfit. And not a lick of it sounds dated. "Stairway to Heaven" is arguably the most popular rock song of all time. And it would be hard to imagine rock radio without "Rock and Roll," "Black Dog," "Kashmir," or a dozen others. The Zep party ended in 1980,

when Bonham died—choking on his own vomit in his sleep—at Page's home in Windsor, England. To their credit, the surviving trio ended the band shortly thereafter and generally stayed apart save for one-off reunions at Live Aid, the Atlantic Records 40th Anniversary concert, and its induction into the Rock and Roll Hall of Fame. In 1994, however, Page and Plant began performing again as a duo, trading on the Led Zep catalog but with promises to pursue their own new music in the future.

what to buy: Led Zeppelin is one of the few rock bands that reward a random selection of its albums, but despite a bevy of box sets and anthologies, nothing betters the individual titles. No collection is complete without the untitled fourth album, commonly known as *Led Zeppelin IV* ✐✐✐✐ (Atlantic, 1971, prod. Jimmy Page) ✐✐✐✐, a uniformly exciting work that's impressive not just for its best-known cuts—"Stairway to Heaven," "Black Dog," "Rock and Roll"—but also for the bluesy "When the Levee Breaks" and the folky "Going to California." *Physical Graffiti* ✐✐✐✐ (Swan Song, 1975, prod. Jimmy Page) is a sprawling, double-length effort that features the enduring epic "Kashmir." *Led Zeppelin* ✐✐✐✐ (Atlantic, 1969, prod. Jimmy Page) and *Led Zeppelin II* ✐✐✐✐ (Atlantic, 1969, prod. Jimmy Page) represent an awesome output for a single year, the latter rating slightly higher due to the arresting "Whole Lotta Love."

what to buy next: There are some fans who will tell you *Houses of the Holy* ✐✐✐✐ (Atlantic, 1973, prod. Jimmy Page) is even better than the fourth album; it's actually a bit less consistent, though it's hard to argue with seminal tracks such as "Dancing Days," "Over the Hills and Far Away," and the reggae number "D'Yer Maker." Somewhat haphazard due to deadline pressures, *Presence* ✐✐✐✐ (Swan Song, 1976, prod. Jimmy Page) is the most underrated title in the Zep canon, with another engaging epic in "Achilles' Last Stand." *BBC Sessions* ✐✐✐✐ (Atlantic, 1997, prod. Jimmy Page) isn't the definitive concert souvenir fans crave, but it's solid nonetheless, tracing Zep's musical development via broadcast sessions between 1969–71.

what to avoid: The soundtrack to the concert film of the same name, *The Song Remains the Same* ✐✐ (Swan Song, 1976, prod. Jimmy Page) is a woeful representation of Led Zeppelin's electrifying live show. So far, there's been no legitimate release to really capture the band's concert prowess.

the rest:
Led Zeppelin III ✐✐✐▽ (Atlantic, 1970)
In through the Out Door ✐✐✐✐ (Swan Song, 1979)
Coda ✐✐✐ (Swan Song, 1982)
Led Zeppelin Box Set ✐✐✐✐ (Atlantic, 1990)
Remasters ✐✐✐▽ (Atlantic, 1992)
Led Zeppelin—Boxed Set 2 ✐✐✐ (Atlantic, 1993)
The Complete Studio Recordings ✐✐✐✐ (Atlantic, 1993)

Robert Plant (l) and Jimmy Page of Led Zeppelin (© Ken Settle)

worth searching for: It's likely that every Led Zeppelin performance has been bootlegged, and extreme caution should be used in delving into this overcrowded market. Representative of the best is *Trampled Underfoot* (Swingin' Pig, 1990), a two-CD set from a 1975 concert in Dallas that boasts strong sound and a good, though incomplete, set of songs.

solo outings:

John Paul Jones:

(With Diamanda Galas) *The Sporting Life* 🎵🎵 (Mute, 1994)

influences:

⏪ Willie Dixon, the Beatles, Chuck Berry, Fairport Convention, Buddy Guy, Howlin' Wolf, Robert Johnson, B.B. King, Little Richard, Joni Mitchell, Elvis Presley, the Rolling Stones, Otis Redding, Sonny Boy Williamson

⏩ AC/DC, Aerosmith, Bad Company, Black Sabbath, Bonham, Alice Cooper, the Cult, Great White, Guns N' Roses, Kingdom Come, Mötley Crüe, Rush, Soundgarden, Whitesnake, Van Halen

see also: *Robert Plant, Page & Plant*

Gary Graff and Sarah Weber

Arthur Lee

See: Love

Brenda Lee

Born Brenda Mae Tarpley, December 11, 1944, in Lithonia, GA.

Brenda Lee was the teenage queen of pre-Beatles rock 'n' roll. Her expressive vocal style allowed her to joyously rave rockabilly one moment, then croon country heartache the next. In 1956, after creating a sensation on the Red Foley, Perry Como, and Ed Sullivan television shows, the 11-year-old Lee signed with Decca Records. Her first discs, including "Jambalaya" and "Dynamite" (which earned her the nickname "Little Miss Dynamite"), were kick-ass performances but minor chart successes. Lee's career didn't really pick up until she toured Europe, where her manager instigated major waves of publicity by starting a rumor that the diminutive teen was actually a 32-year-old midget. After playing packed houses all over the world, Lee returned to the States and began to assault the pop charts with a vengeance in 1960. Adults marveled at her womanly vibrato and emotional command, while teens dug her for being one of them. Though a remarkable vocalist and stage performer, Lee's ordinary looks and plain dress style inspired more loyalty than jealousy among her female fans. As a result, when the British Invasion groups began to dominate the charts, Lee remained a force on Top 40 radio long after many of her American contemporaries had been relegated to obscurity. Though most of her mid- to late '60s output was country-pop in nature, Lee showed some of her old rock verve on "Is It True" (with Jimmy Page on guitar), and the remarkable "Coming on Strong," her final Top 15 hit. After her 1969 single "Johnny One-Time" received more air play on country than pop stations, Lee switched to that genre exclusively. Since the '70s, Lee has maintained a moderately successful solo career, particularly in Europe, where she is rightly acknowledged as one of pop music's greatest all-time performers.

what to buy: All phases of Lee's career as a hit vocalist, from 1956's "Bigelow 6-2000" to 1974's "Big Four Poster Bed," are included on *Anthology, Volumes 1 & 2* ♫♫♫♫ (MCA, 1991, prod. various), a two-disc, 44-song set. *The Brenda Lee Story* ♫♫♫♫ (MCA, 1974/1991, prod. Owen Bradley) is a more concise offering with only her biggest hits.

what to buy next: Lee's Christmas perennial "Rockin' around the Christmas Tree" is on *Jingle Bell Rock* ♫♫♫ (MCA Special Products, 1993, prod. various), along with nine other seasonal favorites. Buy it before you're driven nuts by its constant play on department store easy-listening speakers. Also, there's a good variety of hit tunes and LP tracks on *The EP Collection* ♫♫♫ (See for Miles, 1995, prod. various), a reasonably priced 25-track disc.

what to avoid: Unless you're proficient in German, French, and Spanish and dig Lee's phonetic rendering of her hit songs in those languages, *Weidersehn Ist Wunderschon* ♫♫♫ (Bear Family, 1992, compilation prod. various) will leave you shaking your head or laughing uncontrollably.

the rest:
Brenda Lee ♫♫ (MCA Special Products, 1990)
Brenda Lee ♫♫♫ (Warner Bros., 1991)
A Brenda Lee Christmas ♫♫♫ (Warner Bros., 1991)
Greatest Hits Live ♫♫ (K-Tel, 1992)
Greatest Country Hits ♫♫♫ (MCA Special Products, 1993)
Live Dynamite ♫♫♫ (Charly, 1997)

worth searching for: Everything Lee recorded for Decca between 1956–62 is on *Little Miss Dynamite* (Bear Family, 1995, prod. various), a 122-song box set. Completists might want to check out Lee's contributions to k.d. lang's *Shadowland* (Sire, 1988, prod. Owen Bradley). And Lee sings "You're in the Doghouse Now" with '30s-style sass on the film soundtrack *Dick Tracy* (Sire, 1990, prod. Andy Paley).

influences:
◄◄ Ray Charles, Mahalia Jackson, Teresa Brewer
►► Lesley Gore, Tanya Tucker, LeAnn Rimes

Ken Burke

The Left Banke

Formed 1965, in New York, NY. Disbanded 1969.

Steve Martin, vocals; Michael Brown, keyboards (1966–68); Rick Brand, guitar; Tom Finn, bass; George Cameron, drums.

Single-handedly responsible for the birth of the term Baroque Rock, the Left Banke was the first to graft delicate, classical-influenced melodies and instrumentation onto a standard rock beat for more than just a one-song experiment. Instead, this combination of sensibilities informed just about every song the group recorded. Today the Left Banke is revered by power pop fans not only for its melodic flair but also for its close harmonies and the British-flavored, achingly beautiful vocals of lead singer Steve Martin. Generally acknowledged as the creative genius behind all this (though the band did surprisingly good work without him, too) is keyboardist-songwriter Michael Brown. The son of violinist Harry Lookofsky, Brown (who produced pop acts such as Reparta and the Delrons under the name Hash Brown) called upon his classical training to layer great countermelodies on top of already-superb melodies, embellishing it all with harpsichord and fine string arrangements. Yet it all came out as unmistakably rock 'n' roll, and the group's hits—"Walk away Renee" and "Pretty Ballerina"—never wear out their welcome.

what's available: The original band's entire recorded output—two LPs and assorted non-LP singles—has been collected on a 26-track single CD *There's Gonna Be a Storm: The Complete Recordings, 1966–1969* ♫♫♫♫ (Mercury, 1992).

worth searching for: The song "Two by Two"—a superb post-Banke collaboration between Brown and Martin for the film *Hot Parts*—is on the compilation *Mynd Excursions: A Journey through the Vaults of Buddah and Kama Sutra* (Sequel, 1993).

influences:
◄◄ The Beatles, Gene Pitney, George & Ira Gershwin, Mozart
►► Yes, Procol Harum, the Moody Blues, Genesis, King Crimson

see also: *Stories*

Mike Greenfield

The Legendary Jim Ruiz Group

Formed 1991, in Minneapolis, MN.

Jim Ruiz, vocals, guitar; Stephanie Winter-Ruiz, vocals; Chris Ruiz, bass, keyboards; Danny Sigelman, drums, percussion; Matt Gerzema,

guitar; Charlotte LaBonne, bass; Allison LaBonne, lead guitar; John Crozier, guitar, piano, percussion; Rick Durgin, drums; Bryan Hannah, drums (1993–94).

Imagine Aztec Camera's Roddy Frame fronting the Kingston Trio and you have some idea what to expect from Minneapolis's Legendary Jim Ruiz Group. Its debut, the heart-rending *Oh Brother Where Art Thou?*, happened to bow in the midst of a cocktail craze, prompting many critics to misclassify the record (and the pajama-clad band) as just another bunch of Dino-come-latelies. The more canny scribes picked up on the Everything but the Girl, Orange Juice, and Jazz Butcher influences layered within and reveled in the unique blend of jazz chord progressions, open-hearted lyricism, and throwback innocence.

what to buy: *Oh Brother Where Art Thou?* ♪♪♪♪ (Minty Fresh, 1995, prod. Bryan Hanna) compresses almost four years of songwriting and live performances into a single, nearly flawless album. Featuring lilting guitar, organ, saxophone, agile percussion, and the everyman vocal stylings of frontman-guitarist Ruiz, the record deftly wears its heart on one sleeve and its funny bone on the other.

what to buy next: With just enough variation and polish to show growth but plenty of raw Ruiz zeal to keep longtime fans happy, *Sniff* ♪♪♪ (Minty Fresh, 1998, prod. John Crozier, Tom Herbers, David Trumfio) explores the group's usual jazz-pop terrain but adds more sophisticated production (for better and for worse). Luckily, the songwriting is every bit as solid as on its debut, evidenced by standout tracks "Goodbye to All That" (which features a jaunty call-out to Ruiz's favorite bands, a veritable who's who of earnest popsters) and "Uncle Wienie," a salute to Jim's quirky uncle and his Hispanic roots.

worth searching for: The Minty Fresh seven-inch for *Oh Brother*'s "Mij Amsterdam" contains two charming non-album tracks, "Minneapolis" and "Jody," not to mention an attractive, glossy sleeve.

influences:

◄◄ Aztec Camera, Billy Bragg, the Jazz Butcher, Everything but the Girl, Jonathan Richman, Style Council, Orange Juice

Scott Hess

Legendary Stardust Cowboy

Born Norman Carl Odam, Esq., September 5, 1947, in Lubbock, TX.

He has been hailed as a "cathartic genius"; others call his 1968 recording "Paralyzed" the worst record ever made. Whatever the case may be, this self-described singer-songwriter-dancer-actor-poet and "all 'round whoop-de-do guy" knew by the age of seven that he was destined for fame—just how he would achieve it was not so certain until he acquired his first guitar. He began emulating the styles of his favorite singers (Ray Price, Marty Robbins, and Johnny Cash) and the dance steps of the young Elvis Presley. Joe Ely, who has gone on to pronounce "The Ledge" as no less than "West Texas's greatest jazz musician," remembers watching the teenager singing Everly Brothers songs on the steps of their high school; another friend, Jimmie Dale Gilmore, recalls Odam atop a car with the words "NASA Presents the Legendary Stardust Cowboy" spray-painted across its sides, giving impromptu performances at the local Hi-D-Ho Drive-In. Not surprisingly, in these dark ages before the likes of Willie Nelson, some townsfolk took offense at the sight of a young man with shoulder-length hair, mutton-chop sideburns, and bright orange cowboy get-ups singing the C&W hits of the day at the local burger joint. So in the summer of 1968 the Ledge decided Lubbock could no longer contain a talent and a vision of his magnitude and, with $160 in his pocket and a broken Dobro, and lacking a manager, agent, record contract, and an invitation, he set out for New York City to perform on Johnny Carson's *Tonight Show*. He only made it as far as Fort Worth, though, where some vacuum cleaner salesmen caught his act and immediately took him to their neighbor T-Bone Burnett's recording studio. Gamely offering his services on drums, Burnett began committing the Ledge's repertoire direct to quarter-inch tape, two minutes of which were spliced off and rushed upstairs to the town's only Top 40 radio station. That piece of tape, of a song called "Paralyzed," went on the air that night, and within a week was #38 on KXOL's All-American Hit List. One month later, the Legendary Stardust Cowboy was performing his break-away smash, with every one of its fierce rebel yells and bugle solos intact, on the nation's most popular television show, *Rowan & Martin's Laugh-In*. This appearance, rightly hailed by *Spin* Magazine as one of the 25 Greatest Musical Moments in TV history, led to offers from *American Bandstand*, Joey Bishop, and *The Ed Sullivan Show*. But it was at this most inopportune of moments that a four-month musician's strike, banning live music from network television, halted the phenomenal rise of "Paralyzed" and dealt the Cowboy's momentum a crippling blow. An arrest soon afterwards—on a trumped-up vagrancy charge—only served to add insult to injury, and by decade's end, the Ledge was reduced to working the night shift at the Dunes Hotel in Vegas—and *not* as a performer. His influence festered throughout the 1970s, however. David Bowie, having caught a BBC rerun of the notorious *Laugh-In* episode, admits to being inspired enough to create his Ziggy Stardust persona partially in the Ledge's honor. The Ledge's former classmates Ely and Gilmore continued to sing his praises as their own careers took off, and all of this belated recognition coaxed him back into the studio in the early 1980s to cut his first full-length album, *Rock-It to Stardom*, after which he hit the road for long-awaited tours of the United States, Europe, and Australia.

He was recently the subject of an absolutely delightful documentary film by Anthony Philputt titled *Cotton Pickin' Smash: The Story of the Legendary Stardust Cowboy*, and at last report was sighted opening a Chris Isaak show in San Francisco's Fillmore Auditorium. Unfortunately, he *still* hasn't gotten an invitation to appear on *The Tonight Show*.

what's available: *Retro Rocket Back to Earth* 🎵🎵🎵🎵 (New Rose, 1996, prod. Gary Stillens, Frank Novicki) is a CD reissue of the Ledge's second and third albums, and Norton Records (P.O. Box 646, Cooper Station, New York, NY 10003) also has pressed two singles from these sessions.

worth searching for: *Rock-It to Stardom* (Amazing, 1984, prod. Jim Yanaway) is his first "comeback" album, also issued in Europe on the Big Beat and Virgin labels. As for the song that started it all? "Paralyzed," although it deserves to be made required listening for every man, woman, and child in America, is usually only available on novelty-record compilations, the easiest of which to find is *Wild, Weird & Wacky* (Time/Life, 1990, prod. various).

influences:

◀◀ Elvis Presley, Tom Jones, Herb Alpert

▶▶ Wild Man Fisher, Jandek, Jack Pedler

Gary Pig Gold

The Lemon Pipers

Formed 1967, in Oxford, OH. Disbanded 1970.

Ivan Browne, vocals, guitar; R.G. Nave, organ, green tambourine; Bill Bartlett, guitar; Steve Walmsley, bass; Bill Albaugh, drums.

With their classic bubbledelic hit "Green Tambourine," a shimmering #1 early in 1968, the Lemon Pipers crassly mined the same candy-acid vein already being visited regularly by the likes of John Fred and the incomparable Tommy James. Unlike James, however, the Pipers had only one bona fide hit; as a result, like Fred, the group quickly vanished from the charts and reside to this day in one-hit wonderland. A curious footnote, however: a decade after "Green Tambourine," Bill Bartlett once again visited the Top 20 as leader of the band Ram Jam, another one-hit wonder with "Black Betty." Neither he nor his fellow Lemon Pipers have been heard from since.

what's available: The fine compilation *Golden Classics* 🎵🎵🎵 (Collectables, 1994, prod. Paul Leka) contains not only their groovy gummy hit and its several failed follow-ups, but some surprisingly adventurous tracks (for example, a version of Goffin & King's "Wasn't Born to Follow" that stands in stark, swirling contrast to the Byrds' more rural take), hinting that this band perhaps was capable of more depth and scope than

their hit-fixated bosses at Buddah Records allowed them to explore and develop at the time.

influences:

◀◀ The Beatles, the Move, Tomorrow

▶▶ 10cc, Dukes of Stratosphear, Jellyfish

Gary Pig Gold

Lemonheads

Formed 1986, in Boston, MA.

Evan Dando, vocals, guitar; Ben Deily, vocals, guitar, drums (1986–89); Dave Ryan, drums (1989–present); Jesse Peretz, bass (1986–89); Juliana Hatfield, bass (1991–92); Nic Dalton, bass (1992–present).

Lemonheads began life as a hardcore indie-punk outfit and snagged a major label deal after its hard 'n' fast remake of Suzanne Vega's "Luka" became a college radio hit. But the band didn't really take off until spacey "alterna-hunk" Evan Dando took control in 1990 and began doctoring up its punk with winsome pop and folk styles. But its breakthrough didn't come via Dando; rather, it was a 1992 cover of Simon & Garfunkel's "Mrs. Robinson"—included on home video for *The Graduate*—that vaulted Lemonheads to mass popularity, though it repulsed as many boomers as it intrigued Generation Xers.

what to buy: *It's a Shame about Ray* 🎵🎵🎵🎵 (Atlantic, 1992, prod. Robb Bros., Evan Dando) is a masterful blend of gray ballads such as "My Drug Buddy" and punk-pop raveups like "Alison's Starting to Happen." A second edition added the remake of "Mrs. Robinson."

what to buy next: *Lick* 🎵🎵🎵 (TAANG!, 1989, prod. Tom Hamilton, Terry Katzman) represents the band at its most raucous, especially on "Luka." *Come on Feel the Lemonheads* 🎵🎵🎵 (Atlantic, 1993, prod. Robb Bros., Evan Dando) is a loose, experimental effort with solid songs such as "Big Gay Heart," "Being Around," and "Into Your Arms."

what to avoid: *Create Your Friends* 🎵🎵 (TAANG!, 1989, prod. Tom Hamilton) is a run-of-the-mill post-punk effort.

the rest:

Hate Your Friends 🎵🎵 (TAANG!, 1987)
Creator 🎵🎵 (TAANG!, 1988)
Lovey 🎵🎵 (Atlantic, 1990)
Car Button Cloth 🎵🎵🎵 (Atlantic, 1996)
Best of the Atlantic Years 🎵🎵🎵 (Atlantic, 1998)

worth searching for: *Lemonology: The Study of Specific Songs from Lemonheads' Past* (Tag/Atlantic, 1996) is a sweet 11-song sampler of previous Lemonheads material issued to promote the then-new *Car Button Cloth*.

influences:

◀◀ Replacements, Neil Young, Sex Pistols, Ramones

▶▶ Gin Blossoms, Cracker, Everclear

Thor Christensen

John Lennon

Born October 9, 1940, in Liverpool, England. Died December 8, 1980, in New York, NY.

John Lennon is an icon not only in rock 'n' roll but in all of pop culture. So it's surprising how thin his post-Beatles output turned out to be. In the days when he was more in the news as a social force, his songwriting sometimes sagged. When he spent most of his days as a househusband, his work was simply absent. Still, for the urgent familiarity of his voice and the timelessness of his best material, Lennon's legacy will undoubtedly endure, especially since his tragic murder outside his Manhattan apartment building as he was on the verge of a major comeback with 1980's *Double Fantasy*. It was his partially finished songs, after all, that led to the Beatles' unexpected "reunion" in 1994, with his former bandmates overdubbing his old demo tracks.

what to buy: *Plastic Ono Band* ♪♪♪♪ (Apple, 1970, prod. John Lennon, Phil Spector) is a searing, indelible work that has never been matched even in the days of the most confessional grunge. A collection of songs inspired by the primal scream therapy of Dr. Walter Janov, Lennon's autobiographical songs about his mother (who died when he was a child), his declaration of independence from God (and the Beatles), and his lonely calls for the working-class hero is a tour de force nearly three decades later. Of the several collections available, *Lennon Legend* ♪♪♪♪ (EMI, 1997, prod. various) is the best.

what to buy next: *Rock 'n' Roll* ♪♪♪♪ (Apple, 1975, prod. John Lennon, Phil Spector) is a splendid collection of rock favorites done in a relaxed manner by Lennon, who's in great voice. *Imagine* ♪♪♪♪ (Apple, 1971, prod. John Lennon, Phil Spector) contains the enduring title hymn and a dark stab as his former Beatles partner Paul McCartney in "How Do You Sleep?"

what to avoid: The early experimental albums with Yoko Ono—*Unfinished Music No. 1: Two Virgins* **woof!** (Apple, 1968, prod. John Lennon, Yoko Ono), *Unfinished Music No. 2: Life with the Lions* **woof!** (Zapple, 1969, prod. John Lennon Yoko Ono), and *The Wedding Album* **woof!** (Apple, 1969, prod. John Lennon, Yoko Ono)—are avant garde works comprised of static, spoken word, and repetition. They may have some historical interest or collectors' value—particularly the original nude

cover of *Two Virgins*—but as collectors know, value goes up if the covers aren't opened. And you won't miss much if you don't open these.

the rest:

Live Peace in Toronto ♪♪♪ (Apple, 1969)
Some Time in New York City ♪♪♪ (Apple, 1972)
Mind Games ♪♪♪ (Apple, 1973)
Walls and Bridges ♪♪♪ (Apple, 1974)
Shaved Fish ♪♪♪♪ (Apple, 1975)
Double Fantasy ♪♪♪♪ (Geffen, 1980)
The John Lennon Collection ♪♪♪♪ (Capitol, 1982)
Milk and Honey ♪♪♪ (Polydor, 1984)
John Lennon Live in New York City ♪♪♪ (Capitol, 1986)
Menlove Avenue ♪♪♪♪ (Capitol, 1986)
Imagine: John Lennon (Soundtrack) ♪♪♪♪ (Capitol, 1988)
Lennon ♪♪♪♪ (EMI, 1990)
The John Lennon Anthology N/A (Capitol, 1998)

worth searching for: Yoko Ono did release the entirety of Lennon's demo tapes on a radio series called *The Lost Lennon Tapes*, which were immediately put on the underground market by numerous bootleg labels. They're worth seeking out, especially for "Serve Yourself"—a goof on Dylan's Jesus period—and the original version of "Free As a Bird," which was the first track the surviving Beatles tackled in 1995 for *The Beatles Anthology*.

influences:

◀◀ Gene Vincent, Lonnie Donnegan, Buddy Holly, Chuck Berry, James Joyce

▶▶ Elton John, Billy Joel, Julian Lennon, Lenny Kravitz, Oasis, Sean Lennon

see also: *The Beatles, Yoko Ono*

Roger Catlin

Julian Lennon

Born John Charles Julian Lennon, April 8, 1963, in Liverpool, England.

"Boy, you're gonna carry that weight," sang Paul McCartney on the Beatles' *Abbey Road* album; and although he may not have been singing about Julian Lennon then, he couldn't have better summed up the essential dilemma of this Lennon's creative life. Using his uncanny vocal similarity to his far more talented father as his entree into the big time, Julian scored one Top 10 hit (the bouncy and infectious "Too Late for Goodbyes") and two smaller radio hits (the pretty and nostalgic but ridiculously meandering "Valotte" and the jazzy, Bowie-ish "Say You're Wrong") off his multimillion-selling debut album, *Valotte*. Successive albums failed to follow up that success, and in recent years Lennon has (grudgingly) surrendered his spotlight to his half-brother, Sean, though he continues to release albums abroad.

what to buy: *Valotte* 🎵🎵🎵 (Atlantic, 1984, prod. Phil Ramone) was a fair opening salvo with some decent songs, but it's clear that the young Lennon was still very far from being able to transcend his influences.

what to buy next: With *Help Yourself* 🎵🎵 (Atlantic, 1991, prod. Bob Ezrin), Lennon finally became himself, a mixed-up young singer with a good bit of experience making records but little knowledge gained from it.

what to avoid: His second album, *The Secret Value of Daydreaming* 🎵 (Atlantic, 1986), unmasks his generally weak voice and an even less firm sense of his artistic desires and abilities, while his third, *Mr. Jordan* **woof!** (Atlantic, 1989), is a terrible Bowie ripoff on which he vocally imitates the Thin White Duke. Both titles are justifiably out of print.

worth searching for: If you're a Beatlemaniac, Lennonophile, or—dare we say it?—a Julian fan, you might want to shell out for *Photograph Smile* (Music from Another Room, 1998), which he put out on his own label in the U.K.

influences:

⏪ John Lennon, David Bowie

Bob Remstein

Annie Lennox

See: Eurythmics

Less Than Jake

Formed 1992, in Gainesville, FL.

Chris Domakes, vocals, guitars; Vinnie Fiorello, drums; Roger Manganelli, bass, vocals; Buddy Schaub, trombone; Derron Nuhfer, baritone sax.

The three-chord-happy ska band Less Than Jake may seem to be one of those Third Wave bands manufactured to make some cash off the ska trend. But actually, the band is celebrating its fourteenth release. Less Than Jake, named for Vinnie Fiorello's feeling that his family's dog Jake was being treated better than him, formed in 1992 as a power-pop threesome. The core members tacked on a horn section to boost its sound six months later. Less Than Jake released a series of albums, many of which are no longer available, before signing to Capitol Records for *Losing Streak*, which plays up Less Than Jake's love of blending punk pop and ska. But although it was the band's 13th release, it didn't expand the audience much further than its peers.

what to buy: If only for the sheer humor of it, the eight-song album—number 14—*Greased* 🎵🎵🎵 (No Idea, 1997, prod. Less Than Jake) is worth purchasing. On it, Less Than Jake covers various songs off of the soundtrack to the movie *Grease*.

the rest:
Pez-Core 🎵🎵 (Dill, 1994/Asian Man, 1997)
Losing Streak 🎵🎵🎵 (Capitol, 1996)

influences:

⏪ The Mighty Mighty Bosstones, Operation Ivy, Suicide Machines

⏩ Reel Big Fish, Goldfinger

Christina Fuoco

Let's Active

Formed 1981, in Winston-Salem, NC. Disbanded 1988.

Mitch Easter, vocals, guitar; Faye Hunter, bass, vocals (1981–86); John Heames, bass (1988); Sara Romweber, drums (1981–84); Angie Carlson, vocals, keyboards, percussion (1986–88); Eric Marshall, drums (1986–88).

Through his Drive-In recording studio (so named because it started out in the family garage), Mitch Easter became the center of activity among the so-called "New South" bands and, when several of them moved north, their Hoboken/Manhattan friends. Low-tech but high-concept, Easter's productions were bright and poppy but left room for deeper currents, reflecting his love of '60s pop and the less pretentious '70s underground bands—such as the revered Big Star. Let's Active (the name came from a mangled English-language Japanese T-shirt slogan) embodied the same principles; begun as a band, by the second album it was more Easter-plus-occasional-sidepeople. Since then he has continued to work as a producer and has toured with Velvet Crush.

worth searching for: At this point, the group's catalog requires some work to track down. Easter's talent for fresh sounds and quirky, imaginative hooks stood out most on *Cypress/Afoot* (I.R.S., 1989, prod. Let's Active, Don Dixon), which in its CD version combines the first EP and LP. On the surface it can seem all similarly twinkie, but there's actually plenty of variety, and the male/female vocal split works well. "Blue Line" is Easter's best chorus hook, utterly indelible. *Big Plans for Everybody* (I.R.S., 1986, prod. Mitch Easter) is mostly Easter and contains some appealing sonic experiments. *Every Dog Has His Day* (I.R.S., 1988, prod. John Leckie, Mitch Easter) was the group's heavier swan song, as it returned somewhat to a band structure.

influences:

⏪ The Beatles, Big Star, Move, Nazz/Todd Rundgren

⏩ R.E.M., dB's, Pylon, Bongos/Richard Barone, Velvet Crush, Matthew Sweet, Teenage Fanclub, Guided by Voices

Steve Holtje

Level 42

Formed 1980, in London, England. Disbanded 1994.

Mark King, bass, vocals; Mike Lindup, keyboards, vocals; Phil Gould, drums (1980–87, 1994); Boon Gould, guitar (1980–87); Alan Murphy (died October 19, 1989), guitar (1987–89); Jakko Jacszyk, guitar (1991–94); Gary Husband, drums (1987–94).

Friends on the Isle of Wight, the Gould brothers (Boon and Phil are twins) and Mark King moved to London during 1978. There they met Mike Lindup, a friend of Phil's from college. Inspired by '70s fusion artists such as Chick Corea and Stanley Clarke, Level 42 mixed jazz, funk, and rock in similar ways, with King's mighty, thumping bass sound—borrowed heavily from his idol Clarke—center stage. Although early efforts were mostly instrumental, pressure from the band's record company convinced King to start singing and writing more pop-oriented material. The group found success at home but little interest in America until 1985, when the first of its two most pop-oriented albums appeared on the charts. The hectic touring required by their newfound success proved too much for the Gould brothers, who left the band during 1987, to be replaced by former Go West guitarist Alan Murphy (who died of AIDS in 1989) and ex-Allan Holdsworth sideman Gary Husband. The group remained active, but successive albums never matched the pop appeal of its mid-'80s efforts and the group disbanded in 1994. King is said to be considering a solo career.

what to buy: For well-composed songs matched with funky, cohesive playing, you can't beat the band's two most successful albums, *World Machine* 🎵🎵🎵 (Polydor, 1985, prod. Level 42, Wally Badarou) and *Running in the Family* 🎵🎵🎵 (Polydor, 1987, prod. Level 42, Wally Badarou). Both boast quality pop tunes leavened with jaw-dropping musicianship: "Something about You" and the title track on *World Machine*, "Children Say," and "Fashion Fever" on *Family*. *World Machine* boasts two added hits from a previous album, the dance track "Hot Water" and tribal groove "The Chant Has Begun."

what to avoid: Most of the band's records after *Family* fall into a familiar rut, with the pop muse that delivered such appealing songs on its hit albums conspicuously absent. Of these, *Staring at the Sun* **woof!** (Polydor, 1988, prod. Level 42, Wally Badarou, Julian Mendelsohn) commits the greatest sin, unfolding as a totally uninteresting album assembled by a group of top-notch musicians who should have known better.

the rest:
Early Tapes 🎵🎵 (Polydor, 1981)
Level 42 🎵🎵🎵 (Polydor, 1981)
The Pursuit of Accidents 🎵🎵 (Polydor, 1982)
Standing in the Light 🎵🎵🎵 (Polydor, 1983)
True Colours 🎵🎵🎵 (Polydor, 1984)

A Physical Presence, Pt. 1 🎵🎵 (Polydor, 1985)
A Physical Presence, Pt. 2 🎵🎵🎵 (Polydor, 1985)
Level Best 🎵🎵🎵 (Polydor, 1989)
Guaranteed 🎵🎵 (RCA, 1992)
Forever Now 🎵🎵🎵 (RCA, 1994)
Live at Wembley 🎵🎵🎵 (World Famous, 1996)
Remix Collection 🎵🎵🎵 (Connoisseur, 1996)

worth searching for: The video *Live at Wembley* (PolyGram, 1987), shot during a triumphant four-night stand at Wembley Arena in London, captures the group at its creative best, showcasing all the best things about Level 42's sound and stage show.

influences:

◄◄ Chick Corea, Stanley Clarke, Return to Forever, Herbie Hancock's Headhunters

►► Brand New Heavies

Eric Deggans

Keith Levene

See: Public Image Ltd.

Jerry Lee Lewis

Born September 29, 1935, in Ferriday, LA.

He wasn't the first nor the most successful, but Jerry Lee Lewis was the greatest of the '50s rockers. His blues-drenched bravado, combined with his dramatic feel for country music and sexually charged boogie-woogie, effortlessly created the impression that he was living every moment of each song on a grand scale. Moreover, he has left behind a richer, more variegated catalog of recordings than any of his contemporaries. On stage, he raised rock 'n' roll showmanship to a high, nearly Pentecostal art. After bopping the keyboards with his fists, elbows, feet, and ass (somehow always hitting the right note), he would triumphantly kick back his stool, suggestively wriggle into an upright position while playing one last run and then vault onto the piano top. Then, with his long, peroxide blonde hair hanging in his eyes, he would exhort his ecstatic followers to "Shake it, baby, shake it!" Rebellious kids seeking rhythmic freedom and release loved him. Their parents hated his guts.

Lewis absorbed his stark, personal country style from his father's Jimmie Rodgers and Hank Williams 78 rpm records and experienced the liberating forces of the blues at Haney's Big House. On his own, Lewis learned to transform everything from the cowboy songs of Gene Autry to the overwrought pop of Al Jolson into thrilling cut-time boogie and moving honkytonk ballads. A masterful self-taught pianist, he could attack the keys with frightening energy and power, or softly caress them, cocktail-style. But though his racy (for the time) Sun Records hits

"Whole Lotta Shakin' Goin' On," "Great Balls of Fire," and "Breathless" put him in line to become rock's new king once Presley was inducted into the Army, Lewis was derailed by a controversial marriage to his 13-year-old cousin—which resulted in the banishment of his records from most radio playlists—and, later, by excessive drinking, pill-popping, chronic health problems, the IRS, and complex personal tragedies too numerous to mention. Despite that, his 1995 album *Young Blood* proved he could still transform a stunning array of American musical genres into pulse-pumping, heart-wrenching Jerry Lee Lewis music.

what to buy: To hear why Jerry Lee Lewis was one of the very first inductees into the Rock and Roll Hall of Fame, check out the 19-song *Original Sun Greatest Hits* 𝄢𝄢𝄢𝄢 (Rhino, 1984, compilation prod. Art Fein), which not only contains his legendary '50s hits, but also remarkably wild lesser-known tunes such as "Drinkin' Wine Spo-dee-o-dee," "Put Me Down," "Wild One," and the infamous "Big Legged Woman." Those wishing to take a baby step into his vast country catalog should check out *Killer Country* 𝄢𝄢𝄢𝄢 (Mercury, 1995, compilation prod. Colin Escott), a 20-song collection featuring some of the finest honky tonk performances of this or any other era. Lewis also brings forth a lot of punk energy for *Live at the Star Club, Hamburg* 𝄢𝄢𝄢𝄢 (Rhino, 1992, compilation prod. Siggi Loch), the finest live performance ever captured on tape by any of the original rockers and a must-have item. However, if you feel like spending a few extra dollars, the two-disc, 42-song set *The Jerry Lee Lewis Anthology: All Killer, No Filler* 𝄢𝄢𝄢𝄢 (Rhino, 1993, compilation prod. James Austin) contains every major chart record from his eras with Sun, Smash, Mercury, and Elektra. All four collections are excellent introductions to one of the greatest performers to ever grace rock or country music.

what to avoid: The Killer has never cut a completely bad LP, but there are several discs out there you should be wary of, such as *Duets* **woof!** (Sun Entertainment, 1979/1996, prod. Shelby Singleton), a deceptive package that has Jimmy "Orion" Ellis overdubbing his imitation of the King onto several of Lewis's Sun-era tracks in a cynical attempt to trick fans into believing Presley recorded extensively with Jerry Lee. Other releases demand a discerning eye as well. *The Golden Rock Hits of Jerry Lee Lewis* 𝄢𝄢 (Smash, 1967/1987, prod. Jerry Kennedy, Shelby Singleton) features slick re-recordings of his Sun material taped during his first months at Smash/Mercury. The soundtrack to *Great Balls of Fire* (Polydor, 1989, prod. T-Bone Burnette) 𝄢𝄢𝄢 contains re-recordings of his classic Sun material as well—albeit potent ones. *Great Balls of Fire!* 𝄢𝄢 (Columbia River, 1997) sports a picture of Lewis from the '50s, but contains live tracks from the '70s and '80s that were initially issued on Tomato. *Roots of Rock 'n' Roll* 𝄢𝄢 (Prime Cuts, 1995/Direct Source,

1997) sounds as if were recorded with a hand-held tape-recorder, which is a shame because Lewis really burns through this late '70s concert set.

the rest:
Jerry Lee Lewis 𝄢𝄢𝄢 (Sun, 1958/Rhino, 1989)
Jerry Lee's Greatest! 𝄢𝄢𝄢 (Sun, 1961/Rhino, 1989)
The Greatest Live Shows on Earth 𝄢𝄢𝄢𝄢 (Smash, 1964, 1967/Bear Family, 1992)
(With Johnny Cash and Carl Perkins) *The Survivors* 𝄢𝄢 (Columbia, 1982/Razor & Tie, 1995)
Silver Eagle Presents Jerry Lee Lewis Live 𝄢𝄢 (Silver Eagle, 1984/1997)
Milestones 𝄢𝄢𝄢 (Rhino, 1985)
Live at the Vapors Club 𝄢𝄢𝄢 (SCR, 1985/Ace, 1993)
(With Carl Perkins, Roy Orbison, and Johnny Cash) *Class of '55* 𝄢𝄢 (America/Smash/Mercury, 1986)
20 Classic Jerry Lee Lewis Hits 𝄢𝄢𝄢𝄢 (Original Sound Entertainment, 1986)
The Complete Million Dollar Session 𝄢𝄢𝄢 (Charly/Sun, 1987)
Rare and Rockin'—Original Sun Recordings 𝄢𝄢𝄢 (Charly, 1987)
Up through the Years (1956–1963) 𝄢𝄢𝄢𝄢 (Bear Family, 1988)
Rare Tracks: Wild One 𝄢𝄢𝄢 (Rhino, 1989)
Killer: The Mercury Years, Volume One: 1963–1968 𝄢𝄢𝄢 (Mercury, 1989)
Killer: The Mercury Years, Volume Two: 1969–1972 𝄢𝄢𝄢𝄢 (Mercury, 1989)
Killer: The Mercury Years, Volume Three: 1973–1977 𝄢𝄢𝄢 (Mercury, 1989)
Rocket 88 𝄢𝄢𝄢 (Tomato, 1989/1992)
Heartbreak 𝄢𝄢 (Tomato, 1989/1992)
The Complete Palomino Club Recordings 𝄢𝄢𝄢 (Tomato, 1989/1991)
The EP Collection 𝄢𝄢𝄢 (See for Miles, 1991)
Best of Jerry Lee Lewis 𝄢𝄢 (Curb, 1991)
Rockin' My Life Away: The Jerry Lee Lewis Collection 𝄢𝄢𝄢 (Warner Bros., 1991)
Live in Italy 𝄢𝄢 (Magnum, 1991)
Great Balls of Fire! 𝄢𝄢𝄢𝄢 (Charly, 1992)
Good Rockin' Tonight 𝄢𝄢𝄢 (Charly, 1992)
The Alternate Collection 𝄢𝄢𝄢 (Charly, 1992)
Rockin' My Life Away 𝄢𝄢𝄢 (Tomato, 1992)
Honky Tonk Rock 'n' Roll Piano Man 𝄢𝄢 (Ace, 1992)
Pretty Much Country 𝄢𝄢 (Ace, 1992)
Great Balls of Fire Live! 𝄢𝄢 (Pilz, 1993)
Whole Lotta Shakin' Goin' on Live! 𝄢𝄢 (Pilz, 1993)
The EP Collection, Vol. 2 𝄢𝄢𝄢 (See for Miles, 1994)
Greatest Hits—Finest Performances 𝄢𝄢𝄢 (Sun, 1995)
Young Blood 𝄢𝄢𝄢 (Sire, 1995)
Best of the Best of Jerry Lee Lewis 𝄢𝄢𝄢 (Federal, 1996)
Back to Back 𝄢𝄢𝄢 (K-Tel, 1996)
Mercury & Smash Recordings 𝄢𝄢𝄢 (Collectables, 1997)
The Hits 𝄢𝄢𝄢 (Mercury, 1997)

worth searching for: Box sets were made for someone as prolific as the Killer and *Classic Jerry Lee Lewis (1956–1963)* (Bear Family, 1989/1992, compilation prod. Colin Escott) is one of the best ever. This enormously satisfying and listenable eight-CD, 247-song set collects everything found to date that he cut at Sun, including off-the-cuff jams, alternate takes, and his famous argument with Sam Phillips concerning religion and "Great Balls of Fire." The oddly titled *Locust Years . . . and the Return to the Promised Land* (Bear Family, 1994, compilation prod. Richard Weize) is another eight-CD set that encapsulates all of Lewis's mid-to-late '60s work for Smash Records, including his three brilliant live LPs, experiments in soul, pop, and modern country music. For his later Mercury material, the vinyl-only sets *The Killer 1969–1972* (Bear Family, 1989, compilation prod. Richard Weize) and *The Killer 1973–1977* (Bear Family, 1989, compilation prod. Richard Weize) will have to make do until Bear Family gets around to reissuing them on CD.

influences:

◀◀ Moon Mullican, Merrill Moore, Roy Hall, Amos Milburn, Little Richard, Fats Domino, Hank Williams, Jimmy Rodgers, Freddie Slack, Gene Autry, Big Joe Turner, George Jones, Ray Charles, Bob Wills, Del Wood, B.B. King, Chuck Willis, Billy Lee Riley, Chuck Berry, Carl Perkins, Elvis Presley

▶▶ Linda Gail Lewis, Carl McVoy, Carl Mann, Ray Smith, Charlie Rich, Mickey Gilley, Jimmie Lee Swaggert, Freddie "Fingers" Lee, Jason D. Williams, Tom Jones, Hank Williams Jr., Gary Stewart, Elton John, Billy Joel, Preacher Jack, Becky Hobbes, Marcia Ball, Ben Folds

Ken Burke

Gary Lewis & the Playboys

Formed 1964, in Los Angeles, CA.

Gary Harold Lee Lewis (born July 31, 1945, in Newark, NJ), vocals, drums, guitar; Al Ramsey, guitar (1964–67); John R. West, guitar (1964–67); David Walker, keyboards (1964–67); David Costell, bass (1964–67); Tom Tripplehorn, guitar (1965–67); Charley Carey, guitar, vocals (1968–70); Arnold Rosenthal, bass, vocals (1968–70); Billy Boatman, drums (1968–70); Billy Sullivan, guitar, vocals (1995–present); John Dean, bass, vocals (1995–present); Rich Spina, keyboards, vocals (1995–present); Michal Hadak, drums (1995–present).

As if being the Number One Son of the legendary King of Comedy, Jerry Lewis, wasn't pressure enough, Gary Lewis and his chums the Playboys found themselves signed to a lucrative, long-term deal with Liberty Records, performing to a nationwide audience on *The Ed Sullivan Show,* and topping the American charts with their first-ever release ("This Diamond Ring," co-written by Al Kooper), all within the space of several weeks between November 19, 1964 and January 23, 1965. Just four months earlier the band

had been performing for tips at Disneyland. Such are the Cinderella tales that litter the pop world of the 1960s, but of course the Playboys had more than a simple "in" to the business; without papa Jerry's considerable clout, it's hard to imagine a winsome if mediocre voice like Gary's being heard much outside the family den. Nevertheless, under the watchful ear of studio ace Snuff Garrett and a roomful of the hottest session men royalties could buy (most notably arranger/keyboardist Leon Russell), the Playboys racked up an astonishing run of hits until the bubble inevitably burst in 1967. For the next several years, the fairy tale turned more than grim as Lewis found himself drafted, divorced, and addicted to drugs. Things weren't much brighter as far as his musical career was concerned either, and after several comeback attempts (his album titles of the period tell the story: *New Directions, I'm on the Right Road Now,* and *Listen!*), Lewis retired from the pop scene, dazed and most definitely confused. Still, with his cheery "can-do" attitude returned and an ever-revolving lineup of Playboys at the ready, Lewis can still be heard singing his many carefully crafted hits on the yesteryear circuit and, each and every Labor Day, on Dad's telethon.

what's available: *Legendary Masters Series* ♫♫♫♪ (EMI America, 1990/Gold Rush, 1996, compilation prod. Ron Furmanek) contains more than a dozen hits so infectiously written and performed that you can't help but crack at least half a grin, and "Time Stands Still," in which Gary for one verse does a wickedly accurate imitation of his father, is worth the price of admission alone.

worth searching for: Two of the Playboys' original LP's were briefly issued together on disc as *Everybody Loves a Clown/She's Just My Style* (Liberty, 1965, 1966/EMI America, 1992, compilation prod. Ron Furmanek). Squeezed alongside all the rote-by-note quickie covers of the day herein lurk some true gems: Gary's self-penned "Everybody Loves a Clown," the terrific Beach Boys knock-off "She's Just My Style," and the latter's magnificent B-side "I Won't Make That Mistake Again," one of Leon Russell's greatest arrangements ever.

influences:

◀◀ Buddy Rich, Ricky Nelson, the Beach Boys, the Beatles

▶▶ Dino, Desi & Billy, the Loved Ones, the Clarke Bar Five

Gary Pig Gold

Huey Lewis & the News

Formed 1979, in Marin County, CA.

Huey Lewis (born Hugh Cregg III), vocals, harmonica; Chris Hayes, guitar; Johnny Colla, guitar, saxophone; Sean Hopper, keyboards; Mario Cipollina, bass (1979–95); Bill Gibson, drums.

Commonly viewed as a bar band that made good, Huey Lewis &

the News actually played a mere two live dates before signing a record contract. But the members mainly came from stalwart pillars of the active '70s Marin County club scene, so the impression is not without basis in fact. The band polished up the burgeoning new wave/power pop sound then coming out of England; Lewis and keyboardist Hopper had recently returned from an extended stay in that country with their band Clover, where the group recorded albums of its own and some members participated in Elvis Costello's debut, *My Aim Is True*. Although the News' second album earned the band some respectable FM airplay, it was the third release, the hit-laden *Sports*, that made Lewis and company one of the most popular American rock bands of the day—an album, ironically, that sat on a shelf for almost a year following the record label's bankruptcy. With "Power of Love" from the *Back to the Future* soundtrack scorching up to the top of the singles charts in 1985, the News could do no wrong. Lewis's boy-next-door image played well on MTV (another irony, considering he is the son of a jazz buff father and hippie artist mother). But, live by the hit single—die by the hit single. As the band's commercial marksmanship faltered with the slightly out of character 1988 release *Small World*, the group fell into a popularity decline, hardly spelled by the label change and the sub-par 1991 offering, *Hard at Play*. Its most recent offering, *Four Chords and Several Years Ago*, may have helped restore some credibility to the group's tarnished luster in between lucrative private party and corporate performances and Lewis's vacations at his Montana ranch.

what to buy: Although *Sports* ♪♪♪♪ (Chrysalis, 1983, prod. Huey Lewis & the News) may be the obvious starting point, that multi-platinum monster's predecessor, *Picture This* ♪♪♪ (Chrysalis, 1982/Gold Rush, 1996, prod. Huey Lewis & the News) laid out all the basic architecture to the group's forthcoming hit career.

what to buy next: Unappreciated for its quirky honesty and well-rounded musicality, *Small World* ♪♪♪ (Chrysalis, 1988, prod. Huey Lewis & the News) bounced happily from the jazzy overtones of the two-part title track (illuminated by an extended sax solo from Stan Getz), the New Orleans drive of "Old Antoine's," and one of the most under-appreciated tracks from the group's entire oeuvre, the Marin reggae instrumental "Bobo Tempo," originally recorded for the soundtrack to a short film by the vocalist's mother.

what to avoid: Under pressure to produce another *Sports*, the band labored so long on *Hard at Play* ♪ (EMI, 1991/Gold Rush, 1996, prod. Huey Lewis & the News), the musicians managed to choke out any glimmer of life the mannered songs might have contained in the first place. Hard to Hear is more like it.

the rest:
Huey Lewis and the News ♪♪ (Chrysalis, 1980)

Fore! ♪♪♪ (Chrysalis, 1986)
Four Chords and Several Years Ago ♪♪♪ (Elektra, 1994)
Time Flies: The Best of Huey Lewis & the News ♪♪♪♪ (Elektra, 1996)

worth searching for: An offhand *a capella* track for "People Get Ready: A Tribute to Curtis Mayfield" (Shanachie, 1993) gave the band's moribund radio prognosis new life and spurred the group's agreeable tribute to mid-chart soul records, *Four Chords and Several Years Ago*.

influences:
◀◀ Clover, Brinsley Schwartz, Elvis Costello, doo-wop, Motown

▶▶ Bruce Hornsby, Nick Lowe, Blues Traveler

Joel Selvin

Life of Agony
Formed 1989, in New York, NY.

Keith Caputo, vocals (1989–97) ; Joey Z., guitar; Alan Robert, bass; Sal Abruscato, drums; Whitfield Crane, vocals (1997–present).

Life of Agony is one of the more distinctive metal bands of the '90s; like headbangers from every era, there is a Black Sabbath influence, but LOA eschew the sex and swagger of bands such as AC/DC, Kiss, and Aerosmith for more serious hardcore influences—particularly from the fellow New Yorkers in Sick of It All. But unlike SOIA, LOA developed its sound gradually: after the streetwise concept album *River Runs Red*, the group snuck the novelty cover of Simple Minds' "Don't You (Forget about Me)" onto its sophomore effort, *Ugly*. By *Soul Searching Sun*, LOA even pulled a few power ballads, showing that maybe it isn't so hardcore after all—a move that won some mainstream radio play but also cost the group many of its long-time fans. The band's future is now in question, as singer Keith Caputo has left to form a new group, Absolute Bloom. The band's choice of a replacement—Whitfield Crane, formerly of hair metal group Ugly Kid Joe—seemed like a bad joke when it was announced, but the band apparently plans to record new songs and re-record old tracks with him.

what to buy: *River Runs Red* ♪♪♪ (Roadrunner) is as powerful as metal/hardcore hybrids get, with a story that any depressed kid can relate to.

the rest:
Ugly ♪♪ (Roadrunner, 1995)
Soul Searching Sun ♪♪ (Roadrunner)

influences:
◀◀ Sick of It All, Biohazard, Sepultura

Brian Ives

The Lightning Seeds

Formed 1988, in Liverpool, England.

Ian Broudie, vocals, guitar; Martin Campbell, bass; Chris Sharrock, drums; Paul Hemmings, guitar.

Lightning Seeds founder Ian Broudie began his career playing in Liverpool bands such as Big in Japan, Original Mirrors, and Care before becoming a successful producer for the Fall and Echo & the Bunnymen. However, Broudie the bandleader (the Lightning Seeds are essentially a one-man act) didn't seem to develop musically the same way Broudie the producer did; the group often comes off as the Pet Shop Boys minus the dance beats and cynicism.

what to buy: The group's first album, *Cloudcuckooland* ♪♪♪ (MCA, 1989, prod. Ian Broudie) is a fine display of bouncy pop, though on many of the tracks, it's easy enough to play spot the influence.

the rest:
Sense ♪♪♪ (MCA, 1992)
Jollification ♪♪♪ (Trauma/Interscope, 1994)
Dizzy Heights ♪♪♪ (Epic, 1997)

worth searching for: The import *Like You Do . . . Best of the Lightning Seeds* (Epic, 1997, prod. various) is the best single stop for those who can find it.

influences:
◄◄ The Teardrop Explodes, Elvis Costello, The The
►► Echo & the Bunnymen, Icicle Works

Anna Glen

Limp Bizkit

Formed 1994, in Jacksonville, FL.

Fred Durst, vocals; Sam Rivers, bass; John Otto, drums; Wes Borland, guitars; DJ Lethal, DJ.

Limp Bizkit got its big break when singer Fred Durst inked his art into the skin of Fieldy, bassist for KoЯn, after that band's Jacksonville show in 1995. While in town, KoЯn picked up a copy of Limp Bizkit's demo tape and was so impressed that the band members handed it over to their producer Ross Robinson, who became the quartet's patron and helped it land a major label deal.

what's available: Fans of Pantera, 311, or KoЯn will either love or hate Limp Bizkit's *Three Dollar Bill, Y'all* ♪♪ (Interscope, 1997, prod. Ross Robinson). Right off the bat, the song "Pollution" is a never-ending excuse to swear. The album's whiny cover of George Michael's "Faith" isn't even entertaining.

influences:
◄◄ KoЯn, Pantera

Christina Fuoco

Lincoln

Formed 1986, in New York, NY.

Christopher Temple, vocals, guitar, keyboards; Gonzalo Martinez, drums; Danny Weinkauf, bass; Dan Miller, guitars, keyboards.

Eastern Pennsylvania native Chris Temple formed Lincoln after moving to New York City. Following his move, Temple, a former landscaper, played the city's folk circuit, holding court frequently with his droll story songs and purposely inhibited delivery. And while he never came across as a natural performer, it's that same awkwardness that makes Lincoln so utterly charming. Accompanied by an able band and surrounded by quality power pop hooks and melodies, Temple singspeaks (á la King Missile's John Hall) his way through a variety of topics, including his favorite—cars—in a guileless, disarmingly naive way.

what's available: Spry piano lines and chunky guitar riffs line the length of Lincoln's self-titled debut *Lincoln* ♪♪♪ (London, 1997, prod. Christopher Temple, David Kahne, Roger Greenawalt), an album as much about the singer/lyricist's droll psychotherapy and insecurity as it is about fun, concise pop 'n' roll.

influences:
◄◄ King Missile, the Raspberries, Elton John

Bob Gulla

Lindisfarne

Formed 1969, in Newcastle, England. Disbanded 1974. Re-formed 1978.

Alan Hull (died 1995), lead vocals, guitar (1969–74, 1978–95); Ray Jackson, guitar, mandolin, harmonica (1969–74, 1978–90); Simon Cowe, guitar, mandolin (1969–73, 1978–94); Rod Clements, bass, violin, vocals (1970–73, 1978–present); Roy Laidlaw, drums (1969–73, 1978–present); Marty Craggs, saxophone (1984–present).

Like its contemporaries Steeleye Span and the Strawbs, Lindisfarne had an acoustic, folk-based sound. But it eschewed those bands' medieval and Elizabethan trappings, instead coming off more like a bunch of regular lads from the local ale house. Indeed, many of its songs have a pub-singalong quality to them, complete with harmonica, mandolin, and reedy but engaging harmonies. Others reveal the more sensitive side of Alan Hull's writing, but they remain in most cases refreshingly down-to-earth and free of pretense. After enjoying considerable chart success in England with its first two albums (which also earned it a small cult following in the U.S. based on college-radio airplay), the band went for a less folky, more contemporary sound on its third, to the derision of critics who were always at the ready to take Lindisfarne down a peg. The band never quite recovered from this blow, splitting into two factions in 1973 and breaking up altogether the next year. However, a Christmas reunion show in 1977 led to the reformation of the original band, and members have carried on ever since—albeit at a lower level—releasing albums both commercially and on Lindisfarne's own private label. The band endures to this day with two original members, surviving even Hull's death due to a heart attack in 1995.

what to buy: The title of Lindisfarne's debut, *Nicely out of Tune* ♫♫♫ (Elektra, 1970/Virgin 1988, prod. John Anthony), is marvelously descriptive. Standout tracks include the mysterious "Lady Eleanor," the plaintive Hull solo outing "Winter Song," and the thoroughly wonderful "Clear White Light," which melds a Hollies-sounding verse to an explosive, gospel-style chorus.

what to buy next: The second album, *Fog on the Tyne* ♫♫♫ (Elektra, 1971/Virgin 1988, prod. Bob Johnston), is a bit more introspective but still pleases, particularly the delightfully wheezy "Meet Me on the Corner" and the closing title track.

the rest:
Dingly Dell ♫♫ (Elektra, 1972/Virgin 1988)
Back and Fourth ♫♫♫ (Atco, 1978/Castle, 1991)

influences:
◀◀ Bill Monroe, Davy Graham, Bob Dylan

▶▶ Early Rod Stewart, Del Amitri

Mike Greenfield

David Lindley

Born 1944, in San Marino, CA.

Winner of banjo and fiddle contests as a teenager, long-time sideman to Jackson Browne through the '70s, scraggly-haired solo artist during the '80s, and a world music collaborator during the '90s, David Lindley has never met a stringed instrument he didn't like. His fiddle and explosive lap steel leads ignited Browne concerts and songs (listen to "Redneck Friend" or "Running on Empty"), and his work livened albums by James Taylor (*In the Pocket*), Linda Ronstadt (*Heart like a Wheel*), Graham Nash (*Wild Tales* and *Songs for Beginners*), and Warren Zevon (*Warren Zevon*), among many others. Lindley's solo career offers a different perspective: songs, many of them familiar, but laced with a whimsical sense of humor that matched his rayon/polyester attire and eccentric faux dub reggae/ chunk/ Tex-Mex/pop/rock/dance style. Lindley has spent the '90s recording with Henry Kaiser in Madagascar and Norway, and touring with percussionist Hani Naser. Like Ry Cooder, the L.A. guitarist with whom he collaborates occasionally, Lindley is a musician for all seasons.

what to buy: *El Rayo-X* ♫♫♫♫ (Asylum, 1981, prod. Jackson Browne, Greg Ladanyi) is an album no discriminating rock lover should be without—particularly because of such tunes as "Mercury Blues" and "She Took off My Romeos." *Win This Record* ♫♫♫ (Asylum, 1982, prod. David Lindley, Greg Ladanyi) is almost as good, especially the strangely prophetic "Talk to the Lawyer." *Very Greasy* ♫♫♫ (Elektra, 1988, prod. Linda Ronstadt) offers the tackiest ("Tiki Torches at Twilight") and funkiest ("Papa Was a Rolling Stone") tunes in the Lindley canon. And *A World out of Time: Henry Kaiser and David Lindley in Madagascar* ♫♫♫ (Shanachie, 1992, prod. Birger Gesthuisen, Henry Kaiser) presents a gorgeous romp with the cream of Malagasy musicians topped off with an improbably wonderful "I Fought the Law."

what to buy next: *A World out of Time, Vol. 2: Henry Kaiser and David Lindley in Madagascar* ♫♫♫ (Shanachie, 1993, prod. Birger Gesthuisen, Henry Kaiser) offers more cross-cultural tomfoolery. *Mr. Dave* ♫♫♫ (WEA International, 1985, prod. David Lindley, Greg Ladanyi, Danny Kortchmar) is only slightly less fun than his other solo records.

what to avoid: Steer clear of Lindley's early trippy albums with the late '60s psychedelic folk group Kaleidoscope; they have all the direction of a bad acid trip.

the rest:
The Sweet Sunny North: Henry Kaiser and David Lindley in Norway ♫♫♫ (Shanachie, 1994)

worth searching for: *David Lindley and Hani Naser: Live in Tokyo Playing Real Good* and *David Lindley and Hani Naser: Live All over the Place Playing Even Better!! Official Bootleg* are both self-produced with no official imprint and available only at their live shows. You haven't lived until you've heard their carnivorous reading of Jerry Lee Lewis's "The Meat Man."

influences:
◀◀ Clifton Chenier, Gabby Pahinui, the Pioneers, Yellow Magic Orchestra, Ry Cooder, Duane Eddy, the Ventures, the Fendermen, James Burton, Huey "Piano" Smith, King Curtis, Sam the Sham & the Pharoahs

▶▶ The Black Crowes, the Bottle Rockets, the Hooters, Chris Whitley

Leland Rucker

Arto Lindsay

Born May 28, 1953, in Richmond, VA.

Arto Lindsay came to New York to be an artist but took up guitar to become part of the fermenting No Wave scene. His major impact came as co-founder of DNA, but he also played on the debut albums of the Lounge Lizards, Love of Life Orchestra, and Golden Palominos. Lindsay's Brazilian upbringing, which he first exposed on record in the duo Ambitious Lovers, was an important influence even beyond overt musical borrowings on his recent albums, since that country's free-thinking younger musicians during the '60s used music as a revolutionary tool. Lindsay later produced a number of Brazilian artists, including Caetano Veloso, Marisa Monte, and Gal Gosta, as well as Talking Heads' David Byrne (who came to share Lindsay's interests) and jazz guitarist Bill Frisell.

what to buy: Nine of the 26 tracks on the Arto Lindsay Trio's *Aggregates 1–26* 𝒥𝒥𝒥𝒥 (Knitting Factory Works, 1995, prod. Arto Lindsay) are under a minute long, exploring a looser, heavier version of the DNA sound without tangents into Brazilian or pop music. Worthy of note in addition to Lindsay's unique vision is Rollins Band bassist Melvin Gibbs's playing, functioning as much as a melodic element as a rhythm section with drummer Dougie Bowne.

what to buy next: *Noon Chill* 𝒥𝒥𝒥 (BarNone, 1998, prod. Andres Levin, Arto Lindsay, Melvin Gibbs) is the most adventurous of Lindsay's Brazilian-influenced albums and includes many familiar names, included the other half of Ambitious Lovers, Peter Scherer. The mellower *Mundo Civilizado* 𝒥𝒥𝒥 (BarNone, 1997, prod. Arto Lindsay) includes a striking cover of Prince's "Erotic City."

the rest:
O Corpo Sutil—The Subtle Body 𝒥𝒥𝒥 (BarNone, 1996)
Hyper Civilizado 𝒥𝒥𝒥 (BarNone, 1997)

influences:

◄◄ Caetano Veloso, Gilberto Gil, James Brown, Derek Bailey

►► David Byrne, Cameo

see also: *Ambitious Lovers, DNA, Lounge Lizards, Golden Palominos*

Steve Holtje

Mark Lindsay
See: Paul Revere & the Raiders

Liquorice
See: His Name Is Alive

Little Anthony & the Imperials
Formed as the Duponts, 1956. Became the Chesters, then Little Anthony & the Imperials, 1958. Disbanded 1961. Re-formed 1963.

Anthony Gourdine (born January 8, 1940 in Brooklyn, NY), vocals; Ernest Wright Jr., vocals; Clarence Collins, vocals; Nate Rogers, vocals; Sammy Strain, vocals; Tracy Lord, vocals.

Little Anthony & the Imperials were one of the few '50s doo-wop groups to have an impact during the '60s soul era. Lead singer Anthony Gourdine's vocal style owed much to Frankie Lymon's, with a dash of Dinah Washington thrown in, and the soaring harmonies of the Imperials could emulate the dramatic gospel of the Dells or the comic timing of the Cadets. Dynamic onstage, the group thrilled audiences with a variety of precision steps, knee-drops, and splits without ever missing a note. Gourdine and various members recorded unsuccessfully as the Duponts and the Chesters before legendary producer George Goldner changed their name to the Imperials. (The majority of '50s doo-wop groups had either bird or automobile names.) The first single for Goldner's End label was the ultimate expression of teen heartbreak, "Tears on My Pillow," which became a major smash on both the pop and R&B charts. Disc jockey Alan Freed loved the diminutive lead singer's sound so much he began introducing the group as Little Anthony & the Imperials, which the group's record label quickly adopted. Subsequent heart-tuggers "So Much," "Wishful Thinking," and "A Prayer and a Jukebox" were bigger hits in the New York area (thanks to Freed) than they were nationally, so the group made a brief foray into novelty R&B. Gourdine has jokingly called 1959's "Shimmy, Shimmy, Ko-Ko Bop" (which is thematically similar to "Stranded in the Jungle" by the Cadets) "the stupidest song I ever heard," but it was another major dual market hit. The follow-up singles were nowhere near as successful, and Gourdine left the group for an unsuccessful solo career. A short tenure with DCP Records led to a mid-'60s revival, but when the company was absorbed by United Artists, the run was over. Nowadays the solo Little Anthony and a vastly changed version of the Imperials are much appreciated mainstays at oldies revivals and nostalgia concerts.

what to buy: You can't go wrong with *The Best of Little Anthony & the Imperials* 𝒥𝒥𝒥𝒥 (Rhino, 1989, compilation prod. Bill Martin), a completely enjoyable 18-track collection that includes all the big hits from the '50s through the dramatic soul years of the '60s. An informative booklet with vintage photos and a reminiscence from A&R man Richard Barratt complete a smart package. Those who want only the late '60s incarnation of the group should check out *The Best of Little Anthony & the Imperials* 𝒥𝒥𝒥 (EMI, 1996, compilation prod. Ron Furmanek, Steve Kolanijan), which also features some fine liner notes and crisp digitally remastered sound.

what to buy next: Nearly everything Little Anthony & the Imperials cut during the '50s and early '60s resides on *For Collectors Only* 𝒥𝒥𝒥 (Collectables, 1992, prod. various), a 39-song set that includes the big hits ("Tears on My Pillow," "Shimmy, Shimmy, Ko Ko Bop"), inspired lesser-know tracks such as "I'm All Right" and "Bayou, Bayou Baby," as well as three previously unreleased songs.

what to avoid: It's not a bad album, but those who are expecting Gourdine's trademark vocal pyrotechnics on *Little Anthony Sings the Gospel* 𝄞𝄞 (MCA Special, 1996, prod. B.J. Thomas) will be disappointed.

the rest:

Goin' out of My Head/Payin' Our Dues 𝄞𝄞𝄞 (DCP, 1965/Veep,1967/Beat Goes On, 1996)

The Imperials—Featuring Little Anthony 𝄞𝄞𝄞 (Collectables, 1991)

worth searching for: The group's first two LPs have been reissued on *We Are the Imperials/Shades of the '40s* (End, 1959, 1961/Westside, 1998), a superior English import with fine sound, booklet notes, and vintage photos.

influences:

◀◀ The Dells, Frankie Lymon & the Teenagers, the Cadets

▶▶ Jackson 5, the Stylistics, the Delfonics, the O'Jays

Ken Burke

Little Eva

Born Eva Narcissus Boyd, June 29, 1945, in Bell Haven, NC.

Little Eva is one of the great overnight success stories of early rock 'n' roll. Cookies singer Earl-Jean McCrea introduced teenaged Eva Boyd to songwriter Carole King; the introduction led to jobs as King's live-in babysitter and as an alternate member of the Cookies. She also sang on Ben E. King's "Don't Play That Song for Me (You Lied)." Little Eva eventually got her own single, "The Loco-Motion"—a bright explosion of drums, horns, guitar, and Cookies harmonies that was one of the essential dance hits of the early '60s (and of the mid-'70s, in the hands of hard-rockers Grand Funk Railroad). Little Eva nearly matched the success of "The Loco-Motion" with one other record, "Keep Your Hands off My Baby," but soon fell into recording silly dance retreads such as "Let's Turkey Trot" and "Old Smokey Locomotion."

what to buy: *Best of* 𝄞𝄞𝄞𝄞 (Collectables, 1991, prod. various) covers roughly the same ground as the more concise and more easily accessible *The Loco-Motion* 𝄞𝄞𝄞𝄞 (Rhino, 1996, prod. various), which contains "The Loco-Motion" and "Keep Your Hands off My Baby," as well as Eva's versions of "Will You Love Me Tomorrow," "Breaking up Is Hard to Do" and "Swinging on a Star," recorded with Big Dee Irwin.

the rest:

Back on Track 𝄞𝄞 (San Francisco Sound, 1989)

influences:

◀◀ Mahalia Jackson, LaVern Baker, Carole King

▶▶ Linda Ronstadt, Kylie Minogue

Brian Mansfield

Little Feat

Formed 1969, in Los Angeles, CA. Disbanded 1979. Re-formed 1988.

Lowell George (died 1979), guitar, harmonica, vocals (1969–78); Bill Payne, keyboards, vocals; Richard Hayward, drums, background vocals (1970–present); Roy Astrada, bass, background vocals (1970–73); Paul Barrere, guitars, vocals (1973–present); Kenny Gradney, bass (1972–present); Sam Clayton, percussion, vocals (1973–present); Craig Fuller, guitar, vocals (1988–94); Fred Tackett, guitar (1988–present); Shaun Murphy, vocals (1994–present).

Little Feat sprung from the very fertile California music scene during the early '70s, but its musical influences were all over the map. Led by the brilliant slide guitarist, songwriter, and vocalist Lowell George, Little Feat created a body of music that touched on blues, Southern rock, gospel-influenced harmonies, and country. For a relatively small group of music fans, Little Feat was the most funktabulous rock band on the face of the Earth. At its peak from 1972 to 1974, the band released its three most representative albums—*Sailin' Shoes, Dixie Chicken*, and *Feats Don't Fail Me Now*. While still involved, George's influence diminished, and he left the band in 1978 to produced his only solo album, the under-appreciated *Thanks I'll Eat It Here*. "China White," a song George recorded but chose not to include on that album, foreshadowed his death in 1979 from a heroin overdose. The band went on an extended hiatus, prompting Bonnie Raitt to comment, "I miss Little Feat more than I miss being eight years old." She wasn't alone in that feeling. The Little Feat that emerged in 1988 added vocalist Craig Fuller and Fred Tackett. *Let It Roll* attempted to re-capture the magic of vintage Little Feat and to the surprise of many, succeeded ably. Unfortunately, subsequent albums did not measure up as successfully, and Fuller left, replaced by former Bob Seger backup singer Shaun Murphy, who's brought a welcome new dimension to the group at a time it was in danger of becoming little more than a shell of its past glories.

what to buy: *Sailin' Shoes* 𝄞𝄞𝄞𝄞 (Warner Bros., 1972, prod. Ted Templeman) contains some of the band's best songs, including "Easy to Slip" and "Sailin' Shoes." *Feats Don't Fail Me Now* 𝄞𝄞𝄞𝄞 (Warner Bros., 1974, prod. Lowell George) captures the essence of one of the great American bands of the '70s. *Waiting for Columbus* 𝄞𝄞𝄞𝄞 (Warner Bros., 1978, prod. Lowell George) is a live album that captures the band's particular way with a groove onstage.

what to buy next: *As Time Goes By: The Best of Little Feat* 𝄞𝄞𝄞𝄞 (Warner Communications, 1986, prod. various) is a superb introduction for the casual fan; once an import, it's now available (at a much lower price) as a domestic release. *Hoy-Hoy!* 𝄞𝄞𝄞𝄞 (Warner Bros., 1981, prod. Bill Payne, George Massenburg, Paul Barrere) is a lovingly constructed scrapbook that also serves as a fairly representative retrospective. *Dixie*

Chicken 🎵🎵🎵 (Warner Bros., 1973, prod. Lowell George) boasts delicious melodies and hip-shaking grooves. An instant party.

what to avoid: Outside of the title track, *Down on the Farm* 🎵🎵 (Warner Bros., 1979 prod. Lowell George) doesn't have much to keep you interested.

the rest:
Little Feat 🎵🎵🎵 (Warner Bros., 1971)
The Last Record Album 🎵🎵🎵 (Warner Bros., 1975)
Time Loves a Hero 🎵🎵🎵 (Warner Bros., 1977)
Let It Roll 🎵🎵🎵🎵 (Warner Bros., 1988)
Representing the Mambo 🎵🎵 (Warner Bros., 1990)
Shake Me Up 🎵🎵 (Morgan Creek, 1991)
Ain't Had Enough Fun 🎵🎵 (Zoo/BMG, 1995)
Live from Neon Park 🎵🎵🎵 (Zoo, 1996)
Under the Radar 🎵🎵🎵 (CMC International, 1998)

worth searching for: *Rock and Roll Doctor: A Tribute to Lowell George* (BMG Music, 1997, prod. various) is as good as a tribute album can be. Many tracks feature special duets, such as Little Feat backing up Bonnie Raitt on "Cold Cold Cold" and Randy Newman joining Valerie Carter for a sublime version of "Sailin' Shoes."

solo outings:
Lowell George:
Thanks I'll Eat it Here 🎵🎵🎵 (Warner Bros., 1979)

Paul Barrere:
On My Own Two Feet 🎵🎵🎵 (Atlantic, 1983)
If the Phone Don't Ring 🎵🎵🎵 (Zoo/BMG, 1995)

influences:
◀◀ Hank Williams, the Beatles, the Byrds, Lee Dorsey, the Meters, Muddy Waters, Howlin' Wolf, John Lee Hooker, Canned Heat, the Grateful Dead

▶▶ Elvis Costello, Emmylou Harris, Linda Ronstadt, the Black Crowes, Blind Melon, Daniel Lanois, Uncle Tupelo

Michael Isabella and Simon Glickman

Little Richard

Born Richard Wayne Penniman, December 5, 1935, in Macon, GA.

Not just the king of rock 'n' roll, but the queen, too, Little Richard drove his music with the maniacal energy of an androgenous but unambiguous raw sexuality. He blasted the path for rock 'n' roll, his 1955 hit "Tutti Frutti" shattering the tame tempos of the Eisenhower era. For all his extraordinary impact, Little Richard spent something like a mere 72 hours total over in the recording studio compiling his towering legacy. He cut some sessions in a Roy Brown vein for RCA Victor from 1951 to 1952 and did a couple of R&B sides with producer Johnny Otis

on the Texas-based Duke label. But it wasn't until he hooked up with producer Bumps Blackwell in New Orleans and made "Tutti Frutti" for Specialty Records that Little Richard forever changed the course of pop music history. A man as tall in life as legend, at the height of his popularity he quit show business to study for the ministry and disappeared from the scene. When he returned to rock 'n' roll performances several years later in Europe, his opening acts included some band called the Beatles. He continues to record to this day, almost catching a comeback hit off the 1986 *Down and out in Beverly Hills* soundtrack with "Great Gosh A'Mighty." He has cut some interesting music, everything from gospel to children's records, but nothing he ever committed to tape again would surpass the handful of records he made for Specialty during the '50s.

what to buy: The current owners of the Specialty catalog have made the 25 greatest Little Richard recordings available on *The Georgia Peach* 🎵🎵🎵🎵 (Specialty, 1991, prod. Bumps Blackwell) and, if that isn't enough, an additional 24 lesser-known pieces and alternate takes of hits appear on *Shag on down by the Union Hall* 🎵🎵🎵 (Specialty, 1996, prod. Bumps Blackwell).

what to buy next: For the truly ambitious, there's a three-disc box set, *The Specialty Sessions* 🎵🎵🎵🎵 (Specialty, 1989, prod. Bumps Blackwell), abridged from a five-disc British predecessor. Also, those wishing to either dispute or champion Richard's claim to being the first rock 'n' roller should check out *The Formative Years 1951–1954* 🎵🎵🎵🎵 (Bear Family, 1989, reissue prod. Richard Weize), which collects his jump blues tracks at RCA and his work with Billy Wright on the Peacock label.

what to avoid: Richard re-recorded his classic '50s hits for various labels during the '60s and '70s, and they continue to pop up on budget rack staples such as *20 Greatest Hits* 🎵 (Deluxe, 1994), *Golden Hits* 🎵 (ITC, 1997), *Killer Cuts* **woof!** (Public, 1995), and *Mega-Mix* 🎵🎵 (K-Tel, 1995). Though these discs all have some nice moments, it's best to stick with the Specialty or Rhino collections if you want the authentic brainblasts that kickstarted the music we all know as rock 'n' roll. Also, his gospel recordings turn up from time to time on various labels, including *Sings the Gospel* **woof!** (MCA, 1995). Although his powerful rock 'n' roll singing might lead one to reasonably suspect a great gospel singer lies beneath, Richard records deliberately tame, unexciting ballads sung without any flair or color.

the rest:
Well Alright 🎵🎵🎵 (Specialty 1970)
The Essential Little Richard 🎵🎵🎵🎵 (Specialty, 1985)
18 Greatest Hits 🎵🎵🎵🎵 (Rhino, 1988)
Shake It All About 🎵🎵🎵 (Disney, 1994)
Greatest Songs 🎵🎵 (Curb, 1995)

worth searching for: His 1965 OKeh Records jived-up "live" album that was actually recorded in the studio—Club OKeh, get it?—captures the wild, extravagant personality of the man himself, along with some impossibly intense vocal performances, and was released on a budget-priced CD titled *Little Richard's Greatest Hits* (OKeh, 1967/Epic, 1987, prod. Larry Williams). This is one of the greatest live performances in music history, an underrated masterwork that easily ranks with better known landmarks such as James Brown's *Live at the Apollo* and Otis Redding's *Live in Europe*. Also, if you dig Richard's freaky talk-show personality mixed with a little religious zealotry, check the vinyl bins for *God's Beautiful City* (Black Label, 1982), which mixes gospel music with preaching, and Richard's compelling "testimony" can be viewed by turns as hilarious or deeply moving.

influences:

◀◀ Roy Brown, Cab Calloway, Esquirita, Billy Wright

▶▶ Paul McCartney, Otis Redding, James Brown, John Fogerty, Prince, Michael Jackson

Joel Selvin and Ken Burke

Little River Band

Formed 1975, in Melbourne, Australia.

Beeb Birtles, guitar, vocals (1975–83); Graham Goble, guitar, vocals (1975–92); Glenn Shorrock, vocals (1975–82, 1988–present); Roger McLachlan, bass (1975–77); Derek Pellicci, drums (1975–85, 1988–present); Rick Formosa, guitar (1975–77); David Briggs, guitar, vocals (1977–82); George McArdale, bass (1977–79); Wayne Nelson, bass, vocals (1980-present); Steve Housden, guitar (1982–present); John Farnham, vocals (1982–88); Steven Prestwich, drums (1985–88); David Hirschfelder, keyboards (1985–88); Peter Beckett, guitar (1994–present); Tony Sciuto, guitar (1994–present).

During the mid- and late '70s, Australian rock meant AC/DC (heavy), Split Enz (quirky), and—the Little River Band. To be fair, this middle-of-the-road pop group was not without its virtues: frontman Glenn Shorrock provided a prototype for the kind of singing we'd hear on Phil Collins's solo albums; harmonies were a strong suit; and with three guitarists (!) LRB could step up for the occasional guitar jam à la its first hit, "It's a Long Way There"—though nobody yelled for "Free Bird" at its concerts. Mostly, however, LRB specialized in lite rock and lush pop, at best warmly melodic ("Help Is on Its Way," "Lonesome Loser"), at worst pure piffle ("Reminiscing").

what to buy: The single disc *Greatest Hits* 🎵🎵🎵 (Capitol/EMI, 1982, prod. various) should suffice for most. If this stuff really barbies your shrimp, go for *Reminiscing: The Twentieth Anniversary Collection* 🎵🎵🎵 (Rhino, 1994, prod. various), whose two-CDs leave room for a few of the less-inspiring moments.

the rest:

Little River Band 🎵🎵 (Harvest, 1976/One Way, 1997)
Diamantina Cocktail 🎵🎵🎵 (Harvest, 1977/Capitol, 1996)
Sleeper Catcher 🎵🎵🎵 (Harvest, 1978/One Way, 1996)
First under the Wire 🎵🎵 (Capitol, 1979/One Way, 1996)
Time Exposure 🎵 (Capitol, 1981/One Way, 1996)
The Net 🎵🎵 (Capitol, 1983/One Way, 1997)
No Reins 🎵🎵 (Capitol, 1986/One Way, 1997)
Worldwide Live 🎵 (Curb, 1991)
All-Time Greatest Hits 🎵🎵🎵 (CEMA Special Products, 1992)
It's a Long Way There 🎵🎵🎵 (Diskey, 1997)

influences:

◀◀ The Eagles, the Bee Gees, America

▶▶ Fleetwood Mac, Hootie & the Blowfish, Savage Garden

Gary Graff

Little Steven

Born Steven Van Zandt, November 22, 1950, in Boston, MA.

Steve Van Zandt made a name for himself on the Jersey shore club scene long before he was known to the world at large as Miami Steve or Little Steven. He had played in various bands during the '60s and early '70s, including the early Bruce Springsteen band Steel Mill. After a stint with Southside Johnny & the Asbury Jukes, Van Zandt joined the E Street Band in 1975, where he was dubbed Miami Steve and became an important part of Springsteen's rise to stardom, playing the role of de facto musical director on the road and co-producer in the studio. After releasing his first solo album in 1982, under the name Little Steven—and with an ace band called the Disciples of Soul—Van Zandt began to grow as a songwriter and a political artist. In 1984 he left the E Street Band and started his own solo career. Although his records have never sold well in the United States, he did gain notoriety for his anti-apartheid single "Sun City," which he recorded with more than 50 performers including Springsteen, Bob Dylan, Pete Townshend, Lou Reed, and Bono. A song that soon turned into an album and all-star concert, "Sun City" is a classic sample of Van Zandt's sound of late—heavy rhythms, driving guitars, and pointed lyrics on political issues of the day.

what to buy: *Men without Women* 🎵🎵🎵🎵 (EMI, 1982, prod. Miami Steve Van Zandt), Van Zandt's first solo effort, is a fine collection of soul-drenched rock 'n' roll that's closer to his work with the Jukes than his later efforts, with only a hint of the political tack he would take on those.

what to buy next: By his third album, *Freedom—No Compromise* 🎵🎵🎵🎵 (EMI Manhattan, 1987, prod. Little Steven), Van Zandt's songs carried heavier rhythms, inspired more by Prince's Minneapolis groove than by the Jersey shore rock 'n' roll swing. And even though these are mostly protest songs—

including duets with Springsteen ("Native American") and Ruben Blades ("Bitter Fruit")—Van Zandt still let the music drive the songs rather than the message.

the rest:
Voice of America 🎵🎵🎵 (EMI, 1984)

worth searching for: The hard-to-find *Revolution* (RCA, 1989, prod. Little Steven) continued in the hard hitting political vein of *Freedom—No Compromise*.

influences:
◄◄ Stax, Motown, Hank Williams, the Rolling Stones, the Yardbirds, Cream

►► Southside Johnny, Bon Jovi

see also: *Bruce Springsteen*

Mike Joiner

Little Village

Formed 1987, in Los Angeles, CA.

John Hiatt, vocals, guitar; Ry Cooder, guitar; Nick Lowe, vocals, bass; Jim Keltner, drums.

This quartet first got together to record John Hiatt's 1987 album *Bring the Family*, and the musicians enjoyed the experience so much they decided to make a go of it as a band. Unfortunately, for a band with so much personality and instrumental prowess, not much of it was in evidence on their debut album, which fizzled commercially, leaving the band members to return to their own pursuits. Little Village hasn't officially disbanded, but another record would certainly be a surprise.

what's available: *Little Village* 🎵🎵 (Reprise, 1992, prod. Little Village) lacks the spontaneous creative explosions you'd expect from the assembled talent here. Hiatt handles most of the singing and manages a couple of laughs on "Solar Sex Panel" and "Do You Want My Job." The rest of the album is a disappointment, though, and it comes off not so much like the Traveling Wilburys as a lukewarm Hiatt solo album.

influences:
◄◄ Brinsley Schwarz, Rockpile, Little Feat

see also: *John Hiatt, Nick Lowe, Ry Cooder*

Steve Knopper

Little Willie John

Born William J. Woods, November 15, 1937, in Cullendale, AR. Died May 26, 1968, in Walla Walla, WA.

Little Willie John stood tall in the R&B world of the '50s. His intensity brought his vocal performances to the edge of hysteria. John was a constant presence on the R&B charts for six years, beginning with his 1955 King Records debut, "All around the World." John suffused his signature song, "Fever," with vivid eroticism. He sounded desolate beyond description, moaning, "I Need Your Love So Bad." Whatever he sang, John put the full weight of his feelings behind it. Offstage he was a wild, untamed character who came to a sorry end, dying of a heart attack in Washington State Prison, where he was serving a 20-year sentence for manslaughter after being convicted of stabbing a man to death in a nightclub argument. Though he's not well known these days, Little Willie John inspired and influenced a generation of black musicians whose names became household words. The owner of Harlem's famed Apollo Theater believes John was the best male vocalist he ever heard. And the Rock and Roll Hall of Fame gave John some long overdue notice with an induction in 1996.

what to buy: After years of being impossible to find, John's music finally received the long-overdue treatment it deserves with *Fever: The Best of Little Willie John* 🎵🎵🎵🎵 (Rhino, 1993, prod. H. Glover), a 20-song collection that details his glory years at King Records.

what to buy next: Two of his original albums have also been reissued on CD—*Mister Little Willie John* 🎵🎵🎵 (King, 1958, prod. H. Glover) and *Sure Things* 🎵🎵🎵 (King, 1961, prod. H. Glover).

the rest:
Fever 🎵🎵🎵 (King, 1956/Charly, 1987)
All 15 Chart Hits 🎵🎵🎵 (King, 1996)
Greatest Hits 🎵🎵🎵 (King, 1996)
Talk to Me 🎵🎵🎵 (King, 1997)

worth searching for: Dig through the vinyl bins for the two-LP set *Free at Last* (Bluesway, 1970/Gusto, 1976, prod. Henry Glover) for a deeply satisfying mix of hits and B-sides at a budget price.

influences:
◄◄ Johnny Otis, Willie Dixon, John Lee Hooker

►► Hank Ballard, James Brown, Smokey Robinson, Edwin Starr, Otis Redding

Joel Selvin and Ken Burke

Live

Formed 1985, in York, PA.

Ed Kowalczyk, vocals, guitar; Chad Taylor, guitar, vocals; Patrick Dahlheimer, bass, vocals; Chad Gracey, drums, vocals.

Straight outta York, Pennsylvania, Live is the little garage band that could. Formed when the members were wee lads of 13, the group bears the trademarks of the two most notable bands of the era in which it was born—U2 and R.E.M. Like the former,

Ed Kowalczyk of Live (© **Ken Settle**)

Live sports an agenda that addresses issues of the world and of the spirit. Like the latter, the band's arrangements are often circumspect. Filling its songs with self-importance and the cosmic influence of Indian philosopher J. Krishnamurti, Live leaves itself open to charges of pretentiousness. But the truth is, the band is less preachy than U2, less precious than R.E.M., and its records are valuable as entertainment, if not metaphysics.

what to buy: *Throwing Copper* 𝄞𝄞𝄞 (Radioactive, 1994, prod. Jerry Harrison, Live) is the sound of a band truly coming into its own. They fearlessly take on the big subjects—religion, death, desperation—but rock with an authority that drives the sometimes overreaching lyrics home. The hits "Selling the Drama," "I Alone," and "Lightning Crashes" are every bit as memorable as they are meaningful.

what to buy next: The group's debut, *Four Songs* 𝄞𝄞𝄞 (Radioactive EP, 1991 prod. Jerry Harrison), contained signs of good things to come, most notably the anthemic "Operation Spirit," which later appeared on the debut album, *Mental Jewelry* 𝄞𝄞𝄞 (Radioactive, 1991, prod. Jerry Harrison)—although by then it had grown a parenthetical subtitle, "(The Tyranny of Tradition)." *Mental Jewelry* occasionally bogs down lyrically, but it's the kind of mistakes—oversimplification, for example—that 20-year-olds are apt to make.

what to avoid: Musically strong, *Secret Samadhi* 𝄞𝄞 (Radioactive, 1997, prod. Jay Healey, Live) repeatedly goes for the big statement, but falls woefully short.

influences:
◀◀ U2, R.E.M.

Daniel Durchholz

Live Skull

Formed 1983, in New York, NY. Disbanded 1989.

Thalia Zedek, vocals (1987–89); Mark C, guitar, vocals; Tom Paine, guitar, vocals; Marnie Greenholz, bass, vocals (1983–88); Sonda Andersson, bass, vocals (1988–89); James Lo, drums (1983–87); Rich Hutchins, drums (1987–89).

Arising from the noise-rock center of the world, Manhattan's Lower East Side, Live Skull was generally overlooked outside New York despite having made two albums the equal of Sonic Youth's best. Although the focus was on guitar sounds, monolithic bass lines, and James Lo's tightly wound drumming, the occasional mediocrity of the various members' vocals could be distracting, so Thalia Zedek (Uzi, Dangerous Birds) was brought in and raised the band to new heights with her aggressively droning style. Marnie Greenholz and Lo left shortly after her arrival and were replaced by Sonda Andersson (ex-Rat at Rat R) and Rich Hutchins. When lack of success eventually dis-

solved the band, Zedek went on to found Come. After playing in Wider, Lo turned up in Chavez.

what to buy: Zedek's peak comes on *Positraction* 𝄞𝄞𝄞𝄞 (Caroline, 1989), which includes the EP *Snuffer* 𝄞𝄞𝄞 (Caroline, 1988). The guitars are sharper and less dense than on the earlier records, and the sound bludgeons more effectively.

what to buy next: The best document of the pre-Zedek band, the live *Don't Get Any on You* 𝄞𝄞𝄞𝄞 (Homestead, 1987, prod. Live Skull, Massive Records), is an explosion of angst punctuated by the most chilling version of "Pusherman" ever.

the rest:
Bringing Home the Bait 𝄞𝄞𝄞𝄪 (Homestead, 1985)
Cloud One 𝄞𝄞𝄞 (Homestead, 1986)
Dusted 𝄞𝄞𝄞𝄪 (Homestead, 1987)
Chavez's Gone Glimmering 𝄞𝄞𝄪 (Matador, 1995)

worth searching for: The EP *Live Skull* (Massive, 1984, prod. Live Skull) shows the strength of the group's conception even at the beginning. The 12-inch *Raise the Manifestation* (Homestead, 1986, prod. Live Skull, Massive Records) has the only studio versions of three songs on *Don't Get Any on You*—the title song plus "Swingtime" and "Pusherman."

influences:
◀◀ Joy Division, Killing Joke, Sonic Youth, Swans, Psychedelic Furs

▶▶ Band of Susans, Come, Rein Sanction

Steve Holtje

Living Colour

Formed 1983, in Brooklyn, NY. Disbanded 1995.

Corey Glover, vocals; Vernon Reid, guitar; Muzz Skillings (born Manuel Skillings), bass (1983–92); William Calhoun, drums; Doug Wimbish, bass (1992–95).

Convened by Vernon Reid after stints in Ronald Shannon Jackson's Decoding Society and Defunkt, Living Colour remained a curiosity of the downtown New York rock scene until Rolling Stones frontman Mick Jagger produced a demo tape of two songs by the group in 1987. Though originally marketed as an all-black metal band, the group's brainy, politicized lyrics and razor-sharp instrumental chops showed it had much more to offer. But the MTV support that made its first album a hit never returned, and subsequent forays into subjects of racial pride and social injustice seemed to fly over the heads of many rock fans. By 1992 Muzz Skillings had left the group, replaced by former Sugarhill Gang member Doug Wimbish, and by 1995 tensions between Corey Glover and Reid had blown the band apart for good.

what to buy: The group's sophomore record, *Time's Up* ♫♫♫♪ (Epic, 1990, prod. Ed Stasium) stakes its ground with a muscular mix of songs, from the sorta bluesy, sorta fusion vibe of "Love Rears Its Ugly Head" to the heavy metal funk of "Elvis Is Dead" and the bruising punk of the title track. One listen and it's obvious: no other band in history could have made this record.

what to buy next: Living Colour's last statement as a band, *Stain* ♫♫♫♫ (Epic, 1993, prod. Ron Saint Germain, Andre Betts, Living Colour), also turned out to be one of its best, as Wimbish's bionic bass sounds prove the final link in pushing the band toward new sonic territory. Balancing almost punky rockers like "Go Away" and "Mind Your Own Business" with the tongue-in-cheek rumination "Bi" and the dreamy "Wall," the album offers a tantalizing look at what might have been.

what to avoid: Released when the band couldn't get an album together in time, the collection of live tracks and unreleased tunes that fills the six-song *Biscuits* **woof!** (Epic EP, 1991, prod. Ed Stasium, Living Colour) probably did more harm than good, exposing the public to uninspired playing and half-done compositions far below the standard set by the previous album. Sometimes, there's a reason why tracks are unreleased.

the rest:
Vivid ♫♫♫♪ (Epic, 1988)
Pride (Greatest Hits) ♫♫♫ (Epic, 1995)
Super Hits ♫♫♫♪ (Epic/Legacy, 1998)

worth searching for: The fiery Japanese live album *Dread* (Epic, 1995) provides proof of Living Colour's onstage acumen.

solo outings:
Vernon Reid:
Mistaken Identity ♫♫♫♪ (Sony 550, 1996)

Corey Glover:
Hymns ♫♫♫ (LaFace, 1998)

influences:
◄◄ Jimi Hendrix, Parliament/Funkadelic, Bad Brains, Fishbone
►► The Fugees, Me'Shell NdegeOcello, I Mother Earth

Eric Deggans

Local H

Formed 1987, in Zion, IL.

Scott Lucas, guitar, bass, vocals; Joe Daniels, drums.

Before Zion-Benton Township High School students Scott Lucas and Joe Daniels formed Local H, power-pop heroes the Shoes were Zion's primary contribution to rock history. But Local H broadened the town's reputation (as little-known as it was) to the world of hard rock and metal. As a duo, Lucas and Daniels have a fuller sound than half of the rock bands on the charts. Originally Local H started out as a quartet, but as band members dropped out, Lucas decided to use an octave splitter to transform his American Strat into a bass and guitar. After honing its skills around the Chicago area, Local H was signed to Island Records in May 1994.

what to buy: The band's debut, *Ham Fisted* ♫♫♪ (Island, 1995, prod. Steven Haigler), spawned the hard-driving single "Cynic." The ballad "Grrrlfriend" is a gentle tribute to Bikini Kill vocalist and sometime video star Kathleen Hanna.

the rest:
As Good As Dead ♫♫♪ (Island, 1996)
Pack up the Cats ♫♫♫♫ (Island, 1998)

influences:
◄◄ Stone Temple Pilots, Pearl Jam

Christina Fuoco

Lisa Loeb

Born March 11, 1968 in Bethesda, MD.

Catapulted to stardom by Greenwich Village neighbor Ethan Hawke's placement of her song "Stay (I Missed You)" on the *Reality Bites* soundtrack, Lisa Loeb has used that initial exposure to her advantage, coaxing the funding and the forum necessary for her to grow from a coffeehouse guitar girl into one of the more recognized faces and voices in '90s pop music. Loeb's musical career began in earnest at Brown University, where she and roommate Liz Mitchell (now of the band Ida) spent their undergraduate career in the aptly named outfit Liz & Lisa. After graduation, Loeb moved to Manhattan, went solo, and met producer Juan Patino. With Patino's help, Loeb's acoustically based sensibility has grown fuller in scope, but her real strength lies in her lyrics. When Lilith Fair called in the summer of 1997, Loeb stood up and was counted among the best young female singer-songwriters of the time.

what to buy: *Tails* ♫♫♫ (Geffen, 1995, prod. Juan Patino) was released in the wake of the Grammy-nominated "Stay (I Missed You)." The album is essentially a collection of acoustic numbers with Patino's studio shellac there to bolster them to the point of radio respectability. Not without some snickers, Loeb's lyrics were likened to a page out of a teenage girl's diary. But teenage troubles are just as valid as, and often times more passionate than, those from any other time in life.

what to avoid: On *Firecracker* ♫♫ (Geffen, 1997, prod. Juan Patino, Lisa Loeb), Loeb seems more at home with the production, but her lyrics generally lack the personal connection of her debut.

influences:

◀◀ The Go-Go's, Juliana Hatfield

▶▶ Tara MacLean, Paula Cole

Isaac Josephson

Bill Lloyd

See: Foster & Lloyd

Richard Lloyd

See: Television

Nils Lofgren
/Grin

Born June 21, 1951, in Chicago, IL.

Always the star sideman, never the star—that pretty much sums up the career of guitar wunderkind Nils Lofgren, who at age 17 played on Neil Young's *After the Goldrush* album and was once rumored to be a replacement candidate for Mick Taylor in the Rolling Stones. Lofgren was a member of Crazy Horse for one album and later toured with Young after playing on the album *Tonight's the Night*. As for his own work, Lofgren formed the band Grin in 1969 with Washington D.C. mates Bob Gordon (bass) and Bob Berberich (drums), later adding brother Tom Lofgren on guitar. Unfortunately, Grin never achieved the widespread recognition or critical kudos befitting its taut, melodic rock and tender ballads, and the group's legacy is tough to track these days and not much remains in print. After Grin split up in 1974 Lofgren went on to pursue a solo career marked by stellar guitar work but albums rendered wildly uneven by his weak vocals and frequently poor songwriting. His highest visibility was as a member of Bruce Springsteen's E Street Band from 1984 to 1991. Still, his last few albums are surprisingly strong, suggesting there may be hope yet for this sometimes underrated/sometimes underachieving artist.

what to buy: Lofgren's auspicious solo debut, *Nils Lofgren* 𝄞𝄞𝄞𝄞 (A&M, 1975, prod. Nils Lofgren, David Briggs) is his best, featuring "Keith Don't Go," his plea to self-destructive Rolling Stones guitarist Keith Richards, as well as "Back It Up," "Rock and Roll Crook," and a version of Carole King's "Goin' Back." The 15-track *Classics, Volume 13* 𝄞𝄞𝄞𝄞 (A&M, 1989, prod. various) offers a generous look back at his A&M years and effectively culls the best material from those five albums.

what to buy next: After several spotty albums, *Nils* 𝄞𝄞𝄞 (A&M, 1979, prod. Bob Ezrin) put Lofgren back on his feet thanks to a productive writing session with Lou Reed that yielded the boxing epic "No Mercy" and the beautiful "Shine Silently." *Silver Lining* 𝄞𝄞𝄞 (Rykodisc, 1991, prod. Kevin McCormick, Nils Lof-

gren) offers Lofgren's best batch of songs in years—including the heartfelt ballad "Valentine"—and some all-star help from Springsteen, Clarence Clemons, Billy Preston, and Levon Helm.

what to avoid: When Lofgren's songwriting lets him down, it's not enough for him to try and let his guitar do the talking. Those tendencies reveal themselves on several albums, most notably *I Came to Dance* 𝄞 (A&M, 1977, prod. Nils Lofgren, Andy Newmark).

the rest:
Cry Tough 𝄞𝄞𝄞 (A&M, 1975)
Night after Night 𝄞𝄞𝄞 (A&M, 1977)
Night Fades Away 𝄞𝄞 (Backstreet, 1981)
Wonderland 𝄞𝄞𝄞 (Backstreet, 1983)
The Best of Nils Lofgren 𝄞𝄞𝄞 (A&M, 1985)
Flip 𝄞𝄞𝄞 (Columbia, 1985)
Crooked Line 𝄞𝄞𝄞𝄞 (Rykodisc, 1992)
Damaged Goods 𝄞𝄞𝄞𝄞 (Pure, 1995)
Code of the Road: Greatest Hits Live! 𝄞𝄞𝄞 (The Right Stuff, 1997)
Acoustic Live 𝄞𝄞𝄞 (The Right Stuff, 1998)

worth searching for: *Back It Up!!* (A&M, 1976) was a promotional release of a radio concert that capitalized on Lofgren's incendiary skills as a performer—perhaps to the detriment of the studio album that was current at the time.

solo outings:
Grin:
1+1 𝄞𝄞𝄞𝄞 (Spindizzy, 1972/Epic, 1992)

influences:

◀◀ Neil Young, the Rolling Stones, Chuck Berry

▶▶ Bruce Springsteen, Paul Westerberg, Eric Johnson, Stevie Ray Vaughan

see also: *Neil Young, Bruce Springsteen, Ringo Starr*

Daniel Durchholz

Loggins & Messina
/Kenny Loggins

Formed 1972, in Los Angeles, CA. Disbanded 1976.

Kenny Loggins (born January 7, 1948, in Everett, WA.), guitar, vocals; Jim Messina (born December 5, 1947, in Maywood, CA.), guitar, bass, vocals.

Kenny Loggins, whose claim to fame during the early '70s was the Nitty Gritty Dirt Band's recording of his "House at Pooh Corner," was fortunate to have Jim Messina produce his first solo album. The result, *Sittin' In*, was the first of what was to become a highly successful partnership. Messina's credentials include playing bass, assembling the material for and producing Buffalo Springfield's final record, *Last Time Around,* and being a founding member of Poco, where he remained for their first three albums. A fine technician with a great ear, Messina probably curtailed Loggins's penchant for overly sensitive mush. Together they spun out a long string of hits, including "Danny's Song," their own treatment of "House at Pooh Corner," and "Your Mama Don't Dance." On his own—following the duo's 1976 split—Loggins parlayed his personable image and talent into a successful, if creatively middling, solo career marked by excessively romantic songs, ultra-slick production but also numerous hits, particularly soundtrack smashes such as "Footloose," "Nobody's Fool," and "Danger Zone."

what to buy: Loggins & Messina's debut, *Sittin' In* 𝄞𝄞𝄞𝄞 (Columbia, 1972/1989 prod. Jim Messina), is their best, most fully realized recording. Practically every song is a charmer, from the tightly rockin' country guitar accents on the opening track, "Nobody but You," to Loggins's sweet ballad, "Danny's Song." *On Stage* 𝄞𝄞𝄞𝄞 (Columbia, 1974/Legacy, 1998, prod. Jim Messina) features an excellent backing band and a definitive, extended version of "Angry Eyes."

what to buy next: *Loggins & Messina* 𝄞𝄞𝄞 (Columbia, 1972/1989), the duo's sophomore effort, has the tiresome single "Your Mama Don't Dance," but also the studio version of "Angry Eyes." *Yesterday, Today, Tomorrow: The Greatest Hits of Kenny Loggins* 𝄞𝄞𝄞 (Columbia, 1997, prod. various) is as advertised, containing "Pooh Corner," "I'm Alright," "Danger Zone," "Whenever I Call You 'Friend'," and "Celebrate Me Home," among others.

what to avoid: The duo's *Native Sons* **woof!** (Columbia, 1976/1990) and *So Fine* **woof!** (Columbia, 1975) suffer from severe lapses in songwriting originality. Loggins's *Vox Humana* **woof!** (Columbia, 1985) is so overblown that it leaves one speechless. His most recent album, *The Unimaginable Life* **woof!** (Columbia, 1997), is even worse, full of new-age platitudes and collaborations with his wife. The album is the companion piece to their book of the same name. Come back, Leo Buscaglia, all is forgiven.

the rest:

Loggins & Messina:
Full Sail 𝄞𝄞 (Columbia, 1973)
Mother Lode 𝄞𝄞𝄞 (Columbia, 1974/1990)
Best of Friends 𝄞𝄞𝄞 (Columbia, 1976)

Kenny Loggins:
Nightwatch 𝄞𝄞𝄞 (Columbia, 1978)
Keep the Fire 𝄞𝄞𝄞 (Columbia, 1979)
Alive 𝄞𝄞𝄞 (Columbia, 1980)
High Adventure 𝄞𝄞𝄞 (Columbia, 1982)
Back to Avalon 𝄞 (Columbia, 1988)
Leap of Faith 𝄞 (Columbia, 1991)
Outside: From the Redwoods 𝄞𝄞 (Columbia, 1993)
Return to Pooh Corner 𝄞𝄞𝄞 (Columbia, 1994)

December N/A (Sony, 1998)

worth searching for: Loggins & Messina's *Star Box* (CBS/Sony, 1989) is a Japanese collection whose 20-songs offer a better overview than the domestic *Best of Friends*.

influences:
◀◀ Simon & Garfunkel, Poco, Bread

▶▶ The Captain & Tennille, Buckingham Nicks, Fleetwood Mac

see also: *Poco, Buffalo Springfield*

Patrick McCarty

Lone Justice
/Maria McKee

Formed 1983, in Los Angeles, CA. Disbanded 1987.

Maria McKee (born August 17, 1964), vocals, guitar; Ryan Hedgecock, guitar, vocals (1983–86); Marvin Etzioni, bass, vocals (1983–86); Don Heffington, drums (1983–86); Shayne Fontayne, guitar (1986–87); Gregg Sutton, bass (1986–87); Rudy Richman, drums (1986–87); Bruce Brody, keyboards (1986–87).

Before it was a rock 'n' roll movement, Lone Justice played rock with a countrified twang, taking a spirited, rootsy approach that in 1985 was fresh, not trendy. With her powerful voice and eye-catching presence, it wasn't long before Maria McKee became the group's focal point—and, in fact, the group, as an entirely different band of musicians, came on board for Lone Justice's second and final album. The group split up following a tour on which it opened for U2, and McKee (working with Lone Justice keyboardist Bruce Brody) took a solo path that has been nothing if not fascinating, as she has changed styles from the ethereal *Maria McKee* to the Lone Justice soundalike *You Gotta Sin to Get Saved* and the more eclectic *Life Is Sweet*. Marvin Etzioni, meanwhile, has recorded some albums of his own and produced titles for Peter Case and Toad the Wet Sprocket.

what to buy: *Lone Justice* 𝄞𝄞𝄞𝄞 (Geffen, 1985, prod. Jimmy Iovine) is an exceptional debut, the arrival of a fresh new sound via exuberant performances and a tremendous batch of songs such as "East of Eden," "Sweet, Sweet Baby (I'm Falling)," and Tom Petty's "Ways to Be Wicked."

what to buy next: Lone Justice's *BBC Radio 1 Live in Concert* 𝄞𝄞𝄞𝄞 (Windsong, 1993) gives a sense of the band's—and particularly McKee's—strength on a concert stage. McKee's second solo album, *You Gotta Sin to Get Saved* 𝄞𝄞𝄞𝄞 (Geffen, 1993, prod. George Drakoulias) is nearly as good as *Lone Justice* and features the original band's rhythm section as well as members of the Jayhawks.

what to avoid: McKee's *Life Is Sweet* 𝄞𝄞 (Geffen, 1996, prod. Maria McKee, Bruce Brody, Mark Freegard) is all over the place to the point where even the force of her singing can't bring the album back into focus.

the rest:

Shelter ♫♫♯ (Geffen, 1986)

worth searching for: Check out McKee's guest appearance for a duet on "Temple and Shine" with Marvin Etzioni on his album *Weapons of the Spirit* (Restless, 1994).

solo outings:

Maria McKee:

Maria McKee ♫♫♫ (Geffen, 1989)

Marvin Etzioni:

The Mandolin Man ♫♫♫ (Restless, 1992)

influences:

◄◄ Tom Petty & the Heartbreakers, the Byrds, the Flying Burrito Brothers, Janis Joplin, Aretha Franklin

►► Sheryl Crow, Uncle Tupelo, Jayhawks, Cowboy Junkies

Gary Graff

Roy Loney

See: The Flaming Groovies

Mary Lou Lord

Born March 1, 1965, in Salem, MA.

While Ani DiFranco is heralded as indie-rock's stubborn savior, Mary Lou Lord has been mounting a quieter kind of revolution for years. Despite a brief flurry of gossip-mongering attention in 1993 as one of Courtney Love's favorite targets (Lord was romantically linked to Kurt Cobain before his marriage), the former Boston subway busker defiantly has pursued an underground following, often eschewing formal concerts in favor of impromptu street-corner gigs and releasing singles and EPs on Seattle's iconoclastic Kill Rock Stars label. Although she's a gifted songwriter with a knack for humorous nods to rock history ("His Lamest Flame" is a play on Elvis Presley's "His Latest Flame") and colorful imagery ("I'm Western Union desperate/at a pay phone in the rain"), she prefers to cover artists both legendary (Bob Dylan, Big Star) and obscure (Elliott Smith, Nick Saloman of the Bevis Frond). Now signed to Sony's WORK subsidiary after a ferocious bidding war, Lord is enjoying the fruits of major-label affiliation: The radio success of the jangly "Lights Are Changing" in 1998 allowed her to tour with a band for the first time, resulting in shows that rocked harder but sacrificed the compelling intimacy of her solo acoustic concerts. The key to Lord's appeal remains the disarming impact of her hushed, purring soprano, a weathered voice hovering in the gray areas between confidence and doubt, love and disdain, soft-hearted optimism and hard-luck disappointment. Those differences are communicated not in volume or range, but in her delicate phrasing—the aural equivalent of a wince or a sideways glance that elevates a pop song from melodic to memorable.

what to buy: Lord's major-label debut, *Got No Shadow* ♫♫♫♫ (WORK/Sony, 1998, prod. Tom Rothrock, Rob Schnapf, Fred Maher), fulfills the promise of her indie releases by whisking off on a glorious, Rickenbacker-laced pop excursion propelled by songwriting collaborator-guitarist Nick Saloman and help from Elliott Smith, Shawn Colvin, and Roger McGuinn. Although she covers tunes by Freedy Johnston ("The Lucky One") and Elizabeth Cotten ("Shake Sugaree"), the most moving songs come from her own pen, including the deliciously cryptic "Throng of Blowtown" and fleshed-out remakes of both sides of her 1993 single, "Some Jingle Jangle Morning" and "Western Union Desperate."

what to buy next: The eight-song *Mary Lou Lord* ♫♫♫♯ (Kill Rock Stars, 1995) includes her first stab at a band-arranged "Lights Are Changing" as well as solo acoustic renditions of Saloman's "He'd Be a Diamond" and her funny alt-rock hipness quotient lament, "His Indie World." *Martian Saints* ♫♫♫ (Kill Rock Stars, 1997, prod. John Porter, others) is a five-song EP notable for her tender rendition of Elliott Smith's "I Figured You Out" and Pete Droge's quirky "Sunspot Stopwatch."

worth searching for: The acoustic four-track *The Pace of Change* (WORK/Sony, 1998), featuring covers of Richard Thompson's "1952 Vincent Black Lightning" and Billy Bragg's "Ontario, Quebec and Me," was given away to fans who responded to a postcard questionnaire included in the first run of *Got No Shadow*.

influences:

◄◄ Bob Dylan, Joni Mitchell, Neil Young

►► Shawn Colvin, Elliott Smith

David Okamoto

Lords of Acid

Formed 1988, in Belgium.

Lady Galore (born Ruth McArdle), vocals; Nathalie Delaet, vocals (1988–93); Lord T. Byron (born Frank Vloeberghs), bass; Sai De La Luna, keyboards, vocals; McGuinnes (born Kurt Liekens), drums; Erhan, guitar (1992–present).

Led first by Nathalie Delaet, the Lords of Acid emerged from the hot Belgian techno scene of the late '80s with the hit "I Sit on Acid." The song's tawdry mix of drug subculture and unabashed sexuality established the Lords as club favorites. British vocalist Ruth McArdle took over as frontwoman as of the *Voodoo-U* album, and while the group continues to get their ya ya's out by topping themselves with ever-naughtier lyrics, they're still capable of producing some potent dance music.

what to buy: The first album, *Lust* 𝄞𝄞𝄞 (Caroline, 1991, prod. various), expands on the group's early singles with lush female vocals adding a human sensuality to the electronic samples and sound machines.

what to buy next: With *Voodoo-U* 𝄞𝄞 (American Recordings, 1994, prod. various), the band makes a few changes, not only swapping lead singers and labels, but trading in the slower, mesmerizing club mix for harsh, pounding, guitar-sampled, industrial/rave music. Lady Galore screams throughout the album, ordering submission to the new sound. Songs such as "Do What You Wanna Do" emphasize the new guitar driven noise and are almost metalesque, but the beats are still there—only they're a bit faster and denser.

the rest:
Our Little Secret 𝄞𝄞𝄞 (Antler Subway, 1997)

influences:
◀◀ Front 242, KMFDM, Einstürzende Neubauten

▶▶ Ethyl Meatplow

Bryan Lassner

Lords of the New Church
See: Dead Boys

Los Bravos
Formed 1965, in Spain. Disbanded early 1970s.

Michael Kogel, vocals; Antonio Martinez, guitar; Miguel Luis Vicens Danus, bass; Manuel Fernandez, organ; Juan-Pablo Sanllehi, drums.

During 1966, with the British Invasion in retreat, one of the biggest hits in the United States ("Black Is Back") came from Los Bravos, a rock group from the unlikely locale of Spain. In fact, it sounded more like an American group, with its brassy pop-rock arrangements and Michael Kogel's emphatic vocals, which were tinged with an expressive tenor reminiscent of Gene Pitney's. "Black Is Black" was a Top 5 hit here, but little else happened until the group made a minor impact with "Bring a Little Lovin'," a song written for it by Easybeats members George Young and Harry Vanda.

worth searching for: There's nothing to be found on these shores, but the European collection *All the Best* serves up a generous 30 tracks, most of them sung in English.

influences:
◀◀ Del Shannon, the Animals, Jay & the Americans

▶▶ The Buckinghams, Herb Alpert, Los Lobos, rock en Español

Christopher Scapelliti

Los Lobos
Formed 1974, in Los Angeles, CA.

David Hidalgo, guitar, vocals; Conrad Lozano, bass, vocals; Cesar Rosas, guitar, vocals; Louis Perez, drums, guitar, vocals; Steve Berlin, saxophone, keyboards (1984–present).

One could argue that "La Bamba" was the best thing to ever happen to Los Lobos. Not because their spunky 1987 cover of the Ritchie Valens hit gave this Los Angeles act its 15 minutes of Top 40 fame, but because fear of being labeled a Chicano version of Sha-Na-Na challenged them to put their own weird, wobbly spin on the festive fusing of blues, R&B, rockabilly, and Mexican folk music that originally established them as roots-rock torchbearers. Such twangy T-Bone Burnett–produced efforts as *By the Light of the Moon* and *How Will the Wolf Survive?* introduced a tight garage band that would be happy if it never left the barrios or the bars. But in 1990, prodded by producers Larry Hirsch and Mitchell Froom, Los Lobos transformed into one of rock's most experimental acts. Fuzz, feedback, distortion, and dense percussion blended with lead singer Hidalgo's soulful tenor and Froom's quirky production techniques to create the intoxicating cross-section of rhythms and textures behind *The Neighborhood* and 1992's jaw-dropping *Kiko*. The band that once amazed listeners by deftly handing a variety of genres now blurs the lines so much that it's hard to figure out where it's going next. And that's something that can't be said about most roots-rock bands.

what to buy: Of its early efforts, *How Will the Wolf Survive?* 𝄞𝄞𝄞 (Slash/Warner Bros., 1984, prod. T-Bone Burnett, Steve Berlin) holds up the best. It's a roots-rock primer ranging from savage blues ("Don't Worry Baby") to engaging country-rock ("A Matter of Time," "Will the Wolf Survive?") and traditional Tex-Mex ("Serenata Nortena"). The band begins flexing its experimental muscles on *The Neighborhood* 𝄞𝄞𝄞 (Slash/Warner Bros., 1990, prod. Larry Hirsch, Mitchell Froom, Los Lobos), a rich, riveting effort driven by guest drummer Jim Keltner and a mesmerizing mix of the band's raunchiest ("Jenny's Got a Pony," "Georgia Slop") and prettiest ("Little John of God," "Be Still") performances. All rules go out the window on *Kiko* 𝄞𝄞𝄞𝄞 (Slash/Warner Bros., 1992, prod. Mitchell Froom, Los Lobos), an ambitious, atmospheric patchwork of the Beatles, Tom Waits, New Orleans jazz, country, and blues that never lapses into avant garde pretension. More important, Hidalgo and Louie Perez's songs—which tackle death (the lovely "Saint behind the Glass"), homelessness ("Angels with Dirty Faces"), child abuse ("Two Janes"), and domestic violence ("Reva's House")—are their hardest hitting to date.

what to buy next: *La Pistola y El Corazon* 𝄞𝄞𝄞 (Slash/Warner Bros., 1988, prod. Los Lobos) is a delightful Spanish-language romp through traditional Mexican music played on accordions,

David Hidalgo (top) and Cesar Rosas of Los Lobos (© Ken Settle)

nylon-string guitars, upright bass, bajo sextos, and other folk-loric instruments.

what to avoid: Once you break all the rules on *Kiko*, what do you do for an encore? The bluesy, noisy *Colossal Head* 🎵🎵 (Slash/Warner Bros., 1996, prod. Mitchell Froom, Tchad Blake, Los Lobos) buckles under the pressure of topping its predecessor, sounding more contrived than created.

the rest:
. . . And a Time to Dance 🎵🎵🎵 (Slash/Warner Bros., 1983)
By the Light of the Moon 🎵🎵🎵 (Slash/Warner Bros., 1987)
Just Another Band from East L.A.: A Collection 🎵🎵🎵 (Slash/Warner Bros., 1993)

worth searching for: The soundtrack to Paul Bartel's black comedy *Eating Raoul* (Varese, 1982, prod. Scot Holton, Tom Null) features the then-unknown band rampaging through "Diablo Con Vestido," a Spanish version of "Devil with a Blue Dress."

solo outings:
Latin Playboys (Hidalgo, Perez, Mitchell Froom, and Tchad Blake):
Latin Playboys 🎵🎵 (Slash/Warner Bros., 1994)

influences:
◀◀ Ritchie Valens, Sir Douglas Quintet

▶▶ The Blazers, rock en Español

David Okamoto

Los Straitjackets
/The Raybeats

Raybeats formed 1980, in New York, NY. Disbanded 1983. Los Strait-jackets formed 1994, in Nashville TN.

Los Straitjackets: Danny Amis, guitar; Eddie Angel, guitar; L.J. Lester, drums; E. Scott Esbeck, bass. The Raybeats: Danny Amis, bass, guitar; Jody Harris, guitar; Pat Irwin, alto sax, organ, guitar; Don Christensen, drums.

Who are these guys? With their Mexican wrestling masks, it's impossible to know exactly who these twangy surf-mongers are. If the liner notes are correct, then within its ranks is former Raybeat and altogether fantastic guitarist Danny Amis. As far as instrumental surf music goes, these guys are relative purists—no punk or kitsch sneaks into their loyal string-bending sound. Amis and Eddie Angel split the songwriting tasks fairly evenly with enough cuts for both to showcase their talents. Both of the group's records also have the honor of being produced by the great Ben Vaughn. If you're not a fan of the style, you probably won't be converted. But if you are, then catch a wave and hang ten.

what to buy: On the Raybeats' *Guitar Beat* 🎵🎵🎵🎵 (PVC/Jem, 1981, prod. Martin Rushent), Amis joins with New York No-

Wave veterans (former members of the Contortions and 8 Eyed Spy) Jody Harris, Don Christensen, and Pat Irwin to make one of the better surf records you'll ever hear. Harris is an amazing guitar player, and utility-man Irwin spices up the venture with sax and organ. Check out "International Operator" and "B-Gas Rickshaw" for thrills and chills—as well as "Calhoun Surf," which also appears on the first Los Straitjackets record. The second Los Straitjackets record, *¡Viva! Los Straitjackets* 🎵🎵🎵 (Upstart, 1996, prod. Ben Vaughn), is pretty much what you expect of the genre: snappy beats, one-stringed riffing, and pulsing bass on a raucous journey that, with a repeat button, only ends when you want it to.

what to buy next: *The Utterly Fantastic and Totally Unbelievable Sound of Los Straitjackets* 🎵🎵🎵 (Upstart, 1995, prod. Ben Vaughn) will be only fantastic to those who have heard Amis play before. It's more of the same, with string bends, reverb, respectfully precise bass, and crisp drumming to anchor the tasty sound.

worth searching for: Amis's solo recording *Whiplash* (Coyote EP, 1983, prod. Mitch Easter) is pretty good and in the same vein. Also worth a hunt are two other Raybeats records: the EP *Roping Wild Bears* and *It's Only a Movie.*

influences:
◀◀ The Ventures, Dick Dale, Link Wray, the Surfaris, the Shadows

▶▶ The Mermen, Huevos Rancheros, the Aqua Velvets, the Volcanos, Galaxy Trio, the Phantom Surfers

Barry M. Prickett

Lothar & the Hand People

Formed 1967, in New York, NY. Disbanded 1970.

John Emelin, vocals, theremin; Kim King, moog, guitar, tapes; Paul Conly, keyboards, moog; Rusty Ford, bass; Tom Flye, percussion.

Unrecognized visionary geniuses who boldly attempted to mix rock 'n' roll with the latest advances from the world of electronic music, or second-rate quasi-cosmic doodlers who got blotto watching *The Day the Earth Stood Still* on TV late one night and decided to start a group? History records that Brian Wilson was the first rocker to employ the theremin, a mainstay of horror movie soundtracks ever since Hitchcock's *Spellbound*, using it on *Pet Sounds* and most notably "Good Vibrations." Shortly thereafter, Micky Dolenz was heard tinkering with an early prototype Moog Synthesizer at the end of the fourth Monkees album. But when John Emelin brought his new theremin (which he affectionately nicknamed "Lothar") to rehearsal one day, encouraging his transfixed bandmates to wave their hands around its oscillator stick (by which the pitch of the instrument's tone is manipulated), Lothar & the Hand People were suddenly born. This being 1967, they had little trouble convincing Capitol Records to finance and issue not one, but *two* entire albums of their music until apparently everyone involved came to their senses and the entire project was quickly shuffled under the rug—but not before Emerson, Lake & Palmer picked up the stick, as it were, and kicked off an entire era of bigger-budgeted and severely more pompous career in art rock. Lothar, it seems, has quite a lot to answer for.

what's available: A recent re-release of *Presenting—Lothar & the Hand People* 🎸🎸🎸 (Capitol, 1968/One Way, 1994, prod. Robert Marguleff) presents the original album plus six newly unearthed bonus tracks. Versions of the Everly Brothers' "Bye Bye Love" and possibly the Woody Woodpecker theme reveal these guys may very well have had pop-rock roots, but three of their own compositions, "Machines," "Sex and Violence," and "It Comes on Anyhow," are severely deranged numbers that, depending on how you approach such material, are either brave experimentations for the era or a laughable waste of both time and space. File alongside *Electronic Sound* by George Harrison.

worth searching for: Things get even more totally "out there" on *Space Hymn* (Capitol, 1969), as such song titles as "Sdrawkcab" and "Today Is Only Yesterday's Tomorrow" plainly suggest. A hilarious take on Martha & the Vandellas' "Heat Wave" notwithstanding, Emelin spends the majority of the title track attempting to hypnotize the listener—into doing exactly *what*, however, is never really explained.

influences:

◀◀ Bernard Herrmann, Walter Carlos, Leon Theremin, Roger Ruskin Spear

▶▶ Hawkwind, Pere Ubu, Simply Saucer, Bob Hoffnar

Gary Pig Gold

Lotion

Formed 1991, in New York, NY.

Tony Zajkowski, vocals, guitar; Jim Ferguson, guitar, vocals; Bill Ferguson, bass; Rob Youngberg, drums.

Perhaps it's the group's diversity, but Lotion is one of the more tragically overlooked bands of the '90s. Each record is highly listenable, with myriad variations of power pop. One cut shoegazes, the next wistfully strums, and the next crunches and slams with abandon. Thomas Pynchon and Michael Moore are fans, Buffy the Vampire Slayer loves 'em, and the quartet has even appeared on the Taco Bell compilation (!) *Do Something*. But stardom has avoided Lotion, while the group plugs on with a Cheap Trick-meets-Britpop blend that deserves to be heard blasting from boomboxes and T-topped Camaros.

what to buy: *Nobody's Cool* 🎸🎸🎸🎸 (spinArt, 1995, prod. Jim Rondinelli) should have done the trick. Galloping drums, intricately chiming guitars, understated, yet melodic bass, and pleading vocals make Lotion's second full-length release—for which author Pynchon wrote liner notes—a completely engaging listen.

what to buy next: *Full Issac* 🎸🎸🎸 (spinArt, 1994, prod. Kurt Ralske) is a neat collection of songs by a band that could rule the world. It includes the fine "Dock Ellis," named for the pitcher who reputedly threw a no-hitter on LSD, and many other shoulda-been hits. *The Telephone Album* 🎸🎸🎸 (spinArt, 1998, prod. Lotion, Mark Mason) only suffers in comparison to Lotion's previous work. There's no extensive growth here, but it's still a worthy effort.

the rest:

Lotion 🎸🎸🎸 (KokoPop EP, 1992)
Lotion (Head) 🎸🎸🎸 (KokoPop EP, 1993)
The Agnew Funeral 🎸🎸🎸 (spinArt EP, 1995)

influences:

◀◀ Cheap Trick, the Shoes, the dB's, R.E.M., Echo & the Bunnymen, Pavement, Swervedriver

Barry M. Prickett

Loud Family

See: Game Theory

The Lounge Lizards

Formed 1979, in New York, NY.

John Lurie, soprano and alto saxophones, vocals; Evan Lurie, keyboards (1979–90, 1996–present); Arto Lindsay, guitar (1979–80); Dana Vicek, guitar (1980); Danny Rosen, guitar (1981); Steve Piccolo, bass (1979–81); Anton Fier, drums (1979–81); Peter Zummo, trombone (1983); Tony Garnier, bass (1983); Dougie Bowne, drums (1983–90); Roy Nathanson, saxophone (1984–90); Curtis Fowlkes, trombone (1984–90); Marc Ribot, guitar, trumpet, banjo (1984–90); Eric Sanko, bass (1984–90, 1993–present); E.J. Rodriguez, percussion (1987–90); Michael Blake, saxophone, bass clarinet (1991–present); Steven Bernstein, trumpet, cornet (1991–present); Bryan Carrott, vibraphone, marimba, timpani (1991–92); Michele Navazio, guitar (1991–95); David Tronzo, slide guitar (1993–present); Danny Blume, guitar (1993–95); John Medeski, organ (1993); Oren Bloedow, bass (1991–92); Grant Calvin Weston, drums (1991–present); Billy Martin, percussion (1991–93); Jane Scarpantoni, cello (1991–present); Ben Perowsky, percussion (1996–present).

Once upon a time, John Lurie's self-bestowed description "fake jazz" made ironic sense, but his band long ago graduated to a warped version of the real thing, though it goes beyond jazz boundaries and always has. The key to the band has always been not Lurie (which isn't to say he's not a good saxophonist and composer), but who's playing with him. The first edition with atonal guitarist Arto Lindsay was stellar; it deconstructed familiar tunes by changing their sonic context, while the Lurie brothers' own compositions posited an alternate jazz reality in which cool tunes with jagged edges bespoke a casual yet aware stance. After a couple of changes of guitarist, the band was revamped. The second main lineup with Peter Zummo lost the frenetic, barely contained anarchy and had little to substitute; but starting with the third main lineup, African influences could be heard, both in the less square rhythms and in Lurie's keening tone and phrasing. The fourth lineup, with musical director Steve Bernstein (who leads the post-modernist jazz trio Spanish Fly and the bizarro avant-lounge Sex Mob), emphasized the world beat aspect even more while sometimes adding a funky '60s soul-jazz aspect. After legal tangles with David Byrne's Luaka Bop label over the Lounge Lizards' *Queen of All Ears* in 1996, Lurie started his own label, Strange & Beautiful Music, on which he issued that album along with several new or previously out-of-print items. Outside of the Lounge Lizards, Lurie had earlier hooked up with director Jim Jarmusch, who's not only had him score three films but also act in *Stranger Than Paradise* and *Down by Law*, where his detached presence and iconic good looks work to good noir effect (he has appeared in other films as well). One of Lurie's oddest projects is the *Fishing with John* sports/travel television series, where he and a guest (Tom Waits, Jarmusch, Matt Dillon, Dennis Hopper, and Willem Dafoe, so far) travel to a more or less exotic locale and pursue the native aquatic life, despite the fact that Lurie "knows absolutely nothing about fishing."

what to buy: *The Lounge Lizards* ♪♪♪♪♫ (EG, 1981, prod. Teo Macero) is a brilliant refraction of familiar jazz elements recontextualized. Lindsay's skronk guitar effusions and the covers of two Thelonious Monk tunes and "Harlem Nocturne" stand out. *Live in Berlin 1991, Vol. 1* ♪♪♪♪ (Intuition, 1993, prod. John Lurie) and *Live in Berlin 1991, Vol. 2* ♪♪♪♪ (Intuition, 1995, prod. John Lurie), with the Bernstein-directed lineup, cover all the po-mo bases, and things get stirringly hot or cool according to the circumstance. The overall feeling is looser and more organic than in the earlier versions of the band, and more democratic.

what to buy next: The loose, fun *Voice of CHUNK* ♪♪♪♫ (Lagarto, 1989/Strange & Beautiful Music, 1998, prod. John Lurie) was self-issued by Lurie and originally was sold via an 800-line phone number (which no longer works). Evan Lurie has a strong interest in tango, and his first album as a leader, *Selling Water by the Side of the River* ♪♪♪ (Island, 1990), features Alfredo Pedernera, a respected virtuoso on the bandoneon (an elongated accordion), as well as the versatile Ribot. Evan's an-

gular, off-kilter piano style, rife with pregnant dissonances, fits right in. The many John Lurie tracks on the soundtrack of the hit John Travolta film *Get Shorty* ♪♪♪♪ (Island, 1995), which includes a few tracks by other artists, utilize many Lounge Lizard members, with LL music director Steve Bernstein the orchestrator and conductor. This is where the band's soul-jazz side comes through most clearly.

what to avoid: Some of the compositions on *Live from the Drunken Boat* ♪♪ (Europa, 1983, prod. Teo Macero, John Lurie) are good, but this studio recording finds Lurie between great band lineups and not yet a strong enough player to carry the album himself.

the rest:
Live in Tokyo—Big Heart ♪♪♪ (Island, 1986)
No Pain for Cakes ♪♪♪ (Island, 1987)
Queen of No Ears ♪♪♪♫ (Strange & Beautiful Music, 1998)

worth searching for: *Live 79/81* (ROIR, 1985) is a cassette-only release that offers a valuable glimpse of the original Lindsay lineup in action on three 1979 tracks, including one from the band's very first gig. The next two variations on the original lineup, with Dana Vicek and then Danny Rosen replacing Lindsay, are nearly as good.

solo outings:
Evan Lurie:
How I Spent My Vacation ♪♪♪♫ (Tzadik, 1998)

John Lurie:
Stranger than Paradise/The Resurrection of Albert Ayler ♪♪♪ (Enigma, 1986/Strange & Beautiful Music, 1998)
Down by Law/Variety ♪♪♪♪ (Intuition/Capitol, 1987/Strange & Beautiful Music, 1998)
Mystery Train ♪♪♪ (RCA, 1989)
Fishing with John ♪♪♪ (Strange & Beautiful Music, 1998)

influences:
◄◄ Thelonious Monk, Charles Mingus, Dollar Brand, Peter Apfelbaum's Heiroglyphics Ensemble

►► Ambitious Lovers, Jazz Passengers, Medeski, Martin & Wood, Squirrel Nut Zippers, Golden Palominos, Spanish Fly

Steve Holtje

Love
/Arthur Lee & Love
/Arthur Lee & Band Aid

Formed 1965, in Los Angeles, CA.

Arthur Lee (born Arthur Porter Taylor, March 7, 1945 in Memphis, TN), vocals, guitar, keyboards, harmonica, drums; Bryan MacLean, guitar, vocals (1965–68, 1977–78); Johnny Echols, guitar (1965–68); John

Fleckenstein, bass (1965); Ken Forssi, bass (1965–68); Don Conka, drums (1965, 1991); Alban "Snoopy" Pfisterer, drums, keyboards (1965–67); Michael Stuart, drums (1966–68); Tjay Cantrelli, horns, woodwinds (1966–67); Jay Donnellan (a.k.a. Jay Lewis), guitar (1968–70); Frank Fayad, bass, vocals (1968–73); George Suranovich, drums, vocals (1968–71, 1977–78); Drachen Theaker, drums (1969); Jim Hobson, keyboards (1969–71); Paul Martin, guitar (1969–71); Gary Rowles, guitar, vocals (1970–71); Noony Ricketts, guitar, vocals (1970–71); Charles Karp, guitar (1972–73); Craig Tarwater, guitar (1972–73); Clarence McDonald, keyboards (1972–73); Don Poncher, drums (1972–73); David "Dakota Dave" Hull, "extra bass" (1972–73); Melvan Whittington, guitar (1974–75, 1991); John Sterling, guitar (1974–75, 1977–78); Sherwood Akuna, bass (1974–75, 1987, 1991); Robert Rozelle, bass (1974–75); Joe Blocker, drums (1974–75, 1987); Herman McCormick, percussion (1974–75); Kim Kesterson, bass (1977–78); Shuggie Otis, guitar (1991).

The story of Love is the sad tale of a band with enormous talent and unlimited potential, all of which was squandered by a combination of misguided musical aloofness, bad business decisions, and just plain rotten luck. The same can also be said of its founding member, Arthur Lee. One of Los Angeles' great rock 'n' roll eccentrics (in a league with Neil Young, Frank Zappa, and Brian Wilson), Lee should easily have become one of the true musical icons of his generation; instead, today he is all but forgotten. The tales actually began in 1965 when Lee, after kicking around the periphery of the L.A. music scene with various second-class soul bands, met Beverly Hills golden boy Bryan MacLean, veteran of the burgeoning West Coast folk scene and then working as a roadie for his pal David Crosby's new band. When this affluent young brat hooked up with the self-confessed, R&B-obsessed bad boy from West L.A., the band they formed forged hitherto unimaginable bridges between the high-decibel fervor of the early Stones and the burgeoning jingle-jangle of MacLean's former employers the Byrds. Quickly becoming the top attraction on the Sunset Strip, Love launched Elektra Records' new rock division in 1966 with their eponymously titled debut album and were, everyone agreed, poised to emerge as one of the great musical forces of its time. Instead, Lee's egocentric insularity (which many say bordered on schizophrenia, or at least agoraphobia) stopped Love from touring as much as they should have in support of their landmark early releases, and when hard drugs entered the picture it only served to further isolate the band from not only their core followers, but their record company as well (who decided to concentrate on promoting their *other* L.A. signing, the Doors, instead). Holed up in a decaying horror movie castle high in the Hollywood Hills, Lee broke up this landmark edition of Love in 1968, but without the vital melodic influence of MacLean, his music soon declined into skewed heavy metal (although even at this questionable point in his career Lee could count amongst his most rabid followers the newly famous

Robert Plant and Jimmy Page). Lee spent the next two decades forming, then re-forming, various groups called Love (which have contained everyone from members of the Knack and Das Damen to veteran Lee disciples Baby Lemonade), but other than one brief reunion in the late 1970s, the classic Love lineup remains nothing more than a cherished memory—not to mention one of the most frustratingly tragic cases of "What if?" on record.

what to buy: The landmark *Forever Changes* 𝄞𝄞𝄞𝄞 (Elektra, 1967/1987, prod. Bruce Botnick, Arthur Lee) remains an absolute classic, easily transcending (as few other releases of its time do) the (no pun intended) Summer of Love to exert a continuing influence on countless bands, writers, arrangers, and producers the world over. An intrinsically seamless, nearly flawless work.

what to buy next: Like most bands' debuts, *Love* 𝄞𝄞𝄞 (Elektra, 1966/1988, prod. Jac Holzman, Mark Abramson, Arthur Lee) is a raw, passionate exercise in carefree music making, but this one contains enough flashes of brilliance scattered throughout to hint at wild rides to come. Said potential began to flower fully on *Da Capo* 𝄞𝄞𝄞 (Elektra, 1967/1988, prod. Paul A. Rothchild, Arthur Lee). The first six songs on this sophomore release remain just about the finest half-hour in rock history, though the 19-minute "Revelation" that follows is an abrupt about-taste.

what to avoid: Both *Out Here* 𝄞 (Blue Thumb, 1969/One Way, 1991, prod. Arthur Lee) and *False Start* 𝄞𝄞 (Blue Thumb, 1970/One Way, 1991, prod. Arthur Lee) are thoroughly excessive exercises in bottom-denominator boogie, the likes of which even guest guitarist Jimi Hendrix can't salvage.

the rest:
Four Sail 𝄞𝄞 (Elektra, 1969)
Vindicator 𝄞𝄞 (A&M, 1972/1997)
The Best of Love: Golden Archive Series 𝄞𝄞𝄞 (Rhino, 1980/1986)
Live/Studio 𝄞𝄞𝄞 (MCA, 1982/One Way, 1991)
Out There 𝄞𝄞𝄞 (Chiswick/Big Beat, 1988/1990)
Love Story, 1966–1972 𝄞𝄞𝄞𝄞 (Rhino/Elektra Traditions, 1995)
Comes in Colours 𝄞𝄞𝄞 (Raven, 1997)

worth searching for: The mysterious compilation *Black Beauty and Rarities* (Eva, 1997, prod. various) is sort of the *Arthur Lee Anthology*: Like its bigger-budgeted Beatles equivalent, this is an important collection of demos and unreleased gems, including nine pre-Love productions (such as a 1964 Rosa Lee Brooks track with Hendrix), the entire unreleased *Black Beauty* album from 1973, and some stray tracks from 1977 and 1994. *oncemoreagain* (Distortions, 1996) contains live recordings from one-off 1992 and 1994 London performances, with Lee accompanied on the former by none other than the High Llamas.

solo outings:

Bryan MacLean:

ifyoubelievein ♫♫♫ (Sundazed, 1997)

influences:

◀◀ Booker T. & the MG's, the Rolling Stones, Rising Sons, the Byrds, Billy Roberts

▶▶ The Seeds, the Doors, Jimi Hendrix, Moby Grape, Kaleidoscope, Three O'Clock, Lenny Kravitz

Gary Pig Gold

Darlene Love

Born Darlene Wright, July 26, 1938, in Los Angeles, CA.

When compiling any roster of the most distinctive and influential songstresses of the 1960s, Darlene Love's name undoubtedly ranks alongside those of Diana Ross and Aretha Franklin. However, because she seemed content to toil as a mere backup singer, or in the case of several Phil Spector hits, go totally uncredited for her work, Love's contributions have cruelly gone unrecognized and, to all but the keenest students of pop and R&B, largely unnoticed.

Along with sister Edna (later a member of the chart-topping Honey Cone) and friends Fanita James and Gracia Nitzsche, Love formed the Blossoms in 1957, and the group made several records for Capitol, Challenge, and OKeh before settling into a successful career as Los Angeles' back-up singers of choice. It was in this capacity that Phil Spector hired them in 1962 to record the classic "He's a Rebel," although he released this Number One hit under the name of his Philles Records act the Crystals, not the Blossoms. Sufficiently impressed by Love's voice, however, Spector released six singles by her over the next two years, but ironically none of these sold as well as the Crystals' follow-up "He's Sure the Boy I Love" and a version of the Disney standard "Zip-a-Dee-Doo-Dah" (released under the name Bob B. Soxx & the Blue Jeans), both of which again featured the uncredited lead vocals of Love. The Blossoms spent the remainder of the 1960s performing behind a myriad of acts both in the studio (Doris Day one moment; Jan & Dean the next), on television (the landmark *Shindig* series), and on stage (they were the vocal support behind Elvis Presley's Vegas comeback). Love then spent the ensuing decade vocalizing behind Nancy Sinatra, Dionne Warwick, and Cher, although she seldom stepped into the recording studio under her own name (one bizarre exception being a 1977 single reuniting her with the increasingly erratic Spector). Love pursued an acting career during the 1980s, but more often than not could be found earning $50 a day as a Los Angeles housemaid, embarrassed to show up for assignments driving her 1974 Mercedes sedan. Ellie Greenwich finally tracked Love down singing on a cruise ship and cast her to star in the Broadway musical *Leader of the Pack*, which led to Love's own long-running show at the Bottom Line in New York City, *Portrait of a Singer*. Not only was recognition finally hers, but a successful suit against Spector enabled her for the first time to collect the royalties she's long been due for her work on many of his most groundbreaking records. Love is currently completing her autobiography, with plans being made already to adapt it for the motion picture screen.

what to buy: Phil Spector may have given her the name "Love," but he often neglected to put it on the label. Proudly setting the records straight at last, *The Best of Darlene Love* ♫♫♫♫ (Abkco, 1992, prod. Phil Spector) collects 15 of her greatest Crystals, Bob B. Soxx and—oh yeah!—Darlene Love releases on one concise and illuminating disc. The hits are all here, of course, but so are the equally enjoyable misses ("Not Too Young to Get Married") and even that lone '77 release ("Lord, If You're a Woman") that demonstrates just how fully Spector's gifts had by then abandoned him. Not to worry though: Love still sounded absolutely fabulous on it.

what to buy next: Spector's infamous *A Christmas Gift for You* ♫♫♫♫ (Philles, 1963/Abkco, 1990, prod. Phil Spector) includes Love's blistering "Christmas (Baby, Please Come Home)," which is quickly becoming a Yuletide classic in its own right.

worth searching for: Friends both old (Paul Butterfield, sister Edna) and new (Tom Petty, Joan Jett) provide able if occasionally bombastic support on *Paint Another Picture* (Columbia, 1990, prod. various), but the true highlight of this overlooked gem is Love's soaring, practically *a capella* rendition of "You'll Never Walk Alone."

influences:

◀◀ Marian Anderson, Arlene Smith, the Raelettes

▶▶ Tina Turner, Bill Medley, Whitney Houston

see also: *The Crystals, Phil Spector*

Gary Pig Gold

Love & Rockets

Formed 1985, in Northampton, England.

Daniel Ash, guitar, vocals; David J (born David Haskins), bass, vocals; Kevin Haskins, drums.

Named after the Hernandez underground comic, this band reunites three of the four Bauhaus musicians. Daniel Ash and Kevin Haskins had spent some of the interim with Tones on Tail, while bassist David J recorded two albums with the Jazz Butcher in between solo projects. After Ash became dissatisfied with Campling and former Bauhaus frontman Peter Murphy backed out of a reunion, the three decided to form Love &

Rockets. With Murphy out of the picture, the trio went on to perform varied styles from folk-rock to upbeat dance pop ("So Alive" in 1989 was the group's lone smash) to low, booming drum-based songs to ambient trance music that was a far cry from their beginnings—a diversity that has made Love & Rockets always interesting and occasionally frustrating.

what to buy: *Seventh Dream of Teenage Heaven* 𝄢𝄢𝄢 (Beggars Banquet, 1985/1988, prod. John A. Rivers) is an odd, varied album, ranging from the booming drums in "Haunted When the Minutes Drag" to the light harmonies of "If There's a Heaven Above." *Earth Sun Moon* 𝄢𝄢𝄢 (Beggars Banquet/RCA, 1987, prod. Love & Rockets) is a collection of acoustic-driven songs with sweet melodies and introspective lyrics. On the solo front, two of J's albums—*Crocodile Tears and the Velvet Cosh* 𝄢𝄢𝄢𝄢 (Glass, 1985, prod. David J) and *On Glass* 𝄢𝄢𝄢 (Glass, 1986, prod. David J) show a knack for poetic and light melodies and hold up well next to the group's releases.

what to buy next: *Express* 𝄢𝄢𝄢 (Beggars Banquet/RCA, 1986, prod. John A. Rivers, Love & Rockets) is the band's most upbeat album, including a cover of the Temptations' hit "Ball of Confusion." *Sweet F.A.* 𝄢𝄢𝄢 (American, 1996, prod. Love & Rockets) is a return to the group's beginnings, with its brooding guitars and quiet vocals.

what to avoid: Although it yielded a Top 5 hit with "So Alive," the rest of the songs on *Love and Rockets* 𝄢𝄢 (Beggars Banquet/RCA, 1989, prod. John Fryer, Love & Rockets) are redundant and excessive.

the rest:
Hot Trip to Heaven 𝄢𝄢𝄢 (American, 1994)
Lift 𝄢𝄢𝄢 (Red Ant, 1998)

worth searching for: *The Glittering Darkness* (Beggars Banquet, 1996, prod. Love and Rockets, John Fryer) is an import that collects some previously unreleased tracks.

solo outings:
Daniel Ash:
Coming Down 𝄢𝄢𝄢 (Beggars Banquet, 1991)
Foolish Thing Desire 𝄢𝄢𝄢 (Beggars Banquet, 1992)

David J:
Etiquette of Violence 𝄢𝄢𝄢 (Situation Two, 1983)
V for Vendetta 𝄢𝄢𝄢 (Glass EP, 1984)
Blue Moods Turning Tail 𝄢𝄢𝄢 (Glass EP, 1985)
Songs from Another Season 𝄢𝄢𝄢𝄢 (Beggars Banquet/RCA, 1990)
Fingers in the Grease 𝄢𝄢𝄢 (RCA, 1990)
Candy on the Cross 𝄢𝄢𝄢 (MCA, 1992)
Urban Urbane 𝄢𝄢𝄢 (MCA, 1992)

influences:
◀◀ Bauhaus, Tones on Tail, the Jazz Butcher, New Order, the Smiths

▶▶ Ministry, Sisters of Mercy, Christian Death

see also: *Bauhaus, Tones on Tail*

J.D. Cantarella

G. Love & Special Sauce
Formed 1993, in Boston, MA.

G. Love (born Garrett Dutton, October 3, 1972), vocals, guitar, harmonica; Jeffrey Clemens, drums, backing vocals; Jimmy Prescott, bass (1993–96); King Kane, bass (1996–present).

A contemporary update of Jimmy Page, Keith Richards, Eric Clapton, and all the young British '60s musicians who scavenged old blues records, G. Love offers a surprisingly successful merger of hip-hop and traditional styles. But while Love's stylish sideburns help draw the teenage girls to his shows, he's no sarcastic hipster. In his fire-engine red silk suits and Elvis-like stage presence, Love sings of shooting hoops, hanging out on the street, and enjoying a refreshing drink while making a point of honoring his heroes, from Bob Dylan to Professor Longhair.

what to buy: The young singer-songwriter's style, especially on his debut, *G. Love & Special Sauce* 𝄢𝄢𝄢 (OKeh/Epic, 1994, prod. Stiff Johnson, Special Sauce), mimics the Beastie Boys' bratty rap. Yet, if anything, his music is too tradition-conscious; he titles his first single, "The Things That I Used to Do," closely after Guitar Slim classic "The Things I Used to Do." Still, the group does something that's traditionally avoided blues artists—get their songs on the radio, notably the back-porch rap "Cold Beverage."

what to buy next: The group's sophomore effort, *Coast to Coast Motel* 𝄢𝄢𝄢 (OKeh, 1995, prod. Jim Dickinson, G. Love & Special Sauce), serves up healthy portions of funk ("Sweet Sugar Mama"), New Orleans R&B groove ("Kiss and Tell" and "Bye Bye Baby"), and stripped-down acoustic sounds ("Coming Home").

the rest:
Yeah, It's That Easy 𝄢𝄢 (OKeh, 1997)

influences:
◀◀ Guitar Slim, Professor Longhair, Bob Dylan, Eric Clapton

Steve Knopper and Christina Fuoco

Love Delegation
See: The Fleshtones

Love Spit Love
See: Psychedelic Furs

Love Tractor

Formed 1980, in Athens, GA.

Michael Richmond, guitars, vocals; Mark Cline, guitar, banjo, keyboards, vocals; Armistead Wellford, bass, piano, clarinet, guitars, keyboards, vocals; Kit Swartz, drums, vocals (1980–83); Andrew Carter, drums, percussion (1983–89).

During the late '70s and early '80s, Athens, Georgia, was a veritable hothouse for new wave, post-punk bands. R.E.M., the B-52's, Pylon, and more all took root in the college town's fertile musical soil, and Love Tractor tilled the fields with the best of them. With entrancing percussion and a deft blend of guitar, banjo, and piano, Love Tractor managed to make its energy seem effortless and laid-back. Drawing on lounge, surf-guitar, folk, and rock influences, Love Tractor created a brand of pop that was unique yet instantly identifiable as a product of the New South. The band began its life as an all-instrumental group, and the combo's first, self-titled album, *Love Tractor*, established a multi-textured, propulsive sound that remained, in one form or another, throughout its career. On its second album, *Around the Bend*, the band introduced vocal harmonies, although these were usually not a focal point; instead, they were often unobtrusively blended into the mix. Subsequent albums continued in a similar vein, but unfortunately, Love Tractor's lyrical, intelligent, and eminently danceable music never really took root beyond the kudzu confines of the Georgia scene. The group disbanded in 1989, following the release of its last album, *Themes from Venus*. Armistead Wellford went on to play with Gutterball and Steve Wynn.

what to buy: The re-release of two of the band's better albums on one CD, *Love Tractor/'Til the Cows Come Home* ✍✍✍✍ (DB, 1982,1986/Ichiban, 1998, prod. Love Tractor), is a perfect way to trace the career of this band. The group's earlier, beat-heavy minimalism sparkles on tracks like "Wheel of Pleasure" and "Motorcade," penned by R.E.M.'s Bill Berry. The tracks from *Cows*, including a cover of Kraftwerk's "Neon Lights," offer a good idea of the direction the band was to take on its other releases.

what to buy next: *Around the Bend* ✍✍✍✍ (DB, 1983/Ichiban, 1997, prod. Love Tractor) puts a mellower spin on the band's sound. Several tracks feature the group's early forays into vocal territory, with mixed results. However, the standout track "Spin Your Partner" represents the band at its finest.

the rest:
Wheels of Pleasure ✍✍✍✍ (DB, 1985)
This Ain't No Outer Space Ship ✍✍✍ (Big Time, 1987)
Themes from Venus ✍✍✍✍ (DB, 1989/Ichiban, 1997)

worth searching for: Mike Richmond occasionally joined fellow Athenians Method Actors during breaks from Love Tractor. That band's live EP, *Live in a Room!* (Press, 1983) occasionally turns up in cutout bins. The 1988 video *Athens, GA: Inside/Out* chronicles that city's scene in the early '80s and includes footage of a Love Tractor performance.

influences:
◄◄ The Byrds, Bill Monroe, Raybeats, Duane Eddy, Pylon, dB's
►► Man or Astro-Man?, dumptruck, Game Theory

Lisa M. Moore

Lovemongers

See: Heart

Loverboy

Formed 1979, in Calgary, Alberta, Canada.

Mike Reno, vocals; Paul Dean, guitar; Doug Johnson, keyboards; Matt Frenette, drums; Scott Smith, bass.

Marketed as something of a hard rock glam band, Loverboy was really a slick, mainstream lite rock group, playing anonymous arena rock that's interchangeable with any number of other early '80s outfits. Its rounded-edges approach and constant touring garnered them platinum success and, presumably, enough bucks for a lifetime supply of Moosehead. Relying on party themes and driving, FM-ready singles, the band enjoyed a string of hits without having to change the formula or Mike Reno's headband. And people wonder why punk was necessary.

what to buy: *Loverboy Classics* ✍✍✍ (Columbia, 1994, prod. various) culls most of the more memorable hits into a fairly cohesive picture of the band's output.

what to buy next: The guitar-driven debut *Loverboy* ✍✍✍ (Columbia, 1980, prod. Bruce Fairbairn) contains the radio whopper, "The Kid Is Hot Tonight" and the churning "Turn Me Loose." The title of *Get Lucky* ✍✍✍ (Columbia, 1981, prod. Bruce Fairbairn) is a good explanation of the group's commercial success, although the overlooked "Take Me to the Top" got swept away with the less engaging "Waiting for the Weekend."

what to avoid: *Wildside* **woof!** (Columbia, 1987, prod. Bruce Fairbairn) shows what happens when Reno and Paul Dean can't come up with the hooks that camouflaged their other albums' shortcomings.

the rest:
Keep It Up ✍✍ (Columbia, 1983)
Lovin' Every Minute of It ✍✍ (Columbia, 1985)
VI **woof!** (CMC International, 1997)
Super Hits ✍ (Legacy, 1997)

solo outings:
Paul Dean:
Hardcore ✍✍ (Columbia, 1989)

influences:
◄◄ Boston, Foreigner, Styx
►► Warrant, Poison, Skid Row

Allan Orski

Lyle Lovett

Born November 1, 1957, in Houston, TX.

Originally a Houston folkie, Lyle Lovett went to Nashville during the mid-1980s, when alternative-leaning country acts like Steve Earle, k.d. lang, and Lovett could get a fair hearing. While he did have some country hits and won a country Grammy, Nashville never could figure out what exactly was so intriguing or funny about a guy who wore an "Eraserhead" hairdo instead of a Stetson and sang Tammy Wynette's "Stand by Your Man" with a straight face. It's their loss; Lovett's albums have surveyed jazz, Texas swing, folk, and country with equal aplomb. Stylistically, he is, to use his own words, "What Hank Williams is to Neil Armstrong." But Lovett's lyrical bent—witty, ironic, and sometimes unsettlingly direct—is his music's most memorable quality.

what to buy: *Pontiac* 𝄪𝄪𝄪𝄪 (MCA/Curb, 1987, prod. Tony Brown, Lyle Lovett) is quintessential Lovett. Few could turn the subject matter of a wedding that ends in double murder or a surreal seagoing horseback rider to their advantage, but that's what he accomplishes on "L.A. County" and "If I Had a Boat," respectively. "She's No Lady" and "She's Hot to Go" earned him charges of misogyny, but the songs are as self-deprecating as they are chauvinistic. *Lyle Lovett* 𝄪𝄪𝄪𝄪 (MCA/Curb, 1986, prod. Tony Brown, Lyle Lovett) is a spectacular debut featuring the utterly unsentimental "God Will" and Lovett's wry reportage of nuptials held at a funeral parlor, "An Acceptable Level of Ecstasy (The Wedding Song)." On *Joshua Judges Ruth* 𝄪𝄪𝄪𝄪 (MCA/Curb, 1992, prod. George Massenburg, Billy Williams, Lyle Lovett) the melancholy streak that has run through Lovett's music from the beginning nearly takes over on such songs as "North Dakota" and "She's Already Made up Her Mind," but injections of fiery gospel ("Church") and Lovett's arid wit ("Since the Last Time," which is narrated by a corpse) make the album one of his deepest and most diverse.

what to buy next: *The Road to Ensenada* 𝄪𝄪𝄪𝄪 (MCA/Curb, 1996, prod. Lyle Lovett, Billy Williams) is Lovett's most country-flavored album in a while, and while it contains plenty of upbeat humor ("That's Right (You're Not from Texas),") it's also his most somber album, perhaps reflecting obliquely on his split with ex-wife Julia Roberts. *Lyle Lovett & His Large Band* 𝄪𝄪𝄪𝄪 (MCA/Curb, 1989, prod. Tony Brown, Billy Williams, Lyle Lovett) spotlights his quirkiness with a string of non-sequiturs ("Here I Am") and plays the country numbers strictly for yuks ("I Married Her Just Because She Looks like You," "Stand by Your Man").

what to avoid: Lovett's weakest album, *I Love Everybody* 𝄪𝄪𝄪 (MCA/Curb, 1994, prod. Lyle Lovett, Billy Williams), is the musical proof of your high-school football coach's imprecation that "women weaken legs." Lovett's only recording made during his brief tenure as Mr. Julia Roberts has its moments of wry humor, but it mostly consists of stale leftovers and trifles like "La to the Left" and "Penguins," which are more strange than funny.

the rest:
Step Inside This House 𝄪𝄪𝄪𝄪 (MCA, 1998)

worth searching for: The Oscar-nominated hit "You've Got a Friend in Me" from the soundtrack to *Toy Story* (Disney, 1995, prod. various) is a rollicking duet with Randy Newman.

influences:
◄◄ Townes Van Zandt, Guy Clark, Ray Charles, Randy Newman, Al Green
►► Robert Earl Keen Jr., Walter Hyatt, Eric Taylor, Vince Bell

Daniel Durchholz

Lene Lovich

Born Lili-Marlene Premilovich, March 30, 1949 in Detroit, MI.

Lene Lovich is one of the true originals and enduring influences of the new-wave era, known for an Eastern European fashion sense and an operatic affectation that didn't cover up a keen sense of drama and a phenomenal vocal range. Her jittery and campy but audaciously sophisticated compositions would inspire a plethora of slick and gimmicky early '80s imitators. Still, she enjoyed more success than most visionaries do—partially by flavoring her space-age-bachelor-pad and Balkan sources with an affectionate pop literacy that made her style as recognizable as it was unpredictable. Carrying off the lofty pretensions of a Wagner with the endearing chutzpah of every underdog rocker from Chuck Berry to Courtney Love, Lovich achieved the iconic mixture of artistic authority and sly humor patented by David Bowie (who, in the records he made during her heyday, owed her as much of a stylistic debt as vice-versa). The best pop idols are symbols as well as artists, and Lovich provides all aspiring individualists with the role model of a unique personality who, while open to influences and capable of error, is unshakably herself.

what to buy: Most of Lovich's catalog is collected on two lavish and loving compilations from Rhino. *Stateless . . . Plus* ♫♫♫♫♯ (Stiff, 1978/Rhino, 1991, prod. various) includes her entire first album and a number of uncollected and unreleased tracks. Playing like the Top 40 from a parallel-universe of kitsch-pop history learned phonetically by an alien, it's a landmark of virtuosity and wit. *Flex . . . Plus* ♫♫♫♫ (Stiff, 1979/Rhino, 1991, prod. various) contains all of her second album and the *New Toy* EP, plus most of what Lovich wants you to hear from the record-company-meddled-with *No Man's Land* album. Her most ambitious collection, it extends her vocalese experiments and weird world-music recombinations to extreme but logical conclusions, and avoids the dated arrangements that occasionally crop up on *Stateless*.

what to buy next: As close to a commercial album as she'll ever make of her own free will, *March* ♫♫♫♫ (Evidence, 1989/1995, prod. Les Chappell, Lene Lovich) outlives the rest of late '80s quirk-pop for listenability. The tinny dance-rock production is the kind of thing an artist comes to regret, but the songwriting is superb.

worth searching for: PETA's first *Animal Liberation* album (Wax Trax, 1987, prod. various) contains two exclusive Lovich tracks: the great dance-rant "Supernature" and the mortifying rap duet with Nina Hagen, "Don't Kill the Animals."

influences:

◄◄ Lotte Lenya, Yma Sumac, David Bowie, Devo, Yoko Ono, Buffy Sainte-Marie

►► Cyndi Lauper, Mitchell Froom, Rasputina, David Bowie

Adam McGovern

The Lovin' Spoonful /John Sebastian

Formed 1965, in New York, NY. Disbanded 1968. Re-formed 1991.

John Sebastian, autoharp, guitar, harmonica, vocals (1965–68); Steve Boone, bass, vocals; Zal Yanovsky, guitar, vocals (1965–67); Joe But-ler, drums, vocals; Jerry Yester, guitar (1967–68, 1991–present); John Marrella, drums (1991–present); Lena Yester, keyboards, guitar (1991–present).

Dressed in colorful comic-book duds and singing good-timey folk, love songs, and plugged-in country blues in Greenwich Village coffee houses, the Lovin' Spoonful—named after a Mississippi John Hurt lyric—were the darlings of Greenwich Village and the country between 1965 and 1967. (The band's early days at the Night Owl Cafe are recounted in the Mamas & the Papas' "Creeque Alley.") The Spoonful's loosey-goosey, youthful innocence and engaging folk-rock caught on like a giant happy-day smile; its first seven singles went Top 10, including "Do You Believe in Magic," which used as its lead instrument John Sebastian's electrified Appalachian autoharp, and "Summer in the City," which helped define the summer of 1966 as it rose to Number One. The hits ended as quickly as they had begun, and Zal Yanovsky left the group in 1967, replaced by Jerry Yester. Sebastian, who sang and wrote most of the songs, left soon afterward. With Joe Butler as vocalist, the group managed another record, but the original spirit of the group had already dissipated. Sebastian, meanwhile, released some highly worthwhile solo albums—most recently *I Want My Roots*, a real jug-band album that reaches back to early Spoonful influences with blues legend James "Yank" Rachell as special guest.

what to buy: The Spoonful was a singles group, which means *Anthology* ♫♫♫♫ (Rhino, 1990, prod. Erik Jacobsen), which includes all the hits in chronological order and enough album sides to keep everyone but the most fanatical happy, is a must-have.

what to buy next: *Daydream* ♫♫♫♫ (Kama Sutra, 1966/One Way, 1992, prod. Erik Jacobsen) is one of the few original Spoonful albums in print in this country, with several original hits, their delightful take on blues ("Bald-Headed Lena"), and an alternate take of "Butchie's Tune." Sebastian's solo debut, *John B. Sebastian* ♫♫♫♫ (Reprise/MGM, 1970), is a logical extension of Spoonful ideas along with the hit, "She's a Lady," while *Tarzana Kid* ♫♫♫♫ (Reprise, 1974) is his best solo effort, with Lowell George helping on guitar.

what to avoid: Beyond John Stewart's "Never Goin' Back," there's nothing to recommend on the leftover *Revelation: Revolution '69* ♫ (Kama Sutra, 1968, prod. Bob Finiz).

the rest:
Best-Of ♫♫♯ (UNI, 1994)
Greatest Hits ♫♫♫ (Hollywood, 1996)

worth searching for: Be on the lookout for vinyl. Many of the masters for Spoonful recordings have long been destroyed, which makes more reissues unlikely. The only way to actually hear the group as it originally sounded is to find their records on vinyl, especially *Hums of the Lovin' Spoonful* (Kama Sutra, 1967, prod. Erik Jacobsen) and *Do You Believe in Magic* (Kama Sutra, 1966, prod. Erik Jacobsen).

solo outings:

John Sebastian:

Four of Us ♫♫♫♫ (Reprise, 1971)

Real Live John Sebastian ♫♫♫ (Reprise, 1972)

Welcome Back ♫♫♫ (Reprise, 1976)

The Best of John Sebastian ♫♫♫♫ (Rhino, 1989)

Tar Beach ♫♫♫ (Shanachie, 1993)

King Biscuit Flower Hour Presents ♫♫♫ (King Biscuit Flower Hour, 1996)

I Want My Roots ♫♫♫♫ (Musicmasters, 1996)

influences:

◀◀ Mississippi John Hurt, Fred Neil, the Weavers, Rev. Gary Davis, Yank Rachell

▶▶ Crosby, Stills & Nash, Poco, the Eagles

Leland Rucker

Nick Lowe

Born March 25, 1949, in Suffolk, England.

He produced groundbreaking albums for the Damned, Elvis Costello, and Graham Parker, but Nick Lowe has always been more into pranks than angst. His first American single, 1978's "So It Goes," blatantly ripped off its hook from Steely Dan's "Reeling in the Years"; he named a 1977 EP *Bowi* after David Bowie released *Low*; he put out two straightfaced paeans to the Bay City Rollers under the pseudonym Tartan Horde; and he minced no words criticizing banal pop music in his lyrics ("Do you remember Rick Astley?/He had a big fat hit/It was ghastly"). But ever since his pub-rock days in the band Brinsley Schwarz, Lowe has taken his rock 'n' roll roots very seriously, and his albums reveal a startling command of rockabilly, soul, Motown, bubblegum, country, and blues. A Top 20 hit with 1979's irresistible "Cruel to Be Kind" and a media blitz following an album and tour with longtime co-horts Dave Edmunds, Terry Williams, and Billy Bremner under the banner Rockpile looked to be his only commercial rewards for his efforts. Then it happened: In 1992 a Curtis Stigers cover of Lowe's "(What's So Funny 'Bout) Peace, Love and Understanding" was included on the multiplatinum soundtrack for *The Bodyguard,* netting the composer a seven-figure royalty check. Sometimes there is justice in the world.

what to buy: More send-up than put-down, *Pure Pop for Now People* ♫♫♫♫ (Columbia, 1978, prod. Nick Lowe) mocks everyone from David Bowie ("I Love the Sound of Breaking Glass") to the Jackson 5 ("Nutted by Reality"). It also showcases Lowe's perverse sense of humor by marrying innocuous '60s melodies to "Little Hitler" and "Marie Provost," about an actress whose corpse is devoured by her dog. More importantly, the Chuck

Berry-derived "Heart of the City" and "They Called It Rock" tear it up with a vengeance. Sex and twang are the driving forces behind the Rockpile-backed *Labour of Lust* ♫♫♫♫ (Columbia, 1979, prod. Nick Lowe), which features the saucy rockers "Skin Deep," "American Squirm," and Mickey Jupp's "Switchboard Susan." The introspective *The Impossible Bird* ♫♫♫♫ (Upstart, 1994, prod. Nick Lowe, Neil Brockbank) is a stark, country-flavored collection that finds Lowe confronting his personal demons and the emotional tug-of-war between love and loss. His own version of "The Beast in Me," the haunting centerpiece of Johnny Cash's *American Recordings*, is a revelation.

what to buy next: The 25-track *Basher: The Best of Nick Lowe* ♫♫♫♫ (Columbia, 1989, prod. Nick Lowe, Colin Fairley, others) gathers the essential early classics and the choice cuts from his uneven later albums, specifically "Ragin' Eyes," "Half a Boy and Half a Man," and "The Rose of England."

what to avoid: *Dig My Mood* ♫♫ (Upstart, 1998, prod. Nick Lowe, Neil Brockbank), Lowe's deadpan take on lounge music, is modeled after *The Impossible Bird*. But on that intimate landmark, he sounded torn and tortured; here, he merely sounds tired.

the rest:

Nick the Knife ♫♫♫ (Columbia, 1982)

The Abominable Showman ♫♫♫ (Columbia, 1983)

Nick Lowe & His Cowboy Outfit ♫♫♫ (Columbia, 1984)

16 All-Time Lowes ♫♫♫ (Demon, 1984)

The Rose of England ♫♫♫ (Columbia, 1985)

Nick's Knack ♫♫♫ (Demon, 1986)

Pinker and Prouder than Previous ♫♫ (Columbia, 1988)

Party of One ♫♫♫ (Upstart, 1990)

Live! On the Battlefield (Upstart EP, 1994) ♫♫♫

worth searching for: *The Wilderness Years* (Demon, 1991, prod. Nick Lowe) is an import that collects British B-sides and rarities such as "I Love My Label," a cover of Sandy Posey's "Born a Woman" (from the infamous *Bowi* EP), and "Truth Drug."

influences:

◀◀ Chuck Berry, the Everly Brothers, Johnny Cash, Carl Perkins

▶▶ Francis Dunnery, Don Dixon, Elvis Costello, John Hiatt

see also: *Dave Edmunds/Rockpile*

David Okamoto

L7

Formed 1985, in Los Angeles, CA.

Suzi Gardner, vocals, guitar; Jennifer Finch, vocals, bass (1985–96); Donita Sparks, vocals, guitar; Roy Koutsky, drums (1985–90); Dee Plakas, drums (1990–present).

Direct foremothers—along with Minneapolis peers Babes in

Toyland—of the "riot grrrl" movement, L7 plays lunkheaded, Black Sabbath–style heavy metal with frequently exaggerated social critiques, but almost no guitar solos. The group's best songs, "Shove" and "Pretend We're Dead," have wonderful headbanging hooks and blood-curdling shrieks that eventually begat Courtney Love. To draw attention to itself, L7 does extreme things on stage—Sparks pulled a tampon out of herself and tossed it into the crowd at 1992's Reading Festival in England, for instance. Though the band doesn't come from Seattle, it recorded for that city's influential Sup Pop Records and went along literally with the "grunge" concept, showcasing outfits of rags worthy of Nirvana or the Melvins.

what to buy: *Bricks Are Heavy* ♪♪♪♪ (Slash, 1992, prod. Butch Vig, L7) is either a brilliant punk-metal album that flaunts social convention (the opening track is called "Wargasm") or a sharp satire of Black Sabbath and its legacy of bass-heavy metal bands. Either way, it works. The EP *Smell the Magic* ♪♪♪ (Sub Pop, 1991, prod. Jack Endino), whose title is a euphemism for oral sex, leads off with the pounding kiss-off single "Shove."

what to buy next: *Hungry for Stink* ♪♪♪ (Slash/Reprise, 1994, prod. L7, G.G. Garth) lacks the straightforward punch of *Bricks Are Heavy*, but its highlights, including the single "Andres," rescue it from boredom. By the late '90s, when grunge had given way to shinier bands like Bush and Garbage, L7's beautiful ugliness wasn't quite as big on the radio. The title of *The Beauty Process: Triple Platinum* (Slash/Warner Bros., 1997, prod. Rob Cavallo, Joe Barresi, L7) humorously acknowledges this; if anything, the band's songwriting has grown even stronger though the music sounds exactly the same. "The Masses Are Asses" rails (possibly) at said Bush and Garbage fans, and "Moonshine," "Bitter Wine," and "Off the Wagon" suggest a subplot.

what to avoid: The debut, *L7* ♪♪ (Epitaph, 1987, prod. Brett Gurewitz, L7), is a scratchy, angry mess, with no coherent ideas, good melodies, or decipherable lyrics.

worth searching for: *The Grunge Years: A Sub Pop Compilation* (Sub Pop, 1991, prod. various) puts "Shove" in context, along with early singles by Nirvana, Screaming Trees, the Fluid, Afghan Whigs, and Babes in Toyland.

influences:

◀◀ Black Sabbath, Iggy Pop, the Sex Pistols, Holly & the Italians, X, Babes in Toyland, Nirvana, Motörhead

▶▶ Hole, Alanis Morissette, Bikini Kill, Bratmobile, Pearl Jam

Steve Knopper

Lulu

Born Marie McDonald McLaughlin Lawrie, 1949, in Lennox Castle, Scotland.

The raspy-voiced white lass from the suburbs of Glasgow got her stage name when an early manager, blown away by her 14-year-old pipes, exclaimed "That girl is one lulu of a singer!" And so it was as Lulu that she went on to crack the English charts from 1964 through the early '70s, with fine and rowdy R&B singles performed and produced in the spirit of Dusty Springfield and Aretha Franklin. The peak of Lulu's career came during 1967, when she soared to the top of the U.S. charts with the theme from *To Sir with Love*, a movie in which she also starred. By decade's end, her music had become passé, although an attempted comeback in 1973 resulted in covers of several David Bowie songs performed with and co-produced by Bowie himself.

what's available: *Something to Shout About* ♪♪♪ (Decca, 1965, prod. Micky Most) is a 20-song compilation of her earliest hits, including her raucous debut recording of the Isley Brother's rave-up "Shout," "I'll Come Running Over" (featuring Jimmy Page on guitar), and "Here Comes the Night," which would become a hit for Van Morrison's Them. For a broader retrospective, pick up *From Crayons to Perfume: The Best of Lulu* ♪♪♪♪ (Rhino, 1994, prod. various), which includes the hits, some B-sides, and the Bowie covers.

influences:

◀◀ Etta James, Dusty Springfield, Aretha Franklin

▶▶ Olivia Newton-John, Bonnie Tyler, LeAnn Rimes

Christopher Scapelliti

Luna

Formed 1991, in New York, NY.

Dean Wareham, guitar, vocals; Sean Eden, guitar (1993–present); Justin Harwood, bass; Stanley Demeski, drums (1991–96); Lee Wall, drums (1996–present).

Dean Wareham formed Luna after the break-up of his band Galaxie 500, which was a college radio favorite. To complete the band, Wareham enlisted former Feelies drummer Stanley Demeski and bassist Justin Harwood of the Chills. Luna plays a form of understated, enigmatic rock that goes beyond lo-fi, complementing Wareham's wry lyrics with a masterful weaving of guitars and the band's fluid ensemble playing. Comparisons to the Velvet Underground are unending, and Lou Reed invited to the group to open the VU's 1993 European reunion tour and his own 1996 solo tour.

what to buy: *Lunapark* ♪♪♪♪ (Elektra, 1992, prod. Fred Maher), the group's debut album, is comprised of the leisurely melodic tunes, soft-voiced vocals and ironic humor that give Luna its subtle edge. *Bewitched* ♪♪♪♪ (Elektra, 1994, prod. Victor Vugt, Luna) reaches an even greater level of understatement, with the late VU guitarist Sterling Morrison on two highlight tracks, "Friendly Advice" and "Great Jones Street."

what to buy next: *Pup Tent* ♫♫♫ (Elektra/Asylum, 1997, prod. Pat McCarthy) is a conscious effort on the part of the band to break free of the VU mold, a tag which the members of Luna grow increasingly annoyed of hearing. Throughout *Pup Tent*, Luna experiments with divergent sounds and instruments—keyboards, foreign-sounding percussion, trumpets, xylophones—to produce a more upbeat and boisterous sounding record.

the rest:
Penthouse ♫♫♫ (Elektra, 1995)
Luna ♫♫♫ (Number 6 EP, 1996)

influences:
◄◄ Velvet Underground, Television

see also: *Galaxie 500*

Kim Forster, Anna Glen, and William Harmer

Evan Lurie
See: The Lounge Lizards

John Lurie
See: The Lounge Lizards

Luscious Jackson
Formed 1992, in New York, NY.

Jill Cunniff, bass; Gabrielle Glaser, guitar; Vivian Trimble, keyboards; Kate Schellenbach, drums.

Named after a sports announcer's mispronunciation of NBA star Lucius Jackson's name, this group began with friends Jill Cunniff and Gabrielle Glaser; Vivian Trimble and Kate Schellenbach joined during the making of the debut EP. Schellenbach drummed in an early version of the Beastie Boys (as well as with Lunachicks and Wench), while Trimble has worked with dance companies on the NYC music scene. The group's style suggests an all-female take on the funky sound of the Beastie Boys' *Check Your Head*, and it's certainly had a number of career breaks—including opening for R.E.M. and Live as well as a second stage booking on Lollapalooza.

what to buy: *In Search of Manny* ♫♫♫♫ (Grand Royal/Capitol EP, 1992) is a seductively catchy 24-minute, seven-track EP that blends girl group pop, hip-hop rhythms, and smooth urban attitude into a unique stew.

what to buy next: *Natural Ingredient* ♫♫♫ (Grand Royal/Capitol, 1994, prod. Jill Cunniff, Gabrielle Glaser, Tony Mangurian) develops the EP's sound, perhaps too tightly since it's much less startling. *Fever in Fever Out* ♫♫♥ (Grand Royal/Capitol, 1996, prod. Daniel Lanois) is more of a rock album than the quartet's previous efforts, and much more sonically ambitious,

combining sounds in striking ways. Aside from the beats, which vary from mellow hip-hop to dub, much of the material (often keyed around cheezy Farfisa organ noodling) sounds like dreamy progressive rock (especially "Water Your Garden" with its flute sound, sinuous guitar, and oddly phased synthesizer) or really weird, drugged funk. It doesn't all work, but at least they're not standing still.

worth searching for: The otherwise electronica-oriented soundtrack to the Val Kilmer movie *The Saint* (Virgin, 1997, prod. various) includes "Roses Fade," apparently an outtake from *Fever in Fever Out* but more striking than anything on that album or on the rest of the soundtrack thanks to its flamenco-tinged rhythm and a bit more of a melodic shape. *Ain't Nothing but a She Thing* (FFRR/London, 1995, prod. various) finds Luscious Jackson covering French pop star Serge Gainesbourg's "69 Année Erotique."

influences:
◄◄ Beastie Boys, De La Soul
►► Cibo Matto, Poe, Litany

Steve Holtje

Lush
Formed 1988, in London, England. Disbanded 1998.

Miki Berenyi, guitar, vocals; Emma Anderson, guitar, vocals; Chris Acland (died 1996), drums; Philip King, bass (1992–98); Steve Rippon, bass (1988–92).

Weaving otherworldly harmonies with blurred guitar chords, Lush set a new course for sonic adventure in the British music scene. The group's impeccable string of early singles provided the missing link between the Cocteau Twins and the Beach Boys, between My Bloody Valentine and Phil Spector's '60s girl groups. Lush essentially put a face and some personality to England's blossoming dreampop genre—including a main stage spot on the 1992 Lollapalooza festival—before moving on to a harder-edged pop sound on its later albums. The band scored its biggest hits during 1996 with the aggressive "Single Girl" and "Ladykillers." It was a bittersweet success, however; drummer Chris Acland committed suicide shortly after the release of *Lovelife* in 1996, and the group mourned for nearly two years before officially calling it quits. Emma Anderson is working with a new band called Sing-Sing, Miki Berenyi is composing solo material, and Philip King is touring with the Jesus & Mary Chain.

what to buy: Lush's debut album, *Gala* ♫♫♫♫ (4AD/Reprise, 1990, prod. Tim Friese-Greene, Robin Guthrie, Lush, John Fryer), compiles two early EP's of astral, ambient pop. Among its stellar tracks are the unforgettable "De-luxe" and "Sweetness and

Light." The equally radiant *Spooky* &&& (4AD/Reprise, 1992, prod. Robin Guthrie) captured a worldwide audience, luring listeners with its layers of soothing guitars, cherubic voices, and catchy songs like "Fantasy" and "Untogether."

what to buy next: Even though Lush excelled in the dreampop genre, *Lovelife* &&& (4AD/Reprise, 1996, prod. Pete Bartlett, Lush) shows that the band was equally adept at crunchy new wave ("Ladykillers") and elegiac ballads ("Olympia").

what to avoid: *Split* & (4AD/Reprise, 1994, prod. Mike Hedges, Lush) found the band in a creative wilderness, struggling to balance its opulent melodies with a punkier edge that was emerging in its sound.

worth searching for: Worth seeking out are either of the original British EP's, *Scar* (Nesak, 1989) or *Mad Love* (Nesak, 1990), though *Gala* makes them of interest to collectors only.

influences:

◀◀ Cocteau Twins, Phil Spector, My Bloody Valentine

▶▶ Slowdive, Medicine, the Cranes

Aidin Vaziri

Luxuria
See: Magazine

Annabella Lwin
See: Bow Wow Wow

John Lydon
See: Public Image Ltd.

Frankie Lymon & the Teenagers
Formed 1955, in New York, NY. Disbanded 1956. Reunited 1965.

Frankie Lymon (born September 30, 1942, in New York, NY; died February 28, 1968), lead vocals; Joe Negroni, baritone; Herman Santiago, first tenor; Jimmy Merchant, second tenor.

Possessed of one of the sweetest voices in all of doo-wop, 13-year-old Frankie Lymon brought the Teenagers massive acclaim with the 1956 smash "Why Do Fools Fall in Love?" An enduring number that has not aged one whit, it showcased Lymon's wise-beyond-his-years delivery, thus spawning a number of kid groups and influencing legions of later superstars such as Michael Jackson, Smokey Robinson, Marvin Gaye, and Diana Ross. That was about all she wrote, as Lymon soon left for a disappointing solo career, hampered by the drug addiction that would kill him at age 26. Nasty legal battles among surviving band members over authorship of the hit and over his estate cast a greedy shadow over an already tragic tale.

what to buy: *The Best of Frankie Lymon & the Teenagers* &&&&& (Rhino, 1990, prod. George Goldner) offers classic New York doo-wop and has all the essential songs recorded by the child prodigy.

what to buy next: *At the London Palladium* &&& (Collectables, 1991, prod. George Goldner) captures a performance in front of an ecstatically excited crowd.

worth searching for: *Complete Recordings* (Bear Family, prod. various) is a five-disc import set for hard-core collectors.

influences:

◀◀ The Harlemaires, the Premiers, Bobby Day, Del Vikings

▶▶ Michael Jackson, Smokey Robinson, Marvin Gaye, Maze

Allan Orski

George Lynch/Lynch Mob
See: Dokken

Jeff Lynne
See: Electric Light Orchestra

Lynyrd Skynyrd
Formed 1965, in Jacksonville, FL.

Ronnie Van Zant (died October 20, 1977), vocals; Gary Rossington, guitar; Allen Collins (died January 23, 1990), guitar; Ed King (died 1997), guitar (1973–75, 1987–93); Billy Powell, keyboards; Leon Wilkeson, bass; Bob Burns, drums (1965–74); Artimus Pyle, drums (1974–91); Steve Gaines (died October 20, 1977), guitar (1976–77); Johnnie Van Zant, vocals (1987–present); Randall Hall, guitar (1991–93); Custer, drums (1991–97); Hughie Thomasson, guitar (1996–present); Rickey Medlocke, guitar (1996–present).

Lynyrd Skynyrd was the most commercially successful, critically acclaimed, and hardest rocking of the Allman Brothers–influenced Southern Rock bands to emerge during the early '70s. With fierce regional pride, the Florida natives always evinced tremendous creativity and originality, mixing Allman-esque guitar harmonies with crunchy Stones-y rhythms and overdriven, Cream-style distortion. At the heart of the band's sound was a three-guitar juggernaut of Gary Rossington, Ed King, and Allen Collins, and the forceful presence of vocalist Ronnie Van Zant, who successfully combined a country voice with heavy metal swagger. While some of their Southern Rock peers went over the edge into boogie excess, Skynyrd never did—in large part because, in addition to being a ferocious live band, they wrote great songs, including "Sweet Home Alabama," "Free Bird," "Gimme Three Steps," and "What's Your

Name." After a short dry spell, the band was reenergized by the 1976 addition of the phenomenally talented guitarist Steve Gaines, who infused the band with new energy, leading to their finest album, *Street Survivors*. But before Lynyrd Skynyrd could reap the fruits of their second coming, their charter plane crashed into a Mississippi swamp, killing Van Zant and Gaines and seriously injuring the other members. The group re-formed during the late '80s, with Van Zant's brother Johnnie taking over as a vocalist.

what to buy: It doesn't get much better than *Street Survivors* ♫♫♫♫♫ (MCA, 1977, prod. Lynyrd Skynyrd, Jimmy Johnson, Tim Smith), a molten slab of fiery three-guitar Southern rock, with just the right amount of country and a fantastic collection of songs, including "You Got That Right," "That Smell," and "What's Your Name." *One More from the Road* ♫♫♫♫ (MCA, 1977, prod. Tom Dowd) is an awesome live document and includes the famous "What song is it you want to hear?" "Freeeebird!" dialogue. *Pronounced Leh-Nerd Skin-Nerd* ♫♫♫♫ (MCA, 1973, prod. Al Kooper) introduced the band with a bang, though it is occasionally weighed down by Al Kooper's overproduction. The three-CD *Lynyrd Skynyrd* ♫♫♫♫♫ (MCA, 1991, prod. various) is everything a box set should be; it's not overstuffed and it features all the essential tracks as well as a host of previously unreleased material, most of which is actually *good*, including the demo of "Free Bird."

what to buy next: Both *Second Helping* ♫♫♫♫ (MCA, 1974, prod. Al Kooper) and *Nuthin Fancy* ♫♫♫♫ (MCA, 1975, prod. Al Kooper) continue down the same path as the band's debut. The former includes "Sweet Home Alabama," "Don't Ask Me No Questions," "Call Me the Breeze," and "The Needle and the Spoon," classics all, and the latter includes "Saturday Night Special," and the surprisingly introspective "Am I Losin.'" *Gold & Platinum* ♫♫♫♫ (MCA, 1979, prod. various) is a thorough two-disc greatest hits collection with an annoying lack of notes or credits.

what to avoid: The band was sounding a little strained and creatively dry by *Gimme Back My Bullets* ♫♫♫ (MCA, 1976, prod. Tom Dowd), its fourth album in four years. *Lynyrd Skynyrd 1991* ♫♫ (Atlantic, 1991, prod. Tom Dowd) was an outright embarrassment.

the rest:
Skynyrd's First and . . . Last ♫♫♫♫ (MCA, 1978)
Gold & Platinum ♫♫♫♫ (MCA, 1980)
Best of the Rest ♫♫♫ (MCA, 1986)
Legend ♫♫♫ (MCA, 1987)
Southern by the Grace of God ♫♫♫ (MCA, 1988)
Skynyrd's Innyrds ♫♫♫ (MCA, 1989)
The Last Rebel ♫♫♫♫ (Atlantic, 1992)
Endangered Species ♫♫♫ (Capricorn, 1994)
Freebird: The Movie ♫♫♫♫ (MCA, 1996)

What's Your Name ♫♫♫ (MCA, 1997)
Twenty ♫♫♫ (CMC International, 1997)
Live from Steel Town ♫♫♫ (CMC International, 1998)
Essential ♫♫♫♫ (MCA, 1998)

worth searching for: *The King Biscuit Flower Hour Presents Lynyrd Skynyrd* (KBFH, 1995) was mistakenly released and quickly re-called, making this 1975 concert broadcast a collector's item.

solo outings:
Rossington Collins Band:
Anytime, Anyplace, Anywhere ♫♫♫ (MCA, 1980)

Johnny Van Zant:
Brickyard Road ♫♫♫♫ (Atlantic, 1990)
Collection ♫♫♫ (PolyGram, 1997)
King Biscuit Flower Hour Presents in Concert ♫♫♫ (KBFH, 1997)
Van Zant ♫♫♫ (Unidisc, 1997)
(With Donnie Van Zant) *Brother to Brother* ♫♫♫ (CMC International, 1998)

influences:

◄◄ The Allman Brothers, Cream, Led Zeppelin, the Rolling Stones, the Yardbirds

►► Molly Hatchet, Metallica, the Black Crowes, .38 Special, Todd Snider

Alan Paul

The Lyres
Formed 1983, in Boston, MA.

Jeff Conolly, vocals, keyboards; Rick Coraccio, bass (1983–88, 1993–94); Paul Murphy, drums (1983–86, 1993–94); Danny McCormack, guitar (1983–86); John Bernardo, drums (1986); Matt Miklos, bass (1988); John Smith, drums (1988); Richard Carmal Jr., guitar; Jack Hickey, guitar, harmonica (1988–94); others.

The keepers of the garage-rock flame in Boston, the Lyres formed as a vehicle for organist/singer Jeff Conolly (formerly of DMZ) to pursue his quest for the perfect mix of straight-ahead rock and gritty R&B. He has kept his pursuit up well into the '90s, putting out occasional, and often recycled, releases to a cult audience.

what to buy: *Some Lyres* ♫♫♫ (Taang!, 1994, prod. Jeff Conolly, Richard W. Harte) is a career retrospective, imaginatively packaged as a satire of the Rolling Stones' *Some Girls*. It contains two live cuts, including "She Pays the Rent," one of Conolly's most accessible '60s rewrites. Stiv Bators joins the group for "Here's a Heart."

what to buy next: *On Fyre* ♫♫♫ (Ace of Hearts, 1984, prod. Richard W. Harte) brought the Lyres as close to national prominence as they'd ever come when heavy local airplay of "Don't Give It up Now" prompted a positive review in *Rolling Stone*. The album is a minor classic for garage-rock aficionados.

what to avoid: *A Promise Is a Promise + 9 Bonus/Live Europe* 𝄞𝄞 (Ace of Hearts, 1988, prod. Richard W. Harte) is burdened by its lo-fi live tracks.

the rest:
AHS 1005 𝄞𝄞𝄞 (Ace of Hearts, 1983/Matador, 1998)
Nobody but Lyres 𝄞𝄞 (Taang!, 1992)
Happy Now 𝄞𝄞 (Taang!, 1993)
Those Lyres 𝄞𝄞 (Norton, 1995)
The Early Years—1979–1983: Live at Cantones and WERS-FM 𝄞𝄞𝄞
    (Crypt, 1997)

worth searching for: The Ace of Hearts cassette version of *On Fyre* includes eight bonus tracks. So does the French CD on the New Rose label. It also contains "She Pays the Rent."

influences:
◀◀ The Kinks, the Standells, Shadows of Knight, ? & the Myste-rians

▶▶ Del Fuegos

Brian Mansfield

Kirsty MacColl

Born October 10, 1959, in London, England.

The daughter of British folkie Ewan MacColl (writer of "The First Time Ever I Saw Your Face") has had a long string of hit singles in England, but in the United States she has never gone beyond a cult following, despite her distinctive voice. A songwriter with a knack for organic melodies and clever turns of phrase, she may have handicapped herself commercially by being adept at so many styles, from country and rockabilly to alternative rock, dance-pop, and even the suave Latin arrangement of "My Affair." She also has a good ear for other people's material and has done wonderful covers of the Smiths' "You Just Haven't Earned It Yet Baby," the Kinks' "Days," Billy Bragg's "A New England," Lou Reed's "Perfect Day" (a duet with Lemonheads' Evan Dando), and Cole Porter's "Miss Otis Regrets" (with the Pogues, originally on the *Red, Hot & Blue* AIDS benefit album). After appearing in 1979 on Stiff with her first single, "They Don't Know" (later a hit for Tracey Ullman), she made *Desperate Character* for Polydor (never released in the United States) in 1981 but had the follow-up rejected. MacColl was hardly un-heard from, however, since her vocal talents were in demand

and she did sessions with the Rolling Stones and Van Morrison, among many others. Her 1984 marriage to Steve Lillywhite, a producer noted for the shimmering guitar sounds heard on al-bums by U2 and others, eventually led to him producing her 1989 and 1991 comeback albums. (The couple later split up.) During the time between her Polydor and Charisma albums, MacColl apparently become more politicized (dare we specu-late that Bragg may have had something to do with that?), and several Charisma tracks tackle reactionary British Prime Minis-ter Margaret Thatcher, poverty, and the like, though MacColl's focus remains interpersonal relationships.

what's available: The 18-track best-of *Galore* 𝄞𝄞𝄞𝄞 (I.R.S., 1995, prod. various) is the only MacColl album available in the United States. Not only is it thus the only source for material from her better albums, it also has excellent non-album tracks and a sampling of *Desperate Character* as well as two then-new tracks, including the Dando duet. Highlights include "They Don't Know," "A New England," the rockabilly relation-ship putdown "There's a Guy Works down the Chip Shop Swears He's Elvis," and the Pogues collaboration "Fairytale of New York." The only other MacColl album currently in print is a British import, *What Do Pretty Girls Do?* 𝄞𝄞𝄞 (Hux, 1998, prod. Peter Watts, Chris Whatmough), which collects all 15 tracks of her four 1989–95 BBC sessions. Many of her hits are here, con-siderably stripped down in this live-in-the-studio context.

worth searching for: The best of the out-of-print albums, *Ti-tanic Days* (I.R.S., 1993, prod. various) is janglier and sunnier than the Lillywhite productions, with a bittersweet tone typi-fied by "Soho Square." The Lillywhite-produced "Angel" boasts a mutant dub/hip-hop beat supporting MacColl's ethereal vo-cals. That was as close as the album came to a hit, but every track is strong, with many pretty string arrangements suggest-ing MacColl's calling is as a sophisticated chanteuse. Other-wise unavailable, MacColl's "As Long as You Hold Me" is on the soundtrack to *Mad Love* (Zoo, 1995, prod. various).

influences:
◀◀ Patsy Cline, the Pretenders, Rockpile, the Smiths, Billy Bragg, Elvis Costello

▶▶ Billy Bragg, Tracey Ullman, Shirley Manson

Steve Holtje

Pat MacDonald

See: Timbuk 3

Shane MacGowan & the Popes

See: The Pogues

Ashley MacIsaac

Born February 24, 1975, in Creignish, Cape Breton, Nova Scotia, Canada.

Young Ashley MacIsaac's success in the music industry shouldn't come as much of a surprise. The teenage fiddle phenomenon has been exposed to music all his life; his father, a fiddle player, would play around the house, and MacIsaac himself got a rather early start, learning to stepdance at age five and beginning formal fiddle instruction at the age of nine. A fast learner—and then some—he began touring Canada as well as U.S. cities such as Detroit and Boston by the time he was 13 and has filled venues ranging from local Cape Breton sites to New York's Carnegie Hall. The term "prodigy" come to mind? MacIsaac has won numerous awards, including Best Live Act at the 1995 East Coast Music Awards and Best New Solo Artist and Best Roots and Traditional Album/Solo at the 1996 Juno Awards. He was the subject of a major label feeding frenzy while still in his teens. A&M won out.

what to buy: MacIsaac's major-label debut, *How Are You Today?* 🎵🎵🎵 (A&M, 1995, prod. Michael Phillip Wojewoda, Pete Prilesnik), reflects both his Celtic/Canadian heritage and his youthful exhuberance in its driving, aggressive instrumentation. A perfect, if unlikely combination of ancient Celtic folk songs with punk-rock arrangements and attitude.

the rest:
Fine Thank You Very Much 🎵🎵🎵 (Unisphere, 1998)

worth searching for: MacIsaac's Canadian releases, *Close to the Floor* (Unisphere, 1992) and *A Cape Breton Christmas* (1993) are available as imports.

influences:
◀◀ The Chieftains, the Clash, Charlie Daniels
▶▶ Leahy

Christopher Scanlon

Bryan MacLean

See: Love

Tara MacLean

Born October 25, 1973, in Charlottetown, Prince Edward Island, Canada.

One of the seemingly infinite number of pretty voices (and faces) consigned to pop during the mid- to late '90s, Tara MacLean's particular brand combines throaty vocals with swatches of ethereal guitar and a plodding, unobtrusive rhythm. To her credit, when taken out of the studio and placed onstage with only her voice, her acoustic guitar, and electric guitarist/husband Bill Bell, MacLean is positively captivating.

WHAT ALBUM CHANGED YOUR LIFE?

I'd have to say Rickie Lee Jones was pretty huge to me, her first record, just how young she was and how brilliant she is. You can always use the excuse that you're not trying hard or doing as well as you can or being as good a writer or musician 'cause you're young and there's so much time to learn. Then you turn around and see someone like her, whose first record is so brilliant and so connected.

Tara MacLean

what to buy: *Silence* 🎵🎵 (Nettwerk, 1997, prod. Norm Kerner) tempers MacLean's strong vocals with studio shellac and overdubs that reek of label-inspired attempts to copy the recorded work of Jewel and Sarah McLachlan. On the upside, minimal instrumentation on the haunting "Silence," a song about loss of life, makes room for Tara's voice. Bruce Kaphan's (American Music Club) pedal steel on "Let Her Feel the Rain" also pokes through the polish, but the brightest spot on the album is an acoustic version of the same song tacked onto the end; take two strikes a much better balance between music and vocals, offering a glimpse of MacLean's actual capabilities.

what to avoid: The EP *If You See Me* 🎵 (Nettwerk, 1997, prod. Norm Kerner, Bill Bell) consists of two previously unreleased tracks, two remixes, and a live version of "Evidence" from the 1997 Lilith Fair—the disc's only redeeming point. MacLean herself apologizes for its lack of substance in the liner notes, writing "I promise I'll have new material soon."

influences:
◀◀ Loreena McKennitt, Sarah McLachlan

Isaac Josephson

Jeep MacNichol

See: The Samples

Madder Rose

Formed 1991, in New York, NY.

Billy Cote, guitar, bass; Johnny Kick, drums, vocals; Mary Lorson, vocals, guitar; Matt Verta-Ray, bass, guitar, vocals.

A guitar band with a girl out front, Madder Rose released its first LP the same year Liz Phair captured the hearts, minds, and libidos of America with her *Exile in Guyville*. Regrettably, Madder Rose's *Bring It Down* was lost in Phair's wake. At it's best, Madder Rose's sound falls somewhere in between the Chicago indie-queen's smart and alluring mid-fi melodies and the aggro-guitar sensibilities of '80s alt-rock—most notably, Hüsker Dü and the Pixies. Madder Rose formed when Billy Cote, a post-punk songwriter in search of a singer, auditioned Mary Lorson in his Manhattan apartment. For what Cote had in mind, Lorson fit the bill: solid pitch, but untrained, staccato and a little too angry to be cute. As she gained confidence and tenure, Lorson's voice matured down an octave, growing more robust and warm.

what to buy: Where Madder Rose's first release boasted more excited punk sensibilities, and its later work took on a more subdued and produced feel, *Panic On* ♫♫♫ (Atlantic, 1994, prod. Madder Rose, Mark Freegard) struck a balance between the two. Without dropping its guitar-based melodic structure, Cote & Co. upped its production standards a notch, tacked on some tremelo and added a layer of polish. The agressive and distorted sound on tracks such as "Sleep Forever" and "Black Eye Town" help keep a foot in the past, while "Almost Lost My Mind" and "Mad Dog" come off as terrific jangle pop singles.

what to buy next: *Bring It Down* ♫♫♫ (Seed, 1993, prod. Kevin Salem) is simple, innocent, bare-bones pop. Cote and Lorson's songs sway from melodious and driving ("Lay Down Low," "Beautiful John") to slow and brooding ("Bring It Down") to hook-laden and hypnotic ("Swim"), all flowing together through slick transitions. The only thing that holds this album back is that the band seems to run out of steam on the last four tracks.

what to avoid: *Love You Save* **woof!** (Seed EP, 1995, prod. Billy Cote, Adam Lasus) is an overproduced, lite-rock EP released between albums. The time would have been better spent on vacation.

the rest:
Tragic Magic ♫♫♫ (Atlantic, 1997)

influences:
◀◀ The Go-Go's, Hüsker Dü, the Pixies
▶▶ Veruca Salt, Pee Shy

Isaac Josephson

Madness

Formed 1978, in London, England. Disbanded 1986.

Lee Thompson, saxophone; Chris Foreman, guitar; Mike Barson, keyboards; Dan Woodgate, drums; Mark Bedford, bass; Graham "Suggs" McPherson, vocals; Chas Smash (born Cathal Smythe), emcee, trumpet; others.

Maybe it's the fashions, or maybe the music itself, but there are some trends that Americans just seem destined not to get. So was the ska revival that swept England in the late '70s and early '80s. Purists by no means, Madness crossed all sorts of musical boundaries, from ska and gritty R&B to contemporary pop and near-novelty music for a mix that was anarchic and endlessly entertaining. All of Europe thought so, anyway, making Madness the toast of the Continent for a while, and rightfully so, considering how throughly the group broke down barriers of race, age, and attitude among audience members. Alas, the band's U.S. fortunes were much more modest. Here it's remembered as a new wave one-hit wonder for its pleasant pop song "Our House." The group disbanded in 1986, though some members later tried a comeback as *the* Madness, but by then the group had run its course. Now, a decade later, with another ska revival in full swing, Madness is finally being appreciated for the groundbreaking act it was.

what to buy: *Total Madness: The Very Best of Madness* ♫♫♫ (Geffen, 1997, prod. various) offers a good introduction to the band, with "Our House," "One Step Beyond," and "Michael Caine," but it suffers for lack of the band's early Stiff singles. The compilation *Madness* ♫♫♫ (Geffen, 1983/1993, prod. various) fills in a little more of the story, but there are still some essential tracks missing, and both sets could be longer.

the rest:
Keep Moving ♫♫♫ (Geffen, 1984, 1997)
Mad Not Mad ♫♫ (Geffen, 1985, 1997)

worth searching for: Currently unavailable, the group's first two albums, *One Step Beyond* (Stiff, 1979/Sire, 1980) and *Absolutely* (Stiff/Sire 1980) set a very high entertainment quotient for the band to maintain.

influences:
◀◀ Prince Buster, the Skatalites
▶▶ No Doubt, Save Ferris, Hepcat, Barenaked Ladies

see also: *Voice of the Beehive*

Daniel Durchholz

Madonna

Born Madonna Louise Veronica Ciccone, August 16, 1958, in Bay City, MI.

Madonna's career began as that of any other cute blonde

Madonna (© Ken Settle)

singer making electronic dance music in the '80s. But once she began to wield her amazing talent in earnest—a talent for business and marketing as well as for music—she wound up, alongside Michael Jackson, as one of the biggest pop stars since Elvis Presley. Her early hits were innocent throwaways ("Everybody," "Holiday"), promoted by titillating videos of a scantily clad Madonna dancing hither and yon and rolling around on the floor. She even parlayed her videocentricity into a co-starring role in the hit film *Desperately Seeking Susan*. But once she lured the masses, Madonna began spewing messages. With every record she changed costumes and, like David Bowie in the early '70s, personas. MTV followed her every move, whether she was challenging moral conventions in "Papa Don't Preach," sexual mores in "Like a Virgin," or religious sensibilities with "Like a Prayer." (She gained a quick foothold in the tabloids, too, by marrying and quickly divorcing hot-tempered actor Sean Penn, then having affairs with—depending who you believe—actor/auteur Warren Beatty, and basketball players Charles Barkley and Dennis Rodman.) Her videos, at the time, were consistently more outrageous than her songs, which remained impeccably crafted and well-sung

dance music. As she grew older, Madonna turned into a self-contained entertainment industry, producing the tour documentary *Truth or Dare* and the photo book *Sex*, which shocked millions—though maybe more than anything because it showed her trysting with hip-hop flyweight Vanilla Ice. She started her own label, Maverick, which scored hits with Candlebox and Alanis Morissette. Unlike her contemporaries, Prince and Michael Jackson, Madonna has always managed to stay ahead of the pop curve, embracing gay and club cultures so as to be a leader in bringing them to the mainstream. In 1996 she starred in the film version of *Evita*. Then she decided to have a baby, Lourdes, and entered the matriarchal phase of her career. She shifted to a more sober look, shedding the sexpot image entirely and recording a mature album, the electronica-influenced *Ray of Light*.

what to buy: *The Immaculate Collection* 🐾🐾🐾🐾 (Sire, 1990, prod. various) saves you the trouble of compiling all of Madonna's singles from her sometimes inconsistent albums. *Like a Virgin* 🐾🐾🐾 (Sire, 1984, prod. Nile Rodgers), *True Blue* 🐾🐾🐾 (Sire, 1986, prod. Madonna, Patrick Leonard, Stephen

Bray), and *Like a Prayer* (Sire, 1989, prod. Madonna, Patrick Leonard, Stephen Bray, Prince) are the best of her studio albums, though in retrospect, the electronic touches don't sound as good as they did during the '80s.

what to buy next: *Erotica* 🎵🎵🎵 (Maverick, 1992, prod. Madonna, Shep Pettibone) is Madonna's foray into the world of hypnotic ambient-techno music, and as an added bonus features her sucking on somebody's toe on the back cover. A collection of Madonna's ballads, *Something to Remember* 🎵🎵🎵 (Maverick/Sire, 1995, prod. various) includes two new songs and two versions of her trancey take on "I Want You," originally recorded for the Marvin Gaye tribute album *Inner City Blues*.

what to avoid: As if the movie wasn't painful enough, *Who's That Girl* 🎵 (Sire, 1987, prod. various) is an embarrassment for such an ambitious artist.

the rest:
Madonna 🎵🎵 (Sire, 1983)
You Can Dance 🎵🎵 (Sire, 1987)
I'm Breathless 🎵🎵 (Sire, 1990)
Bedtime Stories 🎵🎵🎵 (Maverick, 1994)
Ray of Light 🎵🎵🎵 (Maverick, 1998)

worth searching for: Sonic Youth's bizarre and hilarious send-up of (mostly) Madonna tunes, *The Whitey Album* (Blast First, 1989, prod. Ciccone Youth) is credited to Ciccone Youth, a sly reference to Madonna's surname.

influences:

◀◀ Donna Summer, the Crystals, Tina Turner, Cyndi Lauper, Blondie, Aretha Franklin, Billie Holiday, Elvis Presley, Michael Jackson, Marilyn Monroe

▶▶ Terence Trent D'Arby, Whitney Houston, TLC, En Vogue, Celine Dion, Alanis Morissette, Mariah Carey

Tracey Birkenhauer and Steve Knopper

Magazine

Formed 1977, in Manchester, England. Disbanded 1981.

Howard Devoto, vocals; John McGeoch, guitar (1977–79); Barry Adamson, bass; Dave Formula, keyboards; Martin Jackson, drums (1977–78); John Doyle, drums (1978–81); Robin Simon, guitar (1979–80); Ben Mandelson, guitar (1980).

Magazine's arty, cerebral post-punk earned a cult following thanks in large part to singer-lyricist Howard Devoto's prodigious wit and the gifted band's utter refusal to honor musical boundaries. A founding member of punk/new-wave innovators the Buzzcocks, Devoto cowrote several songs with that band's leader Pete Shelley; one of these, "Shot by Both Sides," became an early Magazine favorite. Balancing punk's manic energy and questioning attitude with frosty keyboard textures and funky grooves, Magazine quickly set itself apart from the pack. By the release of its third LP, *The Correct Use of Soap*, the band had moved in a poppier direction; though a bit of airplay widened its audience, Magazine dissolved in 1981. Guitarist John McGeoch, who departed for greater fame with Siouxie & the Banshees in 1980, also played with Dave Formula and Barry Adamson in the successful synth-pop band Visage. Devoto released a solo album and subsequently formed a new band, Luxuria, with guitarist Noko; this effort, though periodically impressive, lacked the powerful gestalt of Magazine. Adamson played with Nick Cave & the Bad Seeds and released a string of eclectic solo albums. In the ensuing years, Magazine's influence on a number of younger artists has become even more apparent.

what to buy: The Magazine retrospective *Rays & Hail, 1978–81* 🎵🎵🎵🎵 (Virgin, 1987, prod. various) collects the band's essential tracks. It's the obvious selection for novices.

what to buy next: Fans of the earlier, harder material will gravitate toward Magazine's debut, *Real Life* 🎵🎵🎵 (Virgin, 1978, prod. John Leckie), while those who enjoy the more melodic songs will likely prefer *The Correct Use of Soap* 🎵🎵🎵 (Virgin, 1980, prod. Martin Hannett).

what to avoid: Devoto's solo album *Jerky Versions of the Dream* 🎵🎵 (I.R.S., 1983, prod. Howard Devoto, Greg Walsh) shows flashes of wit but suffers in large part from musical anemia.

the rest:
Secondhand Daylight 🎵🎵🎵 (Virgin, 1979)
Play 🎵🎵🎵 (I.R.S., 1981)
Magic, Murder, and the Weather 🎵🎵🎵 (I.R.S., 1982)
After the Fact 🎵🎵🎵 (I.R.S., 1982)
Scree (Rarities, 1978–81) 🎵🎵🎵 (Blue Plate, 1991)

worth searching for: Fans will want to scope out a furious live version of *The Correct Use of Soap's* "Model Worker" on the film soundtrack *Urgh! A Music War* (I.R.S., 1981, prod. various).

solo outings:
Luxuria (Devoto):
Unanswerable Lust 🎵🎵🎵 (I.R.S., 1985)
Beast Box 🎵🎵 (I.R.S., 1987)

Visage (McGeoch and Adamson):
Visage 🎵🎵🎵 (Polydor, 1980/One Way, 1997)
The Anvil 🎵🎵 (Polydor, 1982/One Way, 1997)
Fade to Grey—The Singles Collection 🎵🎵🎵 (Polydor, 1983)
Beat Boy 🎵🎵 (Polydor, 1984)

Barry Adamson:
Moss Side Story 🎵🎵🎵 (Mute, 1989)
Delusion (Soundtrack) 🎵🎵🎵 (Mute, 1991)
Soul Murder 🎵🎵🎵 (Mute, 1992)
The Negro inside Me 🎵🎵🎵 (Mute, 1993)

Oedipus Schmoedipus 𝄢𝄢𝄢𝄢⁷ (Mute, 1996)
As above, So Below N/A (Mute, 1998)

influences:

◄◄ Sex Pistols, Buzzcocks, Captain Beefheart, Sly & the Family Stone, Franz Kafka, Fyodor Dostoevsky

►► Radiohead, the Negro Problem

see also: *Buzzcocks, Siouxsie & the Banshees, Nick Cave & the Bad Seeds, Barry Adamson*

Simon Glickman

Magnapop
Formed 1987, in Athens, GA.

Linda Hopper, vocals; Ruthie Morris, guitar; Shannon Mulvaney, bass; David McNair, drums (1987–95); Mark Posgay, drums (1996–present).

Magnapop's edgy alternative pop is distinguished by Ruthie Morris's economically powerful guitar work and Linda Hopper's affectless vocals, and by driving rhythms that propel the sweet-and-sour tension of the melodies. The band first courted attention via the high-profile producers of its first two albums—R.E.M.'s Michael Stipe, a fellow Athenian, and Hüsker Dü's Bob Mould, respectively—but the band's fervent post-punk rock stands on its own.

what to buy: *Hot Boxing* 𝄢𝄢𝄢𝄢⁷ (Priority, 1994) is a terrific power-pop-meets-punk rock slamfest with some of the group's most engaging performances on songs such as "Lay It Down" and "The Crush."

the rest:
Play It Again 𝄢𝄢𝄢 (Play it Again Sam, 1992)
Rubbing Doesn't Help 𝄢𝄢𝄢 (Priority, 1996)

influences:

◄◄ Blondie, Hüsker Dü

Simon Glickman

Mallard
See: Captain Beefheart

Yngwie Malmsteen
Born Lars Johann Yngwie Lannerback, June 30, 1963, in Stockholm, Sweden.

By age 21, Yngwie Malmsteen had the rock world praising his blazing speed and impressive dexterity—even if his greatest admirers tended to overlook a certain absence of feeling. Yngwie (pronounced ING-vey, it means "young viking chief") received his first guitar at age five, but it took a 1970 Jimi Hendrix TV special to make him pick it up. He moved to California in 1983—thanks to the patronage of *Guitar Player* editor Mike

Varney, who had heard a Malmsteen demo tape—and quickly established himself as a successor in the lineage of Edward Van Halen and Randy Rhodes. Malmsteen first joined the group Steeler, then recorded two albums with Alcatrazz before moving on to greater notoriety as a solo act. He's struggled through a series of personal setbacks—including a car crash that damaged his picking hand, the death of his mother, and embezzlement of funds by his manager—and his sales don't approach the levels of many of his colleagues. But Malmsteen remains undeterred, playing his particular brand of guitar pyrotechnics for mostly audiences in Europe and Japan, where such shredding has not yet gone out of style.

what to buy: Malmsteen's debut, *Rising Force* 𝄢𝄢𝄢𝄢⁷ (Polydor, 1984, prod. Yngwie Malmsteen), is a call to arms, a non-stop barrage of technique blazing over the leaden drumming of ex-Jethro Tuller Barriemore Barlow. *Odyssey* 𝄢𝄢𝄢𝄢 (Polydor, 1988, prod. Jeff Glixman) signaled his return after the car accident, and with the help of former Rainbow singer Joe Lynn Turner, it's his most successful album to date.

what to buy next: *The Yngwie Malmsteen Collection* 𝄢𝄢𝄢 (PolyGram, 1992, prod. various) is a good sampler that's not quite as satisfying as the other albums.

what to avoid: *Live in Leningrad: Trial by Fire* **woof!** (Polydor, 1992) is one of the most pompous and indulgent hard rock displays this side of Spinal Tap.

the rest:
(With Alcatrazz) *No Parole for Rock & Roll* 𝄢𝄢𝄢 (RCA/Rockshire/Grand Slamm, 1983)
(With Alcatrazz) *Live Sentence* 𝄢𝄢𝄢 (Grand Slamm, 1983)
Marching Out 𝄢𝄢𝄢 (Polydor, 1985)
Trilogy 𝄢𝄢𝄢 (Polydor, 1986)
Odyssey 𝄢𝄢⁷ (Polydor, 1988)
Eclipse 𝄢𝄢𝄢 (Polydor, 1990)
Fire and Ice 𝄢𝄢𝄢 (Elektra, 1992)
Power and Glory 𝄢𝄢 (Pony Canyon, 1994)
The Seventh Sign 𝄢𝄢𝄢 (CMC International, 1994)
I Can't Wait 𝄢⁷ (Pony Canyon, 1994)
Magnum Opus 𝄢𝄢𝄢 (Viceroy/Architect Music, 1995)
Inspiration 𝄢𝄢 (Foundation, 1996)
Facing the Animal 𝄢𝄢𝄢 (Mercury, 1998)

worth searching for: *Steeler* (Shrapnel, 1983, prod. Mike Varney), Malmsteen's first recorded work on these shores, caused an underground sensation.

influences:

◄◄ Ritchie Blackmore, Jimi Hendrix, J.S. Bach, Beethoven, Vivaldi, Paganini, Steve Hillage

►► Jennifer Batten, "Dimebag" Darrell Abbott (Pantera), Zakk Wylde, Slash

Sarah Weber and Eric Deggans

Michelle Malone

Born 1967, in Atlanta, GA.

Certainly one of the more talked-about also-rans of the women's music renaissance, Michelle Malone has yet to really have her day on the pop parade. Through 10 years of recording and constant touring she's made lots of important friends, most notably her mentors, the Indigo Girls, and has existed under several different banded monikers (Drag the River, Band de Soleil). But her drive remains undilluted: an angry urgency of throaty force. Sometimes subtle but more often at the front of the room and staring right in your face, Malone's strength has probably been a large part of her downfall. Her antics translate poorly beyond their rowdy girl-bar framing, and as such, she's had to sit out the more graceful successes of contemporaries such as Sheryl Crow and Shawn Colvin. But through it all she's grown into a confident artist who is today more likely to perform than to just flat out rock. Her 10 years, then, are to her credit.

what to buy: *Beneath the Devil Moon* 𝄢𝄢𝄢 (Velvel, 1997, prod. Michelle Malone, David Ryan Harris) is as good a folk-pop album as any, really. Filled with rural metaphors and themes of natural growth, it's Malone's tour de force, richly textured and spiced by her signature anger and occasional howl. Malone's erstwhile Band de Soleil is featured, as are the Indigo Girls, making for a feast of harmonic convergence. This would be a Heart album if it weren't so sincere.

what to buy next: *Redemption Dream* 𝄢𝄢𝄢 (Daemon, 1994) is actually creditied to the full Band de Soleil, but it rings true as a solid effort from Malone, who seems comfortable in the rich jangle of a band setting.

the rest:
New Experience (Aluminum Jane, 1988)
Relentless (Aluminum Jane, 1990)
For You Not Them (Sister Ruby, 1992)
A Swingin' Christmas in the Attic (Aluminum Jane, 1993)

influences:

⏮ Heart, Stevie Nicks, Linda Ronstadt, Patti Smith

⏭ Kristen Hall, Sheryl Crow, Ani DiFranco

Billy Manes

The Mamas & the Papas

Formed 1964, in New York, NY. Disbanded 1968. Re-formed and disbanded 1971. Re-formed (with new lineup) 1982.

John Phillips, guitar, vocals (1965–68, 1971); Denny Doherty, vocals (1965–68, 1971, 1982–87); "Mama" Cass Elliot (born Ellen Naomi Cohen; died July 29, 1974, in London, England), vocals (1965–68, 1971); Michelle Phillips (born Holly Michelle Gilliam), vocals (1965–68, 1971); MacKenzie Phillips, vocals (1982–88); Spanky McFarlane, vocals (1982–88); Scott McKenzie, vocals (1988).

Though short-lived, this free-spirit vocal group came to embody early Southern California soft rock. Writer-arranger John Phillips's distinct sound was a deft blend of '60s folk, wistful melodies, and lush harmonies. Just as important was the group's romanticized embrace of an emerging California lifestyle unknown to many Americans at the time. As John, his wife Michelle Phillips, Denny Doherty, and "Mama" Cass Elliot grew into roles as likable hippies, fans were also struck by the unusual sight of maverick marrieds and their friends cavorting on album covers and on stage. More striking was the obtuse Michelle Phillips/Cass Elliot visual: winsome blond harmonizing with zaftig earth mother. Ultimately, the breezy image was undone by drugs and acrimony, which led to Phillips firing his wife and the group's bitter split. A 1971 reunion was short and unsuccessful. Meanwhile, Elliot was reclaiming a solo career that once held much promise, but it was not to be. She died in London, officially of a heart attack—though longheld rock lore has it that she choked on a deli sandwich. During 1982 Doherty and Phillips re-teamed to mine the lucrative oldies circuit with Phillips's *One Day at a Time* TV-star daughter MacKenzie Phillips and former Spanky & Our Gang frontwoman Spanky McFarlane playing the fem-leads. John Phillips remained active as a songwriter, and despite years of hard living, survived a 1995 liver transplant. Rarely idle, Michelle Phillips moved quickly from music to movies, the gossip columns, and TV (*Dillinger*, *Bloodline*, CBS's long-running *Knots Landing*), where she still gets plenty of prime-time work. Daughter Chynna Phillips comprised one-third of the early '90s pop group Wilson Phillips, partnered with family friends—the two daughters of Beach Boy Brian Wilson.

what to buy: Though more polished work was to come, *If You Can Believe Your Eyes and Ears* 𝄢𝄢𝄢𝄢 (Dunhill, 1966/MCA, 1998, prod. Lou Adler), with the first innocent hits "California Dreamin'" and "Monday, Monday," remains a keeper. *Deliver* 𝄢𝄢𝄢𝄢 (MCA, 1967, prod. Lou Adler) saw the group indeed evolving in delivery, becoming harmony masters, particularly on the quintessential cover "Dedicated to the One I Love."

what to buy next: There's no end to the hits packages, compilations, and reissues out there for bargain prices, just about all of which feature the identical chart songs (including "I Saw Her Again," "Words of Love," "Dream a Little Dream") and classic tracks. *The Mamas & the Papas—Greatest Hits* 𝄢𝄢𝄢𝄢 (MCA, 1998, prod. various), timed to the group's induction into the Rock and Roll Hall of Fame, distinguishes itself with fresh liner notes—and dishy background material from Michelle Phillips. Other hits sets approved by fans through the years include the packed *Creeque Alley: The History of the Mamas & the Papas*

IJIJ (MCA, 1991, prod. various), which also contains rare Cass Elliot tracks and her earlier work with Doherty from the Mugwumps; the early *Farewell to the First Golden Era IJIJ* (Dunhill, 1968); and *Sixteen of Their Greatest Hits IJIJ* (MCA, 1969, prod. Lou Adler).

what to avoid: Diehards might also want the live set *Monterey International Pop Festival IJ* (One Way, 1967, prod. Lou Adler, John Phillips), but so-so sound makes this one best for buffs only.

best of the rest:
The Mamas & the Papas IJIJ (MCA, 1966)
Golden Era, Vol. 2 IJIJ (Dunhill, 1968)
The Papas & the Mamas IJIJ (Dunhill, 1968)
People like Us IJ (MCA, 1971)

influences:

◀◀ Peter, Paul & Mary, the Lovin' Spoonful, the Hollies, the Byrds, the Beach Boys, the Beatles

▶▶ Crosby, Stills & Nash, the Carpenters, Fleetwood Mac, Bette Midler, Wilson Phillips, Shania Twain

Deborah Wilker

Man or Astro-Man?

Formed 1992, in Auburn, AL.

CoCo the Electronic Monkey Wizard, alternate universe bass; Birdstuff, traps; Star Crunch, guitar; Dr. Delecto & his Invisible Vaportron, bass; Captain Zeno, anti-rhythm guitar.

Pretending to be intergalactic travelers who have ventured back in time to present-day Earth to expose the population of the world slowly to the harmonic evolution, Man or Astro-Man? is actually a group of former Auburn University students prolifically producing some of the finest lounge/surf revival music of the decade. The still-underground band's live shows are already legendary, featuring futuristic costumes—in a fashion sense that recalls Juan Garcia Esquivel's '50s era of "space-age bachelor pad music"—and playing a repertoire of thematic instrumentals saluting everything from spies to drag racing.

what to buy: The debut album, *Is It Man or Astro-Man? IJIJ* (Estrus, 1993) showcases the band's fine licks, sense of humor, and range (within this somewhat limited genre), with slick ditties such as "Taxidermist Surf," "Sadie Hawkins Atom Bomb," and the bizarre sexual tribute to the former *CHiPs* television star, "Eric Estrotica."

what to buy next: *Project Infinity IJIJ* (Estrus, 1995) features the engineering of indie-rock impresario Steve Albini. *Made from Technetium IJIJ* (Touch & Go, 1997) features a couple of interesting vocal tracks and a harder sound for variety.

what to avoid: *Live Transmissions from Uranus IJ* (Touch & Go, 1997) doesn't do justice to the band's otherworldly stage show.

the rest:
Destroy All Astromen!! IJIJ (Estrus, 1994)
Intravenous Television Continuum IJIJ (One Louder, 1995)
Experiment Zero IJIJ (Touch & Go, 1996)
What Remains inside a Black Hole IJIJ (Au-Go-Go, 1997)
Your Weight on the Moon IJIJ (Touch & Go, 1997)

worth searching for: The band from the future goes back to the recent past with a cover of "Interplanet Janet" on *School House Rock! Rocks* (Atlantic, 1996, prod. Andrew Leary, Janet Billig). Its tribute to the "galaxy gal" is one of the better tracks on a CD of '90s rockers covering the three-minute lessons that aired in between *Scooby Doo* and *Hong Kong Phooey* on ABC Saturday mornings.

influences:

◀◀ Dick Dale, Devo, Figrin D'an & the Modal Nodes, the Ventures, Sentinels, Juan Garcia Esquivel, the Tubes, GWAR

▶▶ Combustible Edison, Laika & the Cosmonauts, Southern Culture on the Skids

Alex Gordon

ManBREAK

Formed 1994, in Liverpool, England.

Steve "Swindelli" Swindells, vocals; Snaykee, guitars; Roy Van Der Kerkoff, bass; Stu Boy Stu, drums.

Steve Swindells, the former frontman of the rap-rock band the 25th of May, named his new band ManBREAK after a secret military program of the '50s and '60s in which the British government exposed some of its own soldiers to low-level chemical weapons, then monitored how they performed in the field. That alone says a lot about what to expect from this group.

what's available: Swindelli pontificates about politics in *Come and See IJIJ* (Almo Sounds, 1997, prod. Stephen Hague), a deluge of swirling samples, aggressive guitars, and hook-laden lyrics. The opening track, "Ready or Not," about German atrocities in the Eastern bloc, ranks with Republica's "Ready to Go" in the category of adrenaline-charged sports anthems. Although *Come and See* continues with more of the same, the album is a worthy debut.

influences:

◀◀ The 25th of May, Rage Against the Machine

Christina Fuoco

Melissa Manchester

Born February 15, 1951 in the Bronx, NY.

Hers is the classiest voice in pop music, and it's little wonder: Melissa Manchester acquired a love of fine music from her father, a former bassoonist with the Metropolitan Opera Orchestra; was a published poet and jingle singer by the age of 15; and graduated from New York's prestigious High School of the Performing Arts. How ironic, then, that her first big break professionally should come as one of the original Harlettes, the backup singers for Bette Midler, allowing her to fulfill a childhood dream of playing Carnegie Hall as part of Midler's famous cabaret act. Before that, Manchester had landed a staff writing job at Chappell Music and attended New York University, where she enrolled in a songwriting seminar taught by Paul Simon. She took that experience to the streets, performing as a solo singer-pianist at clubs in Greenwich Village and Manhattan's Upper West Side where she was discovered in 1971 by Midler and her longtime accompanist, Barry Manilow. Manchester's solo recording career began in 1973 with the LP *Home to Myself*, followed in close succession by *Bright Eyes* and *Melissa*, the latter yielding her first Top 10 single in "Midnight Blue." While honing her craft during the '70s, she co-wrote "Whenever I Call You Friend" with Kenny Loggins, which Loggins recorded with Stevie Nicks to create a classic radio duet. Her lyrics increasingly echoing the mounting rise of feminism, Manchester followed her second Top 10 solo hit, 1979's "Don't Cry out Loud," by becoming the first artist in the history of the Academy Awards to be nominated for two movie themes in the same year (*Ice Castles* and *The Promise* in 1980), and performed both works during the ceremony. Manchester received her Grammy Award in 1982 for Best Female Vocal Performance with her biggest hit, "You Should Hear How She Talks about You," before setting her sights on acting—reuniting with Midler in the movie *For the Boys*, playing the wandering birth mother of the series namesake in a recurring TV role on *Blossom*. She continues to record occasionally and has written an off-Broadway musical based on the Bernice Rubens novel, *I Sent a Letter to My Love*.

what to buy: The most comprehensive showcase for Manchester's artistry is contained in *The Essence of Melissa Manchester* ♫♫♫♫♫ (Arista, 1997, prod. various), her second greatest-hits collection but the first for which the singer hand-picked her favorite selections off her 13 previous Arista releases. Beyond the obvious choices ("Whenever I Call You Friend," "Don't Cry out Loud," "Midnight Blue," her Peabo Bryson duet "Lovers after All") are rare gems from her early out-of-print albums, including "Easy" and "It Feels Good" from her debut LP and the gospel-fired "O Heaven" from her 1974 album *Bright Eyes*.

what to buy next: Distressingly few of Manchester's albums remain in print. Of them, *If My Heart Had Wings* ♫♫♫ (Atlantic, 1995, prod. Arif Mardin, Jud J. Friedman, Ron Nevison, Melissa Manchester) is not a great work but is representative of her talent.

the rest:
Joy ♫♫♫ (Angel, 1997)

worth searching for: On her 1989 LP *Tribute* (PolyGram, 1989), Manchester paid vibrant vocal homage to the female singers she says influenced her career, reworking timeless standards from the likes of Judy Garland, Edith Piaf, Ella Fitzgerald, and Barbra Streisand. Two of her other albums, *Hey Ricky* (Arista, 1982) and *For the Working Girl* (Arista, 1980), are available as Japanese imports.

influences:

◄◄ Bette Midler, Barbra Streisand, Barry Manilow, Peter Allen, Carole Bayer Sager, Carole King, Paul Simon

►► Laura Branigan, Rita Coolidge, Sheena Easton

Jeff Hatch and Jim McFarlin

Manic Street Preachers

Formed 1990, in Cardiff, Wales.

James Dean Bradfield, guitar; Sean Moore, drummer; Nicky Wire, bass; Richey Edwards, guitar.

Despite its loud politics and punk image, the Manic Street Preachers played a soft brand of hard rock. Achieving some success in England, the group was mostly ignored in America. The band's legend rests not on music but on the disappearance of guitarist Richey Edwards—who had a history of depression and self-mutilation—before a major U.K. tour in 1995. His car was found, but Edwards is still missing.

what to buy: *Holy Bible* ♫♫♫♫ (CBS U.K., 1994, prod. Steve Brown), the last album before Edwards's disappearance, is the band's strongest, with songs that are angry, political, and, most importantly, well-written.

the rest:
Generation Terrorists ♫♫♫ (Columbia, 1992)
Gold against the Soul ♫♫ (Columbia, 1993)
Everything Must Go ♫♫♫ (Columbia, 1996)

influences:
◄◄ The Clash, the Sex Pistols

Anna Glen

Manitoba's Wild Kingdom

See: The Dictators

Aimee Mann

Born August 19, 1960, in Richmond, VA.

The bassist and vocalist for the now-defunct 'Til Tuesday, Aimee Mann has in recent years distinguished herself as a songwriter of formidable talent, much along the lines of Chrissie Hynde and Elvis Costello. Foregoing the synth-laden pop of her former band, Mann's albums are sonically adventurous affairs that blend catchy melodies with eloquent and dryly humorous observations of relationships and vulnerability. Much credit is due to Jon Brion, Mann's producer and a multi-instrumentalist, who performs much of the material. A perennial darling of both critics and songwriters (including Squeeze's Chris Difford and Glenn Tilbrook), Mann has shown remarkable creative growth over her first two albums and is definitely an artist to keep an eye on.

what to buy: Packed end to end with instantly memorable melodies, *I'm with Stupid* ♪♪♪♪ (Geffen, 1995, prod. Jon Brion) is simply one of the best pop albums to come out in years. From power-distortion rockers such as "Superball" and "Choice in the Matter" to gorgeous ballads like "Amateur" and "Ray," Mann shows a talent for crafting delectable pop candy that occasionally bites back.

what to buy next: *Whatever* ♪♪♪ (Imago, 1993, prod. Jon Brion) is brighter and more pop-oriented than its successor. While nothing here is particularly ground breaking, there are numerous standouts, including "I Should've Known," "Fifty Years after the Fair," and "Could've Been Anyone."

worth searching for: The EP *Say Anything* (Imago, 1993, prod. Jon Brion) offers up an acoustic version of "Say Anything" (from *Whatever*) and adds Mann's capable cover of the Badfinger hit "Baby Blue" and the previously unreleased "Jimmy Hoffa Jokes."

influences:

◀◀ The Beatles, the Byrds, Elvis Costello, the Pretenders, Squeeze

▶▶ Crowded House, Jules Shear, Sam Phillips, Juliana Hatfield, Michael Penn

see also: *'Til Tuesday*

Christopher Scapelliti

Manfred Mann
/Manfred Mann's Earth Band

Formed 1964, in England. Disbanded 1980.

Manfred Mann, keyboards; Paul Jones, vocals, harmonica (1964–66); Mike Hugg, drums; Michael Vickers, guitar (1964–65); Tom McGuinness, bass, guitar; Jack Bruce, bass (1965–66); Klaus Voorman, bass (1967); Michael D'Abo, vocals (1967). Manfred Mann's Earth Band: Manfred Mann, keyboards; Mick Rogers, vocals, guitar (1971–74); Colin Pattenden, bass (1971–76); Chris Slade, drums (1976–78); Chris Thompson, vocals, guitar (1976–80); Geoff Britton, drums (1979); Dave Flett, guitar (1976–78); Pat King, bass (1978–80); Steve Waller, guitar (1979–80); John Lingwood, drums (1980).

Under the calculating eyes of the jazz- and blues-trained Manfred Mann, the band that carried his name first surfaced with trash-pop during the early '60s ("Do Wah Diddy") for the sole purpose of record sales. Although he had a good belter in Paul Jones, Mann then employed Michael D'Abo (notable mostly for writing the lovely "Handbags and Gladrags," which Rod Stewart later nailed), a lesser singer. Mann then disbanded the group before forming the Earth Band and pursuing heavier art-rock ambitions. The group had considerable success with re-makes of Bruce Springsteen's "Blinded by the Light" and "Spirit in the Night." But it did not repeat those successes, and Mann finally put a wedge in the revolving door of members and called it a day in 1980 to pursue his own lofty ambitions. Reports of a new Earth Band began surfacing in Britain during the mid-'90s, however.

what to buy: *Best of—The Definitive Collection* ♪♪♪ (EMI, 1992, prod. various) is the place to start for fans of the early pop material such as "Do Wah Diddy." Also included are first versions of "Pretty Flamingo" (again, covered to greater effect by Stewart and, in early live shows, Bruce Springsteen) and "My Little Red Book."

what to buy next: *The Best of Manfred Mann's Earth Band* ♪♪♪ (Warner Archives, 1996, compilation prod. Greg Geller) highlights Mann's elaborate cover versions during the '70s, which alternate between nifty ("Blinded by the Light") and ponderous ("Quit Your Low Down Ways"), as well as revealing his continued dependence on Bob Dylan material. It also includes one last stab at a Springsteen overhaul, "For You," which has little of the charm of Greg Kihn's version.

what to avoid: The Earth Band's catalog has been recently reissued by Twinbrook Music, but there's really no point to owning anything beyond the above two collections. The same goes for the third-world excursions of *Somewhere in Afrika* ♪ (Arista, 1984/One Way, 1997).

the rest:
The Roaring Silence ♪♪♪ (Warner Bros., 1976)
Chapter Two: The Best of the Fontana Years ♪♪ (Fontana, 1994)
The Manfred Mann Album/The Five Faces of Manfred Mann ♪♪♪ (EMI, 1996)

worth searching for: In 1996 the U.K. label Cohesion re-released Mann's original '70s albums *Nightingales and Bombers* (1975); *Watch* (1976); *Solar Fire* (1973); *Messin'* (1973); *Man-*

fred Mann's Earth Band (1972); *Chance* (1980); *Budapest Live* (1984); and *Angel Station* (1979).

solo outings:
Manfred Mann:
Plains Music ♫♫ (Priority Music, 1991)

influences:
◀◀ Bob Dylan, Bruce Springsteen

▶▶ Emerson, Lake & Palmer, Asia

Allan Orski

Phil Manzanera /801

Born Phillip Targett-Adams, January 31, 1951, in London, England.

Phil Manzanera played experimental music in a rock band called Quiet Sun before Bryan Ferry asked him to join Roxy Music, where Manzanera's frantic, angular guitar lines became a hallmark. By the time the group disbanded after *Avalon* in 1982, Manzanera's guitar playing had become less abstract and more lyrical. Though he had been active in outside projects while Roxy was together, his post-Roxy life freed the South American–raised guitarist to explore any number of directions, from free-form jazz to Latin-flavored progressive rock.

what to buy: A surprising number of Manzanera's daring and occasionally dull solo efforts, including collaborations with Roxy Music reedman Andy Mackay and his avant-garde supergroup 801, are available on CD. But none encapsulates the guitarists' vast stylistic range, not to mention his six-string daring, more than *The Manzanera Collection* ♫♫♫ (Caroline, 1992, prod. various), which touches upon the many stepstones of his career. It offers some of his best recorded work, including the group 801's breathtaking live version of the Beatles' "Tomorrow Never Knows." Speaking of which, *801 Live* ♫♫♫♫ (Polydor, 1976/Editions E.G., 1982) is an electrifying live album with Brian Eno sitting in to perform his "Baby's on Fire."

what to buy next: *Diamond Head* ♫♫♫ (Editions E.G., 1975, prod. Phil Manzanera), a solo recording made while Roxy was still active, features most of the band's players plus all of Quiet Sun and Robert Wyatt. Those are dispirate talents, but Manzanera's fluid playing holds it all together.

what to avoid: *Listen Now* ♫♫ (Editions E.G., 1977, prod. Phil Manzanera), recorded with the side band 801 (including Quiet Sun bassist Bill MacCormick), is a rote letdown—particularly after its exciting predecessor, the out-of-print *801 Live*.

the rest:
K-Scope ♫♫♪ (Editions E.G., 1978)
Primitive Guitars ♫♫♫ (Editions E.G., 1982)

Guitarissimo ♫♫ (Editions E.G., 1986)
(With Andy Mackay) *Crack the Whip* ♫♫ (Relativity)
(With Andy Mackay) *Up in Smoke* ♫♫♪ (Relativity)
(With Sergio Dias) *Mato Grosso* ♫♫ (Black Sun/Celestial Harmonies)

influences:
◀◀ Charlie Christian, Charles Mingus, Edgar Varese

▶▶ Andy Taylor (Duran Duran), Adrian Belew

see also: *Roxy Music*

Doug Pullen and Gary Graff

Teena Marie

Born Mary Christine Brockert, March 5, 1957, in Santa Monica, CA.

With a family full of music lovers supporting her, young Mary Brockert began performing at age eight, eventually taking her nickname, Teena Marie, as her stage name. While in college, she was spotted by Motown Records chief Berry Gordy Jr. and signed to the label; as legend goes, R&B superstar Rick James heard her singing in a studio and offered to produce her first record. Before long, the industry and fans were buzzing about this white girl who could sing funk and soul with convincing passion and rock 'n' roll energy. From 1979 to 1981, she found success with Motown and James, gradually taking over more of her own songwriting and production responsibility as she became the most successful white artist ever to work at Motown. Moving to Epic Records during the early '80s after a royalty dispute with Motown, Marie truly spread her creative wings, refining the rock/funk mix alongside Prince, Cameo, and James. Enjoying her biggest hit in the 1984 single "Lovergirl," Marie crossed into the pop territory that Mariah Carey would later stumble into. But it was a success she would never duplicate again. Releasing a series of ever more ambitious albums that failed to find an audience, she lost her record deal in 1991.

what to buy: *Starchild* ♫♫♫♫ (Epic, 1984, prod. Teena Marie) balances Marie's talents as a multi-instrumentalist, producer, and performer, offering "Lovergirl" and a touching tribute to Marvin Gaye ("My Dear Mr. Gaye"). Marie's records for Motown had a different flavor, shaped less by the Minneapolis influence of Prince than by the grittier Detroit-bred funk of her mentor James. The best album from this period is *It Must Be Magic* ♫♫♫♫ (Motown, 1981, prod. Teena Marie), on which she experiments with Latin-tinged numbers such as "Portuguese Love" and straight-up funk grooves like "Square Biz."

what to buy next: Because no one's yet waded through the legal morass involved in Marie's united Motown and Epic material, you'll have to buy two greatest-hits packages to get her best. Motown's *Greatest Hits* ♫♫♫♫ (Motown, 1985, prod. various) features the James-penned smash "I'm a Sucker for Your Love"—Marie's breakthrough single—along with the surprise disco smash "Behind the Groove." Epic's *Greatest Hits* 🎜🎜🎜 (Epic, 1991, prod. Teena Marie) boasts her less impressive post-Motown work.

what to avoid: Coming after the powerhouse success of *Starchild,* the ambitious experimental funk of *Emerald City* **woof!** (Epic, 1986, prod. Teena Marie) seems like a jagged left turn, offering a host of rock- and jazz-influenced compositions that fell on deaf ears.

the rest:
Wild and Peaceful 🎜🎜🎜 (Motown, 1979)
Lady T. 🎜🎜🎜🎜 (Motown, 1980)
Irons in the Fire 🎜🎜🎜 (Motown, 1980)
Robbery 🎜🎜🎜🎜 (Epic, 1983)
Naked to the World 🎜🎜🎜🎜 (Epic, 1988)
Ivory 🎜🎜🎜 (Epic, 1990)
Passion Play 🎜🎜🎜 (Sarat, 1994)
Lovergirl: The Teena Marie Story 🎜🎜🎜 (Sony, 1997)

influences:
◄◄ Aretha Franklin, Rick James, Prince

►► Mariah Carey, Lisa Stansfield, Madonna, Wendy & Lisa

Eric Deggans

Marillion /Fish

Formed 1979, in London, England.

Steve Rothery, guitars; Mick Pointer, drums (1979–83); Fish (born Derek William Dick), vocals (1980–88); Mark Kelly, keyboards, vocals (1981–present); Pete Trewavas, bass, vocals (1982–present); Ian Mosely, drums (1984–present); Steve Hogarth, vocals, keyboards (1989–present).

Taking its name by shortening the title of the J.R.R. Tolkien novel *The Silmarillion,* Marillion became known for its dramatic art-rock presentations, both in concert and on record. Carrying the torch of theatrical progressive music that was abandoned by Genesis after Peter Gabriel left, Marillion made its name with their lengthy, orchestral opuses and spectacle-driven live shows. Fish, a six-foot-six behemoth, clearly emulated Gabriel in both his vocal styling and early stage antics (like Gabriel, he took to wearing face paint for performances). But while the music often evokes Genesis, Marillion managed to carve its own signature sound into the art-rock mantle. By the late '80s it was one of the most popular touring acts in the United Kingdom. Internal discord prompted Fish's departure in 1988, which left a substantial vacuum that the remaining band members were hard-pressed to fill. Steve Hogarth proved to be the ideal choice in that he em-

bodied many of Fish's best theatrical qualities, was a strong singer, and, perhaps most importantly, sounded nothing like his precursor, thus avoiding backlash for hiring a sound-a-like. Hogarth's arrival marked a gradual shift from the band's Genesis-heavy sound to a leaner template that is still firmly rooted in progressive rock. For his part, Fish led many loyal fans to his solo career, which has flourished in the U.K. but—like Marillion itself—has yet to transcend cult boundaries in America.

what to buy: A record from each vocalist's era is suggested. The album that best defines Fish's tenure with the band is *Misplaced Childhood* 🎜🎜🎜🎜 (Capitol, 1985, prod. Chris Kimsey), which gave Marillion their sole U.S. hit, "Kayleigh." Influenced by Gabriel-era Genesis, this is a concept album that draws heavily from Fish's personal history (as the bulk of his material does). In true art-rock fashion, the songs segue into one another, creating an extended mood piece with multiple parts. Hogarth's debut, *Season's End* 🎜🎜🎜🎜 (Capitol, 1989, prod. Nick Davis, Marillion), retains the band's sense of drama and dynamics, with lengthy songs that start slowly and quietly and gradually build to operatic crescendos. Hogarth's more polished vocals, however, clearly set him apart from Fish's raw energy and emotional immediacy.

what to buy next: Fish's final Marillion studio album, *Clutching at Straws* 🎜🎜🎜 (Capitol, 1987, prod. Chris Kimsey, Marillion), is a good companion piece to *Misplaced Childhood,* following the chronology of its predecessor by picking up with reflections of Fish's adult life—primarily on his love/hate relationship with alcohol. Marillion's latter-day concept album, *Afraid of Sunlight* 🎜🎜🎜🎜 (I.R.S./El Dorado, 1995, prod. Dave Meegan, Marillion), illustrates the extent to which its sound has evolved since Hogarth came on board in 1988. The theme is the toll of celebrity status, with particular attention paid to Elvis Presley, Brian Wilson, John Lennon, and (perhaps presciently) O.J. Simpson. The songs "King," "Out of This World," and "Afraid of Sunrise" still bear elements of Marillion's trademark sound, but other cuts explore new territory; "Cannibal Surf Babe" combines Beach Boys–style vocals with a menacing techno beat for an effect that is quite different from anything the band has previously done.

what to avoid: *Holidays in Eden* 🎜🎜 (Capitol, 1991, prod. Chris Neil), Hogarth's second outing with Marillion, is something of a hit or miss affair—with a good dose of "miss" taking the spotlight.

the rest:
Script for a Jester's Tear 🎜🎜🎜 (Capitol, 1983)
Fugazi 🎜🎜🎜 (Capitol, 1984)
Brief Encounter 🎜🎜🎜🎜 (Capitol EP, 1986)
B'Sides Themselves 🎜🎜🎜 (Capitol, 1988)
The Thieving Magpie (La Gazza Ladra) 🎜🎜🎜 (Capitol, 1988)

Brave ♫♫♫♪ (I.R.S./El Dorado, 1994)
This Strange Engine ♫♫♫ (Velvel, 1997)

worth searching for: Frustratingly, Fish's solo albums are only available as imports. Most are worthwhile and illustrate the singer's creative growth in his years after Marillion, particularly in his broadened lyrical approach and introduction of new music forms. His catalog is well represented by his solo debut, *Virgil in a Wilderness of Mirrors* (EMI, 1989, prod. Fish) and the dual releases *Yin* and *Yang* (Dick Bros., 1995/Renaissance, 1996, prod. Fish). An early Marillion live album, *Real to Reel* (EMI, 1984), is also worth searching out.

influences:

◀◀ Genesis, Yes, Emerson, Lake & Palmer, King Crimson, the Moody Blues

▶▶ Dream Theatre, Dramarama, Queensryche

David Galens

Marilyn Manson

Formed 1990, in Ft. Lauderdale, FL.

Marilyn Manson (Brian Warner), vocals; Daisy Berkowitz (1990–98), guitar; Madonna Wayne Gacy, keyboards; Gidget Gein, bass (1990–93); Twiggy Ramirez, bass (1993–98); Sara Lee Lucas, drums (1991–95); Ginger Fish, drums (1995–present); Zum Zum, guitar (1998–present).

Flaunting a circus horror show-meets-gothic dominatrix vibe, Marilyn Manson's initial claim to fame was its live shows, which feature lots of '90s-style headbanging with touches of Alice Cooper–style theatrics and bandmembers with stage names combining famous starlets and famous serial killers. Discovered by nine inch nails guru Trent Reznor and signed to his nothing label, the band benefited from his production help and guitar playing on its first album. Touring with nine inch nails offered tremendous exposure, but it was a gothic/industrial remake of Eurythmics' "Sweet Dreams" from the second CD that snared radio and mainstream attention. By the time of its third album, Rev. Manson and his band were spreading dark rock 'n' roll myths far and wide—scaring the fundamentalist right with tales of Satan worship while spreading fibs about arrests after gigs to increase their street cred. In 1996 the group released its most ambitious album yet, *Antichrist Superstar*, debuting to mega-sales even as conservative politicians began citing the group as an example of the American dream gone way bad.

what to buy: *Antichrist Superstar* ♫♫♫♪ (Interscope/nothing, 1996, prod. Dave Ogilvie, Trent Reznor, Mr. Manson) refines the band's bombastic sound with killer riffs and a deliciously nihilistic vision.

what to buy next: As a fine record that only hints at what rock fans would soon face, *Portrait of an American Family* ♫♫♫ (In-

terscope/nothing, 1994, prod. Trent Reznor, Mr. Manson) shows off the sequenced keyboards, muscular guitars, and raggedy vocals that would make Rev. Manson and his band teen heroes.

the rest:
Smells like Children ♫♫♫ (Interscope/nothing, 1995)
Mechanical Animals ♫♫♫♪ (Interscope/nothing, 1998)

worth searching for: Given its heavy reliance on sequencers, it might sound like a redundancy to pair Marilyn Manson with an electronica outfit like the Sneaker Pimps, but "Long Hard Road out of Hell," their contribution to *Spawn: The Soundtrack* (Epic, 1997), turned out to be an inspired team-up.

influences:

◀◀ Alice Cooper, Kiss, nine inch nails

▶▶ Filter, KoЯn, Coal Chamber

Eric Deggans

The Mark-Almond Band

Formed 1970, in London, England. Disbanded 1973. Re-formed 1975. Disbanded 1979. Re-formed 1996.

Jon Mark, vocals, guitar; Johnny Almond, reeds, vibes; Dannie Richmond, drums (1970–73); Ken Craddock, keyboards, guitar (1972); Tommy Eyre, keyboards; Colin Gibson, bass (1972); Roger Sutton, bass, cello (1970–73); Geoff Condon, brass, reeds (1972); Alun Davies, guitar (1973); Bobby Torres, percussion (1973).

Jon Mark and Johnny Almond enjoyed their first fame as sidemen to John Mayall on the acclaimed 1969 *Turning Point* album. Banding together, they pursued a non-commercial, highly acoustic folk-rock-jazz fusion. Their light, improvisational sound was among the earliest fusion approaches and a precursor to the new age sound that would rise during the late '70s. The duo came together once again in 1996.

what to buy: Mark-Almond almost always wrote and recorded suites rather than songs; the band's most celebrated pieces, "The City" and "One Way Sunday," are included on the *The Best of Mark-Almond* ♫♫♫♫ (Rhino, 1991, prod. various). An attempt to revive the group, *To the Heart* ♫♫♪ (ABC, 1976/One Way, 1993, prod. Roy Halee) included a bunch of jazz stars and resulted in some pretty melodies but ultimately unengaging music.

the rest:
Nightmusic ♫♫♪ (White Cloud, 1996)

influences:

◀◀ John Mayall, Alan Price, Charles Mingus

▶▶ Tom Scott, Kenny G

Lawrence Gabriel

Marilyn Manson (© Ken Settle)

Bob Marley & the Wailers

Formed as the Wailin' Wailers, 1963, in Kingston, Jamaica.

Robert Nesta Marley (born April 6, 1945, in St. Ann's Parish, Jamaica; died May 11, 1981, in Miami, FL), vocals, guitar; Peter Tosh, vocals, keyboards, guitar (1963–73); Bunny Wailer, vocals (1963–73); Rita Marley, vocals (1973–81); Judy Mowatt, vocals (1973–81); Marcia Griffiths, vocals (1973–81); Carlton Barrett, drums (1963–81); Ashton Barrett, bass (1963–81); Touter, keyboards (1972–74); Tyrone Downie, keyboards (1975–81); Al Anderson, guitar (1972–81); Alvin Patterson, percussion (1972–81); Julian "Junior" Marvin, guitar (1972–81); Earl "Wire" Lindo, keyboards (1978–81); Earl Smith, guitar (1974–76).

Bob Marley's is the one name most associated with reggae worldwide, though the original Wailin' Wailers was a more-or-less equal partnership between him, Peter Tosh, and Bunny Wailer. The Wailers were a moderately successful harmony singing group in Jamaica when they signed with Island records in 1972. The two seminal albums, *Catch a Fire* and *Burnin'*, put reggae and rastas, Jamaica and ganja on the international map with their hard-edged music and uncompromising, socially and spiritually conscious lyrics. When the trio broke up in 1973 Marley took over, added the I-Threes as background singers, and embraced a more rock-oriented sound. Marley's raw charisma and brilliant songwriting led to international superstar status no other reggae musician has equalled, though his biggest hit would come in another's hands—Eric Clapton's 1973 cover of "I Shot the Sheriff." Marley became the revolutionary standard bearer rock musicians of the '60s had been. He was given the United Nations Peace Medal in 1978, the same year he coaxed feuding Jamaican presidential candidates to join hands on stage at a concert. Marley died of cancer in 1981, at age 36.

what to buy: *Burnin'* ♫♫♫♫♫ (Island, 1973, prod. Chris Blackwell, Wailers) features the Wailers' classic harmonies on some of their best material: "Get up, Stand Up," "I Shot the Sheriff," and "Burnin' and Lootin'" took the world by storm. *Legend* ♫♫♫♫♫ (Tuff Gong/Island, 1984, prod. various) is a tightly compiled greatest hits set with "No Woman No Cry," "Is This Love," and the lovely acoustic "Redemption Song."

what to buy next: *Babylon by Bus* ♫♫♫♫ (Island, 1978, prod. Chris Blackwell, Jack Nuber) captures the Marley charisma at various concerts over a three-year period, particularly on a killer version of "War."

what to avoid: It's not actually bad, but *Kaya* ♫♫ (Island, 1978, prod. Bob Marley & the Wailers) is comprised of some of Marley's most forgettable tunes, except for "Easy Skanking" and "Is This Love." Also beware the many cheap repackagings of Marley's work. There are enough quality releases readily available without having to resort to these.

the rest:
Natty Dread ♫♫♫♫♫ (Island, 1974)
Live ♫♫♫♫♫ (Island, 1975)
Rastaman Vibration ♫♫♫♫♫ (Island, 1976)
Exodus ♫♫♫♫ (Island, 1977)
Survival ♫♫♫ (Island, 1979)
Uprising ♫♫♫♫ (Island, 1980)
Confrontation ♫♫ (Island, 1983)
Rebel Music ♫♫♫♫ (Island, 1986)
Talkin' Blues ♫♫♫♫ (Tuff Gong/Island, 1991)
One Love ♫♫♫ (Heartbeat, 1991)
Songs of Freedom ♫♫♫♫♫ (Tuff Gong/Island, 1992)
Natural Mystic ♫♫♫♫ (Tuff Gong/Island, 1995)
Dreams of Freedom: Ambient Translations of Bob Marley in Dub ♫♫ (Island, 1997)
The Complete Wailers 1967–1972, Part 1 ♫♫♫ (Jad/Koch, 1998)

worth searching for: *The Birth of a Legend* (Calla, 1976, prod. C.S. Dodd) features some of the Wailers' 1960s work at the legendary Studio One, including the 1964 Jamaican hit "Simmer Down."

influences:

◄◄ The Skatalites, Desmond Dekker

►► Ziggy Marley & the Melody Makers, UB40, English Beat, Lucky Dube, Tricky

Lawrence Gabriel

Ziggy Marley & the Melody Makers

Formed 1979, in Kingston, Jamaica.

David "Ziggy" Marley, vocals, guitar; Stephen Marley, vocals, percussion; Cedella Marley, vocals; Sharon Marley Prendergast, vocals.

Bearing a striking resemblance, both physically and vocally, to his father—reggae icon Bob Marley—has likely been as much a burden as a boon to Ziggy Marley. But he's borne up under it amazingly well, leading a group including his brother and two sisters. Their father wrote and produced a single for the group, "Children Playing in the Streets," but the Melody Makers' first two albums suffered from their general lack of seasoning and from their record company's focus on making Ziggy a solo star. After moving to Virgin, Ziggy was still out front, but his family's influence grew on each successive album. While the group leans decidedly toward the pop side of reggae, with considerable influence from American R&B and hip-hop, its lyrics continue in the vein of their late father—cautionary, righteous, but ever optimistic. Still, business is business—these days the group is perhaps better known for appearing in a Cover Girl makeup commercial and performing the theme song for the cartoon show *Arthur*.

what to buy: The group's years on Virgin, certainly its most fertile period, are well summed up on *The Best Of (1988–1993)* 𝄞𝄞𝄞𝄞 (Virgin, 1997, prod. various), a 17-track compilation. In terms of individual releases, though, *Conscious Party* 𝄞𝄞𝄞𝄞 (Virgin, 1988, prod. Chris Frantz, Tina Weymouth) fulfills both parts of its title, with lyrics extolling Rastafarianism and liberation, and grooves that just won't quit. The title track and "Tomorrow People" promote awareness and uplift, while "Lee and Molly" recounts the strife encountered by an interracial couple. The production by Weymouth and Frantz doesn't get in the way of the songs, and the Talking Heads–style keyboard textures on "Have You Ever Been to Hell," for example, certainly makes some of them more palatable to American ears. The group's reggae/hip-hop/rock synthesis is picked up again on *Free like We Want 2 B* 𝄞𝄞𝄞𝄞 (Virgin, 1995, prod. Melody Makers), which finds the family's involvement at an all-time high. Backup vocalists Cedella and Sharon (along with Erica Newell) take the lead on "Today," and Stephen steps to the fore on a number of tunes, including "Tipsy Dazy," "Keep On," and "Bygones." Ziggy's presence is still strong, though, especially on the title track and "Power to Move Ya."

what to buy next: *Jahmakya* 𝄞𝄞𝄞 (Virgin, 1991, prod. Melody Makers, Glenn Rosenstein) is perhaps the group's first truly mature album, with a nod to reggae's past, but with an eye more on creating a sound of their own, incorporating riddim-heavy hip-hop and dancehall influences, and adding a harder rock edge to boot. "Raw Riddim," "Kozmik," and "So Good So Right" are standouts.

what to avoid: *Time Has Come . . . The Best of Ziggy Marley & the Melody Makers* 𝄞𝄞 (EMI America, 1988, prod. Rita Marley) captures the best of a developmental period, a treat for the devout fan but few others.

the rest:
One Bright Day 𝄞𝄞𝄞 (Virgin, 1989)
Joy and Blues 𝄞𝄞𝄞 (Virgin, 1993)
Fallen Is Babylon 𝄞𝄞𝄞 (Elektra, 1997)

worth searching for: Die-hard fans or collectors can scour the racks for the original Melody Makers releases: *Children Playing* (EMI America, 1984, prod. Steve Levine), *Play the Game Right* (EMI America, 1985, prod. Grub Cooper, Tyrone Downie, Ricky Walters, David Marley), and *Hey World* (EMI America, 1986, prod. David Marley, Tyrone Downie, Grub Cooper, Ricky Walters).

influences:
◀◀ Bob Marley, the Wailers, Curtis Mayfield, Earth, Wind & Fire
▶▶ Fugees, Spearhead, Big Mountain

Daniel Durchholz

Marmalade
/Dean Ford & the Gaylords
/The Gaylords
/Dave Dee & Marmalade

Formed 1961, in Glasgow, Strathclyde, Scotland.

Dean Ford (born Thomas McAleese), vocals, harmonica, guitar (1961–75); Pat Fairley, guitar (1961–71); Wullie "Junior" Campbell, guitar, piano, vocals (1961–71); Billy Irving, bass (1961–64); Raymond Duffy, drums (1961–66); Graham Knight, bass, vocals (1964–74, 1976–present); Alan Whitehead, drums (1966–71, 1975–80); Hugh Nicholson, guitar, vocals (1971–72); Dougie Henderson, drums (1971–74); Mike Japp, guitar, keyboards, vocals (1974–75); Joe Breen, bass (1974–75); Howie Casey, horns (1974–75); Sandy Newman, guitar, keyboards, vocals (1976–present); Garth Watt-Roy, guitar, vocals (1977–78); Alan Holmes, vocals, keyboards (1978–present); Glenn Taylor, drums; Charlie Smith, drums.

Although best remembered for its shimmering 1970 classic "Reflections of My Life," the story of Marmalade is a long and eventful one, stretching far back to its roots as Scottish Shadows and Motown devotees. Hiring Brian Poole & the Tremeloes' management in 1965, the band, known as the Gaylords, began playing regularly throughout England and were signed to EMI Records by Cliff Richards's producer Norrie Paramor. Unfortunately, its was obliged to record primarily stale versions of American novelty numbers, and a subsequent stint on the British CBS label, under the new name Marmalade, also failed to produce much of merit (despite no less than Jimi Hendrix declaring its 1967 release "I See the Rain" the best single that year). Still, CBS insisted the group continue to record covers for its A-sides, culminating in 1969 with a U.K. chart-topping treatment of the Beatles' "Ob-La-Di, Ob-La-Da." With this, the band may have finally scored a hit, but eager to concentrate on its *own* compositions, Marmalade defiantly decided to go for broke: Negotiating an unprecedented new deal with Decca Records that gave the group total control over its recorded output for the first time, Wullie Campbell and Dean Ford's "Reflections of My Life" became a deserving worldwide hit. Ironically it was at this very point that Campbell, the group's recognized musical director, quit to pursue his studies at the Royal College of Music, dealing the band a crippling blow. Nevertheless, various incarnations of Marmalade continue recording and performing to this day, and "Reflections" remains as beautiful and poignant a number now as it was in 1970.

what's available: The 20 tracks on Marmalade's *Definitive Collection* 𝄞𝄞𝄞 (Castle Communications, 1996, prod. various) concentrate solely on the group's CBS and Decca years, meaning the original material is equally balanced with covers both odd ("I Shall Be Released") and downright ludicrous ("Take a Little

Piece of My Heart"). Still, Marmalade's arranging and vocal skills make most anything they touch well worth a listen, and several numbers herein are absolute pop-rock masterworks.

influences:

◄◄ The Beatles, the Bee Gees, the Hollies

►► Badfinger, the Raspberries, Aaron Skye

Gary Pig Gold

Marry Me Jane

Formed 1993, in New York, NY.

Amanda Kravat, vocals; Dan Petty, guitar; Richard Pagano, drums; Tim Beattie, steel guitar, harmonica; Kevin Augunas, bass.

Film soundtracks are often used by labels to further expose their rosters. Rarely, though, are those soundtracks almost completely comprised of tracks from a single unknown band. Eric Schaeffer's screenplay for the film *If Lucy Fell* was apparently so well accommodated by the music of Marry Me Jane that he decided to buy the whole record as a soundtrack (or at least nine of its 13 tracks). What resulted was a press feast on Amanda Kravat & company and a larger than usual promotion schedule for a brand new band, which was surely happy to have heard the phrase "You"—or at least your music—"oughta be in pictures."

what to buy: *Marry Me Jane* ♫♫♫ (550 Music, 1996) is a pleasant enough revisit to the edgy girl-rock of the Bangles or even Belinda Carlisle in her angrier moments. The softer side of grunge.

the rest:

Tick ♫♫ (550 Music, 1997)

influences:

◄◄ Bangles, Lita Ford, Sheryl Crow

Billy Manes

Chris Mars

See: The Replacements

Amanda Marshall

Born August 29, 1972, in Toronto, Ontario, Canada.

One of several post–Alanis Morissette exports from Canada, Marshall is the antithesis of the wispy folk/pop girls saturating the charts during the '90s. A gutsy vocalist who knows how to tame her bellowing voice when necessary, Marshall began touring and performing at 17, while still attending high school in Toronto. A chance meeting with guitarist Jeff Healy led to an opening gig on a Healy tour—all before Marshall had an album, or even a demo, released. When it came time to record her debut, Marshall assembled a standout cast of studio musi-

cians, including drummer Kenny Aronoff (John Mellencamp, Melissa Etheridge, Bob Dylan) and guitarist Tim Pierce (Tina Turner, Rick Springfield). Growing up with a Canadian father and Trinidadian mother, Marshall was influenced by '60s pop and Caribbean rhythms, both evident on her debut.

what's available: *Amanda Marshall* ♫♫♫♫ (Epic, 1995, prod. David Tyson) is a stunning collection of sturdy pop filled with melodic hooks. Marshall didn't write most of the songs on the album, including her biggest American hit, "Birmingham," but she did pen the rollicking anthem "Sitting on Top of the World," which country star LeAnn Rimes adopted into her live set. Other tunes written for her—"Let it Rain" and "Dark Horse" in particular—would falter under a less capable voice. But Marshall is a peerless belter in the style of '70s soul divas.

worth searching for: The swelling "This Could Take All Night" from *Tin Cup: Music from the Motion Picture* (Epic Soundtrax, 1996, prod. Ron Shelton, Glen Brunman, Kellie Davis, Gary Foster) proves that Marshall's sultry growl is better-suited for titillating rockers than the grimy pop of her debut. However, the emotional "I'll Be Okay" from *My Best Friend's Wedding: Music from the Motion Picture* (WORK/Sony Music Soundtrax, 1997, prod. Glen Brunman, Bonnie Greenberg) is a gorgeous midtempo shuffler on which Marshall is perfectly restrained.

influences:

◄◄ Joan Osborne, Sheryl Crow, Amy Grant

Melissa Ruggieri

The Marshall Tucker Band

Formed 1971, in Spartanburg, SC.

Toy Caldwell (died February 23, 1994), guitar, vocals (1971–83); Doug Gray, vocals; George McCorkle, guitar (1971–83); Paul Riddle, drums (1971–83); Jerry Eubanks, reeds, keyboards, vocals; Tommy Caldwell (died April 28, 1980), bass, vocals (1971–80); Frank Wilkie, bass (1980–83); Rusty Milner, guitar (1983–present); Tim Lawter, bass (1983–present).

The Marshall Tucker Band is a unique entity in Southern rock; the group could boogie with the best of them, but it had a jazzier sensibility that gave Doug Gray's flutes and saxophones a berth alongside the dueling guitars. The group was also a little more Southern and more country, with a bit more twang in its sound than compatriots such as the Allman Brothers Band and Lynyrd Skynyrd; Waylon Jennings was even able to turn MTB's first hit, "Can't You See," into a country hit for himself in 1976. The group's heyday came to an end during the mid-1970s, and it was never the same after the 1983 schism that took three of the original members—including the indispensable Toy Caldwell—out of the picture. You'll still find Marshall Tucker trucking itself out on the road though, stretching hits such as "24 Hours at a Time" to just about that length.

what to buy: With a series of generally interchangeable albums, it's the comprehensive *The Best of the Marshall Tucker Band: The Capricorn Years* &&&& (Era, 1995, prod. various) that gives the band its due, though it chooses the occasional live track over the preferable studio version.

what to buy next: Though the biggest hits are on other albums, *Searchin' for a Rainbow* &&& (Capricorn/AJK, 1975, prod. Paul Hornsby) is the group's most consistent outing.

what to avoid: The criminally skimpy *Greatest Hits* & (Capricorn, 1978/AJK, 1989, prod. Paul Hornsby) offers just eight selections from the band's 1972 through 1977 heyday.

the rest:
The Marshall Tucker Band &&& (Capricorn, 1973/AJK, 1988)
A New Life &&& (Capricorn, 1974/AJK, 1988)
Where We All Belong &&& (Capricorn, 1974/AJK, 1988)
Long, Hard Ride &&& (Capricorn, 1976/AJK, 1988)
Carolina Dreams &&& (Capricorn, 1977/AJK, 1988)
Southern Spirit &&& (Cabin Fever, 1990)
Still Smokin' && (Cabin Fever, 1992)
Walk outside the Lines && (Cabin Fever, 1993)
Country Tucker &&&& (Era, 1996)
MT Blues &&& (Era, 1997)

worth searching for: The out-of-print *Dedicated* (Warner Bros., 1981) finds the band, deeply moved by Tommy Caldwell's death, delving further into the country side of its sound.

solo outings:
Toy Caldwell:
Can't You See && (Pet Rock/BMG, 1998)

influences:
◄◄ The Allman Brothers Band, Waylon Jennings, Johnny Cash, the Grateful Dead

►► Sea Level, the Atlanta Rhythm Section, the Black Crowes

Gary Graff

Martha & the Vandellas

Formed 1962, in Detroit, MI.

Martha Reeves, lead vocals; Annette Beard, vocals (1962–63); Rosalind Ashford, vocals (1962–69); Betty Kelly, vocals (1963–67); Lois Reeves, vocals (1967–73); Sandra Tilley, vocals (1969–73).

A more emotionally forthright alternative to their chief rivals, the Supremes, the Vandellas were led by Martha Reeves's no-nonsense vocals, making it one of the toughest sounding girl groups of the '60s. Possessing an earthy soulfulness and a street-sass charm, the group recorded a string of propul-

---

WHAT ALBUM CHANGED YOUR LIFE?

I'm a huge Bonnie Raitt fan. I remember *Nick of Time* being a big record for me, one of those records I wore out, played over and over and over again.

Amanda Marshall

---

sive dance hits ("Heatwave," "Dancin' in the Streets," and "Quicksand") that stand among some of Motown's finest achievements. Reeves locked horns with Motown and left for a solo career in 1974, though she still performs with different combinations of Vandellas, including Beard and Ashton. The Vandellas were inducted into the Rock and Roll Hall of Fame in 1995.

what to buy: *Motown Milestones* &&&& (Motown, 1995, prod. various) is condensed, definitive, and cheap, an 18-track collection with all the essential hits—including "Jimmy Mack," "Nowhere to Run," "Heatwave," and "Dancin' in the Streets." Though it's full-priced, *The Ultimate Collection* &&&& (Motown, 1998, prod. various) is even better, offering 25 cuts.

what to buy next: *Live Wire! The Singles 1962–1972* &&&& (Motown, 1993, prod. various) is an excellent two-disc package that has numerous B-sides and non-hit singles in addition to the obvious hits.

what to avoid: *Motown Superstar Series, Vol. 2* && (Motown, 1981, prod. various) is a skimpy 11-track sampler.

the rest:
Heatwave &&& (Motown, 1963)
Come and Get These Memories &&& (Motown, 1963/1994)
Greatest Hits &&& (Motown, 1966)

worth searching for: *Martha Reeves: The Collection* (Object Enterprises, 1986) gathers some of her later, though inferior, material.

influences:
◄◄ Della Reese

►► The Supremes, the Pointer Sisters, Salt-N-Pepa, TLC, En Vogue

Allan Orski

The Marvelettes

Formed 1960, in Inkster, MI. Disbanded 1971.

Katherine Anderson, vocals; Gladys Horton, vocals (1960–68); Georgeanna Tillman, vocals (1960–66); Juanita Cowart, vocals (1960–65); Georgia Dobbins, vocals (1960–61); Wanda Young, vocals (1961–71); Anne Bogan, vocals (1968–71).

The only Motown act that could safely be slipped into the "girl group" genre, the Marvelettes' lack of an identifiable frontperson and frequent inter-group shake-ups denied them their fair share of the spotlight during the image-conscious mid-1960s. History, however, records that despite these drawbacks they produced a most solid, credible body of work that easily holds its own against that of their more colorful Motor City counterparts.

Gathering around her a group of friends already adept at vocalizing in local church choirs and talent shows, Gladys Horton formed the initial quintet while still in high school, and it was at a contest there that a scout from the newly formed Motown label first heard them perform (under the name the Marvels; a previous moniker, the Casinyets, as in "can't sing yet," already having been fortunately discarded). Advising the group to seek out new and original material, Dobbins helped rework a song her neighbor—yes, a letter carrier—had composed, and "Please Mr. Postman" not only secured the Marvelettes a contract with Motown, but became the label's very first #1 R&B and pop hit in December 1961. The group continued to score successes the following year with "Playboy" and "Beechwood 4-5789," but in 1963 they turned down the chance to record a new Holland-Dozier-Holland composition titled "Baby Love." Snapped up by the Supremes, this song quickly launched Ross & Co.'s career, and it can be safely argued that the lack of attention afforded the Marvelettes during the ensuing years by Berry Gordy effectively, and irreparably, stalled their momentum. Nevertheless, it was during this comparatively fallow period, sales-wise, that the group cut some of its very best material, thanks to brilliant songwriting and production assists from Smokey Robinson, Marvin Gaye, Ashford & Simpson, and Van McCoy. Reduced to a trio by 1967, falling victim to both changing musical times and continuing inattention from Motown, the group struggled gallantly onwards before unceremoniously calling it a day in the early 1970s. Sadly, Tillman succumbed to sickle-cell anemia in 1980, and subsequent efforts by Horton to reform the group have all been unsuccessful.

what to buy: Their definitive career overview remains *The Marvelettes Deliver: The Singles, 1961–1971* (Motown, 1993, compilation prod. Cary E. Mansfield), a 42-track, double-CD parade of hits, B-sides, key album tracks, and rarities that not only amply showcase the lead vocals of Horton and Young, but demonstrate yet again the absolute wealth of talent operating

under Berry Gordy at the time (for example, that's Marvin Gaye playing drums on "Please Mr. Postman").

the rest:
The Marvelous Marvelettes (Tamla, 1963)
Greatest Hits (Motown, 1966)
Motown Milestones (Motown, 1995)

influences:
◀◀ The Chantels, the Shirelles, Smokey Robinson
▶▶ The Supremes, Tammi Terrell, Deborah Harry

Gary Pig Gold

Richard Marx

Born September 16, 1963, in Chicago, IL.

Earnest pop craftsmanship isn't necessarily a crime, but sometimes it just doesn't hold up to serious scrutiny or over time. We give you Richard Marx—a guy with a pleasant, mellow image, a bit of a rock 'n' roll jones, and a touch for sweeping, romantic balladry. He broke into the business singing backup for Lionel Richie hits, including "All Night Long (All Night)," and writing for Chicago and Kenny Rogers before beginning his own recording career—one that would see numerous smash hits ("Satisfied," "Hold on to the Nights," "Right Here Waiting") that are still waiting for their resurrection in the '80s nostalgia boom.

what to buy: *Greatest Hits* (Capitol/EMI, 1997, prod. various) gives you everything you need, from his promising start with the crunchy "Don't Mean Nothing" to the lush love songs of later years.

what to buy next: His best individual outing remains his first, *Richard Marx* (EMI Manhattan, 1987, prod. David Cole, Richard Marx), which is driven by the palpable exuberance of a man finally making his own music—something that comes through on the hits "Should've Known Better" and the Eagles soundalike "Don't Mean Nothing," with Joe Walsh playing slide guitar and Eagles Randy Meisner and Timothy B. Schmit singing backup.

the rest:
Repeat Offender (EMI, 1989)
Rush Street (Capitol/EMI, 1991)
Paid Vacation **woof!** (Capitol/EMI, 1994)
Flesh and Bone (Capitol/EMI, 1997)

influences:
◀◀ The Eagles, Chicago/Peter Cetera, Bob Seger, Bryan Adams
▶▶ Celine Dion

Gary Graff

Dave Mason

Born May 10, 1946, in Worcester, England.

An excellent guitarist with a smoothly distinctive voice that has just enough strain to suggest emotional intensity, Dave Mason quit Traffic in 1968 (returning briefly in 1971) and eventually moved to California. After hooking up with Delaney & Bonnie for their 1969 tour, he went into the studio the next year with them, fellow tour member Leon Russell, Traffic drummer Jim Capaldi, and others and made by far his best album, *Alone Together*. The same year he made a forgettable duet album with Cass Elliot of the Mamas & the Papas, while in 1971 he appeared in George Harrison's benefit Concert for Bangladesh. But he did little to build on the success of *Alone Together* aside from touring with his crack quartet. Switching to Columbia, his albums appeared more regularly, but the music was so mellow that it left little impression even when it was well done. Despite several catchy tunes on *Let It Flow*, his style had come to seem irrelevant, and during the '80s he could be heard singing in Miller beer commercials. Mason continued touring but has released just one album of new material since 1980. In 1994 he joined the revolving cast of the post-Buckingham/Nicks Fleetwood Mac, joining Delaney & Bonnie's daughter Bekka and performing on the 1995 album *Time*, which includes two songs he co-wrote.

what to buy: *Alone Together* ♫♫♫♫ (Blue Thumb, 1970, prod. Tommy Li Puma, Dave Mason) is a bit deficient in the lyric department (always a Mason problem) but offers music so perfect that here, for once, that shortcoming can be overlooked. There's more forward momentum here than on all his Columbia work combined.

what to buy next: Some of Mason's Columbia albums are decent, but *Long Lost Friend: The Best of Dave Mason* ♫♫♫ (Columbia Legacy, 1995, prod. various) contains the high points required by all but dedicated fans. The half-studio, half-live *Headkeeper* ♫♫♫ (Blue Thumb, 1972, prod. Tommy Li Puma, Dave Mason) is notable for Mark Jordan's electric piano work and Mason's electric guitar solos on the concert half, which includes a cookin' version of Mason's Traffic classic "Feelin' Alright."

what to avoid: *The Very Best of Dave Mason* ♫♫ (MCA, 1978, prod. various) is a shameless rehash of far too much of *Alone Together*, plus filler. At a mere 10 tracks, *Greatest Hits* ♫♫ (Columbia, 1981, prod. various) pales next to the 19-track *Long Lost Friend*.

the rest:
Dave Mason & Cass Elliot ♫♫ (Blue Thumb, 1971)
It's Like You Never Left ♫♫ (Columbia, 1973)
Dave Mason ♫♫♫ (Columbia, 1974)

Split Coconut ♫♫ (Columbia, 1975)
Certified Live ♫♫ (Columbia, 1976)
Let It Flow ♫♫♫ (Columbia, 1977)
Mariposa de Oro ♫♫♫ (Columbia, 1978)
Old Crest on a New Wave ♫♫ (Columbia, 1980)
Two Hearts ♫♫ (MCA/Voyager, 1988)

worth searching for: The live album *Dave Mason Is Alive* (Blue Thumb, 1972, prod. Tommy Li Puma, Dave Mason) may be a bit redundant, but Mark Jordan's electric piano work and Mason's electric guitar solos are once again worth hearing, and the version of "Feelin' Alright" here is even better than the one on *Headkeeper*.

influences:
◄◄ The Beatles, Jimi Hendrix, Stephen Stills, Eric Clapton

►► Joe Cocker, Delaney & Bonnie

see also: *Traffic, Delaney & Bonnie, Fleetwood Mac*

Steve Holtje

Nick Mason

See: Pink Floyd

Massive Attack

Formed 1987, in Bristol, England.

3D; Daddy G; Mushroom; Shara Nelson, vocals (1988–91); Tricky (1988–91).

Strong influences from dub reggae, hip-hop, and classic soul brought Massive Attack to its beginning points, and the fusion resulted in a brand new sound that shot the band to the forefront of the British urban soul movement. It arose out of the Wild Bunch, a loose '80s collective of graffiti artists, breakdancers, and musicians based in Bristol that once featured acclaimed producer Nellee Hooper (Soul II Soul, Madonna). The group made its first splash during 1991 with its debut album *Blue Lines*, which launched three U.K. hits ("Unfinished Sympathy," "Safe from Harm," "Daydreaming") and scored strong underground support in America, which would be solidified in the pop world with 1995's follow-up album *Protection*. Relishing their role as behind-the-scenes producers and music lovers, the members of Massive Attack formed their own record label, Melankolic, during 1997, and collaborated with influential artists such as Radiohead and Everything but the Girl. The group resurfaced in 1998 with its third album, *Mezzanine*, this time with former Cocteau Twins singer Liz Frasier as the spotlighted vocalist.

what to buy: Massive Attack's seminal *Blue Lines* ♫♫♫♫ (Wild Bunch/EMI, 1991, prod. Massive Attack) is an extraordinarily polished debut album. Shara Nelson's vocals on "Unfinished Sympathy" and "Safe from Harm" are breathtaking and unforgettable, while Tricky's smoldering delivery on "Daydreaming" foreshadows his later successes as a solo artist. Similarly, *Mezzanine* ♪♪♪♪ (Virgin, 1998, prod. Massive Attack) presents a group at the peak of refinement. With chilling vocal contributions from Frasier on songs such as "Teardrop," "Black Milk," and "Group Four," it stands alongside the debut as the group's most inspired work.

what to buy next: Everything but the Girl's Tracey Thorn, who appears on *Protection* ♪♪♪♪ (Virgin, 1995, prod. Massive Attack), successfully rekindled her career—and her band's—with her stunning performances on both the title track and "Better Things," while Horace Andy's distinctive voice lends "Light My Fire (Live)" and "Spying Glass" an authentic island flavor. *Protection* has fewer memorable moments than the group's other releases but is definitely a worthwhile selection.

worth searching for: Mad Professor vs. Massive Attack's remix album *No Protection* (Caroline, 1996, prod. Mad Professor, Massive Attack) reworks *Protection* into a dub delight. The mark of a remixer without an ego complex, Mad Professor makes his distinct mark on each track without disturbing the essence of Massive Attack. Songs are stripped down to their most minimal elements and then processed through the dementia of the Professor, which generally means a lot of reverb, delay, random funny sound effects, and a real sense of the value of sparse production. Excellent.

solo outings:
Horace Andy:
Skylarking: The Best of Horace Andy (Melankolic, 1997)

Shara Nelson:
What Silence Knows ♪♪♪♪ (Chrysalis/ERG, 1994)
Friendly Fire ♪♪♪ (Cooltempo/UK, 1995)

influences:
◀◀ Horace Andy, Soul II Soul, Sade

▶▶ Portishead, Erykah Badu, Everything but the Girl

see also: *Tricky*

Tamara Palmer and Aidin Vaziri

Matchbox 20

Formed as Tabitha's Secret, early 1990s, in Orlando, FL.

Rob Thomas, vocals; Kyle Cook, lead guitars; Adam Gaynor, guitars; Brian Yale, bass; Paul Doucette, drums.

Matchbox 20's success is kind of like Pavlov and his dogs; if its music is played enough, music fans are bound to start drooling. That's what happened, thanks to the relentless airplay of the 1997 single "Push," which followed in Hootie & the Blowfish's footsteps to adult-rock radio playlists all over the country. Singer-songwriter Rob Thomas, who was born to parents stationed on a

U.S. Army base in Germany, played in several bands around the Southeast—as he drifted around the region to escape family problems—before scoring with Matchbox 20. Thomas has the ability to write thought-provoking lyrics, although it's either black or white with him; his lyrics are either stereotypical, whiny alternative-rock ("I wish the real world would just stop hassling me") or painfully honest ("Well, I'm surprised that you'd believe/in anything that comes from me"). But the group's tuneful, earnest melodies ("3 A.M.") kept it on the radio for more than a year, making Matchbox 20's debut a multi-radio format success.

what's available: *Yourself or Someone Like You* ♪♪ (Lava/Atlantic, 1996, prod. Matt Serletic) hit gold status because of "Push," which was all over MTV and VH1 for most of 1997. With its chorus of "I want to push you around/when I will/when I will," "Push" tells the story of the emotional abuse Thomas sustained during a former relationship. Of course, it was just as abusive to listen to Thomas's Cher-like vocals wail "when I will/when I will" across the radio dial.

worth searching for: *The Aware 3 Compilation* (Aware, 1995, prod. various) features an early version of "3 A.M.," which Matchbox 20 recorded under its former name, Tabitha's Secret.

influences:
◀◀ Counting Crows, Better Than Ezra, Live, Pearl Jam

Christina Fuoco

Material

See: Bill Laswell

Material Issue

Formed 1985, in Chicago, IL.

Jim Ellison (died June 20, 1996), guitar, vocals; Ted Ansani, bass; Mike Zelenko, drums.

Material Issue was a Chicago power-pop trio in the tradition of such heartland bands as Cheap Trick and the Shoes. With songs characterized by a devotion to tight harmonies, girls, and motor vehicles, the group became one of the premiere power-pop bands of the '90s but never grew its audience outside that circle. The band's label dropped the group after 1994's *Freak City Soundtrack*. The group ended when frontman and chief songwriter Jim Ellison committed suicide in June 1996; Ted Anansi and Mike Zelenko have since played, either separately or together, in such Chicago bands as Hummer, Slink Moss, and Teenage Frames.

what to buy: Material Issue's major label debut, *International Pop Overthrow* ♪♪♪ (Mercury, 1991, prod. Material Issue, Jeff Murphy) occasionally comes close to revolution promised in the title. There's something of a traditionalist bent when four songs feature girls' names in the titles (i.e., "Valerie Loves Me," "Renee Remains the Same"), but Ellison's songs contains the ambition and craftsmanship of the great pop music to which he aspired. *International Pop Overthrow* was also the group's most successful album, selling more than three times the amount of any subsequent album.

what to buy next: If you like one Material Issue record, you'll probably like 'em all, but *Destination Universe* ♫♫♫ (Mercury, 1992, prod. Material Issue, Jeff Murphy) contains what's arguably the group's finest moment, the near-hit "What Girls Want," which more likely is what Ellison wished girls wanted ("love, drugs, sex and affection . . . Rod Stewart's hair and Keith Richards's stagger").

what to avoid: *Freak City Soundtrack* ♫♫ (Mercury, 1994, prod. Mike Chapman) doesn't quite measure up to the group's first two albums, despite assistance from former Sweet producer Chapman. Sometimes it sounds as though the trio is going for the big-success sounds of other power-pop acts such as Gin Blossoms. Guitarists Rick Nielsen (Cheap Trick) and Gilby Clarke (Guns N' Roses) guest.

the rest:
Telecommando Americano ♫♫♫ (Rykodisc, 1997)

worth searching for: Material Issue's six-song EP, *Material Issue* (Big Block/Landmind, 1987, prod. Jeff Murphy, Material Issue), was tacked onto *Telecommando Americano*, but there are also 1,000 copies of the original vinyl version, plus an additional 500 pressed on blue vinyl. MI also contributed fun covers to a number of compilations, among them Sweet's "Little Willy" on *20 Explosive Dynamic Super Smash Hit Explosions!* (Pravda, 1991, prod. Phil Bonnet) and "The Tra La La Song (One Banana, Two Banana)" with Liz Phair on *Saturday Morning Cartoon's Greatest Hits* (MCA, 1995, prod. Material Issue, Jeff Murphy).

influences:
◄◄ Sweet, Cheap Trick, the Shoes, the Hollies, Big Star

►► Liz Phair, Everclear, Fastball

Brian Mansfield

Jas. Mathus & His Knock-Down Society

See: Squirrel Nut Zippers

Eric Matthews

Born 1970, in Gresham, OR.

While Eric Matthews is a native of the Pacific Northwest and records for the Seattle label SubPop, he sounds nothing at all like the grunge stereotype those details imply. A classically

trained trumpet player, Matthews is instead an old-school pop craftsman of the highest order. He first gained notice as half of the duo Cardinal with Richard Davies, former leader of the Australian group the Moles. But the one Cardinal album was just a warmup for Matthews's vastly superior solo work, in which ex-Jellyfish guitarist Jason Falkner serves as his primary foil.

what to buy: Picking up where the Beatles' "Penny Lane" left off, Matthews's solo debut *It's Heavy in Here* ♫♫♫♫ (SubPop, 1995, prod. Eric Matthews) evokes the golden age of mid-'60s English rock, when pop and psychedelia were beginning to mingle. The album's 14 songs have dry, spare arrangements, with each instrument clearly defined and hooks that just won't quit. Matthews's muted trumpet is the perfect embellishment to his own languid croon, and Falkner's multi-instrumental contributions are likewise impeccable. Except for some of the lyrics' hippie-dippie psychobabble ("Trip out on long lost time" and so forth), *It's Heavy in Here* is just about flawless.

what to avoid: *The Lateness of the Hour* ♫♫ (SubPop, 1997, prod. Eric Matthews, Tony Lash) is perhaps a too-quick followup. While all the same elements are in place from the debut, there's a noticeable dropoff in material—too much arranging, not enough songs. Matthews's continuing self-consciousness doesn't help. The opening track "Ideas That Died That Day" declares, "I'd like to be full of unbelievable speech." He succeeds, but not in a good way.

influences:
◄◄ The Beatles, XTC, Richard X. Heyman, High Llamas, World Party, Jellyfish

►► Belle & Sebastian, Ben Folds Five

see also: *Richard Davies*

David Menconi

Iain Matthews
/Matthews Southern Comfort
/Plainsong
/Hamilton Pool

Born Iain Matthew MacDonald, June 16, 1946, in Lincolnshire, England.

Iain Matthews has had two careers, really. The first began during the late '60s when he co-founded the influential British folk group Fairport Convention. He left Fairport after two records and in 1970 started Matthews Southern Comfort, which recorded three albums and had a Top 40 hit with Joni Mitchell's "Woodstock" (a year after Crosby, Stills & Nash's version had charted). In 1971 Matthews embarked on a moderately successful and quite prolific solo career as a singer (and occasional songwriter) of easygoing folk/country-pop songs; he released 10 albums in 10 years, plus a couple with the singers' collective Plainsong. He then vanished from the record bins for eight years, though he spent some time in Seattle playing in a band called Hi-Fi with ex-Pavlov's Dog singer David Surkamp. His second career began in 1988 with the release of *Walking a Changing Line*, an album of Jules Shear covers that was the Windham Hill label's first all-vocal project. Counting various retrospectives and live collections, Matthews has released over 12 records since then, including a new disc with a reunited Plainsong and a one-off with a band called Hamilton Pool (named after a swimming hole just outside Austin, Texas, where Matthews has lived since 1990).

what to buy: CD retrospective collections have been a welcome development for both Matthews and his fans, as his extensive '70s catalog is rather spotty in quality. *The Soul of Many Places: The Elektra Years, 1972–1974* 🎵🎵🎵🎵 (Elektra, 1993, prod. Iain Matthews, Michael Nesmith, Sandy Roberton) gathers the best tracks from what was probably his strongest artistic period; included are richly melodic covers of classics such as Tom Waits's "Ol' 55" and Jesse Winchester's "Biloxi," as well as Matthews's own hauntingly beautiful "For the Second Time" and "You Fell through My Mind." Documenting the best tracks from a slightly earlier period in his career is *The Best of Matthews Southern Comfort* 🎵🎵🎵🎵 (MCA, 1992, prod. various). As for actual albums, his most recent efforts are his best; their cohesiveness reveals a significant artistic growth from the hit-and-miss nature of his '70s records. Particularly strong is *The Dark Ride* 🎵🎵🎵🎵 (Watermelon, 1994, prod. Mark Hallman); a close second is *Skeleton Keys* 🎵🎵🎵 (Mesa, 1992, prod. Mark Hallman).

what to buy next: *Walking a Changing Line* 🎵🎵🎵 (Windham Hill, 1988, prod. Mark Hallman) is an intriguing attempt to bring mainstream accessibility to the brilliant pop songs of Jules Shear, though the record didn't quite live up to its potential. Also of interest to serious fans are four collections of demos and live tracks from throughout Matthews's career: *Orphans and Outcasts, Vol. 1: Demos 1969–1979* 🎵🎵🎵 (Dirty Linen, 1991), *Orphans and Outcasts, Vol. 2: Demos 1981–1989* 🎵🎵🎵 (Dirty Linen, 1993), *Intimate Wash* 🎵🎵🎵 (Perfect Pitch, 1993), and *Camouflage* 🎵🎵🎵 (Perfect Pitch, 1996).

what to avoid: *Stealin' Home* 🎵🎵 (Mushroom, 1978) contains "Shake It," Matthews's highest-charting hit single to date, but that song is also one of the shallowest things he's ever recorded and is indicative of the lack of creativity in his late '70s work—which likely led to his extended sabbatical during the '80s.

the rest:

Iain Matthews
If You Saw thro' My Eyes 🎵🎵🎵 (Vertigo, 1971)
Tigers Will Survive 🎵🎵🎵 (Vertigo, 1972)
Valley Hi 🎵🎵🎵 (Elektra, 1973)
Some Days You Eat the Bear and Some Days the Bear Eats You 🎵🎵🎵 (Elektra, 1974)
Journeys from Gospel Oak 🎵🎵🎵 (Mooncrest, 1974)
Go for Broke 🎵🎵 (Columbia, 1976)
Hit and Run 🎵 (Columbia, 1977)
Siamese Friends 🎵🎵 (Mushroom, 1979)
Spot of Interference 🎵🎵 (RSO, 1980)
Pure and Crooked 🎵🎵🎵 (Gold Castle, 1990/Watermelon, 1995)
God Looked Down 🎵🎵🎵 (Watermelon, 1996)
Seattle Years 1978–1984 🎵🎵 (Varese Sarabande, 1996)
Nights in Manhattan (And Points West) 🎵🎵🎵 (DCC, 1997)

Matthews Southern Comfort:
Matthews Southern Comfort 🎵🎵🎵 (Sire, 1970)
Second Spring 🎵🎵🎵 (Decca, 1970)
Later That Same Year 🎵🎵🎵 (Decca, 1970)

Plainsong:
In Search of Amelia Earhart 🎵🎵🎵 (Elektra, 1972)
Plainsong II 🎵🎵🎵 (Elektra, 1972)
Dark Side of the Room 🎵🎵 (Mesa, 1993)

Hamilton Pool:
Return to Zero 🎵🎵 (Watermelon, 1995)

influences:

◄◄ Simon & Garfunkel, Peter & Gordon, Jimmy Webb

►► Seals & Crofts, England Dan & John Ford Coley, America

see also: *Fairport Convention*

Peter Blackstock

Dave Matthews Band

Formed 1991, in Charlottesville, VA.

Dave Matthews (born January 9, 1967 in Johannesburg, South Africa), vocals, acoustic guitar; Boyd Tinsley, violin; LeRoi Moore, saxophone; Stefan Lessard, bass; Carter Beauford, drums.

Dave Matthews, a regular-joe musician who initially played clubs on the University of Virginia campus, has used constant touring and a hypnotic jazz-rock sound to become one of the biggest rock stars of the late '90s. At age two, he and his family moved from racially divided Johannesburg to the New York City suburb of Yorktown Heights. After relocating to Charlottesville as an adult, he put together a band—picking up Carter Beauford and LeRoi Moore, regular performers at Miller's, a jazz club where Matthews tended bar, 16-year-old bass prodigy Stefan Lessard, and violinist Boyd Tinsley. The Dave Matthews Band played its first gig in front of 40 people on May 11, 1991, on the

Dave Matthews (© Ken Settle)

roof of a Charlottesville apartment building. After performing as part of a 1991 Earth Day Festival, the band found a permanent place to play: the Eastern Standard, a small restaurant, on Tuesday nights. Eventually, the band moved on to a club called Trax and its Tuesday night shows became a "must see." Because the band allows fans to tape shows, the Dave Matthews Band's first recordings were bootlegs; its first official album was the live *Remember Two Things*. From those small beginnings, the Matthews Band won opening concert slots from fellow jam-rockers such as the Samples, then made smash hits out of catchy, bouncy numbers from its breakthrough 1994 album, *Under the Table and Dreaming*.

what to buy: The guitar-heavy *Before These Crowded Streets* ♫♫♫♫ (RCA, 1998, prod. Steve Lillywhite), darker and more political than the DMB's previous efforts, tackles issues of slavery and Native Americans, as well as broader subjects such as death and fear. "The Last Stop" incorporates Egyptian rhythms with banjos (courtesy of Bela Fleck) and includes the urgent lyrics "There you are nailing a good tree/Then say forgive me, forgive me" and "How is this/Hate so deep/Lead us all blindly killing killing." "Don't Drink the Water," which chastises white men for how they treated Native Americans, showcases Matthews's maniacal vocals coupled with an angelic-sounding Alanis Morissette. "Stay (Wasting Time)" is a full-on production featuring the gospel-flavored background vocals of Tawatha Agee, Cindy Myzell, and Brenda White.

what to buy next: *Under the Table and Dreaming* ♫♫♫ (RCA, 1994, prod. Steve Lillywhite) blends world-beat, jazz, folk, and pop styles with the group's fierce jamming skills. The album yielded a string of hits, including the sweet, acoustic "Satellite," the funk-driven "What Would You Say," and the sprightly "Ants Marching."

the rest:
Crash ♫♫♫ (RCA, 1996)
Live at Red Rocks 8.15.95 ♫♫ (RCA, 1997)

influences:
◀◀ The Grateful Dead, Phish, the Samples
▶▶ Agents of Good Roots

Christina Fuoco

Brian May
See: Queen

John Mayall
Born November 29, 1933, in Macclesfield, England.

Two truths about singer/harmonica player John Mayall: He's a survivor, and he's got a keen ear for talent. Mayall was a seminal force in the early British blues scene that produced so many great and influential artists, most notably Eric Clapton. Ol' Slow Hand was working construction after leaving the Yardbirds, a young British rock band that was just starting to have commercial success, when Mayall made him one of his Bluesbreakers, in which Clapton really established his name as one of the pre-eminent guitarists on the scene. Mayall fronted the Bluesbreakers until the '80s, and the roster of artists who passed through the group reads like a who's who of British blues-rock: Mick Taylor (Rolling Stones); John McVie, Mick Fleetwood, and Peter Green (Fleetwood Mac); Colin Allen; Jimmy McCulloch (Wings); Jack Bruce (Cream); journeyman Aynsley Dunbar; and countless others. Mayall is considered one of the fathers of the '60s British blues movement, but unlike his peer, the late Alexis Korner, he was able to make it beyond the small clubs to become a star, releasing some of the most consistent, faithful blues records on either side of the Atlantic. Mayall's longevity—he's still recording and touring and discovering new talent well into his '60s—is attributable largely to his ability to redefine the blues, finding new and challenging ways to interpret and expand the American music he loves so dearly.

what to buy: If ever an artist cried out for a box set, it's Mayall. But there is no such thing, so you're better off checking out a few albums that represent important phases in his career. *Bluesbreakers—John Mayall with Eric Clapton* ♫♫♫ (Deram, 1966, prod. Mike Vernon) captures the legendary singer and guitarist in one of their earliest and grittiest phases (there's a more expensive Mobile Fidelity gold disc version that offers improved sound; the recordings are pretty raw). *The Turning Point* ♫♫♫ (Deram, 1969, prod. John Mayall) is an all-acoustic affair (no drums, even) that included his harmonica showcase "Room to Move." *Archives to Eighties* ♫♫♫ (Deram, 1988, prod. John Mayall) is an unusual and successful late '80s restoration of his 1971 *Back to the Roots* album that featured Clapton and Taylor. Mayall spruced up the drums, added some new material, and essentially came up with a new and fresh-sounding record.

what to buy next: *The Best of John Mayall & the Bluesbreakers* ♫♫♫♫ (Deram, 1997, compilation prod. John Mayall) features 20 digitally remastered songs from the great early Bluesbreakers canon and an unusual twist—between-track interviews with the man himself. The mid-'70s to '80s were mostly fallow for Mayall, who had fallen out of favor with blues and rock fans. But he hung in there and in 1990 came up with one of the most assured and eloquent sets of blues-rock in his career. *A Sense of Place* ♫♫♫ (Island, 1990, prod. R.S. Field) is a little more slick than his fans are used to, but Mayall's wizened vocals and smart song selection proved that the blues don't have to be raw or formulaic.

what to avoid: *Behind the Iron Curtain* ♫♫ (GNP/Crescendo, 1985) is a good idea—it was recorded in Hungary—but not a particularly thrilling or memorable live album.

the rest:

A Hard Road ♫♫♫ (Deram, 1967)
Crusade ♫♫ (Deram, 1967)
Raw Blues ♫♫ (Polydor, 1967)
Diary of a Band, Vol. 1 ♫♫♫ (London, 1968)
Diary of a Band, Vol. 2 ♫♫♫ (London, 1968)
Blues Alone ♫♫♫ (Deram, 1968)
Bare Wires ♫♫♫ (Rebound, 1968)
Blues from Laurel Canyon ♫♫♫ (Deram, 1968)
Looking Back ♫♫♫ (Deram, 1968)
Empty Rooms ♫♫♫ (Polydor, 1969)
USA Union ♫♫♫ (Polydor, 1970)
Memories ♫♫ (Polydor, 1971)
Jazz Blues Fusion ♫♫♫ (Polydor, 1972)
Thru the Years ♫♫ (Deram, 1972)
New Year, New Band, New Company ♫♫ (One Way, 1975)
Notice to Appear ♫♫ (One Way, 1976)
A Banquet of Blues ♫♫ (One Way, 1976)
Lots of People ♫♫ (One Way, 1977)
A Hard Core Package ♫♫ (One Way, 1977)
The Last of the British Blues ♫♫ (One Way, 1978)
Return of John Mayall ♫♫ (Aim, 1982)
Chicago Line ♫♫ (Island, 1988)
Primal Solos ♫♫♫ (Deram, 1988)
John Mayall: London Blues, 1964–1969 ♫♫♫ (Polydor, 1992)
John Mayall: Room to Move, 1969–74 ♫♫♫ (Polydor, 1992)
Wake up Call ♫♫♫ (Silvertone, 1993)
Cross Country Blues ♫♫ (One Way, 1994)
The 1982 Reunion Concert ♫♫ (One Way, 1994)
Spinning Coin ♫♫♫ (Silvertone, 1995)
Drivin' South: The ABC Years (1971–1982) ♫♫♫ (MCA, 1998)

worth searching for: Mayall's first album, *John Mayall Plays John Mayall* (Decca, 1965) was released in England but never made it to these shores, except as an import.

influences:

◀◀ Muddy Waters, Little Walter, Howlin' Wolf

▶▶ The Rolling Stones, Savoy Brown, Foghat, the Fabulous Thunderbirds, Blues Traveler

see also: *Eric Clapton, the Rolling Stones, Cream, the Yardbirds*

Doug Pullen

Curtis Mayfield

Born June 3, 1942, in Chicago, IL.

Curtis Mayfield got his chance to lead the Impressions and made the best of it when Jerry Butler left the group in 1959

WHAT ALBUM CHANGED YOUR LIFE?

Blue Valentine by Tom Waits was one. I was young, 12 or something, and I'd never heard music like that—the poetry, the lyrics, and everything about it. It's a whole package, one whole thing. That's what amazed me about it.

Dave Matthews

after a handful of hits including "For Your Precious Love." Mayfield's songwriting, engaging vocals, and spare arrangements led the group to an early and mid-1960s peak with hits such as "Gypsy Woman" and "I'm So Proud." Unlike many soul artists during the early part of the decade, Mayfield's themes embraced civil rights sentiments; "People Get Ready" and "Choice of Colors" set a musical agenda long before Motown artists, for example, began to address social issues. Mayfield started his own Curtom label in 1968 for Impressions releases and wrote hits for Major Lance, Butler, and others. He left the group (though he continued to manage them), and embarked on a solo career in 1970, reaching the height of fame with his score for the 1972 movie *Superfly*—a gritty souladelic tour de force that yielded the hits "Freddy's Dead," "Pusherman," and the title track. Mayfield even performed in the movie as the leader of a local bar band. Though he began to lose form in the mid-1970s, Mayfield the songwriter, singer, arranger, producer, and label owner stands as a giant of soul music. His performing career ended tragically in 1990, when some stage lights fell on him and left him a quadriplegic. Happily, he's made a triumphant return to recording in recent years.

what to buy: Mayfield was never better than on *Superfly* ♫♫♫♫♫ (Curtom, 1972/Rhino, 1997, prod. Curtis Mayfield), where his falsetto cut through visions of ghetto life like a stiletto blade in a street fight. The wah-wah guitar that drives through this album is exemplary proto-funk. The Rhino reissue is a deluxe two-disc set, complete with previously unreleased music from the movie, studio outtakes, radio spots, and exclusive interview excerpts. Mayfield's tenure with the Impressions—as well as some of his solo highlights—are captured on

Curtis Mayfield & the Impressions: The Anthology 1961–1977 𝄢𝄢𝄢𝄢𝄢 (MCA, 1992, prod. various).

what to buy next: The three-disc box set *People Get Ready* 𝄢𝄢𝄢𝄢𝄢 (Rhino, 1996, prod. various) covers the whole spectrum, from the Impressions to 1970s hits such as "Kung Fu" and "Billy Jack."

what to avoid: Taking on longer forms and conceptual compositions didn't serve Mayfield well on *There's No Place like America Today* 𝄢𝄢 (Curtom, 1975, prod. Curtis Mayfield), which features preachy raps on themes not conducive to partying.

the rest:
The Impressions Greatest Hits 𝄢𝄢𝄢𝄢 (MCA, 1965)
Groots 𝄢𝄢𝄢𝄢 (Curtom, 1971)
Curtis in Chicago 𝄢𝄢𝄢 (Charly, 1973)
Of All Time 𝄢𝄢𝄢𝄢 (Curtom, 1974)
Do It All Night 𝄢𝄢𝄢 (Curtom, 1978)
Living Legend: Heartbeat 𝄢𝄢𝄢𝄢 (Curtom, 1979/1995)
Curtis Mayfield's Chicago Soul 𝄢𝄢𝄢𝄢 (Legacy, 1995)
New World Order 𝄢𝄢𝄢 (Warner Bros., 1996)
The Very Best of Curtis Mayfield 𝄢𝄢𝄢𝄢 (Rhino, 1997)

worth searching for: *Heartbeat* (Curtom, 1979, prod. various) finds Mayfield in a disco mode with dance floor grooves such as "Tell Me, Tell Me (How Ya Like to Be Loved)."

influences:
◀◀ The Drifters, the Soul Stirrers
▶▶ Seal, Maxwell, D'Angelo, Tony Rich

Lawrence Gabriel and Aidin Vaziri

Maypole
Formed 1996, in Los Angeles, CA.

Tobi Miller, guitars; Hugh Mangum, drums; Hans Hitner, guitars, vocals; Miiko Watanabe, bass; Chris Frankfort, tremofect, lap steel.

Tobi Miller was one of the original guitarists in Jakob Dylan's Wallflowers, though he left before the group's breakthrough success. His first post-Wallflowers band was the instrumental band Slue Foot Sue. When he heard a tape of Tucson resident Hans Hitner's vocals, however, Miller ditched that project and approached the singer to form Maypole.

what's available: Heavily influenced by the Rolling Stones and the Replacements, the impressive debut *Product* 𝄢𝄢𝄢 (Work Group, 1997, prod. T.G. Miller, Andrew Slater) begins with breakneck speed and doesn't let up. With raspy vocals, Hitner waxes poetic on the opening track "Going Dutch," while "Concrete Shoes" has Bryan Adams–worthy "na na na na nas."

Product also uses the Chamberlin, an early version of the sampler, as a base for its songs.

influences:
◀◀ The Beatles, the Rolling Stones, the Replacements
see also: *The Wallflowers*

Christina Fuoco

Mazzy Star
Formed 1989, in Los Angeles, CA.

David Roback, guitar; Hope Sandoval, vocals.

A former participant in L.A.'s postpunk psychedelic revival of the 1980s known as the "paisley underground," David Roback split his band Rain Parade in favor of the short-lived Clay Allison, which evolved into Opal, featuring vocalist Kendra Smith. When Smith left that group, Roback teamed up with Going Home singer Hope Sandoval to form Mazzy Star. The group combines Roback's trippy sensibilities with Sandoval's chilly vocals, making for music that, at its best, offers plenty of intrigue, though its lack of variance may become a problem as the years go by.

what to buy: *She Hangs Brightly* 𝄢𝄢𝄢𝄢 (Capitol, 1990, prod. David Roback) is a collection of slow, dreamy songs characterized by Sandoval's detached, cold delivery. The effect can be quite stunning, even as the songs' tempos and lyrical temperatures approach absolute zero. *So Tonight That I Might See* 𝄢𝄢𝄢𝄢 (Capitol, 1993, prod. David Roback) is even better, with a warmer, otherwordly quality and the beautiful hit "Fade into You."

the rest:
Among My Swan 𝄢𝄢𝄢 (Capitol, 1996)

influences:
◀◀ The Velvet Underground, Rain Parade

Anna Glen and Daniel Durchholz

MC 900 Ft. Jesus
Formed 1988, in Dallas, TX.

Mark Griffin, vocals; DJ Zero, mixer.

MC 900 Ft. Jesus, named for the vision Oral Roberts claimed to have had, started as the brainchild of record store clerk Mark Griffin. While working at one of Dallas's best-known independent stores, Griffin started collaborating with local mixer DJ Zero, combining his own interest in the avant-garde post-industrial music of the time with Zero's rap and hip-hop interests. What resulted was one of the first bands to consolidate these two forms of music into something entirely new. Quickly signed to the respectable Canadian Nettwerk Records, Griffin and Zero started releasing singles that were instant club hits. The two later parted ways, but the DJ's impact on Griffin's musical sensibilities is still felt on the most recent releases. Streetwise and cocky, MC 900 Ft. Jesus combines the best elements from Front 242 and Skinny Puppy with Public Enemy and Boo-Ya Tribe; while not technically proficient in the American form of rap, Griffin could easily pass as European. His vocals have a quirky narrative style that can sound like a disembodied voice or someone screaming. Griffin rarely sings in the traditional sense; he just talks to you over thumping music.

what to buy: Griffin begins coming into his own on *Welcome to My Dream* &&&& (Nettwerk/IRS, 1991), which displays greater dynamics and proves Griffin is a competent songwriter—particularly on the eerie "While the City Sleeps," a narrative that tracks the nightly rounds of an arsonist.

what to buy next: Griffin shows off his comical prowess on *One Step Ahead of the Spider* &&&♥ (Nettwerk/I.R.S., 1994). His twisted sarcasm is especially keen on "If I Only Had a Brain."

the rest:
To Hell with the Lid Off &&& (Nettwerk/I.R.S., 1989)

worth searching for: For more MC 900 Ft. Jesus, check the import bins; plenty of remixes, EP's, and singles are available as Canadian and British imports only.

influences:
◄◄ Cabaret Voltaire, Depeche Mode, Skinny Puppy, Public Enemy, Talking Heads

►► Gravity Kills, Beck, Stabbing Westward, 311

Tim Davis

Edwin McCain Band

Formed 1993, in Charleston, SC.

Edwin McCain, lead vocals, acoustic guitar; Scott Bannevich, bass, vocals; Craig Shields, saxophones, keyboards, wind controller; Dave Harrison, drums, percussion; Larry Chaney, lead guitar.

Thanks to the anti-grunge pleasantries of Hootie & the Blowfish and the Dave Matthews Band, Edwin McCain and his band immediately found an audience primed for gentleness and lucid lyrics. With his raspy, soulful vocals and saxophone-tinged acoustic strummers, singer-songwriter-aspiring novelist McCain could become a modern-day James Taylor. Bred on the sounds of Motown and David Wilcox, McCain joined his first band at age 17 and briefly attended the University of South Carolina. After bonding with the Hootie boys, McCain nabbed the opening slot on the band's monster "Cracked Rear View" tour in 1995. McCain's early affiliation with Hootie frontman (and fellow South Carolina native) Darius Rucker, meanwhile, re-

sulted in a minor hit with their gravelly duet, "Solitude," on McCain's first album, giving the band enviable exposure.

what to buy: McCain's debut, *Honor Among Thieves* &&&♥ (Lava/Atlantic, 1995, prod. Paul Fox), isn't only funky and jazzy—it reeks with maturity that belies McCain's 25 years (at the time of release). "Don't Bring Me Down" and "Kitchen Song" bebop along with sizzling horns courtesy of Tower of Power's Greg Adams, while the heartache-laden "Sorry to a Friend" is an easily believable lament—a testament to McCain's superb songwriting skills.

the rest:
Misguided Roses &&& (Lava/Atlantic, 1997)

influences:
◄◄ The Dave Matthews Band, Hootie & the Blowfish, Blues Traveler, Earth, Wind & Fire

Melissa Ruggieri

Paul McCartney /Wings

Born June 18, 1942, in Liverpool, England.

Wings (1971–81): Paul McCartney, bass, vocals; Denny Laine, guitar, vocals; Linda McCartney (died April 17, 1998), keyboards, vocals; Denny Seiwell, drums (1971–73); Henry McCullough, guitar (1972–73); Geoff Britton, drums (1974); Joe English, drums (1974–76); Jimmy McCulloch (died September 27, 1979), guitar (1974–76); Laurence Juber, guitar, vocals (1978–81); Steve Holly, drums (1978–81).

The most steadily active former Beatle, Paul McCartney also seems the most frustrated at his inability to consistently top the group that gave him his fame, although he has certainly been the most commercially successful on his own. As the Beatle who officially announced the breakup of the band as a way to plug his first solo album, he was the first to benefit from the fallout (although all the other band members by then had released solo turns). While *McCartney* was an interesting notebook of leftover Beatles ditties (some of which the band had considered), he hoped to lose himself in the anonymity of the band Wings, which had its ups and downs but was never considered anything but a McCartney project. Because its hit singles were almost always upbeat fluff, he was dismissed as the airhead yin to John Lennon's more serious and politicized yang. Disbanded in 1981, Wings made way for some spectacular McCartney flops, including a film (*Give My Regards to Broad Street*) and a financial slip (he saw his two-time duet partner Michael Jackson buy the rights to the Beatles publishing from under him). McCartney buckled down and even met a co-writer in Elvis Costello to bolster a pair of albums in the late '80s and early '90s that formed the basis for two successful world tours

Paul McCartney (© Ken Settle)

during which he embraced more and more Beatles material. By 1991 he began trying his hand at classical music, so far producing *Liverpool Oratorio* and *Standing Stone*. His 1997 album *Flaming Pie* was well-received and up for a Grammy in 1998, the year wife Linda McCartney died of breast cancer.

what to buy: Wings' *Band on the Run* ♪♪♪♪ (Apple, 1974, prod. Paul McCartney) was the best conceived, least embarrassing album of McCartney's solo career. With just he, Linda, and Denny Laine comprising the band, it was recorded in Nigeria, where the rhythms helped give the tunes a sunny disposition. *Choba B CCCP—The Russian Album* ♪♪♪♪ (Melodiya, 1988/ Capitol, 1991, prod. Paul McCartney) is a freewheeling album of American rock oldies—originally intended only for release in the old Soviet Union—that's as relaxed as McCartney has ever sounded since the Beatles split.

what to buy next: *McCartney* ♪♪♪♪ (Apple, 1970, prod. Paul McCartney) is an intriguing notebook of works in progress— some of which, including "Maybe I'm Amazed," turned out to be among his more fully realized post-Beatles tunes. *Ram* ♪♪♪♪ (Apple, 1971, prod. Paul McCartney, Linda McCartney) of-

fers more fully formed pop tunes that may be fluff, but darn catchy fluff. On *Flaming Pie* ♪♪♪ (Capitol/EMI, 1997, prod. various) he simplifies and suggests his old Beatle craftsmanship to boot.

the rest:
Paul McCartney:
McCartney II ♪♪♪ (Columbia, 1980)
Pipes of Peace ♪♪ (Columbia, 1983)
Give My Regards to Broad Street ♪♪ (Columbia, 1984)
All the Best ♪♪♪ (Capitol, 1987)
Flowers in the Dirt ♪♪♪ (Capitol, 1989)
Tripping the Live Fantastic ♪♪♪ (Capitol, 1990)
Tripping the Live Fantastic—Highlights! ♪♪♪ (Capitol, 1990)
Liverpool Oratorio ♪♪♪ (EMI Classics, 1991)
Off the Ground ♪♪♪ (Capitol, 1993)
Paul Is Live ♪♪♪ (Capitol, 1993)
Standing Stone ♪♪♪ (EMI America, 1997)

Wings:
Wild Life ♪♪♪ (Apple, 1971)
Red Rose Speedway ♪♪ (Apple, 1973)

Venus and Mars 🎵🎵 (Capitol, 1975)
Wings at the Speed of Sound 🎵🎵 (Capitol, 1976)
Wings over America 🎵🎵 (Capitol, 1976)
Thrillington 🎵🎵 (EMI, 1977/1995)
London Town 🎵🎵 (Capitol, 1978)
Wings Greatest 🎵🎵🎵 (Capitol, 1978)
Back to the Egg 🎵 (Columbia, 1979)

worth searching for: *Unplugged* (Capitol, 1991, prod. Paul Mc-Cartney, Geoff Emerick) is a limited edition album meant to fend off bootleggers. It has some wonderful renditions of Mc-Cartney's best material.

influences:

◀◀ Fats Domino, Jim Mac Jazz Band, Eddie Cochran, Buddy Holly, Elvis Presley, George & Ira Gershwin, Sammy Cahn

▶▶ Oasis, Blur, Jellyfish

see also: *The Beatles*

Roger Catlin

Kathy McCarty /Glass Eye

Formed 1983, in Austin, TX. Disbanded 1993.

Kathy McCarty (born February 1, 1961 in Stamford, CT), vocals, guitar; Brian Beattie, bass; Scott Marcus, drums (1985–86, 1989–93); Stella Weir, vocals, keyboards (1985–86, 1989–93); Dave Cameron, drums, (1986–89); Sheri Lane, vocals, keyboards (1986–89).

Kathy McCarty, a terrific guitarist who seems to hear melodies slightly more bent than other musicians, was the heart of the Austin, Texas, indie band Glass Eye. The band was deliberately skronky—fretless bassist Brian Beattie set typically bizarre, hard-to-follow rhythms—and never managed to build more than a loyal cult following in Austin despite some terrifically twisted pop songs, including "Christine." At one point, singer-songwriter Daniel Johnston went to a show, gave McCarty a tape of his *Hi, How Are You* album and begged to open concerts for them. The connection led to much creative respect between Johnston and McCarty, and after Glass Eye broke up in 1993, the singer-songwriter put out a masterpiece comprised of Johnston's songs.

what to buy: McCarty's brilliant *Dead Dog's Eyeball* 🎵🎵🎵🎵 (Bar/None, 1994, prod. Brian Beattie, Kathy McCarty) retools Johnston's "Sorry Entertainer," "Like a Monkey in a Zoo," "Rocket Ship," and "Hey Joe" so they sound purely rocking instead of purely eccentric.

what to buy next: The best Glass Eye albums, *Bent by Nature* 🎵🎵🎵 (Bar/None-Restless, 1988, prod. Brian Beattie) and *Christine* 🎵🎵🎵 (Bar/None-Restless EP, 1989, prod. Brian Beattie), are

straightforward, with enough jagged strangeness to keep listeners on the edge.

what to avoid: The EP *Marlo* 🎵🎵🎵 (1985) shows the band, while talented, still trying to come up with a sound and meandering behind McCarty's then-unfocused voice.

the rest:
Hello Young Lovers 🎵🎵 (Bar/None-Restless, 1989)

worth searching for: *Sorry Entertainer* (Bar/None EP, 1995, prod. various) includes a couple of the best tracks from *Dead Dog's Eyeball* and the unreleased Glass Eye track "Exodus Song."

influences:

◀◀ Daniel Johnston, the Minutemen, the Raincoats, Robyn Hitchcock, Sonic Youth, Talking Heads

▶▶ Yo La Tengo, the Dead Milkmen

Steve Knopper

Scott McCaughey

See: Young Fresh Fellows

Delbert McClinton

Born November 4, 1940, in Lubbock, TX.

Delbert McClinton has been kicking around for years, playing a decidedly unfashionable mix of blues, rock, country, and R&B that has rarely dented the charts. Highly regarded as a raspy, southern-fried vocalist, an adroit songwriter, and a harmonica player and performer par excellence, McClinton got his start on the Texas honky-tonk circuit, where he is still a fixture today. His early years were filled playing blues and breaking racial barriers—one of his bands, the Straitjackets, crossed the color line on a Fort Worth black station in 1960 with a cover of Sonny Boy Williamson's "Wake up Baby." He played harmonica on Bruce Channel's 1962 hit, "Hey Baby," and taught a then-unknown John Lennon a few licks while on tour in England. After fronting the Ron Dels in the 1960s, he formed a duo with Glen Clark, with whom he released two acclaimed albums in the early 1970s. The label-jumping, style-bending singer has been plugging ever since; his songs have been covered by artists as diverse as Emmylou Harris ("Two More Bottles of Wine") and the Blues Brothers ("B Movie Boxcar Blues").

what to buy: Few of McClinton's studio albums have done him justice, because it's onstage where he excels. His *Live from Austin* 🎵🎵🎵 (Alligator, 1989, prod. Delbert McClinton), taped during an *Austin City Limits* appearance, is a rock-solid example of what this guy can do.

what to buy next: McClinton, no doubt frustrated at his lack of commercial success, called in the big guns for *Never Been Rocked Enough* ♫♫♫ (Curb, 1992, prod. Don Was, Jim Horn, Delbert McClinton, Bonnie Raitt), which includes his Grammy-winning version of "Good Man, Good Woman" (sung with Raitt) and guest shots from Melissa Etheridge, Tom Petty, Paul Shaffer, and members of David Letterman's house band.

what to avoid: *Honky Tonk 'n' Blues* ♫♫♪ (MCA, 1994) sounds tired and uninspired.

the rest:
Second Wind ♫♫♫ (Mercury, 1978)
I'm with You ♫♫♪ (Curb, 1990)
The Best of Delbert McClinton ♫♫♫ (Curb, 1991)
Delbert McClinton ♫♫♪ (Curb, 1993)
Classics, Vol. 1: The Jealous Kind ♫♫♪ (Curb, 1994)
Classics, Vol. 2: Plain from the Heart ♫♫♪ (Curb, 1994)
The Great Songs: Come Together ♫♫♪ (Curb, 1995)
One of the Fortunate Few ♫♫♫ (Rising Tide, 1997)

worth searching for: The two Delbert & Glen albums, *Delbert & Glen* (Clean, 1972, prod. Daniel J. Moore, J. Henry T-Bone Burnett) and *Subject to Change* (Clean, 1973, prod. Geoffrey Haslam), foresaw the fusion of country, rock, and blues and hold up well today. They're long out of print and pressings are rare, but they're worth the trouble for completists.

influences:
◄◄ Jimmy Reed, Sonny Boy Williamson I, Bobby "Blue" Bland
►► Lonnie Mack, the Fabulous Thunderbirds

Doug Pullen

David McComb
See: The Triffids

Ian McCulloch
See: Echo & the Bunnymen

Michael McDermott
Born 1969, in Chicago, IL.

By waxing earnest at a time when the poles were more set to the gloss of radio pop and the apathy of grunge, a young Michael McDermott was able to land a spot in MTV's fickle rotation with a plaintive little confessional, "A Wall I Must Climb." Time spent on the Chicago club scene and the always diminishing returns of an honest pop career took their toll on his career. McDermott is currently unsigned and rumored to be playing around Chicago with a new rock act named Pawn Shop.

what to buy: His debut, *620 West Surf* ♫♫♫ (Giant, 1991), had an alienated charm, cast in sepia-toned reverie and with only a guitar strum to hold it all in.

the rest:
Gesthemane ♫♫ (SBK, 1993)
Michael McDermott ♫♫ (Capitol, 1996)

influences:
◄◄ Bob Dylan, John Mellencamp, Jim Croce, Richard Marx
►► Marc Cohn, Billy Mann

Billy Manes

Country Joe McDonald
See: Country Joe & the Fish

Michael McDonald
See: The Doobie Brothers

John McEuen
See: The Nitty Gritty Dirty Band

Eleanor McEvoy
Born in Dublin, Ireland.

That the roots of country and Celtic music are entwined is well known, although contemporary exponents of both Irish and Nashville sensibilities are few and far between. Eleanor McEvoy is one such artist, combining the Celtic-tinged pop/rock of her homeland with the brand of smart, singer-songwriter country-pop of the Mary Chapin Carpenter school. Tragically, McEvoy has thus far fallen through the cracks commercially, as her overall sound may be too rockish for country radio, and too country for rock. Still, someone in Nashville should seriously consider covering her songs, particularly the feminist anthem (and huge Irish hit) "Only a Woman" from her debut album.

what to buy: *What's Following Me?* ♫♫♫ (Columbia, 1996, prod. Kevin Moloney, Eleanor McEvoy) features the sparkling "A Glass Unkissed," which crystallizes heartbreak as well as any honky-tonk song. And the vulnerable ballad "My Own Sweet Bed Tonight" offers pertinent commentary on the subjects of sleeping single and drinking doubles.

the rest:
Eleanor McEvoy ♫♫♫ (Geffen, 1993)

influences:
◄◄ R.E.M., Bob Dylan, Mary Black

Daniel Durchholz

MC5

Formed 1965, in Lincoln Park, MI. Disbanded 1972.

Rob Tyner (died September 17, 1991), vocals; Wayne Kramer, guitar; Fred "Sonic" Smith (died November 4, 1994), guitar; Michael Davis, bass; Dennis Thompson, drums.

The MC5 were so concerned with social revolution—although it was never entirely clear what its members were revolting for—that it forgot to follow through with the musical revolution. For a while, the band's rock 'n' roll was as explosive as its Detroit-area brethren, including Bob Seger's early punk experiments (don't laugh), Ted Nugent's rambling metallic guitar, and Iggy Pop's on-stage self-destruction. The MC5's social figurehead was White Panther John Sinclair, who was always screaming about something, but the band was best known for its enduring anthem, "Kick out the Jams," which even today has the power to make young people run amok in a room full of speakers. After that, the band's work is much more sporadic—the rest of the album *Kick out the Jams* is incoherent and spacey. *Back in the U.S.A.* is much more interesting, if far under-produced, with '50s-style Chuck Berry rock 'n' roll and compact guitar solos that later inspired Television, Richard Hell, the Sex Pistols, X, and Black Flag. Where the punks picked up on the Velvet Underground and the Stooges' overall social-musical legacy, the MC5's meager contributions were one amazing song and a couple of impressive guitar solos. After the group broke up, Tyner became a songwriter and photographer before dying of a heart attack. Smith toured briefly with Iggy Pop before forming his own band, Sonics Rendezvous, and marrying punk songstress Patti Smith; he died in 1994 from heart failure. Kramer, who spent some time in prison for dealing cocaine, resumed his career in 1995 with powerful rock that's occasionally nostalgic for the old revolutionary days but more frequently full of lively, modern punk and metal.

what to buy: *Back in the U.S.A.* ♪♪♪♫ (Atlantic, 1970/Rhino, 1992, prod. Jon Landau) sounds tinny and bassless, but its re-hashing of Elvis Presley and Chuck Berry sensibilities and its theme of "Teenage Lust" is wonderful in its simplicity.

what to buy next: *Kick out the Jams* ♪♪♫ (Elektra, 1969, prod. Jac Holzman, Bruce Botnick) is worth buying for the title track, "Ramblin' Rose," and "Motor City Is Burning," three key songs in the big-guitar-riff Detroit hard-rock tradition.

what to avoid: *High Time* ♪♪ (Atlantic, 1971/Rhino, 1992, prod. MC5, Geoffrey Haslam) contains "Poison" and a few other over-long, unmemorable pre-metal songs.

worth searching for: Sinclair, the band's former manager, after doing time on trumped-up marijuana charges, left prison in the '70s and became a New Orleans blues deejay, musicologist, and author. He's still bitter about former *Rolling Stone* critic and eventual Bruce Springsteen manager Jon Landau taking

over his band in the early '70s, but has made up with his old friend Kramer. The two collaborate on Sinclair's hilarious, wonderful spoken-word-meets-blues-and-rock solo album, *Full Circle* (Alive, 1996, prod. Patrick Boissel). The best track is "Ain't Nobody's Bizness (Just Say Yes)," in which Sinclair gleefully lists a litany of horrific acts (from pot-smoking to suicide) and concludes, "Ain't nobody's business if we do!" The hard-to-find CD is also an entertaining blues history lesson.

solo outings:

Wayne Kramer:

The Hard Stuff ♪♪♪ (Epitaph, 1995)
Dangerous Madness ♪♪♪ (Epitaph, 1996)
Citizen Wayne ♪♪♪ (Epitaph, 1997)

influences:

◄◄ The Rolling Stones, the Velvet Underground, the Stooges, Bob Seger, the Amboy Dukes, Chuck Berry, the New York Dolls, Mitch Ryder & the Detroit Wheels, John Coltrane

►► Modern Lovers, Alice Cooper, the Sex Pistols, Black Flag, Bad Brains, the Presidents of the United States of America, Kiss, Rollins Band, Motörhead, Metallica, Slayer, Guns N' Roses

Steve Knopper

Kate & Anna McGarrigle

Kate McGarrigle, born 1944, in Canada; Anna McGarrigle, born 1946, in St. Sauveur, Montreal, Quebec, Canada.

Canadian sisters Kate and Anna McGarigle gained critical attention with their mid-'70s releases because they played a perfectly pitched type of folksy music that combined their beautifully trilling vocals with a wide-eyed sensual purity that was downright refreshing at a time when punk rock was fermenting (the Patti Smith Group's debut came out the same year as the McGarrigles'), FM album rock was bottoming out, and music in general was becoming more of a commodity. As an antidote, here were two intelligent, whimsical, and decidedly quirky women who wrote songs that were sometimes witty and sometimes wrenching, but always shot straight for the heart. In fact, it was songwriting that snared the McGarrigles their record deal after Maria Muldaur recorded "Work Song" and Linda Ronstadt covered "Heart like a Wheel." Unfortunately, their own records—liberally laced with the evocative fiddles and accordions of their French-Canadian culture (and songs sung in French)—were often brilliant, but never became hits. After a couple of fabulous releases, their songwriting was obscured in misguided attempts to "produce" them for greater commercial effect. But those efforts failed, of course, and the McGarrigles disappeared from the scene for the better part of a decade. Their 1996 album *Matapedia* proved the sisters still had the goods, but couldn't expand their audience beyond a devoted coterie.

what to buy: *Dancer with Bruised Knees* ♫♫♫♫ (Warner Bros., 1977/Hannibal, 1993, prod. Joe Boyd) remains a thrilling recorded moment that transcends its period despite (or because of) its fearless use of goofy sonic elements, from a cornball voice-over on the opening title track to oompah music. Country, gospel, and rock all come into play, and songs such as "No Biscuit Blues," "Be My Baby," and "Kitty Come Home" are all indelible melodies written with the very rare combination of smart, funny, and touching lyrics.

what to buy next: *Kate & Anna McGarrigle* ♫♫♫ (Warner Bros., 1975/Hannibal, 1993 prod. Joe Boyd) got rave reviews upon its release, but its songs don't have the timeless ring that the material on *Dancer* does. But it's a startling record for its time, featuring "Heart like a Wheel" and a lively take of (Kate's then-husband) Loudon Wainwright III's hilarious "Swimming Song."

the rest:
French Record ♫♫♫ (Warner Bros., 1981/Hannibal, 1992)
Love Over and Over ♫♫♫♫ (Polydor, 1983/Hannibal, 1997)
Heartbeats Accelerating ♫♫♫♫ (Private Music, 1990)
Matapedia ♫♫♫ (Hannibal, 1996)

worth searching for: *Pronto Monto,* the McGarrigle's most conventional folk-pop album, is currently out of print.

influences:
◀◀ The Carter Family, Joni Mitchell, Maria Muldaur

▶▶ The Roches, Iris DeMent, Nanci Griffith, Rufus Wainwright

Gil Asakawa

Roger McGuinn /McGuinn, Clark & Hillman /McGuinn & Hillman

See: The Byrds

Barry McGuire

Born October 15, 1935, in Oklahoma City, OK.

The folk-rock protest hit "Eve of Destruction" earned ex–New Christy Minstrel Barry McGuire his first and only solo hit in 1965. A Dylan knockoff, the song featured McGuire trumpeting the certain doom that awaited us all. Trouble is, the apocalypse only comes . . . what, once? That didn't leave much for an encore, and McGuire sank into drug addiction before emerging as a born-again Christian singer during the '70s.

what's available: Besides "Eve," *The Barry McGuire Anthology* ♫♫♫♫ (One Way, 1994, compilation prod. Terry Wachsmuth) contains a number of predictable Dylan covers. And with titles such as "Why Not Stop & Dig It While You Can?," it's probably more McGuire than you need.

influences:
◀◀ Phil Ochs, Bob Dylan, New Christy Minstrels

▶▶ The Mamas & the Papas

Allan Orski

Duff McKagan
See: Guns N' Roses

Maria McKee
See: Lone Justice

Loreena McKennitt
Born February 17, 1957, in Morden, Manitoba, Canada.

Loreena McKennitt isn't so much a pure folk or pop singer as a swirling, ethereal musician who uses elements of folk, pop, and Celtic music to enhance the atmosphere. Though the singer-harpist is more rooted in traditional songcraft than her new age contemporary Enya, McKennitt's music aims for the spiritual much more than the straightforward. She initially planned a career as a veterinarian, but wound up performing in folk clubs and working as a composer, actor, and singer at the Shakespeare Festival in Stratford, Ontario. (This would account for her dabbling in 19th-century poetry, such as the version of Alfred Lord Tennyson's *The Lady of Shalott* she set to music in 1992.) Soon, she began producing and distributing her own albums, finally catching during the late '80s when new age was beginning its run as a music-industry commercial force. McKennitt's soaring voice and her ability to turn any sort of traditional folk tune into an angelic hymn launched her subsequent albums past gold sales levels with very little radio or video play. Though she uses her considerable talent to mix all kinds of lofty musical traditions together, her music is best experienced while sleeping, having sex, or otherwise trying to avoid distractions.

what to buy: "All Souls Night," the opening track of *The Visit* ♫♫♫ (Quinlan Road/Warner Bros., 1992, prod. Loreena McKennitt), is a spooky Celtic tune propelled by rolling percussion and McKennitt's voice blending with a tamboura, balalaika, cello, and accordion. The album is impeccably crafted, well-thought-out (there's a version of the traditional "Bonny Portmore"), and there's nary a bump in the road.

what to buy next: McKennitt can sing with emotional power, as on the soft, fragile folk song "The Dark Side of the Soul," which is a nice break from the swirling new age music that otherwise colors *The Mask and Mirror* ♫♫♫ (Quinlan Road/Warner Bros., 1994, prod. Loreena McKennitt).

what to avoid: "Over a number of years spent ruminating on the distinctive characteristics of the Celts. . . ." So begins

McKennitt's introduction to *The Book of Secrets* ♫♫ (Quinlan Road/Warner Bros., 1997, prod. Loreena McKennitt), which despite these lofty pretensions—and the hit single "The Mummer's Dance"—manages to sound pretty good . . . for background music.

the rest:
Elemental ♫♫♫ (Quinlan Road, 1985)
To Drive the Cold Winter Away ♫♫♫ (Quinlan Road, 1987)
Parallel Dreams ♫♫♫ (Quinlan Road, 1989)
A Winter Garden: Five Songs for the Season ♫♫ (Quinlan Road/Warner Bros., 1995)

influences:
◀◀ Lao Tzu, Johnny Clegg, Peter Gabriel, Alfred Lord Tennyson

▶▶ Enya, Yanni, Erykah Badu, Deep Forest

Steve Knopper

Sarah McLachlan

Born January 28, 1968, in Halifax, Nova Scotia, Canada.

Sarah McLachlan grew up in Halifax studying classical guitar and piano. By the time she had reached 17 Nettwerk Records took notice—particularly of her stunning, dramatic vocals that tiptoe between her normal range, a throaty push, and a soprano falsetto (kind of like Enya without sounding too new agey). McLachlan mixes that with an ethereal combination of layered guitars, keyboards, and ambient percussion, while her lyrics create almost visual images out of feelings and emotions. It's a unique sound that's allowed McLachlan to stand apart from the scores of female singers that long-negligent labels brought to the pop mainstream during the mid-'90s. During the summer of 1997, McLachlan put together the first major tour consisting of female artists. While many promoters were wary, it was the fans that responded best; the Lilith Fair became one of the highest grossing tours of the year, surpassing the perennially successful Lollapolooza tour.

what to buy: Her second album, *Solace* ♫♫♫♫ (Arista/Nettwerk, 1991, prod. Pierre Marchand), is the deepest and most mesmerizing of her releases, from the ambient-Celtic-folk mix of "Drawn to the Rhythm" to the gutsy guitar drive of "Into the Fire."

what to buy next: *Live* ♫♫♫ (Arista/Nettwerk, 1992, prod. Pierre Marchand) covers mostly "Solace" songs and shows McLachlan can replicate all the textures and layers of her studio albums onstage. *Fumbling towards Ecstasy* ♫♫♫♫ (Arista/Nettwerk, 1993, prod. Pierre Marchand) adds some dance rhythms, drum machines, and a more straightforward pop tone to the songs. Multimedia fans should check out *The Freedom Sessions* ♫♫♫♫ (Arista/Nettwerk, 1994, prod. Pierre

WHAT ALBUM CHANGED YOUR LIFE?

Peter Gabriel's *Security,* 'cause I'd been playing folk music all my life, and when I heard that album, it made me think, 'This is exactly what I want to do'—not 'I'm going to copy what he's doing,' but what he made me feel, what he brought out in me. I want to make people feel like he made me feel. It was also the first time I ever listened to lyrics; with folk music, it was always melody that got me. With his songs it was his lyrics as well, how wonderfully they mixed with the melody and how both were very, very important to create a mood.

Sarah McLachlan

Marchand), an eight-song EP featuring alternate versions of her songs, a cover of Tom Waits's "Ol' 55," and CD-ROM footage of interviews, videos, and concerts.

what to avoid: Her debut, *Touch* ♫♫ (Arista/Nettwerk, 1988, prod. Greg Reely)—despite gems such as "Vox" and "Ben's Song"—is definitely the work of a 20-year-old who hasn't quite caught her stride.

the rest:
Surfacing ♫♫♫ (Arista, 1997)

worth searching for: A two-CD edition of *Surfacing* was sold during 1997 at Border's Books & Music stores, one of the Lilith Fair's sponsors. The second disc includes a "jazz versions" of the song "Sweet Surrender," the traditional "Prayer of Saint Francis," and some multi media material.

influences:
◀◀ Joni Mitchell, Joan Baez, the Cure, Kate Bush

▶▶ Tara MacLean, Jewel, Paula Cole, Jars of Clay

Joshua Zarov

Ian McLagan

See: The Faces

Malcolm McLaren

Born January 22, 1946, in London, England.

Known more for his cannily opportunistic posturing as the Sex Pistols' manager than for his musical contributions, Malcolm McLaren manipulated several less controversial acts (Adam & the Ants, Bow Wow Wow) before taking matters into his own non-musical but foxy hands. He has since exploited the marketplace numerous times to varying degrees of success, but never without the stamp of his looming presence.

what to buy: *Fans* 𝄢𝄢𝄢𝄢 (Island, 1984, prod. various) melds opera with rap in an unholy but clever union, particularly his nutso take on "Madam Butterfly." *Duck Rock* 𝄢𝄢𝄢𝄢 (Island, 1983, prod. Trevor Horn) takes hip-hop and African music to novel "heights" in the dance-junk of "Buffalo Gals" and "Double Dutch"; of course, McLaren didn't accord his sources proper credit, further tainting his charlatan image.

the rest:
Paris 𝄢𝄢 (Island, 1984)
Swamp Thing 𝄢𝄢 (Island, 1985)
Waltz Darling 𝄢𝄢 (Epic, 1989)
Round the Outside! Round the Outside! 𝄢𝄢 (Virgin, 1990)

influences:
◀◀ P.T. Barnum, Col. Tom Parker

Allan Orski

Pat McLaughlin

Born September 28, 1950, in Waterloo, IA.

Southern white soul has seldom sounded this good. Pat McLaughlin, a Nashville-based singer-songwriter, can bring to mind Van Morrison and Aaron Neville with his emotional voice, and John Hiatt with his smart songs. He even had a kickass band for the debut record and tour, which featured former Rockpile guitarist Billy Bremner. Capitol signed him with all the fanfare of a star-to-be, but failed to promote him, and his debut album fell by the wayside. He then fell victim to the major-label purgatory syndrome, and they refused to release the follow-up. It took six years before McLaughlin could extricate himself from the label machinery and allow an Austin, Texas, indie label, Dos, to release the album *Get out and Stay Out* in 1995. Most recently McLaughlin has been writing songs and performing in an informal group calling itself Tiny Town, with former members of the subdudes.

what to buy: *Pat McLaughlin* 𝄢𝄢𝄢𝄢 (Capitol, 1988, prod. Mitchell Froom) delivers the goods with some of his best songs and most soulful singing.

the rest:
Unglued 𝄢𝄢𝄢 (dos, 1994)
Get out and Stay Out 𝄢𝄢𝄢𝄢 (dos/Capitol, 1995)

worth searching for: *Party at Pat's* (Apaloosa, 1992) and *Wind It on Up* (Apaloosa, 1996) are only available as imports.
Gil Asakawa

Don McLean

Born October 2, 1945, in New Rochelle, NY.

After graduating from Iona College in 1968, folk-singing troubadour Don McLean enrolled at Columbia Graduate School but didn't attend, choosing instead to work dates with childhood hero Pete Seeger. McLean's first album, *Tapestry*, was released in 1970 on the Mediarts label after being turned down by 34 other companies. It contained the original version of "And I Love You So," a song that became a moderate country hit for Bobby Goldsboro, a pop smash for Perry Como, and an album cut for Elvis Presley. McLean's breakthrough came with his second album, *American Pie*, which spent nearly two months atop the pop album charts in late 1971 and 1972 and was dedicated to Buddy Holly. In addition to the epic title song, that album also contained the hit "Vincent." After *American Pie*, McLean made a series of inspired folk-rock albums but never recaptured the magic of his eight-and-a-half-minute blockbuster, though he was the inspiration for "Killing Me Softly with His Song," a chart-topping smash for Roberta Flack and, more recently, the Fugees. McLean, whose lengthy list of influences includes Hank Williams and Johnny Cash, traveled to Nashville in 1978 to record *Chain Lightning*, the album yielding his only Top 10 country hit, a remake of Roy Orbison's "Crying" that didn't chart until 1981. In 1981 he released another Nashville album, *Believers*, which, like *Chain Lightning*, was engineered by legendary country producer Billy Sherrill and featured some of Music City's prime players. He had one of his last hits with "He's Got You," a remake of Patsy Cline's "She's Got You," in 1987.

what to buy: *The Best of Don McLean* 𝄢𝄢𝄢𝄢 (EMI, 1988, prod. various) is a 10-song career overview containing all of his key tracks as well as his loving remake of hero Buddy Holly's "Every Day."

what to buy next: *American Pie* 𝄢𝄢𝄢𝄢 (EMI, 1971, prod. Ed Freeman) is the original breakthrough album that made such a big noise during the winter of 1971, the pure and unpretentious work of a troubadour who had no idea that a chart-topping classic was in his future.

Sarah McLachlan (© Ken Settle)

the rest:

Tapestry 𝄢𝄢𝄢𝄢 (Mediarts, 1970/Capitol, 1996)

Primetime 𝄢𝄢𝄢 (Arista, 1977/Hip-O, 1997)

Believers 𝄢𝄢𝄢 (Millenium, 1982/Hip-O, 1997)

For the Memories 𝄢𝄢𝄢𝄢 (Gold Castle, 1989/Hip-O, 1997)

Greatest Hits Live! 𝄢𝄢𝄢𝄢 (Gold Castle, 1990/Hip-O, 1997)

Head Room 𝄢𝄢𝄢 (Curb, 1991)

Don McLean Christmas 𝄢𝄢𝄢 (Curb, 1991)

Classics 𝄢𝄢𝄢𝄢 (Curb, 1992)

American Pie & Other Hits 𝄢𝄢𝄢 (Capitol Special Products, 1994)

The River of Love 𝄢𝄢𝄢 (Curb, 1995)

Favorites & Rarities 𝄢𝄢𝄢 (Alliance, 1997)

Don McLean's Christmas Dreams 𝄢𝄢𝄢 (Hip-O, 1997)

worth searching for: *Chain Lightning* (Millennium, 1978/Hip-O, 1997, prod. Larry Butler) features his compassionate vocals on material such as "Crying" and "Your Cheating Heart," recorded in Nashville. A country singer he's not; still, with his impassioned but tasteful deliveries, McLean makes you believe every word he sings.

influences:

⏪ Pete Seeger, Johnny Cash

⏩ Mary Chapin Carpenter, Steve Forbert

David Sokol

Grant McLennan /Robert Forster /The Go-Betweens

The Go-Betweens formed 1977, in Brisbane, Australia. Disbanded 1990.

Grant McLennan, vocals, bass, guitar (1978–90); Robert Forster, vocals, guitar (1978–90); Lindy Morrison, drums (1980–90); Robert Vickers, bass (1983–88); Amanda Brown, violin, oboe, vocals (1986–90); John Willsteed, bass (1988–90).

The story of the Go-Betweens is one that should inspire all young musicians. Starting out as a slightly Dylan-influenced duo, Grant McLennan and Robert Forster flew off to the U.K. in 1982 to take their shot at creating a lasting musical career for themselves. But rather than getting caught up in the syrupy synth-pop scene that held sway in Britain at the time, they blazed their own trail to develop a coarse, bittersweet post-punk sound during the early '80s through tentative ornamentalism in the mid-'80s until they finally produced a mini-classic, *16 Lovers Lane*, for their swan song. Early on, it was Forster, with his frank, occasionally out-of-tune vocals, who dominated; McLennan took over later, as he began to find his compositional and stylistic voice. The band broke up in 1990, and while Forster and McLennan have released several solo albums each,

McLennan has received greater acclaim—particularly for 1995's impressive *Horsebreaker Star*.

what to buy: McLennan's third solo effort, *Horsebreaker Star* 𝄢𝄢𝄢𝄢 (Beggars Banquet, 1995, prod. John Keane) presents the best work of his career—sunny pop melodies, nicely undercut by lyrics reflecting complex emotional situations. Recorded in Athens, Georgia, with a backing band McLennan had never met, *Horsebreaker Star* sounds like an album made by musicians who'd been mates for years. (Note: the import version of the album is a two-disc set with 25 tracks). The Go-Betweens' *16 Lovers Lane* 𝄢𝄢𝄢𝄢 (Beggars Banquet/Capitol, 1988, prod. Mark Wallis) is a gem from start to finish. McLennan's driving, straightforward and jangly pop tunes ("Streets of Your Town," "Is There Anything I Could Do?") are balanced beautifully by Forster's pensive, more puzzling material ("Clouds," "Love Is a Sign"), and producer Wallis helps the band create gorgeously hazy arrangements, using airy backup vocals, warm violin lines, and incisive oboe parts to support a mesmerizing group of songs.

what to buy next: *The Go-Betweens/1978–1990* 𝄢𝄢𝄢 (Beggars Banquet/Capitol, 1990, prod. various) surveys the band's career, though with a bit too much space allotted to early singles and less-than-stunning B-sides.

what to avoid: Poorly recorded and somewhat amateurish in execution, the band's debut, *Send Me a Lullaby* 𝄢𝄢 (Beggars Banquet, 1981), will be of interest only to completists.

the rest:

Grant McLennan:

Watershed 𝄢𝄢𝄢 (Beggars Banquet/RCA)

Fireboy 𝄢𝄢𝄢𝄢 (Beggars Banquet/ADA, 1993)

In Your Bright Ray 𝄢𝄢𝄢𝄢 (Beggars Banquet, 1997)

The Go-Betweens:

Before Hollywood 𝄢𝄢𝄢 (Beggars Banquet, 1983)

Spring Hill Fair 𝄢𝄢𝄢 (Beggars Banquet, 1984)

Liberty Belle & the Black Diamond Express 𝄢𝄢𝄢𝄢 (Beggars Banquet, 1986)

Tallulah 𝄢𝄢𝄢 (Beggars Banquet, 1987)

worth searching for: The Go-Betweens' *Metals and Shells* (PVC, 1985, prod. various) is a pithy but out-of-print compilation drawn from the group's first four albums. McLennan's two albums with the Church's Steve Kilbey (under the moniker Jack Frost) are of some interest. Both *Jack Frost* (Arista, 1991, prod. Steve Kilbey) and *Snow Job* (Beggars Banquet, 1996, prod. Steve Kilbey) feature ethereal, experimental pop that is closer to the Church than the Go-Betweens.

solo outings:

Robert Forster:

Danger in the Past 𝄢𝄢𝄢 (Beggars Banquet/RCA, 1991)

I Had a New York Girlfriend 🎵🎵🎵🎵 (Beggars Banquet, 1994)
Warm Nights 🎵🎵🎵 (Beggars Banquet, 1996)

influences:

⏪ Echo & the Bunnymen, the Cure, Bob Dylan

⏩ Deacon Blue, Downy Mildew, Poi Dog Pondering

Bob Remstein and Daniel Durchholz

James McMurtry

Born March 18, 1962, in Fort Worth, TX.

Son of the *Lonesome Dove* novelist and a university English professor, you'd expect James McMurtry to have a respect for the delicacies of language. And he doesn't disappoint. McMurtry is a fine narrative songwriter, spinning ironic tales of small-town boredom, vagabond loners and lovers, the weight of the past, and the illusions of memory in a style that's spare but finely etched. He sings in a detached world-weary monotone reminiscent of another deadpan non-singer, Lou Reed, and plays guitar with a subtle passion. McMurtry learned to play guitar at seven and after taking courses at the University of Arizona, he began to see the instrument as his meal-ticket, soloing at a local beer garden during happy hour. "I could sort of sing, but I decided I would really play," he says. "In those days, I wanted to be a major flat picker like David Bromberg and Doc Watson. That was before I figured out I didn't really have the speed. I'm more an endurance guitarist." In 1987 he was one of the winners of the prestigious New Folk contest that is part of the Kerrville Folk Festival. When dad Larry and John Mellencamp collaborated on the screenplay for the film *Falling from Grace*, Larry passed a tape of James's music to Mellencamp, who was impressed enough to volunteer his services as producer. Co-produced by Mellencamp band members Michael Wanchic and Larry Crane, that album was released to critical acclaim, leading to a second Mellencamp-sponsored set.

what to buy: McMurtry's debut, *Too Long in the Wasteland* 🎵🎵🎵🎵 (Columbia, 1989, prod. John Mellencamp, Michael Wanchic, Larry Crane), is a compelling collection of short stories set to song, highlighted by the title cut, "Paint by Numbers," and "I'm Not from Here."

what to buy next: *Where'd You Hide the Body* 🎵🎵🎵🎵 (Columbia, 1995, prod. Don Dixon) is a more electric, broader album with one great song ("Levelland") supported by 12 other substantial tunes. Also available is a video compilation of the album directed by a variety of University of Southern Cal and CalArts film students.

the rest:
Candyland 🎵🎵🎵 (Columbia,1992)
It Had to Happen 🎵🎵🎵🎵 (Sugar Hill, 1997)

Walk Between the Raindrops 🎵🎵🎵🎵 (Sugar Hill, 1998)

worth searching for: McMurtry turns in fine acoustic versions of "Too Long in the Wasteland" and "Safeside" on *Columbia Records Radio Hour, Vol. 1* (Columbia, 1995, prod. Mitch Matensky, Paul Rappaport), a superior collection featuring similar turns by Shawn Colvin, Mary Chapin-Carpenter, Roseanne Cash, Leonard Cohen, and Bruce Cockburn in a live/studio setting.

influences:

⏪ Lou Reed, Bruce Springsteen, John Mellencamp, Kinky Friedman

⏩ Darden Smith, Robbie Fulks

Martin Connors and Ken Burke

Ian McNabb
See: The Icicle Works

Christine McVie
See: Fleetwood Mac

MD .45
See: Fear

Meat Beat Manifesto
Formed 1987, in England.

Jack Dangers (born John Corrigan), keyboards, programming; Johnny Stephens, keyboards, programming.

Yet another example of the post-synth pop identity crisis, Meat Beat Manifesto found a new inspiration in the organic anger of hip-hop's oppressive beats and imperative bravado. Jack Dangers and Johnny Stephens had previously worked more traditional pop duties in the little-heard act Perennial Divide before embarking on a series of single side projects under this suggestive moniker. What started as a one-off studio gig turned out to be a scene-defining outfit, as the industrial-dance movement rumbled into underground club scenes on both sides of the Atlantic. Dangers and Stephens became unwilling posterboys to the science-fiction angst of the foot-stomping neogoths and were within a short time driven to redefine their motives. A switch to American living saw the band hooking up with the more politically charged (anti-meat, anti-establishment) noodlings of Consolidated (to the point of Dangers collaborating with Consolidated's Mark Pistel on production of Disposable Heroes of Hiphoprisy) and forming a notable collective of musicians and malcontents alike. Recent years brought the departure of Stephens and the escalation of Dangers' evolution into ambient/experimental techno.

what to buy: *Satyricon* 🎵🎵🎵 (Elektra, 1992, prod. Jack Danger, Johnny Stephens) found Dangers and Stephens bridging the industrial-melodic gap with notable aplomb. This album would later be seen as a seed to the ambient/dance movement of the late '90s.

the rest:
Storm the Studio 🎵🎵🎵 (WaxTrax, 1989)
99% 🎵🎵🎵 (WaxTrax, 1990)
Armed Audio Warfare 🎵🎵🎵 (WaxTrax, 1990)
Subliminal Sandwich 🎵🎵🎵 (Play It Again, 1996)
Actual Sounds and Voices N/A (nothing, 1998)

influences:
◀◀ William Orbit, David Bowie, Public Enemy, Depeche Mode
▶▶ Nitzer Ebb, Ultramarine, Prodigy

Billy Manes

Meat Loaf

Born Marvin Lee Aday, September 27, 1951, in Dallas, TX.

At a time when rock 'n' roll had reached its bloated, bloodless nadir with the unholy trilogy of Styx, Kansas, and Supertramp, Meat Loaf and songwriter Jim Steinman screamed onto the charts with 1977's *Bat out of Hell*. Fueled by shameless bombast and backseat bravado, they offered emotion-starved, hormone-driven teenagers salvation in the form of operatic, Springsteen-derived mini-dramas. The new wave movement would soon render their Wagnerian excess moot, but for one glorious summer, the motorcycle-riding cult hero from *The Rocky Horror Picture Show*—who's previous credits were a role in *Hair*, an album with singer Shaun Murphy as Stoney & Meat Loaf (for Motown, no less), and singing with Ted Nugent—tapped into what it was like to be clumsy, young, and in lust. A fallout with Steinman resulted in the longest sophomore jinx in rock history, which found Meat Loaf floundering from pseudo-Steinman copycats to heavy-metal posing until the duo reunited for 1993's multi-platinum *Bat out of Hell II: Back into Hell*. He continues to be a great voice in search of a vision, and to bide his time Loaf has rekindled his acting career: He recently was seen portraying the Spice Girls' bus driver in *Spice World*.

what to buy: *Bat out of Hell* 🎵🎵🎵🎵 (Epic, 1977, prod. Todd Rundgren), featuring such sweat-soaked anthems as "Paradise by the Dashboard Light," "You Took the Words Right out of My Mouth," and "Two out of Three Ain't Bad," holds up remarkably well. Audiophiles may want to splurge on the gold Master Sound reissue, which adds some much-needed definition to Todd Rundgren's dense production. *Bat out of Hell II* 🎵🎵🎵 (MCA, 1993, prod. Jim Steinman) ably mimics its predecessor's sound and fury, albeit with long-winded song titles like "Objects in the Rear View Mirror May Appear Closer than They Are" and "I'd Do Anything for Love (But I Won't Do That)."

what to buy next: Released in a "limited edition" of 200,000 copies, the two-CD *Live around the World* 🎵🎵🎵 (Tommy Boy, 1996, prod. Meat Loaf, Dave Thoener) is a hefty souvenir from his *Bat out of Hell II* tour. The performances are suitably over the top and overly extended but this is the only place to hear him revive his *Rocky Horror Picture Show* anthem "Hot Patootie" and his 1971 Motown hit as Stoney & Meat Loaf, "What You See Is What You Get."

what to avoid: *Welcome to the Neighborhood* **woof!** (MCA, 1996, prod. Ron Nevison, Sammy Hagar, Steven Van Zandt, Meat Loaf) finds Meat Loaf again abandoned by Steinman and turning to hook-for-hire song doctors such as Diane Warren. The results are the lunkheaded pop-metal anthems "I'd Lie for You (And That's the Truth)" and "Where the Rubber Meets the Road," which is about safe sex (really). When the best song on the disc is written by Sammy Hagar, you know you're in trouble.

the rest:
Dead Ringer 🎵🎵🎵 (Epic, 1981)
Midnight at the Lost and Found 🎵🎵 (Epic, 1983)
Bad Attitude 🎵🎵 (RCA, 1984)
Blind before I Stop 🎵 (Atlantic, 1986)
Hits out of Hell 🎵🎵🎵 (Epic, 1994)
The Very Best of Meat Loaf N/A (MCA, 1998)

worth searching for: *Bad for Good* (Epic, 1981), Steinman's solo debut, is the original sequel to *Bat out of Hell*. Made up of the songs and arrangements originally written for Meat Loaf before he broke off his partnership with Steinman, this album is hampered by some of the weakest lead vocals ever committed to tape. But the teen angst is palpable.

influences:
◀◀ Bruce Springsteen, Phil Spector, Richard Wagner
▶▶ Bon Jovi

David Okamoto

Meat Puppets

Formed 1980, in Phoenix, AZ.

Curt Kirkwood, guitar, vocals; Cris Kirkwood, bass, vocals; Derrick Bostrom, drums.

Many only know this trio's music from Nirvana's *MTV Unplugged* session (the Meat Puppets guested and the CD has three of its songs) and from covers by Minutemen and fIRE-HOSE. Its members' penchant for trading instruments during endearingly sloppy, feedback-drenched concert finales typifies the group's spirited aesthetic. Having come from the punk scene but soon incorporating country twang, psychedelia, and heavy guitar, the group's punk days now are long behind it, as is any apparent urge to try something new. Still, the Puppets are consistently entertaining and unusual—imagine an alternative Blue Öyster Cult, with fat, dark, rumbling guitar riffs. Curt Kirkwood's inimitable vocals make even the most minimal melodies sound catchy; similarly, his lyrics say a lot with simple means and images. That's harder than it seems.

what to buy: *Up on the Sun* ⅃⅃⅃⅃ (SST, 1985) is a conceptual shock and a musical tonic, with a totally warped slacker interpretation of the Byrds' interpretation of country at its center.

what to buy next: *Too High to Die* ⅃⅃⅃ (London, 1994, prod. Paul Leary, Meat Puppets) is the best of the group's major-label albums.

what to avoid: *Huevos* ⅃⅃ (SST, 1987, prod. Meat Puppets, Steven Escallier) offers more evidence for the proposition that inevitably every rock 'n' roll trio tries to sound like ZZ Top at one point or another.

the rest:
In a Car ⅃⅃⅃ (World Imitation EP/SST, 1981)
Meat Puppets ⅃⅃⅃ (SST, 1982)
II ⅃⅃⅃ (SST, 1983)
Out My Way EP (SST, 1986) ⅃⅃
Mirage ⅃⅃⅃ (SST, 1987)
Monsters ⅃⅃⅃ (SST, 1989)
No Strings Attached ⅃⅃⅃ (SST, 1990)
Forbidden Places ⅃⅃⅃ (London, 1991)
No Joke! ⅃⅃⅃ (London, 1995)
Sweet in the Pants ⅃⅃⅃ (Bloodshot, 1997)

influences:
◀◀ Black Flag, the Byrds, Buck Owens, Captain Beefheart, Blue Öyster Cult, ZZ Top

▶▶ Overwhelming Colorfast, Nirvana

Steve Holtje

Medeski, Martin & Wood

Formed 1990, in New York, NY.

John Medeski, Hammond B-3 organ, clavinet, pianos; Billy Martin, drums, percussion; Chris Wood, bass, guitar, harmonica.

Having collaborated with John Zorn, Marc Ribot, the Either/Orchestra, John Scofield, Oren Bloedow, David Byrne, John Lurie, Ken Shaphorst, and numerous other jazz and rock luminaries, Medeski, Martin & Wood bring a wide influence to their improvisational playing. Almost entirely instrumental, the band's sound includes elements of funk, straight jazz, noise, rock, hip-hop, New Orleans, and African music. Unlike many organ trios, MMW allows each player equal time in the spotlight, occasionally augmented by horns and woodwinds.

what to buy: *Shack-man* ⅃⅃⅃⅃ (Gramavision, 1996, prod. Medeski, Martin & Wood, David Baker) is a reasonable start. A bit more funky on the downbeat than previous efforts, *Shack-man* was partially recorded at the band's "shack" in Hawaii. Without the band's typical lineup of accompanying players, the album is often more cohesive and focused than usual.

what to buy next: *Combustication* ⅃⅃⅃⅃ (Blue Note, 1998, prod. Medeski, Martin & Wood, David Baker, Scott Harding, Jason Kibler) adds depth with DJ Logic's presence on a few cuts. Previously used on the remix EP *Bubblehouse* ⅃⅃⅃⅃ (Gramavision, 1996, prod. Medeski, Martin & Wood, others) to great effect, Logic heats up the fiery grooves with scratching and samples. *Combustication* also continues in a more straightforward vein, which for MMW does not mean boring or staid, just a bit more direct.

the rest:
Notes from the Underground ⅃⅃⅃⅃ (hap-Jones, 1992/Accurate, 1995)
It's a Jungle in Here ⅃⅃⅃⅃ (Gramavision, 1993)
Friday Afternoon in the Universe ⅃⅃⅃⅃ (Gramavision, 1995)
Farmers Reserve ⅃⅃⅃⅃ (Indirecto, 1997)

influences:
◀◀ Miles Davis, King Sunny Ade, Sun Ra, Herbie Hancock, James "Blood" Ulmer

▶▶ Critters Buggin, Guru, US3, Charlie Hunter

see also: *The Lounge Lizards, Marc Ribot, David Byrne*

Barry M. Prickett

Joe Meek

Born April 5, 1929, in Glouchestershire, England. Died February 3, 1967, in London, England.

Britain's first independent producer and a believer in the occult, Meek was not above holding seances in the recording studio to summon assistance from beyond the veil from his leading inspiration, Buddy Holly. When he killed himself after murdering his landlady—on the anniversary of Holly's death—Joe Meek assured his place in rock 'n' roll annals, even though his impact in the United States was limited to the 1963 #1 hit by the Tornados, "Telstar," and another modest British Invasion chart entry, "Have I the Right" by the Honeycombs. An engineer trained in the Royal Air Force, Meek helped bring Britain's nascent recording industry into the modern age. His productions employed rudimentary sound effects, celestial choirs, and majestic melodies to evoke worlds from beyond. Eccentric and inventive, Meek made more of a mark with hit records by artists unknown on the North American side of the Atlantic, people like John Leyton, Mike Berry, Heinz, and others. In England he has been the subject of a biography, a remarkable BBC documentary, as well as several reissues devoted to his recordings.

what's available: A 20-track collection of Meek's work was released in this country as *It's Hard to Believe It: The Amazing World of Joe Meek* ♫♫♫ (Razor & Tie, 1995, compilation prod. Rob Kemp), which encompasses his best-known independent productions.

worth searching for: Those fascinated by the sound and story of Meek's career should look for two British imports: *The Joe Meek Story: The Pye Years* (Sequel, 1991) and *The Joe Meek Story* (Decca, 1977); the latter offers even more exhaustive looks at recordings he made for two of the three British labels with which he customarily worked.

influences:

◀◀ Phil Spector, George Martin, Martin Denny, Les Baxter

▶▶ The Tornados, the Honeycombs, David Bowie

Joel Selvin

Mega City Four

Formed 1988, in Farnborough, England.

Wiz, guitar, vocals; Danny Brown, guitar; Gerry Bryant, bass; Chris Jones, drums.

Led by first-rate singer-songwriter-guitarist Wiz, Mega City Four—which has had the same lineup for the decade it's existed—has kept up an admirable standard of superb consistency over five studio albums plus a blizzard of non-LP singles and EP's. Known around its native England for excessive, non-stop tours in a beat-up van (thus the title of its 1989 debut LP, *Tranzophobia*), this Farnborough foursome skirted the punk scene despite the original releases' scruffy, raw assault. This was managed thanks to the melodic pop sensibility it established early on, and as the band matured, it managed to temper the attack with no loss of power. More recent work has shown a decided influence of American '80s bands that made a similar progression, such as the Replacements and Hüsker Dü (the latter of which the

Megas covered on its live LP). This progression briefly resulted in English chart success for the group during 1992, but when the fashion there turned to Oasis and Blur, the group comfortably returned to the clubs and garages from whence it sprang and even redoubled its intensity on its most recent LP.

what to buy: The Megas transformation is best heard on the magnificent *Sebastopol Rd.* ♫♫♫♫ (Big Life/Caroline, 1992, prod. Jessica Corcoran), with its well-rounded variety and non-stop dramatic moments. The glistening "Scared of Cats," the searing disquiet of "Prague," and the pulsing "Ticket Collector" run afoul of the gentle nature of Wiz's empathy, despite the pounding rhythm section. This is a tense, taut, pop mini-masterpiece, with great romantic words from one of the world's best relationship-oriented lyricists. It's also the Megas only album released in the United States, though the other titles are readily accessible. *Magic Bullets* ♫♫♫ (Big Life, 1993, prod. Chris Potter) is barely a fall-off from *Sebastopol Rd.*'s brilliance; any album that includes the punishing single "Iron Sky" is reason enough for purchase, but there are plenty of other hummable gifts, such as the kick-starting opener "Perfect Circle," the also vicious "Enemy Skies," and the quiet passion of "Speck."

what to buy next: It's hard to go wrong with the naive but energetic, souped-up smacking that is the second LP, *Who Cares Wins* ♫♫♫ (Decoy U.K., 1990, prod. Iain Burgess). Although the production mix is too muddy, there's plenty of stinging zingers, such as the slam-bang "Me Not You," the tangy charm of "Messenger," and the great harmonies and hooks of "Who Cares?" The band's latest, *Soulscraper* ♫♫♫ (Fire Records U.K., 1996, prod. Chris Potter), is its most abrasive outing in six years. Once again, Wiz's pen is as sharp as ever despite a three-year layoff, as evidenced by the bopping singles "Android Dreams," "Skidding," and "Superstar." Rocks off!

what to avoid: The first LP, *Tranzophobia* ♫♫♫ (Decoy U.K., 1989, prod. Iain Burgess), is actually not that bad; it's just too rough in spots and overshadowed as a document of the young Megas by *Terribly Sorry Bob*.

the rest:

Inspiringly Titled the Live Album ♫♫♫ (Big Life U.K., 1992)
The Peel Sessions ♫♫♫ (Strange Fruit U.K., 1993)

worth searching for: For those who want the more mainlined stuff, *Terribly Sorry Bob* (Decoy U.K., 1991, prod. various) is a knockout compilation of all 12 non-LP songs from the group's earliest singles and EP's. This hot document is one hot speedy-pop, hook-collision after another; don't miss "Finish."

influences:

◀◀ The Replacements, Hüsker Dü, the Buzzcocks

▶▶ The Doughboys, Les Thugs, Leatherface

Jack Rabid

Dave Mustaine of Megadeth (© **Ken Settle**)

Megadeth

Formed 1983, in Los Angeles, CA.

Dave Mustaine, guitar, vocals; David Ellefson, bass; Chris Poland, guitar (1983–86); Gars Samuelson, drums (1983–86); Jeff Young, guitar (1986-88); Chuck Behler, drums (1986-88); Marty Friedman, guitar (1988-present); Nick Menza, drums (1988–present).

Named for the military term for nuclear war casualties, Megadeth has been laying out arenas full of fans with tactical speed-metal strikes since leader Dave Mustaine was kicked out of Metallica during its early days. And just as that band has balanced its thrash-intensive, chops-heavy attack with measured, radio-ready hard rock, so has Mustaine, and massive popularity has been the reward for both acts, albeit on a significantly smaller scale for Megadeth. A notorious attitude problem, Mustaine was ousted from Metallica in a power struggle over control of the band and, allegedly, over his out-of-control drug use. His abuse of drugs, including heroin, continued until he was arrested for impaired driving in 1990. He cleaned up with the help of a 12-step program and apparently has stayed straight ever since, though his misbehavior got the band bounced from an

opening slot on Aerosmith's 1993 tour. But then, among metal's devoted fans, repentance is rarely seen as a virtue.

what to buy: It may pain long-time fans to read, but *Youthanasia* 𝄞𝄞𝄞𝄞 (Capitol, 1994, prod. Dave Mustaine, Max Norman) is Megadeth's best overall album. With its slower tempos, polished production, and conventional song structures, the album moved the band into the big leagues. Just as good is *Cryptic Writings* 𝄞𝄞𝄞𝄞 (Capitol, 1997, prod. Dan Huff, Dave Mustaine), which is more varied than *Youthanasia* and doesn't scrimp on the power. Meanwhile, *Rust in Peace* 𝄞𝄞𝄞𝄞 (Combat/Capitol, 1990, prod. Dave Mustaine, Mike Clink), the band's first sober effort, plays Mustaine's guitar off that of Friedman and jazz-schooled drummer Menza, allowing the fusion-influenced brand of metal envisioned by Mustaine from the very start.

what to buy next: Like its predecessor *Rust in Peace*, *Countdown to Extinction* 𝄞𝄞𝄞 (Combat/Capitol, 1992, prod. Dave Mustaine, Max Norman) features Megadeth's by-now trademark instrumental twists, but it doesn't shy away from headbanging heaviness. The best of the band's early phase, *So Far, So Good . . . So What!* 𝄞𝄞𝄞 (Capitol, 1988, prod. Paul Lani, Dave

Mustaine) cuts to the bone with Mustaine's razor-sharp guitar and double-time rhythms.

what to avoid: *Peace Sells . . . But Who's Buying?* ♫♫ (Combat/Capitol, 1986, prod. Dave Mustaine Randy Burns) has the fury, but the band seems to be treading water here.

the rest:
Killing Is My Business . . . and Business Is Good! ♫♫♫ (Combat, 1985)
Hidden Treasures ♫♫♫ (Capitol, 1995)

worth searching for: *Maximum Megadeth* (Capitol, 1991, prod. various) is an eight-song promotional sampler with live versions of "Hangar 18" and the Sex Pistols' "Anarchy in the U.K."

influences:
◄◄ Black Sabbath, Iron Maiden, the Dead Boys, the Sex Pistols
►► White Zombie, Pantera, Entombed, Corrosion of Conformity

see also: *Metallica*

Daniel Durchholz

The Mekons

Formed 1977, in Leeds, England.

Jon Langford, guitar, vocals, drums; Tom Greenhalgh, guitar, vocals; Kevin Lycett, guitar (1977–83); Mark White, vocals (1977–83); Sally Timms, vocals (1985–present); Rico Bell, accordion, vocals (1985–present); Steve Goulding, drums (1985–present); Dick Taylor, guitar (1985–91); Brendan Crocker, guitar (1985–91); Lu Edmonds, bass (1985–91, 1996–present); Susie Honeyman, violin (1985–present); Sarah Corina, bass (1994–present).

The Mekons just may be the last—and certainly longest-lived—punk band, not because its plays exclusively hard, fast, three-chord rock (on the contrary, the group has embraced numerous styles, from country to dub reggae), but in the sense that punk is an attitude, an ethic, and a way of defining one's place in the world. The band's first single, "Never Been in a Riot," gored the Clash's sacred cow, "White Riot," and the Mekons have been pursuing a singularly contrary path ever since, undeterred by a constant state of near poverty, abysmal relations with a series of record companies, and frequent lineup changes. In directing the band through a bewildering variety of incarnations, core members Jon Langford, Tom Greenhalgh, and Sally Timms have retained their fondness for biting humor, socialist politics, and buoyant live performances. Several band members relocated to Chicago during the '90s, and Langford and Steve Goulding spun off side projects such as the Waco Brothers and Skull Orchard, which perform more frequently than the Mekons, which confines itself to special appearances. These include stagings of the avant-garde musical *Pussy, King of the Pirates,* a collaboration with the late feminist author Kathy Acker and concerts/readings built around the re-

lease of the Mekons' fractured memoir and experimental CD *Mekons United*.

what to buy: *Fear and Whiskey* ♫♫♫♫♫ (Sin U.K., 1985), also contained in its entirety in the more expansive mid-period compilation *Original Sin* ♫♫♫♫ (Sin-Twin/Tone, 1989, prod. Mekons, Tony Bonner), is the Mekons' bleary, back-against-the-wall attempt to play honky-tonk music as Hank Williams and Ernest Tubb once did. It fails, of course, but it comes up with a rustic sound just as passionate and moving. Ground down by the twin boot of Reagan-Thatcher oppression, the 3 a.m. voices of Greenhalgh, Langford, and the rest sound like the last stand of the dispossessed. In *The Mekons Rock 'n' Roll* ♫♫♫♫♫ (Twin/Tone/A&M, 1989, prod. Mekons, Ian Caple), the subject is Rock 'n' Roll Inc. itself, and the music roars with an energy and vigor not heard on any Mekons record. "Memphis, Egypt," for example, takes its cues from Motörhead, and "Blow Your Tuneless Trumpet" razzes U2's "Dublin messiah" Bono.

what to buy next: *The Edge of the World* ♫♫♫♫ (Sin U.K., 1986 prod. Mekons, Tony Bonner) is nearly the mutant-country equal of *Fear and Whiskey* and introduces the subversively pure and melodious voice of Timms to the Mekons' arsenal. *The Curse of the Mekons* ♫♫♫♫ (Blast First U.K., 1991, prod. Mekons, Ian Caple) sustains the band's touch for diversity, touching on Cajun, country, Stonesy rock, and country-swing rhythms, with plenty of defiant attitude in the aftermath of the group's short-lived major-label deal with A&M Records.

what to avoid: *The Quality of Mercy Is Not Strnen* ♫♫ (Virgin U.K., 1979/Blue Plate, 1990), the band's debut, has its moments of comic relief but musically is pretty much unlistenable, even by the loose standards of punk.

the rest:
Devils Rats and Piggies: A Special Message from Godzilla ♫♫♫ (Red Rhino U.K., 1980)
It Falleth like Gentle Rain from Heaven—The Mekons Story ♫♫♫ (Feel Good All Over, 1982)
Honky Tonkin' ♫♫♫ (Sin-Twin/Tone, 1987)
So Good It Hurts ♫♫♫♫ (Twin/Tone, 1988)
F.U.N. 90 ♫♫♫ (Twin/Tone-A&M EP, 1990)
Wicked Midnight ♫♫♫ (Loud Music EP, 1992)
I ♥ Mekons ♫♫♫ (Quarterstick, 1993)
Millionaire ♫♫♫ (Quarterstick EP, 1993)
Retreat from Memphis ♫♫♫ (Quarterstick, 1994)
Mekons United ♫♫♫ (Quarterstick, 1996)
(With Kathy Acker) *Pussy, King of the Pirates* (Quarterstick, 1996)
me ♫♫♫♫ (Quarterstick, 1998)

worth searching for: *New York* (ROIR, 1987), initially available on cassette only, is an almost too-accurate account of one of the band's typically raucous tours, the mood nailed by a boozy spin through The Band's "The Shape I'm In."

influences:

◄◄ The Band, Johnny Cash, Hank Williams, Ernest Tubb, the Sex Pistols

►► The Pogues, the Palace Brothers, the Ex, the Handsome Family

Greg Kot

Melanie

Born Melanie Safka, February 3, 1947, in Queens, NY.

A guitar-wielding flower child with a sultry rasp of a voice, Melanie combined the winsome folk of late '60s Joni Mitchell with the folk-naif girlishness of England's Mary Hopkin. Somehow she managed to crack the mainstream in a way neither of those artists did. From 1969 to 1971 Melanie landed on pop charts both at home and abroad, establishing herself in the vein of other nonpolitical folk artists (Donovan, John Sebastian) with pleasant sing-alongs such as "What Have They Done to My Song, Ma?" and the chart-topping "Brand New Key." Her music has enjoyed an element of crossover success thanks to covers by Barbra Streisand, Ray Charles, and Mel Tormé, among others. Comebacks during late '80s and again in the mid-'90s showed she hasn't lost her audience or her touch. She remains a sophisticated songwriter of humane and healing themes.

what to buy: *The Best of Melanie* ♪♪♪♪ (Rhino, 1990, prod. various) is certainly the right choice to make. The 18 tracks include all six of her Top 40 hits, as well as her compelling cover of the Rolling Stones classic "Ruby Tuesday."

what to buy next: *Candles in the Rain* ♪♪♪ (Buddah, 1970, prod. Hank Hoffman) is Melanie's premiere album, featuring deft and inspired songwriting ("Lay Down," "Ruby Tuesday," "What Have They Done to My Song, Ma?") and glorious backup vocals from the gospel chorus (and Buddah labelmates) the Edwin Hawkins Singers.

what to avoid: Melanie tried to shed her girlish image on *Ballroom Streets* ♪♪ (RCA/Rhino, 1979), and while the songs are more sophisticated than on previous efforts, nothing here is as strong as her early hits.

the rest:
Leftover Wine ♪♪♥ (Buddah/One Way, 1970)
Freedom Knows My Name ♪♪♥ (Lonestars, 1993)

worth searching for: *Gather Me* (Neighborhood, 1971, prod. Peter Schekeryk), the first release on the label founded by Melanie and husband Peter Schekeryk, was a winning effort that housed "Brand New Key" and the equally wonderful "Ring the Living Bell."

WHAT ALBUM CHANGED YOUR LIFE?

[Bob Dylan's] *Highway 61 Revisited.* It's the greatest record ever made, that's why. I thought everybody knew that, that it's just common knowledge.

John Mellencamp

influences:

◄◄ Joan Baez, Odetta, the Ronettes, Dusty Springfield

►► Olivia Newton-John, Alanis Morissette, Jewel

Christopher Scapelliti

John Mellencamp

Born October 7, 1951, in Seymour, IN.

John Mellencamp is often dismissed as a bantamweight Bruce Springsteen. He too writes guitar-based rock songs about the shattered dreams of America's common folk, but just because Springsteen does a similar job better is no reason to knock Mellencamp. Rebounding from some dismal early recordings under the stage name Johnny Cougar, Mellencamp began in the early '80s to make music that was thoughtful and rollicking, with his Midwest sensibility decidedly on his sleeve. He has also displayed broad musical ambitions, going rootsy in the mid-'80s—well before the so-called No Depression movement hit—and embracing dance rhythms during the '90s. He joined forces with Willie Nelson and Neil Young to launch the Farm Aid concerts during the mid-'80s and tried his hand at record producing (for Mitch Ryder and James McMurtry) and film acting and directing (1992's *Falling from Grace*). Mellencamp suffered a minor heart attack in 1994, but a few months later he was back onstage, playing clandestine club shows and—surely to his doctors' disapproval—chain-smoking cigarettes. In 1998 he switched labels, from Mercury to Columbia, with plans to release a new album during the fall of 1998.

what to buy: Mellencamp's experiment in Appalachian garage-rock, *The Lonesome Jubilee* ♪♪♪♪♪ (Mercury, 1987, prod. John Mellencamp, Don Gehman), produced some of his most durable songs ("Paper in Fire," "Check It Out," "Cherry Bomb"). The earlier *Scarecrow* ♪♪♪♪♪ (Riva, 1985, prod. John Mellen-

John Mellencamp (© Ken Settle)

camp, Don Gehman) mixed protest songs ("Rain on the Scarecrow") with lighter but equally soulful fare such as "R.O.C.K. in the U.S.A" and "Rumbleseat."

what to buy next: *Uh-huh* ⚜⚜⚜ (Riva, 1983, prod. John Mellencamp, Don Gehman) finds the singer in full Stones-inspired glory ("Pink Houses," "The Authority Song"). *American Fool* ⚜⚜⚜ (Riva, 1982, prod. John Mellencamp, Don Gehman) was an eloquent throat-clearing, buoyed by a pair of great pop singles—"Hurt So Good" and "Jack and Diane"—that established the then-Johnny Cougar's star in the pop pantheon.

what to avoid: *Chestnut Street Incident* (Mainman/MCA, 1976/Rhino, 1986, prod. John Cougar) is a dead-end collection of cover songs.

the rest:
A Biography ⚜⚜ (Riva UK, 1978)
John Cougar ⚜⚜ (Riva, 1979)
Nothin' Matters and What If It Did ⚜⚜ (Riva, 1980)
Big Daddy ⚜⚜⚜ (Mercury, 1989)
Whenever We Wanted ⚜⚜⚜ (Mercury, 1991)
Human Wheels ⚜⚜ (Mercury, 1993)
Dance Naked ⚜⚜⚜ (Mercury, 1994)
Mr. Happy Go Lucky ⚜⚜⚜ (Mercury, 1996)
John Mellencamp ⚜⚜⚜ (Columbia, 1998)

worth searching for: Fans will want a promotional-only issue of *Dance Naked* (Mercury, 1994) in book form that featured a second CD of 18 Mellencamp hits.

influences:
◀◀ The Rolling Stones, James Brown, Mitch Ryder & the Detroit Wheels, Van Morrison, Humble Pie

▶▶ Michael McDermott, Uncle Tupelo, James McMurtry

Thor Christensen

The Melvins

Formed 1984, in Aberdeen, WA.

Buzz "King Buzzo" Osborne, vocals, guitars, bass; Dale Crover, drums; Matt Lukin, bass (1984–88); Joe Preston, bass (1988–89); Lori "Lorax" Black, bass (1989–92); Mark Deutrom, bass (1993–present).

Along with Metal Church and, later, Nirvana, the Melvins made an unlikely triptych of bands from the small logging town of Aberdeen, Washington. Musically it was the most influential (if not precisely the first; St. Vitus, perhaps, has that honor) punk band to seize upon the notion of playing as slowly as possible. It was also among the first punk bands not to repudiate their adolescent fondness for Kiss and Black Sabbath. Named for an unpopular co-worker, the group relocated to San Francisco during 1988 (leaving Matt Lukin behind to help form Mudhoney). Only the undying respect of their peers in Seattle—and a belated major

label deal—connected the group to the commercial juggernaut that followed three years later. Among the most musically iconoclastic (and enduring) of bands, the Melvins dart equally between brutal metal moods and neo-musique concrete sound sculptures—an acquired taste, but a good taste to acquire.

what to buy: Recorded in bursts and with a bass player in transition, *Houdini* ⚜⚜⚜ (Atlantic, 1993, prod. Melvins, Kurt Cobain, GGGarth Richardson) may not be the archetypal Melvins outing. It remains, however, one of the finest metal albums of a desultory decade and a singularly straight-forward introduction to the band's distinctive, menacing crunch.

what to buy next: The follow-up, *Stoner Witch* ⚜⚜⚜ (Atlantic, 1994, prod. Melvins, GGGarth Richardson), reflects the band's strongest and most versatile line-up. *Melvins* ⚜⚜⚜ (C/Z, 1986, prod. Chris Hanzsek) features the original powerhouse lineup; it actually comprises alternate takes from its original seven-song seven-inch single. *Ozma* ⚜⚜⚜ (Boner, 1989) is packaged on CD with its predecessor, *Gluey Porch Treatments* (Alchemy, 1987), which makes for a pretty fine document of the Lori "Lorax" Black years.

what to avoid: A fondness for Kiss is a fine thing, and lots of folks were tickled by the Melvins' three solo EP's packaged to resemble the Kiss solo LP's. But you can skip *King Buzzo*, *Dale Crover*, and *Joe Preston* ⚜⚜ (Boner, 1992). And even the band acknowledges that *Prick* ⚜⚜ (Amphetamine Reptile, 1994) was half-meant as a joking exercise in noise.

the rest:
Bullhead ⚜⚜ (Boner, 1991)
Self-Titled ⚜⚜ (Boner, 1992)
Stag ⚜⚜⚜ (Atlantic/Mammoth, 1996)
Honky ⚜⚜⚜ (Amphetamine Reptile, 1997)
Vol. 1—12-96 ⚜⚜ (Amphetamine Reptile, 1997)

worth searching for: If only for the exquisite packaging (and the absurdity of putting a live album on a seven-inch single collection), *Live* (Christmas, 1995), from the 1995 Tora Tora Tora Tour, is a pretty amazing document.

influences:
◀◀ Flipper, Black Sabbath, Alice Cooper, Kiss

▶▶ Nirvana, Soundgarden, Mudhoney, Marilyn Manson

Grant Alden

Men at Work

Formed 1979, in Melbourne, Australia.

Colin Hay, vocals, guitar; Ron Strykert, guitar, vocals; Jerry Speiser, drums, vocals (1979–84); Greg Ham, winds, keyboards, vocals; John Rees, bass, vocals (1979–84).

Scottish-born Colin Hay moved to Australia as a teenager and perfected his guitar skills by performing original work in pubs and universities. In 1978 he met Ron Strykert, and the next year they formed Men at Work. Mixing engaging lyrics and solid guitar playing with melodic synth-pop and a touch of horns proved to be a winning combination. Arriving at a cultural nexus—the new wave revolution was just taking off, Americans became fascinated enough with the Land Down Under to know what "Vegemite" was, and MTV was entering its first golden age of massively popular, if silly, videos—Men at Work scored a series of consecutive #1 hits.

what to buy: *Contraband: The Best of Men at Work* ♫♫♫♫ (Columbia/Legacy, 1995, prod. various) is all you really need to own; it has the hits from the first two albums, as well as some overlooked songs, such as "Hard Luck Story," from the out-of-print third album, *Two Hearts*.

what to buy next: The first album, *Business as Usual* ♫♫♫♫ (Columbia, 1981, prod. Peter Mclan) quickly went multi-platinum, becoming a huge international success, earning the group a Best New Artist Grammy, and spawning the hits "Who Can It Be Now" and "Down Under." The follow-up, *Cargo* ♫♫♫ (Columbia, 1993, prod. Peter Mclan), comes in just a shade behind and contains the hits "It's a Mistake," "Overkill," and "Dr. Heckyll and Mr. Jive."

the rest: *Brazil* ♫♫ (Legacy, 1998)

worth searching for: Men at Work's staunchest fans will likely want to seek out Hay's solo albums *Looking for Jack* (Columbia, 1987) and *Wayfaring Sons* (MCA, 1990), though the general populace will find little of interest there.

influences:
◀◀ The Police, Split Enz, the Beatles
▶▶ Wang Chung, Third Eye Blind, Dave Matthews Band

Bryan Lassner

Men Without Hats

Formed 1980, in Montreal, Quebec, Canada.

Ivan Doroschuk, vocals; Stefan Doroschuk, guitar; Colin Doroschuk, keyboards; Allan McCarthy, drums.

Men Without Hats' first single was "The Safety Dance," which hit #3 in 1983. Its repetitive octave-interval synth riff stuck itself into pop consciousness like a lawn dart; only the Knack's "My Sharona" had the same madness-inducing jumpy repetition. And also like the Knack, Men Without Hats would fail to expand on its initial success. Bound up by serious artistic ambitions, the group's novelty pop songs often suffered from delusions of grandeur, making them a lot less fun than "The

Safety Dance." The band made some headway in 1987 with "Pop Goes the World," a weightlessly engaging ditty that has a fair amount of charm. But the band's career was all but over by the early '90s.

what to buy: *Collection* ♫♫♫ (Oglio, 1996, prod. various) offers the group's two hits and its more listenable fare, such as "I Got the Message" and "I Like," revealing that underneath the pomposity were a few pop songs with more enduring qualities than "The Safety Dance."

the rest: *Rhythm of Youth* ♫♫♫ (MCA, 1983)

influences:
◀◀ The Human League, Duran Duran

Allan Orski

Menswear

Formed 1994, in London, England.

Johnny Dean, vocals; Chris Gentry, guitar; Stuart Black, bass; Simon White, guitar; Mathew Everett, drums.

Formed out of the trendy Camden mod revival scene, Menswear had the distinction of being the first band to play *Top of the Pops* before releasing an album. This was fine with the band members, since in their minds they were born rock stars. Their good looks and cavalier attitude helped convince the press of this delusion, but the love affair was short lived. Critics soon started calling the band an updated version of the Monkees. After just one moderately received album, which went straight to the budget bins in America, Menswear stalled in a mess of nervous breakdowns and substance abuse.

what's available: *Nuisance* ♫♫ (Laurel/London, 1995, prod. Neil King) is not as bad as one would imagine. For every blatant Wire rip-off ("Daydreamer"), there is a song like "Hollywood Girl," which shows a remarkable amount of lyrical and melodic maturity.

influences:
◀◀ Blur, Pulp, Wire

Aidin Vaziri

Natalie Merchant

See: 10,000 Maniacs

Freddie Mercury

See: Queen

Mercury Rev

Formed 1989, in Buffalo, NY.

Jimmy Chambers, drums; Jonathan Donahue, guitar, vocals; Grasshopper, guitar; Suzanne Thorpe, bass, flute; Dave Fridmann, bass (1989–94); David Baker, vocals (1989–94); Jason Russo, bass (1994–present).

Mercury Rev makes voluptuous songs that cavort around with everything from tubas to strings. The band's penchant for experimental space rock, described by some as the "music of entropy," makes it the kind of group people either love or hate—like a chaotic medium between Sun Ra and Sonic Youth. Former bassist Dave Fridmann formed the band in 1989 as his senior project at the University of Buffalo. The group originally began doing scores for their friends' student films, recording directly onto 35mm magnetic film. After finding early critical success in the U.K., the band—which makes its home in the nooks of the Catskill Mountains—didn't quite become a mainstream hit stateside; this is, after all, a group that got booted from the 1993 Lollapalooza tour for being too noisy. Later that year, after two albums, Fridmann and lead singer David Baker left the group, stripping the band, the remaining members said, of the acrimonious tension. Surprisingly, the group maintained all of its artsy moxy, but with less noise and weirdness.

what to buy: Mercury Rev's second album, *Boces* 𝄢𝄢𝄢𝄢 (Columbia, 1993, prod. Mercury Rev), is an amazing audio experience that sonically reveals something new with each listen. The band seemed to have found its voice. However, after lead singer Baker left the group later that year, the remaining members made *See You on the Other Side* 𝄢𝄢𝄢𝄢 (WORK Group, 1994, prod. Mercury Rev), which turned out to be no less intense a piece of work. Devoid of its excesses, Mercury Rev found a more refined identity that somehow seemed to work.

what to buy next: You'll know instantly if Mercury Rev intrigues you or not and, if it does, everything the group puts out is worth getting. While its debut, *Yerself Is Steam* 𝄢𝄢𝄢𝄢 (Columbia, 1992, prod. Mercury Rev), is a bit raw, it is very much worth having for Rev fans.

worth searching for: The singles the group puts out always give people a little something extra for their money. Two in particular are those for "Chasing a Bee" and "Something for Joey": the former includes an intoxicated cover of Sly & the Family Stones' "If You Want Me to Stay," while the latter ends with a lengthy interview with former porn star Ron Jeremy, who also stars in the song's video.

solo outings:
David Baker:
(With Shady) *World* 𝄢𝄢𝄢 (Beggars Banquet, 1994)

influences:
◀◀ Sun Ra, Sonic Youth, Spacemen Three, My Bloody Valentine

▶▶ Tortoise, Ui

Joseph Patel

Mercyland

See: Bob Mould/Sugar

The Mermen

Formed 1986, in San Francisco, CA.

Jim Thomas, guitar; Allen Whitman, bass; Martyn Jones, drums.

Think instrumental surf-rock has run its course? Well, think again. The San Francisco–based Mermen transcend the genre and forge a powerfully unique sound. Jim Thomas's inspired, soaring guitar work is amazing, while Allen Whitman and Martyn Jones add great melodic reach to the songs. Vocals aren't needed by the Mermen, as their sound ranges from aggressively gripping to lush atmospherics—often within a single cut.

what to buy: *Songs of the Cows* 𝄢𝄢𝄢𝄢𝄡 (Mesa, 1996, prod. Jim Thomas) is listed as an EP, yet at nearly 35 minutes it is actually a bargain-priced epic. Led off by the twangy "Curve," which might make Dick Dale lop off his pony-tail, *Songs of the Cows* is almost perfect. While occasionally veering towards prog-rock, the record rips and curls in all the right places.

what to buy next: *A Glorious Lethal Euphoria* 𝄢𝄢𝄢𝄢 (Toadphile/Mesa, 1995, prod. Jim Thomas, Mermen), ponderous title notwithstanding, is amazing. The rhythm section of Whitman and Jones is incredibly precise, as Thomas again puts on a surf-guitar clinic.

the rest:
Krill Slippin' 𝄢𝄢𝄢𝄢 (Kelptone, 1989/Beach, 1995)

worth searching for: Two other sadly out-of-print Mermen LPs exist. The dreamy, ambitious *Food for Other Fish* (Kelptone, 1994, prod. Mermen, Jon Kerr) has an ethereal, sometimes ambient nature. Also of note is *Live at the Haunted House* (Shittone, 1995, prod. Phil Dirt, Mermen), a rollicking live recording from various San Francisco–area venues. *Brine the Anti-Surf Companion* (Beach, 1997, prod. Allen Whitman) is a lovingly assembled compilation by bassist Whitman; it includes tracks by Scenic, the Mermen, DJ Spooky, Loop Guru, and others.

influences:
◀◀ Ennio Morricone, the Ventures, Jimi Hendrix, Dick Dale, Duane Eddy, Martin Denny

▶▶ The Volcanos, Galaxy Trio, Laika & the Cosmonauts, Man or Astro-Man?

Barry M. Prickett

James Hetfield of Metallica (© Ken Settle)

The Merry-Go-Round /Emitt Rhodes

Formed 1965, in Hawthorne, CA. Disbanded 1969.

Emitt Rhodes, vocals, guitar; Gary Kato, guitar, vocals; Bill Rhinehart, bass; Joel Larson, drums.

Perhaps America's best-ever response to the kind of melodic magic wrought by the Beatles came from this California quartet and, later, from frontman Emitt Rhodes as a solo act. At the tender age of 16, Rhodes formed the Merry-Go-Round, whose one album and two additional 45's feature sprightly melodies and Rhodes's English-inflected singing backed by winning harmonies, a crunchy guitar attack, and Paul McCartneyesque bass work. After disbanding the group, Rhodes resurfaced as a solo act for three albums on Dunhill, producing, playing every instrument, and singing every vocal—just like his greatest influence, McCartney, did on his debut solo album. Many of these tracks feature nice keyboard underpinnings as well as the standard guitar backing, and most feature irresistible hooks. Sadly, Rhodes disappeared from view after 1973, recording only for his personal pleasure in his garage studio.

what to buy: *Listen, Listen: The Best of Emitt Rhodes* 🎵🎵🎵🎵 (Varese Sarabande, 1995, compilation prod. Cary Mansfield, Michael Amicone) does a good job of compiling the best of those albums plus key Merry-Go-Round tracks.

what to buy next: The straight reissue of Rhodes's first solo LP, *Emitt Rhodes* 🎵🎵🎵 (Dunhill, 1970/One Way, 1993, prod. Emitt Rhodes, Harvey Bruce), features mostly sunny, upbeat tunes such as "Fresh as a Daisy" and "Live 'till You Die," but also the tougher-sounding "Long Time No See."

worth searching for: The now out-of-print *The Best of the Merry-Go-Round* (Rhino, 1985, prod. Larry Marks) features additional Merry-Go-Round tracks not on the Varese Sarabande collection, as well as fine pre-Dunhill solo work and a superb unreleased track, "Saturday Night."

influences:

◄◄ The Beatles, the Beach Boys, Buddy Holly

►► The Raspberries, Cheap Trick, the Plimsouls, 20/20

Mike Greenfield

Jim Messina

See: Poco, Loggins & Messina

Metallica

Formed 1981, in Los Angeles, CA.

James Hetfield, guitar, vocals; Lars Ulrich, drums; Dave Mustaine, guitar (1981–83); Ron McGovney, bass (1981–83); Kirk Hammett, gui-

WHAT ALBUM CHANGED YOUR LIFE?

At the point when I was first trying to play bass, *Ace of Spades* from Motörhead was a big deal for me, just because it was a big-time production. They really put some money into that one. The way the bass worked, [Lemmy Kilminster] was playing with a pick, and it was distorted. I didn't start playing with a pick until I heard Lemmy.

Jason Newsted (of Metallica)

tar (1983–present); **Cliff Burton (died September 27, 1986), bass (1983–86); Jason Newsted, bass (1986–present).**

A monster band whose ferocious attack defined a new brand of heavy metal during the '80s, Metallica is the closest thing this generation has to a Led Zeppelin. Integrity is the key here; Metallica has always flown a flag of no-compromise, which meant that when the rock 'n' roll mainstream (including radio) finally embraced the group during the early '90s, it was a strong bond built gradually by years of relentless touring and literally headbanging away at every corner of the globe to be heard. The group takes its sonic sledgehammer—replete with stop-start dynamics, doomy ambience and leaden rhythms—from both British metal bands and punk rockers, though it certainly dresses up any lessons taken from the latter in a hellish, heavier sonic garb than you'll generally hear at CBGB. When Kirk Hammett and Cliff Burton joined Metallica in 1983—the former replacing Dave Mustaine, who went on to form Megadeth—the group's sound coalesced. Since then it's only been refined, but strictly on Metallica's terms. That its last several albums have turned the group into and maintained its status as an arena-filling rock radio favorite (and the headliner of the 1996 Lollapalooza tour!) is merely a sign that the audience has met the band half-way, which is the way many a lasting musical relationship has been created.

what to buy: *Metallica* 🎵🎵🎵🎵 (Elektra, 1991, prod. Bob Rock, James Hetfield, Lars Ulrich) is an exceptional hard rock album, retaining the sinister, subversive edge that won the group its underground following amidst considerable growth in craft. "Enter Sandman" and "Sad but True" are pulverizing, but "Nothing Else Matters" is disarmingly pretty and melodic. Metallica really hit stride with the aptly titled *Ride the Lightning* ⅃⅃⅃⅃ (Elektra, 1984, prod. Mark Whittaker), a sizzling, electrifying assault that contains continuing concert favorites such as "For Whom the Bell Tolls," "Fade to Black," and "Creeping Death."

what to buy next: *Master of Puppets* ⅃⅃⅃⅃ (Elektra, 1986, prod. Flemming Rasmussen, Metallica) refined *Ride the Lightning*'s ground-shaking dynamics and was the group's first million-seller. *Live Shit: Binge & Purge* ⅃⅃⅃⅃ (Elektra, 1993, prod. James Hetfield, Lars Ulrich) is an over-the-top live box set—three CDs, three videos, a book, and a stencil of the band's scary guy mascot. Know what? Metallica is such a tremendous live act it's worth it. *Load* ⅃⅃⅃⅃ (Elektra, 1996, prod. Bob Rock, James Hetfield, Lars Ulrich) is darker than *Metallica* and finds the band trying on a few of the sonic stances introduced by so-called alternative rockers after *Metallica* was released. *Re-Load* ⅃⅃⅃⅃ (Elektra, 1997, prod. Bob Rock, James Hetfield, Lars Ulrich) takes the experiments a step further, using acoustic instrumentation, industrial touches, and an amazing cameo by Marianne Faithfull ("The Memory Remains"), all to fine effect.

what to avoid: *. . . And Justice for All* ⅃⅃ (Elektra, 1988, prod. Flemming Rasmussen) is conceptually sound, but the production is too dense and murky to give the songs their due.

the rest:
Kill 'Em All ⅃⅃ (Megaforce, 1983/Elektra, 1987)
Garage Days Inc. N/A (Elektra, 1998)

worth searching for: *The $9.98 CD—Garage Days Revisited* (Elektra EP, 1987, prod. Metallica) is a spirited collection of covers of songs by influences and friends such as the Misfits and Killing Joke. It marks Newsted's first work with the band and is sadly out of print, although for late 1998 the group was planning to reissue it in a new package, *Garage Days Re-Revisited*, fleshed out with other covers and B-sides.

influences:

◀◀ Black Sabbath, Iron Maiden, Queen, the Misfits, Killing Joke, the Sex Pistols

▶▶ Megadeth, Danzig, Slayer

see also: *Megadeth*

Gary Graff

The Meters

Formed 1967, in New Orleans, LA. Disbanded 1977. Re-formed 1990.

Art Neville, keyboards, vocals; Leo Nocentelli, guitar; George Porter Jr., bass; Zig Modeliste, drums (1967–77); Cyril Neville, percussion, vocals (1975–77); David Russell Baptiste, drums (1990–present).

The Meters cooked up some of the most intoxicating grooves in the history of funk, adding the flavor of the syncopated rhythms of the group's hometown, New Orleans. Under the leadership of organist Art Neville—overseen by impresario Allen Toussaint—the quartet assembled during the late '60s as the house band for Toussaint and Marshall Sehorn's label, Josie. Between studio sessions for a panoply of New Orleans soul artists and grueling live work, the Meters honed a funky chemistry that surfaced most distinctively on the instrumental tracks the group cut toward the end of the decade. A few of these recordings became R&B hits, notably "Sophisticated Cissy," "Cissy Strut," "Looka-Py-Py," and "Chicken Strut." After signing with Reprise during the early '70s, the Meters moved into rock-soul territory, with vocals provided by Neville. While none of the band's albums achieved the success of its leaner '60s instrumentals, the Meters have been widely influential and frequently sampled, with a track record of backing up other acts such as Dr. John, Paul McCartney & Wings, the Pointer Sisters, and Robert Palmer. The band broke up in 1977 but has reunited in different configurations into the '90s; legal disputes involving the name of the band and the rights to their recordings were mostly resolved by the middle of that decade. Neville's main gig is with the Neville Brothers, a troupe that has enjoyed some of the commercial success that the Meters never found.

what to buy: A fine introduction to these masters of New Orleans funk can be found on *The Very Best of the Meters* ⅃⅃⅃⅃ (Rhino,1997, prod. Allen Toussaint, others), a 16-song set that features the group's most popular numbers. For those who want even more, the 41-song, two-CD anthology *Funkify Your Life* ⅃⅃⅃⅃ (Rhino, 1995, compilation prod. James Austin, Don Snowden, John Brenes) collects most of the group's important tracks, with one disc devoted to its work for Josie and the other sifting the wheat of the Reprise years from the substantial chaff.

what to buy next: The best album-length collection of Meters instrumentals, *Looka Py-Py* ⅃⅃⅃⅃ (Josie, 1969/Rounder, 1990, prod. Allen Toussaint, Marshall Sehorn), captures the band at its grooving peak.

what to avoid: The band's first farewell album, *New Directions* ⅃⅃ (Reprise, 1977, prod. David Rubinson, others), dilutes its greasy funk with soggy rock tropes and is a far cry from the economy of its best work.

the rest:
The Meters ⅃⅃⅃⅃ (Josie, 1969)

Struttin' ♪♪♪♪ (Josie, 1970)

Cabbage Alley ♪♪♪ (Reprise, 1972)

Fire on the Bayou ♪♪♪ (Reprise, 1975)

The Best of the Meters ♪♪♪♪ (Virgo, 1975/Mardis Gras, 1996)

Trick Bag ♪♪♪♪ (Reprise, 1976)

Good Old Funky Music ♪♪♪ (Rounder, 1990)

Funky Miracle ♪♪♪♪ (Charly, 1991)

The Meters Jam ♪♪♪ (Rounder, 1992)

Uptown Rulers: The Meters Live on the Queen Mary ♪♪♪ (Rounder, 1992)

The Original Funkmasters ♪♪♪ (Instant, 1993/Charly, 1997)

Fundamentally Funky ♪♪♪ (Charly, 1994)

worth searching for: The hard-to-find *Rejuvenation* (Reprise, 1974, prod. Allen Toussaint, Meters) has a few vital tracks that didn't make it to the Rhino anthology. Also, the group's presence is strongly felt on Toussaint's *Life, Love, & Faith* (Charly, 1994, prod. Allen Toussaint) and *The Wild Tchoupioulas* (Mango, 1976, prod. Allen Toussaint).

influences:

◀◀ James Brown, Booker T. & the MG's, Allen Toussaint, Professor Longhair

▶▶ Parliament-Funkadelic, the Neville Brothers, Prince, Red Hot Chili Peppers, Beastie Boys, De La Soul

see also: *The Neville Brothers, Allen Toussaint*

Simon Glickman and Ken Burke

Method Man

See: Wu-Tang Clan

Miami Sound Machine

See: Gloria Estefan

George Michael /Wham! /Andrew Ridgely

Formed 1981, in London, England. Disbanded 1986.

George Michael (born Georgios Kyriacos Panayiotou, June 25, 1963 in London, England), vocals; Andrew Ridgely, vocals, guitar.

When lightweight British pop bands began storming the American charts during the early '80s, it was George Michael's talent that set Wham! apart from its competition. In a glut of synthesizers and hairstyles, it was the songs the honey-voiced singer authored for Wham!'s brief string of albums that gave the duo's music uncommon appeal, with a sound that clinched the U.S. R&B tradition and set it to a contemporary pop beat. Wham!'s exhaustive success caused Michael to disband the group at the height of its popularity in 1986 and head out on a solo career

that proved initially more lustrous, though he has since bogged down in high-minded denouncements of pop music marketing and an unsuccessful lawsuit against his old record company. It didn't help that after a six-year sabbatical, Michael refused to do any promotion work for his 1996 comeback album *Older*. Two years later, he was arrested for masturbating in the rest room at a Los Angeles park and publicly acknowledged the sexuality most had figured out, anyway.

what to buy: Michael did not come into his creative prime until *Listen without Prejudice: Vol. 1* ♪♪♪♪ (Columbia, 1990, prod. George Michael), an album filled with melancholy lyrics and lush, soaring melodies that recalled the great pop and soul hits of the '60s. As Michael's commanding artistic statement, it gave the former teen idol uncharacteristic depth, inspiring comparisons to everyone from Stevie Wonder to Elton John.

what to buy next: Michael's solo debut, *Faith* ♪♪♪ (Columbia, 1987, prod. George Michael), sold nearly 15 million copies worldwide and represented an artistic leap from the pre-fab pop of Wham!, balancing soulful ballads ("Kissing a Fool") with hard-hitting dance numbers ("Monkey," "I Want Your Sex").

what to avoid: Michael's talentless Wham! partner Andrew Ridgely made a dismal attempt at a solo singing career with *Son of Albert* **woof!** (Epic, 1990), which deservingly slipped through the cracks unnoticed.

the rest:

George Michael:

Older ♪♪♪ (DreamWorks, 1996)

Ladies and Gentlemen . . . The Best of George Michael N/A (DreamWorks, 1998)

Wham!:

Fantastic ♪♪ (Columbia, 1983)

Make It Big! ♪♪ (Columbia, 1984)

Music from the Edge of Heaven ♪♪♪ (Columbia, 1986)

worth searching for: Paying tribute to Queen's legendary late singer Freddy Mercury, Michael joined the British group onstage at Wembley with special guest Lisa Stansfield. The resulting EP, *Five Live* (Hollywood, 1992), features several remarkable covers by the assemblage, including a take on Seal's "Killer."

influences:

◀◀ Elton John, Duran Duran, Aretha Franklin

▶▶ Seal, Babyface, Backstreet Boys

Aidin Vaziri

Lee Michaels

Born November 24, 1945, in Los Angeles, CA.

Lee Michaels's organ-heavy soul-rock was an anomaly in guitar-happy California during the mid-'60s. Michaels worked with a number of inconsequential bands until moving to San Francisco during 1965 and coming under the influence of the Jefferson Airplane (Michaels had formerly worked with Airplane drummer John Barbata). A talented producer, Michaels became enamored of overdubbing and began playing all the instruments on his records shortly after garnering a contract. His eponymous third album, a jam between Michaels and drummer Frosty (Bartholomew Eugene Smith-Frost), gave Michaels his first large-scale public notice, and he remained a draw for the next few years, scoring a major hit, "Do You Know What I Mean?," in 1971. When Michaels lost drummer Keith Knudsen to the Doobie Brothers in 1973, he retired for a short while before returning to a lower rung on the music biz ladder.

what to buy: Most of what you want to hear from him—including "Do You Know What I Mean?," "Highty-Hi," and "Stormy Monday"—can be found on *The Lee Michaels Collection* ♪♪♪♪ (Rhino, 1992, prod. various).

the rest:
Carnival of Life ♪♪♪ (A&M, 1968/One Way, 1996)
Recital ♪♪♪♪ (A&M, 1969/One Way, 1996)
Lee Michaels ♪♪♪ (1970/One Way, 1996)
Barrell ♪♪♪ (A&M, 1970/One Way, 1996)
5th ♪♪♪♪ (A&M, 1971/One Way, 1996)
Live ♪♪♪ (A&M, 1972/One Way, 1996)
Space & First Takes ♪♪ (A&M, 1972/One Way, 1996)
The Best of Lee Michaels ♪♪♪♪ (One Way, 1997)

influences:
◀◀ Ray Charles, Booker T. Jones, Huey "Piano" Smith

▶▶ James Taylor Quartet, Sly Stone

Lawrence Gabriel

Mickey & Sylvia

Formed 1955. Disbanded 1965.

Mickey Baker (born McHouston Baker, October 15, 1923 in Louisville, KY), guitar; Sylvia Vanderpool (born March 6, 1936 in New York, NY), vocals.

Individually, or as a duo, Mickey "Guitar" Baker and Sylvia Vanderpool are two extremely important figures in the history of American popular music. During the early to mid-'50s, Baker virtually defined the role of electric rock guitar on sessions for such R&B greats as Big Maybelle, Ray Charles, Ruth Brown, Screamin' Jay Hawkins, Ivory Joe Hunter, the Coasters, and Little Willie John. No stranger to blues, jazz, or even rockabilly (he did sessions with the legendary Joe Clay), Baker's biting lead style is as distinctive as Chuck Berry's, though much more flexible. When he wasn't cutting hit records or playing behind the biggest stars of early rock in Alan Freed's stage shows, Baker

cut many fine blues, jazz, and calypso-flavored sides for the Savoy, Vik, Groove, and Atlantic labels, though few received much notice outside of musician's circles. Baker's collaboration with Sylvia Vanderpool (whom he married and taught to play guitar) provided his commercial breakthrough. Their 1956 hit "Love Is Strange" showcased a sexy and sassy interplay ("Oh Sylvia—How do you call your lover boy?" "I say, 'C'MERE LOVER BOY!'") as well as Baker's stinging guitar fills. Their formula, based loosely on Les Paul and Mary Ford, yielded several more R&B hits, including "There Ought to Be a Law," "What Would I Do," "Bewitched," and "Baby, You're So Fine." The couple divorced in 1961, though they would continue to work together on and off until the mid-'60s. For a time, Baker recorded with Kitty Noble as Mickey & Kitty, but the chemistry wasn't the same. After publishing several highly successful (and widely influential) guitar instruction books, Baker moved to France, where he still records occasionally. Vanderpool, who married producer Jim Robinson, billed herself simply as Sylvia and went on to record the 1973 hit "Pillow Talk." She also founded her own label, Sugar Hill Records, which issued the first rap records by such notables as the Sugarhill Gang and Grandmaster Flash.

what to buy: An excellent mid-priced 18-song disc, *Love Is Strange: A Golden Classics Edition* ♪♪♪♪ (Collectables, 1997, prod. various) features Mickey & Sylvia's biggest hits—"Love Is Strange," "There Oughta Be a Law," and "Bewildered." Baker's guitar work is evident in fills and solos, but it's the duo's sly chemistry that makes this disc such a delight. There are fewer tracks on *Love Is Strange & Other Hits* ♪♪♪♪ (RCA, 1990, prod. various), but it is a strong introductory collection nonetheless.

what to buy next: Many of Baker's early '50s solo recordings for Savoy, Vik, and Groove are on *Rock with a Sock* ♪♪♪ (Bear Family, 1994, reissue prod. Richard Weize), a somewhat pricey 28-song collection. Sharing vocal chores with Larry Dale, Baker effortlessly mixes jazz and blues on such scintillating tracks as "Guitar Mambo," "Riverboat," and "Spinning Rock Boogie." As a bonus, five rare tracks with Sylvia are included. Also, Mickey & Sylvia's recordings for their own label during the '60s are on *The Willow Sessions* ♪♪♪♪ (Sequel, 1996, prod. Mickey & Sylvia), a 19-track compilation that includes the hit "Baby, You're So Fine" as well as Sylvia's first solo recordings for the All Platinum label.

worth searching for: Nearly all the Mickey & Sylvia recordings (1955–64) have been compiled on the German import *Love Is Strange* (Bear Family, 1994, reissue prod. Richard Weize), a two-disc, 60-song set that includes a booklet with extensive recording information. Baker's first non-Sylvia LP, *Wildest Guitar* (Atlantic, 1959, prod. Tom Dowd), is a favorite among guitar snobs and well worth hearing for its transformation of such pop standards as "Night and Day," "Autumn Leaves," and "The Third Man Theme" into inspired jazz/blues work-outs. Baker cut some wild tracks with Joe Clay, which are on *Get Hot or Go Home: Vintage RCA Rockabilly '56–'59* (Country Music Foundation, 1989, prod. Country Music Foundation); it includes tough takes on "Get on the Right Track," "You Look That Good to Me," and "Cracker Jack." Also worth tracking down is Baker's *Blues, Jazz & Rock Guitar: The Legendary Mickey "Guitar" Baker* (Kicking Mule, 1977/Shanachie, 1992), a fine collection of R&B standards and instrumentals originally recorded for Stefan Grossman's label.

influences:

◀◀ Charlie Christian, Little Esther, Les Paul & Mary Ford, Shirley & Lee

▶▶ Steve Cropper, Roy Buchanan, Ike & Tina Turner

Ken Burke

Midnight Oil

Formed 1976, in Sydney, Australia.

Peter Garrett, vocals; Jim Mogine, guitar, keyboards; Rob Hirst, drums; Martin Rotsey, guitar; Andrew "Bear" James, bass (1976–79); Peter Gifford, bass (1979–87); Bones Hillman, bass (1990–present).

A muscular outfit with a burning social conscience, Midnight Oil honed its chops in the Sydney pubs where its incendiary live act has long been revered. Led by the towering, shaven-headed Peter Garret, the band's political messages are raging forces, matched by Jim Mogine's inventive hard-nosed melodies and Rob Hirst's impassioned pounding. Whether standing up for aboriginal Australians' rights or nuclear disarmament, or simply blasting away at suburban complacency, the Oils have maintained individualistic integrity while gradually toning down the musical attack in order to achieve mainstream acceptance.

what to buy: *10, 9, 8, 7, 6, 5, 4, 3, 2, 1* 𝄞𝄞𝄞𝄞 (Columbia, 1983, prod. Nick Launay, Midnight Oil) matches the band's intensity with its strongest (and most articulate) set of songs to date. Starting with the slow burn of "Outside World," the bone-rattling "Only the Strong" follows like a jet whipping through your back yard. And that's just the first two songs. To glimpse the thunder of its live shows, *Scream in Blue* 𝄞𝄞𝄞 (Columbia, 1992, prod. Midnight Oil, Keith Walker) is a raw (and random) selection that includes fierce versions of many lesser-known songs, such as "Brave Faces" and "Progress," as well as "Read about It" and "Only the Strong." *Red Sails in the Sunset* 𝄞𝄞𝄞𝄞 (Columbia, 1985, prod. Nick Launay, Midnight Oil) finds the band at its most ambitious, welding funk and dense atmospheric keyboards to hard-rock roots. Though it's not as cohesive as any of

Midnight Oil's distinctive individual albums, the best-of CD *20,000 Watt R.S.L.* 𝄞𝄞𝄞 (Sony, 1997, prod. various) includes "Blue Sky Mine," "Beds Are Burning," "Back on the Borderline," and "Forgotten Years," saving newcomers the trouble of sifting through the band's big catalog for the key songs.

what to buy next: Softer, muted tones dilute the blow of *Diesel and Dust* 𝄞𝄞𝄞 (Columbia, 1989, prod. Warne Livesy, Midnight Oil), but "Beds Are Burning," "Dreamworld," and "Warakurna" are sturdy enough to support the radio-ready flavor. The softer sound sets in for good on *Blue Sky Mining* 𝄞𝄞𝄞 (Columbia, 1990, prod. Warren Livesey, Midnight Oil); it doesn't match the excitement levels of *Diesel*, although the tuneful title track, "King of the Mountain," and "Forgotten Years" nearly make up for the lulls. *Head Injuries* 𝄞𝄞𝄞 (Columbia, 1978, prod. Leszek J. Karski) is the band's best pre– *10, 9, 8...* work. The pure, lean muscle of "Cold, Cold Change" and "Back on the Borderline" are prime examples of the formative years.

what to avoid: *Earth and Sun and Moon* 𝄞𝄞 (Columbia, 1993, prod. Nick Launay, Midnight Oil) is an ill-conceived attempt to return to the band's early rawness. Short on decent material, it sounds forced and redundant.

the rest:

Midnight Oil 𝄞𝄞 (Powderworks, 1978/Columbia, 1990)
Bird Noises 𝄞𝄞𝄞 (Powderworks EP, 1979/Columbia, 1990)
Place without a Postcard 𝄞𝄞𝄞 (Columbia, 1981/1990)
Species Deceases 𝄞𝄞𝄞𝄞 (Columbia EP, 1985/1990)
Redneck Wonderland N/A (Columbia, 1998)

worth searching for: *The Green Disc* (Columbia, 1989, prod. various) is an exceptional, but promotional-only, retrospective with hits, remixes, and unreleased tracks.

influences:

◀◀ The Clash, the Easybeats, Split Enz

▶▶ Love & Rockets, INXS, Silverchair

Allan Orski

Mighty Blue Kings

Formed 1995, in Chicago, IL.

Ross Bon, vocals; Jimmy Sutton, bass (1995–97); Clark Sommers, bass (1997–present); Gareth Best, guitar; Samuel Burckhardt, saxophone; Jerry Devivo, saxophone, drums; Bob Carter, drums; Donny Nichilo, piano.

At an average age of 26, this charismatic, tuxedoed group of Chicago-based musicians became leaders of the jump-blues resurgence and icons of the new cocktail nation, throwing out timeless tunes to martini-gulping capacity crowds all over the country. Though West Coast cats such as Royal Crown Revue got the jump, so to speak, on the Kings, Ross Bon and Co. kick some serious tail in the class, vitality, and talent departments. Bon, the group's founder and spiritual leader, cut his teeth on the Chicago blues circuit. Taking the dress, audience rapport, and quiet confidence from old-timers such as Willie Smith and Pinetop Perkins, the young baritone teamed up with standouts from the local rock and jazz scenes and secured a weekly gig at noted Chicago jazz hotspot the Green Mill. Drawing crowds that transcended the local social structure, the Mighty Blue Kings soon grew out of the club and took its act on the road, signing with Sony Records in late 1997.

what to buy: *Come One, Come All* 𝄪𝄪𝄪 (R-Jay, 1997, prod. Mighty Blue Kings) showcases the Kings' musicianship with soaring bebop saxophone breaks and cutting, bluesy piano solos. More tight and full than its predecessor, it packs more punch and oozes more charm. The band splits the album between covers and originals, and Bon's songwriting skills have improved tremendously.

what to buy next: It's onomatopoeia unbound on *The Mighty Blue Kings* 𝄪𝄪𝄪 (R-Jay, 1996, prod. Wally Hersom, Mighty Blue Kings), as songs such as "Buzz Buzz Buzz" and "Honey Chile Jump" make the Kings' debut sound like it leaped right out of a postwar juke joint. The album is equal parts covers and originals, and if it weren't for the Chicago references ("Jumpin' at the Green Mill," "Meet Me in Uptown"), it would be hard to tell the difference between the two. The only transgression here is that the Kings spend too much time copying that jump-blues sound and not enough developing its own distinct brand.

influences:

◄◄ Louis Jordan, Louis Armstrong, Pinetop Perkins, Royal Crown Revue

►► Chicago Jump Company, the Big Swing

Isaac Josephson

Mighty Joe Plum

Formed 1995, in Tampa, FL.

Brett Williams, vocals; Marlin Clark, guitar; Mark Mercado, drums; Davy Mason, bass.

Florida is primarily known for heavy metal, so when Mighty Joe Plum formed, its music wasn't an easy sell to record companies. Scraping together money earned from club gigs, Mighty Joe Plum entered the studio to whip out a quick demo. One of the songs, "Live through This (Fifteen Stories)," weaseled its way onto Tampa radio station WXTB and became a hit. Cashing in on the single, Mighty Joe Plum returned to the studio and recorded its debut, the full-length *Aardvark*, which sold as many as 200 copies per week at its peak.

what's available: *The Happiest Dogs* 𝄪 (Atlantic, 1997, prod. Justin Niebank), a dog of an album, is a re-recording of *Aardvark*. Not especially catchy, *The Happiest Dogs* blends the classic rock of Lynyrd Skynyrd with a more modern sound that recalls Matchbox 20 and Hootie & the Blowfish. The jangly "Live through This" includes the curious lyric "what if I were sticky enough to walk the ceiling." "Borderline" begins *a capella* and rambles through two or so minutes of blase rock.

influences:

◄◄ Hootie & the Blowfish, Matchbox 20, Lynyrd Skynyrd

Christina Fuoco

Mighty Lemon Drops

Formed 1985, in Wolverhampton, England.

Paul Marsh, vocals; David Newton, guitar; Keith Rowley, drums; Tony Linehan, bass (1985–89); Marcus Williams, bass (1989–93).

What happens when your "one hit" isn't even really a hit? Well, if you're the Mighty Lemon Drops, you make five other albums of similarly listenable, commercially uninteresting music before futility screams you into silence. Barely holding the torch Echo & the Bunnymen passed along at the end of the '80s, singer Paul Marsh and company hit pay-dust with an inspired, if simply nostalgic, postmodern hit, "Inside Out." The band never really hit the boil of either popular or critical acclaim, which is sad considering the music was actually quite good.

what to buy: *World without End* 𝄪𝄪𝄪 (Sire, 1988, prod. Tim Palmer) punched blister-pop into a well-suited anthemic whirl.

what to buy next: *Laughter* 𝄪𝄪𝄪 (Sire, 1989) showcases a nearly perfect pop synthesis of the dance-rock rumbling going on on the Lemon Drops' home shores. Neither as forlorn as the Stone Roses nor as obscure as Primal Scream, the Lemon Drops merely enhance its already-solid song form on gems such as "Into the Heart of Love" and "Where Do We Go from Heaven?"

the rest:

Happy Head 𝄪𝄪𝄪 (Sire, 1986)
Out of Hand 𝄪𝄪 (Sire, 1987)
Sound 𝄪𝄪 (Sire, 1991)
Ricochet 𝄪𝄪 (Sire, 1992)

influences:

◄◄ Echo & the Bunnymen, the Smiths, Wire

►► The Farm, Inspiral Carpets, the Ocean Blue

Billy Manes

Mighty Mighty Bosstones

Formed 1985, in Boston, MA.

Dicky Barrett, vocals; Nate Albert, guitar; Joe Gittleman, bass; Tim "Johnny Vegas" Burton, saxophone, vocals; Ben Carr (a.k.a. "Bosstone"), dancer; Josh Dalsimer, drums (1985–90); Kevin Lenear, saxophone (1990–present); Dennis Brockenborough, trombone, vocals (1990–present).

One of the most influential and imitated rock bands of the latter half of the '90s, the Mighty Mighty Bosstones were combining ska rhythms and horn playing with hard rock and punk influences back when it seemed like a freakish idea. Fast forward to 1997–98, and half of what used to be garage rock bands are mining their high school marching bands to find horn sections. One of the things that has made the Bosstones so appealing is the fact that the group is, well, a lot of fun. After the brooding music that dominated alternative rock during the early '90s, the Bosstones' fourth wave of ska was a happy way to spell relief without wimping out. Despite critics dogging it for a blue-collar, jock-filled following, frontman Dicky Barrett is the first to point out their music isn't brain surgery. It's of some value to note that, like Bruce Springsteen as well as numerous other punk and ska bands the group has cited as influences, the Bosstones have aligned themselves with several causes, mainly Anti-Racist Action and Safe & Sound, an organization dedicated to preventing violence at abortion clinics.

what to buy: *More Noise and Other Disturbances* 𝄫𝄫𝄫𝄪 (Taang!, 1992, prod. Paul Q. Kolderie, Mighty Mighty Bosstones) is the band's first release with its current lineup and a sign of things to come—though the songs sound even better in concert. *Let's Face It* 𝄫𝄫𝄫𝄪 (Big Rig/Mercury, 1997, prod. Paul Q. Kolderie, Sean Slade) finds the band hitting its stride five albums and nearly a decade into its career. Ska is still a prominent influence, but the Bosstones manage to stay ahead of the pack by using James Brown–style arrangements for the horn section.

what to buy next: *Devil's Night Out* 𝄫𝄫𝄫 (Taang!, 1989, prod. Paul Q. Kolderie), the band's debut, finds it hitting on a winning formula; check out "Hope I Never Lose My Wallet" and "A Little Bit Ugly," a duet with Jimmy Gestapo of hard-core legend Murphy's Law. *Question the Answers* 𝄫𝄫𝄫𝄪 (Big Rig, 1994, prod. Paul Q. Kolderie, Butcher Brothers) is the album that introduced the band to the mainstream via catchy singles such as "Kinder Words" and "Hell of a Hat."

the rest:
Don't Know How to Party 𝄫𝄫𝄪 (Mercury, 1993)

worth searching for: The Bosstones, like Springsteen and a number of punk bands, love putting out EP's and singles with B-sides for completists; some of the best of these are its 1991 self-titled EP with covers of Aerosmith, Metallica, and Van Halen songs, and the 1993 EP with covers of Minor Threat, SSD, and Bob Marley. Also worth finding are the band's covers of Kiss's "Detroit Rock City" on the *Kiss My Ass* tribute and its duet with the vampiric muppet the Count on "The Zig Zag Dance" from *Elmopalooza*.

influences:
◀◀ The Clash, the Specials, Bob Marley, Madness, Aerosmith, Bruce Springsteen

▶▶ No Doubt, Less Than Jake, Reel Big Fish, the Aquabats, the Voodoo Glow Skulls

Brian Ives

Mike & the Mechanics
See: Genesis

Buddy Miles

Born September 5, 1946, in Omaha, NE.

At the apex of his career, he was playing the back line next to Jimi Hendrix in the legendary supergroup Band of Gypsies. At his nadir, he was living in the body-search line next to some guy named Bubba while serving a prison sentence. In between, Buddy Miles has been a buffoonish, occasionally brilliant drummer/singer/bandleader who has shifted easily between hard rock and R&B since the '60s. Learning his heavy-handed, bottom-end drum style as a child, playing his first professional gig with his father's Omaha jazz combo at the age of 12, Miles attracted the interest of touring soul and doo-wop groups and joined Wilson Pickett's live revue while in his teens. Becoming one of the most sought-after session musicians in the business while working with the Wicked One, he was approached in 1967 by guitarist Michael Bloomfield to join a new psychedelic rock band called Electric Flag. That group made one memorable LP before splitting the following year, whereupon Miles formed his own band, the Buddy Miles Express. Renewing a friendship with Hendrix, whom he had met while playing the Monterey Pop Festival, Miles joined him in the studio to collaborate on Jimi's groundbreaking *Electric Ladyland* album and lay down a thick blues backbeat for the tunes "Still Raining, Still Dreaming" and "Rainy Day, Dream Away." (Hendrix repaid the favor by writing the liner notes to the Miles LP *Expressway to Your Skull* and producing cuts on the subsequent Express release *Electric Church*.) When the Jimi Hendrix Experience broke up in 1969, Hendrix recruited Miles for what would become a landmark moment in rock music history: over the objections of his management, Hendrix formed the power trio Band of Gypsys with Miles on drums and Billy Cox on bass, in essence the first true "black rock" group. In their historic 1970 concert recording at Bill Graham's Fillmore East (*Band of Gypsys*), the trio performed the propulsive, prophetic Miles tune "Them Changes," which would become his trademark hit. Since that milestone event, "Booger Bear" (the nickname divulged on a Miles album title) has dabbled in a variety of performing aggregations, and his session playing can still be found in almost every corner of the record store. He has worked with Carlos Santana, the Monkees—he even has a credit on the Priority LP *The California Raisins Sing the Hits*.

what to buy: While none of Miles's albums with the Buddy Miles Express are still in print, the 1997 compilation *The Best of Buddy Miles* ♫♫♫ (Mercury, 1997, prod. various) is a representative assortment of his best moments. "Them Changes" is here, of course, as are his other noteworthy hits: "Wholesale Love," "Dreams (to Remember)," "Memphis Train," "Midnight Rider"—awash in Buddy's melodramatic, over-the-top soul vocals—and the pulsating, previously unreleased "69 Freedom Special."

what to buy next: Trying to recapture the Band of Gypsys magic, Miles entered into a stunning but uneven alliance with P-Funk legend Bootsy Collins and guitarist Stevie Salas as a power trio called Hardware on the LP *Third Eye Open* ♫♫ (Rykodisc, 1994, prod. Bill Laswell). Eccentric, eclectic producer Bill Laswell never seems to quite get a handle on this threesome or where he wants it to go, though the playfulness of "I Got a Feeling" and Buddy's piledriving R&B on "Hard Look" and "Love Obsession" hold promise.

the rest:
Greatest Christmas Hits ♫ (Priority, 1991)
Hell and Back ♫♫♫ (Rykodisc, 1994)
(With Carlos Santana) *Carlos Santana/Buddy Miles Live* ♫♫♫♫ (Legacy, 1994)

worth searching for: Though their focus is clearly on the star, two 1997 Hendrix reissues do give the drummer some spotlight time, featuring Miles at the peak of his energetic prowess. *Electric Ladyland* (Experience Hendrix/MCA, 1997) is a remastered version of the 1968 classic with Miles on drums when Mitch Mitchell is not, and *First Rays of the New Rising Sun* (Experience Hendrix/MCA, 1997) finds Miles one of myriad guest artists including Steve Winwood, Stephen Stills, and the Ronettes.

influences:
◄◄ James Brown, Gene Krupa, Wilson Pickett, Michael Bloomfield, Buddy Rich, Jimi Hendrix, Mitch Mitchell, George Clinton

►► Bus Boys, Maze featuring Frankie Beverly, Fat Boys, Afros

Jim McFarlin

Robert Miles

Born November 3, 1969, in Switzerland.

Beneath the banner of an anti-rave, anti-drug crusade, Robert

Miles set the world to melodic reflection in pulsating 4/4 time with 1996's smash hit, "Children." On its own, the single was an inoffensive continuation of the middle-aged, coffee-table ambience that once elevated Enigma and even Vangelis to international notoriety.

what to buy: "Children" and its host album, *Dreamland* ♫♫♫ (Arista, 1996, prod. Robert Miles), captured the petty cash of millions and sealed Miles in the text of the music-history books (he won several Brit awards to boot). Boring Italian House music with little imagination prevails, but it's rather painless.

what to avoid: *23am* ♫♫ (Arista, 1998, prod. Robert Miles), an ambitious foray into world-beats and R&B, shows Miles's naive tourism taking a turn for the sloppy, issuing platitudes such as "Freedom" and "Everyday Life" to the charm of virtually no one, all the while resting upon twice-heard electronica minus the grit. Yanni, anyone?

influences:
◄◄ Mike Oldfield, Vangelis, Enigma

►► B-Tribe, John Tesh, Yanni

Billy Manes

Milla

Born Milla Jovovich, December 17, 1975, in Kiev, Ukraine.

When they start handing out record contracts to fashion models, conventional wisdom dictates that you head for the hills. Not this time. Ukrainian-born, L.A.-reared Milla Jovovich is as capable a lyricist as one could hope to find in an 18-year-old girl—dreamy and slightly schoolgirlish, perhaps, but look what those attributes have done for a grizzled vet like Tori Amos. Since recording her debut album, Milla has concentrated more on acting, scoring particularly good notices for her portrayal of an alien being in the Bruce Willis vehicle *The Fifth Element*.

what's available: On the ambitiously titled *The Divine Comedy* ♫♫♫ (SBK/ERG, 1994, prod. Rupert Hine, Richard Feldman, Mark Holden), Milla's delicate vocals are surrounded by an intriguing soundscape of gently burbling keyboards, cascading acoustic guitars, and more exotic instruments such as harmonium and kalimba. Milla is hardly revolutionary, but songs such as "It's Your Life" and "The Alien Song (for those who listen)" could mark the beginning of a new genre: Call it New Waif.

influences:
◄◄ Kate Bush, Tori Amos

Daniel Durchholz

Bill Miller

Born 1940, in WI.

Don't trouble yourself trying to label the music of Native American singer-songwriter Bill Miller; he's happy to do it himself. It's not alternative, he's fond of saying: it's alter-Native. And so it is. Miller can shift gears rapidly between Neil Young–style folkie reveries and tradition-based Native American chants. His 1996 release was a rock album, much of which drew on the kind of energy Miller saw when he shared a concert bill with alternative rockers Pearl Jam. Having grown up on a northern Wisconsin reservation, Miller was exposed to the vagaries of racism and all its attendant violence. And while his music occasionally gives in to bitterness and a thirst for revenge, it is mostly about hope, dignity, and compassion. Miller's is an important and genuinely wise voice.

what to buy: On *Raven in the Snow* ♪♪♪♪ (Reprise, 1995, prod. Richard Bennett), Miller switches from his gentle folkie stance to full-bore rock arrangements—a good idea since, for the first time, the music reflects the fury behind such songs as "The Final Word" and the title track. Others—such as the defiant "Brave Heart" and "Listen to Me," which pleads for understanding between generations—are more reflective and have an ethereal quality. Altogether, *Raven* is Miller's most fully realized work. To get a glimpse of Miller's other abilities, check out *The Red Road* ♪♪♪♪ (Warner Western, 1993, prod. Richard Bennett), which combines acoustic-based folk music with Native American flutes and chants. It includes the haunting instrumental "Dreams of Wounded Knee," plus "Praises," which is based on a Menominee prayer to the Creator, and "Reservation Road," a gritty memoir of Miller's birthplace.

the rest:
(With Robert Mirabal & the Smokey Town Singers) *Native Suite* ♪♪♪♪
    (Warner Western, 1996)

worth searching for: Miller's earlier, self-released albums, which he sells at shows and by mail order, include a pair of folk outings: *Old Dreams and New Hopes* (Rosebud, 1987) and *The Art of Survival* (Rosebud, 1990), as well as the Native American/new age–leaning *Loon, Mountain, and Moon: Native American Flute Songs* (Rosebud, 1991).

influences:
◀◀ Neil Young, Dan Fogelberg, XIT

                                        Daniel Durchholz

Buddy Miller

Born Steven Paul Miller, September 6, 1952, in Fairborn, OH.

During the '80s, singer-songwriter-guitarist Buddy Miller played in the bands of Shawn Colvin and Jim Lauderdale. He moved to Nashville during the early '90s with his wife, Julie, who is also a singer-songwriter. Miller proceeded to build a studio in the couple's home; it was there that he made his solo albums for HighTone, two of the most soulful hard-country albums of the '90s. Miller also handles lead guitarist chores in the touring bands of Steve Earle and Emmylou Harris.

what's available: Featuring cameos from Lucinda Williams, Emmylou Harris, and Memphis soul great Dan Penn, *Your Love and Other Lies* ♪♪♪♪ (HighTone, 1995, prod. Buddy Miller) is the finest stone-country LP released since Gary Stewart's *Out of Hand* or Joe Ely's *Honky Tonk Masquerade*. *Poison Love* ♪♪♪♪ (HighTone, 1997, prod. Buddy Miller) is only slightly less magnificent. Even more than its predecessor, it finds Miller exploring the links between country and soul music.

influences:
◀◀ George Jones, Merle Haggard, James Carr

see also: *Julie Miller*

                                        Bill Friskics-Warren

Julie Miller

Born July 12, 1956, in Dallas, TX.

Although Julie Miller had previously recorded four albums of contemporary Christian music (all out of print), her work didn't come to the attention of pop and rock fans until Emmylou Harris included one of her originals, "All My Tears (Be Washed Away)," on her influential *Wrecking Ball* album. After moving to Nashville during the early '90s with her husband Buddy, a solo artist in his own right, Miller released her secular debut, *Blue Pony*, a darkly passionate album that sets country, blues, and Anglo-Celtic folk music to a rock backbeat.

what's available: *Blue Pony* ♪♪♪♪ (HighTone, 1997, prod. Julie Miller, Buddy Miller) is an exquisite testament of faith and resilience.

influences:
◀◀ Valerie Carter, Mark Hurd, Victoria Williams

see also: *Buddy Miller*

                                        Bill Friskics-Warren

Roger Miller

Born January 2, 1936, in Fort Worth, TX. Died October 25, 1992, in Los Angeles, CA.

If he had left us with nothing more than "King of the Road," his place in the pantheon of American musical giants would be assured. But Roger Miller's remarkable body of work contains literally dozens of songs its equal and beyond: songs that remain as vibrant, funny, poignant, and thought-provoking today as they were over three decades ago when they first set the country music world on its ear. To the undiscriminating listener, Miller is best remembered for his mid-1960s string of light-hearted classics ("Dang Me," "England Swings," "Engine Engine No. 9"), which, thanks to their sparse, clever arrangements and Miller's countrypolitan image, sold in Beatle-like quantities to pop and folk audiences alike. His overnight success (six Grammy Awards in 1965) was the result of years spent honing his craft in near obscurity, playing fiddle for Minnie Pearl, drums for Faron Young, and pitching his unique catalog of songs to anyone who'd listen. Few did in the straight-laced Nashville of the early 1960s. In desperation, and in need of quick cash to finance a move to friend Lee Hazelwood's Hollywood garage, Miller took Smash Records' new Nashville A&R chief Jerry Kennedy into the studio on January 11, 1964 to cut a dozen new songs. With accompaniment so bare-boned Miller was forced to scat-sing where the guitar solos would normally have gone, "Chug-a-Lug" and "Dang Me" soon launched a series of hits combining this musical simplicity with wit and wordplay as much Chuck Berry as it was Hank Williams. However, by 1967 things had already started to go awry. First, his loyal label Smash was swallowed up by the giant Mercury corporation, affording Miller less of a free reign inside the studio and less of a promotional push outside of it. A long-rumored amphetamine dependency also began to take its toll, most noticeably on his writing ability. He could still spot and release a good song before anyone else ("Ruby, Don't Take Your Love to Town," "Little Green Apples," "Me and Bobbie McGee"); they just weren't *his* songs anymore. After a lackluster stint at Columbia Records, some film work, and a subsequent exile to the Vegas lounges, Miller wisely lay low in the early 1980s. Surprisingly, when he next popped up it was as a Broadway composer: His score for *Big River* duly won a Tony Award In 1985. Having proved to himself and the world that he still had what it took, Roger spent his remaining years fishing, hanging with friends both old and new (his last hit, "It Only Hurts Me When I Cry," was a collaboration with Dwight Yoakam), and joking about the throat cancer that finally claimed him in 1992. As writer J.R. Taylor so perfectly eulogized, "Having conquered the sticks, the suburbs *and* the city, Roger Miller then put our country in his pocket and took it all with him."

what's available: The three-CD *King of the Road: The Genius of Roger Miller* 𝄢𝄢𝄢𝄢 (Mercury, 1995, compilation prod. Daniel Cooper) has it all. From the early stabs to the mega-hits, the should've-been hits ("My Uncle Used to Love Me But She Died," to name but one), *Big River* highlights, and a version of "Heartbreak Hotel" that is positively demonic, you just owe it to yourself to take the wild and wonderful ride through these 70 songs.

worth searching for: *Roger and Out* (Smash, 1964, prod. Jerry Kennedy), *The Return of Roger Miller* (Smash, 1965, prod. Jerry Kennedy), and *Words and Music by Roger Miller*

(Smash, 1966, prod. Jerry Kennedy) contain the absolute cream of his work, wonderfully veering from the ridiculous ("You Can't Roller Skate in a Buffalo Herd") to the sublime ("Train of Life") and then some. These albums show a man at the absolute peak of his creative and commercial powers, and a musician at least the equal of any operating anywhere, then or now.

influences:

◀◀ Bob Wills, Hank Williams, Sheb Wooley

▶▶ Mel Tillis, Tom Waits, Tylin Whaler

Gary Pig Gold

Steve Miller

Born October 5, 1943, in Milwaukee, WI.

Throughout his prolific and protean journeyman career, Steve Miller has braided together polished pop-rock, straight-ahead blues, and acoustic-flavored pop. Widely regarded as a Top 40 stooge whose '70s hits remain a staple of classic rock radio 20 years later, Miller—usually performing under the Steve Miller Band moniker—has actually made rewarding forays into a broad array of musical styles, displaying a depth and prowess often nothing short of astonishing. His father was a fanatical music buff with a tape recorder, and Les Paul, T-Bone Walker, and Charles Mingus all held sessions in the Miller living room. His first high school band in Dallas included schoolmate Boz Scaggs and backed up visiting R&B stars such as Jimmy Reed at local clubs. Miller left college to pursue a musical career in the Chicago blues realm, where he recorded an unreleased album with the Goldberg-Miller Blues Band. He found his real starting place several years later in the burgeoning San Francisco rock scene. His band appeared at the historic 1967 Monterey Pop Festival and signed to Capitol Records, an association that lasted more than a quarter-century. While Miller's early albums made him an underground radio favorite, he finally found the pop chart stroke in 1973 with *The Joker*; subsequent albums *Fly like an Eagle* and *Book of Dreams* made him one of the top attractions of the day. Although the gleaming hits gave Miller his Top 40 hack reputation, he was still capable of turning out a soulful jazz experiment such as *Born 2B Blue* or a solid blues outing like *Living in the 20th Century*. He *is* Maurice, the Gangster, the Space Cowboy, Stevie "Guitar" Miller—the musician of many faces.

what to buy: His second greatest hits album, *Greatest Hits, 1974–1978* 𝄢𝄢𝄢𝄢 (Capitol, 1978, prod. Steve Miller), has stayed on the best-seller lists since its release. But *Fly like an Eagle* 𝄢𝄢𝄢𝄢 (Capitol, 1976, prod. Steve Miller) contains the best single all-around look at his great gifts.

what to buy next: Samples of his first six albums cover a broad territory, but *The Best Of, 1968–1973* 🎵🎵🎵 (Capitol, 1990, prod. Steve Miller) provides a quick, albeit spotty retrospective of his development. *Book of Dreams* 🎵🎵🎵🎵 (Capitol, 1977, prod. Steve Miller) was actually recorded at the same sessions as *Fly like an Eagle* and released a year later.

what to avoid: Miller remixed and edited many of the tracks on the three-CD collection *Box Set* 🎵🎵 (Capitol, 1994, prod. Steve Miller) without broadening the set's viewpoint beyond much more than a greatest hits album on steroids.

the rest:
Brave New World 🎵🎵🎵 (Capitol, 1969/1994)
Sailor 🎵🎵🎵 (Capitol, 1969)
Your Saving Grace 🎵🎵🎵 (Capitol, 1970)
Number Five (Capitol, 1970/1994)
Anthology 🎵🎵🎵 (Capitol, 1972)
The Joker 🎵🎵🎵 (Capitol, 1973)
Circle of Love 🎵 (Capitol, 1981)
Abracadabra 🎵🎵 (Capitol, 1982)
Steve Miller Band Live 🎵 (Capitol, 1983)
Italian X-Rays 🎵🎵 (Capitol, 1984)
Living in the 20th Century 🎵🎵🎵 (Capitol, 1986)
Born 2B Blue 🎵🎵🎵 (Capitol, 1988)
Living in the U.S.A. 🎵🎵 (Cema Special Products, 1992)
Wide River 🎵🎵🎵 (Polydor, 1993)

worth searching for: The Miller band's debut album, *Children of the Future* (Capitol, 1969, prod. Glyn Johns) is a bluesey Beatlesque undiscovered gem that was briefly available on compact disc.

influences:
◀◀ Jimmy Reed, the Beatles, Cream

▶▶ Omar & the Howlers, Blues Traveler, Spin Doctors, Big Head Todd & the Monsters

see also: *Boz Scaggs*

Joel Selvin

Milli Vanilli

Formed 1988, in Munich, Germany.

Rob Pilatus (died April 2, 1998, in Frankfurt, Germany), vocals; Fabrice Morvan, vocals.

Milli Vanilli almost went down in pop history as one of the most successful—albeit artistically insignificant—groups of the video era. Instead, the duo became perhaps the biggest punchline in pop before tragedy superseded the jokes. Milli Vanilli, of course, first turned the music world on its ear with its 1989 debut album, *Girl You Know It's True*. Though critically reviled, winning both worst band and worst album hon-

ors in the 1989 *Rolling Stone* Critics' Poll, and likened to Alvin & the Chipmunks by *Time* magazine, Milli Vanilli appeared to be having the last laugh, as *Girl You Know It's True* spawned five Top 5 hits, sold more than seven million copies, and even earned the group a Best New Artist Grammy. The giggling suddenly stopped when it was revealed that Pilatus and Morvan hadn't sung a single note on the hit record—that Milli Vanilli was really Charles Shaw, John Davis, and Brad Howe. The group's mastermind, Frank Farian—the German producer known for his work with Boney M—had apparently wanted an attractive look to go with his lightweight dance-pop, and so he hired former breakdancers Pilatus (from Munich) and Morvan (from Paris) to become the faces of Milli Vanilli. The dreadlocked, bare-chested men appeared on the album cover, in videos, and on stage (lip-synching, of course), and were described by the *New York Times* as "exotically sexy." The group also conducted interviews as Milli Vanilli, with Pilatus telling one writer: "Musically, we are more talented than any Bob Dylan. We are more talented than Paul McCartney, Mick Jagger . . . I'm the new Elvis." Following the revelations that they weren't quite ready to build their own Graceland, Pilatus and Morvan were stripped of their Grammy, while their record company was ordered to give partial refunds to anybody who bought Milli Vanilli recordings or attended concerts believing that the duo was actually singing. Ironically, after Pilatus and Morvan sang *a capella* at a press conference, a voice coach said they sounded better than the men who actually were recorded. The duo tried to continue on as Rob & Fab but went nowhere, quickly. In 1991 a despondent Pilatus attempted suicide; five years later, he was charged on eight counts of allegedly attacking and threatening two people in separate incidents. Under court order, he later entered a drug treatment facility. In 1998, a year after Morvan told VH1 that he and Pilatus were deceived into fronting Milli Vanilli, Pilatus was found dead in a Frankfurt hotel room after consuming alcohol and pills.

what to avoid: *Girl You Know It's True* **woof!** (Arista, 1989, prod. Frank Farian) is worth having only to remind you what all the fuss was about. All featherweight lyrics, flat vocals, and standard-issue hip-hop rhythms, the album features the consecutive #1's "Baby Don't Forget My Number," "Girl I'm Gonna Miss You," and "Blame It on the Rain." But still. . . .

the rest:
Quick Moves: The Remix Album 🎵🎵 (Arista, 1990)
Rob and Fab **woof!** (Taj, 1993)

influences:
◀◀ Klaatu, Spinal Tap, the Monkees

Josh Freedom du Lac

Ministry

Formed 1981, in Chicago, IL.

Al Jourgensen, vocals, guitar, keyboards; Lamont Welton, bass (1981–82); Paul Barker, bass, programming (1986–present); Stevo, drums (1981–82); Stephen George, drums (1982–86); William Rieflin, drums (1986–present); Roland Barker, keyboards (1986–present); Mike Scaccia, guitar (1990–present).

nine inch nails might sell more records, but the Al Jourgensen–led Ministry is the most influential American industrial-rock band. The group's 1983 debut, *With Sympathy*, was a forgettable exercise in synth-driven Europop, complete with fake British accents, but by the mid-'80s, Jourgensen and Paul Barker, his chief collaborator, had cooked up a brave new sound, fusing menacing guitar-punk with harsh vocals and factory style rhythms pioneered by European acts such as Einstürzende Neubauten. Ministry defined industrial rock in the United States with albums such as *The Land of Rape and Honey* and *The Mind Is a Terrible Thing to Taste*. Though unquestionably on the cutting edge, the group muscled onto the pop charts with its 1992 album *Psalm 69* and stole the show on that summer's Lollapalooza tour. Meanwhile, Jourgensen and Barker have dabbled in countless projects outside of Ministry, most notably the Revolting Cocks but also 1,000 Homo DJs, Lard (with the Dead Kennedys' Jello Biafra), Pigface, Pailhead (with Fugazi/Minor Threat's Ian MacKaye), and Lead into Gold.

what to buy: *The Land of Rape and Honey* ♫♫♫♫ (Sire, 1988, prod. Al Jourgensen, Paul Barker) is Ministry's most harrowing journey into the sonic apocalypse, featuring the hypnotic scream-fest "Stigmata."

what to buy next: *The Mind Is a Terrible Thing to Taste* ♫♫♫♫ (Sire, 1989, prod. Al Jourgensen, Paul Barker) walks the same path of horrific guitar-punk as *Rape and Honey*, though, as a successor, it doesn't sound quite as groundbreaking. The more experimental *Psalm 69: The Way to Succeed and the Way to Suck Eggs* ♫♫♫♫ (Sire, 1992, prod. Al Jourgensen, Paul Barker) boasts "Jesus Built My Hotrod," a brilliant duet with Butthole Surfer Gibby Haynes.

what to avoid: *Twelve-Inch Singles, 1981–1984* ♫♫ (Wax Trax!, 1987) is a spotty collection of dance remixes from the band's early days.

the rest:
With Sympathy ♫♫♫ (Wax Trax!/Arista, 1983)
Twitch ♫♫♫ (Sire, 1986)
In Case You Didn't Feel Like Showing Up ♫♫♫ (Sire EP, 1990)
Filth Pig ♫♫♫ (Warner Bros., 1996)

worth searching for: The unintentionally amusing debut EP *Cold Life* (Wax Trax!, 1981) casts the band as a Human League wanna-be.

solo outings:
Revolting Cocks:
Big Sexy Land ♫♫♫ (Wax Trax!, 1986)
You Goddamned Son of a Bitch ♫♫♫♫ (Wax Trax!, 1988)
Beers, Steers & Queers ♫♫♫ (Wax Trax!, 1990)
Linger Ficken' Good . . . and Other Barnyard Oddities ♫♫♫ (Sire, 1993)

Lard:
Power of Lard ♫♫♫ (Alternative Tentacles, 1989)
The Last Temptation (Alternative Tentacles, 1990)

Pailhead:
Trait ♫♫♫ (Wax Trax! EP, 1988)

influences:
◄◄ Einstürzende Neubauten, Cabaret Voltaire, Throbbing Gristle, the Sex Pistols

►► nine inch nails, KMFDM, Filter, Gravity Kills

Thor Christensen

Mink DeVille

See: Willy DeVille

Kylie Minogue

Born May 28, 1968, in Melbourne, Victoria, Australia.

As long as there are pretty girls, lonely boys, songs to sing . . . and money to be made, there will be careers like Kylie Minogue's. A young star of Australian television soap operas, she was spotted by producer Pete Waterman in 1987 and brought to London for 10 days to record a zesty piece of dance fluff titled "I Should Be So Lucky." It went #1 in the U.K. the following year, kicking off an unbelievable run of 13 straight British Top 10 hits, most the wares of the Stock-Aitken-Waterman song factory. So pervasive and all-encompassing was her success that Kylie became the favorite name given newborns in Britain during much of the late '80s. A highly publicized fling with the late INXS singer Michael Hutchence kept Minogue in the papers long after she'd fallen from the charts, and while today she continues to record in a more "mature" vein, she's wisely set her career sights back onto television work.

what's available: The budget compilation *Kylie* ♫♫♫ (DGC, 1988/Geffen Goldline, 1996, prod. Mike Stock, Matt Aitken, Pete Waterman) contains 10 of the star's biggest hits, including a remake of her very first Antipodean release, Little Eva's "Loco-Motion." If these productions sound somewhat lifeless beneath all of their digital high-sheen, perhaps the self-confessed Queen of S-A-W's Bubblegum Motown assembly line can help explain why: "You see a song for the first time, and 20 minutes later the red light goes on and you sing. A professional job—just like reading from a script in a soap." 'Nuf said.

Al Jourgensen of Ministry (© Ken Settle)

influences:

◄◄ Olivia Newton-John, Clare Grogan, Sheena Easton, Madonna

►► Vanessa Paradis, Fantastic Everlasting Gobstopper, Dannii Minogue

Gary Pig Gold

Minor Threat

Formed 1980, in Washington, DC. Disbanded 1983.

Ian MacKaye, vocals; Lyle Preslar, guitar; Brian Baker, bass, guitar; Steve Hansgen, bass (1982–83); Jeff Nelson, drums.

Behind its D.C. mentors, the pre-Rasta Bad Brains, Minor Threat was easily the second best thrash band of all time in that peculiar genre of already-fast punk sped up to hyper-warp speeds. Singer Ian MacKaye and drummer Jeff Nelson launched the now-fabled, still prospering independent label Dischord with their former band the Teen Idles, but the raspy Idles were quickly overshadowed by this teen powerhouse—a kick in the ass that also kicked serious butt over the unwashed masses of international hardcore shouters/thrashers that followed in its wake. Besides Fugazi, Minor Threat's members also went on to work in bands such as Bad Religion, Dag Nasty, the Meatmen, Egg Hunt, and Embrace.

what's available: Sometime after Minor Threat's demise, what little the group managed to release was culled together on one handy CD. The force of the jagged juggernaut *Complete* ♫♫♫♩ (Dischord, 1987, prod. Minor Threat) is still fierce. MacKaye's fervor and eyes-open passion approach that of a preacher's, but with a snarl instead of a smile. Railing against the violent, the cement-headed, the drug-dependent, basic hypocrisy, and two-facedness, the man/boy is a human dynamo of rage, sarcasm, morals, and liberating spirit, the howl of the young who want something better (a vision he still perpetuates, a decade and a half later, as a member of Fugazi). This ungodly performance is backed up by some of the most searing rock imaginable, so blistering and raw and sped up it's as if your 45 rpm record is playing at 78 without sounding like the Chipmunks. Such lacerating blips as "Minor Threat," "Bottled Violence," "Guilty of Being White," "Out of Step," and a cover of Wire's "12XU" are awe-striking in their pure, uncut speed and fury. Even when Minor Threat tempers the tempos on the second half—from the 1983 *Out of Step* EP—the force remains a rocket, though with more sing-a-long results; listen to "Cashing In" and the surprising take on the Standells' mid-'60s classic "Good Guys Don't Wear White."

influences:

◄◄ The Ramones, the Stooges, MC5, Sham 69, Bad Brains

►► Fugazi, Bad Religion, Dag Nasty, NOFX, Stanford Prison Experiment, Rage Against the Machine

see also: *Fugazi, Bad Religion*

Jack Rabid

The Minus Five

See: Young Fresh Fellows

Minutemen

Formed 1980, in San Pedro, CA.

D. Boon (born Dennes Dale Boon; died December 23, 1985), guitar, vocals; Mike Watt, bass, vocals; George Hurley, drums.

Operating on the premise that if you can't say it in 60 seconds or less, it ain't worth saying, the Minutemen fired up an original, thought-provoking, and ass-kicking response to '70s punk. With furious ensemble playing that suggested the chaotic energy of free jazz (à la Ornette Coleman's Prime Time or Albert Ayler), lyrical concerns that ventured into agit-prop hell-raising while surfing pop culture for signs of intelligence, and a missionary zeal for touring that brought the trio to every godforsaken hole in the wall in the land, the Minutemen changed lives. Its records steadily improved, and its terse songs eventually expanded past the one-minute barrier to include verses and choruses—and sometimes even genuine melodies. D. Boon's death in a road accident brought the Minutemen to a premature end in 1985. Mike Watt and George Hurley went on to form fIREHOSE, and Watt has since pursued a solo career.

what to buy: *Double Nickels on the Dime* ♫♫♫♫ (SST, 1984, prod. Ethan James) is an '80s landmark, with 45 songs that muse on everything from Michael Jackson to nuclear war, with a cool 38-seconnd Van Halen cover ("Ain't Talkin' 'bout Love") demonstrating that the Minutemen didn't wear punk-rock blinders while pursuing their ideals.

what to buy next: *3-Way Tie for Last* ♫♫♫♩ (SST, 1985, prod. Ethan James) is the band's most polished record, but it still buzzes like a hive of hornets in a bad mood. Boon's tribute to Vietnam veterans, "The Price of Paradise," may be the band's finest song, in a league with similar righteous protest fare from John Fogerty, whose "Have You Ever Seen the Rain?" is also covered.

the rest:

Ballot Result ♫♫♫♩ (SST, 1987)
Post-Mersh, Vol. 1 ♫♫♩ (SST, 1987)
Post-Mersh, Vol. 2 ♫♫♫♩ (SST, 1987)
Post-Mersh, Vol. 3 ♫♫♩ (SST, 1989)

worth searching for: *My First Bells* (SST, 1985) is a 62-track cassette that compiles the terse blasts of Pedro bile that made up the trio's early years.

influences:

◀◀ Blue Öyster Cult, Creedence Clearwater Revival, Meat Puppets, Ornette Coleman

▶▶ Red Hot Chili Peppers, Faith No More, Jane's Addiction, Sublime, the Offspring

see also: fIREHOSE

Greg Kot

The Miracles

See: Smokey Robinson

The Misfits

Formed 1977, in NJ. Disbanded 1983. Re-formed mid-1990s.

Glenn Danzig, vocals, electric piano (1977–83); Jerry Only (born Jerry Caiafa), bass; Manny, drums; Frank Licata, guitar (1978); Jim Catania, drums (1978–79); Bobby Steele, guitar (1979); Joey Image, drums (1979); P.C. Doyle, guitar (1979–83, 1995–present); Arthur Googy, drums (1979–83); Robo, drums (1983); Michael Graves, vocals (1995–98); Dr. Chud, drums (1995–present).

With an evil glee, the Misfits emerged in New York City clubs playing fast and brutal punk, complete with ghoulish makeup and lyrics that splatter like horror flicks. What kept the group out of the dumbbell category was lead singer Glen Danzig's articulate and tuneful bellowing and an undercurrent of humor in its perverted, '50s-style attack. After the band broke up, Danzig formed the short-lived Samhain, then named a band after himself and became an MTV darling briefly during the early '90s. The Misfits reformed, sans Danzig, which seems infinitely more perverse than "Mommy Can I Go out and Kill Tonight?"

what to buy: *Walk among Us* ♫♫♫♫ (Ruby, 1982/1988) is the definitive and highly sought-after album that contains the classics "Vampira" and "Mommy, Can I Go out and Kill Tonight?"; it's offensive, ugly, and indispensable. It's also the only full-length studio album the band ever recorded. *Misfits* ♫♫♫♫ (Plan 9, 1986) packs most of the essential tracks into a melodic roar. *Legacy of Brutality* ♫♫♫ (Caroline, 1985, prod. various) compiles, with a few missteps, some of the band's early recordings and excellent outtakes, notably the bossa-nova "Angelfuck" and "She."

what to buy next: *Misfits Box* ♫♫♫♫ (Caroline, 1996) slams together virtually everything the band recorded into a four-disc, coffin-shaped box.

what to avoid: *Earth A.D./Wolfsblood* ♫♫ (Plan 9, 1982) finds the band attempting to conform to hardcore with stiff and tune-less results. *American Psycho* ♫ (Geffen, 1997) is Danzig-less rehash.

the rest:
Misfits 2 ♫♫♫ (Caroline, 1995)

worth searching for: *Evil Live* (Plan 9, 1982) captures the live thunder shortly after the release of *Walk among Us*.

influences:

◀◀ The Ramones, the Damned, Kiss

▶▶ Samhain, Danzig, Guns N' Roses

Allan Orski

Missing Persons

Formed 1980, in Los Angeles, CA. Disbanded 1986.

Dale Bozzio, vocals; Warren Cuccurullo, guitar; Patrick O'Hearn, bass; Chuck Wild, keyboards; Terry Bozzio, drums.

Whether you love or hate the music of Frank Zappa, you can't deny his knack for assembling talented backup musicians. One of Zappa's most accomplished ensembles—the Bozzios, Patrick O'Hearn, and Warren Cuccurullo—went on to form Missing Persons, whose poppy new wave, marked by Dale Bozzio's hiccup-riddled Kewpie doll vocals, was a far cry from Zappa's avant rock madness. The group scored a handful of hits before breaking up in 1986, with most of the band moving on to other projects—most notably Cuccurullo to Duran Duran.

what to buy: At this point, little of the group's work remains in print. *The Best of Missing Persons* ♫♫♫ (Capitol, 1987, prod. various) is a good starting point, featuring most of the band's singles ("Words," "Destination Unknown," "Walking in L.A.,") and some of its better album tracks ("Mental Hopscotch," "I Can't Think about Dancin'").

the rest:
Missing Persons ♫♫♫ (Capitol, 1982)
Spring Session M ♫♫♫ (Capitol, 1982/One Way, 1995)
Rhyme and Reason ♫♫♫ (Capitol, 1984)
Color in Your Life ♫♫ (Capitol, 1986)

worth searching for: The Japanese release *Late Nights/Early Days* (Bandai, 1997) is a concert recorded in 1982, featuring many of the band's best tunes, as well as their cover of the Doors' "Hello I Love You." If you've never heard drummer Terry Bozzio live, you might want to pick this up.

solo outings:
Terry Bozzio:
(With Polytown) *Polytown* ♫♫♫ (CMP Karakter, 1994)
(With Tony Levin and Steve Stevens) *Black Light Syndrome* ♫♫♫ (Magna Carta, 1997)

Warren Cuccurullo:
Warren Cuccurullo ♪♪♪ (Imago, 1996)
Machine Language ♪♪ (Imago, 1997)

Patrick O'Hearn:
Ancient Dreams ♪♪♪♪ (BMG, 1985)
Between Two Worlds ♪♪♪♪ (BMG, 1987)
Rivers Gonna Rise ♪ (BMG, 1988)
El Dorado ♪♪♪♪ (BMG, 1989)
Indigo ♪♪♪♪ (BMG, 1991)
Private Music ♪♪♪ (BMG, 1992)
Trust ♪♪♪ (Deep Cave, 1995)
Metaphor ♪♪ (Deep Cave, 1996)

influences:

◀◀ Frank Zappa, the Beatles, the Supremes, Twiggy

▶▶ Garbage

Brandon Trenz

Mission of Burma

Formed 1979, in Boston, MA. Disbanded 1983.

Clint Conley, bass, vocals, percussion; Roger Miller, guitar, vocals, piano, trumpet, percussion; Peter Prescott, drums, vocals, percussion; Martin Swope, tape manipulations, loops, percussion.

During its fruitful, extremely loud, four-year existence, Mission of Burma established itself as the best punk band to ever come from Boston, and maybe the most important Beantown band of any genre. "Academy Fight Song," MoB's first single, has frequently been covered, most notably by R.E.M., and "That's When I Reach for My Revolver" is one of the three greatest alternative-rock songs ever. The band was formed by Roger Miller, who had moved to Boston from Ann Arbor, Michigan, in 1978, after he and Conley quit Moving Parts. The relentlessly clanging guitars and the throbbing bass set a standard for intense, dense rock that many bands since have aspired to. In 1983, when Miller's severe hearing damage forced him to cut back on his playing, the band broke up. Prescott went on to form Volcano Suns and, in the '90s, Kustomized. Miller and Swope stayed together in Birdsongs of the Mesozoic. Miller also released a large quantity of work under his own name and with his group No Man, as well as childhood recordings under the name M-3. Conley produced the first Yo La Tengo album and then left the music industry.

what to buy: The seminal EP *Signals, Calls, and Marches* ♪♪♪♪♪ (Ace of Hearts, 1981/Ryko, 1997, prod. Richard W. Harte) includes the classics "That's When I Reach for My Revolver," "Fame and Fortune," "This Is Not a Photograph," and, added to the most recent CD version, the contents of the

"Academy Fight Song" seven-inch. Nobody can understand punk without this CD.

what to buy next: The group's only studio LP, *Vs.* ♪♪♪♪ (Ace of Hearts, 1982/Ryko, 1997, prod. Richard W. Harte) hits hardest on "That's How I Escaped My Certain Fate." Again, extra tracks have been added. *The Horrible Truth about Burma* ♪♪♪♪ (Ace of Hearts, 1985/Ryko, 1997, prod. Richard W. Harte) is a live collection featuring covers of the Stooges' "1970" and Pere Ubu's "Heart of Darkness." The most recent CD version adds four previously unreleased live tracks, including "That's When I Reach for My Revolver."

the rest:
Forget Mission of Burma ♪♪♪♪ (Taang!, 1988)
Peking Spring ♪♪♪ (Taang!, 1988)

worth searching for: The band's final hometown show in 1983 was filmed, and though *Live at the Bradford* (Atavistic Video, 1991, prod. Paul Rachmann) barely breaks the half-hour mark, it's a worthwhile document.

influences:

◀◀ The Velvet Underground, the Stooges, Gang of Four, Pere Ubu

▶▶ Sonic Youth, Nirvana

Steve Holtje

The Mission U.K.

Formed 1985, in Leeds, England.

Wayne Hussey, vocals, guitar; Simon Hinkler, guitar (1985–90); Craig Adams, bass; Mick Brown, drums, Paul Etchells, guitar; others.

Essentially an offshoot of seminal goth band Sisters of Mercy (Wayne Hussey and Craig Adams were both members before parting ways with Andrew Eldritch) and Red Lorry Yellow Lorry (another semi-goth band that included Mick Brown), the Mission U.K. (so-called because a gospel outfit had prior dibs on the Mission moniker in the United States) began with every intention of setting the music world on its ear with its gother-than-thou attitude. It didn't happen though, largely because the group came off as a decidedly second-tier Led Zeppelin clone (Zep bassist John Paul Jones even produced them at one point). Still, they were capable of making some fine music at times—"Garden of Delight" and "Butterfly on a Wheel" spring to mind—with dark, mysterious, angst-ridden vocals and by-the-book goth backing. While the earliest efforts of the Mission were successful, later releases tended to fall flat with goth/atmospheric rock fans and, for better or worse brought the Mission into the mainstream with tracks getting airplay on rock and alternative radio. This marked the beginning of the end as they tried to straddle both sides of the musical fence. Nobody wound up being overly impressed, and the band has splintered and faded into oblivion, though Hussey continues to soldier on, the only original member in an otherwise anonymous lineup.

what to buy: *Sum and Substance: The Best of the Mission U.K.* 🎵🎵🎵🎵 (Polydor, 1994, prod. various) culls tracks from the band's previous releases and leaves out many of the more annoying tunes that fans of this type of music can do without. It's a solid introduction to the band, and makes a dandy Halloween soundtrack.

what to buy next: *God's Own Medicine* 🎵🎵🎵🎵 (Mercury, 1986, prod. Tim Palmer, Mission) is a nice goth record, albeit a somewhat mellow one, with bewitching melodies interrupted by the occasional scream. While not groundbreaking by any stretch, it's very listenable and well produced.

what to avoid: *Grains of Sand* 🎵🎵 (Mercury EP, 1990, prod. various) contains remixes and outtakes from the *Carved in Sand* sessions. *Carved* was a solid release, but this does it little, if any justice.

the rest:
Children 🎵🎵🎵 (Mercury, 1988)
Beyond the Pale 🎵🎵 (Mercury, 1988)
Carved in Sand 🎵🎵🎵🎵 (Mercury, 1990)
Masque 🎵🎵🎵 (Mercury, 1992)

influences:
◀◀ Sisters of Mercy, the Cure, Joy Division, March Violets, Bauhuas, Led Zeppelin, the Beatles

▶▶ White Zombie, Type O Negative, Tea Party, Alice in Chains

see also: *Sisters of Mercy*

Tim Davis

Mr. Big

Formed 1988, in Los Angeles, CA.

Eric Martin, vocals; Paul Gilbert, guitar; Billy Sheehan, bass; Pat Torpey, drums.

When Mr. Big came together during the late '80s, each of its members had done time on the hard rock/lite metal circuit with varying amounts of commercial success (Billy Sheehan was a noted bassist who played for a newly solo David Lee Roth). Swearing allegiance to '70s blues-rock such as the Free song from which the band took its name, Mr. Big's first videos and concerts nevertheless showcased flourescent guitars, flashy shredding, and guitar and bass solos played with electric drills (which eventually led to a Makita power tool sponsorship). As with most lite metal acts of the day, the band's brief moment in the spotlight came thanks to a power ballad, "To Be with You,"

which was a #1 single in 1991. After that blip, however, Mr. Big's impact has been untrackable, and nowadays the band splits its time between the inevitable solo albums and cultivating its popularity in Japan and other overseas markets.

what to buy: *Big, Bigger, Biggest! The Best of Mr. Big* 🎵🎵 (Atlantic, 1998, prod. Kevin Elson) compiles "To Be with You," soundtrack work, and the higher quality album cuts, and it's all the Mr. Big one should really ever need.

the rest:
Mr. Big 🎵🎵 (Atlantic, 1989)
Lean into It 🎵 (Atlantic, 1991)
Bump Ahead 🎵 (Atlantic, 1993)
Hey Man 🎵 (Atlantic, 1996)

influences:
◀◀ Free, David Lee Roth

▶▶ Extreme

Todd Wicks

Mr. Bungle

See: Faith No More

Mr. Mister

Formed 1982, in Los Angeles, CA. Disbanded 1988.

Richard Page, bass, vocals; Steve George, keyboards; Steve Farris, guitar; Pat Mastelotto, drums.

Enjoying pop success that seemed to come from nowhere during the mid-'80s, Mr. Mister actually began as the vision of Richard Page and Steve George, experienced songwriters who had crafted hits for acts such as John Parr and REO Speedwagon. Eager to grab a bit of the spotlight for themselves, they recruited two other session aces to round out the band and concentrated on writing hits for themselves. Despite selling millions of copies of their sophomore album, Mr. Mister flopped on its next outing as its particular brand of synth-pop faded from view. After the group disbanded, Page turned down offers to join both Toto and Chicago, and Pat Mastelotto briefly joined King Crimson.

what's available: The group's sophomore effort, *Welcome to the Real World* 🎵🎵🎵 (RCA, 1985, prod. Mr. Mister, Phil DeVilliers), is all that remains in print, boasting massive, semi-spiritual hits such as the atmospheric ballad "Broken Wings" and "Kyrie."

worth searching for: *Best Selection* (RCA, 1997), a Japanese import, is the closest thing to a greatest hits album you'll find for these guys, putting the best cuts from their three albums into one place.

solo outings:
Richard Page:
Shelter Me ♫♫♫ (Blue Thumb, 1996)

influences:
◄◄ Toto, Berlin, REO Speedwagon
►► Jars of Clay, Hanson

Eric Deggans

The Mr. T Experience
Formed 1985, in Berkeley, CA.

Dr. Frank, guitar, vocals; Joel, bass (1996–present); Jon Von, guitar (1985–92); Aaron, bass (1985–93); Alex, drums (1985–93); Jym, drums (1996–present).

If irony were currency, Mr. T Experience leader Dr. Frank would be a millionaire several times over. The fertile Berkeley punk rock scene, centered around the all-ages venue Gilman Street and the local label Lookout! Records, has given to the world at large the snotty antics and poppy-punk anthems of Green Day. But behind every successful punk band there's the scene that spawned it and the bands that, to the locals, defined that particular culture. In this case, the bands that shouldered the influence load for the East Bay scene were the short-lived-but-hugely influential Operation Ivy and, more durably, the Mr. T Experience. T's 12-year lifespan can be divided neatly into two phases, both of which are characterized by Dr. Frank's smarter-than-your-average-punk sense of often self-deprecating, bittersweet humor and his nimble and clever wordsmithery, but differ in how much pop was mixed into the pop-punk confection. The band snuck into the ranks of the recorded as a quartet with its debut *Everyone's Entitled to Their Own Opinion* in 1986. Band members Von, Alex, Aaron, and Frank didn't let the fact that they couldn't play their instruments get in the way of their enthusiasm. As they improved, well, the music got much better, and Frank's melodic songwriting style started to crystalize. Through 1990's *Making Things with Light* and 1992's *Milk Milk Lemonade*, the group got tighter, tougher, and more accomplished, musically. It was then that guitarist Von left Doc's flock to form the lo-fi, two-chord wonders the Ripoffs, and the MTX regrouped as a trio with Frank, Alex, and Aaron, releasing the fully Dr. Frank–driven *Our Bodies, Our Selves*. The record continued the already well-established tradition of endearing cross-cultural references in MTX songs with the inclusion of the Judy Blume–inspired "Are You There God? It's Me, Margaret," and "Even Hitler Had a Girlfriend." But the stride was not to last as, soon after, both Aaron and Alex left MTX to join the band Samiam. Forced to return to the lab, Dr. Frank re-emerged with a tighter, more poppy, three-headed rock creation evidenced on 1996's anthemic and enthusiastic *Love Is Dead*. Dr.

Frank, the album proved, could outpace his musical offspring and, judging by the proliferation of Web sites run by impressionable teenagers that feature some variation on "Which MTX member is cutest?," Frank and company are still doing it for the kids. And another generation of punks influenced by the good doctor can only be encouraging.

what to buy: Dive right into the modern MTX with *Love Is Dead* ♫♫♫♫ (Lookout!, 1996, prod. Kevin Army). The sound is big but polished, and the hooks will get their barbs under your skin before you can sing along with the first chanting "na na na" chorus. This record is just about as infectious as the pop-punk genre gets, and you'll likely get a chuckle out of the lyrics, too.

what to buy next: Two albums give a good overview of the original Mr. T Experience. *Big Black Bugs Bleed Blue Blood* ♫♫♫♫ (Rough Trade, 1989/Lookout!, 1998, prod. Kevin Army) features 24 additional tracks on the Lookout! reissue, while *Making Things with Light* ♫♫♫♫ (Lookout!, 1990, prod. various), a compilation of live, outtake, and demo tracks, represent a band that's having too much fun to care about whether it's profitable.

what to avoid: *Everyone's Entitled to Their Own Opinion* ♫ (Disorder, 1986/Lookout!, 1995, prod. Mr. T Experience) is the band at its rawest, yes, but that's not enough of a selling point to justify blowing your dough on this album.

the rest:
Night Shift at the Thrill Factory ♫♫♫ (Rough Trade, 1988/Lookout!, 1998)
Milk Milk Lemonade ♫♫♫ (Lookout!, 1992)
Our Bodies Our Selves ♫♫♫♫ (Lookout!, 1993)
And the Women Who Love Them ♫♫♫ (Lookout! EP, 1996)
Revenge Is Sweet, and So Are You ♫♫♫ (Lookout!, 1997)

solo outings:
Bomb Bassetts:
Dress Rehearsal ♫♫♫ (Lookout! EP, 1997)
Take a Trip With . . . ♫♫♫ (Lookout!, 1997)

influences:
◄◄ The Ramones, the Dead Kennedys
►► Green Day, the Offspring, the Hi-Fives

see also: *Samiam*

Chris Handyside

Joni Mitchell
Born Roberta Joan Anderson, November 1943, in Fort Macleod, Alberta, Canada.

Joni Mitchell is one of the most influential singer-songwriters to emerge from the late '60s folk-rock scene, a poet on a par with

Bob Dylan. As a child, Joan Anderson took piano lessons in Saskatoon, Canada, and as a teenager taught herself to play ukulele and later guitar so she could entertain at parties. She first gained notice as a songwriter when Judy Collins turned her song "Both Sides Now" into a Top 10 hit in 1968. That same year, Mitchell's debut album was released to critical acclaim, and the rapid succession of albums that followed peaked with the classic *Court and Spark*. During the mid-'70s, Mitchell shifted gears, dropped the angst-angel image, and stretched out for experimentations in electronic and ethnic music and collaborations with jazz players such as Tom Scott and the legendary Charles Mingus. Though she releases albums infrequently—she also pursues an active career as a painter—Mitchell remains a vital and ambitious artist.

what to buy: *Court and Spark* 𝄢𝄢𝄢𝄢 (Asylum, 1974, prod. Joni Mitchell) remains Mitchell's top achievement, a melding of pop and jazz stylings that netted multiple Grammy nominations and the hit singles "Help Me" and "Free Man in Paris." *Turbulent Indigo* 𝄢𝄢𝄢𝄢 (Warner Bros., 1994, prod. Joni Mitchell, Larry Klein) is an evocative collection of songs that sounds both modern and timeless. With its all-star guest list—including Stephen Stills and James Taylor—*Blue* 𝄢𝄢𝄢𝄢 (Reprise, 1971, prod. Joni Mitchell) is a frank and revealing work, as well as one of Mitchell's finest singing performances. The companion CDs *Hits* 𝄢𝄢𝄢𝄢 (Reprise, 1996, prod. various) and *Misses* 𝄢𝄢𝄢𝄢 (Reprise, 1996, prod. various) go a long way toward summarizing Mitchell's best material, but both ultimately come up short. If Mitchell isn't deserving of a comprehensive box set, no one is.

what to buy next: *Ladies of the Canyon* 𝄢𝄢𝄢𝄢 (Reprise, 1971, prod. Joni Mitchell) houses the Mitchell standards "Big Yellow Taxi," "Woodstock," and "The Circle Game." *For the Roses* 𝄢𝄢𝄢𝄢 (Asylum, 1972, prod. Joni Mitchell) was Mitchell's first gold album and includes her first Top 40 hit "You Turn Me on, I'm a Radio." *The Hissing of Summer Lawns* 𝄢𝄢𝄢𝄢 (Asylum, 1975, prod. Joni Mitchell) finds her exploring a jazzy and impressionistic vein using the same all-star jazz aces who worked on *Court and Spark*.

what to avoid: The guest-laden (Billy Idol?) *Chalk Mark in a Rain Storm* 𝄢𝄢 (Geffen, 1988, prod. Joni Mitchell, Larry Klein) is a surprisingly slight effort, musically bland and lyrically weak.

the rest:
Joni Mitchell 𝄢𝄢𝄢 (Reprise, 1968)
Clouds 𝄢𝄢𝄢 (Reprise, 1969)
Miles of Aisles 𝄢𝄢𝄢 (Asylum, 1974)
Hejira 𝄢𝄢𝄢 (Asylum, 1975)
Don Juan's Reckless Daughter 𝄢𝄢𝄢 (Asylum, 1977)
Mingus 𝄢𝄢𝄢 (Asylum, 1979)
Shadows and Light 𝄢𝄢𝄢 (Asylum, 1980)

Wild Things Run Fast 𝄢𝄢𝄢 (Geffen, 1982)
Dog Eat Dog 𝄢𝄢𝄢 (Geffen, 1985)
Night Ride Home 𝄢𝄢𝄢 (Geffen, 1991)
Taming the Tiger 𝄢𝄢𝄢𝄢 (Warner Bros., 1998)

worth searching for: *Just Ice* (KTS, 1994) is a digital bootleg recording of a rare Mitchell performance in Toronto after *Turbulent Indigo*'s release.

influences:

◄◄ Crosby, Stills & Nash, James Taylor, Motown, Charles Mingus, John Coltrane, Dizzy Gillespie

►► Tori Amos, Tracey Bonham, Shawn Colvin, Milla, Jewel, Alanis Morissette, Sarah McLachlan, Prince, Seal

Hilary Weber

Moby

Born Richard Melville Hall, September 11, 1965, in Darien, CT.

Although Moby (so named because Richard Melville is a distant relative of *Moby Dick* author Herman Melville) is one of techno's brightest stars, he works outside of techno conventions. He's emerged from the studio to put a face with his music in an otherwise anonymous genre. He's frowned upon drug and alcohol consumption while working in a community in which Ecstacy is all the rave. And he's exploded far beyond the sonic boundaries of techno, boldly folding elements of other genres into his cathartic recordings. A born-again Christian who used to play in a hardcore punk band—then worked as a New York club DJ, spinning records for the likes of Run-D.M.C. and Cher—Moby refuses to preach to the converted. Instead, the self-contained studio whiz passionately challenges with his strong ideals and intense, three-dimensional music that contains uplifting messages of faith and strong elements of spirituality.

what to buy: Although you'll find it filed under techno, the masterful *Everything Is Wrong* 𝄢𝄢𝄢𝄢 (Elektra, 1995, prod. Moby) is free from lyrical and musical constraints, incorporating elements of classical, reggae, gospel, hip-hop, funk, industrial, disco, and punk into its restless but cleansing fold. As always, Moby handles almost all of the writing, composing, producing, instrumentation, programming, and engineering, although several disco divas and a dance-hall toaster share much of the vocal load. The hyper "Feeling So Real," "Everytime You Touch Me," and the ambient, album-closing "When It's Cold I'd Like to Die" are standouts.

what to buy next: *Move* 𝄢𝄢𝄢𝄢 (Elektra EP, 1993, prod. Moby), which features the moving "Unloved Symphony," provides a sneak preview of the ground Moby would cover on *Everything Is Wrong*.

the rest:
Moby 𝄢𝄢𝄢𝄢 (Instinct, 1992)
Early Underground 𝄢𝄢𝄢 (Instinct, 1993)
Ambient 𝄢𝄢𝄢 (Instinct, 1993)
Everything Is Wrong: Mixed and Remixed 𝄢𝄢𝄢 (Mute, 1995)
Rare: Collected B-Sides 𝄢𝄢𝄢 (Instinct, 1996)
Animal Rights 𝄢𝄢𝄢𝄢 (Elektra, 1997)
I Like to Score 𝄢𝄢𝄢 (Elektra, 1997)

influences:

◀◀ Brian Eno, Arvo Part, Tangerine Dream, Donna Summer, Bad Brains, the Orb, St. Etienne

▶▶ Tricky, Goldie, Aphex Twin

Josh Freedom du Lac

Moby Grape

Formed 1966, in San Francisco, CA.

Skip Spence, guitar, vocals (1966–68); Jerry Miller, guitar, vocals; Peter Lewis, guitar, vocals; Bob Mosley, bass, vocals; Don Stevenson, drums, vocals.

Though the Grateful Dead, Jefferson Airplane, and Big Brother & the Holding Company are the groups synonymous with the Summer of Love, no finer record emerged from San Francisco in 1967 than *Moby Grape*. Spearheaded by a three-guitar frontline, tight harmonies, and a more propulsive sound than their Bay Area brethren, the Grape mixed equal parts rock, psychedelia, country-funk, and folk on their superb debut. They seemed a band destined for great things; everyone could write, everyone had chops, and they all could sing—from Bob Mosely's gravelly white-soul pipes to the hauntingly plaintive cry of Peter Lewis. Yet, by their second album, ego and excess were beginning to take their toll. *Wow* was a double LP, with one record ("Grape Jam") consisting entirely of aimless studio jammming. Within three years, the group was hopelessly and weirdly splintered—Mosely left to enlist in the Marines (!), Skip Spence was in Bellevue, and the rest were wandering through the wreckage, never to recapture the promise of their fine first album.

what to buy: Perhaps the only Moby Grape you'll ever need to own, *Vintage: Very Best* 𝄢𝄢𝄢𝄢 (Columbia/Legacy, 1993, prod. various) is a well-packaged two-CD retrospective that includes the entire debut album as well as a strong selection of late 60's material, plus unreleased demos, outtakes, and live performances. If, understandably, you'd prefer the debut album alone, *Moby Grape* 𝄢𝄢𝄢𝄢 (San Francisco Sound, 1994, prod. David Rubinson) is available on a single CD.

what to buy next: *Wow/Grape Jam* 𝄢𝄢𝄢 (San Francisco Sound, 1994, prod. David Rubinson) is the band's overblown sopho-

more release, with a few gems among the over-ambitious misses—plus the lackluster set of studio jams. Only available on vinyl as of this writing, *Moby Grape '69* 𝄢𝄢𝄢 (Columbia, 1969, prod. David Rubinson) is the best of the later records, notably for some fine songs by Peter Lewis.

what to avoid: *Moby Grape '83* 𝄢𝄢 (San Francisco Sound, 1983, prod. David Robinson) was a far from successful reunion. For fanatics only.

the rest:
Truly Fine Citizen 𝄢𝄢 (Columbia, 1969)
20 Granite Creek 𝄢𝄢𝄢 (Reprise, 1971)
Live Grape 𝄢𝄢 (Escape, 1978)

worth searching for: During the late 70's, Mosley formed a band called the Ducks, which backed up Neil Young on a brief but notorious back-to-the-bars tour of California. Look for the bootlegs.

solo outings:
Skip Spence:
Oar 𝄢𝄢𝄢 (Columbia, 1969/Collectors, 1993)

Bob Mosley:
Bob Mosley 𝄢 (Warner Bros., 1972)

influences:

◀◀ The Byrds, Buffalo Springfield, Jefferson Airplane, the Beatles

▶▶ Gin Blossoms, Golden Smog, Wilco

Doug Pippin

Modern English

Formed 1979, in Colchester, England. Disbanded 1991. Re-formed 1995.

Robbie Grey, vocals; Ted Mason, guitars, keyboards; Matthew Shipley, keyboards; Nicholas Denton, bass; Robbie Brian, drums; Richard Brown, drums (1979–84); Gary McDowell, guitar; Michael Conroy, bass; Stephen Walker, keyboards (1979–84); Aaron Davidson, keyboards, guitar, vocals (1984–91).

Modern English, comprised of self-taught musicians, played a psychedelic-revival style of new wave. Falling into the "bands with weird haircuts" category, its biggest contribution was a memorable song called "I Melt with You" from its sophomore effort, *After the Snow*. The band has milked the song with unusual success, but it wasn't enough to keep the original lineup together. Robbie Grey gathered a new group of musicians during the mid-'90s and relaunched the band, though even they disavow the resulting album, *Everything's Mad*. Still on the road thanks to a spate of '80s nostalgia, the group is writing songs and seeking a new recording deal.

what to buy: Since all you really need by Modern English is the enduring hit "I Melt with You," *After the Snow* 𝄞𝄞𝄞 (Sire, 1983/1992, prod. Hugh Jones) is the album to get. The CD also includes the whole of the band's *Life in the Gladhouse* EP.

what to avoid: Although it's a serviceable album, *Pillow Lips* 𝄞𝄞 (TVT, 1991) contains an inferior, re-recorded version of "I Melt with You."

the rest:
Mesh and Lace 𝄞𝄞𝄞 (4AD, 1980)
Ricochet Days 𝄞𝄞 (Sire, 1984)
Stop Start 𝄞𝄞 (Sire, 1985)
Everything's Mad 𝄞𝄞 (Imago, 1996)

influences:
◄◄ Joy Division, This Mortal Coil

►► The Psychedelic Furs, Marcy Playground, Everclear

Anna Glen

Modern Lovers

See: Jonathan Richman

Modest Mouse

Formed 1993, in Issaquah, WA.

Isaac Brock, guitar, vocals; Jeremiah Green, drums; Eric Judy, bass.

In the case of Modest Mouse, perception has little to do with reality. Though diminutive in name, age, and stature ('tis a wee trio), the band can sneak up on you with a riff that impacts like a sack full of hammers. Modest Mouse is one of several razor-sharp Pacific Northwest emo-core bands (Satisfact, Linc, Lois) with ties to Calvin Johnson's K Records imprint. The band has careened through two full-length albums and as many EP's since its eponymous nine-song EP in 1996, producing more than 60 individual tracks for stunningly diverse albums that float easily between jagged, diving guitar parts and smoothed-out melodies. Like its predecessors, the Pixies and Built to Spill, the band cranks out an emotion-laden racket that attracts and repels in equal proportions. The result is a deliciously crooked mixture that makes you feel like a teen clenching your teeth on freshly tightened braces. Isaac Brock's vocals, which produce some of the most honest and unsettling strains since David Byrne's early days with the Talking Heads, provide the spark for the band's flame. Meanwhile, his compact and inventive lyrics are served up over a volatile sonic texture created by his own formidable guitar style, Eric Judy's intelligent bass lines, and Jeremiah Green's rhythmic drum volleys.

what to buy: *The Lonesome Crowded West* 𝄞𝄞𝄞𝄞 (Up, 1997, prod. Calvin Johnson, Isaac Brock, Scott Swayze) is a 15-song cranker full of musical whirling dervishes. Tracks such as "Teeth like God's Shoeshine" and "Doin' the Cockroach" showcase the band's ability to start slow, finish hard, and leave you aching for another cut. "Cowboy Dan" and "Styrofoam Boots/It's All Nice on Ice, Alright" bring to the fore Brock's edgy and surreal song writing style.

what to buy next: *Interstate 8* 𝄞𝄞𝄞𝄞 (Up, 1996, prod. Steve Wold) is more of the same, but most of the tracks are recorded live. Brock spins his singular yarns over foot-tapping grooves with the added flavor of slide guitar, mandolin, cello, and some backing vocals provided by Nicole Johnson. "Tundra/Desert" is a fearsome composition that poses to your central nervous system the very real question of whether to fight or flee. An altogether absorbing album.

the rest:
Modest Mouse 𝄞𝄞𝄞𝄞 (K, 1996)
This Is a Long Drive for Someone with Nothing to Think About 𝄞𝄞𝄞𝄞 (Up, 1996)
The Fruit That Ate Itself 𝄞𝄞𝄞 (K, 1997)

influences:
◄◄ The Tree People, Joy Division, Built to Spill, the Pixies, David Byrne

Brandon Barber

moe.

Formed 1990, in Buffalo, NY.

Chuck Garvey, guitars, vocals; Al Schnier, guitars, lapsteel, vocals; Rob Derhak, bass, vocals; Vinnie Amico, drums (1996–present); Chris Mazur, drums (1995–96); Mike Strazza, drums (1995); Jim Loughlin, drums (1992–95); Ray Schwartz, drums (1990–92); Dave Kessler, guitars (1990–92).

Like Phish and the Grateful Dead before it, moe. has constructed its sound and its fanbase from the ground up. Through seasons of grueling tour schedules, internet chatter, and incessant tape trading, this Albany-based quartet has snagged a sizable portion of the neo-hippie masses. A slot on 1997's Furthur Festival and several expansive jam sessions with former Dead rhythm guitarist Bob Weir gave moe. much needed face time in front of the right audience and extended its musicians' playing skills immensely. More than most bands of its ilk, moe. uses the lyrics as a slipcover for the music, powering through a song's prelude—usually of respectable radio length—then veering abruptly off into an indulgent jam.

what to buy: Dominated by zany lyrics, heavy bass, and flowing jams, *Headseed* 𝄞𝄞𝄞 (1994, prod. moe.) captures a young and loose moe. at its very best. Too inexperienced to know better, the band vacillates between styles—from country twang to

Primus-like gashes to guitar noodling—while keeping a consistent, soaring groove through all 10 tracks.

what to buy next: *No Doy* ♫♫ (Sony 550, 1996, prod. John Porter) boasts a tighter sound and an infinitely superior production quality. Unfortunately, growth and unification seem to have squeezed some of the charm out of the music, resulting in a solid, but standard radio rock pastiche.

worth searching for: Troll the internet for armies of moe. tape traders and pick up a live show. *Fatboy* is an out-of-print demo tape recorded during 1992. *Loaf* is moe.'s only live album to date; recorded during 1996 at Wetlands in New York City, it is also out of print, but widely circulated.

influences:

◀◀ The Grateful Dead, Primus, Phish

Isaac Josephson

Mohave 3

See: Slowdive

The Mojo Men /The Mojo /Mojo

Formed 1965, in San Francisco, CA. Disbanded 1970.

Jim Alaimo, vocals, bass; Paul Curcio, guitar; Don Metchik, keyboards; Dennis De Carr, drums (1965–66); Jan Errico, drums, vocals (1966–70).

Having mutated from a vibrant folk scene in the aftermath of the Beatles' arrival, the early Bay Area rock groups were without exception dealt a cruel and unjust fate. Roundly ignored by the big record companies and producers down south in Los Angeles, these bands were left to toil in near total obscurity, only to be trampled underfoot a couple of years later when their higher-profiled, more ruthlessly aggressive descendants (e.g., the Grateful Dead, Jefferson Airplane) finally broke through to national acclaim. The story of the Mojo Men pretty well follows this outline: Beginning life as slavish Animals and Yardbirds devotees, the group scored regional successes with a cover of Jagger/Richard's "Off the Hook" and its self-composed raver "Dance with Me." When drummer Jan Errico joined from fellow Frisco folk-rockers the Vejtables, the Mojo Men became one of several acts from the tiny Autumn label roster absorbed by Warner Bros., where they immediately began work with producer Lenny Waronker and arranger Van Dyke Parks. The first fruit of these labors resulted in a cleverly neo-baroque hit reading of Stephen Stills's "Sit Down, I Think I Love You" and the band's newly adventurous, vocally dependent approach seemed to mesh perfectly alongside such contemporaries as

the Mamas & the Papas and the Association. Unfortunately, save for several exceptional (though seldom heard) follow-up 45's, the Mojo Men released no other material of merit, and sadly seemed to fall through the cracks before their full potential could even begin to be explored, let alone exposed to an audience at large.

what's available: The two distinct stages of this band's career are perfectly chronicled on *Whys Ain't Supposed to Be: The Autumn Sessions* ♫♫♫♫ (Sundazed, 1995, compilation prod. Jud Cost, Bob Irwin), presenting 21 of their pre-Errico, Sly Stone–produced recordings, and *Sit Down: It's the Mojo Men* ♫♫♫♭ (Sundazed, 1995, compilation prod. Jud Cost, Bob Irwin), a splendid collection of the more colorful Warner Bros. material. Both of these discs contain moments of absolute brilliance that will surprise even those familiar with the wonders of the group's one big hit.

influences:

◀◀ The Rolling Stones, Beau Brummels, the Knickerbockers

▶▶ Harpers Bizarre, the Bangles, Richard X. Heyman

Gary Pig Gold

The Moles

See: Richard Davies

Joey Molland

See: Badfinger

Molly Hatchet

Formed 1975, in Jacksonville, FL.

Dave Hlubek, guitar; Duane Roland, guitar; Danny Joe Brown, vocals (1975–80, 1982); Banner Thomas, bass (1975–82); Bruce Cump, drums (1975–82); Jimmy Farrar, vocals (1980–81); Barry Borden, drums (1982–late 1980s); Riff West, bass (1982–late 1980s). Current lineup: Bobby Ingram, guitar, vocals; Phil McCormack, vocals; John Galvin, keyboards, vocals; Bryan Bassett, guitar; Andy McKinney, bass, vocals; Mac Crawford, drums.

Molly Hatchet is one of the *other* Southern rock bands—not the Allman Brothers, not Lynyrd Skynyrd, not even .38 Special. Hell, it only had *two* guitar players. But for a time during the late '70s, the group held its own with a slightly heavier attack than many of its contemporaries, leaning almost toward metal in some spots—appropriate enough considering the group's name was taken from the legend of Hatchet Molly, a prostitute who was said to lure men to her bedroom in order to castrate them. The band's first three albums sold nearly five million copies between them, and that's been enough to insure a waiting audience for any state fair or small bar the band, whose original members are long gone, chooses to play.

what to buy: Though poorly annotated, *Greatest Hits* 🎵🎵🎵 (Epic, 1990, prod. Tom Werman, Pat Armstrong, Andy de-Ganahl) is a concise sampler, with a dozen prime Hatchet cuts that include "Flirtin' with Disaster," "Gator Country," "Ragtop Deluxe," and the epic "Fall of the Peacemakers."

what to buy next: Of its first three efforts, the sophomore *Flirtin' with Disaster* 🎵🎵🎵 (Epic, 1979, prod. Tom Werman) represents the group's finest studio moment, with Werman's production loading on the punch for a big, crunchy, arena-sized attack.

what to avoid: Collections such as *Cut to the Bone* 🎵🎵 (SMSP, 1995, prod. various) and *Super Hits* 🎵🎵 (Epic, 1998, prod. various) are skimpy and superfluous.

the rest:
Molly Hatchet 🎵🎵🎵 (Epic, 1978)
Beatin' the Odds 🎵🎵🎵 (Epic, 1980)
Take No Prisoners 🎵🎵🎵 (Epic, 1981)
No Guts . . . No Glory 🎵🎵🎵 (Epic, 1983/SMSP, 1996)
Double Trouble Live 🎵🎵🎵 (Epic, 1985/1989)
Silent Reign of Heroes 🎵🎵🎵 (CMC International, 1998)

influences:
◀◀ The Allman Brothers Band, Lynyrd Skynyrd, Blackfoot, the Yardbirds

▶▶ Point Blank, Creed

Gary Graff

Mommyheads

Formed 1989, in San Francisco, CA.

Adam Cohen, vocals, guitar, keyboards; Mike Holt, keyboards, guitar, vocals; Jeff Palmer, bass, vocals; Dan Fisherman, drums, vocals.

The Mommyheads' fine whine certainly got better with age. The constraints of indie label recording budgets couldn't contain the band's ultimate goal—which is evidently to sound as much like late-period (and we're talking recent) Paul McCartney.

what to buy: *The Mommyheads* 🎵🎵🎵 (DGC, 1997, prod. Don Was) comes closest to making the band's pop dreams come true. But barely hidden, like darkness at the roots of dyed-blond hair, are strands of pseudo-quirky indie guitar. "Bellhop" evokes Jellyfish at its best; the gorgeous "I'm in Awe" finds the Mommyheads expressing exactly that sentiment about Paul McCartney, sprouting melodic wings as a result.

what to buy next: Each of the albums *Coming into Beauty* 🎵🎵🎵 (Simple Machines, 1992, prod. Perkin Barns) and *Flying Suit* 🎵🎵🎵 (Dromedary, 1994, prod. Dan Rathbun, Mommyheads) catch the band during its awkward transitional stage. But ado-

lescence can be beautiful, too, and that's borne out by the Mommyheads' catchy tunes.

what to avoid: Ultimately, *Bingham's Hole* 🎵🎵 (Dot Dot Dash, 1995, prod. Peter Katis, Mommyheads) is a small step back, with the band's ideas growing faster than its songwriting abilities. Also, *Acorn* 🎵🎵 (Fang, 1989, prod. Mommyheads) isn't bad, just a rough take-off for this band that later took flight with some great songs.

influences:
◀◀ Paul McCartney, XTC

▶▶ The Merrymakers

Jordan Oakes

Eddie Money

Born Edward Mahoney, March 21, 1949, in Brooklyn, NY.

For straight-ahead, shot-and-a-beer barroom rock 'n' roll, it's hard to do better than Eddie Money's 1977 debut album and a few other assorted moments from his career. The son of a police officer, Money attended the New York Police Academy himself but was more interested in the rock he was playing at night. He dropped out of cop school and headed to the Bay Area where, with help from promoter Bill Graham, Money began his music career as an affable palooka with a knack for irresistible hits such as "Two Tickets to Paradise" and "Baby Hold On." But since Money's partnership with guitarist and chief foil Jimmy Lyon splintered during the early '80s, he's floundered, with the occasional hit—such as "Take Me Home Tonight (Be My Baby)," a Top 5 smash during 1986—rising out of a wealth of tepid and forgettable, if well-intentioned, material.

what to buy: *Eddie Money* 🎵🎵🎵 (Columbia, 1977, prod. Bruce Botnick) is a fine debut that remains Money's strongest entry, buoyed by the hits ("Two Tickets to Paradise," "Baby Hold On") and other fine tracks such as his cover of the Miracles' "You've Really Got a Hold on Me."

what to buy next: *Life for the Taking* 🎵🎵🎵 (Columbia, 1978, prod. Bruce Botnick) and *Playing for Keeps* 🎵🎵🎵 (Columbia, 1980, prod. Ron Nevison) are solid, rocking efforts whose key songs—"Gimme Some Water," "Rock and Roll the Place," "Trinidad," "Get a Move On"—still hold up. *Greatest Hits: Sound of Money* 🎵🎵🎵 (Columbia, 1989, prod. various) is a reasonable best-of whose three new songs should have been canned in favor of better songs from his albums.

what to avoid: Judging by *Unplug It In* **woof!** (Columbia EP, 1992), although the unplugged format benefits some artists, Money isn't one of them.

the rest:

No Control ♫♫♫ (Columbia, 1982)

Where's the Party? ♫♫ (Columbia, 1983)

Can't Hold Back ♫♫♫ (Columbia, 1986)

Nothing to Lose ♫ (Columbia, 1988)

Right Here ♫ (Columbia, 1991)

Love and Money ♫♫ (Wolfgang, 1995)

Shakin' with the Money Man ♫♫♫ (CMC International, 1997)

influences:

◀◀ Sam Cooke, Chuck Berry, Elvis Presley, Rod Stewart, Eric Burdon (Animals), Motown, Stax

▶▶ Michael Bolton, Jon Secada, Peter Cetera, John Mellencamp, Bryan Adams

Gary Graff

The Monkees

Formed 1965, in Los Angeles, CA. Disbanded 1970. Reunited 1986–89, 1996.

David "Davy" Jones, vocals; Mickey Dolenz, vocals, drums; Mike Nesmith, vocals, guitar (1965–69, 1996); Peter Tork, bass, guitar, vocals (1965–69, 1989–present).

From the Fab Four it was a quick move to the prefab four. The Monkees didn't form; the band was made—in this case for an American TV show inspired by the Beatles' film *A Hard Day's Night* (among the auditions' more famous rejects were Stephen Stills and Three Dog Night's Danny Hutton). The show retained the movie's zaniness and even went a step or two further into a plotless kind of creative anarchy. Musically, however, the Monkees played tightly constructed, Brill Building–style pop overseen by music biz mogul Don Kirshner. It worked; with songs written by Neil Diamond and the team of Gerry Goffin and Carole King, among others, the Monkees were a chart and radio fixture with "Last Train to Clarksville," "Pleasant Valley Sunday," "I'm a Believer," and "Daydream Believer." The group even enjoyed a bit of influence on the punk scene with "(I'm Not Your) Steppin' Stone," a particular favorite of the Sex Pistols. The hits stopped coming—at least in droves—about the time the group wrested creative control for itself. After the TV show was canceled in 1968, the Monkees tried a movie, the trippy and largely unwatchable *Head*, and slowly splintered—Peter Tork leaving first, then Mike Nesmith. But when MTV started airing episodes of the TV show again in 1986, the Monkees (sans Nesmith) were back, and the revival repeats itself periodically—including a brief 1996 reunion of all four Monkees for an album and TV special.

what to buy: *The Monkees' Greatest Hits* ♫♫♫♫♫ (Rhino, 1995, prod. various) is a 20-song confection of timeless pop hits—something nobody with an ounce of hipness could have expected of the Monkees at the time. For those who want more, *Anthology* ♫♫♫♫ (Rhino, 1998, prod. various) is a two-CD set brimming with everything—and even more than—you'd want.

what to buy next: This is a bit problematic—how much more do you want than the hits? But try the soundtrack to *Head* ♫♫♫ (Colgems, 1968/Rhino, 1994, prod. various), a trippy little souvenir of the times that features poetry, dialogue from the film, and guest appearances by Neil Young, Leon Russell, and Ry Cooder. *Barrel Full of Monkees: Monkees for Kids* ♫♫♫ (Kid Rhino, 1996, prod. various) is considerably more listenable than a Barney tape.

what to avoid: The three-volume series *Missing Links* ♫ (Rhino, 1988/1989/1996, prod. Bill Inglot, Andrew Sandoval) is proof that, although the Monkees made some terrific singles, it wasn't a band whose vault is filled with treasures.

the rest:

The Monkees ♫♫♫ (Colgems, 1966/Rhino, 1994)

More of the Monkees ♫♫♫ (Colgems, 1967/Rhino, 1994)

Headquarters ♫♫♫ (Colgems, 1967/Rhino, 1995)

Pisces, Aquarius, Capricorn & Jones, Ltd. ♫♫♫ (Colgems, 1967/Rhino, 1995)

The Birds, the Bees, and the Monkees ♫♫♫ (Colgems, 1968/Rhino, 1994)

Instant Replay ♫♫ (Colgems, 1969/Rhino, 1995)

The Monkees Present ♫♫ (Colgems, 1969/Rhino, 1994)

Changes ♫ (Colgems, 1970/Rhino, 1994)

Live 1967 ♫♫ (Rhino, 1987)

Pool It ♫♫ (Rhino, 1987/1995)

Listen to the Band ♫♫♫ (Rhino, 1991)

Justus ♫♫ (Rhino, 1996)

worth searching for: Videotapes from the Monkees' TV shows are out there, including a lavish (and expensive) box set from Rhino.

solo outings:

Dolenz & Jones :

(With Tommy Boyce and Bobby Hart) *Concert in Japan* ♫♫ (Varese Sarabande, 1996)

Mike Nesmith:

And the Hits Just Keep Comin' ♫♫♫ (Rio, 1972/1995)

influences:

◀◀ The Beatles, Herman's Hermits, the Hollies

▶▶ The Partridge Family, the Archies, Josie & the Pussycats, Big Star, the Sex Pistols, the Go-Go's

Gary Graff

Monks of Doom

See: Cracker

Mono

Formed 1997, in London, England.

Siobhan De Mare, vocals; Martin Virgo, keyboards, production.

Despite the name, Mono is a London-based stereophonic duo: Martin Virgo supplying the beats and Siobhan De Mare the vocals. Virgo spent time as a member of Nellee Hooper's renowned production team, working with the likes of Massive Attack and Björk before hooking up with De Mare, who was initially headed to Paris to become a disco diva. Mono's sound is deriviative of the Bristol sound as exemplified by their contemporaries Massive Attack, Tricky, and Portishead.

what's available: Listening to *Formica Blues* ♫♫♫♪ (Mercury, 1998, prod. Martin Virgo), one is gently absorbed into a sonic pastiche of late '60s American soul, orchestrally inclined soundtrack collages, and atmospheric, often eerie, electronic haberdashery. The sound is at once familiar yet strangely Promethean, seemingly documenting the collision of a forgotten musical past with an as of yet uncharted melodic future. While it bears striking similarities to other symphonically inclined, heavily atmospheric ambient music, Mono's overall tone is lighter and wispier than that of other bands. Virgo's sonic penchant is to incorporate the productions styles of various producers, such as Phil Spector and soundtrack composers like John Barry; in fact, the song "Life in Mono" actually incorporates portions of Barry's score for *The Ipcress File*.

worth searching for: The import 12-inch single for "Life in Mono" (Echo Label Unlimited/Mercury, 1996) features scathing remixes by the Propellerheads and Lightfoot.

influences:

◀◀ Massive Attack, Tricky, Portishead, John Barry, Phil Spector

Spence D.

The Mono Men

Formed 1988, in Bellingham, WA.

Dave Crider, guitar, vocals; Marx Wright, guitar, vocals (1988–91); Lodge Morrisette, bass; Aaron Roeder, drums; John Mortensen, guitar, vocals (1991–96).

At some point during the early '90s Dave Crider left behind a promising career in the management of used record stores to devote full-time energy to his label, Estrus Records, and to his flagship band, the Mono Men. Named for the cantankerous lead singer of the Lyres (though the name could as easily have come from the monaural records that inspire much of their

sound), the Mono Men tapped into the ugly underbelly of the cocktail revival. That is, their sources are the rumbling, intimidating sounds of Link Wray, the Sonics, and the Ramones: folks who take their liquor straight, and never mind the martini glass. Most of their oeuvre is available on vinyl (much of it on 45's only), and none of it is, uh, nice. The Mono Men have an ugly, inescapably masculine, hard-drinking, and utterly joyous take on garage rock. Album artwork (mostly the creation of legendary Seattle designer Art Chantry; look for alternate covers) draws heavily from the classic men's and hot-rod magazines of the 1950s.

what to buy: *Wrecker* ♫♫♫♪ (Estrus, 1992, prod. Richard Head) is a classic of the genre, replete with snarling pop classics, brutish guitar riffs, and utterly frenzied vocals. On this record Crider's punk sensibility fused neatly with Mortensen's pop impulses producing the same kind of crunch that the meeting of punk and metal were manifesting 90 miles south in Seattle.

what to buy next: After the uninsured Estrus warehouse burned down, taking with it the band's equipment, the label's stock, and a priceless collection of kitsch, they recorded the indelicately titled *Have a Nice Day, Motherfucker* ♫♫♫♪ (Estrus, 1997, prod. Tim Kerr). Stripped down to a trio, and sharpened by an outside producer utterly in tune with their sensibility, it is a concise catharsis. An earlier homage to the almost forgotten tradition of instrumental rock, *Shut Up!* ♫♫♫ (also packaged as

Shut the Fuck Up!) (Estrus, 1993) romps through Link Wray, Dick Dale, and some surprisingly authentic originals.

the rest:
Stop Draggin' Me Down 𝄞𝄞𝄞 (Estrus, 1990)
Sin & Tonic 𝄞𝄞𝄞 (Estrus, 1994)
Live at Tom's Strip n' Bowl! 𝄞𝄞 (Estrus, 1995)
10 Cool Ones 𝄞𝄞𝄞 (Scat, 1996)
Bent Pages 𝄞𝄞𝄞 (AuGoGo, 1997)

worth searching for: The Mono Men have repackaged a number of titles on foreign labels, of which *Back to Mono* (1+2, 1992, prod. Richard Head) is a pretty swell 25-song summation of the band's virtues.

influences:
◀◀ Link Wray, the Sonics, the Lyres
▶▶ The Makers, the Oblivions, the Headcoats

Grant Alden

Country Dick Montana
See: Beat Farmers

Montrose
Formed 1973, in the San Francisco Bay Area, CA. Disbanded late 1970s.

Ronnie Montrose, guitar; Sammy Hagar, vocals (1973–75); Denny Carmassi, drums (1973–78); Bill Church, bass (1973–74); Alan Fitzgerald, bass, keyboards (1974–76); Bob James, vocals (1975–78); Jim Alcivar, keyboards, 1975–late '70s); Randy Jo Hobbs, bass (1976–78); Rick Schlosser, drums (1978); Edgar Winter, keyboards (1978).

Colorado-born Ronnie Montrose was a guitar hero for those in the know, people who appreciated taste and subtlety rather than simply flash. He moved to Los Angeles circa 1970 and made his name playing sessions, including Gary Wright's *Dream Weaver* and Van Morrison's albums *Tupelo Honey* and *St. Dominic's Preview*. A brief membership in the Edgar Winter Group for *They Only Come out at Night* won an offer to take over the guitar spot in Mott the Hoople, but Montrose instead opted to start his own band, a hard rock outfit best known for introducing the world to Sammy Hagar. Montrose itself made minimal commercial impact, though it soldiered bravely through the '70s before finally succumbing towards the end of the decade. Montrose formed another band, Gamma, during the early '80s but has spent most of his time as a solo artist, including scoring the Sega video game *Mr. Bones*. Hagar has had a successful solo career as well as a tenure fronting Van Halen; he also reunited the original Montrose lineup for a track on his *Marching to Mars* album. Carmassi went on to play in Heart.

what to buy: Very little of Montrose's group or solo catalog is in print in the United States these days. *Montrose* 𝄞𝄞𝄞𝄞 (Warner

Bros., 1973/1989, prod. Montrose, Ted Templeman) boasts the sound of a new band hungry and ready to prove itself—before Hagar became too hystrionic. "Rock Candy," "Good Rockin' Tonight," and "Rock the Nations" (sensing a theme here?) are prototypical crunch-rock that's absolutely ageless.

the rest:
Montrose:
Paper Money 𝄞𝄞𝄞 (Warner Bros., 1974)

Ronnie Montrose:
Mr. Bones 𝄞𝄞𝄞𝄞 (Sega Music Group, 1996)

worth searching for: Montrose's best solo album, *Open Fire* (Warner Bros., 1978), is available as a German import.

influences:
◀◀ Jeff Beck, Rick Derringer, Steve Miller, Led Zeppelin
▶▶ Sammy Hagar, Dokken, Poison

see also: *Sammy Hagar, Edgar Winter*

Gary Graff

The Moody Blues /Justin Hayward & John Lodge /Mike Pinder
Formed 1964, in Birmingham, England. Disbanded 1974. Re-formed 1978.

Justin Hayward, vocals, guitar (1966–present); John Lodge, vocals, bass (1966–present); Ray Thomas, vocals, flute; Graeme Edge, vocals, drums; Mike Pinder, vocals, keyboards (1964–78); Patrick Moraz, keyboards (1978–89); Denny Laine, vocals, guitar (1964–66); Clint Warwick, bass, vocals (1964–66).

One of the most enduring bands to emerge during the '60s, the Moody Blues quickly departed from its original blues orientation to adopt the "cosmic" style for which it is best known. The band's work is strongly melodic, ranging from meditative mood pieces—"Isn't Life Strange," "Legend of a Mind"—to driving rock—"Ride My See Saw," "I'm Just a Singer (In a Rock and Roll Band)"— with lyrics that often ponder the Big Questions. The group has enjoyed two periods of great success, one in its initial heyday of the late '60s and early '70s, the other during a period of renewal in the late '70s and early '80s, which brought a string of more straightforward hits such as "Your Wildest Dreams" and "I Know You're Out There Somewhere." The Moodies' latest tack is augmenting its summer amphitheater shows with symphony orchestras, harkening back to the early days of the Hayward-Lodge lineup.

what to buy: *Days of Future Passed* 𝄞𝄞𝄞𝄞 (Deram/Polydor, 1967, prod. Hugh Mendl, Tony Clarke, Michael Dacre-Barclay) is one of the earliest collaborations between a rock band and an orchestra. It's a flowing conceptual piece that houses the hits "Nights in White Satin" and "Forever Afternoon (Tuesday?)." *Seventh Sojourn* ♫♫♫ (Threshold, 1972, prod. Tony Clarke) is one of the Moodies' most consistent albums and its last before an extended hiatus. *This Is the Moody Blues* ♫♫♫ (Polydor, 1974, prod. various) is a good compilation of the group's 1967 through 1972 peak.

what to buy next: *On the Threshold of a Dream* ♫♫♫ (Deram/Polydor, 1969, prod. Tony Clarke) prominently features the band's signature Mellotron sound, while *Every Good Boy Deserves Favour* ♫♫♫ (Polydor, 1971, prod. Tony Clarke) contains some of its best songs, including "Emily's Song" and the upbeat "The Story in Your Eyes." Devotees will have a ball with *Time Traveller* ♫♫♫ (Polydor, 1994, prod. various), an extensive and comprehensive box set; the more modest *The Best of the Moody Blues* ♫♫♫ (PolyGram Chronicles, 1997, prod. various) is another generous best-of featuring digitally remastered tracks.

what to avoid: *The Present* ♫♫ (Polydor, 1983) is mediocre at best; many of its songs sound only half-written.

the rest:
In Search of the Lost Chord ♫♫♫ (Deram/Polydor, 1968)
To Our Children's Children's Children ♫♫♫ (Polydor, 1969)
Question of Balance ♫♫♫ (Polydor, 1970)
Caught Live + 5 ♫♫♫ (PolyGram, 1977)
Octave ♫♫♫ (Polydor, 1978)
Long Distance Voyager ♫♫♫ (Polydor, 1981)
The Other Side of Life ♫♫♫ (Polydor, 1986)
Sur la Mer ♫♫♫ (PolyGram, 1988)
Greatest Hits ♫♫♫ (PolyGram, 1989)
Keys of the Kingdom ♫♫♫ (PolyGram, 1991)
A Night at Red Rocks with the Colorado Symphony Orchestra ♫♫♫♫ (Polydor, 1993)

worth searching for: The import *The Magnificent Moodies* (London, 1965/Polydor, 1989) showcases the earliest edition of the band. *Prelude* (Polydor, 1987) is another import compilation and includes some "lost" tracks and B-sides.

solo outings:
Justin Hayward:
Night Flight ♫♫ (Deram/PolyGram, 1980)

Justin Hayward & John Lodge:
Blue Jays ♫♫♫ (Threshold/Polydor, 1975)

Mike Pinder:
The Promise ♫♫♫ (Threshold, 1975/One Step, 1996)
Off the Shelf ♫♫♫ (Higher & Higher, 1993)
Among the Stars ♫♫♫ (One Step, 1994)

influences:
◀◀ Buddy Holly, Elvis Presley, the Beatles, Motown

WHAT ALBUM CHANGED YOUR LIFE?

A Hard Day's Night by the Beatles, because I'd just broken up with a girl that I thought it would be impossible to ever live without, and that album just summed it all up. A lot of people would say it's lightweight compared to later Beatles albums, but to me every song was a winner. The one thing I learned from it was to always write from the heart. Before then I'd been writing, but not really with any kind of soul behind it.

Justin Hayward (of the Moody Blues)

▶▶ Electric Light Orchestra, Genesis, Yes, Barclay James Harvest, Fairport Convention

Polly Vedder

Keith Moon
See: The Who

Abra Moore
Born June 8, 1966, in Mission Bay, CA.

Although Abra Moore left Poi Dog Pondering—a group she helped form in 1986—durng the early '90s to pursue a solo career, this singer-songwriter-guitarist didn't release a major-label album until 1997's *Strangest Places*. Moore burst onto the music scene amidst an industry focused upon female singers as well as the birth of the Lilith Fair, the first all-female traveling music festival. But it was her powerful lyrics and light, airy vocals that earned a 1997 Grammy nomination for Best Female Rock Vocal Performance for her song "Four Leaf Clover." Moore developed her unique musical style as a teenager living in New York, London, and Paris, but she truly recognized her connection with the Earth while studying at the University of Hawaii, where she met Poi Dog co-founder Frank Orrall. In addition to singing, Moore has appeared in two Richard Linklater movies, *Slacker* and *The Newton Boys*.

what's available: *Strangest Places* ♫♫♫ (Arista Austin, 1997, prod. Mitch Watkins) shows Moore's development as a solo artist. While retaining folky roots, she expands her music into a solid rock sound. The songs contain sharp lyrics and deep guitar licks while at the same time retain the artist's love for folk and R&B. Her major label debut was preceded by the critically acclaimed *Sing* ♫♫♫ (Bohemia Beat, 1995, prod. Mitch Watkins). Moore's softest side shone through on this independent release; she sings of heartache, loss, and her respect for life, especially when sharing her feelings about her mother, who died when Moore was a small child.

influences:
◀◀ Billie Holiday, Chet Baker, Bob Dylan, Tom Petty, Aretha Franklin, Judy Garland

see also: *Poi Dog Pondering*

Ari Bendersky

Gary Moore

Born April 4, 1952, in Belfast, Ireland.

A lively, energetic guitar player, Gary Moore served stints in Coliseum and Thin Lizzy—during the latter's mid-'70s *Jailbreak* peak—before following his own path. He stumbled at first, chasing rock radio with a series of plodding, occasionally contrived albums. But during the late 1980s Moore got the blues, and since then, all has been well. He isn't necessarily about flash, so you have to pay attention to hear his subtle mix of rhythm and lead elements. He's also good for a few hot guests on each album, ranging from blues heroes such as B.B. King and Albert Collins to heavy metal icon Ozzy Osbourne.

what to buy: *Still Got the Blues* ♫♫♫ (Charisma, 1990, prod. Gary Moore) commands an immediate reassessment of Moore's place in the rock pantheon, with guest appearances by Albert King and Albert Collins and Moore's best-known track, "Oh Pretty Woman." He also helmed *Blues for Greeny* ♫♫♫ (Charisma, 1996, prod. Gary Moore, Ian Taylor), an album of deftly played early Fleetwood Mac covers in tribute to that band's troubled founder, Peter Green.

what to buy next: Moore can cut a commanding live figure, though that aspect of his talents has never been captured adequately on record. *Blues Alive* ♫♫♫ (Virgin, 1993, prod. Gary Moore, Ian Taylor) is the best of his concert albums, with estimable—though not quite transcendent—versions of blues staples such as "The Sky Is Crying," "Further on up the Road," and "Walking by Myself."

what to avoid: *Wild Frontier* ♫♫ (Virgin, 1987) is one of those early albums that shows that, for a hard rocker, Moore is a pretty good blues player.

best of the rest:
After the War ♫♫♫ (Virgin, 1989)
Live at the Marquee ♫♫♫ (Griffin, 1994)
Ballads + Blues 1982–94 ♫♫♫ (Charisma, 1995)

worth searching for: There's a plethora of Moore guest appearances in the record racks. Check out his licks on "If Trouble Was Money" from the Albert Collins best-of *Collins Mix* (Pointblank, 1993) or his solo on "She's My Baby" from the Traveling Wilburys' *Vol. III* (Warner Bros., 1990).

influences:
◀◀ Fleetwood Mac, John Mayall's Bluesbreakers, Elmore James, B.B. King, Albert Collins, Hubert Sumlin

▶▶ Stevie Ray Vaughan, Randy Rhoads, Metallica, Colin James, Kenny Wayne Shepherd

Gary Graff

Thurston Moore

See: Sonic Youth

Moose

Formed 1989, in London, England.

Russell Yates, guitar, vocals, bass; Kevin McKillop (a.k.a. Moose), guitar; Damien Warburton, drums (1990–91); Lincoln Fong, bass; Richard Thomas, drums (1991–93); Russell Fong, guitar (1992–94); Mig Morland, drums (1993–present).

Moose's biggest problem has been its inability to get its LP's released in the United States. Upon forming, the band quickly became a star of the exploding English dreampop/shoegaze scene, up there in popularity and camaraderie with Ride, Slowdive, Lush, Boo Radleys, Pale Saints, My Bloody Valentine, Chapterhouse, Catherine Wheel, Kitchens of Distinction, and others. A trio of successful EP's for hip U.K. semi-indie Hut Records established their dreamy but well-defined guitar music, which was always more accessible (but chock full of depth and warm production) than their more blissed-out compatriots. Because of the good looks, smarts, style, and charm of talented songwriter-guitarists Kevin McKillop and Russell Yates, they should have been the biggest and longest lasting of all of the above over here. Instead, they've been the most unjustly overlooked. Hut's parent, Virgin Records, merely tested the water by making a seven-song mini-LP out of the three EP's for release in the United States (oddly minus a few tracks, in contrast to Ride and Lush's similar first U.S. LP's, also made completely out of their initial import singles). But *Sonny & Sam* failed to excite radio and retail, setting off a chain of events—

including an order that Hut drop the group from its roster—that have hamstrung Moose's ability to make inroads in the U.S. Moose fans the Cocteau Twins tried to help by bringing the band on tour with it in the United States, but that still didn't help net a deal. Moose released its latest album, *Twelve New Ways to Fly*, on its own Cool Badge label, with hopes of securing some sort of U.S. distribution.

worth searching for: Virgin U.S. refused to issue . . . *xyz* (Hut U.K., 1992, prod. Mitch Easter) and ordered a shocked and reticent Hut to drop the band from its roster almost immediately upon its import release! Those who have somehow obtained copies have nonetheless attested to its restrained elegance, some surprising hints (only hints) of country—including a cover of Harry Nilsson's *Midnight Cowboy* movie classic "Everybody's Talking"—and to former R.E.M. producer Easter's most sympathetic sound in years. *Honey Bee* (Play It Again Sam Belgium, 1993, prod. Lincoln Fong) not only equals its predecessor, but is an even more elegant, stylized, pretty, and consistent work. Led by the finest song of the band's career to date, the single "I Wanted to See You to See if I Wanted You," the self-produced (by bassist Fong) LP doesn't so much dispense with the tiny country influences as play them down, emitting an extremely pleasant, strongly developed post-punk, post-shoegaze, still dreamy, pop prize.

influences:

⏪ Jimmy Webb, the House of Love, Cocteau Twins, the Sound

⏩ Alison's Halo, Half String, Boo Radleys, Mojave 3

Jack Rabid

Morcheeba

Formed 1995, in London, England.

Skye Edwards, vocals; Paul Godfrey, programming, turntables, drums; Ross Godfrey, guitar, keyboards; Pete Norris, synthesizers (1997–present).

The Godfrey brothers weren't having much luck soliciting their instrumental demos around London until they recruited the honey-voiced Skye Edwards as vocalist. Morcheeba released its debut album, *Who Can You Trust?*, at the same time several bands who fell under the trip-hop tag were infiltrating the airwaves, meaning the group almost got lost in the tide of sameness. But then former Talking Heads frontman David Byrne tapped the group to produce an album, and chart-toppers Fiona Apple and Live invited Morcheeba along for separate and extensive North American tours. The experience translated to a much more refined musical climate on the band's critically acclaimed second album *Big Calm*.

WHAT ALBUM CHANGED YOUR LIFE?

Paul's Boutique by the Beastie Boys. I was so blown away by the concepts and the Dust Brothers' production. It inspired me, gave me the confidence to get on with my own sound.

Paul Godfrey (of Morcheeba)

what to buy: Haunting dub rhythms and vintage spy movie themes provide the backdrop for *Big Calm* ✏✏✏ (Sire, 1998, prod. Morcheeba, Pete Norris). But the group sounds surprisingly ripe. With mesmeric rhythm-and-blues tracks such as "Shoulder Holster" and the meditative "Fear and Love" it is finally allowed to put all those Portishead comparisons to rest.

what to buy next: Morcheeba's debut album, *Who Can You Trust?* ✏✏✏ (Discovery, 1996, prod. Morcheeba), sounds too derivative to be pertinent, but it does showcase some smooth and psychedelic soul gems in "Trigger Hippie" and "Moog Island."

influences:

⏪ Massive Attack, Sade, Lee Scratch Perry

⏩ Sneaker Pimps, Hooverphonic, Baby Fox

Aidin Vaziri

The Morells

See: The Skeletons

Blake Morgan

Born July 10, 1969, in New York, NY.

The son of two writers, Blake Morgan grew up surrounded by music, art, politics, and poetry. Influenced by Bach, Beethoven, and Mozart, he performed his first piano recital at age five, then studied at the United Nations International School in New York City. While he was a student at the Berklee College of Music, however, he realized that rock music was his calling—so he finished college in three years, returned to Greenwich Village, and formed a band.

what's available: *Anger's Candy* ✍✍✍ (N2K Encoded Music, 1997, prod. Terry Manning, Blake Morgan) is a worthy first release because Morgan, a straightforward pop-rock singer, doesn't pretend to be anything that he's not. "Lately" is a catchy tale told to chugging guitars. Lenny Kravitz lends vocals to an otherwise middle-of-the-road rock song, "Why Don't You See." "It's Gone," however, sounds suspiciously like the soundtrack standard "Crazy Love."

influences:

◄◄ Rhythm Corps, Black Crowes, .38 Special, Tom Petty & the Heartbreakers

►► Steve Poltz

Christina Fuoco

Ikue Ile Mori

See: DNA

Alanis Morissette

Born June 1, 1974, in Ottawa, Ontario, Canada.

Americans may think Alanis Morissette came out of nowhere, but Canadians know she came from worse than that. A child actress on the television program *You Can't Do That on Television,* Morissette recorded an independent single when she was 10. That led to a Canadian record deal that produced a pair of dance-pop albums, *Alanis* and *Now Is the Time,* which were successes in the Great White North (even earning her a Juno Award for Most Promising Female Artist) but were ignored everywhere else. (They're now strenuously deleted worldwide). Had that been the end of the story, Morissette would be remembered, if at all, as the Tiffany of Canada. A couple of years and a move to Los Angeles made all the difference in the world, though. Morissette hooked up with slick pop producer/songwriter Glenn Ballard to create *Jagged Little Pill,* a striking if studied alternapop that became the sensation of 1995 and '96, winning her several Grammy Awards, including Album of the Year and Best Rock Album. Morissette's much-anticipated follow-up to *Jagged* was due in the fall of 1998.

what to buy: On *Jagged Little Pill* ✍✍✍✍ (Maverick, 1995, prod. Glen Ballard), Morissette crafts a pensive but volatile persona and a sound that's very attentive to current music but fertile with its own ideas. Her graft of ragged Dylan-esque harmonica to grunge-era guitars sets up a generational dialogue that reflects with witty irony on the simple style-recycling of her peers. Her continuation of the demonic-possession vocal tradition of Buffy Sainte-Marie and Sinéad O'Connor stood out refreshingly at a time of monotone alternarock grumblers, though her singing can tend toward affectedness in the studio and benefits from the rawness and spontaneity of live performance. Ballard's production makes too-frequent use of the stop-short, *a capella* ending, but is satisfyingly gimmick-free otherwise, particularly in the power-folk atmospherics of "Right through You" and "Forgiven."

the rest:

Supposed Former Infatuation Junkie N/A (Maverick, 1998)

worth searching for: You qualify as obsessive, and perhaps worse, if your life is not complete without copies of *Alanis* (MCA Canada, 1991, prod. Leslie Howe) and *Now Is the Time* (MCA Canada, prod. Leslie Howe).

influences:

◄◄ Sinéad O'Connor, Edie Brickell, Joni Mitchell, Melanie

►► Fiona Apple, Jen Trynin, Meredith Brooks

Adam McGovern

Morphine

Formed 1992, in Boston, MA.

Mark Sandman, two-string slide bass, vocals; Dana Colley, baritone saxophone; Billy Conway, drums.

Morphine could easily be dismissed as a gimmick—a rock band with no guitar—were it not for the musicians' skills and their ability to craft great songs from sparse resources. What makes the band's minimalist formula click is each member's keen understanding of his role: Mark Sandman writes insidiously catchy songs that he injects with propulsively cool bass lines (think the *Peter Gunn* theme on peyote) and a sly vocal style; Billy Conway's drumming is a solid anchor; and, most importantly, Dana Colley's sax (or saxes; he occasionally plays two at a time) writhes and slithers with sleazy delight. You never miss the guitar. Morphine has had continued success with this formula. Each of its three records sounds fresh, inventive, and addictively cool.

what to buy: *Yes* ✍✍✍✍ (Rykodisc, 1995, prod. Mark Sandman, Paul Q. Kolderie) is the best so far, with a lexicon of alluring riffs riding beneath Sandman's detached vocals. The best songs ("Honey White," "All Your Way," and "Super Sex") achieve an infectious hybrid of rock and seedy strip-club jazz that perfectly conveys Sandman's world-weary lyrics. Sandman's writing accepts that the world is full of treachery, infidelity, and dangerous sexual curves and, like a New Orleans funeral, finds reason to celebrate anyway.

the rest:

Good ✍✍✍ (Rykodisc, 1992)
Cure for Pain ✍✍✍✍ (Rykodisc, 1993)
Like Swimming ✍✍✍ (DreamWorks, 1997)
B-Sides and Otherwise ✍✍✍ (Rykodisc, 1997)

Alanis Morissette (© Ken Settle)

worth searching for: *Sampilation* (Ryko/DreamWorks, 1997, prod. various) is a promo item that collects eight songs from three of Morphine's albums.

solo outings:

Treat Her Right (Sandman, Conway):

The Anthology 🎵🎵🎵 (Razor & Tie, 1998)

influences:

◀◀ Tom Waits, Duane Eddy, Johnny Burnette, the Who, the Rolling Stones

▶▶ Soul Coughing

David Galens

Morrissey

Born Stephen Patrick Morrissey, May 22, 1959, in Manchester, England.

As lead singer of the Smiths, Morrissey became an icon for a legion of mournful followers. Blending angst with humor, homoerotic swagger with impenetrable attitude, Morrissey carried the Smiths out of the underground and into worldwide alternative music stardom. Releasing a small load of influential albums, the group disintegrated during 1987 after only five years together, but the road had already been paved for Morrissey's solo career; he released his debut album, *Viva Hate*, the following year. But despite his prolific outpouring of singles and albums, his post-Smiths work rarely came close to either the majesty or innovation of his former band. Many of his critics even suggest that he has turned into a caricature of his former self; even though he scored an occasional hit single, his career was on a steady decline—both artistically and commercially—in recent years. A new label deal seemingly rejuvenated his creative spark on 1997's *Maladjusted*.

what to buy: Hot on the heels of the Smiths' death, *Viva Hate* 🎵🎵🎵 (Sire, 1988, prod. Stephen Street) does not drift too far from the group's well-established formula. While lacking the sonic finesse of guitarist Johnny Marr, it still contains some classic Morrissey intellect, particularly on standout tracks such as "Everyday Is like Sunday" and "Suedehead."

what to buy next: *Bona Drag* 🎵🎵🎵 (Sire, 1990, prod. Clive Langer, Stephen Street), a collection of singles, similarly showcased some of Morrissey's finest moments as a solo artist—including the indispensable "Interesting Drug" and "November Spawned a Monster," which come close to capturing the walloping grandeur of the Smiths.

what to avoid: Morrissey's creative flame went out fast after he left the Smiths. Rather than pushing his work into new terrain, he fell into a tired groove on insipid offerings such as *Kill Uncle* 🎵 (Sire, 1991, prod. Clive Langer) and *Southpaw Grammar* 🎵

(Sire, 1995, prod. Steve Lillywhite). Both discs were colorless takes on the former Morrissey sound.

the rest:

Your Arsenal 🎵🎵 (Sire, 1992)
Vauxhall & I 🎵🎵 (Sire, 1994)
World of Morrissey 🎵🎵 (Sire, 1995)
Maladjusted 🎵🎵 (Mercury, 1997)

worth searching for: *Beethoven Was Deaf* (EMI, 1993) is a British live album, recorded with one of his strongest bands cranking through 16 songs from throughout his solo career.

influences:

◀◀ David Bowie, Johnny Ray, the New York Dolls

▶▶ Blur, the Sundays, Radiohead

Aidin Vaziri

Bill Morrissey

Born c. 1952, in NH.

For years critics have called Bill Morrissey America's most literate songwriter, comparing him to authors such as James Carver and Andre Dubus as often as to songwriters like Bob Dylan and Bruce Springsteen. It's fitting, then, that he recently published his first novel, the semi autobiographical *Edson*, about a struggling folksinger scraping by on day-labor and still dreaming—just barely—about making it as a full-time musician. Morrissey himself worked in New England mills and on Alaskan fishing boats both before and after releasing his first album in 1984, a personal history that fills his songs about working-class life with a rare verisimilitude.

what to buy: Morrissey's third album, *Standing Eight* 🎵🎵🎵🎵 (Philo/Rounder, 1989, prod. Darleen Wilson), was his artistic breakthrough. Featuring harmonies by friends Shawn Colvin and Suzanne Vega, it has some of his most moving songs, including the heartbreaking divorce ballad "Last Day of the Last Furlough" and "These Cold Fingers," a hauntingly intimate song about a man who can't quite get a handle on the things he needs most. His next album, *Inside* 🎵🎵🎵🎵 (Philo/Rounder, 1992, prod. John Jennings), was almost as good, branching out into hardbitten blues ("Robert Johnson") and breezy love songs ("Rite of Spring") while continuing to write introspective and incisive ballads ("Man from out of Town" and "Casey, Illinois") as good as any this side of Springsteen's *Nebraska*.

what to buy next: Morrissey re-recorded his eponymous 1984 debut album in 1991, apparently unhappy with his original performance. The new version of *Bill Morrissey* 🎵🎵🎵 (Philo/Rounder, 1991, prod. Bill Morrissey, Ellen Karas) is still a solo album and features three bonus cuts—but it's the songs that were on the original release that stand out. "Barstow," a hard-bitten look at a group of contemporary hobos, and the aching ballad "Rosie" are the best of a fine lot of songs. His second album, *North* ♪♪♪♪ (Philo/Rounder, 1986, prod. Edward Gerhard), was just as good, though at just 30 minutes it's disappointingly short.

what to avoid: *You'll Never Get to Heaven* ♪♪ (Philo/Rounder, 1996, prod. Scott Billington, Ellen Karas) finds Morrissey moving beyond the confines of folk music, but neither the arrangements nor the songs really gel.

the rest:
Night Train ♪♪♪♡ (Philo/Rounder, 1993)
(With Greg Brown) *Friend of Mine* ♪♪♪ (Philo/Rounder, 1993)

worth searching for: Morrissey's novel, *Edson* (Knopf, 1996), is an astonishingly good portrait of a struggling folksinger; for anyone interested in life on the fringes of contemporary music, it's essential reading.

influences:
◀◀ Bob Dylan, Bruce Springsteen, Gordon Lightfoot, Richard Thompson

Jeff Schwager

Van Morrison

Born August 31, 1945, in Belfast, Ireland.

More than anyone's except maybe Jerry Lee Lewis or Little Richard, the mercurial music of Van Morrison explores that most elusive of dichotomies: the tension between the sacred and the profane, the spiritual and the worldly, weird sex and chastity of the heart. Alternately pious and lascivious, Morrison's best albums explore that most tenuous and volatile of life's conflicts, and he has lurched all over the emotional and musical landscape in his search. As a teenager in Them, Morrison screamed lustily, emulating hard-bitten American bluesmen and scoring hits with the proto-rock/blues of "Baby, Please Don't Go" and his own "Gloria," still a garage-band mainstay. After the pop-heavy (but controversial) "Brown-Eyed Girl," which revealed a seemingly endless capacity for hit records, Morrison's first real solo record, *Astral Weeks*, veered away from the mainstream, introducing an inquisitive, introspective, and self-absorbed obsession with folk/jazz, all banging acoustic guitars, strings, impressionistic lyrics, and a grunting, growling scat that would differentiate his voice from all others. He embraced the poetry and mysticism of William Blake and William Butler Yeats with the same enthusiasm as the lyrics of Jackie Wilson and Huddie Ledbetter. His early solo records for Warner Bros., especially the warm country/soul of *Moondance, His Band and Street Choir, Tupelo Honey*, and *St. Dominic's Preview*, reflect the rural hippie aesthetic of the period and his Woodstock, New York, surroundings. After a brief hiatus between 1974 and 1977, his later Warner Bros. albums seemed to tilt in favor of the mystic and spiritual, most notably on *Beautiful Vision* and *Into the Music*. Since moving to Polydor during the mid-'80s, Morrison's music has matured even more but has retained—some might suggest *regained*—its edge. For all his accomplishments and influence, Morrison remains something of a (large) cult artist, and his aversion to show-business mechanisms has been well documented. Eschewing fashion in favor of his muse, wherever it takes him, he displays a rare honesty, tenacity, and willingness for growth and exploration without consideration for commercial trends or fashion. It seems he's forever stalled at the crossroads where the path of righteousness meets the highway to hell. He can make it bumpy and uncomfortable at times, but it's worth getting in the back seat and hanging on for the ride.

what to buy: Choosing the best from someone as prolific and challenging as Morrison is difficult at best, but his first three solo records are absolute musts. *Astral Weeks* ♪♪♪♪♪ (Warner Bros., 1968, prod. Lewis Merenstein) is a song cycle that sounds like a concept album, even if it isn't, as it meanders through the winding alleys and smelly back streets of London's Notting Hill Gate alongside sleazy eccentrics like the unforgettable icon "Madame George." *Moondance* ♪♪♪♪ (Warner Bros., 1970, prod. Van Morrison) and *Van Morrison His Band and the Street Choir* ♪♪♪♪ (Warner Bros., 1970, prod. Van Morrison) would have made an extraordinary double album, with numerous youthful examples of the Morrison acoustic soul magic, including "Into the Mystic," "Caravan," "Crazy Love," "Domino," "Blue Money," and "Call Me up in Dreamland."

what to buy next: *The Healing Game* ♪♪♪♪ (Polydor, 1997, prod. Van Morrison) is a stone James Brown record, with a young band keeping up with the old master at every whimsical mood he can muster. *St. Dominic's Preview* ♪♪♪♡ (Warner Bros., 1972, prod. Van Morrison, Ted Templeman) is filled with wonderful songs such as "Jackie Wilson Said (I'm in Heaven When You Smile)," "Almost Independence Day," and the epochal "Listen to the Lion." *Irish Heartbeat* ♪♪♪♪ (Mercury, 1988/1998, prod. Van Morrison, Paddy Maloney), a collaboration with the Chieftains, is an inspired assortment of contemporary traditional music. *A Night in San Francisco* ♪♪♪♪♡ (Polydor, 1994, prod. Van Morrison) and *It's Too Late to Stop Now* ♪♪♪♪ (Warner Bros., 1974, prod. Van Morrison) both do justice to his high-energy, big-band performances 20 years apart.

what to avoid: *Inarticulate Speech of the Heart* ♪ (Warner Bros., 1983, prod. Van Morrison), as confusing as the title implies and full of synthesized new age blather, was, not surprisingly, his last record for Warner Bros.

the rest:
Blowin' Your Mind ♪♪♪ (Bang, 1967)
Best of Van Morrison ♪♪♪ (Bang, 1970)
Tupelo Honey ♪♪♪♪ (Warner Bros., 1971)

T.B. Sheets ♫♫♫ (Bang, 1972)
Hard Nose the Highway ♫♫ (Warner Bros., 1973)
Veedon Fleece ♫♫ (Warner Bros., 1974)
A Period of Transition ♫♫♫ (Warner Bros., 1977)
Wavelength ♫♫♫♫ (Warner Bros., 1978)
Into the Music ♫♫♫♫ (Warner Bros., 1979)
Common One ♫♫♫ (Warner Bros., 1980)
Beautiful Vison ♫♫♫♫ (Warner Bros., 1982)
A Sense of Wonder ♫♫♫ (Mercury, 1985/1998)
Live at the Grand Opera House Belfast ♫♫♫♫ (Mercury, 1985/1998)
No Guru, No Method, No Teacher ♫♫♫♫ (Mercury, 1986/1998)
Poetic Champions Compose ♫♫♫♫ (Mercury, 1989/1998)
Avalon Sunset ♫♫♫♫ (Mercury, 1989)
Enlightenment ♫♫♫♫ (Mercury, 1990)
The Best of Van Morrison ♫♫♫♫ (Polydor, 1990/1998)
Hymns to the Silence ♫♫♫♫ (Polydor, 1991)
Bang Masters ♫♫♫ (Epic, 1991)
Too Long in Exile ♫♫♫♫ (Polydor, 1993)
The Best of Van Morrison, Vol. 2 ♫♫♫♫ (Polydor, 1993)
Days like This ♫♫♫♫ (Polydor, 1995)
(With Georgie Fame) *How Long Has This Been Going On* ♫♫♫♫ (Verve, 1996)
Brown Eyed Girl & Blue Eyed Soul ♫♫♫ (Sony Music Special Products, 1996)
Tell Me Something: Songs of Mose Allison ♫♫♫♫ (Verve, 1996)
The Philospher's Stone ♫♫♫♫ (PolyGram, 1998)

worth searching for: Morrison's sporadic live sets are generally considered the best way to experience the Belfast Cowboy, as witnessed by his three excellent, authorized live albums. There are literally dozens more available in bootleg form, and since Morrison rarely does the same show twice, many of them are worth the effort. *Can You Feel the Silence?* (Great Dane) is a 1982 show with a great Morrison rant about "Idiot Wind" that tries to explain why he's playing at a rock festival. *Van Morrison Gets His Chance to Wail, Vols. 1 & 2* (Gold Standard) puts you in the studio during 1969 through 1971, with Van on acoustic guitar working out demo versions of "Ballerina," "Domino," "And It Stoned Me," "Wild Night," "Caravan," and many more.

influences:

◀◀ Sonny Boy Williamson, Leadbelly, Muddy Waters, John Lee Hooker, Sam Cooke, Slim Harpo, Solomon Burke, James Brown, Ray Charles, Sonny Terry & Brownie McGhee, Jackie Wilson, Bo Diddley, Curtis Mayfield & the Impressions, Johnny & the Pirates, Alexis Korner, Mose Allison, Bob Dylan

▶▶ Counting Crows, Graham Parker & the Rumour, Dexy's Midnight Runners, Sinéad O'Connor, U2, the Band, Elvis Costello, Rod Stewart, Mark Knopfler, Bob Seger, John Mellencamp, Bruce Springsteen, Joan Armatrading, Rickie Lee Jones

see also: *Them*

Leland Rucker

Bob Mosley
See: Moby Grape

The Motels
Formed 1972, in Berkeley, CA. Disbanded 1986.

Martha Davis, vocals; Dean Chamberlain, guitar (1972–75); Richard D'Andrea, bass (1972–76); Michael Goodroe, bass (1976–86); Marty Jourard, saxophone, keyboards (1976–86); Brian Glascock, drums (1976–86); Jeff Jourard, guitar (1976–79); Tim McGovern, guitar (1979–81); Guy Perry, guitar (1980–86); Scott Thurston, guitar, keyboards (1982–86).

The Motels hovered in L.A. for a decade, sifting through numerous band members before ever releasing a record. In addition to being among the first of the West Coast's new wave groups, the band boasted the dramatic vocals of Martha Davis, evolving into a critically lauded, if only modestly successful, group. The group's main stab at pop mainstream came with the melancholy hit "Only the Lonely" in 1982. Public indifference, constantly shifting personnel and Davis's own health issues all factored into the band's demise during the mid-'80s, though in the late '90s Davis began performing again and was talking about reactivating the band's name.

what to buy: The generous 19-track sampler *No Vacancy: Best of the Motels* ♫♫♫ (Capitol/EMI, 1990/Gold Rush, 1996, prod. various) is a tidy summation of the best of its largely unrecognized career. It contains the hits "Only the Lonely" and "Suddenly Last Summer."

the rest:
Motels ♫♫ (Capitol, 1979, 1996)
Careful ♫♫♫ (Capitol, 1980)
All Four One ♫♫♫ (Capitol, 1982/One Way, 1996)
Little Robbers ♫♫♫ (Capitol, 1983)
Shock ♫ (Capitol, 1985)
XL Series N/A (The Right Stuff, 1998)

solo outings:
Martha Davis:
Policy ♫♫♫ (Capitol, 1987)

influences:
◀◀ Bryan Ferry, Kim Carnes
▶▶ Scandal, Berlin

Allan Orski

Mother Earth
Formed 1990, in London, England. Disbanded 1996.

Matt Deighton, guitar, vocals; Neil Corcoran, bass; Bryn Barklam, organ; Chris White, drums, percussion (1991–95); Shauna Greene, vo-

cals (1991); Bunny, vocals, programming (1991); Famous Jos, drums (1996).

Mother Earth was one of the first bands, along with the James Taylor Quartet and the Brand New Heavies, to sign to Acid Jazz Records. Musically nourished on equal parts of the Jam and rare '70s soul and funk, Mother Earth would become the modern incarnation of the Small Faces. Its debut fit well within the Acid Jazz mold: *Stoned Woman* is a jazz-inflected smooth funk album paying tribute to the members' rare-groove upbringing. It soon became clear, however, that Mother Earth frontman Matt Deighton found the jazz/funk idiom claustrophobic; he wanted to take the group on a more pop/rock course. The band started down this new route during 1993, when it became more like its '60s heroes—trimming the sextet to a quartet (with Deighton assuming lead vocals) and morphing its sound to American soul-influenced English mod rock. The shift caught the ear of Paul Weller, the former Jam and Style Council founder and an unabashed Small Faces aficionado, who lent a hand in the making of its sophomore effort, *The People Tree* (which is dedicated to Small Faces leader Steve Marroitt, who died a year prior). Deighton continued his journey to broaden his sound when he issued a solo modern folk-rock album, *The Villager*. In 1995 Mother Earth hit its stride with its third album, *You Have Been Watching*, which Acid Jazz issued on its new rock boutique, Focus Records. But like the Jam, Mother Earth disbanded soon after reaching the height of its creative output. Deighton would re-emerged in 1997 as a side musician for Weller during his *Heavy Soul* sessions.

what to buy: *You Have Been Watching* ♪♪♪♪ (Focus/Acid Jazz/Hollywood, 1995, prod. Madrak) is the band's finest, the completion of a creative transformation to a modern mix of '60s American R&B and '60s and '70s English mod. Comfortable in their new style, Deighton and company delivered a powerful, passionate work.

what to buy next: *The People Tree* ♪♪♪ (Acid Jazz/Hollywood, 1993, prod. Edward Piller) can be viewed, positively, as a transitional album, or, snidely, as a sophomore slump. It's this album where Mother Earth altered course from jazz/funk to soul/pop. The discomfort in this choice is evident, with sparkless, rote performances of idioms one expects from a mod band. The one glimmer is the track "Jesse," a beautiful mid-tempo piece with Deighton on acoustic guitar. For Deighton, "Jesse" would evolve into a full folk-flavored excursion on his solo effort, *The Villager* ♪♪♪♪ (Acid Jazz/Hollywood, 1995, prod. Matt Deighton), which is marked by beautiful compositions and wonderful, simple instrumentation.

worth searching for: *Stoned Woman* (Acid Jazz U.K., 1992, prod. Edward Piller) is the odd-man-out in ME's catalog, a deep jazz/funk album with haunting female vocals. One walking in at the middle of the album might think it an old S.O.U.L. record. It's a strong outing that belies the group's ultimate course. *The Desired Effect* (Focus/Acid Jazz U.K., 1996) is a live document of the band's 1995 *You Have Been Watching* tour. Featuring only the quartet (studio sessions often included help from side artists), this is a vibrant live album that also serves as a fitting farewell.

influences:
◄◄ Small Faces, the Jam, S.O.U.L., Johnny Hammond

Coqui Toyoda

Mother Love Bone
See: Pearl Jam

Mother's Finest
Formed late 1960s, in Chicago, IL. Disbanded 1983. Re-formed 1989.

Joyce Kennedy, vocals; Garry Moore (a.k.a., Moses Mo), guitar; Glenn Murdock, vocals; Jerry Seay (a.k.a.,Wizzard), bass; Barry Borden (a.k.a., B.B. Queen), drums; Mike Keck, keyboards.

Starting in Chicago, Mother's Finest perfected its potent blend of funk and rock in Atlanta, Georgia, home of seminal funk outfit Cameo. But in the studio, record companies kept trying to turn the band into the next K.C. & the Sunshine Band or the next Rufus, refusing or unwilling to let MF claim its status as one of the first modern-day funk/rock groups. Despite the success of the sultry ballad "Love Changes," the band broke up in 1983, with Joyce Kennedy moving on to a solo career and drummer Barry Borden playing with Molly Hatchet. Though the group re-formed in 1989, it found the same problems in reaching audiences used to either white rock or black funk bands, prompting the irreverent title of its first record in the '90s, *Black Radio Won't Play This*.

what to buy: Though renowned for incendiary live shows and the Chaka Khan–style power of vocalist Kennedy, the band was never able to harness that formula on record, coming closest in its concert album, *Live* ♪♪♪♪ (Epic, 1979, prod. Jimmy Iovine), which melded old-school soul vocals to a riff-laden, bombastic live sound.

what to buy next: *The Very Best of Mother's Finest: Not Your Mother's Funk* ♪♪♪ (Razor & Tie, 1997, prod. various) is a top-notch compilation and a fine introduction to a sadly underrated group.

what to avoid: The title implied lack of attention for dubious reasons, but there was another explanation why some stations slept on *Black Radio Won't Play This* ♪♪ (RCA, 1992, prod. Thom Panunzio); it wasn't any good.

the rest:
Rock Your Soul ♪♪♪ (Sony Special Products, 1996)

influences:

◀◀ Sly & the Family Stone, Rufus, Jimi Hendrix

▶▶ Living Colour, Red Hot Chili Peppers, the Black Rock Coalition

Eric Deggans

Mötley Crüe
/Vince Neil

Formed 1981, in Los Angeles, CA.

Tommy Lee, drums, vocals; Mick Mars, guitar, vocals; Vince Neil, vocals (1981–92, 1996–present); Nikki Sixx (born Frank Carlton Serafino Ferranno), bass, piano, vocals; John Corabi, vocals, guitar (1992–96).

A leader of the "hair metal" movement that dominated MTV and magazine covers briefly during the '80s, Mötley Crüe had several big hits with hard-rock songs and soupy ballads. The band carefully crafted a decadent outlaw image and took concert excess to unprecedented heights, and by the original lineup's last studio album, *Dr. Feelgood*, it was a decent hard-rock outfit with savvy pop sense. But in the early '90s, when Nirvana changed the hard-rock marketplace, the band slipped out of vogue. Vince Neil fared the worst, getting fired, putting out a stinker solo album, and filing a $5 million wrongful termination lawsuit against the band that was quietly settled when he rejoined in 1996. Tommy Lee did better, rebounding from a failed marriage with *Melrose Place* star Heather Locklear by marrying and starting a family with the buxom *Baywatch* bombshell Pamela Anderson. In recent years, Mötley Crüe has been more famous for its members' sex lives than for any of its music. But even that soured, as a porn video featuring Lee and Anderson (already one of the internet's most frequently downloaded dreamboats) somehow slipped into the public's hands. Lee was later convicted of spousal abuse, and Anderson filed for divorce.

what to buy: *Dr. Feelgood* ♫♫♫ (Elektra, 1989, prod. Bob Rock) was a #1 album, featuring the hits "Kickstart My Heart" and "Same Ol' Situation (S.O.S.)." The career retrospective *Decade of Decadence—'81–'91* ♫♫♫ (Elektra, 1991, prod. various) does a good job of showcasing the band's strengths and avoiding its weaknesses.

what to buy next: *Theater of Pain* ♫♫♫ (Elektra, 1985, prod. Tom Werman) has the Crüe's hit remake of Brownsville Station's "Smokin' in the Boys' Room" as well as "Home Sweet Home," which opened the doors for the hit power ballad—a dubious achievement if ever there was one.

what to avoid: The post-Neil *Mötley Crüe* ♫ (Elektra, 1994, prod. Bob Rock) is a desperate, failed stab at regaining the band's former foothold in the hard-rock marketplace.

the rest:

Too Fast for Love ♫♫ (Elektra, 1981)
Shout at the Devil ♫♫ (Elektra, 1983)
Girls, Girls, Girls ♫♫♫ (Elektra, 1987)
Generation Swine ♫♫ (Elektra, 1997)
Greatest Hits ♫♫♫♫ (Mötley Records, 1998)

solo outings:

Vince Neil:
Exposed ♫ (Elektra, 1993)
Carved in Stone ♫♫ (Warner Bros., 1995)

influences:

◀◀ Black Sabbath, Foreigner, Alice Cooper, Boston, Kansas, Kiss, Cheap Trick, Meat Loaf

▶▶ Warrant, Ratt, Ugly Kid Joe, Guns N' Roses

Tracey Birkenhauer and Steve Knopper

M.O.T.O.
/Masters of the Obvious

Formed 1983, in LA.

Paul Caporino, vocals, guitar; Beck Dudley, drums, vocals (1988–94); Dennis Spaag, bass (1995–present).

Paul Caporino had been writing grungy little blasts of low-fi pop since the early '80s, but M.O.T.O. didn't become a band until the songwriter moved from his native Louisiana to Boston in 1987 at the prompting of a long-distance fan, Beck Dudley. With Dudley playing percussion on a sardine can and Caporino strumming Ronettes-meets-Spike Jones ditties at Ramones-like tempos, the band busked in Harvard Square and won a cult following on the college circuit. The duo subsequently moved to Chicago, and its limited-edition homemade records have become collector's items. Dudley eventually quit to pursue architecture in Seattle, but Caporino continues to record prolifically out of his Chicago apartment and plays the occasional live show with a rhythm section.

what's available: *Single File* ♫♫♫♫ (Mind of a Child, 1997, prod. various) compiles all the singles from the Dudley-Caporino duo years. There are—count 'em—28 two-minutes-or-less pop-punk raspberries with titles such as "Crystallize My Penis," "It's So Big It's Fluorescent," and "Satan Always Calls Collect," each guaranteed to make you laugh out loud while pogoing around the living room.

worth searching for: Caporino sells tapes at shows and via mail: M.O.T.O., Box 578912, Chicago IL, 60657. He's amazingly consistent, with each disc containing at least a handful of should-be hits.

Vince Neil of Mötley Crüe (© Ken Settle)

influences:

◄◄ The Ramones, Bread, Looking Glass, Modern Lovers, Daniel Johnston

►► Sebadoh, Liz Phair, Rebecca Gates, Ben Lee

Greg Kot

Motorcaster

See: blackgirls

Motörhead

Formed 1975, in London, England.

Lemmy Kilmister, vocals, bass; "Fast" Eddie Clark, guitar (1975–82); Phil "Philthy Animal" Taylor, drums (1977–83, 1991); Brian Robertson, guitar (1982–83); Mick "Wurzel" Burston, guitar (1983–96); Pete Gill, drums (1983–91); Mikkey Dee, drums (1991–present).

Yes, Motörhead repeats the same three-chord rock song until your head snaps off, flies onto the stage, and rolls into the bass drum with a dull thud. Yes, Lemmy's voice sounds like somebody crammed 27 cigarettes into his mouth and lit them while he sings. Yes, they've been doing this the exact same way (give or take a few personnel changes) for more than two decades. Somebody has to do it. Heavy metal has always flirted with daintiness and pretty-boy showmanship, but Motörhead has always worn leather, stayed in touch with the Harley-driving crowd, and refused to change its sound, no matter what happens. As a result, Lemmy and whoever happens to be playing with him have become one of the most influential metal bands of all time: A few years back, Metallica performed at a Motörhead tribute party under a pseudonym: "The Lemmys."

what to buy: It's tough to build a comprehensive Motörhead CD collection these days, because their original LP's have come out on various British labels, some of which don't distribute to mainstream U.S. record stores. But watch out for *No Sleep 'til Hammersmith* 𝄞𝄞𝄞𝄞𝄞 (Mercury, 1981/Roadracer Revisited, 1992, prod. Vic Maile), the consummate fist-pounding, neighbor-annoying, speaker-exploding, normality-disturbing metal record. It captures the band in full peak live with versions of "Ace of Spades," "Iron Horse," "Overkill," and "Metropolis." *No Remorse* 𝄞𝄞𝄞𝄞 (Bronze, 1984/Roadracer Revisited, 1990, prod. various) advertises itself as "the ultimate Motörhead," and it's no exaggeration.

what to buy next: *Motörhead* 𝄞𝄞𝄞𝄞 (Chiswick U.K., 1977/Roadracer Revisited, 1990, prod. Speedy Keen), *Overkill* 𝄞𝄞𝄞𝄞 (Bronze U.K., 1979/Roadracer Revisited, 1992, prod. Jimmy Miller), and *1916* 𝄞𝄞𝄞 (WTG/Sony, 1992, prod. Peter Solley) all amplify the Motörhead experience. *1916* includes Lemmy's slow, riveting, guitarless anti-war title track.

what to avoid: Despite a good cover of Ted Nugent's "Cat Scratch Fever," *March or Die* 𝄞𝄞 (WTG/Sony, 1992, prod. Peter Solley) is part of the band's slide into boring old age.

the rest:

Bomber 𝄞𝄞𝄞 (Bronze, U.K. 1979/Roadracer Revisited, 1992)
On Parole (Cleopatra, 1980/1992) 𝄞𝄞
Iron Fist 𝄞𝄞 (Mercury, 1982/Roadracer Revisited, 1990)
Orgasmatron 𝄞𝄞𝄞 (GWR/Profile, 1986)
Rock 'n' Roll 𝄞𝄞 (GWR/Profile, 1987)
No Sleep at All 𝄞𝄞 (Enigma, 1988/Roadracer Revisited, 1992)
All the Aces 𝄞𝄞𝄞 (Roadracer Revisited, 1992)
The Best of Motörhead 𝄞𝄞𝄞 (Roadrunner, 1993)
Overnight Sensation 𝄞𝄞𝄞 (CMC International, 1996)
King Biscuit Flower Hour Presents Motörhead 𝄞𝄞𝄞 (KBFH, 1997)
Snake Bite Love 𝄞𝄞𝄞 (CMC International, 1998)
Singles Collection 𝄞𝄞𝄞 (Cleopatra, 1998)

worth searching for: A band billing itself as "Lemmy & the Upsetters," although they suspiciously sound like Motörhead, reveal a hidden rockabilly influence on Carl Perkins's "Blue Suede Shoes" for the British fundraising album *The Last Temptation of Elvis* (New Musical Express, 1990). Classic liner note: "If you bumped into Elvis this very day, what would be your immediate reaction?" Lemmy: "I would be astounded, and I would say, 'Elvis, I'm astounded!'"

influences:

◄◄ Ted Nugent, MC5, the Ramones, the Who, Iggy Pop, Count Five, the Yardbirds, Alice Cooper, Black Sabbath

►► Metallica, Megadeth, Slayer, Anthrax, Soundgarden, Ministry, Bad Religion, Guns N' Roses, Body Count

Steve Knopper

The Motors

Formed 1977, in England.

Nick Garvey, vocals, guitar, bass; Andy McMasters, vocals, keyboards, bass; Bram Tchaikovsky (born Peter Bramall), guitar, vocals (1977–78); Ricky Slaughter, drums, vocals (1977–78).

Journeymen songwriters and performers Nick Garvey and Andy McMasters were already pub-rock veterans by the time they joined forces in the band Ducks Deluxe. After that group split, the two went their separate ways, but they began writing together in 1977 and soon thereafter joined forces with drummer Ricky Slaughter and guitarist Bram Tchaikovsky. The group scored a modest hit on its debut with the unusually long track "Dancing the Night Away," but the original duo then split the group to continue on as a two-piece. Bad move: They did release a fine effort in *Approved by the Motors*, but quickly ran out of ideas after that. Tchaikovsky went on to some degree of success with a series of solo albums, most notably the breezy *Strange Man, Changed Man*.

what to buy: *Airport: The Motors' Greatest Hits* 𝄞𝄞𝄞 (Caroline, 1995, prod. various) offers a generous sampling of the band's best moments, including the driving "Dancing the Night Away," "Airport," and "Forget about You." Its best single album is *Approved by the Motors* 𝄞𝄞𝄞 (Virgin, 1978, prod. Peter Ker, Nick Garvey, Andy McMaster), which contains the latter two U.K. hits.

what to buy next: Tchaikovsky's solo career peaked early with *Strange Man, Changed Man* 𝄞𝄞𝄞 (Polydor, 1979), a remarkably fresh sounding mix of Byrds-influence harmonies and punk-cum-new wave spirit. The singles—"Girl of My Dreams," "I'm the One That's Leaving," and "Sarah Smiles"—were plentiful and tuneful in the extreme. Bet you can still sing the hooky chorus of "Girl of My Dreams" today.

what to avoid: *Tenement Steps* 𝄞 (Virgin, 1980, prod. Jimmy Iovine) was recorded after the band had basically split, though Garvey and McMaster continued to use the name. But by this point they'd clearly run out of gas.

the rest:
The Motors I 𝄞𝄞𝄞 (Virgin, 1977)

solo outings:
Bram Tchaikovsky:
The Russians Are Coming (a.k.a.) *Pressure* 𝄞𝄞𝄞 (Polydor, 1980)
Funland 𝄞𝄞 (Arista, 1981)

Nick Garvey:
Blue Skies 𝄞𝄞 (Virgin, 1982)

influences:
◀◀ Ducks Deluxe, Bruce Springsteen, the Byrds
▶▶ Rockpile

Daniel Durchholz

Mott the Hoople

Formed 1968, in Hereford, England. Disbanded 1977.

Stan Tippens, vocals (1968); Ian Hunter, vocal, piano, guitar (1969–74); Mick Ralphs, guitar, vocals (1969–73); Overend Pete Watts, bass; Dale "Buffin" Griffin, drums; Verden Allen, organ, vocals (1969–73); Ariel Bender, guitar, vocals (1973–74); Morgan Fisher, keyboards (1973–77); Mick Ronson, guitar (1974); Ray Major, guitar (1975–77); Nigel Benjamin, vocals (1975–77).

Mott the Hoople, at least at the beginning, was a somewhat plodding, English Bob Dylan/Rolling Stones clone. Its early efforts on Atlantic went nowhere, and it wasn't until David Bowie wrote "All the Young Dudes," which became Mott's only American hit, that the group enjoyed some mid-level success. The only problem was that although the single (and corresponding

album) became cornerstones of the glitter/glam-rock scene, the Hooples themselves weren't Dudes. Still, the band's killer live shows (check its onstage version of Little Richard's "Keep a Knockin'" on *Wildlife*) took it a long way, and frontman Ian Hunter was inspired to his best songwriting before guitarist Mick Ralphs left to form Bad Company and Mott ran out of gas. Mott is now fondly remembered for some great songs ("All the Way from Memphis," "Ballad of Mott the Hoople," "Roll Away the Stone") and as the great '70s band that might have been. Its music provides a solid link from the '60s to the punk movement that was gathering steam just as Mott broke down.

what to buy: Even if he hated to be involved, the last album with Ralphs, *Mott* 𝄞𝄞𝄞𝄞 (Columbia, 1973/1988, prod. Mott the Hoople), is a splendid example of crunching, post-Bowie British rock. *The Ballad of Mott: A Retrospective* 𝄞𝄞𝄞𝄞 (Columbia Legacy, 1993, prod. various) is a two-disc compilation that gathers all the best Columbia recordings but goes light on the Atlantic albums. *Mott the Hoople* 𝄞𝄞𝄞𝄞 (Atlantic, 1969/Rhino, 1991, prod. Guy Stevens) is a wild, eclectic debut with outlandish covers of Doug Sahm ("At the Crossroads"), Sonny Bono ("Laugh at Me"), the Kinks ("You Really Got Me"), and the band's own outrageous Dylan and Stones tributes, "Backsliding Fearlessly" and "Rock 'n' Roll Queen."

what to buy next: *All the Young Dudes* 𝄞𝄞𝄞𝄞 (Columbia, 1972/1988, prod. David Bowie) could have been titled *All the Wrong Dudes. Backsliding Fearlessly: The Early Years* 𝄞𝄞𝄞𝄞 (Rhino, 1994, prod. various) provides a good sampling of Mott's Atlantic output. *The Hoople* 𝄞𝄞𝄞𝄞 (Columbia, 1974/Columbia Legacy, 1990, prod. Ian Hunter, Dale Griffin, Overend Watts) is the final album with Hunter.

what to avoid: Hardcore fans might disagree, but except for "Walking with a Mountain," *Mad Shadows* ♫♫ (Atlantic, 1970/Rhino, 1991, prod. Guy Stevens) is a muddy, unintelligible mess, the sound of a band backsliding fearfully.

the rest:
Wildlife ♫♫♫ (Atlantic, 1971/Rhino, 1991)
Brain Capers ♫♫♫ (Atlantic, 1972/Rhino, 1991)
Rock 'n' Roll Queen ♫♫♫♫ (Atlantic, 1974/Rhino, 1991)
Mott the Hoople Live ♫♫♫ (Columbia, 1974/1989)
Greatest Hits ♫♫♫ (Columbia, 1976/1987)
London to Memphis ♫♫♫ (Sony Special Products, 1992/1996)
Super Hits ♫♫♫ (Columbia Legacy, 1997)

worth searching for: Hunter's diary of Mott's 1972 American tour, *Reflections of a Rock Star* (Flash Books, London, 1976) is as fascinating as it is rare, breaking down the myths of rock stardom as it shows the day-to-day inner workings of a rock 'n' roll tour. Musically, the bootleg *Hoopling Furiously* (Hiwatt) surveys a series of early live performances that catch Mott making an enjoyably spirited racket.

influences:
◀◀ Little Richard, Bob Dylan, the Rolling Stones, Sir Douglas Quintet

▶▶ The Clash, Generation X, the Sex Pistols

see also: *Ian Hunter*

Leland Rucker

Bob Mould /Sugar

Born October 12, 1960, in Malone, NY. Sugar formed 1992; disbanded 1995.

Sugar: Bob Mould, vocals, guitar; David Barbe, bass; Malcolm Travis, drums.

Though Bob Mould has never had anything close to a hit single, he is the most recognizable and successful ex-member of the great Minneapolis punk trio Hüsker Dü. A brilliant pop melody writer, the singer-guitarist probably could be a solo superstar in the age of big-bucks alternative music if he weren't so (deservedly) suspicious of fame and the music industry. Instead, he deliberately writes cryptic songs and produces albums on which the bass is hard to hear and the treble is fuzzy and jagged. Yet the melodies usually grow into irresistible songs no matter what he does with them. Mould left Hüsker Dü in early 1988; his first solo albums were downbeat and overly confessional, sort of like Hüsker Dü's "Candy Apple Gray." The trio Sugar, like Hüsker Dü with a more catchy pop feel, filtered Mould's raw emotions through an old-fashioned rock 'n' roll lens of loud guitars. That band ended in 1995, when Mould and other band members, surprisingly enough, had a disagreement about pursuing fame.

what to buy: Sugar's *Copper Blue* ♫♫♫♫♫ (Rykodisc, 1992, prod. Bob Mould, Lou Giordano) at first sounds like a scratchy racket, with Mould's nasal voice matching the guitars' exaggerated high pitch. Eventually, the tightly controlled tunes grab you, particularly the melancholy "If I Can't Change Your Mind" and the pleasantly schizoid "A Good Idea." Despite Mould's aversion to fame, the trio's *File Under: Easy Listening* ♫♫♫♫ (Rykodisc, 1994, prod. Bob Mould) is the purest pop record of his career. Bubblegum tunes such as "Your Favorite Thing" and "Believe What You're Saying" came dangerously close to making the band alternative-rock MTV heroes.

what to buy next: Mould's first post-Sugar album, *Bob Mould* ♫♫♫♫ (Rykodisc, 1996, prod. Bob Mould), is wholly suspicious of contemporary post-punk; it includes the self-explanatory "I Hate Alternative Rock" and "Egoverride," which deals with being "burned out in the galaxy." Sugar's *Besides* ♫♫♫ (Rykodisc, 1995, prod. Bob Mould, Nick Giordano) is a relaxed collection of studio outtakes and live recordings, including a stellar version of the Who's "Armenia City in the Sky."

what to avoid: Mould's second album, *Black Sheets of Rain* ♫♫ (Virgin, 1990, prod. Bob Mould) endures mostly for its college-radio hit "It's Too Late," but it's not as coherent or focused as Hüsker Dü or Sugar.

the rest:
Bob Mould:
Workbook ♫♫♫ (Virgin, 1989)
Poison Years ♫♫♫ (Virgin, 1994)
The Last Dog and Pony Show ♫♫♫♫ (Rykodisc, 1998)

worth searching for: Sugar's *Beaster* (Rykodisc EP, 1993, prod. Bob Mould, Nick Giordano) contains longer, angrier songs and more repetitive choruses and solos than *Copper Blue*, peaking with "JC Auto," which melts down images of cars and Jesus Christ into one wonderfully traditional rock 'n' roll song.

solo outings:
Buzz Hungry (David Barbe):
Fried like a Man ♫♫ (Engine, 1994)
At the Hands of Our Intercessors ♫♫♫ (Compulsiv, 1995)

Mercyland (Barbe):
No Feet on the Cowling ♫♫ (Tupelo, 1989)
Enter the Crafty Bear ♫♫ (Planned Obsolescence EP, 1991)
Spillage ♫♫♫ (Rykodisc, 1994)

influences:
◀◀ The Ramones, Richard Thompson, the Sex Pistols, the Minutemen, Television

⚹ Nirvana, the Pixies, the Breeders, the Offspring, Boo
Radlees, Medicine, Magnapop, Junkie XL

see also: *Hüsker Dü*

Steve Knopper

Mountain

Formed 1969, in New York, NY. Disbanded 1972. Re-formed 1974–76,
1985.

**Leslie West (born Leslie Weinstein), guitar, vocals; Felix Pappalardi
(died April 17, 1983), bass, vocals; N.D. Smart II, drums (1969); Steve
Knight, organ (1970–71); Corky Laing, drums (1970–72, 1985–present); Alan Schwartzberg, drums (1974–76); Mark Clarke, bass
(1974–present).**

A heavin', sweatin' beast was Mountain, with its ham-fisted
pounding submerged in barnyard sludge. A brute-strength trio
led by former Cream producer Felix Pappalardi and the mammoth Leslie West, Mountain shook the foundations with heavy
rock excess and greasy jams. The lumbering cowbell-rocker
"Mississippi Queen" started the '70s off with a whomp, and it's
been a sweatshop of hard, grungey guitar noise ever since. The
group has broken up and regrouped many times—West and
Laing even hooked up with Cream's Jack Bruce at one point—
but the seminal lineup was destroyed in 1983 when Pappalardi
was shot and killed by his wife. Although the group performs
occasionally, West can be heard more often as a guest on
Howard Stern's morning radio show.

what to buy: The anthology *Over the Top* ♫♫♫♫ (Columbia,
1995, prod. various) is a bulging monument much like the band
itself. The album stuffs two discs worth of thumping rock and
endless solos into a package of lowbrow glory. It also contains
"Dreams of Milk and Honey" from West's deleted 1969 solo
debut.

what to buy next: *Mountain Climbing!* ♫♫♫♫ (Columbia/Legacy,
1970, prod. Felix Pappalardi) is the group's first and best
album, containing "Mississippi Queen."

what to avoid: *Twin Peaks* ♫♫ (Columbia, 1973/1989, prod.
Felix Pappalardi) is a sprawling two-disc set that runs out of
steam early on.

the rest:
Nantucket Sleighride ♫♫♫ (Columbia/Legacy, 1971/1992)
Flowers of Evil ♫♫♫ (Columbia/Legacy, 1972/1996)
Best of Mountain ♫♫♫♫ (Columbia, 1973/1989)
Go for Your Life ♫♫ (Scotti Bros., 1986)

solo outings:
Leslie West:
Mountain ♫♫♫ (Windfall, 1969/Columbia, 1996)
Dodgin' the Dirt ♫♫ (Blues Bureau International, 1993)

West, Bruce & Laing:
Why Dontcha ♫♫♫ (Columbia, 1972)
Whatever Turns You On ♫♫♫ (Columbia, 1973)

influences:

◀◀ Cream, the Jimi Hendrix Experience, the Who

⚹ Black Sabbath, Uriah Heep, Nazareth, AC/DC

Allan Orski

The Move
/Roy Wood

Formed 1966, in Birmingham, England. Disbanded 1972.

**Roy Wood (born Ulysses Adrian Wood), guitar, vocals; Bev Bevan,
drums, vocals; Jeff Lynne, guitar, keyboards, vocals (1970–72); Carl
Wayne, vocals (1966–70); Trevor Burton, guitar, bass, vocals
(1966–69); Chris "Ace" Kefford, bass, vocals (1966–68); Rick Price,
bass, vocals (1969–71).**

The Move was an early pioneer in the art of power pop. Though
the group followed in the footsteps of the Beatles and Beach
Boys by combining riff-rock with choirboy harmonies, its work
clearly influenced much of the glam and pomp-rock that followed in its wake. Leader Roy Wood, a gifted songwriter,
shared the reins in the group's final incarnation with the similarly talented Jeff Lynne, who would go on to form the far more
successful Electric Light Orchestra. Wood, meanwhile, joined
ELO briefly before moving on to a series of eccentric recordings
with his band Wizzard and as a solo act. Wood's ambition
showed in the use of classical motifs in the earliest works,
which he integrated with English psychedelia, lush chamber
pop, and thundering proto-metallic riffs. Lynne's influence took
the Move in more of a symphonic power-pop direction, though
this, too, was part of Wood's repertoire. Lynne has since become a preeminent producer, most famously with the Traveling
Wilburys and as an engine in the ghostly Beatles "reunion"
during the mid-90s. Wood has traveled more obscure roads but
announced in the mid-'90s that he was starting his own record
label, Woody, and projected the release of a live album.

what to buy: *Shazam* ♫♫♫♫ (A&M, 1970, prod. Roy Wood)
shows the band in all its eclectic glory, from incandescent folk-
pop to full-blown pomp.

what to buy next: *The Collection/The Collector's Series (1967–
70)* ♫♫♫ (Castle Communications, 1986, prod. Roy Wood, Jeff
Lynne) captures a range of delectable, most early, highlights.
Meanwhile, *Great Move! The Best of the Move* ♫♫♫ (EMI,
1994, compilation prod. Ron Furmanek) emphasizes the finest
late-period work.

what to avoid: Wood's *Boulders* ♪♪ (United Artists, 1973, prod. Roy Wood) has one or two lovely moments but for the most part chronicles his artistic schizophrenia, careening from pretense to adolescent retro-rock. Wood played, arranged, and sang everything on the record. He clearly needed a hand.

the rest:
The Move ♪♪♪ (Regal Zonophone, 1968)
Something Else ♪♪♪ (Regal Zonophone, 1968)
Looking On ♪♪♪ (Capitol, 1971)
Message from the Country ♪♪♪♪ (Harvest, 1972)
Split Ends ♪♪♪ (United Artists, 1972)
The Best of the Move ♪♪♪♪ (A&M, 1974)
Shines On ♪♪♪ (A&M, 1979)
Black Country Rock ♪♪♪ (Gold Standard, 1993)
BBC Sessions ♪♪♪ (Band of Joy, 1995)

worth searching for: *You Can Dance the Rock 'n' Roll: The Roy Wood Years 1971–73* (EMI/Harvest, 1989, prod. Roy Wood, Jeff Lynne) is a strong import overview of Wood's work with the Move, ELO, Wizzard, and on his own.

solo outings:
Roy Wood:
Wizzard's Brew ♪♪♪ (Harvest, 1973)
See My Baby Jive ♪♪ (Warner Bros., 1974)
Introducing Eddie & the Falcons ♪♪ (Warner Bros., 1974)
Mustard ♪♪ (Jet, 1975)
Super Active Wizzo ♪♪ (Warner Bros., 1977)
On the Road Again ♪♪ (Warner Bros., 1979)

influences:
◀◀ The Beatles, the Beach Boys, the Kinks, Stax, Motown, J.S. Bach, Donovan

▶▶ David Bowie, T. Rex, Queen, Cheap Trick, Electric Light Orchestra, Elvis Costello, the Posies, Jellyfish, Teenage Fan Club

see also: *Electric Light Orchestra*

Simon Glickman

Moxy Früvous
Formed 1990, in Toronto, Ontario, Canada.

Mike Ford, vocals, guitar, piano, percussion; Murray Foster, vocals, guitar, bass; David Matheson, vocals, guitar, banjo, keyboards, harmonica, saxophone, accordian; Jian (a.k.a. Jean) Ghomeshi, vocals, percussion, drums, flute.

Moxy Früvous started out as street buskers, melding musical styles as diverse as rap, bluegrass, folk, and doo-wop, delivered in four-part, frequently *a capella* harmony or augmented with a variety of eclectic instruments. Its street show incorporated comedy, theatrics, and a well-honed sense of sarcasm

and pop-culture saviness, which the group members dubbed "Rocky-Horror-vaudeville-glam-folk." Or something like that. Like fellow Canadians Barenaked Ladies, Moxy Früvous thrives on musical humor delivered with dazzling virtuosity. Spotted by a CBS radio exec, it put its songs on cassette and went to #1 on the Canadian indie charts, leading to its signing with Warner Bros. in Canada and Atlantic in the United States for *Bargainville*. Next, the group attempted to get "serious" on *Wood*, with less than stellar results. (Atlantic didn't even release it, to Moxy's distress.) So the group recorded another indie, *The B Album*, some of which came from its work writing topical ditties for radio. Its next label release, *You Will Go to the Moon*, offered some of its strongest work to date.

what to buy: *You Will Go to the Moon* ♪♪♪♪ (Bottom Line/ Velvel, 1997, prod. Moxy Früvous, Stephen Traub) oozes catchy cleverness. "Michigan Militia," with a "Last Train to Clarksville" on the banjo intro, is a brilliant bit of sarcasm aimed at the incident in Waco, Texas. "Get in the Car" is worthy of NRBQ. A charged version of the Bee Gee's "I've Gotta Get a Message to You" employs wah-wah guitar, Theramin, doo-wop choruses, and keyboards. Moxy Früvous also cribs slyly from the era of the Cowsills and the Partridge Family, and songs such as "Your New Boyfriend" show strong Beach Boys/NRBQ leanings— with a decidedly Moxy twist, while "Kick in the Ass" is an anthem for anyone who's ever endured incompetence, aggravation, or bad attitudes. *Live Noise* ♪♪♪♪ (Bottom Line, 1998, prod. Moxy Früvous) is an equally good live set that culls some of *Moon*'s best along with other career highlights and preserves a good deal of the witty stage banter that spices Moxy's shows.

what to buy next: *Bargainville* ♪♪♪♪ (Atlantic, 1993, prod. Moxy Früvous) requires use of that darned "Beatlesque" adjective, along with a comparison to the Beach Boys. Moxy's storytelling moxie also is reminiscent of yet another group—the Capitol Steps—thanks to political songs that are as hilarious as they are pithy. Just listen to "Stuck in the '90s," an irresistibly poppy, nearly Simon-&-Garfunkelish tune that manages to attack Patrick Buchanan and right-wingers in flawless harmony. And it's doubtful anyone's ever recorded a cooler version of the *Spiderman* theme.

what to avoid: *Wood* ♪♪ (Warner Music Canada, 1995, prod. Moxy Früvous, Michael Koppelman) seems like an attempt to create more mainstream (i.e., commercial) songs. They're pure pop and pretty enough, but they lack the fun and the bite of the band's more humorous work.

worth searching for: *The B Album* (Warner Music Canada, 1996, prod. Moxy Früvous) is a compendium of pithy Moxy pieces such as "The Greatest Man in America" (Rush Limbaugh) or "Johnny Sauce Pan," a bluegrass ode to what sounds like Southern roadkill cuisine. Some cuts were recorded live—a perfect way to experience them.

influences:

◀◀ The Beatles, the Beach Boys, NRBQ, Barenaked Ladies, the Lettermen, the Bee Gees, Beck

▶▶ Barenaked Ladies

Lynne Margolis

Alison Moyet
/Yaz
/Yazoo

Born Genevieve Alison-Jane Moyet June 18, 1961, in Basildon, Essex, England.

As Yazoo (Yaz in the United States, thanks to a copyright dispute), singer Alison Moyet and former Depeche Mode keyboardist Vince Clark made an argument for synthesizer music with its remarkably emotional pop created amid the often vacuous techno landscapes of the early '80s. Much of the duo's vibrancy belonged to Moyet's rich, passionate voice, a sultry blend of R&B and nervy energy. Her singing, matched with Clarke's quirky keyboard pop, lifted the group's songs to a resonant level above that of their peers. After only a year and a half with Yaz, Clarke went on to form Erasure, while Moyet carved out a solo career that has yet to make significant inroads in America.

what to buy: Yaz's *You and Me Both* ♪♪♪♪ (Sire, 1983), the group's second and last release, is a romantic overture of defiance and desperation with a little joyous bounce thrown in to lighten the load. Moyet has yet to come up with material as strong as "Nobody's Diary," "Good Times," and "Walk away from Love." Moyet's *Hoodoo* ♪♪♪ (Columbia, 1991, prod. Pete Glenister) was a commercial flop, but its diversity creates a better stage for her blazing honesty than any of her previous solo efforts.

what to buy next: Yaz's *Upstairs at Eric's* ♪♪♪ (Sire, 1982, prod. E.C. Radcliffe, Yaz) is the group's ambitious and experimental debut that hits sonic warm spots ("Only You" and "Don't Go") as well as horrendous left-field ditches ("I before E Except after C").

what to avoid: Moyet's *Raindancing* ♪ (Columbia, 1987, prod. Jimmy Iovine) is smothered by formula pop production. And titles such as "I Grow Weak in the Presence of Beauty" add insult to injury.

the rest:
Alf ♪♪♪ (Columbia, 1984)
Essex ♪♪♪ (Columbia, 1994)
Singles ♪♪♪ (Columbia, 1995)

influences:

◀◀ Depeche Mode, Kraftwerk, Joy Division

▶▶ Erasure, the Blue Nile, Eurythmics, Annie Lennox

see also: *Erasure*

Allan Orski

Mud

Formed 1966, in Carshalton, Surrey, England.

Les Gray, vocals; Rob Davis, guitar, vocals; Ray Stiles, bass, vocals; Dave Mount, drums, vocals.

Beneath all of the dry ice, outlandish eyewear, and tall, tall boots (and hairstyles) of the early British glitter bands there always lurked musical roots knee-deep in the similarly innocent passion (not to mention chord progressions) of rock 'n' roll's Golden Age. Mud, a typically unassuming yet mega-selling British quartet of the mid-'70s, was no exception to this rule: Each member woodshed in skiffle and Merseybeat combos, and despite an unwise foray into mock-psychedelia on its earliest releases (such as 1967's "Flower Power"), Mud proudly wore its traditional rock influences on its bandmembers' puffy sleeves—even going so far as to cover Buddy Holly's immortal "Oh Boy" at the height of its chart success. Said string of U.K. Top 10's didn't really kick off until it hooked up with the Nicky Chinn–Mike Chapman songwriting and production team in 1973, culminating a year later with the engagingly affected "Tiger Feet," a song so moronically charming that it not only hit #1, but it even sparked off a brief dance craze throughout the British Isles. The hits continued, even after the band left the "Chinni-Chap" song factory to begin tackling such material as Bill Withers's "Lean on Me," and despite an array of solo projects (for example, Ray Stiles often moonlights in the Hollies). Mud to this day can be found headlining various "70's Glam Rock Weekends," where the Tiger Feet is still enthusiastically danced in certain nostalgic circles.

what's available: Lease-breaking rock at its finest, and better-than-average glitter-rock primers to boot, *Great Mud* ♪♪♪ (Goldies, 1996) and *Let's Have a Party: The Best of Mud* ♪♪♪ (EMI, 1990) are absolutely marvelous collections of the band's greatest and goofiest triumphs. Although these original recordings barely made a dent on the American charts, their influence can nonetheless be heard thudding beneath the post-punk repertoires of all the classiest new wave and power pop combos.

influences:

◀◀ Sweet, Slade, Mungo Jerry, Elvis Presley

▶▶ Bay City Rollers, the Ramones, Joan Jett & the Blackhearts, AC/DC, Leather Tuscadero

Gary Pig Gold

Mudhoney

Formed 1988, in Seattle, WA.

Mark Arm, vocals, guitar; Steve Turner, guitar, vocals; Matt Lukin, bass; Dan Peters, drums.

Mudhoney's summer of 1988 debut brown vinyl 45, "Touch Me, I'm Sick," was the first and most elegant signature song of the post-punk metal fusion that came to be marketed as grunge. Formed in the ashes of seminal Sub Pop act Green River (most of whom became Mother Love Bone, some of whom then became Pearl Jam), Mudhoney was the first Seattle band to fuse down-and-dirty punk with a peculiar pop instinct *and* attract an international audience doing it. Named for a Russ Meyer film, Mudhoney was the first standard-bearer for the Seattle scene; its debut EP, *Superfuzz Bigmuff* (named for two cheap effects pedals they favored, or so the story goes) attracted the "grunge" tag, while the group's spectacularly passionate live shows in support first won over the fickle British press. Despite considerable financial inducements, Mudhoney has stayed true to its anti-corporate roots long after their contemporaries have cashed in. When Mudhoney signed to Reprise in 1992, the Seattle gold rush was clearly over. It was also one of many bands to have benefited from the efficient and sympathetic production of Jack Endino.

what to buy: *Superfuzz Bigmuff* 🎵🎵🎵🎵 (Sub Pop, 1988, prod. Jack Endino) has been repackaged with Mudhoney's first two epic singles—"Touch Me, I'm Sick" and "You Got It (Keep It outta My Face)"—and remains the benchmark by which all future releases might be judged. Here they are at their unequaled best: snide, angry, catchy, brooding, very, very loud, and utterly committed. *My Brother the Cow* 🎵🎵🎵🎵 (Reprise, 1995, prod. Jack Endino, Mudhoney) is a canny, muscular return to form, though its popularity had long since been eclipsed by second- and third-generation grunge imitators.

what to buy next: It's hard to argue against Mudhoney's debut long-player, *Mudhoney* 🎵🎵🎵🎵 (Sub Pop, 1989, prod. Jack Endino), for it's full of vim and vigor and classic songs like "This Gift" and "Here Comes Sickness." Like most Mudhoney records, it is better approached as a collection of singles than as a suite of thematically connected songs.

what to avoid: The seven-song *Five Dollar Bob's Mock Cooter Stew* 🎵 (Reprise, 1993, prod. Kurdt Bloch, Mudhoney) can only be explained by the need to keep product in the pipeline. It is as passionless and unfocused a record as a proud band could make, and is little more than a collection of released and unreleased B-sides.

the rest:
Every Good Boy Deserves Fudge 🎵🎵🎵 (Sub Pop, 1991)
Piece of Cake 🎵🎵🎵 (Reprise, 1992)
Tomorrow Hit Today 🎵🎵🎵 (Warner Bros., 1998)

worth searching for: *Mudhoney* (Reprise, 1993) is an eight-song live promotional CD recorded during the filming of the movie *Hype* at the Oddfellows Hall in Seattle. It's a solid performance—a bit more restrained and professional than they managed when younger, but several songs are unique to this release, and it's a good barometer of how stunning the band could be on a good night.

influences:

◀◀ The Stooges, Billy Childish, the Ramones, Green River

▶▶ Nirvana, Tad, Jon Spencer Blues Explosion

Grant Alden

The Muffs

Formed 1991, in Los Angeles, CA.

Kim Shattuck, vocals, guitar; Ronnie Barnett, bass; Roy McDonald, drums; Melanie Vammen, guitar (1991–94); Cris Crass, drums (1991–94).

A poster child for laryngitis, Kim Shattuck left her mediocre underground '80s band, the Pandoras, to create the Muffs. Their concept is simple—loud guitars, irresistible melodies, and lots of high-pitched, Courtney Love–style shrieking. When they're on, the Muffs can match the concise power and humor of the Ramones. When they're off, they sound like punks making a hideous cacophony. Marketing is the only possible explanation why Green Day became major rock superstars with *Dookie*, which came out not long after the Muffs' similar-sounding, just-as-good 1991 debut.

what to buy: *The Muffs* 🎵🎵🎵🎵 (Warner Bros., 1993, prod. Rob Cavallo, David Katznelson, Muffs) is a glorious collection of catchy kiss-offs—on "Lucky Guy," "Better than Me," "Big Mouth," and "Stupid Jerk," Shattuck sounds like she wants to bash the entire male gender with her big guitar and extremely big voice.

what to buy next: *Blonder and Blonder* 🎵🎵🎵 (Warner Bros., 1995, prod. Rob Cavallo, Muffs), with the band reconfigured into a trio (without Vammen and with a new drummer), has a couple of nice tracks in "Oh Nina" and "Red Eyed Troll." But Shattuck's screeches are starting to wear thin, especially without the spirit of the debut.

what to avoid: Don't bother with anything by the Pandoras, an ultra-horny mid-'80s band led by singer-guitarist Paula Pierce, who put out two albums (including *Stop Pretending* 🎵🎵 (Rhino, 1986, prod. Bill Inglot)), plus two EPs and a live disc—but are mostly notable for giving the world Kim Shattuck.

the rest:
Happy Birthday to Me 🎵🎵🎵 (Reprise, 1997)

worth searching for: The Muffs' version of the suburban electro-hit "Kids in America," on the *Clueless* soundtrack (Capitol, 1995, prod. various), is almost as good as Kim Wilde's 1981 original.

influences:

◀◀ The Ramones, Joan Jett, L7, Bad Religion

▶▶ Hole, Green Day, the Offspring, NOFX

see also: *Pandoras*

Steve Knopper

The Mumps

Formed 1978, in New York, NY.

Lance Loud, vocals; Kristian Hoffman, keyboards; Rob Duprey, guitar; Paul Rutner, drums; Kevin Kiely, bass.

The Mumps expanded on the cheeky aspect of punk, coming on like the '70s Kinks gone punk and loopy—sort of a "Lola"-polooza, if you will. Lead vocalist Lance Loud (who was seen in the PBS documentary *An American Family*) was so extroverted he made Jonathan Richman look like James Taylor. Keyboardist/songwriter Kristian Hoffman came up with sticky new wave ditties that were perfect for Loud's over-the-top exuberance.

what to buy: The 23-track *Fatal Charm* 𝄢𝄢𝄢𝄢 (Eggbert, 1994, prod. Earle Mankey, Mumps) not only includes everything you'll ever need by the Mumps but everything the group ever recorded. It's a strong collection with fawning liner notes by rock icons from Michael Stipe to Cherry Vanilla.

solo outings:

Kristian Hoffman:

I Don't Love My Guru Anymore 𝄢𝄢𝄢 (Eggbert, 1993)

Earthquake Weather (Eggbert, 1997)

influences:

◀◀ The Kinks, Sparks

▶▶ Pulp, the Violent Femmes

Jordan Oakes

Alan Munde

See: Flying Burrito Brothers

The Murmurs

Formed 1991, in New York, NY.

Heather Grody, guitar, vocals; Leisha Haily, guitar, vocals.

Heather Grody and Leisha Haily were studying at the American Academy of Dramatic Arts when they happened upon a mutual interest in irreverent, often loud, acoustic duality. The Murmurs

is more like the upbeat, humorous pop of Voice of the Beehive than the sincere folk of the Indigo Girls, but through a course of ill-advised shock singles, it carries little of either band's prestige. Knocked up the charts by a tuneless directive, "You Suck" ("now there's dust on my guitar/and it's all your fault. . . ."), the band could only fall—which it did rather quickly with a cover of Jefferson Airplane's "White Rabbit." Lesson: songs with titles such as "You Suck" don't usually precede lengthy careers.

what's available: The debut, *The Murmurs* 𝄢𝄢 (MCA, 1994, prod. Roger Greenawalt, Billy Basinski), contains the empty minor radio hit "You Suck," churned with an angst that ultimately missed the mark. By the time the Murmurs got around to a second full-length album, *Pristine Smut* 𝄢𝄢 (MCA, 1997, prod. k.d. lang. Murmurs), it had cast a lesbian hue involving a romantic linking with producer lang. But even that didn't bring much public interest.

influences:

◀◀ Voice of the Beehive, Altered Images, the B-52's

Billy Manes

Elliott Murphy

Born March 16, 1949, in Garden City, NY.

Ernest Hemingway said no man who ever wrote anything of value left his country to work his craft. Elliott Murphy, one of the more gifted practitioners of heartland rock to ever labor under the "new Dylan" tag, is the contradiction to refute such a claim. And of that unlucky lot, Murphy has suffered perhaps the most pervading kind of U.S. indifference. At one point he was actually doing office work in a law firm, such was the lack of attention. Nevertheless, he has retained his songcraft while doggedly forging a career of more than 20 years. His consistency has remained on a higher level than most of his peers, as he continues to craft songs of remarkable intellectual depth while retaining a journeyman's stance. Murphy now resides in the more welcoming environs of Paris, where he has a much larger following.

what to buy: Much of Murphy's output is out of print, but his recent *Selling the Gold* 𝄢𝄢𝄢𝄢 (Dejadisc, 1996, prod. Djoum, Elliott Murphy) is a telling intoduction to his mature subtlety and still active muse. Without resorting to bombast or overly simplistic immediacy, it's also typical Murphy: there's big payoff to be had, but only if you pay attention. Both Bruce Springsteen and the Violent Femmes' Gordon Gano pop up for cameos. Dipping into his past a bit, *Going through Something: The Best of Elliott Murphy* 𝄢𝄢𝄢𝄢 (Dejadisc, 1996, prod. Elliott Murphy, Steve Wilkison) covers highlights from 1978–91 from otherwise deleted albums. A decent run-through of what you missed the first time around.

what to buy next: The title track and a host of others make *Party Girl, Broken Poets* ♫♫♫ (Dejadisc, 1984, prod. Elliott Murphy, Ernie Brooks) a decent spin. Murphy's knack for extended storytelling while adhering to conventional folk and pop song structures flourishes, untouched by the new wave '80s.

the rest:
Diamonds by the Yard: A Career Retrospective ♫♫♫ (Razor & Tie, 1992)
Unreal City ♫♫♫ (Razor & Tie, 1993)

influences:
◀◀ Bob Dylan, Lou Reed, the Velvet Underground
▶▶ Bruce Springsteen, John Mellencamp, Tom Petty, Violent Femmes

Allan Orski

Peter Murphy
/Dali's Car

Born July 11, 1957, in Northampton, England.

Peter Murphy began his career as the singer of the seminal gothic band Bauhaus. Upon that band's breakup in 1983, he joined forces with former Japan member Mick Karn in the group Dali's Car, releasing just one album before going solo. Murphy initially clung to Bauhaus' moody, gloomy approach, and it wasn't until his sophomore effort, *Love Hysteria*, that he found his own way and began to separate himself from that sound. He learned to control his voice, allowing him to sing a rich range of sensual melodies that were backed by dense, layered instrumental attacks.

what to buy: *Love Hysteria* ♫♫♫♫ (Beggars Banquet, 1988, prod. Simon Rogers) is where Murphy realizes he is no longer part of Bauhaus. His upbeat, moving melodies and smooth vocals delicately lure the ear into the music.

what to buy next: *Cascade* ♫♫♫♫ (Beggars Banquet/Atlantic, 1995, prod. Pascal Gabriel) finds a refreshed Murphy singing dramatically with catchy melodies.

what to avoid: *Deep* ♫♫ (Beggars Banquet/RCA, 1990, prod. Simon Rogers) laced Murphy's flare and brought him into adult contemporary radio and easy listening.

the rest:
Should the World Fail to Fall Apart ♫♫♫♫ (Beggars Banquet, 1986)
Holy Smoke ♫♫♫ (Beggars Banquet, 1992)

worth searching for: The lone Dali's Car effort, *The Waking Hour* (Paradox/Beggars Banquet, 1984) is sonically close to Japan, though it never quite reaches that group's heights.

influences:
◀◀ John Cale, David Bowie, Bryan Ferry, Japan

▶▶ David Sylvian, Edwyn Collins

see also: *Bauhaus*

J.D. Cantarella

Music Explosion

Formed mid-1960s, in OH. Disbanded 1969.

Jamie Lyons, vocals, guitar, trombone; Don Tudor Atkins, guitar; Rick Nesta, guitar; Butch (Burton) Stahl, bass, organ; Bob Avery, drums, harmonica.

Sounding like a polished version of ? & the Mysterians—it covered "96 Tears" on its first album—this one-hit Ohio garage band reached #2 in 1967 with "Little Bit o' Soul," a gutsy R&B number with a hooky bass-organ riff. Jamie Lyons sneers out his vocals in what sounds like an earnest tribute to Mick Jagger, but whatever personality the group may have had was subverted by producers Jeff Katz and Jerry Kasenetz, who would go on to create successful bubblegum acts such as the 1910 Fruitgum Co. and the Ohio Express.

what's available: *Anthology* ♫♫ (One Way, 1995, prod. Elliot Cheprut, Jerry Kasenetz, Jeff Katz) is an interesting retro-punk artifact that effectively pulls together the bulk of the Music Explosion's meager catalog. Little of the material stands up today, but some of it ("Little Bit o' Soul," "I See the Light," "96 Tears," and "Sunshine Games") is just offbeat enough to be interesting.

influences:
◀◀ The Rolling Stones, the Box Tops, ? & the Mysterians
▶▶ 1910 Fruitgum Co., the Ohio Express, Elvis Costello & the Attractions, Blondie

Christopher Scapelliti

Music Machine
/Bonniwell Music Machine
/Friendly Torpedoes

Formed 1965, in Los Angeles, CA. Disbanded 1968.

Sean Bonniwell, vocals, guitar; Doug Rhodes, keyboards, vocals; Keith Olsen, bass, vocals; Mark Landon, guitar; Ron Edgar, drums.

Had it not been for the brilliantly dark, twisted mutterings of singer-songwriter Sean Bonniwell, the Music Machine would have been just one of a hundred Rickenbacker and Farfisa-pounding combos slumming as suntanned Stones wannabes along the Sunset Strip circa 1965 (although, to give due credit for originality, each bandmember actually wore one black glove while performing—along with the requisite dark turtlenecks and white Levis, that is). The group's one and only hit, "Talk

Talk," was just about the most furious two minutes of proto-punk to hit the Top 20 in its time, though subsequent recordings failed to fully capture the band's hot, bothered, on-stage fury. As Bonniwell grew more and more experimental in his approach, he brought a sense of curious danger to his music that played to much greater acclaim and success, including admiring comments from the Doors' Jim Morrison. But the original Music Machine slowly drifted away towards other, softer pursuits (such as the Millennium and Sagittarius studio projects). Bonniwell himself recorded a solo album for Capitol in 1969, briefly resurfaced during the '80s with a Christian rock band called Heaven Sent, and remains to this day the proud curator of his tiny but important legacy in the annals of American garage rock history.

what's available: Frustrating in a way—as every Bonniwell treasure seems followed by an unspectacular cover-of-the-day (including even Neil Diamond's "Cherry Cherry")—*(Turn On) The Music Machine* 𝄢𝄢𝄢 (Original Sound, 1966/Repertoire, Performance, 1994, prod. Stephen Kaplan, Arthur Marko) is nevertheless required listening, as it's the only way to savor the legendary "Talk Talk" in its original, black-gloved setting. *Beyond the Garage* 𝄢𝄢𝄢 (Sundazed, 1996, compilation prod. Bob Irwin, Brian Ross, Sean Bonniwell) packages together the seldom-heard 1967 Bonniwell Music Machine album cut for Warner Bros. along with relevant single sides and unreleased tracks.

influences:

◄◄ The Ragamuffins, the Yardbirds, the Leaves, ? & the Mysterians, the Barbarians, the Seeds

►► Chocolate Watch Band, the Amboy Dukes, Blue Cheer, the dB's, the Minstrels

Gary Pig Gold

My Bloody Valentine

Formed 1984, in Dublin, Ireland.

Kevin Shields, vocals, guitars; Colm O'Ciosoig, drums; Tina, keyboards (1984–85); Dave Conway, vocals (1984–87); Deb Googe, bass (1986–present); Belinda Butcher, guitar, vocals (1987–present).

As far as most pop music pundits are concerned, My Bloody Valentine—whose name is derived from a B-grade Canadian horror film—redefined rock music. Following the addition of Butcher's haunting vocals, the group's 1988 debut album, *Isn't Anything*, and its follow-up, 1991's *Loveless*, presented a sound that was fresh and distinctive. Using feedback, tape loops, flutes, pianos, distortion, and drums, along with a variety of skewed production techniques, MBV earned acclaim not only for its warped sound collages but also for its captivating songs.

This quest for innovation has a price, though; the recording of *Loveless* took three years, cost as much as $500,000, and nearly bankrupted the band's British label, Creation Records. The band has not been heard from since.

what to buy: On *Loveless* 𝄢𝄢𝄢𝄢 (Sire, 1991, prod. Kevin Shields), the band perfected its melodic noise pop with richly textured music that's loud and noisy, yet never harsh or abrasive. The closing track, "Soon," "sets a new standard for pop," according to Brian Eno. *Glider* 𝄢𝄢𝄢 (Creation/Sire EP, 1991, prod. Kevin Shields, My Bloody Valentine) contains "Soon," as well as three other songs that aren't as ethereal as *Loveless*—making it perhaps an even better starting point.

what to buy next: *Isn't Anything* 𝄢𝄢𝄢 (Creation/Relativity, 1988, prod. My Bloody Valentine) isn't quite as fully realized as *Loveless*, but it's still mesmerizing—sort of like grunge with eerie overtones. *Tremolo* 𝄢𝄢𝄢 (Creation/Sire EP, 1991, prod. My Bloody Valentine) offers some of the group's most noisy and experimental songs, each loaded with distortion, tape loops, and re-engineering touches.

what to avoid: Lacking Belinda Butcher's vocals and the complex, organic feel of the later releases, *This Is Your Bloody Valentine* 𝄢𝄢 (Tycoon EP, 1985/Dosier EP, 1991, prod. My Bloody Valentine) is a basic, bland rock set. Stick to the more recent records.

worth searching for: *Ecstasy and Wine* (Lazy, 1989, prod. My Bloody Valentine) is an out-of-print EP that finds the group making more strides towards its signature sound.

influences:

◄◄ Cocteau Twins, Sonic Youth, Philip Glass

►► Smashing Pumpkins, Radiohead, Lush

Aidin Vaziri and Bryan Lassner

My Drug Hell

Formed 1992, in London, England.

Tim Briffa, vocals, guitars; Paul Donnelly, bass, backing vocals; Joe Bultitude, drums, backing vocals.

My Drug Hell creates rainswept, enigmatic, and surprisingly infectious back-to-basics rock 'n' roll that draws equally on the goth, psychedelic, punk, and pure-pop traditions. But there's more going on here than meets the ears—MDH's pre-digital recording technique conveys a great homemade intimacy, but its hollowness and hiss are the aural equivalent of yellowing paper. MDH may believe in preserving what's best in popular music's past, but it obviously adheres to living in the present as well: its ear-candy's ineffable undercurrent of creepiness makes it sound like the crooning of nostalgic vampires—a wry if tacit commentary on the logical extreme of looking backward. The band's recipe of one part retro salability to one part promo savvy assures it a deservedly long run—as signaled by the hilarious recent adoption by Miller Genuine Draft (who bring you America's drug hell) of MDH's lovely but unsettling "Girl at the Bus Stop" for a stateside TV ad.

what's available: Dour and delicious, the debut *This Is My Drug Hell* ♫♫♫ (Countdown, 1996, prod. Fellini Retrospective) is the kind of come-from-nowhere critical favorite and alternative-radio hit that keeps up the hopes of aspiring musicians and plain old fans alike.

influences:

◄◄ Gerry & the Pacemakers, the Velvet Underground, Nick Cave, the Psychedelic Furs, the Smiths

Adam McGovern

My Life with the Thrill Kill Kult /The Bomb Gang Girlz

Formed 1987, in Chicago, IL.

Groovie Mann (born Frank Nardiello), vocals; Buzz McCoy (born Marston Daley) vocals, guitar; Levi Levi (born Charles Levi), bass (1991–present); Buck Ryder (born Thomas Thorn), keyboards, samples (1987–93); Otto Mattix, drums (1987–93); Trash K., guitars (1994); Dick Furry, drums (1995–present); Wolfgang Dodge, horns (1995). The Bomb Gang Girlz: Kitty Killdare (born Laura Gomel), keyboards, vocals (1987–95); Jacky Blacque (born Rachel Hollingsworth), vocals; Rhond "Pickles" Bond, vocals; Beat Mistress, drums; Cinderella Pussie, vocals (1995); Linda Lunch, vocals; Arena Rock (born Carmen Marusich), vocals (1995–present); Sekret DeZyre, vocals (1990–95).

In 1987 Frank Nardielo and Marston Daley approached Dannie Flesher of Wax Trax! records with an idea to create a B-grade horror movie titled *My Life with the Thrill Kill Kult*. The project almost got underway; the two went so far as to record a soundtrack to the film, and it became the group's first EP. Incorporating an array of musicians and an ever-changing line-up of female singers (known collectively as the Bomb Gang Girlz), Thrill Kill Kult (TKK) has always sounded just like it intended, a purveyor of kitschy horror-movie music. Even though the band has never made a movie, the music has been used in several motion pictures, and the group generously samples from a wide variety of cult films and television shows.

what to buy: TKK's first outings contain an industrial edge, culminating with *Confessions of a Knife* ♫♫♫♫ (Wax Trax!, 1990, prod. Buzz McCoy), which combines glam, metal, and industrial touches with an electro-dance groove. With the release of *Sex-*

plosion! ♫♫♫♫ (Interscope, 1991, prod. Buzz McCoy), TKK changes not only the labels, but also sounds, becoming even more dance oriented and less harsh. The album launched a club and underground hit, "Sex on Wheels."

what to buy next: For fans of the Wax Trax! era, TKK's original outing, *I See Good Spirits and I See Bad Spirits* ♫♫♫ (Wax Trax! 1988, prod. Buzz McCoy) is sure to please; Satan and samples abound, thrown in with a good mix of disco and industrial backbone. *13 Above the Night* ♫♫♫ (Interscope, 1994, prod. Buzz McCoy) follows *Sexplosion!*'s descent into disco-glam, softening the tinge of distortion that remains.

what to avoid: *Hit and Run Holiday* ♫♫ (Interscope, 1995, prod. Buzz McCoy) is TKK's most dance-oriented album to date, and its most tempered, with relatively subdued guitar and vocal distortion.

the rest:
Kooler than Jesus ♫♫♫ (Wax Trax!, 1989)
A Crime for All Seasons ♫♫♫ (Red Ant, 1997)

solo outings:
Electric Hellfire Club (Buck Ryder and Otto Mattix):
Burn Baby Burn ♫♫ (Cleopatra, 1993)
Satan's Little Helpers ♫♫ (Cleopatra EP, 1994)
Kiss the Goat ♫♫ (Cleopatra, 1995)
Calling Dr. Luv ♫♫♫ (Cleopatra, 1996)
Unholy Roller ♫♫♫ (Cleopatra, 1998)

influences:

◄◄ Big Stick, Death in June, Legendary Pink Dots

►► Pigface, Electric Hellfire Club, Ministry, Luc Van Acker, KMFDM, Lords of Acid, Meat Beat Manifesto

Bryan Lassner

Mysteries of Life

See: Antenna

Naked Eyes

Formed 1982, in London, England. Disbanded 1984.

Pete Byrne, vocals; Rob Fisher, keyboards.

A featherweight addition to the early '80s MTV electro-pop scourge, Naked Eyes is one of the many indistinguishable airy duos that swept across the airwaves. Like the rest, it had one song in it ("Promises, Promises") and a cover (R.B. Greaves's

1970 hit "Always Something There to Remind Me") before it chirped right off the charts. If the latter carries any worth at all, it is to turn listeners back to Dionne Warwick's chiming original.

what's available: *Promises, Promises: The Very Best of Naked Eyes* 𝄢𝄢𝄢 (EMI, 1994, prod. various) offers as full a picture of the band as is necessary, with two versions of "Promises, Promises" plus "Always Something There to Remind Me" and 17 other tracks.

influences:

◀◀ ABC, Adam Ant, Soft Cell

▶▶ a-ha

Allan Orski

Naked Raygun

Formed 1982, in Chicago, IL.

Jeff Pezzati, vocals; Santiago Durango, guitar (1982–83); John Haggerty, guitar (1984–89); Bill Stephens, guitar (1990–present); Marco Pezzati, bass (1982); Camilo Gonzalez, bass (1983); Pierre Kezdy, bass (1984–present); Jim Colao, drums (1982–83); Eric Spicer, drums (1984–present).

Along with Big Black and the Effigies, Naked Raygun shaped a unique, Midwestern response to the British punk of the Buzzcocks, Wire, and Gang of Four. The jack-booted, buzz-cut quartet stood out from the post-punk pack by merging paramilitary aggressiveness with a strong pop sense and unusually thoughtful lyrics. Raygun toured heavily, and its penchant for raucous, "whoah-ay-ohhhh!" harmonies made it a kingpin of the all-ages circuit for much of the '80s. The group went on hiatus in 1991 but regrouped six years later for live appearances.

what to buy: With five studio albums circa 1984–90 out of print, the best option is *The Last of the Demo Hicans* 𝄢𝄢𝄢𝄢 (Dyslexic, 1997, prod. various), a solid if hardly definitive career retrospective composed entirely of unreleased tracks. Live versions of "Metastasis" and "Treason," among others, demonstrate the greatness of Raygun during its mid-'80s prime. These are framed by lesser material: four studio tracks from '92; and dim-sounding, if fascinating, early demos with future Big Black guitarist Santiago Durango.

worth searching for: *All Rise* (Homestead, 1985, prod. Iain Burgess, Naked Raygun) is no-frills aggro-pop perfect for the skateboard punk you once were, still are, or always longed to be.

influences:

◀◀ The Buzzcocks, Wire, Minor Threat, Killing Joke

▶▶ Pegboy, No Empathy, Jack Scratch, Bhopal Stiffs

Greg Kot

Nancy Boy

Formed 1993, in Los Angeles, CA.

Donovan Leitch, vocals; Jason Nesmith, guitars/background vocals; Nigel Mogg, bass; Mike Williams, drums, percussion; Jesse Dorsey, keyboards.

Part-time pouty supermodel Donovan Leitch, Jason Nesmith, and Nigel Mogg were bound to get into the music industry. After all, Leitch's father is "Sunshine Superman" folk singer Donovan, Nesmith's father is ex-Monkee Mike Nesmith, and Mogg is the nephew of a UFO member. But strong lineage doesn't necessarily mean the group can come up with anything creative.

what's available: The band's debut *Nancy Boy* 𝄢 (Sire, 1996, prod. Shel Talmy) simply rehashes the glam rock of David Bowie and T. Rex, with trite lyrics to boot. "Can You Dig It," with its synthesized beeps and blurps, sounds like a bad Flock of Seagulls B-side. In its liner notes, Nancy Boy (the name is British slang for "effeminate") should have thanked Duran Duran for letting it heist "Rio" and re-name it "Johnny Chrome." "W.R.I.P.," a play on the call letters of the seminal Detroit rock station WRIF, honors the city's rock history with embarassingly David Bowiesque vocals. Nancy Boy should leave Brit pop and glam rock to Blur and Pulp.

influences:

◀◀ David Bowie, Mott the Hoople, Charm Farm

▶▶ Harvey Danger

Christina Fuoco

Graham Nash

Born February 2, 1941, in Lancaster, England.

Graham Nash as a solo act seems not only overshadowed by his membership in Crosby, Stills & Nash, but also by his two bandmates. Maybe it's because they both came from hugely influential American bands (Crosby from the Byrds, Stills from Buffalo Springfield) whereas Nash's old band, the Hollies, isn't looked on in as reverential a light. Or maybe it's because Stills records more solo albums and Crosby gets more headlines. But while Nash was often the guiding light in CSN, his solo career hasn't yielded the hits of either Crosby ("Hero") or Stills ("Love the One You're With")—although the then-timely "Chicago," a response to the riotous 1968 Democratic National Convention in that city, comes close. Nash's solo career started off well with 1971's *Songs for Beginners*, which was recorded at a time when CSN members couldn't miss; if one of them was in the studio, talent would just show up and great songs would come out. His other solo albums just aren't as good; Nash seems to prefer being in a band, whether it's CSN, his duo project Crosby/Nash, or his occasional reunions with the Hollies.

what to buy: *Songs for Beginners* ♪♪♪ (Atlantic, 1971, prod. Graham Nash) came out just after CSN&Young's *Deja Vu* period and features guest appearances by Crosby, Neil Young (as "Joe Yankee"), Dave Mason of Traffic, and Jerry Garcia and Phil Lesh of the Grateful Dead stopping by. "Military Madness" and "Chicago" are Nash's best songs with any group of collaborators.

the rest:
Wild Tales ♪♪ (Atlantic, 1973)
Earth and Sky ♪♪ (EMI, 1980)
Innocent Eyes ♪♪ (Atlantic, 1986)

worth searching for: Worth tracking down for severe fans is a single Graham and Neil Young recorded as a duo, called "War Song."

influences:
◀◀ Bob Dylan, Joni Mitchell, the Beatles
▶▶ Jackson Browne, Hootie & the Blowfish, the Indigo Girls

see also: *Crosby, Stills & Nash, the Hollies*

Brian Ives

Nashville Teens

Formed 1962, in Weybridge, Surrey, England. Disbanded 1973.

Arthur Sharpe, vocals; Barry Jenkins, drums (1962–66); Pete Shannon, guitar; Ray Phillips, bass; John Allen, guitar; John Hawken, drums (1966–73).

One of many British Invasion-era bands who refurbished (dare we say improved) the sounds of American blues and R&B, the Nashville Teens were sublime one-hit wonders. Named in such a way to let fans know they played American youth-oriented music, the sound of the Nashville Teens featured dual lead vocals, snarling electric guitar, and stabbing piano triplets. At the start of their career, the group was the backing band for such touring U.S. luminaries as Bo Diddley and Jerry Lee Lewis, and played many of the same European venues as the Beatles. In 1964 they backed the Killer (on "My Baby Don't Want Nobody but Me") and performed "Whatcha Gonna Do" in the seldom seen Brit-teen flick *Be My Guest*. After legendary producer Mickey Most got them signed to Decca Records, the Teens transformed John D. Loudermilk's folksy white-trash survival hymn "Tobacco Road" into a hard-hitting electric blues. A massive hit in Britain and America, "Tobacco Road" quickly became part of garage band repertoires everywhere. Unfortunately it was their only U.S. hit. "Google Eye," which featured a similar approach, was a Top 10 U.K. record, but it didn't register at all here. They capitalized by appearing in low-rent teen exploitation films like *Gonks Go Beat* and *Go Go Mania*, but these poorly made films didn't revive the group's career momentum. The Teens and producer Most had a falling out that resulted in their

being at the mercy of a panicky label who wanted the group to cut more pop-oriented sides. Subsequently their final chart entries "Find My Way Way Back Home" and "This Little Bird" left fans feeling that the Nashville Teens had abandoned the sacred cause of blues-based rock 'n' roll. Neither accomplished writers or producers, the fame of the Teens was short-lived. Just two years after "Tobacco Road," the group had returned to the small-time, backing visiting performers and playing lengthy European gigs. Their lone bright spot, an appearance in the movie *Run with the Wind*, starred Shawn Phillips. Eventually members began defecting from the band—Jenkins joined the Animals in '66, Hawken helped form Renaissance, then the Strawbs. The Teens disbanded in 1973. An early '80s version of the band featured only one original member, but still proved capable of churning out hot blues with a big beat.

what to buy: Their one and only Top 10 American hit resides on *Tobacco Road* ♪♪♪ (One Way, 1995, prod. Mickey Most). This powerful reissue sports great sound and contains such unheralded blues-rockers as "Parchment Farm," "Mona," and their U.K. Top 10 hit "Google Eye." Those who believe the Animals and the Stones cornered the market on tough R&B/Britpop are well-advised to add this stomping aural treat to their collection.

what to avoid: Unless you can't find the One Way disc, steer clear of *With a Girl like You* ♪♪ (Collectables, 1991), a split disc featuring mid-'60s tracks from both the Nashville Teens and the Troggs. For a few more dollars you can get full LP's by both of these worthwhile groups.

worth searching for: You can see the Nashville Teens do "Tobacco Road" on the fine video *Shindig Presents: British Invasion, Vol. 1* (Rhino Home Video, 1992), which also features mid-'60s appearances by Gerry & the Pacemakers, Herman's Hermits, the Searchers, the Honeycombs, Peter & Gordon, and Mannfred Mann. Also, the Nashville Teens are the backup band for the legendary Jerry Lee Lewis on *Live at the Starclub, Hamburg* (Phillips, 1964/Bear Family, 1994, reissue prod. Siggy Loch). At his very best, Lewis is surly, powerful, and intense on this landmark recording. He pushes the Teens to their limits, and they push back with sass and vigor, resulting in the greatest in-concert recording of the early rock era.

influences:
◀◀ Muddy Waters, Bo Diddley, Jerry Lee Lewis, the Swinging Blue Jeans, the Beatles
▶▶ The Searchers, the Honeycombs, Blues Magoos, the Strawbs, Renaissance

see also: *The Animals, Renaissance, the Strawbs*

Ken Burke

Nazareth

Formed 1968, in Dunfermline, Scotland.

Dan McCafferty, vocals; Manny Charlton, guitar (1968–90); Darrel Sweet, drums; Pete Agnew, bass; Zal Cleminson, guitar (1978–80); Billy Rankin, guitar, keyboards (1981–83, 1990–present); John Locke, keyboards (1981–82).

Like a boot slamming on a hardwood floor, Nazareth's rock is hard and heavy. While not overly creative in terms of original material, the group did rework a surprising selection of cover tunes (by Bob Dylan, Joni Mitchell, and Woody Guthrie). Purging the songs of their rustic beauty—the grinding version of the Everly Brothers' "Love Hurts" being the most famous example—the Scots gave 'em a solid stomp, while Dan McCafferty's rip-saw vocals shredded everything in sight without apology. After middling through the '80s without a U.S. label (spending time instead in Canada and Europe), Nazareth returned to the States in 1993 with its thumping style still intact.

what to buy: Since most of its albums are spotty, *Greatest Hits* ✻✻✻✻ (A&M, 1996, prod. various), a distillation of their best material digitally remastered, is a handy intro. Among the 18 tracks, listen for "Love Hurts," "This Flight Tonight," and "Hair of the Dog."

what to buy next: *Hair of the Dog* ✻✻✻✻ (A&M, 1975, prod. Manny Charlton) is the group's most consistent album, with "Love Hurts" and the relentlessly nasty title track.

what to avoid: *Razamanaz* ✻✻ (A&M, 1973/1994, prod. Roger Glover) demonstrates that plodding around without a good tune is just plodding around.

the rest:
Hot Tracks ✻✻✻ (A&M, 1977)
Classics, Vol. 16 ✻✻✻✻ (A&M, 1987)
No Jive ✻✻ (Griffin, 1995/1993)
Singles Collection ✻✻✻ (Griffin, 1994)
Early Years ✻✻ (Griffin, 1995)
Snaz Live ✻✻✻ (Griffin, 1981/1995)

influences:
◀◀ Led Zeppelin, Mountain, Deep Purple, Sensational Alex Harvey Band

▶▶ Mötley Crüe, Krokus

Allan Orski

Me'Shell Ndegéocello

Born August 29, 1969, in Berlin, Germany.

In a way, it may be best to think of Me'Shell Ndegéocello as a modern Patrice Rushen: a child prodigy schooled in music, becoming an accomplished composer, arranger, producer, vocal-

ist, and multi-instrumentalist (bass being primary) who signs to a small label—Madonna's Maverick Recordings—because of the assurances of artistic and creative freedom. And like Rushen, Ndegéocello refuses to follow the claustrophobic course of one specific genre. She blends soul, funk, jazz, rock, pop, and hip-hop (and various hybrids of all of those) to create a sound that's the future of R&B, but a future that thankfully—and unashamedly—knows its past. Ndegéocello has, in a very short period of time, shown herself to be one of the most—if not *the* most—important and vibrant forces in modern R&B. It is clear that she has learned a lot and is more than willing to share that knowledge with us. We'd be wise to pay attention.

what's available: Her debut, *Plantation Lullabies* ✻✻✻✻ (Maverick, 1993, prod. Bob Power, Andre Betts, David Gamson), is a mosaic of black music styles over which she addresses—quite candidly—drugs, love, lust, poverty, and race. It's clear from tracks such as "I'm Diggin' You (like an Old Soul Record)" and "Dred Loc" that Ndegéocello knows how to bring black music's past into the present and mold an enticing future from it. Having made her point on *Lullabies*, Ndegéocello allows herself to relax on the follow-up, *Peace beyond Passion* ✻✻✻✻ (Maverick, 1996, prod. David Gamson). She loosens her grip and allows a host of talented people—including guitar funkmeister Wah Wah Watson, organ grinder Billy Preston, reedsman Joshua Redman, former Revolution guitarist Wendy Melvoin, and concertmaster Gene Page—to share her revolutionary jazz vision. The album is a raw and subtle funk tour de force, a suite of 12 songs (11 originals and one cover) that shows how Ndegéocello has matured as a composer and performer.

worth searching for: The mass pop audience knows Ndegéocello via her spunky (it's the only word for it) duet with John Mellencamp on Van Morrison's "Wild Night." It can be found on Mellencamp's album *Dance Naked* (Mercury, 1994, prod. John Mellencamp).

influences:
◀◀ Marvin Gaye, Teena Marie, Charles Mingus, Bootsy Collins, Prince, George Clinton, Millie Jackson

▶▶ Ambersunshower, Erykah Badu

Coqui Toyoda

Ned's Atomic Dustbin

Formed 1987, in England. Disbanded 1996.

Jonn Penny, vocals; Rat, guitars; Matt Cheslin, bass; Alex Griffin, bass; Dan Warton, drums.

Ned's Atomic Dustbin began as a goth-rock band but evolved into a double-bass swirl of punk and Brit pop. Its first single, the relentlessly addictive "Kill Your Television," embedded

Me'Shell Ndegéocello (© Jack Vartoogian)

Ned's into British rock history. Its commercial success earned the band a contract with Sony Music, but the band never did anything with it. After breaking up in 1996, Penny and Rat formed Groundswell, which played its debut show in September of 1997.

what to buy: It's rare that a band's debut becomes its best album, but such is the case with *God Fodder* ♫♫♫ (Columbia, 1991, prod. Jessica Corcoran, Ned's Atomic Dustbin), on which "Kill Your Television" eventually landed. With fast melodies that will make you jump around the house, it's a heavenly mix of aggressive pop-rock, including the lesser-known song "Less Than Useful."

what to buy next: Ned's last release, *Brainbloodvolume* ♫♫♫ (Work Group, 1995, prod. Tim Palmer) was a pleasing way for the band to say good-bye. "All I Ask of Myself Is That I Hold Together," the CD's lead-off track, is classic Ned's. The name of the closing song, "Song 11 Could Take Forever," is just as comical as the song itself.

the rest:
Are You Normal? ♫♫♪ (Chaos, 1992)

worth searching for: *Bite* (Chapter 22, 1991, prod. Jessica Corcoran) is out of print but offers the interesting "Kill Your Remix."

influences:
◄◄ Carter the Unstoppable Sex Machine, Ethyl Meatplow

►► ManBREAK

Christina Fuoco

Negativland

Formed 1980, in Berkeley, CA.

Mark Hosler, instruments, electronics, vocals; Don Joyce, electronics, vocals; Chris Gregg, instruments, electronics, vocals; David Wills, electronics, vocals; Richard Lyons, vocals.

The members of Negativland are mass-media Robin Hoods, sampling the corporate siren song of ubiquitous ads and bad music and restructuring it into subversive messages and exciting avant-pop. Threading audio garbage into stunning found-sound tapestries along with their own witty, jack-of-all-styles music, the band's albums are like disjointed documentaries you can dance to. Their Information Highwayman activities earned them folk-hero status—and near bankruptcy—when they dared to sample a profane Casey Kasem blooper tape and a hit U2 song right when Kasem was reestablishing himself and U2 had a comeback album on the way. They survived the legal retaliation with some of their best albums and a new-found crusade for the rights of artists in the information age to re-use

what we all have no choice but to hear. Some would call it piracy. But it's genuinely revolutionary and runs very real risks—so call it rock 'n' roll.

what to buy: The intentionally listener-unfriendly *Escape from Noise* ♫♫♫♫ (Rec Rec, 1987, prod. Negativland) is a kind of out-of-sequence opera on media overload that endures as a prescient bit of standup electronica. *Helter Stupid* ♫♫♫♫♫ (Rec Rec, 1989, prod. Negativland) is the band's first masterpiece and the concept album they didn't have to make up, culled from the media circus ensuing when the band dropped hints that an infamous teen mass-murderer was influenced by one of their songs. Both laugh-riot and tear-jerker, the album's moral is plain: If a rock band can get its lies printed verbatim on the front page, why not the government? *DisPepsi* ♫♫♫♫♫ (Seeland, 1997, prod. Negativland) is the band's most side-splitting and savvy indictment of interchangeable art and commerce yet. The album's real title was withheld from its packaging to avert another legal strike, but then the soft drink giant pledged not to sue, which just goes to show you have less to fear from the fascists than you do from your friends.

what to buy next: *Free* ♫♫♫♫ (Seeland, 1993, prod. Negativland)—as in "land of the"—is the band's deceptively "song-based" mock-patriotic pageant, with gallows-humor found-voice collages of guilt, fanaticism, and isolation set between high-lonesome ballads in a karaoke-like spectrum of styles. Negativland hijack the airwaves themselves for three free-form hours a week on KPFA-FM (Berkeley, CA)'s *Over the Edge* broadcast. It's all perfectly licensed, so think of it as "pirate format." Picture a stranger-than-fiction *X-Files* with a laugh track. They're archiving the show on disk; the best include *Over the Edge, Vol. 1: Jam Con '84* ♫♫♫♫ (Seeland, 1984/94, prod. Negativland). But for the hilarious live coverage of Reagan's second inaugural, you'll have trouble believing this smart satire was recorded 15 years ago, and not 15 minutes ago.

the rest:
Negativland ♫♫♫♫ (Seeland, 1980)
"Points" ♫♫♫♫ (Seeland, 1981)
A Big 10-8 Place ♫♫♫♫ (Seeland, 1983)
Over the Edge, Vol. 1.5: The Starting Line ♫♫♫♫ (Seeland, 1985)
Over the Edge, Vol. 2: Pastor Dick ♫♫♫♫♪ (Seeland, 1990)
Over the Edge, Vol. 3: The Weatherman ♫♫♫♫ (Seeland, 1990)
Over the Edge, Vol. 4: Dick Vaughn's Moribund Music of the '70s ♫♫♫♫♪ (Seeland, 1990)
Guns ♫♫♫♫ (SST EP, 1992)
Over the Edge, Vol. 5: Crosley Bendix: The Radio Reviews ♫♫♫♫♪ (Seeland, 1993)
Over the Edge, Vol. 6: The Willsaphone Stupid Show ♫♫♫♫ (Seeland, 1994)
Over the Edge, Vol. 7: Time Zones Exchange Project ♫♫♫♫ (Seeland, 1994)

Over the Edge, Vol. 8: Sex Dirt &&&& (Seeland, 1995)
Death Sentences (Seeland, 1998)

worth searching for: The band's self-published book, *Fair Use: The Story of the Letter U and the Numeral 2* (Seeland, 1995), tells the whole humorous horror story of Negativland's brush with the lawyers. It also comes with an exclusive CD, *Dead Dog Records*. On the band's website (www.negativland.com) you can even download the infamous "U2" single itself, in addition to getting much useful (if scary) info on copyright law and more comic multi-media social commentary.

influences:

◄◄ Tom Lehrer, Firesign Theatre, the Tubes, Devo

►► Emergency Broadcast Network, Consolidated, U2, Pansy Division

Adam McGovern

Fred Neil

Born 1937, in St. Petersburg, FL.

If you've seen the movie *Midnight Cowboy*, you're familiar with the highlight of Fred Neil's career. He wrote the song "Everybody's Talkin'," which was performed by Harry Nilsson on the soundtrack. Unfortunately, this was as close as Neil would come to reaching a broad audience. He became a fixture on the Greenwich Village folk club scene during the early '60s, and his laid-back 12-string guitar style and singing voice, which slipped effortlessly from a mellow tenor to a haunting baritone, influenced everyone from Bob Dylan to Tim Buckley to John Sebastian. After recording four albums from 1965–71, Neil retreated to his home in Florida, where, by all accounts, he lives in virtual seclusion.

what to buy: Neil's recorded output is spotty, but this cult figure really shines on his second release. The moody and introspective, *Fred Neil* &&&& (Capitol, 1966, prod. Nik Venet) is highlighted by the dreamlike "The Dolphins" and Neil's own version of "Everybody's Talkin'."

the rest:
Bleecker and McDougal &&& (Elektra, 1965)
Other Side of This Life &&& (Capitol, 1971)

influences:

◄◄ Pete Seeger, Woody Guthrie, Ramblin' Jack Elliott, Dave Von Ronk

►► Bob Dylan, Tim Buckley, Harry Nilsson, John Sebastian

Dan Weber

Vince Neil

See: Mötley Crüe

Ben Neill

Born in Winston-Salem, NC.

With the "mutantrumpet," a hybrid of a trumpet and electronics, including trigger pads, Ben Neill plays a nifty combination of ambient, jazz, and drum-and-bass music. The instrument in question, also his invention, allows him to play both acoustically and electronically. Collaborating to great effect on occasion with DJ Spooky (That Subliminal Kid), Page Hamilton (Helmet), cellist Jane Scarpantoni, and DJ Olive, Neill remains a visionary and pioneer. He also does performance art and gallery shows.

what to buy: *Goldbug* &&&& (Antilles, 1998, prod. Eric Calvi, Ben Neill) features relatively normal trumpet. Tunefully bleating and braying along with the thumping beats, Neill is ringleader for an often collaborative work. Hamilton appears on three tracks, including the lead cut "Tunnel Vision," which also closes the disc with re-mixes by Spring Heel Jack, X-Ecutioners, and DJ Krust.

what to buy next: *Triptycal* &&&& (Antilles, 1996, prod. Ben Neill, Eric Calvi) is also a good starting point. The mutantrumpet is in effect here, but sounds a bit less traditional than on later work. Less groovy and more spacey, *Tryptical* features a cover of Neil Young's "After the Gold Rush" and stellar assistance from DJ Spooky.

the rest:
Green Machine &&& (Astralwerks, 1995)

influences:

◄◄ Miles Davis, Chet Baker, Spacetime Continuum, the Orb

Barry M. Prickett

Nelson

Formed 1988, in Los Angeles, CA.

Matthew Nelson, vocals, bass; Gunnar Nelson, vocals, guitar.

With a rock star father (teen idol Ricky Nelson) and blonde, blue-eyed, hunky good looks, the Nelson twins jumped onto the pop-metal bandwagon in 1990. Musically active as children, the pair had once recorded a song in a pro studio (courtesy of dad) with the Pointer Sisters singing backup. They kicked around in metal bands throughout the '80s, positioning themselves perfectly for teen idol success in 1990.

what to buy: *After the Rain* && (Geffen, 1990, prod. David Thoener, Mark Tanner) housed a #1 single "(Can't Live without Your) Love and Affection" and another Top 10 hit in the title track—virtually the only Nelson anyone heard. Or wanted to.

the rest:
Because They Can && (Geffen, 1995)

influences:

◀◀ Rick Nelson, Boston, Def Leppard

▶▶ Hanson

Eric Deggans

Bill Nelson

See: Be Bop Deluxe

Rick Nelson

Born Eric Hilliard Nelson, May 8, 1940, in Teaneck, NJ. Died December 31, 1985, in DeKalb, TX.

Unjustly maligned as a pretty-boy teen idol, Rick Nelson actually made records in his early days that rivaled his more "authentic" counterparts in Memphis. He didn't live long enough to receive the recognition he deserved as one of rock 'n' roll's early greats, but he never stopped rocking. He died, in fact, when his plane literally went down in flames on his way to yet another in an endless stream of one-nighters, churning out the oldies for an audience of middle-aged housewives who remembered the adorable, wise-cracking scion of TV's *Ozzie and Harriet.*

what to buy: His string of hit singles pioneering the California rockabilly sound have been commemorated on two worthwhile discs. *Ricky Nelson: The Legendary Masters Series* ♫♫♫ (EMI, 1990, prod. various) showcases the spare, Memphis-influenced rock 'n' roll of his early recordings, with guitarists Joe Maphis and James Burton adding to the instrument's vocabulary on virtually every new side. The subsequent singles, including more pop-oriented pieces such as Gene Pitney's "Hello Mary Lou," Jerry Fuller's "Travelin' Man," and Dave Burgess's "Everlovin'," have been compiled on *The Best of Rick Nelson (Vol. 2)* ♫♫♫♫ (EMI, 1991, prod. Rick Nelson). However, if you want all of Nelson's best early rockers, track down *Rockin' with Ricky* ♫♫♫♫♫ (Ace, 1996, prod. various), a 33-song collection of his biggest '50s hits and hottest B-sides and LP tracks. Finally, Nelson's slow decline into middle-of-the-road '60s pop-rock and eventual resuscitation with the 1972 hit, "Garden Party," is chronicled on *The Best of Rick Nelson 1963–1975* ♫♫♫ (Decca/MCA, 1990, prod. various).

what to buy next: The CD reissue of his 1968 Troubadour engagement, *Rick Nelson in Concert* ♫♫♫♫ (MCA, 1994, prod. Rick Nelson, J. Sutton), teems with the palpable excitement of the Hollywood nightclub shows where former teen idol Ricky reclaimed his position in California rock.

what to avoid: At his most confused, Nelson did a mundane album with Hollywood producer Keith Olsen (Fleetwood Mac, Foreigner), an entirely misguided unreleased project with producer Al Kooper, and a relatively refreshing return to his rockabilly roots recorded in Memphis, also unreleased. Bits of these

are commemorated on *Stay Young: The Epic Recordings* ♫♫ (Epic/Legacy, 1993, compilation prod. Bob Irwin). You should also be aware that *Best of Ricky Nelson* ♫ (Curb, 1991) and *All-Time Greatest Hits* ♡ (Curb, 1991) mix re-recordings of his early hits with originals and are for completists only.

the rest:

Sings for you ♫♫♫ (MCA, 1963/1990)
Live 1983–1985 ♫ (Rhino, 1989)
Lonesome Town ♫♡ (CEMA Special Products, 1992)
Live at the Aladdin ♫♡ (Magnum, 1995)

worth searching for: Nelson's country period—either the early experiments or the country-rock of the Stone Canyon Band—have been digitally documented only overseas. A European set, *Country Music* (Entertainers, 1994, prod. various), combines the two original 1966 country albums. The British release *Rick Nelson & the Stone Canyon Band 1969–1976* (Edsel, 1995, prod. various) is drawn from singles sessions and the Stone Canyon Band's four studio albums. Also, a vinyl version of his third album, *Ricky Sings Again* (Imperial, 1958, prod. J. Haskell), is one of the great, unheralded rock 'n' roll albums of the '50s, easily the match of the best of more highly regarded contemporaries like Eddie Cochran, Gene Vincent, or Buddy Holly.

influences:

◀◀ Carl Perkins, Elvis Presley, Dale Hawkins, Johnny & Dorsey Burnette

▶▶ The Eagles, Fleetwood Mac, Nelson

Joel Selvin and Ken Burke

Shara Nelson

See: Massive Attack

Neurotic Outsiders

See: Guns N' Roses

Neutral Milk Hotel

Formed 1989, in Ruston, LA.

Jeff Mangum, vocals, guitar, bass, tapes; Julian Koster, accordion, singing saw, bass, banjo (1996–present); Scott Spillane, euphonium, bugle, flugelhorn (1996–present); Jeremy Barnes, drums, organ (1996–present).

Neutral Milk Hotel is the *nom de rock* of Jeff Mangum, who with a handful of childhood chums from a Louisiana backwater town formed the Elephant 6 artists collective and recording label (also home to such notables as Apples in Stereo and Olivia Tremor Control). Mangum is among the most eccentric of the Elephant 6 posse, and that's saying something; he recorded his debut album while living in a friend's walk-in closet. Yet his diehard devotion to '60s orchestral pop, '70s psychedelia, and '80s punk is reflected in ambitious recordings that have expanded the boundaries of the low-fi realm.

what to buy: *On Avery Island* 🎵🎵🎵🎵 (Merge, 1996, prod. Robert Schneider) is a kaliedescopic journey filled with shape-shifting psychedelic pop tunes and vivid religious and childhood imagery. Mangum and his producer, Apples in Stereo's Robert Schneider, play virtually all the instruments.

what to avoid: *In the Aeroplane over the Sea* 🎵🎵 (Merge, 1998, prod. Robert Schneider) lacks its predecessor's quirky richness and ear-opening arrangements. It's surprisingly stripped down, with Mangum howling—often tunelessly—over the vigorous strum of his acoustic guitar.

influences:

◀◀ The Beach Boys, the Beatles, Fleetwood Mac

Greg Kot

The Neville Brothers /Aaron Neville

Formed 1977, in New Orleans, LA.

Art Neville, keyboards, vocals; Charles Neville, saxophone, vocals, percussion; Aaron Neville, vocals, percussion; Cyril Neville, percussion, vocals.

The Neville Brothers formed in New Orleans during 1977, though various incarnations of the group had been performing and recording since the early '60s. Indeed, keyboardist Art Neville formed his first band, the Hawketts, in the preceding decade and later achieved some success with the soul/funk quartet the Meters, which had backed up brother Aaron on his solo sides and on some records made under the Neville Sounds moniker. The group's debut as the Neville Brothers came out in 1978, after the brothers had gotten together for their uncle George "Big Chief Jolly" Landry's *Wild Tchoupitoulas* project. The Nevilles' following increased during the 1980s, mostly on the strength of the group's fiery live shows. Aaron's success both as a solo artist and in a series of high-profile, Grammy-winning duets with pop singer Linda Ronstadt and country singer Trisha Yearwood brought the group's name to a larger following. Its upbeat, grooving, often syncopated soul and Mardi Gras vibe owes much to the Meters, though the Nevilles streamlined the sound with pop and, of course, Aaron's sweet, soaring pipes.

what to buy: *Treacherous: A History of the Neville Brothers* 🎵🎵🎵🎵 (Rhino, 1988, prod. various) is, hands-down, the best collection of the group's strongest work. The double-disc set features solo material as well as favorites from the whole group, such as "Fever," "Hey Pocky Way," and "Fear, Hate, Envy, Jealousy."

what to buy next: *Yellow Moon* 🎵🎵🎵🎵 (A&M, 1989, prod. Daniel Lanois) is an impressive, mature album that boasts a kinetic rendition of Link Wray's "Fire and Brimstone." Daniel Lanois's moody production takes the Nevilles' sound into a bold and intriguing new direction.

what to avoid: On Aaron's *Soulful Christmas* 🎵🎵 (A&M, 1993, prod. Steve Lindsey), the fine singer makes lite R&B mush of over-recorded seasonal favorites.

the rest:
The Neville Brothers 🎵🎵🎵 (Capitol, 1978)
Fiyo on the Bayou 🎵🎵🎵🎵 (A&M, 1981)
Neville-Ization 🎵🎵🎵 (Black Top, 1984)
Live at Tipitina's 🎵🎵🎵 (Spindletop, 1985)
Uptown 🎵🎵🎵 (EMI America, 1987)
Brother's Keeper 🎵🎵🎵 (A&M, 1990)
Treacherous Too! 🎵🎵🎵🎵 (Rhino, 1991)
Family Groove 🎵🎵🎵 (A&M, 1992)
Live on Planet Earth 🎵🎵🎵 (A&M, 1994)
Mitakuye Oyasin Oyasin (All My Relations) 🎵🎵🎵🎵 (A&M, 1996)
The Very Best of the Neville Brothers 🎵🎵🎵🎵 (Rhino, 1997)

worth searching for: *The Wild Tchoupitoulas* (Island, 1976, prod. Allen Toussaint, Marshall Sehorn), the Nevilles' soulful collaboration with their older relatives, mines a soulful vein of Louisiana musical history.

solo outings:
Aaron Neville:
Greatest Hits 🎵🎵🎵🎵 (Curb, 1990)
My Greatest Gift 🎵🎵🎵🎵 (Rounder, 1991)
Warm Your Heart 🎵🎵 (A&M, 1991)
The Grand Tour 🎵🎵 (A&M, 1993)
The Tattooed Heart 🎵🎵🎵 (A&M, 1995)
To Make Me Who I Am 🎵🎵🎵 (A&M, 1997)

Art Neville:
His Specialty Records, 1956–58 🎵🎵🎵🎵 (Specialty, 1992)
That Old Time Rock 'n' Roll 🎵🎵🎵 (Specialty, 1993)

Cyrille Neville:
Fire This Time 🎵🎵🎵 (Iguana, 1995)

Charles Neville:
Charles Neville & Diversity 🎵🎵 (Laserlight, 1991)
(With Songcatchers) *Moving in Color* 🎵🎵🎵🎵 (A&M, 1994)

influences:

◀◀ Mahalia Jackson, Andrae Crouch, Professor Longhair, Ray Charles, Lee Dorsey

▶▶ Daniel Lanois, the Dirty Dozen, the Fugees, Maria Muldaur

see also: *The Meters*

Simon Glickman

New Bohemians

See: Edie Brickell

The New Bomb Turks

Formed 1990, in Columbus, OH.

Jim Weber, guitar; Matt Reber, bass; Bill Randt, drums; Eric Davidson, vocals.

Whatever you wanna call it—basement punk, garage, or plain old punk rock—the New Bomb Turks possess that magical bone of contention that transforms three chords and a microphone from tired old formula into truly revelatory NO! Part of the fertile Ohio punk caucus of the '90s that spawned Prisonshake, Gaunt, the Thomas Jefferson Slave Apartments, and Monster Truck 5, the Turks' broad knowledge of the many brands of punk (they've covered the Modern Lovers, the New York Dolls, Thin Lizzy, Thee Headcoats, the Rolling Stones, and Gaunt, to name a few) provides it with a solid foundation on which to build its own invigorating sound.

what to buy: The New Bomb Turks are a singles band; and on each of their records are two or three phenomenal guitar romps that mix the perfect chord combinations with furious hooks and smart, thoughtful lyrics. So it's best to snatch up *Pissin' out the Poison* ♪♪♪♪ (Crypt, 1995, prod. various), a document that collects most of their singles and extant compilation cuts onto one long-player. The collection also serves as a history of the band, moving from their beginnings in the basement to more sophisticated studio recordings, all possessing that bigbang rhythm section and the yowl of lead clown Eric Davidson, who proves that he understands the fury of Iggy and the power of howling from the belly.

what to buy next: *Information Highway Revisited* ♪♪♪♪ (Crypt, 1994, prod. Mike Mariconda) is a beast, an out-of-the-gate windsprint that actually gathers speed as it progresses. It contains one of the Turks' finest moments in "T.A.S.," a (relatively) slow dirge that reveals their strong points—that rhythm, that guitar scrape, and that voice—in all their glory. After switching to punk stalwart Epitaph and creating one relatively overproduced record, they returned to the world of audible hiss with the phenomenal *At Rope's End* ♪♪♪♪ (Epitaph, 1998, prod. Jeff Graham, Tomas Skogsberg, New Bomb Turks), as hard and furious a record as they've ever done. It contains a great song of angst-ridden longing, "Veronica Lake."

the rest:
Destroy Oh-Boy ♪♪♪♫ (Crypt, 1993)
Drunk on Cock ♪♪♪ (Engine, 1993)
Scared Straight ♪♪♪ (Epitaph, 1996)

worth searching for: The seven-inch single "Bottle Island" (Damaged Goods, 1993) was an import-only release on Billy

WHat aLBum CHanGED YOur LiFe?

The first Saints album. I let a friend borrow it and he never gave it back. Years later I found it sealed for 99 cents, in a mall, no less. I didn't have speakers for my stereo at the time, so I would crank it really loud, with the headphones on, and my ears would be ringing afterwards. It's exactly what I liked about punk—the speed of the Ramones, the noise, and kind of the vocals of the Stooges.

Eric Davidson (of the New Bomb Turks)

Childish's label, and contains the Turks' version of fellow Ohioans Thomas Jefferson Slave Apartments' great "Bottle Island," along with a cover of Thee Headcoats' "Youngblood." Another single, "I Wanna Sleep" (Demolition Derby, 1993) contains the Modern Lovers' unreleased classic "I Wanna Sleep in Your Arms" and a glorious version of one of the great punk songs of the '90s, Gaunt's "Jim Motherfucker."

influences:
◄◄ The Stooges, Pagans, Styrenes, the Modern Lovers
►► Supersuckers, Devil Dogs, Rip Offs

Randall Roberts

The New Colony Six

Formed as the Patsmen, 1964, in Chicago, IL. Disbanded 1974.

Gerry Van Kollenburg, guitar; Pat McBride, vocals, harmonica (1964–70); Ray Graffia, vocals, tambourine (1964–69); Wally Kemp, bass (1964–67); James "Chic James" Chitkowski, drums (1964–69); Greg Kemp (nee Kempinski), organ (1964–66); Ronnie Rice, organ (1966–71); Les Kummel, bass (1967–70); Bill Herman, drums (1969–74); Chuck Jobes, keyboards (1969–74); Bruce Gordon, guitar (1969–74).

The matching colonial outfits worn by the New Colony Six invite an obvious comparison to the similarly dressed Paul Revere &

the Raiders. Like the Raiders, the New Colony Six was an honest-to-God rock 'n' roll band disguised as a bubblegum act. Unlike the Raiders, though, the New Colony Six never quite hit the big time, in spite of a string of stellar recordings. The group's early material includes scads of rock-solid nuggets, garage-bred but fully accomplished. "I Confess" (much later covered by the Lyres), the Yardbirdsy "At the River's Edge," the pure pop "Love You So Much," "Let Me Love You," "Cadillac," and "I Lie Awake" are little-known classics that should have found a berth on the charts and on the radio. The New Colony Six did eventually score two Top 40 hits with the ballads "I Will Always Think of You" and "Things I'd Like to Say." While the latter is an amazing, hypnotic record, the group's success with such relatively sedate material has led some oldies historians to miscategorize the Six as the soft-rock group it wound up becoming. 'Twasn't always so.

what to buy: A coin toss here: *Colonized! Best of the New Colony Six* 𝄞𝄞𝄞 (Rhino, 1993, prod. Bill Inglot) is a comprehensive career overview covering both the New Colony Six's early garage-pop recordings and its Mercury-era hit and stiffs; as such, it starts off strong and finishes weak. *At the River's Edge* 𝄞𝄞𝄞𝄞 (Sundazed, 1993, prod. Bob Irwin) eschews the hits and gives us only the early stuff, but offers a more consistent good time.

the rest:
Colonization 𝄞𝄞𝄞 (Sentar, 1967/Sundazed, 1994)

influences:
◀◀ The Beatles, the Rolling Stones, Paul Revere & the Raiders, the Kinks, the Yardbirds, the Searchers, the Zombies

▶▶ The Lyres, Mystic Eyes

Carl Cafarelli

New Kids on the Block

Formed 1985, in Boston, MA. Disbanded 1994.

Jordan Knight, vocals; Donnie Wahlberg, vocals; Joe McIntyre, vocals; Danny Wood, vocals; Jon Knight, vocals.

There was no middle ground with teen sensations New Kids on the Block during the late '80s and early '90s: you either loved 'em or hated 'em. And although prepubescent girls seemed to be the only ones who loved them, that was apparently enough. At their peak, the ubiquitous New Kids had their own line of Hasbro dolls and were named the world's highest-paid entertainers by *Forbes*, earning $115 million in 1990 and 1991. More a marketing ploy than a musical force, the group was formed and controlled by writer-producer-manager Maurice Starr, who wanted to replace his suddenly departed black teen group, New Edition, with a similar group that would appeal to a broader

(read: white) audience. One of his original recruits was Mark Wahlberg, who later decided to pursue a career in rap as Marky Mark instead. However, Wahlberg's brother, Donnie, signed up and was eventually joined by three of his schoolmates (Danny Wood and the Knight brothers) plus Joe McIntyre. The group, which was originally called Nynuk, broke through in 1988 with its chart-topping second album, *Hangin' Tough*, winning over legions of adoring, squealing teenyboppers thanks to their looks and hook-laden, R&B-influenced, bubble-gum pop. Its 1990 tour was one of the biggest-grossing in the history of the concert business, bringing in $74.1 million, but the group was greeted with hard skepticism and intense loathing by nearly everybody over the age of 15, particularly pop critics. During the Milli Vanilli scandal, a disgruntled associate producer for the New Kids accused the group of similar fraudulent practices, saying that Starr and his brother did most of the singing on the New Kids' albums. The group eventually appeared on *The Arsenio Hall Show* to sing *a capella* and prove its detractor wrong. After a four-year hiatus from studio work and a split with Starr, the group attempted to reposition itself in 1994 as tougher and more mature, appearing with facial hair and a changed name, NKOTB. But New Kids simply could not shake the past. (Hey, whatever they call themselves, they're still L-A-M-E, said David Letterman.) They broke up later that year.

what to buy: Although it sounds grossly dated now, if you must see what the New Kids fuss was about, the breakthrough *Hangin' Tough* 𝄞𝄞 (Columbia, 1988, prod. Maurice Starr) is the best place to go with its abundance of hits, including the innocent teen ballads "I'll Be Loving You (Forever)," "Please Don't Go Girl," and the quasi-funk title track, as well as "You Got It (The Right Stuff)" and "Cover Girl."

what to buy next: Hip-hop-informed New Jack production values and tight, layered harmonies make *Face the Music* 𝄞𝄞𝄞 (Columbia, 1994, prod. Teddy Riley, Donnie Wahlberg, Narada Michael Walden, Walter Afanasieff) the most current and vibrant-sounding album in the New Kids catalog, although the group's street-style stance is a bit tough to digest after three albums of sugar-sweet pop.

what to avoid: *Merry, Merry Christmas* **woof!** (Columbia, 1989). Bah, humbug.

the rest:
New Kids on the Block 𝄞 (Columbia, 1986)
Step by Step 𝄞𝄞 (Columbia, 1990)
No More Games: The Remix Album 𝄞𝄞 (Columbia, 1990)

influences:
◀◀ New Edition, Bay City Rollers, the Jackson 5

▶▶ Milli Vanilli, Marky Mark, Spice Girls, Backstreet Boys

Josh Freedom du Lac

New Model Army

Formed 1980, in Bradford, England.

Justin Sullivan ("Slade the Leveller"), guitar, vocals; Rob Heaton, drums; Stuart Morrow, bass (1981–85); Moose, bass (1985–91); Nelson, bass (1990–present).

For nearly two decades the northern English trio New Model Army has outlasted every British music fad/trend, has transcended every snipe from an unsupportive U.K. music press, and has nurtured an enduring, massive European underground cult following that has remained the envy of more industry-respected bands from one generation to the next. It's done all this with a demonstrated conviction that has lasted through 18 years and seven LP's, with an ever-present willingness to stretch past their original post-punk power blasts into a liberal variety of feels and emotions, even releasing an all-acoustic EP before that was fashionable—1985's *Better than Them*—and redoing one of their most harrowing tracks with nothing more than piano and vocal. Such excursions highlight why NMA has prospered and gained such a committed following: Justin Sullivan has remained a master tune-writer and convincing vocalist, which underpins some of the most contentious lyrics the isles have ever produced, from 1982's scathing "Spirit of the Falklands" (an opposition to a public-supported war that is the equivalent to Bad Religion's virulent objection to the also super-popular, cake-walk Gulf War nine years later) to the 1992 single "Here Comes the War," which begins the trio's sixth LP with the memorable lines, "Today as you listen to this song, another 394,000 children were born into this world/They break like waves of hunger and desire upon these eroded shores, carrying the curses of history and a history yet unwritten." But like Billy Bragg, Sullivan and his mates prove equally capable on each release of exploring human relationships with equal poignancy and passion. With the release of its first album in five years, another roller-coaster thriller called *Strange Brotherhood*, NMA serves further notice that they remain vibrant and fresh after such a long time away.

what to buy: *The Ghost of Cain* ♪♪♪♪♫ (Capitol, 1985, prod. Glyn Johns) finds the band at its most hard-hitting, both musically and lyrically, led by the absolutely gargantuan, anti-drug-pusher frontier justice song "The Hunt." Withering! Likewise, through a smorgasbord of clashing styles, the group all but explodes on the post-punk-pop smashers "51st State," "Western Dream," and the sweetly melodic "Poison Street" as effectively as on the quiet, haunting "The Ballad" and the barely restrained wounds-licking of "Heroes."

what to buy next: *The Love of Hopeless Causes* ♪♪♪♪ (Epic, 1993, prod. Niko Bolas) proved a remarkable comeback from a three-year absence, with a rejuvenated attack and brilliant production from old pro Bolas. Ponderous, almost Cure-like brood-

ers such as "Living in the Rose" mix perfectly with more direct bash-em-ups like the angry "Here Comes the War" and the positively gleeful "Bad Old World."

what to avoid: To be fair, the band thought it was their masterpiece at the time, and the majority of their fans agreed, but *Thunder and Consolation* ♪♪♫ (Capitol, 1989, prod. Tom Dowd) is basically too much of a good thing, where drama turns to blustering melodrama.

the rest:
No Rest for the Wicked ♪♪♪♫ (Capitol, 1985)
Radio Sessions '83–'84 ♪♪♪♫ (Abstract U.K., 1988)
Impurity ♪♪♪ (EMI U.K., 1990)
Raw Melody Men (live) ♪♪♪ (EMI U.K., 1991)
BBC Radio 1 Live in Concert ♪♪♪♪ (Windsong U.K., 1993)
Strange Brotherhood ♪♪♪♪ (Attack Germany, 1998)

worth searching for: *B-Sides & Abandoned Tracks* (EMI U.K., 1994, prod. various) may seem on the surface a fans-only curiosity but instead proves that NMA was and is an absolutely extraordinary B-sides and non-LP A-sides band—so much so their heads should have been examined for leaving such five-bone material as the thoughtful "Brave New World," the spitting, anti-Vatican "Ten Commandments," the spiteful "Heroin," the mournful "Prison," and the sentimental "Ghost of Your Father" off their albums. And for those who want to hear the group in its earliest, uncut, fastest and zippiest just-after-punk adrenaline, you can't go wrong with *Vengeance* (Abstract U.K., 1984, prod. Mond Cowie), particularly if you secure the augmented, domestic CD version issued as *Vengeance/The independent Story* (JCI, 1988).

influences:
◀◀ The Ruts, the Clash, Killing Joke, Phil Ochs, Bob Dylan

▶▶ Leatherface, China Drum, Red Letter Day

Jack Rabid

New Order

Formed 1980, in Manchester, England.

Bernard Sumner (born Bernard Albrecht), guitar, vocals; Peter Hook, bass, vocals; Stephen Morris, percussion; Gillian Gilbert, keyboards, vocals.

New Order rose out of the ashes of Joy Division after that group's frontman Ian Curtis took his own life in 1980. The remaining members—Bernard Sumner, Peter Hook, and Stephen Morris—brought in keyboardist Gillian Gilbert and went on to become one of the most pivotal synth-based pop bands of the '80s. Casting away Joy Division's dark overtones, the new group instead embraced disco rhythms and forward-thinking ideals while maintaining an astute sense of emotional alienation. Where Joy Division provided the morbid missing link between the Doors and Nirvana, New Order was all about living for the thrill of the moment—and in the process paved the way for the U.K.'s current techno scene. Most of its singles—from "Age of Consent" to "Bizarre Love Triangle" to "Regret"—remain staples at dance clubs, while the individual musicians have also pursued a variety of side projects.

what to buy: The bulk of New Order's best songs were released as singles, which makes both *(The Best of) New Order* 𝄢𝄢𝄢𝄢 (Qwest, 1995, prod. various) and the more eclectic *Substance 1987* 𝄢𝄢𝄢𝄢 (Qwest, 1987, prod. various) ideal packages for neophytes. For the more discriminating ear, however, New Order's second album, *Power, Corruption, and Lies* 𝄢𝄢𝄢𝄢 (Qwest, 1983, prod. Martin Hannet, New Order) represents the perfect embodiment of the group's original sound, linking Joy Division's dark power with the new group's experimental ambitions.

what to buy next: New Order's debut album, *Movement* 𝄢𝄢𝄢 (Factory/Rough Trade, 1981, prod. New Order), laid the blueprint for the group's innovative sound, making it one of the most pivotal records of the '80s. *Technique* 𝄢𝄢𝄢 (Qwest, 1989, prod. New Order) is the group's most melodic album to date, mixing contemporary club rhythms with acoustic guitars and Hook's exquisite bass lines.

what to avoid: On its fourth album, *Brotherhood* 𝄢 (Qwest, 1986, prod. New Order), it sounded like the band had run out of ideas, despite the indispensable single "Bizarre Love Triangle."

the rest:
Low-Life 𝄢𝄢𝄢 (Qwest, 1985)
Republic 𝄢𝄢 (Qwest, 1993)

worth searching for: *BBC Radio 1 Live In Concert* (Windsong, 1992, prod. Pete Ritzema) features rough renditions of such New Order classics as "Touched by the Hand of God" and "Perfect Kiss." The sound quality and song selection are both excellent.

solo outings:
Revenge (Hook):
One True Passion 𝄢 (Capitol, 1990)
Gun World Porn **woof!** (Capitol, 1992)

Monaco (Hook):
Music for Pleasure 𝄢𝄢𝄢 (Polydor, 1997)

The Other Two (Morris, Gilbert):
The Other Two and You **woof!** (Qwest, 1992)

influences:
◀◀ Kraftwerk, Sylvester, Brian Eno

▶▶ Pet Shop Boys, Underworld, the Stone Roses, Prodigy

see also: *Joy Division, Electronic*

Aidin Vaziri

New Riders of the Purple Sage

Formed 1969, in Marin County, CA.

John "Marmaduke" Dawson, guitar, vocals (1971–81); David Nelson, guitar, vocals (1971–81); Jerry Garcia, guitar, pedal steel (1969–71); Mickey Hart, drums (1969–70); Phil Lesh, bass (1969–70); Spencer Dryden, drums (1970); David Torbert, bass, vocals (1971–75); Skip Battin, bass, vocals (1974–76); Buddy Cage, pedal steel (1972–82); Stephen Love, bass (1976–82); Allen Kemp, guitar (1977–85); Rusty Gauthier, guitar, violin, fiddle, mandolin, Dobro (1982); Gary Vogensen, vocals, guitar (1985–93); Evan Morgan, guitar (1993).

The New Riders of the Purple Sage garnered a substantial cult-like following as the Grateful Dead's warmup band—not to mention a busman's holiday for Jerry Garcia, Mickey Hart, and Phil Lesh—during the Dead's country-oriented, *Workingman's Dead / American Beauty* period. They were offered a recording deal with Columbia, and in 1971 the label released *New Riders of the Purple Sage*, which contained the romantic "Louisiana Lady" and "Henry," a humorous tale about a dope smuggler. Subsequent releases, however, were simply a rehashing of the same hippie-outlaw material.

what to buy: *New Riders of the Purple Sage* 𝄢𝄢𝄢 (Columbia, 1971/1989, prod. various) contains "Louisiana Lady" and John Dawson's gliding "I Don't Know You," which features some tasty steel guitar licks courtesy of Jerry Garcia.

what to buy next: Some early New Riders demos featuring Garcia and Dead-mates Lesh and Hart can be found on *Before Time Began,* which is now packaged as a two-fer with *The Backwards Tapes* 𝄢𝄢 (Relix, 1990).

what to avoid: Pass on such reissued MCA albums as *New Riders* 𝄢 (MCA, 1976/One Way, 1993), *Who Are Those Guys?* 𝄢 (MCA, 1977/One Way, 1993), and *Marin County Line* 𝄢 (MCA, 1978/One Way, 1993).

the rest:
The Adventures of Panama Red 𝄢𝄢𝄢 (Columbia, 1973/1989)
The Best of New Riders of the Purple Sage 𝄢𝄢𝄢 (Columbia, 1976)
Live 𝄢𝄢𝄢 (Avenue, 1982)
Vintage New Riders 𝄢𝄢𝄢 (Relix, 1987)
Midnight Moonlight 𝄢𝄢𝄢 (Relix, 1992)
Live in Japan 𝄢𝄢𝄢 (Relix, 1994)

influences:
◀◀ The Grateful Dead, the Byrds, the Flying Burrito Brothers, Seatrain, Gene Clark

▶▶ The Eagles, Ozark Mountain Daredevils, New Grass Revival, Tony Rice, Bela Fleck

see also: *The Grateful Dead*

Rick Petreycik

The New York Dolls
/Johnny Thunders

Formed 1971, in New York, NY. Disbanded 1977.

David Johansen, vocals (1971–75); Johnny Thunders (born John Anthony Genzale; died April 23, 1991), guitar (1971–75); Arthur Kane, bass (1971–75); Sylvain Sylvain (born Syl Mizrahi), guitar (1974–77); Jerry Nolan (died January 14, 1992), drums (1972–1974); Billy Murcia (died November 6, 1972), drums (1971–72); Rick Rivets, guitar (1971–72).

The visual prototype for many '80s metal bands, the tremendously influential New York Dolls started off acting and sounding like a second-rate Rolling Stones. In glam makeup and nearly full drag, the group came to prominence in the tumultuous New York pre-punk club scene of the mid-'70s via venues such as Max's Kansas City. Though revered by the music press, the band's actual lifespan was fairly short: two unsuccessful albums and a brief, turbulent period with future Sex Pistols (mis)handler Malcom McLaren as its manager, after which the Dolls split up. David Johansen reinvented himself during the '80s as hambone party boy Buster Poindexter and took small roles in several films; he still records occasional solo albums. Johnny Thunders, a notorious junkie, developed cult status as a Keith Richards–styled living zombie, and continued to play and record—with and without backing band the Heartbreakers—up until his drug overdose in 1991. He remains a rock legend more for his abusive habit than any great musical legacy. Drummer Jerry Nolan died of a stroke soon after. Like the Pistols, whom they greatly influenced, there are endless Dolls bootlegs and live shows circulated by succeeding generations of fans who weren't around to see the real thing.

what to buy: *New York Dolls* 🎜🎜🎜🎜 (Mercury, 1973, prod. Todd Rundgren) perfectly captures the group's tongue-in-cheek mix of glam guitar swagger and bleak NYC realism.

the rest:
Too Much Too Soon 🎜🎜🎜 (Mercury, 1974)
Lipstick Killers 🎜🎜 (ROIR, 1981/1990)
Red Patent Leather 🎜🎜🎜 (Restless, 1984)
Rock 'n' Roll 🎜🎜🎜🎜 (Mercury, 1994)

worth searching for: *Paris Burning* (Skydog, 1974) is a live set that does the band better than the flawed, late-career *Red Patent Leather.*

influences:
◀◀ The Rolling Stones, David Bowie, the Stooges

▶▶ The Sex Pistols, Guns N' Roses, D Generation

see also: *David Johansen/Buster Poindexter*

Todd Wicks

Martin Newell
/Brother of Lizards
/Cleaners from Venus

Born in Great Britain.

Martin Newell records the sort of British pop made possible by the KInks' *VIllage Green Preservation Society*, informed by the pastoral side of XTC, and touched by the melodic gestures of Robert Wyatt. XTC's Andy Partridge produced *The Greatest Living Englishman*, the only one of Newell's solo albums to come out in America.

what to buy: *The Greatest Living Englishman* 🎜🎜🎜🎜 (Humbug/Pipeline, 1993, prod. Andy Partridge) is an almost cryptically British pop document, as gentle and breezy as the English countryside. It should appeal to fans of power pop, and literature majors alike (Newell is also a published poet). "Goodbye Dreaming Fields" matches a classic jangle to a quaint old-fashioned melody. The rest follows suit—and hat.

what to buy next: *The Off White Album* 🎜🎜🎜🎜 (1994, Humbug, prod. Louis Philippe) is every bit the equal of its predecessor. "Miss Van Houten's Coffee Shoppe," despite its oh-so-British title, evokes *Pet Sounds* -era Beach Boys. Back to familiar territory, "When the Damsons are Down" has a Who-like feel. Newell somehow manages to transform the Smiths' lyrically vacuous, ridiculously titled "Some Girls Are Bigger than Others" into something spare, poppy, and meaningful. *Lizardland* 🎜🎜🎜🎜 (Long Play, 1995, prod. Brotherhood of Lizards), by Newell's previous two-man combo, the Brotherhood of Lizards, will appeal to any fan of his, though it's more psychedelic than the down-to-green-earth pop he creates on his own.

worth searching for: Two compilations from Newell's old band, the Cleaners from Venus—*Golden Cleaners* (Tangerine, 1993, prod. Martin Newell) and *Back from the Cleaners* (Tangerine, 1995, prod. Martin Newell)—will appeal to those who find Newell's solo releases a genuine pleasure. Devotees will also want the vinyl versions of *The Greatest Living Englishman* and *The Off White Album* on the Pink Lemon label. The former has three bonus tracks, and the latter comes with two bonus tracks and a limited-edition 10-inch containing a live performance by Newell. Even more obscure is the *Let's Kiosk!* EP (Humbug, 1993, prod. Andy Partridge, Martin Newell), which features one track from *The Greatest Living Englishman* and three excellent previously unreleased songs.

influences:
◀◀ The Kinks, XTC, Robyn Hitchcock, the Beatles

▶▶ Apples in Stereo, the Lilys

Jordan Oakes

Randy Newman

Born November 28, 1943, in New Orleans, LA.

Swaggering onto the scene like Jonathan Swift at a Bourbon Street piano bar, Randy Newman thrives on misinterpretation. His biggest hit, 1977's "Short People," drew protests from diminutive listeners who didn't realize he was attacking a larger target—prejudice in general. He sometimes takes on the personae of apartheid-supporting South Africans ("Christmas in Capetown"), insecure gay bashers ("Half a Man"), Southern bigots ("Rednecks"), and right-wing conservatives ("Roll with the Punches") to get his points across. The ultimate irony is that despite his perennial cult-hero status, Newman's wry blend of Tin Pan Alley pop, ragtime, and Crescent City R&B has won over Madison Avenue and Hollywood: he's licensed his songs for commercial jingles ("I Love L.A." for Nike, "I Love to See You Smile" for Colgate), penned soundtracks for *Ragtime, The Natural,* and *Avalon,* and dueted with Lyle Lovett on the catchy theme for 1995's *Toy Story.* His albums barely trickle out—between 1979 and 1996, he released all of four discs—but he hasn't lost his satirical edge or ambitious flair: 1995's *Randy Newman's Faust* is a twisted musical-theater adaptation of Johann Wolfgang von Goethe's classic set in South Bend, Indiana. The Lord is played by James Taylor, the Devil, of course, by Newman.

what to buy: Newman wedges his tongue into his cheek on the gloriously sardonic *Sail Away* ♫♫♫♫ (Reprise, 1972, prod. Russ Titelman, Lenny Waronker) as he entices slaves to America like a sideshow huckster ("Sail Away"); celebrates the polluted Cuyahoga River like it was Walden Pond ("Burn On"); and advocates dropping the Big One ("Political Science"). *Good Old Boys* ♫♫♫♫ (Reprise, 1974, prod. Russ Titelman, Lenny Waronker), a rollicking concept album about the South, is celebrated for skewering redneck ignorance but "Louisiana 1927," "A Wedding in Cherokee County," and "Marie" garner their emotional clout from Newman's sympathetic narrative eye. The engaging *Land of Dreams* ♫♫♫♫ (Reprise, 1988, prod. Mark Knopfler, James Newton Howard, Tommy LiPuma, Jeff Lynne) opens with three autobiographical numbers about his New Orleans childhood and ends with "I Want You to Hurt like I Do," his chilling answer to "We Are the World."

what to buy next: *Trouble in Paradise* ♫♫♫♫ (Reprise,1983, prod. Russ Titelman, Lenny Waronker) is often dismissed as the album that spawned "I Love L.A." But digging deeper uncovers such gems as "Miami," the scathing "Christmas in Capetown," and "My Life Is Good," in which a cocky Newman brags about Bruce Springsteen asking him "How would you like to be the Boss for a while?"

what to avoid: The pinched production and bloated orchestrations of *Randy Newman* ♫♫ (Reprise, 1968, prod. Lenny

Waronker, Van Dyke Parks) make for a tough listen, even with "Davy the Fat Boy" and "I Think It's Going to Rain Today."

the rest:
12 Songs ♫♫♫♫ (Reprise, 1970)
Randy Newman Live ♫♫♫ (Reprise, 1971)
Little Criminals ♫♫♫♫ (Reprise, 1977)
Born Again ♫♫♫ (Reprise, 1979)
Randy Newman's Faust ♫♫♫ (Reprise, 1995)
Guilty: 30 Years of Randy Newman ♫♫♫♫ (Warner Bros., 1998)

worth searching for: For timid beginners, the German-made *Lonely at the Top* (WEA International, 1987, prod. Lenny Waronker, Russ Titelman, Van Dyke Parks) is a 22-track best-of collection that mixes sarcastic favorites like "Rednecks" and "Short People" with such lovely ballads as "Marie," "I Think It's Going to Rain Today," and "Living without You." It's an impressive portrait, though hardly a complete picture.

influences:

◄◄ Stephen Foster, uncles Lionel and Alfred Newman, George and Ira Gershwin, Fats Domino

►► Lyle Lovett, Timbuk 3, Bruce Hornsby

David Okamoto

Olivia Newton-John

Born September 26, 1948, in Cambridge, England.

Olivia Newton-John had all the tools for pop star perfection—good looks, a good voice, and perk to spare. Somebody saw that when she was 16; she won a talent contest in Australia (where she was living at the time) and was sent to England to make her mark. She wasn't always the aerobicized pop diva we came to know during the '80s. In fact, her first hit was a sweetened-up remake of Bob Dylan's "If Not for You"; in England she also scored with re-makes of George Harrison's "What Is Life" and John Denver's "Take Me Home Country Roads." She even used her supple tones to mine the country market for awhile, though she caused a stir when she was named the Country Music Association's Female Vocalist of the Year in 1974. Well, if folks were going to get sassy with her, Newton-John could get sassy right back. Following her starring role in the film *Grease*, she put out two albums—*Totally Hot* and *Physical*—that let her body do the talking right around the time music videos were starting to take hold in the United States. There were more films and more hits, though Newton-John did slow down after marrying actor Matt Lattanzi and giving birth to a daughter. During the early '90s, just after the release of a new greatest hits collection, Newton-John was diagnosed with breast cancer, for which she was successfully treated.

what to buy: Singles are her stock in trade, so *Back to Basics: The Essential Collection 1971–92* ♫♫♫♫ (Geffen, 1992, prod. various) is a good place to start, though it would be much better if the brand new songs were removed to make room for neglected hits such as "If Not for You."

what to buy next: It was a sales bust, but *The Rumour* 𝄞𝄞𝄞 (MCA, 1988/1993, prod. Davitt Sigerson) was a daring, uncommercial twist for Newton-John, who worked with different textures as well as an inspired group of guests that included Elton John, Paulinho Da Costa, and rock troubadour David Baerwald.

what to avoid: *Physical* **woof!** (MCA, 1981, prod. John Farrar) was huge. But it stinks.

the rest:
Have You Ever Been Mellow 𝄞𝄞 (Griffin, 1975/1995)
Come on Over 𝄞𝄞 (MCA, 1976)
Making a Good Thing Better 𝄞𝄞 (MCA, 1977/1990)
Xanadu 𝄞𝄞 (MCA, 1980/1998)
Greatest Hits, Vol. 2 𝄞𝄞𝄞 (MCA, 1982)
Soul Kiss 𝄞 (MCA, 1985/1993)
Warm and Tender 𝄞𝄞𝄞 (Geffen, 1989)
I Honestly Love You 𝄞𝄞𝄞 (MCA, 1998)
Back with a Heart 𝄞𝄞𝄞 (MCA Nashville, 1998)

worth searching for: The out-of-print *Greatest Hits* (MCA, 1977) has the crucial—and far more palatable—early hits.

influences:
◀◀ Sandra Dee, Lulu, Cilla Black

▶▶ Debbie Gibson, Tiffany, Kylie Minogue, Spice Girls, LeAnn Rimes

Gary Graff

Stevie Nicks

Born May 6, 1948, in Phoenix, AZ.

As the tensions in Fleetwood Mac escalated during the late '70s, Stevie Nicks—clearly the most popular member of the *Rumours*-era Mac lineup, then and now—went solo and scored big. Her dramatic vocals, openly vulnerable lyrics, and fantasy images spoke directly to young women. Nicks dresses eccentrically, imagines herself a good witch, and . . . she writes with lots of . . . ellipses. She started her career in a duo with Lindsay Buckingham and has always preferred collaborations. During her solo career, she has worked with Tom Petty (including a cover of "Needles & Pins" released under his name) and his guitarist Mike Campbell, Don Henley, Prince, Kenny Loggins, and Jon Bon Jovi.

what to buy: Nicks's first and best solo album, *Bella Donna* 𝄞𝄞𝄞𝄞 (Modern/Atlantic, 1981, prod. Jimmie Iovine), has successful duets with Petty ("Stop Draggin' My Heart Around") and Henley ("Leather and Lace") and no weak tracks. Waddy Wach-

WHAT ALBUM CHANGED YOUR LIFE?

I was thinking just the other day how much the *Crosby, Stills & Nash* album affected me. It immediately made me know what I wanted to do in my music, that I wanted harmonies—two harmony singers—and I wanted to go after a special sound and I wanted to write, like, really incredible words. I listened to it probably for six solid months.

Stevie Nicks

tel (guitar) and Benmont Tench and Roy Bittan (keyboards) put fire in the arrangements.

what to buy next: Since the single-CD best-of, *Time Space*, is missing three of her Top 40 hits, the three-CD box set *Enchanted* 𝄞𝄞𝄞𝄞 (Modern/Atlantic, 1998, prod. various) is the best place to catch up with the rest of Nicks's non-Mac career. Though it's not as completist as it could be (where's "Needles & Pins"?) it does conveniently gather many of the other collaborations that appeared on other people's albums, as well as demos, B-sides, unreleased tracks, and, aside from the already-mentioned omission, all her Top 40 hits.

what to avoid: Nicks was not at her best, either mentally or physically (i.e., substance abuse), when she made *The Other Side of the Mirror* 𝄞𝄞 (Modern/Atlantic, 1989, prod. Rupert Hine). This time, the house landed on the Good Witch.

the rest:
The Wild Heart 𝄞𝄞𝄞 (Modern/Atlantic, 1983)
Rock a Little 𝄞𝄞𝄞 (Modern/Atlantic, 1985)
Time Space—The Best of Stevie Nicks 𝄞𝄞𝄞 (Modern/Atlantic, 1991)
Street Angel 𝄞𝄞 (Modern/Atlantic, 1994)

worth searching for: At this point, *Buckingham Nicks* (Polydor, 1973, prod. Keith Olsen) is legendary for not yet having appeared on CD, and only one track showed up on *Enchanted*. Perhaps the duo is embarrassed by the Avedonesque nude cover photo, but surely they can't be ashamed of some of the best music either of them has made. Its very California folk-

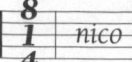
rock sound hasn't dated a bit. The soundtrack to *Twister* (Warner Bros., 1996, prod. various) has the Nicks & Buckingham track, "Twisted" (written by Nicks), which also included Mick Fleetwood on drums—in its final version here, as opposed to the demo Nicks chose to put on *Enchanted*, minus both Buckingham and Fleetwood.

influences:

◀◀ Melanie, Janis Ian

▶▶ Tori Amos, Toni Childs

see also: *Fleetwood Mac*

Steve Holtje

Nico

See: The Velvet Underground

Night Ranger /Damn Yankees /Shaw-Blades

Formed 1981 in San Francisco, CA.

Night Ranger: Jack Blades, bass, vocals (1981–89, 1997–present); Kelly Keagy, drums, vocals; Brad Gillis, guitar, vocals; Alan Fitzgerald, keyboards (1981–88); Jeff Watson, guitar. Damn Yankees: Jack Blades, bass, vocals; Ted Nugent, guitar, vocals; Tommy Shaw, guitar, vocals; Michael Cartellone, drums.

Night Ranger was the transitional rock-radio band between Foreigner, Journey, and the other early '80s hard-rock balladeers and the hair-pop-glam-metal bands that replaced them. Led by charismatic bassist Jack Blades—who's best with a ballad—the band had hits with "Sister Christian" and "(You Can Still) Rock in America." Blades later hooked up with Styx's Tommy Shaw and Motor City Madman Ted Nugent to form the reasonably popular hard-rock band Damn Yankees in 1989. Shaw and Blades have also collaborated on one bland album as a duo.

what to buy: Night Ranger's *Greatest Hits* 🎵🎵 (MCA, 1989, prod. various) is a solid collection of radio-friendly pop-metal, mostly ballads, with bonus tracks "Eddie's Comin' out Tonight" and "Rumours in the Air." It also saves you the trouble of tracking down the band's tepid studio albums. Damn Yankees' two albums, *Damn Yankees* 🎵🎵🎵 (Warner Bros., 1990, prod. Ron Nevison) and *Don't Tread* 🎵🎵 (Warner Bros., 1992, prod. Ron Nevison), have a touch of attitude, thanks to the Nuge's calculated insanity and still-innovative metal guitar licks.

what to avoid: Night Ranger's *Feeding off the Mojo* 🎵 (Drive Entertainment, 1995, prod. David Prater) and *Live in Japan* 🎵 (MCA, 1990, prod. Night Ranger) are excessive no matter how great your Night Ranger jones.

the rest:

Night Ranger:
Dawn Patrol 🎵🎵 (Boardwalk/MCA, 1982)
Midnight Madness 🎵🎵 (MCA, 1983)
7 Wishes 🎵🎵 (Camel/MCA, 1985)
Man in Motion 🎵🎵 (Camel/MCA, 1988)
Neverland 🎵🎵 (Legacy, 1997)
Seven 🎵🎵 (CMC International, 1998)

solo outings:

Shaw-Blades:
Hallucination 🎵🎵 (Warner Bros., 1995)

influences:

◀◀ Kiss, Ted Nugent, Journey, Foreigner, Styx, REO Speedwagon

▶▶ Hootie & the Blowfish, Bon Jovi, Warrant, Mötley Crüe, Poison

see also: *Styx, Ted Nugent*

Tracey Birkenhauer and Steve Knopper

Willie Nile

Born 1949, in Buffalo, NY.

Like Steve Forbert, Willie Nile emerged on the Greenwich Village folk scene at a time when most record companies were more interested in the CBGB punk scene. But even though they weren't as loud, Nile's literate, live-wire compositions—which blended the earnest jangle of the Byrds, the blue-collar angst of Bob Seger, and the rock 'n' roll heart of Bruce Springsteen— matched the emotional clout of anything produced by the new wave movement. After a glowing review in *The New York Times* by the late Robert Palmer, A&R execs flocked to his shows and Nile signed with Arista in 1979. His self-titled debut, which remains one of the most thrilling post-Byrds folk-rock albums of all time, drew the expected critical hosannas, and even caught the attention of Pete Townshend, who invited the rookie rocker to open some stateside dates for the Who. But the sophomore jinx—1983's *Golden Down* was merely a musclebound, FM-radio-ready rehash of the first album—and legal woes derailed his momentum. In 1991 he resurfaced on Columbia with *Places I Have Never Been*, which miraculously picked up right where his first album left off. Now back on the indie track, he continues performing in New York clubs and recently collaborated with singer Andrew Dorff, brother of actor Stephen Dorff, on Dorff's debut album.

what to buy: *Willie Nile* 🎵🎵🎵🎵 (Arista/Razor & Tie, 1980, prod. Roy Halee) is a timeless album that sounds just as vital up against today's twangy Americana movement as it did when it was first released on Arista. From such three-chord raveups as "She's So Cold" and "Dear Lord" to such jangling anthems as

"Vagabond Moon" and a Springsteen-influenced world hunger lament called "Across the River," Nile's youthful idealism is dwarfed only by his enthusiasm. *Archive Alive!* 🎵🎵🎵🎵 (Archive/Paradigm, 1997, prod. Willie Nile, Sam Kopper), recorded live at his Central Park homecoming in 1980 after the Who tour, captures that enthusiasm with rollicking abandon.

what to buy next: Roger McGuinn, Richard Thompson, and members of the Hooters and the Roches help out on the impressive *Places I Have Never Been* 🎵🎵🎵🎵 (Columbia, 1991, prod. Tom Wolk, Stewart Lerman), which finds Nile's guarded optimism and jaded sense of humor (his musical advice to celebrities who don't want tabloid vultures picking at their bones: "Don't Die") intact.

what to avoid: *Hard Times in America* 🎵 (Polaris, 1992, prod. Willie Nile, Martin Briley) is a five-song EP recorded after he was dropped from Columbia. It rocks, but the heartland-hero stances on "Hard Times in America" and "Seeds of a Revolution" are as forced as the song titles.

the rest:
Golden Down 🎵🎵🎵 (Razor & Tie, 1983)

worth searching for: On *A Live Christmas Extravaganza* (Deko Music, 1994, prod. Alan Douches, others), Nile contributes a rollicking "O Come All Ye Faithful" to an an all-star celebration that also includes Marshall Crenshaw, Syd Straw, and Lenny Kaye.

influences:

◀◀ Bruce Springsteen, Bob Dylan, the Byrds, Bob Seger

▶▶ The Hooters, Steve Forbert, John Mellencamp

David Okamoto

Harry Nilsson

Born Harry Edward Nelson III, June 15, 1941, in Brooklyn, NY. Died January 15, 1994, in Augora Hills, CA.

An engaging singer-songwriter whose fluid vocals roamed several octaves, Harry Nilsson was also one of rock's more interesting enigmas: a clever tunesmith who let others sing his best work and an alluring vocalist whose biggest hits were penned by others. Never one to follow protocol, he hopped from dramatic rock to sentimental standards and movie scores, kids' songs, TV themes, and soundtracks. No matter the style, it was almost always intelligently produced and lovely to listen to. Nilsson came of age in Los Angeles, and by the mid-'60s was working a night job in a bank, with songwriting dreams by day. He had some modest success early on, but it wasn't until he caught the ear of Phil Spector in 1967 that he was truly on his way. His debut, *Pandemonium Shadow Show*, included an inventive take on the Beatles' "You Can't Do That," making instant Nilsson fans and lifelong friends out of John Lennon and

Ringo Starr. Soon after he became known to the masses with the 1969 classic, "Everybody's Talkin'," the theme from the Oscar-winning film *Midnight Cowboy*. Though albums and early '70s hits followed, so did hard living and a lack of creative focus. Lennon's death seemed more than he could bear, and—but for sporadic dabbles and anti-gun lobbying—Nilsson dropped from the radar. He returned to composing just before his death, leaving behind his first new songs in years. Despite an unconventional career that never quite followed any path, his contributions as the musical soul of *Midnight Cowboy*, writer of Three Dog Night's "One," Lennon confidant—and, of course, his untimely death—guarantee continued status as near-great.

what to buy: *Personal Best: The Harry Nilsson Anthology* 🎵🎵🎵🎵 (RCA, 1995, prod. various) is a sterling retrospective, a truly comprehensive look at an entire career. The remastered 50-track set also includes a 36-page book. *All Time Greatest Hits* 🎵🎵🎵🎵 (RCA, 1989, prod. various) is also an excellent value, offering 20 satisfying tracks.

what to buy next: Devoted fans say Nilsson hit his stride with *Nilsson Schmilsson* 🎵🎵🎵🎵 (RCA, 1971, prod. Richard Perry), which contains the Beatlesque, Badfinger-penned classic, "Without You." On *A Little Touch of Schmilsson in the Night* 🎵🎵🎵🎵 (RCA, 1973, prod. Derek Taylor), he covered old standards ("You Made Me Love You," "Makin' Whoopie") with surprising appeal.

what to avoid: More noteworthy for who participated than what was created, *Son of Schmilsson* 🎵🎵 (RCA, 1972, prod. Richard Perry, Chick Crumpacker) included performances by George Harrison, Ringo Starr, Nicky Hopkins, a pre-*Comes Alive* Peter Frampton, and others. The result was just so-so; still, it's a keeper for fans.

the rest:
Harry 🎵🎵🎵 (RCA, 1969)
The Point 🎵🎵🎵 (RCA, 1970)
A Touch More Schmilsson 🎵🎵🎵 (1988)

worth searching for: Though Nilsson had recorded previously, *Pandemonium Shadow Show* (RCA, 1967, prod. Rick Jarrard) was his first for a major label and was considered his debut. The record that made Lennon take notice also includes "Cuddly Toy," later a hit for the Monkees. Next came *Aerial Ballet* (RCA, 1968), with "Everybody's Talkin'" and "One." *Pussycats* (RCA, 1974, prod. John Lennon) is Nilsson's Lennon-inspired cover set of off-beat rock classics. He collaborated with Lennon again on *Flash Harry* (1980, prod. Steve Cropper), another eccentric set that includes contributions from Van Dyke Parks and Monty Python comedian Eric Idle.

influences:

◀◀ The Beatles, the Turtles

▶▶ Randy Newman, Ringo Starr

Deborah Wilker

nine inch nails

Formed 1987, in Cleveland, OH.

Trent Reznor (born May 17, 1965, in Mercer, PA), vocals, guitar, bass, drums, electronics, computers; Robin Finck, guitar; Danny Lohner, keyboards, guitar, bass; Charlie Clouser, keyboards; Chris Vrenna, drums.

In the early '90s, as Generation X was starting to gain an over-generalized media identity as a consumer group of alienated, jobless slackers, Trent Reznor's nine inch nails came out with the perfect soundtrack of anger and angst. Originally a hard dance band, NIN built a huge underground buzz by gradually injecting its debut, *Pretty Hate Machine*, into gloomy night-clubs all over the world. Though Reznor's problems with his original record label, TVT, prevented a timely follow-up release, the long-haired young scientist-type gained a cult following that eventually earned NIN a spot on the first Lollapalooza tour. By then, fans and critics were crediting him as the most artistically consistent innovator of throbbing industrial music, at the head of a pack that also included Ministry, Skinny Puppy, and KMFDM. After that, it was only a matter of time before Reznor became a huge alternative-rock superstar, coating himself with mud for Woodstock '94 and scoring huge MTV and radio hits.

what to buy: *Pretty Hate Machine* ♫♫♫♫ (TVT, 1989, prod. Trent Reznor) is most notable for the terrific angry single, "Head like a Hole." The rest was originally intended to sound like a harsh factory of metallic objects slamming into each other, but several years later it sounds (agreeably) goofy.

what to buy next: *The Downward Spiral* ♫♫♫ (TVT/Interscope, 1994, prod. Trent Reznor) took five years to create, but its catchy hits "Closer," "Piggy," and "Hurt" helped create the al-ternative-rock radio format as we know it.

what to avoid: *Fixed* ♫♫ (Nothing/TVT/Interscope, 1992, prod. various) is a bunch of inconsequential remixes from the *Broken* EP.

the rest:
Broken EP ♫♫♫ (Nothing/TVT/Interscope, 1992)
Further down the Spiral ♫♫♫ (TVT/Interscope, 1995)

worth searching for: The soundtrack to *Natural Born Killers* (Nothing/Interscope, 1994, prod. Trent Reznor) has new NIN remixes and artfully stews up bits of violent movie dialogue with harsh industrial music and a couple of folk songs.

influences:

◀◀ Butthole Surfers, Ministry, Black Sabbath, Motörhead, Can, Kraftwerk

▶▶ Filter, Rage Against the Machine, KMFDM, White Zombie

Tracey Birkenhauer and Steve Knopper

Nineteen Wheels

Formed 1995, in East Lansing, MI.

Chris Johnston, vocals, guitars; Tim Mazorati, bass, vocals; Scott Owens, guitars, vocals; Greg Williams, drums.

Former members of the critically acclaimed roots-rock band the Hannibals, Chris Johnston and Scott Owens formed Nineteen Wheels soon after a former bandmate left to attend school in New Mexico. Thanks to the support of Aware Records in Chicago, Nineteen Wheels received national attention, which helped land a distribution deal through Sony.

what's available: An earnest collection of love songs, *Six Ways from Sunday* ♫♫♫ (Aware/Red Ink, 1997, prod. Tim Patalan) is a sweet, rollicking example of countryish pop, fitting nicely with the recent Americana. The chorus of "Colorado"—"Colorado/ Never knew/Skies so blue/Colorado/Never knew/Love so true"—sticks with you like glue. Johnston's vocals have never been more emotional than on "Good Enough," and upon hearing "13 Seconds to Burn," you'll keep your finger on the rewind button to learn the words to the addictive chorus.

worth searching for: The song "Colorado," found on the origi-nal *Six Ways from Sunday* (Aware, 1997, prod. Tim Patalan), is gutsier and sexier than the later Red Ink version.

influences:

◀◀ The Verve Pipe, R.E.M.

Christina Fuoco

Nirvana
/Foo Fighters

Formed 1987, in Aberdeen, WA.

Kurt Cobain (died April 5, 1994), vocals and guitar; Krist Novoselic, bass; Jason Everman, guitar (1987–89); Chad Channing, drums (1987–90); Dave Grohl, drums (1990–94); Pat Smear, guitar (1993–94).

Millions of music fans were shocked to pick up *Billboard* maga-zine one morning in early 1992 to read that Nirvana, a rattily dressed group of anti-authority Seattle kids who made shriek-ing punk rock, had the #1 album in the country. But it shouldn't have been so surprising: Singer-songwriter Cobain, despite his hollering and cryptic, angst-ridden lyrics, had a Paul McCart-

Trent Reznor of nine inch nails (© Ken Settle)

ney-level knack for catchy melodies. And the band's breakthrough album, *Nevermind*, used Butch Vig's big, crisp production to build an inviting rock 'n' roll sound that dragged raw punk rock into the mainstream. Cobain's songs, backed with the stellar rhythm section of Dave Grohl and Krist Novoselic, were downbeat and confusing, and struck a chord with a generation disgusted with baby boomers, happy hippies, and classic-rock radio. The band ushered in the oxymoronic "grunge fashion" movement, paved the way for mass acceptance of Pearl Jam, Stone Temple Pilots, Smashing Pumpkins, and Bush, and was an icon for what became "alternative music" and "modern-rock radio." But the troubled 27-year-old Cobain handled his success poorly and shot himself to death in his Seattle home in 1994. After a brief period of mourning, Grohl formed the Foo Fighters with Nirvana touring guitarist (and ex-Germ) Pat Smear; Novoselic turned to grassroots political activism and put out an uneven Latin-and-grunge album by his band, Sweet 75. Cobain's wife, Hole frontperson Courtney Love, became a love-her-or-hate-her rock star, then changed her image (with obvious plastic surgery) to glamorous movie star, earning accolades as Larry Flynt's wife, Althea, in *The People vs. Larry Flynt*.

what to buy: The opening chords of "Smells like Teen Spirit," the trailblazing single and video from *Nevermind* 𝄞𝄞𝄞𝄞𝄞 (DGC, 1991, prod. Butch Vig), have become as gratifyingly familiar as the whooooos in the Beatles' "She Loves You" or the stuttering in the Who's "My Generation." The album also contained the guitar-rock gems "Lithium," "Polly," "Come as You Are," and "Territorial Pissings." The follow-up, *In Utero* 𝄞𝄞𝄞𝄞 (DGC, 1993, prod. Steve Albini), reflects Cobain's maturing songwriting style ("All Apologies," "Pennyroyal Tea") but also his indulgences with unlistenable noise. The band's postmortem, *MTV Unplugged in New York* 𝄞𝄞𝄞𝄞 (DGC, 1994, prod. Scott Litt, Nirvana), showcases Cobain with his mojo hand in the Leadbelly blues "Where Did You Sleep Last Night?" and intense, slow versions of Nirvana, Meat Puppets, and David Bowie songs. Though posthumous rock albums are traditionally a drag—see Jimi Hendrix and Elvis Presley—Novoselic and Grohl lovingly helped assemble *From the Muddy Banks of the Wishkah* 𝄞𝄞𝄞 (DGC, 1996, prod. various), a collection of fierce live songs from 1989–94 concerts. In addition to powerful versions of "Polly," "Negative Creep," "Smells like Teen Spirit," and "Lithium," it contains Novoselic's inspirational and surprisingly fan-like liner notes.

what to buy next: *Bleach* 𝄞𝄞𝄞 (Sub Pop, 1989, prod. Jack Endino) is the raw, unfocused sound of a band coming together. The inconsistent *Incesticide* 𝄞𝄞𝄞 (DGC, 1992, prod. various) outtakes collection contains the wonderful cover of the Vaselines' "Molly's Lips" plus the originals "Dive" and "Sliver."

the rest:
Blew 𝄞𝄞𝄞 (Tupelo EP, 1989)

worth searching for: *Rare Tracks, Vol. II* is a bootleg with two versions of "Smells like Teen Spirit," including one with the Red Hot Chili Peppers' Flea on trumpet, plus the Who's "Baba O'Riley" and an irritating, moaning duet, "It's Closing Soon," by Cobain and Love.

solo outings:

Foo Fighters (Grohl):
Foo Fighters 𝄞𝄞𝄞𝄞 (Capitol, 1995)
The Colour and the Shape 𝄞𝄞𝄞 (Capitol, 1997)

Sweet 75 (Novoselic):
Sweet 75 𝄞𝄞𝄞 (DGC, 1997)

influences:

◀◀ David Bowie, the Who, Cheap Trick, the Melvins, Leadbelly, Hüsker Dü, Sonic Youth, the Replacements, Flipper, the Vaselines, the Raincoats

▶▶ Pearl Jam, Stone Temple Pilots, Bush, Everclear, Radish, Garbage, Smashing Pumpkins, Hole

Steve Knopper

The Nitty Gritty Dirt Band

Formed 1966, in Long Beach, CA.

Jeff Hanna, vocals, guitar; Jimmie Fadden, vocals, drums; Les Thompson, vocals, mandolin (1966–73); Bruce Kunkel, guitar, violin, vocals (1966–67); Ralph Barr, guitar, clarinet, vocals (1966–68); Jackson Browne, guitar, vocals (1966); John McEuen, banjo, guitar, fiddle, (1967–86); Chris Darrow, guitar, fiddle (1968); Jimmy Ibbotson, bass, vocals (1969–76, 1983–present); John Cable, guitar, bass, vocals (1976–77); Jackie Clark, bass, guitar (1976–77); Michael Buono, drums (1976–77); Bob Carpenter, keyboards, vocals (1979–present); Al Garth, saxophone, violin (1978–82); Richard Hathaway, bass (1978–82); Merle Brigante, drums (1978–79); Vic Mastriani, drums (1980–82); Michael Gardner, bass (1980–82); Bernie Leadon, guitar, banjo (1987–88).

The Nitty Gritty Dirt Band was the group that introduced many second-generation rock 'n' rollers to music outside of the bubblegum pop that AM Top 40 radio served up during the late '60s and early '70s. With hits such as "Mr. Bojangles" (written by Jerry Jeff Walker), the NGDB led interested fans to other singer-songwriters and the country-rock scene. Its sprawling, landmark 1972 three-record set, *Will the Circle Be Unbroken* brought unadulterated folk and roots country stars to rock fans' ears. The collection was a generational gathering of traditional musicians from Mother Maybelle Carter and Doc Watson to Opry founders Roy Acuff and Merle Travis, with the long-haired Dirt Band members playing backup and proving they listened to a wider range of music than many of their fans.

That catholic stylistic sense came from the band's roots in the halcyon L.A. folk-rock scene of the mid-'60s, where the NGDB first formed as a jug-band. When multi-instrumentalist John McEuen joined, the core group was set for most of the rest of its career. Its records at various times were more rock than country (the 1975 *Dream* LP even included a spacey banjo opus that sounded like Pink Floyd for hillbillies), but by the '80s, with myriad personnel changes and a stint officially calling themselves the Dirt Band, the core members settled in as something of a country-music institution; their sound hadn't changed, but in the post-punk era, twangy music found itself unhip and relegated to country radio. Although it wasn't as much of a revelation the second time around, the Dirt Band also released an updated version of *Circle* in 1989, a songfest featuring some of the original legends (Roy Acuff, Earl Scruggs) as well as the new Nashville set (Rosanne Cash, John Hiatt, Emmylou Harris, Bruce Hornsby). Now in its fourth decade, the band has become one of the longest-running bands of the rock era and the end seems nowhere in sight.

what to buy: *Will the Circle Be Unbroken* 𝄞𝄞𝄞𝄞 (Liberty, 1972, prod. William E. McEuen) is the hands-down must-own release by the NGDB, although it's not as much a reflection of the band's own music as it is a testament to its roots. The music was already old by then but sounded fresh in this context. And it hasn't aged in the quarter-century since.

what to buy next: *Uncle Charlie and His Dog Teddy* 𝄞𝄞𝄞 (Liberty, 1970, prod. William E. McEuen) includes the group's biggest hit, "Mr. Bojangles," as well as a minor-hit version of Michael Nesmith's great "Some of Shelley's Blues" that's typical of its hippie eclecticism. The mid-career three-LP compilation *Dirt, Silver & Gold* 𝄞𝄞𝄞 (United Artists, 1976/One Way, 1994, prod. various) collects the good stuff and filters out the dross.

the rest:
Ricochet 𝄞𝄞 (Liberty, 1967/Beat Goes On, 1996)
All the Good Times 𝄞𝄞 (Liberty, 1971)
Stars and Stripes Forever 𝄞𝄞𝄞 (Liberty, 1971/Gold Rush, 1995)
Dream 𝄞𝄞𝄞 (United Artists, 1975)
20 Years of Dirt 𝄞𝄞𝄞 (Warner Bros., 1986)
Hold On 𝄞𝄞 (Warner Bros., 1987)
Best of the Nitty Gritty Dirt Band 𝄞𝄞𝄞 (Liberty, 1987)
Will the Circle Be Unbroken, Vol. 2 𝄞𝄞𝄞 (Curb, 1989)
More Great Dirt 𝄞𝄞 (Warner Bros., 1989)
Greatest Hits 𝄞𝄞𝄞 (Curb, 1990)
Live Two Five 𝄞𝄞 (Capitol Nashville, 1991)
Not Fade Away 𝄞𝄞 (Liberty, 1992)
Best Of 𝄞𝄞𝄞 (Curb, 1993)
Acoustic 𝄞𝄞𝄞 (Liberty, 1994)
The Christmas Album 𝄞𝄞𝄞 (Rising Tide, 1997)
Best Of 𝄞𝄞𝄞 (Capitol, 1997)
Bang Bang Bang 𝄞𝄞𝄞 (Decca, 1998)

solo outings:
John McEuen:
John McEuen 𝄞𝄞 (Warner Bros., 1988)
String Wizards 𝄞𝄞 (Vanguard, 1992)
String Wizards II 𝄞𝄞 (Vanguard, 1993)
Acoustic Traveller 𝄞𝄞𝄞 (Vanguard, 1996)
String Wizard's Picks 𝄞𝄞 (Vanguard, 1997)

Jimmy Ibbotson:
Wild Jimbos 𝄞𝄞 (MCA, 1991)
Wild Jimbos Two 𝄞𝄞 (Resounding, 1993)

influences:
◀◀ The Carter Family, the Weavers, Buddy Holly, the Jim Kweskin Jug Band, the Byrds

▶▶ Rodney Crowell, Rosanne Cash, Foster & Lloyd, Travis Tritt, Hank Williams Jr., Michelle Shocked, Uncle Tupelo

Gil Asakawa

Nitzer Ebb

Formed 1982, in Chelmsford, Essex, England.

Vaughan "Bon" Harris, vocals, programming, bass; Doug McCarthy, lead vocals, guitar; David Gooday, percussion (1982–89); Julian "Joolz" Beeston, percussion (1989–94); Jason Payne, percussion (1994–present).

Despite its Teutonic name, Nitzer Ebb is actually a British group; its three founding members—Essex schoolmates Bon Harris, Doug McCarthy, and David Gooday—created the meaningless words "Nitzer Ebb" by cutting random letters out of a newspaper. With a spartan, beat-heavy electronic dance sound and disturbing militaristic imagery, the proto-industrial trio quickly gained a reputation in their hometown, later releasing their debut single, "Isn't It Funny How Your Body Works," in 1984 on their own Power of Voice Communications label with the help of London producer Phil Harding. It became an underground dance hit in the U.K., leading to five more singles and eventually a deal with Mute Records in Britain and Geffen in the U.S. Nitzer Ebb's 1987 full-length debut *That Total Age* made them famous worldwide thanks to the international dance hits "Murderous" and "Join in the Chant." 1989's *Belief* and 1990's *Showtime* expanded their following with several more club/college radio singles and clever production work by Flood; a landmark world tour opening for Depeche Mode followed, consolidating the trio's underground following. Sadly, after recording 1991's *Ebbhead*, their commercial highpoint, the group became sidetracked—McCarthy worked with Depeche Mode's Alan Wilder on the Recoil project, while Beeston quit the group altogether—and their next release, *Big Hit*, proved anything but when it finally came out in 1995. Since then Nitzer Ebb has been on indefinite hiatus. McCarthy continues to work with Wilder in Recoil, while Harris joined Ethyl Meatplow's John Napier (who worked as a touring musician for Nitzer Ebb in their later days) in the group Maven. Julian Beeston is currently touring with the industrial supergroup C-Tec.

what to buy: *That Total Age* 𝄞𝄞𝄞 (Geffen, 1987, prod. Phil Harding) is a throbbing mass of electro-industrial dance minimalism, replete with monotonous drum beats and angry, chanted, repetitive lyrics. It includes the smash club hit "Join in the Chant," as well as "Murderous" and "Let Your Body Learn."

what to buy next: *Ebbhead* 𝄞𝄞𝄞 (Geffen, 1991, prod. Flood, Alan Wilder), the group's commercial highpoint, is another strong effort, and features the radio singles "Godhead" and "I Give to You." *Belief* 𝄞𝄞𝄞 (Geffen, 1989, prod. Flood) and *Showtime* 𝄞𝄞𝄞 (Geffen, 1990, prod. Flood), which include the singles "Hearts and Minds," "Shame," "Lightning Man," and "Fun to Be Had," finds Nitzer Ebb filling out their sound with excellent production work by Flood. The discs provide an excellent transition from *That Total Age* to *Ebbhead*.

what to avoid: *Big Hit* 𝄞 (Geffen, 1995, prod. Flood, Alan Wilder) is a hopeless, half-hearted attempt by this thoroughly electronic group to incorporate live instruments into their act, probably in response to the rise of grunge (analogous to pal Depeche Mode's failed *Songs of Faith and Devotion*). Not worth the nearly four-year wait.

worth searching for: The *As Is* EP (Geffen, 1991, prod. Jaz Coleman, Flood, Alan Wilder, Barry Adamson, Paul Kendall), which includes four cuts recorded by Nitzer Ebb while preparing for their *Ebbhead* album, is sure to interest devoted fans.

influences:

◀◀ DAF, Bauhaus, the Birthday Party, Killing Joke

▶▶ nine inch nails

Seth Hindin

Mojo Nixon

Born Neill Kirby McMillan Jr., August 2, 1957, in Chapel Hill, NC.

Poking holes in stuffy celebrities and chiding right-wing zealots, Mojo Nixon mashes blues, folk, rock, punk, soul, and country into a steamy stew and serves it up with a rabble-rousing yelp that is part Howlin' Wolf, part Wolfman Jack, part late-night used-car salesman. 1987's "Elvis Is Everywhere," a backhanded tribute to the King, got him on radio, talk shows, and MTV. But he has earned his reputation as the guardian of rock 'n' roll's lunatic fringe with such biting music-industry diatribes as "Stuffin' Martha's Muffin" (a serenade for former MTV VJ Martha Quinn), "Don Henley Must Die" ("He's a tortured artist/used to be in the Eagles/now he whines like a wounded beagle"), and "Don't Want No Foo Foo Haircut on My Head." After three duo projects with washboard-toting partner Skid Roper, Nixon started recording with a full band in 1990, achieving a hard-nosed balance between the musical and the maniacal. In between his politically incorrect collaborations with Jello Biafra (which reached a tasteless nadir with 1993's "Will the Fetus Be Aborted"), he has contributed to a spate of tribute albums honoring everyone from Led Zeppelin to the Sonics.

what to buy: John Doe, the late Country Dick Montana, Bill Davis, and Eric Ambel provide the muscle power on *Otis* 𝄞𝄞𝄞 (I.R.S., 1990, prod. Jim Dickinson). Not only is this Nixon's most savage album, it's also his most consistent, thanks to "Destroy All Lawyers," "You Can Dress 'Em up (But You Can't Take 'Em Out)," and "Don Henley Must Die." *Root Hog or Die* 𝄞𝄞𝄞 (I.R.S., 1989, prod. Jim Dickinson), his swan song with Roper, ups the ante on outrageousness with the James Brown–style "Louisiana Liplock" and the riotous lawsuit-waiting-to-happen "Debbie Gibson Is Pregnant with My Two-Headed Love Child." *Bo-Day-Shus!* 𝄞𝄞𝄞 (I.R.S., 1987, prod. Ron Goudie) offers "Elvis Is Everywhere," "Gin Guzzlin' Frenzy," "Don't Want No Foo-Foo Haircut on My Head," and the surprisingly touching "Wide Open."

what to buy next: *Gadzooks!!!* 𝄞𝄞𝄞 (Needletime, 1997, prod. various) collects 17 riotous 45's, flexidiscs, and other oddities, including the notorious showstopper "Bring Me the Head of David Geffen," "Beer Ain't Drinkin'," and a devastating rewrite of Jonathan Richman's "Roadrunner" called "Death Row Blues."

what to avoid: *Mojo Nixon and Skid Roper* 𝄞𝄞 (I.R.S., 1985, prod. Ron Goudie) captures the duo in their primal stage, flailing away with testosterone-fueled tantrums such as "Jesus at McDonald's," "Mushroom Maniac," and a barely recognizable cover of Bruce Springsteen's obscure "The Big Payback."

the rest:
Frenzy /Get out of My Way 𝄞𝄞𝄞 (I.R.S., 1986)
Horny Holidays 𝄞𝄞𝄞 (Triple X, 1992)
Whereabouts Unknown 𝄞𝄞𝄞 (Ripe & Ready, 1995)

worth searching for: *20 Explosive Dynamic Super Smash Hit Explosions* (Pravda, 1991, prod. various), a various-artists tribute to K-Tel, ends with Nixon's warped remake of Kenny Rogers & the First Edition's "Just Dropped in (to See What Condition My Condition Was In)."

influences:

◀◀ Howlin' Wolf, Foghorn Leghorn, James Brown, Jerry Lee Lewis

▶▶ Reverend Billy C. Wirtz

David Okamoto

The Nixons

Formed 1992, in Oklahoma City, OK.

Zac Maloy, vocals, guitar; Jesse Davis, guitar; Ricky Wolking, bass (1997–present); Ricky Brooks, guitar (1994–97); John Humphrey, drums.

The Nixons fall into the rock end of what is termed modern rock. The band's principal singer-songwriter, Zac Maloy, has music running through his family; his grandfather was a country musician in a band called Buddy White & the Western Aires. Maloy still has his granddaddy's guitar, which he plays to this day. The band rocks hard and was among the most impressive of the acts that had to endure opening for Kiss during its 1996–97 reunion tour. The Nixons' high-energy show combines a stage presence that many of their contemporaries lack, while their songwriting is a combination of old and new rock schools, with a splash of pop. The group's lone hit, "Sister," may have established the band's place among the one-hit wonders of the '90s, but the jury's still out.

what to buy: The title *Foma* ♪♪♪ (MCA, 1995, prod. Mark Dodson, Nixons) is a made-up word to describe "lies that people make up to make themselves feel better." The album's "Sister" is a true-life ballad about Maloy's sister and a tribute to their close sibling relationship—not your typical love song. For the most part, the band rocks out with the title track and the infectious "Jim."

the rest:
The Nixons ♪♪ (MCA, 1997)

worth searching for: The EP *Six* (Dragon Street, 1992), with drummer Tye Robinson, is the band's first recording. *Halo* (self-released, 1994) has the same songs as *Foma* but in a different order and with slightly different production.

influences:
◀◀ Alice in Chains, Goo Goo Dolls, Van Halen, Metallica
▶▶ Days of the New, Creed

Darren Davis

No Doubt

Formed 1987, in Los Angeles, CA.

Gwen Stefani, vocals; Eric Stefani, keyboards (1987–95); Tony Kanal, bass; Adrian Young, drums; Tom Dumont, guitar.

Riding the ska-pop revival and the ubiquitous bellybutton of a blond, halter-topped singer, No Doubt sold millions of records during the mid-'90s. But the overwhelming success of the *Tragic Kingdom* album was preceded by years of indifference that might have broken a less determined group. No Doubt was a ska band, performing with a horn section and a toasting emcee back when ska was being kept alive by pork-pie-hatted scenesters in the Orange County underground and little else.

The quintet cranked out a series of demos, including one produced by their pal Flea from the Red Hot Chili Peppers, but struggled to find a deal. Finally latching on with Interscope, No Doubt's 1992 debut album sank without a trace. Undaunted, the band woodshedded for several years and wrote 60 songs that blended traces of its early ska sound with pop melodies and distinctive hooks, such as the flamenco guitar break in the power ballad "Don't Speak." Singer Gwen Stefani also brought a more personal approach to the lyric writing, and her girl-next-door sassiness offered a sunny alternative to an emerging crop of rock's "angry young women" such as Alanis Morissette, Courtney Love, and Tori Amos.

what to buy: *Tragic Kingdom* ♪♪♪ (Trauma/Interscope, 1995, prod. Matthew Wilder) is a well-crafted pop album, no more and no less. For every indulgence, such as the prog-rock contortions of the title track, there are a handful of snappy melodies, from the ska-tinged anthem "Just a Girl" to the break-up ballad of the mid-'90s, "Don't Speak."

what to avoid: *The Beacon Street Collection* ♪♪ (Sea Creature/Interscope, 1995, prod. No Doubt) is symbolic of an obnoxious trend: relatively new bands dumping their outtakes on the market after scoring a huge commercial success. *Beacon Street* contains solid but unremarkable demos considered for "Tragic Kingdom," but eventually scrapped. Hearing them now only confirms the wisdom of that initial judgment.

the rest:
No Doubt ♪♪ (Interscope, 1992)

influences:
◀◀ Fishbone, English Beat, the Specials, Madness

Greg Kot

NOFX

Formed 1983, in Los Angeles, CA.

Fat Mike (born Mike Burkett), vocals, bass; Eric Melvin, guitar, vocals; El Hefe (born Aaron Abeyta), guitar, trumpet, vocals; Smelly (born Erik Sandin), drums; others.

Punk bands do get old, but rarely as gracefully as NOFX. Perhaps graceful is not exactly right; they are still the same proudly juvenile jerks who pass gas, laugh at pee-pee jokes, and think saying the f-word a lot is cool. As talented as they are funny, NOFX's members write fast and catchy punk ditties that stick like chewing gum in your hair. Leader Fat Mike sings like he has a chronic adenoid problem. El Hefe and Eric Melvin play guitar like closet metalheads who think slow equals bad, and drummer Smelly tears around his kit like he's racing a train. The songs are about idiots, boobs, STDs, long lines (both varieties), drugs, booze, and every other subject that ranks as fun to a teenager. Offensive enough to irritate your dad but humorous enough to win him over, NOFX sets a bad example for everyone. Recommended to anyone who likes loud and fast Southern California punk.

what to buy: *White Trash, Two Heebs and a Bean* ♫♫♫♫ (Epitaph, 1992, prod. NOFX, Donnell Cameron) had to be shaved of an even more offensive title, an unfortunate controversy given the quality of the music. This gem contains the great lesbian love song "Liza and Louise," the skinhead-razzing "Bob," and the more serious "You're Bleeding," about a friend of the band.

what to buy next: The EP *The Longest Line* ♫♫♫♫ (Fat Wreck Chords, 1992, prod. NOFX, Donnell Cameron), released on Fat Mike's own label, introduces El Hefe to the band. His trumpet brings a bit more ska-skank to the mix, while strong harmonies à la old Bad Religion, stop-and-start riffing, and hyperactive drums make this EP a winner. The El Hefe–sung "Kill All the White Man" is a concert favorite.

the rest:
Liberal Animation ♫♫ (Fat Wreck Chords, 1988/Epitaph, 1991)
S&M Airlines ♫♫♫ (Epitaph, 1989)
Ribbed ♫♫♫♫ (Epitaph, 1991)
Punk in Drublic ♫♫♫♫ (Epitaph, 1994)
I Heard They Suck Live ♫♫♫ (Fat Wreck Chords, 1995)
Heavy Petting Zoo ♫♫♫ (Epitaph, 1996)
So Long and Thanks for All the Shoes ♫♫♫ (Epitaph, 1997)

influences:
◀◀ Circle Jerks, Bad Religion, Dead Milkmen, Social Distortion

▶▶ Lagwagon, Green Day, Blink 182, Nuisance, Diesel Boy, Snuff, Less Than Jake

Barry M. Prickett

Heather Nova

Born Heather Frith, 1968, in Bermuda.

Singer-songwriter Heather Nova came out of the proverbial blue to open for Neil Young and Pearl Jam in Europe during 1995, when her debut CD spawned a hit single in "Walk This World." She's no overnight sensation, though. While in college at the Rhode Island School of Design, where she was studying film and painting, Nova began to explore her musical side in creating the soundtracks to her films. According to her, "I got into the studio and doing films where I would make the soundtracks first and then do the Super 8 films to go with the soundtracks; after a while, these films started taking the forms of songs." Finding her way through her songs, Nova went to Europe, where she played the cafes and pubs of London at night and worked in the Bermuda tourism office during the day. At one of those gigs, she was "discovered" by Abbo, president of Big Cat records, which was the European home to the likes of Pavement, Luscious Jackson, and the Palace Brothers.

what to buy: Nova's full-length debut, *Oyster* ♫♫♫ (WORK Group, 1995), showcased a rising young talent at home in the worlds of both pop and rock. The lilting ballads "Maybe an Angel" and "Truth and Bone" mark a sharp but effective contrast from the aggressive sensuality of "Walk This World" and "Sugar." Nova's pop chops are best displayed in the engaging "Blue Black" and "Verona." The threads uniting the diverse tracks are Nova's vocals, which flow freely from riveting to reassuring, depending on the mood and her lyrics.

what to avoid: Nova's follow-up to *Oyster*, *Siren* ♫♫ (WORK Group, 1998) could be used as the definition of sophomore slump. The album lacks all the passion of its predecessor, with 14 totally unmemorable songs that knock Nova's status from Alanis Morissette to Olivia Newton-John.

the rest:
Live from the Milky Way ♫♫♫♫ (Big Cat/WORK Group, 1994)

influences:
◀◀ Patti Smith, Lou Reed

Steve Baltin

Nova Mob
See: Hüsker Dü

NRBQ
Formed 1967, in Miami, FL.

Terry Adams, piano, vocals; Joey Spampinato, bass, vocals; Steve Ferguson, guitar (1967–71); Frankie Gadler, vocals (1967–72); Tom Staley, drums (1967–74); Al Anderson, guitar, vocals (1971–94); Tom Ardolino, drums (1974–present); Johnny Spampinato, guitar (1994–present).

In the liner notes to NRBQ's 1990 retrospective *Peek-a-Boo*, Mark Rowland writes: "Pop music fans generally divide into two camps regarding NRBQ—those who consider them among the great bands of the last two decades, and those who have not yet heard them play." Rowland is right: NRBQ may be the best band you've never heard. The name is an acronym for the New Rhythm and Blues Quartet (Quintet when it formed), although rhythm and blues are just two of the myriad elements that make up its sound. The band's foundation is one of roots-influenced rock with a hearty helping of boogie-woogie ladled on top. Those familiar with NRBQ's eclectic ways, however, know that the band is just as likely to break midsong into free-form jazz, execute an irresistible Motown shuffle, or toss off a letter-perfect country ballad. With lesser outfits, this merry genre-hopping could merely be construed as showing off—a trait at which, granted, NRBQ is quite adept. But the band's encyclopedic knowledge of music styles is most often applied to the delivery of its material. NRBQ has always been about good songs; the fact that they are played with witty irreverence and blinding chops only intensifies their power. While numerous musicians populated the band prior to 1974, the lineup that came together in that year—Anderson, Adams, Ardolino and Joey Spampinato—is generally considered the definitive NRBQ.

what to buy: *Peek-a-Boo* ♫♫♫♫♫ (Rhino, 1990, compilation prod. Bill Inglot) is a superb collection of material from NRBQ's first 20 years of recording. The two-disc set offers prime examples of the band's keen understanding of musical idioms as well as their dedication to fine pop craftsmanship. Standout cuts include the good-time rock 'n' roll of "Flat Foot Flewzy," "RC Cola and a Moon Pie," and "Me and the Boys," which sit comfortably alongside such goofy workouts as "Captain Lou" (with professional wrestling legend Captain Lou Albano contributing enthusiastically atonal vocals) and "Here Comes Terry."

what to buy next: *Message for the Mess Age* ♫♫♫♫ (Rykodisc, 1994, prod. Terry Adams, Joey Spampinato) is another stellar outing that shows the band only improving with age as it sails beyond the quarter century mark. There's not a lot of new ground plowed here (the band's previous excursions left very little uncharted territory), but the material and playing are so good that stylistic freshness isn't really an issue.

what to avoid: OK, it is a hoot for those who like the band's silliness quotient cranked up to "11." But for the rest of us, *Lou and the Q* ♫♫ (Rounder, 1986) is merely a ridiculous outing featuring wrestling cartoon Captain Lou Albano that should be reserved for completists only.

the rest:
Stomp ♫♫♫♫ (CBS, 1968)
Scraps ♫♫♫♫ (Kama Sutra, 1972/Red Rooster/Rounder, 1982)
Uncommon Denominators ♫♫♫ (Red Rooster/Rounder, 1972)
Workshop ♫♫♫ (Kama Sutra, 1973/Red Rooster/Rounder, 1982)
All Hopped Up ♫♫♫ (Red Rooster/Rounder, 1977)
At Yankee Stadium ♫♫♫♫ (Mercury, 1978/1988)
Kick Me Hard ♫♫♫♫ (Red Rooster/Rounder, 1979/1990)
Tiddlywinks ♫♫♫ (Rounder, 1980)
Grooves in Orbit ♫♫♫ (Bearsville, 1983/Bearsville/Rhino, 1990)
Tapdancin' Bats ♫♫♫ (Rounder, 1983/Red Rooster/Rounder, 1990)
(With Skeeter Davis) *She Sings, They Play* ♫♫♫ (Rounder, 1985)
Christmas Wish ♫♫♫ (Rounder, 1985)
RC Cola & a Moon Pie ♫♫ (Rounder, 1986)
God Bless Us All ♫♫♫ (Rounder, 1988)
Diggin' Uncle Q ♫♫ (Rounder, 1988)
Wild Weekend ♫♫♫♫ (Virgin, 1989)
Honest Dollar ♫♫♫♫ (Rykodisc, 1992)
You're Nice People You Are ♫♫♫ (Rounder, 1997)
Tokyo: Recorded Live on Air West Tokyo ♫♫ (Rounder, 1997)
Tapdancin' Bats: The Anniversary Edition ♫♫♫♫ (Rounder, 1998)
Gotta Be Loose ♫♫♫ (Rounder, 1998)

WHAT ALBUM CHANGED YOUR LIFE?

I remember hearing Patti Smith for the first time, her album *Horses*. At that point I realized here was someone who was mixing poetry with rock 'n' roll. I realized that's what I wanted to do.

Heather Nova

worth searching for: NRBQ's early albums on Columbia unfortunately fell out of circulation within a few years of their release. *NRBQ* (Columbia, 1969) is an audacious melding that runs from Eddie Cochran's "C'mon Everybody" to Sun Ra's "Rocket Number 9." Carl Perkins, meanwhile, guests on *Boppin' the Blues* (Columbia, 1970).

solo outings:
Steve Ferguson:
Jack Salmon and Derby Sauce ♫♫♫♫ (Schoolkids, 1993)
Mama U-Seapa ♫♫♫♫ (Schoolkids, 1995)

Al Anderson:
Party Favors ♫♫ (Twin/Tone, 1988)

Terry Adams:
Terrible ♫♫♫ (New World, 1995)

influences:
◄◄ The Beatles, Chuck Berry, Eddie Cochran, Little Richard, Jerry Lee Lewis, the Everly Brothers, Carl Perkins, Elvis Presley, the Rolling Stones, Duane Eddy, Johnny Cash, Hank Williams Sr., Cecil Taylor, Thelonious Monk, Charlie Christian, Spike Jones

►► Steely Dan, Uncle Tupelo, Blue Rodeo, the Jayhawks, Golden Smog

David Galens and Eric Deggans

Ted Nugent
/The Amboy Dukes
Born December 13, 1948, in Detroit, MI.

Though it may seem that Ted Nugent was raised by wolves, he's really just a guy who loves bow-hunting as much as guns, girls, and guitars. Nugent first made waves with his searing, psychedelic guitar wailing on "Journey to the Center of Your Mind" by his first big band, the Amboy Dukes. But the Motor City Madman raised bombast to a fine art during the '70s after he broke up the Dukes to go solo. Known for his squawking lead guitar work, outrageous stage antics, and songs that reveled in macho bravado and blatant sexual imagery, Nugent was one of the most popular hard rock acts in the U.S. during the mid- and late '70s. Though his commercial fortunes have flagged since then, Nugent has managed to survive in the ever-changing wilds of rock 'n' roll while developing side careers as a guitarist with the popular Damn Yankees group and as a hunting advocate, merchandiser, publisher, activist, aspiring radio talk show host, and sponsor of a new brand of beef jerky.

what to buy: With its air-raid guitars and urgent sexual suggestiveness, *Cat Scratch Fever* 🎵🎵🎵 (Epic, 1977, prod. Tom Werman) captures the Nuge in all his outrageous, piledriving, crotch rock glory. He's at the top of his game as both a writer and a player.

what to buy next: Nugent's recorded output has been pretty spotty since his late '70s glory days, and most of what he's released since then has been pretty weak. It's surprising, then, to hear him put it all together again nearly 20 years later on *Spirit of the Wild* 🎵🎵🎵 (Atlantic, 1994, prod. Ted Nugent). It's his first album that balances his love of the outdoors with his love of the indoors (i.e., the bedroom) and includes "Fred Bear," a sincere tribute to the legendary hunter. *Out of Control* 🎵🎵🎵 (Epic/Legacy, 1993, prod. various) is a two-CD box set that encapsulates Nugent's career from his first recordings with the Amboy Dukes.

what to avoid: All of his work with Atlantic during the '80s was tepid, formulaic stuff—a retread of his earlier successes, but the audience had moved on. The worst of the lot is *Nugent* 🎵 (Atlantic, 1982, prod. Ted Nugent).

the rest:
(With the Amboy Dukes) *Journey to the Center of Your Mind* 🎵🎵 (Mainstream, 1968)
(With the Amboy Dukes) *Call of the Wild* 🎵🎵 (Discreet, 1972)
Ted Nugent 🎵🎵🎵 (Epic, 1975)
Free for All 🎵🎵 (Epic, 1976)
Double Live Gonzo 🎵🎵 (Epic, 1977)
Weekend Warriors 🎵🎵 (Epic, 1978)
State of Shock 🎵🎵 (Epic, 1979)
Scream Dream 🎵🎵 (Epic, 1980)
Intensities in Ten Cities 🎵 (Epic, 1980)
Great Gonzos! The Best of Ted Nugent 🎵🎵🎵 (Epic, 1980)
Penetrator 🎵 (Atlantic, 1984)
Little Miss Dangerous 🎵🎵 (Atlantic, 1986)
If You Can't Lick 'Em . . . Lick 'Em 🎵 (Atlantic, 1988)

worth searching for: The vast bulk of the Amboy Dukes' catalog is out of print, and it's as varied in quality as Nugent's solo work. *Survival of the Fittest* (Polydor, 1971) and *Tooth, Fang, and Claw* (Discreet, 1973) come closest to approximating what would become the Nugent solo sound.

influences:
◀◀ Duane Eddy, Chuck Berry, Jimi Hendrix
▶▶ Aerosmith, Jackyl, Cry of Love

Doug Pullen

Nuisance

Formed 1990, in Santa Rosa, CA. Disbanded 1994.

Andrew Asp, vocals, guitar; Kyle Henner, bass; Jesse Wickman, drums.

Timing is everything, but Nuisance had everything but. Its crunchy, Green Day–meets-Nirvana-in-a-pencil-breaking-match punk and classic country songs would have been huge just two or three years after the band broke up. Andrew Asp's two-pack-an-hour vocals and fat guitar melded with Kyle Henner's active bass and Jesse Wickman's intricate, walloping drumming to make two excellent records. While it lasted, Nuisance was a raucous treat that should have made Santa Rosa famous.

what to buy: Tighter than your high school pants, *Sunny Side Down* 🎵🎵🎵🎵 (Lookout!, 1993) tears up phone books and fills out muscle shirts. "Eureka (I Found It)," a clever reference to a California backwater town, leads the record off with an extra-base hit. (Come to think of it, *most* of Nuisance's songs are about California, touring, or cigarettes.) "Sunny Side Down" is a nearly perfect makeout record if your date chain-smokes, shoplifts, skateboards, or has a BMX bike. Stick around at the end for the delayed, add-on cover of the Kiss classic "Beth."

what to buy next: *Confusion Hill* 🎵🎵🎵 (Lookout!, 1991, prod. Kevin Army, Alex Sergay, Nuisance) is not quite as realized as *Sunny Side Down* (and is docked for a lousy cover of "Brown Eyed Girl") but still has ample merits. "Broken Van" and "Nicotine" deserve to be played at parties where beer is served in cans and the only women present are in tattered pin-up photos. It's classic rock for punk geeks.

influences:
◀◀ Roy Acuff, Hank Williams Sr., Rush, Nirvana, Green Day, Crimpshrine, Squirrel Bait
▶▶ Lag Wagon, Diesel Boy

Barry M. Prickett

Gary Numan

Born Gary Anthony James Webb, March 8, 1958, in Hammersmith, London, England.

First appearing on the scene with Tubeway Army in 1978 under the name Valerium, Gary Numan was a sight to behold. With his glum, robotic appearance and vocal delivery, staring eyes, and synthesizer music, he popularized robots as dramatic entities and inspired a cult that exists to this day. Through the course of many albums he has changed his image from that of a cold machine operator to debonair man about town. After establishing the first synth-pop hits of the era (especially "Cars"), he began to pursue his other passion: flying planes. In 1982 Numan attempted to fly around the world in his light aircraft; he was arrested in India on suspicion of spying, charges that were later dropped. Numan still flies planes, fights for animal rights, and records albums in England, recently making a new bid for acceptance with audiences in the United States.

what to buy: All of Numan's U.S. and European hits with Tubeway Army are deftly compiled on *Premier Hits* ♫♫♫♫ (Beggar's Banquet, 1997, compilation prod. Steve Ebbon), an 18-song set boasting digitally remastered sound. *Telekon* ♫♫♫♫ (Atco, 1980/Beggar's Banquet, 1998, prod. Gary Numan) was his first LP to feature guitars, which created intriguing new musical textures. This reissue also includes many revealing bonus tracks that longtime fans will savor. If it's a bargain you're looking for, track down *Telekon/I Assassin* ♫♫♫♫ (Atco, 1980/1982/Beggar's Banquet, 1992, prod. Gary Numan), which features two of his best early LPs.

what to buy next: The reissue of the first album released under his own name, *The Pleasure Principle* ♫♫♫♫ (Atco, 1979/Beggar's Banquet, 1998, prod. Gary Numan) is Numan at his best in the electronic pop realm and contains seven previously unavailable B–sides and alternate takes. The reissue of *Gary Numan & Tubeway Army* ♫♫♫♫ (Atco, 1979/Beggar's Banquet, 1998) features 12 live tracks recorded at the Roxy in 1978, making for a very tasty package indeed. Finally, *Replicas* ♫♫♫♫ (Atco, 1979/Beggar's Banquet, 1998, prod. Gary Numan) features the hit song "Are Friends Electric," and several previously unavailable tracks, which make it worthwhile for fans and novices alike.

what to avoid: The messy Tubeway Army effort *First Album* ♫♫ (Atco, 1978, prod. Gary Numan) was recorded while Numan was still forming what would become his signature sound and should be heard in that spirit.

the rest:
The Other Side of Gary Numan ♫♫ (Receiver, 1992)
Here I Am ♫♫ (Receiver, 1994)
Archive ♫♫ (Rialto, 1996)
Exile ♫♫♫ (Cleopatra, 1998)

WHAT ALBUM CHANGED YOUR LIFE?

The first one I heard was an Ultravox album called *Systems of Romance.* That was probably the most influential one as far as my direction with electronic music was concerned. I was already moving that way, and I found it very, very helpful in indicating how to integrate that much more than anyone else had done.

Gary Numan

White Noise ♫♫ (Cleopatra, 1998)
The Mix ♫♫♫ (Cleopatra, 1998)

worth searching for: The three-disc set *The Story So Far* (Receiver, 1996, prod. Gary Numan) is a very thorough collection of funk, electronic, and synth-pop done simply and elegantly. Also, Numan's batch of self-produced albums on his own label—*Berserker* (Numa, 1984); *White Noise—Live* (Numa, 1985); *The Fury* (Numa, 1985); *Strange Charm* (Numa, 1986); *1978–1979, Vols. 2 & 3* (Numa, 1985); and *Sacrifice* (Numa, 1994)—are scattershot but give him the appearance of being the most prolific, self-contained artist this side of Prince.

influences:

◀◀ Kraftwerk, Brian Eno, David Bowie, Roxy Music

▶▶ Underworld, Orbital, the Orb, Deee-Lite, Human League, A Flock of Seagulls, Berlin, Duran Duran

Anna Glen and Ken Burke

Nuno

See: Extreme

Laura Nyro

Born Laura Nigro, October 18, 1947, in the Bronx, NY. Died April 8, 1997, in Danbury, CT.

One of the best and brightest songwriters of the late '60s, Laura Nyro is essential listening for anyone seeking out the roots of rock's singer-songwriter movement. Nyro was a mere 18 years old when she recorded her first album, *More Than a New Discovery*, a remarkable debut that showcased her prodigious musical talent and swooping, gutsy voice. Throughout a 30-year career, Nyro wrote and released a sterling catalog of angst-bearing confessional music inflected with R&B, soul, and gospel touches. While she had only one recording reach the Top 100 (her cover of the Drifters' "Up on the Roof" in 1970), her own songs have been major hits for artists such as Barbra Streisand ("Stoney End"), the Fifth Dimension ("Wedding Bell Blues"), Blood, Sweat & Tears ("And When I Die"), and Three Dog Night ("Eli's Coming"). With her 1971 album *Gonna Take a Miracle*, Nyro became one of the first rock-era songwriters to release an album of cover material in tribute to past mentors. Tragically, Nyro died from ovarian cancer at the age of 49, just as new compilation and tribute albums were signalling revived interest in her artistry.

what to buy: *Stoned Soul Picnic: The Best of Laura Nyro* ♪♪♪♪ (Sony/Legacy, 1997, prod. various) offers a good point of entry into Nyro's considerable and diverse catalog. True to its name, the two-CD set is a well-stocked portfolio of her strongest and most eclectic material. Those wishing to dive deeply into Nyro's emotional netherlands should check out *The First Songs* ♪♪♪♪ (Columbia, 1973, prod. Milton Okun), Nyro's stellar debut that was recorded when she was all of 18. Featuring numerous songs that later became hits for other artists ("Wedding Bell Blues," "And When I Die," "Flim Flam Man," and "Stoney End"), the album spins out a continuous stream of first-class introspective music. Another bona fide classic. *New York Tendaberry* ♪♪♪♪ (Columbia, 1969, prod. Laura Nyro, Roy Halee) is the culmination of the style Nyro began developing on her debut, a dramatic *noir* journey through love and its loss. Supporting her expressive vocal work with piano and delicate instrumental accompaniment, Nyro explores a vast spectrum of human emotions with music that memorably touches the core of expression.

what to buy next: *Eli & the 13th Confession* ♪♪♪♪ (Sony, 1968, prod. Charlie Calello, Laura Nyro) is a mini-progression from *The First Songs*. Nyro is more soulful and more introspective, presenting a stellar collection of memorable songs that range from R&B ("Stoned Soul Picnic") to gospel ("Poverty Train") and powerful ballads ("Lonely Women"). Nyro changed the pace on her fourth album, *Gonna Take a Miracle* ♪♪♪♪ (Sony, 1971, prod. Kenny Gamble, Leon Huff), teaming with soul-funk group LaBelle for joyful and inspired readings of 1960s R&B hits such as "Jimmy Mack," "Spanish Harlem," and "Nowhere to Run."

what to avoid: Although Nyro's work can never be considered weak, *Mother's Spiritual* ♪♪ (Line, 1984, prod. Laura Nyro) is not among her best works. The urgent passion of her earlier music is replaced here by a cooler, more politically attuned sensibility that's respectable but not compelling.

the rest:
Smile ♪♪♪ (Sony, 1976)
Season of Lights ♪♪♪♪ (Columbia, 1977)
Live at the Bottom Line ♪♪♪ (Cypress, 1990)
Walk the Dog & Light the Light ♪♪♪ (Columbia, 1993)

worth searching for: Given Nyro's considerable influence on contemporary female artists, it only seems fitting that 14 of them (including Suzanne Vega, Rosanne Cash, Phoebe Snow, and Jonatha Brooke) should pay her tribute with *Time and Love: The Music of Laura Nyro* (Astor Place, 1997, prod. Peter Gallway). Recorded just prior to Nyro's death, the album reinterprets her best-known songs in rock, country, blues, and spoken-word arrangements. Few of the entries are as compelling as the originals, but anyone looking for fellowship in Nyro devotion should look no further than here.

influences:

◀◀ Joan Baez, Leonard Cohen, Bob Dylan, LaBelle, Carole King, Judy Collins, Joni Mitchell, Aretha Franklin

▶▶ Todd Rundgren, Barbra Streisand, Carole King, the Fifth Dimension, Blood, Sweat & Tears, Randy Newman, Rickie Lee Jones, Carly Simon, Chaka Khan, Des'ree, Alanis Morissette, Sarah McLachlan, Fiona Apple, Joan Osborne

Christopher Scapelliti

Oasis

Formed 1991, in Manchester, England.

Liam Gallagher, vocals; Noel Gallagher, guitar, vocals; Paul "Bonehead" Arthurs, guitar; Paul "Guigsy" McGuigan, bass; Tony McCarroll, drums (1991–94); Alan White, drums (1994–present).

Oasis set for itself the task of becoming the biggest band in the world. Sure enough, the group went on to release the fastest selling debut album in British history, score several international hits, and play three sold-out concerts at Knebworth during the span of two years. Direct and uncompromising, the Gallagher brothers not only made headlines for their cocky brand of rock 'n' roll, but their penchant for public scandals. The attention from the tabloids waned following the release of the group's difficult third album, but Oasis remains one of England's strongest musical assets.

what to buy: The gritty and melodic guitar pop of *(What's the Story?) Morning Glory* ♪♪♪♪ (Epic, 1995, prod. Owen Morris, Noel Gallagher) captures Oasis in full flight. Giving all the right

Noel Gallagher of Oasis (© Ken Settle)

nods to its influences, the band swaggers through a collection of songs built on familiar melodies with plenty of attitude and aggression.

what to buy next: Oasis' debut album, *Definitely Maybe* 🎵🎵🎵🎵 (Epic, 1994, prod. Oasis, Mark Coyle) started it all. It captures a rawer vibe with essential anthems like "Live Forever" and "Supersonic." The group's third disc, *Be Here Now* 🎵🎵🎵 (Epic, 1994, prod. Oasis, Owen Morris), didn't exactly expand the formula, but it still contains some melodic gems in "D' You Know What I Mean" and "Don't Go Away."

the rest:
Masterplan 🎵🎵🎵 (Epic, 1998)

worth searching for: Oasis has released enough non-album B-sides to fill out another two albums. There'll likely be a collection one day, but the bootleggers already thought of that. The cleverly titled *(That's the Story) behind the Story!* collects 16 of these tracks, including the TV performance of "Come Together" that features Liam Gallagher with Paul McCartney and Paul Weller.

influences:
◀◀ The Beatles, Stone Roses, Paul Weller

▶▶ Cast, Supergrass, Ocean Colour Scene

Aidin Vaziri

Oblivion Express
See: Brian Auger

Oblivious
See: Holly Vincent

Ric Ocasek
See: The Cars

Ocean Colour Scene
Formed 1989, in Manchester, England.

Simon Fowler, vocals, guitar; Steve Cradock, vocals, guitar, keyboards; Damon Minchella, bass; Oscar Harrison, drums, vocals.

Although virtually unknown in the United States, Ocean Colour Scene is riding atop the Britpop wave in its native England. With fans such as Paul Weller and Noel Gallagher of Oasis throwing props toward the band, it was obvious to see why OCS' major label debut, *Moseley Shoals*, was snatched up by thousands of young Brits who sent it to #2 its first week out. However, life wasn't all (Stone) rosey for the band. It took Ocean Colour Scene nearly six years, a split with Fontana Records (which released their poorly received eponymous debut album before dropping OCS in 1993), and years of hustling while unemployed and owing Fontana hundreds of thou-

sands of dollars to achieve top musical status in Britain. OCS' big break came during 1994, when Gallagher offered the band an opening slot on Oasis' first mega tour of the U.K. OCS, which was not signed to a label, joined Oasis on the road and received enough of a buzz to merit a bidding war. The band eventually joined forces with MCA U.K. in 1995.

what to buy: *Moseley Shoals* 🎵🎵🎵🎵 (MCA, 1997, prod. Ocean Colour Scene, Brendan Lynch) is an amalgamation of '60s psychedelic pop, folk, and early '90s British lad rock. Simon Fowler's powerful vocals combined with Steve Cradock's hyped-up, looping guitar licks have enough energy alone to keep this album spinning on a turntable. But the addition of Oscar Harrison's passion on the skins and Damon Minchella's funky, slapping bass lines round out *Moseley Shoals* on songs such as "Riverboat Song" and "You've Got It Bad." While the album is heavily influenced by the Beatles, Allman Brothers, and Stone Roses, it's original enough to merit high praise.

what to buy next: *Marchin' Already* 🎵🎵🎵 (MCA, 1998, prod. Brendan Lynch) more or less picks up where *Moseley Shoals* leaves off—but with a little less enthusiasm. It continues to showcase the band's move toward musical maturity and Fowler's dedication to strong vocals.

influences:
◀◀ The Beatles, the Allman Brothers Band, Stone Roses, the Jam, David Bowie

Ari Bendersky

Phil Ochs
Born December 19, 1940, in El Paso, TX. Died April 9, 1976, in Far Rockaway, NY.

More than two decades after his death, Phil Ochs remains an enigma. He loved John Wayne flicks, country music, and rock 'n' roll, but he became a folk singer. He went to military school but became a radical. He loved John F. Kennedy but despised the social order Kennedy represented. He wanted fame and fortune but chose a path that could never give it to him. As a college journalist at Ohio State University, Ochs began to write regularly. Soon a friendship with a folk-music enthusiast led him to learn to play guitar and write songs that were infused with his growing interest in left-wing politics. In 1962, with just months to go before graduation, he left school for New York's Greenwich Village. There, he set out to make his mark on the scene that was abuzz with a folk music boom. Ochs recorded a number of songs included on folk compilations before he was signed to Elektra Records in 1963. He recorded three albums dominated by protest songs for that label, all the while pulling for Bob Dylan to become a major rock star. Ochs even defended Dylan's stylistic jumps against attacks by outraged folk fans. Dylan insulted Ochs by calling him nothing but a journalist; but there are wells of emotion and insight in Ochs's music that belie Dylan's criticism. Ochs suffered from depression that may have been passed down genetically from his dad, and that probably factored into his inability to turn the corner toward greater popularity. Certainly, "There but for Fortune" and "Changes" showed he was capable of going there. When Ochs moved to A&M records during 1967, his lyrical direction was more poetic and his musical direction orchestral. Part of this was the flavor of the day, but Ochs had always done more than point fingers. For instance, he set Edgar Allan Poe's "The Bells" and Alfred Noyes's "The Highway Man" to music on his first two albums, and "There but for Fortune," with its empathy and neutral politics, also came from the protest days. He went through one other major stylistic change, trying to work a down-home, Elvis Presley approach in 1970. In theory, this finally would bring Ochs in touch with the real people that his protest songs had been about. In practice, it alienated his old folk audience and drew almost no one outside that small circle. It also ended his recording career. Ochs's version of "The Highway Man" may actually be one of the most telling in his catalog. Obviously, a tale of rebellious people should appeal to a protest singer. But more importantly, it's about a romantic who throws his life away in a burst of passion. In his last days, at the end of a five-year downward spiral, with a voice permanently damaged by a mugging in Africa, without a recording contract, and with no firm direction for his muse, Ochs must have felt defeated. Whether as an act of protest or passion, he hung himself on April 9, 1976.

what to buy: Sadly, most of the albums Ochs released in his lifetime are out of print. Of the "protest" albums available, *I Ain't Marching Anymore* ✍✍✍✍ (Elektra, 1965/Hannibal, 1995, prod. Jac Holzman) offers a glimpse of Ochs hitting his stride. And what a stride! Here is his greatest anthem, "I Ain't Marching Anymore," and his best lampoon, "Draft Dodger Rag." (Note that despite the pacifism of the former, he blasts the draft dodger's lack of moral rectitude in the latter.) The non-protest songs—"That Was the President," "The Highway Man," "Hills of West Virginia," and "The Men behind the Guns"—are finely sensitive, and Ochs's voice becomes unusually tender at times. There's nothing of politics when he sings of JFK, "a man so full of life, even death was caught off guard." *In Concert* ✍✍✍✍✍ (Elektra, 1966/Rhino, 1995, prod. Mark Abramson, Jac Holzman) was not a collection of favorites from the past but Ochs's then-most-recent pack of tunes. The set list was strong, starting out with the cocksure "I'm Going to Say It Now" and ending with the melancholy "When I'm Gone." In between those bookends are "There but for Fortune," "Changes," and "Love Me, I'm a Liberal." *Farewells & Fantasies* ✍✍✍✍✍ (Elektra Traditions/Rhino, 1997, compilation prod. Gary Stewart, Michael Ochs, Megan Lee Ochs), a three-CD set, gathers work from his entire major-label

career. Every stand-out tune is here (in fact, all of *In Concert* is here), as well as the long-out-of-print electric version of "I Ain't Marching Anymore" and some previously unissued cuts. More importantly, the set captures the arc of his career—the way his initial optimism and fire gave way to intimations of despair.

what to buy next: *All the News That's Fit to Sing* ✍✍✍ (Elektra, 1964/Hannibal, 1994, prod. Jac Holzman) finds Ochs just shy of the standard he soon would set for himself. Nonetheless it's a good album with evergreen songs such as "One More Parade," "The Bells," and "Bound for Glory" balancing out the more timely (and somewhat more disposable) songs such as "Talking Vietnam" and "Talking Cuban Crisis." *There but for Fortune* ✍✍✍✍ (Elektra, 1989, compilation prod. Michael Ochs) compiles Ochs's first three albums, but unless your budget is tight, it's superseded by *Farewells & Fantasies*. With some important exceptions, the same might be said of *The War Is Over: The Best of Phil Ochs* ✍✍✍✍ (A&M, 1988, prod. Jeffrey Gold, Geoffrey Schulman), which compiles songs from the A&M albums. It also includes two non-album rarities: "Kansas City Bomber," Ochs's rejected attempt to write a theme for the Raquel Welch movie, and a live version of "I Ain't Marching Anymore" from the 1968 Toronto Peace Festival. *A Toast to Those Who Are Gone* ✍✍✍✓ (Rhino, 1986, prod. Michael Ochs) allows listeners to peer into the head of the budding protest writer. It's a collection of demos circa 1964 that are almost as strong as the material he officially released on Elektra.

the rest:
The Broadside Tapes, Volume I ✍✍✍ (Smithsonian/Folkways, 1963)
There and Now: Live in Vancouver ✍✍✍✍ (Rhino, 1991)
Live at Newport ✍✍✍ (Vanguard, 1996)

worth searching for: *Pleasures of the Harbor* (A&M, 1967, prod. Larry Marks); *Tape from California* (A&M, 1968, prod. Larry Marks); and *Rehearsals for Retirement* (A&M, 1969, prod. Larry Marks) are all worth a search for the original vinyl. *Greatest Hits* (A&M, 1970/Edsel, 1993, prod. Van Dyke Parks), the album on which Ochs tried to channel a still-living Elvis, is available as an import CD. Another must is *Gunfight at Carnegie Hall* (A&M Canada, 1974, prod. Phil Ochs), a live album recorded during 1970 that's a startlingly frank chronicle of how his audience reacted to Ochs in gold lamé.

influences:
◄◄ Woody Guthrie, Bob Gibson, Elvis Presley
►► Billy Bragg, John Wesley Harding

Salvatore Caputo

Maura O'Connell

Born September 16, 1958, in Ennis, County Clare, Ireland.

Maura O'Connell is a quality example of the singer as free-wheeling interpreter, unfettered by any genre in particular. Her soulful eclecticism is only fitting in an Irish-born artist who scored her first big musical successes by recording pop albums in Nashville. After starting out singing in clubs for Galway college kids, O'Connell hooked up with the traditional group De Danann for two years. She split in 1983, trekked to Nashville on her manager's advice, and recorded three solo albums that became huge hits in her home country. O'Connell's signing to Warner Bros. sparked a string of meticulously produced albums distinguished by her warm, flexible mezzo and adventuresome song selections from John Hiatt, Tom Waits, and Shawn Colvin, mixed with second looks at standards by Tin Pan Alley and the Beatles. The efforts earned critical raves but modest U.S. sales. Her incandescent live performances have solidified her audience in the U.S., while her star status in Ireland remains assured. Still, Warner Bros. opted not to renew her contract in 1994, so O'Connell launched her own Permanent Records for her album *Stories*, which was released through Hannibal/Rykodisc in 1995.

what to buy: *Helpless Heart* 𝄞𝄞𝄞𝄞 (Warner Bros., 1989, prod. Bela Fleck) probably is the closest O'Connell has flirted with country, but Fleck's thoughtful arrangements deftly blend bluegrass and mountain influences with traditional Irish touches—and in "You'll Never Know," O'Connell demonstrates her authority with standards.

what to buy next: The smokier *A Real Life Story* 𝄞𝄞𝄞𝄞 (Warner Bros., 1991, prod. Greg Penny) continues O'Connell's great sense of song selection for grownups, with such meaty items as Hiatt's "When We Ran" and Hugh Prestwood's "A Family Tie"—a wrenching, ambivalent look at an alcoholic husband.

what to avoid: You won't get burned with any of O'Connell's stuff—it's all at least interesting—but you can skip some of the efforts, such as the folky, low-key *Just in Time* 𝄞𝄞𝄞 (Philo, 1988, prod. Bela Fleck) until after you've bought the Warner Bros. and Hannibal albums.

the rest:
(With De Danann) *The Star-Spangled Molly* 𝄞𝄞𝄞 (Shanachie, 1981)
Maura O'Connell 𝄞𝄞𝄞 (Third Floor Music, 1983)
Blue Is the Colour of Hope 𝄞𝄞𝄞𝄞 (Warner Bros., 1992)
Stories 𝄞𝄞𝄞𝄞 (Hannibal, 1995)
Wandering Home 𝄞𝄞𝄞 (Hannibal, 1997)

worth searching for: *A Woman's Heart* (Dara, 1992, prod. various) is a collection of work by Irish female singers that includes O'Connell's "Trouble in the Fields" and "Western Highway."

influences:
◄◄ Bonnie Raitt, Little Feat

►► Mary Black, Mary Coughlan, Delores O'Riordan (the Cranberries)

Elizabeth Lynch

Sinéad O'Connor
Born December 8, 1966, in Dublin, Ireland.

Despite the double-platinum success of 1990's *I Do Not Want What I Haven't Got*, Sinéad O'Connor remains one of rock 'n' roll's great unsung heroes. Her stubbly dome and piercing sapphire eyes made her an instant icon, but it was O'Connor's signature singing style—a kind of banshee bel canto, by turns redolent of Kate Bush, Siouxsie Sioux, and Sarah Vaughan—that spawned droves of imitators, female *and* male, during the alternative-rock '90s. Yet today O'Connor rarely receives the recognition that is her due, in large part because of the lingering effects of an unpopular public persona, of which verbal recklessness and dubious publicity stunts were the defining features (her infamous 1992 *Saturday Night Live* appearance, during which she ripped up a photograph of the Pope, being the most obvious example). Born into a conservative Irish Catholic family, O'Connor, the third of four children, was discovered at age 15 by Paul Byrne of the Irish group In Tua Nua. Her first big break came in 1986 when U2 guitarist the Edge enlisted her services for the *Captive* film soundtrack. Her full-length debut, *The Lion and the Cobra*, arrived one year later.

what to buy: The only debut album by a female rocker worthy of mention in the same breath as Patti Smith's *Horses* and PJ Harvey's *Dry*, O'Connor's *The Lion and the Cobra* 𝄞𝄞𝄞𝄞𝄞 (Ensign/Chrysalis, 1987, prod. Sinéad O'Connor) is less pretentious than the former and more influential than the latter. From the opening emotional odyssey of "Jackie" through the jagged-edged, synth-bathed ecstasy of "Jerusalem" to the concluding electric dreamscape of "Just Call Me Joe," *The Lion and the Cobra* delivers an arresting melange of art-rock intricacy, post-punk aggression, gorgeous pop melody, hard-thumping street beats, Celtic folk balladry, and, of course, O'Connor's force-of-nature voice. It spawned the minor hits "Mandinka," perhaps the single best showcase of O'Connor's startling vocal acrobatics, and "I Want Your (Hands on Me)," a brazen expression of post-Catholic carnal passion unlike anything else in her oeuvre.

what to buy next: Although it lacks the stylistic cohesion of its predecessor, *I Do Not Want What I Haven't Got* 𝄞𝄞𝄞𝄞 (Ensign/Chrysalis, 1990, prod. Sinéad O'Connor) is no less engrossing an album, not to mention an infinitely more personal one. In contrast to *The Lion and the Cobra*'s sometimes impenetrable lyrics, with their oblique allusions to classical mythology and biblical legend, *I Do Not Want What I Haven't Got* fairly overflows with unabashed autobiography. Indeed, so intrusively intimate and acutely painful are the details recounted in breakup songs such as "The Emperor's New Clothes" and "The Last Day of Our Acquaintance," one feels compelled to blush as a matter of course. Even her reading of Prince's "Nothing Compares 2 U" (a #1 smash co-produced by Nellee Hooper) gets fashioned into something so heart-wrenching as to be almost scandalous. The album—especially the haunting berceuse "Three Babies"—also marks the beginning of O'Connor's preoccupation with the theme of motherhood.

what to avoid: Vanity project or dilatory tactic? Either way, *Am I Not Your Girl?* ♫ (Ensign/Chrysalis, 1992, prod. Phil Ramone, Sinéad O'Connor) proves O'Connor the artist to be susceptible to the same lapses in judgment as O'Connor the celebrity. Featuring big-band cover versions of jazz and pop chestnuts such as "Bewitched, Bothered, and Bewildered" and "I Want to Be Loved by You," *Am I Not Your Girl?* neither provides insight into O'Connor's musical mind nor succeeds in establishing her as an important interpretive artist. Sure, it showcases how supple and powerful a vocal instrument she possesses. But that fact was made plain on O'Connor's first two albums—back when her soul, not her whim, catalyzed her larynx.

the rest:
Universal Mother ♫♫♫ (Ensign/Chrysalis EP, 1994)
Gospel Oak ♫♫♫ (Chrysalis/EMI, 1997)
So Far . . . The Best of Sinéad O'Connor ♫♫♫ (Chrysalis/EMI, 1997)

worth searching for: The CD single *Fire on Babylon* (Ensign/ Chrysalis, 1994) contains three otherwise unavailable cover versions: Bob Dylan's "I Believe in You," the Animals' "House of the Rising Sun," and Ralph McTell's "Streets of London."

influences:
◀◀ Kate Bush, Siouxsie & the Banshees, Sarah Vaughan, Peter Gabriel, Bob Dylan, Van Morrison, Clannad

▶▶ The Cranberries, Tori Amos, Sarah McLachlan, PJ Harvey, Björk, Ani DiFranco, Jeff Buckley

Greg Siegel

The Odds

Formed 1987, in Vancouver, British Columbia, Canada.

Craig Northey, vocals, guitars, keyboards; Doug Elliott, bass, vocals; Pat Steward, drums, percussion; Steven Drake, vocals, guitars, keyboards; Paul Brennan, drums (1987–95).

Like fellow Canadians the Pursuit of Happiness, the Odds specialize in tough-rocking, straight-ahead, '60s-influenced pop songs whose pleasant melodies belie the dark sense of humor in the lyrics. So naturally, the Odds, like TPOH, are merely cult favorites in the U.S., known mostly for a tongue-in-cheek novelty number that cracked college radio, 1993's riotous "Heterosexual Man." That's a shame, because the group has matured from wimpy Squeeze soundalikes into a ferocious torchbearer for Crowded House, layering on louder, fuzzier guitars but also giving co-lead singer Craig Northey more opportunities to showcase the creamy tenor that makes oddball lines like "Let

me lick the dew from the money tree" and "Yes means it's hard to say no to you" sound eerily romantic.

what to buy: *Bedbugs* ♫♫♫ (Zoo, 1993, prod. Jim Rondinelli) channels the group's sardonic humor, sexual innuendo, Beatlesque balladry, and developing alt-rock instincts into a surprisingly cohesive whole. Northey's gorgeous vocal on "Yes (Means It's Hard to Say No)," featuring Warren Zevon on piano, helps balance the raucousness of the Drake-sung "Heterosexual Man" and "The Little Death."

what to buy next: With *Nest* ♫♫♫ (Elektra, 1996, prod. Nigel the Cat), the Odds crank up the guitars and rock out convincingly on "Say You Mean It Wondergirl," "Someone Who's Cool," and the chugging "Make You Mad," bringing them another important step closer to honing their own sound out of their indelible influences.

what to avoid: The debut album, *Neopolitan* ♫♫ (Zoo, 1991, prod. Odds), is more derivative than daring, relying heavily on Squeeze-like harmonies and a clumsy sophomoric viewpoint that reaches its nadir with the unprintable chorus of "Wendy under the Stars."

the rest:
Good Weird Feeling ♫♫♫ (Elektra, 1995)

worth searching for: A faithful treatment of "We Three Kings" shows up on the various-artists holiday compilation *A Lump of Coal* (First Warning, 1991, prod. various).

influences:
◀◀ Squeeze, the Beatles

▶▶ The Pursuit of Happiness, Crowded House

David Okamoto

Off Broadway usa

Formed 1979, in Chicago, IL. Disbanded c. 1981. Re-formed 1995.

Cliff Johnson, vocals; John Ivan, guitar (1979–81); Rob Harding, guitar, vocals; John Pazdan, bass, vocals (1979–80); Ken Harck, drums, cymbals; Mike Gorman, bass, vocals (1980–81); Mimi Betinis, vocals, guitar, keyboards (1995–present).

With one ear tuned into the sound of mid-'60s AM radio and the other locked onto '70s AOR, Off Broadway usa is one of several airplay-friendly Midwest pop-rock groups to flirt with (fleeting) success during the late '70s and early '80s. Cliff Johnson and John Pazdan were original members of Pezband, another well-regarded Chicago pop act, but left that group before its first album; Mike Gorman, Pazdan's replacement in Off Broadway, had been with Pezband for each of its three albums. Off Broadway was the more commercially successful group, with its signature tune "Stay in Time" charting at #51 in *Bill-*

board. But this slight success was insufficient to keep things going, and Off Broadway's show closed after two albums. During 1995 Johnson, Harding, and Gorman formed a group called Black & Blonde with former Pezband frontman Mimi Betinis (initially with Randy Antlept on drums); Ken Harck subsequently returned to the drum seat, and the group reverted to the familiar Off Broadway usa moniker.

what to buy: *On* 🎵🎵🎵🎵 (Atlantic, 1979, prod. Tom Werman) kicks off with "Stay in Time," then bops its way through a winning selection of agreeable rockin' pop numbers. Cheap Trick fans should adore this, as should anyone who digs the sort of melodic rock 'n' roll your radio needs to function properly.

what to buy next: *Fallin' In* 🎵🎵🎵 (Pavement, 1997, prod. Doug McBride, Off Broadway usa) packs enough pop punch to set your giddy heart a-fluttering, but it occasionally succumbs to plodding heaviosity (and not even *total* heaviosity). Still, it's a welcome return, and a fairly encouraging sign of good things yet to come. *Live at Fitzgerald's* 🎵🎵🎵 (NMG, 1998, prod. Doug McBride) reinforces such optimism. Welcome back, guys.

worth searching for: The group's out-of-print second album, *Quick Turns* (Atlantic, 1980, prod. Kyle Lehning, Off Broadway usa), nearly matches the rush of the debut and is well worth a hunt through the bargain LP bin. The 7-inch vinyl EP *Pezband* (Not Lame, 1995, prod. Bruce Brodeen) is an essential historical document, presenting four previously unreleased demos that are the only known recordings of Cliff Johnson's tenure with that group. And speaking of that, where *are* all the Pezband album reissues?

influences:

◄◄ The Beatles, Cheap Trick, Pezband, the Raspberries, Artful Dodger

►► Enuff Z'nuff, Material Issue, Gigolo Aunts

Carl Cafarelli

The Offspring

Formed 1986, in Orange County, CA.

Brian "Dexter" Holland, vocals, guitar; Ron Welty, drums; Greg Kriesel, bass; Kevin "Noodles" Wasserman, guitar.

Toiling away in the punk rock underground for years, it took the Offspring nearly a decade to make its mark via a combination of edgy rock and catchy tunes. In 1994 success came with a vengeance, as the band's third album exploded onto the charts, selling more than four million copies. Though the band chose to hang with its independent label for years, in 1996 it announced a deal with Columbia Records—for an advance reported in the millions of dollars—citing conflicts with Epitaph owner Brett Gurewitz (a former guitarist with punk stalwarts

Bad Religion). But the subsequent record's lackluster material and backlash from punk fans helped bury the album quickly.

what to buy: The Offspring's appropriately titled *Smash* 🎵🎵🎵🎵 (Epitaph, 1994, prod. Thom Wilson) sold several million copies and succeeded mostly on the strength of tunes that weren't punk, including the Nirvana-influenced "Come out and Play" and the grungey-sounding teen anthem "Self Esteem."

what to avoid: Though produced by punk stalwart Thom Wilson (Dead Kennedys, the Vandals), *The Offspring* 🎵🎵 (Nemesis, 1989/Nitro-Epitaph, 1995, prod. Thom Wilson) doesn't offer much.

the rest:

Ignition 🎵🎵🎵 (Epitaph, 1993)
Ixnay on the Hombre 🎵🎵 (Sony, 1997)

worth searching for: The Offspring's punky, blistering take on the Damned's "Smash It Up" was a high point of the soundtrack for the 1995 film *Batman Forever*.

influences:

◄◄ Black Flag, the Damned, Nirvana

►► Bouncing Souls, Pennywise, NOFX

Eric Deggans

Mary Margaret O'Hara

Born in Toronto, Ontario, Canada.

The elusive Mary Margaret O'Hara's only full-length record, *Miss America*, was a critical fave, but following its release the singer all but disappeared from the scene, appearing occasionally to offer songs for a collection here and there, and singing backup on a few obscure titles. Which is no biggie in the general scheme: only the lucky among musicians don't suffer a similar fate. O'Hara's mystique, though, has as its foundation the wondrous, inspired *Miss America*, a record filled with such revelatory vocal acrobatics that it's no wonder her impact has been so immense.

what's available: On *Miss America* 🎵🎵🎵🎵 (Virgin, 1988/Koch International, 1996, prod. Mary Margaret O'Hara, Michael Brook), you can hear her lose herself inside the songs, all originals. At times she stutters and gasps as she attempts to spit out a phrase that's caught in her throat, pausing and breathing and building up steam until the force behind the words is too much for her to handle, and when the levy breaks the result is massive and perfectly timed; perhaps only Van Morrison has achieved a more breathless passion. At others, her voice runs smooth and thick through the flawless duration of a song. And while that voice is the centerpiece of the record, the clean restrained accompaniment is the perfect trampoline for her, providing just enough pizzazz for her to cut loose.

worth searching for: O'Hara's only other solo release was a limited edition Christmas album, *Christmas EP* (Virgin U.K., 1991/Koch International, 1996, prod. Mary Margaret O'Hara), on which she performs "Blue Christmas," "Silent Night," "What Are You Doing New Year's Eve," and an original, "Christmas Evermore."

influences:

◄◄ Van Morrison, Joni Mitchell, Tim Buckley, Cocteau Twins

►► Tanya Donelly, Kristin Hersh, Victoria Williams, Natalie Merchant

Randall Roberts

Patrick O'Hearn

See: Missing Persons

The Ohio Express /Ohio Ltd.

Formed 1966, in Mansfield, OH. Disbanded 1972.

Joey Levine, vocals; Doug Grassel, guitar; Dale Powers, guitar; Jim Pfayler, keyboards; Buddy Bengert, organ; Dean Kastran, bass; Tim Corwin, drums.

Create a vacuum and something must fill it, so goes the Law of the Universe. So as popular music started becoming somewhat grown-up and sophisticated circa *Sgt. Pepper's*, a definite hole appeared where once had thrived such happy-go-lucky popsters as Herman's Hermits and the Dave Clark Five. Realizing as much, the savvy production team of Jerry Kasenetz and Jeff Katz decided to fill this void with something they called bubblegum, and they soon enlisted singer Joey Levine to front not one but two groups for Buddah Records. While one, the 1910 Fruitgum Company, was basically a studio concoction, the Ohio Express had a life of their own prior to Kasenetz-Katz, already having recorded several garage-rock gems on the Cameo label ("Beg, Borrow, and Steal" actually charted at #29). But it was the terrifically gummy "Yummy Yummy Yummy" and its ultra-sticky follow-up, "Chewy Chewy," for which the Ohio Express will forever be remembered. It's perhaps interesting to note that Levine's voice sold more records during 1968 than Mick Jagger's did. Food for thought—just remember to spit out that gum first.

what's available: *The Ohio Express: Golden Classics* 𝄢𝄢𝄢 (Collectables, 1994, prod. various), besides providing roots for the 1970s power-pop movement with such two-minute wonders as "Mercy," could very well lead entire new generations to ponder the possible aural-sexual innuendoes within the "Yummy Yummy Yummy" lyrics.

influences:

◄◄ Tommy James & the Shondells, Lou Christie, Tommy Roe

►► The Archies, the Bay City Rollers, Mini-Pops

Gary Pig Gold

Oingo Boingo /Danny Elfman

Formed 1979, in Los Angeles, CA. Disbanded 1995.

Danny Elfman, vocals, guitar; Steve Bartek, guitar; Kerry Katch, bass (1979–83); Rich Gibbs, keyboards (1979–83); Johnny "Vatos" Hernandez, drums; Sam Phipps, tenor sax; Leon Schneiderman, baritone sax; Dale Turner, trumpet, trombone; John Avila, bass, vocals (1983–95).

Oingo Boingo started out during the late '70s as a new wave outfit, albeit one with a truly impressive horn section and a keen sense of humor. California crowds loved the band, but the rest of the country, except for a few college students, thought little of Oingo Boingo. Frontman Danny Elfman has captured critical acclaim for his side projects—soundtracks to films such as *Batman*, *Edward Scissorhands*, and *The Nightmare before Christmas*, as well as the theme to *The Simpsons* television show. After 16 years of trying to make its mark with little to show except a cult following and one semi-hit, "Dead Man's Party," the group decided to pack it in after its traditional 1995 Halloween blowout in Los Angeles.

what to buy: *Dead Man's Party* 𝄢𝄢𝄢𝄢 (MCA, 1985) is a solid example of how effective and creative this band can be when focused. The title song, a toe-tapping classic, created a small buzz when the band appeared in the Rodney Dangerfield movie, *Back to School*.

what to buy next: *Only a Lad* 𝄢𝄢𝄢 (A&M, 1981), Oingo Boingo's first full-length album, is raw, irreverent, and all the more charming for it.

what to avoid: *Boingo* **woof!** (Giant, 1994, prod. John Avila, Steve Bartek, Danny Elfman) is burdened by a shortened name, a shortened interest in the project, and a shortened list of worthwhile songs.

the rest:
Nothing to Fear 𝄢𝄢 (A&M, 1982)
Good for Your Soul 𝄢𝄢𝄢 (A&M, 1983)
BOI-NGO 𝄢𝄢 (MCA, 1987)
Boingo Alive: Celebration of a Decade 1979–1988 𝄢𝄢𝄢 (MCA, 1988)
Skeletons in the Closet: The Best of Oingo Boingo 𝄢𝄢𝄢 (A&M, 1988)
Dark at the End of the Tunnel 𝄢𝄢𝄢 (MCA, 1990)

Best o' Boingo 🎵🎵🎵 (A&M, 1991)
Farewell: Live from the Universal Amphitheatre, Halloween 1995 🎵🎵🎵 (A&M, 1996)

worth searching for: *Boingo Jr.* (MCA, 1988, prod. Danny Elfman, Steve Bartek, John Avila) is a promotional sampler from the *Boingo Alive* album, a good collector's piece and not a bad distillation of the album.

solo outings:
Danny Elfman:
So Lo 🎵🎵🎵 (MCA, 1984)
Music for a Darkened Theatre 🎵🎵🎵 (MCA, 1990)
Music for a Darkened Theatre: Film and Television Music—·Vol. 2 🎵🎵🎵 (MCA, 1996)

influences:

◀◀ Devo, XTC, Frank Zappa, Madness

▶▶ No Doubt, Mighty Mighty Bosstones, the Presidents of the United States of America

J. Christopher Newberg

Ol' Dirty Bastard
See: Wu-Tang Clan

Old 97's
Formed 1993, in Dallas, TX.

Rhett Miller, guitar, vocals; Philip Peeples, drums; Murry Hammond, vocals, bass; Ken Bethea, guitar.

Country at a time country is starting to be cool again, the Old 97's actually owe more to the cowpunk of hellraisers such as Jason & the Scorchers than to the back porch ruralism of No Depression stalwarts like Wilco and Son Volt. Even its country side takes more from the outlaw moves of Waylon Jennings (with whom the group recorded two songs) than the mournful laments of Hank Williams, and singer Rhett Miller dips into the nervous energy (and, sometimes, the sarcasm) of Elvis Costello as much as the high lonesome sound of Bill Monroe. Raised in Dallas, Miller met Murry Hammond and Ken Bethea in the town's music scene and began playing around town with them in early 1993. By the end of the year, they had chosen a name, added drummer Philip Peeples, and recorded a four-song cassette to sell at shows. The next year, the group gave its country sound a rough rock edge on *Hitchhike to Rhome*, then turned up the electric guitar even more on *Wreck Your Life*, released by Chicago country indie Bloodshot in 1995. After much touring, the band signed to Elektra, where it recorded the sharper but not-slickly smooth *Too Far to Care*.

what to buy: From the propulsive opening riff of "Time Bomb," *Too Far to Care* 🎵🎵🎵🎵 (Elektra, 1997, prod. Wally Gagel) is a blast

of barroom energy—frenetic, affecting, and delightfully lyrically acerbic. On *Wreck Your Life* 🎵🎵🎵🎵 (Bloodshot, 1995, prod. Chuck Uchida) the band's disparate influences come together in songs that convey country's poignancy at punk rock speed.

what to buy next: *Hitchhike to Rhome* 🎵🎵🎵 (Big Iron, 1994, prod. Alan Wooley) doesn't pack quite the punch of the band's later albums, but it's solid, down-home fun, and the band's revved-up cover of Merle Haggard's "Mama Tried" shows they have both the chops and the bad attitude to be a cowpunk contender. (Now sold only over the Web and at the group's concerts.)

worth searching for: A few months after forming, the Old 97's recorded a cassette-only four-song EP, *Old 97's* (self-released, 1993, prod. Ed Miller) that offers a revealing, if primitive, look at its folkie roots. Three of the four songs also appear on *Hitchhike to Rhome*.

influences:

◀◀ Johnny Cash, X, Jason & the Scorchers

▶▶ Whiskeytown

Robert Levine

Mike Oldfield
Born 1953, in Reading, England.

Legendary as he might seem, new age progenitor Mike Oldfield is still mainly known for his one shining moment—and that was 25 years ago. Some argue that Oldfield has spent the bulk of his career trying to alternately eschew and recreate the magic of *Tubular Bells*, going as far as to produce a sequel during the early '90s. He maintains, however, that his is a solid craft of visionary sonic landscapes somewhere on the cutting edge. And he should know—he outsells Michael Jackson in Spain! It is somewhat comedic, really: he is a European instrumental superstar and mythic space guru who has a comet named after him. It was 1968 when Oldfield began playing music with his sister, Sally. The duo released several recordings overseas and amassed minor acclaim. Oldfield had recorded *Tubular Bells* by the age of 19, thus boding well for the rest of his life. But not really; the inclusion of the piece as the theme for the hit film *The Exorcist* brought too much heavy scrutiny upon the young composer, leading him to try and quickly capitalize on the piece's meaning and money. He did so with moderate success on *Hergest Ridge* and the even better *Ommadawn*. The following years, even up to the present, have seen Oldfield riding the shifting tides of, first, punk backlash and later, new age malaise, in search of separate credibility. In truth, though, his offerings have been mired by their ambitious frames of art rock and ambience—more often soundtracks to films never lensed than actual complete works (except for his capable score for *The Killing Fields* soundtrack in 1985). Oldfield's forays into pop at the decade's turn were understandable, given the transitional state of the industry. His songs quickly descended in size and grandeur and became frequented by female vocaists such as Wendy Roberts and Maggie Reilly. Covers of Gershwin's "I Got Rhythm" and ABBA's "Arrival" saw Oldfield straddling schmaltz and innovation with his by then characteristic silliness. But the development of the synthesizer through the era found him seeking all new indulgent muses through the decade's end, trying to procure the most inorganic and universally resonant frippery that money could by. Currently donning a Celtic muse and re-claiming his half-Irish ancestry, Oldfield is still trying to balance trend with his particular clunky classicism. And doing so with little success.

what to buy: *Tubular Bells* 🎵🎵🎵 (Virgin, 1973, prod. Mike Oldfield) is just as awe-inspiring today as it was then, only now it seems more suited to the techno style it alluded to. Profoundly ahead of its time, this is really the only Oldfield album any collection requires.

what to buy next: *The Best of—Elements* 🎵🎵🎵 (Virgin, 1993, prod. various) abridges the overripe *Elements* box set into a standard-issue hits collection.

the rest:
Hergest Ridge 🎵🎵🎵 (Caroline, 1974)
Orchestral Tubular Bells 🎵 (Virgin, 1975)
Ommadawn 🎵🎵🎵 (Caroline, 1975)
Incantations 🎵🎵🎵 (Caroline, 1978)
Exposed 🎵🎵 (Caroline, 1979)
Platinum 🎵🎵🎵 (Caroline, 1979)
QE2 🎵🎵🎵 (Caroline, 1980)
Five Miles Out 🎵🎵 (Caroline, 1982)
Crises 🎵🎵 (Caroline, 1983)
Discovery 🎵🎵 (Caroline, 1984)
The Killing Fields 🎵🎵🎵🎵 (Caroline, 1984)
Islands 🎵🎵 (Virgin, 1987)
Earth Moving 🎵🎵 (Virgin, 1989)
Amarok 🎵🎵 (Caroline, 1990)
Heaven's Open 🎵🎵 (Caroline, 1991)
Elements 🎵🎵🎵 (Virgin, 1992)
Tubular Bells II 🎵🎵🎵 (Reprise, 1992)
The Sound of Distant Earth 🎵🎵 (Reprise, 1994)
Voyager 🎵🎵 (Reprise, 1996)

influences:
◀◀ Mozart, Yes

▶▶ Robert Miles, the Orb, Vangelis

Billy Manes

Will Oldham
See: Palace

Olive
Formed November 1995, in Buxton, England.

Tim Kellett, keyboards; Ruth-Ann Boyle, vocals; Robin Taylor-Firth, programming.

Formed by former Simply Red keyboardist Tim Kellett and programming whiz Robin Taylor-Firth, Olive found its missing ingredient in vocalist Ruth-Ann Boyle, whom Kellett heard when she appeared briefly on a Durutti Column demo. That minute stint was enough to convince him that Boyle was the voice he was looking for. Shortly after joining forces, the trio recorded a three-song demo that included a sparse arrangement of a track called "You're Not Alone," which sparked interest from several major labels in the band's native U.K. The finished version of "You're Not Alone" was an immediate international smash, going to #1 in England as well as in several other countries. The song's success was especially sweet for Kellett, as Olive marked the first group with which he served as the primary songwriter. After the single took off, the band appeared at several prestigious European festivals and toured internationally for several months.

what's available: Olive's debut, *Extra Virgin* 🎵🎵 (RCA, 1997), mixes the most basic elements of trip-hop with Britpop hooks. The sometimes bubbly 12 songs that make up the disc are driven by Kellett's engaging melodies, as he proves himself to be an adept songwriter during his initial turn in the spotlight. But the heart of songs such as the lovely "Falling" and the moving "Safer Hands" is the warmth Boyle's vocals conveys. *Extra Virgin* shows the group can go as far as Boyle will take them.

influences:
◀◀ Portishead, Squeeze, Massive Attack

see also: *Simply Red*

Steve Baltin

Olivia Tremor Control
Formed 1993, in Athens, GA.

Bill Doss, guitar, vocals; W. Cullen Hart, guitar, vocals; Eric Harris, drums; John Fernandes, bass; Peter Erchick (1996–present).

If the Beatles had stayed around long enough to absorb ambient music and indie rock, they might very well have made music like that of Olivia Tremor Control, an Athens, Georgia, band with ambitions of crafting pop like the Beach Boys and spacing out listeners like Brian Eno. Though its most effective material puts its mastery of the recording studio (even when there's only four tracks of it) to work layering psychedelic touches atop irresistible pop, the group has also dabbled in the ambient, the avant-garde, and, occasionally, the absolutely incomprehensible. Though Olivia Tremor Control drifted together gradually in Athens (beginning work on the first album in 1993), the group has its roots in Ruston, Louisiana. The group's songwriters and co-frontmen, Bill Doss and W. Cullen Hart, grew up there, along with Robert Schneider and Jeff Mangum, who would eventually form the Apples in Stereo and Neutral Milk Hotel, respectively. Recording at home and nearly taking over the local college's radio station, the four developed a similar aesthetic that brought together the formalistic experimentation of psychedelia with the DIY ethic of punk. As adults, they formed the Elephant 6 Recording Company, a psychedelic pop "music collective" that now also includes the Clay Bears, Elf Power, and several other groups with equally unlikely names. The groups also share a love for side projects: many appear on each other's albums, and the members of Olivia Tremor Control also make more experimental music as the Black Swan Network.

what to buy: On *Music from the Unrealized Film Script "Dusk at Cubist Castle"* ♪♪♪♪ (Flydaddy, 1996, prod. Robert Schneider), the band's disparate elements and influences come together, creating a masterpiece with both the way-out weirdness and wide-eyed innocence of the Summer of Love–era Beatles.

what to buy next: Initially packaged as a bonus disc with the first copies of *Cubist Castle*, *Explanation to: Instrumental Themes and Dream Sequences* ♪♪♪ (Flydaddy, 1996, prod. Robert Schneider) is a full album's worth of entertaining but hardly groundbreaking ambient music—the interludes in the band's imagined movie. The two 20-minute "pop suites" on the EP *Olivia Tremor Control vs. the Black Swan Network* ♪♪♪♪ (Flydaddy, 1997, prod. Black Swan Network) split the difference between ambient and pop with entertaining but not mind-blowing results. The pop-rooted songs on the vinyl-only EP *Giant Day* ♪♪♪♪ (Drug Racer, 1996, prod. Olivia Tremor Control) are more like *Cubist Castle*—ambitious but still instantly engaging.

worth searching for: Olivia Tremor Control's experimental alter ego, the Black Swan Network, asked fans to send recorded descriptions of their dreams; they layer them over ambient music on *The Late Music* (Camera Obscura, 1997, prod. Black Swan Network).

influences:
◀◀ The Beatles, the Beach Boys, Big Star

Robert Levine

Olympic Death Squad

See: Unrest

OMC

Formed 1995, in Auckland, New Zealand.

Pauly Fuemana, vocals, guitars, drums, bass; others.

OMC, essentially, is Pauly Fuemana, even though at least eight people accompany him on tour. Although best known for a worldwide smash single "How Bizarre," this group live has the ability to give any rave or late-night party a second wind with its funk-a-fied, Polynesian-influenced sound. OMC was born after the Otara Millionaires Club disbanded in 1995. The original group formed in a poor section of Auckland and adopted the name to show naysayers that these kids bred on the tough streets were smart enough to create a unique sound and survive. On the strength of "How Bizarre," OMC does have the unfortunate chance of being a one-hit wonder. However, with Fuemana's strong vision of musical success, OMC may just be around for awhile.

what's available: OMC's debut album, *How Bizarre* ♪♪♪ (Mercury, 1997, prod. Alan Jansson) combines Fuemana's roots of Polynesian flair with hip-hop, jazz, funk, and runaway rock. Although Fuemana is credited with playing the majority of the instruments on the album, he enlisted a host of musicians to contribute their expertise with the likes of pedal steel, violin, cello, piano, trumpet, accordion, French horn, Dobro, and sax.

influences:
◀◀ Marvin Gaye, Prince, Grandmaster Flash, David Bowie, New Order

Ari Bendersky

Omni Trio

Formed 1995, in England.

Rob Haigh; others.

Omni Trio, which is primarily the work of one Rob Haigh, blends various dance-based genres for reasonable home-listening. While certainly more for rug-cutting than quilt-sewing, Omni Trio is quite enjoyable if one is already fond of the jungle/drum-and-bass/ambient phenomena.

what's available: Numerous imports and compilation cuts exist, but stateside there are two records available. *Haunted Science* ♪♪♪ (Sm:)e, 1996, prod. Rob Haigh) is the better, being the more cohesive of the two. Still, containing two versions each of two songs, *Haunted Science* will likely be listened to in pieces rather than in one sitting. *Music for the Next Millennium* ♪♪♪ (Sm:)e, 1995, prod. Rob Haigh) is more of a collection of 12-inch techno/dance singles than a true album, which is fine since some of these tracks are hard to find elsewhere.

influences:
◀◀ Inner City, Juan Atkins, Moby, Aphex Twin

Barry M. Prickett

The Only Ones

Formed 1977, in London, England. Disbanded 1981.

Peter Perrett, vocals, guitar; Mike Kellie, drums; John Perry, guitar; Alan Mair, bass; Adam Maitland, keyboards, sax; Rabbit, keyboards.

It's quite unfortunate that every band out of England in the late '70s had to be tagged as "punk." This label was sadly bestowed upon the pop band the Only Ones who, like the Soft Boys, went tragically unnoticed. Led by the sardonic Peter Perrett, the Only Ones released three records in their short existence. However, these records paved the way for the fledgling pop bands to come. Neither as politically minded as the Clash nor as intense as the Buzzcocks, the Only Ones chose the route of helpless romantics. From the opening cut, "Another Girl, Another Planet," on the debut album *Special View*, the Only Ones cemented their legendary status in the history books of pop music. "Another Girl" never quite hit the masses at the time but has since become a modern rock staple and is constantly being covered by today's pop mainstays such as Paul Westerberg of the Replacements. In fact, after one listen to the Only Ones' debut, you can hear a blueprint for what would become the sound of the Replacements.

what's available: The Only Ones' first record, *Special View* 𝄞𝄞𝄞𝄞 (Epic, 1978, prod. Robert Ash), is a great pop rock record, sounding like an English version of Television, as Perrett's delivery is almost identical to that of Tom Verlaine. *Special View* contains the bulk of what has become the group's most influential songs, including "Another Girl, Another Planet" and "Out There in the Night." Sadly, this is the only domestic record available, and import records are hard to come by.

influences:

◀◀ The Who, the Kinks, the Zombies

▶▶ The Replacments, Alex Chilton, Robyn Hitchcock

Chris Richards

Yoko Ono

Born February 18, 1933, in Tokyo, Japan.

Much vilified and rarely understood, Yoko Ono was already established as an important artist in the Fluxus movement before she met John Lennon; in fact, they met at an exhibit of her work, which was largely conceptual and interactive. As a musician, her disregard for accepted rock practices, complete openness to experimentation, incorporation of the abstract vocal style of traditional Japanese theater, and awareness of avant-garde theories and examples such as John Cage's music made her ahead of her time. She also created books, films, and performance art. Sometimes during the '80s, when she flirted more seriously with mainstream pop, her unwillingness to mediate her sentiment resulted in sappy songs, but they were sometimes beautiful sappy songs—a surprise to those who had filed her away under "unlistenable noise." Granted, the only thing closed-minded rock fans might appreciate about the couple's first release, *Unfinished Music No. 1. Two Virgins*—filled as it is with lo-fi tape recordings of music (and musique concrete) more concerned with sounds than structure, much less harmony or melody—are the nude photos of Lennon and Ono, front and back. The title itself was significant; not only did they feel reborn emotionally, each was a virgin in the other's musical universe. In addition to the work issued under her own name—which sometimes included Lennon, most often on guitar—the couple issued several dually credited albums that were divided evenly between Lennon's music and Ono's. Here, discussion and ratings of the latter albums will only examine her contributions—a slight compensation for the long history of the opposite being the case. Now that Rykodisc has reissued all her albums in well-conceived CDs with plentiful bonus tracks, her legacy is finally available for the re-evaluation it so richly deserves.

what to buy: Far too little of *Fly* 𝄞𝄞𝄞𝄞 (Apple/Capitol, 1971/ Rykodisc, 1997, prod. Yoko Ono, John Lennon) made it onto the compilation *onobox*, and the tracks "Airmale" (10:40), "You" (9:00), and "Fly" (22:53) were shrunk down to a 2:32 medley. This double LP contains some of her most intense longform improvisation and should be heard in its entirety. *Season of Glass* 𝄞𝄞𝄞𝄞 (Geffen, 1981/Rykodisc, 1997, prod. Yoko Ono, Phil Spector) was partly a reaction to Lennon's soul-shattering death. The sheer existential terror of "No No No" and the bottomless despair of "I Don't Know Why" are balanced by the touching "Nobody Sees Me like You Do." This album and the single "Walking on Thin Ice" are her greatest achievements in pop-song form. Ono's first album whose billing didn't include Lennon, *Plastic Ono Band* 𝄞𝄞𝄞𝄞 (Apple/Capitol, 1970/Rykodisc, 1997, prod. John Lennon, Yoko Ono)—not to be confused with the Lennon album of the same title and similar cover design issued at the same time—is a must-own for "AOS," a rehearsal recording of Ono with free jazz legend Ornette Coleman's quartet. Hearing musicians used to totally unstructured improvisation respond to her in an organic rather than mechanical way is a revelation; her work is much more closely allied with their tradition than with the contexts she was usually heard in by rock fans; and in fact this is the sort of thing she was known for before she ever met Lennon.

what to buy next: *Rising* 𝄞𝄞𝄞𝄞 (Capitol, 1996, prod. Yoko Ono, Rob Stevens) is a triumphant return to her "outside" singing style, accompanied by her son (with John) Sean's band IMA. *onobox* 𝄞𝄞𝄞𝄞 (Rykodisc, 1992, prod. Yoko Ono) is a pricey six-CD set that, in design, must be the most beautiful box set ever produced. It contains brief liner notes by Ono for each volume and a booklet with oodles of photos, an extensive essay by

$\begin{smallmatrix} 8 \\ 3 \\ 8 \end{smallmatrix}$ *opal*

critic Robert Palmer and a complete discography. It covers her career from 1968 to 1992. The first two CDs contain some of Lennon's most adventurous, far-out guitar playing—and Eric Clapton's, too. Many listeners will find it a sufficient survey of the albums not yet mentioned, and it includes the entire contents of the LP version of *Feeling the Space* ���� (Apple/Capitol, 1973/Rykodisc, 1997, prod. Yoko Ono) and all of Yoko's songs on both *Double Fantasy* ���� (Geffen, 1980, prod. John Lennon, Yoko Ono, Jack Douglas) and *Milk and Honey* ���� (Polydor, 1984, prod. John Lennon, Yoko Ono).

what to avoid: *It's Alright (I See Rainbows)* � (Polydor, 1983/Rykodisc, 1997, prod. Yoko Ono) and *Starpeace* �� (Polydor, 1985/Rykodisc, 1997, prod. Bill Laswell, Yoko Ono) are studio hackwork and pop pabulum. Worst of all is the cast recording of her musical *New York Rock* **woof!** (Capitol, 1995, prod. Rob Stevens). Though it recycles many of her best songs, it makes them bland and devoid of musical interest, insipid and sentimental in the extreme, with the big, belting show voices and slick band totally inappropriate.

the rest:
(With John Lennon) *Unfinished Music No. 1. Two Virgins* �� (Apple, 1968/Rykodisc, 1997)
(With John Lennon) *Unfinished Music No. 2. Life with the Lions* �� (Zapple, 1969/Rykodisc, 1997)
(With John Lennon) *Wedding Album* �� (Apple/Capitol, 1969/Rykodisc, 1997)
(With John Lennon) *Live Peace in Toronto* ���� (Apple/Capitol, 1969)
(With John Lennon) *Some Time in New York City* ���� (Apple/Capitol, 1972)
Approximately Infinite Universe ���� (Apple/Capitol, 1973/Rykodisc, 1997)
Walking on Thin Ice ���� (Rykodisc, 1992)
(With IMA) *Rising Mixes Plus* ���� (Capitol, 1996)
A Story �� (Rykodisc, 1997)

worth searching for: With all the bonus tracks Rykodisc has added to Ono's albums, there are a lot fewer obscurities to track down than there were just a few years ago. But completists will want *Rock and Roll Circus* (Abkco, 1996, prod. Jimmy Miller, Jody Klein, Lenne Allik), with excerpts from the multi-artist concert the Rolling Stones put on in 1968. It includes "Whole Lotta Yoko," Ono singing wordlessly and avant-gardely over a grungey blues played by the Dirty Mac (Lennon and Clapton on guitars, Keith Richards on bass, Mitch Mitchell on drums) plus violinist Ivry Gitlis.

influences:
◄◄ John Cage, LaMonte Young, Albert Ayler, Cathy Berberian
►► Patty Waters, Diamanda Galas, Lene Lovich, Shonen Knife, B-52's, Nina Hagen, Death of Samantha, Cibo Matto

Steve Holtje

Opal

Formed 1984, in Los Angeles, CA. Disbanded c. 1989.

Kendra Smith, vocals, bass; David Roback, guitars, keyboards, vocals; Suki Ewars, keyboards, vocals; Keith Mitchell, drums.

Although Opal's key members are best known for their work in other bands, the group's small oeuvre is still quite precious and gemlike. There's not much flash and sparkle here, but Kendra Smith (hailing from Dream Syndicate) and David Roback (late of Rain Parade) produced music with a sly, beguiling glimmer that has managed to outshine a subsequent wave of drone-and-moan bands who shared the idea but not the inspiration. Certainly Opal took its cue from the somnambulant side of the Velvet Underground, but that's something of an oversimplification. Part country, part dreamland, the reigning aesthetic of Opal was a hazy, lazy, Sunday-morning sound that drifted into psychedelia at times, but mostly it clung to warm and organic melodies, stretched out long and languid. After Smith's departure, Roback carried on with Hope Sandoval, reshaping the group into Mazzy Star.

what to buy: *Happy Nightmare Baby* ����� (SST, 1987, prod. Dave Roback) is the band's essential work. Not much scariness here, despite the title. Instead, expect graceful, moody guitar-based songs that peek from clouds like a bright sun.

what to buy next: Opal's life was short, as band members wandered off to other projects, but the posthumously released *Early Recordings* ���� (Serpent/Rough Trade 1989, prod. various) ties together a pleasing assortment of odds and ends. The stripped-down production brings a gloomier edge to Opal's usually sweet aesthetic.

solo outings:
Kendra Smith:
Five Ways of Disappearing ����� (4AD, 1995)

influences:
◄◄ The Velvet Underground
►► Low, Bedhead, Cowboy Junkies

see also: *Mazzy Star, Rain Parade, Dream Syndicate*

Amy Weivoda

OP8

Formed 1997, in New Orleans, LA.

Lisa Germano, vocals, piano, guitar; Joey Burns, vocals, guitar, bass; John Convertino, percussion; Howe Gelb, vocals, guitar.

A one-off project between Lisa Germano and the group Giant Sand, OP8 combines the troubled-soul lyrical bent of the former with the minimalist approach and desert sensibility of the latter on an album that couples dry-land country & western with a drenched, drowsy tone that covers each song with weariness and regret.

what's available: "Here on earth, where the wind and rain prevail, it bends what you build and it rusts what you nail," Germano sings on "Cracklin' Water," one of the many fine tunes on the unrecognized masterpiece *Slush* 🎵🎵🎵🎵 (Thirsty Ear, 1997, prod. Howe Gelb). The album is an existential examination, a big-picture slap-in-the-face to the information age—one of those wake-up records that speaks clearly and lovingly about the pits and perils of the natural world that exists beyond the reach of cubicles and car alarms. Case in point: the bitter indictment "The Devil Loves L.A." *Slush* closes with a gorgeous, other-worldly version of Buffalo Springfield's "Round and Round."

influences:

⏮ Neil Young, Victoria Williams, Vic Chesnutt

see also: *Lisa Germano, Giant Sand*

Randall Roberts

Orange 9mm

Formed 1992, in New York, NY.

Chaka Malik, vocals; Chris Traynor, guitars (1992–96); David Gentile, bass (1992–95); Taylor McLam, bass (1995–96), guitar (1997–present); Chris Vitali, bass (1996–present); Matthew Cross, drums.

A product of the New York hardcore scene, Orange 9mm formed after Chaka Malik and Chris Traynor met during a show at Connecticut's Tune Inn club. The band released a live EP in 1993, earning a deal with EastWest records. Traynor left soon after the release of the group's second album, *Tragic*, to join Helmet.

what to buy: *Driver Not Included* 🎵🎵🎵 (EastWest, 1994/Atlantic, 1995, prod. Dave Jerden) is so muscular and aggressive you can almost feel Malik's sweat dripping on you, especially in the bass-heavy opening track "Glistening." The rap/rock collage "High Speed Changer" is an amplified note of encouragement on which Malik growls, "Do you want to watch yourself fly?/Do you want to cling to nothing?/Don't you want to take your chances?"

what to buy next: On the title track for *Tragic* 🎵🎵🎵 (Atlantic, 1996, prod. Dave Sardy), Malik, in front of heavy drums and a slew of guitars, hammers his chorus: "Do you wanna live/do you wanna die/Talk a lotta shit is like a suicide." "Gun to Your Head" is an exercise in contradictions with threats of death told to a slow groove. The only thing *Tragic* about Orange 9mm is that it was dropped from Atlantic.

influences:

⏮ Clutch, Quicksand, Helmet

Christina Fuoco

The Orb

Formed 1988, in London, England.

Dr. Alex Patterson (born Duncan Robert Alex Patterson), electronics; Jimmy Cauty, electronics (1988–90); Thrash (born Kristian Weston), electronics (1991–96); Thomas Fehlman, production, programming, engineering (1992–present); Andy Hughes, production, engineering (1993–present).

Using found sounds and samples, the Orb created (and coined the term) "ambient house"—or snippets of dialogue, loops, and general atmospherics combined with rhythm tracks to form an ethereal sonic collage. The band was essentially the brainchild of former roadie and record label guy Alex Patterson, who took charge after Jimmy Cauty left to record as Space and play with KLF. The other members came on board later. Occasionally joined on record by luminaries such as Jah Wobble (of Public Image Limited) and Steve Hillage (of Gong and System 7), the Orb is continually changing. Today, the band's live set is augmented by actual musicians, leaving Patterson to direct traffic. Not merely music for watching plants grow, nor mindless dance floor tripe, the Orb is always challenging and engaging.

what to buy: *U.F. Orb* 🎵🎵🎵🎵 (Island, 1992, prod. Orb, Steve Hillage, Youth), which contains the U.K. hit "Blue Room," is about as good as the electronica genre gets. Even without the standard verse-chorus-verse pop song structure, the album stays memorable—you can actually hum along a bit. Sounds swoop and soar, with little resemblance to common instruments.

what to buy next: *The Orb's Adventure beyond the Ultraworld* 🎵🎵🎵🎵 (Island 1991/1994, prod. Orb, others) is the band's first actual full-length release. Containing the very cool "Little Fluffy Clouds," with its goofy Rickie Lee Jones talking sample, *Adventure* is an interesting introduction to the Orb's never-static sound.

the rest:

The Aubrey Mixes 🎵🎵🎵 (Big Life, 1991)
Peel Sessions 🎵🎵🎵 (Strange Fruit, 1991)
Live '93 🎵🎵🎵🎵 (Island, 1992)
Pomme Fritz 🎵🎵🎵 (Island, 1994)
Orbus Terrarum 🎵🎵🎵 (Island, 1995)
Orblivion 🎵🎵🎵 (Island, 1997)
U.F. Off: The Best Of N/A (Island, 1998)

influences:

⏮ Brian Eno, Pink Floyd, Tangerine Dream, Robert Fripp, Bill Nelson, Kraftwerk

⏩ Future Sound of London, bt, Omni Trio, Ben Neill, Space-time Continuum, Crystal Method, Chemical Brothers, Keoki, LTK Bukem, DJ Shadow, Underworld

Barry M. Prickett

Roy Orbison

Born April 23, 1936, in Vernon, TX. Died December 6, 1988, in Hendersonville, TN.

Perhaps the greatest pure singer that rock 'n' roll has produced, Roy Orbison brought an unsurpassed sense of melodrama and angst to the music that has had a huge influence on other performers. A native of Texas, Orbison began singing country and rockabilly music but found that the styles weren't particularly suited to his tremendous tenor voice, which seemed to have no upper limit. Orbison recorded for Sun Records during the '50s and then RCA, but he didn't achieve fame until he signed with Monument in 1960 and began working with producer Fred Foster. Together they made records that were miniature pop operas—"Only the Lonely (Know How I Feel)," "Running Scared," "Crying," et al. He also recorded for MGM, Mercury, Elektra, and Virgin. Orbison's 1987 induction into the Rock and Roll Hall of Fame—as well as membership in the superstar group the Traveling Wilburys (with Bob Dylan, George Harrison, Tom Petty, and Jeff Lynne)—helped spark a career revival: he was finishing *Mystery Girl*, his first album of new material in a decade, when he died at his Tennessee home.

what to buy: Take your choice of three worthwhile anthologies. *The Legendary Roy Orbison* 🎵🎵🎵🎵🎵 (CBS Special Products, 1990, prod. various) is a three-disc box set that outshines all other Orbison collections, but *For the Lonely: A Roy Orbison Anthology, 1956–1964* 🎵🎵🎵🎵 (Rhino, 1988, prod. Fred Foster, Sam Phillips) or *The All-Time Greatest Hits of Roy Orbison* 🎵🎵🎵 (Monument, 1972, prod. Fred Foster) will do just fine as a starter set.

what to buy next: *Roy Orbison and Friends: A Black and White Night Live* 🎵🎵🎵 (Virgin, 1989, prod. T-Bone Burnett) is an excellent concert document recorded for an HBO film and featuring guest performances by Bruce Springsteen, k.d. lang, and others. A CD version, *Black & White Night* 🎵🎵🎵🎵 (Orbison, 1997), came out in 1997. *Mystery Girl* 🎵🎵🎵 (Virgin, 1989, prod. various) shows how other performers, such as U2's Bono and the Electric Light Orchestra's Jeff Lynne, viewed his music.

what to avoid: *The RCA Days* 🎵🎵 (RCA, 1988, prod. Chet Atkins) and *Little Richard/Roy Orbison* 🎵🎵 (RCA, 1990, prod. Chet Atkins) cull material from Orbison's time with RCA in Nashville, among the least successful recordings (artistically and commercially) of his career. And if you buy *In Dreams: The Greatest Hits* 🎵🎵🎵 (Virgin, 1987, prod. T-Bone Burnett), know what you're getting; these are re-recordings of Orbison's big songs, inspired by a new version of "In Dreams" for the film *Blue Velvet*. They're quite good as these things go, but they're not the originals.

the rest:
Laminar Flow 🎵🎵 (Elektra, 1979)

(With Johnny Cash, Carl Perkins, and Jerry Lee Lewis) *Class of '55* 🎵🎵🎵 (America/Smash, 1986)
Interviews from the Class of '55 Recording Sessions 🎵🎵 (America/Smash, 1986)
The Sun Years 🎵🎵🎵 (Rhino, 1989)
The Classic Roy Orbison (1965–1968) 🎵🎵🎵 (Rhino, 1989)
Rare Orbison 🎵🎵🎵 (Sony, 1989)
Best Loved Standards 🎵🎵🎵 (Sony, 1989)
Best of His Rare Classics 🎵🎵🎵 (Curb, 1991)
King of Hearts 🎵🎵🎵 (Virgin, 1992)
Crying 🎵🎵 (Collectors' Series, 1993)
In Dreams 🎵🎵🎵 (Collectors' Series, 1993)
Sings Lonely and Blue 🎵🎵🎵🎵 (Collectors' Series, 1993)
Shades Of 🎵🎵🎵 (Sony Music Special Products, 1995)
Super Hits 🎵🎵🎵 (Sony, 1995)
The Hits You Remember 🎵🎵🎵 (Sony Music Special Products, 1996)
The Very Best of Roy Orbison 🎵🎵🎵🎵 (Virgin, 1997)
Combo Concert 🎵🎵🎵 (Orbison, 1997)

worth searching for: *The Sun Story* (Rhino, 1987) is a sampler of Sun's glory days that prominently features early Orbison hits such as "Ooby Dooby" and "Devil Doll."

influences:

◀◀ Elvis Presley, Hank Williams

▶▶ Chris Isaak, Bruce Springsteen, the Mavericks

see also: *The Traveling Wilburys*

Brian Mansfield

Orbit

Formed 1994, in Boston, MA.

Jeff Lowe Robbins, vocals, guitar; Paul Buckley, drums, vocals; Wally Gagel, bass, vocals.

Three Boston-area musicians with a nose for melody and a taste for roaring guitars, Orbit joined together in 1994, rallying around material singer-guitarist Jeff Lowe Robbins had already demoed. Robbins, Paul Buckley, and Wally Gagel clicked instantly and decided to establish Lunch Records, in part to release their own music, but also to issue a string of split singles by Boston bands that shared the same DIY philosophy. In September of 1995 Orbit launched a debut EP on Lunch, *La Mano*, which spawned a video for the song "Come Inside." The track received airtime on MTV and played a significant role in the band signing on with a major label for their debut full-length, *Libido Speedway*.

what to buy: The group's major-label debut, *Libido Speedway* 🎵🎵🎵 (A&M, 1997, prod. Orbit, Ben Grosse) features a dynamic mix of high-energy alt-rock led by tracks such as "Bicycle Song," "Medicine," and the catchy "Paper Bag."

the rest:

La Mano ♫♫♪ (Lunch EP, 1995)

influences:

◀◀ Nirvana, Led Zeppelin, the Beatles

Bob Gulla

William Orbit
/Strange Cargo
/Torch Song

Born December 15, 1956, in London, England.

These days, British techno guru William Orbit is best known as the man who produced Madonna's *Ray of Light* CD. However, Madonna wanted to work with Orbit because he's been one of the most influential and innovative purveyors of techno music for the better part of this decade. Orbit has remixed tracks for everyone from Prince to Peter Gabriel, from Blur to Beth Orton, whom he helped "discover." In addition to his remixing duties, Orbit worked on the score of the Robert DeNiro/Al Pacino vehicle *Heat* at the personal request of director Michael Mann. Orbit also hosted a weekly radio show on L.A. college station KCRW-FM for a few months at the beginning of 1996. Searching through Orbit's discography is akin to scouring through the history of a John Coltrane, as there is so much material, other than his own, where Orbit's presence can be found—including a few titles he recorded under monikers such as Strange Cargo and Torch Song. At the same time, Orbit has had an ambivalent relationship with his potential stardom, and he was reclusive for a time before appearing at Madonna's side.

what to buy: All three of the Strange Cargo albums have their merits, but *Strange Cargo 3* ♫♫♫♫ (I.R.S., 1993, prod. William Orbit) is widely considered Orbit's classic thanks to the opening track, "Water from a Vine Leaf," which features a then-unknown Beth Orton on lead vocals. Orbit used five guest vocalists, including Orton Baby B., Divine Bashim, Cleo Torres, and longtime Orbit associate Laurie Mayer. Much to Orbit's credit, he maintains a continuity by weaving a moody, atmospheric array of sounds through the selections. The same can be said of *Hinterland* ♫♫♫♫ (Discovery, 1996, prod. William Orbit), which also bears the signature of his atmospheric ambiance.

what to buy next: Perhaps even more impressive is the consistency found in *The Best of Strange Cargo* ♫♫♪ (I.R.S., 1996, prod. William Orbit), a 16-song compilation culled from the three Strange Cargo CDs. This provides a good introduction to Orbit and features three previously unreleased mixes, including an Underworld remix of "Water from a Vine Leaf."

what to avoid: Even artists as innovative and consistent as Orbit can make mistakes. *Orbit* ♫♫ (I.R.S., 1987, prod. William Orbit) is Orbit's. Prior to finding his way as an electronica svengali, he released this clumsy CD that featured a variation of the Psychedelic Furs' "Love My Way" and a rare vocal turn by Orbit on "Cluny Ann."

the rest:

Strange Cargo ♫♫♫ (IRS, 1987)
Strange Cargo 2 ♫♫♪ (IRS, 1990)
(As Torch Song) *Toward the Unknown Region* ♫♫♫ (Discovery, 1996)

worth searching for: Of all the rarities Orbit has been involved in, *Superpinkymandy* is the most intriguing. A collaboration between Orbit and Orton, calling themselves Spill, this CD was only released in Japan and is extremely rare. Also worth seeking out for Orbit-philes is Bassomatic's *Set the Control for the Heart of the Bass* (Virgin, 1990), one of several "group" projects Orbit has been involved in.

influences:

◀◀ Brian Eno, Can

▶▶ Chemical Brothers, Goldie, DJ Shadow, Caroline Lavelle, Beth Orton

Steve Baltin

Orbital

Formed 1987, in Kent, England.

Paul Hartnoll, keyboards; Phil Hartnoll, keyboards.

Named after a dreaded stretch of motorway in their native England, Orbital made its grand entrance into the international electronic dance music arena with the debut single "Chime," recorded on home equipment in 1990. Built on minimal loops and a subtle (yet memorable) bass line, its music demonstrated the triumph and proficiency of the bedroom musician, in turn sparking the creativity of a wave of new, young British electronic upstarts with their own homegrown—and low-priced—creations. Orbital's willingness to incorporate any number of disparate musical sources as sampling fodder (anything from ABC to the Butthole Surfers, classical music to Crass), paired with the Hartnolls' unique musical sensibility in sound synthesis, has earned the duo a signature "Orbital sound." This recognizability has garnered praise and remix work for Madonna, Meat Beat Manifesto, Yellow Magic Orchestra and Queen Latifah, among others. Having routinely played the English festival circuit, Orbital was one of the few electronic acts invited to perform at Woodstock '94, and it headlined a portion of the 1997 edition of Lollapalooza. With four albums and numerous singles and EPs behind them, the Hartnoll brothers stand as seasoned veterans in techno's fleeting history.

what to buy: Orbital's first two albums are both called *Orbital;* they are therefore distinguished by their colors. The "green" debut, *Orbital* 𝄢𝄢𝄢𝄢 (ffrr/London, 1992, prod. Paul Hartnoll, Phil Hartnoll), contains the early rave anthems that won the band international repute ("Satan," "Chime," and "Midnight") plus Moby's remix of "Speed Freak." The "brown" *Orbital* 𝄢𝄢𝄢𝄢 (ffrr/London, 1993, prod. Paul Hartnoll, Phil Hartnoll) is a more varied and experimental affair, containing the club hits "Impact," "Halcyon + On + On + On" (a variation on an earlier, rare single), and the two-part opus "Lush."

what to buy next: *Diversions* 𝄢𝄢𝄢 (ffrr/London, 1994, prod. Paul Hartnoll, Phil Hartnoll) is an excellent opportunity for non-vinyl collecting enthusiasts to sample some of the "brown" *Orbital* remixes (previously available only on DJ-oriented 12-inch singles) alongside excerpts from the duo's John Peel Sessions and unreleased bonus tracks. *Snivilisation* 𝄢𝄢𝄢 (ffrr/London, 1994, prod. Paul Hartnoll, Phil Hartnoll) seems to be the album that splits most Orbital fans down the middle as the Hartnoll brothers take their most adventurous foray outside of their expected sound. While it may disappoint some upon initial listen, it takes a few plays to discover the diamonds, such as the piano-driven "Kein Trink Wasser" or the neo-jungle rhythms of "Are We Here?"

the rest:

In Sides 𝄢𝄢𝄢 (ffrr/London, 1996)

worth searching for: Orbital's rare singles and EPs contain some dazzling tracks unavailable elsewhere, many of which capture the true charm of the band. One of the best is *Midnight* (ffrr/London U.K., 1991, prod. Paul Hartnoll, Phil Hartnoll).

influences:

◄◄ The Archies, Kate Bush, Crass, Dead Kennedys, Kraftwerk, Tangerine Dream

►► Pressure of Speech, Drum Club

Tamara Palmer

Orchestral Manoeuvres in the Dark

Formed 1978, in Liverpool, England.

Paul David Humphreys, keyboards, percussion, vocals (1978–86); Andy McCluskey (born George Andrew McCluskey), bass, keyboards, vocals; Malcolm Holmes, drums (1980–86); Michael Douglas, keyboards; Dave Hughes, tape editing (1978–80); Martin Hansley Cooper, saxophone (1980–86).

Starting out as a slick synth-pop outfit, Orchestral Manoeuvres in the Dark was inventive and versatile enough to abandon its sparkling techno sound in favor of more natural instrumenta-tion and, eventually, progressive experimentation. Core members Paul David Humphreys and Andy McCluskey began performing together in school, creating their own four-track tapes and eventually adding drummer Malcolm Holmes. Throughout the group's early years, the presence of a live drummer helped to warm up OMD's techno sound and give the group some distinction among the many synthesizer-driven bands of the period. Other members came and left as the group progressed, first into soundscape experiments (*Architecture & Morality*) and later into rhythm-heavy dance music (*Junk Culture*) and mainstream pop (*Crush*). A mass exodus in 1986 left McCluskey alone to create a new incarnation of OMD. Most of the albums since that period have been tepid though not wholly unenjoy-able rehashings of his group's previous efforts.

what to buy: *The Best of OMD* 𝄢𝄢𝄢𝄢 (Virgin/A&M, 1988, prod. various) is a handy guide to the many stages and sounds of OMD's long and varied career. Featuring 14 A-sides, the album gleans the choice bits from the group's synth periods ("Enola Gay," "Messages"), dance tracks ("Tesla Girls," "Locomotion"), and mainstream romance-oriented singles ("If You Leave," "So in Love"). Start here and decide what you like before digging in too deeply.

what to buy next: *Architecture & Morality* 𝄢𝄢𝄢𝄢 (Virgin/Epic, 1981, prod. Mike Howlett) finds OMD pursuing techno-pop dance music but with an emphasis on natural sounds rather than electronic gimmickry. The standouts are "Souvenir" and a cover of Leonard Cohen's gem "Joan of Arc." *Junk Culture* 𝄢𝄢𝄢𝄢 (Virgin/A&M, 1984, prod. Brian Tench) hones the sound OMD began creating on *Architecture & Morality*, giving it a denser rhythm layer and stronger melodies.

what to avoid: *Dazzle Ships* 𝄢 (Virgin/Epic, 1983, prod. Rhett Davies) eschews songwriting for found-tape sampling and technological doodling. Despite some fine atmospherics, the album has little going for it, and only two tracks, "Genetic Engineering" and "Radio Waves," have any lasting appeal.

the rest:

Orchestral Manoeuvres in the Dark 𝄢𝄢𝄢 (Virgin, 1980)
Organisation 𝄢𝄢𝄢 (Virgin, 1980)
Crush 𝄢𝄢𝄢 (Virgin/A&M, 1985)
Sugar Tax 𝄢𝄢 (Virgin, 1991)
Liberator 𝄢𝄢 (Virgin, 1993)

worth searching for: Although widely panned in Britain, *The Pacific Age* (A&M, 1986) did quite well in the United States; surprisingly, it's no longer available on CD. OMD scored with the hits "(Forever) Live & Die" and "We Love You," but the most interesting nugget here is "Southern," featuring snippets of Martin Luther King Jr.'s speeches played over an instrumental bed.

influences:

◄◄ David Bowie, Roxy Music, Ultravox

►► Duran Duran, Human League, Talk Talk, ABC, A Flock of Seagulls, Gary Numan, Soft Cell, Spandau Ballet, Arcadia, the Buggles

Christopher Scapelliti

The Original Harmony Ridge Creek Dippers

See: The Jayhawks

Orion
/Jimmy Ellis

Born Jimmy Ellis, 1945, in Orrville, AL.

In a most unsettling case of life-imitating-art-imitating-the-King, author Gail Brewer-Giorgio received a phone call in 1978 from a man claiming to be the living, breathing embodiment of the hero of her just-published novel *Orion*, the story of the life and fake death of an internationally famous singing star. Sound vaguely familiar? Although the caller, whose real name was Jimmy Ellis, had been working the nether regions of the music business since 1964 (including, at one point, re-recording Elvis Presley's first-ever single), it wasn't until he'd assumed the identity of Brewer-Giorgio's mythical character that his career too, ironically, showed signs of life. Signed to (you guessed it, Elvis's first label) Sun in 1978, his voice was clandestinely over-dubbed onto a series of Jerry Lee Lewis, Carl Perkins, and Charlie Rich out-takes for the *Duets* and *Trio Plus* compilations, and an electronic duet with Lewis on "Save the Last Dance for Me" actually hit the Top 20 in 1979. That same year Orion appeared—dressed as a ghostly Elvis-like apparition, face masked, rising from a coffin—on his first "solo" LP, *Reborn*. And in one of *Cashbox* magazine's greatest-ever lapses of taste, he was voted one of the world's three most promising country male vocalists in 1980. Several more albums followed before Ellis, understandably beginning to tire of the whole farce, tore off his mask in 1983 and, just to make sure everyone was listening, released a song titled "I'm Trying Not to Sound like Elvis." Problem was, nobody *was* listening: by then, the already booming Cult of Elvis had many more colorful and outrageous characters to concern itself with, relegating Ellis once again into well-earned obscurity. In 1989, however, he reappeared on the tiny Aron label with the optimistically titled *New Beginnings* and, having apparently resigned himself to his fate, once again donned his mask, capes, and dry-ice machine en route to the Rock 'n' Roll Heaven circuit.

what's available: Surprisingly enough, not one of Orion's seven original (gold vinyl!) LPs are in print, though true con-noisseurs of musical necrophilia are directed towards the import-only compilation *Some Think He Might Be King Elvis* **woof!** (Bear Family, 1992, prod. various).

influences:

◄◄ Ryder Preston, Conrad Birdie

►► El Vez, Janice K., Kiss

Gary Pig Gold

Orion the Hunter

See: Boston

Jim O'Rourke

Born 1969, in Chicago, IL.

Since emerging in his teens as something of a new-music guitar prodigy, championed by such postmodern masters as Derek Bailey and Henry Kaiser, Jim O'Rourke has drifted in and out of the rock world, a disruptive figure revered for his innovations and insistent iconoclasm. In this regard, he recalls the impact that fellow Chicagoan Steve Albini had on underground music during the '80s, except that Albini confined himself to punk rock. O'Rourke operates on a much wider playing field; he has participated in the making of more than 200 records as an instrumentalist, songwriter, producer, and tape engineer. These range from esoteric avant-garde projects involving tape-splicing sound experiments and improvised music, to more song-driven efforts. He's worked with rock artists such as Sonic Youth, Tortoise, Chris Connelly, Edith Frost, Braniac, U.S. Maple, and Smog, and he had a hand in the recent comebacks by folk primitive John Fahey, Krautrock legends Faust, and minimalist master Tony Conrad. In addition, he has played an integral role in rock-oriented bands such as Gastr del Sol and the Red Krayola and dabbled in a kind of rock deconstruction experiment known as Brise Glace. What's startling is that none of O'Rourke's work sounds much alike; if there's a guiding impulse in his still-young but already prolific career, it's constant change.

what to buy: *Bad Timing* ♫♫♫♫ (Drag City, 1997, prod. Jim O'Rourke) is the place to begin exploring O'Rourke's far-flung world. It's by far his most pop-friendly work; reference points include the movie soundtrack arrangements of Jack Nietzche and the acoustic guitar playing of John Fahey. Its four long, shape-shifting instrumentals blend O'Rourke's finger-picking with electronic textures and orchestrations for horns and strings that abruptly, mischievously change mood.

what to buy next: *Tomorrow Knows Where You Live* ♫♫♫♫ (Victo, 1992, prod. Henry Kaiser, Jim O'Rourke) is a series of improvised guitar duets between the middle-aged lion (Kaiser) and the young cat snapping at his heels (O'Rourke). Though

Ozzy Osbourne (© Ken Settle)

the disc affirms O'Rourke's mastery as an electric guitarist, it's an indication of his almost perverse iconoclasm that he has seen fit to concentrate on other instruments and approaches ever since.

best of the rest:
Terminal Pharmacy ♫♫♫♪ (Tzadik, 1995)
Happy Days ♫♫♫♪ (Revenant, 1997)

worth searching for: *Dutch Harbor: Where the Sea Breaks Its Back* (Atavistic, 1997, prod. various) is a soundtrack for an independent film that features O'Rourke prominently, including a duet with Palace's Will Oldham.

solo outings:
Brise Glace:
When in Vanitas . . . ♫♫♫ (Skin Graft, 1994)

influences:
◀◀ Derek Bailey, Michael Nyman, Tony Conrad, John Fahey

▶▶ Sonic Youth, Sea & Cake, Tortoise, Smog

Greg Kot

Orquestra Was

See: Was (Not Was)

Benjamin Orr

See: The Cars

Joan Osborne

Born July 8, 1965, in Louisville, KY.

Joan Osborne was studying at New York University when she sat in one night at a local blues club. That led to her being encouraged to perform more often, and she began appearing at similar small clubs and finally put a band together. Her releasing a live album and an EP herself, combined with the buzz about her live show, eventually led to a deal with a subsidiary of Mercury. The New York City roots music circuit had already spawned the Holmes Brothers, Chris Whitley, Curtis Stigers, Blues Traveller, and the Spin Doctors, but the hit "One of Us" made Osborne a household name beyond any of them thanks to its four Grammy nominations. Ironically, it's the one tune on her major label debut, *Relish*, that was written entirely by someone else (Eric Bazilian of the Hooters), and it's atypical of her dark, soulful style. "I felt like that really innocent perspective is one that I didn't have in a lot of other songs that I was working with," Osborne said when it was first released, "but it really dovetailed nicely with a lot of the other themes that were going on." Rather than rushing to duplicate her success, Osborne spent the next few years recording gospel singer Bethenia Rouse and making guest appearances, such as

singing "Raglan Road" on Irish troupe the Chieftains' album *Tears of Stone*, and continuing to expand her musical knowledge. The follow-up to *Relish* was expected by the end of 1998 or early 1999.

what to buy: *Relish* ♫♫♫♫ (Blue Gorilla/Mercury, 1995, prod. Rick Chertoff) has plenty of other great songs besides "One of Us": the eerie "Pensacola," the forcefully soulful "Ladder," the spooky, surreal "Spider Web," the gorgeous "Lumina," Osborne's anguished love song "Crazy Baby," and a cover of Bob Dylan's "Man in the Long Black Coat." The musical sound is often a harder-edged modern variation on classic Muscle Shoals Southern soul, with the shimmering keyboards of Rob Hyman (another Hooters member) a vital component, while lyrically a twilight tone of personal apocalypse and uneasy spirituality dominates.

what to buy next: After Osborne hit it big, Mercury combined most of Osborne's two independent releases—*Soul Show* and the EP *Blue Million Miles* ♫♫♫ (Swimming Pool Blue, 1993)—on *Early Recordings* ♫♫♫♪ (Blue Gorilla/Mercury, 1996) so that new fans could hear them. Here's the proof that, despite *Relish*'s reliance on co-writers, Osborne can pen fine songs by herself. The cover of Captain Beefheart's "His Eyes Are a Blue Million Miles" (made gender-appropriate with a pronoun change) is also interesting.

worth searching for: Not all the tracks on Osborne's self-released debut, *Soul Show* (Womanly Hips, 1991), made it onto *Early Recordings*. *Soul Show* documents a Joan Osborne Band gig at the defunct blues club Delta 88, with the original version of *Relish*'s "Crazy Baby," a better version of Sonny Boy Williamson's "Help Me," and hot covers of "Son of a Preacher Man" (oozing sex from every pore) and "Lady Madonna."

influences:
◀◀ Mavis Staples, Al Green, Aretha Franklin, Etta James, Dusty Springfield, Otis Redding, Van Morrison, Joan Armatrading, Bonnie Raitt, Janis Joplin, Melissa Etheridge

▶▶ Alana Davis, Rebekah

Steve Holtje

Ozzy Osbourne

Born December 3, 1948, in Birmingham, England.

Ozzy Osbourne's descent into self-parody after leaving the seminal thundering of Black Sabbath for the solo path has been painful to witness. At the beginning, the classically influenced guitar work of Randy Rhoads fueled Osbourne to produce some inspired rock that equals Sabbath's in spots. Rhoads's untimely death in a 1982 plane crash derailed Osbourne's sense of purpose, and since then the revolving door of axemen (getting younger every year) has led him to rely on hambone antics, battles with the religious right, and the oldest ploy in the book—a retirement that's quickly rescinded—to court the spotlight. The Ozzman has shown signs of artistic life in the '90s, even getting together with his old Sabbath pals for gigs and a late 1998 live album. But the chances of the "Crazy Train" ever getting back on the rails again seem very slim.

what to buy: *Tribute* ♫♫♫♫ (Epic, 1987, prod. Max Norman) is a blazing double live set showcasing Rhoads's wicked virtuosity and the inspired performances it prodded from Osbourne. His debut, *Blizzard of Ozz* ♫♫♫♫ (Epic, 1981, prod. various), introduces Rhoads's disciplined attack, plus blowtorchers such as "Crazy Train" and the anti-alcohol lament, "Suicide Solution" which was wrongly accused of precipitating three suicides.

what to buy next: Despite the goofy cover, *Diary of a Madman* ♫♫♫♫ (Epic, 1981, prod. various) has signs of artistic growth with "You Can't Kill Rock 'n' Roll" and the rollicking "Flying High Again." *No More Tears* ♫♫♫♫ (Epic, 1991, prod. Duane Baron, John Purdell) finds Osbourne co-writing with Motörhead's Lemmy Kilmister; it's a promising return to form that contains one of his best ballads, "Mama, I'm Coming Home." Sabbath diehards might even thank the lord for *The Ozzman Cometh* ♫♫♫♫ (Epic, 1997, prod. various), a greatest hits collection that includes four unreleased Sabbath rehearsal recordings from 1970.

what to avoid: The faux horror on *No Rest for the Wicked* ♫ (Epic, 1989, prod Keith Olsen, Roy Thomas Baker) is nearly as depressing as hearing the former Sabbath frontman singing in front of airy keyboards on *Bark at the Moon* ♫ (CBS/Epic, 1983, prod various).

the rest:
Speak of the Devil ♫♫♫ (Jet/Epic, 1982)
Just Say Ozzy ♫♫ (Epic, 1990)
Live & Loud ♫♫ (Epic, 1992)
The Ultimate Sin ♫ (Epic 1995)
Ozzmosis ♫♫♫ (Epic, 1996)

worth searching for: Osbourne's duet with Miss Piggy on "Born to be Wild" from *Kermit Unpigged* (Jim Henson, 1994, prod. Robert Kraft, John Boylan) is an oddity even for Ozzy; he didn't even take a bite out of the pig.

influences:
◀◀ Black Sabbath, Alice Cooper, the Tubes
▶▶ Danzig, Wasp, White Zombie

see also: *Black Sabbath*

Allan Orski

The Osmonds /Donny Osmond

Formed 1957, in Ogden, UT.

Alan Osmond, vocals, guitar; Wayne Osmond, vocals, guitar, saxophone, banjo, bass, drums; Merrill Osmond, vocals, bass; Jay Osmond, drums; Donny Osmond, vocals, keyboards; Marie Osmond, vocals; Jimmy Osmond, vocals.

The Osmonds were discovered by Andy Williams while they played a gig at Knott's Berry Farm. Using their goody-goody appeal as a major selling point, they took only what they needed from rock 'n' roll, coated it with sugar, and gave the people—in this case the kids—what they wanted. During the '70s, Donny was the very picture of teen-idoldom, creating a hit-filled solo career, sometimes pairing with sister Marie, while the brother act languished. Through a good part of that decade, he—and especially they—maintained a soda-fountain wholesomeness, but the '80s found Donny grasping at stylistic straws for a hit, while the gone-country Osmonds were relegated to gigs in Branson, Missouri. Donny climbed back on top by starring in the revival of *Joseph and the Amazing Technicolor Dreamcoat* and poking gentle fun at his image, but his recording career remains largely in disarray.

what to buy: Look beyond those smiles, and the Osmonds had a number of golden-throated hits. They're all there on *21 Hits—Special Collection* ♫♫♫♫ (Curb, 1995, prod. various). Highlights include "One Bad Apple (Don't Spoil the Whole Bunch)," which doesn't fall too far from the Jackson 5's tree; the mushy "That's My Girl"; and the near-Spinal Tap hard rock of "Crazy Horses." The most famous of the brothers gets the same treatment on Donny Osmond's *25 Hits—Special Collection* ♫♫♫♫ (Curb, 1995, prod. various), which allows you to cuddle up to "Puppy Love," ponder the lyrically questionable "Why," and sigh along to "Go Away, Little Girl." If it's similar bites of sugar pop you require, this is the musical candy store the kid in you needs to visit.

what to buy next: Christmastime fits the Osmonds like a glove—or a stocking, and the Osmond Family's *Christmas* ♫♫♫ (Curb, 1991, prod. Don Costa) contains 12 yule classics (one to mark each of the 12 days of Christmas, one assumes), including "Silent Night," "White Christmas," and "Silver Bells."

what to avoid: Donny and Marie's *Greatest Hits* ♫♫ (Curb, 1993, prod. Mike Curb) shows that this pair was no Sonny & Cher. *The Best of Donny Osmond* ♫♫ (Curb, 1994, prod. Carl Sturken, Evan Rodgers) represents Donny's '80s phase, when he came on like George Michael for the Family Channel set. *Osmond Boys* ♫ (Curb, 1990, prod. various) and the Osmonds' *Second Generation* ♫ (Curb, 1992, prod. Nigel Wright) show the new breed of Osmonds trying to replicate the success of their fathers, lamely armed with synthesizers and a New Kids on the Block marketing ploy. Their pair of albums are two bad apples.

the rest:
The Osmonds:
Greatest Hits ♫♫♫ (Curb, 1992)

Donny Osmond:
Greatest Hits ♫♫♫ (Curb, 1993)
(With Marie Osmond) *The Best of Donny and Marie* ♫♫ (Capitol, 1993)

influences:
◀◀ Andy Williams, Paul Anka
▶▶ Hanson, Backstreet Boys

Jordan Oakes

Gilbert O'Sullivan

Born December 1, 1946 in Waterford, Ireland.

Had Gilbert O'Sullivan, a resident of Britain since age seven, only recorded only two songs—the stirring "Alone Again (Naturally)" and the jaunty "Clair"—he'd have earned his place in the dainty-pop hall of fame. He's a housewife-friendly substitute for Linda's husband, sort of a non-dairy creamer to McCartney's whole milk. Known in America mainly for the tearjerker "Alone Again (Naturally)," O'Sullivan never managed to sustain much of a career. Caught between one-hit-wonder status and cult-artist reverence, he's still recording, but his star faded long before the blue jeans of the '70s did.

what to buy: *The Best of Gilbert O'Sullivan* ♫♫♫♫ (Rhino, 1991, prod. Gordon Mills, Gilbert O'Sullivan) is absolutely all, and in fact more than, you need from this sappy Brit. All the hits (many struck gold only outside America) are here, including the gooey "Alone Again (Naturally)," "Clair," and "Get Down," along with chewy Badfinger-ish treats such as "I Don't Love You but I Think I Like You."

what to avoid: *In the Key of G* ♫♫ (Festival/Interfusion, 1990, prod. Gilbert O'Sullivan, Ken Gold, Chris Tsangarides, Gus Dudgeon) and *Singer Sowing Machine* ♫♫ (Park, 1998) are lame imports that indicate O'Sullivan's been alone so long that songwriting no longer comes naturally.

influences:
◀◀ The Beatles, Elton John
▶▶ Billy Joel, Ben Folds Five, Barry Manilow

Jordan Oakes

WHAT ALBUM CHANGED YOUR LIFE?

The first two Led Zeppelin albums really changed my life. They were basically a blues root, which is where I come from, but Jimmy Page is brilliant in the studio. I love stereo effects, panning, things like that. There was always a lot of that in the Zeppelin albums, done very well.

Ozzy Osbourne

Johnny Otis

Born John Veliotes, December 28, 1924, in Vallejo, CA.

Orchestra leader Johnny Otis contributed substantially to the development of R&B during the '40s and '50s—more than just his hit, "Willie & the Hand-Jive." His skills as a talent scout were unmatched; among his discoveries were Hank Ballard, Little Willie John, Etta James, and Jackie Wilson. Besides playing on sessions with jazz greats Charlie Parker, Lester Young, and Art Tatum, Otis produced and played drums on Big Mama Thornton's original recording of "Hound Dog" and played vibes on Johnny Ace's "Pledging My Love." Otis's band has featured the likes of Mel Walker, Jimmy Rushing, Bill Doggett, Big Jay McNeely, Little Esther Phillips, and the Robins (who would later become the Coasters). Otis's tenure at Capitol Records began in 1957, when he wrote and recorded his sole Top 10 pop hit, "Willie & the Hand-Jive," which was later featured in the 1959 teen-flick *Jukebox Rhythm* and covered by George Thorogood, Eric Clapton, and dozens of others. In 1994 Otis was voted into the Rock and Roll Hall of Fame as a "non-performer," which in light of all the music he's played seems ill-informed.

what to buy: *The Original Johnny Otis Show* ♫♫♫♫ (Savoy, 1995, prod. Ralph Bass) features the best of Otis and his orchestra backing Jimmy Rushing, Little Esther, and the Robins on "Harlem Nocturne," "Deceiving Blues," "Mambo Boogie," "Rockin' Blues," and others.

what to buy next: Otis's hit years at Capitol are well chronicled on *The Capitol Years* ♫♫♫♫ (Capitol/EMI, 1989, prod. Tom Morgan, Ben Vaughn), which contains 24 tracks, including "Willie & the Hand-Jive," "Crazy Country Hop," and "Castin' My Spell."

what to avoid: *Johnny Otis Presents . . .* ♪ (Laserlight, 1993, prod. Johnny Otis, Tom Morgan) features remakes of big hits cut over the years for Otis's Blues Spectrum label by Amos Milburn, Joe Turner, Joe Liggins, Charles Brown, and Louis Jordan. Although this five-disc set is cheap, it features none of the superior original material and is recommended for completists only.

the rest:
Live at Monterey ♪♪♪ (Epic, 1970/Legacy, 1970/1993)
The New Johnny Otis Show ♪♪♪ (Alligator, 1981)
Good Lovin' Blues ♪♪♪ (Ace, 1990)
Let's Live It Up ♪♪♪ (Charly, 1991)
Spirit of the Black Territory Bands ♪♪ (Arhoolie, 1992)
Live in Los Angeles 1970 ♪♪♪ (Wolf, 1994)
Otisology ♪♪♪ (Kent, 1994)
Too Late to Holler ♪♪♪ (Night Train, 1995)
Hand Jive '85 ♪♪ (Blues Legends, 1998)

worth searching for: From Otis's 1956 to 1975 era, *Creepin' with the Cats . . . Dig Masters, Vol.1* (Ace, 1993, prod. various) contains 22 tracks ("Ali Baba's Boogie," "Hey Hey Hey," etc.) and 10 previously unreleased cuts that are well worth having for serious fans.

influences:
◄◄ Count Basie, Louis Jordan
►► Shuggie Otis, Lucky Otis

Ken Burke

Our Lady Peace
Formed 1993, in Toronto, Ontario, Canada.

Raine Maida, vocals, guitar; Mike Turner, guitar; Jeremy Taggart, drums; Chris Eacrett, bass (1993–95); Duncan Coutts, bass, keyboards, cello (1995–present).

Prior to the 1993 recording of its major-label debut, *Naveed*, the members of Our Lady Peace had played only a handful of shows together; the band was signed to Sony Music Canada on the strength of a modestly recorded three-song demo. During the two-and-a-half years between their first and second albums, OLP kept busy opening for Bush, Elastica, the Ramones, Jimmy Page and Robert Plant, Sponge, Letters to Cleo, Van Halen, and even fellow Canadian Alanis Morissette. Propelled by the Eastern-inflected smash "Starseed," *Naveed* hit multiplatinum pay dirt in Canada. "Starseed" pricked up a few ears in America as well, cracking the Top 10 Modern Rock and Active Rock charts, but it wasn't until 1997's *Clumsy* that things really took off for OLP south of the Canadian border. That album, seven-times platinum in Canada, debuted at #1 on the Canadian SoundScan chart.

what to buy: Released in 1994 in Canada and a year later in the States, *Naveed* ♪♪♪♪ (Relativity, 1995, prod. Arnold Lanni) championed guitar-based alternative rock at a time when that genre's revolutionary spark was being snuffed out by every major label on a quest for the next Nirvana and by every upstart band with an axe to grunge. Nevertheless, *Naveed* is one of the finest rock albums to be released during the mid-'90s, and that's partly because Our Lady Peace never wanted to be Nirvana—it wanted to be U2. On tracks such as "Hope" and "Under Zenith," OLP and producer Arnold Lanni ply the virtues of atmosphere and texture to eerie effect. Elsewhere—"The Birdman," "Supersatellite," "Dirty Walls"—Turner's crunching riffs sharpen the band's attack without overwhelming Maida's spiritually inclined musings on life in the modern world.

what to buy next: Although the substantial radio play garnered by its leadoff single, "Superman's Dead," succeeded in raising Our Lady Peace's visibility in America, *Clumsy* ♪♪♪ (Columbia, 1997, prod. Arnold Lanni) pales in comparison to its predecessor. Where *Naveed* was positively rapturous, *Clumsy* is merely earnest. Moreover, the band could have benefited from a change in producers; Lanni injects into the mix a novel instrument or two, but for the most part *Clumsy* sounds as if it were *Naveed II*. Only Maida seems willing to step out, both as a lyricist (the confessional father-son drama of "4am") and as a vocalist (his wounded-animal falsetto in "Car Crash"). Maybe next time the rest of the band will step with him.

worth searching for: To promote the *Naveed* tour, Sony Music Canada issued *Live 1995*, a promo-only CD featuring live renditions of "Dirty Walls," "Hope," "Naveed," and "Denied."

influences:
◄◄ U2, Led Zeppelin, the Church, Soundgarden

Greg Siegel

The Outfield
Formed 1983, in London, England.

Tony Lewis, vocals, bass; John Spinks, guitar, keyboard, vocals; Alan Jackman, drums.

This smooth power trio achieved its goal—making hits—and managed to stick it out over four albums. Tony Lewis's high-pitched voice (which sounds a lot like the guys from Boston and Styx, only more new wave) and some great catchy tunes, including "For You," were perfect for the radio. Plus, the group's slick outfits and slightly shaggy demeanor fit MTV pretty well. In other words, confident—but you won't mistake it for the Velvet Underground.

what to buy: *Big Innings: Best of the Outfield* ♪♪♪ (Legacy, 1996, prod. various) is exactly what you need—the hits by a hit-oriented band; plus, at 16 songs, it's probably a little more than you might even want.

the rest:
Play Deep 𝄞𝄞𝄞 (Columbia, 1985)
Bangin' 𝄞𝄞𝄞 (Columbia, 1987)
Voices of Babylon 𝄞𝄞 (Columbia, 1989)
Diamond Days 𝄞𝄞𝄞 (MCA, 1990)
Rockeye 𝄞 (MCA, 1992)
Playing the Field 𝄞𝄞 (Columbia Special Products, 1993)

influences:
◀◀ Scorpions, the Alarm, U2, Boston, Styx

▶▶ Hootie & the Blowfish, Bush, Rembrandts

Tracey Birkenhauer and Steve Knopper

The Outlaws

Formed 1974, in Tampa, FL. Disbanded 1996.

Hughie Thomasson, guitar; Billy Jones (died 1995), guitar (1974–81); Henry Paul, rhythm guitar, vocals (1974–77, 1983–86); Monte Yoho, drums (1974–80); Frank O'Keefe (died 1995), bass (1974–77); Harvey Dalton Arnold, bass (1977–80); Freddy Salem, guitar (1978–79); David Dix, drums (1977–mid-'90s); Rick Cua, bass (1979–early '80s); Chris Hicks, guitar (1983–96); Jeff Howell, bass (1983–96); Barry "B.B." Borden, drums (mid-1990s–96); Timothy Cabe, guitar, vocals (c. 1993).

One of the last of the Southern boogie bands to get a record deal during the early '70s, the Outlaws often appeared to exist because Southern deejays could program only so much Lynyrd Skynyrd and Marshall Tucker. The group developed a good reputation for its live, three-guitar jams, which could go on for 20 minutes, but 1975's "There Goes Another Love Song" would be its only original Top 40 hit. Eventually the group became a stopping point for musicians who wanted Southern rock credentials, and some Outlaws alumni went on to respectable careers: Henry Paul formed the platinum-selling country band BlackHawk, bassist Rick Cua became a contemporary Christian artist, and Chris Hicks for a while played with the Marshall Tucker Band. Head Outlaw Hughie Thomasson now plays guitar with Lynyrd Skynyrd.

what to buy: Though many of its songs topped six minutes, the Outlaws was basically a singles band for Southern AOR radio, so *Best of the Outlaws . . . Green Grass & High Tides* 𝄞𝄞𝄞𝄞 (Arista, 1996, prod. various) adequately represents the band's output. With 16 tracks, *Green Grass & High Tides* captures the Outlaws' best stuff—"There Goes Another Love Song," the "Free Bird"–wannabe title track, and its rendition of "(Ghost) Riders in the Sky."

what to buy next: The Outlaws were a fairly consistent band, at least until relegated to the Southern-rock oldies circuit, so any album's as good as another. But the best is probably *Outlaws* 𝄞𝄞𝄞 (Arista, 1975, prod. Paul Rothchild), recorded when the group still seemed like it might develop into something more than just another boogie band.

what to avoid: *Hittin' the Road—Live!* 𝄞𝄞 (Blues Bureau, 1993, prod. Mickey Mulcahy, Hughie Thomasson) is retread Southern rock only for those needing a memento of their redneck youth.

the rest:
Lady in Waiting 𝄞𝄞𝄞 (Arista, 1976)
Hurry Sundown 𝄞𝄞𝄞 (Arista/Collector's Pipeline, 1977)
Playin' to Win 𝄞𝄞𝄞 (Arista, 1978)
Bring It Back Alive 𝄞𝄞𝄞 (Arista, 1978)
In the Eye of the Storm 𝄞𝄞 (Stodys, 1979)
Ghost Riders in the Sky 𝄞𝄞 (Arista/Collector's Pipeline, 1980)
Los Hombres Malo 𝄞𝄞 (Arista, 1982)
Soldiers of Fortune 𝄞𝄞 (Pasha, 1986)
Diablo Canyon 𝄞𝄞 (Blues Bureau, 1994)

solo outings:
BlackHawk (Henry Paul):
BlackHawk 𝄢𝄢𝄢 (Arista, 1994)
Strong Enough 𝄢𝄢𝄢 (Arista, 1995)
Love & Gravity 𝄢𝄢 (Arista, 1997)

Rick Cua:
The Way Love Is 𝄢𝄢 (Reunion, 1995)

influences:
◀◀ Poco, the Eagles, the Allman Brothers Band, Lynyrd Skynyrd

▶▶ Georgia Satellites, Screaming Trees

see also: *Lynyrd Skynyrd*

Brian Mansfield

The Outsiders

Formed 1965, in Cleveland, OH. Disbanded 1968.

Tom King, guitar; Sonny Geraci, vocals; Bill Bruno, lead guitar; Merdin Madsen, bass; Ricky Baker, drums.

Better than the average garage band from that era, the Outsiders were formed by Tom King with an eye on climbing the charts. Signed by Capitol in early 1966, the band sold more than 600,000 copies of its first single "Time Won't Let Me" by April. That summer, the Outsiders reached #1 again with "Girl in Love." With such quick success, the Outsiders seemed destined for more. They hit again with "Respectable," but then the capricious winds of pop blew them into obscurity. Lead singer Sonny Geraci later formed Climax, landing such hits as "Precious and Few" and "Life and Breath."

what's available: *Capitol Collector's Series: The Outsiders* 𝄢𝄢𝄢𝄢 (Capitol, 1991, compilation prod. Ron Furmanek) shows the band was more than a hit-making machine. Through four albums, one of which was a live recording, the Outsiders put together generally cohesive recordings that ran deeper than the singles. *The Best of the Outsiders (1965–1968)* 𝄢𝄢𝄢 (Rhino, 1986, prod. various) also offers a good selection, but it's not nearly as comprehensive as the Capitol set.

influences:
◀◀ The Beatles, the Dave Clark Five, the Kinks

▶▶ Climax, Journey, Ben Folds Five, Matchbox 20

Patrick McCarty

Buck Owens

Born Alvis Edgar Owens Jr., August 12, 1929, in Sherman, TX.

Current industry catch-phrases such as "twang-core" and "alternative country" could just as legitimately be applied in retrospect to the music and the attitude of Buck Owens & His Buckaroos. Owens remained defiantly based in Bakersfield, California, throughout his 40-year career and, even at the height of his mid-1960s successes, never failed to assail the powers-that-be in Nashville for their narrow-mindedness. Owens and his band developed, perfected, then took around the world their own highly characteristic honky-tonking, hard-country sound that to this day can be heard reverberating throughout "modern" C&W and rock. For years remembered, if at all, as little more than the goobering co-star of television's *Hee Haw* series, the innovative Owens and his band are finally being fully appreciated. After years spent playing various instruments in a variety of nondescript bands, Owens began doing recording sessions for Capitol Records in the early 1950s with his newly acquired Fender Telecaster guitar—a revolutionary instrument for its time, especially in the hands of an innovator like Owens. It was one such session, for singer Tommy Collins, that led to Owens's own contract with Capitol in 1957, an association that didn't really begin bearing fruit until several years later. By then, having assembled (with musical right-hand man Don Rich) his first crack outfit of Buckaroos, Owens was ready to fully capitalize upon the hits that soon started coming: 15 consecutive Country #1 songs between 1963 and 1967, not to mention hit duets with Rose Maddox (in the early 1960s), Susan Raye (early 1970s), and Emmylou Harris (in 1979). Under the supervision of producer Ken Nelson, Owens and Rich's lyrically simple, musically focused, and Telecaster-bright sound ensured that their records had sufficient punch on AM radio to take on all that the comparatively meek Music City releases had to offer. So pervasive was Owens's success in those years that Bakersfield was being called, grudgingly in some circles, Nashville West. Be it at Carnegie Hall, *The Ed Sullivan Show,* or the Fillmore West, the Buckaroos' "Freight Train Sound" rolled on unchallenged until 1974, when a tragic motorcycle accident claimed the life of Don Rich, a loss from which the band, and Owens personally, never fully recovered. Independently wealthy from his extensive business holdings, Owens made a few more half-hearted recordings for Warner Bros. in the mid-1970s and continued to ham it up with Roy Clark on *Hee Haw,* but he was clearly just going through the motions before eventually retiring in 1980. He was hardly heard from again for seven years, until Dwight Yoakam drew him back on stage, then into the studio for their 1988 hit duet "Streets of Bakersfield." Owens then triumphantly re-signed with Capitol, re-recorded some old hits (including "Act Naturally" with Ringo Starr), and to this day can be found performing regularly for fans both old and new at his prestigious Crystal Palace club, proudly continuing to play the role of the undisputed, all-encompassing "Baron of Bakersfield." Long may he reign.

what to buy: They don't come much better than *The Buck Owens Collection (1959–1990)* 𝄢𝄢𝄢𝄢 (Rhino, 1992, compilation prod. James Austin), which is not only 62 of the man's greatest recordings, meticulously compiled and annotated with the assistance of Owens himself, but it's also an absolute honky-tonk music primer. In a word: essential.

what to buy next: *The Instrumental Hits of Buck Owens & His Buckaroos* ₰₰₰₰ (Capitol, 1965/Sundazed, 1995, prod. Ken Nelson) puts the spotlight not only on the ingenious Don Rich (guitars, fiddle) but on the remainder of Buck's best-ever set of Buckaroos: Tom Brumley (steel guitar), Doyle Holly (bass), and Willie Cantu (drums). *Live at Carnegie Hall* ₰₰₰₰ (CMF, 1988, prod. Ken Nelson) is an expanded version of the original 1966 Capitol release that captured Bakersfield's Finest, in all their Nudie-suited glory, sockin' it to 'em and at 'em at the corner of 57th and 7th.

best of the rest:
Together Again/My Heart Skips a Beat ₰₰₰₰ (Capitol, 1964/Sundazed, 1995)
I've Got a Tiger by the Tail ₰₰₰ (Capitol, 1965/Sundazed, 1995)
Open up Your Heart ₰₰₰ (Capitol, 1966/Sundazed, 1995)
Buck Owens & His Buckaroos in Japan! ₰₰₰₰ (Capitol, 1976/Sundazed, 1997)

worth searching for: Owens's initial, pre-Buckaroo recordings for the tiny Pep and Chesterfield labels, including the searing rockabilly single "Hot Dog"/"Rhythm and Booze" from 1956 (released under the alias Corky Jones) are sporadically available on several semi-legitimate releases, the best of which is *You're for Me* (Creative Sounds, 1990).

influences:
◀◀ Bob Wills, Chuck Berry

▶▶ John Fogerty, Dwight Yoakam, Ghost Rockets, the Derailers

Gary Pig Gold

The Oyster Band

Formed 1981, in England.

John Jones, lead vocals, melodeon, accordion, piano; Ian "Chopper" Kearey, bass, cello, tiple, vocals; Ian Telfer, fiddle, viola, tenor concertina; Russell Lax (Lee), drums, percussion, hammer, vocals; Alan Prosser, guitar, banjo, mandolin, violin, vocals; Cathy LeSurf, vocals (1981); Chris Taylor (1981–84).

The Oyster Band is a one-of-a-kind punk band of master musicians leaning on Celtic and English dance traditions while rocking harder than most of the mainstream. Criminally underappreciated, the band explores the political and personal landscape with intensity and consistency, generating high-spirited power-folk led by the assertive vocals of Welchman John Jones and the incisive electric fiddle of Ian Telfer. The Oysters are frequently transcendent on disc, though no release has ever ap-

proached the band's incendiary live performance. The Oyster Band had its genesis in two bands, the Whitstable Oyster Co. Ceilidh Band (later the Oyster Celidh Band), which first took the stage in 1975, and Fiddler's Dram, founded in 1972 by violinist David Arbus, known for his work with East of Eden and the Who. Fiddler's Dram, then consisting of Alan Prosser, Telfer, Chris Taylor, and Cathy LeSurf, made the album *To See the Play*, notable for a posthumous hit novelty single, "Day Trip to Bangor" in 1979. The hit's success forced the band to make another album, where they were joined by Ian Kearey, among others. Meanwhile, much of Fiddler's Dram enjoyed a parallel existence in the Oyster Ceilidh Band, with LeSurf, Prosser, Kearey, Telfer, and Taylor joining Jones on the dance hall circuit. In 1981 the band dropped "Ceilidh" from its name, LeSurf departed, and the Oyster Band became essentially the unit that exists today. The Oysters have occasionally collaborated with English folk singer June Tabor.

what to buy: *Ride* ₰₰₰₰ (PolyGram, 1989, prod. Dave Young) comes closest to the glorious assault of their live show. Cuts range from the rollicking "New York Girls" to the pensive "This Year, Next Year," closing with the itchy fiddle cover of New Order's "Love Vigilantes." *The Shouting End of Life* ₰₰₰₰ (Cooking Vinyl, 1995, prod. Pat Collier) is led by the fiddle and guitar pyrotechnics of "Blood-Red Roses" and a pulsating reworking of Bruce Cockburn's "Lovers in a Dangerous Time." *Deserters* ₰₰₰₰ (Rykodisc, 1992, prod. John Ravenhall) is a hard-edged beauty that includes the reeling "All That Way for This" and the working class anthem "Fiddle or a Gun."

what to buy next: The band's one full-fledged experiment with June Tabor, *Freedom and Rain* ₰₰₰₰ (Rykodisc, 1990, prod. Oyster Band), is an atmospheric near-masterpiece that includes tunes by Shane MacGowan, Richard Thompson, and Billy Bragg.

what to avoid: Though a poor Oyster recording is not to be had, *Little Rock to Leipzig* ₰₰₰ (Rykodisc, 1991, prod. Oyster Band, Dave Young) is a less compelling collection of studio and live odds and ends best left to die-hard fans.

the rest:
Step Outside ₰₰₰ (Cooking Vinyl, 1986)
Wild Blue Yonder ₰₰₰ (Cooking Vinyl, 1987)
Holy Bandits ₰₰₰₰ (Rykodisc, 1993)
Trawler ₰₰₰ (Cooking Vinyl, 1994)
Deep Dark Ocean ₰₰₰ (Cooking Vinyl, 1997)

worth searching for: Several early Oyster recordings were released on the band's own Pukka label and are not readily available: *English Rock 'n' Roll—The Early Years 1800–1850*; *Lie Back and Think of England*; *20 Golden Tie Slackeners*; and *Liberty Hall*. The CD single "Cry Cry" (Rykodisc, 1994) from the

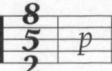

Holy Bandits album includes three previously unreleased tunes, including an astonishing "Star of the County Down."

influences:

◀◀ Fairport Convention, Pentangle, the Clash

▶▶ The Pogues, Spirit of the West

Martin Connors

P

See: Butthole Surfers

Richard Page

See: Mr. Mister

Page & Plant /Jimmy Page

Formed 1994, in London, England.

Jimmy Page (born January 9, 1944, in Heston, Middlesex, England), guitar; Robert Plant (born August 24, 1948, in Bromwich, Staffordshire, England), vocals.

After Led Zeppelin split in the wake of drummer John Bonham's death in 1980, the group's principal songwriters Jimmy Page and Robert Plant went their separate ways—Plant hitting the solo trail almost immediately while Page took a slower route into the Firm with former Bad Company singer Paul Rodgers and, finally, his own solo album, *Outrider*, in 1988. The duo's own relationship was marked by subtle sniping via the media—in-between one-off Led Zeppelin reunions. Things finally thawed in 1994, however, when Page and Plant (to the chagrin of Zep bassist John Paul Jones) re-grouped for an MTV concert project, dubbed *No Quarter*, that led to a seemingly permanent reunion for the two old road warriors.

what to buy: *No Quarter: Jimmy Page & Robert Plant UnLedded* ♫♫♫♫ (Atlantic, 1994, prod. Jimmy Page) finds the duo charting some new sonic territory—delving deeply in the world music realm—as well as rearranging some of Led Zeppelin's most challenging material. The set's highlight is a killer, orchestrated rendition of "Kashmir." *Walking into Clarksdale* ♫♫♫♫ (Atlantic, 1998, prod. Jimmy Page, Robert Plant, Steve Albini) is just as adventurous, albeit in a more straightforward rock direction. Here the duo retains the hard rock majesty that defined Led Zeppelin's appeal during the '70s.

what to buy next: Page's sole solo album, *Outrider* ♫♫♫ (Geffen, 1988, prod. Jimmy Page), is a player's album, with rich instrumentation and not many strong melodies–but that's not what you came for, is it? The album also features guest shots from Plant and Bonham's son Jason on drums.

what to avoid: Page's soundtrack for *Death Wish II* ♫ (Swan Song, 1982, prod. Jimmy Page) is strictly for fans of ambient guitar excursions.

the rest:

Jimmy Page:

(With David Coverdale) *Coverdale/Page* ♫♫ (Geffen, 1993)

worth searching for: The promotional piece *Jimmy Page & Robert Plant: A Songwriting Legacy* (Atlantic, 1995, prod. Jimmy Page) features songs from *No Quarter* and each of the Led Zeppelin albums.

influences:

◀◀ Willie Dixon, the Beatles, Chuck Berry, Fairport Convention, Buddy Guy, Howlin' Wolf, Robert Johnson, B.B. King, Little Richard, Joni Mitchell, Elvis Presley, the Rolling Stones, Otis Redding, Sonny Boy Williamson, Led Zeppelin

▶▶ AC/DC, Aerosmith, Bad Company, Black Sabbath, Bonham, Alice Cooper, the Cult, Great White, Guns N' Roses, Kingdom Come, Mötley Crüe, Rush, Soundgarden, Whitesnake, Van Halen

see also: *Led Zeppelin, Robert Plant*

Gary Graff and Sarah Weber

Pailhead

See: Ministry

Palace /Palace Songs /Palace Music /Palace Brothers

Formed 1992, in Louisville, KY.

Will Oldham, vocals, guitar; others.

The modern-day country-blues entity Palace is the creation of reticent but prolific singer-songwriter Will Oldham. Like many artists, Oldham has an eccentric side that keeps him on the fringe of things, but never out of the spotlight. Oldham also works under the names Palace Songs, Palace Music, and Palace Brothers (after the harmony-happy Everly Brothers). There is no record of a permanent "band" working with him. And because he has often refused interviews and put out records without credits, a complete list of collaborators may be impossible. But Slint, Pale Horse Riders, David Berman (Silver Jews), Liam Hayes (Plush),

David Grubbs (Gastr del Sol), and Brianna Corrigan (Beautiful South) are safe bets. Before he became a recording artist, Oldham had what appeared to be the beginnings of an acting career; at 16 he played a miner in John Sayles's 1987 movie *Matewan*. His brand of post-punk plays on country and folk, which has courted comparisons to Neil Young and Nick Cave. The album that marked the start of a serious career in music was 1993's *There Is No-One What Will Take Care of You,* which, despite the obscure nature of its barren hillbilly dirges—courtesy of Oldham's broken voice and acoustic guitar—still managed to get attention and favorable reviews. In 1995 came a shift in Palace sound; Steve Albini produced Palace Music's *Viva Last Blues*, and critics applauded the record for having a full and more polished sound while maintaining the enchanting roughness of Oldham's pervious work. It appeared on Oldham's newly established imprint Palace Records (still distributed by Drag City).

what to buy: *Viva Last Blues* ♫♫♫♪ (Drag City, 1995, prod. Steve Albini) is a good place to get to know Oldham because of its fuller sound and accessibility. *There Is No-One What Will Take Care of You* ♫♫♫♫ (Drag City, 1993, prod. Will Oldham) is the primitive-sounding debut that won Oldham an immediate following. He recorded the equally compelling *Joya* ♫♫♫♫ (Drag City, 1997, prod. Will Oldham) under his own name with Dave Pajo.

what to buy next: *Hope* ♫♫♫♪ (Drag City EP, 1994, prod. Will Oldham) and *Days in the Wake* ♫♫♫♪ (Drag City, 1994, prod. Will Oldham) are two equally appealing examples of Oldham's odd, brave melding of folk and country. *Arise Therefore* ♫♫♫♫ (Drag City, 1996) is an ingenious collaboration between Oldham and Grubbs that is not to be missed. *Lost Blues and Other Songs* ♫♫♫♪ (Drag City, 1997) offers B-sides and rarities from Palace Music.

worth searching for: Since 1993 Oldham has released a tall stack of seven-inch singles using various names. A few come highly recommended, especially "The Mountain"/"(End of) Travelling" (Drag City/Palace, 1995) and "For the Mekons et al."/"Stable Will" (Palace, 1996).

influences:

◀◀ Nick Cave, Bob Dylan, Woody Guthrie, the Everly Brothers, Neil Young

▶▶ Smog, Silver Jews

Norene Cashen

Pale Saints

Formed 1987, in Leeds, England.

Chris Cooper, drums, percussion; Ian Masters, guitar (1987–94); Graeme Naysmith, guitar; Meriel Barham, vocals, guitar (1990–present); Colleen Browne, bass (1994–present).

Pale Saints never achieved the recognition its sublime compositions deserved, even when the musical climate in England was dictated by like-minded ethereal bands such as Lush and the Boo Radleys. The addition of honey-voiced Meriel Barham helped divert the band from guitar virtuosity and toward succulent pop melodies on its masterpiece, 1992's *In Ribbons*. A partnership between 4AD and Warner Bros. even brought the album to America; unfortunately, it became a casualty in the flood of non-profitable dreampop bands clogging record company rosters. Founder Ian Masters departed shortly after that pivotal album ran its course and the group has pressed forth with less-than-thrilling results.

what to buy: Pale Saints' sophomore release, *In Ribbons* ♫♫♫♫ (4AD, 1992, prod. Hugh Jones), immaculately balances widescreen guitars and soft melodies. "Thread of Light" and "Shell" sound at once ghostly and alluring, cascading on vivid chord changes and exotic percussion, while the longing-filled "Hunted" draws tension from restrained feedback and ascending harmonies.

what to buy next: More jagged and gloomy than its follow-up, *Comforts of Madness* ♫♫♫ (4AD, 1990) is most notable for its psychedelic layers of guitar feedback. Restrained selections such as "Sea of Sound" and "Little Hammer" serve the group best.

the rest:
Slow Buildings ♫♫ (4AD/Warner Bros., 1994)

solo outings:
Spoonfed Hybrid (Masters):
Spoonfed Hybrid ♫♫♫♪ (Guernica, 1994)
Hibernation Shock ♫♫♫♪ (Farrago EP, 1997)

ESP Summer (Masters):
ESP Summer ♫♫♫♪ (Time Stereo, 1996)

influences:

◀◀ My Bloody Valentine, Cocteau Twins, Sonic Youth

▶▶ Slowdive, Seefeel, the Boo Radleys, Half String, Alison's Halo

Aidin Vaziri and Jack Rabid

Robert Palmer

Born Alan Palmer, January 19, 1949, in Bately, England.

Not to be confused with the late rock critic of the same name, Robert Palmer started off in a series of forgettable British groups before going solo during the mid-'70s. With a knack for picking the right cover tunes and an intriguing mix of rootsy, soul-tinged, Caribbean-influenced rock compositions (early albums featured members of the Meters and Toots & the Maytals), Palmer carved out a healthy niche as an eclectic, progressive pop artist. Still, it wasn't until his brief stint with supergroup the Power Station—which featured members of Duran Duran and Chic—that the singer became a bona fide pop star. Refusing to tour after the group's first record, Palmer snagged the Power Station's production team for his own work, rafting a metallized rock/soul sound that brought his biggest solo hits yet. But an unfortunate turn toward the Tin Pan Alley standards of his youth brought commercial disaster—a fate made worse by an ill-advised stab at reforming the Power Station that was hampered by the death of bassist/producer Bernard Edwards and killed by bad material.

what to buy: As one of the few Palmer albums that doesn't sabotage its great material with equally confusing and eclectic indulgences, *Secrets* &&&& (Island, 1979, prod. Robert Palmer) contains classics such as his rocking cover of Moon Martin's "Bad Case of Lovin' You (Doctor, Doctor)" along with a sensitive, soulful take on Todd Rundgren's "Can We Still Be Friends?" Almost as impressive is his solo debut, *Sneakin' Sally through the Alley* &&&& (Island, 1974, prod. Steve Smith). Featuring the Allen Toussaint–penned title cut backed by both Little Feat and the Meters, the record is about as close to New Orleans soul as any British guy will ever get.

what to buy next: For a consistently engaging taste of his '80s pop star incarnation, no album touches all the bases better than Palmer's breakthrough, *Riptide* &&&& (Island, 1986, prod. Bernard Edwards). With a well-crafted, edgy production style courtesy of Power Station–mate Edwards, and with songs ranging from the hormone-addled hit "Addicted to Love" to a synthesizer-laden remake of the blues tune "Trick Bag," Palmer turns in his most creative, confident album in years. To sample the best of his '70s and early '80s work, the hits collection *Addictions, Volume Two* &&&& (Island, 1992, prod. various) isolates highlights such as his inspired cover of the System's funky "You Are in My System" and the dreamy, reggae-tinged ballad "Every Kind of People."

what to avoid: As a tribute to the jazzy pop standards of the '40s, *Ridin' High* **woof!** (EMI, 1992, prod. Teo Macero, Robert Palmer) falls flat, mostly due to Palmer's emotionless, bionic delivery.

the rest:
Pressure Drop &&&& (Island, 1975)
Some People Can Do What They Like &&& (Island, 1976)
Double Fun &&& (Island, 1978)
Clues &&&& (Island, 1980)
Maybe It's Live &&& (Island, 1982)
Pride && (Island, 1983)
Heavy Nova && (EMI, 1988)
Addictions, Volume One &&& (Island, 1989)
Don't Explain **woof!** (EMI America, 1990)
True Romance & (Morgan Creek, 1993)

Honey &&& (EMI America, 1994)
The Very Best of Robert Palmer &&&& (Guardian, 1997)

worth searching for: *Simply Palmer* (EMI, 1988) is a promotional interview CD that has a smooth, suave James Bond quality.

influences:

◄◄ James Brown, Wilson Pickett, Tony Bennett, Mel Tormé, Billie Holiday, Nina Simone, Ronald Isley

►► Toto, Mr. Mister, Jai

see also: *Duran Duran*

Eric Deggans

The Pandoras

Formed 1983, in Los Angeles, CA. Disbanded 1991.

Paula Pierce (died 1991), vocals, guitar; Casey, drums (1983–84); Bambi Conway, bass, vocals (1983–84); Gwynne Kelly, organ, vocals (1983–84); Karen Blankfield, drums, vocals (1984–87); Julie Patchouli, bass, vocals (1984–85); Melanie Vammen, organ, vocals (1984–91); Kim Shattuck, bass, vocals (1985–91); Rita D'Albert, guitar, vocals (1988–91); Sheri Kaplan, drums, vocals (1988–91).

The Pandoras were the only all-female group to achieve any notoriety during the mid-'80s psychedelic/garage-punk revival, an insular scene dominated by male acts imitating the Sonics and the Chocolate Watch Band, desperately seeking to convince you that it was 1966 and this was the now sound. Although the Pandoras were notoriously willing to trade on its members' gender, the group was ultimately memorable because it delivered musically; at its best, the Pandoras were one of the few neo-garage groups to transcend novelty value and rock 'n' roll as convincingly and as engagingly as their *Nuggets/Pebbles*-enshrined heroes. The group ended when Paula Pierce passed away in 1991. Kim Shattuck went on to form the Muffs, initially with organist Melanie Vammen in tow.

what to buy: The first incarnation of the Pandoras recorded *It's about Time* &&&& (Voxx, 1984/Rhino, 1993, prod. Greg Shaw, Gary Stern, Bill Inglot), a growling, grungy slab of garage-bred rock 'n' roll with a belligerent pop sensibility. The expanded reissue adds non-LP tracks.

what to avoid: *Rock Hard* && (Restless, 1988, prod. Stevie Salas) proves that leering, single-entendre odes to sexual prowess and primal horniness are no more palatable when offered by, y'know, grrrls. The live album, *Live Nymphomania* **woof!** (Restless, 1989), is worse.

influences:

◄◄ The Sonics, the Standells, the Rolling Stones, Them, the Pretty Things, the Chocolate Watch Band, the Kinks

▶▶ Hole, 4 Non-Blondes, Babes in Toyland, Lunachicks

see also: *The Muffs*

Carl Cafarelli

influences:

◀◀ The Beatles, Green Day

▶▶ Extra Fancy, Team Dresch

Christina Fuoco

Pansy Division

Formed 1991, in San Francisco, CA.

Jon Ginoli, vocals, guitars; Chris Freeman, bass, vocals; Luis, drums (1996–present); Patrick Goodwin, guitar (1997–present); Dustin Donaldson, drums (1995–97); David Ayer, drums (1991–95).

Jon Ginoli grew up during the '70s, long before homosexuality was a subject anybody spoke about in public. A student of the '70s punk scene, he was called a "fag" because he listened to Blondie, the Clash, and X-Ray Specs. Before forming the openly gay punk band Pansy Division, Ginoli made three "sexually nonspecific albums" in Illinois. He relocated to San Francisco and met Freeman through an ad he placed in the *San Francisco Weekly* looking for "queer musicians into the Ramones, Buzzcocks, and early Beatles." Initially Pansy Division's songs, such as the bouyant "Bill and Ted's Homosexual Adventure" and the satirical "Smells like Queer Spirit," were greeted as novelties. But Pansy Division proved to be innovative and paved the way for other openly gay rock bands, gaining mainstream attention in 1994 when it was chosen as the opening act for Green Day's tour. On some dates, the San Francisco band was booed; on others it was cheered. Later, a DJ at a South Carolina college radio station was fired for playing a Pansy Division song, and the Christian Coalition shut down a show at California State–Fullerton. Later, Ginoli expanded Pansy Division to a quartet, adding the one-named guitarist Luis. One critic dubbed it the "Fag Fab Four."

what to buy: *Pile Up* 𝄢𝄢𝄢 (Lookout, 1995, prod. various), a collection of singles, compilation cuts, and rare tracks, is Pansy Division at its best. The song titles may create a smile— "Smells like Queer Spirit," "Touch My Joe Camel," "Cowboys Are Frequently Secretly Fond of Each Other," "Fem in a Black Leather Jacket," and "Pretty Boy (What's Your Name?)"—but there's nothing funny about the music. Pure punk-pop makes *Pile Up* a quick listen despite the sheer mass of its 20 tracks. The sexually graphic lyrics aren't for the faint of heart, however.

what to buy next: *Wish I'd Taken Pictures* 𝄢𝄢𝄢 (Lookout, 1996, prod. Pansy Division) is Pansy Division's most focused effort. Although tight and polished, the humor is still intact.

the rest:

Undressed 𝄢𝄢𝄢 (Lookout, 1993)
Deflowered 𝄢𝄢 (Lookout, 1994)
More Lovin' from Our Oven 𝄢𝄢𝄢 (Lookout, 1997)
Absurd Pop Song Romance N/A (Lookout, 1998)

Pantera

Formed 1982, in Arlington, TX.

Terrence Lee, vocals (1982–87); Philip Anselmo, vocals (1987–present); "Dimebag" (formerly "Diamond") Darrell Abbott, guitars; Vinnie Paul Abbott, drums; Rex "Rocker" Brown, bass.

Starting out as '80s glam rockers, Pantera hit big when it lost the glitter and found the tattoo parlor. With four independent releases behind it, the band collected an underground following encompassing the punk and metal crowds with the release of *Cowboys from Hell* in 1990. Pantera's full-on but melodic aural assault of power chords, slow grooves, and growling vocals turned the band into million-sellers, while its live performances show no mercy to the audience with a deafening onslaught of volume that acts as a soundtrack for frontman Phil Anselmo, who stalks the stage like an animal ready to pounce on its prey.

what to buy: *Vulgar Display of Power* 𝄢𝄢𝄢𝄢 (EastWest, 1992, prod. Terry Date, Vinnie Paul Abbott) is an impressive display of machine-gun power chords, crafty guitar work, and double-bass drum rhythms. The infectious, anthemic song "Walk" is the standout track.

what to buy next: *The Great Southern Trendkill* 𝄢𝄢𝄢 (EastWest, 1996, prod. Terry Date, Vinnie Paul Abbott) takes an even more brutal approach. Anselmo's furious vocals on the title track open the album as it continues through to the hypnotic groove of "Drag the Waters," the morose (in terms of Pantera) "10's," the somber "Suicide Note Pt. 1," and its inflammatory partner, "Suicide Note Pt. 2."

what to avoid: *Official Live—101 Proof* 𝄢𝄢 (EastWest, 1997, prod. Vinnie Paul Abbott, Dimebag Darrell Abbott) isn't the live album it should be, as it is missing the visceral power of Pantera's concerts.

the rest:

Cowboys from Hell 𝄢𝄢𝄢 (Atco, 1990)
Far beyond Driven 𝄢𝄢𝄢 (EastWest, 1994)

worth searching for: Although out of print—and a far cry from what Pantera sounds like now—the horrific glam-rock albums *Metal Magic* (Metal Magic, 1984, prod. Vinnie Paul Abbott), *Projects in the Jungle* (Metal Magic, prod. Vinnie Paul Abbott), *I Am the Night* (Metal Magic, prod. Vinnie Paul Abbott), and *Power Metal* (Metal Magic, 1988, prod. Vinnie Paul Abbott) are amusing to listen to just to see how far the band has come.

solo outings:

Phil Anselmo:

(With Down) *Nola* 🎵🎵🎵 (Elektra, 1995)

influences:

◀◀ Black Sabbath, Metallica, Suicidal Tendencies

▶▶ Clutch, Prong

Christina Fuoco

Papas Fritas

Formed 1993, in Somerville, MA.

Tony Goddess, guitar, vocals; Shivika Asthana, drums, vocals; Keith Gendel, bass, vocals.

The pun-wielding pop trio Papas Fritas (as in "pop has freed us" or fried potatoes—take your pick) has its roots in a Wilmington, Delaware, high school marching band. It was there that members Tony Goddess and Shivika Asthana discovered their mutual affection for sugar-coated songcraft. After high school, the pair enrolled at Tufts University and discovered still another soulmate in Texan Keith Gendel. Like many a fledgling group, Papas Fritas began a two-year odyssey of basement gigs and homemade recordings. Validation came in the person of indie label owner Matt Hanks (Sunday Driver Records), for whom the group cut a three-song seven-inch single during early 1993. After "Smash This World" received airplay on several college radio stations, Chicago's Minty Fresh Records became the second indie label to take a shine to the Papas, signing the group to a contract later that spring. Papas Fritas released its self-titled debut in 1995; *Helioself*, the hotly anticipated follow-up, bowed in 1997.

what to buy: From the Beatles to the Archies, *Helioself* 🎵🎵🎵🎵 (Minty Fresh, 1997, prod. Papas Fritas) catalogs a whole crateful of airy pop influences to create an organic, indie-pop masterpiece.

the rest:

Papas Fritas 🎵🎵🎵 (Minty Fresh, 1995)

worth searching for: The one-week old band recorded and distributed a Casio-riddled cassette called *Retards/Cowboys* (self-released, 1992) that's so rare that drummer Asthanas doesn't even own a copy. A year later, the Fritas self-released another cassette, the only slightly more available *Careers for Culture Lovers* (self-released, 1993), which the trio sold at its early shows.

influences:

◀◀ The Archies, the Raspberries, the Beatles, Brian Wilson, the Pooh Sticks

Scott Hess

Park Central Squares

See: The Skeletons

Graham Parker /Graham Parker & the Rumor

Born 1950, in East London, England. The Rumor formed 1977; disbanded 1981.

The Rumor: Graham Parker, guitar, harmonica, vocals; Brinsley Schwarz, guitar; Martin Belmont, guitar; Bob Andrews, keyboards; Andrew Bodnar, bass; Stephen Goulding, drums.

Although he seldom gets the credit for it, Graham Parker blazed the trail for punk rock. With his acerbic lyrics, caustic vocals, and angry-young-man stance, Parker bridged the gap between raucous pub rock and punk, creating a prototype for the likes of fellow Brits Joe Jackson and Elvis Costello. At a time when British music had been polarized into Fairport Convention neofolkies and artsy glam acts such as Roxy Music and Sweet, Parker reminded everyone that rock 'n' roll was always, first and foremost, a personal thing. Against a high-octane blend of R&B, soul, and Dylanesque cynicism, Parker churned out memorable attacks against former lovers, hipster poseurs, and record company suits. Little has changed in Parker's music over the years; although his recent songs tend toward more mature themes of marriage and family, his passion, as always, comes through loud and strong.

what to buy: *Passion Is No Ordinary Word: The Graham Parker Anthology, 1976–1991* 🎵🎵🎵🎵 (Rhino, 1993, prod. various) is a terrific introduction to Parker's lengthy career. In addition to pulling the critical cuts from Parker's stronger albums, the compilation culls gems such as "Temporary Beauty," "Life Gets Better," and "Little Miss Understanding" from otherwise mediocre albums and adds the previously unavailable single "Mercury Poisoning."

what to buy next: The touchstone for every British singer-songwriter to come, *Howlin' Wind* 🎵🎵🎵🎵 (PolyGram, 1976, prod. Nick Lowe) demonstrates a breathtaking range of styles and emotions. Parker shows equal parts venom and sensitivity throughout on the finger-snapping R&B number "White Honey," the vitriolic "Back to Schooldays," and the haunting "Don't Ask Me Questions." *The Mona Lisa's Sister* 🎵🎵🎵🎵 (RCA, 1988, prod. Graham Parker, Brinsley Schwarz) shows Parker older, wiser, and in peak form. Backed by Schwarz and former members of Rockpile, Parker delivers a smooth collection of masterful R&B ("Under the Mask of Happiness"), soul ("The Girl Isn't Ready"), and folk ("Blue Highways").

what to avoid: Anxious to get out of his contract with Mercury, Parker released *The Parkerilla* 🎵🎵 (Mercury, 1978, prod. Robert John "Mutt" Lange), three sides of live material plus a second studio version of "Don't Ask Me Questions." Despite strong performances, there's nothing here that isn't better covered on the studio releases.

the rest:
Stick to Me 🎵🎵 (PolyGram, 1977)
Squeezing out Sparks 🎵🎵🎵🎵 (Arista, 1979/1996)
The up Escalator 🎵🎵 (Arista/Razor & Tie, 1980)
Another Grey Area 🎵🎵🎵 (Arista/Razor & Tie, 1982)
The Real Macaw 🎵🎵 (Arista/Razor & Tie, 1983)
Steady Nerves 🎵🎵🎵 (Elektra, 1985)
Live! Alone in America 🎵🎵🎵 (RCA, 1989)
Human Soul 🎵🎵 (RCA, 1989)
Pumpin' It Out 🎵🎵🎵 (Phonogram, 1990)
Struck by Lightning 🎵🎵🎵 (RCA, 1991)
The Best of Graham Parker & the Rumor 🎵🎵🎵 (Vertigo, 1992)
The Best of Graham Parker 1988–1991 🎵🎵🎵🎵 (RCA, 1992)
Burning Questions 🎵🎵 (Demon, 1992)
Live Alone! Discovering Japan 🎵🎵🎵 (Demon, 1993)
Live on the Test 🎵🎵🎵 (Windsong, 1994)
12 Haunted Episodes 🎵🎵🎵 (Razor & Tie, 1995)
Acid Bubblegum 🎵🎵🎵 (Razor & Tie, 1996)
Live from New York 🎵🎵🎵🎵 (Razor & Tie, 1996)
Not If It Pleases Me N/A (Hux, 1998)

worth searching for: *Energetic* (Kisses Deluxe, prod. Ron Wolfe) is a live bootleg emanating from Parker's 1979 gig at San Francisco's Old Waldorf. Recorded by Arista when Parker and the Rumor were sonically at their toughest and leanest, about half the tracks here were also released on the promotion-only LP *Live Sparks* (Arista, 1979, prod. Ron Wolfe), which subsequently surfaced as tracks for the 1996 reissue of *Squeezing out Sparks*. Cuts such as "Passion Is No Ordinary Word," "Protection," and "I Want You Back (Alive)" are worthy reminders that, in concert, Parker and the Rumor were a force to be reckoned with.

influences:
◀◀ Sam Cooke, Dion, Bob Dylan, Van Morrison, Motown, Bruce Springsteen

▶▶ Rockpile, Dave Edmunds, Brinsley Schwarz, Nick Lowe, Elvis Costello, Joe Jackson, the Jam, Tom Petty, the Pretenders, John Hiatt, Billy Bragg, John Wesley Harding, Frank Black

Christopher Scapelliti

Van Dyke Parks
Born January 3, 1943, Hattiesburg, MS.

There are artists who are in it for the money, and then there's Van Dyke Parks. Throughout his career Parks continues to use his own very personal and eclectic musical vision as a guide for al-

bums that often feel like soundtracks to movies that were never made. And that cinematic/Tin Pan Alley approach was developed at an early age. Parks began his professional music career in a very commercial fashion, working on Walt Disney soundtracks in 1963. Since then he has been a writer, producer, arranger, and collaborator with a wide variety of artists such as Lowell George and Little Feat, Harper's Bizarre, Bonnie Raitt, Randy Newman, and Ry Cooder. But he remains most closely associated with Brian Wilson through his contributions to the legendary and never released Beach Boys album *Smile*. Beginning with his critically acclaimed debut release, *Song Cycle* in 1967, through his recent live release in 1998, Parks has created a body of work that is challenging, unique, and—to steal a word from the title of his 1994 compilation—"idiosyncratic." Based on your point of view, you'll find his music exhilarating or exasperating.

what to buy: *Orange Crate Art* 🎵🎵🎵🎵 (Warner Bros., 1995, prod. Van Dyke Parks) is Parks's most accessible work, created and performed in tandem with Brian Wilson. It combines rich yet deceptively simple melodies with lyrics that portray a nostalgic and vivid expression of life in California.

what to buy next: *Moonlighting—Live at the Ash Grove* 🎵🎵🎵 (Warner Bros., 1998, prod. Van Dyke Parks) is a well-produced live album that suffers only from Wilson's absence on the songs included from *Orange Crate Art*.

what to avoid: *Tokyo Rose* 🎵🎵 (Warner Bros., 1989, prod. Van Dyke Parks) was a big hit in Japan (seriously), but it is probably his least accessible album.

the rest:
Song Cycle 🎵🎵🎵 (Warner Bros., 1967)
Discover America 🎵🎵🎵 (Warner Bros., 1972)
Clang of the Yankee Reaper 🎵🎵🎵 (Warner Bros., 1975)
Jump! 🎵🎵🎵 (Warner Bros., 1984)

worth searching for: The British import *Idiosyncratic Path: The Best of Van Dyke Parks* (Demon, 1994, prod. Van Dyke Parks) is a worthy career retrospective and a good place to find out if you want to dig deeper into Parks's catalog.

influences:
◀◀ Bertolt Brecht, Sammy Cahn, Leiber & Stoller, Cole Porter

▶▶ Randy Newman, Paul McCartney, Elvis Costello

Michael Isabella

Parliament /Parliament-Funkadelic
See: George Clinton

Parlor James
See: Amy Allison

Alan Parsons
/Alan Parsons Project

Born 1949, in England.

As one of the engineers on the Beatles' *Abbey Road* album and Pink Floyd's *The Dark Side of the Moon*, Alan Parsons ranks as studio rat supreme. So it was little surprise when, in 1975, he decided to make his own musical expression a studio-based venture. Operated with colleague Eric Woolfson, the Alan Parsons Project became a sonic pop lab, with musicians and singers constantly changing as the two engineers toiled to create the perfect sonic experience. It made for great headphone music—in the '70s that went a long way. But as mass tastes veered away from such sterile endeavors, the Parsons Project's commercial fortunes declined—and so did the quality of the product, degenerating into new agey fluff. By the time Parsons finally decided to take his project on the road during the early '90s, it was well beyond the point where it mattered.

what to buy: *I Robot* 𝄞𝄞𝄞𝄞 (Arista, 1977, prod. Alan Parsons) is the penultimate Parsons Project album. In hindsight it's a little thin on songs, though the hit single "I Wouldn't Want to Be like You," "Some Other Time," and "Breakdown" made for a strong early album set. But put the headphones on while you're listening, and you'll understand why it worked.

what to buy next: *The Definitive Collection* 𝄞𝄞𝄞 (Arista, 1997, prod. Alan Parsons) is a fine, two-CD anthology that winnows Parsons's oeuvre into an all-you-could-want (and maybe even a little more) set. Of the individual efforts, *Tales of Mystery and Imagination—Edgar Allan Poe* 𝄞𝄞𝄞 (20th Century, 1976/Arista, 1987, prod. Alan Parsons) and *The Turn of a Friendly Card* 𝄞𝄞𝄞 (Arista, 1980, prod. Alan Parsons) are the most thematically cohesive.

what to avoid: *Try Anything Once* **woof!** (Arista, 1993, prod. Alan Parsons) has neither thematic unity nor good individual songs to carry it.

the rest:
Pyramid 𝄞𝄞 (Arista, 1978)
Eve 𝄞𝄞𝄞 (Arista, 1979)
Eye in the Sky 𝄞𝄞 (Arista, 1982)
The Best of the Alan Parsons Project 𝄞𝄞𝄞𝄞 (Arista, 1983)
Ammonia Avenue 𝄞 (Arista, 1984/1991)
Vulture Culture 𝄞 (Arista, 1984)
Stereotomy 𝄞 (Arista, 1985/1991)
Gaudi 𝄞 (Arista, 1987/1991)
The Best of the Alan Parsons Project, Vol. 2 𝄞𝄞𝄞 (Arista, 1987)
Very Best—Live 𝄞𝄞 (RCA Victor, 1995)
On Air 𝄞𝄞𝄞 (River North, 1996)

worth searching for: Parsons's approach lends itself well to film music. He recorded a compelling theme and song, "Voyager," for the soundtrack to *Ice Castles* (Arista, 1979/1990).

influences:

◀◀ Pink Floyd, Tangerine Dream, Wings

▶▶ Manfred Mann's Earth Band, Donna Summer, M, Queen

Gary Graff

Gram Parsons

Born Cecil Ingram Connor, November 5, 1946, in Winterhaven, FL. Died September 19, 1973, in Joshua Tree, CA.

A Harvard dropout who played with both the Byrds and the Flying Burrito Brothers before going solo, Gram Parsons gave rock 'n' roll a country martyr it could claim as its own. Parsons serves much the same function for such 1990s "alternative country" acts as Son Volt and the Jayhawks that Hank Williams serves for mainstream country—he drank too much, wrote sad songs, and died before he hit 30. Parsons's storytelling gift is enhanced by his tragic legend, and it didn't hurt that he helped introduce Emmylou Harris to the music world. When Parsons died, his road manager and a friend stole his body, cremated it, and scattered the ashes at Cap Rock, a California national monument.

what to buy: *G.P./Grievous Angel* 𝄞𝄞𝄞𝄞 (Reprise, 1990, prod. Gram Parsons, Rick Grech) is a twofer classic that combines Parsons's two solo albums. Emmylou Harris provides a harmonic foil for Parsons's voice, and great musicians such as guitarist James Burton and fiddler Byron Berline grace the albums. A couple generations' worth of country-rockers look to Parsons's musings and laconic vocals as the standards of country cool. California country-rock doesn't come more influential than this.

what to buy next: *Sleepless Nights* 𝄞𝄞𝄞 (A&M, 1976, prod. various), a posthumous release, was compiled from solo material and tracks from Parsons's days with the Flying Burrito Brothers.

the rest:
Gram Parsons & the Fallen Angels Live 1973 𝄞𝄞𝄞 (Sierra, 1992/Rhino, 1997)
Cosmic American Music 𝄞𝄞𝄞 (Magnum, 1995)

worth searching for: *Safe at Home* (Shiloh, 1968/Sundown, 1991) is an early record with the International Submarine Band that shows the direction Parsons would travel. Also worth uncovering is *Warm Evenings, Pale Mornings, Bottled Blues* (Raven, 1994), an Australian compilation.

influences:

◀◀ Hank Williams, Merle Haggard, Elvis Presley, the Byrds

▶▶ Emmylou Harris, the Eagles, the Jayhawks, Uncle Tupelo, Wilco, Son Volt, the Bottle Rockets

see also: *The Byrds, Flying Burrito Brothers*

Brian Mansfield

The Partridge Family

See: David Cassidy

Passengers

See: U2

Ellis Paul

Born January 14, 1965 in Fort Kent, ME.

More folk singer than rocker, Ellis Paul is likely someone that most of you have missed. Your loss. Paul, who sings and plays guitar and harmonica, spins tales that read nearly as well as they sound. With an English degree from Boston University, a lovely, plaintive tenor, and all-star accompaniment (Patty Griffin, Bill Morrissey, Jerry Marotta, Tony Levin, and others), Paul creates future campfire sing-alongs and topical epics that most other songwriters should envy. Unlike the work of many of his contemporaries, his arrangements are richly rendered. Such accomplished playing though merely provides the backdrop for Paul's thoughtful writing. On-record trappings notwithstanding, he often performs solo, with equal success.

what to buy: *A Carnival of Voices* 🎵🎵🎵🎵 (Philo, 1996, prod. Jerry Marotta) is slightly better than its predecessors, if perhaps only for its lush sound. Paul's voice works as an additional instrument such that his well written lyrics are a bonus to the record. Paul doesn't pen any songs here about anyone we know—just several about folks we might wish we did, as on "All My Heroes Were Junkies," "Deliver Me," and "Weightless."

what to buy next: *Stories* 🎵🎵🎵 (Philo, 1995, prod. Duke Levine, Ellis Paul, Mark Tanner) just misses *Carnival*'s level of achievement due to a couple of weaker tracks ("River," "Who Shot John Lennon"). But "Autobiography of a Pistol" might be his most accomplished work yet. *Say Something* 🎵🎵🎵 (Black Wolf, 1993, prod. Bill Morrissey) is an excellent debut, often compared to producer Bill Morrissey's work.

the rest:
Translucent Soul 🎵🎵🎵 (Philo/Rounder, 1998)

influences:
◀◀ Bob Dylan, Bill Morrissey, Nanci Griffith, John Gorka, James McMurtry, Woody and Arlo Guthrie, Tim Buckley, Paul Simon, Randy Newman, John Lennon

Barry M. Prickett

Les Paul

Born Lester William Polsfuss, June 9, 1915, in Waukesha, WI.

His own musical tastes were consistent with post–World War II, pre–Elvis Presley America, but guitarist and inventor Les Paul made important contributions to the development of the electric guitar and modern recording techniques. Paul started performing at age 13, and his Les Paul Trio was a fixture on Fred Waring's NBC radio and television programs starting in the late '30s. After teaming with (and marrying) singer Mary Ford, the duo became one of the biggest acts in show business, with 37 Top 40 easy-listening hits from 1948 through 1958 and a popular radio program that displayed Paul's guitar and studio innovations as much as his hits with Mary. Always a tinkerer, Paul built a series of solid-body electric guitars beginning in 1934. Paul spent much of 1946 to 1949 working on guitar designs at his garage studio in Hollywood. His experimentation yielded, in 1952, the first commercial Les Paul model Gibson electric guitar, which forever changed the way guitars sound and are played. His pioneering recording techniques, all now basic, taken-for-granted parts of the studio process, include multitracking (which in his case made it sound like he was playing several guitars at once), delay, echo, phase shifting, flanging, and variable tape speeds. The hits dried up long ago, but Paul has remained active, still playing weekly at a New York club. His name and guitars will live forever.

what to buy: *Best of the Capitol Masters* 🎵🎵🎵🎵 (Capitol, 1991, prod. Ron Furmanek) contains absolutely essential stuff for guitar lovers and fans of his fruitful partnership with Mary Ford, including "Viya Con Dios," "Mockin' Bird Hill," "Tiger Rag," and "How High the Moon?" And if you're really interested, *Les Paul: The Legend and the Legacy* 🎵🎵🎵🎵 (Capitol, 1991, prod. Ron Furmanek) includes 100-plus tracks that allows you to hear Paul's guitar experiments chronologically, all the Les Paul/Mary Ford hits, and an entire disc of outtakes with three complete Les Paul/Mary Ford radio shows and commercials from the '50s. A treasure trove of the period and of the history of the electric guitar.

what to buy next: Paul recorded extensively in many genres (jazz, big-band, blues, and country) and formats (small combos, solo, orchestras) for Decca before he met Ford, and *Les Paul: The Complete Decca Trios—Plus (1936–47)* 🎵🎵🎵🎵 (Decca/MCA, 1997, compilation prod. Steven Lasker) gathers many of his best sides from that period. It's a decidedly mixed bag: Paul as Rhubarb Red kicking up hillbilly music with guitar and harmonica; arranging and backing singers as varied as Georgia White, Helen Forrest, Bing Crosby, the Andrews Sisters, and Dick Haymes; recordings with his own trio; even tracks from a Hawaiian album made to please Decca head Jack Kapp. You'll find the very eclectic groundwork for Paul's later work with Ford on these 50 sides, the way he sounded *before* he started taking apart guitars and diddlying with the delay and echo effects.

the rest:
The Fabulous Les Paul and Mary Ford 🎵🎵 (Columbia, 1965)

Les Paul Now ♫♫♫ (London, 1968)

(With Chet Atkins) *Chester & Lester* ♫♫♫♪ (RCA, 1976)

worth searching for: Paul is featured on any number of compilations, from a version of "Moten Swing" on *Jazz Club* (PGD/Verve, 1990) to "The World Is Waiting for the Sunset" included alongside Chuck Berry, Duane Eddy, Link Wray, and Johnny Otis on *Guitar Player Presents Legends of Guitar: Rock: The '50s* (Rhino, 1990, prod. various). To see the elderly Paul playing with those he influenced, seek out the video *He Changed the Music* (Warner Bros.), which pairs him with, among others, Stanley Jordan, Rita Coolidge, Pink Floyd's David Gilmour, B.B. King, Steve Miller, and Eddie Van Halen.

influences:

◀◀ Deford Bailey, Sonny Terry, Gene Autry, Eddie Lang, Django Reinhardt

▶▶ Jeff Beck, George Benson, Michael Bloomfield, James Burton, Eric Clapton, Rick Derringer, Peter Frampton, Jerry Garcia, David Gilmour, Steve Howe, Stanley Jordan, B.B. King, Mark Knopfler, Steve Miller, Steve Morse, Jimmy Page, Joe Perry, Keith Richards, Brian Setzer, Slash, Bruce Springsteen, Billy Squier, Pete Townshend, Eddie Van Halen, Waddy Wachtel, Nancy Wilson, Link Wray, Frank Zappa

Leland Rucker

Pavement

Formed 1988, in Stockton, CA.

Steve Malkmus, vocals, guitar; Spiral Stairs (born Scott Kannberg), guitar, vocals; Gary Young, drums (1989–92); Bob Nastanovich, percussion, keyboards, vocals (1992–present); Mark Ibold, bass (1992–present); Steve West, drums (1992–present).

If there was ever encouragement for do-it-yourself enthusiasts, it's Pavement, whose slurred vocals and minor MTV hits such as "Cut Your Hair" have generated one of the longest prolonged buzzes in post-Nirvana rock. From the early days of noise as an instrument to its later, more refined sound, Pavement is always a challenge. Influences from the Fall to Die Kreuzen exist, but the band had a sound all to itself until Pavement became indie/low-fi rock heroes, earned fawning reviews in *SPIN* and *Details* as the ultimate slacker band, and many acolytes attempted to approach the altar. Steve Malkmus is a lethal songwriting talent, and paired with Scott Kannberg's musical ability, the band is genuinely great. Hummable and quotable—"What about the voice of Geddy Lee/How did it get so high/I wonder if he speaks like an ordinary guy," goes one of the more memorable throwaway lines, in "Stereo"—Pavement has the goods.

what to buy: The landmark is *Slanted and Enchanted* ♫♫♫♫ (Matador, 1992, prod. Pavement), the band's first full-length album. Nothing like this had ever seeped through your college radio station before. Beautiful and sad, raucous and cryptic, *Slanted and Enchanted* knocked shoegazing British rock off the bar and took the gold. "Summer Babe," with its California Delta references, and "Loretta's Scars" were masterpieces of jagged-edge guitars, off-kilter drums, and evocative lyrics.

what to buy next: It was hard to live up to the hype of the previous record, but *Crooked Rain, Crooked Rain* ♫♫♫♪ (Matador, 1994, prod. Pavement) took another tack and nearly equaled *Slanted and Enchanted*. The untamed drummer Gary Young was gone, and a trio of new players was added for depth. Amid high-school shoutouts and disses of more popular bands (including Stone Temple Pilots and Smashing Pumpkins) were more excellent songs. A hit (with video) "Cut Your Hair" emerged, and Pavement was no longer an indie-cred secret. "5-4 = Unity" is an example of the band's growth, with its impressive tribute to fellow Stocktonite Dave Brubeck.

the rest:

Watery Domestic ♫♫♫♫ (Matador EP, 1992)

Westing (By Musket and Sextant) ♫♫♫♫ (Drag City, 1993)

Wowee Zowee ♫♫♫ (Matador, 1995)

Brighten the Corners ♫♫♫♫ (Matador, 1997)

worth searching for: Granted, there are many Pavement singles and rare EPs out there, but many of those were compiled on the *Westing* compilation, which encompasses the early stuff and *Perfect Sound Forever* 10". That would leave the *Pacific Trim EP* (Matador, 1996, prod. Pavement), which was more than a simple stop-gap between albums.

influences:

◀◀ Velvet Underground, Swell Maps, Can, the Replacements, Die Kreuzen, the Fall, Wire, Modern Lovers, Captain Beefheart

▶▶ Guided by Voices, Butterglory, Failure, Creeper Lagoon, Rollerskate Skinny, Red Red Meat

see also: *Silver Jews*

Barry M. Prickett

Paw

Formed 1992, in Lawrence, KS.

Mark Hennessy, vocals; Grant Fitch, guitar, lap-steel, vocals; Peter Fitch, drums, percussion; Charles Bryan, bass (1991–94); Paul Boblett, bass (1994–present).

This nuevo hick-metal quartet spins riff-heavy yarns about dogs, livestock, family, and drinking that can either fuel a binge or occupy a spot on a weight-lifting tape. Paw is not quite roots-rock, not entirely accessible guitar-rock, and it just barely fits radio's definition of "alternative." But the group's music is quite listenable. Brothers Grant and Peter Fitch shift easily from countrified weeping to ass-whooping stomp, and singer Mark Hennessey's distinctive, guttural growl (especially on the first album) complements his roadhouse croon. With dubious indie credentials that include a couple of impossible-to-find singles that were reportedly backed by A&M Records, these guys rode in Nirvana's wake to find a loyal, albeit small audience of their own.

what to buy: *Death to Traitors* 𝄞𝄞𝄞𝄞 (A&M, 1995, prod. Clif Norrell, Paw), named for the apparent betrayal of the band by former bassist Charles Bryan (see the title track for exact details), is an aggressive onslaught of heavy rants like "No Such Luck" and quasi-country balladry such as "Seasoned Glove" that shouldn't work but do. More varied than the debut *Dragline*, and thus more listenable, *Death to Traitors* is a work of considerable though somewhat calculated talent.

what to buy next: *Dragline* 𝄞𝄞𝄞 (A&M, 1993, prod. Mr. Colson, Paw) isn't quite as subtle as *Death to Traitors*. In accordance with the band's reputation for fighting and drinking, this sludgy collection often sounds like the soundtrack to a backwoods snuff film. Replete with a boy, a dog, and a gun on the cover, *Dragline* actually lauched a semi-hit, the anthemic "Jessie," which is, of course, about some mutt in the band's past.

worth searching for: The CD single *Hope I Die Tonight* (A&M, 1995, prod. Clif Norrell, Ed Rose, Paw) adds a neat cover of Nirvana's "School" and the non-album track "Kid Cotton."

influences:
◄◄ Nirvana, the Melvins, Molly Hatchet

Barry M. Prickett

Peach Union

Formed 1991, in London, England.

Pascal Gabriel, keyboards, programming; Paul Statham, keyboards, programming; Lisa Lamb, vocals.

When Garbage rose from the ashes of aging production concerns just two years ago, it seemed a fluke: three veteran industry-ites hire a seductive frontwoman to pursue pure pop in a world of endless drain. The similarities between that situation and the simultaneous formation of Peach Union (or Peach in the U.K.) are notably eerie, though, and almost suggest a trend or even transcendence in the production field (i.e., knobby preponderence eventually gives way to celebratory and painless girlpop). Whatever the case, Peach Union comes with a history that doesn't really match its present. Pascal Gabriel co-penned some of the banner moments of late '8os ambient dance music

with Bomb the Bass and S'Express, while Paul Statham guided the rebirth of Peter Murphy into post-goth enigma with his particular brand of brazen production blur. The two met on the wane of their respective projects and immediately formed Peach Union. Lisa Lamb, a showgirl and poetess with a nomadic history of her own, eeked her way into one of their conversations and together they set out to conquer the . . . studio.

what's available: *Audiopeach* 𝄞𝄞𝄞𝄞 (Epic, 1997, prod. Paul Statham, Pascal Gabriel, Stephen Hague) shimmers with an FM lackadaisy that is as winsome as it is perfect. Set immediately to the tone of Dubstar and St. Etienne, Peach Union marks its territory with its seemingly innocent lack of irony ("On My Own" sounds like Sandy in *Grease* on a bad hair day). The revolution is over, it appears, as these production gurus sit back to simply enhance the greater song with rhythmic variations, white ragga-dub, and bubble texture. Disposable? Sure. But isn't that how it's supposed to be?

influences:
◄◄ Blondie, St. Etienne, Pet Shop Boys

Billy Manes

Pearl Jam
/Mother Love Bone
/Green River
/Temple of the Dog

Formed 1991, in Seattle, WA.

Eddie Vedder, vocals, guitar; Stone Gossard, guitar; Mike McCready, guitar; Jeff Ament, bass; Dave Krusen, drums (1991); Dave Abbruzzese, drums (1991–94); Jack Irons, drums (1994–present).

Seattle's Pearl Jam broke through the door Mudhoney, Nirvana, and Soundgarden kicked open as part of the storied grunge frenzy of the early '90s. Fronted by charismatic singer Eddie Vedder—who swooped from mopey mumble to feral wail, and whose good looks and apparent integrity quickly made him a reluctant media darling—the group's sonic attack owed much to the arena rock of the '70s, filtered though a goodly dose of post-punk attitude and the requisite '90s angst. The group came together after Mother Love Bone members Jeff Ament and Stone Gossard—grieving for the death of their band's singer Andrew Wood—recorded the *Temple of the Dog* album with Soundgarden's Chris Cornell and Matt Cameron, local guitar-slinger Mike McCready, and, at the last moment, Vedder. Vedder, then in San Diego, sent the band a homemade tape of himself singing lyrics over *Temple* instrumental demos (at the behest of Irons). Outspoken on a number of political issues, Pearl Jam earned points with fans—but ultimately spun its wheels—for its quixotic but highly publicized battle with the

Eddie Vedder of Pearl Jam (© Ken Settle)

ticket agency TicketMaster, which the band felt charged extortionate surcharges. The band has also backed rock legend Neil Young several times, notably on his 1995 album *Mirror Ball*.

what to buy: *Ten* &&&& (Epic, 1991, prod. Pearl Jam, Rick Parashar) remains the band's finest collection of songs, several of which—notably "Jeremy," "Alive," and "Evenflow"—were smashes on both radio and MTV ("Evenflow" also has the distinction of being the name of pro wrestler the Raven's signature finishing move). A glorious loud rock record and a conscious homage to the '70s rock anthems that inspired the late Andrew Wood, *Temple of the Dog* &&&& (A&M, 1991, prod. Rick Parashar, Temple of the Dog) is every bit as good, and, written as it was on the heels of their friend's death, is far more emotionally empowered.

what to buy next: *Vs.* &&&& (Epic, 1993, prod. Brendan O'Brien, Pearl Jam) is a solid follow-up that made the band even bigger thanks to the crossover success of the single "Daughter." *Merkin Ball* &&& (Epic EP, 1995, prod. Brendan O'Brien, Pearl Jam) contains two songs, "I Got Id" and "Long Road," recorded during Young's *Mirror Ball* sessions. Vedder re-recorded the latter for the "Dead Man Walking" movie soundtrack. Given Pearl Jam's phenomenal success, fans might find it illuminating to touch on the bands that came before it. Green River output—angrier, punkier, and more raw than Pearl Jam—is summarized on the twin EP reissue *Dry As a Bone/Rehab Doll* &&& (Sub Pop, 1987, 1988/1990, prod. Jack Endino, Bruce Calder). Mother Love Bone's album, *Apple*, and another half-dozen stray tracks comprise *Mother Love Bone* &&& (PolyGram, 1992, prod. Terry Date, Mother Love Bone).

what to avoid: *Vitology* && (Epic, 1994, prod. Brendan O'Brien, Pearl Jam) contains a couple of compositions that are identifiable as songs—two are actually decent—and a great deal of self-indulgent murk.

the rest:
No Code &&& (Epic, 1996)
Yield &&& (Epic, 1998)

worth searching for: The CD-5 for "Dissident" (Epic, 1994, prod. Brendan O'Brien, Pearl Jam) kicked off a three-CD series of tracks recorded during a live radio broadcast from Atlanta—the only way other than the bootleg market to acquire a Pearl Jam live album.

solo outings:
Three Fish (Ament):
Three Fish &&& (Epic, 1996)

influences:
◀◀ Led Zeppelin, Black Sabbath, the Beatles, the Allman Brothers Band

▶▶ Stone Temple Pilots, Bush, silverchair

see also: *Brad, Neil Young*

Grant Alden and Simon Glickman

Dave Pegg & Friends
See: Fairport Convention

Pell Mell
Formed 1980, in Portland, OR.

Bob Beerman, drums, guitar; Greg Freeman, bass, guitar (1982–present); Arni May, guitar (1980–82); Jon-Lars Sorenson, bass (1980–82); Steve Fisk, organ, synthesizer, piano, sampler, (1983–present); David Spalding, guitar, bass (1989–present).

Completely instrumental, yet lumped with surf music by lazy writers, Pell Mell crafts great songs that don't need a singer. The lead instruments shift from guitar to keyboard from cut to cut as the band explores and expands the normal constraints of voiceless rock. Though reputedly recorded via tapes sent by the U.S. Postal Service, each album sounds cohesive. Don't expect a hit single from Pell Mell, but its occasionally twangy and always interesting work merits attention.

what to buy: The major-label debut *Interstate* &&&& (Geffen, 1995, prod. Pell Mell) is well recorded and performed—and aptly named. Perfect for long, boring drives, the album allows you to script movies in your head, with the band's subtle skill providing an inspirational backdrop.

what to buy next: The crisp, clean *Flow* &&&& (SST, 1991, prod. Pell Mell) was what got the band signed, and it's no wonder why. The tracks eliminate the need for any singing, as emotion and perspective are easily discerned from the music.

the rest:
Rhyming Guitars &&& (Indoor EP, 1982/SST, 1990)
The Bumper Crop &&& (SST, 1988)
Star City &&& (Matador, 1997)

influences:
◀◀ The Ventures, Duane Eddy, Link Wray

▶▶ Slint, Tortoise, Don Caballero, Scenic

Barry M. Prickett

Michael Penn
Born August 1, 1958, in New York, NY.

To say that Michael Penn has show business in his blood is to state the obvious: his father is actor/director Leo Penn, his mother actress Eileen Ryan, his brothers Sean and Christopher. Of course, Madonna was once his sister-in-law. But pedigree can only do so much, and Penn's work has amply proved that he's the real deal, even if the public has been somewhat indifferent to his intriguing brand of melodious, sometimes baroque pop.

what to buy: On his debut album, *March* 𝄞𝄞𝄞𝄞 (RCA, 1989, prod. Tony Berg), Penn's lyrics tend toward the willfully obscure—die-hard fans, no doubt, are out there still trying to figure out the meaning of Penn's hit "No Myth," as well as the equally cryptic "This & That" and "Cupid's Got a Brand New Gun"—but no doubt they've got those songs' melodies imprinted deep within their cerebellums, too. Of special note on *March* are the contributions of Penn's keyboardist Patrick Warren, whose manipulation of the Chamberlin, an arcane Mellotron-like instrument, gives many of Penn's songs their distinctive sound.

what to buy next: The follow-up album to *March*, *Free for All* 𝄞𝄞𝄞 (RCA, 1992, prod. Tony Berg, Michael Penn) was nearly as fine an effort, but failed to attract much attention.

the rest:
Resigned 𝄞𝄞𝄞 (Epic, 1997)

influences:
◄◄ John Lennon, Brian Wilson, Paul McCartney

Daniel Durchholz

Pentangle

Formed 1967, in England. Disbanded 1973. Re-formed 1983.

Bert Jansch, guitar, vocals (1967–73, 1983–94); Jacqui McShee, vocals; Terry Cox, drums, percussion (1967–73, 1983–89); John Renbourn, guitar, vocals, sitar (1967–73, 1983–85); Danny Thompson, bass (1967–73, 1983–85); Mike Piggott, guitar (1985–89); Nigel Portman-Smith, bass (1985–89); Gerry Conway, drums (1990–present); Peter Kirtley, guitar (1990–94); Spencer Cozens, keyboards (1995–present).

The original Pentangle grew out of the collaborations of British finger-style guitarists Bert Jansch and John Renbourn. On their own and in their duets they display a great appreciation for the subtle swing and interplay of jazz, and so it now seems a very natural evolution that they added a rhythm section. Danny Thompson played upright bass and had an affinity for Charles Mingus (a favorite of Renbourn and Jansch) and Terry Cox was comfortable playing with brushes at a time when drum sets were growing louder and larger. On top of this, singer Jacqui McShee's crystalline voice sang lyrics and melodies that drew from American and British folk traditions, but her inflections had more in common with the cool trumpet of Miles Davis than Cecil Sharp's ballad singers. The overall combination made for a remarkably elegant hybrid of Celtic, folk, jazz, and blues. In hindsight, the music seems all the more impressive when contrasted with the overwrought studio albums that followed *Sgt. Pepper*

or the roar of the psychedelic sound that dominated the airwaves at that time. After three extremely well-made records, the group struggled along, disbanded in 1973, reforming briefly from 1983 to 1985. Jansch and McShee then kept together one version or another until 1994, when Jansch left. McShee now works with drummer Conway and keyboardist Cousins and the trio continues to use the name Pentangle.

what to buy: There isn't a false step in Pentangle's brief career. *Basket of Light* 𝄞𝄞𝄞𝄞𝄞 (Reprise/Transatlantic, 1969/Castle, 1996, prod. Shel Talmy) is perhaps the most commercially successful effort, yielding two modest hits in the United Kingdom: "Once I Had a Sweetheart" and "Sally Free and Easy."

what to buy next: *Sweet Child* 𝄞𝄞𝄞𝄞 (Reprise, 1968/Castle, 1996, prod. Shel Talmy) is a double album that explores most of the themes found on subsequent releases. It may be their most diverse record, ranging from updated arrangements of traditional Celtic tunes, to a tribute to Manhattan street composer Moondog, to Thompson's solo rendering of Mingus's "Haitian Fight Song."

what to avoid: *Open the Door* 𝄞𝄞 (Varrick, 1985/Shanachie, 1985, prod. Pentangle) is a disappointing return after a lengthy absence and holds none of the magic of the early recordings.

the rest:
The Pentangle 𝄞𝄞𝄞 (Reprise, 1968/Castle, 1996)
In the Round 𝄞𝄞 (Varrick, 1986)
So Early in the Spring 𝄞𝄞𝄞 (Green Linnet, 1990)
Think of Tomorrow 𝄞𝄞𝄞 (Green Linnet, 1991)
People on the Highway (1968–1971) 𝄞𝄞𝄞 (Transatlantic, 1992/1994)
Collection 𝄞𝄞𝄞𝄞 (Castle, 1992)
Live at the BBC 𝄞𝄞𝄞𝄞 (Band of Joy, 1995)

worth searching for: *Cruel Sister* (Reprise, 1971/Castle, 1996, prod. Shel Talmy) introduced electric guitars into the group's arrangements; understated and flowing, its focus is more exclusive of Celtic folk. The 18-minute "Jack Orion" is a highlight. *Early Classics* (Shanachie, 1992, prod. various) is a good overview, but the flow and segues from the original recordings are missed.

influences:
◄◄ Charles Mingus, Davy Graham, Ian Campbell Group, Miles Davis

►► Nick Drake, John Martyn, Clannad

Jared Snyder

Pere Ubu

Formed 1975, in Cleveland, OH. Disbanded 1982. Re-formed 1987.

David Thomas (a.k.a. Crocus Behemoth), vocals; Tom Herman, guitar (1975–79, 1995–present); Peter Laughner, guitar (1975–77); Tim

Wright, bass (1975–78); Allen Ravenstine, synthesizer (1975–89); Scott Krauss, drums (1975–82, 1985–95); Tony Maimone, bass (1978–93); Mayo Thompson, guitar, vocals (1979–85); Anton Fier, drums (1982–85); Jim Jones, guitar (1985–present); Chris Cutler, drums (1985–89); Eric Drew Feldman, synthesizer (1989–91); Garo Yellin, cello (1993–95); Michele Temple, bass (1993–present); Robert Wheeler, synthesizer (1995–present); Scott Benedict, drums (1995); Steven Mehlman, drums (1995–present).

Pere Ubu—named after the hero in the French absurdist play *Ubu Roi* by Alfred Jarry—released a classic debut single, "30 Seconds over Tokyo"/"Heart of Darkness," that prefigured punk rock, then quickly moved on to the more enigmatic terrain staked out by the synthesizer gurgles of Allen Ravenstine and the wheezing, wailing vocals of David Thomas. The group dubbed its synthesis of punk and art-rock "avant-garage," and its early albums were enormously influential, darkly powerful works that barely made a ripple commercially. Ubu disbanded in 1982 only to regroup five years later to pursue a more direct emotional and musical language; "Where do the broken-hearted park their cars?" Thomas asked. By the mid-'90s, the group had virtually been re-made; with Thomas the sole constant and founding member Tom Herman back in the fold, Ubu returned to the oblique soundscapes of its '70s albums.

what to buy: Unfortunately, to own an essential slice of underground-rock history, you'll have to shell out for the five-CD *Datapanik in the Year Zero* ♫♫♫♫ (Geffen, 1996, prod. Pere Ubu, Ken Hamann, Adam Kidron). By all means try to find the original versions of such early Ubu albums as *The Modern Dance* and *Dub Housing*, masterpieces that have been out of print for years. But failing that, *Datapanik* contains all the early albums, the key singles, and a CD's worth of related Cleveland garage rock. This music inspired impressionable would-be alt-rockers by the hundreds, with Ubu quickly graduating from punk singalongs such as "Non-Alignment Pact" to the forbidding avant-garde atmospherics of "Codex." Of the band's comeback discs, *Cloudland* ♫♫♫ (Fontana, 1989, prod. Stephen Hague, Paul Hamann, Dave Meegan, Daniel Miller, Rico Conning) is the most ravishing approximation of pop, especially "Waiting for Mary" and "Bus Called Happiness."

what to buy next: *The Tenement Year* ♫♫♫♫ (Enigma/Mercury, 1988, prod. Pere Ubu, Paul Hamann) bridges the gap between the band's more experimental first phase and the more accessible sound of *Cloudland*. *Pennsylvania* ♫♫♫♫ (Tim Kerr, 1998, prod. David Thomas) is a dynamic return to Ubu's early, twisted sound on the band's 20th anniversary.

the rest:
Worlds in Collision ♫♫♫ (Fontana, 1991)
Ray Gun Suitcase ♫♫♫ (Tim Kerr, 1995)

worth searching for: The limited edition *The Hearpen Singles* (Tim Kerr, 1995, prod. Pere Ubu, Ken Hamann) includes vinyl versions of four groundbreaking early singles with original artwork: "30 Seconds over Tokyo," "Final Solution," "Street Waves," and "The Modern Dance," plus their respective B sides.

influences:
◄◄ The Stooges, Red Crayola, Can, Henry Cow, Captain Beefheart

►► The Pixies, Big Black, R.E.M., Hüsker Dü

Greg Kot

Perfect
See: The Replacements

Carl Perkins
Born April 9, 1932, in Ridgeley, TN. Died January 19, 1998.

Like many Southerners of his generation, Carl Perkins is a country singer who heard the clarion call of rock 'n' roll on the first Elvis Presley record and headed straight for 706 Union Avenue in Memphis to sign up with the suddenly ascendant Sun label. When Sun-owner Sam Phillips sold Presley's contract to RCA Victor, he did so under the assumption that he had another guy as good as Presley—and maybe even a little better, because Perkins wrote his own songs. But Perkins never followed "Blue Suede Shoes"—his version actually beat Presley's RCA debut, "Heartbreak Hotel," into the Top 10—with anything even remotely that earthshaking. He spent the rest of his career making records that hewed closely to his original artistic vision, while the pop music world quickly left rockabilly—and Perkins—behind. He worked extensively in country music, cutting many well-reviewed LPs that sold poorly. His brilliant "Restless" reached the country Top 20 in 1968, but he made a greater mark in that genre writing hit songs for Patsy Cline, Johnny Cash, and the Judds, among others. Like Bill Haley, his career often boiled down to one record—the redoubtable "Blue Suede Shoes"—but Perkins, even more than Elvis, served as a role model for aspiring rockabilly kings. A badly timed car crash on the way to become the second rock 'n' roller ever to appear on *The Perry Como Show* interrupted his career at a crucial juncture, but Perkins churned out a slew of classic sides for Sun, a body of work that stands like a mountain in the tiny realm of authentic rockabilly.

what to buy: His *Original Sun Greatest Hits* ♫♫♫♫♫ (Rhino, 1986, compilation prod. Bill Inglot) eloquently makes the case for Perkins as one of rock 'n' roll's greats. The wealth of material he cut during his few short years at Sun runs far deeper than just "Blue Suede Shoes." His classic performances of "Honey

Don't," "Put Your Cat Clothes On" (with Jerry Lee Lewis on piano), "Boppin' the Blues," and "Gone, Gone, Gone" virtually define the rockabilly movement then and now.

what to buy next: Perkins continued to record in the same style for years to come, without much commercial success, alongside his Sun compatriot Johnny Cash at the Columbia label. *Restless: The Columbia Recordings* ♫♫♫ (Columbia/Legacy, 1992, compilation prod. Bob Irwin) chronicles the next decade of Perkins's recordings, rockabilly-in-exile. Proof of his enduring legacy can be found in his final LP, the 1996 tribute album, *Go Cat Go!* ♫♫♫ (Dinosaur Entertainment, 1996, executive prod. Jim McCullough), wherein the Rockin' Guitar Man jams with such admirers as Paul McCartney, George Harrison, Johnny Cash, John Fogerty, Ringo Starr, Paul Simon, Tom Petty, and others on a strong set of fresh, self-penned tunes. It's a helluva swan song.

what to avoid: Watch out for a chintzy *Best of Carl Perkins* ♫ (Curb, 1993), a 10-song rip-off featuring re-recordings of "Blue Suede Shoes" and lesser known pieces.

the rest:
Country Boy's Dream: The Dollie Masters ♫♫♫ (CBS, 1968/Bear Family, 1994)
Disciple in Blue Suede Shoes ♫ (Astan, 1968/RCA, 1998)
Carl Perkins & NRBQ: Boppin' the Blues ♫♫♫ (Columbia, 1970)
My Kind of Country ♫♫♫ (Mercury, 1973/Rebound, 1998)
Country Soul ♫♫ (Charvan, 1981/Chicago, 1995)
Carl Perkins & Sons ♫♫ (Accord, 1982/RCA, 1998)
Take Me Back ♫♫ (Joker, 1982 /RCA, 1998)
Up through the Years ♫♫♫♫ (Bear Family, 1986)
Honky Tonk Gal: Rare and Unissued Masters ♫♫♫ (Rounder, 1989)
Born to Rock ♫♫♫ (MCA/Universal, 1989/Liberty, 1995)
Jive after Five ♫♫♫ (Rhino, 1991)
Friends, Family, & Legends ♫♫ (Platinum Intl., 1992)
Guitar Legends ♫♫ (Prime Cuts, 1995)
The Man and the Legend ♫♫ (Magnum, 1996)
Carl Perkins Live ♫♫ (Silver Eagle, 1997)
Roots of Rock 'n' Roll ♫♫ (Direct Source, 1997)

worth searching for: All of Perkins's work for Sun and his first runs at Columbia and Decca are included on *The Classic Carl Perkins* (Bear Family, 1994, compilation prod. Richard Weize), a five-disc box set mixing heartbreaking country with blues-drenched rockabilly. Fans of his later work should be on the lookout for an obscure album, *Carl Perkins on Top* (Columbia, 1969, prod. B. Denny), which contains a rare, unreissued track, "Champagne, Illinois," that Perkins co-wrote with Bob Dylan. This bluesy offering was reissued on Columbia's budget-label as *Brown-Eyed Handsome Man* (Harmony, 1972), but Perkins's experiments with funk-style guitar sound like they're full-priced.

influences:
◀◀ Hank Williams, Ernest Tubb, John Lee Hooker, Muddy Waters, Elvis Presley

▶▶ Ricky Nelson, Mac Curtis, the Beatles, John Fogerty

Joel Selvin and Ken Burke

Permanent Green Light
See: The Three O'Clock

Steve Perry
See: Journey

Pet
Formed 1993, in Los Angeles, CA. Disbanded 1997.

Lisa Papineau, vocals; Tyler Bates, guitar; Alex LoCascio, drums.

Like teenage sex, the emotional territory explored by the Los Angeles-based Pet is expansive and risky. Singer/lyricist Lisa Papineau's poetic narratives are stretched taut over a wall of guitar sound, courtesy of principal songwriter Tyler Bates, while drummer Alex LoCascio's precise rhythms pin everything down at the corners. And talk about your serendipitous beginnings; after Bates's brother saw Papineau perform an Ozzy Osbourne cover, he suggested she meet his guitar-toting brother. Within hours, the pair were penning songs together. Bates soon prevailed upon hometown pal LoCascio to relocate from Chicago to L.A., and Pet's nucleus was formed. (The band enlisted the services of several bass players, most recently L.A. punk journeyman Juan Alderete.) After their demo caught the ears of rock biggies Tori Amos and her manager/guru Arthur Spivak, the band signed to Amos's Igloo imprint, recording its debut at her estate in Ireland. After extensive touring in support of the record, the band quietly succumbed to lukewarm audience response.

what's available: Invoking Sonic Youth (minus the arty noodling) and Björk's early vocal calisthenics with the Sugarcubes, Pet's debut, *Pet* ♫♫♫ (TAG/Atlantic, 1996, prod. Tyler Bates), is all creaky atmosphere and fragmented imagery. On the dream-inspired "360 Degrees," Papineau channels a disturbed three-year-old piloting an out-of-control car. "Skin Tight," the single, is an energetic caterwaul that showcases the band's impressive emotional and dynamic range. And "Fatherland" is both possessed and poppy all at once, like Linda Blair in an alley fight with the Spice Girls. Guaranteed to confuse your friends.

influences:
◀◀ Sugarcubes, Sonic Youth, Fetchin' Bones

Scott Hess

Pet Shop Boys

Formed 1983, in London, England.

Neil Tennant, vocals; Chris Lowe, instruments.

Ex-music journalist Neil Tennant and former architecture student Chris Lowe met and discovered they had a mutual love for Eurodisco and pop. The Pet Shop Boys were born and quickly found a successful formula for their music—sardonic lyrics with hypnotic synthesizer melodies and infectious beats—that led to a parade of hits in the U.K. (though somewhat fewer in the United States). The duo maintains a low profile, seeming unemotional and scheming, but with an intuitive sense for blending the artistically subversive and commercially populist. Besides their own music, Tennant and Lowe also lent their skills to diva Liza Minnelli's 1989 album *Results*.

what to buy: *Discography: The Complete Singles Collection* ♫♫♫♫ (EMI, 1991, prod. various) provides ample evidence of the Pet Shop Boys' fine songwriting and musical sophistication. *Very* ♫♫♫ (ERG, 1993, prod. Pet Shop Boys) achieves an effective balance between happiness and melancholy.

what to buy next: *Please* ♫♫♫♫ (EMI, 1986, prod. Stephen Hague) features the hit singles "West End Girls," "Opportunities (Let's Make Lots of Money)," "Love Comes Quickly," and "Suburbia." *Actually* ♫♫♫♫ (Parlophone, 1987, prod. various) includes "It's a Sin," a cover of Elvis Presley's "Always on My Mind," and Tennant's duet with Dusty Springfield on "What Have I Done to Deserve This."

what to avoid: *Disco* ♫♫ (EMI, 1986, prod. various) and *Disco 2* ♫♫ (Capitol, 1994, prod. Pet Shop Boys, Harold Faltermeyer) are a pair of tedious remix albums.

the rest:
Introspective ♫♫♫ (EMI America, 1988)
Behavior ♫♫♫♫ (EMI America, 1990)
Alternative ♫♫♫ (EMI, 1995)
Bilingual ♫♫♫♫ (EMI, 1996)
Essential Pet Shop Boys ♫♫♫ (EMI, 1998)

worth searching for: The special edition of *Very* comes in a textured orange jewel box—a nice way to own one of the essential titles.

influences:

◀◀ Human League, New Order, the Smiths, Kraftwerk

▶▶ Electronic

Anna Glen

Peter & Gordon

Formed 1961, in London, England. Disbanded 1968.

Peter Asher, vocals, guitar; Gordon Waller, vocals, guitar.

Many musical successes are a combination of luck and serendipity, but it's impossible to guess what the fate of British Invaders Peter Asher and Gordon Waller would have been had Asher's sister, Jane, not been dating Paul McCartney. Peter and Gordon were high school friends drawn together by their mutual love of harmony vocals and acoustic guitar-playing, as embodied by their heroes, the Everly Brothers. They didn't take long to discover their ability to harmonize, and they began picking up gigs performing material by the Everlys, Elvis Presley, Buddy Holly, Woody Guthrie, and others. Meanwhile, McCartney, already a Beatle, was basically living in the Asher family home when not on the road. When Peter & Gordon were offered an opportunity to make a record for EMI in 1963, Asher asked McCartney to finish a song he'd been working on—already rejected by the Beatles and Billy J. Kramer, for whom it was written—called "A World without Love." The catchy tune zoomed straight to #1 in America and the U.K., and was quickly followed by several others, including three more written by McCartney—one ("Woman") under a pseudonym in his now-legendary attempt to find out whether it was his name or songwriting ability that was producing so many hits. (The others—"Nobody I Know" and "I Don't Want to See You Again"—are attributed to Lennon/McCartney.) "True Love Ways," "I Go to Pieces," "Nobody I Know," "Lady Godiva," "Knight in Rusty Armour"—all were hits for the duo, which parted ways in 1968. Waller faded into obscurity after showing up on the 1974 MCA soundtrack album of Andrew Lloyd Webber's *Joseph and the Amazing Technicolor Dreamcoat*. Asher went on to become one of the most respected A&R men in rock history, discovering, producing, and/or managing such artists as Linda Ronstadt, James Taylor, Joni Mitchell, Warren Zevon, 10,000 Maniacs, Randy Newman, Cher, Carole King, Bonnie Raitt, and John Wesley Harding.

what to buy: *The Best of Peter & Gordon* ♫♫♫♫ (Rhino, 1991, compilation prod. Bill Inglot) contains all of the duo's hits, plus six tracks unearthed for this release and excellent liner notes.

what to buy next: Those looking to delve deeper might check out *The EP Collection* ♫♫♫♫ (See for Miles, 1995, prod. various), which has the hits plus some esoterica and European versions.

the rest:
I Go to Pieces/True Love Ways ♫♫♫ (Collectables, 1998)
Woman/Lady Godiva ♫♫♫ (Collectables, 1998)
World without Love/I Don't Want to See You Again ♫♫♫ (Collectables, 1998)

influences:

◄◄ The Everly Brothers, Elvis Presley, the Beatles, Buddy Holly, Phil Spector, Del Shannon, Billy J. Kramer, the Searchers, Phil Ochs, Gerry & the Pacemakers

►► Chad & Jeremy, Freddie & the Dreamers, the Searchers, the Zombies, the Byrds, Linda Ronstadt, James Taylor, the Williams Brothers, the Devlins

Lynne Margolis

Mike Peters

See: The Alarm

Petra

Formed 1973, in Fort Wayne, IN.

Bob Hartman, guitar, vocals, synthesizer (1972–95); Greg Hough, guitars, vocals (1972–78); Bill Glover, drums, percussion (1972–79); John DeGeoff, bass, guitars, vocals (1972–81); Rob Frazier, guitars, keyboards, vocals (1979–80); Greg X. Volz, vocals (1979–86); Louie Weaver, drums (1980–present); John Slick, keyboards, vocals (1981–83); Mark Kelly, bass, vocals (1981–87); John Lawry, keyboards, vocals (1984–94); John Schlitt, vocals (1986–present); Ronny Cates, bass (1988–97); Jim Cooper, keyboards (1994–97); David Lichens, guitar (1995–97); Kevin Brandow, keyboards, guitar, vocals (1997–present); Lonnie Chapin, bass (1997–present); Pete Orta, guitar (1997–present).

With a name that means "rock," Petra evokes both rock as a musical form and the Rock, Jesus Christ, to whom all its music is dedicated. Formed when "Christian rock" was an oxymoron and many Christians denounced all rock as evil, the band married scriptural lyrics to a strong rock sound and solid musicianship in a pioneering effort to speak to young people in their own language. Grammy and Dove awards and album sales in the millions attest to their success—Petra is Christian rock's top-selling band, and it has won respect for its integrity and focus on ministry over image. The sound has changed some with the times, and members have come and gone, but one of the most dramatic shifts occurred when singer-songwriter Greg X. Volz left for a solo career and was replaced by John Schlitt, formerly of Head East. While both Volz and Schlitt can wail with the best of 'em, Volz's supple voice finessed the ballads in a way Schlitt's thinner one can't match. Bob Hartman, the band's founder and chief songwriter, has remained the constant, weathering every change, although he gave up touring in 1995. Petra's latest sound fits right into the '90s modern/alternative mode—the band that influenced so many others now taking some direction from its own descendants. The message remains the same, however—as Schlitt says: "Jesus Christ is Lord and He has a plan for your life. Why try it without Him?"

what to buy: To see where it all began, start with *Petra* 𝄢𝄢𝄢 (Myrrh, 1974). Also worth a listen are a couple of Grammy winners: *Beyond Belief* 𝄢𝄢𝄢 (Dayspring, 1990) and *Unseen Power* 𝄢𝄢𝄢 (Dayspring, 1991), all from the band's arena-rock period.

what to buy next: If you're into modern/alternative, give *God Fixation* 𝄢𝄢𝄢 (Word, 1998, prod. John Elefante, Dino Elefante) a listen.

the rest:

Come and Join Us 𝄢𝄢 (Myrrh, 1977)
Petra Means Rock 𝄢𝄢𝄢 (Star Song, 1989)
Petra Praise: The Rock Cries Out 𝄢𝄢 (Dayspring, 1989)
War and Remembrance 𝄢𝄢𝄢 (Star Song, 1990)
Petrafied: The Very Best of Petra 𝄢𝄢𝄢𝄢 (Star Song, 1991)
Wake-up Call 𝄢𝄢 (Dayspring, 1993)
Rock Block 𝄢𝄢𝄢 (Star Song, 1995)
No Doubt 𝄢𝄢𝄢 (Word, 1995)
Petra Praise 2: We Need Jesus 𝄢𝄢𝄢 (Word, 1997)

worth searching for: For excellent early Petra (of the Volz era), look for vinyl or tape versions of *More Power to Ya* (Star Song, 1982, prod. Jonathan David Brown) and *Not of This World* (Star Song, 1983).

solo outings:

John Schlitt:
Shake 𝄢𝄢 (Sony, 1995)
Unfit for Swine 𝄢𝄢𝄢 (Sony, 1996)

influences:

◄◄ The Beatles, Rush, Triumph, Queen, Scorpions

►► Audio Adrenaline, Jars of Clay, Newsboys, Stryper, Whiteheart

Polly Vedder

Tom Petty & the Heartbreakers

Formed 1975, in Los Angeles, CA.

Tom Petty (born October 20, 1952 in Gainseville, FL), vocals, guitar, keyboards; Mike Campbell, guitar; Benmont Tench, keyboards; Ron Blair, bass (1875–82); Howie Epstein, bass, guitar, vocals (1982–present); Stan Lynch, drums (1975–94); Steve Ferrone, drums (1994–present).

If a prototype for a cool rock 'n' roll star were ever drawn up, chances are it would look a lot like Tom Petty. He's a bit of a hippie *and* a bit of a punk; the leather-jacketed look of his first album cover looked new wave, but the songs showed plenty of reverence for his forebears (particularly the jangly guitar sound of the Byrds) while retaining a decidedly modern sensibility. He's equal parts southern and urbane. Petty is undeniably mainstream, but he's no star-machine conformist: after the giant MCA conglomerate swallowed his original label, Petty held back what would be his breakthrough album, *Damn the*

Tom Petty (© Ken Settle)

Torpedoes, until he renegotiated an unacceptable deal; and he fought his new label when it wanted to release the follow-up, *Hard Promises*, for $1 more than what was then the standard list price. Ultimately, Petty wins with songs—tuneful, catchy, hard-hitting—and one of the best bands in the business. The Heartbreakers have their roots in Mudcrutch, a Gainesville band they brought west to Los Angeles. The migration was at first unsuccessful and the group split up, but when Campbell and Tench began working with Blair and Lynch, Petty roped them in to become the Heartbreakers. It's been a trying two decades—replete with personnel changes and the unsettling specter of Petty's solo ambitions—but the group has bent and grown together, incorporating mature, rootsy flavorings while still maintaining an admirable cross-generational appeal. And if you ever worry that Petty is losing his adolescent outlook, he comes up with a song like "You Don't Know How It Feels," with its decidedly un-adult "let's roll another joint" sentiments.

what to buy: *Damn the Torpedoes* 𝄞𝄞𝄞𝄞 (Backstreet, 1979, prod. Tom Petty, Jimmy Iovine) bursts forth with all the pent-up energy of Petty's corporate fight prior to its release. "Don't Do Me like That"—actually a holdover from the old Mudcrutch days—the ferocious "Refugee," the yearning "Even the Losers," and the unapologetically smug "Here Comes My Girl" all sound great coming out of the radio today. *Hard Promises* 𝄞𝄞𝄞𝄞 (Backstreet, 1981, prod. Tom Petty, Jimmy Iovine) is just as good if maybe a touch more mature. "The Waiting" is a winning testament to faith and love, while "Insider"—a duet with Stevie Nicks—is a real heartstring-tugger. Petty's first solo album, *Full Moon Fever* 𝄞𝄞𝄞𝄞 (MCA, 1989, prod. Jeff Lynne, Tom Petty, Mike Campbell), counters its acoustic trappings with the feisty lyrics of "I Won't Back Down" and "Yer So Bad," while "Runnin' down a Dream" is one of the best rockers he's ever recorded. *Greatest Hits* 𝄞𝄞𝄞𝄞 (MCA, 1993, prod. various) is a generous (18 songs), career-spanning collection that makes a case for Petty's spot in the upper echelon of rock songwriting.

what to buy next: Splurge for *Playback* 𝄞𝄞𝄞𝄞 (MCA, 1995, prod. various), a whopping five-volume box set that's well worth the price. The first volume alone is crammed with some of the best rock America has to offer, while the voluminous collection of rarities is unusually strong. For individual albums, you can't miss with *You're Gonna Get It* 𝄞𝄞𝄞𝄞 (Shelter/Gone Gator, 1978, prod. Denny Cordell, Noah Shark, Tom Petty), the semi-concept album *Southern Accents* 𝄞𝄞𝄞𝄞 (MCA, 1985, prod. various), or the underappreciated *Let Me Up (I've Had Enough)* 𝄞𝄞𝄞𝄞 (MCA, 1987, prod. Tom Petty, Mike Campbell).

what to avoid: There's hardly a clunker in Petty's catalog, but his second solo album, *Wildflowers* 𝄞𝄞𝄞 (Warner Bros., 1994, prod. Rick Rubin, Tom Petty, Mike Campbell), is an unusually soft and unfocused work.

the rest:
Tom Petty & the Heartbreakers 𝄞𝄞𝄞 (Shelter/Gone Gator, 1976)
Pack up the Plantation 𝄞𝄞𝄞 (MCA, 1985)
Into the Great Wide Open 𝄞𝄞𝄞 (MCA, 1991)

worth searching for: *Breakdown* (Seagull) and *Straight into Darkness* (Swingin' Pig) are among the several bootlegs that chronicle the Heartbreakers' raucous live show better than the legitimately released *Pack up the Plantation*.

influences:

◀◀ The Byrds, Chuck Berry, Del Shannon, Bob Dylan, the Kingsmen, the Outsiders

▶▶ The Plimsouls, Phil Seymour, Georgia Satellites, Pearl Jam, the Wallflowers

see also: *The Traveling Wilburys*

Gary Graff

Liz Phair

Born Elizabeth Clark Phair, April 17, 1967, in New Haven, CT.

Liz Phair's out-of-nowhere debut, *Exile in Guyville*, caught critics' attention for its blunt sexuality, cryptic but pointed analysis of relationships, and simplistic, barely produced but rocking sound. Chicago singer-songwriter Phair bared her nipples (partially) on the cover and delighted in saying the F-word, for which she got a lot of press. The album is more compelling, though, because it seizes stereotypical rock machismo and spits it back from a woman's perspective. It's intended as a song-by-song response to the Rolling Stones' classic *Exile on Main Street*, and if you actually take the nerdy step of making a tape alternating the two albums' songs, Phair's social critique of traditional rock becomes interesting and subversive. Also, the tunes are damned catchy. Phair's follow-up had its moments, and the modern-rock radio and MTV hit "Supernova" gave her some cash flow, but the much happier album earned more mixed reviews.

what to buy: *Exile in Guyville* 𝄞𝄞𝄞𝄞 (Matador, 1993, prod. Brad Wood, Liz Phair) won the annual *Village Voice* Pazz & Jop Critics' Poll. Its best songs, the Stones-grooved "6'1"," the lonely "Fuck and Run," and the buoyant "Soap Star Joe," validate the critical hype.

what to buy next: *Whip-smart* 𝄞𝄞𝄞 (Matador/Atlantic, 1994, prod. Brad Wood, Liz Phair) isn't a sophomore slump, but the tunes aren't quite as memorable—although "Cinco De Mayo" and "Jealousy" were underrecognized.

what to avoid: The eight-song EP *Juvenalia* 𝄞𝄞 (Matador, 1995, prod. various) contains a boring novelty version (with the Chicago power-pop band Material Issue) of the Vapors' masturbation anthem "Turning Japanese" as well as several songs from Phair's pre-*Guyville* debut, the impossible-to-find Girlysound indie tapes, which don't wear well.

the rest:

whitechocolatespaceegg 🎵🎵🎵♡ (Matador/Capitol, 1998)

worth searching for: *Secretly Timid* (Empire, 1996), a bootleg compilation of her underwhelming Girlysound releases, provides insight if not much enjoyment.

influences:

◀◀ The Rolling Stones, Patti Smith, Suzanne Vega, Urge Overkill, Smashing Pumpkins

▶▶ Alanis Morissette, Ben Lee, Jennifer Trynin, Tracy Bonham

Steve Knopper

Phantom, Rocker & Slick

See: Stray Cats

Sam Phillips

Born Leslie Phillips, 1962, in Los Angeles, CA.

Sam Phillips walks the line between teenage heartache and womanly wisdom. Sporting a throaty and girlishly seductive voice, she sings familiar lines about strained and failed relationships. What separates her from the dross is her ability to write exacting phrases that cut to the heart of the matter, as well as lovely poetic couplets that lend a surprisingly different perspective on familiar emotions. Phillips began her musical career in 1984 as a Christian rock artist performing under her given name. Under the guidance of her husband and producer, T-Bone Burnett, she switched to secular music in 1988. Since then, Phillips has cultivated a sound that shows the strong influence of the Beatles. Her albums are sprightly pop affairs laden with bright guitars and dark atmospherics, a compelling combination that works particularly well with her woman-child persona.

what to buy: *The Indescribable Wow* 🎵🎵🎵🎵 (Virgin, 1988, prod. T-Bone Burnett) is Phillips's stunning secular debut recording. It's the most varied album of her career, offering '60s-influenced pop and lush, heart-wrenching ballads. Many of the tracks here are among her best work, including "What You Don't Want to Hear," "I Don't Know How to Say Good-bye to You," and "What Do I Do?"

what to buy next: *Martinis & Bikinis* 🎵🎵🎵🎵 (Virgin, 1994, prod. T-Bone Burnett, Colin Moulding) shows Phillips emerging as a distinctive songwriter. Despite the obvious Beatles influence here, Phillips imbues the songs with her own pop sensibilities and an original and poetic voice.

what to avoid: Phillips strays from her pop roots on *Cruel Inventions* 🎵🎵 (Virgin, 1991, prod. T-Bone Burnett), and while the

results aren't bad, they aren't nearly as stunning as her earlier and later albums. Of the 10 tracks, only a few make the grade ("Tripping over Gravity," "Where the Colors Don't Go," and "Standing Still"). If you must have it all, those cuts will make the album a necessary addition to your collection.

the rest:

(As Leslie Phillips) *Recollection* 🎵🎵🎵 (Myrhh, 1987)

Omnipop (It's Only a Flesh Wound, Lambchop) 🎵🎵🎵 (Virgin, 1996)

worth searching for: *The Turning* (Myrhh, 1987, prod. T-Bone Burnett) is Phillips's last album of Christian rock and offers a fascinating look at the singer at the height of her pre-secular career. She fills the tracks with lots of guitars and synthesizers, coming up with a sound not unlike Eurythmics or, for that matter, Pat Benatar. Although out of print, this album and Phillips's other Christian albums, *Beyond Saturday Night* (Myrhh, 1984) and *Black & White in a Grey World* (Myrhh, 1985) can still be found in Christian bookstores.

influences:

◀◀ Bob Dylan, the Beatles, Elvis Costello, Squeeze, the Pretenders, T-Bone Burnett, John Hiatt, Fleetwood Mac

▶▶ Stevie Nicks, Suzanne Vega, Crowded House, Aimee Mann, Juliana Hatfield, Joan Osborne, Fiona Apple

Christopher Scapelliti

Phish

Formed 1983, in Burlington, VT.

Trey Anastasio, guitar, percussion, vocals; Mike Gordon, bass, mandolin, vocals; Page McConnell, piano, organ, theremin, vocals; Jon Fishman, drums, vocals.

Although other neo-hippie jam bands may have sold more records, Phish is the leader of the genre in spirit and versatility. Adding a postmodern twist to its brand of psychedelic rock, the Vermont-based quartet has amassed a fanbase whose dedication is matched only by that of the Grateful Dead's itinerant armies. Incidentally, most of those armies and their would-be younger recruits have crossed over to Phish. When the band throws its late-summer weekend festival (two full days of Phish in some remote, East Coast location), the massive tent cities that arise are like a cross between a Civil War encampment and a bonafied Kesey acid test. Like most jam bands, Phish is at its best in the live forum, choosing randomly from its 150+ song repertoire to craft two 90-minute sets filled with covers, originals, and extended jams every time it takes the stage. But where most jam bands' roots lie in the folk tradition, Phish's sound stems more from the counterpoint dissonance of jazz. Each member of the group—all of whom are formally trained musicians—has the uncanny ability to improvise complex, unique melodies that, despite their apparent incompatibility, build off each other. The result is sometimes tedious but mostly lively and engaging on a number of levels. Phish may be a musician's band, but that's not to say it can't write a good stripped-down rock song, either. Or bluegrass, or reggae, lounge, barbershop quartet, or soul. This incessant genre-shifting has gotten the group into trouble on some albums (*Picture of Nectar* veers wildly between genres, sacrificing cohesion for diversity) and in print, where rock critics cry hubris between references to patchouli and weed. Where Phish's detractors may be missing the mark, however, is that the band is not taking the piss out of those genres; they're paying homage to them. And as a famous St. Louis Cardinals pitcher once said, it ain't braggin' if you can do it.

what to buy: More than any of Phish's other recorded work, *Billy Breathes* ❚❚❚❚ (Elektra, 1996, prod. Steve Lillywhite) comes together as an *album*. Avoiding the trappings of earlier efforts, the band concentrates more on ebb and flow than on theme, pace, or diversity, and there is a perfect balance between energy and cohesion—two elements that they had previously been unable to marry in the studio. *Billy Breathes* also retains Phish's trademark genre-shifting without leaving the listener out of breath trying to keep up. Powerful rockers such as "Character Zero" fuse seamlessly with muted acoustic melodies ("Waste," "Trainsong"), and the soaring, latin-inflected grooves of "Taste" blend right into the lively organ jazz of "Cars Trucks Buses." *Slip Stitch and Pass* ❚❚❚❚ (Elektra, 1997, prod. Phish), the band's second live release, is tops when it comes to approximating an actual Phish show. On cuts culled from a Hamburg, Germany, gig earlier that year, Phish powers through a series of cathartic peaks and valleys. Included somewhere in the jam-infested haze are three covers ("Cities" by the Talking Heads, "Jesus Just Left Chicago" by ZZ Top, and a zany *a capella* rendition of "Hello My Baby") and a few otherwise unreleased songs. *Slip Stitch* is fun but lengthy, and not without a few spots where you can leave to use the bathroom, get a beer, or roll a joint—just like an actual Phish show.

what to buy next: *Lawnboy* ❚❚❚ (Absolute a Go Go, 1990/Elektra 1992, prod. Phish), one of Phish's earlier albums, showcases its verve and musical prowess with jokey preludes and frenzied, guitar-and-piano-based musical workouts. "Squirming Coil" and "Reba" both start out with light grooves and trippy lyrics, then float off into epic jams. "Bouncing around the Room," appeared later on the live album *A Live One*, and from there flirted briefly with radio notoriety.

what to avoid: Phish's crack at a concept album, *Rift* ❚ (Elektra, 1993, prod. Barry Beckett), has cohesion but lacks energy. Although it contains a few songs that evolved into frenzied live show favorites ("Maze," "My Friend, My Friend"), even they

come off as stilted and boring here. Appropriately enough, the album's theme centers around sleep and dreams.

the rest:
Junta ❚❚❚ (1988/Elektra, 1992)
Picture of Nectar ❚❚❚ (Elektra, 1992)
Hoist ❚❚ (Elektra, 1994)
(With the Dude of Life) *Crimes of the Mind* ❚ (Elektra, 1994)
A Live One ❚❚ (Elektra, 1995)
The Story of the Ghost N/A (Elektra, 1998)

worth searching for: Phish allows concertgoers to tape shows. Poke around on the internet and you'll find nearly every lick of their live music since the late '80s. Trey Anastasio's senior thesis, a rock musical called *The Man Who Stepped into Yesterday* was never released but is widely circulated. *The White Album* a.k.a. *Phish* is an early set of demos usually found in the collections of the more serious tape traders.

solo outings:
Trey Anastasio:
Surrender to the Air ❚❚ (Elektra, 1996)

influences:
◀◀ Frank Zappa, Funkadelic, Santana, Talking Heads, the Grateful Dead, John Coltrane

▶▶ moe., God Street Wine, Blues Traveler

Isaac Josephson

Phranc

Born Susan Gottlieb, August 28, 1957, in Santa Monica, CA.

Boy, did Phranc emerge at the wrong time. During the mid-'80s, when Ronald Reagan ruled and even punk rock's lesbians and gay men weren't terribly eager to come out of the closet, this self-described "all-American Jewish lesbian folk singer" began inflicting her wonderful sense of humor on society at large. After playing in a few punk bands and co-opting the genre's ironic sense of humor, the former Ms. Gottlieb renamed herself Phranc, and began a solo career. She sang about her love for female mud-wrestlers, a clever obsession with Kim Novak in the Hitchcock film *Vertigo*, and her hatred for punk's misguided emphasis on sexism and Nazism. In one of her most hilarious songs, she also rewrote the Modern Lovers' "Pablo Picasso" as "Gertrude Stein," neatly recasting the feminist icon as a rock 'n' roll rebel. Sadly, when lesbians became hip circa 1996— Ellen DeGeneres, Melissa Etheridge, and even k.d. lang take themselves far more seriously than Phranc ever did—the singer's career suffered personal setbacks. Her brother was murdered in 1991, and she left the music industry for several years, returning with a bizarre Neil Diamond tribute tour and an EP on the gay-friendly riot-grrrl label Kill Rock Stars.

what to buy: Though Phranc's best-known music came out on big record labels, it's hard to find in record stores these days: *Positively Phranc* 𝄞𝄞𝄞 (Island, 1991) includes a song co-written with macho country-rocker Dave Alvin, a gender-bending take on the Beach Boys' "Surfer Girl," and the gleeful "Gertrude Stein"; the highlight of *I Enjoy Being a Girl* 𝄞𝄞𝄞 (Island, 1989) is "Take off Your Swastika," which Phranc used to sing, courageously, to slam-dancers at punk shows.

what to buy next: The EP *Goofyfoot* 𝄞𝄞𝄞 (Kill Rock Stars, 1995), aside from an inexplicable surf-music obsession, is most notable for its backup musicians—Hole's Patty Schemel and Bikini Kill's Tobi Vail, among others. Who says punks don't take care of their own?

the rest:
Folksinger 𝄞𝄞𝄞 (Rhino, 1985/Island, 1990)

influences:

◀◀ Joan Baez, the Sex Pistols, k.d. lang, the Beach Boys, the Ventures, the New York Dolls, Two Nice Girls

▶▶ Melissa Etheridge, Bikini Kill, Hole, Nirvana, Mary Lou Lord

Steve Knopper

Wilson Pickett

Born March 18, 1941, in Prattville, AL.

Among all of soul music's throat-shredding testifiers, none could match Wilson Pickett. From his earliest recordings as lead vocalist with the Falcons, Pickett's voice was unmistakable in its sheer, unsettling power. But until he was sent off to Memphis in 1965 by Atlantic Records, Pickett had not found the right instrumental backing for chart success. He most definitely found it there: using musicians from the Stax house band and from Muscle Shoals, Pickett unleashed a string of incomparable soul classics—"Mustang Sally," "In the Midnight Hour," and "Funky Broadway" among them. His combination of gospel urgency and sexual swagger earned him the nickname "The Wicked Pickett," as his singles ruled the dance floor. But despite a career-reviving stint with Kenny Gamble and Leon Huff's slicker Philadelphia sound during the early '70s, the hits eventually stopped coming. Though the wicked side of Pickett gets him more press these days than his music (he has a fondness for guns, it seems), he still stands as one of the soul era's greatest vocalists.

what to buy: Pickett's best has been thoroughly and admirably documented on the two-CD set *Wilson Pickett: A Man and a Half* 𝄞𝄞𝄞𝄞 (Rhino/Atlantic, 1992, prod. various). Beginning in 1961 with Pickett's vocalizing on "I Found a Love" by the Falcons, this collection offers a comprehensive journey through the Atlantic years and the Philadelphia sides and culminates with a live 1971 performance of "Funky Broadway" from a show in Ghana. And there are a few unreleased songs, alternate versions, and rare live cuts along the way. If you just want the hits and nothing more, *The Very Best of Wilson Pickett* 𝄞𝄞𝄞𝄞 (Rhino, 1993, prod. various) is where to find them on one tight CD.

what to buy next: Of the earlier Atlantic albums available on CD, *The Exciting Wilson Pickett* 𝄞𝄞𝄞𝄞 (Atlantic, 1966, prod. Jerry Wexler) and *The Sound of Wilson Pickett* 𝄞𝄞𝄞𝄞 (Atlantic, 1967, prod. Tom Dowd) are the best. *Wilson Pickett in Philadelphia* 𝄞𝄞𝄞𝄞 (Atlantic, 1970, prod. Kenny Gamble, Leon Huff) is the great soul shouter's final outstanding album.

what to avoid: On *Mr. Magic Man* 𝄞 (RCA, 1973) the voice is still there, but this is the beginning of Pickett's slide into uninspired mediocrity.

the rest:
In the Midnight Hour 𝄞𝄞𝄞𝄞 (Atlantic, 1965)
Wicked Pickett 𝄞𝄞𝄞𝄞 (Atlantic, 1966)
Wilson Pickett's Greatest Hits 𝄞𝄞𝄞𝄞 (Atlantic, 1973)

worth searching for: *American Soul Man* (Motown, 1987) is a brief stop at the legendary Detroit R&B label that finds Pickett in good voice—perhaps inspired by the hallowed surroundings.

influences:

◀◀ The Swan Silvertones, the Soul Stirrers, Hank Ballard & the Midnighters

▶▶ Bobby Womack, Teddy Pendergrass, the Commitments

Doug Pippin

Billy Pilgrim

Formed 1989, in Knoxville, TN.

Andrew Hyra, guitar, vocals; Kristian Bush, guitar, vocals.

Continuing a long line of sensitive strummy harmonic male vocal duos, the winsome songcraft of Billy Pilgrim (originally indie-successes as Hyra-Bush) nearly cracked into the American consciousness with a fair push from Atlantic Records in the Hootie & the Blowfish era. Unfortunately, it was Hootie's more linear band sound that turned heads, and not the complex, optimistic balladry of Hyra and Bush. Still, for a career reportedly on hiatus as of 1998, the duo was able to produce two variably solid albums.

what to buy: *Billy Pilgrim* 𝄞𝄞𝄞𝄞 (Atlantic, 1994, prod. Dan Mc-Collister, Hugh Padgham) benefited greatly from the presence of Indigo Girls Amy Ray and Emily Saliers on the riveting "Insomniac." "Try" and "Get Me out of Here" swung similarly rural swoops around innocence and nature, and drove their simple melodies into soul-rich revivals. This is, by most counts, a cutout male version of the Indigo Girls academic folk, only here the humility of guys on the mend carries it a step away from the candle-dripped bottles of the Girls' poetic indulgences.

what to buy next: Billy Pilgrim sought minor redirection for its sophomore effort, *Bloom* ♫♫♫ (Atlantic, 1995, prod. Richard Dodd), with mixed results. Where strong efforts like the closing "Closed Down" are strong dismal folk-blues, other attempts at BoDeans-style smile-rock, notably the single "Sweet Louisiana Sound," rang hollow with pointless celebration. Ensemble performance with throwbacks of the E Street Band and Tom Petty's Heartbreakers do more to bury the sincerity in mainstream rock-radio dirge than to elevate the duo's obvious power.

influences:

◀◀ Indigo Girls, BoDeans, Simon & Garfunkel

▶▶ Hootie & the Blowfish, Semisonic

Billy Manes

Mike Pinder

See: The Moody Blues

Pink Floyd

Formed 1965, in London, England.

Roger Keith (Syd) Barrett, guitar, vocals (1965–69); David Gilmour, guitar, vocals (1968–present); Nick Mason, drums; Roger Waters, bass, vocals (1965–84); Richard Wright, keyboards (1965–82, 1987–present).

Syd Barrett named Pink Floyd for two bluesmen—Pink Anderson and Floyd Council—but the closest the band came to the blues was the demeanor of its lyrics. The Floyd was among the first of Britain's post–*Sgt. Pepper's* groups, riding the psychedelic pop wave with hits such as "Arnold Layne" and "See Emily Play" before evolving into the more space-age, tripped-out fury of "Astronomy Domine" and "Interstellar Overdrive." Barrett tripped himself out of the band before long, and the Floyd evolved yet again into a more ethereal, ambient style that was enhanced by the group's high-tech, multi-media stage shows. The zenith of this was *Dark Side of the Moon*, one of rock's most original and durable epics. Driven by Roger Waters's bleak lyrical outlook, each succeeding album was a thematic work, examining insanity, fascism, societal decay, and other social and political issues. *The Final Cut* was largely a Waters solo album, after which he decided Pink Floyd was over. But the other Floyds, particularly David Gilmour, weren't quite ready to pack it in, and they continued—fending off Waters's legal and verbal attacks while packing stadiums around the world. The rift hadn't healed by the time Pink Floyd was inducted into the Rock and Roll Hall of Fame in 1996 (Waters didn't show), but rest assured that all concerned are benefiting handsomely from the group's continuing activity.

what to buy: *Dark Side of the Moon* ♫♫♫♫ (Harvest, 1973, prod. Pink Floyd) is the essential piece, a seamless and inventive song cycle bolstered by a three-dimensional soundscape of instruments and special effects—not to mention some first-rate songs like "Money," "Us and Them," and "Time." *Wish You Were Here* ♫♫♫♫ (Columbia, 1975, prod. Pink Floyd) is just as good and a touch more organic, highlighted by the extended piece "Shine on You Crazy Diamond." *The Wall* ♫♫♫♫ (Columbia, 1979, prod. Roger Waters, David Gilmour, Bob Ezrin) is another masterful concept piece that, despite its length, housed more solid songs such as "Comfortably Numb," "Goodbye Blue Sky," and Pink Floyd's biggest hit, "Another Brick in the Wall (Part II)." No collection is complete without a piece of Pink Floyd's early days, and *The Piper at the Gates of Dawn* ♫♫♫ (Capitol, 1967, prod. Norman Smith) fits the bill, even if it now sounds a bit dated.

what to buy next: *Meddle* ♫♫♫ (Harvest, 1971, prod. Pink Floyd) captures Pink Floyd at a crucial, formative juncture just before *Dark Side*'s breakthrough. *Works* ♫♫♫ (Capitol, 1983, prod. various) is a useful collection of early singles and album tracks. *The Division Bell* ♫♫♫ (Columbia, 1994, prod. David Gilmour, Bob Ezrin) shows that the post-Waters Pink Floyd still has something to offer.

what to avoid: *A Collection of Great Dance Songs* ♫ (Columbia, 1981, prod. various) is a misbegotten compilation that's only worthwhile for the wonderfully ironic title.

the rest:

A Saucerful of Secrets ♫♫ (Harvest, 1968)
Tonite Let's All Make Love in London (Soundtrack) ♫♫♫ (Columbia, 1968)
Ummagumma ♫♫♫ (Harvest, 1969)
More (Soundtrack) ♫ (Harvest, 1969)
Atom Heart Mother ♫♫ (Harvest, 1970)
Relics ♫♫♫ (Harvest, 1971)
Obscured by Clouds (Soundtrack) ♫ (Harvest, 1972)
Animals ♫♫♫ (Columbia, 1977)
The Final Cut ♫♫♫ (Columbia, 1983)
A Momentary Lapse of Reason ♫♫ (Columbia, 1987)
Delicate Sound of Thunder ♫♫♫ (Columbia, 1988)
Pulse ♫♫♫ (Columbia, 1995)

worth searching for: *Shine On* (Columbia, 1992, prod. various) is as lavish—and expensive—as box sets come. Eight of Pink Floyd's titles are included, as well as an extra disc of early singles and a hardcover book. An easy way to attain an instant Pink Floyd collection.

solo outings:
David Gilmour:
David Gilmour ♫♫♫ (Columbia, 1978)
About Face ♫♫♫ (Columbia, 1984)

Nick Mason:
Nick Mason's Fictitious Sports 🎵🎵 (Columbia, 1981)
Profiles 🎵🎵🎵 (Columbia, 1985)

Roger Waters:
The Pros and Cons of Hitch Hiking 🎵🎵 (Columbia, 1984)
Radio K.A.O.S. 🎵🎵🎵 (Columbia, 1987)
The Wall: Live in Berlin 🎵🎵🎵 (Mercury, 1990)
Amused to Death 🎵🎵 (Columbia, 1992)

Richard Wright:
Wet Dream 🎵🎵 (Harvest, 1978)
Identity 🎵🎵 (Harvest, 1984)

influences:

◀◀ Early British blues and jazz, the Beatles, the Beach Boys

▶▶ Genesis, Roxy Music, Kansas, Focus, the Orb, Orbital

see also: *Syd Barrett*

Gary Graff

Pistoleros

Formed 1992, in Tempe, AZ.

Lawrence Zubia, lead vocals; Mark Zubia, rhythm guitar, vocals; Scott Andrews, bass; Gary Smith, drums (1993–present); Thomas Laufenberg, guitar (1996–present); Doug Hopkins (died December 5, 1993), lead guitar (1992–93); Peter Milner, lead guitar (1993–96); Mark Riggs, drums (1992–93).

The Pistoleros began life in 1992 as the Chimeras, a Phoenix-area supergroup made up of ex-Gin Blossom Doug Hopkins along with Scott Andrews and Mark Riggs, who had just left local-legend axeman Chuck Hall, and the Zubia brothers from Live Nudes. Hopkins was a major contributor as songwriter after his bitter parting from the Gin Blossoms, and when the band debuted in the since-defunct Edcel's Attic on Tempe's Mill Avenue, the highlight of the set was the band's fierce version of "Hey Jealousy," the Blossoms' Hopkins-penned hit. Hopkins left the group soon after it debuted, his personal demons consuming him almost entirely. (He shot himself to death in December 1993.) Riggs left after that, because his own personal commitments were mounting. Thomas Laufenberg and Gary Smith ably filled the holes, and the Zubias became the dominant songwriters. They had been playing mariachi music since their youth, and they often added those tunes to their sets in the manner of Los Lobos. Upon signing with Hollywood Records in 1996, the band had to change its name because of a conflict with another recording group called Chimera. The Pistoleros' name aptly reflects the Southwestern spin the band gives to heartland rock verities.

what's available: *Hang on to Nothing* 🎵🎵🎵 (Hollywood, 1997, prod. Julian Raymond), the Pistoleros' promising national debut, hinges on a strong mariachi-flavored single "Guardian

Angel," written by Hopkins with the help of Mark Zubia. Lawrence Zubia's impassioned voice and the band's rhythmic kick match the tuneful material. The record company suggested that the band work with Pat DiNizio of the Smithereens (Lawrence's soulful voice sounds eerily like DiNizio's at times), and the collaboration produced three memorable tunes: "Somehow Someway," "Nothing Lasts Forever," and "The Game." Other record-company suggestions led them to write with the Jayhawks' Gary Louris on the title cut and "Wasting My Time," and Radney Foster on "Just to Hold on to You."

worth searching for: *Mistaken for Granted* (Imaginary Music, 1995, prod. Chimeras, Mark Mattson) helped the Chimeras get its big-label contract. It also showcases the essential elements of the Pistoleros' sound—a touch of soul and country woven into rhythmically popping heartland rock and power pop.

influences:

◀◀ Bruce Springsteen, Smithereens

▶▶ Gin Blossoms, Refreshments

Salvatore Caputo

Gene Pitney

Born February 17, 1941, in Hartford, CT.

Gene Pitney had some huge hits during the early '60s, thanks to a vibrant but pained tenor that could give the heartstrings a pretty good tug. Unlike many pop singers of his day, Pitney wrote many of his own songs, established his own record company (Musicor), and worked easily in a variety of styles and with a diversity of artists, including songwriters Burt Bacharach and Hal David (who wrote his wrenching hit "Only Love Can Break a Heart"), the Rolling Stones, and George Jones. Pitney was much bigger in Europe than in the United States, so by the mid-'60s he was concentrating his recording and touring efforts there. The resilient singer had a #1 hit in the U.K. as recently as 1988 ("Something's Gotten Hold of My Heart," a collaboration with Marc Almond) and made a triumphant return to the United States in 1993 with a sold-out show at Carnegie Hall. Mostly a singles artist, Pitney has wracked up more than 20 hits during his career.

what to buy: There is no definitive Pitney collection that deftly covers the singer's long and varied career. The one that comes closest is *More Greatest Hits* 🎵🎵🎵 (Varese Vintage, 1995, prod. various), which rounds up 19 remastered versions of Pitney's biggest hits, including "Town without Pity," "(The Man Who Shot) Liberty Valance," "Only Love Can Break a Heart," and the more recent "Something's Gotten Hold of My Heart."

what to buy next: *Anthology (1961–1968)* 🎵🎵🎵 (Rhino, 1991, prod. various) sums up his most prolific period, the '60s, with the obvious hits but also Pitney's versions of hits he wrote for other artists, including Ricky Nelson's "Hello Mary Lou."

what to avoid: With just 10 songs, *Greatest Hits* 🎵🎵 (Curb, 1995, prod. various) is far too skimpy, particularly compared to what else is available.

the rest:

Best of Gene Pitney 🎵🎵🎵 (K-Tel International, 1991)
Best of Gene Pitney 🎵🎵 (Laserlight Digital, 1995)
Best of Gene Pitney 🎵🎵 (Delta)
Greatest Hits 🎵🎵 (Evergreen)
Greatest Hits, Vols. 1 and 2 🎵🎵🎵 (Eclipse)
His Golden Classics 🎵🎵 (Collectables, 1991)
The Collection 🎵🎵 (Griffin)
The Great Recordings 🎵🎵🎵 (Tomato, 1995)
Great Gene Pitney 🎵🎵 (Goldies, 1996)

influences:

◀◀ George Jones, Johnny Ray

▶▶ Soft Cell, Chris Isaak

Doug Pullen

The Pixies

Formed 1986, in Boston, MA. Disbanded 1993.

Black Francis (a.k.a. Frank Black; born Charles Michael Kitteridge Thompson IV), guitar, vocals; Kim Deal (a.k.a. Mrs. John Murphy), bass, vocals; Joey Santiago, lead guitar; David Lovering, drums.

At a time when rock's more subversive talents (chief among them, Elvis Costello and Joe Jackson) had been declawed, defanged, and preened for mainstream acceptance, the Pixies embraced the raucous chaos at rock's very core: squealing guitars, passable musicianship, sly humor, and disturbing lyrics. As a result, the group brought lively unpredictability to a genre homogenized by commercial interests, giving new hope to the musically disenfranchised. (Nirvana, for example, cited the Pixies as an influence.) As the group's main songwriter, Black Francis crafted short, punchy songs that alternate the noisy anarchy of thrash punk with the melodicism of surf-rock and pop. His lyrics (which frequently incorporate Spanish) are a ride down a decaying Route 66—a cultural malaise of sex, religion, and mutilation that speaks reams about the growing fragmentation of America, always earning a wry smile for the effort. Signed by Britain's alternative label 4AD in 1987, the Pixies became a favorite of the college circuit, eventually scoring a minor hit in 1989 with the single "Here Comes Your Man." With its final album, 1991's *Trompe Le Monde*, the band was looking more and more like a solo project for Francis, and

in early 1993 its members split. Francis went solo three months later under the name Frank Black, David Lovering joined Cracker, and Kim Deal threw her efforts into her side band, the Breeders.

what to buy: A mini-album born out of eight demos financed by Francis's father, *Come on Pilgrim* 🎵🎵🎵🎵 (4AD/Rough Trade, 1988, prod. Gary Smith) is a bold debut that put the Pixies firmly on its own terra firma. "Ed Is Dead" and "The Holiday Song" are headshakingly hooky, while "Isla de Encanta" and "Vamos" are hip little gems fueled by potent rhythms and Francis's effective (and humorous) employment of Spanish. The Pixies' third album, *Doolittle* 🎵🎵🎵🎵 (4AD/Elektra, 1989, prod. Gil Norton) is as close to mainstream as the group ever got. Producer Norton smoothed out the band's rough edges and endearing inconsistencies to craft an album that's never quite punk, never quite pop. Frenetic rants like "Debaser" and "Monkey Gone to Heaven" serve up infectious choruses, while seemingly innocuous tunes such as "Here Comes Your Man" and "La La Love You" show Francis's finely tuned schizophrenic pop sensibilities present and accounted for.

what to buy next: *Surfer Rosa* 🎵🎵🎵🎵 (4AD/Rough Trade, 1988, prod. Steve Albini) is a free-for-all of thrashing punk and innovative pop that still sounds fresh today. Tracks such as Deal's "Gigantic" and Francis's "Bone Machine" harness a manic energy that delights time and time again. (Note: The import version adds the eight tracks from *Come on Pilgrim.*)

what to avoid: *Bossa Nova* 🎵🎵 (4AD/Elektra, 1990, prod. Gil Norton) is a surprisingly lackluster follow-up to the brilliance of *Doolittle*, a smug bit of self-indulgence that just sounds bad.

the rest:

Trompe Le Monde 🎵🎵 (4AD/Elektra, 1993)
Death to the Pixies 🎵🎵🎵 (Elektra, 1997)
At the BBC 🎵🎵🎵 (Elektra, 1998)

worth searching for: Fans will want to scout around for the Japanese version of *Trompe Le Monde*, which adds four live tracks: "Bone Machine," "Cactus," "Debaser," and "Gouge Away."

influences:

◀◀ Dick Dale & His Del-Tones, the Ventures, the Velvet Underground, Iggy Pop, the Ramones

▶▶ Dinosaur Jr., the Feelies, the Flaming Lips, My Bloody Valentine, Nirvana, Sonic Youth, Throwing Muses, Belly, Weezer, the Lemonheads, the Sugarcubes, Hüsker Dü

see also: *Frank Black, Cracker, the Breeders*

Christopher Scapelliti

Pizzicato Five

Formed 1984, in Tokyo, Japan.

Yasuharu Konishi, composer, concept; Maki Nomiya, vocals, style (1991–present); K-Taro Takanami, composer, concept (1984–95).

This Japanese duo is really more of a conceptual-art piece-in-progress than a rock band. Yasuharu Konishi formed P5 during the mid-'80s as an outlet for his fascination with Western pop (especially '70s soul music), sampling snatches of music and creating whacked-out sound collages for dance-crazed Tokyo-ites. He met his perfect visual foil in Maki Nomiya, whose jones for high fashion and low culture includes a dizzying number of costume changes during the group's rare performances. America was finally introduced to P5's filtered view of America through an indie label, Matador, which released a compilation of Japanese hits, *Made in USA*, in 1994. Matador's major-label mentors, Atlantic, helped give the next year's CD, *The Sound of Music By . . .* a bigger push, as well as getting it placed in the documentary about fashion designer Isaac Mizrahi. Give the group a cursory listen and you'll swear you've heard all their music before—probably during the '70s—but upon closer listening, you'll find the songs are all original, even if they evoke another time and place. The group's cultural pilfering doesn't just stop at musical references and retro clothing; each release is a conceptual art piece in itself, with extravagant packaging and prizes like a "Carte Pizzicato" club member card enclosed with the second U.S. release. (The Japanese version of P5 releases are even more complex in their packaging.) These days basically a duo, P5 continues to record prolifically, aiming as much at the feet as at the head. The *Remix* album features other dance producers' homage to and their spin on P5's music.

what to buy: A compilation of tracks from Japanese P-5 albums, *Made in USA* 𝄢𝄢𝄢𝄢 (Matador, 1994, prod. Pizzicato Five) contains kitschy cool tracks such as "Magic Carpet Ride," "Sweet Soul Revue," and "Peace Music." *The Sound of Music by Pizzicato Five* 𝄢𝄢𝄢𝄢 (Matador/Atlantic, 1995, prod. Pizzicato Five) offers similarly retro-minded fun, with "We Love Pizzicato Five" and "If I Were a Groupie."

what to buy next: A handful of U.S. EP releases are worth seeking out, and some of them have lots of music for the money: *Five by Five* 𝄢𝄢𝄢 (Matador, 1994); *Magic Carpet Ride* 𝄢𝄢𝄢 (Matador, 1995); *Sister Freedom Tapes* 𝄢𝄢𝄢 (Matador, 1996); and *Magic Carpet Ride* 𝄢𝄢𝄢 (Matador, 1997).

the rest:
Happy End of the World 𝄢𝄢𝄢 (Matador, 1997)
Remix Album: Happy End of You 𝄢𝄢𝄢𝄢 (Matador, 1998)

worth searching for: Fans can track down any of the many Japanese import singles and albums, including *Overdose* (Triad/Nippon Columbia, 1994, prod. Pizzicato Five), which includes the Japanese version of "Happy Sad." Also, the U.S. CD-single of *Happy Sad* (Matador/Atlantic, 1995) includes both the English "Single Mix" and Japanese "Hot Wax Mix" versions of the song.

influences:
◀◀ Juan Garcia Esquivel, James Bond movie themes, Sly & the Family Stone, disco

▶▶ Deee-Lite, St. Etienne, Juan Garcia Esquivel

Gil Asakawa

Plainsong

See: Iain Matthews

Robert Plant

Born August 20, 1948, in Bromwich, Staffordshire, England.

Robert Plant left home to become a musician at age 16, released a couple of singles, and went through the ranks of such colorful local bands as the New Memphis Bluesbreakers, the Crawling King Snakes, Black Snake Moan, the Banned, the Delta Blues Band, and the Band of Joy, the latter featuring future Led Zeppelin drummer John Bonham. Yardbirds guitar star Jimmy Page was looking for a frontman for his new band and turned up at a Hobbstweedle gig one night in 1968. Page was immediately knocked out by the 20-year-old singer's good looks and sexually charged singing. And for the next 12 years, as Led Zeppelin's lead singer, Plant embodied rock's Golden God fantasy and fashioned a prototypical look for hard-rock singers, from his poses to his testosterone-fueled cries of "Baby, baby, bay-beeee!" After Led Zeppelin splintered, Plant launched the most ambitious of all Led Zeppelin solo careers, exploring a variety of new musical directions—world music, ambient pop, and rockabilly—without ever leaving his Zep-style pomp. He also intermittently tested the Led Zep waters, reuniting with Page and John Paul Jones for one-off gigs and sampling the group's music in his songs. In 1994 he made the plunge and got back together with Page for an extended reunion.

what to buy: Teaming with guitarist Robbie Blunt, a childhood friend, Plant began his solo career with *Pictures at Eleven* 𝄢𝄢𝄢𝄢 (Swan Song, 1982, prod. Robert Plant), an album that rocks hard but also pursues some of the same ambient directions of later Led Zeppelin albums. His next album, *Principle of Moments* 𝄢𝄢𝄢𝄢 (Es Paranza, 1983, prod. Robert Plant, Benji Lefevre, Pat Moran), offered more of a departure by way of moody, textured tracks such as "Big Log" and "In the Mood."

what to buy next: *Now and Zen* 𝄢𝄢𝄢 (Es Paranza, 1989, prod. Robert Plant, Tim Palmer, Phil Johnstone) found Plant re-embracing his Led Zep roots after determinedly straying from them for several years. He samples some Zep pieces on "Tall Cool One," while Page solos on that song and on "Heaven Knows."

The Honeydrippers, Vol. 1 (Es Paranza, 1984) is a spirited five-song oldies workout that features Page and Jeff Beck on guitar.

what to avoid: The socially conscious *Fate of Nations* 🎵🎵 (Es Paranza, 1993, prod. Chris Hughes, Robert Plant) is heavy-handed and inconsistent, the weakest of Plant's otherwise strong solo career.

the rest:
Shaken 'n' Stirred 🎵🎵🎵 (Es Paranza, 1985)
Manic Nirvana 🎵🎵 (Es Paranza, 1990)

worth searching for: The vinyl 12-inch single for "Burning down One Side" (Swan Song, 1982, prod. Robert Plant) from *Pictures at Eleven* features the non-album track "Far Post," a fine song that's well worth owning.

influences:

◄◄ Donovan, Tim Hardin, Little Richard, Keith Relf, Muddy Waters, Howlin' Wolf

►► David Coverdale, Axl Rose, Vince Neil, Bret Michaels

see also: *Led Zeppelin, Page & Plant*

Sarah Weber

Plastikman /Circuit Breaker /Cybersonik /FUSE

Born Richie Hawtin, 1970, in Banbury, England.

If you're inclined to dismiss techno as mindless dance music, then you obviously haven't heard the music of Richie Hawtin. Under a variety of pseudonyms—Plastikman being the most famous—Hawtin has consistently raised the level of achievement in techno and, in the process, has elevated the music beyond its dance floor origins. Hawtin was born in England, but in 1979 his family relocated to Windsor, Ontario, Canada, located just across the border from Detroit. As a child, Hawtin was immersed in the world of computers and electronic kits while his father (who worked as an engineer for a Canadian General Motors robotics division) introduced him to the futuristic sounds of Kraftwerk and Tangerine Dream. Thanks to radio shows by DJs such as Jeff Mills, Hawtin discovered the sounds of Chicago house and Detroit techno around 1987. He soon began making regular trips across the border to Detroit to buy records by original techno pioneers Derrick May, Juan Atkins, and Kevin Saunderson while also attending the clubs where they DJ'd. Unlike the wave of European techno and rave producers that emerged during the '90s, Hawtin was able to experience the birth of techno firsthand. It wasn't long before he began DJ'ing himself and started a club in his hometown.

Hawtin also began making tracks with Kenny Larkin using minimal equipment, and in 1990 he hooked up with John Aquaviva to start the influential Plus 8 label. Since then Hawtin has produced several solo albums and countless 12-inches while continuing to be in demand throughout the world as one of the top techno DJs. What makes Hawtin's work so unique is his ability to create complex rhythms with minimal drum patterns—in a manner similar to Steve Reich's early minimalist compositions—that keep the dance floor moving while also providing plenty of musical material for a listener to dissect.

what to buy: On his first two Plastikman albums, *Musik* 🎵🎵🎵🎵 (Novamute/Plus 8, 1994, prod. Richie Hawtin) and *Sheet One* 🎵🎵🎵🎵 (Novamute/Plus 8, 1993, prod. Richie Hawtin), you'll hear Hawtin construct mind-bending polyrhythms (as opposed to the usual mindless 4/4 pounding of most techno tracks) with his Roland TR-808 and TR-909 drum machines while stabbing your ears with the psychedelic acid squelches of the Roland TB-303 bass synthesizer. Amazingly enough, Hawtin uses those same tools to construct moody ambient pieces on both albums to make them more akin to a sonic journey rather than a collection of dance tracks. The budget conscious can pick up Hawtin's two excellent Plastikman EPs, *Recycled Plastik* 🎵🎵🎵 (Novamute/Plus 8, 1994, prod. Richie Hawtin) and *Sickness* 🎵🎵🎵 (Novamute/Plus 8, 1997, prod. Richie Hawtin).

what to buy next: Originally released as part of Warp's Artificial Intelligence series of albums, FUSE's *dimension Intrusion* 🎵🎵🎵 (TVT/Wax Trax/Plus 8, 1993, prod. Richie Hawtin) is an excellent collection of Hawtin's earlier work that's more melodic and not as trippy as his Plastikman material. *Live! Richie Hawtin* 🎵🎵🎵 (Mixmag/Moonshine, 1995, prod. Richie Hawtin) is a continuous mix of various techno tracks that gives the home listener an approximation of what it would be like to hear Hawtin DJ. *Consumed* 🎵🎵🎵 (Novamute/Minus, 1998, prod. Richie Hawtin) and the *Concept 1 96:CD* 🎵🎵🎵 (Minus, 1998, prod. Richie Hawtin) project are both extremely minimal pieces of electronica that average listeners might find a bit difficult to ingest but are definitely worth the effort.

worth searching for: Hawtin's collaborations with German ambient musician Pete Namlook have resulted in a series of beautiful ambient electronica full of lush synth work and minimal percussion that are currently available only as limited edition imports: *From Within* (FAX/World, 1994, prod. Pete Namlook, Richie Hawtin); *From Within II* (FAX, 1995 prod. Pete Namlook, Richie Hawtin); and *From Within III* (FAX, 1997, prod. Pete Namlook, Richie Hawtin). They're expected be re-released by Hawtin's Minus label sometime in the future.

influences:
◄◄ Derrick May, Juan Atkins, Kevin Saunderson, Jeff Mills, Kraftwerk, Tangerine Dream

Howard Shih

The Platters

Formed 1953, in Los Angeles, CA.

Tony Williams, lead vocals (1953–60); David Lynch, tenor vocals; Herbert Reed, bass vocals; Alex Hodge, baritone vocals (1953–54); Zola Taylor, contralto vocals (1954–61); Paul Robi, baritone vocals (1955–62); Sonny Turner, lead vocals (1961–65); Nate Nelson, baritone vocals (1962–65); Sandra Dawn, contralto vocals (1962–65).

From 1955 to 1960, few vocal groups could touch the Platters' crossover appeal. Featuring Tony Williams's heart-rending lead vocals, the group had several smash hits that are now inarguable classics of the genre. "Only You," "The Great Pretender," and "Smoke Gets in Your Eyes" remain prime examples of head-over-heels romantic R&B. Williams's total emotional immersion in the material is nothing less than overwhelming. As the 1960s wore on, numerous member changes effectively stalled the former hit-makers. The 1970s were marked by court battles over ownership of the group's name; the rights are now held by Paul Robi's widow. The group was inducted into the Rock and Roll Hall of Fame in 1990.

what to buy: *Enchanted: The Best of the Platters* 🎵🎵🎵🎵 (Rhino, 1998, prod. various) is a generous 20-track primer on the group that hits all the highlights of their career. The perfect introduction to the group. *The Very Best of the Platters* 🎵🎵🎵 (Mercury, 1991, compilation prod. Bill Levenson) has the major hits, but offers fewer cuts than the Rhino set.

what to buy next: *The Magic Touch: An Anthology* 🎵🎵🎵🎵 (Mercury, 1991, compilation prod. Harry Weinger) is a more complete two-disc set that includes many lesser-known tracks, making it a more definitive album for those already acquainted.

what to avoid: *Greatest Hits, Vol. 2* 🎵🎵 (Curb, 1996, prod. various) is a skimpy collection devoid of the biggest hits.

the rest:
Greatest Hits 🎵🎵 (Special Music Company)
The Platters 🎵🎵 (King)
Golden Hits Collection 🎵🎵🎵🎵 (Pickwick, 1993)
Christmas with the Platters 🎵🎵🎵 (Mercury, 1994)
The Musicor Years 🎵🎵🎵 (Kent, 1994)

worth searching for: *Four Platters and One Lovely Dish* (Bear Family, 1994, prod. various) is a typical whole-hog, nine-disc set that should appeal to the ultra-completists.

influences:
◀◀ The Ink Spots, Bobby Bland

▶▶ New Edition, Boyz II Men, Huey Lewis & the News

Allan Orski

The Pleasure Barons

See: Dave Alvin, Beat Farmers

The Plimsouls

See: Peter Case

PM Dawn

Formed 1990, in Jersey City, NJ.

Prince Be (born Attrell Cordes), vocals; DJ Minutemix (born Jarrett Cordes), DJ.

"Reality Used to Be a Friend of Mine" is one of the anthems that put PM Dawn on the map; it could also serve as a label for the duo's metaphysical raps and musings. Some take its hippy-dippy attitude as an influence from De La Soul, which has since taken on a more hardcore image. But in music, the tent is big, and the otherworldly excursions of PM Dawn add another ring to the circus.

what to buy: *The Bliss Album . . . ? (Vibrations of Love and Anger and the Ponderance of Life and Existence)* 🎵🎵🎵🎵 (Gee Street/Island, 1993, prod. PM Dawn) proves to be inspired musicianship, whatever the genre, though "Beyond Infinite Affections," "Nocturnal Is in the House," and, especially, "Plastic" show the duo can throw down when the challenge arises (the latter song is inspired by KRS-One's infamous on-stage assault of Prince Be).

what to buy next: Paradoxically, PM Dawn broke in during the height of gangsta rap with *Of the Heart, of the Soul and the Cross: The Utopian Experience* 🎵🎵🎵🎵 (Gee Street/Island, 1991, prod. PM Dawn), an album loaded with interesting samples—and one in which Prince Be croons bona fide soul between rhymes. Built around Spandau Ballet's "True," the breakthrough single "Set Adrift on Memory Bliss" is a glorious slice of dreamy pop. The group's poppish psychedelia begins to wear thin, though, by its third album, *Jesus Wept* 🎵🎵🎵 (Gee Street/Island, 1995, prod. PM Dawn), even though "My Personal Gravity" did hit the airwaves with its haunting "What could be lonely 'bout you?" line. Reportedly, the final product isn't even close to the one PM Dawn wanted to release, (no) thanks to sample-clearance issues—a major problem for a group that thrives on sampling unlikely sources (Spandau Ballet, George Michael, Joni Mitchell, Hugh Masekela, Doobie Brothers).

the rest:
Dearest Christian, I'm So Very Sorry for Bringing You Here. Love, Dad N/A (Gee Street/Island, 1998)

influences:
◀◀ Prince, the Beatles, Donovan, the Beach Boys

▶▶ Me Phi Me, O.M.D., Beck

Lawrence Gabriel

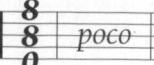
Poco

Formed 1968, in Los Angeles, CA.

Rusty Young, pedal steel, vocals (1968–84, 1989–present); Richie Furay, guitar, vocals (1968–73, 1989–91); Jim Messina, guitar, vocals (1968–70, 1989–91); Randy Meisner, bass, vocals (1968–69, 1989–91); Timothy B. Schmit, bass, vocals (1969–77); George Grantham, drums, vocals (1968–77); Paul Cotton, guitar, vocals (1970–84); Steve Chapman, drums (1977–84); Kim Bullard, keyboards (1977–84); Charlie Harrison, bass (1977–84).

Of all the original groups that tried to combine rock and country music in the wake of the Byrds' *Sweetheart of the Rodeo* album, Poco went farthest in creating a new kind of sound. Instead of just singing with a twang and adding pedal steel—though they did those things, too—Poco incorporated elements of bluegrass music but sang with a high-pitched fervor that was matched by the group's electric performances, both on record and on stage. These guys never sounded like a mere folk-rock band (except in its later, more commercial years). Founded by former Buffalo Springfield members Jim Messina and Richie Furay, the group recruited several Colorado musicians—Randy Meisner, pedal steel specialist Rusty Young (who brought a rock mentality to what was still considered a country instrument), and George Grantham—and cut loose for a handful of breathless albums before attrition and a changing radio climate tamed the sound. Meisner was the first out, joining Rick Nelson's band, then Linda Ronstadt's, then the Eagles (he was replaced by Timothy B. Schmit, who later left to replace Meisner again, in the Eagles). Messina followed his muse to a successful duo career with Kenny Loggins. Furay left to form a "supergroup," the Souther-Hillman-Furay Band, and now is a pastor in Boulder, Colorado. Latter-day releases under Rusty Young's leadership are likable pop albums, with big production touches including horns and synthesizer strings on hits such as "Heart of the Night," "Keep on Tryin'," and "Crazy Love." The original Poco lineup reformed in 1989 for the *Legacy* recording and tour.

what to buy: The group's purity of vision is clear as a bell on *Poco* ♪♪♪♪ (Epic, 1970/Legacy, 1990 prod. Jim Messina). The album's sound is driven by Furay's cutting tenor, which gives the record a sonic edge that other country rockers didn't have. The harmonies especially are unbelievably high. But the music rocks, gets churchy when it needs to, and makes cool use of Young's pedal steel without ever sounding like a rock imitation of country music. *Deliverin'* ♪♪♪♪ (Epic, 1971/Legacy, 1990 prod. Jim Messina) shows how powerful a live group Poco was, even at its start.

what to buy next: *The Very Best of Poco* ♪♪♪♪ (Epic, 1975, prod. various) is a non-stop fun-fest and a great overview of Poco's strengths up to mid-career. As for Poco's later work,

after *Rose of Cimarron* ♪♪♪ (ABC, 1976/One Way, 1993, prod. Poco, Mark Harman) the band sounded increasingly more pedestrian and middle-of-the-road. Then again, this is the period when the big hits came; go figure. *Crazy Loving, the Best of Poco 1975–1982* ♪♪♪ (MCA, 1989, prod. various) is a lean, no-fat collection of those pop chartmakers.

what to avoid: *Legacy* ♪ (RCA, 1989, prod. David Cole) was a calculated move at reigniting the fan base with an reunion of original members, but the music was cynically aimed at middle-of-the-road radio. One of the hits (there were two) was co-written by lukewarm rocker Richard Marx.

the rest:
Pickin' up the Pieces ♪♪♪ (Epic, 1969/Legacy, 1995)
From the Inside ♪♪♪ (Epic, 1971/Legacy, 1995)
A Good Feelin' to Know ♪♪♪ (Epic, 1972)
Crazy Eyes ♪♪♪ (Epic, 1973/Legacy, 1995)
Seven ♪♪♫ (Epic, 1974/Legacy, 1995)
Cantamos ♪♪♫ (Epic, 1974)
Head over Heels ♪♪♫ (Epic, 1975)
Live ♪♪ (Epic, 1976)
Indian Summer ♪♪♫ (ABC, 1977)
Legend ♪♪ (ABC, 1978)
Under the Gun ♪♪ (MCA, 1980)
Blue and Gray ♪♪ (MCA, 1981/One Way, 1993)
Cowboys and Englishmen ♪♪ (MCA, 1982/One Way, 1993)
Ghost Town ♪♪ (Atlantic, 1982)
Inamorata ♪♫ (Atlantic, 1984)
The Forgotten Trail 1969–1974 ♪♪♪♫ (Epic/Legacy, 1990)

worth searching for: The CD single for "Call It Love" (RCA, 1989, prod. David Cole) is worth ferreting out, not so much for the fairly pedestrian song but for the arresting, fold-out graphics that feature a cut-out of the Poco horse emblem on the cover.

solo outings:
Souther-Hillman-Furay Band:
The Souther-Hillman-Furay Band ♪♪♪ (Asylum, 1974)
Trouble in Paradise ♪♪♪ (Asylum, 1975)

Richie Furay:
(With the Richie Furay Band) *I've Got a Reason* ♪♫ (Asylum, 1976)

Jim Messina:
Oasis ♪♫ (Columbia 1979)
Messina ♪ (Warner Bros., 1981)

Rusty Young:
(With the Sky Kings) *The Sky Kings* ♪♪♪ (Warner/Reprise, 1996)

influences:
◀◀ Flatt & Scruggs, the Everly Brothers, the Byrds, the Flying Burrito Brothers, Buffalo Springfield

New Grass Revival, Foster & Lloyd, Alison Krauss & Union Station, Uncle Tupelo, Son Volt, Wilco

see also: *The Eagles, Loggins & Messina*

Gil Asakawa

Poc

Born Annie Danielewski, March 23, 1968, in New York, NY.

One great angry, big-guitar-rock hit—"Trigger Happy Jack," with its eerie "Can't talk to a psycho like a normal human being" chorus—has given singer-songwriter Poe a career. It helped, of course, that she wrote "Hello" about the Internet, did interviews with all the nerdy Web magazines while her contemporaries ignored them, and cultivated a cyber-savvy-sex-symbol image worthy of *The X-Files*' Gillian Anderson. Her debut album, *Hello*, showed a glimpse of potential, although the lyrical mix of cuteness and anger didn't jell, except in "Trigger Happy Jack" and "Angry Johnny." Poe, who named herself after the writer Edgar Allan Poe at the wizened age of 10, followed up *Hello* with a series of Net-simulcast concert tours and backing vocals on Fastball's album *All the Pain Money Can Buy*.

what's available: *Hello* 𝄢𝄢𝄽 (Atlantic, 1995, prod. R.J. Rice, Dave Jerden, Poe, Jeffrey Connor) is another of those prevalent CDs you need for one song: in this case, "Trigger Happy Jack." Its bent chorus and scary ambience finger Poe as a bright young talent, but the rest of the album, with the exception of the slower but just-as-angry "Angry Johnny," is a mess of overpersonal, overproduced folk songs.

influences:

Bush, Garbage, Smashing Pumpkins, Jewel

Smash Mouth, Third Eye Blind, Sugar Ray

Steve Knopper

The Pogues /Shane MacGowan & the Popes

Formed 1982, in London, England. Disbanded 1997.

Peter "Spider" Stacy, vocals, pennywhistle; Jeremy "Jem" Finger, banjo, guitar; Shane MacGowan, vocals (1982–91); Joe Strummer, vocals, guitar (1991–93); James Fearnley, accordion (1982–93); James McNally, accordion (1993–present); Philip Chevron, guitar (1984–93); Jamie Clarke, guitar (1993–97); Andrew Ranken, drums; Cait O'Riordan, bass (1982–86); Darryl Hunt (1986–97).

The Pogues inject the bile of punk rock into traditional Celtic folk music. And at its best—with the brilliant gutter-poet Shane MacGowan on lead vocals—the band was one of England's most original rock acts. But MacGowan, a career alcoholic, be-

came increasingly unstable and left the band in 1991. With Stacy handling lead vocals, the Pogues became a decent Celtic rock outfit, but hardly the revolutionary group it was in the past. The magic was gone without MacGowan, and the band split up after one lackluster album.

what to buy: *Rum, Sodomy & the Lash* 𝄢𝄢𝄢𝄢 (MCA, 1985, prod. Elvis Costello) is MacGowan and the Pogues at the group's peak, thrashing through punk workouts such as "The Sock Bed of Cuchulainn" and switching easily into ballads like "And the Band Played Waltzing Matilda."

what to buy next: MacGowan was still in fine form on *If I Should Fall from Grace with God* 𝄢𝄢𝄢 (Island, 1988, prod. Steve Lillywhite), especially his brawling duet with Kirsty Mac-Coll on "Fairy Tale of New York." But you could practically smell the whiskey in his slurred vocals on *Peace and Love* 𝄢𝄢𝄽 (Island, 1989, prod. Steve Lillywhite), a still-strong effort that foreshadowed the downhill stumble to follow.

what to avoid: *Pogue Mahone* 𝄢𝄽 (Mesa, 1995, prod. Steve Brown) is a pleasant but all-too-safe post-MacGowan effort.

the rest:
Red Roses for Me 𝄢𝄢𝄢 (Enigma, 1984)
Poguetry in Motion 𝄢𝄢𝄽 (MCA EP, 1986)
Hell's Ditch 𝄢𝄢𝄽 (Island, 1990)
Yeah, Yeah, Yeah, Yeah 𝄢𝄢 (Island, 1990)
Essential Pogues 𝄢𝄢𝄢 (Island, 1991)
Waiting for Herb 𝄢𝄢𝄽 (Chameleon, 1993)

worth searching for: The soundtrack for *Straight to Hell* (Enigma Classics, 1987) features the Pogues' version of Ennio Morricone's theme for the Clint Eastwood film *The Good, the Bad, and the Ugly*, as well as the traditional "Danny Boy."

solo outings:
Shane MacGowan & the Popes:
The Snake 𝄢𝄢𝄽 (ZTT/Warner Bros., 1995)

influences:

The Clancy Brothers, the Clash, the Chieftains, the Sex Pistols

The Drovers, the Levellers, the Cranberries

Thor Christensen

Poi Dog Pondering

Formed 1984, in Waikiki, HI.

Frank Orrall, guitar, vocals; Dave "Max" Crawford, keyboards, trumpet, accordion; Susan Voeltz, violin; Brigid Murphy, saxophone; Dag Julan, guitar.

The first question everyone asks is "Where did the name come from?" The answer: from the Hawaiian food Poi, a sort of regional fruit staple—kind of like mashed potatoes on the mainland. The term "Poi Dog" is a Hawaiian slang term for mixed breed or mutt. Seeing themselves as a bit of a thinking mixed-breed of musicians, Poi Dog Pondering was the perfect name. The group kicked around for several years as a street band in Hawaii before attacking the rest of the country. On the way, it picked up new members in California and Austin, until the aggregation eventually ended up in New York. There, the group signed a deal with Texas Hotel records and were quickly picked up by Columbia. But after three albums and an EP, Columbia dropped the band and PDP—since re-located to Chicago—created its own record company, Pomegranate. Its lineup over the years has included more than 30 different musicians, and the sound has remained an exciting combination of roots rock, world music, techno-dance, and disco blended with classically styled arrangements. PDP is more of a modern rock orchestral troupe (with a horn section, strings, keyboards, guitars, bass, drums, percussionists, and soulful background vocals) than a conventional rock band. Its lyrical content may be as simple as what's for breakfast and the joys of walking, or as complex as the embracing of one's mortality and the beauty of love. While so many ingredients could convolute a band, PDP succeeds brilliantly.

what to buy: *Volo Volo* 𝄪𝄪𝄪𝄪 (Columbia, 1992, prod. various), the third and final full-length record with Columbia, best displays the full extent of this band's talents and is wonderfully team-produced by Orall, ex-Talking Head Jerry Harrison, and many others. "Lackluster" and "Jack Ass Ginger" showcase the strong horn section and funky bass lines for a contagiously fun and danceable side, while songs like "Collarbone" showcase Susan Voeltz's amazingly haunting violin layered over a light acoustic guitar and keyboards.

what to buy next: The debut, *Poi Dog Pondering* 𝄪𝄪𝄪𝄪 (Columbia, 1989, prod. Poi Dog Pondering, Mike Stewart), captures the PDP energy and fun before the big-time producers got involved. "Wood Guitar" displays their louder, rocking side, while "Pulling Touch" is quite possibly the group's most beautiful and perfect song. *Liquid White Light* 𝄪𝄪𝄪 (Plate-Tec-Tonic, 1997, prod. Martin Stebbing, Dave Max Crawford), a 23-song, two-disc live record, captures all of the excitement and diversity that is Poi Dog Pondering. It includes a great cover of Brian Eno's and John Cale's "Lay My Love."

what to avoid: *Pomegranate* 𝄪𝄪 (Pomegranate, 1995, prod. Frank Orrall, Martin Stebbing, Poi Dog Pondering) is a disappointment. The production is flat, burying great guitar hooks and dramatic drum sweeps while turning up the hoaky saxophone solo's reminiscent of Kenny G.

the rest:
Wishing like a Mountain and Thinking like the Sea 𝄪𝄪𝄪 (Columbia, 1990)
Electrique Plummegram 𝄪𝄪 (Bar/None/Platetectonic, 1996)

worth searching for: The out-of-print *Fruitless* (Columbia EP, 1990) contains an amazing cover of New Order's "Love Vigilantes" that's alone worth the search, as well as live versions of "Wood Guitar" and "Falling."

solo outings:
Palm Fabric Orchestra:
Vague Gropings in the Slip Stream (Carrot Top, 1994)

influences:
◀◀ Talking Heads, Van Morrison, the Pogues, the Waterboys, Paul Simon

▶▶ Rusted Root, the Dave Matthews Band

see also: *Abra Moore*

Joshua Zarov

Buster Poindexter
See: David Johnansen

Poison
Formed 1983, in Harrisburg, PA.

Bret Michaels (born Bret Michael Sychak), vocals, guitar; **Matt Smith,** guitar (1983–85); **Bobby Dall** (born Robert Kuy Kendall), bass, vocals; **Rikki Rockett** (born Richard Ream), drums; **C.C. Deville** (born Bruce Anthony Johannesson), guitar, vocals (1985–92, 1996–present); **Richie Kotzen,** guitar (1992–93); **Blues Saraceno,** guitar (1992).

The title of Poison's debut, *Look What the Cat Dragged In*, summed up the attitude of this makeup-wearing, hairspray-loving '80s pop-metal band. Bret Michaels, underneath his long, blonde, Mötley Crüe–like hair, was an equally charismatic and cynical frontman who carried his band to the top of the pop charts. Poison had many massive '80s hits, including the power ballad "Every Rose Has Its Thorn," which hit #1 in 1988, and "Unskinny Bop," #3 in 1990. But like all the other hair metal bands, Poison found itself without an audience during the early '90s and, despite a desperate shift of personnel, faded into trivia. Nevertheless, the group planned a comeback for the late '90s, while Michaels kept in the headlines by cavorting with *Baywatch* babe Pamela Anderson in a sex video, then forming a film company with actor Charlie Sheen and signing Marlon Brando to co-star in their first feature project.

what to buy: *Poison's Greatest Hits 1986–1996* 𝄪𝄪𝄪 (Capitol, 1996, prod. various) has all the essentials. Pleasant ear candy when all you want is a musical snack.

what to avoid: *Open up and Say . . . Ahh!* 𝄪 (Enigma/Capitol, 1988, prod. Tom Werman) is a rehash of Poison's debut.

the rest:
Look What the Cat Dragged In 𝄪𝄪𝄪 (Capitol, 1986)
Flesh and Blood 𝄪𝄪 (Enigma/Capitol, 1990)

Swallow This Live 🎸🎸 (Capitol, 1991)
Native Tongue 🎸 (Capitol, 1993)

influences:

◄◄ AC/DC, Kiss, Kansas, Journey

►► Winger, Warrant, Ratt, Cry of Love

Tracey Birkenhauer and Steve Knopper

The Police

Formed 1977, in London, England. Disbanded 1984.

Sting (born Gordon Sumner), bass, vocals, saxophone, keyboards; Stewart Copeland, drums; Henri Pandovani, guitar (1977); Andy Summers (born Andrew Somers), guitar.

Though they arrived amid the fury of England's punk revolution, the members of the Police, while not actual punks themselves, played them on TV. By bleaching their hair so they could appear in a bubblegum commercial, the band may have called its credibility into question from the very beginning, but the fact is, their ability to write songs and actually play their instruments wouldn't have curried much favor in the DIY era anyway. With musical pasts ranging from jazz (Sting) to prog-rock (Stewart Copeland) to all manner of session work (Andy Summers), the Police focused on white reggae (*Reggetta de Blanc*, as their second album's title proclaimed), coating it with a pop sheen that soon enough brought the world to their punky reggae party. Sting's middle-to-highbrow lyrics included some serious pretensions—namechecking novelist Vladimir Nabokov here, attempting to explain Jungian concepts there. But give the guy credit: if he helped sell a few extra copies of *Lolita* or *Psychology of the Unconscious*, then so much the better. The group splintered in 1984 with all three members going on to solo success of varying degrees, led of course by Der Schtingle, who has become one of the world's most famous rock superstars.

what to buy: The group's best album overall was also its swan song. *Synchronicity* 🎸🎸🎸🎸 (A&M, 1983, prod. Hugh Padgham, Police) contains the seamless hit "Every Breath You Take," a song about control that was subtle enough to be mistaken for a love ditty. "King of Pain" laid bare Sting's martyr complex, and "Tea in the Sahara" revealed him to be a man of wealth and taste. But "Synchronicity" is the band's strongest statement, full of exotic elements but played with utter assurance. Alas, the same creative friction that drove them to new heights split them apart in the wake of the album's massive success. *Zenyatta Mondatta* 🎸🎸🎸🎸 (A&M, 1980, prod. Police, Nigel Gray) is the album on which the Police's grasp finally matched its outsized reach. "Don't Stand So Close to Me," and the nonsensical "De Do Do Do, De Da Da Da" turned the group more toward pop, while "Driven to Tears" kept an eye on world events and "When

the World Is Running Down, You Make the Best of What's Still Around" somehow works the topic of entropy into a love song. If you can only afford to buy one Police album, though, let it be *Every Breath You Take: The Singles* 🎸🎸🎸🎸 (A&M, 1986, prod. various), which covers the territory as well as one disc will allow, though it's docked one bone for its pointless remake of "Don't Stand So Close to Me." The album was reissued a decade later with a couple of added remixes as *Every Breath You Take: The Classics* 🎸🎸🎸🎸 (A&M, 1995, prod. various).

what to buy next: For those with plenty of money and a weekend to kill, the four-CD *Message in a Box: The Complete Recordings* 🎸🎸🎸🎸 (A&M, 1993, prod. various) offers just what its title indicates—the whole of the bands oeuvre in one package. The rarities are pretty spare, though, and don't offer enough additional insight into the band to justify the purchase to someone who owns the individual albums. On *Regatta de Blanc* 🎸🎸🎸🎸 (A&M, 1979, prod. Police, Nigel Gray) you can hear Sting's songwriting take a leap forward the moment his self-pity turns to empathy in "Message in a Bottle." The album also contains the equally fine "Bring on the Night" and "Walking on the Moon." *Ghost in the Machine* 🎸🎸🎸🎸 (A&M, 1981, prod. Police, Hugh Padgham) contains the band's most ebullient single, "Every Little Thing She Does Is Magic," as other songs survey themes of media overload ("Too Much Information") and future shock ("Demolition Man") over an increasingly complex instrumental attack.

the rest:

Outlandos d'Amour 🎸🎸🎸 (A&M, 1978)
The Police Live! 🎸🎸🎸🎸 (A&M, 1995)

worth searching for: The two-volume bootleg *Live in Melbourne* (Golden Stars, 1990) captures a fiery 1981 show during a tour that found the Police enthusiastically embracing its new-found arena-sized popularity.

influences:

◄◄ Bob Marley, the Beatles, Miles Davis, Wayne Shorter

►► Wang Chung, Men at Work, the Samples, Rancid, Goldfinger

see also: *Andy Summers, Sting, Stewart Copeland*

Daniel Durchholz

Robert Pollard

See: Guided by Voices

Steve Poltz

See: The Rugburns

Polytown

See: Japan, Missing Persons

Iggy Pop /The Stooges

Formed 1967, in Ann Arbor, MI. Disbanded 1971. Re-formed 1972. Disbanded 1974.

Iggy Pop (born James Jewel Osterberg, April 21, 1947 in Ypsilanti, MI), vocals; Ron Asheton, guitar, bass; Dave Alexander (died February 10, 1975), bass (1967–70); Scott Asheton, drums; James Williamson, guitar (1970–74); Scott Thurston, bass, keyboards (1973–74).

We can only marvel at the sheer resilience Iggy Pop has displayed over the years. Like the Rolling Stones' Keith Richards, Iggy has done enough drugs and engaged in enough self-destructive behavior to wipe out a squadron of lesser pop stars—maybe more, since Richards never spread peanut butter all over himself or rolled around in broken glass onstage. Whatever the case, Iggy keeps at it, and even now he cuts a lean, sinewy figure who, in his music, never seems to have trouble finding something to be angry about or finding a girl to chase. Raised in a trailer park, Iggy was inspired to pursue rock 'n' roll after attending a Doors concert; he formed the Stooges in time for the group to debut, appropriately enough, on Halloween night, 1967. The Stooges will forever be intertwined with fellow Ann Arborites the MC5 as punk rock forebears, and the rock community of the late '60s—with its plethora of love beads and flower power—had neither seen nor heard anything like the Stooges' primal roar and songs about raw power and wanting to be your dog. It wasn't just outrage that made the Stooges legendary, though; it was the sheer, brutal force of its rock, driven not only by James Williamson and Ron Asheton's raging guitars but also by Scott "Rock Action" Asheton's drumming, a combination of rock quarry thud and soulful swing that owed more than a little to the music being made at Motown Records in nearby Detroit. The Stooges lasted just long enough to record some amazing rock 'n' roll albums and secure its legacy, and a year doesn't go by when there isn't some discussion about a reunion. Iggy's solo career, on the other hand, has been more fitful; excepting the electrifying 1977 double dip of *The Idiot* and *Lust for Life*, he's never really approached the Stooges' level of fury. More worrisome is how he flirts with becoming a caricature, playing to an image rather than fully exercising his artistry. He never quite reaches that point, and there's always something on his albums—and certainly in his live shows—that brings you back for more. But at the same time, there's something both invigorating and disconcerting about hearing one of rock's most revered personalities sing about chasing girls in the most base and sophomoric terms.

what to buy: Consider this a grand slam of primal punk rock power. The Stooges' *Fun House* ♫♫♫♫ (Elektra, 1970/1987, prod. Dan Galluci) and *Raw Power* ♫♫♫♫ (Columbia, 1972,

prod. David Bowie/Columbia Legacy, 1997, prod. Iggy Pop) are molten slamfests that are essential touchstones for every form of aggressive rock that came after—from '70s heavy metal to punk to speed metal and thrash. Lots of blitzkrieg, but no bop. (Nike used the song "Search and Destroy" from *Raw Power* during its commercials for the 1996 summer Olympics.) The Legacy version of *Raw Power* finds Iggy reclaiming his vision of the album after the record company called in David Bowie to make it more commercially palatable after the Stooges first recorded it. On the solo front, 1977 wasn't only a good year for British punk; Iggy's *The Idiot* ♫♫♫♫ (RCA, 1977/Virgin, 1990, prod. David Bowie) and *Lust for Life* ♫♫♫♫♫ (RCA, 1977/Virgin, 1990, prod. Bewlay Brothers) are seminal works, capturing the energetic magic of the Stooges but incorporating some dynamic sophistication courtesy of Bowie's influence.

what to buy next: *The Stooges* ♫♫♫ (Elektra, 1968/1988, prod. John Cale) is inconsistent and a bit rough (in the bad sense), but you've got to have songs such as "1969," "I Wanna Be Your Dog," and "No Fun" in the collection. Iggy's *Brick by Brick* ♫♫♫♫ (Virgin, 1990, prod. Don Was) was considered too soft by some; that's a mistake, because it conveys the broadest range of emotions he's ever set on record, in some of the most tuneful settings as well.

what to avoid: Iggy's *Zombie Birdhouse* ♫♫ (I.R.S., 1982/1992, prod. Chris Stein) represents a noble effort by Blondie guitarist Chris Stein to put the singer in some new sonic settings, but he never quite warms to them and, consequently, the album sounds forced.

the rest:
TV Eye ♫♫♫ (RCA, 1978/Virgin, 1994)
Blah, Blah, Blah ♫♫ (A&M, 1986)
American Caesar ♫♫♫ (Virgin, 1993)
Naughty Little Doggie ♫♫♫ (Virgin, 1996)
Nude and Rude: The Best of Iggy Pop ♫♫♫♫ (Virgin, 1996)
The King Biscuit Flower Hour Presents Iggy Pop ♫♫♫♫ (KBFH, 1997)

worth searching for: The Stooges' final concert in 1974 is enshrined on the import *Metallic 2 X KO* (Skydog), a rough-sounding recording that still conveys the band's anarchic zeal. *We Will Fall: The Iggy Pop Tribute* (Royalty, 1997, prod. various) features protégés such as Joey Ramone, the Red Hot Chili Peppers, Monster Magnet, and others paying homage to but never bettering their master.

influences:

◄◄ The Doors, the Animals, Mitch Ryder & the Detroit Wheels, the Rolling Stones, Motown

►► The Ramones, the Sex Pistols, the Damned, Black Flag, the Misfits, Metallica, Danzig

Gary Graff

Iggy Pop (© Ken Settle)

Pop Will Eat Itself

Formed 1986, in Sturbridge, England.

Clint Mansell, vocals, guitar; Adam Mole, guitar, keyboards; Graham Crabb, drums; Richard March, bass.

The anarchic quartet Pop Will Eat Itself developed from ranty jangle-pop into cocksure techno-rap-metal in a relatively short time, marking the development of the technology itself. And while today it sounds painfully dated (shelf life is the problem with technologically inspired music), at the time it rang the revolution and spawned such personalities as Carter the Unstoppable Sex Machine, Jesus Jones, and EMF, while also coloring a gothic-industrial movement that took itself too seriously. After a tumultuous wave of three increasingly indulgent albums, the band was signed to nine inch nails auteur Trent Reznor's nothing label. But soon after, PWEI disbanded, leaving only a remix album in its wake.

what to buy: *This Is the Day, This Is the Hour, This* 🎵🎵🎵 (RCA, 1989, prod. various) is still fun to listen to, although it never seemed to sound like the Beastie Boys as much as it does now. Noted patching of rap with British swagger makes for interesting fare like the anthemic "Inject Me."

the rest:
The PWEI Cure for Sanity 🎵🎵♥ (RCA, 1990)
The Looks or the Lifestyle 🎵🎵♥ (RCA, 1992)
Dos Dedos Mis 🎵🎵 (nothing, 1994)

influences:
◀◀ Public Enemy, Sigue Sigue Sputnik, Beastie Boys, Renegade Soundwave

▶▶ EMF, nine inch nails, Nitzer Ebb

Billy Manes

Porno for Pyros

Formed 1991, in Los Angeles, CA. Disbanded 1998.

Perry Farrell, vocals, percussion, samples, keyboards; Peter DiStefano, guitar; Paul Stephen Perkins, drums; Martyn LeNoble, bass (1991–96); Mike Watt, bass (1996).

In a city choking on bands eager to find that consummate union of funk and metal during the late '80s, it was Perry Farrell's eccentric vision that set Jane's Addiction apart from its competition. But Jane's Addiction's mounting popularity caused Farrell to disband the group in 1991—just after he launched the Lollapalooza tour—and start up Porno for Pyros. The new group left Farrell open to new sonic experimentation set against soul-searching revelations, loose-limbed grooves, and cosmic city and surf themes. Unfortunately, the new stint only lasted two albums before the eccentric frontman became distracted with another Lollapalooza tour, a 1997 Jane's Addiction reunion tour, and the possibility of working in other mediums.

what to buy: The second Porno for Pyros album, *Good God's Urge* 🎵🎵🎵 (Warner Bros., 1996, prod. Perry Farrell, Thomas Johnson, Matt Hyde) attained Farrell's ideal union of jagged rock songs and exotic textures. In songs such as the soaring "Porpoise Head," the whimsical "Tahitian Moon," and the forlorn "Wishing Well," the band conjured up a majestic, oceanic rush of melody and feeling.

what to avoid: *Porno for Pyros* 🎵🎵 (Warner Bros., 1993, prod. Perry Farrell, Matt Hyde) left a lot to be desired; following Jane's superlative string of albums, the record came across as an unfinished sketchbook of ideas, filled with Farrell's mercurial warbling and a hyperkinetic soundtrack that never quite clicked. Still, that's not an entirely bad thing.

influences:
◀◀ Jane's Addiction, the Minutemen, the Beastie Boys, Juan Garcia Esquivel

▶▶ Beck, Air

see also: *Jane's Addiction*

Aidin Vaziri

Portastatic
See: Superchunk

Portishead

Formed 1991, in Bristol, England.

Geoff Barrow, programming, drums, keyboards; Beth Gibbons, vocals; Adrian Utley, musical director, guitar, bass, keyboards.

It's hard to believe now, with so many trip-hop copycats littering the pop landscape, but Portishead was a thoroughly original group when it first arrived in 1994. Created largely by Adrian Utley and prominent British studio worker Geoff Barrow, the reclusive band's debut, *Dummy*, blended spaghetti-Western guitars, cocktail keyboards, and eerie string arrangements with scratchy tape loops, languid hip-hop rhythms, and, of course, Beth Gibbons's melancholy torch vocals about longing and heartbreak. The alluring album was both artistically compelling and emotionally haunting—dark, atmospheric music that would not have sounded out of place in an abandoned cabaret. Three years passed between the debut and a self-titled follow-up, allowing expectations for the sophomore record to blossom, along with the careers of countless groups copying the Portishead sound and guy musician/girl singer setup. Even a dummy could have figured out that the elements were in place for a let-down, which is largely what the sophomore album, *Portishead*, was.

what to buy: It's hard to say what's most compelling about *Dummy* 🎵🎵🎵♥ (Go! Discs/London, 1994, prod. Portishead). Is it Gibbons's detached, disturbed soprano? The dour lyrics in the surprising hit, "Sour Times (Nobody Loves Me)"? The icy, ambient soundscape Barrow and Utley created, using guitars, a Fender Rhodes keyboard, a drum machine, and samples of old records by Weather Report, Isaac Hayes, and Lalo Schifrin? Whatever, it makes for some of the most interesting and original dance music of the '90s.

what to buy next: *Portishead* ♪♪♪ (Go! Discs/London, 1997, prod. Portishead) employs just two traditional samples (from *The Pink Panther* and a Pharcyde record), but it still has the same sample-happy—if emotionally depressed—feel of *Dummy*. Several songs match up well with the first album's best, including "Leslie" and "Only You," but Portishead is already running in place.

the rest:
PNYC N/A (London, 1998)

worth searching for: The EP *Sour Times (Nobody Loves Me)* (Go! Discs/London, 1994, prod. Portishead) features a handful of tracks not included on *Dummy*, but the standout is a lengthy reworking of the title single.

influences:
◀◀ Ennio Morricone, Lalo Schifrin, Shirley Bassey, Edith Piaf, Massive Attack, Björk, Isaac Hayes

▶▶ Sneaker Pimps, Moloko, Lamb, Morcheeba, Hooverphonic, Tricky/Nearly God, Björk

Josh Freedom du Lac

The Posies
Formed 1988, in Seattle, WA.

Ken Stringfellow, guitar, vocals; Jon Auer, guitar, vocals; Rick Roberts, bass (1988–91); Michael Musburger, drums (1988–94); Dave Fox, bass (1992–94); Brian Young, drums (1994–present); Joe "Bass" Howard, bass (1994–present).

The Posies seem to have perfected pop music, almost to the point of sheer brilliance. Formed by childhood friends, the Posies recorded first in Jon Auer's father's house. Strong local sales and good reviews started a bidding war, and the group wound up with DGC for its major label debut. What followed was a string of power pop records that showcased the Posies' incredible talent for knocking out great pop songs that borrow as much from the Who as from its mentors, Big Star—whom Auer and Ken Stringfellow began working with during the early '90s. During mid-1998, however, rumors of a break up began running wild after Stringfellow prepared a solo record.

what to buy: *Dear 23* ♪♪♪♪ (DGC, 1990, prod. John Leckie) is the definitive release in the band's canon, setting the foundation for the Posies' brand of power pop—rich harmonies and sharp arrangements played off of raunchy guitar parts with big

hooks, all gleaned from heroes such as the Beatles, Cheap Trick, the Hollies, and the Move.

what to buy next: Its subsequent releases—*Frosting on the Beater* ♪♪♪ (DGC, 1993, prod. Don Fleming) and *Amazing Disgrace* ♪♪♪ (DGC, 1996, prod. Nick Launey)—have continued in the same vein, while Auer and Stringfellow distinguished themselves as part of a reunited Big Star, performing and recording with Alex Chilton and Jody Stephens beginning in mid-1993.

the rest:
Failure ♪♪♪♪ (Pop Llama, 1988)
Success ♪♪♪ (Pop Llama, 1998)

influences:
◀◀ Big Star, the Beatles, Nick Lowe

▶▶ Young Fresh Fellows, Best Kissers in the World, Flop

see also: *Big Star*

John Nieman and Chris Richards

Robert Poss
See: Band of Susans

Possum Dixon
Formed 1991, in Los Angeles, CA.

Rob Zabrecky, bass, vocals; Celso Chavez, guitar; Robert O'Sullivan, drums; Matt Devine, various instruments.

Stealing its name from an *America's Most Wanted* fugitive, Possum Dixon has spent the bulk of its career pilfering and pasting its own favorite facets of the rock together to create solid American pop. The band found initial acclaim through the single "Watch That Girl Destroy Me" and a moderately successful debut, *Possum Dixon*. With a Knack-like knack for quick-witted bar pop, the group trudged on to concert success on the college circuit.

what to buy: *Star Maps* 𝄢𝄢𝄢 (Interscope, 1996, prod. Tim O'Heir) challenged some of the ready-to-eat styles of the group's debut. By looping similar thickness to that of previous projects with Sebadoh and Dinosaur Jr., producer O'Heir pulled Possum Dixon up to a more attention-sustaining complexity. Radio success didn't really follow, though, and the band went back to the boards to work with former Cars leader Ric Ocasek on its next album, *New Sheets*.

the rest:
Possum Dixon 𝄢𝄢𝄢 (Interscope, 1993)
New Sheets N/A (Interscope, 1998)

influences:
◀◀ The Knack, Crowded House, Weezer

Billy Manes

Poster Children

Formed 1987, in Champaign, IL.

Rick Valentin, guitar, lead vocals; Rose Marshack, bass, vocals; Shannon Drew, drums (1987–89); Brendan Gamble, drums (1989–90); Mike Radar, drums (1990–91); Bob Rising, drums (1991–93); John Herndon, drums (1993–94); Howie Kantoff, drums (1994–present); Jeff Dimpsey, guitar (1991); Jim Valentin, guitar (1992–present).

When guitarist Rick Valentin and bassist Rose Marshack, two escapees from Champaign's corporate computer culture, formed Poster Children in 1987, the term indie rock still meant something. More than a sound, indie rock was a lifestyle, one defined by endless low-budget tours, dogged self-reliance, and a sincere commitment to the fans. The Poster Children took this lifestyle to heart. Despite several lineup changes (the first six years of the band's existence saw an almost Spinal Tap–esque turnover on the drum stool) and a variety of labels, both major and minor, the band members always made music on their terms. The Children's first full-length album, *Flower Plower*, laid its musical and philosophical groundwork—punk and new wave rock that recalled the Pixies and Hüsker Dü. Like those bands, Poster Children toured incessantly, managing to maintain creative control over all aspects of the music, from artwork to recording, promotion and even advertising. In 1997 the band's core struck out in a new musical direction as Salaryman, a critically acclaimed experiment with electronic instrumental music that produced an independently released, self-titled album. However, Poster Children was still the main attraction,

and as of 1998 the group was preparing a new album on its own label, 12 Inch Records.

what to buy: Without a doubt, *Junior Citizen* 𝄢𝄢𝄢𝄢 (Sire/Reprise, 1994, prod. Brian Anderson, Poster Children) is the Poster Children's most accessible album. It's full of catchy, power-pop numbers (the title track, the sarcastic "New Boyfriend," "Get a Life") that are infectious but never disposable. The breakneck delivery of "Revolution Year Zero" digs deep into the band's trademark guitar onslaught, while taut production on all the tracks captures every subtle lyrical and musical nuance. On *RTFM* 𝄢𝄢𝄢 (Sire/Reprise, 1997, prod. Bryce Goggin, Poster Children), the band leaves some of *Junior Citizen*'s pop sound behind and returns the focus to fierce, speed-strummed guitars and muscular bass lines. "Attack" and the album's superb single, "O for 1," build and release tension in cathartic walls of sound.

what to buy next: *Flower Plower* 𝄢𝄢𝄢𝄢 (Limited Potential, 1989/Frontier, 1991, prod. Iain Burgess, Poster Children) is technically the band's first album. On it, PC begin to build its musical lexicon, making bold strides into the world of noisy but melodic pop. *Daisy Chain Reaction* 𝄢𝄢𝄢 (Twin Tone, 1990/Sire, 1992) is a logical progression from *Flower Plower*. The album melds grungy psychedelic pop to roaring guitars and surging rhythm changes; standout tracks include "Chain Reaction" and "If You See Kay."

the rest:
Tool of the Man 𝄢𝄢𝄢 (Sire, 1993)
Just like You EP 𝄢𝄢𝄢 (Sire, 1994)

solo outings:
Salaryman:
Salaryman 𝄢𝄢𝄢 (12 Inch Records/City Slang, 1990)

influences:
◀◀ Big Black, Sonic Youth, the Pixies, Thin White Rope, the B-52's, the Buzzcocks

▶▶ Tsunami, Superchunk, Tortoise

see also: *Hum*

Lisa M. Moore

The Power Station

See: Duran Duran

Powerman 5000

Formed 1989, in Boston, MA.

Mike "Spider" Cummings, vocals; Dorian Heartsong, bass (1991–present); Adam Williams, guitar; Allan Pahanish, drums (1991–present).

Mike "Spider" Cummings and his older brother, Rob, now

legally known as Rob Zombie, didn't come from a musical family, so it's curious both ended up in stellar metal outfits. Spider began writing music at age 14 while his brother became obsessed with film before helming the band White Zombie. Spider's first official project was a single called "Much Evil," which he recorded under the name MC Spider. When the single garnered airplay, Spider brought together several musicians, many of whom attended the Berklee College of Music, and dubbed the group Powerman 5000. During early 1994 the quartet recorded the seven-song EP *True Force* in two days with $600. Capitol Records came calling, but just after the ink dried, the record company withdrew its contract. Frustrated, PM5K returned to the studio to record its debut full-length release, *Blood Splat Rating System*, named after the way a magazine rated films. Writing about suicidal superheroes, circus freaks, shark attacks, and Kung Fu fighters, Spider calls the album "the soundtrack to the life you wish you had."

what's available: *Mega!! Kung Fu Radio* ♫♫♫ (DreamWorks, 1997, prod. Powerman 5000, Mudrock) is a reworking of *Blood Splat Rating System* and includes two new songs "Mega!! Kung Fu Radio" and "Tokyo Vigilante No. 1." A collision of rap and metal, *Mega!! Kung Fu Radio* is as addictive as it is dark and brooding. Spider spins a web of furious, super-charged guitars, heavy pulsating bass, and pounding drums, which, coupled with his melodic vocals, makes Powerman 5000 a force to be reckoned with.

influences:
◄◄ White Zombie, Fun Lovin' Criminals

Christina Fuoco

Johnny Powers

Born John Pavlick, May 25, 1938, in Utica, MI.

Detroit's most well-known rockabilly artist, Johnny Powers rose to regional fame during the '50s, recording for several labels—including the local companies Fortune and Fox, where he had his trademark hit "Long Blond Hair." From there, Powers moved to legendary Sun Records, where he released two singles (including the sublime "With Your Love, with Your Kiss") and soon after made history as the first white artist signed to Motown. As his popularity waned, Powers moved to the producer's chair, where he worked with mostly obscure artists through the '70s. However, as with many lesser-known American rockabilly treasures, European interest prompted a return to the stage, and after several tours overseas, Powers began concentrating on the American market once again, cutting albums and playing fiery live shows with his pompadour aged but intact.

what to buy: The career retrospective *Long Blond Hair* ♫♫♫ (Norton, 1992, prod. various) compiles all of Powers's greatest cuts and proves that there was more to '50s rockabilly than Gene Vincent and Eddie Cochran.

the rest:
New Spark (For an Old Flame) ♫♫♫ (Schoolkids, 1994)
Rockabilly Blast—Live ♫♫ (Over-Eazy, 1997)

influences:
◄◄ Elvis Presley, Gene Vincent, Eddie Cochran
►► Stray Cats

Todd Wicks

Prefab Sprout

Formed 1980, in Newcastle, England.

Paddy McAloon, vocals, guitar; Martin McAloon, bass; Wendy Smith, vocals, percussion (1981–present); Neil Conti, drums (1985–93).

Those people impressed by heavy guitars and raw, intense emotions can go ahead and flip the page. Do it now, because the music and lyrics of this matchless British quartet aim at unraveling the subtleties of romance, guilt, and aspiration, often with a dry sense of humor. Imagine Elvis Costello with less attitude and a better melodic gift, or a weirder Aztec Camera, and you've got a general idea of Prefab's approach. Frontman/mastermind Paddy McAloon has rarely targeted his songs at a particular radio format, and the band has never toured the States, so its following remains limited here. In Britain, though, McAloon is revered as a unique songwriter—on the level of, say, a Tom Waits—and 1990's *Jordan: The Comeback*, was nominated for the British equivalent of a Grammy. The band's 1984 debut, *Swoon*, established it as an offbeat, jazzy sort of pop outfit, but it was the follow-up, *Two Wheels Good* (called *Steve McQueen* in the U.K.), which showed what they were capable of. During the '90s, McAloon laid low, experimenting with different musical concepts. Finally, in 1997, he re-emerged with the lackluster *Andromeda Heights*, a major disappointment. Can Paddy get those creative juices flowing again? Keep your fingers crossed.

what to buy: Brilliantly conceived and executed, *Two Wheels Good* ♫♫♫♫ (Kitchenware/Epic, 1985, prod. Thomas Dolby) easily ranks as the band's crowning achievement. McAloon serves up his best set of tunes here, as well as his most dynamic vocal performances, but it is Dolby who provides the extra spark, supplying unusual synth parts that often add just the right touch to these songs of love and regret. Nineteen songs long and divided into four essentially unrelated thematic segments, *Jordan: The Comeback* ♫♫♫♫ (Kitchenware/Epic, 1990, prod. Thomas Dolby) certainly can be criticized for being sprawling and uneven, yet it features a wide variety of impressive songs. The most moving cuts come near the end, especially the gospel-influenced "One of the Broken" (with McAloon providing the voice of God!) and the upbeat yet strangely haunting "Doo-Wop in Harlem" (dedicated to McAloon's late father).

what to buy next: The group's full-length debut, *Swoon* ✍✍✍ (Kitchenware/Epic, 1984, prod. David Brewis, Prefab Sprout) was a revelation at the time of its release. Jazzy, poetic, and utterly weird without being off-putting, the album features a tribute to chess champion Bobby Fischer ("Cue Fanfare"), and a coolly devastating confession of jealousy ("Cruel"). *The Best of Prefab Sprout: A Life of Surprises* ✍✍✍ (Epic, 1992, prod. various) leaves out most of *Swoon* in favor of too much *Langley Park* (and skips many of the best numbers from *Jordan*), but it's still a worthy overview of the band's more immediate tunes.

what to avoid: Available only as an import, *Andromeda Heights* ✍✍ (Kitchenware, 1997, prod. Paddy McAloon) is a snore and a half. After seven years of diddling around, McAloon holed himself up in the studio and made a limp, uninspiring album that sounds like a solo effort. Neil Conti is sorely missed, and without an outside producer, the record seems stale.

the rest:
Lions in My Own Garden ✍✍✍ (Kitchenware EP, 1983)
From Langley Park to Memphis ✍✍✍ (Kitchenware/Epic, 1988)

worth searching for: Recorded just after *Two Wheels Good*, *Protest Songs* (Kitchenware, 1989, prod. Paddy McAloon) never was released in the United States, and only saw release in the U.K. after *Langley Park* came out. Though the production is a bit plain, the disc reveals an odder side of the band.

influences:

◀◀ Aztec Camera, Steely Dan, Frank Sinatra, Antonio Carlos Jobim

▶▶ Everything but the Girl, Deacon Blue, Lloyd Cole, Gavin Friday

Bob Remstein

Presence
See: The Cure

The Presidents of the United States of America

Formed 1991, in Seattle, WA. Disbanded 1997.

Chris Ballew, vocals, two-string basitar; Dave Dederer, three-string guitbass, vocals; Jason Finn, drums, vocals.

Just as the Knack provided a pure pop answer to the first wave of punk, so too do the Presidents of the United States of America have a response to the triumph of alternative rock. Understandably tagged by some as a novelty band, the Presidents

display a sense of fun and lyrical guile that holds up to repeated listenings—a few, anyway. Sensing (correctly) that, after only two albums, it had had its moment in the sun, the group released a quick odds 'n' ends collection and called it quits in 1997.

what to buy: On their self-titled debut, *Presidents of the United States of America* ✍✍✍ (Columbia, 1995, prod. Chris Ballew, Dave Dederer, Conrad Uno), the group tosses off a few funny lines and then drive them deep into your cerebrum with repeated choruses and irresistible melodies. There's the nonsensical hit "Lump," plus a string of songs ("Kitty," "Peaches," "Boll Weevil") that turns the mundane into three-chord art. The throwaway cover of the MC5's "Kick out the Jams" ultimately reveals the trio to be lightweights, but the album is harmless fun for the whole family. Anything wrong with that?

the rest:
II ✍✍✍ (Columbia, 1996)
Pure Frosting ✍✍✍ (Columbia, 1998)

influences:

◀◀ The Knack, the Nazz, the Beatles, the MC5, They Might Be Giants

Daniel Durchholz

Elvis Presley

Born Elvis Aron Presley, January 8, 1935, in East Tupelo, MS. Died August 16, 1977, in Memphis, TN.

People sometimes forget that Elvis Presley—king of rock 'n' roll, movie star, tragic symbol of garish excess, paragon of moral decay, one of the best-selling pop artists of all time, even a pop-culture Christ figure—actually was talented. Whether or not he invented rock 'n' roll by linking, as myth recalls, white country music and black R&B, he had an innate command of the stage and audience, and he was a terrific singer and interpreter. Born to a poor Southern couple, the shy Presley began greasing his hair into a tall pompadour, wearing long sideburns, and choosing his outlandish outfits carefully in pinks, blacks, and whites. Peers thought he was nuts. Eventually, he was vindicated: After he hung around Memphis's Sun Records studio for a year, confident entrepreneur and record producer Sam Phillips saw an intangible quality in Presley and set him up for a session. (Phillips, a longtime recorder of black bluesmen and minor R&B stars, from Junior Parker to Rufus Thomas, had long predicted that if he could get a white boy with "the Negro look and the Negro feel," he would make a million dollars. That turned out to be a significant understatement.) With hungry session musicians Scotty Moore on guitar and Bill Black on upright bass, the trio performed take after take until, while fooling around, they came up with reworked versions of Arthur

"Big Boy" Crudup's "That's All Right (Mama)" and Bill Monroe's "Blue Moon of Kentucky." An excited Phillips dropped the cuts off to famous Memphis DJ Dewey Phillips, who played "That's All Right (Mama)" countless times in a row, thus creating Presley's first buzz.

For the subsequent two decades, Presley's career moved so fast that he—to say nothing of his friends and family, who were simultaneously excited and suspicious—could barely keep up. "The Colonel," brilliant opportunist and Hank Snow manager Tom Parker, took the young singer under his wing and autocratically began navigating Presley's career trajectory, signing him to RCA Records. As Presley began performing more and more unprecedentedly great concerts, attracting teenage girls by the truckload, his legend started to grow. Then came a rash of tremendous singles: "Hound Dog," "Don't Be Cruel," "Love Me Tender," "All Shook Up," and the classic hits written by the now-legendary songwriting duo of Leiber & Stoller, including "Jailhouse Rock." The King bought a pink Cadillac for his mother, many more Cadillacs for himself and, in 1957, Graceland, a former Memphis church he converted into a mansion. Everything was going perfectly until Presley was inducted into the Army in 1958; shortly after that, a plane carrying Buddy Holly and Richie Valens crashed—that was, as Don McLean later lamented, "the day the music died." But despite all this, as well as the advent of Bob Dylan, the Beach Boys, and the Beatles, Presley never went away. He was rock's first careerist, continuing to release hits ("Little Sister," "It's Now or Never," "Can't Help Falling in Love," "Return to Sender," and "Bossa Nova Baby") throughout the '60s. In that decade of hippies, the Vietnam War, and baby boom counter-culture, Presley focused on innocent movies (and soundtracks), starring in total throwaways such as *It Happened at the World's Fair* and *Girl Happy*, and energetic dance flicks such as *Blue Hawaii* and *Clambake*. Presley began creating an insular world for himself and a close circle of friends and relatives in the garishly decorated Graceland. His 1968 television concert was a tremendous comeback, an explosive show with a smash soundtrack. But Presley inevitably drifted toward Las Vegas, gained much weight, and became a parody of himself. Not a total parody, though—some of Presley's late '60s and '70s songs, including "In the Ghetto," "Suspicious Minds," and the underrated "Burning Love," were explosive and funky. Presley had become more famous for his lifestyle, obesity, and white-fringed costumes than he previously had been for his music. Legions of imitators stepped up to create a bizarre and enduring cottage industry in Vegas, Memphis, and elsewhere. Then Presley died in his Graceland bathroom. Though the cause of death has been frequently disputed, the most reliable diagnosis lists drug-related heart failure, advanced arteriosclerosis, and enlargement of the liver. The King left behind his daughter, Lisa Marie, heir to the $100-

million Graceland mansion and its 675,000 annual visits from tourists; a manager, Parker, who said upon Presley's death that he would "go right on managing him," which he did until his own death in the mid-'90s; 94 gold singles; 40 gold albums; $180 million in movie grosses; millions more in merchandise sales, and, perhaps most important, the entire pop music industry (rock 'n' roll in particular) as his legacy. Some have said the King is still alive—during the late '80s, shoppers in a Kalamazoo, Michigan, grocery store were among many to report Presley sightings. It's possible that, centuries from now, when the rest of American pop culture has decayed and disappeared, the King's velvet image will remain.

what to buy: RCA's three five-disc box sets were a godsend, because without them it was impossible to navigate the record store binfuls of studio albums and greatest-hits collections for the essential stuff. Start with *Elvis—The King of Rock 'n' Roll: The Complete '50s Masters* 𝄞𝄞𝄞𝄞 (RCA, 1992, compilation prod. Ernst Mikael Jorgensen, Roger Semon) and hear the young truck driver transform from raw talent in the early hits "Blue Moon of Kentucky" and "That's All Right" to accomplished showman in "Jailhouse Rock" and "Love Me Tender." Next stop: *From Nashville to Memphis: The Essential '60s Masters I* 𝄞𝄞𝄞𝄞 (RCA, 1994, compilation prod. Ernst Mikael Jorgensen, Roger Semon) proves that, despite the Beatles and his late '50s stint in the Army, Presley was still a vital performer; "Little Sister," "Suspicious Minds," "In the Ghetto," and "Fever" are among the transcendental tracks. *Walk a Mile in My Shoes: The Essential '70s Masters* 𝄞𝄞𝄞𝄞 (RCA, 1995, compilation prod. Ernst Mikael Jorgensen, Roger Semon) and *Command Performances: The Essential '60s Masters II* 𝄞𝄞𝄞𝄞 (RCA, 1995, compilation prod. Ernst Mikael Jorgensen, Roger Semon) compile the best live tracks and soundtrack songs while eliminating most of the chaff. *The Complete Sun Sessions* 𝄞𝄞𝄞𝄞𝄞 (RCA, 1987, prod. Sam Phillips) is mostly revisited on the first box set, but it contains the fascinating sound of Elvis, Moore, Black, and producer Phillips inventing rock 'n' roll in the Sun Records studio; "Milkcow Blues Boogie" finds Elvis stopping a slow blues song, announcing "that don't MOVE me," and proceeding to change it before our ears into something completely different.

what to buy next: The boxes don't necessarily preclude Presley's individual titles. Many are worthwhile, but these are the first to check out: *Loving You* 𝄞𝄞𝄞𝄞 (RCA, 1957, prod. Elvis Presley, Hal Wallis), the first Elvis movie soundtrack; *His Hand in Mine* 𝄞𝄞𝄞𝄞 (RCA, 1960, prod. Elvis Presley), a gospel album that initially confused the record company; *Elvis NBC-TV Special* 𝄞𝄞𝄞𝄞𝄞 (RCA, 1968, prod. Steve Binder), the master's triumphant return to television when everybody thought he was washed up; *From Elvis in Memphis* 𝄞𝄞𝄞𝄞𝄞 (RCA, 1969, prod. Felton Jarvis, Chips Moman), another solid comeback, this time to where he began his career; *Elvis Country* 🎵🎵🎵 (RCA, 1971, prod. Felton Jarvis, Steve Sholes), proof that the '70s Elvis wasn't just a fat druggie awaiting death; *Burning Love* 🎵🎵🎵 (RCA Camden, 1972, prod. various), whose title track still sounds surprisingly fresh and vital; and *The Million Dollar Quartet* 🎵🎵🎵🎵 (RCA, 1990, prod. Sam Phillips), which features Presley, Jerry Lee Lewis, and Carl Perkins (plus a no-show Johnny Cash), sharing classic '50s rockabilly hits with spontaneity, style, and fun.

what to avoid: Most of Presley's schlock, which became almost as famous as his great stuff, was in either the bad-live-performance or icky-movie soundtrack categories. His bad live albums were most prominent during the '70s, including *As Recorded at Madison Square Garden* 🎵🎵 (RCA, 1972, prod. Felton Jarvis), *Recorded Live on Stage in Memphis* 🎵🎵 (RCA, 1974, prod. Felton Jarvis), *Having Fun with Elvis on Stage* 🎵 (RCA, 1974) (just the King making bad jokes), *Elvis in Concert* 🎵 (RCA, 1977, prod. Don Wardell), and *Elvis on Stage* 🎵 (RCA, 1977). Of the soundtracks, stay away from *Fun in Acapulco* 🎵🎵 (RCA, 1963, prod. Elvis Presley), *Live a Little, Love a Little/Charro!/The Trouble with Girls/Change of Habit* 🎵🎵 (RCA, 1995, compilation prod. Ernst Mikael Jorgensen, Roger Semon), *Girl Happy/Harum Scarum* 🎵🎵 (RCA, 1965/1995, prod. Elvis Presley), and *Frankie and Johnny/Paradise, Hawaiian Style* 🎵🎵 (RCA, 1966/1994, prod. Elvis Presley). Also gloriously bad are *Interviews and Memories of: The Sun Years* 🎵 (Sun, 1977, prod. Sam Phillips), *From Elvis Presley Boulevard, Memphis, Tennessee* 🎵 (RCA, 1976, prod. Chick Crumpacker), both volumes of *Our Memories of Elvis* 🎵 (RCA, 1979, prod. various), *I Was the One* 🎵 (RCA, 1983, prod. various), and *The Elvis Presley Interview Record: An Audio Self-Portrait* 🎵 (RCA, 1984). In the tribute category, avoid *It's Now or Never: The Tribute to Elvis* 🎵🎵 (Mercury, 1994, prod. various), which does feature Presley fan Dwight Yoakam but unfortunately has loser hacks such as Michael Bolton, Travis Tritt, and Wet Wet Wet as well.

the rest:
Elvis Presley 🎵🎵🎵🎵 (RCA, 1956)
Elvis 🎵🎵🎵🎵 (RCA, 1956)
Elvis's Christmas Album 🎵🎵🎵🎵 (RCA, 1957)
King Creole 🎵🎵🎵🎵 (RCA, 1958)
Elvis' Golden Records, Vol. 1 🎵🎵🎵🎵🎵 (RCA, 1958)
For LP Fans Only 🎵🎵🎵🎵 (RCA, 1959)
A Date with Elvis 🎵🎵🎵🎵 (RCA, 1959)
Elvis Is Back! 🎵🎵🎵🎵 (RCA, 1960)
G.I. Blues 🎵🎵🎵 (RCA, 1960)
50,000,000 Elvis Fans Can't Be Wrong: Elvis' Golden Records, Vol. 2 🎵🎵🎵🎵 (RCA, 1960)
Something for Everybody 🎵🎵🎵 (RCA, 1961)
Blue Hawaii 🎵🎵🎵 (RCA, 1961)
Pot Luck 🎵🎵🎵 (RCA, 1962)
Girls! Girls! Girls! 🎵🎵🎵 (RCA, 1962)

It Happened at the World's Fair 🎵🎵🎵 (RCA, 1963)
Elvis's Golden Records, Vol. 3 🎵🎵🎵🎵🎵 (RCA, 1963)
Elvis for Everyone 🎵🎵🎵 (RCA, 1965)
Spinout 🎵🎵🎵🎵 (RCA, 1966)
Double Trouble 🎵 (RCA, 1967)
How Great Thou Art 🎵🎵🎵🎵 (RCA, 1967)
Speedway 🎵🎵🎵 (RCA, 1968)
Elvis's Golden Records, Vol. 4 🎵🎵🎵🎵🎵 (RCA, 1968)
Elvis Sings Hits from His Movies 🎵🎵🎵 (RCA, 1969)
From Memphis to Vegas/From Vegas to Memphis 🎵🎵🎵 (RCA, 1969)
Back in Memphis 🎵🎵🎵 (RCA, 1970)
That's the Way It Is 🎵🎵🎵 (RCA, 1970)
Almost in Love 🎵🎵🎵 (RCA, 1970)
On Stage—February 1970 🎵🎵🎵🎵 (RCA, 1970)
Elvis in Person at the International Hotel, Las Vegas 🎵🎵🎵 (RCA, 1970)
World Wide 50 Gold Award Hits, Vol. 1, Nos. 1–4 🎵🎵🎵🎵🎵 (RCA, 1970–71)
I Got Lucky 🎵🎵🎵 (RCA, 1971)
You'll Never Walk Alone 🎵🎵🎵 (RCA, 1971)
Love Letters from Elvis 🎵🎵🎵 (RCA, 1971)
C'mon Everybody 🎵🎵🎵 (RCA, 1971)
Elvis 🎵🎵🎵 (RCA, 1971)
Elvis Sings the Wonderful World of Christmas 🎵🎵🎵🎵 (RCA, 1971)
He Touched Me 🎵🎵🎵🎵 (RCA, 1972)
Elvis Now 🎵🎵🎵 (RCA, 1972)
Separate Ways 🎵🎵🎵 (RCA, 1973)
Elvis: Raised on Rock/For Ol' Times Sake 🎵🎵🎵 (RCA, 1973)
Aloha from Hawaii 🎵🎵🎵 (RCA, 1973)
A Legendary Performer: Vol. 1 🎵🎵🎵🎵 (RCA, 1974)
Let's Be Friends 🎵🎵 (RCA, 1975)
Promised Land 🎵🎵🎵 (RCA, 1975)
Pure Gold 🎵🎵🎵 (RCA, 1975)
A Legendary Performer: Vol. 2 🎵🎵🎵🎵 (RCA, 1976)
Welcome to My World 🎵🎵🎵 (RCA, 1977)
Moody Blue 🎵🎵🎵 (RCA, 1977)
The Elvis Tapes 🎵🎵 (Redwood, 1977)
He Walks beside Me 🎵🎵 (RCA, 1978)
A Canadian Tribute 🎵🎵 (RCA, 1978)
Elvis Sings for Children and Grownups Too! 🎵🎵 (RCA, 1978)
A Legendary Performer: Vol. 3 🎵🎵🎵 (RCA, 1978)
Elvis Aron Presley 🎵🎵🎵🎵 (RCA, 1980)
This Is Elvis 🎵🎵🎵 (RCA, 1981)
Elvis: The Hillbilly Cat 🎵🎵🎵🎵 (Music Works, 1982)
Elvis: The First Live Recordings 🎵🎵🎵 (Music Works, 1982)
Memories of Christmas 🎵🎵🎵 (RCA, 1982)
A Legendary Performer: Vol. 4 🎵🎵🎵🎵 (RCA, 1983)
Elvis—A Golden Celebration 🎵🎵🎵 (RCA, 1984)
Elvis's Gold Records, Vol. 5 🎵🎵🎵 (RCA, 1984)
Reconsider Baby 🎵🎵🎵 (RCA, 1985)
A Valentine Gift for You 🎵🎵🎵 (RCA, 1985)
Always on My Mind 🎵🎵🎵🎵 (RCA, 1985)
Return of the Rocker 🎵🎵🎵🎵 (RCA, 1986)
The Memphis Record 🎵🎵🎵🎵 (RCA, 1987)
The Number One Hits 🎵🎵🎵 (RCA, 1987)

Essential Elvis 🎵🎵🎵 (RCA, 1988)
Stereo '57 (Essential Elvis, Vol. 2) 🎵🎵🎵 (RCA, 1988)
Elvis in Nashville 🎵🎵🎵 (RCA, 1988)
The Alternate Aloha 🎵🎵🎵 (RCA, 1988)
50 World Wide Gold Award Hits, Vol. 1 🎵🎵🎵 (RCA, 1988)
The Top 10 Hits 🎵🎵🎵 (RCA, 1988)
Known Only to Him: Elvis Gospel, 1957–1971 🎵🎵🎵 (RCA, 1989)
The Lost Album 🎵🎵 (RCA, 1990)
The Great Performances 🎵🎵🎵 (RCA, 1990)
Elvis Presley Sings Leiber & Stoller 🎵🎵🎵 (RCA, 1991)
The Essential Elvis, Vol. 3 🎵🎵🎵 (RCA, 1991)
Viva Las Vegas/Roustabout 🎵🎵🎵 (RCA, 1993)
Amazing Grace: His Greatest Sacred Performances 🎵🎵🎵 (RCA, 1994)
Kissin' Cousins/Clambake/Stay Away, Joe 🎵🎵🎵 (RCA, 1994)
Flaming Star/Wild in the Country/Follow That Dream 🎵🎵 (RCA, 1995)
Elvis '56 🎵🎵🎵 (RCA, 1996)
Great Country Songs 🎵🎵 (RCA, 1996)
The Essential Elvis, Vol. 4: 100 Years from Now 🎵🎵🎵 (RCA, 1996)
An Afternoon in the Garden 🎵🎵 (RCA, 1997)
Elvis's Greatest Jukebox Hits 🎵🎵 (RCA, 1997)
Elvis Platinum: A Life in Music 🎵🎵 (RCA, 1997)
Jailhouse Rock/Love Me Tender 🎵🎵🎵 (RCA, 1997)
Love Songs 🎵🎵 (RCA, 1998)
Rhythm 'N' Country: Essential Elvis, Vol. 5 N/A (RCA, 1998)
Tiger Man N/A (RCA, 1998)

worth searching for: If only for sport, try tracking down some of these great songs about Elvis or covering him: "Elvis Is Dead" by Living Colour; "Elvis Is Everywhere" by Mojo Nixon; "My Boy Elvis" by Janis Martin; "Galway to Graceland" by Richard Thompson; "Elvis Ate America" by Passengers (a.k.a. U2, Brian Eno, et al.); "Little Sister" by Dwight Yoakam; "Johnny Bye Bye" by Bruce Springsteen. Also, the entire soundtrack of *Honeymoon in Vegas* (Epic, 1992, prod. Peter Afterman, Glen Brunman), despite the lifeless carbon-copy Billy Joel versions of "All Shook Up" and "Heartbreak Hotel." Finally, one great disc of Elvis songs: the British import *The Last Temptation of Elvis* (New Musical Express, 1990, executive prod. Roy Carr) has Motörhead's Lemmy doing "Blue Suede Shoes," Bruce Springsteen doing "Viva Las Vegas," the Jesus & Mary Chain demolishing "Guitar Man," and Cath Carroll and legendary weirdo punk-noise producer Steve Albini deconstructing "King Creole."

influences:

◄◄ Bill Monroe, Hank Snow, Arthur "Big Boy" Crudup, Little Richard, Chuck Berry, Lowell Fulson, Big Mama Thornton, Frank Sinatra, Hank Williams Sr., Roy Brown, the Carter Family, Jimmie Rodgers, the Ink Spots, Eddy Arnold

►► Buddy Holly, Carl Perkins, Roy Orbison, the Beatles, Johnny Cash, Bob Dylan, the Beach Boys, Janis Martin, Bruce Springsteen, Billy Joel, Mojo Nixon, Dwight Yoakam, the Band, the Blasters, Elvis Hitler, Elvis Costello, U2, Stray Cats, Living Colour, Public Enemy . . . indeed, pretty much everyone ever associated with rock 'n' roll

Steve Knopper

Billy Preston

Born September 9, 1946, in Houston, TX.

Best known for his distinctive bluesy keyboard work on the Beatles' *Let It Be* album, Billy Preston had already established himself on the gospel and R&B circuits before George Harrison pulled him into the Fab Four's fractious recording sessions in 1969. A child prodigy, Preston played organ for gospel queen Mahalia Jackson and landed a role playing songwriter W.C. Handy as a boy in the movie *St. Louis Blues* (1958) to Nat King Cole's portrayal of the adult Handy. Throughout the early '60s, Preston toured with Little Richard and Sam Cooke in Europe, where he first met the Beatles at Hamburg's Star Club. A spot as a backup musician on Britain's *Shindig* TV music program landed him a gig touring the continent with Ray Charles; on that tour, he again met up with Harrison, who promptly signed him to the Beatles' Apple label. Next to Badfinger, Preston was the best-known and most prolific artist in Apple's stable, and he was the only artist to receive a performance credit with the Beatles (the "Get Back" single is credited to "The Beatles with Billy Preston"). After the Fab Four called it quits, Preston worked with John Lennon on a number of his Plastic Ono Band albums and recorded with Ringo Starr and Harrison. He performed at Harrison's Concert for Bangladesh in 1971, where his was among the concert's standout performances. Throughout the '70s, Preston enjoyed a string of hit singles ("Will It Go 'round in Circles," "Outa-Space") while backing up such top acts as the Rolling Stones and Aretha Franklin. Preston continues to write and record, dividing his energies between gospel and secular recordings. Among rock keyboardists, he is an original, a true living legend.

what to buy: *The Best of Billy Preston* 🎵🎵🎵 (A&M, 1988, prod. Billy Preston, George Martin) is an excellent retrospective of Preston's solo work, with all his pop hits along with the moving gospel-rocker "That's The Way God Planned It," originally recorded for Apple.

the rest:
Encouraging Words 🎵🎵 (Apple, 1970)
Minister of Music 🎵🎵 (Pepper Co., 1995)

worth searching for: Among Preston's tours of duty was a stint as organist for Sam Cooke, and nowhere are his keyboard chops better displayed during this period than on Cooke's *Night Beat* (RCA, 1963, prod. Al Schmitt).

influences:

◄◄ W.C. Handy, Ray Charles, Aretha Franklin, Little Richard

►► Stevie Wonder, Gregg Allman, the Beatles, Booker T. & the MG's, Lee Michaels, James Taylor, Ben Folds Five

Christopher Scapelliti

The Pretenders

Formed 1978, in London, England.

Chrissie Hynde (born September 7, 1951, in Akron, OH), vocals, guitar; James Honeyman-Scott (died June 16, 1982), guitar, vocals (1978–82); Pete Farndon (died April 14, 1983), bass, vocals (1978–82); Martin Chambers, drums, vocals (1978–84, 1993–present); Robbie McIntosh, guitar, vocals (1983–87); Malcolm Foster, bass, vocals (1983–84, 1987, 1990); T.M. Stevens, bass (1986–87); Blair Cunningham, drums (1986–90); Billy Bremner (born 1947, in Scotland), guitar, vocals (1990); Dominic Miller, guitar (1990); John McKenzie, bass (1990); Adam Seymour, guitar, vocals (1995–present); Andy Hobson, bass, vocals (1995–present).

The Pretenders have always been Chrissie Hynde's band; even at its most democratic—the short period when the original lineup was together—it was clear that the expatriate Akron, Ohio, native called the shots and set the tone. The Pretenders emerged from London's late '70s punk scene (Hynde even worked for Sex Pistols impresario Malcolm McLaren), but the music it put forth on its debut record was markedly different from its contemporaries. While Hynde's sneering, leather-clad image made it clear that she was no boy-toy, her music was far removed from punk's atonal anger. She was, instead, something altogether new on the pop horizon: a tough, independent woman who was nevertheless unafraid to show that she possessed both a rational mind and human tenderness. The early Pretenders were skilled players whose capabilities encompassed punk aggression and deft pop melodicism; their music was rugged, tuneful, and, with Hynde's punk chanteuse image, widely accessible. The group managed to retain punk credentials while simultaneously appealing to pop radio. By 1982, however, dissension and deaths had fractured the original Pretenders, and the group's membership became volatile, making subsequent albums little more than Hynde solo efforts. But with 1994's *Last of the Independents*, Hynde became interested in a more stable band format, and the Pretenders regained some of the unique energy and interplay of its early years.

what to buy: *The Pretenders* 𝄞𝄞𝄞𝄞 (Sire, 1980, prod. Chris Thomas) is a tour de force of sharp playing and writing, with a range that covers the tough slam of "Tattooed Love Boys" and "Precious," the melodic delights of "Brass in Pocket" and "Mystery Achievement," and the subtle beauty of "Kid" and "Stop Your Sobbing."

what to buy next: Formed from the ashes of James Honeyman-Scott's and Pete Farndon's deaths, the band that came together to record *Learning to Crawl* 𝄞𝄞𝄞𝄞 (Sire, 1984, prod. Chris Thomas) was the closest Hynde would get to the essence of her original lineup. In guitarist Robbie McIntosh, she found a spiritual and ideological descendent of Honeyman-Scott, a guitarist with a gift for melody and sharp accompaniment, while the material showcases Hynde's growing facility with the songwriting craft. *Singles* 𝄞𝄞𝄞𝄞 (Sire, 1987, prod. various) is testament to the body of first-rate music Hynde and her collaborators have produced over the years.

what to avoid: *Packed!* 𝄞𝄞 (Sire, 1990, prod. Chrissie Hynde)—a mundane workout of themes that she exercised better on previous albums—brutally highlights Hynde's need for strong musical accompaniment.

the rest:
Pretenders II 𝄞𝄞𝄞𝄞 (Sire, 1981)
Extended Play 𝄞𝄞𝄞𝄞 (Sire EP, 1981)
Get Close 𝄞𝄞𝄞 (Sire, 1986)
Last of the Independents 𝄞𝄞𝄞𝄞 (Sire, 1994)
The Isle of View 𝄞𝄞𝄞 (Warner Bros., 1995)

worth searching for: Pretenders historians and completists will want to look for Hynde's early material. She worked with a band called the Berk Brothers and recorded a single under the name Moors Murders—a challenging quest, to be sure.

influences:

◄◄ The Kinks, the Byrds, the Beatles, Patti Smith, Suzi Quatro, the Who, Jimi Hendrix, Elvis Costello, Nick Lowe

►► Divinyls, Nick Lowe, Rockpile, Scandal/Patti Smyth, Alanis Morrisette, Elastica

David Galens

Pretty & Twisted

See: Concrete Blonde

Pretty Things

Formed 1963, in London, England. Disbanded 1976.

Phil May, vocals, harmonica; Dick Taylor, guitar (1963–69); Brian Pendleton, guitar (1963–66); John Stax, bass (1963–66); Viv Prince, drums (1963–65); Skip Alan, drums (1965–68, 1970–76); Wally Allen, bass (1966–70); John Povey, keyboards (1966–76); John Alder, drums (1968–70); Victor Unitt, guitar (1969–70); Peter Tolson, guitar (1970–76); Stuart Brooks, bass (1971–73); Gordon Edwards, keyboards, guitar, bass (1974–76); Jack Green, bass (1975–76).

A talented band that garnered heaps of critical praise, the Pretty Things never quite caught on with the buying public—particularly in the United States. The schizophrenic reception to its work helps explain the long list of musicians who have passed through the group as well as the abrupt changes in musical direction during the band's 12-year career. Led by Phil May and Dick Taylor, the Pretty Things started out as R&B roots rockers along the lines of the early Rolling Stones. (Not surprising, since Taylor was the original Stones bassist.) During the late '60s, frustrated by its inability to break through in the United States, the band switched gears, entering the world of psychedelia and progressive rock. The major achievement of this period was *S.F. Sorrow*, which in 1968 was the first rock opera and both a precursor to and influence on the Who's *Tommy*. Entering the '70s, Taylor was gone and May led a more straight-ahead, album-rock version of Pretty Things. These days, most of the group's work has fallen out of print, including *S.F. Sorrow*.

what's available: The group's early years are well chronicled on *Get a Buzz—The Best of the Fontana Years* ♫♫♫ (Fontana, 1982, prod. various), a generous sampler full of chaotic covers and thrashing originals.

worth searching for: The band's best work from its late period is the out-of-print *Silk Torpedo* (Swan Song, 1974, prod. Jimmy Page).

influences:

◄◄ Bo Diddley, Muddy Waters, Chuck Berry

►► Bad Company, UFO

Gary Plochinski

Lloyd Price

Born March 9, 1933, in New Orleans, LA.

Lloyd Price began his career following the stylistic lead of Fats Domino and Roy Perkins; by the end of the '50s, he was a top pop singer with a style all his own. As a teenager, Price incorporated "Lawdy Miss Clawdy!," a catch-phrase by WBOK disc jockey Okey Dokey, into a radio station jingle. After turning it into a full song, he auditioned for Art Rupe of Specialty Records and sang it so emotionally, Rupe thought Price was actually crying. Recorded with Fats Domino on piano, "Lawdy Miss Clawdy" was one of 1952's biggest R&B hits. (Most of Price's early recordings feature Domino's band.) He followed with "Restless Heart," "Ooh, Ooh, Ooh," and "Ain't It a Shame," which were fine performances but lesser hits. Price was drafted into the Army in 1953. When he returned to civilian life, his style of plaintive blues singing had gone out of favor. It was the age of rock 'n' roll, and his place at Specialty had been usurped by his friend Little Richard, whom Price had steered towards the label a few years earlier. After his last session, Specialty hired Price's pianist and valet, Larry Williams, to take his place

on the roster. Late in 1956, Price and partner Harold Logan formed KRC Records and leased "Just Because" to ABC-Paramount; the record hit #29 on the pop charts. Price signed with ABC-Paramount outright in 1958. Working with producer Don Costa, Price's music became more mainstream pop than the raw R&B of a few years earlier. Their first collaboration updated "Stack-O-Lee," the old folk blues about gambling and murder. Though the record was a major smash, Price was forced to cut an alternate version with a happy ending for *American Bandstand* and a few hypercritical radio stations; "Stagger Lee" was a #1 record for four weeks. Price's pop career peaked in 1959 with the bouncy New Orleans double entendre of "Personality" and the teen lament "I'm Gonna Get Married." He continued his hit streak into 1960, but his formula at ABC-Paramount soon wore out its welcome. His final hit record came late in 1969 with the socially conscious "Bad Conditions" on Turntable Records, another label he and Logan formed just before the latter was brutally murdered. (The story of Price's later turbulent years is told in the margins of HBO's Don King biopic *Only in America*.) Price went on to record for a number of other labels without much success. After years in semi-seclusion, Price has returned to music full time, and in 1998 he was inducted into the Rock and Roll Hall of Fame. Lawdy Miss Clawdy, indeed!

what to buy: Price's best ABC-Paramount recordings are on *Greatest Hits* ♫♫♫♫ (MCA, 1994, compilation prod. Bill Inglot), which includes 18 tracks featuring his two versions of "Stagger Lee" (the sanitized version has Billy and Stagger Lee parting friends), "Personality," "Where Were You on Our Wedding Day," "I'm Gonna Get Married," and a sharp remake of his own "Lawdy Miss Clawdy."

what to buy next: The best of Price's earlier, grittier work at Specialty is collected on *Lawdy* ♫♫♫♫ (Specialty, 1991, prod. Art Rupe). The original "Lawdy Miss Clawdy" and its sequel, "Forgive Me Clawdy," are here as well as other chart numbers and alternate takes recorded between 1952 and 1956.

what to avoid: The skimpy budget rack perennial *Personality* ♫♫ (MCA Special Products, 1990, prod. Don Costa) has only eight of Price's ABC-Paramount hits. For a couple of extra dollars, you can get a lot more.

the rest:

Lloyd Price—His Originals ♫♫♫♫ (Specialty, 1959)
Greatest Hits ♫♫♫♫ (Curb, 1990)
Stagger Lee ♫♫♫♫ (Collectables, 1992)
Vol. 2—Heavy Dreams ♫♫♫♫ (Specialty, 1993)
Sings His Big Ten ♫♫♫♫ (Curb, 1994)
Walkin' the Track ♫♫♫♫ (Specialty, 1997)

worth searching for: There's a pleasing variety of material on *Greatest Hits* (Pair U.K., 1991, prod. various), which features some of Price's big ABC-Paramount hits plus surprisingly effective cover versions of "I Count the Tears," "Shop Around," "He Will Break Your Heart," and others.

influences:

◄◄ Roy "Boogie Boy" Perkins, Fats Domino

►► Larry Williams, Freddy Cannon, Wilson Pickett

Ken Burke

Primal Scream

Formed 1986, in Scotland.

Bobby Gillespie, vocals; Denise Johnson, vocals; Robert Young, guitar; Andrew Innes, guitar; Martin Duffy, keyboard; David Hood, bass; Roger Hawkins, drums.

Contrary to popular opinion, Primal Scream has not preyed on the past; it has helped create the future. Although the Scottish group's string of hits—ranging from the trance-dance "Loaded" to the communal, celebratory romp "Come Together"—inevitably brought on comparisons to everyone from the Rolling Stones to T. Rex to Sly & the Family Stone, the band's sound is definitely a product of the times. Primal Scream's free-wheeling, Ecstasy-inspired attitude often gained the band association with England's once-thriving rave scene, which also bred the likes of the Stone Roses, Happy Mondays, and Blur. Founded by former Jesus & Mary Chain drummer Bobby Gillespie, its music definitely set the group apart from the pack: mixing a blues/gospel pace with modern technology, it created an effervescent pop previously unheard.

what to buy: Primal Scream's third album, *Screamadelica* ♫♫♫♫♫ (Sire, 1991, prod. various), is the one to hear, an album that solidifies the band's identity and traces its remarkable creative history—which can best be described as '60s-influenced, slick, melodic, and slightly psychedelic. The album covers a spectrum of styles: "Slip inside This House" is an acid-soaked rocker; "Damaged" is an enchanting lullaby about love gone bad; and "Higher than the Sun" is an ambient killer. All in all, an enthralling mix.

what to buy next: After temporarily losing its footing, Primal Scream got back on track with *Vanishing Point* ♫♫♫♫ (Sire, 1997, prod. various), a wonderful dub-fueled romp through sublime blues. Standout tracks include the expansive "Burning Wheel" and the grinding "Kowalski."

what to avoid: Too much recreation stripped the band of its creative impetus around the time of *Give out but Don't Give Up* **woof!** (Sire, 1994), a dismal rewriting of the Rolling Stones' *Sticky Fingers*.

the rest:

Sonic Flower Groove ♫♫ (Creation, 1987)

Primal Scream ♫ (Creation, 1989)

influences:

◄◄ The Rolling Stones, Lee "Scratch" Perry, T. Rex

►► Oasis, the Stone Roses, the Verve

Aidin Vaziri

Primus /Sausage

Formed 1984, in San Francisco, CA.

Les Claypool, vocals, bass; Larry LaLonde, guitar (1989–present); Todd Huth, guitar (1984–89); Tim "Herb" Alexander, drums.

Primus' bizarre musical vision has two elements: great technical playing with a thrash-funk rhythm section that emulates Rush's machine-like perfection, and a sense of humor that's often purely goofy but sometimes sophisticated enough to impress singer-songwriter Tom Waits. Les Claypool struts on stage like he's auditioning for Monty Python's Ministry of Silly Walks, sings in a clipped cartoonish voice, and writes songs about tragic race car drivers, weird fishermen, and big brown beavers. The songs almost always move aside for long, spacey jams, in which Claypool (who once auditioned for Metallica) shuts off the funk and plays up his chops. The band, whose legions of fans perversely shout "Primus sucks!," scored several terrific concert slots during the early '90s, opening for Jane's Addiction, the Public Enemy–Anthrax tour, and U2's Zoo TV tour, as well as headlining Lollapalooza '93—all of which helped push the band onto alternative radio playlists. The fact that Primus wrote and performs the theme song to Comedy Central's deliriously popular cartoon show *South Park* certainly doesn't hurt, either.

what to buy: *Sailing the Seas of Cheese* ♫♫♫♫ (Interscope, 1991, prod. Primus) is an eccentric masterpiece, despite some showoffy bass-and-guitar jamming that goes on a bit too long, with the hilariously tragic "Jerry Was a Race Car Driver." On the band's one true classic song, "Tommy the Cat," Tom Waits sings the demented cat's part.

what to buy next: *Tales from the Punch Bowl* ♫♫♫ (Interscope, 1995, prod. Primus) contains Primus' biggest hit single, the not-so-subtle "Wynona's Big Brown Beaver." *Pork Soda* ♫♫♫ (Interscope, 1993, prod. Primus) was the big breakthrough, hitting #7 the same summer the band headlined the Lollapalooza tour.

what to avoid: *Riddles Are Abound Tonight* ♫♫ (Interscope, 1994, prod. Sausage), a side project by the group Sausage (Claypool, original Primus guitarist Huth, and drummer Jay Lane), has all the technical prowess with none of Primus' endearing whimsy.

the rest:

Suck on This ♫♫ (Prawn Song, 1989)
Frizzle Fry ♫♫ (Caroline, 1990)
The Brown Album ♫♫ (Interscope, 1997)
Rhinoplasty ♫♫♪ (Interscope EP, 1998)

worth searching for: Waits's apocalyptic single, "Earth Died Screaming," off his 1992 album *Bone Machine* (Island, 1992, prod. Tom Waits) has Claypool returning the "Tommy the Cat" favor with sharp, focused bass playing.

influences:

◀◀ Talking Heads, Rush, Tom Waits, the Dead Milkmen, Metallica, the Red Hot Chili Peppers, the Residents

▶▶ The Presidents of the United States of America, Rage Against the Machine

Steve Knopper

Prince
/♀
/The Artist

Born Prince Rogers Nelson, June 7, 1958, in Minneapolis, MN.

No matter what you call him—Prince, the Artist Formerly Known As Prince, the Artist, or that unpronounceable symbol he used to go by—there's no denying his stature as one of the most influential dance/funk artists in the history of popular music. Named after his father's jazz trio, Prince didn't attract much more than a cult following until after his fifth album, *1999*, was released in 1982, earning him Rock Artist of the Year honors from *Rolling Stone*. The semi-autobiographical movie *Purple Rain* and its soundtrack propelled Prince to the top of the charts and exposed one of music's best-kept secrets to the world. Frequently laced with sexually explicit lyrics and religious overtones, the sound of Prince encompasses a wide range of musical genres—pop, rock, dance, funk, soul, gospel, jazz, rap, world music, and more. The ability of "His Royal Badness" to mesh these many styles into his own unique sound is truly remarkable. Dubbed a musical genius by many, Prince writes all his own material, plays all the instruments on many of his albums, and has never been produced by anyone but himself. With the release of *Chaos & Disorder* in July 1995, Prince officially ended his longtime relationship with Warner Bros. To celebrate the event, he founded his own label, NPG, and released *Emancipation*, an appropriately named three-disc collection that contains some of his best work since *Sign o' the Times*. Prince and Mayte Garcia—one of his backup singers—were married on Valentine's Day, 1996. In October of that year their son was born prematurely and died shortly after birth, reportedly from Pfeiffer syndrome type 2, an extremely rare skull deformity.

what to buy: *Sign o' the Times* ♫♫♫♫ (Paisley Park/Warner Bros., 1987, prod. Prince) is a masterpiece that leads the listener on an incredible journey through the world according to Prince. This double-disc set is Prince at his diverse best and showcases his amazing range as an instrumentalist and singer. *1999* ♫♫♫♫ (Warner Bros., 1982, prod. Prince) gave rockdom its first taste of Prince with the title track and "Little Red Corvette." It's a masterful mix of pop, rock, and funk, and it was Prince's breakthrough project. *Dirty Mind* ♫♫♫♫ (Warner Bros., 1980, prod. Prince) is perhaps the definitive funk/rock album (with a nasty theme) and contains the classics "When You Were Mine," "Uptown," and "Partyup." *Purple Rain* ♫♫♫♫ (Warner Bros., 1984, prod. Prince) may be a bit too mainstream for some (it was #1 for 24 weeks), but this album put Prince over the top, and it's loaded with great dance/pop songs.

what to buy next: *The Hits/The B-Sides* ♫♫♫♫ (Paisley Park/Warner Bros., 1993, prod. Prince) is chock full of hits, though they do lose some of their luster when listened to out of their original context. Nevertheless, this is the only album that contains such legendary Prince B-sides as "Erotic City," "Gotta Stop (Messin' About)," and "How Come U Don't Call Me Anymore." *Parade (Music from the Motion Picture Under the Cherry Moon)* ♫♫♫♫ (Paisley Park/Warner Bros., 1986, prod. Prince) is often dismissed as a failure, largely because of the lack of success of its companion movie. While "Kiss" may be its most familiar track, it contains other great songs—"Girls & Boys," "Mountains," "Anotherloverholenyohead," and the haunting "Sometimes It Snows in April"—that were inexplicably left off the hits packages.

what to avoid: Prince was handpicked to do the soundtrack for *Batman* **woof!** (Warner Bros., 1989, prod. Prince) by one of the film's stars (and Prince fan), Jack Nicholson. That's one phone call Prince should've never answered. A couple of cuts ("The Future," "Partyman") aren't half bad, but the album as a whole is Prince's worst effort to date.

the rest:

For You ♫♫♪ (Warner Bros., 1978)
Prince ♫♫♫♫ (Warner Bros., 1979)
Controversy ♫♫♫♫ (Warner Bros., 1981)
Around the World in a Day ♫♫♫♫ (Paisley Park/Warner Bros., 1985)
Lovesexy ♫♫♫ (Paisley Park/Warner Bros., 1988)
(With others) *Graffiti Bridge (Soundtrack)* ♫♫ (Paisley Park/Warner Bros., 1990)
Diamonds and Pearls ♫♫♫♫ (Paisley Park/Warner Bros., 1991)
♀ ♫♫♫ (Paisley Park/Warner Bros., 1992)
The Hits 1 ♫♫♫♫ (Paisley Park/Warner Bros., 1993)
The Hits 2 ♫♫♫♫ (Paisley Park/Warner Bros., 1993)

Prince (© Ken Settle)

The Black Album 𝄞𝄞𝄞 (Warner Bros., 1994)
Come 𝄞𝄞 (Warner Bros., 1994)
The Gold Experience 𝄞𝄞𝄞 (NPG/Warner Bros., 1995)
(With others) *Girl 6 (Soundtrack)* 𝄞𝄞𝄞𝄞 (Warner Bros., 1996)
Emancipation 𝄞𝄞𝄞𝄞 (NPG/EMI, 1996)
Crystal Ball 𝄞𝄞𝄞𝄞 (NPG, 1998)
The Truth 𝄞𝄞𝄞 (NPG, 1998)
(With the New Power Generation) *New Power Soul* 𝄞𝄞 (NPG, 1998)

worth searching for: *The White Album* (Neutral Zone, 1989), a bootleg live CD recorded in Germany in 1988, is 71 minutes of no-holds-barred funk, made even better by its surprisingly fine sound quality.

influences:

◀◀ Carlos Santana, Sly & the Family Stone, Jimi Hendrix, James Brown, the Beatles, the Rolling Stones

▶▶ The Time, Vanity 6, Tevin Campbell, Madonna, Terence Trent D'Arby

Dean Dauphinais

John Prine

Born October 10, 1946, in Maywood, IL.

One of the first to be strapped as "the new Dylan," John Prine is one of the few to actually outgrow the tag and become a distinct, trenchant songwriting voice. Mostly because of his admittedly limited guitar skills, Prine often gets lumped in the folkie-singer-songwriter genre, but as anyone who has ever listened carefully or heard him play with a band knows, he has the heart and soul of a rock 'n' roller. His 1971 self-titled debut alone includes such astonishing songs as "Sam Stone," the first Vietnam protest song to tackle the war's effect on soldiers' lives; an homage to the elderly wryly titled "Hello in There"; "Donald and Lydia," a touching ode to masturbation; the wicked social satire "Spanish Pipedream," with the oft-repeated chorus, "Blow up your TV/Throw away your paper"; and "Angel from Montgomery," a longtime Bonnie Raitt staple. Major labels gave up on Prine, which led to him to start his own Oh Boy! Records during the early '80s. These days his edge, sharp eye for detail, and feel for simple melodies, common language, and popular culture seems, if anything, more exact—and he's even more effective in concert. His songs have been recorded by many diverse artists, including Joan Baez, Bette Midler, the Everly Brothers, and Cowboy Junkies, but more importantly, Prine's influence can be heard whenever guitars are played on streets and living rooms around the world.

what to buy: *John Prine* 𝄞𝄞𝄞𝄞𝄞 (Atlantic, 1971, prod. Arif Mardin) is filled with raw, harrowing, sometimes goofy tales of life. *The Missing Years* 𝄞𝄞𝄞𝄞𝄞 (Oh Boy, 1991, prod. Howie Epstein) offers the same kind of world-view undaunted by middle age. *Bruised Orange* 𝄞𝄞𝄞𝄞 (Asylum/Oh Boy, 1978, prod. Steve Goodman) adds the twist of Steve Goodman's inspired arrangements. *John Prine Live* 𝄞𝄞𝄞𝄞 (Oh Boy, 1988, prod. John Prine, Dan Einstein, Jim Rooney) and *Live on Tour* 𝄞𝄞𝄞𝄞 (Oh Boy, 1997, prod. Dan Einstein, John Prine) includes the stories and onstage charisma that's missing on his studio albums.

what to buy next: *Storm Windows* 𝄞𝄞𝄞𝄞 (Asylum, 1980, prod. Barry Beckett) is Prine's best-sounding record, courtesy of producer Barry Beckett. *Aimless Love* 𝄞𝄞𝄞𝄞 (Oh Boy, 1984, prod. John Prine, Jim Rooney) is a pleasant, country-flavored record. The best collection to span his Atlantic career is *Great Days* 𝄞𝄞𝄞𝄞 (Rhino, 1993, prod. various), with music from all his albums for that label.

what to avoid: *Common Sense* 𝄞𝄞 (Atlantic, 1975, prod. Steve Cropper) is a classic example of mismatching producer and artist. The songs—and there are some good ones—often sound incomplete, and Prine sounds out of breath at the end of every one.

the rest:
Sweet Revenge 𝄞𝄞𝄞 (Atlantic, 1973)
Prime Prine 𝄞𝄞𝄞 (Atlantic, 1976)
German Afternoons 𝄞𝄞𝄞𝄞 (Oh Boy, 1988)
Diamonds in the Rough 𝄞𝄞𝄞 (Atlantic, 1990)
A John Prine Christmas 𝄞𝄞𝄞𝄞 (Oh Boy, 1993)
Lost Dogs and Mixed Blessings 𝄞𝄞𝄞 (Oh Boy, 1995)

worth searching for: On *Pink Cadillac* (Asylum/Oh Boy, 1979, prod. Knox Phillips, Jerry Phillips), a primal Prine draws from the unique energy and vibe of Memphis' famous Sun Studios—with Sam Phillips's kids at the knobs.

influences:

◀◀ The Carter Family, Hank Williams, Chuck Berry, Jerry Lee Lewis, Bob Dylan

▶▶ Nanci Griffith, Iris DeMent, Cowboy Junkies

Leland Rucker

P.J. Proby
/Jett Powers
/Orville Woods

Born James Marcus Smith, November 6, 1938, in Houston, TX.

The brilliant writer Nik Cohn once described P.J. Proby as a composite of Errol Flynn, Judy Garland, and Jesus Christ. Add to that volatile mix the dripping sexuality of an Elvis Presley crossed with the chest-pounding arrogance of Jerry Lee Lewis, and you can *almost* begin to fathom the magnitude of this man's deep-rooted talent. So why, then, is P.J. Proby unknown p.j. proby

to all but a few record collectors and Swinging '60s buffs? Because, though in possession of a voice and possibly even a talent the equal of Presley's, Proby's litany of professional missteps, which in retrospect seem suspiciously like career self-sabotage, have for the past four decades prevented him, time after time, from achieving the global stardom he will be the first to tell you he deserves. Following a childhood spent singing at talent contests and an adolescence trapped in military school, James Marcus Smith escaped to Hollywood where, adopting the moniker Jett Powers, he scuffled from job to job within the showbiz lower strata. A stint as Paul Newman's chauffeur preceded bit parts in B-movies and TV westerns during the late '50s, while a gig demoing soundtrack filler for Elvis himself led to a series of flop 45's of his very own for a variety of small labels. Proby also served time with such vocal groups as the Mello-Kings and Hollywood Argyles (playing "wine glasses" alongside Kim Fowley on the latter's hit "Alley Oop") while singing back-up behind everyone from B.B. King to Johnny Cash. He formed his own band, the Moon Dogs, and even recorded surprisingly authentic R&B material under the name of Orville Woods before scoring a position with Liberty Records as a songwriter. Rick Nelson, Jackie DeShannon, Johnny Burnette, and the Searchers all recorded his material, to varying degrees of notoriety, but it was not until fellow Liberty writer Sharon Sheeley introduced him to British producer Jack Good (as well as suggesting he rename himself P.J. Proby) that things finally began to connect for the man. Whisked to London to appear in Good's *Around the Beatles* television spectacular, Proby became an instant sensation throughout the U.K., his first release there hitting #3 on the charts and his brazenly theatrical stage act becoming the talk of the country—especially after one night his skin-tight velvet trousers split from knee to crotch during his opening number. When this very same mishap occurred the next night, then the next and then again the next, the ABC Theatre chain, smelling a rat, wasted no time instigating a nationwide ban on live appearances. A week later, both the ATV and BBC networks barred him from radio and television airplay as well. Proby quickly recorded a song called "I Apologise," but the British, he found, were quick to embrace but painfully slow to forget and forgive. It also didn't help much when John Lennon called him "Elvis in a bottle," and Paul McCartney added that "he has the voice of Pluto the Dog barking at Mickey Mouse." (Nevertheless, several weeks later the twosome donated a Beatle outtake, "That Means a Lot," for Proby's exclusive use). Citing dire financial straits, Proby headed back to America, where he enjoyed his only homeland hit, "Niki Hoeky," in 1967. Yet already the man seemed a novelty figure at best—and an unreliably provocative, mistrustful performer at worst ("P.J.," he seemed proud to say at the time, "stands for Perpetually Juiced.") During the 30 years since, Proby has starred in various British musicals (ironi-

cally to greatest acclaim when portraying the Vegas-era Elvis), recorded in a variety of styles for a variety of labels (including an album with Dutch art-rockers Focus), gotten married a few times, toiled as a supermarket cleaner and manure spreader, been thrown in and out of several jails on alcohol and weapons infractions, and suffered six heart attacks. Yet through it all he has somehow managed to survive with his dignity—and, yes, his commanding set of vocal pipes—intact. Living a relatively settled life today in a small North London suburb, he seems light-years apart from that pony-tailed, velvet-encased rabbler-ouser who once taunted British schoolgirls from the stage with cries of "Am I clean? Am I spotless? Am I pure?" Still, to this day his every cocksure sideways glance seems to reinforce the immortal words that, following his first fall from grace in 1966, he distributed as a "testament" to the entertainment industry that once seemed to persecute him: "I am an artist," Proby defiantly proclaimed, "and should be exempt from shit." If only Elvis could have possessed the courage to believe as much.

what to buy: The remarkable two-disc, 51-track *Rough Velvet* ♪♪♪♪ (EMI, 1992, compilation prod. Vic Lanza) provides an ideal overview of Proby's crazed career, concentrating—as it should—on his landmark '60s recordings. Regardless of what you may think of the man's, um, personality deficiencies, it's hard to find fault with what he could do when set in front of a microphone.

what to buy next: Six of his earliest, most illustrative original albums have been packaged together on disc as: *I Am P.J. Proby/P.J. Proby* ♪♪♪ (Liberty, 1964, 1965/C-Five, 1994, prod. Charles Blackwell, Johnny Spence, Ron Richards); *P.J. Proby's in Town/Enigma* ♪♪♪ (Liberty, 1965, 1966/C-Five, 1994, prod. Johnny Spence, Ron Richards, Les Reed, Calvin Carter, Jack Nitzsche); and *Phenomenon/Believe It or Not* ♪♪♪ (Liberty, 1967, 1968/C-Five, 1994, prod. Calvin Carter, Les Reed, Bob Reisdorff). Veering wildly from album to album—and sometimes track to track—between lush, soulful ballads and gaunt, surly rockers, listening *can* be a bumpy ride. But as with all things Proby, that's to be expected. *California License* ♪♪♪ (Liberty, 1969/Freedom, 1994, prod. Bob Reisdorff) contains 22 of the man's seminal Jett Powers recordings, while *Three Week Hero* ♪♪♪ (Liberty, 1969/BGO, 1990, prod. Steve Rowland) will also be of interest to Led Zeppelin collectors, as Jimmy Page, Robert Plant, John Paul Jones, *and* John Bonham battle throughout to remain audible over the Proby roar. Needless to say, the sometimes downright incongruous *Focus Con Proby* ♪♪♪ (Harvest, 1978/EMI, 1988, prod. Yold de Jong) is worth experiencing as well.

the rest:
The Legendary P.J. Proby at His Very Best ♪♪♪ (See for Miles, 1986, 1989)
The Legendary P.J. Proby at His Very Best, Vol. 2 Plus ♪♪♪ (See for Miles, 1987/1990)

The EP Collection 🎵🎵🎵 (See for Miles, 1996)
The Legend 🎵🎵🎵 (EMI Premier, 1997)
If I Loved You 🎵🎵 (Hallmark, 1998)

worth searching for: A series of obscure British releases—
Savoy Digital Angst (Savoy, 1992, prod. David Britton, Michael
Butterworth, Stephen Boyce-Buckley), *Savoy Wars* (Savoy,
1992, prod. David Britton, Michael Butterworth), and *The Savoy
Sessions* (Savoy, 1995, prod. David Britton, Michael Butterworth, Stephen Boyce-Buckley)—contain Proby renditions of
Prince's "Sign o' the Times" and an utterly brilliant, nine-
minute, Pistol-popping tear through "Anarchy in the U.K." Not
since Tiny Tim tackled "White Wedding" and "Highway to Hell"
has anything quite as jaw-dropping been committed to tape.

influences:

◀◀ Slim Whitman, Frank Sinatra, Elvis Presley, Tommy Sands,
James Brown

▶▶ Jim Morrison, Mark Lindsay, the Walker Brothers, the
Cramps, Tom Jones

Gary Pig Gold

The Proclaimers

Formed 1983, in Edinburgh, Scotland.

Craig Reid, vocals; Charlie Reid, guitar, vocals.

A couple of geeky brothers with bizarre rockabilly haircuts,
Buddy Holly glasses, and impossibly thick Scottish burrs (not
to be confused with the Jesus & Mary Chain's Reid brothers),
the Proclaimers wrote some incredibly melodic post-post-new
wave tunes during the '80s. The duo immediately hit the charts
in England and Australia, but it took the 1993 film *Benny and
Joon*, whose soundtrack contained the duo's best-known song
"I'm Gonna Be (500 Miles)," to really make them American one-
hit wonders. The *Hit the Highway* album was disconcertingly
religious, but there's no denying the Reids's crisp pop talent.

what to buy: *Sunshine on Leith* 🎵🎵🎵 (Chrysalis, 1988, prod.
Pete Wingfield), the original home of "I'm Gonna Be (500
Miles)," offers the best evidence of the Proclaimers' strong
melodic skills.

what to buy next: *This Is the Story* 🎵🎵🎵 (Chrysalis, 1987, prod.
John Williams) is a collection of acoustic tunes that produced
the #3 U.K. single "Letter to America."

what to avoid: *Hit the Highway* 🎵🎵 (Chrysalis, 1994, prod. Pete
Wingfield) was a gospel album, and a way-too-preachy one at
that.

the rest:
King of the Road 🎵🎵 (Chrysalis EP, 1990)

worth searching for: The soundtrack to *Benny and Joon* (BMG,
1993, prod. various) provided the band's belated breakthrough; though beyond two versions of the "I'm Gonna Be . . ."
hit, the rest is a bland movie score.

influences:

◀◀ The Everly Brothers, Buddy Holly, Tom Robinson Band, the
Romantics, Buzzcocks, the Plimsouls

▶▶ Lowen & Navarro, Jackopierce, Green Day

Tracey Birkenhauer and Steve Knopper

Procol Harum

Formed 1966, in London, England. Disbanded 1977. Reunited 1991.

**Gary Brooker, piano, vocals; Keith Reid, lyrics; Matthew Fisher,
organ, vocals (1966–70, 1991); Dave Knights, bass (1966–70); Ray
Royer, guitar (1966–67); Bobby Harrison, drums (1966–67); Robin
Trower, guitar (1967–71, 1991); B.J. Wilson (died 1989), drums
(1967–77); Chris Copping, bass, organ (1970–77); Dave Ball, guitar
(1971–72); Alan Cartwright, bass (1971–76); Mick Grabham, guitar
(1972–77); Pete Solley, organ (1976–77); Dave Bronze, bass (1991);
Mark Brzezicki, drums (1991).**

From the ashes of the Paramounts, a commercially unsuccessful
British R&B band, rose Procol Harum, which established itself
early with the landmark single "A Whiter Shade of Pale." Unlike
other "progressive" rock bands of the time, Procol Harum didn't
use string arrangements and classical melodies to disguise the
fact that it couldn't write or as a way to seem more important
than it was. On the contrary, it wrote concise pop songs that
were magnificent, beautiful, haunting, mysterious, and hummable. Gary Brooker and Keith Reid are obvious choices when
discussing what made Procol Harum tick, but B.J. Wilson is possibly one of the most underrated drummers ever (slightly less
manic than Keith Moon and far more stylish), and the many guitarists who played with the band (Robin Trower went on to huge
success as a solo act) all provided flash and taste. Things
tended to sound bombastic or pretentious at times, but you always got the feeling that the band was winking at you all the
while. For example, is "A Salty Dog" a sailing song or is it the
story of conception? Only Reid knows for sure. But Procol
Harum ran out of inspiration a couple of albums before it quit
recording for the first time (the group reunited in 1991). Brooker,
Reid, and Matthew Fisher have recorded and toured together recently, and much of the magic has returned with them.

what to buy: *A Salty Dog* 🎵🎵🎵🎵 (A&M, 1969, prod. Matthew
Fisher) has the title song, "So Much between Us," Fisher's
"Boredom," and probably the strangest drinking song ever
recorded, "The Devil Came from Kansas." *Greatest Hits* 🎵🎵🎵🎵
(A&M, 1996, prod. various) provides a good single-disc
overview of the band, featuring digitally remastered sound.

what to buy next: Powerful production, good songs, great guitar solos, and some wonderful counterpoint singing on "Fires which Burn Brightly" make *Grand Hotel* 𝄞𝄞𝄞𝄞 (Chrysalis, 1973, prod. Chris Thomas) a surprising and consistently fine album.

what to avoid: On *Something Magic* 𝄞𝄞 (Chrysalis, 1977, prod. Procol Harum, Ron Albert, Howie Albert) the band sounds too tired to do anything but go for the formula and hope for the best. It didn't work, and the band broke up shortly after.

the rest:
A Whiter Shade of Pale 𝄞𝄞𝄞 (A&M, 1967)
Shine on Brightly 𝄞𝄞𝄞 (A&M, 1968)
Home 𝄞𝄞𝄞 (A&M, 1970)
Broken Barricades 𝄞𝄞𝄞𝄞 (A&M, 1971)
The Best of Procol Harum 𝄞𝄞𝄞𝄞 (A&M, 1972)
Procol Harum in Concert with the Edmonton Symphony Orchestra 𝄞𝄞𝄞𝄞 (Chrysalis, 1972)
Exotic Birds and Fruit 𝄞𝄞𝄞 (Chrysalis, 1974)
Procol's Ninth 𝄞𝄞𝄞 (Chrysalis, 1975)
The Prodigal Stranger 𝄞𝄞𝄞 (Zoo, 1991)
The Long Goodbye: Symphonic Music of Procol Harum 𝄞𝄞 (RCA Victor, 1995)
30th Anniversary Anthology N/A (Westside, 1998)

worth searching for: Fisher's first solo outing, *Journey's End* (RCA, 1973), is a neat collection of pop tunes—not at all what you might expect after hearing the band's work.

solo outings:
Gary Brooker:
No More Fear of Flying 𝄞𝄞𝄞 (Chrysalis, 1979)
Lead Me to the Water 𝄞𝄞𝄞 (PolyGram, 1982)
Echoes in the Night 𝄞𝄞𝄞 (PolyGram, 1984)

Matthew Fisher:
I'll Be There 𝄞𝄞𝄞 (RCA, 1974)
Matthew Fisher 𝄞𝄞𝄞 (A&M, 1980)

influences:
◀◀ J.S. Bach, the Shangri-Las
▶▶ Electric Light Orchestra, Genesis, Kansas

see also: *Robin Trower*

Shane Faubert

Prodigy

Formed 1991, in Braintree, England.

Liam Howlett, programming; Maxim Reality, MC; Keith Flint, vocals, dancer; Leeroy Thornhill, dancer.

Alongside the Chemical Brothers, Prodigy helped introduce mainstream U.S. audiences to the high-energy thrills of electronic music. But commercial success didn't come instantly to this motley crew. The group, which in essense is ringmaster Liam Howlett's travelling circus, was dropped from Elektra in the United States after its first two albums bombed. But on the strength of its manic "Firestarter" single and escalating British hype, it became the center of a fierce bidding war in 1996, before most the tracks for its breakthrough album *The Fat of the Land* were even written. Madonna's Maverick label came out as the victor, and the group predictably went on to conquer the charts—much to the Elektra A&R department's chagrin. The group is often referred to as the Sex Pistols of the '90s, more for its dramatic stage antics and loud music than for its attitude.

what to buy: *The Fat of the Land* 𝄞𝄞𝄞𝄞 (Maverick, 1997, prod. Liam Howlett) was fueled by video game–style electronic music played hard and fast. Howlett's surprisingly adept compositional skill confirmed this group would last longer than frontman Keith Flint's green haircoloring.

what to buy next: *Music for the Jilted Generation* 𝄞𝄞𝄞 (Elektra, 1994, prod. Liam Howlett) showed the first signs of Howlett's advanced sense for melody and energy. Frantic songs such as "Poison" set the tone for future hits "Breathe" and the controversial "Smack My Bitch Up."

the rest:
The Prodigy Experience 𝄞𝄞 (Elektra, 1995)

influences:
◀◀ Public Enemy, Sex Pistols, Happy Mondays

Aidin Vaziri

Professor Griff

See: Public Enemy

Projekct Two

See: King Crimson

Prong

Formed 1986, in New York, NY.

Tommy Victor, vocals, guitar; Ted Parsons, drums; Mike Kirkland, bass, vocals (1986–90); Troy Gregory, bass, vocals (1991–93); Paul Raven, bass (1993–present).

Brutal and uncompromising, Prong is the rare case of a band starting in the underground and then letting its sound get *harder* when it signs with a major label. The group was put together by guitarist Tommy Victor, who mixed sound at CBGB before deciding to get his own band together. He took a New York brand of thrash and stripped it to its essence—just the song structures and a lot of noise made by the three instrumentalists, but all in service of the tune rather than for shows of speedy virtuosity.

what to buy: *Beg to Differ* ✺✺✺✹ (Epic, 1990, prod. Mark Dodson, Prong) is the major-label debut that caught everyone off guard. Rather than soften its sound, Prong cranks it up yet another notch, making an almost industrial kind of racket.

what to buy next: *Rude Awakening* ✺✺✺ (Epic, 1996, prod. Terry Date, Tommy Victor) imports pal Charlie Clauser from nine inch nails to add keyboards and sampling for an extra layer of density in Prong's already harsh attack.

what to avoid: *Primitive Origins* ✺✺ (Mr. Bear/Sound League, 1987) is invigorating but indistinct from the rest of the thrash pack.

the rest:
Force Fed ✺✺✹ (In-Effect, 1989)
Prove You Wrong ✺✺✺ (Epic, 1991)
Whose Fist Is This Anyway? ✺✺ (Epic, 1993)
Cleansing ✺✺✺ (Epic, 1993)

influences:
◄◄ Black Flag, Metallica, Megadeth, Living Colour

►► nine inch nails, Pantera, White Zombie, Body Count

Gary Graff

Chuck Prophet

See: Green on Red

The Psychedelic Furs /Richard Butler /Love Spit Love

Formed 1978, in London, England. Disbanded 1991.

Richard Butler, vocals; Tim Butler, bass; Duncan Kilburn, sax (1978–81); Mars Williams, horns, saxes (1984–88); Roger Morris, guitar (1978–81); John Ashton, guitar; Knox Chandler, guitar, cello (1989–91); Vince Ely, drums (1979–82, 1987–90); Phil Calvert, drums (1982–83); Paul Garisto, drums (1984–87); Don Yallech, drums (1990–91).

With his ragged, raspy voice, Richard Butler sounded like the prototypical punk, and the Psychedelic Furs band did come from that background. But by the time the group disbanded 13 years later, it had garnered glossy pop hits and been popular in dance clubs—yet with that voice up front, it rarely sounded compromised. The debut recordings were fairly dirgy, but in a catchy way; BBC DJ John Peel played them, and the group was signed by Columbia. It would prove to be popular in its native country but continually have trouble breaking through in the United States, often coming tantilizingly close. For instance, a Furs song was the inspiration for John Hughes's film *Pretty in Pink* and was re-recorded for its soundtrack; Hughes was the

most American of '80s directors, yet the single peaked at #41. The group moved to America and recorded its third album, *Forever Now*, with Todd Rundgren and actually found itself with a gold record and a hit, "Love My Way." Ultimately, the dancey "Heartbreak Beat," from the otherwise uninteresting *Midnight to Midnight*, was the only Top 40 hit the band ever had here. It was all downhill from there, with apparent confusion among band members as to just what they wanted to sound like and represent. Three years after the band was dissolved, Butler was trying to duplicate its rock sound with a new band, Love Spit Love, which has so far gone nowhere.

what to buy: The two-CD *Should God Forget: A Retrospective* ✺✺✺✺ (Columbia Legacy, 1997, prod. various) functions equally well as an overview of the Furs' career for new listeners and as a resource full of tracks previously unreleased or U.K.-only tracks, live or otherwise differing versions of familiar material, and B-sides in addition to the well-known album material. A recording for the BBC of "Mack the Knife" is especially illuminating. It's also a good way of acquiring the better later material from when the group had passed its peak. The albums from the first half of the group's career are definitely worth owning individually, however. *Talk Talk Talk* ✺✺✺✺ (Columbia, 1981, Steve Lillywhite) moves the bleakness of the debut into mainstream territory without compromising. *Forever Now* ✺✺✺✺ (Columbia, 1982, prod. Todd Rundgren) is positively Beatlesque (Rundgren's doing, of course) in its production effects.

what to buy next: *The Psychedelic Furs* ✺✺✺✺ (Columbia, 1980, prod. various) is one of the bleakest documents of the punk era to have actual melodies and hooks—droning yet shiny, and gloriously unnerving. *Mirror Moves* ✺✺✺✺ (Columbia, 1984, prod. Keith Forsey) is the most pop-melodic Furs, with "The Ghost in You," "Heaven," and "High Wire Days."

what to avoid: *World Outside* ✺ (Columbia, 1991, prod. Stephen Street, Psychedelic Furs) is exhausted of new ideas, and the desperate-for-a-hit production makes the sound annoying.

the rest:
Midnight to Midnight ✺✺ (Columbia, 1987)
All of This and Nothing ✺✺✺✺ (Columbia, 1988)
Book of Days ✺✺ (Columbia, 1989)

worth searching for: The import *The Radio-One Sessions* (Strange Fruit, 1997) captures vintage Furs performances on the BBC, including fiery renditions of "Pretty in Pink," "Sister Europe," and "All of This and Nothing."

solo outings:
Love Spit Love (Richard Butler):
Love Spit Love ✺✺ (Imago, 1994)
Trysome Eatone ✺✺✹ (Maverick, 1997)

influences:

◀◀ Velvet Underground, the Beatles, Joy Division, the Sex Pistols

▶▶ Sisters of Mercy, Live Skull, Nirvana

Steve Holtje

Public Enemy

Formed 1982, in Long Island, NY.

Chuck D. (Carlton Ridenhour), vocals; Flavor Flav (William Drayton), vocals; Terminator X (Norman Lee Rogers), DJ; Professor Griff (Richard Griffin), minister of information (1985–89).

Public Enemy seized the still-young hip-hop genre and transformed it from lighthearted, braggy dance music to a politically potent bullhorn news broadcast. Leader Chuck D.'s voice, always the equivalent of yelling "fire!" at a crowded concert, dismissed Elvis Presley as a racist, attacked Hollywood as patronizing, and encouraged revolution. He was often brilliant, but, as egotistical visionaries are wont to do, often shot himself in the foot. He embraced the anti-Semitic Nation of Islam Minister Louis Farrakhan; hired, apologized for, and reluctantly fired the even more anti-Semitic "minister of information" Professor Griff; and his lyrics distorted Biblical passages to hold Jews responsible for Christ's crucifixion. The flip-side was Public Enemy's songs: Chuck D's voice, augmented by sidekick Flavor Flav's high-pitched "Yeeeeehhh booooyyyyyys," and DJ Terminator X's complex collage of funk samples, was as powerful as Johnny Rotten or Mick Jagger (but maybe not Howlin' Wolf) ever were. Public Enemy bestowed upon rap a political conscience and, more importantly, gave hip-hop music and culture a sense of purpose.

what to buy: *It Takes a Nation of Millions to Hold Us Back* ♫♫♫♫ (Def Jam, 1988, prod. Hank Shocklee, Carly Ryder) is the definitive political rap album, establishing Public Enemy's underground power with "Bring the Noise," the anti-media "Don't Believe the Hype," and the searing funk grooves of "She Watch Channel Zero" and "Black Steel (In the Hour of Chaos)." Produced by the so-called Bomb Squad—Hank Shocklee, Carl Ryder, Eric (Vietnam) Sadler, and Keith Shocklee—the follow-up, *Fear of a Black Planet* ♫♫♫♫ (Def Jam, 1990, prod. Bomb Squad), has more filler, but "Fight the Power" (originally heard in Spike Lee's film *Do the Right Thing)*, "Who Stole the Soul?," and "Welcome to the Terrordome" are some of the most forceful songs ever recorded. *Muse Sick-N-Hour Mess Age* ♫♫♫✓ (Def Jam, 1994, prod. Bomb Squad), with the wise-old-soul hit "Give It Up," was tremendously underrated.

what to buy next: P.E.'s debut, *Yo! Bum Rush the Show* ♫♫♫ (Def Jam, 1987, prod. Hank Shocklee, Bill Stephney, others), is not as complex as later stuff, but it contains the buzzing battle cry

"Public Enemy No. 1." *Apocalypse '91 . . . The Enemy Strikes Black* ♫♫♫ (Def Jam, 1991, prod. Stuart Robertz, Cerwin (C-Dawg) Depper, Gary G-Wiz, JBL) meanders with moral messages about the evils of drinking alcohol, but it's worth the price for the Public Enemy–Anthrax metal-rap collaboration "Bring the Noise."

what to avoid: There's almost no redeeming quality to Professor Griff's morally irritating solo albums *Pawns in the Game* ♫ (Luke, 1990) and *Kao's II Wiz*7*Dome* **woof!** (Luke, 1991).

the rest:
Greatest Misses ♫♫ (Def Jam, 1992)
He Got Game ♫♫♫✓ (Def Jam, 1998)

worth searching for: Chuck D.'s brilliant improvised reading of the Charles Mingus poem "Gunslinging Bird (Or If Charlie Parker Were a Gunslinger, There'd Be a Whole Lot of Dead Copycats)," on the Mingus tribute *Weird Nightmare: Meditations on Mingus* (Columbia, 1992, prod. Hal Willner), is not to be missed.

solo outings:
Chuck D.:
Autobiography of Mista Chuck ♫♫♫ (Mercury, 1996)

Terminator X:
Terminator X & the Valley of the Jeep Beets ♫♫♫ (RAL, 1991)
Terminator X & the Godfathers of Threatt: Super Bad ♫♫ (RAL, 1994)

influences:

◀◀ James Brown, Gil Scott-Heron, the Last Poets, Kurtis Blow, Boogie Down, Anthrax

▶▶ Rage Against the Machine, Geto Boys, Boo-Yaa T.R.I.B.E, Tricky

Steve Knopper

Public Image Ltd.
/PiL
/John Lydon

Formed 1978, in London, England. Disbanded 1993.

John Lydon, vocals; Keith Levene, guitar (1978–83); Jah Wobble (born John Wordle), bass (1978–81); Jim Walker, drums (1978–79); Richard Dudanski, drums (1979); Martin Atkins, drums (1979–80); John McGeoch, guitar (1987–92); Lu Edmonds, keyboards, guitar (1987–92); Alan Dias, bass (1987–92); Bruce Smith, drums (1987–92).

Thrown clear of the wreckage of the Sex Pistols, Johnny Rotten soon turned up under his original name of John Lydon and piloting a new vehicle, Public Image Ltd. Known for its offbeat packaging, an industry-mocking presentation, and the occasional violent outburst from uncomprehending concert audiences, as well as for its groundbreaking music, PiL was subversive in a way more subtle and perhaps more durable than that of the Pistols themselves. Early versions of the band included avant-guitarist Keith Levene, drummer Martin Atkins (of later Brian Brain and Pigface fame) and bassist Jah Wobble, who'd been vetoed as a Sex Pistol by that band's guitarist and drummer for his allegedly physical brand of conflict resolution. Dissension after PiL's first U.S. tour in 1980 began its attrition into a Lydon solo project, and in 1993 he deactivated the band, releasing a dance single with Leftfield that year and publishing his autobiography, *Rotten: No Irish—No Blacks—No Dogs*, the next. With a Mountain Dew commercial and pledge-breaking Pistols reunion tour in '96, Lydon seemed to be fulfilling PiL's satirical early claim to be a corporation and not a band. But within a year, his solo-billed debut, *Psycho's Path*, showed that his dip in the mainstream had refreshed him for new expeditions into uncharted artistic territory, and he hasn't settled yet.

what to buy: The band's two best albums are at either end of the pop-to-alternative spectrum. The fascinating *Second Edition* ♫♫♫♫♫ (Virgin, 1979, prod. Public Image Ltd.) intersects dance grooves, ambient structures, and noise guitar in a way hard to imagine in the stylistically sectarian '70s. The album's sound is improvisational but remarkably cohesive, disintegrating and rebuilding before your ears, while Lydon channels a variety of song-specific voices that don't lead the band so much as haunt it. At the opposite extreme, *Album* ♫♫♫♫♫ (Elektra, 1986, prod. Bill Laswell, John Lydon) ferociously updated the Pistols' sound, filtered through the mainstream techniques of the time. It surrounded some of the typical experiments in ranting polyphony ("Rise," "Round") with mid-'80s metal and synth-pop accents and an ironically corporate package (also titled *Cassette* and *Compact Disc* for the appropriate formats), but it was the sound of Reagan-era complacency being blown up from the inside.

what to buy next: The debut, *First Issue* ♫♫♫♫ (Virgin, 1978, prod. Public Image Ltd.), adds a novel, mournful strain to post-Pistols punk while moving toward the band's mature style. *Paris au Printemps* ♫♫♫♫ (Virgin, 1980, prod. Public Image Ltd.) convincingly adapts the band's spontaneity and sense of mischief to the concert setting. On the quietly bizarre solo album *Psycho's Path* ♫♫♫♪ (Virgin, 1997, prod. John Lydon, Mark Saunders, Leftfield), Lydon employs garage techno, world-music tinges, and a kind of stark electronic folk to show an experimentalism his critics had thought no longer in him, and a sensitivity they'd thought was never there.

what to avoid: The nondescript *Live in Tokyo* ♫ (Elektra, 1983, prod. Public Image Ltd.) is inessential and only for die-hards. *9* ♫♫ (Virgin, 1989, prod. Stephen Hague, Eric Thorngren) and *That What Is Not* ♫♫ (Virgin, 1992, prod. Dave Jerden) track a downward curve of idea depletion.

the rest:
The Flowers of Romance ♫♫♫ (Warner Bros., 1981)

This Is What You Want . . . This Is What You Get ♫♫♫ (Elektra, 1984)
Happy? ♫♫♫ (Virgin, 1987)
The Greatest Hits So Far ♫♫♫♫ (Virgin, 1990)

worth searching for: *Metal Box* (Virgin U.K., 1979, prod. Public Image Ltd.) is the original import version of *Second Edition*. It came as three vinyl discs in a round metal canister. Also, the imported version of *Flowers of Romance* (Virgin U.K., 1981, prod. Public Image Ltd.) offers three additional songs not found on other albums.

solo outings:
Keith Levene:
Violent Opposition ♫♫♫♪ (Rykodisc, 1989)

Jah Wobble:
Legend Lives On ♫♫♫ (Blue Plate, 1990)
(With Brian Eno) *Spinner* ♫♫♫ (Gyroscope, 1995)
Heaven and Earth ♫♫♪ (Island, 1996)

Jah Wobble's Invaders of the Heart:
Rising above Bedlam ♫♫♫ (Atlantic, 1992)
Take Me to God ♫♫♫♪ (Island, 1994)
Without Judgement ♫♫♫♪ (Restless, 1994)

influences:
◀◀ Yoko Ono, Sex Pistols, psychedelic rock, Electronica, South African and East European roots and pop

▶▶ Glenn Branca, U2

see also: *The Sex Pistols*

Adam McGovern and Anna Glen

Gary Puckett & the Union Gap

Formed 1967, in San Diego, CA. Disbanded 1971.

Gary Puckett, vocals; Dwight Bement, tenor sax; Kerry Chater, bass; Gary Withem, keyboards; Paul Wheatbread, drums.

Suited up in mock Civil War regimental finery, the San Diego–based Gary Puckett & the Union Gap honed a power-pop formula of earnest love songs performed with full-throttle brass and string arrangements. (Imagine Blood, Sweat & Tears performing endless variations on "You've Made Me So Very Happy.") For all their beseeching quality, the songs were well served by Puckett's full-bodied vocals, which amplified the music's soaring, easy-listening nature. From 1967 to 1968 the group scored a string of hit tunes about young girls ("Young Girl"), young girls becoming young women ("This Girl Is a Woman Now"), and young women with cheating on their minds ("Woman Woman"). It's more than one man could take, but Puckett made it easy to swallow, with memorable melodies and a golden voice.

what's available: *Looking Glass* 🎵🎵🎵 (Sony, 1992, prod. various) is a 20-track retrospective that pulls out the Puckett plums ("Lady Willpower," "Over You," plus the aforementioned hits) and for good measure adds on his solo work (a cover of Paul Simon's "Keep the Customer Satisfied").

influences:

◄◄ The Buckinghams, Paul Revere & the Raiders

►► Blood, Sweat & Tears, Chicago, Rick Astley

Christopher Scapelliti

Pulp

Formed 1980, in Sheffield, England.

Jarvis Cocker, vocals; Russell Senior, guitar, violin; Steve Mackey, bass; Candida Doyle, keyboards; Nick Banks, drums; Mark Webber, guitar, keyboards.

Formed nearly 20 years ago—but only a presence in the United States since 1994—Pulp's music began as synth/pop in the tradition of Roxy Music and David Bowie. Originally, charismatic but nerdish lead singer Jarvis Cocker led the band through gloomy, unremarkable folk-rock songs, with a slowly growing edge of hard rock and even funk. He grew as a songwriter, and *Different Class*, with typical lyrics that chronicle the lives of everyday people from an outsider's perspective, yielded an out-of-nowhere smash single, the very Bowie-influenced "Common People." Thanks to a publicity stunt that involved leaping onstage for an unspecific protest of a Michael Jackson show, Cocker briefly became British rock's bad boy in 1996; as such, he fit perfectly among Oasis' Gallagher brothers and earned a few minutes of fame. *This Is Hardcore*, the band's 1998 follow-up to *Different Class*, earned rave critical reviews but hasn't led to huge sales power.

what to buy: *His 'n' Hers* 🎵🎵🎵🎵 (Island, 1994, prod. Ed Buller) produced a hit single in the U.K., "Do You Remember the First Time?" On the band's breakthrough album, *Different Class* 🎵🎵🎵🎵 (Island, 1995, prod. Chris Thomas), songs such as "Common People," "I Spy," and "Sorted for E's and Wizz" display Pulp's epic crescendos and wry lyrics.

what to buy next: *This Is Hardcore* 🎵🎵🎵🎵 (Island, 1998, prod. Chris Thomas) showcases Cocker's still-growing singing and songwriting, especially on gloomy but catchy tracks such as the cabaret-influenced "TV Movie" and the title song. Though the album sleeve is filled with pictures of naked, busty women, some of them lying dead with Pulp members standing over them, Cocker's lyrics imply that this is merely a social commentary. "Hey, man, how come you treat your woman so bad?" he sings, on "A Little Soul." "That's not the way you do it."

what to avoid: In 1997 Velvel Records put out much of Pulp's considerable British back catalog in the United States. Many of those albums are interesting snapshots of the band's development on the road to "Common People." But some, such as *Masters of the Universe: Pulp on Fire 1985–86* 🎵🎵🎵 (Fire, 1995/Velvel, 1997), show the band aspiring to the gloomy cabaret singing of Nick Cave. Cocker isn't nearly as much of a lunatic as Cave, so loungey ballads such as "Little Girl (With Blue Eyes)" and "Simultaneous" come off as bad Nico imitations—although more aggressive Velvet Underground–style punk occasionally pops up.

the rest:

It 🎵🎵⁷ (Red Rhino, 1983/Fire, 1994/Velvel, 1997)
Freaks 🎵🎵⁷ (Fire, 1986/1993/Velvel, 1997)
Separations 🎵🎵⁷ (Fire, 1992/Razor & Tie, 1995)
1992–83—Countdown 🎵🎵🎵 (Velvel, 1998)

influences:

◄◄ The Kinks, Nick Cave & the Bad Seeds, David Bowie, the Beatles

►► Oasis, Blur

Anna Glen and Steve Knopper

The Pulsars

Formed 1995, in Chicago, IL.

Dave Trumfio, vocals, guitar, bass, keyboards; Harry Trumfio, percussion.

The brainchild of Chicago studio whiz-kid Dave Trumfio, the Pulsars sound like a space-age reanimation of Boston's infamous Cars, replete with tales of robot-addled alienation and lost love. Ably aided by his brother, percussionist Harry Trumfio, Dave creates a Phil Spectorish wall of sound with all manner of electronic textures, including a fair amount of pulsing blips and bleeps.

what to buy: *Pulsars* 🎵🎵🎵🎵 (Almo Sounds, 1997, prod. David Trumfio), the pair's eponymous debut, comes off like a greatest hits album, stacking one perfect single atop another. Velvety pop tunes like "Tunnel Song" and "Owed to a Devil" carve out a perfect middle ground between the Cars' *Candy-O* and OMD's *Crush*. Boy would these guys have been BIG during the '80s!

the rest:

Submission to the Masters 🎵🎵🎵 (Almo Sounds, 1996)

influences:

◄◄ The Cars, the Cure, Gary Numan, OMD, New Order

Scott Hess

Jimmy Purcey

See: Sham 69

Pure Prairie League

Formed 1971, in Cincinnati, OH. Disbanded 1988.

Craig Fuller, vocals, guitars (1971–75, 1985–88); George Powell, guitars, vocals (1971–77); Jim Lanham, bass, vocals (1971–72); Jim Caughlan, drums (1971–72); John David Call, steel guitar (1971–75); Michael Connor, keyboards (1972–88); Michael Reilly, bass, vocals (1972–88); Billy Hinds, drummer (1972–88); Larry Goshorn, guitar (1975–77); Timmy Goshorn, steel guitar (1975–77); Vince Gill, guitar, vocals (1978–81); Patrick Bolin, woodwinds (1979–80); Jeff Wilson, guitar, vocals (1980–88); Gary Burr, vocals (1981–85).

Pure Prairie League, which took its name from a women's temperance group in an Errol Flynn movie, was a Cincinnati country-rock group that drew influences from the California sounds of the Flying Burrito Brothers as well as from the local region's bluegrass. Neither of the group's first two albums, *Pure Prairie League* or *Bustin' Out*, did well upon their release in 1972, prompting RCA to drop the group. Singer Craig Fuller, having draft problems, left the band (Gerald Ford eventually pardoned him). Two years later, "Amie" began receiving national airplay, leaving the group in the unenviable position of having a hit and no frontman. RCA re-signed a revamped group, which continued evolving into the '80s and eventually featured a young Vince Gill on the group's only Top 10 hit, 1980's "Let Me Love You Tonight." Fuller went on to form American Flyer and front a post-Lowell George version of Little Feat before re-joining PPL in 1985.

what to buy: At the time of its release, *Bustin' Out* 🎵🎵🎵 (RCA, 1972, prod. Robert Alan Ringe) didn't quite seem to be either rock or country but rather a blend of the better parts of both. Fuller wrote and sang gentle pop-rock songs that were accented by steel guitar and a largely acoustic background. The "Falling in and out of Love/Amie" medley that appears here became an FM radio hit before "Amie" turned into a Top 40 single on its own, suggesting possibilities to an entire generation of future country singers. Mick Ronson of David Bowie's Spiders from Mars contributed string arrangements.

what to buy next: Fuller left PPL before the group made *Two Lane Highway* 🎵🎵🎵 (RCA, 1975, prod. John Boylan), so the songwriting suffers. But this album showcases the group's country licks, particularly on the concert favorite "Pickin' to Beat the Devil." Even though *Best of Pure Prairie League* 🎵🎵🎵 (Mercury, 1995, prod. various) sequences the "Falling in and out of Love/Amie" medley backwards and favors the band's Mercury days over its better RCA material, the compilation is still the only place to get "Amie" and "Let Me Love You Tonight" on the same disc.

what to avoid: Pure Prairie League hasn't been well served by best-of compilations, partially because the group's two biggest hits came five years apart for different labels. Those singles aside, the band's albums are fairly consistent, *Dance* 🎵🎵 (RCA,

1976, prod. Alan Abrahams) being the weakest album from the early period and *Something in the Night* 🎵🎵 (Mercury, 1981, prod. Rob Fraboni) the weakest from the latter.

the rest:
Pure Prairie League/If the Shoe Fits 🎵🎵🎵 (RCA, 1972/1976/Renaissance, 1997)
Firin' Up 🎵🎵🎵 (Mercury, 1980)
"Amie" and Other Hits 🎵🎵🎵 (RCA, 1990)

worth searching for: *Live! Takin' the Stage* (RCA, 1977) is a live recording from early in the band's career. It's currently out of print and unavailable on CD.

influences:
◀◀ The Byrds, Flying Burrito Brothers, Creedence Clearwater Revival

▶▶ Vince Gill, Little Feat, Garth Brooks, Clint Black

see also: *Little Feat*

Brian Mansfield

The Purple Outside

See: Screaming Trees

The Pursuit of Happiness

Formed 1986, in Edmonton, Alberta, Canada.

Moe Berg, vocals, guitar; Dave Gilby, drums; Kris Abbot, guitar, vocals; John Sinclair, bass (1988–90); Leslie Stanwyck, vocals (1988–90); Brad Barker, bass, vocals (1990–present); Rachel Oldfield, vocals (1993–95); Jenny Foster, vocals (1995–present).

The Pursuit of Happiness is the rare band that delivers visceral and cerebral pleasures in equal doses. Its sound is deceptively simple, with chunky guitars and vigorously solid drums buttressing irresistible pop melodies. The appeal is heightened by sharp arrangements that make adroit use of the group's two female singers; their innocently sweet harmonies render a poignant counter to Moe Berg's everyman vocals. The result is music that is both reassuringly familiar and invitingly fresh. To its further credit, TPOH executes this highly accessible style with a bare minimum of cliché. What truly separates TPOH from other rock bands, however, is Moe's songwriting. His relationship songs offers a bracing hit of reality; Berg has the courage to confront listeners with the bald truth that real romance is rarely perfect and that most people *do* look silly having sex. Berg is well aware when his libido plunges him into typical male behavior, and he's intelligent enough to seek alternative methods of relief. It's fortunate for rock music that one of those methods is his great songwriting.

what to buy: While all of TPOH's releases boast remarkable consistency, *One Sided Story* 🎵🎵🎵🎵 (Chrysalis, 1990, prod. Todd

Rundgren) stands out for Berg's exceptionally strong writing and the band's no-nonsense delivery. "Two Girls in One" and "Food"—which likens intestinal appetite with sexual appetite—brilliantly showcase Berg's sense of humor while "Shave Your Legs" depicts a challenged romance that, while far from story-book, nevertheless finds a redeeming emotional core.

what to buy next: *Love Junk* 🎵🎵🎵🎵 (Chrysalis, 1988, prod. Todd Rundgren) is TPOH's major-label debut and bears the group's major hit, the humorous "I'm an Adult Now." And the single is far from the best the album has to offer.

the rest:
The Downward Road 🎵🎵🎵 (Mercury, 1993)
Where's the Bone? 🎵🎵🎵 (Iron Music, 1995)
Wonderful World of Pursuit of Happiness 🎵🎵🎵 (Iron Music, 1997)

worth searching for: TPOH's first album, an indie release that contains the original versions of "I'm an Adult Now" and "Killed by Love," is difficult to find in the United States but can be ob-tained from the group's fan club, Loveslaves of TPOH, 253 College St., Box 127, Toronto, Ontario M5T 1R5, Canada.

influences:
◀◀ Todd Rundgren, Television

▶▶ The Breeders, Veruca Salt, the Pixies

David Galens

Quarterflash

Formed as Seafood Mama, 1980, in Portland, OR.

Rindy Ross, vocals, saxophone; Marv Ross, vocals, guitar; Jack Charles, vocals, guitar; Rick DiGiallonardo, keyboards; Brian Willis, drums; Rick Gooch, bass.

Rindy and Marv Ross were school teachers who wanted to make a difference—preferably on radio and in concert halls rather than in the classroom. So they went full-time with their avocation and hit fast with singles such as "Harden My Heart" and "Find Another Fool." Quarterflash played dense, polished pop that was near-perfect for radio during the early '80s, fitting just between the arena rock period and the MTV revolution that boosted new wave into the pop mainstream. And Rindy Ross was a compelling frontwoman, brandishing heavy metal—a saxophone—while most women in rock were wearing tight jeans and short skirts. Quarterflash's 15 minutes were tuneful, inoffensive, and ultimately not quite memorable enough to bring the group back during the '80s nostalgia boom.

what to buy: *Harden My Heart: The Best of Quarterflash* 🎵🎵🎵 (Geffen, 1997, prod. various) pretty much does the trick and, if nothing else, shows that the Rosses had at least a handful of good tunes in 'em.

the rest:
Quarterflash 🎵🎵🎵 (Geffen, 1981/1997)
Take Another Picture 🎵🎵 (Geffen, 1983/1997)
Back into Blue 🎵🎵🎵 (Geffen, 1985/1997)

influences:
◀◀ Linda Ronstadt, REO Speedwagon, Hall & Oates

▶▶ Candy Dulfer, the Cranberries, K's Choice

Gary Graff

Suzi Quatro

Born June 3, 1950, in Detroit, MI.

Although best known in the U.S. for her role as Leather Tus-cadero on TV's *Happy Days,* and from "Stumblin' In"—the sappy duet with Chris Norman that was her only American Top 40 hit—Suzi Quatro is a major star in her adopted U.K. home. More importantly, she was the first female rock 'n' roller to rock as hard as the big boys, an androgynous tough girl wrapped in tight leather and wielding a dangerous-looking bass guitar. Quatro's mid-'70s British hits were fashioned in the image of the Sweet (Sweet auteurs Mike Chapman and Nicky Chinn wrote and produced most of her early singles) and were pro-pelled by teenage-rampage hooks and a plodding, clunky charm. It was formula stuff, not all that dissimilar to what Slade, Mud, Hello, T. Rex, Gary Glitter, and scads of other glam/glitter Brits were pounding out at the time, but it was a goofy, catchy formula. Quatro's gender-bending stance may have seemed a novelty at first, but its ground breaking effect was nothing short of revelatory, perhaps even revolutionary. By rocking out on her own aggressive terms, Quatro served as an inspiration to all girls who rejected the idea of just being the rock star's girlfriend—she promoted the idea of being the rock star herself. Just ask Joan Jett. Or Courtney Love.

what to buy: *The Wild One: Classic Quatro* 🎵🎵🎵 (Razor & Tie, 1996, prod. various) is all the Quatro most folks will ever need. Its 20 tracks include a fair amount of dreck (including the ever-limp "Stumblin' In"), but its sins are fully redeemed by the American debut of Quatro's best track, the terrific "Tear Me Apart."

what to avoid: Steer clear of *Your Mama Won't Like Me* 🎵 (Arista, 1975, prod. Mike Chapman, Nicky Chinn), a simply hor-rid stab at fake funk.

influences:
◀◀ The Rolling Stones, David Bowie, the Sweet

▶▶ Joan Jett, the Go-Go's, Sara Lee, Cheri Knight, Courtney Love

Carl Cafarelli

Finley Quaye
Born in Edinburgh, Scotland.

Half Ghanaian, half Scottish, Finley Quaye could hardly have made ordinary music if he had tried. Luckily for us, he didn't, producing a soulful, inventive debut album that crackles with creative energy. Quaye is essentially a reggae artist, but he injects so many different elements into his music—classic soul, hip-hop, electronic dub—that it would be unwise to evaluate him in direct comparison to, say, Ziggy Marley or even Shabba Ranks. The son of a jazz composer and younger brother of a guitarist who played with Elton John, Hall and Oates, and others, Quaye clearly has music in his blood. Supposedly he's also the uncle of British trip-hop pioneer Tricky (remember, Tricky's debut was called *Maxinquaye*), although Tricky and he seem to have vastly different opinions on whether they are at all related. In Britain, the release of "Sunday Shining" put him on the musical map, but it was the more reflective "Even After All" that became his breakthrough hit in the fall of 1997. Soon he was winning awards, and by early 1998 he began scoring some airplay on American radio. Given the mixed reviews that have greeted his early live performances, it remains to be seen how far his star can go, but one thing is for sure: he has made a unique debut album, and that ought to presage even better music in the future.

what's available: Inconsistent and flawed, but often strikingly, utterly original, *Maverick a Strike* 𝄢𝄢𝄢𝄢 (550 Music/Sony, 1997, prod. Kevin Bacon, Jonathan Quarmby, Finley Quaye) easily qualifies as one of the great debut records of the '90s. Whatever you do, look past "Sunday Shining," the first single, which is not necessarily one of the better tracks. From the simmering soul of "It's Great When We're Together" to the booming, hip-hop inflected "Supreme I Preme" to the soaring gospelish chorus of "Ride on and Turn the People On," this album will tickle your eardrums in wonderfully surprising ways.

influences:
◀◀ Bob Marley, Al Green, Shinehead

Bob Remstein

Queen
Formed 1971, in England. Disbanded 1991.

Freddie Mercury (born Frederick Bulsara; died November 24, 1991), vocals, piano; Brian May, guitar, vocals; John Deacon, bass; Roger Meddows Taylor, drums, vocals.

When you think of great rock 'n' roll harmony groups, the Beach Boys or some doo-wop outfits spring to mind. Unless you're a Queen fan. The quartet's unique sound blended glam-rock, heavy metal, disco rhythms, and intricate vocal harmonies inspired more by opera and show tunes than by classic doo-wop or the call-and-response technique most rock bands incorporate. Although it would take until its third album before the Queen sound fully developed, its live act was a hit from the start. Led by one of rocks most outrageous frontmen (Mercury) and anchored by soaring guitar work by May, Queen's concerts rank among some of rock's finest. The group's pomp and bombast won it a worldwide audience, but its U.S. success dwindled during late '80s. In 1991 Mercury died from AIDS, and while the surviving trio has staged a memorial concert and released an album of material culled from Mercury's final sessions, they have no plans to continue on as Queen.

what to buy: No collection is complete without *A Night at the Opera* 𝄢𝄢𝄢𝄢 (Elektra, 1975, prod. Roy Thomas Baker, Queen) and *A Day at the Races* 𝄢𝄢𝄢𝄢 (Elektra, 1976, prod. Queen). From heavy metal powerhouses to operatic ballads, Queen fills these albums with every sound imaginable, including kazoos and ukulele, without even using synthesizers. In fact, each of these albums features one of the band's operatic opuses—the seminal "Bohemian Rhapsody" from *A Night at the Opera* and "Somebody to Love" from *A Day at the Races*.

what to buy next: *News of the World* 𝄢𝄢𝄢𝄢 (Elektra, 1977, prod. Queen, Mike Stone) is as entertaining an album as *Opera* or *Races*. It finds the group moving into the safer regions of rock, marking something of an end to Queen's most adventurous period. *Live Killers* 𝄢𝄢𝄢𝄢 (Elektra, 1979, prod. Queen) features a feisty collection of performances and serves as a pleasant relic of one of rock's great live acts. *Greatest Hits* 𝄢𝄢𝄢𝄢 (Hollywood, 1992, prod. various) gathers the appropriate singles.

what to avoid: The only thing to say about Queen's soundtrack for *Flash Gordon* **woof!** (Elektra, 1980, Brian May, Mack) is that the movie (based on the old comic strip) doesn't deserve anything better.

the rest:
Queen 𝄢𝄢𝄢𝄢 (Elektra, 1973)
Sheer Heart Attack 𝄢𝄢𝄢𝄢 (Elektra, 1973)
Queen II 𝄢𝄢 (Elektra, 1974)
Jazz 𝄢𝄢𝄢 (Elektra, 1978)
The Game 𝄢𝄢𝄢 (Elektra, 1980)
Greatest Hits 𝄢𝄢𝄢𝄢 (Elektra, 1981)
Hot Space 𝄢𝄢 (Elektra, 1982)
The Works 𝄢𝄢𝄢 (Capitol, 1984)
A Kind of Magic 𝄢𝄢𝄢 (Capitol, 1986)
The Miracle 𝄢𝄢𝄢 (Capitol, 1989)
Innuendo 𝄢𝄢𝄢 (Hollywood, 1991)
Classic Queen 𝄢𝄢𝄢𝄢 (Hollywood, 1992)

Live at Wembley '86 𝄞𝄞𝄞 (Hollywood, 1992)
Greatest Hits 𝄞𝄞𝄞 (Hollywood, 1992)
(With George Michael and Lisa Stansfield) *Five Live* (Hollywood EP, 1992)
Queen at the BBC 𝄞𝄞 (Hollywood, 1995)
Made in Heaven 𝄞𝄞𝄞 (Hollywood, 1995)
Rocks, Vol. 1 𝄞𝄞𝄞 (Hollywood, 1997)

worth searching for: The promo-only four-volume *Queen Rocks* (Hollywood, 1990, prod. various) sampler series is a nicely packaged 20th-anniversary set that heralded the group's signing to Hollywood Records.

solo outings:
Freddie Mercury:
Mr. Bad Guy 𝄞𝄞𝄞 (Columbia, 1985)
(With Montserrat Caballe) *Barcelona* 𝄞𝄞 (Hollywood, 1987)
The Great Pretender 𝄞𝄞𝄞 (Hollywood, 1992)

Brian May:
Star Fleet Project 𝄞𝄞𝄞 (Capitol EP, 1983)
Back to the Light 𝄞𝄞𝄞𝄞 (Hollywood, 1993)
Another World 𝄞𝄞𝄞 (Hollywood, 1998)

Roger Taylor:
Fun in Space 𝄞𝄞𝄞𝄞 (Elektra, 1981)
Strange Frontier 𝄞𝄞𝄞 (Capitol, 1984)

influences:

◄◄ Led Zeppelin, David Bowie, Mott the Hoople, Liza Minnelli, Maria Callas

►► Def Leppard, Oasis, Guns N' Roses, George Michael, Annie Lennox, *Wayne's World*

Mike Joiner

Queensryche
Formed 1981, in Bellevue, WA.

Geoff Tate, vocals; Chris DeGarmo, guitar (1981–97); Michael Wilton, guitar; Eddie Jackson, bass; Scott Rockenfield, drums.

This Seattle band, with its art rock pretensions and heavy metal thunder, came along as Kansas, Boston, Styx, and other '70s American progressive rock bands were faltering or disbanding. Formed by guitarists DeGarmo and Wilton, the group skipped the bars and concentrated on writing songs and developing a concert-level stage show. Its first EP, *Queen of Reich*, won a contract with EMI America, which reissued the album in an expanded version as Queensryche's self-titled debut in 1983. A cult favorite for several years, the group finally broke through commercially with the Top 10 hit and video "Silent Lucidity" from its 1990 album, *Empire*.

what to buy: *Empire* 𝄞𝄞𝄞 (EMI, 1990, prod. Peter Collins) moved away from the conceptual approach of previous albums and worked as a flowing collection of arty hard rock, from the pounding to the poignant. The centerpiece is "Silent Lucidity," the Seattle group's answer to "Dust in the Wind."

what to buy next: *Operation: Mindcrime* 𝄞𝄞𝄞 (EMI Manhattan, 1988, prod. Peter Collins) a smart—and fast—concept album about censorship and mind control.

what to avoid: *Queensryche* 𝄞𝄞 (EMI, 1983, prod. Queensryche, Neil Kernan) was an inauspicious debut.

the rest:
The Warning 𝄞𝄞 (EMI, 1984)
Rage for Order 𝄞𝄞 (EMI, 1986)
Promised Land 𝄞𝄞𝄞 (EMI, 1994)
Hear in the New Frontier 𝄞𝄞𝄞 (Virgin, 1997)

worth searching for: *Operation: Livecrime* (EMI, 1991), now out of print, puts Queensryche's concept piece to the concert test with, truth be told, mediocre results.

influences:

◄◄ Kansas, Styx, Pink Floyd

►► Pearl Jam, Alice in Chains

Doug Pullen

The Queers
Formed 1982, in Portsmouth, NH.

Joe King, vocals, guitar; Tulu, bass, vocals, drums (1982–84); Wimpy Rutherford, drums, vocals (1982–84, 1993); Keith, bass (1984); J.J. Rassler, guitar (1985–89); B-Face (born Chris Barnard), bass (1990–97); Geoff Useless, bass (1997–present); Hugh O'Neill Jr., drums (1990–97); Rick Respectable, drums (1998–present).

Despite its name—originally chosen to shock New Hampshire rednecks—the Queers are not a gay pride band. In fact, certain lyrics by this gleefully immature punk rock trio actually border on the homophobic; but clearly, with songs such as "Ursula Finally Has Tits" and "I Can't Stop Farting," the Queers are not for the easily offended. First formed in New Hampshire in 1982, the Queers' earliest years found the trio of Joe King, Tulu, and Wimpy churning out snotty, hastily written, comically offensive two-chord punk tunes in the vein of the Angry Samoans. However, by the mid-'80s all of the band members had left New Hampshire for other parts of the Northeast, ending the group's first phase. King, now living in Boston, took control of the band and struggled to keep it going; musicians quickly came and went during this period, though ex-DMZ guitarist J.J. Rassler lasted longer than most, writing several of the Queers better-known songs. By 1990 the Queers settled into their classic lineup of King, bassist B-Face, and drummer Hugh O'Neill, and adopted their trademark Brian Wilson–meets–Joey Ramone pop-punk sound. With help from Screeching Weasel frontman and longtime Queers fan Ben Weasel, the Queers secured a deal with Lookout! Records of Berkeley, California, which released their classic *Love Songs for the Retarded* in 1993. The warmly received album was supported by a tour with Screeching Weasel, after which the band recorded its 1994 follow-up, *Beat Off*, with Weasel producing, while fellow Weasel member Danny Vapid temporarily became one of a long line of second guitarists for the Queers. Several more albums of Ramones-style punk—increasingly leaning towards '60s pop—followed, making the Queers one of the most popular indie-label punk bands of the mid-'90s. Sadly, in late 1997 the trio was torn apart when B-Face left to join the Groovie Ghoulies and Hugh O'Neill was diagnosed with cancer. Though Joe King announced he was re-forming the Queers with a new bassist and drummer, most fans considered it the end of an era in pop-punk.

what to buy: *Love Songs for the Retarded* ♪♪♪ (Lookout!, 1993, prod. Ben Weasel, Mass Giorgini) is the definitive Queers album, showing off its juvenile side ("Ursula Finally Has Tits"), its rockin' side ("Monster Zero"), and its '60s pop side ("Debra Jean") all at once. One of the key pop-punk albums of the '90s.

what to buy next: *Don't Back Down* ♪♪♪ (Lookout!, 1996, prod. J.J. Rassler, Mass Giorgini) finds the Queers displaying its Beach Boys influences more prominently with songs such as "Don't Back Down" and "Sidewalk Surfin' Girl," though its stupid side still shines through on songs like "No Tit" and "I Only Drink Bud." The raw-sounding *Grow Up* ♪♪♪ (Shakin' Street, 1990/Lookout!, 1994, prod. Sean Slade) features such concert standards as "I Met Her at the Rat" and "Love Love Love," but it's not as consistent as the group's later work (though it's still worth having). To get a feel for the raw, aggressive early days of the Queers, check out *A Day Late and a Dollar Short* ♪♪♪ (Lookout!, 1995, prod. various). Though wildly uneven, it chronicles the Queers' first eight or so years, collecting 30-plus long out-of-print compilation tracks and EP cuts on one CD. Be forewarned that while songs like "This Place Sucks," "I Like Young Girls," "Tulu Is a Wimp," and "Kicked Out of the Webelos" are Queers classics, much of this disc is poorly produced and extremely juvenile.

what to avoid: The title of *Move Back Home* ♪♪ (Lookout!, 1995, prod. Mass Giorgini) could be good advice, since it's clear the Queers needed to get back in touch with its roots of a decade prior.

the rest:
Beat Off ♪♪ (Lookout!, 1994)

worth searching for: Yes, *Rocket to Russia* (Selfless, 1995) is a track-for-track cover of the 1977 Ramones album of the same name, but while this long out-of-print, limited-edition LP is not interesting musically, it's nonetheless highly valued by punk rock record collectors. Original copies of the out-of-print early

7-inches compiled on *A Day Late and a Dollar Short* are collectibles as well.

influences:

◀◀ The Ramones, the Beach Boys, Angry Samoans, Lesley Gore, Black Flag

▶▶ Screeching Weasel, the Vindictives, the Nobodys

Seth Hindin

? and the Mysterians

Formed 1962, in Flint, MI. Disbanded 1968.

? (Question Mark), vocals; Larry Borjas, guitar; Robert Balderrama, guitar; Frankie Rodriguez, keyboards; Frank Lugo, bass; Robert Martinez, drums; Edward Serrato, drums.

The personification of one-hit wonders, this mysterious Michigan group, made up of the sons of migrant farm workers, contributed one of the consummate garage rock anthems of the '60s, "96 Tears," which was recorded in a basement studio in Bay City, Michigan. It featured a cheesy, repetitive organ line (often attributed to a Farfisa, but in actuality it was a Vox Continental) and the emphatic, embittered vocals of the band's enigmatic singer. It became a regional hit in Flint and Detroit, then was picked up by Cameo records and topped the charts in 1966. The band (which at one point included future Grand Funk Railroad bassist Mel Shacher) released two albums and disappeared, though its singer, ?—who legally changed his name and never allows himself to be photographed without his trademark sunglasses—has kept the band alive and makes occasional appearances. "96 Tears" is credited to a Rudy Martinez, though nobody has acknowleged whether that's ?'s real name or not. He signed away the publishing rights to those songs years ago. The company that owns "96 Tears" has allowed other artists, including Aretha Franklin, to record the song, and allowed its use on various compilations, but has not reissued either of the Mysterians' albums—*96 Tears* and *Action*—on CD.

what to buy: *Do You Feel It Baby* ♪♪ (Norton, 1998, prod. ?) is a respectable live set recorded at New York's Coney Island High that shows the original symbol man and his compadres can still rock.

what to avoid: *96 Tears Forever: The Dallas Reunion Tapes* ♪♪ (ROIR, 1984) is an almost bootleg-quality live album featuring ? and a new group of Mysterians. The live version of the song is also available on the compilation *Ten ROIR Years* (ROIR).

influences:

◀◀ Eddie Cochran, Little Richard, the Kingsmen, the Animals

▶▶ The Fleshtones, the Ramones, the New York Dolls

Doug Pullen

Quicksilver Messenger Service

Formed 1965, in San Francisco, CA. Disbanded 1975. Re-formed 1987. Disbanded 1988.

Gary Duncan, guitar, vocals (1965–69, 1970–75, 1987–88); John Cipollina (died May 29, 1989), guitar (1965–71); David Freiberg, bass, vocals (1969–71); Greg Elmore, drums; Jim Murray, harmonica, vocals (1965–67); Nicky Hopkins, keyboards (1969–70); Dino Valente (born Chester Powers), vocals (1970–75); Mark Naftalin, keyboards (1971); Mark Ryan, bass (1971–73); Chuck Steales, keyboards (1971–73); Sammy Piazza, drums (1987–88); W. Michael Lewis, keyboards (1987–88).

Little remembered these days, Quicksilver Messenger Service could, on any given night, easily surpass better-known peers from the San Francisco rock scene such as the Jefferson Airplane or the Grateful Dead. Stacking harmony vocals on top of a charging guitar-driven sound, Quicksilver transformed the band's signature folk-rock material into high-flying electrical improvisations that transported audiences at the Fillmore and Avalon Ballrooms into other realms. Once persuasive vocalist Dino Valente joined the ranks, the band managed a couple of radio hits ("Fresh Air," "What about Me"), but it is the Quicksilver of the band's first two albums that really left its mark on the San Francisco scene.

what to buy: The first two albums say it all: *Quicksilver Messenger Service* ♫♫♫♫ (Capitol, 1968/1994, prod. Nick Gravenites, Harvey Brooks, Pete Welding) and *Happy Trails* ♫♫♫♫ (Capitol, 1969/Beat Goes On, 1994) are both terrific. Especially great is the side-long version of "Who Do You Love" on the second album, which was edited *down* to 25 minutes.

what to buy next: A two-disc retrospective, *Sons of Mercury, 1968–1975* ♫♫♫ (Rhino, 1991, compilation prod. Michael Briggs) lends a complete overview of the band's checkered career, including some rare early material and a second CD that does little more than chronicle the band's decline.

what to avoid: Guitarist Gary Duncan reprised the band name for a hapless heavy metal solo album, *Peace by Piece* **woof!** (EMI, 1987, prod. Gary Duncan, Sammy Piazza, Bob Ohlsson).

the rest:
Shady Grove ♫♫ (Capitol, 1969/One Way, 1995)
Just for Love ♫ (Capitol, 1970/One Way, 1995)
What about Me ♫ (Capitol, 1971/One Way, 1995)
Quicksilver ♫ (Capitol, 1971/One Way, 1995)
Comin' Thru ♫ (Capitol, 1972/One Way, 1995)

solo outings:
Dino Valente:
Dino Valente ♫♫♫ (Epic, 1968)

John Cipollina:
Copperhead ♫♫ (Columbia, 1973)

influences:
◀◀ The Righteous Brothers, Buffy Sainte-Marie, the Charlatans
▶▶ Copperhead, Man, Blues Traveler

Joel Selvin

Quickspace

Formed 1995, in London, England.

Tom Cullinan, vocals, guitar; Nina Pascale, vocals, guitar; Sean Newsham, bass; Chin, drums.

In 1995, when Tom Cullinan saw his critically acclaimed band th' Faith Healers abruptly call it a day, he wasted no time in getting another project together. Though th' Faith Healers had gained a considerable reputation as a worthwhile noise-rock band, having already released three albums on the lauded U.K.-based Too Pure label, Cullinan was intent on moving in a different creative direction. Where his former band enjoyed the mesmerizing sounds of cyclical, occasionally transcendent guitar-based drones, he had decided that his new project would work in differing shades of tonal subtlety. Originally named Quickspace Supersport, Cullinan's first-assembled supporting cast failed quickly. Citing artistic differences, everyone in the original group but bass player Sean Newsham jumped ship. By then, Cullinan had a label, Kitty Kitty, a business partner in bass player Newsham (who had worked a radio promo gig for Too Pure), a handful of songs, and a few upcoming, high-profile gigs, but no band. With an important opening slot for the Grifters the evening following his bandmates' desertion, Cullinan threw together a band in less than a day. His frenzied decisions proved sturdy. Following the gig, the band decided to stay together. After dropping the "Supersport" portion of their name, the band went in to record their self-titled debut.

what's available: Led by songs like the engaging "Friend" and the equally intriguing "Rise," *Quickspace* ♫♫♫ (London, 1997, prod. Quickspace) fuses vertiginous Moog grooves with economical guitar lines, lo-fi atmospherics, and Cullinan and Pascale's sotto voce vocals to achieve a deceptively mesmerizing sonic effect.

influences:
◀◀ The Orb, Velvet Underground, Can
see also: *Th' Faith Healers*

Bob Gulla

Quiet Riot

Formed 1975, in Burbank, CA. Disbanded 1989. Re-formed 1991.

Kevin DuBrow, vocals (1975–87, 1990–present); Randy Rhoads (died March 19, 1982), guitar (1975–79); Kelly Garni, bass (1975–76); Drew

Forsyth, drums (1975–79); Drew Cavazo, guitar (1982–89, 1991–present); Rudy Sarzo, bass (1977–79, 1982–85, 1996–present); Frankie Banali, drums (1981–89, 1993–present); Chuck Wright, bass (1986, 1995); Paul Shortino, vocals (1987–89); Sean McNabb, bass (1987–89); Kenny Hillary (died 1996), bass (1991–94); Bobby Rondinelli, drums (1992).

A quick blip on the pop charts, Quiet Riot helped usher in the mid-'80s era of heavy metal hair bands with its smash cover of Slade's "Cum on Feel the Noize." But the real noteworthy aspect of the band's career is that it was an early stop for guitarist Randy Rhoads, who went on to trend-setting glory at Ozzy Osbourne's side until his death in a 1982 plane crash. Quiet Riot, meanwhile, never equalled its initial success—despite another Slade cover, "Mama Weer All Crazee Now"—and by 1984 its popularity was already on the slide. Frontman DuBrow was axed in one of rock's nastier firings, and the group floundered before taking him back in 1990. Now it flounders on a hard rock club circuit that makes Spinal Tap's itinerary look glamorous.

what to buy: *Metal Health* ♪♪♪ (Pasha, 1983, prod. Spencer Proffer) is Quiet Riot's big moment, spirited and dispensable trash-metal, highlighted by "Cum on Feel the Noize."

what to buy next: *The Randy Rhoads Years* ♪♪♪ (Rhino, 1993) lets Rhoads fans—and they are legion—take a listen to his formative years before hooking up with Osbourne. *Winners Take All* ♪♪♪ (Columbia Special Products, 1993, prod. various) is a compact best-of, probably all the Quiet Riot you'll need.

what to avoid: *Terrified* ♪ (Moonstone, 1993) is absolute junk, like most of the post–*Metal Health* releases.

the rest:
Condition Critical ♪♪ (Pasha, 1984)
QR III ♪ (Pasha, 1986)
QR ♪ (Pasha, 1988)
Down to the Bone ♪ (Kamikaze Records, 1995)
Best Of ♪♪♪ (Pasha, 1996)

influences:
◀◀ Slade, Kiss, Van Halen
▶▶ Winger, Dokken, Ratt

Allan Orski

Robert Quine
Born December 30, 1942, in Akron, OH.

After giving up bands in favor of a law career, Robert Quine reversed his decision after meeting Tom Verlaine and Richard Hell. With Hell & the Voidoids, Quine's abstract, jagged guitar lines had a major influence on the sound of punk; among his influences were early rockabilly, mid-'70s Miles Davis records, and Lou Reed's Velvet Underground work—all of which he dis-

tilled into a flexible, versatile style. Quine subsequently joined Lou Reed's band but has more recently abandoned touring in favor of session work that's kept him on the periphery of public recognition; he has made some notable contributions to several successful Matthew Sweet albums.

what to buy: With fellow guitarist Jody Harris (Raybeats, Contortions), Quine made *Escape* ♪♪♪ (Lust/Unlust, 1981, prod. Jody Harris, Robert Quine), on which they share bass and electronic percussion duties for a stylistically varied, mildly experimental album.

the rest:
Basic ♪♪♪ (EG, 1984)

influences:
◀◀ The Velvet Underground, Miles Davis, Carl Perkins, Cliff Richard & the Shadows

▶▶ Matthew Sweet, Lou Reed, Big Bad Voodoo Daddy

see also: *Richard Hell & the Voidoids*

Steve Holtje

Radiohead
Formed 1991, in Oxford, England.

Thom Yorke, piano, guitar, vocals; Jon Greenwood, guitar, organ, recorder, synthesizer, keyboards; Ed O'Brien, guitar; Colin Greenwood, bass; Phil Selway, drums.

Radiohead broke in America on the strength of a self-loathing anthem called "Creep." Recorded spontaneously in one take and included as the opening cut on its debut album, *Pablo Honey*, the song's undeniable charms made it clear that this group was different from the usual U.K. hype-driven fluff. In fact, no one in Britain even acknowledged Radiohead until the group had already conquered the U.S. charts. While the English music tabloids were trying to shove fey groups such as Suede and the Verve down American throats, Radiohead snuck out and ahead of the ranks by mixing sensitive Britpop jangle with hormone-induced American grunge. Ripe with ambition, Radiohead showed it had the chops for greatness. However, it wasn't until its third album, *OK Computer*, that the group reached its full-strength. Hailed as a *Dark Side of the Moon* for the '90s, the spiraling and dark album earned Radiohead an untouchable reputation.

what to buy: On *OK Computer* ♪♪♪♪♪ (Capitol, 1995, prod. John Leckie), the quintet cast off its faux grunge fur and made an un-

Thom Yorke of Radiohead (© Ken Settle)

usually ambitious musical statement. The disc's first single, the roaming "Paranoid Android" attempted to sonically recreate the sensation of claustrophobia, while its follow-up "Karma Police" was built on doomy nursery rhyme melody. The album was not so much an excersice in being willfully difficult as it was in rejecting routine.

what to buy next: *The Bends* ♫♫♫♫ (Capitol, 1995, prod. John Leckie) is unblinkingly charged, exasperatingly beautiful, full of graceful crevices, glorious melodies and ambitious musical flex.

the rest:
Pablo Honey ♫♫ (Capitol, 1993)

influences:
◀◀ The Pixies, the Stone Roses, U2, Pink Floyd

▶▶ Mansun, Travis

Aidin Vaziri

Rage Against the Machine

Formed 1991, in Los Angeles, CA.

Zack de la Rocha, vocals; Tom Morello, guitar; Tim Bob Commerford, bass; Brad Wilk, drums.

Who says that the revolution will not be televised? Rage Against the Machine has managed to get its fiery brand of revolutionary metal-funk-rap all over MTV (not to mention modern-rock radio), making the dynamic quartet the most-popular politically charged group since Public Enemy. Led by militant spit-fire singer Zack de la Rocha and Harvard-educated guitarist Tom Morello—the son of an American anti-censorship activist/school teacher and a Mau Mau revolutionary from Kenya—the group pounds the status quo with angry lyrics, thunderous riffs, and crushing rhythms, taking on big business, oppressive governments, state corruption, racism, right-wing hatred, police brutality, media manipulation, domestic decay, and inner-city violence. The uncompromising quartet also throws its intense support behind controversial causes (the Zapatista movement in the Chiapas state of Mexico) and figures (Leonard Peltier, Mumia Abu-Jamal). Rage put a photo of Che Guevara on the cover of an import single and included a picture of a Buddhist monk burning himself to death to protest the U.S. invasion of Vietnam on its self-titled debut. Rage has also been known to stage benefit concerts (for the Chiapas) at de la Rocha's house and to stand naked in front of 40,000 (at Lollapalooza) to protest censorship. Morello, who once worked for U.S. Senator Alan Cranston, is even writing a collection of 25 short biographies of figures such as Malcolm X who often are overlooked in U.S. history books.

what to buy: With its visceral guitar attack, thunderous rhythms, and furious social commentary, *Rage Against the Machine* ♫♫♫♫ (Epic, 1992, prod. Rage Against the Machine,

Gggarth) is equal parts Black Sabbath and Public Enemy, with a dash of Sly Stone funk thrown in for good-rocking measure. Of course, while the lyrics are full of sociopolitical relevance, the mesmerizing grooves of such standouts as "Killing in the Name" and "Bullet in the Head" are probably what earned the band most of its fans.

what to buy next: As improbable as it may seem to anybody who's seen Rage live, the thick, raw, frenzied, churning *Evil Empire* ♫♫♫♫ (Epic, 1996, prod. Brendan O'Brien, Rage Against the Machine) manages to capture the intensity of the group's explosive performances. Morello's wah-wah guitar break on "Bulls on Parade," a rant against government misspending, steals the show.

worth searching for: In 1996 the band issued a vinyl seven-inch single to fan-club members featuring an intense live version of "Bombtrack" (from a BBC performance). The spit-fire B-side cover of "Fuck tha Police" (recorded at a benefit concert for Mumia Abu-Jamal) is exceptional. Also, the group's cranked-up version of Bruce Springsteen's "The Ghost of Tom Joad" is included as a CD single with its home video *Rage Against the Machine* (Epic, 1997), which features both clips and live performance footage.

influences:
◀◀ The MC5, the Clash, Ice Cube, Public Enemy, Black Sabbath, Body Count, Minor Threat, Youth of Today, Led Zeppelin, the Beastie Boys, the Sex Pistols, Red Hot Chili Peppers, Fugazi

▶▶ Deftones, KoЯn, Salmon

Aidin Vaziri

Railroad Jerk

Formed 1989, in New York, NY.

Marcellus Hall, vocals, guitar; Tony Lee, bass; Jez Aspinall, drums (1989–91); Steve Cerio, drums (1991–92); Dave Varenka, drums (1992–present); Chris Mueller, guitar (1989–91); Alec Stephen, guitar (1991–present).

"Well, I'm hi-fi and/I'm low-brow" Railroad Jerk singer Marcellus Hall belts out on "Gun Problem," the first song on the band's best album, *One Track Mind*. Frenzied, emotional, and knowingly clever, it could be the New York City band's quintessential moment, only Hall has it all wrong: he's lo-fi and highbrow. Just as the Jon Spencer Blues Explosion uses a rusty pliers from punk's toolbox to rewire the juke joint blues of Junior Kimbrough, Railroad Jerk tackles the more rural sounds of artists such as Bukka White with similarly explosive results—and some of the same semiotics major references. Its first record, *Railroad Jerk*, is raw and lurching, though the shout-outs to rock classics on "Talking RR Jerk Blues" gives a hint as to the group's future direction. Its second album is more artful: its punk moments owe more to the Fall than Iggy Pop, and its inspired cover of White's "Fixin' to Die" proves it can play off of its influences with originality and verve. On the EP *We Understand*, Railroad Jerk added little to the mix besides two new members—drummer Dave Varenka and guitarist Alec Stephen—but their addition helped set the stage for the glorious mess of *One Track Mind* and the less self-referential indie-rock of *The Third Rail*. Hall and Varenka are also involved in an ongoing side project called White Hassle.

what to buy: The band's punk-blues vision is clearest on *One Track Mind* 𝄢𝄢𝄢𝄢 (Matador, 1995, prod. Railroad Jerk, Settly), a frantic blast of bad-attitude fun from start to finish. More mature and less self-consciously postmodern, *The Third Rail* 𝄢𝄢𝄢 (Matador, 1996, prod. Railroad Jerk, Settly) shows the band has both the chops and the songwriting to succeed without depending on its Downtown-meets-the-Delta trope.

what to buy next: Most of the themes on *Raise the Plow* 𝄢𝄢𝄢 (Matador, 1992, prod. Railroad Jerk) come to fruition later, but the record is still revealing and pleasantly raw. Including everything from the frenetic *One Track Mind* outtake "Highway 80" to a clanky, lo-fi hijacking of "Why Don't We Do It in the Road" to several radio performances, the six-song EP *Bang the Drum* 𝄢𝄢𝄢𝄢 (Matador, 1995, prod. Railroad Jerk, Settly) shows the group's more experimental side.

the rest:
Railroad Jerk 𝄢𝄢𝄢 (Matador, 1990)
We Understand 𝄢𝄢𝄢 (Matador EP, 1993)
Sauberes Hemd 𝄢𝄢𝄢𝄢 (Matador, 1996)

worth searching for: A three-song seven-inch record recorded on exactly the day one would think, *02-20-93* (Walt, 1993, prod. Railroad Jerk) offers a glimpse of the band getting the most out of its bluesey influences without taking them too seriously.

solo outings:
White Hassle (Hall and Varenka):
National Chain 𝄢𝄢𝄢 (Matador, 1997)

influences:
◄◄ Bukka White, Pavement, Pussy Galore
►► The Jon Spencer Blues Explosion

Robert Levine

Railway Children

Formed 1986, in Wigan, England.

Gary Newby, vocals, guitars; Stephen Hull, bass (1986–94); Guy Keegan, drums (1986–94); Brian Bateman, guitars (1986–94).

Named after a Victorian English children's book, the Railway Children was formed by childhood friends Gary Newby and

Stephen Hull. After Guy Keegan and Brian Bateman joined, the band started playing around Wigan, a suburb of Manchester, and Liverpool. Before the Railway Children signed with Virgin, they opened for R.E.M. and for Lloyd Cole & the Commotions. The band released its first single, "A Gentle Sound," on Manchester's Factory Records in 1986—it reached #4 on the U.K. indie chart, and the subsequent debut album, *Reunion Wilderness*, hit #2 shortly thereafter. In 1994 Guy Keegan joined the Tansads, and Bateman and Hull left the music business. In spring 1998 one-man band Newby traveled to Japan to play guitar with Cripton but returned to England to possibly reunite with the Railway Children for live dates.

what's available: Unfortunately, the *Railway Children Radio One Sessions Album* 𝄢𝄢𝄢 (Strange Fruit, 1993, prod. BBC) is the only Railway Children album available in the States. Though the music is stripped down, the album is representative of the band's light pop sound.

worth searching for: The 12-song *Native Place* (Virgin, 1990, prod. Steve Lovell, Steve Power) is one of the definitive pop albums of the early '90s. Newby's gentle vocals are flawless, but don't let that fool you; there's a bite to the synth-heavy "Every Beat of the Heart," the Children's biggest single in the U.S. *Dream Arcade* (Ether Records, 1998) is available through Newby's website (http://www.ether.co.uk/trc.html).

influences:
◄◄ The Beatles, R.E.M., Duran Duran
►► Semisonic

Christina Fuoco

The Rain Parade

Formed 1982, in Los Angeles, CA. Disbanded 1985.

David Roback, vocals, guitar, percussion (1982–84); Steven Roback, vocals, bass; Matthew Piucci, vocals, guitar, sitar; Will Glenn, keyboards, violin; John Thoman, guitar, vocals (1984–85); Eddie Kalwa, drums (1982–84); Mark Marcum, drums (1984–85).

A member of the influential "paisley underground" scene of the late '80s—which is to say, a West Coast revival of '60s-style psychedelic rock—the Rain Parade was formed by brothers David and Steven Roback and signed by Enigma Records on the strength of the self-issued first single, "What's She Done to Your Mind?" The band rarely deviated from its influences, such as the Velvet Underground and the Byrds, which frequently made it more respected than loved.

what's available: *Emergency Third Rail Power Trip/Explosions in the Glass Palace* 𝄢𝄢𝄢 (Enigma, 1983/1984, prod. David Roback, Rain Parade, Jim Hill), a CD combining the debut album and a follow-up EP, makes up the group's only in-print material.

The overall mood is quite subdued, with the EP's last two tracks (the quiet "Broken Horse" and the spacey "No Easy Way Down") standing out the most.

influences:

⏪ Buffalo Springfield, the Byrds, Love, Big Star, Pink Floyd, the Beatles

⏩ Dream Syndicate, Mazzy Star

Steve Holtje

Rain Tree Crow

See: Japan

Rainbow

Formed 1975, in Los Angeles, CA. Disbanded 1984. Re-formed 1995.

Ritchie Blackmore, guitar; Ronnie James Dio, vocals (1975–78); Craig Gruber, bass (1975); Mickey Lee Soule, keyboards (1975); Gary Driscoll, drums (1975); Jimmy Bain, bass (1975–77); Tony Carey, keyboards (1975–77); Cozy Powell (died April 5, 1998), drums (1975–80); Bob Daisley, bass (1977–78); David Stone, keyboards (1977–78); Graham Bonnett, vocals (1979–80); Roger Glover, bass (1979–84); Don Airey, keyboards (1979–81); Joe Lynn Turner, vocals (1980–84); Bob Rondinelli, drums (1980–84); David Rosenthal, keyboards (1981–84); Dookie White, vocals (1995–present); Chuck Berge, drums (1995–present); Greg Smith, bass (1995–present); Paul Morris, keyboards (1995–present); Candice Night, vocals (1995–present).

Fed up with the group dynamic in Deep Purple—mostly the other members' desire for democracy—fabulously tempermental guitarist Ritchie Blackmore put together Rainbow as an outlet for his classically based, virtuostic brand of bombast. He initially recruited the little-known band Elf, scoring a captivating frontman in singer Ronnie James Dio. The second version of Rainbow—with powerhouse drummer Cozy Powell—was Blackmore's best, a group of solid players that could pull off the kind of extended pieces Blackmore wanted to perform (without, of course, getting in the guitarist's way). Over the years, Blackmore's temperament made Rainbow something of a musician's lab, even a launching pad for a few careers, such as singers Graham Bonnett and Joe Lynn Turner. Rainbow had its greatest commercial success after Deep Purple bassist Roger Glover joined the fold and took over production chores, and while the group was put on ice for Purple's mid-'80s reunion, Blackmore re-activated it after he left the band again a decade later.

what to buy: Rainbow's best lineup, its second, recorded just one studio album, *Rainbow Rising* ♫♫♫♫ (Polydor, 1976, prod. Martin Birch). With extended pieces such as "Stargazer" and "A Light in the Black," it's the definitive representation of Blackmore's ambitions. *Live in Europe* ♫♫♫♫ (Mausoleum Classix, 1996, prod. Steve Ship, Barry Ehrmann, Evert Wilbrink) cap-

tures the same lineup onstage in 1976, stretching out even further on "Mistreated," "Catch the Rainbow," and the Yardbirds' "Still I'm Sad."

what to buy next: *The Best of Rainbow* ♫♫♫♫ (Polydor, 1981, prod. various) is a good sampling of the band's prime material, with the focus rightly on the Dio years.

what to avoid: *Down to Earth* ♫ (Oyster/Polydor, 1979, prod. Roger Glover), Bonnet's sole effort as Rainbow frontman, is a tepid collection that particularly misses Dio's power as a singer.

the rest:
Ritchie Blackmore's Rainbow ♫♫♫ (PolyGram, 1975)
Onstage ♫♫ (Oyster/Polydor, 1977)
Long Live Rock 'n' Roll ♫♫♫ (Oyster/Polydor, 1978)
Difficult to Cure ♫♫ (Polydor, 1981)
Jealous Lover ♫♫ (Polydor, 1981)
Straight between the Eyes ♫♫♫ (Mercury, 1982)
Bent out of Shape ♫♫ (Mercury, 1982)
Final Vinyl ♫♫♫ (Mercury, 1986)
Stranger in Us All ♫♫♫ (BMG, 1995)

worth searching for: *Live in Tokyo '84* is a Japanese laser disc of what turned out to be Rainbow's temporary farewell. The Tokyo Symphony Orchestra is on hand for a particularly rousing version of "Difficult to Cure" that leads into Beethoven's Ninth Symphony.

influences:

⏪ Deep Purple, Jeff Beck Group, the Yardbirds, Ludwig Van Beethoven, Richard Wagner

⏩ Accept, Metallica, Alcatrazz, Dokken

see also: *Deep Purple, Ronnie James Dio*

Gary Graff

The Raincoats

Formed 1977, in London, England. Disbanded 1984. Reunited 1994.

Ana da Silva, vocals, guitar, bass; Gina Birch, vocals, bass, guitar; Vicky Aspinall, vocals, violin, guitar (1978–84); Palmolive, drums (1978–80); Ingrid Anne Wood, violin, bass (1994–present); Heather Dunn, drums, bass (1994–present).

"If it weren't for the luxury of putting on that scratchy copy of the Raincoats' first record, I would have had very few moments of peace." So wrote Kurt Cobain in 1993, an indication of the devotion the relatively obscure but highly influential Raincoats inspired among a subsequent generation of indie rockers, male and female alike. Contrary to the impression created by all the "women in rock" stories that began proliferating during the '90s, the punk era of the late '70s was the time of true female emancipation in rock 'n' roll. It didn't matter if you were part of the boys club that ran the music industry; it didn't even matter if you could play an instrument—anybody was welcome to form a band, find an audience, and make a record. It was in this liberating atmosphere that the original U.K. riot grrrls appeared: the Au Pairs, the Slits, Delta 5, and Raincoats, among many others. After experimenting with several lineups during 1977, Ana Da Silva and Gina Birch recruited Palmolive (from the Slits) and Vicky Aspinall in '78 for the debut single, "Fairytale in the Supermarket," which declares, "No one teaches you how to live." The band made up its own rules as it went along—and then proceeded to bend and break nearly every one, moving from drone-and-strum punk to increasingly experimental textures over the course of three albums. The group—by now a three piece with a revolving cast of drummers—broke up in 1984, but popular demand (at least from high-profile fans such as Cobain and Sonic Youth) prompted a reunion in 1994. Birch and Da Silva recorded an EP (with Sonic Youth's Steve Shelley on drums), hired a couple of new recruits to play some concerts, then recorded a studio album before disappearing again.

what to buy: *The Raincoats* ♪♪♪♪ (Rough Trade, 1979/Geffen, 1993, prod. Geoff Travis, Mayo Thompson, Raincoats) is not for everyone, especially those who like their pop music resolutely in tune and tightly structured. But this debut's odd song shapes, woozy violin solos, and unvarnished singing are the epitome of punk sincerity and exude a strange beauty that sounds unlike any album of the era.

what to buy next: *Odyshape* ♪♪♪♪ (Rough Trade, 1981/Geffen, 1994, prod. Raincoats) floats into more experimental territory, perhaps because the already adventurous band was working without a full-time drummer. Though less overtly "punk" than the debut, its mood-swing charm is trend-proof.

the rest:
Moving ♪♪♪♪ (Rough Trade, 1984/Geffen, 1994)
The Raincoats ♪♪♪ (Smells Like EP, 1994)
Looking in the Shadows ♪♪♪♪ (Geffen, 1996)

worth searching for: *The Kitchen Tapes* (ROIR, 1983) is a cassette-only live recording of a 1982 performance that captures the band's penchant for finding schoolgirl bliss amid grating noise.

influences:
◀◀ The Velvet Underground, Patti Smith

▶▶ Nirvana, Bikini Kill, the Vaselines, Liz Phair

Greg Kot

Bonnie Raitt

Born November 8, 1949, in Los Angeles, CA.

There are two Bonnie Raitt stories—one in the bottle and one out. From the late '60s to the early '80s, the Quaker-raised, Radcliffe-educated daughter of Broadway star John Raitt was a blues mama who learned her craft at the feet of John Lee Hooker, Mississippi Fred McDowell, and Sippie Wallace. They taught her to play hard and true—and to party hard, too. Raitt made good on their lessons, turning out songs that mined blues, pop, and folk while developing a distinctive, stinging slide guitar style and an aching, honest vocal delivery. An exceptional cover of Del Shannon's "Runaway" unjustly defined the first phase of her career, though Raitt also proved herself a performer of conscience and strong convictions, joining kindred spirits such as Jackson Browne and James Taylor at various benefits and rallies. It was after being dropped by Warner Bros. in 1983 that Raitt decide to clean up, dry out, and, essentially, start over again. Her 1989 release, *Nick of Time,* revealed a smoother pop style that showcased her trademark slide guitar and retained just enough blues touches to make it work; it sold more than four million copies and started a string of Grammy victories that made Raitt—who married actor Michael O'Keefe in 1991—the darling of her peers as well as the mainstream audience. She's explored other styles on subsequent releases, though never straying too far from the proven sound. And in 1995 Fender made her the first female guitarist to have an instrument named after her, with royalties funding a program to provide guitars and music lessons to inner city youths.

what to buy: Smooth, assured, and forthright, *Nick of Time* ♪♪♪♪ (Capitol, 1989, prod. Don Was) is a mature and celebratory effort in which Raitt unveils her new sound and sings with depth and feeling about the tribulations of the past; she even makes Jerry Williams's "I Will Not Be Denied" sound like one of her own songs. *The Bonnie Raitt Collection* ♪♪♪♪ (Warner Bros., 1990, prod. various) is her old label's cash-in on *Nick of Time*'s success, but it's a terrific overview anyway, featuring previously unreleased live duets with Wallace ("Woman Be Wise") and John Prine ("Angel from Montgomery").

what to buy next: *Give It Up* ♪♪♪♪ (Warner Bros., 1973, prod. Michael Cuscuna) is the best of Raitt's Warner albums, a corker that blasts open with her own "Give It up or Let Me Go" and continues through an inspired collection of originals and covers. *Luck of the Draw* ♪♪♪♪ (Capitol, 1991, prod. Don Was, Bonnie Raitt) finds the Raitt of *Nick of Time* exuberantly in love and ready to tell the world about it on "Something to Talk About" and her burning duet with Delbert McClinton, "Good Man, Good Woman."

what to avoid: *Home Plate* ♪ (Warner Bros., 1975, prod. Paul D. Rothchild) is a weak and ill-conceived attempt to take Raitt in a country direction—and it strikes out.

the rest:
Bonnie Raitt ♪♪♪ (Warner Bros., 1971)
Takin' My Time ♪♪♪♪ (Warner Bros., 1973)

Streetlights ♫♫ (Warner Bros., 1974)
Sweet Forgiveness ♫♫ (Warner Bros., 1977)
The Glow ♫♫ (Warner Bros., 1979)
Green Light ♫♫♫ (Warner Bros., 1982)
Nine Lives ♫♫♫ (Warner Bros., 1986)
Longing in Their Hearts ♫♫♫♪ (Capitol, 1994)
Road Tested ♫♫♫ (Capitol, 1995)
Fundamental ♫♫♫♪ (Capitol, 1998)

worth searching for: Raitt's ubiquitous guest shots on her friends' albums have resulted in some fine music. Her Grammy winning duet with Hooker on "In the Mood" from his album *The Healer* (Chameleon, 1989, prod. Roy Rogers) is definitive, while her contributions to her father's *Broadway Legend* (Angel, 1995) are sweet.

influences:

◄◄ Howlin' Wolf, Muddy Waters, Sippie Wallace, Mississippi Fred McDowell, John Lee Hooker, Odetta, Joan Baez

►► Pat Benatar, Melissa Etheridge, Melissa Ferrick, Sheryl Crow, Joan Osborne

Gary Graff

The Ramones

Formed 1974, in Queens, NY. Disbanded 1996.

Joey Ramone (born Jeffrey Hyman), lead vocals; Johnny Ramone (born John Cummings), guitar; Dee Dee Ramone (born Douglas Colvin), bass (1974–89); C.J. Ramone (born Christopher Ward), bass (1989–96); Tommy Ramone (born Tommy Erdelyi), drums (1974–77); Marky Ramone (born Marc Bell), drums (1977–83, 1987–96); Richie Ramone (born Richard Reinhardt), drums (1983–87).

Back in their gabba-gabba-heyday, the Ramones were championed as living, leather-jacketed cartoon characters, a punk band to be adored but not taken seriously. And given the subject matter of such fast, furious two-minute anthems as "Now I Wanna Sniff Some Glue," "Teenage Lobotomy," and "Beat on the Brat," even that might be giving the group too much credit. But what the safety pin crowd loved about the band—its relentless tenacity and ability to play 30 songs in an hour—would have worn thin before you could say "1-2-3-4!" if not for the fact that hidden under the power chords was a genuine affection for '60s icons such as the Beach Boys, the Trashmen, and the Searchers. As punk waned, the Ramones matured—that is, the group learned a couple more chords, extended its songs beyond two minutes, and started writing about topics other than girls and mental disorders (a topic it officially exhausted with 1983's "Everytime I Eat Vegetables It Makes Me Think of You"). But its subsequent records have run all over the map, from the Phil Spector–produced grandeur of *End of the Century* to the headbanging speed metal of *Halfway to*

WHAT ALBUM CHANGED YOUR LIFE?

I think [Bob Dylan's] *The Times They Are a-Changin'* was the most life-altering for me. It was the first time I had ever heard folk music from a modern perspective, talking about issues of today. I decided not to get the new Beatles record immediately but to get the new Bob Dylan record instead.

Bonnie Raitt

Sanity to the '60s covers of *Acid Eaters*. In 1995 the Ramones announced plans to break up, but were still touring a year later on the Lollapalooza caravan. By the time they threw in the towel, they had released three—count 'em, three—"farewell" collections, including *Adios Amigos*, *Greatest Hits Live*, and the CD/video package *We're Outta Here*, which only drove home the point that this was a band that indeed would never say die.

what to buy: The first two albums, *The Ramones* ♫♫♫♪ (Sire, 1976, prod. Craig Leon) and *Leave Home* ♫♫♫♪ (Sire, 1977, prod. Tony Bongiovi, Tommy Erdelyi), are compiled as *All the Stuff (and More)—Vol. 1* (Sire, 1990). But the group's pop roots begin to show on *Rocket to Russia* ♫♫♫♪ (Sire, 1977, prod. Tony Bongiovi, Tommy Erdelyi) and *Road to Ruin* ♫♫♫♫♪ (Sire, 1978, prod. Tommy Erdelyi, Ed Stasium)—compiled on volume two of *All the Stuff*—making it the best place to start, if only for Joey's yearning vocal on the Searchers' "Needles and Pins," the convincing country-rock of "Questioningly," and the fist-pumping guitar attack of "I Wanna Be Sedated" and "I Just Want to Have Something to Do."

what to buy next: Former 10cc member Graham Gouldman helms *Pleasant Dreams* ♫♫♫♪ (Sire, 1981, prod. Graham Gouldman), which turns out to be a protest album driven by the metallic crunch of "We Want the Airwaves," "This Business Is Killing Me," and "The KKK Took My Baby Away."

what to avoid: *Halfway to Sanity* ♫♪ (Sire, 1987, prod. Ramones, Daniel Rey), one of several veerings into hardcore punk and metal, offers all of the volume and none of the charm of its predecessors.

the rest:
It's Alive 🎵🎵 (Sire, 1979)
End of the Century 🎵🎵🎵 (Sire, 1980)
Subterranean Jungle 🎵🎵🎵 (Sire, 1983)
Too Tough to Die 🎵🎵🎵 (Sire, 1984)
Animal Boy 🎵🎵 (Sire, 1986)
Brain Drain 🎵🎵🎵 (Sire, 1989)
Ramones Mania 🎵🎵🎵🎵 (Sire, 1989)
Loco Live 🎵🎵 (Sire, 1991)
Mondo Bizarro 🎵🎵 (Radioactive, 1992)
Acid Eaters 🎵🎵🎵 (Radioactive, 1994)
Adios Amigos 🎵🎵🎵 (Radioactive, 1995)
Greatest Hits Live 🎵🎵🎵 (Radioactive, 1996)
We're Outta Here 🎵🎵🎵 (Radioactive, 1997)

worth searching for: The first-run vinyl pressings of *Leave Home* (Sire, 1977) contain "Carbona Not Glue," which was removed from subsequent pressings after a threatened lawsuit.

solo outings:
Dee Dee Ramone (as Dee Dee King):
Standing in the Spotlight 🎵🎵 (Sire, 1987)

Marky Ramone & the Intruders:
Marky Ramone & the Intruders 🎵🎵🎵 (Thirsty Ear, 1997)

influences:
◄◄ The Trashmen, the Beach Boys, Phil Spector
►► Pansy Division, Green Day, Shonen Knife

David Okamoto

Willis Alan Ramsey

Born March 5, 1951, in Birmingham, AL.

Wielding more influence than the meager sales of his lone album would indicate, Willis Alan Ramsey is seen today as a genuine forbear of the alternative-country scene that has grown up around Austin, Texas, during the past two decades. Only 21 when he recorded his debut album, an effort that teemed with promise and a crack session team (Leon Russell, Ernie Watts, Leland Sklar, Russ Kunkel, Jim Keltner, Carl Radle), Ramsey inexplicably failed to follow it up. For a time he lived in England and Ireland, but has since relocated to Nashville. Rumors of a second album abound, but thus far nothing has appeared.

what's available: *Willis Alan Ramsey* 🎵🎵🎵🎵 (Shelter, 1972/DCC Compact Classics, 1990, prod. Denny Cordell, Willis Alan Ramsey) is an acoustic-based collection of literate and laid-back country/folk tunes, some of which have been covered by Leon Russell, Jimmy Buffett, America, Waylon Jennings, and, most recently, Shawn Colvin. Ramsey's best-known song, "Muskrat

Love," which is included here, was a hit for America and for the Captain & Tennille.

influences:
◄◄ Woody Guthrie, Bob Dylan, Gram Parsons
►► Lyle Lovett, Nanci Griffith, Butch Hancock

Daniel Durchholz

Lee Ranaldo

See: Sonic Youth

Rancid

Formed 1991, in Marin County, CA.

Tim Armstrong, guitar, vocals; Matt Freeman, bass, vocals; Brett Reed, drums, backing vocals; Lars Frederiksen, guitar, vocals (1994–present).

Emerging as the next next big thing in the mid-'90s post-punk media craze, Rancid capitalizes on '70s punk and '80s hardcore in an energized but rote flurry of tough, taut dynamics. The group emerged with a strong pedigree: Tim Armstrong and Matt Freeman hailed from the acclaimed Bay Area ska-punk group Operation Ivy, while Lars Fredericksen spent some time in a latter-day version of the U.K. Subs. With its mohawk haircuts and strident lyrical themes, the group has the familiar feel of the Clash, a comparison that both rattles and flatters the band members. The group earned credibility points by staying with its independent label, Epitaph Records, in the face of intense major-label bidding wars, and in 1996 it played on the Lollapalooza main stage.

what to buy: *. . . And out Come the Wolves* 🎵🎵🎵 (Epitaph, 1995, prod. Jerry Finn, Rancid) tears through hardcore, ska, and '70s-styled punk anthems with loyal abandon. The handful of catchy pounders that highlight the album, "Lock, Step, & Gone," "Ruby Soho," and the radio hit "Time Bomb" are tasty, if a bit disposable. The method gets a touch better on *Life Won't Wait* 🎵🎵🎵🎵 (Epitaph, 1998, prod. Tim Armstrong, Lars Frederiksen), which, even though it was recorded over the better part of 14 months, is still taught and fierce, with frighteningly personal lyrics that focus on Armstrong's battles with substance abuse.

the rest:
Rancid 🎵🎵 (Epitaph, 1993)
Let's Go 🎵🎵🎵 (Epitaph, 1994)

influences:
◄◄ The Clash, U.K. Subs, Operation Ivy, Fishbone
►► Third Eye Blind, КоЯn, Chumbawamba

Allan Orski and Gary Graff

Rank & File

Formed 1981, in Hoboken, NJ. Disbanded 1987.

Chip Kinman, vocals, guitar, harmonica; Tony Kinman, vocals, bass; Alejandro Escovedo, guitar (1981–83); Jeff Ross, guitar (1983–87); Slim Evans, drums (1981–83); Stan Lynch, drums (1983–85); R. Kahr, drums (1986–87).

Long before it became fashionable to hang bolo ties and Telecasters around one's neck, Rank & File were bravely bringing their own ferocious mixture of thrash and twang to an initially bewildered public, and in the process almost single-handedly kick-started the entire alternative-country movement (though they'd likely be loathe to admit to, or take credit for, such an achievement). Following the disbandment of their Bay Area punk combo the Dils in 1980, the Kinman brothers sought refuge in Austin alongside old pal Alejandro Escovedo, and soon afterwards they formed the initial incarnation of Rank & File. Their highly unusual—and at the time highly unfashionable—blend of Bakersfield-style swagger and Ramones-tempo fervor quickly landed them a deal with Warner's upstart Slash division. The band's debut album won widespread praise (no less than the *Los Angeles Times* called it "one of the strongest American debut records in a decade"), a headlining appearance on *Austin City Limits,* and even a cover of one of its songs, "Amanda Ruth," by the Everly Brothers. Before fully capitalizing on this notoriety, however, the band splintered, leaving the Kinmans to record their second album with a bevy of competent, if "uninitiated" sidemen. Nevertheless, this record is even better than its predecessor: richer, more melodically adventurous, and surprisingly more John Fogerty than Johnny Cash in its overall approach. Unfortunately, outside of a small circle of friends and followers (a young Dwight Yoakam among them), nobody seemed to be listening, and after one final record, the Kinmans unceremoniously pulled the plug on the entire endeavor. Though the pair continues to perform and record under various monikers, and original guitarist Escovedo has enjoyed a successful post-Rank career both with the True Believers and as a solo performer, the dust stirred up and shock waves created by Rank & File in its prime are only now becoming obvious deep within the sounds and attitudes of an entire generation of "roots-rock" artists.

what to buy: Their first two albums, *Sundown* ♪♪♪♪ (Slash, 1982, prod. David Kahne) and *Long Gone Dead* ♪♪♪♪♪ (Slash, 1984, prod. Jeff Eyrich), remain vitally important documents of the rebirth of an entire genre of American music that, watered down and pasteurized, resurfaced later in everything from John Mellencamp's first post-Cougar releases to the entire current crop of alterna-twangers. Not only that, they're just damn good records to boot.

what to avoid: The first recorded evidence of the Kinmans' odd but frequent penchant towards style-juggling career suicide is painfully evident on the defiant, metallic *Rank & File* ♪♪ (Rhino, 1987, prod. Bill Pfordresher). Only Neil Young seems ready, willing, and able to self-destruct more enjoyably.

solo outings:
Blackbird:
Blackbird ♪♪ (Iloki, 1988, 1989/Scotti Brothers, 1992)

Cowboy Nation:
Cowboy Nation ♪♪♪ (Demon, 1997)

influences:
◀◀ The Blasters, George Jones, the Everly Brothers
▶▶ The Long Ryders, Lone Justice, Uncle Tupelo

see also: *Alejandro Escovedo*

Gary Pig Gold

Ranking Roger
See: The English Beat

Rare Earth

Formed as the Sunliners, 1964, in Detroit, MI. Disbanded 1983. Reformed late 1980s.

Gil Bridges, reeds, vocals (1964–78); Pete Rivera, drums, vocals (1964–74, 1977–78); John Persh, bass, trombone, vocals (1964–72); Rod Richards, guitars, vocals (1969–70); Kenny James, keyboards (1969–70); Ray Monette, guitar (1971–76, 1978); Ed Guzman, percussion (1970–78); Mark Olson, keyboards, vocals (1971–74, 1978); Michael Urso, bass, vocals (1972–74, 1977–78); Roger McBride, bass, vocals (1975–76); Gabriel Katona, keyboards, vocals (1975); Jerry LaCroix, vocals, reeds (1975–76); Barry Eugene Frost, percussion (1975); Paul Warren, guitar, vocals (1975); Frank Westerbrook, keyboards (1976); Ron Fransen, keyboards (1977); Daniel Ferguson, guitar (1977).

For a long time Motown played around with rock 'n' roll, dabbling—with the Neil Young/Rick James–led Mynah Birds, for instance—but never really making a move until the label signed Rare Earth in 1968. Ironically, the group's first big hit was a remake of the Temptations' "Get Ready" in 1970; it was a workmanlike cover, but it was wholly unrepresentative of Rare Earth's original material, which blended touches of jazz and psychedelic pop. Crammed into the Motown machine, where its songs came from staff songwriters, Rare Earth fit somewhere between Parliament and Blood, Sweat & Tears, which made it a hard sell for any company, much less a label whose primary experience had been in the R&B and pop markets and was a virtual stranger to the newer—and growing—rock community. Rare Earth did hit the Top 20 again with "I Just Want to Celebrate" and "Hey Big Brother," both driven by soulful vocal chorales. But the group never really hit the mainstream in a big way, which has as much to do with the woozy focus of its music as it does with Motown's unfamiliarity with rock. Rare Earth is still around however, led by Bridges and Monette and enjoying particular favor in Europe.

what to buy: With 20 tracks, *Greatest Hits and Rare Classics* ♪♪♪♪ (Motown, 1991, prod. various) is a good introduction to this group's varied body of work.

what to buy next: If *Greatest Hits* really grabs you, go for the two-CD *Anthology* ♪♪♪ (Motown, 1995, prod. various), which is diffuse but provides a sonic smorgasbord for the various sounds being made in pop music as the 1960s became the 1970s.

what to avoid: *Earth Tones: The Essential Rare Earth* ♪ (Motown, 1994, prod. various) is a misleadingly titled collection marked by long, ponderous live cuts and the unfair sense that these guys couldn't play a tightly constructed song.

the rest:
Get Ready ♪♪♥ (Rare Earth/Motown, 1969)
Ecology ♪♪ (Rare Earth/Motown, 1970)
In Concert ♪♪ (Rare Earth, 1971/Motown, 1989)
Ma ♪♪♥ (Motown, 1973/1994)
Different World ♪♪ (Koch International, 1993)

influences:
◀◀ The Temptations, Pink Floyd, Procol Harum, Sly & the Family Stone

▶▶ The Commodores, Was (Not Was), Funkadelic, Mother's Finest

Gary Graff

The Raspberries

Formed 1970, in Cleveland, OH. Disbanded 1975.

Eric Carmen, keyboards, bass, guitar; Wally Bryson, guitar; Dave Smalley, bass, guitar (1970–73); Jim Bonfanti, drums (1970–73); Scott McCarl, bass (1974–75); Michael McBride, drums (1974–75).

Miscast throughout its career as a lightweight singles band, the Raspberries have since gained a rightful place as one of the true pioneers of power pop. Forming in Cleveland from the ashes of local phenoms the Choir and Cyrus Erie, the Raspberries was propelled by Eric Carmen's Paul McCartney–esque songwriting and featured some of the most powerful pop you'd ever want to hear. With producer Jimmy Ienner leading the way, the Raspberries' recorded output is filled with soaring ballads and rock 'n' roll treasures. There were some conflicts between Carmen's teen idol poses and Wally Bryson's harder rock leanings, and the band's fourth album, *Starting Over* found two new Berries in the place of Dave Smalley and Jim Bonfanti. The new personnel didn't ease the tension, and the Raspberries

broke up in 1975. Carmen went on to a solo career marked by soft rock hits such as "All by Myself" and "Hungry Eyes." But with power-pop classics such as "Go All the Way," "Tonight," and "Overnight Sensation (Hit Record)" waiting to be rediscovered by new generations of fans, the Raspberries will continue to be one of the most influential pop bands to come out of the post-Beatles '70s—which makes the lack of Raspberries product on U.S. shelves all the more tragic.

what to buy: *Capitol Collector's Series* ♪♪♪♪ (Capitol, 1991, prod. Jimmy Ienner) is certainly enjoyable—and essential, with 20 songs that cover all the hits and the good album tracks.

the rest:
Greatest Hits ♪♪♪♪ (Capitol/EMI, 1995)

worth searching for: You'll be doing yourself a real favor to scare up *The Raspberries: Power Pop, Vol. 1* (RPM, 1996, prod. Jimmy Ienner) and *The Raspberries: Power Pop, Vol. 2* (RPM, 1996, prod. Jimmy Ienner), import sets that each house two of the original albums, plus extensive liner notes and song commentary from the band members.

solo outings:
Eric Carmen:
Eric Carmen ♪♪ (Arista, 1975/Rhino, 1992)
The Best of Eric Carmen ♪♪♥ (Arista, 1988)
The Definitive Collection ♪♪♪♪ (Arista, 1997)

influences:
◀◀ The Beatles, Badfinger, the Beach Boys

▶▶ Big Star, the Records, Cheap Trick, Gin Blossoms, the Odds

Keith Klingensmith

Rasputina

Formed 1992, in New York, NY.

Melora Creager, cello, vocals; Julia Kent, cello; Carpella Parvo, cello (1996); Agnieszka Rybska, cello (1996–present); Norman Block, drums.

An exclamation of "Rock is Dead! Long Live Rock!" may come to your lips when you hear the incomparable chamber-punk of Rasputina, three cellists who play harder than most bands would with a similar number of electric guitars. In founding this trio (augmented by a drummer and the occasional heavy-metal foot pedal), Melora Creager and her cohorts escaped the narrow job market for non-orchestral cello players and filled an alterna-niche that no one else had realized was even there. Nothing is like the band's live shows, where haunted-house sonics are punctuated with bizarre children's-recital stage patter. Attired archly in the fashions not of this *fin de siecle* but the last, these corseted contrarians play out a musical bloodbath between futuristic freedom and classical control—pre-millennium tension doesn't get tenser than this. Inventive songwriting marks the group as more than a one-joke band, but even if it were, it's literally the joke of the century.

what to buy: The astonishing technique and gallows humor of *Thanks for the Ether* 🎵🎵🎵🎵 (Columbia, 1996, prod. Jimmy Boyle, Melora Creager) make it the kind of pop culture revelation no one ever expects, with advanced tunecraft under the gothic-horror trappings and biting feminist punchlines beneath the wry Victorian mannerisms.

what to avoid: A remix EP with tour mate and patron Marilyn Manson, *Transylvanian Regurgitations* 🎵🎵 (Columbia, 1997, prod. Jimmy Boyle, Melora Creager) injects the latter's less-subtle scare tactics to forgettable effect.

the rest:
How We Quit the Forest 🎵🎵 (Columbia, 1998)

influences:

◄◄ Switchblade Symphony, Johann Sebastian Bach, Stephen Sondheim, Diamanda Galas, Edward Gorey, Anne Rice

Adam McGovern

Ratt

Formed 1981, in Los Angeles, CA. Disbanded 1992.

Bobby Blotzer, drums; Juan Croucier, bass; Robbin Crosby, guitar; Warren De Martini, guitar; Stephen Pearcy, vocals.

Riding the '80s wave of pop-metal, Ratt spent more time mimicking Led Zeppelin licks than developing a Mötley Crüe–like fake rebelliousness or a Poison-like cynicism. This was hardly the high road. Ratt's biggest hit, the high MTV-rotated "Round and Round," gave the musicians some money but wasn't exactly an enduring contribution to American music history. Ratt broke up after Pearcy quit the band.

what to buy: *Ratt & Roll 8191* 🎵🎵🎵 (Atlantic, 1991, prod. various) is a dubious greatest-hits package, showcasing Ratt as little more than a second-rate Aerosmith (or a fourth-rate Rolling Stones).

what to buy next: *Out of the Cellar* 🎵🎵 (Atlantic, 1984, prod. Beau Hill), which contains "Round and Round," and *Invasion of Your Privacy* 🎵🎵 (Atlantic, 1985, prod. Beau Hill) both hit the Top 10 and were two of the band's four platinum albums.

what to avoid: *Detonator* 🎵 (Atlantic, 1990, prod. Sir Arthur Payson) showed that Ratt had worn out its musical welcome by the turn of the decade.

the rest:
Ratt 🎵🎵 (Time Coast, 1983)
Dancing Undercover 🎵🎵 (Atlantic, 1986)

Reach for the Sky 🎵 (Atlantic, 1988)
Collage 🎵🎵 (D Rock, 1997)

influences:

◄◄ Aerosmith, the Rolling Stones, Alice Cooper, Kiss, Styx, Journey, Meat Loaf

►► Ugly Kid Joe, Skid Row

Tracey Birkenhauer and Steve Knopper

Johnnie Ray

Born January 10, 1927, in Dallas, OR. Died February 24, 1990, in Los Angeles, CA.

Something less than the missing link between Frank Sinatra and Elvis Presley, but something more than another Italianate '50s pop crooner, Johnny Ray inhabited a space all his own in the pre-rock 'n' roll pop music universe. His near-hysterical signature melodrama, "Cry," seemed to presage the raw emotionalism of rock 'n' roll, although Ray himself remained true to the supper club esthetics that the advent of rock 'n' roll overturned. He emerged from Detroit's Flame Showbar, where he performed alongside black R&B acts, to be signed by Columbia Records in 1951. His first release, "Whiskey and Gin," was a raucous noise, with Ray accompanying himself on piano. But it was his second single, "Cry," along with "The Little White Cloud That Cried," that blasted Ray into a full-fledged phenomenon. He continued to cut hits through the '50s, including many tunes originally associated with black artists ("Such a Night," "Walkin' in the Rain"). But changing musical styles and his own personal problems led to a decline he never reversed. In his extraordinary Ray biography, *Cry: The Johnnie Ray Story* (Barricade Books, 1994), author Jonny Whiteside paints a portrait of a man haunted by a troubled extra-marital affair with columnist Dorothy Kilgallen, his own homosexuality, deafness, drugs, and alcohol—making Ray sound like the ultimate victim of his own dark and desolate songs.

what to buy: The standard compilation *16 Most Requested Songs* 🎵🎵🎵 (Columbia/Legacy, 1991, compilation prod. Michael Brooks) covers Ray's glory years as one of Columbia's leading record-sellers. *High Drama: The Real Johnnie Ray* 🎵🎵🎵 (Columbia Legacy, 1997, compilation prod. Al Quaglieri) is a noteworthy collection that navigates through the more intense, bluesey highpoints of Ray's catalog and features informative notes from his biographer, Whiteside.

what to avoid: Most of Ray's Columbia Records albums were dull, lifeless affairs, built on lightweight filler. And *Johnnie Ray's Greatest Hits* 🎵 (Columbia, 1958/K-Tel, 1990) was not well mastered when transferred to compact disc.

the rest:
Cry 🎵🎵 (Bear Family, 1990)

worth searching for: His first Columbia album, *Johnnie Ray* (Columbia, 1952, prod. Mitch Miller) was an eight-song, 10-inch record that qualifies as the most consistent collection of his career. The German reissue specialists Bear Family unearthed a live 1954 recording, *Live at the Palladium* (Bear Family, 1993, prod. Richard Weize) that documents the feverish ecstasy Ray could provoke at the height of his powers.

influences:

◀◀ Billie Holiday, Frankie Laine, Ivory Joe Hunter

▶▶ Tom Jones, Anthony Newley, Dexy's Midnight Runners

Joel Selvin

Sean Ray

See: Farmer Not So John

The Raybeats

See: Los Straitjackets

Chris Rea

Born March 4, 1951, in Middlesbrough, England.

Kind of a Mark Knopfler for mellow adult listeners, Chris Rea is a fine guitarist with an inclination toward bluesy slide textures. With his smoky baritone voice, he could have been the poor man's Leonard Cohen, but his musical tastes run too much toward bouncy pop and his lyrics toward wistful sentimentality. Still, he's had a lengthy career in the U.K., and his success shows no signs of abating just yet. He scored his biggest U.S. hit with his debut single back in 1978, the lightly cha-cha infused "Fool (If You Think It's Over)." After a few years of stiffs, he finally started receiving acclaim again with some of his mid-'80s releases. A collection of those tunes was re-recorded for 1988's *New Light from Old Windows*, with the slinky "On the Beach" (kind of like Bryan Ferry singing a Sade number while on summer vacation) being the most memorable. More recently, he's alternated between moodier stuff that begs to be taken seriously and synthy pop-rockers that beg the question, why?

what to buy: *The Road to Hell* ♫♫♫ (Atco, 1989, prod. Chris Rea, Jon Kelly) is a dark semi-concept album, with the wry title track offering a deadpan deconstruction of yuppie mores. Lighter but no less compelling, *Auberge* ♫♫♫ (Atco, 1991, prod. Jon Kelly) finds Rea in a hazy mood, and waxing particularly elegant on "Heaven" and "Looking for the Summer."

what to buy next: *The Best of Chris Rea* ♫♫♫ (EastWest America, 1994, prod. Chris Rea, Jon Kelly) not only includes "Fool" and "On the Beach," it also contains "If You Were Me," the warm pairing between Rea and Elton John found originally on John's otherwise awful *Duets* album.

what to avoid: Perky and occasionally irritating, *Espresso Logic* ♫♫ (EastWest America, 1993, prod. Chris Rea) lacks the charm that makes Rea's better work worth hearing.

the rest:
New Light from Old Windows ♫♫♫ (Geffen, 1988)

influences:

◀◀ Dire Straits, Robert Palmer, Gerry Rafferty, Neil Diamond

▶▶ Del Amitri, Curtis Stigers

Bob Remstein

Eddi Reader

See: Fairground Attraction

Recoil

See: Depeche Mode

The Records /Jude Cole

Formed 1978, in England. Disbanded 1982.

John Wicks, vocals, guitar; Huw Gower, guitar, vocals, harmonica (1978–79); Jude Cole, guitar, vocals (1980); Dave Whelan, lead guitar (1982); Chris Gent, lead vocals (1982); Phil Brown, bass, vocals; Will Birch, drums, vocals.

The Records were noted for cool harmonies and irresistible hooks, as exemplified on "Starry Eyes"—by far the best-known Records record (though the Searchers successfully covered "Hearts in Her Eyes"). John Wicks and Will Birch (who later became a music critic) were the main songwriters and consistently honored the pop-rock verities. After the first album, Huw Gower quit, later serving time in David Johansen's band and putting out a solo EP. American Jude Cole replaced him on the second album and then also quit, putting out two bland solo records. The Records' final lineup lasted long enough to record a so-so swan song. The group surprisingly reunited in 1990 to record "Darlin' " for the Beach Boys tribute *Smiles, Vibes, & Harmony*. The 1988 and 1990 albums, however, are both collections of 1978 demos.

what to buy: With everything else out of print, *Smashes, Crashes, and Near Misses* ♫♫♫♫ (Blue Plate/Caroline, 1995, prod. various) collects this underrated band's many gems as intelligently and thoroughly as possible on one CD, leading off with "Starry Eyes." The first two albums, by far the best, are each represented by seven out of 10 cuts, and this group never recorded a bad song.

what to buy next: Cole scored with his solo album *A View from 3rd Street* ♫♫♫♫ (Reprise, 1990, prod. David Tyson, Michael Ostin). Although the sweet "Baby It's Tonight" and the heartfelt

Anthony Kiedis of the Red Hot Chili Peppers **(© Ken Settle)**

"Time for Letting Go" were Top 40 hits, the album could have spawned three more hits.

the rest:
A Sunny Afternoon in Waterloo 𝄞𝄞 (Waterfront, 1988)
Paying for the Summer of Love 𝄞𝄞 (Skyclad, 1990)

worth searching for: Most trips to a used record store should be able to scare up LP copies of *The Records* (Virgin, 1979, prod. various) and *Crashes* (Virgin, 1980, prod. Craig Leon, Mick Glossop) for the six songs not on the collection. *Music on Both Sides* (Virgin, 1982, prod. Will Birch) also has a few worthy tracks left off the compilation. Huw Gower's four-song EP *Guitarophilia* (X-disque, 1984) boasts his "Calling out the Heretics" and a powerful cover of Eddie & the Hot Rods' "Do Anything You Wanna Do."

solo outings:
Jude Cole:
Jude Cole 𝄞𝄞 (Reprise, 1987)
Start the Car 𝄞𝄞𝄞 (Reprise, 1992)
I Don't Know Why I Act This Way 𝄞𝄞𝄞 (Island, 1995)

influences:
◄◄ The Hollies, the Beatles
►► Oasis

Steve Holtje and Christina Fuoco

Red Hot Chili Peppers

Formed 1983, in Hollywood, CA.

Flea (born Michael Balzary), bass, vocals; Jack Irons, drums (1983–88); Anthony Kiedis, vocals; Hillel Slovak (died June 25, 1988, in Los Angeles, CA), guitar (1983–88); Chad Smith, drums (1989–present); Jack Sherman, guitar (1983–85); Cliff Martinez, drums (1983–85); John Frusciante, guitar (1989–92, 1998–present); Jesse Tobias, guitar (1993); Dave Navarro, guitar (1993–98).

The Red Hot Chili Peppers began as post-punk novelties, a less funny, more funky version of the Dead Milkmen. The group was best known for lunkheaded stunts like posing with socks on their private parts while lampooning the cover of the Beatles' *Abbey Road*. Gradually, thanks to tattooed, crewcutted underwear exhibitionist bassist Flea's growing technical skill, it became a legitimate band of good songwriters and accomplished musicians; Flea's bass, derived from a lifetime of listening to old P-Funk records, gave the funny songs a killer bottom, which was nurtured when the group scored a coup and hired George Clinton himself as an early producer. Through perseverance—including numerous personnel changes and overcoming tragedies such as original guitarist Hillel Slovak's death and Anthony Kiedis's drug addiction—novelties gave way to hits, first with the 1989 singles "Knock Me Down" and a cover of Stevie Wonder's "Higher Ground," then with the breakthrough 1991 album *BloodSugarSexMagik* and its first single, "Give It Away." By 1992 the Chili Peppers were one of the world's most popular rock bands, headlining Lollapalooza, dominating MTV, and helping create alternative-rock radio. Though its music became more serious—the smash "Under the Bridge" was a heroin-hazed walk through the big city—the musicians continued to undress onstage and performed at Woodstock '94 with giant light bulbs on their heads. The Peppers' lineup seemed settled with the addition ex-Jane's Addiction guitarist Dave Navarro, but even he departed recently, making way for the return of John Frusciante.

what to buy: Clocking in at more than 75 minutes, *BloodSugarSexMagik* 🎵🎵🎵🎵 (Warner Bros., 1991, prod. Rick Rubin) is far too long and has plenty of filler, but if you wade towards "Under the Bridge" and the funky "Give It Away," it's an essential part of a modern rock record collection. *What Hits!?* 🎵🎵🎵 (EMI, 1992, prod. various) completes a non-fanatic's essential collection, summarizing the band's career up to *BloodSugarSexMagik*. It includes "Taste the Pain," "If You Want Me to Stay," and "Higher Ground."

what to buy next: *Mother's Milk* 🎵🎵🎵 (EMI, 1989, prod. Michael Beinhorn) is a great transition album, with good jokes ("Magic Johnson"), strong funk ("Higher Ground" and Jimi Hendrix's "Fire"), and powerful punk ("Nobody Weird like Me"). Of the pre-superstar albums, *Freaky Styley* 🎵🎵🎵 (EMI, 1985, prod. George Clinton) is the funniest and most charming.

what to avoid: *Out in L.A.* 🎵 (EMI, 1994, prod. Tom Cartwright, Vincent M. Vero) is a hodgepodge of nasty remixes.

the rest:
The Red Hot Chili Peppers 🎵🎵 (EMI, 1984)
The Uplift Mofo Party Plan 🎵🎵🎵 (EMI, 1987)
Abbey Road EP 🎵🎵 (EMI, 1988)
One Hot Minute 🎵🎵🎵 (Warner Bros., 1995)
Under the Covers 🎵🎵🎵 (Capitol, 1998)

solo outings:
John Frusciante:
John Frusciante 🎵🎵 (Warner Bros., 1994)

influences:
◄◄ Parliament-Funkadelic, Stevie Wonder, Jimi Hendrix, the Sex Pistols, the Minutemen, Flipper

►► Primus, Rage Against the Machine, Fishbone, Anthrax, Onyx, Body Count, Pearl Jam, Jane's Addiction

Tracey Birkenhauer and Steve Knopper

Red House Painters

Formed 1989, in San Francisco, CA.

Mark Kozelek, vocals, guitar; Gordon Mack, guitar (1989–95); Jerry Vessel, bass; Anthony Koutsos, drums, Phil Carney, guitar.

Red House Painters was the brainchild of frontman Mark Kozelek, who formed the group after moving to San Francisco from Massillon, Ohio. Within a year, the band was playing local venues on a regular basis and creating a considerable buzz. One of the people turned on by the Red House Painters' downhearted sound was Mark Eitzel, then a member of American Music Club. He enthusiastically peddled the group's demo tape to various record companies, including Ivo Watts-Russell at the prestigious 4AD label. Watts-Russell signed Red House Painters, selected six tracks from its demo, and released it as the band's debut album, *Down Colorful Hill*, in 1992. This set off a tide of critical acclaim for the group. Although its sound was too unwieldy for radio, the group quickly built up a loyal cult following, sealed with the release of its eponymous 1993 double album and its companion disc, released a few months later. Red House Painters released an EP covering Kiss' "Shock Me" during 1994, then its final album for 4AD in 1995, *Ocean Beach*. After a bout of creative differences with the label, the group bowed out of its deal and signed with filmmaker John Hughes's newly developed Supreme Recordings for its more rock-oriented 1996 release, *Songs for a Blue Guitar*.

what to buy: *Red House Painters (Rollercoaster)* 🎵🎵🎵🎵🎵 (4AD, 1993, prod. Mark Kozelek), the group's double album-length debut, is all about painfully intricate melodies and lyrics. It's a magnificent experiment in stretching out a three-minute pop song into a 75-minute monument that punctuates every chord, word, and beat with mesmerizing desolation. On "Rollercoaster" Kozelek recalls the sights, smell, and abandon of being a kid in an amusement park; on "Mother" he relives an age when his mother would brush his hair, clean his belly button, and breathe unrivaled love. In other words, the singer ached for a world free of adulthood constraints—broken hearts, sexual hang-ups, relationships, etc. Don't we all? *Red House Painters (Bridge)* 🎵🎵🎵🎵🎵 (4AD, 1993, prod. Mark Kozelek), the companion tracks that did not fit the mood of the double-album, continues in the same vein. Released only a few months after its predecessor, it contained such poignant songs as "Evil," "Blindfold," and an aching cover of Paul Simon's "I Am a Rock."

what to buy next: *Down Colorful Hill* 🐾🐾🐾🐾 (4AD EP, 1992, prod. Mark Kozelek), the Red House Painters' majestic debut, includes such striking songs as "24" and "Japanese to English." *Ocean Beach* 🐾🐾🐾🐾 (4AD, 1995, prod. Mark Kozelek) finds a lighter, more grounded group offering irresistible cuts such as "Summer Dress" and "Brockwell Park."

the rest:
Shock Me 🐾🐾🐾 (4AD, 1994)
Songs for a Blue Guitar 🐾🐾🐾 (Supreme, 1996)

influences:

◀◀ Neil Young, John Denver, Kiss

▶▶ Jeff Buckley, Hayden, Wilco

Aidin Vaziri

Redd Kross

Formed 1978, in Hawthorne, CA.

Jeff McDonald, vocals, guitar; Steve McDonald, vocals, bass; Greg Hetson, guitar (1978–82); Ron Reyes, drums (1978–82); Gere Fennelly, keyboards (1993–present); Eddie Kurdziel, guitar (1993–present); Brian Reitzell, drums (1993–present).

Originally named the Tourists, then Red Cross, L.A.'s Redd Kross pioneered punk-fueled power pop long before Green Day and others turned the formula into mainstream success. Formed around the nucleus of the brothers McDonald, the band began plying its trade on the L.A. punk scene at the end of the '70s; its first gig was opening for hardcore heroes Black Flag, and with a partisan in hip local DJ Rodney Bingenheimer, Redd Kross became a staple on the scene. Over the years the McDonalds' pop instincts have sharpened; influenced equally by the good-time punk rock of the Ramones and the Carpenters' aching melodicism, Redd Kross fashioned a delectable pop hybrid of chainsaw guitars and choirboy vocal harmonies. The McDonalds have let the group dabble in everything from metal to adult contemporary without losing its signature sound. After releasing a handful of highly acclaimed indie albums, the band signed to Atlantic in 1990, only to return to an indie when fame continued to elude it. Though they have yet to achieve the success that their acolytes have seen, Redd Kross has stayed true to its fun-loving vision and remains an important influence on '90s alternative rock.

what to buy: *Phaseshifter* 🐾🐾🐾🐾 (This Way Up, 1993, prod. Redd Kross) is a heady confection of uptempo rock and lovely, well-crafted pop, largely eschewing the adolescent fury of the band's earlier work.

what to buy next: *Neurotica* 🐾🐾🐾 (Big Time, 1987, prod. Redd Kross) blends power-pop and psychedelia to splendid effect.

what to avoid: *Born Innocent* 🐾🐾 (Frontier, 1986, prod. Redd Kross) has its share of fine moments but is the band's least consistent album.

the rest:
Red Cross 🐾🐾🐾 (Posh Boy, 1980)
Teen Babes from Monsanto 🐾🐾🐾🐾 (Enigma, 1984)
Third Eye 🐾🐾🐾 (Atlantic, 1990)
Show World 🐾🐾🐾 (This Way Up, 1997)

worth searching for: *The Siren* (Posh Boy, 1980, prod. various) is a three-band sampler album that includes a half-dozen songs from the fledgling Red Cross—when Steven McDonald was all of 13 years old.

influences:

◀◀ The Beatles, the Beach Boys, Phil Spector, the Carpenters, Cheap Trick, Kiss, the Raspberries, the Ramones

▶▶ Jellyfish, Teenage Fanclub, the Lemonheads, Stone Temple Pilots, Green Day

Simon Glickman

Otis Redding

Born September 9, 1941, in Dawson, GA. Died December 10, 1967, in Madison, WI.

Because his approach to '60s soul music was more organic than that of his contemporaries, Otis Redding's popularity has endured and the appreciation of his music has even deepened in the years since his death at age 26. The prince of Memphis soul was blossoming into something only hinted at in his final recording, "(Sittin' on) The Dock of the Bay," recorded only three days before he died. He might not have bothered to learn all the lyrics to a song before recording—the most glaring example is his version of the Rolling Stones' "(I Can't Get No) Satisfaction"—but close scrutiny of his live recordings or the available outtakes indicate it was exactly this spirit of improvisation, this enthusiasm for creativity, that illuminated all his work. From his earliest Little Richard–inspired efforts to the enormous body of work he compiled in four short years at Memphis's Stax/Volt, Redding dominated whatever he recorded with a vivid vision of himself: warm and whimsical, both cornpone and secretly wise.

what to buy: With ace Atlantic engineer Tom Dowd at the board, *Otis Blue: Otis Redding Sings Soul* 🐾🐾🐾🐾🐾 (Stax, 1965/Atlantic, 1991, prod. Jim Stewart) features a rich, resonant sound that, coupled with the single finest selection of songs of any Redding album, makes it one of the greatest soul albums of its era. *The Very Best of Otis Redding* 🐾🐾🐾🐾🐾 (Rhino,

1992, compilation prod. Gary Stewart) is a terrific compilation of the essential material.

what to buy next: The thrilling and historic *Live in Europe* ☆☆☆☆ (Stax, 1967/Atlantic, 1991, prod. Jim Stewart), with Dowd at the controls again, commemorates Redding's greatness as a live performer.

what to avoid: Although compelling in its unvarnished honesty, *Good to Me* ☆☆ (Stax, 1993, prod. Al Jackson Jr.) is not really a very good album. Composed of scraps leftover from *Live at the Whiskey* and featuring Redding's unskilled—and undoubtedly underpaid—road band stumbling through the songs, this is the least interesting of his many live recordings.

the rest:
Pain in My Heart ☆☆☆☆ (Stax, 1964/Atlantic, 1991)
The Great Otis Redding Sings Soul Ballads ☆☆☆☆ (Stax, 1965/Atlantic, 1991)
The Soul Album ☆☆☆✟ (Stax, 1966/Atlantic, 1991)
The Otis Redding Dictionary of Soul ☆☆☆☆ (Stax, 1966/Atlantic, 1991)
Good to Me: Live at the Whiskey a Go Go, Vol. 2 ☆☆✟ (Stax, 1966/Atlantic, 1993)
(With Carla Thomas) *King & Queen* ☆☆☆ (Stax, 1967/Atlantic, 1991)
The Dock of the Bay ☆☆☆☆ (Stax, 1968/Atlantic, 1991)
In Person at the Whiskey a Go Go ☆☆☆✟ (Stax, 1968/Atlantic, 1992)
The Immortal Otis Redding ☆☆☆✟ (Stax, 1968/Atlantic, 1994)
Love Man ☆☆☆☆ (Atco, 1970/Atlantic, 1992)
Tell the Truth ☆☆☆ (Atco, 1970)
The Ultimate Otis Redding ☆☆☆☆ (Warner Special Products, 1986)
Remember Me ☆☆☆ (Stax, 1992)
The Very Best of Otis Redding, Vol. 2 ☆☆☆☆ (Rhino, 1995)
Love Songs ☆☆☆ (Rhino, 1998)

worth searching for: The three-disc box set *The Otis Redding Story* (Atlantic, 1987, prod. various), also released in a six-LP edition, was replaced—but not improved upon—by a pricey, four-disc box *Otis: The Definitive Otis Redding* (Rhino, 1993, compilation prod. Bill Inglot).

influences:
◀◀ Little Richard, Sam Cooke, Solomon Burke

▶▶ Al Green, Janis Joplin, Mick Jagger, Maxwell

Joel Selvin

Rednex

Formed 1994, in Sweden.

Billy the Kid, engineering, mixing; Joe Cartwright, vocals; Anders Hansson, vocals, engineering, mixing; Henrik Janson, guitar.

From the join-our-club glibness of the packaging to the awkward bastardization of bluegrass with techno, Rednex is much more a distant statement about America through a language barrier than a band in its own right. In other words, it's a gimmick with an eye for the pocketbook. Crashing the scene with the insipid, insane "Cotton Eye Joe," the band topped the pop charts worldwide. Novelty noted, it returned with the slightly less successful "Old Pop in an Oak" and quickly followed it with an unneccessary album, *Sex & Violins*.

what to avoid: The generously promoted *Sex & Violins* **woof!** (Jive, 1995, prod. Anders Hansson, Denniz Pop) is so bad it might be considered for the sound of the world ending.

influences:
◀◀ Sigue Sigue Sputnik, Jive Bunny, Disco Duck

▶▶ Los Del Rios, Barney

Billy Manes

Jimmy Reed

Born Mathis James Reed, September 6, 1925, in Dunleith, MS. Died August 29, 1976, in Oakland, CA.

Jimmy Reed was the last of the archetypal blues primitives. His simple electric guitar lines, shrill harmonica playing, and understated vocals forged some of the most unique and enduring records of the '50s and early '60s. After a World War II hitch in the Navy, Reed moved to Indiana, worked in the steel mills, jammed with local bands, and occasionally played for tips on the street. During 1949 he teamed up with his childhood friend Eddie Taylor and began to work Southside Chicago nightclubs. Albert King directed Reed to the fledgling Vee-Jay label, and his first single, "High and Lonesome," was released on the Chance subsidiary. Reed moved to Vee-Jay full time in 1953 but didn't have his first national hit until late 1955 with "You Don't Have to Go." Over the next eight years, Reed scored nearly two dozen R&B hits, several of which crossed over to the middle regions of the pop charts. Reed, a functional illiterate who "made up" many of his best songs, needed his wife Mary (Mama Reed) to cue him by whispering forgotten lyrics while he sang live in the studio. Producer Calvin Carter cleverly turned this handicap into an irresistible facet of the Jimmy Reed sound, and soon Mama Reed was a regular feature of her husband's recordings. Reed's sideman Eddie Taylor (a great performer in his own right) continually added guitar fills and arrangement ideas that gave Reed's records their distinctive hooks. The early to mid-'60s was a peak time for Reed; besides his string of hits and acclaimed performance at Carnegie Hall, many of his songs were being covered with great success by the likes of Elvis Presley, the Animals, and the Rolling Stones. But by then, alcoholism and epilepsy were taking their toll. When the Vee-Jay label crumbled in 1964, Reed's manager Al Smith moved him to ABC-Bluesway. The loss of Calvin Carter behind the glass was a big blow, and Reed seemed to dry up as a songwriter. With Smith (who wrote "Big

Boss Man") producing and writing most of the songs, Reed's recordings developed a cleaner, more professional sound but somehow became a less compelling listening experience. Reed's last recordings mistakenly attempted to put him in the '60s soul/'70s funk bag, and they were artistic disasters as well as commercial flops. Reed finally sobered up when he hit the comeback trail during 1976, but just as bookings were picking up, he died in his sleep after an attack of epilepsy. Reed's work has undergone a revival in the last few years, and several compilations of his Vee-Jay material attest that Reed sounded great in his time, but even better in ours.

what to buy: Some catalogs and stores still carry *Speak the Lyrics to Me Mama Reed* 🐾🐾🐾🐾 (Vee-Jay, 1993, prod. Calvin Carter), which has 25 digitally remastered tracks, all the influential numbers that Reed made famous, plus two previously unissued recordings. A nice starter set. *Best of Jimmy Reed* 🐾🐾🐾🐾 (GNP/Crescendo, 1990, prod. Calvin Carter), *Greatest Hits* 🐾🐾🐾🐾 (Charly, 1992, prod. Calvin Carter), *Big Boss Blues— Original Vee-Jay Recordings* 🐾🐾🐾🐾 (Charly, 1988, prod. Calvin Carter), and *Bright Lights, Big City—Charly Blues Masterworks, Vol. 17* 🐾🐾🐾🐾 (Charly, 1992, prod. Calvin Carter) are equally good sets of hit Vee-Jay material if you're wiling to do without digitally remastered sound.

what to buy next: The three-CD, 44-song set *The Classic Recordings* 🐾🐾🐾🐾 (Tomato, 1995, compilation prod. Pete Welding) features all of his Vee-Jay hits, some top B-sides and LP cuts, interesting liner notes, and a remarkably ugly cover painting. If you want more, *Classic Recordings* 🐾🐾🐾🐾 (Rhino, 1995, prod. Calvin Carter) is a three-CD, 55-song compilation of Reed's Vee-Jay material with most of the hits (though "Honest I Do" is missing) and his best LP sides.

what to avoid: Info is scarce and the packaging is deceptive on *Big Legged Woman* 🐾 (Collectables, 1996), *Jimmy Reed Is Back* 🐾 (Collectables, 1994), and *Cry before I Go* 🐾 (Drive Archives, 1995), budget compilations of slickly over-produced later sides where much of Reed's charm is lost.

the rest:
Rockin' with Reed 🐾🐾🐾 (Charly, 1987)
Ride 'Em on Down 🐾🐾🐾 (Charly, 1989)
Jimmy Reed—1965 🐾🐾🐾 (Paula/Jewel, 1991)
Greatest Hits 🐾🐾 (Hollywood/Rounder, 1992)
Heartaches and Troubles 🐾🐾 (MCA Special Products, 1995)
Rockin' with Reed 🐾🐾🐾 (Eclipse, 1996)
Big Boss Man 🐾🐾🐾 (Ronn, 1996)
New Jimmy Reed Album/Soulin' 🐾🐾🐾 (See for Miles, 1997)
Big Boss Man/Down in Virginia 🐾🐾 (See for Miles, 1997)
Lost in the Shuffle 🐾🐾🐾 (32 Jazz, 1997)
Upside the Wall 🐾🐾 (Dove, 1997)
Bright Lights, Big City 🐾🐾🐾 (Blues Encore, 1998)

WHAT ALBUM CHANGED YOUR LIFE?

Ornette Coleman, *Change of the Century.* To this very day, my favorite song would have to be 'Lonely Woman,' along with a track called 'Ramblin'' that was just incredible. I've never, since the day I heard it, had that album out of my mind; it has a permanent residence in my head. Hearing that free jazz improvisation, it really changed my way of thinking about music.

Lou Reed

worth searching for: Though Reed doesn't perform live at all on *Jimmy Reed at Carnegie Hall* (Mobile Fidelity Sound, 1992, prod. Calvin Carter), he recreates his Carnegie Hall playlist with new recordings cut in 1961 on this tremendous sounding 23-track remastering of the original Vee-Jay double LP on a 24-k gold disc. The rest is Vee-Jay's LP *The Best of Jimmy Reed*, which has original versions of many of his '50s hits and B-sides.

influences:
◄◄ Sonny Boy Williamson, Elmore James, Eddie Taylor
►► Slim Harpo, Lonnie Brooks, Elvis Presley, Dale Hawkins

Ken Burke

Lou Reed
Born Louis Firbank, March 2, 1942, in Brooklyn, NY.

Lou Reed's place in the rock pantheon rests primarily on his role in guiding the commercially ignored but enormously influential Velvet Underground from 1965 to 1970. But his post-VU career, though dizzyingly erratic, contains several notable albums. After quitting the Velvets, he re-emerged as a solo act in England, where he was adopted by admirers such as David Bowie, who produced and performed on his breakthrough hit, "Walk on the Wild Side," and Mott the Hoople, which covered Reed's Velvets classic, "Sweet Jane." Later, he would be em-

Lou Reed (© Ken Settle)

braced by the likes of Johnny Rotten and Patti Smith as the godfather of punk, Nooo Yawk division. Throughout the '70s Reed flirted with self-parody, as his records veered wildly from blatant pop compromises to scarifying song cycles to perverse noise experiments. At the onset of the '80s, he recruited his best post-Velvets band, including guitarist Robert Quine and bassist Fernando Saunders, and uncorked a handful of brilliant ensemble albums. By the '90s he was releasing album-long song cycles such as *New York* and *Magic and Loss*, which approached the level of his Velvets work.

what to buy: *The Blue Mask* ♫♫♫♫ (RCA, 1982, prod. Lou Reed, Sean Fullan) combines delicate melodicism and raging rock, stoked by Quine's incendiary guitar on "Waves of Fear" and Saunders's beautifully buoyant bass on "My House," a tender tribute to the late poet and Reed mentor Delmore Schwartz. *New York* ♫♫♫♫ (Sire, 1989, prod. Lou Reed, Fred Maher) examines a city's moral and spiritual decay in one of Reed's most bluntly political and pissed-off works. *Magic and Loss* ♫♫♫♫ (Sire, 1991, prod. Lou Reed, Mike Rathke) is more subdued, but it's a magnificently moving meditation on dealing with a loved one's death.

what to buy next: *Berlin* ♫♫♫♫ (RCA, 1973, prod. Bob Ezrin) is a jarring song cycle about a modern-day Romeo and Juliet—that is if Romeo were a pusher and Juliet a masochist. Hide the razor blades, but it's among Reed's most fully realized works. *Street Hassle* ♫♫♫♫ (Arista, 1978, prod. Lou Reed, Richard Robinson) is the "Mean Streets" of rock; the three-part title track is a brilliant drama of drugs, degradation, and redemption. *The Bells* ♫♫♫♫ (Arista, 1979, prod. Lou Reed) is among Reed's most underrated releases, with a jazz-oriented backing cast, including Don Cherry, and eloquent, affirming lyrics. *New Sensations* ♫♫♫♫ (RCA, 1984, prod. Lou Reed, John Jansen) noses out *Transformer* as the most enduring and least contrived of Reed's pop-oriented discs. *Between Thought and Expression: The Lou Reed Anthology* ♫♫♫♫ (RCA, 1992, prod. various) is a solid three-CD overview.

what to avoid: The spin cycle of a washing machine has more melodic variation than the electronic drone that was *Metal Machine Music* **woof!** (RCA, 1975, prod. Lou Reed).

the rest:
Lou Reed ♫♫♫ (RCA, 1972)
Transformer ♫♫♫♫ (RCA, 1972)
Rock 'n' Roll Animal ♫♫♫ (RCA, 1974)
Sally Can't Dance ♫ (RCA, 1974)
Lou Reed Live ♫♫ (RCA, 1975)
Coney Island Baby ♫♫♫ (RCA, 1976)
Rock & Roll Heart ♫♫ (RCA, 1976)
Walk on the Wild Side: The Best of Lou Reed ♫♫♫ (RCA, 1977)
Live Take No Prisoners ♫♫ (Arista, 1978)
Growing up in Public ♫♫♫ (Arista, 1980)

Rock & Roll Diary: 1967–1980 ♫♫♫ (Arista, 1980)
Legendary Hearts ♫♫♫♫ (RCA, 1983)
City Lights: Classic Performances ♫♫ (Arista, 1985)
Mistrial ♫♫♫ (RCA, 1986)
(With John Cale) *Songs for Drella* ♫♫♫♫ (Sire, 1990)
Set the Twilight Reeling ♫♫♫ (Sire, 1996)
Perfect Night ♫♫♫ (Reprise, 1998)

worth searching for: *Live in Italy* (RCA, 1984) is an import title featuring Reed with Quine, Saunders, and drummer Fred Maher ripping through a career-spanning series of classics, from "Satellite of Love" to an incendiary "White Light/White Heat."

influences:

◀◀ Andy Warhol, Ornette Coleman, Don Cherry, Bob Dylan, Doc Pomus

▶▶ Patti Smith, Kurt Cobain, Ian Hunter, R.E.M., Nick Cave

Greg Kot

Reef

Formed 1993, in Glastonbury, England.

Gary Stringer, vocals; Kenwyn House, guitar; Jack Bessant, bass; Domenic Greensmith, drums.

Combining the rock 'n' roll swagger of the Rolling Stones with the late '60s grind of Humble Pie, Reef delivers a confident brew of proven, primal blues rock, heavy on the blissed-out, feel-good vibe of the best classic rock, light on pretense and artifice. Originally known as Naked, Reef came together in England's West Country. After solidifying its line-up, the quartet sent a demo to Sony's S2 label, which immediately signed the band. Former Jam guitarist Paul Weller heard the tape and asked them to join his tour, which included three sold-out nights at Royal Albert Hall. From there, there was no turning back. Reef's debut album, *Replenish*, spawned the hit "Naked," which went to #11 on the U.K. charts. That success led to tour dates with the Rolling Stones and Soundgarden. The group finally scored in America with the follow-up, *Glow*, and the best seems yet to come.

what to buy: The group's U.S. debut, *Glow* ♫♫♫♫ (Epic, 1997, prod. George Drakoulias), contains the hit "Place Your Hands," a vintage-sounding Creedence-style riff with gospel choir support. The song earned substantial rotation on MTV and spawned a successful American tour.

the rest:
Replenish ♫♫♫ (S2/Sony, 1995/Epic, 1996)

influences:

◀◀ Led Zeppelin, the Rolling Stones, Creedence Clearwater Revival, Humble Pie

Bob Gulla

Michael Stipe of R.E.M. (© Ken Settle)

The Reegs

See: The Chameleons

The Refreshments

Formed 1993, in Tempe, AZ.

Roger Clyne, rhythm guitar, vocals; Buddy Edwards, bass; Brian Blush, guitar; P.H. Naffah, drums.

At first glance, the Refreshments may seem another in the long line of guitar-oriented college rock bands (it also hails from the same town that gave us Dead Hot Workshop and the Gin Blossoms). But its members' experiences, particularly those of Roger Clyne, add depth. As a child, Clyne spent time on his grandmother's ranch in the desert near the Arizona/Mexico border. Upon graduation, he taught English in Taiwan, where he honed his performance skills busking in the subways. Clyne also lived with the Mariachis of Ensenada and, while visiting Mexico, his best friend died. Clyne returned to Tempe, where he formed the Refreshments in 1994. It didn't take long to lasso in fans around the valley; the same year, the group released its debut, *Wheelie,* and, according to *Billboard,* sold more than 286,000 units and reached the top spot on the magazine's Heatseekers charts before peaking at #97 in August of 1996. Topping off a stellar year, the band was schlepping gear around Tempe watering holes when its members came across an ad for the Ticketmaster national talent search. Chosen for the contest, the Refreshments took first place out of 7,200 bands, earning time in Bad Animals studio in Seattle and a showcase at the prestigious South by Southwest music conference in Austin, Texas, in 1995. After signing with Mercury Records, the band's music was beamed to millions of homes around the United States—as the Refreshments wrote and recorded the country-flavored theme song to the Fox television show *King of the Hill.*

what to buy: *Fizzy Fuzzy Big and Buzzy* 🎵🎵🎵 (Mercury, 1996, prod. Clif Norrell) is fun, a rarity in modern rock. The Refreshments blend alterna-twang with driving beats and witty lyrics. In the snappy "Down Together," Clyne sings, "We could both wear cowboy hats and pretend that we could speak Italian/I could eat some gum and make my breath so minty fresh to kiss you." Later on, he name-checks his neighbors: "We could all wear ripped up clothes/and pretend that we were Dead Hot Workshop." Clyne's lush vocals, accompanied by galloping guitar in "Mekong," sound like a Toad the Wet Sprocket B-side, although that's not necessarily a bad thing. But the real gem of the album is "Mexico," a favorite subject of the Refreshments; "Here comes another song about Mexico," Clyne sings, "but I just can't help myself."

what to avoid: After touring for *Fizzy Fuzzy,* the Refreshments matured, went serious, and produced an album that would make the Gin Blossoms proud. *The Bottle and Fresh Horses* 🎵🎵 (Mercury, 1997, prod. Paul Leary) sounds too much like a Gin Blossoms knock-off to be appreciated. There are a few bright spots, however; "Wanted" could be "Banditos," part II, and "Heaven or the Highway" pays tribute to the Indian casinos around the Phoenix valley.

influences:
◀◀ Toad the Wet Sprocket, Gin Blossoms

Christina Fuoco

Vernon Reid

See: Living Colour

R.E.M.

Formed 1980, in Athens, GA.

Michael Stipe (born John Michael Stipe), vocals; Peter Buck, guitar; Mike Mills, bass, vocals; Bill Berry, drums (1980–97); Barrett Martin, drums (1998).

During the early '80s, R.E.M. created the new Southern rock—ringing guitars, punky rhythms, and oblique, indecipherable vocals. By the end of the decade these erstwhile underground heroes were headlining arenas, a mainstream incision accomplished virtually without artistic compromise. Perhaps the only notable shift in the band's sound was the more pronounced clarity of Michael Stipe's vocals and lyrics, which coincided with his emergence as a political activist. It even could be argued that R.E.M. has actually gotten better and more adventurous the longer it has remained in the game. During the early '90s, the band quit touring and cranked out three of its finest

---

albums and its biggest hit, "Losing My Religion" (from the 1991 *Out of Time* album), before returning to the arenas with new-found purpose in 1995. The tour took its toll, with Berry suffering a brain aneurysm and eventually quitting in 1997. But the remaining three have vowed to carry on and spent 1998 working on a new studio album.

what to buy: The band's full-length debut, *Murmur* 𝄞𝄞𝄞𝄞 (IRS, 1983, prod. Mitch Easter), remains one of the prototypical college-rock albums of the '80s. It insinuates rather than bludgeons, yet also manages to avoid sounding wimpy—which is to say it rocks hard enough to keep a frat party in full swing; but it layers on the melancholy atmosphere and oblique lyricism so thick that a moody sophomore could spend an entire semester plumbing its murky depths. The band's second masterpiece is *Automatic for the People* 𝄞𝄞𝄞𝄞 (Warner Bros., 1993, prod. Scott Litt, R.E.M.), a uniformly downcast, but emotionally transcendent meditation on death and loss. *Document* 𝄞𝄞𝄞𝄞 (IRS, 1987, prod. Scott Litt, R.E.M.) is the band's hardest-rocking disc; Litt introduces a new punch and clarity that presages the jump to arenas. *Out of Time* 𝄞𝄞𝄞𝄞 (Warner Bros., 1991, prod. Scott Litt, R.E.M.) is a sprawling, brilliantly executed tour of pop styles, with the classic "Losing My Religion" as its centerpiece.

what to buy next: *Monster* 𝄞𝄞𝄞𝄞 (Warner Bros., 1994, prod. Scott Litt, R.E.M.) is a bombastically entertaining homage to early '70s glam-rock that finds Stipe cleverly trying on a variety of vocal personas.

what to avoid: *Dead Letter Office* 𝄞𝄞 (IRS, 1987, prod. various) is a batch of B-sides and rarities of interest only to hard-core collectors, redeemed partially by the inclusion of the 1982 *Chronic Town* EP.

the rest:
Reckoning 𝄞𝄞𝄞 (IRS, 1984)
Reconstruction of the Fables 𝄞𝄞𝄞 (IRS, 1985)
Life's Rich Pageant 𝄞𝄞𝄞𝄞 (IRS, 1986)
Eponymous 𝄞𝄞𝄞 (IRS, 1988)
Green 𝄞𝄞𝄞𝄞 (Warner Bros., 1988)
New Adventures in Hi-Fi 𝄞𝄞𝄞𝄞 (Warner Bros., 1996)
Up 𝄞𝄞𝄞 (Warner Bros., 1998)

worth searching for: The EP *Chronic Town* (IRS, 1982, prod. Mitch Easter, R.E.M.) features the title cut without the deadweight of *Dead Letter Office*.

solo outings:
Tuatara (Buck):
Breaking the Ethers 𝄞𝄞𝄞 (Epic, 1997)
Trading with the Enemy 𝄞𝄞𝄞 (Epic, 1998)

influences:
◀◀ Patti Smith, Soft Boys, New York Dolls, Wire, Pere Ubu, Television, the Velvet Underground

▶▶ Gin Blossoms, Hootie & the Blowfish, Toad the Wet Sprocket, For Squirrels, Drivin' N' Cryin'

Greg Kot

The Rembrandts

Formed 1990, in Los Angeles, CA.

Phil Solem, vocals, guitar, banjo, piano, synthesizer, percussion, bass (1990–96); Danny Wilde, vocals, bass, guitar, mandolin, harmonica, synthesizer.

There is an unfortunate possibility that the Rembrandts may one day be remembered (inaccurately) as one-hit wonders for "I'll Be There for You," the massively successful theme song to the popular TV sitcom *Friends*. "I'll Be There for You" is a winning radio-ready track, whose ad-jingle exuberance and Monkees-derived virtues virtually guaranteed it would be played over and over again. Nonetheless, it would be a shame to see the Rembrandts' ultimate legacy reduced to just that song. Phil Solem and Danny Wilde's partnership dates back to the early '80s and the L.A. pop band Great Buildings. Wilde subsequently did some solo albums—often enlisting the aid of Solem—and the pair officially resurfaced at the start of the '90s as the Rembrandts, a pop duo drawing recognizable inspiration from the Beatles and the Everly Brothers. Solem split following the third album, and Wilde currently bills himself as Danny Wilde & the Rembrandts.

what to buy: *The Rembrandts* 𝄞𝄞𝄞 (Atco, 1990, prod. Rembrandts) is a casual, easygoing affair, with hidden hooks and gorgeous vocals. That debut album contains "Just the Way It Is, Baby," a #14 hit. "I'll Be There for You" appears on *LP* 𝄞𝄞𝄞 (EastWest, 1995, prod. Don Smith), which is a touch heavier, mixing heartache and harmony but not scrimping on the hooks. And there are lots of songs on *LP* as good as "I'll Be There for You."

the rest:
Untitled 𝄞𝄞𝄞 (Atco, 1992)
Spin This 𝄞𝄞 (EastWest, 1998)

worth searching for: *Great Buildings* (Columbia, 1981, prod. Ed E. Thacker, John Boylan), the sole album by Wilde and Solem's former band, is a gem.

influences:
◀◀ The Beatles, the Everly Brothers, the Monkees, Squeeze

Carl Cafarelli

Renaissance

Formed 1969, in Surrey, England. Disbanded 1987.

Keith Relf, vocals (1967–69); Jim McCarty, drums (1967–69); Jane Relf, vocals (1967–69); John Hawken, keyboards (1967–69); Louis Cen-

namo, bass (1967–69); Rob Hendry, guitar (1969–72); Annie Haslam, vocals (1969–87); Michael Dunford, guitar (1972–87); Jon Camp, bass (1969–87); John Tout, keyboards (1969–79); Terry Sullivan, drums, percussion (1969–79); Peter Gosling, keyboards (1979–87); Peter Barron, drums (1979–87).

Started by former Yardbirds Keith Relf and Jim McCarty, Renaissance was completely overhauled after its self-titled 1969 album. Unsatisfied with the venture, Relf, McCarty, and the other founding members left and the lineup had completely changed by the time *Prologue* was issued in 1971. That decade of thriving progressive and art rock suited the group, which blended classical, pop, folk, and subtle jazz influences into an almost symphonic form of pop music. It found favor in the U.S., but not much interest abroad, including its native England. Renaissance broke up in 1987, its lush style of music pushed aside by the new punk generation. Annie Haslam resurfaced as a solo artist.

what to buy: Most of the group's material is out of print; fortunately, its home label, Sire, issued some of the group's best-known material—including "Mother Russia," "Ashes Are Burning," and its ambitious "Scheherazade" interpretation—into a two-part CD compilation called *1001 Nights—Vol. 1* 𝄞𝄞𝄞 (Sire, 1990, prod. various) and *1001 Nights—Vol. 2* 𝄞𝄞𝄞 (Sire, 1990, prod. various).

what to buy next: *King Biscuit Flower Hour Presents Renaissance, Part 1* 𝄞𝄞𝄞 (KBFH, 1997) and *King Biscuit Flower Hour Presents Renaissance, Part 2* 𝄞𝄞𝄞 (KBFH, 1997) capture the band during a landmark concert at London's Royal Albert Hall, backed by the Royal Philharmonic Orchestra, which lends an appropriate pomp to its majestic prog-rock.

the rest:
Prologue 𝄞𝄞𝄞 (Elektra/One Way, 1972)
Ashes Are Burning 𝄞𝄞𝄞 (Elektra/One Way, 1973)
Songs from Renaissance Days 𝄞𝄞𝄞 (Mausoleum Classix, 1997)

influences:
◀◀ The Yardbirds, Cream, the Moody Blues

▶▶ Emerson, Lake & Palmer, Electric Light Orchestra, Loreena McKennitt, Sara McLachlan

Doug Pullen

The Rentals

See: Weezer

REO Speedwagon

Formed 1969, in Champaign, IL.

Terry Luttrell, vocals (1969–71); Kevin Cronin, vocals (1972, 1976–present); Mike Murphy, vocals (1973–75); Gary Richrath, guitar (1969–90); Dave Amato, guitar (1990–present); Neal Doughty, keyboards; Jesse Harms, keyboards (1990–91); Gregg Philbin, bass (1969–77); Bruce Hall, bass (1978–present); Alan Gratzer, drums (1969–90); Bryan Hitt, drums (1990–present).

Formed in 1969 by college roommates Neal Doughty and Alan Gratzer, REO Speedwagon evolved from a moderately successful country-rock band to an immensely successful arena rock band to a perennial participant on the '70s nostalgia summer concert circuit. Fraught with personality conflicts, the band's ever-changing lineup finally stabilized in 1978 with Kevin Cronin, Gary Richrath, Doughty, Bruce Hall, and Gratzer; it was this incarnation that produced the band's first big seller, *You Can Tune a Piano but You Can't Tuna Fish*, as well as its hit-laden, multi-million selling mainstream breakthrough *Hi Infidelity*. But after another smash album with *Wheels Are Turnin'*, the tenuous peace that had existed between band members began to crumble, as did its sales. Though it continues to release albums, REO mostly serves to play "Ridin' the Storm Out" and "Keep on Loving You" for the same crowds that have worn out their *Boston* and *Frampton Comes Alive* albums.

what to buy: Though anyone owning a radio in 1981 may have gotten their fill of *Hi Infidelity* 𝄞𝄞𝄞 (Epic, 1981, prod. Kevin Cronin, Gary Richrath, Kevin Beamish), the album still reigns as REO's best effort. While the sappy ballad "Keep on Loving You" sounds a bit dated, most of the album reflects Richrath's and Cronin's ability to weave country, rock, and pop into an eminently listenable collection of tunes.

what to buy next: *You Can Tune a Piano, but You Can't Tuna Fish* 𝄞𝄞𝄞𝄞 (Epic, 1978, prod. Kevin Cronin, Gary Richrath, Paul Grupp) and *Wheels Are Turnin'* 𝄞𝄞𝄞𝄞 (Epic, 1985, prod. Kevin Cronin, Gary Richrath, Alan Gratzer) offer a similar brand of feel-good arena rock, though the latter displays both more maturity and a willingness to stray a bit from the proven pop formula.

what to avoid: Though the title track is one of REO's seminal tunes, *Ridin' the Storm Out* **woof!** (Epic, 1973, prod. John Stronach, Gary Richrath, John Henning) originally featured Cronin on vocals, but partway through recording he was replaced by the soporific Mike Murphy (prompting an 11th-hour album cover reshoot). The last-minute replacement transformed what would have been merely a dull album into a slipshod embarrassment.

the rest:
REO Speedwagon 𝄞𝄞𝄞 (Epic, 1971)
R.E.O./T.W.O. 𝄞𝄞𝄞 (Epic, 1972)
Lost in a Dream 𝄞 (Epic, 1974)
This Time We Mean It 𝄞𝄞 (Epic, 1975)
R.E.O. (C.O.W.) 𝄞𝄞𝄞 (Epic, 1976)
Live: You Get What You Play For 𝄞𝄞𝄞𝄞 (Epic, 1977)
Nine Lives 𝄞𝄞𝄞 (Epic, 1979)
A Decade of Rock and Roll 𝄞𝄞𝄞𝄞 (Epic, 1980)
Good Trouble 𝄞𝄞 (Epic, 1983)

Life As We Know It 🦴🦴🦴 (Epic, 1987)
The Hits 🦴🦴🦴 (Epic, 1988)
The Earth, a Small Man, His Dog, and a Chicken 🦴🦴 (Epic, 1990)
The Second Decade of Rock and Roll 🦴🦴🦴 (Epic, 1991)
Building the Bridge 🦴 (Castle, 1996)

solo outings:
Gary Richrath:
Richrath 🦴🦴 (GNP/Crescendo, 1992)
Only the Strong Survive 🦴 (GNP/Crescendo, 1992)

influences:
◄◄ The Allman Brothers Band, the Beatles, Creedence Clearwater Revival, Chuck Berry

►► Mr. Mister, Eddie Money, Kenny Loggins, Boston, Journey, Starcastle

Brandon Trenz

The Replacements /Paul Westerberg

Formed 1981, in Minneapolis, MN. Disbanded 1991.

Paul Westerberg, guitar, vocals; Bob Stinson (died February 15, 1995), guitar (1980–86); Tommy Stinson, bass, vocals; Chris Mars, drums (1981–90); Slim Dunlap, guitar (1987–91).

The Replacements were widely known for their drunken antics and unpredictable live shows, which ranged from the sublime to the ridiculous—often within the same song. But what set the band apart from its fellows in the burgeoning early '80s modern rock scene was its ability to balance scorching rockers featuring Bob Stinson's crash-and-burn guitar with Westerberg's aching, vulnerable ballads like "Sixteen Blue," "Unsatisfied," and "Here Comes a Regular." It seemed for a time that the 'Ments were the band that would lead the underground into the mainstream. It was among the first alternative bands to sign with a major label, leaving Twin/Tone for Sire in 1985—a full three years before their underground rivals R.E.M. hitched their wagon to Warner Bros. But the band could never quite maintain a level of consistency, and its members drifted apart without ever becoming household names. Which isn't to say the band didn't leave a mark; its melding of punk aggression and pop hooks became a touchstone for legions of alternative bands. Kurt Cobain, for one, was a major acolyte, taking much of his frayed flannel vulnerability, as well as the pained, nicotine-and-vinegar singing, from Westerberg. And the Goo Goo Dolls hit pay dirt in 1996 after years of building on a heavily Replacements-oriented sound.

what to buy: Without a doubt, three albums represent the Replacements' peak: *Let It Be* 🦴🦴🦴🦴 (Twin/Tone, 1984, prod. Steve Fjelstad, Paul Westerberg, Peter Jesperson) is an uneven album, and several songs are almost unlistenable. But the high points are fantastic: "I Will Dare," "Unsatisfied," "Sixteen Blue," and "Answering Machine" are as good as '80s indie rock got. The high points of *Tim* 🦴🦴🦴🦴 (Sire, 1985, prod. Tommy Erdelyi) are almost as good, and it's a more consistent album, the perfect realization of the band's ballad/rocker yin-yang. *Pleased to Meet Me* 🦴🦴🦴🦴 (Sire, 1987, prod. Jim Dickinson) is also top notch, arguably the band's finest, but Stinson's careening, over-the-top guitar leads are sorely missed in some spots.

what to buy next: Both of Westerberg's solo albums—*14 Songs* 🦴🦴🦴🦴 (Sire, 1993, prod. Matt Wallace, Paul Westerberg) and *Eventually* 🦴🦴🦴🦴 (Sire, 1996, prod. Paul Westerberg, Lou Giordano, Brendan O'Brien)—vary in overall quality, but also feature some of his finest writing. You won't go wrong with either.

what to avoid: The band's final two outings are both pretty dispirited affairs. *Don't Tell a Soul* 🦴🦴 (Sire, 1989, prod. Matt Wallace, Replacements) is a lackluster attempt to score a pop hit, while *All Shook Down* 🦴🦴 (Sire, 1990, prod. Scott Litt, Paul Westerberg) is essentially a Westerberg solo album—one which isn't nearly as strong as what has followed.

the rest:
Sorry Ma, Forgot to Take out the Trash 🦴🦴🦴 (Twin/Tone, 1981)
The Replacements Stink 🦴🦴 (Twin/Tone, 1982)
Hootenanny 🦴🦴🦴🦴 (Twin/Tone, 1983)
All for Nothing/Nothing for All 🦴🦴🦴🦴 (Reprise, 1997)

worth searching for: *Live Inconcerated* (Sire, 1989) is a promotional sampling of the Replacements' live show. Its five songs are a bit brief, but it'll certainly whet your appetite for some full-length bootlegs. The staunchest of Replacements fans will also want the rare cassette-only release *The Shit Hits the Fans* (Twin/Tone, 1985), an anarchic live tape of the band in a total drunken stupor. Chances are, you had to be there.

solo outings:
Slim Dunlap:
The Old New Me 🦴🦴🦴🦴 (Medium Cool, 1983)
Times like This 🦴🦴🦴🦴 (Restless, 1996)

Tommy Stinson:
(With Bash & Pop) *Friday Night Is Killing Me* 🦴🦴🦴🦴 (Reprise, 1983)
(With Perfect) *When Squirrels Play Chicken* 🦴🦴🦴 (Medium Cool, 1996)

Chris Mars:
Horseshoes and Hand Grenades 🦴🦴🦴🦴 (Smash, 1992)
75% Less Fat 🦴🦴🦴 (Smash, 1993)
Tenterhooks 🦴🦴🦴 (Bar/None, 1995)
Anonymous Botch 🦴🦴 (Bar/None, 1996)

influences:
◄◄ Big Star, the Sex Pistols, the Faces, the Kinks, Black Flag, the Ramones

▶▶ Nirvana, Goo Goo Dolls, Wilco, Soul Asylum, Cracker

Alan Paul

Republica

Formed 1994, in London, England.

Saffron, lead vocals; Tim Dorney, keyboards; Jonny Male, guitar; Pete Riley, drums; Dave Barborossa, drums (1994–97); Andy Todd, keyboards (1994–97).

A self-described techno-pop-punk-rock band, Republica sought to combine '80s new wave sensibilities with the harsh, electronica dance grooves of the '90s. Call it anti-Britpop. After spending her early 20s frequenting raves in London clubs, the Nigerian-born Saffron, then singing with unknowns N-Joi, was introduced to the writing-engineering duo of Tim Dorney and Andy Todd. Dorney was already known for his work in the underground U.K. band, Flowered Up, while Todd was considered the technical wizard of the trio. The band debuted in 1994 with two massive club hits in England, "Out of This World" and "Bloke," and were soon joined by guitarist Jonny Male and Dave Barborossa, formerly of Bow Wow Wow and Adam & the Ants. Much of the band's attention has focused on the striking stage presence of the ballet-trained Saffron, who descends from Portuguese, Chinese, and English ancestry. The band is best known for its propulsive hits "Ready to Go" and "Drop Dead Gorgeous," featured in the TV show *Baywatch* and the hit flick *Scream*. But Republica also contributed a version of Gary Numan's "Are Friends Electric?" to a Numan tribute album, while Saffron supplied backing vocals to Prodigy's hit *The Fat of the Land*.

what's available: *Republica* ♫♫♫ (RCA, 1996, prod. Republica) is a sonic whirlwind of metallic guitars and razor-sharp drum programming. But what makes Republica stand out from the hordes of British popsters is its sneering yet non-smug attitude. Saffron snakes through the sassy lyrics of "Bitch" and "Drop Dead Gorgeous" with such feminine chutzpah that her arrogance is actually admirable.

influences:

◀◀ The Clash, Blondie, Human League, Prodigy

Melissa Ruggieri

The Residents

Formed 1970, in San Francisco, CA.

Members unknown.

We may never encounter another musical force like the Residents, a band that somehow has sustained a career of more than 25 years built on aural experimentation, enigmatic visu-

als, and a series of myths that has followed it through every stage of its career. The identity of the band's personnel has always been a closely guarded secret, which leaves us with the music, intermittent live performances, and some willfully obscure liner notes from which to glean clues. The group's first full-length release, *Meet the Residents*, laid the groundwork for what was to come: nightmarish nursery-rhyme word-play "sung" over sound collages, sometimes based on familiar melodies. Imagine a twisted, funny, extreme, and musically coherent "Revolution #9," and you get the idea. The band's sound has changed through the years, possibly due to new personnel, but it has always managed to be interesting, inspired, and technologically advanced. Three of the most recent outings are re-worked soundtracks to interactive CD-ROMs. All of the band's recordings are self-produced.

what to buy: *The Commercial Album* ♫♫♫♫ (Ralph, 1980/ESD, 1988, prod. the Residents) is a great place to start. The ESD reissue adds 10 bonus tracks to the original 40.

what to buy next: For early craziness, try *The Residents Present the Third Reich & Roll* ♫♫♫♫ (Ralph, 1975/ESD, 1988, prod. the Residents). Again, the ESD reissue has bonus tracks, this time four. The more musically accessible and emotionally intense later-period Residents are showcased on *The King and Eye* ♫♫♫♫ (Enigma, 1988, prod. the Residents).

what to avoid: *Heaven?* ♫♫♫ (Rykodisc, 1986, prod. the Residents) and *Hell!* ♫♫♫ (Rykodisc, 1986, prod. the Residents) consist of material from various albums. While the songs on both are good choices, they are decidedly less powerful out of context. Also skip the soundtrack *God in Three Persons* ♫♫ (Torso, 1987). The music just doesn't make it on its own.

the rest:

Meet the Residents ♫♫♫♫ (Ralph, 1974)
Fingerprince ♫♫♫♫ (Ralph, 1977)
Not Available ♫♫♫♫ (Ralph, 1978)
Duckstab/Buster & Glen ♫♫♫♫ (Ralph, 1978)
Eskimo ♫♫♫♫♫ (Ralph, 1979)
Mark of the Mole ♫♫♫♫ (Ralph, 1981)
The Tunes of Two Cities ♫♫♫ (Ralph, 1982)
Intermission ♫♫♫ (Ralph, 1983)
The Mole Show ♫♫♫ (Ralph, 1983)
Residue of the Residents ♫♫♫♫ (Ralph, 1983)
George & Jones ♫♫♫♫ (Ralph, 1984)
What Happened to Vileness Fats? ♫♫♫♫♫ (Ralph, 1984)
The Big Bubble ♫♫♫♫ (Ralph, 1985)
Stars and Hank Forever ♫♫♫ (Ralph, 1986)
13th Anniversary Show—Live in Japan ♫♫♫♫ (Ralph, 1986)
The Mole Show Live in Holland ♫♫♫♫ (ESD, 1988)
Liver Music ♫♫♫♫ (U-WEB, 1990)
Cube E Live in Holland ♫♫♫♫ (Enigma, 1990)
Daydream B-Liver ♫♫♫♫ (U-WEB, 1990)

Freak Show 🎜🎜🎜 (Official Products, 1991)
Our Finest Flowers 🎜🎜🎜 (Ralph, 1992)
Gingerbread Man 🎜🎜🎜 (Ralph, 1992)
Hunters 🎜🎜🎜 (Milan, 1995)

influences:

◀◀ The Beatles, Captain Beefheart, Edgard Varese

▶▶ Primus, Half Japanese

Shane Faubert

Paul Revere & the Raiders /Paul Revere & the Raiders Featuring Mark Lindsay /Raiders /Pink Puzz

Formed 1960, in Portland, OR.

Paul Revere (born Paul Revere Dick, January 7, 1938, in Harvard, NE), keyboards; **Mark Lindsay** (born March 9, 1942 in Eugene, OR), vocals, saxophone (1960–75); **Robert White**, guitar (1960–61); **Richard White**, guitar (1960–61); **William Hibbard**, bass (1960–61); **Jerry Labrum**, drums (1960–61); **Leon Russell**, keyboards (1961); **Steve West**, guitar (1962–63); **Ross Allemang**, bass, guitar, piano (1962–63); **Mike "Smitty" Smith**, drums (1962–67, 1971–72); **Dick Walker**, bass, guitar, piano (1963); **Pete Ouellette**, guitar (1963); **Charlie Coe**, bass (1963, 1967–68); **Mike "Doc" Holiday**, bass (1963–65); **Drake "the Kid" Levin**, guitar (1963–66); **Phil "Fang" Volk**, bass (1965–67); **Jim "Harpo" Valley**, guitar (1966–67); **Joe Correro Jr.**, drums (1967–71); **Freddy Weller**, guitar (1967–73); **Keith "Guitar" Allison**, bass (1968–75); **Steve Eaton**, guitar (1971); **Omar Martinez**, drums, vocals (1972–77, 1980s–present); **Robert Wooley**, keyboards (1972–77); **Doug Heath**, guitar (1973–present); **Rusty Smith**, bass (1974); **Ron Foos**, bass (1975–77, 1980–present); **Blair Hill (a.k.a. Louie Fontaine)**, vocals (1978–80); **Neil Rush**, saxophone (1978–80); **Greg Branson**, keyboards (1978–80); **Scott Ellershaw**, bass, guitar (1978–80); **Mervin Kato April**, drums (1978–80); **Dick Gerber**, bass (1979–80); **Michael Bradley**, vocals (1980–83); **Danny Krause**, keyboards (1980–present); **Carl Driggs**, vocals (1983–present); **Jamie Revere**, guitar (1990–present); **Martin Ross**, vocals (1997–present).

The Raiders were among the founders and architects of the early Pacific Northwest rock scene. It released the first rock arrangement of the perennial classic "Louie Louie," recorded Columbia Records' first-ever million-selling rock LP, and was the first rock band to star in a hit television series. Yet it's remembered today primarily for the red, white, and blue Revolutionary War costumes the musician stubbornly wore on stage throughout the entire '60s. Well, hopefully enough time has now passed—and the sight of oddly attired bands singing on TV has become common enough—that the Raiders can finally begin to

be appreciated solely for the abundance of great music written and recorded during its spectacular reign: 15 albums and just about as many Top 20 hits between 1965 and 1971, which puts the group right up with the Beatles, the Beach Boys, the Rolling Stones, and the Supremes in terms of sales. So there! The story really began when Mark Lindsay joined Paul Revere's already locally thriving show band the Downbeats in 1959, but it was not until the mid-'60s, after Dick Clark cast them in his daily *Where the Action Is* series and Columbia had assigned its hot young staff producer Terry Melcher to record the group, that the Raiders finally hit pay-dirt. "Steppin' Out," "Just like Me," "Kicks" (an anti-drug song, highly unusual for the time), "Hungry," "Good Thing," and "Him or Me," Top 10 hits one and all, remain among the best examples of American hard pop you'll ever hear, and even after Melcher's departure, Lindsay continued to write and produce hits for the band, ranging from the innovative bubblegum of "Mr. Sun Mr. Moon" to the proto-metallic "Just Seventeen." Yet it wasn't until 1971 that the band released its biggest seller, "Indian Reservation," which was its only #1 record and, ironically, its very final hit. Several years later Lindsay forever hung up his colonial headgear, but a staunchly determined Revere continues to front new bands of "baby Raiders" to this day, still wears his high-boots and tights, and still insists his "Louie Louie" is not only the first, but the *best*.

what to buy: *The Essential Ride, '63–'67* 🎜🎜🎜🎜 (Sony Legacy, 1995, compilation prod. Bob Irwin) presents a carefully chosen, lovingly annotated 20-song collection of hits, album tracks, and rarities, including the unreleased gastro-sexual tub-fest "Crisco Party" (listeners under the age of 17 should be accompanied by an adult for this track).

what to buy next: *The Legend of Paul Revere* 🎜🎜🎜🎜 (Sony Legacy, 1990, prod. various) is a more in-depth, double disc overview that also contains examples of the band's more R&B-flavored pre-Columbia recordings. And as for the Raiders' legendary sense of the wild and the downright bizarre, *A Christmas Present—and Past* 🎜🎜🎜 (Columbia, 1967/alala music, 1996, prod. Terry Melcher) proves that the Beatles weren't the *only* rock stars creating chemically seasoned greetings for their unsuspecting fans every December.

the rest:
Here They Come! 🎜🎜🎜 (Columbia, 1965)
Midnight Ride 🎜🎜🎜 (Columbia, 1966)
The Spirit of '67 🎜🎜🎜 (Columbia, 1966/Sundazed, 1996)
Greatest Hits 🎜🎜🎜🎜 (Columbia, 1967)
Revolution! 🎜🎜🎜 (Columbia, 1967/Sundazed, 1996)
Something Happening 🎜🎜🎜 (Columbia, 1968/Sundazed, 1996)
Collage 🎜🎜🎜 (Columbia, 1970/alala music, 1996)
Greatest Hits—Live 🎜🎜🎜 (Remember, 1996)
The Best of Paul Revere & the Raiders 🎜🎜 (Sony Special Products, 1997)

Generic Rock Live II ♫♫♫ (Image Designs, 1997)

worth searching for: Both *Goin' to Memphis* (Columbia, 1968, prod. Chips Moman) and *Alias Pink Puzz* (Columbia, 1969, prod. Mark Lindsay) demonstrate just how remarkable a singer Lindsay could be, especially when given material as challenging as "Soul Man" (even Isaac Hayes and David Porter give their praise on the former's liner notes) and "Let Me" (originally released as a single under the nom-de-group Pink Puzz, it tricked even *Rolling Stone* into believing Columbia had signed a hot new rock group of Zeppelin-like ferocity). Meanwhile, the video *The Last Mad Man of Rock & Roll* (MCA Home Entertainment, 1986) captures the later Raiders in all of its crazed, current glory.

solo outings:
Mark Lindsay:
A Golden Classics Edition ♫♫♫ (Collectables, 1996)
Video Dreams ♫♫♫ (alala music, 1996)

influences:
◄◄ Jerry Lee Lewis, Spike Jones, Bill Haley & His Comets

►► The Monkees, the Unknowns, Brotherhood, T.J. Tyler

Gary Pig Gold

The Reverend Horton Heat
See: Heat, The Reverend Horton

Revolting Cocks
See: Ministry

The Rezillos
Formed 1976, in Edinburgh, Scotland. Disbanded 1978.

John Callis, guitar, vocals; Angel Patterson, drums; Eugene Reynolds, vocals; Fay Fife, vocals; William Mysterious, bass, saxophone (1976–78); Gail Warning, backing vocals (1976–77, 1978); Hi-Fi Harris, guitar (1976–77); D.K. Smythe, bass (1976–77); Simon Templar, bass (1978).

One of the relatively few U.K. punk acts to fully embrace trashy pop culture with the same giddy glee as American forebears the Dictators and the Ramones, the Rezillos made records that bounced off the walls and wallowed in their own willful junkiness. It was exactly the sort of band that's never built to last, though Fay Fife and Eugene Reynolds continued for a bit in much the same vein with their next band, the Revillos. John Callis joined the somewhat less wacky Human League and co-wrote the hit "Don't You Want Me."

what's available: *Can't Stand the Rezillos—The (Almost) Complete Rezillos* ♫♫♫ (Sire, 1993, prod. various) includes the group's sole studio album, 1978's *Can't Stand the Rezillos*, both sides of a non-LP single, and all but one track from the group's posthumous live album, *Mission Accomplished . . . but the Beat Goes On.* Whatta friggin' rush! The disc's 15 studio tracks careen with unbridled pop energy, with tunes such as "Top of the Pops," "No," and "I Can't Stand My Baby" demanding that you crank up the stereo and commence to jumping up and down like a big stupidhead having a righteous good time. The live tracks, taken from the group's farewell performance, are a swell souvenir and include otherwise-unavailable Rezillos covers of "Land of 1,000 Dances" and "Ballroom Blitz."

influences:
◄◄ The Dictators, the Ramones, the Kinks, the Dave Clark Five, Gerry & the Pacemakers, the Sex Pistols

►► The B-52's, Shonen Knife, Redd Kross

see also: *Human League*

Carl Cafarelli

Emmit Rhodes
See: The Merry-Go-Round

Marc Ribot
Born May 21, 1954, in Newark, NJ.

This mainstay of the Downtown New York scene, a former member of the Lounge Lizards, is a versatile, inventive guitarist heard frequently and often extensively on albums by Madeleine Peyroux, Medeski, Martin & Wood, Ellery Eskelin, the Klezmatics, John Zorn, David Sanborn, Caetano Veloso, Marisa Monte, Elvis Costello, Tom Waits, Marianne Faithfull, Allen Ginsburg, T-Bone Burnett, and many more. He played in a group called the Real Tones that backed soul singers and other types traveling without a band—people like Wilson Pickett, Solomon Burke (Ribot is on his *Soul Alive!* album), and Chuck Berry. On his own albums, adding many other instruments to his toolbox, Ribot covers an expansive stylistic territory, always in distinctive fashion. Representative of the younger avant-garde that refuses to exclude pop materials, he skews familiar tunes and styles into non-Euclidean shapes, and makes avant-garde techniques listener-friendly.

what to buy: *Rootless Cosmopolitans* ♫♫♫♫ (Island, 1990, prod. Arthur Moorhead) mixes shockingly deconstructed covers of Sammy Cahn's "I Should Care," Jimi Hendrix's "The Wind Cries Mary," George Harrison's "While My Guitar Gently Weeps," and Duke Ellington's "Mood Indigo" with Ribot originals, positing a fresh amalgam of jazz, rock, and avant-garde. Exhibiting a wry humor, Ribot's style has nothing to do with fusion in the genre sense, and sometimes produces oddly beautiful abstract structures.

what to buy next: *Shrek* ♫♫♫ (Avant, 1994, prod. Marc Anthony Thompson, Marc Ribot) is mostly performed by Ribot's group of that name, which here includes Soul Coughing bassist Sebastian Steinberg. Closing with Albert Ayler's "Bells," this instrumental record is more consistently abstract than *Rootless Cosmopolitans*. On many of Ribot's albums his solo recastings of well-known tunes have been highlights. *Don't Blame Me* ♫♫♫ (DIW, 1995, prod. Gert-Jan Blom, Marc Ribot) has only three originals and includes his takes on jazz standards ("I'm in the Mood for Love," "Don't Blame Me," "Body and Soul," "Dinah," "These Foolish Things," etc.) and Albert Ayler's "Ghosts," Duke Ellington's "Solitude," and Charlie Haden's "Song for Che." The level of concentration required to follow the subtle logic of the terrorism he perpetrates on standards sometimes makes this heavy—but rewarding—listening.

the rest:

The Book of Heads ♫♫♫ (Tzadik, 1995)
Shoe String Symphonettes ♫♫♫♫ (Tzadik, 1997)
Marc Ribot Y Los Cubanos Postizos ♫♫♫ (Atlantic, 1998)

worth searching for: Two albums on a small Belgian label are worth hearing. In fact, *Requiem for What's His Name* (Les Disques du Crepuscule, 1992, prod. Kirk Yano, Marc Ribot) is utterly essential. It's built along the same lines as *Rootless Cosmopolitans* but with slightly greater self-assurance. The irreverent "Yo, I Killed Your God" memorably mocks anti-Semitism and perhaps religion itself, while a cover of Howlin' Wolf's "Commit a Crime" displays a stunning array of stinging blues licks. *Solo Guitar Works of Frantz Casseus* (Les Disques du Crepuscule, 1993, prod. Ilana Pelzig Cellum), a tribute to Ribot's Haitian-American guitar teacher, lets him show off impeccable classical guitar technique on lyrical, romantic pieces heavily influenced by the rhythms and harmonies of Haiti. Shrek shows up again on *Subsonic 1* (Subsonic/Sub Rosa, 1994, prod. Anthony Coleman), a confusingly split CD that's half Ribot, half solo Fred Frith. Ribot is at his most avant-garde here.

influences:

◀◀ Derek Bailey, Jimi Hendrix, Eugene Chadbourne, Arto Lindsay, Fred Frith, Frantz Casseus, John Zorn, Bill Frisell, Captain Beefheart

▶▶ Brad Schoeppach, David Tronzo, Danny Blume

Steve Holtje

Cliff Richard

Born Harry Rodger Webb, October 14, 1940, in Lucknow, India.

Cliff Richard has always been big in Britain—the empire's Elvis, if you will. He's had more hits in Britain than anyone but the King, for that matter, and these days he even holds his own alongside more contemporary (and dare we say trendy?) hitmakers such as Oasis and Blur. In America? Hey, we *have* Elvis

(or had him, at least). Richard has never meant much over here—even during his early '60s heyday, when he was backed by his fabulous band the Shadows—a star act in its own right with guitarist Hank Marvin considered a hero amongst protégés such as Jeff Beck and Jimmy Page. In the United States Richard has had all of nine singles in the Top 40, two of them duets with Olivia Newton-John ("A Little in Love" and "Daddy's Home").

whats available: *The Cliff Richard Collection* ♫♫♫♫ (Razor & Tie, 1994, prod. various) is all you'll find in the racks on these shores, and it's a pretty skimpy representation. For the real story, check out any number of import hits sets.

worth searching for: The best of those imports is *40 Golden Greats* (Virgin, 1993, prod. various), a two-CD set that isn't complete but is certainly a more comprehensive introduction. For the Shadows, *The EP Collection* (See for Miles, 1989, prod. various) is the most readily available title on these shores—again not the full story but at least a taste of the magic.

influences:

◀◀ Lonnie Donegan, Frank Sinatra, Bobby Helms, Bill Haley

▶▶ The Beatles, David Essex, Bryan Adams

Gary Graff

The Richards

See: The Flashcubes

Keith Richards

Born November 18, 1943, in Dartford, England.

The Rolling Stones guitarist's solo retaliations to Mick Jagger's mid-'80s "defection" proved once and for all which one of the Glimmer Twins has the piss and vinegar—in case anyone still wondered. Keith Richards's solo work is a raw, sloppy free-for-all that would barely qualify as demo for some rock acts. And Richards's voice, never a honey bear, is now a ravaged strep-throat croak. But if the Stones could still clang and rattle with the disheveled grace at the heart of Richards's solo albums, we'd still think they were the greatest rock 'n' roll band in the world.

what to buy: *Talk Is Cheap* ♫♫♫♫ (Virgin, 1988, prod. Keith Richards, Steve Jordan) features "Take It So Hard" and a grooving rhythm section of Jordan and Charley Drayton.

what to buy next: *Live at the Hollywood Palladium* ♫♫♫ (Virgin, 1991, prod. Keith Richards, Steve Jordan, Don Smith) takes the virtues of *Talk Is Cheap* to stage, where Richards's backup band, the X-pensive Winos, rocks with ragged glory. *Main Offender* ♫♫♫ (Virgin, 1992, prod. Keith Richards, Steve Jordan, Waddy Wachtel) continues in the same vein as the debut, highlighted by "Wicked As It Seems" and the swinging "Eileen."

worth searching for: The CD single *Wicked As It Seems* (Virgin, 1993, prod. Keith Richards, Steve Jordan, Waddy Wachtel) carries live tracks and a previously unreleased version of "Key to the Highway."

influences:

◄◄ Elmore James, Chuck Berry, Jimmy Reed, Buddy Guy

►► Bash & Pop, Izzy Stradlin

see also: *The Rolling Stones, Mick Jagger*

Allan Orski

Kim Richey

Born December 1, 1956, in Zanesville, OH.

Like John Hiatt, Kim Richey has paid enough dues and sold enough songs to make her one of those rare "integrity" artists that a record company signs more for their credibility cachet than sales figures—which means she gets a little more rope creatively and a little less pressure to "deliver." It's a comfortable situation that resulted in an impressive 1995 self-titled solo debut that showcased her natural instincts for blurring the lines between pop, rock, country, and folk and for writing insightful, incisive lyrics about that gray area between heart-fluttering romance and ego-bandaging recovery. She might have leased out two of her catchiest songs to Radney Foster ("Nobody Wins") and Trisha Yearwood ("(Believe Me Baby) I Lied"), but Richey has saved her most personal material for herself, not out of greed but out of necessity. There's something about the way her quavering voice describes running away from a doomed relationship ("It's just me and one good wiper blade up against the rain"), wondering whether to stick it out ("Lately we've been missing something/love is wearing at the seams"), and acknowledging the futility ("After all was said and done/there was nothing left to do") that makes you appreciate the difference between hearing a song and truly feeling it.

what to buy: *Bitter Sweet* 𝄞𝄞𝄞 (Mercury Nashville, 1997, prod. Angelo, John Leventhal) substitutes the jangly crackle that producer Richard Bennett brought to her first album with a softer but equally compelling sound built around acoustic guitars, banjos, and accordions that suits the longing passion of these songs. Her pop savvy comes through on "I Know," which echoes Joni Mitchell's *Court and Spark* era, and "Lonesome Side of Town," which could easily pass for an old Del Shannon hit. More important, Richey's voice hovers over the straight-forward arrangements without reverb or other studio enhancements, lending a natural, comforting intimacy to such moving, melodic numbers as "Fallin'," the retro-country "To Tell the Truth," and the jaunty "I'm Alright."

the rest:

Kim Richey 𝄞𝄞𝄞 (Mercury Nashville, 1995)

worth searching for: Before he formed a duo with Radney Foster, Bill Lloyd released a collection of Beatlesque pop demos recorded between 1983 and 1986, called *Feeling the Elephant* (Throbbing Lobster/Bar None, 1987, prod. Bill Lloyd). The haunting last cut, "Everything's Closing Down," features one of Richey's first recorded vocals.

influences:

◄◄ John Hiatt, Mary Chapin Carpenter, Joni Mitchell

►► Radney Foster, George Ducas, Trisha Yearwood

David Okamoto

Jonathan Richman /Jonathan Richman & the Modern Lovers

Born 1951, in Boston, MA.

If you thought Ronald Reagan's leap from the movie screen to the White House was a stunner, consider Jonathan Richman's left-turn from underappreciated father of punk rock to heel-clicking, soul-baring hopeful romantic. As the leader of an early '70s Boston bar band called the Modern Lovers—which also featured future Talking Heads keyboardist Jerry Harrison and future Cars drummer David Robinson—Richman created a brooding, Velvet Underground–derived sound that yielded such influential three-chord classics as "Roadrunner" and "Pablo Picasso." But even back then he wasn't afraid to express his deepest feelings and darkest fears, an unflinching honesty that pervades his work to this day—even though he's now funneling those emotions through stripped-down '50s- and '60s-inspired ditties that range from offbeat covers (Bette Midler's "The Rose," the theme from *Moulin Rouge*) to disarming paeans to awkward slow dancing ("They're Not Tryin' on the Dance Floor") and dressing down for a date ("Everyday Clothes"). Cynics dismiss him as childish and self-consciously cute, but they haven't been paying attention since the days of "I'm a Little Dinosaur" and "Hey There Little Insect." Even though his recent breakup with his longtime wife darkened his attitude, Richman used 1996's *Surrender to Jonathan* to come to terms with his pain and himself. His world remains full of treasured moments and small pleasures, where growth is measured in wrinkles, not milestones, and where true love is still a quest, not an anachronism.

what to buy: Mopey and minimalistic, *Modern Lovers* 𝄞𝄞𝄞𝄞 (Beserkley/Rhino, 1975, prod. John Cale) is the album that launched a thousand garage bands with "Roadrunner," "Pablo Picasso," and "She Cracked." The mostly acoustic *Back in Your*

Life 🎵🎵🎵 (Beserkley, 1979, prod. Matthew King Kaufman, Glen Kolotkin, Kenny Laguna) contains both his silliest ("I'm Nature's Mosquito," "Party in the Woods Tonight") and most sublime ("Affection," "Back in Your Life") material. *Jonathan Sings!* 🎵🎵🎵🎵 (Sire, 1983, prod. Peter Bernstein) marks an important transition as Richman learns how to celebrate life and love from an adult's perspective and a child's heart. "This Kind of Music," which champions rock 'n' roll as something to be felt and not merely heard, and "The Neighbors," about not letting other people control your life, are as empowering as they are entertaining. *I, Jonathan* 🎵🎵🎵🎵 (Rounder, 1992, prod. Brennan Totten) is the most consistent of the recent work, although it would be worth the price just for the uplifting "A Higher Power" and the funky "I Was Dancing in the Lesbian Bar."

what to buy next: *Surrender to Jonathan* 🎵🎵🎵 (Vapor, 1996, prod. Andy Paley) is an inspiring celebration of finding closure after separating from his wife. A gurgling Hammond organ and a horn section lend a soulful sincerity to such disarmingly honest songs as "Just Look at Me," "My Little Girl's Got a Full-Time Daddy Now," and "Not Just a 'Plus-One' on the Guest List Anymore," an affecting anthem of independence that uses rock-concert terminology not as a gimmick, but as a dead-on metaphor.

what to avoid: The self-indulgent, sonically anemic *Jonathan Richman* 🎵🎵 (Rounder, 1989, prod. Brennan Totten) contains some great tunes—Ronnie Dawson's "Action Packed" and Richman's "Everyday Clothes"—but they're drowned out by droning instrumentals, foreign-language ditties, and a painful spoken-word number called "I Eat with Gusto, Damn! You Bet."

the rest:
Jonathan Richman:
Jonathan, Te Vas a Emocionar 🎵🎵 (Rounder, 1984)
Rockin' and Romance 🎵🎵🎵 (Twin Tone, 1985)
It's Time for Jonathan Richman 🎵🎵🎵 (Upside, 1986)
The Beserkley Years 🎵🎵🎵🎵 (Rhino, 1987)
Jonathan Goes Country 🎵🎵🎵🎵 (Rounder, 1990)
Having a Party with Jonathan Richman 🎵🎵🎵🎵 (Rounder, 1991)
You Must Ask the Heart 🎵🎵🎵 (Rounder, 1995)
I'm So Confused N/A (Vapor, 1998)

Jonathan Richman & the Modern Lovers:
Modern Lovers Live 🎵🎵🎵 (Beserkley/Rhino, 1977)
Jonathan Richman & the Modern Lovers 🎵🎵🎵 (Beserkley, 1977)
Rock 'n' Roll with the Modern Lovers 🎵🎵 (Beserkley/Rhino, 1977)
Modern Lovers 88 🎵🎵🎵 (Rounder, 1988)
Precise Modern Lovers Order 🎵🎵🎵 (Rounder, 1994)

worth searching for: *Chartbusters: The Best of Beserkley 1975–1978* (Rhino, 1986, prod. Matthew King Kaufman, Glen Kolotkin), a reissue of the 1975 compilation of rare tracks by labelmates the Rubinoos, Greg Kihn, and Earth Quake, contains four Richman rarities: "The New Teller," a joyful rocker about his crush on a bank teller; a heartfelt cover of the Showmen's "It Will Stand"; "Government Center"; and a bouncier, post-John Cale rendition of "Roadrunner."

influences:
◀◀ Velvet Underground, Chuck Berry, the Ventures
▶▶ Poi Dog Pondering, Ben Lee, Beck

David Okamoto

Ride

Formed 1988, in Oxford, England. Disbanded 1995.

Mark Gardener, vocals, guitar; Andy Bell, vocals, guitar; Steve Queralt, bass; Laurence Colbert, drums.

After launching its career as the voice of England's blank generation (i.e., the so-called "shoe gazers"), the Oxford quartet went through some interesting changes. From the shiftless sonic layers of feedback on 1990's *Smile* EP to the assured pop bite of 1992's *Going Blank Again* to 1994's rootsy *Carnival of Light*, Ride rarely trod the same ground twice. But as the music became more disparate, so did the band members' individual interests. Ride had split up by the time 1995's *Tarantula* was completed, though hearing a band falling apart at the seams still made for engaging listening.

what to buy: *Nowhere* 🎵🎵🎵🎵 (Sire/Reprise, 1990, prod. Marc Waterman) is a sonic monster, using layers of guitars, wispy vocals, and hard-hitting drums to help re-define British rock at the outset of the decade. The decidedly American rock vibe of *Carnival of Light* 🎵🎵🎵🎵 (Sire/Reprise, 1994, prod. John Leckie) shows that Ride was more than a one-trick pony.

what to buy next: *Going Blank Again* 🎵🎵🎵 (Sire/Reprise, 1992, prod. Ride, Alan Moulder) contains Ride's most pop-oriented and accessible batch of songs, particularly the single "Twisterella."

the rest:
Smile 🎵🎵🎵 (Sire/Reprise, 1990)
Tarantula 🎵🎵 (Sire, 1996)

worth searching for: *Live Light* (Mutiny, 1995) is a sanctioned bootleg released during the awkward interim between *Carnival of Light* and *Tarantula*. The sound quality is superlative, as is the comprehensive selection of songs.

solo outings:
Andy Bell (with Hurricane No. 1):
Hurricane No. 1 🎵 (Sire. 1997)

influences:
◀◀ The Smiths, My Bloody Valentine, House of Love
▶▶ Oasis, Chapterhouse, Slowdive

Aidin Vaziri

Andrew Ridgely

See: George Michael

Amy Rigby

Born Amy McMahon, in Pittsburgh, PA.

At its essence, "pop" music—that irrepressible celebration of romantic yearning marked by chiming Rickenbackers and soaring, Beatlesque harmonies—is considered the province of peach-fuzzed, gung-hopeful youngsters. But the subject matter of classic pop—the rush of infatuation, the crush of disappointment, the fear of trying again—isn't alien to songwriters over age 35: they've just been around long enough to know that while most pop focuses on either falling in love or falling apart, the most fascinating themes lie in-between, which is where most of life is spent. No artist in the past decade has understood that better than Amy Rigby, whose stunning 1996 solo debut, *Diary of a Mod Housewife*, introduced a sharp-eyed, softhearted songwriter who knows that adulthood magnifies, rather than dulls, the ache of broken hearts and unfulfilled dreams. Starting her career in the late '80s with New York cowpunk quartet the Last Roundup, Rigby later became the creative force behind the Shams, a quirky folk-pop trio proudly consisting of three women over age 30 who signed to Matador Records in 1991 but only lasted for one album and an EP. Embracing the full-time responsibilities of raising her daughter as a single mom, Rigby developed the penetrating insight that marks her *Diary*. Whether she's addressing communication-impaired lovers, overwhelmed working women, or giving voice to her unrequited crush on a younger bookstore clerk, Rigby never lapses into self-pity: she writes about her life as it exists, not as she wishes it was, and remains brave enough to face down her fears in public.

what to buy: A pure pop album informed by the soul-searching cycle of hurt and healing, *Diary of a Mod Housewife* ♪♪♪♪ (Koch, 1996, prod. Elliot Easton) loses nothing in melodic accessibility but gains everything in depth and perspective. The hilarious "20 Questions" mixes Nancy Sinatra–like sass with the bluster of *Highway 61*–era Dylan. "Down Side of Love" sets reality ("That tingling feeling when you're first holding hands/gives way to dealing with a list of demands") to an Everly Brothers twang. And the heavenly "Don't Break the Heart" starts as a warning but turns into an achingly vulnerable plea.

the rest:
(With the Last Roundup) *Twister!* ♪♪♪ (Rounder, 1987)
(With the Shams) *Quilt* ♪♪♪ (Matador, 1991)
(With the Shams) *Sedusia* ♪♪♪ (Matador EP, 1993)
Middlescence N/A (Koch, 1998)

worth searching for: The promotional single for "20 Questions" (Koch, 1997, prod. Elliot Easton) boasts two non-LP B-sides: the

solo acoustic "Housecleaning" and "Against the Law," a 1995 live number featuring the World Famous Blue Jays.

influences:

◄◄ Marshall Crenshaw, Everly Brothers, Nancy Sinatra, the Roches

►► Jill Sobule, Kate Jacobs, John Wesley Harding

David Okamoto

Will Rigby

See: The dB's

The Righteous Brothers

Formed 1962, in Los Angeles, CA. Disbanded 1968. Subsequent reunions in 1974 and throughout the 1980s and 1990s.

Bill Medley (born September 19, 1940, in Santa Ana, CA), vocals; Bobby Hatfield (born August 10, 1940, in Beaver Dam, WI), vocals.

The archetypal blue-eyed soul team, the Righteous Brothers churned out a steady procession of classic rock 'n' roll—with "Little Latin Lupe Lu" at the apex—long before even meeting Wagnerian producer Phil Spector, who assured the duo pop immortality on their first collaboration, the epochal 1965 #1 hit "You've Lost That Lovin' Feelin'." By matching Bill Medley's oozing baritone with Bobby Hatfield's ecstatic tenor, the pair could generate sparks with their furious, almost intuitive vocal trade-offs. After splitting with Spector following a string of massive hits with Medley at the helm, the Brothers proved they learned their lessons well, etching a pop perfect recreation of the Spector sound on "(You're My) Soul and Inspiration," which also hit #1. After splitting up and reforming—on a guest appearance on the *Sonny & Cher* television show, no less—the Righteous Brothers returned to the Top 5 in 1974 with "Rock 'n' Roll Heaven," a relatively cheesy piece of formula radio fodder fashioned for them by the songwriting-production team of Dennis Lambert and Brian Potter, who were experiencing similar Top 40 successes at the time with the Four Tops and the Tavares. The re-emergence of the Spector-produced "Unchained Melody" on the 1990 soundtrack of the film *Ghost* led to yet another reformation (Medley, in the meantime, scored a #1 hit on a duet with Jennifer Warnes with "(I've Had) The Time of My Life" from the *Dirty Dancing* soundtrack), leaving the pair headlining oldies but goodies shows and casino main rooms with a slickly produced act honed to a fare-thee-well over four decades of performing.

what to buy: Released in the wake of the *Ghost* soundtrack, *Unchained Melody: The Very Best of the Righteous Brothers* ♪♪♪ (PolyGram, 1990, prod. various) covers the basics of the group's hit repertoire with little chaff amidst the wheat.

what to buy next: Before linking up with Spector, Medley and Hatfield combined on a succession of rollicking R&B-influenced

sides collected on *The Moonglow Years* 𝄫𝄫𝄫 (PolyGram, 1991, prod. various).

what to avoid: The budget-rack perennial *The Best of the Righteous Brothers, Vol. 2* 𝄫 (Curb, 1993) features lackluster re-recordings of their classic '60s material mixed in with weaker later material.

the rest:
Anthology: 1962–1974 𝄫𝄫𝄫𝄫 (Rhino, 1989)
Reunion 𝄫𝄫 (Curb, 1991)
Rock 'n' Roll Heaven 𝄫 (CEMA Special Products, 1992)
The Best of the Righteous Brothers 𝄫𝄫 (Curb, 1993)

worth searching for: *Some Blue-Eyed Soul* (Moonglow, 1964) is the deepest and most consistent of the individual albums from the duo's peak period. If you want to watch the duo strutt their stuff during its prime years, check out *Shindig Presents: The Righteous Brothers* (Rhino Home Video, 1990). Classic stuff.

influences:
◀◀ Don & Dewey, Ray Charles

▶▶ The Walker Brothers, Daryl Hall & John Oates

Joel Selvin and Ken Burke

Rising Sons
See: Ry Cooder

Brian Ritchie
See: Violent Femmes

Rites of Spring
See: Fugazi

Johnny Rivers
Born John Ramistella, November 7, 1942, in New York, NY.

Raised in Baton Rouge, Louisiana, and christened with his stage name by Alan Freed during a summer trip to New York, Johnny Rivers arrived in Los Angeles in 1960 and worked as a record producer and writer before becoming a star as a regular at the Whiskey a Go Go in 1963 during its discotheque incarnation. His version of Chuck Berry's "Memphis," and his debut album, recorded "live, very live" there, became one of 1964's biggest sellers—no mean feat during the first year of the British Invasion. He found great musicians, employing only the best of L.A. sessionists (producer Lou Adler, bassist Joe Osborn, drummer Hal Blaine, and keyboardist Larry Knechtel before they became known as one of rock's master rhythm sections). But Rivers's lasting gift is his taste in songs and writers: Chuck Berry, Sam Cooke, Arthur Alexander, Willie Dixon, Pete Seeger, P.F. Sloan, Jimmy Webb (Rivers discovered him), Holland/Dozier/Holland, Gene Vincent, Van Morrison; Rivers had

hits with songs by all of them. With Adler, Rivers founded Dunhill Records, which helped establish L.A. as a recording center and was home to the Mamas & the Papas, Barry McGuire, Scott McKenzie, Steppenwolf, and the Grass Roots. For his own Soul City imprint, Rivers produced the Fifth Dimension's "Up, up, and Away." The hits slowed after 1973, and Rivers emerged again after the '80s as a born-again soul singer who includes an Elvis tribute in his act.

what to buy: The two discs that make up *Anthology: 1964–1977* 𝄫𝄫𝄫𝄫 (Rhino, 1991, prod. Lou Adler, Johnny Rivers, Bill Inglot) include everything you need—all the hits, a few surprises, and a nice booklet that analyzes Rivers's 13-year chart run. If you don't want to go that deeply in his catalog, try the single-disc *Greatest Hits* 𝄫𝄫𝄫𝄫 (Capitol, 1996).

what to buy next: *Johnny Rivers at the Whiskey a Go Go* 𝄫𝄫𝄫 (Imperial, 1964/Beat Goes On, 1995, prod. Lou Adler) features tight arrangements and the introduction of Hal Blaine, one of rock's all-time great drummers, who really struts his stuff in this trio setting. On disc it's packaged with its sequel, *Here We Go Go Again*. Though his own songs don't measure up to his great cover standards, *Last Train to Memphis* 𝄫𝄫𝄫 (Soul City, 1998) is a pleasant enough light-rock album with blues and gospel overtones.

what to avoid: You can do better than the chintzy 10 tracks on *Greatest Hits* 𝄫 (CEMA Special Products, 1992/1994).

the rest:
At the Whiskey a Go Go/Here We a Go Go Again 𝄫𝄫𝄫 (Imperial, 1964/Beat Goes On, 1995)
Johnny Rivers Rocks the Folk/Meanwhile Back at the Whiskey a Go Go 𝄫𝄫 (Imperial, 1965/Beat Goes On, 1996)
Totally Live at the Whiskey a Go Go 𝄫𝄫𝄫 (EMI-America, 1995)
Last Boogie in Paris 𝄫𝄫𝄫 (Varese Village, 1995)
Greatest Hits 𝄫𝄫𝄫 (Soul City, 1998)
Memphis Sun Recordings 𝄫𝄫𝄫𝄫 (Soul City, 1998)

worth searching for: For the hard-to-find *Johnny Rivers Greatest Hits,* (MCA, 1985, prod. Johnny Rivers), Rivers re-recorded versions of nine early hits, including "Secret Agent Man" and "Summer Rain," and improves on several of the earlier, cloying arrangements. For *Changes/Rewind* (Imperial, 1966–67/1992, prod. Lou Adler), Rivers traded in the suit-and-tie of his Whiskey days for peace-and-love beads and leather, the great outdoors, and the more introspective songs of Jimmy Webb. Unfortunately, the two-fer package is now out of print.

influences:
◀◀ Chuck Berry, Jimmy Reed, Dick Holler, Jimmy Clanton, Elvis Presley, Jerry Lee Lewis, Trini Lopez, Mose Allison

▶▶ John Mellencamp, the Doobie Brothers, Bob Seger

Leland Rucker

Archie Roach

Born in Framingham, Australia.

Archie Roach, an Australian Aborigine, was taken from his parents and told they had died when he was very young. This fiction was also told to the white Cox family that adopted him. (The action was one of thousands that were all part of an Australian campaign to assimilate the Aborigines into the white culture.) Learning of this fundamental deceit sent Roach into a tailspin—rebelling against his foster parents and, perhaps, against himself. He hit the bottle hard, then began a search for his real family and took to wandering, supporting himself by playing guitar. His foster family's love of Hank Williams started him on his musical path. Eventually, he found one of his older sisters in a chance encounter in a bar and began the process of healing. All the while he was writing songs that both reconciled and illustrated the ugliness of his experience. These songs caught the ear of guitarist Steve Connolly and his colleague, singer-songwriter Paul Kelly. They helped get Roach recorded during the early '90s, and Roach has recorded two more albums since. He often performs with his wife, Ruby Hunter.

what to buy: Roach's debut album, *Charcoal Lane* ⅊⅊⅊⅊ (High-Tone, 1992, prod. Steve Connolly, Paul Kelly), remains his best, perhaps because it sums up the experience of an Aborigine in white-run Australia without the refinement of his later efforts. For a songwriter who writes long narratives, Roach has a deft touch with melody, always keeping them interesting. "Took the Children," which recounts the Australian project that took Aborigine children from their parents, is a heartbreaking "protest" song. Roach also deals with just plain heartbreak too, on a wonderfully plaintive country tune called "I've Cried," which resonates with the ghost of Hank Williams.

what to buy next: *Jamu Dreaming* ⅊⅊⅊ (HighTone, 1993, prod. David Bridie) is just incrementally less memorable than *Charcoal Lane*. The intensity of the message and Roach's passionate delivery are just as strong as on the debut album, but the highlights aren't as high. On *Looking for Butter Boy* ⅊⅊⅊ (HighTone, 1997, prod. Malcolm Burn), Roach tightens things up a bit, with a strong collection of tunes that once again revisits his aboriginal lyric themes but with more musical punch.

influences:
◄◄ Hank Williams, Woody Guthrie

►► Paul Kelly, Bruce Springsteen, John Wesley Harding

Salvatore Caputo

Rick Roberts

See: Firefall

Robbie Robertson

See: The Band

Smokey Robinson & the Miracles

Formed 1957, in Detroit, MI.

William "Smokey" Robinson (born February 19, 1940, in Detroit, MI), vocals (1957–72); Ronnie White (died 1997), vocals; Bobby Rogers, vocals; Warren "Pete" Moore, vocals; Claudette Rogers, vocals (1957–64); William Griffin, vocals.

Berry Gordy Jr. owned Motown, but Smokey Robinson was the label's king. A singer and songwriter who befriended Gordy during the late 1950s, Robinson was Motown's go-to guy. He wrote the label's first #1 pop hit, "My Guy," for Mary Wells, and its biggest, "My Girl," for the Temptations. Sensing a theme here? As an artist, Robinson wrote and performed some of the sweetest and most poetic love songs in pop music history. No less than Bob Dylan called him "America's greatest living poet," and the British band ABC celebrated Robinson in song with "When Smokey Sings." In his prime, Robinson was able to convey passion, pain, longing, and any other emotion with just a few words and his own flexible vocals—particularly his ability to sweep into an ear-clutching falsetto. The Miracles were no simple backup group, either; the others—particularly the late Ronnie White (who co-wrote "My Girl") and Bobby Rogers—served as creative foils, while Robinson and Claudette Rogers were married for nearly 25 years. On his own, Robinson coined a whole new pop music genre—the pillow-talk "Quiet Storm"—though his hits have become considerably more sporadic. He actually left Motown during the early '90s, though he remains an occasional ambassador for the label.

what to buy: *Anthology: The Best of Smokey Robinson & the Miracles* ⅊⅊⅊⅊ (Motown, 1995, prod. Smokey Robinson) is a marvelous two-CD distillation that has all the hits—"Ooo Baby Baby," "Going to a Go-Go," "I Second That Emotion," "The Tears of a Clown"—plus some important album tracks. *A Quiet Storm* ⅊⅊⅊ (Motown, 1975/1989, prod. Smokey Robinson) is a landmark solo album, a sexy, whispery affair that launched a whole new realm of music.

what to buy next: While some of the other Motown box sets have their share of filler, *The 35th Anniversary Collection* ⅊⅊⅊⅊ (Motown, 1994, prod. various) reminds us that with a talent like Robinson on board, it's not hard to have four discs worth of wonderful music (including selections from his solo career and from the post-Smokey Miracles). Robinson's *One Heartbeat* ⅊⅊⅊ (Motown, 1987, prod. various) is another fine solo album, a return to form after several fallow years with the hits "Just to See Her" and the title track. *The Ultimate Collection* ⅊⅊⅊ (Motown, 1997, prod. various) is a suitable gathering of Smokey's solo hits, while the like-titled *The Ultimate Collection* 🎵🎵🎵 (Motown, 1998, prod. various) does the same for Robinson with the Miracles.

what to avoid: *Motown Superstar Series, Vol. 18* 🎵🎵 (Motown) is, in this case, a redundancy.

the rest:
Smokey Robinson & the Miracles:
Cookin' with the Miracles 🎵🎵 (Motown, 1962/1994)
Christmas with the Miracles 🎵🎵🎵 (Motown, 1963)
Going to a Go-Go 🎵🎵🎵 (Motown, 1965)
Greatest Hits, Vol. 2 🎵🎵🎵 (Motown, 1968)
The Season for Miracles 🎵🎵🎵 (Motown, 1970)
The Tears of a Clown 🎵🎵🎵 (Motown, 1970)
Whatever Makes You Happy: More of the Best 🎵🎵🎵 (Rhino, 1993)
Motown Legends: The Ballad Album 🎵🎵🎵 (ESX, 1994)

Smokey Robinson:
Blame It on Love & All the Great Hits 🎵🎵🎵 (Motown, 1983/1990)
Double Good Everything 🎵🎵 (SBK/EMI, 1991)
Cruisin'—Being with You 🎵🎵🎵 (ESX, 1995)

worth searching for: Here's a true mark of Robinson's talents: His vocal on "We've Saved the Best for Last" actually makes a Kenny G album—*Silhouette* (Arista, 1988)—worth buying.

influences:
◀◀ Jackie Wilson, Clyde McPhatter, Sam Cooke

▶▶ Paul McCartney, Michael Jackson, Terence Trent D'Arby, Babyface

Gary Graff

Tom Robinson Band /Sector 27

Tom Robinson Band formed 1977, in London, England. Disbanded 1979. Sector 27 formed 1979, in London, England. Disbanded 1980.

Tom Robinson Band: Tom Robinson (born 1951 in Cambridge, England), vocals, bass; Danny Kustow, vocals, guitar; Mark Ambler, keyboards (1977–79); Brian "Dolphin" Taylor, drums (1977–79); Ian Parker, keyboards (1979); Preston Heyman, drums (1979). Sector 27: Tom Robinson, vocals, guitar; Jo Burt, bass; Stevie B., guitar; Derek Quinton, drums.

Though he got more attention for being openly gay and proudly singing his anthem "Glad to Be Gay," Tom Robinson's explosive band contributed to the rich new wave movement that rose in the Sex Pistols' wake. The band's U.K. hit "2-4-6-8 Motorway" is among the finest driving songs ever recorded, and Robinson's explicit politics gave his songs a social punch. Like many of the flag-waving punks, Robinson's muse eventually dissolved, and he spent the rest of his career behind the scenes.

He still puts out an album now and then, and he still contributes to gay rights and anti-AIDS causes, but he now has a young son and a relationship with a woman. Robinson touchingly acknowledged the changes in his life, and the death of punk, in the 1994 Irish-style ballad "Days."

what to buy: The American version of the Robinson Band's debut, *Power in the Darkness* 🎵🎵🎵 (Harvest, 1978/Razor & Tie, 1993, prod. Chris Thomas), captures the group's early spirit and includes the single "2-4-6-8 Motorway."

what to buy next: The band's more polished follow-up, *TRB Two* 🎵🎵🎵 (Harvest, 1979/Razor & Tie, 1993, prod. Todd Rundgren), contains a duet with Peter Gabriel that became a small U.K. hit. Sector 27's only album, *Sector 27* 🎵🎵 (I.R.S., 1980, prod. Steve Lillywhite), isn't quite as good as Robinson's former band incarnation, but it works out OK.

what to avoid: Robinson's string of solo records, many released only outside the U.S.—including *Hope and Glory* 🎵🎵 (Geffen, 1984, prod. Robin Millar, Tom Robinson)—are close to pointless.

the rest:
North by Northwest 🎵🎵🎵 (I.R.S., 1982)
Love over Rage 🎵🎵🎵 (Rhythm Safari, 1994)
Having It Both Ways 🎵🎵🎵 (Cooking Vinyl, 1996)

worth searching for: Most people bought *The Secret Policeman's Ball* (Island, 1980, prod. Martin Lewis) to hear Pete Townshend play Who songs as an acoustic solo act. But Robinson sneaks in two wonderful performances—his strident-and-powerful "Glad to Be Gay" and the wistful "1967 (So Long Ago)."

influences:
◀◀ The Kinks, the Who, Todd Rundgren, Bob Dylan

▶▶ Elvis Costello, John Wesley Harding, Pansy Division, Me'Shell Ndegéocello

Steve Knopper

Robyn

Born Robin Miriam Carlsson, June 12, 1979, in Stockholm, Sweden.

Robyn was born into a family of entertainers—her parents are Willhelm Carlsson, a stage director, and Maria Ericson, an actress, both of whom were members of Scheherazade, a theater group that traveled through Europe. While Robyn was in elementary school, the group disbanded, and her parents joined the Royal Dramatic Theater in Stockholm. Robyn entered the entertainment business at a young age, loaning her voice to characters in Swedish cartoons such as *The Trip to Melonia* and the film *Anglahund*. Her songwriting skills surfaced at age 11, when she wrote "In My Heart" about her parents' divorce. That song led to her record deal with BMG/RCA at age 15. Robyn performed an *a capella* rendition of "In My Heart" during intermission of a Legacy of Sound concert at her secondary school, Eriksdalsskolan; after being "knocked out" by Robyn's performance, Legacy of Sound singer Meja took Robyn's telephone number. The chance meeting led to a recording session with the band's label, Ricochet, which was later acquired by BMG.

what's available: The soulful "In My Heart" appeared on Robyn's debut album *Robyn Is Here* ♫♫♫ (RCA, 1997, prod. Peter Swartling), a collection of spunky, relentlessly addictive pop songs. "In My Heart" is amazingly heart-felt for an 11 year old—"You said that it never should be like this and when/I was a little child I never had this on my mind/But now it is like it is/and I don't think it's gonna be a change." *Robyn Is Here* covers a range of emotions, from puppy love in the syncopated rhythms of "Show Me Love" to questionable relationships in the Janet Jackson–styled "Just Another Girlfriend." At first listen, Robyn could be tagged just another synth-happy Swede, but her deftly written lyrics put her above the rest.

influences:

⏮ Janet Jackson, Amber

Christina Fuoco

The Roches

Formed 1976, in Greenwich Village, NY.

Maggie Roche, guitar, keyboards, vocals; Terre Roche, guitar, vocals; Suzzy Roche, guitar, vocals.

Graduates of the Greenwich Village folk scene, Maggie, Terre, and Suzzy Roche stood out like crewcuts at a Grateful Dead concert when they released their self-titled debut in 1979: Folk was dead, punk was threatening, and the idea of three sisters harmonizing around acoustic guitars was hardly hip. Yet their songwriting was filled with quirky humor, and their voices purposely didn't weave so much as collide, flirting with atonalism and eschewing traditional rules of harmony singing. Alternately pretty ("The Married Men"), powerful ("The Hallelujah Chorus"), and punishing ("Bobby's Song"), their unison sound was so daring and distinctive that the trio spent the better part of a decade harnessing its force and fighting with record companies over the best direction to follow. Such recent albums as *A Dove* and *Can We Go Home Now?* showed they've finally won both battles. But the 1995 death of their father from emphysema and Alzheimer's took an emotional toll on the sisters, and they decided to temporarily take a breather from each other. Suzzy resurfaced in 1997 with a moving solo album called *Holy Smokes*; Terre has been playing New York clubs with her jazz-influenced band, Terre Roche & Her Moodswings.

what to buy: A clarion-calling card if there ever was one, *The Roches* ♫♫♫♫ (Warner Bros., 1979, prod. Robert Fripp) is a mes-

merizing acoustic showcase framed around such striking compositions as "Hammond Song," "Married Men," and the giddy "Mr. Sellack." The immediacy and intimacy of Fripp's "audio verite" production captures every nuance from breathing sounds to the squeaks of sliding fingers on guitar strings. *Keep on Doing* ♫♫♫ (Warner Bros., 1982, prod. Robert Fripp) includes the stunning *a capella* version of "The Hallelujah Chorus" and the strange but endearing "The Largest Elizabeth in the World." The sisters' relentless quest to weave pop elements and band arrangements around their harmonies is finally fulfilled on *A Dove* ♫♫♫♫ (MCA, 1992, prod. Stewart Lerman).

what to buy next: *Nurds* ♫♫♫ (Warner Bros., 1980, prod. Roy Halee) is a brave attempt to shoehorn them into the new-wave movement with such oddities as "Bobby's Girl," "The Boat Family," and the hysterically self-deprecating "Death of Suzzy Roche."

what to avoid: *No Trespassing* **woof!** (Rhino, 1986, prod. Joe Terry, Andy Bloch, Roches) is a lifeless four-song EP recorded after the trio split from Warner Bros.

the rest:
Another World ♫♫♫ (Warner Bros., 1985)
Speak ♫♫♫ (MCA, 1989)
We Three Kings ♫♫♫ (Rykodisc, 1990)
Will You Be My Friend ♫♫♫ (Baby Boom Music, 1994)
Can We Go Home Now ♫♫♫ (Rykodisc, 1995)

worth searching for: *Seductive Reasoning* (Columbia, 1975, prod. Paul Simon, Paul Samwell-Smith), a pre-Suzzy folk album, was co-produced by Simon after Maggie and Terre backed him on *There Goes Rhymin' Simon*.

solo outings:
Suzzy Roche:
Holy Smokes ♫♫♫ (Red House, 1997)

influences:
⏮ Laura Nyro, Simon & Garfunkel, Kate & Anna McGarrigle
⏭ The Murmurs, the Story

David Okamoto

Rock en Español

There's always been a truism in rock 'n' roll: sing it in English or don't bother to sing it at all. Despite fervent cults for German art-rock, French cabaret, and Japanese noise, native English-speakers have relegated most foreign-language pop to the back of the musical bus. But the Spanish-language world is fighting back and it has a potent weapon: rock en Español. As with so much of the globe, many pop/rock musicians in Spain and Latin America (as well as Latino players in the U.S.) merely imitated their Anglo-American counterparts during the '50s through the '70s. There were exceptions, of course. From Ritchie Valens through Santana and Los Lobos, the West Coast began exporting a unique Latino rock subculture—though much of it was in English. That started to change during the '80s, when musicians all over Spain, Latin America, and the United States—raised on rock and ranchera, beatbox and bolero—began mixing it all up and singing about things that mattered to them, in Spanish—global commercialism be damned. Unsurprisingly, rock en Español got its initial start in countries with the closest ties to the Unites States or Europe, namely Mexico, Argentina, and Spain. Despite disdain or outright hostility from local authorities, "los roqueros" flocked around such acts as El Tri, a smoky-voiced Mexican blues-rock outfit whose roots go back to the '60s and Mexico City's working class, and Charly Garcia, a musical rebel with a cause in a clamped-down Argentina. It wasn't until the early '90s, though, that this movement bubbled up from the underground and became a force with which the English-speaking world has had to reckon. Spanish folk-rock duo Duncan Dhu signed to Sire and teamed with Argentinian rocker Miguel Mateos for a small-scale U.S. tour that proved there was an audience outside their home countries. Meanwhile, back home, the socially aware salsa-punk-cumbia-Afro-pop of Maldita Vecindad (Mexico), sassy alternative rock of Soda Stereo (Argentina), dreamy, swirling rock of Caifanes (Mexico), electro-dance grooves of Los Prisioneros (Chile), punk folklorico of Cafe Tacuba (Mexico), punk-funk-ska of Los Fabulosos Cadillacs (Argentina), sublime, quirky pop of Fobia (Mexico), beautiful, post-McCartney pop of Fito Paez (Argentina), lightweight pop-reggae of Mana (Mexico), and the heavy, Doors-like rock of Heroes del Silencio (Spain) began filling clubs and stadiums. No doubt the movement has been helped along by the collapse of the region's military regimes, the introduction of MTV Latino, and the large Spanish-speaking population in los Estados Unidos. By the mid-to late '90s, there was cool stuff coming out of Panama (Los Rabanes), Venezuela (Desorden Publico, Los Amigos Invisibles), Colombia (Aterciopelados), Peru (Pedro Suarez-Vertiz), and the United States (Maria Fatal, Los Olvidados, King Chango, Yeska). In fact, rock en Español could end up being a victim of its own success. With its own Grammy category, at least two slick California-based fanzines (*Retila, La Banda Elastica*), specialty record labels (Aztlan, Grita!), and increased media exposure, the new musical genre could find its unique, fiery cross-cultural musical and political attitudes crushed by hype and a broader, mainstream audience. However, until then, rock en Español—with its often ferocious, soccer game–style live shows, musicians who can skillfully play both sides of the rhythmic border, and lyrics honed by culturally different situations—proves that rock's innate spirit doesn't talk only in English and can speak to everyone.

what to buy: Two compilations are absolute musts—*Silencio= Muerte: Red Hot + Latin* ♪♪♪♪ (PolyGram/Hola, 1996, prod. various) and *Reconquista! The Latin Rock Invasion* ♪♪♪♪ (Rhino/Zyanya, 1997, prod. various). The former, a high point in the anti-AIDS "Red Hot" benefit discs, pairs leading Latin lights with cutting-edge English-language performers: Los Lobos with Money Mark; Cafe Tacuba with David Byrne; and Los Fabulosos Cadillacs with Fishbone. The latter compilation is more of a historical sampler of the genre, though compiler Ruben Guevara keeps things on the punk and political end of the spectrum.

what to buy next: In terms of individual acts, here's the essential list: Maldita Vecindad, *El Circo* ♪♪♪♪ (BMG Latin, 1991, prod. Gustavo Santaolalla), a perfect introduction to the genre with its heady blend of cross-continental styles and social observation; Fito Paez, *Circo Beat* ♪♪♪♪ (WEA Latina, 1994, prod. Phil Manzanera, Fito Paez), the Beatles-meet-Elvis Costello in Buenos Aires; Aterciopelados, *La Pipa de la Paz* ♪♪♪♪ (BMG Latin, 1996, prod. Phil Manzanera), inventive, intelligent rock fronted by the charismatic Andrea Echeverri; Los Fabulosos Cadillacs, *Rey Azucar* ♪♪♪♪ (Sony Discos, 1995, prod. Chris Frantz, Tina Weymouth), a propulsive pastiche of ska, reggae, and punk with some top-shelf guest stars (Mick Jones, Deborah Harry, Big Youth); Caifanes, *El Silencio* ♪♪♪♪ (BMG Latin, 1992, prod. Adrian Belew), moody yet hooky Cure-like art-rock; Soda Stereo, *Cancion Animal* ♪♪♪♪ (CBS Discos, 1990, prod. Gustavo Cerati, Zeta Bosio), muscular pop-psychedelia alt-rock; Los Amigos Invisibles, *The New Sound of the Venezuelan Gozadera* ♪♪♪♪ (Warner Bros./Luaka Bop, 1998, prod. Andres Levin), a party-rocking blend of disco, acid jazz, and bossa-nova lounge; Todos Tus Muertos, *Dale Aborigen* ♪♪♪♪ (Grita!, 1996, prod. Todos Tus Muertos, Guillermo Picolini), ultra-political Bad Brains-ish punk-funk from a group fronted by two Afro-Argentines; Fobia, *Amor Chiquito* ♪♪♪ (BMG Latin, 1995, prod. Gustavo Santaolalla, Fobia), clever and quirky pop-rock; Cafe Tacuba, *Cafe Tacuba* ♪♪♪ (WEA Latina, 1992, prod. Gustavo Santaolalla) and *Avalancha de Exitos* ♪♪♪ (WEA Latina, 1996, prod. Gustavo Santaolalla, Anibal Kerpel), both fun, stylistic hodgepodges, ranging from Mexican traditionalism to Beck-ish post-modernism, marred only by the sometimes screeching vocals of Cosme (who changes names every album); Mana, *Donde Jugaran Los Ninos?* ♪♪♪ (WEA Latina, 1992, prod. Fher, Alex Quintana, Jose Quintana), the best album from the Guadalajara outfit whose mix of Police-lite reggae, environmentalism, and suave good looks has made it a major act at home and the first rock en Español act to move to the arena level in the States. Finally, rock en Español is as diverse as its English counterpart. There's ska, rap, and even Celtic-Hispano rock. One of the best of the ska-influenced bands is Desorden Publico, whose two U.S. albums—*Canto Popular de la Vida y Muerte* ♪♪♪ (Sony Discos, 1995, prod. Carlos Savalla) and *Plomo Revienta* ♪♪♪♪

(Sony Latin, 1997, prod. K.C. Porter)—are breezy and infectious. *Pura Eskañol: Latin Ska Underground* 𝄞𝄞𝄞 (Aztlan, 1997, prod. various) is a solid compilation of U.S.-based acts. Rap en Español exploded in the mid-'90s thanks to albums such as Molotov's *Donde Jugaran Las Ninas?* 𝄞𝄞𝄞 (Universal, 1997, prod. Gustavo Santaolalla), whose title is a take-off on a popular Mana album, and Control Machete's *Mucho Barato* 𝄞𝄞𝄞 (PolyGram Latino, 1996, prod. Jason Roberts, Antonio Hernandez), both albums from Mexican acts very much influenced by Cypress Hill and the Beastie Boys. The best, though, may come from Spain's Latino Diablo, whose *El Mundo No Es de la Gente Humilde* 𝄞𝄞𝄞𝄞 (Grita, 1998, prod. Latino Diablo) pounds hard yet has subtle touches. Also from Spain, Celtas Cortos combine a love of both Celtic and Spanish cultures on the knockout *En Estos Dias Inciertos . . .* 𝄞𝄞𝄞𝄞 (WEA Latina, 1996, prod. Eugenio Munoz, Celtas Cortos).

worth searching for: Some of the most striking music in the genre doesn't get released by American labels, and Latin divisions of U.S. companies are notoriously dim-witted about promoting rock en Español. That means seeking out mom-and-pop or small chains in Latino neighborhoods that carry imports from Latin America to find such gems as Spain's Los Planetas, whose *Super 8* (BMG Mexico, 1995) is an explosion of Replacements/Nirvana–style riff-o-rama.

influences:

◀◀ Santana, Los Lobos, War, Los Brazos, Ritchie Valens

▶▶ Ozomatli, Maria Fatal

Cary Darling

Lee Rocker
/Lee Rocker's Big Blue

See: Stray Cats

Rocker's Hi-Fi

Formed in Great Britain.

Richard Wittingham, samplers, programming; Glyn Bush, samplers, programming.

Rocker's Hi-Fi is a British duo that revels in the sample-heavy, dance-club aesthetic. Mixing everything under the sun—house, hip-hop, techno, and old school reggae dub—the group cultivates a massive, momentous audio sound whose sole intent is to make you dance. Richard Wittingham comes from a punk background, but he also spent lots of time DJing and throwing raves. Bush loves anything musical.

what's available: *Mish Mash* 𝄞𝄞𝄞 (Warner Bros., 1997, prod. Rocker's Hi-Fi) is the group's only U.S. album to date. It features a barrage of media-heavy samples mixed with dub

rhythms and dance grooves. While the music of Rocker's Hi-Fi sounds good in a club, its cluttered, noisy sound can cause headaches at home.

worth searching for: The duo's wide-ranging love of music probably makes them pretty good DJs. As part of the *DJ Kicks* series on K7 Records in the U.K., Rocker's Hi-Fi put together a mix CD of some of its favorite dance tracks, *DJ Kicks: The Black Album*, that comes off as being pretty darn funky.

influences:

◀◀ King Tubby, Double D & Steinski, Cold Cut

▶▶ Crystal Method, Chemical Brothers

Joseph Patel

Rocket from the Crypt

Formed 1989, in San Diego, CA.

Speedo (born John Reis), vocals, guitars; Petey X, bass, vocals; N.D., guitar; Atom, drums; Apollo 9, saxophone (1991–present); J.C. 2000, trumpet (1995–present).

Primarily a seven-inch singles factory (16 between 1991–96), Rocket from the Crypt is a band that abuses rock clichés by masterfully blending punk energy with mainstream accessibility. Its Phil Spector Wall-of-Sound-on-crack production fused with '60s garage gutters and Famous Flames–ish horn attacks has turned RFTC into San Diego's undisputed rock 'n' roll royalty. Named by band leader Speedo as a tribute to Rocket from the Tombs (the late '70s Cleveland band that evolved into Pere Ubu), Rocket's prodigious output of West Coast sonic soul has brought fun and chicanery back to '90s alterna-rock.

what to buy: *All Systems Go* 𝄞𝄞𝄞𝄞 (Headhunter/Cargo, 1993, prod. John Reis) unwittingly is the definitive Rocket. Originally a compilation of B-sides and studio out-takes intended as a Japanese-only tour release, copies were quickly smuggled back into the States (at $30 a pop!), forcing the band to reissue it here. More complete and, where necessary, re-recorded, the domestic version of *All Systems Go* captures the raw, hook-laden RFTC without the studio polish, and it saves one from the maddening task of trying to accumulate the original (and essential) vinyl. *RFTC* 𝄞𝄞𝄞𝄞 (Interscope, 1998, prod. Kevin Shirley) is the studio platter the group has always seemed to have in it. With flight assistance from Jim Dickinson (producer of Big Star, the Replacements, and others), Anton Fig (from David Letterman's band), and Holly Golightly (the Headcoatees), *RFTC* rips, with more hooks than a Squeeze anthology. Don't miss "Eye on You," a duet in which Speedo and Golightly swing better than Nancy Sinatra and Lee Hazelwood ever dreamed of.

what to buy next: A crank-it not spank-it special (see the cover art), *Circa: Now!* 𝄢𝄢𝄢 (Headhunter, 1992/Interscope, 1993 prod. John Reis) offers a more fully fleshed-out Rocket sound to complement its silvery riffs and singsongy chants.

what to avoid: The one-sided single "Gold" **woof!** (Drunken Fish, 1992, prod. John Reis) is pure dreck—a sham, actually. Fans of Lou Reed's grating *Metal Machine Music* might appreciate the grin, but don't bother.

the rest:

Paint As Fragrance 𝄢𝄢𝄢 (Headhunter, 1991)
Scream, Dracula, Scream! 𝄢𝄢𝄢 (Interscope, 1995)
The State of Art Is on Fire 𝄢𝄢𝄢 (Sympathy for the Record Industry, 1995)

worth searching for: The LP-only *Hot Charity* (Perfect Sound, 1995, prod. John Reis) was limited to 5,000 red vinyl copies and introduces J.C. 2000 and his rocking trumpet.

influences:

◀◀ The Beatles, Black Flag, Graham Parker, the Ramones

▶▶ Lucy's Fur Coat, Back off Cupids

Jim Cummer and Barry M. Prickett

Rockpile

See: Dave Edmunds

Paul Rodgers

See: Bad Company

Tommy Roe

Born 1942, in Atlanta, GA.

Best known as one of bubblegum music's biggest hit makers, Tommy Roe began his recording career as a rocker in the same mold as Buddy Holly. During the early '60s, Roe cut a number of top-notch R&B tunes, including the 1962 chart-topper "Sheila" (a song much like Holly's "Peggy Sue"), "Stagger Lee," and "Everybody." As R&B fell behind pop, Roe switched to bubblegum, scoring hits in 1966 with "Sweet Pea" and "Hooray for Hazel." His smash was "Dizzy," a transatlantic hit during 1969. Like other teenybopper idols of the period, Roe switched to country music during the early bloom of the '70s and eventually became a staple of the oldies circuit.

what to buy: *Tommy Roe's Greatest Hits* 𝄢𝄢𝄢 (MCA, 1993, compilation prod. Bill Inglot) is the best of the Roe anthologies, offering 18 hits (including "Sheila," "Hooray for Hazel," "Dizzy," and "Stagger Lee") and excellent liner notes.

the rest:

The Best of Tommy Roe 𝄢𝄢 (Curb, 1990)
Tommy Roe's Greatest Hits 𝄢𝄢 (Curb, 1994)

influences:

◀◀ Buddy Holly

▶▶ 1910 Fruitgum Company, the Music Express, Jimmy Ray

Christopher Scapelliti

The Rolling Stones

Formed 1962, in London, England.

Mick Jagger (born Michael Phillip Jagger), vocals, guitar; Keith Richards, guitar, vocals; Brian Jones (born Lewis Brian Hopkins-Jones; died 1969), guitar (1962–69); Bill Wyman (born William Perks), bass (1962–94); Charlie Watts, drums; Mick Taylor, guitar (1969–74); Ron Wood, guitar (1974–present); Daryl Jones, bass (1994–present).

During its first decade, the Rolling Stones defined the classic rock lineup—two guitars, bass, drums, and a little red rooster crowing out front—and created the enduring standard for how it should sound. The Stones never were much for formal innovation; the group's more experimental tracks and albums sounded contrived next to its expert synthesis of Chicago blues, hard country music, and early rock 'n' roll. Mick Jagger borrowed freely from performers such as James Brown, Jackie Wilson, and Tina Turner, but unlike other British bands smitten by American roots music, the Stones trafficked heavily in irony and distance. Richards succeeded Chuck Berry as rock's primary riff-meister, and Richards and Jagger (a.k.a. the Glimmer Twins) wrote classic melodies and pithy, unsentimental, and frequently just plain cruel lyrics that were the equal of their '60s rivals Bob Dylan and the Beatles. And the group's rhythm section, anchored by the peerless Charlie Watts, made it all swing like nobody's business. Only problem is, the Stones kept the money machine in motion long after the artistic drive waned. Like its blues heroes, the Stones entered their fifties still singing about their overworked mojos and cranking out competent product that bespoke professionalism rather than inspiration.

what to buy: *Aftermath* 𝄢𝄢𝄢𝄢 (London/Abkco, 1966, prod. Andrew Loog Oldham) marked the entry of these erstwhile blues traditionalists into the album-rock pantheon alongside Dylan and the Beatles, with its canny use of sitar, marimba, and dulcimer (all performed by Brian Jones) to augment Jagger's multi-faceted star turn as a vocalist on "Paint It Black," "Lady Jane," and "Under My Thumb." The weakest cuts on *Beggars Banquet* 𝄢𝄢𝄢𝄢 (London/Abkco, 1968, prod. Jimmy Miller) are its best known: "Street Fighting Man" offers a rare political commentary that is musically stirring but lyrically ambivalent; and "Sympathy for the Devil" finds Jagger pandering to the group's bad-boy image. Otherwise, the disc is a tour de force of acoustic-tinged savagery and slumming sexuality, particularly the gleefully flippant "Stray Cat Blues." *Let It Bleed* 𝄢𝄢𝄢𝄢

Mick Jagger of the Rolling Stones (© Ken Settle)

(London/Abkco, 1969, prod. Jimmy Miller) slams the door on the '60s with such harrowing anthems as "Gimme Shelter" and "You Can't Always Get What You Want." *Exile on Main Street* 🎵🎵🎵🎵 (Rolling Stones/Virgin, 1972, prod. Jimmy Miller) got some bum reviews when first issued for its muddy sound and decadent atmospherics. It's now rightly hailed as a masterpiece, and from the passionate yearning of the gospel-tinged "Let It Loose" to the demon fury of "Rip This Joint," it remains a towering survey of the Stones as they reinvent their influences.

what to buy next: *Big Hits/High Tide and Green Grass* 🎵🎵🎵🎵 (London/Abkco, 1966, prod. Andrew Loog Oldham) is an impeccable 12-cut summary of the Stones' pre-*Aftermath* singles; of the hits collections, it's surpassed only by the pricey but worth-it box set, *The Singles Collection* 🎵🎵🎵🎵 (Abkco, 1989, prod. various), which documents the band's first and best decade of music-making. *Sticky Fingers* 🎵🎵🎵🎵 (Rolling Stones/Virgin, 1971, prod. Jimmy Miller) has the most famous cover art of any Stones album (Andy Warhol's zippered crotch shot) and—"Brown Sugar" excepted—among the most darkly weary music. But amid the druggy drama, the luminous beauty of "Sway" and "Moonlight Mile" is redemptive. *Some Girls* 🎵🎵🎵🎵 (Rolling Stones/Virgin, 1978, prod. Glimmer Twins) is the last gasp of greatness, with Richards's "Before They Make Me Run" serving as what should have been a fitting epitaph: "See my tail lights fading/Not a dry eye in the house." Those who insist on owning something from the latter-day, Steel Wheelchairs–era Stones should head straight for *Stripped* 🎵🎵🎵🎵 (Virgin, 1995, prod. Don Was, Glimmer Twins), the first live album by the group that isn't superfluous, with its revelatory "unplugged" treatment of several classic tracks compensating for a tepid cover of Dylan's "Like a Rolling Stone."

what to avoid: Before *Stripped*, the Stones released five live albums, all of them stiffs. None offer tracks that improve upon the studio originals, including: *Got Live if You Want It* 🎵 (London/Abkco, 1966, prod. Andrew Loog Oldham); the overrated *Get Yer Ya's-Ya's Out* 🎵🎵 (London/Abkco, 1970, prod. Glyn Johns, Rolling Stones); *Love You Live* 🎵 (Rolling Stones, 1977, prod. Glimmer Twins); *Still Life* 🎵 (Rolling Stones, 1982, prod. Glimmer Twins); and *Flashpoint* 🎵 (Rolling Stones, 1991, prod. Chris Kimsey, Glimmer Twins).

the rest:
The Rolling Stones: England's Newest Hit Makers 🎵🎵🎵🎵 (London/Abkco, 1964)
12 x 5 🎵🎵🎵🎵 (London/Abkco, 1964)
The Rolling Stones, Now! 🎵🎵🎵🎵 (London/Abkco, 1965)
Out of Our Heads 🎵🎵🎵 (London/Abkco, 1965)
December's Children 🎵🎵🎵🎵 (London/Abkco, 1965)
Between the Buttons 🎵🎵🎵🎵 (London/Abkco, 1967)
Flowers 🎵🎵🎵 (London/Abkco, 1967)

Their Satanic Majesties Request 🎵🎵 (London/Abkco, 1967)
Through the Past Darkly (Big Hits, Vol. 2) 🎵🎵🎵🎵 (London/Abkco, 1968)
Hot Rocks 1964–71 🎵🎵🎵🎵 (London/Abkco, 1972)
More Hot Rocks: Big Hits and Fazed Cookies 🎵🎵🎵 (London/Abkco, 1973)
Goats Head Soup 🎵🎵 (Rolling Stones/Virgin, 1973)
It's Only Rock 'n' Roll 🎵🎵🎵 (Rolling Stones/Virgin, 1974)
Made in the Shade 🎵🎵🎵 (Rolling Stones/Virgin, 1975)
Black & Blue 🎵🎵🎵 (Rolling Stones/Virgin, 1976)
Emotional Rescue 🎵🎵 (Rolling Stones/Virgin, 1980)
Sucking in the Seventies 🎵🎵🎵 (Rolling Stones, 1981)
Tattoo You 🎵🎵🎵 (Rolling Stones/Virgin, 1981)
Undercover 🎵🎵 (Rolling Stones/Virgin, 1983)
Rewind (1971–84) 🎵🎵🎵 (Rolling Stones, 1984)
Dirty Work 🎵🎵🎵 (Rolling Stones, 1986)
Steel Wheels 🎵🎵 (Rolling Stones, 1989)
Voodoo Lounge 🎵🎵🎵 (Virgin, 1994)
Bridges to Babylon 🎵🎵🎵 (Virgin, 1997)
No Security 🎵🎵🎵 (Virgin, 1998)

worth searching for: *Jump Back: The Best of the Rolling Stones* (Virgin, 1993, prod. various) is a sparkling-sounding (20-bit mastered) U.K. compilation spanning 1971 to 1993, with exceptional liner notes.

influences:

◀◀ Willie Dixon, Muddy Waters, Chuck Berry, Buddy Holly, Sam Cooke, the Beatles

▶▶ New York Dolls, Aerosmith, Guns N' Roses, Black Crowes

see also: *Mick Jagger, Keith Richards, Ron Wood*

Greg Kot

Henry Rollins /Rollins

Born Henry Garfield, February 13, 1961, in Washington, DC.

Henry Rollins is a one-man industry, simultaneously the leader of a highly respected rock band, actor, author, tireless spoken word performer, publisher, and executive of two record labels. The product of a broken home, Rollins musically started out in D.C.'s SOA, came to prominence and maturity in Black Flag (which he joined at the age of 20), and began leading his Rollins Band (drummer Simeon Cain, guitarist Chris Haskett, and bassist Andrew Weiss—later replaced by Melvin Gibbs) after Black Flag broke up in 1986. The ensemble melds punk and heavy metal in a way that infuriates some punk purists but which prophetically turned out to be the commercial future of alternative rock. (Mix engineer Theo van Eenbergen, later known as Theo Van Rock, is considered a fifth member of the group.) Rollins's spoken word career has become as important as his music; he began publishing his writings through his book company, 2.13.61, which has issued more than a dozen of his books plus work by Exene Cervenka, Hubert Selby, Nick Cave, and more. His no-BS attitude has also made him a popular guest writer for magazines such as *Details* and *Spin*. The external image—multiple tattoos, including a massive sun face covering his back; body pumped up from weightlifting; scowling visage; black shorts and black T-shirt—certainly reflects genuine aspects of his personality but hardly tells the whole story. Rollins listens to music across a broad spectrum, from John Lee Hooker to John Coltrane. He uses most of his money to make available neglected music he loves via Infinite Zero, a label collaboration with Rick Rubin, and 2.13.61 CD, the sonic arm of his publishing company. During the '90s, Rollins also began getting film roles; though hardly a schooled actor, he was effective as a dumb, macho cop in *The Chase* (despite having no license and never having owned a car, he did his own stunt driving) and an idealist underground doctor in *Johnny Mnemonic*.

what to buy: *Weight* ♪♪♪♪ (Imago, 1994, prod. Theo Van Rock) was a hit on the strength of the sardonic "Liar" and its amusing video, but "Disconnect" is the best track, typical of Rollins's elevated self-analysis. *Come in and Burn* ♪♪♪♪ (Dreamworks, 1997, prod. Steve Thompson) builds on the progress of *Weight*, just as hard-hitting both lyrically and musically as the earlier (pre-Gibbs) albums but increasingly intricate and well-produced. *Do It* ♪♪♪♪ (Texas Hotel, 1988, prod. Ian MacKaye, Theo van Eenbergen) has three good outtakes from *Life Time*—including a cover of the Pink Fairies' title cut—and 12 hot live tracks from a 1987 European tour that improve on the studio versions. The best version of the desolately alienated "Lonely" is the touchstone of Rollins's indie period. The spoken word double CD *Human Butt* ♪♪♪♪♪ (1/4 Stick/Touch & Go, 1992) finds Rollins weaving long stories drawn from his life, by turns hilarious and poignant—a real, complex, compassionate human being eloquently expressing simple truths.

what to buy next: The studio album *The End of Silence* ♪♪♪♪ (Imago, 1992, prod. Andy Wallace) captures the power and passion of the band's epochal performances on the first Lollapalooza tour. "Low Self Opinion" is the pinnacle of a cleaner, more constructive approach that retains the old power. The two-CD spoken word set *The Boxed Life* ♪♪♪♪ (Imago, 1992) nearly positions Rollins as a stand-up comedian (though he'll deny that label), with funny stories and astute observations concentrating on the nomadic existence of touring. *Everything* ♪♪♪♪ (2.13.61, 1996, prod. Alyson Careaga) matches some of Rollins's most intense, best-written spoken word material with occasional musical accompaniment by free jazz greats Charles Gayle (tenor sax, piano) and Rashied Ali (drums).

what to avoid: With all the live Rollins Band music available, *Turned On* ♪♪ (1/4 Stick/Touch & Go, 1990) is unnecessary. The

sound is not as good as elsewhere, and there's no CD indexing—just one long track for 15 songs. Also avoid *Fast Food for Thought* ♪♪ (Chrysalis EP, 1990, prod. Andrew Weiss, Theo Van Rock), a numbing enterprise by Wartime, a duo comprised of Rollins and Weiss.

the rest:
Music:
Hot Animal Machine ♪♪♪ (Texas Hotel, 1987)
Life Time ♪♪♪ (Texas Hotel, 1988)
Hard Volume ♪♪♪ (Texas Hotel, 1989)
Spoken word:
Big Ugly Mouth ♪♪♪ (Texas Hotel, 1987)
Sweat Box ♪♪♪ (Texas Hotel, 1989)
Deep Throat ♪♪♪♪ (1/4 Stick, 1992)
Live at McCabe's ♪♪♪ (1/4 Stick/Touch & Go, 1993)
Get in the Van ♪♪ (Time Warner Audio Books, 1994)
Black Coffee Blues ♪♪♪ (Thirsty Ear, 1997)

worth searching for: A limited edition of *Weight* comes packaged in a round tin designed like a barbell weight.

influences:

◄◄ Led Zeppelin, Black Sabbath, Bad Brains, Charles Bukowski, Iggy Pop

►► Pearl Jam, Soundgarden, Tool

see also: *Black Flag*

Steve Holtje

The Romantics

Formed 1977, in Detroit, MI.

Wally Palmar, guitar, vocals; Mike Skill, guitar, bass, vocals (1977–81, 1985–present); Richard Cole, bass, vocals (1977–85); Jimmy Marinos, drums, vocals (1977–83, 1995–present); Coz Canler, guitar (1977–83); David Patratos, drums (1983–89); Clem Burke, drums (1989).

The Romantics summed up new wave fashion with signature matching suits and skinny ties, and new wave music with the incredibly infectious singles such as "What I Like about You" and "Talking in Your Sleep." The group's hits are perfectly disposable pop songs, built on classic rock 'n' roll major chords that rehash "Gloria" and "Louie Louie" with grand enthusiasm. Though "What I Like about You" hit just #49 when it came out in 1980, it has been played endlessly at school dances and sports arenas, and on Budweiser commercials and HBO movies. The band went to court during the mid-'90s to win ownership of its songs and—re-united with original singer/drummer Jimmy Marinos—planned another round of recording.

what to buy: *The Romantics* ♪♪♪♪ (Nemperor, 1980, prod. Peter Solley) contains "What I Like about You" and a bunch of other explosive, fun pop singles. *National Breakout* ♪♪♪ (Nemperor,

1980, prod. Peter Solley) offers more of the same and is almost as good—with "Tomboy" and "Stone Pony" as standouts.

what to buy next: *Super Hits* 𝄢𝄢𝄢 (Epic, 1998, prod. various) is a serviceable greatest-hits package, but at 10 songs, it's a bit skimpy.

what to avoid: *Strictly Personal* 𝄢𝄢 (Nemperor/Epic, 1981, prod. Mike Stone) is the band's major misstep, trading the explosive Kingsmen-like garage-pop for bland, overproduced schlock.

the rest:
In Heat 𝄢𝄢𝄢 (Nemperor, 1983)
Rhythm Romance 𝄢𝄢𝄢 (Nemperor, 1985)
What I Like about You (and Other Romantic Hits) 𝄢𝄢𝄢 (Nemperor, 1990)
Made in Detroit 𝄢𝄢𝄢 (Westbound EP, 1993)
King Biscuit Flower Hour Presents 𝄢𝄢𝄢 (King Biscuit Entertainment, 1996)

worth searching for: For the proper context, try *Shake It Up! American Power Pop II (1978–80)* (Rhino, 1993, prod. Gary Stewart), which has "What I Like about You" plus "Tell It to Carrie" alongside songs by the Shoes, Plimsouls, Holly & the Italians, 20/20, the Beat, and other kindred spirits.

influences:
◀◀ The Kingsmen, Them, the Easybeats, the Buzzcocks, Rockpile, the Monkees, the Beatles

▶▶ Green Day, the Offspring, the Proclaimers, the Plimsouls, the Shoes

Tracey Birkenhauer and Steve Knopper

Romeo Void

Formed 1979, in San Francisco, CA. Disbanded 1985.

Debora Iyall, vocals; Frank Zincavage, bass; Peter Woods, guitar; Jay Derrah, drums (1979–80); John Stench, drums (1980–81); Larry Carter, drums (1981–84); Ben Bossi, saxophone.

Romeo Void whomped across the post-punk landscape with a wailing sax, a dark dance beat, and Debora Iyall's detached talk-singing. Vacant love was the main thrust of her songs, which gave some relief to the more vacuous and hollow areas of new wave. The crashing emptiness in the lyrics of 1981's "Never Say Never" ("I might like you better if we slept together") sound like they could have lifted from one of Bret Easton Ellis's despairing '80s novels. Yet the group's only chart hit was the slippery pop of "A Girl in Trouble (Is a Temporary Thing)" in 1984.

what's available: The best of the group's output, including "A Girl in Trouble (Is a Temporary Thing)," can be found on the

band's sole remaining title, the compilation *Warm in Your Coat* 𝄢𝄢𝄢 (Columbia, 1992, prod. various).

influences:
◀◀ Blondie, the Sex Pistols, Siouxsie & the Banshees

▶▶ Human League, Bow Wow Wow, the Vapours

Allan Orski

The Ronettes
/Ronnie Spector

Formed 1959, in New York, NY. Disbanded 1967.

Ronnie Spector (born Veronica Bennett, August 10, 1943, in New York, NY), vocals; Estelle Bennett, vocals; Nedra Talley, vocals.

As lead singer of the remarkable Ronettes, Ronnie Spector's precocious vibrato brought an aura of teen vulnerability and eroticism to the 1960s girl-group sound, yet her many releases since as a solo artist have had limited commercial success. Nevertheless, the voice and attitude Spector displayed on her greatest recordings over three decades ago continues to infect and inspire countless performers to this day.

Ronnie, sister Estelle, and cousin Nedra formed their first group, the Darling Sisters, in 1959 and spent the next several years performing semi-professionally around New York City at sock hops and bar mitzvahs. An audition with Brill Building-producer Stu Phillips led to a contract with Colpix Records in 1961 where, as Ronnie & the Relatives, they released several singles and secured regular engagements dancing and singing back-up at Murray the K's Brooklyn Fox revues and with Joey Dee at the Peppermint Lounge. Although still nondescript vocally, the trio was beginning to invoke notice throughout the burgeoning twist scene for their energetic stage show and unmistakable aura of Spanish Harlem "tough-girl chic." One day early in 1963, frustrated by their continuing lack of success on record, Estelle brazenly picked up the phone, called the hottest producer in town, and arranged for an audition: Needless to say, Phil Spector happened to take that call personally, quickly recognized in Ronnie's Frankie Lymon–style voice the perfect blend of virgin and vixen he'd been searching for, and signed the trio, now known as the Ronettes, to his Philles label. "Be My Baby," one of Spector's finest creations and the Ronettes' biggest-ever hit, was nothing less than a defining moment in the careers of both singer and producer. But while the follow-up singles "Baby I Love You" and "(The Best Part of) Breakin' Up" were rife with hungry, radio-ready sexuality, they failed to make as big an impact, and Spector's growing infatuation with Ronnie personally soon began to yield negative results. She had not been allowed to join the Ronettes on their final tour across

America with the Beatles in 1966 (her cousin Elaine substituted), as the increasingly jealous and possessive Spector by now had her living in virtual seclusion inside his Beverly Hills mansion. The pair married shortly afterwards, and for the next several years Ronnie would be allowed to record a single or two for whatever label Phil was then working with, but no more. Divorced in 1974 (though still battling with Spector to this day in the courts), Ronnie continued recording both as a solo artist and with various makeshift "Ronettes," but only her cameo appearance on Eddie Money's 1986 hit "Take Me Home Tonight" has so far returned her to where she works her magic best: on the airwaves of Top 40 radio.

what to buy: Some of Phil Spector's greatest recordings—which is to say, some of the greatest records ever made—were written for, and spectacularly sung by Ronnie Spector, and they're all included on *The Best of the Ronettes* ♪♪♪♪ (Abkco, 1992, prod. Phil Spector). You'll instantly recognize the hits, but if you're not already familiar with the equally stunning misses (such as "Do I Love You" and "You Came, You Saw, You Conquered"), then by all means put this book down immediately and head for the nearest record store.

what to buy next: The Ronettes' versions of "Frosty the Snowman," "Sleigh Ride," and "I Saw Mommy Kissing Santa Claus" off Phil Spector's *A Christmas Gift for You* ♪♪♪♪ (Philles, 1963/Abkco, 1990, prod. Phil Spector) have become Yuletide standards. The pre- and post-Spector recordings are best represented by *The Colpix and Buddah Years* ♪♪♪ (Sequel, 1994, prod. various) and *Dangerous, 1976–1987* ♪♪♪♪ (Raven, 1996, prod. various), both fine overviews that demonstrate, to varying degrees, how a voice as potent as Ronnie's can overcome even the most vacuous of material (the stock, sub-Brill schmaltz of much of the Colpix sides) and accompaniment (Springsteen's bombastic E Street Band only tends to get in the way of a performer as nuanced as Ronnie on their 1970s recordings together).

worth searching for: In a well-meaning if misguided attempt to update Spector's sound, *Siren* (Polish, 1980, prod. Genya Raven) does contain one deliciously sublime moment: a version of the Ramones' "Here Today, Gone Tomorrow" that demonstrates that while Deborah Harry and Chrissie Hynde may have had the money and push behind them at the time, Ronnie still had the talent—and then some.

influences:

◀◀ Frankie Lymon, Hank Ballard, the Chantels, Little Anthony & the Imperials, George Goldner

▶▶ Joey Ramone, the Bangles, SWV

Gary Pig Gold and Ken Burke

Mick Ronson
Born 1946, in Hull, England. Died April 30, 1993, in London, England.

The author of three little-known solo albums, Mick Ronson was also a silent partner in some of rock's finest moments and a guitar hero whose mix of virtuosity and economy was alien to many others more famous and flashy. He was the musical director for David Bowie's *Ziggy Stardust* period (1972–74), co-creating the sound that first brought Bowie superstardom. He was equally influential coproducing Lou Reed's 1972 comeback album *Transformer*, joining Bob Dylan's legendary Rolling Thunder Revue tour in 1975, collaborating with Mott the Hoople and Ian Hunter through 1989's *Y U I Orta*, and producing Morrissey's acclaimed *Your Arsenal* in 1992. When diagnosed with liver cancer in 1991, Ronson had embarked on an all-star solo project that turned out to be his own posthumous tribute album, *Heaven and Hull*. A musician's musician, Ronson worked until his death, facing the future and not just the end.

what to buy: Ronson's first two albums, *Slaughter on 10th Ave.* (RCA, 1974) and *Play Don't Worry* (RCA, 1975), are combined with some bonus tracks on the two-disc set *Only after Dark* ♪♪♪♪ (Griffin, 1995, prod. Mick Ronson). *Slaughter* is ambitious but random, though finely produced, arranged, and played. The lost glam-rock classic "Only after Dark" still holds up, as do the lean, atonal jams of "Pleasure Man." *Play* is Ronson's most cohesive, assured, and individual album. It stands as a prime example of the glam genre, and features some forward-looking machine sonics and clean-but-full production.

what to buy next: The posthumous *Heaven and Hull* ♪♪♪♪ (Epic, 1994, executive prod. Suzanne Ronson, Sam Lederman, Steve Popovich) is solidly crafted but seldom dynamic. Chrissie Hynde fans will want her *tour-de-force* guest vocal on "Trouble with Me," and "Colour Me" is a prize of dexterous fretwork, inventively verse-heavy pop-drone structure, and Prince-inspired choral vocal.

worth searching for: Ronson's album as a duo with Ian Hunter, *Y U I Orta* (Mercury, 1989), is currently out of print.

influences:

◀◀ David Bowie, Marc Bolan

▶▶ Robyn Hitchcock, Morrissey, Suede, Def Leppard

Adam McGovern

Linda Ronstadt /The Stone Poneys
Born July 15, 1946, in Tucson, AZ.

Any assessment of Linda Ronstadt stands or falls on how strongly you feel about songwriting as an artistic credential.

Ronstadt's not a writer; rather, she interprets the songs of others—often in tones so distinctive and authoritative that they sound like they're her own. The profound influence of Ronstadt's singing mandates a place for her, along with Emmylou Harris, as a major voice in the '70s fusion of country and rock. But where Harris leaned toward country's mountain and bluegrass traditions, Ronstadt mined the throbbing, emotional territory once owned by Patsy Cline. In doing so, she established a model for any number of subsequent pop-rock belters. Ronstadt arrived in Los Angeles at the end of the '60s as singer for the Stone Poneys, scoring her first chart success with 1967's "Different Drum" before the group broke up. Ronstadt eventually emerged as princess of the California rock mafia that included the Eagles, John David Souther, and Jackson Browne—sealing her ascension with the #1 hit "You're No Good" in 1974. But as the decade moved on, so would Ronstadt, and succeeding years have found her acting in Broadway's *The Pirates of Penzance*, recording mariachi music, playing pop standards with Nelson Riddle and his orchestra, dueting with New Orleans' angel-voiced Aaron Neville, and, most recently, recasting rock standards as lullabies. With the occasional exception, the hits are in the past, but Ronstadt does enjoy a body of work that speaks of considerable artistic ambition.

what to buy: *Heart Like a Wheel* 𝄞𝄞𝄞𝄞𝄞 (Capitol, 1974, prod. Peter Asher) and *Prisoner in Disguise* 𝄞𝄞𝄞𝄞 (Asylum, 1975, prod. Peter Asher) exemplify Asher's influential production style and Ronstadt's emotional brand of country-rock. In the poignant title tunes, memorable duets with Harris, and carefully chosen remakes (such as Smokey Robinson & the Miracles' "Tracks of My Tears"), Ronstadt successfully walks the line dividing sadness from sappiness. Some of Ronstadt's best singing of the '80s is on the country-traditional *Trio* 𝄞𝄞𝄞𝄞𝄞 (Warner Bros., 1987, prod. George Massenburg), with Harris and Dolly Parton.

what to buy next: *Hasten Down the Wind* 𝄞𝄞𝄞𝄞 (Asylum, 1976, prod. Peter Asher) completes the '70s trio of Ronstadt/Asher mega-successes and spotlights excellent songwriting by Karla Bonoff and Warren Zevon. Ronstadt is not a definitive artist in either big-band sound or mariachi folk, but her experiments are honorable introductions to those genres. *For Sentimental Reasons* 𝄞𝄞𝄞𝄞 (Asylum, 1984, prod. Peter Asher) is the best of the Riddle records; *Canciones de Mi Padre* 𝄞𝄞𝄞𝄞 (Asylum, 1987, prod. Peter Asher, Ruben Fuentes) pays homage to the vibrant art of such singers as Lola Beltran. Those interested in pre-Asher Ronstadt should seek out *A Retrospective* 𝄞𝄞𝄞 (Capitol, 1977, prod. various), which collects the best of her early output.

what to avoid: *Mad Love* 𝄞𝄞 (Asylum, 1980, prod. Peter Asher) is an ill-advised foray into tough-posturing punk, on which she sounds like the Girls' Citizenship club president trying to smoke her first joint—and swallowing instead of inhaling.

the rest:
Linda Ronstadt:
Hand Sown Home Grown 𝄞𝄞𝄞 (Capitol/EMI, 1969)
Silk Purse 𝄞𝄞𝄞𝄞 (Capitol, 1970)
Linda Ronstadt 𝄞𝄞𝄞 (Capitol, 1972)
Don't Cry Now 𝄞𝄞𝄞𝄞 (Capitol, 1973)
Greatest Hits, Vol. I 𝄞𝄞𝄞𝄞 (Asylum, 1975)
Simple Dreams 𝄞𝄞𝄞 (Asylum, 1977)
Living in the USA 𝄞𝄞𝄞 (Asylum, 1978)
Greatest Hits, Vol. 2 𝄞𝄞𝄞 (Asylum, 1980)
Get Closer 𝄞𝄞𝄞 (Asylum, 1982)
What's New 𝄞𝄞𝄞𝄞 (Asylum, 1983)
Lush Life 𝄞𝄞𝄞𝄞 (Asylum, 1984)
(With Aaron Neville) *'Round Midnight: The Nelson Riddle Sessions* 𝄞𝄞𝄞𝄞 (Elektra, 1986)
Cry like a Rainstorm, Howl like the Wind 𝄞𝄞𝄞 (Elektra, 1989)
Mas Canciones 𝄞𝄞𝄞 (Elektra, 1991)
Frenesi (Elektra, 1992)
Winter Light 𝄞𝄞𝄞 (Elektra, 1993)
Dedicated to the One I Love 𝄞𝄞𝄞 (Elektra, 1996)
We Ran 𝄞𝄞𝄞𝄞 (Elektra, 1998)

The Stone Poneys:
Stone Poneys 𝄞𝄞 (Capitol, 1967/1995)
Evergreen, Vol. 2 𝄞𝄞 (Capitol, 1967)
Stone Poneys and Friends, Vol. III 𝄞𝄞𝄞 (Capitol, 1995)

worth searching for: Ronstadt has made myriad guest appearances on an assortment of albums. Two of the most interesting (and varied): Philip Glass's *1000 Airplanes* (Virgin Classics, 1989) on which her singing humanizes Glass's ethereal minimalism; and *Kermit Unpigged* (Jim Henson Records, 1994) on which she and the frog duet on "All I Have to Do Is Dream."

influences:
◀◀ Patsy Cline, Elvis Presley, Lola Beltran

▶▶ Trisha Yearwood, Celine Dion, Rosanne Cash, Sheryl Crow

Elizabeth Lynch

The Rooks

Formed 1990, in New York, NY.

Michael Mazzarella, guitar, vocals; Kristin Pinell, guitar, mandolin, flute, vocals; Annmarie Gatti, bass (1990–94); Jim Riley, drums (1990–93); Patrick Yourell, drums (1993–present); Nancy Leigh, bass, vocals (1995); Anne Benkovitz, bass, vocals (1995–present).

Perhaps the most highly regarded of all current acts in the broad category of pure pop and power pop, the Rooks are primarily the vehicle for Michael Mazzarella's intelligent, densely layered songwriting. Mazzarella's songs are expressive, emotional, and well-versed in both the human condition and pop music tradition. They're propelled in the Rooks' recordings by Kristin Pinell's authoritative, fluid guitar leads, which add a graceful but powerful punch to Mazzarella's words and music. In years to come, it's likely that the Rooks will be recalled in much the same way we recall Big Star now: an accomplished and influential act whose stature can only grow with the passing of time. Pinell also plays with the Grip Weeds, a superb pop band that took its name from John Lennon's character in the film *How I Won the War*.

what to buy: The Rooks share billing with Twenty Cent Crush on *A Double Dose of Pop!* ♫♫♫♪ (Not Lame, 1995, prod. Michael Mazzarella), a split CD offering nine tracks by the Rooks and eight by Twenty Cent Crush. Although there's nothing wrong with Twenty Cent Crush (a fine pop group in its own right), the Rooks tracks are why you'll buy this, and it's the best-available introduction to their wonderful world. The soaring chorus of "Reasons," the group's signature tune, sounds like some beyond-this-mortal-coil collaboration between Big Star's Chris Bell and the Byrds' Gene Clark, perhaps with Graham Nash chiming in from the land of the living. "Love Said to Me" and "Glitter Best" are equally efficient at inspiring goose pimples.

what to buy next: The five-song EP *Chimes* ♫♫♫ (Not Lame, 1995, prod. Michael Mazzarella) offers a nice stopgap while the band works on the long-delayed *A Wishing Well*. Credited to Mazzarella, *Memories of a Mad Rook* ♫♫♫ (Not Lame, 1997, prod. Michael Mazzarella) is a limited-edition collection of his songwriting demos—get it while you can.

worth searching for: *The Rooks* (Guardian, 1993, prod. Michael Mazzarella), the group's out-of-print debut, includes the first appearance of "Reasons," "Love Said to Me," and "Steeplechase," each of which was subsequently remixed for *A Double Dose of Pop!* It also includes a bunch of tracks not available elsewhere, and some enterprising label should reissue it as a public service.

solo outings:
The Grip Weeds:
House of Vibes ♫♫♫♪ (Ground Up, 1994)

influences:
◀◀ The Beatles, the dB's, Big Star, the Byrds, Brian Wilson

Carl Cafarelli

Diana Ross

Born March 26, 1944, in Detroit, MI.

Smokey Robinson was the king of Motown; Diana Ross was the label's queen. As the focal point of the Supremes, her delicate features, doe-eyed expressions, and clear—if sometimes thin—vocals became symbols for the company's desired image of sophistication and glamour. Motown lore is filled with trash talk about Ross: ego, ambition, *esprit de Me*. And when you read her self-celebratory autobiography, *Secrets of a Sparrow*, or look at the photo of magazine covers she's graced in the booklet for *The Ultimate Collection*, it does seem that modesty is not among Ross's virtues. But she must be given her due as a distinctive talent, with a drive that established her star not only in music but also in movies (*Lady Sings the Blues, Mahogany*). She left Motown to record for RCA in 1981, but eight years later she was back "home," and whatever else is said about her, it's certain that no one would be talking unless she was a star.

what to buy: With only six of its 20 songs overlapping with Supremes anthologies, *The Ultimate Collection* ♫♫♫♫ (Motown, 1994, prod. various) is a good way to sample Ross's solo career, from the epic schmaltz of "Ain't No Mountain High Enough" to heartfelt ode to Marvin Gaye's "Missing You." *Diana* ♫♫♫♫ (Motown, 1980, prod. Nile Rogers) was a smart move forward, bringing in Chic's Nile Rodgers and Bernard Edwards to modernize Ross's sound and launch two of her biggest solo hits, "Upside Down" and "I'm Coming Out."

what to buy next: *Diana & Marvin* ♫♫♫♪ (Motown, 1973, prod. various) is a pleasant summit from two of Motown's brightest lights that was reportedly driven by some real sparks (of anger) in the studio.

what to avoid: The box set *Forever Diana* ♫♫ (Motown, 1993, prod. various) is a padded vanity project that was initially withdrawn from sale due to its poor sound quality (which was corrected upon reissue).

the rest:
Lady Sings the Blues ♫♫♫♫ (Motown, 1972)
Touch Me in the Morning ♫♫♫ (Motown, 1973)
Ain't No Mountain High Enough ♫♫♫♪ (Motown, 1979/1989)
The Boss ♫♫♫ (Motown, 1979)
Diana's Duets ♫♫♫ (Motown, 1982)
Anthology ♫♫♫♫ (Motown, 1986)
Diana Ross ♫♫♫♫ (Motown, 1989)
Live at Caesar's Palace ♫♫♪ (Motown, 1990)
All the Great Hits ♫♫♫♫ (Motown, 1991)
An Evening with Diana Ross ♫♫♪ (Motown, 1991)
The Force behind the Power ♫♫ (Motown, 1991)
Diana Ross's Greatest Hits ♫♫♫♫ (Motown, 1991)
Stolen Moments: The Lady Sings Jazz & Blues ♫♫ (Motown, 1993)
Extended—The Remixes ♫♫♪ (Motown, 1994)
Take Me Higher ♫♫♫ (Motown, 1995)
Greatest Hits: The RCA Years ♫♫♫♫ (RCA, 1997)

worth searching for: Diana, Placido, and Jose? That's Domingo and Carreras to you non-opera buffs, and they make for a classy kind of Supremes on *Christmas in Vienna* (Sony Classical, 1993).

influences:

◀◀ Billie Holiday, Ella Fitzgerald, Smokey Robinson

▶▶ Donna Summer, Cher, Dionne Warwick, Brandy

see also: *The Supremes*

Gary Graff

David Lee Roth

See: Van Halen

Patti Rothberg

Born in New York, NY.

The story goes that while attending art school in New York, Patti Rothberg began playing her music at subway stops in Manhattan. With the '90s record-company interest in riot grrrls, Rothberg managed to parlay her history and a high-quality demo tape into a contract with EMI. No neophyte, Rothberg began her musical education with piano lessons at age three. College (at Boston University) presented a dilemma between her music and her artwork, but she chose art. While studying in Paris, she wrote songs to pass the time. These personal vignettes formed the main body of what she was singing when her manager "discovered" her in the subway.

what to buy: On *Between the 1 and 9* ♫♫♫♫ (EMI-America, 1996, prod. Little Dave Greenberg), Rothberg shows her artistic sophistication both with the self-portraits that adorn the album cover and insert, and with her tight, eclectic songwriting. Certainly, she can be tough as nails ("This One's Mine"), but honesty prevails over posturing. Unlike many others, she can create characters aware of their own foibles: "As long as you're a stranger/You'll stay perfect to me."

influences:

◀◀ Rickie Lee Jones, Joni Mitchell

▶▶ Tracy Bonham, Jewel, Meredith Brooks

Salvatore Caputo

Roxette

Formed 1986, in Sweden.

Marie Fredriksson, vocals; Per Gessle, guitar, vocals.

As Sweden's hottest musical export since ABBA, Roxette has developed a worldwide fan base via its success in America. Per Gessle, a member of popular Scandinavian rocker group Gyllene Tider, first used the name Roxette on a 1984 record by his band, which aspired to crack the more lucrative U.S. market. The gambit failed, but former ABBA manager Thomas Johannson suggested Gessle team with vocalist Marie Fredriksson for a record under the same name in 1986. Although that album was only released in Sweden and Canada, the next album in 1988 brought blockbuster sales in America, fueled by hit singles such as "The Look" and "It Must Have Been Love," the latter from the soundtrack for the film *Pretty Woman*. Combining catchy pop/rock tunes with a new wave–influenced image, the pair enjoyed a string of hits: "Dressed for Success," "Dangerous," and "Joyride." The onset of modern rock during the early '90s spelled doom for the group's commercial ambitions in the States, though it continues to crank out the hits overseas.

what to buy: Grounding catchy pop melodies in the spirit of classic rock and new wave, Roxette's giddy hits connected with the tenor of the late '80s on *Look Sharp* ♫♫♫♫ (EMI, 1988, prod. Clarence Ofwerman), which veers effortlessly from rockers such as "The Look" to soaring ballads such as "Listen to Your Heart" and perky, percolating pop such as "Dressed for Success."

what to buy next: As a further refinement of the formula that conquered the world, *Joyride* ♫♫♫ (EMI, 1991, prod. Clarence Ofwerman, Anders Herlin) is the perfect Roxette follow-up. Songs such as "Knock on Every Door" and "Watercolors in the Rain" pick up exactly where the last album left off.

what to avoid: A confusing collage of live performances and new studio material, *Tourism: Songs from Studios, Stages, Hotel Rooms, and Other Strange Places* **woof!** (EMI, 1992, prod. Clarence Ofwerman), proves a directionless mishmash. And hearing thousands of fans sing along to hits such as "It Must Have Been Love" highlights just how lunkheaded Gessle's lyrics can be.

the rest:

Pearls of Passion ♫ (EMI Sweden, 1986)
Queen of Rain ♫♫ (EMI America, 1992)
Crash! Boom! Bang! ♫♫ (EMI America, 1994)
Baladas en Español ♫♫ (EMI International, 1996)

worth searching for: *Greatest Hits: Don't Bore Us, Get to the Chorus* (EMI, 1995) is an import collection that features the new-look Roxette: Gessle bleached blond and Fredriksson sporting a Susan Powter–style buzz cut.

influences:

◀◀ Eurythmics, the Beatles

▶▶ Ace of Base

Eric Deggans

Roxy Music

Formed 1971, in London, England. Disbanded 1983.

Bryan Ferry, vocals, keyboards; Andy Mackay, saxophone, oboe; Brian Eno, synthesizers, treatments (1971–73); Dexter Lloyd, drums (1971); Roger Bunn, guitar (1971); Graham Simpson, bass (1971–72); Paul Thompson, drums (1971–80); David O'List, guitar (1972); Phil

Manzanera (born Philip Targett-Adams), guitar (1972–83); Rik Kenton, bass (1972); John Porter, bass (1972); Sal Maida, bass (1972–73); John Gustafson, bass (1972–75); Eddie Jobson, violin, synthesizer (1973–78); John Wetton, bass (1975–76); Rick Wills, bass (1976–78); Gary Tibbs, bass (1978); David Skinner, keyboards (1978–83); Paul Carrack, keyboards (1978–80); Alan Spenner, bass (1978–83); Andy Newmark, drums (1980–83).

Roxy Music's sense of style—by turns effete, subversive, sexy, and confounding—was exceeded only by its brilliance as one of the '70s finest art-rock bands. It featured inventive instrumentalists in Andy Mackay and Phil Manzanera, and two bonafide musical visionaries in Bryan Ferry and Brian Eno, whose brief, tumultuous, and enormously influential collaboration was reminiscent of the sparks generated by Lou Reed and John Cale in the Velvet Underground. Roxy never achieved commercial success in America on par with its artistic achievement, in part because of its genre- and gender-bending cool and wicked humor—Ferry at times sang like a tremulous lounge crooner, and his lyrical obsession with unrequited love/lust extended in at least one instance to a blow-up doll on "In Every Dream Home a Heartache." The group burnished some of those edges after a brief hiatus in the mid-'70s, and it scored a few unremarkable hits before calling it quits in 1983.

what to buy: *Siren* 𝄢𝄢𝄢𝄢 (EG/Reprise, 1975, prod. Chris Thomas) is the ultimate synthesis of the group's arty experimentation and adroit, wide-ranging pop instincts. Ferry cruises the land of one-night stands with equal parts fascination and revulsion, and the epiphanies are numerous: "Both Ends Burning," "Just Another High," "Love Is the Drug," "Sentimental Fool."

what to buy next: *Roxy Music* 𝄢𝄢𝄢𝄢 (EG/Reprise, 1972, prod. Peter Sinfield) introduced a twisted pop fabulousness to the U.K. music scene that would resonate for decades. *For Your Pleasure* 𝄢𝄢𝄢𝄢 (EG/Reprise, 1973, prod. Chris Thomas, John Anthony), the second and final Ferry-Eno collaboration, is weirder still, and nearly as good. *Stranded* 𝄢𝄢𝄢𝄢 (EG/Reprise, 1973, prod. Chris Thomas) is a showcase for Ferry's increasingly theatrical vocals. *Avalon* 𝄢𝄢𝄢𝄢 (Warner Bros., 1982, prod. Rhett Davies, Roxy Music) sounds like a new age album in comparison to the early stuff, but Ferry's nuanced vocal performance and the shimmering, sculpted beauty of the arrangements are undeniable.

what to avoid: *The High Road* 𝄢𝄢 (Warner Bros. EP, 1983, prod. Rhett Davies, Roxy Music) finds the band sounding stiff and glossy near the end of its life, redeemed only by a strangely moving cover of John Lennon's "Jealous Guy."

the rest:
Country Life 𝄢𝄢𝄢 (EG/Reprise, 1974)
Viva! 𝄢𝄢𝄢 (EG/Reprise, 1976)
Greatest Hits 𝄢𝄢𝄢 (EG/Reprise, 1977)
Manifesto 𝄢𝄢𝄢 (EG/Reprise, 1979)
Flesh + Blood 𝄢𝄢 (EG/Reprise, 1980)
The Atlantic Years 𝄢𝄢𝄢 (Atco, 1983)
Street Life: 20 Greatest Hits 𝄢𝄢𝄢𝄢 (Reprise, 1989)
Heart Still Beating 𝄢𝄢𝄢 (EG/Reprise, 1990)

worth searching for: *The Thrill of It All* (Virgin U.K., 1995, prod. various) is a four-CD set from Britain that covers plenty of ground, though it doesn't replace the most essential individual albums.

influences:

◀◀ Velvet Underground, Brecht-Weill, Humphrey Bogart, King Crimson, Billie Holiday

▶▶ New York Dolls, Adam & the Ants, Duran Duran, the Cars, ABC, Combustible Edison

see also: *Bryan Ferry, Brian Eno, Phil Manzanara, Paul Carrack*

Greg Kot

Royal Crescent Mob

Formed 1985, in Columbus, OH. Disbanded 1994.

David Ellison, lead vocals, harmonica; B, guitar, vocals; Harold Chichester, bass, vocals; Billy Schwers, drums (1985); Carlton Smith, drums (1986–94).

Royal Crescent Mob garnered critical acclaim for combining dirty rock guitar and a funky backbeat. David Ellison was fond of pointing out that he mowed the lawn of the Ohio Players' Leroy "Sugar" Bonner while growing up and absorbed both funk and punk. The band was put together from the pieces of two groups competing in a local battle of the bands, so they could better use the contest prize: studio time. After two small releases the band was signed by Sire records. But its producers on Sire, Richard Gottehrer and Eric Calvi, were not well suited to funk and whitewashed the proceedings. Despite critical appreciation record sales were disappointing, and Sire dropped the group. Royal Crescent Mob, always hot live, continued gigging and put out a 1992 concert recording, *Destruction 13*, on its own Mobco imprint. The band then retreated to its hometown, playing within driving range on weekends, and managed to put out a final album before Harold Chichester left to spend more time with his family, which ultimately ended the band's run. Chichester later showed up in Howlin' Maggie, playing in a related but inferior style.

worth searching for: None of the band's releases are currently in print. *Omerta* (Moving Target, 1987, prod. Jonathon Myner, Royal Crescent Mob, Montie Temple) is by far the band's best work, with "Get on the Bus" and covers of "Fire" and "The Big Payback." Funky, hard-driving, showing no mercy, it's the must-own album. Fortunately, it was reissued on CD just before the band's demise. Funky but even harder-to-find collections such as *Good Lucky Killer* (Enemy, 1993, prod. Royal Crescent Mob, Montie Temple), the early compilation *Something New, Old, and Borrowed* (Moving Target, 1988), and the live *13 Destruction* (Mobco, 1992, prod. Royal Crescent Mob, Montie Temple) are also consistently rewarding.

solo outings:

Howling Maggie (Harold Chichester):

Honeysuckle Strange 🎵🎵 (Columbia, 1996)

influences:

◀◀ Ohio Players, James Brown, the Stooges, the Dead Kennedys

▶▶ Red Hot Chili Peppers, Infectious Grooves, Mind Funk

Steve Holtje

Royal Crown Revue

Formed 1989, in Los Angeles, CA.

Eddie Nichols, vocals; James Achor, guitar; Daniel Glass, drums; Mando Dorame, tenor sax; Bill Ungerman, baritone sax; Scott Steen, trumpet; Veikko Lepiston, bass.

Royal Crown Revue is one of the oldest bands of the current swing revival. Put together during 1989, it plays straight swing with a touch of jump blues, all to the tune of its self-styled "gangster-bop." With its sharp nice suits and '40s hep-talk, the act came off as a novelty, but one that earned the group opening spots for both Kiss and Neil Diamond. But with the surge of interest in swing culture, RCR suddenly found itself taken seriously for the music and spoken of as one of the forerunners of an old craze suddenly sweeping the country again.

what to buy: *Mugzy's Move* 🎵🎵🎵 (Warner Bros., 1995, prod. Ted Templemann) zips right along, filled with gangster riffs and hoodlum talk, a full set of Louis Jordan–inspired swing that, while coming across occasionally as kitschy, still manages to produce enough energy to satisfy.

what to buy next: Like any true swing band, the canned stuff is great, but the live stuff is even better. All the more reason to pick up *Caught in the Act* 🎵🎵🎵 (Surfdog, 1997, prod. Royal Crown Revue). Although not as polished as *Mugzy's Move,* some of the solos here are worth the price of admission alone.

the rest:

Kings of Gangster Bop 🎵🎵🎵 (BYO/Big Daddy, 1991)
The Contender 🎵🎵🎵 (Warner Bros., 1998)

influences:

◀◀ Louis Jordan, Benny Goodman

▶▶ Big Bad Voodoo Daddy

Anders Wright

Royal Trux

Formed 1987, in New York, NY.

Neil Hagerty, guitar, vocals; Jennifer Herrema, vocals.

Neil Hagerty formed Royal Trux with fellow Washington, D.C., native Jennifer Herrema while he was still a member of the notorious slop-core band Pussy Galore. Pussy Galore once released a song-by-song desecration of the Rolling Stones' walk on the wild side, *Exile on Main Street,* and that aesthetic carried over into the raunch 'n' boogie of Trux. The duo's self-titled debut includes an inner-sleeve photograph that gives a chilling twist to rock's obsession with phallic symbols: a big-city skyscraper as hypodermic needle. Yet Trux's music was championed by tastemakers such as Sonic Youth and Pavement, and in the great indie-rock signing spree of the mid-'90s, the duo found itself briefly employed by Virgin Records. Soon after, Hagerty and Herrema returned to the indie-rock world from which they came and continued to release distinctively sleazy recordings.

what to buy: *Cats and Dogs* 🎵🎵🎵🎵 (Drag City, 1993, prod. Neil Hagerty, Jennifer Herrema) takes the corpse of the Rolling Stones' *Sticky Fingers,* hitches it to the back bumper of a rusty station wagon with bad shocks, and clatters down the highway trailing smoke, syringes, and whiskey bottles.

what to buy next: *Singles, Live, Unreleased* 🎵🎵🎵🎵 (Drag City, 1997, prod. various) is a career retrospective that drifts through the duo's many phases, from tape-loop alchemists to barbed-wire boogie monsters.

what to avoid: *Twin Infinitives* 🎵 (Drag City, 1989, prod. Neil Hagerty, Jennifer Herrema) arrived at the height of the drug daze: an impenetrable mulch of warped guitars, primitive synthesizers, tape loops, and muffled voices.

the rest:

Royal Trux 🎵🎵🎵 (Royal Records, 1988/Drag City, 1993)
Untitled 🎵🎵🎵 (Drag City, 1991)
Thank You 🎵🎵 (Virgin, 1995)
Sweet Sixteen 🎵🎵 (Virgin, 1996)
Accelerator 🎵🎵🎵🎵 (Drag City, 1998)

influences:

◀◀ Butthole Surfers, the Rolling Stones, Blue Öyster Cult

▶▶ Hole, Come, Urge Overkill

Greg Kot

RTZ

See: Boston

The Rubinoos

Formed 1973, in San Francisco, CA. Disbanded 1980.

Jon Rubin, vocals, guitar; Donn Spindt, drums; Royse Ader, bass; Tommy Dunbar, guitars, keyboards, vocals.

There were the Archies, the 1910 Fruitgum Co., and the De-Franco Family—but bubblegum rarely got sweeter, stickier, and unabashedly more goo-goo-eyed than the three-minute outbursts of puppy love songs and schoolboy rock practiced by the Rubinoos–a short-lived group that nevertheless made sweet pop music that stuck in your ears long after the group was gone.

what to buy: The quartet's footnote contribution to the power-pop pantheon was the Raspberries-influenced *Back to the Drawing Board* ✍✍✍✍ (Beserkley, 1979, prod. Matthew King Kaufman, Gary Phillips), a luscious collection of harmony-laden, heel-clicking anthems like "Operator," "Promise Me," "Fallin' in Love," and the irresistible "I Wanna Be Your Boyfriend." The sugar-coated, Stridex-scented sentiments may make your teeth ache, but your heart will never feel so young.

what to buy next: The Rubinoos debuted with the cheesy but cheerful *Rubinoos* ✍✍✍ (Berserkley, 1977, prod. Matthew King Kaufman, Glen Kolotkin, Gary Phillips). Highlights included a wicked Who parody called "Rock and Roll Is Dead" and a heartfelt cover of Tommy James's "I Think We're Alone Now" that rivaled the original and actually grazed the Top 40.

the rest:
Party of Two ✍✍ (Warner Bros., 1983)
Basement Tapes ✍✍✍ (One Way, 1993)
Garage Sale ✍✍✍ (Big Deal, 1994)

influences:
◀◀ The Beatles, the Raspberries, the Modern Lovers
▶▶ Matthew Sweet, the Plimsouls

David Okamoto

ruby

Formed 1994, in Scotland.

Leslie Rankine, vocals, guitar, programming; Mark Walk, guitar, bass, keyboards, programming.

Leslie Rankine used to be the lead singer of the aggro-industrial band Silverfish, but that was before she got her groove on as ruby. Just before electronic dance music shimmied its way into the mainstrem, Rankine and musical partner Mark Walk (with whom she played in the rotating member industrial supergroup Pigface) dropped *Salt Peter* to a perplexed record industry. Soon after, Garbage released its self-titled debut, introducing a dark but fun, funky middle ground between rock

music and electronic dance sounds to the pop charts. Since then, not only is electronic music more widely accepted, but Rankine has appeared in a soda commercial, and ruby has appeared on Lollapalooza's second stage and on a few soundtracks. Hopefully the stars are aligned to help take the group past its cult following on its next release.

what to buy: *Salt Peter* ✍✍✍ (Creation/Work/Columbia, 1995, prod. Mark Walk, Leslie Rankine) is one of the few funky dance albums that would also sound great on just an acoustic guitar; one of the most successful (artistically if not commercially) mergers of beats, samples, and songs.

what to buy next: *Stroking the Full Length* ✍✍✍ (Creation/Work/Columbia, 1996, prod. Varopis) contains remixes by the likes of ruby's own Walk, ruby collaborator William Rieflin (formerly of Ministry), and members of Girls Against Boys and Goldie's Metalheadz.

worth searching for: ruby's bizarre collaboration with Tom Jones on a cover of the Carl Douglas hit "Kung Fu Fighting" on the *Supercop* film soundtrack is worth tracking down.

influences:
◀◀ Pigface, Ministry, nine inch nails

Brian Ives

David Ruffin

See: The Temptations

The Rugburns /Steve Poltz

Formed mid-1990s, in San Diego, CA.

Steve Poltz, vocals; Robert "Doc" Driscoll, guitars; Gregory Page, bass; Stinky, drums.

This San Diego–based quirky pop band has the rare talent of coupling humor with serious issues—sex and love, political righteousness, and baseball. The songwriting team of Steve Poltz and Robert Driscoll has written a cache of smart pop songs, including "The ABC's of Love," which uses each letter of the alphabet to describe a stage of a relationship. In 1997 the group went on hiatus, while Poltz, who holds a political science degree and spent time busking in Europe, began pursuing a solo career jump-started by his contributions—particularly the song "You Were Meant for Me"—to his ex-girlfriend Jewel's multimillion-selling debut album.

what to buy: Poltz's relentlessly charming solo debut *One Left Shoe* ✍✍✍✍ (Mercury, 1998, prod. J.J. Steven Soles) shines above his work with the Rugburns. The California native wears his heart on his sleeve throughout the album, confessing he's "Got to buy baby diamond rings/Keep it simple/Just don't brag/Got to be high speed low drag/Impala of my love" to the percolating accompaniment of acoustic guitar and the Mighty Mighty Bosstones' brassmen. On the album's highlight, "Leavin' Again"—used during the 1998 season finale of the Fox TV drama *Party of Five*—Poltz begs his lover to make her choice "So I can start my grievin'." His humor is intact, too; in "Impala," during which he harmonizes with Jewel, Poltz sings "Everything these days is so high tech/Why can't we just park by the lake and neck?"

what to buy next: Humor is the forte of the Rugburns, especially on *Taking the World by Donkey* ♫♫♫ (Priority, 1995). "Suburbia" has become the theme song for angst-ridden, skateboarding teenagers, while "Tree Hugger" pokes fun of environmentally correct activists. The group's *Morning Wood* ♫♫♫ (Planet 3, 1994) contains just as many catchy pop songs that will stick in your mind long after the CD ends.

influences:
◄◄ Barenaked Ladies, XTC

Christina Fuoco

Run-D.M.C.

Formed 1981, in Hollis, Queens, NY.

Run (born Joseph Simmons), vocals; D.M.C. (born Darryl McDaniels), vocals; Jam Master Jay (born Jason Mizell), turntables, programming.

No group was more responsible for taking hip-hop into the pop culture mainstream than Run-D.M.C. The trio did it with a canny mixture of streetwise image (a casual, jock-inspired look and attitude known as b-boy), clever, conversational wordplay, and, most of all, stripped-down beats that drew as much on hard rock as funk. On its 1984 self-titled debut album, Run-D.M.C. established its signature sound; nothing in rap sounded quiet so hard and minimalist as "Sucker M.C.'s" and "It's like That," reprised from the trio's groundbreaking 1983 single. The debut also introduced the wailing, P-Funk–styled guitar of Eddie Martinez, who returned on the title track of the 1985 album *King of Rock*—a boast the group would make good on the next year. That's when Aerosmith's Steven Tyler and Joe Perry collaborated with the rappers on a remake of Aerosmith's cock-rock standard "Walk This Way," a team-up that launched Aerosmith's comeback and, as the cornerstone of the multimillion-selling *Raising Hell* album, established Run-D.M.C. as an arena act. Unfortunately, the group's attempt to expand its success with a 1988 movie and album of the same name, *Tougher Than Leather*, bombed, and the increasing political militancy and verbal explicitness of a new breed of hip-hop groups eventually made Run-D.M.C. sound quaint and dated. But the group continued to tour and cemented its reputation as among the best live acts hip-hop has ever produced. A 1997 techno remake of

"It's like That" by dance deejay Jason Nevins became a hit throughout Europe.

what to buy: *Raising Hell* ♫♫♫♫ (Profile, 1986, prod. Russell Simmons, Rick Rubin) has its thin moments, but the initial burst of "Peter Piper," "It's Tricky," "My Adidas," and "Walk This Way" is as powerful an opening sequence as you'll find on any rap or rock record of the '80s. While *Raising Hell* is as much a cultural milestone as a musical one, the aural pleasures are packed wall to wall on the thumping *Together Forever: Greatest Hits 1983–1991* ♫♫♫♫ (Profile, 1991, prod. various).

what to buy next: The debut, *Run-D.M.C.* ♫♫♫♫ (Profile, 1984, prod. Russell Simmons, Larry Smith) is another milestone, the first true hip-hop album—though it may sound a tad too stripped-down and insular to rap non-believers. With its minimal but meaty rhythms and strident vocal cadences, even the tracks without electric guitar still rock.

what to avoid: *Back from Hell* ♫♫ (Profile, 1990, Run-D.M.C., Jam Master Jay) is a transparent attempt to keep up with foul-mouthed gangsta rappers. For the first time, the group is chasing trends rather than starting them.

the rest:
King of Rock ♫♫♫ (Profile, 1985)
Tougher Than Leather ♫♫ (Profile, 1988)
Down with the King ♫♫♫ (Profile, 1993)

worth searching for: The debut 12-inch single, *"It's like That"/"Sucker M.C.'s"* (Profile, 1983, prod. Russell Simmons, Larry Smith), is a hip-hop classic, with an extended mix of "It's like That" and instrumental versions of both tracks perfect for your own karaoke party.

influences:
◄◄ Grandmaster Flash, Parliament-Funkadelic, James Brown, Afrika Bambaataa, Kool DJ Herc, Queen, Aerosmith

►► Public Enemy, N.W.A., the Beastie Boys, Rage Against the Machine

Greg Kot

Run On

Formed 1994, in New York, NY.

Rick Brown, drums, percussion, synthesizer/programs, vocals; Sue Garner, guitar, bass, piano, vocals; Alan Licht, guitar, organ, vocals; David Newgarden, organ, synthesizer, percussion (1994–96); Katie Gentile, violin, organ, backing vocals (1996–present).

Since its formation, Run On has become one of the smartest melting pots currently bubbling. Rick Brown and Sue Garner started the band a year after their previous joint venture, Fish & Roses, quietly disappeared. Run On is in many ways a distillation of the better qualities of its predecessor, as well as encompassing forays explored throughout the history of their various other bands (the Shams, V-Effect, Timber, and many others). Brown's approach to percussives provides the ensemble with a subtly unique voice; his playing is more orchestral than just about anyone plying their trade in the rock marketplace, and his always well-mixed playing is left to shimmer on the strength of each strike, with virtually no interference from the ringing of any cymbals. On top of that is Alan Licht's more overt guitar/noise freakouts and Garner's crystalline singing. The departure of David Newgarden and his replacement with violinist Katie Gentile brought additional colors into the picture.

what to buy: *No Way* 𝄢𝄢𝄢𝄢 (Matador, 1997, prod. Run On) shows that if people will listen, Run On can do this indefinitely. The group manages a deft balancing act that sounds both naturally intuitive and carefully orchestrated, with neither tendency ever getting the upper hand.

what to buy next: *On/Off* 𝄢𝄢𝄢𝄢 (Matador, 1995, prod. Gene Holder, Run On) offers just five songs, but they lay claim to an enormous territory with this impressive debut. The group followed it less than a year later with *Start Packing* 𝄢𝄢𝄢𝄢 (Matador, 1996, prod. Run On), which startles the listener with the group's ability to carry out its agenda over the course of a long-player.

worth searching for: Run On released two EPs of new songs and remixes, both of which demonstrate the sturdy inventiveness of its approach to writing and arranging: *Sit Down* (Matador, 1997, prod. Nicholas Vernhes, Warren Defever, Casey Rice, Jerry Teel, Run On); and *Scoot* (Sonic Bubblegum, 1998, prod. Nicholas Vernhes, Jerry Teel, Run On).

solo outings:
Sue Garner:
To Run More Smoothly 𝄢𝄢𝄢𝄢 (Thrill Jockey, 1998)

influences:
◀◀ Fred Frith, Yo La Tengo, Brian Eno

David Greenberger

The Runaways

Formed 1975, in Los Angeles, CA. Disbanded 1979.

Joan Jett, guitar, vocals; Sandy West, drums; Micki Steele, bass, vocals (1975); Cherie Currie, vocals (1975–77); Lita Ford, guitar (1975–79); Jackie Fox, bass (1975–77); Vickie Blue, bass (1977–79).

Launched as manager Kim Fowley's jailbait fantasy of lingerie and leather-clad vixens, the Runaways never truly took hold commercially anywhere except Japan. The band's lasting contribution is not its brand of hyped-up shriek rock but rather its role as a forebear to girl groups such as the Go-Go's and the

Bangles—as well as a launching pad for Joan Jett's solo career (and, to a lesser extent, Lita Ford's).

what to buy: *Best of the Runaways* 𝄢𝄢𝄢 (Mercury, 1982/1987, prod. Kim Fowley) culls the best from the group's two albums. The signature blast of "Cherry Bomb" from their debut typifies the crass, barely legal sex appeal Fowley was after.

what to buy next: *Queens of Noise* 𝄢𝄢𝄢 (Mercury, 1977/Collectors Pipeline, 1994, prod. Kim Fowley), the Runaways' second album, is a touch better than the debut thanks to Jett exerting a little more control.

what to avoid: *The Runaways* 𝄢 (Mercury, 1976/Collectors Pipeline, 1994, prod. Kim Fowley) is a dead end of a debut that's insulting in its blatant titillation.

the rest:
Little Girls Lost 𝄢𝄢 (Rhino, 1981)
Neon Angels 𝄢𝄢 (PolyGram Special Products)

worth searching for: The spirited import *Live in Japan* (Mercury, 1977, prod. Kent J. Smythe, Runaways) shows that every band can find an audience.

solo outings:
Cherie Currie/Marie Currie:
Messin' with the Boys 𝄢𝄢 (Renaissance, 1997)

influences:
◀◀ T. Rex, Slade, Suzi Quatro

▶▶ The Go-Go's, the Bangles, L7

see also: *Joan Jett, Lita Ford*

Allan Orski

Todd Rundgren /Utopia

Born June 22, 1948, in Upper Darby, PA.

Utopia: Todd Rundgren, guitars, vocals; John Siegler, bass, cello (1974–76); Kasim Sulton, bass, vocals (1977–present); Mark "Moogy" Klingman, keyboards (1974–76); Ralph Shuckett, keyboards (1974–76); M. Frog Labat, synthesizers (1974); Roger Powell, keyboards, vocals (1975–present); Kevin Ellman, drums (1974); John Wilcox, drums, vocals (1975–present).

As pretentious as it sounds, Renaissance man may be the most accurate description befitting Todd Rundgren. A musician, songwriter, producer, and techno-dabbler, Rundgren is the da Vinci of rock 'n' roll, having left no corner of the music industry untouched. From his early work with the Nazz (1968–70), Rundgren showed a tremendous melodic gift and an ability to craft a sophisticated sound fused from various genres. While his music ranges from Beatles-influenced pop to Hendrix-inspired rock and Philadelphia soul, he retains a gift for honest sentiment, inspiring lyrics, and laconic wit throughout his ample body of work. Proficient on no end of instruments, Rundgren has frequently displayed his ample chops by performing all vocals and instruments on some of his albums (well before digital sampling was possible). His adventurous use of synthesizers during the early '70s helped to usher that instrument into widespread use in popular music, and while at times he could use it to the point of distraction, he also showed what was possible. If his musical dexterity has at times bordered on grandstanding, it has also clearly inspired many artists, most notably Prince, to follow suit. As a producer, Rundgren can be most likened to Phil Spector: brilliant, innovative, and at times wildly erratic. Despite his self-indulgent tendencies with such acts as the Patti Smith Group, Hall & Oates, Grand Funk Railroad, and XTC, he has more often than not helped musicians score chart hits (most notably Meat Loaf's mega-hit *Bat out of Hell*). With the advent of digital recording techniques during the late '70s, Rundgren began breaking new ground in music technology, producing some of the most advanced rock videos and exploring new possibilities in digital technology with interactive CD-ROMs (such as his 1993 release, *No World Order*). Beginning in 1975, Rundgren released a number of albums in the progressive-rock mode with his band Utopia; despite his best efforts to blend in, Rundgren's character permeates the band's catalog, making it at times indistinguishable from his solo work.

what to buy: Roundly considered one of rock's more important albums, the double-CD extravaganza *Something/Anything?* 🎵🎵🎵🎵🎵 (Bearsville/Rhino, 1972, prod. Todd Rundgren) is a landmark work, filled with lovely pop confections, pristine production, and a lighthearted sense of humor. Rundgren performs and sings the first three-quarters of the album, a nervy feat that's still breathtaking to behold. Those looking for the hits will find them here ("I Saw the Light," "It Wouldn't Have Made Any Difference," "Hello, It's Me") along with a host of stellar though lesser-known treasures ("Torch Song" and "Breathless"). Rundgren's follow-up effort, *A Wizard, a True Star* 🎵🎵🎵🎵 (Bearsville/Rhino, 1973, prod. Todd Rundgren), is a fascinating sonic collage that skews his pop star image 180 degrees. Opening with a dizzying 30-minute medley of short songs and musical skits, the album catches its breath midway, relaxing into the Philly soul number "Sometimes I Don't Know What to Feel," a clever medley of '60s tunes, and the hit anthem "Just One Victory." Rundgren never hit the mark so solidly again until *Nearly Human* 🎵🎵🎵🎵 (Warner Bros., 1989, prod. Todd Rundgren). Sliding into the soul groove he knows so well, Rundgren turns in an emotional and inspiring effort. Although none of the songs here are as well known as his earlier hits, a few of them—"The Want of a Nail," "The Waiting Game," and "Parallel Lines"—are among his best work.

what to buy next: The double CD *Anthology (1968–1985)* 🎵🎵🎵🎵 (Rhino, 1989, prod. various) is a tidy retrospective of Rundgren's career dating back to his days with the Nazz. Rhino does a first-class job here, compiling and remastering all the essential Rundgren tunes from a nearly 20-year period, among them "A Dream Goes on Forever," "Love of the Common Man," "Can We Still Be Friends?," and "Bang the Drum All Day." *The Best of Todd Rundgren* 🎵🎵🎵🎵 (Rhino, 1994) is a single-disc distillation for those who don't want quite as much Rundgren in one sitting.

what to avoid: The interactive CD (CD-I) *No World Order* 🎵 (Forward/Rhino, 1993, prod. Todd Rundgren) is an intriguing idea that never quite takes off. Rundgren offers some four hours of musical snippets for listeners to manufacture into new songs via their CD-I. For those without the required hardware, the disk includes 10 lackluster dance tracks on which Rundgren ventures unsuccessfully into rap. *No World Order Lite* **woof!** (Forward/Rhino, 1994, prod. Todd Rundgren) excludes the interactive element and, with it, what little enjoyment it offered.

the rest:
Todd Rundgren:
Runt 🎵🎵🎵 (Bearsville/Rhino, 1970)
The Ballad of Todd Rundgren 🎵🎵🎵🎵 (Bearsville/Rhino, 1971)
Todd 🎵🎵🎵 (Bearsville/Rhino, 1974)
Initiation 🎵🎵 (Bearsville/Rhino, 1975)
Faithful 🎵🎵🎵🎵 (Bearsville/Rhino, 1976)
Hermit of Mink Hollow 🎵🎵🎵 (Bearsville/Rhino, 1978)
Back to the Bars 🎵🎵🎵 (Bearsville/Rhino, 1978)
Healing 🎵🎵 (Bearsville/Rhino, 1981)
The Ever Popular Tortured Artist Effect 🎵🎵🎵 (Bearsville/Rhino, 1983)
A Cappella 🎵🎵🎵 (Warner Bros./Rhino, 1985)
Second Wind 🎵 (Bearsville/Rhino, 1991)
Individualist 🎵🎵 (Digital Entertainment Enhanced CD, 1995)
With a Twist 🎵🎵🎵 (Guardian, 1997)

Utopia:
Todd Rundgren's Utopia 🎵🎵 (Bearsville/Rhino, 1974)
Another Live 🎵🎵 (Bearsville/Rhino, 1975)
RA 🎵 (Bearsville/Rhino, 1977)
Oops! Wrong Planet 🎵🎵 (Bearsville/Rhino, 1977)
Deface the Music 🎵🎵🎵 (Bearsville/Rhino, 1980)
Adventures in Utopia 🎵 (Bearsville/Rhino, 1980)
Utopia 🎵🎵 (Network/Rhino, 1982)
Swing to the Right 🎵🎵 (Bearsville/Rhino, 1982)
Oblivion, P.O.V. & Some Trivia 🎵🎵🎵 (Rhino, 1986)
Anthology 1974–1985 🎵🎵🎵 (Rhino, 1989)

worth searching for: If there is a Holy Grail for Rundgren fans, it's the test pressing release of his solo debut, *Runt* (Ampex, 1970, prod. Todd Rundgren), of which some 500 copies were erroneously issued back in 1970. Although the cover and track listing are identical to the official release, the rare *Runt* features numerous differences, including a complete version of "Baby Let's Swing," an unlisted and haunting track called "Say No More," and an early recording of "Hope I'm Around," a later version of which appeared on *The Ballad of Todd Rundgren*.

influences:

⏮ The Beach Boys, the Beatles, Jimi Hendrix, Stevie Wonder, the Move, Motown, Doo-Wop

⏭ Electric Light Orchestra, Meat Loaf, Hall & Oates, the Tubes, Queen, XTC, Prince, Madonna

Christopher Scapelliti

Rush

Formed 1969, in Toronto, Ontario, Canada.

Geddy Lee (born Gary Lee Weinrib), bass, vocals, keyboards; Alex Lifeson (born Alex Zivojinovich), guitar; Neil Peart, drums (1974–present); John Rutsey, drums (1969–74).

Starting out as a flashy, power chord–slinging hard rock trio, Rush gradually moved into egghead territory—first with the addition of Neil Peart's Ayn Rand–inspired lyrics, then with the introduction of keyboards, which resulted in a sonic straddle of the metal and progressive rock lines. Remaining intact for nearly three decades, Rush has become something of a rite of passage band, celebrated by successive generations for its instrumental prowess and state-of-the-art stage performances. Modern rockers such as Primus regularly sing Rush's praises, giving the trio a hip credential most of its '70s counterparts lack.

what to buy: *Retrospective I, 1974–1980* 𝄞𝄞𝄞𝄞 (Anthem/Mercury Chronicles, 1997, prod. various) and *Retrospective II, 1981–1987* 𝄞𝄞𝄞𝄞 (Anthem/Mercury Chronicles, 1997, prod. various) tell, on two separate, sonically enhanced albums, the story of Rush's peak years and allow for sampling without having to wade through individual albums whose concepts are often ponderous and oblique. *All the World's a Stage* 𝄞𝄞𝄞𝄞 (Mercury, 1976, prod. Rush, Terry Brown) is the first and best of Rush's three live albums, an energetic outing that (fortunately) focuses more on punch than intellect. *Moving Pictures* 𝄞𝄞𝄞𝄞 (Mercury, 1981, prod. Rush, Terry Brown) is the most consistent of the studio sets, featuring some of Rush's most memorable songs ("Tom Sawyer," "Limelight") and most ambitious instrumental excursions ("YYZ," "Red Barchetta").

what to buy next: *Permanent Waves* 𝄞𝄞𝄞𝄞 (Mercury, 1980, prod. Rush, Terry Brown) is on par with *Moving Pictures* and includes the seminal Rush radio hits "Spirit of Radio" and "Freewill." *2112* 𝄞𝄞𝄞 (Mercury, 1976, prod. Rush, Terry Brown) houses the sidelong title suite. *Presto* 𝄞𝄞𝄞 (Anthem/Atlantic, 1989), for which Rush switched labels, showcases a more spacious, organic approach.

what to avoid: *Grace under Pressure* 𝄞 (Mercury, 1984, prod. Rush, Peter Henderson) is an unusually stiff and graceless entry in the Rush catalog.

the rest:
Rush 𝄞𝄞 (Mercury, 1974)
Fly by Night 𝄞𝄞𝄞 (Mercury, 1975)
Caress of Steel 𝄞𝄞𝄞 (Mercury, 1975)
A Farewell to Kings 𝄞𝄞𝄞 (Mercury, 1977)
Hemispheres 𝄞𝄞 (Mercury, 1978)
Exit . . . Stage Left 𝄞𝄞𝄞 (Mercury, 1981)
Signals 𝄞𝄞𝄞 (Mercury, 1982)
Power Windows 𝄞𝄞𝄞 (Mercury, 1985)
Hold Your Fire 𝄞𝄞𝄞 (Mercury, 1987)
A Show of Hands 𝄞𝄞𝄞 (Atlantic/Anthem, 1989)
Chronicles 𝄞𝄞𝄞𝄞 (Anthem/Mercury, 1990)
Roll the Bones 𝄞𝄞𝄞 (Atlantic/Anthem, 1991)
Counterparts 𝄞𝄞 (Atlantic/Anthem, 1993)
Test for Echo (ECD) 𝄞𝄞𝄞 (Atlantic, 1996)
Different Stages 𝄞𝄞𝄞𝄞 (Atlantic, 1998)

worth searching for: *Rush Profiled* (Atlantic/Anthem 1990) is a promotional interview CD that finds the three musicians in an expansive and reflective mood as they switch labels after 15 years with Mercury.

solo outings:
Alex Lifeson:
Victor 𝄞 (Atlantic/Anthem, 1996)

Neil Peart:
Burning for Buddy: A Tribute to the Music of Buddy Rich 𝄞𝄞𝄞 (Atlantic/Anthem, 1994)

influences:

⏮ Led Zeppelin, Yes, King Crimson, the Move, the Guess Who, Buddy Rich

⏭ Triumph, Primus, Zebra

Gary Graff

Ed Rush /Hydro

Born Ben Settle.

Ed Rush has been one of jungle's most important DJ/producers since the release of his influential 12-inch "Bloodclot Artattack" in early 1993. Created with the help of his long-time friend and neighbor, producer/engineer Nico Sykes, "Bloodclot Artattack" fused horror movie samples, eerie synths, and elements of hip-hop and dub with the fast and funky breakbeats of U.K. hardcore. (Sykes, a.k.a. Nico, would continue to collaborate and assist Rush on the majority of Rush's releases.) "Bloodclot"'s dark vibe laid the foundation for the jungle sub-genre known as tech-step,

Alex Lifeson of Rush (© Ken Settle)

which was virtually created by Rush, Sykes, and fellow DJ/producer Duncun Hutchinson (a.k.a. Trace) with the 1995 release of their collaborative remix of T-Power's jungle hit "Mutant Jazz" (which was released under Trace's name). The track, better known as "The Mutant," replaced jungle's slowly throbbing sub-bass sounds with bludgeoning bass lines that sound something like a swarm of killer bees on steroids mixed with the distorted sound of a Hoover vacuum cleaner run through a stack of Marshall amps. Thanks to a steady stream of 12-inches for labels such as Emotif/Sour, Goldie's Metalheadz, and Sykes's own No U-Turn, tech-step became the sound of jungle in 1996 and 1997 with virtually every jungle/drum-and-bass artist creating tracks that followed in its footsteps.

what to buy: The definitive Ed Rush document, *Torque* ♫♫♫ (No U-Turn, 1997, prod. Nico Sykes, Ed Rush, Trace) has not been released domestically in the United States, but is readily available in any store that stocks imports from the U.K. *Torque* is a double-CD compilation that features the dark and brutal tech-step sounds of Rush, Nico, and Trace. The second disc is a continuous DJ mix of No U-Turn's best tracks by Rush that provides the proper context for which the music was originally created: the dance floor.

what to buy next: On the domestic front, Rush has one track on each of the following compilations: *Platinum Breakz II* ♫♫♫ (Metalheadz/FFRR, 1998, prod. various) ("The Raven"); *V Classic: Volume II* ♫♫♫ (V Classic/Ultra, 1998, prod. various) ("Naked Lunch"); and *Grooverider Presents: The Prototype Years* ♫♫♫ (Prototype/Columbia, 1998, prod. various) ("Locust").

worth searching for: Two other important, import-only compilations featuring Rush tracks are *Techsteppin* (Emotif, 1996, prod. various) and *Routes from the Jungle* (Circa/Virgin U.K., 1995, prod. various), which contains "Bloodclot Artattack."

influences:
◀◀ Doc Scott, Two Bad Mice

Howard Shih

Leon Russell

Born April 2, 1941, in Lawton, OK.

In addition to his idiosyncratic solo career of swampy gospel blues, Leon Russell has an amazing résumé as a session player on Phil Spector's masterpieces along with guest spots for Bob Dylan, the Beach Boys, and Jerry Lee Lewis; leader of Joe Cocker's epochal Mad Dogs & Englishmen band; part of a touring gig with the Rolling Stones; and, for a time, owner of his own label, the now-defunct Shelter Records. His work has been well covered by others, notably "A Song for You," which has been done by Ray Charles and every piano-bar performer

going. With his menacing stare and cheese-grater voice, Russell's own albums may be a bit rough for the timid, but his material has a strong individuality that warrants a listen.

what to buy: His major-label debut album, *Leon Russell* ♫♫♫ (Shelter/A&M, 1970/Right Stuff, 1995, prod. Denny Cordell, Leon Russell) contains many of his best songs, including "Delta Lady," "A Song for You," and "Shoot Out at the Plantation." The reissue adds a bizarre take of Dylan's "Masters of War" sung to the tune of "The Star-Spangled Banner." *Leon Russell & the Shelter People* ♫♫♫ (Shelter, 1971/Right Stuff, 1995, prod. Denny Cordell, Leon Russell) is a rollicking follow-up of backyard blues and well-chosen covers. For those seeking a good overview of Russell's Shelter period, you can't go wrong with the two-disc set *Gimme Shelter! The Best of Leon Russell* ♫♫♫ (EMI, 1996, prod. various).

what to buy next: On *Hank Wilson's Back!* ♫♫♫ (Shelter, 1973/Right Stuff, 1995, prod. various), Russell predates The The's Matt Johnson by 20-odd years with a joyously executed tribute to Hank Williams. *Carney* ♫♫♫ (Shelter, 1972/Right Stuff, 1995, prod. Denny Cordell, Leon Russell) is his biggest seller thanks to the single "Tightrope."

what to avoid: *Anything Can Happen* ♫♫ (Virgin, 1992, prod. Bruce Hornsby) is an unheralded comeback. Despite Hornsby's presence, much of the material feels like a car stalling uphill.

the rest:
Asylum Choir ♫♫♫ (Shelter, 1971/Right Stuff, 1995)
Leon Live ♫♫♫ (Shelter, 1973/Right Stuff, 1996)
Stop All That Jazz ♫♫ (Shelter, 1974/Right Stuff, 1995)
Retrospective ♫♫♫ (Shelter, 1977/Right Stuff, 1997)
Legend in My Time: Hank Wilson, Volume III ♫♫♫ (Ark 21, 1998)

worth searching for: His debut, *Look inside the Asylum Choir* (Smash, 1968) was good enough to attract admirers such as Delaney & Bonnie and Joe Cocker to Russell's camp.

influences:
◀◀ Bob Dylan, Clarence "Gatemouth" Brown, Jerry Lee Lewis

▶▶ Richie Havens, Joe Cocker, Bruce Hornsby

Allan Orski

Rusted Root

Formed 1990, in Pittsburgh, PA.

Mike Glabicki, lead vocals, acoustic guitar; Liz Berlin, vocals, percussion; Patrick Norman, bass, vocals, percussion; Jim Donovan, drums, percussion, vocals; Jenn Wertz, vocals, percussion (1990–95); John Buynak, woodwinds, percussion, hand drums, vocals; Jim DiSpirito, percussion, hand drums (1993–present).

The first band in decades to break out of Pittsburgh onto the national scene, Rusted Root had its genesis in the coffee-house folk duo of Mike Glabicki and Liz Berlin, who added Patrick Norman and Jim Donovan before entering a band contest. On the strength of their first public performance, they made it to the semi-finals of that event. The second year they entered the group placed second overall. By then they'd added Jenn Wertz and John Buynak and begun building up a large, enthusiastic following for their tribal-organic-Afro-hippie-funk-meets-David-Byrne sound. On the strength of their independent release, *Cruel Sun*, and huge turnouts for their live shows, the band caught the ears of Mercury Records, which signed it in '94. It wasn't long before they found themselves attracting the Grateful Dead crowd—and the band itself, which gave Rusted Root the opening act spot for the Pittsburgh date of its final tour. By then Rusted Root had already traveled with the Dave Matthews Band and the Allman Brothers and become the opening act on the heralded Page & Plant reunion tour. Fans say in order to truly experience Rusted Root, one has to attend the band's live shows; there, the hallucinogenic-influenced twirlers mix with the suburban high-schoolers and parents trying to recall the feel-good days of their hippie youth. While commanding frontman Glabicki's rooster-walk is something to see, it's the instrumental dexterity and percussion interludes that tend to send those fans into trances of ecstasy. Most listeners fall into two camps: love 'em or hate 'em. Though Glabicki's sometimes hiccupy falsetto can get grating after awhile, the percussion generally tends to set enough of a hypnotic tone to lure in those skeptics who find themselves at a live Rusted Root show.

what to buy: *Cruel Sun* ♪♪♪♪ (Blue Duck, 1992, prod. Dave Bryan, Rusted Root) is an incredibly well-realized indie debut from a band that was still quite young at the time. Besides displaying Glabicki's songwriting promise, it also brought forth a sense of free-form experimentation that fit right in with the H.O.R.D.E. festival gang. Rusted Root got some of its earliest national exposure as a H.O.R.D.E. act, and now, like fellow H.O.R.D.E. vets Matthews and Phish, couldn't lose the twirlers if it wanted to.

what to buy next: *When I Woke* ♪♪♪ (Mercury, 1994, prod. Bill Bottrell) features a few of the best cuts from *Cruel Sun* but is not merely a re-release. Curiously, it also contains a song titled "Cruel Sun," which the album of that name does not. Go figure. But that's just one of the quirks this band rather delights in displaying. Perhaps the best cut is the exuberant country-cajun romp of "Rain," though the hits of this platinum-seller were the lilting "Send Me on My Way" and "Ecstasy." *Remember* ♪♪♪♪ (Mercury, 1996, prod. Jerry Harrison) has a more grown-up sound, with fewer references to the world's traumas and more love-related themes. Glabicki's lyrics, however, inevitably are written more in a rhymical pattern than in linear concepts, so it's often hard to determine just what the heck he's jabbering about. Which may be the point.

worth searching for: Though the band's "Virtual Reality" (from *Remember*) also made it onto the soundtrack of the blockbuster film *Twister,* the better cut is one from the soundtrack of *Home for the Holidays:* both are on *Evil Ways* (1996, prod. Tim Bomba, others), an EP that also contains three live tunes.

influences:

◄◄ Talking Heads, David Byrne, Santana, Grateful Dead, Lenny Kravitz

Lynne Margolis

The Rutles

Formed 1978, in England.

Neil Innes, guitar, keyboards, vocals; Ollie Halsall, guitar, keyboards, vocals; Ricky Fataar, guitar, bass, sitar, tabla, vocals; Andy Brown, bass; John Halsey, drums, vocals.

As Beatles parodies go, none have been as good-naturedly hilarious, dead-on accurate, or tuneful as the Rutles. The group originated from an idea by Monty Python troupe member Eric Idle, who recruited British musician/songwriter (and ex–Bonzo Dog Band member) Neil Innes to perform his Beatles sound-alike song "I Must Be in Love" for a Python TV skit. The sketch went down well enough that Idle decided to pursue a full-length TV "documentary" (titled *All You Need Is Cash*) chronicling the rise and fall of the Rutles, a.k.a. the Prefab Four. Innes played Ron Nasty (John Lennon), Ricky Fataar portrayed Stig O'Hara (George Harrison), and John Halsey appeared as Barry Wom (Ringo Starr). Although he plays no instruments on the soundtrack, Idle portrayed the Paul McCartney character, Dirk McQuickley, in the film. The group reassembled in 1996 for *Archaeology,* an album that—with its "lost" and "rare" tracks—spoofs the much ballyhooed "Anthology" series of unreleased Beatles tracks issued during this same period.

what to buy: Basically a soundtrack from Idle's movie, *The Rutles* ♪♪♪♪ (WEA/Atlantic/Rhino, 1978, prod. Neil Innes) presents Innes's 20 dead-on pastiches of key songs from the Beatles' career, including "Hold My Hand" ("All My Loving"), "Doubleback Alley" ("Penny Lane"), and "Piggy in the Middle" ("I Am the Walrus"). At least half the fun is listening for the original sources within the Rutles' parodies. Vinyl owners note: The CD version includes six worthwhile bonus tracks from the movie. For *Archaeology* ♪♪♪♪ (Virgin, 1996, prod. Neil Innes, Steve James), Innes took a handful of tracks he'd written in the intervening years and gave them the Rutles treatment. It's a fun and well-done effort, although *The Rutles* will suffice for most fans.

worth searching for: Collectors may also want to look for the out-of-print CD *Rutles Highway Revisited* (Shimmy Disc, 1990, prod. various), a "tribute" album containing the 20 tracks from

The Rutles performed by Syd Straw, Marc Ribot, and Shonen Knife, among others.

influences:

◄◄ The Beatles, Bonzo Dog Band, Monty Python, Todd Rundgren, Utopia

►► XTC, the Dukes of Stratosphear

Christopher Scapelliti

Matthew Ryan

Born November 7, 1971, in Chester, PA.

Like Steve Earle and Bruce Springsteen before him, Matthew Ryan is that rare breed of songwriter who can sound barroom tough, yet still sing with the tenderness and intelligence of a sensitive '90s guy. With a poet's sense of detail and the charred voice of a coal miner, the Pennsylvania-born bard sings of losers and loss, longing and melancholy, desperation and frustration. When it comes to the unredemptive life, Ryan's eyes have seen it all. He moved to Nashville at age 21, and, with a few original tunes on hand, began playing with a hard honky-tonk group known as the Caustics. They gigged nonstop, but Ryan longed for a sparer, more contemplative mode of musical expression, which eventually led to *Mayday*, his debut.

what's available: "One day soon that dam is gonna break/It'll wash you away from me," Ryan sings on "Dam," one of the many enduring lyrics on *Mayday* 𝄢𝄢𝄢 (A&M, 1997, prod. David Ricketts). The critically acclaimed album offers a solid foundation for Ryan to build his career on, featuring a dozen songs that turn even the most downcast personal predicaments into jubilant musical events.

influences:

◄◄ Steve Earle, Bruce Springsteen, Bob Dylan, Leonard Cohen

Bob Gulla

Bobby Rydell

Born Robert Ridarelli, April 26, 1942, in Philadelphia, PA.

Sixties teen idol Bobby Rydell didn't so much rock as swing. His output seldom (if ever) featured an electric guitar, and for the most part he was saddled with cutesy material and cloying musical arrangements. The fact that his music is listenable today is entirely due to Rydell's ability as a vocalist. Applying the same Sinatraesque phrasing that Bobby Darin brought to teen pop (sans the finger-popper's innate surliness), Rydell made everything sound as if he were the hippest boy-next-door/lounge lizard-in-training of his era. Something of a child prodigy, at age seven Rydell played drums, sang, and did imitations in Philadelphia nightclubs before becoming the regular

WHAT ALBUM CHANGED YOUR LIFE?

Every once in awhile a new one pops up that sort of helps me regain my faith in songwriting and helps me expand my mind as far as that goes. Fiona Apple did that for me recently, when I first got hooked on her [debut] album. I know there's all this weird talk and weird energy about her as far as just people not thinking she's for real or people thinking she's on some pop star thing. I just think she's a brilliant songwriter. It's helped me regain some faith in the industry that she actually got picked by the powers that be to become this popular, that her music has been accepted that widely.

Liz Berlin (of Rusted Root)

drummer on Paul Whiteman's local TV show. As a teenager, he and trumpeter/future teen idol Frankie Avalon were part of Rocco & the Saints, a popular Philadelphia dance band. Avalon's later success opened the doors for Rydell, who scored his first hit with "Kissin' Time" (a cha-cha tempoed remake of "Sweet Little Sixteen"). Alternating uptempo ear candy such as "Wild One" and "Swingin' School" with the adult contemporary sounds of "Volare," "Forget Him," and "That Old Black Magic," Rydell placed 24 records on the charts between 1959 and 1965. A blonde alternative to Avalon and Fabian (and a better singer than either), Rydell was also featured regularly on Dick Clark's *American Bandstand* and appeared with the host in the 1960 teen flick *Because They're Young*. The role of Hugo in the 1963 film version of *Bye Bye Birdie* represents Rydell's final moment of glory as a teen idol; the following year, the Beatles arrived and made him and his type irrelevant to young record buyers. Rydell survived better than most; after signing with Capitol, he scaled the lower regions of the charts with "I Just Can't Say Goodbye" and "Diana," and later became a first-rate cabaret/

lounge performer. Nowadays, Rydell performs on the oldies circuit, where he still swings more than he rocks.

what's available: Rydell re-recorded his greatest hits for *Best of Bobby Rydell* ♪♪ (Dominion, 1996), and the more mature renditions of "Volare" and "Forget Him" are actually quite pleasing. But the uptempo numbers lack the snap and hustle of his original versions.

worth searching for: You can find Rydell's original Cameo-Parkway hits on the French import *Bobby's Biggest Hits* (Cameo, 1997, prod. various) or the Italian release *18 Greatest Hits* (Cameo, 1990, prod. various), which feature all his best teen idol chart-toppers. Until comparable domestic compilations are released, these are the ones to get.

influences:

◀◀ Bobby Darin, Frankie Avalon, Jimmy Clanton

▶▶ Johnny Tillotson, James Darren, Bobby Sherman

Ken Burke

Mitch Ryder

Born William Levise Jr., February 26, 1945, in Hamtramck, MI.

Mitch Ryder's music of the mid-'60s was the *other* Motown sound—the sound of the auto plants, the shot-and-a-beer bars, the raucous, industrial, violent roots of his hometown. He never conveyed it better than he did with the Detroit Wheels, a band driven by one of the great drummers in rock 'n' roll history (Johnny "Bee" Badanjek) and given spice by the lethal guitar licks of Jimmy McCarty. Ryder and the Wheels cranked out two years of hits—"Jenny Take a Ride!," "Little Latin Lupe Lu," "Shake a Tail Feather," the "Devil with a Blue Dress On/Good Golly Miss Molly" medley (an encore favorite of Bruce Springsteen & the E Street Band)—before producer Bob Crewe convinced him to go solo in 1967. The move met with limited success, but Ryder caught the fire once again when he, Badanjek, and McCarty reunited for one album as Detroit. Since then Ryder has made his living touring Europe, particularly Germany, and releasing records in Europe with only occasional attempts to crack the U.S. market again. His 1994 album *Rite of Passage* featured the song "Mercy," which voiced support for assisted suicide advocate Dr. Jack Kevorkian.

what to buy: *Rev Up: The Best of Mitch Ryder & the Detroit Wheels* ♪♪♪♪ (Rhino, 1989, prod. various) is a generous (21 tracks) must-have that surveys not only the Wheels' best but also includes highlights from Ryder's solo career and from Detroit. The original *Breakout!!!* ♪♪♪♪ (New Voice, 1966/Sundazed, 1993, prod. Bob Crewe) lives up to its multiple exclamation points.

what to buy next: *Sock It to Me!* ♪♪♪♪ (New Voice, 1967/Sundazed, 1993, prod. Bob Crewe) is another four-on-the-floor blowout; the reissue betters it with some singles that weren't on the original album. *Detroit with Mitch Ryder* ♪♪♪♪ (Paramount, 1971/MCA, 1987) boasts considerable hard rock muscle heard in the pumped-up treatment of the Velvet Underground's "Rock and Roll."

what to avoid: *The Rockin' Hits* ♪♪ (Special Music, 1993, prod. Bob Crewe) pales in comparison to the collection on *Rev Up*.

the rest:
Take a Ride ♪♪♪ (New Voice, 1966/Sundazed, 1993)
All Hits! ♪♪♪♪ (Sundazed, 1994)
Devil with the Blue Dress On ♪♪♪ (Rhino, 1995)

worth searching for: At this point, Ryder has released more albums in Europe than he has in the States. The most interesting is one that actually did come out here. *Never Kick a Sleeping Dog* (Riva, 1983/Line, 1987, prod. John Mellencamp) was longtime fan John Mellencamp's noble effort to give Ryder another shot in the United States, and the producer's spare, energetic aesthetic worked well on a cover of Prince's "When You Were Mine" as well as originals such as "The Thrill of It All," "Code Dancing," and "B.I.G.T.I.M.E."

influences:

◀◀ Big Joe Turner, Little Richard, Gary U.S. Bonds, Jackie Wilson

▶▶ John Mellencamp, Bruce Springsteen, the Rockets, the Iron City Houserockers

Gary Graff

Doug Sahm /Sir Douglas Quintet

Born November 6, 1941, in San Antonio, TX. Sir Douglas Quintet formed 1964, in CA. Disbanded 1972.

Doug Sahm, guitar, vocals; Augie Meyers, organ, vocals; Francisco Moran, saxophone; Harvey Kagan, bass; Johnny Perez, drums.

Although it was Augie Meyers's carnival organ that would define the unique sound of the Sir Douglas Quintet's biggest hits, the group was the brainchild of the original cosmic cowboy, Doug Sahm, who has kept the name going on and off whenever feasible. A steel-guitar prodigy, Sahm began performing as Little Doug Sahm at age six. During 1964, after moving to California and recruiting Meyers, Sahm started the Quintet. Although the music of the group's first big single, "She's about a Mover," produced by Cajun wildman Huey Meaux, was a mixed bag of border conjunto and San Francisco psychedelia (especially Meyers's primal organ licks), the long hair and quasi-royal name had many thinking the Texans hailed from England. After one more hit, 1969's "Mendocino," Sahm began a fascinating, checkered solo career that has included recordings with Bob Dylan, Dr. John, Flaco Jimenez, David "Fathead" Newman, Yusef Lateef, and most recently with Freddie Fender, Jimenez, and Meyers as the Texas Tornados. Sahm's wry blend of country, border rock, soul, and horn-based R&B has grown even better with age, and he remains an understated master of stringed instruments. In whatever incarnation, Doug Sahm represents Texas blues and rock at its finest.

what to buy: Two solo albums capture the heady ambience of Sahm's mix. *Juke Box Music* 𝄞𝄞𝄞𝄞 (Antone's, 1988/Musicraft, 1997, prod. Doug Sahm) offers a refreshing set of pure Texas soul classics, including Sahm's unforgettably tasty cover of Little Sunny's "Talk to Me." *The Last Real Texas Blues Band* 𝄞𝄞𝄞𝄞 (Antone's, 1994/Musicraft, 1997, prod. Doug Sahm, Derek O'Brien) forms a perfect bookend, reprising the R&B of the big horn bands that Sahm chewed up in San Antonio during the '50s. It was recorded live with a fine big band at Antone's, one of Sahm's favorite Austin haunts. You can almost taste the margaritas and jalapenos. *Best of Doug Sahm and the Sir Douglas Quintet* 𝄞𝄞𝄞𝄞 (Mercury, 1990, prod. Doug Sahm) includes 22 tracks that fill in many of the gaps in Sahm's canon before the Antone's discs.

what to buy next: *Best of Doug Sahm and Friends: Atlantic Sessions* 𝄞𝄞𝄞 (Rhino, 1992) offers an eclectic selection from Sahm's two early '70s Atlantic albums and includes his collaborations with Dylan.

what to avoid: *Daydreaming at Midnight* 𝄞𝄞 (Elektra, 1994, prod. Doug Sahm, Doug Clifford) is a heavy-metal version of the Quintet that just didn't work, with Sahm's son Shawn on second guitar.

the rest:
Amos Garrett, Doug Sahm, Gene Taylor 𝄞𝄞𝄞 (Rykodisc, 1989)
Live 𝄞𝄞𝄞𝄞 (Bear Family, 1994)
The Early Years 𝄞𝄞𝄞 (Collectables, 1997)

Sir Douglas Quintet:
Quintessence 𝄞𝄞𝄞 (Varrick, 1995)
Texas Fever 𝄞𝄞𝄞 (AIM, 1998)

worth searching for: You can't go wrong with most of the Quintet's long-out-of-print vinyl albums, especially *Honkey Blues* (Smash, 1968) or *1+1+1=4* (Philips, 1970). Sahm's *Groover's Paradise* (Warner Bros., 1974) is a stoned, wacky-tobaccy, Tex-

Mex period piece recorded with the Creedence Clearwater Revival rhythm section. And watch the vinyl sections as well for *Border Wave* (Takoma, 1981), a Quintet update for the new wave era with Alvin Crow on guitar and vocals and Speedy Sparks on bass.

influences:

◀◀ Hank Williams, Freddie Fender, Santiago Jimenez Sr., Little Sunny & the Skyliners, T-Bone Walker, Junior Parker, Bobby "Blue" Bland, Howlin' Wolf, Jimmy Reed, Bob Wills & His Texas Playboys, Carl Perkins, Chuck Berry, Little Richard, Guitar Slim, James Brown, the Beatles, the Rolling Stones

▶▶ Sam the Sham & the Pharoahs, ? & the Mysterlans, Mouse & the Traps, Creedence Clearwater Revival, Joe (King) Carrasco & the Crowns, Elvis Costello & the Attractions, Uncle Tupelo, BoDeans, Bruce Springsteen, Gram Parsons, the Byrds, James McMurtry, Jimmie Dale Gilmore, Joe Ely, John Hiatt, Stevie Ray Vaughan, Los Lobos, Flying Burrito Brothers, Long Ryders, Kris Kristofferson

see also: *Texas Tornados*

Leland Rucker

St. Etienne

Formed 1990, in Croydon, England.

Bob Stanley, keyboards, programming; Pete Wiggs, keyboards, programming; Sarah Cracknell, vocals (1991–present).

Disillusioned with the state of pop records, Bob Stanley—who at the time was writing for Britain's *Melody Maker* magazine—teamed up with school-mate Pete Wiggs to form St. Etienne, intending to show people how to do pop right. Their stated goal was to incorporate the feeling of the fantasy-happy '60s and '70s into pop songs that nonetheless felt current. Originally intending to write for specific individuals instead of having one constant singer, St. Etienne's first singles include vocals from Kyle Minouge, Shara Nelson, and Mora Lambert. Sarah Cracknell became a permanent member after the release of the first album, *Foxbase Alpha*. Thanks to a frantic release of singles since then, St. Etienne has quickly risen to the forefront of Britpop.

what to buy: *Foxbase Alpha* 𝄞𝄞𝄞𝄞 (Warner Bros., 1991, prod. Bob Stanley, Pete Wiggs) at first sounds familiar because St. Etienne draws from a vast collection of pop sources. But the album quickly demonstrates its uniqueness because of the special way the group effortlessly combines those many influences, blending warmer sounds and samples with its electronic orientation. *So Tough* 𝄞𝄞𝄞𝄞 (Warner Bros., 1993, prod. St. Etienne) continues the foray into techno/synth pop, and although the band seems to follow the popular dance whims of the moment, it consistently values musical expertise over trendy stylings. *So Tough* also contains its biggest hit (though probably not one of its best songs), "You're in a Bad Way."

what to buy next: The third album, *Tiger Bay* ♫♫♫♫ (Warner Bros., 1995, prod. St. Etienne), is a bit of a departure from the previous releases, experimenting with folk songs laid out on techno and other electronic beats. It's a bit darker than its predecessors. U.S. fans might want to look into the British version since Warner Bros. slightly altered the format of *Tiger Bay* in the U.S. to make it more "American sounding" and, in the process, removed a few good tracks.

worth searching for: St. Etienne releases a large number of singles and remixes in England, often containing some of its finest work. The import compilation album, *Too Young to Die* (Heavenly, 1995, prod. St. Etienne) features the best singles from all three albums, as well as two extra tracks, including the hit "He's on the Phone."

influences:

◄◄ The Fall, the Jam, Neil Young, Bee Gees, Adam Ant, ABBA, the Monkees

►► Boo Radleys, Shara Nelson, the Charlatans

Bryan Lassner

Kate St. John

See: Dream Academy

Buffy Sainte-Marie

Born February 20, 1941, in Saskatchewan, Canada.

A sizable early output followed by a 20-year low profile has made Buffy Sainte-Marie one of those artistic icons who's more respected than known, but she beat everyone to some of the most fertile and enduring trends in contemporary music. Though most remembered as a folkie, you'll hear the very earliest stirrings of world music, goth, electronica, and new age on her albums, as well as explorations in almost any other style you can name. The folk revitalizations heralded by such artists as Suzanne Vega and Tracy Chapman during the '80s and Ani DiFranco in the '90s were actually resumptions of the uncompromising and borderless music movement Sainte-Marie had begun before most of them were born. Her unique, melismatic vocal style introduced a histrionic, revelatory extremity that has revolutionized rock every time it has been expanded on, from Yoko Ono and Patti Smith to John Lydon and Sinéad O'Connor. With her *Illuminations* album, she also ushered in the era of electronic rock, a year before Kraftwerk. The secret is an absolute disregard of limits, which sometimes takes her music over the top but overall has sustained her as a Native American woman in a white-male-dominated field, and yielded a contribution to the twentieth-century musical canon that few have paralleled.

what to buy: Sainte-Marie's debut, *It's My Way!* ♫♫♫♫♫ (Vanguard, 1964, prod. Buffy Sainte-Marie), takes the gloves right off with the Native rights anthem "Now That the Buffalo's Gone" and never stops slugging, through prime blues-gospel and Hindi standards, window-rattling feminist laments, joyous Americana, and the exhilarating, iconoclastic title track. *The Best of Buffy Sainte-Marie* ♫♫♫♫ (Vanguard, 1970, compilation prod. Maynard Solomon) and *The Best of Buffy Sainte-Marie, Vol. 2* ♫♫♫♫ (Vanguard, 1971, compilation prod. Maynard Solomon) are solid, satisfying collections that rescue many great songs from her out-of-print albums and salvage what's good from her lesser in-print ones.

what to buy next: Even were its ambitious folk/Scottish/Muzak instrumental track to be erased, *Little Wheel Spin and Spin* ♫♫♫♫♫ (Vanguard, 1966, prod. Buffy Sainte-Marie) would stand as one of the most harrowing and virtuosic vocal performances of the rock era. On *Moonshot* ♫♫♫♫ (Vanguard, 1972, prod. Buffy Sainte-Marie, Norbert Putnam), Sainte-Marie's damn-the-torpedoes experimentation results in perhaps the most enigmatically bizarre pop album of all time.

what to avoid: The quasi-Nashville approach of *I'm Gonna Be a Country Girl Again* ♫♫♫ (Vanguard, 1968, prod. Bob Lucie, Maynard Solomon) ranges from pedestrian to gauche, with little in between. *She Used to Wanna Be a Ballerina* ♫♫ (Vanguard, 1971, prod. Jack Nitzsche, Buffy Sainte-Marie) is a strained and dated attempt at commerciality. *Up Where We Belong* ♫♫♫ (Angel, 1996, prod. Chris Burkett, Buffy Sainte-Marie) has a few moments of bracing pow-wow pop that aren't worth its many listless hits remakes, though the better tracks would make a great EP.

worth searching for: Inexplicably out of print, *Illuminations* (Vanguard, 1969, prod. Buffy Sainte-Marie) electronically processed Sainte-Marie's vocals and guitar to add a kind of proto-sampling and eerie instrumental atmosphere to her haunting folk balladry, prescient worldbeat, and banshee-wail psychedelia. Three decades ahead of its time, it's still a striking listen. On *Coincidence and Likely Stories* (Ensign, 1992, prod. Rick Marvin, Chris Burkett, Buffy Sainte-Marie), also revolutionary and out of print, Sainte-Marie synthesized pissed-off political pop with a radical, pow-wow–influenced singing style that yet again expanded the horizons of what the rock vocal could be.

influences:

◄◄ Woody Guthrie, Pete Seeger, Bob Dylan, Joan Baez, Ben Blackbear

►► Yoko Ono, Patti Smith, Suzanne Vega, Sinéad O'Connor, Tracy Chapman, Diamanda Galas, John Lydon, Morrissey, Ani DiFranco, Mary Ann Farley, Jim Wilson/Little Wolf, Robbie Robertson

Adam McGovern

The Saints

Formed 1973, in Brisbane, Australia.

Chris Bailey, vocals, guitar; Ed Kuepper, guitar (1973–78); Ivor Hay, drums (1973–78, 1980, 1986); Kym Bradshaw, bass (1973–76); Algy Ward, bass (1977–78); Barrington Francis, guitar (1979–81, 1985–88); Janine Hall, bass (1979–84); Mark Birmingham, drums (1979–81); Ian Shedden, drums (1981–85, 1987–88); Archie Larizza, bass (1986–88).

"Rock music of the '70s was changed by three bands—The Sex Pistols, the Ramones and the Saints," according to Sir Bob Geldof. The world now realizes that the once-reviled Pistols and the marginalized Ramones left behind crucial, trailblazing work that inspired thousands of young people to buy instruments and play, and spawned true musical revolutions in their respective countries. But too many still are not aware that the Saints did likewise, not only in their native Australia (mostly), but abroad as well—where most of the Saints' albums are available. In fact, along with countrymen Radio Birdman, the Saints were totally unprecedented in their continent, whereas the Pistols and Ramones quickly found supportive scenes they could thrive in. During the Saints' first four years, the group encountered total resistance—from clubowners to labels to fans—before the worldwide punk explosion recognized their fiery genius; and even then, the group had to move to England in 1977, where it had one Top 40 hit with "This Perfect Day." The three albums the original incarnation made are classic rock records, displaying great variety; the third, *Prehistoric Sounds*, is not even faintly a punk record. Even without inflammatory lyrics, the Saints managed to threaten the status quo (and Status Quo) just as much. And even when incredible singer Chris Bailey co-opted the Saints name for himself with an entirely different lineup, he released from 1980 to 1988 four superb—if totally different—rock albums and one final so-so one. Bailey has since retreated to a series of also-excellent solo albums. So has original guitarist and songwriter extraordinaire Ed Kuepper, who returned to Australia in 1978 and formed the Laughing Clowns—one of the most uncompromising bands of the early '80s, an ensemble that is spoken of in awed whispers Down Under to this day thanks to his use of jazz structures and soul horns. Kuepper's solo career began in 1985, and his nine solo LPs are what he does best: solid and soulful rock with an emphasis on his guitar talents and songwriting abilities.

what to buy: *Eternally Yours* ♪♪♪♪ (Sire, 1978, prod. Chris Bailey, Ed Kuepper) picks up on every rock 'n' roll influence of the genre's first 20 years and ups the throttle considerably to absolutely torch a series of knockout songs. In addition to the crushing hit "This Perfect Day," the album is particularly remembered for the first "punk with Stax horns" experiment—with god-like results—on its opening track, "Know Your Product." Punk historians and all fans of the dirtiest rock sounds

marvel over the sheer grit and determination of the band's rough debut, *(I'm) Stranded* ♪♪♪♪ (Sire, 1977, prod. Rod Coe). Originally intended as merely a demo—and two of its songs were greatly bettered when re-recorded properly for an EP called *1-2-3-4*—this album is still so blistering, uncompromising, and raw that it's a bit of a purist statement of intent and is punishing as all get-out. *All Fool's Day* ♪♪♪♪ (TVT, 1987, prod. Hugh Jones), by the Bailey-led Saints, finds a singer-songwriter at the height of his powers. The opening "Just Like Fire Would" even matches the multi-instrumental prowess of "Ghost Ships," and Jones's production positively crackles.

what to buy next: The final record of the Kuepper-era Saints, *Prehistoric Sounds* ♪♪♪♪ (EMI U.K., 1978, prod. Chris Bailey, Ed Kuepper) was a brave post-punk album for its time, the first indication of where Bailey would take the band without his original guitar player. Stacks of horns dominate whole sides on a mixture of soul-raveups and rockers with terrific lyrics. A cover of Otis Redding's "Security" fits in particularly well with this swinging Saints. As for the rest of the Bailey oeuvre, *Out in the Jungle* ♪♪♪♪ (New Rose Records France, 1982, prod. Ricardo Mentalban (a.k.a. Chris Bailey)) is the most outright simple rock 'n' roll record he attempted, with the Damned's Brian James even guesting on "Animal" and "Out of Sight." *The Monkey Puzzle* ♪♪♪♪ (New Rose Records France, 1981, prod. Chris Bailey) is a similar record with more dense production and less economical playing. Finally, fans of the early Bailey-Kuepper Saints are well served by the compilation *Scarce Saints* ♪♪♪♪ (Raven Records Australia, 1989, prod. Chris Bailey, Ed Kuepper), which culls together the quality B-sides and EP tracks of this halcyon legend and adds a bunch of smoking live tracks.

what to avoid: *Prodigal Son* ♪♪♪ (TVT Records, 1988, prod. Chris Bailey), the last true album of Bailey Saints, does its best to tear down some typically wonderful songs in uncharacteristic, overblown production.

the rest:
Paralytic Tonight, Dublin Tomorrow ♪♪♪♪ (New Rose Records France EP, 1979)
Prehistoric Songs ♪♪♪♪ (Harvest France, 1981)
Live in a Mud Hut ♪♪♪ (New Rose Records France, 1985)
Best of the Saints ♪♪♪♪ (Razor Records Australia, 1986)
Box Set ♪♪♪♪♪ (Mushroom Australia, 1989)
The New Rose Years ♪♪♪♪ (Fan Club Records France, 1989)
Songs of Salvation 1976–1988 ♪♪♪♪ (Raven Records Australia, 1991)
Permanent Revolution ♪♪♪♪ (Mushroom Records Australia, 1991)
The Most Primitive Band in the World, Live '74 ♪♪♪♪ (Restless Records, 1995)

worth searching for: Bailey's Saints' *A Little Madness to Be Free* (New Rose Records France, 1984, prod. Chris Bailey) is the penultimate work of the post-Kuepper era. Still working with heavy guitars, the more reflective and bluesy Bailey washes in whole oceans of strings, barking brass, and a bleakly romantic worldview. The icy chill that storms through the tour-de-force "Ghost Ships" is just the final thought of an LP that also encompasses the neo–New Orleans jump of "Imagination" and the beautiful, turgid horror of "The Hour." Remarkable.

solo outings:
Chris Bailey:

Casablanca 𝄢𝄢𝄢𝄢 (New Rose Records France, 1983)

What We Did on Our Holidays 𝄢𝄢𝄢𝄢 (New Rose Records France, 1984)

Demons 𝄢𝄢𝄢 (Mushroom Records Australia, 1991)

Savage Entertainment 𝄢𝄢𝄢𝄢 (New Rose Records France, 1992)

54 Days at Sea 𝄢𝄢𝄢 (Mushroom Records U.K., 1994)

Ed Kuepper:

Electrical Storm 𝄢𝄢𝄢𝄢 (Hot Records Australia, 1986)

Rooms of the Magnificent 𝄢𝄢𝄢𝄢 (Hot Records Australia, 1987)

Everybody's Got To 𝄢𝄢𝄢𝄢 (Capitol Records, 1989)

Today Wonder 𝄢𝄢𝄢 (Rattlesnake Records Germany, 1990)

Honey Steel's Gold 𝄢𝄢𝄢𝄢 (Restless Records, 1992)

Black Ticket Day 𝄢𝄢𝄢 (Hot Records Australia, 1992)

Serene Machine 𝄢𝄢𝄢𝄢 (Hot Records Australia, 1993)

Character Assassination 𝄢𝄢𝄢𝄢 (Restless Records, 1994)

The Butterfly Net 𝄢𝄢𝄢𝄢𝄢 (Restless Records, 1994)

A King in the Kindness Room 𝄢𝄢𝄢 (Hot Records Australia, 1995)

I Was a Mail Order Bridegroom 𝄢𝄢𝄢𝄢 (Hot Records Australia, 1995)

Exotic Mail Order Moods 𝄢𝄢𝄢𝄢 (Hot Records Australia, 1995)

Sings His Greatest Hits for You 𝄢𝄢𝄢𝄢 (Hot Records Australia, 1995)

influences:
◀◀ Eddie Cochran, Easybeats, Pretty Things

▶▶ Celibate Rifles, Leaving Trains, White Flag

Jack Rabid

Ryuichi Sakamoto
Born January 17, 1952, in Nakano, Japan.

Along with Peter Gabriel and Brian Eno, Ryuichi Sakamoto occupies an extremely rare position in the world of contemporary popular music: that of a world-class artist who has created a unique, truly global form of music and whose every move is viewed with excitement and trepidation by fans all over the planet. Schooled in Western classical music but influenced by both Japanese music and Western pop, Sakamoto is an international leader in the melding of synth-pop and dance music with folk elements from not only Japan but also Africa, Brazil, India, and even (gulp) North America. After an initial solo album in 1978 (*Thousand Knives*), the keyboardist-composer formed the Yellow Magic Orchestra (YMO) with drummer-vocalist Yukihiro Takahashi and bassist-producer Haruomi Hosono. The three took Japan by storm with

their arty and sometimes downright silly disco-ish synth-pop. Sakamoto left the trio in 1983 and immediately placed himself squarely on the map with his lovely, synth-inflected score to the film *Merry Christmas, Mr. Lawrence*, the first of close to a dozen such works. In 1984, he took the first step toward the extraordinary synthesis of styles that now characterizes his music, releasing *Illustrated Musical Encyclopedia*. By 1987's *Neo Geo*, he had developed his concept to a level that still stands as a benchmark for world-music fusion, and a year later his portion of the score to Bernardo Bertolucci's *The Last Emperor* won him both an Oscar and a Grammy for best motion picture soundtrack. Since then he has furthered both his pop and film-scoring careers, honing the advancements of *Neo Geo* on *Heartbeat* and re-working themes from his scores on *Playing the Orchestra* and the chamber-music album *1996*. Given his interest in using technology to serve the creative process, it's not surprising that his latest release, *Discord*, is also a "CD Extra," with visual tracks and a hyperlink to a special *Discord* web site. But the music on *Discord*, a four-movement tone poem leading from "Grief" to "Salvation," continues his shift back towards orchestral writing. No matter where Sakamoto's interests lead, however, he will certainly keep on producing quirky, dazzling, beautiful, and ultimately meaningful music of lasting value.

what to buy: From start to finish, *Neo Geo* 𝄢𝄢𝄢𝄢𝄢 (Epic, 1987, prod. Bill Laswell, Ryuichi Sakamoto) is a knockout. Framed by gentle, Satie-like instrumental pieces, the album shifts through Okinawan/hip-hop combinations, rocketing dance-funk and cool 'n' jazzy alternative rock ("Risky," sung by collaborator Iggy Pop). Of his soundtracks, *Merry Christmas, Mr. Lawrence* 𝄢𝄢𝄢𝄢 (London/Milan, 1983) is the best starting point, as the main theme illustrates his singular ability to mix Asian modality with a rather French, impressionistic style of classical music.

what to buy next: *Heartbeat* 𝄢𝄢𝄢𝄢 (Virgin, 1991, prod. Ryuichi Sakamoto, David Sylvian) is in many ways a more listenable affair than *Neo Geo*, although it seems more of a stylistic grab bag. Still, no matter what genres he dances through, Sakamoto's composing, arranging, and producing skills are in tip-top form here. The best-known cut from *Illustrated Musical Encyclopedia* 𝄢𝄢𝄢𝄢 (Midi, 1984) is the bouncy Thomas Dolby collaboration "Field Work," but that track doesn't begin to reveal the cross-cultural wonders hidden within this disc, which ties together big-band jazz lines, Asian beats, rugged classical passages, light funk, and Japanese and Brazilian motifs.

what to avoid: Because Sakamoto has never been much of a singer, he (like Carlos Santana) has often been at the mercy of the vocalists with whom he's collaborated. On *Media Bahn Live* 𝄢𝄢𝄢 (Midi, 1986, prod. Ryuichi Sakamoto) he depends on Bernard Fowler to carry most of the melodies, and Fowler is little more than a middle-of-the-road R&B singer. Even the band seems rather stiff on this dismissable double-album.

the rest:

Thousand Knives 𝄞𝄞𝄞 (Alfa, 1978)
Miraiha Yaro 𝄞𝄞𝄞𝄞 (Midi, 1985)
(With David Byrne and Cong Su) *The Last Emperor (Soundtrack)* 𝄞𝄞𝄞𝄞 (Virgin, 1988)
A Handmaid's Tale (Soundtrack) 𝄞𝄞𝄞 (GNP Crescendo, 1989)
Beauty 𝄞𝄞𝄞𝄞 (Virgin, 1990)
The Sheltering Sky (Soundtrack) 𝄞𝄞𝄞 (Virgin, 1991)
High Heels (Soundtrack) 𝄞𝄞𝄞𝄞 (Island, 1992)
Little Buddha (Soundtrack) 𝄞𝄞𝄞𝄞 (Milan, 1993)
(With Yosuke Yamashita and Bill Laswell) *Asian Games* 𝄞𝄞𝄞𝄞 (Verve, 1993)
Sweet Revenge 𝄞𝄞𝄞𝄞 (Elektra, 1994)
1996 𝄞𝄞𝄞𝄞 (Milan, 1996)
Discord 𝄞𝄞𝄞𝄞 (Sony Classical, 1998)

worth searching for: *Playing the Orchestra* (Virgin, 1988, prod. Aki Ikuta, Ryuichi Sakamoto) features a suite of material from the score to *Merry Christmas, Mr. Lawrence* and one from *The Last Emperor,* performed live by an orchestra. The music is gripping, poignant, and marvelously played. Rarity seekers may want to search for the special promo-only boxed version of this album, which includes an extra three-song CD-single highlighted by an orchestral version of "Before Long," the opening cut from *Neo Geo.*

influences:

◄◄ Brian Eno, Bill Nelson, Prince, David Byrne, Material, Sergio Mendes, Erik Satie, Maurice Ravel, Japanese, African, and Arabian folk music

►► Pizzicato Five, Deee-Lite, Soul Coughing, Air

Bob Remstein

Walter Salas-Humara

See: The Silos

Sam & Dave

Formed 1961, in Miami, FL. Disbanded in 1970.

Sam Moore (born October 12, 1935, in Miami, FL), vocals; Dave Prater (born May 9, 1937, in Ocilla, GA; died April 11, 1988, in Atlanta, GA), vocals.

Soul men indeed, Sam Moore and Dave Prater could trade vocals with both ease and urgency that seemed almost instinctive. Using the call-and-response technique that harkened back to their beginnings as gospel singers, Prater and Moore slipped around each other's vocal lines like cracking bullwhips. Their Stax/Volt recordings, largely written and produced by the team of Isaac Hayes and David Porter, rank with the finest works in the field, records that have been covered by a disparate group of artists such as Elvis Costello, Fabulous Thunderbirds, Tom Jones, and Carl Wilson of the Beach Boys. The duo first paired in 1961 and recorded several unsuccessful singles for the Roulette label before producer Jerry Wexler of Atlantic Records signed them and put the duo in the bosom of Memphis soul, where Hayes and Porter supervised a string of hit singles beginning with the timeless "Hold on I'm Coming," one of the definitive records of '60s soul and a title allegedly inspired by repeated calls for songwriter Hayes to return to a session from the bathroom. After Stax folded its tent, the duo continued to record for Atlantic under a procession of different producers—notably Wexler and Tom Dowd, and Miami's Brad Shapiro and Dave Crawford—although without much success. Personal conflicts led to a split in 1970. They rejoined a number of times, briefly, but nothing they ever did again on their own or as a team matched the incendiary force of their Stax/Volt recordings. Prater died in a 1988 car crash, after the Blues Brothers hit version of their "Soul Man" reignited interest in their work. Moore continues to ply his trade, notably singing harmonies on the 1992 Bruce Springsteen album *Human Touch,* a 1994 duet with Conway Twitty on the country and soul collaboration *Rhythm Country and Blues,* and a terrific live performance with John Fogerty at the Concert for the Rock and Roll Hall of Fame in 1995.

what to buy: The double-disc retrospective, *Sweat 'N' Soul: Anthology, 1965–1971* 𝄞𝄞𝄞𝄞 (Rhino, 1993, prod. various) combines all the duo's famed highspots with rewarding gems plucked from the dusty corners of their estimable body of work.

what to buy next: All the individual original Stax albums boast non-single tracks steeped in that greasy fatback sound of Memphis soul, but *Soul Men* 𝄞𝄞𝄞𝄞 (Stax, 1967/Atlantic, 1992, prod. Isaac Hayes and David Porter) holds a slight edge with cuts such as "Broke Down Piece of Man" (later covered by Southside Johnny & the Asbury Jukes), "May I Baby," and their delicious take on the Everly Brothers' "Let It Be Me."

what to avoid: The later re-recordings of their hits on *Sweet & Funky Gold* 𝄞 (Hollywood/Rounder, 1994) are as insulting as they are unnecessary.

the rest:

Hold on I'm Coming 𝄞𝄞𝄞𝄞 (Stax, 1966/Atlantic, 1991)
Double Dynamite 𝄞𝄞𝄞𝄞 (Stax, 1966/Atlantic, 1991)
I Thank You 𝄞𝄞𝄞 (Stax, 1968/Atlantic, 1992)
Best of Sam & Dave 𝄞𝄞𝄞𝄞 (Atlantic, 1987)
Greatest Song 𝄞𝄞 (Curb, 1995)
The Very Best of Sam & Dave 𝄞𝄞𝄞𝄞 (Rhino, 1995)
Soul Man 𝄞𝄞 (Remember, 1996)

worth searching for: *The Stax/Volt Revue, Volume One—Live in London* (Stax, 1967, prod. Jim Stewart) contains a spellbinding live version of their drop-dead soul ballad "When Something Is Wrong with My Baby" alongside another pair of Sam & Dave performances, not to mention cuts by Otis Redding, Booker T. & the MG's, Eddie Floyd, and others.

influences:

◀◀ Sam Cooke, Jackie Wilson, the Sims Twins

▶▶ The Righteous Brothers, the Blues Brothers

Joel Selvin and Ken Burke

Sam the Sham & the Pharaohs /Sam the Sham Revue

Formed 1963, in Dallas, TX. Disbanded 1968.

Sam the Sham (born Domingo Samudio, 1940, in Dallas, TX), lead vocals, organ; David Martin, bass (1963–66); Ray Stinnet, guitar (1963–66); Jerry Patterson, drums (1963–66); Butch Gibson, saxophone (1965–66); Frank Carabetta, guitar, saxophone, keyboards (1966–68); Andrew Kouha, guitar (1966–68); Tony Gerace, bass (1966–67); Billy Bennett, drums (1966–67); Ronnie "Spiderman" Jacobsen, bass (1967–68); Louis Vilardo, drums (1967–68); Fran Curcio, vocals (1967–68); Loraine Genero, vocals (1967–68); Jane Anderson, vocals (1967–68).

With the crazed yelp "Uno, dos, one-two-tres-quatro!" Sam the Sham burst into the spotlight seemingly out of nowhere with the classic "Wooly Bully," the second-best–selling single of 1965. The sight of his band, festooned in garish mock-Egyptian garb, was a refreshing if somewhat bizarre distraction from the Merseybeat and Motown-infested mid-1960s. Unfairly categorized even then as a novelty act despite solid, groundbreaking musicianship, Sam the Sham, with roots deep-set in Southern-fried R&B, can rightfully lay claim today to being one of the principle architects of the entire Tex-Mex genre.

After a four-year Navy stint and time spent at Arlington State College studying classical music by day (and club-hopping by night), Samudio formed his first band in the early 1960s and began performing sets full of John Lee Hooker, Jimmy Reed, and Elmore James tunes before the denizens of Dallas juke joints. However, quickly tiring of the five-dollar-per-man-per-night regimen, Samudio disbanded this outfit soon afterwards, but not before acquiring the moniker "Sam the Sham" due to his penchant for enthusiastically emceeing the act (a.k.a. "shamming") as opposed to simply planting himself dourly behind his organ on stage. With his old school pal David Martin, Samudio later assembled his first set of Pharaohs and released "Haunted House" in May 1964. This record fared well enough on local radio to bring them to the attention of Sun Records alumnus Stan Kesler, who arranged to cut a version of a new song (about Sam's cat) that the band had ad-libbed on stage one night. Li-

censed to MGM Records in 1965, "Wooly Bully" went on to sell 3.5 million copies, and the Pharaohs toured the world in their trademark turban outfits as well as making frequent television appearances and even walk-ons in a couple of quickie MGM movie musicals. The original quintet disbanded the following year however, leaving Sam to cut his second-biggest hit, "Little Red Riding Hood," with a New York band previously known as the Gypsies. This arrangement, later augmented by a chorus of back-up singers and dancers ("the Shamettes") grew into the full-scale Sam the Sham Revue, which cut an additional album for MGM in 1967 before Sam went totally solo with the wonderful *Sam, Hard and Heavy* album in 1970. Cut with Duane Allman and the Dixie Flyers for Atlantic Records, it won Sam his first and only Grammy Award—for its liner notes. Samudio resurfaced over a decade later alongside Ry Cooder, composing music for *The Border* soundtrack. Today offering his services strictly in the name of the Lord, Sam can be found preaching on Memphis street corners and performing for the inmates of Tennessee jails when not readying and recording new songs at home on his acoustic guitar. He was recently honored with the prestigious Desi Award in recognition of his achievements as a Mexican American, and at the gala presentation ceremonies leapt on stage to perform a blistering "Wooly Bully" accompanied by, appropriately enough, one of his many heirs-apparent, the Texas Tornados.

what to buy: The stupendous *Pharaohization: The Best of Sam the Sham and the Pharaohs* ♫♫♫♫ (Rhino, 1985, prod. various) demonstrates that this band had far more to offer than the mere novelties of its two biggest hits. Left to its own devices, the band's rockabilly-infused Louisiana R&B was practically without precedent in the mid-1960s, and greatly influenced many artists to come.

what to buy next: With every single one of their spectacular MGM albums sorrowfully out of print, and until some visionary soul decides to issue Sam's newest recordings, we'll have to make due with the fine, fun *Turban Renewal: A Tribute to Sam the Sham & the Pharaohs* ♫♫♫ (Norton, 1994, compilation prod. Billy Miller, Mark Natale), in which 26 acts (28 on the double-vinyl edition) pay homage to one of Tex-Mex's founding fathers.

influences:

◀◀ Louis Jordan, Hank Williams, Otis Rush, Screamin' Jay Hawkins, Booker T. & the MG's

▶▶ Sir Douglas Quintet, Joe "King" Carrasco, Texas Tornados

Gary Pig Gold

Richie Sambora

See: Bon Jovi

Samhain

See: Danzig

Samiam

Formed 1988, in Berkeley, CA.

Jason Beebout, vocals; Sergie Loobkoff, guitar; James Brogan, guitar; Martin Brohm, bass (1988–93); Aaron Rubin, bass (1993–98); Sean Kennerly, bass (1998–present); Mark Mortensen, drums (1988–90, 1993–94); David Ayer, drums (1990–93); Victor Indrizzo, drums (1994–96); M.P., drums (1996–present).

The melodic punk quintet Samiam is a veritable East Bay supergroup, initially comprising Jason Beebout (vocals) and Martin Brohm (bass) of the defunct group Isocracy, Social Unrest guitarist James Brogan, ex–Sweet Baby guitarist Sergie Loobkoff, and local drummer Mark Mortensen. Mortensen left the band to return to college in 1990 and was replaced by David Ayer, while ex–Mr. T. Experience bassist Aaron Rubin replaced Brohm during mid-1993. Thanks to a heavy tour schedule during the early '90s, Samiam quickly developed a large European following; in America, the group was careful to avoid being typecast as a "punk" band, and was more closely aligned with the alternative rock scene than the underground punk scene. In 1994 Samiam became the subject of a post-*Dookie* bidding war, eventually signing with Atlantic Records. Unlike its contemporary, Jawbreaker, Samiam survived its troubled major label experience, resurfacing in 1998 on the independent label Ignition Records with *You Are Freaking Me Out*. Beebout currently divides his time between Samiam and the indie rock group Knapsack.

what to buy: *Soar* &&&& (New Red Archives, 1991, prod. Brett Gurewitz) is the cream of Samiam's high-quality catalog, a shining example of its unique blend of emotional, melodic punk and intense, dynamic vocals. Production by Bad Religion's Brett Gurewitz is a plus. A classic of '90s punk.

the rest:

Samiam &&& (New Red Archives, 1990)
Billy &&&& (New Red Archives, 1992)
Clumsy &&& (Atlantic, 1994)
You Are Freaking Me Out &&& (Ignition, 1998)

solo outings:

Knapsack (Beebout):
Silver Sweepstakes &&& (Alias, 1995)
Day Three of My New Life &&& (Alias, 1997)

influences:

◄◄ Hüsker Dü, the Goo Goo Dolls, the Doughboys

►► Knapsack

Seth Hindin

The Samples

Formed 1987, in Boulder, CO.

Sean Kelly, vocals, guitar; Andy Sheldon, bass, vocals; Jeep MacNichol, drums, vocals (1987–96); Al Laughlin, keyboards, vocals (1987–96); Charles Hambleton, guitar (1987–91); Rob Somers, guitar, backing vocals (1997–present); Kenny James, drums, backing vocals (1997–present); Alex Matson, keyboards (1997–present).

In an odd twist, the Samples started with a major label deal (on Arista), then switched to the small indie W.A.R.? (What Are Records?). But this backwards career path worked, since the band's frequent touring slowly built a solid grassroots following, especially in college towns. Named for the band's early survival technique of making meals from free supermarket samples, the group offers airy, jazzy pop, a singer who sounds eerily like Sting, sincere lyrics, and CDs that come packaged in environmentally friendly cardboard. The band restructured during the late '90s, losing two founding members and adding three new members.

what to buy: The Samples' recordings have a certain similarity to them, but *Underwater People* &&&& (W.A.R.?, 1992, prod. Jim Scott, the Samples)—a collection of demos, live tracks, and leftovers from an aborted second album—rises above the rest with lots of energetic reggae rhythms and more consistent songwriting, as well as a guest shot from Branford Marsalis.

what to buy next: *The Samples* &&&& (Arista/W.A.R.?, 1990, prod. Walt Beery) is the band's first and only major label record and, perhaps because of that, is one that still sells after all these years. *No Room* &&&& (W.A.R.?, 1992, prod. Jim Scott) is a solid effort with a spacious, jazzy feel and strong songs.

what to avoid: *The Last Drag* ♫♫♫ (W.A.R.?, 1993, prod. Marc DeSisto, the Samples) is indeed a drag due to plodding, mediocre songs.

the rest:
Autopilot ♫♫♫ (W.A.R.?, 1994)
Still Water ♫♫♫ (W.A.R.?, 1994)
Outpost ♫♫♫ (W.A.R.?, 1996)
Transmissions from the Sea of Tranquility ♫♫♫♫ (W.A.R.?, 1997)
Here and Somewhere Else N/A (W.A.R.?, 1998)

worth searching for: Before *No Room*, the Samples recorded *The Sigma Album*. It went unreleased, though it's available via bootlegs. And some of the tracks appear on "Underwater People."

solo outings:
Sean Kelly:
Light House Rocket ♫♫♫♫ (W.A.R.?, 1995)

Jeep MacNichol:
With a Fist ♫♫ (W.A.R.?, 1996)

Andy Sheldon (with Häzard):
Science Fiction ♫♫ (W.A.R.?, 1996)

influences:
◀◀ The Police, Bob Marley, the Grateful Dead
▶▶ The Why Store, Ugly Americans

Jill Hamilton

Sand Rubies
See: Sidewinders

Santana
/Carlos Santana
Formed 1967, in San Francisco, CA. Carlos Santana born July 20, 1947, in Autlan de Navarro, Mexico.

Carlos Santana, guitar; Gregg Rolie, organ, vocals; David Brown, bass; Michael Shrieve, drums; Jose "Chepito" Areas, timbales; Michael Carabello, congas; others.

Unknowns who took Woodstock by storm—literally, since the band played during a downpour—Santana could have stopped recording after its third album and its legacy would still be secure. But guitarist Carlos Santana continued to ply the group's trademark Latin-tinged rock sound to increasingly lesser effect during the next three decades, using an uncountable array of players and even regrouping with the original band members during 1988 in an attempt to recapture the majestic magic of those early days. His piercing, stinging guitar set against the roiling clatter of Latin percussion led the attack; when future Journey lead guitarist Neal Schon joined the band for the third

album, his bluesy fusillades gave Santana a latticework to play against. Although he recorded umpteen albums, in a wide variety of variations of the basic formula, Santana never again equaled the power and sweep of those first three albums.

what to buy: On the heels of the original band's 1998 induction into the Rock and Roll Hall of Fame, Columbia Legacy gave the cornerstone first three albums a complete going over with previously unreleased bonus tracks that weren't even part of the examplary box set *Dance of the Rainbow Serpent* ♫♫♫♫ (Columbia Legacy, 1997, compilation prod. Bob Irwin). The new set includes the sparkling debut, *Santana* ♫♫♫♫ (Columbia, 1969, prod. Brent Dangerfield), *Abraxas* ♫♫♫♫♫ (Columbia, 1970, prod. Fred Catero), and *Santana III* ♫♫♫♫ (Columbia, 1971, prod. Santana).

what to buy next: The band's first attempt at recording the debut album—a December 1968 show at the Fillmore West—is featured on *Live at the Fillmore '68* ♫♫♫♫ (Columbia Legacy, 1998, prod. David Rubinson, Bill Irwin), and why this wasn't released in the first place is an utter mystery. Confident to the point of being cocky, this strutting, menacing band manhandles its fiery fusion of blues, Latin, jazz, and rock like masters.

what to avoid: The so-called *Lotus* **woof!** (Columbia, 1973, prod. New Santana Band) album, a three-record set recorded live in Japan but unreleased in this country for nearly 20 years, is the guru guitarist's jazz-fusion conceit at its highest.

the rest:
Carvanserai ♫♫ (Columbia, 1972)
Welcome ♫ (Columbia, 1973)
Greatest Hits ♫♫ (Columbia, 1974)
Borboletta ♫ (Columbia, 1974)
Amigos ♫ (Columbia, 1976)
Festival ♫ (Columbia, 1977)
Moonflower ♫ (Columbia, 1977)
Inner Secrets (Columbia, 1978)
Marathon ♫♫ (Columbia, 1979)
Zebop! ♫♫ (Columbia, 1981)
Shango **woof!** (Columbia, 1982)
Havana Moon ♫♫♫♫ (Columbia, 1983)
Beyond Appearances ♫ (Columbia, 1985)
Freedom **woof!** (Columbia, 1987)
Viva Santana! ♫♫♫ (Columbia, 1988)
Spirits Dancing in the Flesh ♫ (Columbia, 1990)
Milagro ♫ (Polydor, 1992)
The Best of Santana ♫♫♫ (Columbia Legacy, 1998)

worth searching for: The only time the most ferocious Santana band ever performed the Miles Davis classic "In a Silent Way" happened to also be the final time the illustrious lineup played together, closing night at the Fillmore West in 1971. Ironically,

Carlos Santana (© Ken Settle)

this serene benediction was recorded live and included on the box set *Fillmore: The Last Days* (Epic, 1972/ Legacy, 1995).

solo outings:
Carlos Santana:
(With Mahavishnu John McLaughlin) *Love, Devotion and Surrender* 𝄞𝄞𝄞 (Columbia, 1973)
(With Turiya Alice Coltrane) *Illuminations* **woof!** (Columbia, 1974)
Oneness, Silver Dreams—Golden Reality **woof!** (Columbia, 1979)
The Swing of Delight 𝄞 (Columbia, 1980)
Blues for Salvador 𝄞𝄞 (Columbia, 1987)
Sacred Fire: Live in South America 𝄞𝄞𝄞 (Polydor, 1993)
Brothers 𝄞𝄞 (Island, 1994)
Dance of the Rainbow Serpent 𝄞𝄞𝄞𝄞 (Columbia, 1995)

influences:
◀◀ Willie Bobo, Tito Puente, Olatunji, John Coltrane, Miles Davis, Peter Green

▶▶ Malo, Azteca, Journey

Joel Selvin

Satchel
See: Brad

Joe Satriani
Born July 15, 1957, in Carle Place, NY.

Joe Satriani's six-string wizardry leaves guitar fans gasping for breath, but he's also one of the few rock instrumentalists who has cracked the mainstream charts. That's because the former guitar teacher, whose pupils included Steve Vai, jazz ace Charlie Hunter, and Metallica's Kirk Hammett, never neglects melody or arrangement when he puts his jaw-dropping technique to work. A guitar *player,* Satriani gave lessons and sold his own recordings through ads in guitar magazines until Vai, who by then was playing with David Lee Roth's band, persuaded Relativity Records to sign his former instructor. Satriani's first recording with Relativity produced the platinum-selling hit *Surfing with the Alien* and landed him a spot in Mick Jagger's solo band. Satriani is undeniably one of rock's quickest, most creative guitarists; his imagination sometimes takes him to the outer limits—as seen on songs with titles such as "The Mystical Potato Head Groove Thing" and "Luminous Flesh Giants." But he can pluck, whammy, hammer, or tap his way through a maelstrom of metal, blues, boogie, or funk, then squeeze the most delicate and emotional notes out of his Ibanez. Satriani's vocals and harmonica, which he began adding on 1989's *Flying in a Blue Dream*, are adequate but unexceptional.

what to buy: *Crystal Planet* 𝄞𝄞𝄞𝄞 (Epic, 1998, prod. Mike Fraser) offers everything an axe-aholic could want: layers of lightning-fast electric guitars, futuristic tones, ingenious grooves, and enough flash to light up Times Square. The 15 instrumentals range from riveting space-metal jammers ("Crystal Planet" and "Psycho Monkey") to radically inventive ballads ("A Piece of Liquid" and "Trundrumbalind"). The steady pulse and swirling riffs of "A Train of Angels" is a highlight.

what to buy next: *Flying in a Blue Dream* 𝄞𝄞𝄞𝄞 (Relativity, 1989, prod. Joe Satriani, John Cuniberti) bows to the guitar Mount Rushmore of Hendrix, Page, Clapton, and Beck, then blasts ahead with state-of-the-art effects and dazzling technique on such rockers as "Back to Shalla-Bal" and "Can't Slow Down." *Surfing with the Alien* 𝄞𝄞𝄞𝄞 (Relativity, 1987, prod. Joe Satriani, John Cuniberti) opens with swooshing jet guitars on the title cut and keeps the afterburners red-hot, hitting a sonic boom on the explosive "Satch Boogie." One complaint: the 10 instrumentals measure up to a relatively paltry 37 minutes. *Satriani* 𝄞𝄞𝄞𝄞 (Relativity, 1995, prod. Glyn Johns) comes through as a delayed sequel to *Flying in a Blue Dream*, showing the same brilliant technique but no new vision.

what to avoid: Though Satriani hasn't released a loser yet, *Not of This Earth* 𝄞𝄞𝄞 (Relativity, 1986) treads a bit too much of the same ground as *Surfing with the Alien*. In 1996, Satriani shared the stage with former student Vai and Texas ace Eric Johnson for the "G3 Tour," captured on *Joe Satriani, Eric Johnson, Steve Vai—G3 Live in Concert* 𝄞𝄞 (Epic, 1997, prod. Mike Fraser). What was a great experience in concert translates into guitar overkill on CD.

the rest:
Dreaming #11 𝄞𝄞𝄞𝄞 (Relativity EP, 1988)
The Extremist 𝄞𝄞𝄞 (Relativity, 1992)
Time Machine 𝄞𝄞𝄞𝄞 (Relativity, 1993)

worth searching for: *Joe Satriani* (Rubina EP, 1984), the guitarist's low-budget debut EP, is out of print but not impossible to find.

influences:
◀◀ Jimmy Page, Jeff Beck, Pat Metheny, Jimi Hendrix, Johnny Winter, Eric Clapton

▶▶ Steve Vai, Metallica, Megadeth, Pantera

David Yonke

Sausage
See: Primus

Savage Garden
Formed 1993, in Brisbane, Australia.

Darren Hayes, vocals; Daniel Jones, instruments.

In what is becoming a more and more familiar tale, Darren Hayes and Daniel Jones met through an ad Jones placed for a singer. They connected immediately and began writing songs.

In 1996, the synth-pop–influenced "I Want You" and its identifying line "chic-a-cherry cola" was the top-selling Australian single. After its follow-up single "To the Moon and Back" hit #1, Columbia Records knocked on the door and offered Savage Garden an international record deal.

what's available: The debut, *Savage Garden* &&& (Columbia, 1997, prod. Charles Fisher), shows the band isn't just a throwaway pop act. Savage Garden's lyrics are deeper than your average Europop, and *Savage Garden* is an exercise in contradictions. In the aforementioned "I Want You," Hayes seductively raps "Come stand a little bit closer/Breathe in and get a bit higher/You'll never know what hit you/When I get to you" over a bed of pulsating drum beats and cascading keyboards. On the opposite side is "Truly Madly Deeply," a heartfelt love song told to the tune of a slowed-down drum beat. In a different direction is "Tears of Pearls," a potential disco dance hit.

influences:
◄◄ Depeche Mode, the Thompson Twins

Christina Fuoco

Save Ferris

Formed 1995, in Orange County, CA.

Monique Powell, vocals; Brian Mashburn, guitar, vocals; Bill Uechi, bass; Marc Harismendy, drums; Jose Castellanos, trumpet; Eric Zamora, saxophone; Brian Williams, trombone.

See if this sounds familiar: ska band from Orange County, female lead singer, melodies that stick like bubblegum, bouncy horns, and unassuming guitars. But despite frequent and obvious comparisons to the much more successful No Doubt, Save Ferris obliviously plays upbeat jump-ska music and even a cover of Dexy's Midnight Runners' 1983 hit "Come on Eileen." They're thoroughly unoriginal—right down to the name, derived from the '80s movie *Ferris Bueller's Day Off*—but more fun than Puff Daddy. Monique Powell, who Brian Mashburn badgered into joining by constantly calling her parents' house, is a solid vocalist and the band's live focal point. Mashburn writes most of the songs, which lean towards the goofy (he describes Spam as "pink and it's oval/I buy it at the Mobil" in one song), and supplies the rhythmic backbone.

what's available: *It Means Everything* &&& (Epic, 1997, prod. Peter Collins, Craig Nepp, Save Ferris) won't win any preservation-of-Jamaican-music awards, but it's rewarding in a playful way. At the very least, the band never takes itself too seriously.

influences:
◄◄ The Specials, Madness, Dexy's Midnight Runners, No Doubt, the Mighty Mighty Bosstones, Cherry Poppin' Daddies

Steve Knopper

Savoy Brown

Formed 1966, in London, England.

Kim Simmonds (born December 5, 1947, in Wales, Great Britain), guitar, vocals; Bryce Portius, vocals (1966–68); Martin Stone, guitar (1966–68); Ray Chappell, bass (1966–68); Leo Mannings, drums (1966–68); Bob Hall, keyboards (1966–70); Chris Youlden, vocals (1968–70); Lonesome Dave Peverett, guitar, vocals (1968–70); Rivers Job, bass (1968); Tone Stevens, bass (1968–70); Roger Earl, drums (1968–70); Dave Walker, vocals (1971–72, 1988–90); Paul Raymond, keyboards (1971–74); Andy Pyle, bass (1971, 1972–74); Andy Sylvester, bass (1971–72); Dave Bidwell, drums (1971–72); Jackie Lynton, vocals (1972–74); Ron Berg, drums (1972–74); Stan Webb, guitar, vocals (1974); Miller Anderson, guitar, vocals (1974); Jimmy Leverton, bass (1974); Eric Dillon, drums (1974); Andy Rae, bass, vocals (1975); Ian Ellis, bass, vocals (1976–78); Tom Farnell, drums (1975–78); Jim Dagnesi, bass (1988–89); Al Macomber, drums (1988–89); Rick Jewett, keyboards, vocals (1990); Lou Kaplan, bass, vocals (1990); Pete Mendillo, drums (1990); Pete McMahon, vocals, harmonica (1994–95); Jim Heyl, bass (1994–96); Dave Olson, drums (1994–95); Nathaniel, bass, vocals (1996–present).

Kim Simmonds might just be the Rodney Dangerfield of the blues world. It's not that there's anything comedic about his music, but who could blame him for pulling nervously at the neck of his guitar and complaining that he gets "no respect." Simmonds is no whiner, but the fact is he's been dealt with dismissively, if at all, in blues circles, and frequently has fared only marginally better amid the rock 'n' roll cognoscenti—this despite his having stayed relatively true to his (admittedly imported) blues roots through a career that has spanned 30-plus years and more than 20 albums. He keeps the Savoy Brown logo active, continuing to make new music, while pleasing old fans through regular touring on the club circuit. At its inception, Savoy Brown was part of an important if imitative British blues movement that helped popularize blues in America by introducing the music in an acceptable boogie and rock-fusion setting. Always more pleasing to American than British audiences, Savoy Brown first appeared in 1966 with the long out-of-print *Shake Down*. In a move that signaled a career pattern of constantly changing line-ups, Simmonds was soon found playing with a whole new group of musicians. Lacking a particularly strong voice, Simmonds usually opted to front the vocals to someone more capable. During Savoy's salad days in the late '60s, Simmonds found two truly exceptional vocalists in Chris Youlden and Dave Peverett.

what to buy: In a six-month period in 1970 the band released two outstanding albums. *Raw Sienna* &&&& (Deram, 1970, prod. Kim Simmonds, Chris Youlden) features Youlden's world-weary, sometimes anguished, always satisfying croak and a full horn section that gives it a hard-edged R&B feel. *Looking In* &&&& (Deram, 1970, prod. Kim Simmonds) is a more stripped-down, hard-rocking affair with Peverett rising to the occasion. *The Savoy Brown Collection* ♫♫♫♪ (Deram/Chronicles, 1993, prod. various) is a well-chosen, nicely annotated, chronologically arranged two-disc overview that starts at the earliest days of the band and ends two-and-a-half hours later with material recorded in the late 1970s, including more than half an hour of material from *Raw Sienna* and *Lookin' In.* A return to roots, *Bring It Home* ♫♫♫♪ (Viceroy, 1995, prod. Kim Simmonds) offers straight-ahead rocking blues.

what to buy next: *Getting to the Point* ♫♫♫♪ (Deram, 1968, prod. Mike Vernon), *Blue Matter* ♫♫♫♪ (Deram, 1968, prod. Mike Vernon), and *A Step Further* ♫♫♫♪ (Deram, 1969, prod. Mike Vernon), Savoy's second, third, and fourth albums respectively, are all worthwhile, showing a band gaining in skill and confidence and developing the group voice that came to fruition on *Raw Sienna* and *Lookin' In.* *Street Corner Talking* ♫♫♫♪ (Deram, 1971, prod. Neil Slaven) seems a boogie-based step in the direction of commerciality and mainstream acceptance with some memorable original songs like "Tell Mama" and "All I Can Do (Is Cry)."

what to avoid: During the late '80s, Simmonds reunited with Dave Walker. The two resulting studio efforts, *Make Me Sweat* **woof!** (GNP Crescendo, 1988) and *Kings of Boogies* **woof!** (GNP Crescendo, 1989) have a high boogie-bombast quotient, hoarsely brayed vocal histrionics by Walker, and period arena rock trappings like the annoying and pointless synthesizer washes on the latter.

the rest:
Hellbound Train ♫♫♫ (Deram, 1972)
Lion's Share ♫♫♫ (Deram, 1972)
Jack the Toad ♫♫♫ (Deram, 1973)
Live and Kickin' ♫♫♪ (GNP Crescendo, 1990)
Archive Alive!—Live at the Record Plant, 1975 N/A (Archive, 1998)

worth searching for: One of the biggest reasons for Simmonds's longevity has been his willingness to tour and perform live. Thus, it's fitting that there are several live albums worth hearing. The concert recorded for *Live in Central Park* (Relix, 1989) was voted the best of New York's 1972 summer concert series by the *Village Voice,* and mostly features material from *Street Corner Talking* and *Lion's Share.* *Slow Train* (Relix, 1987), an all-acoustic set, includes solo studio recordings by Simmonds and several live numbers recorded with harmonica and bass backing in 1986 at New York City's Lone Star Cafe.

solo outings:
Kim Simmonds:
Solitaire ♫♫♫ (Blue Wave, 1997)

influences:
◀◀ Freddie King, Howlin' Wolf, Hubert Sumlin, Willie Dixon, Earl King, Eric Clapton, Peter Green

▶▶ Foghat, the Allman Brothers Band, Cactus, George Thorogood & the Destroyers

see also: *Foghat*

Michael Dixon

Savuka
See: Johnny Clegg & Savuka

Saxon
Formed 1977, in Yorkshire, England.

Biff Byford, vocals; Paul Quinn, guitar; Graham Oliver, guitar (1977–96); Steve Dawson, bass; Pete Gill, drums; Nigel Glockler, drums; Doug Scarrat, guitar; Nibbs Carter, bass.

A few members of the new wave of British heavy metal—Iron Maiden, Judas Priest—made their mark on western shores. Not so Saxon. And that's ironic, since this quintet was, and remains, perhaps the loudest and proudest of the bunch, playing a snarling, aggressive, and deafening pub-style brand of hard rock that frequently sounds like an airplane landing—appropriate, since one of its British hits is titled "747 (Strangers in the Night)." The truth is that if you haven't yet heard Saxon, you're not really missing much. On the other hand, if you have a taste for the heavy stuff, and can forgive a band that covers Christopher Cross's "Ride Like the Wind" (honest), this might just be a group for you to investigate.

what to buy: Saxon live beats the studio most every day, and *The Eagle Has Landed, Pt. 2* ♫♫♫ (CMC International, 1998) houses the right songs, conveying the group's loutish attitude in abundance.

the rest:
Dogs of War ♫♫♫ (Mayhem, 1995)
Unleash the Beast ♫♫ (CMC International, 1997)
Live at Donnington ♫♫♪ (Castle, 1998)

worth searching for: *The Best of Saxon* (Griffin, 1994, prod. various) is a worthwhile, out-of-print sampler. The group's best albums, 1980's *Wheels of Steel* and 1981's *Denim & Leather,* are available only via German import.

influences:
◀◀ Deep Purple, Black Sabbath, Judas Priest, Motörhead

▶▶ Guns N' Roses, Metallica, Quiet Riot

Gary Graff

Leo Sayer
Born May 21, 1948, in Shore Ham-on-Sea, England.

The '70s twisted many a promising career into a pretzel by the decade's end; proof positive of that lies in the recorded output of Leo Sayer. A talented songwriter, Sayer, aided by fellow Brit David Courtney, got his start on a slightly edgier note fronting Patches, a hard-pop outfit featuring Sayer out front in a clown's costume, of all things. Sayer's "Giving It All Away" caught the attention of Roger Daltrey, who covered it and other Sayer/Courtney tunes on his debut solo album. Moving into more mainstream turf by the mid-'70s, Sayer found an American audience when "Long Tall Glasses" went Top 10. His mass acceptance came full flower a few years later with an onslaught of unabashedly MOR hits—"You Make Me Feel Like Dancing," "When I Need You," "How Much Love," all of which are well-written and right in step with the times—and now hopelessly dated. One final smash, "More Than I Can Say," ushered in the '80s for Sayer, but he was unable to follow up that success and faded unceremoniously away.

what to buy: For those who must have some Sayer for the home, your one-stop shopping source is *The Show Must Go On: Anthology* ♫♫♫ (Rhino, 1996, prod. Adam Faith, Richard Perry, Alan Tarney), which samples all of Sayer's works, starting with his 1974 debut *Silverbird* and including all the hits, misses, and then some.

the rest:
Endless Flight ♫♫♫ (Chrysalis, 1976)
Collection ♫♫♫ (Castle, 1992)
All the Best ♫♫♫ (Chrysalis, 1993)

influences:
◀◀ The Beatles, David Bowie, Elton John

▶▶ Sheena Easton, Robert John

David Simons

Boz Scaggs

Born June 8, 1944, in Canton, OH.

The cool, urbane sound of Boz Scaggs's brand of white soul was more than just the soundtrack to '70s singles bars: his R&B blood runs a tad bit deeper. Prior to his emergence as a sophisticated soulful crooner, he was Steve Miller's cohort in a Dallas prep school during the late '50s. After their shared college years in Wisconsin, they made blues-based R&B, culminating in his appearances on the first two Steve Miller albums, which in turn fueled Scaggs to go the solo route. His debut was earthy blues, with some stellar slide guitar from the late Duane Allman on the track "Loan Me a Dime." Gradually eschewing rockers for ballads while picking up top L.A. studio pros along the way, Scaggs created the slick adult soul that hit its peak with *Silk Degrees* during the mid-'70s. That five-million seller set the course for all his later recordings, although he has never reached that level of success since. Recently, he's spent more time nurturing his Bay Area club, Slim's, than recording or touring, although he's surfaced sporadically during the '90s with some promising work.

what to buy: *Silk Degrees* ♫♫♫♫ (Columbia, 1976, prod. Joe Wissert) represents an obvious creative and commercial peak, with the laid-back cool elegance of "Lowdown" and the chugging "Lido Shuffle," both staples of '70s FM radio. *Boz Scaggs* ♫♫♫♫ (Atlantic, 1969/1988, prod. Jan Wenner, Marlin Greene) is highlighted by the Muscle Shoals house band, which provides hot backing on this rootsy debut, and also by the fiery Allman solos on "Loan Me a Dime."

what to buy next: For latter-day Scaggs, *Some Change* ♫♫♫ (Virgin, 1994, prod. Boz Scaggs, Ricky Fataar) is a sincere comeback that has a down-home comfort. Scaggs sounds assured and inspired, and Booker T. Jones on the organ doesn't hurt either. As his back catolog has yet to be remastered, *My Time: A Boz Scaggs Anthology, 1969–1997* ♫♫♫♫ (Legacy, 1997, prod. various) offers newly mixed versions of most of his essential tracks.

what to avoid: His first release after an eight-year hiatus, *Other Roads* ♫♫ (Columbia, 1988, prod. Bill Schnee, Stewart Levine) is so anti-climactic it makes you wonder if he shouldn't stick to running his restaurant. Scaggs's voice is in fine form, but the material is unchallenging, and the wimp-chops of backing band Toto squash out any remaining life.

the rest:
Slow Dancer ♫♫♫ (Columbia, 1974)
Down Two Then Left ♫♫♫ (Columbia, 1977)
Hits ♫♫♫♫ (Columbia, 1980)
Come on Home ♫♫♫♫ (Virgin, 1997)

worth searching for: *My Time* (Columbia, 1972, prod. Boz Scaggs) has the last of the rockers, "Full-Lock Power Slide" and "Dinah Flo." Pretty charged-up stuff, considering what the following 20 years held.

influences:
◀◀ Lou Rawls, Ray Charles, Dan Penn, Motown, Steve Miller Band

▶▶ Phil Collins, Huey Lewis and the News, Michael Bolton

see also: *Steve Miller*

Allan Orski

Scandal
See: Patty Smyth

The Scene Is Now
Formed 1983, in Hoboken, NJ. Disbanded 1990.

Dick Champ, various instruments; Philip Dray, various instruments; Chris Nelson, various instruments; Jeff McGovern, drums (1983–88);

Will Rigby, drums (1988–90); Tony Maimone, bass, synthesizer (1988–90); Rusty Jones, bass (1990); others.

In the heyday of post No Wave New York City, while bands like the Swans, Sonic Youth, and Live Skull were detuning and deconstructing guitar rock, Hoboken's The Scene Is Now was gently and affectionately examining guitar pop with a similar curiosity, in the process creating magical bits of dust out of the remains. Founding member Philip Dray is an author whose works include books on the ozone layer, the Civil Rights movement, and cinema in the '60s and '70s, and his book-smarts occasionally leave us rock 'n' roll ape-heads at a loss; but taken as a whole, it matters less what the hell the band is talking about than that they're saying something so angular and engaging.

what to buy: That anything by the Scene Is Now is available is a victory in itself. *The Oily Years* 🎵🎵🎵 (Bar/None, 1995, prod. the Scene Is Now) is a wonderful collection, but on first listen somewhat of a tough sell: you gotta distort your brain to hum along and lose your trained-on-Beatles melodic sense to whistle. It pays off, though, after your ears adjust, and the next challenge is figuring out the meaning of ditties like "Voltaire's Repair to the Organ," "Bank," and "Tofu Golf Course."

worth searching for: Any of the band's three original releases, *Burn All Your Records* (Lost Records, 1985, prod. the Scene Is Now), *Total Jive* (Lost Records, 1986, prod. the Scene Is Now), and *Tonight We Ride* (Lost Records, 1988, prod. the Scene Is Now) are worth owning, and can be obtained by scouring the cheapy bin at your local record store. Their final release was the cassette-only *Shotgun Wedding* (Lost Records, 1990, prod. the Scene Is Now).

influences:

◀◀ Captain Beefheart, Red Krayola, DNA, Pere Ubu

▶▶ Yo La Tengo, Mofungo, $2 Guitar

see also: *The dB's*

Randall Roberts

Peter Scherer

Born July 22, 1953, in Zurich, Switzerland.

Peter Scherer is best known as Arto Lindsay's former partner in Ambitious Lovers. He studied classical and avant-garde music, and his teachers include Gyorgy Ligeti, Terry Riley, and Robert Ashley. After working on Kashif's debut album and touring with him during 1980, Scherer came to New York. He has had a fertile production career, working with everyone from the World Saxophone Quartet, Laurie Anderson, and Jaron Lanier to Caetano Veloso, Nile Rodgers (Chic), and Cameo (on the smash *Word Up!* album).

what to buy: The low-key intensity of *Very Neon Pet* 🎵🎵🎵 (Metro Blue/Capitol, 1995, prod. Peter Scherer) combines avant-garde techniques with dance, ambient, and worldbeat influences, sporting an especially pronounced Middle Eastern flavor. Collaborators include Anderson, Vasconcelos, Gibbs, Lou Reed bassist Fernando Saunders, and electric harpist Zeena Parkins. Lindsay plays guitar on the first track.

the rest:
Cronologia 🎵🎵🎵 (Tzadik, 1996)

influences:
◀◀ Robert Ashley, Laurie Anderson, Jaron Lanier

see also: *Ambitious Lovers*

Steve Holtje

John Schlitt
See: Petra

Adam Schmitt
Born June 16, 1968.

Champaign, Illinois, has always fostered impressive pop talent. Adam Schmitt is arguably the heart of that scene, despite his reclusive, not-very-prolific nature. After a disappointing stint on Warner Bros., Schmitt has been focusing on producing lately, though he recently returned to recording a project of his own.

what to buy: *The Race of All Races* 🎵🎵🎵🎵 (Parasol, 1998, prod. Adam Schmitt) is pure pop, as perfect as it gets. Tight melodies prevail, with very few loose ends in the production department.

worth searching for: The compilation *Yellow Pills: Volume One* (Big Deal, 1993) contains the only other example of Schmitt's work currently in print, the song "Speed Kills," which some fans consider his best. *World So Bright* (Warner Bros., 1991, prod. Greg Edward, Adam Schmitt) is a flawless disc, one great song after another, comparable in quality to Emitt Rhodes's first album. The title track in particular is a symmetrical diamond. *Illiterature* (Warner Bros., 1993, prod. Adam Schmitt) is almost as good, but it offers a few loud, distorted concessions to alt-rock. Still, the melodies come through loud and clear. *Trademark of Quality* (1993) is a multi-label promo disc containing unreleased songs from many alt-rockers, including Schmitt's cover of "I Know You're All Mine," a song by fellow Champaign popster Nick Rudd. Schmitt sounds unlike himself, opting for a ragged delivery and rowdy Big Star riffing.

influences:
◀◀ Emitt Rhodes, the Raspberries, 20/20

▶▶ The Andersons

Jordan Oakes

Neal Schon

See: Journey

School of Fish
/Josh Clayton-Felt

Formed 1990, in Los Angeles, CA. Disbanded 1993.

Josh Clayton-Felt, vocals, guitar; Michael Ward, guitar, vocals; Dominic Nardini, bass; M.P., drums.

In 1991, School of Fish tasted fleeting success with an electrifying alternative radio hit called "Three Strange Days." The former Guitar Institute graduates couldn't keep it together after success came, however. The group's second album fizzled on the charts and School of Fish disbanded shortly thereafter. Clayton-Felt launched a solo career, while Ward joined Jakob Dylan as a songwriting partner in the Wallflowers.

what to buy: *School of Fish* ♫♫♫ (Capitol, 1991, prod. John Porter) paired strong songwriting with innovative playing. It was as adventurous as rock records got around the time of its release.

what to avoid: School of Fish's second and final release, *Human Cannonball* **woof!** (Capitol, 1993, prod. Matt Wallace, School of Fish) was burdened by lackluster songs lost in layers of ringing feedback and a mess of haphazard ideas.

solo outings:
Josh Clayton-Felt:
Inarticulate Nature Boy ♫♫ (A&M, 1996)

influences:
◀◀ Prince, the Beatles, Steely Dan
▶▶ Beck, Jellyfish

Aidin Vaziri

The Schramms

Formed 1987, in Hoboken, NJ.

Dave Schramm, vocals, guitar, harmonica, piano, organ, accordion; Ron Metz, drums, percussion; Terry Karydes, organ, accordion, vocals (1987–93); Al Greller, bass; George Usher, organ, vocals (1994–97); Andy Burton, keyboards (1997–present); Jon Graboff, guitar (1997–present).

After a stint as guitarist with Hoboken neighbors Yo La Tengo, Dave Schramm put together his namesake band. Their releases have all appeared first in Germany, sometimes not coming out in their homeland until four years later. But with bands such as the Wallflowers selling millions of records, if even a small portion of those multitudes would take the small step into the similar world of the Schramms, they'd be amply rewarded. Steeped in the sense of place and simplicity of country music, then filtered through '60s rock, it all lands rather near the forest that Bob Dylan hiked through with the Band.

what to buy: *Little Apocalypse* ♫♫♫♫♪ (ESD, 1994, prod. the Schramms), the band's debut, has always been more or less easy to find in the U.S. It contains "Little American Hymn," one of the most gorgeously introspective instrumentals this side of John Hartford's "Presbyterian Guitar."

the rest:
Dizzy Spell ♫♫♫♪ (Blue Rose, 1996/Checkered Past, 1998)

worth searching for: *Walk to Delphi* (ESD, 1995, prod. the Schramms) was originally released in Germany on OKra in 1990 and is a subtly powerful set of songs steeped in world-weary optimism, community concerns, love, and longing. Two years later (in Germany, anyway, again on OKra) came the richer, more confident *Rock, Paper, Scissors, Dynamite* (ESD, 1995, prod. the Schramms).

solo outings:
Dave Schramm:
Folk und die Folgen ♫♫♫♫ (Normal, 1994)

influences:
◀◀ The Band, Gram Parsons, Richard Thompson

David Greenberger

Paul Schütze
/Uzect Plaush
/Seed

Born 1958, in Melbourne, Australia.

While it has become hip for '90s indie rockers to namecheck Brian Eno and previously obscure Krautrock bands such as Can, Paul Schütze actually grew up listening to that music during the early '70s and was inspired to become one of the most innovative and exciting musician/composers to emerge from the ambient/electronic music scene of the '90s. Currently based in London, England, Schütze's musical career began during the early '80s, when he joined the Australian experimental rock band the Laughing Hands before moving on to compose film scores for the better part of the decade. Despite his success in that field (he won the 1985 AFI award for best score), Schütze was not happy with his work and embarked on a solo career. Since 1989 he has released more than 14 solo albums and has worked with the likes of Bill Laswell, Main's Robert Hamson, and trombonist Julian Priester, a former Herbie Hancock associate. Utilizing ethnic percussion, microtonal tuning, synthesizers, samplers, and digital sound technology (for post-performance editing of other musicians' playing), Schütze crafts spacious, three-dimensional soundscapes full of sensuous sounds, unusual rhythms, and organic textures that cover a wide spectrum of music—ranging from Eno-like ambiance to futuristic gamelan percussion pieces to dark and explosive cyber-jazz reminiscent of Miles Davis's mid-'70s albums such as *Agharta*. Besides its stylistic diversity, what sets Schütze's music apart from other ambient musicians is his ability to build a sonic vocabulary from album to album that defines specific locations (earthly or unearthly) for the listener to explore, whereas most ambient music of the '90s just wanders around aimlessly with some strange sounds thrown in the mix.

what to buy: Because Schütze is incredibly prolific, a newcomer to his music has a lot to choose from. Rock-oriented listeners are directed to *Site Anubis* ✍✍✍✍ (Big Cat, 1996, prod. Paul Schütze), *New Maps of Hell* ✍✍✍✍ (Extreme, 1992/Big Cat, 1996, prod. Paul Schütze), or *The Annihilating Angel* ✍✍✍ (Extreme, 1990/Tone Casualties, 1997, prod. Paul Schütze). All three albums have a similar feel to them—drifting between relaxed ambient atmospheres to sonic nightmares where shrieking guitars and shrill horns pierce the air and dense percussion lines collide with taped sounds of the city in a sonic embodiment of urban paranoia. Those who are curious about ambient but are turned off by anything remotely resembling new age music should check out *New Maps of Hell II: The Rapture of Metals* ✍✍✍✍ (SDV, 1993/Big Cat, 1996, prod. Paul Schütze), *Regard: Music by Film* ✍✍✍ (Multimood/Tone Casualties, 1991/1997, prod. Paul Schütze), or *Isabelle Eberhardt, the Oblivion Seeker* ✍✍✍✍ (SDV, 1994/Tone Casualties, 1997, prod. Paul Schütze). *New Maps of Hell II* has a distinct gamelan feel to it while *Regard* and *Isabelle Eberhardt* feature Schütze's lush, understated synthesizer work.

what to buy next: People who aren't put off by "background music" or "music that doesn't go anywhere" should investigate Schütze's more experimental ambient works, particularly *Deus Ex Machina Extreme* ✍✍✍ (Extreme, 1989/Tone Casualties, 1997, prod. Paul Schütze). Those with slightly deeper pockets should pick up *Stateless* ✍✍✍ (Big Cat, 1997, prod. Paul Schütze), which is Schütze's contribution to Big Cat's moderately priced *Driftworks* four-CD box set of experimental contemporary composers. But perhaps the least accessible of Schütze's domestic albums is *Nine Songs from the Garden of Welcome Lies* ✍✍✍ (Tone Casualties, 1997, prod. Paul Schütze), on which Schütze explores the acoustic sounds of church organs and percussion.

the rest:
The Surgery of Touch ✍✍✍✍ (Sentrax, 1994/Tone Casualties, 1997)
(With Uzect Plaush) *More Beautiful Human Life* ✍✍✍ (R&S, 1994)
(With Seed) *Vertical Memory* ✍✍✍✍ (Beyond, 1995)
Apart ✍✍✍ (Virgin/Caroline, 1995)

worth searching for: Schütze has several albums that were released in the U.K. or Europe and are worthy of your attention should you come across them: *Shiva Recoil* (Virgin U.K., 1997); *Abysmal Evenings* (Virgin U.K., 1996); and *Second Site* (Virgin U.K., 1997).

influences:
◀◀ Jon Hassell, '70s Miles Davis, early '70s Herbie Hancock, Can, Fripp/Eno, Arab, Indian, and South Asian musics

Howard Shih

Scorpions

Formed 1971, in Hanover, Germany.

Klaus Meine, vocals; Michael Schenker, guitar (1971–73, 1978–79); Rudolf Schenker, guitar; Lother Heimberg, bass (1971–73); Jurgen Rosenthal, drums (1971–73); Francis Buccholz, bass (1973–93); Wolfgang Dziony, drums (1973–76); Ulrich Rother, guitar (1973–78); Rudy Lenners, drums (1976–77); Herman Rarebell, drums (1977–present); Matthias Jabs, guitar (1978–present); Ralph Rieckermann, bass (1993–present).

The members of Scorpions have long contended that prior to 1980, its record companies wouldn't fork over the bucks to help the group tour in the U.S., therefore rendering the hard rock band obscure on these shores even as it won a following in Europe. That may have been to the group's benefit in the long run: when it finally began touring in the U.S., Scorpions roared forth with a fully finished sound, honed and polished by the band and its longtime producer Dieter Dierks. It was slick but not Teflon, mixing crunch and melody in a recipe that was perfect for the '80s pop-metal market. Scorpions delivered the goods with raging rockers such as "Rock You Like a Hurricane" and "No One Like You," as well as Bic-lighter power ballads like "Still Loving You" and "You Give Me All I Need." Always a part of the various Monsters of Rock festivals, Scorpions have been more like Rodan than Godzilla. Then again, this group is still around, and where are Guns N' Roses?

what to buy: *Love at First Sting* ✍✍✍ (Mercury, 1984, prod. Dieter Dierks) is Scorpions' best, the full realization of their sound in a powerful, radio-friendly package. *Best of Rockers 'n' Ballads* ✍✍✍ (Mercury, 1989, prod. Dieter Dierks, Bruce Fairbairn) fills the gaps with hits from the rest of the band's '80s albums.

what to buy next: *Hot + Heavy* ✍✍✍ (RCA, 1993, prod. Dieter Dierks, Scorpions) offers up tracks from the '70s, when the Scorpions were a decidedly underground attraction in the U.S. For that matter, metal fans might want to check out the group's debut, *Lonesome Crow* ✍✍✍ (Brain, 1972/Rhino, 1989, prod. Conny Plank), which features Michel Schenker during his short tenure with Scorpions, before he went off to join UFO.

Michael Schenker of Scorpions (© Ken Settle)

what to avoid: *Live Bites (1988–1995)* ♩ (Mercury, 1995) suffers for being the second live album in a decade, without enough top-shelf songs to support it.

the rest:
In Trance ♫♫ (RCA, 1976/1991)
Tokyo Tapes ♫♫ (RCA, 1979/1993)
Love Drive ♫♫ (Mercury, 1979)
Animal Magnetism ♫♫♫ (Mercury, 1980)
Blackout ♫♫♫ (Mercury, 1982)
Best of Scorpions, Vol. 2 ♫♫♫ (RCA, 1984/1992)
World Wide Live ♫♫♫ (Mercury, 1985)
Savage Amusement ♫♫♫ (Mercury, 1987)
Crazy World ♫♫♫ (Mercury, 1990)
Feel the Heat ♫♫ (Mercury, 1993)
Pure Instinct ♫♫♫ (Atlantic, 1996)

worth searching for: When former Pink Floyder Roger Waters staged an all-star performance of *The Wall* to celebrate the fall of the Berlin Wall, he invited Scorpions to open the show. The group's celebratory version of "In the Flesh?" is captured on *The Wall Live in Berlin* (Mercury, 1990, prod. Nick Griffiths, Roger Waters).

influences:
◀◀ The Beatles, the Rolling Stones, the Kinks, the Who

▶▶ Metallica, Dokken, Def Leppard, Warrant, Spinal Tap

Gary Graff

Jack Scott

Born Jack Scalfone Jr., January 28, 1936, in Windsor, Ontario, Canada.

Jack Scott is best remembered for his pop hits "My True Love" (1958), "What in the World's Come over You" (1960), and the equally fine "Goodbye Baby (Bye Bye)" (1958). These staples of oldies radio are clever hybrids of country music and doo-wop, but the fierce rockers found on the B-sides are Scott's true legacy. His ABC-Paramount recording of "Baby She's Gone" (1957) snarls and stutters with rockabilly perfection, "Leroy" (1958) is a top-notch rocker despite a pop chorus and sax, and "The Way I Walk" (1959) seethed with iconoclastic rebellion. Like Conway Twitty, Jack Scott reshaped Elvis Presley's sound, adding a groaning bass to the ballads, and wrote many of his best-known numbers. Handsome and greasy with a powerful physique, Scott's run of hits should have made him a much bigger star, but Top Rank and Carlton seldom promoted him with any genuine vigor. Though these small labels did little to advance his career, at least they left his music alone. At Capitol, where he recorded his last charting records, producers made him stop rocking, and concentrated largely on ballads such as "My Dream Come True" and "A Little Feeling." Eventually, the British Invasion artists of the mid-'60s ended Scott's string of

19 chart hits. A transplanted Canadian with a fan base in the Midwest and Northeast, Scott wasn't able to get a foothold in the regions where his style of country music would've prolonged his career. His years at RCA/Groove produced some fine country sides but not much airplay or sales, and a stint at Dot fared even worse. Scott never gave up; he stayed busy playing country music bars around the Detroit and Cleveland areas and recording for small labels. After Presley's death, Scott's early sides were rediscovered by neo-rockabillies such as the Cramps and Robert Gordon, and tours of England and Europe re-energized the career of this underrated, original rocker.

what to buy: The easy-to-find *The Greatest Hits of Jack Scott* ♫♫♫ (Curb, 1990, prod. Harley Hatcher) is a concise, budget-priced collection of Scott's best-known recordings including "What in the World's Come over You," "My True Love," and others. However, the Canadian 24-track compilation *The Best of Jack Scott (1957–1960)* ♫♫♫ (Stardust, 1995) is more comprehensive and includes Scott's tough, lesser-known Presleyesque rockers "Geraldine" and "Two-Timin' Woman" as well as wild demo versions of "Geraldine" and "Greaseball" (the unsanitized version of "Leroy"). The latter can be found in some mail-order catalogs.

worth searching for: Everything Scott recorded for ABC-Paramount, Carlton, Top Rank, Capitol, RCA/Groove, and Dot are compiled on *Classic Scott—The Way I Walk* (Bear Family, 1994, prod. Richard Weize), a five-disc set. It's a bit much, but all the hits and the great rockers, as well as early demos, are here. Scott's mid-'60s RCA/Groove period is neatly compiled on *On Groove* (Bear Family, 1992, prod. Richard Weize), a solo disc with great liner notes, but not much rockin'. Also, the vinyl-only *Four Rock 'n' Roll Legends* (EMI Harvest, 1978) features Scott, Warren Smith, Charlie Feathers, and Buddy Knox thrilling a worshipful crowd of English teddy boys with live versions of their classic rockabilly sounds.

influences:
◀◀ Elvis Presley, Sonny James, Buddy Knox

▶▶ Conway Twitty, Robert Gordon, the Cramps, Dwight Yoakum

Ken Burke

Screaming Trees

Formed 1984, in Ellensburg, WA.

Mark Lanegan, vocals; Gary Lee Conner, guitars, backing vocals; Van Conner, bass, backing vocals; Barrett Martin, drums (1992–present); Mark Pickerel, drums (1984–92).

Ellensburg, Washington, is a small college and cow town in the Cascade Mountains. In such a place young men with musical tastes that are at all removed from what is played on the local radio station are compelled to hang out together, if only for mutual protection. Screaming Trees, originally formed as the Explosive Generation (in which guise they played new wave covers), were intended to be a punk band, in which incarnation none of the original members played the instrument they finally settled on. Instead they found a neo-psychedelic voice—the middle ground of their myriad prog and punk instincts—which they explored prolifically during the initial stages of their career, frequently aided by producer Steve Fisk (Pell Mell, Pigeonhed). The Trees were one of the first Northwest underground bands to sign with a national label (SST, at the time a dominant indie), and then had more in common with the Olympia scene (Beat Happening, with whom they recorded an early EP) and Portland, Oregon's Wipers than with the harder punk-metal sounds evolving in Seattle. In the end, they, too, were swept up in the grunge signing frenzy; by dint of the *Singles* soundtrack, tighter songcraft, and a more self-assured lead singer, the Trees at last dented the charts with *Sweet Oblivion*. Coincidentally this was the first recording to feature Barrett Martin, late of Skin Yard, on drums. Throughout, Lee Conner's guitars have given the band a distinctive, swirling sound.

what to buy: *Sweet Oblivion* 🎵🎵🎵🎵🎵 (Epic, 1992, prod. Don Fleming) is the first record in years to feature songwriting from the band as an ensemble, rather than as individuals. Bolstered by the critical success of his first solo album, Lanegan's vocals are confident and no longer compete for space in the mix with Lee's guitar. "Nearly Lost You" became the hit single off the hit *Singles* soundtrack, but "Dollar Bill" and "Butterfly" are equally vibrant pop songs, with Lanegan's deep vocals playing hard and sad against keening guitars. Their second full-length album, *Even If and Especially When* 🎵🎵🎵🎵 (SST, 1987, prod. Steve Fisk, Screaming Trees), is full of raw enthusiasm, innocently complicated musical structures, and, as announced by the opener "Transfiguration," an alienated view of life. *Buzz Factory* 🎵🎵🎵 (SST, 1989, prod. Jack Endino, Screaming Trees) is the best known of their indie releases, but the songs are less spontaneous and energetic, having been recorded twice. *Buzz Factory* was originally recorded as a double-LP, with Donna Dresch on bass; Dresch left for Dinosaur Jr.—and Team Dresch—and Van rejoined the band.

what to buy next: *Invisible Lantern* 🎵🎵🎵 (SST, 1988, prod. Steve Fisk, Screaming Trees) and the EP *Change Has Come* 🎵🎵🎵 (Sub Pop, 1990, prod. Steve Fisk, Jack Endino, Screaming Trees) are fine frolics through the Trees' woody world. *Anthology* (SST, 1992, prod. various) is a two-disc compilation of their years in the indie world.

what to avoid: Sometimes everybody tries just too hard and the stakes are just too high. *Uncle Anesthesia* 🎵🎵 (Epic, 1991, prod. Terry Date, Chris Cornell) came at the height of the grunge frenzy. Produced by Date, better known for his work with metal bands, and Soundgarden singer Cornell, *Uncle Anesthesia* is stiff and awkward, and the band plays for the first time as if it were aware of a potential audience.

the rest:
Clairvoyance 🎵🎵🎵 (Velvetone, 1986)
Other World 🎵🎵 (SST, 1988)
Beat Happening/Screaming Trees 🎵🎵 (Homestead EP, 1988)
Something about Today 🎵🎵🎵 (Epic EP, 1990)
Dirt 🎵🎵 (Epic, 1996)

worth searching for: A sterling cover of the Youngbloods' "Darkness Darkness" on the soundtrack for *True Lies* (Lightstorm Music/Epic, 1994, prod. John Agnello) is all that remains of the initial sessions for the Trees' 1996 release. It's an odd soundtrack—a few pop songs and a long batch of incidental music (and nobody's exactly sure where in the movie the song might have been heard, anyway)—but this one number is quite spectacular.

solo outings:
Mark Lanegan:
The Winding Sheet 🎵🎵🎵🎵 (Sub Pop, 1990)
Whiskey for the Holy Ghost 🎵🎵🎵🎵 (Sub Pop, 1993)
Scraps at Midnight 🎵🎵🎵 (Sub Pop, 1998)

The Purple Outside (Gary Lee Conner):
Mystery Lane 🎵🎵🎵 (New Alliance, 1990)

Solomon Grundy (Van Conner):
Solomon Grundy 🎵🎵🎵 (New Alliance, 1990)

influences:
◀◀ Love, Leonard Cohen, Lee Hazelwood, the Wipers
▶▶ Luna, Darkside

Grant Alden

Screeching Weasel

Formed 1986, in Prospect Heights, IL. Disbanded 1989. Re-formed 1991. Disbanded 1994. Re-formed 1996.

Ben Weasel (born Ben Foster), vocals, guitar; Johnny Jughead (born John Pierson), guitar; Vinnie Bovine, bass (1986–87); Warren "Fish" Ozzfish, guitar (1987–88); Dan Vapid (born Dan Schafer), bass, guitar, vocals (1988–89, 1991–93, 1996–97); Doug Ward, bass (1989); Dave Naked, bass (1991); Johnny Personality, bass (1992); Steve Cheese, drums (1986–88); Brian Vermin, drums (1988–89); Dan Panic (born Dan Sullivan), drums (1991–97); Zac Damon, guitar (1998–present); Mass Giorgini, bass (1998–present); Dan Lumley, drums (1998–present).

One of the most popular and influential pop-punk bands of the '90s, and easily the most famous punk group to emerge from Chicago since Naked Raygun, Screeching Weasel is largely the effort of its controversial frontman, Ben Weasel, a punk-scene celebrity and pariah due to his uncompromising, if often contradictory, beliefs. Along with high school pal Johnny Jughead, the only other permanent member of the group, Weasel has guided Screeching Weasel from garage band to underground superstar status, while also promoting punk shows (at McGregor's and elsewhere), writing for the 'zines *MaximumRockNRoll* and his own *Panic Button,* running the now-defunct Roadkill Records label, guesting with other Chicago-area bands, and working a variety of crappy day jobs to boot. As a student at Prospect High School in suburban Prospect Heights, Illinois, Weasel was inspired to start a punk band after seeing the Ramones in 1986; the fact that neither he nor Jughead could play an instrument didn't stop them from forming All Night Garage Sale with local drummer Steve Cheese. Several tours followed, as well as a second album, 1988's *Boogadaboogadaboogada!,* but ongoing lineup problems and difficulty finding a reliable record label caused Screeching Weasel to break up in late 1989. In 1991, the band re-formed as a quintet and recorded the snotty pop-punk tour-de-force *My Brain Hurts.* Unexpectedly, in 1996, after breaking up for the second time, Screeching Weasel released *Bark Like a Dog,* which mostly consisted of recycled songs.

what to buy: *Anthem for a New Tomorrow* ♫♫♫♫ (Lookout!, 1993, prod. Mass Giorgini), the last album with Screeching Weasel as a fully functioning band, is easily its most consistent, mature effort. Unlike every other Screeching Weasel full-length, there is not one bad song here, making this one of the best pop-punk albums of the '90s. Still, many prefer *My Brain Hurts* ♫♫♫♫ (Lookout!, 1991, prod. Andy Ernst, Larry Livermore), recorded at the height of the group's popularity and containing such classics as "Slogans," "Guest List," "The Science of Myth," and "What We Hate."

what to buy next: *Boogadaboogadaboogada!* ♫♫♫ (Roadkill, 1988/Lookout!, 1992, prod. Ben Weasel) marks the true beginning of Screeching Weasel as a serious band. Though rather poorly produced, the 26-song album does contain several vital Weasel classics, including "Supermarket Fantasy," "I Wanna Be Naked," and "Hey Suburbia." *Wiggle* ♫♫♫ (Lookout!, 1992, prod. Mass Giorgini, Eric Spicer) is a darker effort that includes some of the group's best songs—including the Steve Albini–engineered "Going Home"—but also a lot of filler. *Kill the Musicians* ♫♫♫ (Lookout!, 1995, prod. Screeching Weasel, Mass Giorgini, Mike Potential, Eric Spicer) is a compilation of various out-of-print EPs, compilation tracks, and four live cuts recorded at Berkeley's 924 Gilman Street.

what to avoid: The tepid *How to Make Enemies and Irritate People* ♫♫ (Lookout!, 1994, prod. Mass Giorgini) has one or two standout cuts but is most valuable for its liner notes that include a (nearly) complete Screeching Weasel discography. *Bark*

Like a Dog ♫ (Fat, 1996, prod. Mass Giorgini) is a shoddy, cash-in collection of second-rate Riverdales songs put out under the Screeching Weasel name when the group hastily reunited in 1996. Also avoid the recent reissue of *Screeching Weasel* **woof!** (Underdog, 1987/VML, 1998, prod. Ben Weasel), the group's long-forgotten debut album. Ben Weasel kept this piece of juvenalia out of print for years for a very good reason—it's horrid.

the rest:
Television City Dream N/A (Fat Wreck Chords, 1998)

worth searching for: Screeching Weasel has issued a string of long-out-of-print vinyl EPs. Most of these are collected on *Kill the Musicians,* but for the original vinyl, the best of the lot are the split 7-inch *Screeching Weasel/Pink Lincolns* (VML, 1993, prod. Mass Giorgini, Eric Spicer), featuring "Stab Stab" and "Going Home," and *Radio Blast* (Underdog, 1993, prod. Mass Giorgini).

influences:

◄◄ The Ramones, Adrenalin O.D., Teenage Head, Forgotten Rebels, the Buzzcocks, Circle Jerks, the Dickies, Angry Samoans, Black Flag

►► Sludgeworth, the Riverdales, the Vindictives, Squirtgun, Teen Idols

Seth Hindin

Scritti Politti

Formed 1977, in Leeds, England.

Green Gartside, vocals, guitar, keyboards; Nial Jinks, bass; Tom Morley, drums; David Gamson, keyboards; Fred Maher, drums.

Few bands have changed identity so dramatically as Scritti Politti. Starting out as an avant-garde rock band in the post-punk mold, the group recorded a handful of singles that were heavy on scratchy guitar, weird tempo changes, and situational lyrics. After frontman Green Gartside suffered from a heart ailment and took some time off to recover and write, the band's focus turned toward soul-influenced pop. By the mid-'80s, he and his partner David Gamson were penning songs for such R&B and adult-contemporary heavyweights as Chaka Khan and Al Jarreau; even jazz legend Miles Davis covered one of their compositions.

A couple of bubbly pop records made the band a presence in '80s dance clubs, after which the reclusive Gartside once again submerged, returning sometime later to assemble a series of soul covers with such reggae artists as Shabba Ranks and Sweetie Irie.

what to buy: *Cupid & Psyche '85* ♫♫♫ (Warner Bros., 1985, prod. Green Gartside, David Gamson) is an effervescent collection of dance-pop tunes. Though Gartside's wispy vocals can be terribly cloying, the strength of the material wins out.

what to avoid: *Provision* 🎵🎵 (Warner Bros., 1988, prod. Green Gartside, David Gamson), the less-than-illustrious follow-up to *Cupid*, boasts a couple of strong tracks but generally falls flat.

the rest:
The Peel Sessions 🎵🎵🎵 (Rough Trade, 1979)
Songs to Remember 🎵🎵🎵 (Rough Trade, 1982)

worth searching for: The EP *4 A Sides* (St. Pancras/Rough Trade, 1979, prod. various) is a smashing example of the group's idiosyncratic but compelling early work—a completely different animal from its better-known, squeaky-clean pop, and reminiscent of fellow Leeds post-punkers Gang of Four, but with a more developed melodic sense and off-kilter arrangements.

influences:
◀◀ The Beatles, Gang of Four, the Fall, Al Green, Motown, Kraftwerk

▶▶ Ace of Base, Madonna, Pet Shop Boys

Simon Glickman

Seal

Born Sealhenry Samuel, February 19, 1963, in Paddington, England.

Seal strikes an imposing figure—six-foot-plus, shaved head, odd facial scars, swathed in black leather. His music is only slightly less imposing, mixing Seal's sweet voice, Trevor Horn's impeccable production, and a blend of polyrhythmic dance rhythms and soaring melodies for something close to pop perfection. Like Peter Gabriel, he's self-titled each of his two albums *Seal*.

what to buy: The infectious single "Crazy" was the calling card for the first *Seal* 🎵🎵🎵🎵 (ZTT/Sire, 1991, prod. Trevor Horn), a wholly splendid effort in which every song carries weight and significance.

what to buy next: The second *Seal* 🎵🎵🎵 (ZTT/Sire, 1994, prod. Trevor Horn) shows songwriting maturity, with tunes that are mellower and a bit deeper. The single "Kiss from a Rose," used in the film *Batman Forever,* was a worldwide smash.

the rest:
Human Being N/A (Sire, 1998)

worth searching for: Worth hunting down is *The Acoustic Session* (ZTT/Sire, 1991, prod. Dick Meanie), a promotional CD that features wonderfully stripped-down reinterpretations of songs from his debut.

influences:
◀◀ George Michael, Peter Gabriel, Joni Mitchell

▶▶ Maxwell, D'Angelo, Erykah Badu, Ali

Aidin Vaziri

Seals & Crofts

Formed 1969, in Los Angeles, CA.

Jim Seals, vocals, guitar, saxophone, fiddle; Dash Crofts (born Darnell Crofts), vocals, mandolin, keyboards, guitar, drums.

Seals and Crofts are both Texas natives who met on the club circuit during the '50s. They both wound up playing in the Champs ("Tequila") and later moved to Los Angeles, where they worked sessions, formed bands, and finally settled into working as a duo. Devout followers of the Baha'i faith, they scored a recording contract in 1971 and were on radio in short order with seminal soft-rock hits such as "Summer Breeze," "Hummingbird," "Diamond Girl," and the high-school yearbook special "We May Never Pass This Way Again." These days, Seals and Crofts rarely play together; the former farms coffee in Costa Rica, while the latter was last seen around Nashville.

what to buy: You'll find all the key tracks on *Greatest Hits* 🎵🎵🎵🎵 (Warner Bros., 1975, prod. Louie Shelton), a collection of tuneful, sturdy melodies.

the rest:
Summer Breeze 🎵🎵 (Warner Bros., 1972/1994)

influences:
◀◀ The Weavers, Crosby, Stills & Nash, the Lettermen, the Walker Brothers

▶▶ Indigo Girls

Gary Graff

Seam

Formed 1990, in Chapel Hill, NC.

Sooyoung Park, guitar, vocals; Lexi Mitchell, bass (1990–94); Mac McCaughan, drums (1990–92); Bob Rising, drums (1992–93); Craig White, guitar (1992–93); Chris Manfrin, drums (1993–present); Reg Shrader, guitar (1993–present); William Shin, bass (1994–present).

Despite a history filled with continual upheaval in personnel, Seam has been able to maintain its trademark sound, full of brooding and melancholy. Still, there is much passion beneath the surface, and the group's albums are hard rocking and richly textured.

what to buy: After Mac McCaughan left to concentrate on his other band, Superchunk, Seam relocated to Chicago and signed with Touch & Go Records. *The Problem with Me* 🎵🎵🎵 (Touch & Go, 1993, prod. Brad Wood) is a bit more optimistic than the group's debut, *Headsparks*, but it's still characteristically grim. *Are You Driving Me Crazy* 🎵🎵🎵 (Touch & Go, 1995, prod. Brad Wood) came after another full re-haul of the Seam lineup, with Sooyoung Park and his new cohorts still holding firm to the languid, contemplative music Seam began making five years before.

the rest:
Headsparks 🎵🎵🎵 (Homestead, 1992)
Kernel 🎵🎵🎵 (Tough & Go, 1993)

influences:
◀◀ The Bats, Mercury Rev

see also: *Superchunk*

Kim Forster

The Searchers

Formed 1961, in Liverpool, England.

Mike Pender (born Mike Prendergast), guitar, vocals (1961–85); John McNally, guitar, vocals; Tony Jackson, bass, vocals (1961–64); Chris Curtis (born Chris Crummey), drums, vocals (1961–66); Frank Allen, bass, vocals (1964–present); John Blunt, drums (1966–68); Billy Adamson, drums (1968–present); Spencer James, guitar, vocals (1985–present).

Remembered by most Americans as a Top 40 group with a few hits—most everyone knows "Needles and Pins"—the Searchers were somewhat more successful in Britain. But listeners on either side of the Atlantic seldom give the band the credit it deserves as an influence on more highly regarded bands that came later—particularly the Byrds, whose vocal and instrumental sound owe much to the Searchers. It should be noted that the Searchers electrified a folk song ("What Have They Done to the Rain") several months before the Byrds released "Mr. Tambourine Man." Always a tight and very professional band, the Searchers' guitars rang out nicely and their vocals were crystal-clear. Perhaps their relatively scant output of original songs (though the group picked some great ones to cover, often altering their arrangements radically, and usually for the better) and lack of a clearly defined image have kept them out of the ranks of more highly esteemed '60s rockers. But anyone who takes a listen will walk away impressed with how forward-looking the band was.

what to buy: There are two choices for the curious these days. *The Best of the Searchers* 🎵🎵🎵🎵 (Rhino, 1988, prod. various) covers all the necessary hits and also includes an exceptional version of Jackie DeShannon's "Each Time." For the more adventurous, there's *The Searchers 30th Anniversary Collection* 🎵🎵🎵🎵 (Sequel, 1992, prod. various), a three-CD set that comprises all of the hit singles, prime LP tracks, and a generous selection of rarities.

worth searching for: After spending much of the '70s in cabaret, the Searchers revived themselves at decade's end with two fine albums of contemporary-sounding material, *The*

Searchers (Sire, 1979, prod. Pat Moran) and *Love's Melodies* (Sire, 1981, prod. Pat Moran, Ed Stasium), earning plaudits from both original and new fans. Both are now available with bonus tracks on the import single CD, *Sire Sessions—Rockfield Record* (Raven).

influences:
◀◀ The Clancy Brothers, the Weavers, Buddy Holly & the Crickets

▶▶ The Byrds, Manfred Mann, Fairport Convention

Mike Greenfield

Sebadoh /The Folk Implosion

Formed 1987, in Amherst, MA.

Lou Barlow, vocals and guitars; Eric Gaffney, percussion (1987–93); Jason Loewenstein, bass (1989–present); Bob Fay, drums (1990–present).

Getting fired from Dinosaur Jr. was the most creatively lucrative thing Lou Barlow ever did. The singer-guitarist, long frustrated with J. Mascis's control obsession, collaborated with his friend Eric Gaffney in 1987 on a folky, poorly produced demo tape called *Weed Forestin*. The songs were all short, mostly catchy and wrapped in spontaneous noise distortions that sometimes made them more powerful and sometimes made them incomprehensible. For a while, Dinosaur Jr. brought Sebadoh tapes to concerts and sold them to fans along with the latest Dinosaur albums. Then Mascis dumped Barlow, who weathered various Sebadoh personnel changes (Gaffney left and returned several times before exiting for good in 1993), and let his project gradually ferment into a great rock 'n' roll band. Beginning with *Sebadoh III*, a wonderful if unfocused mix of folk, rock, and pop, the trio started a streak of records so great it had to spin off two entirely new bands. The Folk Implosion, and its expanded alter-ego, the Deluxx Folk Implosion, helped cement Barlow's legend as the leader of the "lo-fi" production trend that inspired Liz Phair producer Brad Wood, among several others. Despite Barlow's naturally anti-commercial tendencies, the Folk Implosion actually had a minor modern-rock radio hit, "Natural One," in 1995.

what to buy: *Sebadoh III* 🎵🎵🎵 (Homestead, 1991) and *Bakesale* 🎵🎵🎵 (Sub Pop, 1994) gut the '90s big-guitar alternative-rock trends by featuring well-written songs that were recorded in the sloppiest way possible. *Sebadoh vs. Helmet* 🎵🎵🎵 (20/20, 1992) and *Smash Your Head on the Punk Rock* 🎵🎵🎵 (Sub Pop, 1992) are explosive punk records that pay homage to Flipper and Hüsker Dü. *Harmacy* 🎵🎵🎵 (Sub Pop, 1996) is Barlow's tightest collection of pop-like songs to date, including the beautiful "Too Pure" and "Willing to Wait."

what to buy next: At 41 songs, *Freed Weed* ♫♫♪ (Homestead, 1990, prod. Lou Barlow) is hard to pore through, but it compiles the band's first two tapes, *Freed Man* ♫♫♪ (Homestead, 1989, prod. Lou Barlow) and *Weed Forestin* ♫♫♪ (Homestead, 1990, prod. Lou Barlow).

what to avoid: The live album *. . . In Tokyo* ♫♫ (Bolide, 1995) is full of irony and sneering punk-rock pyrotechnics, but it's not much fun to listen to.

the rest:
Rocking the Forest ♫♫♫ (20/20, 1992)
Bubble & Scrape ♫♫♪ (Sub Pop, 1993)
Four Song CD ♫♫ (Domino, 1994)

worth searching for: The Folk Implosion was the big story on the soundtrack *Kids* (London/PolyGram, 1995, prod. various), when "Natural One" became a much bigger hit than any single Dinosaur Jr. ever released. The soundtrack, in addition to nine songs by the Folk Implosion, Deluxx Folk Implosion, and Sebadoh, contains tracks by Daniel Johnston and Slint.

solo outings:
The Folk Implosion:
Folk Implosion ♫♫♫ (Communion EP, 1996)
Dare to Be Surprised ♫♫♫♪ (Communion, 1997)

influences:
◄◄ Flipper, Hüsker Dü, the Sex Pistols, Dinosaur Jr., the Replacements, the Minutemen, the Velvet Underground, the Stooges, Neil Young

►► Liz Phair, Superchunk, Nirvana, Smashing Pumpkins

Steve Knopper

John Sebastian

See: Lovin' Spoonful

Jon Secada

Born Juan Secada, October 4, 1962, in Havana, Cuba.

Even more emphatically than his mentor, Gloria Estefan, Jon Secada has each foot planted triumphantly in two different musical worlds: American adult contemporary and Afro-Cuban pop. Estefan may be a bilingual singing superstar, but Secada is a doe-eyed Cuban crooner, able to bend (and compose) the most sensitive ballad to the strengths of his sweet, exhilarating tenor. And Latin lovers have a way of sustaining stardom for a long, long time. A two-time Grammy winner, Secada emerged as one of the most successful AC artists of the '90s on the wings of his eponymous first album alone, selling more than six million copies worldwide. He came to the U.S. at the age of nine, after his father served a year and a half in a Cuban work camp for daring to ask permission to leave Castro's country legally. Secada learned English quickly upon arriving in the States, but his singing talent didn't begin to show itself until the 11th grade, when he won the part of a young Scrooge in a school musical version of *A Christmas Carol*. Secada went on to earn a master's degree in jazz vocal performance at the University of Miami and took a job teaching music theory and voice training at Miami Community College while shopping his own demo tapes. One of them fell into the hands of Gloria's husband, Emilio Estefan, who signed him as a backup singer; soon Secada was co-writing several of the songs for Gloria's *Into the Light* LP (including the memorable "Coming out of the Dark") and singing on her subsequent concert tour before striking out on his own. Unquestionably one of the top Latin solo singer-songwriters of his era, his albums *Otro Dia Mas Sin Verte* and *Amor* each won Grammy Awards in the Best Latin Pop categories in 1992 and 1996, respectively. Respected as one of the nice guys in pop music, Secada also starred as Danny Zuko on Broadway in a 1995 production of *Grease* and frequently performs on behalf of UNICEF, music education, and AIDS-related charities.

what to buy: Five singles were eventually released from his debut album, *Jon Secada* ♫♫♫♫ (Capitol, 1992, prod. Emilio Estefan Jr., Jorge Casas, Clay Ostwald), but none established his sound or catapulted his career as much as the soaring "Just Another Day," one of the most radio-friendly hits of the decade. Of course, the other four—"Angel," "Do You Believe in Us," "I'm Free," and "Do You Want Me"—ain't exactly Menudo, either.

what to buy next: After a two-year hiatus from recording, Secada returned in 1997 with *Secada* ♫♫♫♫ (Capitol, 1997, prod. James Harris III, Terry Lewis), his most self-assured, focused musical collection. Needing a boost to re-enter U.S. record charts that had become female-dominated during his absence, Secada joined forces with Minneapolis megaproducers Jimmy Jam and Terry Lewis to create a soundscape that mixes his trademark mid-tempo romantic ballads (led by "Too Late, Too Soon") with the dancefloor zest of "I Live for You" and the Latin-spiced beat of "After All Is Said and Done."

the rest:
Otro Dia Mas Sin Verte ♫♫♫♫ (EMI Latin, 1992)
Heart, Soul & a Voice ♫♫♫ (Capitol, 1994)
Si Te Vas ♫♫♫ (EMI Latin, 1994)
Amor ♫♫♫♫ (Capitol, 1995)

worth searching for: The movie soundtrack to *The Specialist* (Sony, 1994, prod. various) features three songs written by Secada, including the track "Mental Picture," which he also performs.

influences:
◄◄ Emilio Estefan, Gloria Estefan, Stevie Wonder, Billy Joel, Elton John, Johnny Mathis, Luther Vandross, Earth, Wind & Fire

►► Mellow Mellow, Eddie Santiago, Todd Terry

Jim McFarlin

Sector 27

See: Tom Robinson Band

Neil Sedaka

Born March 13, 1939, in Brooklyn, NY.

A child prodigy at nine years of age, worldwide star at 20, has-been at 25, and defiant comeback kid a decade after that, Neil Sedaka's story is full of typical showbiz ups and downs. But despite what one might think of the man and his music—and there seems to be no critical middle ground here—you have to give Sedaka credit for not only persevering whenever all seemed lost, but for carrying on fearlessly to this day, serenading all who'll listen with his own eunuch style of Tin Pan Alley rock.

Fresh into Lincoln High School, Sedaka was already composing with 16-year-old neighbor Howard Greenfield and singing in local vocal groups such as the Tokens (later of "The Lion Sleeps Tonight" fame) when no less an authority than Arthur Rubinstein chose him as New York City's outstanding classical pianist, resulting in a scholarship at the prestigious Juilliard School of Music. He and Greenfield were soon afterwards brought to the attention of music publishers Don Kirshner and Al Nevins, who helped them place songs with such reputable artists as Clyde McPhatter and LaVern Baker, though it was Connie Francis who first hit with their "Stupid Cupid" in 1958. Nevins then played a demo of "The Diary" to RCA Victor, who were impressed enough with Sedaka's voice to sign him as a recording artist in his own right, launching a run of worldwide smashes that lasted four years. However, unable to compete with the challenge of the Beatles-led musical revolution of the mid-1960s, Sedaka spent the remainder of that decade composing primarily, performing sporadically, and recording even less. A successful club tour of Northern England in 1971 led Sedaka to relocate to London, where he began writing with a new lyricist, Phil Cody, and recording with a Manchester group who would soon become better known as 10cc. Several successful U.K.-only releases, culminating in 1974 with "Laughter in the Rain," brought an offer from long-time fan Elton John to release these recordings in the U.S. on his new Rocket label. Within a year Sedaka was back atop the American charts with not only "Laughter" but also a remake of his 1962 classic "Breaking up Is Hard to Do," a hit duet with Elton himself on "Bad Blood," and a Grammy-winning cover of "Love Will Keep Us Together" as sung by the Captain & Tennille. Although Sedaka last visited the Top 20 in 1980 with "Should've Never Let You Go," sung alongside his daughter Dara, he remains active to this day recording and performing, and through it all found time to write a surprisingly candid autobiography entitled, most prophetically it turned out, "Laughter in the Rain."

what to buy: The early triumphs are best collected on *Neil Sedaka Sings His Greatest Hits* ♫♫♫ (RCA, 1992, compilation prod. Herman Diaz Jr.), while *Laughter in the Rain: The Best of Neil Sedaka, 1974–1980* ♫♫♫ (Varese Vintage, 1994, compilation prod. Cary E. Mansfield) ably covers the highlights of his 1970s renaissance.

what to avoid: Caveat emptor: the invitingly titled *Tuneweaver* ♫♫ (Varese Vintage, 1995, compilation prod. Cary E. Mansfield, Leba Sedaka) actually contains 10 1990s re-recordings of old Sedaka/Greenfield chestnuts mixed with 10 lackluster new compositions.

the rest:
All-Time Greatest Hits ♫♫ (RCA, 1975)
Oh! Carol and Other Big Hits ♫♫ (RCA, 1989)

influences:
◀◀ Cole Porter, Johnnie Ray, the Penguins, Hotlegs
▶▶ Frankie Valli, Barry Manilow, George Michael

Gary Pig Gold

The Seeds

Formed 1965, in Los Angeles, CA. Disbanded 1970.

Sky Saxon (born Richard Marsh), vocals; John Savage, guitar; Daryl Hooper, keyboards; Rick Andridge, drums.

A garage band with a psychedelic/punk attitude, the Seeds made an impact with cheesy-sounding instruments and the long, annoying whine of Sky Saxon; ultimately, when it came to skills, the Seeds were low on the food chain. The group is best remembered for its 1967 hit "Pushin' Too Hard," after which it had little success for its succession of soundalike songs. That's not to say the band didn't experiment; in 1969 it released a blues album, albeit an ill-advised one, *Full Spoon of Seedy Blues*. But as the psychedelic movement was making way for blues-based hard-rock bands, the Seeds' limitations became more obvious, leading to diminishing record sales, smaller audiences, and ultimately a breakup—though Saxon still periodically trots out a new version of the Seeds.

what to buy: *Future* ♫♫♫ (Crescendo, 1967, prod. Marcus Tybalt) is the pinnacle of the Seeds' enchantment with psychedelic music, a true time warp with "March of the Flower Children," "Travel with Your Mind," and "Where Is the Entranceway to Play," as well as the hit "Thousand Shadows."

what to buy next: *Seeds* ♫♫♫ (GNP Crescendo, 1966) includes the first two albums, *The Seeds* and *Web of Sound*. The band's best-remembered hits are here.

what to avoid: *A Full Spoon of Seedy Blues* **woof!** (GNP Crescendo, 1969) is dismal stuff from a band that should have never played the blues.

Bob Seger (© Ken Settle)

the rest:

Raw & Alive: Merlin's Music Box ♪♪ (GNP Crescendo, 1968)
Fallin' off the Edge ♪ (GNP Crescendo, 1977)

influences:

◄◄ The Rolling Stones, Shadows of Knight, the Yardbirds, the Standells, the Electric Prunes

►► Soul Asylum, the Replacements, Green River, the Dukes of Stratosphear

Patrick McCarty

Jonathan Segel

See: Cracker

Bob Seger

Born May 6, 1945, in Detroit, MI.

Bob Seger is the consummate Midwestern rocker—earnest but (mostly) apolitical, sentimental but not maudlin, and creatively steeped in soul, country, and pounding rock 'n' roll. His songs are honest and occasionally philosophical musings, remem-brances of backseat maneuvers ("Night Moves," "Brave Strangers"), working on the line ("Making Thunderbirds"), and struggling for perspective ("Hollywood Nights," "Against the Wind"). Raised in Ann Arbor, Seger is indelibly marked by the departure of his father, who abandoned the family when his youngest son was 12, and by the near-poverty conditions he grew up in. Seger's songs are the paeans of an outsider, the "Beautiful Loser" he started singing about in 1975; even after he became successful, Seger retained a shiftless spirit, the hall-mark of the insecure and distrustful who, as he sings, will "al-ways be running against the wind." Only on his most recent al-bums, *The Fire Inside* and *It's a Mystery*, has Seger revealed any sense of comfort, singing warmly about his wife and children—but also taking sharp aim at the violent and capricious elements of society that he fears can undermine his family's well being. A little wariness makes for great songs, of course, and Seger has written them by the bushel—dating back to the 1966 street nar-rative "East Side Story" and the late '60s frat party favorites "Ramblin' Gamblin' Man" and "Heavy Music." And when Seger and his Silver Bullet Band get cooking, they're—still—as formi-dable a rock 'n' roll outfit as you'll find treading the boards.

what to buy: Maybe it was the bicentennial, but 1976 was a great year for Seger. First, *Live Bullet* ♫♫♫♫ (Capitol, 1976, prod. Bob Seger, Punch Andrews) showed the world what the middling production of Seger's eight prior albums couldn't: that he could rock with a fury to match anyone in rock's upper echelon. Playing in front of the partisan hometown brethren at Detroit's Cobo Arena, Seger and the Silver Bullet Band delivered a storming barn-burner of a show that—thanks to some radio play for "Katmandu"—finally made the rest of the country notice. Then he delivered *Night Moves* ♫♫♫♫ (Capitol, 1976, prod. Bob Seger, Punch Andrews, Jack Richardson, the Muscle Shoals Rhythm Section), a masterful collection of songs that retains the energy of *Live Bullet*—particularly on the ferocious rockers "The Fire Down Below," "Sunspot Baby," and "Rock and Roll Never Forgets." Recorded with a trimmed-down Silver Bullet Band, *The Distance* ♫♫♫♫ (Capitol, 1972, prod. Jimmy Iovine) is a loosely themed collection of soaring affirmations, with Seger exulting in triumphing over adversity in "Roll Me Away," "Little Victories," and "Even Now."

what to buy next: *Stranger in Town* ♫♫♫♫ (Capitol, 1978, prod. Bob Seger, Punch Andrews, the Muscle Shoals Rhythm Section) and *Against the Wind* ♫♫♫♫ (Capitol, 1980, prod. Bob Seger, Punch Andrews, the Muscle Shoals Rhythm Section) are of a piece, cementing the mass success grasped by *Night Moves* without really advancing the craft. Despite a couple of rockers that remain concert favorites ("The Horizontal Bop," "Betty Lou's Gettin' out Tonight"), *Against the Wind* is a notably softer album, marked by medium tempo hits such as "Fire Lake," "You'll Accomp'ny Me," and the title track.

what to avoid: Despite a bunch of terrific songs, the single-volume *Greatest Hits* ♫♫ (Capitol, 1994, prod. various) is really a slight overview of Seger's career. He deserves better.

the rest:
Ramblin' Gamblin' Man ♫♫♫ (Capitol, 1969)
Noah ♫♫ (Capitol, 1969)
Mongrel ♫♫ (Capitol, 1970)
Smokin' O.P.'s ♫♫♫ (Capitol, 1972)
Back in '72 ♫♫♫ (Capitol, 1973)
Seven ♫♫♫ (Capitol, 1974)
Beautiful Loser ♫♫♫♫ (Capitol, 1975)
Nine Tonight ♫♫♫♫ (Capitol, 1981)
Like a Rock ♫♫♫ (Capitol, 1986)
The Fire Inside ♫♫♫ (Capitol, 1991)
It's a Mystery ♫♫♫♫ (Capitol, 1995)

worth searching for: *The Silver Seger Sampler* (Capitol, 1993, prod. various) is a six-song promotional release containing some of the cream from Seger's pre–*Live Bullet* albums.

influences:
◀◀ Van Morrison, Wilson Pickett, Chuck Berry, John Fogerty, Hank Williams, Bob Dylan, Rodney Crowell

▶▶ The Eagles (Glenn Frey), Bruce Springsteen, John Mellencamp, Michael Stanley, Garth Brooks

Gary Graff

The Selecter

Formed 1979, in Coventry, England. Disbanded 1981. Re-formed 1992.

Noel Davies, guitar; Charley Anderson, bass (1979–81); Pauline Black, vocals; Charley "H" Bembridge, drums (1979–81); Compton Amanor, guitar (1979–81); Arthur Hendrickson, vocals (1979–81); Desmond Brown, keyboards (1979–81); Perry Melius, drums (1992–present); Martin Stewart, keyboards (1992–present); Nick Welsh, bass (1992–present).

In an effort to get its ska brew heard, the Selecter band started its own company, 2-Tone, a label that went on to considerable success with kindred spirits such as the Specials. Like most of its ska-revivalist peers, the Selecter focused mainly on brittle and propulsive tunes with a political edge, highlighted by the jumpy drama of Pauline Black's vocals. The Selecter wrongly played second fiddle as England embraced the Specials and Madness. Black and Noel Davies regrouped in 1992 to no greater recognition, just a bit too early for the new ska movement in the U.S.

what to buy: *Selected Selecter Selections* ♫♫♫♫ (Chrysalis, 1989, prod. Errol Ross) is a potent reminder of the band's best work, culled from its first two albums, *Too Much Pressure* and *Celebrate the Bullet*. Selections such as "Too Much Pressure," "Murder," "On My Radio," "Three Minute Hero," and "Celebrate the Bullet" all reveal, again, that the Selecter was an unjustly neglected part of the early '80s ska scene.

the rest:
Out on the Streets ♫♫ (Triple X, 1992)
The Happy Album ♫♫ (Triple X, 1994)
Back out on the Streets ♫♫ (Triple X, 1996)

influences:
◀◀ Bob Marley, Jimmy Cliff, Skatalites, Delroy Wilson, Derrick Morgan, Desmond Dekker

▶▶ Smash Mouth, Chumbawamba, Sublime, 311, Sugar Ray

Allan Orski

Semisonic

Formed 1994, in Minneapolis, MN.

Dan Wilson, vocals, guitar; John Munson, bass, vocals; Jake Slichter, drums, keyboards.

This power-pop trio revisits the legendary "Minneapolis sound," but updates it with the friendliest pop hooks heard anywhere in a long time. Not too many bands play pure pop songs for rock-tempered ears, and Semisonic's attention to craft rather than attitude is a great relief after the feel-bad grunge years. The three musicians survived many years in various Twin Cities outfits (including the folk-rock band Trip Shakespeare) before coming together, and their tight playing and dedication promise a future as one of the next great rock 'n' roll stories.

what to buy: Wilson has a penchant for writing catchy, perennially sweet boy-likes-girl radio songs with original hooks and loads of appeal. *Feeling Strangely Fine* 𝄢𝄢𝄢𝄢 (MCA, 1998, prod. Nick Launay) offers a generous mix of driving rockers, winsome popcraft, and a few surprisingly good ballads. The single "Closing Time," with its sing-along refrain, lit up nationwide sales of the album, and deservedly so, but it's not the whole story.

what to buy next: In many ways more sophisticated than *Feeling Strangely Fine*, *The Great Divide* 𝄢𝄢𝄢𝄢 (MCA, 1996, prod. Paul Fox) features exhilarating guitar work, smarter lyrics, and a road-song spirit. In terms of overall effect, though, it's not quite the equal of its successor.

worth searching for: *Pleasure EP* (Cherrydisc EP, 1995) shows the promise of things to come.

influences:

◀◀ The Beatles, the Beach Boys, Elton John, Matthew Sweet, the Replacements

see also: *Trip Shakespeare*

Amy Weivoda

Sepultura

Formed 1984, in Belo Horizonte, Brazil.

Max Cavalera, vocals, guitar (1984–97); Andreas Kisser, guitar; Paulo Jr., bass; Igor Cavalera, drums.

Following the late '80s success of Metallica, Slayer, Anthrax, and Megadeth, it seemed heavy metal had no place new to go. Hailing from Brazil, Sepultura's spin on the music gave the genre a shot in the arm. Combining the speed of thrash metal with the do-it-yourself ethic of hardcore, Sepultura became one of the first metal acts to attract a punk-rock audience. Although Sepultura has occasionaly collaborated with artists from other genres (punk icon Jello Biafra, Jonathan Davis of KoЯn, Mike Patton of Faith No More, DJ Lethal of House of Pain), the band has always kept its sound fast and heavy. Where most bands from the metal underground say they are "expanding their sound" but mean "do a power ballad to get on the radio," Sepultura became the rare metal band to truly experiment—incorporating the music of the indigenous people of Brazil to its thrash on "Ratamahatta" from *Roots*, its most ambitious and

best album. The band's future, unfortunately, is in doubt, because singer Max Cavalera has departed to make music with his wife, the band's now-former manager, in what seems to be a John Lennon/Yoko Ono scenario.

what to buy: *Roots* 𝄢𝄢𝄢𝄢 (Roadrunner, 1996, prod. Ross Robinson) shows that Sepultura is best when it's most ambitious. "Roots Bloody Roots" is as heavy as anything the band ever did, and "Ratamahatta" is so catchy it actually earned airplay on conservative alternative-rock (gasp!) radio stations.

what to buy next: With *Chaos A.D.* 𝄢𝄢𝄢 (Epic/Roadrunner, 1993, prod. Andy Wallace), the band made no concessions to its new major record label. Sepultura begins using indigenous influences here, on "Kaiowas," but "Refuse/Resist," "Territory," and a version of New Model Army's "The Hunt" are as brutal as ever.

the rest:

Morbid Visions 𝄢𝄢𝄢 (Roadrunner, 1986)
Bestial Devastation 𝄢𝄢 (Roadrunner, 1986)
Schizophrenia 𝄢𝄢𝄢 (Roadrunner, 1987)
Beneath the Remains 𝄢𝄢𝄢 (Roadrunner, 1989)
Arise 𝄢𝄢𝄢 (Roadrunner, 1991)
Against N/A (Roadrunner, 1998)

influences:

◀◀ Black Sabbath, Metallica, Voivod, Dead Kennedys, Black Flag

▶▶ KoЯn, Deftones, Life of Agony

Brian Ives

Brian Setzer

See: Stray Cats

Seven Mary Three

Formed 1992, in Williamsburg, VA.

Jason Ross, vocals, guitar; Jason Pollock, guitars; Giti Khalsa, drums; Casey Daniel, bass.

Named for Larry Wilcox's radio code name on the TV series *CHiPs,* Seven Mary Three came together as a collaboration between two Jasons—Ross and Pollock—who earned degrees together at the College of William and Mary in Williamsburg, Virginia. Playing around the college and in Ross and Casey Daniel's hometown of Orlando, Florida, the band eventually recorded an independent CD dubbed *Churn.* Its manager prevailed upon radio station WJRR-FM, which had jumped on Collective Soul's "Shine" before it was a hit, to play the band's Pearl Jam–influenced single, "Cumbersome." It worked; moving back to Florida, the band had a deal.

what to buy: Its debut CD, *American Standard* ♪♪♪ (Atlantic, 1995, prod. Jason Ross, Jason Pollock, Tom Morris), presented a catchy mix between Pearl Jam's bombast and Stone Temple Pilots' '90s-style classic rock, selling more than a million copies and taking "Cumbersome" nationwide.

what to avoid: On the follow-up, *Rock Crown* ♪♪ (Atlantic, 1997, prod. Tom Morris), the band is weighed down by pretentious material and its unfailingly derivative sound.

the rest:
Orange Ave ♪♪♪ (Atlantic, 1998)

worth searching for: With only a small number of copies pressed, the band's 1994 independent release, *Churn* (1994, prod. Seven Mary Three), serves as a rare, impressive find for any collector.

influences:
◄◄ Pearl Jam, Stone Temple Pilots
►► Sponge, Our Lady Peace

Eric Deggans

Sevendust

Formed as Crawlspace, 1995, in Atlanta, GA.

Lajon Witherspoon, vocals; Clint Lowery, guitars; John Connolly, guitar; Vinnie Hornsby, bass; Morgan Ross, drums.

Sevendust is a collective of veteran Atlanta players who came together after a gig in late 1994. Vinnie Hornsby and Morgan Ross were members of Snake Nation, whose opening act was Body and Soul, a local R&B band fronted by Lajon Wither-spoon. Impressed by Witherspoon's vocals, Hornsby and Rose invited him to start a band with them. They asked John Connolly, then the drummer for Peacedog, to join them. First known as Rumblefish, then as Crawlspace, the band found a mentor in Jay Jay French, guitarist for Twisted Sister, who produced its first demos in August 1995. Thanks to its song "My Ruin," Crawlspace was introduced to a mass audience through its participation in the *Mortal Kombat: More Kombat* soundtrack. After a West Coast band named Crawlspace objected to sharing the name, the group hit on Sevendust.

what's available: The debut, *Sevendust* ♪♪ (TVT, 1997, prod. Jay Jay French), is a collision of ear-throbbing drums, chugging guitars, and Witherspoon's aggressive vocals. Unfortunately, it's not that much different from its peers. The song "Face," with the lyrics "Rape me/don't make me wait/I love the pain," seems added as a desperate way of getting attention. (For the record, the band says the song was written about a woman who wants "to be taken aggressively.") "Black," however, is a poignant look at racism.

influences:
◄◄ Living Colour, Clutch, White Zombie

Christina Fuoco

The Sex Pistols

Formed 1975, in London, England. Disbanded 1978. Re-formed 1996.

Johnny Rotten (born John Lydon), vocals; Glen Matlock, bass (1975–77, 1996); Sid Vicious (born Simon Ritchie; died 1979), bass (1977–78); Steve Jones, guitar; Paul Cook, drums.

The band that defined the punk rock revolution, the Sex Pistols thrived on a notorious reputation earned by angry, irreverent songs (a blitz-speed "God Save the Queen" doesn't endear you to most British folks) and outrageous on- and off-stage antics, many manipulated by the group's manager-of-sorts, Malcolm McLaren. Though only teenagers when they formed, the Pistols almost single-handedly launched the punk movement in Britain and opened the door for new wave; like the Ramones before them, the Sex Pistols told disaffected youth that you could indeed pick up a guitar and, without technical prowess, just start bashing it to make a valid noise. Reacting to the complacency of dinosaur rock bands and bland popular music, the group set out to shock and antagonize people out of their musical apathy. Taking on subjects such as the royal family, anarchy, and corporate irresponsibility—as well as giving voice to the rising mood of hopelessness John Lydon sensed in his country—the Pistols were raw, angry, violent, and alive. Unfortunately, the Sex Pistols were destined to be short-lived. The group broke up following a dismal and unorganized U.S. tour in 1978; its members went on to an assortment of solo projects—Lydon's Public Image Ltd. being the most durable—and Sid Vicious died of a drug overdose in 1979 after being arrested for the murder of his girlfriend. But in 1996, amidst cynicism and accusations of sell-out—which the group readily fessed up to—the Sex Pistols reunited for a brief tour with original bass player Glen Matlock, which Lydon said would be the last he'd ever do with his former bandmates. We'll see.

what to buy: *Never Mind the Bollocks Here's the Sex Pistols* ♪♪♪♪♪ (Warner Bros., 1977, prod. Chris Thomas) was the great punk-rock wake-up call whose resonance still echoes in the modern-rock community.

what to buy next: *The Great Rock & Roll Swindle* ♪♪♪ (Warner Bros., 1979, prod. various), from the crappy movie of the same name, is filled with muddled garbage but just enough noteworthy live and studio cuts to make it a worthwhile addendum to *Bollocks*.

what to avoid: *Better Live Than Dead* ♪♪ (Restless, 1988) is interesting for its energetic performance and selection of covers (the Who's "Substitute," the Monkees' "Stepping Stone"), but the poor fidelity is grating.

the rest:
The Swindle Continues ♪♪♪ (Restless, 1988)
Live at Chelmsford Top Security Prison ♪♪♪ (Restless, 1990)
Filthy Lucre Live ♪♪♪ (Virgin, 1996)

worth searching for: *Kiss This* (Virgin, 1992, prod. various) is a U.K. compilation that should be, for most, a one-stop Pistols collection.

solo outings:
Steve Jones:
(With Chequered Past) *Chequered Past* ♪♪ (EMI, 1984)
Mercy ♪♪ (Gold Mountain/MCA, 1987)
Fire and Gasoline ♪ (Gold Mountain/MCA, 1989)

Malcolm McLaren:
Duck Rock ♪♪ (Island, 1983)
Would Ya Like More Scratchin'? ♪ (Island, 1984)
Fans ♪♪♪♪ (Island, 1984)
Swamp Thing ♪ (Island, 1985)
Waltz Darling ♪ (Epic, 1989)
Round the Outside! Round the Outside! ♪♪♪ (Virgin, 1990)
Paris ♪♪ (Gee Street/Island, 1995)

Sid Vicious:
Never Mind the Reunion: Here's Sid Vicious ♪♪ (Cleopatra, 1997)
Sid Vicious & Friends N/A (Caroline, 1998)

influences:
◀◀ The Ramones, the Who, the Monkees

▶▶ Black Flag, Minutemen, Nirvana, Green Day, any band that operates under the punk umbrella

see also: *Public Image Ltd.*

Anna Glen and Gary Graff

WHAT ALBUM CHANGED YOUR LIFE?

I definitely love the first New York Dolls album. I loved it. That was one of the albums I'd always listen to a lot. I really got off on it, y'know?

Steve Jones (of the Sex Pistols)

Ron Sexsmith

Born c. 1964, in Ontario, Canada.

Canadian Ron Sexsmith formed his first band during the late '70s and earned a local following during the '80s with a group called the Uncool. Originally signed to Interscope Records as a songwriter, some of Sexsmith's demos caught the ear of label head Jimmy Iovine, who gave the singer-songwriter a recording contract.

what to buy: When his eponymous debut, *Ron Sexsmith* ♪♪♪♪ (Interscope, 1995, prod. Mitchell Froom, Daniel Lanois), finally came out in 1995, it was an instant cult favorite, earning critical plaudits and raves from fellow artists, including Elvis Costello, who called it "a modest and elegant gem." Moody and understated, it recalls Frank Sinatra as much as Costello, focusing on sad ballads and yearning to create a haunting atmosphere wholly at odds with contemporary pop music. "Secret Heart" is as innocent as the Beach Boys' "In My Room," while "There's a Rhythm" mixes the melancholy and the spiritual in a way not unlike Sexsmith's fellow Canadian Leonard Cohen. Often-heavyhanded producer Mitchell Froom (Elvis Costello, Richard Thompson, Suzanne Vega) is smart enough to let Sexsmith do his own thing, though the final cut, a shimmering alternate version of "There's a Rhythm" produced by Daniel Lanois, hints at an even greater record that might have been.

what to buy next: Sexsmith's sophomore effort, *Other Songs* ♪♪♪♪ (Interscope, 1997, prod. Michell Froom, Tchad Blake), is almost as good, though a couple of slightly more upbeat numbers prevent it from sustaining the cohesive mood of its predecessor.

influences:
◀◀ The Kinks, Leonard Cohen, Harry Nilsson, Leonard Cohen, Elvis Costello, Daniel Lanois

Jeff Schwager

Charlie Sexton

Born August 11, 1968, in San Antonio, TX.

A guitar phenom from an early age, this San Antonio and Austin product was touring with fellow Texan Joe Ely's band at age 13. He won a recording contract two years later, hobnobbing with the likes of Bob Dylan and Keith Richards. Charlie Sexton de-emphasized his guitar prowess for a pouty, pretty-boy look (with a faux British accent to boot) for his debut album, released when he was 17. It was a hit, but a second album flopped. Sexton dropped the glam-rock facade to join the late Stevie Ray Vaughan's rhythm section in Arc Angels, a gutsy blues rock band that released one album and toured extensively, but broke up soon after. A more mature and focused Sexton convened a new band and began performing and writing more strong, autobiographical materal—sometimes with help from the enigmatic songwriter Tonio K.

what to buy: *Under the Wishing Tree* ♫♫♫ (MCA, 1995, prod. Malcolm Burn, Charlie Sexton) finds Sexton purging some personal demons and making the kind of big, open, rangy roots rock that fits his lyrical motifs.

the rest:
Pictures for Pleasure ♫ (MCA, 1985)
Charlie Sexton ♫ (MCA, 1985)

influences:
◀◀ Chuck Berry, the Rolling Stones, Bryan Adams, David Bowie

see also: *Arc Angels*

Doug Pullen

Phil Seymour

See: Dwight Twilley

S.F. Seals

Formed 1993, in San Francisco, CA. Disbanded 1995.

Barbara Manning, guitars, bass, vocals; Brently Pusser, guitars, vocals; Melanie Clarin, drums, vocals, accordion; Margaret Murray, bass, guitar.

S.F. Seals was the creation of the enchanting Barbara Manning, a songwriter whose work with 28th Day, World of Pooh, and Glands of External Secretion has solidified her status as one of the most curious and head-scratchingly unpredictable pop songwriters around. At her core is a devotion to the three-minute pop song, but she will happily toss a blast of pure noise or random act of violence smack dab in the middle of a song just to mess with the listener's head. S.F. Seals was her more straight-ahead guitar-pop band, and over the course of two LPs and numerous singles, they created solid, roller-coaster pop with patches of found sound and montage snippets juggled in.

what to buy: The *Baseball Trilogy EP* ♫♫♫ (Matador, 1993, prod. Greg Freeman) contains three songs devoted to baseball, most notably the phenomenally catchy "Dock Ellis," about the pitcher who threw a no-hitter while tripping on acid. *Nowhere* ♫♫♫ (Matador, 1994, prod. Greg Freeman) is as screwy as a pop album can be, containing, among the glorious originals, covers of Badfinger, the Holy Modal Rounders, Faine Jade, and Goblin Mix.

what to buy next: The final album, *Truth Walks in Sleepy Shadows* ♫♫♫ (Matador, 1995, prod. Greg Freeman, S.F. Seals), is a moving, somewhat thematic album concerned with the sea. It contains a marvelous version of the John Cale and Terry Riley song "Soul of Patrick Lee."

influences:
◀◀ Suzanne Vega, the Beatles, John Cale
▶▶ Spinanes, Liz Phair, Thinking Fellers Union Local 282

Randall Roberts

The Shadows

See: Cliff Richard

The Shadows of Knight

Formed 1964, in Arlington Heights, IL.

Jimmy Sohns, lead vocals, percussion; Norm Gotsch, bass (1964–66); Warren Rodgers, guitar, bass (1964–66); Jerry McGeorge, guitar, vocals (1964–67); Tom Schiffour, drums, vocals (1964–67); Joe "Red" Kelley, guitar, bass, harmonica, vocals (1966–67); Dave "The Hawk" Wolinski, bass, keyboards (1966–67); Jeffrey "Woody" Woodruff, guitar (1968–70); Dan Baughman, guitar (1968–70); John Fisher, bass (1968–70); Kenny Turkin, drums (1968–70); Jack "Hawkeye" Daniel, guitar (1970); Charlie Hess, bass (1970–71); Bob Harper (1970–71); Eric Blomquist (1970–71); Gary Levin, guitar (1970–71); Bob Bostanche, drums (1972–74); Lee Brovitz, bass, vocals (1972–78, 1987–present); Paul Roy, guitar, vocals (1972–78, 1995–97); Michael Gotshall, guitar (1987–97); Michael Campbell, drums, vocals (1995–present); Ray Nesbit, guitar, vocals (1997–present).

The Shadows of Knight, undisputed Garage Rock Kings of Illinois, said it best themselves more than 30 years ago: "The Stones, Animals, and Yardbirds took the Chicago blues and gave it an English interpretation. We've taken the English version of the blues and re-added a Chicago touch." That the group most certainly did—and then some—as its Benzedrine-tempo takes on the Bo Diddley songbook more than demonstrate. But it was its show-stopping version of Van Morrison's "Gloria," recorded and released on the tiny Dunwich label in early 1966, that spread their Chicago-by-way-of-London sound high up the charts and forever into the Garage Hall of Infamy. "If you invited them over for dinner," the liner notes on the debut album warned, "your parents would, at first, have you examined or call the police or run screaming to the neighbors." Awright! "If your parents stayed around," however, "they would find that the Shadows are polite, quiet, considerate and that they might even grow to like them." Uh-oh. Sure enough, lead vocalist Jimmy Sohns's *second* band of Knights surfaced several years later on the bubblegum-lite Super K label, with nary a fuzz box in sight nor a hint of Diddley left to their sound. Subsequent Shadows dabbled with heavier proto-metal, defiantly declining to cash in on the mid-'70s punk rock movement the group did its fair share to inspire. The group proudly continues performing and recording to this day with a sound right back in the garage where it belongs. Ready now? Repeat after me: "Gee-El-O-Are-I-Ay!"

what to buy: The band's story may best be told overall on *Dark Sides: The Best of the Shadows of Knight* ♪♪♪♪ (Rhino, 1994, compilation prod. Bill Inglot, David McLees), but for a *real* taste of what these guys could do in their prime, try *Raw 'n' Alive at the Cellar, Chicago 1966!* ♪♪♪♪ (Sundazed, 1993, prod. Bob Irwin). A surprisingly well-recorded, amazingly raw tape of the Shadows in action deep down inside Chicago's very own Cavern Club, this record demonstrates, as few others do, the pure, uninhibited, unbounded joy to be had bashing out your favorite songs on electric guitars and drums in front of your friends in some stinky basement on a Saturday night. Timeless, spirited, and tons of fun.

what to buy next: Both *Gloria* ♪♪♪♪ (Dunwich, 1966/Sundazed, 1998, prod. Bill Traut, George Badonsky) and *Back Door Men* ♪♪♪♪ (Dunwich, 1967/Sundazed, 1998, prod. Bill Traut, George Badonsky) show the band at its earliest, snarling best, while *Shake!* ♪♪♪ (One Way, 1994, prod. Joey Levine, Arthur Resnick) focuses on their more sticky-sweet Super K material.

the rest:
Live in Rockford, 1972 ♪♪♪♪ (Performance, 1993)
Super K Kollection ♪♪♪ (Collectables, 1994)

influences:
◀◀ The Yardbirds, Them, Eric Burdon, the Kinks, the Wheels

▶▶ The Syndicate of Sound, the Stooges, Chesterfield Kings, the Cheepskates, the Lyres

Gary Pig Gold

Shady
See: Mercury Rev

Shakespear's Sister
See: Bananarama

Sham 69

Formed 1977, in Hersham (London), England. Disbanded 1981.

Jimmy Pursey, vocals; Dave Parsons, guitar; Dave "Kermit" Tregunna, bass; Albie "Slider" Maskell, drums (1977); Mark "Dodie" Cain, drums (1978–79); Ricky Goldstein, drums (1980).

Of all the late '70s original U.K. punk legends, none was more maligned (and more beloved by a Sham Army of fans) than Sham 69. Like its equally great and also roundly dismissed contemporaries the U.K. Subs, Sham's crime was to take the intellectual edge out of this once vibrant movement, bringing the music down to the level of the average kid concert-goer, complete with football stadium–style chants for all to sing along with. In this sense, the group completely anticipated the coming '80s hardcore explosion, particularly the American branch (note that Ian MacKaye and Henry Rollins migrated all the way to New York to attend the two '79 East Coast Sham shows before singing for Minor Threat and Fugazi (MacKaye), and Black Flag (Rollins)). But in so doing, Sham traded industry respect and credibility for simplistic and crude yet honestly affecting and enduring punk. Those purchasing Dojo Records' reissues of the first four albums (only the spotty debut *Tell Us the Truth* enjoyed an American release back then) will be struck by the band's saving graces, the kind that inspired such a loyal, albeit thuggish (and exclusive) audience that the band racked up seven U.K. Top 40 singles (including three Top 10s) during those first three years. For a bunch of bellowing, braying Joes, there was no denying that motormouth man-of-the-people singer Jimmy Pursey was a hardworking, committed, and charismatic leader, and that sidekick Dave Parsons came up with effective guitar riffs, making them more than just punks becoming popular after the original innovators left the scene. Sham 69 has reunited periodically, but without the notoriety of its original incarnation.

what to buy: The 1980 swan song *The Game* ♪♪♪♪ (Dojo, 1996, prod. Jimmy Pursey, Pete Wilson) sent Sham out in a blaze of surprising glory with its most convincing and workmanlike album, punctuated by a hot single "Give a Dog a Bone." The 1978 release *That's Life* ♪♪♪♪ (Dojo, 1996, prod. Jimmy Pursey, Pete Wilson), the first punk-rock concept LP (a day in the life of a working-class teen, complete with a pub fight over a girl) is not quite the Kinks but still succeeds thanks to the abundance of big hooks in "Leave Me Alone," "That's Life," and the U.K. hit "Hurry up Harry."

what to buy next: On 1979's *Hersham Boys* ♪♪♪ (Dojo, 1996, prod. Jimmy Pursey, Pete Wilson), the group stepped away from the narrow dictates of its violent crowd by donning cowboy gear for a country-western homage, along with a tribute to James Dean ("Lost on Highway 46"), and by solidly covering the Yardbirds' "You're a Better Man Than I." Another 1978 effort, *Tell Us the Truth* ✷✷✷ (Dojo, 1996, prod. Jimmy Pursey, Pete Wilson), is too formulaic, which made many miss the band's later improvement, though it has some good moments such as the oft-covered "Borstal Breakout."

what to avoid: If ever there was a band that shouldn't have attempted a comeback, it was Sham 69. Though admirable in intent, the new direction it hit upon—a crap rap/boogie/metal/dance trip without edge—on *Volunteer* **woof!** (Legacy U.K., 1988, prod. Jimmy Pursey) was just awful.

the rest:
The First, Best, and Last ✷✷✷ (Polydor U.K., 1980)
Angels with Dirty Faces: The Best of Sham 69 ✷✷✷ (Receiver U.K., 1986)
Live and Loud! Volume 2 ✷✷✷ (Link U.K., 1988)
Sham's Last Stand ✷✷✝ (Link U.K., 1989)
Live at the Roxy ✷ (Receiver U.K., 1990)
Rare and Unreleased ✷✷✷ (Limited Edition U.K., 1991)

worth searching for: *Live and Loud!* (Link U.K., 1987) is a scorching concert LP recorded during 1979 that proves the band was far better than its reputation and was in fact a hot group of musicians by the end of its tenure.

solo outings:
Jimmy Pursey:
Imagination Camouflage ✷✷✷✷ (Polydor U.K., 1980)
Alien Orphan ✷✷✝ (Epic U.K., 1982)
Revenge Is Not the Password ✷✷ (Turbo U.K., 1983)
The Lord Divides ✷ (Eskimo Green U.K., 1983)

influences:
◀◀ Sex Pistols, Chelsea, the Yardbirds

▶▶ Minor Threat, Cockney Rejects, Angelic Upstarts

see also: *Lords of the New Church*

Jack Rabid

The Shams

See: Amy Rigby

The Shangri-Las

Formed 1964, in Queens, NY. Disbanded 1968.

Mary Weiss, lead vocals; Elizabeth "Betty" Weiss, vocals (1964–65); Marge Ganser, vocals; Mary Ann Ganser, vocals.

Part cheerleading squad, part biker moll convention, the Shangri-Las bravely crossed the sugar-sweetness of the New York girl group sound with a sordid, tough underbelly of heartbreak and anguish that has always been a crucial part of the teen experience. The two sets of sisters had long been harmonizing informally between classes at Andrew Jackson High, but it was not until they began singing demos for producer George

"Shadow" Morton that their career really got underway. The brilliantly ego-eccentric Morton, in the grand tradition of Joe Meek and Phil Spector, took a bold cinematic approach to record making, and in the four girls from Queens he found the ideal mouthpieces for his little slices of acned melodrama (and, on Jerry Leiber and Mike Stoller's new Red Bird label, the perfect creative outlet for his masterpieces). Their very first song together was the epic "Remember (Walkin' in the Sand)" which, awash in seagulls and mock-operatic back-up choruses, cleverly set *West Side Story* on the beach and had no difficulty whatsoever hitting #5 during the height of Beatlemania. The all-time death-rock classic "Leader of the Pack" quickly followed, one of the most bombastically effective—and effect-laden—chart-toppers ever. But a host of legal problems (some allegedly involving the girls' deportment while on tour), culminating with the dissolution of Red Bird Records in 1966, forced a premature end to the Shangri-Las' brief but extremely colorful existence. However, such is the everlasting power of the music and the myth they left behind that, despite the deaths of both Ganser sisters, various trios and quartets continue performing to this day under the hallowed Shangri-Las' name, while the group's original recordings have lost absolutely none of their grit, spit, or sparkle.

what's available: After decades with their catalog in disarray, *The Best of the Shangri-Las* ✷✷✷✷ (Mercury, 1996, compilation prod. Bas Hartong, Bill Levenson) finally presents a domestic collection worthy of this group's indelible, far-reaching legacy. Every musical and lyrical base is touched herein, from the spirited buoyancy of "Give Him a Great Big Kiss" to the haunting, other-worldly "Past, Present, and Future" (reportedly one of Pete Townshend's all-time favorites). Of course, the majority of the Shangri-Las' time was spent brooding over deception, debauchery, and death, and outside of Johnny Cash's darker moments such themes have rarely been portrayed in song with more, uh, spirit than in "He Cried," "Dressed in Black," and "Give Us Your Blessings." You already know about "Leader of the Pack," but the other two dozen tracks on this spectacular disc each deserve your undivided attention as well.

influences:
◀◀ The Ronettes, the Angels, the Four Seasons, Jay & the Americans, Rachmaninov

▶▶ The New York Dolls, the Pandoras, Twinkle, Coyote Shivers, the Detergents

Gary Pig Gold

Del Shannon

Born December 30, 1939, in Coopersville, MI. Died February 8, 1990, in Santa Clarita, CA.

Del Shannon is Exhibit A of pre–British Invasion American rock 'n' roll. While rock historians would have you believe that everyone was just piddling around before the Fab Four arrived, Shannon was releasing seething and imaginative music ("Runaway," "Little Town Flirt," "Hey! Little Girl") as early as 1961. Along with Roy Orbison, he is virtually the first white U.S. artist to write dark, paranoid love songs that offered no light at the end of the tunnel. Focusing on aggressive minor key verses that shifted dramatically to major key choruses, Shannon seemed incapable of playing with anything less than gripping urgency. A versatile singer, he leapt to falsetto with startling effect and stayed on the charts throughout the first half of the '60s. In a grievous effort to mold him into a teen idol, the production team at Liberty all but snuffed out his career. Suffering from alcoholism and depression, he nonetheless made several attempts to return to music during the late '70s and early '80s, some with the help of Tom Petty and members of the Heartbreakers. Shannon was a candidate to replace Orbison in the Traveling Wilburys at the time of his suicide in 1990.

what to buy: *Greatest Hits* 𝄚𝄚𝄚𝄚 (Rhino, 1990, prod. various) is a perfectly riveting compilation of Shannon's teen heartbreak tragedies. His signature smash "Runaway" is here, along with essential material such as "Hats off to Larry," "Stranger in Town," "Keep Searchin' (We'll Follow the Sun)," and a kicking rendition of the Beatles' "From Me to You."

what to buy next: The posthumous *Rock On* 𝄚𝄚𝄚 (MCA, 1991, prod. Jeff Lynne, Mike Campbell) is a competent return to form with various members of Tom Petty's Heartbreakers lending strong support.

what to avoid: There's nothing on *Greatest Hits* 𝄚𝄚 (Curb, 1996, prod. Harry Balk) that's not on the Rhino compilation, so why bother?

the rest:
Sings Hank Williams 𝄚𝄚𝄚 (Rhino, 1990)
Little Town Flirt 𝄚𝄚𝄚 (Rhino, 1990)

worth searching for: The out-of-print *Drop down and Get Me* (Elektra, 1981) is the first Petty-induced comeback attempt and runs closer to country than to his '60s rock.

influences:
◄◄ Roy Orbison, Billy Haley, Buddy Holly, Bobby Freeman

►► Nirvana, Bruce Springsteen, Tom Petty

Allan Orski

Feargal Sharkey
See: The Undertones

Dave Sharp
See: The Alarm

Elliott Sharp
Born March 1, 1951, in Cleveland, OH.

Elliott Sharp is a virtuoso of not only electric guitar but also his unique doubleneck guitarbass, his self-designed "slab," lapsteel, dobro, bass clarinet, and saxophones (he also sings on occasion in a basso growl). Classically trained at the University of Buffalo, Sharp came to New York City during 1979 and quickly became an integral part of its downtown avant-garde scene, sometimes documenting it on his Zoar label with intelligently compiled surveys of various artists' works. Sometimes E# (as he refers to himself in type) functions purely as a composer, writing for ensembles that don't include him as a player; sometimes he goes in the opposite direction and plays the blues. He is equally at home in either context, or in his many disparate groups: Carbon, a rock band that includes electric harpist Zeena Parkins; the trio Boodlers, with a pair of ex-NYC stalwarts who now live in Portland, Oregon, plus six-string bassist Fred Chalenor and drummer Henry Franzoni; Hoosegow, a blues duo with singer Queen Esther; Terraplane, an instrumental blues trio; 'Dyners Club, a guitar quartet; and more. In the past he also led or participated in such ensembles as Bootstrappers, Mofungo, Hi-Sheriffs of Blue, and I/S/M.

what to buy: *Amusia* 𝄚𝄚𝄚𝄚 (Atavistic, 1995, prod. Elliott Sharp) may be Carbon's most accessible album, putting Sharp's array of guitar textures into rock structures (and his singing is less growly than before). On *Psycho-Acoustic* 𝄚𝄚𝄚𝄚 (Victo, 1994, prod. Michel Levasser) Sharp and Carbon harpist Parkins duet on a series of sonic assaults/sculptures (including a few downright pretty tracks) that utilize space more than most of his work. Another fine piece of sonic mayhem from Carbon, *Interference* 𝄚𝄚𝄚𝄚 (Atavistic, 1995, prod. Elliott Sharp) is the aural equivalent of spider webs built from strands of jagged metal—a combination of tensile beauty and brutal power. The subtleties are sometimes buried in the mix, but Sharp's skittering guitar solos, often developing in near-cyclic fashion, are fascinating.

what to buy next: Sharp's loose collaborative group I/S/M included at various times such downtown all-stars as cornetist Olu Dara, bassist Bill Laswell, and drummers Bobby Previte and Philip Wilson. They played truly improvised music in which texture is explored freely but groove isn't ruled out. *Arc 1: 1980–1983* 𝄚𝄚𝄚𝄚 (Atavistic, 1996, prod. Elliott Sharp) collects out-of-print records and previously unreleased material; its closest familiar analogy is the first Golden Palominos album. For E# the bluesman, start with Hoosegow's *Mighty* 𝄚𝄚𝄚𝄚 (Homestead, 1996, prod. Elliott Sharp). Accompanying Queen Esther's soulful, subtly inflected singing, Sharp is both a fantastic slide guitarist and a fingerpicking wizard thanks to digital dexterity and harmonic imagination. Showcasing Sharp's trio of the same name, *Terraplane* 𝄚𝄚𝄚𝄚 (Homestead, 1994) mixes four originals with such blues classics as "Killing Floor," "Dust My Broom," "Mystery Train," and the like in instrumental arrangements. Sharp draws an effective connection between avant-garde and blues uses of microtonal pitch-bending and tunings that's gutsy, not academic.

what to avoid: *K!L!A!V!* ♫♫ (Newport Classic, 1990) is subtitled "Extreme Music for Various Keyboards." Though it contains some interesting compositional ideas, it lacks the textural variety of Sharp's best work.

the rest:

Elliott Sharp:

Virtual Stance ♫♫♫ (Dossier, 1986)

Nots ♫♫♫♫ (Atonal, 1992)

Beneath the Valley of the Ultra-Yahoos ♫♫♫ (Sulpher/Silent, 1992)

(With the Soldier String Quartet) *Cryptid Fragments* ♫♫♫♪ (Extreme/Cargo, 1993)

'Dyners Club ♫♫♫♪ (Intakt, 1995)

ARC 2: 1972–1979 ♫♫♫ (Atavistic, 1997)

Carbon:

Datacide ♫♫♫♪ (Enemy, 1990)

Tocsin ♫♫♫♪ (Enemy, 1991)

Truthtable ♫♫♫♪ (Homestead, 1993)

Autoboot ♫♫♫ (Zoar, 1995)

Orchestra Carbon:

Abstract Repressionism: 1990–99 ♫♫♫♫ (Victo, 1992)

Boodlers:

Boodlers ♫♫♫ (Cavity Search, 1995)

Bootstrappers:

GI=GO ♫♫♫ (Atonal, 1992)

worth searching for: The avant-garde jazz/improvisation ensemble the New York Composer's Orchestra's *First Program in Standard Time* (New World, 1992, prod. Wayne Horvitz, Hans Wendl) includes Sharp's piece "Skew," with all-star solos by Wayne Horvitz (ring modulated prepared piano) and drummer Bobby Previte. "Skew" is a pure exploration of sound, an abstract tone poem.

influences:

◀◀ John Cage, Harry Partch, Jimi Hendrix, Albert Ayler, Pharoah Sanders, Cecil Taylor, Otis Rush

▶▶ Sonic Youth, Material

Steve Holtje

Sandie Shaw

Born Sandra Goodrich, 1947, in Dagenham, England.

Shaw's career divides neatly into two periods: that of the cool London Swinging Girl of the '60s who sang her way through a string of #1 songs, and that of the cool '80s chanteuse who briefly returned to fame with tasteful renditions of songs by the Smiths and Lloyd Cole. From 1964 to 1967, Shaw epitomized the London sound on hit records such as "Long Live Love" and "There's Always Something There to Remind Me." "Puppet on a String," her entry in the 1967 Eurovision Song Contest, also went #1, resulting in endless European imitations of her unique pop style. Shaw disappeared during the late '60s to raise a family with British fashion designer Jeff Banks, but she returned to the spotlight with a guest appearance on Heaven 17's *Music of Quality and Distinction* (1981). Her career got a minor boost from the Smiths when Morrissey, a longtime fan, brought Shaw in to sing lead vocals on reprised versions of his group's hits "Hand in Glove" and "I Don't Owe You Anything." Shaw continued collaborating with contemporary artists throughout the '80s, although her output had thinned out considerably by the end of the decade.

what to buy: *Collection* ♫♫♫♫ (Castle, 1991, prod. various) is a fairly comprehensive retrospective, from the early hits to her collaborations with the Smiths. An excellent introduction to one of Britain's original pop singers.

what to buy next: *Reviewing the Situation* ♫♫♫♫ (RPM, 1996, prod. various) is an excellent reissue compiled with Shaw's assistance that features elaborate packaging, including photos and extensive liner notes. The compilation couples her last album of the '60s with five contemporary singles. Shaw tackles songs by the Rolling Stones, Bob Dylan, and even Led Zeppelin, and while not all the results are flattering, she shines on the bulk of the material. *The Sandie Shaw Supplement* ♫♫♫ (RPM, 1996, prod. various) is the reissue of her 1968 album of the same name, featuring songs performed during Shaw's six-week BBC TV series that same year. The selections read like a cross-section of greatest hits from the day, including Simon & Garfunkel's "Homeward Bound" and "Scarborough Fair," the Rolling Stones' "(I Can't Get No) Satisfaction" and the Mary Hopkin hit "Those Were the Days." Like all the RPM reissues of Shaw's work, *Supplement* features deluxe packaging and a good eye for historical detail.

what to avoid: After a long absence from the music scene and before recording with the Smiths, Shaw privately released *Choose Life* ♫♫ (RPM, 1996, prod. Sandie Shaw) as a limited-edition album on her own label. Although her voice is in excellent form, Shaw's choice of material lacks focus and her themes of mysticism and empowerment, while worthy, come off as strident and forced.

the rest:

Sandie/Me ♫♫♫ (See for Miles, 1996)

Long Live Love ♫♫♫ (Sequel, 1996)

Love Me, Please, Love Me ♫♫ (RPM, 1996)

worth searching for: *64/67 Complete Sandie Shaw Set* (Sequel, 1994, prod. various) is an excellent but hard-to-find double-disc set featuring all of Shaw's essential '60s hits plus minor chart entries. The definitive portrait of London's Swinging Girl vocalist.

influences:

◄◄ Cilla Black, Dusty Springfield, Dionne Warwick

►► Petula Clark, Marianne Faithfull, Nico, Mary Hopkin, the Smiths

Christopher Scapelliti

Tommy Shaw

See: Styx

Shaw-Blades

See: Night Ranger

Jules Shear

Born March 7, 1952, in Pittsburgh, PA.

Like John Hiatt, Jules Shear's songs are more familiar to the masses than his name, thanks to the Bangles ("If She Knew What She Wants"), Cyndi Lauper ("All through the Night"), and Alison Moyet ("Whispering Your Name"). After false starts as a member of L.A.'s woefully misnamed Funky Kings (a laid-back sextet featuring ex-Eagle Jack Tempchin) and the leader of the new wave act Jules & the Polar Bears, Shear hit his stride as a songwriter with such superb solo albums as 1983's Todd Rundgren–produced *Watch Dog* and 1985's *The Eternal Return*. His passionate, nasal singing is an acquired taste, but his knack for expressing complex emotions within simple song structures laced with '60s-inspired melodies, jangling guitars, and heavenly harmonies has resulted in an impressive catalog overflowing with small but significant treasures. Footnote: He was the original host and brainstormer behind *MTV Unplugged*.

what to buy: *Watch Dog* ♫♫♫♫ (EMI, 1983, prod. Todd Rundgren) drapes such edgy love songs as "Whispering Your Name," "Never Fall," and "All through the Night" against Rundgren's dense, swirling sonic pastiche of textures drawn from the Beatles and Roy Orbison. Tougher guitars and tasteful keyboards bring a fuller sound to *The Great Puzzle* ♫♫♫♫ (Polydor, 1992, prod. Jules Shear, Stewart Lerman), which is highlighted by "The Sad Sound of the Wind" and the Lovin' Spoonful–influenced "The Mystery's All Mine." The first pressing was packaged with a bonus CD titled *Unplug This*, featuring acoustic versions of "If She Knew What She Wants," "All through the Night," and six others. *Between Us* ♫♫♫♫ (High Street, 1998, prod. Jules Shear, Stewart Lerman) is an intimate acoustic

duets project teaming Shear with pals such as Paula Cole, Ron Sexsmith, Susan Cowsill, Carole King, and Amy Rigby.

what to buy next: *Horse of a Different Color: The Jules Shear Collection* ♫♫♫ (Razor & Tie, 1993, prod. various) samples his solo career and short-lived stints with the Funky Kings, Jules & the Polar Bears, and Reckless Sleepers. The majestic "If We Never Meet Again," recorded with the Sleepers and covered by ex-Byrd Roger McGuinn, is one of the most touching songs about faith and devotion ever written.

what to avoid: For all the critical accolades, Jules & the Polar Bears' *Got No Breeding* ♫♫ (Columbia, 1978, prod. Larry Hirsch, Stephen Hague) and *Fenetiks* ♫♫ (Columbia, 1979, prod. Stephen Hague, Jules Shear) sound distressingly dated, the work of a maturing artist reaching for notes out of his range and straining for new-wave credibility.

the rest:
The Eternal Return ♫♫♫♫ (EMI, 1985)

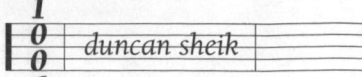

Demo-Itis ♪♪♫ (Enigma, 1987)
The Third Party ♪♪♪ (I.R.S., 1989)
Healing Bones ♪♪♪ (Island, 1994)

worth searching for: Long before tribute albums were cool, Ian Matthews covered 12 Shear compositions on *Walking a Changing Line: The Songs of Jules Shear* (Windham Hill, 1988, prod. Ian Matthews, Mark Hallman). His crisp tenor brings out the elegance of "Standing Still," "Following Every Finger," and "On Squirrel Hill."

influences:
◄◄ The Beatles, the Byrds, Roy Orbison

►► Jonny Polonsky, Ron Sexsmith, Freedy Johnston

David Okamoto

Duncan Sheik

Born November 18, 1970, in Montclair, NJ.

Singer-songwriter Duncan Sheik was inspired early to play music. Until the age of five, Sheik lived in New Jersey with his grandfather and grandmother, a former piano student at Juilliard. Sitting in front of a piano, Sheik soon mastered the instrument, then took up guitar. He spent his pre-teen years playing classical and jazz music at summer camps and experimented with rock music during high school with a Van Halen/Def Leppard cover band called Slightly Off. By the 10th grade, he switched gears to the synth-pop of New Order and Depeche Mode. After graduating from high school, Sheik studied at Brown University and performed with a schoolmate, singer-songwriter Lisa Loeb. Sheik, who didn't start singing until his freshman year of college, began shopping demos of his own after earning his degree and landed in the band His Boy Elroy, which released an album on Epic during 1993. Two years later he met musician/producer Rupert Hine and, after recording his self-titled debut, notched a few low-key radio hits.

what to buy: *Duncan Sheik* ♪♪♪ (Atlantic, 1996, prod. Rupert Hine) shows a star in the making, although the album hits several spots of turbulence—limited, perhaps, by Sheik's decision to play most of the instruments himself. A song such as the heartbreaking "In the Absence of Sun" loses its impact when it disappears into a fog of strings. "Barely Breathing," on the other hand, starts strong and stays that way. "Out of Order" should have been a follow-up hit single; the bouncy piano and fading distorted guitars make it one of the jazzier numbers on the album.

the rest:
Humming N/A (Atlantic, 1998)

worth searching for: *Live at the Reservoir* (Atlantic, 1997), a promotional release sent to radio stations, features the highlight of his live shows, a cover of Radiohead's "Fake Plastic

Trees," and stripped-down, satisfying renditions of his songs that he perfected during two years of touring.

influences:
◄◄ Bruce Hornsby, Radiohead, Nirvana

►► Steve Poltz

Christina Fuoco

Shellac

Formed 1993, in Chicago, IL.

Steve Albini, vocals, guitar; Bob Weston, bass, vocals; Todd Trainer, drums.

Steve Albini's '80s band, Big Black—with its rugged sonics and extreme subject matter—was a major influence on what became known as alternative rock. During the '90s, Albini became better known as a recording engineer, enlisted by the likes of Nirvana, Helmet, PJ Harvey, the Pixies, Bush, and Robert Plant and Jimmy Page. But in between studio assignments he continued to make abrasive indie-rock records with fellow underground veterans Bob Weston (Volcano Suns) and Todd Trainer (Riflesport) in Shellac. The band records and tours infrequently, but remains a diehard exponent of the do-it-yourself aesthetic.

what to buy: *Shellac at Action Park* ♪♪♪♪ (Touch & Go, 1994, prod. Shellac) is pristinely recorded power-trio rock. Albini's guitar plays with space and provides texture while Weston and Trainer plow deep, skull-crushing grooves.

what to buy next: *Terraform* ♪♪♪♫ (Touch & Go, 1998, prod. Shellac) is slightly more restrained, with unusually nuanced vocals from Albini and an emphasis on hypnotic rhythms that suggest the influence of '70s Krautrock bands such as Can and Neu.

worth searching for: The band's debut singles, "The Rude Gesture (A Pictorial History)" and "Uranus," are beautiful collector's items with individually made cover art by the band members.

influences:
◄◄ Wire, Can, Gang of Four

►► Tar, U.S. Maple

see also: *Big Black*

Greg Kot

Pete Shelley
See: Buzzcocks

Vonda Shepard

Born July 7, 1963, in New York, NY.

Unfairly pegged as an overnight sensation, singer-songwriter-pianist Vonda Shepard became ingrained in the music scene when she was 20 and toured as a backing vocalist and keyboardist with Rickie Lee Jones before serving similar tenures with Al Jarreau and Jackson Browne. But it was with the debut of the 1997 television series *Ally McBeal* that Shepard was finally introduced to millions of viewers, thanks to her role as the resident singer in the show's fictional bar. Longtime followers, however, remember Shepard's lilting 1987 duet with softie Dan Hill, "Can't We Try," which became a Top 10 single. Despite critical praise, Shepard, who began playing piano at age six and writing songs in her teens, never achieved much commercial success, mostly because of record company snafus. She recorded two albums for Reprise Records during the late '80s and early '90s, and a third on her own. Throughout her career, Shepard often performed in half-filled clubs, unaware that one loyal follower was television producer/writer David E. Kelley. After Kelley married Hollywood actress Michelle Pfeiffer, a longtime friend and fan of Shepard's, he was introduced to Shepard and approached her about contributing music to *Ally*. Shepard's insightful piano pop soon became an integral part of the show, finally bringing her commercial success. Though Shepard was born in Manhattan, she and her three sisters were raised in Southern California, mostly by their father, a struggling actor and mime.

what to buy: *The Radical Light* ℐℐℐℐ (Reprise, 1992/Vesper Alley, 1996, prod. Michael Ostin) exemplifies Shepard's knack for writing lyrically bright tunes buoyed by her big, blustery voice. The initial version of the theme song for *Ally McBeal*, "Searchin' My Soul," makes its first appearance, but newer fans might be cautious to embrace the drowsy, mandolin-heavy read originally given to the song. Contributions from '80s one-hit-wonder-turned-producer Matthew Wilder ("Break My Stride") turn the title track into a finger-snapping pop ditty, while guest musicians drummer Jeff Porcaro (Toto) and keyboardist Benmont Tench (Tom Petty & the Heartbreakers) layer songs such as "Wake up the House" and "Dreamin'" with snappy musicianship. Though some of Shepard's earlier work tends to drag when she gets ballad-happy, here her oft-somber piano playing isn't the focus, giving the album a mirthful cast.

what to buy next: On *It's Good, Eve* ℐℐℐ (Vesper Alley, 1996, prod. Vonda Shepard, Michael Landau), Shepard sums up her childhood with the toss-off line, "I was born in a cardboard box, New York City, 1963, poetry readings and bohemians, now inspiration floats around me like a cloud" ("Naiveté"). It is this simple poignancy that renders *It's Good* its heart. Taking a page from the Paul Simon Book of Good Songwriting, Shepard isn't ashamed of her emotional bleeding, from the weepy "Long Term Boyfriend" to the observational, tempo-shifting "This Steady Train," which boasts background vocals from Jackson Browne. It is painfully apparent here that Shepard is aching to be heard.

what to avoid: Unfortunately, by the time success found Shepard, *Songs from Ally McBeal* ℐℐ (Sony 550 Music, 1998, prod. Vonda Shepard) found her forced to succumb to being a corporate sell-out. Yes, her updated version of "Searchin' My Soul" is a breezy, up-with-life anthem that makes for a tidy, 30-second television intro, but here, Shepard is forced to become the lounge singer she plays on *Ally* and spends far too much time mucking through cover songs. Her debut, *Vonda Shepard* ℐℐ (Reprise, 1989/Vesper Alley, 1996, prod. Vonda Shepard, Art Munson), features nothing more than a twentysomething voice that was too helium-inflected to matter. Shepard's promising songwriting and piano skills hinted at the gems that would soon come, but here she is trapped in thin '80s production and pseudo dance songs.

worth searching for: Shepard's duet with Dan Hill on his "Can't We Try" (Columbia, 1987) is the first glimpse at her awesome ability to convey more emotion with the flicker of her voice than most artists can on an entire album.

influences:

◀◀ Rickie Lee Jones, Jackson Browne, Joni Mitchell

▶▶ Paula Cole, Sheryl Crow

Melissa Ruggieri

Kenny Wayne Shepherd

Born June 12, 1977, in Shreveport, LA.

Just as the mantle of "next Dylan" has been placed on the shoulders of countless unlucky folksingers, the term "next Ste-

Kenny Wayne Shepherd (© Jack Vartoogian)

vie Ray" has been thrown around carelessly in blues circles, most recently in the direction of young gun Kenny Wayne Shepherd. Maybe it's their use of middle names, or the nearly complete shadow Vaughan's ghost casts over Shepherd's playing, in terms of tone, feel, phrasing—you name it. But there is more than a little spark of originality in his playing, and hell, he's young. Chances are he'll grow out of it and into his own style like every guitarist of note before him. Shepherd is not a vocalist, however, and must rely on his guitar to do his talking for him. So far, it's doing just fine.

what to buy: An unexpected hit, *Ledbetter Heights* ♪♪♪♪ (Giant, 1995, prod. David Z) caught on with blues fans looking for a Stevie Ray fix and rock fans seeking out a bluesier alternative. Both sides can be sated with this impressive debut, featuring "Born with a Broken Heart," which pays tribute to Vaughan without mentioning his name, and the rock steady "Deja Voodoo." Shepherd tackles country-style blues on "Aberdeen" and shines on the live instrumental "While We Cry." He even takes tentative steps toward becoming a vocalist on "Riverside." Altogether an impressive outing.

what to buy next: The follow-up, *Trouble Is . . .* ♪♪♪♪ (Revolution, 1997, prod. Jerry Harrison) is billed to the Kenny Wayne Shepherd Band, which indicates a bit of a shift in power in the band, and also signals a move more toward hard rock, though there's still plenty of blues in Shepherd's playing. Singer Noah Hunt's gruff emoting is not completely convincing, but the album did yield the hit "Blue on Black."

influences:
◀◀ Stevie Ray Vaughan, Albert King, Jimi Hendrix

Daniel Durchholz

The Shirelles

Formed 1957, in Passaic, NJ.

Shirley Owens, vocals (1957–75); Addie "Micki" Harris, vocals (1957–82); Doris Coley, vocals (1957–68, 1975–present); Beverly Lee, vocals.

One of the first and defining practitioners of the girl group sound, and one of the few who actually had a hand in writing their own material, the Shirelles were rarely out of the Top 10 between 1960 and 1963, and their songs and style had a major impact on the way rock 'n' roll sounded during the early 1960s.

Originally formed as the Poquellos in high school, the quartet sang semi-professionally at dances and parties where one of their own compositions, "I Met Him on a Sunday," came to the attention of a fellow classmate named Mary Jane Greenberg. Greenberg's mother, Florence, became the group's manager, formed a record company called Scepter with writer/producer

WHAT ALBUM CHANGED YOUR LIFE?

I've studied [Jimi] Hendrix, man. He's one of my mentors. I close my set every night with "Voodoo Chile"; that's one of hardest songs by Hendrix to really cover and do justice. I've always loved Hendrix's way of playing.

Kenny Wayne Shepherd

Luther Dixon, and released the newly renamed Shirelles' version of the Five Royales' "Dedicated to the One I Love" in 1959. Lacking national distribution, the record stalled at #83, but a year later, the Owens/Dixon composition "Tonight's the Night" became a Top 40 pop and R&B success. The hits continued with "Will You Still Love Me Tomorrow" (the first-ever girl group chart-topper), "Mama Said," and even a reissue of "Dedicated," which this time soared to #3. In 1962, both the Burt Bacharach/Hal David–composed "Baby It's You" and "Soldier Boy," the latter written in a matter of minutes by Greenberg and Dixon as mere album filler, continued the group's remarkable string of hits, but following Dixon's departure from Scepter in '63 the group placed only one final release in the Top 20. By now their impact internationally was already being acknowledged (for example, the Beatles recorded two Shirelles songs on their first album), but competition at home increased dramatically as producers like Phil Spector and Berry Gordy began flooding the charts with artists and records fashioned on the Shirelles' sound. A three-year legal dispute with Greenberg prevented the band from recording new material until 1967 (though Scepter continued to release old masters—with little success—in the interim) and the group, now reduced to a trio with the temporary departure of Coley, spent the majority of their time touring the rock 'n' roll revival circuit while recordings for Mercury, Bell, and RCA failed to chart. Following one such appearance in 1982, Harris died of heart failure, and it was not until a decade later that the group, after a prolonged court case, were awarded $1 million in royalties owed them and former Scepter labelmates Gene Pitney and B.J. Thomas. In 1994, the three surviving original Shirelles reunited for the first time in 19 years to perform at the Rhythm and Blues Foundation's Pioneer Awards show, and were subsequently inducted into the Rock and Roll

Hall of Fame in recognition of not only their ground-breaking initial successes, but for their decades spent on the road continuing to bring the sound they helped fashion to new generations of eager students and listeners the world over.

what to buy: Exquisitely assembled, *The Shirelles Anthology (1959–1964)* ♫♫♫♫ (Rhino, 1986, compilation prod. Bill Inglot, Gary Stewart) contains all of their greatest recordings, many tastefully remixed into digital stereo for the first time from the original multi-track tapes.

what to buy next: With access to some of the greatest songwriters of the time (i.e., Goffin and King) and the winning combination of Owens's lead vocals and Dixon's arrangements and production, *Shirelles Sing to Trumpets and Strings* ♫♫♫ (Scepter, 1961/Sundazed 1994, prod. Luther Dixon), *Baby It's You* ♫♫♫ (Scepter, 1962/Sundazed, 1993, prod. Luther Dixon), and *Foolish Little Girl* ♫♫♫ (Scepter, 1963/Sundazed, 1994, prod. Luther Dixon) are surprisingly free of the clutter that padded most albums during the early 1960s, though the promisingly titled *Shirelles and King Curtis Give a Twist Party* ♫♫♯ (Scepter, 1962/Sundazed, 1993, prod. Luther Dixon) contains only one real "duet" between the group and their sax player.

best of the rest:
The World's Greatest Girl Group ♫♫♫ (Tomato/Rhino, 1995)
For Collectors Only ♫♫♫ (Collectables, 1995)

worth searching for: *The Shirelles* (RCA Victor, 1972) is a more-than-competent return to form for the group, no doubt bolstered by the presence of strong material from Bill Withers, Marvin Gaye, and even the Bee Gees.

influences:
⏪ The Chantels, the Five Royales

⏩ The Crystals, Martha & the Vandellas, the Shangri-Las

Gary Pig Gold

Michelle Shocked

Born Michelle Johnston, February 24, 1962, in Dallas, TX.

One of the most gifted and outspoken artists to emerge from the late '80s singer-songwriter movement that spawned Tracy Chapman and Suzanne Vega, Michelle Shocked can be a captivating storyteller: she possesses a sassy, soulful voice and an endearing blend of East Texas charm and New York street savvy. But she also exhibits a stubborn commitment to her art that sometimes overwhelms her good intentions and rubs against the greedy grain of the music industry. Discovered playing around a campfire in 1986 at Texas' legendary Kerrville Folk Festival, Shocked became an instant overseas sensation after a Walkman-recorded tape of her songs was released by London's Cooking Vinyl Records. She signed to Mercury in 1988, but the relationship was

acrimonious at best: the two parties bickered over everything from album-cover art (she proposed posing in blackface on the cover of 1991's *Arkansas Traveler* to drive home the belabored point that black musicians have been robbed of their legacy by white artists) to the stylistic direction of her jazzy *Captain Swing*. When Mercury balked at releasing the dark, brooding songs she proposed for *Kind Hearted Woman*, she filed suit against the label, citing a California labor law that sets a seven-year term limit on personal services contracts. The feud was settled out of court in April 1996. Her devious parting shot was a retrospective called *Mercury Poise*—a sly twist on Graham Parker's infamous diatribe against the label, "Mercury Poisoning."

what to buy: *Kind Hearted Woman* ♫♫♫♫ (Private Music, 1996, prod. Bones Howe), inspired by the death of her grandmother, is a soul-stirring, intensely personal work about loss and the painful search for closure. The howling midwife crisis of "Stillborn" and the dark-humored blues of "Eddie" are startling, but her stark, hushed delivery of the mournful "A Child like Grace" is both riveting and revelatory. Her poignant major-label debut, *Short Sharp Shocked* ♫♫♫♫ (Mercury, 1988, prod. Pete Anderson), blends rustic reminiscences about her East Texas childhood with chugging country-rockers and the Dylanesque "Anchorage," which remains her most touching and timeless song.

what to buy next: *The Texas Campfire Tapes* ♫♫♫ (Mercury, 1986, prod. Pete Lawrence) contains the now-mythical Kerrville recordings, complete with crickets chirping and low-fidelity sound. Three songs—"Fogtown," "Don't You Mess around with My Little Sister," and "The Secret to a Long Life"—would be re-recorded on later albums.

what to avoid: *Captain Swing* ♫♫♯ (Mercury, 1989, prod. Pete Anderson) has its nostalgic charms, but much of the material crosses the line between lighthearted and lightweight.

the rest:
Arkansas Traveler ♫♫♫♯ (Mercury, 1991)
Mercury Poise: 1988–95 ♫♫♫ (Mercury, 1996)

worth searching for: Since leaving Mercury, Shocked has been recording limited-edition CDs in her New Orleans home and selling them exclusively at her shows. *Kind Hearted Woman* (1994) is a solo electric guitar version of the album that came out on Private Music in 1996. *Artists Make Lousy Slaves* (1996) is a direct-to-DAT effort that finds her sharing lead vocals with Fiachna O'Braonain of Hothouse Flowers and includes the jaunty "Laundry Day" and an *a capella* reading of "The Water Is Wide."

influences:
⏪ Guy Clark, Woody Guthrie, Jean Ritchie

⏩ Liz Phair, Ani DiFranco

David Okamoto

Shoes

Formed 1974, in Zion, IL.

Jeff Murphy, vocals, guitar, keyboards, percussion; John Murphy, vocals, bass, guitar, keyboards, percussion; Gary Klebe, vocals, guitars, keyboards, percussion; Skip Meyer, drums.

During the mid-'70s, in the middle-of-nowhere town of Zion, Illinois, Shoes took the Beatles' blueprint and built its own model of pure pop on it. The four musicians taught themselves how to play as they wrote songs, practically guaranteeing a fresh approach. Unlike so-called skinny-tie bands that took new wave shortcuts (and haircuts) by replicating Beatles harmonies with a retro cynicism, Shoes' sound meshed hard guitars and soft harmonies—a commercially promising middle ground between Big Star and Boston. The lyrics sidestepped clichés, reflecting the heartbreak and anger of lost romance, deftly making art out of therapy.

what to buy: Musically, Shoes' albums vary little; this is not a band that tries on new styles with each album. For the value conscious, *Present Tense/Tongue Twister* ✍✍✍✍ (Elektra, 1979, 1981/Black Vinyl, 1988, prod. Mike Stone, Richard Dashut) combines two of the very best titles. *Propeller* ✍✍✍✍ (Black Vinyl, 1995, prod. Shoes) and the darker, more ethereal *Black Vinyl Shoes* (Black Vinyl, 1978/1994, prod. Shoes) are also landmark pop works.

what to buy next: *Boomerang/Shoes on Ice* ✍✍✍✍ (Elektra, 1982/Black Vinyl, 1990, prod. Shoes) is another solid two-fer, the second part recorded live at the Zion Ice Arena (*Shoes on Ice*—get it?). *Fret Buzz* ✍✍✍✍ (Black Vinyl, 1996) is a good live album (with much better fidelity than *Shoes on Ice*), while *Shoes' Best* ✍✍✍✍ (Black Vinyl, 1987, prod. various) provides a fine, if overly long, overview. The two-disc *As Is* ✍✍✍ (Black Vinyl, 1996, prod. Shoes), like the title implies, is a come-as-you-are assemblage of unpolished Shoes—demos, outtakes, and embarrassing noodling—but it marks the CD debut of the nascent *One in Versailles* and the first time the obscure early work *Bazooka* ever appeared outside of a hard-to-score cassette tape. Kicking off the collection are the previously unreleased "A Voice inside Me," "Rugged Terrain," and "Jetset," each representing one of the three songwriters—Jeff Murphy, John Murphy, and Gary Klebe, respectively—at his peak. The demos of "Feel the Way That I Do" (later to appear on *Stolen Wishes*) and "Karen" (from *Tongue Twister*) are superior to their finished counterparts, but much of *As Is* sounds like cleaning out the old-Shoes closet. That, and its high price tag, make it an either-or proposition—essential for diehard fans but a hard bill to foot for casual Shoes admirers.

what to avoid: The rare *Un dans Versailles* ✍✍ (self-released, 1975, prod. Shoes) (also known as *One in Versailles*) is an early

four-track recording that contains no input from Klebe. It's a raw, nascent work that shows how far the band has come and how quickly the group grew.

the rest: *Silhouette* ✍✍✍ (Demon, 1984/Black Vinyl, 1991)

worth searching for: A great bit of ethereal hard-pop, "Like I Told You," appears only on the cassette *Trouser Press Presents the Best of America Underground* (ROIR, 1983).

influences:

◀◀ The Beatles, the Raspberries, Badfinger, Grin

▶▶ Material Issue, DM3, Game Theory

Jordan Oakes

Shonen Knife

Formed 1982, in Osaka, Japan.

Naoko (a.k.a. Nancy) Yamano, vocals, guitar; Michie Nakatani, vocals, bass; Atsuko Yamano, drums, vocals.

This Japanese trio distills the DIY spirit of punk across the generations—not just the Buzzcocks, the Ramones, and XTC, but also the early Beatles. Naoko Yamano writes most of its songs, Michie Nakatani writes a few, and Atsuko Yamano, Naoko's sister, designs the group's trademark pop-Mondrianesque clothes. Unlike the vast majority of Japanese bands, Shonen Knife isn't prepackaged and—even more shocking—is from Osaka, not Tokyo (its original Japanese label, Zero, is based in Kyoto). The utterly unironic songs gained the three women cult status in Los Angeles, resulting in the two-LP 1989 tribute album, *Every Band Has a Shonen Knife Who Loves Them*, with Sonic Youth and other underground groups. And for that matter, California bubblegum punks Redd Kross put their ode "Shonen Knife" on 1990's *Third Eye*. (The name, by the way, basically means "toy knife"; "shonen" literally translates as "little boy.") The first three Knife albums and some EP tracks were repackaged for America on the two 1990 Gasatanka releases listed below, after which the Japanese and American releases are more or less parallel—aside from some language differences. A U.K. tour with Nirvana in 1991 and some small U.S. excursions spread the group's name enough that Virgin began issuing its albums here, allowing the trio to afford higher production values and more studio time. After Virgin lost interest, the group moved to MCA Victor in Japan, with Big Deal licensing the albums for the U.S.

what to buy: *Let's Knife* ✍✍✍ (Virgin, 1992, prod. Shonen Knife) features many of the group's best early songs redone at a level of genuine competence, but they're just as charming and tuneful and pop-iconic as ever.

what to buy next: On *Rock Animals* 🎜🎜🎜 (Virgin, 1993, prod. Page Porrazzo, Shonen Knife), the trio stops recycling its old material, coming up with simple, often sitarish guitar riffs (leaning more towards '60s pop than punk), while the lyrical focus on fauna and flora are surreal enough to forgive the stolid drumming. *Brand New Knife* 🎜🎜🎜 (Big Deal, 1997) continues the progression and throws in seven Japanese tracks as a bonus. The group's jangly, slightly punky guitar pop is less imitative of obvious role models, yet the hooks are still instantly memorable. The vocals and lyrics remain so off-center that the Knife remains distinctive and unique.

what to avoid: *Pretty Little Baka Guy + Live in Japan* 🎜🎜 (Gasatanka/Rockville, 1990) isn't bad, but it's the least necessary of the group's output.

the rest:
Shonen Knife 🎜🎜🎜 (Gasatanka/Rockville, 1990)
712 🎜🎜 (Gasatanka/Rockville, 1991)
The Birds & the B-Sides 🎜🎜🎜 (Virgin, 1996)
Explosion! 🎜🎜🎜 (Big Deal EP, 1997)
Happy Hour 🎜🎜 (Big Deal, 1998)

worth searching for: The Carpenters tribute *If I Were a Carpenter* (A&M, 1994, prod. various) finds Shonen Knife transforming the sappy "Top of the World" into a fresh and sincere Ramonesish ditty. Another pop icon, Burt Bacharach, is the subject of the tribute album *What the World Needs Now* (Big Deal, 1998, prod. various), which leads off with Shonen Knife's take on "Raindrops Keep Falling on My Head." And every fan should pick up a copy of *Every Band Has a Shonen Knife Who Loves Them* (Gasatanka/Giant, 1989, prod. various).

influences:
◄◄ The Beatles, the Byrds, the Beach Boys, Ramones, XTC, Buzzcocks

►► Boredoms, Nirvana, Redd Kross

Steve Holtje

Shriekback
See: Gang of Four

Shudder to Think
Formed 1988, in Washington, DC.

Craig Wedren, vocals, guitar, keyboards; Stuart Hill, bass, vocals; Chris Matthews, guitar (1988–92); Nathan Larson, guitar, keyboards, vocals (1992–present); Mike Russell, drums (1988–93); Adam Wade, drums (1993–97).

The nearly indescribable Shudder to Think began recording for Dischord in 1990. How sexually ambiguous singer Craig Wedren fit in with the Dischord hardcore punk crowd, however, is a mystery—especially since his operatic trill often makes him sound like an aspiring diva. At the beginning, at least, Shudder to Think made some fairly incredible music. Chris Matthews's biting guitar was sympathetic to Wedren's alto, and something kept Matthews in check on those early records. Drummer Adam Wade formerly played with fellow Dischord alumnus Jawbox.

what to buy: *Funeral at the Movies/Ten Spot* 🎜🎜🎜 (Dischord, 1990/1991, prod. Shudder to Think, Kenny Inouye), a CD that contains both records (originally released separately), is completely confounding. While not entirely recommended, the great cuts "Chocolate" and "Jade Dust Eyes" make up for absolute garbage like "Ride That Sexy Horse." That's the problem with Dischord—the label is too politically correct to have an A&R guy there to say "no way" to this kind of crap. The cover of Jimi Hendrix's "Crosstown Traffic" is better than you'd expect given such a posturing singer.

what to buy next: *Get Your Goat* 🎜🎜🎜 (Dischord, 1992, prod. Eli Janney) is somewhat tolerable if you like the band's *La Boheme*-meets-Fugazi shtick. Wedren is more out of control here, but the still-tight playing reigns him in on occasion.

what to avoid: The only redeeming quality to *Pony Express Record* **woof!** (Epic, 1994, prod. Ted Nicely) is that you probably don't own it.

the rest:
50,000 B.C. 🎜 (Epic, 1997)
High Art N/A (Reel Sounds/Velvel, 1998)

influences:
◄◄ Queen, Madame Butterfly, your cousin's singing lessons

see also: *Jawbox*

Barry M. Prickett

Jane Siberry
Born October 12, 1955, in Toronto, Ontario, Canada.

Although every one of her albums have their shortcomings, this Canadian singer-songwriter-experimental artiste is an utterly unique figure whose importance should not be underestimated. Jane Siberry has always been an innovative arranger and composer, using breathy vocal clusters and a wide vibrato, and often ending melodic lines on a dissonant note to create alluring, off-putting, or comical effects. Sometimes shrill, sometimes self-indulgent, her work is consistently original, frequently demanding several listens to be comprehended fully. When she released *Maria*, an odd jaunt into concept-heavy jazziness, Reprise thanked her by dropping her from the label in early 1996; Siberry bounced back by starting her own label, Sheeba, kicking things off with *Teenager*, on which she recorded a series of the first songs she ever wrote, and *Child*, a live two-disc set of Christmas (and Hanukkah) material. Once again, she continues to carve out her own path; expect more of the (not the) same from her.

what to buy: *When I Was a Boy* ♫♫♫♫ (Reprise, 1993, prod. Jane Siberry, Brian Eno, Michael Brook) is in some ways her most straightforward effort, and yet it ranges from Peter Gabriel–like lushness to cuts that make use of hip-hop and operatic ideas. Heartbreak seems to have been her inspiration; she makes it seem like the off-ramp into heaven.

what to buy next: With its Linn drums and thin keyboard sounds, *No Borders Here* ♫♫♫ (Duke Street/Open Air, 1984, prod. Jo Goldsmith, Kerry Crawford, Jane Siberry, John Switzer) sounds a bit dated now, but it's still mighty involving, with the lovely, sardonic "I Muse Aloud," the half-whimsical, half-spooky "Dancing Class," and the extended revenge fantasy of "Mimi on the Beach." *Bound by the Beauty* ♫♫♫ (Duke Street/Reprise, 1989, prod. Jane Siberry, John Switzer) marked a turning point for Siberry away from the near prog-rock of its immediate predecessors. The Latin touches may remind some of later k.d. lang.

what to avoid: Although its highlights include two of Siberry's best songs (the bouncy "One More Colour" and the devastating ballad "The Taxi Ride"), *The Speckless Sky* ♫♫♫ (Duke Street/Open Air, 1985, prod. Jane Siberry, John Switzer) seems especially dated now. You'll want to hear several of her other records first.

the rest:
The Walking ♫♫♫♫ (Duke Street/Reprise, 1987)
Maria ♫♫♫ (Reprise, 1995)
Teenager ♫♫♫ (Sheeba, 1996)
Child ♫♫♫♫ (Sheeba/Blackbird/Elektra, 1997)

worth searching for: Siberry's debut, *Jane Siberry* (Can. Street, 1981/ESD, 1991, prod. Jane Siberry, David Bradstreet, Carl Keesee), finds her already in impressive command of the wryly humorous side of her sound. If you can track it down, *A Day in the Life* (Sheeba EP, 1997, prod. Jane Siberry) offers a funny and inventive look at Siberry's busy NYC life, complete with taxi rides, phone messages, workout classes, and snippets from recording sessions.

influences:
◄◄ Kate Bush, Laurie Anderson, Joni Mitchell

►► Sarah McLachlan, Jonatha Brooke & the Story, the Innocence Mission

Bob Remstein

Sick of It All

Formed 1985, in New York, NY.

Lou Koller, vocals; Pete Koller, guitar; Rich Cipriano, bass (1985–90); Craig Ahead, bass (1990–present); Armand Majidi, drums (1985–90).

Sick of It All is, to many, the definitive East Coast hardcore band. Playing brutal mosh-pit anthems well before it was fashionable to slam dance, this band, like fellow New Yorkers the Ramones, practically created a genre. And like the Ramones (who sound nothing like SOIA despite the New York punk influences), when Sick of It All releases an album, you know what you're going to get. At 10 years old, the band sounds pretty much like it did at the start: loud, fast, and pissed. This is great for keeping a fan base, but not necessarily helpful for attracting new fans outside of the genre (which is never the point with hardcore, anyway).

what to buy: The debut *Blood, Sweat, and No Tears* ♫♫♫ (In Effect/Relativity, 1989, prod. Sick of It All) is near the top of any list of seminal hardcore punk albums. It's more explosive than any of the subsequent releases (but not by much). And it has a guest appearance from the group's neighbor, hip-hop legend KRS-One.

what to buy next: *Scratch the Surface* ♫♫♫ (EastWest/Atlantic, 1994, prod. Sick of It All) shows that major labels don't always force bands to mellow out; but why Atlantic would sign such a raw band remains a mystery.

the rest:
Sick of It All ♫♫♫ (Revelation, 1987)
Just Look Around ♫♫♫ (Relativity EP, 1992)
Live in a World Full of Hate ♫♫♫ (Lost & Found, 1993)
Spreading the Hardcore Reality ♫♫♫ (Revelation, 1997)
Built to Last ♫♫♫ (EastWest, 1997)

influences:
◄◄ Black Flag, Minor Threat, the Cro-Mags

►► Biohazard, Civ, Quicksand, Helmet, Rancid, the Beastie Boys

Brian Ives

The Sidewinders /The Sand Rubies

Formed 1985, in Tucson, AZ. Disbanded 1994.

David Slutes, vocals, guitar; Rich Hopkins, guitar; Mark Perrodin, bass; Andrea Curtis, drums, vocals (1987–89); Diane Padilla, drums (1989); Bruce Hapler, drums (1990).

Even when Neil Young was floundering during the mid-'80s, bands bearing his stamp kept popping up—like the Sidewinders, an Arizona quartet that picked up where Crazy Horse left off. The group very quietly dropped a great little record right out of the box with its full-length debut and made a solid follow-up before coming to a bad end, running into heinous legal difficulties about the time its second album was released. Eventually, the Sidewinders lost their name to a similarly monikered

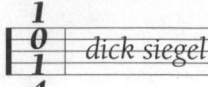

cover band from North Carolina. Leaders Rich Hopkins and David Slutes lost the rest of the band, too, finally re-emerging a few years later as the Sand Rubies. But the damage had been done by then, and the Sand Rubies split after one album.

what to buy: *Witch Doctor* ♪♪♪♪ (Mammoth/RCA, 1989, prod. Rich Hopkins, David Slutes) still sounds pretty terrific, an album full of anthemic-sounding buzzsaw originals that stick ("What She Said," "What Am I Supposed to Do?"). A terrific cover of Neil Diamond's "Solitary Man" is an added bonus, proving that great songs are where you find 'em.

what to buy next: The follow-up, *Auntie Ramos' Pool Hall* ♪♪♪ (Mammoth/RCA, 1990, prod. Rich Hopkins, David Slutes), is a decent riff-rock record that comes up a bit short on material.

what to avoid: Given all the different producers, it's no surprise that *Sand Rubies* ♪♪ (Atlas/PolyGram, 1993, prod. Larry Hirsch, Waddy Wachtel, David Briggs, Mike Campbell, Rich Hopkins, David Slutes) is a patchwork that doesn't quite hang together.

influences:
◀◀ Neil Young
▶▶ Giant Sand

David Menconi

Dick Siegel

Born December 28, 1948, in Newark, NJ.

A veteran of several semi-successful Midwest bands during the '70s and '80s (most notably Siegel Schwal), Dick Siegel didn't really hit his stride until he went solo during the mid-'70s. His work is based on folk music, but the folk is taken uptown and uptempo with a big jolt of finger-snapping jive. His songs have an old-fashioned feel—his venues are "joints," and they're usually "jumpin'." Lyrically, Siegel sticks with the simple subjects such as listening to a favorite band or the joys of eating breakfast at a favored Ann Arbor, Michigan, hangout. In 1992 he won a New Folk award at the Kerrville Folk Festival and has since become a popular fixture on the folk circuit.

what to buy: Siegel first released *Snap!* ♪♪♪♪ (Schoolkids, 1992, prod. Neil Scott, Dick Siegel) on his own tiny Boo-Kay records in 1980, but it wasn't until its re-release over a decade later that the record found a wider audience for its jazzy swing sound.

what to buy next: On *Angels Aweigh* ♪♪♪ (Schoolkids, 1994, prod. Paul Pearcy, Dick Siegel), Siegel loses some of the jazziness and puts the emphasis on a gentler folk sound.

what to avoid: Siegel's turn with '80s party band Tracy Lee & the Leonards on the cassette-only *Tomorrow Morning* ♪

(Schoolkids, 1993, prod. Dick Siegel, George Bedard, Greg Ward) sounds dated now.

worth searching for: During the '80s, Siegel made a compilation of his live performances with his band, the Ministers of Melody, on the cassette-only *Dick Siegel Live* (Boo-Kay, 1984, prod. Dick Siegel).

influences:
◀◀ Dr. John, Bob Dylan
▶▶ Townes Van Zandt, Mark Eitzel, John Doe (X)

Jill Hamilton

Silkworm

Formed as Ein Heit, 1987, in Missoula, MT.

Tim Midgett, bass, vocals; Andrew Cohen, guitar, vocals; Michael Dahlquist, drums; Joel Phelps, guitar, vocals (1987–94).

After relocating from Missoula to Seattle, Silkworm cut a swath of indie rock that starts somewhere with Mission of Burma and adds a dash of Pavement to the twisted, arty mix. With plaintive vocals and edgy, sometimes brittle guitars, the band has had some left-of-the-dial success. College-rock champions, Silkworm don't rock hard enough to scare your girlfriend; rather, they plead with her to leave you. The playing is hardly precision, but catchy songs with occasionally humorous overtones stick comfortably in your memory. Tim Midgett, Andrew Cohen, and Joel Phelps have all shared songwriting duties, with Michael Dahlquist an occasional contributor. Since paring down to a trio, Silkworm sounds even more cohesive, with greater subtlety in the guitar work.

what to buy: *Developer* ♪♪♪♪ (Matador, 1996, prod. Steve Albini) is an uneven stroke of occasional genius. Softer as a trio and capable of memorable cuts such as "Never Met a Man I Didn't Like," Silkworm explores the cold and strident with casual aplomb.

what to buy next: To witness the group's growth, check out *Even a Blind Chicken Finds a Kernel of Corn Now and Then* ♪♪♪ (Matador, 1998, prod. various). Tracking the band 1990–94, this double-CD set collects odds and ends that reach back to the band's early days as Ein Heit. This flawed but charming collection includes, among other things, most of the early release *L'ajre* (Temporary Freedom, 1992) and nifty covers of Fleetwood Mac, Comsat Angels, and Tom Petty songs. Probably not for the uninitiated, but a fun ride for fans.

the rest:
Libertine ♪♪♪ (El Recordo, 1994)
The Marco Collins Sessions ♪♪♪♪ (Matador EP, 1995)
Firewater ♪♪♪ (Matador, 1996)
Blueblood N/A (Touch & Go, 1998)

worth searching for: The promotional-only release *New School/Old School* (Matador, 1997, prod. various) is a similar, stronger, and shorter version of *Even a Blind Chicken* . . . . With additional covers of Bob Dylan and a song made known by George Jones, *New School/Old School* is a neat find.

solo outings:

Joel Phelps:

Warm Springs Night 🎵🎵🎵 (El Recordo, 1996)

influences:

◄◄ Wire, Mission of Burma, Dream Syndicate, Gang of Four, Pavement, Giant Sand

►► Varnaline

Barry M. Prickett

The Silos
/Vulgar Boatmen
/Walter Salas-Humara

Formed 1985, in New York, NY.

The Silos: Bob Rupe, guitar, vocals (1985–91); Walter Salas-Humara, guitar, vocals; Mary Rowell, violin (1985–90, 1991–present). Vulgar Boatmen: Walter Salas-Humara, guitar, vocals; Robert Ray, guitar, vocals; Dale Lawrence, guitar, vocals.

As musicians in Florida—Walter Salas-Humara in Gainesville, Bob Rupe in Ft. Lauderdale—the future principals of the Silos took a defiantly independent route to distributing the unadorned country-tinged pop sound of their separate bands. The two moved to New York within six months of each other and got together in 1985, continuing their independent course until the major labels came courting—which led to a short-lived and unpleasant experience with RCA. The two went their separate ways in 1991, with Salas-Humara carrying on the Silos name, as well as recording under his own name and with the Vulgar Boatmen.

what to buy: The offhand, ramshackle recklessness of the Silos' *Susan across the Ocean* 🎵🎵🎵🎵 (Watermelon, 1994, prod. Walter Salas-Humara, David McNair) is beguiling, with choice covers such as "Let's Take Some Drugs and Drive Around" fitting alongside the group's originals.

what to buy next: The Boatmen's *You and Your Sister* 🎵🎵🎵🎵 (Safe House, prod. Walter Salas-Humara) is a sterling debut of winsome melodic hooks and jittery charm ("Fallen Down," "Drive Somewhere"), introducing the songwriting talents of Robert Ray and Dale Lawrence. The Silos/Salas-Humara release *Ask the Dust* 🎵🎵🎵🎵 (Watermelon, 1995, prod. Walter Salas-Humara) is a generous sampler of early solo recordings and previously unreleased Silos work, much of which was origi-

nally recorded at friends' lofts and other intimate locales, lending the album an organic immediacy.

what to avoid: On Salas-Humara's solo album *Radar* 🎵🎵 (Watermelon, 1995, prod. Walter Salas-Humara), the fuller, harsher waves of discord overtake his melodic sensibilities.

the rest:

The Silos:

Cuba 🎵🎵🎵 (Watermelon, 1987)

Hasta La Victoria! 🎵🎵🎵 (Watermelon, 1992)

worth searching for: *The Silos* (RCA, 1990), the band's out-of-print major label debut, is engaging and sacrifices none of the lean pull of its earlier work. The Boatmen's *Please Panic* (Safe House, 1992, prod. Jonathan Isley, Robert Ray) is arguably a stronger and better-sounding record than *You and Your Sister*, with the Boatmen's light touch zeroing in like a homing pigeon.

influences:

◄◄ Buddy Holly, Johnny Cash, Waylon Jennings, Buffalo Springfield

►► Beat Happening, Uncle Tupelo, Son Volt, Wilco

Allan Orski

Silver Jews

Formed 1989, in Charlottesville, VA.

David Berman, vocals, guitar; Steve Malkmus, guitar (1989–95); Bob Nastanovich, drums (1989–95); Steve West, drums (1989–95); Matt Hunter (1995–present); Peyton Pinkerton (1995–present); Rian Murphy (1995–present); Michael Deming (1995–present).

Because of the presence of Steve Malkmus, Bob Nastanovich, and Steve West in the Silver Jews, many people made the mistake of thinking of the band as a Pavement side-project. The fact is, this band's mastermind always has been singer-guitarist David Berman. When the other members made it big with Pavement, Berman used the opportunity to make the sloppy country aesthetics of the Silver Jews even more his own. A graduate student, writer, and university lecturer, Berman infused the band's music with sharp, heady observations delivered from a lax, joint-smoking pose on an old couch in somebody's basement. With the Pavement trio, Berman made *The Arizona Record* EP, the band's first recording that was cohesive enough to be acknowledged. *Starlight Walker* followed the next year and was incessantly compared with the savvy indie sounds of Pavement's *Crooked Rain, Crooked Rain*. The inevitable falling away of the Pavement members happened in 1995, when Berman set out to record *The Natural Bridge*.

what to buy: *Starlite Walker* 🎵🎵🎵🎵 (Drag City, 1994, prod. Doug Easley, Davis McCain, Silver Jews) is a remarkable record that

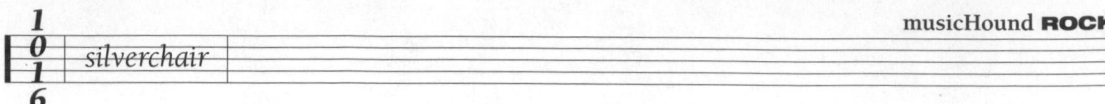

Berman wrote alone in a remote cabin in Mississippi and recorded with the Pavement trio. *The Natural Bridge* 🎵🎵🎵 (Drag City, 1996, prod. Rian Murphy, Shadwell Cougars) is a quirky introduction to the new Silver Jews: Matt Hunter and Peyton Pinkerton (both of New Radiant Storm King), Rian Murphy, and Michael Deming.

what to buy next: *The Arizona Record* 🎵🎵🎵 (Drag City EP, 1993) is the band's fuzzy debut (with the Pavement members), a loosely structured pop experiment that has an improvisational feel and sounds barely produced.

influences:

◀◀ Neil Young, Sebadoh

▶▶ Pavement

see also: *Pavement*

Norene Cashen

silverchair

Formed 1992, in Newcastle, Australia.

Daniel Johns, vocals, guitar; Ben Gillies, drums; Chris Joannou, bass, vocals.

silverchair is Australia's answer to grunge. Its powerfully deep lyrics, seething guitars, and pulsating drums have earned this trio a place in music history—much of which could be attributed to the fact that when the trio released its debut album, *Frogstomp*, all three members were unable to legally drive a car in America. silverchair, which was originally named the Innocent Criminals, gained notoriety in its homeland during 1994 after winning a radio contest for the single "Tomorrow." Following a fierce label-bidding war, silverchair signed to Murmur/Sony and released the single, which then quickly soared to #1 and became the fourth top-selling single in Australian history. During 1995, the band recorded *Frogstomp* in the span of one week. The album was the first to ever debut at #1 in Australia, and during that summer it crossed the Pacific and went on to achieve platinum status in the U.S. The band returned to the studio in 1996 and released its sophomore attempt, *Freak Show*, the following year.

what to buy: *Frogstomp* 🎵🎵🎵 (Epic, 1995, prod. Kevin Shirley) launched silverchair to international acclaim. Steeped in Cobain-esque lyrics and Zeppelin-styled guitar riffs, the album also showed the innocence of three teenagers wanting to have a fun time and meet chicks. It wasn't until the second album, *Freak Show* 🎵🎵🎵🎵 (Sony, 1997, prod. Nick Launay), that silverchair proved its ability to grow as musicians and songwriters. Johns's vocals and lyrics—while still gripping and painful—also became more contemplative, allowing the listener to enter a world of anguish only a teenager could know. The band wasn't afraid to experiment on *Freak Show*, demonstrated by its use of Far Eastern instruments like sitars, tamboura, and tablas, displaying a more wistful and psychedelic side.

influences:

◀◀ Nirvana, Pearl Jam, Soundgarden, Metallica, Led Zeppelin, You Am I

Ari Bendersky

Kim Simmonds

See: Savoy Brown

Patrick Simmons

See: The Doobie Brothers

Carly Simon

Born June 25, 1945, in New York, NY.

Carly Simon's career began more than 30 years ago when she dueted with her sister, Lucy, on "Winken Blinken and Nod," a modest hit on the Kapp label. After a couple of false starts, Simon—whose father cofounded the Simon & Schuster publishing house—landed a deal with Elektra and her self-titled debut was released in 1971. Since then she has released over two dozen albums on which her warm, often vulnerable-sounding vocals share romantic intimacies, child-like wonders, and bold observations. The '70s remain her most accomplished decade. Part of the problem with her career, though it is also a source of her appeal, is that no one knows quite what to expect from one recording to the next. Her uneven *Hotcakes* album is a case in point; she scored a hit with the buoyant "Mockingbird" (a duet with then-husband James Taylor), but it was her more introspective and heartfelt songs such as "Haven't Got Time for the Pain" that rang the truest. Since then, Simon has explored pop standards, children's music, and has even written some children's books, which is thoroughly appropriate given her literary lineage.

what to buy: Simon's first three albums remain her best. *No Secrets* 🎵🎵🎵🎵 (Elektra, 1972, prod. Richard Perry) is forthright, passionate, and wonderfully outspoken, particularly on the great put-down classic "You're So Vain." Her debut, *Carly Simon* 🎵🎵🎵🎵 (Elektra, 1971, prod. Eddie Kramer), is a fine melding of rock, pop, blues, country, and ballads. She landed a deserved Top 10 hit with the lead track, "That's the Way I Always Heard It Should Be." *Anticipation* 🎵🎵🎵🎵 (Elektra, 1971, prod. Paul Samwell-Smith) is not as varied and lacks the instrumental depth of Simon's debut, but her vocals carry the album in an increasingly confident and at times confidential manner.

what to buy next: *Coming around Again* 🎵🎵🎵 (Arista, 1987, prod. various) is a mature, confident work with hits in the title track, "All I Want Is You," and "Give Me All Night." *Letters Never Sent* ⚬⚬⚬ (Arista, 1994) takes an interesting concept—notes and letters that Simon had stashed away turned into songs—and turns it into a rich, personal musical outing.

what to avoid: Simon's two attempts to cover American popular standards generally wound up in failure. Though her heart may be in *Torch* **woof!** (Warner Bros., 1981) and *My Romance* **woof!** (Arista, 1990), her pipes and tone are incompatible, so removed from the high quality of the real thing as to be an embarrassment.

the rest:
Hotcakes ⚬⚬⚬ (Elektra, 1974)
Playing Possum ⚬⚬ (Elektra, 1974)
The Best of Carly Simon ⚬⚬⚬ (Elektra, 1975)
Another Passenger ⚬⚬⚬ (Elektra, 1976)
Boys in the Trees ⚬⚬ (Elektra, 1978)
Spy ⚬⚬ (Elektra, 1979)
Come Upstairs ⚬⚬⚬ (Elektra, 1980)
Hello Big Man ⚬⚬ (Warner Bros., 1983)
Spoiled Girl **woof!** (Epic, 1985)
Heartburn (Soundtrack) ⚬⚬ (Arista, 1986)
Working Girl (Soundtrack) ⚬⚬ (Arista, 1988)
Greatest Hits Live ⚬⚬⚬ (Arista, 1988)
Have You Seen Me Lately ⚬ (Arista, 1990)
Postcards from the Edge (Soundtrack) ⚬⚬ (Arista, 1990)
This Is My Life (Soundtrack) ⚬⚬ (Qwest, 1992)
Clouds in My Coffee: 1965–1995 ⚬⚬⚬ (Arista, 1995)
Film Noir ⚬⚬⚬ (Arista, 1997)

influences:
◀◀ James Taylor, Cat Stevens, Joni Mitchell, Carole King, Laura Nyro, Judy Collins, William Butler Yeats

▶▶ Melissa Manchester, Olivia Newton-John, Helen Reddy, Yvonne Elliman

Patrick McCarty

Paul Simon

Born October 13, 1941, in Newark, NJ.

Riding high on the success of Simon & Garfunkel's "Bridge over Troubled Water"—the duo's last gasp—Paul Simon began strong as a solo artist, churning out five hits from his first three albums. His attempt at a movie about the life of a touring rock act (*One Trick Pony*) flopped, and his 1983 *Hearts and Bones*—which started as a reunion album with Art Garfunkel—is still his worst-seller and least-respected album. In 1986 he took a chance, recording with South African musicians and then added his own lyrics to the instrumental tracks. The resulting collaboration, *Graceland*, became one of the most influential albums of the '80s, a dazzling mix of pop lyricism and African rhythms.

More recently, *The Capeman*, his first attempt at a musical, closed in 1998 after a short Broadway run. Still, he remains one of the rock era's most accomplished and ambitious artists.

what to buy: *Graceland* ⚬⚬⚬⚬ (Warner Bros., 1986, prod. Paul Simon) is an amazing comeback record and arguably the best collaboration between a Western songwriter and African musicians. *Paul Simon* ⚬⚬⚬ (Warner Bros., 1972, prod. Paul Simon, Roy Halee) picks up the world music groove—which he lightly pursued with Garfunkel—on the hits "Mother and Child Reunion" and "Me and Julio down by the Schoolyard."

what to buy next: *Live Rhymin'* ⚬⚬⚬ (Columbia, 1974, prod. Phil Ramone) is a well-recorded live set that featured the Dixie Hummingbirds singing back-up and the Peruvian folk troupe Urubamba providing instrumental support. *Still Crazy after All These Years* ⚬⚬⚬ (Warner Bros., 1975, prod. Paul Simon) features classy songs caught in a rich, '70s-styled production.

what to avoid: *Hearts and Bones* ⚬⚬ (Warner Bros., 1983, prod. Paul Simon, Russ Titelman, Roy Halee, Lenny Waronker) contains one great song ("The Late Great Johnny Ace") but also features selections such as "When Numbers Get Serious" and "Cars Are Cars," which are as silly as their titles imply.

the rest:
There Goes Rhymin' Simon ⚬⚬⚬ (Columbia, 1973)
Greatest Hits, Etc. ⚬⚬⚬ (Columbia, 1977)
One Trick Pony ⚬⚬ (Warner Bros., 1980)
Negotiations and Love Songs ⚬⚬⚬ (Warner Bros., 1988)
The Rhythm of the Saints ⚬⚬⚬ (Warner Bros., 1990)
Paul Simon's Concert in the Park ⚬⚬⚬ (Warner Bros., 1991)
Paul Simon 1964/1993 ⚬⚬⚬ (Warner Bros., 1993)
Songs from the Capeman ⚬⚬⚬ (Warner Bros., 1997)

worth searching for: *Paul Simon: The Collection* (Warner Bros., 1991), a three-volume Japanese set, includes a selection of Simon's hits, a live set from his "Graceland" tour, and an interview.

influences:
◀◀ Pete Seeger, the Weavers, Peter, Paul & Mary, Bob Dylan, the Kingston Trio, the Beach Boys, the Everly Brothers

▶▶ James Taylor, George Harrison, Jim Croce, Jackson Browne, Mary Chapin Carpenter, Joe Henry, Sheryl Crow

see also: *Simon & Garfunkel*

Leland Rucker

Simon & Garfunkel

Formed 1956, in New York, NY. Disbanded 1970.

Paul Simon, vocals, guitar; Art Garfunkel, vocals.

Never mind that their first hit happened after they had broken up a second time; Paul Simon and Art Garfunkel proved one of

Paul Simon (© Ken Settle)

the most durable of the folk groups of the '60s—and all-time. Boyhood friends who had a minor hit ("Hey, Schoolgirl") during 1957 as Tom & Jerry, they recorded on and off, including a folk album, *Wednesday Morning, 3 A.M.*, in 1964 before Simon headed off to England. It might have ended there but for producer Tom Wilson; the rock backing that he added to "The Sounds of Silence" sounds more forced and intrusive today than it did back then, but it proved perfect radio fare alongside the chiming guitars of the Byrds' "Turn, Turn, Turn" and the Beatles' "We Can Work It Out." Simon returned and came up with ambitious lyrics such as "Homeward Bound," "I Am a Rock," "The Dangling Conversation," "The Boxer," and "Mrs. Robinson"—the latter a massive hit in the soundtrack for *The Graduate*. With equally ambitious production, those songs became some of the era's biggest hits and threaded together the folk/protest movement of the early '60s, Simon's earlier Brill Building apprenticeship, and the burgeoning singer-songwriter movement. If Simon's confessional lyrics often seemed pretentiously literary (see "Richard Cory") and were considered sophomoric tripe by some critics, they were considered poetry by the baby-boom generation. The obvious disparity and tension in the act—Simon was musically adept, wrote the songs, and sang most of them; Garfunkel played no instrument, sang harmony and occasional lead—resulted in their parting while at a creative and commercial peak after *Bridge over Troubled Water*, their most successful album and the title track (their last #1) Garfunkel's best moment. Garfunkel went on to films (*Catch-22, Carnal Knowledge*) and a part-time recording career; Simon went on to bigger and better things. They have collaborated occasionally since then, including a massive reunion concert in New York's Central Park during 1981. After Simon & Garfunkel, any nerd with a sensitive lyric, a few guitar moves, and a friend singing would become fair game for the pop market.

what to buy: *Bookends* 𝄞𝄞𝄞𝄞𝄞 (Columbia, 1968, prod. Paul Simon, Art Garfunkel, Roy Halee) holds together like a concept album, with the film hit "Mrs. Robinson" crassly tacked on at the end. *Parsley, Sage, Rosemary and Thyme* 𝄞𝄞𝄞𝄞 (Columbia, 1966, prod. Bob Johnston) is their real first album together as S&G, and almost works as well as *Bookends*.

what to buy next: *Bridge over Troubled Water* 𝄞𝄞𝄞𝄞 (Columbia, 1970, prod. Paul Simon, Art Garfunkel, Roy Halee) is considered their masterpiece, though today it sounds top-heavy, overproduced, and too precious for its own good. *Sounds of Silence* 𝄞𝄞𝄞𝄞 (Columbia, 1966, prod. Bob Johnston) is basically an electric reworking of *The Paul Simon Songbook* (CBS UK, 1965), adding the Wilson-electrified "Sounds of Silence."

what to avoid: Yes, *The Graduate* 𝄞 (Columbia, 1968, prod. Teo Macero) was an important soundtrack; no, it doesn't have anything new on it except "Mrs. Robinson." *The Concert in Central Park* 𝄞 (Warner Bros., 1982, prod. Paul Simon, Art Garfunkel, Roy Halee, Phil Ramone) is a too-late attempt to recapture the magic.

the rest:
Wednesday Morning, 3 A.M. 𝄞𝄞𝄞 (Columbia, 1966)
Greatest Hits 𝄞𝄞𝄞 (Columbia, 1972)
Old Friends 𝄞𝄞𝄞𝄞 (Columbia, 1997)

worth searching for: *Collected Works* (Columbia, 1990, prod. various) collects all the studio albums chronologically on three compact discs.

influences:

◀◀ Pete Seeger, the Weavers, Peter, Paul & Mary, Bob Dylan, the Kingston Trio, the Beach Boys, the Everly Brothers

▶▶ James Taylor, George Harrison, Jim Croce, Jackson Browne, Mary Chapin Carpenter, Joe Henry, Sheryl Crow

see also: *Paul Simon, Art Garfunkel*

Leland Rucker

Simple Minds

Formed 1977, in Glasgow, Scotland.

Jim Kerr, vocals; Charlie Burchill, guitar, keyboards; Duncan Barnwell, guitar (1977–78); Tony Donald, bass (1977–78); Derek Forbes, bass (1978–84); Brian McGee, drums (1977–80); Kenny Hyslop, drums (1980); Mike Ogletree, drums (1980–82); Mel Gaynor, drums (1982–present); Michael McNeil, keyboards (1977–89); John Giblin, bass (1984–89); Robin Clark, vocals (1984–89); Sue Hadjopoulos, percussion (1984–89); Peter Vitesse, keyboards (1989–93).

Simple Minds sprang out of the English punk scene of the late '70s, but they were a punk band with good musical skills. The band originally started with Jim Kerr and Charlie Burchill as Johnny & the Self Abusers, with a 7-inch single featuring the tracks "Saints and Sinners" and "Dead Vandals." While Simple Minds' first album, *Life in a Day*, proved to be more influenced by psychedelic pop, the band's roots were firmly entrenched in a post-punk feel, even before punk had died. Simple Minds rode through many phases—including industrial, new wave, the short-lived New Romantic movement, and a hearty foray into arena rock during the mid-'80s thanks to the massive hit "Don't You (Forget about Me)" from the film *The Breakfast Club*. It wasn't until the early '90s that the band—by this point a duo—found its own groove, moving into new territory really only navigated by the likes of Peter Gabriel and a handful of others, with a slant toward world music and influences from early Celtic folk songs. Despite minimal commercial success at this point, the band is still together; Virgin Records UK has a long-term commitment to the band, and Kerr and company seem anxious to continue to provide new material. It's interesting to note that Kerr lost his second wife (his first was Chrissie

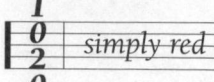
Hynde of the Pretenders who left Ray Davies of the Kinks for him), Patsy Kensit, to Noel Gallagher of Oasis.

what to buy: *New Gold Dream* ✍✍✍✍ (Virgin/A&M, 1983, prod. Peter Welsh) is as solid a post–new wave album as you can find. Ranging from gloomy to introspective, the one word that seems to best describe this record is grandiose. The sound of the recording, even on vinyl, has the ability to fill a room with a glow.

what to buy next: *Glittering Prize* ✍✍✍✍ (A&M, 1993, prod. various) is a safe bet. It's a rather impressive singles collection that offers a nice overview of the band's history, although it's rather stunted in that it includes just one song prior to *New Gold Dream*. *Sparkle in the Rain* ✍✍✍✍ (Virgin/A&M, 1984, prod. Peter Welsh) was the band's stylistic follow-up to *New Gold Dream*. Showing a smarter but less open sound than previous efforts, this record has moments when it almost rocks. The second half (second *side* in the old days) shows the band's experimental bent, with instrumentals and a Lou Reed cover ("Street Hassle"). The modern side of Simple Minds is revealed on *Good News from the Next World* ✍✍✍✍ (Virgin, 1995, prod. Keith Forsey, Simple Minds), which, while not as good as the mid-'80s material, makes an effort to recapture that vibe. Hitting the charts with "She's a River," the album goes a long way toward returning the band to the limelight.

what to avoid: *Real Life* ✍✍ (A&M, 1991, prod. Stephen Lipsey) shows the band trying to live up to the commercial success of the massive *Once upon a Time* and falling flat.

the rest:
Life in a Day ✍✍✍ (Virgin, 1979)
Real to Real Cacophony ✍✍✍✍ (Virgin, 1980)
Empires and Dance ✍✍✍✍✍ (Virgin, 1980)
Sons and Fascination/Sister Feelings Call ✍✍✍ (Virgin, 1981)
Once upon a Time ✍✍✍✍ (A&M, 1985)
Live in the City of Lights ✍✍✍ (A&M, 1987)
Street Fighting Years ✍✍✍✍ (A&M, 1989)

influences:
◀◀ Roxy Music, Peter Gabriel, Genesis, King Crimson
▶▶ The Call, U2, Jars of Clay, Zerra One, Tears for Fears

Tim Davis

Simply Red

Formed 1982, in Manchester, England.

Mick Hucknall, vocals; Sylvan Richardson, guitar (1985–89); Fritz McIntyre, keyboards; Tony Bowers, bass; Chris Joyce, drums; Tim Kellett, horns, keyboards; Aziz Ibrahim, guitar (1989–91); Ian Kirkham, sax (1989).

With its polished commercial soul sound and R&B riffs, Simply Red was a fresh-sounding new force when it landed in the U.S.

during the 1980s. Lead singer and band leader Mick Hucknall, who sang in punk bands during the late '70s and early '80s, was the key to this success, singing in a plaintive high tenor that evokes yearning and loss and has just enough texture to make it interesting. It continues to provide a good counter to the band's slick and slightly tame arrangements, which have worked for the occasional hit—"Holding Back the Years" in 1985 and its cover of Harold Melvin & the Blue Notes' "If You Don't Know Me by Now" four years later.

what to buy: *Picture Book* ✍✍✍ (Elektra, 1985, prod. Stewart Levine), the band's debut, was a revelation that showcased Sylvan Richardson's classical background and Hucknall's tremendously emotional singing. The result is Stax/Volt meets Philly soul and two of the year's best singles in "Holding Back the Years" and the group's rendition of "Money$ Too Tight to Mention." *Greatest Hits* ✍✍✍ (EastWest, 1996, prod. various) isn't quite as cohesive, but it has all the songs you should own.

what to buy next: After some middling releases in between, *Stars* (EastWest, 1991) is Simply Red's strongest album since its debut.

what to avoid: Coming after such a stellar debut, *Men & Women* ✍✍ (Elektra, 1987, prod. Alex Sadkin) is a significant sophomore slump—even though Hucknall had Motown great Lamont Dozier as a collaborator.

the rest:
A New Flame ✍✍✍ (Elektra, 1989)
Life ✍✍✍ (EastWest, 1995)
Blue ✍✍ (EastWest, 1998)

influences:
◀◀ Bobby Purify, Smokey Robinson, the Dells, Harold Melvin & the Blue Notes
▶▶ Lisa Stansfield, Rick Astley, the Commitments

Patrick McCarty

Martin Simpson

Born May 5, 1953, in Scunthorpe, Lincolnshire, England.

A versatile guitarist, Martin Simpson was one of the most sought-after accompanists on the British folk scene prior to moving to America in 1987 with his wife, singer-songwriter Jessica Radcliffe Simpson. He started playing guitar at the age of 12 but his earliest influences came as a result of his father's singing and his mother's record collection. Simpson was playing in folk clubs throughout his teens and recording his first solo album relatively soon after that. Soon he was opening up for established acts such as Steeleye Span, associating with stars like Martin Carthy, Ashley Hutchings, and June Tabor, and joining that free-floating musical ensemble known as the Albion Country Band. By 1980, Tabor and Simpson had formed an intermittent musical partnership that has lasted for decades, recording several albums together—including the masterful *Abyssinians* and *A Cut Above*. Since Simpson moved to America he has worked with the bluegrass hybrid group Metamora, as an accompanist for blues pianist Henry Gray, and, of course, on tours as a solo act and with his wife and their group, Band of Angels.

what to buy: *Cool and Unusual* 🎵🎵🎵 (Red House, 1997, prod. Martin Simpson) is a superb instrumental album that features Simpson displaying his fret and plectrum wizardry in the company of fellow guitar luminaries David Lindley and Kelly Joe Phelps. "Prelude/Santa Cruz," featuring three musicians from the Malagasy group Tarika Sammy, is particularly interesting from the standpoint of cultural cross-pollination. *Live* 🎵🎵🎵 (Beautiful Jo, 1995/Red House, 1997) is taken from a solo concert recorded during 1994 and showcases Simpson's superb guitar playing and sensitive vocals in a mixture of traditional British folk material and original tunes with some exquisite slide work tossed in as a bonus.

what to buy next: Anyone wishing to explore Simpson's earlier work should look to *The Collection* 🎵🎵🎵🎵 (Shanachie, 1994, prod. Tony Engle, Martin Simpson, Jessica Simpson), which selects cuts from three albums that he recorded for Britain's Topic label during the mid-'80s. While it hovers close to the folk end of the spectrum, there is still some stunning slide guitar playing to be heard in "Green Linnet/Grinning in Your Face," and some fine clawhammer-style banjo workouts in "Moonshine." *Leaves of Life* 🎵🎵🎵 (Shanachie, 1989, prod. Martin Simpson, Jessica Simpson), while filled with wonderful guitar playing, is a relaxed instrumental setting for arrangements of traditional Celtic-influenced folk tunes. It veers uncomfortably close to Celtic-influenced new age music at times, but the overall integrity of Simpson's playing saves it from being trite background music.

the rest:
When I Was on Horseback 🎵🎵🎵 (Shanachie, 1992)
(With Jessica Simpson) *Band of Angels* 🎵🎵🎵 (Red House, 1996)
(With Wu Man) *Music for the Motherless Child* 🎵🎵🎵 (Water Lily Acoustics, 1997)

worth searching for: According to Simpson, folk fanatics and blues freaks both recoiled from *Smoke and Mirrors* (Thunderbird, 1995, prod. Martin Simpson) because he dared to play the blues. Folk adherents feared he had deserted them, and blues fans rejected his playing as if it were coming from outside the idiom (despite featuring noted blues guitarist Ronnie Earl on half the tunes). The album is effectively out of print at present, which is too bad because Simpson just wails on this sucker. His version of "Spoonful" stacks up well against some of the stuff

put out as blues these days, and Simpson's dobro playing on "Gone Fishing" is a stone cold delight. He also has a video, *Martin Simpson in Concert*, which was released through Vestapol Video and takes him through a tasteful batch of traditional medleys.

influences:

◄◄ Davey Graham, Martin Carthy, Paul Robeson, Big Joe Williams, Henry Gray, John Renbourn, Richard Thompson

►► Jessica Simpson, June Tabor

Garaud MacTaggart

Nancy Sinatra

Born June 8, 1940, in Jersey City, NJ.

It's unlikely Nancy Sinatra would have enjoyed much of a music career were it not for her famous father. Sporting a set of average-sounding pipes, she passed muster on a slew of uneven albums that today play like deliciously kitschy novelties. With producer Lee Hazelwood, Sinatra found success, first in tough, sex-kitten "go-go" music (typified by her 1966 hit "These Boots Are Made for Walkin'") and later on a string of bizarre modern Western tunes penned by Hazelwood. Whatever one makes of her singing, Sinatra's musical backing (including Hal Blaine, James Burton, and Larry Knechtel) was impeccable, and her lightweight pop was masterfully performed. Without exception, Sinatra's albums follow a prescribed formula: a hit title track, a few adequate remakes of contemporary hits, and a whole passel of Hazelwood's disquieting country-western songs.

what to buy: *Hit Years* 🎵🎵🎵🎵 (WEA/Atlantic/Rhino, 1986, prod. Lee Hazelwood) is the album to own, containing all of Sinatra's solo hits, her duets with dad, plus the best of her output with Hazelwood ("Some Velvet Morning," "Sugar Town," and the head-bobbin' truckin' song "Jackson").

what to avoid: Even Sinatra's worst album qualifies as a camp classic. Let's just say that *Country My Way* 🎵🎵 (Sundazed, 1967, prod. Lee Hazelwood) has the least enjoyable selection of cuts, but that's not to say you won't love Nancy's game attempt at covering the country-western genre.

the rest:
Boots 🎵🎵 (Sundazed, 1966)
How Does That Grab You? 🎵🎵 (Sundazed, 1966)
Nancy in London 🎵🎵 (Sundazed, 1966)
Sugar 🎵🎵 (Sundazed, 1967)
Movin' with Nancy 🎵🎵 (Sundazed, 1968)
Nancy 🎵🎵 (Sundazed, 1969)

worth searching for: The Australian release *Lightning's Girl* (Raven, 1986, prod. Lee Hazelwood) ups the *Hit Years* ante with a few more tracks.

influences:

◀◀ Petula Clark, Dusty Springfield, Cilla Black

▶▶ Blondie, X, Exene Cervenka

Christopher Scapelliti

Siouxsie & the Banshees

Formed 1976, in London, England. Disbanded 1996.

Siouxsie Sioux (born Susan Dallion), vocals; Steve Severin, bass; Marco Pirroni, guitar (1976–77); Peter Fenton, guitar (1977); John McKay, guitar, 1977–79); Robert Smith, guitar (1979–80, 1983–84); John McGeoch, guitar (1980–83); John Carruthers, guitar (1984–87); Jon Klein, guitar (1987–96); Sid Vicious, drums (1976–77); Kenny Morris, drums (1977–79); Budgie, drums (1979–96); Martin McCarrick, cello, keyboards (1987–96).

The spiritual godmother of gothic rock, Siouxsie Sioux was a British punk fan who turned her admiration into action, forming the Banshees for a 1976 English punk festival, with future Sex Pistols bassist Sid Vicious on drums. Group membership changed frequently, particularly in the guitar position, which has included Marco Pirroni (later of Adam & the Ants) and Robert Smith (the Cure founder, who appeared on *Hyaena* and the live *Nocturne*). Originally a punk band with arty pretensions, the Banshees gradually evolved into a more dance-oriented group. The group's lofty status among the future alternative crowd rarely translated into mainstream success in the United States, but its egos and record sales got a big boost by its inclusion on the first Lollapalooza tour in 1991. Sioux, who dabbled with a side project called the Creatures in the 1980s, broke up the Banshees in 1996; she and Budgie, her husband, plan to continue the Creatures.

what to buy: Most of the band's albums sound dated now, but the second hits collection, *Twice upon a Time—The Singles* 𝄢𝄢𝄢 (Geffen, 1992, prod. various), at least displays a clarity of vision and conviction that runs through the group's groovy gothic-art-punk rock. This set rounds up singles released between 1981 and 1992, after the band signed with Geffen.

what to buy next: Some of the crude punk trappings had worn off by the time the Banshees released *Juju* 𝄢𝄢𝄢 (Geffen, prod. the Banshees, Nigel Gray), a dark, mysterious, sometimes sensual record that combined Sioux's pained lyrics with smartly evocative grooves.

what to avoid: The live album *Nocturne* 𝄢𝄢 (Geffen, 1983, prod. Siouxsie Sioux, the Banshees) was recorded during one of Smith's tenures in the band but isn't compelling beyond that.

the rest:
The Peel Sessions 𝄢𝄢𝄢 (Dutch East India, 1977/Strange Fruit, 1991)
The Scream 𝄢𝄢𝄢 (Polydor, 1978/Geffen, 1992)

Join Hands 𝄢𝄢 (Geffen, 1979)
Kaleidoscope 𝄢𝄢 (PVC, 1980/Geffen, 1992)
Once upon a Time: The Singles 𝄢𝄢𝄢 (PVC, 1981/Geffen, 1984)
A Kiss in the Dreamhouse 𝄢𝄢 (Polydor U.K., 1982/Geffen, 1984)
Hyaena 𝄢𝄢 (Geffen, 1984)
Tinderbox 𝄢𝄢 (Geffen, 1986)
Through the Looking Glass 𝄢𝄢 (Geffen, 1987)
Peepshow 𝄢𝄢 (Geffen, 1988)
Superstition 𝄢𝄢𝄢 (Geffen, 1991)
The Rapture 𝄢𝄢 (Geffen, 1995)

worth searching for: The British CD-5 single for "Cities in Dust" from the *Tinderbox* album features five extra non-album songs.

influences:

◀◀ The Sex Pistols, New York Dolls, the Ramones, Ann Rice

▶▶ The Cure, Alanis Morissette, Hole

see also: *The Cure, the Sex Pistols, Adam Ant*

Doug Pullen

Sir Douglas Quintet
See: Doug Sahm

Sister Hazel

Formed 1994, in Gainesville, FL.

Ken Block, lead vocals, acoustic guitar; Andrew Copeland, vocals, acoustic guitar; Jeff Beres, bass, vocals; Ryan Newell, guitar (1996–present); Mark Trojanowski, drums.

Sister Hazel has earned a well-deserved reputation as nice guys who write nice, happy songs and put on happy shows. Named after an African American woman who ran Sister Hazel's Rescue Mission in Gainesville during the '70s and '80s, Sister Hazel released its self-titled debut cassette in 1994; it became a regional hit that led to a national recording deal.

what to buy: The group was shuttled to Memphis to re-record *. . . Somewhere More Familiar* 𝄢𝄢𝄢 (Universal, 1997, prod. Paul Ebersold), which was originally released on the group's own label, Croakin' Poets Records. The result of the new, improved *. . . Somewhere More Familiar* is a collection of happy roots-rock songs. The giddy first single "All for You" has one of 1997's most memorable choruses: "Hard to say what it is I see in you/Wonder if I'll always be with you/Words can't say/What I can't do/Enough to prove it's all for you." "Superman" flaunts a Memphis soul groove, while Andrew Copeland's honest, emotive vocals on "Cerilene," a potential country crossover hit, make the song a gem.

the rest:
Sister Hazel 𝄢𝄢 (Croakin' Poets, 1994/Universal, 1997)

influences:

◀◀ Toad the Wet Sprocket, Phish

▶▶ The Why Store, Matchbox 20

Christina Fuoco

Sisters of Mercy

Formed 1980, in Leeds. England.

Andrew Eldritch, vocals, guitar; Wayne Hussey, guitar (1980–85); Craig Adams, bass (1980–85); Gary Marx, guitar (1980–85); Patricia Morrison, bass (1987–90); Tim Bricheno, guitar (1990–present); Andreas Bruhn, guitar (1990–present); Tony James, bass (1990–present).

When you think goth, chances are Sisters of Mercy make your short list. Rightfully, the Sisters can claim to be the most influential band for the more Prozac-prone listener. Along with contemporaries such as Bauhaus, Joy Division, and other bands that were either more arty or industrial, the Sisters painted a soundscape of bleak urban blight and tenous graspings of reality. Before the term gothic rock had even been truly invented, the Sisters were paving the way. Both pretentious and inspirational, Andrew Eldritch and his crew made the soundtrack to your nightmare before you'd even gone to sleep. With a rotating roster around him that has changed so much it makes your head spin, Eldritch's Sisters contributed directly to various outfits, including the Mission U.K., the Batfish Boys, the March Violets, All about Eve, Ghost Dance, and the Sisterhood (actually Eldritch's project while the lawyers were deciding who got to keep the Sisters of Mercy name after the group's first breakup). The Sisters' music is everything you would expect from a goth outfit—at times it's brooding, dark swirls of sound (synth, acoustic guitar, exotic strings, hypnotic percussion, and angst-ridden vocals), and at other times it's loud, abrasive, and angry (screaming vocals, loud screeching guitars, driving drums, and layers of feedback and white noise). The Sisters were as at home in a pretentious dance club as they were in a loud heavy-metal bar. If you like this style, you can't go wrong by exploring the import bins for anything on Merciful Release—Eldritch's own label, which he used to release Sisters material from and help launch other up-and-comers who followed his lead.

what to buy: *Some Girls Wander by Mistake* 𝄢𝄢𝄢𝄢 (Elektra, 1992, prod. various) isn't a proper greatest hits. Rather, it's a collection of the band's material from 1980 to 1983 that was available only on import EPs. This album will give you the creeps—dark, snarling vocals over stripped-down drum tracks and swirling guitars. It's goth at its earliest stage, garage/punk with a biblical twist. Not-to-be-missed tracks include "Alice," an amazing cover of "Gimme Shelter" as only the Sisters could do it, and "Kiss the Carpet" from 1983's legendary *Reptile House* EP.

what to buy next: *A Slight Case of Overbombing: Greatest Hits, Volume 1* 𝄢𝄢𝄢 (Elektra, 1993, prod. various) is the band's token singles collection and pulls songs almost exclusively from its 1985–90 catalog (only a newer version of "Temple of Love" is duplicated here and on *Some Girls*). This collection shows that the Sisters *are* Eldritch, and very little has been lost since the band's inception more than a decade before. The production values are higher than earlier—almost slick, in fact—and the atmospherics are amazing. A dandy CD for all of your seance needs.

the rest:
First & Last & Always 𝄢𝄢𝄢 (Elektra, 1985)
(As Sisterhood) *Gift* 𝄢𝄢𝄢 (Merciful Release EP, 1986)
Floodland 𝄢𝄢𝄢 (Elektra, 1987)
Vision Thing 𝄢𝄢𝄢 (Elektra, 1992)

worth searching for: The promotional-only *Tour Thing* (Elektra, 1992) came out during the band's tour in support of *Vision Thing* and features alternate takes on several tracks from that album as well as *Floodland*—and, most notably, a lengthy interview with Eldritch.

influences:

◀◀ The Sex Pistols, the Cure, Cabaret Voltaire, Alice Cooper, Black Sabbath, Led Zeppelin

▶▶ Marilyn Manson, nine inch nails, Alice in Chains, Ministry, Type O Negative

see also: *Mission U.K.*

Tim Davis

6 String Drag

Formed 1993, in Clemson, SC.

Kenny Roby, guitar, vocals; Rob Keller, bass, vocals; Ray Duffey, drums; Glenn Cannon, guitar; Scott Miller, guitar.

Keeping up with 6 String Drag can be an exhausting task. Acolytes of the play-all-night-long school of bar-band rock, 6 String Drag is as likely to cover AC/DC as the Louvin Brothers onstage, and the group's name comes from the Stanley Brothers' "Five String Drag." 6 String Drag's originals draw from just as broad a palette; Drivin' N' Cryin' talks the talk about playing "heavy metal bluegrass," but 6 String Drag really pulls it off and adds a heavy dose of earthy country soul to boot. While frontman Kenny Roby's soulful rasp is the band's most obvious attribute, its secret weapon is bassist Rob Keller's mournful harmony vocals. Together, Roby and Keller make 6 String Drag sound like the world's loudest country brother vocal duo.

what to buy: Had Elvis Costello continued in a roots rock vein after 1986's *King of America*, he might've made a record like 6 String Drag's *High Hat* 𝄢𝄢𝄢 (E Squared, 1997, prod. Steve

Earle, Ray Kennedy). *High Hat* is as far flung an album as you'll ever hear, yet still takes in only a fragment of the band's on-stage live sprawl. Country blues rests alongside pure pop, fervid gospel, ragtime, and, in "Elaine," the best Sir Douglas Quintet rip that anyone not named Doug Sahm has ever done. When the horns kick in on "Gasoline Maybelline," it's pure heaven.

what to buy next: 6 String Drag's large ambitions were also evident on its debut *6 String Drag* ♫♫♫ (Fundamental, 1994, prod. Michael Hayes), but the band couldn't yet back 'em up. It's a good-but-not-quite-great record with some fine songs that aren't quite developed, either in terms of writing or performance.

worth searching for: If you still own a turntable, track down the "Bottle of Blues" 7-inch vinyl single (E Squared, 1997). The B-side is a cover of the Louvin Brothers' "Lorene" and shows off one of 6 String Drag's key influences in Roby and Keller's eerie vocal harmonies. Also noteworthy is *Tonebenders* (Yep Roc, 1997, prod. Mike Beard, Bryon Settle, Tonebenders) by the group of the same name, which includes members of 6 String Drag's part-time horn section. *Tonebenders* is a sort of Pavement-esque indie-rock take on Booker T. & the MG's–style funk vamps.

influences:

◀◀ Doug Sahm, Elvis Costello, the Band, the Louvin Brothers, Delbert McClinton, the LeRoi Brothers

▶▶ Tonebenders, the V-Roys, Mercury Dime

David Menconi

16 Horsepower

Formed 1992, in Denver, CO.

David Eugene Edwards, vocals, guitars, banjo, bandoneon, lap steel; Jean-Yves Tola, drums, backup vocals, piano; Kevin Soll, stand-up bass, acoustic bass, cello, backup vocals (1992–96); Jeffrey Paul, backup vocals, fiddle, guitar, cello, organ (1997–present); Pascal Humbert, bass, bass fiddle, guitar (1996–present).

David Eugene Edwards moved to Los Angeles in 1990 as guitarist for the Denver Gentlemen. They broke up. He ended up working on the set of a Roger Corman movie, where he met Jean-Yves Tola, who'd moved to L.A. from France with the band Passion Fodder, which had also broken up. They played a few dates together in Los Angeles, then reconvened in Denver with an evolving set of friends. (Jeffrey Paul had been a Denver Gentleman as well, and had actually played with the nascent band in Los Angeles.) The resulting ensemble is a half-French, half-American aggregation devoted to vintage acoustic instruments, Appalachian gothic musics, and Edwards's nineteenth-century religious convictions (he's the grandson of a traveling Nazarene minister). Theirs is a striking, eerie sound that seems altogether dislocated from any temporal roots. Edwards sings

with a distinct howl, the vintage instruments play at odd dissonances (but within conventional frameworks), and it's all carried off with the ferocity of a punk-rock fire and brimstone preacher. And, yes, Edwards writes songs from a Christian perspective, but they have absolutely nothing to do with the contemporary Christian rock movement.

what to buy: The sophomore effort *Low Estate* ♫♫♫♫ (A&M, 1997, prod. John Parish) reflects the efforts of an enormously versatile ensemble that has become less a foil for Edwards's songs and more an integral portion of that creative process. And it somehow feels like Ann Rice's New Orleans at 4 a.m.

what to buy next: *Sackcloth and Ashes* ♫♫♫ (A&M, 1995, prod. Warren Bruleigh, 16 Horsepower) is a fine opening statement, filled with Edwards's complex religious imagery and minor key phrasing.

the rest:

16 Horsepower ♫♫♪ (Ricochet/A&M, 1995)

worth searching for: A&M sent the song "For Heaven's Sake" to college radio with an unreleased B-side from the *Low Estate* sessions, a spectacularly unsettling version of Creedence Clearwater Revival's "Bad Moon Rising."

influences:

◀◀ Nick Cave, Bob Dylan, Dorsey Dixon, PJ Harvey

▶▶ Freakwater, Johnny Dowd

Grant Alden

The 6ths

Formed 1995.

Stephin Merritt, vocals, various instruments; others.

It seems unlikely that there will ever be another 6ths album. The merits of the collective's lone album, *Wasps Nests*, make that a pity, but consolation can be found in the fact that these talents will be brewing something else somewhere else under another name. Part supergroup, part vision of mad genius, the 6ths were an inspired gathering of some of the most interesting and provocative musicians working on the edge of alternative pop. Brought together by Stephin Merritt, best known for his troubled pop tapestries with the Magnetic Fields, his partners in the project included Sebadoh's Lou Barlow, Yo La Tengo's Georgia Hubley, famed producer Mitch Easter, and singer-songwriters Chris Knox and Barbara Manning, among others.

what's available: *Wasps Nests* ♫♫♫♫♪ (London, 1995, prod. Stephin Merritt) is a 14-song pop masterpiece that, unfortunately, flew under the radar screens of the record-buying public. Each track features a different voice, most of whom share impeccable indie pedigrees. Yo La Tengo's Georgia Hubley is sweetly present on one of the best tracks, "Looking for Love (In the Hall of Mirrors)," a song that in many ways explains the whole project: it's slightly goofy and cracked, a little unsettling, but put together with aching tenderness and an ear for intimacy. The end result is the perfect soundtrack for the end of the alternative era.

influences:

◄◄ Magnetic Fields, Yo La Tengo, Sebadoh

Amy Weivoda

Roni Size /Reprazent

Formed 1992, in Bristol, England.

Roni Size; DJ Krust; Suv; Die; MC Dynamite; Onallee.

Roni Size and his drum 'n' bass collective emerged during the early '90s as part of the underground dance scene in Bristol, England—a coastal town that spawned such innovators as Massive Attack, Tricky, Nellee Hooper, and Smith & Mighty. An influx of immigrants from the Caribbean during the '50s brought black culture to Bristol and laid the groundwork for the musical revolution to come. Size, Krust, Suv, and the rest of the Reprazent posse were part of a multi-culti generation of DJs and producers who grew up in England's dance clubs, drawing on the influence of American hip-hop and Jamaican reggae and blending them with new, readily available recording and mixing technology. The result has been a new kind of urban music: the spooky, neo-psychedelic street grooves of trip-hop; and the skittering snare beats and thick, reverberating bass lines of drum 'n' bass. Though it was Goldie, a London native, who produced the first drum 'n' bass landmark with the *Timeless* album in 1995, it was Size who brought the sound to a new level of mainstream recognition—in England, at least—when *Newforms*, his double-CD debut, won the coveted Mercury Prize, England's equivalent of the album of the year, in 1997.

what to buy: *Newforms* ✍✍✍✍ (Mercury, 1997, prod. Roni Size) is a cut above most of the drum 'n' bass discs that flooded the market after Goldie's *Timeless* broke through during 1995. Size's use of plush soul vocals, upright bass, and other live instruments gives the disc a warmth that evokes early hip-hop, the funk of James Brown, and the dub innovations of King Tubby even as it emphasizes beats and texture over melody and dispenses with conventional pop-song structure. The more vocal-oriented first disc is the perfect introduction for drum 'n' bass novices, while the more abstract second disc should thrill aficionados.

influences:

◄◄ James Brown, Lee "Scratch" Perry, King Tubby, Public Enemy

Greg Kot

WHAT ALBUM CHANGED YOUR LIFE?

I think AC/DC was probably the first thing that got me into wanting to play music. I just loved them. There was always something there. I didn't go with whatever their message was; I thought it was ridiculous even when I was a kid. It was just something about them, their music, the way they played it. They just really went for it. I still like it.

David Eugene Edwards (of 16 Horsepower)

The Skeletons /The Morells

The Skeletons formed 1979, in Springfield, MO. The Morells formed 1983, in Springfield, MO. Disbanded 1987.

The Skeletons: Lou Whitney, bass, vocals; D. Clinton Thompson, guitar, vocals; Bobby Lloyd Hicks, drums, vocals; Randle Chowning, guitar, harmonica, vocals (1979); Nick Sibley, keyboards, guitar, harmonica, vocals (1979, 1988); Joe Terry, keyboards, vocals (1988, 1990–present); Kelly Brown, keyboards, vocals (1990–96). The Morells: Lou Whitney, bass, vocals; D. Clinton Thompson, guitar, vocals; Maralie, keyboards, vocals; Ron Gremp, drums, vocals; Joe Terry, keyboard, vocals (1983–87).

Purveyors of roots rock in nearly all its myriad guises, the Skeletons and Morells—different incarnations of roughly the same sensibility—are the greatest bar bands you never heard. Their members have assimilated an astounding array of influences—rockabilly, country, R&B, beach music, frat rock, and Phil Spector are all in there someplace—making for an eclecticism that has cost them commercial success but left their fans agape on countless occasions. The Skeletons formed from the ashes of the Springfield, Missouri, group the Original Symptoms, then took a hiatus when Lou Whitney, D. Clinton Thompson, and Bobby Lloyd Hicks backed Steve Forbert for a spell. Whitney and Thompson then chose to start the Morells before re-activating the Skeletons during the late '80s. The Skeletons continue to work on their own and as a popular backing band for such artists as Dave Alvin, Jonathan Richman, Boxcar Willie, and Syd Straw. And when the Skeletons are on hiatus, Thompson leads the roots-pop trio Park Central Squares.

what to buy: The Morells' *Shake and Push* 🎵🎵🎵🎵 (Borrowed Records, 1982/East Side Digital, 1989, prod. Morells) is an absolute masterpiece of what was not then called roots rock. Drawing on obscure sources from across the musical spectrum, *Shake and Push* is a rockin' dance floor delight, with lyrics that are smart and funny to boot. Of special note is "Red's," which pays tribute to Route 66's finest roadside diner, and a high-stepping version of the Maddox Brothers & Rose's hilarious "Ugly and Slouchy."

what to buy next: The Skeletons' *In the Flesh!* 🎵🎵🎵🎵 (East Side Digital, 1991, prod. Skeletons) compiles two albums issued during the 1980s on the Scottish label Next Big Thing. Featured numbers include Whitney's brilliant car anthem "Trans Am" and "Thirty Days in the Workhouse," as great a Johnny Cash–style tune as Cash ever wrote himself, plus Thompson's percussive pop gem "Outta My Way" and covers of Little Jimmy Dickens's "I'm Little but I'm Loud" and the Flying Burrito Brothers' "Older Guys."

the rest:
The Skeletons:
Waiting 🎵🎵🎵 (Alias, 1993)
Nothing to Lose 🎵🎵🎵🎵 (HighTone, 1997)

worth searching for: The Skeletons turn in a rockin' Christmas classic by combining "Do You Hear What I Hear?" with the Kinks' "You Really Got Me" on the holiday compilation album *Christmas Party with Eddie G* (Strikin' It Rich/Columbia, 1990, prod. Jeff Rosen).

solo outings:
D. Clinton Thompson (with The Park Central Squares):
Park Central Squares 🎵🎵🎵🎵 (Fabius/Blueberry Hill)

influences:
◀◀ Swingin' Medallions, Arthur Conlee, Moon Mullican, Sonny Bono, Johnny Cash

▶▶ Ben Vaughan, Del Lords, Dave Alvin, Marshall Crenshaw

Daniel Durchholz

Skid Row

Formed 1986, in NJ.

Matt Fallon, vocals (1986–87); Dave "Snake" Sabo, guitar; Scotti Hill, guitar; Rachel Bolan, bass; Rob Affuso, drums; Sebastian Bach (born Sebastian Bierk), vocals (1987–present).

Owing first to Bon Jovi and then to MTV, Skid Row achieved a derivative sort of success. But it didn't last long. Signing Bon Jovi's original guitarist proved to be one of the band's smartest moves, since it earned them an opening berth for Jon and the boys in 1989. After a few hits from the first album—including MTV's embrace of "Youth Gone Wild"—and a lucrative spot opening a tour for Guns N' Roses, the band plummeted into obscurity, making headlines more for Sebastian Bach's homophobic statements and rowdy antics than for any alleged musical gifts.

what to buy: *Skid Row* 🎵🎵 (Atlantic, 1989, prod. Michael Wagener) is the apex of Skid Row's existence, selling four million copies thanks to Bach's more-operatic-than-Bon-Jovi voice and a Guns N' Roses–inspired bad-boy image.

what to buy next: The EP *B-Sides Ourselves* 🎵🎵🎵 (Atlantic, 1992, prod. Skid Row) is the band's most interesting album, playing up its punk fascination with covers of the Ramones' "Psycho Therapy" and Jimi Hendrix's "Little Wing."

what to avoid: By *Subhuman Race* 🎵 (Atlantic, 1995, prod. Randy Staub), the band's commercial health mercifully took a turn for the worse.

the rest:
Slave to the Grind 🎵🎵 (Atlantic, 1991)

influences:
◀◀ Poison, Bon Jovi, Warrant, Mötley Crüe, Guns N' Roses, the Ramones, Jimi Hendrix, the Sex Pistols

▶▶ Ugly Kid Joe, Bush, Alanis Morissette

Tracey Birkenhauer and Steve Knopper

Skinny Puppy

Formed 1983, in Vancouver, British Columbia, Canada. Disbanded 1995.

cEVIN Key, percussion; Nivek Ogre, vocals; Wilhelm Schroeder, keyboards (1985–86); Dwayne Goettel (died August 23, 1995), keyboards (1986–95).

Skinny Puppy was born out of the dark imaginations of cEVIN Key (yes, that's how he spells it) and Nivek Ogre, who discovered that they shared a taste for bizarre, eerie music and films. The band pioneered a brand of industrial music that used electronics and samples to create not only music but also a mood—usually dark and menacing. Sometimes criticized for borrowing too much from forefathers such as Cabaret Voltaire and Throbbing Gristle, Skinny Puppy has nonetheless left its own stamp on terror-industrial/dance music. The group's mix of thunderous percussion, howling vocals, distorted lyrics, and searing electronics resulted in a generally brutal sound that was picked up by such contemporary mainstream bands as Ministry and nine inch nails.

Sebastian Bach of Skid Row (© Ken Settle)

what to buy: *VIVI SectVI* 𝄞𝄞𝄞𝄞 (Nettwerk, 1988, prod. David Ogilvie, cEVIN Key) is the most listenable, danceable, and satisfying of Skinny Puppy's albums—as well as an overtly political record that attacks crimes against humanity, animals, and the world at large. *ain't it dead yet?* 𝄞𝄞𝄞𝄞 (Nettwerk, 1991, prod. David Ogilvie, cEVIN Key) is a live recording of a ferocious 1989 show at the Toronto Concert Hall that was also released on video. The distorted Barbra Streisand samples that open the show are a nice touch. The band ended on a high note with *The Process* 𝄞𝄞𝄞𝄞 (Americana, 1996, prod. David Ogilvie, Skinny Puppy), a furious collection completed just before Dwayne Goettel's untimely death.

what to buy next: *Cleanse Fold and Manipulate* 𝄞𝄞𝄞𝄗 (Nettwerk, 1987, prod. David Ogilvie, cEVIN Key), Skinny Puppy's third full-length release, was the first full realization of the band's horrific sonic assault—the first that actually sounds as scary as they want it to. *Too Dark Park* 𝄞𝄞𝄞 (Nettwerk, 1990, prod. David Ogilvie, cEVIN Key) is a dense, bass-heavy album with a richer sound and lyrics that paint a more dismal than usual vision of an apocalyptic, decaying world. *Rabies* 𝄞𝄞𝄞 (Nettwerk, 1989, prod. David Ogilvie, cEVIN Key, Al Jourgensen) is distinguished only by the powerful presence of Ministry's Al Jourgensen, whose thunderous guitar, angry vocals, and expert production add a bone to its rating.

what to avoid: *Last Rites* 𝄞𝄞 (Nettwerk, 1992, prod. David Ogilvie, cEVIN Key) was recorded just before the band temporarily broke up, and the lack of originality and enthusiasm comes through loud and clear.

the rest:
Bites 𝄞𝄞𝄗 (Nettwerk, 1985)
Mind: The Perpetual Intercourse 𝄞𝄞𝄗 (Nettwerk, 1986)
12 Inch Anthology 𝄞𝄞𝄗 (Nettwerk, 1990)
Brap (Back and Forth, Vols. 3 & 4) 𝄞𝄞𝄞 (Nettwerk, 1996)

influences:
◀◀ Cabaret Voltaire, Chrome, Throbbing Gristle

▶▶ Ministry, nine inch nails, Marilyn Manson

Christopher Scanlon

Skunk Anansie

Formed 1994, in London, England.

Skin (born Deborah Dyer), vocals; Cass Lewis, bass; Ace, guitar; Mark Richardson, drums (1995–present).

Skunk Anansie transforms turn-of-the-century London's multicultural ferment into an explosive world-punk that has many recognizable sources but whose synthesis is like nothing you've ever heard. (That's Skunk Anansie appropriately portraying the band of the future in the sci-fi thriller *Strange Days*.) Skunk's spectrum of styles embraces the tumult of electronica without adopting much of its technology—the working-class quartet's approach is as down-to-earth as its roots, powering experimentation with some of the most direct and energetic rock to emerge in years. The band's acclaim and notoriety is propelled by lead singer Skin (the first known black woman to lead a heavy rock outfit), an exhilarating and truly dangerous persona on the order of Johnny Rotten, Chuck D, and Sinéad O'Connor. Everything's grounded by bassist Cass Lewis's solid syncopation, drummer Mark Richardson's seismic steadiness, and guitar-strangler Ace's alien crunch. Only seemingly indifferent promotion has kept the band from becoming nearly as huge as possible in the age of chart-climbing aggro such as Rage Against the Machine.

what to buy: Unprecedented and unsurpassed, Skunk's debut, *Paranoid and Sunburnt* 𝄞𝄞𝄞𝄞𝄞 (One Little Indian/Epic, 1995, prod. Sylvia Massey, Skunk Anansie), epitomizes both the fleeting fury of youth and the staying power of art. Sounding like a tuneful 747 engine, the band melts down punk, pop, metal, rap, funk, soul, and gospel into a new sonic alloy.

what to buy next: With the acoustic, classical, and Caribbean textures of *Stoosh* 𝄞𝄞𝄞𝄞𝄗 (Epic, 1997, prod. Garth Richardson), the band branches out even further in style and tone, moving from the decade's most bracing post-punk to the shock of the subtle.

influences:
◀◀ Bad Brains, Public Enemy, the Sex Pistols, the Clash, Living Colour, Stevie Wonder

Adam McGovern

Patrick Sky

Born Patrick Lynch, October 2, 1940, in Liveoak Gardens, GA.

The strange and sometimes sordid saga of Patrick Sky can be interpreted in many ways, most obviously as a musical David and Goliath fable, but one thing is without question: unlike countless numbers of his contemporaries in the so-called 1960s "protest movement," when push came to shove, Sky was never once afraid to put his mouth where his harmonica was, nor to risk it all—career, reputation and peace of mind—for songs and stands he truly believed in.

Sky's musical background is not that much different from those of his fellow Greenwich Villagers: disillusioned with what society was offering the college-age man of the era, he found solace and then inspiration as much in the writings of Will Rogers as in the songs of Woody Guthrie, and no less an authority than Dave Van Ronk was soon proclaiming Sky to be "one of the best storytellers I know." His live sets from the time were alternately moving and annoying, witty and scatological, bitter and bittersweet, but never less than memorable, and by the time of his first album release in 1965, he was already becoming a force to be reckoned with in folk music circles. As the decade progressed, and Sky (along with girlfriend Buffy Sainte-Marie) became more involved with issues pertaining to the plight of the Native American, his songwriting became more biting and his performances, now legendary for their unpredictability, less frequent. When he did sing in those days, his shows consisted more and more of a series of songs that were so very confrontational in their lyrical stance that many wondered if the acceptable bounds of satire had somehow been breached. The song titles themselves, "Bake Dat Chicken Pie," "Ramblin' Hunchback," "Vatican Caskets," and "Child Molesting Blues," were enough to frighten away many listeners, to say nothing of the dozen record companies who outright rejected an album's worth of such material recorded during March 1971. Despite a high-profile campaign in *The New York Post* by journalist Al Aronowitz begging for its release, the album languished unheard for two years until it was finally picked up by a small label called Adelphi and unleashed upon an incredulous world under the title *Songs That Made America Famous*. It has since become legendary, as much for its cover art and label design (two butt cheeks proudly pressed flat together in a parody of the Apple Records logo) as for its musical content. Not surprisingly, Sky hasn't been heard from much since, though he remains active in record production (i.e., he supervised Mississippi John Hurt's final sessions) and was given a grant by the Irish government to make aeolian pipes. While there, he happened upon a village pub where the townsfolk gather, every Friday night, to sing *Songs That Made America Famous* in its entirety, word for word and note for note. Vindication is sweet, it seems—even if it is overdue and comes from far, far away.

what to buy: The album that was simultaneously being hailed as "*the* social commentary disc of the decade" and scorned as "a disgrace to the nation" when it was first issued in 1973, *Songs That Made America Famous* 🎵🎵🎵🎵🎵 (Adelphi/GENES, 1997, prod. Alex Bennett, Patrick Sky), sounds no less offensively brilliant today. The daddy of all things politically incorrect, the album proves Sky did much more than simply walk the social-commentary walk when it came to confronting Nixonian America, and he did it with a hearty if suspect smile. Meanwhile, Dylan was shopping for pottery and scoring Peckinpah westerns, just to put things in their proper historical perspective.

what to buy next: His debut disc *Patrick Sky* 🎵🎵 (Vanguard, 1965) is a comparatively meek and mild offering, sweet and competent but, in comparison to what lay ahead, inconsequential. Call it "The Freewheelin' Pat Sky."

worth searching for: Although they're becoming increasingly hard to find, *A Harvest of Gentle Clang* (Vanguard, 1966), *Real-*

ity Is Bad Enough (Verve/Forecast, 1968, prod. Barry Karnfeld), and *Photographs* (Verve/Forecast, 1969) are all worth acquiring as important elements of the overall Sky experience.

influences:

◀◀ Bertolt Brecht, Lenny Bruce, the Marquis de Sade

▶▶ John Butler Train, G.G. Allin, Lenny Molotov

Gary Pig Gold

Sky Cries Mary

Formed 1988, in Paris, France.

Roderick Romero, vocals, drum programming; Anisa Romero, vocals, harmonium, bells, finger cymbals, castanets (1991–present); Jon Auer, guitar, drum programming (1988–89); Ken Stringfellow, bass (1988–89); Ivan Kral, guitar (1990–92); Kevin McCoy, guitar, bass, piano (1990); Marc Olsen, guitar, vocals (1992–93); Michael Cozzi, guitar (1993–present); Joe Howard, bass (1990–93); Juano, bass (1993–present); Gordon Raphael, keyboards, guitar (1991–98); Todd Robbins (a.k.a. DJ Fallout, TR), DJ, drum programming (1991–present); Bennet James, drums, percussion (1990–91); Ben Ireland, drums, percussion (1991–present).

With line-up changes that equal its touring appearance as a band of gypsies, Sky Cries Mary makes slightly pretentious, heavy music that, mysticism aside, is often very original and inspiring. Misnamed for a Hendrix song, this eclectic collective combines DJ/ambient sounds with strong beats and classically inspired rock. Dreamy and swirling, the songs of Sky Cries Mary envelop the listener with a hippie-tinged flow that is ultimately uplifting. The Romeros' vocals, meanwhile, often entwine in a manner that borders on eroticism; also an accomplished artist, Anisa Romero paints much of the group's cover art. Not recommended for those who find "serious" music annoying.

what to buy: The group's varying sound is a bit more reigned in on *Moonbathing on Sleeping Leaves* 🎵🎵🎵 (Warner Bros., 1997, prod. Paul Fox, Sky Cries Mary). An ethereal experience, it's docked a half-bone for occasionally resembling the Moody Blues. The album is best on its louder, more beat-driven numbers; "Deep River" even kinda rocks. Krist Novaselic (Nirvana, Sweet 75) adds acoustic bass to one track.

what to buy next: *A Return to the Inner Experience* 🎵🎵🎵 (World Domination, 1994, prod. Norman Kerner) features covers of the Rolling Stones' "2000 Light Years from Home" and the Stooges' "We Will Fall," along with a remake of the group's own "When the Fear Stops."

the rest:
Exit at the Axis 🎵🎵🎵 (World Domination EP, 1992)
This Timeless Turning 🎵🎵🎵 (World Domination, 1994)
Fresh Fruits for the Liberation 🎵🎵🎵 (World Domination, 1998)

worth searching for: A promotion-only disc, *Moonbathing Remixes EP* (World Domination, 1997, prod. Paul Fox, Sky Cries Mary, others) features five remixes of the title song.

influences:

◀◀ Pink Floyd, Moody Blues, Jefferson Airplane, the Velvet Underground and Nico, Hawkwind, Stevie Nicks, Dead Can Dance, Cocteau Twins

▶▶ Kula Shaker, Cornershop

see also: *The Posies*

Barry M. Prickett

Sky King

See: Poco

Slade

Formed 1966, in Wolverhampton, England.

Noddy Holder, vocals, guitar; Dave Hill, guitar; Jimmy Lea, bass, piano; Don Powell, drums.

Wildly successful in its homeland during the '70s, Slade pulverized cheesy glam rock into tight anthems of simplistic power chords and thumping backbeats. The band's in-your-face approach and Noddy Holder's raw vocals provided an influence for a number of hard and punk rockers that came in its wake. With deliberately misspelled song titles that nodded to its working-class roots, Slade's hits, such as "Cum on Feel the Noize" and "Mama Weer All Crazee Now," became cornerstones of the glam-rock movement and were given second lives when covered by Quiet Riot during the '80s—which allowed Slade an opportunity for its own U.S. hits with "Run Runaway" and "My Oh My."

worth searching for: Inexplicably, nothing remains in print stateside, although Slade continues its trash-rock career across the pond. It's well worth looking for the compilations *Sladest* (Polydor, 1973) and *Keep Your Hands off My Power Supply* (unrated).

influences:

◀◀ New York Dolls, Alice Cooper, the Sweet, Black Sabbath

▶▶ Quiet Riot, Twisted Sister

Allan Orski

Slash's Snakepit

See: Guns N' Roses

Slayer

Formed 1982, in Los Angeles, CA.

Tom Araya, bass, vocals; Jeff Hanneman, guitar; Kerry King, guitar; Dave Lombardo, drums (1982–92); Paul Bostaph, drums (1992–present).

The albums are called *Reign in Blood* and *Hell Awaits*. There are songs with titles such as "Die by the Sword," "The Antichrist," and "Serenity in Murder." Clearly it's not the Carpenters we're talking about here. Slayer is your parent's worst nightmare for the '90s—brutal music, brutal subject matter (death, serial killers, death, Satanism, death), brutal imagery. This is dark, mean, and humorless stuff, played at breakneck speed with the same kind of on-a-dime dynamics practiced by early speed metal scene-mates Metallica and Megadeth. Unlike those bands, however, Slayer has little chance—or desire—of slipping itself into the pop culture mainstream, though its audience remains a sizable, arena-filling cult. Now *that's* scary.

what to buy: For the timid, might we suggest *Haunting the Chapel* 🎵🎵🎵 (Metal Blade EP, 1993), a nugget-sized portion of Slayer music that gives a clear indication of what awaits on the full-length albums. An all-star production team makes *Seasons in the Abyss* 🎵🎵🎵🎵 (Def American, 1990, prod. Rick Rubin, Andy Wallace) Slayer's best-sounding album, with crackling sonics to support the band's aural assault. Rubin came back on board for *Diabolus in Musica* 🎵🎵🎵 (American/Columbia, 1998, prod. Rick Rubin), another sonically superior outing that also flaunts more intricate dynamics and even leaner—but not less aggressive—arrangements.

what to buy next: *Divine Intervention* 🎵🎵🎵 (American, 1994, prod. Slayer) is a slightly—ever so slightly—more accessible outing, with the tempos slowed down just a tad and songs that veer away from the horrific to take on the occasional issue, such as "SS-3"'s indictment of war criminals.

what to avoid: The debut, *Show No Mercy* 🎵🎵 (Metal Blade, 1983/1994, prod. Slayer), is a spirited but not-ready-for-prime-time outing.

the rest:
Live Undead 🎵🎵 (Metal Blade, 1984/1994)
Hell Awaits 🎵🎵 (Metal Blade, 1985/1994)
Reign in Blood 🎵🎵🎵 (Def Jam, 1985)
South of Heaven 🎵🎵🎵 (Def Jam, 1988)
Decade of Aggression Live 🎵🎵 (Def American, 1991)
Undisputed Attitude 🎵🎵🎵 (American, 1996)

worth searching for: The sampler *Metal Massacre III* (Metal Blade, 1983) features Slayer's auspicious debut, "Aggressive Perfector."

influences:

◀◀ Black Sabbath, Deep Purple, the Minutemen

▶▶ Cannibal Corpse, Sepultura, Entombed

Gary Graff

Sleater-Kinney

Formed 1994, in Olympia, WA.

Corin Tucker, vocals, guitar; Carrie Brownstein, guitar, vocals; Misty Farrell, drums (1994); Lora Macfarlane, drums (1994–96); Toni Gogin, drums (1996); Janet Weiss, drums (1996–present).

Had Sleater-Kinney emerged during the '80s, among Hüsker Dü, the Minutemen, and other independent-label punk rockers, its proudly raw albums wouldn't have seemed so out of place. But punk was different during the mid-'90s—it sounded big, polished, ready for major radio play, and Sleater-Kinney's shrieking passion and emotion seemed a refreshing throwback. The trio, which formed around former Heavens to Betsy singer Corin Tucker, former Excuse 17 guitarist Carrie Brownstein, and a progression of drummers, immediately established a distinctively eerie vocal style to go with its aggressive guitars and well-written words and melodies. On one level, Sleater-Kinney sounds angry and prepared not to take any crap, like the riot grrrls it's occasionally been associated with. But the more you listen to Tucker's high-pitched yodel, with Brownstein's clearer voice coming underneath as an anchor, the warmer the sound becomes. Like its punk forebears, the band builds terrific pop songs and subverts them with pointed social commentary. On "Little Babies," one of the band's best songs, the chorus of "dum dum dee dee dee dum dum dee dum do" is as irresistible as any early rock hit, but the words are a critique of supposedly enlightened men who rely too much on their women. Snarls Tucker, as if she can't think of a worse fate than this: "I peeled potatoes, set the table, washed the floor." The band has become a critics' darling surpassed only by Beck; Sleater-Kinney's two best albums, *Call the Doctor* and *Dig Me Out*, hit the Top 3 in the influential *Village Voice* Pazz & Jop poll in 1996 and 1997.

what to buy: *Dig Me Out* 𝄞𝄞𝄞𝄞 (Kill Rock Stars, 1997, prod. John Goodmanson) is both accessible and repellant, which was an apt description of the Sex Pistols, Hüsker Dü, the Pixies, the Jesus and Mary Chain, and Hole. All the songs are great, beginning with the title track, in which Tucker sings about bleeding skin and sores above a fast rhythm section and a jagged guitar line. But once you hit "Little Babies," it will be impossible to proceed to the rest of the CD, because you'll be repeating the song over and over. Just when punk seemed ready to die, Sleater-Kinney's masterpiece gave it life yet again.

what to buy next: "This is love—and you can't make it!" Tucker shouts during the first minute of *Call the Doctor* 𝄞𝄞𝄞𝄞 (Kill Rock Stars, 1996, prod. John Goodmanson, Sleater-Kinney). There's a compelling contradiction of attractive things (a dozen red roses, rock 'n' roll pictures on a bedroom door, a boyfriend, a car) and vicious destruction of same (a heart attack, a hit-and-run, throwing up, "sticky stupid running down my legs").

On the album's best songs, such as "I Wanna Be Joey Ramone"—which sounds nothing like the fun, straightforward Ramones—Sleater-Kinney attacks and soothes at the same time.

the rest:
Sleater-Kinney 𝄞𝄞𝄞 (Chainsaw, 1995)

influences:
◀◀ Hüsker Dü, Babes in Toyland, Hole, the Slits, Replacements, Nirvana, the Sex Pistols, the Jesus & Mary Chain

Steve Knopper

Sleeper

Formed 1993, in London, England.

Louise Wener, vocals, guitar; Jon Stewart, guitar; Diid Osman, bass; Andy McClure, drums.

Louise Wener and Jon Stewart decided to start their own band after meeting at Manchester University. Frustrated with the tight-knit, P.C. attitudes of the local music scene, they moved to London and formed Sleeper—a forum for Wener's outspoken views on feminism and sex, delivered within bright, pop-rock tunes. Although the band was a darling of London's Brit-pop scene, its favor waned as the scene lost its glow toward the end of 1997. Sleeper's 1997 release, *Pleased to Meet You*, was greeted with poor sales and underattended live shows, fueling rumors that Wener might ditch the boys and go solo.

what's available: Sleeper's debut, *Smart* 🦴🦴🦴 (Arista, 1995, prod. Sleeper, Paul Corkett, Ian Broudie), covers the complexities of relationships with a cynical twist. *The It Girl* 🦴🦴🦴🦴 (Arista, 1996, prod. Stephen Street) goes over the same territory, but with lyrics that are more introspective and less cynical and boasting a greater sense of humor.

worth searching for: Having been thoroughly (and inexplicably) trashed by the British press, *Pleased to Meet You* (BMG, 1997, prod. Stephen Street, Cenzo Townsend, Sleeper) was denied a U.S. release. Too bad, because it features some of Wener's most tuneful and developed writing to date, with songs like "You Got Me," "She's a Good Girl," and "Romeo Me" sounding quite reminiscent of the Pretenders circa *Learning to Crawl*. The CD is available as a British import, and a Japanese version purports to offer new tracks in addition to the 13 already here.

influences:

◀◀ The Kinks, the Pretenders, the Replacements, Elvis Costello

▶▶ PJ Harvey, Aimee Mann

Anna Glen and Christopher Scapelliti

Grace Slick

See: Jefferson Airplane, Jefferson Starship

The Slits

Formed 1976, in London, England. Disbanded 1981.

Arri Up, vocals; Palmolive, drums (1976–78); Kate Korus, guitar (1976); Viv Albertine, guitar (1977–81); Tessa Pollit, bass (1977–81); Budgie, drums (1978–79).

In the early days of punk, encouraged by friends like the Clash's Joe Strummer and Mick Jones, the Slits began performing when former Flowers of Romance members Viv Albertine and Tessa Pollit joined with Arri Up—fresh out of German boarding school at the ripe age of 14. Armed with a raucous and chaotic attitude, if no other discernible talent, the Slits played their first gig on the 1977 White Riot tour with the Buzzcocks, Subway Sect, and the Clash. Drummer Palmolive left the group to form the influential band the Raincoats.

what to buy: The dub-influenced *Cut* 🦴🦴🦴🦴 (Antilles, 1979, prod. Dennis Bovell) is surprisingly more sophisticated than anarchic, probably owing more to reggae dubmaster Bovell's production. The album is still probably better known for its cover, with the bandmembers in thongs and covered with mud, than it is for the music, though.

the rest:
In the Beginning 🦴🦴🦴 (Cleopatra, 1997)

influences:

◀◀ The Sex Pistols, the Clash

▶▶ Hole, L7, riot grrls of every stripe

Anna Glen

Sloan

Formed 1991, in Nova Scotia, Canada.

Jay Ferguson, guitars, vocals; Chris Murphy, bass, vocals; Patrick Pentland, guitars, vocals; Andrew Scott, drums, vocals.

Sloan's brand of pop sounds at times like a science experiment gone wrong and at other times so sugary-sweet it makes your molars ache. Either way you can't go wrong. This Great White North foursome has released three full-length albums and an EP, and while perfectly accessible guitar pop is Sloan's game, the buying public hasn't quite played along. Lost in the Geffen Records' power-packed early '90s roster (Nirvana, Guns N' Roses, Counting Crows), Sloan's slow sales ended its brief American major label experience.

what to buy: The band sounds absolutely liberated on *One Chord to Another* 🦴🦴🦴🦴 (Murderecords, 1996, prod. Sloan), a work of exuberant pop and mature style that renders everything else in its catalog almost irrelevant. Sloan takes listeners on a musical trip through decades of pop music from the Who-sounding "Anyone Whose Anyone" to the almost Chicago-styled "Everything You've Done Wrong."

what to buy next: *Navy Blues* 🦴🦴🦴🦴 (Murderecords, 1998, prod. Sloan, Daryl Smith) should almost be called *One Chord to Another, Part 2*, because the similarities are just incredible. The songs just keep getting better and better, from the *White Album*–sounding "Sinking Ships" to the classic Sloan-sounding, and incredibly clever, "She Says What She Means."

the rest:
Peppermint 🦴🦴🦴 (Murder EP, 1992)
Smeared 🦴🦴🦴 (Geffen, 1992)
Twice Removed 🦴🦴🦴🦴 (Geffen, 1994)

worth searching for: Be on the lookout for the limited issue of *One Chord to Another* (The Enclave, 1997, prod. Sloan), issued in the U.S. in 1997 with an extra disc of live covers.

influences:

◀◀ The Beatles, the Who, Sonic Youth

▶▶ Thrush Hermit, Super Friendz, Johan

Chris Richards

P.F. Sloan

Born September 18, 1945, in Kew Gardens, Queens, NY.

One of the music business' most successful bottom-feeders ever, Phil "P.F." Sloan's career began with a series of nondescript singles released, to zero acclaim, in the New York area during the very early '60s. He relocated to Los Angeles in 1963 and teamed with Steve Barri, the two becoming staff writers for the Trousdale Music Company, churning out upwards of 35 demos a week for, most notably, Johnny Rivers, Jan & Dean, the Turtles, and Herman's Hermits. Sloan and Barri also released dozens of their own novelty records under such names as the Rally Packs, Lifeguards, Street Cleaners, and Willie & the Wheels. But it was not until the duo decided to turn their sights on the burgeoning "protest music" market that they struck paydirt big-time, with the ridiculous sub-Dylan pastiche "Eve of Destruction" (a #1 hit for Barry McGuire in 1965). It was then that Sloan began pursuing his *own* recording career again, filling two entire albums with similarly earnest yet misguided Top 40 sloganeering. When these too sank without a trace, Sloan returned to New York, apparently taking up residence in the infamous Chelsea Hotel alongside Nico, Lou Reed, and other hep Warholians. (Keep in mind, however, that P.F. also claims to have produced "Paint It, Black" for the Rolling Stones, gotten the Beatles their first American record deal, and been taught his first guitar chords in a music store by Elvis Presley.) Valiant stabs at flower power ("Sunflower, Sunflower"), raga-rock ("Karma: A Study of Divinations") and R&B-lite (his 1968 *Measure of Pleasure* LP) failed to produce anything meaningful in the way of royalties, relegating Sloan to the Where Are They Now file until a recent "comeback" album titled—wouldn't you just know it—*(Still on The) Eve of Destruction*.

what's available: If you've ever wondered what John Lennon meant by there being an immense distinction between a songwriter and a song *craftsman*, cue up any of the 18 tracks on *Anthology* 🎵🎵🎵 (One Way, 1993, compilation prod. Terry Wachsmuth). Sure, Sloan concocted his fair share of catchy tunes back in the Swinging '60s, but Tiny Tim did "Eve of Destruction" best.

the rest:

The Fantastic Baggys:

Tell 'Em I'm Surfin' 🎵🎵🎵 (Imperial, 1964/EMI America, 1992)

The Rincon Surfside Band:

The Surfing Song Book 🎵🎵 (Dunhill, 1965/Varese Vintage, 1994)

influences:

◄◄ Bobby Darin, Brian Wilson, Paul Simon, Lou Adler

►► Lou Reed, Tom Goodkind, Jon Tiven, the Spokesmen

see also: *The Grass Roots*

Gary Pig Gold

Slowburn

See: Kyuss

Slowdive
/Mojave 3

Formed 1989, in Reading, Britain.

Slowdive (1989–94): Rachel Goswell, vocals, guitar; Nick Chaplin, bass; Neil Halstead, vocals, guitar; Ian McCutcheon, drums (1994–present); Christian Saville, guitar; Simon Scott, drums (1989–94). Mojave 3 (1995–present): Rachel Goswell, vocals, guitar; Neil Halstead, vocals, guitar; Ian McCutcheon, drums.

Started as a noise-tinged My Bloody Valentine/Sonic Youth clone by school friends Neil Halstead and Rachel Goswell, Slowdive did not take long to evolve into its own wondrous entity. Taking the inventive aesthetics of its progenitors, Slowdive quickly gained acclaim in Britain as a moving force of the so-called dream-pop pack, alongside bands such as Chapterhouse, Ride, and the Pale Saints. When the fickle British audience cooled to that sound, however, Slowdive took a dive, trying in vain to re-invent itself as an ambient outfit. The group fizzled to an end, while Halstead, Goswell, and drummer Ian McCutcheon breathed new life into their music-making in the new band Mojave 3.

what to buy: Slowdive's debut album, *Just for a Day* 🎵🎵🎵🎵 (Creation/SBK, 1991, prod. Chris Hufford, Neil Halstead), was the definitive dreampop record, channeling droning guitars, lush melodies, and velvety textures into an astral musical mix.

what to buy next: Mojave 3's debut, *Ask Me Tomorrow* 🎵🎵🎵 (4AD, 1996, prod. Paul Tipler, Mojave 3), casts away Slowdive's daydreaming ways in favor of stirring up the sum and substance of languid pop greats such as Neil Young, Leonard Cohen, and Lee Hazelwood.

what to avoid: The U.K.-only *Pygmalion* 🎵🎵 (Creation, 1994, prod. Slowdive) is a tired and bleary album that got the band dropped from its record label.

the rest:

Slowdive:

Souvlaki 🎵🎵🎵 (Creation/SBK, 1994)

influences:

◄◄ Cocteau Twins, My Bloody Valentine, the Byrds

►► Chapterhouse, Garbage, Seefeel

Aidin Vaziri

Sly & the Family Stone

Formed 1967, in San Francisco, CA.

Sly Stone (born Sylvester Stewart), keyboards, guitar, vocals; Freddie Stone, guitar, vocals; Larry Graham, bass, vocals (1967–72); Rosie

Stone, keyboards, vocals; Greg Errico, drums (1967–72); Jerry Martini, saxophone; Cynthia Robinson, trumpet.

Sly Stone dragged black music into the modern era. He bridged the worlds of traditional R&B and the new '60s rock sound with a dazzling amalgam of rock, soul, and gospel, and music was never the same again. By the time Sly and his Family Stone burst onto the radio with the 1968 hit, "Dance to the Music," the bandleader had already amassed an extraordinary background in music. His recording career dates back to a childhood 78 rpm gospel record he made with his family, the Stewart Family Four, and he notched a regional doo-wop hit before he was out of high school in Vallejo, California. As a disc jockey, he was the fastest talking, jivingest spieler on two Bay Area soul stations. As a house producer for San Francisco–based Autumn Records, he supervised hit records by Bobby Freeman ("C'mon and Swim"), the Beau Brummels ("Laugh Laugh"), and an assortment of lesser-knowns such as the Great Society, which featured a young, pre-Airplane Grace Slick. But with the Family Stone—the rich, throbbing thump-and-pluck bass of Larry Graham, colorful contrapuntal vocal harmonies, and sassy, brassy, downright uppity sloganeering songs—Sly led his band to the mountain of Woodstock and beyond before succumbing to massive drug abuse and titanic flights of ego. One of the most talented musicians to ever tackle the soul scene, Stone himself was reduced to a cocaine-ravaged wraith, a fugitive from justice for several years during the late '80s and into the '90s. But his vast influence becomes only more pervasive as the years pass.

what to buy: The band's fourth album, *Stand!* 🎵🎵🎵🎵 (Epic, 1969, prod. Sly Stone), remains Stone's towering achievement, an album by turns militant ("Don't Call Me Nigger, Whitey"), paranoid ("Somebody's Watching You"), and inspirational ("Everyday People," "You Can Make It If You Try").

what to buy next: Although the band's record label has done an abysmal job of introducing the Family Stone's full body of work to the digital domain, the unheralded first three albums— *A Whole New Thing* 🎵🎵🎵 (Epic, 1967/Legacy 1995, prod. Sly Stone), *Life* 🎵🎵🎵 (Epic 1968/Legacy, 1995), and *Dance to the Music* 🎵🎵🎵 (Epic, 1968/Legacy, 1995, prod. Sly Stone)—have been made available with previously unreleased bonus tracks. His epic, angry, and sarcastic masterpiece, *There's a Riot Goin' On* 🎵🎵🎵🎵 (Epic, 1971/1990, prod. Sylvester Stewart), is a snarling diatribe that presaged his downfall.

the rest:
Greatest Hits 🎵🎵🎵🎵 (Epic, 1970)
Fresh 🎵🎵🎵🎵 (Epic, 1973/Legacy, 1991)
Anthology 🎵🎵🎵🎵 (Epic, 1981/1989)

worth searching for: A collection of largely unreleased Autumn Records solo recordings and productions, *Precious Stone: In the Studio with Sly Stone 1963–1965* (Ace, 1994, prod. Sly Stone) was released in England. In used record stores, it is still possible to find the Billy Preston album, *The Wildest Organ in Town* (Capitol, 1966, prod. Steve Douglas), with Sly playing piano and the original version of what later became the Sly & the Family Stone standard, "I Want to Take You Higher."

solo outings:
Larry Graham/Graham Central Station:
Graham Central Station 🎵🎵🎵 (Warner Bros., 1973/O' Skool, 1996)
Release Yourself 🎵🎵 (Warner Bros., 1974/Ol' Skool, 1975)
Ain't No Doubt about It (Warner Bros., 1975/Ol' Skool, 1997)
The Best of Larry Graham and Graham Central Station . . . Vol. 1 🎵🎵🎵 (Warner Bros., 1996)

influences:
◀◀ Otis Redding, Lenny Bruce, Swan Silvertones

▶▶ Temptations, Stevie Wonder, Miles Davis, Graham Central Station, Funkadelic, Prince, Red Hot Chili Peppers

Joel Selvin

Small Faces
See: The Faces

Smash Mouth
Formed 1994, in San Jose, CA.

Steve Harwell, vocals; Greg Camp, guitars; Paul De Lisle, bass; Kevin Coleman, drums.

The beginnings of Smash Mouth, whose hit "Walkin' on the Sun" was unavoidable to any MTV watcher or radio listener throughout 1997, can be traced back to when Steve Harwell and Kevin Coleman were junior high school kids jamming to Van Halen. Influenced by '80s metal, the two formed a garage band; Harwell, who had previously formed the rap band F.O.S. but had a Scotti Bros. record deal fall apart, returned home to call on Coleman. Harwell's manager hooked up the pair with Greg Camp and, by association, Camp's former bandmate Paul De Lisle. As Smash Mouth, the band recorded a demo in Camp's apartment and impressed producer Eric Valentine, who had turned knobs for Third Eye Blind and Steve Vai. The band went in the studio with Valentine and produced a two-song demo including "Nervous in the Alley." Although Smash Mouth didn't have a deal, "Nervous in the Alley" found its way into regular rotation on radio station KOME. Before long, the band had signed a lucrative contract with Interscope Records, recorded *Fush Yu Mang*, and began flogging its hit everywhere from clubs to opening spots on U2's PopMart tour.

what's available: *Fush Yu Mang* 🎵🎵 (Interscope, 1997, prod. Eric Valentine) is a hybrid of ska, punk, and speed metal, although Smash Mouth's music falls flat despite attempts at humor. "Beer Goggles" tells the worn-out story of drunken sex. With a title like "The Fonz" you'd think the band had a winner, but with its "Wild Things" and "Walk like a Man" samples and uninspired lyrics, it's a dud. Within the haze of punk and ska music, though, comes a gem: the psychedelic '60s-flavored "Walkin' on the Sun," a brilliant use of samples and quick, short drum beats that makes you want to do the swim.

influences:

◀◀ Mighty Mighty Bosstones, Rancid

Christina Fuoco

Smashing Pumpkins

Formed 1989, in Chicago, IL.

Billy Corgan, vocals, guitar; James Iha, guitar; D'arcy Wretzky, bass, vocals; Jimmy Chamberlin, drums (1989–96).

The Smashing Pumpkins were among the first groups to dive through the alternative-rock portal Nirvana opened during the early '90s. Then, after Kurt Cobain died and Nirvana broke up, the Pumpkins found themselves de facto leaders of a popular youth culture hungry for loud guitars and unhappy anthems. In his songs, singer-songwriter Billy Corgan sometimes whines like a spoiled brat and other times screeches in an exhilarating complement to James Iha's grunge noise. Racked with personal problems almost from the beginning—most notably over Corgan's tight-fisted control and Jimmy Chamberlin's reported drug use—the Pumpkins held together and wound up co-headlining the third Lollapalooza tour. The Technicolor videos for "Today" and "Cherub Rock" resulted in smash hits and shot 1993's *Siamese Dream* album well past platinum. For an encore, Corgan drew from such reviled rock sources as Emerson, Lake & Palmer and Boston to come up with a double-disc concept album titled *Melon Collie and the Infinite Sadness*. Despite a couple of irritating art-rock indulgences, including a concept about a boy growing up, the songs "Bullet and Butterfly Wings" (with its memorable "despite all my rage, I am still just a rat in a cage" chorus) and "1979" were forceful and strong. But in July 1996, near the start of the band's North American tour to support the album, touring keyboardist Jonathan Melvoin died after an alleged heroin overdose in his New York City hotel room. Shortly thereafter, the band fired drummer Chamberlin, who had been in the same room and was arrested for heroin possession. The band, employing members of the Frogs and other underground bands, has continued to tour and speak out against drugs in general (and Chamberlin specifically) in high-profile magazine interviews.

what to buy: *Siamese Dream* 𝄞𝄞𝄞𝄞 (Virgin, 1993, prod. Butch Vig, Billy Corgan) is the (sometimes overwrought) sound of a maniac shrieking his discontent to the sound of sympathetic grunge guitars. When Corgan sings, "Today is the greatest day I've ever

WHAT ALBUM CHANGED YOUR LIFE?

Recently, that Radiohead album, *OK Computer,* really changed the way I think about songwriting. Anything goes [with] us, anyway, but after listening to that record, I thought really, *really* anything goes. I couldn't believe it, how insanely it was produced. Some of the songs don't have any structure to them. That's great.

Greg Camp (of Smash Mouth)

known," you wonder if maybe he just murdered or ate somebody. *Melon Collie and the Infinite Sadness* 𝄞𝄞𝄞 (Virgin, 1995, prod. Flood, Alan Moulder, Billy Corgan) is irritating only if you can't stand "concept albums" in any form; otherwise, it's a decent record with lots of angst and Corgan believably shrieking that he's a rat in a cage. It's also the biggest-selling double-CD of all time.

what to buy next: *Gish* 𝄞𝄞𝄞 (Caroline, 1991/Virgin, 1994, prod. Butch Vig) is a good record, but its '60s garage-band sound gave few hints that the Pumpkins would turn to '70s hard- and art-rock for later inspiration.

what to avoid: The Pumpkins, and Corgan in particular, have an arrogant streak and occasionally foist much crappy rare tracks and minutiae onto their fans. The most blatant attempt to cash in on this was the five-disc box set *Aeroplane Flies High* 𝄞𝄞 (Virgin, 1996), which has a few interesting tracks but nothing to merit the collection's far-too-high price.

the rest:

Pisces Iscariot 𝄞𝄞𝄞 (Virgin, 1994)
Adore 𝄞𝄞𝄞 (Virgin, 1998)

worth searching for: The Pumpkins, like R.E.M. and Bruce Springsteen, are generous about doling outtakes and obscure studio experiments to their fans. Among the best of these are *Zero* (Virgin EP, 1995) and *Tonight, Tonight* (Virgin EP, 1996), two CD singles loaded with extra tracks that didn't appear on *Melon Collie.*

Billy Corgan of Smashing Pumpkins (© Ken Settle)

solo outings:

James Iha:

Let It Come Down ✗✗✗ (Virgin, 1998)

influences:

◀◀ Nirvana, Black Sabbath, Kiss, Boston, Pixies, Velvet Underground, Cheap Trick, Soundgarden

▶▶ Bush, Sponge, Alanis Morissette, Dig, Tripping Daisy, silverchair, Stone Temple Pilots

Steve Knopper

Curtis Smith

See: Tears for Fears

Darden Smith

Born March 11, 1962, in Brenham, TX.

A veteran of the fertile early '80s Austin scene that also spawned Lyle Lovett and Nanci Griffith, Darden Smith is a pop craftsman with a folksinger's eye for detail and ear for the truth. In concert, he can be both elegant and electrifying, prefacing his songs with wry parables and often jumping offstage to serenade fans row by row. That rousing attitude translates to his uplifting music, which evokes a reflective, philosophical warmth that is poetic but never preachy, gung-ho but rarely giddy in his quest for true love and redemption.

what to buy: Hometown fans rightly revere *Native Soil* ✗✗✗ (Watermelon, 1986, prod. Darden Smith, Larry Seyer) for touching country-folk vignettes such as "Two Dollar Novels" and "Painter's Song," as well as for harmony help from Griffith and Lovett. But Smith's most affecting hybrid of farm-boy dreams and city-boy polish is *Trouble No More* ✗✗✗ (Columbia, 1990, prod. Darden Smith, Martin Lascelles, Pete Anderson), which utilizes gospel, country, folk, and pop as disarmingly bouncy backdrops for touching narratives about everything from heel-clicking lovers ("Frankie and Sue") to disillusioned Vietnam vets ("Johnny Was a Lucky One").

the rest:

Darden Smith ✗✗✗ (Epic, 1988)

(With Boo Hewerdine) *Evidence* ✗✗✗✗ (Compass, 1989)

Little Victories ✗✗ (Chaos/Columbia, 1993)

Deep Fantastic Blue ✗✗✗ (Plump, 1996)

influences:

◀◀ Bruce Cockburn, Townes Van Zandt, Robert Earl Keen

▶▶ Boo Hewerdine, Hal Ketchum

David Okamoto

Elliott Smith

Born 1969, in Dallas, TX.

Singer-songwriter Elliott Smith epitomizes the Portland sound. Originally part of the hard-rocking band Heatmiser, which broke up in 1996, Smith began performing his own material—slow, acoustic, and, like the city he calls home, somewhat depressing. In 1997, Portland filmmaker Gus Van Sant tapped him to write music for the Academy Award–nominated *Good Will Hunting,* including "Miss Misery," for which Smith was nominated for an Oscar, too. Although he didn't take home a statue, there was nothing quite like seeing the indie rocker taking a bow with fellow nominees Celine Dion on one arm and Trisha Yearwood on the other.

what to buy: *Either/Or* ✗✗✗✗ (Kill Rock Stars, 1997, prod. Elliott Smith) doesn't actually stand out all that much from Smith's other solo albums—actually, all of them are good. But this record cements the fact that even though Smith's singing voice is sometimes not much more than a nasal whine, you still pull for him and believe in what he's saying.

what to buy next: It's worth picking up *Good Will Hunting* ✗✗✗ (Capitol, 1997, prod. various) just to hear "Miss Misery." The rest of Smith's songs are also strong, but you'll find yourself amazed that Hollywood, so full of bloated budgets and special effects, would embrace this simple, sweet song.

the rest:

Roman Candle ✗✗✗ (Cavity Search, 1994)

Elliott Smith ✗✗✗✗ (Kill Rock Stars, 1995)

XO ✗✗✗ (DreamWorks, 1998)

Heatmiser:

Dead Air ✗✗✗ (Frontier, 1993)

Cop and Speeder ✗✗✗ (Frontier, 1994)

Mic City Sons ✗✗✗✗ (Caroline, 1996)

influences:

◀◀ Art Garfunkel, Cat Stevens

▶▶ Pete Krebs

Anders Wright

Huey "Piano" Smith

Born October 10, 1924, in New Orleans, LA.

Huey "Piano" Smith's best records were group-sung nonsense songs that sounded as if they were recorded at a New Orleans rent party. Smith's first hit, the oft-covered "Rockin' Pneumonia and the Boogie Woogie Flu" in 1957, showcases all the best elements of his sound: a loping second-line rhythm, half-chanted vocals, good-humored, funny lyrics, and a superb rolling piano. Before Smith began his solo career, he played in

Patti Smith (© Ken Settle)

Lloyd Price's and Earl King's road bands, and worked on recording sessions for such notables as Smiley Lewis and Little Richard (who can only play in one key). In 1955, Smith played piano on one of Ace Records' first hits, Earl King's "Those Lonely Lonely Nights." Various incarnations of Smith's band, the Clowns, featured some of the best musicians (Lee Allen, Alvin Tyler, Robert Parker, Mac Rebennack/Dr. John) in the New Orleans area. Smith supplemented his erratic singing with a series of vocalists (the great Bobby Marchan, Bobby Roosevelt, Gerry Hall, Eugene Francis, Junior Gordon, and Roland Cook, among others), and they gave his records a sense of good-humored variety. After "Rockin' Pneumonia" in 1957, Smith and the Clowns hit the pop Top 10 in 1958 with the two-sided smash "Don't You Just Know It" b/w "High Blood Pressure." Their follow-up, "Don't You Know Yockomo," was every bit as entertaining and danceable, but a lesser hit (perhaps it was too funny). Smith wrote inventive lyrics, but he continually reprised his musical arrangements from his big hits. On LP, this method is a bit tedious, but in the days of the 45 rpm single, this repetition just seemed like a periodic continuation of the last recorded party. When he wasn't touring, Smith and his band did session work behind Jimmy Clanton and Frankie Ford (whose hits "Sea Cruise" and "Roberta" were actually Huey Smith tracks with Smith's vocals erased). During the late '60s, Smith tried to retool his sound for the soul generation, and he recorded for a variety of labels under the names Shindig Smith & the Soul Shakers, the Pitter Pats, and the Hueys. Smith's last chart entry was "Coo Coo over You" for the Cotillion label in 1968. During the 1970s, Smith became a Jehovah's Witness, and he seldom plays music anymore. Don't you just know it?

what to buy: *Rock 'n' Roll Revival* ♪♪♪♪ (Ace, 1991, prod. Johnny Vincent) has all the big hits ("Rockin' Pneumonia," "High Blood Pressure," "Don't You Just Know It") and others, plus two previously unreleased tracks. Frankie Ford and Bobby Marchan guest.

what to buy next: *Good Ole Rock 'n' Roll* ♪♪♪♪ (Ace, 1991, prod. Johnny Vincent) contains 16 non-hit tracks, showcasing some fine New Orleans–style party music including "Educated Fool," "Won't You Turn Me On," and "At the Mardi Gras."

what to avoid: *Huey "Piano" Smith & Friends* ♪♪ (Charly, 1987, prod. various) features several '60s soul-style remakes of Smith's hits from the '50s. The original recordings are still the best.

the rest:
Pitta Pattin' ♪♪♪ (Charly, 1988)
Snag-A-Tooth Jeannie ♪♪▽ (Night Train, 1996)

worth searching for: *Serious Clownin'—The Best of Huey Piano Smith* (Rhino, 1989, prod. Johnny Vincent) is a 14-track

WHAT ALBUM CHANGED YOUR LIFE?

Every single Bob Dylan album did something for me—*Highway 61 Revisited, Blonde on Blonde,* all of them. I think each one of his records gave me what I needed at the time, especially in the '60s. I can't tell you exactly what 'Desolation Row' meant or what he meant in 'Like a Rolling Stone,' but it didn't matter. Bob Dylan just had a way of speaking for you; I felt less estranged, less like a stranger in the world.

Patti Smith

compilation of quality. It's out of print, but some stores still have it on their stock lists if you prefer vinyl.

influences:
◄◄ Earl King, Professor Longhair
►► Frankie Ford, Bobby Marchan, Dr. John

Ken Burke

Kendra Smith
See: Dream Syndicate

Patti Smith
/Patti Smith Group

Patti Smith born 1946, in Chicago, IL. Patti Smith Group formed 1976, in New York, NY. Disbanded 1979.

Patti Smith, vocals, guitar; Lenny Kaye, guitar, bass, vocals; Ivan Kral, bass, guitar, vocals; Richard Sohl (died June 3, 1990, in Long Island, NY), keyboards; Bruce Brody, keyboards (1978); Jay Dee Daugherty, drums.

Like the great rock poets before her, Patti Smith writes music that is defiantly original and emotionally raw; what makes her stand out from the meager pack is her bare aggression. Smith was already an established poet, playwright, and music critic when she entered New York's underground music scene during the mid-'70s. In short course, she became the underground's figurehead, and her trademarks—poetic ramblings, vocal wailings, and sonic distortion—became the sound of the movement. With its passionate rage, rudimentary musicianship, and audio verite production, Smith's 1975 debut album, *Horses*, established the protocol that punk music would follow when it emerged two years later. Ironically, Smith and her band (galvanized on subsequent albums as the Patti Smith Group) had tightened up their performances and expanded their sonic palette by the time punk came along. Although Smith served to inspire the likes of Michael Stipe and U2, her own band eventually peaked out. In 1979 she took a lengthy sabbatical and settled in suburban Detroit to raise a family with ex-MC5 guitarist Fred "Sonic" Smith, who died in 1995. Her recent albums show a more resolved and peaceful artist at work. But the music, as always, comes from the heart and hits you right in the gut. In 1996, Arista released re-mastered versions of Smith's albums, filled out with bonus tracks.

what to buy: Smith's debut album, *Horses* ♫♫♫♫ (Arista, 1995, prod. John Cale), is required listening for anyone interested in her music—or in the evolution of rock music into the genres of punk and grunge. From the album's opening refrain ("Jesus died for somebody's sins, but not mine"), Smith creates an edgy and disconcerting standoff between artistic expression and listener expectations that's troubling even today. Tracks such as "Redondo Beach" and "Free Money" still stand up quite nicely. Her second effort, *Radio Ethiopia* ♫♫♫♫ (Arista, 1976, prod. Jack Douglas), hits a palatable balance between the idiosyncrasies of *Horses* and her later, more commercialized releases. The band is tighter, the arrangements are strong and the songs—in particular "Ask the Angels," "Pumping (My Heart)," "Poppies," and "Distant Fingers"—show how quickly Smith made the leap from punk poet to accomplished songwriter.

what to buy next: The union of Patti Smith Group and rock producer Jimmy Iovine resulted in *Easter* ♫♫♫ (Arista, 1978, prod. Jimmy Iovine), a swaggering rock album that only begins to border on strident overconfidence. Although songs such as "Till Victory," "Ghost Dance," and "We Three" rehash some of the group's earlier (and better) efforts, the album earns high points for the gorgeous Top 20 hit "Because the Night" (co-written with Bruce Springsteen).

what to avoid: If it's hard to imagine a boring Patti Smith album, take a listen to *Wave* ♫ (Arista, 1979, prod. Todd Rundgren). The band sounds dispirited, and Rundgren's production is a loathsome distraction. While "Frederick" and "Dancing Barefoot" are among the best songs Smith has written, the rest

of the material suggests her passion had shifted from her art to her marriage.

the rest:
Dream of Life ♫♫♫ (Arista, 1988)
Gone Again ♫♫♫ (Arista, 1996)
The Patti Smith Masters: The Collective Works ♫♫♫♫ (Arista, 1996)
Peace & Noise ♫♫♫ (Arista, 1997)

worth searching for: *Live in Paris* (Golden Stars-Italy, 1978) is a well-recorded bootleg that presents the Patti Smith Group in peak form. In addition to offering a wealth of the band's best cuts—"Ask the Angels," "Till Victory," "Because the Night"—the CD tacks on three *Horses*-era television performances from *The Mike Douglas Show* along with a 1978 performance of "I Was Working Real Hard" from NBC's *The Today Show*.

influences:

◀◀ Bob Dylan, the Rolling Stones, the Velvet Underground, Nico, the Doors, Jimi Hendrix, Joni Mitchell, Leonard Cohen, Plastic Ono Band, Iggy & the Stooges

▶▶ Lou Reed, John Cale, Iggy Pop, Television, Bruce Springsteen, the Pretenders, Marianne Faithfull, R.E.M., the Sugarcubes, Björk, Nirvana, Hole, PJ Harvey, Liz Phair, Alanis Morissette, Yoko Ono

Christopher Scapelliti

The Smithereens

Formed 1980, in Carteret, NJ.

Pat DiNizio, guitar, vocals; Jim Babjak, guitar, vocals; Dennis Diken, drums, vocals; Mike Mesaros, bass, vocals.

The Smithereens play latter-day British Invasion pop with a decidedly American garage band edge. While it's not hard to pick out the Beatles and Kinks references in their tunes, the Smithereens can also roar with the force of the Stooges. That effortless balance of noise and melody makes the group one of America's best post-punk outfits, though the mass audience seems to have noticed only on all-too-rare occasions.

what to buy: *Especially for You* ♫♫♫♫ (Enigma, 1986, prod. Don Dixon) contains the brooding-pop gems "Blood and Roses" and "Behind the Wall of Sleep." *Blown to Smithereens: The Best of the Smithereens* ♫♫♫♫ (Capitol, 1995, prod. various) shows what a great singles band the group is with an absolutely awesome parade of should-have-been radio smashes.

what to buy next: *Green Thoughts* ♫♫♫ (Capitol, 1988, prod. Don Dixon) is the band's second full-length LP, filled with near-perfect downer pop tunes such as "Only a Memory" and "Drown in My Own Tears."

the rest:
Beauty and Sadness 𝄢𝄢𝄢 (Enigma EP, 1983)
Smithereens Live 𝄢𝄢𝄢 (Restless EP, 1987)
11 𝄢𝄢𝄢 (Capitol, 1990)
Blow Up 𝄢𝄢𝄢𝄢 (Capitol, 1991)
Date with the Smithereens 𝄢𝄢𝄢 (RCA, 1994)

worth searching for: The British CD-5 for "Top of the Pops" (Capitol, 1991, prod. various) includes covers of "One after 909," "Shakin' All Over," and the *MTV Unplugged* version of the hit "A Girl like You."

solo outings:
Pat DiNizio:
Songs and Sounds 𝄢𝄢𝄢 (Velvel, 1997)

influences:
◀◀ The Beatles, the Kinks, the Beach Boys, the Hollies, Black Sabbath

▶▶ Better Than Ezra, Weezer, Muzzle

Thor Christensen

The Smiths

Formed 1983, in Manchester, England. Disbanded 1987.

Morrissey (born Stephen Patrick Morrissey), vocals; Johnny Marr (born John Maher), guitar; Andy Rourke, bass; Mike Joyce, drums; Craig Gannon, guitar (1985–87).

The Smiths excelled in bucking trends. While the rest of England was infatuated with new-wave synthesizer pop and other transient movements at the outset of the '80s, the Smiths came along with a more traditional guitar sound that seemed eerily out of place. But their songs, bolstered by Johnny Marr's exquisite guitar playing and Morrissey's sharp lyrics, were so enchanting that the group didn't really need to fit in. Embracing poetry and a sound reminiscent of '60s beat groups, the Smiths laid the groundwork for modern alternative rock. Morrissey's contemplative lyrics brought the group a die-hard cluster of fans who connected with his tales of torment and loneliness. In its four years together, the group released an abundance of original material in various formats, all of it consistently solid, breaking up just prior to the release of its last album, *Strangeways Here We Come.* Morrissey went on to a fruitful solo career, while Marr played with The The, Bryan Ferry, and the Pretenders before making Electronic—originally a side project for him and New Order's Bernard Sumner—a full-time endeavor. Andy Rourke and Mike Joyce joined Sinéad O'Connor's band, and Joyce later sat in with the reunited Buzzcocks.

what to buy: *The Queen Is Dead* 𝄢𝄢𝄢𝄢𝄢 (Sire, 1986, prod. John Porter, Johnny Marr, Morrissey) represents the Smiths' artistic peak, blending an impeccable set of songs with Morrissey's ex-

ceptional wit and Marr's most accomplished guitar playing. Its highlights include "The Boy with the Thorn in His Side" and the stirring "There Is a Light That Never Goes Out." The Smiths' first two albums, *The Smiths* 𝄢𝄢𝄢𝄢𝄢 (Sire, 1984, prod. John Porter) and *Hatful of Hollow* 𝄢𝄢𝄢𝄢𝄢 (Rough Trade, 1984, John Porter), are important because they capture the group as it develops its sound—a heady mix of Byrdsy jangle, gritty glam, and old school British pop—along with seminal songs such as "How Soon Is Now?," "This Charming Man," and "Hand in Glove."

what to buy next: You really can't go wrong with the two-part Smiths greatest hits collections, *Best . . . I* 𝄢𝄢𝄢𝄢 (Sire, 1992, prod. various) and *Best . . . II* 𝄢𝄢𝄢𝄢 (Sire, 1992, prod. various). While not as cohesive as the group's proper albums, they are great testaments to the Smiths' fantastic vision.

what to avoid: *Rank* 𝄢𝄢 (Sire, 1988, prod. Pete Dauncey) is a posthumous live release recorded a bit too late to capture the Smiths in peak form.

the rest:
Hatful of Hollow 𝄢𝄢𝄢𝄢 (Rough Trade, 1984/Sire, 1993)
Meat Is Murder 𝄢𝄢𝄢𝄢 (Sire, 1985)
Louder Than Bombs 𝄢𝄢𝄢𝄢 (Sire, 1987)
Strangeways Here We Come 𝄢𝄢𝄢 (Sire, 1987)
Singles 𝄢𝄢𝄢𝄢 (Sire, 1995)

worth searching for: The Japanese EP for "This Charming Man" (WEA, 1992, prod. various) includes seven surprisingly decent versions of the song plus the B-sides from the song's original 1983 release.

influences:
◀◀ David Bowie, Roxy Music, New York Dolls

▶▶ Jeff Buckley, Ride, the Sundays

see also: *Electronic, Morrissey, New Order, The The*

Aidin Vaziri

Smoking Popes

Formed 1989, in Crystal Lake, IL.

Josh Caterer, vocals and guitar; Eli Caterer, guitar; Matt Caterer, bass; Mike Felumlee, drums.

The Popes—three brothers and a neighbor—emerged as part of a thriving punk scene in the Chicago suburbs, playing in basements for friends and graduating to sold-out shows at rock clubs long before they had a record deal. The quartet blends the sound of two Johnnys: Ramone and—believe it or not—Mathis. While his bandmates pump out driving three-minute pop-punk, Josh Caterer croons lovestruck lyrics that acknowledge a debt to the saloon singers and country weepers in his parents' record collection; an un-ironic version of Willie Nelson's "Angel Flying Too Close to the Ground" was a standard part of the Popes' live set for years.

what to buy: *Destination Failure* 🎜🎜🎜🎜 (Capitol, 1997, prod. Jerry Finn) blends classic pop-punk ("Before I'm Gone") with a nod to Anthony Newley ("Pure Imagination")—no kiddin'. Want bratty attitude with your punk? Get a Green Day record. The Popes specialize in revved-up, ultra-sincere love songs.

what to buy next: *Born to Quit* 🎜🎜🎜 (Capitol, 1995, prod. Phil Bonnet) is a reissue of the band's second independent release. It's over in 28 punk-rock minutes, but its 10 songs—especially "Rubella," "Gotta Know Right Now," and the minor hit "Need You Around"—will stick with you for weeks.

worth searching for: *Get Fired* (Johann's Face, 1993, prod. Smoking Popes, Mass Giorgini), the Popes' full-length debut, is nearly as addictive as "Born to Quit"; it includes the original version of "Let's Hear It for Love," later re-recorded on *Destination Failure.*

influences:

◄◄ The Ramones, the Buzzcocks, Willie Nelson, Johnny Mathis

Greg Kot

Patty Smyth /Scandal

Born June 26, 1957, in New York, NY.

Patty Smyth, vocals; Zachary Smith, guitar; Keith Mack, guitar; Ivan Elias, bass; Frankie LaRocca, drums (1982–83); Thommy Price, drums (1983–84).

Built around the core of Patty Smyth and Zachary Smith, and with studio musicians augmenting the group, Scandal rode a video showcasing Smyth's girl-next-door good looks into the middle of the charts with "Goodbye to You," one of the earliest MTV-propelled hits, in 1982. It made the debut EP Columbia's best-seller in that format, ironically conceived as a way of selling less commercial music (such as the Clash) in a cheaper package. Frankie LaRocca left for an A&R position, and the group fell apart after releasing its only full-length album. Smyth went on to a more successful solo career, though one that seems built around her relationships. In the mid-'80s, Smyth married rocker Richard Hell (imagine: "Darling, I'd like you to meet Mrs. Hell . . . ") and had a daughter with him; during the mid-'90s she set up house-keeping with tennis star John McEnroe and sometimes sang in his ad-hoc performances (he plays guitar; one jam included fellow tennis pro Jim Courier on drums). Through it all, her un-abashed pop style has offered catchy nuggets, with her voice—and a native New Yorker's don't-mess-with-me attitude—carrying the less memorable moments.

what to buy: *Patty Smyth* 🎜🎜🎜 (MCA, 1992, prod. Roy Bittan) was a hit on the strength of the anthemic #2 smash "Sometimes Love Just Ain't Enough," a duet with Don Henley that, like several other tracks here, Smyth co-wrote with gun-for-hire and onetime Styx member Glen Burtnik. Springsteen keyboardist Roy Bittan, who also plays on the album, fortunately can't smooth the rough edges off Smyth's voice, but he polishes everything else—though some numbers ("My Town") have a tougher impact and "River of Love" is darn near funky.

what to buy next: The five-song EP *Scandal* 🎜🎜🎜 (Columbia, 1982, prod. Vini Poncia) contained two hits, "Goodbye to You" and "Love's Got a Line on You." Smyth's *Never Enough* 🎜🎜🎜 (Columbia, 1987, prod. Rick Chertoff, William Wittman) contains an effective version of Tom Waits's "Downtown Train" (three years before Rod Stewart covered it). As with many Chertoff productions, Hooters Rob Hyman and Eric Bazilian have songwriting input and play extensively. Some of the synthesizer sounds here are dated, but guitar riffs power most of the refrains.

the rest:
Scandal:
The Warrior 🎜🎜🎜 (Columbia, 1984)

influences:

◄◄ Pat Benatar, Bonnie Raitt

►► Sheryl Crow, Alanis Morissette, Joan Osborne, Magnapop, Garbage

Steve Holtje

Sneaker Pimps

Formed 1995, in Manchester, England.

Kelli Dayton, vocals; Chris Corner, guitar; Liam Howe, keyboards.

Childhood pals Liam Howe and Chris Corner started working together in 1992, first calling themselves F.R.I.S.K. and then Line of Flight. A few years later, they heard Kelli Dayton singing in a pub, asked her to join them, and the Sneaker Pimps were born. With the release of *Becoming X*, the trio's impressive 1996 debut, the genre of trip-hop received a significant kick in the pants. Adding fairly aggressive guitar parts to the more orderly beats of British trip-hop, the group snagged a sizable share of the limelight, scoring big early in 1997 with the CD's sensuous hit single, "6 Underground." Later in the year, an orchestra-and-vibes-enhanced remix of the song also garnered some airplay. Unfortunately, that cut was one of the few highlights on *Becoming Remixed*, a collection of largely irritating and repetitive club mixes. At this point, the world awaits a true second album.

what to buy: Rather than feature a signature sonic approach, as the albums of fellow trip-hoppers Portishead have, *Becoming X* 🎜🎜🎜🎜 (Clean Up/Virgin, 1996, prod. Line of Flight) finds the Sneaker Pimps mixing and matching sounds according to the demands of individual songs. The result, while not always right on target, is often fresh, and certainly dynamic.

the rest:

Becoming Remixed ♫♫ (Clean Up/Virgin, 1998)

influences:

◀◀ Portishead, Tricky, Massive Attack, Garbage, John Barry

▶▶ Mono, Air, Lamb

Bob Remstein

The Sneakers

Formed late 1970s, in Chapel Hill, NC.

Mitch Easter, guitars, vocals, bass, drums, keyboards; Chris Stamey, vocals, guitars, keyboards; Will Rigby, drums; Robert Keely, bass.

The Sneakers were the power-pop brainchild of Chris Stamey and Will Rigby, the eventual duo at the heart of the great dB's, plus guest-star Mitch Easter, who went on to form Let's Active and produce R.E.M. (Another eventual R.E.M. producer, Don Dixon, was the Sneakers' prominent engineer.) The band put out two influential releases during the mid-'70s, then moved on to more prominent projects. Easter and Stamey reunited during the early '90s to remix old tracks for a new CD, *Racket*, and dug up unreleased songs as well. They also spontaneously re-recorded several songs—which proved to be quite an amazing feat, given that hearing the pair sing together again was every jangle-pop fan's dream come true. From a historic point of view, *Racket* contains some of the earliest pop music from the important Chapel Hill, North Carolina, power-pop scene.

what to buy: *Racket* ♫♫♫♫ (East Side Digital, 1992, prod. Mitch Easter) contains the Sneakers' entire recorded output. The songs sound like they were recorded during the heydays of both the dB's and Let's Active, from the opening guitar riff of "Decline and Fall" to the simple beauty of "S'il Vous Plait." A campy but incredibly rare radio jingle sung by Mitch Easter is one of the previously unreleased tracks thrown in as a bonus.

worth searching for: The Sneakers' original LPs, including the EP *Sneakers* (Carnivorous, 1976, prod. Don Dixon) and *In the Red* (Car, 1978, prod. Don Dixon), include classics such as "Love's Like a Cuban Crisis" and a superb version of Bo Diddley's "Roadrunner," respectively. Both are out of print.

influences:

◀◀ The Beatles, Led Zeppelin

▶▶ The Windbreakers, R.E.M.

see also: *The dB's, Let's Active, Don Dixon*

Chris Richards

WHat aLBUM CHaNGeD YOUr LiFe?

I was gonna be in ninth grade. The summer between eighth and ninth grade, music and girls and all that kind of comes at once. That summer, there was this kid from the college who needed a place to stay, and he moved in with our family. He broke out Lynyrd Skynyrd's *One More from the Road,* the live record. About six months later I had my entire bedroom covered with pictures of this one band, and I had all their records. I think that's maybe when I first realized I loved music more than I think my dad thought was healthy.

Todd Snider

Todd Snider

Born October 11, 1966, in Portland, OR.

One of the freshest voices on the alternative country scene, Todd Snider successfully mixes Dylanesque wordplay, Springsteen and Mellencamp populism, and Steve Earle's renegade country rock. He's a bit of an uncomfortable fit for Nashville, since he has no trouble occasionally tweaking the Religious Right, and, in "I Believe In," goes even farther than Garth Brooks–sanctioned tolerance ("I believe in gangsta rap, gays, and geeks, and ghosts"). Snider is an adept storyteller, a moralist with a sense of humor and a ragged-but-right vocalist. Accordingly, Snider has followed Lyle Lovett away from MCA's Nashville office to their pop division. A talent to watch, for sure.

what to buy: True to its title, Snider's debut, *Songs for the Daily Planet* ♫♫♫♫ (Margaritaville/MCA, 1994, prod. Tony Brown, Michael Utley), reads like dispatches from the newspaper of a modern Metropolis. The sardonic "My Generation (Part 2)" tweaks Generation X with a laundry list of its flash-in-the-pan iconography. "Easy Money" details a scam artist's dealings over a brassy R&B backing. On the serious side, the tempestuous rocker "This Land Is Our Land" offers the Native American spin on the white man's idea of progress. But lest he get too deep, Snider offers "Alright Guy," perhaps the ultimate "What? Me worry?" anthem. The album may be rough around the edges, but that's part and parcel of Snider's considerable charm.

the rest:
Step Right Up ☾☾☾☿ (Margaritaville/MCA, 1996)
Viva Satellite ☾☾☾☿ (MCA, 1998)

worth searching for: Snider portrays a naive hitchhiker in the radio play–style audio version of Hunter Thompson's classic gonzo journalism screed, *Fear and Loathing in Las Vegas* (Margaritaville/Island, 1996, prod. Laila Nabulsi). He also wrote and performed incidental music for the production.

influences:
⏮ Bruce Springsteen, Bob Dylan, John Mellencamp, Steve Earle

Daniel Durchholz

Phoebe Snow
Born July 17, 1952, in New York, NY.

The purity of Phoebe Snow's instrument has always been disarming. A rich contralto with versatility of nearly limitless proportions, she has never been properly established as the major talent she is. The problem has always been where and how to house her fluid chops. Similarly, poor production, nasty label relations, and her own decision (albeit admirable) to provide home-care for her autistic daughter have seriously hampered her commercial viability. From her jazzy-folk beginnings in the '70s all the way up to her solid return in 1989, Snow has been an undeniable talent in search of worthy surroundings. After a long dry spell, Snow returned to recording in 1998 through a deal with the House of Blues label.

what to buy: *Phoebe Snow* ☾☾☾☾ (Shelter-A&M, 1974/Right Stuff, 1995, prod. Dino Airali) is an auspicious coffeehouse folk debut that reveals an emotional assuredness underneath her considerable vocal range. It contains her biggest hit, "Poetry Man," as well as the gutsy "Harpo's Blues" and an interesting cover of Sam Cooke's "Good Times."

what to buy next: Snow's emotional urgency on the title track alone makes *Something Real* ☾☾☾ (Elektra, 1989, prod. Rob Fraboni, Ricky Fataar) cost-effective. Overall, the album's tone is surprisingly relaxed, given that this was her first recording in eight years. Elektra apparently expected desperation and dropped her quick.

what to avoid: Snow is clearly not a singles-churning hit machine, making brief best-of efforts such as *The Best of Phoebe*

Snow ☾☾☾ (Columbia, 1981, prod. Phil Ramone) a bit shortsighted and unrevealing.

the rest:
Second Childhood ☾☾☾ (Columbia, 1976/1988)
It Looks Like Snow ☾☾☾ (Columbia, 1976/1989)
Never Letting Go ☾☾☾ (Columbia, 1977/1990)
I Can't Complain ☾☾☾☿ (House of Blues, 1998)

worth searching for: *Against the Grain* (Columbia, 1978) is a bit slick, but has a good version of Paul McCartney's "Every Night." On *Rock Away* (Mirage/Atlantic, 1981) Snow tries her hand at rock, covering everything from Rod Stewart's "Gasoline Alley" to Bob Dylan's "I Believe in You."

influences:
⏮ Sarah Vaughan, Bob Dylan, Paul Simon, Joan Baez, Judy Collins, Joni Mitchell

⏭ Dionne Farris, Tracy Chapman

Allan Orski

Jill Sobule
Born January 16, 1959, in Denver, CO.

Jill Sobule, whose family is full of storied characters (for example, the grandfather who was a Jack Dempsey sparring partner), got an electric guitar when she was in the sixth grade and within a year was composing her own songs. While in college she began busking in Spain and dropped out to continue at a long-term gig there. She developed a fine eye for telling details, but her first album, on which she sang serious relationship songs, went nowhere, and her follow-up album, produced by Joe Jackson, was rejected by MCA and never issued. It wasn't until she communicated her scenarios with humor that she broke through. Aided by its trendy, stripped-down production, "I Kissed a Girl" garnered attention not only through its subject but also by being catchy and full of wit. But Sobule was dropped by Atlantic after *Happy Town*, which opens with "Bitter," the lyrics of which say "And the one who made it/made it 'cuz her breasts were really big," a comment widely perceived as a swipe at labelmate Jewel. While label-less, Sobule became lead guitarist in Lloyd Cole's band.

what to buy: *Jill Sobule* ☾☾☾ (Lava/Atlantic, 1995, prod. Brad Jones, Robin Eaton) contains not only "I Kissed a Girl" but also the hilarious "Good Person Inside." After Sobule's "Supermodel" from the soundtrack to *Clueless* got radio play, it was added to her album. Despite Sobule's girlish voice and the wacky persona and lightweight pop emphasized on this album, she's a keen observer of idiosyncracy and irony, so this is more than a few funny songs.

what to buy next: *Happy Town* 🎵🎵🎵 (Lava/Atlantic, 1997, prod. Brad Jones, Robin Eaton) is less effervescent than its predecessor, and certainly does seem bitter at times, but still contains some good material. *Things Here Are Different* 🎵🎵🎵 (MCA, 1990, prod. Todd Rundgren) includes some fine songs ("Sad Beauty," "So Kind") but lacks the goofy humor that fans of her later hits might be looking for.

what to avoid: Used-bin cruisers should be careful not to buy the early version of *Jill Sobule* that doesn't include "Supermodel."

influences:
◀◀ Cyndi Lauper

Steve Holtje

Social Distortion

Formed 1979, in Fullerton, CA.

Mike Ness, vocals, guitar; Dennis Danell, guitar; Brent Liles, bass (1979–88); Derek O'Brien, vocals, drums (1979–88); Chris Reece, drums (1988–96); Chuck Biscuits, drums (1996–present); John Maurer, bass (1988–present).

Mike Ness and his rebel-rock pals, like so many suburban Los Angeles teens in the late '70s, picked up guitars and learned how to rock with them. At first, they rehashed Clash-Sex Pistols-X chords with youthful exuberance. Then they hit a creative wall until Ness discovered country music and figured out how to write good songs. By 1990, the tattooed, Elvis-haircutted Ness was heavily into Johnny Cash and making music (with the Mekons, among others) that predated the country-punk fusion that led indirectly to Uncle Tupelo, Wilco, and Son Volt. A couple of early '90s college-radio hits gave Social D. a spot opening for Neil Young and Sonic Youth in a high-profile arena tour, and Ness's skills steadily improved after that.

what to buy: *Social Distortion* 🎵🎵🎵🎵 (Epic, 1990, prod. Dave Jerden) has a killer version of Cash's "Ring of Fire" plus the enduring college-radio hits "Ball and Chain" and "Story of My Life." The debut *Mommy's Little Monster* 🎵🎵🎵🎵 (Time Bomb, 1982, prod. Chaz Ramirez, Social Distortion) is all smash and thrash, and the nine songs are over before you know it.

what to buy next: *Somewhere between Heaven and Hell* 🎵🎵🎵 (Epic, 1992, prod. Dave Jerden) sacrifices some of Social Distortion's sloppy firepower but adds a nice dimension of lonely-loser country music.

the rest:
Prison Bound 🎵🎵 (Sticky Fingers, 1988)
White Light, White Heat, White Trash 🎵🎵🎵 (Epic, 1996)
Live at the Roxy 🎵🎵🎵 (Time Bomb, 1998)

worth searching for: The promotional CD for the single "Story of My Life" (Epic, 1990) includes two versions of the track plus four energetic live recordings.

influences:
◀◀ The Ramones, X, Avengers, Johnny Cash, Carl Perkins
▶▶ Jason & the Scorchers, Uncle Tupelo, Wilco, Son Volt

Steve Knopper

The Soft Boys

Formed 1976, in Cambridge, England. Disbanded 1981.

Robyn Hitchcock, vocals, guitar; Alan Davies, guitar, vocals (1976–77); Kimberley Rew, guitar, vocals (1977–81); Morris Windsor, drums, vocals; Andy Metcalfe, bass, vocals (1976–79); Matthew Seligman, bass, vocals (1979–81).

Formed in the midst of a folk boom in Cambridge (that immediately preceded punk and new wave), the Soft Boys featured the surreal and psychedelic songwriting of Robyn Hitchcock (twin muses: Syd Barrett and Bob Dylan) and the blazing guitar prowess of Kimberly Rew (who went on to Katrina & the Waves, among others). It was not an altogether happy marriage of sensibilities and was certainly commercially unrewarding—not to mention utterly out of step with the surrounding music scene by the time their records finally came out. The Soft Boys' discography is filled with mysterious singles, EPs, repackages, live fan club cassettes, and other oddments.

what to buy: *Underwater Moonlight* 🎵🎵🎵🎵 (Armageddon, 1980/Rykodisc, 1992, prod. Pat Collier) was the Soft Boys' last gasp. The band was in trouble, knew it, and agreed simply to cooperate long enough to make one good record before calling it a day. Instead, they managed a minor masterpiece. Recorded for 600 British pounds on the fly, it includes such pop classics as "I Wanna Destroy You," "Kingdom of Love," and the title track.

what to buy next: The course of least resistance leads to the two-disc compilation *The Soft Boys 1976–81* 🎵🎵🎵🎵 (Rykodisc, 1993), which neatly compiles an assortment of tracks from the Soft Boys' three long-players, rarities, unreleased tracks, obscurities, etc. It's a cagey enough collection—and Hitchcock's songwriting is strong enough—to make for a fine summary.

what to avoid: Why would you want to?

the rest:
A Can of Bees 🎵🎵🎵 (Two Crabs, 1979/Rykodisc, 1992)
Invisible Hits 🎵🎵🎵 (Armageddon, 1983/Rykodisc, 1992)

worth searching for: Nah, leave the rest of 'em be. If Hitchcock didn't put tracks on the Ryko reissues, there's probably a good reason.

influences:

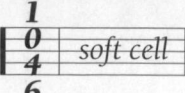 John Lennon, Syd Barrett, Bob Dylan

▶▶ Robyn Hitchcock & the Egyptians, Katrina & the Waves, R.E.M.

see also: *Robyn Hitchcock*

Grant Alden

Soft Cell
/Marc Almond

Formed 1979, in Leeds, England. Disbanded 1984.

Marc Almond, vocals, keyboards; Dave Ball, synthesizers.

Very few outside observers ever realized just how sexually twisted Marc Almond was. Soft Cell is best known for the now irritatingly common "Tainted Love"—still one of the best-selling singles ever in the U.S. and England. However, Soft Cell's perversions go far beyond the odd cover tune that's plagued the world for almost two decades. Almond, as lead singer and lyricist for the band, seems to take great pleasure in mixing as many sexual metaphors as possible, and often leaving very little to the imagination. His overt femme attitude made Soft Cell the idols of the underground scene during the '80s, all the while counting only "Tainted Love" as a brush with commercial success. With numerous EPs and re-mix releases to its credit, Soft Cell's discography seems somewhat lengthy, as the band only released two proper albums before parting ways in 1984. Those two albums, however, managed to set the trend for the U.K.'s Some Bizarre Records, with "Tainted Love" footing the bill for numerous other ground-breaking acts (including Depeche Mode, The The, Cabaret Voltaire, the Swans, and many other influential acts of the British indie scene). Most Some Bizarre releases were similiar in their twisted, albeit accessible, styles. Not too dissimilar from the fashionable labels of the era like Factory (Joy Division, New Order), 4AD (Cocteau Twins, Dead Can Dance), Beggars Banquet (Cult, Bauhaus), and Mute (Depeche Mode, Erasure), you always had a good idea of what a Some Bizarre release was about without ever hearing it—they were that consistent. Writing Soft Cell off as a one-hit wonder, then, is presumptuous. While "Tainted Love" is representative of the band's sound, it's not all it was capable of. The band did create some amazingly entertaining music, at least lyrically, and while most of its songs are simple, catchy synth tunes, peeling away the layers reveals some very erotic, almost perverse imagery. One hidden gem in the Soft Cell repertoire was the inclusion of the Vicious Pink Phenomenon, a group Almond discovered, for backing vocals on Soft Cell's first album. Later known simply as Vicious Pink, the band scored numerous club hits on its own with blatantly sexual lyrics and grinding pseudo-indus-

trial dance beats. Once the duo split, Dave Ball was relagated to, well, an apt comparison would be Andrew Ridgley to George Michael. Almond, on the other hand, has had a prolific solo career, releasing more than half a dozen full-length albums, some meeting with critical praise and commercial success. Best known for the shiny pop song "Tears Run Rings" from *Stars We Are*, Almond continued his pursuit for almost show tune–style performances and cabaret textures, all the while inserting as much sexual energy as possible. While many of his own releases incorporated sex regularly, it's his uncredited appearances with other artists that reveal the madman behind the curtain and show the true depths of depravity that Almond wallows in. A good portion of Almond's solo efforts have been reissued by Thirsty Ear Records in the last two years. He has performed under the monikers Marc & the Mambas and Marc Almond & the Willing Sinners in addition to his solo material.

what to buy: *Non-Stop Erotic Cabaret* 🎵🎵🎵🎵 (Sire, 1981/Pendulum, 1996, prod. Mike Thorne) frankly makes for good dancing music and can also set the romantic mood with the strong sexual innuendo of the lyrics. It contains the crispy "Tainted Love" and not-to-be missed-classic "Sex Dwarf." For Marc Almond, *Treasure Box* 🎵🎵🎵 (Thirsty Ear, 1995, prod. various) covers the basics and then some. The only downside is that some odd remixed versions of songs were included, not as bonus tracks, but in lieu of the originals. Many of the remixes don't stand up to the originals and seem to be afterthoughts. However, it covers Almond's solo career throughly and is worth the investment.

what to buy next: *Memorabilia: The Singles* 🎵🎵🎵 (Phongram–Some Bizarre, 1986/Polydor, 1991, prod. various) highlights the best of the band's past. In an odd twist, the later domestic release features several additional tracks, remixes, and an excellent version of "Sex Dwarf," which was not included on the original import. From Almond's repertoire, the painfully romantic *Stars We Are* 🎵🎵🎵 (Capitol, 1986, prod. Marc Almond) is a fine listen through and through. While a bit precious at times, and a tad overly effeminate, it's fun and emotive, and half the songs harken back to Soft Cell's best work. It's torch songs with a Depeche Mode twist.

what to avoid: *This Last Night in Sodom* 🎵🎵 (Sire, 1984, prod. various) was the last Soft Cell album and does little more than revisit previously encountered themes and melodies.

worth searching for: Released as an import only, try to hunt down Almond's collaboration with Jim "Foetus" Thirwell under the name Flesh Volcano. The union resulted in a 12-inch single called "Slut" that is as lyrically twisted and musically harsh as a release from this pairing would suggest.

solo outings:
Marc Almond:

Mother Fist . . . and Her Five Daughters 🎵🎵🎵 (Some Bizarre, 1987/
Thirsty Ear, 1997)
Jacques 🎵🎵🎵 (Some Bizarre, 1989/Thirsty Ear, 1996)
Enchanted 🎵🎵🎵 (Capitol, 1990)
Tenement Symphony 🎵🎵🎵 (Sire, 1991)
A Virgin's Tale 🎵🎵🎵 (Thirsty Ear, 1998)
Violent Silence/A Woman's Story 🎵🎵 (Thirsty Ear, 1998)

Marc & the Mambas:
Untitled 🎵🎵🎵 (Some Bizarre, 1983)
Torment and Toreros 🎵🎵 (Some Bizarre, 1983)

Marc Almond & the Willing Sinners:
Vermine in Ermine 🎵🎵🎵 (Some Bizarre)
Stories of Johnny 🎵🎵🎵🎵 (Some Bizarre, 1984/Thirsty Ear, 1997)

influences:

◄◄ Cabaret music, torch songs, Depeche Mode, Yaz, Alison
Moyet

►► Culture Club, Jeff Buckley, Ke, Human League, Alphaville

Tim Davis

Soft Machine
Formed 1966, in Canterbury, England.

**Mike Ratledge, keyboards (1966–76); Robert Wyatt, drums, vocals
(1966–71); Kevin Ayers, guitar, vocals, bass (1966–69); David Allen,
guitar, vocals (1966–67); Hugh Hopper, bass, guitar (1968–73). Other
members: Larry Nolan, guitar; Elton Dean, saxophone; Marc Charig,
trumpet; Nick Evans, trombones; Lyn Dobson, flute, saxophone; Rob
Spall, violin; Phil Howard, drums; John Marshall, drums; Karl Jenkins,
saxophone, keyboards; Roy Babbington, bass; Allan Holdsworth, guitar; John Etheridge, guitar; Alan Wakeman, saxophone; Steve Cook,
bass; Jack Bruce, bass, vocals; Dick Morrissey, saxophone; Alan
Parker, guitar; Ray Warleigh, saxophone; Dave Macrae, keyboards.**

The Soft Machine was a band to catch in its early days, since
the band's revolving door was spinning from the get-go. Before
the self-titled debut, original guitarist David Allen had left to
form the trippy, evolving group Gong. After the first album, vocalist and bassist Kevin Ayers quit, taking with him a fine sense
of absurd humor. At least vocalist-drummer Robert Wyatt hung
around for a few years, though it would be keyboardist Mike
Ratledge whose vision would guide the band longer than any
of his cohorts. Blending snippets of pop, jazz, rock, and just
plain weirdness throughout its career, Soft Machine offered
sonic adventure with every new bar of notes—which delighted
bolder listeners and confused the more timid. In that way, Soft
Machine's constantly in-flux lineup works to the group's benefit, bringing new ideas into a system that can't wait to try them.

what to buy: Saxophonist Elton Dean, trumpeter Marc Charig,
flutist/saxophonist Lyn Dobson, and violinist Rob Spall joined

for *Third* 🎵🎵🎵🎵🎵 (Columbia, 1970/1991), a double album with
one composition per side—well before Yes came forth with
Tales from Topographic Oceans. Wyatt's equally ethereal and
dramatic composition "Moon in June" is a must for any serious
popular music collection.

what to buy next: *The Soft Machine* 🎵🎵🎵🎵🎵 (Probe, 1968/One
Way, 1993) and *The Soft Machine, Volume Two* 🎵🎵🎵🎵🎵 (Columbia, 1969/One Way, 1993) each boast quirky charm and a fistful
of music styles to create floating, *Alice in Wonderland*–style
pastiches.

what to avoid: *Fifth* 🎵🎵 (Columbia, 1972/One Way, 1993), *Sixth*
🎵🎵 (Columbia, 1973/One Way, 1995), and *Seventh* 🎵🎵🎵 (Columbia, 1974/One Way, 1995) are burdened by uncommitted, journeyman musicians, and they pale against the ground-breaking
Third.

the rest:
Fourth 🎵🎵 (Columbia, 1971/One Way, 1993)
Land of Cockayne 🎵🎵🎵 (EMI, 1981/One Way, 1996)
Peel Sessions 🎵🎵🎵🎵 (Dutch East India, 1991)
BBC Live 🎵🎵🎵🎵 (Windsong, 1993)
Live in France 🎵🎵🎵 (One Way, 1995)
Live at the Paradiso 🎵🎵🎵 (Blueprint, 1996)
Spaced 🎵🎵🎵 (Cuneiform, 1996)
Virtually N/A (Cuneiform, 1998)
Rubber Riff N/A (Blueprint, 1998)

worth searching for: *The Soft Machine* and *Volume Two* are
combined on a single two-fer CD, *Soft Machine I & II* (Big Beat,
1989), making for some wonderful, uninterrupted listening.

influences:

◄◄ Pink Floyd, Miles Davis, Ornette Coleman

►► Sting, Kansas, Steely Dan

see also: *Kevin Ayers, Robert Wyatt*

Patrick McCarty

Solomon Grundy
See: Screaming Trees

The Someloves /DM3
Someloves formed 1985. Disbanded 1991. DM3 formed 1992.

**Someloves: Dom Mariani, vocals, guitar; Darryl Mather, guitar; Rob-
bie Scorer, drums; Tony Italiano, bass, vocals, guitar; Mitch Easter,
guitar, keyboards, tambourine. DM3: Dom Mariani, vocals, guitar;
Pascal Bartolone, drums, percussion; Tony Italiano, bass, keyboards.**

Australian post-punk figure Dom Mariani veered from the pop-
sweetened garage rock of the Stems to the garage-cleaned

power-pop of the Someloves, which began as a studio band existing concurrently with the Stems. Currently, he purveys the slightly rawer tunefulness of DM3.

what to buy: The Someloves' *Something or Other* ✍✍✍✍ (White Label, 1989, prod. Mitch Easter, John Villani, the Someloves) is a rock-melody tour de force. Sharing the songwriting burden with Darryl Mather (late of the Lime Spiders), the band comes up with something (or other) that the Plimsouls' younger brothers might have concocted. "Melt," "Back on Side with You," "Girl Soul," and most of the others match prettiness and grittiness in just the right proportions. *One Time, Two Times, Three Red Light* ✍✍✍✍ (Citadel, 1989, prod. DM3) bodes well for Mariani's new band and carries on the Someloves' turbo-charged pop. Songs like "Foolish" are anything but.

what to buy next: *Road to Rome* ✍✍✍ (Citadel, 1996, prod. Mitch Easter, DM3) is almost as good as DM3's debut, but a perfect song like "Second Floor" really rises above most of the others. *Dig It the Most* ✍✍✍ (Bomp!, 1997, prod. Mitch Easter, DM3), the only DM3 album in print in America, is a collection of tracks from both imports, plus various alternate versions.

worth searching for: A slew of import CD and vinyl singles exist by both the Someloves and DM3, usually pairing up an album track with live versions, cover tunes (including the Plimsouls' "Zero Hour"), and B-sides. The Someloves' long-out-of-print *Sunshine's Glove* EP has some exclusive studio recordings that are among its purest pop.

influences:

◀◀ The Plimsouls, the Shoes, Paul Collins's Beat

Jordan Oakes

Jimmy Somerville /Bronski Beat /Communards

Born June 22, 1961, in Glasgow, Scotland. Bronski Beat formed 1982. Disbanded 1986. Communards formed 1985. Disbanded 1987.

Bronski Beat: Jimmy Somerville, vocals (1982–85); Steve Bronski, keyboards, percussion; Larry Steinbachek, keyboards, percussion; John Jon Foster, vocals (1985–86). Communards: Jimmy Somerville, vocals; Richard Coles, keyboards.

Although Boy George, Morrissey, the Pet Shop Boys, and Frankie Goes to Hollywood each struck musical blows on behalf of gay rights in England during the 1980s, none made as extreme an impact as the voice of Jimmy Somerville, original lead singer of Bronski Beat, co-leader of the Communards, and, finally, a successful solo artist. When the singles "Smalltown Boy" and "Why?" pounded dance floors in 1984, nothing had existed to compare with his piercing, yet not quite unpleasant,

falsetto voice—except perhaps an operatic countertenor. By 1985, he had left Bronski Beat to form the Communards; he had (along with Billy Bragg and Paul Weller, among others) become an active part of the socialist Red Wedge movement that was sweeping Britain at the time, and though politics didn't play a direct role in the group's music, he was clearly developing his art. In 1990, he put out his first solo album, and it expressed an even wider musical scope. His hitmaking days may be over at this point, but his sonic and stylistic influence cannot be overstated. His voice and genre may not be for all tastes, but without him, dance-club music would be very different.

what to buy: Somerville's career retrospective *The Singles Collection, 1984–90* ✍✍✍✍ (FFRR/London, 1990, prod. various) offers nearly everything you could possibly want, including wistful Bronski Beat hits such as "Why?" and "Smalltown Boy," plenty of Communards cuts (especially the furious dance remake of "Never Can Say Goodbye"), and five from his first solo disc, *Read My Lips*.

what to buy next: Although most of the best cuts from *Read My Lips* ✍✍✍✍ (London, 1990, prod. Jimmy Somerville, Pascal Gabriel, Stephen Hague) are contained on *The Singles Collection*, *Lips* features quite a stylistic range and makes for an impressive listening experience on its own.

what to avoid: More than 10 years after Bronski Beat first astonished the dance-pop scene with its hyper-trebliness, Somerville's *Dare to Love* ✍✍✍ (London, 1995, prod. various) sounds behind the times. He's a pro, and his voice is as cutting as ever, but the new songs just don't measure up.

the rest:
Bronski Beat:
The Age of Consent ✍✍✍✍ (MCA, 1984)
Truthdare Doubledare ✍✍✍ (MCA, 1986)

Communards:
Communards ✍✍ (MCA, 1986)
Red ✍✍✍✍ (MCA, 1987)

influences:

◀◀ Donna Summer, Giorgio Moroder, Thelma Houston, Alison Moyet, Q-Feel

▶▶ Cece Peniston, Cathy Dennis

Bob Remstein

Son Volt

Formed 1994, along the Mississippi River.

Jay Farrar, vocals, guitar; Jim Boquist, bass, vocals; Mike Heidorn, drums; Dave Boquist, guitar, fiddle, banjo, lap steel.

After splitting from Uncle Tupelo in 1994, Jay Farrar formed Son Volt, which, in terms of the bandmembers' hometowns, must be as equitable a representation of middle-America as exists in a rock 'n' roll band. While putting the group together, Farrar lived in New Orleans (he's since moved to St. Louis); Heidorn, Tupelo's original drummer, continues to live in that band's initial home base of Belleville, Illinois; the Boquist brothers, meanwhile, call Minneapolis home. Farrar's material for Son Volt doesn't stray far from the formula he created while in Tupelo—alternately fast and slow songs with richly poetic (if sometimes puzzling) lyrics and an engaging, finely textured acoustic/electric instrumental attack. But that's okay. Over the course of the band's two albums, you get the feeling that Farrar has found a place where he's comfortable but not altogether settled with his music, and that it's a good place to be—for him and for listeners alike.

what to buy: Farrar wrote the songs for *Trace* ✺✺✺✺ (Warner Bros., 1995, prod. Brian Paulson, Son Volt) during long, searching sojourns up and down the highways along the Mississippi River, and the album accurately reflects the countryside that inspired it. Though lyrically obtuse, Farrar's tunes hit home hard, particularly the hard-country/folk numbers "Windfall" and "Tear Stained Eye," and the slashing rockers "Drown" and "Loose String." Next to one of Tupelo's own near-masterpieces, *Trace* is perhaps the finest album the so-called "alternative country" movement has yet produced.

what to buy next: Though not a step backwards, the group's sophomore album *Straightaways* ✺✺✺✺ (Warner Bros., 1997, prod. Brian Paulson, Son Volt) has a slight feel of attempting to maintain the status quo, which is only a problem if, like Son Volt, you set the bar so high on your debut. Still, songs like "Caryatid Easy" and "Cemetery Savior" offer lyrical intrigue, and the music—particularly the multi-instrumental contributions of Dave Boquist—is terrific.

the rest:
Wide Swing Tremelo ✺✺✺✺ (Warner Bros., 1998)

influences:
◀◀ Merle Haggard, Gram Parsons, Neil Young, the Clash

see also: *Uncle Tupelo*

Daniel Durchholz

Sonic Youth
/Thurston Moore
/Lee Ranaldo
/Ciccone Youth
/Bewitched

Sonic Youth formed 1981, in New York, NY.

Thurston Moore, vocals, guitar; Kim Gordon, vocals, bass; Lee Ranaldo, guitar; Richard Edson, drums (1981–82); Jim Sclavunos, drums (1982–83); Bob Bert, drums (1983–85); Steve Shelley, drums (1985–present).

One of the most innovative, inconsistent, influential, annoying, cathartic, and frustrating groups in rock history, Sonic Youth has spent its years exploring guitar sounds and ways to confuse the public (and critics). Along the way, it has made some of the most intensely dark yet ecstatic and accessible albums to come out of the pop underground. Thurston Moore and Lee Ranaldo met while playing in one of avant-gardist Glenn Branca's multiple-guitar ensembles (Sonic Youth's first two efforts initially came out on Branca's label). Ranaldo's love of pure sound in its infinite variety combined with Moore's rudimentary songcraft for a sound that extended the experiments of the New York No Wave scene into somewhat more accessible (if still uncompromised) rock territory. Gradually combining the members' varying musical impulses more coherently, the group hit its stride in 1986–88 when, having settled on Steve Shelley as drummer, it made the great indie trilogy of *Evol*, *Sister*, and *Daydream Nation*. Its signing to DGC was supposed to open mainstream doors for the underground, though that breakthrough was achieved not by the group but rather by a band Moore and company touted highly to Geffen: Nirvana. The members of Sonic Youth are so relentlessly hip that there's been a constant backlash against them ever since SY joined the major-label ranks, but their work—with the band and with myriad outside projects—has remained rewarding, even if it's returned to more erratic expression (probably deliberately).

what to buy: *Sister* ✺✺✺✺✺ (SST, 1987, prod. Sonic Youth) combines a great vocabulary of guitar sounds, a modicum of avant daring, and the most memorable songs of SY's career ("Schizophrenia," "Catholic Block," "Hot Wire My Heart"). The sprawling, 71-minute *Daydream Nation* ✺✺✺✺✺ (Blast First/Enigma, 1988, prod. Sonic Youth, Nicholas Sansano) consolidated the group's many innovations within a consistent mood. The glinting walls of guitar produce an unmatched spooky edge.

what to buy next: *Evol* ✺✺✺✺ (SST, 1986, prod. Sonic Youth, Martin Bisi) was the first SY album with no failed experiments, its dreamlike mood haunting and disturbing. *Washing Machine* ✺✺✺ (DGC, 1995, prod. Sonic Youth, John Siket) explores the nuances within SY's ample niche, cohering better than previous '90s SY albums. The 1986 soundtrack to the indie film *Made in USA* ✺✺✺ (Rhino, 1995, prod. Sonic Youth) includes much that was dropped in the final edit of the movie. The short, often instrumental cues provide a surprisingly good setting in which to appreciate the textures that make this band great.

what to avoid: The debut *Sonic Youth* ✺ (Neutral EP, 1982/SST, 1987, prod. Sonic Youth) gets points for trying something new, but its mechanical processes and clunky rhythms pale compared to future works. *The Whitey Album* **woof!** (Blast

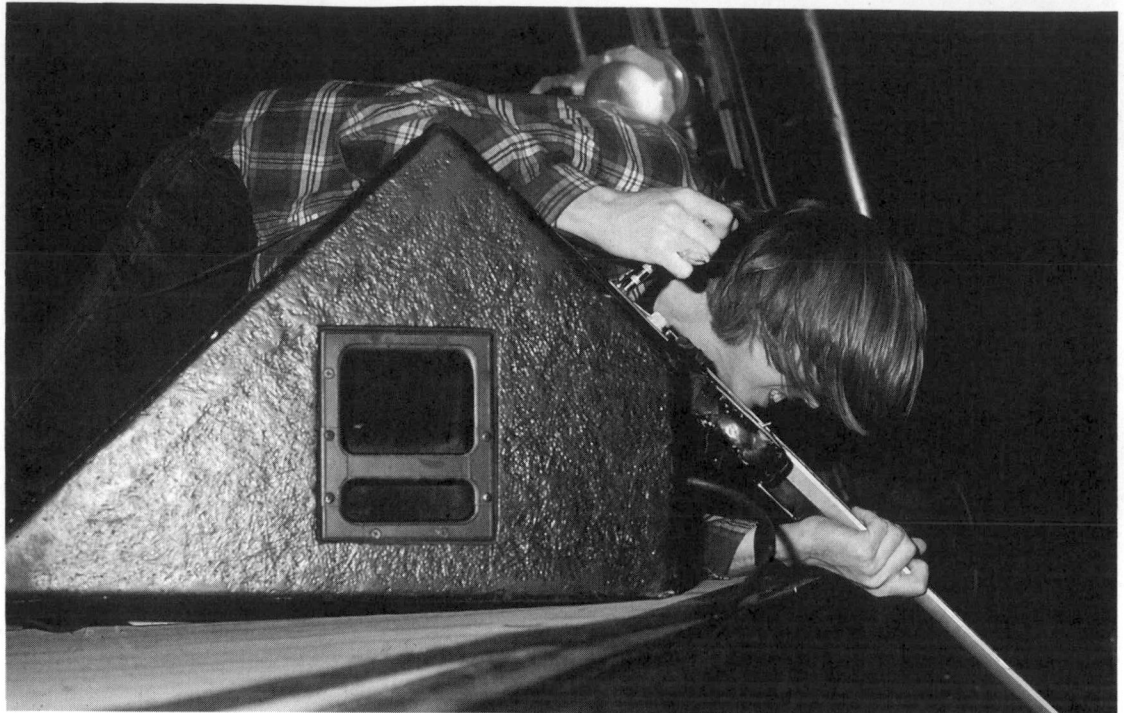

Thurston Moore of Sonic Youth (© Ken Settle)

First/Enigma, 1988, prod. Ciccone Youth), SY's sole full-length album as Ciccone Youth, includes a massive amount of shamelessly pointless goofing around. The curious should stick to their Madonna covers 12-inch.

the rest:
Sonic Death: Sonic Youth Live ♫♫ (Ecstatic Peace, 1984/SST, 1988)
Bad Moon Rising ♫♫♫ (Homestead, 1985)
Death Valley '69 ♫ (Homestead EP, 1985)
The Master-Dik ♫♫ (SST EP, 1988)
Goo ♫♫♫ (DGC, 1990)
Dirty Boots ♫♫♫ (DGC EP, 1991)
Dirty ♫♫♫ (DGC, 1992)
TV Shit ♫♫ (Ecstatic Peace EP, 1993)
Screaming Fields of Sonic Love ♫♫♫ (Geffen, 1994)
Experimental Jet Set, Trash, and No Star ♫♫♫ (DGC, 1994)
Confusion Is Sex /Kill Yr. Idols ♫♫♫ (Geffen, 1994)
A Thousand Leaves ♫♫♫ (DGC, 1998)

worth searching for: Sonic Youth has begun releasing instrumental EPs on its own label that may be hard to find. *Perspectives Musicales* (SYR, 1997) and *Muzikale Vergezichten* (SYR, 1997) are well worth tracking down, as unlike other side projects, the group has clearly put some care and thought into these guitarscapes. Sonic Youth has also been very active in contributing to tribute albums. One of the few good tracks on the British collection *Sgt. Pepper Knew My Father* (NME, 1988, prod. various), which offers new versions of the songs on the Beatles' classic album, is the quartet's striking version of "Within You without You." The Neil Young tribute *The Bridge* (No. 6/Caroline, 1989, prod. various) finds SY roughing up "Computer Age." Its version of Brian Wilson's "I Know There's an Answer" is one of the highlights of the uneven *Smiles, Vibes & Harmony* (DeMilo, 1990, prod. various). The Carpenters tribute *If I Were a Carpenter* (A&M, 1994, prod. various) includes a fine cover of "Superstar" with Moore on vocals.

solo outings:
Ciccone Youth:
Into the Groove(y)/Burnin' Up ♫♫♫ (Blast First 12-inch, 1986)

Thurston Moore:
Psychic Hearts ♫♫♫ (DGC, 1995)

Lee Ranaldo:
From Here to Infinity ♪♪♪ (SST, 1987)
East Jesus ♪♪♪ (Atavistic, 1995)

William Hooker & Lee Ranaldo:
Envisioning ♪♪♪ (Knitting Factory Works, 1994)
(With William Hooker, Jim O'Rourke, and Gianni Gebbia) *Clouds: Victoriaville Concert, May 1997* ♪♪♪♪ (Victo, 1997)

Bewitched (Bob Bert):
Brain Eraser ♪♪♪ (No.6/Rough Trade, 1990)

influences:

◄◄ DNA, Television, Richard Hell & the Voidoids, Sonny Sharrock, Sun Ra, John Coltrane, Glenn Branca, Rhys Chatham, Einstürzende Neubauten, Velvet Underground

►► Live Skull, Nirvana, Sloan, Hole, Neil Young

Steve Holtje

Sonny & Cher /Cher

Formed 1964, in Los Angeles, CA.

Salvatore "Sonny" Bono (born February 16, 1935, in Detroit, MI; died January 5, 1998, in South Lake Tahoe, CA), vocals; Cher (born Cherilyn Sarkasian La Pier, May 20, 1946, in El Centro, CA), vocals.

Sonny and Cher met while working for producer Phil Spector. She was a 19-year-old backup singer; he was a glorified go-fer with a variety of dubious accomplishments. They recorded a couple of singles under the name Caesar & Cleo but only started to click when, as Sonny & Cher, they scored a modest regional hit with "Baby Don't Go." After a switch to Atco Records and the #1 hit "I Got You Babe," Sonny and Cher became the Ozzie and Harriet of the Flower Power set, invariably garbed in mod rags. Bono cut Spectorian duo records for one label and even tossed off one immortal protest record of his own, "Laugh at Me," after being asked to leave a restaurant because he wasn't wearing a tie. Cher did solo records for Liberty (notably "Bang Bang"). Their decline from Top 40 popularity may have been inevitable, but their '70s resurrection as a kind of Louis Prima–Keely Smith comedic pop vocal team could hardly have been predicted. With a top-rated weekly TV program and a series of hit records produced by the sage veteran Snuff Garrett (Bobby Vee, Gary Lewis & the Playboys), Sonny and Cher were back entertaining the parents of the people who only a few years before were buying their records. In the wake of their divorce, personal and professional, Cher established herself as one of Hollywood's leading ladies. Music dropped to little more than a sideline for her; in fact, her albums became more noteworthy for fleshy covers than the music inside. Bono, meanwhile, opened a restaurant and entered politics in sleepy Palm Springs, where he was serving as a two-term Republican congressman when he died in a ski accident.

what to buy: Because of the number of different labels involved, no single set comprehensively covers the career of Sonny & Cher, but *The Beat Goes On* ♪♪♪ (Atco, 1991, prod. Sonny Bono) covers their most fruitful period.

what to buy next: If the double-CD set *All I Ever Need Is You: The Kapp/MCA Anthology* ♪♪ (MCA, 1995, compilation prod. Todd Everett) is more from their TV years than you truly need, then the single disc *Greatest Hits* ♪♪♪ (MCA, 1998, prod. various) should do nicely.

what to avoid: On the other hand, there is an abundance of mediocre recordings in their *oeuvre.* Take your pick from: *Allman and Woman* ♪ (Capricorn, 1976), a bizarre collaboration between Cher and her second husband, Gregg Allman (of *those* Allmans); any of the Kapp/Uni albums with one of the hit songs in the title—*Gypsies, Tramps, and Thieves* ♪ (MCA, 1971), *All I Ever Need Is You* ♪ (MCA, 1972), *Half Breed* ♪ (MCA, 1973)—or choose from her disco-era excesses, currently collected on one convenient set, *The Casablanca Years* **woof!** (Polydor, 1996, compilation prod. Bill Levenson).

the rest:
Sonny and Cher:
All I Really Want to Do/The Sonny Side of Cher ♪♪ (EMI, 1992)
In Case You're in Love ♪ (Sundazed, 1998)
Look at Us ♪♪ (Sundazed, 1998)
The Wondrous World of Sonny & Cher ♪ (Sundazed, 1998)

Cher:
Cher ♪♪ (Geffen, 1987)
Heart of Stone ♪♪ (Geffen, 1989)
Bang Bang and Other Hits ♪♪ (Capitol Special Products, 1992)
It's a Man's Man's World ♪♪ (Geffen, 1996)

worth searching for: Two bona fide Phil Spector–produced singles, both collector's items, feature Cher as lead vocalist: "Ringo I Love You" by Bobbie Jo Mason (Annette, 1964), her first record, and "A Love Like Yours" (Warner Spector, 1975), a duet with Harry Nilsson.

influences:

◄◄ Louis Prima and Keely Smith, Phil Spector

►► ABBA, the Captain & Tennille, Madonna

Joel Selvin

Sons of Champlin

Formed 1965, in Marin County, CA. Disbanded 1978.

Bill Champlin, vocals, guitar, keyboards; Terry Haggerty, guitar; Geoff Palmer, vibes, saxophone; David Shallock, bass (1972–77); James Preston, drums (1972–79).

Little known outside the San Francisco music scene, the Sons of Champlin were widely regarded in that provincial circle as

Dave Pirner of Soul Asylum (© Ken Settle)

the most accomplished set of musicians around. Bill Champlin, a triple-threat vocalist-keyboardist-guitarist, went on to write two Grammy-winning R&B songs ("After the Love Is Gone" for Earth, Wind & Fire and "Turn Your Love Around" for George Benson) after he finally gave up, left the band, and moved to Los Angeles, where he eventually joined multi-platinum popsters Chicago. But this band of staunch hippies, who released a debut album without either a photo of the group or any musicians' names, left behind some stunning, soul-infused acid rock, unmatched by many more famous groups of the era.

what to buy: The double-record set that introduced the band to an unsuspecting and, ultimately, unsympathetic world, *Loosen up Naturally* ₰₰₰₰ (Capitol, 1969/One Way, 1995, prod. Sons of Champlin), was finally released in its entirety on CD, after Capitol, the band's old label, put together a budget-priced compilation, *The Best of the Sons of Champlin* ₰₰₰ (Capitol, 1993, prod. various), drawing from the first three albums.

what to avoid: Don't waste your money on Bill Champlin solo albums.

the rest:
Live ₰₰₰₰ (GDR, 1998)

worth searching for: In the band's second incarnation, the Sons allowed Hollywood producer Keith Olsen to distill the group's often uncontrollable instincts into a svelte, sonically superb package, *Circle Filled with Love* (Ariola America, 1976), which actually launched a Top 50 hit, "Hold On." *Seeds and Stems* (1970) was a private pressing of around 500 copies of demos highly prized by aficionados. Also, the Sons made Capitol send out a free 7-inch 33 1/3-rpm disc of "Jesus Is Coming"—a track Capitol insisted be deleted from the debut album—to anyone who wrote in.

influences:
◀◀ Lou Rawls, Bobby Bland, Johnny Smith
▶▶ Chicago, Tower of Power, Lee Ritenour

Joel Selvin

Soul Asylum

Formed 1981, in Minneapolis, MN.

Dave Pirner, vocals, guitar, piano, saxophone, drums; Dan Murphy, guitar, vocals; Karl Mueller, vocals, bass; Pat Morley, drums (1984–85); Grant Young, drums (1985–94); Sterling Campbell, drums (1995–97).

Starting as the teenage punk band Loud Fast Rules, Soul Asylum's mid-'80s incorporation of country into its sound helped set it apart from hometown heroes Hüsker Dü (whose Bob Mould produced Soul Asylum's first two albums) and the Re-

WHAT ALBUM CHANGED YOUR LIFE?

The first one that came to my mind was *Rock and Roll Diary,* which is a collection of Lou Reed stuff from the Velvet Underground through to his solo career. I consequently went back and got all the Velvet Underground records and all the Lou Reed records.

Dave Pirner (of Soul Asylum)

placements. Dave Pirner, who began as the group's drummer, was frontman by the time of the debut. Writing the vast majority of the group's material (guitarist Dan Murphy contributes a song occasionally), he set the tone for the group's image as passionate, rowdy losers hiding a sensitive side on masterpieces such as "Never Really Been" (from *Made to Be Broken*). Frequent touring honed the band into a powerful force, just sloppy enough to avoid slickness. Its years on the Minneapolis label Twin/Tone, which eventually entered into a distribution deal with A&M, brought the band critical and underground respect but little commercial success. Switching to Columbia certainly changed that, with Pirner's sappy ballad "Runaway Train" reaching #5 on *Billboard*'s pop chart and the album *Grave Dancers Union* breaking the platinum sales barrier. The band became ubiquitous, with Pirner (then sporting dreadlocks) making the gossip pages by dating actress Winona Ryder for several years. That symbolized for many old fans of the band how mainstream it had become, smoothing out the group's rough edges—though its live appearances remain exciting. Murphy's work with the side group Golden Smog is more interesting than anything on *Grave Dancers* ' follow-up, *Let Your Dim Light Shine* (Pirner also sang on one of the *Backbeat* film soundtracks). Three years went by before the release of the next album, which, musically at least, proved to be a heartening comeback.

what to buy: Soul Asylum's second album, *Made to Be Broken* ₰₰₰₰ (Twin/Tone, 1986, prod. Bob Mould), was a huge leap forward, with improved production and more pointed songs. Pirner's country music interests surfaced here (usually tinging rather than transforming the songs) and made for some of the most memorable tracks. "Ship of Fools," "Can't Go Back," the punky "Whoa!," "New Feelings," and the emotional "Never Really Been" are the work of a masterful songwriter. *Hang Time* ♪♪♪♪ (Twin/Tone/A&M, 1988, prod. Lenny Kaye, Ed Stasium) put major-label dollars to good use with sparkling production that honed the group's strengths rather than glossing them over. Though the sound's clear, there's an edge to the music, and "Endless Farewell" shows Pirner can do heartwrenching ballads without losing his edge. Murphy's "Cartoon" is another highlight and suggests Pirner's not the only appreciator of country twang.

what to buy next: *Grave Dancers Union* ♪♪♪ (Columbia, 1993, prod. Michael Beinhorn) may have the group's first hit, "Runaway Train," but there's a loss of identity here: "April Fool" could be Kiss, and "Sun Maid" is just plain wimpy. Enough of the old sound remains ("Somebody to Shove," "Growing into You") to save it. *Candy from a Stranger* ♪♪♪♪ (Columbia, 1998, prod. Chris Kimsey) may not meet the energetic standards of the group's best work, but its cheery guitar pop sound has enough of a dark undercurrent that it's not cloying, and Pirner's songs (especially "No Time for Waiting") are chock-full of catchy hooks.

what to avoid: *Let Your Dim Light Shine* ♪ (Columbia, 1995, prod. Butch Vig, Soul Asylum) is even more mainstream than *Grave Dancers Union*; worse, it sounds formulaic and tired.

the rest:
What You Will, Clarence . . . Karl Sold the Truck ♪♪♪ (Twin/Tone, 1984)
While You Were Out ♪♪ (Twin/Tone, 1986)
Clam Dip & Other Delights ♪♪♪♪ (Twin/Tone EP, 1989)
Soul Asylum and the Horse They Rode in On ♪♪♪ (Twin/Tone/A&M, 1990)
Runaway Train ♪♪ (Columbia EP, 1993)

worth searching for: The "Standing in the Doorway"/"James at 16 (Heavy Medley)" 12-inch single (Twin/Tone/A&M, 1988) is a must-own for the B-side's unbelievably eclectic live medley of songs by Prince, Buffalo Springfield, the Velvet Underground, Wild Cherry, Ted Nugent, the Bee Gees, and others. Soul Asylum has appeared on both of the Sweet Relief benefit albums: *Sweet Relief: A Benefit for Victoria Williams* (Chaos/Columbia, 1993, prod. various) finds the group covering their friend Williams's "Summer of Drugs"; and on *Sweet Relief II: Gravity of the Situation: The Songs of Vic Chesnutt* (Columbia, 1996, prod. various) it covers "When I Ran off & Left Her." There's a Pirner original, "Motel Notell," on yet another charity album, the uneven two-CD *Honor: A Benefit for the Honor the Earth Campaign* (Daemon, 1996, prod. various). The band also shows up on the soundtrack to *Twister* (Warner Bros., 1996, prod. various) with another original, "Miss This."

influences:
◀◀ Hüsker Dü, the Replacements, Buck Owens, the Rolling Stones

▶▶ Afghan Whigs, Gin Blossoms, Dharma Bums

see also: *Golden Smog*

Steve Holtje

Soul Coughing
Formed 1993, in New York, NY.

M. Doughty, vocals, guitar; Sebastian Steinberg, upright bass; Yuval Gabay, drums; Mark De Gli Antoni, keyboards, samples.

Led by M. Doughty—a white T-shirt–wearing, chain-smoking, shaved-headed product of the poetry department at New York's New School—Soul Coughing nestles nasal word jazz in tight rhythms and mind-bending samples, single-handedly cobbling together a neo-beat aesthetic that's so hip it's almost cartoonish. The band was born out of Manhattan's renowned avant-garde jazz club the Knitting Factory, where Doughty was taking tickets and tossing off asides to Sebastian Steinberg, Yuval Gabay, and Mark De Gli Antoni, all veterans of the underground jazz and hip-hop scenes. It was partially because of these origins that Soul Coughing appealed initially to the emerging set of overeducated, hyperexperienced urbanites of the mid-'90s. But the band's searing rock groove and Doughty's insightful non-sequitor observations quickly propelled them onto the national scene.

what to buy: *Ruby Vroom* ♪♪♪♪ (Warner Bros./Slash, 1994, prod. Soul Coughing, Tchad Blake) was the East Coast version of Beck's *Mellow Gold*, a lazy and ingenious volley against the self-absorbed guitar rock of the time. M. Doughty's barely discernable character sketches range from biting and poignant ("Screenwriters Blues" comments stolidly on the plastic culture of Los Angeles) to delightfully absurd, like "Is Chicago, Is Not Chicago" and "Blueeyed Devil," the latter of which could've and should've been the biggest single of the year.

the rest:
Irresistible Bliss ♪♪♪ (Warner Bros./Slash, 1996)
El Oso ♪♪♪♪ (Warner Bros./Slash, 1998)

worth searching for: Soul Coughing has made several one-off recording appearances, including the Red Hot Organization's *Offbeat* compilation, the *X-Files* television soundtrack *Songs in the Key of X*, and a Baby Gap commercial ("Get into the Gap. Get into the Gap. Get into the Gap" ad infinitum).

influences:
◀◀ Ken Nordine, Allen Ginsberg, Beastie Boys, Beck, Medeski, Martin & Wood

Isaac Josephson

The Soul Survivors

Formed 1966, in New York, NY. Disbanded 1970. Re-formed 1974.

Kenneth Jeremiah, vocals; Richard Ingui, vocals; Charles Ingui, vocals; Paul Venturini, organ; Edward Leonetti, guitar; Joey Forigone, drums.

The Soul Survivors had only one hit, but it was a big one. In 1967, "Expressway to Your Heart" reached the Top 5 on both the pop and R&B charts. That song was one of the early works of producers/songwriters Kenny Gamble and Leon Huff, the team that would later give the world the much-vaunted "Philly Sound."

worth searching for: If you've gotta have a copy of "Expressway," you'll need to search for the group's now out-of-print album *When the Whistle Blows Anything Goes* (Collectables, 1993), but prepare to be disappointed, even if you find it. The Soul Survivors couldn't write and, except for the one hit, made poor song selections. Better to find "Expressway" on a good oldies collection.

influences:

◄◄ Gamble & Huff, Jerry Butler

Patrick McCarty

Soul II Soul

Formed 1982, in London, England.

Jazzie B (born Beresford Romeo), producer, vocals; Nellee Hooper, producer, arranger (1985–91).

Soul II Soul started out as a traveling sound system modeled after the mobile dub crews of the Caribbean. After years of supplying DJs and equipment to warehouse parties around England on a freelance basis, the collective started organizing its own events. Things took off for the group after Nellee Hooper, a member of Bristol's Massive Attack, joined the fold in 1985. After securing a residency at the Africa Centre in Covent Garden, the group started making its own demos, which attracted the attention of Virgin. Releasing a pair of singles ("Fairplay," "Feel Free") with modest success in 1988, Soul II Soul struck paydirt with "Keep on Movin'," a song that featured the band's trademark sound in full: lush strings, soaring vocals, and an inescapable rhythm. The group's debut album, *Club Classics, Vol. I*, went platinum shortly thereafter, and Hooper and Jazzie B became coveted producers, scoring their biggest success arranging Sinéad O'Connor's "Nothing Compares 2 U" in 1990. Soul II Soul became one of the most influential dance acts on Britain's early '90s scene. The band released its second album *Vol. II: 1990—A New Decade* to much critical and commercial acclaim, but started to disintegrate shortly thereafter. Hooper, arguably the most talented member of the collective, returned to his

Massive Attack duties, while Jazzie B pressed forth with a pair of dismal follow-up albums (*Volume III: Just Right* and *Volume V: Believe*). The group was abruptly dropped by Virgin in 1995, closing the chapter on one of England's most important musical movements of the decade.

what to buy: Caron Wheeler's astral vocals and the Jazzie B/Hooper production team make *Club Classics, Vol. I* 🎵🎵🎵🎵 (Virgin, 1989, prod. Soul II Soul) an indispensable document of the innovation coming out of England at the beginning of the decade. Mixing dub and R&B influences with contributions from Wheeler and the Reggae Philharmonic Orchestra, this album justifiably made Soul II Soul an international sensation at the time of its release, launching hit singles with "Keep on Movin'" and "Back to Life (However Do You Want Me)."

what to buy next: While not as startlingly brilliant as its predecessor, *Vol. II: 1990—A New Decade* 🎵🎵🎵 (Virgin, 1990, prod. Soul II Soul) further established Soul II Soul's distinctive sound. Although it lacks Wheeler's voice, the album features some of Soul II Soul's most innovative work, particularly the symphonic "Get a Life" and "A Dream's a Dream."

what to avoid: When Hooper left Soul II Soul after its second album, the group lost its spark. *Volume III: Just Right* ♪ (Virgin, 1992, prod. Jazzie B) and *Volume V: Believe* ♪ (Virgin, 1995, prod. Jazzie B) are tiresome listens, fruitlessly rehashing the textures of the first two albums without gelling into anything beyond ear candy.

worth searching for: Released only in the U.K., *Vol IV: The Classic Singles* (Virgin UK, 1993, compilation prod. Jazzie B) compiles all the band's best material on one convenient disc and tacks on some remixes as bonus tracks. It's a good way to avoid the filler on the second and third albums.

influences:

◄◄ Augustus Pablo, Sade, James Brown

►► Portishead, Massive Attack, Madonna

see also: *Massive Attack*

Aidin Vaziri

Soundgarden

Formed 1984, in Seattle, WA. Disbanded 1997.

Chris Cornell, vocals, guitar; Kim Thayil, guitar; Scott Sundquist, drums (1985–86); Matt Cameron, drums (1986–97); Hiro Yamamoto, bass (1984–89); Jason Everman, bass (1989–90); Ben Shepherd (born Hunter Shepherd), bass (1990–97).

The members of Soundgarden use to grouse about being regarded as a metal band, and you have to agree that they did have a point. After all, they played an important role in creating the '90s Seattle scene of grunge and alternative rock, and their EP *Screaming Life* was the very first release on the Sub Pop label, which eventually brought the Seattle sound to the world. Plus, much of their hard rock bluster was tongue-in-cheek, even if their audience didn't necessarily notice. But like Blue Öyster Cult a generation before them, what began as an ironic comment on metal became the thing itself. Soundgarden's intelligence kept the quality of their music from descending to metal's clichéd excess. Unabashedly Zeppelinesque, Chris Cornell's keening vocals reach operatic heights, slicing through the wall-o-sludge guitar cranked out by Kim Thayil. Its roots may have been as much in punk as in '70s AOR, but Soundgarden made it safe for Seattlites and fellow grungesters everywhere to shake their hair down in their face and rock out. Sensing the cresting of the wave in 1997, though, Soundgarden quietly disbanded.

what to buy: From the apocalyptic "Black Hole Sun" to the contemplative "Fell on Black Days," to the downright desperate "The Day I Tried to Live," *Superunknown* ♪♪♪♪♪ (A&M, 1994, prod. Michael Beinhorn, Soundgarden) is lyrically complex and packs the sonic wallop of a tsunami. It's the best hard-rock album of the '90s. *Badmotorfinger* ♪♪♪♪ (A&M, 1991, prod.

Terry Date, Soundgarden) is the album on which the band truly found its voice. Songs like "Rusty Cage," "Jesus Christ Pose," and "Outshined" feature well-tempered hard rock and razor-sharp lyrics.

what to buy next: *Louder Than Love* ♪♪♪♪ (A&M, 1989, prod. Terry Date, Soundgarden) convincingly updates '70s hard rock, but the band's sense of irony is subtle enough that not everyone got the joke of macho anthems like "Big Dumb Sex." The follow-up to *Superunknown*, *Down on the Upside* ♪♪♪♪ (A&M, 1996, prod. Soundgarden, Adam Kasper) further refines the band's attack, featuring shimmering pop-metal ("Pretty Noose"), Ramones-inspired punk ("Ty Cobb"), and Lennonesque psychedelia ("Blow up the Outside World").

what to avoid: The individual EPs *Screaming Life* ♪♪♪ (Sub Pop EP, 1987) and *Fopp* ♪♪♪ (Sub Pop EP, 1988) were combined by Sub Pop in 1990 for a more value-efficient single disc.

the rest:
Ultramega OK ♪♪♪ (SST, 1988)
A-Sides ♪♪♪♪ (A&M, 1997)

worth searching for: *Alive in the Superunknown* (A&M, 1995) is a multimedia CD-Plus featuring tracks and videos from *Superunknown* and unreleased material.

solo outings:
Ben Shepherd and Matt Cameron:
(With Hater) *Hater* ♪♪ (A&M, 1993)

influences:

◄◄ Led Zeppelin, Black Sabbath, Killing Joke, the Melvins

►► Alice in Chains, Screaming Trees, Mudhoney, Pearl Jam, Bush, silverfish

see also: *Pearl Jam*

Daniel Durchholz

Sounds of Life

See: Source Direct

Epic Soundtracks

Born Kevin Paul Godfrey, March 23, 1959, in London, England. Died November 6, 1997, in West Hampstead, England.

His friends were often punks and hardcore noise people, but Epic Soundtracks emulated good old-fashioned soul and pop singing. An ex-member of a buffet of underground bands—he drummed in the Swell Maps, played in Red Crayola, Crime and the City Solution, These Immortal Souls, and the Jacobites—Soundtracks began performing during the '70s and went solo in 1992. He often listed his influences as hardcore punk bands and legendary rock 'n' rollers, from Big Star to Dion, but you can hear Carole King, Billy Joel, and Queen creeping up in his

Chris Cornell of Soundgarden (© Ken Settle)

lush, sometimes syrupy piano pop. The brother of cult-rocker Nikki Sudden, Soundtracks's somber music, in retrospect a tuneful death knell, was overlooked in his lifetime. Soundtracks committed suicide before he had a chance to become at least a cult icon, a status he deserved every bit as much as his brother.

what to buy: By the time he recorded *Change My Life* 𝄢𝄢𝄢𝄢 (Bar/None, 1996, prod. Henry Olsen), Soundtracks showed he could leap from the fine-tuned Televisionisms of "You Can Be My Baby" to the Beach Boys' Phil Spector phase in "Steal Away," to the John Lennon-ish "Something's Wrong."

the rest:
Rise Above 𝄢𝄢𝄢 (Bar/None, 1992)
Sleeping Star 𝄢𝄢𝄢 (Bar/None, 1994)

influences:

◀◀ Big Star, Dion, Carole King, Billy Joel, Queen

▶▶ Juliana Hatfield, Lemonheads

Steve Knopper and Jordan Oakes

The Soup Dragons

Formed 1985, in Belshill, Scotland.

Sean Dickson, vocals; Jim McCulloch, guitar (1985–94); Sushil Dade, bass (1985–94); Paul Quinn, drums (1985–94).

This mid-'80s punk/pop band had little to no success during the early years with its edgy guitar-driven albums. But thanks to the late '80s success of Manchester chums Happy Mondays and the Stone Roses, the Soup Dragons found their talents were in infusing funky rhythms with psychedelic, '60s-style guitars. The band's success was short-lived, and their most memorable recorded work was their remake of the Rolling Stones' "I'm Free."

what to buy: *Love God* 𝄢𝄢𝄢𝄢 (Big Life/Mercury, 1990) is the Generation X handbook to what the Manchester sound is all about. It contains the mega smash "I'm Free," complete with a reggae-rap segment by Jamaican artist Junior Reid and a gospel choir that's a nice touch.

what to buy next: *Hot Wired* 𝄢𝄢𝄢𝄢 (Big Life/Mercury, 1992) is spotty but worthwhile for "Divine Thing." Imagine "I'm Free" with different words; the potential is limitless.

what to avoid: On *Hydrophone* 𝄢 (Raw T.V./Mercury, 1994), a pretentious lead singer thinks the way to bring back the hipness is to fire the entire band and do it himself. Wrong.

the rest:
Hang Ten 𝄢𝄢𝄢 (Sire, 1987)
This Is Our Art 𝄢𝄢𝄢 (Sire, 1988)

influences:

◀◀ Procol Harum, the Rolling Stones, Pretty Things, Thompson Twins

▶▶ Jesus Jones, Happy Mondays, Charlatans U.K., the Stone Roses

J. Christopher Newberg

Source Direct /Sounds of Life

Formed 1994, in St. Albans, England.

Jim Baker, samplers, sequencer, synthesizers; Phil Aslet, samplers, sequencer, synthesizers.

In the realm of breakbeat science—the art of cutting up and re-arranging sampled drum breaks into completely different beats—Source Direct's breaks are rivaled in their complexity by their friend and label-mate, Photek. If Goldie and Roni Size are the kings of the U.K. jungle scene, then the members of Source Direct are among its deadliest assassins. Jim Baker and Phil Aslet befriended each other while attending school in St. Albans, England (where Photek also hails from) during the early '90s. While they had divergent musical taste—Baker's love was hip-hop, Aslet was into early breakbeat, acid house, and techno—they found common ground in jungle's precursor, the U.K. hardcore scene. During 1994, Aslet and Baker released their first 12-inches under the Sounds of Life moniker for the tiny Certificate 18 label, the success of which led to further releases on respected jungle labels such as Metalheadz and LTJ Bukem's Good Looking Records, while also allowing the group to form its own label, Source Direct Recordings. Source Direct's music mixes harsh, almost atonal sounds with complex breakbeat patterns that dazzle and strike the listener with the speed and dexterity of an expert martial artist. Indeed, many of Source Direct's records take their names from kung-fu styles ("The Crane," "Snake Style") or employ samples from martial arts films ("The Cult"). Despite the increasingly experimental nature of its music, Source Direct's tracks retain a link to the dance floor that allows them to be embraced by jungle's more influential DJs such as Fabio, Doc Scott, and LTJ Bukem, whereas breakbeat mutants such as Squarepusher and Plug are rejected outright.

what to buy: Source Direct were among jungle's heavy hitters (like Goldie, Photek, and Roni Size) signed to major labels after jungle exploded in popularity in the U.K. during 1994. *Controlled Developments* 𝄢𝄢𝄢𝄢 (Astralwerks/Science, 1997, prod. Source Direct) is a collection of singles from Source Direct's U.K. label, Science/Virgin, that brilliantly demonstrates the duo's ability to blend dark sci-fi atmospheres with lightning-fast drum beats that twist, turn, and strike the listener like a clan of ninjas doing battle with a squadron of hi-tech commandos.

worth searching for: Sadly, almost all of Source Direct's earlier works were only released on now-out-of-print import 12 inches. Three of their tracks, however, are available on the two excellent jungle compilations from Goldie's Metalheadz label, *Platinum Breakz* (Metalheadz/FFRR, 1997, prod. various) and *Platinum Breakz II* (Metalheadz/FFRR, 1998, prod. various). *Platinum Breakz II* features two Source Direct tracks ("Stonekiller" and "Dark Metal (remix)") similar in style to *Controlled Developments*. However, "Your Sound," on the first volume, displays Source Direct's trademark killer drum breaks in a lighter, jazzier context that sharply contrasts with the majority of their works.

influences:
◄◄ Ultramagnetic MCs, Boogie Down Productions, Joey Beltram, Lalo Schiffrin, Photek

Howard Shih

Joe South

Born Joe Souter, February 28, 1940, in Atlanta, GA.

Considering how many timeless pop music classics were crafted during 1968, you could win a ton of bar bets asking people to name the Song of the Year. It was the sing-songy, Grammy-winning single "Games People Play," the moralistic solo high ground for Joe South—who until that point had been known primarily as a session musician and songwriter who created memorable hits for artists ranging from Deep Purple ("Hush") to Billy Joe Royal ("Down in the Boondocks"). Not surprisingly, South began his career as a country musician, performing on an Atlanta radio station during the mid-'50s. After recording the novelty sequel "The Purple People Eater Meets the Witch Doctor" in 1958, he became a session guitarist in Muscle Shoals and Nashville, working on records by Eddy Arnold, Aretha Franklin, Bob Dylan, and Simon & Garfunkel ("The Sounds of Silence"). After his own chart breakthrough with "Games People Play," South went on to notch the country-tinged hits "Don't It Make You Want to Go Home" and "Walk a Mile in My Shoes," while penning a million-selling crossover single for Lynn Anderson in 1971 with "I Never Promised You a Rose Garden." His brother's suicide that same year sent South into semi-retirement and self-imposed seclusion in Hawaii. Despite a drug bust and a notorious reputation as an antisocial artist, he made a brief comeback in 1975 with his *Midnight Rainbows* LP, but retired from performing permanently during the early '90s to concentrate on music publishing.

worth searching for: The South may rise again, but Joe South will have a much harder time. The years have not been kind to the singer's discography: all of his 11 solo LPs are out of print,

and the compilation *The Best of Joe South* (Rhino, 1990, prod. various) is no longer offered in the Rhino catalog. Oh, the games people play.

influences:
◄◄ Pete Drake, Eddy Arnold, Marty Robbins, Bob Dylan, Glen Campbell
►► Billy Joe Royal, Kris Kristofferson, Michael Martin Murphy

Jim McFarlin

Souther-Hillman-Furay Band
See: Poco

Southern Culture on the Skids
Formed 1985, in Chapel Hill, NC.

Rick Miller, guitar, vocals; Mary Huff, bass, vocals; David Hartman, drums, percussion, whip.

It's unclear what grand artistic statement Rick Miller is making when he sings about eating tasty snack crackers while simultaneously submitting to a dominatrix's pointy boots. But the riddle is just part of the band's hillbilly mystique. Miller, who wears overalls and the occasional Conway Twitty wig (which looks surprisingly like Kurt Cobain's hair), is the guiding force behind this mostly instrumental surf-and-rockabilly trio. Though some critics say the band is nothing more than a few inside jokes—such as the weirdly sexual finger-licking in the Kentucky Fried Chicken tribute "8 Piece Box"—the secret of SCOTS is the music. Miller is a superb guitarist, with an encyclopedic knowledge of Duane Eddy and Dick Dale licks, and the rhythm section of big-haired bassist Mary Huff and nebbishy drummer David Hartman matches him without drawing attention to itself. The trio took years to get even a tiny taste of fame, and once signed to the major label DGC/Geffen Records it made the same record twice in a row. For a "joke band," though, SCOTS' music stands up surprisingly well.

what to buy: Though many diehard fans swear by the pre-Geffen independent releases, *Dirt Track Date* ♫♫♫♫ (DGC, 1995, prod. Mark Williams, Southern Culture on the Skids) is a well-rounded display of tight rock 'n' roll instrumentals ("Camel Walk"), a dry, reddeckish sense of humor ("8 Piece Box," a live staple re-recorded for this album), and a bit of greasy soul ("Soul City," "Firefly").

what to buy next: With three live tracks (including "Daddy Was a Preacher but Mama Was a Go-Go Girl" and Link Wray's "Run Chicken Run"), *Peckin' Party* ♫♫♫ (Feed Bag EP, 1993), recorded live at Chicago's Lounge Ax nightclub, captures SCOTS at its least polished.

the rest:

For Lovers Only 𝄞𝄞𝄞 (Safe House, 1992)
Ditch Diggin' 𝄞𝄞𝄞 (Safe House, 1994)
Plastic Seat Sweat 𝄞𝄞𝄞 (DGC, 1997)

worth searching for: The band's Chapel Hill–based record company, Moist, folded shortly after releasing the landmark Southern Culture on the Skids album *Too Much Pork for Just One Fork* (Moist, 1992), which contains the greasy original version of "8 Piece Box," plus "Voodoo Cadillac," another classic later retooled for the DGC debut.

influences:

◀◀ Link Wray, Dick Dale, Duane Eddy, the Cramps, X, Elvis Presley

▶▶ Laika & the Cosmonauts, Los Fabulosos Cadillacs, Man or Astro-Man?

Steve Knopper

Southside Johnny & the Asbury Jukes

Formed 1974, in Asbury Park, NJ.

Southside Johnny (born John Lyon, December 4, 1948, in Neptune, NJ), vocals, harmonica; Billy Rush, guitar (1974–85); Kevin Kavanaugh, keyboards; Al Berger, bass (1974–80); Kenny Pentifallo, drums (1974–77); Carlo Novi, tenor sax (1974–77); Eddie Manion, baritone sax (1974–82); Tony Palligrosi, trumpet (1974–78); Ricky Gazda, trumpet (1974–82); Richie (La Bamba) Rosenberg, trombone (1974–82); Steve Becker, drums (1977–91); Bob Muckin, trumpet (1978–80); Stan Harrison, tenor sax (1978–80); Joel Gramolini, guitar (1979–82); Gene Boccia, bass (1980–85); Mike Spencer, trumpet (1980–82); Joey Stann, baritone sax, tenor sax (1980–82, 1986–91); Rusty Cloud, keyboards (1983–present); Mark Pender, trumpet (1983–86); Al Torrente, trumpet (1983–85); Bobby Ferrel, trombone (1983–86); Frank Elmo, saxophone (1983–86, 1991); George L. Ruiz, bass (1986); Bobby Bandiera, guitar (1986–present); Barry Danielian, trumpet; Dan Levine, trombone; Jerry Vivino Jr., tenor sax; others.

Southside Johnny & the Asbury Jukes came out of the same Asbury Park, New Jersey, scene that produced Bruce Springsteen, and at roughly the same time. In fact, the group's leader, Southside Johnny Lyon, and Springsteen occasionally played in the same bands during the early '70s. But where Springsteen leaned toward '50s rock and Phil Spector records, Lyon preferred urban blues and horn-band R&B, leading him to form the Jukes. Lyon is an excellent, gravel-voiced white-soul singer, but the Springsteen connection has been a double-edged sword. Springsteen has written much of the Jukes' best-known material ("Hearts of Stone," "The Fever"), which has gained the group fans while creating a shadow from which

it has not been able to emerge. And when the group has abandoned the Springsteen connection (as on 1979's *The Jukes*, when guitarist Billy Rush became the primary songwriter), it has faltered. But it remains a great band in the New Jersey R&B/rock vein, if more limited in appeal than their more famous colleague.

what to buy: *The Best of Southside Johnny and the Asbury Jukes* 𝄞𝄞𝄞𝄞 (Epic/Legacy, 1992) collects the best material from the Jukes' three Epic albums, along with some live material. It's a wonderful white-soul, horn-band album that features tunes by Springsteen and cameos by Ronnie Spector and Lee Dorsey. *Havin' a Party with Southside Johnny* 𝄞𝄞𝄞𝄞 (Epic, 1979, prod. Miami Steve) is a skimpier—but cheaper—collection from the same era.

what to buy next: The Jukes' records after leaving Epic were more uneven, but almost all of them contained good songs. *All I Want Is Everything: The Best of Southside Johnny & the Asbury Jukes* 𝄞𝄞𝄞𝄞 (Rhino, 1993, prod. various) compiles material from 1979 to 1991 and gets nearly all the good stuff, much of which is otherwise hard to find now. *Live/Reach up and Touch the Sky* 𝄞𝄞𝄞𝄞 (Epic, 1981, prod. John Lyon, Stephan Galfas) shows the band in its natural element.

what to avoid: *Trash It Up* 𝄞𝄞 (Mirage, 1983, prod. Nile Rogers) totally removes Southside from his Jersey bar roots and places him in some parallel MTV-spawned R&B universe. Instead of sounding passionate, he sounds merely lascivious.

the rest:

I Don't Want to Go Home 𝄞𝄞𝄞𝄞 (Epic, 1976)
This Time It's for Real 𝄞𝄞𝄞 (Epic, 1977)
Hearts of Stone 𝄞𝄞𝄞𝄞 (Epic, 1978)
The Jukes 𝄞𝄞 (Mercury, 1979/Off Beat, 1995)
Jukes Live at the Bottom Line 𝄞𝄞𝄞𝄞 (Image, 1996)
Rockin' with the Jukes 𝄞𝄞𝄞 (Sony Music Special Products, 1996)

worth searching for: *Better Days* (Impact, 1991, prod. Little Steven) finds Southside Johnny making his peace with his place in New Jersey music—and with Springsteen's shadow—reuniting with the Miami Horns for one of his toughest, most exciting albums. Little Steven returned to the production board, and Springsteen and Jon Bon Jovi contributed guest vocals. *At Least We Got Shoes* (Atlantic, 1986, prod. John Lyon, John Rollo) contains a marvelous rendition of "I Only Want to Be with You."

influences:

◀◀ Bruce Springsteen, the Coasters, the Drifters, Gary U.S. Bonds, James Brown, Wilson Pickett

▶▶ Little Steven & the Disciples of Soul, Jack Mack & the Heart Attack, Iron City Houserockers

Brian Mansfield

Space

Formed 1993, in Liverpool, England.

Tommy Scott, vocals, bass; Jamie Murphy, vocals, guitars; Franny Griffiths, keyboards (1995–present); Andy Parle, drums (1994–97); Leon Caffrey, drums (1997–present); Carl "Yorkie" Brown, bass (1997–present).

Space is pop noir at its finest, but when the band formed it wanted to follow in the footsteps of the Beatlesque La's. Jamie Murphy got his first crack at pairing up with Tommy Scott when he was 14. Scott, then 22, dismissed Murphy as a young punk. Three years later, however, he heard Murphy play guitar and relented. Legend has it that Franny Griffiths was in a Liverpool nightclub when someone delivered an empty pack of cigarettes to him. Scrawled on the box was an invitation to join Space. Skeptical at first, Griffiths came on board. Space released its first single, "Money," and sold out of its first pressing. Its follow-up single, "Neighborhood," was, according to a British music magazine, "temporarily banned because it mentioned a serial killer during the week a shooting massacre occurred at a Scottish school." Space found its niche, however, when the Latin-meets-techno-meets-Sinatra single "Female of the Species" became a minor alternative-rock radio hit in 1997. Unfortunately, Space wasn't able to capitalize on its success as sickness forced the cancellation of many concert dates after Griffiths developed an ulcer and Scott lost his voice due to stress. Murphy had a nervous breakdown and subsequently stopped drinking and began taking anti-depressants.

what to buy: Space's debut album, *Spiders* 🎵🎵🎵 (Gut, 1996/Universal, 1997, prod. Steve Lironi), recalls every musical style under the sun and tips its hat to a host of pop culture stars, including Frank Sinatra and cartoon character Speedy Gonzales. Apparently confused about its hit potential, Space originally recorded "Female of the Species" as a B-side. "Mister Psycho," featuring a sampled laugh of Vincent Price, is as entertaining as *Plan B from Outer Space,* too funny to take seriously. On the serial killer front, Charles Manson even gets his own song, called, appropriately enough, "Charlie M." But again, it's hard to be offended by such an entertaining song. Leading off with samples of villains saying "moog a laka, moog a laka," "Charlie M." continues with lyrics that name-check Madonna, John F. Kennedy ("Someone blew his head off/And now he's in a cemetery"), and Mickey Mouse ("I can see Mickey Mouse/sitting on a shrink's couch/Tryin' to cure his hang-up/'bout screwin' Minnie Mouse").

the rest:
Tin Planet N/A (Gut, 1998)

influences:
◄◄ Fun Boy Three, Black Grape, Happy Mondays, Combustible Edison

Christina Fuoco

WHAT ALBUM CHANGED YOUR LIFE?

The white album, I think, by the Beatles. I came to it really late; I knew the Beatles and everything, but I'd never heard the white album. Same with Led Zeppelin's fourth album. I'd managed to avoid that album for quite a long time, too. Both of them completely blew me away. I couldn't stop playing either one of them. I think the white album was on the turntable for four months, at least, or maybe even six, 'cause there's a lot on it, isn't there? Lots of juicy stuff.

Richard Steel (of Spacehog)

Spacehog

Formed 1994, in New York, NY.

Royston Langdon, lead vocals, bass guitar; Anthony Langdon, guitar, vocals; Richard Steel, lead guitar; Jonny Cragg, drums.

Formed by British expatriates Royston and Anthony Langdon in New York's East Village, Spacehog is a purveyor of a poppy pastiche of glam-rock sonic theatrics and minimal prog-rock anthemics. Drawing heavily upon the '70s musical terrain once explored by David Bowie, T. Rex, and countless other Britons, Spacehog created a flurry of buzz when it debuted during 1995 with the insta-hit "In the Meantime."

what to buy: The quartet's sophomore effort, *The Chinese Album* 🎵🎵🎵 (Sire, 1998, prod. Bryce Goggin, Spacehog), is pure glam fetish, the band sounding like some bastard, polysonic offspring of Queen's Freddie Mercury, David Bowie, and the Kinks' Ray Davies. It's also more sonically ambitious than the group's debut album. From the eerie quietude of the opening track, "One of These Days," to the late '70s/early '80s arena rock retro-fit of the radio smash "Mungo City," Spacehog proves to be all about catchy guitar riffs, off-kilter melodies, and finger-poppin' rock attitude. Additionally they drop mod be-bop vocals and chug rhythm happiness on "Captain Freeman," as well as some cheery soft pop ("Almond Kisses") and even some twanged-out honky tonk ("Anonymous").

what to buy next: The band's first album, *Resident Alien* 𝄞𝄞𝄞 (Sire, 1995, prod. Bryce Goggin, Spacehog), contains "In the Meantime," which expertly combines twisted yodeling with burbling bass and electronic atmospheria to create a post-Mod prog-inspired ditty. The rest of the album follows suit, dipping into unfiltered NYC rock ("Spacehog"), impassioned vocal exercises ("Candyman"), and two-part epics ("Never Coming Down" Parts I and II). The album creeps under your skin with its excellent grasp of late '70s Brit rock theory and inescapably catchy verve, but it ultimately has no succinct identity of its own.

influences:

◀◀ David Bowie, Mott the Hoople, T. Rex, the Kinks

Spence D.

Spacemen 3

Formed 1982, in Rugby, England. Disbanded 1991.

Pete Kember (a.k.a. The Mainliner, Peter Gunn, Sonic Boom), guitar, vocals; Jason Pierce (a.k.a. J Spaceman), guitar, vocals; Pete Bain (a.k.a. Bassman), bass (1985–89); Will Caruthers, bass (1989–91); Natty Brooker (a.k.a. Gnatty), drums (1982–86); Stewart Roswell, drums (1986–89); John Mattock, drums (1989–91).

One of the progenitors of neo-space rock and early '90s shoegazing bands, Spacemen 3 cooked up extended narcotic guitar drones and tied them off with the languid vocals of two drug-dependent friends. The band, low on rhythm and high on ambient wash, was wholly off-the-wall for its time and location. While punk was in its final death pangs and new wave was percolating to prominence, these British blokes were covering songs by '60s Texas psychedelic cult legends the Red Krayola and 13th Floor Elevators. As they grew, Jason Pierce and Sonic Boom developed distinct styles, with the former focusing on more intricate, spiritual melodies. Sonic Boom moved towards foreboding, minimalist, one-chord jams; when allowed to indulge that penchant too much, he led the group on endless, pulsating, hypnotic journeys geared toward the heavily drugged listener. The almost entirely ambient *Dreamweapon*, subtitled "An Evening of Contemporary Sitar Music," is an excellent example. The liner notes even contain a miniature treatise on the "disappearance of melody." Infighting between Pierce and Sonic Boom eventually sank the band. Both sold or sanctioned unreleased tapes of their own volition, turning the band's catalog into a quagmire of "official" vs. "unofficial" releases, rights issues, and outright bootlegs. Pierce took the remnants of Spacemen 3 and formed Spiritualized, while Sonic Boom went on to a number of different projects, Spectrum being the most recent and most suc-

cessful. Now, despite a flurry of reissues and the recent commercial success of Spiritualized, Spacemen 3 have been relegated almost exclusively to college radio hero status.

what to buy: When *The Perfect Prescription* 𝄞𝄞𝄞𝄞 (Glass, 1987/Fire, 1987/Genius, 1987/Taang!, 1996) was recorded, Pierce and Sonic Boom had just begun to move in separate musical directions. At this *Perfect* moment, the two temper each other rather than clash: Pierce adds structure, beauty, and melody, while Sonic Boom injects life and passion. "Walking with Jesus," the two-chord, organ-led single, is both hypnotic and transcendent. "Call the Doctor," dark and oozing, eloquently captures the post-euphoric depression of a drug trip. When the shimmering ambiance of "Ecstasy Symphony" gives way to the trippy symphonic grandeur of "Transparent Radiation (flashback)" (a Red Krayola cover), Spacemen 3 come closest in form to Pierce's breathtaking compositions a decade later with Spiritualized.

what to buy next: The split between the band's two styles emerges on *Playing with Fire* 𝄞𝄞𝄞 (Fire, 1989/Bomp!, 1989/Taang!, 1994). Pierce's compositions, which comprise one-third of the album, are a little more lush and delicate; Sonic Boom's are more dominant and woozy. The track sequence is carefully crafted, creating a hypnotic ebb and flow, with one delightful exception: the soft and narcotic "I Believe It" segueing into the frenzied "Revolution" is the most jarring wakeup call on an album since Pink Floyd's "On the Run" segued into "Time."

what to avoid: Recorded in 1984, *For All the Fucked up Children of This World We Give You Spacemen 3* woof! (SFTRI, 1995) showcases the band in its earliest garage rock stages—something only the members' mothers or diehard fans should have to hear. Other than a headache and some neat liner notes, the only thing that comes out of this release is the realization of how far "Walking with Jesus" came by the time it was recorded for *Perfect Prescription*.

the rest:

Sound of Confusion 𝄞𝄞𝄞 (Glass, 1986/Fire, 1986/Taang!, 1995)
Performance—Live at the Melkweg 6/2/88 𝄞𝄞𝄞 (Glass, 1988/Fire, 1988/Genius, 1988/Taang!, 1996)
Taking Drugs to Make Music to Take Drugs To 𝄞𝄞 (A Father Yod, 1990/Bomp!, 1994)
Dreamweapon 𝄞𝄞𝄞 (SFTRI, 1993)
Spacemen Are Go!—Live in Europe, 1989 𝄞𝄞 (Bomp!, 1995)
The Singles 𝄞𝄞𝄞 (Taang!, 1995)

worth searching for: On *Recurring* (Fire, 1991), the band's out-of-print breakup album, Sonic Boom and Pierce split the songwriting evenly, each recording his half at separate times, in separate studios. *Losing Touch with Your Mind* (1991) is an unofficial but widely circulated album. The limited edition *Walking with Jesus/Transparent Radiation* (1993), was re-released by

Taang! as *The Singles* two years later with three extra tracks. *Revolution or Heroin* (Fierce, 1995), an unsanctioned live release, is allegedly from a 1986 show.

influences:

◀◀ Velvet Underground, Syd Barrett, the Red Krayola, the Doors, Hawkwind, Joy Division

▶▶ Galaxy 500, My Bloody Valentine, the Verve, Sonic Youth, Stereolab, Underworld

see also: *Stereolab*

Isaac Josephson

Spacetime Continuum

Formed 1993, in San Francisco, CA.

Jonah Sharp, DJ, electronics, sampling.

DJ, drummer, producer, stoner—call him what you want, but under the moniker Spacetime Continuum, Jonah Sharp is an electronic wizard. Combining ambient and techno sounds that work well on your Walkman and on the dance floor, Sharp is in pursuit of the eternal headrush. Nearly entirely "artificial," Spacetime Continuum is still quite listenable, with an occasional new age feel—though Sharp will probably never record live at the Acropolis. Best of all, his records don't require a club setting or a good buzz to be enjoyable.

what to buy: Sharp is at his best on *Sea Biscuit* ✶✶✶✶ (Astralwerks, 1994, prod. Jonah Sharp), where he doesn't seem particularly driven to move the crowd. The tracks are long, but shift in tempo and mood enough to keep all but the most jaded raver enthralled.

what to buy next: *Emit Ecaps* ✶✶✶ (Astralwerks, 1996, prod. Jonah Sharp) ups the BPMs a bit, urging listeners to get their rave on. It's not likely to convert your neighborhood metalhead, but for the believers it's a groove-laden pleasure.

what to avoid: *Alien Dreamtime* ✶✶ (Astralwerks, 1993, prod. Jonah Sharp) would be OK were it not for the monotonous ramblings of psilocybin maverick Terence McKenna that waste the intriguing performances of Trance Mission's didgeridoo player Stephen Kent.

the rest:

Spacetime Continuum ✶✶✶ (Astralwerks EP, 1997)

worth searching for: The debut EP *Fluresence* (Reflective, 1993, prod. Jonah Sharp) is only essential to fanatics, yet is worth a listen.

influences:

◀◀ Kraftwerk, Tangerine Dream, Future Sound of London, Underworld, Aphex Twin, Moby, the Orb, Orbital

▶▶ Keoki, DJ Shadow, bt, Spring Heel Jack, Plug

see also: *Bill Laswell*

Barry M. Prickett

Spain

Formed 1995, in Los Angeles, CA.

Josh Haden, vocals, bass; Ken Boudakian, guitar, organ; Merlo Podlewski, guitar; Evan Hartzell, drums.

Spain emerged from L.A.'s sunny vistas with a slow-motion, somnolent sound that conjured up love-torn bedrooms, smoke filled cabarets, and hazy states of mind. Josh Haden, the son of legendary jazz bassist Charlie Haden and brother of that dog.'s Rachel and Petra Haden, got his start playing art-damaged punk in the Treacherous Jaywalkers, then took an abrupt turn with Spain, a band that wears matching dark suits and never seems to crank its amps above five. Its first album, *The Blue Moods of Spain*, had rock critics breathing heavy, but for some reason it has yet to follow up with a second effort, apparently applying its slow and steady approach to its career, as well.

what's available: Like you have to ask? *The Blue Moods of Spain* ✶✶✶✶ (Restless, 1995, prod. Norman Kerner, Josh Haden) is a quiet masterpiece, from the brooding "It's So True" to the stately "Untitled #1" and the dreamy "Her Used-to-Been." And the noirish cover portrait is perfect.

influences:

◀◀ Charlie Haden, Red House Painters, Spiritualized, the Velvet Underground

Marc Weingarten

Spandau Ballet

Formed 1980, in London, England. Disbanded 1990.

Tony Hadley, vocals; Gary Kemp, guitars; Martin Kemp, bass; Steve Norman, saxophones; John Keeble, drums.

Starting out as one of the many New Romantic bands to emerge from England's late new wave scene, this glossy, puffy pop group (which, according to some, took its name from an expression used to describe the paroxysmic flailings of a person's body as they were being gassed in a Nazi concentration camp) eventually made its mark as an overheated middle-of-the-road outfit before quickly burning out and slowly disintegrating throughout the '80s.

what to buy: The quintet hit it big worldwide with the title track of its third album, *True* ✶✶✶ (Chrysalis, 1983, prod. Tony Swain, Steve Jolley, Spandau Ballet). Here the group was recast as a proto-lounge band, only with none of the needed irony.

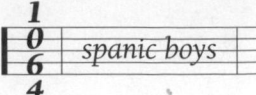
Granted, "Lifeline" and "Gold" were decent enough attempts at funky pop lite, and "True" did ultimately serve as the basis for PM Dawn's rap-lite breakthrough *Set Adrift on Memory Bliss* in 1991. But the group has to answer for its role as a prototype for mellow bellowers such as King and Cutting Crew, and even Spandau's better material always seemed false and unabashedly annoying.

what to avoid: For diehards, there's always *The Singles Collection* ♫♫ (Chrysalis, 1985, prod. various), but let's just say there's not much there to collect.

influences:

◀◀ Gary Numan, the Cars, Bauhaus

▶▶ PM Dawn, King, Cutting Crew

Bob Remstein

Spanic Boys

Formed 1987, in Milwaukee, WI.

Ian Spanic, vocals, guitar; Tom Spanic, vocals, guitar; Mike Fredrickson, bass (1987–93); Teddy Freese, drums (1987–91); Paul Schroeder, bass (1993–present); Curt Lefevre, drums (1991–present).

Best known as the band that replaced Sinéad O'Connor when she refused to perform on *Saturday Night Live* with host Andrew Dice Clay in 1990, the Spanic Boys know exactly how to rock. The father-and-son team—both wearing horn-rimmed glasses goofier than Buddy Holly's—rehashes rockabilly and other roots music, but adds wailing, raging guitars that wouldn't seem out of place on some Metallica songs. Tom, the elder Spanic, played in rock 'n' roll cover bands during the '60s, then taught guitar lessons for two decades before forming the band with his son in early 1987. Though the Boys have never produced a follow-up as powerful as the self-titled debut or *Strange World*, they deserve far more commercial attention than they've received.

what to buy: *Strange World* ♫♫♫♫ (Rounder, 1991, prod. Ian Spanic, Mike Hoffman) is a wonderfully catchy mix of sharp rockabilly rhythms, spooky harmonies, and fierce guitar playing. *Spanic Boys* ♫♫♫ (Rounder, 1990, prod. Scott Billington) is an out-of-nowhere update of Everly Brothers harmonies and '50s-style rock 'n' roll songwriting.

what to buy next: *Dream Your Life* ♫♫♫ (Rounder, 1992, prod. Ian Spanic, Mike Hoffman) has "That Train" and a few other stomping songs, but it's not as explosive as *Strange World* or the debut.

the rest:

(With the Spanic family) *Family Album* ♫♫♫ (ESD, 1994)

worth searching for: *Early Spanic Boys* (Rounder, 1992, prod. Mike Hoffman), a reissue of the band's tiny-label debut, showcases its developing Buddy Holly and Chet Atkins influences.

influences:

◀◀ Buddy Holly, Chet Atkins, Elvis Presley, the Everly Brothers, Jimi Hendrix, Richie Valens, X, Los Lobos

▶▶ The Blazers, Wayne Hancock, Rosie Flores, Big Sandy & His Fly-Rite Boys, Radio Kings

Steve Knopper

Sparklehorse

Formed 1995, in Richmond, VA.

Mark Linkous, vocals, guitar; others.

Although nominally a band, Sparklehorse is the brainchild of Mark Linkous, a pop eccentric fond of surging guitar anthems and crepuscular ballads whose songs would be worth hearing even without the hooks and the flourishes of banjo and steel guitar. Sex and nature are Linkous's best subjects, and he renders them with a voice, poetically and musically, that's as inscrutable as it is evocative.

what to buy: *Vivadixiesubmarinetransmissionplot* ♫♫♫♫ (Capitol, 1995, prod. Mark Linkous, David Lowery) is one of the more enchanting rock albums released during the mid-'90s. Darkness and whimsy abound, but with a humanity that's as indelible as Linkous's alternately shimmering and muted melodies.

the rest:

Chords I've Known ♫♫♫ (Slow River/Capitol EP, 1996)

influences:

◀◀ John Lennon, Soft Boys, Vic Chesnutt

Bill Friskics-Warren

Sparks

Formed 1971, in Los Angeles, CA.

Russell Mael, vocals; Ron Mael, keyboards.

Brothers Ron and Russell Mael are a half-musical, half-comic duo; in that respect, they could almost be a pop-rock incarnation of Gilbert and Sullivan. Between Ron's operatic near-falsetto and Russell's deft and comic keyboard flourishes, the two have created their own niche in the music industry, in which excellent keyboard-pop music melds seamlessly with humorously insightful lyrics. The duo (including an ever-changing backup band) made a significant impact in England during the mid-'70s with the singles "This Town Ain't Big Enough for the Both of Us" and "Amateur Hour." Success has been more elusive in its homeland, where the bulk of the group's largely terrific body of work is now out of print.

what to buy: *Profile: The Ultimate Sparks Collection* 𝄞𝄞𝄞𝄞 (Rhino, 1991, prod. various) is certainly the best Sparks album available at this time. The generous double-CD package offers all the group's best material, including "This Town Ain't Big Enough for the Both of Us," "Amateur Hour," "Hasta Manana, Monsieur," "Big Boy," "Cool Places" (which features the Go-Go's Jane Wiedlin), and "Change."

what to buy next: *Angst in My Pants* 𝄞𝄞𝄞𝄞 (Atlantic, 1982, prod. Mack) marks the point in Sparks' history when their music and lyrics achieved an equal measure of cleverness. The album contains some of the best songs from the group's middle period, including "Eaten by the Monster of Love," "Mickey Mouse" (a bizarre tribute to the Disney gang), and "Moustache" (a history of brother Ron's facial hair). In a terrific return to form, the Mael brothers bounced back from nowhere with *Gratuitous Sax and Senseless Violins* 𝄞𝄞𝄞𝄞 (Logic, 1995, prod. Sparks), perhaps the best album from the duo since *Angst* and reminiscent of the group's earliest and most inventive work.

what to avoid: *Sparks in Outer Space* 𝄞𝄞 (Atlantic, 1983, prod. Ron Mael, Russell Mael) is too self-consciously cute, and the songs are less inventive—though "Cool Places" did sneak into the Top 50.

worth searching for: *Kimono My House* (Island, 1974, prod. Sparks) is one of the best of Sparks' early albums, though it was way too quirky for the times.

influences:

◄◄ Captain Beefheart, Frank Zappa, Todd Rundgren, Commander Cody

►► The B-52's, Talking Heads, Soft Cell, Beck

Christopher Scapelliti

Spearhead /Disposable Heroes of Hiphoprisy

Spearhead formed 1993, in Oakland, CA. Disposable Heroes of Hiphoprisy formed 1990, in Oakland, CA. Disbanded 1990.

Spearhead: Michael Franti, vocals; Mary Harris, vocals (1993–95); Le Le Jamison, keyboards; Keith McArthur, bass; David James, guitar; James Gray, drums. Disposable Heroes: Michael Franti, vocals; Rono Tse, DJ, percussion.

Singer-rapper Michael Franti gained attention—first as a member of the Beatnigs, and then with the more visible Disposable Heroes of Hiphoprisy—for his confrontational but articulate political rapping, which owed a massive debt to Gil Scott-Heron and the Last Poets. The Disposables, who sought to replace the boasting and misogyny of mainstream rap with substantive argument, essayed such topics as U.S. foreign policy, homophobia, and the corrosive effects of television. Franti's tract-like rhymes were placed in a sonic collage influenced by punk and free jazz more than R&B. The result, though admirable in its intent, was too mired in political correctness and in-your-face indie cred to be very enjoyable. As with the Beatnigs before them, Franti dissolved the Heroes after one release and returned in 1994 with something entirely different—and better. Spearhead allowed him to mingle the political and the personal in a powerful new way, and instead of samples and *musique concrete,* his new musical context was a band that played warm, emotionally powerful soul and funk. Unable to capture the gangsta-loving rap audience, Spearhead was marketed to the alternative-rock crowd with some success, thanks in part to its insinuating single and video "Hole in the Bucket." Despite the departure of the band's other main vocalist, Mary Harris, after the release of the debut *Home,* the group remained together to record a second album—a first for Franti.

what to buy: On Spearhead's *Home* 𝄞𝄞𝄞𝄞 (Capitol, 1994, prod. Joe Nicolo, Michael Franti), Franti stretches out lyrically and displays a surprisingly effective singing voice. Harris, meanwhile, provides powerhouse accompaniment and a wry, sly counterpoint to Franti's sincere persona.

the rest:
Spearhead:
Hole in the Bucket 𝄞𝄞𝄞 (Capitol EP, 1995)
Chocolate Supa Highway 𝄞𝄞𝄞𝄞 (Capitol, 1997)

Disposable Heroes of Hiphoprisy:
Hiphoprisy Is the Greatest Luxury 𝄞𝄞𝄞𝄞 (4th &Broadway, 1992)

worth searching for: Franti's first group, the Beatnigs, lasted for just one hard-to-find recording. But what an album. *The Beatnigs* (Alternative Tentacles, 1988, prod. the Beatnigs) is the most interesting and innovative album any of Franti's three groups has made, loaded with sonic twists and turns (buzzsaws! chains whipped against tire rims!). Despite the industrial album's strong political bent, though, Franti generally manages to avoid the sort of pedantry that too often marks similar groups. Like, say, the Disposable Heroes of Hiphoprisy.

influences:

◄◄ Gil Scott-Heron, Last Poets, Einstürzende Neubauten, Public Enemy, Bob Marley, Stevie Wonder, Marvin Gaye

►► Paris, Consolidated

Simon Glickman and Josh Freedom du Lac

The Specials

Formed 1977, in Coventry, England. Disbanded 1981. Re-formed 1994.

Jerry Dammers, keyboards (1977–81); Lynval Golding, guitar; Sir Horace Gentleman (born Horace Panter), bass; Terry Hall, vocals (1978–81); Neville Staples, vocals, percussion; Roddy "Radiation" Byers, guitar; Siverton, drums (1977–78); John Bradbury, drums (1979–81); Mark Adams, keyboards, vocals (1994–present); Adam Birch, horns (1994–present); Aitch Hyatt, drums (1994–present).

A ska revival group, the Specials were the showpiece band of the U.K.'s short-lived two-tone movement of the late '70s and early '80s. Two-tone referred to the racially mixed groups that formed partly as a reaction to emerging skinhead racial violence in England. Evolving from various bands known as Coventry, the Coventry Specials, and the Specials AKA, the group had a number of U.K. singles and EP hits with their bouncy, party-friendly ska songs. The band shattered in 1981, when Neville Staples, Terry Hall, and Lynval Golding formed Fun Boy Three and Roddy Byers formed Roddy Radiation & the Tearjerkers. Jerry Dammers led a revamped lineup known as Specials AKA, then re-formed the band under its original moniker in 1994. Today, ska fans refer to the Specials' peak period as the genre's "second wave"—the first being the originals, Jamaicans such as the Skatalites, and the third being recent hit modern rock bands such as the Mighty Mighty Bosstones and No Doubt.

what to buy: *The Specials* 𝄞𝄞𝄞𝄞 (Chrysalis, 1979, prod. Elvis Costello) is the group's peak, with party favorites such as "A Message to You, Rudy," "Monkey Man," "Gangsters," and "Too Much, Too Young." The best set in print is *Singles Collection* 𝄞𝄞𝄞𝄞𝄞 (Capitol, 1991, prod. various), which includes "Ghost Town" and "Free Nelson Mandela," two of the group's best songs.

what to buy next: After the band regrouped, *Today's Specials* 𝄞𝄞𝄞𝄞 (Virgin, 1996, prod. various) gets back on the ska track with a number of covers—particularly a scorching version of "Take Five"—but doesn't quite match the unbridled exuberance of the first album.

what to avoid: *More Specials* 𝄞𝄞𝄞 (Chrysalis, 1980/Alliance, 1986, prod. Jerry Dammers, Dave Jordan), the follow-up to *The Specials*, lost the beat as the group veered into lounge music.

the rest:
Guilty 'til Proved Innocent 𝄞𝄞𝄞 (MCA, 1998)

influences:
◀◀ The Skatalites, the Wailers, Madness
▶▶ No Doubt, Mighty Mighty Bosstones

see also: *Fun Boy Three*

Lawrence Gabriel

Phil Spector

Born December 24, 1940, in the Bronx, NY.

The trademark mulched sound of Phil Spector's glorious productions—borrowed equally from Frank Guida and Leiber and Stoller—didn't survive the transfer into the digital domain with all their majesty intact. But his landmark work, probably best heard on the original 45s, commands an incomparable position in the realm of rock's history. His story is well known and, in fact, reads like fiction—the high school senior who wrote a #1 record (the Teddy Bears' "To Know Him Is to Love Him") from his father's epitaph and "retired" at age 25 to live the life of a reclusive Beverly Hills millionaire, only to return to the studio to remix the tapes from the Beatles' arduous *Let It Be* sessions. Spector was rock's ultimate *auteur,* a visionary—and a notorious eccentric, to be kind—who imprinted his artistic signature so thoroughly on the records he made during the early '60s for his own Philles Records that they are universally known as Phil Spector records and not by the name of the titular artists—who, by the way, included Gene Pitney, the Crystals, the Ronettes, Darlene Love, and the Righteous Brothers' "You've Lost That Lovin' Feelin'." According to legend, after his Tina Turner–sung production of "River Deep—Mountain High" bombed domestically, Spector quit the business in protest. More likely, he sensed his Wall of Sound teen dramas (mostly recorded in three-channel mono) would sound anachronistic amid late '60s musical trends. Spector kept his hand in, releasing an LP by famed "sick" comedian Lenny Bruce, leasing masters to the fledgling A&M label and making a cameo appearance in the hippie film classic *Easy Rider.* Since Spector seldom paid his artists their due royalties, he had plenty of money to pick and choose projects as a producer for hire during the '70s and '80s. His work with the Beatles, John Lennon, Leonard Cohen, the Ramones, and others were modest commercial successes but drew critical jeers. Moreover, in every case, his eccentric behavior served to estrange him from artists and record labels alike. Most recently, he produced sessions for Canadian chanteuse Celine Dion that she chose not to use. As a result, Spector has threatened to put out *his* version of the album. Though Spector appears finished as a creative force, his early productions are perpetual staples of oldies radio, and virtually every musician who has stepped into a recording studio in his wake owes him a massive debt.

what's available: Spector personally oversaw the production of the four-disc box set *Back to Mono (1958–1969)* 𝄞𝄞𝄞𝄞 (Abkco, 1991, prod. Phil Spector), so he has nobody else to blame for the indifferent, cloudy digital transfers of his masterpieces. In addition to his brilliant 1963 Christmas album, included on its own disc, the set spans his entire career—from "To Know Him Is to Love Him" to Tina Turner's "River Deep—

Mountain High" and a selection of rare and unissued latter-era studio experiments.

worth searching for: Spector so carefully rewrites his own history, he breezes through his wilderness years hitting just a few successful highpoints. But a Japanese import, *Twist and Shout* (WEA, 1989, prod. Phil Spector), collects 12 early productions he did for Atlantic Records that capture the artist in transition. They aren't uniformly great records, but the original singles are so hard to find that this set offers an unparalleled glimpse of the young Spector. You collectors should know that the ultra-rare *Lenny Bruce Is out Again* (Philles, 1965, prod. Phil Spector) fetches a high prices at auctions, even though it is one of Bruce's lesser works.

influences:

◄◄ Leiber & Stoller, Gary U.S. Bonds, the Drifters, Frankie Lymon & the Teenagers

►► Joe Meek, the Beach Boys, the Beatles, the Ramones, U2, Steve Lillywhite, Don Was, James "Jimmy Jam" Harris III & Terry Lewis, Kenneth "Babyface" Edmonds

Joel Selvin and Gary Graff

Ronnie Spector
See: The Ronettes

Speech
See: Arrested Development

Spell
See: The Fluid

Skip Spence
See: Moby Grape

Jon Spencer Blues Explosion
Formed 1991, in New York, NY.

Jon Spencer, vocals, guitar; Judah Bauer, guitar; Russell Simins, drums.

A brainy white guy from New England who attended Brown University and is obsessed with discordant noise and low-fi recording techniques, Jon Spencer would qualify as a prototypical indie-rocker if only he wasn't obsessed with the perverted, oily side of the blues. While his previous band, Pussy Galore, made noisy and occasionally offensive sleaze-rock, Spencer's Blues Explosion makes noisy and compellingly chaotic sleaze-blues that matches an amped-up, two-guitar boogie crunch with a punch-drunk vocal delivery. Sounding at once urgent and kitschy, Spencer is a combustible, idiosyncratic showman whose crude

WHAT ALBUM CHANGED YOUR LIFE?
The first side of Terry Reid's *River*. It's just seamless, funky. It was sort of spare and minimal. Also an album called *This Is Soul* on Atlantic. It was a sampler. It had Wilson Pickett on it, and Joe Tex and Otis Redding and Aretha Franklin.

Sir Horace Gentleman (of the Specials)

playing and singing is unpredictable and therefore exciting. By no means a blues trio, the Blues Explosion did close the gap between its ironic, postmodern music and the primitive blues when it backed R.L. Burnside on the elderly bluesman's fascinating *A Ass Pocket of Whiskey* in 1996. Significantly less interesting—and generally worth avoiding—is the work of wife Christina Martinez's band, Boss Hog, to which Spencer contributes.

what to buy: On the fierce and sludgy *Orange* ◊◊◊◊ (Matador, 1994, prod. Jon Spencer, Jim Waters), the Blues Explosion finally (and thankfully) grasps the notion of song structure, making it the most accessible Blues Explosion album yet—not that you'll be hearing the *Orange* standout "Bell Bottoms" alongside the latest from the Backstreet Boys or anything. Lyrically, though, it's still often difficult to figure out exactly what the hell Spencer is so hopped-up about.

what to buy next: *Experimental Remixes* ◊◊◊ (Matador, 1995, prod. various) features dueling versions of "Greyhound" (one by techno auteur Moby, the other by Wu-Tang Clan's Genius, with a menacing rap by Killah Priest), plus a double dip of "Flavor" by Beck, Beastie Boy Mike D, and Beasties producer Mario Caldato Jr. The boot-stompin' *Extra Width* ◊◊◊ (Matador, 1993, prod. Jon Spencer) isn't quite as structured as *Orange*, but it does show the trio finally finding its bearings—not to mention a funky undertone on the breakthrough "Afro."

what to avoid: *Mo Width* ◊◊ (Au-Go-Go, 1994) isn't terrible. It's just Spencer's worst.

the rest:
Jon Spencer Blues Explosion ◊◊◊ (Caroline, 1992)

Crypt Style ♫♫♫ (Crypt, 1993)
Now I Got Worry ♫♫♫ (Capitol, 1996)
(With R.L. Burnside) *A Ass Pocket of Whiskey* ♫♫♫♫ (Matador, 1996)
Acme N/A (Matador, 1998)

influences:

◄◄ Hound Dog Taylor, Elvis Presley, the Cramps, Jerry Lee Lewis, Johnny Burnette, the Stooges, Gibson Brothers, Stax/Volt, James Brown, Curtis Mayfield, New York Dolls, Velvet Underground

►► Big Ass Truck, Beck, Mac Swanky Trio, Delta 72, Royal Trux

see also: *Boss Hog*

Josh Freedom du Lac

The Spice Girls

Formed 1994, in London, England.

Geri "Ginger Spice" Halliwell, vocals (1994–98); Victoria "Posh Spice" Adams, vocals; Melanie "Sporty Spice" Chisolm, vocals; Melanie "Scary Spice" Brown, vocals; Emma Lee "Baby Spice" Bunton, vocals.

So tell us what you want, what you really really want. If it's radio-ready pop pap of the most disposable variety, wrapped in a pretty package and run up the flagpole with the most calculating of marketing schemes, the Spice Girls may just be the group for you. The Spice Girls scored the highest-charting British debut single ever with "Wannabe" in 1996. But that accomplishment was only a modest warning of the media tempest that followed them afterwards. The story goes that the five young women were brought together by a greedy producer (or a would-be team of svengalis—such are the vagaries of marketing, you know), but upon meeting one another broke out on their own, eschewing the virtues of "Girl Power!" and crafting their catchy but disposable debut album *Spice*. In reality, the whole thing was contrived, from the image to the sloganeering to the music. But that didn't stop the group from scoring several international hits with adult-contempo synth songs like "Say You'll Be There" and "2 Become 1." Crass, maybe, but on the other hand, don't hate them because they're (relatively) beautiful. Sometimes, as in the tradition of the Monkees, New Edition, Wham!, and countless other manufactured bands, the Spice Girls rise above their very real limitations and create some of the most enticing ear and eye candy in recent pop music history. And if we forget them tomorrow, what harm will have been done?

what to buy: The hype accompanying the Spice Girls' megaselling worldwide smash *Spice* ♫♫♫ (Virgin, 1996, prod. Richard Stannard, Matt Rowe, Absolute) has been so enduring and so fevered, that the experience of sitting down and actually listening to the thing, as opposed to merely having an opinion about it, seems almost irrelevant. But no; *Spice*, it turns out, is actually an enjoyable pop trifle, full of hooky choruses, danceable grooves, and yes, tolerable singing. The girl-power anthem "Wannabe" is an obvious winner, and the follow-up, "Say You'll Be There" charms with a surprising touch, a Stevie Wonder–like harmonica in the instrumental break.

what to buy next: *Spiceworld* ♫♫♫ (Virgin, 1997, prod. Richard Stannard, Matt Rowe, Absolute) accompanied the group's leap to the silver screen, and while it yielded a hit in the lightly Latinized "Spice up Your Life," the album as a whole suggests that the clock is running on the Spice Girls' 15 minutes of fame.

influences:

◄◄ Madonna, Wham!, Motown, Margaret Thatcher

Daniel Durchholz and Aidin Vaziri

Spill

See: William Orbit

Spin Doctors

Formed 1988, in New York, NY.

Chris Barron (born Christopher Barron Gross), vocals; Aaron Comess, drums; Mark Burton White, bass; Eric Schenkman, guitar (1988–94); Anthony Krizan, guitar, vocals (1994–97); Erin Tabib, guitar (1997–present).

Born from the same fertile New York City blues-rock scene that also produced Joan Osborne and Blues Traveler (whose members went to the same Princeton, New Jersey, high school as Chris Barron), Spin Doctors built their reputation as a tireless live band that jammed to a funky, elastic groove while rubber-boned frontman Barron bounced up and down reciting his sometimes catchy, sometimes quizzical lyrics. Despite the members' instrumental prowess, it was a tightly written hit single, "Little Miss Can't Be Wrong," that broke the band nationally. Subsequent albums have failed to repeat that success, and Barron's lyrics have grown prolix. For a time, Spin Doctors were compared to the Grateful Dead for their extended live jams and dedicated audience, which would follow them around the country. But maybe the real similarity is that, as with Deadheads and the Dead, dyed-in-the-wool Spin Docs fans should not—repeat, should not—listen to the band after they've run out of dope. A rude awakening awaits. Plus, that audience has dwindled considerably, to the point where the band's label, Epic, dropped them in 1997. A new album featuring contributions from keyboardist/vocalist Ivan Neville is reportedly in the can, but as of this writing, no record deal has been announced.

what to buy: *Pocket Full of Kryptonite* ♫♫♫ (Epic, 1991, prod. Spin Doctors, Peter Denenberg, Frankie LaRocka) shows off both sides of the band. Its instrumental attack is varied, and what jamming goes on is well thought out and executed. The album also contains the band's two best and most concise singles, "Two Princes" and "Little Miss Can't Be Wrong." The latter song sounds so much like a Steve Miller Band smasheroo, it should have been titled "Little Miss Can't Miss"—despite its misogynistic lyric directed at Barron's former stepmother.

what to buy next: The concert recording *Homebelly Groove* ♪♪♪ (Epic, 1992, prod. Peter Denenberg, Aaron Comess, Eric Schenkman, Frankie LaRocka, Spin Doctors) bears witness to Spin Doctors' appeal as a live act. The emphasis is squarely on jamming, with Eric Schenkman's guitar leading the way and some impressive rhythmic interplay between Aaron Comess and Mark White. This release adds a handful of new and previously unreleased tracks to the 1990 *Up for Grabs* EP, including a live version of "Little Miss Can't Be Wrong."

what to avoid: *Turn It Upside Down* **woof!** (Epic, 1994, prod. Frankie LaRocka) is the very definition of a sophomore slump; it makes all the same moves as *Pocket Full of Kryptonite*, only not half as well. The downward spiral continues with *You've Got to Believe in Something* **woof!** (Epic, 1996, prod. Danny Kortchmar, Peter Denenberg), which features moronically pseudopoetic lyrics ("Riches and the roads bring brigands hither . . . ") and even less musical oomph than *Turn It Upside Down*.

worth searching for: Fanatics and collectors may want to search used CD bins for the now-deleted original version of *Up for Grabs* (Epic EP, 1990), just so they can say they knew 'em when.

influences:

◀◀ The Grateful Dead, the Steve Miller Band, Parliament-Funkadelic, Blues Traveler

▶▶ Screaming Cheetah Wheelies, the Why Store, Ugly Americans

Daniel Durchholz

Spinal Tap

Formed 1984, in Los Angeles, CA.

David St. Hubbins (Michael McKeon), vocals/guitar; Nigel Tufnel (Christopher Guest), guitar/vocals; Derek Smalls (Harry Shearer), bass.

Spinal Tap is really two bands: the fictional heavy metal dinosaurs featured in director Rob Reiner's brilliant 1984 rockumentary satire *This Is Spinal Tap*, and the film's writers/actors, who wrote and performed the music for the film's soundtrack and one other album. *This Is Spinal Tap* documented the waning years of a British hard rock outfit that never quite made it over the course of two decades, numerous name changes, dozens of albums with titles such as *Brain Hammer*, *Shark Sandwich*, *Intravenus de Milo*, and *The Sun Never Sweats*, and a succession of drummers, all of whom seem to die under mysterious circumstances (including one who choked on vomit—

somebody else's—and several who spontaneously combusted). It's all great fun, and occasionally an all too accurate portrayal of real-life music industry experiences.

what to buy: The soundtrack for *This Is Spinal Tap* ♪♪♪ (Polydor, 1984, prod. Spinal Tap) contains passable musicianship and hilarious metal send-ups such as "Sex Farm," "Hell Hole," and "Big Bottom" ("The bigger the cushion/The sweeter the pushin'"), as well as the psychedelic "(Listen to the) Flower People."

the rest:
Break Like the Wind ♪♪♪ (MCA, 1992)

influences:

◀◀ Black Sabbath, Deep Purple, Motörhead, the Rutles

Brandon Trenz

The Spinanes

Formed 1992, in Eugene, OR.

Rebecca Gates, guitar, vocals; Scott Plouf, drums (1992–97).

When the Spinanes were signed to Sub Pop Records in 1991, subtlety wasn't in the label's vocabulary, and the duo was viewed curiously by the longhairs and grunge kids used to snatching up everything on the label, racing home, and rocking their bedroom. The Spinanes illustrated to these losers that other emotions besides anger and frustration could be discussed in a song, and that volume and superfuzz weren't necessarily essential ingredients for tension, but they can work in a pinch. Using only guitar, vocals, and drums, the Spinanes—who since 1997 are Rebecca Gates plus whoever—create gorgeous folk songs that have grown more lush over the years. More recent albums have featured mellotron, moog, organ, bass, and percussion. At their heart, though, is Gates's whispery yet mighty voice, a voice that, regardless of the distortion pedal she's using for her guitar, remains steady and consistent. When she relocated to Chicago in 1997, she left Scott Plouf behind to pound for Built to Spill and gathered a bevy of locals to accompany her.

what to buy: Each successive Spinanes record has shown a marked variance over the previous, making *Arches and Aisles* ♪♪♪♪ (Sub Pop, 1998, prod. Rebecca Gates) Gate's most accomplished and interesting work. Partly recorded in Memphis with engineer du jour Doug Easley and partly in Chicago with Tortoise brainiac John McEntire, the record moves on a dime from thick and complex to simple and elegant.

what to buy next: *Manos* ♪♪♪ (Sub Pop, 1993, prod. Brian Paulson), the Spinanes' debut, manages to tread between folk and hard-rock songs with an ease that usually takes artists years to develop, and it's this feat, along with marvelous songs—especially the title track—that make the album desirable to anyone curious about the winding paths behind the whole "Women in

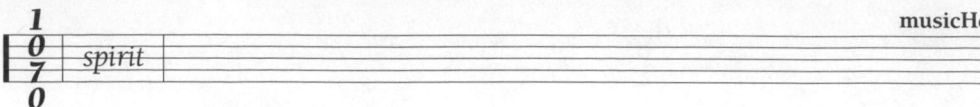
Rock" thing. *Strand* ✍✍✍♥ (Sub Pop, 1996, prod. Spinanes) is nearly as consistent as *Manos*, but lacks the devotion and backbone of the others. It does, however, feature a couple of phenomenal tracks with genius-of-the-moment Elliott Smith.

influences:

◀◀ Beat Happening, the Raincoats, Throwing Muses

▶▶ Elliott Smith, Sleater-Kinney, Liz Phair

Randall Roberts

Spirit

Formed 1969, in Los Angeles, CA.

Randy California (born Randy Wolfe; died January 1997), vocals, guitar (1967-70, 1974-97); Ed Cassidy, drums (1967-97); Jay Ferguson (born John Ferguson), vocals, guitar, keyboards (1967-70, 1984); John Locke, keyboards, vocals (1967-72, 1976-77, 1984); Mark Andes, bass, vocals (1967-70, 1976-77, 1984); Chris Staehely, vocals, guitar (1970-74); Al Staehely, bass, vocals (1970-74); Matt Andes, guitar (1976-77); Larry Knight, bass (1977-97).

Spirit was very much a band of its time—that being the psychedelic late '60s. All of the original members encountered each other in and around Los Angeles before settling into the group; Ed Cassidy, Spirit's oldest member by at least 25 years, was Randy California's stepfather. Though its musical scope was impressive—mixing rock, blues, jazz, and country in a trippy stew that foreshadowed the genre blending of '90s rock—Spirit was a second-division fixture at best, though it did produce one enduring hit in "I Got a Line on You." Numerous personnel changes led to an original lineup reunion in 1984. Mark Andes and Jay Ferguson co-founded the band Jo Jo Gunne; Andes moved on to Firefall and Heart, while Ferguson had a couple of solo hits ("Thunder Island," "Shakedown Cruise"). California and Cassidy kept Spirit on the oldies circuit with a revolving series of bassists until California's accidental drowning in 1997.

what to buy: *The Twelve Dreams of Dr. Sardonicus* ✍✍✍✍ (Epic, 1970/Legacy, 1996, prod. David Briggs) was Spirit's crowning moment and one of the era's great underrated albums. Loosely conceptual, it housed songs that were Spirit's prettiest ("Nature's Way"), funkiest ("Mr. Skin"), and hippiest ("Animal Zoo," "Nothin' to Hide"). Rather than dated, it still sounds fresh today.

what to buy next: Everyone needs to own "I Got a Line on You" in some form. The best is probably *Time Circle (1968–1972)* ✍✍✍✍ (Epic/Legacy, 1991, prod. Bob Irwin), a double-length compilation of music from Spirit's first four albums. Some of the 41 songs haven't aged as well as "Line" or the "Sardonicus" material, but it's still better than any of the individual albums.

what to avoid: Do you need more than the title to know to stay away from *The Adventures of Kaptain Kopter & Commander Cassidy in Potatoland* **woof!** (Rhino, 1981, prod. Randy California)?

the rest:

Spirit ✍✍ (Ode, 1968/Legacy, 1996)
The Family That Plays Together ✍✍✍ (Ode, 1968/Legacy, 1996)
Clear ✍✍✍ (Ode, 1969/Legacy, 1996)
Feedback ✍✍ (Epic, 1972)
The Best of Spirit ✍✍✍✍ (Epic, 1973)
Spirit of '76 ✍✍ (Mercury, 1975)
Son of Spirit ✍✍ (Mercury, 1975)
Farther Along ✍ (Mercury, 1976)
Future Games ✍ (Mercury, 1977)
Spirit of '84 ✍✍ (Mercury, 1984)
Rapture in the Chambers ✍✍ (I.R.S., 1989)
Tent of Miracles ✍ (Dolphin/Caroline, 1990)
The Mercury Years ✍✍✍♥ (Mecury Chronicles, 1997)

worth searching for: *Live Spirit* (Potato, 1979, prod. Randy California) offers an inspired trio performance with an additional verse in "Nature's Way" and expanded versions of "Looking Down" and "All the Same."

solo outings:

Randy California:
Kaptain Kopter & the Fabulous Twirlybirds ✍✍ (Epic, 1972)
Euro-American ✍ (Beggars Banquet, 1982)
Shattered Dreams ✍✍ (Line, 1987)

Jo Jo Gunne (Ferguson and Andes):
Jo Jo Gunne ✍✍✍ (Asylum, 1972)
Bite Down Hard ✍ (Asylum, 1973)
Jumping the Gunne **woof!** (Asylum, 1973)
So . . . Where's the Snow? ✍ (Asylum, 1974)

Jay Ferguson:
All Alone in the End Zone ✍ (Asylum, 1976)
Thunder Island ✍✍ (Asylum, 1977)
Real Life Ain't This Way ✍ (Asylum, 1979)
White Noise ✍ (Capitol, 1982)

influences:

◀◀ The Weavers, Gerry Mulligan, Thelonious Monk, Rising Sons, Jimi Hendrix

▶▶ Jo Jo Gunne, Beck, Cake

see also: *Firefall, Heart*

Gary Graff

Spiritual Cowboys

See: Eurythmics

Spiritualized

Formed 1990, in Rugby, England.

Jason Pierce, vocals, guitars; Kate Radley, keboards, vocals; Sean Cook, guitars, harmonica; Mark Refoy, guitars (1990–95); John Mat-

tock, percussion (1990–95); Damon Reece, percussion (1996–present); John Coxon, guitars, melodica (1996–present).

Born out of the hypnotic guitar drones and drug posturing of Spacemen 3, this neo-psychedelic band has grown up to craft some of the most organic and dynamic headphone symphonies of the '90s. Jason Pierce, the band's creative center, pens lyrics about love, loss, anger, and escape, and he wraps them in music that's equal parts polish (from trained gospel voices to symphony orchestras) and raw, visceral energy (Captain Beefheart–school harmonica, saxophone squonks, etc.). The music is sometimes melodious and sometimes dissonant, but nearly always cold. Although rife with peaks and valleys, Pierce's compositions are somehow almost completely devoid of catharsis. But Spiritualized's music is not unfeeling; rather, it is what is left after all the feeling has been drained.

what to buy: At its best, *Ladies and Gentlemen We Are Floating in Space* ✍✍✍ (Arista, 1997, prod. Jason Pierce, John Coxon) is hypnotic and staggeringly beautiful. At its worst, it's noisy and self-indulgent. Still, it's hard not to give Pierce props even for his self-indulgence: the more trying parts come on songs such as "No God Only Religion" where a 58-piece orchestral arrangement careens through four full minutes of utter dissonance. At the bottom of all that sonic garbage sits the gentle gospel tune "Cool Waves," which blends into the album's final track, "Cop Shoot Cop," a 17-minute blues-inflected exploration led by Dr. John. Find that in a rock record these days.

what to buy next: *Pure Phase* ✍✍✍ (Dedicated, 1995, prod. Jason Pierce) is less about peaks and valleys and more about ebb and flow. Guitar drones more reminiscent of Syd Barrett than the Velvet Underground are prevalent, structured neatly around occasional smatterings of gospel and horns.

the rest:
Laser Guided Melodies ✍✍✍ (Dedicated, 1992)

influences:
◄◄ Spacemen 3, Velvet Underground, Syd Barrett/Pink Floyd

see also: *Spacemen 3*

Isaac Josephson

Split Enz /Tim Finn /Alt

Formed 1972, in Auckland, New Zealand. Disbanded 1984. Re-formed 1993.

Tim Finn, vocals (1972–83); Phil Judd, guitars, vocals (1972–77); Eddie Rayner, keyboards; Malcolm Green, drums (1972–82); Noel Crombie, percussion, drums (1972–84); Phil Chunn, bass (1974–77); Nigel

Griggs, bass (1977–84); Neil Finn, guitar, lead vocals (1977–84); Paul Hester, drums (1984).

Split Enz's history begins with the band's art-school genesis in 1972. Not quite fitting into the burgeoning punk scene of the mid-'70s, the band did little to distinguish itself. But in 1977, following the departure of co-founder Phil Judd, singer Tim Finn brought his younger brother Neil aboard as the band's guitarist and second vocalist, thus beginning Split Enz's most commercially fruitful period. Where the band had previously explored odd song structures and artistic indulgences, Neil's influence added a leaner pop sensibility to the mix. With the release of the 1980 album *True Colors*, Split Enz achieved a balance between its past quirks and an increasing talent for hooks that brought the group to the fore of the new wave movement bubbling up in punk's wake. Tim Finn left the group for a solo career in 1983, and in the early '90s he formed the group Alt with Liam O'Maonlai from Hothouse Flowers and Irish recording star Andy White. Split Enz broke up a year later, and Neil Finn led the group Crowded House—which included Tim on its excellent album *Woodface*. Split Enz re-formed for a reunion tour in 1993, and in '94 Neil and Tim Finn got together as the Finn Brothers in the U.S. and as Finn everywhere else.

what to buy: Regrettably, almost all of the Split Enz catalog has been deleted in the U.S.—a pity given the quality that its best albums displayed. Of the remaining choices, the retrospective *History Never Repeats* ✍✍✍ (A&M, 1987, prod. various) is the most representative of the band's range. The collection focuses on the more pop-friendly material in the band's oeuvre, and, as a result, Neil Finn's material gets a greater proportion of the spotlight than it did on the group's albums.

what to buy next: The group's landmark album *True Colors* ✍✍✍ (A&M, 1980, prod. David Tickle) saw the first flourish of Neil's pop sensibility (the hit "I Got You"), while Tim still managed to infuse the album with plenty of nervous, arty energy ("Shark Attack").

what to avoid: Tim Finn's solo album *Big Canoe* ✍ (Virgin, 1988, prod. Nick Launay) is an unruly, self-indulgent mess, missing his characteristic knack for melody.

the rest:
Anniversary ✍✍✍ (Fuel, 1996)

worth searching for: With so much of the Split Enz catalog available on import only, there are lots of choices here. *Waiata* (A&M, 1981, prod. David Tickle), featuring the stellar Neil Finn compositions "One Step Ahead" and "History Never Repeats," is particularly worth the hunt.

solo outings:
Tim Finn:
Tim Finn ✍✍✍ (Capitol, 1989)

Before and After 🎵🎵 (Capitol, 1993)
(With Alt) *Altitude* 🎵🎵🎵 (Cooking Vinyl, 1995)

influences:

◄◄ Roxy Music, David Bowie, the Beatles

►► Phil Keaggy, Schnell Fenster, That Petrol Emotion, Boom Crash Opera, Crowded House

see also: *Crowded House*

David Galens

Sponge

Formed 1993, in Detroit, MI.

Vinnie Dombroski, vocals; Mike Cross, guitar; Joey Mazzola, guitars; Tim Cross, bass; Jimmy Paluzzi, drums (1993–95); Charlie Grover, drums (1995–present).

Blending glam attitude and traditional blue-collar Detroit rock, Sponge is no overnight sensation. Most of the band members sharpened their teeth in Loudhouse, which was dropped by Virgin Records after one album. The bad news motivated Vinnie Dombroski and brothers Mike and Tim Cross into creative success with Sponge—a spirit reflected in songs such as "Plowed" and "Molly (Sixteen Candles)" off its hit debut, *Rotting Pinata*.

what to buy: The follow-up to *Rotting Pinata*, *Wax Ecstatic* 🎵🎵🎵 (Columbia, 1996, prod. Sponge, Tim Patalan) really has the goods, with grinding guitars, relentlessly hook-laden lyrics and melodies, and Dombroski's raw vocals. Originally meant to be a concept album about a drag queen, the band's departure didn't bode well with singleminded fans who expected more Bush-like alternative rock—and that's unfortunate. With its acerbic guitars, the title track is trashy yet beautiful. Memphis blues is sprinkled throughout the album. "I Am Anastasia," during which Dombroski duets with ex–Psychedelic Furs frontman Richard Butler, is a stellar effort.

what to buy next: *Rotting Pinata* 🎵🎵🎵 (Work, 1994, prod. Sponge, Tim Patalan) was the band's breakthrough hit, though it sounded like dozens of existing bands on MTV and the radio at the time.

worth searching for: The Australian CD-5 for "Wax Ecstatic" (Columbia, 1996, prod. Sponge, Tim Patalan) features two non-album tracks, including a cover of the Stooges' "No Fun."

influences:

◄◄ Iggy Pop, MC5, Bush, Smashing Pumpkins, Pearl Jam

►► Hoarse

Christina Fuoco

The Spongetones

Formed c. 1980, in Charlotte, NC.

Jamie Hoover, vocals, guitar, bass, mandolin, recorder, harmonica; Steve Stoeckel, vocals, bass, guitar; Rob Thorne, drums, percussion; Patrick Walters, vocals, keyboards, guitar, harmonica, dulcimer.

The early Beatles reborn, or merely an incredible simulation (or maybe Klaatu in disguise)? Dismissed by some as too slavishly derivative of the Fab Four, the Spongetones have delighted discerning pop fans with avowedly Beatlesque hooks and harmonies. The group's earliest efforts were engaging pastiches of *Beatles '65*—much like the Rutles played straight—with each tune a familiar-sounding rummage through the British Invasion songbook. While it's certainly fun playing Name That Tune, the appeal of the Spongetones' recordings lies not in where the group nicks its hooks and melodies, but in the self-assured manner in which it assembles such thefts into appealing new pop confections. Later recordings have downplayed the Mersey factor but have generally retained an unspoiled, irresistible pop charm.

what to buy: *Beat & Torn* 🎵🎵🎵🎵 (Black Vinyl, 1994, prod. Jamie Hoover) combines the group's first two releases, *Beat Music* (Ripete, 1982) and *Torn Apart* (Ripete, 1984), on one CD, along with a bonus song. This means 19 tracks of heart-stopping ersatz merseybeat, performed with a sense of gusto and accomplishment that makes the music's second-hand roots an irrelevant point. *Oh Yeah!* 🎵🎵🎵🎵 (Black Vinyl, 1991, prod. Jamie Hoover) assimilates the Spongetones' influences into a brilliant work that's still beholden to the Beatles, but less slavish in its devotion.

what to buy next: On *For Textural Drone Thing* 🎵🎵🎵 (Black Vinyl, 1995, prod. Jamie Hoover) the Spongetones cut back on the Beatlemania moves in an attempt to forge a new group identity. The result lacks the immediate rush of the group's faux Liverpudlian material but succeeds in the easygoing pop style familiar to fans of Marshall Crenshaw.

what to avoid: Recorded without participation from Steve Stoeckel, *Where-Ever-Land* 🎵🎵 (Triapore, 1987, prod. Jamie Hoover, Don Dixon) was the group's first attempt to get away from imitation Britboom, a stumble despite the superior tracks "Anna" and "Talk to the Girl."

worth searching for: The Spongetones have contributed worthwhile non-album tracks to a few sampler albums, including "Christmasland" on *Yuletunes* (Black Vinyl, 1991, prod. various), "Skinny" on *Yellow Pills, Volume One* (Big Deal, 1993, prod. various), and "Eyedoan Geddit" on *Hit the Hay, Volume 2* (Sound Asleep, 1996, prod. various).

solo outings:

Jamie Hoover:

Coupons, Questions and Comments 🎵🎵 (Triapore, 1990)

Vinnie Dombroski of Sponge (© **Ken Settle**)

influences:

⏪ The Beatles, the Hollies, the Knickerbockers, the Searchers, the Dave Clark Five

⏩ Marshall Crenshaw, Jellyfish

Carl Cafarelli

Spooky Tooth

See: Gary Wright

Spoonfed Hybrid

See: Pale Saints

Dusty Springfield

Born Mary O'Brien, April 16, 1939, in London, England.

Dusty Springfield was part of the female pop vocalist explosion of the mid-'60s that was fueled by artists from both sides of the Atlantic. As lead singer of the Springfields, she scored her first hit with "Silver Threads and Golden Needles" during 1962. From there she went solo and recorded a slew of Top 40 hits through the rest of the decade. What separated British-born Springfield from the pack was her willingness to perform well-chosen material from a wide variety of songwriters. She lacked the sheer vocal ability of some of her contemporaries but overcame that with inspired phrasing and performances; it's hard to imagine anyone delivering a sexier performance of Burt Bacharach and Hal David's "The Look of Love." Her syncopated delivery of "I Just Don't Know What to Do with Myself" is inspired and soulful. With the help of legendary producers Jerry Wexler and Tom Dowd, she stretched in a new direction with 1969's *Dusty in Memphis*, an album that melded R&B instrumentation and background vocals with contemporary pop. Springfield and the album's producers also selected material from Randy Newman, Gerry Goffin and Carole King, Bacharach and David, and Michael Legrand. But other than the single "Son of a Preacher Man," the album did not make much of a commercial impact. Today, it's widely regarded as a classic, and artists such as Joan Osborne cite it as a musical touchstone. Springfield got even more soulful on *A Brand New Me* in 1970, teaming up with Kenny Gamble, Leon Huff, and others who were shaping the emerging Philly Sound. Springfield recorded sporadically through the '70s and '80s, with mixed results. In 1987, she contributed vocals to the Pet Shop Boys' single "What Have I Done to Deserve This," which was a hit on both sides of the Atlantic. She remains a national treasure in her native Great Britain.

what to buy: *The Dusty Springfield Anthology* ♪♪♪♪ (Mercury Chronicles, 1997, prod. various) is a well-thought-out three-disc retrospective, starting with "Silver Threads and Golden Needles" and concluding with two late '80s collaborations with the Pet Shop Boys. In between you'll find a wealth of hits and some rare tracks, although with this volume, some of the material on the final disc gets a bit thin. Also, some key tracks, such as "24 Hours from Tulsa," are omitted. Those wanting a smaller taste of Springfield may do better with *The Very Best of Dusty Springfield* ♪♪♪♪ (Mercury Chronicles, 1998, prod. various), a single disc that covers the appropriate highlights. And don't overlook *Dusty in Memphis* ♪♪♪♪ (Atlantic/Rhino, 1969, prod. Jerry Wexler, Tom Dowd, Anif Mardin), a bona fide classic and the most ambitious project Springfield ever put on record.

Stay Awhile—I Only Want to Be with You/Dusty ♪♪♪♪ (PolyGram/Taragon, 1997, prod. various) is a great-sounding disc that combines two 1964 Springfield albums and includes some of her most well-known songs ("I Only Want to Be with You," "24 Hours from Tulsa," "Anyone Who Had a Heart").

what to avoid: On *A Very Fine Love* ♪♪ (Columbia/Sony, 1995, prod. Tom Shapiro), Springfield's voice is still in fine form, but the material is strictly mediocre and the production is bloated and already sounds dated. Her duet with Daryl Hall on "Wherever Would I Be" is perfunctory.

the rest:

A Brand New Me ♪♪♪ (Atlantic/Rhino, 1970)

influences:

⏪ Doris Day, Aretha Franklin, Patti Page, Connie Francis

⏩ Joan Osborne, Vonda Shepard, Celine Dion, Mariah Carey

Michael Isabella

Rick Springfield

Born Richard Springthorpe, August 23, 1949, in Sydney, Australia.

Music fans may chuckle, but if you grew up during the '80s, there's no doubt that Rick Springfield's music had an effect on you. Women swooned when he pointed at them and sang "Where can I find a woman like that?"—especially if your boyfriend's name was Jessie. The ultimate '80s revenge song—besides "You Give Love a Bad Name" by Bon Jovi—was "I've Done Everything for You (You've Done Nothing for Me)." But what most '80s teenyboppers don't know is that his career began long before that. Born to a father in the military, Springfield bopped around the world with his family, living in Australia and England. Settling in Australia, Springfield played in Rock House and the pop band Zoot before the '60s were over. After Zoot broke up, Springfield went solo and scored a hit with "Speak to the Sky" from his now out-of-print album *Comic Book Heroes*. But as quickly as his star rose, it fell. As a back-up, Springfield tried his hand at acting, but that too fell flat. His musical career was revived, however, when RCA Records gave him a shot. Following the cliché "when it rains it pours," Springfield got the part of Dr. Noah Drake on the ABC soap opera *General Hospital* in 1981, a fortuitous opportunity to cross-promote that gave him a few years' worth of superstardom.

what to buy: Springfield's first CD for RCA, *Working Class Dog* ♫♫♫ (RCA, 1981, prod. Rick Springfield, Keith Olsen), is by far his best. The power-pop of "Jessie's Girl" and "I've Done Everything for You" pushed Springfield into teen idoldom. "Love Is Alright Tonight" showed the singer's gritty side.

what to buy next: *Success Hasn't Spoiled Me Yet* ♫♫♫ (RCA, 1982, prod. Keith Olsen), featuring Mr. Mister frontman Richard Page on back-up vocals, is nearly as satisfying. In the melancholy "Don't Talk to Strangers," Springfield urged a lover not to date others ("Don't talk to strangers/You know he'll only use you"). The mid-tempo pop hit "What Kind of Fool Am I?" was another gem.

what to avoid: The title of *Beautiful Feelings* **woof!** (Mercury, 1984) is exactly what you don't have after listening to this dog of an album, a repackaging that tried to cash in on his then-current success.

the rest:
Living in Oz ♫♫♫ (RCA, 1983)
Hard to Hold ♫♫ (RCA, 1984)
Tao ♫♫♪ (RCA, 1985)
Rock of Life ♫♫ (RCA, 1988)
Greatest Hits ♫♫♫ (RCA, 1989)

worth searching for: Those wishing a taste of Springfield's early work—which wasn't nearly as compelling as his '80s material—can keep an eye out for *Beginnings* (Capitol, 1972), *Comic Book Heroes* (Capitol Tie, 1973), *Mission Magic* (Wizard, 1974), and *Wait for the Night* (Chelsea, 1976).

influences:
◀◀ Rick Nelson, Fabian, Bobby Vee, the Beatles
▶▶ Jamie Walters, Gerald Collier

Christina Fuoco

Springhouse
Formed 1988, in New York, NY.

Mitch Friedland, guitar, lead vocals, hammer dulcimer; Jack Rabid (born Paul Corradi), drums, vocals; Larry Heinemann, bass, guitar, Chapman Stick, mandolin, backing vocals.

Combining the talents of Blue Man Group music director Larry Heinemann, music critic and ex–Even Worse leader Jack Rabid, and guitar-sound-obsessed ambulance driver Mitch Friedland, Springhouse became a downtown Manhattan favorite via opening for many of the British bands *MusicHound Rock* contributor

Jack Rabid champions in his long-running fanzine, *The Big Takeover*. Those bands' fans are exactly the audience most likely to appreciate Springhouse's pastel-tinted sound, akin to some British "shoegazer" bands. Friedland constructs shimmering walls of plectral tintinnabulation by running gut-strung acoustic guitars through effects boxes and then singing over it all with yearning and angst. After releasing an indie single, the group signed with Caroline Records and released a debut album that did moderately well thanks to a little MTV play. The group experienced a disastrous cross-country tour during early 1993; its equipment was stolen and its van was damaged so badly in a robbery that it couldn't be driven and, as a result, shows were cancelled. After Caroline dropped the band, Springhouse disbanded, but reunited in 1998 to record a third album.

what to buy: On *Postcards from the Arctic* ♫♫♫♫ (Caroline, 1993, prod. Joe Chiccarelli), the best song among many great slices of atmospheric, melodic pop is "Alley Park," a.k.a. "Twilight."

what to buy next: *Land Falls* ♫♫♫♫ (Caroline, 1991, prod. Mike McMackin, Springhouse), featuring "Layers," is slightly more straightforward and less baroquely dark than *Postcards*, but perhaps even more melodic. The highlight of the five-song EP *Eskimo* ♫♫♫♪ (Caroline, 1991, prod. Mike McMackin, Springhouse) is the only cover song the group has released, the Saints' "Angels." Also featured are a different mix of the title song and two non-album tracks.

worth searching for: The "Menagerie Keeper"/"Soul Astray" 7-inch single (Singles Only, 1990, prod. Mike McMackin, Springhouse) sounds tentative compared to later work, but it's still well written.

influences:
◀◀ R.E.M., the Saints, the Buzzcocks, the Who, Bert Jansch, John Martyn, Nick Drake, Richard Thompson

Steve Holtje

Bruce Springsteen /Bruce Springsteen & the E Street Band
Born September 23, 1949, in Freehold, NJ.

E Street Band: Clarence Clemons, saxophone, vocals (1972–89); Garry Tallent, bass (1972–89); Danny Federici, keyboards (1972–89); Vini "Mad Dog" Lopez, drums (1972–73); Ernest "Boom" Carter, drums (1973–74); David Sancious, keyboards (1972–74); Max Weinberg, drums (1974–89); Roy Bittan, keyboards (1972–89); "Miami"

Steve Van Zandt, guitar, vocals (1975–84); Nils Lofgren, guitar, vocals (1984–89); Patti Scialfa, vocals, guitar (1984–89).

Bruce Springsteen didn't set out to be the new Bob Dylan or the future of rock 'n' roll or any of the other hyperbole attached to him when he began recording during the early '70s. He was, in fact, a prototypical Jersey shore rocker—big guitars and bouncy tunes with at least a little bit o' soul—who also had an appreciation for poetry and the great, sweeping narratives of American literature; Springsteen understood the art in *The Grapes of Wrath,* in "Like a Rolling Stone," and in "Louie, Louie," and he funneled those sensibilities into his own body of work. Besides the "new Dylan" tag, Springsteen also survived having his picture appear simultaneously on the cover of *Time* and *Newsweek,* being used as a crass campaign tool by Ronald Reagan, and experiencing a troubled (and short) first marriage that ended amidst paparazzi photos of his affair with current wife Patti Scialfa. That's a testament to the credibility of his music—with and without the E Street Band—which has proven more durable than the transient aspects of image-building and marketability. Springsteen's common-man touch never stood in the way of strong, vivid writing; "Baby this town rips the bones from your back" is a killer image, and Springsteen has dozens of 'em. Springsteen made a name for himself during the '70s as the ultimate bar-rocker on a big stage, but there've been considerable growth and stylistic diversions that have been fascinating to witness, from his full-on embrace of big, stadium rock on *Born in the U.S.A.* to the stripped-down, folky orientation of *Nebraska* and *The Ghost of Tom Joad* to the more personal ruminations of *Lucky Town.* Through it all, Springsteen has upheld the notion of rock 'n' roll as spiritual salvation, something that can help you through the worst of times and celebrate the best. He's a True Believer who's been able to convey that faith both on record and onstage.

what to buy: Springsteen hit a prolific creative peak between 1975 and 1980, turning out three seminal albums and a wealth of castoffs that—as myriad bootlegs attest—were of equally high quality. *Born to Run* 𝄢𝄢𝄢𝄢 (Columbia, 1975, prod. Bruce Springsteen, Jon Landau, Mike Appel) mines themes of escapism (the title track, "Thunder Road") and nostalgia ("Backstreets"), and delivers a rare four-on-the-floor love song in "She's the One" and an epic street tale in "Jungleland." Coming after a long legal battle to extricate himself from a management deal, *Darkness on the Edge of Town* 𝄢𝄢𝄢𝄢 (Columbia, 1978, prod. Bruce Springsteen, Jon Landau) is indeed darker but not without redemptive hope in songs such as "Badlands" and "The Promised Land." This may well be Springsteen's best batch of songs, though the production is criminally flat. *The River* 𝄢𝄢𝄢𝄢𝄢 (Columbia, 1980, prod. Bruce Springsteen, Jon Landau, Steve Van Zandt) is a sprawling, double-length collection that sweeps from the frat rock of "Sherry Darling" and

"Cadillac Ranch" to the more somber "Independence Day" and "The Price You Pay" to the endlessly moving title track. An epic aural journey. Fifteen years later, Springsteen's spare, folky *The Ghost of Tom Joad* 𝄢𝄢𝄢𝄢 (Columbia, 1995, prod. Bruce Springsteen, Chuck Plotkin) finds him examining many of the same themes—namely the state of the American Dream and where it's left ordinary Joes and Janes—in hushed and vividly cinematic narratives.

what to buy next: *The Wild, the Innocent & the E Street Shuffle* 𝄢𝄢𝄢𝄢 (Columbia, 1973, prod. Mike Appel, Jim Cretecos) is loose and expansive, with Springsteen and the original E Streeters really stretching out on "Kitty's Back" and the seminal "Rosalita (Come out Tonight)." The multi-million-selling magnitude of *Born in the U.S.A.* 𝄢𝄢𝄢𝄢 (Columbia, 1984, prod. Bruce Springsteen, Jon Landau, Chuck Plotkin, Steve Van Zandt) sometimes obscures the disturbing vision that exists within this crafted, radio-friendly batch of songs. *Lucky Town* 𝄢𝄢𝄢𝄢 (Columbia, 1992, prod. Bruce Springsteen, Jon Landau, Chuck Plotkin) came out as a twin to the poppier *Human Touch,* but this one digs deeper into Springsteen's emotional revitalization following his divorce and subsequent marriage to Scialfa.

what to avoid: On his debut, *Greetings from Asbury Park, N.J.* 𝄢𝄢𝄢 (Columbia, 1973, prod. Mike Appel, Jim Cretecos), Columbia thought it had a troubadour, not a rocker, and this set sounds more stiff and mannered with each passing year.

the rest:
Nebraska 𝄢𝄢𝄢𝄢 (Columbia, 1982)
Live, 1975–1985 𝄢𝄢𝄢𝄢 (Columbia, 1986)
Tunnel of Love 𝄢𝄢𝄢𝄢 (Columbia, 1987)
Human Touch 𝄢𝄢𝄢𝄢 (Columbia, 1992)
Greatest Hits 𝄢𝄢𝄢 (Columbia, 1994)
Tracks: 1973–1998 𝄢𝄢𝄢𝄢 (Columbia, 1998)

worth searching for: Along with the Beatles, Bob Dylan, and Prince, Springsteen is one of rock's most bootlegged artists. There are lots of worthwhile titles, but two live releases stand out: *The Saint, the Incident & the Main Point Shuffle* (Great Dane, 1990), from a 1975 show that features violinist Suki Lahav, an E Street short-timer; and the three-disc *Piece de Resistance* (Great Dane, 1990), the best of many radio broadcasts during Springsteen's 1978 tour. Also worthwhile is *The Early Years* (Early, 1994, prod. Mike Appel, Jim Cretecos), a legitimate collection of early recordings and demos that slipped out overseas before Springsteen put the legal clamps on it.

solo outings:
Clarence Clemons:
Peacemaker 𝄢𝄢 (Zoo, 1995)

Danny Federici:
Flemington 𝄢𝄢𝄢 (Deadeye/MusicMasters, 1998)

Bruce Springsteen (© Ken Settle)

influences:

◀◀ Roy Orbison, Chuck Berry, Bob Dylan, Van Morrison, Creedence Clearwater Revival

▶▶ Bryan Adams, John Mellencamp, John Cafferty, Will T. Massey, Melissa Etheridge

see also: *Nils Lofgren, Little Steven*

Gary Graff

Tobin Sprout
See: Guided by Voices

Squeeze
/Difford & Tilbrook
/Jools Holland

Formed 1974, in London, England. Disbanded 1982. Re-formed 1985.

Chris Difford, guitar, vocals; Glenn Tilbrook, guitar, vocals; Julian "Jools" Holland, keyboards, vocals (1974–80, 1985–90); Harry Kakoulli, bass (1974–79); Gilson Lavis, drums (1974–93); John Bentley, bass (1979–82); Paul Carrack, vocals, keyboards (1981–82, 1993); Don Snow, keyboards, vocals (1982, 1995–present as John Savannah); Keith Wilkinson, bass, vocals (1985–present); Andy Metcalfe, keyboards (1985–90); Matt Irving, keyboards, accordion (1985–90); Pete Thomas, drums (1993); Kevin Wilkinson, drums (1995–present).

Lousy promotion, comparisons to the Beatles, and regular lineup changes have kept this plucky bunch at cult status in the U.S., but to its fans, music critics, and fellow musicians, Squeeze was one of the most important bands to emerge from the British new wave scene of the early '80s. The songwriting duo of Chris Difford (lyrics) and Glenn Tilbrook (music) has been crafting sublime music together for nearly 25 years; they've often been mentioned in the same breath as Lennon and McCartney and Gilbert and Sullivan. Unsettled by such lofty comparisons and the constant turnover of keyboardists, Difford and Tilbrook folded up the tent in 1982 to pursue a career as a duo. They restarted Squeeze's engines in 1985, and the band has been rolling along ever since. Through all the ups and downs, Difford and Tilbrook have remained remarkably loyal to each other, and their place in pop history is secure.

what to buy: *Argybargy* 𝄢𝄢𝄢𝄢 (A&M, 1980, prod. John Wood, Squeeze) features clever, driving pop songs such as "Pulling Mussels from the Shell" and "If I Didn't Love You" that showcase Jools Holland's considerable piano skills, Difford's wordsmithery, and Tilbrook's meaty guitar hooks. The equally impressive and Beatlesque *East Side Story* 𝄢𝄢𝄢𝄢𝄢 (A&M, 1981, prod. Roger Bechirian, Elvis Costello, Dave Edmunds) was the band's breakthrough album stateside, with a broad pop style

embracing country and classical undertones—as well as ace songs such as "Tempted," "In Quintessence," and "Piccadilly," the last a masterful pop portrait of London life. *Singles—45's and Under* 𝄢𝄢𝄢𝄢𝄢 (A&M, 1982, prod. various) offers a classy dollop of the band's early years.

what to buy next: *Sweets from a Stranger* 𝄢𝄢𝄢𝄢 (A&M, 1982, prod. Squeeze, Phil McDonald) is another finely crafted pop album that contains the enduring fan favorites "Black Coffee in Bed" (with background vocals by Costello and Paul Young).

what to avoid: *Frank* (A&M, 1989, prod. Eric (E.T.) Thorngren, Glenn Tilbrook) 𝄢𝄢 isn't one of Difford's best efforts lyrically, and his voice is pressed to its limit during his lead vocals on "Slaughtered, Gutted, and Heartbroken" and "Love Circles."

the rest:
U.K. Squeeze 𝄢𝄢 (A&M, 1978)
Cool for Cats 𝄢𝄢𝄢 (A&M, 1979)
Babylon and On 𝄢𝄢𝄢𝄢 (A&M, 1987)
Classics, Volume 25 𝄢𝄢𝄢 (A&M, 1988)
A Round and a Bout 𝄢𝄢𝄢 (I.R.S., 1990)
Play 𝄢𝄢𝄢 (Reprise, 1990)
Some Fantastic Place 𝄢𝄢𝄢𝄢 (A&M, 1993)
Ridiculous 𝄢𝄢𝄢𝄢 (I.R.S., 1996)

worth searching for: *Cosi Fan Tutti Frutti* (A&M, 1985), the reformed band's lush, complex comeback, features the haunting "Last Time Forever" and Motown-influenced "Hits of the Year."

solo outings:
Difford & Tilbrook:
Difford & Tilbrook 𝄢𝄢𝄢 (A&M, 1984)

Jools Holland:
A World of His Own 𝄢𝄢𝄢𝄢 (I.R.S., 1990)
The A–Z of the Piano 𝄢𝄢𝄢 (Bugle, 1993)

influences:

◀◀ The Beatles, Motown, 10cc, Todd Rundgren

▶▶ Gin Blossoms, Crowded House, the Odds, Del Amitri

see also: *Paul Carrack*

William Hanson

Billy Squier
Born May 12, 1950, in Wellesley Hills, MA.

Squier's blown-dry shag and rock-star good looks, coupled with semi-aggressive thumpers of macho lust, eventually computed to national success in 1981. Although he recoiled from the teen idol popularity that ensued, subsequent recordings (and videos) did little to dissuade his beef-boy image. Resolutely sticking to a sexist one-two grind, he pushed his horny telecaster against an increasingly politically correct social climate while record sales dropped in proportion. His recent recordings include increasingly cranky rockers that lack the melodic hooks that redeem his early material—though to his credit, he's refused to latch onto the '70s/'80s retro tours that trot out on the road every summer.

what to buy: *Don't Say No* 🎸🎸🎸 (Capitol/EMI, 1981, prod. Mack, Billy Squier) is unquestionably his finest moment as well as his commercial breakthrough, with the not-so-subtle wordplay of "The Stroke" and enduring radio faves like "Lonely Is the Night," "In the Dark," and "My Kinda Lover." *The Best of Billy Squier: 16 Strokes* 🎸🎸🎸 (Capitol/EMI, 1995, prod. various) is the most economical overview available, though it curiously omits "Lonely Is the Night."

what to buy next: *Reach for the Sky: The Anthology* 🎸🎸🎸 (Poly-Gram, 1996, prod. various) will reward those with more than a passing interest. The truly devoted will welcome the two-and-a-half hours worth of material, which includes a good chunk of material from out-of-print albums as well as two tracks from his fledgling band, Piper. Even so, a 41-year-old man jerking around with nonsense such as "She Goes Down" is just plain sad. Not to mention creepy.

what to avoid: The sophomoric pitfalls of *Here and Now* 🎸🎸 (Capitol/EMI, 1989, prod. Godfrey Diamond, Billy Squier) are summed up by titles such as "Rock Out/Punch Somebody." It's redeemed slightly by "Don't Say You Love Me," but then again it's hard to mess up a Bo Diddley beat.

the rest:
Emotions in Motion 🎸🎸🎹 (Capitol/EMI, 1982)
King Biscuit Flower Hour Presents 🎸🎸🎹 (KBFH, 1996)

worth searching for: *Enough Is Enough* (Capitol, 1986) features a guest appearance from Queen's Freddie Mercury, as well as "Love Is the Hero" and "Lady with a Tenor Sax," Squier's best songs since *Don't Say No.*

influences:
◀◀ Kiss, Led Zeppelin, Rick Springfield, Queen
▶▶ Bon Jovi, Def Leppard, Winger, Dokken, Quiet Riot

Allan Orski

Squire

Formed 1978, in England. Disbanded 1983.

Anthony Meynell, vocals, guitar; Enzo Esposito, bass, vocals (1978–80); Jon Bicknell, bass, vocals (1982–84); Steve Baker, vocals, rhythm guitar; Ross Di'Landa, drums (1978–79); Kevin Meynell, drums (1979–84).

Superficially part of the Jam-typified neo-mod movement, Squire—mainly a vehicle (though not a scooter) for Anthony

Meynell's sophisticated pop songs—transcended that fad. In 1978, Meynell joined the already-existent Squire, an average combo lacking a great songwriter and charismatic leader, thus forming the band as it will be remembered. The group ostensibly split up around 1980, with the original drummer leaving and Meynell entangled in the mess left by a bad manager. Meynell formed Hi-Lo Records in an attempt to regain control over Squire's output and subsequently released a batch of Squire demos under his own name. In 1982, he issued a new single under his band's moniker—the *Revolver*-influenced "No Time Tomorrow." His mod skin shed, Meynell released more records that showed his ability to craft timeless pop, reminiscent of everyone from the Beatles and the Byrds to the Three O'Clock.

what's available: *Big Smashes* 🎸🎸🎸🎸 (Tangerine, 1992) is the only in-print CD of Squire's latter-day power-pop. Fortunately, this import has almost everything you need by this overlooked mod squad, including two covers that assure Meynell's spot in the pop-hipster echelon: Big Star's "September Gurls" and Shoes' "Boys Don't Lie." Neither adds anything to the originals, but they show an astute interpreter with the right influences. *Get Ready to Go* 🎸🎸🎸🎸 (Tangerine, 1994) rescues Squire's early recordings from the pit of obscurity. Songs like "It's a Mod Mod World" show how Meynell kept his distance from the movement with which he was associated, while using its accoutremental aspects for surface appeal. "Don't Cry to Me" is a Merseybeat-ish ditty that was originally the B-side of "No Time Tomorrow," hinting at the later years covered on *Big Smashes*.

worth searching for: Under the name Sugarplum, Meynell issued a wonderful import EP of jangly pop songs called *Crazy Feeling* (Antenna, 1992/1997).

influences:
◀◀ The Beatles, the Who, Big Star
▶▶ Three O' Clock, the Velvet Crush, the La's

Jordan Oakes

Squirrel Bait

Formed 1984, in Louisville, KY. Disbanded 1986.

Peter Searcy, vocals; David Grubbs, guitar; Brian McMahan, guitar; Clark Johnson, bass; Britt Walford, drums (1984); Ben Daughtrey, drums (1984–86).

Louisville's gloriously warped underground scene traces part of its heritage to Squirrel Bait, a teenagers' punk band that lasted barely two years, recorded two records, and never played west of Minneapolis or south of Virginia. Yet the quintet's influence was incalculable, if only for sowing the seeds for such future Louisville luminaries as Slint, the Palace Brothers, and Bastro.

what to buy: *Squirrel Bait* ♫♫♫♫ (Dexter's Cigar, 1997) is an eight-song, 18-minute EP originally issued in 1985 on the now-defunct Homestead label, and it remains a pure, cleansing blast of hurtling, post-adolescent energy. Worth it if only to hear the record's opening seconds, in which David Grubbs snarls at Peter Searcy: "I'm gonna beat you up at the end of this." On its cover is a snapshot of guitarist Brian McMahan as a bespectacled, heavy-lidded 12-year-old sucking on a portable tape player—an indelible image of alien innocence.

what to buy next: *Skag Heaven* ♫♫♫ (Dexter's Cigar, 1997, prod. Squirrel Bait) is more ambitious than the debut, the songs less about barreling rancor and more about arrangement, texture, and cleverness.

influences:

◄◄ Circle X, Hüsker Dü, Minutemen, Meat Puppets, Gun Club, Misfits

►► Slint, Palace Brothers, Rodan, King Kong, Bastro

Greg Kot

Squirrel Nut Zippers
/Jas. Mathus
& His Knock-Down Society

Formed 1993, in Chapel Hill, NC.

Tom Maxwell, guitar, horns, vocals; James Mathus, guitar, piano, vocals; Katherine Whalen, banjo, vocals; Chris Phillips, drums; Ken Mosher, horns, guitar, vocals; Stacy Guess, trumpet (1993–95); Je Widenhouse, trumpet (1996–present); Don Raleigh, bass (1993–96); Stu Cole, bass (1996–present).

The Squirrel Nut Zippers originally came together as a lark—people from a wide variety of alternative rock bands playing prohibition-vintage "hot jazz." Certainly, it's a schtick with a lot of inherent commercial appeal, although you'd figure it would only get the group as far as NPR, not MTV. Yet MTV was precisely where the Zippers found themselves in 1997, with a hit single in the Calypso shout-along "Hell" (which was omnipresent enough that it showed up as a sample on a rap single before the end of the year, Funkdoobiest's "Papi Chulo"). That resulted in one of the unlikeliest platinum albums in recent memory. One can only hope that the Zippers' spirit and ragged-but-right chemistry will withstand the skewed expectations that inevitably accompany success.

what to buy: *Hot* ♫♫♫♫ (Mammoth, 1996, prod. Brian Paulson, Mike Napolitano) is the album that benefited from the hit status of the aforementioned single "Hell," and it's a wonderful listen. Recorded in New Orleans for that Crescent City feel, the album also works in a bit of Memphis and Las Vegas—and

swings with a vengeance. The Bessie Smith–styled "Put a Lid on It" stands as Katherine Whalen's finest on-record vocal moment. On his own, James Mathus comes by his bluesier leanings honestly, having grown up in Clarksdale, Mississippi, where Rosetta Patton (daughter of the legendary bluesman Charley Patton) was his nanny. Her ailing health was the impetus behind the benefit record *Jas. Mathus & His Knock-Down Society Play Songs for Rosetta* ♫♫♫♫ (Mammoth, 1997, prod. Jas. Mathus). Recorded in Mathus's hometown with a large crew of friends and associates, *Songs for Rosetta* has a free-wheeling house-party vibe similar to those old sides from the *Anthology of American Folk Music*.

what to buy next: While not quite as solid as *Hot*, the full-length debut *The Inevitable Squirrel Nut Zippers* ♫♫♫♫ (Mammoth, 1995, prod. Brian Paulson) is still tremendous fun. The group's chemistry was evident even then, a balance between Whalen's Betty Boop, Mathus's soul man, and Tom Maxwell's Fred Schneider. *Sold Out* ♫♫♫ (Mammoth EP, 1997, prod. various) is a stopgap live record. Rough but nevertheless charming, it includes a recording that dates back to the group's second-ever rehearsal. Among the unlisted bonus tracks are the hilarious "Santa Claus Is Smoking Reefer" and some vintage radio spots for Squirrel Nut Zippers candy, from whence came the group's name. Also charmingly rough is *Roasted Right* ♫♫♫ (Merge EP, 1993), the Zippers' debut four-song single. As a measure of how quickly the Zippers progressed, compare the *Roasted Right* rendition of "Anything but Love" with the more polished version of the song that appears on *Inevitable* (the latter version is the one that plays over the opening credits of the 1995 Ben Stiller film *Flirting with Disaster,* by the way).

the rest:
Perennial Favorites ♫♫♫♫ (Mammoth, 1998)
Christmas Caravan N/A (Mammoth, 1998)

worth searching for: Prior to forming the Zippers, Mathus played in the twangy rockabilly band Metal Flake Mother, which left behind the album *Beyond the Java Sea* (Moist 1991/Hep-Cat 1997, prod. Lou Giordano). Maxwell played drums in the art rock band What Peggy Wants, whose lone album *Death of a Sailor* (Moist, 1992, prod. Tim Harper) will probably have you scratching your head wondering how he got from there to the Zippers. Drummer Chris Phillips can also be heard on the $2 Pistols' *On down the Track* (Scrimshaw, 1997, prod. John Plymale), a fabulous album of straight honky tonk à la Lefty Frizzell. Go figure.

influences:

◄◄ B-52's, Red Clay Ramblers, Fats Waller, Louis Prima, Bessie Smith, Billie Holiday, Django Reinhardt

►► Asylum Street Spankers, Blue Rags

David Menconi

Stabbing Westward

Formed 1985, in Chicago, IL.

Christopher Hall, vocals, guitars; Walter Flakus, keyboards, programming; Jim Sellers, bass; David Suycott, guitars (1991–94); Mark Eliopulos, guitar (1996–present); David Suycott, drums (1991–94); Andy Kubiszewski, drums, programming, backing vocals.

Stabbing Westward began In a much different form than what it is now, with former Western Illinois University students Chris Hall and Walter Flakus on bass and keyboards, respectively. Hall moved over to guitar when Jim Sellers came on board. Stabbing Westward went through a series of drummers—including Chris Vrenna of nine inch nails—before settling on Andy Kubiszewski. Ironically, Vrenna returned in the summer of 1998 to replace Kubiszewski after he was injured while in-line skating. After the success of a four-song EP in 1990, Hall put Stabbing Westward on hiatus so he could tour as a percussionist with Die Warzau. Realizing what he left behind, Hall returned to Chicago, re-formed Stabbing Westward, and went in the studio, coming out with a debut album, *Ungod*, that made enough impact to earn the band a spot opening for Depeche Mode during the summer of 1993.

what to buy: Stabbing Westward didn't break until it released *Wither Blister Burn + Peel* 𝄞𝄞𝄞 (Columbia, 1996, prod. John Fryer). "Shame" is the epitome of a perfect moshing song; it builds slowly from tribal drums to an all-out chaotic onslaught of grinding guitars, chest-beating drums, and keyboards, climaxing with the line "how can I exist without you?" "What Do I Have to Do" is a desperate attempt to persuade a lover to return, and the accompanying guitar-heavy music is just as desperate (although the keyboards at the end sound suspiciously like nine inch nails' "Terrible Lie" from *Pretty Hate Machine*).

what to buy next: *Darkest Days* 𝄞𝄞𝄞 (Columbia, 1998, prod. Dave Jerden, Stabbing Westward) is moodier than *Wither Blister Burn + Peel*. Although still dark, some of the songs offer a glimmer of hope.

the rest:
Ungod 𝄞𝄞𝄞 (Columbia, 1993)

influences:
◄◄ nine inch nails, Ministry
►► Gravity Kills, Filter

Christina Fuoco

Chris Stamey

See: The dB's

The Standells

Formed 1964, in Los Angeles, CA. Disbanded 1967.

Dick Dodd, drums, vocals; Larry Tamblyn, organ, vocals; Tony Valentino, guitar, vocals; Gary Lane, bass, vocals (1964–66); Dave Burke, bass, vocals (1966); John Fleck, bass, vocals (1966–67).

Beloved TV personality Herman Munster said it best: "I'm going to sleep a lot easier tonight knowing that the future of America is in the hands of fine young men like the Standells." What a testimonial! The Standells were the definitive American punk band of the '60s; never mind that they'd started out as just another Los Angeles teen cover act, or that Dick Dodd had been a Mouseketeer on TV's *Mickey Mouse Club* (or that Larry Tamblyn's brother Russ played Riff in *West Side Story*). On record, these guys projected themselves as the American Rolling Stones, seething with attitude and daring you to tempt their wrath. The confidant swagger of "Dirty Water" scored a #11 hit single and a permanent entry in the Punk Rock Hall of Fame. No other big hits followed, but equally sneering efforts such as "Why Pick on Me," "Sometimes Good Guys Don't Wear White," the salacious "Try It," "Riot on Sunset Strip," "Have You Ever Spent the Night in Jail," and "Rari," the ferocious punk B-side of "Dirty Water," ensure the Standells a place in the heart of anyone with a chip on his shoulder and a song in his (or her) heart.

what to buy: *Best of the Standells* 𝄞𝄞𝄞 (Rhino, 1989, prod. Ed Cobb, Sonny Bono) collects all of the essential Standells sides in one package and packs the most potent punch of any Standells disc.

what to buy next: Though it's hard to keep track of the many Standells reissues on the market, *Dirty Water* 𝄞𝄞𝄞 (Tower, 1966/Sundazed, 1994, prod. Ed Cobb), *Hot Ones* 𝄞𝄞 (Sundazed, 1994), *Why Pick on Me* 𝄞𝄞𝄞 (Tower, 1966/Sundazed, 1994, prod. Ed Cobb), and *Try It* 𝄞𝄞𝄞 (Tower, 1967/Sundazed, 1994, prod. Ed Cobb) are well worthwhile.

what to avoid: *The Hot Ones* 𝄞𝄞 (Tower, 1966/Sundazed, 1994, prod. Ed Cobb) is an ill-advised collection of then-contemporary covers.

the rest:
The Very Best of the Standells 𝄞𝄞𝄞𝄞 (Hip-O/MCA, 1998)

worth searching for: The Standells, along with Count Five and the Seeds, are at the heart of the famous *Nuggets* series. "Dirty Water" leads off the original, *Nuggets: Classics from the Psychedelic Sixties* (Rhino, 1986, prod. various), which also includes the Count Five's "Psychotic Reaction," the Amboy Dukes' "Journey to the Center of the Mind," the Easybeats' "Heaven and Hell," and the Monkees' "Valleri." *More Nuggets: Classics from the Psychedelic Sixties* (Rhino, 1987, compilation prod. Bill Inglot) includes another Standells gem, the funnier but slightly less powerful "Sometimes Good Guys Don't Wear White."

influences:

◀◀ The Beatles, the Rolling Stones, the Who, Elvis Presley, Carl Perkins

▶▶ The Ramones, Bruce Springsteen, the Sex Pistols, Lester Bangs, Count Five

Carl Cafarelli

Lisa Stansfield

Born April 11, 1966, in Rochdale, England.

Lisa Stansfield had all the makings of another teen diva, coming up through the talent contest and TV show ranks. But her tastes ran not towards pop but to soul, which isn't surprising considering that she hung around R&B-loving Manchester quite a bit. She started out in a group called Blue Zone with former schoolmates Andy Morris and Ian Devaney; the group—or, rather, Stansfield's—break came when the British production team Coldcut recorded its "People Hold On," which became a Top 20 hit. Arista Records signed Stansfield, and Morris and Devaney stayed on as her producers, songwriters, and backing musicians. Her career has been sporadic; she never really capitalized after a big beginning with *Affection*, and a five-year break during the mid-1990s left her in an unenviable comeback position when she re-emerged during 1997.

what to buy: Her debut, *Affection* 𝄢𝄢𝄢𝄢 (Arista, 1989, prod. Ian Devaney, Andy Morris) was a deserving smash—lush, sultry, and buoyant all at the same time. The songs—including the hits "All around the World" and "You Can't Deny It"—are deft pop confections, and Stansfield's performance is absolutely outstanding. *Lisa Stansfield* 𝄢𝄢𝄢𝄢 (Arista, 1997, prod. Ian Devaney) marked a welcome return to form, with lush production and improved songwriting.

the rest:

Real Love 𝄢𝄢𝄢 (Arista, 1991)
So Natural 𝄢𝄢 (Arista, 1993)
#1 Remixes 𝄢𝄢𝄢 (Arista EP, 1998)

influences:

◀◀ Barry White, Annie Lennox, Tracy Thorn (Everything but the Girl)

▶▶ Ambersunshower, Maxwell, D'Angelo, Spice Girls

Gary Graff

Ringo Starr

Born Richard Starkey, July 7, 1940, in the Dingle, Liverpool, England.

One of the best rock 'n' roll drummers ever, a most engaging show business personality, or one of the luckiest men on earth? There seems no easy way to categorize the Beatles' little drummer boy, and even a superficial gaze over his long and spotty post-Fab career confirms that Ringo Starr perhaps, in struggling to be all things to all people, ultimately turns out disappointing us all—and probably himself as well. Hindsight confirms he *was* a great drummer (session tapes from the Beatle years reveal Starr to be both as creative on his instrument as the rest of the band and as consistent in his time-keeping as a metronome), and while he may pose no immediate threat to Tony Bennett, his vocal abilities, when set against a sympathetic backdrop, can be pleasant enough. For his first album, *Sentimental Journey*, producer George Martin helped the soon-to-be-ex-Beatle record a dozen standards from the '40s and '50s (apparently as a present for Ringo's mum). A country LP cut in Nashville with the cream of Music City's session men (including D.J. Fontana of Elvis Presley's original band on drums—not Ringo) was followed by two strong singles produced by George Harrison, "It Don't Come Easy" and "Back off Boogaloo," both of which were deserving Top 10 hits. In 1973, producer Richard Perry surrounded Ringo with an all-star cast, including all three ex-Beatles, and the *Ringo* album became the drummer's biggest sales success, spawning three hit singles. Since then, however, ill-advised attempts to repeat this once-winning formula have resulted in a steadily decreasing quality of both material and execution—not to mention sales. Today, he lugs various editions of B-level rockers on the road with him under the moniker of "The All-Starr Band," but what worked so easily in 1973 doesn't seem to apply to today's marketplace. Still, the man remains a perennial favorite amongst graying boomers and their children everywhere, and so long as he continues riding the Yellow Submarine of nostalgia, Starr will continue to get by—with a little help from his friends, that is.

what to buy: All even the most fervent Beatle completist need really own from the Ringo department is his first hits collection *Blast from Your Past* 𝄢𝄢𝄢 (Apple, 1975/Gold Rush, 1996), though were the wonderful *Beaucoups of Blues* 𝄢𝄢𝄢𝄢 (Apple, 1970/Gold Rush, 1996, prod. Pete Drake) released today, it would hopefully give Garth Brooks a run in the country crossover sweepstakes.

what to buy next: Prior to their *Anthology* series, the closest the Beatles ever came to an electronic reunion was on the million-selling *Ringo* album (Apple, 1973/DCC Gold Disc, 1994/Gold Rush, 1996, prod. Richard Perry) 𝄢𝄢𝄢. Recommended for those who like their rock 'n' roll Hollywood-style, it includes Ringo's, uh, theme song, "I'm the Greatest" (one of John Lennon's best, most sarcastic creations ever), and the addition of "It Don't Come Easy" on the Gold Rush edition makes it practically a de facto best-of itself.

what to avoid: Both *Ringo Starr & His All-Starr Band* **woof!** (Rykodisc, 1990, prod. Joe Walsh, Jim Nipar) and *Ringo Starr &*

His All-Starr Band, Volume 2: Live from Montreux **woof!** (Rykodisc, 1993, prod. Ringo Starr) are the in-concert equivalent of a celebrity AA meeting (Burton Cummings? Nils Lofgren?? Timothy B. Schmit?!!), while the recent studio efforts *Time Takes Time* ⅃⅃ (Private Music, 1992, prod. Jeff Lynne, Don Was, Peter Asher, Phil Ramone) and *Vertical Man* ⅃⅃⅃ (Mercury, 1998, prod. Mark Hudson) find everyone from Jellyfish and the Posies (on the former) to Steven Tyler and Alanis Morissette (on the latter's remake of Dobie Gray's "Drift Away") desperately attempting to drag Ringo and his once-popular formula into the '90s. Oasis does it better, believe it or not.

the rest:
Sentimental Journey ⅃⅃⅃ (Apple, 1970/Gold Rush, 1996)
Goodnight Vienna ⅃⅃⅃⅄ (Apple, 1974/Gold Rush, 1996)
Ringo's Rotogravure ⅃⅃ (Atlantic, 1976)
Ringo the 4th ⅃⅃ (Atlantic, 1977)
Bad Boy ⅃⅄ (Portrait, 1978/Epic, 1991)
Stop and Smell the Roses ⅃⅃⅄ (Boardwalk, 1981/The Right Stuff, 1994)
Old Wave ⅃⅃ (RCA Canada, 1983/The Right Stuff, 1994)
Starr Struck: The Best of Ringo Starr, Volume 2 ⅃⅃⅄ (Rhino, 1989)

worth searching for: The soundtrack from *Magic Christian Music* (Commonwealth-United, 1969)—deleted shortly after its issue to avoid confusion with the Badfinger album of the same name—contains some of Ringo's dialogue from the film dubbed over background music.

influences:
◀◀ Roy Rogers, Rory Storm, Anthony Newley
▶▶ Micky Dolenz, Phil Collins, Barry Wom

see also: *The Beatles*

Gary Pig Gold

Status Quo
Formed 1962, in Beckenham, Kent, England.

Francis "Mike" Rossi, guitar, vocals; Alan Lancaster, bass, vocals (1962–84); Alan Key, guitar (1962); Jess Jaworski, keyboards (1962–63); Barry Smith, drums (1962–63); John Coghlan, drums (1963–82); Roy Lynes, keyboards (1964–70); Rick Parfitt (born Richard Harrison), guitar, vocals (1967–present); Andrew Bown, keyboards, guitar (1976–present); Pete Kircher, drums (1982–84); John "Rhino" Edwards, bass (1986–present); Jeff Rich, drums (1986–present).

How is it possible that one of Britain's longest-established bands, having sold more than 120 million records, performed more than 4,500 shows, and even been immortalized in wax at Madame Tussaud's Wax Museum and preserved for the ages on a limited edition Royal Doulton china mug series be remembered in America, if at all, only for a harmless piece of vintage

1967 camp psychedelia? Perhaps because, since abandoning its foppish Carnaby Street roots and dumbing down severely circa 1970, this self-proclaimed Number One 12-Bar Boogie Band in the World can really inspire no interest whatsoever in the land that gave birth to lowest-common-denominator rock. Nevertheless, from Hamburg to Holland, Tottenham to Tokyo and beyond, "the Quo" is nothing short of the first and last rude word in loud, denim-clad, beer-soaked, and stripped-to-the-basics music-making. While trends duly come and go, and myriad challengers to its throne rise to briefly boogie then vanish, Status Quo seems destined to persevere well into the next century at least. "So what if we're boring and only do three chords?," asks Frank Rossi after nearly four decades spent E-chording. "There's no point in getting hung up about it." And you know what? He's absolutely right.

what to buy: The 41-track double disc *Whatever You Want: The Very Best of Status Quo* ⅃⅃⅃ (PolyGram/Vertigo, 1997, prod. various) follows the story from "Pictures of Matchstick Men," that first innocent piece of Top 20 bubblegum, onward through several decades of increasingly meat 'n' potatoes *rawk*. To be very highly commended for its consistency, if nothing else.

what to buy next: Taking time out from its boogiework to sing some oldies with famous friends, *Don't Stop: The 30th Anniversary Album* ⅃⅃⅃ (PolyGram, 1996, prod. Pip Williams) is a surprisingly eclectic (The Beach Boys! Timbuk 3! Men Without Hats!) collection of songs the Quo have long loved and performed regularly at rehearsals and soundchecks the world over. If you've ever wondered what Buddy Holly might sound like had he lived to collaborate with Bad Company, here's your chance. Meanwhile, from the Skeletons in the Closet department, *Picturesque Matchstickable: Messages from the Status Quo* ⅃⅃⅃ (Cadet Concept, 1968/Castle Classics, 1991, prod. John Schroeder) reveals that this band's repertoire once proudly consisted of Bee Gees, Lemon Pipers, and Tommy Roe songs.

the rest:
Spare Parts ⅃⅃⅄ (Pye, 1969/Castle Classics, 1991)
Ma Kelly's Greasy Spoon ⅃⅃ (Janus, 1971/Castle Classics, 1991)
Dog of Two Head ⅃⅃⅄ (Janus, 1971/Castle Classics, 1991)
Rockin' All over the Years: The Greatest Hits ⅃⅃⅄ (Alex, 1991)
B-Sides and Rarities ⅃⅃⅃ (Castle Communications, 1991)
The Collection ⅃⅃⅃ (Castle Communications, 1991)
Early Works ⅃⅃⅃ (Castle Communications, 1994)
Early Years ⅃⅃⅃ (Castle Communications, 1994)

worth searching for: With a pulverizing, leaden thud that the Who's *Live at Leeds* and Deep Purple's *Made in Japan* only hint at, *Live!* (Capitol, 1977/Vertigo, 1977/1984, prod. Status Quo, Pip Williams) captures the Quo in all of its boogie glory, doing battle with a typically uproarious audience in Glasgow, Scotland. The Doors' "Roadhouse Blues" never sounded so beatific.

influences:

◄◄ Chuck Berry, Iron Butterfly, Bob Young

►► Grand Funk Railroad, Motörhead, Bachman-Turner Overdrive, Bad News

Gary Pig Gold

Tommy Steele

Born Thomas Hicks, December 17, 1936, in Bermondsey, London, England.

Britain's very first rock star per se, Tommy Steele was an inspiration less for the records he made (which were hack pieces at best) than for the career direction he provided dozens of English several-hit-wonders who followed in his wake—namely, score a few big hits quick, have a laugh or two, then humbly graduate into the world of "legitimate" theater and supper club work. Steele's early material, such as "Rock with the Caveman" and "Elevator Rock," sound at best like novelty numbers today, but in 1956 this was actually the closest England could get to producing homegrown rock 'n' roll. After a very generous couple of years in the limelight, Steele wisely escaped to Australia where, assembling a 28-piece orchestra and two hours of "real music," he fashioned a future as a more mature, well-rounded entertainer. While his 1959 film *Tommy the Toreador* makes even *G. I. Blues* look Oscar-worthy, Steele soon enough found his footing on the London stage, and eventually on Broadway and even in Hollywood, starring in such musicals as *Half a Sixpence*, *Finian's Rainbow*, and *Singin' in the Rain*. Meanwhile, back home, such comparatively accomplished mock-Elvii as Cliff Richard were left to fill any leftover spaces in the British Top 20—that is, until the Beatles arrived to save the day.

worth searching for: Not surprisingly, Steele's earliest recordings are out of print, but true fans of British kitsch will find either *Tommy Steele's Greatest Hits* (Deram, 1990, prod. various) or *The EP Collection* (See for Miles, 1995, prod. various) worth the hunt required to unearth a copy.

influences:

◄◄ Elvis Presley, Guy Mitchell, Danny Kaye

►► Adam Faith, Peter Noone, Davy Jones, Gerry Marsden

Gary Pig Gold

Steely Dan

Formed 1972, in Los Angeles, CA.

Walter Becker, bass, guitar, vocals; Donald Fagen, vocals, keyboards; Jim Hodder (died June 5, 1990), drums (1972–74); Denny Dias, guitar (1972–79); David Palmer, vocals (1972–73); Jeff "Skunk" Baxter, guitar (1972–75); Michael McDonald, vocals, keyboards (1974–75).

Steely Dan was one of rock's first "projects"—a group in name only. Walter Becker and Donald Fagen, friends at Bard College in upstate New York during the late '60s, shared a fondness for jazz, blues, pop, R&B, and beatnik culture. They brought all this to Steely Dan, named after the talking dildo in William Burrough's *Naked Lunch*. From the get-go, Steely Dan's brand of rock was more sophisticated than most, blending catchy hooks with jazz chordings and tricky instrumental arrangements. As band members gradually departed—many of them frustrated by their leaders' reluctance to tour—Becker and Fagen's chief cohort became producer Gary Katz; employing dozens of session musicians, they steered Steely Dan's sound more towards jazz, and set standards for sonic perfectionism along the way. Becker and Fagen parted company during the early '80s but began working together again during the early '90s. Ironically, Steely Dan came back via tours and a live album, while Becker and Fagen kept their studio collaborations to each other's solo albums.

what to buy: As sophisticated as Steely Dan became, it never really beat its debut effort, *Can't Buy a Thrill* ♫♫♫♫♫ (ABC, 1972, prod. Walter Becker, Donald Fagen, Gary Katz). Becker and Fagen showed a clear gift for pop melodicism with instantly memorable tracks such as "Do It Again," "Dirty Work," "Midnight Cruiser," and "Brooklyn." Elliot Randall's guitar solos on "Reelin' in the Years" would be worth the price of admission alone. *Aja* ♫♫♫♫♫ (ABC, 1977, prod. Walter Becker, Donald Fagen, Gary Katz) has songs that are just as infectious ("Peg," "Black Cow") but also showcases expansive moments such as the title track and "Deacon Blue." *Pretzel Logic* ♫♫♫♫♫ (ABC, 1974, prod. Walter Becker, Donald Fagen, Gary Katz) has some of Steely Dan's best songs ("Rikki Don't Lose That Number," "Any Major Dude Will Tell You"), as well as early steps toward jazz fusion such as "Parker's Band" and the title track.

what to buy next: The four-volume *Citizen Steely Dan* ♫♫♫♫ (MCA, 1993, prod. Walter Becker, Donald Fagen, Gary Katz) packages the group's seven albums plus a couple of rarities. If you're hooked by the essential recordings, it's worth having the entire oeuvre.

what to avoid: Despite a couple of fine songs ("Hey Nineteen," "Time out of Mind"), the stiff and tired *Gaucho* ♫ (MCA, 1980, prod. Walter Becker, Donald Fagen, Gary Katz) shows why Becker and Fagen brought the curtain down on Steely Dan after this album.

the rest:

You Got to Walk It Like You Talk It (Soundtrack) ♫ (Spark, 1971)
Countdown to Ecstasy ♫♫♫ (MCA, 1973)
Katy Lied ♫♫♫♫ (MCA, 1975)

The Royal Scam 🐾🐾🐾 (MCA, 1976)
Greatest Hits 🐾🐾🐾🐾 (MCA, 1978)
Steely Dan Gold 🐾🐾🐾 (MCA, 1982)
Live 🐾🐾🐾 (Giant, 1995)

worth searching for: *Catalyst* (Thunderbolt, 1994) is a sterling-sounding, two-CD British import of early Becker and Fagen recordings made between 1968 and 1971. Included are early versions of "Brooklyn," "Parker's Band," and "Barrytown."

solo outings:
Walter Becker:
11 Tracks of Whack 🐾🐾🐾🐾 (Giant, 1994)

Donald Fagen:
The Nightfly 🐾🐾🐾🐾 (Warner Bros., 1992)
Kamakiriad 🐾🐾🐾🐾 (Reprise, 1993)

influences:

◀◀ Stax-Volt, Duke Ellington, Charlie Parker, B.B. King

▶▶ Rickie Lee Jones, Deacon Blue, China Crisis

Gary Graff

Steppenwolf

Formed 1967, in Los Angeles, CA. Disbanded 1972. Re-formed 1974–76, 1980–present.

John Kay (born Joachim F. Krauledat), vocals, guitar; Jerry Edmonton (born Jerry McCrohan; died 1993), drums (1967–76); Goldy McJohn (born John Goadsby), organ (1967–75); Michael Monarch, guitar (1967–69); Rushton Moreve (died 1991), bass (1967–68); John Russell Morgan, bass (1968–69); Larry Byrom, guitar (1969–71); Nick St. Nicholas (born Klaus Karl Kassbaum), bass (1969); George Biondi, bass (1969–72, 1974–76); Kent Henry, guitar (1971–72); Bobby Cochran, guitar (1974–76); Andy Chapin, keyboards (1975); Wayne Cook, keyboards (1975–76); others.

If the youth of the day wore flowers in their hair in San Francisco during the late '60s, Los Angeles' Steppenwolf countered with denim, leather, dark shades, and the biker anthem "Born to Be Wild." Used to great effect in the film *Easy Rider*, that song alone insured Steppenwolf a place in rock history. Steppenwolf began as the Sparrows, which united folk singer John Kay—an East German native who immigrated to Canada in 1958 and later moved to southern California—with former members of the Mynah Birds, the Toronto group that was led by Neil Young and Rick James. The Sparrows recorded an early version of the Steppenwolf hit "The Pusher"; after the band split up, producer Gabriel Mekler prevailed upon Kay to reunite the players and christened the aggregate Steppenwolf, after the Herman Hesse novel. For five years, Steppenwolf cranked out an agreeable blend of hard rock and psychedelia, following "Born to Be Wild"—written by Jerry Edmonton's brother Dennis

(under the moniker Mars Bonfire)—with "The Pusher," "Magic Carpet Ride," "Rock Me," and "Hey Lawdy Mama." Kay's lyrics were pointedly political, producing one entire album—1969's *Monster*—of social commentary. The group split up in 1972, and subsequent incarnations haven't been nearly as successful, though "Born to Be Wild" still gets 'em on their feet at the summer amphitheater oldies shows.

what to buy: The concise, well-annotated *Born to Be Wild: A Retrospective, 1969–1990* 🐾🐾🐾🐾 (MCA, 1991, compilation prod. Andy McKaie) renders almost everything else in the catalog unnecessary. Opening with a taste of the Sparrows and closing with "The Wall," Kay's reflection on the dismantling of the Berlin Wall, it's the Steppenwolf story in a satisfying nutshell.

what to buy next: *Tighten up Your Wig: The Best of John Kay & Sparrow* 🐾🐾🐾 (Columbia Legacy, 1993, compilation prod. Bob Irwin) suffers for its fodder, but the collection does provide an insightful look at the strains of folk, blues, and rock that became the sound not only of Steppenwolf but also of one segment of the late '60s rock community. Similarly, *Monster* 🐾🐾🐾 (Dunhill, 1969, prod. Gabriel Mekler) is a dated but fascinating period piece that captures the counter-culture political sensibility.

what to avoid: Such latter-day Steppenwolf albums as *Rock 'n' Roll Rebels* 🐾🐾 (Qwil, 1987, prod. John Kay, Michael Wilk, Rocket Ritchotte) and *Rise and Shine* 🐾 (I.R.S., 1990, prod. John Kay, Michael Wilk, Rocket Ritchotte), miss the character and energy of the original band.

the rest:
Steppenwolf 🐾🐾🐾🐾 (Dunhill, 1968)
Steppenwolf the Second 🐾🐾🐾🐾 (Dunhill, 1968)
Early Steppenwolf 🐾🐾 (Dunhill, 1969)
Steppenwolf at Your Birthday Party 🐾🐾🐾 (Dunhill, 1969)
Steppenwolf Live 🐾🐾🐾 (Dunhill, 1970)
Steppenwolf 7 🐾🐾🐾 (Dunhill, 1970)
Steppenwolf Gold 🐾🐾🐾🐾 (Dunhill, 1971)
For Ladies Only 🐾🐾 (Dunhill, 1971)
Rest in Peace 🐾🐾🐾 (Dunhill, 1972)
16 Greatest Hits 🐾🐾🐾 (Dunhill, 1973)
Slow Flux 🐾🐾🐾 (Mums, 1974)
Hour of the Wolf 🐾🐾🐾🐾 (Epic, 1975)
Skullduggery 🐾🐾 (Epic, 1976)
Reborn to be Wild 🐾🐾🐾 (Epic, 1977)
Wolftracks 🐾🐾🐾 (Allegiance, 1982)
Paradox 🐾🐾 (Attic, 1984)
Live at 25 🐾🐾🐾 (ERA, 1994)
Feed the Fire 🐾🐾 (Winter Harvest, 1996)

worth searching for: Kay's autobiography, *Magic Carpet Ride* (Quarry Press, 1994), co-written with John Einarson, gives the skinny on the band and the '60s L.A. rock scene.

solo outings:

John Kay:

Forgotten Songs and Unsung Heroes ♫♫♫ (Dunhill, 1972)

My Sportin' Life ♫♫ (Dunhill, 1972)

All in Good Time ♫♫ (Mercury, 1978)

Lone Steppenwolf ♫♫♫ (MCA, 1987)

influences:

◄◄ Sonny Boy Williamson, Chuck Berry, the Animals, Bob Dylan, Pete Seeger, the Yardbirds

►► Led Zeppelin, Blue Öyster Cult, Kiss, Boston

Gary Graff

Stereo MC's

Formed late 1980s, in East London, England.

Rob B. (born Rob Bich), vocals; the Head (born Nick Hallam), DJ; Owen If (born Owen Rossiter), drums.

While many groups have attempted to bridge the gap between funk, hip-hop, and dance music, few have done it as well as the Stereo MC's. Maintaining a musical vibe that was simultaneously upbeat and down 'n' dirty soulful, the group perfected the synthesis of hip-hop beats and milky acid-jazz–infused dance grooves. While the popular Manchester sound of the time supplied slinky dance grooves and rock 'n' roll, the Stereo MC's cast its eye not on rock, but on the traditional trappings of American hip-hop. Rapper Rob B., DJ-remixer the Head, and drummer Owen If may have lacked the hardcore posturing of their New York rap contemporaries, but they more than made up for it with sheer sonic verve. Indeed, whatever you thought of their Euro-Anglo accents (and Rob B. does deserve credit for staunchly refusing to emulate his East Coast counterparts by copping a fake inner-city drawl), you simply couldn't front on their impeccable production. Giving a nod to the New York old school, the group featured not only a real DJ, but also an actual drummer both on their studio recordings and in their live sets (a practice that was later adopted by the likes of the Digable Planets, the Roots, and Snoop Doggy Dogg). Yet despite their links to the old school and, more significantly, the endorsement of both the Beatnuts and the Jungle Brothers' Afrika Baby Bam, the Stereo MC's failed to connect with the American hip-hop community, which has traditionally ignored European artists. The crew subsequently turned its attention to production under the moniker Ultimatum and remixed songs for the likes of U2, the Jungle Brothers, PM Dawn, and the Disposable Heroes of Hiphoprisy.

what to buy: *Supernatural* ♫♫♫♫ (4th and B'way/Island, 1990, prod. Afrika Baby Bambaataa, the Beatnuts, Stereo MC's) comes in two flavors: the original, 16-track album and a re-

duced, 12-track "American Mix." The 16-track version is far superior, containing the Afrika Baby Bam-and-Beatnuts-produced "Watcha Gonna Do?" and Baby Bam's nearly eight-minute funk jam, "Smokin' with the Motherman." The Stereo MC's shake things up, too, with "Two Horse Town" (which grabs the now-popular cowboy/outlaw thematic by the reigns), "Goin' Back to the Wild" (which offers a verbal link between Baby Bam and Rob B.), and "Lost in Music" (a shuffling, jazzy rump-shaker supreme). But the true star here is the upbeat, dancy "Elevate My Mind," whose electro-charged BPMs match perfectly with Rob B.'s slinky, decidedly British flow. The "American Mix" album is most notable for its Groove Holmes–styled remix of "Lost in Music."

what to buy next: *Connected* ♫♫♫ (Gee Street/Island, 1992, prod. Stereo MC's) is not a hip-hop album in the pure sense. As if in frustration over the lack of support it received from stateside hip-hop heads, the Stereo MC's shift to a more dance-oriented approach here. Yet, where many dance groups might pump out soulless music tailored for the masses, the Stereo MC's infuse theirs with plenty of earthy soul and even a touch of down-in-the-gutter funk. This time out, the trio is joined by the sultry singers Cath Coffey, Andrea Groves, and Verona Davis, who provide sensuous backing vocals.

worth searching for: The five-song EP *Stereo MC's* (4th and B'Way/Island, 1989, prod. Stereo MC's) is the group's most hip-hop–oriented release, featuring the Run-D.M.C.-meets-Van McCoy turntablized funk of "What Is Soul," the rapid-fire lyrical assault of "Bring It On," and the old-school beat snatching of "Neighborhood."

influences:

◄◄ Massive Attack, Hijack, PM Dawn

►► Orchestral Manoeuvers in the Dark, Jamiroquai

Spence D.

Stereolab

Formed 1991, in London, England.

Tim Gane, guitar, bass, keyboards, percussion; Laetitia Sadier, vocals, percussion, keyboards; Martin Kean, bass (1990–92); Joe Dilworth, drums (1990–92); Gina Morris, vocals (1990–92); Mary Hansen, vocals, guitar, keyboards, percussion (1993–present); Sean O'Hagan, keyboards, bass (1993–present); Duncan Brown, bass (1993–96); Andy Ramsay, drums (1993–present); Katharine Gifford, keyboards, vocals (1994); Morgane Lhöte, keyboards (1995–present); Richard Harrison, bass (1996–present).

The '90s aren't about formal innovation in rock so much as ever more refined recombinations of the past. Stereolab was ahead of the pack in looking beyond traditional rock sources for inspiration, plundering the cut-out bins for Moog (and mood) music, lounge combos, novelty numbers, and even stereo equipment test records. Stereolab's albums—essentially the work of London underground rocker Tim Gane, French chanteuse Laetitia Sadier, and an army of vintage synthesizers and organs—meld insidiously catchy pop melodies, avant-garde electronics, Caribbean textures, and cheesy sound effects into percolating songs that shouldn't work but somehow do. This unlikely pastiche is summed up in the title of one of the group's EPs: *John Cage Bubblegum*. Striking a balance between the cerebral and the silly, the synthetic and organic, Stereolab anticipated the lounge and post-rock scenes that have sprung up in the rock underground, but has made pop music durable enough to outlast them both.

what to buy: *Transient Random-Noise Bursts with Announcements* 𝄞𝄞𝄞𝄞 (Elektra, 1993, prod. Phil Wright) is an ungainly title for an album that glides effortlessly on a bed of electronic rhythms worthy of early '70s Kraut-rockers Neu! while percolating with a sensuality at times worthy of Antonio Carlos Jobim. Sadier's lulling, lilting French-accented vocals keep the melodic hooks flowing, but it's the group's command of the groove, particularly on the 18-minute "Jenny Ondioline," that makes this a trance-pop milestone.

what to buy next: *Switched on Stereolab* 𝄞𝄞𝄞𝄞 (Slumberland, 1992, prod. various) collects the early, self-produced, and highly addictive singles from the group's Duophonic label. *Emperor Tomato Ketchup* 𝄞𝄞𝄞𝄞 (Elektra, 1996, prod. Paul Tipler, John McEntire, Stereolab) is the band's deepest excursion yet into analog-synthesizer esoterica, without skimping on the melodic allure.

the rest:
Peng! 𝄞𝄞𝄞 (Too Pure, 1992)
Low Fi 𝄞𝄞𝄞 (Too Pure, 1993)
The Groop Played "Space Age Batchelor Pad Music" 𝄞𝄞𝄞𝄞 (Too Pure, 1993)
Crumb Duck 𝄞𝄞𝄞 (Clawfist, 1993)
Mars Audiac Quintet 𝄞𝄞𝄞𝄞 (Elektra, 1994)
Dots and Loops 𝄞𝄞𝄞𝄞 (Elektra, 1997)

worth searching for: *Music for the Amorphous Study Center* (Duophonic, 1995, prod. Stereolab) is one of numerous import EPs, this for an exhibit by artist Charles Long. It introduces live strings to the Stereolab studio machinery.

influences:
◀◀ Martin Denny, Neu!, Kraftwerk, Throbbing Gristle, Brian Wilson, the Velvet Underground, Antonio Carlos Jobim

▶▶ Tortoise, the Sea & Cake, Ui, LaBradford, Cardigans

Greg Kot

Cat Stevens

Born Steven Demetri Georgiou, July 21, 1947, in London, England.

Despite immensely popular folk-rock songs that have become international standards, Cat Stevens is the ultimate reluctant pop star. In 1966, just a year after he started performing professionally, he had his first hit; by 1968, he was semi-retired and suffering from tuberculosis. Stevens was turned off by the pop star life, and when he resurfaced in 1970 with *Mona Bone Jakon*, the music was more developed and the lyrics more mature and sensitive. Stevens's fame grew during the next few years, as he added orchestrations and spiritually concerned lyrics to his work. By 1973, Stevens was even more reclusive; he moved to Brazil as a tax exile and donated the savings to charities. His record sales eventually flagged, and by decade's end Stevens became a Muslim, changed his name to Yusef Islam, and retired from music altogether. He stirred controversy in 1989 by endorsing the Ayatollah Khomeini's *fatwa* against *The Satanic Verses* author Salman Rushdie for alleged blasphemies in the book. He has since softened his hardline positions slightly and in 1997 he organized and sang on an album benefiting Bosnian Muslims.

what to buy: Even though he'd had a few hits, *Tea for the Tillerman* 𝄞𝄞𝄞𝄞 (A&M, 1971, prod. Paul Samwell-Smith) blasted Stevens into international superstardom. "Wild World," "Father and Son," "Where Do the Children Play," "Hard Headed Woman," and others made Stevens an album-rock radio staple. The album's cartoon cover art and the innocence expressed in the songs were perfect for the flower-child ethos. *Teaser and the Firecat* 𝄞𝄞𝄞𝄞 (A&M, 1971, prod. Paul Samwell-Smith) is almost as good, particularly the (then) side-two combination of "Morning Has Broken," "Bitterblue," "Moonshadow," and "Peace Train."

what to buy next: *Foreigner* 𝄞𝄞𝄞𝄞 (A&M, 1973, prod. Cat Stevens) offers a taste of the more orchestral side of Stevens's music. The composition "Foreigner Suite" is a complex long form that veers away from lyrics and displays his talent as a musician. *Classics: Vol. 24* 𝄞𝄞𝄞𝄞𝄞 (A&M, 1987, prod. various) is an aptly titled hits collection, including songs he recorded for the darkly comedic cult film *Harold and Maude*.

what to avoid: *Izitso* 𝄞𝄞 (A&M, 1977, prod. Cat Stevens, Dave Kershenbaum) delves into period electronics to little avail, though there are some revealing personal tales on a couple of songs.

the rest:
New Masters 𝄞𝄞𝄞 (Deram, 1967)
Mona Bone Jakon 𝄞𝄞𝄞𝄞 (A&M, 1970)
Very Young and Early Songs 𝄞𝄞𝄞 (Deram, 1972)
Catch Bull at Four 𝄞𝄞𝄞𝄞 (A&M, 1973)

Buddah and the Chocolate Box 🎵🎵🎵🎵 (A&M, 1974)
Greatest Hits 🎵🎵🎵🎵 (A&M, 1975)
Numbers 🎵🎵🎵🎵 (A&M, 1976)
Back to Earth 🎵🎵 (A&M, 1979)

worth searching for: *Matthew and Son* (Deram, 1967) provides an early earful of the straight folk sound of one guy with a guitar and a song to sing.

influences:

◄◄ Bob Dylan, Paul Simon

►► Jackson Browne, James Taylor, Joe Henry, 10,000 Maniacs

Lawrence Gabriel

Shakin' Stevens

Born Michael Barratt, March 4, 1948, in Ely, Wales, England.

One of Britain's finest rock revivalists, Shakin' Stevens has managed to imbue his music with the joy found in Elvis Presley's early records without stooping to outright imitation. His movie-star good looks, intensely physical stage act, and vocal pyrotechnics (which owe as much to R&B as rockabilly), made him a major European star during the '80s, though he is scarcely known in America. Stevens spent the early part of his career with the Sunsets (Carl Petersen, Steve Percy, Paul Dolan, Rockin' Louis, Trevor Hawkins, and, later, Ace Skudder), a dedicated rock revival group that found a solid audience among British Teddy Boys and Dutch rockabilly fanatics. After Stevens left the band, producer Jack Good hired him as one of three actors (including Tim Whitnall and P.J. Proby) to play Elvis Presley at the various stages of his career in the award-winning London theater production of *Elvis*. Good (who produced the breakthrough '60s musical series *Shindig*), was impressed enough by Stevens's performance to cast him in his TV shows *Oh Boy!* and *Let's Rock* (the latter was shown in the U.S. and featured Lulu, Freddie "Fingers" Lee, Joe Brown, and others). High-powered management and a contract with Epic Records resulted in Stevens's hitting the top of Britain's pop charts with rockabilly remakes of Jim Lowe's "Green Door," Rosemary Clooney's "This Ole House," and, from his own pen, "Oh Julie." At Epic, Stevens's sound was slicker, but he employed first-rate roots musicians such as Mickey Gee, Albert Lee, Stuart Coleman, Eddie Jones, and fellow revivalists Matchbox to achieve an early-rock feel that few artists of the '80s possessed. His archivist instincts gave him access to diverse song material (Irma Thomas's "It's Raining," John Fred's "Shirley," the Blasters' "Marie Marie") to which he added impressive zeal and credible interpretive skill. Stevens scored nearly three dozen British hits by the early '90s, then everything seemed to fall apart in a series of lawsuits, management disputes, and declining fortunes. However, his fans are just as faithful to him (and as eager for a comeback) as "Shaky" has been to the heroes of original rock 'n' roll, so you can't count him out yet.

worth searching for: Domestically, there is nothing in print by Shakin' Stevens. However, some on-line services and catalogs carry the British imports *The Hits of Shakin' Stevens* (Epic, 1995, prod. various) and *The Singles Collection* (Arcade, 1994, prod. various). Both are solid collections, and the Arcade set has a few more tracks and includes Shaky's excellent version of Billy Swan's "I Can Help."

influences:

◄◄ Elvis Presley, Gene Vincent, Big Joe Turner, Little Richard, the Sunsets

►► Freddie "Fingers" Lee, Crazy Cavan & the Rhythm Rockers, Matchbox, Jimmy Ray

Ken Burke

Al Stewart

Born September 5, 1946, in Glasgow, Scotland.

With his cerebral lyrics, light vocal delivery, and understated guitar work, Al Stewart was something of an antidote for the disco-crazed '70s. His recordings were pleasant-sounding excursions that delved into such unusual topics as Nostradamus. With roots in folk and arid vocals, Stewart needed somebody to push him over the top. Who better than the over-the-top producer himself, Alan Parsons? Each complemented the other: Stewart sang with greater confidence and had lush multi-tracked layers of sound backing him, while Parsons was limited to the amount of sound he could produce lest he squash Stewart's sensitive sensibilities. Despite a few hits—"Year of the Cat," "Song on the Radio," "Time Passages"—Stewart's older material doesn't time-travel well. But he continues to make new music that's gripping and forward looking.

what to buy: *Between the Wars* 🎵🎵🎵🎵 (Messa/Bluemoon, 1995, prod. Al Stewart, Lawrence Juber) is a terrific album that doesn't sound much like the older Stewart. He and guitarist/co-producer Lawrence Juber fashion 13 songs that conjure up musical memories of '30s swing-time Paris, with looser arrangements and a full backing band that includes bass, drums, strings, reeds, and percussion.

what to buy next: *The Best of Al Stewart* 🎵🎵🎵 (Arista, 1988, prod. various) is a 13-track thumbnail sketch of his work with Parsons and others. It includes material from *Year of the Cat*, *Time Passages*, *24 Carrots*, and the rest of his most well-known, if not best, periods.

what to avoid: The thematic bent of *Russians and Americans* 🎵🎵 (Passport, 1984/Mesa-Bluemoon, 1994) is a noble concept, but it ends up interfering with the album's musical flow.

the rest:

Past, Present, and Future ♪ (Columbia, 1974/Rhino, 1992)
Modern Times ♪♪ (Janus, 1975/Rhino, 1992)
Year of the Cat ♪♪♪ (Arista, 1976)
Time Passages ♪♪♪ (Arista, 1978)
24 Carrots ♪♪♪ (Arista, 1980/Razor & Tie, 1993)
Rhymes in Rooms ♪♪♪♪ (Messa/Blue Moon, 1992)
Famous Last Words ♪♪♪ (Mesa/Bluemoon, 1994)

worth searching for: Stewart was more of a lovelorn folkie when he recorded *Orange* (Columbia, 1972/Beat Goes On, 1993), but guests Rick Wakeman and Brinsley Schwarz brought some muscle to his muse.

influences:

◄◄ Donovan, Bob Dylan, King Crimson, Alan Parsons Project

►► Sting, Rupert Holmes, Nick Gilder

Patrick McCarty and Gary Graff

Dave Stewart

See: Eurythmics

John Stewart

Born September 5, 1939, in San Diego, CA.

John Stewart took a giant step upon leaving the Kingston Trio in 1967. His first album, *California Bloodlines*, remains a classic and set the foundation for a lengthy solo career. Working from the enthusiasm of the Kennedy years—with the Trio, he wrote "New Frontier" for John F. Kennedy, and the songs he composed while traveling with the 1968 Robert Kennedy presidential campaign are a continuing thread through his later work—Stewart has written with an unabashed love of humanity and country and sings with good humor and compassion in a deep, resonant voice that has always seemed older than its years. He bounced from major label to major label through 1980, with the strangely ironic "Gold," recorded for RSO—a label that marketed him alongside the Bee Gees and *Saturday Night Fever*—as his only real hit. Many of his songs have been recorded by others, the most famous being the Monkees' 1967 #1 "Daydream Believer." Stewart's later albums, on small labels and often for his own Homecoming imprint, continue in the same vein, and he stays busy as a live and recording act. Though his optimism has been shaken and his images have turned darker and more impressionistic over the decades, Stewart remains a durable and formidable songwriter and performer.

what to buy: *The Phoenix Concerts—Live* ♪♪♪♪ (Capitol, 1974/One Way, 1997, prod. Nick Venet) is a superb live recording with one of Stewart's best ensembles, and the new reissue adds two songs to the original two-album set. Recorded with his wife, Buffy Ford, and with only a 12-string guitar for accom-

paniment, *Live at the Turf Inn Scotland* ♪♪♪♪ (Folk Era, 1996) is a warm and generous introduction/retrospective to Stewart's career.

what to buy next: *Airdream Believer: A Retrospective* ♪♪♪♪ (Shanachie, 1995, prod. John Stewart) includes several new songs and even reaches back into his Trio days for the pre-rap "The Rev. Mr. Black." *Bullets in the Hourglass* ♪♪♪♪ (Shanachie, 1992, prod. John Hoke, John Stewart) shows the ever-widening direction and more subjective imagery of his more recent songwriting. *The Last Campaign* ♪♪♪♪ (Homecoming, 1985/Laserlight, 1996, prod. John Stewart) gathers together some songs written specifically about and during the Robert Kennedy presidential campaign, most of which had ended up as pieces of other albums. It's now packaged with *American Folk Song Anthology* and *Trio Years* as a budget, three-disc set, *American Journey* ♪♪♪♪ (Laserlight, 1996, prod. various).

what to avoid: On the heels of the success of "Gold," RSO pushed for another *Bombs Away Dream Babies*, and Stewart attempted to retain some dignity while going Hollywood with *Dream Babies Go Hollywood* **woof!** (RSO, 1980, prod. John Stewart). That he failed was perhaps best for all parties concerned.

the rest:

Cannons in the Rain/Wingless Angels ♪♪♪ (Capitol, 1973/1975/Bear Family, 1990)
Fire in the Wind ♪♪♪♪ (RSO, 1977)
Bombs Away Dream Babies ♪♪♪ (RSO, 1979/Razor & Tie, 1994)
Blondes ♪♪♪♪ (Allegiance, 1982)
Trancas ♪♪♪♪ (Affordable Dreams, 1984)
Secret Tapes '86 ♪♪♪♪ (Homecoming, 1986)
Punch the Big Guy ♪♪♪ (Shanachie, 1987)
Secret Tapes II ♪♪♪ (Homecoming, 1987)
American Sketches ♪♪♪ (Laserlight, 1991)
American Originals ♪♪♪ (Capitol, 1992)
Chilly Winds (Trio Years & Revenge of the Budgie) ♪♪♪♪ (Folk Era, 1994)
An American Folk Song Anthology ♪♪♪ (Laserlight, 1996)
Rough Sketches (of Route 66) ♪♪♪♪ (Folk Era, 1997)
Bandera ♪♪♪ (Folk Era, 1997)
(With Buffy Ford) *Signals through the Glass* ♪♪ (Capitol, 1968)
(With Buffy Ford) *The Essential John and Buffy* ♪♪♪ (Feegie, 1994)
(With Cumberland Three) *Songs of the Civil War* ♪♪ (Rhino, 1991)

worth searching for: Stewart's early albums are available on compact disc mostly in European import configurations. The best is still *California Bloodlines/Willard Minus 2* (Bear Family, 1989, prod. Nick Venet), which captures the yin and yang of that period as well as anything. Now packaged with all but two songs of its equally charismatic 1970 follow-up, *Willard*, on one CD, it's an incredible bargain even at import prices. *Lonesome Picker Rides Again* (Warner Bros., 1971/Line, 1990, prod. Michael Stewart) and *Sunstorm* (Warner Bros., 1972/Line,

1995, prod. Michael Stewart) are Americana song collections in the manner of *California Bloodlines* that got lost in the shuffle but still hold up well. *Neon Beach* (Line, 1992, prod. John Stewart) is a ragged, hard-to-find, one-night-only live tape with a loose band that includes some classic '80s songs and weird, yet affecting, covers—"Lady Came from Baltimore," "Shake, Rattle, and Roll," even Paul Simon's "The Boy in the Bubble."

influences:

◄◄ Cumberland Three, Kingston Trio, Dave Guard

►► Lindsey Buckingham, Beat Farmers, Long Ryders

Leland Rucker

Rod Stewart

Born January 10, 1945, in London, England.

A former frontman for the Jeff Beck Group and Faces, Rod Stewart has been written off so many times that rock critics could use him as a tax deduction. Granted, consistency has never been his forte: Even *Foolish Behaviour*, *Tonight I'm Yours*, and *A Night on the Town*—his best, hardest-rocking albums since his early '70s heyday with the Faces—were uneven, reneging on the promise of his classic 1972 album title, *Never a Dull Moment*. But "Maggie May," "You Wear It Well," and "Stay with Me" still sound great on classic-rock radio, and even in middle age, that soulful howl can wring emotion from sappy love songs. Credit Stewart's longevity to a thrilling live show (save for his yawn-inducing 1996 tour that inexplicably found him performing his hits in chronological order) and an impeccable taste in cover songs that over the years has included Eddie Cochran's "Cut across Shorty," Bobby Womack's "It's All Over Now," Jimi Hendrix's "Angel," Cat Stevens's "The First Cut Is the Deepest," Tom Waits's "Downtown Train," and the Blue Nile's "Downtown Lights."

what to buy: *Every Picture Tells a Story* 𝄢𝄢𝄢𝄢 (Mercury, 1971, prod. Rod Stewart) and *Never a Dull Moment* 𝄢𝄢𝄢𝄢 (Mercury, 1972, prod. Rod Stewart) make up one of the most overwhelming one-two punches in rock history. Acoustic guitars, mandolins, organs, and drums collide with Stewart's potent, scruffy pipes. Gloriously reckless but never sloppy, these two classics throw off even more sparks on their newly remastered 1998 editions, part of Mercury's "Rod Stewart Remasters" series.

what to buy next: *The Rod Stewart Album* 𝄢𝄢𝄢𝄢 (Mercury, 1969, prod. Lou Reizner) offers a formative glimpse of his songwriting ("An Old Raincoat Won't Ever Let You Down") and interpretive prowess (the Rolling Stones' "Street Fighting Man," Michael D'Abo's "Handbags and Gladrags"). *A Night on the Town* 𝄢𝄢𝄢𝄢 (Warner Bros., 1976, prod. Tom Dowd) plays to his strengths as a balladeer ("Tonight's the Night," "The First Cut Is the Deepest") and barroom rocker ("The Balltrap," "The Wild

Side of Life"). *Absolutely Live* 𝄢𝄢𝄢 (Warner Bros., 1982, prod. Rod Stewart) is a sweat-soaked document of one of his strongest post-Faces tours, with roof-raising versions of "Hot Legs," Chuck Berry's "Sweet Little Rock 'n' Roller," and a smoking medley of "Little Queenie" and "She Won't Dance with Me."

what to avoid: *If We Fall in Love Tonight* 𝄢 (Warner Bros., 1996, prod. various) could easily be subtitled *Lamest Hits*, as it collects such goopy favorites as "You're in My Heart" and "Tonight's the Night" alongside mundane remakes of Leo Sayer's "When I Need You," Carole King's "So Far Away," and a new arrangement of "Forever Young."

the rest:

Gasoline Alley 𝄢𝄢𝄢 (Mercury, 1970)
Smiler 𝄢𝄢𝄢 (Mercury, 1974)
Sing It Again Rod 𝄢𝄢𝄢 (Mercury, 1972)
Atlantic Crossing 𝄢𝄢𝄢 (Warner Bros., 1975)
Footloose and Fancy Free 𝄢𝄢𝄢 (Warner Bros., 1977)
Blondes Have More Fun 𝄢𝄢𝄢 (Warner Bros., 1978)
Greatest Hits 𝄢𝄢𝄢 (Warner Bros., 1979)
Foolish Behaviour 𝄢𝄢𝄢 (Warner Bros., 1980)
Tonight I'm Yours 𝄢𝄢𝄢 (Warner Bros., 1981)
Body Wishes **woof!** (Warner Bros., 1983)
Camouflage 𝄢𝄢 (Warner Bros., 1984)
Rod Stewart 𝄢𝄢𝄢 (Warner Bros., 1986)
Out of Order 𝄢𝄢 (Warner Bros., 1988)
Storyteller: The Complete Anthology, 1964–1990 𝄢𝄢𝄢𝄢 (Warner Bros., 1989)
Downtown Train: Selections from Storyteller 𝄢𝄢𝄢 (Warner Bros., 1990)
Vagabond Heart 𝄢𝄢 (Warner Bros., 1991)
The Mercury Anthology 𝄢𝄢𝄢𝄢 (Polydor, 1992)
Unplugged . . . and Seated 𝄢𝄢𝄢 (Warner Bros., 1993)
A Spanner in the Works 𝄢𝄢𝄢 (Warner Bros., 1995)
When We Were the New Boys 𝄢𝄢𝄢 (Warner Bros., 1998)

worth searching for: The European import *Lead Vocalist* (Warner Bros., 1993, prod. various) mixes hits with five tracks from an aborted Trevor Horn–produced album, including covers of Stevie Nicks's "Stand Back" and the Stones' "Ruby Tuesday."

influences:

◄◄ Sam Cooke, Otis Redding, Bob Dylan

►► Dan Baird, the Black Crowes, Bash & Pop, Melissa Etheridge

see also: *The Faces*

David Okamoto

Chris Stills

Born April 19, 1974, in Boulder, CO.

Not many musicians are blessed with having two famous singers as parents, but Chris Stills was not only graced with a

Rod Stewart (© Ken Settle)

great last name, but fantastic genes to boot. His mother, French pop singer Veronique Sanson, taught Stills to play piano at age five, and he started playing drums around age 10. However, it wasn't until one of his father's (Stephen Stills) guitar techs taught him a few chords that his fate was sealed. From that moment, for Stills, it was all about music. The young musician was living in Paris at age 16 with his mother when he wrote his first blues-influenced song, "If I Were a Mountain." Only seven years later, he released his debut album, *100 Year Thing*, on Atlantic Records, the same label that has sold millions of Crosby, Stills & Nash albums, as well as Stephen Stills solo recordings. Chris may have good genes and a famous last name, but it's his dedication and creativity on the guitar and fluid lyrics that will have people snapping up his music for years to come.

what's available: Although it didn't come out with a bang or a buzz, it won't take long for *100 Year Thing* 𝄢𝄢𝄢𝄢 (Atlantic, 1998, prod. Ethan Johns) to pick up a lot of steam. With his debut, Stills carries the torch of hippie singers, while being straightforward and grounded—a real '90s guy. He sings about the problems of racial boundaries, lost dreams, and the need to roam throughout one's life. Stills has a vocal range that parallels his father's and combines it with the ability to translate his talents from electric and acoustic guitar to drums, piano, and pump organ—and he even sings backup.

influences:

◀◀ Buffalo Springfield, Jimi Hendrix, the Beatles, the Police, Beck

Ari Bendersky

Stephen Stills

Born January 3, 1945, in Dallas, TX.

The best thing that never happened to Stephen Stills was getting a role as a Monkee. Had he been picked as a member of the prefab four, a central part of rock 'n' roll history—the folk-inflected Southern California sound popularized by Linda Ronstadt, Jackson Browne, and the Eagles—might have evolved quite differently. Fortunately, Stills instead founded Buffalo Springfield (first called the Herd) with Neil Young, Richie Furay, Bruce Palmer, and Dewey Martin, and later, Crosby, Stills & Nash with David Crosby and Graham Nash (and sometimes, Young). The latter band was formed after Stills turned down another opportunity: fronting Blood, Sweat & Tears following Al Kooper's departure. To say Stills is a brilliant guitarist might undercut his equal—if not greater—worth as a songwriter. The composer of a slew of late '60s and early '70s anthems such as "For What It's Worth," "Bluebird," "Suite: Judy Blue Eyes," and "Love the One You're With," Stills definitely was on a roll for a period of time. His solo efforts do vary wildly in quality, though

his first, *Stephen Stills*, has many moments that still sound thrilling nearly three decades later. Stills also did some dynamite session work on some of the best albums of the '60s and '70s, sharing credits with everyone from Eric Clapton and Jimi Hendrix (who appeared on *Stephen Stills*) to Joni Mitchell, Loggins & Messina, Bill Withers, John Sebastian, and even . . . the Monkees. (He also extended this run into the '90s, when the strident rap band Public Enemy invited him to sing "For What It's Worth" on the hit "He Got Game.") If for nothing else than "For What It's Worth"—which, though written about a bar-closing that party police mistook for a riot, turned into a prescient description of the 1968 Democratic National Convention—Stills would have a cemented place in rock music history. But his post-Springfield work with CSN raised folk-rock to a new level, and his work with Manassas again brought his bluegrass/southern soul roots to a wider audience. In 1997, Stills was inducted into the Rock and Roll Hall of Fame twice on the same night: with Buffalo Springfield and with Crosby, Stills & Nash.

what to buy: *Stephen Stills* 𝄢𝄢𝄢𝄢 (Atlantic, 1970, prod. Stephen Stills, Bill Halverson) is a stunning solo debut, featuring both down-and-dirty jams ("Go Back Home," "Black Queen") and longing, soulful ballads ("To a Flame, We Are Not Helpless"). Stills had a lot of help from his friends here: Clapton, Coolidge, Crosby, Mama Cass, Sebastian, and Hendrix, to name a few. *Stephen Stills Live* 𝄢𝄢𝄢 (Atlantic, 1975/1992, prod. Bill Halverson) shows both the electric and "wooden" sides of Stills, and the solo acoustic side is particularly charming.

what to buy next: *Manassas* 𝄢𝄢𝄢 (Atlantic, 1972, prod. Stephen Stills, Chris Hillman, Dallas Taylor) has a tendency to meander, but its Byrds/bluegrass bent is delightful. *Stephen Stills 2* 𝄢𝄢𝄢 (Atlantic, 1971, prod. Stephen Stills, Bill Halverson) reveals just how hopelessly hokey some of Stills's lyrics sound, mired as they are in the hippie-love-peace language of their time ("Fishes and Scorpions"). Yet other cuts manage to transcend their era to become anthems for any generation.

what to avoid: Manassas' *Down the Road* 𝄢𝄢 (Atlantic, 1973/1988, prod. Stephen Stills, Chris Hillman, Dallas Taylor) conveys just how uneven Stills's output can be, even when he's backed by the fine musicians in Manassas. It was reissued as *Manassas Down*.

the rest:

Stills 𝄢𝄢 (Columbia, 1975/1993)
Illegal Stills 𝄢𝄢 (Columbia, 1976/1990)
(With the Stills-Young Band) *Long May You Run* 𝄢𝄢𝄢 (Reprise, 1976/1988)
Right by You 𝄢𝄢 (Atlantic, 1984)
Stills Alone 𝄢𝄢𝄢 (Vision, 1991)

worth searching for: *Supersession* (Columbia, 1968, prod. Al Kooper), in which Stills sat in for an unexpectedly AWOL Michael Bloomfield, contains a version of "Season of the Witch" that outdoes Donovan's by miles. *The Best of Stephen Stills* (Atlantic, 1977, prod. various) is a fine summation of his solo work that's unfortunately out of print.

influences:

◀◀ The Beatles, Jimi Hendrix, Eric Clapton, the Byrds, Ritchie Havens, Bob Dylan

▶▶ The Eagles, Chris Stills, Poco, Joni Mitchell, Rita Coolidge

see also: *Buffalo Springfield, Crosby, Stills & Nash*

Lynne Margolis

WHAT ALBUM CHANGED YOUR LIFE?

I think probably *Bitches Brew* by Miles Davis. That was, I suppose, the beginning of rock 'n' roll and jazz mixed up, which thrilled me. It still does, actually.

Sting

Sting

Born Gordon Matthew Sumner, October 2, 1951, in Newcastle, England.

Given Sting's massive worldwide success in the wake of the Police's mid-'80s demise, it's hard to remember the rending of garments and tearing of hair that greeted his hiring an all-black jazz band to back him on his solo debut, *The Dream of the Blue Turtles.* You think that someone would have remembered that Sting actually began his career playing jazz in the pubs of his native Newcastle, whiling away his days as a schoolteacher. Luckily, charges of cultural imperialism didn't stick, and Sting's solo act went on to surpass his success with the Police both in terms of success and artistic vitality. The music hews close to the Police's formula—a little reggae here, a little jazz there, and solid pop melodies throughout. Lyrically, Sting has always had much to answer for, invoking mythological beasties and occasionally slipping into a foreign tongue. But give him this much—few pop stars have taken as many risks and have scored as many hits with such challenging material. Sting has always been willing to stick his neck out far enough for his critics to chop it off, and they have, with relish. But his albums are consistently marked by intelligence, wit, political savvy, and, yes, an intense fascination with the importance of being Sting. So sue him already—but not without giving his albums a fair listen.

what to buy: An obvious place to start is *Fields of Gold: The Best of Sting, 1984–1994* ✈✈✈✈✈ (A&M, 1994, prod. various), a 14-song compilation that hits the highlights of his solo career and includes the new songs "When We Dance" and "This Cowboy Song." Recording a live album after only one studio effort was a bold move, but *Bring on the Night* ✈✈✈✈ (A&M, 1986, prod. Kim Turner, Sting) offers ample justification, with expansive versions of songs from *Blue Turtles* plus some well-chosen and reworked Police selections. Further, *Bring on the Night* offers a more accurate portrait of Sting's jazz-oriented group than does his debut. Dauntingly verbose, *Nothing Like the Sun* ✈✈✈✈✈ (A&M, 1987, prod. Neil Dorfsman, Sting) scores on the basis of its joyous polyrhythmic groove, thanks in large part to drummer Manu Katche. Dedicated to Sting's late father, *The Soul Cages* ✈✈✈✈✈ (A&M, 1991, prod. Hugh Padgham, Sting) is an extraordinarily moving album and his most emotionally rewarding work, filled with autobiographical details and provocative (for pop music) philosophy.

what to buy next: *The Dream of the Blue Turtles* ✈✈✈✈ (A&M, 1985, prod. Sting, Pete Smith) offers a departure from Sting's work with the Police, though not as radical a one as the makeup of his band might indicate. The album opening "If You Love Somebody Set Them Free" is a curious sentiment coming from the man who wrote the smash "Every Breath You Take"; "Fortress around Your Heart," the album's closer, is more on the same beam. Showing less ambition than the albums that preceded it, but no less quality or style, *Ten Summoner's Tales* ✈✈✈✈ (A&M, 1993, prod. Hugh Padgham, Sting) features 11— ha,ha—pop songs that entertain more and preach less than is usual for Sting. As musically accomplished as anything he's done, yet slightly less fun for its relentless sobriety, *Mercury Falling* ✈✈✈✈ (A&M, 1996, prod. Hugh Padgham, Sting) contains one grim tale after another, though the album is redeemed with the hopeful "Let Your Soul Be Your Pilot" and the sly "All Four Seasons in One Day."

the rest:

The Very Best of Sting & the Police ✈✈✈✈ (A&M, 1997)

worth searching for: From the same sessions that produced *Nothing Like the Sun, Nada Como el Sol* (A&M EP, 1991, prod. Neil Dorfsman, Sting) offers Spanish-language versions of "We'll Be Together," "Little Wing," and "Fragile," plus a version of "Fragile" sung in Portuguese.

Sting (© Ken Settle)

influences:

◄◄ Gilberto Gil, Gil Evans, Bob Marley, the Beatles

►► The Samples, Peter Himmelman, Dave Matthews Band

see also: *The Police*

Daniel Durchholz

The Stone Poneys

See: Linda Ronstadt

The Stone Roses

Formed 1985, in Manchester, England. Disbanded 1996.

Ian Brown, vocals; John Squire, guitar (1985–96); Andy Couzens, guitar (1985–87); Pete Garner, bass (1985–87); Gary "Mani" Mounfield, bass (1987–present); Alan "Reni" Wren, drums (1985–95).

Formed out of the dubious ashes of a Clash-copy band, the Patrol, and an equally sketchy mod-revival act English Rose, this quartet nevertheless went on to become the biggest band to hit England during the late '80s, a phenomenon so fast and so unprecedented it went from playing small clubs to selling out an entire island (just under 100,000 at Spike Island) in the space of a year. But the Stone Roses didn't catch on in America because the band failed to play a single date in the U.S., even canceling what dates were booked. Instead, they sued their way out of their record contract, and the protracted legal fight resulted in a five-year vacation between LPs. By the time the Roses convened to record a proper follow-up for their new label, Geffen, the air had exited the balloon. Drummer Reni followed producer John Leckie's lead and walked before the world tour. A year later, guitarist John Squire also bolted to form his own band, the unbelievably awful Seahorses, and the Stone Roses effectively ceased to exist.

what to buy: Considering how patchy its earliest singles were, the band's debut *The Stone Roses* ♫♫♫♫ (Silvertone, 1989, prod. John Leckie) is a shocking LP, as close to perfection as stylish, edgy English pop gets. Songs that had seemed ordinary in original (later bootlegged) demos became minor wonder-rockets, a mixture of styles segueing beautifully thanks to Leckie's mellifluous production, so flawless it's as if the producer was playing a violin. Right from the opening, dramatic moments of the anthemic "I Wanna Be Adored" through to the vaguely funk/Hendrix psychedelic groove of "I Am the Resurrection," going from grandiose pop to backwards-tape-looped melanges, this LP weaves an atmospheric spell without ever sounding nostalgic.

what to buy next: During the band's protracted legal wranglings, two decent B-sides albums were issued, *Turns to Stone* ♫♫♫ (Silvertone, 1992, prod. John Leckie, Peter Hook) and the

more generous *The Complete Stone Roses* ♫♫♫♫ (Silvertone, 1995, prod. John Leckie, Peter Hook).

what to avoid: *Second Coming* ♫♫ (Geffen, 1994, prod. Simon Dawson, Paul Schroeder) showed the band still had plenty of aplomb, but it's easy to see why an exasperated John Leckie, the original producer, walked off in a huff. The LP is nothing more than bombastic, overblown, tired rockisms, with Squire reduced to ripping off Jimmy Page's Led Zeppelin licks on top of way-too-long dance jams crying out for an editor. The Seahorses' *Do It Yourself* **woof!** (Geffen, 1997, prod. Tony Visconti) contains all of Squire's horrific, overbearing Page worship from that fatal second Roses LP, without the textural interest and with a vocalist that makes one yearn for Ian Brown.

worth searching for: Brown's solo debut, *Unfinished Monkey Business* (Polydor U.K., 1998, prod. Ian Brown), appeared in Britain only upon its release in the hopes of building a homeland buzz before trying to bring it to the U.S. Singles such as "My Star" (with guest guitar from old Stone Roses admirer, Oasis guitarist Noel Gallagher) and "Corpses" are winners, although Brown is not a real match for the 1989 Squire as a writer.

influences:

◄◄ The Smiths, Deep Purple, Mach I

►► Suede, Oasis, Smash Mouth

Jack Rabid

Stone Temple Pilots
/Talk Show
/Scott Weiland

Formed as Mighty Joe Young, 1987, in San Diego, CA.

Scott Weiland, vocals; Dean DeLeo, guitar; Robert DeLeo, bass; Eric Kretz, drums.

Alternarock's favorite whipping boy, Stone Temple Pilots never could win with critics. Damned for its success and for its sonic similarity to Seattle grungesters Soundgarden, Alice in Chains, and Pearl Jam, STP took its case straight to the people, who made each of STP's three albums—each one better than its predecessor—platinum-plus affairs. It was largely a bum rap, though. Anyone who does the math can see that STP, Alice, and Pearl Jam are roughly contemporaries, and that it's nigh unto impossible that the group ripped off its sound from anyone except the same folks as Alice and Pearl Jam—that is, purveyors of '70s rock and '80s punk, from Led Zeppelin to Black Flag. So sue STP for its hooky, concise alternametal if you want—it'll never hold up in court. What will hold up in court, however, is lead singer Scott Weiland's recidivist history of drug abuse, which forced

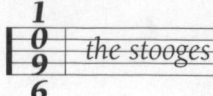

cancellation of an STP tour and left the band's future uncertain. For their part, the DeLeo brothers and Eric Kretz picked up singer Dave Couts and formed the band Talk Show. Weiland, meanwhile, went on to record a solo album. Both were worthwhile efforts, but tanked commercially, leading one to wonder if STP was a band whose whole was greater than the sum of its parts.

what to buy: *Tiny Music . . . Songs from the Vatican Gift Shop* 🎵🎵🎵 (Atlantic, 1996, prod. Brendan O'Brien) lessens the metallic grind of previous efforts (though it's still evident in "Trippin' on the Hole in a Paper Heart" and "Big Bang Baby") in favor of a lighter touch; "Lady Picture Show," for example, is downright Beatlesque, while "And So I Know" finds Weiland crooning over some smooth cocktail jazz.

what to buy next: The group's debut, *Core* 🎵🎵🎵 (Atlantic, 1992, prod. Brendan O'Brien), scored with the grim "Creep," stirred controversy with "Sex Type Thing"—a song about date rape told from a seemingly unironic, first-person point of view—and otherwise delivered heavy, arena-ready anthems such as "Plush" and "Wicked Garden." The follow-up, *Purple* 🎵🎵🎵 (Atlantic, 1994, prod. Brendan O'Brien), was equally reviled by critics, but fans rallied around it. "Vasoline," "Interstate Love Song," and the acoustic "Pretty Penny" are the standout tracks.

solo outings:
Talk Show:
Talk Show 🎵🎵🎵 (Atlantic, 1997)

Scott Weiland:
12 Bar Blues 🎵🎵🎵 (Atlantic, 1998)

influences:
◄◄ David Bowie, Led Zeppelin, the Beatles, Black Flag, Brecht & Weill

Daniel Durchholz

The Stooges
See: Iggy Pop

Stories
Formed 1971, in New York, NY. Disbanded 1975.

Michael Brown (born Michael Lookofsky), keyboards (1971–73); Ian Lloyd (born Ian Buoncocglio), vocals, bass; Steve Love, guitar, vocals; Bryan Madey, drums, vocals (1971–75); Kenny Aaronson, bass (1971–75); Ken Bichel, keyboards (1971–75); Rick Ranno, drums (1974–75).

After the dissolution of the Left Banke and his stint as songwriter for the group Montage, keyboardist/songwriter Michael Brown co-founded Stories. Lead singer Ian Lloyd's raspy, Rod Stewart–like vocals don't complement Brown's melodic compo-

sitions quite as well as Steve Martin's in the Banke, but Stories still managed to produce two enjoyable albums.

what to buy: The second LP, *About Us* 🎵🎵🎵 (Kama Sutra, 1973/Original Buddah Classics, 1996), is regarded as a power pop classic. Ironically, Stories hit it big with a #1 cover of Hot Chocolate's "Brother Louie" after Brown left the group, and the song was subsequently appended to the album.

worth searching for: *Stories* (Kama Sutra, 1972) is out of print but worth seeking out for the unlikely Top 40 hit "I'm Coming Home," as well as strong tracks such as "Hello People," "Step Back," and "Take Cover."

influences:
◄◄ The Left Banke, Hot Chocolate, the Spinners, Rod Stewart
►► The Black Crowes, Michael Bolton

see also: *The Left Banke*

Mike Greenfield

Stormtroopers of Death
See: Anthrax

The Story
See: Jonatha Brooke

Storyville
See: Arc Angels

Izzy Stradlin
See: Guns N' Roses

Strange Cargo
See: William Orbit

The Strangeloves
Formed 1964, in New York, NY.

Bob Feldman, vocals; Jerry Goldstein, vocals; Richard Gottehrer, vocals.

During the summer of '64, the songwriting team of Bob Feldman, Jerry Goldstein, and Richard Gottehrer was in trouble. They'd had a string of hits—not the least of which was the Angels' teen classic "My Boyfriend's Back"—during the Brill Building pop era, the last vestiges of the Tin Pan Alley days of songwriters. But the Beatles had arrived in New York that February, and the mop-topped sensations had re-written the rules. Record companies were only interested in acts that wrote their own material—especially if the act came with British accents. So the trio invented Brit-accented alter-egos as a goof, calling themselves the Strangeloves: Miles, Niles, and Giles Strangelove, brothers from Australia. They wore a hodgepodge of tribal costumes from several continents and beat out variations of the primitive Bo Diddley beat on drums supplied by a friend, the acclaimed African percussionist Olatunji. They went on the TV show *Hullabaloo* and faked their way through a performance, like some sort of primal Milli Vanilli. The wonder of it was that a couple of the trio's phony Brit-Invasion singles—"I Want Candy" and "Night Time"—were kicking rock songs and became staples of garage-bands everywhere. Once the Strangeloves' masquerade was over, the FGG songwriting and production team returned to what it knew best: finding talent and recording great songs (Gottehrer went on to produce some of the best music of the punk era, including Blondie's early tracks).

what's available: *I Want Candy* ♪♪♪♪ (Bang, 1965/Legacy, 1995, prod. Bob Feldman, Jerry Goldman, Richard Gottehrer) is a glorious and twisted document of the British Invasion era. The songs sound fresh—and still convincingly British—and the beats are as big as they could be. The album also includes the Strangeloves' original version of "Hang on Sloopy," later recorded by the McCoys, a band discovered by the trio.

influences:

◀◀ Elvis Presley, Bo Diddley, the British Invasion

▶▶ Lydia Lunch, Bow Wow Wow

Gil Asakawa

The Stranglers
Formed 1974, in Guilford, England.

Hugh Cornwell, guitar, vocals (1974–90); Dave Greenfield, keyboards; Jet Black (born Brian Duffy), drums (1974–93); Jean-Jacques Burnel, bass; John Ellis, guitar (1990–present); Paul Roberts, vocals (1990–present); Tikake Tobe, drums (1993–present).

Credibility and respect were in short supply for the Stranglers. Positioning themselves in the punk bad-boy mode, they found moderate success in England and Europe with hits such as "Something Better Change," "Peaches," "No More Heroes," "Nice 'n' Sleazy," "Golden Brown," and "Skin Deep." But America ignored the Stranglers; the band had a good name and an appropriately insufferable punk attitude, but little to no compelling material. From punk to some arty miscues and desperate grabs at other songwriters' material, the Stranglers became bad boys to whom no one paid any attention. In some ways the band was ahead of its time, in that such early Stranglers' songs as "Peaches" were refused airplay because of crude lyrics. Ultimately, the Stranglers' success was more due to hype than talent—nothing new for the pop business, but this band made

quite a long run of it. Even after the departure of cult hero Hugh Cornwell, the rest of the band remained determined (and signed, in America, to the goth-ish Cleopatra imprint), and brought on Paul Roberts as a replacement, along with John Ellis on guitar. Perhaps mired by its own nostalgia, the band is hardly the vital force it used to be, but still maintains a loyal (if not desperate) fan base of black-wearers. Cornwell continues to perform as a solo artist, but with little notoriety to carry his aging grudgery.

what to buy: *Greatest Hits, 1977–1990* ♪♪♪♪ (Epic, 1990, prod. various) might have been a sign-off to an illustrious career had the group decided to end it there. Regardless, this is the essential music legacy of a band whose legacy is only partially comprised of music.

what to buy next: *No More Heroes* ♪♪♪ (A&M, 1977) is as punk as the Stranglers got, and for a minute it suited them fine. "No More Heroes" is genius, as is the stomper "Something Better Change." *Dreamtime* ♪♪♪ (Epic, 1986) departed from the typical buzz and grind. With its haunting keyboard beds and soft edges, it could well have been from a different group.

what to avoid: The big record company push on the lumbering *Feline* ♪♪ (Epic, 1982/1991) left lots of folks wondering what the fuss was about.

best of the rest:
IV (Rattus Norvegicus) ♪♪♪ (A&M, 1977)
Black and White ♪♪♪ (A&M, 1978)
The Raven ♪♪♪' (EMI America, 1979)
Aural Sculpture ♪♪ (Epic, 1984)
All Live and All of the Night ♪♪ (Epic, 1989)

influences:

◀◀ Blue Öyster Cult, the Sex Pistols, the Beatles

▶▶ The Clash, the Cramps, Social Distortion

Billy Manes and Patrick McCarty

Syd Straw
Born in Los Angeles, CA.

Singer-songwriter Syd Straw's music has been described as "jangle-pop" and "alternative pop-rock," though she's so quirky she slips through pigeonholes. Originally a backing vocalist for Pat Benatar and later a member of the Golden Palominos, Straw has since been a guest on many other artists' recordings, a favor several return on her own frustratingly rare releases. In fact, Straw has given her fans only two solo discs to date—*Surprise* and *War and Peace* (so called, she jokes, because it took so long to happen and because, with 14 songs, it's almost an epic). Straw, daughter of actor Jack Straw (*The Pajama Game*), has also done some acting, appearing in Nickelodeon's *The Ad-*

ventures of Pete and Pete and the BBC/PBS co-production of Armistead Maupin's *Tales of the City.* Her tune "People of Earth" made it onto the soundtrack of the TV show *Party of Five.*

what to buy: *Surprise* 🎵🎵🎵🎵 (Virgin, 1989, prod. Syd Straw, Anthony Moore, Van Dyke Parks, Daniel Lanois) features an A-list of accompanists, including Michael Stipe, John Doe, Don Was, Richard Thompson, Marshall Crenshaw, Peter Holsapple, Ry Cooder, Antion Fier, Chris Stamey, Jim Keltner, Tony Levin, Bernie Worrell, Marc Ribot, and Dave Alvin. But it's her voice—so beautifully exhibited on "Golden Dreams" and Stephen Foster's "Hard Times," a famous Civil War–era folk hymn—that shines through all the exemplary arrangements and instrumentation.

what to buy next: *War and Peace* 🎵🎵🎵 (Capricorn, 1996, prod. Syd Straw) is full of rootsy, gutsy rock, country, and blues, and at least a few should-have-been-hits. Straw hits a nerve on "Love, and the Lack of It," "The Toughest Girl in the World," and "CBGB's," with able assistance by the bone-clanking Skeletons. When she sings "A woman of uneasy virtue taking her chances when she can sits on the edge of the bed explaining her scars to another stupid man," there's not a single woman of a certain age who doesn't know exactly how it feels.

worth searching for: The Golden Palominos' *A History (1982–1985)* (Metrotone/Restless, 1992) includes eight cuts from *Visions of Excess* (Metrotone, 1985, prod. Anton Fier), several of which include vocals by Straw. They cook, with Fier's propulsive drumming, elements of funk, folk, and whatever else Bill Laswell and the band's ever-changing crew threw in. All of Straw's cuts can also be found on *Thundering Herd: The Best of the Golden Palominos* (Oceana, 1991, prod. John Matarazzo). Finally, "People of Earth," from *Music from Party of Five* (Reprise, 1996, prod. various), is a humorous but pointed plea for courtesy and environmental consciousness.

influences:

◀◀ Carly Simon, John Hiatt, Richard Thompson, Exene Cervenkova, Loudon Wainwright III

▶▶ Kacy Crowley, Kim Fox

Lynne Margolis

The Strawberry Alarm Clock

Formed 1967, in Santa Barbara, CA. Disbanded 1971.

Ed King, guitar, vocals; Lee Freeman, guitar, bass, horns, drums, vocals; Mark Weitz, keyboards; Gary Lovetro, bass, vocals (1967–68); George Bunnel, bass (1967–69); Randy Seol, drums, vocals (1967–69); Jimmy Pitman, guitar, vocals (1969–70); Gene Gunnels, drums (1969–71); Paul Marshall, guitar, vocals (1970–71).

With flowers, beads, and hippie dreams, the Strawberry Alarm Clock tapped into a psychedelic vein with the album and hit single "Incense and Peppermints." Better-than-average arrangements and proficient instrumentation—guitarist Ed King went on to join Lynyrd Skynyrd—helped make up for such ludicrous songs as "Strawberries Mean Love."

what's available: *Anthology: Strawberry Alarm Clock* 🎵🎵 (One Way, 1993, compilation prod. Steve Bartek) makes for an easy, if dated, listen. Though the band is mostly notable today for its groovy psychedelic name and the occasional nostalgic radio hit from the '60s, the Alarm Clock regained credibility briefly when Camper Van Beethoven covered its violin-heavy arrangement of "Pictures of Matchstick Men" during the late '80s.

what to avoid: *Incense & Peppermints* 🎵🎵 (MCA Special Products, 1994) isn't exactly a proud portrait of the psychedelic era. Aside from the title track, this is lightweight, rambling stuff—as pretentious song titles such as "Sit with the Guru" indicate.

influences:

◀◀ The Beatles, the Rolling Stones, the Grateful Dead, Jefferson Airplane

▶▶ Camper Van Beethoven

Patrick McCarty

The Strawbs /Dave Cousins

Formed as the Strawberry Hill Boys, 1967, in Leicester, England. Disbanded 1980. Re-formed 1983.

David Cousins, vocals, guitar; Tony Hooper, vocals, guitar (1967–72, 1983–present); Dave Lambert, vocals, guitar (1972–79); Arthur Philips, mandolin (1967–68); Ron Chesterman, bass (1968–69); John Ford, vocals, bass (1969–73, 1983–present); Chas Cronk, bass, vocals (1974–79); Sandy Denny, vocals, guitar (1968); Rick Wakeman, keyboards (1969–71); Blue Weaver, keyboards (1971–73, 1983–present); John Hawken, keyboards (1974–79); Richard Hudson, drums (1969–73, 1983–present); Rod Coombes, drums, vocals (1974–79); Brian Willoughby, guitar (1979, 1983–present); Rod Demick, bass (1985–present); Chris Parren, keyboards (1985–present).

Eclectic and ever evolving, the Strawbs started out as the folk collective the Strawberry Hill Boys during the mid-'60s and metamorphosed into a strong folk-rock-progressive band. While a constantly changing stream of musicians has passed through the group—including keyboard wizard Rick Wakeman, later of Yes, and pop-rock duo Hudson-Ford—its constant has always been singer-songwriter-guitarist Dave Cousins. His voice isn't for all tastes (the sound lies somewhere between that of Jethro Tull's Ian Anderson and Bob Dylan), but as a folk instrument, it's more than adequate to convey a wide range of viewpoints and emotions. His imaginative and literate lyrics, which often take either a personal or a bardic, folktale tack, encompass satires; searching treatments of life, death, spirituality, and ethical problems; lullabies; and love songs running from earthy to humorous to lush. The music is sometimes consciously ancient-sounding, sometimes straight-ahead rock 'n' roll—at various times intimate, folky, or grand—and characterized by an intricate mix of acoustic guitar and electric backing. Various members of the group, including Cousins, Wakeman, Hudson-Ford, and Dave Lambert, released independent projects either during or outside their time with the Strawbs. (Note: Much of the Strawbs' back catalog is scheduled for reissue in 1998.)

what to buy: *From the Witchwood* ♫♫♫ (A&M, 1971, prod. Tony Visconti), from the Strawbs' "ancient music" period, features lush harmonies on traditional-style ballads with a semi-medieval lyric setting as well as more contemporary folk-rock arrangements played on dulcimer, harpsichord, recorder, banjo, sitar, and autoharp in addition to rock instruments. *Bursting at the Seams* ♫♫♫ (A&M, 1973, prod. Strawbs) is one of the Strawbs' most accessible and contemporary-sounding albums, with the hits "Lay Down" and "Part of the Union" (a satirical look at the inordinate power of British labor unions).

what to buy next: *A Choice Selection of Strawbs* ♫♫♫ (A&M, 1992, prod. various) has much of the group's best out-of-print material. *Greatest Hits Live!* ♫♫♫ (Road Goes on Forever, 1993) captures the best of the band's long history in a concert setting.

the rest:
Just a Collection of Antiques and Curios ♫♫♫ (A&M, 1970)
Grave New World ♫♫♫♫ (A&M, 1972)
Hero and Heroine ♫♫♫♪ (A&M, 1974)
Ghosts ♫♫♫♫ (A&M, 1975)
Deadlines ♫♫♪ (Arista, 1978/One Way, 1997)
Preserves Uncanned ♫♫♪ (Road Goes on Forever, 1991)
Sandy Denny and the Strawbs ♫♫♫♪ (Hannibal, 1991)
Heartbreak Hill ♫♫♫♫ (Road Goes on Forever, 1995)
Deep Cuts/Burning for You ♫♫♫ (Road Goes on Forever, 1996)
Don't Say Goodbye/Ringing down the Years ♫♫♫ (Road Goes on Forever, 1998)
Halcyon Days: The A&M Years ♫♫♫♪ (A&M, 1998)

solo outings:
Dave Cousins:
(With Brian Willoughby) *Old School Songs* ♫♫♪ (Road Goes on Forever, 1979)
The Bridge ♫♫♪ (Road Goes on Forever, 1994)

influences:
◀◀ Leadbelly, Lonnie Donegan, Flatt & Scruggs, Watersons, Young Tradition, Bob Dylan, the Beatles, Pete Townshend

▶▶ Fairport Convention, Alan Parsons Project, Jethro Tull

see also: *Yes*

Polly Vedder

WHAT ALBUM CHANGED YOUR LIFE?

I picked up the second Gene Vincent record, and I couldn't believe it. I heard that guitar playing and the slap bass and the sound—I was just, 'Oh my God; this is what I want to sound like!' Then I saw a picture of Eddie Cochran and said, 'That's what I want to look like!'

Brian Setzer

Stray Cats
/Brian Setzer
/Lee Rocker
/Lee Rocker's Big Blue
Formed 1979, in Massapequa, NY.

Brian Setzer, vocals, guitar; Lee Rocker (born Lee Drucker), upright bass, vocals; Slim Jim Phantom (born Jim McDonell), drums.

A definite anomaly in the synth-heavy early '80s, the pompadoured, tattooed, and bowling-shirted Stray Cats can be credited with introducing rockabilly to a whole new audience. After scuffling around the New York scene, the band moved to the more rockabilly-receptive England, where it enjoyed the patronage of Dave Edmunds, who produced its first two albums. Returning to the U.S. in 1982—after opening some shows on the Rolling Stones 1981 tour—the Cats scratched the U.S. with hits such as "Rock This Town" and "Stray Cat Strut." Suddenly teenagers who wouldn't even think about buying an old Elvis Presley record were interested in a sound that was more akin to their parents' generation than their own. The Cats' popularity quickly faded, however, and while the group hasn't disbanded, it gets together only sporadically while its members pursue their own interests—Setzer crooning big band standards and the odd Stray Cats tune for swing-dancing revivalists with the 16-piece Brian Setzer Orchestra, Rocker with the more traditional rockabilly outfit Big Blue, whose first album featured Presley guitarist Scotty Moore.

what to buy: *Built for Speed* 𝄞𝄞𝄞𝄞 (EMI America, 1982, prod. Dave Edmunds) compiles the best of the Stray Cats' two British releases for a powerhouse introduction.

what to buy next: The unjustly ignored *Blast Off* 𝄞𝄞𝄞𝄞 (EMI America, 1989, prod. Dave Edmunds) is a corker, with nine exhilarating rockabilly workouts and an anthemic, swinging closer, "Nine Lives." Of the solo albums, the Brian Setzer Orchestra's classy *Guitar Slinger* 𝄞𝄞𝄞𝄞 (Interscope, 1996, prod. Phil Ramone) is a bright, brassy romp through a variety of styles, with Setzer's stinging guitar keeping the energy level high.

what to avoid: *Rock Therapy* 𝄞𝄞 (EMI, 1986, prod. Stray Cats) finds Setzer and Co. staying true to their sound but so desperate for a comeback that the songwriting is flawed and the performances tentative.

the rest:
Rant 'n' Rave 𝄞𝄞𝄞 (EMI America, 1983)
Rock This Town: The Best of the Stray Cats 𝄞𝄞 (EMI America, 1989)
Choo Choo Hot Fish 𝄞𝄞𝄞𝄞 (JRS/Great Pyramid, 1992)
Greatest Hits 𝄞 (Curb, 1992)
Runaway Boys: A Retrospective '81–'92 𝄞𝄞𝄞 (EMI, 1997)

worth searching for: *Original Cool* (Griffin Music, 1993, prod. Stray Cats, Jeff "Skunk" Baxter) is a Japanese import of the still-kicking Cats blazing through 15 rockabilly and early rock standards.

solo outings:
Brian Setzer:
The Knife Feels Like Justice 𝄞𝄞𝄞 (EMI, 1986)
Live Nude Guitars 𝄞𝄞𝄞𝄞 (EMI Manhattan, 1988)
The Brian Setzer Orchestra 𝄞𝄞𝄞 (Hollywood, 1994)
The Dirty Boogie 𝄞𝄞𝄞𝄞 (Interscope, 1998)

Phantom, Rocker & Slick:
Phantom, Rocker & Slick 𝄞𝄞𝄞 (EMI America, 1985)
Cover Girl 𝄞𝄞 (EMI America, 1986)

Lee Rocker:
(With Big Blue) *Lee Rocker's Big Blue* 𝄞𝄞𝄞 (Black Top, 1994)
No Cats 𝄞𝄞𝄞 (Up Right, 1998)

influences:
◀◀ Eddie Cochran, Gene Vincent, Elvis Presley
▶▶ Uncle Tupelo, Bottle Rockets, Royal Crown Revue

Todd Wicks

John P. Strohm & the Hello Strangers
See: Antenna

Joe Strummer
See: The Clash

Dan Stuart
See: Green on Red

Style Council
Formed 1983, in London, England. Disbanded 1989.

Paul Weller, guitar, bass, keyboards, vocals; Mick Talbot, keyboards, vocals; Dee C. Lee, vocals (1986–89).

If the Jam's punk-rock roots were too confining for Paul Weller's expanding musical interests, the Style Council gave him an open door to unrestricted excess. Backed by an army of jazz and funk session musicians, Weller and keyboardist Mick Talbot (formerly of the Merton Parkas and Dexy's Midnight Runners) fused R&B, soul, funk, and jazz, straining it all through European elitism and Weller's growing leftist political ideology. While the music was highly polished and sophisticated, it could be wildly pretentious and slick as well, produced at times with layered synth brass and drum machines. Nevertheless, the Style Council demonstrated what could be done with a palette of divergent styles, setting a trend that was echoed in the work of other former punk artists, including the Clash's Mick Jones (in Big Audio Dynamite) and Bow Wow Wow's Matthew Ashman (in Chiefs of Relief). By 1988, the Style Council was tripping over its own self-importance, and, as slipping album sales indicated, no one really cared anymore. Weller wisely abandoned the project, married vocalist Dee C. Lee, and, following a lengthy sabbatical, launched a successful solo career.

what to buy: Of the Style Council's albums, *Our Favourite Shop* 𝄞𝄞𝄞𝄞 (Polydor, 1985, prod. Peter Wilson, Paul Weller) is more consistent than anything that preceded it and more optimistic than anything that would follow it. (Weller admits he lost interest in the band after this release.) For once the group's varied styles worked together in a surprisingly coherent mix of funk ("The Lodgers"), soul ("Shout to the Top"), and classic instrumentation ("A Stone's Throw Away"). (Note: This album was also released as *Internationalists* 𝄞𝄞𝄞𝄞 (Geffen, 1985), with a different cover, alternate mixes, and a slightly revised track list. It is currently not available on CD.)

what to buy next: As greatest-hits offerings go, *The Style Council Collection* 𝄞𝄞𝄞𝄞 (Polydor, 1996, prod. Peter Wilson, Paul Weller) is just about perfect, emphasizing the band's early hits ("Speak Like a Child," "Long Hot Summer," "My Ever Changing Moods") and tossing in several excellent non-LP tracks ("It Just Came to Pieces in My Hands," "Ghosts of Dachau") for good measure. Oddly, some of the Style Council's best work appeared not on albums but on singles and EPs. *Here's Some*

That Got Away ✲✲✲ (Pony Canyon, 1994, prod. Peter Wilson, Paul Weller) serves them up on one fine disc. Among the treats are the lovely and wistful "The Piccadilly Trail" and Talbot's rousing instrumental "Party Chambers."

what to avoid: Weller's disgust with everything (including the Style Council) comes across loud and clear on *Confessions of a Pop Group* ✲ (Polydor, 1988, prod. Peter Wilson, Paul Weller). Opening with a toilet flush, the album wearily concludes with a 10-minute orchestral suite, complete with doo-wop chorus.

the rest:
Cafe Bleu ✲✲✲ (Polydor, 1984)
My Ever Changing Moods ✲✲✲ (Geffen, 1984)
Live! The Style Council, Home & Abroad ✲✲ (Polydor, 1986)
The Singular Adventures of the Style Council (Greatest Hits, Vol. 1) ✲✲✲
   (Polydor, 1989)

worth searching for: The seven-song CD *Introducing the Style Council* (Polydor, 1983, prod. Peter Wilson, Paul Weller) brims with enthusiasm and breezy soul. Standouts include the group's debut single, "Speak Like a Child," the moody hit "Long Hot Summer," and an excellent alternate version of "The Paris Match."

influences:
◀◀ Curtis Mayfield, Marvin Gaye, Steely Dan, Modern Jazz Quartet, Dexter Gordon

▶▶ Big Audio Dynamite, Chiefs of Relief, Everything but the Girl, Communards, Us3, Guru

see also: *The Jam*

Christopher Scapelliti

Styx

Formed 1963, in Chicago, IL. Disbanded 1984. Re-formed 1990 and 1996.

Dennis DeYoung, vocals, keyboards; James Young, guitar, vocals (1970–present); Tom Naridni, guitar (1963–69); John Curulewski, guitar (1969–74); Chuck Panozzo, bass; John Panozzo (died July 17, 1996), drums (1963–94); Tommy Shaw, guitar, vocals (1974–84, 1996–present); Glen Burtnik, guitar, vocals (1990).

Styx took its name from the mythical river to Hades, and more than a few critics have equated the group's music with a journey in that direction. Styx's response? Keep paddling, guys. A 1979 Gallup poll named Styx the favorite rock band among the 13-to-18-year-old set, which the group fed throughout the late '70s and early '80s with a string of hits that combined elements of Midwestern hard rock, British art rock, and lush melodicism that would make Barry Manilow proud—a wide sweep from the grind of "Renegade" to the sap of "Babe" and "The Best of Times" to the downright silliness of "Mr. Roboto." Styx scored

its breakthrough hit in 1974 with "Lady" (a song that had actually come out two years prior), but it was 1977's loosely conceptual *The Grand Illusion* that put the group over the top and began a string of commercial successes that didn't stop until Styx splintered in 1984, following another bloated conceptual work, *Kilroy Was Here*. The subsequent reunions have produced little music of new consequence, though Styx's 1996 summer tour with Kansas was one of that season's hottest tickets.

what to buy: Save yourself the individual albums and go straight for *Styx Greatest Hits* ✲✲✲✲ (A&M, 1995, prod. Styx, Dennis DeYoung), a replay of late '70s rock radio. The only downside is that the group had to re-record "Lady" rather than include the original version, which was recorded for another label.

what to buy next: *Styx Greatest Hits, Part 2* ✲✲✲ (A&M, 1996, prod. Styx, Dennis DeYoung) is the best of the rest, with two new songs that don't add much to the story. *Pieces of Eight* ✲✲✲ (A&M, 1978, prod. Styx) is the best of the individual albums, with durable rockers such as "Renegade" and "Blue Collar Man (Long Nights)."

what to avoid: Don't bother with *Kilroy Was Here* **woof!** (A&M, 1983, prod. Styx). Two words: "Mr. Roboto."

the rest:
Styx ♪♪ (Wooden Nickel/RCA, 1972)
Styx II ♪♪ (Wooden Nickel/RCA, 1973)
The Serpent Is Rising ♪ (Wooden Nickel/RCA, 1973)
Man of Miracles ♪♪ (Wooden Nickel/RCA, 1974)
Equinox ♪♪♪ (A&M, 1975)
Crystal Ball ♪♪ (A&M, 1976)
The Grand Illusion ♪♪♪ (A&M, 1977)
Cornerstone ♪♪ (A&M, 1979)
The Best of Styx ♪♪♪ (RCA, 1980)
Paradise Theater ♪♪♪ (A&M, 1981)
Caught in the Act—Live ♪♪ (A&M, 1984)
Edge of the Century ♪♪ (A&M, 1990)

worth searching for: *Radio-Made Hits, 1975–1991,* (A&M, 1991, prod. Styx, Dennis DeYoung) is a promotion-only sampler that includes the original "Lady" and most of the big hits—though it does have three selections from the lackluster *Edge of the Century.*

solo outings:
Dennis DeYoung:
Desert Moon ♪♪ (A&M, 1984)
Back to the World ♪ (A&M, 1986)
Boomchild ♪♪ (A&M, 1988)
10 on Broadway ♪♪♪ (Atlantic, 1994)

Tommy Shaw:
Girls with Guns ♪♪ (A&M, 1984)
What If ♪ (A&M, 1985)
Seven Deadly Sings ♪♪♪ (CMC International, 1998)

James Young (with Jan Hammer):
City Slickers ♪♪ (Whitehouse, 1985/1995)
Raised by Wolves ♪♪ (Absolute/Whitehouse, 1995)

influences:
◀◀ The Beatles, Yes, Chicago

▶▶ A Flock of Seagulls, Starcastle, Asia, Smashing Pumpkins, the Cure, Depeche Mode

Gary Graff

The subdudes

Formed 1987, in New Orleans, LA. Disbanded 1997.

John Magnie, keyboards, accordion, vocals; Tommy Malone, guitar, vocals; Johnny Ray Allen, bass, vocals; Steve Amedee, percussion.

The subdudes played music that was both simple and pure in its roots, but also hybridized with a pragmatic, non-purist's sense of style. Like the group's percussive gimmick—Steve Amedee pounded his funky polyrhythms on a tambourine, not a full drum set—the group was willing to try, and use, whatever worked. But the music's essential purity came from its deep base in New Orleans funk and R&B, Tommy Malone's understated, bluesy guitar playing, and the soulful vocal interplay between Malone and John Magnie, which recall nothing if not the Band in its glory days. The 'dudes had known each other so long they played almost intuitively with each other. Malone, Ray Allen, and Amedee all grew up together in the up-river town of Edgard, Louisiana, before running off to New Orleans, eventually playing in a group called the Continental Drifters. Magnie, a Colorado native, relocated to New Orleans during the '70s, attracted by the city's indigenously funky piano playing. The subdudes formed out of necessity: Magnie played a regular Tuesday solo gig at Tipitina's, and the only way the rest could sit in was as an acoustic outfit. Hence Amedee's tambourine and Malone's acoustic guitar, which he played more often than not at the start. The band moved as a unit, families and all, to northern Colorado in late '87 and began tearing up the Denver-area club scene with its acoustic-based grooves and original songs that already sounded like timeless R&B classics. Every album included a couple of these classic-sounding songs, but the group's live show was what made converts out of skeptics, partly because producers found it hard to capture the enormous live sound of the tambourine on tape. The band added touring member and studio session guitarist Willie Williams in 1994 as an unofficial member. Unable to break through commercially, the group disbanded in 1997.

what to buy: *The subdudes* ♪♪♪♪ (Atlantic, 1989, prod. Don Gehman), the group's debut, includes some of its best songs, which are also staples of its live shows: "Light in Your Eyes," "Got You on His Mind," and "Need Somebody." *Annunciation* ♪♪♪♪ (High Street, 1994, prod. subdudes, Keith Keller, Glyn Johns) is the best-produced of the 'dudes' albums, featuring strong songs and passionate, churchy performances.

what to buy next: *Primitive Streak* ♪♪♪ (High Street, 1996, prod. Clark Vreeland) finds the band establishing itself as a recording group, with balanced studio performances but some weaker songs. Malone's "Carved in Stone" is a beautiful tribute to a deceased friend.

the rest:
Lucky ♪♪♪ (EastWest, 1991)
Live at Last ♪♪♪ (High Street, 1997)

influences:
◀◀ The Band, Eric Clapton, the Neville Brothers, Wild Tchoupitoulas, Earl King, Bonnie Raitt

▶▶ The Continental Drifters

Gil Asakawa

Sublime

Formed 1988, in Long Beach, CA.

Bradley Nowell (died May 1996), vocals, guitar, percussion, sampler; Eric Wilson, bass, percussion, organ; Bud Gaugh, drums.

In one of the great tragedies of '90s rock, Sublime leader Bradley Nowell didn't live to see his band's major label debut album released, and legions of fans—many of whom weren't even aware that he was no longer alive—embraced Sublime's unique blending of reggae, hip-hop, punk rock, ska, and folk. Nowell, who'd long battled heroin addiction, overdosed and died shortly before Sublime's major label debut and third album overall, *Sublime*, came out. No one predicted that Sublime, thanks to the catchy first single "What I Got," would be a best-selling act for the next three years, or that the band would spawn imitators months after its distinctive music began hitting alternative, Top 40, and even adult-contemporary airwaves. It did, however, ensure a legacy that's included vault-raiding albums of outtakes and live recordings, the curse of many a rocker who's died before their time.

what to buy: The band's debut, *40 Oz. to Freedom* 🎵🎵🎵🎵 (Skunk, 1992, prod. Elephant Levitation), includes covers of both Bad Religion ("We're Only Gonna Die for Our Arrogance") and the Grateful Dead ("Scarlet Begonias," a rewrite of "Sugar Magnolia") on one record, both done with reverence while adding something to the originals. Add to that an acoustic ode to one of the founders of hip-hop ("KRS-One") and a hit single about a rapist football jock who gets his in jail ("Date Rape"), plus taped conversations and a bunch of most likely uncleared samples, and this is one winner of a record. *Sublime* 🎵🎵🎵🎵 (MCA, 1996, prod. Paul Leary, David Kahne) shows the band dropping the taped conversations and the uncleared samples but not conceding much else for mainstream considerations. Thanks to Nowell's incredibly soulful vocals, "What I Got" was such an infectious hit that even soft-rock stations were playing it, and "Wrong Way" and "Santeria" became almost as successful.

what to avoid: *Robbin' the Hood* 🎵🎵 (Skunk/MCA, 1995, prod. Sublime) is a little too stoned and bugged out; the taped conversations are too long to be funny time after time, and the songs aren't as good as their other two albums. But it's nearly redeemed by a cover of Peter Tosh's "Steppin' Razor," "Lincoln Highway Dub" (which is the seed of the later hit "Santeria"), and a duet with a pre-famous No Doubt singer Gwen Stefani on "Saw Red."

the rest:
Second Hand Smoke 🎵🎵🎵 (Gasoline Alley/MCA, 1997)
Stand by Your Van Live 🎵🎵🎵 (Gasoline Alley/MCA, 1998)

worth searching for: Two other Sublime cover versions are available on compilations: Peter Tosh's classic "Legalize It" on

Hempilation—Freedom Is Norml (Capricorn, 1995, prod. various) and the theme from the cartoon *Hong Kong Phooey* on *Saturday Morning Cartoons' Greatest Hits* (MCA, 1995, prod. Ralph Sall). And the "Doin' Time" CD single features remixes by members of the Pharcyde and the Fugees.

influences:
◀◀ The Beastie Boys, Peter Tosh, Bad Religion, Grateful Dead, Bad Brains, Boogie Down Productions
▶▶ Sugar Ray, Smash Mouth

Brian Ives

Subrosa
See: For Squirrels

Suede
/Bernard Butler

Formed 1990, in London, England.

Brett Anderson, vocals; Bernard Butler, guitar, keyboards (1990–94); Justine Frischmann, guitar (1990–91); Richard Oakes, guitar (1994–present); Mat Osman, bass; Simon Gilbert, drums; Neil Codling, keyboards.

Launched by an obnoxious barrage of U.K. music-press hype then unprecedented (but later matched by Blur and Oasis), this quartet sounded so much like early '70s *The Man Who Sold the World* David Bowie—an influence the group at least owned up to—that it was quickly introduced to him for a master/pupil interview in one music magazine. Add in decided punk influences and hints of the Smiths and the T. Rex/New York Dolls camp-glam, and this decidedly sassy group more or less ushered in the "Britpop" movement that later almost eclipsed it. Having already survived the departure of original second guitarist (and Brett Anderson's former girlfriend) Justine Frischmann—who proved herself a considerable talent in her own right by forming and leading Elastica—perhaps it's not surprising that Suede further continued after the shocking (to outsiders) defection of prime songwriter and main talent Bernard Butler for a solo career.

what to buy: Underneath the worn-on-the-sleeve influences, the debut LP *Suede* 🎵🎵🎵🎵 (Columbia, 1993, prod. Ed Buller) displays a rich world of inventive tunes and textures, thanks to Butler's masterful guitar—a true heir to Mick Ronson and the Stone Roses' John Squire—over which Anderson plays his ribald, funny, and strangely touching lyrics (several homoerotic, though Anderson himself is straight). Given the fickle mantle of English stardom, Suede rose to the challenge on the breakthrough second LP, *Dog Man Star* 🎵🎵🎵🎵 (Columbia, 1994, prod. Ed Buller), which advances the band to Bowie's *Aladdin Sane* but otherwise shucks the more obvious influences in favor of

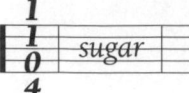
expanding on them. Butler's first solo LP, *People Move On* 𝄞𝄞𝄞 (Columbia, 1998, prod. Bernard Butler) is as lush and deeply involving as his final Suede work—hear the sparks fly out of his guitar again on "You Just Know"—and Butler is even a credible and capable studio vocalist, as it turns out. That he lacks Anderson's gift for (melo)drama holds the weight of the compositions back.

what to buy next: Suede's sole effort to date with Butler's replacement, Richard Oakes (and new keyboardist and fifth member Neil Codling), *Coming Up* 𝄞𝄞𝄞 (Columbia, 1996, prod. Ed Buller) produces mixes results. There are a number of strong tunes, such as the vintage-sounding "Trash" and "She," but other selections go for the slow and moody over the band's previously consistent razzle-dazzle. And Oakes, while a strong player, can in no way make up for the loss of Butler's wild string-pounding any more than Kenny Jones could replace Keith Moon in the Who. The disparity in talent (and to a lesser degree in song composition) is particularly evident on the double-CD of all Suede's English EP B-sides called *Sci-Fi Lullabies* 𝄞𝄞𝄞𝄞 (Columbia, 1997, prod. Ed Buller). While the first half of Butler-era material sparkles with the same flash and raunch, as well as hooks, as the two proper Butler LPs, the remainder from the Oakes era is a downgrade similar to that of *Coming Up*. On the other hand, considering the critical member the group lost, it's perhaps a miracle that Suede remains as vibrant and enjoyable as it does, and Anderson remains a refreshing star.

influences:

◀◀ David Bowie, T. Rex, New York Dolls, the Smiths

▶▶ Mansun, the Verve, Travis

see also: *Elastica*

Jack Rabid

Sugar

See: Bob Mould

Sugar Ray

Formed mid-1990s, in Orange County, CA.

Mark McGrath, vocals; Rodney Sheppard, guitars; Murphy Karges, bass; Craig "DJ Homicide" Bullock, DJ (1995–present); Stan Frazier, drums.

Perhaps the most interesting fact about Sugar Ray is culled from an event before frontman Mark McGrath was born. His mother was a *Jeopardy* champion, and he went on to win a similar game show on VH1 in the spring of 1998. If his mother's winnings influenced him, then so did McGrath's experiences as a latch-key kid listening to the Sex Pistols and Black Flag. Sugar Ray's debut album was a commercial flop, but millions of people still saw and heard Sugar Ray when its single, "Mean Machine," began popping up at sporting events and was given a thumbs-up by Beavis and Butt-head. The band was also chosen by film director Ivan Reitman to appear in his Robin Williams–Billy Crystal vehicle, *Fathers' Day*. One important change that happened during the first national tour was the addition of Craig "DJ Homicide" Bullock, a former hip-hop DJ who dabbled in production and brought an exciting—and lucrative—new element to Sugar Ray's sound.

what to buy: Bullock was instrumental in the success of *Floored* 𝄞𝄞𝄞 (Atlantic, 1997, prod. David Kahane). His turntable scratching and the freestyling of Jamaican toaster Super Cat laid the foundation for the hip-hopping hit "Fly." Unfortunately, like Smash Mouth's *Fush Yu Mang*, *Floored* had only one big hit. But there are a few winners. The opening track, "RPM," is a rush of adrenaline injected with rolling drums, race car-sound guitar licks, and melodic vocals that would rival any KoЯn or deftones song. The schizophrenic *Floored* also includes a dead-on cover of Adam & the Ants' "Stand and Deliver"—complete with the hiccuped vocals—and a pointless, Super Cat–less rendition of "Fly."

the rest:

Lemonade and Brownies 𝄞𝄞 (Lava/Atlantic, 1995)

influences:

◀◀ KoЯn, the Clash

▶▶ Smash Mouth, deftones

Christina Fuoco

Sugarcubes

See: Björk

Suicidal Tendencies

Formed early 1980s, in Venice, CA.

Mike "Cyko Mico" Muir, vocals; Grant Estes, guitar (1983–96); Louiche Mayorga, bass (1983–87); Mike Clark, guitar; Rocky George, guitar (1987–94); Robert Trujillo, bass (1992–94); R.J. Herrara, drums (1987); Jimmy Degrasso, drums; Amery Smith, drums (1983).

Suicidal Tendencies rumbled out of the West Coast hardcore scene with a potent and expressive brand of punk rock. Spearheaded mainly by Mike Muir, a forceful singer, the band released one of hardcore's best debuts ever in 1983. As the '80s metal bell tolled, Suicidal salivated as if on cue, abandoning its hardcore roots for a far less imaginative form of heavy metal, with Muir picking up the unfortunate handle "Cyco Miko" along the way. Black Flag this band is not. Muir and Trujillo also work together in the band Infectious Grooves.

what to buy: A rushing debut of articulate isolation, detachment, and alienation in a galloping but clean hardcore setting, *Suicidal Tendencies* 🎵🎵🎵 (Frontier, 1983/1993, prod. Glen E. Friedman) features the half-hilarious, half-unsettling "Institutionalized" and "Suicide's an Alternative," which give the album an appealing tempo-shifting recklessness.

what to buy next: On *Join the Army* 🎵🎵🎵 (Caroline, 1987, prod. Lester Claypool), the swing to metal already has begun, though the band still cultivates a skate-punk image. Muir's hardened vocals and the warp-speed punk peel off into the netherworld between hardcore and heavy metal.

what to avoid: The raging but formless *Suicidal for Life* 🎵🎵 (Epic, 1994, prod. Paul Northfield) features Cyco Miko bellowing like a football lineman in a steroid rage.

the rest:

How Will I Laugh Tomorrow When I Can't Even Smile Today 🎵🎵🎵 (Epic, 1988)
Feel Like Shit . . . Deja Vu/Controlled by Hatred 🎵🎵 (Epic, 1989)
Lights . . . Camera . . . Revolution 🎵🎵🎵 (Epic, 1990)
The Art of Rebellion 🎵🎵 (Epic, 1992)
Still Cyco after All These Years 🎵🎵 (Epic, 1993)
Prime Cuts 🎵🎵🎵 (Epic, 1997)

solo outings:

Infectious Grooves (Muir and Trujillo):
The Plague That Makes Your Booty Move . . . It's the Infectious Groove 🎵🎵 (Epic, 1991)
Sarsippius' Ark 🎵🎵🎵 (Epic, 1993)
Groove Family Cyco 🎵🎵 (550, 1994)

influences:

◀◀ Black Flag, D.R.I.

▶▶ Anthrax, Faith No More, Corrosion of Conformity

Allan Orski

The Suicide Machines

Formed 1991, in Redford, MI.

Jason Navarro, vocals; Dan "Suicide Machine" Lukacinsky, guitars, vocals; Derek Grant, drums, vocals, keyboards (1991–97); Erin Pitman, drums (1998–present); Royce Nunley, bass, backing vocals.

The Suicide Machines' first gig—opening for the Mighty Mighty Bosstones in 1992—was an appropriate beginning. The foursome—once known as Jack Kevorkian & the Suicide Machines—honed its frenetic, adrenalized power-punk/ska skills supporting acts such as Rancid and by appearances on the Vans Warped Tour.

what to buy: The Suicide Machines captured the punk-ska sound on its full-length debut, *Destruction by Definition* 🎵🎵🎵 (Hollywood, 1996, prod. Julian Raymond, Phil Kaffel), a collection of songs about youth angst, broken relationships, and the horror of murdered peers.

what to avoid: *Battle Hymns* 🎵🎵 (Hollywood, 1998, prod. Julian Raymond) is a 22-song, 28-minute lesson on the band's thoughts on racism ("Hating Hate," "Black and White World"), friendships gone sour ("Give," "Pins and Needles"), war ("Confused"), the environment ("DDT"), and trust ("Empty Room"). Although the issues are depressing, the music, which weaves back and forth between ska, punk, and hardcore, keeps the mood upbeat. The problem with *Battle Hymns* is it lacks most of what made *Destruction by Definition* a success—melodic songs laced with horns.

worth searching for: A split CD with California's Rudiments, *Skank for Brains* (Dill, 1995, prod. Dan Lukacinsky, Derek Grant, Steve Presti), spawned the Detroit radio hit "New Girl" and piqued the attention of major labels.

influences:

◀◀ Jack Kevorkian, Rancid, Mighty Mighty Bosstones, Less Than Jake

Christina Fuoco

Sukia

Formed 1995, in Somis, CA.

Ross Harris, vocals, coronet, guitar, Vox organ, bass pedals; Craig Borrell, vocals, trumpet, trombone, accordion, sampler; Sasha Fuentes, guitar, bass, vocals, Moog synthesizer, bass pedals, sampler; Grace Marks, drum machine, congas, bass pedals; others.

Sukia is not your average dark-side-of-the-lounge cult band. The collective contains an aesthetic brain trust of musicians, artists, actors, graphic designers, and photographers. Based in the southern California town of Camarillo, the self-described "experiment in mood enhancement" began in the desert air in 1994. Sukia's rare live appearances (it opened select dates for Beck and toured the U.K. in 1997) are events in absurdist theater as much as mere performances, with the band members appearing on stage in astronaut suits with earmuffs, or maybe a jock strap—or less (60-year-old sax player Chuck performs nude). With its overall visual message of omnisexuality, the group has even been encouraged to get off the stage during performances in front of rowdy crowds at such otherwise liberal havens as Stanford University, and it's been shut down by more than one chamber of commerce. But in the U.K., where Sukia's record was released by the influential MoWax label, the band was well received opening for Stereolab. Pop-culture vultures, take note: Sukia member Ross Harris is said to have been the boy in the movie *Airplane!* reading *Nun's Life* magazine and the son of the station sergeant on the late '70s television series *CHiPs*.

what to buy: Sukia's manifesto as we know it—love, lounge, and intergalactic horizontal samba—congeals on its debut, *Contacto Espacial con el Tercer Sexo* 🎵🎵🎵🎵 (Nickel Bag, 1996, prod. Jerry Finn, the Dust Brothers). On the surface, the album evokes images of cocktail culture, Muzak, and '50s mainstream America with instrumentation that includes the Moog synthesizer, plunger-muted trombone, surf guitar, congas, and other artifacts of past pop musics. Lurking just below this ironic sheen, though, are much scarier and funnier sexual and technological themes.

worth searching for: *Gary Super Macho* (Nickel Bag, 1997, prod. Dust Brothers, DJ Me DJ You, Kudo, Toshi) is a remix album.

influences:

◄◄ Juan Garcia Esquivel, Dick Hyman, Ennio Morricone

►► Beck

Chris Handyside

Andy Summers

Born Andrew Sommers, December 31, 1942, in Blackpool, England.

A well-known professional who'd worked with Eric Burdon's Animals and Neil Sedaka, Andy Summers was recruited by drummer Stewart Copeland and bassist Sting to add instrumental heft with founding guitarist Henry Padovani in the then-fledgling group the Police. Soon Padovani was gone, jettisoned to make room for Summers's flights of echo-laden guitar noise and sideways tonal excursions. Like Copeland, Summers grew frustrated with frontman Sting's control jones, venting his songwriting work in collaborations with art-rock guitar king Robert Fripp during the early '80s. After the Police went on indefinite hiatus in 1985, Summers released a number of solo records that veer from experimental rock guitar bombast to unconventional jazz-fusion work.

what to buy: A master of many styles of playing, Summers suffers from two weaknesses as a recording artist—an amazing inability to write good material and an annoying habit of downplaying his own instrumental talents. His best solo outing, *Charming Snakes* 🎵🎵🎵 (Private Music, 1990, prod. Andy Summers, David Hentschel), avoids those faults. Featuring such august sidemen as Herbie Hancock, Bill Evans, and the Sting-man himself, this record marks Summers's first and best turn from ambient rock guitar noise to artful jazz fusion.

what to buy next: For fans of great guitar playing, there are few better records than Summers's collaboration with Robert Fripp, *I Advance Masked* 🎵🎵🎵 (A&M, 1982, prod. Robert Fripp, Andy Summers). While Summers leaps off melodic cliffs Fripp dares

not approach, Fripp's echo-drenched fretwork provides the perfect bedrock for his partner's sonic flights.

what to avoid: There's nothing more tedious than a bad jazz/rock fusion record—which is what Summers's first post-Police outing is. *XYZ* **woof!** (MCA, 1987, prod. Andy Summers) is a boring mishmash of tired themes and conventionally unconventional playing.

the rest:
(With Robert Fripp) *Bewitched* 🎵🎵🎵 (A&M, 1984)
Mysterious Barricades 🎵🎵🎵 (Private Music, 1988)
The Golden Wire 🎵🎵🎵 (Private Music, 1989)
World Gone Strange 🎵🎵🎵 (Private Music, 1991)
Andy Summers 🎵🎵 (Private Music, 1991)
(With John Etheridge) *Invisible Threads* 🎵🎵🎵 (Mesa/Blue Moon, 1993)
Synaesthesia 🎵🎵🎵 (CMP, 1995)
Last Dance of Mr. X **woof!** (RCA, 1997)
Retrospective N/A (Private Music /Windham Hill, 1998)

worth searching for: Back in the days when Sting would let someone else from the band intrude on his creative vision, Summers composed a love poem for a blow-up doll, dutifully inserted in the punky workout "Be My Girl" from the Police's first album, *Outlandos d'Amour*. Hearing him describe the object of his affection in a thick cockney accent is worth the price of admission.

influences:

◄◄ Steve Howe, Allan Holdsworth, Syd Barrett, David Gilmour

►► Adrian Belew, Steve Farris (Mr. Mister), the Samples

see also: *Robert Fripp, the Police*

Eric Deggans

Elaine Summers

Born November 19, 1959, in Washington, DC.

She may seem like a newcomer, but Elaine Summers is no rookie. After spending several years on the record-label side of the biz, Summers transplanted herself up to the Pacific Northwest and in 1993 became a primary member of rocker Pete Droge's band. It's not surprising, then, that when she decided to set her coolly raggedy voice to some tunes of her own, she had Droge produce them. The result, *Transplanting*, is uneven, but it sports a fun, sassy spirit and a willingness to try new ideas and sounds. Frankly, Droge ought to step out of the way for the follow-up and really let Summers shine.

what's available: With its loosey-goosey production and occasionally goofy vocal effects, *Transplanting* 🎵🎵🎵 (Loosegroove, 1997, prod. Pete Droge) has the feel in spots of a souped-up demo. But "Ain't No Way" features some potent, soulful lead vocals, and "Fly" is an excellent bit of balladry that does Sheryl

Crow one better. A few too many tunes are strongly derivative of Bob Dylan, but that's not unusual for a first effort. Besides, who would you rather have her emulate?

influences:

◀◀ Sheryl Crow, Bob Dylan, Joan Osborne, Pete Droge, the Black Crowes

Bob Remstein

Sun Ra

Born Herman Blount, May 14, 1914, in Birmingham, AL. Died May 30, 1993, in Birmingham, AL.

During the '50s, when revolutionary figures such as Ornette Coleman and Cecil Taylor began carving out niches for their singular sounds, Herman Blount, a little-known pianist, changed his name to Sun Ra, claimed to be from Saturn, and set about rearranging the entire concept of big band jazz. Ra's early years playing around Chicago, both solo and with the Fletcher Henderson band, were undistinguished. Even after assembling his Arkestra, their music—increasingly based on African-style polyrhythms, radical harmonics, and Ra's unorthodox compositions—seldom found large audiences until the late '60s when the psychedelic youth culture connected with the music, colorful costumes, and Ra's mystic philosophy. More than 100 musicians graced the Arkestra over the years, including Craig Harris, Julian Priester, Billy Bang, and Vincent Chauncey. But a core that included reed players John Gilmore, Marshall Allen, and Laurdine "Pat" Patrick, bassist Ronald Boykins, and vocalist June Tyson stayed with the group for decades. For a period during the '60s and '70s, the band lived together communally in Philadelphia, and Ra's most consistent label work was for his own Saturn Records. Sources show that there are more than 500 Sun Ra albums. Ra's work breaks roughly into three periods: big band/hard bop exotica during the '50s; outer-and-outer free jazz during the '60s; and swing from the mid-'70s until his death. Ra's longtime saxophonists (John Coltrane acknowledged Gilmore as an influence) were a key element of his sound as he pushed the music further into mystical abstractions without forgetting that it was the beat that made peoples' asses shake. While the music seemed advanced, the Arkestra's stage presence, complete with singers and dancers that sometimes cavorted in the audience, was straight out of vaudeville.

what to buy: The free-jazz landmark *The Magic City* ♫♫♫♫♫ (Saturn, 1965/Evidence, 1993, prod. Infinity Inc., Alton Abraham, reissue prod. Jerry Gordon) is a high point for Ra—and for anyone else. Its mysterious ebbs and flows slowly build to musical tidal waves with eerie synthesizer work, agitated piano, and exultant saxophone solos.

what to buy next: *Mayan Temples* ♫♫♫♫ (Black Saint, 1990, prod. Giovanni Bonandrini) was one of Ra's final studio albums and offers a fine summation of his late period, mixing up standards ("Alone Together"), big-band exotica, and one long, exploratory piece. Included is a wonderful reading of "El Is the Sound of Joy," which prefigured Coltrane's "Giant Steps."

best of the rest:
Supersonic Jazz ♫♫♫♫♫ (Saturn, 1956/Evidence, 1991)
Sun Song ♫♫♫♫ (Delmark, 1957/1990)
Sound of Joy ♫♫♫♫ (Delmark, 1957)
Jazz in Silhouette ♫♫♫♫♫ (Saturn, 1958/Evidence, 1991)
Sun Ra Visits Planet Earth/Interstellar Low Ways ♫♫♫♫ (Saturn, 1958/1960/Evidence, 1992)
Angels and Demons at Play/The Nubians of Plutonia ♫♫♫♫ (Saturn, 1959, 1960/Evidence, 1993)
Sound Sun Pleasure ♫♫♫♫ (Saturn, 1960/1973/Evidence, 1991)
We Travel the Spaceways/Bad and Beautiful ♫♫♫♫ (Saturn, 1960/1961/Evidence, 1992)
Fate in a Pleasant Mood/When Sun Comes Out ♫♫♫♫♫ (Saturn, 1961/1963/Evidence, 1993)
Cosmic Tones for Mental Therapy/Art Forms of Dimensions Tomorrow ♫♫♫ (Saturn, 1962/1963/Evidence, 1992)
Other Planes of There ♫♫♫♫ (Saturn, 1964/Evidence, 1992)
The Heliocentric Worlds of Sun Ra, Vol. 1 ♫♫♫♫ (ESP, 1965)
Monorails and Satellites ♫♫♫ (Saturn, 1966/Evidence, 1991)
Pictures of Infinity ♫♫♫ (Black Lion, 1968)
Holiday for Soul Dance ♫♫♫ (Saturn, 1969/Evidence, 1991)
Atlantis ♫♫♫♫ (Saturn, 1969/Evidence, 1993)
Solar Myth Approach ♫♫♫♫ (Affinity, 1970)
My Brother the Wind II ♫♫♫ (Saturn, 1970/Evidence, 1992)
Space Is the Place ♫♫♫♫ (Blue Thumb, 1972/Impulse!, 1998)
Unity ♫♫♫♫♫ (Horo, 1977)
Solo Piano ♫♫♫♫ (Improvising Artists, Inc., 1977)
St. Louis Blues ♫♫♫♫ (Improvising Artists, 1978)
Visions ♫♫♫♫ (SteepleChase, 1978)
Sunrise in Different Dimensions ♫♫♫♫♫ (hat HUT, 1981)
Strange Celestial Road ♫♫♫♫ (Rounder, 1985)
Reflections in Blue ♫♫♫♫ (Black Saint, 1987)
Live at Pitt-Inn ♫♫♫♫♫ (DIW, 1988)
Hours After ♫♫♫♫ (Black Saint, 1989)
Out There a Minute ♫♫♫♫ (Enigma, 1990)
Somewhere Else ♫♫♫♫ (Rounder, 1993)
Soundtrack to Space Is the Place ♫♫♫♫♫ (Evidence, 1993)
Live at the Hackney Empire ♫♫♫ (Leo, 1994)
Live from Soundscape ♫♫♫♫ (DIW, 1994)
The Singles ♫♫♫ (Evidence, 1996)
Calling Planet Earth N/A (Freedom, 1998)

worth searching for: There are literally hundreds of Sun Ra LPs that are either out of print or were distributed by Saturn only at Arkestra concerts. Here's a trio of noteworthy gems. On a German label, *It's after the End of the World* (MPS, 1972, prod.

Joachim Berendt) captures the Arkestra at two 1970 festival concerts in Germany during a particularly strong and fertile period. Ra is playing an especially wide variety of keyboards and the band stretches out on three of the five tracks. *Pathways to Unknown Worlds* (Saturn, 1973/Impulse!, 1975, prod. Alton Abraham) is a bit easier to find because it's one of the Saturn albums Impulse! licensed in the 1970s (when it was owned by ABC). It's a screaming, totally out-there session with Marshall Allen going off on some long, scorching solos—just about as close as Sun Ra ever got to the energy stream of free jazz. The double LP *Live at Montreux* (Inner City, 1976, prod. Sun Ra) documents one of the larger versions of the Arkestra—20 pieces—and drummer Clifford Jarvis really drives the group. Sun Ra's lengthy solo piano intro to the side-long "Take the 'A' Train" is a must-hear, as is Marshall Allen's impassioned second solo on "Of the Other Tomorrow."

influences:

◀◀ Fletcher Henderson, Duke Ellington

▶▶ Art Ensemble of Chicago, John Coltrane, Michael Ray and the Cosmic Krewe, Medeski, Martin & Wood, Parliament-Funkadelic

Lawrence Gabriel and Steve Holtje

The Sundays

Formed 1987, in London, England.

David Gavurin, guitar; Harriet Wheeler, vocals; Paul Brindley, bass; Patrick Hannan, drums.

Emerging during the late '80s, the Sundays scored a minor hit with its debut single—an enchanting tune about bittersweet love called "Here's Where the Story Ends"—and bounced around in the college charts with the accompanying debut album. Taking five-year breaks between records, the group eventually built up a solid coffeehouse following with its successive albums.

what to buy: *Reading, Writing and Arithmetic* 🎵🎵🎵🎵 (DGC, 1989, prod. the Sundays, Ray Shulman) is a jangly, sweet, and invigorating effort that blends melancholy moods with uplifting melodies. It includes unforgettable tracks such as "Can't Be Sure" and the big breakthrough "Here's Where the Story Ends."

what to buy next: *Blind* 🎵🎵🎵 (DGC, 1992, prod. David Gavurin, Harriet Wheeler, Dave Anderson) is just as exquisite as its predecessor, though it's slightly more downhearted. It includes a fine cover of the Rolling Stones' "Wild Horses," as well as stellar originals such as "Love" and "Blood on My Hands." *Static & Silence* 🎵🎵🎵🎵 (DGC, 1997, prod. the Sundays) faithfully revisits the formula on tracks such as "Summertime" and "Cry."

influences:

◀◀ The Smiths, the Stone Roses, Aztec Camera

▶▶ Cranberries, Mazzy Star, Björk

Aidin Vaziri

Sunny Day Real Estate

Formed 1992, in Seattle, WA. Disbanded 1995.

Jeremy Enigk, vocals, guitar; Dan Hoerner, guitar, vocals; William Goldsmith, drums; Nate Mendel, bass.

Jeremy Enigk can tell a moody tale unlike any other songwriter before him. The depressed tone and pure rock-bottom sympathetic nature of his lifelike lyrics can send you off to contemplate your own fears. Appropriately layered underneath the montage of lyrics are some of the most intricate song structures that give the band an almost transcendent quality. It was this unique quality that eventually put Sunny Day Real Estate on the map. Despite not giving interviews or the members' intent refusal to play live in California, Sunny Day Real Estate proved to the faithless that a moderate success can be achieved on one's own terms. The Sunny Day Real Estate saga is a long and sordid tale that touches on elements of prosperity and, of all things, religion. After its first record, *Diary*, frontman Jeremy Enigk committed himself wholly and somewhat obsessively to God. This announcement came right as the band was recording its second record, and as you could probably guess this revelation came as a shock to both the band and to its ever-growing fan base. Unfortunately, Sunny Day Real Estate broke up right before the release of its second record. William Goldsmith and Nate Mendel found greener pastures in joining ex-Nirvana drummer Dave Grohl in the band Foo Fighters. Enigk, with guidance from a higher power, found the time to release his first solo record, *Return of the Frog Queen*. From the time Sunny Day Real Estate released its first record to its untimely breakup, the group was an ongoing inspiration to the world of indie rock. Meanwhile, rumors have been rampant about a reunion in the very near future.

what to buy: *Diary* 🎵🎵🎵 (Sub Pop, 1994, prod. Sunny Day Real Estate) was an incredibly influential record, filled with amazing arrangements of somewhat simple songs draped around Enigk's nonsensical, apocalyptic lyrics.

what to buy next: *Sunny Day Real Estate* 🎵🎵🎵 (Sub Pop, 1995, prod. Sunny Day Real Estate, Brad Wood) is a fitting follow-up to *Diary* and an appropriate last record for the boys. Filled to the rim with slow and introspective songs of controlled rage, *Sunny Day Real Estate* lived up to the fans' ever-growing expectations.

influences:

◀◀ Nirvana, the Posies, the Seeds, Green River

▶▶ Foo Fighters

see also: *Jeremy Enigk*

Chris Richards

Super Deluxe

Formed mid-1990s, in Seattle, WA.

Braden Blake, vocals, guitars; John Kirsch, guitar, vocals; Jake Nesheim, bass; Chris Lockwood, drums.

Those who can't get enough Posies might want to investigate this Seattle band whose slacker power-pop skills aren't quite enough to sustain it. True to the name, Super Deluxe offers the immediate satisfaction of a fast-food hamburger, but after the hour put into hearing one of its albums, you're hungry for something better. The songwriting falls short of its idols, and its heart doesn't seem to be in it.

what to buy: The wishful-thinking *Famous* 𝄞𝄞𝄞 (Revolution, 1995, prod. Gavin Guss, Martin Feveyer, Super Deluxe) connects the Hollies, the Posies, and angst but fails to completely connect with its audience. The hooks are pretty good, particularly in "She Came On," but the songs generally feel less the product of an original pop band than plain old product. Super Deluxe sounds tentative and faceless, affected by the specter of feedback and grunge that breathes down its power-pop neck.

the rest:

Via Satellite 𝄞𝄞𝄞 (Revolution, 1997)

influences:

◀◀ The Posies, Teenage Fanclub

Jordan Oakes

Super Furry Animals

Formed 1993, in Cardiff, Wales.

Gruff Rhys, vocals, guitar; Huw Bunford, guitars, vocals; Cian Ciaran, electronics; Guto Pryce, bass; Dafydd Leuan, drums.

Beginning as a mad electronica outfit in the early '90s, Super Furry Animals turned, for reasons known only to them, to a high-spirited brand of offbeat psychedelic pop. The sound of Cardiff's favorite misfits is led by fuzzy guitars, Cian Ciaran's slightly askew electronic underpinnings, and the band's decidedly Welsh approach. (Though their English label, Creation, insisted they do their songs in English to maximize appeal, the band still enjoys performing at home in their native tongue.) Their debut album, released in 1996—and seen as a forerunner in a resurgence of rock 'n' roll from Wales—saw considerable commercial and critical success in the U.K.

what's available: SFA's splashy debut, *Fuzzy Logic* 𝄞𝄞𝄞𝄞 (Epic/Creation, 1996, prod. Super Furry Animals, Gorwel Owen), traverses a vast expanse of musical terrain, held in place by the band's unadulterated, and unorthodox, love of distorted psychedelia.

influences:

◀◀ 13th Floor Elevators, My Bloody Valentine, the Beatles

Bob Gulla

Superchunk

Formed 1989, in Chapel Hill, NC.

Mac McCaughan, guitar, vocals; Jack McCook, guitar (1989–91); Jim Wilbur, guitar (1991–present); Laura Ballance, bass; Jon Wurster, drums (1991–present); Chuck Garrison, drums (1989–91).

Occasionally likened to a happier Nirvana, Superchunk combines '80s punk (à la the Buzzcocks and Hüsker Dü) with pop melodies. The band manages to remain an important indie band, and the only thing that separates Superchunk from "Alternative Nation" stardom is the band's fear of major labels; thus the group formed its own record company, Merge, when former distributors were purchased by a conglomerate. While the group isn't breaking any new ground and the music may be somewhat static, Superchunk still scores with authentic, high-energy, and hard-rocking tales of suburban angst.

what to buy: *Tossing Seeds: Singles 89–91* 𝄞𝄞𝄞𝄞 (Merge, 1992, prod. Superchunk) is a compilation of 19 tracks that highlight what Superchunk does best: create good, fast, hard-hitting hooks. The music does seem to blend together after awhile, but *Tossing Seeds* highlights the group's transition from noisy garage band to tight pop/punk ensemble. *On the Mouth* 𝄞𝄞𝄞𝄞 (Matador, 1992, prod. Superchunk) catches Superchunk at one of its best and most accessible periods; the sound is starting to get cleaned up, though it retains its garage-inspired immediacy and rawness.

what to buy next: *No Pocky for Kitty* 𝄞𝄞𝄞 (Matador, 1991, prod. Superchunk) is a solid album with a number of good punk anthems, catching Superchunk as it moved to a more song-oriented approach. *Incidental Music 1991–1995* 𝄞𝄞𝄞 (Merge, 1995, prod. Superchunk) is a collection of rare singles and B-sides from the group's later, more accessible period.

what to avoid: With its crisper sound, *Here's Where the Strings Come In* 𝄞𝄞 (Merge, 1995, prod. Superchunk) sounds a bit watered down and less vital than its predecessors.

the rest:
Superchunk ♫♫♫ (Matador, 1990)
Foolish ♫♫♫ (Merge, 1995)
Indoor Living ♫♫♫♫ (Merge, 1997)

worth searching for: Superchunk's split seven-inch single titled "She Cracked" (Honey Bear, 1995, prod. Superchunk) shares the vinyl with another indie fave, Tsunami.

solo outings:
Portastatic (Mac McCaughan):
I Hope Your Heart Is Not Brittle ♫♫ (Merge, 1993)
Slow Note from a Sinking Ship ♫♫♫ (Merge, 1995)
Scrapbook ♫♫♫ (Merge EP, 1995)
The Nature of Sap ♫♫♫ (Merge, 1997)

influences:
◀◀ Hüsker Dü, the Buzzcocks, the Sex Pistols, the Ramones

▶▶ Polvo, Tsunami, Helium

Bryan Lassner

Supergrass
Formed 1993, in Oxford, England.

Gaz Coombes, vocals, guitar; Mickey Quinn, bass; Danny Goffey, drums.

As teenagers, Gaz Coombes and Danny Goffey started their first band, the Jennifers. Modeled on trendy British shoegazers such as Ride and Chapterhouse, the band released one unimpressive single and quickly disappeared. The duo then spent several years soaking in new influences such as the Buzzcocks and Small Faces and befriending the elder, and therefore more sophisticated, Mickey Quinn. They reintroduced themselves as Supergrass in 1994, just as the Britpop phenomena was hitting a fever pitch on a global scale. Built on infectious guitar hooks and bright melodies, *I Should Coco* became the soundtrack for the zeitgeist. The album showed impressive musical maturity, but it was the band members' carefree public image that helped them transcend age, culture, and gender barriers. Director Steven Speilberg even offered Supergrass a Monkees-style TV show, which the group politely turned down in order to focus on their music. By the time the group released its sophomore album, *In It for the Money*, during 1996, it had turned stoic, downplaying the wild antics and tackling darker themes. The album, while gaining critical acclaim, failed to repeat the widespread commercial success of the debut.

what to buy: Perfectly paced, *I Should Coco* ♫♫♫♫ (Capitol, 1995, prod. Sam Williams) moves through exciting guitar licks, menacing teenage manifestos, and warm ballads with equal gusto. It works as well at a party as it does on headphones. The uplifting "Alright" should be considered the unofficial summer anthem, while the more introspective "She's So Loose" offers an entrancing respite from the noisy celebration.

what to buy next: Even though the band's sophomore record, *In It for the Money* ♫♫♫ (Capitol, 1996, prod. Supergrass, John Cornfield), shies away from the urgent pop-punk licks of its predecessor, it still has something to offer beneath its layers of expansive, orchestral terrain. A detectable Beatles influence works particularly well on kaleidoscopic tracks such as "Late in the Day" and "Hollow Little Reign."

worth searching for: The Japanese-only *Alright* (Capitol, 1996) features several hard-to-find live recordings and B-sides. Most notable is a fierce version of the Kinks' "Where Have All the Good Times Gone" and the kitschy "Je Suis Votre Papa." Not so great is the country parody "Sex."

influences:
◀◀ The Buzzcocks, the Kinks, the Beatles

▶▶ Foo Fighters, Ash, Kula Shaker

Aidin Vaziri

Supertramp
Formed 1969, in London, England. Disbanded 1989. Re-formed 1996.

Rick Davies, keyboards, vocals; Roger Hodgson, guitar, keyboards, vocals (1969–83); Richard Palmer, guitar (1969–70); Bob Miller, drums (1969–70); Dave Winthrop, saxophone (1970–74); Frank Farrell, bass (1970–74); Kevin Currie, drums (1970–74); Bob Siebenberg, drums (1974–present); John Anthony Helliwell, saxophone, reeds, vocals (1975–present); Dougie Thompson, bass (1975–89); Mark Hart, vocals, keyboards, guitar (1996–present); Cliff Hugo, bass (1996–present); Lee R. Thornburg, horns (1996–present); Carl Verheyen, guitar (1996–present); Tom Walsh, percussion (1996–present).

Thanks to the financial support of a young, eccentric Dutch millionaire, Supertramp was able to muddle through the first few years of its existence pursuing a ponderous art/rock sound. After its first two records went virtually unnoticed, the group's patron withdrew his backing, forcing Rick Davies and Roger Hodgson to come up with something more appealing in order to keep the band alive. They recruited a new line-up and created the tightly produced, high-voiced, sax-and-keyboard-dominated pop style that became Supertramp's trademark. After four successful records with this formula, culminating in the platinum-selling *Breakfast in America*, the band changed directions yet again, this time to a more R&B flavored sound. This move cost it most of its following, as well as Hodgson, who left to pursue a solo career. After Hodgson left, the band put out two more undistinguished efforts before calling it quits. After a 10-year break, the band, led by Davies, John Helliwell, and Bob Siebenberg, re-formed during 1996 for a new album and tour. Unfortunately, this jazzier incarnation failed to attract much attention.

what to buy: *Crime of the Century* 🎵🎵🎵 (A&M, 1974, prod. Ken Scott, Supertramp) is worth owning, if only for the piano solo on the opening track, "School." This is the album where the band first put its sound together, and it remains its best, with other highlights such as "Bloody Well Right" and "Dreamer." *Crisis? What Crisis?* 🎵🎵🎵 (A&M, 1975, prod. Ken Scott, Supertramp) was a strong follow-up, from the jangly guitars on "Sister Moonshine" to the final lilting chords of "Two of Us," as well as lots of first-rate work that was never subjected to radio overkill.

what to buy next: *Breakfast in America* 🎵🎵🎵 (A&M, 1979, prod. Supertramp, Peter Henderson) was the band's biggest success—with hits such as "The Logical Song," "Take the Long Way Home," and the title track—and probably the album that most casual fans would label their favorite. *Even in the Quietest Moments* 🎵🎵🎵 (A&M, 1977, prod. Supertramp) is another compelling effort that occasionally offers a taste of the band's art/rock beginnings.

what to avoid: The band's first two albums, *Supertramp* 🎵 (A&M, 1970, prod. Supertramp) and *Indelibly Stamped* 🎵 (A&M, 1971, prod. Supertramp), like so much early '70s art/rock, were neither art nor rock.

the rest:
Paris 🎵🎵🎵 (A&M, 1980)
Famous Last Words 🎵🎵 (A&M, 1982)
Brother, Where You Bound 🎵🎵 (A&M, 1985)
Free as a Bird 🎵🎵 (A&M, 1987)
Classics, Volume 9 🎵🎵🎵 (A&M, 1987)
The Very Best of Supertramp 🎵🎵🎵 (A&M, 1993)
Some Things Never Change 🎵🎵🎵 (Oxygen, 1997)

worth searching for: Though Supertramp couldn't really cut it in the studio after Hodgson left, the import-only *Supertramp Live '88* (A&M, 1988, prod. Rick Davies, Norman Hall) shows the group still had something to offer in concert.

solo outings:
Roger Hodgson:
In the Eye of the Storm 🎵🎵 (A&M, 1984)
Hai Hai 🎵🎵 (A&M, 1987)
Rites of Passage 🎵🎵🎵 (Unichord, 1998)

influences:
◄◄ Willie Dixon, the Beatles, Dusty Springfield
►► Jellyfish, the Judybats

Gary Plochinski

The Supremes
Formed as the Primettes, 1959, in Detroit, MI.

Diana (Diane) Ross, vocals (1959–69); Florence Ballard (died February 22, 1976), vocals (1959–67); Mary Wilson, vocals; Betty McGlown,

WHAT ALBUM CHANGED YOUR LIFE?

Traffic had a big influence on me, the early albums of Traffic. They just had a looseness and a vibe and a feel about them that were just really raw. It wasn't very sophisticated. The songs were great. They took risks. They jammed. They had long sections at the end of songs that just went on and on and jammed, and sometimes it was great and sometimes it was kind of average, but they just took risks. I just love the looseness of that band.

Roger Hodgson
(of Supertramp)

vocals (1959–60); Barbara Martin, vocals (1960–63); Cindy Birdsong, vocals (1967–71, 1974–76); Jean Terrell, vocals (1970–74); Lynda Laurence, vocals (1972–74); Scherrie Payne, vocals (1974–77); Susaye Greene, vocals (1976–77).

The Supremes were as much about sugary pop confection and image as about R&B; they were Berry Gordy Jr.'s ticket to the Copacabana and the other mainstream trappings he craved, which (along with his romance with Diana Ross) helps explain why they were the most successful of Motown's female vocal groups. It's hard to overstate the magic of Holland-Dozier-Holland's hits and, to a slightly lesser extent, Ross's dynamic and striking lead vocals. Balancing choreographed stage glamour with alternatingly cool and flirty coyness, the Supremes' sweet vocals epitomized the everyone-welcome crossover nature of the Motown sound. Along with the Beatles, the Supremes defined Top 40 pop during the 1960s. But after Ross's departure for a career as a solo artist and movie star, the Supremes were placed on Motown's back burner; the gradual departure of Holland-Dozier-Holland's songs and the label's decreased support left the group floundering until it folded in 1977, though Mary Wilson continues to tour using the Supremes moniker.

what to buy: *Anthology* 🎵🎵🎵🎵 (Motown, 1970, prod. various) contains every single Motown hit the group recorded—an awesome display of timeless music-making that's still amazing to behold.

what to buy next: *Greatest Hits and Rare Classics* 🎵🎵🎵 (Motown, 1991, prod. various) is an informative supplement to *Anthology* for those interested in the post-Ross years.

what to avoid: *The Best of the Supremes & the Four Tops* 🎵🎵 (Motown, 1991, prod. various) is a skimpy compilation that sells both groups short.

the rest:
Merry Christmas 🎵🎵🎵 (Motown, 1965)
The Supremes Sing Country, Western & Pop 🎵🎵 (Motown, 1965/1994)
I Hear a Symphony 🎵🎵🎵 (Motown, 1966)
Supremes a-Go-Go 🎵🎵🎵 (Motown, 1966/1989)
Reflections 🎵🎵🎵 (Motown, 1968/1991)
Live at London's Talk of the Town 🎵🎵🎵 (Motown, 1968)
Captured Live on Stage 🎵🎵🎵 (Motown, 1970)
Every Great #1 Hit 🎵🎵🎵🎵 (Motown, 1974)
Motown Superstar Series, Vol. 1 🎵🎵🎵🎵 (Motown, 1979)
Great Songs & Performances That Inspired Motown 25 🎵🎵 (Motown, 1983/1991)
Greatest Hits, Vol. I 🎵🎵🎵 (Motown, 1986)
Greatest Hits, Vol. II 🎵🎵🎵 (Motown, 1989)
Greatest Hits, Vol. III 🎵🎵🎵 (Motown, 1991)
Motown Legends: Stoned Love 🎵🎵🎵 (ESX Entertainment, 1995)
The Ultimate Collection 🎵🎵🎵🎵 (Motown, 1997)

worth searching for: Look for *Where Did Our Love Go* (Motown, 1964), the trio's sophomore effort and one of Ross's great pre-vanity showcases.

influences:
◄◄ The Shangri-Las, the Chiffons

►► The J. Geils Band, TLC, SWV, the Braxtons, Luther Vandross, Brandy

see also: *Diana Ross*

Allan Orski

Surf Music

During the late '50s and early '60s, just before John F. Kennedy was assassinated, everybody was (seemingly) having fun. On California beaches, anyhow. The first major surf character was Dick Dale (born Richard Monsour), who approximated the crashing sound of a tidal wave on his guitar. Dale, with the early '60s hits "Let's Go Trippin'" and "Misirlou," stole a bit of funky country style from Link Wray and Duane Eddy and a lot of fun-loving teen attitude from Chuck Berry and invented a fingernails-down-the-fretboard style that could explode and shiver at will. Soon the beaches of Malibu were filled with surfboards, bikinis, hot rods, and . . . guitars. Not only that, but rockers-to-be in such non-surfing fiefdoms as New York City and Boulder, Colorado, were listening to the sounds and deciding they could make surf music their own way. The most famous surf offspring were, of course, the Beach Boys, who drew from Berry, doo-wop, and the blues to make "Surfin' U.S.A.," "Fun Fun Fun," "California Girls," "In My Room," and the rest. Also breaking out were Jan & Dean ("Drag City"), the Trashmen ("The Bird"), the Ventures ("Diamond Head"), the Chantays ("Pipeline"), the Surfaris ("Wipe Out"), the Astronauts ("Baja"), and countless underground bands that picked up guitars and tried to rock—similar to the phenomenon of the '60s garage bands. The obscure surf rockers, too, put out some wonderful records, often hilarious in the most campy possibly way: the Del-Vettes' "Ram Charger," Brian Lord's "The Big Surfer," the Honeys' "Shoot the Curl," the Tradewinds' "New York's a Lonely Town," and Eddie & the Showmen's "Mr. Rebel," to name just a few. It all wiped out after the Beach Boys lost their hegemonic battle for creative superiority with the Beatles. After the Boys' landmark 1966 album *Pet Sounds*, surf-rockers' days in the sun were numbered. It wasn't until the late '70s, when punks recaptured some of its sounds, that surf returned to anything beyond oldies stations. During the early '90s, such bands as Laika & the Cosmonauts, the Mermen, Man or Astro-Man?, and Dale himself picked up the torch once again.

what to buy: The four-disc set *Cowabunga! The Surf Box* 🎵🎵🎵🎵🎵 (Rhino, 1996, prod. various), with 82 songs and samplings of most of the aforementioned bands' repertoire, is the most comprehensive and well-packaged surf collection to date. Other good compilations include: *Wild City* 🎵🎵🎵🎵 (Capitol, 1991, prod. various), *Drag City* 🎵🎵🎵🎵 (Capitol, 1991, prod. various), *Pebbles, Vol. 4: Surf N Tunes!* 🎵🎵🎵🎵 (Archive International, 1992, prod. various), and *Rock Instrumental Classics, Vol. 5: Surf* 🎵🎵🎵🎵 (Rhino, 1994, prod. Gary Stewart, James Austin, David McLees).

what to buy next: An assortment of collections from individual surf practitioners that are diverse and fascinating, if spotty, include the Honeys' *Collectors Series* 🎵🎵🎵 (Capitol, 1992, prod. Ron Furmanek), which showcases an all-girl surf band whose members were '60s pals of Beach Boy Brian Wilson (and featured his first wife, Marilyn); the Ventures' *Ventures in Space* 🎵🎵🎵 (Dolton, 1964/EMI, 1992, reissue prod. Ron Furmanek) and *Play Telstar—The Lonely Bull and Others* 🎵🎵🎵 (Dolton, 1963/EMI, 1992, reissue prod. Ron Furmanek), offering spacey, explosively performed psychedelic instrumentals that influenced the Who's Keith Moon, among many others; *Surfin' Bird* 🎵🎵🎵 (Soma, 1964/Sundazed, 1995, prod. Bob Irwin), a surprisingly fresh argument that the Trashmen were more talented than their novelty place in rock history. Jan & Dean, whose tragedy-filled career is documented in the '70s movie *Dead-*

man's Curve, were Beach Boys' imitators, but good ones. Their music is showcased best on *The Little Old Lady from Pasadena* 🎵🎵🎵 (Liberty, 1964/EMI, 1992, reissue prod. Ron Furmanek).

worth searching for: Some of the best contemporary surf music can be heard on Man or Astro-Man?'s *Is It Man . . . or Astro-Man?* (Estrus, 1993, prod. Jim Marrer, Birdstuff) and Laika and the Cosmonauts' straight-outta Finland *The Amazing Colossal Band* (Upstart, 1994, prod. Laika, the Cosmonauts).

see also: *The Beach Boys, Dick Dale, Jan & Dean, Man or Astro-Man?*

Steve Knopper

Swamp Dogg

Born Jerry Williams Jr., July 12, 1942, in Portsmouth, VA.

Even if he hadn't reinvented himself as Swamp Dogg in 1970, the former Jerry Williams Jr. would still have a musical career of considerable note. Over the years, Williams has produced records by Gene Pitney, Patti LaBelle, and the Commodores; written hits for Conway Twitty, Irma Thomas, and Johnny Paycheck; and charted R&B singles under his own name. Still, nothing could have prepared the pop music world for his emergence as Swamp Dogg, a persona that sprang from the cultural upheaval of the '60s. With his visionary synthesis of social protest, humor, and Southern-style funk, Swamp Dogg has, over the course of three decades and at least a dozen albums, wielded his brassy bullhorn of a bark to affirm life and decry anything that threatens it.

what to buy: *The Excellent Sides of Swamp Dogg* 🎵🎵🎵🎵 (S.D.E.G., 1996, prod. Swamp Dogg) reissues Swamp's first two LPs, the lost 1970 classic *Total Destruction to Your Mind* and the uneven *Rat On* from 1971.

what to buy next: *Best of 25 Years of Swamp Dogg . . . or F*** the Bomb, Stop the Drugs* 🎵🎵🎵🎵 (Pointblank/Virgin, 1995, prod. Swamp Dogg) collects 18 recordings from at least eight different labels. And yet with only one cut from the epochal *Total Destruction*, it is far from representative. It does, however, unearth three Swamp Dogg tracks from Faberge's short-lived Brute label, including the searing statement of purpose, "Call Me Nigger."

the rest:
Surfin' in Harlem 🎵🎵🎵🎵 (Volt/Fantasy, 1991)

worth searching for: *Generations I: A Punk Look at Human Rights* (Ark 21, 1997, prod. Jason Rothberg) is a various artists compilation that benefits ex–Amnesty International head Jack Healey's Human Rights Action Center. The album features Swamp Dogg and the British punk band Moon Dogg re-making "Synthetic World," a song that Swamp originally recorded for *Total Destruction.*

influences:

◀◀ Johnny Ace, Jackie Wilson, Sly & the Family Stone, Joe South, the Mothers of Invention

▶▶ The Commodores, Freddie North, Johnny Paycheck, George and Gwen McCrae

Bill Friskics-Warren

Billy Swan

Born May 12, 1942, in Cape Girardeau, MO.

"A modern-day 1950s" is how no less an expert than Elvis Presley producer Felton Jarvis described Billy Swan upon the release of his 1974 chart-topper "I Can Help." True enough, Swan's roots reach deep into the sounds and styles of classic country and rockabilly. While still in high school and a member of Mirt Mirley's Rhythm Steppers, Swan wrote "Lover Please," and it became a huge hit for Clyde McPhatter in 1962. Soon afterwards, Swan moved to Nashville on the recommendation of Kris Kristofferson (who offered him his job as janitor at the Columbia studios) and recorded several singles for the MGM and Rising Sons labels. His initial success, however, came as producer of Tony Joe White's early records, including the hit "Polk Salad Annie." Swan stayed active on-stage as well, joining old pal Kristofferson's road band (he continued to record and tour with him well into the 1990s). Then came the international country-crossover sensation "I Can Help," a song so charmingly absolute in its treatment of early rock that it earned Swan not only a cover version by Elvis himself, but an actual pair of the King's socks! Not bad for a kid who, not long before, had been crashing on Presley's uncle's living-room couch. It was his last major hit, though he's continued to work both in the studio and on the road with everyone from Kinky Friedman (in the mid-1970s) to Randy Meisner (with the band Black Tie a decade later) and, most recently, Peter Case.

what to buy: *The Best of Billy Swan* 🎵🎵🎵 (Epic/Legacy, 1998, compilation prod. Nick Shaffran) includes not only the still timeless "I Can Help" but Swan's own "Lover Please," the rollicking "Vanessa" (Dave Edmunds, for one, has made a career out of recycling this gem), plus a genuinely otherworldly reading of his idol's "Don't Be Cruel."

influences:

◀◀ Sun Records, the Crickets, Sir Douglas Quintet

▶▶ Nick Lowe, Bill Lloyd, the Muffins, Rick Harper

Gary Pig Gold

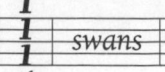

Swans

Formed 1982, in New York, NY. Disbanded 1997.

Michael Gira, guitars, vocals, tapes; Jarboe, vocals, keyboards (1987–present).

The most horrible experience of your life? Early Swans might have qualified. Born in the belly of the noise-rock beast that was New York's Lower East Side during the early '80s, Swans set out to brutalize the listener in a manner that makes current terrormongers such as Marilyn Manson and Tool sound positively effete. But after definitive statements of degradation such as "Raping a Slave," the group shifted gears, even playing up its latent goth-rock side by covering Joy Division's "Love Will Tear Us Apart." Such odd concessions to the mainstream aside, the ultra-prolific Swans were producing a rich, heavily textured brand of near-ambient music by the time the duo called it quits in 1997. Michael Gira and Jarboe then continued in the same direction with their new project, the Body Lovers.

what to buy: *Children of God/World of Skin* ♪♪♪♪ (Young God/Atavistic, 1998, prod. Michael Gira, Rico Conning) is a double-CD repackaging of work originally released from 1986 to 1988. It marks a major turning point in the Swans' sound, with the golden-voiced, classically trained Jarboe making her debut on a series of stately, acoustic-laden tracks that evoke a medieval sense of beauty and horror.

what to buy next: *Soundtracks for the Blind* ♪♪♪♪ (Young God/Atavistic, 1997, prod. Michael Gira) is a different beast than early Swans but equally intense and consuming: dense, epic-length tracks that suggest an ambient symphony for a vampire movie.

best of the rest:
Swans Are Dead ♪♪♪ (Young God/Atavistic, 1998)

worth searching for: The 12-inch single version of "Love Will Tear Us Apart" (Caroline, 1988) is easily the most conventional work in the Swans' canon and also a port of entry for the noise-phobic. The flip side includes a stripped-down alternate version, with lead vocal by Jarboe, that bests the Gira-sung A-side.

solo outings:
The Body Lovers:
Number One of Three ♪♪♪ (Young God/Atavistic, 1998)

influences:
◀◀ Frank Zappa, Pink Floyd, Can, Art Ensemble of Chicago
▶▶ Godflesh, Tool, Ministry, Cop Shoot Cop

Greg Kot

The Sweet

Formed 1968, in London, England. Disbanded 1981.

Brian Connolly, vocals; Mick Tucker, drums, vocals; Andy Scott, guitar, keyboards, vocals; Steve Priest, bass, vocals.

As catchy as they were stupid, the Sweet's hits led the raunchy, glam cheese pack during the '70s. Developed as a bubblegum teenybopper sensation by British producers Nicky Chinn and Mike Chapman (who wrote most of the group's biggest hits), the Sweet charted with insistent, trashy singles such as "Little Willy," "Blockbuster," and "Ballroom Blitz," all of which make for guilty pleasures. Fueled by fat power chords, nitro-vocals, and bone-snappingly crisp production (often covering the group's musical slightness)—not to mention obvious, crude lyrics—these coiffed pretty boys were just obnoxious enough to offend your mother but safe enough to cultivate a mass success. Apparently there may have been a real band lurking in there somewhere, as some of the Sweet's own material—such as its biggest hit, "Fox on the Run"—stands up to Chinn-Chapman's.

what's available: With the individual albums long out of print, *The Best of Sweet* ♪♪♪♪ (Capitol, 1992, prod. various) packs all the Sweet you'd ever want to hear onto a 16-track set.

influences:
◀◀ The Monkees, the New York Dolls, the Beatles, the Rolling Stones
▶▶ The Ramones, Kiss, Cheap Trick, Nirvana, Urge Overkill

Allan Orski

Matthew Sweet

Born October 6, 1964, in Lincoln, NE.

Matthew Sweet (yes, it's his real name) came out of the Athens, Georgia, scene and was first heard on EPs by Oh-OK (with Linda Stipe, Michael's sister) and Buzz of Delight. A masterful songwriter and talented multi-instrumentalist ironically known for the superb performances of his sidemen (especially guitarists Robert Quine and Richard Lloyd), Sweet was dropped by Columbia and then A&M after fine albums attracted little attention. But when A&M declined his third album, *Girlfriend*, Zoo picked it up and it rocketed onto the charts on the strength of the Japanese animation video for the song "Divine Intervention." The best songwriting and most Beatlesque production of his career didn't hurt either, and it could be that the tuneful success of *Girlfriend* (full of classic rock verities) paved the way for the acceptance of the like-minded rock melodists such as Gin Blossoms and Goo Goo Dolls. However, Sweet's creativity has subsequently been infected by a slight sense of formula and routine; he still sounds good, but he's not advancing, although at least *Blue Sky on Mars* regained the freshness of his second and third albums.

what to buy: If Sweet never again equals *Girlfriend* 🎸🎸🎸🎸 (Zoo, 1991, prod. Fred Maher, Matthew Sweet), it's nothing to be ashamed of. It's that good. Lloyd's trademark freak-out solos on "Divine Intervention" followed by the wistful "I've Been Waiting" set the album's tone of alternating guitar aggression with twangy ballads, while Sweet overdubs angelic harmonies all over the place.

what to buy next: *Earth* 🎸🎸🎸🎸 (A&M, 1989, prod. Fred Maher, David M. Allen, Matthew Sweet) has a slightly lusher pop sound than *Girlfriend*, but with hooks galore and enough crunch ("Underground" and "The Alcohol Talking") to not cloy. Members of Trip Shakespeare add rich harmony vocals to a batch of Sweet's most poignant tunes, and Quine, Lloyd, and Gary Lucas contribute scintillating guitar work.

what to avoid: *Inside* 🎸🎸 (Columbia, 1986, prod. Scott Litt, David Kahne, Stephen Hague, Dave Allen, Matthew Sweet, Simon Hanhart, Don Dixon, Alan Tarney, Francois Kevorkian, Ron St. Germain) was good for a debut but is slick and bland compared to Sweet's later work. The multiplicity of producers couldn't have helped.

the rest:
Time Capsule 🎸🎸🎸 (Zoo EP, 1993)
The Ugly Truth 🎸🎸🎸 (Zoo EP, 1993)
Altered Beast 🎸🎸🎸🎸 (Zoo, 1993)
Son of Altered Beast 🎸🎸🎸 (Zoo EP, 1994)
100% Fun 🎸🎸🎸 (Zoo, 1995)
Blue Sky on Mars 🎸🎸🎸🎸 (Zoo, 1997)

worth searching for: The 13-track, promo-only *Goodfriend* (Zoo, 1992) has live, radio, and home recordings. Mostly it focuses on *Girlfriend* material, but there's also an early version of *Altered Beast* 's "Someone to Pull the Trigger" as well as superb covers of Neil Young's "Cortez the Killer" (with the Indigo Girls) and John Lennon's "Isolation." Another promo item, the four-song EP *I've Been Waiting* (Zoo, 1992), has live versions of *Girlfriend* 's "Does She Talk," the Beatles' "She Said She Said," and Neil Young's Buffalo Springfield tune "Mr. Soul," with Voidoids guitarist Ivan Julian. Sixteen *Girlfriend* demos show up on the Taiwanese bootleg *Supervixen*, including six unreleased songs; sound is tinny but clear and listenable.

influences:
◄◄ The Beatles, the Raspberries, Neil Young, Television, the dB's

►► Velvet Crush, Teenage Fanclub, Gin Blossoms, Goo Goo Dolls

Steve Holtje

Rachel Sweet

Born 1963, in Akron, OH.

A big-voiced teenager who signed to Stiff Records at the age of 16, Rachel Sweet recorded several albums in the late '70s and early '80s that were stylistic mish-mashes of new wave mixed with country rock, MOR rock, and just enough punk thrown in to make her seem a bit naughty. Her big American hit was "Everlasting Love," a duet with teen heartthrob Rex Smith. Sweet was certainly talented, penning and producing the whole of her 1982 album *Blame It on Love*, but her career fizzled, and she faded away until the late '80s, when film director John Waters plucked her out of obscurity to record the title song for his campy flick *Hairspray*.

what's available: All that remains in print from Sweet's brief moment in the sun is *Fool Around: The Best of Rachel Sweet* 🎸🎸🎸 (Rhino, 1992, compilation prod. Liam Stewart, Gary Stewart). It contains both "Everlasting Love" and "Hairspray," as well as the minor hits "Who Does Lisa Like?" and "B-A-B-Y," a cover of the old Carla Thomas chestnut.

influences:
◄◄ Linda Ronstadt, Brenda Lee

►► LeAnn Rimes

Daniel Durchholz

Sweet 75

See: Nirvana

Swervedriver

Formed 1988, in Oxford, England.

Adam Franklin, vocals, guitar; Jim Hartridge, guitar; Adi Vines, bass (1988–92); Steve George, bass, vocals (1992–present); Graham Bonnar, drums (1988–91); Danny, drums (1991–92); Jez, drums (1991–present).

Few groups that aren't metal bands are as beautifully punishing as Swervedriver. Combining the heaviness of that genre with the smack-slap attack of punk, the hiss of hardcore, the dreamy soundscapes of shoegaze, the pop smarts of Britpop (the Who seem to be a large influence), and the simple, vaguely psychedelic jams of the Stooges (another major checkpoint here), Swervedriver lashes with edge, but in the most laconic blast of heat imaginable. Toss in lyrics obsessed with cars (and motorbikes), science fiction, and film noir cinema, and you have one of the more intriguing groups Britain has produced during the '90s.

what to buy: A fresh rhythm section improved things on the smashing *Mezcal Head* 🎸🎸🎸🎸 (A&M, 1993, prod. Alan Moulder, Swervedriver), an album of pure, adrenalized, souped-up rock complete with the deceptive, harsh hooks of "Duel" and "Blowin' Cool."

what to buy next: Perhaps *Raise* ♫♫♫♪ (A&M, 1991, prod. Swervedriver) is a bit ragtag—it was made up of a number of different sessions that produced the earliest EPs—but the main tracks ("Son of Mustang Ford," "Rave Down," "Sandblasted") remain some of the band's signature power-moments. A fourth LP was recorded for new label Geffen, but it never appeared on that label. The group asked for and obtained their release after Geffen fired the woman who had initially signed the album. Instead, almost a year later, the album, *99th Dream* ♫♫♫♪ (Zero Hour, 1998, prod. Swervedriver, Alan Moulder), appeared as Swervedriver's first U.S. release in five years. If not as superb as *Ejector Seat Reservation* due to a small drop-off in hooks, or as well-produced as the still-scorching *Mezcal Head*, it still furthers the band's record of sterling releases, led by the laconic-to-pretty "These Times" and the more roller-coaster distortion-driven thrills of the title track and "Behind the Scenes of the Sounds and the Times."

worth searching for: Sadly, Swervedriver's best album, *Ejector Seat Reservation* (Creation U.K., 1995, prod. Swervedriver, Alan Moulder), wasn't released in the U.S. But with its tempered rushes and greater emphasis on developed pop songs—as well as a masterly use of strings and horns in a supporting role—it remains one of the most quietly ambitious albums of the decade.

influences:

◀◀ The Who, the Stooges, the MC5, Hüsker Dü

▶▶ Oasis, Radiohead, Catherine Wheel

Jack Rabid

Swing out Sister

Formed 1986, in Manchester, England.

Corinne Drewery, lead vocals; Andy Connell, keyboards; others.

Evoking the jet-set, not acid, trips of the '60s, England's Swing out Sister soars from Burt Bacharach–inspired elegance to easygoing funk with the ease of a Concord. The ghosts of classic pop haunt its sound, and the band's airy soulfulness makes for good background music. But Swing out Sister's rich melodies put the band at the forefront of the mellow-dramatic pop movement.

what to buy: *Kaleidoscope World* ♫♫♫♫ (Fontana, 1989, prod. Paul S. O'Duffy) is Swing out Sister's loving portrait of '60s pop as they see it. They take their cues from Burt Bacharach, Dusty Springfield, John Barry, the Fifth Dimension, and Jimmy Webb (who arranges and conducts a couple of tracks). This is great

easy-listening music years before anyone realized how cool it was.

what to buy next: *Get in Touch with Yourself* ♫♫♫ (Fontana, 1992, prod. Paul S. O'Duffy, Swing out Sister, Stuart James) includes "Not Gonna Change"—Bacharach meets modern easy-funk; "Am I the Same Girl," which sounds like a well-preserved '60s classic; and "I Can Hear You but I Can't See You," an instrumental with light blaxpoitation-soundtrack underpinnings and an overlay of Bacharach. Much of *The Living Return* ♫♫♫♪ (PolyGram, 1994, prod. Ray Hayden, Swing out Sister) evokes a less forceful Laura Nyro, with sultry Marvin Gaye grooves. *Shapes and Patterns* ♫♫♫♪ (Mercury, 1997, prod. Paul S. O'Duffy) runs the gamut from Todd Rundgren–esque pop bounce to feather-light soul. "Somewhere in the World," "Here and Now," and "Better Make It Better" are standouts on this career-affirming release, which shows Swing out Sister to be more swinging than ever.

what to avoid: *It's Better to Travel* ♫♫ (Fontana, 1987, prod. Paul S. O'Duffy) is a pleasant debut, but should be your last purchase by this adult-friendly pop band. The melodies here are thinner than Twiggy.

worth searching for: *Live at the Jazz Café* (Fontana, 1993, prod. Swing out Sister) is an import with a breezy ambiance that should blow away fans.

influences:

◀◀ Dionne Warwick, Motown, Burt Bacharach

▶▶ Cardigans, High Llamas

Jordan Oakes

The Swinging Blue Jeans /The Bluegenes /Ray Ennis & the Blue Jeans

Formed 1958, in Liverpool, England.

Ray Ennis, guitar, vocals; Paul Moss, banjo (1958–61); Ralph Ellis, guitar (1961–66); Les Braid, bass, keyboards (1961–66, 1973–present); Norman Kuhlke, drums (1961–68); Terry Sylvester, guitar, vocals (1966–68); Mike Gregory, bass (1966–68); Mike Pynn, guitar (1973–88); John Lawrence, drums (1973–82); Colin Manley, guitar, vocals (1983–present); John Ryan, drums (1983–88); Phil Thompson, drums (1989–present).

Back when Messrs. Lennon, McCartney, and Harrison were still skiffling their way around local talent contests, the Swinging Blue Jeans (though admittedly an early "trad-jazz" incarnation) were already headlining at Liverpool's legendary Cavern Club. By 1963, following a high-profile ad campaign for "swinging blue" Lybro jeans, the band was right atop the U.K. charts alongside those very same Beatles, although chances for similar success in America were thwarted the following year when they unwisely turned down an invitation to appear on *The Ed Sullivan Show*. Perhaps what ultimately led the Blue Jeans down the road to obscurity, however—alongside practically every other non-Beatle combo from Liverpool—was their lack of in-house songwriting ability: their several hits ("The Hippy Hippy Shake," "Good Golly Miss Molly," and "You're No Good") were all competent if unspectacular covers of stage-tested chestnuts, which is not the way to ensure a lasting recording career. As a result, they've spent the past three decades back on the club circuit, happily playing their "Shaking" medley at European pubs and resort clubs.

what's available: *Hippy Hippy Shake: The Definitive Collection* ♫♫♫♫ (EMI, 1993/Gold Rush, 1996, compilation prod. Ron Furmanek) demonstrates, if nothing else, what a powerhouse unit these guys must've been back at the Cavern. Keen students of Merseybeat can hear, in the later material, the first tentative strummings of Hollie-to-be Terry Sylvester.

influences:

◄◄ Lonnie Donegan, Little Richard, Chan Romero, Johnny Kidd & the Pirates

►► The Rattles, Ducks Deluxe, Teenage Head, the Georgia Satellites

Gary Pig Gold

David Sylvian

Born David Batt, February 23, 1958, in Beckenham, Kent, England.

While his former band, Japan, was largely a collaborative effort, David Sylvian is generally regarded as the group's primary creative force. This is borne out by Sylvian's solo career, which is easily the most successful and diverse of the post-Japan projects. Despite the fact that all of his solo albums feature significant contributions from Japan drummer Steve Jansen and keyboardist Richard Barbieri, Sylvian's catalog boasts a stamp that is singular and distinctive. His first solo album, *Brilliant Trees*, has lingering elements of Japan's trademark Eastern sound but is more focused on introducing jazz overtones and acoustic instruments. Contributions from notable musicians such as Ryuichi Sakamoto, Robert Fripp, and former Bebop Deluxe guitarist Bill Nelson made Sylvian's subsequent outings even more discrete.

what to buy: Two Sylvian albums do a nice job of illustrating the primary thrusts of his solo career. *Secrets of the Beehive* ♫♫♫♫ (Virgin, 1987, prod. David Sylvian) showcases his contemplative side with sumptuous mood pieces buoyed by rich acoustic tones, luxurious string arrangements, and Sylvian's striking vo-

cals. (Note: later editions of the album omit "Forbidden Colors," Sylvian's collaboration with Sakamoto.) Partnering with seminal art rock guitarist Fripp (King Crimson, League of Crafty Guitarists), Sylvian shifted gears with the release of the more aggressive *The First Day* ♫♫♫♫ (Virgin, 1993, prod. Robert Fripp, David Sylvian). A true collaboration, the album successfully grafts Fripp's angular guitar style to Sylvian's mellifluous vocals and ambient inclinations for a work that is both driving and ethereal, at times recalling middle period King Crimson.

what to buy next: *Gone to Earth* ♫♫♫♫ (Virgin, 1986, prod. David Sylvian, Steve Nye) is really two releases in one. The first half of the recording features vocals and the significant guitar work of Nelson and Fripp; this material, particularly "Taking the Veil" and the title track, offer a transitional view of Sylvian as he moves from Japan toward the quieter sounds he would pursue on *Secrets of the Beehive*. The second half of *Gone to Earth* comprises instrumental mood pieces that draw heavily from Brian Eno's atmospheric canon to create a dreamlike tapestry. (Note: The CD version of the album excises half the instrumental tracks.)

what to avoid: *Plight and Premonition* ♫♫ (Virgin, 1988, prod. David Sylvian, Holger Czukay) is the first of two nearly identical collaborations that Sylvian undertook with former Can bassist Holger Czukay, and, if a distinction can be made, is the worst of the two. Like the most insipid new age music, the instrumentals on this album are vacuous and without direction.

the rest:

Brilliant Trees 𝄢𝄢𝄢𝄢 (Virgin, 1984)

(With Holger Czukay) *Flux and Mutability* 𝄢𝄢 (Virgin, 1989)

(With David Mills) *Ember Glance: The Performance of Memory* 𝄢𝄢𝄢 (Venture, 1991)

worth searching for: *Damage* (Virgin, 1994, prod. David Sylvian, Robert Fripp), a limited-edition import, is a live recording of the tour that Sylvian and Fripp undertook in support of *The First Day* and is well worth hearing. If you're looking for the definitive Sylvian collection, *Weatherbox* (Virgin, 1989) is the ticket; now out of print, the box set contains all of Sylvian's full-length albums, his EPs—*Alchemy, An Index of Possibilities,* and *Words with the Shaman*—and, for the first time on CD in the U.S., the complete instrumental half of *Gone to Earth.*

influences:

◀◀ Roxy Music, Brian Eno, David Bowie, King Crimson, Can, Gong

▶▶ Holger Czukay, Bill Nelson/Bebop Deluxe, Depeche Mode, Moby, Aphex Twin

see also: *Japan*

David Galens

Sylvian & Fripp

See: Robert Fripp

Symposium

Formed 1994, in London, England.

Ross Cummins, vocals; Hagop Tchaparian, guitar; William McGonagle, guitars; Wojtek Godzisz, bass; Joe Birch, drums.

With more exuberance than inhibition, more ambition than self-consciousness, the nearly adolescent quintet known as Symposium has in four very short, very formative years, gone from a bunch of unknown funseekers to "the best live band in Britain," a tagline concocted by the U.K. weekly *Melody Maker.* Superlatives aside, Symposium does indeed bring an abundance of high-spirited energy to both its recordings and performances. One particularly righteous example of this occurred when singer Ross Cummins broke his leg onstage, finished the set singing flat on his back, and returned the next night to sing from his wheelchair. Together since 1994, the members of Symposium first met as Catholic schoolmates. Helmed by songwriter Wojtek Godzisz and his keen social observations, and buttressed by the passionately simple guitar chords of Hagop

Tchaparian and William McGonagle, the band began making a name for itself almost immediately with its intensely melodic songcraft and infectious energy. Since forming, it has released a few EPs and a couple of acclaimed singles that are only available as imports. Symposium's only U.S. release is *One Day at a Time*, produced by the team behind Bush's American success.

what to buy: *One Day at a Time* 𝄢𝄢𝄢 (Red Ant Entertainment, 1997, prod. Clive Langer, Alan Winstanley) reflects the band's fondness for rebellion, skateboarding, the Beatles, and punk rock. It's as good an introduction to the band as you'll get short of seeing a performance.

the rest:

On the Outside 𝄢𝄢𝄢 (Red Ant Entertainment, 1998)

influences:

◀◀ The Beatles, the Sex Pistols, the Buzzcocks, Nirvana

Bob Gulla

T. Rex

Formed 1967, in London, England. Disbanded 1975.

Marc Bolan (born Mark Feld, September 30, 1947; died September 16, 1977), vocals, guitar; Steve Peregrine Took, drums, bass, percussion, vocals (1967–69); Mickey Finn, guitar, percussion, vocals (1969–74); Steve Currie, bass (1970–75); Bill Legend, drums (1970–74); Jack Green, guitar (1973–74); Davy Lutton, drums (1974–75); Dino Dins, keyboards (1974–75).

Along with David Bowie, no act symbolizes '70s glam rock better than Marc Bolan and T. Rex. Begun as Tyrannosaurus Rex, Bolan's acoustic strumming and whispered nonsense lyrics about wizards, dragons, and other mystical topics became popular with a hippie audience in England. However, the band didn't come into its own until Bolan plugged in; with a full group behind him (and the moniker shortened to T. Rex) he recorded the masterful *Electric Warrior* and its international hit, "Bang a Gong (Get It On)." With his curly hair and impish demeanor, Bolan inspired a fanatical following documented by Ringo Starr in the film *Born to Boogie.* Other U.K. hits—"Telegram Sam," "The Groover"—didn't make much sense lyrically but were highly addictive glitter goodies. Beyond "Bang a Gong," American success eluded Bolan, and after a few more stellar albums he slipped into making watery, synth-dominated disco that showcased singer/girlfriend Gloria Jones. Bolan eventually got his own British TV series, *Marc*, which introduced several new wave acts to the nation as well as showcasing his own music—often on ridiculously lavish sets. On the eve of a supposed comeback in 1977, he died when his car, driven by Jones, hit a tree. Dozens of posthumous best-ofs and compilations of unreleased material have been issued, and caution is urged when building a collection.

what to buy: *Electric Warrior* 🎵🎵🎵🎵 (Reprise, 1971, prod. Tony Visconti) remains T. Rex's seminal work—saucy, playful, and filled with A-material such as "Bang a Gong," "Jeepster," and "Rip Off."

what to buy next: The slightly more restrained *The Slider* 🎵🎵🎵🎵 (EMI, 1972/Chronicles, 1996, prod. Tony Visconti) came at a time when even Bolan's lesser songs were brilliant. A glam-rock superstar at his peak.

what to avoid: *Dandy in the Underworld* 🎵 (EMI, 1977/Chronicles, 1996, prod. Marc Bolan) has frustrating flashes of excitement among the trash that make Bolan's downfall even more disappointing.

the rest:
Tanx 🎵🎵🎵🎵 (EMI, 1973/Chronicles, 1996)
Zinc Alloy and the Hidden Riders of Tomorrow 🎵🎵🎵 (EMI, 1974/Chronicles, 1996)
Zip Gun Boogie 🎵🎵 (EMI, 1975/Chronicles, 1996)
Futuristic Dragon 🎵🎵 (EMI, 1976/Chronicles, 1996)
BBC Live 🎵🎵🎵 (Windsong, 1993)
Great Hits 1972–1977: The A-Sides 🎵🎵🎵 (Chronicles, 1996)
Great Hits 1972-1977: The B-Sides 🎵🎵🎵 (Chronicles, 1996)
Messing with the Mystic 🎵🎵 (Chronicles, 1996)
T. Rex Unchained—Unreleased Recordings, Vol. 1: 1972, Part 1 🎵 (Chronicles, 1997)
T. Rex Unchained—Unreleased Recordings, Vol. 2: 1972, Part 2 🎵 (Chronicles, 1997)
Live 1977 🎵🎵 (Chronicles, 1996)
T. Rex Unchained—Unreleased Recordings, Vol. 3: 1973, Part 1 🎵 (Chronicles, 1998)
T. Rex Unchained—Unreleased Recordings, Vol. 4: 1973, Part 2 🎵 (Chronicles, 1998)

worth searching for: *The Essential Collection* (PolyGram TV, 1995, prod. various), a 24-track British best-of, serves as a fine introduction and is the only compilation that has "Bang a Gong" *and* the group's later hits.

influences:
◀◀ David Bowie, Gary Glitter
▶▶ The Replacements, Oasis, Def Leppard

Todd Wicks

Talk Show
See: Stone Temple Pilots

Talk Talk
Formed 1981, in London, England.

Mark Hollis, vocals, keyboards; Simon Brenner, keyboards; Paul Webb, bass; Lee Harris, drums.

You couldn't swing a stick in the early '80s without whacking a slick pretty boy synth-pop outfit, and you wouldn't have to swing very long before connecting with Talk Talk. Not content as foppish new wavers, the band soon ditched the echoing angst in favor of art-rock, which led to experimental ambient music whose lack of texture or inspiration led to the group's eventual demise.

what to buy: *Natural History: The Very Best of Talk Talk* 🎵🎵🎵 (EMI, 1990, prod. Rhett Davis, Tim Friese-Greene) contains its best song, "Talk Talk," which gave the band a promising future in 1982. But those hopes rapidly diminished as a misguided Roxy Music/Brian Eno fixation took over.

the rest:
It's My Life 🎵🎵 (EMI America, 1984)
Laughing Stock 🎵🎵 (Polydor, 1991)

influences:
◀◀ Roxy Music, Brian Eno
▶▶ Duran Duran, the Fixx

Allan Orski

Talking Heads
/Jerry Harrison
/Tom Tom Club
/The Heads
Formed 1975, in New York, NY.

David Byrne, vocals, guitar; Chris Frantz, drums; Tina Weymouth, bass; Jerry Harrison, keyboards, guitar, vocals (1977–present).

This is what happens at art school, when you bring together high thinkers with a taste for forms that lean towards the baser instincts. Talking Heads specialize in colliding sensibilities, cutting a wide swath from cheesey pop to African rhythms, punk to funk, and bringing them all together around the quirky high tenor of frontman David Byrne. Initiated at the Rhode Island School of Design, where Byrne and Chris Frantz met, Talking Heads was one of the most original-sounding bands to play the burgeoning scene at New York's CBGB during the mid-'70s; not the Ramones or Blondie or Television, the group was much more spare and halting in its delivery, kind of like the tentative younger sibling trying to step into an older brother's football game. The sound got a little more meat after former Modern Lover Jerry Harrison joined the band, and Talking Heads set out on a stylistic journey that delivered 15 years of some of pop's

David Byrne of Talking Heads (© Jack Vartoogian)

most original and tuneful music—dropping into the mass consciousness just once, with the roiling 1983 hit "Burning down the House." Byrne's ambitions in theater, film, and photography rendered the band inactive after 1992, but it's never officially called it quits; though Byrne says he's out, Harrison, Weymouth, and Franz re-grouped as the Heads in 1996 to record an album with guest vocalists that included former Concrete Blonde singer Johnette Napolitano, Live's Ed Kowalczyk, the Violent Femmes' Gordon Gano, and Blondie's Debbie Harry. Harrison, meanwhile, has also become an in-demand producer, working with BoDeans, Live, and the Verve Pipe.

what to buy: In three consecutive years (1978–80), Talking Heads—along with producer Brian Eno—released three remarkable albums of incredible growth and adventure. *More Songs about Buildings and Food* ✍✍✍✍ (Sire, 1978, prod. Brian Eno, Talking Heads) was firmly rooted in pop but added world music touches and electronic sound experiments; it also got the band some radio play with its cover of Al Green's "Take Me to the River." *Fear of Music* ✍✍✍✍ (Sire, 1979, prod. Brian Eno, Talking Heads) was darker and denser, employing more polyrhythms to drive the chanted vocals of "I Zimbra" and Byrne's apocalyptic visions in "Life during Wartime." *Remain in Light* ✍✍✍✍ (Sire, 1980, prod. Brian Eno) brought everything to a tightly focused peak, resulting in a groove-driven group of songs so powerful they explode from the speakers.

what to buy next: Apart from Eno, *Speaking in Tongues* ✍✍✍✍ (Sire, 1983, prod. Talking Heads) takes the spirit of *Remain in Light* in a slightly more straightforward direction, capping a bold era with the percolating "Burning down the House" and the delicately sweet "This Must Be the Place (Naive Melody)." *Popular Favorites 1976–1992: Sand in the Vaseline* ✍✍✍✍ (Sire, 1992, prod. various) is an exemplary two-disc retrospective, with the best songs from those four landmark albums plus the highlights from the rest of the group's catalog.

what to avoid: *True Stories* ✍✍✍ (Sire, 1986, prod. Talking Heads) was hampered by dual agendas, since it also served as a de facto soundtrack album for the Byrne-directed movie of the same name. But lots of bands would love to have something this good as their least-essential offering.

the rest:
Talking Heads 77 ✍✍✍✍ (Sire, 1977)
Stop Making Sense ✍✍✍✍ (Sire, 1984)
Little Creatures ✍✍✍✍ (Sire, 1985)
Naked ✍✍✍ (Sire, 1988)

worth searching for: *The Name of This Band Is Talking Heads* (Sire, 1982, prod. Talking Heads) is an innovative, career-spanning (to that point) live album that shows the development of the Heads' stage prowess. It has yet to appear on CD.

solo outings:
The Heads:
No Talking Just Head ✍✍✍ (Radioactive, 1996)

Tom Tom Club (Frantz and Weymouth):
Tom Tom Club ✍✍✍ (Sire, 1981)
Close to the Bone ✍✍✍ (Sire, 1983)
Boom Boom Chi Boom Boom ✍✍✍ (Sire, 1989)
Dark Sneak Love Action ✍✍✍ (Sire, 1992)

Jerry Harrison:
The Red and the Black ✍✍✍ (Sire, 1981)
Casual Gods ✍✍✍ (Sire, 1988)
Walk on Water ✍✍✍ (Sire, 1990)

influences:
◀◀ The Ramones, Modern Lovers, Mothers of Invention, John Cage, Parliament-Funkadelic

▶▶ R.E.M., Big Audio Dynamite, Blancmange, Love & Rockets, Rusted Root

see also: *David Byrne*

Gary Graff

Tall Dwarfs
See: Chris Knox

Tangerine Dream
Formed 1967, in Berlin, Germany.

Edgar Froese, synthesizer, bass, guitars; Volker Hombach, flute, violin (1967–69); Kurt Herkenburg (1967–69); Lance Hapshash, drums (1967–68); Charlie Prince (1967–69); Sven Ake Johannson (1968–69); Klaus Schulze, drums, keyboards (1969–70); Conrad Schnitzler, flute (1969–70); Steve Schroyder, organ (1971–73); Christoph Franke, synthesizer, keyboards (1971–88); Peter Baumann (1972–77); Steve Jollieffe (1978); Klaus Krieger (1978–79); Johannes Schmoelling (1980–86); Paul Haslinger (1985–90); Paul Wdephul (1988); Jerome Froese (1989–present); Zlatko Perica, guitar (1992–94); Unda Spa, keyboards, saxophone (1993–94).

The influence Tangerine Dream has had upon modern music cannot be overstated; everything from pop to modern movie scores have all been influenced by its expressive, electronic approach. The group practically invented new age and ambient music, and synth-pop groups such as Kraftwerk and Devo are direct descendants. In fact, *anyone* who uses electronic instruments to create music owns some debt to Tangerine Dream. For a concept band its range is massive: early material can sound like anything from textured space odysseys to synthesized classical music, while recent albums explore a variety of music from structured pop songs to cutting-edge techno. No matter which genre or style they take on, Tangerine Dream has always understood how to manipulate its instruments to the fullest degree. After 30 highly productive years, it's still crafting well-made, innovative records.

what to buy: The 19-track, two-disc compilation *Dream Sequence* ♫♫♫♫ (Virgin, 1984, prod. Edgar Froese) contains excerpts of the best Tangerine Dream has to offer; a good introduction to its vast catalog. *Rubycon* ♫♫♫♫ (Virgin, 1975, prod. Tangerine Dream) is a 35-minute masterpiece of sonic layers that offers a thick blanket of sound as complex as any classical symphony and rich enough to yield new enjoyment with every listen. Coming in at just under 60 tracks, *Tangents: 1973–1983* ♫♫♫♫ (Virgin, 1994, prod. Tangerine Dream) collects all the great early electronic works from the group's most experimental and innovative period. *Ricochet* ♫♫♫♫ (Virgin, 1976, prod. Tangerine Dream), a live album on a par with the sequencer masterpiece *Rubycon*, conclusively proves electronic music doesn't have to be a studio-only experience.

what to buy next: *Dream Mixes* ♫♫♫♫ (Miramar, 1995, prod. Edgar Froese) updates classic songs with a house beat, but these tracks are more than the standard techno beat; they have a rhythm and feeling lacking in most dance music. *Hyperborea* ♫♫♫♫ (Virgin, 1983, prod. Edgar Froese) explores the band's classical influences—baroque to Celtic music is emulated in new age style. *Zeit* ♫♫♫♫ (Relativity, 1972, prod. Tangerine Dream) offers the best of the group's early explorations into space-age ambient music. Box set lovers will especially appreciate *The Brick: The Grammy Nominated Albums* ♫♫♫♫ (Miramar, 1997, prod. Tangerine Dream), a five-CD set contaning the LP's *Canyon Dreams*, *Rockoon*, *220 Volt Live*, *Turn of the Tides*, and *Tyranny of Beauty*. An instant collection of superior work.

what to avoid: Extremely short production schedules and pathetic use of vocals bury *Shy People* ♫ (Atlantic, 1987, prod. Tangerine Dream) and *Near Dark* ♫ (Varese Sarabande, 1987, prod. Tangerine Dream), two soundtracks that never should have been released.

the rest:
Electronic Meditation ♫♫♫ (Relativity, 1970)
Alpha Centari ♫♫♫ (Relativity, 1971)
Atem ♫♫♫ (Relativity, 1973)
Green Desert ♫♫♫ (Relativity, 1973)
Paedra ♫♫♫♫ (Virgin, 1974)
Stratosfear ♫♫♫♫ (Virgin, 1977)
Sorcerer ♫♫♫ (MCA, 1977)
Encore: Tangerine Dream Live! ♫♫♫♫ (Virgin, 1977)
Cyclone ♫♫♫ (Virgin, 1978)
Force Majeure ♫♫♫♫ (Virgin, 1979)
Tangerine Dream: 1970–1980 ♫♫♫♫ (Virgin, 1980)
Tangram ♫♫♫ (Blue Plate, 1980)
Quichotte—Live East Berlin '80 ♫♫♫ (Virgin, 1980)
Exit ♫♫♫ (Elektra, 1981)

Thief ♫♫♫ (Asylum, 1981)
White Eagle ♫♫♫ (American Gramaphone, 1982)
Logos—Live at the Dominion ♫♫♫♫ (A&M, 1982)
Wavelength ♫♫♫ (Varese Sarabande, 1983)
Risky Business ♫♫♫ (Virgin, 1983/1995)
Poland ♫♫♫ (Combat, 1983)
Firestarter ♫♫♫ (Varese Sarabande, 1984)
Flashpoint ♫♫♫ (One Way, 1984)
Le Park ♫♫♫♫♫ (Relativity, 1985)
Heartbreakers ♫♫♫ (Virgin, 1985)
In the Begining ♫♫♫♫ (Relativity, 1986)
Legend ♫♫ (MCA, 1986)
Underwater Sunlight ♫♫♫ (Relativity, 1986)
Pergamon—Live at the Palace ♫♫♫ (Caroline, 1986)
Tyger ♫♫ (Relativity, 1987)
Collection ♫♫♫♫ (A&M, 1987)
Three O'Clock High ♫♫ (Atlantic, 1987)
Deadly Care ♫♫ (Silva America, 1987)
Canyon Dreams ♫♫♫ (Miramar, 1987)
Live Miles ♫♫♫ (Caroline, 1988)
Optical Race ♫♫♫ (Private Music, 1988)
Lily on the Beach ♫♫♫ (Private Music, 1989)
Optical Race ♫♫♫♫ (Atlantic, 1989)
Miracle Mile ♫♫♫ (Private Music, 1989)
The Best of Tangerine Dream! ♫♫♫ (Jive, 1989)
Destination Berlin ♫♫♫ (American Gramaphone, 1989)
Melrose ♫♫♫ (Private Music, 1990)
Dead Solid Perfect ♫♫ (Silva Screen, 1990)
From Dawn 'til Dusk - Tangerine Dream 1973–1988 ♫♫♫♫ (Alex, 1991)
The Park Is Mine ♫♫♫ (Silva America, 1991)
Rockoon ♫♫♫ (Miramar, 1992)
Deadly Care ♫♫♫ (Silva America, 1992)
The Private Music of Tangerine Dream ♫♫♫ (Private Music, 1992)
Dream Music: The Movie Music of Tangerine Dream ♫♫♫♫ (Silva America, 1992)
220 Volt Live ♫♫♫ (Miramar, 1993)
Turn of the Tides ♫♫♫ (Miramar, 1994)
Tyranny of Beauty ♫♫♫ (Miramar, 1995)
Dream Music 2 ♫♫♫♫ (Silva America, 1995)
Oasis ♫♫ (Miramar, 1997)
Tournado ♫♫♫ (Blueprint, 1997)
The Analogue Space Years ♫♫♫ (Purple Pyramid/Cleopatra, 1998)

worth searching for: The group's work with the Moog synthesizer is especially expressive on *Stratosfear* (Virgin, 1976/Gold Rush, 1996, prod. Tangerine Dream), an out-of-print reissue featuring superior sound.

influences:

◄◄ Klaus Schulze, Frank Zappa

►► Brian Eno, Kraftwerk, New Order, Dancing Fantasy, Software, Devo

Bryan Lassner and Ken Burke

Tar

Formed late 1980s, in Chicago, IL.

John Mohr, guitar, vocals; Mark Zablocki, guitar, e-bow; Tom Zaluckyi, bass, guitar; Mike Greenlees, drums.

With its pummeling two-guitar attack, Tar was long one of Chicago's finest bands and something of an underground secret. John Mohr's vocals are hardly melodic, but he's not just a shouter; he shows a fine sense of dynamic contrast reflected in the band's music. That and the unhackneyed chord progressions keep the rather basic ingredients from growing overly repetitious. Slowly built structures make this group a slightly more complex Chicago version of Mission of Burma.

what to buy: If there was ever a disc made to be played loud, the EP *Clincher* 🎵🎵🎵 (Touch & Go, 1993, prod. Brad Wood, Tar) is it. A monolithic block of sound, its parts can't be differentiated unless you turn the volume way up. The quartet's sound on *Over and Out* 🎵🎵🎵 (Touch & Go, 1995) is stripped down compared to earlier efforts, with a new, menacing darkness that occasionally resembles Sonic Youth.

the rest:
Handsome EP (Amphetamine Reptile, 1989) 🎵🎵
Roundhouse 🎵🎵 (Amphetamine Reptile, 1990)
Toast 🎵🎵🎵 (Touch & Go, 1993)

influences:
◀◀ Mission of Burma, Eleventh Dream Day
▶▶ Liz Phair, Red Red Meat, Tortoise

Steve Holtje

Tar Babies

Formed 1982, in Madison, WI. Disbanded early '90s.

Bucky Pope, guitars, vocals; Daniel Bitney, drums, piano, vocals; Robin Davies, bass, vocals; Steve Lewis, bass (1988–92); Tony Jarvis, alto sax, clarinet, flute, guitar, vocals, piano (1987–88); Bobby Vienneau, guitar (1991–92).

On the Tar Babies' final album is this declaration: "God grant us the blissfulness to change the things we want, blow up the things we can't and the money to cover the difference." You'd feel like that, too, if you had pioneered the intersection of funk, punk, and heavy guitar, only to see lesser bands get rich off the style. The Tar Babies are like a funky '90s version of the Voidoids, thanks to Robert Quine–like snarling guitar lines and some stuffy-nosed, half-spoken vocals.

what to buy: *Death Trip* 🎵🎵🎵 (Sonic Noise, 1992, prod. Tar Babies, Mr. Colson) isn't the best introduction to the band, but it's the easiest album to find at this point.

the rest:
Face the Music 🎵🎵 (Bone Air EP, 1982)
Respect Your Nightmares 🎵🎵🎵 (Bone Air/Paradise, 1985)
Honey Bubble 🎵🎵🎵 (SST, 1989)

worth searching for: *Fried Milk* (SST, 1987, prod. Robin Davies) has 19 tracks—averaging two minutes apiece—of the funkiest punk ever committed to vinyl. It's a must own, and not too hard to find. *No Contest* (SST, 1988) adds hornman Tony Jarvis for a somewhat more traditional sound. The songs are also longer, though little about the guitar/bass/drums interaction has changed.

influences:
◀◀ James Brown, Parliament-Funkadelic, Richard Hell & the Voidoids, Golden Palominos, the Minutemen
▶▶ Red Hot Chili Peppers, Infectious Grooves, Victim's Family

Steve Holtje

Tarnation

Formed 1992, in San Francisco, CA.

Paula Frazer, vocals; Lincoln Allen, guitar (1992–95); Michael Cernuto, bass, drums, vocals (1992–95); Matt Sullivan, pedal steel (1992–95); Jamie Meagan, bass (1996–present); Joe Byrnes, drums (1996–present); Alex Oropez, guitar (1996–present).

Originally a collaboration between Southern-bred vocalist Paula Frazer, two former S.F. Seals, and a steel player, Tarnation has evolved into a backing group for Frazer's country-flavored operatic visions. While the first incarnation evidently couldn't agree on an single approach, it was also briefly poised on the edge of a distinct and compelling sound. Somewhere between Mazzy Star and Cowboy Junkies, and betraying Frazer's time with a Bulgarian women's choir, Tarnation's debut offered a singular texture and fine songwriting. Inevitably Frazer's voice, a limber instrument capable of high, breathy swoops and darts against the melody line, drew attention, and deservedly so. Minus the strong and competitive voices of her first band, Frazer has yet to approach that height in subsequent work.

what to buy: No question: *I'll Give You Something to Cry About!* 🎵🎵🎵 (Nuf Sed, 1993) may have been recorded under less than state-of-the-art circumstances, but it's a delightful debut. The highlight, "Game of Broken Hearts," has the same moody (foggy?) quality of Chris Isaak's early work, but less obviously reflects the adoration of Roy Orbison.

what to buy next: *Gentle Creatures* 🎵🎵 (4AD, 1995, prod. Tarnation, Joshua Heller, Warren Defever, Wally Sound) reprises many of the best songs from Tarnation's debut, but, as often happens, much of the life was wrung out in the re-recording. *Mirador* 🎵🎵 (Reprise, 1997, prod. David Katznelson, Tarnation)

James Taylor (© Jack Vartoogian)

is Frazer's first outing as unquestioned leader, and (minus other input) comes across as an indulgent exercise in showing off her voice, exceptional though it may be.

worth searching for: *Live* (1995) is an import promo.

influences:

◄◄ Cowboy Junkies, Patsy Cline

►► Beth Orton

Grant Alden

Andy Taylor

See: Duran Duran

James Taylor

Born March 12, 1948, in Boston, MA.

Regardless of what he says in the song "Steamroller," of the many things that James Taylor is, has been, or may someday be, a "churnin' urn of burnin' funk" is not one of them. Perhaps the dictionary definition of the sensitive male singer-song-writer, Taylor's confessional odes and gentle, folk-inflected R&B covers to this day make whole amphitheaters full of boomers swoon. One of the Beatles' initial signings to Apple Records, Taylor ushered in an era of—depending on your point of view—ruthless self-examination or hopeless navel-gazing. It's telling that he actually began his career as a songwriter after checking himself into a mental institution. Songs such as "Fire and Rain" were the result, but Taylor (who once was married to singer Carly Simon) actually had greater success covering the work of others, notably Carole King's "You've Got a Friend." Once a dependable hit maker, if an erratic songwriter, Taylor has for the most part vanished from the scene, save for semi-annual summer tours, political campaigns, and public-television pledge drives. If that doesn't sum up the mellow music of the '70s, what does?

what to buy: *Greatest Hits* ✈✈✈✈ (Warner Bros., 1976, prod. various) would seem the natural place to start, but "Carolina in My Mind" and "Something in the Way She Moves" are re-recorded versions, not the originals. If you're looking for Taylor's best single album, you have to go all the way back to *Sweet Baby*

James ♫♫♫ (Warner Bros., 1970, prod. Peter Asher), which contains a number of songs that became his fans' favorites, including the title track, "Fire and Rain," "Country Road," and "Steamroller Blues"—which in concert becomes Taylor's own personal "Freebird." Since Taylor lacks a hits collection that covers his entire career (excepting the import *Classic Songs*), *Live* ♫♫♫ (Columbia, 1993, prod. Don Grolnick, George Massenburg) has to do. All the requisite songs are here, but Taylor's performance is disappointingly subdued. The set is also available in an abridged one-disc version, *Best Live* ♫♫♫ (Columbia, 1994, prod. Don Grolnick, George Massenburg).

what to buy next: Taylor's debut, *James Taylor* ♫♫♫ (Apple, 1969/Alliance, 1997, prod. Peter Asher), lets you feel his pain as he helps establish the singer-songwriter genre with "Rainy Day Man," "Carolina in My Mind," and "Something in the Way She Moves," as well as the upbeat "Knockin' around the Zoo." *Gorilla* ♫♫♫ (Warner Bros., 1975, prod. Lenny Waronker, Russ Titelman) was Taylor's comeback album after a self-imposed exile during the early '70s; it contains the delightful original "Mexico" but also eased his transition from confessional singer-songwriter to craftsman-like cover man with Marvin Gaye's "How Sweet It Is (to Be Loved by You)." One of his better mid-period albums, *J.T.* ♫♫♫ (Columbia, 1979, prod. Peter Asher) includes the sunny hit "Your Smiling Face," the requisite R&B cover "Handy Man," and the charming "Secret o' Life," plus "Bartender's Blues," which Taylor wrote for George Jones. More recently, *New Moon Shine* ♫♫♫ (Columbia, 1991, prod. Danny Kortchmar, Don Grolnick) offers Taylor's sharpest and most relevant set of lyrics in some time, notably on "Slap Leather" and "Shed a Little Light."

what to avoid: *Never Die Young* ♫♫ (Columbia, 1988, prod. Don Grolnick) is a slight collection, even by Taylor's sometimes lightweight standards.

the rest:
Mud Slide Slim and the Blue Horizon ♫♫♫ (Warner Bros., 1971)
One Man Dog ♫♫ (Warner Bros., 1972)
Walking Man ♫♫ (Warner Bros., 1974)
In the Pocket ♫♫ (Warner Bros., 1976)
Flag ♫♫♫ (Columbia, 1979)
Dad Loves His Work ♫♫♫ (Columbia, 1981)
That's Why I'm Here ♫♫ (Columbia, 1985)
Never Die Young ♫♫♫ (Columbia, 1988)
Hourglass ♫♫♫ (Columbia, 1997)

worth searching for: *James Taylor and the Original Flying Machine 1967* (Euphoria, 1971/Gadfly, 1996) is an interesting curio (but not much else) that contains demos—studio chatter included—of "Night Owl," "Rainy Day Man," and "Brighten Your Night with My Day" that Taylor and guitarist Danny Kortchmar recorded in 1967. The seven-song album saw the light of day only after Taylor hit pay dirt elsewhere and was released without his permission.

influences:
◀◀ Simon & Garfunkel, Bob Dylan, Carole King, the Beatles
▶▶ Jackson Browne, Duncan Sheik, Garth Brooks

Daniel Durchholz

John Taylor
See: Duran Duran

Roger Taylor
See: Queen

James Taylor Quartet
Formed 1986, in London, England.

James Taylor, Hammond organ, piano, synthesizer, keyboards; David Taylor, guitar (1986–89; 1993–present); Allan Crockford, bass (1986–89); Simon Howard, drums (1986–89); Steve White, drums (1989); Chris Jenkins, percussion (1989); Paul Carr, guitar (1989); Steve Walters, bass (1989); Lawrence Cottle, bass (1989); Paul Francis, bass (1989); Robert Gordon, bass (1989); Cleveland Watkiss, vocals (1989); Guy Barker, trumpet (1989); Laurence Parry, trumpet (1989); James McMillan, trumpet (1989); John Wallace, saxophone (1989); Steve Williamson, saxophone (1989); Joe de Jesus, trumpet, trombone, flute (1993–95); John Wilmott, saxophone, flute (1993–present); Mark Cotgrove, percussion (1993); Neil Robinson, drums (1993–present); Noel McCoy, vocals (1993); Gary Crockett, bass (1993–present); Alison Limerick, vocals (1995).

When the Style Council, Paul Weller and Mick Talbot's British Soul Express, derailed in a gorge of new age jazz and half-assed house during the late '80s, the James Taylor Quartet, with its Hammond organ-driven soul gumbo, was there to fill the void. At the start of the decade, the JTQ had risen from the ashes of two influential '60s-revival garage bands: the Prisoners (home to Taylor and Allan Crockford) and the Daggermen (James's brother David's and Simon Howard's aggregate). But the group's history belies the musical direction it would pursue. The Quartet burst on the scene during 1986 with a raucous organ-and-guitar cover of Herbie Hancock's "Blow Up," the theme from the 1966 film, on Eddie Piller's Re-Elect the President Records. Later that year the group issued an eight-song EP of film music instrumentals, *Mission: Impossible*, which included the title track and "Mrs. Robinson." Around this time, London deejays Gilles Peterson and Chris Bangs started to heat up the scene with their jazz-dance discos; They called their dance-floor blend of old jazz/funk and rare groove Acid Jazz, taking their cue from Acid House, another hugely popular European disco genre. Knowing the James Taylor Quartet would be the band this crop of jazz dancers would flock to, Piller quickly changed Re-Elect the President Records to Acid Jazz Records, making the JTQ the first official Acid Jazz artist. While Piller was building a roster to reflect the direction of his newly christened imprint (including the Brand New Heavies, Style Council drummer Steve White's Jazz Renegades, and Mother Earth), his vanguard group jumped ship for Polydor's new acid jazz boutique, Urban Records, an association that would last until the label closed up shop during the early '90s. During this time, Taylor broadened his sound and his band, adding a horn section and vocalists to the mix. After three years of silence, Taylor reinvented himself, reuniting with brother David and re-signing to Acid Jazz Records in 1995, where he continues to record to this day.

what to buy: *In the Hand of the Inevitable* ♫♫♫ (Acid Jazz/Hollywood, 1995, prod. James Taylor) is the JTQ's "comeback" album, announcing its return to Acid Jazz. The album seamlessly runs the gamut from '80s groove ("Love Will Keep Us Together") and smooth modern jazz/soul ("Free Your Mind") to the soul grind of the title track and an insane Booker T.-on-acid cover of Led Zeppelin's "Whole Lotta Love." *Creation* ♫♫♫♫ (Acid Jazz/Hollywood, 1997, prod. James Taylor, Simon Booth) is a return to his roots, incorporating tunes from the U.K. version of the album, titled *A Few Useful Tips for Living Underground* supplemented by tracks issued only on Acid Jazz's sampler series, *Totally Wired*, and an edit of 1988's "Theme from *Starsky & Hutch*," featuring the original quartet with the JB Horns' Fred Wesley and Pee Wee Ellis. *Creation* strips away the sheen of *Inevitable*, leaving a raw, funky, and delightfully nasty album.

what to buy next: The CD issue of *Mission: Impossible* ♫♫♫ (Acid Jazz/Hollywood, 1997, prod. James Taylor Quartet) expands the original eight-cut EP to a 13-track album, adding to the Booker T.–like covers of film and TV themes the flip of the "Blow Up" 45 (a cover of Ray Charles's "One Mint Julep"), early versions of songs that would appear on the debut LP *The Money Spyder*, and a couple of previously unreleased pieces. During the mid-'90s, Taylor played down his association with acid jazz (the genre), claiming what he plays is pop-funk, not acid jazz. His fascination with spy 'n' cop film music would be no better realized than on *The Money Spyder* ♫♫♫♫ (Acid Jazz/Hollywood, 1987, prod. James Taylor Quartet), which musically the quartet pulls off effortlessly and convincingly, and which was foisted as the original soundtrack to a James Bond-type spy film. On *Get Organized* ♫♫♫ (Urban/Verve, 1989, prod. John Williams), Taylor's second album for the Urban imprint, he disbanded the quartet and worked with a host of studio musicians (including Style Council drummer Steve White) and, for the first time, vocalists. With this new collective, Taylor created a cosmopolitan jazz organ album, much in the vein of Jimmy Smith's work for Verve during the '60s. What the album has in

cool sophistication it lacks in raw vitality, an element many had come to expect from the JTQ.

worth searching for: *Wait a Minute* (Urban/Polydor U.K., 1988, prod. Pete Wingfield, Simon Booth), sadly never issued domestically and out-of-print overseas, is the group's finest work. Being the last album by the original quartet, it features fatback, *fonky* originals, in-the-pocket homages to Brother Jack McDuff and Gene Ammonds (whose "The Natural Thing" and "Jungle Strut," respectively, get a loving JTQ treatment) and the original extended version of "Theme from *Starsky & Hutch*." The Japanese pressing of *Inevitable* includes two bonus tracks: the beautiful "Love Ballad;" and the Shaft-esque "Europa." *The BBC Sessions* (Nighttracks U.K., 1995, prod. various) is a sort-of greatest hits album, collecting 10 tracks from six years of live-in-the-studio performances done for the BBC. An excellent pre-*Inevitable* overview of the group.

influences:

◀◀ Jimmy McGriff, Brother Jack McDuff, Jimmy Smith, Lalo Schifrin, John Barry, Small Faces, Booker T. & the MG's

▶▶ Mother Earth

Coqui Toyoda

Bram Tchaikovsky

See: The Motors

The Tea Party

Formed 1991, in Windsor, Ontario, Canada.

Jeff Martin, vocals, guitars; Stuart Chatwood, bass, keyboards; Jeff Burrows, drums, percussion.

Growing up in Windsor, Ontario didn't arouse any musical feelings in Jeff Martin, so he looked across the Detroit River and found blues and industrial music at legendary Detroit hangouts such as the Soup Kitchen and City Club. Frustrated when techno took over the clubs, Martin and friends Stuart Chatwood and Jeff Burrows formed the Tea Party.

what to buy: *Transmission* ♫♫♫ (Atlantic, 1997, prod. Jeff Martin) uses a 50-second acoustic guitar solo, heavy drum beats, sweeping guitars, and programmed keyboards to slide along Martin's vocals in the opening track "Temptation." The 11-song album is an eclectic mix of Middle Eastern-inspired melodies and Indian-style percussion, while hanging on tightly to stomping drum beats. The dramatic "Psychopomp" is sensual and operatic.

what to buy next: *The Edges of Twilight* ♫♫♫ (Chrysalis, 1995, prod. Ed Stasium, Jeff Martin) is an amalgamation of exotic instruments and heavy rock. "Correspondences" opens tenderly with gentle piano playing and winds its way through a maze of mystery. The orchestration of "Fire in the Head" will strike a chord with fans of Led Zeppelin's "Kashmir." Still, it's the use of strings, sitars, and bongos that sets the Tea Party apart.

the rest:
Splendor Solis ♪♪ (Chrysalis, 1994)

influences:
◀◀ The Doors, Jane's Addiction

▶▶ The Gandharvas

Christina Fuoco

Team Dresch
Formed 1993, in Portland, OR.

Donna Dresch, guitar, bass; Jody Bleyle, vocals, guitar, bass; Kaia Wilson, guitar, vocals; Marci Martinez, drums (1994–95); Melissa York, drums, percussion (1995–present).

Spare yourself the pain, homophobes; the all-lesbian Team Dresch is well-versed in the martial arts and can hurt you more than you ever could hurt them. With a history that includes Hazel, Screaming Trees, Adickdid, Calamity Jane, and more, Team Dresch make really good records that beckon you to sing or scream along with their tales of same-sex love, ostracism, and mad crushes.

what to buy: *Personal Best* ♪♪♪ (Candy-Ass/Chainsaw,1994, prod. John Goodmanson, Team Dresch) is cooler than Mariel Hemingway and name-checks the Smiths. Singers Kaia Wilson and Jody Bleyle (the very excellent Hazel drummer) achingly spin tales of lesbian life that can extend to anyone with open ears (and minds). Drummer Marci Martinez provides varied beats that give each track a distinctive flavor.

what to buy next: *Captain My Captain* ♪♪♪ (Candy-Ass/Chainsaw, 1996, prod. John Goodmanson) brightly continues on, but, despite the worthy effort of new drummer Melissa York, suffers a bit with the loss of Martinez. "Yes I Am Too, but Who Am I Really?" communicates the band's issues effectively enough to win over the stoutest non-believers.

worth searching for: *Free to Fight* (Candy-Ass, 1995, prod. various) is a cool compilation CD that comes with a self-defense book for women.

influences:
◀◀ The Slits, Motörhead, Tribe 8, Bikini Kill, Tiger Trap, Hole, Phranc, Tom Robinson, Scrawl, Tilt, the Yeastie Girls, Spinanes, Heavens to Betsy

▶▶ The Donnas, Sleater-Kinney

see also: *Hazel*

Barry M. Prickett

The Tearaways
Formed early 1990s, in Santa Barbara, CA.

Greg Brallier, guitar, vocals; Fin Seth, bass, vocals; Jesse Benenati, drums, percussion; Perry Benenati, piano, organ; Dave Hekhuis, guitar.

On Rhino's pop anthology *Poptopia! Power Pop Classics of the '90s*, "Jessica Something" by the Tearaways was the one track no one had heard—by the band no one had heard of. While that track's inclusion on *Poptopia!* presumably turned a few folks on to the Tearaways, its quiet, effective grace offers little clue to the amazing motherlode of powerful pop nuggets in the group's repertoire. Songwriters Greg Brallier and Fin Seth had previously been in a pop trio called the Volcanos, and with the Tearaways they've formed the sort of act that could rule the radio if the pop movement ever amounts to anything popular. Less consistent (but still impressive) follow-ups qualify praise for the Tearaways somewhat, but this is most definitely an act to keep an eye on.

what to buy: *The Ground's the Limit* ♪♪♪♪ (Perfect Hit, 1997, prod. Earle Mankey, Tom Werman) is a resequenced, remixed, and expanded version of the group's 1993 debut, *See the Sound*. It's flat-out terrific, with "Jessica Something" offering an opportunity to sway in tribute to love's lost opportunity, while "Can't Get Through," "For Free," "It Could Take Years," "In Time," and "Four Letter Man" keep the party moving and the dance floor crowded. And "Nowhere Left to Turn" is a masterpiece, one of the two or three best power-pop records of the whole decade, the kind of my-God-where-did-*this*-come-from?! tune that stops you dead in your tracks and convinces you there really is hope for the future of rock 'n' roll.

the rest:
See the Sound ♪♪♪ (Fried, 1993)
De la Vina ♪♪♪ (Fried, 1996)

influences:
◀◀ The Plimsouls, the Beatles, the Beat, 20/20, the Romantics

Carl Cafarelli

The Teardrop Explodes
See: Julian Cope

Tears for Fears
Formed 1982, in Bath, England.

Roland Orzabal (born Roland Jaime Orzabal de la Quintana), guitar, vocals, keyboards; Curt Smith, bass, vocals, keyboards (1982–92).

Bonded by early friendship, tough childhoods, and an interest in psychotherapist Arthur Janov's primal scream therapy, Roland Orzabal and Curt Smith founded Tears for Fears in an ef-

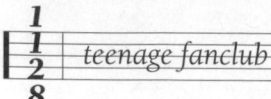

fort to give Janov's concepts a musical voice. Though their sound began as a typically overwrought blend of new wave synthesizers and despondent British nilhism, later albums revealed a knack for songcraft and textured, complex arrangements that brought swift commercial success. Unfortunately, creative differences forced Smith out of the band during the early '90s, allowing Orzabal to craft increasingly self-absorbed and pointless albums that, not surprisingly, have reached fewer and fewer fans.

what to buy: Combining flawless, forward-looking pop tunes with innovative production and accomplished musicianship, *Songs from the Big Chair* ♪♪♪♪♪ (Mercury, 1985, prod. Chris Hughes) provided the group's commercial breakthrough. From the drum machine-fueled hit "Shout" to the percolating, dreamy vibe of "Everybody Wants to Rule the World" and the mechanized, percussive "Mothers Talk," the album proved a perfect blend of inspired songwriting and creative arrangements.

what to buy next: The next effort, *The Seeds of Love* ♪♪♪♪ (Mercury, 1989, prod. David Bascombe, Tears for Fears), enlarged the band's vision to an epic canvas, with help from a veritable army of support players that included Oleta Adams and Phil Collins. The inspired Beatles update "Sowing the Seeds of Love" references the best of '60s psychedelic pop without resorting to empty mimicry, while the atmospheric "Woman in Chains" and expansive rock/gospel workout "Badman's Song" affixes Adams's spine-tingling vocals to even better melodies.

what to avoid: Despite two interesting songs—"Pale Shelter" and "Mad World"—the group's debut, *The Hurting* ♪♪ (Mercury, 1983, prod. Chris Hughes, Ross Cullum) is mostly a tired, formulaic melding of pop angst and dated keyboard sounds.

the rest:
Tears Roll Down (Greatest Hits, 1982–1992) ♪♪♪♪ (Mercury, 1992)
Elemental ♪♪♪ (Mercury, 1993)
Raoul and the Kings of Spain ♪♪♪ (Epic, 1995)
Saturnine Martial and Lunatic ♪♪♪ (PolyGram, 1996)

worth searching for: The import CD-5 for *Laid So Low (Tears Roll Down)* (Mercury/Fontana, 1992) includes two new songs that signaled the transition into the Smith-less Tears.

solo outings:
Curt Smith:
Soul on Board ♪♪♪ (Mercury, 1993)

influences:
◄◄ The Beatles, Bauhaus, Kraftwerk

►► Oleta Adams

Eric Deggans

Teenage Fanclub

Formed 1989, in Glasgow, Scotland.

Norman Blake, guitars, vocals; Raymond McGinley, guitar, vocals; Gerard Love, bass, vocals; Francis McDonald, drums (1989–90); Brendan O'Hare, drums (1990–94); Paul Quinn, drums (1994–present).

Listen to Teenage Fanclub for 15 seconds and it's obvious these guys are huge fans of Alex Chilton and Neil Young (not to mention the Beach Boys and the Beatles). But the quartet is much greater than the sum of its influences; carrying the best of '60s-rock styles into the noisy '90s, Teenage Fanclub's distorted punk-pop tunes are nothing short of intoxicating.

what to buy: *Bandwagonesque* ♪♪♪♪♪ (DGC, 1991, prod. Don Fleming, Paul Chisholm, Teenage Fanclub) was greeted as Album of the Year by *Spin* magazine, and while that might be pushing it (after all, Nirvana's *Nevermind* also came out in '91), the album *is* a brilliant melange of post-punk guitar gauze and classic pop melodies, particlarly "The Concept."

the rest:
A Catholic Education ♪♪♪ (Matador, 1990)
Thirteen ♪♪♪ (DGC, 1993)
Grand Prix ♪♪♪♪ (DGC, 1995)
Songs from Northern Britain ♪♪♪♪ (Columbia, 1997)

influences:
◄◄ Neil Young, the Beatles, the Beach Boys, Big Star/Alex Chilton

►► Weezer, Third Eye Blind

Thor Christensen

DJ Towa Tei

See: Deee-Lite

Television

Formed 1973, in New York, NY. Disbanded 1978. Re-formed 1991. Disbanded 1993.

Tom Verlaine (born Thomas Miller), guitar, vocals; Richard Lloyd, guitar; Billy Ficca, drums; Richard Hell (born Richard Myers), bass (1973–75); Fred Smith, bass (1975–78, 1991–93).

Despite a marked lack of commercial success, the two albums Television recorded for Elektra Records during the late '70s are among the most important and influential of the post-punk era. While Television was born to the punk scene, it quickly set itself apart with a successful combination of intellectual lyrical themes and stunningly creative musical applications. The group appropriated the intensity and raw energy of punk, the introspective lyrical style of the city's thriving poetry community, and sense of musical freedom enjoyed by the jazz scene. Unlike most rock bands, Television eschewed a blues foundation, resulting in a loud, guitar-based sound that was complex and often beautifully lyrical, with balanced measures of improvisation and painstaking structure. The result was music that matched art rock's intricacy and invention and yet retained the accessibility and immediate pleasures of the best garage rock: manna for the thinking guitar freak. Unfortunately, the band's skill at music was accompanied by strong personalities that often clashed. It disbanded after the release of its second album, reuniting in 1991 for an album and tour before the old problems surfaced and split the group again.

what to buy: *Marquee Moon* 🎵🎵🎵🎵 (Elektra, 1977, prod. Andy Johns, Tom Verlaine) is Television's undisputed masterpiece and a landmark in modern rock. Tom Verlaine and Richard Lloyd achieve guitar nirvana; drawing on the Allman Brothers' technique of harmonized guitar lines, the pair limn songs such as "See No Evil" and "Torn Curtain" with delicate melodic passages that soothe the angular attack of the rhythm parts and countermelody the vocals. *Marquee Moon* manages to simultaneously evoke the influence of mediative acts such as the Velvet Underground and Talking Heads and the aggressive virtuosity and arranging skills of bands like the Allmans and Led Zeppelin.

what to buy next: *Adventure* 🎵🎵🎵 (Elektra, 1978, prod. John Jansen, Tom Verlaine) is an over-produced, watered-down version of *Marquee Moon* that still manages to be brilliant and commanding.

what to avoid: Released four years after the band broke up, *The Blow Up*, 🎵🎵 (ROIR, 1982) attempts to provide some kind of insight into Television's volatile live shows. Recorded live at the band's New York base, CBGB, the album's poor sound quality makes it only of interest for die-hard Television/Verlaine fans.

the rest:
Television 🎵🎵🎵 (Capitol, 1992)

worth searching for: There are two early Television recordings that predate *Marquee Moon* and are worthwhile as precursors to that opus: the single, "Little Johnny Jewel" (Ork, 1976) and the British EP *Television* (Stiff, 1976).

solo outings:
Tom Verlaine:

Tom Verlaine 🎵🎵🎵🎵 (Elektra, 1979)
Dreamtime 🎵🎵🎵 (Warner Bros., 1981)
Words from the Front 🎵🎵🎵 (Warner Bros., 1982)
Cover 🎵🎵🎵🎵 (Warner Bros., 1984)
Flashlight 🎵🎵🎵🎵 (I.R.S., 1987)
Warm and Cool 🎵🎵🎵🎵 (Rykodisc, 1992)

Richard Lloyd:
Alchemy 🎵🎵🎵🎵 (Elektra, 1980)

Field of Fire 🎵🎵🎵 (Celluloid, 1985)
Real Time 🎵🎵🎵 (Celluloid/Grand Slamm, 1987)

influences:

◀◀ Bob Dylan, Roky Erikson, the Velvet Underground, Neil Young, Allman Brothers Band, Led Zeppelin, the Beach Boys, David Bowie, John Coltrane, Charlie Parker, Miles Davis

▶▶ Matthew Sweet, the Heartbreakers, Robyn Hitchcock/Soft Boys, Blondie, the Pixies, Sonic Youth, R.E.M., the Feelies, XTC, Eleventh Dream Day, My Bloody Valentine, the Breeders, the Cars, Durutti Column, Material Issue, the Posies, Game Theory, Urge Overkill, the dB's, Big Star

see also: *Richard Hell & the Voidoids*

David Galens

Temple of the Dog
See: Pearl Jam

The Temptations
Formed 1961, in Detroit, MI.

Otis Williams (born Otis Miles), vocals; Eddie Kendricks (died October 5, 1992), vocals (1961–72); Paul Williams (died August 17, 1973), vocals (1971–72); Melvin Franklin (born David English; died February 23, 1995), vocals (1971–95); Elbridge Bryant, vocals (1961–63); David Ruffin (died June 1, 1991), vocals (1963–68); Dennis Edwards, vocals (1968–77, 1979–83, 1986–87); Ricky Owens, vocals (1972); Damon Harris, vocals (1972–75); Richard Street, vocals (1972–93); Glenn Leonard, vocals (1975–83); Louis Price, vocals (1977–79); Ron Tyson, vocals (1983–present); Ali Ollie Woodson, vocals (1983–86, 1987–97); Theo Peoples, vocals (1993–97); Ray Davis, vocals (1995–97); Barrington Henderson, vocals (1997–present); Terry Weeks, vocals (1997–present); Harry McGillberry, vocals (1997–present).

With respect to the Four Tops—who deserve much credit for their longevity and wonderful body of work—the Temptations are *it* when it comes to Motown male vocal groups. The visceral power of the Tempts' five voices combined with its high-stepping stage show (a cross between the Tops' smooth 'n' natural and the Contours' chaos) super-charged the vocal group model to another level; when you hear "Get Ready," it's not just a song—it's a command. The Tempts' history is both blessed and cursed. It's been blessed with some otherwordly lead singers (Paul Williams, David Ruffin, Eddie Kendricks, Dennis Edwards) and some of Motown's top producers and writers (Smokey Robinson, Norman Whitfield). The group has had some luck, too; Robinson and Ronnie White could have kept "My Girl" for their own group, the Miracles. But the Tempts' dominance came with a price; four members are dead from tragic circumstances (suicide, drug OD, lung cancer, a brain seizure). Otis

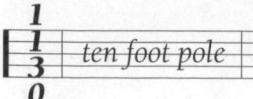
Williams, the band's biographer, is the sole founding member left, but he's been carrying the torch through decades of internal squabbling and ego battles. The Temptations of today surely aren't on a par with the classic lineup of the 1960s, but the incredible battery of songs—"The Way You Do the Things You Do," "Girl (Why You Wanna Make Me Blue)," "Ain't Too Proud to Beg," "I Wish It Would Rain," "Cloud Nine," "Just My Imagination (Running Away with Me)"—usually will out.

what to buy: *The Temptations Anthology* 𝄞𝄞𝄞𝄞 (Motown, 1995, prod. various) packs 46 hits onto two CDs, with not a bad note to be found.

what to buy next: A more total—and worthwhile—immersion can be made with *Emperors of Soul* 𝄞𝄞𝄞𝄞 (Motown, 1995, prod. various), a regally titled box set that, at five discs, needs to be considered before purchase. *One by One* 𝄞𝄞𝄞𝄞 (Motown, 1995, prod. various) offers a well chosen collection of solo recordings by Kendricks, Ruffin, Edwards, and Paul Williams. *The Temptations Sing Smokey* 𝄞𝄞𝄞𝄞 (Motown, 1965/1989, prod. Smokey Robinson) is a nicely conceived collaboration between the Tempts and one of the group's chief patrons.

what to avoid: After all that great music, it's hard to swallow *For Lovers Only* 𝄞𝄞 (Motown, 1995, prod. Richard Perry) and its lush covers of "Some Enchanted Evening," "Night and Day," and "You Send Me."

the rest:
Meet the Temptations 𝄞𝄞𝄞 (Motown, 1964/1992)
The Temptin' Temptations 𝄞𝄞𝄞 (Motown, 1965/1990)
Gettin' Ready 𝄞𝄞𝄞𝄞 (Motown, 1966/1989)
Greatest Hits, Vol. 1 𝄞𝄞𝄞𝄞 (Motown, 1966)
In a Mellow Mood 𝄞𝄞𝄞 (Motown, 1967/1969)
I Wish It Would Rain 𝄞𝄞𝄞 (Motown, 1968)
Cloud Nine 𝄞𝄞𝄞 (Motown, 1969)
Psychedelic Shack 𝄞𝄞𝄞 (Motown, 1970/1989)
Puzzle People 𝄞𝄞𝄞𝄞 (Motown, 1970/1989)
Christmas Card 𝄞𝄞𝄞 (Motown, 1970/1989)
Give Love at Christmas 𝄞𝄞𝄞 (Motown)
Greatest Hits, Vol. 2 𝄞𝄞𝄞𝄞 (Motown, 1970)
Sky's the Limit 𝄞𝄞𝄞 (Motown, 1971/1990)
All Directions 𝄞𝄞𝄞 (Motown, 1972)
Masterpiece 𝄞𝄞𝄞𝄞 (Motown, 1973/1989)
A Song for You 𝄞𝄞𝄞 (Motown, 1975)
All the Million Sellers 𝄞𝄞𝄞𝄞 (Motown, 1981)
Reunion 𝄞𝄞𝄞 (Motown, 1982)
Great Songs & Performances That Inspired Motown 25 𝄞𝄞𝄞𝄞 (Motown, 1983)
Truly for You 𝄞𝄞 (Motown, 1984/1989)
To Be Continued 𝄞𝄞𝄞 (Motown, 1986)
Special 𝄞𝄞 (Motown, 1989)
Milestone 𝄞𝄞𝄞 (Motown, 1991)

Hum Along and Dance: More of the Best (1963–1974) 𝄞𝄞𝄞𝄞 (Rhino, 1993)
Motown Legends: My Girl—(I Know) I'm Losing You 𝄞𝄞𝄞 (ESX, 1994)
Motown Legends: Just My Imagination—Beauty Is Only Skin Deep 𝄞𝄞𝄞 (ESX, 1994)
The Ultimate Collection 𝄞𝄞𝄞𝄞 (Motown, 1997)
Phoenix Rising: Temptations 4-ever 𝄞𝄞 (Motown, 1998)

worth searching for: You may not be able to see 'em, but the Tempts' voices on *Temptations Live!* (Motown, 1967) convey enough of the show's excitement to compensate.

solo outings:
Eddie Kendricks:
People Hold On 𝄞𝄞𝄞 (Motown, 1972/1991)
At His Best 𝄞𝄞𝄞𝄞 (Motown, 1990)

David Ruffin:
At His Best 𝄞𝄞𝄞𝄞 (Motown, 1991)

Jimmy & David Ruffin
Motown Superstar Series, Vol. 8 𝄞𝄞𝄞 (Motown)

influences:
◀◀ The Soul Stirrers, the Falcons, the Drifters
▶▶ The Jackson 5, the Commodores, the Ohio Players, Maze

Gary Graff

Ten Foot Pole /Scared Straight

Formed 1983, in Simi Valley, CA.

Dennis Jagard, vocals, guitar; Scott Radinsky, vocals (1986–95); Steve Carnan, guitar (1984–present); Peter Inu, bass (1992–96); Glen, bass (1996–present); Jordan Lieberman, drums (1983–93); Tony Smurd, drums (1993–present).

The West Coast power punk band Ten Foot Pole sounds similar to a host of other fast, melodic bands on the Fat Wreck Chords/Epitaph record label, but in fact, it was formed years before most of the others. For the first decade of its career, TFP was Scared Straight and played Oxnard, California–style hardcore. Scared Straight recorded and toured on and off for a decade, though its schedule was extremely limited because frontman Scott Radinsky's day-job (pitching for the Chicago White Sox), restricted the band's activities to the off-season. Before touring behind its 1993 Fat Wreck Chords debut *Swill*, on which the band adopted its current style, Scared Straight changed its name to Ten Foot Pole. Later, Radinsky, who currently pitches for the Los Angeles Dodgers, split with the group so it could spend more time on the road; he currently plays with the Epitaph supergroup Pulley during the off-season.

what to buy: *Rev* 🎵🎵🎵 (Epitaph, 1994, prod. Sally Browder, Ten Foot Pole) captures TFP at its height, shortly before the departure of founding member Radinsky. With philosophical lyrics (mostly penned by guitarist Dennis Jaggerd) atypical of West Coast punk bands, TFP shines in songs like the reflective "Old Man" and "Closer to Grey" and the breakneck punk anthem "My Wall."

what to buy next: *Unleashed* 🎵🎵 (Epitaph, 1997, prod. Ryan Greene) is the full-length debut by the latest incarnation of the band, with Jaggerd taking over vocal duties in addition to playing guitar. Its "character study" lyrics continue to prove that TFP's strength is its interesting lyrics, not its run-of-the-mill West Coast punk music.

what to avoid: Scared Straight's little-known debut album *You Drink, You Drive, You Die* 🎵 (Mystic, 1988, prod. Scared Straight) was recorded in 1985, but Mystic released it in 1988 while the band was on hiatus. Without the band's input, the label chose a title and picked photographs that attempted to portray it as a straight-edge band. This prompted Scared Straight to later change its name to the less-confusing moniker Ten Foot Pole.

worth searching for: Sweden's Bad Taste Records released a 1995 split seven-inch single featuring TFP and the acclaimed Swedish garage band Satanic Surfers. Avid Pole fans will appreciate this final recording made by the band's classic lineup. Out of print, *Swill* (Ten Foot/Fat Wreck Chords, 1993, prod. Ten Foot Pole) was recorded shortly before Scared Straight changed its name to Ten Foot Pole and features Radinsky on vocals. Only 10,000 were pressed.

influences:

◀◀ Bad Religion, NOFX

▶▶ Pulley, Strung Out

Seth Hindin

10,000 Maniacs /Natalie Merchant

Formed 1981, in Jamestown, NY.

Natalie Merchant (born October 26, 1963 in Jamestown, NY), vocals (1981–93); Mary Ramsey, vocals (1995–present); John Lombardo, guitar (1981–86, 1995–present); Robert Buck, guitar; Steven Gustafson, bass; Dennis Drew, keyboards; Jerry Augustyniak, drums.

Rarely in rock history has there been an ensemble more woefully misnamed than 10,000 Maniacs. Starting out as a reggae-influenced dance band mixing originals with everything from the Andrews Sisters' "Rum and Coca Cola" to obscure Roxy Music and Gang of Four covers, the group eventually jelled into a melodic, politically minded folk-pop act that brought a refreshing dose of depth and discipline to the mid-'80s college-rock scene. Lead singer Natalie Merchant, always the visual focus with her giddy spins, sang with a soothing, seductive clarity that softened her commentaries on alcoholism ("Don't Talk"), poverty ("Dust Bowl"), and media pandering ("Candy Everybody Wants"). That precarious balance shifted on 1992's *Our Time in Eden* as Merchant's heavy-handed lyrics weighed down the band's denser, more-brooding sound. Her 1993 departure to launch a solo career suggested that she would move in a different direction, but her pensive solo debut, *Tigerlily*, was surprisingly similar to her Maniacs work, even though her live performances were sparked by energetic romps through Aretha Franklin's "Baby I Love You" and the Rolling Stones' "Sympathy for the Devil." The group continues without her, drafting violinist-vocalist Mary Ramsey and original Maniacs guitarist John Lombardo (who had recorded two albums for Rykodisc as John & Mary) for 1996's pleasant but underwhelming *Love among the Ruins*.

what to buy: Despite such heavy-handed topics as child abuse ("What's the Matter Here?"), war ("Gun Shy"), alcoholism ("Don't Talk"), and illiteracy ("The Cherry Tree"), *In My Tribe* 🎵🎵🎵🎵 (Elektra, 1987, prod. Peter Asher) is surprisingly melodic and upbeat. Driven more by resilience than resignation, the songs gain impact from Merchant's ability to put a face on her platforms, telling compelling stories rather than just telling us what to think. Original pressings contained a cover of Cat Stevens's "Peace Train" that was removed at the band's request after the author, a devout Muslim, put a bounty on the head of *The Satanic Verses* author Salman Rushdie.

what to buy next: *The Wishing Chair* 🎵🎵🎵 (Elektra, 1985, prod. Joe Boyd), the band's major-label debut, foreshadows Merchant's socio-political concerns but also exudes an infectious innocence on "Can't Ignore the Train" and "Back o' the Moon."

what to avoid: *Hope Chest* 🎵🎵 (Elektra, 1990, prod. Albert Garzon, 10,000 Maniacs) is a remixed compilation of the band's sonically anemic indie releases — 1982's *Human Conflict No. 5* EP and 1983's *Secrets of the I Ching* — that find it zig-zagging from reggae to pop to punk.

the rest:

Blind Man's Zoo 🎵🎵🎵 (Elektra, 1989)
Our Time in Eden 🎵🎵🎵 (Elektra, 1992)
MTV Unplugged 🎵🎵🎵 (Elektra, 1993)
Love among the Ruins 🎵🎵🎵 (Geffen, 1997)

worth searching for: The CD single for "Few and Far Between" (Elektra, 1993) sports non-LP live duets with Michael Stipe on Lulu's "To Sir with Love" and David Byrne on Iris DeMent's "Let the Mystery Be."

Natalie Merchant of 10,000 Maniacs (© Ken Settle)

solo outings:

Natalie Merchant:

Tigerlily 🎵🎵🎵 (Elektra, 1995)
Ophelia 🎵🎵🎵 (Elektra, 1998)

John & Mary:

Victory Gardens 🎵🎵🎵 (Rykodisc, 1991)
The Weedkiller's Daughter 🎵🎵🎵 (Rykodisc, 1993)

influences:

◀◀ R.E.M., Fairport Convention, Patti Smith, Bob Marley

▶▶ The Nields, Innocence Mission, Freedy Johnston

David Okamoto

Ten Years After

Formed 1967, in Nottingham, England. Disbanded 1974. Re-formed 1989.

Alvin Lee, guitar, vocals; Chick Churchill, keyboards; Leo Lyons, bass; Ric Lee, drums.

Before there was "Stairway to Heaven" or "Free Bird," Ten Years After held the Bic lighter-inducing crown for "I'm Going Home," a crunching, bruising blues-rocker that lit up the Woodstock festival in a 13-minute version that featured seemingly endless (and if you were on acid, it probably was) improvised riffing by Alvin Lee. Playing electrifying blues at a peace 'n' love gathering is kind of the way TYA does things; it'll crank up the volume with something like "Baby Let Me Rock 'n' Roll You," but then the group will glide into something fuzzy and trippy like its biggest hit, "I'd Love to Change the World." Always a workhorse, Lee has kept playing with his own band, though he did bring TYA together for an album and tour in 1989.

what to buy: *Cricklewood Green* 🎵🎵🎵🎵 (Deram, 1970, prod. Ten Years After) is the group's most mature and varied effort, striding from the bravado of "Love like a Man" through the psychedilia of "50,000 Miles beneath My Brain" to the almost jazzy swing of "Me and My Baby."

what to buy next: *Essential Ten Years After* 🎵🎵🎵 (Chrysalis, 1991, prod. various) gets you most of what you'd want—with a nicely annotated booklet, too—although it leaves some good tracks off and includes a live rendition of "I'm Going Home" recorded somewhere other than Woodstock.

what to avoid: Take your pick of a fair share of leaden, same-sounding albums—a category that holds both *Stonehenge* 🎵🎵 (Deram, 1969, prod. Mike Vernon) or *Watt* 🎵🎵 (Deram/Chrysalis, 1970, prod. Chris Wright)

the rest:

Undead 🎵🎵 (Deram, 1968)
A Space in Time 🎵🎵 (Columbia, 1971/Chrysalis, 1989)
Greatest Hits 🎵🎵🎵 (Deram)

Rock & Roll Music to the World 🎵🎵🎵 (Columbia, 1972/Chrysalis, 1989)
Recorded Live 🎵🎵🎵 (Columbia, 1973/Chrysalis, 1989)
Live at Reading 🎵🎵🎵 (Dutch East India, 1983)
Collection 🎵🎵🎵 (Griffin, 1994)

worth searching for: What else would a fan want—"I'm Going Home" live at Woodstock, either via one of the Woodstock albums or on the out-of-print TYA collection *Universal* (Chrysalis, 1987)

solo outings:

Alvin Lee:

Zoom 🎵🎵🎵 (Viceroy, 1992)
Nineteen Ninety Four 🎵🎵 (Thunderbolt, 1993)
I Hear You Rockin' 🎵🎵 (Viceroy, 1994)
Pure Blues 🎵🎵🎵 (EMI, 1995)
Live in Vienna 🎵🎵 (Viceroy, 1996)

influences:

◀◀ John Lee Hooker, John Mayall's Bluesbreakers, Jimi Hendrix

▶▶ George Thorogood & the Destroyers, Molly Hatchet, Stevie Ray Vaughan

Gary Graff

10cc

Formed 1972, in London, England. Disbanded 1982. Re-formed 1991.

Lol Creme, guitars, keyboards, vocals (1972–76); Kevin Godley, drums, vocals (1972–76); Graham Gouldman, guitars, keyboards, vocals; Eric Stewart, guitars, keyboards, vocals; Paul Burgess, drums (1976–77); Rick Fenn, guitars, vocals (1977–82); Tony O'Malley, keyboards (1977–82); Stuart Tosh, drums, vocals (1977–82).

Taking its name from the average volume of fluid produced by a certain procreative act, 10cc's chief tools were witty lyrics, hooky songwriting, and tight harmonies. When the group was able to avoid a certain proclivity towards sappiness, it produced some of the more distinctive pop of the middle '70s. 10cc hit the charts quickly in its native England, but U.S. recognition didn't come until 1975's "I'm Not in Love" became a pillow talk smash. Unfortunately, the band followed this success with only one more album before splitting into two camps: Kevin Godley and Lol Creme recorded as a duo and directed some groundbreaking music videos, scoring their own hit with 1985's "Cry," while Graham Gouldman and Eric Stewart kept the 10cc moniker alive. But neither fragment lived up to the commercial or artistic promise of the foursome.

what to buy: The fact that it contains the biggest hit isn't the only reason to grab *The Original Soundtrack* 🎵🎵🎵🎵 (PolyGram, 1975, prod. 10cc). A solid effort top to bottom, it showcases the band at its literate best, including "The Second Sitting for the Last Supper" and the quirkily metaphorical "Life Is a Minestrone." *Two Classic Albums* 𝄢𝄢𝄢 (DCC Compact Classics, 1990, prod. 10cc) puts the band's first two records—*10cc* and *Sheet Music*—on a single CD containing the U.K. hits "Rubber Bullets," "The Wall Street Shuffle," and "Silly Love."

what to buy next: *The Very Best of 10cc* 𝄢𝄢𝄢 (Mercury, 1997) is arranged chronologically, so you can have fun charting the band's progress from magnificence to mush. *How Dare You* 𝄢𝄢𝄢 (PolyGram, 1976, prod. 10cc) was the last effort by the complete band. There isn't a standout track, but it holds its own with the essential titles.

what to avoid: Virtually everything else is only for hardcore fans, particularly *The King Biscuit Flower Hour Presents 10cc in Concert* 𝄢 (KBFH, 1995), a live radio show from 1975 that proves that the band's complex vocal arrangements were best kept to the safe confines of the studio.

the rest:
Deceptive Bends 𝄢 (PolyGram, 1977)
Mirror, Mirror 𝄢 (Critique, 1995)

worth searching for: Collectors may be interested in the recently re-mastered import versions of *The Original Soundtrack* and *How Dare You*. They contain, respectively, one and two previously unreleased bonus tracks.

influences:

◀◀ The Beach Boys, the Hollies, Badfinger, the Beatles

▶▶ Barenaked Ladies, They Might Be Giants

Gary Plochinski

Terminator X
See: Public Enemy

Tesla
Formed 1984, in Sacramento, CA. Disbanded 1996.

Jeff Keith, vocals; Tommy Skeoch, guitar (1984–95); Frank Hannon, guitar; Brian Wheat, bass; Troy Luccketta, drums.

Although labeled a hair-metal band, Tesla had more in common with the unadorned, workmanlike '70s classic rock of Led Zeppelin and Aerosmith than the slick, processed pop-metal of Whitesnake, Poison, and Ratt. And it scores a point or two for naming itself after the groundbreaking but little-known scientist Nikola Tesla. One of the most faceless million-selling bands to come out of the '80s hard rock scene, Tesla's vigorous, big-bottomed music had a fierce rock 'n' roll energy and demonstrated a studied sense of '70s-style rock dynamics. But it lacked both the flamboyance and cutting-edge style of the most popular '80s rock. As such, the band's melodic, blues-influenced output has held up better than that of most of its less-than-conservative contemporaries. Called City Kidd at first, the five-piece band

was one of the first rock groups to record an acoustic album; its 1990 hit release, *Five Man Acoustical Jam*, anticipated the *MTV Unplugged* trend. After sales of its next two albums sagged and guitarist Tommy Skeoch was kicked out for substance abuse problems, Tesla released a greatest hits album in 1995 that included the only song it ever recorded as a four-piece, the new "Steppin' Over." The following year the band broke up.

what to buy: While the ballad "Love Song" was the album's big hit, *The Great Radio Controversy* 𝄢𝄢𝄢𝄢 (Geffen, 1988, prod. Steve Thompson, Michael Barbiero) is highlighted by the backwater-flavored swagger of "Heaven's Trail (No Way Out)," the piano-flavored "Lazy Days, Crazy Nights," and the winsome "Paradise."

what to buy next: The unplugged *Five Man Acoustical Jam* 𝄢𝄢𝄢𝄢 (Geffen, 1990, prod. Dan McClendon) features a wide array of covers—the Five Man Electrical Band's "Signs," Creedence Clearwater Revival's "Lodi," the Grateful Dead's "Truckin'," and reworked originals including the hit "Modern Day Cowboy."

what to avoid: *Bust a Nut* 𝄢𝄢 (Geffen, 1994, prod. Terry Thomas) is bland, tasteless, corporate rock—and a lousy title to boot. *Psychotic Supper* 𝄢 (Geffen, 1991) is even worse.

the rest:
Mechanical Resonance 𝄢𝄢𝄢 (Geffen, 1986)
Time's Makin' Changes: The Best of Tesla 𝄢𝄢𝄢 (Geffen, 1995)

worth searching for: *Electric, Acoustic and Psychotic* (Geffen, 1992, prod. various), a 12-song promotional sampler from the fist four albums, makes a nice collector's piece.

influences:

◀◀ Queen, Led Zeppelin, Rolling Stones, Aerosmith, Def Leppard, AC/DC, Rush

▶▶ Poison, Guns N' Roses

Josh Freedom du Lac

Texas
Formed 1987, in Glasgow, Scotland.

Sharleen Spiteri, vocals, guitar; Ally McErlaine, guitar; John McElhone, bass; Stuart Kerr, drums, vocals.

Don't expect any roots music from this band; Texas has as much to do with the moody textures and boxed-in sound of Scottish '80s pop/rock as it does with the sort of open-desert blues-rock that the name would suggest. The focus of the group is vocalist Sharleen Spiteri's spectacular voice, though it's debatable whether the band's sometimes bland modern-rock backing and often undistinguished material is the best showcase for it. Still, the group has enjoyed much worldwide success, though to a lesser degree in the United States.

what to buy: The band's debut, *Southside* 🎵🎵🎵 (Mercury, 1989, prod. Tim Palmer) is the best starting point, with the strongest set of songs. Spiteri was already in fine voice by this point, sounding like a more contained Bonnie Raitt/Linda Ronstadt hybrid, and the then-19-year-old McErlaine had already developed quite a hang for the slide guitar. "I Don't Need a Lover" is a solid single, with a tight beat and technopop production reminiscent of the Eurythmics.

what to buy next: *Ricks Road* 🎵🎵🎵 (Mercury, 1994, prod. Paul Fox) contains the semi-hit "So-called Friend," which serves as a looser sequel to "I Don't Need a Lover."

the rest:
Mothers Heaven 🎵🎵 (Mercury, 1991)
White on Blonde 🎵🎵🎵 (Mercury, 1997)

influences:
◀◀ Lone Justice, Linda Ronstadt, the Eurythmics

Bob Remstein

The Texas Tornados

Formed 1989, in San Francisco, CA.

Doug Sahm, vocals, guitar; Freddy Fender, vocals, guitar; Flaco Jimenez, accordion, vocals; Augie Meyers, keyboards, vocals.

For those in pursuit of encyclopedic knowledge of Texas music over the past three decades or so, you could do a lot worse than to begin your search with a serious study of the Texas Tornados. From the Anglo side come rockers Doug Sahm and Augie Meyers, who brought arid border breezes to the rest of the nation during the '60s with the Sir Douglas Quintet and songs like "She's about a Mover" and "Mendocino." From the Latino side come balladeer non pareil Freddy Fender, who charted with "Wasted Days and Wasted Nights" and "Before the Next Teardrop Falls," and accordionist Flaco Jimenez, who has enjoyed crossover success by rocking up traditional Mexican conjunto and Norteno styles. The Tornados play party music, pure and simple, with an occasional Fender ballad thrown in like a couple of swigs of cerveza between bites of hot Texas chili. As mercurial as the individual members of the group are, that they can get together to make music that is this engaging—aw, hell, just plain fun—is nothing short of awe-inspiring.

what to buy: The Tornados' best individual album is their debut, *Texas Tornados* 🎵🎵🎵 (Reprise, 1990, prod. Bill Halverson, Texas Tornados). Mixing Spanish and English throughout, the group scores with the Sir Douglas–style "Who Were You Thinkin' Of" and the high-stepping conjunto number "(Hey Baby) Que Paso." Fender contributes the heart-tugging ballad "A Man Can Cry," and Sahm takes an admirable run at Butch Hancock's brilliant "She Never Spoke Spanish to Me." The album is also available in a Spanish-only version, *Los Texas Tornados* 🎵🎵🎵🎵 (Reprise, 1990, prod. Bill Halverson, Texas Tornados).

what to buy next: *The Best of Texas Tornados* 🎵🎵🎵🎵 (Reprise, 1994, prod. Bill Halverson, Texas Tornados) is just that, collecting tunes from each of their albums, including updates of Fender's "Wasted Days and Wasted Nights" and Sahm's "Is Anybody Goin' to San Antone."

what to avoid: *The Nada Mixes* **woof!** (Reprise, 1997) contains dance remixes of "A Little Bit Is Better than Nada" from 1995's *4 Aces*. In this case, nada would have been better.

the rest:
Hangin' on by a Thread 🎵🎵🎵🎵 (Reprise, 1991)
Zone of Our Own 🎵🎵🎵 (Reprise, 1992)
4 Aces 🎵🎵🎵🎵 (Reprise, 1995)

influences:
◀◀ Santiago Jimenez, the Dave Clark Five, Ritchie Valens, Bob Dylan

▶▶ Emilio, Los Lobos, Santiago Jimenez Jr.

see also: *Doug Sahm*

Daniel Durchholz

that dog.

Formed 1993, in Los Angeles, CA. Disbanded 1997.

Anna Waronker, lead vocals, piano, guitar; Petra Haden, vocals, violins; Rachel Haden, vocals, bass; Tony Maxwell, drums, percussion, guitar.

The group that dog. shouldn't have been able to pull off its catchy mix of dilettantish pop-rock and prefab image-mongering. Like Redd Kross, with whom it shares an adjunct member, that dog. pre-dated the L.A. pop resurgence but broke up before it had a chance to catch on. That's a shame, because despite the familiar ingredients in its sound, that dog. could have taught newer bands some old tricks.

what to buy: *Retreat from the Sun* 🎵🎵🎵🎵 (Geffen, 1997, prod. Brad Wood, that dog.) finds a nifty new area that sounds like a looser, less-angular Breeders. It's tainted only by the band's amateurish playing and barely twining vocals—if that dog. sounds this way on record, you'd swear their live shows must be held together by scotch tape. Still, the album is full of buzzing hooks and a wider array of influences than usually found in alt-rock—everything from new wave synthesizers on "Never Say Never" to West Coast harmonies on the title track, with violins and cellos stringing it all along. A tremendous record in spite of itself.

what to buy next: *Totally Crushed Out* 🎵🎵🎵 (DGC, 1995, prod. Tom Grimley, Rob Cavallo, Paul du Gre') is a wonderful leap forward from that dog.'s debut. Although the chord changes still sometimes sound illogical and the vocals slip off the on-key chain, the charm of that dog.—sort of the Left Banke infested with the Roches, all on the Ramones' turf—begins to sparkle. The baroque-in-half "She Doesn't Know How" and the high harmonies on songs like "Ms. Wrong" lift that dog. above its amateurism like an air balloon.

what to avoid: *that dog.* ♪ (DGC, 1994, prod. that dog.) is the band's cuddly-but-untrained puppy, on a new leash that didn't let that dog. wander far from melody and discipline.

influences:

◀◀ The Go-Go's, Salem 66, Blondie

▶▶ The Donnas

Jordan Oakes

That Petrol Emotion

Formed 1985, in London, England.

Sean O'Neill, guitar (1985–88); Damian O'Neill, bass, guitars; Reamann O'Gormain (a.k.a. Raymond Gorman), guitar; Ciaran McLaughlin, drums; Steve Mack, vocals; John Marchini, bass (1989–92); Brendan Kelly, bass (1992–94).

When legendary Irish punk-pop band the Undertones disbanded in 1983, two of that band's members, brothers Sean and Damian O'Neill, moved to London. There, they enlisted the talents of fellow Irishmen Reamann O'Gormain and Ciaran McLaughlin and American Steve Mack to form That Petrol Emotion in 1985. Fueled by political ardor and a dual-guitar attack, the Petrols melded the pop sensibilities of the Undertones into something much more visceral. And, although the Petrol's members made no bones about their political sympathies—the liner notes to early albums contained excerpts from essays on England's oppression of the Irish—their lyrics generally avoided overt political rhetoric. Over the course of five albums, TPE cut a wide swath through its musical influences, drawing from punk, funk, blues, and everything in between. Of course, such diversity and experimentation often meant that the band was not always in the right musical place at the right time—the effervescent rock-oriented dance hits "Big Decision" and "Hey, Venus" were notable exceptions. Critics gushed over the band's first two albums, *Manic Pop Thrill* and *Babble*, and its last, the unexpectedly solid *Fireproof*, but it wasn't enough. The Petrols' efforts to synthesize the language and attitude of dance music with traditional guitar rock had limited commercial appeal. The band called it quits in 1994 and only two of the members, Sean and Steve, graduated to work with other bands (Rare and Anodyne, respectively) in any permanent fashion.

what to buy: *Fireproof* ♪♪♪♪ (Rykodisc, 1994, prod. That Petrol Emotion) ranks with the band's finest work, opening with "Detonate My Dreams," a return to the band's trademark bruising guitar-driven sound, then going uphill from there to "Last of the True Believers" and "Shangri-La." It's not all bombast, though, as the dreamy "7th Wave" and yearning "Heartbeat Mosaic" prove. As always, Steve Mack's tart, cynical voice is the perfect vehicle for the razor-sharp lyrics.

the rest:

Live ♪♪ (Dutch East India, 1988)
End of the Millennium Psychosis Blues ♪♪♪ (Virgin, 1988)
Peel Sessions ♪♪♪ (Dutch East India, 1989)
Sensitize ♪♪ (Virgin EP, 1990)

worth searching for: The title of *Manic Pop Thrill* (Demon, 1996, prod. Hugh Jones) set the bar high, and although the album was stylistically diverse, it stands as a solid debut. The album was released in the U.K. to critical success, but for reasons unknown was only ever available in the United States as an import. The out-of-print *Babble* (Polydor, 1987, prod. Rolli Mosimann) is packed with smart, angry songs that showcased a band in tight control of its eclectic sound. Finally, the band's first album following the departure of founding member Sean O'Neill, *Chemicrazy* (Virgin, 1990, prod. Scott Litt), was hailed by many critics as one of the best rock albums of the year when it was released in 1990. It still holds up well.

influences:

◀◀ Buzzcocks, the Mekons, Midnight Oil, the Fall, the Alarm, Gang of Four, the Clash, the Sex Pistols, Stiff Little Fingers, Television, Screaming Blue Messiahs, the Jam

▶▶ Black 47, the Young Dubliners

see also: *The Undertones*

Lisa M. Moore

The The

Formed 1980, in London, England.

Matt Johnson; others.

Matt Johnson's The The originally started out as a studio project with no real band, though he would shortly begin using other players. The group's early '80s ties to the 4AD label, which released the group's early singles and first album, were enough to give Johnson the inspiration and acclaim he needed to progress to the next level. The keystone for The The has always been Johnson's lyrics; fancying himself a philosopher, he writes songs that transcend the immediate meaning and pursue loftier topics—often railing against the evils of mankind. The key to dealing with The The's records is to always expect the unexpected; just when a song feels comfortable, it takes a massive twist either musically or lyrically. Johnson's songs generally pursue an alternative rock-pop course, but he likes to flavor them with touches of dance, blues, jazz, and psychedelia. An enormously talented musician and songwriter, Johnson has been party to a number of side projects throughout his career as well as attracting top notch musicians to his stable. Cohorts have included Johnny Marr of the Smiths and Neneh Cherry. He has even tried his hand at film, creating a series of connected videos for the songs on the *Infected* album and linking them together into a critically acclaimed movie.

what to buy: *Mind Bomb* 𝄞𝄞𝄞𝄞 (Epic, 1989, prod. Wayne Livesey, Rolli Mossiman, Matt Johnson) shows a much darker side of Johnson (partly influenced by producer Rolli Mossiman of the Swans), with songs that present a philosophical treatise on the state of man and religion. The album features a stunningly beautiful duet with Sinéad O'Connor on "Kingdom of Rain" and also finds Johnson reaching into more experimental rhythmic patterns from Africa and the Middle East.

what to buy next: *Infected* 𝄞𝄞𝄞𝄞 (Epic, 1986, prod. Wayne Livesey, Matt Johnson) is a rare treat, a pretentious concept album about good vs. evil loaded with pop nuggets that consistently entertain.

what to avoid: While entertaining as a novelty album, *Hanky Panky* 𝄞𝄞 (Epic, 1995, prod. Matt Johnson, Bruce Lampcov)—Johnson's collection of Hank Williams covers—is not for the faint of heart. His versions are certainly unique, but the album doesn't measure up to any of the band's previous efforts.

the rest:
Burning Blue Soul 𝄞𝄞𝄞𝄞 (4AD, 1982)
Soul Mining 𝄞𝄞𝄞𝄞 (Epic, 1983)
Dusk 𝄞𝄞𝄞 (Epic, 1993)

worth searching for: *The The vs. The World* (Epic, 1989, prod. various) is a wonderful promotional compilation of songs from *Soul Mining*, *Infected*, and *Mind Bomb*.

influences:
◀◀ Hank Williams, Julian Cope, Teardrop Explodes, the Doors, Pink Floyd

▶▶ Echo & the Bunnymen, the Smiths, XTC

Tim Davis

Thelonious Monster

Formed mid-1980s, in Los Angeles, CA.

Bob Forrest, vocals; Peter Weiss, drums, vocals; Jon Huck, bass; K.K., guitar; Bill Stobaugh, guitar; Chris Handsone, guitar; Dix Denney, guitar; Mike Marty, guitar, vocals; Rob Graves, bass; Martyn LeNoble, bass; Zander Schloss, guitar.

Given the sodden, punk-rock origins of what was originally

dubbed Thelonious Monster Mellencamp, little of historical accuracy may be said about this band, save that leader Bob Forrest is a prodigiously talented songwriter. And that his penchant for self-destruction more than equals his talent. The child of a 15-year-old, adopted by his grandparents (none of whom he knew until much later), Forrest's musical frame of reference runs from '70s FM radio to Blind Lemon Jefferson to his long-running friendship with the Red Hot Chili Peppers. All that said, drunk, stoned, or sober, Forrest is a compelling performer, reminiscent of Janis Joplin. His best songs are poignant portraits of the underclass who now inhabit America's original suburbs and have little to aspire to save management positions in the fast food empire.

what to buy: Produced during a brief storm of sobriety *Stormy Weather* 𝄞𝄞𝄞𝄞 (Relativity, 1989, prod. John Doe) is an all but forgotten classic album of stunning honesty. From the tender "My Boy" to the furious portrait of his (grand)father, "Colorblind" to the reckless joy of "Sammy Hagar Weekend" to covers of Tracy Chapman's "For My Lover" and Blind Lemon's "See That My Grave Is Kept Clean," *Stormy Weather* captures the full gamut of Forrest's brilliance. It is also packaged, on CD, with *Next Saturday Afternoon* 𝄞𝄞𝄞 (Relativity, 1987, prod. J.B., Thelonious Monster), a less even outing that's highlighted by "Walk on Water" and the goofy wonder of "Michael Jordan."

what to buy next: Recorded about as many times as Lucinda Williams's *Sweet Old World* (and originally for the same label, RCA), the aptly named *Beautiful Mess* 𝄞𝄞𝄞 (Capitol/Signal, 1992, prod. Joe Hardy, others) is a mixed blessing. "Blood Is Thicker than Water" and other cuts retain the confessional urgency of his best work, but there's a pop sheen to the album that doesn't quite fit the songs.

what to avoid: *You're Bummin' My Life out in a Supreme Fashion* 𝄞𝄞 (Epitaph, 1986, prod. Brett Gurewitz, Thelonious Monster) is too clearly in the thrall of the Chili Peppers.

worth searching for: The three-song 12-inch *The Boldness of Style* (Relativity, 1987) is worth digging up just for the live version of the Doobie Brothers' "Listen to the Music."

influences:
◀◀ Red Hot Chili Peppers, X, Gun Club

▶▶ Mark Lanegan, Weezer

Grant Alden

Them

Formed 1963, in Belfast, Northern Ireland.

Van Morrison, vocals; Billy Harrison, guitar; Alan Henderson, bass; Ronnie Millings, drums.

Them was a bruising R&B unit, featuring the gruff vocals of a young Van Morrison. The group's recording career was brief (three years) and spawned few singles, but Morrison's fierce passion and the raw power of the hits left a more significant impression in the United States than many of the other British Invasion acts with whom they were grouped. There were a handful of lunges at the charts ("Baby Please Don't Go," "Here Comes the Night") and spirited covers ("I Got a Woman," "It's All Over Now Baby Blue," and "Turn on Your Lovelight"), but it's the classic "Gloria" that remains its defining moment—just three chords and feral growls, but its mark can be felt not only in its stomping performance but the inumerable cover versions that have surfaced since then (not counting every garage and bar band that peels through the song at a moment's notice).

what to buy: The record is finally set straight with the two-disc set *The Story of Them Featuring Van Morrison* 𝄞𝄞𝄞𝄞 (Deram, 1998, prod. Dorian Wathen). Containing virtually everything you need, both discs offer exceptionally clean sound which heightens the brash attack. But where are the liner notes?

what to buy next: *Them Featuring Van Morrison* 𝄞𝄞𝄞𝄞 (Deram, 1965/1998) is a less thorough compilation, though it does contain their best-known work, such as "Gloria" and the crashing "Mystic Eyes," as well as the searing "Baby, Please Don't Go."

influences:

◀◀ Ray Charles, Bobby Bland, Fats Domino, Bob Dylan

▶▶ U2, Patti Smith, Thin Lizzy, the Pogues

see also: *Van Morrison*

Allan Orski

Therapy?

Formed 1989, in Belfast, Northern Ireland.

Fyfe Ewing, drums (1989–96); Andrew James Cairns, vocals, guitar; Michael McKeegan, bass; Graham Hopkins, drums (1996–present); Martin McCarrick, guitar (1996–present).

The Northern Irish band Therapy? effectively mixes headbanging thrash-metal rhythms with Alice in Chains–style downbeat vocals and catchy, chanting choruses. "I've got nothing to do, 'cept hang around and get screwed up on you," Andrew Cairns sings on "Screamager," Therapy?'s best song—which almost became a radio hit. His lyrics deal with religious depression, psychoses, liars, and sexual frustration, which, content-wise, puts Therapy? among Nirvana, Slayer, Metallica, and Black Sabbath in the gloomy rock club.

what to buy: *Troublegum* 𝄞𝄞𝄞 (A&M, 1994, prod. Chris Sheldon) contains "Screamager" and is a strong, tight sampling of the band's heavy-guitar sound and tortured lyrics.

what to buy next: *Nurse* 𝄞𝄞𝄞 (A&M, 1993, prod. Harvey Birrell) occasionally gels as well as *Troublegum*, but Therapy? hadn't yet effectively honed its sound. The compilation *Caucasian Psychosis* 𝄞𝄞𝄞 (Quarterstick, 1992, prod. Mudd, Therapy?, Harvey Birrell, John Loder) comprises two early EP's and a single.

what to avoid: *Hats off to the Insane* 𝄞𝄞 (A&M EP, 1993, prod. Chris Sheldon, Therapy?) sounds like any other Soundgarden wannabe, just characterless metal and angst-ridden screaming.

the rest:
Nurse 𝄞𝄞 (A&M, 1993)
Teethgrinder 𝄞𝄞 (A&M, 1992)
Infernal Love 𝄞𝄞𝄞 (A&M, 1996)

worth searching for: The band backs Ozzy Osbourne on a terrific version of Black Sabbath's "Iron Man" on *Nativity in Black: A Tribute to Black Sabbath* (Columbia, 1994).

influences:

◀◀ Soundgarden, Black Sabbath, Nirvana, Metallica, Slayer, Alice in Chains, Faith No More

▶▶ Bush, Stone Temple Pilots, Gravity Kills, Type O Negative, White Zombie, Biohazard

Steve Knopper

They Might Be Giants

Formed 1983, in Brooklyn, NY.

John Linnell, vocals, accordion, keyboards, horns; John Flansburgh, vocals, guitar, bass; Tony Maimone, bass (1993–95); Brian Doherty, drums (1993–present); Graham Maby, bass (1996–present); Eric Schermerhorn, guitar (1996–present).

A couple of arty geeks from Brooklyn outfitted with accordion, guitar, and drum machine—not exactly a blueprint for success in the world of rock 'n' roll. Nevertheless, in 1983 John Linnell and John Flansburgh made the awkward apparatus take flight, playing clubs in Manhattan's East Village and setting up their own Dial-a-Song service (a standard answering machine featuring They Might Be Giants tunes). Emboldened by the anything-goes possibilities of life in the aftermath of punk, the Giants devised an inimitable, low-budget (though not lo-fi) style that set absurdist wordplay to McCartneyesque melodies and neo-Beefheartian arrangements. When it works, as it does on the first few albums and some later ones as well, TMBG come off as wildly inventive musicians with a knack for droll deconstruction. In other words, just the right antidote for all that noisy guitar angst.

what to buy: The perfect encapsulation of the world according to John and John, *Lincoln* 𝄞𝄞𝄞𝄞 (Restless/BarNone, 1988, prod. Bill Krauss) pulls off an irresistible pop song ("Ana Ng"), an ersatz-jazz ode to booze ("Lie Still, Little Bottle"), an Aquarian Age send-up ("Cage & Aquarium"), a surrealist military march ("Pencil Rain"), and a Gershwinesque ditty about, of all things, the exploitation of the working class ("Kiss Me, Son of God"). For those who want complete immersion in the early-Giants experience, *Then: The Earlier Years* 🎵🎵🎵 (Restless, 1997, prod. Bill Krauss, They Might Be Giants) provides a deep well. The two-CD set brings together the entirety of the duo's three albums for Restless/BarNone—1986's self-titled debut, *Lincoln* and 1991's B-sides compilation, *Miscellaneous T*—as well as 19 rare and otherwise unavailable tracks.

what to buy next: Thank goodness the jump to a major label didn't warp TMBG's worldview into something, well, *normal*. On the contrary, *Flood* 🎵🎵🎵 (Elektra, 1990, prod. They Might Be Giants, Clive Langer, Alan Winstanley) manages more than its share of inspired lunacy, including a deliciously twisted reading of "Instanbul (Not Constantinople)," the kindergarten sing-along "Particle Man," the "Raw-Hide"-inspired "Minimum Wage," and the semi-hit "Birdhouse in Your Soul." Six years and a couple of mediocre albums later, *Factory Showroom* 🎵🎵🎵 (Elektra, 1996, prod. Pat Dillett, They Might Be Giants), which features such tuneful shenanigans as "S-E-X-X-Y" and "James K. Polk," marks a welcome return to form.

what to avoid: *John Henry* 🎵🎵 (Elektra, 1994, prod. Paul Fox, They Might Be Giants) boldly goes where no Giants album had gone before: full-thrust into the realm of living, breathing backing musicians. Although it boasts the agile accompaniment of former Pere Ubu bassist Tony Maimone and drummer Brian Doherty, the album's revised modus operandi lacks the cheesy charm of vintage TMBG. Then again, perhaps not even the duo's trademark synthesizer-and-beatbox aesthetic could invigorate this batch of anemic songs.

the rest:
They Might Be Giants 🎵🎵🎵 (Restless/BarNone, 1986)
Miscellaneous T 🎵🎵🎵 (Restless/BarNone, 1991)
Apollo 18 🎵🎵🎵 (Elektra, 1992)
Severe Tire Damage N/A (Elektra, 1998)

worth searching for: One of several indispensable TMBG EP's, *Why Does the Sun Shine?* (Elektra, 1993, prod. They Might Be Giants), contains the Giants' hilarious, straight-faced reading of the title track and a 1959 educational jingle, as well as nerdified stabs at the Allman Brothers' "Jessica" and the Meat Puppets' "Whirlpool."

influences:
◀◀ The Beatles, Captain Beefheart, Spike Jones, the Beach Boys, the Residents, XTC, Talking Heads, Frank Zappa, Dadaism, Tin Pan Alley, burlesque, polka, cartoons

▶▶ The Presidents of the United States of America, the Dead Milkmen, Ween, Barenaked Ladies, the Rentals

Greg Siegel

Thin Lizzy
Formed 1970, in Dublin, Ireland. Disbanded 1983.

Phil Lynott (died January 4, 1986), vocals, bass; Brian Downey, drums; Eric Bell, guitar (1970–73); Gary Moore, guitar (1974, 1977–79); Andy Gee, guitar (1974); John Cann, guitar (1974); Scott Gorham, guitar, vocals (1974–83); Brian Robertson, guitar, vocals (1974–77); Midge Ure, guitar (1979); Snowy White, guitar (1980–82); Darren Wharton, keyboards (1981); John Sykes, guitar (1982–83); Darren Wharton, keyboards (1982–83).

Driven by the underrated Phil Lynott—a wonderfully literate songwriter—Thin Lizzy is best remembered for its carefully constructed melodic dual guitar leads and Lynott's throaty, soulful vocals. The scope of Lynott's ambition led to vaguely thematic albums, alternating between macho pounders and soaring, working-class ballads. Highly romanticized and often insightful writing mixed too often with pretentious, obtuse male bonding, and the band failed to break through to a higher level of stardom and broke up in 1983. After recording a solo album and publishing two books of poetry, Lynott suffered a drug overdose that led to a fatal bout of pneumonia and heart failure in 1986. A Lynott/Thin Lizzy tribute concert was held in 1995—with Henry Rollins and others joining surviving band members—with an album of the show expected to be released at some point.

what to buy: On *Jailbreak* 🎵🎵🎵 (Mercury, 1976/1990, prod. John Alcock), Lynott's sensitivity and swagger gel like shots and beers with his strongest set of tunes—notably, "The Boys Are Back in Town," a violent summertime paean to male camaraderie. *Dedication: The Very Best of Thin Lizzy* 🎵🎵🎵 (PolyGram, 1991, prod. various) offers a streamlined view of the band's pub punch, starting with its first hit, "Whiskey in the Jar," through to the final three albums on Warner Bros., which are now unavailable.

what to buy next: *Live and Dangerous* 🎵🎵🎵 (Warner Bros., 1978, 1989, prod. Thin Lizzy, Tony Visconti) is a bare-knuckled tour de force that's arguably the best showcase for the band's power. Swirling guitars, Lynott's thick delivery, and a tight rhythm section illuminate even the obscure tunes.

what to avoid: *Thin Lizzy* 🎵 (Mercury, 1971/Deram, 1990, prod. Scott English, Nick Tauber) is buried in mystical murk with titles such as "The Friendly Ranger at Clontarf Castle"—a rambling mess that offers few hints of things to come.

the rest:

Shades of a Blue Orphanage ♪ (Mercury, 1972/Deram, 1990)
Vagabonds of the Western World ♪♪ (Mercury, 1973/Deram, 1991)
Night Life ♪♪♪ (Mercury, 1974/Polydor, 1990)
Fighting ♪♪♪ (Mercury, 1975, 1990)
Johnny the Fox ♪♪♪ (Mercury, 1976, 1990)
Bad Reputation ♪♪♪♪ (Mercury, 1977, 1990)

worth searching for: *Solo in Soho* (Warner Bros., 1980), Lynott's first solo effort, is spotty, but contains "Ode to a Black Man," which ranks with the best songs he wrote for the band.

influences:

◄◄ Van Morrison, Bob Seger

►► Graham Parker, Metallica, Bon Jovi

Allan Orski

Thin White Rope

Formed 1982, in Davis, CA. Disbanded 1993.

Guy Kyser, vocals, guitar; Roger Kunkel, guitar,vocals, bass; Kevin Staydohar, bass (1982–83), Stephen Tesluk, bass, vocals, guitar (1983–88); John Von Veldt, bass (1988–90); Stooert Odom, bass, vocals (1990–93) Jozef Becker, drums (1983–88); Frank French, drums (1988); Matthew Abourezk, drums, percussion, vocals (1988–93).

The Central Valley of California has spawned many a band, but none quite so wonderfully eclectic as Davis's Thin White Rope. Named for a William Burroughs reference to semen, this challenging quartet has left much behind for your listening pleasure. Singer Guy Kyser sounds like a botany scholar (which he is) channeling the spirit of Howling Wolf. Roger Kunkel's guitars slither and crawl around enough to make Indiana Jones very afraid. The various rythym sections have all been stirring and sympathetic. From a college town, but not quite college rock, Thin White Rope never attained a substantial following in the United States but was bigger in Europe. Often as dry as desert air and with broad soundscapes that sound like scores to not-yet filmed movies, these guys are, like the Velvet Underground, destined for greater appreciation since their demise. Kyser has performed in several outfits with his wife, Johanna, while Kunkel and Matthew Abourezk played together for a while after the breakup, in a band called Plow. And Jozef Becker has drummed for Game Theory and the Loud Family.

what to buy: Thin White Rope doesn't have any bad records, but *Sack Full of Silver* ♪♪♪♪ (RCA/Frontier, 1990, prod. Tom Mallon) wins the title of "best" by a nose. With stellar drummer Abourezk behind the kit, *Sack Full of Silver* is an incredibly dynamic sliver of tight, odd rock. New addition Stooert Odom's elliptical bass playing also adds an increased complexity to the already lurid sound. "Whirling Dervish" and "Americana" are amazing, and the cover of Can's "Yoo Doo Right" gives the original a good pummeling. This was Thin White Rope's only foray on a major label.

what to buy next: *Exploring the Axis* ♪♪♪♪ (Frontier, 1985, prod. Jeff Eyrich) makes for an amazing debut. Not since Television had the electric guitar been so well used to its capacity. Kyser sings as if his water had been long shut off to great effect. His and Kunkel's playing melds as if welded and original member Becker was no slouch of a drummer, either.

the rest:

Moonhead ♪♪♪♪ (Frontier, 1987)
In the Spanish Cave ♪♪♪♪ (Frontier, 1988)
The Ruby Sea ♪♪♪♪ (Frontier, 1991)
The One That Got Away ♪♪♪♪ (Frontier, 1993)
Spoor ♪♪♪♪ (Frontier, 1995)

worth searching for: *When Worlds Collide* (Munster, 1995, prod. various) is a Spanish compilation that contains 19 tracks spanning the career of Thin White Rope.

solo outings:

Roger Kunkel:
(With Acme Rocket Quartet) *S/T* ♪♪♪♪ (Lather, 1996)

influences:

◄◄ Howling Wolf, the Velvet Underground, Can, Television

►► Calexico, Don Caballero, the Popealopes

Barry M. Prickett

Third Eye Blind

Formed 1994, in San Francisco, CA.

Stephan Jenkins, vocals; Kevin Cadogan, guitars; Arion Salazar, bass; Brad Hargreaves, drums.

A University of California—Berkeley graduate, Stephan Jenkins dabbled in a variety of bands before forming Third Eye Blind. A production deal with Atlantic Records led to an international hit with the Braids' hip-hop cover of Queen's "Bohemian Rhapsody" in 1996. Jenkins's hip-hop resume also includes a stint with the group Puck & Zen. Not satisifed with where his music career was leading, Jenkins sought out to find "people who weren't trying to fit into some scene," eventually joining with other players in the area to form Third Eye Blind. Sharing management with Counting Crows, the fledgling group was able to land some choice bookings in the Bay Area—opening for Oasis, for instance—and conduct its pre-label career at an already high level.

what's available: Third Eye Blind is kind of like a dream lover—cute, peppy, and somewhat annoying on the outside, but when you dig deeper he or she is dark and brooding on the inside.

After a quick listen to *Third Eye Blind* ♫♫♫ (Elektra, 1997, prod. Stephan Jenkins), it's easy to dismiss the group as some fluffy pop band. The snotty inflection of the opening track "Losing a Whole Year" is perfectly coupled with equally snotty lyrics: "Well this drama is a bore/And I don't want to play no more/I remember you and me used to spend/The whole goddamned day in bed/losing a whole year." Musically, the song is just as enjoyable with its distorted bass and rollicking beat. In 1997 the "do do do/ do do do do"'s of "Semi-Charmed Life" quite possibly, crossed the lips of every pop fan. But it's that song that best represents Third Eye Blind's appeal to the thinking listener; the tune's light-hearted arrangement contradicts the mood of the song: "Some place back there/Smiling in the pictures you would take/Doing crystal meth/Will life you up until you break."

influences:

◀◀ Cracker, Blur

Christina Fuoco

Third Eye Foundation
Formed early 1990s, in Bristol, England.

Matt Elliot, sampler, guitars, drum machines, sequencing; Deborah Parsons, vocals, noises, other (early 1990s–96).

Third Eye Foundation's stunning 1995 debut, *Semtex*, was perhaps the first recorded attempt to marry My Bloody Valentine's wall of feedback guitar playing with rhythmic intricacy of jungle breakbeats. The group is a prime example of the '90s post-rock trend of bands who've managed to combine indie-rock sensibility with post-techno studio technology. Although Third Eye Foundation used to include the eerie, wordless vocals and guitar playing of Matt Elliot's ex-girlfriend, Deborah Parsons (who now records as Foehn), the group should be more accurately described as the work of Elliot, a veteran of Bristol's indie-rock scene. (Elliot's old group, Linda's Strange Vacation, included members of Movietone and Flying Saucer Attack.) The second Third Eye Foundation album, *In Version*, was a collection of remixes of groups such as AMP, Flying Saucer Attack, and Crescent. The album moved Elliot further away from guitars and rock stylings and deeper into the realm of samplers, fractured beats, and the dark ambience of a group like Main. Those who find Elliot's Third Eye output to be too dark and oppressive should check out his work with Movietone, whose somber, introspective, and folksy songs are anything but oppressive.

what to buy: *Ghost* ♫♫♫♫ (Domino/Merge, 1997, prod. Matt Elliot) is far and away the best Third Eye Foundation album. A nightmarish masterpiece of shrieking sounds and complex rhythms, *Ghost* is the album Aphex Twin or Squarepusher would have made had they grown up listening to industrial groups like Coil or Nurse with Wound.

what to buy next: The EP *The Sound of Violence* ♫♫♫ (Domino/Merge, 1997, prod. Matt Elliot) further refines Elliot's avant-jungle sensibilities.

worth searching for: Unfortunately, the first two Third Eye Foundation albums, *Semtex* (Linda's Strange Vacation, 1996, prod. Matt Elliot) and *In Version* (Linda's Strange Vacation, 1996, prod. Matt Elliot), are available only as imports from the U.K. The 12-inch single *Semtex/Science Fiction* (Domino, 1996, prod. Matt Elliot) and seven-inch single *Universal Cooler* (Planet, 1996, prod. Matt Elliot) feature Elliot at his most twisted.

solo outings:

Movietone:

Movietone ♫♫♫ (Planet E, 1996)
Day and Night ♫♫♫♫ (Drag City/Domino, 1997)

influences:

◀◀ My Bloody Valentine, Disco Inferno, Psychic TV, Nurse with Wound, Aphex Twin, Plug, Squarepusher, Autechre

Howard Shih

3rd Party
Formed 1996, in New York, NY.

Maria Christensen, vocals; Karmine, vocals; Elaine Borja, vocals.

As is customary with most acts of patently disposable dance-pop ilk, the members of 3rd Party are not tortured muses of storied artistry. They do, however, effectively capture the very same naivety, charm, and, yes, talent that brought such gems as the Supremes and on the flipside, Expose, into public recognition. 3rd Party is three women of varying ethnicity and upbringing, each with a strong taste for dance music and a slight knowledge of songcraft (Maria Christensen attempted a solo-diva career prior to her involvement here), artifically assembled and then organically nurtured into a functioning packet of pop.

what's available: The band's debut, *3rd Party* ♫♫ (DV8, 1997, prod. Ric Wake), is a collection more notable for its producer's prior credits (including Taylor Dayne and Celine Dion) than for any real sonic direction of its own. It does define the modern, carefree New York woman in the cursory gaze of a disco involvement. "Can You Feel It?" was the requisite singalong single's rhetorical question, but having been fooled before, the American public answered in quiet decline.

influences:

◀◀ Expose, Bananarama, Pointer Sisters

Billy Manes

.38 Special

Formed 1974, in Jacksonville, FL.

Donnie Van Zant, vocals; Don Barnes, guitar, vocals (1975–87, 1992–present); Jeff Carlisi, guitar; Ken Lyons, bass (1975–78); Jack Grondin, drums (1974–75); Steve Brookins, drums (1975–87); Larry Junstrom, bass, guitar, (1978–present); Danny Chauncey, guitar (1987–present); Max Carl, drums (1987–91); Scott Hoffman, drums (1991–96); Bobby Capps, keyboards (1991–present).

.38 Special worked for years in the shadow of Southern rock giants Lynyrd Skynyrd. (Donnie Van Zant, the group's frontman, was the younger brother of Skynyrd's Ronnie Van Zant.) In fact, the group didn't have a Top 40 hit until 1980, well after Southern rock had peaked. But once it hit, with "Hold on Loosely," .38 Special became the top Southern rock act of the decade, with three consecutive platinum albums. The band achieved this by turning its Southern boogie roots into an accessible pop formula for radio. Where other bands played loose jams, .38 Special was tight; instead of being dominated by guitar solos, .38 Special lived and died by the hooky chorus. It wasn't Lynyrd Skynyrd by any standards, but, then again, it wasn't intended to be.

what to buy: *Flashback* 𝅘𝅥𝅘𝅥𝅘𝅥𝅘𝅥 (A&M, 1987, prod. various) celebrates the fact that .38 Special was one of the best singles bands of the early and mid-'80s, evolving from rough-hewn anthems such as "Rockin' into the Night" to melodic masterpieces such as "If I'd Been the One" and "Caught up in You."

what to buy next: *Tour de Force* 𝅘𝅥𝅘𝅥𝅘𝅥 (A&M, 1983, prod. Rodney Mills, Don Barnes, Jeff Carlisi) is, start to finish, the most consistent of the band's albums, containing the singles "If I'd Been the One" and "Back Where You Belong."

what to avoid: If you have to choose between underdeveloped Southern power and an overworked formula for radio success, choose the former. *Bone against Steel* 𝅘𝅥𝅘𝅥 (Charisma, 1991, prod. Rodney Mills) is the latter.

the rest:
Rockin' into the Night 𝅘𝅥𝅘𝅥𝅘𝅥 (A&M, 1979)
Wild-Eyed Southern Boys 𝅘𝅥𝅘𝅥𝅘𝅥 (A&M, 1981)
Special Forces 𝅘𝅥𝅘𝅥𝅘𝅥 (A&M, 1982)
Strength in Numbers 𝅘𝅥𝅘𝅥 (A&M, 1986)
Rock & Roll Strategy 𝅘𝅥𝅘𝅥 (A&M, 1988)
Resolution 𝅘𝅥𝅘𝅥 (Razor & Tie, 1997)

worth searching for: The promotional vinyl release *.38 Special at the Rainbow Music Hall,* (A&M, 1980, prod. Rodney Mills) features four songs performed live in Denver.

influences:
◄◄ The Allman Brothers Band, Lynyrd Skynyrd, Molly Hatchett, the Beatles

►► Garth Brooks, Travis Tritt, the Mavericks

Brian Mansfield

Thirty Ought Six

Formed 1992, in Portland, OR.

Sean Roberts, vocals, bass; David Blunk, guitar, vocals, organ; Ryan Paravecchio, drums.

Gleefully propelled by bassist Sean Roberts, Thirty Ought Six tears up the great Northwest rock scene. David Blunk's understated, yeomanlike guitar colorizes the songs, while Ryan Paravecchio's staccato, chop-shop drumming pins them to the mat. Dynamically intense, with the loudest whispered tracks ever, Thirty Ought Six's sonic blast could give Helen Keller tinnitus.

what to buy: The first record, *Bosozoku* 𝅘𝅥𝅘𝅥𝅘𝅥𝅘𝅥 (Candy Ass, 1994) is an eccentric gem. Oddly mixed so Roberts can barely be heard above the din, it's an organized racket, with Paravecchio's advanced-calculus drumming hemming in the songs. At times—such as on "Wading," when Hazel and Team Dresch all-star Jody Bleyle sings along—it can be sublimely beautiful. Maddeningly varied in volume, the cacophony can harm tender ears.

what to buy next: *Hag Seed* 𝅘𝅥𝅘𝅥𝅘𝅥 (Mute, 1995, prod. John Goodmanson) is more polished, but with less impact. The songs have goofy names, probably inspired from some nerdy role-playing game, but on the title track it's the playing that matters. Roberts's singing is fine, and when joined by Sunny Day Real Estate vocalist Jeremy Enigk on "Tourmaline," it can be neatly melodic.

influences:
◄◄ Cop Shoot Cop, Three Shades of Dirty, Beefeater, Jones Very, Bastro, Bitch Magnet, Slint, Girls Against Boys, Jawbox

Barry M. Prickett

This Mortal Coil

Formed 1984, in London, England.

This Mortal Coil is a rare thing in the music world, the whole being greater than sum of its parts. Normally these supergroup confabs are nothing more than an attempt to bring in a few extra bucks with name-brand recognition—and with the end product being marginal at best. In the case of TMC, none of the featured members truly has an enormous presence in the music world to begin with. Their unifying factor is that they are all part of Ivo Watts-Russell's vision for what modern music should sound like. Being on 4AD Records is the only thing needed to join This Mortal Coil for most—the lineup features members of the Cocteau Twins, Dead Can Dance, Colourbox, the Wolfgang Press, Modern English, the Pixies, Throwing Muses, the Breeders, and a few minor-league studio musicians who frequent 4AD studio sessions for the aforementioned bands. The only artists of note who contribute significantly to the projects are Dominic Appleton of Breathless, an English band that sells thousands of records in Italy, Gordon Sharp of Cindytalk and, most notably, the Buzzcocks' Howard Devoto. This "all-star" lineup formed as a one-off project conceived by Watts-Russell, who writes, plays, and acts as producer to some extent on each of the band's albums. While no real departure is found from the usual murky 4AD fare, the records are noteworthy simply because of the quality of each album; if you like the Cocteau Twins and Dead Can Dance, you will love TMC. The project allows the band members to cross-pollinate and experiment away from their usual surroundings, and the musicians clearly feel liberated in the TMC fold—as evidenced by wild covers such as Tim Buckley's "Song to the Siren," Big Star's "Kangaroo," and the Talking Heads' "Drugs," all done in the inimitable 4AD style. For lush atmospheres and moody, gothic-style arrangements, very little competes with the quality and consistency of TMC. In June 1998, Watts-Russell decided to revive the This Mortal Coil approach and released a self-titled album under the name Hope Blister (U.K. release only, so far) rather than TMC, since it was not intended as a showcase of 4AD stars but rather featured many of the session musicians from earlier TMC releases. It features a number of cover versions and runs a dispondent, meloncholy tone throughout.

what to buy: Strong from start to finish, *Filigree & Shadow* 𝄞𝄞𝄞𝄞 (4AD, 1986, prod. Ivo Watts-Russell) is a double album that more than makes up for its extra cost by being a true work of art. While not as traditionally stylized as the band's first effort, it shows TMC actually coming into its own as a band, rather than a studio project of label mates. Weighing in at 74 minutes, it's long enough to be a good candlelight dinner record.

the rest:
It'll End in Tears 𝄞𝄞𝄞 (4AD, 1984)
Blood 𝄞𝄞𝄞 (4AD, 1991)
Box Set 𝄞𝄞𝄞 (4AD, 1993)

worth searching for: A self-titled promotional-only sampler released to introduce the United States to the band's material when 4AD opened an American office and prepared to release a TMC box set, the 12-song *This Mortal Coil* (4AD, 1993) culls tracks from all three of the band's albums and a contribution to a 4AD compilation album.

influences:
◄◄ Bauhaus, Breathless, Modern English, Legendary Pink Dots
►► Cocteau Twins, Dead Can Dance, Wolfgang Press, Colourbox, the Pixies

see also: *Cocteau Twins, Dead Can Dance*

Tim Davis

Mickey Thomas
See: Jefferson Starship

Richard Thompson
/Linda Thompson
/Richard & Linda Thompson
Formed 1972, in England.

Richard Thompson (born April 3, 1949, in London, England), vocals, guitar; Linda Thompson (born 1948), vocals.

Richard Thompson was an original member of the innovative folk-rock band Fairport Convention and has in the intervening years carved out a niche as a supremely gifted songwriter and guitarist. With his deep, burnished vocals and generally dark songs, he has modernized the British folk idiom in several ways; his expressive, often baroque fretwork joins a number of different traditions—imagine a Celtic Hendrix in Morocco—and has hugely influenced Mark Knopfler of Dire Straits, among many others. Thompson met Linda Peters while working with the group Bunch, a loose aggregation of Fairport alumni; they married during the early '70s, converted to Islam in 1974, and divorced in 1982 (Richard subsequently married Nancy Covey). Richard began his solo career first, with 1972's *Henry the Human Fly*, then joined forces with Linda for some of the most emotionally bare music ever produced in the pop idiom. After they split up, Richard reactivated his solo career, worked with avant-gardists Fred Frith, Henry Kaiser, and John French, was a busy gun-for-hire (Nick Drake, J.J. Cale, Robert Plant, Bonnie Raitt, Crowded House, Suzanne Vega, the Golden Palominos, Syd Straw), and wielded enough influenced to inspire a 1994 tribute album featuring a bevy of cutting-edge acts. Linda moved into theater before releasing a solo album in 1985 and a retrospective in 1996.

what to buy: The couple's *Shoot out the Lights* 𝄞𝄞𝄞𝄞 (Hannibal, 1982, prod. Joe Boyd)—the release of which barely preceded their divorce—is a devastating, virtually flawless set of performances and the last of their collaborations. Their first release, *I Want to See the Bright Lights Tonight* 𝄞𝄞𝄞 (Hannibal, 1974/Rykodisc, 1991, prod. Richard Thompson, John Wood), is an equally gripping and somewhat happier dialogue. Richard's *Rumour and Sigh* 𝄞𝄞𝄞 (Capitol, 1991, prod. Mitchell Froom) is his personal masterpiece, highlighted by the ironic "I Feel So Good" and the updated Irish ballad "1952 Vincent Black Lightning."

what to buy next: Richard's best solo work is collected in the hefty but consistently engaging three-disc set *Watching the Dark: The History of Richard Thompson* 𝄞𝄞𝄞 (Rykodisc/Hannibal, 1993, prod. various). Linda's *Dreams Fly Away* 𝄞𝄞𝄞𝄞 (Rykodisc/Hannibal, 1996, prod. various) is a 20-track overview of her career, from before Richard to her post-divorce work.

what to avoid: *Richard Thompson Live! (More or Less)* 𝄞𝄞 (Island, 1977, prod. Joe Boyd) was originally paired with *I Want to See the Bright Lights Tonight* as a double album—but didn't deserve to be.

the rest:
Richard Thompson:
Henry the Human Fly 𝄞𝄞𝄞 (Warner Bros., 1972/Rykodisc-Hannibal, 1991)
(Guitar, Vocal) 𝄞𝄞𝄞 (Island, 1976/Rykodisc-Hannibal, 1991)
Strict Tempo! 𝄞𝄞𝄞 (Hannibal, 1981)
Hand of Kindness 𝄞𝄞𝄞𝄞 (Hannibal, 1983/Rykodisc-Hannibal, 1991)
Small Town Romance 𝄞𝄞𝄞 (Hannibal, 1984)
Across a Crowded Room 𝄞𝄞𝄞 (Polydor, 1985)
Daring Adventures 𝄞𝄞𝄞𝄞 (Polydor, 1986)
Amnesia 𝄞𝄞𝄞𝄞 (Capitol, 1988)
Mirror Blue 𝄞𝄞𝄞 (Capitol, 1994)
You? Me? Us? 𝄞𝄞𝄞 (Capitol, 1996)
(With Danny Thompson) Industry 𝄞𝄞𝄞𝄞 (Hannibal/Carthage, 1997)

French, Frith, Kaiser, & Thompson:
Live, Love, Larf and Loaf 𝄞𝄞𝄞 (Rhino, 1987)
Invisible Means 𝄞𝄞𝄞 (Windham Hill, 1990)

Richard & Linda Thompson:
Hokey Pokey 𝄞𝄞𝄞 (Hannibal, 1975/Rykodisc-Hannibal, 1991)
Pour down like Silver 𝄞𝄞𝄞𝄞 (Hannibal, 1975/Rykodisc-Hannibal, 1991)
First Light 𝄞𝄞𝄞 (Carthage, 1978/Rykodisc, 1992)
Sunnyvista 𝄞𝄞𝄞 (Carthage, 1979/Rykodisc, 1992)

Linda Thompson:
One Clear Moment 𝄞𝄞𝄞 (Warner Bros., 1978)

worth searching for: *Lonely Hearts* (Silver Rarities, 1995) is a wonderful two-disc bootleg set that captures Richard and Linda's performances from 1981 and 1982, with a few Fairporters guesting on the latter.

solo outings:
Philip Pickett with Richard Thompson and the Fairport Rhythm Section:
The Bones of All Men (Hannibal, 1998) 𝄞𝄞

influences:
◀◀ Wes Montgomery, Django Rheinhardt, Jimi Hendrix, Nick Drake, Van Morrison, Bob Dylan

▶▶ Dire Straits, Elvis Costello, Jeff Buckley, Womack & Womack

see also: *Fairport Convention*

Simon Glickman and Gary Graff

Thompson Twins
/Babble

Thompson Twins formed 1977, in Chesterfield, England. Disbanded 1992. Babble formed 1993.

Thompson Twins: Tom Bailey, vocals, keyboards, guitar; John Roog (1977–82), guitar; Pete Dodd, guitar (1977–82); Chris Bell, drums (1977–82); Alannah Currie, percussion, saxophone, vocals (1981–92); Joe Leeway, percussion, vocals (1982–86); Matthew Seligman, bass (1981–82). Babble: Tom Bailey (1993–present); Alannah Currie (1993–present).

With its MTV-ready haircuts and bouncy synth-pop, the Thompson Twins hit big in the early '80s after spending its earliest years as a kind of tribal collective formed amid London's squatter culture. Its 15 minutes of fame came via the hit 1984 album *Into the Gap*, a commercial zenith the Twins would never again hit. By 1986 the group was down to the husband-wife duo of Tom Bailey and Alannah Currie; they soldiered on for a few years, pursuing exotic and rhythmic music until they finally decided the Thompson Twins moniker (which came from a British cartoon) was an albatross. Jettisoning it, they continue to record as Babble, plowing wholeheartedly into Eastern-oriented ambient styles.

what to buy: The synth sounds on *Into the Gap* 𝄞𝄞𝄞𝄞 (Arista, 1984, prod. Alex Sadkin, Tom Bailey) are a bit dated today, but in a charming way, and the hits—"Hold Me Now," "Sister of Mercy," "You Take Me Up"—still sound great. *Love, Lies . . . and Other Strange Things* 𝄞𝄞𝄞𝄞 (Arista, 1996, prod. various) is the greatest-hits collection that the U.S. market was missing for so many years.

what to buy next: Babble is a compelling new venture for Bailey and Currie, but an acquired taste for those hooked by the Thompson Twins' more accessible pop fare. Either *The Stone* 𝄞𝄞𝄞𝄞 (Reprise, 1994, prod. Alannah Currie, Tom Bailey) or *Ether* 𝄞𝄞𝄞 (Reprise, 1996, prod. Tom Bailey, Alannah Currie, Keith Fernley) reward repeated listenings with their deep grooves and subtle melodicism.

what to avoid: The bulk of the Thompson Twins' catalog is out of print, and the remix collection *Greatest Mixes: Best of the Thompson Twins* 𝄞𝄞 (Arista, 1988, prod. various) is an inadequate and misleadingly titled representation of the group's work.

the rest:
Big Trash 𝄞𝄞 (Warner Bros., 1989)
Queer 𝄞𝄞 (Warner Bros., 1991)

influences:
◀◀ David Bowie, Roxy Music, Talking Heads

▶▶ Depeche Mode, Neneh Cherry, Howard Jones, Thomas Dolby

Gary Graff and Allan Orski

Paul Thorn

Born in Tupelo, MS.

By 1987 Paul Thorn had reached the peak of his career, but not as a musician. A talented regional boxing champion, Thorn found himself in Atlantic City facing fearsome champion Roberto Duran for the world title. Thorn lost the fight, but soon after found a way to make a living that involved making hits as opposed to getting hit. As the son of a Church of God Minister, Thorn had been playing music since age three, banging on a tambourine at religious revival meetings. Though it took him a while to understand music as his true calling—he'd boxed since his teens and worked 14 years as an assembly line worker in a chair-making factory—Thorn eventually took a solo acoustic apprenticeship playing a house gig in a local tavern for a primarily blue collar audience. Through his brother Stan, a professional musician himself, Thorn met Nashville songwriter Billy Maddox, who helped Thorn develop his own distinct writing style: rural, country-rock-based songs full of grit and hard luck, with a decidedly offbeat perspective. Partnering with Maddox, Thorn succeeded in placing songs with the bigtime country likes of Joe Diffie, Tanya Tucker, and Ronnie Milsap, and eventually secured him a solo deal of his own.

what to buy: Thorn has a poet's eye for detail on his gutsy debut, *Hammer & Nail* 𝄢𝄢𝄢𝄢 (A&M, 1997, prod. Wyatt Easterling, Gregg Wells, Billy Maddox) an earthy, roots-rock collection that shuttles between satisfying gallops and acoustic introspections, from the literate blues rock of "A Heart with Four Wheel Drive" to the infectious metaphor of "800 Pound Jesus" and the mellow, radio-friendly boogie of "I Bet He Knows."

influences:

◄◄ Hank Williams Sr., Lynyrd Skynyrd, Bob Dylan

Bob Gulla

George Thorogood & the Destroyers

Formed 1973, in Wilmington, DE.

George Thorogood, guitar, vocals; Michael Lenn, bass (1973–75); Jeff Simon, drums; Billy Blough, bass (1975–present); Hank Carter, saxophone (1980–present).

George Thorogood blew a breath of fresh air into the studied poses of the new wave era with a blast of unexpurgated, unrepentant blues and boogie on a series of albums for the tiny Boston-based indie label, Rounder. His faithful, frankly derivative attack on blues classics made up in splashy conviction and hard-wrought passion what it lacked in originality. As Thorogood caught fire with radio and the public, he honed his approach, supplying himself with effective originals alongside the vintage R&B numbers and emphasized the boogie side of his mix somewhat more heavily. But in general, Thorogood has remained true to his initial vision after more than 20 years of recording.

what to buy: His breathtaking debut album, *George Thorogood & the Destroyers* 𝄢𝄢𝄢𝄢 (Rounder, 1975, prod. J. Nagy), retains its fresh, ferocious feel, as Thorogood introduces a style that would remain constant—blues, boogie, and lots of slashing slide guitar.

what to buy next: *The Baddest of George Thorogood & the Destroyers* 𝄢𝄢𝄢 (EMI, 1992, prod. Terry Manning, Delaware Destroyers) contains only one track from that original release and collects the highlights of his dozen subsequent albums.

what to avoid: His 1974 demo recordings found their way into release as *Better than the Rest* 𝄢𝄢 (MCA, 1979, prod. D. Lipman) and more recently as *Nadine* 𝄢𝄢 (MCA Special Products, 1998, prod. D. Lipman). The band was unformed and Thorogood himself rather green, and these early experiments offer no pointers towards his imminent success. Tsk, tsk.

the rest:

Move It on Over 𝄢𝄢𝄢 (Rounder, 1978)
More George Thorogood & the Destroyers 𝄢𝄢𝄢 (Rounder, 1980)
Bad to the Bone 𝄢𝄢𝄢 (EMI, 1982)
Maverick 𝄢𝄢 (EMI, 1985)
Live 𝄢𝄢 (EMI, 1986)
Born to Be Bad 𝄢𝄢 (EMI, 1988)
Boogie People 𝄢𝄢 (EMI, 1991)
Haircut 𝄢𝄢𝄢 (EMI, 1993)
Let's Work Together Live 𝄢𝄢 (EMI, 1995)
Rockin' My Life Away 𝄢𝄢𝄢 (EMI, 1997)

worth searching for: *Greatest Hits* (Rounder, 1988, prod. various) is a Japanese import that provides a good summation of Thorogood's Rounder years.

influences:

◄◄ John Lee Hooker, Bo Diddley, Chuck Berry, Duane Eddy, Elmore James

►► The Nighthawks, the Fabulous Thunderbirds, the Black Crowes, Hank Williams Jr.

Joel Selvin

Three Dog Night

Formed 1967, in Los Angeles, CA. Disbanded 1977. Re-formed 1981.

Danny Hutton, vocals (1967–76, 1981–present; Chuck Negron, vocals (1967–77, 1981–83); Cory Wells, vocals; Mike Allsup, guitar (1967–76); Jimmy Greenspoon, keyboards; Joe Schermie, bass (1967–73); Jack Ryland, bass (1973–76); Floyd Sneed, drums (1967–76); Skip Konte, keyboards (1973–76); Jay Gruska, vocals (1976–77).

Three Dog Night was a hit-making machine. From 1969–75, the

George Thorogood (© Ken Settle)

group charted more than 20 times, thanks to terrific lead vocals and harmonies, a keen ear for selecting good songs by great songwriters, and an ability to arrange these songs in a dynamic fashion. A full-fledged seven-piece band, Three Dog Night began as a group of rockers with strong soul and R&B influences; initially the band was as comfortable covering Otis Redding's "Try a Little Tenderness" as Argent guitarist Russ Ballard's "Liar." In so doing, Three Dog Night aided the careers of such songwriters as Randy Newman, Elton John, Bernie Taupin, and Harry Nilsson, to name a very few. What made the group immensely popular also cost it credibility in the burgeoning underground radio market, however. But it was a respect the band could forgo, as 10 of its albums sold more than a million copies each. The hits wound down in the mid-'70s, and these days Danny Hutton and Cory Wells keep the band out on the oldies circuit.

what to buy: *Celebrate: The Three Dog Night Story 1965–1975* ♫♫♫♫ (MCA, 1993, prod. various) has all the hits, plus the better album stuff and two previously unreleased tracks. It's an interesting listen as Three Dog Night grows into its own, at first fumbling but then clicking with precision.

what to buy next: *Harmony* ♫♫♫ (Dunhill, 1971/MCA Special Products 1994, prod. Richard Podolor) is the group's best studio effort, with the early hits "Old Fashioned Love Song," "Family of Man," and Hoyt Axton's "Never Been to Spain."

what to avoid: *Joy to the World: Their Greatest Hits* ♫ (Dunhill, 1974/MCA, 1989) is burdened by haphazard digital transfers and makes for a dull-to-aggravating listening experience. *Captured Live at the Forum* ♫♫ (Dunhill, 1969/MCA, 1989) is not a compelling live performance and does little to enhance the original studio versions.

the rest:
Naturally ♫♫♫ (Dunhill, 1970/MCA Special Products, 1989)
Seven Separate Fools ♫♫♫♫ (Dunhill, 1972/MCA Special Products, 1989)
Cyan ♫♫♫ (Dunhill, 1973/MCA, 1990)
Hard Labor ♫♫ (Dunhill, 1974/MCA, 1990)
Best Of ♫♫♫ (MCA, 1982)

worth searching for: *Around the World with Three Dog Night* (Dunhill, 1973) is a better-sounding concert document than the *Captured Live at the Forum* set.

solo outings:
Chuck Negron:
Am I Still in Your Heart ♫♫ (Viceroy, 1995)

influences:
◀◀ Otis Redding, Laura Nyro, the Four Tops, the Beatles
▶▶ America, Bo Donaldson & the Heywoods, Paper Lace

Patrick McCarty and Gary Graff

WHAT ALBUM CHANGED YOUR LIFE?

Urban Dance Squad's *Mental Thoughts for the Globe* was an underappreciated, groundbreaking album. So much has been culled from that album, idea-wise, not only by us, but Rage [Against the Machine] and anyone who interprets rap and rock has listened to Urban Dance Squad for sure.

S.A. Martinez (of 311)

311

Formed 1990, in Omaha, NE.

Nick Hexum, vocals, guitars; Doug "S.A." Martinez, vocals, turntables; Aaron "P-Nut" Wills, bass; Timothy J. Mahoney, guitars; Chad Sexton, drums.

Music has been in the blood of 311's members since they were young. Chad Sexton caught the bug during the late '70s after his uncle caught a towel "bloodied" by Gene Simmons during a Kiss concert. Later, he honed his drumming skills as a member of a drum-and-bugle corps in Nebraska. 311 is one of those bands that was fortunate enough not to play grimy, low-paying clubs before getting its first high-profile gig. Instead, the band's first show was a spot opening for punk DIY kings Fugazi in the not-so-punk town of Omaha. Unwilling to play off of that, 311 hit the road in 1992 and hasn't given up since, blending rock, hip-hop, and ska with lyrics that are sometimes politically charged and sometimes delve into science-fiction theory. A breakthrough with its 1995 album *311* put the group on the modern rock map, but its follow-up was a failure, making it appear—for the moment—like just another one-hit wonder of the '90s.

what to buy: *311* ♫♫♫♫ (Capricorn, 1995, prod. Ron St. Germain, 311) is a confident amalgamation of hard rock, hip-hop, funk, and reggae. Frontman Nick Hexum's smooth melodic delivery, accented by S.A. Martinez's raps, adds color to the brilliant canvas of songs such as "Random" and "Jackolantern's Weather." The toe-tapping "All Mixed Up" proves that five

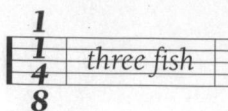

white Midwesterners can pull off dancehall. The pro-hemp band disses hard drug users and violence-prone gangbangers in the groove-heavy "Hive" and "Guns." More than just a momentary success, *311* is one of the finest hip-hop/rock albums of the '90s.

what to buy next: *Music* ♫♫♫ (Capricorn, 1993, prod. Eddy Offord) is an in-your-face jam. Reggae influences peek through a pile of chugging guitars, funky grooves, and rapped vocals, as in the opening song "Welcome." The self-serving "Nix Hex" is reminiscent of spending muggy summer nights on a deck watching world beat bands.

what to avoid: The 21-song mess *Transistor* ♫ (Capricorn, 1997, prod. Scotch Ralston, 311) offers only an EP's worth of good songs. When 311 went into the studio to make *Transistor*, its members must have said "Let's use every influence we can and see what comes out." The result is a pretentious collection of monotone songs.

the rest:
Grassroots ♫♫♫ (Capricorn, 1994)

worth searching for: The band's first three independent albums–*Unity*, *Hydroponic*, and *Dammit* –all released on 311's own What Have You Records—are collector's items. Selected tracks from each of the albums is scheduled to be available by the end of 1998 as part of a compilation CD to be released on What Have You Records. It will be available through 311's website, http://www.311music.com, and to fan club members.

influences:
◀◀ The Beastie Boys, Bad Brains, Red Hot Chili Peppers
▶▶ The Urge

Christina Fuoco

Three Fish
See: Pearl Jam

The Three O'Clock
Formed 1980, in Los Angeles, CA. Disbanded 1988.

Michael Quercio, vocals, bass; Louis Gutierrez, guitar, vocals (1980–86); Jason Faulkner, guitar (1987–88); Danny Benair, drums; Mickey Mariano, keyboards.

When the Three O'Clock arrived on the fledgling L.A. Paisley Underground scene in the early '80s, they were more than just a psychedelic band. But each label that released a Three O'Clock record decided to overplay their psychedelic tendencies, drawing attention away from their merits as a great pop band. Led by Michael Quercio, who had a knack for writing three-minute pop gems, the group was hampered somewhat by his falsetto vocal delivery, which tended to polarize listen-

ers. Still, the Three O'Clock rode the wave of the Paisley movement, sharing the bill with the Bangles, Rain Parade, and the Dream Syndicate, spending some quality time on the then-nascent MTV. The group released four proper records and one amazing EP (not including the repackaging of the Salvation Army records, an early incarnation of the Three O'Clock). All their major-label records, those for I.R.S. Records and Paisley Park, are sadly, long out of print. Since 1988 Quercio has formed a new group in Permanent Green Light, serving the pop needs of the Three O'Clock fans that are remaining.

what's available: The Three O'Clock's most revered recordings were released on the 1982 EP *Baroque Hoedown*, which has been graciously included on the reissue of 1983's *Sixteen Tambourines* ♫♫♫♫ (Frontier, 1993, prod. Earle Mankey). The album includes pretty much everything you need from the band, and makes plain their tight harmonies and the incredible guitar tones of Louis Gutierrez. The songs from *Baroque* include the unforgettable "With a Cantaloupe Girlfriend" and the anthemic "I Go Wild." The group's unique brand of '60s-influenced pop is augmented by cover versions of songs by the Easybeats and the Bee Gees.

solo outings:
Permanent Green Light (Michael Quercio):
Permanent Green Light ♫♫♫ (Giant/Rockville, 1998)

influences:
◀◀ The Easybeats, the Nazz, the Beatles
▶▶ Game Theory, the Bangles, Rain Parade

Chris Richards

Throbbing Gristle
Formed 1975, in Manchester, England. Disbanded 1981.

Cosey Fanni Tutti, vocals, guitar, synthesizer; Chris Carter, synthesizer, vocals; Peter Christopherson, vibraphone, cornet, vocals; Genesis P-Orridge, bass, violin, synthesizer.

So you wanna check out something "truly" industrial? Throbbing Gristle should definitely make your short list. As the founders of Industrial Records (home to Cabaret Voltaire, Clock DVA, and others) TG was the embodiment of the industrial movement of the late '70s and early '80s. In fact, the band had already been together almost half a decade and broken up before Depeche Mode, Ministry, or many other electronically influenced bands had released albums. By modern standards, much of TG's material sounds underproduced and a bit disoriented. Partly to blame are technological advancements in sampling, recording, and instruments, but mostly that was the band's intent. Just because it was electronic didn't mean it didn't have soul; in fact, a large chunk of the TG catalog was never properly written songs—they were free-form improvisation, whether on stage or in a studio. The band's musical style ranges from the barrage of guitar noise and screaming commonly associated with this genre to songs that show the seeds of what would later become known as techno/ambient music. And TG did—on occasion—write a mean pop song, with solid hooks and catchy lyrics cushioning the bent, deviant imagery. While P-Orridge is the de-facto frontman of the band, the other members all went on to higher (relatively) levels of commercial success. P-Orridge still maintains the band's catalog and is constantly digging up some live show, unreleased track, or other to put out in some form. As with many bands that maintain a ferocious cult following, TG has posthumously released a body of work in excess of what came out while the band was still together. In TG's case, the volume is literally almost 100 times more material since the band broke up! After the split in 1981, P-Orridge went on to form Psychic TV and was joined for a brief period by Peter Christopherson. Their parting was so bad, however, that P-Orridge has removed Christopherson from the credits on many later reissues and live releases. Carter and Fanni-Tutti went on to release a number of solo albums but did their best work as Chris & Cosey—actually garnering some commercial success in the U.K. and Canada after signing to Nettwerk Records. After his split with P-Orridge, Christopherson formed the highly influential Coil.

what to buy: *Greatest Hits: Entertainment through Pain* ♫♫♫♫ (Rough Trade, 1980/Mute-Restless, 1990, prod. various) gives an solid introduction to the band. The album culls tracks from the TG's first four releases—the only *real* albums so to speak.

what to buy next: *D.o.A.* ♫♫♫♫ (Industrial, 1979/Mute, 1991) is a bit more developed than the band's first effort and frankly, more listenable. With dissonant vocals, tape loops, found sounds, and William S. Burroughs-influenced themes, this is avante garde/experimental music at one of its best moments—if you don't mind the pain that occasionally comes with listening to it. *Twenty Jazz Funk Greats* ♫♫♫♫ (Industrial, 1979/Mute, 1991) is the band's third release and finds it actually attempting to record proper songs. There are some listenable, industrial-style gems here. It's not as adventurous as the first two releases, but shows great promise and is easily the most influential in terms of relating the spate of post-industrial bands that would follow. Not much pain here.

what to avoid: Try to steer clear of cassettes of live shows—and live shows in general. Many are filled with instrumental jams that have no real focus. If you like hour-long songs with no beginning, middle, or end, then these may be for you.

best of the rest:
Second Annual Report ♫♫♫ (Industrial, 1978/Mute, 1993)

Heathen Earth ♫♫♫ (Industrial, 1979/Mute, 1991)
Mission of Dead Souls ♫♫♫ (Fetish, 1981/Mute, 1991)
TG CD1 ♫♫ (Mute, 1986)
GiftGas (A Children's Story) ♫♫♫ (Dossier, 1995)
Assume Power Focus ♫♫♫ (Hollow Hills Sound, 1997)
Kreeme Horn ♫♫♫ (Caroline, 1997)

worth searching for: *Five Albums* (Zick-Zak, 1981) fetches a pretty penny in the collectors market, but if you're a Throbbing Gristle fan, it's essential. All of the band's early albums were reissued on Fetish Records during the early '80s, and this box collects them all in one place, with excellent sound quality.

influences:

◀◀ Cabaret Voltaire, William S. Burroughs, Kraftwerk

▶▶ Ministy, nine inch nails, Depeche Mode, Coil, Skinny Puppy, SPK

Tim Davis

Throwing Muses /Kristin Hersh

Formed 1980, in Newport, RI. Disbanded 1997.

Kristin Hersh, vocals, guitar; Tanya Donelly, vocals, guitar (1980–92); David Narcizo, drums; Elaine Adamedes, bass (1980–86); Leslie Langston, bass (1986–91, 1992–94); Fred Abong, bass (1991–92); Bernard Georges, bass (1994–97).

Kristin Hersh and Tanya Donelly, stepsisters inspired by punk and turned off by corny '80s new wave, built a noisy sound out of fuzz guitars and high-pitched, dreamy vocals. At their peak, the Hersh-Donelly duo produced a raw tension—Donelly liked catchy pop songs, Hersh was more into confessional singer/songwriting and Led Zeppelin–style heavy metal that made the band's sound thick and jagged. The Muses' early albums, notably the self-titled debut and *Hunkpapa*, lurch from soft folk to roaring rock and take in some reggae and waltz rhythms along the way. Eventually, the team unraveled; *The Real Ramona* is the sound of two strong personalities tugging against each other, but it lacks any central vision or coherence. Donelly—who was already working in a side band, the Breeders—left to form Belly, a more straightforward guitar-pop band. Hersh kept Throwing Muses a trio and put out a few confessional folk-rock solo albums.

what to buy: *Hunkpapa* ♫♫♫♫ (Sire, 1989, prod. Gary Smith) echoes the Beatles in its give-and-take between raw, screeching punk and glorious little melodies. The hard-to-find debut, *Throwing Muses* ♫♫♫♫ (4AD, 1986, prod. Gil Norton), is the fresh sound of energetic young women trying all kinds of (mostly noisy) combinations before coming up with their own musical identity. On *Limbo* ♫♫♫♫ (Rykodisc, 1996, prod. Throwing Muses) Hersh often sounds like she's come around to Donelly's way of thinking; it's the most melodic Muses collection yet, still deeply personal and tortured, but with a greater range of moods and an agreeably spare instrumental approach.

what to buy next: Hersh's solo debut, *Hips and Makers* 𝄢𝄢𝄢 (Sire, 1994, prod. Lenny Kaye, Kristen Hersh, Steve Rizzo) lacks Donelly's Paul McCartney that always supplemented Hersh's John Lennon so nicely. Despite some good spooky lyric-writing, it can often be a downer.

what to avoid: Hersh's pretensions become tedious on her EP *Strings* 𝄢𝄢 (Sire, 1994), which actually includes a Led Zeppelin song arranged with cello and violins.

the rest:
House Tornado 𝄢𝄢𝄢 (Sire, 1988)
The Real Ramona 𝄢𝄢𝄢 (Sire, 1991)
Red Heaven 𝄢𝄢 (Sire, 1992)
University 𝄢𝄢𝄢 (Sire, 1995)
In a Doghouse N/A (Rykodisc, 1998)

worth searching for: *The Fat Skier* (Sire EP, 1987, prod. Mark Van Hecke) and *Chains Changed* (4AD EP, 1987) are less meandering, harder-rocking portraits of the Muses in the careening-genre stage of their career.

solo outings:
Kristin Hersh:
Strange Angels 𝄢𝄢𝄢 (Rykodisc, 1998)

influences:
◀◀ The Beatles, Siouxsie & the Banshees, X-Ray Spex, the Sex Pistols, the Modern Lovers, Led Zeppelin, Joni Mitchell, the Velvet Underground, Sonic Youth

▶▶ The Pixies, P.J. Harvey, Voice of the Beehive, Veruca Salt, Sebadoh, Superchunk, Buffalo Tom

see also: *Breeders, Belly/Tanya Donelly*

Steve Knopper

Thunderclap Newman

Formed 1969, in London, England. Disbanded 1970.

John "Speedy" Keen, vocals, drums; Jimmy McCulloch (died September 27, 1979), guitar; Bijo Drains (a.k.a. Pete Townshend), bass; Andy Newman, keyboards.

An oddly assembled one-hit wonder brought to life by Pete Townshend, Thunderclap Newman enjoyed brief success in the early '70s with the song "Something in the Air," which shot to #1 in England, before rapidly calling it quits. Speedy Keen, the quartet's primary songwriter, wrote dramatic, soaring compositions that derived much of their impact from the eccentric bar-

relhouse piano stylings of Andy Newman, a former postal clerk (apparently no inspiration for the barrel-shaped mailman on *Seinfeld*). With Townshend at the production helm and filling in on bass under the pseudonym Bijou Drains, the group released *Hollywood Dream* in 1970. Touring in support of the album with an altered lineup, the band never achieved a proper live sound and quickly disbanded. Keen and Newman went on to establish solo careers while Jimmy McCulloch kicked around with Stone the Crows and John Mayall before working a stint with Paul McCartney's Wings from 1975 to 1978; he died of a drug overdose a year later. "Something in the Air" was covered memorably during the '90s by Tom Petty & the Heartbreakers.

what to buy: The group's sole release, *Hollywood Dream* 𝄢𝄢𝄢𝄢 (Track, 1970/PolyGram, 1991/Touchwood, 1997, prod. Pete Townshend) is something of a lost classic, featuring "Something in the Air," plus Keen's other fine contributions, "The Reason," "Accidents," and "Look Around." The disc also sports a cover of Bob Dylan's "Open the Door, Homer." The recent Touchwood version of the album includes six bonus tracks, the A and B sides of the band's three singles.

influences:
◀◀ John Mayall & the Bluesbreakers, the Who, Bob Dylan

▶▶ Badfinger, Tom Petty

see also: *Pete Townshend, Paul McCartney & Wings*

Jeff Hatch

Tiffany

Born Tiffany Renee Darwisch, October 2, 1971, in Norwalk, CA.

Tiffany's story has all the necessary elements of a bonafide rags-to-riches showbiz fable: As a young child, she escaped the trauma of an unhappy homelife by singing for tips in a local country bar, where she was spotted by Hoyt and Mae Axton and whisked to Nashville for an appearance on *The Ralph Emery Show*. After brief tours with George Jones and Jerry Lee Lewis—not to mention a totally disheartening plow through the Alaskan nightclub circuit—Darwisch returned to California and spent her out-of-school hours doing voice-overs in a local demo studio. George E. Tobin, the studio's owner, immediately commandeered the teenager's career and several years later secured a deal with MCA Records. Her first album, however, spent months languishing unheard in the label's warehouses until the newly rechristened Tiffany determinedly set out on the coast-to-coast "Beautiful You: Celebrating The Good Life Shopping Mall Tour '87." An undeniably brilliant promotional gimmick, these appearances soon sparked the album to life, helping it eventually sell an unprecedented four million copies and spawn two consecutive #1 singles—including a remake of

Tommy James's "I Think We're Alone Now." With this, Tiffany may have become the youngest female ever to hit the top of the album charts, but unlike her East Coast counterpart Debbie Gibson, she did not compose her own material or have any control whatsoever over her career, on stage or off. Any money she was able to squirrel away was quickly spent in a series of legal battles with both her family and Tobin, but upon freeing herself from both by the age of 21 her days as a chart-topper were already long past. In recent years Tiffany has released records in the Far East, toiled in the Vegas lounges, supplied the voice of Daughter Judy for *The Jetsons* movie, and briefly considered a return to her country roots before recently hiring Adult Contemporary producer Michael Lloyd to help mastermind a return to the domestic pop charts.

what to buy: The dozen tracks on Tiffany's *Greatest Hits* 𝄞𝄞 (Hip-O, 1996, compilation prod. Cary E. Mansfield, Andy McKaie) are really only for students of late '80's white teen dance-pop—if such students actually exist anywhere, that is. Tiffany's voice may be capable enough, but the choice of material veers from the cloying ("Could've Been," "Feelings of Forever") to the annoying ("Radio Romance") to the downright abominable ("I Think We're Alone Now," "I Saw *Him* Standing There").

the rest:
Tiffany 𝄞𝄞 (MCA, 1987)
Hold an Old Friend's Hand 𝄞𝄞 (MCA, 1988)
New Inside 𝄞 (MCA, 1990)

worth searching for: *Dreams Never Die* (MCA Japan, 1993) is a recent offering for anyone who might have an interest in what Tiffany is up to now. Don't all raise your hands at once.

influences:
◀◀ Tanya Tucker, Anne Murray, Bonnie Tyler, Belinda Carlisle, Patty Duke

▶▶ Martika, Robyn, Chynna Phillips, LeAnn Rimes, Charlotte's Bionic Blimp

Gary Pig Gold

'Til Tuesday
Formed 1984, in Boston, MA. Disbanded 1988.

Aimee Mann, bass, acoustic guitar, vocals; Michael Hausman, drums, percussion; Robert Holmes, guitars, background vocals; Joey Pesce, keyboards, background vocals (1984–87); Michael Montes, keyboards (1987–88).

'Til Tuesday most likely would be long forgotten if it weren't for the solo career of its frontwoman, Aimee Mann. A synth-pop quartet of average talent, 'Til Tuesday was blessed with Mann's gift for writing engaging melodies and sophisticated lyrics. The group scored a mega-hit early on with the single "Voices Carry,"

then promptly joined the rank and file of one-hit wonders. Despite Mann's obvious talents, the songs on all of the band's three albums are swamped by what was for the mid-'80s formulaic production: shimmering synths and stadium-size reverb. While critics praised the group and luminaries such as Elvis Costello gave creative input, 'Til Tuesday was largely ignored by its label and broke up shortly after releasing its third album.

what to buy: *Coming up Close: A Retrospective* 𝄞𝄞𝄞𝄞 (Sony, 1996, prod. various) has everything you could want from the group's catalog (and more). In addition to featuring the band's best material ("Voice Carry," "On Sunday," "The Other End of the Telescope"), the CD-Extra format offers up video clips for several tracks (including "Voices Carry") and other scrapbook items.

what to buy next: Rhett Davies's production was decidedly wrong for *Everything's Different Now* 𝄞𝄞𝄞 (Epic, 1988), but the album is made worthy by its mature songwriting and confident vocal work. Penned by Mann and songwriter/former *MTV Unplugged* host Jules Shear, the album chronicles the couple's relationship and breakup through such gems as "J for Jules," "Limits to Love," and the bouncy title track. Notable among the tunes is "The Other End (of the Telescope)," written by Mann and Elvis Costello and featuring supporting vocals from the latter.

what to avoid: *Voices Carry* 𝄞𝄞 (Epic, 1985) is a decent first effort that sounded hopelessly dated within a few years of its release. In addition to the brittle synths and glossy production, Mann's songwriting talent had yet to emerge.

the rest:
Welcome Home 𝄞𝄞𝄞 (Epic, 1986)

worth searching for: Back when 'Til Tuesday was part of MTV's regular rotation, Sony Video capitalized on the group's success (and Mann's good looks) with the music video *'Til Tuesday* (Sony, 1987), featuring videos for "Voices Carry," "What about Love," "Looking over My Shoulder," and others.

influences:
◀◀ The Beatles, the Byrds, Elvis Costello, the Pretenders, Squeeze

▶▶ Crowded House, Jules Shear, Sam Phillips, Juliana Hatfield

see also: *Aimee Mann*

Christopher Scapelliti

Timbuk 3
Formed 1978, in Madison, WI. Disbanded 1995.

Pat MacDonald, vocals, guitar, harmonica, bass; Barbara Kooyman MacDonald, vocals, guitar, harmonica, violin, mandolin; Wally Ingram, drums (1991–95); Courtney Audain, bass (1991–95).

Ever since their bluesy anti-nuclear diatribe "The Future's So

Bright, I Gotta Wear Shades" was adopted as a yuppie-lifestyle anthem in 1986, this Austin, Texas-based husband & wife duo has been thwarted by the Randy Newman Principle: If you use tongue-in-cheek humor to get under the skin, you'll wind up going over the heads of most listeners. Their compelling blend of hypnotic rhythms, clever wordplay, stinging guitars, and sweet-and-sour harmonies helped them score big on college radio with underdog-championing commentaries on homelessness ("Dirty Dirty Rice"), the religious right ("Prey"), jingoism ("National Holiday"), and shallow values ("Hairstyles and Attitudes"). Once relying on a beatbox for backing, Timbuk 3 expanded to four-piece band on its last two albums. But lack of commercial success and personal strife led to the MacDonalds breaking up both their band and their marriage. Barbara continues performing as Barbara K. in the Austin club scene; Pat has been collaborating with artists ranging from Cher to Brazilian singer Marina Lima and recently signed with I.R.S. founder Miles Copeland's new Ark 21 label.

what to buy: The MacDonalds' bluesy cynicism runs rampant through *Greetings from Timbuk 3* 🎵🎵🎵 (I.R.S., 1986, prod. Dennis Herring), the launchpad of such college favorites as "The Future's So Bright," "Life Is Hard," and "Just Another Movie." *Eden Alley* 🎵🎵🎵 (I.R.S., 1988, prod. Dennis Herring) broadens their musical base and expands their targets to include "Sample the Dog" (which predicted technology's chilling effect on education and the arts), the ska-flavored "Too Much Sex, Not Enough Affection," and a reggae-tinged hymn of devotion called "A Sinful Life." *Edge of Allegiance* 🎵🎵🎵 (I.R.S., 1989, prod. Denardo Coleman, Timbuk 3) boasts some of Pat MacDonald's darkest compositions, including "Standard White Jesus," "Daddy's Down in the Mine," "B-Side of Life," and "Acid Rain."

what to buy next: *Espace Ornano* 🎵🎵🎵 (Watermelon, 1993, prod. Timbuk 3) is a live band album recorded in France that mixes longtime favorites like "Tarzan Was a Bluesman" and "Reckless Driver" with the previously unreleased "Rage of Angels," "Throw down Gun," and "Bleeding Heart."

what to avoid: *Looks like Dark to Me* 🎵🎵 (Windham Hill, 1994, prod. Timbuk 3) is a stopgap EP with alternate versions of two songs found on *A Hundred Lovers*, a spooky rearrangement of "The Future's So Bright," and a bland cover of Steppenwolf's "Born to Be Wild."

the rest:
Big Shot in the Dark 🎵🎵🎵 (I.R.S., 1991)
Field Guide: Some of the Best of Timbuk 3 🎵🎵🎵 (I.R.S., 1992)
A Hundred Lovers 🎵🎵🎵 (Windham Hill, 1995)

worth searching for: *Just in Time for Christmas* (I.R.S., 1990, prod. various) includes Timbuk 3's bluesy diatribe against children's war toys, "All I Want for Christmas (Is World Peace)."

solo outings:
Pat MacDonald:
Pat MacDonald Sleeps with His Guitar 🎵🎵🎵 (Ark 21, 1997)

influences:
◄◄ Muddy Waters, Talking Heads, Leonard Cohen, Jim Kweskin Jug Band

►► Penelope Houston, Luscious Jackson, Sheryl Crow

David Okamoto

Tin Machine
See: David Bowie

Tindersticks
Formed 1992, in Nottingham and Kilburn, England.

Stuart Staples, vocals, guitar; Neil Fraser, guitar; Dickon Hinchcliffe, violin; Dave Boulter, keyboards; Mark Colwill, bass; Al Macaulay, drums.

The solitudinous, morning-after yang to Nick Cave's demonic, shot-through-with heroin yin, England's Tindersticks are one of today's most intriguing pop curios. Rivaled only by Scotland's Belle & Sebastian in their fragile but buoyant arrangements and intoxicating, supple etherealness—a jazzier sort, though, not so much like the Cocteau Twins'—this publicity shy sextet creates mysterious, moody music that in its tone harkens as much to the acidic humor of the Velvet Underground as to the instrumental panache of Ennio Morricone or Angelo Badalamenti. The band's first two efforts (both self-titled) rely equally on macabre drama and soothing shading—a tough mix—and vocalist Stuart Staples's rumbling mumble remains the source of much consternation for casual fans. Push past the exterior, however, and what's uncovered is an intricate web of tear-stained emotions that counterbalance the supposed spookiness. Smart, highbrow, self-sufficient, exquisitely outfitted (by London's Timothy Everest, as the band routinely mentions) but never stuffy, Tindersticks were formed from the ashes of the short-lived Asphalt Ribbons. By the start of 1993 they were issuing now-rare singles and EP's on the independent British label Tippy Toe. Critical accolades for the group's striking sound and live performances quickly elevated it to cult status, where it has remained. The group's fourth proper album (not counting the soundtrack *Nenette et Boni*, was due in 1998.

what to buy: The debut, *Tindersticks* 🎵🎵🎵🎵 (London, 1993, prod. Tindersticks), is the blueprint for the whole. Conceived as a musical evening in four parts, it's the soundtrack to a dinner party at which most guests would become extremely antsy. The second self-titled work, *Tindersticks* 🎵🎵🎵🎵 (London, 1995, prod. Tindersticks), introduces elements of Spanish guitar and lush orchestration to a decidedly far-reaching proceeding. The standout is Boulter's tragic, sardonic "My Sister," an eight-minute year of childhood trauma. But cuts such as "She's Gone" and "A Night In," with their assured sense of melody, constitute bolder steps forward for the band. *Curtains* ♪♪♪♪ (London, 1997, prod. Tindersticks) finds the 'Sticks beginning to tread water with their formula, though a newfound crispness to the songwriting and arranging offers hope of a progressive breakthrough.

what to buy next: Easy-listening fans will enjoy *Nenette et Boni* ♪♪♪ (BarNone, 1997, prod. Tindersticks), the soundtrack to a mostly unknown Claire Denis film from 1996. Though too fragmented for pure pop classicists, it nevertheless serves as a fine sampler for someone just beginning to get into darkly textured instrumental work. Staples's unique baritone, for many the element that makes Tindersticks great, is largely absent, but the atmospheric slowness (think *Twin Peaks*) still intrigues.

worth searching for: They're hard to find in stores, but two live imports are worth tracking down. *Amsterdam* (Tindersticks, 1994, prod. Tindersticks) was initially available only through mail order. It has several shining moments. *The Bloomsbury Theater 12-3-95* (Tindersticks, 1995, prod. Tindersticks) benefits greatly from the addition of a 24-piece orchestra. There are several vinyl-only singles as well—notably Sub Pop's amusing "The Smooth Sounds of Tindersticks"—but they're exceedingly difficult to acquire.

influences:

◄◄ Nick Cave & the Bad Seeds, Birthday Party, the Velvet Underground, Nico, Angelo Badalamenti

►► Julee Cruise, Friends of Dean Marinez, Belle & Sebastian

Ben Wener

Toad the Wet Sprocket

Formed 1988, in Santa Barbara, CA.

Glen Phillips, vocals, guitars; Todd Nichols, guitars; Dean Dinning, bass, keyboards, backing vocals; Randy Guss, drums.

Folk-style songwriting with a toe-tapping, guitar-pop beat, Toad the Wet Sprocket is one of the few bands that successfully used early R.E.M. as a model and went on to create a sound of its own. Formed by childhood friends, Toad began as a college band but moved up to the major leagues after the release of the beautifully melodic album *fear*. A laudable live band, Toad also enjoys a warm—and hardly harmful—relationship with Hootie & the Blowfish; the two bands have toured together, and frontman Glen Phillips lent his hand to Hootie's second album.

what to buy: *fear* ♪♪♪♪ (Columbia, 1991, prod. Gavin MacKillop) is as perfect as an album can get. A poet laureate of the modern pop scene, Phillips sings his lyrics with equal amounts of grace

and unleashed emotion. "I Will Not Take These Things for Granted," "Before You Were Born," and the shimmering mandolin in "Walk on the Ocean" are the highlights of the album.

what to buy next: *Dulcinea* ♪♪♪ (Columbia, 1994, prod. Gavin MacKillop) is even poppier than previous releases. The singles "Fly from Heaven," "Something's Always Wrong," and "Fall Down" are tasty, well-crafted songs, but the gems of the album are "Stupid" and "Nanci," the latter a sing-around-the-campfire folk ode to Nanci Griffith and Loretta Lynn. But a dark cloud floats over *Coil* ♪♪♪ (Columbia, 1997, prod. Gavin MacKillop, Toad the Wet Sprocket). On previous albums, Toad took the most heartbreaking situations and turned them into an upbeat song (see the anti-rape song "Hold Her Down" on *fear*). But on *Coil*, a song like "Dam Would Break" is musically dark and shows what can happen when you hold feelings in.

what to avoid: With the exception of "Good Intentions," it's easy to see why the songs on *In Light Syrup* ♪♪♪ (Columbia, 1995, prod. various) were either not used or consigned to B-sides and movie soundtracks.

the rest:
Bread and Circus ♪♪♪ (Columbia, 1989)
Pale ♪♪♪ (Columbia, 1990)

worth searching for: The sweet-tempered *Acoustic Dance Party* (Columbia EP, 1994, prod. Toad the Wet Sprocket), a five-song CD sold at Toad concerts, offers a nibble of the band's outstanding live shows.

influences:

◄◄ R.E.M., Nanci Griffith, the Beatles, Crosby, Stills & Nash

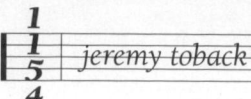 Hootie & the Blowfish, the Verve Pipe, Gin Blossoms, Better than Ezra

Christina Fuoco

Jeremy Toback

Born June 18, 1968 in Los Angeles, CA.

An Ivy League humanities student turned singer-songwriter, Jeremy Toback dabbled in the L.A. avant garde jazz scene for a few years before surfacing on pop culture radar with Stone Gossard's (Pearl Jam) side project, Brad. There, the dexterous Princeton graduate transcended his role as bass player, taking on organ, guitar, and production duties on the band's 1993 debut *Shame*. He also played on the group's second album, *Interiors*, but skipped the tour in order to pursue his own career.

what's available: Toback's own first record, *Perfect Flux Thing* (RCA, 1997, prod. Craig Street), 🎵🎵🎵 is a sturdy rock work with casual folk undertones. On it, Toback moves from low-impact, jangly guitar play with minimal band backup to songs where percussion and bass chime in big like an acoustic Soundgarden. Toback's voice, though not particularly strong, is always on pitch, and lilts without being whiny. Smart lyrics, neat little production tricks, and a few well-placed post-punk guitar licks round things out.

worth searching for: In 1996 Jeremy released a self-titled EP on Boston-based CherryDisc Records.

influences:

◀◀ Matthew Sweet, Neil Young, Soundgarden, Afghan Whigs

see also: *Brad*

Isaac Josephson

Toenut

See: Drivin' N' Cryin'

The Tokens
/The Tokens Featuring Mitch Margo
/The Four Winds
/The Buddies
/The Coeds
/Cross Country

Formed 1960, in Brooklyn, NY.

Jay Siegel, lead baritone vocals; Hank Medress, first tenor vocals (1960–70); Mitch Margo, second tenor and baritone vocals, guitar, keyboards, drums; Phil Margo, bass vocals, guitar, percussion; Joseph Ven-

neri, vocals (1961–65); Jay Leslie, vocals, horns, percussion (1990–present); Mike Johnson, vocals, keyboards, bass (1990–present); Noah Margo, drums, "merchandise" (1990–present); Damien Margo.

Although best remembered for its 1961 chart-topping classic "The Lion Sleeps Tonight," the Tokens actually did more than any other vocal group to not only update the sounds and styles of authentic doo-wop vocalizing, but also ensure its pedigree survive the horrors of the '70s and beyond. An early incarnation of the Tokens briefly included Neil Sedaka, but upon his departure for greener (solo) pastures and the subsequent recruitment of angel-voiced Jay Siegel, the freshly re-formed quartet scored quickly with "Tonight I Fell in Love," a one-off release on Morty Kroft's tiny Warwick label. When Kroft decided not to pay up after the record hit the Top 20, the Tokens moved on to RCA, where the group not only released several international hits but wisely set up its own publishing, production, and recording concerns. This ensured the group remained active with other artists, such as the Chiffons and the Happenings, while the majority of its contemporaries languished under the onslaught of the British Invasion. After a Tokens revival of Brian Wilson's "Don't Worry Baby" flopped in 1970, Medress left the group to work behind the scenes with Tony Orlando & Dawn, while the Margo brothers and Siegel enjoyed a final chart entry in 1973 with their innovative remake of Wilson Pickett's "In the Midnight Hour." Nevertheless, both Siegel *and* the Margos have kept rival groups of Tokens active on the corporate nostalgia circuit to this day, while "The Lion Sleeps Tonight" remains an indelible presence in everything from Disney movies to R.E.M. songs.

what to buy: There are many harmony-drenched joys to be found on *Wimoweh! The Best of the Tokens* 🎵🎵🎵 (RCA, 1994, compilation prod. Paul Williams), not the least of which is the never-less-than-awe-inspiring vocals of Siegel. With the possible exception of the Four Seasons, this was the music that best bridged the '50s to the '60s.

what to buy next: One of the most criminally overlooked treasures in all of rock, *Intercourse* 🎵🎵🎵🎵 (B.T. Puppy, 1971/1995, prod. Tokens) boldly succeeded, as none other even attempted, in welding the Brooklyn doo-wop aesthetic to a post-*Sgt. Pepper* framework. This still-progressive-sounding song cycle, originally recorded for Warner Bros. in 1968 but left unreleased until several years later, is thankfully now available in wide release for the first time ever. Don't you dare miss it.

what to avoid: The title shouldn't fool you: *The Lion Sleeps Tonight* 🎵🎵 (RCA, 1994, compilation prod. Paul Williams) is *not* a reissue of the group's debut album, but a skimpy 10-song collection rendered more than superfluous by the 1994 *Wimoweh!* package.

the rest:

Oldies Are Now 🎵🎵🎵 (B.T. Puppy, 1993)

Merry Merry ♫♫♪ (B.T. Puppy, 1995)

Tonight, the Lion Dances (Esta Noche, el Leon Baila) ♫♫♪ (B.T. Puppy, 1996)

All Time Greatest Hits N/A (Taragon, 1998)

influences:

◀◀ The Weavers, Dion & the Belmonts, Darryl & the Oxfords

▶▶ Frankie Valli & the Four Seasons, Robert John, Tight Fit, the Nylons

Gary Pig Gold

Tommy Tutone

Formed late 1970s, in San Francisco, CA.

Tommy Heath, vocals; Jim Keller, guitar; others.

This duo first surfaced with "Angel Say No" in 1980, but it was 1981's indelible "867-5309/Jenny" that earned Tommy Heath and Jim Keller their footnote in pop history, at the same time spawning innumerable crank calls to the title number. The obsessive ditty opens with a guy so immobilized with passion for a girl whose name and number he got off a wall—a girl he's never met, mind you—that he can only sit by the phone in torment. What happens next is anybody's guess, though it probably involves stalking. Tutone is now led by Heath alone.

what's available: The only material currently available on the band is *Golden Classics* ♫♫♪ (Collectables, 1997), which contains the first two albums, *Tommy Tutone* and *Tommy Tutone 2*, in their entirety. Both "Angel Say No" and "867-5309/Jenny" are here, though. At press time, their new album, *Rich Text Files*, was scheduled for release in 1998.

influences:

◀◀ The Beatles, the Outsiders, Cheap Trick

▶▶ 1-800-COLLECT

Allan Orski

Tones on Tail

Formed 1981, in Northhampton, England. Disbanded 1984.

Daniel Ash, vocals, guitar; Glen Campling, bass; Kevin Haskins, drums.

Tones on Tail began as a Bauhaus side project for Daniel Ash and roadie Glen Campling; after Bauhaus split in 1983, Kevin Haskins joined as drummer. Tones on Tail was completely different than its parent band, with a poppier and more modern feel in contrast to Bauhaus' gloomy gothic sound. Tones on Tail ended after a U.S. tour in 1984, as Ash and Haskins were preparing to step into yet another project, Love & Rockets.

what to buy: *Everything* ♫♫♫♫ (Beggar's Banquet, 1998, prod. Tones on Tail) is just what it says–everything Tones on Tail released on a two-CD set with beautifully remastered sound that gives the song a sharper, punchier quality. Tones' only proper release, *The Album Pop* ♫♫♫♫ (Vertigo/PolyGram, 1984, prod. Tones on Tail) sounds genuinely contemporary, giving Ash the kind of free creative rein he didn't have in Bauhaus. The single "Go!" hit big in U.S. dance clubs.

the rest:

Tones on Tail ♫♫♫ (Situation Two, 1985)

Night Music ♫♫♫♫ (Beggars Banquet, 1987)

Tones on Tail ♫♫♫♪ (Beggars Banquet, 1990)

influences:

◀◀ Siouxsie & the Banshees, Nick Cave & the Bad Seeds

▶▶ Sisters of Mercy, Marilyn Manson

see also: *Bauhaus, Love & Rockets*

J.D. Cantarella

Tonic

Formed 1993, in Los Angeles, CA.

Emerson Hart, vocals, guitars; Jeff Russo, guitar; Dan Rothchild, bass (1993–95); Dan Lavery, bass (1995–present); Kevin Shepard, drums.

Growing up in New Jersey, Emerson Hart had no problems with his neighbors when he was rehearsing with his band. After all, E Street Band drummer Max Weinberg lived next door. Hart, the son of Sandra Hart of the television show *Romper Room*, started fiddling around with the guitar when he was seven and began to take music seriously 12 years later. He packed up, moved west, and ran into childhood acquaintance Jeff Russo in an L.A. deli. The duo began writing songs and inked a publishing deal with EMI. While visiting L.A.'s Kibitz Room, they met house drummer Kevin Shepard and bassist Dan Rothchild, the son of Doors' producer Paul Rothchild. Thus Tonic, originally known as Radio Flyer, was formed. To round out Tonic's credentials, Russo starred in one of the first TV condom commercials.

what's available: For *Lemon Parade* ♫♫ (A&M, 1996, prod. Jack Joseph Puig), Tonic could have squeezed out a few more hooks. The band's ability to do that is best shown in the singles "If You Could Only See" and "Open up Your Eyes." Soaring guitars coupled with Hart's cascading vocals show that Tonic can rise above the mush that is "Casual Affair" and the title track. "Thick" opens with wailing à la Robert Plant and continues with a mess of distorted guitars. Tonic should stick with the formula that made the hits work so well.

influences:

◀◀ The Beatles, Counting Crows, Dishwalla

Christina Fuoco

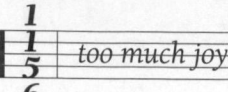

Too Much Joy

Formed 1983, in Scarsdale, NY.

Tim Quirk, vocals; Jay Blumenfield, guitar, vocals; Sandy Smallens, bass, vocals (1983–93); Tommy Vinton, drums; William Wittman, bass, vocals (1993–present).

Tim Quirk is a genuinely funny guy, which is a good thing for a rock 'n' roll band—except on those occasions when he's not funny. Too Much Joy's first two or three albums are hilarious; Quirk's clever, simple knack with words results in lines like "People wore dumb hats/And they fell in love," his thumbnail take on the year 1964. His wonderfully weird lyrics drop the names Genghis Khan, Edgar Allan Poe, Red Riding Hood, the Mekons, the Clash ("Hugo" deservedly lampoons *Combat Rock*), and all long-haired guys from England. It helps that the band backs up Quirk's sarcastic musings with loud, explosive rock 'n' roll, particularly Tommy Vinton's Keith Moon–like drumming, Alas, Too Much Joy has never received the attention it deserves, despite inspired stunts like following up the 2 Live Crew's famous arrest by playing the controversial rap song "Me So Horny" in Florida and getting arrested for it, too. After business problems with Giant Records, which never figured out how to market the band, Too Much Joy wandered around labelless before putting out a lukewarm return, . . . *Finally*, in 1996.

what to buy: *Son of Sam I Am* 🎵🎵🎵🎵 (Alias, 1988/Giant/Warner Bros., 1990, prod. Michael James) is the definitive Too Much Joy album, with the classic "Hugo" and 15 funny songs that never get old. Some critics said the band finally lost its edge on *Mutiny* 🎵🎵🎵🎵 (Giant-Warner Bros., 1992, prod. William Wittman), but they weren't listening carefully enough. With a snappy, rewritten version of the Records' "Starry Eyes" and a tremendous femme-fatale song, "Donna Everywhere," the album should have made at least a commercial blip.

what to buy next: *Cereal Killers* 🎵🎵🎵 (Alias/Giant/Warner Bros., 1991, prod. Paul Fox) is more notable for its jokes (a parody of the TV ad "King of Beers," among them) than its music, but it's still fun listening.

what to avoid: On . . . *Finally* 🎵🎵 (Discovery, 1996, prod. William Wittman), Quirk downplays humor for rebellious introspection—like James Taylor fronting a punk band or something.

worth searching for: The debut, *Green Eggs and Crack* (Stonegarden, 1987, prod. Al Hemburger, Too Much Joy), is hard to find, but it's full of electric tunes and songs about James Dean.

influences:
◀◀ The Who, the Clash, the Records, Tom Petty, the Dead Milkmen

▶▶ The Presidents of the United States of America, Cracker, Weezer

Steve Knopper

Tool
/The Replicants

Formed 1991, in Los Angeles, CA.

Maynard James Keenan, vocals; Adam Jones, guitars; Paul D'Amour, bass (1991–95); Justin Chancellor, bass (1995–present); Danny Carey, drums.

Maynard James Keenan spent his formative years among the dairy farms and dirt roads of rural Western Michigan. Still, rock, metal, and horror films eeked into his blood, creating the base for Tool. Schlepping gear around the Los Angeles area, Keenan played in a variety of bands before meeting his neighbor, Danny Carey, the former drummer for Green Jellÿ, best known for its in-your-face rendition of the "Three Little Pigs." Artist and guitarist Adam Jones moved to L.A. from Illinois in 1986 and learned the art of stop-motion camera techniques before moving into the rock realm. A booking on Lollapalooza's first second stage during the summer of 1992 gave Tool a strong start; by 1997 it was one of the festival's headliners.

what to buy: On *Undertow* 🎵🎵🎵🎵 (Zoo, 1993, prod. Sylvia Massy, Tool), a rape victim tells the gritty tale of physical retribution in "Prison Sex," a hypnotic blend of guitars and drums that ironically became a hit in alternative dance clubs. Keenan jumped on his soap box for the dramatic first single "Sober," where he wails "Why can't we not be sober?" Jones's talent came in handy as he created creepy award-winning videos for "Sober" and "Prison Sex."

what to buy next: The debut EP *Opiate* 🎵🎵🎵 (Zoo, 1992, prod. Sylvia Massy, Steve Hansgen, Tool) hinted at the dark crunge that would surface on *Undertow*.

what to avoid: The long wait for Tool's sophomore full-length effort culminated with the dismal, unfocused *Aenima* 🎵🎵 (Zoo, 1996, prod. Dave Bottrill, Tool), a dense, dour and ponderous disc that lacks the best qualities of *Undertow*. Also skipable is the album by the Replicants, former Tool bassist Paul D'Amour's side project with members of Failure. *The Replicants* 🎵 (Zoo, 1995, prod. Replicants) offers an acerbic assortment of covers, including guest vocalist Keenan on Wings' "Silly Love Songs."

influences:
◀◀ Rollins Band, Rage Against the Machine

▶▶ Sevendust, Coal Chamber

Christina Fuoco

Torch Song

See: William Orbit

Tornados

Formed 1961, in London, England. Disbanded 1966.

George Bellamy, guitar; Heinz Burt, bass; Alan Caddy; Clem Cattini, drums; Roger LaVern, keyboards.

The English instrumental band the Tornados was actually the product of eccentric Brit Joe Meek, an early independent producer who wrote their biggest hit, "Telstar," created the sound, and engineered their recordings, which made innovative use of keyboards in a pre-synthesizer world. They backed singer Billy Fury in between studio sessions, even while "Telstar" became an international hit. The Tornados were lumped into the surf music craze, though they were based far from any beach. Within a year of the group's break-up (precipitated by the Mersey invasion), Meek, despondent over business failures, murdered his landlady and then turned the rifle on himself. "Telstar," however, lives on, having been recorded by the Ventures, Ashley Hutchings with Richard Thompson, Simon Nicol, and bandleader Billie Vaughn.

what's available: "Telstar" is readily available on many collections of period music. If you want more, you'll need to find *The Very Best of the Tornados: "Telstar" & Other Joe Meek Productions* 𝄞𝄞𝄞𝄞 (Musical Collection International, 1997), which contains their signature tracks as well as 14 other ghostly instrumental tracks, including the lovely "Hymn for Teenagers."

worth searching for: For the fanatic only: another version of "Telstar"—this one credited to the Tornados 74 on *Kahuna Classics: A Collection of Surf Music* (K-Tel, 1997), alongside 31 other surf classics, from "Wipe Out" to "The Little Old Lady (From Pasadena)." Evan Johns and the H-Bombs' killer guitar version of "Telstar" appears on *Please Mr. Santa Claus* (Rykodisc, 1990), and you can hear Elvis Costello quote the song near the end of "Little Atoms," on *All This Useless Beauty* (Warner Bros., 1996).

influences:

◀◀ The Ventures, the Surfaris, the Marketts, Santo & Johnny

▶▶ Elvis Costello, the Sir Douglas Quintet, the Ventures

Leland Rucker

Tortoise

Formed 1991, in Chicago, IL.

Doug McCombs, bass, lap steel; John Herndon, drums, vibraphone, keyboards; John McEntire, drums, keyboards, marimba, programming (1992–present); Bundy K. Brown, bass (1992–95); Dan Bitney, percus-sion, keyboards, bass, programming (1994–present); Dave Pajo, bass, guitar (1995–present); Jeff Parker, guitar (1996–present).

Begun as a side project by Doug McCombs and John Herndon, Tortoise evolved into a veritable indie-rock all-star band of Chicago musicians representing notable outfits such as Eleventh Dream Day, the Poster Children, the Sea and Cake, Gastr del Sol, Slint, and even the free-jazz bastion the Association for the Advancement of Creative Musicians. The quintet, which at first may have appeared to be an esoteric indulgence with its guitarless, double-bass lineup and all-instrumental compositions, emerged as a leading light in the mid-'90s post-rock wave in which bands formed by rock musicians looked to non-rock sources for inspiration. Following a pair of singles, the group's self-titled debut album established its vocabulary: a blend of fusion jazz, progressive rock, dub reggae, and avant-garde electronic music in which melody is on equal footing with texture, mood, and dynamics, and in which linear song structure is not a concern.

what to buy: The studio-as-instrument aesthetic was fully realized on the 21-minute "Djed" that opens *Millions Now Living Will Never Die* 𝄞𝄞𝄞𝄞 (Thrill Jockey, 1996, prod. John McEntire), in which the band creates mood music that refuses to be shoved into the background. The addition of AACM member Jeff Parker broadens the sonic spectrum even further on *TNT* 𝄞𝄞𝄞𝄞 (Thrill Jockey, 1998, prod. John McEntire).

the rest:

Tortoise 𝄞𝄞𝄞 (Thrill Jockey, 1994)
Rhythms, Resolutions, and Clusters 𝄞𝄞𝄞 (Thrill Jockey EP, 1995)

influences:

◀◀ John Zorn, Frank Zappa, the Residents

see also: *Eleventh Dream Day*

Greg Kot

Toto

Formed 1976, in Los Angeles, CA.

David Paich, keyboards, vocals; Steve Lukather, guitar, vocals; Steve Porcaro, keyboards (1976–86); Jeff Porcaro (died August 5, 1992), drums, percussion (1976–92); David Hungate, bass (1976–83); Michael Porcaro, bass (1983–present); Simon Phillips, drums (1993–present); Bobby Kimball, vocals (1976–84); Fergie Fredericksen, vocals (1984–86); Joseph Williams, vocals (1986–90); Jean-Michel Byron, vocals (1990–92).

Based around a core of high school buddies who eventually became Los Angeles' hottest '70s and '80s-era session musicians—David Paich, Steve Lukather, and brothers Steve and Jeff Porcaro—Toto emerged as an instrumentally slick, endlessly evolving rock band whose soft side scored big with the adult contemporary audience. Starting out as a group of hopeful rockers—the band formed while cutting tracks for Boz Scaggs's *Silk Degrees*—Toto started strong but really went through the roof when it won six Grammys for its 1982 album *Toto IV*. But success took its toll, bringing an endless string of lead singers that kept the group off-balance, unable to assemble more than two or three quality tunes for any one album. By 1993 the band gave up, installing Lukather as lead singer and chief songwriter and developing a Bon Jovi-ish rock sound just as the grunge revolution made that style passe. Founding drummer Jeff Porcaro's 1992 death prompted the band to recruit studio whiz Simon Phillips for the drum chair, but by then Toto's popularity had shifted to Japan and Europe, the only places where a post-grunge disdain for its well-crafted sound hadn't made the group irrelevant.

what to buy: Few Toto records offer more than a couple of good cuts among an album's worth of seamless playing, which is why the debut record, *Toto* 🎵🎵🎵 (Columbia, 1978, prod. Toto), stands out. Offering a range of material, from the AOR hit "Hold the Line" to the urban radio single "Georgy Porgy" (with R&B diva Cheryl Lynn helping out on vocals), this record is the band's most consistent.

what to buy next: It took the slick rock/pop of *Toto IV* 🎵🎵🎵 (Columbia, 1982, prod. Toto) to put the group over the top, with five hits and the six Grammy awards. But even as well-produced, middle-of-the-road tunes such as "Rosanna," "Africa," and "I Won't Hold You Back" were creating a new niche for easygoing rockers, their seamless sound was becoming less and less popular. *Past to Present 1977–1990* 🎵🎵🎵 (Columbia, 1990, prod. various) fails as a retrospective—missing several cool tunes never released as singles—but remains the best way to get the wheat without the chaff.

what to avoid: *Kingdom of Desire* **woof!** (Combat, 1993, prod. Toto, Danny Kortchmar) stands as the worst Toto album ever—no mean feat. It's primarily an ego-stroking showcase for Lukather, who gets to strut his limited vocal range and limited songwriting chops in a metal-tinged setting that emphasizes his guitar playing. Great for chasing stray cats out of your yard.

the rest:
Hydra 🎵🎵🎵 (Columbia, 1979)
Turn Back 🎵🎵 (Columbia, 1981)
Isolation 🎵🎵 (Columbia, 1984)
Fahrenheit 🎵🎵🎵 (Columbia, 1986)
The Seventh One 🎵🎵🎵 (Columbia, 1988)
Absolutely Live 🎵🎵🎵 (Alex, 1993)
Tambu 🎵🎵🎵 (Legacy, 1996)

worth searching for: Numerous albums by the likes of Scaggs, Pink Floyd, Steely Dan, Bruce Springsteen, Earth, Wind & Fire, and others feature the session contributions of Toto's core members.

influences:

◀◀ The Shadows, Jimi Hendrix, the Beatles

▶▶ The Tubes, Mr. Mister

Eric Deggans

Allen Toussaint

Born January 14, 1938, in New Orleans, LA.

Through the course of his five-decade career, outside influences never interfered with the basic integrity of Allen Toussaint's brilliant, evocative productions and songwriting. Deeply rooted in the traditional jazz and parade rhythms of his native New Orleans, Toussaint has always evolved and grown based on his own artistic premises. He rarely leaves New Orleans, which is why artists as distinguished as the Band and Paul McCartney have traveled to Toussaint to help them make records. His productions have ranged from '70s hits with Dr. John and Labelle to minor masterpieces by a galaxy of homegrown New Orleans R&B stars such as Irma Thomas, Ernie K-Doe, Lee Dorsey, Chris Kenner, the Meters, and virtually anyone who mattered after Fats Domino came on that city's rich and colorful scene. But Toussaint's own recordings have been quizzical affairs, undermined by his own insecurities as a vocalist, although artists such as Bonnie Raitt, Esther Phillips, Boz Scaggs, and others have covered songs from his solo albums. But his solid sense of craftsmanship and his own slightly florid but mellifluous piano playing always informs his own records with a scrupulous sense of purpose and powerful musicality.

what to buy: His lack of commercial success as a recording artist has left Toussaint's infrequent solo outings largely out of print and difficult to find, so most people will have to make do with *The Allen Toussaint Collection* 🎵🎵🎵 (Reprise, 1991, compilation prod. Bill Bentley, Charlie Springer), a selection drawn from solo albums recorded from 1970–78.

what to buy next: His first two solo albums, *From a Whisper to a Scream* 🎵🎵🎵 (Scepter, 1970, prod. Allen Toussaint, C. Greene) and *Life, Love, and Faith* 🎵🎵🎵 (Reprise, 1972/Charly, 1994, prod. Allen Toussaint) are readily available in the import racks and well worth owning.

what to avoid: His instrumental work under the name Tousan resides on *The Complete "Tousan" Sessions: The Wild Sound of New Orleans* 🎵🎵 (Bear Family, 1992, compilation prod. Rick Coleman) and is largely an uninteresting—if jaunty—exercise in Prof. Longhairish pianistics. For collector's only.

the rest:
Connected 🎵🎵🎵 (NYNO, 1996)
A New Orleans Christmas 🎵🎵 (NYNO, 1997)

worth searching for: His album *Southern Nights* (Reprise, 1975, prod. Allen Toussaint, Marshall Sehorn) is a marvel, Toussaint's vocals bathed in shimmering vocals effects, the supple majesty of the production lighting each of the intricately wrought compositions.

influences:

◄◄ Professor Longhair, Fats Domino

►► The Neville Brothers, Boz Scaggs

Joel Selvin

Tower of Power

Formed 1968, in Oakland, CA.

Rufus Miller, vocals (1969–70); Rick Stevens, vocals (1970–72); Lenny Williams, vocals (1973–75); Hubert Tubbs, vocals (1975–76); Edward McGee, vocals (1976); Michael Jeffries, vocals (1977–79); Ellis Hall, vocals, keyboards, guitar (1987–96); Tom Bowes, vocals (1991–94); Brent Carter, vocals (1995–present); Emilio Castillo, alto sax, tenor sax, vocals; Greg Adams, trumpet, flugelhorn, vocals (1968–93); Lenny Pickett, reeds, vocals (1973–79); Steve Kupka, baritone sax, oboe, English horn, vocals; Skip Mesquite, tenor sax, flute, vocals (1968–72); Richard Elliot, alto sax, tenor sax, lyricon (1987); David Mann, sax (1994–96); John Scarpulla, alto & tenor saxophones (1997–present); David Padron, trumpet (1968–70); Mic Gillette, brass, vocals (1970–79); Lee Thornburg, brass, vocals (1987–93); Barry Danielian, trumpet, flugelhorn (1995–present); Bill Churchville, trumpet, flugelhorn, trombone (1995–present); Jay Spell, keyboards (1972); Chester Thompson, keyboards, vocals (1973–79); Nick Milo, keyboards (1991–present); Willie Fulton, guitar, vocals (1968–72, 1987); Bruce Conte, guitar, vocals (1973–78); Danny Hoefer, guitar (1979); Carmen Grillo, guitar, vocals (1991–96); Jeff Tamelier, guitar, background vocals (1997–present); Francis Rocco Prestia, bass (1968–76, 1991–present); Victor Conte, bass (1978); Vito San Filippo, bass, vocals (1979); Dave Garibaldi, drums, vibes, vocals (1968–76, 1979); Brent Byars, percussion (1972–74); David Bartlett, drums (1975); Ronnie Beck, drums, vocals (1976–78); Mick Mestek, drums (1987); Russ McKinnon, drums, piano (1991–93); Herman Matthews, drums (1995–present).

When Lenny Williams was its florid lead vocalist, Tower of Power was in the first rank of funk, artistically and commercially. Even without him, its funky rhythm section and tight, jazzy horns are always worth hearing. Throughout the group's many personnel changes, most of the horn section has been constant (though Mic Gillette no longer tours with the band, he's still on its albums); however, its best-known member, Lenny Pickett, went to New York, joined the *Saturday Night Live* band, and worked with avant-garde musicians. (As a guest he took five solos on 1993's *T.O.P.*, the pinnacle of the group's comeback.) TOP's horn sound was especially distinctive thanks to Steve Kupka's use of baritone sax for a fat low end, and the

arrangements at their best emphasized intricately interlocking parts. The horn section found itself an in-demand brand-name entity, spicing up countless sessions by bands across the rock and R&B spectrums—including Huey Lewis & the News and the Rolling Stones. During the dark decade of the '80s, in fact, the group practically disbanded while the horns worked more away from the band than with it. The challenge for T.O.P. has always been to retain its trademark sound yet stay up-to-date, a challenge that has been met with varying degrees of success during the past two decades. Throughout all the ups and downs, however, TOP has been a thrilling live band with a huge repertoire of classic funk to sustain it.

what to buy: *Urban Renewal* ♪♪♪♪ (Warner Bros., 1975, prod. Emilio Castillo, Tower of Power) has the amazingly tight rhythm section interplay among Chester Thompson, Bruce Conte, Francis Ricco Prestia, and David Bartlett that makes "Maybe It'll Rub Off," "Give Me the Proof," "Only So Much Oil in the Ground," and "It's Not the Crime" so funky they hurt. Williams's fervid singing is front and center on the ballads "I Won't Leave unless You Want Me To" and "Willing to Learn."

what to buy next: *Tower of Power* ♪♪♪♪ (Warner Bros., 1973) contains "What Is Hip?" and the ultra-funky "Soul Vaccination." *Back to Oakland* ♪♪♪♪ (Warner Bros., 1974) offers "Don't Change Horses (In the Middle of a Stream)." Both albums feature Williams on vocals.

what to avoid: *Ain't Nothin' Stoppin' Us Now* ♪ (Columbia, 1976, prod. Emilio Castillo, Tower of Power) has dated production along with the annoying vibrato and thin voice of Edward McGee, who oozes insincerity. *Power* ♪ (Cypress/A&M, 1987, prod. Emilio Castillo, Ellis Hall) fails not only because Ellis Hall is a forced, unsoulful singer, but also because there's too much unidiomatic synthesizer and formulaic arranging.

the rest:

East Bay Grease ♪♪♪ (San Francisco/Atlantic, 1971)
Bump City ♪♪♪ (Warner Bros., 1972)
In the Slot ♪♪♪ (Warner Bros., 1975)
Live in Living Color ♪♪♪♪ (Warner Bros., 1976)
We Came to Play! ♪♪♪ (Columbia, 1978)
Back on the Streets ♪♪♪♪ (Columbia, 1979)
Direct ♪♪♪ (Sheffield Lab, 1981)
Monster on a Leash ♪♪♪♪ (Epic, 1991)
T.O.P. ♪♪♪♪ (Epic, 1993)
Souled Out ♪♪ (Epic, 1995)
Rhythm & Business ♪♪♪ (Epic, 1997)

worth searching for: Huey Lewis & the News' albums *Picture This* (Chrysalis, 1982) and *Fore!* (Chrysalis, 1986) testify to the supple versatility of the TOP horns as they shift gears into a pop format.

Pete Townshend (© Ken Settle)

influences:

◀◀ Stan Kenton, James Brown, Sam & Dave, Otis Redding, Sly & the Family Stone

▶▶ Cameo, the Uptown Horns, Incognito, Weapon of Choice, Liquid Soul

Steve Holtje

Pete Townshend

Born Peter Dennis Blandford Townshend, May 19, 1945, in London, England.

One of rock's premiere architects and one of its major theoreticians—on his own and as the leader of the Who—Pete Townshend's solo career has often suggested he's too smart for his own good. At times his solo work has been a worthy addendum to his Who catalog, but his albums have grown increasingly bogged down in conceptual trappings that need further fleshing out. Townshend, of course, is the one who penned the now-infamous line "Hope I die before I get old" from the Who song "My Generation," and since he didn't, his albums have continued to address his ever-changing feelings on the relationship between rock and maturity. Some of the songs on *Empty Glass* in particular bespeak something of a mid-life crisis, and his most recent conceptual piece, *Psychoderelict,* concerns the tribulations of a washed-up rock star; it hits a little too close to home for comfort. On *Empty Glass*, Townshend proved he could respond when he feels he's been challenged as a spokesman for rock 'n' roll, but most often, his solo work is at its best when he simply relaxes and delves into what truly interests him. Still, Townshend's ambitions have always been outsized, so much so that in recent years rock 'n' roll by itself couldn't contain them. He has also published *Horse's Neck*, a book of short fiction, worked as an editor at the London publishing house Faber & Faber, and helped turn the Who's rock opera *Tommy* into a Tony-winning Broadway hit. His interest in the album as the proper format for his work seems to have waned, but he remains an artist that nearly everyone in rock 'n' roll has either emulated and rejected, or rejected and then emulated.

what to buy: *Rough Mix* ♫♫♫♪ (MCA, 1977/Atco, 1983, prod. Glyn Johns) is the model of what a solo album from a member of a superstar act should be. The atmosphere is easy and assured, the host and his guests (in this case, the Faces' Ronnie Lane, Rolling Stone Charlie Watts, and Eric Clapton) step out of their familiar roles, and the songs are great. *Empty Glass* ♫♫♫♪ (Atco, 1980, prod. Chris Thomas) on the other hand, is quite in the opposite direction. An attempt to reconcile with the punks that abhorred him, the roaring, homoerotic "Rough Boys" finds Townshend leaping into the breach with abandon. Similarly, "Jules and Jim" angrily answers his critics. The hit sin-

gle "Let My Love Open the Door" and "A Little Is Enough" return to more familiar territory, but they would have made terrific Who songs. *The Best of Pete Townshend: Coolwalkingsmoothtalkingstraightsmokingfirestoking* ♫♫♫ (Atlantic, 1996, prod. various) provides a useful thumbnail sketch of Townshend's solo career, and it performs a real service in gathering up songs such as "Slit Skirts," "English Boy," and "Face the Face" from Townshend's less listenable albums.

what to buy next: *Who Came First* ♫♫♫♪ (Decca, 1972/Rykodisc, 1993, prod. Pete Townshend) is not the star trip you'd imagine from the guitarist and songwriter from (at the time) the world's biggest band. It's a collection of odds and sods in which Townshend occasionally turns lead vocals over to Ronnie Lane and Billy Nichols, sets other people's poems to music, and even performs his guru's favorite Jim Reeves tune. The highlights are "Pure & Easy" and "Let's See Action" from the Who's abandoned "Lifehouse" project. The Rykodisc reissue offers six bonus tracks. Who obsessives will likely want both *Scoop* ♫♫♫ (Atco, 1983, prod. Spike) and *Another Scoop,* ♫♫♫ (Atco, 1987, prod. Pete Townshend, Spike), which comprise many of Townshend's demos and early song sketches for an intriguing glimpse into the creative process.

what to avoid: Despite the presence of good songs such as "Slit Skirts" and "Stardom in Acton," most of *All the Best Cow-*

boys Have Chinese Eyes 🎜🎜 (Atco, 1982, prod. Chris Thomas) is simply impenetrable.

the rest:

White City—A Novel 🎜🎜🎜 (Atco, 1985)

Pete Townshend's Deep End Live! 🎜🎜🎜 (Atco, 1986)

The Iron Man 🎜🎜 (Atco, 1989)

Psychoderelict **woof!** (Atlantic, 1993)

Psychoderelict: Music Only 🎜🎜 (Atlantic, 1993)

worth searching for: For fans with deep pockets and great contacts, look for the limited-edition, privately issued albums *Happy Birthday* (1970) and *I Am* (1971). Both are tributes to Townshend's guru, Meher Baba, and contain some tracks eventually used on *Who Came First*.

influences:

◀◀ Sonny Boy Williamson, Meher Baba, the Rolling Stones, Stephen Sondheim

▶▶ U2, the Jam, Nirvana, Pearl Jam

see also: *The Who, Thunderclap Newman*

Daniel Durchholz

Traffic

Formed 1967, in Berkshire, England. Disbanded 1974. Re-formed 1994.

Steve Winwood, vocals, guitar, keyboards; Jim Capaldi, drums, vocals; Chris Wood (died July 12, 1983), reeds; Dave Mason, guitar, vocals (1967–68, 1971); Rick Grech, bass (1970–71); Jim Gordon, drums (1971); Reebop Kwaku Baah, percussion (1971–73); Roger Hawkins, drums (1971–73); David Hood, bass (1971–73); Rosco Gee, bass (1973–74, 1994).

Steve Winwood was already famous as Little Stevie Winwood, the child prodigy of "Gimme Some Lovin'," before he left the Spencer Davis Group in search of something more mature and foreward looking. He, Jim Capaldi, Chris Wood, and Dave Mason retired to a rural cottage to craft the Traffic sound, a blend of rock, psychedelia, blues, R&B, and folk that was wholly unique for the times—but also completely in step with the adventurous spirit of the times. The group enjoyed instant radio success with "Paper Sun," but it was the winding, textured "Dear Mr. Fantasy" and "Heaven Is in Your Mind" that were harbingers of things to come as Traffic explored different arranging and instrumental sensibilities. It was a volatile outfit, changing membership and even taking a mid-term hiatus—during which Winwood played in the supergroup Blind Faith—before recording the masterful *John Barleycorn Must Die*. Ultimately, Traffic assembled a broad musical palette from which other bands would draw inspiration for decades to follow. The recent reunion of Winwood and Capaldi didn't produce any new music of note, but it was good to hear them play "40,000

Headmen," "Feelin' Alright," and "Low Spark of High-Heeled Boys" again.

what to buy: *John Barleycorn Must Die* 🎜🎜🎜🎜 (United Artists, 1970/Island, 1987, prod. Steve Winwood, Chris Blackwell) is an exceptionally cohesive piece, tapping into the acoustic vibe of the time but still offering plenty of bite in "Freedom Rider," "Glad," and the wonderful "Empty Pages." The excellent retrospective *Smiling Phases* 🎜🎜🎜🎜 (Island, 1991, prod. various) contains every crucial track and serves as the best guide for subsequent album purchases.

what to buy next: The epic title track alone makes *The Low Spark of High-Heeled Boys* 🎜🎜🎜🎜 (United Artists, 1971/Island, 1987, prod. Steve Winwood) worthwhile, but it's just one of several aces as Traffic sets out on a new, more expansive musical path.

what to avoid: *Welcome to the Canteen* 🎜🎜 (United Artists, 1971/Island, 1988, prod. Jimmy Miller) is a tepid live album that contains a particularly vapid version of "Gimme Some Lovin'."

the rest:

Mr. Fantasy 🎜🎜🎜 (United Artists, 1968/Island, 1987)

Traffic 🎜🎜🎜 (United Artists, 1968/Island, 1987)

Last Exit 🎜🎜🎜 (United Artists, 1969/Island, 1988)

Shoot out at the Fantasy Factory 🎜🎜🎜 (United Artists, 1973/Island, 1988)

Traffic on the Road 🎜🎜🎜 (United Artists, 1973/Island, 1988)

When the Eagle Flies 🎜🎜🎜 (Asylum, 1974)

Far from Home 🎜🎜🎜 (Virgin, 1994)

worth searching for: *The Perfumed Garden,* (Gold Standard, 1994), a bootleg of early BBC performances, boasts exceptionally strong sound quality.

influences:

◀◀ Ray Charles, the Spencer Davis Group, the Beatles, Procol Harum, the Zombies, Fairport Convention

▶▶ Steely Dan, Fleetwood Mac, the Grateful Dead, Toad the Wet Sprocket, the Tragically Hip

see also: *Steve Winwood, Spencer Davis, Blind Faith*

Gary Graff

The Tragically Hip

Formed 1986, in Kingston, Ontario, Canada.

Gordon Downie, vocals; Paul Langlois, guitar; Bobby Baker, guitar; Gord Sinclair, bass; Johnny Fay, drums.

The members of the Tragically Hip were high school friends prior to forming the band. Since the beginning, the Hip has been a Canadian favorite, filling arenas and regularly earning its country's gold and platinum awards; it has become more popular as the sound has evolved from bluesy, guitar-driven rock to more textured and ambient but equally energetic fare. No matter the direction, singer Gordon Downie's yearning, expressive vocals are the band's calling card, a distinctive characteristic that gives the Hip an identity in much the same way Bono and Michael Stipe help define U2 and R.E.M., respectively. The U.S. pop audience has yet to really embrace the Hip, but it's their loss.

what to buy: *Road Apples* ♫♫♫♫ (MCA, 1991, prod. Don Smith) is the Hip's finest release to date, a stirring collection of straightforward, blues-inspired rock exemplified by "Little Bones," "The Luxury," and "Three Pistols." Its predecessor, *Up to Here* ♫♫♫♪ (MCA, 1989, prod. Don Smith), is another strong and straight-ahead work, with such favorites as "Blow at High Dough" and "New Orleans Is Sinking."

what to buy next: *Fully Completely* ♫♫♫♪ (MCA, 1993, prod. Chris Tsangarides) follows the Hip as it moves forward, striving for and achieving a more intimate recording than its predecessors, with more varied musical approaches—from the edgy rock of "Courage" to the gentle acoustic feel of "Wheat Kings"—to Downie's masterful stream-of-consciousness lyrics on songs such as "Fifty Mission Cap."

the rest:
The Tragically Hip ♫♫♫♪ (MCA, 1987)
Day for Night ♫♫♫♪ (MCA, 1994)
Trouble at the Hen House ♫♫♫♪ (Atlantic, 1996)
Phantom Power ♫♫♫♪ (Sire, 1998)

worth searching for: *Between Us* (Universal, 1997, prod. Tragically Hip, Mark Vreeken) is a band-issued live album recorded during an energetic 1996 concert at Detroit's Cobo Hall in front of an enthusiastic border crowd.

influences:
◄◄ Neil Young, Joni Mitchell, Gordon Lightfoot, the Rolling Stones, the Yardbirds, the Band

►► Live, Our Lady Peace

Kim Forster

Tranquility Bass

Born Mike Kandel, 1968, in Chicago, IL.

After producing ambient music for the Exist Dance music label, which he helped create, and causing a buzz among L.A.'s underground dance scene with the trip-hop single "Cantamilla," Chicago native Tranquility Bass gave up the fast-paced lifestyle of the Land of Fruits and Nuts and headed north to Washington State's San Juan Islands. Holed up for two years in the wilderness in a rented cabin with nothing much more than his turntables, guitars and an axe to chop wood, Bass created his debut

album, *Let The Freak Flag Fly*. He returned to Chicago in 1996 and the following spring released his first full-length album on Astralwerks Records.

what to buy: *Let The Freak Flag Fly* ♫♫♫ (Astralwerks/Caroline, 1997, prod. Mike Kandel) is the product of two reclusive years of peace, quiet, and the great outdoors. In attempting to create a sound somewhere between rock and electronic music, Tranquility Bass combined light, fun guitar riffs with heavy dance overdubs and trippy lyrics laden with hippie wisdom. It works, dude.

the rest:
Beep! ♫♫♪ (Astralwerks/Caroline, 1998)

influences:
◄◄ House music, psychedelics, the Simpsons, the Grateful Dead, Ted Nugent

Ari Bendersky

Transglobal Underground

Formed 1991, in London, England.

Alex Kasiek, keyboards, vocals, flute, melodica, programming; **Hamid Mantu,** drums, percussion, keyboards, programming; **T.U.U.P.,** vocals, congas; **Natacha Atlas,** vocals; **Coleridge,** vocals, djembe; **Johnny Kalsi,** dhol; others.

Transglobal Underground, a loose-knit collective that has involved numerous players, creates a sound whose influences read longer than its cast. Middle Eastern vocals and chants, Latin lyrics and percussion, Indian drumming, British hip-hop, drum-and-bass, African music, and reggae are the basics, but are also just a few of the many styles the band embraces. Call it dance music for clubs in exotic locales, perfect for those that can't make it to a WOMAD concert or for those who like a wide variety of ethnic pop, yet don't have a multi-disc CD player. It's worth hearing just for Natacha Atlas's sublimely lovely voice. The evolving ensemble also adds strings, guitar, bass, woodwinds, and other implements to its sound, depending on the occasion.

what to buy: *Psychic Karaoke* ♫♫♫♪ (MCA, 1996, prod. Transglobal Underground) has more variety than you can shake a drum stick at, including layers of percussion and strings. Atlas's soaring vocals often carry the disc, as she is probably the one element essential to Transglobal Underground's diverse pastiche of sound.

what to buy next: *International Times* ♫♫♫♪ (Epic, 1994, prod. Transglobal Underground) is similar—dance music with an emphasis on true ethnic instrumentation. With more ingredients than a good curry, *International Times* is a spicy concoction guaranteed to liven up your house party.

the rest:
Rejoice, Rejoice 🎵🎵🎵 (MCA, 1998)

solo outings:
Natacha Atlas:
Diaspora 🎵🎵🎵 (Beggars Banquet, 1995)

influences:
◀◀ Yma Sumac, Nusrat Fateh Ali Khan, Ofra Haza

▶▶ Morcheeba, Talvin Singh, Bally Sagoo

Barry M. Prickett

Transister

Formed 1996, in London, England.

Keely Hawkes, vocals; Gary Clark, guitar; Eric Pressly, bass.

A self-professed product of drunk conversation, Transister's ambitious beginnings do seem a bit precarious. Eric Pressly met Gary Clark in a Los Angeles bar and, as legend has it, instantly invited him to return to his London studio for collaboration. The two would often recess to a local pub, where fate would place petite Keely Hawkes on the stage for their repeated entertainment. And as if it had happened before, the two studio guys asked the seductive singer to collaborate on a series of electronic pop songs.

what's available: *Transister* 🎵🎵 (Interscope, 1997, prod. Gary Clark, Eric Pressly) began life as a radio leak through one of Pressly's friends. The band was quickly courted by major labels and signed to Interscope. The music itself is both surprising and familiar. Where the jagged edges work, as they do on single and eerily Hitchcockian video for "Look Who's Perfect Now," they seem to crack the same staged indifference as Shirley Manson. But too often Hawkes comes off as overwrought and artless, opting for histrionics where a quiet stare might better fit. The background is insincere, sampled loopery that, although apocalyptic at times, sounds awkwardly sterile to today's trained ears.

influences:
◀◀ Eurythmics, Garbage, Curve, Alanis Morissette

Billy Manes

Translator

Formed 1979, in Los Angeles, CA. Disbanded 1986.

Steve Barton, vocals, guitar; Robert Darlington, vocals, guitar; Larry Decker, bass; David Scheff, drums.

Translator was one of the best guitar pop bands nobody heard during the '80s. Although the band never had a hit or made much of a ripple outside the San Francisco Bay Area in its time,

it has been the subject of numerous anthologies, which may be evidence enough of the music's durability. What keeps resurfacing is the before-its-time alternative jangle and tuneful pop smarts held aloft by sharp emotional insistence. Translator's most striking song—"Everywhere That I'm Not," written the day after John Lennon's assassination—is a riveting lament that certainly beats the pants off Elton John's "Empty Garden" gurglings.

what to buy: *Everywhere That We Were: The Best of Translator* 🎵🎵🎵🎵 (Columbia/Legacy, 1996, prod. various) rounds up 17 memorable tracks, including the band's signature song as well as "Oh Lazurus" and "Everywhere"; both boast similarly strong melody lines and are nearly as gripping.

what to buy next: *Translation* 🎵🎵🎵 (Oglio, 1995, prod. various) is docked a half bone for having slightly fewer tunes and less extensive liner notes, but it does have a number of tracks not included on the Columbia compilation.

influences:
◀◀ The Cars, the Modern Lovers

▶▶ Simple Minds

Allan Orski

The Traveling Wilburys

Formed 1988, in Los Angeles, CA.

Bob Dylan, vocals, guitar; George Harrison, vocals, guitar; Roy Orbison (died December 6, 1988), vocals, guitar (1988); Tom Petty, vocals, guitar, bass; Jeff Lynne, vocals, guitar, bass, keyboards; Jim Keltner, drums.

Checking their egos at the door, the superstar lineup of the Traveling Wilburys surprised everyone with their status-shedding debut on which they reveled in the relative anonymity of adopted identities (Otis Wilbury, Nelson Wilbury, etc.), and in some cases, turned in stronger performances here than they had on their own recent albums. Roy Orbison, for example, cemented his late-career comeback by adding his gorgeous unearthly voice to the Wilburys' chorus; Tom Petty is uncommonly jocular and Bob Dylan whipped out the most playful lyrics he'd penned in years. Orbison's sudden death after the release of the first album put a damper on the project, though, and while a second album was released, nothing has been heard from the Wilburys collective since—although in 1998 there were rumblings about investigating some unused tracks by the late Carl Perkins for Wilburys usage.

what to buy: *Traveling Wilburys, Vol. 1* 🎵🎵🎵 (Warner Bros., 1988, prod. Otis Wilbury, Lucky Wilbury) is a welcome delight, featuring songs such as "Handle with Care," "Dirty World," and "Last Night."

the rest:
Traveling Wilburys, Vol. 3 🎝🎝 (Warner Bros., 1990)

worth searching for: The CD single for "She's My Baby" (Warner Bros., 1990) from *Vol. 3* features the group's cover of Del Shannon's "Runaway."

influences:
◀◀ Elvis Presley, the Beatles, Little Richard, the Highwaymen

▶▶ The Notting Hillbillies

Allan Orski

Travis
Formed 1996, in Glasgow, Scotland.

Francis Healy, vocals; Andrew Dunlop, guitar; Douglas Payne, bass; Neil Primrose, drums.

Apart from being Noel Gallagher from Oasis's favorite new band, these young Scots made an impressive showing with their debut album *Good Feeling*. Critics have even compared Francis Healy's songwriting with that of Thom Yorke from Radiohead and even John Lennon. While consistently named as one of the best releases of 1997 in the U.K., the album failed to make much of an impact on American ears.

what's available: *Good Feeling* 🎝🎝🎝 (Epic, 1997, prod. Steve Lillywhite) is a relaxed and ambitious debut, showcasing Healy's wide musical range. "All I Wanna Do Is Rock" is seemingly the band's mission statement.

influences:
◀◀ Radiohead, the Beatles, Oasis

Aidin Vaziri

Treadmill Trackstar
Formed 1993, in Columbia, SC.

Angelo Gianni, guitars, vocals; Katie Hamilton, cello; Chris Grigg, bass; Tony Lee, drums.

This South Carolina quartet features the capable songwriting of guitarist Angelo Gianni, who dabbles in open acoustic-guitar tunings and overlays some fiery electric leads for good measure. Cellist Katie Hamilton, who'd never played rock prior to joining the band, adds an air of distinction. The band's incessant Southern touring eventually found it opening for Hootie & the Blowfish, who were impressed enough to sign Treadmill Trackstar to the Blowfish's upstart Breaking Records label.

what to buy: *Only This* 🎝🎝🎝 (Breaking/Atlantic, 1997, prod. Joe Hardy) is an impressive debut, with Gianni paying obvious homage to hero Michael Hedges and filling the record with tasteful guitar colorations. Hardy's production is smooth and restrained.

the rest:
Excessive Use of the Passive Voice 🎝🎝🎝 (self-released, 1994)

influences:
◀◀ Michael Hedges, Hüsker Dü

David Simons

Treat Her Right
See: Morphine

Treble Charger
Formed 1993, in Toronto, Ontario, Canada.

Greig Nori, vocals, guitar; Bill Priddle, vocals, guitar; Rosie Martin, bass; Morris Palter, drums (1993–97); Trevor Macgregor, drums (1997–present).

Formed from the like intentions of childhood friends Greig Nori and Bill Priddle, Treble Charger's knack for askew lyrical perspectives set to energetic, if not similarly skewed guitar pop, won the group a respectable following in its native Canada long before its recent foray into the major label alt-rock circuit. As a result, the band's current sound stands as a deserved testament to the evolution of its more obscure beginnings, growing from the wistful and incongruous moments of Sebadoh-style mope-rock into more textured, populist power pop. Most notable are the variations in tone inherent in a band with two equal songwriters; the blend of Priddle's slow indie affectations with Nori's more accessible punk-fueled roots results in a sort of scruffy Lennon and McCartney of the new age.

what to buy: *Maybe It's Me* 🎝🎝🎝🎝 (RCA, 1997, prod. Lou Giordano) rings with the kind of sincerity usually reserved for guarded moments. Here Treble Charger attempts to make sadness fun again, and in the process it creates some of the most engaging pop songs ever written. From the orchestral impressionism of "Chris Is on the Lawn" to the tongue-biting release of "Mercury Smile," the whole affair is a messy celebration of metaphor and noise—one that benefits greatly from the arid production wizardry of Lou Giordano (Sugar, Yo La Tengo), who has apparently tried to make sadness fun before.

what to buy next: *Self=Title* 🎝🎝🎝 (Sonic Unyon/RCA, 1994, prod. Rob Sanzo) combines the meandering tones of the broken art-rock promise with a few unexpected catchy hooks to make a thick, ultimately engaging listen. It also includes enhanced CD-ROM video footage of the band, as well as some of its favorite unsigned bands and a flatulent, antimated rodent (!?).

worth searching for: *NC-17* (Sonic Unyon, 1994, prod. Rob Sanzo), Treble Charger's debut, is a largely minimal affair, with bent Byrds-y harmonies and Michael Stipe-influence aplenty to decorate a solidy wisply mood. Although never officially released Stateside, it is still marginally available in Canada.

influences:

◀◀ Sugar, Green Day, R.E.M., Sebadoh, Pavement, Nirvana, Cheap Trick

▶▶ Foo Fighters, Our Lady Peace

Billy Manes

The Tremeloes
/Brian Poole & the Tremeloes
/Chip Hawkes' Tremeloes

Formed 1959, in Dagenham, Essex, England.

Dave Munden, drums, vocals; Alan Blakley (died 1996), guitar, keyboards, vocals (1959–96); Brian Poole, vocals, guitar (1959–66); Alan Howard, bass, saxophone (1959–66); Graham Scott, guitar (1959–61); Rick West (born Richard Charles Westwood), guitar (1961–present); Mick Clark, bass (1966); Leonard Donald "Chip" Hawkes, bass, vocals (1966–74; 1990–91); Bob Benham, guitar, keyboards, vocals (1975–92); Aaron Woolley, guitar, vocals (1975–88); Rob Fisher, keyboards, guitar, vocals (1990–92); Jodie Hawkes, drums, vocals (1990–91); Davey Fryer; Joe Gillingham.

Literally hundreds of teenagers who witnessed Buddy Holly's 1958 tour of England were duly inspired to throw down their schoolbooks and pick up guitars, and one of the best Holly imitators of all turned out to be young Brian Poole. The group of mock-Crickets he drafted from amongst his classmates became an instant success playing local youth clubs and radio shows, and the group actually beat the Beatles out of a recording contract with Decca on New Year's Day, 1962. The following year however, Poole was forced to trade in his Holly eyewear for contact lenses—and the Tremeloes' repertoire was similarly toughened up—in order to compete with the Merseybeat and London R&B suddenly in vogue. The group's lack of in-house songwriting ability also forced it to rely too heavily upon the material of others, both before Poole went solo in 1966 and well on through the Trems' string of European hits later in the decade. Still, despite a de rigueur detour into heaviness circa 1970 (during which time the group declared all of its hits to date "rubbish"—and all who bought them "morons"!), the Tremeloes are today approaching a fourth decade of active duty on the British dancehall circuit, despite the recent death of founding member Alan Blakley.

what's available: There are two things that make listening to *The Best of the Tremeloes* ✏✏✏✏ (Rhino, 1992, compilation prod. Bill Inglot) such a treat for pure pop fans both old and new: The band's often inspired choice of cover material (for example, a version of the Four Seasons' "Silence Is Golden" that actually eclipses the original), and the way its luscious vocal blend makes even a seriously silly piece of fluff such as Cat Stevens's "Here Comes My Baby" sound damn near substantial. Meanwhile, for a taste of what Decca's 1962 A&R division turned down the Fab Four for, *The World of Brian Poole & the Tremeloes* ✏✏✏ (Spectrum, 1996, prod. Mike Smith) contains 20 early recordings full of exuberant—if sometimes stilted—twisting and shouting. Buddy Holly fan(atic)s take note: Crickets producer Norman Petty was actually imported to play piano on the Trems' version of "Someone, Someone" included herein.

influences:

◀◀ Buddy Holly & the Crickets, the Everly Brothers, the Beatles

▶▶ The Dave Clark Five, the Hollies, Sweet, the Corporation (a.k.a. Travelling Wrinklies)

Gary Pig Gold

The Treniers

Formed as the Trenier Twins, 1945. Became the Treniers in 1949.

Claude Trenier, vocals; Clifford Trenier (died March 2, 1983), vocals; Buddy Trenier, vocals; Milt Trenier, vocals; Skip Trenier, vocals.

The Treniers were the first group to openly and proudly refer to themselves as rock 'n' roll artists. A boisterous, chanting R&B quartet with a highly visual stage style, the Treniers scored only one national hit, but their influence has spread to several generations of rock and soul performers. Inspired by their older brother Buddy Trenier (a small-time club singer at the time), twins Claude and Clifford toured with their own band, the Alabama State Collegians during the early '30s. Claude joined Jimmie Lunceford's Orchestra as a ballad singer in 1943, brother Clifford was hired the following year, and Lunceford began billing them as the Trenier Twins. The duo recorded some first-rate jump-blues (which owed much to Louis Jordan's sound) for Decca, but due to the shellac shortage of the war years, the sides weren't released until much later. After Claude and Clifford struck out on their own, brothers Buddy and Milt (a fine jivey recording artist in his own right) joined the group. Their raucous stage antics, zany interplay, and constant shifting of song styles made them major nightclub attractions where, as early as 1949, they were billed as "The Rockin' Rollin' Treniers." Throughout their career, the Treniers have had great difficulty transferring their dynamic live act to the recording studio. Stints at Mercury, Chord, and London yielded no chart action. In 1951 the group moved to OKeh, where "Go! Go! Go!" (driven by the leering saxophone playing of Don Hill) blasted up the R&B charts. Subsequent records such as "Rockin' Is My Business," "Hadacol (That's All)," "Sugar-Doo," and the salacious "Poon-Tang" were strong regional sellers and jukebox favorites, but mainstream success eluded them. Their 1954 tribute to baseball great Willie Mays, "Say Hey" (featuring the Say Hey Kid himself), captured some of the group's live interplay, but was mainly popular among New York Giants fans. During the rock 'n' roll boom of the mid-to-late '50s, the Treniers appeared in such teen-oriented musicals as *Don't Knock the Rock*, *The Girl Can't Help It*, *Calypso Heat Wave*, and *Jukebox Rhythm*. With a few exceptions, next to the stiff, lipsynching white teens populating these films, the Treniers appeared to be the only ones having any fun. One of the group's career highlights was their 1958 tour of England with Jerry Lee Lewis. When the furor over Lewis's child bride resulted in canceled bookings and the ruination of the piano pumper's career, the Treniers filled all his British dates to great critical acclaim. After OKeh dissolved, the Treniers recorded for Epic, and through the years moved on to Vik, Brunswick, Dot, Dom, Ronn, Hermitage, TT, and finally their own label, Mobile. They never sold many records, but by virtue of their exciting club act (these guys just never stop moving), the Treniers have been booked solid in top showrooms (particularly in Las Vegas) for over 40 years. Though Clifford Trenier died in 1983 and brothers Buddy & Milt left the act, Claude Trenier, assisted by their nephew Skip and original band members Don Hill, Gene Gilbeaux, Henry Green, Herman Washington, and Shifty Green, still pump out the rhythm and joy to standing-room-only crowds.

what to buy: The cream of the Treniers work for the OKeh label resides on *They Rock! They Roll! They Swing! The Best of the Treniers* 🎵🎵🎵 (Epic/Legacy, 1995, compilation prod. Bob Irwin), which features "Go! Go! Go!," "Rockin' Is Our Business," "Say Hey (The Willie Mays Song)," and the notorious "Poon-Tang!" Many of these tracks were produced by the young Quincy Jones, who of course went on to produce Michael Jackson and hundreds of hit records for artists from all genres. Informative liner notes by Nick Tosches, vintage photos and ads, as well as five previously unreleased tracks make this a must-have item for all fans of jump blues and early rock 'n' roll.

worth searching for: For even more of the fabulous Treniers check the import racks and specialty catalogs for *Hey Sister Lucy* (Bear Family, 1988, reissue prod. Richard Weize) and *Cool It Baby* (Bear Family, 1988, reissue prod. Richard Weize), two 18-track discs covering their 1947–56 output for Mercury and RCA-Groove, including brother Milt Trenier's work with His Solid Six. Worthwhile jive for all you knowledgeable R&B cats who know where rock 'n' roll really originated.

influences:

◀◀ Jimmie Lunceford, Louis Jordan, Joe Liggins & the Honeydrippers

▶▶ Bill Haley & the Comets, the Coasters, Freddy & the Bellboys

Ken Burke

Tricky

Born Adrian Thaws, 1968, in Bristol, England.

Tricky started out as a featured rapper in Bristol's influential Massive Attack, but the group could not contain him for long. Ambitious and outspoken, the smoky-voiced rapper and producer made his proper solo debut during 1995, with the critically fawned-over *Maxinquaye*. The disc expanded on Massive Attack's urban blues formula with cut-and-paste effects, scratchy guitars, and a variety of stylistic cribbing. The artist's unusual cockiness and unique features instantly won him a heap of attention from the music press. He was tagged as the spearhead of a new genre briefly referred to as trip-hop. Unfortunately, Tricky was never able to follow up the artistic freshness of the debut on any of his successive releases. However, he did continue to experiment with different vocalists (including Björk, Neneh Cherry, and Alison Moyet on *Nearly God*) and genres, admirably pushing his work in new directions.

what to buy: With exquisite singing partner Martina's smooth voice fronting the claustrophobic backdrop of twisted blues, hip-hop, and metal, *Maxinquaye* 🎵🎵🎵 (Island, 1995, prod. Tricky) set the mood for mid-'90s urban funk. It contains the phenomenal string-driven "Aftermath" single as well as several other genre-crashing cuts.

what to buy next: While not as inspired as the debut, *Pre-Milennium Tension* 🎵🎵🎵 (Island, 1996, prod. Tricky) did expand on Tricky's raw, loop-based format. The hallucinatory "Vent" and the resonant "Christiansands" are highlights.

what to avoid: *Tricky Presents Grassroots* 🎵 (Payday, 1996), Tricky's overwrought attempt at staight hip-hop, suggests his ambition has outstripped his actual skills.

the rest:
Nearly God 🎵🎵 (Island, 1996)
Angels with Dirty Faces 🎵🎵 (Island, 1998)

influences:

◀◀ Public Enemy, Kate Bush, John Barry, Massive Attack

▶▶ Sneaker Pimps, Morcheeba, Howie B

see also: *Massive Attack*

Aidin Vaziri

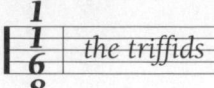
The Triffids

Formed 1980, in Perth, Australia. Disbanded 1989.

David McComb, vocals, guitar, piano; Robert McComb, violin, guitar, keyboards, vocals; Martin Casey, bass, vocals; Phil Kakulas, keyboards (1980–83); Jill Birt, keyboards, vocals (1983–89); Alsy McDonald, drums, vocals; "Evil" Graham Lee, slide guitar (1986–89).

Although influenced by American music ranging from country to the Velvet Underground, the Triffids crafted songs as resolutely Australian as a long, hot drive across the Outback's ochre desolation. Its early albums, *Treeless Plain* in 1983 and *Raining Pleasure* in 1984, were a bit spare and underproduced, but garnered the group a cult following, especially in Europe. But it wasn't until the next album, the haunting and majestic *Born Sandy Devotional* in 1986, that David McComb's poetically detailed, sublimely literate pop took full flight. In fact, the album's first single, "Wide Open Road," with its shimmering sense of space and endless horizons, is arguably the best, and most intrinsically Australian, song to come out of the Triffids' home country during the rock era. The next album, *In the Pines*, also from 1986 and recorded in a shearing shed in rural Western Australia, was a more casual, down-home affair. For 1987's *Calenture*, McComb and the gang returned to their more sumptuous sound, and the approach yielded some gems such as the despairing "Jerdacuttup Man." The group took another musical turn in 1989 on *The Black Swan* to a more basic country-rock style. Unfortunately, outside of Scandinavia the Triffids never sold many records and, before the new decade dawned, they decided to call it a day. But their lyrical, sunburnt legacy lives, thanks to McComb's solo career and Phil Kakulas's Blackeyed Susans.

worth searching for: Unfortunately, the Triffids' catalog is now only available on import, but *Born Sandy Devotional* (White/Hot, 1986, prod. Gil Norton) and *Calenture* (Island, 1987, prod. Gil Norton) are the Triffids' finest moments, at once as wise and warm as a good novel. Also worth seeking out are the best-of sets, *Love in Bright Landscapes* (Megadisc, 1985, prod. various), a collection of early material, and the more all-encompassing *Australian Melodrama* (White, 1994, prod. various).

solo outings:
David McComb:
Setting You Free 𝄠𝄠𝄠𝄠 (White, 1993)
Love of Will 𝄠𝄠𝄠 (White, 1994)

Lawson Square Infirmary:
Lawson Square Infirmary 𝄠𝄠𝄠 (Hot, 1984)

The Blackeyed Susans:
Welcome Stranger 𝄠𝄠𝄠 (Waterfront, 1992)
All Souls Alive 𝄠𝄠𝄠𝄠 (Frontier, 1994)
Mouth to Mouth 𝄠𝄠𝄠 (American, 1996)

influences:
◀◀ The Velvet Underground, Bob Dylan, Tom Verlaine
▶▶ The Whitlams, Paul Kelly

Cary Darling

Trio

Formed 1979, in West Germany. Disbanded 1984.

Stephan Remmler, vocals, keyboards; Kralle Krawinkel, guitar; Peter Behrehns, percussion.

The Teutonic new wave group Trio is the consummate one-hit wonder, virtually synonymous with its sole international success, "Da Da Da (I Don't Love You You Don't Love Me Aha Aha Aha)." Formed in West Germany at the close of the '70s, Trio established its trademark minimalist, monotone-vocals-with-drum machine sound with its self-titled debut album, released in Germany in 1981. The following year Trio rose to international prominence with the release of "Da Da Da," which charted across Europe and reached #2 in the U.K. The song also appeared on Trio's 1982 U.S. debut, *Trio*, an EP that found the three-member group beginning to use (stilted) English lyrics in its fractured dance songs. The following year's full-length *Trio and Error* also featured a version of "Da Da Da." The follow-up, the presciently titled *Bye Bye*, proved to be the group's swan song. Though Trio seemed destined to be forgotten, and "Da Da Da" relegated to cut-rate '80s compilations, during the summer of 1997 the band made a remarkable comeback when Volkswagen featured "Da Da Da" in a high-profile TV commercial. The song returned to radio playlists and a Trio compilation album was hastily assembled. Mercifully, the band didn't go so far as to reunite.

what's available: *Da Da Da* 𝄠𝄠 (Mercury, 1997, prod. Klaus Voormann, compilation prod. Bill Levenson, Bas Hartong) is all that's currently available in the United States. A hastily assembled best-of compilation rushed to stores in the wake of the famous Volkswagen commercial, *Da Da Da* is easily the only Trio album anyone needs. Besides two versions of the title track (is an extended remix really necessary?), *Da Da Da* includes 12 other Trio songs, which are both better and worse than one might imagine—few sound quite like "Da Da Da" but only a handful (the proto-industrial "Anna Letmeinletmeout," the call-and-response "Sunday You Need Love Monday Be Alone," and the Nintendo oompah tune "Hearts Are Trump") are memorable or enjoyable. The minimalist packaging compliments Trio's sparse sound, but the complete lack of liner notes ensures this enigmatic group will forever remain known solely as "that 'Da Da Da' band."

worth searching for: Really hardcore Trio fans might be interested in hunting down the group's original U.S. records: *Trio*

(Mercury, 1982, prod. Klaus Voormann), *Trio and Error* (Mercury, 1983, prod. Klaus Voormann), and *Bye Bye* (Mercury, 1983, prod. Klaus Voormann).

influences:

◀◀ Kraftwerk, Devo

▶▶ Fahrfegnugen

Seth Hindin

Trip Shakespeare

Formed mid-1980s. Disbanded 1991.

Elaine Harris, drums; John Munson, bass, vocals; Dan Wilson (1988–91), guitar, piano, vocals; Matt Wilson, guitar, piano, vocals.

More people have heard Trip Shakespeare's backing vocals on Matthew Sweet's *Earth* than on the group's own albums. Matt Wilson's quirky, often whimsical songs built on '70s psychedelia in an energetic, pop-minded way. The original trio was quickly augmented by Matt's brother Dan, who enriched the fabled harmonies. Elaine Harris, though not singing, was distinctive nonetheless for a Moe Tucker–esque style and for drumming standing up rather than sitting on a stool. The band broke up when A&M dropped it, releasing the EP (*Volt*), containing six well-chosen covers as a farewell gesture.

what to buy: With the A&M albums out of print, the sophomore album *Are You Shakespearienced* 𝄞𝄞𝄞 (Clean, 1989, prod. Trip Shakespeare) is the place to start. It has some of Wilson's best songs, including "Two Wheeler, Four Wheeler," with sparer production than the A&M material.

what to buy next: *Applehead Man* 𝄞𝄞𝄞 (Clean, 1988, prod. Jay Leigh) was the band's first album and is extremely quirky. The original version of "Pearle" and the similarly pretty "Rose" stand out.

the rest:

Volt 𝄞𝄞𝄞 (Black Hole/Clean, 1992)

worth searching for: *Across the Universe* (A&M, 1990, prod. Fred Maher, Trip Shakespeare) gained considerable polish (at no expense to energy) from having a major-label recording budget, filling out the sound without smoothing over the eccentricities. The result sounds like Jefferson Airplane played by a jangly new wave guitar-pop band. The B-side of *The Crane* (A&M EP, 1990, prod. Fred Maher, Trip Shakespeare) has three live versions of material from the two Clean albums. *Lulu* (A&M, 1991, prod. Trip Shakespeare, Justin Niebank) isn't at the exalted level of the other A&M album but contains a solid set of songs.

influences:

◀◀ The Beatles, Jefferson Airplane, the Zombies, Elvis Costello

Steve Holtje

Triumph

Formed 1975, in Toronto, Ontario, Canada.

Rik Emmett, guitar, vocals (1975–88); Gil Moore, drums, vocals; Mike Levine, keyboards, bass; Phil X, guitar (early 1990s).

A Canadian hard rock trio with high-pitched singing—where have we heard that before? The Rush shadow loomed long over Triumph throughout its career, and it's something the group never really came out of. Nevertheless, it made a commercial dent during the late '80s and early '90s with radio hits such as "Hold On," "Magic Power," and "Never Surrender," and it had a good live reputation thanks to its flashy stage show. Ultimately, the group never really regained its bearings after frontman Rik Emmett went solo, and it remains mostly a footnote from arena rock's golden age.

what to buy: The title of *Classics* 𝄞𝄞𝄞 (MCA, 1989/TRC, 1995, prod. various) is something of a misnomer, but this 11-track collection is a fine sampler that has all the crucial cuts, as well as a couple of album tracks that merit repeated play.

what to buy next: *Allied Forces* 𝄞𝄞𝄞 (RCA, 1981, prod. Triumph, David Thoener) is Triumph's best—and most commercially successful—studio album, thanks to the radio hits "Magic Power" and "Fight the Good Fight."

what to avoid: Like many trios with sharp studio facility, Triumph had some trouble filling out its live sound, a shortcoming that's documented on *Stages* 𝄞𝄞 (MCA, 1985/TRC, 1995) and *The King Biscuit Flower Hour Presents* 𝄞𝄞 (KBFH, 1996).

the rest:

In the Beginning 𝄞𝄞 (RCA, 1976/TRC, 1995)
Rock & Roll Machine 𝄞𝄞𝄞 (RCA, 1977/TRC, 1995)
Just a Game 𝄞𝄞𝄞 (RCA, 1979/TRC, 1995)
Progressions of Power 𝄞𝄞𝄞 (RCA, 1980/TRC, 1995)
Never Surrender 𝄞𝄞𝄞 (RCA, 1983/TRC, 1995)
Thunder Seven 𝄞𝄞𝄞 (RCA, 1984/TRC, 1995)
The Sport of Kings 𝄞𝄞 (MCA, 1986/TRC, 1995)

solo outings:

Rik Emmett:

The Spiral Notebook 𝄞𝄞 (Vanguard, 1993)

influences:

◀◀ Led Zeppelin, Rush

▶▶ Zebra, Skid Row, Saga, Dream Theater

Gary Graff

The Troggs

Formed 1965, in Andover, England.

Reg Presley, vocals; Chris Britton, guitar; Peter Staples, bass (1965–69); Ronnie Bond, drums (1965–92); Tony Murray, bass

(1972–76); Colin Fletcher, guitar; Peter Lucas, bass (1976–present); Dave Maggs, drums (1976–present).

The Troggs stood out from most of the British Invasion bands because of its total lack of pretension; the group made a crude thumping so devoid of art that it's not unreasonable to view the band as an embryonic forerunner to the late '70s punk explosion. Its classic "Wild Thing"—perhaps the fundamental non-singing garage-rocking anthem of the '60s—shot the group to rock 'n' roll immortality. Although its commercial success was brief, the Troggs have soldiered on through the decades and remain a popular attraction in England, though in 1992 the group recorded *Athens Andover* with admiring members of R.E.M.

what to buy: *Archeology* 🎵🎵🎵 (Fontana/Chronicles, 1992, prod. various) gives the band its due with 52 tracks comprising the lewd, crude anthems as well as excursions into hard pop and flowery ballads. Obscurities and B-sides are thrown in as well, making this the definitive Troggs statement.

what to avoid: *Best of the Troggs* 🎵🎵 (Fontana, 1994, prod. various) is a decent collection, but nothing compared to *Archeology*.

the rest:
Live at Max's Kansas City 🎵🎵🎵 (Griffin)
Athens Andover 🎵🎵 (Rhino, 1992)

influences:
◀◀ The Who, the Rolling Stones, the Beatles, the Yardbirds, the Animals, Elvis Presley

▶▶ Count Five, the New York Dolls, the Modern Lovers, the Stooges, the Sex Pistols, Kiss, Nirvana, the Fluid

Allan Orski

Robin Trower

Born March 9, 1945, in London, England.

Procol Harum may be remembered mostly for its ruminative chamber pop, but within the band seethed the roiling guitar ambitions of longtime blues devotee Robin Trower. Hooked by Jimi Hendrix's sonic pyrotechnics, Trower began to assert himself more in the band—check out "Whiskey Train" on Procol's *Home*—and finally decided to step out on his own after 1971's *Broken Barricades*. On his own, Trower first specialized in distorted electric blues that came so close to the Hendrix model—right down to bassist Jimmy Dewar's husky vocals—that it was at once skillful and derivative. Ultimately, when the songs were good ("Day of the Eagle," "Too Rolling Stoned," "Alethea"), the skill won out. There's been a journeyman nature to much of Trower's solo career, including a brief early '80s collaboration with Cream's Jack Bruce and participation in the 1991 Procol

Harum reunion. These days you're most likely to find Trower doing session work (most notably for Bryan Ferry) and playing the blues, hewing a bit closer to the original root but never leaving those lightning-fast Hendrix riffs too far behind.

what to buy: *Bridge of Sighs* 🎵🎵🎵🎵 (Chrysalis, 1974/1985, prod. Matthew Fisher) is the epochal Trower album, with his best batch of songs ("Day of the Eagle," "Too Rolling Stoned," "Lady Love," the title track) and empathetic backing from Dewar and drummer Reggie Isadore. *BBC Radio 1 Live in Concert* 🎵🎵🎵🎵 (Griffin, 1995, prod. Jeff Griffin) and *The King Biscuit Flower Hour Presents Robin Trower* 🎵🎵🎵🎵 (KBFH, 1996) are solid concert documents—the latter with some funkier touches—on which Trower stretches out into longer, even more Hendrixian solos.

what to buy next: *Essential Robin Trower* 🎵🎵🎵 (Chrysalis, 1991, prod. various) is a good sampling of his first eight albums, though the absence of "Day of the Eagle" really weakens the set.

what to avoid: *Passion* 🎵🎵 (GNP/Crescendo, 1987, prod. Neil Norman), a transitional album, is often just the opposite of its title.

the rest:
For Earth Below 🎵🎵🎵 (Chrysalis, 1975/1991)
Live 🎵🎵🎵 (Chrysalis, 1976)
Victims of the Fury 🎵🎵🎵 (Chrysalis, 1980/1989)
(With Jack Bruce) *Truce* 🎵🎵 (Chrysalis, 1982/One Way, 1981)
(With Jack Bruce) *No Stopping Anytime* 🎵🎵🎵 (Chrysalis, 1989/Rodolphe Opera Viva, 1989)
20th-Century Blues 🎵🎵 (V12, 1994)
Someday Blues 🎵🎵🎵 (V12, 1997)

worth searching for: *The Robin Trower Portfolio* (Chrysalis, 1987) a British import anthology, bests its U.S. counterpart, though the CD version lopped off the live tracks that were part of the original double-LP.

influences:
◀◀ Jimi Hendrix, Jimmy Page, Robert Johnson

▶▶ Steve Vai, Joe Satriani, Eric Johnson, Vernon Reid

see also: *Procol Harum*

Gary Graff

True Believers

See: Alejandro Escovedo

Jennifer Trynin

Born December 27, 1963.

For the few minutes after Liz Phair's *Exile in Guyville* made it hip to be a frank, angry female singer-songwriter and before Alanis

Morissette made millions doing it, Jennifer Trynin was considered "the next big thing," with major labels battling over her album, *Cockamamie*. (She had financed and released the debut on her own Squint Records label.) For whatever reason, after winning a bidding war, Warner Bros. didn't put much effort into promoting the album. Or maybe radio stations didn't see her as marketable to their demographic audiences. Speculation as to why neither Trynin's debut album nor her follow-up, *Gun Shy Tiger Happy*, has achieved mass success is like trying to second-guess an umpire's wrong, game-changing call. It happened, and that's it. But she's a talented singer and songwriter, and with luck that will translate into deserved commercial success.

what to buy: *Cockamamie* 𝄪𝄪𝄪𝄪 (Squint, 1994/Warner Bros. 1995, prod. Mike Denneen) is a fine album and a lesson to aspiring singer-songwriters: You *can* make a major label record on a small budget.

what to buy next: *Gun Shy Trigger Happy* 𝄪𝄪𝄪 (Warner Bros., 1997, prod. Mike Denneen) is another overlooked gem: solid songwriting, tasteful production. Trynin deserves a shot with the successful all-woman traveling festival Lilith Fair so fans and radio programmers can finally give her a listen.

influences:

◀◀ The Pretenders, the Rolling Stones, Marvin Gaye, Joni Mitchell

▶▶ Tracy Bonham, Natalie Imbruglia

Brian Ives

Tsunami

Formed 1990, in Arlington, VA.

Jenny Toomey, vocals, guitars; Kristin Thomson, guitars, vocals; Andrew Webster, bass, vocals; John Palmer, drums.

One of the major leaders in the indie rock movement, Tsunami has worked with practically every respected band in the scene: Superchunk, Velocity Girl, Jawbox, Seaweed, and, of course, spiritual leader Fugazi. In true indie spirit, Jenny Toomey and Kristin Thomson not only lead the band but run their own record label and produce all of their label-mates' albums. In her spare time, Toomey shows up in a number of other bands, including Liquorice and Grenadine. Like many indie acts, Tsunami began by releasing a tidal wave of seven-inch records and compilation singles before plunging into full-length albums.

what to buy: *The Heart's Tremolo* 𝄪𝄪𝄪𝄪 (Simple Machines, 1994, prod. Brian Paulson) boasts complex and lyrically intriguing songs, combined with a darker mood than the band's debut album, *Deep End*. *World Tour and Other Destinations* 𝄪𝄪𝄪𝄪 (Simple Machines, 1995) puts together the huge collection of Tsunami's singles and seven-inch recordings in one convenient

album, providing a musical timeline that displays not only Tsunami's musical range but also the steady maturation of an excellent band.

what to buy next: *Deep End* 𝄪𝄪𝄪𝄪 (Simple Machines, 1992) is Tsunami's first full-length album, a danceable disc that showcases the group's ability to create an instantly catchy tune while still remaining musically complex.

the rest:
Brilliant Mistake 𝄪𝄪𝄪𝄪 (Simple Machines, 1997)

influences:
◀◀ The Sex Pistols, the Pixies

▶▶ Superchunk, Velocity Girl

Bryan Lassner

Tuatara

See: R.E.M.

The Tubes

Formed 1972, in San Francisco, CA.

Fee Waybill, vocals; Bill Spooner, guitar; Roger Sheen, guitar; Vince Welnick, keyboards; Michael Cotten, keyboards; Prairie Prince, drums; Rick Anderson, bass; Re Styles, vocals; Gary Cambra, keyboards (1993); Jennifer McFee, vocals (1993); Amy French, vocals (1993).

From the mid-'70s through the early '80s, the Tubes pedaled a live show that verged on soft porn and gave the group's proto-metal lumberings a theatrical infamy. As its albums whiffed one right after the other, the band chiseled off the satirical excess for MTV, recording a series of radio friendly pop-rockers during the early '80s ("Talk to Ya Later," "She's a Beauty") that achieved their commercial goals. The Tubes' handle on catchy melodies was short-lived, and the decade soon forgot them. The group still pops up for occasional appearances of Waybill's alter ego, Quay Lewd.

what to buy: *The Best of the Tubes* 🎵🎵🎵 (Capitol/EMI, 1992, compilation prod. Mark Dix) covers all the Tubes you'll need to hear, the undeniably catchy mainstream pop breakthroughs as well as the plundering of Curtis Mayfield's "The Monkey Time," which probably has oodles of soul men flipping in the grave.

what to buy next: *The Tubes* 🎵🎵 (A&M, 1975), the band's debut, contains the mocking metal anti-anthem "White Punks on Dope" and the lesser-known (but just as crude) "Mondo Bondage."

what to avoid: Even producer Todd Rundgren's skills couldn't redeem the melodic monotony of *Remote Control* 🎵 (A&M, 1988/1979, prod. Todd Rundgren).

the rest:
Best of the Tubes 🎵🎵 (CEMA, 1992)
Genius of America **woof!** (Popular, 1996)

worth searching for: *What Do You Want from Live?* (A&M, 1978, prod. John Anthony) documents the group's stage antics, many of which are lost in an audio-only format. *Outside/Inside* (Capitol, 1983, prod. David Foster, Tubes) is the most listenable studio album, with "She's a Beauty," "The Monkey Time" and "Out of the Business." The import collection *Goin' Down* (A&M, 1996, prod. various) is a thorough look at the twisted, pre-hit singles years.

influences:
◀◀ Frank Zappa, New York Dolls, Kiss
▶▶ Meat Loaf, Pet Shop Boys

Allan Orski

Maureen Tucker
See: The Velvet Underground

Turn On
See: High Llamas

Big Joe Turner
Born Joe Vernon Turner, May 18, 1911, in Kansas City, MO. Died November 24, 1985, in Los Angeles, CA.

When Atlantic Records signed Big Joe Turner in 1952, he was the first top artist to be associated with the fledgling R&B company. The Atlantic partners knew Turner well from the minor boogie-woogie craze the barrel-chested vocalist stirred in New

York during the early '40s with pianist Pete Johnson. In fact, Turner was probably deemed past his commercial prime at the time, although he went on to make his greatest records with Atlantic during the '50s. Turner was the last bastion of the Kansas City school of blues shouting, a relaxed, easy moaning style, swung with a voice that sounded like it came from the bottom of a well. He was an unlikely teenage rock 'n' roll star, but after Bill Haley transformed Turner's "Shake, Rattle, and Roll" into a rock evergreen—recorded subsequently by everyone from Elvis Presley to Huey Lewis & the News—Turner himself followed Haley into the Top 40 with "Corinna Corrina" in 1956. At the same time, Atlantic showed good taste by reteaming Turner and pianist Johnson for an album, *The Boss of the Blues*, now recognized as a classic.

what to buy: If you're just looking for Turner's most popular R&B jumpers from the '50s in crisp digital sound, you're sure to dig *The Very Best of Big Joe Turner* 🎵🎵🎵🎵 (Rhino, 1998, compilation prod. Billy Vera), a smart collection featuring such cool jive as "Shake Rattle, and Roll," "Flip, Flop, and Fly," "Corrina, Corrina," and the infamous "T.V. Mama." Looking for more? It took a three-disc retrospective to encompass the breadth of Turner's almost 50 years of recording. *Big, Bad & Blue: The Big Joe Turner Anthology* 🎵🎵🎵🎵 (Rhino, 1994, compilation prod. Bob Porter) runs from his 1939 sessions with pianist Johnson through a 1983 date with jump band revivalists Roomful of Blues.

what to buy next: While he was touring on package rock 'n' roll tours with the teen heartthrobs of the day, Turner took time to re-create the classic Kansas City jazz sound of his youth on *The Boss of the Blues* 🎵🎵🎵🎵 (Atlantic, 1956/1981, prod. Neshui Ertegun, Jerry Wexler), an utterly magnificent chapter in American music.

what to avoid: Turner recorded extensively during the '80s, often with indifferent results, and was not at his best in the informal, jazz-like settings he received on *Stormy Monday* 🎵🎵 (Pablo, 1976/1991, prod. Norman Granz).

the rest:
Big Joe Rides Again 🎵🎵🎵🎵 (Atlantic, 1959/Rhino, 1987)
Texas Style 🎵🎵🎵 (Evidence, 1971/1992)
(With T-Bone Walker) *Bosses of the Blues* 🎵🎵🎵 (RCA Bluebird, 1972/1989)
Life Ain't Easy 🎵🎵🎵 (Pablo, 1974/Original Jazz Classics, 1994)
Everyday I Have the Blues 🎵🎵🎵 (Pablo, 1975/Original Jazz Classics, 1991)
The Trumpet Kings Meet Joe Turner 🎵🎵🎵 (Pablo, 1975/Original Jazz Classics, 1990)
In the Evening 🎵🎵🎵 (Pablo, 1976/Original Jazz Classics, 1996)
Things That I Used to Do 🎵🎵🎵 (Pablo, 1977/Original Jazz Classics)
Best of Joe Turner 🎵🎵 (Pablo, 1980/1987)
The Midnight Special 🎵🎵🎵 (Pablo, 1980/1987)

Have No Fear, Big Joe Turner Is Here 🎵🎵🎵 (Savoy, 1984/1995)
Kansas City Here I Come 🎵🎵🎵 (Pablo, 1984/Original Jazz Classics, 1992)
Patcha, Patcha All Night Long 🎵🎵🎵 (Pablo, 1985/Original Jazz Classics, 1996)
Rhythm and Blues Years 🎵🎵🎵🎵 (Rhino, 1986)
Flip, Flop, and Fly 🎵🎵 (Pablo, 1989)
Greatest Hits 🎵🎵🎵🎵🎵 (Rhino, 1989)
I've Been to Kansas City 🎵🎵🎵 (Decca, 1990)
Tell Me Pretty Baby 🎵🎵🎵🎵 (Arhoolie, 1992)
Every Day in the Week 🎵🎵🎵 (Decca, 1993)
Let's Boogie: The Freedom Records Story 1959–64 🎵🎵🎵 (Collectables, 1992)
Jumpin' with Joe: The Complete Aladdin & Imperial Recordings 🎵🎵🎵 (EMI, 1993)
I Don't Dig It (1946–1949) 🎵🎵🎵🎵 (Mr. R&B, 1994)
Shake, Rattle, and Roll 🎵🎵🎵🎵 (Tomato, 1994)
Shoutin' the Blues 🎵🎵🎵 (Eclipse, 1996)
Joe Turner's Blues 🎵🎵🎵 (Pearl, 1998)

worth searching for: The rollicking backdrop provided by relative youngsters Roomful of Blues made *Blues Train* (Muse, 1983/1995, prod. Doc Pomus, Bob Porter) one of the most satisfying Turner outings since he left Atlantic 20 years earlier.

influences:

◄◄ Pete Johnson, Jimmy Rushing

►► James Brown, Chuck Berry, Wynonie Harris, Little Richard, Mick Jagger, Otis Redding, Sam & Dave, Bruce Springsteen

Joel Selvin and Ken Burke

Ike & Tina Turner
/Tina Turner
/Ike Turner

Ike Turner (born November 5, 1931, in Clarksdale, MS), guitar, vocals; Tina Turner (born Annie Mae Bullock, November 26, 1938, in Nutbush, TN), vocals.

Considering the dramatic saga behind Tina Turner's escape from an abusive relationship with husband Ike, it's not surprising that the duo's role as seminal rock 'n' roll pioneers is sometimes obscured. Ike first came to prominence as leader of the Kings of Rhythm, a group that recorded "Rocket 88"—a tune widely cited as the first rock 'n' roll tune—in 1951 at Sun Studios. Taking the Kings of Rhythm on the club circuit, Ike met Tina at an East St. Louis, Illinois club and eventually she convinced him to let her sing with the band. In 1956 she became a sometime-member, moving into full-time and eventually marrying Ike. When a singer failed to show for a session in 1960, Tina sang lead vocals on the band's first hit, "A Fool in Love." Ike decided to focus the show on Tina after that, hiring a trio of back-ing singers and creating the Ike & Tina Turner Revue, a roaring R&B act that delivered killer covers of rock tunes such as "Proud Mary" and "Come Together." The Rolling Stones invited the Turner Revue to open its 1969 North American tour, while Phil Spector wooed Tina for her first solo hit, "River Deep, Mountain High." But the beatings Tina received from Ike and his escalating drug use eventually prompted her to leave him in 1976, sneaking away with just 36 cents in her pocket. Although Tina's comeback was rocky at first, her friendship with members of British synth-popsters Heaven 17 led to a cover of Al Green's "Let's Stay Together" that launched her new solo career. With help from other friends—Bryan Adams, Eric Clapton, Robert Cray, David Bowie—Tina's star rose higher than ever during the '80s, as she released hit after hit and became an MTV staple. Her autobiography, *I, Tina,* detailed her years with Ike and was the main source for the feature film *What's Love Got to Do with It.* Meanwhile, Ike's continuing drug problems led to a short prison stay, further damaging his already-diminishing prospects.

what to buy: For an accurate take on the arc of this amazing duo's career, the greatest-hits collection *Proud Mary: The Best of Ike and Tina Turner* 🎵🎵🎵🎵 (EMI International, 1991, prod. various) pulls together seminal cuts such as "A Fool in Love" and Tina's rendition of "The Acid Queen" for the Who's film version of *Tommy.* Fortified by impressive liner notes, this collection is a must for any fan seeking a full history. On her own, Tina's best outing remains *Private Dancer* 🎵🎵🎵🎵 (Capitol, 1984, prod. various), which bounds effortlessly from the midtempo hit "What's Love Got to Do with It?" to the moody, Mark Knopfler–penned title track and the rocking "Better Be Good to Me."

what to buy next: As their most successful album, Ike & Tina's *Workin' Together* 🎵🎵🎵🎵 (Liberty, 1970, prod. Ike Turner) contains the breakthrough hit "Proud Mary," along with tasty nuggets of the group's R&B/early rock sound—including a masterful cover of "Ooh Poo Pah Doo." For the soundtrack to *What's Love Got to Do with It* 🎵🎵🎵🎵 (Virgin/EMI, 1993, prod. various), Tina re-records some of the classic Ike & Tina cuts with a better band and better production. Although some later hits are here, updated versions of tunes such as "A Fool in Love," "Nutbush City Limits," and "Rock Me Baby" are the real reason to get this one.

what to avoid: Marrying Tina's earthy, powerful vocals with producer Phil Spector's wall of sound proved a deadly, misguided combination, sinking half the material on *River Deep, Mountain High* 🎵🎵 (A&M, 1969, prod. Phil Spector, Ike Turner). It's no wonder that, when the record failed to do well in the United States, Spector went into a three-year seclusion. On her own, Tina loses more of her distinctive soul flair and rock energy with every record, sublimating those distinctive qualities in

Tina Turner (© Ken Settle)

favor of a generic pop appeal. Small wonder that her last two solo albums, *Foreign Affair* **woof!** (Capitol, 1989, prod. Tina Turner, Dan Hartman) and *Wildest Dreams* ♪ (Virgin, 1997, prod. various), are her worst, just a bunch of generic pop tunes linked solely by Tina's vocals.

the rest:

Ike & Tina Turner:
The Soul of Ike & Tina Turner ♪♪♪ (Sue 1960/Collectable, 1994)
Dance with Ike & Tina Turner ♪♪♪ (Sue 1962/Collectable, 1996)
It's Gonna Work out Fine ♪♪♪ (Sue 1963/Collectables)
The Great Rhythm & Blues Sessions ♪♪♪ (Tomato 1968/1991)
Come Together ♪♪♪ (Liberty 1970/Laserlight, 1995)
What You Hear Is What You Get: Live at Carnegie Hall ♪♪♪ (United Artists, 1971)
Nutbush City Limits ♪♪♪ (United Artists, 1973)
Greatest Hits, Vol. 1 ♪♪♪ (Saja, 1989)
Greatest Hits, Vol. 2 ♪♪♪ (Saja, 1989)
Greatest Hits, Vol. 3 ♪♪♪ (Saja, 1989)
The Collection ♪♪♪ (Castle, 1990)
Greatest Hits ♪♪ (Curb, 1990)
The Best of Ike & Tina Turner ♪♪♪ (CEMA, 1992)
Too Hot to Hold ♪♪♪ (Charly, 1992)
Sexy, Seductive, Provocative ♪♪♪ (Paula, 1993)
Shake, Rattle, and Roll ♪♪ (Laserlight, 1994)
Rockin' and Rollin' ♪♪ (Laserlight, 1995)
Living for the City ♪♪ (Laserlight, 1995)
Keep on Pushing ♪♪♪ (Laserlight, 1995)
Ike & Tina Turner ♪♪♪ (King, 1996)
Back in the Day ♪♪♪ (32 Records, 1997)
Golden Classics ♪♪♪ (Collectable)
Bold Soul Sister: The Best of the Blue Thumb Recordings ♪♪♪ (Hip-O, 1997)

Tina Turner:
Break Every Rule ♪♪♪ (Capitol, 1986)
Tina Live in Europe ♪♪ (Capitol, 1988)
Simply the Best ♪♪♪ (Capitol, 1991)
Collected Recordings: '60s to '90s ♪♪♪ (Capitol, 1994)

Ike Turner:
1958–1959 ♪♪♪ (Paula, 1993)
I Like Ike! The Best of Ike Turner ♪♪♪ (Rhino, 1994)

worth searching for: *I, Tina*, Tina's spellbinding autobiography, is a must-read as it recounts her abusive relatironship with Ike, a near-miraculous escape, and her subsequent career rehabilitation. And she narrates the book-on-tape version herself.

influences:

◀◀ Cab Calloway, Bessie Smith, Big Mama Thornton

▶▶ Sly & the Family Stone, Nona Hendryx, Chaka Khan, Donna Summer

Eric Deggans

The Turtles

Formed 1963, in Inglewood, CA. Disbanded 1970.

Howard Kaylan, vocals; Mark Volman, vocals, guitar, saxophone, "special effects;" Al Nichol, guitar, keyboards; Chuck Portz, bass (1963–66); Don Murray, drums (1963–66); Jim Tucker, guitar (1964–67); John Barbata, drums (1966–69); Chip Douglas, bass (1966–67); Jim Pons, bass (1967–70); John Selter, drums (1969–70).

What ultimately prevented this extremely talented band from receiving the success and recognition it so richly deserved—and fought throughout its entire career to obtain—was a basic confusion amongst the band's record company, its audiences worldwide, and the band members themselves. Was the Turtles merely a happy-go-lucky, witless pop group capable of producing Top 10 hits at the drop of the hat and innocuous enough to procure an invitation to entertain at the Nixon White House? Or was it a seriously visionary group of musicians dedicated to pushing the frontiers of mid-'60s rock as far out there as possible? (One listen to tracks such as "Sound Asleep" and "Grim Reaper of Love" prove there were few equals in the recording studio at the time). Well, the Turtles tried to be both—this musical schizophrenia best illustrated on its classic *Battle of the Bands* album, where in 12 songs it skillfully adopted the personas of *12* different "Turtles"–but after nine Top 40 hits in less than four years, these guys just couldn't shake the teeny-bop tag. To this day, "Happy Together," "She'd Rather Be with Me," and "Elenore" remain staples of oldies radio, and whenever group leaders Mark Volman and Howard Kaylan step on stage—whether with their latest batch of mock-Turtles or under the guise of their acid-fractured alter-egos Flo & Eddie–it's the hits, and nothing but the hits, everyone's come to hear. But what the group may be lacking in respect, it continues to more than make up for with buckets full of happy, self-deflationary, rockin' good fun. Should we ever ask for more?

what to buy: *20 Greatest Hits* ♪♪♪♪ (Rhino, 1984, compilation prod. Mark Volman, Howard Kaylan) contains all the hits *and* all the misses, though with music as varied as the Turtles', the misses often reign supreme. The aforementioned *Battle of the Bands* ♪♪♪♪♪ (White Whale, 1968/Sundazed, 1994, prod. Chip Douglas, Turtles), with tracks such as "I'm Chief Kamanawanalea (We're the Royal Macadamia Nuts)," absolutely beats *Sgt. Pepper's* at its own game.

what to buy next: The Crossfires' *Out of Control* ♪♪♪♪ (Rhino, 1981/Sundazed, 1995, compilation prod. Mark Volman, Howard Kaylan) is actually the pre-Turtles in a surf-rockin' incarnation, though even this early on the insanity was rearing its head (i.e., "Santa and the Sidewalk Surfer"). *Turtle Wax: The Best of the Turtles, Vol. 2* ♪♪♪♪ (Rhino, 1988, compilation prod. Mark Volman, Howard Kaylan) contains key tracks there just wasn't room enough for on *20 Greatest Hits*, while *The Turtles, featuring Flo*

& *Eddie: Captured Live* 𝄞𝄞𝄞 (Rhino, 1992, prod. Steve Remote, David Nelson) presents a perfect mixture of Turtles hits, Vegas schlock, and Flo & Eddie madness, recorded live one raucous New Year's Eve at the Bottom Line in New York City.

what to avoid: *Elenore* 𝄞𝄞 (Laserlight, 1995, prod. various), *Eve of Destruction* 𝄞𝄞 (Laserlight, 1995, prod. various), *Let Me Be* 𝄞𝄞 (Laserlight, 1995, prod. various), *She's My Girl* 𝄞𝄞 (Laserlight, 1995, prod. various), and *The Story of Rock 'n' Roll* 𝄞𝄞 (Laserlight, 1995, prod. various)—all five of which are also available as the box set *30 Years of Rock 'n' Roll: Happy Together* 𝄞𝄞 (Laserlight, 1995, prod. various)—are skimpy, poorly sequenced compilations that pale greatly in comparison to the far superior Rhino and especially Sundazed packages.

the rest:
It Ain't Me Babe 𝄞𝄞𝄞 (White Whale, 1965/Sundazed, 1994)
You Baby 𝄞𝄞𝄞𝄞 (White Whale, 1966/Sundazed, 1994)
Happy Together 𝄞𝄞𝄞𝄞 (White Whale, 1967/Sundazed, 1994)
Turtle Soup 𝄞𝄞𝄞 (White Whale, 1969/Sundazed, 1997)
Wooden Head 𝄞𝄞𝄞 (White Whale, 1970/Sundazed, 1997)

worth searching for: A spectacular collection of songs originally intended for the Turtles' post–"Happy Together" concept album-slash-masterpiece was, like its closest cousin *Smile* by the Beach Boys, never released in its intended form or context but instead dribbled out as B-sides and album tracks over the next several years. Many of these long lost anti-classics, such as "Can't You Hear the Cows" and "Chicken Little Was Right," were gathered together alongside similar overlooked treasures of the period (i.e., "Outside Chance") and briefly issued as *Chalon Road* (Rhino, 1987, compilation prod. Harold Bronson, Howard Kaylan, Mark Volman). Not only is this one of the finest Turtles collections ever, but a brilliant look back at that one brief, shining moment in pop when absolutely *anything* seemed possible. Conversely, a series of motel room sing-alongs and other "road tapes" of dubious intent snuck out on various seven-inch vinyl EP's as the *Rhythm Butchers* series on Rhino during the early '80s, while the whole crazy Turtles saga is lovingly, laughingly portrayed in song and dance on *Happy Together* (Rhino Home Video, 1991), hosted by none other than—need I say more?—Flo & Eddie. The final scene, where the two explain in front of a chalkboard, pointer in hand, just what apparently happened to the millions of dollars the band *supposedly* earned during its salad daze, is at once hilarious, heartbreaking, and a lesson to all musicians out there thinking of going into the business without a team of lawyers by their side.

solo outings:
Flo & Eddie:
Illegal, Immoral, and Fattening 𝄞𝄞𝄞𝄞 (Columbia, 1975/One Way, 1993)
Rock Steady with Flo & Eddie 𝄞𝄞𝄞 (Epiphany, 1981)
The Best of Flo & Eddie 𝄞𝄞𝄞𝄞 (Rhino, 1987)

influences:
◀◀ Stan Freberg, the Four Preps, the Trashmen, Mothers of Invention

▶▶ Cheap Trick, Barnes & Barnes, Strawberry Shortcake & the Care Bears, the Evaporators

Gary Pig Gold

20/20

Formed 1977, in Los Angeles, CA. Disbanded 1983. Re-formed 1995.

Steve Allen, vocals, guitar; Ron Flynt, vocals, bass, keyboards; Mike Gallo, drums (1977–79); Chris Silagyi, vocals, guitar, synthesizer (1979–81); Joel Turrisi, drums (1979–81); Dean Korth, drums (1982–83); Keith Clark, drums (1983); Bill Belknap, drums (1995–present).

Neither hitmaker nor massive seller, 20/20 is a mere footnote in the rock history books. But its legend looms large in the world of power pop, where its first two Beatles-influenced albums should appear on any short list of albums that define the form. Incorporating all the tools on the popcraft workbench—buzzing guitars, three-part harmonies, and energy to spare—20/20 was a breath of fresh air during the days of disco and pompous progressive rock. But pop songs were a hard sell during the late '70s and early '80s, and 20/20 called it quits in 1983. But when artists such as Matthew Sweet showed the '90s to be much more pop friendly, Ron Flynt and Steve Allen decided to give 20/20 another shot.

what to buy: The band's debut, *20/20* 𝄞𝄞𝄞𝄞 (Portrait/Epic, 1979, prod. Earle Mankey) is practically a power pop primer. Tracks such as "Yellow Pills," "Remember the Lightning," and "Jet Lag" stand among the best of the era. Its successor, *Look Out* 𝄞𝄞𝄞 (Portrait/CBS, 1981, prod. Richard Podoor), while not as drop-dead great as the first, features some of 20/20's strongest songs: "Nuclear Boy," one of the great lost singles of the early '80s, and the simply perfect "The Night I Heard a Scream." Both titles have been reissued on a single CD collection *20/20, Look Out!* 𝄞𝄞𝄞𝄞 (Oglio, 1995). *Interstate* 𝄞𝄞𝄞𝄞 (Oglio, 1995, prod. 20/20) takes 20/20 a long way from its streetwise debut and *Look Out*. In more of a worldly wise mood, the band flirts with country—falls in love with it, actually—on "Land of the Free," kicks up J. Geils–style vamp-rock on "What Do You Feel?," and rescues a lost early song called "I Never Did No Hitler." The dance-grooving "Cool White Laura" is almost eerie, with a chorus that seems to drift away. Featuring organ contributions from the Mavericks' Jerry Dale McFadden, *Interstate* is the tour-de-force 20/20 always wanted to make.

what to buy next: Time off seems to have mellowed 20/20 on *4 Day Tornado* 𝄞𝄞𝄞 (Oglio, 1995, prod. 20/20), but the album proves the trio still has the basic stuff that earned its reputation.

what to avoid: After *Look Out*, 20/20 released an independent album called *Sex Trap* ♫♫ (1997), which was a significant letdown from the first two albums. The songs are stripped to shells and sound more like a collection of lukewarm demos.

worth searching for: 20/20 contributed a terrific song, "Drive," to the sampler *Waves* (Bomp, 1979).

influences:

The Beatles, the Raspberries, the Dwight Twilley Band

Adam Schmitt, Tommy Keene, Martin Luther Lennon, Matthew Sweet

Keith Klingensmith and Jordan Oakes

Dwight Twilley /Dwight Twilley Band /Phil Seymour

Formed 1973, in Tulsa, OK. Disbanded 1973.

Dwight Twilley, guitar, vocals (born June 6, 1951 in Tulsa, OK); Phil Seymour (died August 17, 1993), bass, drums, vocals; Roger Lynn, bass, keyboards; Bill Pitron IV, guitar.

Dwight Twilley was one of the first singer-songwriters to crawl from the disco demolition and arena rock stiffness of the '70s. Twilley and Phil Seymour, his partner in crime, set out to preserve guitar pop during the mid-'70s with the now legendary albums *Sincerely* (1976) and *Twilley Don't Mind* (1977), seminal works that combined Twilley's straightforward, Tom Petty–style rock and Seymour's sweeter pop sensibilities. After the second Twilley Band album, Seymour split and Twilley went on to record three somewhat mediocre solo albums.

what to buy: Twilley and Seymour's work is represented these days by anthologies. Twilley's *XXI* ♫♫♫♫ (Right Stuff, 1996, prod. various) is a comprehensive anthology of his band and solo work, featuring the cult power pop hits "I'm on Fire," "Looking for the Magic," and the 1982 Top 20 solo hit "Girls" (which features Petty on vocals).

what to buy next: In late 1997 the Right Stuff label reissued Dwight's first two records, *Sincerley* ♫♫♫ (Shelter, 1976/Right Stuff, 1997, prod. Dwight Twilley, Phil Seymour) and *Twilley Don't Mind* ♫♫♫ (Arista, 1977/Right Stuff, 1997, prod. various), with a couple of rare bonus tracks on each reissue. The Seymour collection *Precious to Me* ♫♫♫ (Right Stuff, 1996, prod. various) gathers songs from the Twilley Band, his own solo albums, as well as the previously unreleased Petty tune "Save Me."

influences:

The Beatles, Elvis Presley, Brian Wilson

Tom Petty, Tommy Keene, Marshall Crenshaw

Chris Richards

Twisted Sister

Formed 1973, in Ho-Ho-Kus, NJ.

Dee Snyder, vocals; Jay Jay French (born John Segall), guitar; Mark "The Animal" Mendoza, bass; Eddie Ojeda, guitar; Tony Petri, drums (1973–81); A.J. Pero, drums (1982–86); Joe Franco, drums (1987).

Taking nothing from the New York Dolls except the rouge, Twisted Sister was like a screaming, last-gasp-of-the-'70s, barband, bird-flipping, metal mediocrity that capitalized on MTV's willingness to showcase its outrageously obnoxious appearance. Nuclear meltdown makeovers notwithstanding, the band's grade-school mentality masked a lack of true hard-rock aggressiveness; those who questioned such half-baked rock were bitten in the face, which says more than "I Wanna Rock" ever did. Lead shriek Dee Snider—now a syndicated radio personality when he's not fronting the latest version of Twisted Sister—did win points for testifying in the famous congressional hearings on rock lyrics in the mid-'80s.

what to buy: *Big Hits and Nasty Cuts: The Best of Twisted Sister* ♫♫ (Atlantic, 1992, prod. various) chronicles the Alice Cooper-wannabe wall of smeared mascara starting with the early "Shoot 'Em Down" and continuing through the attempted anthems "I Am (I'm Me)" and "You Can't Stop Rock 'n' Roll." "We're Not Gonna Take It" is fist-pumping rock at its dumbest, but of course, some folks like it that way.

the rest:

You Can't Stop Rock 'n' Roll ♫ (Atlantic, 1983/1990)
Stay Hungry ♫ (Atlantic, 1984)
Live ♫♫ (CMC, 1994)
Live at Hammersmiths N/A (CMC, 1998)

influences:

Kiss, the Dictators, Alice Cooper

Poison, Warrant

Allan Orski

Two

See: Judas Priest

Type O Negative

Formed 1991, in Brooklyn, NY.

Peter Steele, vocals, bass; Josh Silver, keyboards; Kenny Hickey, guitar; Sal Abruscato, drums (1991–93); John Kelly, drums (1993–present).

Any death-rock band can sing about despair, ingest blood, and taunt religious icons, but how many can cover a Seals & Crofts tune? Type O Negative can; it turned "Summer Breeze" into a haunting horror story. The twisted, talented, and unpredictable quartet is led by Peter Steele, a former heavy-equipment oper-

ator for the City of New York, a former member of Carnivore, and the band's chief songwriter. Type O Negative creates slickly orchestrated gothic metal from the dark side, featuring layered keyboards, slashing guitars, and Steele's ominously slow, brooding vocals. The music is embellished with background nuances, including bubbling liquids, heavy breathing, and sobbing women.

what to buy: *Bloody Kisses* 𝄞𝄞𝄞𝄞 (Roadrunner, 1993, prod. Peter Steele, Josh Silver) is positively evil but sonically compelling gloom-and-doom metal with actual melodies, intriguingly theatrical arrangements, and superb production techniques that include allusions to the Beatles and M.C. Hammer.

what to avoid: The title of *Origin of the Feces* **woof!** (Roadrunner EP, 1992) is indicative of the quality of the music therein.

the rest:
Slow, Deep, and Hard 𝄞𝄞 (Roadrunner, 1991)
October Rust (Roadrunner, 1996)

influences:
 Black Sabbath, the Cure, the Church

David Yonke

U

UB40

Formed 1978, in Birmingham, England.

Ali Campbell, guitar, vocals; Robin Campbell, lead guitar; Astro, vocals; Earl Falconer, bass; Mickey Virtue, keyboards; Brian Travers, saxophone; James Brown, drums; Norman Hassan, percussion.

UB40 widened the audience for reggae by blending the rhythm-heavy, traditional, Caribbean music with a British pop sensibility. Taking its name from the English unemployment form, (something with which the eight band members were quite familiar), UB40 received its first major exposure opening for the Pretenders during that band's first U.S. tour. UB40 rapidly became a college radio favorite, and its 1983 rendition of Neil Diamond's "Red, Red Wine" scored with the masses. Socially conscious on and off record, UB40 was particularly proud to be one of the first Western acts to perform in the Soviet Union. With its lineup remarkably intact, the band enjoys a true worldwide following, taking its typical tours to no less than six continents. One tip: you can find UB40's albums in the reggae rather than the pop sections in more than a few record stores.

what to buy: Sitting squarely in the middle of the discography, the self-titled *UB40* 𝄞𝄞𝄞𝄞 (Virgin, 1988, prod. UB40) finds the

band at a career peak with pointed songs such as "Come Out to Play," "Where Did I Go Wrong," and "Breakfast in Bed," a duet with early benefactor Chrissie Hynde of the Pretenders. The band's first album, *Signing Off* 𝄞𝄞𝄞𝄞 (Virgin, 1980/1994, prod. Roy Falconer, Bob Lamb, UB40), features its first U.K. hit, "King," as well as the standouts "Food for Thought" and "Tyler." *Labour of Love* 𝄞𝄞𝄞𝄞 (Virgin, 1983, prod. Roy Falconer, UB40) showcases the band applying its reggae-pop flavoring to 10 covers, including "Red, Red Wine" and "Please Don't Make Me Cry."

what to buy next: Two strong best-of compilations were released simultaneously. *Volume One* 𝄞𝄞𝄞 (Virgin, 1995, prod. various) features earlier, edgier work, while *Volume Two* 𝄞𝄞𝄞 (Virgin, 1995, prod. UB40) features more radio-friendly fare from the recent past.

what to avoid: *Little Baggaridm* 𝄞𝄞 (A&M EP, 1985, prod. Ray Falconer, UB40) is an unsatisfying winnowing of the *Baggaridm* album that went unreleased in the U.S.

the rest:
Present Arms 𝄞𝄞𝄞 (Virgin, 1981/1992)
Present Arms in Dub 𝄞𝄞 (A&M, 1981)
Live 𝄞𝄞𝄞 (Virgin, 1983)
1980–83 𝄞𝄞𝄞𝄞 (A&M, 1983)
Geoffrey Morgan 𝄞𝄞𝄞 (A&M/Virgin, 1984)
Rat in the Kitchen 𝄞𝄞𝄞𝄞 (A&M/Virgin, 1986)
CCCP—Live in Moscow 𝄞𝄞𝄞 (A&M, 1987)
Labour of Love II 𝄞𝄞 (Virgin, 1989)
Promises and Lies 𝄞𝄞𝄞 (Virgin, 1993)
Guns in the Ghetto 𝄞𝄞𝄞 (Virgin, 1997)

worth searching for: The import *Best of UB40, Volume 1* (Virgin U.K., 1987, prod. various) is a thorough representation of the group's prime period.

solo outings:
Ali Campbell:
Big Love 𝄞𝄞𝄞 (Virgin, 1995)

influences:
 Bob Marley, Gregory Isaacs, Bim Sherman
▶▶ Rancid, Big Mountain, Chrissie Hynde

Gary Plochinski

Ugly Kid Joe

Formed c. 1990, in Isla Vista, CA. Disbanded 1996.

Whitfield Crane, vocals; Cordell Crockett, bass; Klaus Eichstadt, guitar; Roger Lahr, guitar (1990–92); Dave Fortman, guitar (1992–96); Mark Davis, drums.

Ugly Kid Joe has the distinction of having the first multi-platinum short-form album under the then-new category in 1991.

And, yes, you might listen to the *Ugly As They Wanna Be* EP and ask . . . "Why?" Actually, it's not that hard to figure out; Ugly Kid Joe had the same kind of snot-appeal as the Beastie Boys, though without the cleverness. Despite that, the group scored two Top 10 hits, including a cover of Harry Chapin's "Cat's in the Cradle," and had a 15-minute tenure of popularity that's left little in the way of legacy except the couple of albums that remain in print. Lead singer Whitfield Crane has moved on to the Ozzfest favorite Life of Agony.

what to buy: *America's Least Wanted* 𝄢𝄢 (Stardog, 1992, prod. Mark Dodson, Ryan Dorn, Ugly Kid Joe) is about as good as it gets with this group. It does contain "Cats in the Cradle" and the other hit, "Everything about You," and it features guest shots by ex-Judas Priest frontman Rob Halford and Jane's Addiction/Porno for Pyros drummer Stephen Perkins.

what to avoid: The edited version of *America's Least Wanted* **woof!**—it's not like it's that great an album in the first place; who wants it sanitized?

the rest:
Menace to Sobriety 𝄢 (Mercury, 1995)

worth searching for: The platinum-grabbing *Ugly As They Wanna Be* (Stardog EP, 1991) started the whole buzz in the first place. It's out of print but has minor collector's value (God help us).

influences:
◀◀ Kiss, the Beastie Boys, Judas Priest, Ratt, Harry Chapin
▶▶ Koяn, Coal Chamber, Life of Agony

Gary Graff

Tracey Ullman
Born December 30, 1959, in Slough, Berkshire, England.

As a multifaceted actress and comedian, Tracey Ullman is known for her ability to take on myriad personalities, nailing each one with a startling degree of nuance and individual quirks. During her brief singing career, Ullman took on the role of a singer in the classic girl-group mold, though most of her material was drawn from more contemporary sources such as Blondie's "(I'm Always Touched by Your) Presence Dear," Madness's "My Guy," and Reunion's "(Life Is a Rock) But the Radio Rolled Me." Ullman stopped recording after her film and TV career took off, which is acting's gain but music's loss.

what to buy: *The Best of Tracey Ullman* 𝄢𝄢𝄢 (Rhino, 1992, prod. Peter Collins) includes her wonderful debut album in its entirety, plus selected tracks from the follow-up and a few B-sides.

the rest:
You Broke My Heart in 17 Places 𝄢𝄢𝄢 (Stiff/MCA, 1983)
You Caught Me Out 𝄢𝄢𝄢 (Stiff/MCA, 1984)

influences:
◀◀ the Beatles, the Ronettes, Blondie

Daniel Durchholz

Peter Ulrich
See: Dead Can Dance

Ultra Vivid Scene
Formed late 1980s, in New York, NY.

Kurt Ralske, various instruments; various guest musicians.

Ultra Vivid Scene—essentially multi-instrumentalist Kurt Ralske with a revolving cast of guest musicians—matches the soft side of Lou Reed to catchy pop-rock, modern-style. Ralske moved back to New York City after living in London, where he was inspired by bands like My Bloody Valentine. Drawing some blood from that group's sound, it wasn't long before he formed his own combo, which was subsequently signed to 4AD. What followed was a series of capable and sometimes brilliant records, each of which offer a glimpse into Ralske's dark and often pessimistic world.

what to buy: *Joy 1967–1990* 𝄢𝄢𝄢𝄢 (4AD/Columbia, 1990, prod. Hugh Jones) adds some luster to Ralske's pseudo-sado-pop concepts, which remain catchily original except for the near-theft of Big Star's "September Gurls" for "Special One" (featuring guest vocals by the Breeders' Kim Deal). *Rev* 𝄢𝄢𝄢𝄢 (Chaos, 1993) has a T. Rex/Led Zeppelin feel on many tracks. Regardless, it continues Ralske's gift for pessimism, power-pop minimalism, and neo-sexual imagery. One version of the album included a bonus CD with the single remix of "Blood and Thunder" and three other non-LP tracks.

what to buy next: *Ultra Vivid Scene* 𝄢𝄢𝄢 (4AD/Columbia, 1988, prod. Kurt Ralske) is another decent way to peer into the chilly landscape of Ralske's desolate vision. A dense meshing of many instruments with the singer's Peter Perrett–like (Only Ones) vocals, the album starts off interesting but soon wears as thin as an icicle in the springtime.

influences:
◀◀ Game Theory, House of Love, the Velvet Underground
▶▶ Brendan Benson

Jordan Oakes

Ultravox
Formed 1973, in London, England. Disbanded 1987.

John Foxx, vocals, synthesizers (1973–79); Steve Shears, keyboards, vocals (1973–77); Billy Currie, keyboards, synthesizers, violin; Chris Cross, bass; Warren Cann, drums (1973–86); Robin Simon, guitar

(1978–79); **Midge Ure, guitar, vocals (1980–87); Mark Brzezicki, drums (1986–87).**

Ultravox was one of the first new wave bands to let synthesizers dominate its arrangements, though when Midge Ure came on board he not only brought guitar back into the mix but also gave the group a poppier, more accessible flavor. Ultravox landed numerous hits and top-selling albums in Britain, but never quite hit stride in the U.S. More's the pity, since the band recorded some imaginative and fresh-sounding material. Their disbandment spawned the solo careers of Ure and Billy Currie. Original vocalist John Foxx recorded solo albums throughout the early '80s.

what's available: *If I Was: The Very Best of Midge Ure & Ultravox* ♫♫♫♫ (Chrysalis, 1993, prod. various) is a comprehensive, solid selection of hits, though Ure's voice might wear you out.

worth searching for: Nearly all of the Ultravox catalog is currently out of print, necessitating a search for *Ultravox* (Island, 1977), one of three albums that featured Foxx. The best album of the Ure years is *Vienna* (Chrysalis, 1980), which features the title song and "Passing Strangers." Of Foxx's solo albums, seek out the synthed-up *Metalmatic* (Virgin, 1980); Currie's instrumental *Transportation* (IRS No Speak, 1988) is for guitar junkies only.

solo outings:
Midge Ure:
Breathe ♫♫♫ (RCA 1996)

influences:
◀◀ Brian Eno, David Bowie, T. Rex

Patrick McCarty

Uncle Tupelo

Formed 1987, in Belleville, IL. Disbanded 1994.

Jeff Tweedy, vocals, guitar, bass; Jay Farrar, vocals, guitar, banjo, harmonica, mandolin; Mike Heidorn, drums (1987–92); Bill Belzer, drums (1992); Ken Coomer, drums (1992–94); John Stirratt, bass; Max Johnston, banjo, fiddle, mandolin, steel guitar (1993–94).

Like many important bands before them, Uncle Tupelo's reputation spread fastest after its breakup, and its influence far outdistanced the number of units sold, to the point where the band is now seen by some as the Rosetta stone of the alternative/roots/country movement casually known as No Depression after their debut album. Rising from the factory- and farm-belt community of Belleville, Illinois (near St. Louis), the band drew equally on hardcore country and hardcore punk. Songwriting chores were split between Jay Farrar, whose tunes are oblique and wistful, and Jeff Tweedy, who speaks more directly but is no less profound in describing the pair's favorite subject—small-town ennui. Just as the band was gaining steam

with new members, a major-label contract, and *Anodyne*, its best album, Farrar left in 1994 to form Son Volt with Heidorn. Tupelo, with Tweedy at the helm, changed its name to Wilco.

what to buy: *Anodyne* ♫♫♫♫ (Sire/Reprise, 1993, prod. Brian Paulson) is the group's swan song but also it's finest hour. Alternating between yearning, hard-bitten country-folk ("Slate," "Anodyne") and careening rockers ("The Long Cut," "We've Been Had"), it epitomizes the sound, pacing, and texture of Tupelo's memorable live shows.

what to buy next: The group's first two albums, *No Depression* ♫♫♫♫ (Rockville, 1990, prod. Paul Kolderie, Sean Slade) and *Still Feel Gone* ♫♫♫♫ (Rockville, 1991, prod. Paul Kolderie, Sean Slade), are both raucous affairs featuring numerous anthems to booze and boredom. *March 16–20, 1992* ♫♫♫♫ (Rockville, 1992, prod. Peter Buck) is a fine acoustic effort featuring Buck's minimal production and spotlighting dour white-gospel tunes and equally grim originals.

worth searching for: *The Long Cut + Five Live* (Sire/Reprise, 1993, prod. Brian Paulson, Tim Powell) contains the single from *Anodyne* plus a handful of rare live cuts featuring the full five-piece band.

influences:
◀◀ Gram Parsons, Neil Young, Black Flag, Merle Haggard, the Clash

▶▶ The Bottle Rockets, Blue Mountain, Whiskeytown, Old 97's

see also: *Son Volt, Wilco, Golden Smog*

Daniel Durchholz

The Undertones

Formed 1975, in Derry, Northern Ireland. Disbanded 1983.

Feargal Sharkey, vocals; John O'Neill, guitar; Damian "Dee" O'Neill, guitar; Mike Bradley, bass; Billy Doherty, drums.

It took the U.K. press a couple of years to discover the Irish music scene; when it did, the Undertones were one of the more distinctive acts. With a style that was partially influenced by glam rock, its sound was punky pop, with Feargal Sharkey's quavering vocal chords sounding as if they were about to give out. The group broke up in 1983, spawning Sharkey's solo career and the O'Neill brothers' band, That Petrol Emotion.

what to buy: *The Undertones* ♫♫♫♫ (Sire, 1979/Rykodisc, 1994, prod. the Undertones, Roger Bechirian) is filled with perfect pop gems such as "Jimmy Jimmy," "Teenage Kicks," "Here Comes the Summer," and "Get over You."

what to buy next: *The Very Best of the Undertones* ♫♫♫♫ (Rykodisc, 1994, prod. various) is a solid and generous overview of the group's too-brief career.

the rest:

Hypnotized 🎵🎵🎵🎵 (Sire, 1980/Rykodisc, 1994)
Positive Touch 🎵🎵🎵 (Harvest, 1981/Rykodisc, 1994)
The Sin of Pride 🎵🎵🎵 (Ardeck U.K., 1983/Rykodisc, 1994)

worth searching for: *The Peel Sessions Album* (Strange Fruit, 1989) offers a nice shot of live Undertones recorded at the BBC. Sharkey's solo albums, including the quite good debut, *Feargal Sharkey* (Virgin, 1985), and *Wish* (Virgin, 1988), which is more slick and less memorable, have slipped out of print.

influences:

◄◄ Them, the Beatles, the Kinks, the Stooges, the Ramones

►► Supergrass, Oasis, the La's

see also: *That Petrol Emotion*

Anna Glen

Underworld

Formed 1986, in London, England.

Karl Hyde, vocals, guitar, electronics; Rick Smith, keyboards, programming; Darren Emerson, DJ (1992–present).

There was once this band who's name was a symbol (before the Artist . . .). The band eventually came around to calling itself Freur, released a couple of records and had a minor hit, "Doot Doot." So what? So the key members of that forgotten band formed Underworld, which, with a DJ in tow, took dance floors by storm with an ambient drum and bass blend that is equally listenable for those who can't cut a rug with a knife. Most tracks are beat-driven and have vocals, but don't look anywhere but the grooves for their depth. Not recommended for those adverse to predominately synthetic music.

what to buy: *Second Toughest in the Infants* 🎵🎵🎵🎵 (Wax Trax!/TVT, 1996, prod. Underworld) is really all you need. With the inclusion of the dance/rave smash "Pearl's Girl," which can also be found on numerous 12-inch singles and *The Saint* soundtrack, *Second Toughest* is a winner and a fine addition to a electronica starter-set.

what to buy next: *dudnobasswithmyheadman* 🎵🎵🎵 (Wax Trax!/TVT, prod. Underworld) is fairly good as well, but not quite as realized. Some tracks need headphones, a light show, or chemical enhancement to be memorable, but that's what this sort of thing is about. Note: "Spoonman" is not a Soundgarden cover.

the rest:

Pearl's Girl 🎵🎵🎵 (Wax Trax!/TVT EP, 1997)

worth searching for: Much more of a modern rock effort, *Underneath the Radar* (Sire, 1988, prod. Rupert Hine) is the group's out-of-print first record. Little promise of what's to come in here, but if you find it cheap, buy it, as it's a bit of a collector's item now.

influences:

◄◄ Ministry, A Flock of Seagulls, INXS, Modern English, Soft Cell, Heaven 17, Kraftwerk

►► Roni Size, Propellerheads, bt

Barry M. Prickett

Unrest

Formed 1985, in Washington, DC. Disbanded 1994.

Mark Robinson, vocals, guitar; Bridget Cross, bass; Phil Krauth, drums.

Through his role as founder of Teenbeat Records and as an influential producer, Mark Robinson helped shape American indie-rock culture. But his true talent could be found in Unrest. Mixing post-punk insurrection with vivid melodies, Robinson and his revolving crew of musicians turned out a series of definitive college radio discs. It wasn't until Bridget Cross joined the group in 1991, however, that the band finally started to break out of the alternative underground. Signing a deal with trendsetting English label 4AD, Unrest released its biggest critical and commercial success, 1993's *Perfect Teeth*. The group disbanded a year later, however, citing road wear. Phil Krauth made several critically praised solo albums, while Robinson and Cross regrouped as Air Miami.

what to buy: The material on *Perfect Teeth* 🎵🎵🎵🎵 (4AD/Teenbeat, 1993, prod. Simon LeBon, Brian Paulson) explores more straightforward pop terrain, revealing Robinson as a first-rate songwriter, particularly on the brooding "Soon It Is Going to Rain" and the infectious "Six Layer Cake."

what to buy next: While not quite as developed as its successor, *Imperial f.f.r.r.* 🎵🎵🎵 (Teenbeat, 1992, prod. Unrest, Wharton Tiers) offers more variety. From the punk curl of "Yes She Is My Skinhead Girl" to the urban slant of "Isabel," this album perfectly set Unrest apart from the rest of the indie-rock pack.

the rest:

Tink of S.E. 🎵🎵 (Teenbeat, 1988)
Malcolm X Park 🎵🎵🎵 (Caroline, 1988)
Kustom Karnal Blackxploitation 🎵🎵 (Caroline, 1990)
Fuck Pussy Galore . . . 🎵🎵 (Matador/Teenbeat, 1993)

solo outings:

Olympic Death Squad:
Blue 🎵🎵🎵 (Teenbeat, 1996)

Phil Krauth:
Cold Morning 🎵🎵 (Teenbeat, 1995)
Silver Eyes 🎵🎵🎵 (Teenbeat, 1996)

One Two Three 𝄞𝄞𝄞 (Teenbeat, 1998)

influences:

◀◀ Stereolab, Fugazi, Throwing Muses

see also: *Air Miami*

Aidin Vaziri

The Upper Crust

Formed 1994, in Boston, MA.

Lord Bendover, guitar, vocals; Lord Rockingham, guitar, vocals; the Duc d'Istortion, guitar; the Marquis de Roque, bass; Jackie Kickassis, drums.

Veteran Beantown rock 'n' rollers bored with their then-current band (the surf-inspired Satanics), the members of the Upper Crust decided it'd be more fun to dress like foppish 18th-century aristocracy, talk like them, act like them, and combine the theatrics with an AC/DC-cum-Buzzcocks-cum-Ramones hybrid that rails against the bourgeoisie while extolling the virtues of powdered wigs, "Old Money," "Rock and Roll Butler"s, and other endemic themes. Net result: a brilliant mix of comedic shtick, glam-rock campiness, and catchy melodic hard rock that's propelled by uproariously witty lyrics.

what's available: *Let Them Eat Rock* 𝄞𝄞𝄞𝄞 (Upstart/Rounder, 1995, prod. Sean Slade, Paul Q. Kolderie) is unrelentingly funny, benefitting from stalwart musicianship and a thick, guitar-heavy wall of sound. Its follow-up, *The Decline and Fall of the Upper Crust* 𝄞𝄞𝄞𝄞 (Emperor Norton, 1997, prod. Brian Charles), is only slightly marred by a somewhat muddy mix and songs that aren't quite as immediate as those on the debut.

influences:

◀◀ AC/DC, the Ramones, *Les Miserables*

Mike Bieber

Midge Ure

See: Ultravox

The Urge

Formed 1987, in St. Louis, MO.

Steve Ewing, vocals; Karl Grable, bass; Jerry Jost, guitar; Matt Kwiatkowski, trombone (1992–present); Todd Painter, trombone (1992–present); John Pessoni, drums (1993–present); Bill Reiter, saxophone (1993–present); others.

The Urge plays a potent mix of punk/funk/hardcore/ska, but don't accuse this St. Louis septet of being newbies to the genre that's swept Skateboard Nation in the wake of bands such as 311 and the Mighty Mighty Bosstones. The Urge has been at it for more than a decade, building a solid regional following (in

an area that's less hospitable to its sound than to meat-and-potatoes rock and alt-country), enduring shifting lineups (Steve Ewing and Karl Grable are the only constants throughout the band's history), and releasing several albums on its own before *receiving the gift of flavor* was picked up for distribution by the Immortal label in 1996. The group's roots are still strictly old-school, following the lead of such trailblazers as Fishbone and Bad Brains. But what's most impressive about the Urge is its ability to seamlessly mix styles, going from a furious metal tirade to a chilled-out reggae riddim or a punkish snarl, often in the space of a single song. Best get on board with this powerful crew or get out of the way.

what to buy: *Master of Styles* 𝄞𝄞𝄞 (Immoral/Epic, 1998, prod. GGGarth) is the sound of a band truly coming into its own. The opening track, "If I Were You," opens with grinding metallic chords that give way to a punchy, horn-driven verse that veers back into a crunching chorus. "Straight to Hell" combines hip-hop, hard rock, and jazzy Miles Davis–flavored horn accents on a song that tracks the band's gathering momentum. "Jump Right In," a cautionary tale about sexual indiscretion in the era of AIDS, features a guest vocal by 311's Nick Hexum. Other standouts include the skacore classic-to-be "Played Out," a paint-peeling cover of the Bad Brains's hardcore workout "Gene Machine," and the humble nod to Marcus Garvey, "Divide and Conquer."

the rest:

receiving the gift of flavor 𝄞𝄞𝄞 (Neat Guy/Immortal/Epic, 1996)

worth searching for: Chances are you'd have to be in a St. Louis used-record store to find one, but fans who like the band's major-label releases may want to seek out its early, self-released efforts. They include *Fat Babies in the Mix: The Urge Live*, *Magically Delicious*, *Puttin' the Backbone Back*, and *Bust Me Dat Forty*.

influences:

◀◀ Bad Brains, Fishbone, George Clinton

Daniel Durchholz

Urge Overkill

Formed 1986, in Evanston, IL.

National "Nash" Kato, guitar, vocals; Eddie "King" Roeser, guitar, bass, vocals (1986–96); Pat Byrne, drums (1987); Blackie Onassis, drums (1990–present); Nils St. Cyr, guitar (1997–present).

If nothing else, give Urge Overkill credit for chutzpah. While every other band in America was wearing flannel shirts and singing about teenage angst, the Chicago trio was proudly sporting matching velvet jackets and medallions, swilling martinis, and talking unashamedly about Rock with a capital R. Too bad, then, that Urge ultimately became better known for its fashion sense than its music, because its three mid-period recordings are all majestic restatements of the pure glory of rocking out. Principals Nash Kato and Eddie Roeser met at college in the mid-'80s and soon began releasing noisy, Steve Albini–produced records that were hardly endearing—especially to critics, who largely dogged the band throughout its lifespan. Urge hit its musical stride with the addition of ultracool (and drug-addled) drummer Blackie Onassis, settling on a pleasing blend of the current alternative rock sound and gritty '70s guitar vibe. The mid-'90s saw Urge score several radio hits, climaxing with the inclusion of its faithful cover of Neil Diamond's "Girl, You'll Be a Woman Soon" in the film *Pulp Fiction*. However, the momentum didn't last; the band's last album to date was poorly received, and drug habits and egos led to Roeser's departure from the band in 1996. (He now co-leads the band Electric Airlines with brother John.) Kato and Onassis quickly drafted a replacement guitarist and signed a new record deal, but rumors and recent reports have the once-proud Urge on its last legs.

what to buy: Releasing *Saturation* 🎧🎧🎧 (Geffen, 1993, prod. the Butcher Brothers) during the summer of 1993 was perfect timing; the sun-drenched anthems "Sister Havana" and "Positive Bleeding" lead off an album that was built to shake stadiums.

what to buy next: *Stull* 🎧🎧🎧 (Touch & Go EP, 1992, prod. Urge Overkill, Kramer) is the band's darkest record, but the opening seconds of "Now That's the Barclords" are a textbook exercise in rhythm guitar/drum interplay.

the rest:
Strange, I 🎧🎧 (Ruthless, 1986)
Americruiser/Jesus Urge Superstar 🎧🎧🎧 (Touch & Go, 1990)
The Supersonic Storybook 🎧🎧🎧🎧 (Touch & Go, 1991)
Exit the Dragon 🎧🎧🎧🎧 (Geffen, 1995)

influences:
◀◀ The Rolling Stones, Neil Diamond, Parliament-Funkadelic, Cheap Trick, the Sweet

▶▶ Superdrag, Stone Temple Pilots

Todd Wicks

Uriah Heep

Formed 1970, in London, England.

David Byron, vocals (1970–76); Mick Box, guitar; Ken Hensley, keyboards (1970–80); Paul Newton, bass (1970–71); Alex Napier, drums (1970–71); Keith Baker, drums (1971); Lee Kerslake, drums (1971–78, 1981–present); Mark Clarke, bass (1971–72); Gary Thain, bass (1972–76); John Wetton, bass, vocals (1975–76); John Lawton, vocals (1976–78); Trevor Bolder, bass, vocals (1976–81, 1985–present); John Sloman, vocals, (1978–81); Chris Slade, drums (1978–81); Greg Dechert, keyboards (1980–81); Bob Daisley, bass (1981–83); Pete Goalby, vocals (1981–88); Bernie Shaw, vocals (1988–present); John Sinclair, keyboards (1981–88); Phil Lanzon, keyboards (1988–present).

The heavy metal community cuts its bands a pretty wide berth; that's one way to explain the '70s success of Uriah Heep. Some will tell you this was the worst band in the history of rock 'n' roll, which is overstating the case a bit. But the Heep—named after a Charles Dickens character—displayed particularly lumbering quality, dynamic but seldom supple (evidence the suite-like sonic circus of "The Magician's Birthday"). And the late singer David Byron's voice could be grating over extended listenings. That said, the group churned out a fair amount of workmanlike hard rock, especially during its 1970 to 1974 heyday. Call it a poor man's Deep Purple. The group—now led by guitarist Mick Box and drummer Lee Kerslake—still has pockets of fans around the world, but it's been quite awhile since it released anything of more than middling quality.

what to buy: *The Best of Uriah Heep* 🎧🎧🎧 (Mercury, 1975, prod. Gerry Bron) though a bit skimpy—it lacks the big radio hit "Stealin'"—is still the best first, cautious step into the Heep realm.

what to buy next: The Heep peaked with the one-two punch of *Demons and Wizards* 🎧🎧🎧 (Mercury, 1972/1989, prod. Gerry Bron) and *The Magician's Birthday* 🎧🎧🎧 (Mercury, 1972/1989, prod. Gerry Bron), albums that straddle the line between hard and art rock. They can be enjoyable or painful, depending on your taste.

what to avoid: The latest Heep lineup is responsible for *Still 'Eavy, Still Proud: Two Decades of Uriah Heep* **woof!** (Griffin, 1990/1994), a misleadingly titled rip-off on which the old hits are reprised in concert versions.

the rest:
Uriah Heep 🎧🎧 (Mercury, 1970/1989)
Salisbury 🎧🎧 (Mercury, 1971/1989)
Look at Yourself 🎧🎧🎧 (Mercury, 1971/1989)
Live 🎧🎧 (Mercury, 1973/1989)
Sweet Freedom 🎧🎧🎧 (Mercury, 1973/Roadrunner, 1990)
Wonderworld 🎧🎧🎧 (Mercury, 1974/Roadrunner, 1990)
Fallen Angel 🎧🎧 (Warner Bros., 1978/Castle, 1989)
Abominog 🎧 (Peak, 1982/1992)
Live in Moscow 🎧🎧 (Griffin, 1988/1994)
Raging Silence 🎧 (Griffin, 1989/1994)
Different World 🎧🎧 (Griffin, 1991/1994)
The King Biscuit Flower Hour Presents Uriah Heep 🎧🎧 (KBFH, 1997)
Classic Heep: An Anthology N/A (Mercury, 1998)

worth searching for: If you like the Heep, go big; the British box set *A Time of Revelation* (Essential, 1996, prod. various) takes a luxurious (?) four-CD stroll through the band's career. And in a true Spinal Tap move, early copies misspelled the group name Uriah Heap on the spine.

Bono of U2 (© Ken Settle)

influences:

◄◄ Deep Purple, the Yardbirds, Led Zeppelin, Emerson, Lake & Palmer

►► Queen, Scorpions, Dokken, Winger, Spinal Tap

Gary Graff

U2

Formed 1978, in Dublin, Ireland.

Bono (born Paul Hewson), vocals, guitar; the Edge, guitar, keyboards, vocals; Adam Clayton, bass; Larry Mullen Jr., drums.

Let the story of U2 be a lesson to you: if you're gonna dream, dream big. How else to account for the accomplishments of four lads from Dublin's Mount Temple High School, who grew up to be the biggest band in the world and then used their power to (in Bono's words) "f*** with the mainstream?" Their early work drew on the energy of punk, but exchanged the genre's no-future ni-hilism for an interest in progressive politics and Charismatic Christianity. After three albums of thundering arena rock (made, interestingly, before they played arenas), U2 began a long and fruitful collaboration with producers Brian Eno and Daniel Lanois, who tempered their bombast with washes of warm, am-bient sound, and later, clanging metallic racket. Their early '90s albums are among their most successful, but are also their most challenging sonically, which speaks to U2's continuing ability to reinvent themselves and to shape rather than merely react to current musical trends. Of late they've suffered a degree of criti-cal and commercial backlash—their PopMart tour was a success, but not the raging juggernaut everyone expected. Still, as time goes on, the members of U2 are finding ways to score artistically without having to make such grand gestures, like the side pro-ject Passengers, which the band formed with Brian Eno, Howie B, and others in 1995 to record "imaginary soundtracks."

what to buy: A dark turn for a band known for its open-heart-edness, *Achtung Baby* 𝄞𝄞𝄞𝄞𝄞 (Island, 1991, prod. Daniel Lanois, Brian Eno) is the band's most complex and sophisti-cated work. Taking irony, excess, and media overload as its guiding principals, the album is still shot through with genuine emotion, most notably on songs such as "One" and "Love Is Blindness." *The Joshua Tree* 𝄞𝄞𝄞𝄞𝄞 (Island, 1987, prod. Daniel Lanois, Brian Eno), which marked the band's critical and com-mercial apotheosis, is a heady mix of chiming anthems exam-ining the realms of self-analysis ("With or Without You," "I Still Haven't Found What I'm Looking For"), politics ("Bullet the Blue Sky"), and drug addiction ("Running to Stand Still"). *War* 𝄞𝄞𝄞𝄞𝄞 (Island, 1983, prod. Steve Lillywhite) is the culmination of the band's early period, finding in Ireland's troubles the per-fect subject for their message of peace, compassion, and out-

rage as heard in "New Year's Day," "Sunday Bloody Sunday," and "40."

what to buy next: *The Unforgettable Fire* 𝄞𝄞𝄞𝄞 (Island, 1984, prod. Brian Eno, Daniel Lanois) is a moody gem whose rich, at-mospheric aura is rent by the Martin Luther King Jr. tribute "Pride" and the equally passionate "Bad." *Rattle and Hum* 𝄞𝄞𝄞𝄞 (Island, 1987, prod. Jimmy Iovine), the soundtrack to the band's uninten-tionally self-deflating documentary, features the furious "Desire" plus nods to Billie Holiday, John Lennon, and Bob Dylan, and "When Love Comes to Town," with a brilliant cameo by B.B. King. *Zooropa* 𝄞𝄞𝄞𝄞 (Island, 1993, prod. Flood, Brian Eno, the Edge) is U2's most diffuse and chaotic effort, yet it keeps the band on rock's cutting edge with the Edge's techno-rap "Numb" and a strikingly appropriate guest vocal by Johnny Cash. *Boy* 𝄞𝄞𝄞𝄞 (Is-land, 1980, prod. Steve Lillywhite), their auspicious debut, intro-duced the band's soaring sonic architecture and Bono's (then) guileless lyrics on "I Will Follow" and "Into the Heart."

the rest:

October 𝄞𝄞𝄞 (Island, 1981)
Under a Blood Red Sky 𝄞𝄞𝄞 (Island, 1983)
Wide Awake in America 𝄞𝄞𝄞 (Island EP, 1985)
Pop 𝄞𝄞𝄞𝄞 (Island, 1997)
The Best Of: 1980–90 𝄞𝄞𝄞𝄞 (Island, 1998)

worth searching for: *Melon* (Island, 1995, prod. various) and *Kiwi* (Island, 1995, prod. various) were remix collections re-leased only to the band's fan club and are notable for how thor-oughly the songs are recast while remaining remarkably true to the originals. The former is absolutely essential for hardcore fans, the latter somewhat less so. Bono and the Edge sing

"One" and sit in with pal Luciano Pavarotti for a version of the Passengers' "Miss Sarajevo" on *Luciano Pavarotti and Friends: For the Children of Bosnia* (London, 1996), a wildly uneven but well-meaning collection.

solo outings:
The Edge:
(With Michael Brook) *Captive* 𝄢𝄢𝄢 (Virgin, 1987)
(With Jah Wobble and Holger Czukay) *Snake Charmer* 𝄢𝄢 (Island EP, 1983)

Passengers:
Passengers: Original Soundtracks 1 𝄢𝄢𝄢𝄢 (Island, 1995)

influences:
◀◀ David Bowie, Brian Eno, Van Morrison, Bob Dylan, John Lennon, Massive Attack

▶▶ The Alarm, the Cult, Simple Minds, Our Lady Peace

Daniel Durchholz

Steve Vai

Born June 6, 1960, in Carle Place, NY.

One of the most talented musicians to survive the fret-shredding guitar explosion of the '80s, Steve Vai is a virtuoso instrumentalist whose ability to meld artistic sensitivity with heavy metal chops has placed him among the most sought-after studio musicians in the business, as well as a popular solo artist. After picking up the guitar at age 14, Vai attended Berklee College of Music in Boston, augmenting his classwork by transcribing arrangements for Frank Zappa. That led to a job with Zappa's touring band, and appearances on the Zappa albums *Ship Arriving Too Late to Save a Drowning Witch*, *The Man from Utopia*, and *Thingfish*. Vai's own career began with 1984's *Flex-Able*, which sold more than 250,000 copies without any promotion. Along with his solo albums, Vai has worked with the bands Alcatrazz and Whitesnake, as well as with former Van Halen singer David Lee Roth, John Lydon's Public Image Ltd., Ozzy Osbourne, and Alice Cooper. Of late, however, Vai has concentrated on his own music, augmenting his albums with a highly regarded series of instructional books and videotapes. He and axe colleague Joe Satriani have also helmed the popular G3 tour, while Vai organized a six-string Christmas album, *Merry Axemas*, during 1997.

what to buy: Fans of melodic, well-crafted solo guitar will want to make *Passion & Warfare* 𝄢𝄢𝄢𝄢 (Relativity, 1990, prod. Steve

Vai) part of their collections. The expressive, almost symphonic quality of tracks such as "Liberty," "The Riddle," and "Blue Powder" reflect the reverence and spirituality with which Vai approaches his playing. There are also plenty of searing examples of Vai's rock chops, including "The Animal," "The Audience Is Listening," and "Greasy Kid's Stuff."

what to buy next: Though inconsistent, *Flex-Able* 𝄢𝄢𝄢𝄢 (Urantia, 1984, prod. Steve Vai) contains the foundation that Vai has built his reputation upon.

what to avoid: Whitesnake's *Slip of the Tongue* 𝄢 (Geffen, 1989, prod. Mike Clink, Keith Olsen) is a tired rehashing of the band's already derivative sound, with Vai simply stepping in to copy the playing of Adrian Vandenberg, who departed the band in mid-recording.

the rest:
Sex & Religion 𝄢𝄢𝄢 (Relativity, 1993)
Alien Love Secrets 𝄢𝄢𝄢𝄢 (Relativity, 1995)
Fire Garden 𝄢𝄢𝄢 (Sony, 1996)
(With Joe Satriani and Eric Johnson) *G3 Live in Concert* 𝄢𝄢𝄢 (Sony, 1997)
(With various artists) *Merry Axemas* 𝄢𝄢𝄢𝄢 (Sony, 1997)

worth searching for: *Flex-Able Leftovers* (Relativity, 1984, prod. Steve Vai) contains the songs Vai recorded for *Flex-Able* but elected not to include on that release, despite the fact that they are more ambitious and enjoyable than most solo guitar albums released during the '80s.

influences:
◀◀ Frank Zappa, Jeff Beck, Ritchie Blackmore, Tony Iommi

▶▶ Dweezil Zappa, Tony MacAlpine, David Chastain, Joe Satriani, Eric Johnson

see also: *Whitesnake, Frank Zappa, Van Halen/David Lee Roth*

Brandon Trenz

Ritchie Valens

Born Richard Steve Valenzuela, May 13, 1941, in Los Angeles, CA. Died February 3, 1959, in Mason City, IA.

Despite the lionizing his reputation received following his tragic early death in the plane crash that also killed Buddy Holly, Ritchie Valens was a minor figure in rock 'n' roll, and when that plane went down in a snowy Iowa cornfield he had just a couple of singles under his belt and his first hit on the charts. But selling the first Chicano rock star short is unfair to the Mexican-American rock musicians in East Los Angeles and San Bernardino for whom, like Los Lobos, Valens is an important cultural symbol. Valens was an unschooled, intuitive 18-year-old musician when he went into Hollywood's historic Gold Star Studios to hold his first recording session with a band of seasoned professional sidemen. A year later, he was dead, leaving behind frustrating traces of promise, a couple of certi-fied classics ("La Bamba," "Come On, Let's Go," "Donna"), and a legend that continues to grow. Interest in his life and art was revived by the (largely inaccurate) 1987 film *La Bamba.*

what to buy: The 22-song set *Rockin' All Night: The Best of Ritchie Valens* ♫♫♫ (Del-Fi, 1995, compilation prod. Bob Perry, Rob Santos) covers all the bases with hits, early demos, and some instrumental jams. Art Fein's notes are thorough, if per-haps a bit enthusiastic. The 19-song *The Ritchie Valens Story* ♫♫♫ (Rhino, 1993, prod. Bob Keene) is equally fine and boasts a spoken intro by Valens's producer Bob Keene, a vintage radio ad, and a 12-page booklet.

what to buy next: The brand new three-disc box set *Ritchie Valens* ♫♫♫ (Del-fi, 1998, compilation prod. Gary Tannenbaum) features every note he ever committed to tape—including home demos, alternate takes, and a live concert at his local high school. Worthwhile for serious fans and completists.

what to avoid: Revisionism rears it's ugly head on *La Bamba '87 and Other Rock 'n' Roll Classics* **woof!** (Original Sound, 1987, prod. various), which adds modern Latin instrumentation and dance mixes to Valens's original classics. Yeeesh!

worth searching for: You can catch Valens's only on-screen ap-pearance in the 1958 Alan Freed teen-flick on *Go, Johnny Go!* (Video Treasures, 1987), where his "Oh My Head" outrocks cameo efforts by Eddie Cochran, Jackie Wilson, and Jimmy Clanton.

influences:

◀◀ Buddy Holly, the Penguins, Little Richard

▶▶ Chris Montez, Los Lobos, the Blazers

Joel Selvin and Ken Burke

Dino Valente

See: Quicksilver Messenger Service

Frankie Valli

See: The Four Seasons

Van Halen /David Lee Roth

Formed 1974, in Pasadena, CA.

Eddie Van Halen, guitar, keyboards, vocals; Alex Van Halen, drums; Michael Anthony, bass, vocals; David Lee Roth, vocals (1974–84, 1996); Sammy Hagar, vocals, (1984–96); Gary Cherone, vocals, (1996–present).

With the possible exception of Aerosmith, Van Halen was the most important American hard rock band to emerge during the

'70s. Edward Van Halen's blitzkrieg guitar style and string-tap-ping technique launched a thousand imitators, while Roth added a sense of comedy to a genre that generally took itself too seriously. But Roth left the band in 1985 to try to be a movie star (and wound up with a fading solo career) and was replaced by Sammy Hagar, a competent hard rock belter who'd honed his pipes with another guitar wizard, Ronnie Montrose. But while the Hagar-era Van Halen has been immensely popular, its meat-and-potatoes albums aren't as interesting as the band's spicy earlier output. Hagar left the band in 1996 after a spat over the rest of the group's decision to record some new tracks with Roth to include in a planned greatest hits album. His re-placement, ex-Extreme vocalist Gary Cherone, added intelli-gent lyrics to the mix, but his blatant vocal imitation of Hagar was just plain dumb.

what to buy: *Van Halen* ♫♫♫♫ (Warner Bros, 1978, prod. Ted Templeman) is a headbanger's paradise, brimming with muscu-lar romps such as "Runnin' with the Devil," the Kinks' "You Re-ally Got Me," "Jamie's Crying," and Eddie's brilliant guitar-gasm, "Eruption." *1984* ♫♫♫♫ (Warner Bros., 1984, prod. Ted Templeman) found the band experimenting with synthesizers on the #1 hit "Jump" but still cranking out blazing guitar an-thems like "Hot for Teacher" and "Panama."

what to buy next: *Women and Children First* ♫♫♫ (Warner Bros., 1980, prod. Ted Templeman) showed Roth at his most en-tertaining on "Everybody Wants Some" and "And the Cradle Will Rock." *OU812* (Warner Bros, 1988, prod. Van Halen, Don Landee), the best of the Hagar era albums, contains the stun-ning country-metal fusion "Finish What You Started." For a taste of Roth's solo career, pick up *The Best* ♫♫♫ (Rhino, 1997, prod. various), which does a fine job of harvesting the wheat (a distinct minority) from the chaff.

what to avoid: *Van Halen Live: Right Here, Right Now* ♫♫ (Warner Bros., 1993, prod. Van Halen, Andy Johns) is an all-too-typical live album complete with self-indulgent drum and bass solos.

the rest:

Van Halen II ♫♫♫♫ (Warner Bros., 1979)
Fair Warning ♫♫♫♫ (Warner Bros., 1981)
Diver Down ♫♫♫ (Warner Bros., 1982)
5150 ♫♫♫ (Warner Bros., 1986)
For Unlawful Carnal Knowledge ♫♫♫ (Warner Bros., 1991)
Balance ♫♫♫♫ (Warner Bros. 1995)
III ♫♫ (Warner Bros., 1998)

worth searching for: The import CD-5 of "Jump" (Warner Bros., 1993) from the live album features selections not included on the live album; it works as an abbreviated version of the Van Halen live experience.

Eddie Van Halen (© Ken Settle)

solo outings:
David Lee Roth:
Crazy from the Heat ✍✍✍✍ (Warner Bros. EP, 1985)
Eat 'em and Smile ✍✍✍ (Warner Bros., 1986)
Skyscraper ✍✍✍ (Warner Bros., 1987)
A Little Ain't Enough ✍✍✍ (Warner Bros., 1991)
Your Filthy Little Mouth ✍✍✍ (Reprise, 1994)
The Best ✍✍✍✍ (Rhino, 1997)
The DLR Band ✍✍✍ (Wawazat!!, 1998)

influences:
◄◄ Led Zeppelin, Jimi Hendrix, Cream, Louis Prima

►► Randy Rhoads, Steve Vai, Joe Satriani, Skid Row, Bulletboys

see also: *Sammy Hagar, Extreme*

Thor Christensen

Vanilla Fudge
Formed as the Pigeons, 1967, in New York, NY. Disbanded 1970.

Vince Martell, vocals, guitar; Mark Stein, keyboards; Tim Bogert, bass; Carmine Appice, drums.

Along with Iron Butterfly, Vanilla Fudge helped lay the foundation for heavy metal. Stressing production over songwriting, the group layered guitars, organ, and thundering drums into a thick cloud of sonic excess. Vanilla Fudge began its recording career as a cover band, performing slow, drowsy versions of hits in an attempt to mimic the time-distorting effect of drugs. The formula eventually paid off with the Top 10 cover "You Keep Me Hangin' On," which was performed at about half the speed of the Supremes' hit. Nothing else by the group made much of a dent in the charts, and by 1969 the heavy music torch had been passed to Deep Purple and Led Zeppelin. Bogert and Appice went on to form Cactus and later recorded with Jeff Beck.

what to buy: *Psychedelic Sundae: The Best of Vanilla Fudge* ✍✍✍✍ (Rhino, 1993, prod. Shadow Morton, Vanilla Fudge, Adrian Barber) is the premier collection of the group's proto-heavy metal music. The album emphasizes covers ("You Keep Me Hangin' On," "The Look of Love," "Ticket to Ride," and "Season of the Witch"), but then half the fun is hearing these twisted variations on familiar themes. The compilation also contains an album and non-album singles discography as well as track annotations.

what to buy next: To hear much of the same material performed live, try *The Best of Vanilla Fudge Live* ✍✍✍ (Rhino, 1991, prod. Shadow Morton), or check out the first record, *Vanilla Fudge* ✍✍✍ (Atco/Rhino, 1967, prod. Shadow Morton), to hear heavy metal as God intended, a blistering sonic workout from start to finish.

solo outings:
Cactus (Bogert and Appice):
Cactology: The Cactus Collection ✍✍✍ (Rhino, 1996)

influences:
◄◄ The Troggs, Iron Butterfly

►► Deep Purple, Led Zeppelin, Black Sabbath, Dinosaur Jr.

Christopher Scapelliti

The Vapors
Formed 1978, in England. Disbanded 1981.

David Fenton, vocals, guitar; Howard Smith, drums; Edward Bazalgette, guitar; Steve Smith, bass, vocals.

The Vapors helped usher in a new pop era with its hit, the essential "Turning Japanese"—a tightly wound, disturbing ode to masturbation. Surprisingly, the exuding sense of paranoia and isolation carries over throughout its out-of-print debut, *New Clear Days*, which married brittle pop smarts with an aura of madness. Somehow connecting themes of war, adolescent pathos, and Japan, it's strangely disquieting and bears little resemblance to the lightweight new wave frenzy of the period.

what's available: *The Vapors Anthology* ✍✍✍✍ (One Way, 1995, prod. Vic Coppersmith-Heaven) is something of a misnomer, as it actually contains the entire debut plus a few extra songs tacked on at the end and cheap, redundant packaging. It does, however, keep "Turning Japanese" available.

influences:
◄◄ The Beatles, the Kinks

►► The Hooters, Men at Work, Mr. Mister, Men Without Hats

Allan Orski

Varnaline
Formed 1994, in Portland, OR.

Anders Parker, vocals, guitar, bass, drums, piano, keyboards; John Parker, bass; Jud Ehrbar, drums, vocals.

Basically the vision of Anders Parker—who, with Jud Ehrbar, is also in the band Space Needle—Varnaline is often simply Parker's vocals accompanied by guitar. While not the greatest singer, his voice is pleasant enough to succeed with such spartan arrangements, though when the full band is deployed, it is generally an improvement. Varnaline plays impassioned indie rock, with occasional droning and/or whacked-out guitar parts and very slight whiffs of country. The rhythm section, whether real or dubbed in by Parker, generally stays in the background, providing a framework for his typically melancholy songs.

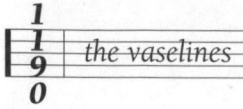

what to buy: *Varnaline* ♫♫♫♪ (Zero Hour, 1997, prod. Adam "Red" Lasus, Jason Cox, Varnaline) is a true college rock pleaser. Certainly college DJs, both male and female, found much to like in the somber ambience of this album, and Parker's songwriting remains strong throughout, particularly on "Meet Me on the Ledge" and "Really Can't Say."

what to buy next: *Man of Sin* ♫♫♫♪ (Zero Hour, 1996, prod. Varnaline) was recorded in 1994 almost entirely by Parker (Bob MacKay played bass on four cuts). Not released until 1996, *Man of Sin* offers no great variance from other Varnaline efforts. It's not essential, but songs such as "Gary's Paranoia" are reason enough to own this.

the rest:
A Shot and a Beer ♫♫♫♪ (Zero Hour, 1997)

influences:
◀◀ The Velvet Underground, the Feelies, Pavement, Guided by Voices, Sebadoh, the Replacements, Uncle Tupelo

Barry M. Prickett

The Vaselines /Eugenius

Formed 1987, in Glasgow, Scotland.

Eugene Kelly, vocals, guitar; Francis McKee, vocals, guitar; James Seenan, bass; Charles Kelly, drums.

It's doubtful that anyone expected the brilliantly catchy/ supremely silly Vaselines to become one of alternative rock's most influential bands. If a young Kurt Cobain had never discovered Kelly and McKee's sunny style of primitive-but-effective hooks and seemingly nonsensical lyrics, he might have never transformed his little sub-Melvins band Nirvana into the pop wunderkind that changed the world. At its best, the Vaselines utilized a variety of styles to create an emptyheaded pop excitement ("Jesus Doesn't Want Me for a Sunbeam," "Rory Rides Me Raw"); at its worst, the group made typical garage noise ("Sex Sux (Amen)"). Luckily, examples of the former outnumber the latter. Kelly went on to form Eugenius, a band whose greatest publicity came from a legal dispute with Marvel Comics over its original name, Captain America. Its two albums deal in the same power-pop vein as the Vaselines, but with less of its predecessor's shambling, unsteady charm.

what's available: The title of *The Way of the Vaselines: A Complete History* ♫♫♫ (Sub Pop, 1992, prod. various) says it all.

the rest:
Eugenius:
Oomalama ♫♫♫ (Atlantic, 1992)
Mary, Queen of Scots ♫♫♫♪ (Atlantic, 1994)

influences:
◀◀ The Beatles, the Velvet Underground
▶▶ Nirvana, Beat Happening, the Raincoats

Todd Wicks

Jimmie Vaughan

Born March 20, 1951, in Dallas, TX.

The older sibling of the more famous Stevie Ray Vaughan, Jimmie kicked around Texas blues and rock bands such as the Chessmen and the Swinging Pendulums during his teen years, eventually forming the Fabulous Thunderbirds with vocalist/harmonica player Kim Wilson in the early '70s. The Thunderbirds developed a reputation as a road-ready rockin' blues unit that was as palatable to purists as it was to new wave fans (the group toured with Rockpile, and Nick Lowe produced one of their albums). Wilson may have been the frontman, but Vaughan's lean, loud guitar lines were the band's defining characteristic. The group topped out in 1986 with the hit "Tuff Enuff," which broke the blues-rock scene wide open in the mid-to-late '80s. But as the Thunderbirds struggled to repeat that success, Vaughan grew restless and left the band in 1990. Jimmie and Stevie Ray recorded *Family Style*, a long awaited collaboration whose joyous tunes are tempered by Stevie Ray's death in a helicopter accident. In 1996, Jimmie and a wide array of guests, including Eric Clapton, Bonnie Raitt, Buddy Guy, and Robert Cray recorded a moving tribute album to the late guitarist. On his own, Jimmie is a less-than-spectacular vocalist, but as long as the focus is kept on the grooves and the guitar, everything's cool.

what to buy: Vaughan came into his own with *Strange Pleasure* ♫♫♫♪ (Epic, 1994, prod. Nile Rodgers), an impressive solo bow that featured hard-charging raveups ("Boom-Bapa-Boom"), strutting instrumentals ("Tilt a Whirl"), and smoky blues ("Love the World"). But the album's emotional centerpiece is "Six Strings Down," a harrowing acoustic number that envisions Stevie Ray as the newest member of an all-star blues band jamming in the hereafter.

the rest:
(With Stevie Ray Vaughan) *Family Style* ♫♫♫♪ (Epic/Associated, 1990)
A Tribute to Stevie Ray Vaughan ♫♫♫♪ (Epic, 1996)
Out There ♫♫♫♪ (Epic, 1998)

influences:
◀◀ Eric Clapton, Jimi Hendrix, and all three Kings: B.B., Freddie, and Albert
▶▶ Stevie Ray Vaughan, Ian Moore, Jonny Lang

see also: *The Fabulous Thunderbirds*

Daniel Durchholz

Stevie Ray Vaughan (© Ken Settle)

Stevie Ray Vaughan

Born October 3, 1954, in Dallas, TX. Died August 26, 1990, in East Troy, WI.

Stevie Ray Vaughan burst onto the national scene in 1983 with *Texas Flood*, a scorching, overdriven blues tornado that followed his guest appearance on David Bowie's *Let's Dance* album, blew down the doors of popular music, and proclaimed loud and clear that blues could actually be a potent force in the marketplace. Playing with deep blues feeling and a roof-shaking rock energy and virtuosity—and volume—Stevie Ray became a certified guitar hero and once again shone a light on many of his own heroes, notably Buddy Guy and Albert King. His rise also paved the way for the return of blues-based rockers such as the Allman Brothers Band. One thing that separated Vaughan from other earnest young bluesmen was that he also worshipped at the house of Jimi, and while his attempts at slavish Hendrix imitation were destined to fall flat, his understanding of Jimi's more subtle, chordal elements informed all of his playing, allowing him to write gorgeous instrumentals such as "Lenny" and "Riviera Paradise." Vaughan's career shot like a skyrocket before hitting some turbulence as he wrestled with drug and alcohol abuse. In 1989, a new, clean SRV came out swinging for the fences, and his last two albums were by far his most focused, hinting that he was on the verge of reaching a whole new level of greatness when he died in a 1990 helicopter crash following a concert jam with Eric Clapton and others.

what to buy: Though it's at times downright jittery, Vaughan's debut, *Texas Flood* ♫♫♫ (Epic, 1983, prod. Stevie Ray Vaughan, Richard Mullen, Double Trouble), remains a gritty summation of his strengths: hard-rocking shuffles ("Pride and Joy," "Love Struck Baby"); slow, nasty blues ("Texas Flood," "Dirty Pool"); overdriven guitar workouts ("Rude Mood," "Testify"); and shimmeringly gorgeous instrumental masterpieces ("Lenny"). His last solo album, *In Step* ♫♫♫♫ (Epic, 1989, prod. Jim Gaines, Stevie Ray Vaughan, Double Trouble), is just as passionate while also reflecting a new-found lyrical maturity and musical and vocal confidence, highlighted by "Riviera Paradise," probably Vaughan's most serene recording. *Family Style* ♫♫♫♫ (Epic, 1990, prod. Nile Rogers) is as much brother Jimmie's album as Stevie's—which doesn't make it any less great.

Quite the contrary, in fact; the album contains some of the Vaughans's finest songs, more of *In Step*'s maturity and confidence, and, of course, lots of serious guitar slinging. The posthumous *The Sky Is Crying* 🎸🎸🎸 (Epic, 1991, prod. various) sketches out the contours of Vaughan's talents and influences, including Hubert Sumlin, Albert King, jazzman Kenny Burrell, and, of course, Hendrix. Stevie's breathtaking, instrumental "Little Wing" is here, as is his first recorded slide ("Boot Hill") and acoustic ("Life by the Drop") playing.

what to buy next: *Soul to Soul* 🎸🎸🎸 (Epic, 1985, prod. Stevie Ray Vaughan, Double Trouble, Richard Mullen) is a fine, relatively relaxed outing. Once you're hooked, you'll also want to own *In the Beginning* 🎸🎸🎸 (Epic, 1992, prod. Wayne Bell), a rough, ragged, thoroughly intense 1980 live performance. The packaging even includes a rare photo of a bare-headed SRV!

what to avoid: *Live Alive* 🎸🎸 (Epic, 1986, prod. Stevie Ray Vaughan, Double Trouble) is, at times, downright painful to listen to, reflecting as it does a great artist's deterioration. Stevie Ray was a mess, strung out on drugs and alcohol, necessitating more overdubs than is proper for a live album, particularly for this fine a performer. Only SRV's subsequent resurgence prevents this from being a tragic album.

the rest:
Couldn't Stand the Weather 🎸🎸🎸 (Epic, 1984)
Greatest Hits 🎸🎸🎸 (Epic, 1995)
Live at Carnegie Hall 🎸🎸🎸 (Epic, 1997)

worth searching for: *Interchords* (Epic, 1992), a promotional CD released with *The Sky Is Crying*, features interviews with Jimmie Vaughan and the members of Double Trouble, as well as snippets of songs and a few quotes from SRV interviews.

influences:

◀◀ Albert King, Otis Rush, Buddy Guy, Jimi Hendrix, Lonnie Mack, Cream, Kenny Burrell

▶▶ Kenny Wayne Shephard, Big Head Todd & the Monsters, Blues Traveler, Jonny Lang

Alan Paul

Ben Vaughn

Born April 6, 1955, in Camden, NJ.

Part musicologist, part goofball, and all heart, Ben Vaughn is a rock 'n' roll purist who worships Sonny Bono and prefers AM radio to Surround Sound, the Goodwill to Tower Records, and Duane Eddy to Eddie Vedder. Ever since forming the short-lived Ben Vaughn Combo in 1984, the New Jersey singer-songwriter-producer has merged odes to facial hair ("Growin' a Beard"), vintage cars ("El Rambler Dorado"), convenience stores ("Lookin' for a 7-11"), and garage bands ("Big Drum Sound,"

"Rhythm Guitar"), with hooks liberally lifted from rockabilly, surf music, British Invasion pop, and Muscle Shoals R&B. And while Vaughn's quirky sense of humor makes him easy to shrug off as a clever novelty act, there's a genuine soul bubbling beneath the smirk: His affection for rock's roots shine through, whether he's recording basement tapes of vintage '60s instrumentals or producing the late Arthur Alexander or the masked surf band Los Straitjackets. His penchant for pop culture metaphors can be as obscure as comedian Dennis Miller's ("I'm Sorry but So Is Brenda Lee"), but there hasn't been any pop song in the last 10 years that has communicated the joyful buzz of puppy love like "Jerry Lewis in France" ("I feel like Jerry Lewis in France/when you hold me in your arms").

what to buy: The presence of Marshall Crenshaw, Alex Chilton, Foster & Lloyd, John Hiatt, Peter Holsapple, and Gordon Gano on *Dressed in Black* 🎸🎸🎸 (Enigma, 1990, prod. Ben Vaughn) lends a boys'-night-out exuberance to the Memphis undertones of "The Man Who Has Everything," the twangy lament of "Doormat," the unrequited crush of "Cashier Girl," and the greasy punch of "Words Can't Say What I Want to Say." The low-fi, high-concept *Rambler '65* 🎸🎸🎸 (Rhino, 1996, prod. Ben Vaughn) gives new meaning to "mobile studio"; Vaughn recorded the entire album inside his aqua-blue 1965 Rambler American. Among the standout tracks are "Beautiful Self Destruction," a haunting condemnation of the glamorization of heroin addiction, and the rollicking "Rock Is Dead," about a kid who falls asleep in front of MTV only to wake up in a world littered with abandoned tour buses and empty record stores.

what to buy next: *Mood Swings ('90–'85 & More)* 🎸🎸🎸 (Restless, 1992, prod. Ben Vaughn) is a handy compilation drawn from his four Restless/Enigma releases and features such essentials as "Jerry Lewis in France," "I'm Sorry but So Is Brenda Lee," "Daddy's Gone for Good," and both sides of his rare first single, "My First Band"/"Vibrato in the Grotto."

what to avoid: *Kings of Saturday Night* 🎸 (Sector 2, 1995, prod. Ben Vaughn, Kim Fowley) is a raucous, *Duets*-like collaboration between Vaughn and rock svengali Fowley in which the latter simply rants over backing tracks that Vaughn mailed to him. We assume Sinatra wasn't available.

the rest:
The Many Moods of Ben Vaughn 🎸🎸🎸 (Restless, 1986)
Ben Vaughn Blows Your Mind 🎸🎸🎸 (Restless, 1988)
Mono U.S.A. (Bar/None, 1993) 🎸🎸🎸
Instrumental Stylings 🎸🎸🎸 (Bar/None, 1995)

worth searching for: *Bonograph: Sonny Gets His Share* (Bogus, 1991, prod. Carl M. Grefenstette), a tribute album to Sonny Bono, includes Vaughn's one-man version of "Koko Joe" and his liner notes that ask, "He wrote 'I Got You Babe' and still collects money from it. What've you done lately?"

influences:

◄◄ Link Wray, Sonny Bono, Chuck Berry, the Kingsmen, Willie DeVille

►► Pete Droge, Jack Logan, the Skeletons, Los Straitjackets

David Okamoto

Bobby Vee
/Bobby Vee & the Shadows

Born Robert Thomas Velline, April 30, 1943, in Fargo, ND.

Although a young Bobby Vee and his schoolyard rock 'n' roll combo may have gotten their big break in the most unfortunate of ways (hired at the last minute by a local promoter desperate to fill holes after that plane carrying Buddy Holly, Ritchie Valens, and the Big Bopper went down), he nonetheless enjoyed quite a career as one of the more substantial performers of the teen idol era. Vee's early band of Shadows (among whom, briefly, was an odd little piano pumper name of Elston Gunnn—yes, with three "n"s—who would later be known as Bob Dylan) quickly parlayed its Crickets connections into a recording contract with Liberty Records, where an eager new producer named Snuff Garrett helped Vee rack up an impressive string of pre-Beatle confections. After one last chart entry with the surprisingly mature "Come Back When You Grow Up" in 1967, Vee remained active in various facets of the business, and when not on tour today (he retains a loyal following in England especially), he can be found working in his own Rockhouse Studios facility, busy recording not only himself but also his sons' remarkably authentic rockabilly band.

what's available: Bobby Vee's *Legendary Masters Series* 🎵🎵🎵 (EMI America, 1990/ Gold Rush, 1996, compilation prod. Ron Furmanek, Steve Kolanijan) contains a better-than-average selection of Brill Building–style pop. "Rubber Ball," "Devil or Angel," "The Night Has a Thousand Eyes," and particularly "Take Good Care of My Baby" were fine achievements for their time: well structured, slickly produced, and as such destined for sock hop immortality. Bobby & the Shadows' first recordings, collected on *The Early Rockin' Years* 🎵🎵🎵 (Era, 1995, prod. Bobby Vee, Tommy "Snuff" Garrett, the Shadows), show a hot young quartet from the Northlands trying its darndest to sound just like that band from Lubbock, Texas. Speaking of which. . . .

worth searching for: Both *Bobby Vee Meets the Crickets* (Liberty, 1962/EMI America, 1991, prod. Snuff Garrett) and *I Remember Buddy Holly* (Liberty, 1963/EMI America, 1991, prod. Snuff Garrett) are fitting tributes to the singer's prime influ-

ence, while *Bobby Vee Sings the New Sound from England!* (Liberty, 1964, prod. Snuff Garrett) demonstrates Vee was certainly paying attention to his opening acts in Britain during his first tours there.

influences:

◄◄ Hank Snow, Buddy Holly, Johnny Burnette, Del Shannon, Rick Nelson

►► Johnny Tillotson, Brian Hyland, Gene Pitney, Leo Sayer, Andrew Lloyd Webber

Gary Pig Gold

Suzanne Vega

Born July 11, 1959, in Santa Monica, CA.

Suzanne Vega grew up in New York, attending the prestigious High School of the Performing Arts. She continued at Barnard, where she began playing her own brand of folk songs at small clubs in Greenwich Village. Her light, whispery voice blended with haunting melodies and vivid imagery, building an underground following and, eventually, a larger audience. In 1984 she signed with A&M Records, and since then her career has evolved dramatically. Like Tom Waits, Vega began with sparse coffeehouse folk and has firmly moved forward into new territory. Her 1985 debut revealed insightful lyrics, acoustic guitar playing reminiscent of Joni Mitchell, and the solitary feel of her folk roots. Three albums later, her musical influences have provided her with the skill of successful risk-taking, with expanded instrumentation, more intricate melodies, and even a collaboration with the dance-music group DNA. While this growth may not be fattening anybody's pockets, her influence as a creative force is incalculable. Her 1987 hit "Luka" helped female performers gain the recognition they long deserved, paving the way for artists such as Tracy Chapman, 10,000 Maniacs, and Sarah McLachlan.

what to buy: Her debut, *Suzanne Vega* 🎵🎵🎵🎵 (A&M, 1985, prod. Steve Addabbo, Lenny Kaye), is still her most consistently moving work. This folkish album opens with the lyrically wonderful "Cracking," a depiction of someone who is often on the edge of breaking down. The sparse "Straight Lines," the poppy "Marlene on the Wall," and the dark fable "Queen and the Soldier" make this album a complete gem.

what to buy next: *Nine Objects of Desire* 🎵🎵🎵 (A&M, 1996) continues the sonic experiments Vega began with her 1992 album *99.9 Degrees*, using driving, urban-style drum sounds, strong electric guitars, and keyboards atop the poetic images that are her trademark. More than ever before, she uses eclectic layering of backing vocals, experimental beats, and exotic melodies as a vehicle to emphasize and complement the incredible images that her songs evoke. *Days of Open Hand* ✍✍✍✍ (A&M, 1990, prod. Anton Sanko, Suzanne Vega) is another of her most ambitious albums. Here Vega successfully makes the jump from accomplished folkster to extraordinary musical artist, flaunting a string arrangement from Philip Glass, heavy use of a Hammond organ and synthesizers for ambient effect, and the eclectic rhythms of drums from around the world. *Solitude Standing* ✍✍✍ (A&M, 1987, prod. Steve Addabbo, Lenny Kaye) contains her two biggest hits, "Luka" and "Tom's Diner." The latter actually gained its notoriety three years later, when DNA took Vega's vocal and added a strong techno beat and a few sound loops.

the rest:

99.9 Degrees ✍✍✍ (A&M, 1992)

worth searching for: One of Vega's greatest attributes is her stage presence, which, of course, can never really be captured in her studio work. On the Australian import *Live in London* (A&M, 1986) we get to hear her sense of humor and excellent storytelling talents, as well as wonderful versions of "Left of Center," "Neighborhood Girls," and other songs.

influences:

◀◀ Tom Waits, Rickie Lee Jones, Joni Mitchell, DNA

▶▶ Shawn Colvin, Tori Amos, 10,000 Maniacs, Tracy Chapman, Sarah McLachlan

Joshua Zarov

Velo-Deluxe

See: Antenna

Velocity Girl

Formed 1990, in Silver Spring, MD. Disbanded 1996.

Sarah Shannon, vocals; Brian Nelson, guitar; Archie Moore, guitar, bass; Kelly Riles, guitar, bass; Jim Spellman, drums.

Velocity Girl took its name from an obscure Primal Scream B-side, and this tempted some early critics to dismiss the group as just another bunch of noise-addicted Anglophiles. True, Velocity Girl relied on squalling guitars and fuzzed-out feedback to give its songs an emotive edge, but the quintet offset this with solid, memorable hooks and Sarah Shannon's sweet soprano. The band's performances gave this duality a chance to shine. Unfortunately, Velocity Girl was caught in the crossfire as the alterna-pop sound began to lose appeal during the mid-'90s, and the band's members called it quits in 1996.

what to buy: *Simpatico* ✍✍✍✍ (Sub Pop, 1994, prod. John Porter) was perhaps the most well-rounded of all the Velocity Girl recordings. The album yielded the alternative radio hit "Sorry Again" and the hook-laden "I Can't Stop Smiling."

what to buy next: *Copacetic* ✍✍✍ (Sub Pop, 1993, prod. Bob Weston), the band's first full-length album, served as a fine introduction, but it also contained tracks such as "A Change" and "Lisa Librarian" that seemed like contrived efforts to break out of the sweet/rough formula. Still, the title track and "57 Waltz" went a long way toward restoring the balance. *Gilded Stars and Zealous Hearts* ✍✍✍ (Sub Pop, 1996, prod. Cliff Norrell, Velocity Girl) found Archie Moore contributing more often in the vocal department, and his voice added a natural counterpart to Shannon's stylized, operatic warblings.

the rest:

Velocity Girl ✍✍✍ (Slumberland, 1992)

influences:

◀◀ The Beatles, R.E.M., Throwing Muses, Lush, the Pixies, Blake Babies, the Wedding Present

▶▶ Belly, Madder Rose, Letters to Cleo, Veruca Salt, Helium

Lisa M. Moore

Velvet Crush

Formed late 1980s, in Providence, RI.

Paul Chastain, bass, vocals; Jeffrey Borchardt, guitar; Ric Menck, drums.

Among all the retro bands of the mid-'90s, here's a group that's every bit as fresh as the original product. Velvet Crush fashions power-pop country-rock that combines the Anglo-pop stylings of Big Star with blazing Rickenbacker hooks redolent of the Byrds, dousing it liberally in the southern mysticism of R.E.M.

what's available: The group's first and (to date) only full-length album, *Teenage Symphonies to God* ✍✍✍✍ (550 Music/Epic, 1994, prod. Mitch Easter, Velvet Crush), is a stellar effort featuring a dozen indelible pop masterpieces. Whether performing crunchy rockers ("Hold Me Up," "My Blank Pages," "Atmosphere"), wistful Byrds-like psychedelia ("Time Wraps Around You," "Weird Summer"), or lilting country (a moving cover of Gene Clark's "Why Not Your Baby"), Velvet Crush brings new life to its musical traditions. This is a compelling and important work that deserves attention.

worth searching for: The trio's debut, *In the Presence Of* (Ringers Lactate, 1991, prod. Matthew Sweet, Velvet Crush), shows a loose, free-form structure in which the group gamely practices its talent for writing hook-filled tunes.

influences:

◀◀ The Byrds, the Monkees, Big Star, R.E.M.

▶▶ Son Volt, Uncle Tupelo, Wilco

Christopher Scapelliti

The Velvet Underground
/Nico
/Maureen Tucker

Formed 1965, in New York, NY. Disbanded 1972.

Lou Reed, vocals, guitar (1965–70); John Cale, viola, bass, keyboards (1965–68); Nico (born Christa Paffgen; died July 18, 1988), vocals (1966–67); Sterling Morrison (died 1995), bass, guitar (1965–71); Maureen "Moe" Tucker, drums, vocals (1965–70); Doug Yule, bass, vocals (1968–72); Billy Yule, drums (1970–72); Walter Powers, vocals (1970–72); Willie Alexander, guitar (1971–72).

No '60s band had a greater influence on post-punk rock than the Velvet Underground. The group's musical innovations are as numerous as its record sales are minuscule, but perhaps most influential was its attitude: a single-minded, uncompromising, and ultimately self-destructive vision that put the band at odds with everyone from recording engineers to record executives. Even its sole benefactor, Andy Warhol, got the boot after guiding the formation of the Velvets' notorious multimedia concerts, dubbed the Exploding Plastic Inevitable, and designing the famed banana cover for its first album, the 1967 *The Velvet Underground and Nico*. At a time when even major bands such as the Beatles and Rolling Stones were genuflecting toward flower-power psychedelia and the ideal of a youth community, the Velvets sang about junkies and transvestites with dispassionate, almost clinical insight, and they spiked Reed's sublime three-chord melodies with feedback, drones, and white noise. More than 20 years after the Velvets' dissolution (discounting a brief reunion tour of Europe in 1993), countless indie-rock bands have built and continue to build entire careers around a single aspect of their wide-screen sound.

what to buy: The band's four studio albums are essential to any complete rock library, beginning with *The Velvet Underground and Nico* ♫♫♫♫ (MGM/Verve, 1967, prod. Andy Warhol), virtually a blueprint of post-punk styles from pitiless noise-rock to poignant ballads such as the stunning "I'll Be Your Mirror," sung with icy efficiency by the German chanteuse Nico, whose inclusion was the sole concession to Warhol's managerial whims. With Nico and Warhol both out of the way, *White Light/White Heat* ♫♫♫♫ (MGM/Verve, 1968, prod. Tom Wilson) is an unsurpassed guitar exorcism, highlighted by the 17-minute landmark "Sister Ray." With the abrasive John Cale gone, Reed was left free to explore his more melodic, subdued side on the gorgeous *The Velvet Underground* ♫♫♫♫ (MGM, 1968, prod. the Velvet Underground). *Loaded* ♫♫♫♫ (Atlantic, 1970, prod. Geoffrey Haslam, Shel Kagan, the Velvet Underground) is the band's most determinedly pop-oriented effort, featuring the Reed masterpieces "Rock and Roll" and "Sweet Jane."

what to buy next: The five-CD box *Peel Slowly and See* ♫♫♫♫ (Polydor, 1995, prod. various) contains the four studio albums in

their entirety, plus crucial unreleased material, live tracks, and an hour's worth of (often tedious) 1965 rehearsals involving Reed, Cale, and Sterling Morrison. *1969 Live* ♫♫♫♫ (Mercury, 1974) captures the band at its best in lower-key, post-Cale mode.

what to avoid: The European-only release *Squeeze* woof! (Polydor, 1972) is essentially a Doug Yule solo album even though it was released under the Velvet Underground moniker.

the rest:

Live at Max's Kansas City ♫♫ (Atlantic, 1972)
V.U. ♫♫♫♫ (Verve, 1985)
Another View ♫♫♫ (Verve, 1986)
The Best of the Velvet Underground: Words and Music of Lou Reed ♫♫♫ (Verve, 1989)
Live MCMXCIII ♫♫♫ (Sire, 1993)

solo outings:

Nico:

Chelsea Girl ♫♫♫ (Verve, 1967)
The Marble Index ♫♫♫♫ (Elektra, 1969)
Desertshore ♫♫♫ (Reprise, 1971)
The End . . . ♫♫♫ (Island, 1974)
Drama of Exile ♫♫ (Aura, 1981)
Do or Die! Nico—in Europe—1982 Diary ♫♫♫♫ (ROIR, 1982)
Camera Obscura ♫♫♫ (Beggars Banquet/PVC, 1985)
The Blue Angel ♫♫♫♫ (Aura, 1985)
Behind the Iron Curtain ♫♫♫ (Dojo, 1986)
Live in Tokyo ♫♫♫ (Dojo, 1986)
Live Heroes ♫♫♫ (Performance, 1986)
The Peel Sessions ♫♫ (Strange Fruit EP, 1988)
Hanging Gardens ♫♫♫ (Restless, 1990)
The Classic Years N/A (Chronicles, 1998)

Maureen Tucker:

Playin' Possum ♫♫♫ (Trash, 1981)
MoeJadKateBarry ♫♫♫ (50 Skidillion Watts EP, 1987)
Life in Exile After Abdication ♫♫♫♫ (50 Skidillion Watts, 1989)
I Spent a Week There the Other Night ♫♫♫♫ (Sky, 1994)
Dogs Under Stress ♫♫♫♫ (Sky, 1994)

influences:

◀◀ John Cage, La Monte Young, '50s doo-wop, "Louie Louie"

▶▶ David Bowie, Mott the Hoople, Brian Eno, Roxy Music, Patti Smith, R.E.M., Sonic Youth, the Feelies, Luna, the entire punk-rock class of 1976, countless others

see also: *Lou Reed, John Cale*

Greg Kot

The Ventures

Formed 1959, in Seattle, WA.

Don Wilson, guitar; Bob Bogle, guitar, bass; Noel "Nokie" Edwards, guitar, bass (1960–67, 1970–85); Howie Johnson, drums (1959–61);

Mel Taylor, drums (1961–96); Gerry McGee, guitar (1968–72, 1985–present); Johnny Durrill, keyboards (1969–80); Leon Taylor, drums (1996–present).

The Ventures have released more then 250 albums during their undisputed, three decades–plus reign as kings of instrumental rock, influencing scores of musicians around the world to pick up electric guitars and strum along to the nearest TV theme or dance craze. Without question the most popular and influential band of its kind in history, with over 90 million records sold (40 million in Japan alone), the Ventures are nothing less than the inventors and chief practitioners of a style of rock 'n' roll that is almost too cool for words. The group's story began humbly enough on a construction site in Seattle when two young aspiring guitarists, Don Wilson and Bob Bogle, met and decided to perform together at local sock hops. They soon added a rhythm section and, as the Versatones, recorded two songs that Don's mother Josie released on her newly founded Blue Horizon Records. The second single, a cover of Johnny Smith's "Walk, Don't Run," was the first released under the name the Ventures and the first to be issued on the local Dolton label. When a disc jockey friend began using it as background music behind his hourly news bulletins, the song caught on in a big way and eventually soared to #2 nationwide. Eager to cash in on what everyone assumed to be fleeting notoriety, the band relocated to Los Angeles to record a quickie instrumental album of contemporary hits, and soon this too was lodged firmly in the Top 20, setting the formula for dozens upon dozens of long-players to follow. Throughout the '60s, the Ventures' dance, surf, pops, stage, and TV theme albums sold millions of copies worldwide: In London, for example, a young drummer named Keith Moon learned to play along with an eerie pedal-steel-on-Mars collection entitled *The Ventures in Space*, while a trip by the band to the Orient in 1965, coinciding with the first mass-marketing there of electric guitars, propelled the Ventures to a near Beatle-like status that remains intact to this day. But perhaps most influential of all was the group's *Play Guitar with the Ventures* series of instructional LPs, upon which an entire generation of would-be axe-wielders cut its teeth using, if they were lucky, brand new Venture-model Mosrite guitars. When these musicians themselves began coming of age during the early '80s, they provided the Ventures with an entirely fresh fan base of new wavers and surf punks, and the band continues to inspire and entertain legions of listeners of every age, race, creed, and musical stripe the world over—while continuing to outsell the Beatles two-to-one throughout the Orient. But while their guitars may hang proudly in the Smithsonian Institution, the Ventures have yet to be duly honored by the Rock and Roll Hall of Fame.

what to buy: There's not a single style of music the Ventures haven't tried to bend to its own twangy designs at least once,

and the cream of this crop can be found on the exemplary *Walk, Don't Run: The Best of the Ventures* 🎵🎵🎵 (EMI America, 1990, compilation prod. Steve Kolanijan, Ron Furmanek). Also essential is *Live in Japan '65* 🎵🎵🎵 (Capitol, 1995, prod. Bruce Harris), a long-overdue domestic release of a blistering double-LP concert wherein the boys absolutely *smoke* through all of their hits—and then deliver a version of Duke Ellington's "Caravan"!

what to buy next: Dick Dale may have done it first, and probably even better, but *Surfing* 🎵🎵🎵 (GNP Crescendo, 1995, prod. various) shows that the Ventures could hang 10 (at least 10) whenever the group tried. *Play Guitar with the Ventures* 🎵🎵🎵 (Dolton, 1965/One Way, 1997, prod. various) is a wonderful three-disc reissue of the entire instructional record series, while *Tele-Ventures: The Ventures Perform the Great TV Themes* 🎵🎵🎵 (EMI, 1996, compilation prod. Steve Kolanijan, Ron Furmanek), although somewhat marred by kitschy-at-best renditions of *Charlie's Angels*–calibre material from '76, contains sleek, Mosrite-powered versions of *Batman, The Man from U.N.C.L.E.*, and other small-screen '60s classics. Similarly, *The Ventures' Christmas Album* 🎵🎵🎵🎵 (Dolton, 1965/Razor and Tie, 1996, prod. Joe Saraceno) presents the band's clever weave of holiday standards and non-Yule hits.

best of the rest:

Walk, Don't Run/Walk, Don't Run, Volume 2 🎵🎵🎵 (Dolton, 1960, 1964/ One Way, 1996)

Surfing/The Colorful Ventures 🎵🎵🎵 (Dolton, 1961, 1963/One Way, 1996)

Let's Go!/The Ventures Play the Country Classics 🎵🎵🎵 (Dolton, 1963/One Way, 1997)

TV Themes/Bobby Vee Meets the Ventures 🎵🎵🎵 (Liberty, 1963/United Artists, 1977/One Way, 1997)

Guitar Freakout/Wild Things! 🎵🎵🎵🎵 (Dolton 1966, 1967/One Way, 1997)

Super Psychedelics/$1,000,000 Weekend 🎵🎵🎵 (Dolton, Liberty, 1967/ One Way, 1996)

Flights of Fantasy/Underground Fire 🎵🎵🎵🎵 (Liberty, 1968/One Way, 1996)

Hawaii Five-O/Swamp Rock 🎵🎵🎵 (Liberty, 1968/One Way, 1996)

Wild Again 🎵🎵🎵🎵 (GNP Crescendo, 1997)

influences:

◀◀ Les Paul, Duane Eddy, Chet Atkins, Johnny & the Hurricanes

▶▶ The Who, Jorma Kaukonen, Teisco Del Rey, Shadowy Men on a Shadowy Planet, the Aqua Velvets, the Mermen

Gary Pig Gold

Verbow

Formed 1993, in Evanston, IL.

Jason Narducy, vocals, guitar; Alison Chesley, cello; Luke Rothchild, bass, backing vocals; Mark Doyle, drums.

This straight-ahead rock quartet was born out of the musical relationship between Chicago punk scene refugee Jason Narducy and classically trained cellist Alison Chesley. Under the name Skinny, the pair (with some help on drums and bass) released the independent *Woodshed* in 1994, which won them opening slots on tours with Live and Morphine. Narducy's churning, explosive guitar and the oddity of a cello in rock had the critics swooning, but it was Verbow's relationship with post-punk magnate Bob Mould, the band's biggest and best fan, that finally hooked them a record deal.

what's available: *Chronicles* ♫♫♪ (Sony 550, 1997, prod. Bob Mould) was a long time coming—perhaps too long, since the hype that accumulated in the four years since Verbow/Skinny's inception had reached such a point that critics would have been underwhelmed by the resurrection of the Beatles. Still, with the exception of the single "Holiday" (slick and punchy, it comes off like something out of a Sugar songbook), the sometimes tuneful but mostly distended *Chronicles* falls far short of expectations.

the rest:
Skinny:
Woodshed ♫♫♪ (Whitehouse, 1994)

influences:
◀◀ Bob Mould, the Beatles, Smashing Pumpkins

Isaac Josephson

Tom Verlaine

See: Television

The Verlaines

Formed 1979, in Dunedin, New Zealand. Disbanded 1994.

Graeme Downes, vocals, guitar, keyboards, oboe, piano; Jane Dodd, bass (1979–88); Greg Kerr, drums (1981–82); Alan Haig, drums (1982–84); Robbie Yeats, drums (1984–89); Mike Stoodley, bass (1991–93); Greg Cairns, drums (1991–92); Darren Stedman, drums, (1993); Paul Winders, guitar, vocals (1993).

An ambitious band, the Verlaines set its sights above the usual pop-punk standards, creating a sound both romantic and furious. Like the symbolist poet the group is both named after and inspired by, the classically trained frontman Graeme Downes spun sweeping tales of imploding relationships, drunks, and melancholy outcasts with engaging melodicism. Largely ignored in the U.S., the band's output was remarkably consistent, and Downes's songwriting skills always hovered around the flawless level. Rather than endure more commercial failure, Downes pulled the plug on the band after 1993's *Way Out Where*.

what to buy: *Juvenilia* ♫♫♫♪ (Flying Nun, 1993, prod. various) is a potent collection of the band's first EPs and a few extras. With the hammering immediacy of punk coupled with Downes's already poetic lyrics, it's a solid introduction to the band's early years. Keeping an eye on the mainstream, *Ready to Fly* ♫♫♫♪

(Slash, 1991, prod. the Verlaines, Victor Grbic) bears an acoustic-tinged grandeur that allows the scope of Downes's tales to reach an unencumbered vastness.

what to buy next: The group's final release, *Way Out Where* ♫♫♫♪ (Slash, 1993, prod. Joe Chiccarelli), finds the band existing in name only, with Downes the only original member left. The darker and tougher edge of his doomed love songs here are truly the stuff to empty the Remy bottle by.

what to avoid: Lumbering under pretentious airs, *Hallelujah All the Way Home* ♫♫♪ (Homestead, 1989) lets most of the album's tunefulness simply get bogged down under its own artiness. For dedicated fans only.

worth searching for: The out-of-print *Bird Dog* (Homestead, 1987) is arguably the band's creative peak.

influences:
◀◀ The Chills

▶▶ Guided by Voices, Chris Knox, the Waterboys

Allan Orski

Versus

Formed 1991, in New York, NY.

Fontaine Toups, bass, vocals; Richard Baluyut, guitar, vocals; Ed Baluyut, drums; James Baluyut, guitar, sampler (1995–present).

Versus draws its name and primary inspiration from Boston noise-pop pioneers Mission of Burma. The foursome's music isn't as anthemic or as angular as that of its hero; rather it leans more toward tensive, mid-tempo barrages that oscillate between the tender and the tortured. At its best, as on "Linus" and the title track from *Deep Red*, Versus' music borders on transcendent.

what to buy: *Deep Red* ♫♫♫♪ (TeenBeat, 1995, prod. Richard Baluyut, Nicholas Vernhes, James Baluyut) is a five-song EP that displays the band's noisy charms to best advantage. The dissonant strings on the title track merely serve to heighten the group's intensity.

what to buy next: *The Stars Are Insane* ♫♫♪ (TeenBeat, 1994, prod. Richard Baluyut, Adam Lasus) is a relatively subdued trio record featuring some of Toups's most affecting vocals.

the rest:
Dead Leaves ♫♫♪ (TeenBeat, 1995)
Secret Swingers ♫♫♪ (TeenBeat/Caroline, 1996)
two cents plus tax ♫♫♪ (Caroline, 1998)

influences:
◀◀ Mission of Burma, New Order

▶▶ Air Miami

Bill Friskics-Warren

Veruca Salt

Formed 1993, in Chicago, IL.

Louise Post, guitars, vocals (1992–98); Stephen L. Lack, bass; Nina Gordon, guitars, vocals (1992–98); Jim Shapiro, drums, vocals (1992–96); Stacy Jones, drums (1996–present).

Louise Post and Nina Gordon met on December 31, 1992 through a mutual friend and soon formed Veruca Salt, named after a character in *Charlie and the Chocolate Factory*. Eight months later, bassist Steve Lack answered an ad and became Veruca Salt's bassist. For a drummer, Gordon kept it in the family by bringing her older brother, Jim Shapiro, on board. In January 1994, the band recorded its debut album, *American Thighs*, with veteran producer Brad Wood for the indie Chicago label Minty Fresh Records. Thanks to regional success for its first recordings, Veruca Salt was picked up by Geffen Records and hit quickly with the song "Seether." It has been a bit of a rocky road, though, with the departures of Shapiro and Gordon throwing curveballs into Veruca Salt's upward trajectory.

what to buy: The aptly titled sweetie-pie hit "Seether" from Veruca Salt's debut album, *American Thighs* ♫♫♫ (Minty Fresh/Geffen, 1994, prod. Brad Wood), furiously hit college radio and slithered onto the charts. If nothing else, you have to give credit to any band that can write a sexy ode to a comic book hero ("Spiderman '79"). But Veruca Salt succeeds in borrowing from fellow Chicago rockers Cheap Trick the ability to meld hard rock with bubblegum pop.

what to buy next: Post and Gordon stripped away their innocent persona and replaced it with a bad-girl image on *Eight Arms to Hold You* ♫♫♫♪ (Outpost, 1997, prod. Bob Rock). Filled with hand claps, double-time drums, and funny lyrics, "With David Bowie" is one of the best songs Veruca Salt has recorded. And at long last, the sassy, hard-rocking first single, "Volcano Girls," solves a mystery—the seether is Post.

the rest:
Blow It Out Your Ass . . . It's Veruca Salt ♫♫♫ (Geffen, 1996)

influences:
◄◄ Cheap Trick, the Go-Go's

►► Hole, Garbage

Christina Fuoco

The Verve

Formed 1991, in England. Disbanded 1995. Re-formed 1996.

Richard Ashcroft, vocals, guitar; Nick McCabe, guitars; Peter Salisbury, drums; Simon Jones, bass; Simon Tong, guitar, keyboards.

The Verve (or simply Verve) evokes a number of influences without actually sounding like any of them—including Jimi Hendrix (especially his psychedelic outings), the Allman Brothers Band, Pink Floyd, and Brian Eno. Most importantly, the group uses these artists as inspirations and not as models to slavishly mimic. The Verve's sound is defined by vast swirls of atmospheric guitars and reverb-drenched vocals atop subtle bass and drums. To say that this music is dreamy and psychedelic is an understatement; it is hypnotic and haunting and, at times, nearly hallucinatory. Techno artists such as the Aphex Twin and Moby have achieved sonic psychotropy on a par with this, but what raises the Verve above such trance artists is its dedication to melody and song structure, and its use of traditional rock instruments. The band—particularly singer Ashcroft—also became at least as well known for its indulgences and mercurial behavior as for its music, which led to a split in 1995; though when it reconvened the following year, it put together its greatest commercial triumph with the album *Urban Hymns*.

what to buy: The Verve's debut album, *A Storm in Heaven* ♫♫♫♫ (Vernon Yard, 1993, prod. John Leckie), is an enveloping ride that is most effective if listened to in a single sitting. While songs such as "Blue," "Butterfly," and "Slide Away" stand well enough on their own, the album as a whole works as a kind of psychedelic tone poem. The "comeback" album, *Urban Hymns* ♫♫♫♫ (Virgin, 1997, prod. Youth, Chris Potter, the Verve), is a mature, dynamic effort that indicates a break was just what the band needed. The majestic opening track, "Bitter Sweet Symphony," was a worldwide smash, though the Verve didn't see much for it. The song was built on a portion of the Andrew Oldham Orchestra's treatment of the Rolling Stones' "The Last Time," and Oldham claimed 100 percent of the royalties—even selling the song for advertising purposes.

what to buy next: *A Northern Soul* ♫♫♫♫ (Vernon Yard, 1995, prod. Owen Morris, the Verve) will not disappoint fans of *A Storm in Heaven*, with sure signs of progress that makes the band's breakup all the more distressing.

the rest:
No Come Down ♫♫♫♪ (Vernon Yard, 1994)

worth searching for: The imported *The Verve EP* (Vernon Yard, 1992) is relatively easy to find and worth the extra cash.

influences:
◄◄ Jimi Hendrix, Pink Floyd, Brian Eno, the Allman Brothers Band

►► Aphex Twin, Moby, Beck

David Galens and Gary Graff

The Verve Pipe

Formed 1991, in East Lansing, MI.

Brian Vander Ark, vocals, guitar; Brian Stout, guitar, vocals (1992–93); A.J. Dunning, guitars (1993–present); Doug Corella, percussion, keyboards (1995–present); Donny Brown, drums, vocals.

A merging of two popular western Michigan bands—Johnny with an Eye and Water 4 the Pool—the melodic power-pop band the Verve Pipe attracted a grass roots following via tours and independent releases well before the release of its platinum-selling major label debut in 1996. The efforts clearly paid off; the single "The Freshman" was a smash, vaulting the Verve Pipe into the prosperous middle level of modern rock success—not quite Pearl Jam, but far better than 99 of every 100 bands that put out a record during the post-alternative signing boom of the mid-'90s.

what to buy: On *Villains* &&&& (RCA, 1996, prod. Jerry Harrison), frontman Brian Vander Ark passionately delivers his shockingly vivid, cynical, and bittersweet tales of love, while edgy, subtle keyboard textures and hypnotic bass and drums swirl around his effortlessly lush vocals. A mature effort that was one of that year's finest debuts.

the rest:
I've Suffered a Head Injury &&& (LMNOPop!, 1992/RCA, 1996)
Pop Smear &&&&& (LMNOPop!, 1993/RCA, 1996)

worth searching for: Fans of the Verve Pipe have two CDs to find. The first pressing of *I've Suffered a Head Injury* (LMNOPop!, 1992) has a few extra tracks, including an early rendition of "The Freshmen" during which Vander Ark sings accompanied only by his acoustic guitar. The promotion-only CD *85 on 31* (RCA, 1997, prod. Jerry Harrison, Michael A. Hoffmann) features a stripped-down demo version of "Photograph"—without Vander Ark's seductive "picture this"—live tracks, and covers of XTC's "Blue Beret" and the Beatles' "Strawberry Fields Forever," a staple in the band's live shows. The highlight of the disc, however, is "Cup of Tea" done acoustically as a ballad.

influences:
◀◀ The Beatles, Blur, XTC
▶▶ Matchbox 20, Semisonic

Christina Fuoco

The Vibrators

Formed 1976, in London, England.

Knox, vocals; Eddie, guitar; Pat Collier, bass (1977–78, 1982–85); John Ellis, guitar (1977–86); Gary Tibbs, bass (1978–80); Noel Thompson, bass (1985–86); Nigel Bennett, guitar (1990).

Opportunistic (and older) punkers, the Vibrators made one ripping album at the crest of the punk explosion. Unlike others, the band didn't split up when it fell out of favor; instead it released a number of now-deleted albums featuring streamlined chargers that lost a little of the group's speed and fury along the way.

what's available: The startling debut, *Pure Mania* &&& (Columbia, 1977/Legacy, 1991), features rudimentary but catchy songs, along with rude riffs that lend it a punch that bears the test of time. *The Power of Money: The Best of the Vibrators* &&&& (Continuum, 1991) collects highlights from the debut as well as material from the later, otherwise out-of-print, work.

influences:
◀◀ The Stooges, the MC5, the Ramones, Blue Cheer
▶▶ The Clash, Operation Ivy, Green Day

Allan Orski

Sid Vicious
See: The Sex Pistols

Vigilantes of Love

Formed 1989, in Athens, GA.

Bill Mallonee, vocals, guitar; Mark Hall, accordion (1989–91); "Dogmess" Jonny Evans, harmonica (1989–91); Billy Holmes, mandolin, guitar (1989–92); Travis McNabb, guitar (1992–94); Newton Carter, drums (1992–94); David LaBruyere, bass (1992–94); Chris Donohue, bass, guitar (1994–95); Tom Crea, drums (1994–97); Chris Bland, bass (1995–98); Kenny Hutson, guitars (1997–present); Scott Klopfenstein, drums (1997–present); Jake Bradley, bass (1998–present).

Having taken its name from a New Order song ("Love Vigilantes"), Vigilantes of Love might reasonably be assumed to hold a dim social outlook. To some degree, it does: many of this Georgia folk-rock band's songs deal with the state of fallen man, though they usually hold out hope for redemption. The group has had a fluid membership since forming as an acoustic duo in 1989 and has always revolved around the urgent voice of singer-songwriter Bill Mallonee. Mallonee comes off like a righteous, ragged street preacher—a little crazed, but fascinating to hear. VOL signed with Capricorn after recording three independent albums during the early '90s. It left the label after three albums and released the mail-order-only *To the Roof of the Sky* in 1998. Guitarist Travis McNabb, who played in VOL's most electric incarnation, joined Better than Ezra after leaving the band in 1994.

what to buy: *Blister Soul* &&&& (Capricorn, 1995, prod. John Keane) is VOL's most fully realized album, with arrangements that incorporate sitar, violin, and steel guitar. *Blister Soul* contains a version of what's arguably the band's most popular song ("Real Down Town"), as well as some of its best, from the tender "Certain Slant of Light" to the scorching "Balaam's Ass."

what to buy next: *Welcome to Struggleville* ♪♪♪♪ (Capricorn, 1994, prod. Jim Scott) features a more electric version of VOL. For Christian rock fans, *V.O.L.* ♪♪♪♪ (Warner Resound, 1996, prod. various), the band's official introduction to the Christian bookstore marketplace, contains a spiritually oriented sampler from several albums.

the rest:
Killing Floor ♪♪♪ (Fingerprint, 1992)
Slow Dark Train ♪♪♪ (Capricorn, 1997)
To the Roof of the Sky ♪♪♪ (Meat Market, 1998)

worth searching for: Mallonee doesn't like to talk much about *Driving the Nails* (Core, 1992, prod. Bill Mallonee, Keith Dressel, Preston Samford) following a soured business relationship with the label, but it contains some of his finest, most accessible songs—including the troubling but brilliantly drawn "Odious," written from the vantage point of an abortion-clinic bomber. VOL re-recorded this album's "Real Down Town" for *Blister Soul* with a slyly rewritten jab at Core's owner.

influences:
◀◀ Bob Dylan, T-Bone Burnett, R.E.M., Mark Heard
▶▶ Better than Ezra, Rusted Root, Sister Hazel

Brian Mansfield

The Village People

Formed 1977, in New York, NY.

Felipe Rose, the Indian; Alexander Briley, the G.I.; Glenn Hughes, the Leatherman (1977–95); David Hodo, the Construction Worker (1977–82, 1987–present); Randy Jones, the Cowboy (1977–80); Victor Willis, the Cop (1977–79); Ray Simpson, vocals (1979–82, 1987–present); Miles Jaye, vocals (1982–85); Jeff Olsen, vocals (1980–present); Eric Anzalone, vocals (1995–present).

The Village People, one of the shrewdest, most cleverly manufactured groups ever, really do deserve to be remembered—if only for putting an unforgettable, if cartoony, face on that most faceless of genres: mid-'70s disco. Beginning as a sly mockery of New York's gay subculture, they ended up—for two years anyway—becoming one of the most successful groups on the planet, and their very exclusive sense of musical and visual humor helped initiate countless millions of unsuspecting listeners into the exotic world of hardcore dance music. Wandering the streets of Greenwich Village late one night in 1976, French record producer Jacques Morali encountered a dancer dressed in full Native Indian regalia en route to his job at the notorious Anvil Club. Intrigued, he followed the man inside where he was joined at the bar by another dancer, this one resplendent in an outrageous Wild West outfit. This incongruous image—a cowboy and an Indian drinking and dancing together at four in the morning—led Morali to form a group that, in its image especially, parodied stereotypes of American masculinity. Running an ad in the trade papers ("Macho Types Wanted: Must Have Mustache"), Morali quickly cast the remaining four "characters" for the group, and their very first live appearance together at Brooklyn's 2001 Odyssey club, where much of *Saturday Night Fever* had just been filmed, was an overwhelming success. The songs Morali wrote for his creations—"Macho Man," "YMCA," and "In the Navy"—were all huge international hits, and the Village People as a result became the first act of its kind to mount and sell out a worldwide stadium tour. However, their movie *Can't Stop the Music* only helped the group fall victim to the gigantic anti-disco backlash that soon engulfed the business, and a 1981 album for RCA, *Renaissance*, was nothing but a feeble attempt to cash in on the burgeoning New Romantic movement. The band all but disappeared for the next several years (though each of its remaining members, thanks to Morali's exceedingly generous contract with them, were well-off financially). Then, inspired by the 20th anniversary reunion tours of that other great prefabricated group, the Monkees, the Village People began performing again during 1987, and in the decade since have carved out a lucrative career entertaining at business conventions, sporting events, and nostalgia fests. Disco now being cool (or at least "camp") again, their story, along with that of the late Morali, is currently under development at Columbia Pictures, and not a week goes by that doesn't find the Village People playing to increasingly large and enthusiastic crowds of insurance agents, baseball fans, and even families at Disney World, all of whom innocently stand on their seats, arms in the air, spelling out the letters "YMCA" as each show comes to a boisterous end.

what to buy: It's sometimes hard to believe that the songs contained on *The Best of the Village People* ♪♪♪ (Casablanca/Mercury, 1994, prod. Jacques Morali, Henri Belolo) sold more than 40 million records between 1977 and 1980, but if you let your guard down (and let your legs do the thinking), it's not very hard at all to be swept up in the good, semi-clean fun these 14 tracks (including several sizzling 12-inch dance mixes) represent.

what to buy next: If the *Best Of* doesn't satisfy, try also *Cruisin'* ♪♪♪ (Casablanca, 1978/Mercury, 1996, prod. Jacques Morali) and *Macho Man* ♪♪♪ (Casablanca, 1978/Mercury, 1996, prod. Henri Belolo). The oh-so-accurately-titled *Live and Sleazy* ♪♪♪ (Casablanca, 1979/Rebound, 1994, prod. Jacques Morali) also makes for an interesting evening's entertainment—while we wait for Columbia's bio-pic, that is.

what to avoid: In retrospect, the title *Can't Stop the Music* ♪♪ (Casablanca, 1980/Mercury, 1996) seems more of a threat than a promise.

the rest:

Village People 🎵🎵 (Casablanca, 1977 / Mercury, 1996)

Go West 🎵🎵 (Casablanca, 1979 / Mercury, 1996)

Live and Sleazy N/A (Mercury, 1998)

solo outings:

Miles Jaye:

Miles 🎵🎵🎵 (Island, 1987)

Irresistible 🎵🎵🎵 (Island, 1989)

Strong 🎵🎵 (Island, 1991)

influences:

◀◀ Bette Midler, Disco Tex & the Sex-O-Lettes, *The Boys in the Band*

▶▶ Culture Club, David Lee Roth, Pet Shop Boys

Gary Pig Gold

Gene Vincent

Born Eugene Vincent Craddock, February 11, 1935, in Norfolk, VA. Died October 12, 1971, in Los Angeles, CA.

Gene Vincent, whose sad, lonely life ended in an early death, is mostly forgotten these days; even his gravesite is so neglected the inscription on his marker is virtually unreadable. But how good were the early rock 'n' roll sides he cut for Capitol Records during the late '50s? Ask any collector who routinely pays hundreds of dollars for clean copies of his original albums. Although the success of his 1956 Top 10 hit, "Be-Bop-A-Lula," would never be repeated, Vincent scored with two solid Top 20 entries "Lotta Lovin'" and "Dance to the Bop." Among his remarkably fine recordings reside some of the most openly erotic rock of its day. ("Woman Love," the B-side to "Be-Bop-A-Lula," was banned from radio because of his "suggestive" vocal.) At his peak, Vincent appeared in such films as *The Girl Can't Help It!* and *Hot Rod Gang* and became the first rock singer to be awarded a star on the Hollywood Walk of Fame. When the hits and lucrative bookings dried up in America, he moved to England, where legendary TV producer Jack Good dressed him in black leather and encouraged him to openly display the brace on his right leg, badly injured in either the navy or in a motorcycle accident, depending upon who you believe. An icon of greasy, primal rockabilly, he paradoxically cut mostly pop sides in England, where he scored his final chart records. The emergence of the Beatles, poor health, and a wide array of soul-wracking personal problems forced Vincent to return to the U.S. for an ill-fated comeback. He cut some well-reviewed, low-selling country and modern rock LPs during the late '60s, but nothing could revive his failing health or career. Vincent died of a bleeding ulcer at age 36, but his influence casts a long shadow upon popular music. Country star Buck Owens started out as an original member of his backup band, the Blue Caps,

whose original guitarist Cliff Gallup remains one of the most uncredited originators of the music. In 1993, guitar maestro Jeff Beck cut an entire album of Vincent oldies, faithfully reproducing Gallup's original work on every track for one of the most sober and reverential tribute albums ever. Like his frequent sidekick Eddie Cochran—who was killed in the car crash that left Vincent's already crippled leg mangled for the rest of his life—Vincent occupied only a small corner of the world of rock 'n' roll in his time. But, man, did he hold that little corner down. After much lobbying from his diligent fans, he was finally inducted into the Rock and Roll Hall of Fame in 1998. A major biography on Vincent's life and music is due out in 1999.

what to buy: One of the great CD reissues of '50s rock 'n' roll, *Capitol Collector's Series* 🎵🎵🎵🎵 (Capitol, 1990, compilation prod. Ron Furmanek), collects 21 tracks from his 1956 to 1959 Capitol sessions, prime cuts from five albums. The *Capitol Collector's Series* edition has a slight edge over the easier-to-find *The Screaming End: The Best of Gene Vincent & His Blue Caps* 🎵🎵🎵🎵 (Razor & Tie, 1997, compilation prod. Matt Goldman, Dave "Daddy Cool" Booth) for sonics, selection, and sequence. In either case, Vincent runs high-octane fuel through a finely tuned engine in some of the finest performances of the classic rock and roll era.

what to buy next: Vincent's original Capitol LPs have recently been reissued on some very strong 2-on-1 compilations including *Bluejean Bop!/Gene Vincent & His Blue Caps* 🎵🎵🎵 (Capitol, 1956, 1957/Collectables, 1998, prod. Ken Nelson), *Gene Vincent Rocks & the Blue Caps Roll/A Gene Vincent Record Date* 🎵🎵🎵 (Capitol, 1958/Collectables, 1998, prod. Ken Nelson), and *Sounds Like Gene Vincent/Crazy Times* 🎵🎵🎵 (Capitol, 1959, 1960/Collectables, 1998, prod. Ken Nelson). Also, longtime fans will definitely want to own *The Lost Dallas Sessions '57–'58* 🎵🎵 (Dragon Street, 1998, compilation prod. David Dennard), which contains previously unreleased demos, alternate takes, and a driving live appearance on the *Big D Jamboree* radio show we have all waited too long to hear.

what to avoid: The budget racks are glutted with releases featuring Vincent's final recordings, such as *Be-Bop-A-Lula* 🎵 (Prime Cuts, 1997), *Be-Bop-A-Lula* 🎵 (Columbia River, 1998), and *Roots of Rock 'n' Roll* 🎵 (Direct Source, 1997). These discs all feature a late '60s remake of "Be-Bop-A-Lula" as well as "The Story of the Rockers," "Pickin' Puppies," and a sickly version of "Hi Lilli Hi Lo." If you absolutely must own these sides, track down *The Gene Vincent Tapes* 🎵🎵 (Jerden, 1995, prod. Red Robinson), which also contains a nice interview with the Black Leather Rebel, or dig through the scraps and oddities contained on Magnum's *Rebel Heart* series (see below).

the rest:

Shakin' up a Storm 🎵🎵🎵 (EMI, 1964/1998)

Ain't That Too Much 𝄢𝄢𝄢 (Challenge, 1967/Sundazed, 1993)
I'm Back & I'm Proud 𝄢𝄢 (Dandelion, 1970/See for Miles, 1995)
Greatest Hits 𝄢𝄢𝄢 (Curb, 1993)
Rebel Heart 𝄢𝄢 (Magnum, 1994)
Rebel Heart, Vol. 2 𝄢𝄢 (Magnum, 1996)
Rebel Heart, Vol. 3 𝄢𝄢 (Magnum, 1996)
Rebel Heart, Vol. 4 𝄢𝄢 (Magnum, 1996)
The EP Collection 𝄢𝄢𝄢𝄢 (See for Miles, 1996)
Rebel Heart, Vol. 5 𝄢𝄢 (Magnum, 1998)

worth searching for: Some import services may still carry *The Gene Vincent Collection* (EMI, 1996, compilation prod. Roger Nunn, Steve Aynsly), a six-disc, 151-song box set that includes everything Vincent recorded for Capitol and England's Columbia label during the '50s and early '60s.

influences:

◀◀ Buddy Holly, Ivory Joe Hunter, Elvis Presley

▶▶ The Beatles, Johnny Carroll, Ronnie Dawson, Billy Fury, Vince Taylor, Jim Morrison

Joel Selvin and Ken Burke

Holly Vincent
/Holly & the Italians
/Oblivious

Born Holly Beth Vincent, late 1950s, in Chicago, IL.

The Italians: Holly Vincent, guitar, vocals; Steve Dalton, drums; numerous bass players.

Author of one true rock 'n' roll classic, the 1980 single "Tell That Girl to Shut Up," Holly Vincent formed the Italians in Los Angeles, then moved to England to sign a recording contract and earn her few minutes of fame. Though "Tell That Girl to Shut Up" is a terrific punk-rock kiss-off song, the band had severe personnel problems and couldn't find a compatible producer, and Vincent's career more or less dwindled into obscurity. She resurfaced occasionally with her '90s band Oblivious and on a duet album with former Concrete Blonde singer Johnette Napolitano.

what's available: Vincent's first two albums—*The Right to Be Italian* 𝄢𝄢𝄢𝄢 (Virgin-Epic, 1981, prod. George "Shadow" Morton, Richard Gottehrer) and *Holly and the Italians* 𝄢𝄢𝄢 (Virgin-Epic, 1982) (the latter's a solo album despite the title)—are out of print, so the curious have only *Shake It Up! American Power Pop II* 𝄢𝄢𝄢𝄢 (Rhino, 1993, compilation prod. Gary Stewart) for a taste, via "Tell That Girl to Shut Up." With Oblivious, Vincent released *America* 𝄢𝄢𝄢 (Daemon, 1993), and with Napolitano she recorded *Vowel Movement* 𝄢𝄢𝄢 (Mammoth, 1995).

influences:

◀◀ The Slits, Patti Smith, the Sex Pistols

▶▶ The Pretenders, the Muffs, Hole, Bikini Kill, Seven Year Bitch, Concrete Blonde

Steve Knopper

Violent Femmes

Formed 1981, in Milwaukee, WI.

Gordon Gano, guitar, vocals; Brian Ritchie, bass, guitar; Victor De-Lorenzo, drums (1981–92); Guy Hoffman, drums (1992–present).

Other acts flirted with the idea, but the Violent Femmes perfected acoustic punk rock. Preacher's kid Gordon Gano doctored up country/gospel styles with his whacked-out poetry, while Brian Ritchie thumped out funky jazz rhythms on a mariachi-styled bass and Victor DeLorenzo scratched propulsive beats on a single snare drum. The trio experimented with different sounds on later albums, with varying degrees of success. But its most lasting style remains the twisted folk-punk it invented in the early '80s while busking on the sidewalks of Milwaukee's East Side.

what to buy: A true word-of-mouth sensation, *Violent Femmes* 𝄢𝄢𝄢𝄢 (Slash, 1983, prod. Mark Van Hecke) sold a million copies over 10 years without ever scratching the *Billboard* charts. Gano's nasal whine of a voice is an acquired taste, but psycho-nerd anthems such as "Add It Up," "Blister in the Sun," and "Kiss Off" have universal appeal.

what to buy next: *The Blind Leading the Naked* 𝄢𝄢𝄢𝄢 (Slash, 1986, prod. Jerry Harrison) adds hard-core punk and R&B to the mix with grand results. Don't judge *Why Do Birds Sing?* 𝄢𝄢𝄢𝄢 (Slash/Reprise, 1991, prod. Michael Beinhorn, the Violent Femmes) by the tepid remake of Culture Club's "Do You Really Want to Hurt Me"; the rest of the album, especially the PG-13 "Girl Trouble" and "American Music," is the Femmes in full glory.

what to avoid: Aside from the album-opening "Don't Start Me on the Liquor," there's little to be intoxicated by on *New Times* 𝄢𝄢 (Elektra, 1994, prod. Brian Ritchie, Gordon Gano).

the rest:
Hallowed Ground 𝄢𝄢𝄢 (Slash, 1984)
3 𝄢𝄢𝄢 (Slash, 1989)
Add It Up: 1981–1993 𝄢𝄢𝄢𝄢 (Slash, 1993)
Freak Magnet 𝄢𝄢𝄢𝄢 (1998)

worth searching for: *Debacle: The First Decade* (Liberation/ Slash, 1990) is an import collection that's a bit more straightforward than the domestic *Add It Up. Rock* (Liberation, 1995), an Australian import, features 12 unreleased songs—including a blistering ditty about the murder of a serial killer, "Dahmer Is Dead."

solo outings:
Gordon Gano:
(With Mercy Seat) *Mercy Seat* 𝄢𝄢 (Slash, 1987)

Brian Ritchie:
The Blend ♫♫♫ (SST, 1987)
I See a Noise ♫♫♫ (Chameleon/Dali 1990)

Victor DeLorenzo:
Peter Corey Sent Me ♫♫ (Dali, 1990)

influences:

◄◄ Jonathan RIchman, the Velvet Underground, the Carter Family

►► Frank Black, Jonny Polonsky, Liz Phair, Hammell on Trial

Thor Christensen

Visage

See: Magazine

Voice of the Beehive

Formed 1987, in London, England. Disbanded 1991.

Tracey Bryn (Belland), vocals, guitar; Melissa Brooke Belland, vocals; Martin Brett, bass, piano (1987–91); Mike Jones, guitar, vocals, keyboards, programming (1987–91); D.M. (Woody) Woodgate, drums, percussion, programming (1987–91).

Sisters and expatriate Californians Tracy Bryn and Melissa Belland front this group, which was conceived as a delightful amalgamation of West Coast and U.K. pop approaches. The original Voice of the Beehive incorporated elements of '60s girl-group sugar, post-punk spice, and a recognition that the world ain't always everything nice. The rest of the band splintered after its second album, *Honey Lingers*, leaving the sisters to carry on on their own.

what to buy: The approach is best realized on *Let It Bee* ♫♫♫♫ (London, 1988, prod. Pete Collins, Hugh Jones, Marvin Etzioni), an uneven but winning foray into the realm of hooks and heartache, with spunk and sass to spare.

the rest:
Honey Lingers ♫♫♫ (London, 1991)
Sex & Misery ♫♫ (Discovery, 1995)

influences:

◄◄ The Angels, the Ronnettes, Suzi Quatro, the Go-Go's

►► L7, Hole

Carl Cafarelli

Chris von Sneidern

Born December 6, 1965, in Syracuse, NY.

Although virtually unknown outside the insular world of pure pop fandom, Chris von Sneidern (or CVS, as he's known) is a bona fide star among the pop cognoscenti, and he achieved this status in a staggeringly short period of time. After leaving his native central New York during the mid-'80s, CVS served his apprenticeship with San Francisco–area bands the Sneetches and Flying Color before becoming friends with power pop legend Paul Collins. At Collins's urging, CVS began fronting his own Pop Gem Factory and releasing solo albums of unerring brilliance. His work demonstrates that it's possible to be overtly influenced by the classic pop of the past and still create new work that is not a simple rehash. Pop Gem Factory, indeed.

what to buy: Buy 'em all! But start with *Sight & Sound* ♫♫♫♫ (Heyday, 1993, prod. Chris von Sneidern), which sounds like some beyond-this-mortal-coil collaboration between Badfinger's Pete Ham and Big Star's Chris Bell. Presumably named after a dB's lyric, *Wood and Wire* ♫♫♫♫ (Mod Lang, 1998, prod. Chris von Sneidern) offers further proof that Chris von Sneidern is one of the most accomplished and vital performers working in the pop idiom today.

what to buy next: *Big White Lies* ♫♫♫ (Heyday, 1994, prod. Chris von Sneidern) and *Go!* ♫♫♫♫ (Mod Lang, 1996, prod. Chris von Sneidern) are likewise mandatory listening for anyone who fancies himself a devotee of heart-stoppin', swoon-inducin' pop music. You gotta love this guy.

influences:

◄◄ The Beatles, Badfinger, Big Star, the Paul Collins Beat, the Raspberries, Emitt Rhodes, the Flamin' Groovies, the Flashcubes, the Hollies

Carl Cafarelli

Vowel Movement

See: Concrete Blonde

Vulgar Boatmen

See: The Silos

The Waco Brothers

Formed 1995, in Chicago, IL.

Jon Langford, vocals, guitar; Dean Schlabowske, guitar; Tom Ray, bass (1995); Steve Goulding, drums; Tracy Dear, mandolin, vocals; Alan Doughty, bass (1995–present); Mark Durante, pedal steel.

The Waco Brothers come not to praise country music—well, sorta, maybe—but to bury it. A barroom brawl of a band, the

Wacos are a ragtag outfit comprised of British and German rockers on holiday from groups such as the Mekons (Jon Langford, Steve Goulding), Jesus Jones (Alan Doughty), and KMFDM (Mark Durante), plus a couple of Americans (Tom Ray, who left to play full-time with the Bottle Rockets, and Dean Schlabowske of Wreck), all of whom are drunk on Hank Williams, Johnny Cash, and, likely, a few pints of their favorite brew. The result has been described as half Cash/half Clash, and that's pretty accurate. But it's a combination that makes sense: after all, country's hell-raising honky-tonk heroes and punk rock's first generation had a lot more in common than either would care to admit. But be warned: the group's yowling vocals, ragged arrangements and relentlessly bleak outlook are more appropriate for those more inclined to pass out in a beer than cry in it. Langford has also recorded similar material under the names Jonboy Langford & the Pine Valley Cosmonauts and Skull Orchard.

what to buy: The country music that appeals to the Wacos' sensibilities is full of grim circumstances and losers with no future—but with terrific barroom stories. *Cowboy in Flames* ♫♫♫♫ (Bloodshot, 1997) declares the "Death of Country Music" on one track, but their covers of Roy Acuff's "Wreck on the Highway," George Jones's "White Lightning," and Johnny Cash's "Big River" swear that it just ain't so. Harder, more musical and less cynical than their debut.

the rest:
. . . To the Last Dead Cowboy ♫♫♫♪ (Bloodshot, 1995)
Do You Think about Me? ♫♫♫ (Bloodshot, 1997)

solo outings:
Jon Langford:
(As Jonboy Langford & the Pine Valley Cosmonauts) *Misery Loves Company* ♫♫♫ (Scat, 1994)
Skull Orchard ♫♫♫♫ (Sugar Free, 1998)

influences:
◀◀ Hank Williams, Johnny Cash, the Sex Pistols

see also: *Mekons*

Daniel Durchholz

John Waite
/The Babys
/Bad English

John Waite born July 4, 1955, in Lancashire, England. The Babys formed 1976. Disbanded 1981. Bad English formed 1988. Disbanded 1991.

The Babys: John Waite, bass, vocals; Wally Stocker, guitar, vocals; Mike Corby, keyboards, vocals (1976–77); Tony Brock, drums, vocals; Jonathan Cain, (1978–81); Ricky Phillips, bass (1978–81). Bad English: John Waite, bass, vocals; Jonathan Cain, keyboards, guitar, vo-cals; Ricky Phillips, bass; Neal Schon, guitar; Deen Castronovo, drums.**

The focal point for all three of these entities is John Waite, a reedy singer and self-styled bad boy who brings abundant attitude—a palpable vocal sneer—to even the prettiest songs. The Babys are the best of this lot, a melodic power pop (a.k.a. Beatlesque) outfit that became an arena-styled act—introducing the world to future Journey member Jonathan Cain—before splitting up. Waite's solo career was relatively routine, save for the 1984 chart-topper "Missing You." Bad English was a bust, which sent Cain and guitarist Neal Schon—and, more recently, drummer Deen Castronovo—back to Journey while Waite continued to pursue his own muse.

what to buy: It's no accident that 14 of the 20 songs on *The Essential John Waite* ♫♫♫♫ (Chrysalis, 1992, prod. various) are Babys selections, including modest hits such as "Isn't It Time," "Back on My Feet Again," and "Head First," as well as his own smash, "Missing You." For any collection, it provides a sufficient taste of Waite at his best.

the rest:
John Waite:
Temple Bar ♫♫♫ (Imago, 1995)
When You Were Mine ♫♫ (Mercury, 1997)

The Babys:
Anthology ♫♫♫♪ (Chrysalis, 1981/1995)

Bad English:
Bad English ♫♫ (Epic, 1989)
Backlash ♫♫ (Epic, 1991)

worth searching for: Though misleadingly titled after a hit that's not on it, the collection *Isn't It Time* (Disky, 1997, prod. various) offers a nice taste of the early Babys, when the group's pop leanings were still intact.

influences:
◀◀ The Beatles, the Raspberries, Mott the Hoople, T. Rex
▶▶ Ratt, Poison, Guns N' Roses, D Generation, Sponge

see also: *Journey*

Gary Graff

The Waitresses

Formed 1979, in Akron, OH.

Patty Donahue (died December 6, 1996), vocals; Mars Williams, reeds; Chris Butler, guitar; Dan Klayman, organ; David Hofstra, bass; Tracy Wormworth, bass; Billy Ficca, drums.

Boasting an armful of smart-aleck one-liners and a funkified pop beat, the Waitresses became a surprise, albeit short-lived, sensation with the teasing "I Know What Boys Like" in 1982. Although Chris Butler wrote the material, it was the pragmatic voice of Patty Donahue that stamped the smirking but no-fooling demeanor that identified the Waitresses. Long after their hitmaking period had subsided, Donahue died of lung cancer at age 40.

what to buy: *The Best of the Waitresses* ♫♫♫♪ (Polydor, 1980/1990, compilation prod. Bill Levenson, Chris Butler) is all that's left and contains everything essential, including the anti-yuletide "Christmas Wrapping" and the theme song to the '80s TV show *Square Pegs*.

influences:

◀◀ Blondie, the Crystals

▶▶ Madonna, Bow Wow Wow

Allan Orski

Tom Waits

Born December 7, 1949, in Pomona, CA.

With a voice that sounds like it was soaked in a vat of bourbon, left hanging in the smokehouse for a few months and then taken outside and run over with a car a few times, Tom Waits is something of an acquired taste. Yet it's his songs that are the real selling point, and Waits's detailed accounts of losers with hearts of gold have won over the likes of Bruce Springsteen, Rod Stewart, Bette Midler, the Eagles, Screamin' Jay Hawkins, the Ramones, Johnny Cash, Bob Seger, and Dion, all of whom have recorded his material. Starting out as the embodiment of dissipated hipster slackness, Waits reached a creative dead-end with that persona and proceeded to reinvent himself as a ravaged-voiced Howlin' Wolf acolyte backed by a combination of avant-rock and traffic noise. Not only did the change reinvigorate his music, it expanded his horizons; Waits has since performed in a stage production he wrote with his wife, Kathleen Brennan, and a filmed cabaret-style concert. He has also acted in a number of films, including *Short Cuts, Ironweed, Bram Stoker's Dracula, Mystery Train*, and *Rumblefish*. Considering the risks he takes in all facets of his career, it's to Waits's credit that nearly every move he makes is worth paying attention to.

what to buy: The first two installments of a loose trilogy (that also includes *Franks Wild Years*), *Swordfishtrombones* ♫♫♫♫ (Island, 1983, prod. Tom Waits) and *Raindogs* ♫♫♫♫♫ (Island, 1985, prod. Tom Waits) find Waits writing the strongest material of his career. The sound is unsettling, to say the least, yet even through the odd instrumental textures, sprung rhythms, and barked vocals, Waits's songs (including the original version of the Rod Stewart hit "Downtown Train") come through loud and clear. *Bone Machine* ♫♫♫♫ (Island, 1992, prod. Tom Waits) ups

the clatter quotient even further, and the material is Waits's most harrowing ever, including "Earth Died Screaming," "Dirt in the Ground," and "Jesus Gonna Be Here." On his debut album, *Closing Time* ♫♫♫♫ (Asylum, 1973, prod. Jerry Yester), the singer may be sentimental in the way people are after a few too many cocktails, and his voice slightly ravaged (though not so much as it would get on later albums), yet songs such as "Ol' 55," "Midnight Lullabye," and "Martha" are so good they transcend his shortcomings. *Beautiful Maladies: The Best of the Island Years* ♫♫♫♫ (Island, 1998, prod. Tom Waits) credibly collects the cream of Waits's later work, including a couple of rare live tracks. But Waits's albums are usually best experienced straight, no chaser.

what to buy next: Many find Waits's monologue-laden live album *Nighthawks at the Diner* ♫♫♫♪ (Asylum, 1975, prod. Bones Howe) hopelessly schticky, but it's the album on which his early beatnik persona came into full flower, for good or ill. Waits tells hilarious tall tales and one-liners, cranks out some sidewalk sociology in verse form, and even performs a few songs—notably a memorable version of Red Sovine's trucker epic "Big Joe and Phantom 309." *Small Change* (Asylum, 1976, prod. Bones Howe) kicks off with the syrupy yet effective "Tom Traubert's Blues," but things pick up fast with "Step Right Up," which finds Waits improvising a huckster's jive at a mile a minute. *Anthology of Tom Waits* ♫♫♫♫ (Asylum, 1985, prod. Jerry Yester, Bones Howe) offers a serviceable selection of Waits's years on Asylum, but there are too many omissions to make it essential.

what to avoid: *The Early Years* ♫♫ (Bizarre/Straight, 1991, prod. Bob Duffey) includes four songs that Waits re-recorded for *Closing Time*, but it's ultimately for curiosity seekers and die-hard fans only—as is *The Early Years, Volume 2* ♫♫ (Bizarre/Straight, 1992, prod. Bob Duffey).

the rest:
The Heart of Saturday Night ♫♫♫ (Asylum, 1974)
Foreign Affairs ♫♫♫ (Asylum, 1977)
Blue Valentine ♫♫♫ (Asylum, 1978)
Heart Attack and Vine ♫♫♫♫ (Asylum, 1980)
Franks Wild Years ♫♫♫♫ (Island, 1987)
Big Time ♫♫♫♪ (Island, 1988)
Night on Earth (Soundtrack) ♫♫♫ (Island, 1992)
The Black Rider ♫♫♫ (Island, 1993)

worth searching for: The soundtrack from Francis Ford Coppola's *One from the Heart* (Columbia, 1982, prod. Bones Howe) pairs Waits's gutter growl against the honeyed crooning of country-music chanteuse Crystal Gayle—a terrible idea on paper, perhaps, but magic on disc.

influences:

◀◀ Chet Baker, Charles Bukowski, Captain Beefheart, Howlin' Wolf

▶▶ Rickie Lee Jones, Beck, Soul Coughing, Holly Cole

Daniel Durchholz

Dave Wakeling

See: The English Beat

Rick Wakeman

Born May 18, 1949, in London, England.

Like his on-again, off-again band Yes, keyboardist Rick Wakeman is the type of artist you either love or hate. In documentaries of '70s music, whenever the narrators start saying things such as "and as progressive rock became more bloated, punk rock rose up to tear it down," you'll almost always see images of Wakeman, dressed in a long robe, standing behind walls of keyboards. If that image of Wakeman makes you want to hide behind stacks of Ramones records, you probably won't be a fan of his solo material. But if your reaction is, "What's wrong with that?" you may want to search out some of Wakeman's solo material—but probably not all of it. It should be mentioned that Wakeman's contributions to certain Yes albums, notably *Fragile, Close to the Edge, Tales from Topographic Oceans*, and *Going for the One*, were considerable, and he also played on such classic albums as David Bowie's *Space Oddity, Hunky Dory*, and *The Man Who Sold the World*, as well as Black Sabbath's *Sabbath Bloody Sabbath* and Elton John's *Madman across the Water*—not to mention his co-starring role in the critically maligned early '90s Yes reunion venture, Anderson, Bruford, Wakeman, and Howe.

what to buy: *The Six Wives of Henry VIII* ♪♪♪ (A&M, 1973, prod. Rick Wakeman) and *Journey to the Centre of the Earth* ♪♪♪ (A&M, 1974, prod. Rick Wakeman), Wakeman's first two solo albums, are also his most listenable projects.

what to avoid: *Greatest Hits* **woof!** (Herald Records, 1994, prod. Rick Wakeman) is a two-CD set of new versions of Wakeman "hits." One disc features him performing new-age instrumental versions of Yes songs, and the other disc has new versions of his own solo material, none of which could really be called hits.

the rest:
The Myths and Legends of King Arthur and the Knights of the Round Table ♪♪ (A&M, 1975)
Lisztomania ♪ (A&M, 1975)
No Earthly Connection ♪♪ (A&M, 1976)
White Rock ♪♪ (A&M, 1977)
Criminal Record ♪♪ (A&M, 1977)
Rhapsodies ♪♪ (A&M, 1979)
The Burning ♪ (Varese Sarabande, 1981)
1984 ♪♪ (Griffin, 1981)
Rock 'N Roll Prophet ♪ (Moon, 1982)

Cost of Living ♪ (Charisan, 1983)
G'Ole! ♪ (Charisan, 1983)
Black Knights in the Court of Ferdinand IV ♪ (Ambient Music, 1984)
Silent Knights ♪ (TBG/President Records, 1985)
Live at the Hammersmith ♪♪ (TBG/President Records, 1985)
Country Airs ♪ (Coda, 1986)
Crimes of Passion ♪♪ (TBG/President Records, 1986)
The Gospels ♪ (Stylus Music, 1987)
Family Album ♪ (President Records, 1987)
Time Machine ♪ (President Records, 1988)
A Suite of Gods ♪ (Relativity, 1988)
Zodiaque ♪ (Relativity, 1989)
Sea Airs ♡ (President Records, 1989)
In the Beginning ♪ (ASAPH Records, 1990)
Phantom Powers ♡ (Ambient Records, 1990)
Aspirant Sunrise ♡ (Roi Digital Records, 1990)
Aspirant Sunset ♡ (Ambient Records, 1990)
Aspirant Sunshadows ♡ (Ambient Records, 1991)
The Classical Connection ♪♪ (Ambient Records, 1991)
2000 AD into the Future ♡ (Ambient Records, 1991)
Soft Sword ♡ (Roi Digital Records, 1991)
African Bach ♪♪ (Quarto Records, 1991)
The Private Collection ♡ (Roi Digital Records, 1991)
Country Airs ♡ (President Records, 1992)
The Classical Connection II ♪ (Ambient Records, 1993)
The Heritage Suite ♡ (President Records, 1993)
No Expense Shared ♡ (President Records, 1993)
Light up the Sky ♡ (President Records, 1994)
Almost Live in Europe ♪ (Griffin, 1995)
The Piano Album ♪♪ (Castle Records, 1995)
The Seven Wonders of the World ♡ (President Records, 1996)
Fields of Green ♡ (Griffin, 1996)
The King Biscuit Flower Hour Presents Rick Wakeman ♪♪ (KBFH, 1996)

influences:
◀◀ Brahms, Beethoven, Bach, Yes, the Beatles, the Who

▶▶ Vangelis, Yanni, John Tesh

see also: *Yes*

Brian Ives

The Walkabouts

Formed 1984, in Seattle, WA.

Chris Eckman, vocals, guitar; Carla Torgerson, vocals, guitar, cello; Glenn Slater, keyboards; Grant Eckman, drums (1984–93); Terri Moeller, drums (1993–present); Michael Wells, bass (1986–96); Baker Saunders, bass (1996–present).

Before Uncle Tupelo burst on the scene in the late '80s with their patented brand of country-flavored punk, there were the Walkabouts, a Seattle outfit intent on bringing the American folk idiom into rock music. As far back as 1984, Chris Eckman, Carla Torgerson, and company were experimenting with mandolin, fiddle, and pedal steel in a rock context, blending their dark vision of electric music with an equally bleak country perspective; imagine the Carter Family coming of age in grunge-era Seattle. Led by Torgerson's and Eckman's dueling vocal parts, usually singing of backwoods tragedies or some other rural misery, the Walkabouts refined their sound by the early '90s to become one of the underground's most acclaimed, and unfortunately, one of its most overlooked, bands. Buttressed by Eckman's hefty electric guitar sound and the band's riveting chord changes, the Walkabouts had everything it took to become a premier alternative-rock band. All, that is, but good timing. By the time the band had hit its stride with records like *Scavenger* and *New West Motel*, grunge had become Seattle's dominant idiom, and the Walkabouts' Crazy Horse–meets–Velvet Underground racket was left out in the rain. But while their deal with Sub Pop's American division soured due to poor domestic sales, the label's European division hung on to the band, and their following grew steadily on the Continent. Between 1993 and 1995, the Walkabouts issued seven recordings overseas—three studio albums by the band, a limited-edition live collection, and three more releases by the duo of Chris & Carla. An impressive run, but had the band emerged a few years later with the same sound, the Walkabouts would be as essential stateside as they are abroad.

what to buy: The entire extant catalog of the band qualifies as essential listening, though a good place to start is *New West Motel* ♫♫♫♫ (Cargo/Creative Man, 1993, prod. Ed Brooks, the Walkabouts), which contains their cover of Townes Van Zandt's "Snake Mountain Blues" and the scorching "Drag This River." Also don't hesitate to pick up the inspired *Setting the Woods on Fire* ♫♫♫♫ (Cargo, 1994, prod. Ed Brooks, the Walkabouts). If that's not enough, go back to their Sub Pop debut, *Scavenger* ♫♫♫♫ (Sub Pop, 1991, prod. Gary Smith), a set that includes guest appearances by Natalie Merchant on the exquisite "Where the Deep Water Goes," and Brian Eno (!) on "Train to Mercy."

what to buy next: The band's covers project, *Satisfied Mind* ♫♫♫♫ (Cargo/Creative Man/Sub Pop Germany, 1993, prod. the Walkabouts, Kevin Suggs), Includes songs by Nick Cave, Patti Smith, Gene Clark, Charlie Rich, the Carter Family, and the traditional "Will You Miss Me When I'm Gone."

the rest:
Cataract/Rag & Bone EP ♫♫♫♫ (Sub Pop, 1992)

worth searching for: *Devil's Road* (Virgin Import, 1996), recorded with the Warsaw Philharmonic, and *Nighttown* (Virgin Import, 1997) will be pricey, but the band is firing in that kind of sublime territory that few rock bands ever reach. Also don't pass by their import odds and sods collection *Death Valley Days: Lost Songs and Rarities, 1985–1995* (Virgin Import, 1996), which is essential at any cost.

influences:

◄◄ Velvet Underground, Neil Young & Crazy Horse, Hank Williams, the Carter Family.

►► Uncle Tupelo, Whiskeytown, 16 Horsepower

Bob Gulla

Junior Walker & the All-Stars

Formed 1964, in Detroit, MI.

Original members: Junior Walker (born Oscar G. Mixon, a.k.a. Autry DeWalt III, June 14, 1931, in Blytheville, AR; died December 23, 1995, in Battle Creek, MI), tenor sax, vocals; Vic Thomas, keyboards; Willie Woods, guitar; James Graves, drums.

Mixing southern fatback funk with gritty vocals and hard-blowing tenor sax straight from the roadhouse, Arkansas-born Junior Walker became an unlikely mid-'60s star at Motown. His wasn't the assembly-line "Sound of Young America" that Berry Gordy had envisioned: In the beginning, Junior & the All Stars' groove was rawer and raunchier than anything else on the label (their single, "Shoot Your Shot," was banned from the airwaves during the Detroit riots in the summer of 1967). The group had immediate success with a series of classic singles—"Shotgun" and "Road Runner" among them—that established Walker, along with King Curtis and New Orleans' Lee Allen, as one of the legends of rock 'n' roll sax. Though he never again reached the frenetic heights of those early singles, Walker enjoyed a successful career with Motown well into the 1970s, recording more mainstream fare such as "What Does It Take" and "These Eyes." He continued to play and tour until his death in 1995.

what to buy: One of the most influential R&B albums of the '60s is *Shotgun* ♫♫♫♫ (Motown, 1965, prod. Berry Gordy, Lawrence Horn). The first side alone includes "Road Runner," "Shotgun," "Shake and Fingerpop," "Shoot Your Shot," and the much-covered, moody instrumental "Cleo's Mood." Aside from James Brown's band, this was the tightest, most raucous funk outfit around during the mid-1960s. For a complete career overview, *Nothing but Soul: The Singles (1962–1983)* ♫♫♫♫ (Motown, 1994, prod. various) contains all the essential early singles, as well as more polished later hits like "What Does It Take," "Do You See My Love," "These Eyes," and "Way Back Home."

what to buy next: For a taste of Walker's late 1960s live shows, check out *Junior Walker & the All-Stars—Live!* ♫♫♫ (Motown, 1969).

what to avoid: There are numerous and needlessly duplicated "best-of" sets Motown has churned out over the years; there are currently six Junior Walker "greatest hits" collections on CD. Stick with *Nothing but Soul*.

the rest:
Road Runner 🎵🎵🎵 (Motown, 1966)
Gotta Hold on to This Feeling 🎵🎵🎵 (Motown, 1967)
Home Cookin' 🎵🎵🎵 (Motown, 1968)
The Ultimate Collection 🎵🎵🎵🎵 (Motown, 1997)

worth searching for: It's worth digging for an original vinyl pressing of the *Shotgun* album—a strong argument for the sonic superiority of the LP vs. the CD.

influences:

◀◀ Illinois Jacquet, Louis Jordan, Coleman Hawkins, Ray Charles

▶▶ Maceo Parker, Morphine, Prince, David Sanborn

Doug Pippin

The Walker Brothers /Scott Walker

Formed 1964, in London, England. Disbanded 1968. Re-formed 1975.

John Maus, vocals, guitars; Scott Engel, bass, vocals, guitars; Gary Leeds, drums, vocals.

Not a duo, not a Walker in sight, and definitely not British, the Walker Brothers—Americans John Maus, Scott Engel, and Gary Leeds—found sudden fame in the midst of British pop mania of the mid-'6os. Lush production and rich vocals made for a romantic swoon, and "The Sun Ain't Gonna Shine (Anymore)" and "Make It Easy on Yourself" are two certified and worthy hits from the era. Although success was short-lived, Scott Walker (Engel) had a fairly successful solo career in England through the '70s.

what to buy: *Anthology* 🎵🎵🎵🎵 (One Way, 1995, prod. various) is the Walker Brothers album available at the moment, and its 15 songs do a good job of preserving the pop specialness during the group's short tenure.

what to buy next: *It's Raining Today: The Scott Walker Story (1967–70)* 🎵🎵🎵🎵 (Razor & Tie, 1996, prod. various) preserves the height of Scott Walker's solo career.

worth searching for: An excellent overview of the Walker Brothers' hits period can also be found on the German import *Collection* (Musicrama, 1997, prod. various), which includes "The Sun Ain't Gonna Shine (Anymore)" and an interesting version of Wilson Pickett's soul classic, "Land of 1,000 Dances" (but not the group's first hit, "Make It Easy on Yourself").

solo outings:
Scott Walker:
Til the Band Comes In 🎵🎵🎵 (1970/Beat Goes On, 1996)
Tilt 🎵🎵🎵 (Drag City, 1997)

influences:

◀◀ The Beatles, the Standells, Phil Spector, the Crystals

▶▶ Spice Girls, Oasis, Wilson Phillips

Patrick McCarty and Gary Graff

Wall of Voodoo /Stan Ridgway

Formed 1978, in Los Angeles, CA. Disbanded 1989.

Stanard Ridgway, vocals, keyboards, harmonica (1978–83); Marc Moreland, guitar; Chas T. Gray, keyboards, bass, vocals; Bruce Moreland, bass, keyboards (1978–81, 1984–89); Joe Nanini, drums, percussion, vocals (1978–83); Andy Prieboy, vocals, keyboards (1983–89); Ned Leukhardt, drums, percussion (1983–89).

With a sound that combined Devo and Ennio Morricone with frontman Stan Ridgway's sarcastic, sardonic delivery, Wall of Voodoo was (with the original lineup) a West-Coast film-noir treat. Percussionist Joe Nanini was reputedly a former junk dealer, and he banged on a variety of items while an antique rhythm machine played along. Keyboardist Chas T. Gray seemingly used only about four of his fingers, often employing the arpeggio that is featured in the group's lone hit, "Mexican Radio." Marc Moreland generally stayed on the top strings of his guitar to add to the spaghetti-western simplicity that Wall of Voodoo extolled. Ridgway's songs were like B-movie scripts, paintings of losers and wanderers that likely embodied the band. The less said about Andy Prieboy (his replacement and imitator) the better. More unlikely pop stars you'd be hard pressed to find, however, as no member of the band was easy on the eyes.

what to buy: *Call of the West* 🎵🎵🎵🎵 (I.R.S., 1982, prod. Richard Mazda), notable for containing the still-popular hit "Mexican Radio," is the group's high point. Having refined its atonal, clattering sound to include melodies, *Call of the West* is a neat time capsule of Wall of Voodoo. Showcasing the band at what they do best, the album contains the epic title song travelogue, the gloomy "Factory," and a noirish TV news intro for "On Interstate 15."

what to buy next: For fans, *Dark Continent* 🎵🎵🎵🎵 (I.R.S., 1981, prod. Jim Hill, Paul McKenna, Wall of Voodoo) is likely the favorite. Ridgway is at his cynical, side-of-mouth singing peak, with his bleak tales of revolution, dead-end jobs, and angst. The band provides a stark, biting sound in accompaniment, where the rhythm machine is nearly the lead instrument. A live version of the record's "Back in Flesh," with a lame rewording of an expletive for a PG audience, was included in the I.R.S. compilation *Urgh, a Music War*.

what to avoid: Basically anything after Ridgway and Nanini left should be left alone; *Seven Days in Sammy's Town* 🎵🎵 (I.R.S.,

1985, prod. Ian Broudie) is inexplicably still in print. Prieboy is subtraction by addition, as his low-budget imitation of his predecessor simply makes those who stuck around look stupid.

the rest:
The Index Masters &&&& (Index/IRS, 1980/Restless, 1991)

worth searching for: *Granma's House* (I.R.S., 1984, prod. various) is an import that wisely recaps only the Ridgway years. Coolly ignoring chronological order of the tracks in sequence, this set is crucial for admirers and a good purchase for even the casually interested. The "hits" are all here, including the nervy cover of Johnny Cash's "Ring of Fire."

solo outings:
Stan Ridgway:
Mosquitos && (Geffen, 1989/1997)
Songs That Made This Country Great &&& (I.R.S., 1992)
Black Diamond &&& (Birdcage, 1995)
(With Drywall) *Work the Dumb Oracle* && (I.R.S., 1995)

Andy Prieboy:
. . . Upon My Wicked Son && (Dr. Dream, 1990)
Montezuma Was a Man of Faith & (Dr. Dream EP, 1991)
Sins of Our Fathers && (Dr. Dream, 1991)

influences:
◀◀ Ennio Morricone, Johnny Cash, X, Devo, Hugo Montenegro, Kraftwerk, Tom Waits, Leonard Cohen, the Residents

▶▶ Oingo Boingo, the Refreshments, Soul Coughing

Barry M. Prickett

The Wallflowers

Formed 1990, in Los Angeles, CA.

Jakob Dylan, vocals, guitar; Rami Jaffee, piano, organ; Barrie Maguire, bass (1990–93); Peter Yanowitz, drums (1990–93); Tobi Miller, guitar (1990–95); Michael Ward, guitar (1995–present); Greg Richling, bass (1993–present); Mario Calire, drums (1995–present).

The Wallflowers were the sleeper surprise hit of 1997, eventually touted as the best "new" band of the year. Trouble is, the lads have been around since the turn of the decade and had already released an album that nobody paid much attention to. When the world decided to embrace the band's organic authenticity and dense dramatic overtones, Jakob Dylan (yes, *his* son) became the year's unlikely pinup idol, a guarded songwriter whose image isn't so much titillating as it is weary. That weariness seeps through the pores of the entire band, which seems much more downtrodden than their youth might suggest.

what to buy: A lengthy disappearance from the public eye (due to label and lineup changes) proved fruitful, as the band displays signficant growth on *Bringing down the Horse* &&&& (Interscope, 1996, prod. T-Bone Burnett). From the opening bars

WHAT ALBUM CHANGED YOUR LIFE?

There are some that I consider to be the heaviest influences on me. Van Morrison's *T.B. Sheets* can always turn me inside-out. When I think about rock 'n' roll, I think about *London Calling* by the Clash; I think that's what it should be like. And when I think of songs, maybe I think of Charlie Rich or I think of Hank Williams or something. There's something you take from all different people.

Jakob Dylan (of the Wallflowers)

on the sultry groove of "One Headlight" on, it's a fully realized return. A tighter, cleaner sound serves the band well, as does Dylan's songwriting, which appears to be just hitting its stride.

what to buy next: The self-titled debut, *The Wallflowers* &&& (Virgin, 1992, prod. various), is a sprawling and indulgent snapshot recorded live in the studio. With many of the songs clocking in at epic length, the near 70-minute total becomes a test of one's attention span. The more concise and sturdy songs such as "Ashes to Ashes," "Sugarfoot," and "Asleep at the Wheel" make the case for further inspection.

worth searching for: The Wallflowers' reverent rendition of David Bowie's "Heroes" was the first single from the modern rock all-star soundtrack for *Godzilla* (Epic/Sony Music Soundtrax, 1998, prod. various).

influences:
◀◀ The Band, Neil Young, the Clash

Allan Orski

Joe Walsh
/The James Gang
/Barnstorm

Born November 20, 1947, in Wichita, KS.

Part guitar ace and part court jester, Joe Walsh is one of the

Jakob Dylan of the Wallflowers (© Ken Settle)

many unique personalities rock 'n' roll has produced. He's scored hits on his own and with every band he's been in, from the James Gang to the Eagles. And his wobbly slide guitar signature has been hooked for sessions by Steve Winwood, B.B. King, Ringo Starr, Bob Seger, Richard Marx, and Wilson Philips. Walsh is capable of writing some terrific songs ("Rocky Mountain Way," "Walk Away," "Help Me through the Night," "Turn to Stone") but too often he lets his comic persona get the best of him, sometimes to the detriment of the music.

what to buy: Walsh did right by *Look What I Did: The Joe Walsh Anthology* 𝄞𝄞𝄞𝄞 (MCA, 1995, prod. various). While his individual albums run the gamut from inconsistent to wretched, this 34-song set snares the best from James Gang, Barnstorm, and his solo albums, showing both the fluid rocker and the rock 'n' roll funny man. The only glaring deletion is his taut rocker "In the City," which he recorded for *The Warriors* soundtrack and for the Eagles' *The Long Run* album. *Little Did He Know* 𝄞𝄞𝄞𝄞 (MCA, 1997, prod. various) is a truncated single-disc collection that, with its comparative brevity, makes an even stronger case for Walsh's virtues.

what to buy next: Not much, really. *The Smoker You Drink, the Player You Get* 𝄞𝄞𝄞 (ABC/Dunhill, 1973, prod. Joe Walsh, Bill Szymczyk) is Barnstorm's defining moment, housing hot tracks such as "Rocky Mountain Way" and "Meadows." Humor dominates on *But Seriously Folks* 𝄞𝄞𝄞 (Asylum, 1978, prod. Bill Szymczyk)—presumably because Walsh's more serious music was being made with the Eagles—but at least the jokes, particularly "Life's Been Good," are funny.

what to avoid: Despite the popular title track, *Ordinary Average Guy* **woof!** (Pyramid/Epic 1991) is a bottom-feeder on which Walsh seems to have run out of ideas on all fronts.

the rest:
Joe Walsh:
So What 𝄞𝄞𝄞 (ABC/Dunhill, 1975)
You Can't Argue with a Sick Mind 𝄞𝄞𝄞 (ABC, 1976)
There Goes the Neighborhood 𝄞𝄞 (Asylum, 1981)
You Bought It . . . You Name It 𝄞𝄞 (Warner Bros., 1983)
The Confessor 𝄞𝄞 (Warner Bros., 1985)
Got Any Gum? 𝄞𝄞 (Warner Bros., 1987)
(With Albert Collins and Etta James) *Jump the Blues* 𝄞𝄞 (Verve, 1989)
Songs for a Dying Planet 𝄞 (Pyramid/Epic, 1992)
Robocop: The Series (Soundtrack) 𝄞𝄞 (Pyramid, 1995)

The James Gang:
Yer Album 𝄞𝄞𝄞 (Bluesay, 1968)
Rides Again 𝄞𝄞𝄞 (ABC/Dunhill, 1970)
Thirds 𝄞𝄞 (ABC/Dunhill, 1970)
Live at Carnegie Hall 𝄞𝄞 (ABC/Dunhill, 1971)

Barnstorm:
Barnstorm 𝄞𝄞 (ABC/Dunhill, 1972)

influences:
◀◀ Chuck Berry, B.B. King, Albert Collins, T-Bone Walker, Pete Townshend, Keith Richards, Chet Atkins

▶▶ Georgia Satellites, Lynyrd Skynyrd, .38 Special, Brother Cane

see also: *The Eagles*

Gary Graff

Jamie Walters

Born James Walters, June 1969, in Boston, MA.

Influenced by Neil Young and Van Morrison, Jamie Walters picked up the guitar at age 12. By high school, he was kicking around in a rock band that gigged in the school. The multiple-tattooed Walters quickly switched gears and turned toward Boston's hardcore scene and, as a 17-year-old college freshman, joined a punk band. That too had a short run; in 1991 he left school and moved west to pursue a career in filmmaking. Shortly thereafter, he landed a role opposite John Travolta in the 1991 movie *Shout* and subsequently joined the cast of the Fox TV show *The Heights*. Little did he know that would boost his career in music as well. In 1992, Walters's song "How Do You Talk to an Angel" from *The Heights* soundtrack dethroned Boyz II Men's record-breaking "End of the Road" reign at #1. Two years later he joined the cast of *Beverly Hills 90210* as Ray Pruit, a musician (what else?) who was also the abusive boyfriend of Donna (Tori Spelling). Although he was frustrated with being compared to his character, Walters used a few seasons of *90210* as a springboard for his music career.

what to buy: Walters opted for a stripped-down, lightly produced approach with *Ride* 𝄞𝄞𝄞 (Atlantic Records, 1997, prod. Steve Tyrell). The country-flavored roots rock song "Reckless" is a good indication of what the rest of the album sounds like; it's confident and it shows in the lyrics: "It looks like I really led myself astray/And even I don't believe half the things I say." The Matthew Sweet–endorsed cover of "Winona" is right on. And "I'd Do Anything for You," which also carries a pronounced country influence, could serve as part two to "Hold On," which appears on his debut.

what to buy next: Listening to *Jamie Walters* 𝄞𝄞𝄞 (Atlantic Records, 1994, prod. Steve Tyrell), you'd never believe this is the product of a guy who gigged with punk bands. The lyrics are stereotypical pop but his intentions are well meaning. Laced with the twinklings of a Hammond B-3 organ, "Hold On" is an honest portrayal of a supportive boyfriend: "Did you call on every saint you know/But still you feel like you're on your own/Can you see through your tears/I will always be here." Fellow Fox TV thespian Vonda Shepard, who found fame with the *Ally McBeal* soundtrack, joins Walters in harmony on the ballad "The Distance." Dr. John lends his vocals to the bluesy "Release Me."

influences:

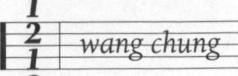 Rick Springfield, Matthew Sweet

Christina Fuoco

Wang Chung

Formed as Huang Chung, 1982, in London, England.

Jack Hues, vocals, keyboards, guitar; Nick Feldman, bass, keyboards, vocals; Darren Costin, drums, percussion, keyboards (1982–84).

The catchy "Dance Hall Days" made a big splash in 1984, with its awkward simplicity, deceptively sinister lyrics, and sanitized synthesizer hooks. Along with its airs of pomposity, it neatly captures the '80s—at least the part of the '80s saluted in today's "retro flashback" radio shows and on CD compilations among Kajagoogoo, Naked Eyes, and Dexy's Midnight Runners.

what to buy: The soundtrack for *To Live and Die in L.A.* 𝄢𝄢𝄢𝄢 (Geffen, 1984, prod. Wang Chung) finds the band playing above its own mediocre level. Besides the fine title track, Wang Chung's best song, the album blends atmospheric electronics into a chilly picture of L.A.'s underside. It's a tense and convincing album that successfully avoids most of singer Jack Hues's arty ambitions.

what to buy next: *Everybody Wang Chung Tonight: Wang Chung's Greatest Hits* 𝄢𝄢𝄢 (Geffen, 1997, prod. various) collects both good ("To Live and Die in L.A.") and bad ("Everybody Have Fun Tonight") material, plus the new song "Space Junk" and a remix of "Dance Hall Days." Also, though it sounds dated today, *Points on the Curve* 𝄢𝄢𝄢 (Geffen, 1983) is notable for the original version of "Dance Hall Days."

what to avoid: *Mosaic* 𝄢𝄢 (Geffen, 1986) isn't the band's worst album, but it contains Wang Chung's most insufferable pop hit, the maddening "Everybody Have Fun Tonight," and sounds ridiculous removed from its '80s context.

influences:

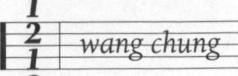 Human League, Men Without Hats, Cyndi Lauper, Gary Numan, the Cars

▶▶ Right Said Fred, Wham!, RuPaul

Allan Orski

The Wannabes

Formed 1988, in Austin, TX.

Jennings Crawford, vocals, guitar; Kevin Carney, vocals, guitar; Hunter Darby, vocals, bass; Thad Swiderski, drums.

Behind the heaps of so-called alterna-power pop bands clog-

ging up college charts and buzz bins with cookie-cutter angst lurk the Wannabes. The band displays a surging rock dynamic in a pop context that packs a melodic wallop where others merely whimper. But with the lamented demise of Austin's Dejadisc Records, the Wannabes have had trouble spreading the good news. And as the band rarely ventures outside of its homebase, it's likely to remain in the shadows.

what to buy: *Popsucker* 𝄢𝄢𝄢𝄢 (Dejadisc, 1995, prod. John Croslin) is a watershed of post-punk prowess. The congenial attack is immediately arresting, powered by a sure-fire melodic sense that soars over the distortion buzz. Packed with strong tunes, from the reeling search of "Keys" to the sneering whomp of "I Am God," there's also a hilarious desecration of ELO's "Don't Bring Me Down" (if it's possible to desecrate ELO).

what to buy next: *Mod Flower Cake* 𝄢𝄢𝄢 (Dejadisc, 1994, prod. John Croslin) is a sweet Telecaster crunch of a debut that displays the combined songwriting talents and vocal harmonies of this energetic bunch.

influences:

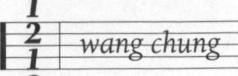 The Replacements, Velvet Crush, Tommy Keene

Allan Orski

War

Formed 1969, in Long Beach, CA.

Lonnie Jordan, vocals, keyboards, bass; Howard Scott, vocals, guitar; Charles Miller, woodwinds (1969–79); B.B. Dickerson, vocals, bass (1969–78); Harold Brown, drums, percussion (1969–83, 1993–present); Papa Dee Allen (died August 30, 1988, in Vallejo, CA), vocals, keyboards (1969–88); Lee Oskar, harmonica (1969–92); Pete Rosen (died 1969), bass (1969); Luther Rabb, bass (1978–84); Ricky Green, bass (1984–89); Pat Rizzo, reeds (1979–86); Ron Hammon, percussion (1979–present); Alice Tweed Smyth, vocals (1978–82); Tetsuya "Tex" Nakamura, harmonica (1993–present); Rae Valentine (born Harold Rae Brown Jr.), programming (1993–present); Kerry Campbell, saxophone (1993–present); Sal Rodriguez, drums, vocals (1993–present); Charles Green, reeds (1993–present).

Some of the best groove music ever laid down was done by War during the 1970s. With its Latin percussion and Angelino concerns, War was the southwest's flagship entry into the funk fray. And it represented it well with memorable jams such as "Low Rider," "The Cisco Kid," "The World Is a Ghetto," and more. War initially formed as a backup group for pro-footballer Deacon Jones and got the attention of U.K. rocker Eric Burdon, who was also looking for a backup group. Adding the Danish-born Lee Oskar, whose harmonica brought a trademark sound to the band, Burdon and War had a smash hit with "Spill the Wine." After two years and two albums, during which the group jammed with Jimi Hendrix the night before he died, the band bid Burdon adieu and went on to even greater accomplishments on its own. Despite numerous personnel changes and flagging sales—particularly during the 1980s—War kept touring until the hip-hop community began embracing its old records. The group then set up an innovative lend-lease kind of arrangement, ensuring that a) it was compensated for the use of its music, and b) that it would be able to cash in on the newfound exposure.

what to buy: *All Day Music* 𝄞𝄞𝄞𝄞 (United Artists, 1971/Avenue, 1994, prod. Jerry Goldstein, Chris Huston, War) is an awesome coming-of-age album, with "Slippin' into Darkness" leading the way. *Anthology, 1970–1994* 𝄞𝄞𝄞𝄞 (Avenue, 1994, prod. various) touches all the essential moments and includes a version of "Don't Let No One Get You Down" that was recorded with hip-hop's Hispanic MC's.

what to buy next: *The World Is a Ghetto* 𝄞𝄞𝄞𝄞 (United Artists, 1972/Avenue, 1992, prod. Jerry Goldstein, Lonnie Jordan, Howard Scott) has "The Cisco Kid" and the pointed, poignant title track as cornerstones for another superlative album. *Rap Declares War* 𝄞𝄞𝄞𝄞 (Avenue, 1992, prod. various) is a fascinating look—through the vantage point of one group's music—at how hip-hop cleverly appropriates and blends older sounds into its mix.

what to avoid: *The Best of War . . . and More* 𝄞 (Priority, 1987/Avenue, 1991, prod. various) is a skimpy, poorly chosen (no "The World Is a Ghetto"?) collection that deserves instant deletion from the catalog.

the rest:
(With Eric Burdon) *Eric Burdon Declares War* 𝄞𝄞𝄞 (MCA, 1970/Avenue, 1992)
(With Eric Burdon) *The Black-Man's Burdon* 𝄞𝄞 (MCA, 1970/Avenue, 1992)
War 𝄞𝄞𝄞 (United Artists, 1971/Avenue, 1992)
Deliver the Word 𝄞𝄞𝄞𝄞 (United Artists, 1973/Avenue, 1992)
War Live 𝄞𝄞𝄞𝄞 (United Artists, 1974/Avenue, 1992)
Why Can't We Be Friends? 𝄞𝄞𝄞 (United Artists, 1975/Avenue, 1992)
Greatest Hits 𝄞𝄞𝄞𝄞 (United Artists, 1976/Avenue, 1995)
(With Eric Burdon) *Love Is All Around (Early Recordings)* 𝄞𝄞 (ABC, 1976/Avenue, 1992)
Platinum Jazz 𝄞𝄞𝄞 (Blue Note, 1977/Avenue Jazz, 1993)
Galaxy 𝄞𝄞𝄞 (MCA, 1977/Avenue, 1993)
Outlaw 𝄞𝄞 (RCA, 1982/Avenue, 1995)
Peace Sign 𝄞𝄞𝄞𝄞 (Avenue, 1994)
(With Eric Burdon) *Best of Eric Burdon and War* 𝄞𝄞𝄞𝄞 (Avenue, 1995)
The Best of War . . . and More, Vol. 2 𝄞𝄞 (Avenue, 1996)
Coleccion Latina 𝄞𝄞𝄞 (Avenue/Rhino, 1997)

worth searching for: The late 1970s couplet *The Music Band* (MCA, 1979, prod. Jerry Goldstein, Lonnie Jordan, Howard Scott) and *The Music Band 2* (MCA, 1979, prod. Jerry Goldstein, Lonnie Jordan, Howard Scott) gave War a bit of a revival in the midst of its commercial doldrums.

influences:
◄◄ Sly & the Family Stone, Los Bravos
►► Groove Collective, Los Lobos

Lawrence Gabriel and Gary Graff

Jennifer Warnes

Born March 3, 1947, in Seattle, WA.

A former background singer, *Smothers Brothers Comedy Hour* regular, and soundtrack diva, Jennifer Warnes has lived to tell the tale. Her singing style through the years has remained appealingly understated, yet it has left her at the mercy of her material, which has ranged from superb to merely middling. After a couple of early hits, including the enduring "Right Time of the Night," Warnes hit it big with songs from a pair of popular films, "Up Where We Belong," sung with Joe Cocker, from *An Officer and a Gentleman*, and "(I've Had) The Time of My Life," a duet with Righteous Brother Bill Medley, from *Dirty Dancing*. While that paid the bills, Warnes's own albums revealed a taste for stronger stuff, notably rich interpretations of Leonard Cohen songs. Despite such triumphs as her album *Famous Blue Raincoat*, Warnes remains a generally underrated artist.

what to buy: *Famous Blue Raincoat: The Songs of Leonard Cohen* 𝄞𝄞𝄞𝄞 (Cypress, 1986/Private, 1991, prod. C. Roscoe Beck, Jennifer Warnes) is a stunning collection that makes Cohen's brooding material accessible without prettifying it too much. Stevie Ray Vaughan adds a tasty guitar solo to "First We Take Manhattan," and Cohen himself sits in on "Joan of Arc."

the rest:
Best of Jennifer Warnes 𝄞𝄞𝄞 (Arista, 1982)
The Hunter 𝄞𝄞𝄞𝄞 (Private, 1992)

influences:
◄◄ Leonard Cohen, Joe Cocker, John Prine
►► Indigo Girls, Mary Lou Lord

Daniel Durchholz

Warrant

Formed 1984, in Los Angeles, CA. Disbanded 1992. Reunited 1994.

Jani Lane (born John Patrick Oswald), vocals, guitar (1986–present); Eric Turner, guitar; Jerry Dixon, bass (1986–present); Rick Steir, guitar (1994–present); Bobby Borg, drums (1995–present); Steven Sweet, drums (1986–92); Joey Allen, guitar (1987–92); David White, keyboards (1994–present); James Kottak, drums (1994–95).

Warrant will forever be linked to the downfall of the '80s hard rock scene, which some dubbed the "hair metal" era. The band was actually formed in 1984 by guitarist Eric Turner, but the lineup that enjoyed success wasn't born until 1986, when Jani

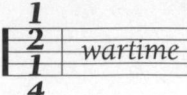

Lane took over the vocal duties. Two years later, Warrant was close to the top of the pop/rock world as MTV exposed its power ballad "Heaven" to the masses. Luckily, the group also had some bona fide party rock hits. As a live act, Warrant was tight and energetic, much better than its songwriting. But by the time the group wrote a "respectable" rock song, "Uncle Tom's Cabin," the pop-metal scene had started to overdose, and by the time the group released "Dog Eat Dog," Warrant and others of its ilk had been replaced by grunge kingpins such as Alice in Chains, though '80s nostalgia has given the group a new lease on life.

what to buy: *Dirty Rotten Filthy Stinkin' Rich* 𝄪𝄪𝄪 (Columbia, 1989, prod. Beau Hill) was neither groundbreaking nor sensitive, but it fit into the popular pop-metal party rock formula that worked for Poison and others. With songs such as the title track, "DRFSR," "Down Boys," and the power ballad "Heaven," Warrant garnered an adoring fan base and plenty of female attention, despite photos, songs, and videos that some interpreted as being degrading to women.

what to buy next: While *Dirty Rotten Filthy Stinkin' Rich* established the band as a force on MTV, 1990's *Cherry Pie* 𝄪𝄪𝄫 (Columbia, 1990, prod. Beau Hill) took that momentum and exploded out of the gate. The album quickly sold more than 2.5 million copies on the strength of the title track, the somewhat serious "Uncle Tom's Cabin," and the heartbreaking "I Saw Red." *The Best of Warrant* 𝄪𝄪𝄪 (Legacy, 1996, prod. various) is a reasonable sampler, though not as cohesive as *Dirty Rotten...*.

what to avoid: By the time grunge hit and '90s techno/industrial was coming into vogue, Warrant tried an about-face and changed to suit the times. *Ultraphobic* **woof!** (CMC, 1995/1998) was a bad move, period.

the rest:
Dog Eat Dog 𝄪𝄫 (Columbia/RoadRunner, 1992)
Belly to Belly, Vol. 1 𝄫 (CMC, 1996)
Live, '86–'97 𝄫 (CMC, 1997)

influences:
◀◀ Kiss, Dokken, Poison, Mötley Crüe

▶▶ D Generation, Ugly Kid Joe

Darren Davis

Wartime
See: Henry Rollins

Was (Not Was)
Formed 1980, in Detroit, MI. Disbanded 1993.

Don Fagenson (a.k.a. Don Was), bass, etc.; David Weiss (a.k.a. David Was), reeds, etc.; Sweet Pea Atkinson, vocals; Sir Harry Bowens, vocals; Donald Ray Mitchell, vocals; others.

Utterly unclassifiable, Was (Not Was) is a combination studio project and rock/R&B/funk collective whose offbeat lyricism—mostly from Weiss—nods to beat culture, Frank Zappa, and Captain Beefheart. The Was brothers' anything-goes sensibility brought together a wildly eclectic group of guests for its albums, including Ozzy Osbourne, Frank Sinatra Jr., Iggy Pop, Mel Tormé, Leonard Cohen, Mitch Ryder, Marshall Crenshaw, and members of the Knack, the MC5, Parliament-Funkadelic, and Wild Cherry. A Top 10 hit with "Walk the Dinosaur" in 1989 took the group on the road, but Fagenson's Grammy-winning production work—his credits include the Rolling Stones, Bonnie Raitt, Bob Dylan, the B-52's, Willie Nelson, Ringo Starr, and the Highwaymen—put the group on ice, while Weiss went on to his own production career, as well as commercial work. By the early 1990s Was (Not Was) was on an extended hiatus—though there was reunion talk during 1997 and 1998—while Don Was stayed busy with assorted production duties and David Was helmed two albums of music for *The X-Files* TV show and movie.

what to buy: *What up, Dog?* 𝄪𝄪𝄪𝄪 (Chrysalis, 1988, prod. Don Was, David Was) is Was (Not Was)'s shining moment. The guest list was interesting—Sinatra Jr. and a co-writing credit to Elvis Costello—but this is the album where a true band identity surfaced, thanks to the singers and to an ace group of Detroit players. The songwriting is solid, particularly on "Spy in the House of Love" and "Boy's Gone Crazy," and Weiss's psycho tone-poem, "Dad, I'm in Jail," is tremendous comedy.

what to buy next: Either of *Dog's* predecessors—*Was (Not Was)* 𝄪𝄪𝄪 (Ze/Island, 1981, prod. Don Was, David Was) and *Born to Laugh at Tornadoes* 𝄪𝄪𝄪 (Ze/Geffen, 1983, prod. Don Was, David Was)—are worthwhile. The latter is guest-drenched; check out Osbourne rapping on "Shake Your Head." The first album is a bit funkier and more subversive, with dance club hits such as "Out Come the Freaks" and "Tell Me That I'm Dreaming."

what to avoid: *Are You Okay?* 𝄪𝄪𝄪 (Chrysalis, 1990, prod. Don Was, David Was) isn't awful, but it's more convoluted than the group's other offerings—particularly a rapified version of the Temptations' "Papa Was a Rolling Stone"—and is therefore the last one to acquire.

worth searching for: *Hello, Dad . . . I'm in Jail* (Fontana, 1992, prod. Don Was, David Was) is a British best-of that captures the essential tracks and includes the updated "Shake Your Head," featuring Osbourne and actress Kim Basinger.

influences:
◀◀ 1960s classic rock, Motown, Stax, Parliament-Funkadelic, Duke Ellington, Charlie Parker, John Coltrane, various world musics

▶▶ 2 Skinnee Js, Red Hot Chili Peppers, Royal Crescent Mob

Gary Graff

The Waterboys

Formed 1981, in London, England. Disbanded 1993.

Mike Scott, vocals, guitar, piano, organ; Steve Wickham, fiddle, organ, vocals; Anthony Thistlethwaite, saxophone, mandolin, organ, harmonica; Colin Blakey, whistle, flute, organ, piano; Noel Bridgeman, drums, percussion; Jay Dee Daugherty, drums; Sharon Shannon, accordion, fiddle; Trevor Hutchinson, bass, bouzouki; Karl Wallinger, bass, keyboards; Roddy Lorimer, trumpet.

The history of the Waterboys is the story of Mike Scott's ever-evolving musical and spiritual quest. "I've always followed my heart or where my latest musical fascination is, which is rarely where popular trends have been going," says Scott. The band was characterized by a continually changing cast of musicians supporting Scott, with one anchor being the musical versatility of Anthony Thistlethwaite. The Waterboys originated the Big Music, an epic, sprawling, feverish sound of layered acoustic guitars, ecstatic horns, and charging, obscure, expansive poetics reminiscent of the myth making of Yeats and Blake. At its best, the music was transcendent, leading the listener into a new, exotic land brimming with imagery and feeling, and owed a debt to the earlier work of fellow shamans Patti Smith, Van Morrison, and Bruce Springsteen, as well as the Beatles. Scott then changed tactics for the band's fourth album, the astounding *Fisherman's Blues*, bringing his Celtic passions to the forefront and toning down the Big Music. That particular "raggle taggle" version of the band broke up after two albums; the Waterboys became Scott and a slew of session players, and music returned to harder guitar riffs, with disappointing results. The first solo outing by Scott is much closer to the spiritual essence he sought with *Fisherman's Blues*, and on the tour supporting that album, Scott promised that next time around, he'd return with a band. So perhaps a new generation of the Waterboys is just around the corner.

what to buy: Different eras of the Waterboys produced distinctly different music. Early Waterboys is best sampled on *A Pagan Place* &&&& (Chrysalis, 1984, prod. Mike Scott), featuring the strumming acoustic majesty of the title cut. *This Is the Sea* &&&&& (Chrysalis, 1985, prod. Mike Scott, Mick Glossop) is a fully realized epic that showcases the Scott-Wallinger partnership and includes the shimmering "This Is the Sea," "The Whole of the Moon," "Spirit," and "Old England." Late Waterboys is captured in all its glory on *Fisherman's Blues* &&&&& (Chrysalis, 1988, prod. John Dunford, Mike Scott), with its embrace of the Celtic tradition. Commencing with the luminous title cut, the album includes a stirring cover of Van Morrison's "Sweet Thing" and the last recorded song written by Scott and Wallinger (with Trevor Hutchinson), "World Party." A masterpiece from start to finish.

what to buy next: *Best of the Waterboys* &&&& (Chrysalis, 1991, prod. Mike Scott) is a good retrospective of the band, with the addition of "Killing My Heart," an early electric version of "When Ye Go Away," and a live take on "Old England." *The Secret Life of the Waterboys* &&&& (Chrysalis, 1994, prod. Mike Scott) is a collection of unreleased Waterboys studio recordings, radio sessions, live tracks, and "lost" B-sides recorded between 1981 and 1985.

what to avoid: *Dream Harder* && (Geffen, 1993, prod. Mike Scott, Bill Price) is a lackluster attempt to do the Waterboys without the Waterboys and is hopefully Scott's last attempt to become a guitar god.

the rest:
The Waterboys &&&&▽ (Ensign, 1983)
Room to Roam &&& (Ensign, 1990)
The Best of the Waterboys, '81–'90 &&&&▽ (Alliance, 1997)

worth searching for: A variety of CD singles and 12-inch releases exist, most prominently from the *Fisherman's Blues* era on forward. They include: *And a Bang on the Ear/Raggle Taggle Gipsy* (1989); *The Whole of the Moon/Golden Age Medley* (1991); *Fisherman's Blues/Medicine Bow* (1991); and *Bring 'Em All In* (with three previously unreleased songs), all on Chrysalis; and *The Return of Pan/Karma/Mister Powers* (Geffen, 1993).

solo outings:
Mike Scott:
Bring 'Em All In &&&& (Chrysalis, 1995)

Anthony Thistlethwaite:
Aesop Wrote a Fable &&& (Rolling Acres, 1993)

influences:
◀◀ Bob Dylan, Patti Smith, the Beatles, Bruce Springsteen, Van Morrison, the Chieftains

▶▶ U2, Sinéad O'Connor, World Party

see also: *World Party*

Martin Connors

Crystal Waters

Born 1964, in Philadelphia, PA.

Crystal Waters's "la da dee, la da dah" chorus, from her 1991 summer dance hit "Gypsy Woman (She's Homeless)," was intensely catchy, and it made this unknown Washington, D.C., singer-songwriter—the daughter of jazz musician Jr. Waters and niece of singer Ethel Waters—a star. Waters has at least as much dance-hall savvy as Paula Abdul, and she's a better lyricist, but she still hasn't been able to click for more than a hit or two per album. "100% Pure Love," a catchy song from her second album, hit #11 on the pop singles charts, but it was "I Believe I Love You," buried between mostly overproduced dance music on that same album, that truly showcased her talent. The song is a Stax-Motown–style soul classic, with perfect sound effects, a funky groove and a Janet Jackson–style delivery.

what to buy: The sophomore album *Storyteller* 𝄢𝄢𝄢 (Mercury, 1994, prod. Basement Boys) is full of much stronger songwriting, especially the wonderful "I Believe I Love You," but its electro-dance-funk production wears thin too fast.

what to buy next: Waters's debut, *Surprise* 𝄢𝄢 (Mercury, 1991, prod. Basement Boys), went gold on the strength of "Gypsy Woman," a story-song told from the perspective of a Washington, D.C., homeless woman.

the rest:
Crystal Waters 𝄢𝄢𝄢 (PolyGram, 1997)

influences:

◀◀ Diana Ross, Donna Summer, Janet Jackson

▶▶ TLC, En Vogue

Steve Knopper

Muddy Waters

Born McKinley Morganfield, April 4, 1915, in Rolling Fork, MS. Died April 30, 1983, in Chicago, IL.

"The blues had a baby," Muddy Waters sang in 1977, "and they named it rock and roll." It was *his* baby. Inspired by Robert Johnson, Son House, and other talented local bluesmen in his home state of Mississippi, the young McKinley Morganfield picked up an acoustic guitar and immediately established himself as a peer. Even as a young man, his voice was deep and charismatic; his untrained guitar tones on "Honey Bee" and "Rollin' Stone"—the latter inspired both the band and the Bob Dylan hit—sounded so new and out of the ordinary that they influenced such torch-carriers as Charlie Parker, Chuck Berry, Elvis Presley, and Keith Richards. At a time when pop music was still defined by George and Ira Gershwin, such "black music" was considered dirty and uncouth, and Waters's gravelly voice and forthright lyrics did little to combat this perception. He didn't earn his legend until the '50s, when he moved to Chicago and picked up an electric guitar. Recording for Chess Records, the label with the right owners at the right place at the right time, Waters developed a sharp, piercing blues sound that influenced generations of blues and rock players and launched the careers of harpist James Cotton and pianist Otis Spann, who both played in Waters's band. He reeled off countless classics—"Hoochie Coochie Man," "You Shook Me," "Got My Mojo Workin'," "Mannish Boy"—many written by Chess session bassist Willie Dixon. His career sagged slightly, and ironically, after Elvis Presley merged Waters's electric blues with Kentucky bluegrass music, but it picked up again when

the Rolling Stones began dropping his name. Waters performed with his protégés several times, including once at Chicago's still-thriving Checkerboard Lounge, and was a prominent figure in the '60s blues revival. In the '70s, he hooked up with guitar hero Johnny Winter and, playing his distinctive electric tones off Winter's spastic solos, found renewed creative power. He died in 1983 as perhaps the world's best-known and most influential bluesman. Others still base their entire career on the fact that they once played with him. And many thriving blues clubs, including Antone's in Austin, Texas, market themselves with huge pictures and T-shirts of Muddy Waters.

what to buy: It's tough to navigate Waters's 20-plus albums, many of which were released simply to promote a single or two, so the best starting point is the comprehensive career retrospective *The Chess Box* 𝄢𝄢𝄢𝄢 (MCA/Chess, 1989, prod. various), which has simply everything, plus the late critic Robert Palmer's must-read liner notes. Other worthwhile collections are *Muddy Waters: His Best, 1947–1955* 𝄢𝄢𝄢𝄢 (MCA/Chess, 1997, compilation prod. Andy McKaie) and *His Best, 1956–1964* 𝄢𝄢𝄢𝄢 (MCA/Chess, 1997, compilation prod. Andy McKaie), which include all the great stuff, from "Got My Mojo Workin'" to "Honey Bee." The *His Best* sets aren't quite as thorough as the box set, but they effectively replace *The Best of Muddy Waters* 𝄢𝄢𝄢𝄢 (MCA/Chess, 1958/1987, prod. various), which contains "I Can't Be Satisfied" and other studio tracks from 1948 to 1954, in the marketplace.

what to buy next: To build a good Waters collection, it's advisable to sample a key album from every phase of his career. *Down on Stovall's Plantation* 𝄢𝄢𝄢𝄢 (Testament, 1966, prod. Alan Lomax) is a collection of folklorist Alan Lomax's acoustic 1941 field recordings; the scholar was trying to find Robert Johnson in the Delta but failed, and was referred to the then-similar-sounding Waters instead. The '50s sides are best collected on *Trouble No More (Singles, 1955–1959)* 𝄢𝄢𝄢𝄢 (MCA/Chess, 1989, prod. various). Waters's '60s material is less spontaneous, though *The Real Folk Blues* 𝄢𝄢𝄢𝄢 (Chess, 1966/MCA/Chess, 1988, prod. Marshall Chess) contains "40 Days & 40 Nights" and "Mannish Boy," which influenced the Stones, Led Zeppelin, Bo Diddley, and every living bluesman. The better-known version of "Mannish Boy," at least the one rock radio stations still play from time to time, is from *Muddy Mississippi Waters Live* 𝄢𝄢𝄢𝄢 (Blue Sky, 1979, prod. Johnny Winter), a fiery collection with Winter's electric guitar smashing dangerously into Waters's confident, perfectly timed chiming notes and friendly vocal growl.

what to avoid: Even Waters put out some lemons, most notably *The Muddy Waters Woodstock Album* 𝄢 (MCA/Chess, 1975, prod. Henry Glover), which gives the legendary upstate New York town a bad name. And it's unclear, aside from archival purposes, why MCA decided to reissue *Electric Mud* ♫♪ (MCA/Chess, 1968/1996), which Waters himself admitted was an awkward attempt to cash in on psychedelic rock. He extends the jams so long you barely recognize the classics "I Just Want to Make Love to You" and "Mannish Boy," and the improvisation isn't particularly interesting. Plus, there's a ridiculous photo montage of Waters, his hair in curlers, getting a bad hipster hairdo.

the rest:

At Newport ♫♫♫♫ (MCA/Chess, 1960/1986)
Sings Big Bill Broonzy ♫♫♫♫ (MCA/Chess, 1960)
Folk Singer ♫♫♫♫ (MCA/Chess, 1964)
Muddy, Brass, and the Blues ♫♫ (MCA/Chess, 1966/1989)
Mud in Your Ear ♫♫♫ (MCA/Chess, 1967/1989)
More Real Folk Blues ♫♫♫♫ (MCA/Chess, 1967/1988)
Fathers and Sons ♫♫♫♫ (MCA/Chess, 1969)
They Call Me Muddy Waters ♫♫♫ (MCA/Chess, 1971/1990)
The London Muddy Waters Sessions ♫♫♫ (MCA/Chess, 1972/1989)
Can't Get No Grindin' ♫♫ (MCA/Chess, 1973/1990)
Hard Again ♫♫♫ (Blue Sky, 1977)
I'm Ready ♫♫♫ (Blue Sky, 1978)
Sweet Home Chicago ♫ (Quicksilver/Intermedia, 1982)
Muddy & the Wolf ♫♫ (MCA/Chess, 1982/1986)
Rolling Stone ♫♫♫ (MCA/Chess, 1982/1984)
Rare and Unissued ♫♫♫ (MCA/Chess, 1982/1991)

worth searching for: The two-on-one CD combination of *Folk Singer* and *Sings Bill Broonzy* (MCA/Chess, 1987), two of Waters's finest albums from the early '60s, is a nice collection if you can find it.

influences:

◀◀ Robert Johnson, Son House, Charley Patton

▶▶ Buddy Guy, Jimi Hendrix, Bob Dylan, the Rolling Stones, Led Zeppelin, PJ Harvey, Johnny Winter, Elvin Bishop, the Paul Butterfield Blues Band, the Allman Brothers Band, Eric Clapton

Steve Knopper

Roger Waters

See: Pink Floyd

Jack Waterson

See: Green on Red

Mike Watt

See: fIREHOSE

Weather Report

Formed 1970, in New York, NY. Disbanded 1985.

Josef Zawinul, keyboards; Wayne Shorter, saxophones; Miroslav Vitous, bass (1970–73); Alphonse Mouzon, drums (1970); Airto Moreira, percussion (1970); Eric Gravatt, drums (1971–72); Dom Um Romao, percussion (1971–73); Ishmael Wilburn, drums (1972); Andrew N. White III, bass, French horn (1973); Herschel Dwellingham, drums (1973); Muruga, percussion (1973); Alphonso Johnson, bass (1973–75); Alyrio Lima, drums (1974); Ndugu (Leon) Chancler, percussion (1974); Chester Thompson, drums (1975); Jaco Pastorius (died September 21, 1987), bass (1976–79); Alex Acuna, percussion (1976); Manola Badrena, percussion (1976); Peter Erskine, drums (1978–81); Victor Bailey, bass (1982–85); Jose Rossy, percussion (1982–85); Omar Hakim, drums (1982–85).

Led by Josef Zawinul and Wayne Shorter—both part of Miles Davis's landmark jazz-rock experiments during the late '60s—Weather Report was a visionary band that managed to infuse its high-voltage jazz with rock 'n' roll excitement and world-music exoticism. Unlike many fusion experiments that fizzled, Weather Report's sound was compelling and seemed to sweep the listener along, prompting Zawinul to dub it "parade music." The unique sound and accessibility quickly earned a following beyond normal jazz aficionados. Zawinul, classically trained on the piano in his native Austria, created a vibrant, full-bodied sound using layers of cutting-edge synthesizers, while the rhythm section built deep, complex foundations. Shorter, with his bebop jazz background, soared above and through the mix with sharp, angular saxophone lines. When the late Jaco Pastorius added his compositional skill and darting jazz-funk flourishes on fretless bass, Weather Report experienced its greatest commercial success, earning a gold record with 1977's *Heavy Weather* and the hit "Birdland."

what to buy: *Heavy Weather* ♫♫♫♫♫ (Columbia, 1977, prod. Josef Zawinul, Jaco Pastorius, Wayne Shorter) is a compelling blend of ebullience ("Birdland," "Teen Town") and beauty ("A Remark You Made," "Harlequin"). The energy level nears meltdown status on *Mysterious Traveler* ♫♫♫♫ (Columbia, 1974, prod. Josef Zawinul), with its adventurous title track and the mesmerizing "Nubian Sundance."

what to buy next: *Black Market* ♫♫♫♫ (Columbia, 1976, prod. Josef Zawinul, Jaco Pastorius) bristles with Latin and African rhythms and exotic melodies. The triumvirate of Zawinul-Shorter-Pastorius hits its compositional peak on *Mr. Gone* ♫♫♫♫ (Columbia, 1978, prod. Josef Zawinul, Jaco Pastorius), creating high drama with instrumental music.

what to avoid: It took a few albums for Weather Report to find its form amid all those influences, so the first two discs, *Weather Report* ♫♫ (Columbia, 1971, prod. Josef Zawinul, Wayne Shorter) and *I Sing the Body Electric* ♫♫ (Columbia, 1972, prod. Josef Zawinul, Wayne Shorter), offer too few glimpses into the magic ahead.

the rest:

Sweetnighter ♫♫♫ (Columbia, 1973)
Tale Spinnin' ♫♫ (Columbia, 1975)

8:30 🎵🎵 (Columbia, 1979)
Night Passages 🎵🎵🎵 (Columbia, 1980)
Procession 🎵🎵 (Columbia, 1983)
Domino Theory 🎵🎵🎵🎵 (Columbia, 1984)
Sportin' Life 🎵🎵🎵 (Columbia, 1985)
This Is This 🎵🎵🎵🎵 (Columbia, 1986)

worth searching for: Though Weather Report's best albums are unified pieces, a couple best-of collections allow for sampling of different periods in the group's evolution. Both Japan's *Star Box* (Sony, 1993, prod. various) and Britain's *Weather Report: The Collection* (Castle, 1990, prod. various) offer key tracks and good introductions to the group.

influences:

◄◄ Miles Davis, Charlie Parker, Dizzy Gillespie, John Coltrane

►► Full Circle, Herbie Hancock, Chick Corea, Steps Ahead

David Yonke

Jimmy Webb

Born August 15, 1946, in Elk City, OK.

Jimmy Webb's accomplishments as a songwriter span the worlds of rock, country, and pop music, and his songs have been recorded by a diverse lot, ranging from Glen Campbell, Art Garfunkel, and Frank Sinatra to Barbra Streisand and R.E.M. But he'll always be a hero to lounge lizards and Cheez Whiz connoisseurs for penning the bizarre and grandiose epic "MacArthur Park," a '60s chart hit for actor Richard Harris, and a '70s dance-floor triumph for disco diva Donna Summer. As a recording artist, Webb's accomplishments are far more modest. His voice is warm and intimate, but very limited, which has no doubt contributed to the commercial failure of nearly all of his albums, most of which are out of print. Generally, he has given his best material to others, and the work that appears on his own albums is perhaps more personal, but maddeningly erratic. Webb's place in history is assured, yet some enterprising record company needs to drive the point home with a collection of his best songs done by the artists that made them hits.

what to buy: Webb had to be dragged to the project, but he finally agreed to record an album of his songs with which others had massive hits. *Ten Easy Pieces* 🎵🎵🎵🎵 (Guardian, 1996, prod. Jay Landers) features simple, heartfelt arrangements of "Galveston," "Wichita Lineman," "All I Know," and "MacArthur Park," among others. Webb's singing is not up to that of the original artists, but the overall effect is that of studio-quality demos, or a private recital at an intimate gathering.

the rest:
Angel Heart 🎵🎵 (Columbia, 1982)
Suspending Disbelief 🎵🎵🎵 (Elektra, 1993)

worth searching for: Richard Harris's *A Tramp Shining* (MCA, 1993, prod. Jimmy Webb) is a re-release of the oddball classic from 1968, featuring the original version of "MacArthur Park" and other songs written by Webb.

influences:

◄◄ Elvis Presley, the Beatles, George & Ira Gershwin

►► Glen Campbell, the Fifth Dimension, Linda Ronstadt

Daniel Durchholz

The Wedding Present

Formed 1985, in Leeds, England.

David Gedge, vocals, guitar; Peter Solowka, guitar (1985–91); Paul Dorrington, guitar (1991–95); Simon Cleave, guitar (1996–present); Keith Gregory, bass (1985–93); Darren Belk, bass, guitar (1993–96); Jayne Lockley, bass, vocals (1995–present); Shaun Charman, drums (1985–88); Simon Smith, drums (1988–present); Hugh Kelly, drums (1995–96).

The Wedding Present has scored numerous hits in its homeland yet remains a cult rock band, its (waning) following confined to college campuses and indie rock circles. Though they are British, the Wedding Present's music is more similar to American indie rock than Britpop; in addition, the band shares the indie rock predilection for issuing and reissuing numerous limited-release EPs and albums in various formats on numerous labels, so as to encourage record collecting; in fact, in 1992 the group released a new single every month, each with an original A-side and B-side cover tune (and every one made the U.K. Top 30, tying the Guinness World Record previously set by Elvis Presley). Formed in Leeds by frontman David Gedge in 1985, the Weddoes—as the group is popularly called—was the "band of the moment" for about six months in Britain's fickle music press following the 1987 release of its debut album. Lineup problems have also plagued the band, though it's resolve seems strong even if interest isn't anymore.

what to buy: *Bizarro* 🎵🎵🎵 (RCA, 1989/Manifesto, 1996, prod. Chris Allison, Steve Albini) is perhaps the Weddoes finest hour, with the hooky "Brassneck" and "Kennedy" singles as well as the quirky nine-minute opus "Take Me!," which borrows a riff from the Velvet Underground's "What Goes On." The 1996 reissue on Manifesto adds the contents of the U.K.-only "Brassneck" single (engineered by Steve Albini), which includes a rougher, darker version of "Brassneck" as well as a cover of Pavement's "Box Elder."

what to buy next: The often discordant *Seamonsters* 🎵🎵🎵 (First Warning, 1991/Manifesto, 1996, prod. Steve Albini) is another strong effort by Gedge and company. It includes

"Dalliance," frequently voted by fans as their favorite Wedding Present song. *Watusi* 𝄞𝄞𝄞 (Island, 1994, prod. Steve Fisk) is even more strongly influenced by American indie rock, as evidenced by production work by Steve Fisk and a cameo appearance by Heather Lewis of Beat Happening. *George Best Plus* 𝄞𝄞𝄞 (Reception, 1987/Cooking Vinyl, 1997) is a reissue of the group's Smith-influenced, out-of-print 1987 debut LP *George Best* (named for a British soccer star), but adds nine tracks from their 1988 U.K.-only EPs *Nobody's Twisting Your Arm* and *Why Are You Being So Reasonable Now?*.

the rest:

Tommy 𝄞𝄞 (Reception, 1988/Cooking Vinyl, 1997)
Hit Parade I 𝄞𝄞 (First Warning, 1992/Manifesto, 1996)
Hit Parade II 𝄞𝄞 (First Warning, 1992/Manifesto, 1996)
Mini Plus 𝄞𝄞 (Cooking Vinyl, 1995)
Saturnalia 𝄞𝄞𝄞 (Cooking Vinyl, 1996)
The Wedding Present: John Peel Sessions, 1992–1995 N/A (Cooking Vinyl, 1998)

worth searching for: The now out-of-print U.S. reissue of *Seamonsters* on the First Warning label includes "Niagara," "Dan Dare," and "Fleshworld" from the U.K.-only "Dalliance" and "Lovenest" singles. Very dedicated Wedding Present fans are sure to seek out the group's numerous U.K.-only singles, which occasionally turn up in U.S. import bins; for the rest of us, most of the singles are available on album reissues and the *Hit Parade* series.

influences:

◄◄ Gang of Four, the Velvet Underground, the Smiths, the Replacements, Joy Division, the Fall

►► Oasis, Blur, Mansun, Travis

Seth Hindin

Ween

Formed 1985, in New Hope, PA.

Dean Ween (born Mickey Melchiondo), vocals, instruments; Gene Ween (born Aaron Freeman), vocals, instruments.

This terminally wacky duo has the musical chops and wiseass sensibility that could have made them millions had they gone the Weird Al Yankovic route. But the brothers Ween are far more subversive than that. Rather than simply parody individual songs, they turn whole genres inside-out and upside-down, exterminating the boundaries of good taste with extreme prejudice and a 4-track tape deck. Their humor is sophomoric—the name Ween, they say, is a combination of the words wuss and penis—but in fairness, they may have been sophomores when they formed the group. Still, if the mood catches you, these guys can be absolutely hilarious. And whether or not you like what they do, Ween can, at the very least, be a test case for a debate about what cheap recording equipment has wrought: is it the democratization of the music industry, or the end of music altogether?

what to buy: A hilarious goof from beginning to end, *God Ween Satan—The Oneness* 𝄞𝄞𝄞𝄞 (Twin/Tone, 1990, prod. Andrew Weiss) has something to offend nearly everyone. But ease off the PC meter and notice how deftly this duo deconstructs genres as various as gospel (in a hilarious hymn to their god, Boognish), mariachi, heavy metal, and funk (a leering cover of Prince's "Shockadelica"). A work of near-genius not despite its excess, but because of it.

what to buy next: The duo's technique was considerably refined by the time it recorded *Chocolate and Cheese* 𝄞𝄞𝄞 (Elektra, 1992, prod. Andrew Weiss), and it takes on Philly soul ("Freedom of '76"), boneheaded '70s rock ("Take Me Away"), and Pink Floyd–style instrumental excursions ("A Tear for Eddie"). "Spinal Meningitis (Got Me Down)" is more creepy than funny, though, and the happy carnival music in "The HIV Song" is either incredibly stupid or their bravest move yet. *The Pod* 𝄞𝄞𝄞 (Shimmy-Disc, 1991, prod. Andrew Weiss)—recorded at the Weens' apartment (hence the title)—is full of bad vibes, distorted vocals, and near-stationary grooves. Still, "Strap on That Jammypac" is a merciless take on the blues, "Demon Sweat" a slab o' neo-Princian bedroom funk, and "Pork Roll Egg and Cheese" offers a bit of twisted psychedelia.

what to avoid: The fact that Ween actually went out and hired a bunch of notable Nashville pros to record the country album *12 Golden Country Greats* 𝄞𝄞 (Elektra, 1996, prod. Ben Vaughan) is actually funnier than anything that resulted from the sessions. It's a good joke, but one joke does not an album make.

the rest:

Pure Guava 𝄞𝄞𝄞 (Elektra, 1992)
The Mollusk 𝄞𝄞𝄞 (Elektra, 1997)

worth searching for: Good luck finding it, but 500 copies of Ween's debut album, *Live Brain Wedgie!* (Bird o' Pray, 1987, prod. Ween), exist out there somewhere. Actually, only half is live, recorded in Trenton, N.J. The rest consists of early 4-track recordings, including "I Got a Weasel."

influences:

◄◄ Prince, Captain Beefheart, Ozzy Osbourne, Alvin & the Chipmunks

►► Beck, Soul Coughing

Daniel Durchholz

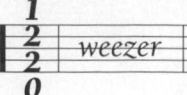
Weezer
/The Rentals

Formed 1992, in Los Angeles, CA.

Rivers Cuomo, vocals, guitar; Brian Bell, guitar, vocals; Matt Sharp, bass, vocals; Pat Wilson, drums.

The missing link between Nirvana and nerdiness, Weezer came out of nowhere to become *the* spotlight-resisting stars of alternative rock. Though none of the band members looked like movie stars (unless you consider *Revenge of the Nerds*), Weezer scored several smash hits, beginning with the slowly unraveling "Undone—The Sweater Song" and running through "Buddy Holly," which has nothing to do with Buddy Holly no matter how hard you listen to the lyrics. Despite a barrage of surprisingly sarcastic magazine profiles and a gradual tilt away from bubblegum and towards Nirvana-like angst, the band maintained its sense of humor even as its second album failed to smash with the same force. While the guitars raised a ruckus and the vocals lifted to strained falsettos, leader Rivers Cuomo kept the melodies down-to-earth, giving punk a bridle instead of sounding suicidal.

what to buy: *Weezer* ♪♪♪♪ (DGC, 1994, prod. Ric Ocasek) was an unexpected hit, especially for a debut album, and it took these recalcitrant rock stars by surprise. Combining noisy chords, geeky lyrics, and jaw-droppingly pretty melodies ("Buddy Holly"), Weezer invented a novel sound that was a great chaser for grunge, and a subtle tracer to classic pop. Influences such as the Beach Boys and Kiss lurked just under the surface of their nerds-on-punk veneer. "Undone—The Sweater Song," with its hardly dyed-in-the-wool lyrics and cotton-candy melody, broke the band to a generation that wanted its grunge to wear a smile.

what to buy next: *Pinkerton* ♪♪♪ (DGC, 1996, prod. Weezer) was far from a dud, but coming after the left-field vibrancy of the debut, it was clearly a disappointment—not just critically, but commercially. The album, showing Weezer without emotional sweaters to bundle its nerves, reeks of celebrity-induced isolation. Weary of the star trip after just one hit album, Cuomo is also "Sick of Sex." On the catchiest *Pinkerton* track, Cuomo sings about there being "No Other One," but the song, like so many of the band's ditties, can't resist coating its sentiment in candy-flavored irony. Despite the messy stabs at seriousness, the album's main flaw is the dirty production. Weezer's first album just *sounded* dirty—producer Ric Ocasek gave a hon-eyed glaze to the post-grunge swarm of guitars—but on *Pinkerton*, Weezer sounds like it wants to resemble the Seattle brigade more than make light of it. In between Weezer's two albums, bassist Matt Sharp and drummer Pat Wilson joined that dog. violinist Petra Haden and three others for *Return of the*

Rentals ♪♪♪ (Maverick, 1995, prod. Matt Sharp, Tom Grimley). The Moog-laden pop tracks repay the aesthetic favor to *Weezer* producer Ocasek by partially resembling the Cars. Unsurprisingly, a couple of songs sound like Weezer, while others come off like a portent for some unwelcome new wave revival. Sharp proves to be a decent songwriter, though, and it's a fun collection—less grating than Weezer's heavy-handed goofiness, but far less exciting than Weezer at its best.

the rest:
The Rentals:
Seven More Minutes N/A (Maverick/Reprise, 1998)

worth searching for: The British single for "Undone—The Sweater Song" contains two non-LP songs; the British single for "Buddy Holly" contains two live tracks and a song otherwise only available on a compilation; and the Australian single for "The Good Life" has two previously unreleased songs and two acoustic live tracks.

influences:
◀◀ The Beach Boys, the Ramones
▶▶ Nerf Herder, Nada Surf

Jordan Oakes

Scott Weiland
See: Stone Temple Pilots

The Weirdos

Formed 1976, in Los Angeles, CA.

John Denney, vocals; Dix Denney, guitar; Clif Roman, guitar, bass; Dave Trout, bass (1977–78); Bruce Moreland, bass (1978); Billy Ford Persons, bass (1979); Greg Williams, bass (1980); Flea (born Michael Balzary), bass (1989); Nickey Beat, drums (1977–78, 1989); Danny Benair, drums (1979); Art Fox, drums (1980); Cliff Martinez, drums (1981); Jerry Angel, drums (1989).

Simply put, the Weirdos were the most explosive punk rock band in America during the pre-hardcore late '70s. Let anyone who doubts it simply hear both sides of the group's classic 1977 single on Dangerhouse records, "We Got the Neutron Bomb"/"Solitary Confinement," and feel the burning hugeness of its attack. Along with the never-released Screamers, the Weirdos were also the top dogs and biggest draws on the pioneering L.A. punk scene of the time, its bizarre and zany clothing even landing the group national exposure in U.S. news-magazines; singer John Denney was known to dress in space-age astronaut gear to frequent record label A&R offices with demo tapes and promotional material. And his characteristic arms-swinging, head-down, chicken-strut has often been thought of as the precursor to the silly "skank" dance favored by later '80s mosh-pit slam-dancers. More importantly, the true stars of that burgeoning time and scene left behind just enough music to document their raw, tumultuous power, incredible cool, and amusing but keen and penetrating intelligence.

what to buy: The curious are well served by the knockout retrospective *Weird World: Vol. 1, 1977—1981* 𝄢𝄢𝄢𝄢𝄢 (Frontier Records, 1991, prod. various). In addition to the "Neutron Bomb" double-sided detonation and the highlights of its other releases, more than half of this 14-track collection is comprised of unreleased demos, providing a slice of history for even the oldest fan. Anyone wishing to hear pure punk power should check out the Dix Denney/Cliff Roman guitar assault on such previously undocumented juggernauts as "Message from the Underworld" and "Teenage." The unadulterated spirit of John Denney's wild voice throughout is another comet of sorts.

what to buy next: Though for some reason *Weird World: Vol. 2* has never appeared as promised, those blown away by the Weirdos' sound are further advised to seek out *Live from the Masque: Forming* 𝄢𝄢𝄢𝄢 (Year One, 1996), which features six live tracks from the Weirdos (as well as the Bags, the Germs, and the Skulls) and also captures the band in its vintage 1977–78 furious, wild glory. Novices should approach the band's lone comeback album, *Condor* 𝄢𝄢𝄢 (Frontier Records, 1990, prod. Dix Denney, John Denney, Cliff Roman), with caution; though certainly no dud, the set fails to completely rekindle the band's prior greatness. As an extra piece, however, the still fast and frenzied "Cyclops Helicopter" and "Shining Silver Light" can please.

influences:

◀◀ The Stooges, the Ramones, the Troggs

▶▶ Bad Religion, the Offspring, Green Day, NOFX

Jack Rabid

Bob Welch

Born July 31, 1946, in Los Angeles, CA.

Bob Welch was a member of Fleetwood Mac for a few years (1971—74) but departed before the band went multi-platinum, making him only slightly better off than ex-Beatles drummer Pete Best. He first formed the short-lived group Paris, then launched a solo career that started strong with his hit remake of the Fleetwood Mac song "Sentimental Lady," which he followed with the peppy "Ebony Eyes." The hits dried up soon after, and Welch drifted into obscurity while his former bandmates went through the roof with almost unparalleled success.

what to buy: *The Best of Bob Welch* 𝄢𝄢𝄢 (Rhino, 1991, prod. various) collects his charting numbers, plus material from Paris. Taken together, Welch's talents as a guitarist and songwriter are evident; he just never parlayed them much to his benefit.

the rest:

Three Hearts 𝄢𝄢 (Capitol/EMI, 1978/1996)
Greatest Hits 𝄢𝄢𝄢 (Curb, 1994)

influences:

◀◀ Steve Miller, the Yardbirds, Jeff Beck, James Taylor, the Eagles

▶▶ Jewel, Duncan Sheik

see also: *Fleetwood Mac*

Allan Orski

Paul Weller

See: The Jam

Mary Wells

Born May 13, 1943, in Detroit, MI. Died July 26, 1992, in Los Angeles, CA.

Motown's first bona fide star, Mary Wells is remembered, perhaps unfairly, for her 1964 smash "My Guy." The song, one of many collaborations with Smokey Robinson, became her biggest seller and overshadowed everything else she did. Wells didn't have much luck after her bitter split with Motown, but she continued to record and perform until her death from throat cancer.

what to buy: *Looking Back: 1961–1964* 𝄢𝄢𝄢 (Motown, 1993, prod. various) is a two-disc set that offers the best representation of the singer's most famous period; all her hits came from the Motown years. "The One Who Really Loves You," "You Beat Me to the Punch," and "My Guy" are all here, in addition to interviews with friends and associates.

what to buy next: *Never, Never Leave Me/The 20th Century Sides* 𝄢𝄢𝄢 (Ichiban, 1996, prod. various) reveals that Wells had more to say after "My Guy." Compiling material from sessions immediately after her Motown split, this has no big hits but plenty of decent, lightweight soul. Wells's chirpy innocence had begun to subside a bit by this point, leading to more versatile interpretations.

what to avoid: *Greatest Hits* 𝄢𝄢 (Motown, 1964/1989, prod. various) is inadequate given the depth of *Looking Back*.

the rest:

My Guy 𝄢𝄢𝄢 (Motown, 1964/1989)
Motown Legends: You Beat Me to the Punch–My Guy 𝄢𝄢𝄢 (ESX, 1994)
Ain't It the Truth 𝄢𝄢𝄢 (Varese Vintage, 1994)
Dear Lover: The Atco Sessions 𝄢𝄢𝄢 (Ichiban, 1995)
The Ultimate Collection 𝄢𝄢𝄢𝄢 (Motown, 1998)

influences:

◀◀ Della Reese, Judy Garland, Smokey Robinson

▶▶ The Supremes, Diana Ross, Martha & the Vandellas

Allan Orski

wendy & lisa

Wendy & Lisa

Formed 1986, in Los Angeles, CA.

Wendy Melvoin, guitar, bass, vocals; Lisa Coleman, keyboards, backing vocals.

One of the first and most interesting spinoffs from Prince's backup band, the Revolution, Wendy Melvoin and Lisa Coleman started their act shortly after their royal employer gave them a pink slip in 1986. Friends since childhood, the two hooked up musically in the Revolution when Melvoin replaced guitarist Dez Deckerson in 1984 (Coleman had been backing Prince since 1979). Playing almost all the instruments on their self-named debut, the two presented a slick neo-psychedelic sound with just enough R&B to hint at their musical roots. Though their five albums progressed toward a rockier, band approach—with notables such as Michael Penn and k.d. lang helping out on *Eroica*—their work went largely unnoticed commercially, despite presaging a nod toward funky psychedelia that artists continue to mint today. The pair have gained a reputation as song doctors, co-writing tunes for soulful pop-singer Seal's first two records.

what to buy: Their debut, *Wendy & Lisa* 𝄞𝄞𝄞 (Columbia, 1987, prod. Bobby Z., Wendy Melvoin, Lisa Coleman), remains the pair's finest work, featuring an atmospheric blend of psychedelic rock and soul that goes down like a gentle dream. Songs such as "Chance to Grow" and "Blues Away" ride a sophisticated groove with spot-on playing. Then things get funky with the wah-wah guitar-spiced "Light."

what to avoid: Though notable for the famous cameos, *Eroica* **woof!** (Virgin, 1990) is pretty much a confused mishmash.

the rest:
Fruit at the Bottom 𝄞𝄞𝄞 (Columbia, 1989)
Re-Mix-in-a-Carnation 𝄞𝄞𝄞𝄞 (Virgin, 1991)
Are You My Baby? 𝄞𝄞𝄞 (Disky, 1996)
Girl Bros. 𝄞𝄞𝄞 (Girl Bros., 1998)

worth searching for: The pair light up Joni Mitchell's 1988 record, *Chalk Mark in a Rainstorm* (Geffen, 1988).

influences:
◄◄ Prince, A Taste of Honey
►► Edna Swap, Alisha's Attic

Eric Deggans

Leslie West

See: Mountain

West, Bruce & Laing

See: Mountain

Wham!

See: George Michael

Whipping Boy

Formed 1989, in Dublin, Ireland.

Ferghal McKee, vocals; Paul Page, guitar; Myles McDonnell, bass; Colm Hassett, drums.

Though they're at present virtually unknown here, this Irish quartet's second album, *Heartworm*, indicates it's one of the most important new bands to emerge from the U.K. The group was introduced to the English public when the album's second single, "We Don't Need Nobody Else," caught fire behind some nervy, controversial lyrics on the subject of domestic violence. The single hit the charts, and its success helped propel *Heartworm* into several "year's best" lists in the U.K. press at the end of 1996. Those fans who were thus enticed to pick up the album found that song—as well as succeeding hits "Twinkle" and "When We Were Young"—were cogs in a dramatic, gripping, varied album; the sort that unfolds for an hour and must be taken in as a flowing whole. Beyond the intelligence and the memorable songwriting, one encounters elusive undercurrents that have always defined the finest U.K. post-punk bands, including "154" Wire, Joy Division, early Echo & the Bunnymen, the Sound, early Stone Roses, and Pale Saints.

what's available: The sonic moods on *Heartworm* 𝄞𝄞𝄞𝄞 (Columbia, 1996, prod. Wayne Livesey) are so enticing and oddly foreboding that they make this a truly special album.

influences:
◄◄ U2, Echo & the Bunnymen, the Cure

Jack Rabid

Whiskeytown

Formed 1993, in Raleigh, NC.

Ryan Adams, vocals, guitars; Phil Wandscher, guitars, vocals (1993–97); Caitlin Cary, violin, vocals; Skillet Gilmore, drums (1993–96); Steve Terry, drums (1996–97); Steve Grothman, bass (1993–96); Jeff Rice, bass (1996–97).

If to be contemporary is to be misunderstood, then rock artists don't get much more contemporary than Ryan Adams, poster boy for the late '90s No Depression set. For all intents and purposes, Adams *is* Whiskeytown because he's never been able to keep a stable lineup together for long (at the time of this writing, ex-fIREHOSE guitarist Ed Crawford is a member, though he has yet to surface on a Whiskeytown recording). Adams is a frightfully charismatic young man given to obsessive ruminations on doomed romance, drinking, and why George Jones is more of a punk than those poseurs in Rancid.

Country provides some of his music's most striking flourishes, but Adams is still a punk at heart. After doing time in the band Patty Duke Syndrome as a teenager, Adams put together Whiskeytown as a vehicle for the increasingly country-sounding direction of his songwriting and quickly outgrew his early Uncle Tupelo enthusiasms. Whiskeytown owes as much to the Replacements as Gram Parsons—a double-edged sword, given the band's reputation for onstage confrontational wooziness. That said, the records are impeccable, as long as one is not inclined to be puritanical about what does and does not count as country music.

what to buy: Whiskeytown's big-league debut, *Strangers Almanac* ♫♫♫♫ (Outpost, 1997, prod. Jim Scott), is a staggeringly ambitious album that shimmers with hooks and mood. Adams's songs stand up to the studio polish exceedingly well, especially the pathos-laden "Excuse Me While I Break My Own Heart Tonight" (a duet with Alejandro Escovedo) and the megaton hook to "Sixteen Days." A landmark in '90s alternative country.

what to buy next: Whiskeytown's debut, *Faithless Street* ♫♫♫♫ (MoodFood, 1995, prod. Whiskeytown, Greg Woods), served notice that Adams was capable of delivering the goods even as a tender lad of 20—his age when he recorded these extraordinarily mature-sounding songs. The album-opening "Midway Park" (a song Freedy Johnston would kill to have written) remains one of Adams's best compositions and performances. *Rural Free Delivery* ♫♫♫ (MoodFood, 1997, prod. Greg Elkins) is a for-the-fans collection of early demos. It's most notable for the countrypolitan version of Black Flag's "Nervous Breakdown."

worth searching for: Whiskeytown is a band that will drive completists insane, in part because the hyper-prolific Adams writes far more songs than the albums can accommodate. The group recorded three dozen songs for the 13-track *Strangers Almanac*, and two of the outtakes plus two earlier demos wound up on the promo-only *In Your Wildest Dreams* (Outpost EP, 1997, prod. Jim Scott, Chris Stamey). One of the demos is a marvelous version of the old True Believers signature, "The Rain Won't Help You When It's Over." Whiskeytown has also made ace contributions to numerous compilations, including a haunting cover of Moon Mullican's 1948 chestnut, "Bottom of the Glass," on *Straight Outta Boone County* (Bloodshot, 1997, prod. various), and a brilliant hayride hoedown deconstruction of "Blank Generation" on *Who the Hell: A Tribute to Richard Hell* (Cred Factory, 1995, prod. various). Finally, the soundtrack album to Wim Wenders's *The End of Violence* (Outpost, 1997, prod. various) includes "Theme for a Trucker," Adams's downcast ode to his one-time Patty Duke Syndrome bandmate Jere McIlwean.

influences:

◀◀ Uncle Tupelo, the Replacements, Fleetwood Mac, Bruce Springsteen, Gram Parsons, Freedy Johnston

▶▶ Slobberbone, the Old 97's

David Menconi

Ian Whitcomb

Born July 10, 1941, in Woking, Surrey, England.

Proving that with the right accent (British) and the right hairstyle (over the ears) at the right time (summer of 1965) *anything* was possible on the U.S. charts, Whitcomb—while still ostensibly studying political science at Trinity College in Dublin—had a Top 10 hit with an innocuous little song full of barrelhouse piano and heavy breathing called "You Turn Me On." He was duly summoned to Hollywood to appear on all the pop shows of the day and to tour with all the other pop stars of the moment. He never again visited the Top 40, but Whitcomb remained in southern California, carving out a career for himself as a record producer, television producer, radio host (currently on NPR), and all-round musicologist. His 1983 book, *Rock Odyssey,* remains a definitive study of popular music during the '60s, and his best-selling *After the Ball* covers every aspect of pop from rock to his beloved ragtime. He has continued making records of a decidedly non-rock nature since 1965, and continues to sell his wares through a post office box high in the California hills.

what to buy: *The Very Best of the Rock and Roll Years* ♫♫♫♫ (Varese Vintage, 1998, compilation prod. Cary E. Mansfield, Ian Whitcomb) contains "You Turn Me On," the many failed but delightful attempts at a follow-up hit, Whitcomb's own unique twists on psychedelia ("Sally Sails the Sky") and social commentary ("Notable Yacht Club of Staines"), his earliest dabblings in ragtime and music-hall, and even an early, test-pressing version of the "Turn On" song, complete with lots of extra grunts and pants at the end.

what to buy next: *You Turn Me On!/Ian Whitcomb's Mod, Mod Music Hall!* ♫♫♫ (Tower, 1965,1966/Sundazed, 1997, compilation prod. Bob Irwin) combines his first two releases, showing just how quickly—and entertainingly—Whitcomb metamorphosized from the self-proclaimed Father of Irish Rock to the lovable if eccentric savior of British musical traditions. The best of his full-fledged explorations into the world of ragtime and Tin Pan Alley have pointedly been compiled as *The Golden Age of Lounge* ♫♫♫ (Varese Vintage, 1997, compilation prod. Ian Whitcomb, Cary E. Mansfield).

the rest:

Happy Days Are Here Again ♫♫♫ (Audiophile, 1989)
Ragtime America ♫♫♫ (ITW Industries, 1992/Audiophile, 1995)
Comedy Songs ♫♫♫ (ITW Industries, 1992/Dove Music, 1996)
Lotus Land ♫♫♫ (ITW Industries, 1992/Audiophile, 1995)
Spread a Little Happiness ♫♫♫ (ITW Industries, 1993)
Titanic: Music As Heard on the Fateful Voyage ♫♫ (Rhino, 1997)

influences:

◄◄ Jerry Lee Lewis, Irving Berlin, Rudy Vallee, Dick Zimmerman

▶▶ Tiny Tim, mid-period Kinks, David Bowie

Gary Pig Gold

White Hassle

See: Railroad Jerk

White Zombie

Formed 1985, in New York, NY.

Rob Zombie (born Robert Straker), vocals; John Ricci, guitar (1985–89); Sean Yseult, bass; Ivan dePrume, drums (1985–93); Jay "J." Yuenger, guitar (1989–present); Phil "Philo" Buerstatte, drums (1993–95); John Tempesta, drums (1995–present).

It's no wonder MTV's Beavis and Butt-head championed this band; it's the realization of every headbanger's wet dream, a blazing, over-the-top band that can't seem to create enough spectacle in its live shows and that hasn't met an album title too long to like. White Zombie first made its mark in the New York rock/industrial underground, putting some groove and swing behind its crunchy guitar licks and sledgehammer drums. It eventually found a more mainstream metal path, still bringing in subversive noises and creating lots of its own "samples" to be looped throughout the songs. "Thunder Kiss '65" and "More Human Than Human" brought White Zombie to the masses, but after its multimillion-selling triumph, 1995's *Astro-Creep 2000 . . .*, the group has been laying low while Rob Zombie gets his new record label up and running.

what to buy: *La Sexorcisto: Devil Music, Vol. 1* ♪♪♪♪ (Geffen, 1992, prod. Andy Wallace) offers a tough, roiling soundscape best realized on the Grammy winning "Thunder Kiss '65" and "Black Sunshine," which features a guest vocal by Iggy Pop. *Astro-Creep 2000: Songs of Love, Destruction and Other Synthetic Delusions of the Electric Head* ♪♪♪♪ (Geffen, 1995, prod. Terry Date, White Zombie) loads up with samples, tape loops, and a variety of sound effects, never obscuring the group's playing but dressing it up in darker, more visceral moods.

the rest:
Make Them Die Slowly ♪♪♪ (Caroline, 1989)
Supersexy Swingin' Sounds ♪♪♪ (Geffen, 1996)

solo outings:
Rob Zombie:
Hellbilly Deluxe ♪♪♪♪ (Geffen, 1998)

influences:

◄◄ Metallica, Megadeth, Einstürzende Neubauten

Gary Graff

Whitesnake

Formed 1978, in Yorkshire, England.

David Coverdale, vocals; Micky Moody, guitar (1978–83); Bernie Marsden, guitar (1978–82); Brian Johnston, keyboards (1978); Neil Murray, bass (1978–82, 1983–87); David Dowle, drums (1978–79); Jon Lord, keyboards (1978–84); Ian Paice, drums (1979–82); Mel Galley, guitar (1982–84); Colin Hodgkinson, bass (1982–83); Cozy Powell (died April 5, 1998), drums (1982–85); John Sykes, guitar (1983–87); Richard Bailey, keyboards (1984–85); Don Airey, keyboards (1985–present); Aynsley Dunbar (died 1998), drums (1985–87); Adrian Vandenberg, guitar (1987–present); Vivian Campbell, guitar (1987–88); Rudy Sarzo, bass (1987–94); Tommy Aldridge, drums (1987–90); Steve Vai, guitar (1988–90); Denny Carmassi, drums (1994–present); Warren DeMartini, guitar (1994).

Whitesnake was actually the name of David Coverdale's first solo album after leaving Deep Purple in 1976; two years later, he figured it would also make a good name for a band. Whitesnake went through a few phases of development, taking a bluesy hard rock approach at first, then coming closer to the Purple sound after the addition of Ian Paice and Jon Lord from that band. Whitesnake finally hit pay dirt in 1987 with the multiplatinum *Whitesnake* album—whose sales were driven by catchy pop-metal songs from the Coverdale–John Sykes team and by videos that featured Coverdale's attractive then-fiancé, Tawny Kitaen. The ride didn't last long, though; one more album and the band was on hiatus while Coverdale—long lambasted as a Robert Plant wannabe—recorded an album and toured with former Led Zeppelin guitarmeister Jimmy Page. Another version of the band toured Europe after that venture, however, so we may still have Whitesnake to kick around.

what to buy: Three years before *Whitesnake*, the group's *Slide It In* ♪♪♪♪ (Geffen, 1984, prod. Martin Birch) was a harbinger of things to come, but without the slick pop sheen that rendered the group's later albums a bit anonymous. *Greatest Hits* ♪♪♪♪ (Geffen, 1994, prod. various) is a good overview of the Whitesnake radio experience.

what to buy next: *Whitesnake* ♪♪♪ (Geffen, 1987, prod. Mike Stone, Keith Olsen) is tuneful enough, and a definitive piece from one of those odd periods when mainstream tastes turned towards hard rock.

what to avoid: The ballyhooed addition of super-guitarist Steve Vai for *Slip of the Tongue* ♪♪ (Geffen, 1989, prod. Mike Clink, Keith Olsen) was a mixed blessing, as his freewheeling style wasn't a crisp fit with Whitesnake's more regimented direction.

the rest:
Snakebite ♪♪♪ (Geffen, 1978)
Saints and Sinners ♪♪♪ (Geffen, 1982)

worth searching for: *Live . . . In the Heart of the City* (Mirage, 1980) is a good document of the early, more rough 'n' tumble Whitesnake.

influences:

◀◀ Deep Purple, Led Zeppelin

▶▶ Extreme, Queensryche, Spinal Tap

see also: *Deep Purple, Page & Plant*

Gary Graff

Chris Whitley

Born August 31, 1960, in Houston, TX.

Chris Whitley's modest number of albums belies the long road his career has taken. Constantly uprooted and moved throughout the South as a child, he began playing guitar and eventually discovered the National Steel guitar and dobro. Whitley served a long stint busking in New York, then moved to Belgium and experimented with blues and funk. Upon returning to America, he met producer Daniel Lanois (U2, Peter Gabriel), scored a record deal, and recorded his heralded debut, *Living with the Law*. Critics loved the stark majesty of Whitley's music, so it was surprising when he did a sharp about-face on later albums, fronting a loud, metallic trio with mixed results. Although the buzz around Whitley dies down a bit more with each successive album, he remains an original and his music is always uncompromising.

what to buy: *Dirty Floor* ♫♫♫♫ (Messenger, 1998, prod. Craig Street) is Whitley at his best, in a spare, acoustic setting that's at once fragile and granite strong, with some of his most starkly drawn songs and affecting performances. *Living with the Law* ♫♫♫ (Columbia, 1991, prod. Daniel Lanois) may not be truly indicative of Whitley's overall style, as his later works attest, but remains a stark, gorgeous album that explores a rusty, burned-out Americana.

what to buy next: *Terra Incognita* ♫♫♫ (Work/Sony, 1996, prod. various) is a good compromise between the beauty of Whitley's debut and the harsh, sometimes droning electric rock he experimented with on its follow-up. It also contains "Automatic," the addictive first single that should have been a smash hit.

the rest:

Poison Girl ♫♫♫♡ (Columbia EP, 1992)
Din of Ecstasy ♫♫♡ (Columbia, 1995)

influences:

◀◀ Hank Williams, Bob Dylan, Tim Buckley, Jimi Hendrix, Daniel Lanois, Richard Thompson, Jimmie Dale Gilmore

▶▶ Jeff Buckley, Jon Spencer Blues Explosion

Todd Wicks and Gary Graff

The Who

Formed 1964, in London, England. Disbanded 1982. Re-formed 1989, 1996.

Peter Townshend, guitar, vocals; Roger Daltrey, vocals; John Entwistle, bass, vocals; Keith Moon (died September 7, 1978), drums (1964–78); Kenney Jones, drums (1979–82); Simon Phillips, drums (1989); Zak Starkey, drums (1996–97); Simon Townshend, guitars (1996–97).

Originally a straightforward R&B band that played for England's short-lived mod subculture, the Who gradually developed a creative and forceful style that led the British Invasion's second wave and gave them lasting fame. Chief songwriter Pete Townshend, an angry young Brit with a big nose and an inferiority complex, spontaneously began smashing his electric guitar at London's Marquee Club; Keith Moon, who joined the band after vaulting on stage and announcing he could best the Who's original drummer, Doug Sandom, followed Townshend's cue and regularly destroyed his drum kits. Roger Daltrey and John Entwistle, the band's talented role players, watched the smoke and violence with bemusement. Eventually Townshend went from writing powerful little pop songs—always with Moon's barely controlled percussion explosions in the background—to more lofty artistic ventures. He wrote *Tommy*, a high-minded "rock opera," then followed it with the failed spiritual project *Lifehouse*, whose remnants eventually became the classic album *Who's Next*. As the Who's live show grew legendary and lured stadium crowds, Townshend's maturity overcame him; he tried to sing about growing up, spirituality, and his personal drug and drinking problems. Some of this inspiration produced great rock 'n' roll, but after Moon died of a drug overdose in 1978, Townshend's vibrancy dwindled away. After several uninspired tours with ex-Faces drummer Kenney Jones, the Who broke up in 1982, then did a bloated reunion tour full of professional backup musicians in 1989. Townshend still puts out solo albums and has turned his attention to the theater; he recreated *Tommy* as a surprisingly successful Broadway musical in 1994. Beginning in 1996, the Who took its other rock opera, *Quadrophenia*, on a world tour; with Ringo Starr's son, Zak Starkey, on drums, and bizarre guest cameos by Billy Idol and Gary Glitter, the band briefly rediscovered its muse. Still, Entwistle and Daltrey have no careers without Townshend—Daltrey's solo tour (with Entwistle on bass) and Entwistle's solo albums were commercial flops.

what to buy: Many of the Who's original CDs (first released in the late '80s) are poorly remastered; watch for the newer, mid-'90s versions, which contain beefed-up liner notes, great archival pictures, and a generous sampling of strong bonus tracks. Also, there are a zillion Who "best of" sets, so let the buyer beware. But you can't go wrong with the original: *Meaty*

Roger Daltrey of the Who (© Ken Settle)

Beaty Big and Bouncy ♫♫♫♫ (MCA, 1971, prod. various) collects "My Generation," "Substitute," "Magic Bus," "I Can't Explain," and all the Who's exhilarating '60s singles. *Who's Next* ♫♫♫♫♫ (MCA, 1971/1995, prod. Glyn Johns, the Who), the band's best studio album, with "Baba O'Riley" and "Won't Get Fooled Again," gave the Who rock-radio staying power. The rock opera *Tommy* ♫♫♫♫ (MCA, 1969/1996, prod. Kit Lambert) is valuable more for the concept than the music, though Moon's brilliant, propulsive drumming overcomes weak production. Townshend's confessional *The Who by Numbers* ♫♫♫♫ (MCA, 1975/1996, prod. Glyn Johns), the still-fresh *The Who Sell Out* ♫♫♫♫ (MCA, 1967/1995, prod. Kit Lambert), and one of the best live albums in rock history, *Live at Leeds* ♫♫♫♫ (MCA, 1970/1995, prod. the Who, reissue prod. Jon Astley), are also essential. And the band's explosive early '70s live period, during which Moon was in prime form and the band was still inspired by *Tommy*, has finally been showcased in non-bootleg form with the two-disc *Live at the Isle of Wight Festival, 1970* ♫♫♫♫♡ (Columbia/Legacy, 1996, prod. Jon Astley, Andy Macpherson). Even the obscure songs, such as "Water" and Entwistle's hilarious "Heaven and Hell," have tremendous power, and the band's disc-long performance of *Tommy* is even more definitive than the original album. The Who was meant to be experienced live, and this is even more rewarding than the too-short classic *Live at Leeds*.

what to buy next: The soundtrack from the film *The Kids Are Alright* ♫♫♫ (MCA, 1979, prod. John Entwistle) is a charming, funny collection of outtakes and concert weirdness, including highlights from the band's Woodstock performance. *Who Are You* ♫♫♫ (MCA, 1978/1996 prod. Glyn Johns, Jon Astley), recorded just before Moon's death, is the original band's last gasp. Completists will enjoy the thorough box set *Thirty Years of Maximum R&B* ♫♫♫♫ (MCA, 1994, compilation prod. Jon Astley, Chris Charlesworth, Bill Curbishley), which includes everything you need plus hilarious live Townshend diatribes.

what to avoid: Don't bother with anything from the Kenney Jones era, including *Face Dances* ♫♡ (MCA, 1981/1996, prod. Bill Szymczyk) and *It's Hard* ♫ (Warner Bros., 1982/1996, prod. Glyn Johns). Also, both *Who's Last* ♫♡ (MCA, 1984) and *Join Together* ♫ (MCA, 1990), which document the band's uninspired, almost embarrassing 1982 and 1989 tours, respectively, make excellent coasters.

the rest:
The Who Sings My Generation ♫♫♫ (Decca, 1965/MCA, 1988)
Happy Jack ♫♫♫ (Decca, 1966/MCA, 1988)
A Quick One, While He's Away ♫♫♫♫ (Decca, 1966/MCA, 1995)
Magic Bus: The Who on Tour ♫♫♡ (Decca, 1968/MCA, 1988)
Quadrophenia ♫♫♫♫ (MCA, 1973/MCA, 1996)
Odds and Sods ♫♫♫♫ (MCA, 1974/1998)
Who's Greatest Hits ♫♫ (MCA, 1983)

Who's Missing ♫♫♫ (MCA, 1985/1987)
Two's Missing ♫♫♡ (MCA, 1987)
Who's Better, Who's Best ♫♫ (MCA, 1988)
My Generation: The Very Best of the Who ♫♫♡ (MCA, 1996)

worth searching for: Though some of the artists are obscure and there are a few disappointing tracks, the British import *Who Covers Who* (CM, 1993) effectively captures the band's lasting influence. Standout tracks include Blur's "Substitute," Alex Chilton's carbon copy of "Anyway, Anyhow, Anywhere," and the Mess' take on the pre-*Tommy* rock opera song "Glow Girl."

solo outings:
Keith Moon:
Two Sides of the Moon ♫♡ (MCA, 1975)

Roger Daltrey:
Daltrey ♫ (MCA, 1973)
Ride a Rock Horse ♡ (MCA, 1977)
One of the Boys ♫ (MCA, 1977)
McVicar (Soundtrack) ♫ (Polydor, 1980)
Under a Raging Moon ♫ (Atlantic, 1985)
Can't Wait to See the Movie ♫ (Atlantic, 1987)
The Best of Rockers and Ballads ♫♡ (Polydor, 1991)
Rocks in the Head ♫♡ (Atlantic, 1992)
A Celebration: The Music of Pete Townshend and the Who ♫ (Continuum, 1994)
Martyrs and Madmen: The Best of Roger Daltrey ♫♫♡ (Rhino, 1997)

influences:
◀◀ James Brown, Mose Allison, Sonny Boy Williamson, the Rolling Stones, the Kinks, the Beatles, the Ventures, Gene Krupa

▶▶ Iggy & the Stooges, the Sex Pistols, the Jam, Too Much Joy, Nirvana, Pearl Jam

see also: *Pete Townshend, John Entwistle*

Steve Knopper

The Why Store

Formed 1989, in Muncie, IN.

Chris Shaffer, vocals, guitar; Michael David Smith, guitar, vocals; Charlie Bushor, drums, percussion; Greg Gardner, bass, vocals; Jeff Pederson, keyboards (1995–present).

While students at Ball State University in Muncie, Indiana, Chris Shaffer, Greg Gardner, and David Smith called themselves Emerald City and quickly became local favorites. The band shifted when, in New York City, it met Charlie Bushor. As a consequence, Smith went from behind the kit to lead guitarist, and Bushor took over the drums. It changed its name to the Why Store and, thanks to the uniqueness and ambivalence of the name, made a mint off of merchandise. After releasing two independent albums, the Why Store signed with MCA's Way Cool Music, scored a couple of radio hits with "Lack of Water" and "Father," and built a following that straddled the Top 40 and H.O.R.D.E. crowds.

what to buy: On *Two Beasts* 𝄞𝄞𝄞 (Way Cool/MCA, 1998, prod. Mike Wanchic, the Why Store), the Why Store strays from the melancholy tone of its major label debut and takes greater advantage of keyboardist Jeff Pederson's abilities. "Working" is a funky head-bobber, while "No Matter" swings with a rollicking beat. "Who Is Your Love" makes for an easy listen thanks to Shaffer's warm, natural vocals, and "When You're High" has a bouncy energy that transcends its silly lyrical imagery.

what to avoid: *The Why Store* 𝄞𝄞 (Way Cool/MCA, 1996, prod. Mike Wanchic, the Why Store) stocks itself with the band's penchant for jam rock. Shaffer's vocals vary between earnest and overdone. "Lack of Water," buried as "bonus" track number 27, should have appeared earlier in the album to attract attention with its staccato guitars and lush harmonies.

influences:

◀◀ Hootie & the Blowfish, Phish, the Black Crowes

Christina Fuoco

Widespread Panic

Formed 1986, in Athens, GA.

John "J.B." Bell, vocals, guitar; John "JoJo" Hermann, keyboards, vocals; Michael Houser, guitars, vocals; Todd Nance, drums; Domingo "Sunny" Ortiz, percussion, vocals; David Schools, bass, vocals.

Widespread Panic can arguably be called of one of the finest live jam bands around. Since its raw beginnings during the early '80s in the college town of Athens, Georgia, the group has toured incessantly, not only fine-tuning the members' abilities to read each other's next musical step during a live performance, but also gathering one of the most devoted fan bases of any touring band. During the early '90s, neo-hippie jam bands began to sprout up around college campuses across America. A few of those bands—Blues Traveler, Phish, Col. Bruce Hampton & the Aquarium Rescue Unit, the Spin Doctors, and Widespread Panic—sought to locate the "Horizons of Rock Developing Everywhere." These five pioneers produced the idea of a traveling hippie music festival that would more commonly become known as the H.O.R.D.E. tour. Although Panic participated in H.O.R.D.E. for the first two years, it then decided to branch off and continue to build its own following. Up until 1998, the band had only produced studio albums, leaving many non-Panic fans clueless as to how intense a live show could be. However, in April of 1998, the band released its first-ever live collection, the two-CD set ti-

tled *Light Fuse . . . Get Away*. That album gave the band—and its fans—considerable leverage when calling Panic an incredible live group. Many have said Panic inherited the Grateful Dead's legacy when Jerry Garcia died in 1995. However, looking to the Dead for much of its early inspiration, Panic only built upon the foundation of the Dead's already solid penchant for the jam. Where R.E.M. put Athens on the map for alternative, college radio–type bands, Widespread Panic established it as a mecca for flower children.

what to buy: Culled from more than 100 shows recorded over the course of two years, *Light Fuse . . . Get Away* 𝄞𝄞𝄞𝄞 (Capricorn, 1998, prod. John Keane) allows veteran fans and newbies alike the ability to enter the realm of a live Widespread Panic show—without actually being there. Although all the songs were taken from independent performances, John Keane's three-month production process created a full-on live experience. Through the course of the long, space-like guitar solos and lively, tribal drum jams, the listener has no choice but to believe *Light Fuse . . . Get Away* was one full, two-set show. But Panic could never have produced such a captivating live collection had it not been for the dramatic roots planted on their first album, *Space Wrangler* 𝄞𝄞𝄞𝄞 (Capricorn, 1988, prod. John Keane). This album housed such concert favorites as the happy, upbeat "Porch Song," the trance-like "Driving Song," "Chilly Water," and, of course, the one that put Panic on the map, "Coconut."

what to buy next: No Panic collection would be complete without *Bombs & Butterflies* 𝄞𝄞𝄞𝄞 (Capricorn, 1996, prod. John Keane). Panic revisited its roots on this album, almost reproducing the strong lineup of songs on *Space Wrangler*. For *Bombs*, Panic enlisted the help of longtime friend and fellow musician Vic Chesnutt, who co-wrote and shared vocal duties on the haunting ballad "Aunt Avis." The band also pays homage to a hero, Pops Staples, on the melancholy "Hope in a Hopeless World." But it's on the songs "Greta," "Glory," and "Rebirtha" that Panic translates to music its strong storytelling ability and love for a great jam.

the rest:
Widespread Panic 𝄞𝄞𝄞𝄞 (Capricorn, 1991)
Everyday 𝄞𝄞𝄞𝄞 (Capricorn, 1993)
Ain't Life Grand 𝄞𝄞𝄞𝄞 (Capricorn, 1994)

worth searching for: *Radio Child* (Capricorn, 1997, prod. various) is an import compilation of studio recordings that winnows down that sector of Panic's career for those who just want to sample.

influences:

◀◀ The Grateful Dead, the Allman Brothers Band, Sea Level

Ari Bendersky

Jane Wiedlin

See: The Go-Go's

Wig

Formed 1989, in Ann Arbor, MI.

Preston Long, vocals (1989–91); Clark S. Nova (born Shawn Jimmerson), vocals (1991–present); Rob Schurgin, guitars; Fran Falls (born Fran Fazzina), bass; John Burke, drums; Wayne Faler, guitar, keyboards (1997–present).

Wig is one of the few bands that changed lead singers and still continued to thrive. Ann Arborite Preston Long led Wig through a maze of punk rock and rap sounds until shortly after the band released its debut EP, *Lying Next to You*, in 1989. Although the EP was named Record of the Week by the BBC's John Peel, Long left the band to form Mule. Clark S. Nova, a member of the band Morsel, was signing copies of his book, *Bone Cold,* when he met Rob Schurgin, Fran Falls, and John Burke. But after two major label CDs, Wig—by this time relocated to Los Angeles—found itself on the street again, showcasing itself in hopes of landing a new deal.

what to buy: *Wireland* 🎵🎵🎵 (Island, 1997, prod. Wig, Andy Johns, Chris Varady, Keith Cleversley) is more melodic and sultry than its predecessor, 1994's *Deliverance*. "California Poppy" wraps Echo & the Bunnymen–like soaring guitars around the toe-tapping, hook-laden lyrics. Twinkling guitars and Nova's distorted vocals on "Negativland" also have elements of Mercury Rev.

what to buy next: *Deliverance* 🎵🎵🎵 (Island, 1994, prod. Chris Varady) opens with the furious "Gun Groove" and continues through a landscape of hip-hop–like rhythms ("Tender Assassin"), quick time changes ("Cedric"), and metal ("Rant"). The highlight of the album is the song "10 Seconds," which doesn't allow the listener one second to breathe before it kicks into a flurry of acerbic guitars and chest-pounding drums and bass.

influences:
◀◀ Jane's Addiction, Pink Floyd

Christina Fuoco

Wilco

Formed 1994, in Chicago, IL.

Jeff Tweedy, vocals, guitar; Ken Coomer, drums; John Stirratt, bass, vocals, guitar, piano, organ; Max Johnston, guitar, vocals, fiddle, mandolin, banjo (1994–96); Jay Bennett, guitar (1995–present).

After Jay Farrar left Uncle Tupelo to form Son Volt in 1994, the rest of the band soldiered on under a new moniker and the leadership of singer-songwriter Jeff Tweedy. Initially, Wilco was

WHAT ALBUM CHANGED YOUR LIFE?

Nick Drake, *Pink Moon.* I listened to that record a lot. It made me a lot more interested in being able to write songs that were not just what you could play on an acoustic guitar but could stand on their own as an acoustic guitar and vocal. I don't think there's many records that achieve that as well as *Pink Moon.* Also just how interesting the arrangements are, considering there *is* no arrangements; it's all just vocal and acoustic guitar.

Jeff Tweedy (of Wilco)

content to follow along in the alternative-country footsteps of the mighty Tupelo, but Tweedy soon made it clear that he had something much more ambitious and musically challenging in mind. In the wake of the group's sophomore set, Wilco became a star vehicle for their leader, while the rest of the band—creative souls in their own right—stretched out by backing singers Steve Forbert and Jeff Black on their albums and recording some material on their own under the name Courtesy Move.

what to buy: If only for its engaging treatment of one of rock's hoariest conceits—the "life-on-the-road" album—*Being There* 🎵🎵🎵🎵 (Reprise, 1996, prod. Wilco) is deserving of the accolades that greeted it upon release. From full-tilt freakout of the opening cut ("Misunderstood") and gritty, Stonesy rock 'n' roll ("Monday," "I Got You (at the End of the Century)"), to gripping Gram Parsons–inspired country rock ("Someday Soon") and two radically different treatments of the song "Outtasite (Outta Mind)," the sprawling two-CD set is a brave statement for a still-young band to make.

what to buy next: On *Mermaid Avenue* 🎵🎵🎵🎵 (Elektra, 1998, prod. Wilco, Billy Bragg, Grant Showbiz), Wilco teams with British singer-songwriter Billy Bragg to bring life to songs left unfinished by folk legend Woody Guthrie. A daunting prospect

for any artist, the album works thanks to the sympatico pairing of the band and Bragg, and the seeming ease with which they make manifest the work of a long-dead prophet whose words are as vital as ever. *A.M.* ✓✓✓ (Reprise, 1995, prod. Brian Paulson, Wilco) contains a preponderance of breakup tunes (directed at Farrar, perhaps?), including "I Must Be High" and "Box Full of Letters."

worth searching for: The band, sans-Tweedy, backs singer-songwriter Jeff Black on his stirring debut, *Birmingham Road* (Arista Austin, 1998).

influences:

◄◄ The Rolling Stones, Gram Parsons, the Replacements, the Band

see also: *Uncle Tupelo, Golden Smog*

Daniel Durchholz

Kim Wilde

Born 1960, in Chiswick, England.

Awkwardly donning the ripped jeans and bleached roots of a well-packaged new wave attempt, Kim Wilde's initial assault on the global charts owed more to the swagger of Debbie Harry than to the washed-over glitz of Diana Ross (who she later successfully covered). "We're the kids in America!" she facetiously belted in 1981, and the irony was quietly noted. Her working-class pout quickly gave way in the face of decreasing impact, though, and a severe image reworking brought the mid-'80s gloss-pop rendition of the Supremes' "You Keep Me Hanging On" as a means of reinvention. The song worked, reaching the Top 10 worldwide. It was, however, to be the last of such successes for the typically lukewarm bleating of Wilde, who after several dips lower into the late '80s tart mode turned up with predictably diminished returns on the charts. Slight single successes in the U.K. ("Who Do You Think You Are?") and their diva-posed host albums (*Now and Forever*) have kept her in the black, but with little chance of musical levity left to promise.

what's available: *The Singles Collection, 1981–1993* ✓✓✓ (MCA, 1993, prod. various) is worthwhile, if only for the novelty of hearing our generation's musical Barbie doll. Sincerity is, as expected, not to be discussed here. But fun does abound throughout, with a candy lip-gloss flavoring that lasts as long as . . . candy, really.

influences:

◄◄ Blondie, Donna Summer, Diana Ross, the Go-Go's

►► Cathy Dennis, Martika, St. Etienne, the Spice Girls

Billy Manes

Webb Wilder

Born May 19, 1954, in Hattiesburg, MS.

A tall, balding, bespectacled white guy in a state trooper's hat might seem a man least likely to be a wild rock 'n' roller, but Wilder has turned his odd looks into an effective schtick. Playing deadpan with his deep baritone voice, Wilder has created a body of work he sometimes calls "hillbilly gothic"—a weird mixture of country, blues, and psychedelic-era rock. His band has evolved from Webb Wilder & the Beatnecks to simply Webb Wilder, and most recently Webb Wilder & the NashVegans. But the elements have remained largely the same: power chords, wild twangy guitar, and a large dose of novelty. He's also come up with one of the best credos in the business: "work hard, rock hard, eat hard, sleep hard, grow big, wear glasses if you need 'em."

what to buy: *It Came from Nashville* ✓✓✓ (Watermelon, 1986/1993, prod. R.S. Field), Wilder's first album, combines instrumentals and songs filled with deadpan southern humor. The best is "Poolside" (co-written by Kevin Welch), in which Wilder lists his summertime rules: "no running, no pushing, no profanity, and no dogs." The updated version of the album includes four extra tracks.

what to buy next: *Town & Country* ✓✓✓ (Watermelon, 1995, prod. R.S. Field, Mike Janas, Webb Wilder, the NashVegans) was originally conceived as a driving tape on which one band performs all the songs. The result is a wild cover album that ranges from the Flamin' Groovies ("Slow Death") to Rodney Crowell ("I Ain't Living Long like This").

what to avoid: The vinyl version of *It Came from Nashville* (Racket, 1986, prod. R.S. Field) is improved with the CD version's extra tracks.

the rest:
Hybrid Vigor ✓✓✓ (Demon, 1984)
Doo Dad ✓✓✓ (Praxis/Zoo, 1991)
Acres of Suede ✓✓✓ (Watermelon, 1996)

influences:

◄◄ The Rolling Stones, ZZ Top, Howlin' Wolf

►► Omar & the Howlers, the LeRoi Brothers

Brian Mansfield

Dar Williams

Born Dorothy Snowdon Williams, April 19, 1967, in Mt. Kisco, NY.

Dar Williams is the quintessential female folk singer of the '90s, capturing society's awkward social transitions as well as the timeless "big questions" with graceful melodies and intelligent, often wry, lyrics. The daughter of a Yale-educated medical writer and a Vassar grad who raises funds for Planned Parenthood, Williams enjoyed a cozy childhood in an upscale Manhattan suburb. A sensitive soul with a crystalline alto voice and a keen eye for the comical, she wrote her first song at age 11, but shied away from performing until age 23, when she managed to overcome a serious case of stage fright and hit the Boston coffeehouses. Gender roles, relationships, and stereotypes— from the innocence of childhood androgyny to a sexist boyfriend with roving eyes—are prime targets for Williams's lyrical twists. But she just as easily spins metaphorical tales about the deeper, more subtle tensions and pleasures of life, with either a delicate tug at the heartstrings or a humorous elbow in the ribs. Although arrangements are generally kept simple, focusing on Williams's silky voice underpinned by her acoustic guitar, some tunes feature a full band (and on one you'll even hear a digeridoo).

what to buy: *Mortal City* ♫♫♫♫ (Razor & Tie, 1996, prod. Steven Miller) offers a brilliant balance of depth and levity, delicacy and strength. On the boisterous "As Cool As I Am," the narrator dumps her lecherous boyfriend and regains her pride. "This Was Pompeii" likens one of history's most deadly, unforeseen disasters with the ashes of a failed relationship. Williams's third release, *End of the Summer* ♫♫♫♪ (Razor & Tie, 1997, prod. Steven Miller), displays a natural evolution from her previous work, with a mature, subtle, and sly touch that doesn't lose its zing. "Party Generation" puts a mirror to the face of all those baby boomer Peter Pans out there, while "Teenagers, Kick Our Butts" humorously delivers a serious challenge for youths to accomplish more than her thirtysomething generation has. The title track captures the hope and regrets of transition, symbolized by the seasons.

what to buy next: Williams's debut, *The Honesty Room* ♫♫♫ (Burning Field Music, 1994/Razor & Tie, 1995, prod. Dar Williams, Adam Rothberg, David Seitz, Brooks Williams), has charm and wit, but is much more straightforward and less ambitious than her later releases.

influences:
◀◀ Joan Baez, Joni Mitchell

David Yonke

Lucinda Williams

Born January 26, 1953, in Lake Charles, LA.

Unfortunately, the same qualities that make Lucinda Williams's music so great also insure that more of it isn't put out for public consumption. The daughter of a poet/university professor, Williams is notoriously headstrong and has an artistic temperament ill-suited to issues of career logistics—stories of her clashes with labels and producers are legendary in the music business.

Yet she is also one of the finest songwriters of her generation, with a writerly gift for nailing a character or situation with the perfect detail, and a great singer whose earthy voice makes Williams her own best interpreter; if only we got to hear more of her music! Alas, in close to 20 years, she has put out a total of just five albums. Perhaps the pace will pick up in the future.

what to buy: Williams made two albums before finding her own voice as a writer and singer, and those early records are most notable as acts of homage to her country and Delta blues roots. Her third album, *Lucinda Williams* ♫♫♫♫ (Rough Trade, 1988/Koch, 1998, prod. Lucinda Williams, Gurf Morlix), is one of the signpost albums of post-punk Americana. Drawing on Williams's failed marriage (to Long Ryders drummer Greg Sowders) and eight years of pent-up career frustrations, these songs cut with an unbelievable intensity. The tough-minded feminine perspective of "I Just Wanted to See You So Bad" and "Passionate Kisses" rings absolutely true, and it's as unusual as it is emotionally rich. A triumph. One measure of this album's songcraft is how frequently other singers raid it for material: Mary Chapin Carpenter had a pop hit with "Passionate Kisses" and Patty Loveless a country hit with "The Night's Too Long," while Tom Petty covered "Changed the Locks" on his soundtrack album for the 1996 movie *She's the One* and Emmylou Harris did "Crescent City" on her 1993 album *Cowgirl's Prayer.* Koch's 1998 reissue of *Lucinda Williams* also includes six bonus tracks, including the songs from Rough Trade's out-of-print 1989 *Passionate Kisses* EP, as well as liner notes by both the artist and her father, Miller Williams.

what to buy next: The *Lucinda Williams* follow-up, *Sweet Old World* ♫♫♫♫ (Chameleon, 1992, prod. Lucinda Williams, Gurf Morlix, Dusty Wakeman), is more self-conscious than its predecessor, but still damned fine. It's also grim, coursing with images of suicide, death, and despair. It's fitting, then, that it closes with a cover of the late English cult folkie Nick Drake's "Which Will." While it took six years and several false starts for Williams's next record to see the light of day, the oft-delayed *Car Wheels on a Gravel Road* ♫♫♫♫♪ (Mercury, 1998, prod. Roy Bittan, Lucinda Williams) proved to be worth the wait. Less country and more bluesy than its two predecessors, *Car Wheels* finds Williams easing into her role of weary, wise soul woman. As usual, the songwriting is fabulous. "I Lost It" (rescued from 1980's *Happy Woman Blues*), the mournful "Lake Charles," the feisty "Joy," and the wonderfully detailed title track are just some of the standouts.

the rest:
Ramblin' on My Mind ♫♫♫ (Smithsonian/Folkways, 1979/1991)
Happy Woman Blues ♫♫♪ (Smithsonian/Folkways, 1980/1990)

worth searching for: Williams's cover of "Main Road" is one of the high points of the Victoria Williams tribute *Sweet Relief*

(Chaos, 1993, prod. various). During the six-year gap between *Sweet Old World* and *Car Wheels*, Williams showed up as a duet partner with Steve Earle on "You're Still Standin' There," from his 1996 album *I Feel Alright*, and on two tracks on Terry Allen's 1996 album *Human Remains*. The soundtrack album to Robert Redford's *The Horse Whisperer* (MCA, 1998, prod. various) also includes a version of "Still I Long for Your Kiss" different from the one on *Car Wheels*. Finally, there are bootleg tapes floating around of earlier versions of *Car Wheels*, most notably the one produced by Earle and his Twangtrust partner Ray Kennedy.

influences:

◄◄ Bob Dylan, Flannery O'Connor, Emmylou Harris, Robert Johnson, Rosanne Cash, Bonnie Raitt, Chrissie Hynde

►► Victoria Williams, Joe Henry, Mary Chapin Carpenter, Iris DeMent, Amy Rigby, Sheryl Crow

David Menconi

Victoria Williams

Born 1959, in Forbing, LA.

With her unusual, high-pitched voice and obviously quirky sensibility, Victoria Williams might seem at first like another indie-pop novelty. A few spins of her records, however, reveal a profound, major artist. A superb songwriter and distinctive vocalist, Williams achieved a great deal of press coverage during 1993 and 1994, when her battle with multiple sclerosis gained attention. Though her struggle against the disease has been an inspiring one—some major rock artists contributed versions of her songs to the tribute/benefit album *Sweet Relief* in 1993, which launched the Sweet Relief charity to help needy musicians with their medical expenses—her work has been somewhat overshadowed by the story. She grew up in Louisiana and attended college there. After trekking around the country, playing her songs for hikers, punks, and anyone else who'd listen, she made her way to Los Angeles, where she waited tables and performed when she could. At last she signed with Geffen, but her debut album sold poorly, as did her subsequent, critically acclaimed effort for Rough Trade. It wasn't until the release of *Sweet Relief*—featuring contributions from Lou Reed, Pearl Jam, Soul Asylum, and many others—that she became better known in the pop world. Her subsequent albums have enjoyed greater attention, though she has remained a bit too unique for the mainstream. Even so, her version of the standard "What a Wonderful World" graced a commercial for Microsoft. She is the subject of the song "Miss Williams' Guitar," by the Jayhawks, of which her husband Marc Olson was a member. A progressive, homespun Christian, Williams spins compassionate tales of friends, family, and nature that evince both childlike

wonder and old-soul wisdom. Musically, she draws from an extraordinary pool of influences—gospel, country, folk, acid-rock, pop—to create works that never seem derivative. Her live performances reach levels of intimacy and spontaneity that are rare in contemporary music.

what to buy: *Loose* ♪♪♪♪ (Mammoth, 1994, prod. Paul Fox) is Williams's most engaging collection—which is saying something. While it is governed, like the earlier albums, by her luminous world view, her experiences with illness and loss give everything greater heft.

what to buy next: On *Musings of a Creekdipper* ♪♪♪◊ (Mammoth, 1998, prod. Victoria Williams, Trina Shoemaker), Williams displays maturity and wisdom. The spare, folky production highlights the richness of her lyrics as she explores issues of life, love, and mortality.

the rest:
Happy Come Home ♪♪♪ (Geffen, 1987)
Swing the Statue! ♪♪♪◊ (Rough Trade, 1990)
This Moment: Live in Toronto ♪♪♪◊ (Mammoth, 1995)

worth searching for: Though Williams doesn't sing a word on it, *Sweet Relief* (Sony, 1993, executive prod. Sylvia Reed, Kelley Walker) launched the singer-songwriter from little-known cult artist to reasonably big star. (It also helped her raise money for health care.) Highlights are Soul Asylum's Rod Stewart–like "Summer of Drugs," Lucinda Williams's "Main Road," Pearl Jam's reverential "Crazy Mary," and Lou Reed's skronky "Tarbelly and Featherfoot."

influences:

◄◄ Joni Mitchell, Kate Bush, the Roches

►► Jewel, Leah Andreone, Soul Asylum

Simon Glickman and Amy Weivoda

Brian Wilson

Born Brian Douglas Wilson, June 20, 1942, in Inglewood, CA.

His younger brother Dennis, in his own inimitable fashion, said it best many, many years ago: "Brian Wilson *is* the Beach Boys. We're his messengers. He's everything. We're nothing. Period." Yet such is the indelible impact of the work Brian Wilson created for his messengers during the mid-'60s that it remains nothing short of an inescapable, insurmountable musical albatross which continues to haunt both the band and its creator to this day. Every note sung or played by Brian and the Beach Boys, who have spent the better part of the last decade primarily working apart, is inevitably compared—usually unfavorably—to their triumphs together 30-plus years ago, and every Brian Wilson solo album is invariably preceded by a press release proclaiming it to be his greatest work since *Pet Sounds*, that crowning achievement from 1966. Nevertheless, those waiting for another all-encompassing masterpiece from either Brian *or* the Boys at this late date are likely looking for a disappointment. That is not to say Wilson isn't still capable of producing works of true beauty: his flair for both vocal and instrumental arrangement remains unparalleled, his voice is now more mature but still as achingly expressive as it was in its prime, and magnificent melodies still seem to spill from him with impossible ease. Unfortunately, Wilson's career has forever been subject to the control of an unsympathetic parade of characters (from his tyrannical father/first manager Murry to the infamous psycho-svengali Dr. Eugene E. Landy to, during the '90s, a host of hotshot producers-of-the-moment), all of whom seem only too willing to take advantage of Wilson's gifts—and most malleable of personalities—solely for their own personal, and, of course, financial gain. It's hardly the kind of atmosphere one could call conducive to the creative spirit. Still, despite all of these adversities and others besides, Wilson has somehow continued to write and record wonderful new music and remains an inspiration to continuing generations of musicians and composers who, rather than wishing this particular Beach Boy return to former glories and "Do It Again," realize the man long ago earned his place as one of America's greatest-ever musical figures and should finally be left alone to now create only what—and *when*—he wants to.

what to buy: Oddly enough, perhaps the best way to grasp the music and the magic of Brian Wilson is through a short soundtrack album entitled *I Just Wasn't Made for These Times* ♫♫♫♫ (MCA, 1995, prod. Don Was, Brian Wilson). Actually recordings made for a documentary film, it captures Wilson and a sympathetic cast of accompanists revisiting both the best of his solo work ("Love and Mercy" remains one of Wilson's greatest statements ever) and overlooked Beach Boy gems (from the tiny opening "Meant for You" to the gorgeous "Warmth of the Sun"). The film itself also does much to reveal the inner workings of this sometimes most inscrutable of artists, and as such should be considered required viewing.

what to buy next: Both *Brian Wilson* ♫♫♫ (Sire/Reprise, 1988, prod. Brian Wilson, Russ Titelman, Andy Paley, Lenny Waronker, Jeff Lynne) and the collaboration with Van Dyke Parks, *Orange Crate Art* ♫♫♫ (Warner Bros., 1995, prod. Van Dyke Parks), contain fine Wilson performances that are routinely buried beneath track upon track of needless studio bombast and artificial sweetening. Thankfully, Wilson's talents are sturdy enough to withstand even this sort of punishment. *Imagination* ♫♫♫ (Giant, 1998, prod. Brian Wilson, Joe Thomas) finds Wilson's voice the strongest it's been in decades, but again the production is wholly overwrought and the presence of Jimmy Buffett, for one, smacks of misguided opportunism.

WHAT ALBUM CHANGED YOUR LIFE?

Joni Mitchell, *Blue.* I listened to *Blue* once for months at a time. It's so real, I felt that she was totally giving. It's a very giving record. She shared a lot on that record.

Victoria Williams

worth searching for: It is a little-known fact that some of Wilson's best work of the '60s was done *outside* of the Beach Boys, and *Still I Dream of You: Rare Works of Brian Wilson* (M & M Enterprise, 1993, compilation prod. Chu Takahashi) is a magnificent, revelatory, 32-track collection of sides he wrote, produced, and/or performed on between 1962 and 1970 for a myriad of artists ranging from Glen Campbell ("Guess I'm Dumb" sports a *Pet Sounds* –like sophistication a year before the fact) to Dino, Desi & Billy. Also necessary is *Sweet Insanity* (Vigotone, 1993, prod. Brian Wilson), Wilson's second record for Sire, which sadly fell victim to a spate of lawsuits and was left "officially" unreleased. Those who were too quick in dismissing some of this album's more, um, "eccentric" moments (such as the duet with Bob Dylan and the surf-rap monstrosity "Smart Girls") are obviously unfamiliar with the key role humor has played in some of Wilson's greatest moments, from "I'm Bugged at My Ol' Man" to *The Beach Boys Love You*—not to mention that so-fittingly-titled Holy Grail of all unreleased albums, the Beach Boys' very own *Smile*.

influences:

◄◄ Phil Spector, George Gershwin, the Four Freshmen

►► Paul McCartney, Eric Carmen, Andy Partridge, Sean O'Hagan

see also: *The Beach Boys, Van Dyke Parks, Wilson Phillips*

Gary Pig Gold

Chris Wilson

See: The Flamin' Groovies

Jackie Wilson

Born June 9, 1934, in Detroit, MI. Died January 21, 1984.

Reputedly the most exciting, acrobatic live performer of his time, Jackie Wilson could sizzle when he sang. His darting, arching shrieks sound like exposed nerves. His greatest recording, "(Your Love Keeps Lifting Me) Higher and Higher," could well be the best single ever made. But Wilson's body of work is riddled with material far less sublime. Under the dubious influence of a manipulative manager and insensitive record label, this great vocal talent was wasted on projects as odious as an entire album of Al Jolson songs. His longings for conventional show business respectability may have mirrored the mores of his generation of black entertainers, but it meant that Wilson would leave behind a recorded legacy more frustrating for what might have been than what he actually accomplished. A one-time professional boxer, he apprenticed as lead tenor with Billy Ward & the Dominoes, replacing the estimable Clyde McPhatter in the lineup. His earliest rock 'n' roll records, which were also the first hits for fledgling songwriter and future Motown chief Berry Gordy Jr., throbbed with his incessant pleading vocals. But after parting ways with Gordy, Wilson fell under the unenlightened artist and repertoire direction of Brunswick Records, the same people that gave you Buddy Holly with strings. Wilson's singles had stopped making the charts at all when "Higher and Higher," a record he cut with moonlighting Motown sidemen behind him, blasted off in 1965, setting the stage for what could have been one of the more extraordinary comebacks in soul history. His decision the following year to leave his longtime, mob-affiliated manager—who also owned Brunswick Records—may have helped sabotage that possibility. The 1969 murder of his 16-year-old son, Jackie Wilson Jr., turned Wilson into a further tragic figure. But the story gets downright Dickensian after his onstage collapse from an apparent heart attack in 1975 at the Latin Casino in Cherry Hill, New Jersey. Shipped out of the emergency room in a coma, possibly the product of improper medical care, Wilson lay speechless and motionless in a hospital bed while a long-forgotten ex-wife and attorneys began fighting over his inert body. When it became apparent there was no money anyway, Wilson wound up a ward of the state—alone, abandoned, and comatose for eight years before he finally died.

what to buy: The high points of 15 years of recording can all be found on *The Jackie Wilson Story* 𝄢𝄢𝄢𝄢 (Epic, 1983, prod. various), a 24-song collection that qualifies as one of the backbones of modern soul music.

what to buy next: The three-disc box set *Mr. Excitement* 𝄢𝄢𝄢𝄢 (Rhino, 1992, prod. various) covers the Jackie Wilson legacy in considerable detail that mixes his key singles with album tracks, including collaborations with Count Basie and the Chi-Lites.

what to avoid: *Merry Christmas from Jackie Wilson* 𝄢 (Brunswick, 1963/Rhino, 1991, prod. Nat Tarnapol) is not only a lame Jackie Wilson album, recorded at the nadir of his career, but it's not a very good Christmas album, either.

the rest:
The Very Best of Jackie Wilson 𝄢𝄢𝄢 (Ace, 1989)
Live at the Copa 𝄢𝄢 (Brunswick, 1962/Rhino, 1995)
The Very Best of Jackie Wilson 𝄢𝄢𝄢 (Rhino, 1994)
Higher and Higher 𝄢𝄢𝄢𝄢 (Rhino, 1995)
Vol. 1: The Chicago Years 𝄢𝄢𝄢𝄢 (Charly, 1995)
Vol. 2: The Chicago Years 𝄢𝄢𝄢 (Charly, 1996)
Vol. 1: The New York Years 𝄢𝄢𝄢 (Charly, 1996)
Vol. 2: The New York Years 𝄢𝄢𝄢 (Charly, 1996)

worth searching for: An X-rated version of the duet with LaVern Baker, "Think Twice," has been only infrequently bootlegged. Plus, if you want to see Jackie Wilson in action, check out *Shindig! Presents Jackie Wilson* (Rhino Home Video, 1991), 30 minutes of classic singing and dynamic footwork from America's best ever live music TV show.

influences:

◄◄ Clyde McPhatter, Little Willie John, Roy Hamilton

►► Elvis Presley, Marv Johnson, Michael Jackson, Chuckii Booker

Joel Selvin

Wilson Phillips

Formed 1989, in Los Angeles, CA. Disbanded 1993.

Chynna Phillips, vocals; Carnie Wilson, vocals; Wendy Wilson, vocals.

They came from a 24-karat gene pool that had already spawned "God Only Knows" and "California Dreaming"; the trio's parents included Beach Boy Brian Wilson and the Mamas & the Papas' John and Michelle Phillips. But theirs was a quick flight; the million-selling 1990 debut, *Wilson Phillips*, proved to be a one-time smash, and after a disappointing sophomore effort the trio went their separate ways. The Wilson sisters have spent some time recording with their father, including contributing backup vocals on his 1995 documentary project, *I Just Wasn't Made for These Times*.

what to buy: The debut, *Wilson Phillips* 𝄢𝄢𝄢𝄢 (SBK, 1990, prod. Glenn Ballard), is a collection of tautly constructed pop tunes, mesmerizing vocal harmonies, and flawless production. It isn't the second coming of anything profound, but a recording that sounds this good and effortless deserves praise.

what to avoid: *The Wilsons* ♪ (Mercury, 1997, prod. various) is a misbegotten attempt by the Wilson sisters to revive their career, including another collaboration with their father. Surf's out.

the rest:
Shadows and Light ♪♪♪ (SBK, 1992)

solo outings:
Chynna Phillips:
Naked and Sacred ♪♪ (EMI, 1995)

Carnie and Wendy Wilson:
Hey Santa! ♪♪♪ (SBK, 1993)

influences:
◀◀ The Beach Boys, the Mamas & the Papas, the Ronettes

▶▶ Hanson, Brandy

Patrick McCarty and Gary Graff

Marty Wilson-Piper

See: The Church

Jesse Winchester

Born May 17, 1944, in Shreveport, LA.

Jesse Winchester is a marvelous songwriter whose tunes straddle the borderline between country and rock. The list of performers that have covered his songs includes Emmylou Harris, Jimmy Buffett, the Amazing Rhythm Aces, Nicolette Larson, Ted Hawkins, the Weather Girls, New Grass Revival, Joan Baez, the Everly Brothers, and Jonathan Edwards, while composing luminaries such as Bob Dylan, Elton John, and Elvis Costello all mention him as an admired contemporary. Even though tunesmithing has provided a relatively steady source of income for Winchester, he first made his mark with a superb eponymous debut album containing such classics as "The Brand New Tennessee Waltz" and "Yankee Lady." The road taken to his vinyl unveiling has its dramatic elements. Winchester grew up in Memphis, Tennessee, when his military family was stationed there. After graduating from Williams College in 1966 he went to Germany to further his studies, and it was there that he received his draft notice in 1967. Winchester, after much agonizing, opted to evade the draft by moving to Montreal, where he eventually married and started a family. His earliest songs are filled with wistful, bittersweet reflections of Americana, but after President Jimmy Carter's amnesty program for draft resisters became a reality in 1977, Winchester (who became a Canadian citizen in 1973) visited Memphis again and came away disillusioned with the changes in his old stomping grounds.

what to buy: *The Best of Jesse Winchester* ♪♪♪♪ (Rhino, 1989, prod. various) is an 18-song collection that extracts well-chosen samples from Winchester's first seven albums. While aficionados may quibble about including this and excluding that, anyone dipping into Winchester's repertoire for the first time should have no complaints. *Jesse Winchester* ♪♪♪♪ (Ampex, 1970/Stony Plain, 1995, prod. Robbie Robertson) is the first album Winchester made and some of the songs found here are little masterpieces that are consistently covered by discerning, big-name fans, including Jimmy Buffett ("Biloxi") and Emmylou Harris ("The Brand New Tennessee Waltz"). It doesn't hurt that Winchester's backup musicians for this release include members of the Band.

what to buy next: *Humor Me* ♪♪♪ (Sugar Hill, 1988, prod. Jesse Winchester, Bil Vorn Dick) is more of a country/bluegrass album than any of the other releases Winchester has put out. It was recorded in Nashville with an awesome lineup of players, including Bela Fleck on banjo, Jerry Douglas on dobro, and Mark O'Connor on fiddle. The warm compositional style Winchester is known for can be heard all through this release, with special favorites such as "Well-A-Wiggy" and "Willow" showing, respectively, the fun and thoughtful sides of the writer.

the rest:
Third Down, 110 to Go ♪♪♪♪ (Bearsville, 1972/Stony Plain, 1995)
Learn to Love It ♪♪♪ (Bearsville, 1974/Stony Plain, 1995)
Let the Rough Side Drag ♪♪♪♪ (Bearsville, 1976/Stony Plain, 1996)
Nothing but a Breeze ♪♪♪ (Bearsville, 1977/Stony Plain, 1995)
A Touch on the Rainy Side ♪♪♪ (Bearsville, 1978/Stony Plain, 1996)
Talk Memphis ♪♪♪ (Bearsville, 1981/Stony Plain, 1996)

influences:
◀◀ Hank Williams, Bob Dylan

▶▶ Mac McAnally

Garaud MacTaggart

Winger
/Kip Winger

Formed 1986, in New York, NY.

Kip Winger, vocals, bass; Reb Beach, guitar; Paul Taylor, guitar (1986–89); Rod Morgenstein, drums; John Roth, guitar (1990–93).

Sporting a studmuffin's hunk appeal and a pop metal safety valve, Kip Winger emerged from Alice Cooper's band all set to charge the MTV airwaves with his new group. Like most hair bands of the same vintage, Winger found its niche in power ballads; Winger could pen reasonably engaging melodies, but there was no disguising the generic rockers. The metal backlash overtook the band as the decade drew to a close, leaving Winger as an '80s footnote—though he's still trying to rekindle the public's flame for him.

what to buy: *Winger* ♪♪ (Atlantic, 1989, prod. Beau Hill) is the group's most successful album and contains Kip Winger's best

ballad, "Headin' for a Heartbreak." There is no excuse for attempting Hendrix's "Purple Haze," however.

the rest:
In the Heart of the Young ♪♪ (Atlantic, 1990)
Pull ♪ (Atlantic, 1993)

worth searching for: Winger's best work actually appears on Alice Cooper albums, of which the hit-laden *Trash* (Epic, 1989, prod. Desmond Child) remains in print.

solo outings:
Kip Winger:
This Conversation Seems like a Dream ♪♪♪ (Domo, 1997)

influences:
◄◄ Boston, Journey, Alice Cooper

Allan Orski

Wings
See: Paul McCartney

Edgar Winter
Born December 28, 1946, in Beaumont, TX.

Edgar Winter may have composed "Frankenstein," that monster of hard-rock redundancy, but fans should rejoice that he first formed White Trash. The band was meaner looking than a half-dozen Jerry Lee Lewises, and twice as rocking. Winter, who is guitar great Johnny Winter's younger brother, is a multi-instrumentalist; his sax and keyboard work is complex, and his technique sways between subtle and ferocious. His vocals could peel a banana or soothe a fevered baby. His take of "Tobacco Road" from his debut album, *Entrance*, is nearly unhinged and completely unforgettable. But for all of his talents, Winter's recordings since the '70s have been sporadic in both volume and quality.

what to buy: *Edgar Winter's White Trash* ♪♪♪♪ (Epic, 1971/1989/Mobile Fidelity, 1997, prod. Rick Derringer) covers hard rock, soul, funk, and blues—often at a blistering pace. The impassioned "Save the Planet" and melodic "Where Would I Be" accompany a salvo of rocking R&B in "I've Got News for You" and "Give It Everything You Got."

what to buy next: *The Edgar Winter Collection* ♪♪♪♪ (Rhino, 1989, prod. various) samples Winter's '70s catalog and highlights his most familiar work. "Frankenstein" is part of Winter's hard rocking *They Only Come out at Night* ♪♪♪ (Epic, 1972, prod. Rick Derringer), which also spawned the play-it-'til-it-melts "Free Ride."

what to avoid: Flawless playing can't overcome the sterile recording on *The Real Deal* ♪♪ (Intersound, 1996), which is as clinical as a jingle house.

the rest:
Entrance ♪♪♪ (Epic, 1970/1992)
Roadwork ♪♪♪♪ (Epic, 1972/1989)
Shock Treatment ♪♪♪ (Epic, 1974/Legacy, 1990)
(With Johnny Winter) *Together: Live* ♪♪♪ (Blue Sky, 1970/Epic, 1992)
I'm Not a Kid Anymore ♪♪ (Thunderbolt, 1994)

worth searching for: On Johnny Winter's *Hey, Where's Your Brother?* (Pointblank, 1992), Edgar provides keyboard, sax, and vocal support on his big brother's strongest showing of the '90s.

influences:
◄◄ Johnny Winter, Blood, Sweat & Tears, the Blues Project, Sly & the Family Stone, Them
►► Stevie Wonder, Rare Earth

Patrick McCarty

Johnny Winter
Born February 23, 1944, in Leland, MS.

Albino blues guitarist Johnny Winter was already a journeyman in 1968, when fame beckoned from the rock 'n' roll crowd via a feature in *Rolling Stone* magazine. Raised in Texas, Winter helped familiarize white rock audiences with traditional blues by incorporating rock into his music. Winter's first few rock recordings made him a top draw, and he played at the Woodstock festival and other high-profile gigs. While Winter semi-retired in 1972 to recover from heroin addiction, his brother Edgar formed White Trash with the rest of Johnny's band; they had a bright but brief rock career that actually eclipsed Johnny's fame, and Johnny didn't repeat his early success until he started working with Muddy Waters in 1977 as a sideman and producer. Two Winter-produced Waters albums won Grammys, and Winter stayed with the elder bluesman until Waters's death in 1983. Winter has continued touring and recording for various labels with varying degrees of success. Not a prolific writer, Winter's skill lies mostly in putting his stamp on other people's tunes. In 1986, he became the first white artist inducted into the Blues Foundation's Hall of Fame.

what to buy: *Johnny Winter and . . . Live* ♪♪♪♪ (Columbia, 1970, prod. Johnny Winter, Rick Derringer) busted him out as big as he would get. With the help of backup guitar ace Derringer, Winter rips through "Jumping Jack Flash" and rocks out the blues on "Good Morning Little Schoolgirl." *Guitar Slinger* ♪♪♪♪ (Alligator, 1983, prod. Bruce Iglauer, Dick Shurman) avoids the rock pyrotechnics as a group of veteran blues sidemen give full support to Winter's rootsier side. Check out his slide guitar on "It's My Life, Baby" and "Iodine in My Coffee." *White Hot Blues* ♪♪♪♪ (Columbia/Legacy, 1997, prod. Johnny Winter) is a good sampler of his early acumen.

what to buy next: After laying off to kick heroin, Winter sent a message with *Still Alive and Well* 🐾🐾🐾 (Columbia, 1973, prod. Rick Derringer). He rocks hard, and even though "Too Much Seconal" and "Cheap Tequila" warn against substance abuse, the album doesn't preach. *Serious Business* 🐾🐾🐾 (Alligator, 1985/1993, prod. various) is solid Texas roadhouse music. "Master Mechanic" proves Winter a master guitarist.

what to avoid: *Captured Live* 🐾🐾 (Blue Sky, 1976, prod. Johnny Winter) finds Winter still trying to climb the rock mountain before turning back to the blues. It's journeyman work, and unexciting.

best of the rest:

Johnny Winter 🐾🐾🐾 (Columbia, 1969/1990)
Second Winter 🐾🐾🐾 (Columbia, 1970/1990)
Johnny Winter And . . . 🐾🐾🐾 (Columbia, 1971)
Nothin' but the Blues 🐾🐾🐾 (Blue Sky, 1977/1987)
Third Degree 🐾🐾🐾 (Alligator, 1986)
The Winter of '88 🐾🐾🐾 (MCA, 1988)
Let Me In 🐾🐾🐾 (Charisma, 1991)
Hey, Where's Your Brother? 🐾🐾🐾 (Pointblank, 1992)
Scorchin' Blues 🐾🐾🐾 (Legacy, 1992)
A Rock 'n' Roll Collection 🐾🐾 (Columbia/Legacy, 1994)
Live in NYC '97 🐾🐾🐾 (Pointblank, 1998)

worth searching for: The bootleg *Texas International Pop Festival* (Oh Boy) captures a seminal Winter performance on home turf, highlighted by a burning, nearly 13-minute take of "Mean Mistreater."

influences:

◄◄ T-Bone Walker, Albert Collins, Chuck Berry, Muddy Waters, Keith Richards

►► Stevie Ray Vaughan, Jimmie Vaughan, Eric Johnson, Edgar Winter

Lawrence Gabriel

Steve Winwood

Born May 12, 1948, in Birmingham, England.

Stevie Winwood belted out "Gimme Some Lovin'" and "I'm a Man" with the Spencer Davis Group when he was still a teenager. Schooled in jazz and R&B, Winwood clearly had ambitions, and he pursued them with zest, leaving Davis for the adventurous Traffic, during which time he also collaborated with Cream's Eric Clapton and Ginger Baker in Blind Faith. Following Traffic's demise, Winwood worked with Japanese composer Stomu Yamashta before launching a solo career that would go from halting to enormously successful—first hitting with his *Arc of a Diver* album in 1980 and then in an even bigger way six years later with *Back in the High Life*. Over the years, Winwood perfected a seamless blend of his jazz and R&B roots

with pop, rock, folk, and world music; at its best, Winwood's music is transcendent, at its worst it seems stiff and formulaic. In 1994 he re-formed Traffic with singer-drummer Jim Capaldi, but it was short-lived, and he returned to solo work thereafter.

what to buy: The box set *The Finer Things* 🐾🐾🐾🐾 (Island/Chronicles, 1995, prod. various) is so comprehensive it's absolutely essential, tracing Winwood's career from Spencer Davis to his latest solo ventures. That may be the one piece you need own, but *Arc of a Diver* 🐾🐾🐾🐾 (Island, 1980, prod. Steve Winwood)—an evocative, one-man-band project—should be heard in its entirety, too.

what to buy next: *Back in the High Life* 🐾🐾🐾 (Island, 1986, prod. Russ Titelman, Steve Winwood) provided Winwood's commercial breakthrough with a string of hits such as "Higher Love," "The Finer Things," and the title track, and even the non-hits—"Wake Me up on Judgment Day," "Split Decision"—rank high in his songbook.

what to avoid: *Junction Seven* 🐾 (Virgin, 1997, prod. Narada Michael Walden, Steve Winwood) is slick, polished, and soulless—and the latter flaw is something Winwood's never had to worry about.

the rest:

Steve Winwood 🐾🐾🐾 (Island, 1977)
Talking Back to the Night 🐾🐾 (Island, 1983)
Chronicles 🐾🐾🐾 (Island, 1987)
Roll with It 🐾🐾🐾 (Virgin, 1988)
Refugees of the Heart 🐾🐾 (Virgin, 1990)

worth searching for: *Go* (Island, 1976), Winwood's first collaboration with Yamshta, is an intriguing exploration of world music and pre-techno ambience.

influences:

◄◄ Ray Charles, the Beatles, Stax, Derek & the Dominos, Fairport Convention

►► Michael Penn, Michael Bolton, Bryan Adams, Tina Turner

see also: *Blind Faith, Spencer Davis, Traffic*

Gary Graff

The Wipers
/Greg Sage

Formed 1977, in Portland, OR.

Greg Sage, guitar, bass, vocals; Dave Koupal, bass (1977–81); Greg Davidson, bass (1981–89); Sam Henry, drums (1977–81); Brad Naish, drums (1981–86); Steve Plouf, drums (1986–present).

Despite 10 extraordinary studio albums over 18 years and having been covered on record by Nirvana (twice!), Hole, Sonic

Steve Winwood (© Ken Settle)

Youth's Thurston Moore, and Dinosaur Jr.'s J. Mascis (some as part of a tribute LP, *Fourteen Songs for Greg Sage & the Wipers*), most people have (likely) never heard of Greg Sage. His 10 albums—eight with the Wipers and two under his own name—form a body of consistently mind-blowing work unmatched over such a long period of time in this country. So why is Sage such a no-name, despite being misleadingly tagged as a "Godfather of Northwest Grunge?" Simply put, the lanky, incredibly talented guitarist is one of the last fiercely independent punk-era nonconformists still running afoul of the bogus, ludicrous star-making machine that is alternative rock. He hates it and shuns it; the man won't even sit for publicity photos. But if his music must speak for itself, it speaks in deafening tones. From his earlier, punk-influenced albums to his more moody, methodical works of the late '80s and early '90s, Sage is a veritable guitar magician, producing his own rough-and-ready records in studios he builds. Eighteen years into his career, Sage's later work is every bit as aggressive, vital, and stunning as his earlier output. In fact, *The Herd* was one of 1996's finest rock albums, a rare and underappreciated knockout. When will anyone outside of continental Europe, where Sage is a loved legend who packs halls and theaters, notice?

what to buy: Hands down, *Youth of America* ♫♫♫♫ (Restless, 1981, prod. Greg Sage) is a monster; the 11-minute title track ranks with the finest, most awe-inspiring pieces of music ever released in America. *The Herd* ♫♫♫♫ (Tim Kerr, 1996, prod. Greg Sage) smolders from start to finish; don't miss "Psychic Vampire" and "Wind the Clock Slowly." For the more reflective side of Sage's piston-pumping rock, *Follow Blind* ♫♫♫♫ (Restless, 1987, prod. Greg Sage) is highlighted by Sage's doomsday chords on the title track and surprising neo–Joy Division bass tones.

what to buy next: Sub Pop smartly reissued the Wipers' rockin' debut, *Is This Real?* ♫♫♫♫ (Park Ave., 1979, prod. Greg Sage). The album produced two songs Kurt Cobain and Co. covered on record ("Return of the Rat" and "D7"), plus the pop gem "Mystery." *Silver Sail* ♫♫♫♫ (Tim Kerr, 1993, prod. Greg Sage) is more of the reflective bent, mixing in surf and spaghetti western. *The Best of the Wipers & Greg Sage* ♫♫♫♫ (Restless, 1990, prod. Greg Sage) provides a solid overview for newcomers, mixed with a few rare singles tracks for old fans.

what to avoid: *Wipers Live* ♫♫♫ (Enigma, 1985, prod. Greg Sage) is the least essential, though even this is of interest since it includes three songs never recorded in the studio.

the rest:
Land of the Lost ♫♫♫♫ (Restless, 1986)
The Circle ♫♫♫♫ (Restless, 1988)

worth searching for: The first three songs on the Wipers' hard-to-find third album, *Over the Edge* (Braineater, 1983, prod. Greg Sage), contain consummate Wipers blowout guitar hooks.

solo outings:
Greg Sage:
Straight Ahead ♫♫♫♫ (Enigma, 1985)
Sacrifice (For Love) ♫♫♫♫ (Restless Records, 1991)

influences:

◀◀ Jimi Hendrix, Dick Dale, the Ventures, the Yardbirds, the Wailers, the Kingsmen, the Raiders

▶▶ Nirvana, Hole, Sonic Youth, Dinosaur Jr., Mudhoney, the Melvins, Screaming Trees, Pearl Jam

Jack Rabid

Wire

Formed 1976, in London, England. Disbanded 1980. Re-formed 1986.

Colin Newman, vocals; Bruce Gilbert, guitar; Graham Lewis, bass, vocals; Robert Gotobed (born Mark Field), drums (1976–91).

In contrast to the working-class snarl of most British punk circa 1977—all you needed to form a band was bad teeth, a couple of strategically inserted safety pins, and three chords—Wire offered a more distanced, coolly cerebral, but no less enthralling approach. Befitting the members' art-school backgrounds, the group recorded songs with titles such as "French Film (Blurred)" and "Reuters," the latter about a news agency reporter whose last dispatch closes the song: "This is your correspondent, running out of tape, gunfire's increasing, looting, burning, rape." The minimalist music was as terse as most punk bands', particularly on the debut album, *Pink Flag*. But the group's debt to the avant-garde quickly became evident with the more experimental textures on the increasingly expansive follow-ups, such as the superb *Chairs Missing* and the less involving *154*. After releasing these three poor-selling but highly influential discs, the group broke up, only to reconvene in 1986 as an angular synth-pop band. Refusing to indulge fans with its punk-era "hits" while on tour, Wire even went so far as to hire an opening band, the Ex-Lion Tamers (named after a song on *Pink Flag*), to play them. Drummer Robert Gotobed, frustrated by the machine-dominated approach, quit in 1991, and the group dropped the last letter of its name to record *The First Letter*.

what to buy: *Pink Flag* ♫♫♫♫ (Restless Retro, 1977, prod. Mike Thorne) is one of the essential documents of British punk, though it's not really a punk record. Whereas bands such as the Sex Pistols and the Clash viewed punk as a means of reclaiming rock 'n' roll's essence, Wire was arty minimalism lumped in with punk by default because of a fondness for fat-free arrangements, terse melodies, and fast, stuttering rhythms. The 21 tracks span all of 35 perfect minutes. The follow-up, *Chairs Missing* ♫♫♫♫ (Restless Retro, 1978, prod. Mike Thorne), lengthens the songs and broadens the sonic palette to include

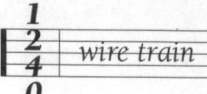

keyboards, synthesizers, and even flutes, while lending credence to Newman's declaration, "I am the fly in the ointment."

what to buy next: *On Returning (1977–79)* ♪♪♪♪ (Restless Retro, 1989, prod. Mike Thorne) collects most of the best of the first three discs (with the crucial exception of "Map Ref. 41° N 93° W" from *154*) and assorted singles from the band's most critical phase. *Wire, 1985–1990: The A List* ♪♪♪♪ (Mute, 1993, prod. various) is an insidiously catchy collection of singles and album tracks from the synth-pop years.

what to avoid: One would think that a document of the band's final live performance from its punk era would be riveting, but instead it's a sham. *Document and Eyewitness* ♪ (Mute, 1991), the bulk of which is from a 1980 concert, is a stunningly dreary avant-garde experiment.

the rest:

154 ♪♪♪♪ (Restless Retro, 1979)
Snakedrill ♪♪♪ (Mute/Enigma EP, 1987)
The Ideal Copy ♪♪♪♪ (Mute/Enigma, 1987)
Ahead ♪♪♪ (Mute/Enigma EP, 1987)
The Peel Sessions ♪♪♪ (Strange Fruit EP, 1987)
A Bell Is a Cup Until It Is Struck ♪♪♪ (Mute/Enigma, 1988)
Kidney Bongos ♪♪♪ (Mute/Restless EP, 1988)
Silk Skin Paws ♪♪ (Mute/Restless EP, 1989)
It's Beginning to and Back Again ♪♪♪ (Mute/Enigma, 1989)
The Peel Sessions Album ♪♪♪ (Strange Fruit/Dutch East India, 1991)
Manscape ♪♪ (Mute/Enigma, 1990)
The Drill ♪♪ (Mute/Elektra, 1991)
(As Wir) *The First Letter* ♪♪ (Mute/Elektra, 1991)
Coatings ♪ (Mute/WMO Limited, 1997)

worth searching for: Though at 18 tracks it contains 13 fewer cuts than the *On Returning* CD compilation, the vinyl-only *And Here It Is . . . Again . . . Wire* (Sneaky Pete Records, 1984) is a more judiciously chosen overview of the band's crucial early years, including some key songs left off the later collection.

influences:

◄◄ John Cage, Kraftwerk, the Stooges, the MC5, the Ramones

►► R.E.M., Sonic Youth, Hüsker Dü, the Cure, Big Black, the Minutemen, Elastica

Greg Kot

Wire Train

Formed 1982, in San Francisco, CA.

Kevin Hunter, vocals, guitar; Anders Runblad, bass; Kurt Herr, guitar (1982–85); Frederico Gil-Sola, drums (1982–84); Brian MacLeod, drums (1985–92); Jeffrey Trott, guitar (1986–92).

Wire Train's pre-industry guitar jangle was noticeably out of sync with the emotionally repressed new wave scene of the early '80s. Despite the group's capability to produce hit singles whose sincerity against the backdrop of the Ronald Reagan years was admirable, it remained more of a local phenomenon than a national act. With whirling guitars and heartfelt messages of societal ills, Wire Train came along at least five years too early.

what to buy: *Last Perfect Thing: A Retrospective* ♪♪♪♪ (Columbia/Legacy, 1996, prod. various) sets the Wire Train record straight, starting off with the ringing "Chamber of Hellos"—surely one of the best forgotten pop songs of 1984. *In a Chamber/Between Two Worlds* ♪♪♪♪ (Oglio Records, 1995, prod. David Kahne, Peter Maunu) contains both of the band's first two releases, which gives pop miners a good bang for their buck. The latter's leaner edge contains some singles as fine as "Chamber," notably "Last Perfect Thing" and "Skills of Summer," as well as a warm version of Bob Dylan's "With God on Our Side."

what to buy next: Despite a strong return in 1992 with *No Soul No Strain* ♪♪♪ (MCA, 1992, prod. Bill Bottrell), the band remained stuck between the cracks of new wave and the then-burgeoning alternative rock sound.

influences:

◄◄ Bob Dylan, the Clash, Billy Bragg

►► Rage Against the Machine

Allan Orski

Wishbone Ash

Formed 1969, in England.

Andy Powell, guitar; David Allen "Ted" Turner, guitar (1969–74, 1987–89); Martin Turner, vocals, bass (1969–80, 1987–89); Steve Upton, drums (1969–89); Laurie Wisefield, guitar (1974–86); others.

Wishbone Ash turned an inability to decide between two auditioning guitarists into a trademark harmonizing twin lead sound. At the forefront of the early '70s progressive rock movement, its guitar-heavy excursions regularly jumped between blues and folk. Lyrics that weren't about boy/girl relationships tended to be heavy-handed and ponderous odes to various English myths and legends, which—in addition to some pretty leaden singing—may be why many of the band's best-liked works are its instrumentals. It was a hot stage act, which explains why live albums make up an unusually high percentage of its catalog. The band's peak years were from 1969 to 1977; since then, Andy Powell has kept the name going with a variety of personnel, but he hasn't been able to recapture the glory days.

what to buy: Although much of the work seems dated, guitar fans will still find some treasures in a couple of collections. *The Best of Wishbone Ash* ♪♪♪♪ (MCA, 1997, prod. Andy Powell,

Andy McKaie) concentrates heavily on the band's first four albums, its best period. Those interested in digging a little deeper should get *Time Was: The Wishbone Ash Collection* 🎵🎵🎵 (MCA, 1993, prod. Andy McKaie), which expands its exploration of the band's catalog across two CDs.

what to buy next: Those interested in sampling a non-best-of Wishbone Ash CD should probably start with *Argus* 🎵🎵🎵 (MCA, 1972, prod. Derek Lawrence), generally acknowledged to be its best piece. *Wishbone Ash* 🎵🎵🎵 (MCA, 1970, prod. Derek Lawrence) is a more straightforward, bluesier effort. To get a taste of the band in concert, pick up *Live Dates* 🎵🎵🎵 (MCA, 1973, prod. Wishbone Ash), a double-CD live set recorded during its prime.

what to avoid: Almost everything put out after 1980, mostly released on various small labels, is only for extremely hard-core fans.

best of the rest:
Pilgrimage 🎵🎵🎵 (MCA, 1971)
Wishbone Four 🎵🎵🎵 (MCA, 1973)
There's the Rub 🎵🎵 (MCA, 1974)
Front Page News 🎵🎵 (MCA, 1977)

worth searching for: Original manager Miles Copeland reunited the founding members during the late '80s to do a couple of instrumental albums for the "No Speak" series on his I.R.S. label. Now out of print, *Nouveau Calls* (I.R.S., 1987, prod. Martin Turner) and *Hear to Hear* (I.R.S., 1989, prod. Martin Turner) house the band's best work since its first four studio albums.

influences:
◀◀ The Yardbirds, Renaissance, Savoy Brown

▶▶ Thin Lizzy, Iron Maiden, Lynyrd Skynyrd

Gary Plochinski

Jah Wobble
See: Public Image Ltd.

Peter Wolf
Born Peter Blankfield, March 6, 1946, in the Bronx, NY.

The J. Geils Band's white-boy R&B ran toward the music's roots, but singer Peter Wolf, a supporter of Boston's R&B scene since his days as a DJ at WBCN, looked toward more modern sounds after leaving the group in 1983. He had some initial success with his solo outings—more, certainly, than the Wolf-less J. Geils Band—and placed three singles ("Lights Out," "I Need You Tonight," and "Come As You Are") in the Top 40. Subsequent releases have not been received as well, however, and have become more infrequent.

what to buy: Wolf had been writing songs with R&B singer Don Covay ("Lights Out") and Michael Jonzun of Boston hip-hoppers the Jonzun Crew when he was squeezed out of J. Geils. Those songs emerged on *Lights Out* 🎵🎵🎵 (EMI America, 1984, prod. Michael Jonzun, Peter Wolf), whose playful approach to the music proved an excellent foil for Wolf's white-funk jive.

what to buy next: On *Come As You Are* 🎵🎵🎵 (EMI America, 1987, prod. Peter Wolf, Eric "E.T." Thorngren), Wolf continued to work with hot hip-hop producers—this time with Eric Thorngren, who had come to fame remixing Grandmaster Flash's records. Wolf and Thorngren turn up the guitars while retaining the grooves, but beyond the title track and a couple other cuts, they can't maintain the party atmosphere in which Wolf has cut his best records.

what to avoid: Written and co-produced with two Nashville songwriters, *Up to No Good* 🎵🎵 (MCA, 1990, prod. Peter Wolf, Robert White Johnson, Taylor Rhodes) doesn't have the spark of his work with R&B musicians.

the rest:
Long Line 🎵🎵🎵 (Reprise, 1996)
Fool's Parade 🎵🎵🎵 (Mercury, 1998)

worth searching for: The 12-inch dance mixes of "Lights Out" and "Come As You Are" are among the best rock remixes of the mid-'80s.

influences:
◀◀ The J. Geils Band, Bobby Womack, the Rolling Stones, Blondie, doo-wop

▶▶ Robert Palmer, Mick Jagger

Brian Mansfield

Wolfgang Press
Formed 1982, in London, England.

Mick Allen, vocals, guitar; Mark Cox, keyboards; Andrew Gray, drums.

A founding member of the 4AD Records roster, the Wolfgang Press has long been enigmatic in regards to its roots and influences. Every album is different from the others, although Mick Allen's vocal style is nothing short of consistently recognizable. The band has ranged from the brooding, dark, swirling pop that 4AD is so well known for to an almost funk-based outfit. The one word that always works to describe this trio is probably "weird." From the band's earliest incarnations (called Rema Rema, then later Mass), the group has espoused a kind of dark and brooding style that's neither properly goth, like label mates Bauhaus, nor as lush and beautiful as Dead Can Dance and the Cocteau Twins. The Press has bludgeoned out its own sound—tribal rhythms and heavy percussion with light synth washes, pounding bass, and occasional walls of guitar noise, all accompanied by Allen's distinct vocal style. Describing Allen's voice would be a thesis; think Nick Cave meets Tom Waits with an odd sarcastic snarl. Rather than staying in a dark psuedo-goth mode, however, the group has ventured forth into an almost funk/dance style on the last few releases. While this has brought the band more attention in the U.S., it alienated some longtime fans. None of the members have ventured off into other projects, and the once prolific Press has been still for quite some time.

what to buy: *The Legendary Wolfgang Press & Other Tall Stories* ♫♫♫♫ (4AD U.K., 1985/4AD, 1995, prod. various) is the band's second full-length release, comprised of three import-only EPs that were released between 1984 and 1985. The tracks were in many cases remixed or edited from their original versions, all to excellent effect. From dark, somber passages to almost silly, playful efforts, it's an excellent sample of what the band is about and, for sheer originality of music and vocal style, stands out from the pack of other '80s English bands.

what to buy next: *Queer* ♫♫♫ (4AD, 1992, prod. Ivo Watts Russell, the Wolfgang Press) was the band's first full-blown U.S. release and showed it taking its music and itself less seriously. Featuring the club hit "A Girl like You," this album shows those pop sensibilities the group had been hinting at for years but never let surface. An excellent listen from end-to-end, this album brought the band some much-deserved attention on the other side of the Atlantic. *Burden of Mules* ♫♫♫ (4AD, 1983, prod. Drostan Madden, the Wolfgang Press) is as dark a record as you'll find without a snarling, vampire-worshipping lead singer. Bleak and brown in its music, this album avoids many pitfalls other Nosferatu-inspired bands fell into. These boys know rhythm and song structure and how to make music you feel as well as hear. It's not for everyone, but those who enjoy a musical challenge will find *Burden* very rewarding.

the rest:
Standing up Straight ♫♫♫ (4AD, 1986)
Bird Wood Cage ♫♫♫ (4AD, 1988)
Funky Little Demons (4AD, 1995)) ♫♫♫

worth searching for: Check out any of the band's now out-of-print 12-inch singles that went toward the development of *The Legendary Wolfgang Press & Other Tall Stories*. These singles contain the original versions of the songs (many were reworked for the re-release on the LP) and show a somewhat more raw version of the band—especially the *Scarecrow* EP, with an interesting, to say the least, cover of Otis Redding's "Respect." The artwork on these EPs is also amazing enough to warrant the search.

influences:
◀◀ Tom Waits, Mass, the Buzzcocks, the Sex Pistols, Bauhaus, Cocteau Twins, XTC

▶▶ This Mortal Coil, the Dave Matthews Band, Our Lady Peace, Gene Loves Jezebel

see also: *This Mortal Coil*

Tim Davis

Bobby Womack

Born March 4, 1944, in Cleveland, OH.

Helping to fill the void left by Sam Cooke's death in 1964, Bobby Womack—who had been Cooke's guitar player—embarked on a solo career. He wrote or co-wrote some key rock 'n' roll songs, played guitar on a lot of crucial sessions, and had rumblings of R&B success, with a gritty soul voice and an advanced sense of soul writing and arrangement. When he and his brothers were signed to Cooke's label as the Womack Brothers, he changed their name to the Valentinos, and they tasted their first success with "Looking for a Love" and "It's All Over Now," which later became hits for the J. Geils Band and the Rolling Stones, respectively. Lapses in Womack's career were said to be caused by drug abuse; pronounced comebacks accompanied several clean-ups. After he helped out on more than a couple of Stones albums, the band repaid him when Ron Wood issued Womack's 1994 comeback on his own label and enlisted superstar rock friends to help out. Womack sees himself as a soul survivor in a field decimated over the decades. He's certainly been able to maintain a major-label career as his peers struggled, although superstardom has so far eluded him.

what to buy: The numbers of Womack titles currently in print are conspicuously spotty, with early 1970s recordings much more readily available than mid- to late 1980s successes. There's never been a lack of Womack compilations, though. *Only Survivor: The MCA Years* ♫♫♫ (MCA, 1996, prod. various) stands out because it collects such otherwise unavailable songs as "I Wish He Didn't Trust Me So Much" and the stirring "I'll Still Be Looking up to You (No Matter How High I Get)." *The Soul of Bobby Womack: Stop on By* ♫♫♫ (EMI, 1996, compilation prod. Leo Sacks) gathers 15 solid favorites from the early and mid-1970s.

what to buy next: *The Poet* ♫♫♫ (Beverly Glen Music, 1981/Razor & Tie, 1993, prod. Bobby Womack) was the first of two strong albums (along with *The Poet II*) that mounted a comeback of sizzling R&B tracks, such as "If You Think You're Lonely Now." *Midnight Mover: The Bobby Womack Collection* ♫♫♫ (EMI, 1993, prod. various) covers a lot of ground: the first nine years of his solo recording career, which included over 11 albums for Minit, Liberty, and United Artists, from 1967 to 1975.

what to avoid: Although it boasts grittier production and a wonderful remake of the Temptations' "I Wish It Would Rain,"

Womack's last album for United Artists, *Safety Zone* ♫♫♪ (United Artists, 1972/The Right Stuff, 1994, prod. David Rubinson), ended with a dismal eight-minute disco stab, "I Feel a Groove Coming On."

the rest:
Communication ♫♫♫ (United Artists, 1971/The Right Stuff, 1994)
Understanding ♫♫♫ (United Artists, 1972/The Right Stuff, 1994)
The Facts of Life ♫♫♪ (United Artists, 1973/The Right Stuff, 1994)
Lookin' for a Love Again ♫♫♪ (United Artists, 1974/ The Right Stuff, 1994)
The Poet II ♫♫♫ (Beverly Glen Music, 1984)
Lookin' for a Love: The Best of Bobby Womack, 1968–1975 ♫♫♫ (Razor & Tie, 1993)
Resurrection ♫♫♫ (Slide/Continuum, 1994)
The Soul of Bobby Womack: Stop on By ♫♫♫ (EMI, 1996)

worth searching for: *Someday We'll All Be Free* (Beverly Glen Music, 1985, prod. Bobby Womack, Patrick Moten) may be the best of the many out-of-print Womack titles. This could have been *The Poet III*, since it was his next album in that series on that small label and boasted workouts such as "I Wish I Had Someone to Go Home To" and the Donny Hathaway–penned title song.

influences:
◄◄ Sam Cooke, Wilson Pickett, Friendly Womack

►► Womack & Womack, the Tony Rich Project, Babyface

Roger Catlin

Stevie Wonder

Born Steveland Morris, May 13, 1950, in Saginaw, MI.

Of all the stars that came out of the Motown stable, Stevie Wonder's has shined the brightest and the longest. Already a sensation as Little Stevie Wonder throughout the '60s, the maturing musician fought Motown president Berry Gordy in 1971 for artistic control of his music—and won. Wonder went on to become a genius of pop invention during the 1970s, with a distinctive sound that borrowed freely from funk, rock, classical, jazz, country, and even reggae. His precisely layered and melodic music was peerless. From "Fingertips, Pt. 2," his first hit at the age of 13, to "I Just Called to Say I Love You" and beyond, Wonder's oeuvre encompasses a treasure trove of ageless songs—"My Cherie Amour," "You Are the Sunshine of My Life," "Superstition," "Golden Lady." Paul Simon put it all in perspective when accepting a Grammy for 1975's *Still Crazy After All These Years*: he thanked Wonder for not putting out a record that year. Wonder was instrumental in the campaign to get Martin Luther King Jr.'s birthday declared a national holiday and has been active in exposing African and Caribbean musicians to American audiences. Though not in the spotlight as much as before, Wonder is still a top pop star with the ability to put his finger on the pulse of the people and compose a tune that goes right to the heart of the matter.

what to buy: Wonder seemed an absolute pop music genius during the '70s, and *Innervisions* ♫♫♫♫ (Motown, 1973, prod. Stevie Wonder) is the pinnacle of that sensibility. Nearly every song—"Too High," "Golden Lady," "Don't You Worry 'bout a Thing," "All in Love Is Fair"—is a classic. But it was the gritty "Living for the City" that really set folks on their ears. *Talking Book* ♫♫♫♫ (Motown, 1972, prod. Stevie Wonder) is almost as good; "Superstition" and "You Are the Sunshine of My Life" gave an inkling of what was to come.

what to buy next: A lot of folks thought Wonder had gone off the deep end when he released the double album *Songs in the Key of Life* ♫♫♫♫ (Motown, 1976, prod. Stevie Wonder). But with its blend of funk and jazz influences, the album yielded hits such as "Sir Duke" and "Isn't She Lovely" to turn minds around. *Where I'm Coming From* ♫♫♫ (Motown, 1972, prod. Stevie Wonder) is the first album that Wonder had complete creative control over and the only one of his adult years on which he gave significant songwriting space to someone else—then-wife Syreeta Wright. The album gave us "If You Really Love Me" and "Never Dreamed You'd Leave Me in Summer." *Song Review: A Greatest Hits Collection* ♫♫♫♫ (Motown, 1997, prod. various) can't tell the whole story, even with two discs, but it's a solid gathering of most of his best-known material.

what to avoid: *Journey Through the Secret Life of Plants* ♫♫ (Motown, 1979, prod. Stevie Wonder) has well-crafted instrumentals that lean toward the new age vibe, but was outside the pop mainstream. It's a testament to Wonder's clout that Gordy even allowed this to be released.

the rest:
The Jazz Soul of Little Stevie Wonder ♫♫♫ (Motown, 1963)
With a Song in My Heart ♫♫♫ (Motown, 1966)
Down to Earth ♫♫♫ (Motown, 1967)
I Was Made to Love Her ♫♫♫ (Motown, 1967)
Someday at Christmas ♫♫♫ (Motown, 1967)
For Once in My Life ♫♫♫♫ (Motown, 1968)
Greatest Hits, Vol. 1 ♫♫♫♫♫ (Motown, 1968)
My Cherie Amour ♫♫♫ (Motown, 1969)
Signed, Sealed and Delivered ♫♫♫♫ (Motown, 1970)
Greatest Hits, Vol. 2 ♫♫♫♫ (Motown, 1972)
Music of My Mind ♫♫♫♫ (Motown, 1972)
Fulfillingness' First Finale ♫♫♫♫ (Motown, 1974)
Hotter Than July ♫♫♫♫ (Motown, 1980)
Original Musiquarium I ♫♫♫♫ (Motown, 1982)
The Woman in Red ♫♫♫ (Motown, 1984)
In Square Circle ♫♫♫ (Motown, 1985)
Characters ♫♫♫ (Motown, 1987)
Jungle Fever ♫♫♫ (Motown, 1991)

Stevie Wonder (© Ken Settle)

Motown Legends: I Was Made to Love Her/Uptight 𝄞𝄞𝄞𝄞 (ESX Entertainment, 1994)
Conversation Peace 𝄞𝄞𝄞𝄞 (Motown, 1995)
Natural Wonder 𝄞𝄞𝄞 (Motown, 1995)

worth searching for: The import *Essential Stevie Wonder* is the only comprehensive collection of Wonder's 1963–71 work, a period no single domestic release covers completely.

influences:

◀◀ Ray Charles, Duke Ellington, Smokey Robinson, Marvin Gaye, Frankie Lymon, Miles Davis

▶▶ Lionel Richie, Lenny Kravitz, Luther Vandross, Howard Jones, Michael Jackson

Lawrence Gabriel

The Wonder Stuff

Formed 1987, in Birmingham, England. Disbanded 1994.

Miles Hunt, vocals, guitar, harmonica; Malc Treece, guitar, vocals; Martin Gilks, drums; Rob Jones, bass (1987–89); Paul Clifford, bass (1990–94); Martin Bell, fiddle, accordion, mandolin, guitar, sitar, keyboards (1989–94).

More wise-ass than wise, the Wonder Stuff got by on cheekiness and cynicism, giving the ravenous British music press a focal point in the arrogant self-confidence of frontman Miles Hunt. That's not to say that when it came to music the band couldn't deliver the goods. Indeed, the Wonder Stuff made a strong case for itself with strong melodies, killer pop hooks, and a sharp, if mean-spirited, sense of humor. A superstar act in England, the Stuffies never scored in the States and disbanded, though several members continue to perform together in the group We Know Where You Live.

worth searching for: All of the Stuffies' albums are currently out of print, but several are definitely worth seeking out. *The Eight Legged Groove Machine* (Polydor, 1988, prod. Pat Collier) was a terrific punk-pop debut filled with strong wit and equally strong melodies. *Hup* (Polydor, 1989, prod. Pat Collier) moved a bit towards the psychedelia, though the foundation remained rooted in power pop. *Never Loved Elvis* (Polydor, 1991, prod. Mick Glossop) contains "Welcome to the Cheap Seats," which enjoyed modest airings on MTV. *Construction for the Modern Idiot* (Polydor, 1993, prod. Pat Collier) was a bit off the mark from previous releases, while the retrospective *If the Beatles Had Read Hunter . . . The Singles* (Polydor, 1994 prod. Pat Collier, Mick Glossop) delivered the U.K. singles in one package.

influences:

◀◀ The Beatles, the Psychedelic Furs, the Clash

▶▶ Oasis, Cast, Travis

John Nieman

The Wondermints

Formed c. 1993, in Los Angeles, CA.

Darian Sahanaja, keyboards, vocals; Nick Walusko, guitar, vocals; Michael D'Amico, drums, vocals; Brian Kassan, bass, vocals (1993–95); Jim Mills, bass (1995–present).

It's likely even the Wondermints are getting sick of this quote, but when former Beach Boy Brian Wilson said, "If I had the Wondermints back in 1967, I would have taken *Smile* out on the road," the pop world was compelled to pay attention. Amazingly enough, the Wondermints live up to Wilson's high praise. The leading light on the Los Angeles pop scene, the group has already served as Wilson's live backing band and recorded scads of worthy tracks, most of which are relatively difficult to track down. Their recorded work has been characterized by irresistibly lush pop textures, creating a dense, gorgeous sound that draws on every band you ever loved on AM radio during the '60s, filtered through a post–new wave sensibility. Founding member Brian Kassan left the Wondermints before the release of their debut album and has since formed his own group, Chewy Marble.

what to buy: Originally issued in 1995 on a Japanese label, *Wondermints* 𝄞𝄞𝄞𝄞 (Big Deal, 1996, prod. Darian Sahanaja, Nick Walusko) is the kind of dreamy pop album you just want to lose yourself in forever. From the opening "Proto-Pretty" through the closing "Carnival of Souls," *Wondermints* presents a non-stop program of giddy, exhilarating pop music that is crisp and fully realized without seeming obsessive. Brian Wilson and the Wondermints *should* record together, and they should take their work on the road.

worth searching for: In addition to several self-released cassettes, the Wondermints recorded an all-covers album, *The Wonderful World of the Wondermints* (Toy's Factory, 1996, prod. Darian Sahanaja, Nick Walusko), which thus far has been issued only in Japan.

solo outings:

Chewy Marble:
Chewy Marble 𝄞𝄞𝄞 (Permanent Press, 1997)

influences:

◀◀ The Beach Boys, Burt Bacharach, the Beatles, the Monkees, the Zombies, Jellyfish

Carl Cafarelli

Ron Wood

Born June 1, 1947, in Hillingdon, England

A consummate support player, Ron Wood has made a career out of playing second-fiddle to bigger stars with bigger egos.

He was the original bass player in the Jeff Beck Group, largely because Beck didn't want another guitarist in the band and Wood was no match for Beck's six-string virtuosity. He did switch to guitar when he joined the Small Faces in 1968 with another disgruntled Beck Group member, singer Rod Stewart. They guided their new group, renamed the Faces, to fame and fortune from 1969 to 1975, perfecting a scuzzy, boozy, ballroom-style rock 'n' roll. The rooster-haired Wood happily served as the ostentatious Stewart's foil, quietly becoming a formidable rhythm and slide player. But Stewart's solo work proved more popular than the band's, particularly in America, turning the Faces' smiles to frowns. Wood released his own solo album, *I've Got My Own Album to Do*, in 1974. But his output has been sporadic since then, largely because he left the Faces to become Mick Jagger and Keith Richards's junior partner in the Rolling Stones in time for their North American tour in 1975. Wood ended a 12-year gap between solo albums with the release of *Slide on This* in 1992. Unfortunately, collector's will have some trouble finding Wood's solo stuff, since most of it is out of print.

what to buy: *Slide on This* 𝄢𝄢𝄢 (Continuum, 1992/Koch, 1998) is the most accomplished of Wood's six solo efforts; louder, brasher, bluesier, and more confident than anything he's ever done—largely because he enlisted the soulful Bernard Fowler, who ably assisted the Stones on their past few albums and tours, as a songwriting partner and singer.

what to buy next: *I've Got My Own Album to Do* 𝄢𝄢 (Warner Bros., 1974/1994, prod. Ron Wood, Garry Kellgren) features guest appearances by Jagger and Richards.

the rest:
Now Look 𝄢𝄢 (Warner Bros., 1975/1994)
(With Ronnie Lane) *Mahoney's Last Stand* 𝄢𝄢 (Atco, 1976)
Gimme Some Neck 𝄢𝄢 (Columbia, 1979/1989)
Slide on Live: Plugged in and Standing 𝄢𝄢 (Continuum, 1993/Koch, 1998)

worth searching for: Hardcore Wood fans should track down *Live at the Ritz* (Victory Music, 1987), an out-of-print concert album taken from Wood's 1986 club tour with his idol, Bo Diddley. It includes Diddley classics such as "Who Do You Love" and Wood's own howling version of "Honky Tonk Women."

influences:
◀◀ Bo Diddley, Howlin' Wolf, Muddy Waters, Keith Richards

▶▶ The Black Crowes, Oasis

see also: *The Rolling Stones, the Faces*

Doug Pullen

Roy Wood

See: The Move

World Party

Formed 1986, in London, England.

Karl Wallinger, vocals, keyboards, guitars, bass; Chris Sharrock, drums (1992–present); Dave Catlin-Birch, guitars (1992–93).

Derivative and hippyesque, yet well-crafted and often soulful, the music of World Party ranks about as high as pop can get without actually seeming to have lasting value. It's doubtful that anyone will ever have a hit cover version of any of Karl Wallinger's songs, yet there's much to enjoy on each of his group's five official releases. He has been knocked for his lyrics, which often fancifully chide mankind for wreaking environmental havoc and being generally inconsiderate to each other, and yet he has stuck to his guns, keeping his focus throughout his career. For the most part, World Party is a Wallinger solo project on whose albums several guests have appeared (including a very young Sinéad O'Connor on backing vocals for one cut on the group's 1986 debut). After a stint as keyboardist for Scottish/Irish rockers the Waterboys around the time of their gloriously over-the-top *This Is the Sea* album in 1985, Wallinger concocted *Private Revolution* as World Party's debut in 1986, pulling stylistic elements from Bob Dylan, Van Morrison, the Beatles, and the Stones. He leaned a little more toward Morrison and the Beatles on 1990's *Goodbye Jumbo*, before taking a turn towards the sassy funk of Prince, first on 1991's "Thank You World" EP, then more so on 1993's riskier but less accomplished *Bang!* After a four-year hiatus, World Party returned in 1997 with the highly derivative but occasionally tantalizing *Egyptology*. Frankly, it's beginning to sound as if Wallinger needs to open a window and get some fresh air into the studio.

what to buy: The first half of *Private Revolution* 𝄢𝄢𝄢 (Ensign/Chrysalis, 1986, prod. Karl Wallinger) remains Wallinger's greatest achievement to date. Haunting, soulful, and brimming with convincingly righteous indignation, the first six tunes run the gamut from sassy dance-pop (the title track) to moody R&B-rock (the wonderful "Ship of Fools") to the beautiful but almost creepy "All Come True." The rest of the album slips a bit—the cover of Dylan's "All I Really Want to Do" only proves once again that Dylan wrote most of his stuff with his own style in mind, and that most others can't hack it—but not enough to tarnish the work as a whole.

what to buy next: Although it lacks the level of atmospheric cohesion that made the first half of *Private Revolution* so compelling, *Goodbye Jumbo* 𝄢𝄢𝄢 (Ensign/Chrysalis, 1990, prod. Karl Wallinger) includes several standout songs and a great deal of heart. The Stonesy R&B-pop of "Way Down Now" and the Van Morrison–like balladry of "Sweet Soul Dream" are highlights, but perhaps most impressive is the surprisingly soulful "Ain't Gonna Come Till I'm Ready."

what to avoid: With Chris Sharrock and Dave Catlin-Birch on board, *Bang!* 🎸🎸🎸 (Ensign/Chrysalis/ERG, 1993, prod. Karl Wallinger, Steve Lillywhite) is Wallinger's attempt at developing a more band-based sound. Somehow, though, the album drags, as too many songs go on too long. Still, "Give It All Away" is the group's wildest funk-dance workout, and "Is It like Today" makes for good, melancholy pop.

the rest:

Thank You World 🎸🎸🎸🎸 (Chrysalis EP, 1991)
Egyptology 🎸🎸🎸 (The Enclave, 1997)

worth searching for: The promo-only *History of the World* (Ensign/Chrysalis/ERG, 1993, prod. Karl Wallinger, Steve Lillywhite) serves as a well-balanced greatest hits package of sorts, though the moody flow of the individual albums is somewhat lost.

influences:

◀◀ The Beatles, Bob Dylan, Van Morrison, Prince, the Rolling Stones, the Beach Boys

▶▶ Lenny Kravitz, Ben Folds Five

Bob Remstein

Link Wray

Born Lincoln Wray, May 2, 1935, in Dunn, NC.

Though he didn't exactly invent the concept of fuzz-tone guitar (that distinction belongs to Willy Kizart, who played on Jackie Brenston's "Rocket 88" in 1951), Link Wray's imaginative use of distortion, tremolo, and sustain revolutionized rock 'n' roll. Initially the frontman for a country band called Lucky Wray & the Palomino Ranch Hands, he cut several singles for the Starday label during the mid-'50s. A bout with tuberculosis necessitated the removal of one of Wray's lungs and forced him to concentrate more on his guitar playing. While experimenting with loosened amplifier tubes and slashed speakers, he stumbled upon his trademark raunchy guitar style, which was embraced by Washington, D.C, DJ and TV host Milt Grant, who helped get Wray signed to Cadence records. Link Wray & the Raymen's first single—the ominous, Bolero-style strut "Rumble"—conjured images of leather-jacketed juvenile delinquency and greasy teen violence. As a result, just as it was hitting the pop Top 20, "Rumble" became the first instrumental to face a radio ban. Intimidated, Cadence owner Archie Bleyer refused to issue follow-up records, and Wray moved his group (which included his brothers Vernon and Doug) to Epic. Hoping to duplicate Duane Eddy's mainstream success, Epic encouraged Wray to record more dance-oriented material, but DJs flipped over the Eddyish "Dixie Doodle" and turned the blistering "Raw-Hide" into a solid hit. Subsequent singles "Comanche," "Slinky," and

"Ramble" (an inside-out version of "Rumble") featured exemplary guitar work but sold poorly. As the era of the rock instrumental was dying, Wray cut his final hit, "Jack the Ripper," for his own label, Rumble. Never idle, Wray has continued to tour and record for a variety of labels, and the inclusion of his music on the *Pulp Fiction* and *Desperado* movie soundtracks has led to major reissues of his early work by the New York–based Norton label. Still intense and edgy, guitar cult heroes don't come any hotter than Link Wray.

what to buy: Wray's most influential singles are collected on *Rumble! The Best of Link Wray* 🎸🎸🎸🎸 (Rhino, 1993, compilation prod. James Austen, Cub Koda), a powerful 20-track disc which includes "Rumble," "The Swag," "Raw-Hide," "Ramble," and the cartoony "Batman Theme." Cub Koda's liner notes and cool period photos make this a must-have item for even casual fans of hot guitar raunch. A fine second step, *Walkin' with Link* 🎸🎸🎸🎸 (Legacy, 1992, prod. Bob Irwin) is a mid-priced 20-track disc which chronicles Wray's work for Epic/OKeh and includes danceable power chord rockers galore, seven previously unreleased cuts, and informative booklet notes by Billy Miller (who later compiled the Norton series). Wild stuff, indeed!

what to buy next: You could get a serious case of guitar envy listening to *Mr. Guitar* 🎸🎸🎸🎸 (Norton, 1995, prod. Ray Vernon), a two-disc, 67-song set which includes all of Wray's non-Epic hits and just about every decent commercial note he struck during the '50s and early '60s. Wray's inventiveness and energy are brilliantly highlighted here. If you still can't get enough, dig deeper into Norton's "Missing Links" series.

what to avoid: One of his most disappointing albums, *Bullshot* 🎸🎸 (Visa, 1979/Line, 1994, prod. Richard Gottehrer) attempts to bring Wray kicking and screaming into the modern age with contemporary sounds and recording techniques. The result is an unconvincing mish-mosh which only completists will appreciate.

the rest:

Jack the Ripper 🎸🎸🎸🎸 (Swan, 1963/FMS, 1997)
(With Robert Gordon) *Robert Gordon with Link Wray* 🎸🎸🎸 (Private Stock, 1977/One Way, 1997)
(With Robert Gordon) *Fresh Fish Special* 🎸🎸🎸🎸 (Private Stock, 1977, 1978/ Raven, 1997)
Live at the Paradiso 🎸🎸 (Visa, 1982/Line, 1994)
The Original Rumble Plus 22 Other Storming Guitar Instrumentals 🎸🎸🎸🎸 (Ace, 1990)
Apache/Wild Side of the City 🎸🎸🎸 (Ace, 1990)
Golden Classics 🎸🎸🎸 (Collectables, 1993)
Growling Guitar/Live in '85 🎸🎸🎸🎸 (Big Beat, 1994)
Born to Be Wild: Live in the U.S.A, 1987 🎸🎸 (Line, 1995)
Hillbilly Wolf: Missing Links, Vol. 1 🎸🎸🎸🎸 (Norton, 1996)
Big City After Dark: Missing Links, Vol. 2 🎸🎸🎸 (Norton, 1996)
Some Kinda Nut: Missing Links, Vol. 3 🎸🎸🎸🎸 (Norton, 1996)

Streets of Chicago: Missing Links, Vol. 4 ♬♬♬ (Norton, 1997)
Shadowman ♬♬♬ (Hip-O Records, 1997)
Swan Singles Collection ♬♬♬ (Rollercoaster, 1997)
Walking down a Street Called Love ♬♬ (Cleopatra, 1997)

worth searching for: The cream of Wray's '70s output is compiled on *Guitar Preacher: The Polydor Years* (Polydor, 1995, prod. Bill Levenson), a two-disc, 37-track set which includes guest appearances by Jerry Garcia, Commander Cody, Boz Scaggs, and the Tower of Power Horns. Also, those who want to see Wray pull off some nasty power chords and screaming leads in a live setting are well-advised to track down *The Rumble Man* (Cleopatra, 1997), a concert video/documentary featuring his first ever on-camera interview and some wild jams. Both are available through various import services.

influences:

◀◀ Chet Atkins, Merle Travis, Bill Doggett, Howlin' Wolf

▶▶ Duane Eddy, Junior Raymen, Pete Townshend, Jimi Hendrix, Flat Duo Jets

Ken Burke

Wreckless Eric

Born Eric Goulden, 1954, in Newhaven, England.

Wreckless Eric's entry into the music world came about when he sent a demo tape to Stiff Records in 1977. Shortly after submitting the tape, however, he moved and left no forwarding address. The label heads were interested in what they had heard and spent weeks tracking Eric down to offer him a contract. That's a telling incident, as Eric Goulden has subsequently displayed a propensity for burning bridges as fast as he can light the matches. With the exception of his endearing hit single, "Whole Wide World," his initial burst of releases are proudly scruffy and not altogther successful (though by the time of *Big Smash* things were taking a turn for the tighter without losing any of the edge). An attempt to slick things up a bit with the Captains of Industry proved unsuccessful both artistically and commercially, and by the mid-'80s Eric moved to France. Two releases from his Len Bright Combo (an ensemble that, of course, included no one by that name) sought refuge in the tipsy comfort of lo-fi. For this trio, Eric strummed exuberantly while the rhythm section of ex-Milkshakes responded in kind. From then on there have been assorted one-offs under his given name, his adopted name, and a fine outfit that came and went, calling itself the Hitsville House Band. Reportedly, Eric moved back to England in 1997; what this will do for his career and recorded output is anybody's guess, but staying tuned to find out is strongly recommended.

what's available: Domestically there's a pretty shallow pool of Wreckless Eric releases to choose from. *The Donovan of Trash*

♬♬♬ (Sympathy for the Record Industry, 1993, prod. Wreckless Eric) leans heavily on casual charm, while *12 O'Clock Stereo* ♬♬♬ (Casino, 1994, prod. Eric Goulden), the release by his Hitsville House Band, is a peak. It's rich with spare and always appropriate exuberance matched to a winning set of songs.

worth searching for: *Karaoke* (Silo EP, 1997, prod. Eric Goulden) appeared as Eric departed France for a return to the U.K. and was released under his given name (although a banner across the top of the front cover called him "the artist formerly known as Wreckless Eric"). This time out Eric opted to be his own band, and he even managed to make the beat box sound like a smart aleck punk. For Eric's terrific original Stiff recordings, including the hit "Whole Wide World," the spooky "Semaphore Signals," and the greedy "Take the Cash (K.A.S.H.)," check out the four-disc *Stiff Records Box Set* (Stiff/Rhino, 1992, prod. various). This collection also includes Elvis Costello, Nick Lowe, Graham Parker, Desmond Dekker, and many other can't-miss artists of the late '70s.

influences:

◀◀ John Otway, the Kinks, Ian Dury

▶▶ Billy Childish, Clay Harper, Ottoman Empire

David Greenberger

Gary Wright /Spooky Tooth

Gary Wright born April 26, 1943, in Creskill, NJ. Spooky Tooth formed 1967, in London, England. Disbanded 1975.

Spooky Tooth: Gary Wright, keyboards, vocals (1967–70, 1972–75); Mike Harrison, vocals, keyboards (1967–75); Luther Grosvenor, guitar (1967–72); Greg Ridley, bass (1967–69); Mike Kellie, drums (1967–72); Andy Leigh, bass; Henry McCullough, guitar (1970–72); Chris Stainton, keyboards (1970–72); Alan Spenner, bass (1970–72); Mick Jones, guitar (1972–75); Chris Stewart, bass (1972–75); Bryson Graham, drums; Mike Patto (died March 4, 1979), keyboards, vocals (1975); Val Burke, bass, vocals (1975).

New Jersey native Gary Wright was a child actor who performed on Broadway in the musical *Fanny* before attending college in Berlin and eventually working his way to England. As a founding member of Spooky Tooth, his keyboard technique brought an experimental edge to the band; to further his vision, he hired French electronic music pioneer Pierre Henry to participate on Spooky Tooth's 1970 album, *Celebration*, marking a huge but successful departure both artistically and commercially. Spooky Tooth suffered from frequent lineup changes and a lack of commitment to recording, which resulted in lots of weak albums. Wright enjoyed the most notable solo career, but guitarist Mick Jones had the most success, forming the group Foreigner and producing albums for Billy Joel and Van Halen. Luther Grosvenor joined Stealers Wheel and, later, Mott the Hoople.

what to buy: *Spooky Two* 🎵🎵🎵 (A&M, 1969/1988, prod. Jimmy Miller) is the band's best and most focused album. When Spooky Tooth truly called it quits in 1975, Wright followed with his platinum-selling solo effort, *The Dream Weaver* 🎵🎵🎵 (Warner Bros., 1975, prod. Gary Wright), which garnered two Top 10 hits in the title track and "Love Is Alive."

what to avoid: *The Mirror* 🎵 (Island/Griffin, 1974) showed the reconstituted Spooky Tooth had little to say and nowhere to go. On *First Signs of Life* **woof!** (Worldly Music, 1995, prod. Gary Wright), Wright spoils the Brazilian-flavored percussive edge with his penchant for naval-gazing and keyboard-noodling, wasting guest appearances by George Harrison and Terry Bozzio.

the rest:
Gary Wright:
First Signs of Life 🎵🎵 (Triloka, 1995)
Best of the Dream Weaver 🎵🎵🎵 (Rhino, 1998)

influences:
◀◀ Spencer Davis Group, Terry Reid

▶▶ Deep Purple, Uriah Heep, the Waterboys, Talk Talk

see also: *Foreigner, Mott the Hoople*

Patrick McCarty

Rick Wright
See: Pink Floyd

Wu-Tang Clan
Formed 1992, in Staten Island, NY.

Prince Rakeem/The RZA (born Robert Diggs), vocals, producer; Method Man (Clifford Smith), vocals; U-God (Lamont Hawkins), vocals; Inspektah Deck (Jason Hunter), vocals; Chef Raekwon (Corey Woods), vocals; Ghost Face Killa (Dennis Coles), vocals; Ol' Dirty Bastard (Russell Jones), vocals; Genius/GZA (Gary Grice), vocals; Masta Killa (Elgin Turner), vocals.

They began as nine MCs who were either unknowns or major-label cast-offs, but together as the Wu-Tang Clan, RZA, Method Man, U-God, Inspektah Deck, Raekwon, Ghost Face Killa, ODB, Genius, and Masta Killa have transformed into the most dominant crew in hip-hop. Though the numbers may not match rap's biggest sellers (with each Wu-related album selling between 500,000 and 2 million copies), the Clan has established a franchise that will surely pay dividends for many years to come. There are only officially nine in the immediate crew, but the Wu-Tang Clan apparently consists of more than 200 members, all from the fifth—and sometimes "forgotten"—New York borough of Staten Island. The unifying principle of the Wu is based on an Asiatic philosophy and mythology developed by the Buddhist monks of the Shao Lin Monastery in ancient times; the Wu-Tang was regarded as one of the deadliest combat techniques that was more mental than physical. Shrouding yourself in an Asiatic discipline may be interpreted as a marketing gimmick. But is it? The Wu gambinos frequently quote text from the likes of Sun Tzu's *Art of War,* the I Ching, and the Koran; chess has become the crew's favorite pastime; and headmaster RZA—who not only organized the Clan but also drew up its guiding principles and has produced almost all of the group's influential beats—can fully explain to you the philosophy at any time.

what to buy: Not everybody had been sold on the Wu-Tang Clan with its debut single, re-released as "Protect Ya Neck" b/w "Method Man." When the group's full-length debut came out, though, everything changed. *Enter the Wu-Tang (36 Chambers)* 🎵🎵🎵🎵 (Loud/RCA, 1993, prod. RZA) is one of those landmark records, a truly original creation that changed people's perception of music. It's a gritty, grimy record that goes against all conventions—and indeed, that's its charm. Songs such as "C.R.E.A.M. (Cash Rules Everything Around Me)" and "Can It Be All So Simple" became street anthems, while the other cuts highlighted the crew's many different personalities. After the first record, a steady stream of solo records were issued, keeping the Wu-Tang on the forefront of the hip-hop nation's minds from 1993 on—for better or for worse. After Method Man and Ol' Dirty Bastard issued their albums (both acquired tastes), Raekwon dropped *Only Built for Cuban Linx . . .* 🎵🎵🎵🎵 (Loud/RCA, 1995, prod. RZA, 4th Disciple), a recording that truly surprised. Arguably even better than the first Wu album, it's tight, concise, and highly cinematic, with "Incarcerated Scarfaces," "Rainy Dayz," and other sonically—if not visually—stunning tunes. And who knew that Raekwon and his partner, Ghost Face Killa, were the two best lyricists in the crew?

what to buy next: Genius/GZA's first (pre-Wu) album, *Words from the Genius* 🎵🎵🎵 (Cold Chillin', 1991/1994, prod. Genius, Prince Rakeem, Easy Mo Bee, others), is a great recording, but the rapper lost his initial label deal when sales didn't live up to expectations. Still, the title track and "Phony As You Want to Be" established the Genius as a gifted MC—one who has always lurked in the Wu shadows. Cold Chillin' reissued the album to capitalize on Wu-mania, replacing "Come Do Me" with "Pass the Bone," which features Prince Rakeem/The RZA. Genius maintains his understated, smooth, and compelling style—albeit in a darker fashion—on his post-Wuxplosion solo record, *Liquid Swords* 🎵🎵🎵 (Geffen, 1995, prod. RZA). Though a little more chaotic-sounding than Raekwon's, Genius's lyrical flow is rivaled by few. Ghost Face Killa, meanwhile, may have played a secondary role on Raekwon's record, but it's the other way around on his own solo debut, *Ironman* 🎵🎵🎵🎵 (Epic, 1996, prod. RZA, True Masta). Wucomer Cappadonna (born Darryl

Hill), first introduced on Raekwon's album, also plays a significant role here. Though you'd think people might be getting a little Wu-zy after hearing five Wu-related albums in just over three years, hearing Ghost Face go off on "Wildflower," and Ghost Face, Raekwon, and Cappadonna exchange verses on "Camay" and "Daytona 500," is simply intoxicating.

what to avoid: In the summer of 1997, the Wu-Tang Clan regrouped for a sophomore album that was one of the most highly anticipated hip-hop records ever. But *Wu-Tang Forever* ♫♫𝅙 (Loud/RCA, 1997, prod. RZA, others) is a dramatic disappointment. RZA's production on some songs ("Reunited" with its flipping violins, the haunting "The City") proves that he has an ear for music. But part of what made Wu-Tang Clan so good initially was its grittiness, and that's abandoned on this slick, seemingly made-for-profit record. The album's length (two hours of music spread out over two discs) is excessive. This easily could have been a tight, single album.

worth searching for: In 1991, RZA released the single "Ooh! I Love You Rakeem" (with "Deadly Venoms" and "Sexcapades") on Tommy Boy. If you can find the single, you'll also find some of the first Wu-Tang remixes.

solo outings:
Method Man:
Tical ♫♫♫ (Def Jam, 1994)

Ol' Dirty Bastard:
Return to the 36 Chambers ♫♫𝅙 (Elektra, 1995)

Killah Priest:
Heavy Mental ♫♫ (Geffen, 1998)

Cappadonna:
The Pillage ♫♫♫ (Epic/Razor Sharp, 1998)

Gravediggaz:
6 Feet Deep ♫♫♫𝅙 (Gee Street, 1994)
The Pick, the Sickle, and the Shovel ♫♫♫ (Gee Street, 1997)

Wu-Tang Killa Bees:
The Swarm, Vol. 1 ♫♫𝅙 (Wu-Tang Records, 1998)

influences:
◄◄ Prince Paul, Kool G Rap, Public Enemy, Cypress Hill

►► GP-Wu, Killarmy, Shyheim, Capone-N-Noreaga, AZ, King Just, Cappadonna, Mobb Deep

Joseph Patel

Robert Wyatt

Born 1945, in Bristol, England.

Almost wholly undiscovered by Americans throughout his 30-year career, Wyatt is among the most durable of Britain's musical artists, having transited his years as the drummer for the progressive art-rock group Soft Machine to build a solo career of lush, meditative music punctuated by the occasional odd British hit. Wyatt's music is almost always pleasantly eccentric, graced by his distinctive, frail tenor, a lovely voice that has a child's bold-faced, unassuming honesty. His solo career suffered an immediate setback when, shortly after the release of his debut, 1970's *The End of an Ear*, a fall from a window left him permanently paralyzed from the waist down. Wyatt devoted his talents to keyboards and returned with back-to-back oddities, the star-studded *Rock Bottom* (1974) and *Ruth Is Stranger than Richard* (1975). For all the frequently primal eccentricities of his music, Wyatt has scored several mainstream U.K. hits over the years, first with a straight version of the Monkees' "I'm a Believer" in 1974, and again during the early '80s with "Shipbuilding," a song about the Falklands War written for him by producer Clive Langer and Elvis Costello. His music became more stridently political during Margaret Thatcher's tenure as Britain's prime minister, but he kept clear of vicious sniping, focusing instead on the human costs of politics and war. Wyatt continues to write, paint, and make music when he wants to, seemingly oblivious to the expectations of the music industry. He remains today as he was in the Soft Machine, an uncommonly devoted artist marching to a different drummer.

what to buy: *Shleep* ♫♫♫♫♫ (Thirsty Ear, 1998, prod. Robert Wyatt, Brian Eno) is a lovely reminder that some artists get better with age. Full of soothing, hypnotic melodies and lovely electronic weirdness, *Shleep* is Wyatt's most pop-friendly effort and an excellent place to start investigating his catalog. *Rock Bottom/Ruth Is Stranger than Richard* ♫♫♫♫ (Virgin, 1981, prod. Nick Mason, Robert Wyatt) is a highly prized repackaging of Wyatt's second and third solo albums. *Rock Bottom* is a quiet and, at times, haunting record dealing (as the title suggests) with Wyatt's recovery from his paralyzing fall. *Ruth/Richard* is, by comparison, a lively and much brighter record on which Wyatt further experiments with jazz and pop. The jaunty opener, "Soup Song," is a particularly fun and memorable track.

what to buy next: If the above CDs motivate you, then dig deep into your pockets for *Going Back a Bit: A Little History of Robert Wyatt* ♫♫♫♫ (Virgin, 1994, prod. various). Although a somewhat pricey offering (a double CD and an import), it more than compensates with 29 tracks that span Wyatt's career from Soft Machine and Matching Mole to his solo years, including collaborations with Brian Eno and others. It's an excellent overview of a wide and varied career, providing a sense of chronology and strong recognition of Wyatt's unique talents.

what to avoid: Despite its value to hard-core Wyatt fans, neophytes will probably be put off by *Flotsam Jetsam* ♫♫♫♫ (Rough Trade, 1994, prod. various), a terrific collection of outtakes and oddities from 1968 to 1990. The CD does a fine job filling in the cracks in Wyatt's career, serving up snippets of his work with avant-garde artists Dagmar Krause and Lol Coxhill, as well as with Jimi Hendrix (with whom Soft Machine toured America during 1968); unfortunately, Wyatt takes a back seat to the many stellar talents in evidence throughout the album.

the rest:

Rock Bottom 🎵🎵🎵 (Blue Plate, 1974)
The Animals Film (Soundtrack) 🎵🎵🎵 (Rough Trade, 1982)
The Peel Sessions 🎵🎵🎵🎵 (Dutch East India EP, 1987)
Dondestan 🎵🎵🎵🎵 (Gramavision, 1991)
A Short Break 🎵🎵🎵 (UK Voiceprint, 1992)
Mid-Fighties 🎵🎵🎵🎵 (Gramavision, 1994)
Nothing Can Stop Us Now/Old Rotten Hat 🎵🎵🎵🎵 (Gramavision, 1994)

worth searching for: *The End of an Ear* (Sony Belgium, 1970, prod. Robert Wyatt) is Wyatt's wonderful solo debut. Featuring a loose improvisational jazz style and plenty of odd scat singing, it's a tempting and enjoyable listen.

influences:

◀◀ David Allen, Pink Floyd, Soft Machine, Matching Mole, Gong, Caravan

▶▶ Fred Frith, Ivor Cutler, Henry Cow, Kevin Ayers, Steve Hillage, John Cale, Brian Eno, Phil Manzanera, Elvis Costello, the Residents, Ozric Tentacles

see also: *Soft Machine*

Christopher Scapelliti

Steve Wynn

See: Dream Syndicate

X
/John Doe
/Exene Cervenka
/The Knitters

Formed 1977, in Los Angeles, CA.

John Doe, vocals, bass; Exene Cervenkova, vocals; Billy Zoom, guitar (1977–85, 1997–present); Don "D.J." Bonebrake, drums; Tony Gilkyson, guitar (1985–97); Dave Alvin, guitar (1987).

Not since the Who has any rock 'n' roll band crashed its individual parts together with such force. When word of British punk rock leaked to America's coasts, Los Angeles suburban teens were among the first to embrace it. X, led by the husband-wife team of regular guy John Doe and tortured poet Exene Cervenka (who has since changed her name to the more traditional Cervenkova), became the shining star of West Coast punk. It helped that guitarist Zoom, once a member of Gene Vincent's bands, could play rockabilly riffs straight from old Link Wray records but juiced up so fast they were exhilaratingly incomprehensible. Bonebrake's metronomic drumming was worthy of his forebear, Elvis Presley drummer D.J. Fontana. And the whole group had, with influence from the Blasters' Dave Alvin and early patron Ray Manzarek of the Doors, a keen sense of American music history to make everything more interesting. For awhile, Doe and Cervenka sang Johnny Cash–June Carter ballads at L.A. coffeehouses—appropriate, because X's music sometimes sounds like a sped-up, angst-ridden version of "Jackson." Eventually, Zoom left the band, replaced by the talented but more professional Gilkyson, and after a few of rock's most propulsive albums, the band eased slowly into older age. Its social conscience, always bubbling under the surface, grew into sometimes preachy ballads. Cervenka and Doe divorced during the late '80s, and their relationship regularly drove the members apart, then brought them back together. The group reunited for good in 1994 and still has interesting things to say, even if, regrettably, there will never be another "The Phone's off the Hook, but You're Not."

what to buy: X's first four albums are up there with the peak runs of Bob Dylan, the Rolling Stones, and the Beatles in terms of career consistency. *Los Angeles* 🎵🎵🎵🎵 (Slash, 1980, prod. Ray Manzarek), with its barely decipherable stories of underground L.A. life and contempt for boring people, has the tracks "Sex and Dying in High Society" and "Johnny Hit and Run Paulene." *Wild Gift* 🎵🎵🎵🎵 (Slash, 1981, prod. Ray Manzarek) is a fine sequel, with even more great songs, including the L.A. punk anthem "We're Desperate" plus "Adult Books" and "Back 2 the Base." In *Under the Big Black Sun* 🎵🎵🎵🎵 (Elektra, 1982, prod. Ray Manzarek) you can actually start understanding the lyrics. *More Fun in the New World* 🎵🎵🎵🎵 (Elektra/Asylum, 1983, prod. Ray Manzarek) is X's most effective blending of standing-up-for-the-oppressed ideals and rock 'n' roll—"The New World" name-drops Detroit and Gary, Indiana, in the most blunt way possible.

what to buy next: *Beyond and Back: The X Anthology* 🎵🎵🎵🎵 (Elektra, 1997, prod. D.J. Bonebrake, John Doe, Exene Cervenkova, Tom DeSavia, John Roecker) has enough original classics (such as "Los Angeles," "Burning House of Love," and "4th of July") and never-before-released live tracks and demos (including the tremendous 1978 outtake "Delta 88") for both completists and newcomers. Though the band never received even a fraction of the commercial success it has always deserved, this two-disc set makes a case for X as one of the best groups in rock history. Liner-note remembrances by Pee-wee Herman, Dave Alvin, Jakob Dylan, Matthew Sweet, and Pleasant Gehman are a bonus. *See How We Are* 🎵🎵🎵🎵 (Elektra/Asylum, 1987, prod. Alvin Clark) reunites an older X, musing poignantly about the plight of the poor. Dave Alvin's classic "4th of July" appears for the first time on record. *Ain't Love Grand* 𝄢𝄢𝄢 (Elektra/Asylum, 1985, prod. Michael Wagener) is pristinely polished, which is jarring for an X album, but its wonderful love song "Burning House of Love" almost makes up for it. The Knitters, the band's short-lived country alter ego, seemed weird at the time, but *Poor Little Critter on the Road* 𝄢𝄢𝄢 (Slash, 1985, prod. the Knitters) holds up surprisingly well today.

what to avoid: *Hey Zeus!* 𝄢𝄢 (Big Life/Mercury, 1993, prod. Tony Berg) is another reunion album, which means trouble and weak, blandly political songs about war and other controversial subjects. *Live at the Whisky A Go-Go on the Fabulous Sunset Strip* 𝄢𝄢 (Elektra/Asylum, 1988, prod. Alvin Clark) goes downhill right after Doe drawls his funny introduction; it was the wrong concert to record.

the rest:
Unclogged 𝄢𝄢𝄢 (Infidelity Records, 1995, prod. X)

worth searching for: Both compilations titled *Dangerhouse* (Frontier, 1991, 1992, prod. various) contain just one X classic each, but they are presented in their historical context—Los Angeles's vibrant late '70s/early '80s punk scene. That context is provided by tracks from Randoms, Weirdos, Avengers, Bags, Alley Cats, Black Randy, and Eyes.

solo outings:
Exene Cervenka:
Twin Sisters 𝄢𝄢 (Freeway, 1985)
Old Wives' Tales 𝄢𝄢𝄢 (Rhino, 1989)
Running Scared 𝄢𝄢𝄢 (Rhino, 1990)
Surface to Air Serpents 𝄢𝄢 (213CD, 1995)

John Doe:
Meet John Doe 𝄢 (DGC, 1990)
Kissingsohard 𝄢𝄢 (Rhino/Forward, 1995)

influences:
◀◀ Johnny Cash and June Carter, the Sex Pistols, the Ramones, the Clash, the Who, the Blasters, Elvis Presley, the Patti Smith Group

▶▶ Hole, Uncle Tupelo, the Mekons, Sonic Youth, the Minute Men, Social Distortion, the Pixies

Steve Knopper

XC-NN

Formed 1992, in London, England.

Tim Bricheno, guitars, samples; David Tomlinson, vocals, samples; Neill Lambert, drums; Nick Witherick, bass (1996–present).

They're named after the TV network that gave us Larry King and Wolf Blitzer, but XC-NN (which had to change its moniker after the threat of litigation) wouldn't know news if it bit them on the ass. "Young, Stupid & White" is its call to arms—relax, it's meant ironically, though it doesn't come off that way as much as the band would like. The group brings together former Sisters of Mercy guitarist Tim Bricheno and ex–Jellyfish Kiss vox David Tomlinson in a band that is all high concept and bluster without much to back it up.

what to buy: *XC-NN* 𝄢𝄢 (550 Music, 1994, prod. Caleb Kadesh, XC-NN) has its share of metallic guitar riffs and ominous samples, but it's mostly alt-rock by-the-numbers. "Young, Stupid & White" has all the style of good punk rock, but not the substance.

the rest:
Lifted 𝄢𝄢 (550 Music, 1996)

influences:
◀◀ Killing Joke, PiL

see also: *Sisters of Mercy*

Daniel Durchholz

X-Ray Spex

Formed 1977, in London, England. Disbanded 1980.

Poly Styrene, vocals; Jak Airport, guitar; Steve Rudan, sax; Paul Dean, bass; B.P. Hurding, drums; Laura Logic, sax (1977).

Though only a band for three years, X-Ray Spex made a lasting impact on the punk scene. Poly Styrene's wild, banshee-style singing was punctuated by saxophones and fast pop melodies; and the song "Oh Bondage Up Yours" announced the group's punk attitude with a bang. Styrene went solo with the jazz-toned *Transluscence* and later joined a Hare Krishna sect in London.

what to buy: It was "Identity" from *Germ Free Adolescents* 𝄢𝄢𝄢𝄢 (EMI/Caroline, 1978, prod. Falcon Stuart) that transcended raw aggression and sent it into hyperspace—albeit for a short journey.

influences:
◀◀ The Stooges, the New York Dolls, the Dictators

▶▶ The Go-Go's, Nirvana, Hole,

Anna Glen

XTC
/The Dukes of Stratosphear

Formed 1977, in Swindon, Wiltshire, England.

XTC: Andy Partridge, guitar, vocals; Colin Ivor Moulding, guitar, bass, vocals; Barry Andrews, keyboards (1977–79); Dave Gregory, guitar, keyboards, vocals (1979–present); Terry Chambers, drums (1977–83). The Dukes of Stratosphear: Sir John Johns (Andy Partridge), guitar,

vocals; the Red Curtain (Colin Moulding), bass, vocals; Lord Cornelius Plum (Dave Gregory), guitar, keyboards, vocals; E.I.E.I. Owen (Ian Gregory), drums.

It's hard to put a finger on XTC. It is either one of the most creative rock bands to come along or simply a capable reinventor of rock's more original creators. Like John Lennon and Paul McCartney (who are obvious influences), Andy Partridge and Colin Moulding write in distinctively different but complementary styles. Partridge is usually quirky and more rock-influenced, while Moulding is the quieter, folk-touched member of the pair. During its lengthy career, XTC has pursued a broad range of styles, including new wave (1977–79), pop-rock (1979–81), neo-folk (1982–83), and a synthesis of Beatles and Beach Boys influences (1984–present). Despite such obvious derivation, the group has produced hook-laden and highly durable music at each stage of its development. Since Chambers's departure in 1983, XTC has performed as a trio, with drumming support from such notable sidemen as the Tubes' Prairie Prince and former Glitter Band member Pete Phipps. The Dukes of Stratosphere is a pseudonymous project undertaken by XTC and producer John Leckie in 1985. With meticulous detail and a good deal of humor, the group creates mock psychedelic music in the same self-conscious way the Rutles ransacked the Beatles' legacy. What could have been a one-joke farce turns out to be an enjoyable and highly listenable romp. Interestingly, for all of its tongue-in-cheek nature, the Dukes' first release (a six-song EP) actually outsold XTC's previously released album, *The Big Express*. XTC's legal problems with their label have prevented the group from releasing new material since 1992's *Nonsuch*, although a resolution was reportedly at hand in late 1997. The band has continued writing and recording in the intervening years, so there's every reason to anticipate a flood of new releases in the near future.

what to buy: *Skylarking* ♫♫♫♫ (Geffen, 1986, prod. Todd Rundgren) is a masterful collection of songs seamlessly woven in one continuous thread, à la *Sgt. Pepper's Lonely Hearts Club Band*. Rundgren's production is well attuned to the group's own influences and offbeat sensibilities. More to the point, the songs—a mixture of pop-rock, neofolk, and lush orchestrations—are simply superb, particularly "Earn Enough for Us," "Big Day," and the surprising hit single "Dear God." Of XTC's early catalog, *Drums & Wires* ♫♫♫♫ (Geffen, 1979, prod. Steve Lillywhite) is among the best. Partridge tones down his idiosyncratic tendencies ever so slightly to turn in terrific and lively pop on "Life Begins at the Hop," "When You're Near Me I Have Difficulty," and "Roads Girdle the Globe." Moulding's stellar offerings include "Ten Feet Tall" and the British hit "Making Plans for Nigel."

what to buy next: *The Compact XTC—The Singles 1978-85* ♫♫♫♫ (Virgin, 1985, prod. various) is a handy repackaging of 18

A-sides from the group's output of singles, including the hyperkinetic rave-up "Science Friction," "Statue of Liberty," and Partridge's beautifully bucolic "Senses Working Overtime." It's a great way to investigate the group's earlier work without making a huge investment. For a fun time, check out *Chips from the Chocolate Fireball* ♫♫♫♫ (Geffen, 1988, prod. John Leckie), a one-disc compilation of the two Dukes of Stratosphear releases—the EP *25 O'Clock* and the album *Psonic Psunspot*, both of which were also released as individual CDs. For all of the group's intended satire, many of the songs ("Vanishing Girl," "Have You Seen Jackie," and "Brainiac's Daughter") are brilliantly rendered and stand up quite nicely on their own.

what to avoid: Released in the same year as the group's wonderfully frenetic debut LP, *Go 2* ♫ (Geffen, 1978, prod. John Leckie) sounds forced and uneven. Aside from the infectious single "Are You Receiving Me?," the songs are merely curious reminders of punk's quirkier side.

the rest:
White Music ♫♫♫ (Geffen, 1978)
Black Sea ♫♫♫♫ (Geffen, 1980)
English Settlement ♫♫♫ (Geffen, 1982)
Waxworks: Some Singles 1977–1982 ♫♫♫♫ (Geffen, 1982)
Mummer ♫♫♫♫ (Geffen, 1984)
The Big Express ♫♫♫ (Geffen, 1984)
Oranges & Lemons ♫♫ (Geffen, 1989)
Rag & Bone Buffet (B-Side & Rarities) ♫♫♫ (Geffen, 1990)
Nonsuch ♫♫♫♫ (Geffen, 1992)
Upsy Daisy Assortment ♫♫♫♫♫ (Geffen, 1997)

The Dukes of Stratosphear:
25 O'Clock ♫♫♫♫ (Virgin, 1985)
Psonic Psunspot ♫♫♫♫ (Geffen, 1987)

worth searching for: *Skylarking Demos and Others* (Extatic, 1995, prod. various) reconstructs nearly the entire *Skylarking* album in demo form, adding on, for good measure, a number of studio outtakes from various projects, including the Dukes of Stratosphear. Good performances and high-quality recording make this a particularly interesting look behind one of XTC's best albums.

solo outings:
Andy Partridge:
Mr. Partridge: Take Away/The Lure of Salvage ♫♫ (Virgin, 1980)
(With Harold Budd) *Through the Hill* ♫♫♫♫ (Gyroscope/Caroline, 1994)

influences:
◄◄ The Beach Boys, the Beatles, Bob Dylan, Pink Floyd, Todd Rundgren

►► The B-52's, the Buzzcocks, Wire, Hüsker Dü, the La's, the Pursuit of Happiness, Blur

Christopher Scapelliti

Xymox

Formed 1983, in Nijmegan, Holland.

Ronny Moorings, vocals, guitars; Anke Wolbert, bass, vocals; Pieter Nooten, synthesizers.

Xymox, founded as Clan of Xymox, was a mid-'80s signing to the 4AD label; if not for that, we may have never heard of the band. After all, being from the Netherlands isn't exactly conducive to making it in the music business. Unique for the spacious synthesizer sounds with an overtly baroque lean, the band differentiated itself from the pack of other arty industrial bands by introducing lush string arrangements and relying heavily on a acoustic steel guitar to customize its sound. While critically accused of overt pretentiousness and lack of talent, the band creates amazing atmospheres with minimal machinery and imbibes all of its work with an amazing emotional pull. No explanation has surfaced to explain the dropping of "Clan of" from the band's third album, which marked its departure from 4AD and its first U.S. release. The first two albums are hard to find, and after the band was dropped from PolyGram in the U.S., all subsequent releases have been through varying European independent labels.

what to buy: *Clan of Xymox* ♪♪♪♪ (4AD, 1985, prod. Xymox, Ivo Watts Russell) is the band's first full-length effort, solid from start to finish, with everything art-dance music lovers look for—angst-ridden lyrics, stunning synth washes, and brooding guitar sounds. "Stranger" and "A Day" are dance floor classics. The band's first release, *Subsequent Pleasures* ♪♪ (Psuedonym/1994), came in 1984 and had only 500 copies pressed; it has been reissued along with some early demo recordings.

the rest:
Medusa ♪♪♪♪ (4AD, 1986)
Twist of Shadows ♪♪♪♪ (Wing/PolyGram, 1989)
Phoenix ♪♪♪ (Wing/PolyGram, 1991)
Headcloudes ♪♪ (Off Beat, 1994)

influences:
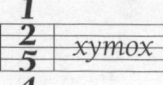 New Order, Joy Division, Sisters of Mercy, Cabaret Voltaire, Kraftwerk

▶▶ Mission U.K., Alice in Chains, Filter, Dust Brothers, Mark Snow

Tim Davis

Yamo

See: Kraftwerk

Weird Al Yankovic

Born Alfred Matthew Yankovic, October 23, 1959, in Lynwood, CA.

A rocker or a mocker? The latter, thank you—and a damn good one at that. Figuring that he wouldn't be the next Elton John on his instrument of choice—accordion—Weird Al Yankovic chose the parody path and for the past 17 years has been twisting the biggest hits of the day into clever and wickedly twisted ditties. It started with "My Bologna," his rewrite of the Knack's "My Sharona," that received airplay from syndicated radio host Dr. Demento. By the time Demento aired "Another One Rides the Bus" (Queen's "Another One Bites the Dust"), Yankovic had his own recording deal. Over the years he's taken on Michael Jackson, Madonna, Nirvana—you're not a pop phenomenon until Weird Al has messed with one of your songs. And his assorted polka medleys of rock 'n' roll classics are even better than the individual parodies. Yankovic only missteps with his originals, which are occasionally funny but never quite hit the zeniths of his whacko covers.

what to buy: *In 3-D* ♪♪♪♪ (Scotti Bros., 1984/1991, prod. Rick Derringer) made Yankovic a phenomenon as he grabbed Jackson's coattails with "Eat It" ("Beat It") and scored with "I Lost on Jeopardy" (Greg Kihn's "Jeopardy"). *The Food Album* ♪♪♪♪ (RCA, 1993, prod. Al Yankovic, Rick Derringer) and *The TV Album* ♪♪♪♪ (Scotti Bros., 1995, prod. Al Yankovic, Rick Derringer) are hysterical thematic albums that are considerably better than Yankovic's skimpy greatest hits collections.

what to buy next: If you're willing to splurge for more than one Yankovic collection, live large with the box set *Permanent Record* ♪♪♪♪ (Scotti Bros., 1994, prod. Al Yankovic, Rick Derringer). Is four discs a bit much? Yeah, but too much Weird Al is better than too little.

what to avoid: He decided to push the originals a bit too hard on *Even Worse* ♪♪ (Scotti Bros., 1988/1991, prod. Rick Derringer), and it's tough to compete with a good parody like "Fat" (Jackson's "Bad").

the rest:
Weird Al Yankovic ♪♪♪ (Rock 'n' Roll/Scotti Bros., 1983/1991)
Dare to Be Stupid ♪♪♪♪ (Scotti Bros., 1985/1991)
Polka Party! ♪♪♪ (Scotti Bros., 1986/1991)
UHF/Original Motion Picture Soundtrack and Other Stuff ♪♪ (Scotti Bros., 1989)
Greatest Hits ♪♪ (Scotti Bros., 1991)
Off the Deep End ♪♪♪ (Scotti Bros., 1992)
Alapalooza ♪♪♪ (Scotti Bros., 1993)
Greatest Hits, Volume II ♪♪♪ (Scotti Bros., 1994)
Bad Hair Day ♪♪♪ (Scotti Bros., 1996)

worth searching for: Weird Al speaks—yes, speaks—as a narrator for a high-minded children's recording of Prokofiev's—

yes, Prokofiev's—*Peter & the Wolf* (CBS Masterworks, 1992). There's not an accordion within earshot.

influences:

⏪ Alan Sherman, Barnes & Barnes, Frankie Yankovic (no relation)

⏩ The Presidents of the United States of America

Gary Graff

The Yardbirds

Formed 1963, in London, England. Disbanded 1968.

Keith Relf (died May 14, 1976), harmonica, vocals; Paul Samwell-Smith, bass; Chris Dreja, guitar, bass, vocals; Jim McCarty, drums; Anthony "Top" Topham, guitar (1963); Eric Clapton, guitar (1963–64); Jeff Beck, guitar (1964–67); Jimmy Page, guitar (1966–68).

If only for featuring Eric Clapton, Jeff Beck, and Jimmy Page as successive lead guitarists, the Yardbirds earned a place in rock history. But—primarily due to that guitar god trinity—the band also brought an inventiveness to British Invasion blues-rock that would only be surpassed by the Rolling Stones and Cream. Clapton left the band early, complaining of commercialism, though not before contributing to its first hit, "For Your Love." Beck took over, and the Yardbirds sound took off with a series of classic singles built around his groundbreaking guitar leads, feedback textures, and experiments with Eastern scales— "Shapes of Things" and "Over Under Sideways Down" among them. For a short time, Beck and Page shared lead guitar duties, creating the band's last great single, "Happenings Ten Years Time Ago." Page took over for one final album before departing for Led Zeppelin (originally billed as the New Yardbirds). Relf went on to form Renaissance, and Samwell-Smith became a producer—though he, McCarty, and Dreja formed a new band, Box of Frogs, during the mid-'80s. Over time, however, the Yardbirds' music continues to influence countless guitar slingers.

what to buy: Two collections provide a good introduction to the Yardbirds' music. *Greatest Hits, Vol. 1: 1964–1966* 🎵🎵🎵🎵 (Rhino, 1986, prod. Giorgio Gomelsky) contains essential tracks—"For Your Love", "Heart Full of Soul," "I'm a Man," "Shapes of Things"—through the band's mid-career. *Vol. 2: Blues, Backtracks & Shapes of Things* 🎵🎵🎵 (Sony, 1991, prod. various) is a two-CD set that fills in many of the remaining gaps, with a number of live and rare cuts as a bonus. Perhaps the Yardbirds' finest album, *Roger the Engineer* 🎵🎵🎵🎵 (1966/Warner Archives, 1997, prod. Paul Samwell-Smith, Simon Napier Bell) finds Beck and Page together at the helm and the band making its most successful experimental forays.

what to buy next: To hear the gritty, pre-hits Yardbirds live, with Clapton on guitar, check out *Five Live Yardbirds* 🎵🎵🎵 (Epic U.K.,

1964/Rhino, 1988, prod. Giorgio Gomelsky). The Beck-Page incarnation of the group turns in an awesome instrumental, "Stroll On," on the soundtrack to *Blow-Up* 🎵🎵🎵 (1966/Rhino, 1996). *BBC Sessions* 🎵🎵🎵 (Warner Archives, 1997, compilation prod. Gregg Geller) picks up some memorable broadcast performances by the Beck and Page lineups, including originals and covers ranging from "Dust My Broom" to "Hang on Sloopy."

what to avoid: A number of not-so-great greatest-hits collections are out there. Stick with the recommendations.

the rest:

Vol. 1: Smokestack Lightning 🎵🎵🎵 (Sony, 1991)
Yardbirds Little Games Sessions & More 🎵🎵🎵 (EMI, 1992)

worth searching for: *Train Kept A-Rollin': The Complete Giorgio Gomelsky Productions* (Charly, 1993, prod. Giorgio Gromelsky) is the kind of sweeping four-disc box set—with a T-shirt, no less—that U.S. Yardbird fans have been waiting for, with excellent sound. Less stunning, but of some historical value, is the Yardbirds' collaboration with hero Sonny Boy Williamson on the import-only *With Sonny Boy Williamson* (Edsel U.K., 1966).

influences:

⏪ Sonny Boy Williamson, Jimmy Reed, Alexis Korner

⏩ Jeff Beck Group, Led Zeppelin, the Allman Brothers Band, the Grateful Dead

see also: *Led Zeppelin, Jeff Beck, Eric Clapton, Jimmy Page, Cream, Renaissance*

Doug Pippin

Yaz/Yazoo

See: Alison Moyet

Yello

Formed 1979, in Zurich, Switzerland.

Boris Blank, various instruments; Dieter Meier, vocals; Carlos Peron, tapes, sound effects (1979–83).

One of the oddest groups ever recorded, Yello combines campy vocals and lyrics with synthetic sounds that span the globe with multicultural sound bites. It's essentially a synth-band, but Chico Hablas regularly adds guitar and Beat Ash contributes real drums when needed. Dieter Meier sounds and looks as if he's moved elegantly into middle age (even on the early records), and if the hyperbole is to believed, is also a millionaire industrialist. Boris Blank looks like the missing member of Sparks yet fills each and every cut with jungle noises, bossa nova beats, and other sonic detritus. The result is a fascinating sound that is danceable and soundtrack-ready—kind of like a Martin Denny record remixed by Moby. Strangely enough it works, though it's difficult at times to discern if the band is in on the joke.

what to buy: *You Gotta Say Yes to Another Excess* ♫♫♫ (Mercury, 1983, prod. Yello, Ursli Weber) is perhaps the weirdest major-label record that you can still dance to. Meier never really sings but rather speaks in a suave, guttural manner. A partial lyric sheet is included, which makes one hope that some intended meaning was lost somewhere in the translation. Even with such silliness, Yello brings the groove. Tracks such as "Smile on You" and "No More Words" rival the band Trio in depth, yet are undeniably catchy.

what to buy next: *One Second* ♫♫♫ (Mercury, 1987, prod. Yello) contains the *Ferris Bueller's Day Off* gem "Oh Yeah"—you know, "Oh Yeah . . . chick-a chick-ahh" (recite that aloud if unclear). Former Associate Billy Mackenzie and James Bond diva Shirley Bassey are present on a couple tracks to add to the strangeness. Eclectic and different, *One Second* continued the evolution of Yello into a more melodic and (somewhat) disciplined group.

the rest:
Solid Pleasure ♫♫♫ (Ralph, 1980/Mercury, 1988)
Claro Que Si ♫♫♫ (Ralph 1981/Mercury 1988)
Bostich ♫♫♫♪ (Stiff EP, 1982)
Stella ♫♫♫ (Elektra, 1985/Mercury, 1988)
The New Mix in One Go: 80–85 ♫♫♫ (Mercury, 1986)
Flag ♫♫♫ (Mercury, 1988)
Essential ♫♫♫ (Smash, 1992)
Zebra 4th & B'way, 1994) ♫♫♫♪
Hands on Yello ♫♫♪ (Mercury, 1995)

influences:
◀◀ Kraftwerk, William S. Burroughs, Tangerine Dream, Martin Denny, Juan Garcia Esquivel, the Residents, M, Tuxedomoon, science fiction and James Bond movies

▶▶ Depeche Mode, Men without Hats, Trio, Taco, Ministry, nine inch nails, Prodigy

Barry M. Prickett

Yes

Formed 1968, in London, England. Disbanded 1980. Re-formed 1983.

Jon Anderson, vocals (1968–80, 1983–89, 1991–present); Chris Squire, bass, vocals; Peter Banks, guitar (1968–69); Tony Kaye, keyboards (1968–71, 1983–95); Bill Bruford, drums (1968–72, 1991); Steve Howe, guitar, vocals (1969–81, 1991–present); Rick Wakeman, keyboards (1971–74, 1976–80, 1991–97); Alan White, drums (1972–present); Patrick Moraz, keyboards (1974–76); Trevor Horn, vocals (1980); Geoff Downes, keyboards (1980); Trevor Rabin, guitar

(1983–94); Billy Sherwood, guitar, keyboards, vocals (1996–present); Igor "Ivan" Khoroshev, keyboards (1997–present).

A shining example of both the zeniths and nadirs of progressive rock, Yes has plied its symphonic, fussy craft since the late '60s with a rotating crew of players. Initially influenced by the Beatles and Simon and Garfunkel, singer Jon Anderson, bassist Chris Squire, and others began work on a rock-jazz-folk-classical hybrid during the peak of psychedelia; indeed, the group's first major gig was an opening spot for acid-rock trio Cream's farewell concert. By the time Yes emerged as an arena-filling act, the '70s had begun and pomp-rock was in full flower. The arrival of keyboardist Rick Wakeman, whose incessant noodling on the synthesizer was unshackled by taste, pushed the band to previously unimagined peaks of pretension. With its lengthy, mind-expanding excursions, instrumental pyrotechnics, and trippy Roger Dean album covers, the band became poster children of progressive rock alongside Pink Floyd, Emerson, Lake & Palmer, Genesis, Jethro Tull, and other kindred spirits. That said, Yes also made some transcendently lovely music. Lineup changes have affected the sound over the years—the new wave touches provided by ex-Buggles Trevor Horn and Geoff Downes, Trevor Rabin's slick album-rockcraft—and for a while some members (Anderson, Bill Bruford, Wakeman, and Steve Howe) struck out on their own rather than be part of all that. But Yes remains, though its most recent output makes one wonder if that's such a good thing.

what to buy: *The Yes Album* ♫♫♫♫ (Atlantic, 1971, prod. Eddie Offord) is crammed with inventive, dynamic rock that borrows from jazz, English folk, and myriad other forms. It's notable especially for the long-form rockers "Starship Trooper" and "Yours Is No Disgrace."

what to buy next: Despite the ominous import of their excesses, *Fragile* ♫♫♫♪ (Atlantic, 1971, prod. Eddie Offord) and *Close to the Edge* ♫♫♫♪ (Atlantic, 1972, prod. Eddie Offord) show Yes at a creative and commercial peak, and both include some of their most majestically beautiful work. The earlier *Time and a Word* ♫♫♫ (Atlantic, 1970, prod. Tony Colton) shows the band in an ambitious but not overweening stage of its development.

what to avoid: Start by dodging the high school reunion–style *Union* **woof!** (Arista, 1991, prod. Jonathan Elias), which suggests that the quality of a modern Yes recording may be inversely proportional to the number of players (eight) on it. And stay far, far away from *Symphonic Music of Yes* **woof!** (RCA, 1993, prod. Alan Parsons), which features the London Philharmonic and English Chamber Orchestras and is an object lesson in why progressive rock died of its own bloat.

the rest:
Yes ♫♫♫ (Atlantic, 1969)

Yessongs 🎵🎵🎵 (Atlantic, 1973)
Tales from Topographic Oceans 🎵🎵 (Atlantic, 1973)
Relayer 🎵🎵🎵 (Atlantic, 1974)
Yesterdays 🎵🎵🎵 (Atlantic, 1975)
Going for the One 🎵🎵🎵 (Atlantic, 1977)
Tormato 🎵🎵 (Atlantic, 1978)
Drama 🎵🎵🎵 (Atlantic, 1980)
Yesshows 🎵🎵🎵 (Atlantic, 1980)
Classic Yes 🎵🎵🎵 (Atlantic, 1982)
90125 🎵🎵🎵 (Atco, 1983)
Big Generator 🎵🎵 (Atco, 1987)
Yesyears 🎵🎵🎵🎵 (Atco, 1991)
Yesstory 🎵🎵🎵🎵 (Atco, 1992)
Highlights: The Very Best of Yes 🎵🎵🎵🎵 (Atlantic, 1993)
Talk **woof!** (Victory, 1994)
Keys to Ascension 🎵🎵🎵 (CMC, 1996)
Keys to Ascension 2 🎵🎵🎵 (Purple Pyramid/Cleopatra, 1997)
Open Your Eyes 🎵🎵🎵 (Beyond, 1997)

worth searching for: *Affirmative: The Yes Solo Family Album* (Connoisseur, 1993, prod. various) is an import with some of the best material from the individual Yes members' myriad solo albums.

solo outings:
Anderson, Wakeman, Bruford & Howe:
Anderson, Wakeman, Bruford and Howe 🎵 (Arista, 1989)
An Evening of Yes Music Plus 🎵🎵🎵 (Herald, 1994)

Jon Anderson:
Olias of Sunhillow 🎵🎵 (Atlantic, 1976)
In the City of Angels 🎵🎵🎵 (Columbia, 1988)
Change We Must 🎵🎵 (Angel/EMI, 1994)
Deseo 🎵🎵 (Windham Hill, 1994)
Angels Embrace 🎵🎵 (Higher Octave, 1995)
Toltec 🎵🎵 (High Street, 1996)
The Promise Ring 🎵🎵🎵 (OM Town, 1997)
Each Mother Earth 🎵🎵🎵 (Ellipsis Arts)
The More You Know 🎵🎵 (Purple Pyramid/Cleopatra, 1998)

Jon & Vangelis:
Short Stories 🎵🎵 (Mercury, 1980)
The Friends of Mr. Cairo 🎵🎵 (Mercury, 1982)
Private Collection 🎵 (Mercury, 1983)
The Best of Jon and Vangelis 🎵🎵 (Mercury, 1984)

Steve Howe:
Beginnings 🎵🎵 (Atlantic, 1975/1994)
The Steve Howe Album 🎵🎵 (Atlantic, 1979/1994)
Turbulence 🎵🎵 (Relativity, 1994)
Not Necessarily Acoustic 🎵🎵🎵 (Herald, 1994)

Trevor Rabin:
Can't Look Away 🎵🎵 (Elektra, 1989)

Chris Squire:
Fish out of Water 🎵🎵🎵🎵 (Atlantic, 1975)

influences:

◄◄ The Beatles, the Byrds, Simon & Garfunkel, Move, the Moody Blues, Genesis, post-bop jazz

►► Rush, Starcastle, Dream Theater, Queensryche

see also: *Asia, King Crimson, the Moody Blues, Rick Wakeman*

Simon Glickman and Gary Graff

Yo La Tengo
Formed 1985, in Hoboken, NJ.

Ira Kaplan, guitar, vocals; Georgia Hubley, drums, vocals; James McNew, bass (1991–present); Dave Rick, bass (1985); Mike Lewis, bass (1986); Stephan Wichnewski, bass (1986–89); Wilbo Wright, bass (1990); Gene Holder, bass (1990–91).

Ira Kaplan and Georgia Hubley spent their early dates playing songs together in a New Jersey apartment and ended up with a marriage and a band. Named for the way a Spanish baseball player says "I've got it," Yo La Tengo is a perennial indie band, a favorite among serious music fans and college radio types. Like a new version of the Velvet Underground (Yo La Tengo members actually portrayed the VU in the film *I Shot Andy Warhol*), the band vacillates between gentle folk pop and noise, often ending up with a hybrid of understated vocals, layered guitar drone experiments, and the occasional noise squall.

what to buy: Smooth transitions between a hushed ballad like "Don't Say a Word (Hot Chicken #2)" and the noisy "(Straight Down to the) Bitter End" on *Electr-O-Pura* 🎵🎵🎵🎵 (Matador, 1995, prod. Roger Moutenot) show Yo La Tengo at peak form. *I Can Hear the Heart Beating As One* 🎵🎵🎵🎵 (Matador, 1997, prod. Roger Noutenot) is a prototypical Yo La Tengo record—churning guitar mixed low into submission, low-key vocals, and the occasional oddity such as the retro bossa nova of "Center of Gravity."

what to buy next: Kaplan was a former music critic, and it shows on his selections of songs for *Fakebook* 🎵🎵🎵🎵 (Bar None, 1990, prod. Gene Holder), a collection of mostly cover tunes filled with obscurities by the Flamin' Groovies, NRBQ, and Daniel Johnston. It's not especially representative of the band, but it is a lot of fun.

what to avoid: *May I Sing with Me* 🎵🎵🎵 (Alias, 1992, prod. Gene Holder) is weighed down with too many lengthy guitar solos.

the rest:
Ride the Tiger 🎵🎵🎵 (Matador, 1986)
President Yo La Tengo/New Wave Hot Dogs 🎵🎵🎵 (Matador, 1989)
Painful 🎵🎵🎵🎵 (Matador, 1993)

worth searching for: *Camp Yo La Tengo* (Matador EP, 1995, prod. Roger Moutenot) is a four-song set that includes interesting remakes of two songs from *Electr-o-Pura*.

influences:

◄◄ The Velvet Underground, Sonic Youth

►► Luna, Spiritualized

Jill Hamilton

Dwight Yoakam

Born October 23, 1956, in Pikesville, KY.

When Yoakam released his debut album in 1986, the Nashville establishment branded him a punk. True, he did cut his teeth doing gigs with noisy L.A. roots-rockers like the Blasters, and he was openly hostile in interviews toward mainstream country music. But that hardly qualified him as a punk. His music has always been pure country, in the mode of Buck Owens and Merle Haggard. Working closely with guitarist-producer Pete Anderson, the singer has turned out some of the best neo-traditional country albums of the past decade. He branched out into acting during the late '90s, with roles in *Sling Blade* and *The Newton Boys,* but he still manged to crank out a new album every year.

what to buy: *Gone* 𝄢𝄢𝄢𝄢 (Reprise, 1996, prod. Pete Anderson) is Yoakam's most fully realized collection—an ambitious mix of hard-core country, psychedelic guitars, string sections, and mariachi horns. The more traditional *If There Was a Way* 𝄢𝄢𝄢𝄢 (Reprise, 1990, prod. Pete Anderson) boasts such gems as "You're the One" and "Nothing's Changed Here," while *Buenos Noches from a Lonely Room* 𝄢𝄢𝄢𝄢 (Reprise, 1988, prod. Pete Anderson) is Yoakam's melancholy masterwork, featuring loving remakes of Owens's "Streets of Bakersfield" and Johnny Cash's "Home of the Blues."

what to buy next: *Hillbilly Deluxe* 𝄢𝄢𝄢𝄢 (Reprise, 1987, prod. Pete Anderson) Yoakam's second album, spawned a flurry of hits, including "Always Late with Your Kisses," "Little Ways," and Elvis Presley's "Little Sister." *Just Lookin' for a Hit* 𝄢𝄢𝄢𝄢 (Reprise, 1989, prod. Pete Anderson) is a fine primer, with a bonus remake of the Flying Burrito Brothers' "Sin City" as a duet with k.d. lang.

what to avoid: None of the songs on *Dwight Live* 𝄢𝄢 (Reprise, 1995, prod. Pete Anderson) come close to matching the versions on his studio albums.

the rest:

Guitars, Cadillacs, etc., etc. 𝄢𝄢𝄢𝄢 (Reprise, 1986)
This Time 𝄢𝄢𝄢𝄢 (Reprise, 1993)
Come on Christmas 𝄢𝄢 (Reprise, 1997)
Under the Covers 𝄢𝄢𝄢 (Reprise, 1997)

A Long Way Home 𝄢𝄢𝄢 (Reprise, 1998)

worth searching for: The soundtrack *White Sands* (Morgan Creek, 1992) features music composed by Yoakam.

influences:

◄◄ Buck Owens, Hank Williams, Hank Snow

►► Travis Tritt, the Mavericks, Uncle Tupelo

Thor Christensen

You Am I

Formed 1990, in Sydney, Australia.

Tim Rogers, vocals, guitar, organ, harmonica, xylophone; Andy Kent, bass, vocals; Russell Hopkinson, drums, percussion, vocals.

The pronouns in its moniker aside, this Sydney-based pop combo has a highly personal touch that pairs riffy rock with spiffy tunes. You Am I sounds like nobody else, and it lets its influences float on the surface of the music instead of penetrating it. The trio sounds '60s-ish without coming off as revivalists, and it siphons some energy from the late '70s power pop movement while peppering the songs with grunge, but without leaving an aftertaste of angst. You Am I, despite any hints inferred by the moniker, doesn't suffer from split personalities— it creates a singular one.

what to buy: *Hourly, Daily* 𝄢𝄢𝄢𝄢𝄢 (Sire, 1997, prod. You Am I, George Drakoulias) is perhaps *the* late '90s lost pop masterpiece. Touches of the Who, XTC, the Left Banke, and the Byrds never overwhelm You Am I's distinctive onslaught. At times the band seems far more English than Australian—its lyrics evoke Ray Davies at his most caustically observational. Hand claps, horns, and a king's ransom of hooks propel ditties such as "Trike" and the Jam-flavored "Opportunities." The somewhat paradoxical "Heavy Comfort" relaxes on a fluffy cushion of baroque, recalling the gentleness of Squeeze's "Vanity Fair." The disparity between the artistic success of the sadly shelved *#4 Record* 𝄢𝄢𝄢𝄢 (Warner Bros., 1998) is nourished by Cheap Trick and soul-rock influences and displays further growth in You Am I's flowering beauty. "Fifteen" agelessly blends the charm of mid-period Kinks with the raucousness of their early work. "Heavy Heart" proves You Am I doesn't lose the beat when it goes balladic.

what to buy next: *Hi Fi Way* 𝄢𝄢𝄢 (Warner Bros., 1994, prod. Lee Ranaldo) is good, chunky power-pop but lacks the songwriting flavor the band cooked up later. Still, fans of the group will want to pick this up.

what to avoid: Since You Am I is clearly a band that got better with age, you'd be wise to avoid *Sound As Ever* 𝄢𝄢 (Warner Bros., 1993, prod. Lee Ranaldo), their nascently charming

American debut. The band's pop instincts are shrouded under a sandpapery sheath of grunge.

influences:

⏪ The Who, the Kinks, the Smithereens, XTC

Jordan Oakes

Jesse Colin Young

Born November 22, 1941, in New York, NY.

Like many a folkie who frequented the acoustic circuit of the New York's Greenwich Village during the early '60s, Jesse Colin Young eventually caught the rock bug, switched to bass, and formed the Youngbloods, a band that lasted a half-dozen years and produced a handful of enduring tracks ("Darkness, Darkness," "Sunlight"). Out on his own again by the early '70s, Young slipped into a smooth-rock persona, writing tunes that reflected the serenity of his Colorado mountain home ("Ridgetop"), his love of family life ("Song for Juli"), and general bliss ("Light Shine"). Though pleasant and well recorded, a lot of these songs are of their time—the mellowness just doesn't transfer all that well into the modern era. Nevertheless, Young maintains a loyal fan base, and he remains active as a performer to this day.

what to buy: Rather than getting caught in the laid-back bedrock of any single Young album, *The Best of Jesse Colin Young: The Solo Years* 𝄞𝄞𝄞 (Rhino, 1991, prod. Jesse Colin Young) extracts the occasional highlights—and taken in this form shows that the man knew how to put together a good light pop song. *Best* includes "Four in the Morning," "Sugar Babe," and "Morning Sun," in addition to his own live (if less effective) version of the Youngbloods classic "Sunlight." Young gets stellar backing along the way from the likes of Hank De-Vito, Timothy B. Schmit, John Sebastian, and Mike Porcaro.

the rest:

Together 𝄞𝄞𝄞 (Warner Bros., 1972)
Song for Juli 𝄞𝄞 (Warner Bros., 1973)
Light Shine 𝄞𝄞 (Warner Bros., 1974)
Songbird 𝄞𝄞 (Warner Bros., 1975)
On the Road 𝄞𝄞 (Warner Bros., 1976)

influences:

⏪ Bob Dylan, the Beatles

⏩ Dan Fogelberg, Pure Prairie League

David Simons

Neil Young

Born November 12, 1945, in Toronto, Ontario, Canada.

Few musicians have been as influential in as broad a manner as Neil Young, whose three-decade-plus career has been remarkably varied. He's both the godfather of grunge and the uncle of unplugged. As a member of Buffalo Springfield, he helped create the folk-rock genre. With Crazy Horse, he introduced the ragged, powerful, three-chords-and-a-cloud-of-dust approach that mutated into grunge. His 1972 album *Harvest* cross-pollinated country and rock. And his "Old Man" and "Heart of Gold" are essential sensitive-guy-on-the-beach acoustic fare. Though some of Young's incursions into alien fields—such as rockabilly and straight country—have been less than successful, each foray has reenergized him, allowing him to return to his classics with renewed vigor. After a long fallow period, Young returned with a vengeance with 1989's *Freedom* and has been more or less going strong ever since.

what to buy: *Decade* 𝄞𝄞𝄞𝄞 (Reprise, 1977, prod. Neil Young, David Briggs) was a box set before its time, a three-album, two-CD summation of Young's career from 1966 to 1975 that gives an excellent overview and should help guide you through the rest of the early catalog. He's planning a sweeping, multi-volume retrospective of his career in the near future, but he has yet to commit to a release date. *After the Gold Rush* 𝄞𝄞𝄞𝄞 (Reprise, 1970, prod. Neil Young, David Briggs) is a great mix of Young's two selves, with rockers such as "Southern Man" and ballads like "Tell Me Why," not to mention the glorious title track. *Everybody Knows This Is Nowhere* 𝄞𝄞𝄞𝄞 (Reprise, 1969, prod. Neil Young, David Briggs) is Young's quintessential Crazy Horse album, featuring the extended guitar workouts of "Down by the River," "Cinnamon Girl," and "Cowgirl in the Sand." *Weld* 𝄞𝄞𝄞𝄞 (Reprise, 1991, prod. Neil Young, David Briggs) is a startlingly good live album, Young's great statement at the time of release that he was back with a vengeance.

what to buy next: *Harvest* 𝄞𝄞𝄞𝄞 (Reprise, 1972, prod. Elliott Mazer, Neil Young) is Young's most popular album, for good reason. It's docked one bone for the presence of two horribly overwrought orchestral numbers, but the rest is pure gold. *Rust Never Sleeps* 𝄞𝄞𝄞𝄞 (Reprise, 1979, prod. Neil Young, David Briggs, Tim Mulligan) is a great live album. *Tonight's the Night* 𝄞𝄞𝄞𝄞 (Reprise, 1975, prod. Neil Young, David Briggs) is one of rock's scariest efforts ever. And *Harvest Moon* 𝄞𝄞𝄞𝄞 (Reprise, 1992, prod. Neil Young, Ben Keith) is a delightful return to acoustic music.

what to avoid: Young has made many missteps along the way. His biggest failures were wild stabs at different genres, such as electronic music—*Trans* 𝄞𝄞 (Geffen, 1982, prod. Neil Young, David Briggs, Tim Mulligan)—and rockabilly—*Everybody's Rockin'* 𝄞𝄞𝄞 (Geffen, 1983, prod. Neil Young, David Briggs, Tim Mulligan). *Mirror Ball* 𝄞𝄞 (Reprise, 1995, prod. Neil Young, David Briggs), his collaboration with Pearl Jam, was also a failure, a leaden bore with undeveloped songs to boot.

Neil Young (© Ken Settle)

the rest:

Neil Young ♫♫ (Reprise, 1969)

Journey through the Past ♫♫ (Reprise, 1972)

Time Fades Away ♫♫♫ (Reprise, 1973)

On the Beach ♫♫♫ (Reprise, 1974)

Zuma ♫♫♫♫ (Reprise, 1975)

(With the Stills-Young Band) *Long May You Run* ♫♫ (Reprise, 1976/ 1988)

American Stars 'n Bars ♫♫♫♫ (Reprise, 1977)

Comes a Time ♫♫♫ (Reprise, 1978)

Live Rust ♫♫♫♫ (Reprise, 1979)

Hawks & Doves ♫♫♫ (Reprise, 1980)

Old Ways ♫♫♫ (Geffen, 1985)

Landing on Water ♫♫ (Geffen, 1986)

Life ♫♫ (Geffen, 1987)

This Note's for You ♫♫♫ (Geffen, 1987)

Freedom ♫♫♫♫ (Reprise, 1989)

Ragged Glory ♫♫♫♫ (Reprise, 1990)

Arc ♫♫ (Reprise, 1991)

Unplugged ♫♫♫♫ (Reprise, 1993)

Sleeps with Angels ♫♫ (Reprise, 1994)

Broken Arrow ♫♫♫♫ (Reprise, 1996)

Year of the Horse ♫♫ (Reprise, 1997)

worth searching for: Besides Young contributions to some recent Randy Bachman records (we just had to throw that in), there are myriad bootlegs of Young concerts and unreleased material. One of the great ones is *Chrome Dreams*, an acetate copy of an album Young worked on during 1975 and 1976. The album never came out, but the songs—including "Pocahontas," "Too Far Gone," "Sedan Delivery," and "Powderfinger"—made their way onto other albums.

influences:

◀◀ Bob Dylan, Jimi Hendrix, Gram Parsons

▶▶ Dinosaur Jr., Joe Henry, Uncle Tupelo, Sonic Youth, Pearl Jam, the Replacements

see also: *Buffalo Springfield, Crosby, Stills & Nash*

Alan Paul

Paul Young

Born January 17, 1956, in Luton, England.

The son of an auto plant worker who logged some time in the factory himself, Paul Young merged a simultaneous affection for new wave rock and '60s soul into a singular solo voice during the '80s. Gaining early notice as lead vocalist for the British soul/horn band the Q-Tips, Young was signed to a solo deal by CBS Records in 1981 and immediately presented an expert blend of the new wave and dance sounds of the day with old-time soul vocal gymnastics. His next efforts further refined that signature sound, blunting the force of his soul sources with increasing amounts of pop flavor. Though a passable songwriter himself, most of Young's big hits were covers of other artists' material, from Marvin Gaye to Hall & Oates. Unfortunately, the proportion of slickness to soul in his records kept tilting toward pop blandness until U.S. listeners—who had never fully embraced him, anyway—stopped caring.

what to buy: Young's debut, *No Parlez* ♫♫♫♫ (Columbia, 1983, prod. Laurie Latham), is both his most eclectic and impressive recorded effort, bridging the gap between arty new wave and funky soul sounds in a vibrant new way. From the dreamy cover of Marvin Gaye's obscure ballad "Wherever I Lay My Hat" to the drum machine and sequencer-fed dance excursion "Sex" and atmospheric lead-off single "Come Back and Stay," this record offers an inspired mix of styles unified by Young's own impassioned blue-eyed soul vocal licks.

what to buy next: His second album, *The Secret of Association* ♫♫♫♫ (Columbia, 1985, prod. Laurie Latham), is the only other Young record that doesn't completely sacrifice passion for precision, as the singer allows a little funky heat to build on cuts like the fretless bass-fueled dance workouts "I'm Gonna Tear Your Playhouse Down," "Bite the Hand That Feeds," and "Hot Fun." But the only hit here, a pop-ified cover of Daryl Hall's "Everytime You Go Away," hints of the mistakes to come.

what to avoid: Basically, steer clear of the rest of Young's catalog. The singer seemed to turn his back on the very soul influences that made him a success in the first place. *Between Two Fires* **woof!** (Columbia, 1986, prod. Hugh Padgham, Paul Young, Ian Krewley) drowns in its own pop slickness (and a preponderance of Young-penned tunes), and *Other Voices* **woof!** (Columbia, 1990, prod. various) tries to rock out on a collection of forgettable songs.

the rest:

From Time to Time/The Singles Collection ♫♫♫♫ (Columbia, 1991)

Crossing ♫♫ (Columbia, 1993)

Reflections ♫♫ (Vision Music, 1995)

Love Hurts ♫♫ (Columbia, 1997)

worth searching for: A rare recording of a pre-stardom Young performing with the Q-Tips in concert, *Live at Last* (Stoic Records/Rewind Records, 1984), is available as an import and offers early versions of the singer's take on Smokey Robinson's "Tracks of My Tears" and his own strongest original tune, "Broken Man."

influences:

◀◀ Rod Stewart, Paul Rodgers, Robert Palmer, Smokey Robinson, Marvin Gaye, Daryl Hall

▶▶ George Michael, Maxwell, Tony Rich

Eric Deggans

Rusty Young
See: Poco

Young Fresh Fellows /Scott McCaughey /The Minus Five
Formed 1983, in Seattle, WA.

Scott McCaughey, guitar, vocals; Jim Sangster, bass; Tad Hutchison, drums; Chuck Carroll, guitar (1983–88); Kurt Bloch, guitar (1989–present).

When Young Fresh Fellows released *The Fabulous Sounds of the Pacific Northwest* in 1984, the Seattle scene was but a glimmer in the eyes of future Sub Pop moguls Bruce Pavitt and Jonathan Poneman. By the time Sub Pop, Nirvana, Soundgarden, and the like entered the picture during the late '80s, the Fellows had already put out a couple of records on a homegrown indie label (PopLlama) and were touring the country, helping to lay a foundation for the flurry of Seattle activity that followed. The Fellows were often as loud and raucous as any band in town, but instead of relying on punk and metal, the music drew inspiration from '60s pop and garage-rock sounds both classic (the Kinks) and obscure (the Flamin' Groovies). Furthermore, the group's attitude has always forsaken angst-ridden doom 'n' gloom in favor of happy-go-lucky hijinks à la the Replacements (it's fitting, then, that the Fellows played at Mats frontman Paul Westerberg's wedding reception). During the early '90s, one of the group's songs was the theme song of the short-lived *Higgins Boys & Gruber* television program on Comedy Central. Though YFF is still a going concern, the group's recorded output has slowed in recent years as its members have become more involved with other projects: Kurt Bloch with his long-running (formed in 1979) Fastbacks punk-pop band; Jim Sangster with original Flamin' Groovy Roy Loney as well as with country-rockers the Picketts; and Scott McCaughey as a sideman with R.E.M. The latter two also have an additional combo, The Lowebeats, whose repertoire consists of only Nick Lowe–penned songs. Tad Hutchison has been pursuing a career in animation.

what to buy: *This One's for the Ladies* ♫♫♫♫ (Frontier, 1989, prod. Conrad Uno) captures the group at its best and makes a solid argument that it deserves to be considered among the finest rock 'n' roll bands of its day. McCaughey originals such as "Carrothead" and "Miss Lonelyhearts" are would-be pop classics that fit right alongside a perfect cover of the Kinks' "Picture Book." *The Men Who Loved Music* ♫♫♫♫ (Frontier, 1987, prod. Conrad Uno) is a close second and a bit more whimsical, offering up the hilarious "Hank, Karen and Elvis"

plus the classic anthem "My Friend Ringo" (the latter written by Charlie Chesterman of Scruffy the Cat). *Electric Bird Digest* ♫♫♫♫ (Frontier, 1991, prod. Butch Vig) may be the strongest of the bunch strictly in terms of songwriting.

what to buy next: The band's first two albums—*The Fabulous Sounds of the Pacific Northwest* ♫♫♫ (PopLlama, 1984, prod. Conrad Uno) and *Topsy Turvy* ♫♫♫ (PopLlama, 1985, prod. Conrad Uno)—find its songwriting abilities not quite fully developed, but both albums contain a sense of youthful innocence that make them wholeheartedly enjoyable outings. *A Tribute to Music* ♫♫♫♫ (Rock & Rock Inc., 1997, prod. Norge/Shrag) is everything anyone's come to love and expect from this band, written and played with verve and finesse. A decade and a half on, and they're in peak form.

what to avoid: *Totally Lost* ♫♫♫ (Frontier, 1988, prod. Conrad Uno), recorded shortly before original member Chuck Carroll decided to leave the band, is the most uneven of the band's efforts, though it still contains a handful of worthwhile songs.

the rest:
Refreshments ♫♫♫ (Frontier EP, 1986)
It's Low Beat Time ♫♫♫ (Frontier, 1992)
Love Battery ♫♫♫ (Popllama, 1993)

worth searching for: *Somos Los Mejores* (Munster, 1991, prod. various) is a Spanish import that collects many highlights from the Fellows' catalog. *Take It Like a Matador* (Impossible Records, 1994) is another Spanish release, recorded live in Madrid. It starts off with the quintessential album-opener, "Live in Spain." *Gleich Jetzt* (1+2, 1993, prod. Conrad Uno, Young Fresh Fellows) is a Japanese release featuring some re-recorded chestnuts from the group's own back pages, along with a few selections previously available only as singles.

solo outings:
Scott McCaughey:
My Chartreuse Opinion ♫♫♫ (East Side Digital, 1989)

The Minus Five (McCaughey, R.E.M.'s Peter Buck, and the Posies' Ken Stringfellow):
Old Liquidator ♫♫♫♫ (East Side Digital, 1994)
Emperor of the Bathroom ♫♫♫ (East Side Digital, 1995)
The Lonesome Death of Buck McCoy ♫♫♫ (Malt/Hollywood, 1997)

influences:
◀◀ The Kinks, the Flamin' Groovies, the Sonics, the Beatles, the Replacements

▶▶ Presidents of the United States of America, the Posies, Scruffy the Cat, Stumpy Joe

see also: *Fastbacks*

Peter Blackstock and David Greenberger

Young Marble Giants

Formed late 1970s, in Cardiff, Wales. Disbanded 1981.

Alison Statton, vocals; Philip Moxham, bass; Stuart Moxham, guitar, organ.

Taking its cue from some idealized notion of a beatnik coffee house, Young Marble Giants confabulate in a hushed, candle-lit mood of studied bohemian minimalism. Alison Statton's gentle, low-key vocals mesh neatly with the Moxham brothers' jazz stylings in a manner that anticipates Everything but the Girl. The group broke up after one album. Under the guise of Gist, Stuart Moxham released *Embrace the Herd* (out of print) with assistance from brother Phil, Statton, and others. Statton went on to form the neo-avante-garde jazz group Weekend and later teamed up with Ian Devine as one half of Devine & Statton.

what's available: *Colossal Youth* 𝄢𝄢𝄢 (Crepuscule, 1980, prod. Young Marble Giants, Dave Anderson) is an off-beat slip of an album whose lo-fi ambience makes scarcely a ripple in your double latte. Apparently the members couldn't keep their blood pressure low enough to pursue another album.

influences:

◀◀ John Cage, LaMonte Young, minimalist jazz

▶▶ Sade, Everything but the Girl, Cassandra Wilson

Christopher Scapelliti

The Young Rascals /The Rascals

Formed 1965, in New York, NY. Disbanded 1972.

Felix Cavaliere, vocals, keyboards; Dino Danelli, drums; Eddie Brigati, vocals (1965–71); Gene Cornish, guitar (1695–71); Buzzy Feiten, guitar (1970–71); Robert Popwell, bass (1971–72); Ann Sutton, vocals (1971–72).

With three-part vocal harmonies rooted in R&B and floating atop an ocean of sound from Felix Cavaliere's Hammond B-3 organ, the Young Rascals were one of the original "blue-eyed soul" bands, bringing the energy and excitement of R&B to the masses by covering Wilson Pickett, Sir Mack Rice, and other soul stirrers. Wearing Little Lord Fauntleroy outfits at nightclub gigs across Long Island, Manhattan, and New Jersey, the Young Rascals offered an American alternative to the British invaders. The band's uptempo cover of the Olympics' "Good Lovin'," its first #1 single, erupts with such rhythmic fury that it endures as one of the greatest dance-rock numbers ever recorded. The band tried a softer touch with the syrupy "Groovin'," another chart-topper that, unfortunately, marked a shift away from raw R&B to polished pop. In 1967, the Rascals dropped the "Young" from its name and the knickers from their stage show, seeking a maturity and awareness appropriate to the times. It was a good fit for a while, as heard in "See," "Ray of Hope," and "People Got to Be Free," the group's last #1 hit. The Rascals experimented with lengthy jazz episodes—working with guests such as Dave Sanborn, Ron Carter, Hubert Laws, and Alice Coltrane—before fading in the charts and dissolving in 1972. There have been periodic, short-term reunions since, and the group was inducted into the Rock and Roll Hall of Fame in 1996.

what to buy: *Time Piece: The Rascals' Greatest Hits* 𝄢𝄢𝄢𝄢 (Atlantic, 1968, prod. the Rascals) crystallizes the band's most exuberant years into one tidy package of essentials ("Good Lovin'," "Mustang Sally," "I Ain't Gonna Eat Out My Heart Anymore," "You Better Run," and "Groovin'"). The two-disc, 44-song set *The Rascals Anthology 1965–1972* 𝄢𝄢𝄢𝄢 (Rhino, 1992, prod. various) is also a superb overview of the Young Rascals, covering everything from the old, the good, the not-so-good, and the awful ("Real Thing," "Brother Tree").

what to buy next: Even though the group only wrote one of the tunes, its debut album, *The Young Rascals* 𝄢𝄢𝄢𝄢 (Atlantic, 1966/Warner Special Products, 1988, prod. the Young Rascals, Tom Dowd, Arif Mardin), can't be beat for sheer energy and exuberance.

what to avoid: After Eddie Brigati and Gene Cornish left, the Rascals lost its R&B heart and replaced it with an artificial jazz pump. Pull the plug on the lifeless *Peaceful World* **woof!** (Atlantic, 1971, prod. Felix Cavaliere) and *The Island of Real* **woof!** (Atlantic, 1972, prod. Felix Cavaliere).

the rest:

Collections 𝄢𝄢𝄢 (Atlantic, 1966/Warner Special Products, 1988)
Groovin' 𝄢𝄢𝄢 (Atlantic, 1967)
Once upon a Dream 𝄢𝄢 (Atlantic, 1968/Rhino, 1993)
Freedom Suite 𝄢𝄢𝄢 (Atlantic, 1969/Rhino, 1993)
See 𝄢𝄢 (Atlantic, 1969)
Search and Nearness 𝄢 (Atlantic, 1971)
The Ultimate Rascals 𝄢𝄢𝄢𝄢 (Warner Special Products, 1986)
Groovin' 𝄢𝄢𝄢𝄢 (Warner Special Products, 1988)
The Very Best of the Rascals 𝄢𝄢𝄢𝄢𝄢 (Rhino, 1993)
Good Lovin' 𝄢𝄢𝄢𝄢 (Rhino, 1993)

solo outings:

Felix Cavaliere:
Felix Cavaliere 𝄢𝄢𝄢 (Bearsville, 1974)
Destiny 𝄢𝄢 (Bearsville, 1975)
Treasure 𝄢𝄢𝄢 (Epic, 1976)
Castles in the Air 𝄢𝄢 (Epic, 1980)
Dreams in Motion 𝄢𝄢 (Karambolage, 1994)

Eddie Brigati:
Brigati 𝄢𝄢 (Elektra, 1976)

influences:

◀◀ Ray Charles, Booker T. Jones, Stax-Volt, Motown

Yum-Yum

Chris Holmes, vocals, guitar, keyboards; Barbara Gretsch, vocals; Jim Newberry, organ; Michael Kirts, drums; Marina Petersen, cello; Darcy Vaughn, viola; Hilary Poriss, violin.

Fronted by sometime underground space rocker Chris Holmes (who, like his fellow Chicagoans—members of the Sea & Cake and Tortoise—plays in a myriad of offshoot bands and side projects), Yum-Yum conjures up bittersweet pop songs that are built around quirky pop melodica and lushly vivid sonic structures created by the alluring mellotron, chugging organ, and a healthy dose of warm fuzzy guitar tones.

what's available: *Dan Loves Patti* ♪♪♪♪ (Tag/Atlantic, 1996) is filled with sweeping orchestral melancholy, catchy pop-psychedelia, lilting melodies, and plenty of neo-fuzz warmness. Yum-Yum is all about creating subtle, endearing ambience, and the whole album glistens with reflective, introspective sonic ruminations on love, life, and the never-ending pursuit of enchantment.

worth searching for: One of Holmes's many side projects, Sabalon Glitz, released *Ufonic* (Trixie, circa 1995), an album of space-rock dimensions. Filled with clamoring guitars, rich cascading organ tones, and found sounds, it is a prog-inclined sonic rumination focussing on Holmes's fascination with UFOs (Holmes majored in UFO-related studies at University of Chicago). Look for the hidden 23rd track.

influences:
◀◀ Sea & Cake, Tortoise, Labradford, Robyn Hitchcock, Yes

Spence D.

Z
/Dweezil Zappa
Formed 1994, in Los Angeles, CA.

Ahmet Zappa, vocals; Dweezil Zappa, guitar, vocals; Mike Keneally, guitar, vocals; Bryan Beller, bass; Scott Thunes, bass; Joe Travers, drums.

Being the children of Frank Zappa is likely a singular experience, as the first names of Zappas Ahmet and Dweezil will at-test. Yet there's nothing like the career boost offered by growing up around a genius who happens to have his own record company, thus giving rise to several solo albums by Dweezil, and when Ahmet joined him, the group Z. The pair are definitely their father's sons, taking no prisoners lyrically while presenting a fierce musical attack (though they lean more toward legitimizing heavy metal, while their dad merely parodied it). The pair are real cut-ups as well, and have become favorite guests on *Late Night with Conan O'Brien*. If they don't watch it, though, they're going to be more famous for that than for their music. Think of Zsa Zsa Gabor, guys.

what to buy: *Shampoohorn* ♪♪♪ (Barking Pumpkin, 1994, prod. Dweezil Zappa) contains plenty of crunch and funky metal shenanigans, with inside joke lyrics of the sort the old man used to do—and flash guitar courtesy of Dweezil, who's a chip off the old block, or at least a chip off the old block's sidemen, like Steve Vai.

the rest:
Music for Pets ♪♪♪ (Zappa, 1995)

solo outings:
Dweezil Zappa:
Havin' a Bad Day ♪♪ (Chrysalis, 1986/Rykodisc, 1987)
My Guitar Wants to Kill Your Mama ♪♪ (Chrysalis, 1988)
Confessions ♪♪ (Barking Pumpkin, 1991)

influences:
◀◀ Frank Zappa, Steve Vai, Van Halen

Daniel Durchholz

Robin Zander
See: Cheap Trick

Dan Zanes
See: Del Fuegos

Dweezil Zappa
See: Z

Frank Zappa
Born Frank Vincent Zappa, December 21, 1940, in Baltimore, MD. Died December 4, 1993, in Los Angeles, CA.

Singer, songwriter, conceptualist, composer, theoretician, would-be politician, guitar god, satirist, record-company scofflaw, ruthless bandleader, and all-around iconoclast: There were many Frank Zappas, but still not enough of him to go around. His groundbreaking works from the mid- to late '60s with the Mothers of Invention blew open the doors for rock experimentalism, and, while others succeeded in work of a similar vein, no one ever bettered him, save perhaps his old running buddy Captain Beefheart. Zappa's muse took him far afield from rock's limiting instrumentation and 4/4 beat; before there was such a thing as fusion, his work approached electrified jazz, and as early as *Freak Out!* he was flirting with orchestral compositions. His talent in that genre would come into full flower on *London Symphony Orchestra* and *The Yellow Shark*. Yet, however complex his music got, Zappa never lost touch with some of rock 'n' roll's cornerstones, such as doo-wop music and "Louie Louie," which he would occasionally sprinkle into his music, if only as a humorous aside. An intimidating and demanding bandleader, Zappa brought the best out of his musicians, and today, time spent in a Zappa band is an accolade worn like a badge of honor. His list of sidemen includes Lowell George, Aynsley Dunbar, Steve Vai, Adrian Belew, Terry Bozzio, and Vinnie Colaiuta. Zappa's controversial material and sometimes scatological humor made him too hot to handle for most mainstream record companies, so he formed his own label during the late '70s and continued to release his music through it for the remainder of his life. Undeniably one of rock's most influential guitarists, in the '80s Zappa put down the instrument for good in favor of the synclavier, a computerized keyboard on which he could realize his compositions all by himself; *Jazz from Hell* is the most impressive display of his prowess on the instrument. A passionate advocate of free speech, Zappa took part in the infamous congressional hearings in 1985, which led to the stickering of rock albums with parental warnings. The hearings are excerpted to hilarious effect on a cut from *Frank Zappa Meets the Mothers of Prevention*. As beloved in Europe as he was scorned in America, Zappa was named Czechoslovakia's cultural liaison to the West by President Vaclav Havel in 1990. A relentless workaholic who smoked cigarettes and drank coffee incessantly, Zappa died of prostate cancer at age 52. There will never be another like him.

what to buy: Less than a year after the Summer of Love, Zappa stepped forward to report he had met the enemy and it is us. *We're Only in It for the Money* ♪♪♪♪♪ (Verve, 1968/Rykodisc, 1995, prod. Frank Zappa) is a savage attack on all things smelling of patchouli; the cover satirizes *Sgt. Pepper*, but the music—spoken sections, white noise, and sound-bite montages—scores a direct hit on the America that so desperately wanted to be hip. A year before Miles Davis's *Bitches Brew*, Zappa's *Hot Rats* ♪♪♪♪ (Bizarre/Reprise, 1969/Rykodisc, 1995, prod. Frank Zappa) presaged jazz-rock fusion with some of Zappa's best instrumental tracks, including "Peaches En Regalia." Captain Beefheart contributes vocals on "Willie the Pimp." Not necessarily one of his best albums, *Apostrophe* ♪♪♪♪ (DiscReet, 1974/Rykodisc, 1995, prod. Frank Zappa) is certainly among his best known, thanks

in large part to the FM rock staples "Cosmik Debris" and the suite comprising "Don't Eat the Yellow Snow" and "St. Alphonso's Pancake Breakfast." *Apostrophe* was Zappa's sole gold record, and the only one to crease the Top 10. Of Zappa's orchestral recordings, *The Yellow Shark* ♪♪♪♪♪ (Barking Pumpkin, 1993/Rykodisc, 1995, prod. Frank Zappa) is the most entertaining; performed by the 26-member Ensemble Modern, the album was released just a month before Zappa's untimely death. It includes "Uncle Meat," "Welcome to the United States," and a breathtaking version of "G-Spot Tornado." The long experimental pieces and obscure personal references make *Uncle Meat* ♪♪♪♪ (Bizarre/Reprise, 1968/Rykodisc, 1995, prod. Frank Zappa) Zappa's most demanding opus outside of his strictly classical work. It includes "Dog Breath Variations" and "King Kong." Novices, on the other hand, may want to begin with *Strictly Commercial: The Best of Frank Zappa* ♪♪♪♪ (Rykodisc, 1995, prod. Frank Zappa), a collection of his humor-oriented vocal material. Zappa's expansive material resists abridgment, though, and true Frank-ophiles will likely want the uncut stuff.

what to buy next: The most audacious debut album in rock history, *Freak Out!* ♪♪♪♪ (Verve, 1966/Rykodisc, 1995, prod. Tom Wilson) was originally released as a double album, one of them containing deft parodies of the teen exploitation music of the day and the other a wildly anarchic experimental piece featuring tape collage experiments and moments of sheer brilliance. *Burnt Weeny Sandwich* ♪♪♪♪ (Bizarre/Reprise, 1969/Rykodisc, 1995, prod. Frank Zappa) and *Weasels Ripped My Flesh* ♪♪♪♪ (Bizarre/Reprise, 1970/Rykodisc, 1990, prod. Frank Zappa) are two volumes of a projected career retrospective that never materialized, but they're Zappa's most consistently great albums. *Weeny* contains "WPLJ" and "The Little House I Used to Live In," while *Weasels* has "Eric Dolphy Memorial Barbecue" and "My Guitar Wants to Kill Your Mama." An extraordinary display of Zappa's instrumental prowess can be found on *Shut up 'N Play Yer Guitar* ♪♪♪♪ (Barking Pumpkin, 1981, prod. Frank Zappa), *Shut up 'N Play Yer Guitar Some More* ♪♪♪♪ (Barking Pumpkin, 1981, prod. Frank Zappa), and *Return of Son of Shut up 'N Play Yer Guitar* ♪♪♪♪ (Barking Pumpkin, 1981, prod. Frank Zappa), a collection of solos laid end-to-end that's now available as the two-CD set *Shut up 'N Play Yer Guitar* (Rykodisc, 1995). You can argue with the methodology of Zappa's *You Can't Do That on Stage Anymore*, a six-volume retrospective (available separately) of his live work; performances from different concerts (different years, even) were spliced together, resulting in a performance that never was. You can't argue with the consistently high quality of the set, however. *Vol. 1* ♪♪♪♪ (Barking Pumpkin, 1988/Rykodisc, 1995, prod. Frank Zappa) is representative of the series.

what to avoid: The compilations *Mothermania* 🎵🎵 (Verve, 1969) and *The Worst of the Mothers* **woof!** (Verve, 1969) unsuccessfully attempt to excerpt Zappa's long-form experiments; they are justifiably out of print. *The Man from Utopia* 🎵 (Barking Pumpkin, 1983/Rykodisc 1995, prod. Frank Zappa) has some interesting instrumental work, but mainly it features Zappa in an annoying sing-song vocal mode. Zappa's long-winded Broadway parody, *Thing-Fish* 🎵 (Barking Pumpkin, 1983/Rykodisc, 1995, prod. Frank Zappa) never really takes off. On *Francesco Zappa* **woof!** (Barking Pumpkin, 1984/Rykodisc, 1995, prod. Frank Zappa) the 20th-century Zappa performs the music of the 18th-century Zappa on the synclavier keyboard. Beware: This recording may induce fond memories of *Switched on Bach*.

the rest:
Absolutely Free 🎵🎵🎵 (Verve, 1967/Rykodisc, 1995)
Lumpy Gravy 🎵🎵🎵 (Bizarre/Reprise, 1967/Rykodisc, 1995)
Cruising with Reuben & the Jets 🎵🎵🎵 (Verve, 1968/Rykodisc, 1995)
Chunga's Revenge 🎵🎵🎵 (Bizarre/Reprise, 1970/Rykodisc, 1990)
The Mothers: Fillmore East, June 1971 🎵🎵 (Bizarre/Reprise, 1971/Rykodisc, 1990)
200 Motels 🎵🎵 (United Artists, 1971/Rykodisc, 1997)
Just Another Band from L.A. 🎵🎵 (Bizarre/Reprise, 1972/Rykodisc, 1995)
Waka/Jawaka 🎵🎵🎵 (Bizarre/Reprise 1972/Rykodisc, 1995)
The Grand Wazoo 🎵🎵🎵 (Bizarre/Reprise 1972/Rykodisc, 1995)
Over-Nite Sensation 🎵🎵🎵 (DiscReet, 1973, Rykodisc, 1995)
Roxy & Elsewhere 🎵🎵🎵 (DiscReet, 1974/Rykodisc, 1995)
One Size Fits All 🎵🎵🎵 (DiscReet, 1975/Rykodisc, 1995)
(With Captain Beefheart) *Bongo Fury* 🎵🎵🎵 (DiscReet, 1975/Rykodisc, 1995)
Zoot Allures 🎵🎵🎵 (DiscReet, 1976/Rykodisc, 1995)
Zappa in New York 🎵🎵🎵 (Barking Pumpkin, 1977/Rykodisc, 1995)
Studio Tan 🎵🎵🎵 (DiscReet, 1978/Rykodisc, 1995)
Sleep Dirt 🎵🎵🎵 (DiscReet, 1979/Rykodisc, 1995)
Sheik Yerbouti 🎵🎵🎵 (Zappa, 1979/Rykodisc, 1995)
Orchestral Favorites 🎵🎵🎵 (DiscReet, 1979/Rykodisc, 1995)
Joe's Garage Acts I, II & III 🎵🎵🎵 (Zappa, 1979, Rykodisc, 1995)
Baby Snakes 🎵🎵 (Barking Pumpkin, 1979/Rykodisc, 1995)
Tinseltown Rebellion 🎵🎵🎵 (Barking Pumpkin, 1981/Rykodisc, 1995)
You Are What You Is 🎵🎵🎵 (Barking Pumpkin, 1981/Rykodisc, 1995)
Ship Arriving Too Late to Save a Drowning Witch 🎵🎵 (Barking Pumpkin, 1982/Rykodisc, 1995)
London Symphony Orchestra 🎵🎵🎵 (Barking Pumpkin, 1983/Rykodisc, 1995)
The Perfect Stranger: Boulez Conducts Zappa 🎵🎵🎵 (Angel/EMI, 1984/Rykodisc, 1995)
Them or Us 🎵🎵🎵 (Barking Pumpkin, 1984/Rykodisc, 1995)
Does Humor Belong in Music? 🎵🎵🎵 (EMI Europe, 1984/Rykodisc, 1995)
Frank Zappa Meets the Mothers of Prevention 🎵🎵🎵 (Barking Pumpkin, 1985/Rykodisc, 1995)
Jazz from Hell 🎵🎵🎵 (Barking Pumpkin, 1986/Rykodisc, 1995)

Guitar 🎵🎵🎵 (Barking Pumpkin, 1988/Rykodisc, 1995)
You Can't Do That on Stage Anymore, Vol. 2: The Helsinki Concert 🎵🎵🎵 (Barking Pumpkin, 1988/Rykodisc, 1995)
Broadway the Hard Way 🎵🎵🎵 (Barking Pumpkin, 1989/Rykodisc, 1995)
You Can't Do That on Stage Anymore, Vol. 3 🎵🎵🎵 (Barking Pumpkin, 1989/Rykodisc, 1995)
Make a Jazz Noise Here 🎵🎵🎵 (Barking Pumpkin, 1991/Rykodisc, 1995)
You Can't Do That on Stage Anymore, Vol. 4 🎵🎵🎵 (Barking Pumpkin, 1991/Rykodisc, 1995)
The Best Band You Never Heard in Your Life 🎵🎵🎵 (Barking Pumpkin, 1991/Rykodisc, 1995)
Playground Psychotics 🎵🎵🎵 (Barking Pumpkin, 1992/Rykodisc, 1995)
You Can't Do That on Stage Anymore, Vol. 5 🎵🎵🎵 (Barking Pumpkin, 1992/Rykodisc, 1995)
You Can't Do That on Stage Anymore, Vol. 6 🎵🎵🎵 (Barking Pumpkin, 1992/Rykodisc, 1995)
Ahead of Their Time 🎵🎵🎵 (Rykodisc, 1993)
Civilization Phaze III 🎵🎵🎵 (Barking Pumpkin, 1994)
Rare Meat 🎵🎵 (Del-Fi, 1995)
The Lost Episodes 🎵🎵🎵 (Rykodisc, 1996)
Läther 🎵🎵🎵 (Rykodisc, 1996)
Have I Offended Someone? 🎵🎵🎵 (Rykodisc, 1997)
Strictly Genteel 🎵🎵🎵 (Rykodisc, 1997)
Cucamonga 🎵🎵 (Del-Fi, 1998)
Cheap Thrills 🎵🎵🎵 (Rykodisc, 1998)

worth searching for: In an attempt to outflank bootleggers, Zappa pulled a number of illegal recordings off the market and rereleased them himself, resulting in a series his most devoted fans will want to own. They include *Piquantique* (Foo-Eee, 1991), *Saarbrucken* (Foo-Eee, 1991), *Tis the Season to Be Jelly* (Foo-Eee, 1991), *Unmitigated Audacity* (Foo-Eee, 1991), *Any Way the Wind Blows* (Foo-Eee, 1991), *Freaks & Motherfu#@%!* (Foo-Eee, 1991), *The Ark* (Foo-Eee, 1991), and *As An Am* (Foo-Eee, 1991). A second batch is available in the box set *Beat the Boots #2* (Foo-Eee, 1992).

influences:

◀◀ Edgard Varese, Spike Jones, Eric Dolphy, Karlheinz Stockhausen, Johnny "Guitar" Watson, Thomas Paine

▶▶ Captain Beefheart, Matt Groening, Eugene Chadbourne, Uz Jsme Doma, the Persuasions, Wild Man Fischer, Pulnoc

Daniel Durchholz

Martin Zellar /Gear Daddies

Born June 14, 1963, in Austin, MN.

Since they hailed from Minnesota, the Gear Daddies were often lumped in with the Replacements, Hüsker Dü, and Soul Asylum. That left leader Martin Zellar compared to such alt-rock pillars as Paul Westerberg, Bob Mould, and Dave Pirner, even though his tastes were more country and his viewpoint was more compassionate. The raspy-voiced Zellar's twangy ruminations on the battered egos and shattered dreams of blue-collar middle America include compelling portraits of blissfully naive housewives, abandoned mothers, self-pitying alcoholics, and bored teenagers that never deteriorate into caricatures. Since the 1992 breakup of the Gear Daddies, Zellar has launched a promising solo career that reflects a focused sound and an authoritative point of view. And while he's abandoned old habits (he quit drinking in 1990) and a healthy portion of his older material (don't ever expect to hear "Zamboni" again), Gear Daddies fans will still recognize his staunch roots-rock allegiance and unrivaled ability to mine that fertile gray area that lies between desperation and hope.

what to buy: Zellar's solo debut, *Born Under* 𝄢𝄢𝄢 (Rykodisc, 1995, prod. Martin Zellar, Steve McKinstry), broadens his barband roots with cellos, organs, accordions, and mandolins. "Problem Solved," "Something's Gotta Happen," and "Cross My Heart" aren't about lonesome losers so much as ego-bruised, guilt-wracked underdogs trying to muster the inner strength for one last stand. After his commercially disappointing stint with Rykodisc, Zellar formed his own label, Owen/Lee, in 1998 and released *The Many Moods of Martin Zellar and the Hardways* 𝄢𝄢𝄢 (Owen/Lee, 1998, prod. Patrik Tanner), a deceptively uptempo album buoyed by strings and horns but fueled by the seam-tearing effects of distance, both emotional and geographical, on relationships.

what to buy next: Of the Gear Daddies' output, it's a tossup between the twangy *Let's Go Scare Al* 𝄢𝄢𝄢 (PolyGram, 1988, prod. Jim Walsh), which includes "She's Happy" and "Boys Will Be Boys," and *Billy's Live Bait* 𝄢𝄢𝄢 (PolyGram, 1990, prod. Tom Herbers, Gear Daddies), which rocks much harder and offers the hockey-rink anthem "Zamboni" as an unlisted bonus track.

the rest:
(With the Gear Daddies) *Can't Have Nothin' Nice* 𝄢𝄢𝄢 (Crackpot, 1992)
Martin Zellar and the Hardways 𝄢𝄢𝄢 (Rykodisc, 1996)

worth searching for: The promotional "Lie to Me" CD single (Rykodisc, 1995, prod. Martin Zellar, Steve McKinstry) adds Zellar's straight-faced cover of Neil Diamond's "If You Know What I Mean" and spirited take on the Cars' "My Best Friend's Girl" as B-sides.

influences:
◀◀ The Band, Buck Owens, Bruce Springsteen

▶▶ Steve Earle, Paul Westerberg

David Okamoto

Warren Zevon

Born January 24, 1947, in Chicago, IL.

You couldn't blame Warren Zevon if he regards the term singer-songwriter as an epithet. Unlike his terminally mellow El Lay brethren Jackson Browne (who produced Zevon's early albums), the Eagles, J.D. Souther, et al., Zevon's tales of life on the left coast are fraught with excess, violence, and nearly every sort of mayhem imaginable. But his songs are literate and literary (novelists Thomas McGuane and Carl Hiaasen have been cowriters), and Zevon seems more influenced by other media, such as the films of Sam Peckinpah or the novels of F. Scott Fitzgerald and Raymond Chandler, than he is by other musicians. And while there's plenty of macho posturing on his albums, he has his tender side, too. Besides, his bluster is almost always accompanied by some of the darkest humor to be had in rock 'n' roll. He's Hunter S. Thompson with a 4/4 beat. In addition to his own albums, Zevon released one disc with the short-lived supergroup Hindu Love Gods, which included R.E.M. members Peter Buck, Mike Mills, and Bill Berry.

what to buy: *Warren Zevon* 𝄢𝄢𝄢𝄢 (Asylum, 1976, prod. Jackson Browne) is one of the great albums of the '70s, a virtual concept album about a culture and its individual inhabitants spinning out of control. Some of the songs were first popularized by Linda Ronstadt ("Hasten Down the Wind," "Poor Poor Pitiful Me," "Mohammed's Radio"), but Zevon's versions are grittier and more desperate. Zevon's dark streak runs rampant on *Excitable Boy* 𝄢𝄢𝄢 (Asylum, 1978, prod. Jackson Browne, Waddy Wachtel), notably on the title track about an eternally coddled sociopath. A prescient warning about O.J. Simpson? You decide. The album is uneven, but it contains some of his best-known songs, including the hit "Werewolves of London," "Roland the Headless Thompson Gunner," and "Lawyers, Guns, and Money." *I'll Sleep When I'm Dead: The Warren Zevon Anthology* 𝄢𝄢𝄢𝄢 (Rhino, 1996, prod. various) is a career-spanning retrospective that hits all the high points and includes some tracks from the highly sought-after live album *Stand in the Fire* (see below).

what to buy next: *Sentimental Hygiene* 𝄢𝄢𝄢𝄢 (Virgin, 1987, prod. Warren Zevon, Andrew Slater, Niko Bolas) finds Zevon back in fighting form after a long struggle with alcoholism. "Detox Mansion," "Trouble Waiting to Happen," and "Bad Karma" offer an unblinking and often hilarious account of his ordeal. "The Factory" veers into Springsteen territory, while "Boom Boom Mancini" offers a more concise sketch of boxing's attraction/repellence than Joyce Carol Oates or Norman Mailer could ever dream of. *Bad Luck Streak in Dancing School* 𝄢𝄢𝄢𝄢 (Asylum, 1980, prod. Warren Zevon, Greg Ladanyi) finds him reworking themes of mercenary violence ("Jungle Work") and personal demons ("Bad Luck Streak in Dancing School"), but

Zevon's wit buoys the album, particularly on "Play It All Night Long," a devastating caricature of the popular notion of going "back to the country."

what to avoid: Zevon's first album *Wanted—Dead or Alive* **woof!** (Imperial, 1969/One Way, 1996, prod. Kim Fowley) is so bad that, after it flopped, Zevon turned to writing jingles for the likes of Chevrolet and Gallo wine.

the rest:
A Quiet Normal Life: The Best of Warren Zevon 🎵🎵🎵🎵 (Asylum, 1986)
Transverse City 🎵🎵🎵 (Virgin, 1989)
Mr. Bad Example 🎵🎵🎵 (Giant, 1991)
Learning to Flinch 🎵🎵🎵 (Giant, 1993)
Mutineer 🎵🎵🎵 (Giant, 1995)

worth searching for: *Stand in the Fire* (Asylum, 1980, prod. Warren Zevon, Greg Ladanyi) and *The Envoy* (Asylum, 1982, prod. Waddy Wachtel, Greg Ladanyi, Warren Zevon) are two albums from Zevon's early period that are inexplicably unavailable on CD. *Stand* is one of the great live albums—Zevon and his band of unknowns can barely contain their excitement. Never one to settle for the usual rock 'n' roll subjects, Zevon wrote the title track of *The Envoy* as a tribute to shuttle diplomat Philip Habib.

solo outings:
Hindu Love Gods:
Hindu Love Gods 🎵🎵🎵 (Giant, 1990)

influences:
◀◀ Bob Dylan, Jackson Browne, Leonard Cohen

▶▶ Linda Ronstadt, Don Henley, R.E.M., Counting Crows, Camper Van Beethoven

Daniel Durchholz

The Zombies

Formed 1961, in St. Albans, England. Disbanded 1968.

Rod Argent, keyboards, vocals; Paul Atkinson, guitar; Colin Blunstone, vocals, guitar; Hugh Grundy, drums; Christopher White, bass, vocals.

Formed while the boys were still in high school, the Zombies went from being a tentative, tremulous bunch of teens to a fully realized, ground-breaking professional unit that hit during the height of the British Invasion. Unusual because it pushed Rod Argent's piano to the forefront, the group also drew attention because their songs had more depth than many of those by their counterparts—and because those songs were gorgeous. To this day, few pop tunes sound as perfect as "Time of the Season," "Tell Her No," or "She's Not There." The blend of vocal harmonies, R&B and pop sensibilities, and songwriting

talent, combined with Argent's jazz- and classical-influenced keyboard work, made the Zombies a hit on American radio; they were far bigger here than in their native land, in fact. It wasn't for lack of trying, however; a string of singles never managed to take off after the early success of "She's Not There" and "Tell Her No," and by the time the Zombies went into the studio to record their second album—and first real studio effort (their first disc, *Begin Here*, was a conglomeration of singles and covers)—the Zombies knew they were close to the end of their time together. *Odessey and Oracle*, considered by some to be a pop masterpiece, wasn't even released in the States until 1968, after the band had split up. CBS decided to release "Time of the Season" as a toss-off single, and to everyone's surprise the song became the band's biggest hit in 1969. By then Argent was already forming his next, self-titled band. Singer Colin Blunstone went solo (at first under the name Neil MacArthur), but didn't find much stateside success. Chris White went into record-producing with Argent. Paul Atkinson became an A&R man, eventually working with Abba, Aerosmith, and Paul McCartney.

what to buy: The four-disc box set *Zombie Heaven* 🎵🎵🎵🎵 (Big Beat, 1997, prod. Alec Palao) contains virtually everything the band ever recorded. Like most box sets, it could be cut by a disc, but the various alternate versions and live BBC sessions are worthwhile listening—and the first disc is a gem. If it's just one disc you want, get *Odessey & Oracle: 30th Anniversary Edition* 🎵🎵🎵🎵 (Big Beat, 1998, prod. Rod Argent, Chris White), which features the full landmark album plus alternate takes of "Time for Emily" and "Time of the Season."

the rest:
Odessey & Oracle 🎵🎵🎵 (Rhino, 1987)
Singles A's and B's 🎵🎵🎵 (See for Miles, 1990)
Greatest Hits, Greatest Recordings 🎵🎵🎵 (Transluxe, 1995)

solo outings:
Colin Blunstone:
Some Years: It's the Time of Colin Blunstone 🎵🎵🎵 (Epic/Legacy, 1995)
Echo Bridge 🎵🎵 (Permanent, 1995)
The Light Inside N/A (Mystic, 1998)

influences:
◀◀ Elvis Presley, the Beatles, Buddy Holly, the Shirelles, Jerry Lee Lewis, Ray Charles, Curtis Mayfield, Holland-Dozier-Holland, the Kinks, the Searchers, Little Anthony & the Imperials

▶▶ The Hollies, the Beach Boys, the Guess Who, Gerry & the Pacemakers, Herman's Hermits, the Left Banke, the Verve, Oasis

see also: *Argent*

Lynne Margolis and Patrick McCarty

Zumpano

Formed 1991, in Vancouver, British Columbia, Canada.

Carl Newman, vocals, guitar; Mike Ledwidge, guitar, keyboards; Jason Zumpano, drums; Stefan Niemann, bass.

The members of Zumpano have taken it upon themselves to take up where another Z band—the Zombies—left off. Leaving the rock 'n' roll brawn to those who lift ideas from heavier influences, these soft-rockers are neither modernists nor garage-rock taxidermists. Instead, they stuff their songs with a life-affirming joy—occasionally expressed through a lens of melancholia—that suggests an immersion in some older brother's record collection.

what to buy: Song-for-song, *Going through Changes* ♫♫♫♫ (Sub Pop, 1996, prod. Keith Cleversley) almost matches the high standard set by Zumpano's pop predecessors, bands like the Zombies, the 5th Dimension, and the Left Banke. The album, devoid of the occasional rawness that makes their debut sound unfinished, is a masterpiece; it's worthwhile for the brilliant "Sylvia Hotel" alone.

what to buy next: *Look What the Rookie Did* ♫♫♫ (Sub Pop, 1994, prod. Kevin Kane, Zumpano) is an album done by baroque-pop rookies, all right, but it's a solid, unusual piece of work made even better by the definitive version of Jimmy Webb's "Rosecrans Boulevard." Otherwise, the unrealized production and chunky rhythms are unbefitting of the group's intrinsic delicacy.

influences:
◄◄ The Left Banke, the Zombies, Jimmy Webb, the Sneetches

Jordan Oakes

Zuzu's Petals

Formed late 1993, in Minneapolis, MN.

Coleen Elwood, bass, vocals; Laurie Lindeen, guitar, vocals; Linda Pitmon, drums, percussion.

Zuzu's Petals is a three-piece band comprised of friends who have released only a couple of singles and two albums, joining the prolific scene of indie-rockers that reached an apex during the early to mid-'90s.

what to buy: Zuzu's Petals' debut album, *When No One's Looking* ♫♫♫ (Twin/Tone, 1992, prod. Lou Giordano), is a melancholic and beautiful blending of folk and pop-rock that earned the band some well-deserved underground praise. The songs range from the serene ("Johanne") to the aggressive ("Psycho Tavern") to the silly ("Dork Magnet"), often within minutes of each other. Through it all, Laurie Lindeen and Coleen Elwood's songwriting remain strong.

the rest:
The Music of Your Life ♫♫♫ (Twin/Tone, 1994)

influences:
◄◄ Throwing Muses, the Breeders
►► Hole, Velocity Girl

Joseph Patel

ZZ Top

Formed 1969, in Houston, TX.

Billy Gibbons Jr., guitar, vocals; Frank Beard, drums; Dusty Hill, bass, vocals.

Few bands have enjoyed the longevity and steady personnel of this "li'l old band from Texas." And working together has paid off, as the trio has improved over the years rather than fading away. Its psychedelic blues-rock led it to national stardom with 1973's *Tres Hombres,* and it stayed on the charts until 1976 when, due to label problems, the group stopped playing and even jamming together. After changing labels, it tossed off a killer blues-rock album, *Deguello,* then recreated itself. Gibbons's trademark licks were still in there, but the sound embraced synthesizers and the band adapted to the MTV generation with its huge beards and humorous videos filled with leggy models. The resultant *Eliminator* in 1983 pumped the trio to superstar status with the hits "Legs," "Sharp Dressed Man," and "Gimme All Your Lovin'." ZZ Top rode that formula until it sputtered out during the early '90s, at which point it began reverting back to its blues-rock roots.

Billy Gibbons of ZZ Top (© Ken Settle)

what to buy: Coming off a two-year layoff, the guys laid it on the line for *Deguello* 🎵🎵🎵🎵 (Warner Bros., 1979, prod. Bill Ham), showcasing deep blues such as "Dust My Broom" and funky fun on "Cheap Sunglasses"—kink, kitsch, and some searing guitar riffs. They just kept rolling, and *Eliminator* 🎵🎵🎵🎵 (Warner Bros., 1983, prod. Bill Ham) let anybody who hadn't heard of them yet in on the secret.

what to buy next: *Tres Hombres* 🎵🎵🎵🎵 (London, 1973/Warner Bros., 1987 prod. Bill Ham) catches the band as it was coming into the spotlight, when its idea of a jam was "Beer Drinkers and Hell Raisers." If you just want to skim the hits, *ZZ Top's Greatest Hits* 🎵🎵🎵🎵 (Warner Bros., 1992, prod. Bill Ham) covers all the bases and adds a cover of Elvis Presley's "Viva Las Vegas."

what to avoid: The only questionable product is *Six Pack* 🎵🎵 (Warner Bros., 1987, prod. Bill Ham), a CD compilation of the first six albums remixed with drum samples that robbed some of the earthiness from the group's sound.

the rest:
ZZ Top 🎵🎵🎵 (London, 1970/Warner Bros., 1987)
Rio Grande Mud 🎵🎵🎵🎵 (London, 1972/Warner Bros., 1987)
Fandango! 🎵🎵🎵🎵 (London, 1975/Warner Bros., 1987)
Tejas 🎵🎵🎵 (London, 1976/Warner Bros., 1987)
The Best of ZZ Top 🎵🎵🎵🎵 (London, 1977/Warner Bros., 1987)
El Loco 🎵🎵🎵 (Warner Bros., 1981)
Afterburner 🎵🎵🎵🎵 (Warner Bros., 1985)
Recycler 🎵🎵🎵 (Warner Bros., 1990)
Antenna 🎵🎵🎵 (RCA, 1994)
One Foot in the Blues 🎵🎵🎵 (Warner Bros., 1994)
Rhythmeen 🎵🎵🎵 (RCA, 1996)

worth searching for: *A Taste of the ZZ Top Six Pack* (Warner Bros., 1987, prod. Bill Ham) is a lively 13-song promotional sampler from the first six albums.

influences:

◄◄ Johnny Winter, Lightnin' Hopkins, T-Bone Walker, Cream

►► Stevie Ray Vaughan, Big Head Todd & the Monsters

Lawrence Gabriel

musicHound ROCK

Resources and Other Information

Compilation Albums

Books and Magazines

Web Sites

Record Labels

Radio Stations

Various artist compilation albums are a particularly volatile area of the music industry. They float in and out of print with disarming speed and with neither rhyme nor reason. What follows is a list of the most important, popular, and available compilations at the time we were compiling this edition of MusicHound Rock. *We cannot vouch for their availability as you read this, but we do stand by their ratings. (List compiled by Gary Graff, Daniel Durchholz, and Ken Burke.)*

Alternative Rock

Alternative Rock Hits 𝄞𝄞 (CEMA Special Products, 1995)

Aware 3: The Compilation 𝄞𝄞𝄞 (Aware, 1995)

Aware 4: The Compilation 𝄞𝄞𝄞𝄞 (Aware, 1996)

Aware 5: The Compilation 𝄞𝄞𝄞𝄞 (Aware, 1997)

The Box Presents Big Ones of Alternative Rock, Volume 1 𝄞𝄞𝄞 (BOXTunes, 1996)

Deep Six 𝄞𝄞𝄞𝄞 (A&M, 1994)

Freedom of Choice: Yesterday's New Wave Hits As Performed by Today's Stars 𝄞𝄞𝄞 (Caroline, 1992)

Genrecide: A Compilation, Vol. One 𝄞𝄞𝄞 (Columbia, 1993)

The Grunge Years 𝄞𝄞 (Sub Pop, 1991)

KCRW Rare on the Air, Volume 1 𝄞𝄞𝄞 (Mammoth, 1994)

KCRW Rare on the Air, Volume 2 𝄞𝄞 (Mammoth, 1995)

KCRW Rare on the Air, Volume 3 𝄞𝄞𝄞 (Mammoth, 1997)

MTV Buzz Bin 𝄞𝄞𝄞𝄞 (Mammoth, 1997)

MTV Buzz Bin, Volume 2 𝄞𝄞𝄞 (Mammoth, 1997)

Reconquista! The Latin Rock Invasion 𝄞𝄞𝄞 (Rhino, 1997)

Road Rash 3D: The Album 𝄞𝄞𝄞 (Atlantic, 1998)

Six Sided Single, Vol. 1 𝄞𝄞𝄞 (I.R.S., 1994)

Six Sided Single, Vol. 2 𝄞𝄞 (I.R.S., 1995)

This Is Fort Apache 𝄞𝄞𝄞𝄞 (MCA, 1995)

Benefits

Ain't Nothin' but a She Thing 𝄞𝄞𝄞 (London, 1995)

Alternative NRG 𝄞𝄞𝄞𝄞 (Hollywood, 1994)

Amazing Grace 𝄞𝄞𝄞 (Island, 1997)

Born to Choose 𝄞𝄞𝄞𝄞 (Rykodisc, 1993)

The Bridge School Concerts, Vol. One 𝄞𝄞𝄞𝄞 (Reprise, 1997)

Come All Ye Faithful: Rock 4 Choice 𝄞𝄞𝄞 (Columbia, 1996)

Generations I: A Punk Look at Human Rights 𝄞𝄞𝄞 (Ark 21, 1997)

Help 𝄞𝄞𝄞 (Go! Discs, 1995)

Hempilation: Freedom is NORML 𝄞𝄞𝄞 (Capricorn, 1995)

Home Alive: The Art of Self-Defense 𝄞𝄞𝄞 (Epic, 1996)

If a Tree Falls 𝄞𝄞 (EarthBeat!, 1996)

In Defense of Animals: A Benefit Compilation 𝄞𝄞𝄞 (Restless, 1993)

Jabberjaw: Good to the Last Drop 𝄞𝄞𝄞 (Mammoth, 1994)

Knebworth: The Concert 𝄞𝄞𝄞 (Polydor, 1990)

MOM: Music for Our Mother Ocean 𝄞𝄞𝄞𝄞 (Interscope, 1995)

MOM II: Music for Our Mother Ocean 𝄞𝄞𝄞 (Interscope, 1997)

No Alternative 𝄞𝄞𝄞𝄞 (Arista, 1993)

No Nukes: The MUSE Concerts for a Non-Nuclear Future 𝄞𝄞𝄞 (Elektra, 1979/1997)

Nobody's Child: Romanian Angel Appeal 𝄞𝄞𝄞𝄞 (Warner Bros., 1990)

Offbeat: A Red Hot Sound Trip 𝄞𝄞𝄞𝄞 (Red Hot/Wax Trax!, 1996)

Peace Together 𝄞𝄞𝄞 (Island, 1993)

Red Hot + Blue 𝄞𝄞𝄞𝄞 (Chrysalis, 1990)

Red Hot + Rio 𝄞𝄞𝄞𝄞 (Antilles, 1996)

Safe and Sound 𝄞𝄞𝄞 (Mercury, 1995)

Silencio = Muerte: Red Hot + Latin 𝄞𝄞𝄞𝄞 (Island, 1996)

Spirit of '73: Rock for Choice 𝄞𝄞𝄞 (550 Music/Epic, 1995)

Sun City: Artists United Against Apartheid 𝄞𝄞𝄞𝄞 (EMI, 1985/Razor & Tie, 1993)

Tame Yourself 𝄞𝄞𝄞 (RNA, 1991)

Tibetan Freedom Concert 𝄞𝄞𝄞 (Grand Royal/Capitol, 1997)

Women for Women 𝄞𝄞𝄞 (Mercury, 1994)

Women for Women 2 𝄞𝄞𝄞 (Mercury, 1996)

British Invasion

The British Invasion: The History of British Rock, Vol. 1 𝄞𝄞𝄞𝄞 (Rhino, 1988)

The British Invasion: The History of British Rock, Vol. 2 𝄞𝄞𝄞𝄞 (Rhino, 1988)

The British Invasion: The History of British Rock, Vol. 3 𝄞𝄞𝄞𝄞 (Rhino, 1988)

The British Invasion: The History of British Rock, Vol. 4 𝄞𝄞𝄞𝄞 (Rhino, 1988)

The British Invasion: The History of British Rock, Vol. 5 𝄞𝄞𝄞 (Rhino, 1988)

The British Invasion: The History of British Rock, Vol. 6 𝄞𝄞𝄞 (Rhino, 1988)

The British Invasion: The History of British Rock, Vol. 7 𝄞𝄞𝄞 (Rhino, 1991)

The British Invasion: The History of British Rock, Vol. 8 ♫♫♫ (Rhino, 1991)

The British Invasion: The History of British Rock, Vol. 9 ♫♫♫ (Rhino, 1991)

British Rock ♫♫♫ (Box Set) (Original Sound, 1991)

British Rock, Vol. 2 ♫♫♫ (Original Sound, 1991)

British Rock, Vol. 3 & 4 ♫♫♫ (Original Sound, 1996)

The Sullivan Years: British Invasion ♫♫♫ (TVT, 1990)

32 Merseybeat Nuggets ♫♫♫ (Collectables, 1994)

Christmas

The Best of Cool Yule ♫♫♫♫ (Rhino, 1988)

Billboard Greatest Christmas Hits: 1955–Present ♫♫ (Rhino, 1989)

Christmas Hits ♫♫♫ (MCA Special Products, 1991)

Christmas of Hope ♫♫♫ (Columbia, 1995)

Christmas Party with Eddie G. ♫♫♫♫ (Rhino, 1990)

Dr. Demento: Holidays in Dementia ♫♫♫♫ (Rhino, 1995)

Dr. Demento Presents the Greatest Christmas Novelty CD of All Time ♫♫♫ (Rhino, 1989)

Doo Wop Christmas ♫♫♫ (Rhino, 1992)

Hardcore Holiday ♫♫♫ (Essential Noise, 1996)

A Home for the Holidays ♫♫♫♫ (Mercury, 1997)

Hot Rod: Hot Rod Holiday ♫♫♫ (The Right Stuff, 1997)

Just Can't Get Enough: New Wave Xmas ♫♫♫ (Rhino, 1996)

Just Say Noël ♫♫♫ (Geffen, 1996)

A Lump of Coal ♫♫♫♫ (First Warning, 1991)

Merry Axemas: A Guitar Christmas ♫♫♫♫ (Epic, 1997)

Merry Axemas 2: A Guitar Christmas N/A (Epic, 1998)

Punk Rock Xmas ♫♫♫♫ (Rhino, 1995)

Rockin' Little Christmas ♫♫♫♫ (MCA Special Products, 1993)

Snow Angels ♫♫♫ (Hear/Compass, 1996)

Superstars of Christmas, 1995 ♫♫♫ (Capitol, 1995)

A Very Special Christmas ♫♫♫♫ (A&M, 1989)

A Very Special Christmas 2 ♫♫♫♫ (A&M, 1992)

A Very Special Christmas 3 ♫♫♫ (A&M, 1997)

You Sleigh Me! ♫♫♫ (Atlantic, 1995)

Doo-Wop

Art LaBoe Presents: 13 of the Best Doo Wop Love Songs ♫♫♫ (Original Sound, 1992)

The Ballad Era: Harlem, N.Y. ♫♫♫ (Collectables, 1993)

The Best of Acapella ♫♫♫ (Relic, 1993)

The Best of Acappella, Vol. 3 ♫♫ (Relic, 1995)

The Best of Candlelite Records, Vol. 1 ♫♫♫ (Juke Box Treasures, 1993)

The Best of Candlelite Records, Vol. 2 ♫♫♫ (Juke Box Treasures, 1994)

The Best of Candlelite Records, Vol. 3 ♫♫♫ (Juke Box Treasures, 1994)

Best of Chess Vocal Groups, Vol. 2 ♫♫♫ (Chess, 1988)

The Best of Doo Wop Ballads ♫♫♫♫♫ (Rhino, 1989)

The Best of Doo Wop Uptempo ♫♫♫♫♫ (Rhino, 1989)

Bim Bam Boom: 28 Rockin' Doo Wops ♫♫♫ (Instant, 1993)

Blue Moon ♫♫♫ (Crimson, 1997)

Blue Moon ♫♫♫ (Rhino, 1997)

Dedicated to the 1950s ♫♫ (Relic, 1995)

The Doo Wop Box ♫♫♫♫♫ (Rhino, 1993)

The Doo Wop Box II ♫♫♫♫ (Rhino, 1996)

Doo Wop Car & Doo Wop Angel Songs ♫♫♫ (Juke Box Treasures, 1996)

Doo Wop Classics ♫♫♫ (PolyGram Special Markets, 1995)

Doo Wop Classics ♫♫♫ (Rebound, 1994)

Doo Wop Delights ♫♫♫ (Relic, 1992)

Doo Wop Delights: The Boston Groups ♫♫ (Relic, 1996)

Doo Wop Delights: The Hartford Groups ♫♫ (Relic, 1994)

Doo Wop Delights: The Los Angeles Groups ♫♫♫ (Relic, 1994)

The Doo-Wop Era: Harlem, N.Y. ♫♫♫ (Collectables, 1993)

The Doo-Wop Era: Harlem, N.Y., Vol. 2 ♫♫ (Collectables, 1993)

The Doo-Wop Era: Harlem, N.Y., Vol. 3 ♫♫ (Collectables, 1993)

Doo Wop from Dolphin's of Hollywood, Vol. 1 ♫♫♫ (Specialty, 1992)

Doo Wop from Dolphin's of Hollywood, Vol. 2 ♫♫ (Specialty, 1992)

Doo Wop Heaven: Streetcorner Vocalists ♫♫♫ (Columbia Special Products, 1994)

Doo Wop: Honey for Sale ♫♫ (Del-Fi, 1998)

Doo Wop: Sh-Boom ♫♫♫ (Rhino, 1997)

Doo Wop Shop ♫♫♫♫ (Ace, 1992)

Doo Wop, Vol. 1: To Be Loved Forever ♫♫ (Del-Fi, 1998)

Doo Wop, Vol. 2: One Tear Drop Too Late ♫♫ (Del-Fi, 1998)

Doo Wop's Greatest Hits ♫♫♫ (K-Tel, 1997)

Dootone Doo-Wop, Vol. 1 ♫♫♫♫ (Ace, 1996)

Dootone Rhythm & Blues: Golden Classics ♫♫♫ (Collectables, 1990)

Echoes Down the Hall: 16 Doo-Wop Classics ♫♫♫ (Arista, 1989)

Eddie Brian Presents: Doo Wop ♫♫ (Relic, 1995)

Excello Vocal Groups ♫♫♫ (Excello, 1995)

For Collectors Only, Volume 1: The Rarities ♫♫ (Collectables, 1993)

The Golden Era of Doowops: Apollo Records, Pt. 1 ♫♫♫ (Relic, 1996)

The Golden Era of Doowops: Apollo Records, Pt. 2 ♫♫ (Relic, 1996)

The Golden Era of Doowops: Apollo Records, Pt. 3 ♫♫ (Relic, 1996)

The Golden Era of Doowops: Apollo Records, Pt. 4 ♫♫ (Relic, 1996)

The Golden Era of Doowops: Atlas Records ♫♫ (Relic, 1996)

The Golden Era of Doowops: Celeste Records ♫♫♫ (Relic, 1994)

The Golden Era of Doowops: Class Records ♫♫♫ (Relic, 1996)

The Golden Era of Doowops: Club Records ♫♫ (Relic, 1996)

The Golden Era of Doowops: Ember Records, Pt. 1 ♫♫ (Relic, 1995)

The Golden Era of Doowops: Ember Records, Pt. 2 ♫♫ (Relic, 1995)

The Golden Era of Doowops: Everlast Records ♫♫ (Relic, 1995)

The Golden Era of Doowops: Fargo Records ♫♫ (Relic, 1996)

The Golden Era of Doowops: Flash Records ♫♫♫ (Relic, 1995)

The Golden Era of Doowops: Fury Records ♫♫♫ (Relic, 1995)

The Golden Era of Doowops: Fury Records, Pt. 2 ♫♫ (Relic, 1995)

The Golden Era of Doowops: Grand Records ♫♫♫ (Relic, 1995)

The Golden Era of Doowops: Herald Records ♫♫♫ (Relic, 1995)

The Golden Era of Doowops: Herald Records, Pt. 2 ♫♫ (Relic, 1995)

The Golden Era of Doowops: Holiday Records ♫♫♫ (Relic, 1995)

The Golden Era of Doowops: Johnson Records ♫♫ (Relic, 1994)

The Golden Era of Doowops: Joyce Records ♫♫ (Relic, 1996)

The Golden Era of Doowops: Len Records ♫♫ (Relic, 1994)

The Golden Era of Doowops: Lummtone Records ♫♫ (Relic, 1995)

The Golden Era of Doowops: Lupine Records ♫♫♫ (Relic, 1996)

The Golden Era of Doowops: Premium Records ♪♪ (Relic, 1994)

The Golden Era of Doowops: Rainbow Records ♪♪ (Relic, 1994)

The Golden Era of Doowops: Red Robin Records, Pt. 1 ♪♪♪ (Relic, 1994)

The Golden Era of Doowops: Red Robin Records, Pt. 2 ♪♪ (Relic, 1994)

The Golden Era of Doowops: Relic Records, Vol. 1 ♪♪♪ (Relic, 1995)

The Golden Era of Doowops: Stanford Records ♪♪ (Relic, 1992)

The Golden Era of Doowops: The Groups of Onyx Records ♪♪½ (Relic, 1993)

The Golden Era of Doowops: The Groups of Parrot Records ♪♪½ (Relic, 1993)

The Golden Era of Doowops: The Groups of Vita Records ♪♪½ (Relic, 1993)

The Golden Era of Doowops: Times Square Records ♪♪ (Relic, 1995)

The Golden Era of Doowops: Tip Top Records ♪♪ (Relic, 1994)

The Golden Era of Doowops: V-Tone Records ♪♪ (Relic, 1995)

The Golden Era of Doowops: Winley Records ♪♪½ (Relic, 1994)

Golden Groups: Specialty's Greatest! ♪♪♪ (Specialty, 1993)

The Greatest Brooklyn Doo-Wops, Vol. 1 ♪♪♪ (Juke Box Treasures, 1994)

The Greatest Brooklyn Doo-Wops, Vol. 2 ♪♪ (Juke Box Treasures, 1994)

The Greatest Hits of Acapella ♪♪♪ (Juke Box Treasures, 1995)

Gus Grossert's 25 Favorite New York Doo Wop Groups ♪♪♪ (Relic, 1994)

Hardcore Doo-Wop: In the Hallway–Under the Street Lamp ♪♪♪ (Specialty, 1993)

I Dig Acapella, Vol. 1 ♪♪ (Relic, 1994)

Legends of Doo-Wop, Vol. 1 ♪♪♪ (Juke Box Treasures, 1996)

Memories of Times Square Record Shop, Vol. 1 ♪♪ (Collectables, 1993)

Memories of Times Square Record Shop, Vol. 2 ♪♪ (Collectables, 1993)

Memories of Times Square Record Shop, Vol. 3 ♪♪ (Collectables, 1993)

Memories of Times Square Record Shop, Vol. 4 ♪♪ (Collectables, 1993)

Memories of Times Square Record Shop, Vol. 5 ♪♪ (Collectables, 1993)

Memories of Times Square Record Shop, Vol. 6 ♪♪ (Collectables, 1993)

Memories of Times Square Record Shop, Vol. 7 ♪♪♪ (Collectables, 1995)

Memories of Times Square Record Shop, Vol. 8 ♪♪♪ (Collectables, 1995)

Memories of Times Square Record Shop, Vol. 9 ♪♪ (Collectables, 1995)

Memories of Times Square Record Shop, Vol. 10 ♪♪ (Collectables, 1995)

Memories of Times Square Record Shop, Vol. 11 ♪♪ (Collectables, 1995)

One Million Years of Doo-Wop ♪♪♪ (Jamie/Guiden, 1997)

The Original New York Doo-Wop Album, Vol. 1 ♪♪♪ (Juke Box Treasures, 1994)

The Paragons & the Jesters Meet the Shells & the Dubs ♪♪♪ (Juke Box Treasures, 1994)

Spotlite on Apollo Records, Vol. 1 ♪♪ (Collectables, 1995)

Spotlite on Apollo Records, Vol. 2 ♪♪ (Collectables, 1995)

Spotlite on Blast & Cheer Records, Vol. 1 ♪♪ (Collectables, 1996)

Spotlite on Capitol Records, Vol. 1 ♪♪ (Collectables, 1995)

Spotlite on Capitol Records, Vol. 2 ♪♪ (Collectables, 1995)

Spotlite on Carlton Records, Vol. 1 ♪♪ (Collectables, 1996)

Spotlite on Class Records, Vol. 1 ♪♪ (Collectables, 1996)

Spotlite on Class Records, Vol. 2 ♪♪ (Collectables, 1996)

Spotlite on Colpix Records, Vol. 1 ♪♪♪ (Collectables, 1995)

Spotlite on Ember Records, Vol. 1 ♪♪♪ (Collectables, 1995)

Spotlite on End Records, Vol. 1 ♪♪♪ (Collectables, 1993)

Spotlite on End Records, Vol. 2 ♪♪♪ (Collectables, 1994)

Spotlite on End Records, Vol. 3 ♪♪ (Collectables, 1994)

Spotlite on End Records, Vol. 4 ♪♪ (Collectables, 1994)

Spotlite on Epic Records, Vol. 1 ♪♪ (Collectables, 1996)

Spotlite on Gee Records, Vol. 1 ♪♪♪ (Collectables, 1993)

Spotlite on Gee Records, Vol. 2 ♪♪♪ (Collectables, 1994)

Spotlite on Gee Records, Vol. 3 ♪♪♪ (Collectables, 1994)

Spotlite on Gee Records, Vol. 4 ♪♪ (Collectables, 1994)

Spotlite on Goldisc Records, Vol. 1 ♪♪ (Collectables, 1995)

Spotlite on Gone Records, Vol. 1 ♪♪♪ (Collectables, 1993)

Spotlite on Gone Records, Vol. 2 ♪♪♪ (Collectables, 1993)

Spotlite on Gotham Records, Vol. 1 ♪♪½ (Collectables, 1996)

Spotlite on Herald Records, Vol. 1 ♪♪♪ (Collectables, 1996)

Spotlite on Herald Records, Vol. 2 ♪♪♪ (Collectables, 1996)

Spotlite on Hull Records, Vol. 1 ♪♪♪ (Collectables, 1994)

Spotlite on Hull Records, Vol. 2 ♪♪ (Collectables, 1994)

Spotlite on Josie Records, Vol. 1 ♪♪ (Collectables, 1993)

Spotlite on Josie Records, Vol. 2 ♪♪½ (Collectables, 1994)

Spotlite on Josie Records, Vol. 3 ♪♪ (Collectables, 1994)

Spotlite on Josie Records, Vol. 4 ♪♪½ (Collectables, 1994)

Spotlite on Jubilee Records, Vol. 1 ♪♪♪ (Collectables, 1995)

Spotlite on Jubilee Records, Vol. 2 ♪♪ (Collectables, 1995)

Spotlite on Jubilee Records, Vol. 3 ♪♪♪ (Collectables, 1995)

Spotlite on Mainline Records, Vol. 1 ♪♪ (Collectables, 1996)

Spotlite on Mainline Records, Vol. 2 ♪♪ (Collectables, 1996)

Spotlite on Melba Records, Vol. 1 ♪♪ (Collectables, 1995)

Spotlite on Port Records, Vol. 1 ♪♪ (Collectables, 1996)

Spotlite on Rainbow Records, Vol. 1 ♪♪ (Collectables, 1995)

Spotlite on Rainbow Records, Vol. 2 ♪♪ (Collectables, 1995)

Spotlite on Rama Records, Vol. 1 ♪♪♪ (Collectables, 1993)

Spotlite on Rama Records, Vol. 2 ♪♪♪ (Collectables, 1993)

Spotlite on Rama Records, Vol. 3 ♪♪ (Collectables, 1995)

Spotlite on Rama Records, Vol. 4 ♪♪ (Collectables, 1995)

Spotlite on Roulette Records, Vol. 1 ♪♪♪ (Collectables, 1993)

Spotlite on Roulette Records, Vol. 2 ♪♪♪ (Collectables, 1994)

Spotlite on Warwick Records, Vol. 1 ♪♪♪ (Collectables, 1995)

Spotlite on Warwick Records, Vol. 2 ♪♪♪ (Collectables, 1995)

Teenage Party ♪♪ (Collectables, 1991)

Your Doo-Wop Hit Parade! ♪♪♪ (Juke Box Treasures, 1994)

The '80s

Alterno-Daze: The '80s ♪♪ (Rebound, 1995)

Arena Rock: The '80s ♪♪♪ (K-Tel, 1997)

Best of '80s Rock 1 ♪♪ (Priority, 1994)

Best of '80s Rock 2 ♪ (Priority, 1994)

Best of '80s Rock 3 ♪½ (Priority, 1994)

Best of '80s Rock 4 ♪ (Priority, 1994)

Best of '80s Rock 5 ♪ (Priority, 1994)

Best of '80s Rock 6 ♪½ (Priority, 1996)

Best of Grunge Rock ♪♪ (Priority, 1993)

Billboard Album Rock Hits: 1981 ♪♪♪ (Rhino, 1997)

Billboard Album Rock Hits: 1982 ♫♫ (Rhino, 1997)

Billboard Album Rock Hits: 1983 ♫♫ (Rhino, 1997)

Billboard Album Rock Hits: 1984 ♫♫ (Rhino, 1997)

Billboard Top Dance Hits: 1981 ♫♫ (Rhino, 1998)

Billboard Top Dance Hits: 1982 ♫♫ (Rhino, 1998)

Billboard Top Dance Hits: 1983 ♫♫ (Rhino, 1998)

Billboard Top Dance Hits: 1984 ♫♫ (Rhino, 1998)

Billboard Top Dance Hits: 1985 ♫♫♫ (Rhino, 1998)

Chart Toppers: Dance Hits of the '80s ♫♫ (Priority, 1998)

Chart Toppers: Modern Rock Hits of the '80s, Vol. 1 ♫♫ (Priority, 1998)

Chart Toppers: Modern Rock Hits of the '80s, Vol. 2 ♫♫ (Priority, 1998)

Chart Toppers: Rock Hits of the '80s ♫♫ (Priority, 1998)

Class Reunion: Greatest Hits of 1981 ♫♫ (Rebound, 1996)

Classic MTV: Class of 1983 ♫♫♫ (Rhino, 1995)

CMC Presents the Rockin' '80s ♫ (CMC, 1998)

18 Modern Rock Classics from the '80s ♫♫♫ (JCI, 1996)

'80s Greatest Rock Hits: Arena Rock ♫♫♫ (Priority, 1992)

'80s Greatest Rock Hits 1: Passion & Power ♫♫ (Priority, 1992)

'80s Greatest Rock Hits 4: Party On ♫♫ (Priority, 1994)

'80s Greatest Rock Hits 5: From the Heart ♫♫ (Priority, 1994)

'80s Greatest Rock Hits 8: Dance Party ♫ (Priority, 1993)

'80s Greatest Rock Hits 10: Dance All Night ♫♫ (Priority, 1994)

'80s Greatest Rock Hits 11: Teen Idols ♫ (Priority, 1994)

'80s Greatest Rock Hits 12: Singers & Songwriters ♫♫♫ (Priority, 1994)

The '80s Hit(s) Back 3 ♫♫ (Hip-O, 1997)

The '80s Hot Rock ♫ (K-Tel, 1996)

The '80s Mega Hits ♫♫ (K-Tel, 1997)

The '80s: Number One Pop Hits ♫♫ (K-Tel, 1997)

Essential '80s: 1980–84 ♫♫ (Hip-O, 1998)

Essential '80s: 1985–89 ♫♫ (Hip-O, 1998)

Fizz Pop Modern Rock, Vol. 1 ♫♫ (Legacy, 1997)

Fizz Pop Modern Rock, Vol. 2 ♫♫ (Legacy, 1997)

Flashback Cafe, Vol. 1 ♫♫ (Oglio, 1994)

Flashback Cafe, Vol. 2 ♫♫ (Oglio, 1995)

Geffen Vintage '80s, Vol. 1 ♫♫ (Geffen, 1995)

Geffen Vintage '80s, Vol. II ♫♫ (Geffen, 1995)

Geffen Vintage '80s Presents It Rocks! ♫♫ (Geffen, 1998)

Greatest Hits of the '80s, Vol. 1 ♫♫♫ (Sony Music Special Products, 1996)

Greatest Rock Hits of the '80s ♫♫ (MCA Special Products, 1996)

I Love Rock & Roll: Hits of the '80s, Vol. 3 ♫♫♫ (Priority, 1996)

Living in Oblivion: The '80s Greatest Hits, Volume 1 ♫♫♫ (EMI, 1993)

Living in Oblivion: The '80s Greatest Hits, Volume 2 ♫♫♫ (EMI, 1993)

Living in Oblivion: The '80s Greatest Hits, Volume 3 ♫♫♫ (EMI, 1994)

Living in Oblivion: The '80s Greatest Hits, Volume 4 ♫♫ (EMI, 1994)

Living in Oblivion: The '80s Greatest Hits, Volume 5 ♫♫ (EMI, 1995)

Modern Rock 1986: Hang the DJ ♫♫♫ (Rhino, 1996)

Modern Rock 1987: Hang the DJ ♫♫♫ (Rhino, 1996)

Modern Rock 1988: Hang the DJ ♫♫♫ (Rhino, 1996)

Nipper's Greatest Hits: The '80s ♫♫♫ (RCA, 1990)

Only Rock 'N' Roll, 1980–1984: #1 Radio Hits ♫♫♫ (JCI, 1996)

Only Rock 'N' Roll, 1984–1989: #1 Radio Hits ♫♫ (JCI, 1996)

Poptopia! Power Pop Classics of the '80s ♫♫♫ (Rhino, 1997)

Radio Daze: Pop Hits of the '80s, Vol. 1 ♫♫ (Rhino, 1995)

Radio Daze: Pop Hits of the '80s, Vol. 2 ♫♫ (Rhino, 1995)

Radio Daze: Pop Hits of the '80s, Vol. 3 ♫♫ (Rhino, 1995)

Radio Daze: Pop Hits of the '80s, Vol. 4 ♫♫ (Rhino, 1995)

Radio Daze: Pop Hits of the '80s, Vol. 5 ♫♫ (Rhino, 1995)

Read the Hits: Best of the '80s ♫♫♫ (Sony Music Special Products, 1994)

Rock of the '80s 1 ♫♫ (Priority, 1991)

Rock of the '80s 2 ♫♫ (Priority, 1993)

Rock of the '80s 3 ♫♫ (Priority, 1993)

Rock of the '80s 4 ♫♫ (Priority, 1993)

Rock of the '80s 5 ♫♫ (Priority, 1993)

Rock of the '80s 6 ♫♫ (Priority, 1993)

Rock of the '80s 7 ♫♫ (Priority, 1993)

Rock of the '80s 8 ♫♫ (Priority, 1993)

Rock of the '80s 9 ♫♫ (Priority, 1993)

Rock of the '80s 10 ♫♫ (Priority, 1993)

Rock of the '80s 11 ♫♫ (Priority, 1994)

Rock of the '80s 12 ♫♫ (Priority, 1994)

Rock of the '80s 13 ♫♫ (Priority, 1994)

Rock of the '80s 14 ♫♫ (Priority, 1994)

Rock of the '80s 15 ♫♫ (Priority, 1994)

Sedated in the Eighties ♫♫♫ (The Right Stuff, 1993)

Sedated in the Eighties No. 2 ♫♫♫ (The Right Stuff, 1994)

Sedated in the Eighties No. 3 ♫♫♫ (The Right Stuff, 1994)

Sedated in the Eighties No. 4 ♫♫♫ (The Right Stuff, 1994)

Sedated in the Eighties No. 5 ♫♫♫ (The Right Stuff, 1994)

That Sound from Down Under ♫♫♫ (Hip-O, 1996)

VH1: More of the Big '80s ♫♫♫ (Rhino, 1997)

VH1 The Big '80s: The Big Movies ♫♫ (Rhino, 1998)

Electronica

Axiom Ambient: Lost in the Translation ♫♫♫♫ (Axiom, 1994)

Counterforce: A Collection of Deep Beats ♫♫♫♫ (FFRR, 1995)

Digital Empire: Electronica's Best ♫♫♫ (Cold Front, 1998)

Excursions in Ambience: The Second Orbit ♫♫♫ (Astralwerks, 1993)

Excursions in Ambience: The Third Dimension ♫♫♫♫ (Astralwerks, 1994)

Future: A Journey Through the Electronic Underworld ♫♫♫ (Virgin, 1997)

Future Perfect ♫♫♫ (Gyroscope, 1994)

A Journey into Ambient Groove 3 ♫♫♫ (Quango, 1996)

MTV's Amp ♫♫♫♫ (Astralwerks/Caroline, 1997)

MTV's Amp 2 ♫♫♫♫ (Astralwerks/Caroline, 1998)

Offbeat: A Red Hot Sound Trip ♫♫♫♫ (Red Hot/Wax Trax, 1996)

Synth Me Up: 14 Classic Electronic Hits ♫♫♫♫ (Hip-O, 1997)

Technomancer: The Hard Edition ♫♫♫ (Astralwerks, 1994)

Trance Planet, Volume 1 ♫♫♫♫ (Triloka, 1994)

Trance Planet, Volume 3 ♫♫♫♫ (Triloka, 1996)

The '50s

All Time Greatest Hits of Rock 'n' Roll ♫♫♫ (Curb, 1990)

All Time Greatest Hits of Rock 'n' Roll, Volume 2 ♫♫ (Curb, 1991)

All Time Greatest Hits of Rock 'n' Roll, Volume 3 ♫♫ (Curb, 1991)

At the Hop: '50s Rock 'N Roll ♫♫♫ (K-Tel, 1997)

A Barrel of Oldies ♫♫♫ (Del-Fi, 1994)

Be Bop Boogie ♫♫ (Collectables, 1990)

Best of the Jukebox ♫♫ (Priority, 1990)

Best of Shakin' '50s ♫♫♫ (Priority, 1990)

Bop City: Red Hot Early Rock ♫♫♫ (Collectables, 1995)

'50s Hits: Great Records of the Decade, Vol. 1 ♫♫ (Curb, 1990)

'50s Rock-N-Roll, Vol. 2: Here to Stay ♫♫♫♫ (Dominion, 1997)

'50s Rock-N-Roll, Vol. 3: Whole Lotta Shakin' ♫♫♫ (Dominion, 1997)

Forefathers of Rock ♫♫♫ (K-Tel, 1997)

Great Groups of the '50s, Vol. 1 ♫♫♫ (Collectables, 1994)

Great Groups of the '50s, Vol. 2 ♫♫♫ (Collectables, 1994)

Great Groups of the '50s, Vol. 3 ♫♫♫ (Collectables, 1994)

I Love Rock & Roll: Hits of the '50s, Volume One ♫♫♫♫ (Priority, 1996)

The King's Record Collection: The Original Versions of Songs Later Recorded by Elvis Presley, Vol. 1 ♫♫♫♫ (Hip-O, 1998)

The King's Record Collection: The Original Versions of Songs Later Recorded by Elvis Presley, Vol. 2 ♫♫♫♫ (Hip-O, 1998)

More '50s Jukebox Favorites ♫♫ (K-Tel, 1989)

Number One Hits of the '50s ♫♫ (Rebound, 1994)

Only Dance, 1955–1959 ♫♫♫ (Esx, 1996)

Only Rock 'N' Roll, 1955–1959 ♫♫♫ (JCI, 1994)

Only Rock 'N' Roll, 1955–1959: #1 Radio Hits ♫♫♫ (JCI, 1996)

Risque Rhythms: Nasty '50s R&B ♫♫♫♫ (Rhino, 1991)

Rock Around the Oldies ♫♫♫ (MCA Special Products, 1994)

Rock Before Elvis: The Hoy Hoy Collection ♫♫♫ (Stash, 1995)

Rock 'N' Roll Relix: 1954–1959 ♫♫♫♫ (Eclipse, 1997)

Rock 'N' Roll Fever: The Wildest from Specialty ♫♫ (Specialty, 1994)

Shout Baby, Shout: Roots of Rock In Texas Boogie ♫♫♫ (Collectables, 1993)

Sounds Like Elvis: Early Imitators, 1956–77 ♫♫♫ (Collectables, 1996)

The Sullivan Years: Rock 'N' Roll Pioneers, 1955–1959 ♫♫♫ (TVT, 1993)

Treasure Isle ♫♫ (Heartbeat, 1994)

Ultimate '50s R&B Smashes ♫♫♫♫ (Rhino, 1998)

WCBS FM-101 History of Rock: The '50s, Pt. 1 ♫♫♫ (Collectables, 1990)

WCBS FM-101 History of Rock: The '50s, Pt. 2 ♫♫♫♫ (Collectables, 1990)

WCBS FM-101 History of Rock: The '50s, Pt. 3 ♫♫♫♫ (Collectables, 1997)

WODS-FM 10th Anniversary: Best of the '50s, Vol. 1 ♫♫♫♫ (Collectables, 1997)

WODS-FM 10th Anniversary: Best of the '50s, Vol. 2 ♫♫♫♫ (Collectables, 1997)

WOGL-FM 10th Anniversary: Best of the '50s ♫♫♫ (Collectables, 1997)

Girls and Women

The Best of the Girl Groups, Vol. 1 ♫♫♫♫♫ (Rhino, 1990)

The Best of the Girl Groups, Vol. 2 ♫♫♫♫ (Rhino, 1990)

The Best of the '70s: Legendary Ladies ♫♫ (K-Tel, 1997)

Detroit Girl Groups ♫♫♫ (Relic, 1994)

'80s Greatest Hits 2: Leather & Lace ♫♫ (Priority, 1992)

The '80s Hot Ladies ♫♫ (K-Tel, 1997)

Great Rockin' Girls ♫♫♫ (Collector, 1997)

Growin' up Too Fast: The Girl Group Anthology ♫♫♫ (Mercury, 1996)

Just Can't Get Enough: New Wave Women ♫♫♫ (Rhino, 1997)

Lilith Fair: A Celebration of Women in Music ♫♫♫ (Arista, 1998)

Listen to the Music: '70s Female Singer/Songwriters ♫♫♫ (Rhino, 1996)

More Great Rockin' Girls ♫♫ (Collector, 1997)

Motown Legends: Motown Girl Groups ♫♫♫ (PolyGram Special Markets, 1995)

Rock She Said: Guitars & Attitudes ♫♫♫ (Hip-O, 1998)

Rock She Said: On the Pop Side ♫♫♫ (Hip-O, 1998)

Rolling Stone's Women in Rock ♫♫♫♫♫ (Razor & Tie, 1998)

She's a Rebel ♫♫ (Shanachie, 1997)

'60s Girl Groups ♫♫♫ (Ol' Skool, 1998)

'60s Girl Groups ♫♫♫♫ (Warner Bros., 1998)

Hard Rock/Heavy Metal

The Beavis and Butt-Head Experience ♫♫♫ (Geffen, 1993)

Best of '80s Metal: Bang Your Head, Volume 1 ♫♫ (Priority, 1997)

Best of '80s Metal: Bang Your Head, Volume 2 ♫ (Priority, 1997)

Best of '80s Metal: Bang Your Head, Volume 3 ♫ (Priority, 1997)

The Best of Hard Rock ♫♫♫ (MCA Special Products, 1997)

Classic Rock Anthems ♫♫♫ (Crimson, 1998)

CMC Presents the Best of Metal ♫ (CMC, 1997)

18 Headbangers from the '80s ♫♫♫ (JCI, 1995)

Hard Rock Cafe: '80s Heavy Metal ♫♫ (Hard Rock/Rhino, 1998)

Hard Rock Essentials: The '80s ♫♫ (Rebound, 1994)

Heavy Metal Hits of the '80s, Vol. 1 ♫♫♫ (Rhino, 1996)

Heavy Metal Hits of the '80s, Vol. 2 ♫♫♫ (Rhino, 1996)

Heavy Metal Hits of the '80s, Vol. 3 ♫♫ (Rhino, 1996)

Killer Metal ♫♫ (Priority, 1992)

Monsters of Rock ♫♫♫ (Razor & Tie, 1998)

Monsters of Rock 1: Heaven and Hell ♫♫ (Priority, 1994)

Monsters of Rock 2: Metal Madness ♫♫ (Priority, 1994)

Power Chords: Volume 1 ♫♫♫ (Hip-O, 1997)

Power Chords: Volume 2 ♫♫♫ (Hip-O, 1997)

Power Chords: Volume 3 ♫♫♫ (Hip-O, 1997)

Power Chords Live ♫♫ (Hip-O, 1997)

Summerdaze ♫♫ (CMC International, 1997)

Youth Gone Wild: Heavy Metal Hits of the '80s ♫♫ (Rhino, 1998)

Hits Compilations

Angel Hits ♫♫♫ (Scotti Brothers, 1995)

Art LaBoe Presents: Best Love Songs, Vol. 1 & 2 ♫♫♫ (Original Sound, 1994)

Art LaBoe Presents: Best Love Songs, Vol. 3 ♫♫ (Original Sound, 1993)

Art LaBoe Presents: Best Love Songs, Vol. 4 ♫♫ (Original Sound, 1993)

Art LaBoe Presents: Dedicated to You, Vol. 1 ♫♫♫ (Original Sound, 1991)

Art LaBoe Presents: Dedicated to You, Vol. 2 ♫♫ (Original Sound, 1993)

Art LaBoe Presents: Dedicated to You, Vol. 3 ♫♫ (Original Sound, 1993)

Art LaBoe Presents: Dedicated to You, Vol. 4 ♫♫♫♫ (Original Sound, 1994)

Art LaBoe Presents: Dedicated to You, Vol. 5 ♫♫♫ (Original Sound, 1994)

Art LaBoe Presents: Dedicated to You, Vol. 6 ♫♫ (Original Sound, 1995)

Art LaBoe Presents: Dedicated to You, Vol. 7 ♫♫ (Original Sound, 1995)

Art LaBoe Presents: Dedicated to You, Vol. 8 ♫♫♫ (Original Sound, 1996)

Art LaBoe Presents: Killer Oldies, Vol. 2 ♫♫♫ (Original Sound, 1994)

Art LaBoe Presents: Memories of El Monte ♫♫ (Original Sound, 1991)

Back to the '50s ♫♫♫ (K-Tel, 1990)

Back to the '70s ♫♫ (K-Tel, 1990)

Beach Music Hits ♫♫ (MCA Special Products, 1997)

Beach Party ♫♫♫ (Madacy, 1997)

Believe in Music ♫♫ (K-Tel, 1996)

The Best of Louie Louie ♫♫♫ (Rhino, 1983/1988)

The Best of Louie Louie, Vol. 2 ♫♫ (Rhino, 1989)

The Best of '60s & '70s Rock: Protest Rock ♫♫ (Priority, 1992)

Billboard Top Rock 'n' Roll Hits: 1955 ♫♫♫ (Rhino, 1988)

Billboard Top Rock 'n' Roll Hits: 1956 ♫♫♫ (Rhino, 1988)

Billboard Top Rock 'n' Roll Hits: 1957 ♫♫♫ (Rhino, 1988)

Billboard Top Rock 'n' Roll Hits: 1958 ♫♫♫ (Rhino, 1988)

Billboard Top Rock 'n' Roll Hits: 1959 ♫♫♫ (Rhino, 1988)

Billboard Top Rock 'n' Roll Hits: 1960 ♫♫♫ (Rhino, 1988)

Billboard Top Rock 'n' Roll Hits: 1961 ♫♫♫ (Rhino, 1988)

Billboard Top Rock 'n' Roll Hits: 1962 ♫♫♫ (Rhino, 1988)

Billboard Top Rock 'n' Roll Hits: 1963 ♫♫♫ (Rhino, 1988)

Billboard Top Rock 'n' Roll Hits: 1964 ♫♫♫ (Rhino, 1989)

Billboard Top Rock 'n' Roll Hits: 1965 ♫♫♫ (Rhino, 1989)

Billboard Top Rock 'n' Roll Hits: 1966 ♫♫♫ (Rhino, 1989)

Billboard Top Rock 'n' Roll Hits: 1967 ♫♫♫ (Rhino, 1989)

Billboard Top Rock 'n' Roll Hits: 1968 ♫♫♫ (Rhino, 1989)

Billboard Top Rock 'n' Roll Hits: 1969 ♫♫♫ (Rhino, 1989)

Billboard Top Rock 'n' Roll Hits: 1970 ♫♫♫ (Rhino, 1989)

Billboard Top Rock 'n' Roll Hits: 1971 ♫♫♫ (Rhino, 1989)

Billboard Top Rock 'n' Roll Hits: 1972 ♫♫♫ (Rhino, 1989)

Billboard Top Rock 'n' Roll Hits: 1973 ♫♫♫ (Rhino, 1989)

Billboard Top Rock 'n' Roll Hits: 1974 ♫♫♫ (Rhino, 1989)

Billboard Top Hits: 1975 ♫♫♫ (Rhino, 1991)

Billboard Top Hits: 1976 ♫♫♫ (Rhino, 1991)

Billboard Top Hits: 1977 ♫♫♫ (Rhino, 1991)

Billboard Top Hits: 1978 ♫♫ (Rhino, 1991)

Billboard Top Hits: 1979 ♫♫ (Rhino, 1991)

Billboard Top Hits: 1980 ♫♫♫ (Rhino, 1992)

Billboard Top Hits: 1981 ♫♫♫ (Rhino, 1992)

Billboard Top Hits: 1982 ♫♫♫ (Rhino, 1992)

Billboard Top Hits: 1983 ♫♫♫ (Rhino, 1992)

Billboard Top Hits: 1984 ♫♫ (Rhino, 1992)

Billboard Top Hits: 1985 ♫♫ (Rhino, 1994)

Billboard Top Hits: 1986 ♫♫♫ (Rhino, 1994)

Billboard Top Hits: 1987 ♫♫ (Rhino, 1994)

Billboard Top Hits: 1988 ♫♫♫ (Rhino, 1994)

Billboard Top Hits: 1989 ♫♫ (Rhino, 1994)

Brown Eyed Soul: East L.A., Vol. 1 ♫♫♫ (Rhino, 1997)

Brown Eyed Soul: East L.A., Vol. 2 ♫♫♫ (Rhino, 1997)

Brown Eyed Soul: East L.A., Vol. 3 ♫♫ (Rhino, 1997)

Bubble Gum Classics ♫♫ (MCA Special Products, 1997)

Bubblegum Classics, Volume 4 ♫♫♫ (Varese Vintage, 1998)

Bubblegum Classics, Volume 5 ♫♫♫ (Varese Vintage, 1998)

Classic Rock from San Antonio, Texas, 1958–1979 ♫♫♫ (Collectables, 1995)

Classic Rock 1: Highway Rockers ♫♫♫ (Priority, 1993)

CMC Presents Superstar Hits ♫♫♫ (CMC, 1998)

Cruisin': 1955 ♫♫ (Increase, 1988)

Cruisin': 1956 ♫♫♫ (Increase, 1988)

Cruisin': 1957 ♫♫♫ (Increase, 1988)

Cruisin': 1958 ♫♫♫ (Increase, 1988)

Cruisin': 1959 ♫♫♫ (Increase, 1988)

Cruisin': 1960 ♫♫♫ (Increase, 1988)

Cruisin': 1961 ♫♫♫ (Increase, 1988)

Cruisin': 1962 ♫♫♫ (Increase, 1988)

Cruisin': 1963 ♫♫♫ (Increase, 1988)

Cruisin': 1964 ♫♫♫ (Increase, 1988)

Cruisin': 1965 ♫♫ (Increase, 1988)

Cruisin': 1966 ♫♫♫ (Increase, 1988)

Cruisin': 1967 ♫♫ (Increase, 1988)

Cruisin': 1968 ♫♫♫ (Increase, 1988)

Cruisin': 1969 ♫♫ (Increase, 1988)

Dick Bartley: On the Radio, Vol. 1 ♫♫♫ (Varese Vintage, 1997)

Dick Bartley: On the Radio, Vol. 2 ♫♫♫ (Varese Vintage, 1997)

Do You Wanna Dance ♫♫♫ (K-Tel, 1994)

Dynamite ♫ (K-Tel, 1996)

Easyriders ♫♫♫ (Thump, 1997)

Easyriders, Vol. 2 ♫♫♫ (Thump, 1997)

Easyriders, Vol. 3 ♫♫♫ (Thump, 1997)

Easyriders, Vol. 4 ♫♫♫ (Thump, 1998)

Electric Currents, Vol. 4 (1967–1975) ♫♫♫ (Island, 1998)

Essential Hits Collection ♫♫♫ (Crimson, 1998)

The Essential Pebbles Collection ♫♫♫♫ (AIP, 1997)

Fast Cars and Southern Stars ♫♫♫ (Critique, 1997)

Golden Dozen Hits ♫♫ (Jin, 1996)

Golden Oldies, Vol. 1 ♫♫♫ (Original Sound, 1988)

Golden Oldies, Vol. 2 ♫♫♫ (Original Sound, 1988)

Golden Oldies, Vol. 3 ♫♫♫ (Original Sound, 1988)

Golden Oldies, Vol. 4 ♫♫ (Original Sound, 1988)

Golden Oldies, Vol. 5 ♫♫ (Original Sound, 1988)

Golden Oldies, Vol. 6 ♫♫♫ (Original Sound, 1988)

Golden Oldies, Vol. 7 ♫♫♫ (Original Sound, 1992)

Golden Oldies, Vol. 8 ♫♫ (Original Sound, 1989)

Golden Oldies, Vol. 9 ♫♫ (Original Sound, 1992)

Golden Oldies, Vol. 10 ♫♫♫ (Original Sound, 1992)

Golden Oldies, Vol. 11 ♫♫♫ (Original Sound, 1992)

Golden Oldies, Vol. 12 ♫♫ (Original Sound, 1989)

Golden Oldies, Vol. 14 ♫♫ (Original Sound, 1992)

Golden Years: 1956 ♫♫♫ (K-Tel, 1993)

Golden Years: 1959 ♫♫♫ (K-Tel, 1993)

Golden Years: 1960 ♫♫ (K-Tel, 1993)

Golden Years: 1961 ♫♫ (K-Tel, 1993)

Golden Years: 1964 ♫♫ (K-Tel, 1993)

*Good Sh*t: 100% Pure Hits* ♫♫♫ (Drive Archive, 1995)

*Good Sh*t: Red Hot & Juicy* ♫♫♫ (Drive Archive, 1995)

Grammy's Greatest Moments, Vol. 1 ♫♫♫ (Atlantic, 1994)

Grammy's Greatest Moments, Vol. 2 ♫♫♫ (Atlantic, 1994)

Grammy's Greatest Moments, Vol. 4 ♫♫ (Atlantic, 1994)

The Greatest Classic Rock Hits ♫♫♫ (MCA Special Products, 1994)

Groove 'N' Grind: '50s & '60s Dance Hits ♫♫♫♫ (Rhino, 1990)

Hard to Find Hits of Rock 'n' Roll, Vol. 1 ♫♫♫ (Curb, 1995)

Hard to Find Hits of Rock 'n' Roll, Vol. 2 ♫♫♫ (Curb, 1995)

Hi Octane: Hard Drivin' Hits! ♫♫ (RCA, 1996)

Hot Rod: Back Seat Movers ♫♫♫ (The Right Stuff, 1997)

Hot Rod: Hot Rod Rebels ♫♫♫♫ (The Right Stuff, 1997)

Hot Rod: Rev It Up ♫♫♫♫ (The Right Stuff, 1997)

I Got Rhythm ♫♫♫ (K-Tel, 1996)

It's Just a Matter of Time ♪♪♪ (Eclipse, 1996)

Kings of New Orleans Rock 'n' Roll ♪♪♪♪ (Music Club, 1998)

Leader of the Pack ♪♪ (Eclipse, 1997)

Let It Rock ♪♪♪ (Quality, 1995)

Louie Louie: The Best of the Northwest Originals ♪♪ (Jerden, 1994)

Love Songs of the Rock 'n' Roll Era ♪♪ (K-Tel, 1994)

Max Weinberg Presents: Let There Be Drums, Vol. 1 (The '50s) ♪♪♪♪ (Rhino, 1994)

Max Weinberg Presents: Let There Be Drums, Vol. 2 (The '60s) ♪♪♪♪ (Rhino, 1994)

Max Weinberg Presents: Let There Be Drums, Vol. 3 (The '70s) ♪♪♪ (Rhino, 1994)

Monster Summer Hits: Drag City ♪♪♪♪ (Capitol/EMI, 1996)

More Stadium Rock ♪♪♪ (Rhino, 1996)

More Sun Splashin': 16 Hot Summer Hits ♪♪♪ (Madacy, 1997)

Murray the K Sings Along with the Original Golden Gassers ♪♪♪ (Collectables, 1991)

New Orleans Party Classics ♪♪♪ (Rhino, 1992)

Oldies but Goodies: Legendary Hits ♪♪♪ (Original Sound, 1990)

Oldies but Goodies, Vol. 1 ♪♪♪ (Original Sound, 1989)

Oldies but Goodies, Vol. 2 ♪♪♪ (Original Sound, 1989)

Oldies but Goodies, Vol. 3 ♪♪♪ (Original Sound, 1989)

Oldies but Goodies, Vol. 4 ♪♪♪ (Original Sound, 1989)

Oldies but Goodies, Vol. 5 ♪♪♪ (Original Sound, 1989)

Oldies but Goodies, Vol. 6 ♪♪ (Original Sound, 1989)

Oldies but Goodies, Vol. 7 ♪♪ (Original Sound, 1989)

Oldies but Goodies, Vol. 8 ♪♪♪ (Original Sound, 1989)

Oldies but Goodies, Vol. 9 ♪♪ (Original Sound, 1990)

Oldies but Goodies, Vol. 10 ♪♪♪ (Original Sound, 1989)

Oldies but Goodies, Vol. 11 ♪♪ (Original Sound, 1989)

Oldies but Goodies, Vol. 12 ♪♪ (Original Sound, 1989)

Oldies but Goodies, Vol. 13 ♪♪♪ (Original Sound, 1992)

Oldies but Goodies, Vol. 14 ♪♪♪ (Original Sound, 1987)

Oldies but Goodies, Vol. 15 ♪♪ (Original Sound, 1989)

Oldies but Goodies: 21 #1 Hits ♪♪♪ (Original Sound, 1989)

Oldies 103-FM WODS: History of Rock, Vol. 2 ♪♪♪♪ (Collectables, 1990)

One Hit Wonders ♪♪ (Rebound, 1994)

Only Dance, 1965–1969 ♪♪♪ (Esx, 1996)

Orbit Records Story: History of Texas Garage Bands, Vol. 2 ♪♪ (Collectables, 1995)

Out of Sight ♪♪♪ (K-Tel, 1996)

Paisley Pop: Pye Psych & Other Colurs, 1966–1969 ♪♪ (Collectables, 1994)

Rock and Roll Festival, Vol. 1 ♪♪♪ (Black Tiger, 1995)

Rock 'n' Roll: All #1 Hits ♪♪♪ (Original Sound, 1994)

Rock the First, Vol. 1 ♪♪♪ (Sandstone, 1992)

Rock the First, Vol. 2 ♪♪♪ (Sandstone, 1992)

Rock the First, Vol. 3 ♪♪♪ (Sandstone, 1992)

Rock the First, Vol. 4 ♪♪♪ (Sandstone, 1992)

Rock the First, Vol. 5 ♪♪ (Sandstone, 1992)

Rock the First, Vol. 6 ♪♪♪ (Sandstone, 1992)

Rock the First, Vol. 7 ♪♪ (Sandstone, 1993)

Rock the First, Vol. 8 ♪♪ (Sandstone, 1993)

Rockin' '50s & '60s ♪♪♪ (Jewel, 1996)

Rumble ♪♪ (Collectables, 1993)

Runway Hits: Music from the Catwalk ♪♪ (Rhino, 1998)

RuPaul's Go-Go Classics ♪♪♪ (Rhino, 1998)

San Francisco: Sound Then & Now, Vol. 1 ♪♪ (San Francisco Sound, 994)

'60s Rock ♪♪♪ (K-Tel, 1997)

Solid Gold Rock & Roll ♪♪ (MCA Special Products, 1996)

Stadium Rock ♪♪ (Rhino, 1995)

Story Songs ♪♪ (K-Tel, 1997)

Summer and Sun ♪♪♪♪ (Rhino, 1989)

Teen Idols ♪♪ (MCA Special Products, 1993)

Texas Music, Vol. 3: Garage Bands & Psychedelia ♪♪♪ (Rhino, 1994)

Three Decades of Rock (60s, '70s, '80s) ♪♪ (Priority, 1990)

Tossin' & Turnin' ♪♪♪ (K-Tel, 1996)

21 Legendary Superstars ♪♪♪ (Original Sound, 1989)

The Ultimate Rock 'n' Roll Collection ♪♪♪♪ (Epic, 1996)

Vintage Collectibles: Vol. 1 (1962–1969) ♪♪ (MCA Special Products, 1986/1994)

Vintage Collectibles: Vol. 2 (1963–1969) ♪♪ (MCA Special Products, 1986/1994)

Vintage Collectibles: Vol. 3 (1956–1966) ♪♪ (MCA Special Products, 1987/1994)

Vintage Collectibles: Vol. 4 (1955–1969) ♪♪ (MCA Special Products, 1987/1994)

Vintage Collectibles: Vol. 5 (1954–1969) ♪♪ (MCA Special Products, 1987/1994)

Vintage Collectibles: Vol. 6 (1958–1967) ♪♪ (MCA Special Products, 1987/1994)

Vintage Collectibles: Vol. 7 (1955–1958) ♪♪ (MCA Special Products, 1995)

Vintage Collectibles: Vol. 8 (1954–1959) ♪♪ (MCA Special Products, 1995)

Vintage Collectibles: Vol. 9 (1958–1963) ♪♪ (MCA Special Products, 1995)

Vintage Collectibles: Vol. 10 (1957–1963) ♪♪ (MCA Special Products, 1995)

Vintage Collectibles: Vol. 11 (1956–1969) ♪♪ (MCA Special Products, 1995)

WCBS FM-101 History of Rock: The '60s, Pt. 2 ♪♪♪ (Collectables, 1991)

What's Shakin' ♪♪♪ (Elektra, 1993)

WODS Jukebox Giants, Vol. 2 ♪♪♪ (Collectables, 1993)

WODS Jukebox Giants, Vol. 3 ♪♪♪ (Collectables, 1993)

Working for a Living ♪♪♪ (Scotti Brothers, 1997)

Your Favorite Songs ♪ (Curb, 1991)

Instrumentals

(Almost) Everybody Slides ♪♪♪ (Rykodisc, 1996)

Classic Rock & Roll Instrumental Hits ♪♪♪ (MCA, 1996)

Classic Rock & Roll Instrumental Hits, Vol. 2 ♪♪♪ (MCA Special Products, 1997)

Everybody Slides, Vol. 2 ♪♪♪ (Rykodisc, 1996)

Guitars That Rule the World, Vol. 1 ♪♪ (Priority, 1994)

Guitar Zone ♪♪♪ (Times Square, 1998)

Guitarrorists ♪♪♪ (No. 6 Records, 1991)

Hot Rod: Big Boss Instrumentals ♪♪♪ (The Right Stuff, 1997)

Legends of Guitar: Rock the '70s, Vol.1 ♪♪♪ (Rhino, 1991)

Legends of Guitar: Rock the '50s, Vol.2 ♪♪♪♪ (Rhino, 1991)

Legends of the Ukulele ♪♪♪ (Rhino, 1998)

Psychedelic Guitar Circus ♪♪♪♪ (Rykodisc, 1994)

Rebel Rouser: Greatest Rock Instrumental Hits ♪♪ (Laserlight, 1994)

Rock Instrumental Classics, Vol. 1: The '50s ♫♫♫♫ (Rhino, 1994)

Rock Instrumental Classics, Vol. 2: The '60s ♫♫♫♫ (Rhino, 1994)

Rock Instrumental Classics, Vol. 3: The '70s ♫♫♫ (Rhino, 1994)

Rock Instrumental Classics, Vol. 4: Soul ♫♫♫♫ (Rhino, 1994)

Rock Instrumental Classics, Vol. 5: Surf ♫♫♫ (Rhino, 1994)

Rock Instrumental Classics ♫♫♫♫ (Box Set) (Rhino, 1995)

Rock 'n' Roll Guitar Classics ♫♫ (K-Tel, 1990)

Rockin' Guitars ♫♫ (MCA Special Products, 1997)

Slide Crazy! ♫♫♫ (Rykodisc, 1992)

The Ultimate Guitar Survival Guide ♫♫♫ (Relativity, 1993)

Kids

Barrelful of Monkees: Monkees Songs for Kids ♫♫♫ (Kid Rhino, 1996)

Beach Blanket Bash ♫♫♫♫ (Nick at Nite, 1997)

Blue Suede Sneakers: Elvis Songs for Kids! ♫♫ (Lightyear, 1995)

Bug & Friends Sing the Beatles ♫♫ (Kid Rhino, 1995)

A Child's Celebration of Rock 'n' Roll ♫♫♫♫ (Music for Little People, 1996)

Fun Rock! Kooky, Crazy, Classic Rock for Kids ♫♫♫ (Kid Rhino, 1992)

Kid Rock! More Kooky, Crazy, Classic Rock for Kids! ♫♫♫ (Kid Rhino, 1993)

Lullabies for Little Dreamers: Soft Rock Classics ♫♫♫ (Kid Rhino, 1993)

Patio Pool Party ♫♫♫ (Nick at Nite, 1997)

Primary Colors: A Rain Forest Rock Musical ♫♫♫ (Kid Rhino, 1993)

Saturday Morning Cartoons' Greatest Hits ♫♫♫ (MCA, 1995)

Schoolhouse Rock! ♫♫♫♫ (Rhino, 1996)

School House Rock: America Rock ♫♫♫♫ (Rhino, 1996)

Schoolhouse Rock: Grammar Rock ♫♫♫♫ (Rhino, 1996)

Schoolhouse Rock: Multiplication Rock ♫♫♫♫ (Rhino, 1996)

Schoolhouse Rock: Science Rock ♫♫♫♫ (Rhino, 1996)

Schoolhouse Rock! Rocks ♫♫♫ (Lava, 1996)

Schoolhouse Rocks the Vote ♫♫♫ (Rhino, 1998)

Space Ghost's Musical Bar-B-Que ♫♫♫ (Kid Rhino, 1997)

Space Ghost's Surf & Turf ♫♫♫ (Kid Rhino, 1998)

Label Retrospectives

All American Rock 'n' Roll from Fraternity Records (1959–61) ♫♫♫ (Ace, 1994)

Atlantic Records 50 Years: The Gold Anniversary Collection ♫♫♫♫ (Atlantic, 1998)

Atlantic Rock & Roll ♫♫♫ (Box Set) (Atlantic, 1991)

Atlantic's Hit Singles, 1958–1977 ♫♫♫♫ (Atlantic, 1988)

Atlantic's Hit Singles, 1980–1988 ♫♫ (Atlantic, 1988)

The Best of Impact Records ♫♫♫ (Collectables, 1998)

The Best of Loma Records: The Rise and Fall of a 1960s Soul Label ♫♫♫ (Warner Archives, 1995)

The Best of Red Bird/Blue Cat Records ♫♫♫ (Taragon, 1998)

The Best of Spade Records ♫♫ (Collectables, 1990)

The Best of Sue Records ♫♫♫ (Collectables, 1989)

Bloodshot! The Gaity Records Story, Volume 1 ♫♫♫ (Norton, 1994)

Bloodshot! The Gaity Records Story, Volume 2 ♫♫♫ (Norton, 1994)

The Blue Rock Records Story ♫♫♫♫ (Chronicles, 1998)

The Brunswick Years, Vol. 1 ♫♫♫♫ (Brunswick, 1995)

Buy-Product 2: Revelations from 20 Underexposed Artists ♫♫♫♫ (DGC, 1996)

Carnival Time: The Best of Ric Records, Vol. 1 ♫♫ (Rounder, 1988)

Casablanca Records Greatest Hits ♫♫♫ (Casablanca/Mercury, 1996)

The Casablanca Records Story ♫♫♫ (Box Set) (Casablanca/Mercury, 1994)

Chess Rhythm & Roll ♫♫♫♫ (Box Set) (Chess, 1994)

The Chiswick Story: Adventures of an Independent Label, 1975–1982 ♫♫♫ (Chiswick, 1994)

The Class & Rendezvous Story ♫♫♫ (Ace, 1994)

Classic Rock Box ♫♫♫♫ (Chronicles, 1992)

Cleveland International Records, 1977–1983 ♫♫♫ (Cleveland International, 1995)

Colossus Gold ♫♫ (Jerden, 1994)

The Colpix-Dimension Story ♫♫♫ (Rhino, 1994)

Columbia Records Radio Hour ♫♫♫♫ (Columbia, 1996)

Columbia Records Radio Hour, Vol. 2 ♫♫♫♫ (Columbia, 1996)

The Complete Stax-Volt Singles: 1959–1968 ♫♫♫♫ (Box Set) (Atlantic, 1991)

The Complete Stax-Volt Singles, Vol. 2: 1968–1971 ♫♫♫♫ (Box Set) (Atlantic, 1993)

The Complete Stax-Volt Singles, Vol. 3: 1972–1975 ♫♫♫ (Box Set) (Atlantic, 1994)

The Complete Sun Singles Collection ♫♫♫ (Bear Family, 1998)

Crystal Ball Records: The 45 RPM Days, Vol. 1 ♫♫♫ (Dee Jay, 1998)

Crystal Ball Records: The 45 RPM Days, Vol. 2 ♫♫♫ (Dee Jay, 1998)

Crystal Ball Records: The 45 RPM Days, Vol. 3 ♫♫ (Dee Jay, 1998)

DGC Rarities, Vol. 1 ♫♫♫♫ (DGC, 1994)

The Dootone Story ♫♫♫ (Ace, 1994)

Dot Rock 'N' Roll ♫♫♫ (Ace, 1996)

Duke-Peacock's Greatest Hits ♫♫♫♫ (MCA, 1992)

East Side Story, Vol. 3 ♫♫ (ESD, 1997)

East Side Story, Vol. 7 ♫♫♫ (ESD, 1997)

East Side Story, Vol. 8 ♫♫♫ (ESD, 1997)

East Side Story, Vol. 9 ♫♫♫ (ESD, 1997)

East Side Story, Vol. 10 ♫♫♫ (ESD, 1997)

East Side Story, Vol. 11 ♫♫♫ (ESD, 1997)

East Side Story, Vol. 12 ♫♫♫ (ESD, 1997)

Every Great Motown Song: The First 25 Years, Vol. 1 (The 1960s) ♫♫♫ (Motown, 1988)

Every Great Motown Song: The First 25 Years, Vol. 2 (The 1970s) ♫♫♫ (Motown, 1989)

Geffen Vintage '80s, Vol. 1 ♫♫♫ (Geffen, 1995)

HighTone Records: The First 10 Years ♫♫♫ (HighTone, 1994)

The History of Cadence Records, Vol. 1 ♫♫ (Varese Vintage, 1996)

The History of Cadence Records, Vol. 2 ♫♫ (Varese Vintage, 1996)

The History of Dot, Vol. 1 ♫♫♫ (Varese Vintage, 1996)

The History of Dot, Vol. 2 ♫♫♫ (Varese Vintage, 1996)

Hitsville USA: The Motown Singles Collection, 1959–1971 ♫♫♫♫♫ (Motown, 1992)

Hitsville USA II: The Motown Singles Collection, 1972–1991 ♫♫♫♫ (Motown, 1993)

If You're Ready! The Best of Dunwich Records, Vol. 2 ♫♫ (Sundazed, 1994)

Island Records: Acoustic Waves ♫♫♫♫ (Island, 1998)

Island Records: Electric Currents ♫♫♫♫ (Island, 1998)

The Monument Story ♫♫♫♫ (Sony Music Special Products, 1994)

Motown Classic Hits, Volume 1 ♫♫♫ (Motown, 1994)

Motown Classic Hits, Volume 2 ♫♫♫ (Motown, 1994)

Motown Classic Hits, Volume 3 (Motown, 1995)

Motown Classic Hits, Volume 4 (Motown, 1995)

Motown Classic Hits, Volume 5 (Motown, 1995)

Motown 40 Forever (Motown, 1998)

Motown Leading Ladies (Motown, 1995)

Motown Legends, Volume 1 (PolyGram Special Products, 1994)

Motown Legends, Volume 2 (PolyGram Special Products, 1994)

Motown Legends, Volume 3 (PolyGram Special Products, 1994)

Motown Legends, Volume 4 (PolyGram Special Products, 1996)

Motown Legends, Volume 5 (PolyGram Special Products, 1996

Motown Love Songs (Motown, 1995)

Motown Meets the Beatles (Motown, 1995)

Motown Year by Year: The Sound of Young America, 1966 (Motown, 1995)

Motown Year by Year: The Sound of Young America, 1968 (Motown, 1995)

Motown Year by Year: The Sound of Young America, 1969 (Motown, 1995)

Motown Year by Year: The Sound of Young America, 1970 (Motown, 1995)

Motown Year by Year: The Sound of Young America, 1973 (Motown, 1995)

Motown Year by Year: The Sound of Young America, 1975 (Motown, 1995)

Motown Year by Year: The Sound of Young America, 1976 (Motown, 1995)

Motown Year by Year: The Sound of Young America, 1980 (Motown, 1995)

Motown Year by Year: The Sound of Young America, 1982 (Motown, 1995)

Motown Year by Year: The Sound of Young America, 1985 (Motown, 1995)

Motown Year by Year: The Sound of Young America, 1987 (Motown, 1995)

Oh Yeah! The Best of Dunwich Records (Sundazed, 1991)

On the Charts: IRS Records, 1979–1994 (IRS, 1994)

The Quill Records Story: The Best of the Chicago Garage Bands (Collectables, 1997)

The Raging Teens, Vol. 1 (Norton, 1992)

The Raging Teens, Vol. 2 (Norton, 1992)

The Red Bird Story (Charly, 1991)

The Return of the Del-Fi & Donna Story (Del-Fi, 1994)

Rig Rock Deluxe: A Musical Salute to the American Truck Driver (Upstart, 1996)

Rig Rock Juke Box: A Collection of Diesel Only Records (First Warning, 1992)

Rock Around the Clock: The Decca Rock 'n' Roll Collection (Decca/MCA, 1994)

Rubaiyat: Elektra's 40th Anniversary (Elektra, 1990)

16 #1 Hits from the Early '60s (Motown, 1987)

16 #1 Hits from the Late '60s (Motown, 1987)

Spotlite on Sun Records, Vol. 1 (Collectables, 1996)

Spotlite on Sun Records, Vol. 2 (Collectables, 1996)

The Stiff Records Box (Rhino, 1992)

The Sun Kings (Johnny Cash, Jerry Lee Lewis, Carl Perkins) (Rhino, 1998)

Tonnage: A Compilation (Epic Records Group, 1995)

Tonnage 2: A Compilation (Epic Records Group, 1995)

This Are Two Tone (Chrysalis, 1983/1989)

12 #1 Hits from the '70s (Motown, 1991)

Twin/Tone: More Hits from Mid-America (Restless, 1992)

We Got a Party: The Best of Ron Records (Rounder, 1988)

New Wave

Classic MTV: Class of 1983 (Rhino, 1994)

Hard Rock Cafe: New Wave (Hard Rock/Rhino, 1997)

Just Can't Get Enough: New Wave Dance Hits of the '80s (Rhino, 1997)

Just Can't Get Enough: New Wave Hits of the '80s, Volume 1 (Rhino, 1994)

Just Can't Get Enough: New Wave Hits of the '80s, Volume 2 (Rhino, 1994)

Just Can't Get Enough: New Wave Hits of the '80s, Volume 3 (Rhino, 1994)

Just Can't Get Enough: New Wave Hits of the '80s, Volume 4 (Rhino, 1994)

Just Can't Get Enough: New Wave Hits of the '80s, Volume 5 (Rhino, 1994)

Just Can't Get Enough: New Wave Hits of the '80s, Volume 6 (Rhino, 1994)

Just Can't Get Enough: New Wave Hits of the '80s, Volume 7 (Rhino, 1994)

Just Can't Get Enough: New Wave Hits of the '80s, Volume 8 (Rhino, 1994)

Just Can't Get Enough: New Wave Hits of the '80s, Volume 9 (Rhino, 1994)

Just Can't Get Enough: New Wave Hits of the '80s, Volume 10 (Rhino, 1994)

Just Can't Get Enough: New Wave Hits of the '80s, Volume 11 (Rhino, 1995)

Just Can't Get Enough: New Wave Hits of the '80s, Volume 12 (Rhino, 1995)

Just Can't Get Enough: New Wave Hits of the '80s, Volume 13 (Rhino, 1995)

Just Can't Get Enough: New Wave Hits of the '80s, Volume 14 (Rhino, 1995)

Just Can't Get Enough: New Wave Hits of the '80s, Volume 15 (Rhino, 1995)

Smash Alternatives: 14 Classic New Wave Hits (Hip-O, 1996)

The '90s

Alterno-Daze: The '90s (Rebound, 1995)

Best of MTV's 120 Minutes, Vol. 1 (Rhino, 1991)

Best of MTV's 120 Minutes, Vol. 2 (Rhino, 1991)

The Best of the Columbia Records Radio Hour (Columbia, 1994)

The Best of the Columbia Records Radio Hour, Volume 2 (Columbia, 1994)

Bop Boys! (Interhit, 1998)

Billboard Top Modern Rock Tracks: 1990 (Rhino, 1997)

Billboard Top Modern Rock Tracks: 1991 (Rhino, 1997)

Billboard Top Modern Rock Tracks: 1992 (Rhino, 1997)

The Concert for the Rock and Roll Hall of Fame (Columbia, 1996)

Live from 6A: Great Musical Performances from Late Night with Conan O'Brien (Mercury, 1997)

Live on Letterman: Music from the Late Show (Reprise, 1997)

1996 Grammy Nominees (Sony, 1996)

1997 Grammy Nominees (PolyGram, 1997)

1998 Grammy Nominees (MCA, 1998)

Poptopia! Power Pop Classics of the '90s (Rhino, 1997)

VH1: Crossroads (Atlantic, 1996)

Woodstock 94 (A&M, 1994)

Yellow Pills: The Best of American Pop! Volume 1 (Big Deal, 1993)

Yellow Pills: The Best of American Pop! Volume 2 (Big Deal, 1994)

Yellow Pills, Volume 3 (Big Deal, 1995)

Yellow Pills, Volume 4 (Big Deal, 1997)

Novelty

A Box of Funny Wacky Favorites (Dominion, 1998)

Cra-a-zy Hits 🎵🎵 (MCA Special Products, 1989)

Dr. Demento 20th Anniversary Collection: The Greatest Novelty Records of All Time 🎵🎵🎵🎵 (Rhino, 1991)

Dr. Demento 25th Anniversary Collection: More of the Greatest Novelty Records of All Time 🎵🎵🎵🎵 (Rhino, 1995)

Dumb Ditties 🎵🎵 (K-Tel, 1993)

Golden Throats 4: Celebrities Butcher Songs of the Beatles 🎵🎵🎵🎵 (Rhino, 1997)

Goofy Greats 🎵🎵 (K-Tel, 1992)

Lounge-A-Palooza 🎵🎵🎵 (Hollywood, 1997)

16 Magazine: Who's Your Fave Rave? 🎵🎵🎵🎵 (Rhino, 1997)

Spy Magazine Presents, Vol. 1: Spy Music 🎵🎵🎵 (Rhino, 1994)

Spy Magazine Presents, Vol. 2, White Men Can't Wrap 🎵🎵🎵 (Rhino, 1994)

Wild & Crazy Tunes 🎵🎵 (Priority 1994)

Party on, Dudes
Frat Rock 🎵🎵🎵🎵 (Rhino, 1987)

Grandson of Frat Rock 🎵🎵🎵 (Rhino, 1991)

More Party Classics 🎵🎵🎵 (Warner Special Products, 1987)

'70s Party Classics 🎵🎵 (Rhino, 1998)

'70s Party Killers 🎵🎵 (Rhino, 1998)

Son of Frat Rock 🎵🎵🎵🎵 (Rhino, 1988)

Punk
Best of Punk Rock 1 🎵🎵🎵 (Priority, 1993)

Best of Punk Rock 2 🎵🎵 (Priority, 1993)

Best of Punk Rock 3 🎵🎵 (Priority, 1993)

Burning Ambition: History of Punk 1 🎵🎵🎵 (Cleopatra, 1996)

Burning Ambition: History of Punk 2 🎵🎵🎵 (Cleopatra, 1996)

Burning Ambition: History of Punk 3 🎵🎵 (Cleopatra, 1997)

Cupid's Revenge: The World's Most Romantic Punk Songs 🎵🎵🎵 (Continuum, 1994)

D.I.Y.: Anarchy in the U.K.: U.K. Punk I (1976–77) 🎵🎵🎵🎵 (Rhino, 1993)

D.I.Y.: Blank Generation: The New York Scene (1975–78) 🎵🎵🎵🎵 (Rhino, 1993)

D.I.Y.: Mass. Ave.: The Boston Scene (1979–83) 🎵🎵🎵🎵 (Rhino, 1993)

D.I.Y.: The Modern World: U.K. Punk II (1977–78) 🎵🎵🎵🎵 (Rhino, 1993)

D.I.Y.: We're Desperate: The L.A. Scene (1976–79) 🎵🎵🎵🎵 (Rhino, 1993)

Faster & Louder: Hardcore Punk, Vol. 1 🎵🎵🎵 (Rhino, 1993)

Faster & Louder: Hardcore Punk, Vol. 2 🎵🎵🎵 (Rhino, 1993)

Generations 1: A Punk Look at Human Rights 🎵🎵 (ARK, 1997)

Guns Classics: The Greatest Punks All Stars 🎵🎵🎵🎵 (Century, 1994)

Live at CBGB's 🎵🎵🎵 (Atlantic, 1976/1994)

Live from the Masque: Forming 🎵🎵🎵 (Year One, 1996)

Live from the Masque: Dicks Fight Banks Hate 🎵🎵🎵 (Year One, 1996)

Live from the Masque: We Can Do Do What We Wanna Do 🎵🎵🎵🎵 (Year One, 1996)

Max's Kansas City, 1976 🎵🎵 (Roir, 1996)

Notes from the Underground 1 🎵🎵🎵 (Priority, 1995)

Notes from the Underground 2 🎵🎵🎵 (Priority, 1995)

Punk: Lost & Found 🎵 (Shanachie, 1996)

Punk-O-Rama 🎵🎵🎵 (Epitaph, 1994)

Punk University 🎵🎵🎵 (Oglio, 1994)

Punk University, Vol. 2 🎵🎵🎵 (Oglio, 1995)

Punk You: Music for the Discerning Slacker, Vol. 1 🎵🎵🎵🎵 (Rhino, 1995)

Real Punk 🎵 (Cleopatra, 1996)

Reggae, Ska, and Other Island Musics
Live from Planet Ska 🎵🎵🎵🎵 (Music Club, 1998)

Ranking & Skanking: The Best of Punky Reggae 🎵🎵🎵 (Rhino, 1995)

Roots of Reggae, Volume One: Ska 🎵🎵🎵🎵 (Rhino, 1996)

Roots of Reggae, Volume Two: Rock Steady 🎵🎵🎵🎵 (Rhino, 1996)

Ska After Ska After Ska 🎵🎵🎵🎵 (Heartbeat, 1998)

Ska Down Her Way: Women of Ska 🎵🎵🎵🎵 (Shanachie, 1997)

The Ska Parade: Runnin' Naked Through the Cornfield 🎵🎵🎵 (A toY, 1996)

Spliff Relief 🎵🎵🎵 (Mesa, 1994)

Rockabilly
Automatic Bop: 31 Rockabilly Burners 🎵🎵🎵 (Collector, 1996)

Best of Lin/Kliff: Rockabilly 🎵🎵 (Collectables, 1994)

Best of Sun Rockabilly, Vol. 1 🎵🎵🎵 (Charly, 1991)

Best of Sun Rockabilly, Vol. 2 🎵🎵🎵 (Charly, 1992)

Cat Music 🎵🎵 (HighTone, 1998)

El Primitivo American Rock 'N' Roll & Rockabilly 🎵🎵 (Ace, 1994)

Essential Sun Rockabilly 🎵🎵🎵🎵 (Charly, 1995)

Essential Sun Rockabilly, Vol. 2 🎵🎵🎵 (Charly, 1995)

Essential Sun Rockabilly, Vol. 3 🎵🎵🎵🎵 (Charly, 1997)

Essential Sun Rockabilly, Vol. 5 🎵🎵🎵 (Charly, 1998)

Fifties Rockabilly Fever 🎵🎵🎵 (Ace, 1992)

Get Hot or Go Home: Vintage RCA Rockabilly, '56–'59 🎵🎵🎵 (CMF, 1990)

Let's Bop! Sun Rockabilly, Volume 1 🎵🎵🎵🎵 (AVI, 1995)

Memphis Rocks: Rockabilly in Memphis, 1954–1968 🎵🎵🎵 (Smithsonian/Folkways, 1992)

Miami Rockabilly 🎵🎵 (Ace, 1998)

Pushing the Norton: The Ace Cafe Compilation 🎵🎵🎵 (Norton, 1995)

Rarest Rockabilly & Hillbilly Boogie: The Best of Ace Rockabilly 🎵🎵🎵 (Ace, 1991)

Rock Baby Rock It! Sun Rockabilly, Volume 2 🎵🎵🎵🎵 (AVI, 1995)

Rock Boppin' Baby! Sun Rockabilly, Volume 3 🎵🎵🎵 (AVI, 1996)

Rock This Town: Rockabilly Hits, Vol. 1 🎵🎵🎵🎵 (Rhino, 1991)

Rock This Town: Rockabilly Hits, Vol. 2 🎵🎵🎵 (Rhino, 1991)

Rockabilly 🎵🎵🎵 (Life, Times, & Music, 1996)

Rockabilly Psychosis & the Garage Disease 🎵🎵🎵 (Big Beat, 1994)

Rockabilly Riot 🎵🎵🎵 (K-Tel, 1995)

Rockabilly Shakedown 🎵🎵 (Buffalo Bop, 1998)

Rockabilly Shakeout 🎵🎵🎵 (Ace, 1992)

Rockabilly Stars, Vol. 1 🎵🎵🎵 (Epic, 1981/Collectors, 1993)

Rockabilly Stars, Vol. 2 🎵🎵🎵 (Epic, 1981/Collectors, 1993)

Rockabilly Stars, Vol. 3 🎵🎵🎵 (Epic, 1982/Collectors, 1996)

Rockin' in the Farmhouse: Original Rockabilly and Chicken Bop, Vol. 2 🎵🎵 (Sundazed, 1992)

The Sun Records Collection 🎵🎵🎵🎵 (Rhino, 1994)

Sun Rockabilly: Classic Recordings 🎵🎵🎵 (Rounder, 1995)

Sun Singles, Vol. 1 🎵🎵🎵🎵 (Bear Family, 1994)

Sun Singles, Vol. 2 🎵🎵🎵🎵 (Bear Family, 1995)

Sun Singles, Vol. 3 🎵🎵🎵🎵 (Bear Family, 1996)

Sun Singles, Vol. 4 🎵🎵🎵🎵 (Bear Family, 1997)

The Sun Story 🎵🎵🎵🎵🎵 (Rhino, 1987)

That'll Flat Git It!, Vol. 1 🎵🎵🎵🎵 (Bear Family, 1992)

That'll Flat Git It!, Vol. 2 🎵🎵🎵🎵 (Bear Family, 1992)

That'll Flat Git It!, Vol. 3 🎵🎵🎵 (Bear Family, 1992)

That'll Flat Git It!, Vol. 4 🎵🎵 (Bear Family, 1994)

That'll Flat Git It!, Vol. 5 🎵🎵 (Bear Family, 1994/1997)

That'll Flat Git It!, Vol. 6 🎵🎵🎵 (Bear Family, 1994)

That'll Flat Git It!, Vol. 7 🎵🎵🎵 (Bear Family, 1996)

That'll Flat Git It!, Vol. 8 🎵🎵 (Bear Family, 1996)

That'll Flat Git It!, Vol. 12 🎵🎵 (Bear Family, 1997)

That'll Flat Git It!, Vol. 14 🎵🎵 (Bear Family, 1997)

Very Best of Sun Rockabilly 🎵🎵🎵🎵 (Charly, 1997)

Wail Man Wail! Original Rockabilly & Chicken Bop, Vol. 3 🎵🎵 (Sundazed, 1993)

Wild Men Ride Wild Guitars: Original Rockabilly & Chicken Bop, Vol.1 🎵🎵🎵 (Sundazed, 1990)

The '70s

Alive Down South 🎵🎵🎵 (White Clay, 1997)

Behind Closed Doors: '70s Swingers 🎵🎵 (Rhino, 1997)

The Best of the '70s Rock Chart Toppers 🎵🎵🎵 (Priority, 1996)

The Best of the '70s Rock Chart Toppers, Volume Two 🎵🎵 (Priority, 1997)

CBS Classics: Pop Classics of the '70s 🎵🎵 (Columbia, 1989)

Chart Toppers: Dance Hits of the '70s 🎵🎵 (Priority, 1998)

Chart Toppers: Rock Hits of the '70s 🎵🎵🎵 (Priority, 1998)

Class Reunion '71: Greatest Hits of 1971 🎵🎵🎵 (Rebound, 1996)

Class Reunion '74: Greatest Hits of 1974 🎵🎵 (Rebound, 1994)

Class Reunion '76: Greatest Hits of 1976 🎵🎵 (Rebound, 1996)

Class Reunion '79: Greatest Hits of 1979 🎵🎵 (Rebound, 1996)

Classic Rock, Vol. 5: Glitter Bands 🎵🎵 (Priority, 1993)

Collector's Essentials, Vol. 2: The '70s 🎵🎵 (Varese Vintage, 1996)

D.I.Y.: Come Out and Play: American Power Pop (1975–78) 🎵🎵🎵 (Rhino, 1993)

D.I.Y.: Shake It Up: American Power Pop II (1978–80) 🎵🎵🎵 (Rhino, 1993)

D.I.Y.: Starry Eyes: UK Pop II (1978–79) 🎵🎵🎵 (Rhino, 1993)

D.I.Y.: Teenage Kicks: UK Pop (1976–79) 🎵🎵🎵 (Rhino, 1993)

8-Track Flashback: The One-Hit Wonders 🎵🎵🎵 (Rhino, 1997)

18 Free and Easy Hits from the '70s 🎵🎵🎵 (JCI, 1995)

18 Rock Classics 🎵🎵 (JCI, 1994)

18 Screamers from the '70s 🎵🎵🎵 (JCI, 1995)

Greatest Tour Bands Ever Recorded 🎵🎵 (MCA Special Products, 1996)

Hard Rock Cafe: Classic Rock 🎵🎵🎵 (Rhino, 1997)

Hard Rock Essentials: The '70s 🎵🎵🎵 (Rebound, 1994)

Hard Rockin' '70s 🎵🎵🎵 (Priority, 1991)

Harley-Davidson: Road Songs 🎵🎵🎵🎵 (The Right Stuff, 1994)

Have a Nice Decade: The '70s Pop Culture Box 🎵🎵🎵 (Rhino, 1998)

I Love Rock 'n' Roll: Hits of the '70s, Volume Three 🎵🎵🎵 (Priority, 1996)

Listen to the Music: '70s Male Singer/Songwriters 🎵🎵🎵 (Rhino, 1996)

Listen to the Music: The '70s California Sound 🎵🎵🎵 (Rhino, 1996)

Message to Love: The Isle of Wight Festival 🎵🎵🎵🎵 (Legacy, 1996)

Nipper's Greatest Hits: The '70s, Vol. 1 🎵🎵 (RCA, 1988)

#1 Hits, 1975–1979 🎵🎵🎵 (GNP/Crescendo, 1996)

#1 Hits, 1980–1984 🎵🎵🎵 (GNP/Crescendo, 1995)

Only Dance, 1970–1974 🎵🎵🎵 (Esx, 1996)

Only Rock 'N' Roll, 1970–1974 🎵🎵🎵 (JCI, 1994)

Only Rock 'N' Roll, 1970–1974: #1 Radio Hits 🎵🎵🎵 (JCI, 1996)

Poptopia! Power Pop Classics of the '70s 🎵🎵🎵 (Rhino, 1997)

Remasterpieces 🎵🎵🎵🎵 (Atlantic, 1994)

Rock for the Ages 🎵🎵🎵 (Hip-O, 1997)

Rock of the '70s, Vol. 1 🎵🎵🎵 (DCC, 1992)

Rock of the '70s, Vol. 2 🎵🎵 (DCC, 1992)

Rock of the '70s, Vol. 4 🎵🎵 (DCC, 1992)

Rock of the '70s, Vol. 5 🎵🎵🎵 (DCC, 1992)

Rock of the '70s, Volume 1 🎵🎵 (CEMA Special Products, 1995)

Rockin' Down the Highway 🎵🎵 (K-Tel, 1997)

Rockin' '70s 🎵🎵 (BMG, 1997)

Rockin' '70s 🎵🎵🎵 (Eclipse, 1997)

Rockin' '70s 🎵🎵 (MCA Special Products, 1996)

Rockin' '70s, Vol. 2 🎵🎵 (MCA Special Products, 1996)

'70s Biggest Hits 🎵🎵🎵 (MCA Special Products, 1997)

The '70s Come Alive Again 🎵🎵 (MCA Special Products, 1995)

'70s Folk Rock 🎵🎵🎵 (K-Tel, 1995)

'70s Greatest Rock Hits, Vol. 1: Hard 'N' Heavy 🎵🎵 (Priority, 1991)

'70s Greatest Rock Hits, Vol. 3: High Times 🎵 (Priority, 1991)

'70s Greatest Rock Hits, Vol. 5: Kickin' Back 🎵 (Priority, 1991)

'70s Greatest Rock Hits, Vol. 6: FM Hits 🎵🎵 (Priority, 1991)

'70s Greatest Rock Hits, Vol. 9: #1 Hits 🎵🎵 (Priority, 1971)

'70s Greatest Rock Hits, Vol. 10: Hitchin' a Ride 🎵🎵 (Priority, 1991)

'70s Greatest Rock Hits, Vol. 11: Heavy Hitters 🎵🎵🎵 (Priority, 1992)

'70s Greatest Rock Hits, Vol. 14: Kings of Rock 🎵🎵 (Priority, 1992)

'70s Heavy Hitters: Arena Rockers 1970–1974 🎵🎵🎵 (K-Tel, 1998)

'70s Heavy Hitters: Arena Rockers, 1975–1979 🎵🎵🎵 (K-Tel, 1998)

'70s Heavy Hitters: Summer of Love 🎵🎵 (K-Tel, 1997)

'70s Hit(s) Back 🎵🎵 (Hip-O, 1998)

'70s Hits: Great Records of the Decade, Vol. 1 **woof!** (Curb, 1990)

'70s Hits: Great Records of the Decade, Vol. 2 🎵🎵 (Curb, 1990)

'70s Teen Heart-Throbs 🎵 (K-Tel, 1995)

Super Hits of the '70s: Have a Nice Day, Vol. 1 🎵🎵🎵 (Rhino, 1990)

Super Hits of the '70s: Have a Nice Day, Vol. 2 🎵🎵 (Rhino, 1990)

Super Hits of the '70s: Have a Nice Day, Vol. 3 🎵🎵 (Rhino, 1990)

Super Hits of the '70s: Have a Nice Day, Vol. 4 🎵🎵 (Rhino, 1990)

Super Hits of the '70s: Have a Nice Day, Vol. 5 🎵🎵 (Rhino, 1990)

Super Hits of the '70s: Have a Nice Day, Vol. 6 🎵🎵 (Rhino, 1990)

Super Hits of the '70s: Have a Nice Day, Vol. 7 🎵 (Rhino, 1990)

Super Hits of the '70s: Have a Nice Day, Vol. 8 🎵🎵 (Rhino, 1990)

Super Hits of the '70s: Have a Nice Day, Vol. 9 🎵🎵 (Rhino, 1990)

Super Hits of the '70s: Have a Nice Day, Vol. 10 🎵🎵🎵 (Rhino, 1993)

Super Hits of the '70s: Have a Nice Day, Vol. 11 🎵🎵🎵 (Rhino, 1990)

Super Hits of the '70s: Have a Nice Day, Vol. 12 🎵🎵 (Rhino, 1990)

Super Hits of the '70s: Have a Nice Day, Vol. 13 🎵🎵 (Rhino, 1990)

Super Hits of the '70s: Have a Nice Day, Vol. 14 🎵🎵 (Rhino, 1990)

Super Hits of the '70s: Have a Nice Day, Vol. 15 🎵🎵 (Rhino, 1990)

Super Hits of the '70s: Have a Nice Day, Vol. 16 🎵🎵 (Rhino, 1993)

Super Hits of the '70s: Have a Nice Day, Vol. 17 🎵🎵🎵 (Rhino, 1993)

Super Hits of the '70s: Have a Nice Day, Vol. 18 🎵🎵🎵 (Rhino, 1993)

Super Hits of the '70s: Have a Nice Day, Vol. 19 🎵🎵 (Rhino, 1993)

Super Hits of the '70s: Have a Nice Day, Vol. 20 🎵🎵 (Rhino, 1993)

Super Hits of the '70s: Have a Nice Day, Vol. 21 𝄞𝄞 (Rhino, 1993)

Super Hits of the '70s: Have a Nice Day, Vol. 22 𝄞𝄞 (Rhino, 1993)

Super Hits of the '70s: Have a Nice Day, Vol. 23 𝄞𝄞 (Rhino, 1996)

Super Hits of the '70s: Have a Nice Day, Vol. 24 𝄞𝄞 (Rhino, 1996)

Super Hits of the '70s: Have a Nice Day, Vol. 25 𝄞 (Rhino, 1996)

Ultimate Rock 'n' Roll Collection 𝄞𝄞𝄞𝄞 (Epic/Legacy, 1996)

Under My Wheels: 12 Road-Trippin' Tracks 𝄞𝄞 (Hip-O, 1997)

WCBS-FM 25th Anniversary: Best of the '70s 𝄞𝄞𝄞 (Collectables, 1997)

WDAS-FM Philadelphia: Hits of the '70s 𝄞𝄞𝄞 (Collectables, 1996)

WODS-FM 10th Anniversary: Best of the '70s 𝄞𝄞𝄞 (Collectables, 1997)

WOGL-FM 10th Anniversary: Best of the '70s 𝄞𝄞𝄞 (Collectables, 1997)

The '60s

Best of Folk Rock 𝄞𝄞𝄞 (K-Tel, 1995)

Biggest Summer Hits 𝄞𝄞𝄞 (MCA Special Products, 1996)

The Brill Building Sound 𝄞𝄞𝄞𝄞 (Era, 1993)

Bubblegum Classics, Volume 1 𝄞𝄞𝄞𝄞 (Varese Vintage, 1995)

Bubblegum Classics, Volume 2 𝄞𝄞𝄞 (Varese Vintage, 1995)

Bubblegum Classics, Volume 3 𝄞𝄞𝄞 (Varese Vintage, 1996)

CBS Classics: Pop Classics of the '60s 𝄞𝄞 (Columbia, 1989)

Chart Busters: All-Time AM/FM Hits 𝄞 (Laserlight, 1994)

Chicago Garage Band Greats: The Best of Rembrandt Records, 1966–69 𝄞𝄞 (Collectables, 1993)

The Cicadelic '60s, Vol. 1 𝄞𝄞 (Collectables, 1993)

The Cicadelic '60s, Vol. 2 𝄞𝄞 (Collectables, 1993)

The Cicadelic '60s, Vol. 3 𝄞𝄞 (Collectables, 1993)

The Cicadelic '60s, Vol. 4 𝄞𝄞 (Collectables, 1993)

The Cicadelic '60s, Vol. 5 𝄞 (Collectables, 1994)

The Cicadelic '60s, Vol. 6 𝄞 (Collectables, 1994)

The Cicadelic '60s, Vol. 7 𝄞𝄞 (Collectables, 1997)

Collector's Essentials, Vol. 1: The '60s 𝄞𝄞𝄞 (Varese Vintage, 1996)

Dick Bartley Presents: One Hit Wonders of the '60s, Vol. 1 𝄞𝄞 (Rhino, 1990/1993)

Dick Bartley Presents: One Hit Wonders of the '60s, Vol. 2 𝄞𝄞 (Rhino, 1990)

Even More Nuggets 𝄞𝄞𝄞 (Rhino, 1989)

Feelin' Groovy: 12 Breezy Rock Hits of the '60s 𝄞𝄞𝄞 (Buddah, 1996)

Fillmore: The Last Days 𝄞𝄞𝄞 (Epic/Associated/Legacy, 1972)

The Golden Age of Underground Radio 𝄞𝄞𝄞 (DCC, 1989)

Greatest Hits of the '60s 𝄞𝄞𝄞 (Sony Music Special Products, 1996)

Happy Days of Rock 'n' Roll 𝄞𝄞𝄞 (Madacy, 1998)

Hard Rock Essentials: The '60s 𝄞𝄞𝄞 (Rebound, 1994)

Highs of the '60s: R&R Classics in Digital 𝄞𝄞𝄞 (Warner Special Products, 1986)

History of Connecticut Garage Bands, Vol. 1 𝄞𝄞 (Collectables, 1995)

History of Texas Garage Bands, Vol. 3: The AOK Story 𝄞𝄞 (Collectables, 1995)

History of Texas Garage Bands, Vol. 4: West Texas Rarities 𝄞𝄞 (Collectables, 1995)

History of Texas Garage Bands, Vol. 5: Corpus Christi 𝄞 (Collectables, 1995)

History of Texas Garage Bands, Vol. 6: Psychedelic Flower Power 𝄞𝄞 (Collectables, 1995)

Hits of the '60s 𝄞𝄞 (CEMA Special Products, 1992)

Hooked on the '60s **woof!** (K-Tel, 1994)

I Feel Good 𝄞𝄞𝄞 (Eclipse, 1996)

I Love Rock & Roll: Hits of the '60s, Volume Two 𝄞𝄞𝄞𝄞 (Priority, 1996)

Land of a Thousand Dances 𝄞𝄞𝄞 (Dominion, 1996)

Let's Twist! 𝄞𝄞 (K-Tel, 1994)

Monster Rock 'N' Roll Show 𝄞𝄞𝄞 (DCC, 1990)

More Nuggets 𝄞𝄞𝄞 (Rhino, 1987)

Near #1 Hits: The Magic Touch 𝄞𝄞 (Eclipse, 1995)

Nuggets: Classics from the Psychedelic '60s 𝄞𝄞𝄞𝄞 (Rhino, 1986)

Nuggets: Original Artyfacts from the First Psychedelic Era, 1965–1968 𝄞𝄞𝄞𝄞 (Rhino, 1998)

Number One Hits of the '60s 𝄞𝄞 (Rebound, 1993)

Only Rock 'N' Roll, 1960–1964 𝄞𝄞𝄞 (JCI, 1994)

Only Rock 'N' Roll, 1960–1964: #1 Radio Hits 𝄞𝄞𝄞 (JCI, 1996)

Only Rock 'N' Roll, 1964–1969 𝄞𝄞𝄞 (JCI, 1994)

Only Rock 'N' Roll, 1964–1969: #1 Radio Hits 𝄞𝄞𝄞 (JCI, 1996)

Pittsburgh: Rhythm & Blues/Rock & Roll (1959–1963) 𝄞𝄞 (Alanna, 1993)

Psychedelic Mind Trip 𝄞𝄞𝄞 (K-Tel, 1993)

Psychedelic Moods, Vol. II 𝄞𝄞 (Collectables, 1993)

Psychedelic Pop: 12 Spaced-Out '60s Classics 𝄞𝄞𝄞𝄞 (Buddah, 1996)

Quick Before They Catch Us: Pop Era, Vol. 1 𝄞𝄞 (Collectables, 1994)

Rhythm of the Rain 𝄞𝄞𝄞𝄞 (Varese Vintage, 1994)

Rock Around the Oldies, Vol. 1 𝄞𝄞𝄞 (MCA Special Products, 1994)

Rock Around the Oldies, Vol. 2 𝄞𝄞𝄞 (MCA Special Products, 1994)

Rock Around the Oldies, Vol. 3 𝄞𝄞𝄞 (MCA Special Products, 1995)

Rock Around the Oldies, Vol. 4 𝄞𝄞 (MCA Special Products, 1995)

Rock 'n' Roll Relix, 1966–67 𝄞𝄞𝄞 (Eclipse, 1997)

Rockin' '60s 𝄞𝄞𝄞 (BMG Special Products, 1997)

Sensational '60s, Vol. 1 𝄞𝄞𝄞 (Dominion, 1993)

Sensational '60s, Vol. 2 𝄞𝄞𝄞 (Dominion, 1993)

Sensational '60s, Vol. 3 𝄞𝄞𝄞 (Dominion, 1993)

Sensational '60s, Vol. 4 𝄞𝄞𝄞 (Dominion, 1993)

Sensational '60s, Vol. 5 𝄞𝄞𝄞 (Dominion, 1994)

'60s Hits: Great Records of the Decade, Vol. 1 𝄞𝄞 (Curb, 1990)

'60s Pop, Volume 1: Those Were the Days 𝄞𝄞𝄞 (Dominion, 1997)

'60s Rock Bands: Wild Thing 𝄞𝄞𝄞𝄞 (Dominion, 1997)

'60s Rock-N-Roll, Volume 1: It's My Party 𝄞𝄞𝄞 (Dominion, 1997)

Sixties Rule! Chapter One 𝄞𝄞𝄞𝄞 (One Way, 1991)

Sixties Rule! Chapter Two 𝄞𝄞𝄞 (One Way, 1993)

Songs of Protest 𝄞𝄞𝄞𝄞 (Rhino, 1991)

Stoned Sixties 𝄞𝄞𝄞 (Collectables, 1995)

The Sullivan Years: Rock Classics 𝄞𝄞𝄞 (TVT, 1991)

The Sullivan Years: Sixties Rock 𝄞𝄞𝄞 (TVT, 1990)

The Sullivan Years: The Mod Sound 𝄞𝄞𝄞 (TVT, 1990)

Summer of Love, Vol. 1: Tune In: Good Times & Love Vibrations 𝄞𝄞𝄞𝄞 (Rhino, 1987/1992)

Summer of Love, Vol. 2: Mind Expansion & Signs of the Times 𝄞𝄞𝄞 (Rhino, 1987/1992)

Sun & Surf, Cars & Guitars 𝄞𝄞𝄞 (Del-Fi, 1994)

Sunshine Days: Pop Classics of the '60s, Vol. 1 𝄞𝄞𝄞 (Varese Sarabande, 1997)

Sunshine Days: Pop Classics of the '60s, Vol. 2 𝄞𝄞𝄞 (Varese Sarabande, 1997)

Sunshine Days: Pop Classics of the '60s, Vol. 3 𝄞𝄞 (Varese Sarabande, 1997)

Watch Your Step: The Beat Era, Vol. 1 (Collectables, 1994)

WCBS FM-101 History of Rock: The '60s, Pt. 1 (Collectables, 1990)

WCBS FM-101 History of Rock: The '60s, Pt. 2 (Collectables, 1990)

WCBS FM-101 History of Rock: The '60s, Pt. 3 (Collectables, 1990)

WCBS FM-101 History of Rock: The '60s, Pt. 4 (Collectables, 1990)

WCBS FM-101 History of Rock: The '60s, Pt. 5 (Collectables, 1990)

WCBS-FM 25th Anniversary: Best of the '60s (Collectables, 1997)

WODS-FM 10th Anniversary: Best of the '60s (Collectables, 1997)

WOGL-FM 10th Anniversary: Best of the '60s (Collectables, 1997)

Woodstock Diary (Atlantic, 1994)

Woodstock: 3 Days of Peace and Music: The 25th Anniversary Collection (Atlantic, 1994)

Yummy Yummy: Best of Bubble Gum Music (K-Tel, 1995)

Soft Rock

Best of Love: 16 Great Soft Rock Hits (Madacy, 1998)

Billboard Soft Rock Hits: 1970 (Rhino, 1997)

Billboard Soft Rock Hits: 1971 (Rhino, 1997)

Billboard Soft Rock Hits: 1972 (Rhino, 1997)

Billboard Soft Rock Hits: 1973 (Rhino, 1997)

Billboard Soft Rock Hits: 1974 (Rhino, 1997)

Chart Toppers: Romantic Hits of the '70s (Priority, 1998)

Chart Toppers: Romantic Hits of the '80s (Priority, 1998)

'80s Greatest Rock Hits 6: Agony & Ecstasy (Priority, 1993)

'80s Greatest Rock Hits 7: Light & Easy (Priority, 1993)

'80s Greatest Rock Hits 13: Soft Sounds (Priority, 1994)

The Glory of Love: '50s Sweet & Soulful Love Songs (Hip-O, 1997)

The Glory of Love: '60s Sweet & Soulful Love Songs (Hip-O, 1997)

The Glory of Love: '70s Sweet & Soulful Love Songs (Hip-O, 1997)

The Glory of Love: '80s Sweet & Soulful Love Songs (Hip-O, 1997)

God, Love and Rock & Roll (Varese Vintage, 1998)

Have A Nice Night: Romantic Hits of the '70s (Rhino, 1998)

Heartthrob Hits (Rhino, 1998)

Hot & Sexy 3: Love & Romance (Priority, 1995)

Keep on Loving You (Columbia Special Products, 1993)

Mellow Rock (MCA Special Products, 1997)

Mellow Rock Hits of the '70s: Summer Breeze (Rhino, 1997)

Mellow Rock Hits of the '70s: Sundown (Rhino, 1997)

Mellow Rock Hits of the '70s: Ventura Highway (Rhino, 1997)

Only Love, 1955–1959 (Esx, 1996)

Only Love, 1965–1969 (JCI, 1996)

Only Love, 1985–1989 (JCI, 1996)

Power of Love: 16 Great Soft Rock Hits (Madacy, 1996)

Retro Lunchbox: Gooey Love Songs (Intersound, 1997)

The Slow Jams: The '60s, Volume 1 (The Right Stuff, 1993)

The Slow Jams: The '60s, Volume 2 (The Right Stuff, 1993)

The Slow Jams: The '60s, Volume 3 (The Right Stuff, 1993)

The Slow Jams: The '60s, Volume 4 (The Right Stuff, 1995)

The Slow Jams: The '70s, Volume 1 (The Right Stuff, 1993)

The Slow Jams: The '70s, Volume 2 (The Right Stuff, 1994)

The Slow Jams: The '70s, Volume 3 (The Right Stuff, 1994)

The Slow Jams: The '70s, Volume 4 (The Right Stuff, 1995)

Thinking About You: A Collection of Modern Love Songs (Hip-O, 1996)

WCBS FM-101 History of Rock: For Lovers Only, Pt. 1 (Collectables, 1993)

WCBS FM-101 History of Rock: For Lovers Only, Pt. 2 (Collectables, 1993)

WCBS FM-101 History of Rock: For Lovers Only, Pt. 3 (Collectables, 1993)

WCBS FM-101 History of Rock: For Lovers Only, Pt. 4 (Collectables, 1993)

Special Occasions

Bar-B-Que Soul-A-Bration! (Rhino, 1998)

Drew's Famous Fang-Tastic Grooves (Turn up the Music, 1997)

Elvira Presents Monster Hits (Rhino, 1994)

Halloween Hits (Rhino, 1991)

Halloween Party Music (Turn up the Music, 1996)

Just Can't Get Enough: New Wave Halloween (Rhino, 1998)

Modern Bride Presents the Wedding Album (Columbia, 1998)

Rock & Rollin' Wedding Songs, Vol. 1 (Rhino, 1992)

Rock & Rollin' Wedding Songs, Vol. 2 (Rhino, 1992)

Sports

Baseball's Greatest Hits, Vol. 1 (Rhino, 1989)

Baseball's Greatest Hits, Let's Play II (Rhino, 1990)

Basketball's Greatest Hoops Hits (Rhino, 1998)

ESPN Presents Jock Jams, Volume 1 (Tommy Boy, 1995)

ESPN Presents Jock Jams, Volume 2 (Tommy Boy, 1996)

ESPN Presents Jock Jams, Volume 3 (Tommy Boy, 1998)

ESPN Presents Jock Rock, Volume 1 (Tommy Boy, 1994)

ESPN Presents Jock Rock, Volume 2 (Tommy Boy, 1995)

Greatest Sports Rock and Jams (Cold Front, 1997)

Greatest Sports Rock and Jams, Volume 2 (Cold Front, 1997)

Greatest Sports Rock and Jams, Volume 3 (Cold Front, 1998)

NBA at 50: A Musical Celebration (Mercury, 1996)

Wrestlemania: The Album (RCA, 1993)

WWF Full Metal: The Album (Edel America, 1996)

WWF: The Music, Volume 2 **woof!** (Edel America, 1997)

Surf

Best of the Hot Rod Hits (CEMA Special Products, 1992)

Big Surf Hits (Del-Fi, 1994)

Bustin' Surfboards: 14 Smash Hits (GNP/Crescendo, 1989)

California Beach Music (K-Tel, 1995)

California USA (Columbia Special Products, 1992)

Cowabunga! The Surf Box (Box Set) (Rhino, 1996)

Hard Rock Records: Surf (Rhino/Hard Rock Records, 1998)

Hot Rod City (Sundazed, 1995)

Jenny McCarthy's Surfin' Safari (I.D., 1996)

Kahuna Classics: A Collection of Surf Music (K-Tel, 1997)

KFWB's Battle of the Surf Bands (Del-Fi, 1994)

Monster Summer Hits: Wild Surf (Capitol/EMI, 1991/1996)

More Surf Legends (and Rumors) (Garland, 1997)

Pulp Surfin' (Del-Fi, 1995)

Revenge of the Surf Instrumentals (MCA, 1995)

Rock Don't Run (Spinout, 1996)

Rock N Roll Beach Party (Madacy, 1997)

Surf & Drag, Volume 2 (Sundazed, 1993)

Surf Legends (and Rumors) (Garland, 1989)

Surf War: The Battle of the Surf Groups (Sundazed, 1995)

Surf's up at Banzai Pipline (Sundazed, 1995)

Wax, Board and Woodie (Varese Sarabande, 1996)

Tribute Albums

Adios Amigo: A Tribute to Arthur Alexander (Razor & Tie, 1994)

Back to the Streets: Celebrating the Music of Don Covay (Shanachie, 1993)

Basskraft: A Tribute to Kraftwerk N/A (Pandisc, 1998)

Beat the Retreat: Songs by Richard Thompson (Capitol, 1994)

Beatlejuice: A Big Apple Tribute to the Beatles (Raven/Palmetto, 1995)

Bespoke Songs, Lost Dogs, Detours & Rendezvous: Songs of Elvis Costello (Rhino, 1998)

Black on White: Great R&B Covers of Rock Classics (Rhino, 1993)

Blue Order: A Trance Tribute to New Order (Cleopatra, 1997)

Bonograph: Sonny Gets His Share (Bogus, 1991)

Borrowed Tunes: A Tribute to Neil Young (Sony, 1994)

Brace Yourself! A Tribute to Otis Blackwell (Shanachie, 1994)

The Bridge: A Tribute to Neil Young (Caroline, 1989)

Burning for Buddy: A Tribute to the Music of Buddy Rich (Atlantic, 1997)

Burning for Buddy: A Tribute to the Music of Buddy Rich, Volume II (Atlantic, 1997)

A Call to Irons: A Tribute to Iron Maiden (Dwell, 1998)

Chairman of the Board: Interpretations of Songs Made Famous by Frank Sinatra (Grass, 1993)

Chuck B. Covered: A Tribute to Chuck Berry (Hip-O, 1998)

The Concert for the Rock and Roll Hall of Fame (Columbia, 1996)

Come Together: America Salutes the Beatles (Liberty, 1995)

Come Together: Motown Sings the Beatles (Razor & Tie, 1994)

Comemorativo: A Tribute to Gram Parsons (Rhino, 1993)

Common Thread: The Songs of the Eagles (Giant, 1993)

Cover Me (Bruce Springsteen Tribute) (Rhino, 1989)

Cover You: The Rolling Stones Songbook (Hip-O, 1998)

Covered in Black: An AC/DC Tribute (Cleopatra, 1996)

Deadicated: A Tribute to the Grateful Dead (Arista, 1991)

Delicacy & Nourishment: Lyrics by Ernest Noyes Brookings, Vol. 3 (ESD, 1993)

Delphonic Sounds Today! (Del-Fi, 1998)

Diana Princess of Wales Tribute (Columbia, 1997)

Do Me Baby: Austin Does Prince (Fume, 1998)

Duran Duran Tribute Album (Mojo, 1997)

Encomium: A Tribute to Led Zeppelin **woof!** (Atlantic, 1996)

Folkways: A Vision Shared: A Tribute to Woody Guthrie and Leadbelly (Columbia, 1988)

For the Love of Harry: Everybody Sings Nilsson (Musicmasters, 1995)

For the Love of Todd: A Tribute to Todd Rundgren (Third Lock, 1997)

For the Masses (Depeche Mode) (1500/A&M, 1998)

The Fox Lies Down: A Tribute to Genesis (Purple Pyramid/Cleopatra, 1998)

Freedom Sounds: A Tribute to the Skatalites (Shanachie, 1997)

Gabba Gabba Hey: A Tribute to the Ramones (Triple X, 1991)

Golden Throats 4: Celebrities Butcher the Beatles (Rhino, 1997)

Gumby (Buena Vista, 1989)

Harry Chapin Tribute (Relativity, 1990)

Here, There and Everywhere N/A (Windham Hill, 1998)

I Only Wrote this Song for You: A Tribute to Johnny Thunders (Essential, 1997)

I Shall Be Unreleased: The Songs of Bob Dylan (Rhino, 1991)

If I Were a Carpenter **woof!** (A&M, 1994)

I'm Your Fan (Tribute to Leonard Cohen) (Atlantic, 1991)

Inner City Blues: The Music of Marvin Gaye (Motown, 1995)

The Inner Flame: A Rainer Ptacek Tribute (Atlantic, 1997)

It's Now or Never: The Tribute to Elvis (Mercury, 1994)

Jackie Robinson, Stealing Home: A Musical Tribute (Legacy, 1997)

Jeffology: A Guitar Chronicle (Shrapnel, 1996)

Jesus Christ Superstar: A Resurrection (Long Play, 1994)

John Fogerty Wrote a Song for Everyone (Pravda, 1995)

Kiss My Ass: Classic Kiss Regrooved (PolyGram, 1994)

Legacy: A Tribute to Fleetwood Mac's Rumours (Lava, 1998)

Legend of a Madman: A Tribute to Ozzy Osbourne N/A (Slipdisc/Mercury, 1998)

Lost in the Stars: The Music of Kurt Weill (A&M, 1985)

Love Gets Strange: The Songs of John Hiatt (Rhino, 1993)

A Means to an End: The Music of Joy Division (Virgin, 1995)

Minneapolis Does Denver: 18 Songs by John Denver Performed by Minneapolis Artists (October, 1995)

Nativity in Black: A Tribute to Black Sabbath (Columbia, 1994)

No Prima Donna: The Songs of Van Morrison (Polydor, 1994)

Not Fade Away (Remembering Buddy Holly) (Decca/MCA)

One Step Up/Two Steps Back: The Songs of Bruce Springsteen (The Right Stuff, 1997)

Outlandos d'Americas (The Police) (Ark 21, 1998)

Outstandingly Ignited: Lyrics by Ernest Noyes Brookings, Vol. 4 (ESD, 1995)

The Passion of Covers: A Tribute to Bauhaus (Cleopatra, 1996)

People Get Ready: A Tribute to Curtis Mayfield (Shanachie, 1993)

Piss & Vinegar: The Songs of Graham Parker (Buy or Die, 1997)

Regatta Mondatta: A Reggae Tribute to the Police (Ark 21, 1996)

Regatta Mondatta II: A Reggae Tribute to the Police (Ark 21, 1997)

September Songs: The Music of Kurt Weill (Sony Classical, 1997)

Shared Vision: The Songs of the Beatles (Mercury, 1994)

Simply Mad About the Mouse (Columbia, 1991)

Sing Hollies in Reverse (Eggbert, 1995)

Skynyrd Frynds (MCA, 1994)

Smoke on the Water: A Tribute to Deep Purple (Shrapnel, 1994)

The Songs of Bob Dylan (Start, 1989)

Songs of Janis Joplin: Blues Down Deep (House of Blues, 1997)

The Songs of Jimmie Rodgers: A Tribute (Egyptian, 1997)

The Songs of West Side Story 𝄞𝄞𝄞 (RCA Victor, 1996)

Stay Awake: Various Interpretations of Music from Vintage Disney Films 𝄞𝄞𝄞𝄞 (A&M, 1988)

Stone Free: Tribute to Jimi Hendrix 𝄞𝄞𝄞 (Reprise, 1993)

Sweet Relief: A Benefit for Victoria Williams 𝄞𝄞𝄞𝄞 (Thirsty Ear/Chaos/Columbia, 1993)

Sweet Relief II: Gravity of the Situation: The Songs of Vic Chesnutt 𝄞𝄞𝄞𝄞 (Columbia, 1996)

Tangerine Ambience: A Tribute to Tangerine Dream 𝄞𝄞 (Cleopatra, 1996)

Tapestry Revisited: A Tribute to Carole King 𝄞𝄞 (Lava, 1995)

A Testimonial Dinner: The Songs of XTC 𝄞𝄞 (Thirsty Ear, 1995)

That's Fats: A Tribute to Fats Domino 𝄞𝄞𝄞 (EMI, 1996)

This Is a Wonderful Place: The Songs of Richard Thompson 𝄞𝄞𝄞𝄞 (Green Linnet, 1993)

Till the Night Is Gone: A Tribute to Doc Pomus 𝄞𝄞𝄞𝄞 (Rhino, 1995)

Tower of Song: The Songs of Leonard Cohen 𝄞𝄞𝄞 (A&M, 1995)

Tribute to Black Sabbath: Eternal Masters 𝄞𝄞 (Priority, 1994)

A Tribute to Curtis Mayfield 𝄞𝄞 (Warners Bros., 1994)

A Tribute to Judas Priest: Legends of Metal 𝄞𝄞 (Century Media, 1997)

A Tribute to Marc Bolan & T-Rex: Resurrection of the Warlock 𝄞𝄞 (Pavement, 1998)

A Tribute to Norman Whitfield 𝄞𝄞𝄞 (Hot Productions, 1996)

A Tribute to Stevie Ray Vaughan 𝄞𝄞𝄞 (Epic, 1996)

Turban Renewal: A Tribute to Sam the Sham & the Pharoahs 𝄞𝄞𝄞 (Norton, 1994)

Twang! A Tribute to Hank Marvin & the Shadows 𝄞𝄞𝄞𝄞 (Ark 21/Pangea, 1996)

Twisted Willie 𝄞𝄞𝄞 (Justice, 1996)

Two Rooms: Celebrating the Songs of Elton John & Bernie Taupin 𝄞𝄞𝄞 (Polydor, 1991)

We Love Bobby: A Tribute to Bobby Bland 𝄞𝄞𝄞 (Collectables, 1992)

We Will Fall: The Iggy Pop Tribute 𝄞𝄞𝄞 (Royalty, 1997)

Working Class Hero: A Tribute to John Lennon 𝄞𝄞𝄞 (Capitol, 1995)

Zappa's Universe 𝄞𝄞𝄞 (Verve, 1993).

Can't get enough rock and roll? Here are some books and magazines you can check out for further information. Happy reading!

Books

BIOGRAPHICAL

ABBA: The Name of the Game
Andrew Oldham (Music Book Services, 1996)

Aerosmith: The Fall and the Rise of Rock's Greatest Band
Martin Huxley (St. Martin's Press, 1995)

All You Need Is Ears
George Martin and Jeremy Hornsby (St. Martin's Press, 1995)

American Bandstand: Dick Clark and the Making of a Rock 'N' Roll Empire
John A. Jackson (Oxford University Press, 1997)

The American Book of the Dead: The Definitive Grateful Dead Encyclopedia
Oliver Trager (Simon & Schuster, 1997)

American Woman: The Story of the Guess Who
John Einarson (Quarry Press, 1995)

And the Beat Goes On
Sonny Bono (Pocket Books, 1992)

The Arrival of B.B. King
Charles Sawyer (Da Capo Press, 1980)

As I Am: ABBA Before & Beyond
Agnetha Faltskog, with Brita Ahman (Virgin, 1997)

Babes in Toyland: The Making and Selling of a Rock and Roll Band
Neal Karlen (Avon Books, 1994)

Back to the Beach: A Brian Wilson and the Beach Boys Reader
Kingsley Abbot, ed. (Helter Skelter Ltd., 1998)

The Backstreet Boys: Official Biography
Rob McGibbon (Trans-Atlantic Publications, 1997)

Bad Seed: The Biography of Nick Cave
Ian Johnston (Little, Brown & Co., 1997)
The B.B. King Companion: Five Decades of Commentary
Richard Kostelanetz and Anson John Pope, ed. (Schirmer Books, 1997)

The Beach Boys: How Deep Is the Ocean
Paul Williams (Omnibus Press, 1997)

Beach Boys: In Their Own Words
Nick Wise, ed. (Omnibus Press, 1995)

The Beatles
Hunter Davies (W.W. Norton & Company, 1996)

The Beatles: The Ultimate Recording Guide
Allen J. Wiener (Facts on File, 1992)

Before I Get Old: The Story of the Who

Dave Marsh (St. Martin's Press, 1983)

Being Frank: My Time With Frank Zappa
Nigey Lennon, et al (California Classics Books, 1995)

Black Diamond: The Unauthorized Biography of Kiss
Dale Sherman (Collector's Guide, 1997)

Black Sabbath: An Oral History (For the Record)
Mike Stark and Dave Marsh (Avon Books, 1998)

Blues All Around Me: The Autobiography of B.B. King
B.B. King, with David Ritz (Avon Books, 1996)

Bob Dylan: A Life in Stolen Moments Day by Day, 1941–1995
Clinton Heylin (Schirmer Books, 1996)

Bob Dylan: American Poet and Singer: An Annotated Bibliography and Study Guide of Sources and Background Materials, 1961–1991
Richard D. Wissolik (Scholars Bibliography Series, No. 2)

Bob Dylan: Watching the River Flow— Observations on His Art-In-Progress, 1966–1995
Paul Williams (Omnibus Press, 1996)

Bob Marley: Songs of Freedom
Adrian Boot and Chris Salewicz (Penguin Studio, 1995)

Bonnie Raitt: Just in the Nick of Time
Mark Bego (Birch Lane Press, 1996)

Born in the U.S.A.: Bruce Springsteen and the American Tradition
Jim Cullen (HarperCollins, 1997)

Break on Through: The Life and Death of Jim Morrison
James Riordan and Jerry Prochnicky (Quill, 1992)

Brian Eno: His Music and the Vertical Color of Sound
Eric Tamm (Da Capo Press, 1995)

Brother Ray: Ray Charles' Own Story
Ray Charles, with David Ritz (Da Capo Press, 1992)

Bruce Springsteen: The Rolling Stones File—The Ultimate Compendium of Interviews, Articles, Facts and Opinions from the Files of Rolling Stones
Editors of *Rolling Stone* magazine, ed. (Hyperion, 1996)

Building a Mystery: The Story of Sarah McLachlan & Lilith Fair
Judith Fitzgerald (Quarry Press, 1998)

Cash: The Autobiography
Johnny Cash and Patrick Carr (Harper San Francisco, 1997)

Catch a Fire: The Life of Bob Marley
Timothy White (Henry Holt & Co., 1989)

Clapton! An Authorized Biography
Ray Coleman (Warner Books, 1988)

Come As You Are: The Story of Nirvana
Michael Azerrad (Main Street Books, 1993)

Come Together: John Lennon in His Time
Jon Wiener (University of Illinois Press, 1991)

Confusion Is Next: The Sonic Youth Story
Alec Foege (St. Martin's Press, 1994)

Dancing in the Street: Confessions of a Motown Diva
Martha Reeves and Mark Bego (Hyperion, 1994)

The Dave Matthews Band: Step into the Light
Morgan Delancey (ECW Press, 1998)

A Day in the Life: The Music and Artistry of the Beatles
Mark Hertsgaard (Delta Books, 1996)

Dead to the Core: An Almanack of the Grateful Dead
Eric F. Wybenga (Delta Books, 1997)

Divided Soul: The Life of Marvin Gaye
David Ritz (Da Capo Press, 1991)

Dylan: World Gone Wrong
Bob Dylan (Music Sales Corporation, 1994)

El Sid: Saint Vicious
David Dalton (St. Martin's Press, 1997)

Elvis
Albert Goldman (McGraw-Hill, 1981)

Elvis
Dave Marsh (Times Books, 1982)

Elvis and Me
Priscilla Beaulieu Presley, with Sandra Harmon (Berkley Books, 1991)

The Elvis Encyclopedia
David E. Stanley and Frank Coffey (General Publishing Group, 1994)

Elvis Presley: A Life in Music—The Complete Recording Sessions
Ernst Jorgensen (St. Martin's Press, 1998)

Eric Clapton: Lost in the Blues
Harry Shapiro (Da Capo Press, 1992)

Everyday I Sing the Blues: The Story of B.B. King
David Shirley (Franklin Watts, 1995)

The Frank Zappa Companion: Four Decades of Commentary
Richard Kostelanetz, ed. (Schirmer Books, 1997)

Frank Zappa: The Negative Dialectics of Poodle Play
Ben Watson (St. Martin's Press, 1996)

George Clinton and P-Funk: An Oral History (For the Record)
Dave Marsh (Avon Books, 1998)

Glory Days: The Bruce Springsteen Story
Dave Marsh (Thunder's Mouth Press, 1996)

Hammer of the Gods: The Led Zeppelin Saga
Stephen Davis (Boulevard Books, 1997)

Hellfire: The Jerry Lee Lewis Story
Nick Tosches (Grove Press, 1998)

Hendrix: Setting the Record Straight
John McDermott, with Eddie Kramer (Warner Books, 1992)

Henry Rollins: The First Five
Henry Rollins (Two Thirteen Sixty-One Publications, 1997)

Hickory Wind: The Life and Times of Gram Parsons
Ben Fong-Torres (Pocket Books, 1991)

I Need More
Iggy Pop (Two Thirteen Sixty-One Publications, 1997)

Into the Heart: The Stories Behind Every U2 Song
Niall Stokes (Thunder's Mouth Press, 1998)

Invisible Republic: Bob Dylan's Basement Tapes
Greil Marcus (Henry Holt & Co., 1997)

Iron Maiden: Run to the Hills—The Official Biography
Mick Wall (Harvill Press, 1998)

It's Only Rock 'N' Roll: The Ultimate Guide to the Rolling Stones
James Karnbach and Carol Bernson (Facts on File, 1997)

Jackie Wilson: Lonely Teardrops
Tony Douglas (Omnibus Press, 1997)

James Brown: The Godfather of Soul
James Brown, with Bruce Tucker (Thunder's Mouth Press, 1997)

Janis Joplin: A Performance Diary, 1966–1970
John Byrne Cooke (Acid Test, 1997)

Jimi Hendrix: Electric Gypsy
Harry Shapiro and Caesar Glebbeek (St. Martin's Press, 1991)

The Jimi Hendrix Experience
Jerry Hopkins (Arcade, 1996)

Jimi Hendrix: Inside the Experience
Mitch Mitchell, with John Platt (Harmony Books, 1990)

Jimi Hendrix: The Final Days
Tony Brown (Omnibus Press, 1997)

The Jimmy Buffett Scrapbook
Mark Humphrey, with Harris Lewine (Citadel Press, 1996)

Johnny Cash
Sean Dolan (Chelsea House, 1995)

Joni Mitchell: Both Sides Now
Brian Hinton (Harvill Press, 1997)

Joni Mitchell: The Complete Poems and Lyrics
Joni Mitchell (Crown Publishers, 1997)

Judy Collins Anthology
Judy Collins and Frank Metis (Music Sales Corp., 1988)

k.d. lang: An Illustrated Biography
David Bennahum (Omnibus Press, 1995)

Kiss and Sell: The Making of a Supergroup
C. K. Lendt (Watson-Guptill, 1997)

Kurt Cobain: The Cobain Dossier
Andrew Dent (Plexus Publishing, 1998)

Last Train to Memphis: The Rise of Elvis Presley
Peter Guralnick (Little, Brown & Co., 1994)

Lennon: The Definitive Biography
Ray Coleman (Harper Perennial, 1992)

The Life and Times of Little Richard
Charles White (Harmony Books, 1984)

Living in America: The Soul Saga of James Brown
Cynthia Rose (Serpents Tail, 1991)

Living with the Dead: Twenty Years on the Bus with Garcia and the Grateful Dead
Rock Scully, with David Dalton (Little, Brown & Co., 1996)

The Long and Winding Road: An Intimate Guide to the Beatles
Ted Greenwald (Michael Friedman/Fairfax Publishing, 1995)

The Long Hard Road Out of Hell
Marilyn Manson, with Neil Strauss (HarperCollins, 1998)

The Long Run: The Story of the Eagles
Marc Shapiro (Omnibus Press, 1995)

Madonna: Bawdy and Soul
Karlene Faith (University of Toronto Press, 1997)

Madonna: The Rolling Stone Files—The Ultimate Compendium of Interviews, Articles, Facts, and Opinions from the Files of Rolling Stone
Editors of *Rolling Stone* magazine, ed. (Hyperion, 1997)

The Man in Black
Johnny Cash (Warner Books, 1975)

Marilyn Manson
Kurt Reighley (St. Martin's Press, 1998)

Marilyn Manson: The Unauthorized Biography
Kalen Rogers (Omnibus Press, 1997)

Metallica: The Frayed Ends of Metal
Chris Crocker (St. Martin's Press, 1993)

Metallica Unbound: The Unofficial Biography
K.J. Doughton (Warner Books, 1993)

Midnight Riders: The Story of the Allman Brothers Band
Scott Freeman (Little, Brown & Co., 1996)

Mother! The Frank Zappa Story
Michael Gray (Plexus Publishing, 1994)

Neil Diamond
Diana Karanikas Harvey and Jackson Harvey (Metro Books, 1996)

Nirvana Tribute: The Life and Death of Kurt Cobain—The Full Story
Suzi Black (Omnibus Press, 1995)

No One Here Gets Out Alive: The Biography of Jim Morrison
Jerry Hopkins and Danny Sugerman (Warner Books, 1995)

Oasis. Definitely.
Tim Abbot (Fireside, 1997)

Oasis: Supersonic Supernova
Michael Krugman (St. Martin's Press, 1997)

Oasis: What's the Story?
Ian Robertson (Delta Books, 1997)

Patti Smith: A Biography
Nick Johnstone (Omnibus Press, 1997)

Pearl Jam: Live
Joey Lorenzo (Omnibus Press, 1995)

Phish Book
Richard Gehr (Villard Books, 1998)

The Phishing Manual: A Compendium to the Music of Phish
Dean Budnick (Hyperion, 1996)

Poison Heart: Surviving the Ramones
Dee Dee Ramone (Helter Skelter Ltd., 1998)

Positively Bob Dylan: A Thirty-Year Discography, Concert, and Recording Session Guide, 1960–1991
Michael Krogsgaard (Popular Culture Ink, 1991)

Prince: Inside the Purple Reign
Jon Bream (Collier Books, 1984)

Queen Live: A Concert Documentary
Greg Brooks (Omnibus Press, 1995)

Ramones: An American Band
Jim Bessman (St. Martin's Press, 1993)

The Real Frank Zappa Book
Frank Zappa, with Peter Occhiogrosso (Poseidon Press, 1990)

The Red Hot Chili Peppers
Dave Thompson (St. Martin's Press, 1993)

R.E.M. Inside Out: The Stories Behind Every Song
Craig Rosen (Thunder's Mouth Press, 1997)

R.E.M.: The Rolling Stone Files—The Ultimate Compendium of Interviews, Articles, Facts, and Opinions from the Files of Rolling Stone
Editors of *Rolling Stone* magazine, ed. (Hyperion, 1995)

Rock Lives: Profiles and Interviews
Timothy White (Henry Holt & Co., 1991)

The Rolling Stones Chronicle: The First Four Decades
Massimo Bonanno (Plexus Publishing, 1997)

Rotten: No Irish, No Blacks, No Dogs— The Authorized Autobiography of Johnny Rotten of the Sex Pistols
John Lydon, with Keith and Kent Zimmerman (Picador USA, 1995)

Route 666: On the Road to Nirvana
Gina Arnold (St. Martin's Press, 1993)

Rimbaud and Jim Morrison: The Rebel As Poet
Wallace Fowlie (Duke University Press, 1994)

Saucerful of Secrets: The Pink Floyd Odyssey
Nicholas Schaffner (Delta Books, 1992)

Save the Last Dance for Me: The Musical Legacy of the Drifters, 1953–1993 (Rock & Roll Remembrances, No. 11)
Tony Allan and Faye Treadwell (Popular Culture Ink, 1994)

'Scuse Me While I Kiss the Sky: The Life of Jimi Hendrix
David Henderson (Bantam Doubleday Dell, 1996)

Skeleton Key: A Dictionary for Deadheads
David Shenk and Steve Silberman (Main Street Books, 1994)

Slowhand: The Life and Music of Eric Clapton
Marc Roberty (Harmony Books, 1991)

Soundgarden: New Metal Crown
Chris Nickson (St. Martin's Press, 1995)

The Spice Girls
Anna Louise Golden (Ballantine Books, 1997)

Stevie Ray: Soul to Soul
Keri Leigh (Taylor, 1993)

Stevie Ray Vaughan: Caught in the Crossfire
Joe Nick Patoski and Bill Crawford (Little, Brown & Co., 1993)

Stone Temple Pilots
Mick Wall and Malcolm Dome (Ominbus Press, 1995)

The Stones
Philip Norman (Penguin, 1994)

The Story of Marilyn Manson
Doug Small (Omnibus Press, 1996)

Take Me Home: An Autobiography
John Denver, with Arthur Tobier (Harmony Books, 1994)

The Temptations
Ted Cox (Chelsea House, 1997)

There's Something Happening Here: The Story of Buffalo Springfield—For What It's Worth
John Einarson and Richie Furay (Quarry Press, 1997)

To the Limit: The Untold Story of the Eagles
Marc Eliot (Little, Brown & Co., 1998)

The True Adventures of the Rolling Stones
Stanley Booth (Vintage, 1984)

Two Times Intro: On the Road with Patti Smith
Michael Stipe (Little, Brown & Co., 1998)

U2 at the End of the World
Bill Flanagan (Delta Books, 1996)

U2: Faraway So Close
B.P. Fallon (Little, Brown & Co., 1994)

U2 Live! A Concert Documentary
Chris Charlesworth, ed. (Omnibus Press, 1995)

U2: The Road to Pop
Carter Alan (Faber & Faber, 1997)

U2: The Ultimate Compendium of Interviews, Articles, Facts, and Opinions from the Files of Rolling Stone
Editors of *Rolling Stone* magazine, ed. (Hyperion, 1994)

Walk This Way: The Autobiography of Aerosmith
Aerosmith, with Stephen Davis (Avon Books, 1997)

Wanted Man: In Search of Bob Dylan
John Bauldie, ed. (Citadel Press, 1991)

We All Shine On: The Stories Behind Every John Lennon Song, 1970–1980
Paul Du Noyer (Harper Perennial, 1997)

Wheels of Confusion: The Story of Black Sabbath
Steven Rosen (Harvill Press, 1997)

The Who: Concert File
Joe McMichael and "Irish" Jack Lyons (Omnibus Press, 1998)

The Who: Maximum R&B
Richard Barnes (Plexus Publishing, 1996)

Whole Lotta Shakin' Going On: Jerry Lee Lewis
Robert Cain (Dial Press, 1981)

With a Little Help from My Friends: The Making of Sgt. Pepper
George Martin and William Pearson (Little, Brown & Co., 1995)

Without You: The Tragic Story of Badfinger
Dan Matovina (Frances Glover Books, 1998)

Yesstories: Yes in Their Own Words
Tim Morse, ed. (St. Martin's Press, 1996)

You Send Me: The Life and Times of Sam Cooke
Daniel Wolff, S.R. Crain, Clifton White, and G. David Tenenbaum (Quill, 1996)

GENERAL INTEREST

A wop bop a loo bop, A lop bam boom: The Golden Age of Rock
Nik Cohn (Da Capo Press, 1996)

Abbey Road: The Story of the World's Most Famous Recording Studios
Brian Southall, et al (Omnibus Press, 1997)

The Accidental Evolution of Rock 'N' Roll: A Misguided Tour Through Popular Music
Chuck Eddy (Da Capo Press, 1997)

The Aesthetics of Rock
Richard Meltzer, et al (Da Capo Press, 1988)

All Music Guide: The Experts' Guide to the Best CDs, Albums & Tapes
Michael Erlewine, Vladimir Bogdanov, Chris Woodstra, and Stephen Thomas Erlewine, ed. (Miller Freeman, 1997)

All Music Guide to Rock
Michael Erlewine, Vladimir Bogdanov, and Chris Woodstra, ed. (Miller Freeman, 1995)

Amps!: The Other Half of Rock 'N' Roll
Ritchie Fliegler and Jon F. Eiche (Hal Leonard Publishing, 1993)

Anti-Rock: The Opposition to Rock 'N' Roll
Linda Martin, et al (Da Capo Press, 1993)

The Art of Rock and Roll
Charles T. Brown (Prentice Hall)

Backstage Pass: Catering to Music's Biggest Stars
John Crisafulli (Cumberland House, 1998)

Bat Chain Puller: Rock and Roll in the Age of Celebrity
Kurt Loder (St. Martin's Press, 1991)

Behind the Hits: Inside Stories of Classic Pop and Rock and Roll
Bob Shannon and John Javna (Warner Books, 1986)

Behind the Song: The Stories of 100 Great Pop & Rock Classics
Michael Heatley and Spencer Leigh (Sterling Publications, 1998)

Beneath the Diamond Sky: Haight-Ashbury, 1965–1970
Barney Hoskyns (Simon & Schuster, 1997)

The Billboard Book of One-Hit Wonders
Wayne Janick (Billboard, 1998)

The Billboard Book of Top 40 Hits
Joel Whitburn (Billboard, 1992)

The Billboard Illustrated Encyclopedia of Rock
Colin Larkin (Watson-Guptill, 1998)

Bootleg: The Secret History of the Other Recording Industry
Clinton Heylin (St. Martin's Press, 1995)

The British Invasion
Nicholas Schaffner (McGraw-Hill, 1982)

Christgau's Record Guide: The '80s
Robert Christgau (Da Capo Press, 1994)

Classic Rock Stories: The Stories Behind the Greatest Songs of All Time
Tim Morse (Griffin, 1998)

The Dark Stuff: Selected Writings on Rock Music, 1972–1995
Nick Kent (Da Capo Press, 1995)

Deep Blues
Robert Palmer (Viking Press, 1981)

Encyclopedia of Pop, Rock, and Soul
Irwin Stambler (St. Martin's Press, 1989)

Encyclopedia of Rock Stars
Dafydd Rees and Luke Crampton (Dorling Kindersley, 1996)

England's Dreaming
Jon Savage (Faber & Faber, 1991)

Feel Like Going Home: Portraits in Blues and Rock 'n' Roll
Peter Guralnick (Little, Brown & Co., 1998)

Fender Amps: The First Fifty Years
John Teagle and John Sprung (Hal Leonard Publishing, 1995)

The Fender Book: A Complete History of Fender Electric Guitars
Tony Bacon and Paul Day (Miller Freeman, 1992)

Fender: The Sound Heard 'Round the World
Richard R. Smith (Music Sales Corp., 1996)

Fodor's Rock & Roll Traveler USA: The Ultimate Guide to Juke Joints, Street Corners, Whiskey Bars and Hotel Rooms Where Music History Was Made
Tim Perry and Ed Glinert (Fodor's, 1996)

Follow the Music: The Life and High Times of Elektra Records in the Great Years of American Pop Culture
Jac Holzman and Gavan Daws (First Media Books, 1998)

Fortunate Son: The Best of Dave Marsh
Dave Marsh (Random House, 1985)

From the Velvets to the Voidoids: A Pre-Punk History for a Post-Punk World
Clinton Heylin (Penguin, 1993)

Getting High: The Adventures of Oasis
Paolo Hewitt (Hyperion, 1997)

Gibson Guitars: 100 Years of an American Icon
Walter Carter (General Publishing Group, 1996)

Girl Groups: The Story of a Sound
Alan Betrock (Delilah, 1982)

Goin' Back to Memphis: A Century of Blues, Rock 'n' Roll, and Glorious Soul
James Dickerson (Simon & Schuster, 1996)

Good Rockin' Tonight: Sun Records and the Birth of Rock 'n' Roll
Colin Escott, with Martin Hawkins (St. Martin's Press, 1991)

The Haight-Ashbury
Charles Perry (Rolling Stone Press, 1984)

The Heart of Rock and Roll
Dave Marsh (Penguin, 1989)

The History of Marshall: The Illustrated Story of "the Sound of Rock"
Michael Doyle (Hal Leonard Publishing, 1993)

Hollywood Rock
Marshall Crenshaw (Harper Perennial, 1994)

Jazz-Rock: A History
Stuart Nicholson (Schirmer Books, 1998)

Kaleidoscope Eyes: Psychedelic Rock from the '60s to the '90s
Jim DeRogatis (Citadel Press, 1996)

Kiss This: Punk in the Present Tense
Gina Arnold (St. Martin's Press, 1997)

Lords of Chaos: The Bloody Rise of the Satanic Metal Underground
Michael Moynihan and Didrik Soderlund (Feral House, 1998)

Lost Highway
Peter Guralnick (Vintage, 1979)

Louie, Louie
Dave Marsh (Hyperion, 1993)

Make the Music Go Bang: The Early L.A. Punk Scene
Don Snowden, ed. (St. Martin's Press, 1997)

The Mansion on the Hill: Dylan, Young, Geffen, Springsteen, and the Head-On Collision of Rock and Commerce
Fred Goodman (Times Books, 1997)

Martin Guitars: An Illustrated Celebration of America's Premier Guitarmaker
Jim Washburn and Richard Johnston (Rodale Press, 1997)

The Midnight Special, 1972–1981: Late Night's Original Rock & Roll Show
B.R. Hunter (MTV Books, 1997)

Music Festivals from Bach to Blues
Tom Clynes (Visible Ink Press, 1996)

MusicHound Blues: The Essential Album Guide
Leland Rucker, ed. (Visible Ink Press, 1998)

MusicHound Country: The Essential Album Guide
Brian Mansfield and Gary Graff, ed. (Visible Ink Press, 1997)

MusicHound Folk: The Essential Album Guide
Neal Walters and Brian Mansfield, ed. (Visible Ink Press, 1998)

MusicHound Jazz: The Essential Album Guide
Steve Holtje and Nancy Ann Lee, ed. (Visible Ink Press, 1998)

MusicHound Lounge: The Essential Album Guide to Martini Music and Easy Listening
Steve Knopper, ed. (Visible Ink Press, 1998)

MusicHound R&B: The Essential Album Guide
Gary Graff, Josh Freedom du Lac, and Jim McFarlin, ed. (Visible Ink Press, 1998)

The Music's All That Matters: A History of Progressive Rock
Paul Stump (Quartet Books, 1998)

The New Book of Rock Lists
Dave Marsh and James Bernard (Fireside, 1994)

The New Rolling Stone Encyclopedia of Rock & Roll
Patricia Romanowski and Holly George-Warren, ed. (Rolling Stone Press, 1995)

Off the Record: An Oral History of Popular Music
Joe Smith, with Mitchell Fink (Warner Books, 1988)

Please Kill Me: The Uncensored Oral History of Punk
Legs McNeil and Gillian McCain (Penguin USA, 1997)

Punk Diary 1970–1979
George Gimarc (St. Martin's Press, 1994)

Punk: The Illustrated History of a Music Revolution
Adrian Boot and Chris Salewicz (Penguin, 1997)

The Rhino History of Rock 'N' Roll: The '70s
Eric Lefcowitz (Pocket Books, 1997)

Rock Albums of the '70s: A Critical Guide
Robert Christgau (Da Capo Press, 1990)

Rock and Roll: A Social History
Paul Friedlander (Westview Press, 1996)

The Rock & Roll Almanac
Mark Bego (Macmillan, 1996)

Rock 'N' Roll Babylon
Gary Herman (Plexus Publishing, 1994)

Rock and Roll Hall of Fame and Museum: Rock Facts
James Henke, ed. (Universe, 1997)

The Rock and Roll Reader's Guide: A Comprehensive Guide to Books by & about Musicians and Their Music
Gary M. Krebs (Watson-Guptill, 1997)

Rock 'n' Roll Road Trip: The Ultimate Guide to the Sites, the Shrines, and the Legends Across America
A.M. Nolan (Pharos, 1992)

Rock Bottom: Dark Moments in Music Babylon
Pamela Des Barres (St. Martin's Press, 1996)

Rock Names: From ABBA to ZZ Top—How Rock Bands Got Their Names
Adam Dolgins (Citadel Press, 1995)

Rock Odyssey: A Chronicle of the Sixties
Ian Whitcomb (Limelight, 1994)

Rock on Film
David Ehrenstein and Bill Reed (Delilah, 1982)

The Rock Pack
James Henke, ed. (Universe, 1997)

The Rock Song Index
Bruce Pollock (Schirmer Books, 1997)

Rock: The Rough Guide
Jonathan Buckley and Mark Ellingham, ed. (Rough Guides, 1996)

Rocking the Classics: English Progressive Rock and the Counterculture
Edward L. MacAn (Oxford University Press, 1996)

Rockonomics: The Money Behind the Music
Marc Eliot (Citadel Press, 1993)

Rolling Stone Album Guide
Anthony DeCurtis and James Henke, ed., with Holly George-Warren (Random House, 1992)

The Rolling Stone Illustrated History of Rock & Roll
Anthony DeCurtis and James Henke, with Holly George-Warren (Straight Arrow, 1992)

The Rolling Stone Interviews, 1967–1980: The Classic Oral History of Rock and Roll
Editors of *Rolling Stone* magazine, ed. (St. Martin's Press, 1989)

Rolling Stone's Alt-Rock-A-Rama: An Outrageous Compendium of Facts, Fiction, Trivia, and Critiques on Alternative Rock
Scott Schinder and the editors of Rolling Stone Press (Delta Books, 1996)

San Francisco Nights: The Psychedelic Music Trip, 1965–1968
Gene Sculatti and Dave Seay (St. Martin's Press, 1985)

She's a Rebel: The History of Women in Rock & Roll
Gillian G. Gaar (Seal Press, 1992)

Solo: Women Singer-Songwriters in Their Own Words
Marc Woodworth, ed. (Delta Books, 1998)

Songs in the Rough: From "Heartbreak Hotel" to "Higher Love"—Rock's Greatest Songs in Rough-Draft Form
Steven Bishop (St. Martin's Press, 1996)

The Sound of the City: The Rise of Rock and Roll
Charlie Gillett (Da Capo Press, 1996)

Spin Underground U.S.A.: The Best of Rock Culture Coast to Coast
Duncan Bock, ed. (Vintage Books, 1997)

Stars of Soul and Rhythm & Blues: Top Recording Artists and Showstopping Performers, from Memphis and Motown to Now
Lee Hildebrand (Watson-Guptill, 1994)

Stranded: Rock and Roll for a Desert Island
Greil Marcus, ed. (Da Capo Press, 1996)

Summer of Love
Joel Selvin (Dutton, 1994)

That Old Time Rock and Roll: A Chronicle of an Era, 1954–1963
Richard Aquila (Schirmer Books, 1989)

A Time to Rock: A Social History of Rock 'N' Roll
David P. Szatmary (Simon & Schuster, 1996)

Trouble Girls: The Rolling Stone Book of Women in Rock
Barbara O'Dair (Random House, 1997)

The Trouser Press Guide to '90s Rock: The All-New Fifth Edition of The Trouser Press Record Guide
Ira A. Robbins (Fireside, 1997)

The Trouser Press Record Guide
Ira A. Robbins (Collier, 1991)

Unknown Legends of Rock 'N' Roll: Psychedelic Unknowns, Mad Geniuses, Punk Pioneers, Lo-Fi Mavericks & More
Richie Unterberger (Miller Freeman, 1998)

Unsung Heroes of Rock 'n' Roll
Nick Tosches (Scribner's Sons, 1984)

VideoHound's Soundtracks: Music from the Movies, Broadway, and Television
Didier Deutsch (Visible Ink Press, 1998)

The Virgin Encyclopedia of Popular Music
Colin Larkin (Virgin Books, 1997)

What Was the First Rock 'n' Roll Record?
Jim Dawson and Steve Propers (Faber & Faber, 1992)

Where Did Our Love Go? The Rise and Fall of the Motown Sound
Nelson George (St. Martin's Press, 1987)

Will You Still Love Me Tomorrow? Girl Groups from the '50s On
Charlotte Greig (Virago, 1989)

The Worst Rock-and-Roll Records of All Time: A Fan's Guide to the Stuff You Love to Hate
Jimmy Guterman and Owen O'Donnell (Citadel Press, 1991)

Magazines

Acoustic Guitar
PO Box 767
San Anselmo, CA 94979
(415) 485-6946

Alternative Press
6516 Detroit Ave., Ste. 5
Cleveland, OH 44102-3057
(216) 631-1510

BAM
3470 Buskirk Ave.
Pleasant Hill, CA 94523
(510) 934-3700

Bass Player
411 Borel Ave., Ste. 100
San Mateo, CA 94402
(415) 358-9500

Billboard
1515 Broadway
New York, NY 10036
(212) 764-7300

Blues Access
1455 Chestnut Pl.
Boulder, CO 80304
(303) 443-7245

Both Sides Now (newsletter)
PO Box 384
Fairfax Station, VA 22039

Cake
2401 University Ave. NE
Minneapolis, MN 55418
(612) 788-2253

Circus
6 W. 18th St.
New York, NY 10011
(212) 242-4902

CMJ New Music Monthly
11 Middleneck Rd., Ste. 400
Great Neck, NY 11021
(516) 466-6000

Country Music
329 Riverside Ave.
Westport, CT 06880
(203) 221-4950

Details
632 Broadway
New York, NY 10012
(212) 598-3710

Dirty Linen
PO Box 66600
Baltimore, MD 21239-6600
(410) 583-7973

Discoveries
PO Box 1050
Dubuque, IA 52004-1050
(319) 588-2073

Goldmine
700 E. State St.
Jola, WI 54990
(715) 445-4612

Guitar
10 Midland Ave.
Port Chester, NY 10573
(914) 935-5200

Guitar Player
411 Borel Ave., Ste. 100
San Mateo, CA 94402
(415) 358-9500

Guitar World
1115 Broadway
New York, NY 10010
(212) 807-7100

Hit Parader
40 Violet Ave.
Poughkeepsie, NY 12601
(914) 454-7420

ICE
PO Box 3043
Santa Monica, CA 90408
(800) 647-4ICE

Keyboard
411 Borel Ave., Ste. 100
San Mateo, CA 94402
(415) 358-9500

Living Blues
Hill Hall, Rm. 301
University of Mississippi
University, MS 38677
(800) 390-3527

Maximum Guitar
1115 Broadway
New York, NY 10010
(212) 807-7100

Melody Maker
King's Reach Tower
Stamford St.
London SE1 9LS, England
44-171-261-5000

Metal Edge
233 Park Ave. S, 5th Fl.
New York, NY 10003
(212) 780-3500

Modern Drummer
12 Old Bridge Rd.
Cedar Grove, NJ 07009
(973) 239-4140

Mojo
Mappin House
4 Winsley St.
London W1N 7AR, England
44-171-436-1515

Musician
1515 Broadway
New York, NY 10036
(212) 536-5208

New Musical Express
King's Reach Tower
Stamford St.
London SE1 9LS, England
44-171-261-5000

No Depression
PO Box 31332
Seattle, WA 98103
(206) 706-7342

Option
1522 Cloverfield Blvd., Ste. B
Santa Monica, CA 90404-3502
(310) 449-0120

Pulse!
2500 Del Monte St.
West Sacramento, CA 95691
(916) 373-2450

Q
Mappin House
4 Winsley St.
London W1N 7AR, England
44-171-436-1515

Rap Pages
8484 Wilshire Blvd.
Beverly Hills, CA 90211
(213) 651-5400

Raygun
2110 Main St., Ste. 100
Santa Monica, CA 90405-2276
(310) 452-6222

Request
10400 Yellow Circle Dr.
Minnetonka, MN 55343
(612) 931-8740

The Rocket
2028 Fifth Ave.
Seattle, WA 98121
(206) 728-7625

Rolling Stone
1290 Avenue of the Americas, 2nd Fl.
New York, NY 10104
(212) 484-1616

The Source
215 Park Ave. South, 11th Fl.
New York, NY 10003
(212) 253-8700

Spin
6 W. 18th St., 8th Fl.
New York, NY 10011-4608
(212) 633-8200

URB
1680 N. Vine St., Ste. 1012
Los Angeles, CA 90028

Vibe
205 Lexington Ave., 3rd Fl.
New York, NY 10016
(212) 522-7092

Vox
King's Reach Tower
Stamford St.
London SE1 9LS, England
44-171-261-5000

Wired
520 Third St., 4th Fl.
San Francisco, CA 94107-1815
(415) 276-5000

Rock and roll is everywhere, even out in cyberspace. Point your Web browser to these sites for more information on your favorite artists or the music in general.

Artists

a-ha
a-ha.wwiv.com
www.ricochetweb.com/a-ha
mason.gmu.edu/~kkasmai/a-ha.html

ABBA
www.polydor.com/polydor/artists/abba
www.sirius.com/~funnyguy/abba.html
www.grrtech.com/brians/abba.htm

ABC
www.path.unimelb.edu.au/~new_wave/
   abc.html
ourworld.compuserve.com/homepages/
   Melomania
www.geocities.com/SunsetStrip/
   Palladium/6871/hmcastle.html

Paula Abdul
www.virginrecords.com/artists/VR.cgi?
   ARTIST_NAME=Paula_Abdul
wavecom.net/~mike/paula.html
www.itech.cup.edu/~jakallis/paula.htm

AC/DC
www.elektra.com/metal_club/acdc/
   acdc.html
home1.swipnet.se/~w-10078/acdc
www.teleport.com/~jhjh/papmain.html

The Accelerators
www.pacificnet.net/~nicoteen/
   accelerators

Johnny Ace
www.mara.nl/artists/johnny_ace.htm

Ace of Base
www.aristarec.com/aristaweb/AceofBase
aobl.simplenet.com
www.eden.com/~wgunter

Acetone
homepage.interaccess.com/~bmaki/
   acetone/home.html

Bryan Adams
www.Bryanadams.com
bryanadams.NET
www.qlcomm.com/adams

Barry Adamson
web.inter.nl.net/users/dvdhaven/
   adamson
www2.southwind.net/~markw/barry/
   barry.html
www.mutelibtech.com/mute/adamson/
   adamson.htm

The Adverts
www.comnet.ca/~rina/adverts.html

Aerosmith
www.aerosmith.com
www.geocities.com/SunsetStrip/3364
www.geocities.com/SunsetStrip/Stage
   /3496/aerosmith.html
wings.dartmouth.edu/~aero/

The Afghan Whigs
www.elektra.com/alternative_club/
   afghanwhigs/afghan.html
dolphin.upenn.edu/~borakove/whigs
www.geocities.com/SunsetStrip/7030

A.F.I.
members.aol.com/Saba29/index.html

Agent Orange
www.geocities.com/SunsetStrip/Palms/
   4640
www.peakpeak.com/~krazykat/list/
   agent.htm

Agents of Good Roots
www.agentsofgoodroots.com
www.wlu.edu/~tilitzen/agr.html
www.vt.edu:10021/A/apathwic/agr.html

Agnes Gooch
www.revolution-online.com/gooch
users.dicksonstreet.com/~silverc/
   ag.html

Air Supply
www.airsupplymusic.com
www.geocities.com/SunsetStrip/Towers/
   4473/index.htm

The Alarm
www.thealarm.com
www.demon.co.uk/alarmpo
www.net-resource.com/mpo/svarty/
   alarm.html

Alice in Chains
www.music.sony.com/Music/ArtistInfo/
   AliceInChains
www.mtl.net/solidarite/pio/aic.htm
www.privat.katedral.se/~nv95mnar/aic

All
www.allcentral.com
www.tetranet.net/users/allroy/ALL/
   all.html
www2.hawaii.edu/~sanner/Descendents
   _all

All Saints
maxoft.hypermart.net/AllSaints
website.lineone.net/~tonk/all-saints
www.fortunecity.com/tinpan/agnetha/
   246/main.html

The Allman Brothers Band
www.epiccenter.com/EpicCenter/docs/
   artistupdate.qry?artistid=6
www.netspace.org/allmans
www.fas.harvard.edu/~needlem/allman

Alphaville
www.netville.de/alphaville/index.html
alphaville.netcns.com
home4.inet.tele.dk/mtp/alpha

Altan
www.altan.ie
we.got.net/docent/altan/altan.htm
www.ceolas.org/artists/Altan.html

Altered Images
www.sukeplow.demon.co.uk/altered/
altered.htm

Dave Alvin
bullwinkle.as.utexas.edu/scot/dave.
html

Ambrosia
www.ambrosiamusic.com
www.ambrosiaweb.com/ambrosia/
index.htm
www.geocities.com/SunsetStrip/Towers/
7661

America
www.horsewithnoname.com
www.pacificrim.net/~wahlgren
MissionImprobable.com/america

American Music Club
www.iuma.com/Warner/html/American
_Music_Club.html

Tori Amos
www.tori.com
www.aye.net/~mikewhy/toriamos.html
www.toriamos.org
pw2.netcom.com/~sgrizzo/toriint.html

Eric Andersen
www.execpc.com/~henkle/fbindex/a/
ander_eric.html

Laurie Anderson
www.cc.gatech.edu/~jimmyd/laurie-
anderson
labserver.kuntrynet.com/~wart/la
hem1.passagen.se/igth64

Leah Andreone
www-scf.usc.edu/~dheller/andreone/
andre1.html
www.geocities.com/SunsetStrip/Towers/
2625/andreone.html
www.xs4all.nl/~robinw/artists/index.
htm?artists/leah

Angel
www.webaccess.net/~arwood/thesight
ofblood/Angel/bats.htm

The Angels
www.theangels.com.au
www.lastbandit.com/angels.html
www.unlv.edu/~carranza/angels

The Animals
www.theanimal.com

Paul Anka
www.geocities.com/SunsetStrip/Lounge/
7824/paulanka.html
www.crl.com/~tsimon/anka.htm
www.allmusic.com/cg/x.exe?p=amg&sql
=B3557

Another Girl
www.bugjuice.com/anothergirl

Adam Ant
www.adam-ant.net
www.esteem.demon.co.uk/html/
adamant/adamant.htm
www.uhs.uga.edu/~john/adam_ant

Anthrax
www.elektra.com/metal_club/anthrax/
anthrax.html
www.enter.net/~jrcville/anthrax
www.netexp.net/~delpi

Aphex Twin
www.elektra.com/ambient_club/aphex/
aphex.html
www.fas.harvard.edu/~jkestler/aphex.
html
www.hyperreal.org/music/artists/afx

Fiona Apple
www.epiccenter.com/EpicCenter/work/
FionaApple
www.fionahaswings.com
members.aol.com/FionaAO/fiona.html
www.pcisys.net/~jrb/fiona

Apples in Stereo
www.applesinstereo.com

Aqua
www.fortunecity.com/tinpan/blur/300/
aqua.htm
home.sol.no/~oeysoere/aqua/aqua.
htm
members.xoom.com/aquariumweb/
aqua.html

The Aquabats
www.theaquabats.com
sanborn.simplenet.com/eNoise/
aquabats/index.shtml
chapz.com/aquabats

Archers of Loaf
www.elektra.com/alternative_club/
archers/archers.html
www.wku.edu/~bob/archers
weber.u.washington.edu/~huevos/aol/
aolhome.html

Jann Arden
www3.sk.sympatico.ca/bakab
www.citw.com/jannarden
www.geocities.com/SunsetStrip/
Lounge/7824/jannarden.html

Arkarna
www.repriserec.com/arkarna
www.angelfire.com/ak/arkarna/index.
html

Joan Armatrading
www.rcavictor.com/rca/joan/index.html
www.rahul.net/hrmusic/artists/jaart.
html

Army of Lovers
www.enqueue.com/aol
www.torget.se/users/d/daha6439/
Home.htm

The Art of Noise
rtt.colorado.edu/~baur/aon/aon.html
ww4.choice.net/~billgert
www.erols.com/dcrouch/aon.htm

Artificial Joy Club
www.artificialjoyclub.com
www.geocities.com/SunsetStrip/
Lounge/7824/artificialjoyclub.html
home.istar.ca/~alamarch/index.shtml

Asia
www.asiaworld.org

Ass Ponys
www2.eos.net/knownuniverse

The Associates
www.path.unimelb.edu.au/~new_wave/
Associates.html
www.cs.uit.no/Music/ViewGrp?grp_id=
2449

The Association
members.aol.com/warp1
members.aol.com/oldies1/associat.htm

Atari Teenage Riot
members.aol.com/nirvana073
www.freek.com/~freek/index.html
www.geocities.com/Augusta/2269/atr.
html

A3
www.geffen.com/a3
www.elemental.music.co.uk/alabama3

Atlanta Rhythm Section
www.lowerymusic.com/arshome.htm
bbuie.home.mindspring.com/ars.html

Audio Adrenaline
www.audioa.com
www.greenapple.com/~kgroves/audioa.
html
www.uidaho.edu/~wits9690/aa/aa.
html

Autechre
subnet.virtual-
pc.com/~sk393820/autechre.html
www.southern.com/mmm/music/
uktechno/artists/autechre.html
trout.sputcorp.com/reviews/autechre.
htm

The Auteurs
home1.swipnet.se/~w-10098/auteurs/
index.htm

The Avengers
members.aol.com/aytab2/houston.html

Average White Band
www.averagewhiteband.com
www.uni-potsdam.de/u/germanistik/
ls_dgs/awb/awb.htm
www.paulin.demon.co.uk/index.htm

Hoyt Axton
www.sixcats.com/axton/hoyt.htm
www.avertsystems.com/hoytaxton

Kevin Ayers
musart.co.uk/ayers1.htm
www.ping.be/~ping8683
www.users.globalnet.co.uk/~marwak/
index.html

Aztec Camera
www.aoinfo.com/aztec/html

Howie B
www.howieb.co.uk

The B-52s
www.RepriseRec.com/theb52s
www.aarondaniels.com/b52s
www.ozemail.com.au/~peterv/b52s/
index.html

Babe the Blue Ox
www.btbo.com

Babes in Toyland
www.RepriseRec.com/reprise_html_
pages/babesintoyland
www.quietroom.com
www.nvg.unit.no/~hersir/babes.html

Baby Bird
www.echo.co.uk/htmlpages/BIRD/
BIRD1.html
www.breakfast.demon.co.uk/feathers_
index.html

Bachman-Turner Overdrive
home1.swipnet.se/~w-15184/bto.html

Backstreet Boys
www.backstreetboys.com
www.geocities.com/SunsetStrip/
Amphitheatre/8671
www.geocities.com/SunsetStrip/Palms/
4622

Bad Brains
home.dti.net/joly/brains/index.html

Bad Company
www.elektra.com/rock_club/badco/
badco.html
www.geocities.com/SunsetStrip/Venue/
9685/bad_company.html

Bad Livers
www.hyperweb.com/badlivers

Bad Religion
www.atlantic-records.com/bad_religion

www.geocities.com/SunsetStrip/Palms/
4466/br.html
thebrpage.tierranet.com

Badfinger
www.badfinger.com

Joan Baez
baez.woz.org
www.afn.org/~afn31658/baez
www.execpc.com/~henkle/fbindex/b/
baez_joan.html

Bailter Space
www.matador.recs.com/bios/bio_
bailter.html
www.turnbuckle.com/Bailter.htm

Merrill Bainbridge
www.geocities.com/SunsetStrip/
Lounge/4112

Bananarama
www.curb.com/Artists/br.html
www.bananaramaweb.com
www.geocities.com/SunsetStrip/Venue/
4699

Banco de Gaia
www.banco.co.uk

The Band
theband.hiof.no
www.geocities.com/SunsetStrip/
Lounge/7824/theband.html

The Bangles
biron.usc.edu/~clare/Bangles.html
www.banglesfan.demon.co.uk
www.geocities.com/SunsetStrip/Studio/
8655/index.html

Barclay James Harvest
www.ftech.net/~harvest/bjh-home.htm

Barenaked Ladies
www.bnl.org
www.FisherTowne.com/Barenaked
www.cs.mun.ca/~craig/gp

Barnes & Barnes
www.inetworld.net/platypus/barnes

Syd Barrett
www.geocities.com/SunsetStrip/Stage/
2607
www.geocities.com/Vienna/Strasse/
2724
www.mtnlake.com/%7erobp/floyd6.
html

John Barry
members.aol.com/mysoundtrx/barry.
html

Basia
basia.techwood.org
djav.simplenet.com/personal/music/
basia

Bauhaus
www.geocities.com/SunsetStrip/Palms/
4349/index.html
www.waste.org/bauhaus
www.bauhaus.org

Bay City Rollers
www.baycityrollers.com
users.aol.com/buesken/bcr/bcr.htm
www.vidwizard.com/BCR/frmain.htm

Be Bop Deluxe
billnelson.com/bebopdeluxe/main.htm

The Beach Boys
www.mindspring.com/~sfrazier/bbfc.
htm
www.personal.u-net.com/~pcworld5/
index.htm
www.prairienet.org/~dauber/cap.html

Beastie Boys
www.grandroyal.com/BeastieBoys
beastieshrine.isontheweb.com/
beastiality/index-n.htm
www.flash.net/~korner

Beat Farmers
sdam.com/artists/bf

Beat Happening
www.subpop.com/bands/bhappening/
bhappening.html

The Beatles
www.primenet.com/~dhaber/beatles.
html
www.dreamscape.com/southrup/apple/
index.shtml
www.geocities.com/SunsetStrip/Alley/
3961
www.mindspring.com/~stewarts/
homepage.htm
members.aol.com/jsweeney/pepper.
htm

The Beautiful South
www.beautiful-south.co.uk
www-public.tu-bs.de:8080/~y0003231/
b_south/b_south.html
www.healey.com.au/~eva/hm

Beck
www.geffen.com/beck
www.rain.org/~truck/beck
earth.vol.com/~debber
www.geocities.com/SunsetStrip/Club/
5444/beck.html

Jeff Beck
www.wsvn.com/~staff/beck
home.dti.net/warr/beck.html

The Bee Gees
www.bgwoc.org
www.geocities.com/SunsetStrip/Alley/
5870/bg.html
www.ping.be/bgi

Bel Canto
math-www.uio.no/bel-canto
www.ozone.de/belcanto
zenith.no/belcanto

Adrian Belew
www.murple.com/adrianbelew

Belle & Sebastian
www.bigspace.co.uk/belleandsebastian
freespace.virgin.net/chris.hall5/index.htm
www.jeepster.co.uk/belleandsebastian

Belly
suze.ucs.usl.edu/~kaj9864/belly.html
www.geocities.com/SunsetStrip/
   Palladium/1994/belly.html
www.geocities.com/Hollywood/1625/
   belly.html

Pat Benatar
www.benatar.com/home.html
www2.southwind.net/~jcross/benatar
www.magpage.com/~bnsc/sandy/pb.htm

Berlin
www.serve.com/rja/berlin.htm
www.total.net/~mmachine/BigF

Dan Bern
www.eskimo.com/~wyiwndr/dan_bern.html

Chuck Berry
shell.ihug.co.nz/~mauricef/frames9.htm

Heidi Berry
www.evo.org/html/group/berryheidi.html

Richard Berry
www.netuser.com/~erp/R_Berry.html

Better Than Ezra
www.elektra.com/alternative_club/
   better/better.html
pages.prodigy.com/ezra
expert.cc.purdue.edu/~kojetin/
   betterthanezra

Bettie Serveert
www.matador.recs.com/bios/bio_bettie.html
home.pi.net/~vincentb/bettie/betindex.html
www.xs4all.nl/~gdvlugt/bettie/head1.html

Big Ass Truck
www.bigasstruck.com

Big Audio Dynamite
www.radioactive.net/BANDS/BAD/bad.html
hsfstud.hisf.no/~964289/bad.htm

Big Bad Voodoo Daddy
www.coolsvillerecords.com/bbvd/index.htm
members.tripod.com/~swingkid21/
   index.htm

Big Black
www.southern.com/Southern/band/
   BIGBL/index.html
www.olywa.net/pasha90/bigblack.htm
www.crl.com/~rfleming/big_black/bb_
   index.html

Big Chief
www.biddeford.com/~gighag

Big Country
www.bigcountry.co.uk
www.flash.net/~barcrow/BigC.htm
www.intercenter.net/~jnu/bc

Big Head Todd & the Monsters
www.bigheadtodd.com
www.revolution-online.com/bhtm

Big Rude Jake
www.bigrudejake.com
www.geocities.com/SunsetStrip/
   Lounge/7824/bigrudejake.html

Big Star
www.geocities.com/SoHo/6770

Big Wreck
www.bigwreck.com
members.xoom.com/BigWreck
www.geocities.com/SunsetStrip/
   Frontrow/1992

Bikini Kill
rebelgirl.simplenet.com/BikiniK.html
www.geocities.com/SoHo/Studios/6831/
   bikini.htm
www.skapunx.ml.org/~BikiniKill

Birddog
www.sugarfreerecords.com/birddog

The Birthday Party
www.alphalink.com.au/~kateb
www.iae.nl/users/maes/cave/disc/bp.html

Bis
homepages.force9.net/bisnation
members.aol.com/lurgeegirl/index.html
www.fortunecity.com/tinpan/sunra/186/
   bis.htm

Björk
www.elektra.com/alternative_club/
   bjork/bjork.html
bjork.mmedia.is
www.xnet.com/~wtchoi/bjork

Cilla Black
www.geocities.com/SunsetStrip/
   Amphitheatre/6370

Frank Black
beaker.nmsu.edu/spaceman/fb

www.cruzio.com/~drg/frank_black/
   index.html

The Black Crowes
www.blackcrowes.com

Black Dog
www.feedback.com/tbd

Black Flag
www.ipass.net/~jthrush/rollflag.htm
www.asan.com/users/crunch/bf
www.geocities.com/SunsetStrip/3694/
   blackflg.htm

Black 47
www.black47.com

Black Grape
home.sol.no/~runeth/musblack.htm

Black Lab
www.geffen.com/blacklab
www.blacklab.sf.ca.us
www.geocities.com/SunsetStrip/Cabaret/
   5080/index.html

Black Oak Arkansas
www.blackoakarkansas.com
www3.ns.sympatico.ca/rmacisaa

Black Sabbath
www.black-sabbath.com
www.geocities.com/SunsetStrip/Studio/
   9009
www.gr-lakes.com/~djgolus/bs.html

blackgirls
www.mammoth.com

Ritchie Blackmore
www.ritchieblackmore.com

Ruben Blades
home.dti.net/warr/colonblades.html

Blake Babies
www.mammoth.com

The Blasters
bullwinkle.as.utexas.edu/scot/blasters.html

Blessid Union of Souls
www.blessidunion.com

Blind Melon
www.blind-melon.com
www.oberlin.edu/~mbadanes/
   melonhome.html
members.aol.com/andrew1800/
   blindmelon.html

Blink 182
www.blink182.com
www.geocities.com/SunsetStrip/Studio/
   5661
www.geocities.com/SunsetStrip/
   Amphitheatre/7913/index.html

Blondie
www.primenet.com/~lab/blondie.html

www.thehub.com.au/~bchudso/blondie.
html
www2.carolina.net/kasey/INDEX.HTM

Blood, Sweat & Tears
members.tripod.com/~marshmallow
man/weird.htm

Bloodhound Gang
www.geffen.com/bloodhoundgang
www.bloodhoundgang.com
students.vassar.edu/~brgrosz/
BloodhoundGang.html

Luka Bloom
www.totalweb.co.uk/dweb/jan/jbloom.
htm

Michael Bloomfield
www.bluespower.com/arbn01.htm

The Blue Aeroplanes
www.foresight.co.uk/blueplanes

Blue Cheer
outland.cyberwar.com/~prw//blue_
cheer

Blue Meanies
www.soundz.com/bluemeanies

Blue Mountain
www2.msstate.edu/~sgn1/blue.html

Blue Nile
www.wco.com/~jkrose/craig/Nile.html
www.wbr.com/bluenile

Blue Öyster Cult
www.sonymusic.com/artists/BOC
www.geocities.com/SunsetStrip/Towers/
1615/index.html
members.aol.com/vegas4boc/index.
htm

Blue Rodeo
www.bluerodeo.com

The Blues Brothers
bluesbrothers.damp.com/bb
www.wfu.edu/~bwilson/bb/index.html
www.geocities.com/Hollywood/Lot/
8246

Blues Traveler
www.bluestraveler.com
www.sgi.net/bluestraveler
www.eagnet.com/baileyml/bt/blues.
htm

The Bluetones
www2.gol.com/users/quez/thebluetones.
html
www.geocities.com/SunsetStrip/1597/
bluetone.html

Blur
www.virginrecords.com/artists/VR.cgi?
ARTIST_NAME=Blur
www.blur.co.uk
blur.cream.org

home6.swipnet.se/~w-69908/
blur-index.html

BMX Bandits
tony.geog.aca.mmu.ac.uk/~junge/
junge/bandits

BoDeans
www.RepriseRec.com/reprise_HTML_
pages/bodeansdir/blenda.html

Body Count
www.geocities.com/SunsetStrip/Club/
9364/bc.html
www.virginrecords.com/artists/VR.cgi?
ARTIST_NAME=Body_Count

The Bogmen
www.resnet.uconn.edu/staff/fletch/
doubt
www.bogmen.com
www.aristarec.com/aristaweb/
TheBogmen/index.html

Tommy Bolin
www.tbolin.com

The Bolshoi
members.aol.com/shriekman/MUSIC/
BOLSHOI/Bol1.html

Michael Bolton
www.beachlife.net/rothrock/onthenet.
htm

Bomb the Bass
www.quango.com/bomb.htm

Bon Jovi
www.geocities.com/SunsetStrIp/Alley/
4685
www.info.tampere.fi/~lhearok/bonjovi
www.jonbonjovi.com

Bonham
www.shelbynet.net/~jbonham

Tracy Bonham
www.ozemail.com.au/~msafier/
TracyBonham/tracyb.html

Karla Bonoff
www.bryndle.com

The Bonzo Dog Band
www.anglia.ac.uk/~systimk/music/
bonzos/index.html
www.provide.net/~strickland/bonzo.
htm

Betty Boo
www-personal.umich.edu/~ferdt/betty.
html
home.dti.net/warr/boo.html

The Boo Radleys
www.geocities.com/Broadway/3308/
boorad.htm

James Booker
offbeat.com/booker/bookerhome.html

Booker T. & the MG's
www.sonymusic.com/artists/
BookerTAndTheMGs.html

Boom Crash Opera
www.bco.com.au

Pat Boone
www.geocities.com/TheTropics/9325/
patmetal.html

Boston
www.boston.org

Bouncing Souls
www.seas.upenn.edu/~markd/bsouls.
html
www.nyct.net/~damaged/bsouls.html
www2.lycoming.edu/~colrebe/index.
htm

Jean-Paul Bourelly
www.bourelly.com

Bow Wow Wow
www.geocities.com/SunsetStrip/Arena/
4970/index.html

David Bowie
www.virginrecords.com/artists/VR.cgi?
ARTIST_NAME=Bowie
www.davidbowie.com/2.0
www.etete.com/Bowie
www.algonet.se/~bassman/BOWIE.
html
ourworld.compuserve.com/homepages/
mbh

Boymerang
www.caroline.com/astralwerks/
boymerang

Brad
www.geocities.com/SunsetStrip/Towers/
1854/index.html

Robert Bradley's Blackwater Surprise
www.rbblackwatersurprise.com

Billy Bragg
www.billybragg.co.uk
home.clara.net/rlang
www.mindspring.com/~usul/billy-bragg.
html

Laura Branigan
www.ee.surrey.ac.uk/Contrib/music/
laura-branigan

Brave Combo
www.brave.com/bo

Bread
www.ktb.net/~insync/BREADtitle.html

The Breeders
www.i1.net/~noaloha/breeders.htm
www.big.du.se/~hedman/breeders/
info.html
home.i1.net/~noaloha/amps1.htm

Edie Brickell & New Bohemians
www.bodyofwater.com/edie
www.nis.za/~cschutte/edie.htm
www.crl.com/~phantom/edie/edie.html

Bronski Beat
bela.fei.tuke.sk/~bencr/bbeat

Johnatha Brooke
www.jonathabrooke.com

Meredith Brooks
hollywoodandvine.com/meredithbrooks
www.meredithbrooks.com
www.ecst.csuchico.edu/~rvanatta/
mbrooks

Greg Brown
gregbrown.wing.net
www.flemtam.com/gb.html

James Brown
www.onlinetalent.com/MRBrown_
homepage.html

Jackson Browne
www.elektra.com/rock_club/browne/
browne.html
www.west.net/~jrpprod/jackson_
browne.html

Jack Bruce
www.jackbruce.com

bt
www.albany.net/~bt

Roy Buchanan
sicel-home-2-19.urbanet.ch:8080/
Music/rbuch.html

Lindsey Buckingham
members.tripod.com/~rhiannon2/index.
html
users.aol.com/lindseyfan/goinsane.htm

Jeff Buckley
www.jeffbuckley.com
www.tiac.net/users/rfuller/buckley
www.geocities.com/SunsetStrip/Towers/
1085

Tim Buckley
pantheon.cis.yale.edu/~bodoin/
tbarchives.html
www.indirect.com/www/phahn/buckley.
html
www.ozemail.com.au/~hektor/buckley.
html

Richard Buckner
home.earthlink.net/~doubters/buckner.
html

Buffalo Springfield
home.dti.net/warr/buffalo.html

Buffalo Tom
www.buffalotom.com/home.html

Jimmy Buffett
www.geocities.com/TheTropics/2902

www.cobo.org
www.geocities.com/TheTropics/3502/
parrot.html
www.parrotkey.com

The Buggles
www.southside.org/~rush/buggles

Built to Spill
www.wbr.com/builttospill

Bulletboys
home.sprynet.com/sprynet/bronco1/
bullet.htm

Sonny Burgess
www.deltaboogie.com/deltamusicians/
burgess.htm

T-Bone Burnett
www.tmtm.com/sam

The Burns Sisters
204.255.183.201/web/Burns

Tony Burrows
www.asahi-net.or.jp/~tm9h-asd/tvotb.
htm

Bush
www.bushnet.com/intro
www.geocities.com/SunsetStrip/8845/
index.html
www.geocities.com/SunsetStrip/Alley/
4260

Kate Bush
www.gaffa.org
www.white-man-killer.com/kate/the_
muse.html
www.clubi.ie/twomey/katebush.htm

Bush Tetras
imusic.com/showcase/indie/busht.html

Jon Butcher
www.jonbutcher.com

Butthole Surfers
www.buttholesurfers.com
www.aristotle.net/~jmcfadden/bhs.html
web.wt.net/~szuckero

Buzzcocks
www.buzzcocks.demon.co.uk
www.mylist.net/SecretPublic

The Byrds
www.geocities.com/SunsetStrip/Palms/
2522/byrds.html
www.uark.edu/~kadler/rmcguinn
members.aol.com/byrdsonlne/
byrdsstuff/byrds.htm

David Byrne
www.talking-
heads.net/davidbyrne/index.html

Cabaret Voltaire
www.brainwashed.com/cv

Cactus
www.icono.org/cactus

Cake
members.aol.com/storage737/index.
html
www.geocities.com/SunsetStrip/Towers/
4534/cakef.htm
www.geocities.com/SouthBeach/
Marina/2986/cake.htm

Cake Like
www.cakelike.com

J.J. Cale
www.jjcale.com

John Cale
www.beggars.com/cale/johncale.html

The Call
www.erols.com/kdrew/call.html
users.vnet.net/misnomer/thecall/
homepage.html

Camel
ng.netgate.net/~jsp/camel/camelpage.
html

Glen Campbell
www.glencampbellshow.com

Camper Van Beethoven
reality.sgi.com/relph/campervan-etc

Can
www.io.com/~jwc/rock/can.html

Candlebox
www.wbr.com/maverick/candlebox96
www.boxheads.com/index.html

The Captain & Tennille
www.vcnet.com/moonlight

Captain Beefheart & His Magic Band
www.shiningsilence.com/hpr
www.cybercomm.nl/~tiotoa

The Cardigans
cardigans.net
www.mhv.net/~kev/cardig/index.html
www.geocities.com/CollegePark/Quad/
2567

Cardinal
www.geocities.com/SunsetStrip/Stage/
8391/davies.html

Mariah Carey
www.sonymusic.com/artists/Mariah
Carey
www.mariah.net
www.geocities.com/SunsetStrip/Palms/
4892

Kim Carnes
www.geocities.com/SunsetStrip/Towers/
1500

The Carpenters
www.mirai.or.jp/~gpda/cp/index3.htm

www.eee.hku.hk/~h9502296/carpenters.
html

Paul Carrack
www.carrack.com
www.ark21.com/paul_carrack/index.
html

Joe "King" Carrasco & the Crowns
www.joeking.com

Johnny Carroll
www.athenet.net/~genevinc/JohnCrrll.
html

The Cars
www.usats.com/dale/thecars
www.vsb.cz/~l91447/cars/ocars.htm
www.evansville.net/~smokey

Lori Carson
www.geocities.com/SoHo/Museum/
8563/home.html

Daniel Cartier
imusic.com/showcase/modern/cartier.
html

Peter Case
www.buzznet.com/petercase

Johnny Cash
www.johnnycash.com
maninblack.net
www.users.csbsju.edu/~sjfische/Cash.
html
www.wallofsound.com/artists/johnny
cash/index.html

David Cassidy
www.hardlink.com/~cassidy

Cat Power
www.net-quest.com/~arne/catpower/
catpower.shtml
www.matador.recs.com/bands/bands.
html#cat

Catatonia
easyweb.easynet.co.uk/~durandal/
catatonia

Catherine Wheel
www.catherinewheel.com
www.MercuryRecords.com/mercury/
artists/catherine_wheel/catherine_
wheel.html
www.netacc.net/~terpstra/CWJuke.html

The Caulfields
www.odyssee.net/~dore/rye/index2.
html

Nick Cave
www.zephyr.net/users/cave
www.geocities.com/SunsetStrip/
Palladium/7428
www.iae.nl/users/maes/cave/index.
html
www.mutelibtech.com/mute/cave/cave.
htm

Celibate Rifles
www.tt.net/hot/rifles

Chad & Jeremy
members.aol.com/bocad/cj.htm

Eugene Chadbourne
wymple.gs.net/~aaswell/eugene.html

The Chameleons
www.indigo.ndirect.co.uk/chameleons
www.geocities.com/SunsetStrip/
Underground/3255
www.trouser.demon.co.uk/chamhome.
html

The Champs
www.iuma.com/IUMA-2.0/ftp/volume3/
Champs,_The

Harry Chapin
members.aol.com/mcmen/home.html

Beth Nieslen Chapman
beth.trends.net
www.RepriseRec.com/BethNielsen
Chapman
users.bart.nl/~jad/nielsen.html

Tracy Chapman
www.elektra.com/alternative_club/
chapman/chapman.html
rzsunhome.rrze.uni-erlangen.de:81/
~sz1526/tracy.html
www.geocities.com/SunsetStrip/Palms/
9541

The Charlatans
www.stud.ifi.uio.no/~eirikg/Charlatans

The Charlatans UK
www.stud.ifi.uio.no/~eirikg/Charlatans

Chalk FarM
www.sonymusic.com/artists/ChalkFarM

Ray Charles
www.raycharles.com
www.celebsite.com/people/raycharles

Charm Farm
imusic.com/showcase/modern/cfarm.
html

Chavez
www.matador.recs.com/bios/bio_
chavez.html

Cheap Trick
www.cheaptrick.com
www.geocities.com/SunsetStrip/
Palladium/1582/OhmSweetOhm.html
www.netins.net/showcase/begeland/
ctrick/ctrick.htm

Chubby Checker
www.ozemail.com.au/~facerg/chubby.
htm

The Chemical Brothers
raft.vmg.co.uk/chemicalbros/index.html
uffa.incyberspace.com/Chemical

www.muohio.edu/~larsonaj/chemical

Neneh Cherry
www.sheenaweb.com/neneh

Cherry Poppin' Daddies
www.bitech.com/daddies/index.html
weber.u.washington.edu/~flooby/
daddies.html
www.jb.com/~henley/cpd.html

Chicago
www.chirecords.com
www.geocities.com/SunsetStrip/
Backstage/2375
www.cjnetworks.com/~chicago

Billy Childish
www.psychogarage.demon.co.uk/
childish

Toni Childs
www.eskimo.com/~wayneld/tonichilds.
html

The Chills
www.btinternet.com/~chills

Alex Chilton
members.aol.com/dammarie/
alexchilton.html

China Crisis
www.geocities.com/SunsetStrip/Towers/
3059/China1.htm

The Choir
www.cm-online.net/the-choir

Chopper
members.aol.com/poppower/chopper

Chumbawamba
www.chumba.com
www.ndh.com/home/chumba

The Church
church.sausage.com

Cibo Matto
www.wbr.com/cibomatto/index.html

Cinderella
www.cinderella.net

The Circle Jerks
www.geocities.com/SunsetStrip/
Amphitheatre/8903/circlejerks.html
www.geocities.com/SunsetStrip/
Cabaret/1472

CIV
www.tumyeto.com/tydu/music/profile/
civ/civ.html

Eric Clapton
www.xs4all.nl/~slowhand
www.geocities.com/SunsetStrip/Towers/
8488
www.celebsite.com/people/ericclapton/
index.html

www.geocities.com/SunsetStrip/Palms/
4538/ec.html
mars.superlink.net/user/wnuck/clapton.
html

Dave Clark Five
www2.excelr8.net/allowell/dcf.html

Petula Clark
www.geocities.com/~petulaclark

The Clarks
www.clarksonline.com

The Clash
www.geocities.com/SunsetStrip/
Palladium/1028

Johnny Clegg
www.globalmusic.com/Scatterlist.html

George Clinton
ourworld.compuserve.com/homepages/
PJebsen/homepage.htm
www.wallofsound.com/artists/
georgeclintonthepfunkallstars/index.
html
www.mediaspec.com/pfunk/index.html

The Coasters
t-e-i.com/coasters.html

Bruce Cockburn
www.kingsfield.com/cockburn
www.fish.com/music/bruce_cockburn

Joe Cocker
www.cocker.com
www.epiccenter.com/EpicCenter/docs/
artistupdate.qry?artistid=37
www.rockinwoman.com/cocker.html

Cockeyed Ghost
members.aol.com/TheGostGrl/index.htm

Cocteau Twins
www.cocteautwins.com
bbaer.rccden.com/~leesa/cocteautwins/
cHTML
www.bogo.co.uk/daisy/home.htm

Leonard Cohen
www.leonardcohen.com
nebula.simplenet.com/cohen
www.terabit.net/icho/cohen.htm

Cold
come.to/Cold
www.flip-records.com/Cold/coldframe.
htm
www.geocities.com/Hollywood/Studio/
1872

Coldcut
www.obsolete.com/pipe/coldcut/error.
html

Holly Cole
www.hollycole.com

Jude Cole
www.castle.net/~becker/music/
judecole/judecole.htm

Lloyd Cole
www.songwriting.com/lloydcole

Paula Cole
www.wbr.com/paulacole
www.geocities.com/SoHo/Coffeehouse/
1686
www.geocities.com/SunsetStrip/Arena/
2414/paulacole.html

Collective Soul
www.csoul.com
www.geocities.com/SunsetStrip/Stage/
8384/soul.html
www.geocities.com/SunsetStrip/Palms/
9334

Bootsy Collins
www.wbr.com/bootsy

Edwyn Collins
www.epiccenter.com/EpicCenter/edwyn

Judy Collins
digink.com/home/jcollins

Phil Collins
members.aol.com/nearlyphil/index.htm
www.geocities.com/SouthBeach/Shores/
1560/newphil.html
www.followme.demon.nl

Colony
members.aol.com/wwwcolony

Colourfield
members.tripod.com/~qroyd/
TheColourfield.html

Shawn Colvin
www.shawncolvin.com
members.aol.com/xiaoqinxu/Shawn/
shawn.html

Combustible Edison
www.subpop.com/bands/combustible/
comed/index.html

Come
www.matador.recs.com/bios/bio_come.
html

Commander Cody
www.awpi.com/CommanderCody
www.globerecords.com/Cody.html

Concrete Blonde
gopher://wiretap.spies.com/oo/Library/
Music/Disc/concrete.dis

The Connells
miavx1.muohio.edu/~ajjipson/connells2.
htmlx

Chris Connelly
blackcat.brynmawr.edu/~kimberly/CC

Consolidated
imusic.com/showcase/indie/
consolidated.html
Continental Drifters

Ry Cooder
www.addict.com/issues/1.01/Features/
Ry_Cooder

Sam Cooke
www.engr.uky.edu/~naowono1/SAM/
sam.html

Alice Cooper
www.alicecoopershow.com
home.sol.no/~embla/alice
www.pathcom.com/~omega/alicecop.
html
village.vossnet.co.uk/s/sihalley/tindex.
html

Cop Shoot Cop
www.lap.umd.edu/harper/csc/csc.html

Julian Cope
www.fsa.ulaval.ca/personnel/gaumondp/
cope/index.html

Cornershop
www.wbr.com/cornershop

Corrosion of Conformity
www.coc.net
hubcap.clemson.edu/~bmullin

The Corrs
www.thecorrs.org/home

Elvis Costello
www.lipa.ac.uk/~people/students/
c_ratliff/EC.htm
www.east.isx.com/~schnitzi/ec/index.
html
www.alphalink.com.au/~ever/ec
www.geocities.com/SunsetStrip/Studio/
7093/index.html

Mary Coughlan
www.cnotes.com/cnotes.artists/mary.
html

Counting Crows
www.countingcrows.com
www.geocities.com/SunsetStrip/Studio/
4110/index.htm
www.monmouth.com/~jkochel/crows.
html

Country Joe & the Fish
www.countryjoe.com
www.well.com/user/cjfish

Cowboy Junkies
www.geocities.com/SunsetStrip/Palms/
7573
members.aol.com/ivey/junkies.htm
www.geffen.com/cowboyjunkies

Cowboy Mouth
www.cowboymouth.com

The Cows
www.billions.com/cows

The Cowsills
www.cowsill.com

The Cramps
users.uniserve.com/~bwray/cramps.
html

The Cranberries
www.cranberries.ie
www.bright.net/~shwendel
www.student.nada.kth.se/~d90-fgi/
Cranberries

Cranes
www.unm.edu/~curemi2/.cranes1.html
www.cranes-fan.com

Crash Test Dummies
www.crashtestdummies.com
home.earthlink.net/~netzoomer

Robert Cray
www.rosebudus.com/cray
patriot.net/~rwhiffen/cray

Cream
www.fas.harvard.edu/~daraujo/cream.
html

Creed
www.creednet.com

Creedence Clearwater Revival
www.jyu.fi/~petkasi/ccr.htm
www.xs4all.nl/~wdw
ourworld.compuserve.com/homepages/
peter_koers

Marshall Crenshaw
www.marshallcrenshaw.com

Jim Croce
www.jim-croce.com
www.timeinabottle.com

Crosby, Stills & Nash
www.alpha.nl/CSN

Christopher Cross
www.christophercross.com

Sheryl Crow
www.wlink.net/~heuvel/sheryl/index.
html
www.geocities.com/SunsetStrip/Alley/
8457/main.html
pages.intnet.mu/jellybaby/home.htm

Crowded House
www.amws.com.au/c/crowded-house
ourworld.compuserve.com/homepages/
jraymond2
www.lr.tudelft.nl/~lr193174/house/index.
html

Kacy Crowley
www.atlantic-
records.com/nonframes/Artists_
Music/index.html?artistID=259

members.aol.com/flickergrl/kacyindex.
html

Cry of Love
www.cryoflove.com

The Crystal Method
www.randommedia.com/
thecrystalmethod
www.outpostrec.com/thecrystalmethod

The Cult
chaos.iagnet.net/.sacredsoul/goto.html
www.coastnet.com/~jtaylor/cult.html

Culture Club
www.geocities.com/SunsetStrip/
Palladium/9726/index3.html
www.geocities.com/SoHo/5816/Boygeo.
html

The Cure
www.thecure.com
miso.wwa.com/~anaconda/cure2.html
ourworld.compuserve.com/homepages/
ChainofFlowers
www.rhumba.pair.com/cure

Mark Curry
www.markcurry.com
rcip.com/markcurry

Mac Curtis
www.athenet.net/~genevinc/MacCurtis.
html

Curve
www.curve.co.uk
www.geocities.com/SunsetStrip/Palms/
5768/curve.html

Cypress Hill
www.sonymusic.com/artists/CypressHill/
index.html
www.citenet.com/users/ctsj1160/
cypress.htm
www.geocities.com/SunsetStrip/
Underground/9146/frameset.html

D Generation
members.aol.com/DGen
www.sonymusic.com/artists/
DGeneration/main.html
www.nytrash.com/dgeneration.html

dada
www.icorp.net/dada

Daft Punk
www.mygale.org/~maxtoan/daftpunk.
htm

Dick Dale
www.dickdale.com

Dambuilders
www.bcpl.lib.md.us/~hoch/dam.html

The Damned
www.geocities.com/SunsetStrip/Towers/
4359/damned.html

Dance Hall Crashers
www.crashers.com
dhc.vfive.com

Dandy Warhols
www.dandywarhols.com

Danzig
www.geocities.com/SunsetStrip/Club/
2373/danzig.html
www.smg-
webworks.com/MrBlond/danzig.htm

Vanessa Daou
members.aol.com/sundayaft/
vanessadaou.htm

Terence Trent D'Arby
home3.inet.tele.dk/hgaarde/TTDArby

Dash Rip Rock
www.dashriprock.com

Alana Davis
www.elektra.com/alternative_club/
alana_davis/alana_davis.html
members.tripod.com/~alana_davis/
index.html
members.aol.com/luv4qryche/page1.
htm

Ronnie Dawson
www.athenet.net/~genevinc/RonnieD.
htm

Taylor Dayne
www.taylordayne.com

Days of the New
www.angelfire.com/md/dotn/index.
html

DC Talk
www.dctalk.com
www.arches.uga.edu/~mcjohns/dctalk.
htm

Chris de Burgh
www.crl.com/~jderouen/cdeb

Deacon Blue
www.fortunecity.com/tinpan/fitzgerald/
275

Dead Boys
www.uta.fi/~csmape/bator.html

Dead Can Dance
www.nets.com/dcd
www.maths.monash.edu.au/~rjh/music/
eyesore/html/interview/
DeadCanDance.biography.html
www.geocities.com/SoHo/7773/
DCDLinks.html

Dead Kennedys
www.geocities.com/Athens/Forum/3111/
dk.htm
www.geocities.com/SunsetStrip/Palms/
1845/deadkennedys-g2.html

www.geocities.com/SunsetStrip/6558/
DKPAGE.HTM
www.geocities.com/SunsetStrip/Club/
5321/dk.html

The Dead Milkmen
www.deadmilkmen.com
www.worldchat.com/public/jeremyh/
3dm

Joey Dee
www.websessions.com/joeydee.htm

Deee-Lite
www.vudu.com/Deee-lite/index.cfm

Deep Forest
www.sonymusic.fr/DeepForest/mainuk.
htm

Deep Purple
www.deep-purple.com
www.pathcom.com/~omega/deeppurc.
html

Def Leppard
www.mercuryrecords.com/mercury/
artists/def_leppard/def_leppard.html
www.senff.demon.nl/leppard.html
www.geocities.com/SunsetStrip/8982
www.qlcomm.com/deflep

deftones
www.wbr.com/maverick/deftones
www.geocities.com/SunsetStrip/6280
www.loudside.com/deftones

Del Amitri
del-amitri.linex.com

Iris DeMent
members.aol.com/jarmode/DeMent.
html

Cathy Dennis
www.gpl.net/users/emove

John Denver
www.geocities.com/SunsetStrip/
Mezzanine/7341/denver.html
www.johndenver.net/mic_net.html
www.austin1.com/JD

Depeche Mode
www.depechemode.com
www.depeche-mode.com
home1.swipnet.se/~w-17595
www.geocities.com/SunsetStrip/Palms/
6631/dm.html

Rick Derringer
www.rickderringer.com

Descendents
listen.to/descendents
www2.hawaii.edu/~sanner/Descendents
_all
www.tetranet.net/users/allroy/
DESCENDENTS/descend.html

Willy DeVille
www.discoveryrec.com/artists/ville/
index.html

The Devlins
www.thedevlins.com
www.monterey.edu/students/
devlinrobertc/world
www.angelfire.com/il/SteMc/devlins.
html

Devo
www-unix.oit.umass.edu/~vndibere/
devo.html
www.spudland.com
fly.hiwaay.net/~drdunlap/devo

Dexys Midnight Runners
www.spiritonline.com/dexys

Neil Diamond
www.sonymusic.com/artists/
NeilDiamond/index3.html
www.diamondville.com
www.imagcom.co.uk/TDC/tdc.html

The Dickies
home.earthlink.net/~dickies

The Dictators
www.furious.com/perfect/dictators.html

Bo Diddley
www.inergy.com/Originator

Ani DiFranco
www.anidifranco.net
www.geocities.com/SoHo/Gallery/1915/
winw.html
www.rit.edu/~apso104/ani
www.gettysburg.edu/~s330544/ani.
html

Dinosaur Jr.
www.iwaynet.net/~keeblin/dinosaur.
html
freakscene.simplenet.com
www.geocities.com/SunsetStrip/Palms/
6440/index.html

Dio
hem1.passagen.se/diomagic
www.hut.fi/~dio/bio
members.aol.com/mikek48/dio.htm

Celine Dion
www.celineonline.com
www.geocities.com/~c-e-l-i-n-e
members.tripod.com/~celineh

Dire Straits
www.users.wineasy.se/daniel/index.html
www.geocities.com/Nashville/3399

Dirty Three
www.billions.com/dirty3

Dishwalla
www.amrecords.com/artists/dishwalla
www.geocities.com/Paris/1529
www.geocities.com/Tokyo/Towers/5997

Divine Comedy
www.thedivinecomedy.com

Divinyls
www.divinyls.com/indextemp.html

The Dixie Dregs
www.stevemorse.com

DJ Krush
www.sme.co.jp/Music/Info/SonyTechno/
othersE/krush/index.html

DNA
www.sonicstate.com/DNA

Dr. Feelgood
ourworld.compuserve.com/homepages/
dr_feelgood_info_service/feelgood.
htm

Dr. John
www.drjohn.com
www.blueflamecafe.com/Dr_John.html

Dr. Octagon
imusic.com/showcase/club/droct.html

Dodgy
www.ftech.net/~nebula/dodgy/dodgy.
html

Dogma
www.geocities.com/SunsetStrip/Alley/
3395

Dog's Eye View
www.dogseyeview.com

Dogstar
www.dogstarfan.com

Dokken
www.dvdol.com/~kirsten/dokken.html

Thomas Dolby
flatearth.tdolby.com

Donner Party
home.earthlink.net/~polpins/index2.
html

Donovan
www.dur.ac.uk/~d416bb/don/index.
html

The Doobie Brothers
www.DoobieBros.com/IndexWin.html

The Doors
www.elektra.com/rock_club/doors/
doors.html
www.geocities.com/SunsetStrip/Palms/
2914/index.html
www.insanetheatre.com
www.insanetheatre.com/Paris/7850/frame.
html
www.ipb.pt/~rufino/doors/doors.html

Down by Law
www.csclub.uwaterloo.ca/u/sstackho/
dbl/dbl.html

Nick Drake
www.algonet.se/~iguana/DRAKE/
DRAKE.html

Dramarama
raven.cybercomm.net/~flem/Drama

Dread Zeppelin
www.dreadzeppelin.com
www.greenheart.com/birdcage/
planetdread.html

The Dream Academy
www.geocities.com/SunsetStrip/Studio/
3983
www.serve.com/brenta/dreamac
pw2.netcom.com/~riple/dream.html

Dream Theater
www.dreamt.org
www.rsabbs.com/dt

Drivin' N' Cryin'
www.drivinncryin.com

Pete Droge
members.xoom.com/bates67/
PeteDroge.htm

Drugstore
www.drugstore-voodoo.co.uk
ssl.pro-net.co.uk/home/wolfg_l/
drugstore
www.roblang.demon.co.uk/Drgstore/
index.html

Chris Duarte
chrisduartegroupfans.org

Dubstar
easyweb.easynet.co.uk/~neilh/index.
htm

Frances Dunnery
www.dunnery.com

Duran Duran
www.guy123.force9.co.uk/duran.htm
www.duranie.com
www.cyberqueens.com
duran.hypermart.net

Bob Dylan
www.bobdylan.com
www.uvm.edu/~ksherloc/dylan
hudson.idt.net/~kharro19
www.geocities.com/Athens/Oracle/6752
e2.empirenet.com/~plong/main.htm

The Eagles
www.dreamscape.com/esmith/dansm/
eagles.htm
members.aol.com/ivyrain/fastlane.htm
www.geocities.com/SunsetStrip/Towers/
7026/longrun.htm
home.worldonline.nl/~annetted/eagles.
html

Fred Eaglesmith
www.panix.com/~tneff/eaglesmith

Steve Earle
http://www.wbr.com/steveearle
www.mcs.net/~lisa/EARLE/steve.htm

The Easybeats
www.algonet.se/~jonwar/easybeats.html

Echo & the Bunnymen
www.bunnymen.com
www.dez.com/doug/bunnymen.html

Echobelly
www.echobelly.com

Eddie & the Hot Rods
members.aol.com/gsfeelgood/hotrods/
welcome.htm

Dave Edmunds
www.pacemaker.com/peter/edmunds
www.harborside.com/home/a/aowens/
dave.htm

eels
www.dhhall.demon.co.uk/eels/eels.htm

Effigies
www.effigies.com

The Egg
discoveryrec.com/artists/egg/index.html

808 State
www.808state.com

Einstürzende Neubauten
www.geocities.com/SunsetStrip/Club/
7442/index.html

El Vez
www.geocities.com/Hollywood/Hills/
5017

Elastica
www.actwin.com/lineup

Electric Light Orchestra
www.spaceportelo.com

Electronic
slashmc.rice.edu/ceremony/electronic/
electronic.html

The Elevator Drops
www.timebombrecordings.com/elhome.
html

Eleventh Dream Day
centerstage.net/chicago/music/
whoswho/EleventhDreamDa.html

Joe Ely
www.ely.com

Elysian Fields
elysianfield.org

Embarassment
www.contrib.andrew.cmu.edu/user/wall/
embos/embos.html

Emergency Broadcast Network
waxtrax.com/bands/ebn.html

Emerson, Lake & Palmer
www.dynrec.com/elp

EMF
www.emf-theband.com/emfindex.html

An Emotional Fish
hsfstud.hisf.no/~964289/aef.htm

Alec Empire
home.msen.com/~liz/destroy

Engine 88
www.best.com/~eknight/engine88

The English Beat
www.best.com/~sirlou/ukbeat.html

Jeremy Enigk
hubcap.clemson.edu/~bpmccal/hollow.
html
www.subpop.com/bands/jeremy/
website-docs

Enigma
www.enigma3.com
www.enigmafan.com

Brian Eno
www.hyperreal.org/music/artists/
brian_eno
www.spies.com/Eno/EnoFAQ.html

Enormous
www.access.digex.net/~gold/e/
enormous.html

John Entwisle
www.eden.com/~theox

Enuff Z'Nuff
www.fh-landshut.de/~holger1/enuff.
html

Erasure
www.maverickent.com/erasure
home.swbell.net/dan-o/index2.htm

Roky Erickson
www.hyperweb.com/roky/roky.html

Eric's Trip
www.subpop.com/bands/ericstrip/et.
html

Gloria Estefan & Miami Sound Machine
www.epiccenter.com/EpicCenter/
custom/56
www.gloriafan.com
dspace.dial.pipex.com/town/estate/
hv18/gloria.html

Maggie Estep
members.aol.com/zoespage/index.html

Melissa Etheridge
www.wowdx.net/~tbird/melissa
members.aol.com/slntlgcy/page2.htm
www.wallofsound.com/artists/
melissaetheridge/index.html

Eurythmics
wwwperso.hol.fr/~tmalaval

Everclear
www.geocities.com/Paris/2068
www.geocities.com/~theafterglow/
index2.html
www.colby.edu/personal/pjoneil/
firemaple.html

Everything but the Girl
www.ebtg.com

Extra Fancy
members.aol.com/exfancy/index.html

Extreme
www.kramerskorner.com/extreme.html

The Fabulous Thunderbirds
www.austinlinks.com/Music/tbirds.html

Face to Face
www.unm.edu/~junelson/facetoface.
htm

John Fahey
www.fantasyjazz.com/fahey.html
www.execpc.com/~henkle/fbindex/f/
fahey_john.html

Fairport Convention
www.NovPapyrus.com/fairport

Faith No More
www.fnm.com
web.access.net.au/~ghendric/faith/
frames.htm
www.geocities.com/SunsetStrip/
Palladium/5113

Marianne Faithfull
www.planete.net/~smironne

The Fall
www.dcs.ed.ac.uk/home/cxl/fall

Chris Farlowe
personal.inet.fi/private/tapani.taka/
chris_farlowe.htm

Mylene Farmer
www.arrakis.es/~advent/mylene.htm

Dion Farris
www.sonymusic.com/artists/DionneFarr
is

Fastbacks
www.subpop.com/~scottl

Fatboy Slim
www.caroline.com/astralwerks/fbs

Faust
www.webquest.com/faust

Melissa Ferrick
www.best.com/~kluce/www.htm

Bryan Ferry
www.dlc.fi/~hope
www.its.caltech.edu/~bryan/roxy

Fig Dish
www.hia.net/bcd/figdishinfo.htm

The Figgs
www.rocknet.com/nov96/figgs.html

Filter
www.hevanet.com/hubka/FILTER

Fine Young Cannibals
www.dsv.su.se/~mats-bjo/fyc/fychome.
html

fIREHOSE
www.mindspring.com/~plant2000/
firehose.htm

Fishbone
gladstone.uoregon.edu/~cschatz/
fishbone.html
www.risingsun.com/fishbone

Five Americans
www2.1starnet.com/west5am

Five-Eight
www.mindspring.com/~fiveeight

The Fixx
byrneweb.com/Fixx

The Flamin' Groovies
www.webcom.com/~smholt/groovies

The Flaming Lips
www.wbr.com/flaminglips

Flat Duo Jets
members.aol.com/Flatdjets/index.html

Fleetwood Mac
cyberpenguin.net/penguin
homepages.udayton.edu/~macdouse/
fmac
www.repriserec.com/fleetwoodmac
members.aol.com/steviewitz/illusion.
htm

The Fleshtones
www.pro-net.co.uk/scaf/fhof.html

A Flock of Seagulls
www.oz.net/~davester/AFOS/AFOS.html

Flop
www.sonymusic.com/artists/Flop.html

Flotsam & Jetsam
www.geocities.com/SunsetStrip/Palms/
9054
www.mca.com/mca_records/amp4/
feature1.html
www3.nf.sympatico.ca/randall.flagg

The Fluid
members.tripod.com/~fluidgeek/index.
html

Fluke
raft.vmg.co.uk/fluke

Fly
www2.ledfeather.com/ledfeather/fly

Focus
www.mindspring.com/~jtymecki/focus
www.student.wau.nl/~nol/focus
www.geocities.com/SunsetStrip/Alley/
8267/index.html

Dan Fogelberg
www.treehouse.org/fogelberg

John Fogerty
www.wbr.com/johnfogerty

Foghat
www.foghat.com

Ben Folds Five
www.epiccenter.com/EpicCenter/
Benfoldsite/index.qry?artistid=274
www.geocities.com/Hollywood/Lot/
5009
www.globaldialog.com/~sschneid/bff

Foo Fighters
www.foofighters.com/foo
foofighters.tierranet.com
www.imagebusiness.com/mikec/foo.
html

For Against
cyclone.swa.com/for_against

For Squirrels
www.epiccenter.com/EpicCenter/docs/
artistupdate.qry?artistid=61

Steve Forbert
www.dip.ee.uct.ac.za/~brendt/music/
forbert

Lita Ford
members.aol.com/ironladies/index2.
html

Julia Fordham
www.virginrecords.com/artists/VR.cgi?
ARTIST_NAME=Julia_Fordham

Foreigner
home.att.net/~DragonFrost
www.geocities.com/SunsetStrip/8471

Forest for the Trees
www.dreamworksrec.com/
forestforthetrees

Fountains of Wayne
www.scratchie.com/fountainsofwayne
www.mlode.com/~zippy

The Four Seasons
www.srv.net/~roxtar/valli_frankie.html

The Four Tops
home.dti.net/warr/fourtops.html

Kim Fox
dreamworksrec.com/kimfox

Samantha Fox
members.aol.com/foxrocks/index.html
newman.simplenet.com/samantha_fox/
samantha_fox2.htm

Peter Frampton
www.frampton.com

Frankie Goes to Hollywood
www.cs.rulimburg.nl/~antal/fgth/
fgth-home.html

Aretha Franklin
www.globalserve.net/~ebutler
www.wallofsound.com/artists/
arethafranklin/index.html

Frente!
www.geocities.com/SoHo/6850/
index.html

Gavin Friday
www.gavinfriday.com

Friends of Dean Martinez
www.subpop.com/bands/fodm/
fodm-bio.html

Robert Fripp
www.cs.man.ac.uk/aig/staff/toby/et

Bill Frisell
www.geocities.com/Hollywood/2251/
frisell.html

Front 242
www.front242.com

Fugazi
www.southern.com/southern/band/
FUGAZ/index.html
www.people.cornell.edu/pages/jma15/
fugazi/fugazi.htm
members.wbs.net/homepages/g/u/f/
gufazi.html

Fun Boy Three
members.tripod.com/~qroyd/
TheFunBoyThree.html

Fun Lovin' Criminals
www.lcity.com/flc/index.htm

Future Sound of London
olohof.et.tudelft.nl/~pteppic/FSOL.html

Peter Gabriel
soundbot.ml.org/pg
www.primenet.com/~carmina/pg
www.mindbridge.com/~jen/jenspage.
html
ourworld.compuserve.com/homepages/
rrakoczy/main.htm

Galaxie 500
users.ox.ac.uk/~ba93013/Galaxie_500.
html

Rory Gallagher
www.hut.fi/~khagelbe/rory.html

Game Theory
www.loudfamily.com/lfgame.html

Gang of Four
trouserpress.com/bandpages/GANG_OF
_FOUR.html

Garbage
www.garbage.com
www.geocities.com/SunsetStrip/Palms/
2290
www.halcyon.com/cantwell/nkm/
garbage.html
www.geocities.com/SunsetStrip/Club/
2221

Art Garfunkel
www.djmegan.com

Greg Garing
www.paladinrecords.com/garing2/
welcome.html

Gas Huffer
weber.u.washington.edu/~gringo/
huffer.htm

Gastr del Sol
www.cen.uiuc.edu/~khoury/sb/gastr.
html

The Gathering Field
www.sgi.net/gathering

Danny Gatton
www.bandpages.com/gatton/index_
main.html

Marvin Gaye
www.calvin.edu/~cdykho15/marvin
www.sedgsoftware.com/marvin

Geggy Tah
www.wbr.com/geggytah

Gene
www.geocities.com/SunsetStrip/Stage/
6124/index.html

Genesis
www.congo.demon.co.uk/genesis.html
www.pacificcoast.net/~pollux/kids.htm
www.genesis-web.com

Gentle Giant
www.cs.umass.edu/~barrett/
gentlegiant.html

Georgia Satellites
fly.hiwaay.net/~dderrick/sats.html

Geraldine Fibbers
www.best.com/~djsq/fibbers.html

Lisa Germano
www.geocities.com/CollegePark/3992/
lisa.html

The Germs
www.best.com/~dru1d/music/germs

Lisa Gerrard
www.wbr.com/lisagerrard/d-index3.htm

Gerry & the Pacemakers
www.geocities.com/SunsetStrip/Palms/
6315

Giant Sand
www.restless.com/gsand.html
infosoc.informatik.uni-bremen.de/mad/
giant.htm

Deborah Gibson
www.truemagic.com/dg

Jimmie Dale Gilmore
monsterbit.com/jdg

Gin Blossoms
www.geocities.com/~eharty/gin_
blossoms.html

Ginger
www.globalserve.net/~hither/ginger
www.eden.com/~gregandi/gow/ginger.
html
www.geocities.com/SunsetStrip/Club/
3179/ginger.htm

Girls Against Boys
www-personal.umich.edu/~egery/GVSB/
index.html
gvsb.simplenet.com

Gladhands
www.gladhands.com

Glitterbox
www.fineran.demon.co.uk/ANTPAGES/
page2.html

The Go-Go's
www.gogosfan.demon.co.uk
www.ee.surrey.ac.uk/contrib/music/
go-gos

Go West
www.worldmachine.com/gowest

God Street Wine
www.godstreetwine.com

The Godfathers
www.unc.edu/~marmbru/godfathers/
index.html

Golden Earring
www1.tip.nl/~t118815/earring.htm

The Golden Palominos
www.goldenpalominos.com

Golden Smog
www.rykodisc.com/RykoInternal/
Features/209

Goldfinger
www.mojorecords.com/goldfinger/
index.html
www.hevanet.com/johnh/frames.htm

Goldie
www.ulster.net/~hmcgowan/saturn.htm

Goo Goo Dolls
www.wbr.com/googoodolls
soong.heinous.net/~goo/index.html

Steve Goodman
www.hepcat.com/goodman/good.html
www.execpc.com/~henkle/fbindex/g/
goodman_steve.html

Robert Gordon
www.athenet.net/~genevinc/Robert
Gordon.html

Lesley Gore
www.flash.net/~pswayne/lgore.htm

Gov't Mule
www.mule.net

Grand Funk Railroad
www.grandfunkrailroad.com

Amy Grant
www.myrrh.com/amygrant
www.geocities.com/Hollywood/9706/
index.html

Grant Lee Buffalo
www.uq.net.au/~zzsmiffs/GLB/grant.
html

The Grapes of Wrath
www.eden.com/~gregandi/grapes.html
www.geocities.com/SunsetStrip/Club/
3179/ginger.htm

The Grateful Dead
www.dead.net
arts.ucsc.edu/gdead/agdl
www.erols.com/jockomo/jockomo.htm
www.taco.com/roots
www.frognet.net/~scott/dead.html

Gravity Kills
www.geocities.com/SunsetStrip/7133

David Gray
members.tripod.com/~Tower

Great Big Sea
www.greatbigsea.com

Great White
web.syr.edu/~reharnoi/gw.html

Al Green
members.tripod.com/~hvredeveld/
voxerotica.html

Green Day
www.RepriseRec.com/GreenDay
www.geocities.com/SunsetStrip/Towers/
4848
www.geocities.com/~pennimrod/
greenday.html

Green Jellÿ
www.greenjelly.com
www.csam.montclair.edu/~cameron/gj
members.xoom.com/cluckin/hellojello.
html

Green on Red
home3.swipnet.se/~w-33845/cpgor/
gor/gor.htm

Greenberry Woods
www.splitsville.com

Patty Griffin
nw3.nai.net/~zigmont

Guadalcanal Diary
winston.tusc.net/gd

The Guess Who
www.theguesswho.com/theguesswho

Guided by Voices
www.gbv.com

Gun Club
www.geocities.com/SunsetStrip/Palms/
2381/gunclub.htm

Guns N' Roses
www.geocities.com/Hollywood/Hills/
1101/gnr1.htm
www.geocities.com/SunsetStrip/Palms/
4551
www.teleport.com/~boerio/gnr
www.bzzt.com/gnrbar

GWAR
www.brainlink.com/~ragnarok/gwar.
html
www.carnivalofchaos.com

Sammy Hagar
clubcabo.simplenet.com
www2.bc.edu/~worboys/sammy.html

Nina Hagen
www.primenet.com/~spork/nina

Haircut 100
www-unix.oit.umass.edu/~gokey/
heyward.html

Bill Haley
rockhall.com/induct/halebill.html

Half Japanese
www.concentric.net/~slug/HalfJapanese.
htm

Kristen Hall
home.intranet.org/kristen_hall

Hall & Oates
iwc.pair.com/hall_oates

Handsome
www.geocities.com/SunsetStrip/Stage/
8694

Hanoi Rocks
where.com/~jkd/hanoi/hanoi.html

Hanson
www.mercuryrecords.com/mercury/
artists/hanson/hanson_homepage.
html
www.hansonline.com
www.geocities.com/SunsetStrip/Venue/
1506

John Wesley Harding
www.wesweb.net

Françoise Hardy
ourworld.compuserve.com/homepages/
geroki/fhdooo.htm

Ben Harper
www.wwpro.com/benharper
www.geocities.com/SunsetStrip/
Lounge/7795/index.html
www.virginrecords.com/ben_harper

Emmylou Harris
www.nashville.net/~kate

George Harrison
web.mit.edu/scholvin/www/harrison/
harrison.html
www.wallofsound.com/artists/
georgeharrison/index.html

P.J. Harvey
pjh.org
http://209.132.53.103/pj/index.html
www.geocities.com/SunsetStrip/
Underground/5190/dryecstasy.html

Harvey Danger
www.blarg.net/~hdanger

Juliana Hatfield
www.geocities.com/SunsetStrip/8579/
index.html
www.satchmo.com/juliana/index.html

Hayden
www.outpostrec.com/hayden/index.
html

Lili Haydn
www.geocities.com/SunsetStrip/
Palladium/3635/lilihaydn.html

Ronnie Hawkins
www.worldchat.com/public/mdgeorge/
hawkins.htm

Screamin' Jay Hawkins
www.crl.com/~tsimon/jhawkins.htm
homepages.uel.ac.uk/K.Eley/screamin.
htm

Sophie B. Hawkins
www.vudu.com/Sophie

Hawkwind
www.geocities.com/SunsetStrip/Towers/
1637/hawkwind.html

Hazel
www.subpop.com/bands/hazel/hazel.
html

The Jeff Healey Band
www.geocities.com/BourbonStreet/
Delta/5180
www.geocities.com/SunsetStrip/Alley/
3670

Heart
www.imt.net/~scooter/Heart.html

www.AnnandNancy.com

The Reverend Horton Heat
www.reverendhortonheat.com
www.cs.utexas.edu/users/jwetzler/rev/
revframe.htm
www.geocities.com/SunsetStrip/Palms/
1682

Heatmiser
www.cs.trinity.edu/~ntrankli/heatmiser/
heatmiser.html

Heaven 17
www.nerosoft.com/Heaven17
www.path.unimelb.edu.au/~new_wave/
17.html
members.aol.com/H17page

Helium
www.princeton.com/sbatten/helium/
index.html

The Hellecasters
www.hellecasters.com
www.flexquarters.com/casters.htm

Helmet
www.interscoperecords.com/hel1.html
www.helmet.org

Jimi Hendrix
www.jimi-hendrix.com
spectra.net/~craig/jimi.html
www.lionsgate.com/music/hendrix
www.captaincrunch.com/jimi/faq
www.geocities.com/SunsetStrip/Studio/
1035/index.html

Don Henley
members.aol.com/ivyrain/don.htm

Joe Henry
www.mammoth.com

Herman's Hermits
members.aol.com/bocad/hh.htm

Richard X. Heyman
www.richardxheyman.com

John Hiatt
www.tiac.net/users/pfl/sor.htm

Dan Hicks
www.ns.net/~chaler/hicks.html

High Llamas
www.cabinessence.com/high-llamas

Peter Himmelman
www.unc.edu/~shlny/ph

His Name Is Alive
www.apocalypse.org/pub/u/friday/
breath.html

Robyn Hitchcock
www.wbr.com/robynhitchcock

Hoarse
www.hoarse.com

Hole
www.geocities.com/SunsetStrip/Alley/
3119/Hole.html
www.geocities.com/SunsetStrip/Club/
5014/index.html
www.geocities.com/SunsetStrip/Studio/
2575

The Hollies
www.proweb.co.uk/~rhaywood

Buddy Holly
www.cmgww.com/music/holly/holly.
html
www.geocities.com/SunsetStrip/Palms/
8334
206.151.68.40:80/kdwilt

The Hoodoo Gurus
www.hoodoogurus.com

John Lee Hooker
www.virginrecords.com/jlhooker
www.rosebudus.com/hooker

The Hooters
melodica.com
users.aol.com/drldeboer/hoo/althoot.
htm

Hootie & the Blowfish
www.hootie.com
www.clarkson.edu/~hinescj/hootie.htm
www.geocities.com/Athens/1995/
blowfish.html

Hooverphonic
www.hooverphonic.com

Bruce Hornsby & the Range
members.aol.com/brhornsby/index.html

Hot Tuna
www1.mhv.net/~federici/jorma2.htm

Hothouse Flowers
home.clara.net/pranksta/hothouse

House of Freaks
curry.edschool.virginia.edu/~jef2e/
freaks/freaks.html

House of Love
www.teleport.com/~luna/hol/hol.html

House of Pain
www1.minn.net/~wkoerner/hoppub/
index.html
www.geocities.com/SouthBeach/Sands/
8501
www.du.edu/~szitnak/mainpain.html

The Housemartins
www.healey.com.au/~eva/hm/hm.html

Penelope Houston
members.aol.com/aytab2/houston.html

Whitney Houston
www.aristarec.com/aristaweb/Whitney
Houston/index.html
www.whitney-fan.com

www.wallofsound.com/artists/
whitneyhouston/index.html

Howlin' Wolf
www.nicom.com/~machare/wolf
www.novia.net/~cedmunds
hob.com/essential/howl.html

H2O
www.h2ogo.com
members.aol.com/h2osmurf/Me/h2o.
html

Huevos Rancheros
www.huevosrancheros.com

Huffamoose
www.interscoperecords.com/huff.html
www.huffamoose.com

Hum
freezone.exmachina.net/cosmos/hum
www.prairienet.org/~hum/homepage.
html

Human League
www.escritoire.demon.co.uk/human.htm

Ian Hunter
www.mv.com/ipusers/mottthehoople/ih.
htm

Hunters & Collectors
www.backmeup.net.au/~ghost/h+c.html

Hüsker Dü
www.ncl.ac.uk/~n4262587/husker.html

Janis Ian
www.songs.com/janisian

Icehouse
www.spellbound-icehouse.org

The Icicle Works
www.geocities.com/SunsetStrip/Studio/
7829
www.beggars.com/icicle/icicle.html

Idaho
web.mit.edu/kcvkk/idaho

Billy Idol
www.billyidol.com
www.geocities.com/SunsetStrip/6464

Incubus
www.epiccenter.com/EpicCenter/Incubus
userzweb.lightspeed.net/~kornyone/
incubus

Indigo Girls
www.epiccenter.com/EpicCenter/
IndigoGirls/index.html
home.earthlink.net/~underdog/index.
html
www.geocities.com/CollegePark/5482/
indigo.html

Insane Clown Posse
www.insaneclownposse.com

www.geocities.com/SunsetStrip/Stage/
1640/index.html

Inspiral Carpets
www.geocities.com/SunsetStrip/9091/
moo.htm

The Interpreters
www.geocities.com/SunsetStrip/
Mezzanine/6871/index.html

INXS
www.umdnj.edu/~kotharne/inxs.html
www.geocities.com/SunsetStrip/Club/
7790
www.netwiz.net/~jhutch/inxs/inxs.html

Iron Butterfly
www.ironbutterfly.com

Iron Maiden
www.ironmaiden.co.uk
www.geocities.com/SoHo/5482/irons.
html

Chris Isaak
www.RepriseRec.com/Reprise_HTML_
Pages/chrisisaakfolder/baja/baja.
html
fly.hiwaay.net/~mdlatham/isaak.html

Ken Ishii
www.sme.co.jp/Music/Info/SonyTechno/
KI/index.html

The Isley Brothers
www2.uic.edu/~wcloyd1/Isley.html
www.geocities.com/SunsetStrip/Alley/
1973

Ivy
members.aol.com/theivyvine
www.cyberramp.net/~lilith/ivy/ivy.html
www.tweekitten.com/ivy.ny

Janet Jackson
www.janet-jackson.com
friendsofjanet.com
www.csun.edu/~mcc59224/janet1.html

Joe Jackson
www.joejackson.com

Michael Jackson
www.histeria.com
www.sonymusic.com/artists/
MichaelJackson
www.telepath.com/skywalk/mj/mj.htm
www.geocities.com/SunsetStrip/Stage/
2943

Jackson 5
www.motown40.com/motown40/
history/j/jackson_5/bio/
jack_5_bio.html
members.aol.com/valsadie/mjphoto2.
htm
www.geocities.com/~jacksonline/
jackson5.htm

Kate Jacobs
members.aol.com/JacobsKate/index.html

Mick Jagger
www.celebsite.com/people/mickjagger/
index.html

Jai
www.jai.co.uk
www.bugjuice.com/jai

Jale
www.dlcwest.com/~gkohut/jale/jale1.
html

The Jam
www.skynet.co.uk/~kefansu/the_jam/
frames.html

James
james.wattyco.com
www.eclipse.net/~stutter

Elmore James
hob.com/essential/ejames.html

Tommy James & the Shondells
www.tommyjames.com

Jamiroquoi
www.netlink.co.uk/users/funkin/
jamiroquai
www.jamiroquai.co.uk
hem1.passagen.se/errkki

Jandek
www.cs.nwu.edu/~tisue/jandek

Jane's Addiction
www.one-percent.com
www.mokum.pair.com/xine/janes_xine
members.aol.com/piginzen/index.html

Jars of Clay
www.jarsofclay.com
www.geocities.com/SunsetStrip/Alley/
2679

Jason & the Scorchers
jasonandthescorchers.com
www.geocities.com/Nashville/3301
fly.hiwaay.net/~dderrick/scorchers/
scorch.html

Jawbox
www.his.com/~desoto/jawbox.html

Jawbreaker
wsrv.clas.virginia.edu/~epk8c

The Jayhawks
www.execpc.com/~tolkien/index
www.geocities.com/SunsetStrip/Studio/
2389/jayhawks.html

Jefferson Airplane
grove.ufl.edu/~number6/Jefferson.
Airplane/airplane.html

Jefferson Starship
grove.ufl.edu/~number6/Jefferson.
Airplane/airplane.html

Garland Jeffreys
www.garlandjeffreys.com

Jellyfish
bubblegum.uark.edu/Jellyfish
millennianet.com/dumyhead/Fanindex.
html

Jane Jensen
www.geocities.com/CollegePark/Quad/
1652/TEST.HTML

The Jesus & Mary Chain
www.zip.com.au/~niina/jamc

Jesus Jones
www.jesusjones.com
home.clara.net/cmap

Jesus Lizard
jhunix.hcf.jhu.edu/~dbm/jesliz.html

Jethro Tull
www.geocities.com/Hollywood/2510/
tull.htm
ourworld.compuserve.com/homepages/
laufi/jethro_e.htm

Joan Jett
www.pipeline.com/~jetthead/joanjett.
htm
www.joanjett.com

Jewel
www.cs.mun.ca/~colins/jewel.html
www.smoe.org/lists/jewel/angels
www.jeweljk.com

Jimmie's Chicken Shack
www.fowl.com/jimmies
www.angelfire.com/tx/JimmiesChicken
Shack/intro.html
members.aol.com/BiGRed1510/
chickenshack.html

Billy Joel
www.sonymusic.com/artists/BillyJoel
www.orlowski.com/joel
members.aol.com/bjwebpage/private/
bjweb.htm
users.aol.com/jdsweeney/fire.html

Elton John
www.eltonfan.com
www.public.usit.net/artboy/ejfan.html
www.ozemail.com.au/~ckratzin/elton/
index.html
ej.kylz.com

Eric Johnson
www.ericjohnson.com
www.inetport.com/~jdekan/eric

Mike Johnson
members.aol.com/mjbluer/index.html

Daniel Johnston
www.oberlin.edu/~lgumpp/danj.html

Freedy Johnston
www.elektra.com/alternative_club/
freedy/freedy.html

Howard Jones
www.wenet.net/~trivera/hojo

Tom Jones
www.catch.com/snack/tomjones
www.geocities.com/SunsetStrip/
Backstage/2175/index.html

Janis Joplin
www.planete.net/~smironne/JANIS/
JOPLIN/index.html
www.geocities.com/SunsetStrip/Palms/
3948/joplin.htm
www.dartmouth.edu/~modred/janis.
html
www.geocities.com/Hollywood/5312
www.bbhc.com/BigBrother.htm

Sass Jordan
www.enter.net/~godofwar/sassy.html

Journey
journey.simplenet.com
www.serve.com/journey

Joy Division
www.wbr.com/joydivision/index.html
www.users.globalnet.co.uk/~liden/joyd.
html
www.geocities.com/SunsetStrip/Studio/
2376/joy.html

Judas Priest
www.webrasilia.com.br/priest/news2.
htm
www.judas-priest.com

Junkster
www.junkster.com
www.bugjuice.com/junkster

Brenda Kahn
www.womanrock.com

Kajagoogoo
www.geocities.com/SunsetStrip/Club/
3346/index.html
www.kajagoogoo.co.uk

Kansas
www.progrock.org/kansas/index.html

Kara's Flowers
www.repriserec.com/karasflowers

Katell Keineg
www.users.interport.net/~slambert/
katell/katell.html

Katrina & the Waves
www.katw.com

KC & the Sunshine Band
www.heykcsb.com

Tommy Keene
www.matador.recs.com/bios/bio_
tommy.html

Paul Kelly
www.amws.com.au/pk

Kenickie
www.kenickie.com

Nik Kershaw
www.ida.com.au/~drew/kershaw

Kid Creole & the Coconuts
www.geocitles.com/SunsetStrlp/Studlo/
7054/coconuts.html

Greg Kihn
www.msn.fullfeed.com/~dale/kihn.html

Albert King
www.hub.org/bluesnet/artists/albert.
king.html

B.B. King
www.worldblues.com/bbking/default.
asp
bbking.mca.com
www.island.net/~blues/bb.html
Prairie.Lakes.com/~jkerekes
www.geocities.com/BourbonStreet/
1242/index.htm

Carole King
www.injersey.com/~joer/bob/carole.
html

Freddie King
www.mazeppa.com/fking.html
www.rounder.com/rounder/catalog/
byartist/k/king_freddie

Sid King & the Five Strings
www.athenet.net/~genevinc/SidKing.
html

King Crimson
www.eazy.net/sws1/band.html
www.elephant-talk.com

King Curtis
www.zoo.co.uk/~primer

King Missle
www.geocities.com/SunsetStrip/Towers/
2441

King's X
www.compassnet.com/grump
users.aol.com/poetx2/KX.HTM

The Kingsmen
www.eskimo.com/~craigb/kingsmen.
html

The Kingston Trio
www.brugold.com/kitmain.html

The Kinks
www.kinks.org/home.htm
www.raydavies.com

Kiss
www.kissasylum.com
www.geocities.com/SunsetStrip/Venue/
5555

members.aol.com/mkayx69/KISS.html
198.93.194.14/~arwood/thesightofblood

Kitchens of Distinction
www.umsl.edu/~s931656

Klaatu
www.mdc.net/~db65/klaatufr.html

KMFDM
www.kmfdm.net
members.kconline.com/chris/kmfdm

KoЯn
students.cec.wustl.edu/~jam2/korn.htm
www.public.asu.edu/~ispawn/korn.htm
www.infectious.com/korn

Leo Kottke
www.windham.com/artists/Leo_Kottke.
html

Kraftwerk
www.kraftwerk.com
sun1.bham.ac.uk/busbykg/kraftwerk/
FAQ

Lenny Kravitz
www.virginrecords.com/kravitz/index3.
html
outer-net.com/circus/index.html
www.geocities.com/SunsetStrip/Stage/
5948

Chantal Kreviazuk
www.kensai.com/chantal

K's Choice
www.kschoice.com

Kula Shaker
www.kulashaker.co.uk/kulashaker/
index.html
www.geocities.com/Hollywood/
Bungalow/4421

Kyuss
207.113.214.3/~dbg/stuff/txt/music/
kyuss

L.A. Guns
www.geocities.com/SunsetStrip/9059/
index.html

Laika
www.netwiz.net/~aleister/laika/home.
html
www.toopure.com/artists/laika/biog.htm
www.students.uiuc.edu/~j-javen/
moonshake

Lamb
www.geocities.com/SoHo/Lofts/3328

Lambchop
www.geocities.com/Nashville/Opry/
4267

Sonny Landreth
www.avi-entertainment.com/landreth.
html

Jonny Lang
www.amrecords.com/artists/jonnylang
home.allgaeu.org/wgeierst/jonny/index.
html

k.d. lang
www.wbr.com/kdlang
www.kdlang.com

Daniel Lanois
www.sfbayconcerts.com/lanois/home.
html

The La's
www.geocities.com/CapeCanaveral/Lab/
8958/las.html

Last Exit
www.geocities.com/SoHo/Lofts/8764

Bill Laswell
www.hyperreal.org/music/labels/axiom

Cyndi Lauper
www.cyndilauper.com
www.House-of-Cyn.com

Led Zeppelin
www.led-zeppelin.com
www.wfu.edu/~derbyjw5/music/
zeppelin
www.dnaco.net/~buckeye/ifmtl.html
www.capecod.net/~rcooke/ledzeppelin
members.aol.com/hartman9/zeppl.htm

Brenda Lee
www.geocities.com/Nashville/4481

The Left Banke
members.aol.com/bocad/leftbank.htm

Legendary Stardust Cowboy
www.hear.com/hollow/paralyzed

Lemonheads
www.geocities.com/SunsetStrip/
Backstage/6037

John Lennon
www.merseyworld.com/imagine
members.aol.com/pop1rock1/john.html

Julian Lennon
www.geocities.com/Hollywood/Bouleva
rd/2801/index.html

Less Than Jake
ltj.ml.org
www.geocities.com/Area51/Dimension/
2251/index.html
www.geocities.com/SunsetStrip/Arena/
4388

Level 42
www.level42.com

Jerry Lee Lewis
www.ciagri.usp.br/~gmsenato/jerry2.
html
www.student.tdb.uu.se/~m93aum/jerry.
html

www.generation.net/~elbonne/fcjllewis/
ejerry.htm

Huey Lewis & the News
www.geocities.com/SunsetStrip/Club/
3922
www.hln.org
www.geocities.com/Hollywood/Set/
3884

Life of Agony
www.lifeofagony.com
listen.to/loa

Gordon Lightfoot
www.geocities.com/Athens/Oracle/
2714/index.html

The Lightning Seeds
www.penna.demon.co.uk/pureseeds
www.lightningseeds.com

Limp Bizkit
www.lightningseeds.com
www.limpbizkit.com

Lincoln
www.thebandlincoln.com
lincoln.tickertape.net
members.aol.com/Aethyrr/Lincoln.html

Little Feat
www.littlefeat.net

Little Richard
home.kolumbus.fi/timrei/lre.htm
fame2.clever.net/fame/richard.htm

Little River Band
www.lrb.net

Live
www.personal.psu.edu/users/g/r/
gra104
home.sol.no/~emeyerla
www.students.uiuc.edu/~g-jaros/live.
html

Living Colour
www.willamette.edu/~cwick/lc
www.geocities.com/Hollywood/Hills/
9892

Local H
www.1starnet.com/localh
pages.prodigy.com/Local_H/home.htm

Locust
www2.netdoor.com/~gorbash/locust

Lisa Loeb
www.lisaloeb.com
members.aol.com/nJhd4/index.htm
ccwf.cc.utexas.edu/~rbecker/lisaloeb.
html

Nils Lofgren
www.rawks.com/nils

Loggins & Messina
www.kennyloggins.com

Lone Justice
www.mariamckee.com
ttlc.net/little_diva

Mary Lou Lord
pages.nyu.edu/~rkb200

Lords of Acid
www.ee.fit.edu/users/ccurtis/lords
www.geocities.com/Area51/Vault/2746/
Lords.html

Los Lobos
www.wbr.com/loslobos

Los Straitjackets
los.straitjackets.com

Lotion
www.ilovelotion.com

Loud Family
www.loudfamily.com

Love
www.ozemail.com.au/~hektor/@love.
html

Love and Rockets
www.eof.net/lr
www.geocities.com/SunsetStrip/Club/
1771

G. Love & Special Sauce
users.ids.net/~kiselka/g-love

Loverboy
www.wcmr.com/loverboy
www.geocities.com/SunsetStrip/Venue/
4689
www.geocities.com/SunsetStrip/
Frontrow/3650

Lyle Lovett
www.geocities.com/SoHo/1192/lyle.
html

Lene Lovich
www.delcom.com/john/lovich/default.
html

The Lovin' Spoonful
www.onlinetalent.com/Spoonful_
homepage.html

Nick Lowe
www.cnet-sa.or.jp/s/sa013916/nick.htm

L7
www.smellL7.com
www.geocities.com/SunsetStrip/
Lounge/4764/L7.html

Lucious Jackson
members.tripod.com/~lusciousjackson/
LUS.HTM
www.grandroyal.com/Bands/
LusciousJackson
www.mygale.org/01/luscious

Lulu
www.oberlin.edu/~gjohnson/lulu/lulu1.
html

Luna
www.triangle23.com/luna
www.elektra.com/alternative_club/luna/
luna.html

Lush
www.geocities.com/TheTropics/8910/
lush.html
www.angelfire.com/oh/Lush/index.html

Brendan Lynch
www.brendanlynch.com

Lynyrd Skynyrd
home.ici.net/~tsoares/skynyrd.html
www.angelfire.com/ar/FeebsSkynyrd
Page

Kirsty MacColl
www.geocities.com/SunsetStrip/4591/
kirsty.htm
www.iag.net/~akoustic/kirsty/kirsty.
html

Ashley MacIssac
www.davebo.way2fast.com/ashley

Madness
www.madness.co.uk
www.mindspring.com/~bowendp
huizen.dds.nl/~dag/madness

Madonna
www.madonnanet.com/mland
www.wbr.com/madonna
www.stanford.edu/~jwb/Madonna
www.joking.com/madonna.html

Magnapop
www.prismnet.com/~darrend/magnapop

Yngwie Malmsteen
www.lewisentertainment.com/yngwie/
ym_home.htm

The Mamas & the Papas
www.interlog.com/~jman
www.rockhall.com/induct/mamaspapas.
html

Man or Astro-Man?
www.astroman.com/Frames/frames.
html
www.edmonton.shaw.wave.ca/~gmillar/
moa

ManBREAK
www.almosounds.com/manbreak

Melissa Manchester
www.melissa-manchester.com

Manic Street Preachers
www.manics.co.uk/manics/perfect/
manics
www.repeat.demon.co.uk
freespace.virgin.net/andrew.barber2

Aimee Mann
songwriting.com/aimeemann

Manfred Mann
www.manfredmann.co.uk

Marilyn Manson
www.marilyn-manson.net
www.binary.net/wicked/manson/index.
html
www.marilyn-manson.com

Mansun
www.parlophone.co.uk/mansun/main.
html

Marcy Playground
www.marcyplayground.com
www-scf.usc.edu/~beardsle/
playground/index.html

Marillion
www.marillion.com
www.empire.net/~freaks

Bob Marley
www.bobmarley.com
www.won.nl/dsp/usr/svketel/Music/
bmarley.html
www.geocities.com/SunsetStrip/9162
www.geocities.com/SunsetStrip/Arena/
4464
www.wallofsound.com/artists/
bobmarley/index.html

Ziggy Marley
www.melodymakers.com
www.elektra.com/randb_club/zmarley/
zmarley.html

Marry Me Jane
www.epiccenter.com/EpicCenter/
MarryMeJane/index.html

Amanda Marshall
ourworld.compuserve.com/homepages/
Adam_Klein
www.geocities.com/SunsetStrip/Palms/
5130/amanda.html

The Marshall Tucker Band
www.marshalltucker.com

Richard Marx
www.richardmarx.com
www.repeatoffenders.com

Dave Mason
members.aol.com/ditum/index.htm

Massive Attack
www.massiveattack.co.uk
ccwf.cc.utexas.edu/~jh/massive/intro98.
html
webhome.idirect.com/~grynberg

Matchbox 20
www.geocities.com/SunsetStrip/Stage/
6968
www.geocities.com/SunsetStrip/Alley/
1478

Material Issue
freakcity.slu.edu

Dave Matthews Band
www.dmband.com
www.naples.net/~nfn01005/dmb
baynet.com/aron/dmb.html
www.geocities.com/SunsetStrip/Alley/
6457/index.html

Eric Matthews
www.bio.vu.nl/home/vwielink/matthews/
matthews.htm

Curtis Mayfield
www.hh.se/stud/d96join/cm/curtis.
html

Maypole
www.sonymusic.com/artists/Maypole
members.aol.com/BSHmaypole

Mazzy Star
hem.passagen.se/bratt/mazzystar.htm
www.thegrid.net/loststar/mazzy/mazzy.
htm
www.geocities.com/SunsetStrip/Palms/
9191

Edwin McCain
www.edwin.com

Paul McCartney
www.geocities.com/SunsetStrip/7003/
paul.html
www.geocities.com/SunsetStrip/Towers/
6264/macca.html
www.wallofsound.com/artists/
paulmccartney/index.html

Eleanor McEvoy
www.dojo.ie/eleanor

MC5
ourworld.compuserve.com/homepages/
rauk/mc-5.htm
members.aol.com/emilbacill/imc5page.
htm
www.ubl.com:80/artists/002016.html

Maria McKee
www.mariamckee.com

Loreena McKennitt
ourworld.compuserve.com/homepages/
leefamily/loreena.htm

Sarah McLachlan
www.sarahmclachlan.com
www.aquezada.com/sarah
www.geocities.com/SouthBeach/Sands/
5645/sarah.htm
www.geocities.com/SunsetStrip/Venue/
6842/heaven.htm

Don McLean
www.mbhs.edu/~bconnell/cty/
american-pie.html

Grant McLennan
we.got.net/~gareth/mclennan

James McMurtry
www.mcmurtry.net

Holly McNarland
www.angelfire.com/ak/hollymcnarland/
index.html
webhome.idirect.com/~markswi/holly.
html

Meat Beat Manifesto
www.brainwashed.com/mbm

Meat Loaf
www.meatloaf.mca.com
www.soton.ac.uk/~gpam196/meat/
meat.htm
www.voicenet.com/~jrls/index.html

Meat Puppets
www.amug.org/~bsandig/puppets
members.xoom.com/kirkwood/puppets

Medeski, Martin & Wood
www.mmw.net/menu.html

Joe Meek
www.concentric.net/~meekweb/telstar.
htm

Megadeth
hollywoodandvine.com/megadeth
www.megadeth.com
home.earthlink.net/~beadil

The Mekons
www.ellipsis.com/mekons/index.html

Melanie
ourworld.compuserve.com/homepages/
David_Boldinger/melanie.htm

John Mellencamp
www.mellencamp.com
www.geocities.com/SunsetStrip/Palms/
7245/index.html
www.icss.net/~BandR/jm.htm

The Melvins
www.community.net/~buster/melvins.
html

Men at Work
members.aol.com/babsjdonne/
menatwrk.htm

Men Without Hats
www.oz.net/~goreal/menwithouthats

Mercy Rule
www.acton.com/bernie/mercy

The Mermen
www.mermen.com

Metallica
www.jcave.com/~poorer/metallica.html
www.metclub.com
www.geocities.com/SunsetStrip/Studio/
6108
www.stop.se/metallica/index.html

George Michael
hem1.passagen.se/eos/gm
members.aol.com/YOGfanclub/index.
htm
www.geocities.com/SunsetStrip/Palms/
9988

Midnight Oil
www.midnightoil.com
www.geocities.com/SunsetStrip/Alley/
1348/mopage.htm
pat.nyser.net/oilbase

Mighty Joe Plum
www.mindspring.com/~brettstu/
mjplum.htm

Mighty Mighty Bosstones
desensitized.simplenet.com/new.htm
mass-pc.wpi.edu/~wuss/bosstones
www.angelfire.com/ia/mmbosstone/
index.html

Robert Miles
www.geocities.com/SunsetStrip/
Palladium/3775
www.aristarec.com/aristaweb/
RobertMiles/index.html

Bill Miller
www.Nashville.Net/~raven

Buddy Miller
www.telalink.net/~kate/buddym.html

Julie Miller
www.GeoCities.com/SunsetStrip/Alley/
1717/jm-index.html
www.nashville.net/~kate/jmiller.html

Steve Miller
www.stevemillerband.com
www.cae.wisc.edu/~conover/html/
miller.html
www.serve.com/joker

Milli Vanilli
www.geocities.com/Tokyo/Temple/
4853/milli.htm

Ministry
www.wbr.com/Ministry
village.cyberbrain.com/ministry

Kylie Minogue
www.kylie.com
ourworld.compuserve.com/homepages/
orth/kylie.htm

Minor Threat
www.crackedass.com/minorthreat
www.angelfire.com/ok/endall
www.southern.com/southern/band/
MTHRT/index.html

Minutemen
www.teleport.com/~billder/minutemen

The Misfits
members.xoom.com/android138/index.
html

www.geocities.com/SunsetStrip/Towers/
9826/misfits.html
www.geocities.com/SunsetStrip/Palms/
1138

Mr. Big
www.geocities.com/SunsetStrip/Club/
4848
www.geocities.com/SunsetStrip/Towers/
3292

Mr. Mister
w1.1364.telia.com/~u136401400/
MrMister
www.itv.se/~va106/mrpages
users.skynet.be/sky67891

The Mr. T Experience
members.aol.com/Brentstv3/MTX/MTX.
html
www.mindspring.com/~schmick/mtx.
htm
www.execpc.com/~wood/mtx.htm

Joni Mitchell
www.jonimitchell.com
members.aol.com/KyBoy1327/
JoniMitchell.html

Moby
www.moby.org
www.xmission.com/~damian/moby.html
www.mnsinc.com/nuwave

Moby Grape
www.mobygrape.com
www.geocities.com/SunsetStrip/1256

Modern English
www.evo.org/html/group/modernenglish.
html

Modest Mouse
www.kimbanet.com/~JohnF/JaySite/
modest
www.geocities.com/SoHo/7644/
ModestMouse.HTM
www.uprecords.com/up/bands/mmouse

moe.
www.moe.org

Mommyheads
www.geffen.com/mommyheads

The Monkees
www.flexquarters.com/monkees.htm
www17.pair.com/sandauer
members.tripod.com/~Weeping_
Willowly

Mono
www.polygram-us.com/mono
www.mercuryrecords.com/mercury/
artists/mono

Monochrome Set
www.algonet.se/~elegans/mono/
m.html

Monster Magnet
www.amrecords.com/artists/
monstermagnet
www.utu.fi/~mikkoski/rock/moma

The Moody Blues
www.moodyblueworld.org
www.moodies-magazine.com/index.asp

Abra Moore
www.abramoore.com

Gary Moore
www.bourgoin.holowww.com/GM

Moose
www.puc.edu/Departments/Art/gallery/
James_Reeder/moose/index.html

Morcheeba
www.obsolete.com/china/morcheeba

Blake Morgan
www.blakemorgan.com/2.0

Alanis Morissette
www.geocities.com/SunsetStrip/9052
www.geocities.com/SunsetStrip/Alley/
3866
virpster.simplenet.com/mtws/frame.
html

Morphine
www.morphine3.com
hadfiiw.simplenet.com/tos/index.html

Van Morrison
intothemusic.interspeed.net/vanbest.
htm
www.harbour.sfu.ca/~hayward/van/
van.html

Morrissey
members.tripod.com/~hotyf/home.html
yi.com/home/ColvinNaomi/Battersea.
htm
www.europa.com/~circe/moz.html

The Motels
members.tripod.com/~TheMotels/index.
html
www.geocities.com/SunsetStrip/Towers/
9991
www.nwlink.com/~mikey/Indexpg.html

Mötley Crüe
www.motley.com
www.geocities.com/SunsetStrip/Palms/
3010/motley.html
www2.sbbs.se/hp/onne/motley/crue.
htm

Motörhead
www.imotorhead.com
www.motorhead.com
freespace.virgin.net/oliver.cornfield

Mott the Hoople
public.logica.com/~perkinsa/hunter-mott
www.nic.com/~dzien/mottthehoople.
html

Moxy Früvous
www.fruvous.com

Bob Mould
www.math.nwu.edu/~richeson/
bricklayer.html

Mountain
www.lewisentertainment.com/mountain/
mtnhome.htm

Mouse on Mars
www.xs4all.nl/~pjoe/mouse.html

The Move
www.roywood.com/move.html

Alison Moyet
www.scu.edu/kscu/webpage/bandpage/
alf

Mudhoney
www.RepriseRec.com/reprise_html_
pages/mudhoney
www.unofficial-mudhoney.com/
mudhoney.htm

The Muffs
www.RepriseRec.com/TheMuffs
www.geocities.com/SunsetStrip/9543

Mule
www.southern.com/southern/band/
MULEo/index.html

The Mumps
www.eggbert.com/eggbert/mumps.html

The Murmurs
www.themurmurs.com
www.geocities.com/SunsetStrip/Towers/
9235

Elliott Murphy
www.mygale.org/03/murphy

Peter Murphy
www.itis.com/murphy

My Bloody Valentine
www.triplo.com/mbv/index.html

My Drug Hell
www.voltone.com/vir/mydrughell
www.cyberpoint.co.uk/mdh

My Life Story
homepages.uel.ac.uk/2212l

My Life with the Thrill Kill Kult
www.thrillkill.com

Nada Surf
www.flotsam.com/~nadanet

Naked
www.nakedtheband.com
members.aol.com/Clayton727/naked.
html

Naked Eyes
www.mindspring.com/~dosswerks/
nakedeyes

www.algonet.se/~jonwar/naked-eyes.
html

Naked Raygun
www.tezcat.com/~gdd/raygun.html

Nancy Boy
www.elektra.com/alternative_club/
nancyboy/nancyboy.html
www.geocities.com/Hollywood/Hills/
4757/nancyboy.htm

Nazareth
rocksolid-inc.com/nazareth
www.pathcom.com/~omega/nazareth.
html

Me'Shell Ndegéocello
www.wbr.com/maverick/meshell
www.geocities.com/BourbonStreet/
Delta/2833/index.html

Ned's Atomic Dustbin
w3.nai.net/~scrawl/dustbin.html

Negativland
www.negativland.com

Nelson
members.aol.com/NelsonInfo/
NelsonInfoHomePage.htm
www.aros.net/~gr8escap/Welcome.
html
members.aol.com/NelsonLovr/
TheNelsonNews.html

Rick Nelson
www.athenet.net/~genevinc/
RickyNelson.html

The Neville Brothers
www.nevilles.com
www.his.com/~georgeg/neville.html

The New Bomb Turks
home.sprintmail.com/~chadvan/nbt/
home.html

New Kids on the Block
www.nkotb.com
www.geocities.com/SunsetStrip/
Underground/1843
tsunami.anime.net/arim/nkotb/nkotb.
html

New Model Army
www.interlog.com/~cb
www.newmodelarmy.org

New Order
www.mindspring.com/~jcabarcos/
neworder.html
slashmc.rice.edu/ceremony/neworder/
neworder.html
home.bc.rogers.wave.ca/alau/neworder
home.nordnet.fr/~abarbet/neworder.
html

The New York Dolls
www.nyrock.com/misc/nydolls.htm

home.echo-on.net/~ifftay/thunders.
htm

Martin Newell
monsterbit.com/longplay/bol.html

Randy Newman
www.RepriseRec.com/reprise_html_
pages/randyfolder/randynewman
www.inet-images.com/mightykymm/
randy.html

Stevie Nicks
nicksfix.com
members.aol.com/WildestHrt/index.html
members.aol.com/N1ghtb1rd/index.html

Nico
www.netpoint.be/abc/nico
www.geocities.com/Paris/1781

Night Ranger
members.aol.com/lilsistrjo/nr.htm
home.sol.no/~spin/night_ranger

Harry Nilsson
www.magicnet.net/~rasmith/nilsson.ht
ml

nine inch nails
rustynails.hypermart.net
attila.stevens-tech.edu/~jhallora/nailz.
html
uslink.net/~cpunut/nin.html
home.thezone.net/~becoming

Nineteen Wheels
www.19wheels.com
www.wgrd.com/19/wheels.htm
www.engin.umd.umich.edu/~jafreema/
19/19.html

Nirvana
www.geocities.com/SunsetStrip/Palms/
3385/title.html
www.geocities.com/SunsetStrip/Towers/
3790
www.geocities.com/~dperle/ms
www.seds.org/~smiley/nirvana
www.geocities.com/SunsetStrip/
Palladium/3715

Nitzer Ebb
www.purplenet.net/~ebbhead

The Nixons
www.nixons.com
www.geocities.com/SunsetStrip/Towers/
6429

No Doubt
www.geocities.com/SunsetStrip/4925/
nodoubt.html
virpster.simplenet.com/nodoubt
www.geocities.com/SunsetStrip/Studio/
1444
pages.prodigy.com/doubt/doubt.htm

NOFX
www.kiss.uni-lj.si/~k4fe0443/index3.
html

www.geocities.com/SunsetStrip/Venue/
9195
www.couch.com/nofx

Noise Addict
www.grandroyal.com/Bands/NoiseAddict

NRBQ
www.geocities.com/BourbonStreet/
7935/index.html
users.loa.com/~ceol/nrbq.html

Ted Nugent
www.thewild.com/jngonzo/nuge.html
www.usmo.com/~jonlaura/nuge.htm
www.dtahou.com/~duane/nugent.html

Gary Numan
www.numan.co.uk
afe.simplenet.com
members.aol.com/Replicant6/index.htm

Laura Nyro
LauraNyro.net

Oasis
www.geocities.com/SunsetStrip/Towers/
4626
members.xoom.com/oasisace
www.oasisinet.com
members.aol.com/mjwood777/oasis.htm

Ocean Colour Scene
osiris.sund.ac.uk/~ca4lba/ocs/ocsmain.
htm
www.geocities.com/SunsetStrip/Towers/
2166/ocs.htm

Phil Ochs
www.cs.pdx.edu/~trent/ochs
home.dti.net/warr/ochs.html

Sinéad O'Connor
www.sinead-oconnor.com
www.geocities.com/SunsetStrip/
Backstage/9922
www.telebyte.nl/~bobbink/sinead/
sinead.htm

The Odds
www.wam.umd.edu/~oddsman/Odds.
html

Offspring
www.offspring.com
www.geocities.com/SunsetStrip/Alley/
4737/index.html
www.geocities.com/SunsetStrip/
Lounge/7860

Oingo Boingo
www.oingoboingo.com
www.isc.rit.edu/~elnppr
www.boingo.com

Old 97s
www.old97s.com
www.geocities.com/~landings/old97s.
html
www.angelfire.com/tx/FunnyLikeOnTV/
index.html

Mike Oldfield
www.geocities.com/SunsetStrip/8565
www.csd.uwo.ca/~pettypi/mike_
oldfield/the_bell.html

Olivia Tremor Control
home1.gte.net/mushaman/olivia.htm

The Only Ones
mh102.infi.net/~redo

Yoko Ono
www.cam.org/~rjoly/yoko/onoweb.html

Opal
www.mazzystar.net/opal/index.htm

Orange 9mm
www.geocities.com/SunsetStrip/Alley/
5076

The Orb
www.theorb.com

Roy Orbison
www.orbison.com
stm1.chem.psu.edu/~krk/orbison/
RoyOrbison.html

Orbit
www.lunch.com/orbit

William Orbit
www.orbit.ndirect.co.uk

Orbital
www.york.ac.uk/~wjb101/orbital.htm
www.geocities.com/Vienna/7087

Orchestral Manoeuvres in the Dark
www.accessone.com/~fester
www.csu.edu.au/faculty/commerce/
account/omd/omd.htm
www.free.cts.com/crash/s/seraphim/
omdone.html

Orion
www.geocities.com/SunsetStrip/2590/
index.html

Orlando
www.totalweb.co.uk/orlando
members.tripod.com/~pulpfreak/
orlando

Jim O'Rourke
www.cs.nwu.edu/~tisue/orourke

Beth Orton
homepages.enterprise.net/jbromley/
beth.html

Joan Osborne
www.mercuryrecords.com/mercury/
artists/osborne_j/osborne_joan.html
members.aol.com/drldeboer2/htm/
jo.htm

Ozzy Osbourne
Clear.lakes.com/~guitar
www.cyberpunk.ca/ozzy

www.geocities.com/SunsetStrip/
Palladium/3992
free.prohosting.com/~bh/index2.html

The Osmonds
www.geocities.com/~feelin-groovy/
meet_osmonds.htm
voyager.osmond.com/donny

Gilbert O'Sullivan
www.gosullivan.com

Our Lady Peace
www.ourladypeace.com
www.ourladypeace.net
www.globalserve.net/~fluflu

The Outfield
www.theoutfield.com

The Outlaws
www.geocities.com/~black-hawk/
outlaws.html
idt.net/~tomg4/outlaws.htm

Overkill
www.wreckingcrew.com

Buck Owens
www.geocities.com/Heartland/Plains/
5040

The Oyster Band
www.sussex.ac.uk/Users/kcci1/
Oysterband

Page & Plant
www2.msstate.edu/~bcp4/page.html

Palace
lookandfeel.thehub.com.au/thepulpit

Pale Saints
www.evo.org/html/group/palesaints.
html

Robert Palmer
casi.simplenet.com/j/oldsite/music/
palmer
www.fortunecity.com/tattooine/ellison/
2/rp.html

Pantera
www.elektra.com/metal_club/pantera/
pantera.html
www.binary.net/wicked/pantera/index.
html
www.csusm.edu/public/guests/pantera/
pantera.htm

Papas Fritas
www.fritas.com

Graham Parker
www.punkhart.com/gparker/index.html
www-nw.uni-regensburg.de/~.dej09534.
rz.uni-regensburg.de/gparker/index.
htm

Van Dyke Parks
www.brerwabbit.com/parks

Alan Parsons
www.roadkill.com/APP
home1.gte.net/gaudi/index.htm

Gram Parsons
www.primenet.com/~klugl/gramhome.
html
www.nashville.net/~kate/gram.html

Ellis Paul
hugse1.harvard.edu/~library/ellispau.
htm

Pavement
www.matador.recs.com/bios/
bio_pavement.html
www.pitt.edu/~rabst59/pave/Index.
html
www-leland.stanford.edu/~jasepiol/
pavement/pavement.html

Paw
www.inergy.com/paw
www.novia.net/~gilgut/paw.html
www.geocities.com/Area51/Rampart/
5538/paw.html

Peach Union
easyweb.easynet.co.uk/~clrlogic/
peachpit.htm

Pearl Jam
www.fivehorizons.com
www.sonymusic.com/artists/PearlJam/
index.html
www.jayd.com/pearljam
www.pauserecord.com/john/pjvault

Pell Mell
www.geffen.com/pellmell

Michael Penn
www.epiccenter.com/EpicCenter/
MichaelPenn
www.people.cornell.edu/pages/tfl1/
penn/penn.html

Pentangle
www.pavilion.co.uk/fdt/pent/old_home.
htm

Pere Ubu
www.dnai.com/~obo/ubu/index.html

Pet
www.atlantic-records.com/pet

Pet Shop Boys
www.unimaas.nl/~mathysen/psb
www.geocities.com/SunsetStrip/Towers/
3458/pets.html
www.clay.co.uk/psb/psb.html

Peter & Gordon
members.aol.com/DosHoss/
PeterGordonHomePage.htm
members.aol.com/GWPA1234/
PeterGordonWebPage.htm

Petra
www.wordrecords.com/petra

www.geocities.com/SunsetStrip/Palms/
1331

Tom Petty & the Heartbreakers
www.gettysburg.edu/~s359420/tom_
petty_and_other_stuff.html
www.indiana-girl.se
www-personal.interkan.net/~tomrat/
Tom_Petty.html
www.uncg.edu/~jcbramwc
www.wallofsound.com/artists/tompetty/
index.html

Liz Phair
www.matador.recs.com/bios/bio_liz.
html
www.geocities.com/SunsetStrip/
Palladium/2834/index.html
www.geocities.com/SunsetStrip/Club/
2471

Sam Phillips
www.tmtm.com/sam

Phish
www.nd.edu/~pjohnso8/hpb.html
www.phish.com
www.phish.net

Photek
www.caroline.com/astralwerks/photek/
default.html

Phranc
www.rahul.net/hrmusic/artists/part.
html

Pink Floyd
clusterone.tibcom.com
utopia.knoware.nl/users/ptr/pfloyd/
start.html
www.memes.com/~tristandcw/breathe.
html
www.dragonfire.net/~echoes/entry.htm
www.xnet.com/~arkiver/dsotr.shtml

Gene Pitney
members.tripod.com/~colli/pitney/
pitney.html

The Pixies
www.pixies4ad.com
beaker.nmsu.edu/spaceman/pixies
www.geocities.com/SiliconValley/Pines/
7537/pixies.html

Pizzicato Five
www.matador.recs.com/bios/bio_p5.
html
www2.hawaii.edu/~evaldez/pizzicato5/
pizzicato5.htm
www.clark.net/pub/fan/pizz.html

Robert Plant
www.geocities.com/Hollywood/Lot/
1691/plant.htm

Plastikman
m-nus.com
www.geocities.com/SoHo/2187

PM Dawn
www.eelab.newpaltz.edu/~harple31/
pm.dawn/index.html

Poco
www.geocities.com/SunsetStrip/8385/
index.html

Poe
poe.cyberfan.com
www.cantnot.org/poe
students.cec.wustl.edu/~ljk1/poe.html

The Pogues
www.dzm.com/pogues
www.ferrie.demon.co.uk/pogues/
pogues.htm
users.terabit.net/todea

Poi Dog Pondering
www.poiHQ.com/poi
reality.sgi.com/employees/relph/
poi-pounders

Poison
wcafe.com/poison
members.aol.com/poisonol/home.htm
www.fandom-paradise.com/Poison

The Police
www.jsp.umontreal.ca/~larochej/police.
html
www.geocities.com/Hollywood/Hills/
3125/police.html
home1.swipnet.se/~w-11561

Steve Poltz
www.mercuryrecords.com/mercury/
artists/steve_poltz
www.angelfire.com/ut/therugburns/
index.html
home1.gte.net/ericj1/rugburns/index.
html

Iggy Pop
virginrecords.com/iggy_pop
www.contrib.andrew.cmu.edu/~jacquez/
iggy
www.delanet.com/~eyeball/modvamp/
iggy1.htm
www.kweb.it/iggy/frameigct.htm

Pop Will Eat Itself
kzsu.stanford.edu/uwi/pwei/pwei.html

Porno for Pyros
www.wbr.com/pornoforpyros
www.westol.com/~straw123/pyros.htm
www.angelfire.com/nj/sublimed/pyros.
html

Portishead
www.portishead.co.uk
portishead.hypermart.net
www.geocities.com/SunsetStrip/Studio/
8424
www.cls.dk/~jqj/portishead

The Posies
www.slumberland.seattle.wa.us/dear23.
html

Possum Dixon
www.possumdixon.com
cc.usu.edu/~slqqc/pd/possum.htm

Poster Children
www.prairienet.org/posterkids

Powerman 5000
www.geocities.com/SunsetStrip/Studio/
8858
www.conscience.com/pm5k

Prefab Sprout
www.xs4all.nl/~elfasih/muziek/prefabs.
html

**The Presidents of the United States of
America**
www.geocities.com/SunsetStrip/Towers/
9616
www.geocities.com/SunsetStrip/
Lounge/5961/pusatitl.htm
www.sonymusic.com/artists/Presidents/
main.html

Elvis Presley
www.elvis-presley.com
users.aol.com/petedixon/elvis/index.
html
sunsite.unc.edu/elvis/elvishom.html
www.pathfinder.com/people/sp/elvis
wsrv.clas.virginia.edu/~acs5d/elvis.
html

The Pretenders
www.pretenders.org
www.wbr.com/pretenders
members.tripod.com/~Pretenders
Archives

Pretty Things
www.mindspring.com/~us000091/
pretties.htm
musik.freepage.de/pretties/index.htm

Primal Scream
www.dreamspace.com/astron/
primalscream/index.html
www.repriserec.com/primalscream
www.creation.co.uk/primal

Primus
www.primussucks.com
www.geocities.com/SunsetStrip/
Palladium/8766/index.html
www.ram.org/music/primus/primus.
html

Prince
www.love4oneanother.com
www.geocities.com/SunsetStrip/9477
www.sevenmag.com.au
www.emale.com/chi-nation
www.thedawn.demon.co.uk/experience/
index.htm
www.uptown.se

John Prine
www.geocities.com/Heartland/1985/
prine1.htm
www.ohboy.com/OBR_Artists.html

The Proclaimers
www.proclaimers.co.uk

Procol Harum
www.procolharum.com
www.geocities.com/Area51/2202/
procol.htm

Prodigy
www.theprodigy.com
members.aol.com/prodigyuk/index.htm
pro.simplenet.com

Prong
www.geocities.com/CapeCanaveral/
7839/old.html

Chuck Prophet
home3.swipnet.se/~w-33845/cpgor/
prophet/cp.htm

The Psychedelic Furs
www.algonet.se/~silverup
www.wbr.com/maverick/lovespitlove
www.geocities.com/SunsetStrip/Palms/
3625

Public Enemy
www.defjam.com/artists/pe/enemy.
html
louis.ecs.soton.ac.uk/~rvn95r/public_e/
pe.html

Public Image Ltd.
www.publicimageltd.com
www.isolation.la.ca.us/pil

Pulp
www.rise.co.uk/pulp
www.geocities.com/SouthBeach/7648/
pulp.htm
rhumba.pair.com/pulp
www.geocities.com/SunsetStrip/Stage/
4996

The Pulsars
www.almosounds.com/pulsars

Pure
www.geocities.com/SunsetStrip/Palms/
7235/pure.html
www.purescape.com
www.geocities.com/Hollywood/1289/
pure.html

The Pursuit of Happiness
www2.excite.sfu.ca/jot/tpoh

Quarterflash
members.aol.com/stlrams4/qflash.htm

Suzi Quatro
www.ozemail.com.au/~suziq
apci.net/~djdenny

Finley Quaye
www.finleyquaye.com

Queen
queen-fip.com
www.geocities.com/Broadway/8033/
home.htm
www.iinet.net.au/~orchard
www.aha.ru/~meddows
www.geocities.com/SunsetStrip/Stage/
9575

Queensryche
www.queensryche.com
www.inspires.com/qryche
www.geocities.com/SunsetStrip/
Palladium/1579

? & the Mysterians
www.96tears.com
ddi.digital.net/~pharaoh/96tears.htm

Quicksand
www.geocities.com/SunsetStrip/8833/
index.htm

Quicksilver Messenger Service
www.penncen.com/quicksilver

Quiet Riot
www.vegasland.com/QRIOT.html

Radiohead
www.radiohead.co.uk
sac.uky.edu/~jsmooro/radio-head2.
html
www.underworld.net/radiohead
www.geocities.com/SunsetStrip/Alley/
8023

Rage Against the Machine
www.ratm.com
www.geocities.com/SunsetStrip/Towers/
6327/rage.html
www.musicfanclubs.org/rage

Railroad Jerk
www.matador.recs.com/bios/
bio_railroad.html

Railway Children
www.ether.co.uk/trc/index.html

Rain Parade
www.sirius.com/~roback/rainparade.
html

Rainbow
www.stat.washington.edu/brandon/
music/rainbow.html

The Raincoats
www.comnet.ca/~rina/raincoats.html

Bonnie Raitt
www.musick.com/BonnieRaitt
home.worldonline.nl/~dalmeier/bonnie.
htm
www.wallofsound.com/artists/
bonnieraitt/index.html

The Ramones
www.the-ramones.com
www.kauhajoki.fi/~jplaitio/ramones.
html
www.geocities.com/SunsetStrip/Palms/
6100
www.calweb.com/~jpeoples/ramones.
htm
hem1.passagen.se/ak5/ramones

Rancid
www.geocities.com/SunsetStrip/Stage/
8874
www.oncontact.com/anton/rancid/main.
htm
www.geocities.com/SoHo/Coffeehouse/
7606/rancid.html
www.spacestar.net/users/medwyn/
rancid/rancidindex.html

The Raspberries
www.geocities.com/Hollywood/Lot/
9440
www.geocities.com/Paris/3863/fresh.
htm
www.ericcarmen.com

Rasputina
www.rasputina.com
www.geocities.com/SunsetStrip/Stage/
3388

Ratt
www.ratt-n-roll.com

Chris Rea
www.helsinki.fi/~wikgren/chrisrea.html

Red Hot Chili Peppers
www.elee.calpoly.edu/~ercarlso/rhcp.
htm
www.wbr.com/chilipeppers
www.algonet.se/~forsg/rhcp

Red House Painters
www.geocities.com/Paris/LeftBank/
1854
206.24.114.3/rusted/rhp

Redd Kross
www.musick.com/ReddKross

Otis Redding
ourworld.compuserve.com/homepages/
Luke_THE_GR8

Rednex
www.bahnhof.se/~rednex

Lou Reed
www.loureed.org
www.wbr.com/loureed/index.html
www.wallofsound.com/artists/loureed/
index.html
members.aol.com/olandem4/reed.html
w3.mtci.or.jp/~wildside/lou_reed/index.
html

Reef
www.compura.com/martbean/reef

www.geocities.com/SunsetStrip/Stage/
6188

The Refreshments
www.therefreshments.com
www.popenema.com
www.geocities.com/SunsetStrip/5881/
refresh.html

Terry Reid
pilot.msu.edu/user/hernan49/links/
terry/tr_index.htm

R.E.M.
www.retroweb.com/rem.html
www.murmurs.com
www2.s-gimb.lj.edus.si/peter/rem/rem.
html
www.angelfire.com/biz/nitegarden/rem.
html

The Rembrandts
april29.simplenet.com/danspage.htm
members.aol.com/PhilnDanny/
Rembrandts.html

Renaissance
user.mc.net/~jtl/nlights/index.htm

REO Speedwagon
www.speedwagon.com
www.zwebsite.com/Tom/reolib.html

The Replacements
tt.net/twintone/mats.html
www.novia.net/~matt/sky/skyway.html

The Residents
www.residents.com

Paul Revere and the Raiders
www.paulrevereraiders.com

Cliff Richard
www.starnet.com.au/sheppard/2cliff.
html

Keith Richards
www.acc.umu.se/~krl/keef.html
www.mainquad.com/web/b/Burgess/
keith.htm

Kim Richey
www.geocities.com/Nashville/3235

Jonathan Richman
www.base.com/jonathan/jonathan.html
members.aol.com/gustoeater/jojo/
jojohome.htm

Ride
www.elektra.com/alternative_club/ride/
ride.html
irix.bris.ac.uk/~dm5751/ride/ride.html

Amy Rigby
www.geocities.com/~20questions

Robbie Robertson
theband.hiof.no/band_members/robbie.
html

Smokey Robinson & the Miracles
www.srv.net/~roxtar/robinson_smokey.
html
www3.edgenet.net/smokey_miracles
home.dti.net/warr/smokey.html

Tom Robinson Band
www.tomrobinson.com

Robyn
www.globalcom.se/robyn
www.geocities.com/Hollywood/
Academy/1446

The Roches
www.roches.com/Roches

Rocket from the Crypt
www.rftc.com

The Rolling Stones
www.the-rolling-stones.com
homepage.seas.upenn.edu/~demarco/
stones/breakfast.html
www.stonesworld.com/2.0
camel.conncoll.edu/ccother/sf.folder/
exile/exile.html
ourworld.compuserve.com/homepages/
ElChae

Henry Rollins
www.cit.nepean.uws.edu.au/~rollins
www.two1361.com/rband/rollins.html
www.ipass.net/~jthrush/rollins.htm

Romeo Void
members.aol.com/romeovoids/
romeovoid.html

The Ronettes
www.geocities.com/SunsetStrip/Studio/
2469
www.crl.com/~tsimon/ronettes.htm
home.ica.net/~phil/thegirls/ronettes.
htm

Mick Ronson
www.hotshotdigital.com/WellAlways
Remember/MickRonson.html

Linda Ronstadt
www.ais-gwd.com/~tpartridge
users.powernet.co.uk/skeyes/
dedicatedtolinda/index.html
www.reno.quik.com/stanpren/linda.htm

Diana Ross
dianaross.com
utopia.knoware.nl/users/ross/ross1.
htm
www.geocities.com/Hollywood/
Boulevard/8612/ross.html

David Lee Roth
www.davidleeroth.com
mflwp.bhcom1.com
www2.cybernex.net/~gambito/dave.
html

Patti Rothberg
www.geocities.com/SunsetStrip/
Palladium/3658/index.html

Roxette
www.geocities.com/SunsetStrip/Alley/
1855/roxintro.html
www.geocities.com/SunsetStrip/Palms/
7244
www.geocities.com/SunsetStrip/Palms/
1828

Roxy Music
www.dlc.fi/~hope
www.cco.caltech.edu/~bryan/roxy

Royal Crown Revue
www.rcr.com

Royal Trux
www.royaltrux.com

The Rubinoos
www.marturo.com/rubinoos

Rule 62
www.wbr.com/maverick/rule62

Run-D.M.C.
www.users.interport.net/~tjbeat/code/
rdmain.html
home.earthlink.net/~tgmoren/rundmc/
index.html
www.geocities.com/SouthBeach/4334/
rundmc.html

Run On
www.matador.recs.com/bios/bio_runon.
html

The Runaways
www.ite.his.se/~c95chrha/secrets.html
members.tripod.com/~KenSternation/
runawaysstory.html

Todd Rundgren
www.tr-i.com
www.roadkill.com/todd/trconn

Rush
oceanrush.com
www.geocities.com/SunsetStrip/Towers/
5318/rush.htm
web2.airmail.net/pscott/perchance.html

Leon Russell
members.aol.com/leonrussel

Rusted Root
www.rustedroot.com
www.geocities.com/SunsetStrip/Palms/
7250
www.public.iastate.edu/~thinker/
rusted.html

The Rutles
www.pythonline.com/unoff/rutles/
index.html
www-bcf.usc.edu/~hazelton/rutles.html
www.primenet.com/~dhaber/rutles

Mitch Ryder
www.esientertainment.com/ryder.htm
members.aol.com/RyderRock

St. Etienne
www.saint.etienne.net

Buffy Sainte-Marie
www.aloha.net/~bsm

Saints
www.xs4all.nl/~cjbailey
members.tripod.com/~saint_jude
www.geocities.com/SunsetStrip/Towers/
4009

Ryuichi Sakamoto
www.sitesakamoto.com
oswald.pages.de/disc/sakamoto

Sam the Sham & the Pharaohs
www.tiac.net/users/rkruse/samudio/
intro.html

The Samples
www.thesamples.org
conk.com/world/thesamples

Santana
www.santana.com
www.csv.warwick.ac.uk/~amuet/
santana.html
www.geocities.com/SunsetStrip/Palms/
6009/santana.html
www.sonymusic.com/artists/Santana/
index.html

Joe Satriani
www.satriani.com
www.cybersatch.com
www.alienkarma.com

Savage Garden
www.savagegarden.com
www.geocities.com/SunsetStrip/Arena/
4909
members.aol.com/Graviton13

Save Ferris
www.geocities.com/Area51/4623/
sferris.htm
www.secant.net/kara/saveferris
www.geocities.com/SunsetStrip/Palms/
6567/ferris.html

Saxon
hz-cis.hzeeland.nl/~wwirtz

Leo Sayer
www.wesjen.simplenet.com/sayer/
leomenu.htm

Boz Scaggs
www.tiac.net/users/kepler/boz.html

School of Fish
www-rcf.usc.edu/~mmaramot/
sof_homepage.html

Klaus Schulze
www.klaus-schulze.com

Paul Schütze
www.hyperreal.org/music/exclusive/
discogs/paul_schutze

Scorpions
www.scorps.com/index2.html
www.pathcom.com/~omega/scorpion.
html

Jack Scott
www.athenet.net/~genevinc/JackScott.
html

Screaming Trees
www.proaxis.com/~elcurte/oblivion
www.lehigh.edu/~jhs2/trees.html

Screeching Weasel
www.screechingweasel.com
www.mindspring.com/~schmick/weasel.
htm
www.geocities.com/SunsetStrip/Alley/
5472/willy.htm
www.crackedass.com/sw

Scritti Politti
www.mindspring.com/~dosswerks/scc
www.brainlink.com/~taliesin/AREAS/
sp/index.html
www.asaponline.com/scritti

Seal
www.ultim.demon.co.uk/seal
www.wbr.com/Seal

Seam
www.frognet.net/~mick/index.htm

The Searchers
www.users.zetnet.co.uk/searchers

Sebadoh
www.subpop.com/bands/sebadoh/
website
www.midheaven.com/fi/midheaven%20
FI.html
www.smoky.org/~darris/loubarlow

Jon Secada
www.geocities.com/CollegePark/Quad/
9411
www.almetco.com/secada/jon-1.html

Neil Sedaka
members.aol.com/sedaka1/index.html

The Seeds
www.wrongway.cc/sky/index.htm
www.theseeds.com
www.jetlink.net/~jim/seeds/seeds.htm

Bob Seger
www4.ncsu.edu/~krreimer/WWW/
seger.html
members.aol.com/wellcomein/
LinerNotes/Directory.html
www-personal.engin.umich.edu/
~jwopdyke/seger.html

Sepultura
www.sepultribe.com

www.geocities.com/SunsetStrip/Alley/
8221/Main.html
www.roadrunnerrecords.com/artists/
sepultura/homepage.htm

Seven Mary Three
www.7m3.com
www.rockpark.com/7mary3

Sevendust
www.sevendust.com
members.tripod.com/~elrancor/index.
html
www.geocities.com/Pipeline/6727

The Sex Pistols
www.virginrecords.com/sex_pistols/
home.html
www.users.wineasy.se/ludde
pcstraining.uts.ohio-state.edu/consult/
decarlo.7/pistols.htm
www.atlas.co.uk/tibco/indexsp.html

Ron Sexsmith
ronsexsmith.com

The Shadows
scofa.muse.com.au
www.stockportmbc.gov.uk/daved

The Shadows of Knight
members.aol.com/bass1lee/
shadowsofknight

Elliot Sharp
www.algonet.se/~repple/esharp/es.
html
www.acns.nwu.edu/jazz/artists/sharp.
elliott/discog.html

Duncan Sheik
www.duncansheik.com
www.geocities.com/SoHo/Studios/6918
www.geocities.com/SunsetStrip/
Lounge/6271/duncan.html

Shellac
www.southern.com/southern/band/
SHLAC/index.html
chicagomusic.com/actionpark/shellac

Kenny Wayne Shepherd
www.kwsband.com
www.geocities.com/BourbonStreet/
2201

Michelle Shocked
www.shellshock.com

Shoes
www.blackvinyl.com/3shoes.htm
www.geocities.com/SunsetStrip/9859

Shonen Knife
www.netropolis.net/shonen/knife/
shrine.htm
www.sentex.net/~sardine/shonen.knife.
html
walden.mo.net/~mckenzie/shonen.htm

Shudder to Think
users.aol.com/phofo/2.shudder.htm

Jane Siberry
www.RepriseRec.com/reprise_html_
pages/janesiberry
www.smoe.org/nbh
www.sheeba.ca

Sick of It All
www.chem.mtu.edu/~tgschaef/soia.
html
www.geocities.com/SunsetStrip/Alley/
4979/index.html
www.geocities.com/SunsetStrip/Alley/
1494

Silkworm
www.matador.recs.com/bios/bio_
silkworm.html
www.cnw.com/~elephant/skwm

The Silos
world.std.com/~silos

Silver Jews
www.xs4all.nl/~pjoe/silver.html

silverchair
www.geocities.com/SunsetStrip/Alley/
3445
www.angelfire.com/hi/MySilverchair
Page
www.geocities.com/SunsetStrip/Towers/
6584

Carly Simon
www.aristarec.com/aristaweb/
CarlySimon
www.zlva.com/carly

Paul Simon
www.wbr.com/paulsimon
www.best.com/~rlai/Paul-Simon.html
www.wallofsound.com/artists/
paulsimon/index.html

Simon & Garfunkel
www3.mistral.co.uk/rkent
www.geocities.com/SunsetStrip/
Backstage/6638

Simple Minds
www.simpleminds.com
www.simple-minds.demon.co.uk
www.geocities.com/~smfiles/index.htm

Simply Red
www.simplyred.com
www.elektra.com/randb_club/red/
slmplyred.html

Siouxsie & the Banshees
siouxsie.simplenet.com
www.citynet.net/personal/banshees/
index.html
members.aol.com/grnfingers/
dreamhouse

Sir Douglas Quintet
catalog.com/arts/sdq_hist.htm

members.aol.com/Sirdoug/index.html

Sister Hazel
www.sisterhazel.com

Sisters of Mercy
www.geocities.com/SunsetStrip/Studio/
8946
www.cs.cf.ac.uk/Sisters.Of.Mercy
tsom-tour.ml.org

6 String Drag
www.6stringdrag.com

Sixteen Horsepower
listen.to/16horsepower
www.paonline.com/heatherm/16hp/
main.htm

The 6ths
neon.cchem.berkeley.edu/~skinner/mf/
6ths.html

The Skeletons
members.aol.com/muzzi/morell.html

Skid Row
www.geocities.com/SunsetStrip/3909
www.netdreams.com/~tamis/skidrow

Skinny Puppy
jamcarr.linknet.net/SkiPu/index.htm
www.geocities.com/SunsetStrip/
Underground/4140/puppy.html
members.aol.com/ia5c23gz/main.htm

Skunk Anansie
www.indian.co.uk/skunk
www.geocities.com/SunsetStrip/Club/
6622
www.angelfire.com/ct/skunka

Sky Cries Mary
www.wbr.com/skycriesmary
www.ac.wwu.edu/~n9610899/scm/
scm_home.html
weber.u.washington.edu/~maximill/scm

Slade
www.mrscsi.com/slade/home.htm

Slayer
www.slayerized.com
www.slaytanic.com
members.tripod.com/~slaypage

Sleater-Kinney
www.napanet.net/~lina/sk
www.intersurf.com/~sisk
www.geocities.com/Wellesley/5419

Sleeper
www.alockton.demon.co.uk/sleeper/
index.html
www.geocities.com/SunsetStrip/Towers/
1545
www2.bitstream.net/~sleeper/index.htm

The Slits
www.comnet.ca/~rina/slits.html

Sloan
www.webgate.net/~maenon/sloan
home.echo-on.net/~tatyos
www.iaw.on.ca/seant/sloan/sloan.html

P.F. Sloan
www.ALLTHEBESTRECORDS.com

Slowdive
www.lysator.liu.se/~chief/slowdive.html

Sly & the Family Stone
www.slyfamstone.com
www.gcsweb.org
home.dti.net/warr/sly.html

Smash Mouth
www.interscoperecords.com/smash1.
html
www.geocities.com/SunsetStrip/
Lounge/1638/smashmouth.html
www.geocities.com/SunsetStrip/Club/
3256/smhome.html

Smashing Pumpkins
www.smashingpumpkins.org
www.starla.org
www.smashing-pumpkins.net
www.geocities.com/SunsetStrip/Club/
1785

Darden Smith
www.execpc.com/~henkle/fbindex/s/
smith_darden.html

Elliott Smith
members.tripod.com/~skylash
www.cs.trinity.edu/~nfrankli/es

Patti Smith
www.aristarec.com/psmith/home.html
www.oceanstar.com/patti
gopher1.bu.edu/PRC/Oar/Exhibitions/
Smith/ps-promo-1.htm
www.phtp.com

The Smithereens
www.main.com/~persails
home.dn.net/~smsnow

The Smiths
cleveohio.simplenet.com/TheSmiths/
smiths.htm
moz.pair.com
www.cyberstreet.com/users/sjw2000/
smiths.htm

Smoke
monsterbit.com/longplay/smoke.html

Patty Smyth
people.delphi.com/ryley/patty.htm

Sneaker Pimps
www.virginrecords.com/sneaker_pimps/
index.html
www.secant.net/kara/sneakerpimps
www.cleanup.music.co.uk/pimps

Todd Snider
www.todd-snider.com

Phoebe Snow
www.flash.net/~vdebolt/phoebehome/
phoebehome.html

Jill Sobule
members.aol.com/ammorrison/jsobule.
html

Social Distortion
www.socialdistortion.com
www.clash.net/socialdistortion

The Soft Boys
www.flash.net/~mmoore72/softboys.
htm

Son Volt
www.wbr.com/SonVolt
www.geocities.com/SunsetStrip/Towers/
6433
www.geocities.com/SunsetStrip/Towers/
2218

Sonic Youth
www.geocities.com/SunsetStrip/9526/
syindex.html
www.angelfire.com/sd/psykogert/index.
html
www.techline.com/~loser/sonichi.htm

Soul Asylum
www.sonymusic.com/artists/SoulAsylum
www.achilles.net/~tedd/sapage.html
home.sprynet.com/sprynet/cagedrat

Soul II Soul
www.soul2soul.co.uk

Soundgarden
www.imusic.com/soundgarden
home.earthlink.net/~superu/limowreck
www.wallofsound.com/artists/
soundgarden/index.html

Epic Soundtracks
members.tripod.com/~swellmap/index.
html
www.geocities.com/~chamberstrings/
epic.html

The Soup Dragons
www.geocities.com/CollegePark/Quad/
3145/soupdragons.html

Source Direct
www.caroline.com/astralwerks/
source_direct

Southern Culture on the Skids
www.scots.com
www.billions.com/scots
www.geffen.com/scots

Southside Johnny & the Asbury Jukes
pease1.sr.unh.edu/1/southside

Space
www.amherst.edu/~bgjohnso/space
www.aspire.co.uk/space
www.geocities.com/SoHo/Lofts/1899/
space.htm

Spacemen 3
www.no-fi.com/spacemen3/index.html

Spandau Ballet
www.geocities.com/SunsetStrip/
Palladium/7994

Spanic Boys
www.spanicboys.com

Sparks
www.doremi.co.uk/sparks

Spearhead
www.euronet.nl/users/ovdgp

The Specials
www.eyeontomorrow.com/specials/
index.htm
pw2.netcom.com/~miles.1/thespecials.
html
www.waycoolmusic.com/artists/
thespecials

Speedball
acm.cps.msu.edu/~hahnpaul/speed2
members.xoom.com/Spotaz/Speedball.
html

Jon Spencer Blues Explosion
www.megalink.net/~jbean/jsbe/jsbe.
html
www.matador.recs.com/bios/bio_jsbx.
html
www.geocities.com/SunsetStrip/9932/
index.htm

The Spice Girls
www.march.force9.co.uk/abspice.html
www.geocities.com/~spicegirlscafe
biscorp.prohosting.com

Spin Doctors
hem1.passagen.se/staff1/Spindoctors.
html
member.aol.com/Markmez/spindoctors.
html
www.spindoctors.com/index.html

Spinal Tap
www.spinaltap.com
www.voyagerco.com/catalog/spinaltap/
indepth
www.geocities.com/Hollywood/
Academy/9177

Spirit
kspace.com/spirit

Spirit of the West
spiritofthewest.bc.ca
www.geocities.com/Athens/Parthenon/
8887/spiritdex.html
duckwurks.web2010.com/sotw/sotw.
html

Spiritualized
www.spiritualized.com:81
www.aristarec.com/aristaweb/
Spiritualized
www.angelfire.com/ca/spiritualized

Split Enz
www.frenz.com
easyweb.easynet.co.uk/~david.brown/
splitenz.htm

Sponge
www.sponge-online.com
www.geocities.com/SunsetStrip/Palms/
7235/index.html
www.deadmedia.com/sponge

Dusty Springfield
www.rainbow.net.au/~dusty
www.srv.net/~roxtar/springfield_dusty.
html
www.isd.net/mbayly

Rick Springfield
www.geocities.com/Hollywood/Hills/
9905
members.tripod.com/~amy1970
home.earthlink.net/%7Eultravox/rlsrox.
html

Springhouse
cyclone.swa.com/springhouse

Bruce Springsteen
fhis.gcal.ac.uk/PSY/Pete/Bruce
www.sonymusic.com/artists/
BruceSpringsteen
www.msn.fullfeed.com/~ptblank/boss
www.mygale.org/11/ggougeon/
Bruce_Springsteen
www.wallofsound.com/artists/
brucespringsteen/index.html

Squarepusher
www.sme.co.jp/Music/Info/SonyTechno/
featureE/9704/index.html
www.northernnet.com/jesterby/spindex.
html
www.warp-net.com/warp/file/sqpsh

Squeeze
www.squeezefan.com

Billy Squier
www.geocities.com/SunsetStrip/5163

Squirrel Bait
www.cen.uiuc.edu/~khoury/sb/index.
html
www.southern.com/ultra/ultra1.1/squirr.
htm

Squirrel Nut Zippers
www.squirrelnutzippers.com
www.geocities.com/SunsetStrip/
Lounge/6666
www.geocities.com/SouthBeach/
Marina/6316

Lisa Stansfield
www.aristarec.com/aristaweb/
LisaStansfield/index.html

Star 69
www.radioactive.net/BANDS/STAR/
discs.html

Ringo Starr
web2.airmail.net/gshultz
www.ringotour.com
www.wpcusrgrp.org/~hshorr/beatles/
webdoc4.html

Status Quo
ourworld.compuserve.com/homepages/
quofrance
home.sol.no/~qwerty/quo.html
www.bath.ac.uk/~ma5jw/quo/sqhome.
html

Steely Dan
www.steelydan.com
pages.prodigy.com/sdresource
www.seanet.com/Users/stalfnzo/
steeldan.html

Steppenwolf
www.steppenwolf.com

Stereolab
www.elektra.com/alternative_club/
stereolab/stereolab.html
www.maths.monash.edu.au/~rjh/
stereolab

Cat Stevens
catstevens.com

Corey Stevens
www.webtozen.com
members.aol.com/dejavudu97/
coreystevens.html

Shakin' Stevens
www.euronet.nl/users/playsoft/shakin.
htm
www.mlbo.com/shaky.htm

Al Stewart
www.fish.com/music/al_stewart

John Stewart
www.sfo.com/~wondrdog/jstewart

Rod Stewart
members.aol.com/maggie1971/rasar.
html
members.aol.com/smilerfrg/rod/sminfo.
htm
ttlc.net/storyteller

Sting
easyweb.easynet.co.uk/~wendavey/
home.html
members.aol.com/omega305/sting/
index.htm
www.wallofsound.com/artists/sting/
Index.html

The Stone Roses
www.umr.edu/~mquinn/music/stone.
roses/sro01.html
www.geocities.com/SunsetStrip/Alley/
6364/index.html
www.freestyle.com/roses

Stone Temple Pilots
www.stonetemplepilots.com

www.illuminet.net/~pwrfouru/stp.html
www.geocities.com/SunsetStrip/Palms/
9125

The Stranglers
www.wwdc.com/~adrian/stranglers
www.btinternet.com/~in.black/st1.htm

Syd Straw
www.paye.org/sydstraw

The Strawbs
www.strawbpage.ndirect.co.uk/index.htm

Stray Cats
www.liglobal.com/ent_fun/music/
li-rock/straycats.html
seaisle.com/BuiltforSpeed/setzerpage.
html
www.interscoperecords.com/setzer1.
html

Styx
ParadiseTheatre.com
www.tiac.net/users/kat/Styx
www2.southwind.net/~tice

Subcircus
www.geffen.com/dreamworks/subcircus

The subdudes
www.gibson.com/fog/artists/n2z/
subdudes/subdudes.html
www.windham.com/ourmusic/artist_
pages/subdudes.empty.byartist.html

Sublime
sublimespot.simplenet.com
www.geocities.com/SunsetStrip/
Cabaret/7868/main.html
tech.simplenet.com/sublime

Suede
www.thelondonsuede.com
www.geocities.com/SunsetStrip/Palms/
2560/index.htm
www.geocities.com/SouthBeach/Sands/
7654/suede.html

Sugar Ray
www.deadmedia.com/sugarray
www.angelfire.com/ca/sugarray/index.
html
www.geocities.com/SunsetStrip/Palms/
2794

Suicidal Tendencies
members.aol.com/stfl/index.htm
www.geocities.com/SoHo/1538/st.htm

The Suicide Machines
www.thesuicidemachines.com
lost.simplenet.com/suicidemachines
www.hollywoodrec.com/suicidemachines
members.tripod.com/~sam6025/suma/
main.html

Sukia
www.nickelbag.com/sukia.html

Summercamp
www.maverickrc.com/summercamp

Sun Ra
www.eyeneer.com/Jazz/Sunra
www.fusebox.com/~jimr
www.holeworld.com/stellar.html

The Sundays
www.geffen.com/sundays
www.huan.com/sundays

Sunny Day Real Estate
hubcap.clemson.edu/~bpmccal/sdre.
html
www.oklahoma.net/~jlondon/sdre.html
pw2.netcom.com/~steadmad/index.
html

Super Deluxe
www.revolution-online.com/superdeluxe
microcosm.simplenet.com/superdeluxe
www.oz.net/~lauried

Super Furry Animals
www.creation.co.uk/superfurry/index.
html
www.come.to/sfa
www.best.com/~gweather/sfamain.htm

Superchunk
www.monkey.org/~chunk/superchunk
www.geocities.com/SunsetStrip/2605/
chunkfaq.html

Supergrass
www.supergrass.com
homepages.enterprise.net/bsm/
Supergrass
www.geocities.com/Hollywood/5085

Supertramp
www.supertramp.com/index2.shtml
www.microtec.net/~sylvn/tramp
www.microtec.net/~corny

The Supremes
homebrew.si.edu/supremes.html
www.mvprecords.com/supremes.html
www.marywilson.com

Billy Swan
www.athenet.net/~genevinc/SwanBilly.
html

Swans
www.swans.pair.com
www.sfs.utoledo.edu/students/Aw/
index.html
www.geocities.com/SoHo/6892/swans.
html

The Sweet
www.algonet.se/~sweetfa
www.personal.u-net.com/~thesweet

Matthew Sweet
www.afn.org/~afno4314/msweet.htm
bubblegum.uark.edu/Matthew_Sweet
www.geocities.com/SoHo/Gallery/1491/
ultrasuede.html

Rachel Sweet
www.angelfire.com/nj/rachelsweet/
index.html
bch48.bch.ncsu.edu/rsweet/index.html

Swell
www.psycho-specific.com
www.angelfire.com/mn/gethigh

Swervedriver
www.swervedriver.com
members.tripod.com/~kidneyboy/
page2.htm
www.odc.net/~ssharma/swerve/main.
shtml

Swing out Sister
www.rit.edu/~kbk4834/swingout/
swing.html

David Sylvian
web.inter.NL.net/users/K.vanBunningen/
music/sylvian/index.html

Symposium
www.sympomania.com

T. Rex
www.epix.net/~valley/trex.html
www.inforamp.net/~ivank/marc_bolan.
html
easyweb.easynet.co.uk/~rthomas/
HROT.html

Talk Talk
home.earthlink.net/~landrvr

Talking Heads
www.talking-heads.net
penguin.cc.ukans.edu/Heads/Talking_
Heads.html
members.xoom.com/DailyGhost/theads/
covers.htm

Tall Dwarfs
www.lancs.ac.uk/postgrad/blairb/
TALLDW/talldwar.htm

Tangerine Dream
www.tadream.com
www.hyperreal.org/music/exclusive/
discogs/tangerine_dream/discog
home.sol.no/~mmoen/tadream

James Taylor
www.james-taylor.com
www.sonymusic.com/artists/
JamesTaylor/jt/index.html
www.westworld.com/~gregb/jtindex.
html

The Tea Party
www.teaparty.com

Team Dresch
members.aol.com/ringard/team.htm
www.monsterbit.com/candyass/td.html

Tears for Fears
homepage.rconnect.com/travzila

www.uni-muenster.de/WiWi/home/
vdhardt/tears.htm?TearsForFears
Corner=Tears+For+Fears+Corner
users.aimnet.com/~markg/tears4fears

Teenage Fanclub
www.teenagefanclub.com
bubblegum.uark.edu/teenage_fanclub

Television
www.slip.net/~rivethed/tvsite.htm
www.aston.ac.uk/~taylorar/tv.htm

The Temptations
ballcom.com/~mrshouse/tempts.html

Ten Foot Pole
www.tenfootpole.com
www.agora.dk/users/c.fw/footpole.htm
www.dlc.fi/~salliha/tfp_index.htm

10,000 Maniacs
www.maniacs.com
www.brsite.com/10kmaniacs/10km.htm
fly.to/natalie
www.nataliemerchant.org

Ten Years After
www.execpc.com/~torrey/tya.html
www.bekkoame.or.jp/~tadatk/music/
tenyrsaftr.html

10cc
www.pacifier.com/~mikes/10cc/10cc.
html

Tesla
www.teslaweb.com

Texas
www.chez.com/texasonline
www.geocities.com/SunsetStrip/
Underground/4850
www.cs.vu.nl/~bernsti/texas

The Texas Tornados
www.RepriseRec.com/Reprise_HTML_
Pages/TexasTDir/TexasTornados.
html
www.xanadu2.net/rrogers/tornados.
html

that dog.
www.geocities.com/SunsetStrip/
Lounge/3465/index.html
www.geocities.com/Heartland/Ranch/
5012/tdmain.htm
www.verinet.com/~thompson

That Petrol Emotion
hsfstud.hisf.no/~964289/tpe.htm

The The
www.tezcat.com/~juanyen/mick/thethe.
htm
www.ingsoc.com/thethe
www.io.com/~fabiol/the_the.html

Therapy?
uktherapy.neverworld.com
www.destructive.demon.co.uk/Therapy

huizen.dds.nl/~whaley/therapy/heavy/
index.htm

They Might Be Giants
www.tmbg.com
earth.vol.com/~uni//tmbg/index.html
www.tmbg.org

Thin Lizzy
members.tripod.com/~Mr_Harrington
www.uncg.edu/~edpoole
ds.dial.pipex.com/thinlizzy

Thin White Rope
www.media.ku.dk/students/anya/ROPE.
HTM

Thinking Fellers Union
www.matador.recs.com/bios/bio_tful.
html
www.wco.com/~raydavis/tful282.html

Third Eye Blind
www.geocities.com/SunsetStrip/Venue/
6661/thirdeyeblind.html
www.geocities.com/SunsetStrip/
Underground/6102/3eb.html
www.geocities.com/SunsetStrip/Towers/
1105/main.html

.38 Special
www.38special.com

Thirty Ought Six
www.mutelibtech.com/mute/thirty/
thirty.htm
www.teleport.com/~ruckus/oregon/
thirty.htm

This Mortal Coil
www.evo.org/html/group/thismortalcoil.
html

Richard Thompson
www.alphalink.com.au/~sfy/RT

The Thompson Twins
www.interlog.com/~ditko37/ttwins.html

George Thorogood & the Destroyers
qlink.queensu.ca/~4bgs/index.html

Three Dog Night
www.threedognight.com

311
www.geocities.com/SoHo/9992/311.
html
www.duke.edu/~bak4/311.html
www.idir.net/~scoryell/311/311.html

Throbbing Gristle
www.brainwashed.com/tg
www.gl.umbc.edu/~vijay/tg/tg.html

Throwing Muses
www.throwingmusic.com/newer/
mainmenu.html
www.repriserec.com/reprise_html_
pages/throwingmuses
members.aol.com/lonls/muses.html

Tiffany
www.tiffany.org
www.indyramp.com/music/tiffany.html
www.northcoast.com/~wahl/title.htm

Timbuk 3
www.iit.edu/~diazrob/timbuk3/index.
html

Tindersticks
huizen.dds.nl/~totos/tinder.htm

Toad the Wet Sprocket
www.geocities.com/SunsetStrip/Stage/
6602
www.prairienet.org/toad
www.houseoftoad.com

Jeremy Toback
www.geocities.com/SunsetStrip/Towers/
1854/jtindex.html

Tommy Tutone
www.tutone.com

Tonic
www.tonic-online.com
www.polygram.com/polydor/artists/
tonic
members.xoom.com/tonic

Too Much Joy
www.discoveryrec.com/artists/tmj/
index.html
www.cybercom.net/~jesse/tmj
www.joybuzzer.com

Tool
toolshed.down.net
www.toolband.com
ww4.choice.net/~raidr

William Topley
www.MercuryNashville.com/mercury_
nashville/artists/topley_wm

Tortoise
www.brainwashed.com/tortoise
trout.sputcorp.com/reviews/tortoise.htm
www.cpedu.rug.nl/~evert/bands/st/
tortoise.htm

Toto
www.sonymusic.com/artists/Toto
www.schwaben.de/home/ninetynine
home1.swipnet.se/~w-10128/toto/
index.html

Tower of Power
www.bumpcity.com
www.rock.n.roll.com/TOP

Traffic
web.syr.edu/~mdentin

The Tragically Hip
www.thehip.com
www.tabbweb.com/thehip/index.html
www.geocities.com/SunsetStrip/Alley/
5440/index.html

Tranquility Bass
www.caroline.com/astralwerks/
tranquility

Transglobal Underground
www.t-g-u.com
www.geocities.com/SunsetStrip/Alley/
5444/Transglobal_Underground.html

The Traveling Wilburys
qlink.queensu.ca/~6djm/Wilburys/
main.htm

Travis
www.scooter.demon.co.uk/travis/index.
htm

Treadmill Trackstar
www.treadmilltrackstar.com

Treble Charger
www.voicenet.com/~mintzer/tc.html
www.treblecharger.com
www.odyssee.net/~zarifah/treble.htm

Treehouse
www.breakingrecords.com/treehouse

The Triffids
www.crosswinds.net/antwerp/~triffids/
triffids.htm

Robin Trower
www.angelfire.com/ca/RobinTrower
www.inforamp.net/~suth/trower/index.
html

Jennifer Trynin
www.wbr.com/jennifertrynin

Tsunami
www.southern.com/southern/band/
TSUNA

The Tubes
www.pacificnet.net/~datalus/tubes

Ike & Tina Turner
www.digiwing.com/tina
www.las.es/tina
www.wallofsound.com/artists/
tinaturner/index.html

The Turtles
www.bymgroup.com/smbwebpage/
smbturtles/turtlecrossing.html

20/20
www.geocities.com/SunsetStrip/9859

Twisted Sister
www.geocities.com/SunsetStrip/2774
weber.u.washington.edu/~warlock2/
twisted.html
www.netusa.net/~hal-j/twisted

Type O Negative
bravedave.com/type
www.geocities.com/SunsetStrip/Alley/
1732
www.geocities.com/~glycerin/typeo.htm

UB40
www.ub40-dep.com
www.d.umn.edu/~chouse/cd_player/
ub40.html
home.wxs.nl/~keizeo25/home.html

Ugly Kid Joe
home.sol.no/~khalguns/ukj.htm
jags.co.uk/~chuck/ukj/index.htm

Ultra Vivid Scene
www.evo.org/html/group/
ultravividscene.html

Ultravox
www.ultravox.org.uk
www.geocities.com/SiliconValley/9463/
fixion.html
www.path.unimelb.edu.au/~new_wave/
ultravox.html

Uncle Tupelo
www.gumbopages.com/uncle-tupelo.
html

Underworld
www.swankarmy.net/transmit/
underworld
dirty.org
www.noord.bart.nl/~pbaars/new/index.
html

Unrest
www.evo.org/html/group/unrest.html

The Urge
www.geocities.com/SunsetStrip/
Lounge/7359
skafunk.ml.org/urge
www.urge.net

Urge Overkill
www.flash.net/~lkras/uo

Uriah Heep
www.uriah-heep.com
www.en.com/users/dhw
www.geocities.com/SunsetStrip/Palms/
2930/uhpages.htm

U2
www.henrywagner.org/zootv
www.vaxxine.com/U2
www.netexp.net/~mldunne
www.geocities.com/SoHo/Lofts/2527/
exit.html

Steve Vai
www.netsonic.fi/~micke/FireGarden
www.dennison.clara.net/svc
www.epiccenter.com/EpicCenter/docs/
artistupdate.qry?artistid=257

Ritchie Valens
www.sonic.net/~damien/index.html

Van Halen
www.van-halen.com
web.wt.net/~vh5150
vanhalen.strafford.com

www.geocities.com/SunsetStrip/Alley/
6190/index.html

Vanilla Fudge
www.vanillafudge.com

The Vapors
hem.passagen.se/pareng/vapors.htm

Varnaline
www.angelfire.com/ny/varnaline
www.wizvax.net/clubland/varnaline

The Vaselines
www.geocities.com/SunsetStrip/Towers/
7085/index.html

Jimmie Vaughan
www.epiccenter.com/EpicCenter/
custom/artistupdatefan.qry?
artistid=176

Stevie Ray Vaughan
www.sonymusic.com/artists/
StevieRayVaughan
w4.lns.cornell.edu/~jjo/srv.html
www.geocities.com/SunsetStrip/7299
www.uark.edu/~scherry/srv
www.fortunecity.com/tinpan/bonehead/
267/rude_mood.html

Ben Vaughn
www.bar-none.com/bios/bv_bio.html

Bobby Vee
www.bobbyvee.net

Suzanne Vega
www.vega.net
www.win.bright.net/~jcprince/svega.
html

Velocity Girl
www.subpop.com/bands/velocitygirl/
velocitygirl.html
www.subpop.com/bands/velocitygirl/
gszh/index.html

Velvet Crush
www.thenet.co.uk/~mikehind

The Velvet Underground
outland.cyberwar.com/~zoso/velvets
members.aol.com/olandem/vu.html
www.poihq.com/loureed
www.angelfire.com/ny/vu1

The Ventures
www.theventures.com
www.kscon.com/lvent/index.htm
www.geocities.com/CapeCanaveral/
3098/venture.htm

Verbow
www.epiccenter.com/EpicCenter/
Verbow/index.qry
www.math.nwu.edu/~richeson/
candy.car.main.html
www.housedog.com/waterdog/
whitehou/verbow/text/verbmain.html

Versus
kickbright.com/versus/index.html
www.caroline.com/caroline/versus

Veruca Salt
www.interlog.com/~drambeau/vs
pages.prodigy.com/vsalt/salt.htm
home.ptd.net/~eric/veruca/veruca.html

The Verve
raft.vmg.co.uk/theverve
www.geocities.com/SunsetStrip/Venue/
3869/index.html
www.virginrecords.com/theverve

The Verve Pipe
www.thevervepipe.com
www-personal.umich.edu/~aclemnts/
vervepipe.html
members.aol.com/vpipeings/homepage.
html

The Vibrators
www.slamdance.co.uk/thevibrators/
index.html

Vigilantes of Love
www.coaster.com/VOL

The Village People
www.geocities.com/TheTropics/4210
www.gryphon.com/village-people

Gene Vincent
www.athenet.net/~genevinc/index20.
html

Violent Femmes
www.vfemmes.com

Chris Von Sneidern
www.iuma.com/IUMA/band_html/Von_
Sneidern,_Chris.html

John Waite
www.johnwaite.com
shakti.trincoll.edu/~jgilbert/jwstuff/
jwpage.html

The Waitresses
www.hardcafe.co.uk/waitresses
webx.trouserpress.com/bandpages/
WAITRESSES.html

Tom Waits
www.tomwaits.com
www.front.net/gtausch/waits.html
www.gameverse.com/music/waits
www.geocities.com/SoHo/7587
www.wallofsound.com/artists/tomwaits/
index.html

Rick Wakeman
www.rwcc.com

The Walkabouts
www.hooked.net/~cbhall

The Walker Brothers
home.sprintmail.com/~chadvan/scott

Wall of Voodoo
www.wallofvoodoo.com
www4.linknet.net/Vieuxdo

The Wallflowers
www.interscoperecords.com/wallflower.
html
www.geocities.com/~6th_Avenue/index.
html
www.gcocitics.com/SunsetStrip/Stage/
4139/wallflowers.html

Joe Walsh
www4.ncsu.edu/eos/users/s/saclodfe/
homepage/jamesgang.html

Jamie Walters
www.geocities.com/SunsetStrip/
Palladium/4542

Wang Chung
www.public.asu.edu/~z001995/wc.html

The Wannabes
www.eden.com/~dejadisc/wannabes.
html

Jennifer Warnes
www.jennifer-warnes.com

Warrant
www.warrant96.com
www2.bitstream.net/~beowulf/warrant.
htm
www.geocities.com/SunsetStrip/
Lounge/4619

The Waterboys
www.ceolas.org/artists/Waterboys.html

Muddy Waters
www.blueflamecafe.com/Muddy_
Waters.html
www.island.net/~blues/morgan.html
www.deltablues.com/muddy.htm

Jimmy Webb
www.jimmywebb.com

The Wedding Present
huizen.dds.nl/~chester/wpindex.htm
www.westnet.com/weddoes

Ween
www.ween.org
www.geocities.com/SunsetStrip/
Palladium/7030
www.geocities.com/SunsetStrip/Palms/
1673/ween.html

Weezer
shakti.trincoll.edu/~cchatter/weezer.
html
www.weezer.a-d-n.com
cloneworld.simplenet.com/Weezer

Wendy & Lisa
www.geocities.com/SunsetStrip/
Lounge/4074/soulsisters.html

Whiskeytown
www.mindspring.com/~bdjackson/
whiskeytown/index.htm

White Courtesy Telephone
www.monsterisland.com/wct/wct.html

White Town
www.white-town.com

White Zombie
www.chez.com/zombie
www.5000volt.com/zombie666
www.gac.edu/~dkuster/zombie/index.
html

Chris Whitley
www.sonymusic.com/artists/
ChrisWhitley
www.phpad.com/whitley
www.geocities.com/SunsetStrip/
Lounge/7760/whitley.html

The Who
www.thewho.net
members.aol.com/TheWho4/index.html
www.geocities.com/Broadway/Stage/
6654/index.html
www.sahr.com/thewho/joe
www.wallofsound.com/artists/thewho/
index.html

The Why Store
php.indiana.edu/~ceinfalt/whystore.htm
pubweb.acns.nwu.edu/~jjb365/
whystore

Widespread Panic
www.widespreadpanic.com
gabriel.cvm.msstate.edu/~chess
www.netspace.org/Widespread

Wig
www.wig.com

Wilco
www.wilcoweb.com
www.geocities.com/Hollywood/Hills/
3965/wilco1.htm
www.wallofsound.com/artists/wilco/
index.html

Kim Wilde
members.aol.com/guko56/kimhome/
index.htm
kimwilde.go4it.net
perso.club-internet.fr/lwheeler/
kimwilde.html

Webb Wilder
www.webbwilder.com
www.nd.edu/~kdrew/WW.html
www.geocities.com/SunsetStrip/Palms/
5540

Dar Williams
www.panix.com/~tneff/dar

Lucinda Williams
www2.bitstream.net/~acs/music/lw

www.lonestarwebstation.com/lucinda.
html

Victoria Williams
www.victoriawilliams.com
traaacy.com/victoria

Brian Wilson
www.cabinessence.com/brian
www.mca.com/mca_records/library/
bios/bio.wilson.html

Jackie Wilson
www.angelfire.com/ok/Hildavid

Wilson Phillips
www.cdc.net/~bpar/wilsonphillips.html
www.geocities.com/SunsetStrip/Stage/
5968/index.htm
www.geocities.com/SunsetStrip/3424/
WP.htm

Winger
www.i2.i-2000.com/~deeprice/wws.htm

Edgar Winter
www.instantimaging.com/edgar

Johnny Winter
sicel-home-2-19.urbanet.ch:8080/
Music/winter.html
www.seachange.com:8010/jwinter

Steve Winwood
www.stevewinwood.com

The Wipers
members.tripod.com/~WIPER/wipers.
html
www.geocities.com/SunsetStrip/Club/
7895/wiper.html
www.cs.uml.edu/~jpenney/wipers

Wire
www.contrib.andrew.cmu.edu/~qwerty/
wire

Wire Train
hsfstud.hisf.no/~964289/wire.htm

Wishbone Ash
skymarshall.com/argus/index.html

Stevie Wonder
student-
www.uchicago.edu/users/jrgenzen/
stevie.html
darkwing.uoregon.edu/~thierry/
wonder/wonder.html
www.xmission.com/~dan_nan/wonder/
stevie.html
www.wallofsound.com/artists/
steviewonder/index.html

World Party
www.world-party.net
www2.cybernex.net/~vijayr/WPhome.
html
www.kamome.or.jp/koji

Gary Wright
www.thedreamweaver.com/index.htm

Wu-Tang Clan
www.algonet.se/~blindman/index.html
www.geocities.com/Colosseum/Field/
4311
www.geocities.com/NapaValley/4035/
wu.html

Robert Wyatt
www.strongcomet.com/wyatt
www.mindspring.com/~us000091/
wyatt3.htm
prog.ari.net/prog/Bands/Gongwyatt/
wyatt.home.html

X
www.zzapp.org/usaronso/x/x.htm
home1.gte.net/havasu/index.html

X-Ray Specs
www.comnet.ca/~rina/xrayspex.html
www.terrapin.co.uk/xrayspex/index.
html

XTC
www.charm.net/~duke/xtc/beatown.
html
www.users.dircon.co.uk/~nonsuch/
bungalow.htm
reality.sgi.com/employees/relph/
chalkhills

Xymox
www.cybercomm.nl/~xymox/xymox.
html
www.evo.org/html/group/clanofxymox.
html

Weird Al Yankovic
www.weirdal.com
www.emsphone.com/Al
www.webspan.net/~dprossi

The Yardbirds
www.idsonline.com/yardbirds

Yello
www.yello.ch
www.totalobscurity.com/yello/index.
html
unet.univie.ac.at/~a9103394/yello/
pgyell.htm

Yes
pages.preferred.com/~pete/fy.htm
www.smartlink.net/~yesman/yesman.
html
www.nfte.org

Yo La Tengo
www.muohio.edu/~plattgj/ylt
www.matador.recs.com/bands/ylt/
index.html

Dwight Yoakam
www.dwightsite.com
www.tpoint.net/~wallen/country/
dwight-yoakam.html

members.aol.com/Zenyram/dwight.html
www.wbr.com/nashville/dwightyoakam

You Am I
www-personal.usyd.edu.au/
~metherde/you_am_i
users.hunterlink.net.au/~ddlpp/youami.
html
www.geocities.com/SunsetStrip/Towers/
4061/youami.html

Neil Young
HyperRust.org
www.geocities.com/SunsetStrip/6734
www.capetech.co.uk/Aurora_Borealis/
ny_index.html
ourworld.compuserve.com/homepages/
nyas
www.wallofsound.com/artists/
neilyoung/index.html

Young Fresh Fellows
www.yff.com/yff

The Young Rascals
www.wesjen.simplenet.com/rascals/
rascals.html
members.aol.com/BrianMac48/rascals.
htm
www.liglobal.com/ent_fun/music/
li-rock/rascalsdisc.html

Z
www.geocities.com/CollegePark/2025/
dweezil.htm

Frank Zappa
www.zappa.com
www.geocities.com/SunsetStrip/6095
darkwing.uoregon.edu/~splat/
zappapage.html
www.catalog.com/mrm/zappa.html
members.aol.com/Doodah999/dog.html

Martin Zellar
www.stolaf.edu/people/anderswa/
martin/main.html
www.martinzellar.com

Warren Zevon
www.eecs.tulane.edu:80/www/Morris.
Ashley/zevon.html
members.aol.com/zevonfan1/private/
zevon.htm

The Zombies
members.aol.com/bocad/zom.htm

ZZ Top
www.integra.hu/private/horvath/zz.htm
www.cjnetworks.com/~leis/album/
zztop
users.iafrica.com/p/pa/pantsula/zztop.
htm

Other Rock and Music-Related Sites

Addicted to Noise
www.addict.com

All Music Guide
www.allmusic.com

Amazon.com
www.amazon.com/music

a2b music
www.a2bmusic.com

Billboard Magazine
www.billboard.com

The Blue Flame Cafe
www.blueflamecafe.com

The Blue Highway
www.thebluehighway.com

BMG Music Service
www.bmgmusicservice.com

Borders.com
www.borders.com/music

Broadcast.com
www.broadcast.com

CD Jukebox
www.broadcast.com/jukebox

CD Universe
www.cduniverse.com

CDnow
www.cdnow.com

CMJ Online
www.cmjmusic.com

Columbia House Music Club
www.columbiahouse.com

Compact Disc Connection
www.cdconnection.com
www.hyperreal.com

ICE Magazine
www.icemagazine.com

iMusic Newsagent
www.imusic.interserv.com/newsagent

International Lyrics Server
www.lyrics.ch

Jam TV
www.jamtv.com

Liquid Audio
www.liquidaudio.com

MTV
www.mtv.com

Music Boulevard
www.musicblvd.com

Music Newswire
www.musicnewswire.com

Muzic.com
www.muzik.com

Pollstar
www.pollstar.com

RealAudio
www.real.com

Rock and Roll Hall of Fame and Museum
www.rockhall.com

RockDaily.com
www.rockdaily.com

RockNews.com
www.rocknews.com

RockOnTV
www.rockontv.com

Rocktropolis
www.rocktropolis.com

Rolling Stone Network
www.rollingstone.com

SonicNet
www.sonicnet.com

Spinner
www.spinner.com

Total E
www.totalE.com

Tower Records
www.towerrecords.com

Tunes.com
www.tunes.com

Ultimate Band List
www.ubl.com

unfURLed
www.unfurled.com

USA Today (Music Index)
www.usatoday.com/life/enter/music/
lem99.htm

VH1
www.vh1.com

Wall of Sound
www.wallofsound.com

The following record labels are just some of the labels that have substantial rock catalogs. You may want to contact them if you have questions regarding specific releases.

A&M Records
1416 N. La Brea Ave.
Hollywood, CA 90028
(213) 469-2411
Fax: (213) 856-2600

ABKCO Records
1700 Broadway, 41st. Fl.
New York, NY 10019
(212) 399-0300
Fax: (212) 582-5090

Alias Records
2815 W. Olive Ave.
Burbank, CA 91505
(818) 566-1034
Fax: (818) 566-6623

All American Music Group
808 Wilshire Blvd.
Santa Monica, CA 90401
(310) 656-1100
Fax: (310) 656-7430

Alligator Records
PO Box 60234
Chicago, IL 60660
(312) 973-7736
Fax: (312) 973-2088

Almo Sounds
360 N. La Cienega Blvd.
Los Angeles, CA 90048
(310) 289-3080
Fax: (310) 289-8662

Alternative Tentacles Records
PO Box 419092
San Francisco, CA 94141-9092
(415) 282-9782
Fax: (415) 282-9786

American Recordings
3500 W. Olive Ave., Ste. 1550
Burbank, CA 91505-4628
(818) 973-4545
Fax: (818) 973-4571

Amphetamine Reptile Records
2200 4th St. NE, Ste. 1
Minneapolis, MN 55418
(612) 781-6120
Fax: (612) 781-9320

Arista Records
6 W. 57th St.
New York, NY 10019
(212) 489-7400
Fax: (212) 830-2238

Ark 21 Records
14724 Ventura Blvd., Penthouse
Sherman Oaks, CA 91403
(818) 461-1700
Fax: (818) 461-1745

Astralwerks Records
104 W. 29th St., 4th Fl.
New York, NY 10001
(212) 886-7500
Fax: (212) 643-5573

Atlantic Recording Corp.
1290 Avenue of the Americas
New York, NY 10104
(212) 707-2000
Fax: (212) 405-5507

Barking Pumpkin Records
PO Box 5265
North Hollywood, CA 91616-5265
(818) 755-3700
Fax: (818) 761-7773

Bar/None Records
1 Newark St., Ste.9
Hoboken, NJ 07030
(201) 795-9424
Fax: (201) 795-5048

Bear Family Records
PO Box 1154
27727 Hambergen, Germany
(49) 04794-93000
Fax: (49) 04794-930020
E-mail: bear@bear-family.de

Beggars Banquet Records
580 Broadway, Ste. 1004
New York, NY 10012
(212) 343-7010
Fax: (212) 343-7030

Bellmark Records/Life Records
7060 Hollywood Blvd., 10th Fl.
Hollywood, CA 90028
(213) 464-8492
Fax: (213) 464-0785

Big Beat Records
14 E. 60th St., 8th Fl.
New York, NY 10022
(212) 508-5400
Fax: (212) 527-0950

Black Top Records
PO Box 56691
New Orleans, LA 70156
(504) 895-7239
Fax: (504) 891-1510

Blue Note Records
1290 Avenue of the Americas, 35th Fl.
New York, NY 10104
(212) 492-5300
Fax: (212) 492-5458

Capricorn Records
1100 Spring St. NW, Ste. 103.
Atlanta, GA 30309-2823
(404) 873-3918
Fax: (404) 873-1807

CherryDisc Records
PO Box 120089
Boston, MA 02112-0089
(617) 350-9966
Fax: (617) 422-0121

CMC International Records
5226 Green Dairy Rd.
Raleigh, NC 27616-4612
(919) 875-3500
Fax: (919) 875-3550

Collectables Records
2320 Haverford Rd.
Ardmore, PA 19003
(800) 446-8426
(610) 649-7650
Fax: (610) 649-0315

Collectors Choice Music
PO Box 838
Itasca, IL 60143-0838
(800) 923-1122

Columbia Records
550 Madison Ave.
New York, NY 10022-3211
(212) 833-8000
Fax: (212) 833-7731

Cooking Vinyl Records
PO Box 311

Port Washington, NY 11050
(516) 484-2863
Fax: (516) 484-6179

Crave Records
20 W. 55th, 9th Fl.
New York, NY 10019
(212) 893-1855
Fax: (212) 893-1860

Creation Records
109X Regents Park Rd.
London, England NW1 8UR
44-171-722-8866
Fax: 44-171-722-3443

Critique Records
50 Cross St.
Winchester, MA 01890-1257
(617) 729-8137
Fax: (617) 729-2320

The Curb Group
47 Music Sq. E.
Nashville, TN 37203
(615) 321-5080
Fax: (615) 327-1964

Death Row Records
9171 Wilshire Blvd., Ste. 302
Beverly Hills, CA 90210
(310) 786-8459
Fax: (310) 786-8467

Decca Records
60 Music Sq. E.
Nashville, TN 37203
(615) 244-8944
Fax: (615) 880-7475

Dedicated Records
580 Broadway, Ste. 1002
New York, NY 10012
(212) 334-5959
Fax: (212) 334-5963

Def Jam Music Group
160 Varick St.
New York, NY 10013
(212) 229-5200
Fax: (212) 675-3588

Delicious Vinyl
6607 Sunset Blvd.
Los Angeles, CA 90028
(213) 465-2700
Fax: (213) 465-8926

Dischord Records
3819 Beecher St. NW
Washington, DC 20007-1802
(703) 351-7507
Fax: (703) 351-7582

Walt Disney Records
350 S. Buena Vista St.
Burbank, CA 91521
(818) 973-4370
Fax: (818) 953-9910

DreamWorks Records
9268 W. Third St.
Beverly Hills, CA 90210
(310) 234-7700
Fax: (310) 234-7750

Earache Records
295 Lafayette St., Ste. 915
New York, NY 10012
(212) 343-9090
Fax: (212)343-9244

EastWest Records
75 Rockefeller Plz.
New York, NY 10019
(212) 275-2500
Fax: (212) 974-9314

Elektra Entertainment Group
75 Rockefeller Plz.
New York, NY 10019-6907
(212) 275-4000
Fax: (212) 974-9314

EMI-Capitol Records
1750 N. Vine St.
Hollywood, CA 90028
(213) 462-6252
Fax: (213) 467-6550

Epic Records
550 Madison Ave.
New York, NY 10022-3211
(212) 833-8000
Fax: (212) 833-5134

Epitaph Records
2798 Sunset Blvd.
Los Angeles, CA 90026
(213) 413-7353
Fax: (213) 413-9678

Fat Possum Records
PO Box 1923
Oxford, MS 38655
(601) 236-3110
Fax: (601) 236-6300

57 Records/Shotput Records
1770 Century Blvd., Ste. B
Atlanta, GA 30345
(404) 633-2800
Fax: (404) 633-2882

Flying Fish Records
One Camp St.
Cambridge, MA 02140-1103
(617) 354-0700
Fax: (617) 491-1970

ForeFront Records
201 Seabord Ln.
Franklin, TN 37067
(615) 771-2900
Fax: (615) 771-2902

4AD Records
PO Box 46187
Los Angeles, CA 90046
(310) 289-8770

Fax: (310) 289-8680

Fox Music
PO Box 900
Beverly Hills, CA 90213-0900
(310) 369-3349
Fax: (310) 369-1516

Geffen Records/DGC Records
9130 Sunset Blvd.
Los Angeles, CA 90069-6197
(310) 278-9010
Fax: (310) 273-9389

Giant Records
1514 South St.
Nashville, TN 37212
(615) 256-3110
Fax: (615) 742-1560

Grand Royal Records
PO Box 26689
Los Angeles, CA 90039
(213) 663-3000
Fax: (213) 663-5726

GRP Recording Co.
555 W. 57th St., 10th Fl.
New York, NY 10019
(212) 424-1000
Fax: (212) 424-1007

HighTone Records
220 Fourth St., Ste. 101
Oakland, CA 94607
(510) 763-8500
Fax: (510) 763-8558

Hollywood Records
500 S. Buena Vista St.
Burbank, CA 91521
(818) 560-5670
Fax: (818) 841-5140

House of Blues Music
8439 Sunset Blvd., Ste. 404
West Hollywood, CA 90069
(213) 848-2508
Fax: (213) 848-7211

Ichiban Records
PO Box 724677
Atlanta, GA 31139-1677
(770) 419-1414
Fax: (770) 419-1230

Interscope Records
10900 Wilshire Blvd.
Los Angeles, CA 90024
(310) 208-6547
Fax: (310) 208-7343

Intersound Records/Branson Entertainment
PO Box 1724
Roswell, GA 30077
(770) 664-9262
Fax: (770) 664-7316

Island Records
825 Eighth Ave., 24th Fl.
New York, NY 10019
(212) 333-8000
Fax: (212) 603-3965

Jive Records/Silvertone Records
137-139 W. 25th St., 11th Fl.
New York, NY 10001
(212) 727-0016
Fax: (212) 645-3783

JVC Music
3800 Bartham Blvd., Ste. 305
Los Angeles, CA 90068
(213) 878-0101
Fax: (213) 878-0202

K Records
PO Box 7154
Olympia, WA 98507
(360) 786-5024

Kill Rock Stars
120 N.E. State Ave., Ste. 418
Olympia, WA 98501
(360) 357-9732
Fax: (360) 357-6408

Kinetic Records
75 Rockefeller Plaza, 21st Fl.
New York, NY 10019
(212) 275-4647
Fax: (212) 247-2638

King Biscuit Flower Hour Records
18 E. 53rd St., 11th Fl.
New York, NY 10022
(212) 758-4636
Fax: (212) 758-4704

Knitting Factory Works
74 Leonard St.
New York, NY 10013
(212) 219-3006
Fax: (212) 219-3401

Koch Records USA
2 Tri Harbor Ct.
Port Washington, NY 11050-4617
(516) 484-1000
Fax: (516) 484-4746

K-Tel International Records
2605 Fernbrook Ln. N.
Minneapolis, MN 55447-4736
(612) 559-6800
Fax: (612) 559-6803

LaFace Records
3350 Peachtree Rd., Ste. 1500
Atlanta, GA 30326
(404) 848-8050
Fax: (404) 848-8051

Laserlight Digital
Delta Music Company

1663 Sawtelle Blvd.
Los Angeles, CA 90025
(310) 268-1205
Fax: (310) 268-1279

Lava Records
75 Rockefeller Plz.
New York, NY 10019
(212) 265-3440
Fax: (212) 265-7706

Little Dog Records
223 W. Alameda Ave., Ste. 101
Burbank, CA 91502
(818) 557-1595
Fax: (818) 557-0524

London Records
825 Eighth Ave., 23rd Fl.
New York, NY 10019
(212) 333-8000
Fax: (212) 333-8030

Loud Records
8360 Melrose Ave., 2nd Fl.
Los Angeles, CA 90069
(213) 653-0891
Fax: (213) 653-6250

Luaka Bop
PO Box 652, Cooper Station
New York, NY 10276
(212)255-2714
Fax: (212) 255-3809

Magnatone Records
1516 16th Ave. S.
Nashville, TN 37212
(615) 383-3600
Fax: (615) 383-0020

Mammoth Records
101 B St.
Carrboro, NC 27510
(919) 932-1882
Fax: (919) 932-1885

Mardi Gras Records
3331 St. Charles Ave.
New Orleans, LA 70115
(504) 895-0441
Fax: (504) 891-4214

Matador Records
625 Broadway, 12th Fl.
New York, NY 10012
(212) 995-5882
Fax: (212) 995-5883

Maverick Records
8000 Beverly Blvd.
Los Angeles, CA 90048
(213) 852-1177
Fax: (213) 852-1505

MCA Records
70 Universal City Plz.
Universal City, CA 91608
(818) 777-4000
Fax: (818) 733-1407

MCG Records/Curb Records
3907 W. Alameda Ave., Ste.
    101
Burbank, CA 91505
(818) 843-1616
Fax: (818) 843-5429

Mercury Records
 World Wide Plz.
825 Eighth Ave.
New York, NY 10019
(212) 333-8000
Fax: (212) 333-1093

Metal Blade Records
2828 Cochran St., Ste. 302
Simi Valley, CA 93065
(805) 522-9111
Fax: (805) 522-9380

MJJ Records
2100 Colorado Ave.
Santa Monica, CA 90404
(310) 449-2960

Mobile Fidelity Sound Lab
105 Morris St.
Sebastopol, CA 95472
(707) 829-0134
Fax: (707) 829-3746

Monument Records
34 Music Sq. E.
Nashville, TN 37203
(615) 742-5724
Fax: (615) 254-3879

Moon Ska NYC
84 E. 10th St.
New York, NY 10003
(212) 673-5538
Fax: (212) 673-5571

Motown Records
825 Eighth Ave., 28th Fl.
New York, NY 10019
(212) 294-9516
Fax: (212) 946-2615

Mute Records
140 W. 22nd, Ste. 10-A
New York, NY 10011
(212) 255-7670
Fax: (212) 255-6056

Neurodisc Records
4592 N. Hiatus Rd.
Fort Lauderdale, FL 33351
(954) 572-0289

Next Plateau Entertainment
530 Broadway, 2nd Fl.
New York, NY 10012
(212) 941-0460
Fax: (212) 941-0509

Nothing Records
2337 W. 11th St.
Cleveland, OH 44113
(216) 781-3300

Fax: (216) 781-9240

N2K Encoded Music
55 Broad St., 18th Fl.
New York, NY 10004
(212) 378-6100
Fax: (212) 742-1775

Oh Boy Records
33 Music Sq. W., Ste. 102-B
Nashville, TN 37203
(800) 521-2112
(615) 742-1250
Fax: (615) 742-1360

Outpost Recordings
7072 Blue Sails Dr.
Huntington Beach, CA 92647
(310) 285-7373
Fax: (310) 276-2690

PNP Records
8455 Beverly Blvd., Ste. 600
Los Angeles, CA 90048
(213) 966-2560
Fax: (213) 966-2589

Polydor Records
1416 N. La Brea Ave.
Hollywood, CA 90028
(213) 856-6600
Fax: (213) 856-6610

Private Music
8750 Wilshire Blvd.
Beverly Hills, CA 90211
(310) 358-4500
Fax: (310) 358-4520

Qwest Records
3800 Barham Blvd., Ste. 503
Los Angeles, CA 90068
(213) 874-7770
Fax: (213) 874-5049

Radioactive Records
8570 Hedges Pl.
Los Angeles, CA 90069
(310) 659-6598
Fax: (310) 659-1679

Razor & Tie Records
214 Sullivan St., #4A
New York, NY 10012
(212) 473-9173
Fax: (212) 473-9174

RCA Records
1540 Broadway
New York, NY 10036
(212) 930-4000
Fax: (212) 930-4468

Red Ant Entertainment
9720 Wilshire Blvd., 4th Fl.
Beverly Hills, CA 90212
(310) 247-1133
Fax: (310) 247-2233

Relativity Records
79 Fifth Ave., 16th Fl.
New York, NY 10003
(212) 337-5300
Fax: (212) 337-5373

Relix Records
PO Box 98
Brooklyn, NY 11229
(718) 258-0009

Reprise Records
3300 Warner Blvd.
Burbank, CA 91505-4694
(818) 846-9090
(818) 953-3223
Fax: (818) 953-3211

Restless Records
1616 Vista Del Mar Ave.
Hollywood, CA 90028
(800) 573-7853
(213) 957-4357
Fax: (213) 957-4355

Reunion Records
2908 Poston Ave.
Nashville, TN 37202
(615) 320-9200
Fax: (615) 320-1734

Revolution Records
8900 Wilshire Blvd., Ste. 200
Beverly Hills, CA 90211-1906
(310) 289-5500

Rhino Records
10635 Santa Monica Blvd.
Los Angeles, CA 90025-4900
(310) 474-4778
Fax: (310) 441-6575

The Right Stuff
1750 N. Vine St.
Hollywood, CA 90028
(213) 960-4634
Fax: (213) 960-4666

Righteous Babe Records
PO Box 95, Ellicott Station
Buffalo, NY 14205-0095
(716) 852-8020
Fax: (716) 852-2741

Rip-It Records
1221 W. Colonial Dr., Ste. 300
Orlando, FL 32804
(407) 648-9889
Fax: (407) 649-6767

Rising Tide Records
48 Music Sq. E.
Nashville, TN 37203-4323
(615) 254-5050
Fax: (615) 313-3700

River North Records
1222 16th Ave. S., 3rd Fl.
Nashville, TN 37212
(615) 327-0770

Fax: (615) 327-0011

Roadrunner Records
536 Broadway
New York, NY 10012
(212) 274-7500
Fax: (212) 334-6921

Rounder Records
One Camp St.
Cambridge, MA 02140
(617) 354-0700
Fax: (617) 491-1970

Ruffhouse Records
129 Fayett St.
Conshohocken, PA 19428
(610) 940-9533
Fax: (610) 940-6667

Ruthless Records
21860 Burbank Blvd., Ste. 100
Woodland Hills, CA 91367
(818) 710-0060
Fax: (818) 710-1009

Rykodisc
27 Congress St.
Salem, MA 01970
(508) 744-7678
Fax: (508) 741-4506

Scamp/Caroline Records
104 West 29th St.
New York, NY 10001
(212) 886-7500

Scotti Brothers Records
808 Wilshire Blvd.
Santa Monica, CA 90401
(310) 656-1100
Fax: (310) 656-7430

Scratchie Records
1914 N. Milwaukee Ave.
Chicago, IL 60647
(773) 342-6196
Fax: (773) 342-6198

Shanachie Entertainment Corp.
37 E. Clinton St.
Newton, NJ 07860
(201) 579-7763
Fax: (201) 579-7083

Shimmy-Disc Records
c/o Knitting Factory
74 Leonard St.
New York, NY 10013
(212) 219-3401
Fax: (212) 219-3006

Sire Records
75 Rockefeller Plz., 17th Fl.
New York, NY 10019
(212) 275-2500
Fax: (212) 275-3562

Slash Records
7381 Beverly Blvd.
Los Angeles, CA 90036
(213) 937-4660
Fax: (213) 933-7277

Solar Records
1635 N. Cahuenga Blvd.
Los Angeles, CA 90028
(213) 461-0390
Fax: (213) 461-9032

Sony 550 Music
550 Madison Ave.
New York, NY 10022
(212) 833-8000
Fax: (212) 833-7120

SpinART Records
PO Box 1798
New York, NY 10156-1798
(212) 343-9644
Fax: (212) 343-1970

SST Records
PO Box 1
Lawndale, CA 90260
(562) 590-8853
Fax: (562) 590-8513

Sub Pop Records
1932 First Ave., Ste. 1103
Seattle, WA 98101
(206) 441-8441
Fax: (206) 441-8245

Sugar Hill Records
PO Box 55300
Durham, NC 27717
(919) 489-4349
Fax: (919) 489-6080

Thirsty Ear Recordings
274 Madison Ave., Ste. 804
New York, NY 10016
(212) 889-9595
Fax: (212) 889-3641

Tim/Kerr Records
PO Box 42423
Portland, OR 97242
(503) 233-1056

Time Bomb Records
31652 Second Ave.
Laguna Beach, CA 92677
(714) 499-8338

Touch and Go Records/Quarterstick Records
PO Box 25520
Chicago, IL 60625
(773) 388-8888

Trauma Records
15165 Ventura Blvd., Ste. 320
Sherman Oaks, CA 91403
(818) 382-2515

TVT Records
23 E. Fourth St., 3rd Fl.
New York, NY 10003
(212) 979-6410
Fax: (212) 979-6489

Universal Records
1755 Broadway, 7th Fl.
New York, NY 10019
(212) 373-0600
Fax: (212) 247-3954

Varese Sarabande Records
11846 Ventura Blvd., Ste. 130
Studio City, CA 91604
(818) 753-4143

Velvel Records
740 Broadway, 11th Fl.
New York, NY 10003
(212) 353-8800
Fax: (212) 228-0660

Verve Records
825 Eighth Ave., 26th Fl.
New York, NY 10019

(212) 333-8000
Fax: (212) 333-8194

Virgin Records
338 N. Foothill Rd.
Beverly Hills, CA 90210
(310) 278-1181
Fax: (310) 278-6231

V2 Records
14 E. 4th St.
New York, NY 10012
(212) 320-8500
Fax: 212-320-8600

Warner Bros. Records
3300 Warner Blvd.
Burbank, CA 91510
(818) 846-9090
(818) 953-3223
Fax: (818) 846-8474

Watermelon Records
1201 W. 24th, Ste. 204
Austin, TX 78765-9056
(512) 472-6192
Fax: (512) 472-6249

Wax Trax Records
23 E. Fourth St.
New York, NY 10003
(212) 979-6410
Fax: (212) 979-6489

Windham Hill Records
8750 Wilshire Blvd.
Beverly Hills, CA 90211-2713
(310) 358-4800
Fax: (310) 358-4805

The WORK Group
2100 Colorado Ave.
Santa Monica, CA 90404
(310) 449-2666
Fax: (310) 449-2095

Zero Hour Records
14 W. 23rd St., 4th Fl.
New York, NY 10010-5203
(212) 337-3200
Fax: (212) 337-3701

The following are some of the U.S. radio stations that serve up fine rock and roll. These stations cover a variety of formats, including Rock, Classic Rock, Classic Hits, Album Oriented Rock, Modern Rock, Alternative, Adult Rock, and Adult Album Alternative. Please be advised that radio station formats often change like the weather. Your best bet would be to check the local radio listings in the cities below. (Radio station listings courtesy of BIA Research Inc.'s MediaAccess Pro.)

Alabama

Birmingham
WRAX (107.7 FM)
WZRR (99.5 FM)

Dothan
WESP (102.5 FM)

Huntsville
WTAK (106.1 FM)

Mobile
WRKH (96.1 FM)
WZEW (92.1 FM)

Montgomery
WRWO (96.1 FM)
WXFX (95.1 FM)

Tuscaloosa
WRTR (105.5 FM)

Alaska

Anchorage
KBFX (100.5 FM)
KKRO (102.1 FM)
KWHL (106.5 FM)

Arizona

Phoenix
KDDJ (100.3 FM)
KDKB (93.3 FM)
KEDJ (106.3 FM)
KGLQ (96.9 FM)
KSLX (100.7 FM/1440 AM)
KUPD (97.9 FM)
KZON (101.5 FM)
KZZP (104.7 FM)

Tucson
KFMA (92.1 FM)
KLPX (96.1 FM)

Arkansas

Fayetteville
KBRS (104.9 FM)
KJEM (93.3 FM)
KKEG (92.1 FM)
KMXF (101.9 FM)

Ft. Smith
KLSZ (102.7 FM)
KZBB (97.9 FM)

Little Rock
KDRE (101.1 FM)
KKPT (94.1 FM)
KMJX (105.1 FM)

Texarkana
KYGL (106.3 FM)

California

Bakersfield
KKBB (99.3 FM)
KRAB (106.1 FM)

Chico
KFMF (93.9 FM)
KRQR (106.7 FM)
KZAP (96.7 FM)

Fresno
KFRR (104.1 FM)
KJFX (95.7 FM)
KRZR (103.7 FM)

Los Angeles
KCBS (93.1 FM)
KLOS (95.5 FM)
KLYY (107.1 FM)
KROQ (106.7 FM)

Merced
KVRQ (92.5 FM)

Modesto
KDJK (103.9 FM)
KHKK (104.1 FM)
KHOP (95.1 FM)

Monterey-Salinas-Santa Cruz
KCDU (93.5 FM)
KMBY (104.3 FM)
KPIG (107.5 FM)

Oxnard-Ventura
KOCP (95.9 FM)
KVYY (107.1 FM)
KXBS (96.7 FM)

Palm Springs
KCLB (93.7 FM)

Redding
KEGR (102.7 FM)
KRRX (106.1 FM)

Riverside-San Bernardino
KBHR (93.3 FM)
KCAL (96.7 FM)
KCXX (103.9 FM)

Sacramento
KRXQ (98.5 FM)
KSEG (96.9 FM)
KWOD (106.5 FM)
KZZO (100.5 FM)

San Diego
KGB (101.5 FM)
KIOZ (105.3 FM)
KKSM (1320 AM)
KPLN (103.7 FM)
KSYY (107.1 FM)
KXGL (94.1 FM)
KXST (102.1 FM)
XHRM (92.5 FM)
XTRA (91.1 FM)

San Francisco
KFOG (104.5 FM)
KITS (105.3 FM)
KSAN (107.7 FM)

San Jose
KFFG (97.7 FM)
KOME (98.5 FM)
KSJO (92.3 FM)
KUFX (104.9 FM)

San Luis Obispo
KOTR (94.9 FM)
KSLY (96.1 FM)
KXTZ (95.3 FM)
KZOZ (93.3 FM)

Santa Barbara
KHTY (97.5 FM)
KJEE (92.9 FM)
KTYD (99.9 FM)

Santa Rosa
KGRP (100.9 FM)
KHBG (95.9 FM)
KRSH (98.7 FM)
KTOB (1490 AM)
KXFX (101.7 FM)

Visalia-Tulare-Hanford
KIOO (99.7 FM)

Colorado

Colorado Springs
KILO (94.3 FM)
KKFM (98.1 FM)

Denver-Boulder
KBCO (97.3 FM)
KBPI (106.7 FM)
KKHK (99.5 FM)
KRFX (103.5 FM)
KTCL (93.3 FM)
KXPK (96.5 FM)

Ft. Collins-Greeley
KRKI (102.1 FM)

Grand Junction
KSTR (96.1 FM)

Connecticut

Danbury
WRKI (95.1 FM)

Hartford-New Britain-Middletown
WCCC (106.9 FM/1290 AM)
WHCN (105.9 FM)
WKZE (98.1 FM)
WMRQ (104.1 FM)
WZMX (93.7 FM)

New Haven
WPLR (99.1 FM)

New London
WNLC (98.7 FM)

Stamford-Norwalk
WEFX (95.9 FM)

Delaware

Salisbury
WZBH (93.5 FM)

District of Columbia

Washington
WARW (94.7 FM)
WHFS (99.1 FM)
WWDC (101.1 FM)

Florida

Daytona Beach
WHOG (95.7 FM)
WKRO (93.1 FM)

Ft. Myers-Naples-Marco Island
WARO (94.5 FM)
WJBX (99.3)
WRXK (96.1 FM)

Ft. Pierce-Stuart-Vero Beach
WSTU (1450 AM)
WZZR (92.7 FM)

Ft. Walton Beach
WKSM (99.5 FM)
WWAV (102.1 FM)

Gainesville-Ocala
WAJD (1390 AM)
WNDD (95.5 FM)
WNDT (92.5 FM)
WRUF (103.7 FM/850 AM)
WSKY (97.3 FM)

Jacksonville
WBGB (106.5 FM)
WFYV (104.5 FM)
WPLA (93.3 FM)
WWRR (100.7 FM)

Miami-Ft. Lauderdale-Hollywood
WBGG (105.9 FM)
WZTA (94.9 FM)

Orlando
WHTQ (96.5 FM)
WJRR (101.1 FM)

Panama City
WSHF (99.3 FM)
WMXP (103.5 FM)
WYYX (97.7 FM)

Pensacola
WTKX (101.5 FM)
WWRO (100.7 FM)

Sarasota-Bradenton
WYNF (107.9 FM)

Tallahassee
WGLF (104.1 FM)
WWFO (99.9 FM)
WXSR (101.5 FM)

Tampa-St. Petersburg-Clearwater
WHPT (102.5 FM)
WTBT (105.5 FM)
WXTB (97.9 FM)

West Palm Beach-Boca Raton
WKGR (98.7 FM)
WPBZ (103.1 FM)

Georgia

Albany
WJAD (103.5 FM)

Atlanta
WKLS (96.1 FM)
WNNX (99.7 FM)

WZGC (92.9 FM)

Augusta
WEKL (102.3 FM)
WGUS (1380 AM)
WRXR (96.3 FM)

Columbus
WVRK (102.9 FM)

Macon
WQBZ (106.3 FM)

Savannah
WFXH (106.1 FM)
WIXV (95.5 FM)
WRHQ (105.3 FM)

Hawaii

Honolulu
KAOI (95.1 FM)
KPOI (97.5 FM)

Idaho

Boise
KARO (103.3 FM)
KFXJ (94.9 FM)
KJOT (105.1 FM)
KKGL (96.9 FM)
KQXR (100.3 FM)

Illinois

Bloomington
WIHN (96.7 FM)

Champaign
WEBX (93.5 FM)
WGKC (105.9 FM)
WPGU (107.1 FM)
WZNF (95.3 FM)

Chicago
WCBR (92.7 FM)
WCKG (105.9 FM)
WFXW (1480 AM)
WIIL (95.1 FM)
WKQX (101.1 FM)
WLLI (96.7 FM)
WLUP (97.9 FM)
WRCX (103.5 FM)
WXCD (94.7 FM)
WXRT (93.1 FM)

Danville
WRHK (94.9 FM)

Marion-Carbondale
WTAO (105.1 FM)
WXLT (95.1 FM)

Peoria
WGLO (95.5 FM)
WIXO (99.9 FM)
WWCT (105.7 FM)

Rockford
WXRX (104.9 FM)

WZOK (97.5 FM)

Springfield
WCVS (96.7 FM)
WQLZ (92.7 FM)
WYMG (100.5 FM)

Indiana

Evansville
WABX (107.5 FM)
WGBF (103.1 FM)
WSWI (820 AM)
WTRI (94.9 FM)

Ft. Wayne
WBYR (98.9 FM)
WEJE (96.3 FM)
WFWI (92.3 FM)
WXKE (103.9 FM)
WYSR (94.1 FM)

Indianapolis
WFBQ (94.7 FM)
WRZX (103.3 FM)
WTTS (92.3 FM)

Lafayette
WGBD (95.7 FM)
WKHY (93.5 FM)

South Bend
WAOR (95.3 FM)
WRBR (103.9 FM)
WZOW (97.7 FM)

Terre Haute
WZZQ (107.5 FM/1230 AM)

Iowa

Cedar Rapids
KKRQ (100.7 FM)
KRNA (94.1 FM)

Des Moines
KAZR (103.3 FM)
KGGO (94.9 FM)
KKDM (107.5 FM)
KLRX (96.1 FM)
KRKQ (98.3 FM)

Dubuque
KGRR (97.3 FM)
KXGE (102.3 FM)

Quad Cities
KCQQ (106.5 FM)
KORB (93.5 FM)
WXLP (96.9 FM)

Sioux City
KSEZ (97.9 FM)

Waterloo-Cedar Falls
KCRR (97.7 FM)
KFMW (107.9 FM)

Kansas

Kansas City
KLZR (105.9 FM)
KQRC (98.9 FM)
KYYS (99.7 FM)

Topeka
KDVV (100.3 FM)
KMKF (101.5 FM)

Wichita
KICT (95.1 FM)
KRZZ (96.3 FM)

Kentucky

Ashland
WAMX (106.3 FM)
WFXN (107.1 FM)
WMGG (101.5 FM)

Lexington-Fayette
WKQQ (100.1 FM)
WLRO (101.5 FM)
WXZZ (103.3 FM)

Louisville
WLSY (94.7 FM)
WQMF (95.7 FM)
WSFR (107.7 FM)
WTFX (100.5 FM)

Owensboro
WKTG (93.9 FM)
WXCM (97.1 FM)

Louisiana

Alexandria
KZMZ (96.9 FM)

Baton Rouge
WDGL (98.1 FM)

Lafayette
KFTE (96.5 FM)

Lake Charles
KKGB (101.3 FM)

Monroe
KCTO (103.1 FM)

New Orleans
KKND (106.7 FM)
KLRZ (100.3 FM)
WCKW (92.3 FM/1010 AM)
WKSY (106.1 FM)

Shreveport
KTAL (98.1 FM)
KTUX (98.9 FM)

Maine

Augusta-Waterville
WTOS (105.1 FM)

Bangor
WKIT (100.3 FM)

Portland
WBLM (102.9 FM)
WCLZ (98.9 FM)
WCYI (93.9 FM)
WCYY (94.3 FM)
WMGX (93.1 FM)
WXGL (95.5 FM)

Maryland

Baltimore
WIYY (97.9 FM)
WRNR (103.1 FM)

Hagerstown
WKMZ (97.5 FM)
WQCM (96.7 FM)

Salisbury
WQJZ (97.1 FM)

Massachusetts

Boston
WAAF (107.3 FM)
WBCN (104.1 FM)
WBOS (92.9 FM)
WFNX (101.7 FM)
WXRV (92.5 FM)
WZLX (100.7 FM)

Cape Cod
WKPE (104.7 FM/1170 AM)
WMVY (92.7 FM)
WPXC (102.9 FM)
WWKJ (101.1 FM)

Springfield
WAQY (102.1 FM/1600 AM)
WHMP (99.3 FM)
WRNX (100.9 FM)

Michigan

Ann Arbor
WIQB (102.9 FM)

Detroit
CIDR (93.9 FM)
CIMX (88.7 FM)
WCSX (94.7 FM)
WKRK (97.1 FM)
WPLT (96.3 FM)
WRIF (101.1 FM)
WWBR (102.7 FM)
WXDG (105.1 FM)

Flint
WWBN (101.7 FM)
WWGZ (103.1 FM)

Grand Rapids
WGRD (97.9 FM)
WKLQ (94.5 FM)
WLAV (96.9 FM)
WMRR (101.7 FM)

Kalamazoo
WFAT (96.5 FM)

WRKR (107.7 FM)
WZUU (92.3 FM)

Lansing-East Lansing
WJXQ (106.1 FM)
WMMQ (94.9 FM)
WWDX (92.1 FM)

Northwest Michigan
WCKC (107.1 FM)
WGFM (105.1 FM)
WGFN (98.1 FM)
WKLT (97.5 FM)
WKLZ (98.9 FM)

Saginaw-Bay City-Midland
WKQZ (93.3 FM)

Minnesota

Duluth
KQDS (94.9 FM/1490AM)
KUSZ (107.7 FM)

Minneapolis-St. Paul
KKMS (980 AM)
KQRS (92.5 FM)
KTCZ (97.1 FM)
KUOM (770 AM)
KXXR (93.7 FM)
KZNR (105.1 FM)
KZNT (105.3 FM)
KZNZ (105.7 FM)
WRQC (100.3 FM)

St. Cloud
KLZZ (103.7 FM)

Mississippi

Biloxi-Gulfport-Pascagoula
WCPR (97.9 FM)
WLNF (95.3 FM)
WXRG (105.9 FM)

Jackson
WSTZ (106.7 FM)
WTYX (94.7 FM)

Laurel-Hattiesburg
WKNZ (107.1 FM)
WXRR (104.5 FM)

Meridian
WTUX (102.1 FM)

Tupelo
WSMS (99.9 FM)

Missouri

Columbia
KBXR (102.3 FM)
KCMQ (96.7 FM)
KFMZ (98.3 FM)
KLSC (93.9 FM)

Joplin
KXDG (97.9 FM)

Kansas City
KNRX (107.3 FM)

St. Louis
KPNT (105.7 FM)
KSD (93.7 FM)
KSHE (94.7 FM)
WALC (104.1 FM)
WVRV (101.1 FM)

Springfield
KKLH (104.7 FM)
KTOZ (95.5 FM)
KWTO (98.7 FM)
KXUS (97.3 FM)
KZRQ (104.1 FM)

Montana

Billings
KMHK (95.5 FM)
KRKX (94.1 FM)

Great Falls
KQDI (106.1 FM)

Nebraska

Lincoln
KIBZ (106.3 FM)
KKNB (104.1 FM)
KTGL (92.9 FM)

Omaha
KEZO (92.3 FM)
KKCD (105.9 FM)
KZFX (101.9 FM)

Nevada

Las Vegas
KKLZ (96.3 FM)
KOMP (92.3 FM)
KXPT (97.1 FM)
KXTE (107.5 FM)

Reno
KDOT (104.5 FM)
KLCA (96.5 FM)
KOZZ (105.7 FM)
KRZQ (100.9 FM)
KTHX (100.1 FM)
KZZF (102.9 FM)

New Hampshire

Manchester
WGIR (101.1 FM)
WNHI (93.3 FM)
WRCI (107.7 FM)

Portsmouth-Dover-Rochester
WHEB (100.3 FM)
WQSO (96.7 FM)
WWNH (1340 AM)
WXBB (105.3 FM)
WXBP (102.1 FM)
WXHT (95.3 FM)

New Jersey

Atlantic City-Cape May
WDOX (93.1 FM)
WJSE (102.7 FM)
WJSX (102.3 FM)
WSAX (99.3 FM)
WZXL (100.7 FM)

Monmouth-Ocean
WHTG (106.3 FM)
WRAT (95.9 FM)

Morristown
WDHA (105.5 FM)

New Brunswick
WMGQ (98.3 FM)

Sussex
WNNJ (103.7 FM)

Trenton
WPRB (103.3 FM)

New Mexico

Albuquerque
KABG (98.5 FM)
KLSK (104.1 FM)
KTEG (107.9 FM)
KZRR (94.1 FM)

Santa Fe
KBAC (98.1 FM)

New York

Albany-Schenectady-Troy
WEQX (102.7 FM)
WPYX (106.5 FM)
WQBJ (103.5 FM)
WQBK (103.9 FM)
WRVE (99.5 FM)
WXCR (102.3 FM)
WXLE (104.5 FM)

Binghamton
WAAL (99.1 FM)
WKGB (92.5 FM)
WLTB (101.7 FM)

Buffalo-Niagara Falls
WEDG (103.3 FM)
WGRF (96.9 FM)

Elmira-Corning
WGMF (1490 AM)
WGMM (97.7 FM)
WNGZ (104.9 FM)
WPHD (94.7 FM)

Ithaca
WIII (99.9 FM)
WVBR (93.5 FM)

Nassau-Suffolk
WBAB (102.3 FM)
WDRE (98.5 FM)
WEHM (96.7 FM)
WHFM (95.3 FM)

WLIR (92.7 FM)
WRCN (103.9 FM)
WRHD (1570 AM)

New York
WAXQ (104.3 FM)
WNEW (102.7 FM)
WXRK (92.3 FM)

Newburgh-Middletown
WRRV (92.7 FM)

Poughkeepsie
WDST (100.1 FM)
WPDA (106.1 FM)
WPDH (101.5 FM)
WRRB (96.9 FM)

Rochester
WCMF (96.5 FM/990AM)
WLLW (93.7 FM)
WNNR 103.5 FM)
WNVE (95.1 FM)
WQRV (93.3 FM)

Syracuse
WAQX (95.7 FM)
WKRH (106.5 FM)
WKRL (100.9 FM)
WTKV (105.5 FM)
WTKW (99.5 FM)

Utica-Rome
WKLL (94.9 FM)
WOUR (96.9 FM)
WRCK (107.3 FM)

Watertown
WCIZ (93.3 FM)
WWLF (106.7 FM)

North Carolina

Asheville
WZLS (96.5 FM)

Charlotte-Gastonia-Rock Hill
WEND (106.5 FM)
WRFX (99.7 FM)
WSSS (104.7 FM)
WXRC (95.7 FM)

Fayetteville
WKQB (106.9 FM)
WRCQ (103.5 FM)

Greensboro-Winston Salem-High Point
WKRR (92.3 FM)
WXRA (94.5 FM)

Greenville-New Bern-Jacksonville
WSFL (106.5 FM)
WXNR (99.5 FM)
WXQR (105.5 FM)

Raleigh-Durham
WBBB (96.1 FM)
WNNL (103.9 FM)
WRDU (106.1 FM)

Wilmington
WAHH (1340 AM)
WRQR (104.5 FM)
WSFM (107.5 FM)

North Dakota

Bismarck
KBYZ (96.5 FM)

Fargo
KPFX (107.9 FM)
KQWB (98.7 FM)

Grand Forks
KJKJ (107.5 FM)

Ohio

Akron
WONE (97.5 FM)

Canton
WRQK (106.9 FM)

Cincinnati
WAQZ (107.1 FM)
WEBN (102.7 FM)
WOFX (92.5 FM)
WOXY (97.7 FM)
WYLX (97.3 FM)

Cleveland
WENZ (107.9 FM)
WMMS (100.7 FM)
WNCX (98.5 FM)

Columbus
WAZU (107.1 FM)
WBZX (99.7 FM)
WKFX (105.7 FM)
WLVQ (96.3 FM)
WWCD (101.1 FM)
WZAZ (98.9 FM)

Dayton
WTUE (104.7 FM)
WXEG (103.9 FM)

Marietta
WRZZ (106.1 FM)

Toledo
WBUZ (106.5 FM)
WIOT (104.7 FM)
WJZE (97.3 FM)
WMTR (96.1 FM)
WXKR (94.5 FM)

Youngstown-Warren
WNCD (106.1 FM)
WYFM (102.9 FM)

Oklahoma

Lawton
KZCD (94.1 FM)

Oklahoma City
KATT (100.5 FM)
KRXO (107.7 FM)

Tulsa
KMOD (97.5 FM)
KMYZ (104.5 FM)

Oregon

Eugene-Springfield
KEHK (102.3 FM)
KNRQ (95.3 FM/1320 AM)
KZEL (96.1 FM)

Medford-Ashland
KBOY (95.7 FM)
KZZE (106.3 FM)

Portland
KGON (92.3 FM)
KINK (101.9 FM)
KNRK (94.7 FM)
KUFO (101.1 FM)

Pennsylvania

Allentown-Bethlehem
WZZO (95.1 FM)

Altoona
WBRX (94.7 FM)
WBXQ (94.3 FM)

Erie
WMDE (94.3 FM)
WRKT (100.9 FM)

Harrisburg-Lebanon-Carlisle
WRVV (97.3 FM)
WTPA (93.5 FM)

Johnstown
WPCL (97.3 FM)
WQKK (99.1 FM)

Philadelphia
WMGK (102.9 FM)
WMMR (93.3 FM)
WPLY (100.3 FM)
WYSP (94.1 FM)

Pittsburgh
WDRV (96.1 FM)
WDVE (102.5 FM)
WELA (104.3 FM)
WRRK (96.9 FM)
WXDX (105.9 FM)
WZPT (100.7 FM)

State College
WBUS (93.7 FM)
WGMR (101.1 FM)
WQWK (97.1 FM)
WUBZ (105.9 FM)

Wilkes Barre-Scranton
WCNR (930 AM)
WEMR (107.7 FM)
WEZX (106.9 FM)
WKQV (95.7 FM)
WQFM (92.1 FM)
WZMT (97.9 FM)

Williamsport
WCXR (103.7 FM)
WZRZ (98.7 FM)
WZXR (99.3 FM)

York
WEGK (92.7 FM)
WQXA (105.7 FM)

Rhode Island

Providence-Warwick-Pawtucket
WBRU (95.5 FM)
WERI (99.3 FM)
WHJY (94.1 FM)
WHKK (100.3 FM)
WWRX (103.7 FM)
WXEX (99.7 FM)

South Carolina

Charleston
WAVF (96.1 FM)
WYBB (98.1 FM)

Columbia
WARQ (93.5 FM)
WMFX (102.3 FM)

Florence
WBZF (100.5 FM)
WHSC (98.5 FM)

Greenville-Spartanburg
WROQ (101.1 FM)
WTPT (93.3 FM)

Myrtle Beach
WKZQ (101.7 FM/1450 AM)
WWSK (107.1 FM)
WYAV (104.1 FM)

South Dakota

Rapid City
KDDX (101.1 FM)
KFXS (100.3 FM)
KSQY (95.1 FM)

Sioux Falls
KRRO (103.7 FM)
KYBB (102.7 FM)

Tennessee

Chattanooga
WDOD (96.5 FM)
WSKZ (106.5 FM)

Johnson City-Kingsport-Bristol
WQUT (101.5 FM)
WRZK (105.9 FM)

Knoxville
WIMZ (103.5 FM)
WOKI (100.3 FM)
WXVO (98.7 FM)

Memphis
WEGR (102.7 FM)
WMFS (92.9 FM)
WRXQ (95.7 FM)
WSRR (98.1 FM)

Nashville
WDBL (94.3 FM)
WKDF (103.3 FM)
WNRQ (105.9 FM)
WRLG (94.1 FM)
WRLT (100.1 FM)
WYYB (93.7 FM)

Texas

Abilene
KEYJ (107.9 FM)
KFQX (102.7 FM)
KHXS (106.3 FM)

Amarillo
KARX (95.7 FM)
KBZD (99.7 FM)
KZRK (107.9 FM/1550 AM)

Austin
KAHK (107.7 FM)
KGSR (107.1 FM)
KLBJ (93.7 FM)
KPEZ (102.3 FM)
KROX (101.5 FM)

Beaumont-Port Arthur
KIOC (106.1 FM)

Bryan-College Station
KHLR (103.9 FM)
KTSR (92.1 FM)
KZTR (101.9 FM)

Corpus Christi
KBTE (102.3 FM)
KNCN (101.3 FM)
KRAD (105.5 FM)
KTKY (106.1 FM)

Dallas-Ft. Worth
KDGE (94.5 FM)
KEGL (97.1 FM)
KKZN (93.3 FM)
KTXQ (102.1 FM)
KZPS (92.5 FM)

El Paso
KLAQ (95.5 FM)
KROD (600 AM)

Houston-Galveston
KKRW (93.7 FM)
KLOL (101.1 FM)
KTBZ (107.5 FM)

Killeen-Temple
KLFX (107.3 FM)
KRYL (98.3 FM)

Lubbock
KCRM (99.5 FM)
KFMX (94.5 FM)

KLZK (104.3 FM)

McAllen-Brownsville-Harlingen
KESO (92.7 FM)
KFRQ (94.5 FM)
KVPA (101.1 FM)

Odessa-Midland
KBAT (93.3 FM)
KCDQ (102.1 FM)
KQRX (95.1 FM)

San Angelo
KWFR (101.9 FM)

San Antonio
KISS (99.5 FM)
KZEP (104.5 FM)

Tyler-Longview
KKTX (96.1 FM/1240 AM)

Waco
KBRQ (102.5 FM)

Utah

Salt Lake City-Ogden
KBER (101.1 FM)
KENZ (107.5 FM)
KQMB (102.7 FM)
KRAR (106.9 FM)
KUMT (105.7 FM)
KURR (99.5 FM)
KXRK (96.3 FM)

Vermont

Burlington
WBTZ (99.9 FM)
WCPV (101.3 FM)
WIZN (106.7 FM)
WNCS (104.7 FM)

Virginia

Blacksburg-Christiansburg-Radford-Pulaski
WBNK (100.7 FM)

Charlottesville
WWWV (97.5 FM)

Harrisonburg
WBOP (106.3 FM)

Norfolk-Virginia Beach-Newport News
WAFX (106.9 FM)
WKOC (93.7 FM)
WNOR (98.7 FM/1230 AM)
WROX (96.1 FM)

Richmond
WBZU (106.5 FM)
WKLR (96.5 FM)
WRXL (102.1 FM)

Roanoke-Lynchburg
WROV (96.3 FM/1240 AM)

Washington

Richland-Kennewick-Pasco
KEGX (106.5 FM)
KTHK (97.9 FM)
KXRX (97.1 FM)

Seattle-Tacoma
KISW (99.9 FM)
KMIH (104.5 FM)
KMTT (103.7 FM)
KNDD (107.7 FM)
KZOK (102.5 FM)

Spokane
KAEP (105.7 FM)
KEZE (96.9 FM)
KKZX (98.9 FM)
KNJY (103.9 FM)

Yakima
KATS (94.5 FM)

West Virginia

Beckley
WMTD (102.3 FM)

Charleston
WCOZ (1300 AM)
WKLC (105.1 FM)

Huntington
WAMX (106.3 FM)
WFXN (107.1 FM)
WMGG (101.5 FM)

Morgantown-Clarksburg-Fairmont
WCLG (100.1 FM)
WFBY (106.5 FM)
WRLF (94.3 FM)

Parkersburg
WRZZ (106.1 FM)

Wheeling
WEGW (107.5 FM)
WZNW (105.5 FM)

Wisconsin

Appleton-Oshkosh
WAPL (105.7 FM)
WOZZ (93.5 FM)

Eau Claire
WCCN (107.5 FM)
WEIO (1050 AM)
WISM (98.1 FM)
WMEQ (92.1 FM)

Green Bay
WJLW (106.7 FM)

La Crosse
WFBZ (105.5 FM)
WKBH (100.1 FM)
WRQT (95.7 FM)

radio stations

Madison
WIBA (101.5 FM)
WJJO (94.1 FM)
WMAD (92.1 FM)
WMMM (105.5 FM)

Milwaukee-Racine
WJYI (1340 AM)

WKLH (96.5 FM)
WLUM (102.1 FM)
WLZR (102.9 FM)

Wausau-Stevens Point
WGLX (103.3 FM)
WKQH (104.9 FM)
WMZK (104.1 FM)

Wyoming

Casper
KASS (106.9 FM)

Cheyenne
KIGN (97.9 FM)
KRQU (102.9 FM)
KZCY (104.9 FM)

musicHound ROCK

Indexes

Five-Bone Album Index

Band Member Index

Category Index

Series Index

The following albums achieved the highest rating possible—♪♪♪♪♪—from our discriminating MusicHound *Rock writers. You can't miss with any of these recordings. (Note: Albums are listed under the name of the entry (or entries) in which they appear and are not necessarily albums by that individual artist or group. The album could be a compilation album, a film soundtrack, an album on which the artist or group appears as a guest, etc. Consult the artist or group's entry for specific information.)*

AC/DC
Back in Black (Atlantic, 1980)
Bonfire (Atlantic, 1997)

Aerosmith
Rocks (Columbia, 1976)

Arthur Alexander
The Ultimate Arthur Alexander (Razor & Tie, 1993)

The Allman Brothers Band
At Fillmore East (Capricorn, 1971/1997)

Altan
Horse with a Heart (Green Linnet, 1989)

aMiniature
Murk Time Cruiser (Restless, 1995)

The Animals
The Best of the Animals (MGM, 1966/Abkco, 1987)

Joan Armatrading
Greatest Hits (A&M, 1996)

Joan Armatrading (A&M, 1976)

Arrested Development
3 Years, 5 Months & 2 Days in the Life of . . . (Chrysalis/EMI, 1992)

The Astronauts
Cowabunga! The Surf Box (Rhino, 1996)
Legends of Guitar—Rock: The '60s, Vol. 1 (Rhino, 1990)

Aswad
Aswad (Island, 1976)

Autechre
Tri Repetae++ (TVT/Wax Trax/Warp, 1996)

The Auteurs
New Wave (Hut, 1993)

Bad Brains
Bad Brains (ROIR, 1982/1996)

Bad Religion
Generator (Epitaph, 1992)

Badfinger
No Dice (Apple, 1970/Gold Rush, 1992)
Straight Up (Apple, 1971/Gold Rush, 1996)

Hank Ballard
Sexy Ways: The Best of Hank Ballard and the Midnighters (Rhino, 1993)

The Band
The Band (Capitol, 1969)
Moondog Matinee (Capitol, 1973)
Music from Big Pink (Capitol, 1968)
Rock of Ages (Capitol, 1972)

The Barracudas
Drop Out with the Barracudas (Voxx, 1981/1984)

Dave Bartholomew
The Spirit of New Orleans: The Genius of Dave Bartholomew (EMI, 1992)

The Bats
Compiletely Bats (Flying Nun, 1987/Communion, 1991)
Daddy's Highway (Flying Nun, 1988/Flying Nun/Mammoth, 1994)

Bauhaus
Mask (Beggars Banquet, 1981/1995)

The Beach Boys
Good Vibrations (Capitol, 1993)
Pet Sounds (Capitol, 1966)

The Beatles
Abbey Road (Apple, 1969)
The Beatles: 1967–1970 (Apple, 1973)
Past Masters: Volume Two (Parlophone, 1988)
Sgt. Pepper's Lonely Hearts Club Band (Parlophone, 1967)

The Beau Brummels
The Best of the Beau Brummels, 1964–1968 (Rhino, 1987)

Chuck Berry
The Chess Box (Chess/MCA, 1988)
Chuck Berry's Golden Decade (Chess, 1967)
Chuck Berry's Golden Decade, Vol. 2 (Chess, 1973)
The Great Twenty-Eight (Chess/MCA, 1982)
St. Louis to Liverpool (Chess, 1964)

Big Star
#1 Record/Radio City (Stax, 1992)

Country Joe & the Fish
Electric Music for the Mind and Body (Vanguard, 1967)

Cream
Those Were the Days (Polydor, 1997)
Wheels of Fire (Polydor, 1968)

Creedence Clearwater Revival
Cosmo's Factory (Fantasy, 1970)

Marshall Crenshaw
Marshall Crenshaw (Warner Bros., 1982)

Crosby, Stills & Nash
Deja Vu (Atlantic, 1970)

Crowded House
Woodface (Capitol, 1991)

The Cure
Staring at the Sea (Elektra, 1986)

Cypress Hill
Cypress Hill (Ruffhouse/Columbia, 1991)

Dick Dale
King of the Surf Guitar: The Best of Dick Dale and His Del-Tones (Rhino, 1989)

The Damned
Damned, Damned, Damned (Stiff U.K., 1977/Frontier, 1993)
Machine Gun Etiquette (Chiswick/Roadrunner, 1979)

Terence Trent D'Arby
Introducing the Hardline According to Terence Trent D'Arby (Columbia, 1987)

Bobby Darin
As Long As I'm Singing: The Bobby Darin Collection (Rhino, 1995)
The Bobby Darin Story (Atco, 1961/Atlantic, 1989)

Dead Can Dance
Spleen and Ideal (4AD, 1985)

Deep Purple
Machine Head (Warner Bros., 1972)

Del Fuegos
Cool Down Time (Private, 1995)

Iris DeMent
Infamous Angel (Philo/Warner Bros., 1992)
My Life (Warner Bros., 1994)

Rick Derringer
All American Boy (Blue Sky, 1973)

Neil Diamond
Classics: The Early Years (Columbia, 1983)

Dire Straits
Making Movies (Warner Bros., 1980)

Fats Domino
Antoine "Fats" Domino (Tomato, 1992)
Fats Domino—The Fat Man: 25 Classics (EMI, 1996)
My Blue Heaven (EMI, 1990)
They Call Me the Fat Man (EMI, 1991)

Dramarama
Live at the China Club (Chameleon EP, 1990)

The Drifters
1959–1965 All-Time Greatest Hits and More (Atlantic, 1988)

Duran Duran
Decade (Capitol, 1991)
Rio (Capitol, 1982)

Bob Dylan
Blonde on Blonde (Columbia, 1966)
Blood on the Tracks (Columbia, 1975)
The Bootleg Series, Vol. 4: Live 1966—The "Royal Albert Hall" Concert (Columbia/Legacy, 1998)
Highway 61 Revisited (Columbia, 1965)

The Eagles
Hotel California (Asylum, 1976)
Their Greatest Hits, 1971–75 (Asylum, 1975)

Duane Eddy
Twang Thing: The Duane Eddy Anthology (Rhino, 1993)

Dave Edmunds
Get It (Swan Song, 1977)

808 State
Utd. State 90 (Tommy Boy, 1990)

Einstürzende Neubauten
Volume 1: Strategies against Architecture (Mute, 1984/Homestead, 1986/Mute-Restless, 1991)

Emergency Broadcast Network
Telecommunication Breakdown (TVT, 1995)

The English Beat
I Just Can't Stop It (Slre, 1980)

The Everly Brothers
Cadence Classics: Their 20 Greatest Hits (Rhino, 1985)

John Fahey
America (Takoma, 1969/1997)
The Return of the Repressed: The John Fahey Anthology (Rhino, 1994)

Fairport Convention
Liege and Leaf (A&M, 1969)

The Fall
Live at the Witch Trials (Step Forward, 1978/I.R.S., 1979)

Fine Young Cannibals
The Raw & the Cooked (I.R.S., 1989)

The "5" Royales
Monkey Hips and Rice: The "5" Royales Anthology (Rhino, 1994)

The Flamin' Groovies
Groovies' Greatest Grooves (Sire, 1989)

The Flaming Lips
Transmissions from the Satellite Heart (Warner Bros., 1993)

Fleetwood Mac
Rumours (Warner Bros., 1977)

Flipper
Album—Generic Flipper (Subterranean, 1982/Warner Bros., 1992)

The Four Tops
Anthology (Motown, 1974/1989)
Greatest Hits (Motown, 1967/1987)

Aretha Franklin
30 Greatest Hits (Atlantic, 1968)
I Never Loved a Man (The Way I Loved You) (Atlantic, 1967)
The Queen of Soul (Rhino/Atlantic, 1992)

Robert Fripp
Exposure (EG, 1979)

Bill Frisell
Have a Little Faith (Nonesuch, 1993)

Front 242
Official Version (Wax Trax!, 1987/Epic, 1992)

Fugazi
Fugazi (Dischord, 1988)

The Bobby Fuller Four
Never to Be Forgotten (Del-Fi, 1998)

Reeves Gabrels
The Sacred Squall of Now (Upstart, 1995)

Danny Gatton
88 Elmira St. (Elektra, 1990)

Marvin Gaye
Anthology (Motown, 1995)
The Master, 1961–1984 (Motown, 1995)
What's Going On (Motown, 1971)

Giant Sand
Center of the Universe (Restless, 1992)

Jimmie Dale Gilmore
After Awhile (Elektra, 1991)

The Golden Palominos
The Golden Palominos (Celluloid, 1981)
A History (1982–1985) (Metrotone/Restless, 1992)
Visions of Excess (Celluloid, 1985)

Steve Goodman
No Big Surprise (Red Pajamas, 1994)

The Grateful Dead
American Beauty (Warner Bros. 1970)
Two from the Vault (Grateful Dead Records, 1992)
Workingman's Dead (Warner Bros., 1970)

Nanci Griffith
Last of the True Believers (Rounder/Philo, 1986)
One Fair Summer Evening (MCA, 1988)
Other Voices, Other Rooms (Elektra, 1993)

The Guess Who
The Best of the Guess Who (RCA, 1971)

Gun Club
Fire of Love (Ruby, 1981/Slash, 1993)

Guns N' Roses
Appetite for Destruction (Geffen, 1987)

Hall & Oates
Sacred Songs (RCA, 1980)

Emmylou Harris
At the Ryman (Reprise, 1992)
Last Date (Warner Bros., 1982)
Wrecking Ball (Asylum, 1995)

George Harrison
All Things Must Pass (Apple, 1970)

PJ Harvey
To Bring You My Love (Island, 1995)

Ronnie Hawkins
The Best of Ronnie Hawkins and the Hawks (Rhino, 1990)

Ted Hawkins
The Final Tour (Evidence, 1998)

Jimi Hendrix
Are You Experienced? (Reprise, 1967/Experience Hendrix/MCA, 1997)
Axis: Bold As Love (Reprise, 1968/Experience Hendrix/MCA, 1997)
Electric Ladyland (Reprise, 1968/Experience Hendrix/MCA, 1997)

Joe Henry
Short Man's Room (Mammoth, 1992)

The Hollies
The Hollies Anthology (Epic, 1990)

Buddy Holly
The Buddy Holly Collection (MCA, 1993)

John Lee Hooker
Chill Out (Pointblank, 1995)
The Ultimate Collection, 1948–1990 (Rhino, 1991)

Hothouse Flowers
People (London, 1988)

The Housemartins
Carry on up the Charts: The Best of the Beautiful South (Mercury, 1995)

Howlin' Wolf
Change My Way (MCA/Chess, 1990)
Howlin' Wolf: His Best (MCA/Chess, 1997)
Howlin' Wolf Rides Again (Flair/Virgin, 1991)
Moaning at Midnight (MCA/Chess, 1989)

The Hudson Brothers
So You Are a Star: The Best of the Hudson Brothers (Varese Sarabande, 1995)

Michael Jackson
Thriller (Epic, 1982)

Jackson 5
The Ultimate Collection (Motown, 1995)

The Jam
Compact Snap! (Polydor, 1983)
Sound Affects (Polydor, 1980)

Elmore James
The Sky Is Crying: The History of Elmore James (Rhino, 1993)

Jan & Dean
All the Hits, from Surf City to Drag City (EMI America, 1996)

Jawbreaker
Unfun (Shredder, 1990/92)

Jefferson Airplane
Surrealistic Pillow (RCA Victor, 1967)

Billy Joel
The Complete Hits Collection, 1973–1997 (Columbia, 1997)
Greatest Hits, Volume I & II (Columbia, 1985)
The Stranger (Columbia, 1977)

Janis Joplin
Cheap Thrills (Columbia, 1968)

Joy Division
Closer (Factory, 1980)

Paul K
Love Is a Gas (Alias, 1997)

Tommy Keene
Places That Are Gone (Dolphin, 1984)

Katell Keineg
O Seasons O Castles (Elektra, 1994)

The Kennedys
Angel Fire (Philo, 1998)

Killing Joke
Killing Joke (EG, 1980)

B.B. King
The Best of B.B. King, Vol. 1 (Flair/Virgin, 1991)
Live at the Regal (MCA, 1971)

Carole King
A Natural Woman: The Ode Collection 1968–1976 (Legacy, 1994/1998)
Tapestry (Ode, 1971)

King Crimson
Red (Atlantic, 1974/EG, 1989)

King Sunny Ade
Juju Music (Mango, 1982)

The Kingston Trio
The Capitol Years (Capitol, 1995)

The Kinks
Arthur (or the Decline and Fall of the British Empire) (Reprise, 1969/Velvel, 1998)
Face to Face (Reprise, 1966/Castle U.K., 1998)
The Kinks' Greatest Hits (Rhino, 1989)

Leo Kottke
Six- and 12-String Guitar (Takoma, 1969/Rhino, 1994)

Laika
Sounds of the Satellites (Too Pure/Sire, 1997)

Last Exit
The Noise of Trouble: Live in Tokyo (Enemy, 1987)

Led Zeppelin
The Complete Studio Recordings (Atlantic, 1993)
Led Zeppelin IV (Atlantic, 1971)

The Left Banke
There's Gonna Be a Storm: The Complete Recordings, 1966–1969 (Mercury, 1992)

John Lennon
Plastic Ono Band (Apple, 1970)

Jerry Lee Lewis
Live at the Star Club, Hamburg (Rhino, 1992)
Original Sun Greatest Hits (Rhino, 1984)

David Lindley
El Rayo-X (Asylum, 1981)

Arto Lindsay
Aggregates 1–26 (Knitting Factory Works, 1995)

Little Richard
The Georgia Peach (Specialty, 1991)

Little Willie John
Fever: The Best of Little Willie John (Rhino, 1993)

FIVE-BONE ALBUM INDEX

Robert Wyatt
Going Back a Bit: A Little History of Robert Wyatt (Virgin, 1994)
Shleep (Thirsty Ear, 1998)

X
Los Angeles (Slash, 1980)
More Fun in the New World (Elektra/Asylum, 1983)
Wild Gift (Slash, 1981)

XTC
Skylarking (Geffen, 1986)
Upsy Daisy Assortment (Geffen, 1997)

Dwight Yoakam
Gone (Reprise, 1996)

Neil Young
After the Gold Rush (Reprise, 1970)
Decade (Reprise, 1977)
Everybody Knows This Is Nowhere (Reprise, 1969)
Tonight's the Night (Reprise, 1975)

The Young Rascals
Time Piece: The Rascals' Greatest Hits (Atlantic, 1968)

Frank Zappa
Uncle Meat (Bizarre/Reprise, 1968/Rykodisc, 1995)
We're Only in It for the Money (Verve, 1968/Rykodisc, 1995)

Warren Zevon
Warren Zevon (Asylum, 1976)

The Zombies
Zombie Heaven (Big Beat, 1997)

Zumpano
Going through Changes (Sub Pop, 1996)

ZZ Top
Deguello (Warner Bros., 1979)

Can't remember what band a certain musician is in? Wondering if a person has been in more than one band? The Band Member Index will guide you to the appropriate entry (or entries).

A., Tod *See* Cop Shoot Cop/Firewater

Aaron *See* The Mr. T Experience

Aaronson, Kenny *See* Stories

Abbey, John *See* Dog's Eye View

Abbot, Gary *See* The Kingsmen

Abbot, Kris *See* The Pursuit of Happiness

Abbot, Tim *See* The Chocolate Watch Band

Abbott, "Dimebag" Darrell *See* Pantera

Abbott, Jacqueline *See* The Housemartins/The Beautiful South/Beats International

Abbott, Jude *See* Chumbawamba

Abbott, Pete *See* Average White Band

Abbott, Vinnie Paul *See* Pantera

Abbruzzese, Dave *See* Pearl Jam/Mother Love Bone/Green River/Temple of the Dog

Abong, Fred *See* Belly/Tanya Donelly; Throwing Muses/Kristin Hersh

Abourezk, Matthew *See* Thin White Rope

Abrahams, Mick *See* Jethro Tull/Ian Anderson

Abruscato, Sal *See* Life of Agony; Type O Negative

Abts, Matt *See* Gov't Mule

Ace *See* Skunk Anansie

Achor, James *See* Royal Crown Revue

Ackerson, Ed *See* Antenna/Velo-Deluxe/The Mysteries of Life/John P. Strohm & the Hello Strangers

Acland, Chris *See* Lush

Acuna, Alex *See* Weather Report

Adamedes, Elaine *See* Throwing Muses/Kristin Hersh

Adams, Billy *See* Dexy's Midnight Runners/Kevin Rowland & Dexy's Midnight Runners

Adams, Craig *See* The Cult/The Holy Barbarians; The Mission U.K.; Sisters of Mercy

Adams, Greg *See* Tower of Power

Adams, Mark *See* The Specials

Adams, Ryan *See* Whiskeytown

Adams, Terry *See* NRBQ

Adams, Victoria "Posh Spice" *See* The Spice Girls

Adamson, Barry *See* The Birthday Party; Nick Cave & the Bad Seeds; Magazine

Adamson, Billy *See* The Searchers

Adamson, Stuart *See* Big Country

Ader, Royse *See* The Rubinoos

Adler, Steven *See* Guns N' Roses

Advert, Gaye *See* The Adverts

Affuso, Rob *See* Skid Row

Agell, Karl *See* Corrosion of Conformity

Agnew, Pete *See* Nazareth

Aguilar, Dave *See* The Chocolate Watch Band

Ahead, Craig *See* Sick of It All

Aimone, Tony *See* Blue Meanies

Airey, Don *See* Rainbow; Whitesnake

Airport, Jak *See* X-Ray Spex

Ajile *See* Arrested Development/Speech/Dionne Farris

AK, Eric *See* Flotsam & Jetsam

Akkerman, Jan *See* Focus

Akuna, Sherwood *See* Love/Arthur Lee & Love/Arthur Lee & Band Aid

Alaimo, Jim *See* The Mojo Men/The Mojo/Mojo

Alan, Skip *See* Pretty Things

Albarn, Damon *See* Blur

Albaugh, Bill *See* The Lemon Pipers

Albers, Eef *See* Focus

Albert, Nate *See* Mighty Mighty Bosstones

Alberti, Doris *See* The Chordettes

Albertine, Viv *See* The Slits

Albin, Peter *See* Janis Joplin/Big Brother & the Holding Company

Albini, Steve *See* Big Black; Shellac

Albrecht, Bernard *See* Joy Division

Alcivar, Jim *See* Montrose

Alcock, Dave *See* Chixdiggit!

Alden, Gene *See* The Champs

Alder, John *See* Pretty Things

Aldrich, Thomas *See* Black Oak Arkansas

Aldridge, Tommy *See* Whitesnake

Alessi, Salvatore "Salv" *See* Carter the Unstoppable Sex Machine

Alex *See* The Mr. T Experience

Alexakis, Art *See* Everclear

Alexander, Dave *See* Iggy Pop/The Stooges

Alexander, Gary *See* The Association

Alexander, George *See* The Flamin' Groovies

Alexander, Scot *See* Dishwalla

Alexander, Tim "Herb" *See* Primus/Sausage

Alexander, Willie *See* The Velvet Underground/Nico/Maureen Tucker

Ali *See* A Flock of Seagulls

Ali, Jimmy Pop *See* The Bloodhound Gang

Allan, Chad *See* The Guess Who

Allandale, Eric *See* The Foundations

Allcock, Martin *See* Fairport Convention/Fairport/Sandy Denny/Fotheringay; Jethro Tull/Ian Anderson

Allemang, Ross *See* Paul Revere & the Raiders/Paul Revere & the Raiders Featuring Mark Lindsay/Raiders/Pink Puzz

Allen, Colin *See* Focus

Allen, Dan *See* Junk Monkeys

Allen, Dave *See* Gang of Four/Shriekback

Allen, David *See* Soft Machine

Allen, Eric *See* Apples in Stereo

Allen, Frank *See* The Searchers

Allen, Joey *See* Warrant

Allen, John *See* Nashville Teens

Allen, Johnny Ray *See* The subdudes

Allen, Lincoln *See* Tarnation

Allen, Mick *See* Wolfgang Press

Allen, Papa Dee *See* War

Allen, Pappy *See* Giant Sand

Allen, Rick *See* Def Leppard

Allen, Rod *See* The Fortunes

Allen, Steve *See* 20/20

Allen, Tommy *See* The Flashcubes/Gary Frenay

Allen, Verden *See* Mott the Hoople

Allen, Wally *See* Pretty Things

Allenberg, Reinhard *See* Einstürzende Neubauten

Alletzhauser, Bill *See* Ass Ponys

Allibut, Barbara *See* The Angels

Allibut, Phyllis "Jiggs" *See* The Angels

Allison, Keith "Guitar" *See* Paul Revere & the Raiders/Paul Revere & the Raiders Featuring Mark Lindsay/Raiders/Pink Puzz

Allman, Duane *See* The Allman Brothers Band

Allman, Gregg *See* The Allman Brothers Band

Allocco, Phil *See* Dogma

Allsup, Mike *See* Three Dog Night

Allum, Rob *See* High Llamas

Almo, Michael *See* Kid Creole & the Coconuts/Dr. Buzzard's Original Savannah Band

Almond, Johnny *See* The Mark-Almond Band

Almond, Marc *See* Soft Cell/Marc Almond

Alston, Andy *See* Del Amitri

Alston, Barbara *See* The Crystals

Alton, Kenny *See* Fingerprintz

Alvarez, Karl *See* All; Descendents

Alvin, Dave *See* The Blasters; X/John Doe/Exene Cervenka/The Knitters

Alvin, Phil *See* The Blasters

Amanor, Compton *See* The Selecter

Amato, Dave *See* REO Speedwagon

Ambel, Eric *See* The Del Lords/Eric Ambel/Scott Kempner

Ambler, Mark *See* Tom Robinson Band/Sector 27

Amedee, Steve *See* The subdudes

Ament, Jeff *See* Pearl Jam/Mother Love Bone/Green River/Temple of the Dog

Amico, Vinnie *See* moe.

Amis, Danny *See* Los Straitjackets/The Raybeats

Amphlett, Christina *See* Divinyls

Anastasio, Trey *See* Phish

Anater, Brian "Crusher" *See* The Flashcats

Anderson, Al *See* Bob Marley & the Wailers; NRBQ

Anderson, Brett *See* Suede/Bernard Butler

Anderson, Charley *See* The Selecter

Anderson, Emma *See* Lush

Anderson, Ian *See* Jethro Tull/Ian Anderson

Anderson, Jane *See* Sam the Sham & the Pharaohs/Sam the Sham Revue

Anderson, Jim *See* The Choir

Anderson, John *See* The Fugs

Anderson, Jon *See* Yes

Anderson, Katherine *See* The Marvelettes

Anderson, Miller *See* Savoy Brown

Anderson, Rick *See* The Tubes

Anderson, Skip *See* The Accelerators

Anderson, Tich *See* Altered Images

Andersson, Benny *See* ABBA

Andersson, Sonda *See* Live Skull

Andes, Mark *See* Firefall; Heart/Lovemongers; Spirit

Andes, Matt *See* Spirit

Andrew, Sam *See* Janis Joplin/Big Brother & the Holding Company

Andrews, Barry *See* Gang of Four/Shriekback; XTC/The Dukes of Stratosphear

Andrews, Bob *See* Brinsley Schwarz; Billy Idol/Generation X; Graham Parker/Graham Parker & the Rumor

Andrews, Scott *See* Pistoleros

Andridge, Rick *See* The Seeds

Andrijasevich, Gary *See* The Chocolate Watch Band

Angel *See* Enigma

Angel, Eddie *See* Los Straitjackets/The Raybeats

Angel, Jerry *See* The Blasters; The Weirdos

Anonymous, Rodney *See* The Dead Milkmen

Ansani, Ted *See* Material Issue

Block, Ken *See* Sister Hazel

Block, Norman *See* Rasputina

Blocker, Joe *See* Love/Arthur Lee & Love/Arthur Lee & Band Aid

Bloedow, Oren *See* Dog's Eye View; Elysian Fields; The Lounge Lizards

Blomquist, Eric *See* The Shadows of Knight

Blood, Dave *See* The Dead Milkmen

Bloodvessel, Buster *See* Bad Manners

Bloom, Eric *See* Blue Öyster Cult

Bloomfield, Brett *See* Jefferson Starship/Starship

Bloomfield, Michael *See* Paul Butterfield Blues Band

Bloss *See* The Darling Buds

Blotto, Blanche *See* Blotto

Blotto, Bowtie *See* Blotto

Blotto, Broadway *See* Blotto

Blotto, Cheese *See* Blotto

Blotto, Chevrolet *See* Blotto

Blotto, Lee Harvey *See* Blotto

Blotto, Sergeant *See* Blotto

Blotzer, Bobby *See* Ratt

Blough, Billy *See* George Thorogood & the Destroyers

Blue, Buddy *See* The Beat Farmers

Blue, Vickie *See* The Runaways

Bluechel, Ted *See* The Association

Blume, Danny *See* The Lounge Lizards

Blumenfeld, Roy *See* Blues Project

Blumenfield, Jay *See* Too Much Joy

Blunk, David *See* Thirty Ought Six

Blunstone, Colin *See* The Zombies

Blunt, John *See* The Searchers

Blunt, Martin *See* The Charlatans UK

Blush, Brian *See* The Refreshments

Blythe, Geoffrey *See* Black 47

Boatman, Billy *See* Gary Lewis & the Playboys

Bob, Simon *See* Corrosion of Conformity

Boblett, Paul *See* Paw

Boccia, Gene *See* Southside Johnny & the Asbury Jukes

Bodine, Michelle *See* Brainiac

Bodnar, Andrew *See* Graham Parker/Graham Parker & the Rumor

Boff *See* Chumbawamba

Bogan, Anne *See* The Marvelettes

Bogdan, Henry *See* Helmet

Bogert, Tim *See* Vanilla Fudge

Bogle, Bob *See* The Ventures

Bohay-Nowell, Vernon Dudley *See* The Bonzo Dog Band

Bolan, Marc *See* T. Rex

Bolan, Rachel *See* Skid Row

Bolder, Trevor *See* Uriah Heep

Boles, Tom *See* The Choir

Bolin, Patrick *See* Pure Prairie League

Bolin, Tommy *See* Deep Purple

Bolles, Don *See* The Germs

Bon Jovi, Jon *See* Bon Jovi/Jon Bon Jovi

Bon, Ross *See* Mighty Blue Kings

Bonaccorsi, Jim *See* Freddy Jones Band

Bonaccorsi, Rob *See* Freddy Jones Band

Bond, Rhond "Pickles" *See* My Life with the Thrill Kill Kult/The Bomb Gang Girlz

Bond, Ronnie *See* The Troggs

Bonebrake, Don "D.J." *See* X/John Doe/Exene Cervenka/The Knitters

Bones *See* L.A. Guns

Bonfanti, Jim *See* The Choir; The Raspberries

Bonham, Jason *See* Bonham/Jason Bonham Band/Motherland

Bonham, John *See* Led Zeppelin

Bonilla, Don Armando *See* Kid Creole & the Coconuts/Dr. Buzzard's Original Savannah Band

Bonnar, Graham *See* Swervedriver

Bonnecaze, Cary *See* Better Than Ezra

Bonnett, Graham *See* Rainbow

Bonniwell, Sean *See* Music Machine/Bonniwell Music Machine/Friendly Torpedoes

Bono *See* U2

Bono, Salvatore "Sonny" *See* Sonny & Cher/Cher

Bonta, Peter *See* Artful Dodger

Boon, Clint *See* Inspiral Carpets

Boon, D. *See* Minutemen

Boone, Joe *See* Big Ass Truck

Boone, Michael *See* Kid Creole & the Coconuts/Dr. Buzzard's Original Savannah Band

Boone, Steve *See* The Lovin' Spoonful/John Sebastian

Booth, Tim *See* James

Boquist, Dave *See* Son Volt

Boquist, Jim *See* Son Volt

Borchardt, Jeffrey *See* Velvet Crush

Borden, Barry "B.B." *See* Molly Hatchet; Mother's Finest; The Outlaws

Borden, Terrence *See* Idaho

Bordin, Mike *See* Faith No More/Mr. Bungle/Imperial Teen

Borg, Bobby *See* Warrant

Borja, Elaine *See* 3rd Party

Borjas, Larry *See* ? and the Mysterians

Borland, Wes *See* Limp Bizkit

Born, Dennis Conroy *See* Cryan' Shames

Borrell, Craig *See* Sukia

Borschied, Tommy *See* The Honeydogs

Bosco, Jimmy *See* The Fleshtones

Bossi, Ben *See* Romeo Void

Bostanche, Bob *See* The Shadows of Knight

Bostaph, Paul *See* Slayer

Bostrom, Derrick *See* Meat Puppets

Bott, Jimmy *See* The Fabulous Thunderbirds

Botts, Mike *See* Bread

Bottum, Roddy *See* Faith No More/Mr. Bungle/Imperial Teen

Bouchard, Albert *See* Blue Öyster Cult

Bouchard, Joe *See* Blue Öyster Cult

Boucher, Andy *See* The Housemartins/The Beautiful South/Beats International

Boudakian, Ken *See* Spain

Boulter, Dave *See* Tindersticks

Boulter, Roy *See* The Farm

Boutette, Dave *See* Junk Monkeys

Bovine, Vinnie *See* Screeching Weasel

Bowens, Sir Harry *See* Was (Not Was)

Burke, Dave *See* The Choir; The Standells

Burke, John *See* Wig

Burke, Noel *See* Echo & the Bunnymen/Electrafixion

Burke, Pat *See* The Foundations

Burke, Sean *See* The Atlanta Rhythm Section/ARS

Burke, Val *See* Gary Wright/Spooky Tooth

Burkum, Tyler *See* Audio Adrenaline

Burnel, Jean-Jacques *See* The Stranglers

Burness, Joe *See* The Champs

Burnett, Larry *See* Firefall

Burnette, Billy *See* Fleetwood Mac

Burnham, Hugo *See* Gang of Four/Shriekback

Burns, Annie *See* The Burns Sisters

Burns, Bob *See* Lynyrd Skynyrd

Burns, Jeannie *See* The Burns Sisters

Burns, Joey *See* Friends of Dean Martinez; Giant Sand; OP8

Burns, Karl *See* The Fall

Burns, Marie *See* The Burns Sisters

Burns, Sheila *See* The Burns Sisters

Burns, Terry *See* The Burns Sisters

Burnz, Cha *See* Fingerprintz

Burr, Clive *See* Iron Maiden/Bruce Dickinson

Burr, Gary *See* Pure Prairie League

Burrell, Boz *See* Bad Company; King Crimson

Burrows, Chris *See* The Godfathers

Burrows, Jeff *See* The Tea Party

Burston, Mick "Wurzel" *See* Motörhead

Burt, Heinz *See* Tornados

Burt-Martin, Wes *See* Edie Brickell & New Bohemians

Burtnik, Glen *See* Styx

Burton, Andy *See* The Schramms

Burton, Cliff *See* Metallica

Burton, Tim "Johnny Vegas" *See* Mighty Mighty Bosstones

Burton, Trevor *See* The Move/Roy Wood

Buschman, Carol *See* The Chordettes

Bush, David *See* The Fall

Bush, Glyn *See* Rocker's Hi-Fi

Bush, John *See* Anthrax; Edie Brickell & New Bohemians

Bush, Kristian *See* Billy Pilgrim

Bush, Roger *See* Flying Burrito Brothers

Bushkin, Scott *See* Agnes Gooch

Bushor, Charlie *See* The Why Store

Bushy, Ron *See* Iron Butterfly

Butch *See* eels; Music Explosion

Butcher, Belinda *See* My Bloody Valentine

Butcher, Damon *See* The Housemartins/The Beautiful South/Beats International

Butcher, Jon *See* Jon Butcher Axis

Butler, Bernard *See* Suede/Bernard Butler

Butler, Chris *See* The Waitresses

Butler, Colin *See* Big Ass Truck

Butler, Joe *See* The Lovin' Spoonful/John Sebastian

Butler, Richard *See* The Psychedelic Furs/Richard Butler/Love Spit Love

Butler, Rod *See* The Honeycombs/The New Honeycombs

Butler, Terry "Geezer" *See* Black Sabbath

Butler, Tim *See* The Psychedelic Furs/Richard Butler/Love Spit Love

Butler, Tony *See* Big Country

Butt Boy *See* Dread Zeppelin

Butterfield, Paul *See* Paul Butterfield Blues Band

Buynak, John *See* Rusted Root

Byars, Brent *See* Tower of Power

Byers, Marilyn *See* The Crystals

Byers, Roddy "Radiation" *See* The Specials

Byfield, Joe *See* Gallon Drunk

Byford, Biff *See* Saxon

Byrne, Chris *See* Black 47

Byrne, David *See* Talking Heads/Jerry Harrison/Tom Tom Club/The Heads

Byrne, Dermot *See* Altan

Byrne, Pat *See* Urge Overkill

Byrne, Pete *See* Naked Eyes

Byrne, Sean *See* Count Five

Byrnes, Joe *See* Tarnation

Byrom, Larry *See* Steppenwolf

Byron, David *See* Uriah Heep

Byron, Jean-Michel *See* Toto

Byron, Lord T. *See* Lords of Acid

Byworth, Ali *See* The Godfathers

C, Mark *See* Live Skull

Cabe, Timothy *See* The Outlaws

Cable, John *See* The Nitty Gritty Dirt Band

Cacavas, Chris *See* Giant Sand; Green on Red

Caddy, Alan *See* Tornados

Cadena, Dez *See* Black Flag/Greg Ginn

Cadogan, Kevin *See* Third Eye Blind

Caffey, Charlotte *See* The Go-Go's

Caffrey, Leon *See* Space

Cage, Buddy *See* New Riders of the Purple Sage

Cahill, Tony *See* The Easybeats

Caiati, Manny *See* The Del Lords/Eric Ambel/Scott Kempner

Cain, Jonathan *See* Journey; John Waite/The Babys/Bad English

Cain, Mark "Dodie" *See* Sham 69

Cairns, Andrew James *See* Therapy?

Cairns, Greg *See* The Verlaines

Calderone, Lenny *See* The Fleshtones

Caldwell, Tommy *See* The Marshall Tucker Band

Caldwell, Toy *See* The Marshall Tucker Band

Cale, John *See* The Velvet Underground/Nico/Maureen Tucker

Calhoun, Dave *See* Bow Wow Wow

Calhoun, William *See* Living Colour

California, Randy *See* Spirit

Calio, Joie *See* dada

Calire, Mario *See* The Wallflowers

Call, John David *See* Pure Prairie League

Callahan, Ken *See* The Jayhawks/The Original Harmony Ridge Creek Dippers

Callier, Alex *See* Hooverphonic

Callis, Jo *See* Human League

Callis, John *See* The Rezillos

Cheng, Chi *See* deftones

Cher *See* Sonny & Cher/Cher

Cherone, Gary *See* Extreme; Van Halen/David Lee Roth

Chesley, Alison *See* Verbow

Cheslin, Matt *See* Ned's Atomic Dustbin

Chesterman, Ron *See* The Strawbs/Dave Cousins

Chesters, Eds *See* The Bluetones

Chevron, Phllp *See* The Pogues/Shane MacGowan & the Popes

Chichester, Harold *See* Royal Crescent Mob

Childers, Lenny *See* Antenna/Velo-Deluxe/The Mysteries of Life/John P. Strohm & the Hello Strangers

Childress, Ross *See* Collective Soul

Childs, Euros *See* Gorky's Zygotic Mynci

Childs, Megan *See* Gorky's Zygotic Mynci

Chilton, Alex *See* Big Star/Chris Bell

Chin *See* Quickspace

Chipperfield, Sheila *See* Elastica

Chisolm, Melanie "Sporty Spice" *See* The Spice Girls

Chitkowski, James "Chic James" *See* The New Colony Six

Chmiel, J.C. *See* The Hangdogs

Chown, Nick *See* The Bolshoi

Chowning, Randle *See* The Skeletons/The Morells

Christ, John *See* Danzig/Samhain

Christensen, Don *See* Los Straitjackets/The Raybeats

Christensen, Maria *See* 3rd Party

Christian, Van *See* Friends of Dean Martinez; Green on Red

Christina, Fran *See* The Fabulous Thunderbirds

Christopherson, Peter *See* Throbbing Gristle

Chrome, Cheetah *See* Dead Boys/Stiv Bators/Lords of the New Church

Chryssaphis, Chris *See* A Flock of Seagulls

Chu, Bryan *See* Farside

Chud, Dr. *See* The Misfits

Chung, Mark *See* Einstürzende Neubauten

Chunn, Phil *See* Split Enz/Tim Finn/Alt

Church, Bill *See* Montrose

Churchill, Chick *See* Ten Years After

Churchville, Bill *See* Tower of Power

Churilla, Scott *See* The Reverend Horton Heat

Chylinski, Mike *See* Drugstore

Ciaran, Cian *See* Super Furry Animals

Ciarlante, Randy *See* The Band

Ciner, Al *See* The American Breed

Cipollina, John *See* Quicksilver Messenger Service

Cipollina, Mario *See* Huey Lewis & the News

Cipriano, Rich *See* Sick of It All

Circuit Breaker *See* Plastikman/Circuit Breaker/Cybersonik/FUSE

Cissell, Ben *See* Audio Adrenaline

Civorelli, Anthony "Civ" *See* CIV

Clapton, Eric *See* Blind Faith; Cream; The Yardbirds

Clarin, Melanie *See* S.F. Seals

Clark, "Fast" Eddie *See* Motörhead

Clark, Alan *See* Dire Straits

Clark, Andrew *See* Be Bop Deluxe

Clark, Dave *See* The Dave Clark Five

Clark, Gary *See* Transister

Clark, Gene *See* The Byrds

Clark, Jackie *See* The Nitty Gritty Dirt Band

Clark, Keith *See* The Circle Jerks; 20/20

Clark, Marlin *See* Mighty Joe Plum

Clark, Mick *See* The Tremeloes/Brian Poole & the Tremeloes/Chip Hawkes' Tremeloes

Clark, Mike *See* Suicidal Tendencies

Clark, Nigel *See* Dodgy

Clark, Paul *See* The Bolshoi

Clark, Peter *See* AC/DC

Clark, Robin *See* Simple Minds

Clark, Steve *See* Def Leppard

Clark, Tony *See* Blessid Union of Souls

Clark, Vince *See* Depeche Mode

Clarke, Allan *See* The Hollies

Clarke, Gilby *See* Guns N' Roses

Clarke, Jamie *See* The Pogues/Shane MacGowan & the Popes

Clarke, Mark *See* Mountain; Uriah Heep

Clarke, Michael *See* The Byrds; Firefall; Flying Burrito Brothers

Clarke, Nobby *See* The Bay City Rollers

Clarke, Vince *See* Erasure

Clawson, Dan *See* Firefall

Claypool, Les *See* Primus/Sausage

Clayton, Adam *See* U2

Clayton, Keith *See* The Feelies

Clayton, Sam *See* Little Feat

Clayton-Felt, Josh *See* School of Fish/Josh Clayton-Felt

Clayton-Thomas, David *See* Blood, Sweat & Tears

Clean, Dean *See* The Dead Milkmen

Cleave, Simon *See* The Wedding Present

Cleaver, Chuck *See* Ass Ponys

Clegg, Johnny *See* Johnny Clegg & Savuka/Juluka

Clemens, Jeffrey *See* G. Love & Special Sauce

Clements, Rod *See* Lindisfarne

Cleminson, Zal *See* Nazareth

Clemons, Clarence *See* Bruce Springsteen/Bruce Springsteen & the E Street Band

Clempson, David "Clem" *See* Humble Pie

Clench, Jim *See* Bachman-Turner Overdrive

Cleuver, Hans *See* Focus

Clifford, Doug *See* Creedence Clearwater Revival

Clifford, Paul *See* The Wonder Stuff

Cline, Mark *See* Love Tractor

Cline, Nels *See* Geraldine Fibbers

Cloud, Rusty *See* Southside Johnny & the Asbury Jukes

Clouser, Charlie *See* nine inch nails

Clower, James *See* The Fluid

Club, Billy *See* The Dickies

D'Amico, Michael *See* The Wondermints

Dammers, Jerry *See* The Specials

Damon, Zac *See* Screeching Weasel

D'Amour, Paul *See* Tool/The Replicants

Dancey, Mark *See* Big Chief

D'Anda, Jimmy *See* Bulletboys

Dando, Evan *See* Blake Babies; Lemonheads

D'Andrea, Richard *See* The Motels

Danell, Dennis *See* Social Distortion

Danelli, Dino *See* The Young Rascals/The Rascals

Dangers, Jack *See* Meat Beat Manifesto

Daniel, Casey *See* Seven Mary Three

Daniel, Jack "Hawkeye" *See* The Shadows of Knight

Danielian, Barry *See* Southside Johnny & the Asbury Jukes; Tower of Power

Daniels, Charlie *See* Charlie Daniels Band

Daniels, Joe *See* Local H

Danko, Rick *See* The Band

Dannemann, Don *See* The Cyrkle

Danner, Mike *See* Big Chief

Danny *See* Swervedriver

Danny Boy *See* House of Pain

Dante, Ron "Archie" *See* The Archies

Danus, Miguel Luis Vicens *See* Los Bravos

Danzig, Glenn *See* Danzig/Samhain; The Misfits

Darby, Hunter *See* The Wannabes

Darlington, Jay *See* Kula Shaker

Darlington, Robert *See* Translator

Darrow, Chris *See* The Nitty Gritty Dirt Band

Darvill, Benjamin *See* Crash Test Dummies

Daugherty, Jay Dee *See* The Beat/Paul Collins; The Church; Patti Smith/Patti Smith Group; The Waterboys

Daugherty, Pat *See* Black Oak Arkansas

Daughtrey, Ben *See* Squirrel Bait

Daughtry, Dean *See* The Atlanta Rhythm Section/ARS

Davenport, Billy *See* Paul Butterfield Blues Band

David, John "Jay" *See* Dr. Hook & the Medicine Show/Dr. Hook

David, Stuart *See* Belle & Sebastian

Davidowski, Steve *See* The Dixie Dregs/The Dregs

Davidson, Aaron *See* Modern English

Davidson, Eric *See* The New Bomb Turks

Davidson, George *See* Paul Butterfield Blues Band

Davidson, Greg *See* The Wipers/Greg Sage

Davidson, Lenny *See* The Dave Clark Five

Davies, Alan *See* The Soft Boys

Davies, Alun *See* The Mark-Almond Band

Davies, Dave *See* The Kinks

Davies, Iva *See* Icehouse

Davies, Noel *See* The Selecter

Davies, Ray *See* The Kinks

Davies, Rick *See* Supertramp

Davies, Robin *See* Tar Babies

Davies, Saul *See* James

Davis, Bill *See* Dash Rip Rock

Davis, Jeff *See* The Balancing Act

Davis, Jesse *See* The Nixons

Davis, Jonathan Houseman *See* Koяn

Davis, Mark *See* Ugly Kid Joe

Davis, Martha *See* The Motels

Davis, Michael *See* MC5

Davis, Paul *See* Happy Mondays/Black Grape

Davis, Ray *See* The Temptations

Davis, Rob *See* Mud

Dawes, Tom *See* The Cyrkle

Dawn, Sandra *See* The Platters

Dawson, Al *See* Cryan' Shames

Dawson, John "Marmaduke" *See* New Riders of the Purple Sage

Dawson, Steve *See* Saxon

Day, Mark *See* Happy Mondays/Black Grape

Daye, Corey *See* Kid Creole & the Coconuts/Dr. Buzzard's Original Savannah Band

Dayton, Kelli *See* Sneaker Pimps

De Beer, Derek *See* Johnny Clegg & Savuka/Juluka

De Borg, Jerry *See* Jesus Jones

De Carr, Dennis *See* The Mojo Men/The Mojo/Mojo

de Castro, Dave *See* The Health & Happiness Show

De Freitas, Pete *See* Echo & the Bunnymen/Electrafixion

de Homem-Christo, Guy-Manuel *See* Daft Punk

de Jesus, Joe *See* James Taylor Quartet

De La Cour *See* Army of Lovers

De la Cruz, Vince *See* Katrina & the Waves

De La Luna, Sai *See* Lords of Acid

de la Rocha, Zack *See* Farside; Rage Against the Machine

De Lisle, Paul *See* Smash Mouth

De Mare, Siobhan *See* Mono

De Martini, Warren *See* Ratt

De Meyer, Jean-Luc *See* Front 242

De Oliveira, Lauder *See* Chicago/Peter Cetera

de Ronde, Peter *See* Golden Earring

Deacon, John *See* Queen

Deal, Kelley *See* The Breeders/The Amps

Deal, Kim *See* The Pixies

Deal, Steven *See* Chopper

Dean, Elton *See* Soft Machine

Dean, John *See* Gary Lewis & the Playboys

Dean, Johnny *See* Menswear

Dean, Mike *See* Corrosion of Conformity

Dean, Paul *See* Loverboy; X-Ray Spex

Deane, Sandy *See* Jay & the Americans

Dear, Tracy *See* The Waco Brothers

Deasy, Bill *See* The Gathering Field

Decharne, Max *See* Gallon Drunk

Dechert, Greg *See* Uriah Heep

Decker, Larry *See* Translator

Decloedt, Mark *See* EMF

Dederer, Dave *See* The Presidents of the United States of America

DiNizio, Pat *See* The Smithereens

Dinning, Dean *See* Toad the Wet Sprocket

Dins, Dino *See* T. Rex

Dinwiddie, Gene *See* Paul Butterfield Blues Band

Dio, Ronnie James *See* Black Sabbath; Rainbow

Dirnt, Mike *See* Green Day

DiSpirito, Jim *See* Rusted Root

DiStefano, Peter *See* Porno for Pyros

Dix, David *See* The Outlaws

Dixon, Jerry *See* Warrant

Dixon, Peter *See* Combustible Edison

DJ Krust *See* Roni Size/Reprazent

DJ Lethal *See* House of Pain; Limp Bizkit

DJ Minutemix *See* PM Dawn

DJ Muggs *See* Cypress Hill

DJ On-e *See* Deee-Lite

D.J. Q-Ball *See* The Bloodhound Gang

DJ Towa Tei *See* Deee-Lite

DJ Zero *See* MC 900 Ft. Jesus

D.M. *See* Voice of the Beehive

D.M.C. *See* Run-D.M.C.

Dmochowski, Wojtek *See* The Blue Aeroplanes

Dobbins, Georgia *See* The Marvelettes

Dobson, Lyn *See* Soft Machine

Dr. Delecto & his Invisible Vaportron *See* Man or Astro-Man?

Dr. Frank *See* The Mr. T Experience

Dr. Know *See* Bad Brains

Dodd, Dick *See* The Standells

Dodd, Jane *See* The Verlaines

Dodd, Pete *See* Thompson Twins/Babble

Dodge, Wolfgang *See* My Life with the Thrill Kill Kult/The Bomb Gang Girlz

Doe, John *See* X/John Doe/Exene Cervenka/The Knitters

Dogbowl *See* King Missile

Doherty, Billy *See* The Undertones

Doherty, Brian *See* Big Wreck; They Might Be Giants

Doherty, Denny *See* The Mamas & the Papas

Doiron, Jane *See* Eric's Trip/Elevator to Hell

Dokken, Don *See* Dokken

Dole, Bobby *See* Blood, Sweat & Tears

Dolenz, Mickey *See* The Monkees

Dollimore, Kris *See* Del Amitri; The Godfathers

Domakes, Chris *See* Less Than Jake

Dombroski, Vinnie *See* Sponge

Dominici, Charlie *See* Dream Theater

Domrose, Bret *See* Dogstar

Donahue, Jerry *See* Fairport Convention/Fairport/Sandy Denny/Fotheringay; The Hellecasters

Donahue, Jonathan *See* The Flaming Lips; Mercury Rev

Donahue, Patty *See* The Waitresses

Donahue, Tim *See* Cherry Poppin' Daddies

Donald, Tony *See* Simple Minds

Donaldson, Dustin *See* Pansy Division

Donato, Dave *See* Black Sabbath

Donegan, Lawrence *See* The Bluebells

Donelly, Tanya *See* Belly/Tanya Donelly; The Breeders/The Amps; Throwing Muses/Kristin Hersh

Donnellan, Jay *See* Love/Arthur Lee & Love/Arthur Lee & Band Aid

Donnelly, Paul *See* My Drug Hell

Donnelly, Pete *See* The Figgs

Donohue, Chris *See* Vigilantes of Love

Donovan, Bazil *See* Blue Rodeo

Donovan, Dan *See* Big Audio Dynamite/B.A.D. II/Big Audio

Donovan, Jim *See* Rusted Root

Doody, Tom *See* Cryan' Shames

Doom, Lorna *See* The Germs

Dope, L.B. *See* A3/Alabama 3

Dope, Shaggy 2 *See* Insane Clown Posse

Dorame, Mando *See* Royal Crown Revue

Dorge, Michel *See* Crash Test Dummies

Dorman, Lee *See* Iron Butterfly

Dorney, Tim *See* Republica

Doroschuk, Colin *See* Men Without Hats

Doroschuk, Ivan *See* Men Without Hats

Doroschuk, Stefan *See* Men Without Hats

Dorough, Howie *See* Backstreet Boys

Dorrington, Paul *See* The Wedding Present

Dorsey, Jesse *See* Nancy Boy

Doss, Bill *See* Olivia Tremor Control

Dotson, Ward *See* Gun Club

Doucette, Paul *See* Matchbox 20

Dougan, Brian *See* Future Sound of London/Amorphous Androgynous

Dougherty, Jim *See* Evan Johns & His H-Bombs

Doughton, Shannon *See* The Breeders/The Amps

Doughty, Alan *See* The Waco Brothers

Doughty, M. *See* Soul Coughing

Doughty, Neal *See* REO Speedwagon

Douglas, Chip *See* The Turtles

Douglas, Graeme *See* Eddie & the Hot Rods

Douglas, Michael *See* Orchestral Manoeuvres in the Dark

Douglas, Mike *See* The Diamonds

Dowd, Christopher Gordon *See* Fishbone

Dowle, David *See* Whitesnake

Downes, Geoff *See* Asia; The Buggles; Yes

Downes, Graeme *See* The Verlaines

Downey, Brian *See* Thin Lizzy

Downey, Rick *See* Blue Öyster Cult

Downie, Gordon *See* The Tragically Hip

Downie, Tyrone *See* Bob Marley & the Wailers

Downing, K.K. *See* Judas Priest

Doyle, Candida *See* Pulp

Doyle, John *See* Magazine

Doyle, Mark *See* Verbow

Doyle, P.C. *See* The Misfits

Dozy *See* Dave Dee, Dozy, Beaky, Mick & Tich/Dozy, Beaky, Mick & Tich

Dragon, Daryl *See* The Captain & Tennille

Drake, Adam *See* The Grapes of Wrath/Ginger

Drake, Steven *See* The Odds

Draper, Terry *See* Klaatu

Edgar, Ron *See* Music Machine/Bonniwell Music Machine/Friendly Torpedoes

Edge, Graeme *See* The Moody Blues/Justin Hayward & John Lodge/Mike Pinder

The Edge *See* U2

Edmonds, Lu *See* The Mekons; Public Image Ltd./PIL/John Lydon

Edmondson, Tim *See* Dramarama

Edmonton, Jerry *See* Steppenwolf

Edmunds, Dave *See* Dave Edmunds/Rockpile

Edmunds, Doug *See* Gladhands

Edson, Richard *See* Sonic Youth/Thurston Moore/Lee Ranaldo/Ciccone Youth/Bewitched

Edward, Terry *See* Gallon Drunk

Edwards, Buddy *See* The Refreshments

Edwards, David Eugene *See* 16 Horsepower

Edwards, Dennis *See* The Temptations

Edwards, Gordon *See* Pretty Things

Edwards, John "Rhino" *See* Status Quo

Edwards, Johnny *See* Foreigner

Edwards, Mike *See* Electric Light Orchestra/Jeff Lynne/ELO II; Jesus Jones

Edwards, Noel "Nokie" *See* The Ventures

Edwards, Richey *See* Manic Street Preachers

Edwards, Simon *See* Fairground Attraction/Eddi Reader

Edwards, Skye *See* Morcheeba

Egan, Bob *See* Freakwater

Egerton, Stephen *See* All; Descendents

Eggermont, Jaap *See* Golden Earring

Eggermont, Mike *See* Chixdiggit!

Ehart, Phil *See* Kansas

Ehrbar, Jud *See* Varnaline

Ehrenfeld, Nathan *See* Agnes Gooch

Eichstadt, Klaus *See* Ugly Kid Joe

Einheit, F.M. *See* Einstürzende Neubauten

Eisenstrager, Thor *See* Cows

Eitzel, Mark *See* Mark Eitzel/American Music Club

Ekberg, Ulf Gunnar "Buddha" *See* Ace of Base

Eklund, Greg *See* Everclear

Eldon, Thor *See* Björk/Sugarcubes

Eldritch, Andrew *See* Sisters of Mercy

Elefante, John *See* Kansas

Elfman, Danny *See* Oingo Boingo/Danny Elfman

Elias, Hanin *See* Atari Teenage Riot

Elias, Ivan *See* Patty Smyth/Scandal

Eliopulos, Mark *See* Stabbing Westward

Elkins, Craig *See* Huffamoose

Ellefson, David *See* Megadeth

Ellenis, Theothorous Athanasious *See* Dramarama

Ellershaw, Scott *See* Paul Revere & the Raiders/Paul Revere & the Raiders Featuring Mark Lindsay/Raiders/Pink Puzz

Elliot, Dennis *See* Foreigner

Elliot, Joe *See* Def Leppard

Elliot, "Mama" Cass *See* The Mamas & the Papas

Elliot, Matt *See* Third Eye Foundation

Elliot, Richard *See* Tower of Power

Elliott, Doug *See* The Odds

Elliott, Jim *See* The Cruel Sea

Elliott, Mike *See* The Foundations

Elliott, Robert *See* The Hollies

Elliott, Ron *See* The Beau Brummels

Ellis, Ian *See* Savoy Brown

Ellis, John *See* Judas Priest; The Stranglers; The Vibrators

Ellis, Ralph *See* The Swinging Blue Jeans/The Bluegenes/Ray Ennis & the Blue Jeans

Ellis, Warren *See* Dirty Three

Ellison, David *See* Royal Crescent Mob

Ellison, Jim *See* Material Issue

Ellman, Kevin *See* Todd Rundgren/Utopia

Ellner, Ken *See* Count Five

Elm, Bill *See* Friends of Dean Martinez

Elmo, Frank *See* Southside Johnny & the Asbury Jukes

Elmore, Greg *See* Quicksilver Messenger Service

Elswit, Rick *See* Dr. Hook & the Medicine Show/Dr. Hook

Eltringham, Fred *See* Gigolo Aunts

Elvis, Brad *See* The Elvis Brothers

Elvis, Graham *See* The Elvis Brothers

Elvis, Rob *See* The Elvis Brothers

Elwood, Coleen *See* Zuzu's Petals

Ely, Jack *See* The Kingsmen

Ely, Joe *See* The Flatlanders

Ely, Vince *See* The Psychedelic Furs/Richard Butler/Love Spit Love

Emelin, John *See* Lothar & the Hand People

Emerson, Darren *See* Underworld

Emerson, Keith *See* Emerson, Lake & Palmer/Emerson, Lake & Powell

Emery, Jill *See* Hole

Emil *See* Black Flag/Greg Ginn

Emmett, Rik *See* Triumph

Empire, Alec *See* Atari Teenage Riot

Engel, Scott *See* The Walker Brothers/Scott Walker

Engelhard, Paul *See* For Against

Englert, Mark "Mr. E. Boy" *See* Dramarama

English, Joe *See* Paul McCartney/Wings

English, Richard *See* The Flaming Lips

Enigk, Jeremy *See* Sunny Day Real Estate

Ennis, Ray *See* The Swinging Blue Jeans/The Bluegenes/Ray Ennis & the Blue Jeans

Eno, Brian *See* Roxy Music

Entner, Warren *See* The Grass Roots

Entwistle, John *See* The Who

Epstein, Howie *See* Tom Petty & the Heartbreakers

Erchick, Peter *See* Olivia Tremor Control

Erhan *See* Lords of Acid

Erhardt, John *See* Ass Ponys

Eriksen, Andreas *See* Bel Canto

Erikson, Duke *See* Garbage

Erlandson, Eric *See* Hole

Ernie-C *See* Body Count

Errico, Greg *See* Sly & the Family Stone

Errico, Jan *See* The Mojo Men/The Mojo/Mojo

Fripp, Robert *See* King Crimson

Frischmann, Justine *See* Elastica; Suede/Bernard Butler

Froese, Edgar *See* Tangerine Dream

Froese, Jerome *See* Tangerine Dream

fROMOHIO, Ed *See* fIREHOSE/Mike Watt/Banyan/Dos

Frost, Barry Eugene *See* Rare Earth

Frost, Craig *See* Grand Funk Railroad

Frusciante, John *See* Red Hot Chili Peppers

Fry, Martin *See* ABC

Fryer, Davey *See* The Tremeloes/Brian Poole & the Tremeloes/Chip Hawkes' Tremeloes

Fuemana, Pauly *See* OMC

Fuentes, Sasha *See* Sukia

Fuller, Bobby *See* The Bobby Fuller Four

Fuller, Craig *See* American Flyer; Little Feat; Pure Prairie League

Fuller, Randy *See* The Bobby Fuller Four

Fulton, Willie *See* Tower of Power

Funaro, Frank *See* The Del Lords/Eric Ambel/Scott Kempner

Funichello, Ross "The Boss" *See* The Dictators

Furay, Richie *See* Buffalo Springfield; Poco

Furious, Danny *See* The Avengers

Furry, Dick *See* My Life with the Thrill Kill Kult/The Bomb Gang Girlz

Furuholmen, Magne "Mags" *See* a-ha

FUSE *See* Plastikman/Circuit Breaker/Cybersonik/FUSE

Fusillo, Dylan "the Rifleman" *See* Big Rude Jake

Futter, Brian *See* Catherine Wheel

Gabay, Yuval *See* Cop Shoot Cop/Firewater; Soul Coughing

Gabriel, Gilbert *See* The Dream Academy

Gabriel, Pascal *See* Peach Union

Gabriel, Peter *See* Genesis

Gacy, Madonna Wayne *See* Marilyn Manson

Gadler, Frankie *See* NRBQ

Gadson, James *See* Booker T. & the MG's

Gaer, Herschel Mark *See* The Interpreters

Gaffney, Eric *See* Sebadoh/The Folk Implosion

Gagel, Wally *See* Orbit

Gagliardi, Ed *See* Foreigner

Gahan, David *See* Depeche Mode

Gaines, Steve *See* Lynyrd Skynyrd

Gale, Gretchen *See* The Crystals

Gale, Melvyn *See* Electric Light Orchestra/Jeff Lynne/ELO II

Gallagher, Jim *See* The Astronauts

Gallagher, Liam *See* Oasis

Gallagher, Mickey *See* Ian Dury/Ian Dury & the Blockheads

Gallagher, Noel *See* Oasis

Galley, Mel *See* Whitesnake

Gallimore, Stan *See* The Grifters

Gallo, Mike *See* 20/20

Gallucci, Don *See* The Kingsmen

Gallup, Simon *See* The Cure

Galvin, John *See* Molly Hatchet

Galvin, Matt *See* Eva Trout

Gamble, Brendan *See* Poster Children

Gamson, David *See* Scritti Politti

Gane, Tim *See* Stereolab

Gannon, Craig *See* Aztec Camera; The Bluebells; The Smiths

Gannon, Mike *See* The Electric Prunes

Gano, Gordon *See* Violent Femmes

Ganser, Marge *See* The Shangri-Las

Ganser, Mary Ann *See* The Shangri-Las

Ganucheau, Ray *See* The Continental Drifters

Garber, Scott *See* Giant Sand

Garcia, Dean *See* Curve

Garcia, Jerry *See* The Grateful Dead; New Riders of the Purple Sage

Garcia, John *See* Kyuss

Gardener, Mark *See* Ride

Gardner, Carl *See* The Coasters

Gardner, Greg *See* The Why Store

Gardner, Michael *See* The Nitty Gritty Dirt Band

Gardner, Suzi *See* L7

Garduno, Max *See* El Chicano

Garfat, Jance *See* Dr. Hook & the Medicine Show/Dr. Hook

Garfunkel, Art *See* Simon & Garfunkel

Gargiulo, Lulu *See* Fastbacks

Garibaldi, Dave *See* Tower of Power

Garisto, Paul *See* The Psychedelic Furs/Richard Butler/Love Spit Love

Garner, Pete *See* The Stone Roses

Garner, Sue *See* Run On

Garni, Kelly *See* Quiet Riot

Garnier, Tony *See* The Lounge Lizards

Garrett, Peter *See* Midnight Oil

Garrett, Scot *See* The Cult/The Holy Barbarians

Garriga, Charlie *See* CIV

Garrison, Chuck *See* Superchunk

Garrity, Freddie *See* Freddie & the Dreamers

Garth, Al *See* The Nitty Gritty Dirt Band

Gartside, Green *See* Scritti Politti

Garvey, Chuck *See* moe.

Garvey, Nick *See* The Motors

Garvey, Steve *See* Buzzcocks

Garvey J. *See* The Elevator Drops

Gary, Bruce *See* The Knack

Gaskill, Jerry *See* King's X

Gaskins, Jeff *See* For Against

Gaster, Jean Paul *See* Clutch

Gates, David *See* Bread

Gates, Rebecca *See* The Spinanes

Gatti, Annmarie *See* The Rooks

Gaudet, Mark *See* Eric's Trip/Elevator to Hell

Gaudio, Bob *See* The Four Seasons/Frankie Valli

Gaugh, Bud *See* Sublime

Gauthier, Rusty *See* New Riders of the Purple Sage

Gavin, Jack *See* Charlie Daniels Band

Gavurin, David *See* The Sundays

Gay, David *See* Freakwater

Gaydon, Dave *See* The Egg

Gaynor, Adam *See* Matchbox 20

Gaynor, Mel *See* Simple Minds

Gayol, Rafael "Danny" *See* BoDeans

Gazda, Ricky *See* Southside Johnny & the Asbury Jukes

Geary, Paul *See* Extreme

Geddes, Chris *See* Belle & Sebastian

Gedge, David *See* The Wedding Present

Gee, Andy *See* Thin Lizzy

Gee, Rosco *See* Traffic

Geerts, Raymond *See* Hooverphonic

Geils, J. *See* J. Geils Band/Bluestime

Gein, Gidget *See* Marilyn Manson

Gelb, Howe *See* Giant Sand; OP8

Geldof, Bob *See* The Boomtown Rats/Bob Geldof

Gelling, Eelco *See* Golden Earring

Gen *See* Jesus Jones

Gendel, Keith *See* Papas Fritas

Genero, Loraine *See* Sam the Sham & the Pharaohs/Sam the Sham Revue

Genius/GZA *See* Wu-Tang Clan

Gent, Chris *See* The Records/Jude Cole

Gent, Mike *See* The Figgs

Gentile, David *See* Orange 9mm

Gentile, Katie *See* Run On

Gentleman, Sir Horace *See* The Specials

Gentling, Matt *See* Archers of Loaf/Eric Bachmann

Gentry, Chris *See* Menswear

Genus, James *See* Elysian Fields

Geordie *See* Killing Joke

George, Lowell *See* Little Feat

George, Rocky *See* Suicidal Tendencies

George, Stephen *See* Ministry

George, Steve *See* Mr. Mister; Swervedriver

George, Tryan *See* The Dambuilders

Georges, Bernard *See* Throwing Muses/Kristin Hersh

Gerace, Tony *See* Sam the Sham & the Pharaohs/Sam the Sham Revue

Geraci, Sonny *See* The Outsiders

Gerber, Dick *See* Paul Revere & the Raiders/Paul Revere & the Raiders Featuring Mark Lindsay/Raiders/Pink Puzz

Germano, Lisa *See* OP8

Gerrard, Lisa *See* Dead Can Dance

Gerritsen, Rinus *See* Golden Earring

Gers, Janick *See* Iron Maiden/Bruce Dickinson

Gerzema, Matt *See* The Legendary Jim Ruiz Group

Gessle, Per *See* Roxette

Getz, David *See* Janis Joplin/Big Brother & the Holding Company

Ghomeshi, Jian *See* Moxy Früvous

Ghost Face Killa *See* Wu-Tang Clan

Giallombardo, Phil *See* The Choir

Giannarese, Carl *See* The Buckinghams

Gianni, Angelo *See* Treadmill Trackstar

Gibb, Barry *See* The Bee Gees

Gibb, Maurice *See* The Bee Gees

Gibb, Robin *See* The Bee Gees

Gibbins, Mike *See* Badfinger/Joey Molland

Gibbons, Beth *See* Portishead

Gibbons, Billy Jr. *See* ZZ Top

Gibbons, Ian *See* The Kinks

Gibbs, Dave *See* Gigolo Aunts

Gibbs, Rich *See* Oingo Boingo/Danny Elfman

Giblin, John *See* Simple Minds

Gibson, Bill *See* Huey Lewis & the News

Gibson, Butch *See* Sam the Sham & the Pharaohs/Sam the Sham Revue

Gibson, Colin *See* The Mark-Almond Band

Gibson, Deborah *See* Debbie Gibson/Deborah Gibson

Gibson, Mike *See* The Godfathers

Gibson, Wilf *See* Electric Light Orchestra/Jeff Lynne/ELO II

Giessmann, Brent *See* Del Fuegos/Dan Zanes; The Embarrassment

Gifford, Katharine *See* Stereolab

Gifford, Peter *See* Midnight Oil

Gift, Roland *See* Fine Young Cannibals

Giguere, Russ *See* The Association

Gil-Sola, Frederico *See* Wire Train

Gilbeau, Floyd "Gib" *See* Flying Burrito Brothers

Gilbert, Bruce *See* Wire

Gilbert, Danny *See* The Fleshtones

Gilbert, Gillian *See* New Order

Gilbert, Michael *See* Flotsam & Jetsam

Gilbert, Paul *See* Mr. Big

Gilbert, Ronnie *See* The Blues Magoos

Gilbert, Simon *See* Suede/Bernard Butler

Gilby, Dave *See* The Pursuit of Happiness

Giles, Michael *See* King Crimson

Gilks, Martin *See* The Wonder Stuff

Gilkyson, Tony *See* X/John Doe/Exene Cervenka/The Knitters

Gill, Andy *See* Gang of Four/Shriekback

Gill, Craig *See* Inspiral Carpets

Gill, Peter *See* Frankie Goes to Hollywood; Motörhead; Saxon

Gill, Vince *See* Pure Prairie League

Gillan, Ian *See* Black Sabbath; Deep Purple

Gillard, Doug *See* Guided by Voices

Gillen, Ray *See* Badlands

Gillespie, Bobby *See* The Jesus & Mary Chain; Primal Scream

Gillette, Mic *See* Tower of Power

Gillies, Ben *See* silverchair

Gillingham, Joe *See* The Tremeloes/Brian Poole & the Tremeloes/Chip Hawkes' Tremeloes

Gillis, Brad *See* Night Ranger/Damn Yankees/Shaw-Blades

Gilmore, Jimmie Dale *See* The Flatlanders

Gilmore, Skillet *See* Whiskeytown

Gilmour, David *See* Pink Floyd

Gingrich, Ken "King Kenny" *See* Flash Cadillac/Flash Cadillac & the Continental Kids

Ginn, Greg *See* Black Flag/Greg Ginn

Ginoli, Jon *See* Pansy Division

Ginsberg, Jennifer *See* KMFDM

Giorgianni, Joe *See* Blood, Sweat & Tears

Giorgini, Mass *See* Screeching Weasel

Gira, Michael *See* Swans

Gittleman, Joe *See* Mighty Mighty Bosstones

Giuffria, Gregg *See* Angel

Glabicki, Mike *See* Rusted Root

Glad, Jens *See* Enigma

Glascock, Brian *See* The Motels

Glascock, John *See* Jethro Tull/Ian Anderson

Glaser, Gabrielle *See* Luscious Jackson

Glass, Daniel *See* The Dambuilders; Royal Crown Revue

Glen *See* Ten Foot Pole/Scared Straight

Glenn, Will *See* The Rain Parade

Glennie, Jim *See* James

Glockler, Nigel *See* Saxon

Glover, Bill *See* Petra

Glover, Corey *See* Living Colour

Glover, Roger *See* Deep Purple; Rainbow

Gluck, Jeremy *See* The Barracudas

Goalby, Pete *See* Uriah Heep

Goble, Graham *See* Little River Band

Godchaux, Donna *See* The Grateful Dead

Godchaux, Keith *See* The Grateful Dead

Goddard, Paul *See* The Atlanta Rhythm Section/ARS

Goddess, Tony *See* Papas Fritas

Godfrey, Paul *See* Morcheeba

Godfrey, Ross *See* Morcheeba

Godin, Nicolas *See* Air

Godley, Kevin *See* 10cc

Godzisz, Wojtek *See* Symposium

Goettel, Dwayne *See* Skinny Puppy

Goffey, Danny *See* Supergrass

Goffrier, Bill *See* The Embarrassment

Gogerty, Patrick *See* The Charlatans

Gogin, Toni *See* Sleater-Kinney

Gold, Marian *See* Alphaville

Goldberg, Devon *See* aMiniature

Goldflies, David *See* The Allman Brothers Band

Golding, Lynval *See* Fun Boy Three; The Specials

Goldsmith, William *See* Sunny Day Real Estate

Goldstein, Jerry *See* The Strangeloves

Goldstein, Ricky *See* Sham 69

Gomez, Tony *See* The Foundations

Gomm, Ian *See* Brinsley Schwarz

Gonzales, Manuel *See* The Blazers

Gonzalez, Camilo *See* Naked Raygun

Gonzalez, Ruben C. *See* The Blazers

Gooch, Rick *See* Quarterflash

Goodall, Jim *See* Flying Burrito Brothers

Gooday, David *See* Nitzer Ebb

Goodell, Scott *See* Dance Hall Crashers

Goodman, Jerry *See* The Dixie Dregs/The Dregs

Goodridge, Robin *See* Bush

Goodroe, Michael *See* The Motels

Goodsight, Andrew *See* Black 47

Goodwin, Dan *See* Kitchens of Distinction

Goodwin, Jim *See* The Call

Goodwin, Patrick *See* Pansy Division

Googe, Deb *See* My Bloody Valentine

Googy, Arthur *See* The Misfits

GoolKasian *See* The Elevator Drops

Gordon, Bruce *See* The New Colony Six

Gordon, Jim *See* Bread; Traffic

Gordon, Kim *See* Sonic Youth/Thurston Moore/Lee Ranaldo/Ciccone Youth/Bewitched

Gordon, Mike *See* Phish

Gordon, Nina *See* Veruca Salt

Gordon, Robert *See* James Taylor Quartet

Gore, Martin *See* Depeche Mode

Gorham, Scott *See* Thin Lizzy

Gorman, Chris *See* Belly/Tanya Donelly

Gorman, Leigh *See* Bow Wow Wow

Gorman, Mike *See* Off Broadway usa

Gorman, Steve *See* The Black Crowes

Gorman, Thomas *See* Belly/Tanya Donelly

Gorman, Tim *See* Jefferson Starship/Starship

Gormly, Ken *See* The Cruel Sea

Gorrie, Alan *See* Average White Band

Goshorn, Larry *See* Pure Prairie League

Goshorn, Timmy *See* Pure Prairie League

Gosling, John *See* The Kinks

Gosling, Peter *See* Renaissance

Gossard, Stone *See* Brad/Satchel; Pearl Jam/Mother Love Bone/Green River/Temple of the Dog

Gotobed, Robert *See* Wire

Gotsch, Norm *See* The Shadows of Knight

Gotshall, Michael *See* The Shadows of Knight

Gott, Larry *See* James

Gottehrer, Richard *See* The Strangeloves

Goudreau, Barry *See* Boston

Gould, Billy *See* Faith No More/Mr. Bungle/Imperial Teen

Gould, Boon *See* Level 42

Gould, Darby *See* Jefferson Starship/Starship

Gould, Phil *See* Level 42

Goulding, Steve *See* The Mekons; Graham Parker/Graham Parker & the Rumor; The Waco Brothers

Gouldman, Graham *See* Wayne Fontana & the Mindbenders; 10cc

Gourdine, Anthony *See* Little Anthony & the Imperials

Gower, Huw *See* The Records/Jude Cole

Goyette, Michael *See* Artificial Joy Club

Grabham, Mick *See* Procol Harum

Grable, Karl *See* The Urge

Graboff, Jon *See* The Schramms

Gracey, Chad *See* Live

Gradney, Kenny *See* Little Feat

Graffia, Ray *See* The New Colony Six

Graffin, Greg *See* Bad Religion

Graham, Bryson *See* Gary Wright/Spooky Tooth

Graham, Glen *See* Blind Melon

Graham, Larry *See* Sly & the Family Stone

Graham, Robby *See* Hoarse

Graham, Terry *See* Gun Club

Gramm, Lou *See* Foreigner

Gramolini, Joel *See* Southside Johnny & the Asbury Jukes

Grant, Bob *See* Bad Livers

Grant, Derek *See* The Suicide Machines

Grant, Jim *See* The Five Americans

Grant, Malcolm *See* The Bats

Grant, Robby *See* Big Ass Truck

Grantham, George *See* Poco

Grassel, Doug *See* The Ohio Express/Ohio Ltd.

Grasshopper *See* Mercury Rev

Gratzer, Alan *See* REO Speedwagon

Graupner, Kurt *See* Faust

Gravatt, Eric *See* Weather Report

Gravem, Dag F. *See* Euro Boys

Graves, James *See* Junior Walker & the All-Stars

Graves, Michael *See* The Misfits

Graves, Rob *See* Thelonious Monster

Gray, Andrew *See* Wolfgang Press

Gray, Chas T. *See* Wall of Voodoo/Stan Ridgway

Gray, Doug *See* The Marshall Tucker Band

Gray, Eddie *See* Tommy James & the Shondells

Gray, James *See* Blue Rodeo; Spearhead/Disposable Heroes of Hiphoprisy

Gray, Les *See* Mud

Gray, Paul *See* Eddie & the Hot Rods

Graziano, Lee *See* The American Breed

Grebb, Marty *See* The Buckinghams

Grech, Rick *See* Blind Faith; Traffic

Greco, Paul *See* Chumbawamba

Green, Bob *See* The Grassy Knoll/Bob Green

Green, Charles *See* War

Green, Dave *See* The Icicle Works

Green, Gary *See* Gentle Giant

Green, Jack *See* Pretty Things; T. Rex

Green, Jeremiah *See* Modest Mouse

Green, Johnny *See* Glitterbox

Green, Karl *See* Herman's Hermits

Green, Malcolm *See* Split Enz/Tim Finn/Alt

Green, Mick *See* Billy J. Kramer & the Dakotas

Green, Peter *See* Fleetwood Mac

Green, Ricky *See* War

Greenall, Rupert *See* The Fixx

Greenberg, Peter *See* DMZ

Greene, Al *See* Big Ass Truck

Greene, Jessy *See* Geraldine Fibbers; The Jayhawks/The Original Harmony Ridge Creek Dippers

Greene, Shauna *See* Mother Earth

Greene, Susaye *See* The Supremes

Greenfield, Dave *See* The Stranglers

Greenhalgh, Tom *See* The Mekons

Greenholz, Marnie *See* Live Skull

Greenlees, Mike *See* Tar

Greensmith, Domenic *See* Reef

Greenspoon, Jimmy *See* Three Dog Night

Greenwich, Ellie *See* The Archies

Greenwood, Al *See* Foreigner

Greenwood, Colin *See* Radiohead

Greenwood, Gail *See* Belly/Tanya Donelly

Greenwood, Jon *See* Radiohead

Greer, Billy *See* Kansas

Greer, "Gentleman" Hal *See* Big Rude Jake

Greer, Jim *See* Guided by Voices

Grefenstette, Carl M. *See* The Flashcats

Gregg, Chris *See* Negativland

Gregorian, F. *See* Enigma

Gregory, Dave *See* XTC/The Dukes of Stratosphear

Gregory, Glenn *See* Heaven 17

Gregory, Keith *See* The Wedding Present

Gregory, Mike *See* The Swinging Blue Jeans/The Bluegenes/Ray Ennis & the Blue Jeans

Gregory, Pam *See* The Cramps

Gregory, Troy *See* Flotsam & Jetsam; Prong

Gregson, Clive *See* Any Trouble; Clive Gregson & Christine Collister/Clive Gregson/Christine Collister

Greller, Al *See* The Schramms

Gremp, Ron *See* The Skeletons/The Morells

Gretsch, Barbara *See* Yum-Yum

Grey, Charles *See* The Aquabats

Grey, Paul *See* The Damned

Grey, Robbie *See* Modern English

Griego, Jack *See* For Squirrels/Subrosa

Griego, Thomas Jacob Jr. *See* For Squirrels/Subrosa

Griffin, Alex *See* Ned's Atomic Dustbin

Griffin, Bob *See* BoDeans

Griffin, Dale "Buffin" *See* Mott the Hoople

Griffin, James *See* Bread

Griffin, Kevin *See* Better Than Ezra

Griffin, Mark *See* MC 900 Ft. Jesus

Griffin, William *See* Smokey Robinson & the Miracles

Griffith, John Thomas *See* Cowboy Mouth

Griffiths, Franny *See* Space

Griffiths, Marcia *See* Bob Marley & the Wailers

Griffiths, Ron *See* Badfinger/Joey Molland

Grigg, Chris *See* Treadmill Trackstar

Griggs, Nigel *See* Split Enz/Tim Finn/Alt

Grill, Rob *See* The Grass Roots

Grilling, Charles *See* Counting Crows

Grillo, Carmen *See* Tower of Power

Grimaldi, John *See* Argent

Grimes, Steve *See* The Farm

Grimm, Matthew *See* The Hangdogs

Grissom, Sean *See* The Health & Happiness Show

Grody, Heather *See* The Murmurs

Grogan, Clare *See* Altered Images

Grohl, Dave *See* Nirvana/Foo Fighters

Grondin, Jack *See* .38 Special

Groothuizen, Chris *See* The House of Love

Grossman, Eric *See* K's Choice

Grossman, Rick *See* Divinyls; The Hoodoo Gurus

Grosvenor, Luther *See* Gary Wright/Spooky Tooth

Grotberg, Karen *See* The Jayhawks/The Original Harmony Ridge Creek Dippers

Grothman, Steve *See* Whiskeytown

Hay, Ivor *See* The Saints

Hay, Roy *See* Culture Club/Boy George

Haydock, Eric *See* The Hollies

Hayes, Chris *See* Huey Lewis & the News

Hayes, Darren *See* Savage Garden

Hayes, Pete *See* The Figgs

Haynes, Gibby *See* Butthole Surfers

Haynes, Warren *See* The Allman Brothers Band; Gov't Mule

Hayward, Justin *See* The Moody Blues/Justin Hayward & John Lodge/Mike Pinder

Hayward, Richard *See* Little Feat

Haywood, Charlie *See* Charlie Daniels Band

Hazley, James *See* Cockeyed Ghost

Head, Bryan *See* Black Lab

The Head *See* Stereo MC's

Headliner *See* Arrested Development/Speech/Dionne Farris

Headon, Nicky "Topper" *See* The Clash

Healey, Jeff *See* The Jeff Healey Band

Healy, Francis *See* Travis

Healy, Wayne *See* Freddy Jones Band

Heames, John *See* Let's Active

Hearn, Kevin *See* Barenaked Ladies

Heartsong, Dorian *See* Powerman 5000

Heath, Doug *See* Paul Revere & the Raiders/Paul Revere & the Raiders Featuring Mark Lindsay/Raiders/Pink Puzz

Heath, Jim *See* The Reverend Horton Heat

Heath, Tommy *See* Tommy Tutone

Heaton, Rob *See* New Model Army

Heckel, Dan *See* The Choir

Hedford, Eric *See* Dandy Warhols

Hedgecock, Ryan *See* Lone Justice/Maria McKee

Hedges, Eddie *See* Blessid Union of Souls

Hefe, El *See* NOFX

Heffington, Don *See* Lone Justice/Maria McKee

Heggie, Will *See* Cocteau Twins

Heidorn, Mike *See* Son Volt; Uncle Tupelo

Heimberg, Lother *See* Scorpions

Heinemann, Larry *See* Springhouse

Heitman, Dana *See* Cherry Poppin' Daddies

Hekhuis, Dave *See* The Tearaways

Hell, Richard *See* Richard Hell & the Voidoids; Television

Helliwell, John Anthony *See* Supertramp

Hellman, Nina *See* Cake Like

Helm, Levon *See* The Band

Hemingway, Dave *See* The Housemartins/The Beautiful South/Beats International

Hemmings, Courtney *See* Aswad

Hemmings, Paul *See* Cast/The La's; The Lightning Seeds

Henderson, Alan *See* Them

Henderson, Andy *See* Echobelly

Henderson, Barrington *See* The Temptations

Henderson, Dougie *See* Marmalade/Dean Ford & the Gaylords/The Gaylords/Dave Dee & Marmalade

Henderson, James *See* Black Oak Arkansas

Hendricks, Bobby *See* The Drifters

Hendrickson, Arthur *See* The Selecter

Hendry, Rob *See* Renaissance

Henley, Don *See* The Eagles

Henneman, Brian *See* The Bottle Rockets

Henner, Kyle *See* Nuisance

Hennessy, Mark *See* Paw

Henning, David *See* Big Wreck

Henrit, Bob *See* Argent; The Kinks

Henry *See* Brownsville Station/Cub Koda

Henry, Dave "Thumper" *See* Flash Cadillac/Flash Cadillac & the Continental Kids

Henry, Kent *See* Steppenwolf

Henry, Sam *See* The Wipers/Greg Sage

Hensley, Ken *See* Uriah Heep

Henssler, Barry *See* Big Chief

Herdman, Bob *See* Audio Adrenaline

Herkenburg, Kurt *See* Tangerine Dream

Herman, Bill *See* The New Colony Six

Herman, Gus *See* Bad Manners

Herman, Maureen *See* Babes in Toyland

Herman, Tom *See* Pere Ubu

Hermann, John "JoJo" *See* Widespread Panic

Hernandez, Alfredo *See* Kyuss

Hernandez, Andy "Coati Mundi" *See* Kid Creole & the Coconuts/Dr. Buzzard's Original Savannah Band

Hernandez, Bubba *See* Brave Combo

Hernandez, Johnny "Vatos" *See* Oingo Boingo/Danny Elfman

Hernandez, Sugar Coated Andy *See* Kid Creole & the Coconuts/Dr. Buzzard's Original Savannah Band

Herndon, John *See* Poster Children; Tortoise

Herr, Kurt *See* Wire Train

Herrara, R.J. *See* Suicidal Tendencies

Herrema, Jennifer *See* Royal Trux

Herren, John *See* The Electric Prunes

Herrera, David *See* The Cheepskates

Herrewig, Gary *See* Artful Dodger

Hersh, Kristin *See* Throwing Muses/Kristin Hersh

Herskell, Jeff *See* Judybats

Heseltine, Miles *See* Glitterbox

Hess, Charlie *See* The Shadows of Knight

Hester, Paul *See* Crowded House; Split Enz/Tim Finn/Alt

Heston, Greg *See* The Circle Jerks

Hetfield, James *See* Metallica

Hetson, Greg *See* Bad Religion; Redd Kross

Heukamp, Andrea *See* The House of Love

Hewitt, Steve *See* The Boo Radleys

Hexum, Nick *See* 311

Heyl, Jim *See* Savoy Brown

Heyman, Preston *See* Tom Robinson Band/Sector 27

Heyward, Nick *See* Nick Heyward/Haircut 100

Hiatt, John *See* Little Village

Hibbard, William *See* Paul Revere & the Raiders/Paul Revere & the Raiders Featuring Mark Lindsay/Raiders/Pink Puzz

Hickel, Ned Rathbone Jr. *See* Dash Rip Rock

Hickenbotham, Matt *See* Colony

Hickey, Jack *See* The Lyres

Hickey, Kenny *See* Type O Negative

Hickman, Johnny *See* Cracker/Camper Van Beethoven

Hicks, Anthony *See* The Hollies

Hicks, Bobby Lloyd *See* The Skeletons/The Morells

Hicks, Chris *See* The Outlaws

Hicks, Dan *See* The Charlatans

Hicks, Glenn *See* Antenna/Velo-Deluxe/The Mysteries of Life/John P. Strohm & the Hello Strangers

Hicks, Rod *See* Paul Butterfield Blues Band

Hidalgo, David *See* Los Lobos

Higgs, Dave *See* Eddie & the Hot Rods

Hill, Blair *See* Paul Revere & the Raiders/Paul Revere & the Raiders Featuring Mark Lindsay/Raiders/Pink Puzz

Hill, Brendan *See* Blues Traveler

Hill, Dave *See* Slade

Hill, Dusty *See* ZZ Top

Hill, Greg *See* For Against

Hill, Ian *See* Judas Priest

Hill, Jayne *See* Bran Van 3000

Hill, Joe Scott *See* Flying Burrito Brothers

Hill, John *See* Apples in Stereo

Hill, Lauryn *See* Fugees/Wyclef Jean

Hill, Roger *See* Fairport Convention/Fairport/Sandy Denny/Fotheringay

Hill, Scotti *See* Skid Row

Hill, Stuart *See* Shudder to Think

Hilland, Derek *See* Iron Butterfly

Hillary, Kenny *See* Quiet Riot

Hiller, Steve *See* Dubstar

Hillman, Bones *See* Midnight Oil

Hillman, Chris *See* The Byrds; Flying Burrito Brothers

Hils, Cliff *See* The Champs

Hinch, John *See* Judas Priest

Hinchcliffe, Dickon *See* Tindersticks

Hinds, Billy *See* Pure Prairie League

Hines, Pete *See* Handsome

Hingley, Tom *See* Inspiral Carpets

Hinkler, Simon *See* The Mission U.K.

Hinrichs, Steven "Mave" *See* For Against

Hinsche, William Ernest Joseph "Billy" *See* Dino, Desi & Billy

Hirsch, Jason *See* Chixdiggit!

Hirschfelder, David *See* Little River Band

Hirsh, Chicken *See* Country Joe & the Fish

Hirst, Rob *See* Midnight Oil

Hitchcock, Robyn *See* Robyn Hitchcock/Robyn Hitchcock & the Egyptians; The Soft Boys

Hitchcock, Russell *See* Air Supply

Hite, Bob "Bear" *See* Canned Heat

Hite, Richard *See* Canned Heat

Hitner, Hans *See* Maypole

Hitt, Bryan *See* REO Speedwagon

Hlubek, Dave *See* Molly Hatchet

Hobbs, Randy Jo *See* Rick Derringer/The McCoys; Montrose

Hobson, Andy *See* The Pretenders

Hobson, Jim *See* Love/Arthur Lee & Love/Arthur Lee & Band Aid

Hodder, Jim *See* Steely Dan

Hodge, Alex *See* The Platters

Hodgens, Robert *See* The Bluebells

Hodges, Jeff *See* Chris Duarte Group

Hodges, Warner *See* Jason & the Scorchers

Hodgkinson, Colin *See* Whitesnake

Hodgson, Roger *See* Supertramp

Hodo, David *See* The Village People

Hoefer, Danny *See* Tower of Power

Hoerner, Dan *See* Sunny Day Real Estate

Hoffman, Christian *See* aMiniature

Hoffman, Guy *See* BoDeans; Violent Femmes

Hoffman, Kristian *See* The Mumps

Hoffman, Kurt *See* Cop Shoot Cop/Firewater

Hoffman, Scott *See* .38 Special

Hoffs, Susanna *See* The Bangles/Susanna Hoffs

Hofstra, David *See* The Waitresses

Hogan, Mike *See* The Cranberries

Hogan, Noel *See* The Cranberries

Hogarth, Steve *See* Marillion/Fish

Holbrook, Mike *See* Hampton Grease Band

Holdaway, Marcus *See* High Llamas

Holden, Randy *See* Blue Cheer

Holder, Gene *See* The dB's/Peter Holsapple/Will Rigby; Yo La Tengo

Holder, Jack *See* Black Oak Arkansas

Holder, Noddy *See* Slade

Holdsworth, Allan *See* Soft Machine

Holiday, Mike "Doc" *See* Paul Revere & the Raiders/Paul Revere & the Raiders Featuring Mark Lindsay/Raiders/Pink Puzz

Holland, Annie *See* Elastica

Holland, Brian "Dexter" *See* The Offspring

Holland, Dave *See* Judas Priest

Holland, Julian "Jools" *See* Squeeze/Difford & Tilbrook/Jools Holland

Holland, Kelly *See* Cry of Love

Holland, Tony *See* Glitterbox

Hollis, Mark *See* Talk Talk

Holly, Steve *See* Paul McCartney/Wings

Holmes, Alan *See* Marmalade/Dean Ford & the Gaylords/The Gaylords/Dave Dee & Marmalade

Holmes, Billy *See* Vigilantes of Love

Holmes, Chris *See* Yum-Yum

Holmes, Malcolm *See* Orchestral Manoeuvres in the Dark

Holmes, Robert *See* 'Til Tuesday

Holmstrom, Peter *See* Dandy Warhols

Holsapple, Peter *See* The Continental Drifters; The dB's/Peter Holsapple/Will Rigby

Holt, Mike *See* Mommyheads

Holt, Stephen *See* Inspiral Carpets

Hombach, Volker *See* Tangerine Dream

Homer, Jenny *See* Downy Mildew

Homme, Josh *See* Kyuss

Honda, Yuka *See* Cibo Matto

Honeyman, Susie *See* The Mekons

Honeyman-Scott, James *See* The Pretenders

Hood, David *See* Primal Scream; Traffic

Hook, Peter *See* Joy Division; New Order

Hooke, J.C. *See* Cryan' Shames

Hoon, Shannon *See* Blind Melon

Hooper, Chris *See* The Grapes of Wrath/Ginger

Hooper, Daryl *See* The Seeds

Hooper, Nellee *See* Soul II Soul

Hooper, Tom *See* The Grapes of Wrath/Ginger

Hooper, Tony *See* The Strawbs/Dave Cousins

Hooton, Peter *See* The Farm

Hoover, Jamie *See* The Spongetones

Hope, Dave *See* Kansas

Hopkin, Ben *See* Th' Faith Healers

Hopkins, Bil *See* Firefall

Hopkins, Doug *See* Gin Blossoms; Pistoleros

Hopkins, Graham *See* Therapy?

Hopkins, Nicky *See* Quicksilver Messenger Service

Hopkins, Rich *See* The Sidewinders/The Sand Rubies

Hopkinson, Russell *See* You Am I

Hopper, Hugh *See* Soft Machine

Hopper, Linda *See* Magnapop

Hopper, Sean *See* Huey Lewis & the News

Hoppus, Mark *See* Blink 182

Hopwood, Keith *See* Herman's Hermits

Horn, Trevor *See* The Buggles; Yes

Hornsby, Vinnie *See* Sevendust

Horovitz, Adam *See* Beastie Boys

Horowitz, Ted *See* Richard Hell & the Voidoids

Horrocks, Simon *See* Freddy Jones Band

Horton, Gladys *See* The Marvelettes

Hoskins, David *See* Chavez

Hosler, Mark *See* Negativland

Hossack, Michael *See* The Doobie Brothers

Hott, Johnny *See* Cracker/Camper Van Beethoven

Hough, Greg *See* Petra

Housden, Steve *See* Little River Band

House, Kenwyn *See* Reef

Houser, Brad *See* Edie Brickell & New Bohemians

Houser, Michael *See* Widespread Panic

Houston, Penelope *See* The Avengers

Hovis, Matt *See* Cotton Mather

Howard, Alan *See* The Tremeloes/Brian Poole & the Tremeloes/Chip Hawkes' Tremeloes

Howard, Jack *See* Hunters & Collectors

Howard, Joe *See* Sky Cries Mary

Howard, Joe "Bass" *See* The Posies

Howard, Pete *See* The Clash

Howard, Phil *See* Soft Machine

Howard, Rowland S. *See* The Birthday Party

Howard, Simon *See* James Taylor Quartet

Howe, Brian *See* Bad Company

Howe, Leslie *See* Artificial Joy Club

Howe, Liam *See* Sneaker Pimps

Howe, Steve *See* Asia; Yes

Howell, Jeff *See* The Outlaws

Howland, Keith *See* Chicago/Peter Cetera

Howlett, Liam *See* Prodigy

Howlett, Mark *See* The Chantays

H.R. *See* Bad Brains

Hubbard, Preston *See* The Fabulous Thunderbirds

Hubley, Georgia *See* Yo La Tengo

Huck, Jon *See* Thelonious Monster

Hucklenut, Dewey Roy *See* Carpetbaggers

Hucknall, Mick *See* Simply Red

Hudson, Bill *See* The Hudson Brothers

Hudson, Brett *See* The Hudson Brothers

Hudson, Cary *See* Blue Mountain

Hudson, Earl *See* Bad Brains

Hudson, Garth *See* The Band

Hudson, Mark *See* The Hudson Brothers

Hudson, Randolph A. *See* Bongwater

Hudson, Richard *See* The Strawbs/Dave Cousins

Hues, Jack *See* Wang Chung

Huey *See* Fun Lovin' Criminals

Huff, Mary *See* Southern Culture on the Skids

Huff, Steven *See* The Beat/Paul Collins

Huffman, Aaron *See* Harvey Danger

Huffman, Joey *See* Drivin' N' Cryin'/Kevn Kinney/Kathleen Turner Overdrive/Toenut; Georgia Satellites/Dan Baird

Hugg, Mike *See* Manfred Mann/Manfred Mann's Earth Band

Hughes, Andy *See* The Orb

Hughes, Dave *See* Orchestral Manoeuvres in the Dark

Hughes, Glenn *See* Black Sabbath; Deep Purple; The Village People

Hughes, Jimmy *See* The Darling Buds

Hughes, Leon *See* The Coasters

Hughes, Lynne *See* The Charlatans

Hugo, Cliff *See* Supertramp

Hull, Alan *See* Lindisfarne

Hull, David "Dakota Dave" *See* Love/Arthur Lee & Love/Arthur Lee & Band Aid

Hull, Stephen *See* Railway Children

Humbert, Pascal *See* 16 Horsepower

Hummell, Andy *See* Big Star/Chris Bell

Humphrey, John *See* The Nixons

Humphreys, Paul David *See* Orchestral Manoeuvres in the Dark

Humphries, Ross *See* The Clean

Hungate, David *See* Toto

Hunt, Darryl *See* The Pogues/Shane MacGowan & the Popes

Hunt, Miles *See* The Wonder Stuff

Hunt, Tommy *See* The Flamingos

Hunter, Carl *See* The Farm

Hunter, Dave *See* Drugstore

Hunter, Faye *See* Let's Active

Hunter, Ian *See* Mott the Hoople

Hunter, Karl *See* Big Bad Voodoo Daddy/BBVD

Hunter, Kevin *See* Wire Train

Hunter, Mark *See* James

Hunter, Matt *See* Silver Jews

Huntley, George *See* The Connells

Hurding, B.P. *See* X-Ray Spex

Hurley, Steve *See* Gigolo Aunts

Hurley, George *See* fIREHOSE/Mike Watt/Banyan/Dos; Minutemen

Hurley, Phil *See* Gigolo Aunts

Husband, Gary *See* Level 42

Huseman, Brandt *See* Greenberry Woods/Splitsville

Huseman, Matt *See* Greenberry Woods/Splitsville

Husic, Anne *See* Band of Susans/Robert Poss

Hussey, Wayne *See* The Mission U.K.; Sisters of Mercy

Hutchence, Michael *See* INXS

Hutchings, Ashley "Tyger" *See* Fairport Convention/Fairport/Sandy Denny/Fotheringay

Hutchins, Rich *See* Live Skull

Hutchinson, Keith *See* Johnny Clegg & Savuka/Juluka

Hutchinson, Trevor *See* The Waterboys

Hutchison, Tad *See* Young Fresh Fellows/Scott McCaughey/The Minus Five

Huth, Todd *See* Primus/Sausage

Hutson, Kenny *See* Vigilantes of Love

Hütter, Ralf *See* Kraftwerk

Hutton, Danny *See* Three Dog Night

Huxley, Rick *See* The Dave Clark Five

Hyatt, Aitch *See* The Specials

Hyde, Karl *See* Underworld

Hyman, Jerry *See* Blood, Sweat & Tears

Hyman, Rob *See* The Hooters/Largo

Hymen, Slymenstra *See* GWAR

Hynde, Chrissie *See* The Pretenders

Hynes, Nick *See* Bran Van 3000

Hyra, Andrew *See* Billy Pilgrim

Hyslop, Kenny *See* Simple Minds

I Quit *See* Faith No More/Mr. Bungle/Imperial Teen

Ian, Scott *See* Anthrax

Ibbotson, Jimmy *See* The Nitty Gritty Dirt Band

Ibold, Mark *See* Pavement

Ibrahim, Aziz *See* Simply Red

Ice-T *See* Body Count

Idol, Billy *See* Billy Idol/Generation X

If, Owen *See* Stereo MC's

Iha, James *See* Smashing Pumpkins

Illsley, John *See* Dire Straits

Image, Joey *See* The Misfits

Imboden, Tris *See* Chicago/Peter Cetera

Immaculate, Johnny *See* Greenberry Woods/Splitsville

Indrizzo, Victor *See* Samiam

Inez, Mike *See* Alice in Chains

Infante, Frank *See* Blondie/Deborah Harry/Jimmy Destri

Ingle, Doug *See* Iron Butterfly

Ingram, Bobby *See* Molly Hatchet

Ingram, Wally *See* Timbuk 3

Ingui, Charles *See* The Soul Survivors

Ingui, Richard *See* The Soul Survivors

Innes, Andrew *See* Primal Scream

Innes, Neil *See* The Bonzo Dog Band; The Rutles

Inspektah Deck *See* Wu-Tang Clan

Intveld, James *See* The Blasters

Inu, Peter *See* Ten Foot Pole/Scared Straight

Iommi, Tony *See* Black Sabbath

Ireland, Ben *See* Sky Cries Mary

Irmler, Hans Joachim *See* Faust

Irons, Jack *See* Pearl Jam/Mother Love Bone/Green River/Temple of the Dog; Red Hot Chili Peppers

Irvin, Russell *See* The Bluebells

Irving, Billy *See* Marmalade/Dean Ford & the Gaylords/The Gaylords/Dave Dee & Marmalade

Irving, Matt *See* Squeeze/Difford & Tilbrook/Jools Holland

Irwin, Catherine *See* Freakwater

Irwin, Pat *See* Los Straitjackets/The Raybeats

Isley, Ernie *See* The Isley Brothers

Isley, Marvin *See* The Isley Brothers

Isley, O'Kelly *See* The Isley Brothers

Isley, Ronald *See* The Isley Brothers

Isley, Rudolph *See* The Isley Brothers

Israel Joseph-I *See* Bad Brains

Italiano, Tony *See* The Someloves/DM3

Ittner, Stephen *See* The Hang Ups

Ivan, John *See* Off Broadway usa

Ivins, Michael *See* The Flaming Lips

Iyall, Debora *See* Romeo Void

J, David *See* Bauhaus; Love & Rockets

J., John *See* The Feelies

J.C. 2000 *See* Rocket from the Crypt

Jabs, Matthias *See* Scorpions

Jackson, Al Jr. *See* Booker T. & the MG's

Jackman, Alan *See* The Outfield

Jackson, Bob *See* Badfinger/Joey Molland; The Fortunes

Jackson, Eddie *See* Queensryche

Jackson, Jackie *See* Jackson 5/The Jacksons

Jackson, Janet *See* Jackson 5/The Jacksons

Jackson, Jermaine *See* Jackson 5/The Jacksons

Jackson, LaToya *See* Jackson 5/The Jacksons

Jackson, Marlon *See* Jackson 5/The Jacksons

Jackson, Martin *See* Magazine

Jackson, Maureen *See* Jackson 5/The Jacksons

Jackson, Michael *See* Jackson 5/The Jacksons

Jackson, Randy *See* Jackson 5/The Jacksons

Jackson, Ray *See* Lindisfarne

Jackson, Roger *See* Robyn Hitchcock/Robyn Hitchcock & the Egyptians

Jackson, Ronald Shannon *See* Last Exit

Jackson, Stevie *See* Belle & Sebastian

Jackson, Tito *See* Jackson 5/The Jacksons

Jackson, Tony *See* The Searchers

Jacobs, Christian *See* The Aquabats

Johnson, Matt *See* 54.40; The The

Johnson, Michael "Stonewall" *See* Big Rude Jake

Johnson, Mike *See* Dinosaur Jr./J Mascis; The Tokens/The Tokens Featuring Mitch Margo/The Four Winds/The Buddies/The Coeds/Cross Country

Johnson, Nate *See* Flop

Johnson, Robert *See* KC & the Sunshine Band

Johnson, Scott *See* Gin Blossoms

Johnson, Terry *See* The Flamingos

Johnson, Wilco *See* Ian Dury/Ian Dury & the Blockheads

Johnson, William "Holly" *See* Frankie Goes to Hollywood

Johnston, Brian *See* Whitesnake

Johnston, Bruce *See* The Beach Boys

Johnston, Chris *See* Nineteen Wheels

Johnston, James *See* Gallon Drunk

Johnston, Max *See* Freakwater; Uncle Tupelo; Wilco

Johnston, Sara *See* Bran Van 3000

Johnston, Tom *See* The Doobie Brothers

Jollieffe, Steve *See* Tangerine Dream

Joncknee, Richard 23 *See* Front 242

Jone *See* Faith No More/Mr. Bungle/Imperial Teen

Jones, Adam *See* Tool/The Replicants

Jones, Anthony *See* Humble Pie

Jones, Billy *See* The Outlaws

Jones, Booker T. *See* Booker T. & the MG's

Jones, Brian *See* Agents of Good Roots; The Rolling Stones

Jones, Busta "Cherry" *See* Gang of Four/Shriekback

Jones, Chris *See* Mega City Four

Jones, Daniel *See* Savage Garden

Jones, Daryl *See* The Rolling Stones

Jones, David "Davy" *See* The Monkees

Jones, Graham *See* Nick Heyward/Haircut 100

Jones, Jim *See* Pere Ubu

Jones, John *See* The Oyster Band

Jones, John Paul *See* Led Zeppelin

Jones, Kendall Rey *See* Fishbone

Jones, Kenney *See* The Faces/The Small Faces; The Who

Jones, Martyn *See* The Mermen

Jones, Mick *See* Big Audio Dynamite/B.A.D. II/Big Audio; The Clash; Foreigner; Gary Wright/Spooky Tooth

Jones, Mickey *See* Angel

Jones, Mike *See* Voice of the Beehive

Jones, Norman *See* The English Beat/General Public

Jones, Paul *See* Catatonia; Manfred Mann/Manfred Mann's Earth Band

Jones, Randy *See* The Village People

Jones, Raymond *See* Billy J. Kramer & the Dakotas

Jones, Rob *See* The Wonder Stuff

Jones, Ronald *See* The Flaming Lips

Jones, Royce *See* Ambrosia

Jones, Rusty *See* The Scene Is Now

Jones, Sandra "Puma" *See* Black Uhuru

Jones, Simon *See* The Verve

Jones, Stacy *See* Veruca Salt

Jones, Steve *See* The Sex Pistols

Jones, Vincent *See* The Grapes of Wrath/Ginger

Jones, Will "Dub" *See* The Coasters

Jordan, Cyril *See* The Flamin' Groovies

Jordan, John *See* Chris Duarte Group

Jordan, Ken *See* The Crystal Method

Jordan, Lonnie *See* War

Jorgenson, John *See* The Hellecasters

Joseph, Greg *See* The Clarks

Joseph, Paul *See* The Blue Nile

Josephsberg, Mark *See* Kid Creole & the Coconuts/Dr. Buzzard's Original Savannah Band

Jost, Jerry *See* The Urge

Jourard, Jeff *See* The Motels

Jourard, Marty *See* The Motels

Jourgensen, Al *See* Ministry

Joyce, Chris *See* Simply Red

Joyce, Don *See* Negativland

Joyce, Mike *See* The Smiths

Juano *See* Sky Cries Mary

Juber, Laurence *See* Paul McCartney/Wings

Judd, Phil *See* Split Enz/Tim Finn/Alt

Judy, Eric *See* Modest Mouse

Jugg, Roman *See* The Damned

Jughead, Johnny *See* Screeching Weasel

Julan, Dag *See* Poi Dog Pondering

Julian, Ivan *See* The Health & Happiness Show; Richard Hell & the Voidoids

Junstrom, Larry *See* .38 Special

Jurgensen, Jens *See* Boss Hog

Justman, Seth *See* J. Geils Band/Bluestime

Justo, Rodney *See* The Atlanta Rhythm Section/ARS

Jym *See* The Mr. T Experience

K., Eshan *See* Bow Wow Wow

Kaballero, Karlos *See* The Dickies

Kagan, Harvey *See* Doug Sahm/Sir Douglas Quintet

Kahr, R. *See* Rank & File

Kakoulli, Harry *See* Squeeze/Difford & Tilbrook/Jools Holland

Kakulas, Phil *See* The Triffids

Kalb, Danny *See* Blues Project

Kale, Jim *See* The Guess Who

Kalicki, Jan *See* The Bolshoi

Kalsi, Johnny *See* Transglobal Underground

Kalwa, Eddie *See* The Rain Parade

Kaminsky, Mik *See* Electric Light Orchestra/Jeff Lynne/ELO II

Kanal, Tony *See* No Doubt

Kane, Arthur *See* The New York Dolls/Johnny Thunders

Kane, Chris *See* Bad Manners

Kane, Howie *See* Jay & the Americans

Kane, Kevin *See* The Grapes of Wrath/Ginger

Kane, King *See* G. Love & Special Sauce

Kantner, Paul *See* Jefferson Airplane; Jefferson Starship/Starship

Kantoff, Howie *See* Poster Children

Kerley, Lenny *See* Cryan' Shames

Kerns, Kurt *See* Gravity Kills

Kerr, Greg *See* The Verlaines

Kerr, Jim *See* Simple Minds

Kerr, Stuart *See* Texas

Kerslake, Lee *See* Uriah Heep

Kessler, Dave *See* moe.

Kesterson, Kim *See* Love/Arthur Lee & Love/Arthur Lee & Band Aid

Kettley, Baz *See* The Charlatans UK

Key, Alan *See* Status Quo

Key, cEVIN *See* Skinny Puppy

Key, Ted *See* The Housemartins/The Beautiful South/Beats International

Keyser, Alex *See* Echobelly

Kezdy, John *See* Effigies

Kezdy, Pierre *See* Naked Raygun

Khalsa, Giti *See* Seven Mary Three

Khan, Steve *See* The Chantays

Khichi, Shal *See* The Bouncing Souls

Khoroshev, Igor "Ivan" *See* Yes

Kibby, Walter Adam *See* Fishbone

Kick, Johnny *See* Madder Rose

Kickassis, Jackie *See* The Upper Crust

Kiedis, Anthony *See* Red Hot Chili Peppers

Kiely, Kevin *See* The Mumps

Kienlen, Bryan "Papillon" *See* The Bouncing Souls

Kilbey, Steven *See* The Church

Kilburn, Duncan *See* The Psychedelic Furs/Richard Butler/Love Spit Love

Kilgour, David *See* The Clean

Kilgour, Hamish *See* Bailter Space; The Clean

Kilkenny, Giorgio *See* Dexy's Midnight Runners/Kevin Rowland & Dexy's Midnight Runners

Killdare, Kitty *See* My Life with the Thrill Kill Kult/The Bomb Gang Girlz

Kilmister, Lemmy *See* Motörhead

Kim, Andy *See* The Archies

Kimball, Bobby *See* Toto

Kimball, Jennifer *See* Jonatha Brooke/Jonatha Brooke & the Story

Kimball, Jim *See* Cop Shoot Cop/Firewater; DK3/Denison/Kimball Trio; The Jesus Lizard; Laughing Hyenas

Kimble, Paul *See* Grant Lee Buffalo

Kincaid, Mark *See* The Electric Prunes

Kinchla, Chan *See* Blues Traveler

King, Ben E. *See* The Drifters

King, Billy *See* Sid King & the Five Strings

King, Ed *See* Lynyrd Skynyrd; The Strawberry Alarm Clock

King, Joe *See* The Queers

King, Jon *See* Gang of Four/Shriekback

King, Kerry *See* Slayer

King, Kim *See* Lothar & the Hand People

King, Mark *See* Level 42

King, Philip *See* Lush

King, Sid *See* Sid King & the Five Strings

King, Stu Boy *See* The Dictators

King, Tom *See* The Outsiders

Kingsmill, Mark *See* The Hoodoo Gurus

Kinman, Chip *See* Rank & File

Kinman, Tony *See* Rank & File

Kinney, Kevn *See* Drivin' N' Cryin'/Kevn Kinney/Kathleen Turner Overdrive/Toenut

Kinney, Sean *See* Alice in Chains

Kirby, Lady Miss Kier *See* Deee-Lite

Kirchen, Bill *See* Commander Cody & His Lost Planet Airmen

Kircher, Pete *See* Status Quo

Kirk, Richard H. *See* Cabaret Voltaire

Kirke, Simon *See* Bad Company; Free

Kirkham, Ian *See* Simply Red

Kirkland, Mike *See* Prong

Kirkland, Scott *See* The Crystal Method

Kirkman, Terry *See* The Association

Kirkwood, Cris *See* Meat Puppets

Kirkwood, Curt *See* Meat Puppets

Kirsch, John *See* Super Deluxe

Kirtley, Peter *See* Pentangle

Kirts, Michael *See* Yum-Yum

Kirwan, Danny *See* Fleetwood Mac

Kirwan, Larry *See* Black 47

Kisser, Andreas *See* Sepultura

K.K. *See* Thelonious Monster

Klaus, Ron *See* The Embarrassment

Klawon, Dann *See* The Choir

Klawon, Randy *See* The Choir

Klayman, Dan *See* The Waitresses

Klebe, Gary *See* Shoes

Klein, Danny *See* J. Geils Band/Bluestime

Klein, Jon *See* Siouxsie & the Banshees

Kleingers, Don *See* Ass Ponys

Kleinow, "Sneaky" Pete *See* Flying Burrito Brothers

Klett, Peter *See* Candlebox

Kletter, Dana *See* blackgirls/Dish

Klingman, Mark "Moogy" *See* Todd Rundgren/Utopia

Klopfenstein, Scott *See* Vigilantes of Love

Knechtel, Larry *See* Bread

Knight, Graham *See* Marmalade/Dean Ford & the Gaylords/The Gaylords/Dave Dee & Marmalade

Knight, Jon *See* New Kids on the Block

Knight, Jordan *See* New Kids on the Block

Knight, Larry *See* Spirit

Knight, Stanley *See* Black Oak Arkansas

Knight, Steve *See* Mountain

Knight, Warren "Butch" *See* Flash Cadillac/Flash Cadillac & the Continental Kids

Knights, Dave *See* Procol Harum

Knopfler, David *See* Dire Straits

Knopfler, Mark *See* Dire Straits

Knox *See* The Vibrators

Knox, Nick *See* The Cramps

Knudsen, Keith *See* The Doobie Brothers

Koda, Cub *See* Brownsville Station/Cub Koda

Kogel, Michael *See* Los Bravos

Koller, Lou *See* Sick of It All

Koller, Pete *See* Sick of It All

Konietzko, Sascha *See* KMFDM

Konishi, Yasuharu *See* Pizzicato Five

Konte, Skip *See* Three Dog Night

Kooper, Al *See* Blood, Sweat & Tears; Blues Project

Kootch, Dan *See* The Fugs

Kooymans, George *See* Golden Earring

Koppes, Peter *See* The Church

Korpi, Mark *See* Evan Johns & His H-Bombs

Korth, Dean *See* 20/20

Korus, Kate *See* The Slits

Kossoff, Paul *See* Free

Koster, Julian *See* Neutral Milk Hotel

Kottak, James *See* Warrant

Kotzen, Richie *See* Poison

Kouha, Andrew *See* Sam the Sham & the Pharaohs/Sam the Sham Revue

Koupal, Dave *See* The Wipers/Greg Sage

Koutsky, Roy *See* L7

Koutsos, Anthony *See* Red House Painters

Kowalczyk, Ed *See* Live

Kowalski, Ted *See* The Diamonds

Kozelek, Mark *See* Red House Painters

Kral, Ivan *See* Sky Cries Mary; Patti Smith/Patti Smith Group

Kramer, Billy J. *See* Billy J. Kramer & the Dakotas

Kramer, Joey *See* Aerosmith

Kramer, Mark *See* Bongwater

Kramer, Mike "Animal" *See* Anti-Nowhere League

Kramer, Phil *See* Iron Butterfly

Kramer, Wayne *See* MC5

Krassenburg, Frans *See* Golden Earring

Krause, Danny *See* Paul Revere & the Raiders/Paul Revere & the Raiders Featuring Mark Lindsay/Raiders/Pink Puzz

Krauss, Scott *See* Pere Ubu

Krauth, Phil *See* Unrest

Kravat, Amanda *See* Marry Me Jane

Krawinkel, Kralle *See* Trio

Krebs, Pete *See* Hazel

Kresge, Geoff *See* A.F.I./Asking for It

Kretmar, Don *See* Blues Project

Kretschmer, Robert *See* Icehouse

Kretz, Eric *See* Stone Temple Pilots/Talk Show/Scott Weiland

Kreutzmann, Bill *See* The Grateful Dead

Krieger, Klaus *See* Tangerine Dream

Kriesel, Greg *See* The Offspring

Krizan, Anthony *See* Spin Doctors

Krukowski, Damon *See* Galaxie 500

Krummenacher, Victor *See* Cracker/Camper Van Beethoven

Krusen, Dave *See* Candlebox; Pearl Jam/Mother Love Bone/Green River/Temple of the Dog

Kubiszewski, Andy *See* Stabbing Westward

Kuepper, Ed *See* The Saints

Kuhl, J.C. *See* Agents of Good Roots

Kuhlke, Norman *See* The Swinging Blue Jeans/The Bluegenes/Ray Ennis & the Blue Jeans

Kulberg, Andy *See* Blues Project

Kulnick, Bruce *See* Kiss

Kulwicki, Richard *See* The Fluid

Kummel, Les *See* The New Colony Six

Kunkel, Bruce *See* The Nitty Gritty Dirt Band

Kunkel, Roger *See* Thin White Rope

Kupferberg, Tuli *See* The Fugs

Kupka, Steve *See* Tower of Power

Kurdziel, Eddie *See* Redd Kross

Kurth, Rob *See* Face to Face

Kustow, Danny *See* Tom Robinson Band/Sector 27

Kwaku Baah, Reebop *See* Traffic

Kwesi *See* Arrested Development/Speech/Dionne Farris

Kwiatkowski, Matt *See* The Urge

Kyser, Guy *See* Thin White Rope

La Camilla *See* Army of Lovers

Labat, M. Frog *See* Todd Rundgren/Utopia

LaBonne, Allison *See* The Legendary Jim Ruiz Group

LaBonne, Charlotte *See* The Legendary Jim Ruiz Group

LaBrie, James *See* Dream Theater

Labrum, Jerry *See* Paul Revere & the Raiders/Paul Revere & the Raiders Featuring Mark Lindsay/Raiders/Pink Puzz

LaBruyere, David *See* Vigilantes of Love

Lack, Stephen L. *See* Veruca Salt

LaCroix, Jerry *See* Blood, Sweat & Tears; Rare Earth

Ladd, Rob *See* The Continental Drifters

Lady Galore *See* Lords of Acid

Laff, Mark *See* Billy Idol/Generation X

Lagerberg, Bengt *See* The Cardigans

Lahr, Roger *See* Ugly Kid Joe

Laidlaw, Roy *See* Lindisfarne

Laine, Denny *See* The Moody Blues/Justin Hayward & John Lodge/Mike Pinder

Laing, Corky *See* Mountain

Laird-Clowes, Nick *See* The Dream Academy

Lake, Greg *See* Asia; Emerson, Lake & Palmer/Emerson, Lake & Powell; King Crimson

LaKind, Bobby *See* The Doobie Brothers

Lally, Joe *See* Fugazi

LaLonde, Larry *See* Primus/Sausage

Lamarche, Andrew *See* Artificial Joy Club

Lamb, Lisa *See* Peach Union

Lambert, Ben *See* Carter the Unstoppable Sex Machine

Lambert, Dave *See* The Strawbs/Dave Cousins

Lambert, Graham *See* Inspiral Carpets

Lambert, Neill *See* XC-NN

Lamble, Martin *See* Fairport Convention/Fairpolt/Sandy Denny/Fotheringay

Lamkins, Tripp *See* The Grifters

Lamm, Robert *See* Chicago/Peter Cetera

Lancaster, Alan *See* Status Quo

Landon, Mark *See* Music Machine/Bonniwell Music Machine/Friendly Torpedoes

Lane, Anita *See* Einstürzende Neubauten

Lane, Gary *See* The Standells

Lane, Jani *See* Warrant

Lane, Ronnie *See* The Faces/The Small Faces

Lunsford, Bret *See* Beat Happening

Lupus *See* The Bloodhound Gang

Lurie, Ben *See* The Jesus & Mary Chain

Lurie, Evan *See* The Lounge Lizards

Lurie, John *See* The Lounge Lizards

Lussenden, Bill *See* Blues Project

Lutton, Davy *See* T. Rex

Luttrell, Terry *See* REO Speedwagon

Lutz, Michael *See* Brownsville Station/Cub Koda

Lux Interior *See* The Cramps

Lwin, Annabella *See* Bow Wow Wow

Lyall, Susan *See* Band of Susans/Robert Poss

Lycett, Kevin *See* The Mekons

Lydon, John *See* Public Image Ltd./PiL/John Lydon

Lymon, Frankie *See* Frankie Lymon & the Teenagers

Lynch, David *See* The Platters

Lynch, Dermot *See* Dog's Eye View

Lynch, George *See* Dokken

Lynch, Stan *See* Tom Petty & the Heartbreakers; Rank & File

Lynch, Tim *See* The Flamin' Groovies

Lynes, Roy *See* Status Quo

Lyngstad, Anni-Frid "Frida" *See* ABBA

Lynn *See* Faith No More/Mr. Bungle/Imperial Teen

Lynn, Roger *See* Dwight Twilley/Dwight Twilley Band/Phil Seymour

Lynne, Jeff *See* Electric Light Orchestra/Jeff Lynne/ELO II; The Move/Roy Wood; The Traveling Wilburys

Lynott, Phil *See* Thin Lizzy

Lynton, Jackie *See* Savoy Brown

Lyons, Guy *See* The Figgs

Lyons, Jamie *See* Music Explosion

Lyons, Ken *See* .38 Special

Lyons, Leo *See* Ten Years After

Lyons, Richard *See* Negativland

Lyons, Toby *See* The Colourfield

Maby, Graham *See* The Health & Happiness Show; They Might Be Giants

Macaulay, Al *See* Tindersticks

MacBeth, Peter *See* The Foundations

MacDonald, Barbara Kooyman *See* Timbuk 3

MacDonald, Pat *See* Timbuk 3

MacDonald, Robin *See* Billy J. Kramer & the Dakotas

Macfarlane, Lora *See* Sleater-Kinney

MacGowan, Shane *See* The Pogues/Shane MacGowan & the Popes

Macgregor, Trevor *See* Treble Charger

MacGregor, Craig *See* Foghat

Mache, Robert *See* The Continental Drifters

Mack, Gordon *See* Red House Painters

Mack, Keith *See* Patty Smyth/Scandal

Mack, Steve *See* That Petrol Emotion

Mackay, Andy *See* Roxy Music

MacKaye, Ian *See* Fugazi; Minor Threat

Macken, Niall *See* The Devlins

MacKendrick, Keith *See* The Champs

Mackenzie, Billy *See* The Associates/Associates

Mackey, Steve *See* Pulp

MacLean, Bryan *See* Love/Arthur Lee & Love/Arthur Lee & Band Aid

MacLeod, Brian *See* Dramarama; Wire Train

MacMaster, Daniel *See* Bonham/Jason Bonham Band/Motherland

MacMillan, Doug *See* The Connells

MacNichol, Jeep *See* The Samples

MacNicol, Alex *See* Green on Red

Macomber, Al *See* Savoy Brown

Macpherson, James *See* The Breeders/The Amps

Macrae, Dave *See* Soft Machine

MacRae, Shel *See* The Fortunes

Madaio, Steve *See* Paul Butterfield Blues Band

Madan, Sonya Aurora *See* Echobelly

Madden, Mickey *See* Kara's Flowers

Madey, Bryan *See* Stories

Madondo, Scorpion *See* Johnny Clegg & Savuka/Juluka

Madsen, Merdin *See* The Outsiders

Mael, Ron *See* Sparks

Mael, Russell *See* Sparks

Maffei, Frank *See* Danny & the Juniors/Danny & the Juniors Featuring Joe Terry

Maggs, Dave *See* The Troggs

Magic Dick *See* J. Geils Band/Bluestime

Maginnis, Tom *See* Buffalo Tom

Magnie, John *See* The subdudes

Magnus, Jeff *See* Dead Boys/Stiv Bators/Lords of the New Church

Magnuson, Ann *See* Bongwater

Magnuson, John *See* Carpetbaggers

Magoo *See* Anti-Nowhere League

Maguire, Barrie *See* The Wallflowers

Maguire, Les *See* Gerry & the Pacemakers

Maher, Fred *See* Richard Hell & the Voidoids; Scritti Politti

Maher, George *See* The Farm

Maher, John *See* Buzzcocks

Mahoney, Timothy J. *See* 311

Maida, Raine *See* Our Lady Peace

Maida, Sal *See* Roxy Music

Maiella, Jim *See* The Cyrkle

Mailhouse, Rob *See* Dogstar

Maimone, Tony *See* Pere Ubu; The Scene Is Now; They Might Be Giants

Maines, Dan *See* Clutch

Mair, Alan *See* The Only Ones

Maitland, Adam *See* The Only Ones

Majewski, Hank *See* The Four Seasons/Frankie Valli

Majidi, Armand *See* Sick of It All

Major, Ray *See* Mott the Hoople

Male, Jonny *See* Republica

Malik, Chaka *See* Orange 9mm

Malin, Jesse *See* D Generation

Malinin, Mike *See* Goo Goo Dolls

Malkmus, Steve *See* Pavement; Silver Jews

Malley, Matt *See* Counting Crows

Mallinder, Stephen *See* Cabaret Voltaire

Mallon, Tim *See* Mark Eitzel/American Music Club

Mallonee, Bill *See* Vigilantes of Love

Malone, Tom *See* Blood, Sweat & Tears

Malone, Tommy *See* The subdudes

Maloy, Zac *See* The Nixons

Mandel, Harvey *See* Canned Heat

Mandelson, Ben *See* Magazine

Manfrin, Chris *See* Seam

Manganelli, Roger *See* Less Than Jake

Mangrum, Jim (Dandy) *See* Black Oak Arkansas

Mangum, Hugh *See* Maypole

Mangum, Jeff *See* Neutral Milk Hotel

Maninger, Hank *See* The Aqua Velvets

Manion, Eddie *See* Southside Johnny & the Asbury Jukes

Manitoba, Handsome Dick *See* The Dictators

Mankey, Jim *See* Concrete Blonde

Manley, Colin *See* The Swinging Blue Jeans/The Bluegenes/Ray Ennis & the Blue Jeans

Mann, Aimee *See* 'Til Tuesday

Mann, David *See* Tower of Power

Mann, Groovie *See* My Life with the Thrill Kill Kult/The Bomb Gang Girlz

Mann, Manfred *See* Manfred Mann/Manfred Mann's Earth Band

Manning, Barbara *See* S.F. Seals

Manning, Chris *See* Jellyfish

Manning, Roger *See* Jellyfish

Mannings, Leo *See* Savoy Brown

Manny *See* The Misfits

Manresa, Mick "Flash" *See* Flash Cadillac/Flash Cadillac & the Continental Kids

Mansell, Clint *See* Pop Will Eat Itself

Mansfield, Tony *See* Billy J. Kramer & the Dakotas

Manshel, Stephen Thomas *See* Firefall

Manson, Marilyn *See* Marilyn Manson

Manson, Shirley *See* Garbage

Mantu, Hamid *See* Transglobal Underground

Manuel, Richard *See* The Band

Many, Trey *See* His Name Is Alive/Liquorice

Manzanera, Phil *See* Roxy Music

Manzarek, Ray *See* The Doors

Maralie *See* The Skeletons/The Morells

Marasse, Mike *See* Downy Mildew

March, Kevin *See* The Dambuilders

March, Richard *See* Pop Will Eat Itself

Marchini, John *See* That Petrol Emotion

Marcum, Mark *See* The Rain Parade

Marcus, Scott *See* Kathy McCarty/Glass Eye

Margaret *See* Björk/Sugarcubes

Margo, Damien *See* The Tokens/The Tokens Featuring Mitch Margo/The Four Winds/The Buddies/The Coeds/Cross Country

Margo, Mitch *See* The Tokens/The Tokens Featuring Mitch Margo/The Four Winds/The Buddies/The Coeds/Cross Country

Margo, Noah *See* The Tokens/The Tokens Featuring Mitch Margo/The Four Winds/The Buddies/The Coeds/Cross Country

Margo, Phil *See* The Tokens/The Tokens Featuring Mitch Margo/The Four Winds/The Buddies/The Coeds/Cross Country

Margolis, Kenny *See* The Choir

Marhevka, Glen "The Kid" *See* Big Bad Voodoo Daddy/BBVD

Mariani, Dom *See* The Someloves/DM3

Mariano, Mickey *See* The Three O'Clock

Marimba, Ed *See* Captain Beefheart & His Magic Band

Marini, Lou Jr. *See* Blood, Sweat & Tears

Marinos, Jimmy *See* The Romantics

Mark, Jon *See* The Mark-Almond Band

Markes, Steve *See* Garbage

Marks, David *See* The Beach Boys

Marks, Grace *See* Sukia

Marks, Toby *See* Banco De Gaia

Marley, Cedella *See* Ziggy Marley & the Melody Makers

Marley, David "Ziggy" *See* Ziggy Marley & the Melody Makers

Marley, Rita *See* Bob Marley & the Wailers

Marley, Robert Nesta *See* Bob Marley & the Wailers

Marley, Stephen *See* Ziggy Marley & the Melody Makers

The Marquis de Roque, *See* The Upper Crust

Marr, Johnny *See* Electronic; The Smiths

Marrella, John *See* The Lovin' Spoonful/John Sebastian

Marriott, Steve *See* The Faces/The Small Faces; Humble Pie

Mars, Chris *See* Golden Smog; The Replacements/Paul Westerberg

Mars, Mick *See* Mötley Crüe/Vince Neil

Marsden, Bernie *See* Whitesnake

Marsden, Freddie *See* Gerry & the Pacemakers

Marsden, Gerry *See* Gerry & the Pacemakers

Marsh, Carl *See* Gang of Four/Shriekback

Marsh, Ian Craig *See* Heaven 17; Human League

Marsh, Paul *See* Mighty Lemon Drops

Marshack, Rose *See* Poster Children

Marshall, Brian *See* Creed

Marshall, Chan *See* Cat Power

Marshall, Eric *See* Let's Active

Marshall, John *See* Soft Machine

Marshall, Maurice "Mo" *See* The Champs

Marshall, Paul *See* The Strawberry Alarm Clock

Marshall, Rob *See* The Chantays

Marsland, Adam *See* Cockeyed Ghost

Marson, Andrew *See* Bad Manners

Martell, Vince *See* Vanilla Fudge

Martin, Barbara *See* The Supremes

Martin, Bardi *See* Candlebox

Martin, Barrett *See* R.E.M.; Screaming Trees

Martin, Billy *See* The Lounge Lizards; Medeski, Martin & Wood

Martin, Chris *See* Jon Butcher Axis

Martin, David *See* Sam the Sham & the Pharaohs/Sam the Sham Revue

Martin, Dean Paul Jr. "Dino" *See* Dino, Desi & Billy

Martin, Dewey *See* Buffalo Springfield

Martin, Eric *See* Mr. Big

Martin, Jeff *See* Badlands; Idaho; The Tea Party

Martin, Jim *See* Faith No More/Mr. Bungle/Imperial Teen

Martin, Kevin *See* Candlebox

Martin, Orestes *See* Bitch Magnet

Martin, Paul *See* Love/Arthur Lee & Love/Arthur Lee & Band Aid

Martin, Rosie *See* Treble Charger

Martin, Sarah *See* Belle & Sebastian

Martin, Steve *See* The Left Banke

Martin, Tony *See* Black Sabbath

Martinez, Anthony *See* Black Flag/Greg Ginn

Martinez, Antonio *See* Los Bravos

Martinez, Christina *See* Boss Hog

Martinez, Cliff *See* Red Hot Chili Peppers; The Weirdos

Martinez, Doug "S.A." *See* 311

Martinez, Gonzalo *See* Lincoln

Martinez, Marci *See* Team Dresch

Martinez, Omar *See* Paul Revere & the Raiders/Paul Revere & the Raiders Featuring Mark Lindsay/Raiders/Pink Puzz

Martinez, Robert *See* ? and the Mysterians

Martini, Jerry *See* Sly & the Family Stone

Martini, Sleazy P. *See* GWAR

Martsch, Doug *See* Built to Spill

Marty, Mike *See* Thelonious Monster

Marvin, Julian "Junior" *See* Bob Marley & the Wailers

Marx, Gary *See* Sisters of Mercy

Masciarelli, Scott *See* Chavez

Mascis, J *See* Dinosaur Jr./J Mascis

Mashburn, Brian *See* Save Ferris

Masino, John "Ricco" *See* Flash Cadillac/Flash Cadillac & the Continental Kids

Maskell, Albie "Slider" *See* Sham 69

Maslen, Peter *See* Boom Crash Opera

Mason, Bob *See* The Fugs

Mason, Dave *See* Fleetwood Mac; Traffic

Mason, Davy *See* Mighty Joe Plum

Mason, Nick *See* Pink Floyd

Mason, Robert *See* Cry of Love

Mason, Steve *See* Gene; Jars of Clay

Mason, Ted *See* Modern English

Massey, Graham *See* 808 State

Massey, Ken *See* Sid King & the Five Strings

Massi, Nick *See* The Four Seasons/Frankie Valli

Masta Killa *See* Wu-Tang Clan

Mastelotto, Pat *See* King Crimson; Mr. Mister

Masters, Barrie *See* Eddie & the Hot Rods

Masters, Ian *See* Pale Saints

Mastriani, Vic *See* The Nitty Gritty Dirt Band

Mastro, James *See* The Health & Happiness Show

Masunaga, Eric *See* The Dambuilders

Mather, Darryl *See* The Someloves/DM3

Matheson, David *See* Moxy Früvous

Mathews, Donna *See* Elastica

Mathus, James *See* Squirrel Nut Zippers/Jas. Mathus & His Knock-Down Society

Matlock, Glen *See* The Sex Pistols

Matson, Alex *See* The Samples

Mattacks, Dave *See* Fairport Convention/Fairport/Sandy Denny/Fotheringay; Jethro Tull/Ian Anderson

Matthews, Cerys *See* Catatonia

Matthews, Chris *See* Shudder to Think

Matthews, Dave *See* Dave Matthews Band

Matthews, Herman *See* Tower of Power

Matthews, Iain *See* Fairport Convention/Fairport/Sandy Denny/Fotheringay

Mattix, Otto *See* My Life with the Thrill Kill Kult/The Bomb Gang Girlz

Mattock, John *See* Spacemen 3; Spiritualized

Maudsley, Frank *See* A Flock of Seagulls

Maugeri, Rudi *See* The Crew Cuts

Maugh, Bugsy *See* Paul Butterfield Blues Band

Maurer, John *See* Social Distortion

Maurice, Brian *See* Dexy's Midnight Runners/Kevin Rowland & Dexy's Midnight Runners

Mauro, Frank *See* Richard Hell & the Voidoids

Maus, John *See* The Walker Brothers/Scott Walker

Mavers, Lee *See* Cast/The La's

Mavers, Neil *See* Cast/The La's

Mavuso, Steve *See* Johnny Clegg & Savuka/Juluka

Maxfield, Mike *See* Billy J. Kramer & the Dakotas

Maximus, Flattus *See* GWAR

Maxwell, Aaron *See* God Street Wine

Maxwell, Tom *See* Squirrel Nut Zippers/Jas. Mathus & His Knock-Down Society

Maxwell, Tony *See* that dog.

May, Arni *See* Pell Mell

May, Brian *See* Queen

May, Phil *See* Pretty Things

Mayell, Norman *See* Blue Cheer

Mayer, Andrew *See* Blake Babies

Mayhew, John *See* Genesis

Mayorga, Louiche *See* Suicidal Tendencies

Mazorati, Tim *See* Nineteen Wheels

Mazur, Chris *See* moe.

Mazur, George *See* The Godfathers

Mazzarella, Michael *See* The Rooks

Mazzola, Joey *See* Sponge

MC Dynamite *See* Roni Size/Reprazent

MC Wildski *See* The Housemartins/The Beautiful South/Beats International

McAlinden, Joe *See* The BMX Bandits

McAllister, George *See* The Fortunes

McAloon, Martin *See* Prefab Sprout

McAloon, Paddy *See* Prefab Sprout

McArdale, George *See* Little River Band

McArdle, Willie *See* The BMX Bandits

McArthur, Keith *See* Spearhead/Disposable Heroes of Hiphoprisy

McBrain, Nicko *See* Iron Maiden/Bruce Dickinson

McBride, Bob *See* The Choir

McBride, Michael *See* The Raspberries

McBride, Pat *See* The New Colony Six

McBride, Roger *See* Rare Earth

McCabe, Nick *See* The Verve

McCabe, Zia *See* Dandy Warhols

McCafferty, Dan *See* Nazareth

McCain, Edwin *See* Edwin McCain Band

McCarl, Scott *See* The Raspberries

McCarrick, Martin *See* Siouxsie & the Banshees; Therapy?

McCarroll, Tony *See* Oasis

McCarthy, Allan *See* Men Without Hats

McCarthy, Doug *See* Nitzer Ebb

McCartney, Linda *See* Paul McCartney/Wings

McCartney, Paul *See* The Beatles; Paul McCartney/Wings

McCarty, Jim *See* Renaissance; The Yardbirds

McCarty, Kathy *See* Kathy McCarty/Glass Eye

McCaughan, Mac *See* Seam; Superchunk

McCaughey, Scott *See* Young Fresh Fellows/Scott McCaughey/The Minus Five

McCloud, Scott *See* Girls Against Boys

McClure, Andy *See* Sleeper

McClure, Ron *See* Blood, Sweat & Tears

McCluskey, Andy *See* Orchestral Manoeuvres in the Dark

McCluskey, David *See* The Bluebells

McCluskey, Kenneth *See* The Bluebells

McCollum, Rick *See* The Afghan Whigs

McComb, David *See* The Triffids

McComb, Robert *See* The Triffids

McCombs, Douglas *See* Eleventh Dream Day; Tortoise

McCook, Jack *See* Superchunk

McCorkle, George *See* The Marshall Tucker Band

McCormack, Danny *See* The Lyres

McCormack, Phil *See* Molly Hatchet

McCormick, Herman *See* Love/Arthur Lee & Love/Arthur Lee & Band Aid

McCoy, Andy *See* Hanoi Rocks/Michael Monroe

McCoy, Buzz *See* My Life with the Thrill Kill Kult/The Bomb Gang Girlz

McCoy, Kevin *See* Sky Cries Mary

McCoy, Nancy *See* Downy Mildew

McCoy, Noel *See* James Taylor Quartet

McCracken, Chet *See* The Doobie Brothers

McCrea, John *See* Cake

McCready, Mike *See* Pearl Jam/Mother Love Bone/Green River/Temple of the Dog

McCulloch, Ian *See* Echo & the Bunnymen/Electrafixion

McCulloch, Jim *See* The BMX Bandits; The Soup Dragons

McCulloch, Jimmy *See* The Faces/The Small Faces; Paul McCartney/Wings; Thunderclap Newman

McCullough, Danny *See* The Animals/Eric Burdon & the Animals/Eric Burdon/Alan Price

McCullough, Henry *See* Paul McCartney/Wings; Gary Wright/Spooky Tooth

McCutcheon, Ian *See* Slowdive/Mojave 3

McDaid, Tony *See* Altered Images

McDermott, Brian *See* Del Amitri

McDonald, Alsy *See* The Triffids

McDonald, Bill *See* Frente!

McDonald, Clarence *See* Love/Arthur Lee & Love/Arthur Lee & Band Aid

McDonald, Country Joe *See* Country Joe & the Fish

McDonald, Eddie *See* The Alarm

McDonald, Francis *See* The BMX Bandits; Teenage Fanclub

McDonald, Ian *See* Foreigner; King Crimson

McDonald, Jeff *See* Redd Kross

McDonald, Michael *See* The Doobie Brothers; Steely Dan

McDonald, Roy *See* The Muffs

McDonald, Steve *See* Redd Kross

McDonnell, Myles *See* Whipping Boy

McDonogh, Chris *See* The Darling Buds

McDougall, Don *See* The Guess Who

McDowell, Gary *See* Modern English

McDowell, Hugh *See* Electric Light Orchestra/Jeff Lynne/ELO II

McElhone, Gerry *See* Altered Images

McElhone, John *See* Altered Images; Texas

McElroy, Sollie *See* The Flamingos

McEntee, Mark *See* Divinyls

McEntire, John *See* Tortoise

McErlaine, Ally *See* Texas

McEuen, John *See* The Nitty Gritty Dirt Band

McFarlane, Spanky *See* The Mamas & the Papas

McFee, Jennifer *See* The Tubes

McFee, John *See* The Doobie Brothers

McGee, Brian *See* Simple Minds

McGee, Edward *See* Tower of Power

McGee, Gerry *See* The Ventures

McGeoch, John *See* Magazine; Public Image Ltd./PiL/John Lydon; Siouxsie & the Banshees

McGeorge, Jerry *See* The Shadows of Knight

McGillberry, Harry *See* The Temptations

McGinley, Raymond *See* Teenage Fanclub

McGinniss, Will *See* Audio Adrenaline

McGlown, Betty *See* The Supremes

McGlynn, Pat *See* The Bay City Rollers

McGonagle, William *See* Symposium

McGovern, Jeff *See* The Scene Is Now

McGovern, Tim *See* The Motels

McGovney, Ron *See* Metallica

McGrath, Mark *See* Sugar Ray

McGraw, Pat *See* Gladhands

McGuigan, Paul "Guigsy" *See* Oasis

McGuinn, Roger *See* The Byrds

McGuinnes *See* Lords of Acid

McGuinness, Tom *See* Manfred Mann/Manfred Mann's Earth Band

Mchunu, Sipho *See* Johnny Clegg & Savuka/Juluka

Meyers, Augie *See* Doug Sahm/Sir Douglas Quintet; The Texas Tornados

Meynell, Anthony *See* Squire

Meynell, Kevin *See* Squire

Miccolis, Dennis *See* The Buckinghams

Michael, George *See* George Michael/Wham!/Andrew Ridgely

Michael, Prakazrel *See* Fugees/Wyclef Jean

Michaels, Bret *See* Poison

Michalski, John *See* Count Five

Mick *See* Dave Dee, Dozy, Beaky, Mick & Tich/Dozy, Beaky, Mick & Tich

Mickle, Dale *See* The Dixie Cups

Midgett, Tim *See* Silkworm

Migdol, Brian *See* Black Flag/Greg Ginn

Mihm, Danny *See* The Flamin' Groovies

Miklos, Matt *See* The Lyres

Milchem, Glenn *See* Blue Rodeo

Miles, Buddy *See* Jimi Hendrix/The Jimi Hendrix Experience/Band of Gypsys

Miles, Kevin *See* Gene

Milhizer, Bill *See* The Fleshtones

Millar, Glenda *See* Johnny Clegg & Savuka/Juluka

Miller, Andy *See* Dodgy

Miller, Bob *See* Supertramp

Miller, Charles *See* War

Miller, Dan *See* Lincoln

Miller, Dominic *See* The Pretenders

Miller, Jerry *See* Moby Grape

Miller, Rhett *See* Old 97's

Miller, Rick *See* Southern Culture on the Skids

Miller, Rob *See* The Hooters/Largo

Miller, Roger *See* Mission of Burma

Miller, Rufus *See* Tower of Power

Miller, Scott *See* Agent Orange; Game Theory/The Loud Family/Scott Miller; 6 String Drag

Miller, Steph *See* Eva Trout

Miller, Tobi *See* Maypole; The Wallflowers

Miller, Vern *See* Barry & the Remains

Millings, Ronnie *See* Them

Million, Bill *See* The Feelies

Mills, Crispian *See* Kula Shaker

Mills, Jim *See* The Wondermints

Mills, Mike *See* R.E.M.

Millward, Mike *See* The Fourmost/The Four Jays/The Four Mosts/Format

Milner, Peter *See* Pistoleros

Milner, Rusty *See* The Marshall Tucker Band

Milo, Nick *See* Tower of Power

Minardi, Gianni *See* The English Beat/General Public

Minardi, Mario *See* The English Beat/General Public

Minarik, Dave *See* The Clarks

Minchella, Damon *See* Ocean Colour Scene

Minnear, Kerry *See* Gentle Giant

Miranda, Danny *See* Blue Öyster Cult

Mitchell, Billy *See* The Clovers

Mitchell, Donald Ray *See* Was (Not Was)

Mitchell, Ian *See* The Bay City Rollers

Mitchell, Keith *See* Green on Red; Opal

Mitchell, Lexi *See* Seam

Mitchell, Mike *See* The Kingsmen

Mitchell, Mitch *See* Guided by Voices; Jimi Hendrix/The Jimi Hendrix Experience/Band of Gypsys

Mize, Ben *See* Counting Crows

Mnculwana, Cyril *See* Johnny Clegg & Savuka/Juluka

Modeliste, Zig *See* The Meters

Moe, Kris "Angelo" *See* Flash Cadillac/Flash Cadillac & the Continental Kids

Moeller, Terri *See* The Walkabouts

Moen, John *See* Dharma Bums

Mogg, Nigel *See* Nancy Boy

Mogine, Jim *See* Midnight Oil

Mohr, John *See* Tar

Mohr, Todd Park *See* Big Head Todd & the Monsters

Mole, Adam *See* Pop Will Eat Itself

Molina, Ralph *See* Crazy Horse

Molla, Chris *See* Cracker/Camper Van Beethoven

Molland, Joey *See* Badfinger/Joey Molland

Moller, Anders *See* Euro Boys

Monarch, Michael *See* Steppenwolf

Monasterio, Juan *See* Brainiac

Monette, Ray *See* Rare Earth

Money, Zoot *See* The Animals/Eric Burdon & the Animals/Eric Burdon/Alan Price

Monigold, Danny *See* The E-Types

Monroe, Michael *See* Hanoi Rocks/Michael Monroe

Montana, Country Dick *See* The Beat Farmers

Monteith, Mark *See* aMiniature

Montero, Isobel *See* Drugstore

Montes, Michael *See* 'Til Tuesday

Monti, Steve *See* The Jesus & Mary Chain

Montoya, Craig *See* Everclear

Montrose, Emmy-Kate *See* Kenickie

Montrose, Ronnie *See* Montrose

Moody, Micky *See* Whitesnake

Moon, Keith *See* The Who

Mooney, Eddie *See* Billy J. Kramer & the Dakotas

Mooney, Tim *See* Mark Eitzel/American Music Club

Moore, Alan *See* Judas Priest

Moore, Angelo Christopher *See* Fishbone

Moore, Archie *See* Velocity Girl

Moore, Garry *See* Mother's Finest

Moore, Gary *See* Thin Lizzy

Moore, Gil *See* Triumph

Moore, Jimmy *See* The "5" Royales

Moore, John *See* The Jesus & Mary Chain

Moore, Johnny *See* The Drifters

Moore, Kevin *See* Dream Theater

Moore, LeRoi *See* Dave Matthews Band

Moore, Sam *See* Sam & Dave

Moore, Sean *See* Manic Street Preachers

Moore, Thurston *See* Sonic Youth/Thurston Moore/Lee Ranaldo/Ciccone Youth/Bewitched

Moore, Warren "Pete" *See* Smokey Robinson & the Miracles

Moorings, Ronny *See* Xymox

Moose *See* New Model Army

Mooseman *See* Body Count

Moraille, Stephane *See* Bran Van 3000

Moran, Chris *See* The Accelerators

Moran, Francisco *See* Doug Sahm/Sir Douglas Quintet

Moraz, Patrick *See* The Moody Blues/Justin Hayward & John Lodge/Mike Pinder; Yes

More, Jonathan *See* Coldcut

Moreira, Airto *See* Weather Report

Moreland, Bruce *See* Wall of Voodoo/Stan Ridgway; The Weirdos

Moreland, Marc *See* Wall of Voodoo/Stan Ridgway

Morello, Tom *See* Rage Against the Machine

Moreno, Chino *See* deftones

Moreve, Rushton *See* Steppenwolf

Morgan, Evan *See* New Riders of the Purple Sage

Morgan, John Russell *See* Steppenwolf

Morgan, Mark *See* Jefferson Starship/Starship

Morgan, Ron *See* The Electric Prunes

Morgan, Stephen *See* Icehouse

Morgenstein, Rod *See* The Dixie Dregs/The Dregs; Winger/Kip Winger

Mori, Ikue Ile *See* DNA

Mori, Romi *See* Gun Club

Morland, Mig *See* Moose

Morley, Pat *See* Soul Asylum

Morley, Tom *See* Scritti Politti

Morris, Bobby *See* The Champs

Morris, Gina *See* Stereolab

Morris, Jeff *See* The Barbarians

Morris, Keith *See* Black Flag/Greg Ginn; The Circle Jerks

Morris, Kenny *See* Siouxsie & the Banshees

Morris, Paul *See* Rainbow

Morris, Roger *See* The Psychedelic Furs/Richard Butler/Love Spit Love

Morris, Ruthie *See* Magnapop

Morris, Scotty *See* Big Bad Voodoo Daddy/BBVD

Morris, Stephen *See* Joy Division; New Order

Morrisette, Ledge *See* The Mono Men

Morrison, David *See* Ass Ponys

Morrison, James *See* Richard Hell & the Voidoids

Morrison, James "Jimbob" *See* Carter the Unstoppable Sex Machine

Morrison, Jim *See* The Doors

Morrison, Lindy *See* Grant McLennan/Robert Forster/The Go-Betweens

Morrison, Patricia *See* Gun Club; Sisters of Mercy

Morrison, Sterling *See* The Velvet Underground/Nico/Maureen Tucker

Morrison, Van *See* Them

Morriss, Mark *See* The Bluetones

Morriss, Scott *See* The Bluetones

Morrissey *See* The Smiths

Morrissey, Dick *See* Soft Machine

Morrow, Stuart *See* New Model Army

Morse, Steve *See* Deep Purple; The Dixie Dregs/The Dregs; Kansas

Morse, Toby *See* H2O

Morse, Todd *See* H2O

Mortensen, John *See* The Mono Men

Mortensen, Mark *See* Samiam

Morton, Everett *See* The English Beat/General Public

Morton, Rockette *See* Captain Beefheart & His Magic Band

Morvan, Fabrice *See* Milli Vanilli

Mosely, Chuck *See* Faith No More/Mr. Bungle/Imperial Teen

Mosely, Ian *See* Marillion/Fish

Mosher, Ken *See* Squirrel Nut Zippers/Jas. Mathus & His Knock-Down Society

Mosley, Bob *See* Moby Grape

Moss, Jason *See* Cherry Poppin' Daddies

Moss, Jon *See* Culture Club/Boy George; The Damned

Moss, Paul *See* The Swinging Blue Jeans/The Bluegenes/Ray Ennis & the Blue Jeans

Mothersbaugh, Bob *See* Devo

Mothersbaugh, Mark *See* Devo

Mould, Bob *See* Hüsker Dü; Bob Mould/Sugar

Moulding, Colin Ivor *See* XTC/The Dukes of Stratosphear

Moulton, Victor "Moulty" *See* The Barbarians

Mounfield, Gary "Mani" *See* The Stone Roses

Mount, Dave *See* Mud

Mouquet, Eric *See* Deep Forest

Mouzon, Alphonse *See* Weather Report

Mowatt, Judy *See* Bob Marley & the Wailers

Moxham, Philip *See* Young Marble Giants

Moxham, Stuart *See* Young Marble Giants

M.P. *See* Samiam; School of Fish/Josh Clayton-Felt

Muckin, Bob *See* Southside Johnny & the Asbury Jukes

Mueller, Chris *See* Railroad Jerk

Mueller, Karl *See* Soul Asylum

Muir, Barry *See* The Blue Shadows

Muir, Jamie *See* King Crimson

Muir, Mike "Cyko Mico" *See* Suicidal Tendencies

Mulholland, Dave *See* Aztec Camera

Mullen, Keith *See* The Farm

Mullen, Larry Jr. *See* U2

Mulligan, Declan *See* The Beau Brummels

Mullin, Reed *See* Corrosion of Conformity

Mulvaney, Shannon *See* Magnapop

Mumy, Bill *See* Barnes & Barnes

Munde, Al *See* Flying Burrito Brothers

Munden, Dave *See* The Tremeloes/Brian Poole & the Tremeloes/Chip Hawkes' Tremeloes

Muñoz, Eddie *See* Peter Case/The Plimsouls

Munro, Jane *See* The Au Pairs

Munroe, James "Mugshot" *See* Big Rude Jake

Pahoa, Dave *See* Peter Case/The Plimsouls

Paice, Ian *See* Deep Purple; Whitesnake

Paich, David *See* Toto

Paine, Tom *See* Live Skull

Painter, Simon *See* Carter the Unstoppable Sex Machine

Painter, Todd *See* The Urge

Pajo, Dave *See* Tortoise

Pakulski, Jan Marek *See* The Fleshtones

Paliselli, Billy *See* Artful Dodger

Palladino, Patsy Pasquale *See* The Interpreters

Palligrosi, Tony *See* Southside Johnny & the Asbury Jukes

Palm, Mike *See* Agent Orange

Palmar, Wally *See* The Romantics

Palmer, Bruce *See* Buffalo Springfield

Palmer, Carl *See* Asia; Emerson, Lake & Palmer/Emerson, Lake & Powell

Palmer, David *See* ABC; Jethro Tull/Ian Anderson; Steely Dan

Palmer, Geoff *See* Sons of Champlin

Palmer, Jeff *See* Mommyheads

Palmer, John *See* Tsunami

Palmer, Richard *See* Supertramp

Palmer-James, Richard *See* King Crimson

Palmolive *See* The Raincoats; The Slits

Palter, Morris *See* Treble Charger

Paluzzi, Jimmy *See* Hoarse; Sponge

Pandovani, Henri *See* The Police

Panic, Dan *See* Screeching Weasel

Pankler, Mark "Vudi" *See* Mark Eitzel/American Music Club

Pankow, James *See* Chicago/Peter Cetera

Panozzo, Chuck *See* Styx

Panozzo, John *See* Styx

Panter, Horace *See* The English Beat/General Public

Papineau, Lisa *See* Pet

Pappalardi, Felix *See* Mountain

Paravecchio, Ryan *See* Thirty Ought Six

Parazaider, Walter *See* Chicago/Peter Cetera

Parcells, Fred *See* Black 47

Parfitt, Rick *See* Status Quo

Park, Sooyoung *See* Bitch Magnet; Seam

Parker, Alan *See* Soft Machine

Parker, Alister *See* Bailter Space

Parker, Anders *See* Varnaline

Parker, Chris *See* Big Ass Truck

Parker, Ian *See* Tom Robinson Band/Sector 27

Parker, Jeff *See* Tortoise

Parker, John *See* Varnaline

Parker, Graham *See* Graham Parker/Graham Parker & the Rumor

Parker, Tom *See* The Animals/Eric Burdon & the Animals/Eric Burdon/Alan Price

Parkin, Ian *See* Be Bop Deluxe

Parkinson, Bill *See* The Fourmost/The Four Jays/The Four Mosts/Format

Parks, Chris *See* Any Trouble

Parle, Andy *See* Space

Parr, Tom *See* The Bottle Rockets

Parra, Adolpho "Fito" de la *See* Canned Heat

Parren, Chris *See* The Strawbs/Dave Cousins

Parrish, Mark *See* The Dixie Dregs/The Dregs

Parry, Dick *See* The Bonzo Dog Band

Parry, Laurence *See* James Taylor Quartet

Parsons, Dave *See* Bush; Sham 69

Parsons, Deborah *See* Third Eye Foundation

Parsons, Gene *See* The Byrds; Flying Burrito Brothers

Parsons, Gram *See* The Byrds; Flying Burrito Brothers

Parsons, Ted *See* Prong

Partington, Darren *See* 808 State

Partridge, Andy *See* XTC/The Dukes of Stratosphear

Parvo, Carpella *See* Rasputina

Pascale, Nina *See* Quickspace

Passalacqua, Tony *See* The Archies

Pastorini, Ed *See* Elysian Fields

Pastorius, Jaco *See* Weather Report

Patchouli, Julie *See* The Pandoras

Patratos, David *See* The Romantics

Patrick, Richard *See* Filter

Patterson, Dr. Alex *See* The Orb

Patterson, Alvin *See* Bob Marley & the Wailers

Patterson, Angel *See* The Rezillos

Patterson, Big Jimmy *See* Dexy's Midnight Runners/Kevin Rowland & Dexy's Midnight Runners

Patterson, Jason *See* Cry of Love

Patterson, Jerry *See* Sam the Sham & the Pharaohs/Sam the Sham Revue

Patterson, Jon "Stormy" *See* The Astronauts

Pattinson, Les *See* Echo & the Bunnymen/Electrafixion

Patto, Mike *See* Gary Wright/Spooky Tooth

Patton, Mike *See* Faith No More/Mr. Bungle/Imperial Teen

Paul, Curtis *See* The Champs

Paul, Henry *See* The Outlaws

Paul, Jeffrey *See* 16 Horsepower

Pauling, Lowman *See* The "5" Royales

Paulo Jr. *See* Sepultura

Paulson, Charlie *See* Goldfinger

Paumgardhen, Mike *See* Richard Hell & the Voidoids

Pawlett, Yvonne *See* The Fall

Payne, Bill *See* Little Feat

Payne, Douglas *See* Travis

Payne, Jason *See* Nitzer Ebb

Payne, John *See* Asia

Payne, Scherrie *See* The Supremes

Payton, Dennis *See* The Dave Clark Five

Payton, Lawrence *See* The Four Tops

Pazdan, John *See* Off Broadway usa

Pearcy, Stephen *See* Ratt

Pearson, Danny *See* Mark Eitzel/American Music Club

Pearson, Jack *See* The Allman Brothers Band

Pearson, Joshua *See* Emergency Broadcast Network

Pearson, Mike *See* Blue Meanies

Pearson, Tony *See* The Flatlanders

Peart, Neil *See* Rush

Peckham, George *See* The Fourmost/The Four Jays/The Four Mosts/Format

Pederast, Chavo *See* Black Flag/Greg Ginn

Pedersen, Kare Joao *See* Euro Boys

Pederson, Chris *See* Cracker/Camper Van Beethoven

Pederson, Jeff *See* The Why Store

Peek, Dan *See* America

Peeples, Philip *See* Old 97's

Pegg, Dave *See* Fairport Convention/Fairport/Sandy Denny/Fotheringay; Jethro Tull/Ian Anderson

Pegg, Matt *See* Jethro Tull/Ian Anderson

Pellicci, Derek *See* Little River Band

Pelligro, J.H. *See* Dead Kennedys

Pence, Jeff *See* Blessid Union of Souls

Pender, Mark *See* Southside Johnny & the Asbury Jukes

Pender, Mike *See* The Searchers

Pendergast, George *See* Dishwalla

Pendleton, Brian *See* Pretty Things

Pengilly, Kirk *See* INXS

Penna, Erik Della *See* The Health & Happiness Show

Penny, Jonn *See* Ned's Atomic Dustbin

Penrod, Jerry *See* Iron Butterfly

Pentifallo, Kenny *See* Southside Johnny & the Asbury Jukes

Pentland, Patrick *See* Sloan

Peoples, Theo *See* The Temptations

Perano, Greg *See* Hunters & Collectors

Peretz, Jesse *See* Lemonheads

Perez, Johnny *See* Doug Sahm/Sir Douglas Quintet

Perez, Louis *See* Los Lobos

Perica, Zlatko *See* Tangerine Dream

Peris, Don *See* The Innocence Mission

Peris, Karen *See* The Innocence Mission

Perkins, Al *See* Flying Burrito Brothers

Perkins, John *See* The Crew Cuts

Perkins, Paul Stephen *See* Porno for Pyros

Perkins, Ray *See* The Crew Cuts

Perkins, Stephen *See* Jane's Addiction/Deconstruction

Perkins, Tex *See* The Cruel Sea

Perlman, Marc *See* Golden Smog; The Jayhawks/The Original Harmony Ridge Creek Dippers

Pero, A.J. *See* Twisted Sister

Peron, Carlos *See* Yello

Peron, Jean-Herve *See* Faust

Perowsky, Ben *See* Elysian Fields; The Lounge Lizards

Perreira, Joseph *See* El Chicano

Perrett, Peter *See* The Only Ones

Perri, Kevin *See* Junk Monkeys

Perrodin, Mark *See* The Sidewinders/The Sand Rubies

Perry, Brendan *See* Dead Can Dance

Perry, Doane *See* Jethro Tull/Ian Anderson

Perry, Guy *See* The Motels

Perry, Joe *See* Aerosmith

Perry, John *See* The Only Ones

Perry, Steve *See* Cherry Poppin' Daddies

Perry, Steve *See* Journey

Persh, John *See* Rare Earth

Personality, Johnny *See* Screeching Weasel

Persons, Billy Ford *See* The Weirdos

Persson, Nina *See* The Cardigans

Pesce, Joey *See* 'Til Tuesday

Pessoni, John *See* The Urge

Peters, Chris *See* Getaway Cruiser

Peters, Dan *See* Mudhoney

Peters, Drew *See* Getaway Cruiser

Peters, Joey *See* Grant Lee Buffalo

Peters, Mike *See* The Alarm

Petersen, Dickie *See* Blue Cheer

Petersen, John *See* The Beau Brummels; Harpers Bizarre

Petersen, Marina *See* Yum-Yum

Peterson, Debbi *See* The Bangles/Susanna Hoffs

Peterson, Garry *See* The Guess Who

Peterson, Robert *See* Rick Derringer/The McCoys

Peterson, Sylvia *See* The Chiffons

Peterson, Vicki *See* The Bangles/Susanna Hoffs; The Continental Drifters

Petersson, Tom *See* Cheap Trick

Petkovic, John *See* Guided by Voices

Petri, Tony *See* Twisted Sister

Petrucci, John *See* Dream Theater

Petty, Dan *See* Marry Me Jane

Petty, Tom *See* Tom Petty & the Heartbreakers; The Traveling Wilburys

Peverett, "Lonesome" Dave *See* Foghat; Savoy Brown

Pew, Tracey *See* The Birthday Party

Pezzati, Jeff *See* Naked Raygun

Pezzati, Marco *See* Naked Raygun

Pfaff, Kristen *See* Hole

Pfayler, Jim *See* The Ohio Express/Ohio Ltd.

Pfeiffer, Darrin *See* Goldfinger

Pfisterer, Alban "Snoopy" *See* Love/Arthur Lee & Love/Arthur Lee & Band Aid

Phaler, Adam *See* Jawbreaker

Phantom, Slim Jim *See* Stray Cats/Brian Setzer/Lee Rocker/Lee Rocker's Big Blue

Phay, Danny *See* The Chocolate Watch Band

Phelps, Joel *See* Silkworm

Philbin, Gregg *See* REO Speedwagon

Philips, Arthur *See* The Strawbs/Dave Cousins

Phillip Dwight *See* Fishbone

Phillips, Anthony *See* Genesis

Phillips, Chris *See* Squirrel Nut Zippers/Jas. Mathus & His Knock-Down Society

Phillips, Chynna *See* Wilson Phillips

Phillips, Glen *See* Toad the Wet Sprocket

Phillips, Glenn *See* Hampton Grease Band

Phillips, Grant Lee *See* Grant Lee Buffalo

Phillips, John *See* The Mamas & the Papas

Phillips, Leonard Graves *See* The Dickies

Phillips, Linn III "Spike" *See* Flash Cadillac/Flash Cadillac & the Continental Kids

Phillips, MacKenzie *See* The Mamas & the Papas

Phillips, Martin *See* The Chills

Phillips, Michelle *See* The Mamas & the Papas

Phillips, Ray *See* Nashville Teens

Phillips, Ricky *See* John Waite/The Babys/Bad English

Phillips, Scott *See* Creed

Phillips, Simon *See* Judas Priest; Toto; The Who

Phipps, Sam *See* Oingo Boingo/Danny Elfman

Piazza, Sammy *See* Hot Tuna; Quicksilver Messenger Service

Picciotto, Guy *See* Fugazi

Piccolo, Steve *See* The Lounge Lizards

Pickens, Earl *See* The Cyrkle

Pickerel, Mark *See* Screaming Trees

Pickett, Lenny *See* Tower of Power

Pickup, Howard *See* The Adverts

Pierce, Jason *See* Spacemen 3; Spiritualized

Pierce, Jeffrey Lee *See* Gun Club

Pierce, Paula *See* The Pandoras

Pierson, Kate *See* The B-52's/Fred Schneider

Pifer, Dan *See* God Street Wine

Pig *See* KMFDM

Piggott, Mike *See* Pentangle

Pihl, Gary *See* Boston

Pilatus, Rob *See* Milli Vanilli

Pilson, Jeff *See* Dokken

Pinder, Mike *See* The Moody Blues/Justin Hayward & John Lodge/Mike Pinder

Pine, Ken *See* The Fugs

Pinell, Kristin *See* The Rooks

Pinera, Mike *See* Iron Butterfly

Pinkerton, Peyton *See* Silver Jews

Pinkus, Jeff "Tooter" *See* Butthole Surfers

Pinnick, Chris *See* Chicago/Peter Cetera

Pinnick, Doug *See* King's X

Pipien, Sven *See* The Black Crowes

Pirner, Dave *See* Soul Asylum

Pirroni, Marco *See* Siouxsie & the Banshees

Pistachio, Rusty *See* H2O

Pistel, Mark *See* Consolidated

Pitman, Erin *See* The Suicide Machines

Pitman, Jimmy *See* The Strawberry Alarm Clock

Pitmon, Linda *See* Zuzu's Petals

Pitrelli, Al *See* Asia

Pitron, Bill IV *See* Dwight Twilley/Dwight Twilley Band/Phil Seymour

Pittam, Tommy *See* Bulletboys

Pitts, Billy *See* Georgia Satellites/Dan Baird

Piucci, Matthew *See* The Rain Parade

P.J. *See* Anti-Nowhere League

Place, Pat *See* Bush Tetras

Plakas, Dee *See* L7

Plant, Robert *See* Led Zeppelin; Page & Plant/Jimmy Page

Pleasance, Richard *See* Boom Crash Opera

Ploog, Richard *See* The Church

Plouf, Scott *See* Built to Spill; The Spinanes

Plouf, Steve *See* The Wipers/Greg Sage

Plum, Lord Cornelius *See* XTC/The Dukes of Stratosphear

Plummer, Joe Ben *See* Cop Shoot Cop/Firewater

Podlewski, Merlo *See* Spain

Poe, John *See* Guadalcanal Diary/Murray Attaway

Poindexter, Buster *See* David Johansen/Buster Poindexter

Pointer, Mick *See* Marillion/Fish

Poirier, Cheryl *See* Kid Creole & the Coconuts/Dr. Buzzard's Original Savannah Band

Poison Ivy Rorschach *See* The Cramps

Poland, Chris *See* Megadeth

Pollack, Courtney *See* The Aquabats

Pollard, Jim *See* Guided by Voices

Pollard, Robert *See* Guided by Voices

Pollit, Tessa *See* The Slits

Pollock, Jason *See* Seven Mary Three

Poltz, Steve *See* The Rugburns/Steve Poltz

Poncher, Don *See* Love/Arthur Lee & Love/Arthur Lee & Band Aid

Ponder, Ed *See* Flying Burrito Brothers

Pons, Jim *See* The Leaves; The Turtles

Poole, Brian *See* The Tremeloes/Brian Poole & the Tremeloes/Chip Hawkes' Tremeloes

Pop, Dee *See* Gun Club

Pop, Iggy *See* Iggy Pop/The Stooges

Pope, Bucky *See* Tar Babies

Popper, John *See* Blues Traveler

Popwell, Robert *See* The Young Rascals/The Rascals

Porcaro, Jeff *See* Toto

Porcaro, Michael *See* Toto

Porcaro, Steve *See* Toto

Poriss, Hilary *See* Yum-Yum

Porter, George Jr. *See* The Meters

Porter, John *See* Roxy Music

Porter, Tiran *See* The Doobie Brothers

Portius, Bryce *See* Savoy Brown

Portman-Smith, Nigel *See* Pentangle

Portnoy, Mike *See* Dream Theater

Portz, Chuck *See* The Turtles

Posgay, Mark *See* Magnapop

Posner, Jay *See* The Barracudas

Poss, Robert *See* Band of Susans/Robert Poss

Post, Gardner *See* Emergency Broadcast Network

Post, Louise *See* Veruca Salt

Potak, Steve *See* The Connells

Potter, Graeme *See* The Barracudas

Potts, Steve *See* Booker T. & the MG's

Poulos, Jon-Jon *See* The Buckinghams

Ragsdale, David *See* Kansas

Railton, Michael *See* The English Beat/General Public

Rainford, Simone *See* All Saints

Rainier, Tony *See* Blue Cheer

Raleigh, Don *See* Squirrel Nut Zippers/Jas. Mathus & His Knock-Down Society

Ralphs, Mick *See* Bad Company; Mott the Hoople

Ralske, Kurt *See* Ultra Vivid Scene

Ramirez, Lou *See* Peter Case/The Plimsouls

Ramirez, Twiggy *See* Marilyn Manson

Ramone, C.J. *See* The Ramones

Ramone, Dee Dee *See* The Ramones

Ramone, Joey *See* The Ramones

Ramone, Johnny *See* The Ramones

Ramone, Marky *See* The Ramones

Ramone, Richie *See* The Ramones

Ramone, Tommy *See* The Ramones

Ramos, Kid *See* The Fabulous Thunderbirds

Ramos, Michael *See* BoDeans

Ramos, Terry *See* The Association

Ramsay, Andy *See* Stereolab

Ramsey, Al *See* Gary Lewis & the Playboys

Ramsey, Mary *See* 10,000 Maniacs/Natalie Merchant

Ranaldo, Lee *See* Sonic Youth/Thurston Moore/Lee Ranaldo/Ciccone Youth/Bewitched

Ranchero, Richie *See* Huevos Rancheros

Randell, Buddy *See* The Knickerbockers

Randt, Bill *See* The New Bomb Turks

Raney, Jerry *See* The Beat Farmers

Ranken, Andrew *See* The Pogues/Shane MacGowan & the Popes

Rankin, Billy *See* Brinsley Schwarz; Nazareth

Rankine, Alan *See* The Associates/Associates

Rankine, Leslie *See* ruby

Ranking Roger *See* The English Beat/General Public

Ranno, Rick *See* Stories

Raphael, Gordon *See* Sky Cries Mary

Rapp, Danny *See* Danny & the Juniors/Danny & the Juniors Featuring Joe Terry

Rarebell, Herman *See* Scorpions

Rasa Don *See* Arrested Development/Speech/Dionne Farris

Rassler, J.J. *See* DMZ; The Queers

Rasta Li-Mon *See* Dread Zeppelin

Rasted, Soren *See* Aqua

Rat *See* Ned's Atomic Dustbin

Rathbone, Donald *See* The Hollies

Ratledge, Mike *See* Soft Machine

Raven, Paul *See* Killing Joke; Prong

Ravenstine, Allen *See* Pere Ubu

Ray, Amy *See* Indigo Girls

Ray, Brian *See* Farmer Not So John

Ray, East Bay *See* Dead Kennedys

Ray, Robert *See* The Silos/Vulgar Boatmen/Walter Salas-Humara

Ray, Sean *See* Farmer Not So John

Ray, Tom *See* The Bottle Rockets; The Waco Brothers

Ray, Will *See* The Hellecasters

Raymond, Paul *See* Savoy Brown

Raymonde, Simon *See* Cocteau Twins

Rayner, Eddie *See* Split Enz/Tim Finn/Alt

Raynor, Scott *See* Blink 182

Razzle *See* Hanoi Rocks/Michael Monroe

Rea, David *See* Fairport Convention/Fairport/Sandy Denny/Fotheringay

Reader, Eddi *See* Fairground Attraction/Eddi Reader

Readman, Alice *See* The Auteurs

Reality, Maxim *See* Prodigy

Reame-James, Milton *See* Be Bop Deluxe

Reber, Matt *See* The New Bomb Turks

The Red Curtain *See* XTC/The Dukes of Stratosphear

Redding, Noel *See* Jimi Hendrix/The Jimi Hendrix Experience/Band of Gypsys

Reding, Greg *See* Black Oak Arkansas

Redmen, Brian *See* The Fourmost/The Four Jays/The Four Mosts/Format

Reece, Chris *See* Social Distortion

Reece, Damon *See* Echo & the Bunnymen/Electrafixion; Spiritualized

Reed, Bill *See* The Diamonds

Reed, Brett *See* Rancid

Reed, Dizzy *See* Guns N' Roses

Reed, Herbert *See* The Platters

Reed, Lou *See* The Velvet Underground/Nico/Maureen Tucker

Reeder, Scott *See* Kyuss

Rees, John *See* Men at Work

Reese, Jim *See* The Bobby Fuller Four

Reeves, Keanu *See* Dogstar

Reeves, Lois *See* Martha & the Vandellas

Reeves, Martha *See* Martha & the Vandellas

Refoy, Mark *See* Spiritualized

Regaldado, Rudy *See* El Chicano

Reid, Charlie *See* The Proclaimers

Reid, Craig *See* The Proclaimers

Reid, Delroy "Junior" *See* Black Uhuru

Reid, Ellen *See* Crash Test Dummies

Reid, Jim *See* The Jesus & Mary Chain

Reid, Keith *See* Procol Harum

Reid, Matt *See* Berlin

Reid, Vernon *See* Living Colour

Reid, William *See* The Jesus & Mary Chain

Reilly, Michael *See* Pure Prairie League

Reiner, Robert *See* The Leaves

Reinhardt, Larry "Rhino" *See* Iron Butterfly

Reiter, Bill *See* The Urge

Reitzell, Brian *See* Redd Kross

Reitzes, Howard *See* Iron Butterfly

Relf, Jane *See* Renaissance

Relf, Keith *See* Renaissance; The Yardbirds

Remmler, Stephan *See* Trio

Renbourn, John *See* Pentangle

Reno, Mike *See* Loverboy

Respectable, Rick *See* The Queers

Reuter, Bert *See* Focus

Revell, Mark *See* The Egg; The Icicle Works

Sampler Sound-EFX, *See* GWAR

Samuelson, Gars *See* Megadeth

Samwell-Smith, Paul *See* The Yardbirds

San Filippo, Vito *See* Tower of Power

Sanborn, David *See* Paul Butterfield Blues Band

Sanchez, Freddie *See* El Chicano

Sanchez, Michel *See* Deep Forest

Sanchez, Paul *See* Cowboy Mouth

Sancious, David *See* Bruce Springsteen/Bruce Springsteen & the E Street Band

Sanders, Ed *See* The Fugs

Sanders, Ric *See* Fairport Convention/Fairport/Sandy Denny/Fotheringay

Sanderson, Nick *See* Gun Club

Sandman, Mark *See* Morphine

Sandoval, Hope *See* Mazzy Star

Sangster, Jim *See* Young Fresh Fellows/Scott McCaughey/The Minus Five

Sanko, Eric *See* The Lounge Lizards

Sanllehi, Juan-Pablo *See* Los Bravos

Santana, Carlos *See* Santana/Carlos Santana

Santiago, Herman *See* Frankie Lymon & the Teenagers

Santiago, Joey *See* The Pixies

Santiglia, Peggy *See* The Angels

Saraceno, Blues *See* Poison

Sarzo, Rudy *See* Quiet Riot; Whitesnake

Saunders, Baker *See* The Walkabouts

Saunders, Marty *See* Jay & the Americans

Sauter, Brenda *See* The Feelies

Savage, Conway *See* Nick Cave & the Bad Seeds

Savage, John *See* The Seeds

Savage, Rick *See* Def Leppard

Savage, Scott *See* Jars of Clay

Saville, Christian *See* Slowdive/Mojave 3

Savoy, Rob *See* Cowboy Mouth

Sawyer, Ray *See* Dr. Hook & the Medicine Show/Dr. Hook

Saxa *See* The English Beat/General Public

Saxon, Sky *See* The Seeds

Scabies, Rat *See* The Damned

Scaccia, Mike *See* Ministry

Scala, Ralph *See* The Blues Magoos

Scalavunos, Jim *See* The Cramps

Scalzo, Tony *See* Fastball

Scanlan, Craig *See* The Fall

Scanlan, Glynn *See* Junk Monkeys

Scarbrough, Toby *See* Chalk FarM

Scarlet, Will *See* Hot Tuna

Scarpantoni, Jane *See* The Lounge Lizards

Scarpulla, John *See* Tower of Power

Scarrat, Doug *See* Saxon

Schacher, Mel *See* Grand Funk Railroad

Schade, Jan Tilman *See* Einstürzende Neubauten

Schaub, Buddy *See* Less Than Jake

Schayer, Bobby *See* Bad Religion

Scheel, Jeff *See* Gravity Kills

Scheff, David *See* Translator

Scheff, Jason *See* Chicago/Peter Cetera

Schelhaas, Jan *See* Camel

Schellenbach, Kate *See* Beastie Boys; Luscious Jackson

Scheme, Patty *See* Hole

Schenker, Michel *See* Scorpions

Schenker, Rudolf *See* Scorpions

Schenkman, Eric *See* Spin Doctors

Scherer, Peter *See* Ambitious Lovers

Schermerhorn, Eric *See* They Might Be Giants

Schermie, Joe *See* Three Dog Night

Schier, Johnny *See* aMiniature

Schiffour, Tom *See* The Shadows of Knight

Schlabowske, Dean *See* The Waco Brothers

Schlesinger, Adam *See* Fountains of Wayne; Ivy

Schlitt, John *See* Petra

Schloss, Zander *See* The Circle Jerks; Thelonious Monster

Schlosser, Rick *See* Montrose

Schmersal, John *See* Brainiac

Schmid, Dan *See* Cherry Poppin' Daddies

Schmit, Timothy B. *See* The Eagles; Poco

Schmoelling, Johannes *See* Tangerine Dream

Schneider, Florian *See* Kraftwerk

Schneider, Fred *See* The B-52's/Fred Schneider

Schneider, Robert *See* Apples in Stereo

Schneiderman, Leon *See* Oingo Boingo/Danny Elfman

Schnier, Al *See* moe.

Schnitzler, Conrad *See* Tangerine Dream

Schock, Gina *See* The Go-Go's

Schofield, Marcia *See* The Fall

Scholz, Tom *See* Boston

Schon, Neal *See* Journey; John Waite/The Babys/Bad English

Schools, David *See* Widespread Panic

Schott, Peter *See* Kid Creole & the Co-conuts/Dr. Buzzard's Original Savannah Band

Schramm, Dave *See* The Schramms

Schreiner, Knut *See* Euro Boys

Schroeder, Paul *See* Spanic Boys

Schroeder, Wilhelm *See* Skinny Puppy

Schroyder, Steve *See* Tangerine Dream

Schulman, Mark *See* Foreigner

Schultz, Steve *See* For Against

Schulz, Gunter *See* KMFDM

Schulze, Klaus *See* Tangerine Dream

Schurgin, Rob *See* Wig

Schurr, Paul *See* Flop

Schwartz, Adam *See* DMZ

Schwartz, Dorothy *See* The Chordettes

Schwartz, Ray *See* moe.

Schwartzberg, Alan *See* Mountain

Schwarz, Brinsley *See* Brinsley Schwarz; Graham Parker/Graham Parker & the Rumor

Schwarzenbach, Blake *See* Jawbreaker

Schwers, Billy *See* Royal Crescent Mob

Scialfa, Patti *See* Bruce Springsteen/Bruce Springsteen & the E Street Band

Sciuto, Tony *See* Little River Band

Sherburne, Adam *See* Consolidated

Sherinian, Derick *See* Dream Theater

Sherman, Jack *See* Red Hot Chili Peppers

Shernoff, Andy *See* The Dictators

Sherwood, Billy *See* Yes

Shields, Craig *See* Edwin McCain Band

Shields, Kevin *See* My Bloody Valentine

Shiflett, Scott *See* Face to Face

Shin, William *See* Seam

Shipley, Matthew *See* Modern English

Shirley, Jerry *See* Humble Pie

Shogren, Dave *See* The Doobie Brothers

Shorrock, Glenn *See* Little River Band

Shorter, Wayne *See* Weather Report

Shortino, Paul *See* Quiet Riot

Shouse, David *See* The Grifters

Shrader, Reg *See* Seam

Shrieve, Michael *See* Santana/Carlos Santana

Shubat, Shu *See* Eleventh Dream Day

Shuckett, Ralph *See* Todd Rundgren/Utopia

Shuffield, Joey *See* Fastball

Shulman, Derek *See* Gentle Giant

Shulman, Phil *See* Gentle Giant

Shulman, Ray *See* Gentle Giant

Shumake, Ron *See* Canned Heat

Shumaker, Dirk *See* Big Bad Voodoo Daddy/BBVD

Sibley, Nick *See* The Skeletons/The Morells

Sice *See* The Boo Radleys

Sidney, Hillarie *See* Apples in Stereo

Siebenberg, Bob *See* Supertramp

Siegel, Jay *See* The Tokens/The Tokens Featuring Mitch Margo/The Four Winds/The Buddies/The Coeds/Cross Country

Siegler, John *See* Todd Rundgren/Utopia

Siegler, Sammy *See* CIV

Siewert, Christine *See* KMFDM

Sigelman, Danny *See* The Legendary Jim Ruiz Group

Sighrue, Johnny *See* Judybats

Sigtryggur *See* Björk/Sugarcubes

Silagyi, Chris *See* 20/20

Silver, John *See* Genesis

Silver, Josh *See* Type O Negative

Silveria, David *See* KoЯn

SilverShower Raven *See* Dread Zeppelin

Simins, Russell *See* Jon Spencer Blues Explosion

Simmonds, Kim *See* Savoy Brown

Simmons, Gene *See* Kiss

Simmons, Patrick *See* The Doobie Brothers

Simms, Mike *See* Mark Eitzel/American Music Club

Simms, Nick *See* Cornershop

Simon, Jeff *See* George Thorogood & the Destroyers

Simon, Paul *See* Simon & Garfunkel

Simon, Robin *See* Magazine; Ultravox

Simonon, Paul *See* The Clash

Simons, Ed *See* The Chemical Brothers

Simper, Nick *See* Deep Purple

Simpson, Derrick "Duckie" *See* Black Uhuru

Simpson, Gerald *See* 808 State

Simpson, Graham *See* Roxy Music

Simpson, Mike *See* The Caulfields

Simpson, Ray *See* The Village People

Sims, David Wm. *See* The Jesus Lizard

Sims, Neil *See* Catherine Wheel

Sims, Orlando *See* Chalk FarM

Sinclair, David *See* Caravan

Sinclair, Gord *See* The Tragically Hip

Sinclair, John *See* Uriah Heep

Sinclair, Richard *See* Camel; Caravan

Sinfield, Peter *See* King Crimson

Singer, Eric *See* Badlands; Black Sabbath; Kiss

Singh, Avtar *See* Cornershop

Singh, Tjinder *See* Cornershop

Singleton, Stephen *See* ABC

Sioux, Siouxsie *See* Siouxsie & the Banshees

Siverton *See* The Specials

Sixx, Nikki *See* Mötley Crüe/Vince Neil

Size, Roni *See* Roni Size/Reprazent

Skeen, Jim "Snake" *See* The Choir

Skeoch, Tommy *See* Tesla

Skibic, Jon *See* Gigolo Aunts

Skill, Mike *See* The Romantics

Skillings, Muzz *See* Living Colour

Skin *See* Skunk Anansie

Skinner, David *See* Roxy Music

Skopelitis, Micky *See* The Golden Palominos

Slade, Chris *See* AC/DC; Uriah Heep

Slash *See* Guns N' Roses

Slater, Glenn *See* The Walkabouts

Slater, Rodney *See* The Bonzo Dog Band

Slaughter, Ricky *See* The Motors

Slaven, Michael *See* Del Amitri

Sledge, Robert *See* Ben Folds Five

Sley, Cynthia *See* Bush Tetras

Slichter, Jake *See* Semisonic

Slick, Grace *See* Jefferson Airplane; Jefferson Starship/Starship

Slick, John *See* Petra

Sloan, Allen *See* The Dixie Dregs/The Dregs

Sloan, Eliot *See* Blessid Union of Souls

Sloman, John *See* Uriah Heep

Slovak, Hillel *See* Red Hot Chili Peppers

Slutes, David *See* The Sidewinders/The Sand Rubies

Smallens, Sandy *See* Too Much Joy

Smalley, Dave *See* All; The Choir; The Raspberries

Smalls, Derek *See* Spinal Tap

Smart, N.D. II *See* Barry & the Remains; Mountain

Smash, Chas *See* Madness

Smear, Pat *See* The Germs; Nirvana/Foo Fighters

Smelly *See* NOFX

Smilios, Arthur *See* CIV

Smith, "Legs" Larry *See* The Bonzo Dog Band

Smith, Adrian *See* Iron Maiden/Bruce Dickinson

Smith, Amery *See* Suicidal Tendencies

Smith, Anthony *See* Icehouse

Smith, Barry *See* Status Quo

Smith, Blake *See* Fig Dish

Smith, Brad *See* Blind Melon

Smith, Brady *See* Hazel

Smith, Brantley *See* Hootie & the Blowfish

Smith, Brix *See* The Fall

Smith, Bruce *See* Public Image Ltd./PiL/John Lydon

Smith, Carlton *See* Royal Crescent Mob

Smith, Chad *See* Red Hot Chili Peppers

Smith, Charlie *See* Marmalade/Dean Ford & the Gaylords/The Gaylords/Dave Dee & Marmalade

Smith, Curt *See* Tears for Fears

Smith, Debbie *See* Echobelly

Smith, Earl *See* Bob Marley & the Wailers

Smith, Fran Jr. *See* The Hooters/Largo

Smith, Fred *See* Television

Smith, Fred "Sonic" *See* MC5

Smith, Garth *See* Buzzcocks

Smith, Gary *See* Pistoleros

Smith, Greg *See* Rainbow

Smith, Howard *See* The Vapors

Smith, Jake *See* Antenna/Velo-Deluxe/The Mysteries of Life/John P. Strohm & the Hello Strangers

Smith, Jeremy *See* Hunters & Collectors

Smith, Jerome *See* KC & the Sunshine Band

Smith, John *See* The Lyres

Smith, Kelly David *See* Flotsam & Jetsam

Smith, Kendra *See* The Dream Syndicate/Steve Wynn/Opal/Guild of Temporal Adventurers/Kendra Smith; Opal

Smith, Kevin *See* DC Talk

Smith, Mark E. *See* The Fall

Smith, Martin *See* Gentle Giant

Smith, Matt *See* Poison

Smith, Michael David *See* The Why Store

Smith, Mike *See* The Dave Clark Five

Smith, Mike "Smitty" *See* Paul Revere & the Raiders/Paul Revere & the Raiders Featuring Mark Lindsay/Raiders/Pink Puzz

Smith, Patti *See* Patti Smith/Patti Smith Group

Smith, Phil *See* Nick Heyward/Haircut 100

Smith, Rick *See* Underworld

Smith, Robert *See* The Cure; Siouxsie & the Banshees

Smith, Ronnie *See* KC & the Sunshine Band

Smith, Rusty *See* Paul Revere & the Raiders/Paul Revere & the Raiders Featuring Mark Lindsay/Raiders/Pink Puzz

Smith, Scott *See* Loverboy

Smith, Shawn *See* Brad/Satchel

Smith, Simon *See* The Wedding Present

Smith, Steve *See* Focus; Journey; The Vapors

Smith, Terry *See* The Barracudas

Smith, Tim *See* Jellyfish

Smith, Tim "T.V." *See* The Adverts

Smith, Toby *See* Jamiroquai

Smith, Wendy *See* Prefab Sprout

Smith, Zachary *See* Patty Smyth/Scandal

Smithies, Reg *See* The Chameleons

Smithson, John *See* Bonham/Jason Bonham Band/Motherland

Smothers, Smokey *See* Paul Butterfield Blues Band

Smurd, Tony *See* Ten Foot Pole/Scared Straight

Smyth, Alice Tweed *See* War

Smyth, Patty *See* Patty Smyth/Scandal

Smythe, D.K. *See* The Rezillos

Snaykee *See* ManBREAK

Sneed, Floyd *See* Three Dog Night

Snow, Don *See* Squeeze/Difford & Tilbrook/Jools Holland

Snyder, Dee *See* Twisted Sister

Soan, Ashley *See* Del Amitri

Sobrante, Al *See* Green Day

Sodergren, Kurt *See* Big Bad Voodoo Daddy/BBVD

Sohl, Richard *See* Patti Smith/Patti Smith Group

Sohns, Jimmy *See* The Shadows of Knight

Solem, Phil *See* The Rembrandts

Soll, Kevin *See* 16 Horsepower

Solley, Pete *See* Procol Harum

Soloff, Lew *See* Blood, Sweat & Tears

Solowka, Peter *See* The Wedding Present

Somers, Andrew *See* The Animals/Eric Burdon & the Animals/Eric Burdon/Alan Price

Somers, Rob *See* The Samples

Somerville, Jimmy *See* Jimmy Somerville/Bronski Beat/Communards

Somerville, Dave *See* The Diamonds

Sommers, Clark *See* Mighty Blue Kings

Sonefeld, Jim "Soni" *See* Hootie & the Blowfish

Sorenson, Jon-Lars *See* Pell Mell

Sorum, Matt *See* The Cult/The Holy Barbarians; Guns N' Roses

Sosna, Rudolf *See* Faust

Sotak, "Miss Cindy" *See* The Flashcats

Soto, Steve *See* Agent Orange

Soule, Mickey Lee *See* Rainbow

Southside Johnny *See* Southside Johnny & the Asbury Jukes

Spa, Unda *See* Tangerine Dream

Spaag, Dennis *See* M.O.T.O./Masters of the Obvious

Spaeth, Brian *See* The Fleshtones

Spaeth, Gordon *See* The Fleshtones

Spagnola, James "Weasel" *See* The Electric Prunes

Spalding, David *See* Pell Mell

Spall, Rob *See* Soft Machine

Spampinato, Joey *See* NRBQ

Spampinato, Johnny *See* NRBQ

Spanic, Ian *See* Spanic Boys

Spanic, Tom *See* Spanic Boys

Spanky G *See* The Bloodhound Gang

Sparks, Donita *See* L7

Stenger, Susan *See* Band of Susans/Robert Poss

Stephen, Alec *See* Railroad Jerk

Stephen, Roxanne *See* Th' Faith Healers

Stephen, Tom *See* The Jeff Healey Band

Stephens, Bill *See* Naked Raygun

Stephens, Bruce *See* Blue Cheer

Stephens, Leigh *See* Blue Cheer

Stephens, Jody *See* Big Star/Chris Bell

Stephens, Johnny *See* Meat Beat Manifesto

Stephenson, Carl *See* Forest for the Trees

Stephenson, Jimmy *See* The Chills

Sterling, John *See* Love/Arthur Lee & Love/Arthur Lee & Band Aid

Steve *See* Fun Lovin' Criminals

Stevens, Rick *See* Tower of Power

Stevens, Rogers *See* Blind Melon

Stevens, T.M. *See* The Pretenders

Stevens, Tone *See* Savoy Brown

Stevens, Tony *See* Foghat

Stevenson, Bill *See* All; Black Flag/Greg Ginn; Descendents

Stevenson, Don *See* Moby Grape

Stevo *See* Ministry

Steward, Pat *See* The Odds

Stewart, Bek-Jean *See* Eva Trout

Stewart, Chris *See* Genesis; Gary Wright/Spooky Tooth

Stewart, Dave *See* Eurythmics/Annie Lennox/Dave Stewart

Stewart, Duglas *See* The BMX Bandits

Stewart, Eric *See* Wayne Fontana & the Mindbenders; 10cc

Stewart, Jamie *See* The Cult/The Holy Barbarians

Stewart, Jeff "Wally" *See* Flash Cadillac/Flash Cadillac & the Continental Kids

Stewart, John *See* The Kingston Trio

Stewart, Jon *See* Sleeper

Stewart, Martin *See* Bad Manners; The Selecter

Stewart, Rod *See* The Faces/The Small Faces

Stewart, Tyler *See* Barenaked Ladies

Stiles, Ray *See* Mud

Stills, Stephen *See* Buffalo Springfield; Crosby, Stills & Nash/Crosby, Stills, Nash & Young/The Stills-Young Band

Sting *See* The Police

Stinky *See* The Rugburns/Steve Poltz

Stinnet, Ray *See* Sam the Sham & the Pharaohs/Sam the Sham Revue

Stinson, Bob *See* The Replacements/Paul Westerberg

Stinson, Tommy *See* The Replacements/Paul Westerberg

Stipe, Michael *See* R.E.M.

Stips, Rober-Jan *See* Golden Earring

Stirratt, John *See* Uncle Tupelo; Wilco

Stirratt, Laurie *See* Blue Mountain

Stobaugh, Bill *See* Thelonious Monster

Stocker, Wally *See* John Waite/The Babys/Bad English

Stoeckel, Steve *See* The Spongetones

Stoker *See* The English Beat/General Public

Stone, David *See* Rainbow

Stone, Freddie *See* Sly & the Family Stone

Stone, Gerry *See* Cryan' Shames

Stone, Martin *See* Savoy Brown

Stone, Rosie *See* Sly & the Family Stone

Stone, Sly *See* Sly & the Family Stone

Stone, Steve *See* The Atlanta Rhythm Section/ARS

Stoodley, Mike *See* The Verlaines

Stopholese, Markus *See* A.F.I./Asking for It

Stout, Brian *See* The Verve Pipe

Stout, Gabriel *See* Air Miami

Stradlin, Izzy *See* Guns N' Roses

Strain, Sammy *See* Little Anthony & the Imperials

Strazza, Mike *See* moe.

Street, Richard *See* The Temptations

Streng, Keith *See* The Fleshtones

Strickland, Keith *See* The B-52's/Fred Schneider

Strickland, Kevin *See* Laughing Hyenas

Strickland, Larissa *See* Laughing Hyenas

Stringer, Gary *See* Reef

Stringfellow, Ken *See* The Posies; Sky Cries Mary

Strohm, John *See* Antenna/Velo-Deluxe/The Mysteries of Life/John P. Strohm & the Hello Strangers; Blake Babies

Strongman, Phil *See* The Farm

Strummer, Joe *See* The Clash; The Pogues/Shane MacGowan & the Popes

Strykert, Ron *See* Men at Work

Stu Boy Stu, *See* ManBREAK

Stuart, Chad *See* Chad & Jeremy

Stuart, Dan *See* Green on Red

Stuart, Hamish *See* Average White Band

Stuart, Lee *See* The Blazers

Stuart, Mark *See* Audio Adrenaline

Stuart, Michael *See* Love/Arthur Lee & Love/Arthur Lee & Band Aid

Stuart, Peter *See* Dog's Eye View

Stubblefield, John *See* Big Ass Truck

Stubbs, Levi *See* The Four Tops

Stuller, John *See* Colony

Sturmer, Andy *See* Jellyfish

Styles, Re *See* The Tubes

Styrene, Poly *See* X-Ray Spex

Such, Alec John *See* Bon Jovi/Jon Bon Jovi

Sulley, Suzanne *See* Human League

Sullivan, Billy *See* Gary Lewis & the Playboys

Sullivan, Jacqui *See* Bananarama/Shakespear's Sister

Sullivan, Jeff *See* Drivin' N' Cryin'/Kevn Kinney/Kathleen Turner Overdrive/Toenut

Sullivan, Justin *See* New Model Army

Sullivan, Matt *See* Tarnation

Sullivan, Terry *See* Renaissance

Sult, Evan *See* Harvey Danger

Sult, Tim *See* Clutch

Sulton, Kasim *See* Todd Rundgren/Utopia

Summers, Andy *See* The Police

Sumner, Bernard *See* Electronic; New Order

Sundholm, Norm *See* The Kingsmen

Sundquist, Scott *See* Soundgarden

Super DJ Dmitry *See* Deee-Lite

Suranovich, George *See* Love/Arthur Lee & Love/Arthur Lee & Band Aid

Sutcliffe, Stuart *See* The Beatles

Sutton, Ann *See* The Young Rascals/The Rascals

Sutton, Graham *See* Boymerang

Sutton, Gregg *See* Lone Justice/Maria McKee

Sutton, Jimmy *See* Mighty Blue Kings

Sutton, Roger *See* The Mark-Almond Band

Suv *See* Roni Size/Reprazent

Suycott, David *See* Stabbing Westward

Sveningsson, Magnus *See* The Cardigans

Svensson, Peter *See* The Cardigans

Swain, Jean *See* The Chordettes

Swales, Julian *See* Kitchens of Distinction

Swalla, Todd A. *See* Laughing Hyenas

Swanson, Dave *See* Guided by Voices

Swarbrick, Dave *See* Fairport Convention/Fairport/Sandy Denny/Fotheringay

Swartz, Bill *See* Flg Dlsh

Swartz, Kit *See* Love Tractor

Sweda, Mick *See* Bulletboys

Sweeney, Matt *See* Chavez

Sweet, Darrel *See* Nazareth

Sweet, Steven *See* Warrant

Swiderski, Thad *See* The Wannabes

Swift, David *See* Inspiral Carpets

Swindells, Steve "Swindelli" *See* Man-BREAK

Swisher, Phil *See* Corrosion of Conformity

Swope, Martin *See* Mission of Burma

Sykes, David *See* Boston

Sykes, John *See* Thin Lizzy; Whitesnake

Sylvain Sylvain *See* The New York Dolls/Johnny Thunders

Sylvester, Andy *See* Savoy Brown

Sylvester, Terry *See* The Hollies; The Swinging Blue Jeans/The Bluegenes/Ray Ennis & the Blue Jeans

Sylvian, David *See* Japan/Rain Tree Crow/Mick Karn/Polytown

Tabib, Erin *See* Spin Doctors

Tabor, Ty *See* King's X

Tackett, Fred *See* Little Feat

Taff *See* Killing Joke

Taggart, Jeremy *See* Our Lady Peace

Tait, Michael *See* DC Talk

Takac, Robby *See* Goo Goo Dolls

Takanami, K-Taro *See* Pizzicato Five

Talbot, Matt *See* Hum

Talbot, Mick *See* Style Council

Talbott, Billy *See* Crazy Horse

Talcum, Joe Jack *See* The Dead Milkmen

Tallent, Garry *See* Bruce Springsteen/Bruce Springsteen & the E Street Band

Talley, Nedra *See* The Ronettes/Ronnie Spector

Tallman, Susan *See* Band of Susans/Robert Poss

Talstra, Jim *See* Dharma Bums

Tamblyn, Larry *See* The Standells

Tamelier, Jeff *See* Tower of Power

Tanas, Andy *See* Black Oak Arkansas

Tandy, Richard *See* Electric Light Orchestra/Jeff Lynne/ELO II

Tanner, Eugene *See* The "5" Royales

Tanner, John *See* The "5" Royales

Tanner, Trevor *See* The Bolshoi

Tanzin, Joe *See* Badfinger/Joey Molland

Taree, Aerle *See* Arrested Development/Speech/Dionne Farris

Tarver, Clay *See* Chavez

Tarwater, Craig *See* Love/Arthur Lee & Love/Arthur Lee & Band Aid

Tashian, Barry *See* Barry & the Remains

Tate, Geoff *See* Queensryche

Tate, Troy *See* Julian Cope/The Teardrop Explodes

Tatuaka, Eric *See* Chris Duarte Group

Taul, Matt *See* Days of the New

Taupin, Bernie *See* Farm Dogs

Taylor, Andy *See* Duran Duran/Arcadia/The Power Station/John Taylor/Andy Taylor

Taylor, Bo *See* blackgirls/Dish

Taylor, Brian "Dolphin" *See* Tom Robinson Band/Sector 27

Taylor, Chad *See* Live

Taylor, Chris *See* The Oyster Band

Taylor, Courtney *See* Dandy Warhols

Taylor, David *See* James Taylor Quartet

Taylor, Dick *See* The Mekons; Pretty Things

Taylor, Gene *See* The Blasters; The Fabulous Thunderbirds

Taylor, Glenn *See* Marmalade/Dean Ford & the Gaylords/The Gaylords/Dave Dee & Marmalade

Taylor, James *See* James Taylor Quartet

Taylor, John *See* Duran Duran/Arcadia/The Power Station/John Taylor/Andy Taylor

Taylor, Larry *See* Canned Heat

Taylor, Leon *See* The Ventures

Taylor, Mel *See* The Ventures

Taylor, Mick *See* The Rolling Stones

Taylor, Paul *See* Winger/Kip Winger

Taylor, Phil "Philthy Animal" *See* Motörhead

Taylor, Roger *See* Duran Duran/Arcadia/The Power Station/John Taylor/Andy Taylor

Taylor, Roger Meddows *See* Queen

Taylor, Scott *See* The Grifters

Taylor, Tim *See* Brainiac

Taylor, Zola *See* The Platters

Taylor-Firth, Robin *See* Olive

Tchaikovsky, Bram *See* The Motors

Tchaparian, Hagop *See* Symposium

Techno-Destructo *See* GWAR

Teel, Jerry *See* Boss Hog

Teeter, Richie *See* The Dictators

Telfer, Ian *See* The Oyster Band

Tempesta, John *See* White Zombie

Templar, Simon *See* The Rezillos

Temple, Brannen *See* Chris Duarte Group

Temple, Christopher *See* Lincoln

Temple, Johnny *See* Girls Against Boys

Temple, Michele *See* Pere Ubu

Templeman, Ted *See* Harpers Bizarre

Tench, Benmont *See* Tom Petty & the Heartbreakers

Tench, Bobby *See* Humble Pie

Tennant, Neil *See* Pet Shop Boys

Tennille, Toni *See* The Captain & Tennille

Tepper, Jeff Morris *See* Captain Beefheart & His Magic Band

Terminator X *See* Public Enemy

Terranova, Joe *See* Danny & the Juniors/Danny & the Juniors Featuring Joe Terry

Terrell, Jean *See* The Supremes

Terry, Boyd *See* The Aquabats

Terry, Isaiah "Buzzy" *See* The Flamingos

Terry, Joe *See* The Skeletons/The Morells

Terry, Steve *See* Whiskeytown

Thain, Gary *See* Uriah Heep

Thayil, Kim *See* Soundgarden

Theaker, Drachen *See* Love/Arthur Lee & Love/Arthur Lee & Band Aid

Theilhelm, Emil "Peppy Castro" *See* The Blues Magoos

Theo *See* Faith No More/Mr. Bungle/Imperial Teen

Thibeaux, Greg *See* Cotton Mather

Thistlethwaite, Anthony *See* The Waterboys

Thoman, John *See* The Rain Parade

Thomas, Banner *See* Molly Hatchet

Thomas, Bruce *See* Elvis Costello/Elvis Costello & the Attractions

Thomas, David *See* Pere Ubu

Thomas, Jim *See* The Mermen

Thomas, Mary *See* The Crystals

Thomas, Mickey *See* Jefferson Starship/Starship

Thomas, Pete *See* Elvis Costello/Elvis Costello & the Attractions; Squeeze/Difford & Tilbrook/Jools Holland

Thomas, Ray *See* The Moody Blues/Justin Hayward & John Lodge/Mike Pinder

Thomas, Richard *See* The Jesus & Mary Chain; Moose

Thomas, Rob *See* Matchbox 20

Thomas, Tim *See* Babe the Blue Ox

Thomas, Vic *See* Junior Walker & the All-Stars

Thomasson, Hughie *See* Lynyrd Skynyrd; The Outlaws

Thompson, Bert *See* Eva Trout

Thompson, Chester *See* Tower of Power; Weather Report

Thompson, Chris *See* Eric's Trip/Elevator to Hell

Thompson, D. Clinton *See* The Skeletons/The Morells

Thompson, Danny *See* Pentangle

Thompson, Dennis *See* MC5

Thompson, Dougie *See* Supertramp

Thompson, Lee *See* Madness

Thompson, Les *See* The Nitty Gritty Dirt Band

Thompson, Linda *See* Richard Thompson/Linda Thompson/Richard & Linda Thompson

Thompson, Mayo *See* Pere Ubu

Thompson, Noel *See* The Vibrators

Thompson, Paul *See* Concrete Blonde; Roxy Music

Thompson, Phil *See* The Swinging Blue Jeans/The Bluegenes/Ray Ennis & the Blue Jeans

Thompson, Porl *See* The Cure

Thompson, Richard *See* The Association; Fairport Convention/Fairport/Sandy Denny/Fotheringay; Richard Thompson/Linda Thompson/Richard & Linda Thompson

Thomson, Kristin *See* Tsunami

Thomson, Rose *See* Babe the Blue Ox

Thorn, Christopher *See* Blind Melon

Thorn, Tracey *See* Everything but the Girl

Thornburg, Lee *See* Supertramp; Tower of Power

Thornbury, James *See* Canned Heat

Thorne, Rob *See* The Spongetones

Thornhill, Leeroy *See* Prodigy

Thornley, Ian *See* Big Wreck

Thornton, Blair *See* Bachman-Turner Overdrive

Thorogood, George *See* George Thorogood & the Destroyers

Thorpe, Suzanne *See* Mercury Rev

Thrall, Pat *See* Asia

Thrash *See* The Orb

Thrasher, Don *See* Guided by Voices

3D *See* Massive Attack

Thunders, Johnny *See* The New York Dolls/Johnny Thunders

Thunes, Scott *See* Fear; Z/Dweezil Zappa

Thurston, Scott *See* The Motels; Iggy Pop/The Stooges

Tibbs, Gary *See* Roxy Music; The Vibrators

Tich *See* Dave Dee, Dozy, Beaky, Mick & Tich/Dozy, Beaky, Mick & Tich

Tichy, John *See* Commander Cody & His Lost Planet Airmen

Tickner, George *See* Journey

Tighe, Brian *See* The Hang Ups

Tilbrook, Glenn *See* Squeeze/Difford & Tilbrook/Jools Holland

Tilley, Ian *See* Boom Crash Opera

Tilley, Sandra *See* Martha & the Vandellas

Tillman, Georgeanna *See* The Marvelettes

Timmins, Margo *See* Cowboy Junkies

Timmins, Michael *See* Cowboy Junkies

Timmins, Peter *See* Cowboy Junkies

Timms, Sally *See* The Mekons

Timony, Mary *See* Helium

Timson, John *See* Cast/The La's

Tina *See* My Bloody Valentine

Tinsley, Boyd *See* Dave Matthews Band

Tippens, Stan *See* Mott the Hoople

Tipton, Glenn *See* Judas Priest

Toback, Jeremy *See* Brad/Satchel

Tobe, Tikake *See* The Stranglers

Tobias, Jesse *See* Red Hot Chili Peppers

Todd, Andrew *See* The Chills

Todd, Andy *See* Republica

Tola, Jean-Yves *See* 16 Horsepower

Tolby, Sean *See* The Chocolate Watch Band

Toler, Dan *See* The Allman Brothers Band

Toler, David "Frankie" *See* The Allman Brothers Band

Tolhurst, Kerryn *See* The Health & Happiness Show

Tolhurst, Laurence "Lol" *See* The Cure

Tolland, Bryan *See* Del Amitri

Tolman, Cache *See* CIV

Tolson, Peter *See* Pretty Things

Tomlinson, David *See* XC-NN

Tommy *See* eels

Tomo *See* God Street Wine

Tonadge, Gary *See* Big Audio Dynamite/B.A.D. II/Big Audio

Tong, Simon *See* The Verve

Toohey, Dan *See* Guided by Voices

Took, Steve Peregrine *See* T. Rex

Tooke, Travis Michael *See* For Squirrels/Subrosa

Toomey, Jenny *See* Tsunami

Topham, Anthony "Top" *See* The Yardbirds

TopTen *See* The Dictators

Torbert, David *See* New Riders of the Purple Sage

Torgerson, Carla *See* The Walkabouts

Torien, Marq *See* Bulletboys

Tork, Peter *See* The Monkees

Torpey, Pat *See* Mr. Big

Torrence, Dean Ormsby *See* Jan & Dean

Torrente, Al *See* Southside Johnny & the Asbury Jukes

Torres, Bobby *See* The Mark-Almond Band

Torres, Tico *See* Bon Jovi/Jon Bon Jovi

Tortelvis *See* Dread Zeppelin

Tosh, Peter *See* Bob Marley & the Wailers

Tosh, Stuart *See* 10cc

Toups, Fontaine *See* Versus

Tourish, Cíarán *See* Altan

Tout, John *See* Renaissance

Touter *See* Bob Marley & the Wailers

Towe, John *See* The Adverts; Billy Idol/Generation X

Townshend, Peter *See* Thunderclap Newman; The Who

Townshend, Simon *See* The Who

Trainer, Todd *See* Shellac

Trash K. *See* My Life with the Thrill Kill Kult/The Bomb Gang Girlz

Travers, Brian *See* UB40

Travers, Joe *See* Z/Dweezil Zappa

Travis, Abby *See* Elastica

Travis, Malcolm *See* Bob Mould/Sugar

Travis, Scott *See* Judas Priest

Traynor, Chris *See* Orange 9mm

Traynor, John "Jay" *See* Jay & the Americans

Treece, Malc *See* The Wonder Stuff

Tregunna, Dave *See* Dead Boys/Stiv Bators/Lords of the New Church; Sham 69

Tremonti, Mark *See* Creed

Trenier, Buddy *See* The Treniers

Trenier, Claude *See* The Treniers

Trenier, Clifford *See* The Treniers

Trenier, Milt *See* The Treniers

Trenier, Skip *See* The Treniers

Trent, Tyler *See* Brainiac

Trewavas, Pete *See* Marillion/Fish

Tricky *See* Massive Attack

Trimble, Vivian *See* Luscious Jackson

Tripplehorn, Tom *See* Gary Lewis & the Playboys

Troiano, Dominic *See* The Guess Who

Trojanowski, Mark *See* Sister Hazel

Trombatore, John *See* The Champs

Trombino, Mark *See* aMiniature

Trondson, Robert *See* Blue Meanies

Tronzo, David *See* The Lounge Lizards

Trott, Jeffrey *See* Wire Train

Trout, Dave *See* The Weirdos

Trower, Robin *See* Procol Harum

Troyer, Eric *See* Electric Light Orchestra/Jeff Lynne/ELO II

Trucks, Butch *See* The Allman Brothers Band

Trujillo, Robert *See* Suicidal Tendencies

Trumfio, Dave *See* The Pulsars

Trumfio, Harry *See* The Pulsars

Tse, Rono *See* Spearhead/Disposable Heroes of Hiphoprisy

Tubbs, Hubert *See* Tower of Power

Tucker, Clive *See* The Bogmen

Tucker, Corin *See* Sleater-Kinney

Tucker, Jim *See* The Turtles

Tucker, Maureen "Moe" *See* The Velvet Underground/Nico/Maureen Tucker

Tucker, Mick *See* The Sweet

Tufano, Dennis *See* The Buckinghams; Farm Dogs

Tufnel, Nigel *See* Spinal Tap

Tuitti, Brian *See* Bad Manners

Tulin, Mark *See* The Electric Prunes

Tulu *See* The Queers

Tumahai, Charles *See* Be Bop Deluxe

Turbin, Neil *See* Anthrax

Turgon, Bruce *See* Foreigner

Turkin, Kenny *See* The Shadows of Knight

Turnbull, John *See* Ian Dury/Ian Dury & the Blockheads

Turner, C.F. (Fred) *See* Bachman-Turner Overdrive

Turner, Dale *See* Oingo Boingo/Danny Elfman

Turner, David Allen "Ted" *See* Wishbone Ash

Turner, Eric *See* Warrant

Turner, Ike *See* Ike & Tina Turner/Tina Turner/Ike Turner

Turner, Joe Lynn *See* Deep Purple; Rainbow

Turner, John *See* The Buckinghams

Turner, Martin *See* Wishbone Ash

Turner, Mick *See* Dirty Three

Turner, Mike *See* Our Lady Peace

Turner, Nick *See* Dead Boys/Stiv Bators/Lords of the New Church

Turner, Nicky *See* The Barracudas

Turner, Sonny *See* The Platters

Turner, Steve *See* Mudhoney

Turner, Tina *See* Ike & Tina Turner/Tina Turner/Ike Turner

Vincent, Holly *See* Holly Vincent/Holly & the Italians/Oblivious

Vincent, Vinnie *See* Kiss

Vines, Adi *See* Swervedriver

Ving, Lee *See* Fear

Vinton, Tommy *See* Too Much Joy

Violent J *See* Insane Clown Posse

Vipond, Douglas *See* Deacon Blue

Virgo, Martin *See* Mono

Virtue, Mickey *See* UB40

Visser, Peter *See* Bettie Serveert

Vitali, Chris *See* Orange 9mm

Vitesse, Peter *See* Simple Minds

Vito, Rick *See* Fleetwood Mac

Vitous, Miroslav *See* Weather Report

Vivino, Jerry Jr. *See* Southside Johnny & the Asbury Jukes

Voeltz, Susan *See* Poi Dog Pondering

Vogelsang, Michael "Popeye" *See* Farside

Vogensen, Gary *See* New Riders of the Purple Sage

Volk, Phil "Fang" *See* Paul Revere & the Raiders/Paul Revere & the Raiders Featuring Mark Lindsay/Raiders/Pink Puzz

Volman, Mark *See* The Turtles

Volz, Greg X. *See* Petra

Von, Eerie *See* Danzig/Samhain

Von, Jon *See* The Mr. T Experience

Von Veldt, John *See* Thin White Rope

Voorman, Klaus *See* Manfred Mann/Manfred Mann's Earth Band

Votel, Freddy *See* Cows

Vrenna, Chris *See* nine inch nails

Waaktaar, Pal *See* a-ha

Wade, Adam *See* Jawbox; Shudder to Think

Wade, Brett *See* The Electric Prunes

Wadenius, Georg *See* Blood, Sweat & Tears

Wadhams, Tad *See* Farm Dogs

Wagner, Kurt *See* Lambchop

Wagner, Rick *See* The dB's/Peter Holsapple/Will Rigby

Wagner, Steve *See* The Balancing Act

Wagon, Chuck *See* The Dickies

Wahlberg, Donnie *See* New Kids on the Block

Wailer, Bunny *See* Bob Marley & the Wailers

Waite, John *See* John Waite/The Babys/Bad English

Wakeling, Dave *See* The English Beat/General Public

Wakeman, Alan *See* Soft Machine

Wakeman, Rick *See* The Strawbs/Dave Cousins; Yes

Walford, Britt *See* Squirrel Bait

Walk, Mark *See* ruby

Walker, Colin *See* Electric Light Orchestra/Jeff Lynne/ELO II

Walker, Dave *See* Fleetwood Mac; Savoy Brown

Walker, David *See* Gary Lewis & the Playboys

Walker, Dick *See* Paul Revere & the Raiders/Paul Revere & the Raiders Featuring Mark Lindsay/Raiders/Pink Puzz

Walker, Jim *See* Public Image Ltd./PiL/John Lydon

Walker, Jimmy *See* The Knickerbockers

Walker, Mick *See* The Flashcubes/Gary Frenay

Walker, Junior *See* Junior Walker & the All-Stars

Walker, Scott *See* The Walker Brothers/Scott Walker

Walker, Simon *See* The House of Love

Walker, Stephen *See* Modern English

Wall, Lee *See* Luna

Wallace, Bill *See* The Guess Who

Wallace, Ian *See* King Crimson

Wallace, Jim *See* The Reverend Horton Heat

Wallace, John *See* James Taylor Quartet

Waller, Gordon *See* Peter & Gordon

Wallinger, Karl *See* The Waterboys; World Party

Walls, Jeff *See* Guadalcanal Diary/Murray Attaway

Walmsley, Steve *See* The Lemon Pipers

Walsh, Joe *See* The Eagles

Walsh, Martyn *See* Inspiral Carpets

Walsh, Steve *See* Kansas

Walsh, Tom *See* Supertramp

Walters, John *See* Dr. Hook & the Medicine Show/Dr. Hook

Walters, Patrick *See* The Spongetones

Walters, Steve *See* James Taylor Quartet

Walton, Mark *See* The Continental Drifters; The Dream Syndicate/Steve Wynn/Opal/Guild of Temporal Adventurers/Kendra Smith

Walusko, Nick *See* The Wondermints

Wandscher, Phil *See* Whiskeytown

Warburton, Damien *See* Moose

Ward, Alan *See* The Honeycombs/The New Honeycombs

Ward, Algy *See* The Saints

Ward, Alistair *See* The Damned

Ward, Andy *See* Camel

Ward, Bill *See* Black Sabbath

Ward, Billy *See* The Knack

Ward, Doug *See* Screeching Weasel

Ward, Jason B. *See* Flotsam & Jetsam

Ward, Michael *See* School of Fish/Josh Clayton-Felt; The Wallflowers

Ware, Martyn *See* Heaven 17; Human League

Wareham, Dean *See* Galaxie 500; Luna

Warleigh, Ray *See* Soft Machine

Warner, Allan *See* The Foundations

Warner, Les *See* The Cult/The Holy Barbarians

Warner, Sieb *See* Golden Earring

Warnick, Kim *See* Fastbacks

Warning, Gail *See* The Rezillos

Waronker, Anna *See* that dog.

Warren, Paul *See* Fairport Convention/Fairport/Sandy Denny/Fotheringay; Rare Earth

Warton, Dan *See* Ned's Atomic Dustbin

Warwick, Clint *See* The Moody Blues/Justin Hayward & John Lodge/Mike Pinder

Was, David *See* Was (Not Was)

Weston, Bob *See* Fleetwood Mac; Shellac

Weston, Grant Calvin *See* The Lounge Lizards

Weston, Joyce *See* The Chordettes

Wetton, John *See* Asia; King Crimson; Roxy Music; Uriah Heep

Weymouth, Tina *See* Talking Heads/Jerry Harrison/Tom Tom Club/The Heads

Whalen, Katharine *See* Squirrel Nut Zippers/Jas. Mathus & His Knock-Down Society

Whaley, Paul *See* Blue Cheer

Wharton, Darren *See* Thin Lizzy

Wheat, Brian *See* Tesla

Wheatbread, Paul *See* Flash Cadillac/Flash Cadillac & the Continental Kids; Gary Puckett & the Union Gap

Wheeler, Harriet *See* The Sundays

Wheeler, Paul *See* Icehouse

Wheeler, Robert *See* Pere Ubu

Whelan, Dave *See* The Records/Jude Cole

Whelan, Gary *See* Happy Mondays/Black Grape

Whelan, Gavan *See* James

Whetstone, Richard *See* The Electric Prunes

Whitaker, Hugh *See* The Housemartins/The Beautiful South/Beats International

White, Alan *See* Oasis; Yes

White, Andrew N. III *See* Weather Report

White, Bubs *See* The Bonzo Dog Band

White, Charlie *See* The Clovers

White, Chris *See* Mother Earth

White, Christopher *See* The Zombies

White, Clarence *See* The Byrds

White, Craig *See* Seam

White, Dave *See* Sid King & the Five Strings

White, David *See* Danny & the Juniors/Danny & the Juniors Featuring Joe Terry

White, David *See* Warrant

White, Dennis *See* Charm Farm

White, Dookie *See* Rainbow

White, James *See* James Chance/James White

White, Jim *See* Dirty Three

White, Kevin *See* The English Beat/General Public

White, Mark *See* ABC

White, Mark *See* The Mekons

White, Mark Burton *See* Spin Doctors

White, Ralph *See* Bad Livers

White, Richard *See* Paul Revere & the Raiders/Paul Revere & the Raiders Featuring Mark Lindsay/Raiders/Pink Puzz

White, Rick *See* Eric's Trip/Elevator to Hell

White, Robert *See* Paul Revere & the Raiders/Paul Revere & the Raiders Featuring Mark Lindsay/Raiders/Pink Puzz

White, Ronnie *See* Smokey Robinson & the Miracles

White, Seth *See* Blake Babies

White, Simon *See* Menswear

White, Snowy *See* Thin Lizzy

White, Steve *See* James Taylor Quartet

White, Tara *See* Eric's Trip/Elevator to Hell

White, Vince *See* The Clash

White, William Richard *See* For Squirrels/Subrosa

Whitehead, Alan *See* Marmalade/Dean Ford & the Gaylords/The Gaylords/Dave Dee & Marmalade

Whitener, Todd *See* Days of the New

Whitford, Brad *See* Aerosmith

Whitman, Allen *See* The Mermen

Whitman, Larry *See* The Beat/Paul Collins

Whitney, Lou *See* The Skeletons/The Morells

Whittaker, Mark *See* The Chocolate Watch Band

Whitted, Dennis *See* Paul Butterfield Blues Band

Whitten, Danny *See* Crazy Horse

Whittington, Melvan *See* Love/Arthur Lee & Love/Arthur Lee & Band Aid

Whitwam, Barry *See* Herman's Hermits

Wichnewski, Stephan *See* Yo La Tengo

Wickham, Steve *See* The Waterboys

Wickman, Jesse *See* Nuisance

Wicks, John *See* The Records/Jude Cole

Wiczling, Bogdan *See* Fingerprintz

Widenhouse, Je *See* Squirrel Nut Zippers/Jas. Mathus & His Knock-Down Society

Wiedlin, Jane *See* The Go-Go's

Wiggs, Josephine *See* The Breeders/The Amps

Wiggs, Pete *See* St. Etienne

Wike, Mark *See* The Bogmen

Wilbur, Jim *See* Superchunk

Wilburn, Ishmael *See* Weather Report

Wilcox, Jimmy *See* Blue Öyster Cult

Wilcox, John *See* Todd Rundgren/Utopia

Wilcox, Kathi *See* Bikini Kill

Wild, Chuck *See* Missing Persons

Wilde, Danny *See* The Rembrandts

Wilder, Alan *See* Depeche Mode

Wildwood, Michael *See* D Generation

Wilhelm, Mike *See* The Flamin' Groovies

Wilk, Brad *See* Rage Against the Machine

Wilkeson, Leon *See* Lynyrd Skynyrd

Wilkie, Chris *See* Dubstar

Wilkie, Frank *See* The Marshall Tucker Band

Wilkinson, Keith *See* Squeeze/Difford & Tilbrook/Jools Holland

Wilkinson, Kevin *See* China Crisis; Squeeze/Difford & Tilbrook/Jools Holland

Wilkinson, Peter *See* Cast/The La's

Will *See* Faith No More/Mr. Bungle/Imperial Teen

Willems, "Buddha" Jerry *See* Big Rude Jake

Williams, Adam *See* Powerman 5000

Williams, Boris *See* The Cure

Williams, Brett *See* Mighty Joe Plum

Williams, Brian *See* Save Ferris

Williams, Charles *See* KC & the Sunshine Band

Williams, Cliff *See* AC/DC

Williams, Forrest *See* Big Wreck

Williams, Greg *See* Nineteen Wheels; The Weirdos

Williams, Joel *See* Black Oak Arkansas

Williams, Joseph *See* Toto

Williams, Ken *See* The Electric Prunes

Williams, Lamar *See* The Allman Brothers Band

Williams, Lenny *See* Tower of Power

Williams, Leo *See* Big Audio Dynamite/B.A.D. II/Big Audio

Williams, Marcus *See* Mighty Lemon Drops

Williams, Mars *See* The Psychedelic Furs/Richard Butler/Love Spit Love; The Waitresses

Williams, Mike *See* Nancy Boy

Williams, Otis *See* The Temptations

Williams, Paul *See* The Temptations

Williams, Richard *See* Kansas

Williams, Robert Arthur *See* Captain Beefheart & His Magic Band

Williams, Simon *See* Goldfinger

Williams, Terry *See* Dire Straits; Dave Edmunds/Rockpile

Williams, Tony *See* The Platters

Williams, Victoria *See* Giant Sand

Williams, Whit *See* Cotton Mather

Williamson, James *See* Iggy Pop/The Stooges

Williamson, Steve *See* James Taylor Quartet

Willis, Brian *See* Quarterflash

Willis, Pete *See* Def Leppard

Willis, Victor *See* The Village People

Willison, Mike *See* Fig Dish

Willoughby, Brian *See* The Strawbs/Dave Cousins

Willoughby, Rusty *See* Flop

Wills, Aaron "P-Nut" *See* 311

Wills, David *See* Negativland

Wills, Rick *See* Bad Company; The Faces/The Small Faces; Foreigner; Roxy Music

Wills, Robin *See* The Barracudas

Willson-Piper, Marty *See* The Church

Willsteed, John *See* Grant McLennan/Robert Forster/The Go-Betweens

Wilmott, John *See* James Taylor Quartet

Wilsey, James Calvin *See* The Avengers

Wilson, Al "Blind Owl" *See* Canned Heat

Wilson, Ann *See* Heart/Lovemongers

Wilson, B.J. *See* Procol Harum

Wilson, Brian *See* The Beach Boys

Wilson, Carl *See* The Beach Boys

Wilson, Carnie *See* Wilson Phillips

Wilson, Chris *See* The Barracudas; The Flamin' Groovies

Wilson, Cindy *See* The B-52's/Fred Schneider

Wilson, Dan *See* Semisonic; Trip Shakespeare

Wilson, Dennis *See* The Beach Boys

Wilson, Don *See* The Ventures

Wilson, Eric *See* Sublime

Wilson, Jeff *See* Pure Prairie League

Wilson, Jeremy *See* Dharma Bums

Wilson, Joe *See* Classics IV

Wilson, Kaia *See* Team Dresch

Wilson, Kim *See* The Fabulous Thunderbirds

Wilson, Mary *See* The Supremes

Wilson, Matt *See* Trip Shakespeare

Wilson, Nancy *See* Heart/Lovemongers

Wilson, Pat *See* Weezer/The Rentals

Wilson, Paul *See* The Flamingos

Wilson, Philip *See* Paul Butterfield Blues Band

Wilson, Ray *See* Genesis

Wilson, Ricky *See* The B-52's/Fred Schneider

Wilson, Robin *See* Gin Blossoms

Wilson, Wendy *See* Wilson Phillips

Wilton, Michael *See* Queensryche

Wimberley, Peele *See* The Connells

Wimbish, Doug *See* Living Colour

Wimbush, Doug *See* Gang of Four/Shriekback

Winders, Paul *See* The Verlaines

Windsor, Morris *See* Robyn Hitchcock/Robyn Hitchcock & the Egyptians; The Soft Boys

Wine, Toni *See* The Archies

Winer, Marty *See* The Elvis Brothers

Winfield, Chuck *See* Blood, Sweat & Tears

Winger, Kip *See* Winger/Kip Winger

Winley, Harold *See* The Clovers

Winn, Andrew *See* Agents of Good Roots

Winston *See* Anti-Nowhere League

Winston, Jimmy *See* The Faces/The Small Faces

Winter, Edgar *See* Montrose

Winter, Kurt *See* The Guess Who

Winter-Ruiz, Stephanie *See* The Legendary Jim Ruiz Group

Winterhart, Paul *See* Kula Shaker

Winters, Ed *See* Judybats

Winthrop, Dave *See* Supertramp

Winwood, Steve *See* Blind Faith; Traffic

Wire, Nicky *See* Manic Street Preachers

Wisefield, Laurie *See* Wishbone Ash

Wiseman, Bob *See* Blue Rodeo

Withem, Gary *See* Gary Puckett & the Union Gap

Witherick, Nick *See* XC-NN

Withers, Pick *See* Dire Straits

Witherspoon, Lajon *See* Sevendust

Withrow, Kenny *See* Edie Brickell & New Bohemians

Wittingham, Richard *See* Rocker's Hi-Fi

Wittman, William *See* Too Much Joy

Wiz *See* Mega City Four

Wobble, Jah *See* Public Image Ltd./PiL/John Lydon

Wolbert, Anke *See* Xymox

Wolf, Bill *See* The Fugs

Wolf, Kurt *See* Boss Hog

Wolf, Peter *See* J. Geils Band/Bluestime

Wolf, Roland *See* Einstürzende Neubauten

Wolinski, Dave "The Hawk" *See* The Shadows of Knight

Wolking, Ricky *See* The Nixons

Woloschuk, John *See* Klaatu

Wolstencroft, John Simon *See* The Fall

Wood, Chris *See* Medeski, Martin & Wood; Traffic

Wood, Chuck *See* Richard Hell & the Voidoids

Wood, Danny *See* New Kids on the Block

Wood, Ingrid Anne *See* The Raincoats

Wood, Peter *See* Dramarama

Wood, Ron *See* The Faces/The Small Faces; The Rolling Stones

Wood, Roy *See* Electric Light Orchestra/Jeff Lynne/ELO II; The Move/Roy Wood

Wood, Stuart *See* The Bay City Rollers

Woodgate, Dan *See* Madness

Woodruff, Jeffrey "Woody" *See* The Shadows of Knight

Woods, Adam *See* The Fixx

Woods, Leslie *See* The Au Pairs

Woods, Orville *See* P.J. Proby/Jett Powers/Orville Woods

Woods, Peter *See* Romeo Void

Woods, Steve *See* Antenna/Velo-Deluxe/The Mysteries of Life/John P. Strohm & the Hello Strangers

Woods, Willie *See* Junior Walker & the All-Stars

Woodson, Ali Ollie *See* The Temptations

Woodward, Karen *See* Bananarama/Shakespear's Sister

Woodward, Kaye *See* The Bats

Woody, Allen *See* The Allman Brothers Band; Gov't Mule

Wooley, Robert *See* Paul Revere & the Raiders/Paul Revere & the Raiders Featuring Mark Lindsay/Raiders/Pink Puzz

Woolley, Aaron *See* The Tremeloes/Brian Poole & the Tremeloes/Chip Hawkes' Tremeloes

Wormer, Chris *See* Charlie Daniels Band

Wormworth, Tracy *See* The Waitresses

Wren, Alan "Reni" *See* The Stone Roses

Wretzky, D'arcy *See* Smashing Pumpkins

Wright, Chuck *See* Quiet Riot

Wright, David *See* The Flamin' Groovies

Wright, Ernest Jr. *See* Little Anthony & the Imperials

Wright, Gary *See* Gary Wright/Spooky Tooth

Wright, Jimmy *See* The Five Americans

Wright, Marx *See* The Mono Men

Wright, Patricia *See* The Crystals

Wright, Richard *See* Pink Floyd

Wright, Simon *See* AC/DC

Wright, Stevie *See* The Easybeats

Wright, Stuart *See* The Dambuilders

Wright, Tim *See* DNA; Pere Ubu

Wright, Wilbo *See* Yo La Tengo

Wurster, Jon *See* The Accelerators; Superchunk

Wusthoff, Gunther *See* Faust

Wyatt, Robert *See* Soft Machine

Wydler, Thomas *See* Nick Cave & the Bad Seeds

Wylie, Dermot *See* A House

Wyman, Bill *See* The Rolling Stones

Wynn, Steve *See* The Dream Syndicate/Steve Wynn/Opal/Guild of Temporal Adventurers/Kendra Smith

X, Johnny *See* Kenickie

X, Petey *See* Rocket from the Crypt

X, Phil *See* Triumph

Xavier, John *See* Richard Hell & the Voidoids

Xefos, Chris *See* King Missile

Yaffa, Sam *See* Hanoi Rocks/Michael Monroe

Yale, Brian *See* Matchbox 20

Yallech, Don *See* The Psychedelic Furs/Richard Butler/Love Spit Love

Yamamoto, Hiro *See* Soundgarden

Yamano, Atsuko *See* Shonen Knife

Yamano, Naoko *See* Shonen Knife

Yamauchi, Tetsu *See* The Faces/The Small Faces; Free

Yang, Naoimi *See* Galaxie 500

Yanovsky, Zal *See* The Lovin' Spoonful/John Sebastian

Yanowitz, Peter *See* The Wallflowers

Yaro, Chad *See* Face to Face

Yarritu, David *See* ABC

Yates, Russell *See* Moose

Yauch, Adam *See* Beastie Boys

Yeager, Roy *See* The Atlanta Rhythm Section/ARS

Yeats, Robbie *See* The Verlaines

Yellin, Garo *See* Pere Ubu

Yester, Jerry *See* The Lovin' Spoonful/John Sebastian

Yester, Jim *See* The Association

Yester, Lena *See* The Lovin' Spoonful/John Sebastian

Yoder, Gary *See* Blue Cheer

Yoho, Monte *See* The Outlaws

York, Andy *See* Jason & the Scorchers

York, John *See* The Byrds

York, Melissa *See* Team Dresch

Yorke, Thom *See* Radiohead

Yost, Dennis *See* Classics IV

Youlden, Chris *See* Savoy Brown

Young, Adrian *See* No Doubt

Young, Angus *See* AC/DC

Young, Brian *See* The Posies

Young, Colin *See* The Foundations

Young, Gary *See* Pavement

Young, George *See* The Easybeats

Young, Grant *See* Soul Asylum

Young, James *See* Styx

Young, Jeff *See* Megadeth

Young, Malcolm *See* AC/DC

Young, Neil *See* Buffalo Springfield; Crosby, Stills & Nash/Crosby, Stills, Nash & Young/The Stills-Young Band

Young, Robert *See* Primal Scream

Young, Rusty *See* Poco

Young, Wanda *See* The Marvelettes

Youngberg, Rob *See* Lotion

Yount, Dick *See* Harpers Bizarre

Yourell, Patrick *See* The Rooks

Youth *See* Killing Joke

Youth, Todd *See* D Generation

Youtz, Ralf *See* Built to Spill

Yow, David *See* The Jesus Lizard

Yseult, Sean *See* White Zombie

Yuenger, Jay "J." *See* White Zombie

The Category Index represents an array of categories put together to suggest some of the many groupings under which rock music and rock artists can be classified. The Hound welcomes your additions to the existing categories in this index and also invites you to send in your own funny, sarcastic, prolific, poignant, or exciting ideas for brand new categories.

All-Girl Groups
The Angels
Babes in Toyland
Bananarama
The Bangles
The Go-Go's
Indigo Girls
L7
Martha & the Vandellas
The Shirelles
The Slits
The Spice Girls
The Supremes

All in the Family
The Allman Brothers Band
The Beach Boys
The Black Crowes
The Burns Sisters
The Chambers Brothers
The Connells
Cowboy Junkies

Creedence Clearwater Revival
Crowded House
The Everly Brothers
Hanson
The Hudson Brothers
The Isley Brothers
Jackson 5
The Jesus & Mary Chain
The Kinks
The Mamas & the Papas
The Marshall Tucker Band
Nelson
The Neville Brothers
Oasis
The Osmonds
The Replacements
Screaming Trees
Throwing Muses
Van Halen
Wilson Phillips

Amazin' Adjectives
Ambitious Lovers
Average White Band
Bad Brains
The Beautiful South
Cheap Trick
Combustible Edison
The Cruel Sea
The Flamin' Groovies
Happy Mondays
Inspiral Carpets
Luscious Jackson
Pale Saints
Pretty Things
The Psychedelic Furs
Simple Minds
The Swinging Blue Jeans

Twisted Sister
Violent Femmes

American Folk Rock
America
American Flyer
Tori Amos
Joan Baez
The Beau Brummels
Luka Bloom
Buffalo Springfield
The Byrds
Tracey Chapman
Shawn Colvin
Crosby, Stills & Nash
Bob Dylan
Dan Fogelberg
Steve Forbert
Janis Ian
Indigo Girls
Love
The Lovin' Spoonful
James McMurtry
John Mellencamp
Joni Mitchell
Phil Ochs
Peter, Paul & Mary
Simon & Garfunkel
Cat Stevens
Neil Young

American Neo-Punk
All
Babes in Toyland
Fugazi
Green Day
Hole
L7
Offspring

Prong
Rancid
Roches
Rocket from the Crypt
Superchunk

American Punk
Agent Orange
Bad Religion
Black Flag
Blondie
Butthole Surfers
The Circle Jerks
Dead Kennedys
Mink DeVille
Devo
Richard Hell & the Voidoids
Hüsker Dü
The Jesus Lizard
Meat Puppets
Minor Threat
Minutemen
The Misfits
Mission of Burma
Modern Lovers
Naked Raygun
New Model Army
The New York Dolls
Pere Ubu
Iggy Pop
The Ramones
The Residents
Patti Smith
Social Distortion
Sonic Youth
Talking Heads
Television
X

George Clinton
Alice Cooper
Marshall Crenshaw
The Four Tops
Aretha Franklin
Marvin Gaye
Grand Funk Railroad
Iggy & the Stooges
The Knack
Madonna
Martha & the Vandellas
MC5
Ted Nugent
? & the Mysterians
Rare Earth
Smokey Robinson & the Miracles
The Romantics
Mitch Ryder & the Detroit Wheels
Jack Scott
Bob Seger & the Silver Bullet Band
Patti Smith
Sponge
The Supremes
The Temptations
The Verve Pipe
Junior Walker & the All-Stars
Was (Not Was)
Jackie Wilson
Stevie Wonder

Dixieland Jams
The Allman Brothers Band
The Atlanta Rhythm Section
The Black Crowes
Charlie Daniels Band
The Dixie Dregs
Georgia Satellites
Lynyrd Skynyrd
The Marshall Tucker Band
Molly Hatchet
The Outlaws
Phish
.38 Special
Widespread Panic

Dr. Kevorkian's Lonely Hearts Club Band
Barry & the Remains
Body Count
Dead Boys
Dead Can Dance
Dead Kennedys
The Dead Milkmen
The Grateful Dead
Gravity Kills
Killing Joke
Megadeth

Stormtroopers of Death
Suicidal Tendencies
The Suicide Machines
White Zombie
The Zombies

Don't Ask, Don't Tell
Marvin Gaye
Nancy Boy
Pansy Division
Queen
The Queers

Don't Bug Me
Adam Ant
The Beatles
The Buggles
Iron Butterfly
Archie Roach
The Roches

Double Vision
ABBA
C.C. Adcock
The Bee Gees
J.J. Cale
Duran Duran
The Go-Go's
Goo Goo Dolls
Kajagoogoo
B.B. King
Mr. Mister
Oingo Boingo
Talk Talk
The The
20/20
Was (Not Was)
ZZ Top

Down on the Farm
Boss Hog
Cowboy Junkies
Cows
The Cowsills
The Farm
Farm Dogs
Farmer Not So John
Love Tractor
The Seeds
The Silos

Dubbed "Loudest" Band
Einstürzende Neubauten
Fugazi
Led Zeppelin
Pantera
Rage Against the Machine
The Ramones
Sonic Youth
Spinal Tap
The Who

Everything Old Is New Again
Edie Brickell & New Bohemians
Lords of the New Church
Modern English
Modern Lovers
The New Bomb Turks
The New Colony Six
New Kids on the Block
New Model Army
New Order
New Riders of the Purple Sage
The New York Dolls
Old 97's

Experimental
Laurie Anderson
Ginger Baker
Beck
David Bowie
Dead Can Dance
Einstürzende Neubauten
Brian Eno
Robert Fripp
Peter Gabriel
King Missile
Kraftwerk
Yoko Ono
Tangerine Dream
They Might Be Giants
The Velvet Underground
Frank Zappa

Fiction 101
Babes in Toyland
The Boo Radleys
Cinderella
Cotton Mather
Divine Comedy
Elysian Fields
The Grapes of Wrath
John Wesley Harding

For the Birds
Baby Bird
The Black Crowes
The Byrds
Counting Crows
Cranes
Sheryl Crow
Dr. Buzzard's Original Savannah Band
The Eagles
Fred Eaglesmith
Charlie Feathers
A Flock of Seagulls
The Jayhawks

Fruit
Fiona Apple
Apples in Stereo

Bananarama
Chuck Berry
Dave Berry
Heidi Berry
Richard Berry
Black Grape
Neneh Cherry
Cherry Poppin' Daddies
The Cranberries
The Figgs
The Lemon Pipers
Lemonheads
Moby Grape
The Raspberries
The Strawberry Alarm Clock

Games People Play
Chubby Checker
Derek & the Dominos

Garage
The Chocolate Watch Band
Count Five
The Electric Prunes
The Kingsmen
MC5
Music Machine
The New Colony Six
New York Dolls
The Pandoras
? & the Mysterians
The Seeds
The Shadows of Knight
The Standells
The Stooges
Them
The Troggs

Geography 101
Air Miami
Asia
The Atlanta Rhythm Section
The Bay City Rollers
The Beautiful South
Berlin
Black Oak Arkansas
Boston
Buffalo Tom
Chicago
China Crisis
Cypress Hill
Euro Boys
Frankie Goes to Hollywood
Future Sound of London
Georgia Satellites
Go West
Grant Lee Buffalo
Hanoi Rocks
Idaho
Japan

Kansas
L.A. Guns
The Left Banke
Miami Sound Machine
Mountain
Nashville Teens
Nazareth
The New York Dolls
The Ohio Express
Mitch Ryder & the Detroit
    Wheels
Spain

Georgia on My Mind
The Allman Brothers Band
Arrested Development
The Atlanta Rhythm Section
The B-52's
The Black Crowes
Ray Charles
Georgia Satellites
Indigo Girls
Leo Kottke
Little Richard
Otis Redding
R.E.M.
Joe South

Glam Rock
Bon Jovi
Cinderella
Def Leppard
Extreme
Gary Glitter
Great White
Kiss
Mötley Crüe
The New York Dolls
Poison
Suzi Quatro
Skid Row
Slade
The Sweet
T-Rex
Tesla
Twisted Sister
Warrant
White Lion
Whitesnake
Winger

Good Gig
The Astronauts
The Au Pairs
The Carpenters
The Dambuilders
The Drifters
Th' Faith Healers
The Grifters
The Waitresses

The Waterboys

Gothic Rock
Bauhaus
The Birthday Party
Nick Cave & the Bad Seeds
The Church
Cocteau Twins
The Cure
Dead Can Dance
The Jesus & Mary Chain
Joy Division
Love & Rockets
Marilyn Manson
Ministry
The Mission U.K.
Peter Murphy
nine inch nails
Siouxsie & the Banshees
Sisters of Mercy
Skinny Puppy
Swans
This Mortal Coil
Tones on Tail

Great Balls o' Fire
Firefall
fIREHOSE
The Flamin' Groovies
The Flaming Lips
Porno for Pyros

Green
Green Day
Green Jellÿ
Green on Red
Green River
Greenberry Woods

Ground Control to Major Tom
The Astronauts
The Bottle Rockets
Cleaners from Venus
Galaxie 500
Heaven 17
King Missle
Love & Rockets
Man or Astro-Man?
Mazzy Star
Heather Nova
Orion
Orion the Hunter
Rocket from the Crypt
Spacemen 3

**Guns, Knives, & Other
Instruments of Torture**
Gun Club
Guns N' Roses
Iron Maiden
L.A. Guns

nine inch nails
The Sex Pistols
Shonen Knife
Violent Femmes

Hardcore
The Avengers
Bad Brains
Bad Religion
Bikini Kill
Black Flag
The Circle Jerks
Dead Kennedys
Fear
Flipper
Fugazi
The Germs
Hüsker Dü
Minor Threat
Minutemen
The Misfits
Suicidal Tendencies

Head Honchos
Big Chief
The Captain & Tennille
Captain Beefheart
Commander Cody
The Dictators
Col. Bruce Hampton
Mr. Big
The Presidents of the United
    States of America

Heavy Metal
AC/DC
Aerosmith
Alice in Chains
The Amboy Dukes
Anthrax
Black Sabbath
Blue Cheer
Blue Öyster Cult
Alice Cooper
Deep Purple
Def Leppard
Lita Ford
Guns N' Roses
Jimi Hendrix
Iron Butterfly
Iron Maiden
Judas Priest
Kiss
L.A. Guns
Led Zeppelin
Marilyn Manson
MC5
Megadeath
Metallica
Mötley Crüe

Motörhead
Mountain
Nazareth
Ozzy Osbourne
Pantera
Quiet Riot
Sepultura
Skid Row
Slayer
Soundgarden
Spinal Tap
Thin Lizzy
Tool
Twisted Sister
Uriah Heep
Van Halen
White Zombie
The Who

Holy Harmony
All Saints
Angel
The Angels
Arc Angels
Blessid Union of Souls
Blind Faith
The Call
The Choir
The Church
Collective Soul
Creed
The Cult
The Damned
Deacon Blue
Dharma Bums
Divine Comedy
Dogma
Th' Faith Healers
Faith No More
Marianne Faithfull
The Fall
Genesis
God Street Wine
Guided by Voices
The Reverend Horton Heat
Heaven 17
Richard Hell
High Llamas
His Name Is Alive
Holy Barbarians
The Hoodoo Gurus
Billy Idol
The Jesus & Mary Chain
Jesus Jones
The Jesus Lizard
Judas Priest
Lords of the New Church
Madonna
Manic Street Preachers

Arrested Development
The Art of Noise
The B-52's
Bananarama
The Bee Gees
Chubby Checker
Neneh Cherry
Culture Club
Deee-Lite
Enigma
Erasure
Everything but the Girl
Frankie Goes to Hollywood
Future Sound of London
Janet Jackson
Michael Jackson
KC & the Sunshine Band
Lords of Acid
The Orb
Orbital
Plastikman
Primal Scream
Prince
Diana Ross
The Village People

Radio Waves
Antenna
Thomas Dolby
Radiohead
Wilco

Relatively Speaking
Big Brother & the Holding
    Company
The Blues Brothers
The Chemical Brothers
dada
The Doobie Brothers
Flying Burrito Brothers
Gear Daddies
Gigolo Aunts
Mommyheads
Mother Earth
Mother Love Bone
The Mothers of Invention
The Offspring
The Partridge Family
The Righteous Brothers
Shakespear's Sister
Sister Hazel
Sisters of Mercy
Swing out Sister
Twisted Sister
Uncle Tupelo
The Waco Brothers
The Walker Brothers

Rhythm Nations
America

Asia
Gary U.S. Bonds
China Crisis
Japan
Mission of Burma
The Mission U.K.

Rockabilly
Hasil Adkins
The Blasters
Johnny Burnette
Eddie Cochran
Bill Haley
Dale Hawkins
The Reverend Horton Heat
Buddy Holly
Jerry Lee Lewis
Rick Nelson
Roy Orbison
Carl Perkins
Elvis Presley
Stray Cats/Brian Setzer
Gene Vincent

Rockin' & Rollin'
Drivin' N' Cryin'
Enuff Z'Nuff
Fun Lovin' Criminals
Gov't Mule
Guns N' Roses
Screamin' Jay Hawkins
Howlin' Wolf
The Lovin' Spoonful

Roots Rock
The Band
The Blasters
Blue Rodeo
BoDeans
Gary U.S. Bonds
T-Bone Burnett
John Cafferty & the Beaver
    Brown Band
Peter Case/The Plimsouls
Eddie Cochran
The Connells
Cowboy Junkies
Cracker/Camper Van
    Beethoven
Marshall Crenshaw
Sheryl Crow
The dB's/Chris Stamey/Peter
    Holsapple
Willy DeVille
Bo Diddley
Dire Straits
Drivin' N' Cryin'
Pete Droge
Bob Dylan
Steve Earle
The Everly Brothers

The Fabulous Thunderbirds
John Fogerty/Creedence
    Clearwater Revival
Steve Forbert
Foster & Lloyd
Danny Gatton
Gin Blossoms
The Grass Roots
Joe Grushecky & the Iron City
    Rockers
John Wesley Harding
John Hiatt
The Hooters
Chris Isaak
Jason & the Scorchers
The Jayhawks
Freedy Johnston
Marti Jones
Nils Lofgren
Lyle Lovett
The Lovin' Spoonful
Dave Matthews Band
Maria McKee/Lone Justice
James McMurtry
John Mellencamp
Randy Newman
Willie Nile
Graham Parker
Michael Penn
Tom Petty & the Heartbreak-
    ers
John Prine
Bob Seger
Del Shannon
Michelle Shocked
Social Distortion
Southside Johnny & the As-
    bury Jukes
Spanic Boys
Bruce Springsteen
Syd Straw
Timbuk 3
The Traveling Wilburys
Uncle Tupelo/Son Volt/Wilco
Lucinda Williams

'Round Midnight
Hank Ballard & the Mid-
    nighters
Dexy's Midnight Runners
Midnight Oil

The Royal Treatment
The Amboy Dukes
Joe "King" Carrasco
The Del Lords
Albert King
B.B. King
Ben E. King
Carole King

Freddie King
Sid King & the Five Strings
King Crimson
King Curtis
King Missle
King Sunny Ade
King's X
The Kingsmen
The Kingston Trio
Mary Lou Lord
Lords of Acid
Lords of the New Church
Mighty Blue Kings
Palace
Prince
Queen
Royal Crescent Mob
Royal Crown Revue
Royal Trux

Say It with Flowers
Madder Rose
Pansy Division
The Posies
Guns N' Roses
Zuzu's Petals

The Seattle Sound
Alice in Chains
Candlebox
Judy Collins
Foo Fighters
Heart
Jimi Hendrix
Mudhoney
Nirvana
Pearl Jam
Screaming Trees
Sebadoh
Soundgarden

See Ya at CBGB's
Blondie
The Cramps
Dead Boys
Mink DeVille
Richard Hell
The Ramones
Patti Smith
Talking Heads
Television

Sex & Drugs & Rock 'n' Roll
Barenaked Ladies
Bongwater
Buzzcocks
Carter the Unstoppable Sex
    Machine
Cheap Trick
Come
Gary Lewis & the Playboys

Green Day
Helium
Hole
The Hooters
Huffamoose
Jane's Addiction
Lords of Acid
Loverboy
The Lovin' Spoonful
My Drug Hell
Prong
The Sex Pistols
Sham 69
The Slits
Steely Dan
10cc
Tool

Shoe Gazers
Blur
The Charlatans UK
Happy Mondays
Inspiral Carpets
My Bloody Valentine
Portishead
The Stone Roses
Suede

Size Doesn't Matter
aMiniature
Big Ass Truck
Big Audio Dynamite
Big Bad Voodoo Daddy
Big Black
The Big Bopper
Big Brother & the Holding
    Company
Big Chief
Big Country
Big Head Todd & the Monsters
Big Rude Jake
Big Star
Big Wreck
Lee Rocker's Big Blue
Little Anthony & the Imperials
Little Eva
Little Feat
Little Richard
Little River Band
Little Steven
Little Village
Little Willie John
Massive Attack
Mr. Big
Small Faces

Sonic Boom
The Amps
Helmet
The Jesus & Mary Chain

Kyuss
Live Skull
Lush
My Bloody Valentine
The Pixies
Ride
Smashing Pumpkins
Sonic Youth
Swervedriver
Tsunami

Southern Alternative Rock
Agents of Good Roots
The B-52's
Edie Brickell & New Bohemi-
    ans
Collective Soul
The Connells
Creed
The dB's
Don Dixon
Gin Blossoms
The Golden Palominos
The Grapes of Wrath
Hootie & the Blowfish
Bruce Hornsby
Indigo Girls
Jason & the Scorchers
Marti Jones
Let's Active
Marilyn Manson
Matchbox 20
Dave Matthews Band
Edwin McCain Band
The Sidewinders
Darden Smith
Syd Straw
Treadmill Trackstar
Uncle Tupelo/Son Volt/Wilco
Victoria Williams

Spirit of the West
Cowboy Junkies
Go West
Pure Prairie League

Stax-Volt/Motown
Booker T. & The Mgs
James Brown
Ray Charles
Sam Cooke
The Four Tops
Aretha Franklin
Marvin Gaye
The Isley Brothers
Jackson 5
Albert King
Ben E. King
Martha & the Vandellas
Curtis Mayfield

Wilson Pickett
Rare Earth
Otis Redding
Smokey Robinson
Diana Ross/The Supremes
Sam & Dave
The Temptations
Jackie Wilson
Stevie Wonder

Surf Groups
The Astronauts
The Beach Boys
The Chantays
Dick Dale & the Del-Tones
Jan & Dean
Man or Astro-Man?
The Tornados
The Ventures

Sweets for the Sweet
Sugar
Sugar Ray
The Sugarcubes
The Sweet
Matthew Sweet
Rachel Sweet
Sweet 75

Take a Number
The B-52's
Black 47
Blink 182
Bran Van 3000
808 State
54.40
The Five Americans
The "5" Royales
Ben Folds Five
The Four Seasons
The Four Tops
The Fourmost
Front 242
The Bobby Fuller Four
Fun Boy Three
Galaxie 500
Gang of Four
Haircut 100
Heaven 17
Jackson 5
Level 42
L7
Matchbox 20
MC 900 Ft. Jesus
MC5
Mega City Four
Omni Trio
OP8
Orange 9mm
Pizzicato Five

Powerman 5000
Sham 69
Spacemen 3
Ten Foot Pole
10,000 Maniacs
10cc
.38 Special
311
Timbuk 3
20/20
UB40
U2

Tangled up in Blue
Babe the Blue Ox
The Blue Aeroplanes
Blue Cheer
Blue Meanies
Blue Mountain
The Blue Nile
Blue Öyster Cult
Blue Rodeo
The Bluebells
The Blues Brothers
The Blues Magoos
Blues Project
Blues Traveler
The Bluetones
Paul Butterfield Blues Band
Deacon Blue
Indigo Girls
The Moody Blues
Jon Spencer Blues Explosion
The Swinging Blue Jeans

Teen Heartthrobs
Paul Anka
Rick Astley
The Beatles
Johnny Burnette
Bobby Darin
Dion & the Belmonts
Donovan
Fabian
Hanson
The Monkees
Rick Nelson
New Kids on the Block
Gene Pitney
Del Shannon
Bobby Vee

Texas
Arc Angels
Edie Brickell & New Bohemi-
    ans
T-Bone Burnett
Butthole Surfers
Steve Earle
Joe Ely

Alejandro Escovedo
The Fabulous Thunderbirds
Jimmie Dale Gilmore
Nanci Griffith
Buddy Holly
Janis Joplin
Lyle Lovett
James McMurtry
Charlie Sexton
Michelle Shocked
Sir Douglas Quintet
Jimmie Vaughan
Stevie Ray Vaughan
Edgar Winter
Johnny Winter
ZZ Top

There's No One Here by That Name
Agnes Gooch
The Beau Brummels
Bettie Serveert
Cocteau Twins
Commander Cody & His Lost Planet Airmen
Derek & the Dominos
Dr. Buzzard's Original Savannah Band
Frankie Goes to Hollywood
Harvey Danger
Hootie & the Blowfish
Jethro Tull
Kid Creole & the Coconuts
Luscious Jackson
Lynyrd Skynyrd
The Marshall Tucker Band

Mr. Bungle
Mr. Mister
Pink Floyd
Steely Dan
Thompson Twins
The Traveling Wilburys

They're Coming to Take Me Away
The Crazy World of Arthur Brown
Crazy Horse
Insane Clown Posse
Madness
Primal Scream
Therapy?
The Weirdos
Weird Al Yankovic

Things You May Find in or Around Your House
A House
The Bottle Rockets
The Box Tops
Bread
Cactus
The Clovers
Pavement
The Raincoats
Shellac
Tool
Wig

TV and Movies
The Boo Radleys
Cinderella
Dash Rip Rock

Duran Duran
Fine Young Cannibals
Guadalcanal Diary
Klaatu
Mudhoney
My Bloody Valentine
The Stooges
Veruca Salt
Zuzu's Petals

Umlaut Overdose
Björk
Blue Öyster Cult
Einstürzende Neubauten
Green Jellÿ
Hüsker Dü
Mötley Crüe
Motörhead
Moxy Früvous

Under the Sea
The Aquabats
The Barracudas
eels
Fishbone
Flipper
Great White
Hootie & the Blowfish
Hot Tuna
Jellyfish
The Mermen
Moby
The Oyster Band
Phish
Reef

U.S.A.! U.S.A.!
America
American Breed
American Music Club
The Presidents of the United States of America

We Just Like the Name
Barenaked Ladies
Big Ass Truck
Bitch Magnet
Cherry Poppin' Daddies
Chixdiggit!
Chumbawamba
Friends of Dean Martinez
Huffamoose
Insane Clown Posse
Kathleen Turner Overdrive
Meat Puppets
Ned's Atomic Dustbin
Smoking Popes
Squirrel Nut Zippers
The Teardrop Explodes
Throbbing Gristle
The Tragically Hip

Wet Behind the Ears
Aqua
H2O
Katrina & the Waves
Ocean Colour Scene
The Waterboys
Crystal Waters
Muddy Waters
Roger Waters

This index is a guide to all of the artists and groups included in the MusicHound series of books (Music-Hound Rock, MusicHound Country, MusicHound Blues, MusicHound R&B, MusicHound Lounge, Music-Hound Folk, *and* MusicHound Jazz*). Following the artist or group's name you'll find the book (or books) they appear in.*

a-ha *See* MH Rock

A House *See* MH Rock

A. Robic and the Exertions *See* MH Folk

Aaliyah *See* MH R&B

Greg Abate *See* MH Jazz

ABBA *See* MH Lounge, MH Rock

Gregory Abbott *See* MH R&B

ABC *See* MH Rock

Paula Abdul *See* MH R&B, MH Rock

Ahmed Abdul-Malik *See* MH Jazz

Ahmed Abdullah *See* MH Jazz

John Abercrombie *See* MH Jazz

Above the Law *See* MH R&B

Colonel Abrams *See* MH R&B

Muhal Richard Abrams *See* MH Jazz

Rick Abrams *See* MH Folk

Nathan Abshire *See* MH Folk

Absolute Zeros *See* MH Rock

AC/DC *See* MH Rock

The Accelerators *See* MH Rock

Ace *See* MH Rock

Johnny Ace *See* MH Blues, MH R&B, MH Rock

Ace of Base *See* MH R&B, MH Rock

The Aces *See* MH Blues

Acetone *See* MH Rock

Barbara Acklin *See* MH R&B

Acoustic Alchemy *See* MH Jazz

Acousticats *See* MH Folk

Roy Acuff *See* MH Country, MH Folk

Adam & the Ants *See* MH Rock

Bryan Adams *See* MH Rock

George Adams *See* MH Jazz

Johnny Adams *See* MH Blues, MH Jazz, MH R&B

Oleta Adams *See* MH R&B

Pepper (Park) Adams *See* MH Jazz

Barry Adamson *See* MH Lounge, MH Rock

C.C. Adcock *See* MH Rock

Eddie Adcock *See* MH Country, MH Folk

Julian "Cannonball" Adderley *See* MH Jazz, MH Lounge

Nat Adderley *See* MH Jazz

Trace Adkins *See* MH Country

Hasil Adkins *See* MH Rock

Helen Folaasade Adu *See* MH Lounge

The Adverts *See* MH Rock

Aengus *See* MH Folk

Aerosmith *See* MH Rock

Ron Affif *See* MH Jazz

The Afghan Whigs *See* MH Rock

A.F.I./Asking for It *See* MH Rock

The Afro Blue Band *See* MH Jazz

Afro Rican *See* MH R&B

Agent Orange *See* MH Rock

Agents of Good Roots *See* MH Rock

Agnes Gooch *See* MH Rock

Eden Ahbez *See* MH Lounge

Ahmad *See* MH R&B

Caroline Aiken *See* MH Folk

Air *See* MH Rock

Air Miami *See* MH Rock

Air/New Air *See* MH Jazz

Air Supply *See* MH Rock

Kei Akagi *See* MH Jazz

David "Stringbean" Akeman *See* MH Country, MH Folk

Garfield Akers *See* MH Blues

Rhett Akins *See* MH Country

Akinyele *See* MH R&B

Toshiko Akiyoshi *See* MH Jazz

Alabama *See* MH Country

Scott Alarik *See* MH Folk

The Alarm *See* MH Rock

Joe Albany *See* MH Jazz

Albion Band *See* MH Folk

Albion Country Band *See* MH Rock

Gerald Albright *See* MH Jazz, MH R&B

Alcatrazz *See* MH Rock

Howard Alden *See* MH Jazz

Ronnie Aldrich *See* MH Lounge

Brian Ales *See* MH Jazz

Alessi *See* MH Lounge

Alger Alexander *See* MH Blues

Arthur Alexander *See* MH R&B, MH Rock

Eric Alexander *See* MH Jazz

John Marshall Alexander Jr. *See* MH Blues

Monty Alexander *See* MH Jazz

Texas Alexander *See* MH Blues

Pat Alger *See* MH Country, MH Folk

Alice in Chains *See* MH Rock

Tha Alkaholiks *See* MH R&B

All *See* MH Rock

All-4-One *See* MH R&B

The All Girl Boys *See* MH Folk

All Saints *See* MH Rock

Gary Allan *See* MH Country

Carl Allen *See* MH Jazz

Fulton Allen *See* MH Blues

Geri Allen *See* MH Jazz

Harley Allen *See* MH Country

Harry Allen *See* MH Jazz

Henry "Red" Allen *See* MH Jazz

Peter Allen *See* MH Lounge

Red Allen *See* MH Country, MH Folk

Rex Allen *See* MH Country

Rex Allen Jr. *See* MH Country

Steve Allen *See* MH Jazz, MH Lounge

Terry Allen *See* MH Country, MH Folk

Red Allen & Frank Wakefield *See* MH Country

Jenny Allinder *See* MH Folk

Amy Allison/Parlor James *See* MH Country, MH Rock

Ben Allison *See* MH Jazz

Luther Allison *See* MH Blues, MH Folk

Mose Allison *See* MH Blues, MH Folk, MH Jazz, MH Lounge

The Allman Brothers Band *See* MH Blues, MH Rock

Alloy Orchestra *See* MH Jazz

Karrin Allyson *See* MH Jazz

Laurindo Almeida/Laurindo Almeida & the Bossa Nova All-Stars *See* MH Jazz, MH Lounge

Almighty RSO *See* MH R&B

Herb Alpert *See* MH Jazz, MH Lounge

Alphaville *See* MH Rock

Peter Alsop *See* MH Folk

Gerald Alston *See* MH R&B

Alt *See* MH Rock

Altan *See* MH Folk, MH Rock

John Altenburgh *See* MH Jazz

Altered Images *See* MH Rock

Joey Altruda with the Cocktail Crew/Jump with Joey *See* MH Lounge

Barry Altschul *See* MH Jazz

Dave Alvin *See* MH Blues, MH Country, MH Folk, MH Rock

Phil Alvin *See* MH Blues, MH Country, MH Rock

Amazing Blondel *See* MH Folk

The Amazing Rhythm Aces *See* MH Country, MH Folk

Eric Ambel *See* MH Rock

Ambitious Lovers *See* MH Rock

Franco Ambrosetti *See* MH Jazz

Ambrosia *See* MH Rock

America *See* MH Folk, MH Rock

The American Breed *See* MH Rock

The American Cafe Orchestra *See* MH Folk

American Flyer *See* MH Rock

American Music Club *See* MH Rock

The Ames Brothers/Ed Ames *See* MH Lounge

The Amidons *See* MH Folk

aMiniature *See* MH Rock

Albert Ammons *See* MH Jazz

Gene "Jug" Ammons *See* MH Jazz

Tori Amos *See* MH Rock

The Amps *See* MH Rock

Eric Andersen/Andersen, Danko, Fjeld *See* MH Folk, MH Rock

Al Anderson *See* MH Country

Bill Anderson *See* MH Country

Chris Anderson *See* MH Jazz

Clifton Anderson *See* MH Jazz

Ernestine Anderson *See* MH Jazz

Fred Anderson *See* MH Jazz

Ian Anderson *See* MH Rock

John Anderson *See* MH Country

Laurie Anderson *See* MH Rock

Leroy Anderson *See* MH Lounge

Little Willie Anderson *See* MH Blues

Lynn Anderson *See* MH Country

Pete Anderson *See* MH Country

Pink Anderson *See* MH Blues, MH Folk

Ray Anderson *See* MH Jazz

Wessell Anderson *See* MH Jazz

Leah Andreone *See* MH Rock

Ernie Andrews *See* MH Jazz

Julie Andrews *See* MH Lounge

Molly Andrews *See* MH Folk

The Andrews Sisters *See* MH Lounge

Horace Andy *See* MH Rock

Angel *See* MH Rock

Maya Angelou *See* MH Lounge

The Angels *See* MH Rock

Fela Anikulapo-Kuti *See* MH Jazz

The Animals/Eric Burdon & the Animals/Eric Burdon/Alan Price *See* MH Blues, MH Rock

Paul Anka *See* MH Lounge, MH Rock

Ann-Margret *See* MH Lounge

Anotha Level *See* MH R&B

Another Girl *See* MH Rock

Adam Ant/Adam & the Ants *See* MH Rock

Antenna/Velo-Deluxe/The Mysteries of Life/John P. Strohm & the Hello Strangers *See* MH Rock

Ray Anthony *See* MH Lounge

Anthrax *See* MH Rock

Anti-Nowhere League *See* MH Rock

Any Old Time String Band *See* MH Folk

Any Trouble *See* MH Rock

Apache *See* MH R&B

Peter Apfelbaum *See* MH Jazz

Aphex Twin *See* MH Rock

A+ *See* MH R&B

Scott Appel *See* MH Folk

Fiona Apple *See* MH Rock

Apples in Stereo *See* MH Rock

Peter Appleyard *See* MH Jazz

Aqua *See* MH Rock

The Aqua Velvets *See* MH Rock

The Aquabats *See* MH Rock

The Cure *See* MH Rock

Dick Curless *See* MH Country

Clifford Curry *See* MH R&B

Tim Curry *See* MH Lounge

Ted Curson *See* MH Jazz

Catie Curtis *See* MH Folk

Mac Curtis *See* MH Rock

Curve *See* MH Rock

Cusan Tan *See* MH Folk

Frankie Cutlass *See* MH R&B

Cybotron *See* MH Rock

Cypress Hill *See* MH R&B, MH Rock

Andrew Cyrille *See* MH Jazz

The Cyrkle *See* MH Rock

Billy Ray Cyrus *See* MH Country

Chuck D. *See* MH Rock

D Generation *See* MH Rock

Da Brat *See* MH R&B

Da Bush Babees *See* MH R&B

Da Lench Mob *See* MH R&B

Da Youngsta's/Illy Funkstas *See* MH R&B

dada *See* MH Rock

Daft Punk *See* MH Rock

Lisa Daggs *See* MH Country

Paul Daigle *See* MH Folk

Bruce Daigrepont *See* MH Folk

Dick Dale *See* MH Rock

Malcolm Dalglish *See* MH Folk

Lacy J. Dalton *See* MH Country

Roger Daltrey *See* MH Rock

Jackie Daly *See* MH Folk

Maria D'Amato *See* MH Blues

The Dambuilders *See* MH Rock

Tadd Dameron *See* MH Jazz

Damn Yankees *See* MH Rock

The Damned *See* MH Rock

Vic Damone *See* MH Lounge

Dana Dane *See* MH R&B

Dance Hall Crashers *See* MH Rock

Dandy Warhols *See* MH Rock

D'Angelo *See* MH R&B

Davis Daniel *See* MH Country

Eddie Daniels *See* MH Jazz

Charlie Daniels Band *See* MH Country, MH Rock

Harold Danko *See* MH Jazz

Rick Danko *See* MH Rock

Johnny Dankworth *See* MH Lounge

Danny & the Juniors/Danny & the Juniors Featuring Joe Terry *See* MH Rock

Danzig/Samhain *See* MH Rock

Vanessa Daou *See* MH Rock

James Dapogny *See* MH Jazz

Terence Trent D'Arby *See* MH R&B, MH Rock

Darby and Tarlton *See* MH Folk

Bobby Darin *See* MH Lounge, MH R&B, MH Rock

Mason Daring/Jeanie Stahl and Mason Daring *See* MH Folk

Dark Sun Riders Featuring Brother J *See* MH R&B

Erik Darling *See* MH Folk

Helen Darling *See* MH Country

The Darling Buds *See* MH Rock

Das EFX/Bobby Sichran *See* MH R&B

Dash Rip Rock *See* MH Rock

Dave & Deke Combo *See* MH Country

Billy Davenport *See* MH Blues

Charles "Cow Cow" Davenport *See* MH Blues

Jeremy Davenport *See* MH Jazz

Lester Davenport *See* MH Blues

Kenny Davern *See* MH Jazz

Shaun Davey *See* MH Folk

David + David/David Baerwald *See* MH Rock

Hal David *See* MH Lounge

Lowell Davidson *See* MH Jazz

Debbie Davies *See* MH Blues

Gail Davies *See* MH Country

Richard Davies/Cardinal/The Moles *See* MH Lounge, MH Rock

Alana Davis *See* MH Rock

Anthony Davis *See* MH Jazz

Billy Davis Jr. *See* MH Lounge

CeDell Davis *See* MH Blues

Eddie "Lockjaw" Davis *See* MH Jazz

Guy Davis *See* MH Blues, MH Folk

James "Thunderbird" Davis *See* MH Blues

Jesse Davis *See* MH Jazz

Jimmie Davis *See* MH Country, MH Folk

Julie Davis *See* MH Folk

Larry Davis *See* MH Blues

Linda Davis *See* MH Country

Mac Davis *See* MH Country, MH Lounge

Maxwell Davis *See* MH Blues

Maxwell Street Jimmy Davis *See* MH Blues

Miles Davis *See* MH Jazz, MH Lounge

The Rev. Gary Davis *See* MH Blues, MH Folk

Richard Davis *See* MH Jazz

Sammy Davis Jr. *See* MH Lounge, MH R&B

Skeeter Davis *See* MH Country

Spencer Davis/The Spencer Davis Group *See* MH Rock

Steve Davis *See* MH Jazz

Thornetta Davis *See* MH Rock

Tyrone Davis *See* MH R&B

Walter Davis *See* MH Blues

Walter Davis Jr. *See* MH Jazz

Wild Bill Davison *See* MH Jazz

Jimmy Dawkins *See* MH Blues

Julian Dawson *See* MH Folk

Ronnie Dawson *See* MH Country, MH Rock

Curtis Day *See* MH Country

Doris Day *See* MH Lounge

Morris Day *See* MH R&B

Taylor Dayne *See* MH R&B, MH Rock

Days of the New *See* MH Rock

Jesse Dayton *See* MH Country

The Dayton Family *See* MH R&B

The Dazz Band *See* MH R&B

The dB's/Peter Holsapple/Will Rigby *See* MH Rock

DC Talk *See* MH R&B, MH Rock

Chris de Burgh *See* MH Rock

De Danann/De Dannan *See* MH Folk

De La Soul *See* MH R&B

Deacon Blue *See* MH Rock

Dead Boys/Stiv Bators/Lords of the New Church *See* MH Rock

Dead Can Dance *See* MH Folk, MH Rock

Dead Kennedys *See* MH Rock

The Dead Milkmen *See* MH Rock

EMF *See* MH Rock

Emilio *See* MH Country

The Emotions *See* MH R&B

En Vogue *See* MH R&B

Enchantment *See* MH R&B

Ty England *See* MH Country

The English Beat/General Public *See* MH Rock

Norma Delores Engstrom *See* MH Lounge

Jeremy Enigk *See* MH Rock

Enigma *See* MH Rock

Lyman Enloe *See* MH Folk

Séamus Ennis *See* MH Folk

Brian Eno *See* MH Lounge, MH Rock

Bobby Enriquez *See* MH Jazz

Ensemble Galilei *See* MH Folk

John Entwistle *See* MH Rock

Enuff Z'Nuff *See* MH Rock

Enya *See* MH Folk

Epic Soundtracks *See* MH Rock

EPMD *See* MH R&B

Erasure *See* MH Lounge, MH Rock

Wayne Erbsen *See* MH Folk

Roky Erickson *See* MH Rock

Eric's Trip/Elevator to Hell *See* MH Rock

Peter Erskine *See* MH Jazz

Booker Ervin *See* MH Jazz

Ron Eschete *See* MH Jazz

Alejandro Escovedo *See* MH Country, MH Rock

Pete Escovedo *See* MH Jazz

Ellery Eskelin *See* MH Jazz

ESP Summer *See* MH Rock

Tom Espinola and Lorraine Duisit *See* MH Folk

Juan Garcia Esquivel *See* MH Lounge

David Essex *See* MH Rock

Gloria Estefan/Miami Sound Machine *See* MH R&B, MH Rock

Maggie Estep *See* MH Rock

Sleepy John Estes *See* MH Blues, MH Folk

Etchingham Steam Band *See* MH Folk

Melissa Etheridge *See* MH Rock

The Ethnic Heritage Ensemble *See* MH Jazz

E.U. (Experience Unlimited) *See* MH R&B

Kevin Eubanks *See* MH Jazz

Robin Eubanks *See* MH Jazz

Eugenius *See* MH Rock

Euro Boys *See* MH Rock

Eurythmics/Annie Lennox/Dave Stewart *See* MH R&B, MH Rock

Bill Evans *See* MH Jazz

Gil Evans *See* MH Jazz

Terry Evans *See* MH Blues

Gerald Evans & Joe Mullins *See* MH Country

Everclear *See* MH Rock

Everlast *See* MH Rock

The Everly Brothers *See* MH Country, MH Folk, MH Rock

Everything but the Girl *See* MH Lounge, MH R&B, MH Rock

Douglas Ewart *See* MH Jazz

Skip Ewing *See* MH Country

Exile/Les Taylor/J.P. Pennington *See* MH Country

Extreme *See* MH Rock

Fabian *See* MH Lounge, MH Rock

Bent Fabric *See* MH Lounge

The Fabulous Thunderbirds *See* MH Blues, MH Rock

Face to Face *See* MH Rock

The Faces/The Small Faces *See* MH Rock

Jon Faddis *See* MH Jazz

Eleanora Fagan *See* MH Lounge

Donald Fagen *See* MH Lounge

John Fahey *See* MH Folk, MH Rock

Barbara Fairchild *See* MH Country

The Fairfield Four *See* MH Folk

Fairground Attraction/Eddi Reader *See* MH Rock

Fairport Convention/Fairport/Sandy Denny/Fotheringay *See* MH Folk, MH Rock

Adam Faith *See* MH Rock

Percy Faith *See* MH Lounge

Th' Faith Healers *See* MH Rock

Faith No More/Mr. Bungle/Imperial Teen *See* MH Rock

Marianne Faithfull *See* MH Folk, MH Lounge, MH Rock

Joseph Falcon and Cleoma Breaux Falcon *See* MH Folk

The Falcons *See* MH R&B

Jason Falkner *See* MH Rock

The Fall *See* MH Rock

Charles Fambrough *See* MH Jazz

Georgie Fame *See* MH Lounge, MH Rock

Donna Fargo *See* MH Country

Richard and Mimi Fariña/Mimi Fariña *See* MH Folk

Mary Ann Farley *See* MH Rock

Tal Farlow *See* MH Jazz

Chris Farlowe/Chris Farlowe & the Thunderbirds/The Hill *See* MH Rock

The Farm *See* MH Rock

Farm Dogs *See* MH Rock

Art Farmer *See* MH Jazz

Farmer Not So John *See* MH Rock

Farmer's Daughters *See* MH Folk

Allen Farnham *See* MH Jazz

Joe Farrell *See* MH Jazz

Dionne Farris *See* MH Rock

Farside *See* MH Rock

Fastbacks *See* MH Rock

Fastball *See* MH Rock

Zusaan Kali Fasteau *See* MH Jazz

Fat Boys *See* MH R&B

Fat Joe Da Gangsta *See* MH R&B

Fatback Band/Fatback *See* MH R&B

Faust *See* MH Rock

Pierre Favre *See* MH Jazz

Fear *See* MH Rock

Stephen Fearing *See* MH Folk

Charlie Feathers *See* MH Country, MH Rock

John Fedchock *See* MH Jazz

Danny Federici *See* MH Rock

The Feelies *See* MH Rock

Michael Feinstein *See* MH Lounge

Jerome Felder *See* MH Blues

Lee Feldman *See* MH Rock

Jose Feliciano *See* MH Lounge

Narvel Felts *See* MH Country

Freddy Fender *See* MH Country

Mike Fenton *See* MH Folk

H-Bomb Ferguson *See* MH Blues

Jay Ferguson *See* MH Rock

Maynard Ferguson *See* MH Jazz

Ferrante & Teicher *See* MH Lounge

Rachelle Ferrell *See* MH Jazz, MH R&B

Melissa Ferrick *See* MH Rock

Glenn Ferris *See* MH Jazz

Ferron *See* MH Folk

Bryan Ferry *See* MH Lounge, MH Rock

Garrison Fewell *See* MH Jazz

Fiddle Fever *See* MH Folk

Arthur Fiedler/The Boston Pops Orchestra *See* MH Lounge

Dale Fielder *See* MH Jazz

The Fifth Dimension *See* MH Lounge, MH R&B

54.40 *See* MH Rock

Fig Dish *See* MH Rock

The Figgs *See* MH Rock

Figgy Duff/Pamela Morgan *See* MH Folk

Fight *See* MH Rock

Fiji Mariners *See* MH Rock

Filé *See* MH Country, MH Folk

Filter *See* MH Rock

Fine Young Cannibals *See* MH R&B, MH Rock

Sally Fingerett *See* MH Folk

Fingerprintz *See* MH Rock

Cathy Fink and Marcy Marxer *See* MH Folk

Alec Finn *See* MH Folk

Neil Finn *See* MH Rock

Tim Finn *See* MH Rock

Finn Brothers *See* MH Rock

Firefall *See* MH Country, MH Rock

fIREHOSE/Mike Watt/Banyan/Dos *See* MH Rock

The Firm *See* MH Rock

First Edition *See* MH Lounge

Fish *See* MH Rock

Fishbone *See* MH R&B, MH Rock

Archie Fisher *See* MH Folk

Eddie Fisher *See* MH Lounge

Matthew Fisher *See* MH Rock

Steve Fisher *See* MH Folk

Ella Fitzgerald *See* MH Jazz, MH Lounge, MH R&B

David Fiuczynski *See* MH Jazz

The Five Americans *See* MH Rock

Five Chinese Brothers *See* MH Country, MH Folk

The Five Keys *See* MH R&B

The "5" Royales *See* MH R&B, MH Rock

The Fixx *See* MH Rock

Roberta Flack *See* MH R&B

The Flamin' Groovies *See* MH Rock

The Flaming Lips *See* MH Rock

The Flamingos *See* MH Rock

Tommy Flanagan *See* MH Jazz

Fred Flange *See* MH Lounge

Flash Cadillac/Flash Cadillac & the Continental Kids *See* MH Rock

The Flashcats *See* MH Rock

The Flashcubes/Gary Frenay *See* MH Rock

Flat Duo Jets *See* MH Rock

The Flatlanders *See* MH Country, MH Folk, MH Rock

Flatlinerz *See* MH R&B

Lester Flatt *See* MH Country

Flatt & Scruggs *See* MH Country, MH Folk

Béla Fleck/Béla Fleck and the Flecktones *See* MH Country, MH Folk, MH Jazz

Mick Fleetwood/Mick Fleetwood's Zoo *See* MH Rock

Fleetwood Mac *See* MH Blues, MH Rock

The Fleetwoods *See* MH Lounge

The Fleshtones *See* MH Rock

Flim & the BB's *See* MH Jazz

Matt Flinner *See* MH Folk

Benton Flippen *See* MH Country, MH Folk

Flipper *See* MH Rock

A Flock of Seagulls *See* MH Rock

Flop *See* MH Rock

Myron Floren *See* MH Lounge

Bob Florence *See* MH Jazz

Rosie Flores *See* MH Country, MH Folk

Flotsam & Jetsam *See* MH Rock

Robin Flower *See* MH Folk

Eddie Floyd *See* MH Blues, MH R&B

The Fluid *See* MH Rock

Flying Burrito Brothers *See* MH Country, MH Folk, MH Rock

Focus *See* MH Rock

Dan Fogelberg *See* MH Country, MH Folk, MH Rock

John Fogerty *See* MH Country, MH Rock

Foghat *See* MH Rock

Ben Folds Five *See* MH Rock

Red Foley *See* MH Country, MH Folk

Sue Foley *See* MH Blues, MH Folk

The Folk Implosion *See* MH Rock

David Folks *See* MH Folk

Frank Fontaine *See* MH Lounge

Wayne Fontana & the Mindbenders *See* MH Rock

Canray Fontenot *See* MH Folk

Foo Fighters *See* MH Rock

For Against *See* MH Rock

For Squirrels/Subrosa *See* MH Rock

Steve Forbert *See* MH Folk, MH Rock

The Forbes Family *See* MH Country, MH Folk

Force M.D.'s *See* MH R&B

Aleck Ford *See* MH Blues

Frankie Ford *See* MH Rock

Lita Ford *See* MH Rock

Mary Ford *See* MH Country, MH Lounge

Ricky Ford *See* MH Jazz

Robben Ford *See* MH Blues

Tennessee Ernie Ford *See* MH Country

Charles Ford Band/Ford Blues Band/Robben Ford *See* MH Blues

Ford Blues Band *See* MH Blues

Julia Fordham *See* MH Folk, MH Rock

Foreigner *See* MH Rock

The Foremen *See* MH Folk

Forest for the Trees *See* MH Rock

The Forester Sisters *See* MH Country

Helen Forrest *See* MH Lounge

Jimmy Forrest *See* MH Jazz

Joel Forrester *See* MH Jazz

John Forster *See* MH Folk

Robert Forster *See* MH Rock

Fort Apache Band *See* MH Jazz

Jesse Fortune *See* MH Blues

Sonny Fortune *See* MH Jazz

The Fortunes *See* MH Rock

Frank Foster *See* MH Jazz

Gary Foster *See* MH Jazz

Radney Foster *See* MH Country

Foster & Lloyd/Bill Lloyd *See* MH Country, MH Rock

Fotheringay *See* MH Folk, MH Rock

The Foundations *See* MH Rock

Pete Fountain *See* MH Jazz

Fountains of Wayne *See* MH Rock

James Founty *See* MH Blues

Four Bitchin' Babes *See* MH Folk

The Four Dukes *See* MH Lounge

The Four Freshmen *See* MH Lounge

The Four Lads *See* MH Lounge

The Four Preps *See* MH Folk, MH Lounge

4 Runner *See* MH Country

The Four Seasons/Frankie Valli *See* MH Lounge, MH R&B, MH Rock

The Four Tops *See* MH R&B, MH Rock

The Fourmost/The Four Jays/The Four Mosts/Format *See* MH Rock

Fourplay *See* MH Jazz

Kim Fox *See* MH Rock

Samantha Fox *See* MH Rock

The Fox Family *See* MH Country

Jeff Foxworthy *See* MH Country

Michael Fracasso *See* MH Country, MH Folk

Amy Fradon and Leslie Ritter/Amy Fradon *See* MH Folk

J.P. & Annadeene Fraley *See* MH Country, MH Folk

Peter Frampton *See* MH Rock

Carol Fran & Clarence Hollimon *See* MH Blues

Connie Francis *See* MH Country, MH Lounge, MH Rock

Jackson C. Frank *See* MH Folk

Keith Frank *See* MH Folk

The Frank & Walters *See* MH Rock

Bob Franke *See* MH Folk

Frankie Goes to Hollywood *See* MH Rock

Aretha Franklin *See* MH R&B, MH Rock

Kirk Franklin & the Family *See* MH R&B

Michael Franks *See* MH Jazz, MH Lounge

Rebecca Coupe Franks *See* MH Jazz

Alasdair Fraser *See* MH Folk

Gail Fratar *See* MH Folk

Rob Fraynor *See* MH Jazz

Calvin Frazier *See* MH Blues

Frazier River *See* MH Country

Freakwater *See* MH Country, MH Rock

Stan Freberg *See* MH Lounge

Freddie & the Dreamers *See* MH Rock

Henry St. Claire Fredericks *See* MH Blues

Free *See* MH Rock

Free Hot Lunch! *See* MH Folk

Free Music Quintet *See* MH Jazz

Nnenna Freelon *See* MH Jazz

Alan Freeman *See* MH Folk

Bud Freeman *See* MH Jazz

Chico Freeman *See* MH Jazz

George Freeman *See* MH Jazz

Russ Freeman *See* MH Jazz

Von Freeman *See* MH Jazz

Freestyle Fellowship *See* MH Jazz, MH R&B

Freewill Savages *See* MH Folk

The Freight Hoppers *See* MH Folk

Gary Frenay *See* MH Rock

John French *See* MH Rock

French, Frith, Kaiser & Thompson *See* MH Folk, MH Rock

Frente! *See* MH Rock

Doug E. Fresh *See* MH R&B

Gideon Freudmann *See* MH Folk

Glenn Frey *See* MH Folk

Freyda and Acoustic AttaTude *See* MH Folk

Janie Fricke *See* MH Country

Gavin Friday *See* MH Rock

Don Friedman *See* MH Jazz

Kinky Friedman *See* MH Country, MH Folk

Friends of Dean Martinez *See* MH Lounge, MH Rock

Friends of Distinction *See* MH R&B

Johnny Frigo *See* MH Jazz

Robert Fripp/League of Crafty Guitarists/Fripp & Eno/Sylvian & Fripp/Fripp & Summers *See* MH Rock

Bill Frisell *See* MH Jazz, MH Rock

David Frishberg *See* MH Jazz

David Frizzell & Shelly West *See* MH Country

Lefty Frizzell *See* MH Country, MH Folk

The Front Porch String Band *See* MH Country, MH Folk

Front Range *See* MH Country, MH Folk

Front 242 *See* MH Rock

Jack Frost *See* MH Rock

Frank Frost & Sam Carr *See* MH Blues

John Frusciante *See* MH Rock

Fu-Schnickens *See* MH R&B

Fugazi *See* MH Rock

Fugees/Wyclef Jean *See* MH R&B, MH Rock

The Fugs *See* MH Folk, MH Rock

Robbie Fulks *See* MH Country

Full Force *See* MH R&B

Full Time Men *See* MH Rock

Blind Boy Fuller *See* MH Blues

Curtis Fuller *See* MH Jazz

Jesse Fuller *See* MH Blues, MH Folk

The Bobby Fuller Four *See* MH Rock

Lowell Fulson *See* MH Blues

Fun Boy Three *See* MH Rock

Fun Lovin' Criminals *See* MH Rock

John Funchess *See* MH Blues

Anson Funderburgh & the Rockets Featuring Sam Myers *See* MH Blues

Funkadelic *See* MH Rock

Funkdoobiest *See* MH R&B

Funkmaster Flex *See* MH R&B

Richie Furay/Richie Furay Band *See* MH Rock

Tret Fure *See* MH Folk

Tony Furtado *See* MH Country, MH Folk

Billy Fury *See* MH Rock

Future Sound of London/Amorphous Androgynous *See* MH Rock

Fuzzy Mountain String Band *See* MH Folk

Kenny G *See* MH Jazz

Warren G *See* MH R&B

Reeves Gabrels *See* MH Rock

Charles Gabriel *See* MH Jazz

Ethel Gabriel *See* MH Lounge

Peter Gabriel *See* MH Rock

Steve Gadd *See* MH Jazz

Chris Gaffney *See* MH Country

Slim (Bulee) Gaillard *See* MH Jazz, MH Lounge

Jon Gailmor *See* MH Folk

Earl Gaines *See* MH Blues

Grady Gaines *See* MH Blues

Rosie Gaines *See* MH R&B

Serge Gainsbourg *See* MH Lounge

Galaxie 500 *See* MH Rock

The Galaxy Trio *See* MH Lounge

Eric Gale *See* MH Jazz

Rory Gallagher *See* MH Blues, MH Rock

Les & Gary Gallier *See* MH Folk

Gallon Drunk *See* MH Rock

Annie Gallup *See* MH Folk

Hal Galper *See* MH Jazz

James Galway *See* MH Lounge

Frank Gambale *See* MH Jazz

Beppe Gambetta *See* MH Folk

Game Theory/The Loud Family/Scott Miller *See* MH Rock

Ganelin Trio/Vyacheslav Ganelin *See* MH Jazz

Gang of Four/Shriekback *See* MH Rock

Gang Starr *See* MH Jazz, MH R&B

Gordon Gano *See* MH Rock

Cecil Gant *See* MH Blues

Gap Band *See* MH R&B

Garbage *See* MH Rock

Jan Garbarek *See* MH Jazz

Art Garfunkel *See* MH Folk, MH Rock

Greg Garing *See* MH Rock

Hank Garland *See* MH Country

Judy Garland *See* MH Lounge

Red Garland *See* MH Jazz

Erroll Garner *See* MH Jazz, MH Lounge

Larry Garner *See* MH Blues

Kenny Garrett *See* MH Jazz

Nick Garvey *See* MH Rock

John Gary *See* MH Lounge

George Garzone *See* MH Jazz

Giorgio Gaslini *See* MH Jazz

Edith Giovanna Gassion *See* MH Lounge

Marvin Gaster *See* MH Country, MH Folk

Gastr del Sol *See* MH Rock

David Gates/Bread *See* MH Country, MH Rock

Gateway *See* MH Jazz

The Gathering Field *See* MH Rock

Larry Gatlin & the Gatlin Brothers *See* MH Country

Keith Gattis *See* MH Country

Danny Gatton *See* MH Rock

Dick Gaughan *See* MH Folk

Frankie Gavin *See* MH Folk

Marvin Gaye *See* MH Lounge, MH R&B, MH Rock

Charles Gayle *See* MH Jazz

Crystal Gayle *See* MH Country

Gloria Gaynor *See* MH R&B

Gear Daddies *See* MH Rock

J. Geils Band/Bluestime *See* MH Blues, MH R&B, MH Rock

Howe Gelb *See* MH Rock

Bob Geldof *See* MH Rock

Gene *See* MH Rock

General Humbert *See* MH Folk

General Public *See* MH Rock

Generation X *See* MH Rock

Genesis *See* MH Rock

Genius/GZA *See* MH R&B

Gentle Giant *See* MH Rock

The Gentle People *See* MH Lounge

Bobbie Gentry *See* MH Country

Frank George *See* MH Folk

Georgia Satellites/Dan Baird *See* MH Rock

Christopher Geppert *See* MH Lounge

Geraldine Fibbers *See* MH Rock

Gerardo *See* MH R&B

Paul Geremia *See* MH Folk

Lisa Germano *See* MH Rock

Mark Germino *See* MH Country, MH Folk

The Germs *See* MH Rock

Alice Gerrard *See* MH Country, MH Folk

Lisa Gerrard *See* MH Rock

Gerry & the Pacemakers *See* MH Rock

George & Ira Gershwin *See* MH Lounge

Bruce Gertz *See* MH Jazz

Getaway Cruiser *See* MH Rock

Geto Boys *See* MH R&B

Stan Getz *See* MH Jazz, MH Lounge

Ghost Face Killa *See* MH R&B

Giant Sand *See* MH Rock

Gerry Gibbs *See* MH Jazz

Terri Gibbs *See* MH Country

Terry Gibbs *See* MH Jazz

Banu Gibson *See* MH Jazz

Bob Gibson *See* MH Folk

Clifford Gibson *See* MH Blues

Debbie Gibson/Deborah Gibson *See* MH Rock

Don Gibson *See* MH Country

Lacy Gibson *See* MH Blues

Gibson Brothers Band *See* MH Folk

The Gibson/Miller Band *See* MH Country

Kathie Lee Gifford *See* MH Lounge

Gigolo Aunts *See* MH Rock

Ronnie Gilbert *See* MH Folk

Vance Gilbert *See* MH Folk

Astrud Gilberto *See* MH Lounge

João Gilberto *See* MH Jazz, MH Lounge

Johnny Gill *See* MH R&B

Vince Gill *See* MH Country

Dizzy Gillespie *See* MH Jazz, MH Lounge

Steve Gillette & Cindy Mangsen *See* MH Folk

Mickey Gilley *See* MH Country

Bill "Jazz" Gillum *See* MH Blues

Jimmie Dale Gilmore *See* MH Country, MH Folk, MH Rock

David Gilmour *See* MH Rock

Gin Blossoms *See* MH Rock

Greg Ginn *See* MH Rock

Girls Against Boys *See* MH Rock

Egberto Gismonti *See* MH Jazz

Jimmy Giuffre *See* MH Jazz

Gladhands *See* MH Rock

Glass Eye *See* MH Rock

Jackie Gleason *See* MH Lounge

Gary Glitter *See* MH Rock

Glitterbox *See* MH Rock

Globe Unity Orchestra *See* MH Jazz

The Glove *See* MH Rock

Corey Glover *See* MH Rock

The Go-Betweens *See* MH Rock

The Go-Go's *See* MH Rock

Go West *See* MH Rock

Goats *See* MH R&B

God Street Wine *See* MH Rock

The Godfathers *See* MH Rock

The Goins Brothers *See* MH Country

Julie Gold *See* MH Folk

Barry Goldberg *See* MH Blues

Ben Goldberg *See* MH Jazz

Samuel Goldberg *See* MH Lounge

Golden Earring *See* MH Rock

Golden Gate Quartet/Golden Gate Jubilee Quartet *See* MH Folk

The Golden Palominos *See* MH Rock

Golden Ring *See* MH Folk

Golden Smog *See* MH Country, MH Rock

Goldfinger *See* MH Rock

Goldie *See* MH Rock

Larry Goldings *See* MH Jazz

Vinny Golia *See* MH Jazz

Mac Gollehon *See* MH Jazz

Benny Golson *See* MH Jazz

Eddie Gomez *See* MH Jazz

Paul Gonsalves *See* MH Jazz

Jerry Gonzalez & the Fort Apache Band *See* MH Jazz

Goo Goo Dolls *See* MH Rock

Good Ol' Persons *See* MH Country, MH Folk

Goodie Mob *See* MH R&B

Cuba Gooding *See* MH R&B

Benny Goodman *See* MH Jazz, MH Lounge

Steve Goodman *See* MH Country, MH Folk, MH Rock

Mick Goodrick *See* MH Jazz

Ron Goodwin *See* MH Lounge

Bobby Gordon *See* MH Jazz

Dexter Gordon *See* MH Jazz, MH Lounge

Robert Gordon *See* MH Country, MH Rock

Berry Gordy Jr. *See* MH R&B

Lesley Gore *See* MH Lounge, MH Rock

Martin Gore *See* MH Rock

John Gorka *See* MH Country, MH Folk, MH Rock

Gorky's Zygotic Mynci *See* MH Rock

Skip Gorman *See* MH Country, MH Folk

Eydie Gorme *See* MH Lounge

Vern Gosdin *See* MH Country, MH Folk

Danny Gottlieb *See* MH Jazz

Susan Gottlieb *See* MH Folk

Barry Goudreau *See* MH Rock

Morton Gould *See* MH Lounge

Robert Goulet *See* MH Lounge

Gov't Mule *See* MH Rock

Lawrence Gowan/Gowan *See* MH Rock

Dusko Goykovich *See* MH Jazz

The GP's *See* MH Folk

Davey Graham *See* MH Folk

Graham Central Station/Larry Graham *See* MH R&B

Lou Gramm *See* MH Rock

Grand Daddy I.U. *See* MH R&B

Grand Funk Railroad *See* MH Rock

Grandmaster Flash & the Furious Five/Melle Mel & the Furious Five *See* MH R&B

Grandpa Jones *See* MH Country, MH Folk

Jerry Granelli *See* MH Jazz

Amy Grant *See* MH Rock

Bill Grant *See* MH Folk

Darrell Grant *See* MH Jazz

Grant Lee Buffalo *See* MH Rock

Grant Street *See* MH Folk

The Grapes of Wrath/Ginger *See* MH Rock

Stephane Grappelli *See* MH Jazz

The Grass Is Greener *See* MH Country, MH Folk

The Grass Roots *See* MH Rock

Lou Grassi *See* MH Jazz

The Grassy Knoll/Bob Green *See* MH Jazz, MH Rock

The Grateful Dead *See* MH Country, MH Folk, MH Rock

Blind Roosevelt Graves *See* MH Blues

Josh Graves *See* MH Folk

Milford Graves *See* MH Jazz

Gravity Kills *See* MH Rock

David Gray *See* MH Rock

Dobie Gray *See* MH R&B

Henry Gray *See* MH Blues

Wardell Gray *See* MH Jazz

Great Plains *See* MH Country

Great White *See* MH Rock

Buddy Greco *See* MH Lounge

Al Green *See* MH Blues, MH R&B

Benny Green *See* MH Jazz

Cal Green *See* MH Blues

Cornelius Green *See* MH Blues

Grant Green *See* MH Jazz

Peter Green *See* MH Blues

Green Day *See* MH Rock

Green Jellÿ *See* MH Rock

Green on Red *See* MH Rock

Green River *See* MH Rock

Greenberry Woods/Splitsville *See* MH Rock

The Greenbriar Boys *See* MH Country, MH Folk

Bruce Greene *See* MH Folk

Dodo Greene *See* MH Jazz

Jack Greene *See* MH Country

Richard Greene/The Grass Is Greener *See* MH Country, MH Folk

Phillip Greenlief *See* MH Jazz

Greg Greenway *See* MH Folk

Lee Greenwood *See* MH Country

Ricky Lynn Gregg *See* MH Country

Clinton Gregory *See* MH Country

Clive Gregson & Christine Collister/Clive Gregson/Christine Collister *See* MH Folk, MH Rock

Adie Grey *See* MH Folk

Al Grey *See* MH Jazz

Sara Grey *See* MH Folk

Grianan *See* MH Folk

David Grier *See* MH Country, MH Folk

James Griffin *See* MH Rock

Johnny Griffin *See* MH Jazz

Patty Griffin *See* MH Folk, MH Rock

Grace Griffith *See* MH Folk

Nanci Griffith *See* MH Country, MH Folk, MH Rock

The Grifters *See* MH Rock

John Grimaldi *See* MH Blues

Henry Grimes *See* MH Jazz

Lloyd "Tiny" Grimes *See* MH Jazz

David Grisman *See* MH Country, MH Folk

Don Grolnick *See* MH Jazz

Groove Collective *See* MH Jazz

Groove Theory *See* MH R&B

SERIES INDEX

George Harrison *See* MH Rock

Wilbert Harrison *See* MH Blues

Deborah Harry *See* MH Rock

Alvin Youngblood Hart *See* MH Blues

Antonio Hart *See* MH Jazz

Billy Hart *See* MH Jazz

Freddie Hart *See* MH Country

Grant Hart *See* MH Rock

Lorenz Hart *See* MH Lounge

John Hartford *See* MH Country, MH Folk

Johnny Hartman *See* MH Jazz, MH Lounge

Mick Harvey *See* MH Lounge, MH Rock

PJ Harvey *See* MH Rock

Harvey Danger *See* MH Rock

Tony Hatch & Jackie Trent *See* MH Lounge

Hater *See* MH Rock

Juliana Hatfield *See* MH Rock

Donny Hathaway *See* MH R&B

Lalah Hathaway *See* MH R&B

Havana 3 A.M. *See* MH Rock

Richie Havens *See* MH Folk, MH R&B, MH Rock

Hampton Hawes *See* MH Jazz

Ginny Hawker & Kay Justice *See* MH Folk

Buddy Boy Hawkins *See* MH Blues

Coleman Hawkins *See* MH Jazz, MH Lounge

Dale Hawkins *See* MH Rock

Erskine Hawkins *See* MH Jazz

Hawkshaw Hawkins *See* MH Country

Jamesetta Hawkins *See* MH Blues

Ronnie Hawkins *See* MH Country, MH Rock

Screamin' Jay Hawkins *See* MH Blues, MH R&B, MH Rock

Sophie B. Hawkins *See* MH Rock

Ted Hawkins *See* MH Blues, MH Country, MH Folk, MH R&B, MH Rock

The Edwin Hawkins Singers *See* MH R&B

Hayden *See* MH Rock

Lili Haydn *See* MH Rock

Isaac Hayes *See* MH Lounge, MH R&B

Louis Hayes *See* MH Jazz

Martin Hayes *See* MH Folk

Wade Hayes *See* MH Country

Dick Haymes *See* MH Lounge

Graham Haynes *See* MH Jazz

Roy Haynes *See* MH Jazz

Justin Hayward & John Lodge *See* MH Rock

Hazard *See* MH Rock

Hazel *See* MH Rock

Hazel & Alice/Hazel Dickens/Alice Gerrard *See* MH Country, MH Folk

Roy Head *See* MH R&B, MH Rock

Topper Headon *See* MH Rock

The Jeff Healey Band *See* MH Rock

The Health & Happiness Show *See* MH Country, MH ROCK

Bill & Bonnie Hearne *See* MH Folk

Heart/Lovemongers *See* MH Rock

The Heartbeats/Shep & the Limelites *See* MH R&B

Johnny Heartsman *See* MH Blues

The Reverend Horton Heat *See* MH Rock

Jimmy Heath *See* MH Jazz

Percy Heath *See* MH Jazz

Tootie Heath *See* MH Jazz

Heatmiser *See* MH Rock

Heatwave *See* MH R&B

Heaven 17 *See* MH Rock

Heavy D. & the Boyz *See* MH R&B

Bobby Hebb *See* MH R&B

Hedgehog Pie *See* MH Folk

Michael Hedges *See* MH Folk, MH Rock

The Hee Haw Gospel Quartet *See* MH Country, MH Folk

Neal Hefti *See* MH Lounge

Gail Heil *See* MH Folk

Mark Helias *See* MH Jazz

Helicon *See* MH Folk

Helium *See* MH Rock

Richard Hell & the Voidoids *See* MH Rock

Hellbenders *See* MH Folk

Jonas Hellborg *See* MH Jazz

The Hellecasters *See* MH Country, MH Rock

Neal Hellman *See* MH Folk

Levon Helm *See* MH Rock

Helmet *See* MH Rock

Heltah Skeltah *See* MH R&B

Jessie Mae Hemphill *See* MH Blues

Julius Hemphill *See* MH Jazz

Bill Henderson *See* MH Jazz

Eddie Henderson *See* MH Jazz

Fletcher Henderson *See* MH Jazz

John William Henderson *See* MH Blues

Joe Henderson *See* MH Jazz

Michael Henderson *See* MH R&B

Mike Henderson *See* MH Blues, MH Country, MH Rock

Wayne Henderson *See* MH Folk

Jimi Hendrix/The Jimi Hendrix Experience/Band of Gypsys *See* MH Blues, MH R&B, MH Rock

Nona Hendryx *See* MH R&B

Mel Henke *See* MH Lounge

Don Henley *See* MH Folk, MH Rock

Margo Hennebach *See* MH Folk

Clarence "Frogman" Henry *See* MH Blues

Ernie Henry *See* MH Jazz

Joe Henry *See* MH Country, MH Rock

Priscilla Herdman *See* MH Folk

Herm *See* MH R&B

Woody Herman *See* MH Jazz, MH Lounge

Herman's Hermits *See* MH Rock

Ty Herndon *See* MH Country

Fred Hersch *See* MH Jazz

Kristin Hersh *See* MH Rock

Monika Herzig *See* MH Jazz

Hesperus *See* MH Folk

Carolyn Hester *See* MH Folk

Howard Hewett *See* MH R&B

Richard X. Heyman *See* MH Rock

Nick Heyward/Haircut 100 *See* MH Rock

Hi-Five *See* MH R&B

The Hi-Lo's *See* MH Lounge

Hi Records *See* MH R&B

John Hiatt *See* MH Rock

Al Hibbler *See* MH Jazz, MH Lounge

Sara Hickman *See* MH Folk

Dan Hicks *See* MH Country, MH Folk, MH Rock

John Hicks *See* MH Jazz

Otis Hicks *See* MH Blues

Robert Hicks *See* MH Blues

Billy Higgins *See* MH Jazz

Johnson Mountain Boys *See* MH Country, MH Folk

Daniel Johnston *See* MH Rock

Freedy Johnston *See* MH Folk, MH Rock

Phillip Johnston /Big Trouble *See* MH Jazz

Randy Johnston *See* MH Jazz

Tom Johnston *See* MH Rock

The Johnstons *See* MH Folk

Jolene *See* MH Country

Al Jolson *See* MH Lounge

Casey Jones *See* MH Blues

Curtis Jones *See* MH Blues

Eddie Lee Jones *See* MH Blues

Edward Jones *See* MH Blues

Elvin Jones *See* MH Jazz

Etta Jones *See* MH Jazz, MH Lounge

Floyd Jones *See* MH Blues

George Jones *See* MH Country, MH Folk

Glenn Jones *See* MH R&B

Grace Jones *See* MH R&B

Hank Jones *See* MH Jazz

Howard Jones *See* MH Rock

Jack Jones *See* MH Lounge

Jo Jones *See* MH Jazz

Johnny Jones *See* MH Blues

Linda Jones *See* MH R&B

Little "Sonny" Jones *See* MH Blues

Marti Jones *See* MH Rock

Mick Jones *See* MH Rock

Oliver Jones *See* MH Jazz

Paul "Wine" Jones *See* MH Blues

"Philly" Joe Jones *See* MH Jazz

Quincy Jones *See* MH Jazz, MH Lounge, MH R&B

Rickie Lee Jones *See* MH Folk, MH Rock

Robert Lewis Jones *See* MH Blues

Ruth Lee Jones *See* MH Blues

Sam Jones *See* MH Jazz

Spike Jones *See* MH Jazz, MH Lounge

Steve Jones *See* MH Rock

Thad Jones *See* MH Jazz

Tom Jones *See* MH Lounge, MH Rock

Tutu Jones *See* MH Blues

Carol Elizabeth Jones & James Leva *See* MH Folk

Diane Jones and Hubie King *See* MH Folk

Freddy Jones Band *See* MH Rock

Betty Joplin *See* MH Jazz

Janis Joplin/Big Brother & the Holding Company *See* MH Blues, MH R&B, MH Rock

Scott Joplin *See* MH Jazz

Al Jordan *See* MH Lounge

Charley Jordan *See* MH Blues

Clifford Jordan *See* MH Jazz

Duke Jordan *See* MH Jazz

Louis Jordan *See* MH Blues, MH Jazz, MH Lounge, MH R&B

Marlon Jordan *See* MH Jazz

Montell Jordan *See* MH R&B

Ronny Jordan *See* MH Jazz

Sheila Jordan *See* MH Jazz

Stanley Jordan *See* MH Jazz

Margie Joseph *See* MH R&B

Pleasant "Cousin Joe" Joseph *See* MH Blues

Scott Joss *See* MH Country

Journey *See* MH Rock

Joy Division *See* MH Rock

JT the Bigga Figga *See* MH R&B

Judas Priest *See* MH Rock

Cledus "T." Judd *See* MH Country

Wynonna Judd *See* MH Country

The Judds *See* MH Country

Judybats *See* MH Rock

Jules & the Polar Bears *See* MH Rock

Juluka *See* MH Rock

Jungle Brothers *See* MH R&B

Junior *See* MH R&B

Junior M.A.F.I.A./Lil' Kim *See* MH R&B

Junk Monkeys *See* MH Rock

Vic Juris *See* MH Jazz

Just Ice *See* MH R&B

Barbara K *See* MH Rock

Paul K/Paul K & the Weathermen/Paul K & the Prayers *See* MH Rock

Ernie K-Doe *See* MH R&B

Ledward Kaapana *See* MH Folk

Bert Kaempfert *See* MH Lounge

Brenda Kahn *See* MH Folk, MH Rock

Si Kahn *See* MH Folk

George Kahumoku Jr. *See* MH Folk

Moses Kahumoku *See* MH Folk

Henry Kaiser *See* MH Jazz

Kajagoogoo/Kaja/Limahl *See* MH Rock

Connie Kaldor *See* MH Folk

Cindy Kallet *See* MH Folk

Kathy Kallick *See* MH Country, MH Folk

Kam *See* MH R&B

Rev. Dennis Kamakahi *See* MH Folk

Michael Kamen *See* MH Lounge

Candye Kane *See* MH Blues

Kieran Kane/The O'Kanes/Jamie O'Hara *See* MH Country, MH Folk

Ray Kane/Raymond Kane *See* MH Folk

Kansas *See* MH Rock

Paul Kantner *See* MH Rock

Lucy Kaplansky *See* MH Folk

Doris Kappelhoff *See* MH Lounge

Kara's Flowers *See* MH Rock

Mick Karn *See* MH Rock

Kashif *See* MH R&B

Kathleen Turner Overdrive *See* MH Rock

Katrina & the Waves *See* MH Rock

Bruce Katz *See* MH Jazz

Mickey Katz *See* MH Lounge

Steve Kaufman *See* MH Folk

Jorma Kaukonen *See* MH Folk, MH Rock

Connie Kay *See* MH Jazz

Sammy Kaye *See* MH Jazz, MH Lounge

KC & the Sunshine Band *See* MH R&B, MH Rock

Dolores Keane *See* MH Folk

James Keane *See* MH Folk

Seán Keane *See* MH Folk

William David Kearney *See* MH Blues

John P. Kee *See* MH R&B

James Keelaghan *See* MH Folk

Robert Earl Keen Jr. *See* MH Country, MH Folk

Tommy Keene *See* MH Rock

Geoff Keezer *See* MH Jazz

Garrison Keillor *See* MH Folk

Katell Keineg *See* MH Rock

Doyle Lawson/Quicksilver *See* MH Country, MH Folk

Hugh Lawson *See* MH Jazz

Lazy Lester *See* MH Blues

Bernadette Lazzaro *See* MH Lounge

Leadbelly/Huddie Ledbetter *See* MH Blues, MH Folk

The Leaders *See* MH Jazz

Leaders of the New School/Busta Rhymes *See* MH R&B

The League of Crafty Guitarists *See* MH Rock

Paul Leary *See* MH Rock

The Leaves *See* MH Folk, MH Rock

Led Zeppelin *See* MH Blues, MH Rock

Chris LeDoux *See* MH Country

Arthur Lee *See* MH Folk, MH Rock

Brenda Lee *See* MH Country, MH Lounge, MH Rock

Bryan Lee *See* MH Blues

Frankie Lee *See* MH Blues

Johnny Lee *See* MH Country

Lorraine Lee *See* MH Folk

Lovie Lee *See* MH Blues

Peggy Lee *See* MH Jazz, MH Lounge

Rick Lee *See* MH Folk

Tracey Lee *See* MH R&B

Raymond Lefevre *See* MH Lounge

The Left Banke *See* MH Rock

Brad Leftwich/Brad Leftwich & Linda Higginbotham *See* MH Folk

Legendary Blues Band *See* MH Blues

The Legendary Jim Ruiz Group *See* MH Rock

Legendary Stardust Cowboy *See* MH Country, MH Rock

Adrian Legg *See* MH Folk

Michel Legrand *See* MH Jazz, MH Lounge

Tom Lehrer *See* MH Lounge

Keri Leigh *See* MH Blues

Peter Leitch *See* MH Jazz

John Leitham *See* MH Jazz

Eddie LeJeune *See* MH Folk

Iry LeJeune *See* MH Folk

Peter Lemer *See* MH Jazz

The Lemon Pipers *See* MH Rock

Lemonheads *See* MH Rock

Overton Lemons *See* MH Blues

Ute Lemper *See* MH Lounge

John Lennon *See* MH Rock

Julian Lennon *See* MH Rock

The Lennon Sisters *See* MH Lounge

Annie Lennox *See* MH Lounge, MH Rock

J.B. Lenoir *See* MH Blues

Lotte Lenya *See* MH Lounge

The LeRoi Brothers *See* MH Country

Less Than Jake *See* MH Rock

Sonny Lester *See* MH Lounge

Let's Active *See* MH Rock

The Lettermen *See* MH Lounge

James Leva & Carol Elizabeth Jones *See* MH Folk

Level 42 *See* MH Rock

Keith Levene *See* MH Rock

Dan Levenson *See* MH Folk

Levert *See* MH R&B

Lou Levy *See* MH Jazz

Ron Levy *See* MH Blues

Furry Lewis *See* MH Blues, MH Folk

George Lewis (clarinet) *See* MH Jazz

George Lewis (trombone) *See* MH Jazz

Jerry Lewis *See* MH Lounge

Jerry Lee Lewis *See* MH Country, MH Rock

John Lewis *See* MH Jazz

Laurie Lewis/Grant Street *See* MH Country, MH Folk

Linda Gail Lewis *See* MH Country

Meade "Lux" Lewis *See* MH Jazz

Mel Lewis *See* MH Jazz

Ramsey Lewis *See* MH Jazz, MH R&B

Smiley Lewis *See* MH Blues

Tom Lewis *See* MH Folk

Walter Lewis *See* MH Blues

Huey Lewis & the News *See* MH Rock

Gary Lewis & the Playboys *See* MH Rock

The Lewis Family *See* MH Country, MH Folk

Liberace *See* MH Lounge

Ottmar Liebert/Luna Negra *See* MH Jazz

Dave Liebman *See* MH Jazz

Life of Agony *See* MH Rock

Lifers Group *See* MH R&B

Jimmy Liggins *See* MH Blues

Joe Liggins *See* MH Blues

Enoch Light *See* MH Lounge

Lighter Shade of Brown (LSOB) *See* MH R&B

Gordon Lightfoot *See* MH Folk, MH Lounge

Lightnin' Slim *See* MH Blues

The Lightning Seeds *See* MH Rock

Kirk Lightsey *See* MH Jazz

Lil' Ed & the Blues Imperials *See* MH Blues

Lil' Kim *See* MH R&B

Lilly Brothers/Lilly Brothers & Don Stover *See* MH Country, MH Folk

The Limeliters *See* MH Folk, MH Lounge

Limp Bizkit *See* MH Rock

Lincoln *See* MH Rock

Abbey Lincoln *See* MH Jazz

Lincoln Center Jazz Orchestra *See* MH Jazz

Colin Linden *See* MH Folk

Lindisfarne *See* MH Rock

David Lindley *See* MH Folk, MH Rock

Arto Lindsay *See* MH Rock

Mark Lindsay *See* MH Rock

Hip Linkchain *See* MH Blues

Lipps, Inc. *See* MH R&B

Mance Lipscomb *See* MH Folk

Liquid Soul *See* MH Jazz

Liquorice *See* MH Rock

Lisa Lisa & Cult Jam *See* MH R&B

Melba Liston *See* MH Jazz

Booker Little *See* MH Jazz

Little Anthony & the Imperials *See* MH Rock

Little Charlie & the Nightcats *See* MH Blues

Little Eva *See* MH R&B, MH Rock

Little Feat *See* MH Rock

Little Milton *See* MH Blues, MH R&B

Little Richard *See* MH R&B, MH Rock

Little River Band *See* MH Rock

Little Sonny *See* MH Blues

Little Steven/Little Steven & the Disciples of Soul *See* MH R&B, MH Rock

Little Texas/Brady Seals *See* MH Country

Mabsant *See* MH Folk

Joel Mabus *See* MH Folk

Margaret MacArthur *See* MH Folk

Ewan MacColl *See* MH Folk

Kirsty MacColl *See* MH Rock

Jeanette MacDonald *See* MH Lounge

Pat MacDonald *See* MH Folk, MH Rock

Rod MacDonald *See* MH Folk

Machito *See* MH Jazz

Ashley MacIsaac *See* MH Folk, MH Rock

Craig Mack *See* MH R&B

Mack 10 *See* MH R&B

Kate MacKenzie *See* MH Country, MH Folk

Bryan MacLean *See* MH Rock

Dougie MacLean *See* MH Folk

Tara MacLean *See* MH Rock

Kate MacLeod *See* MH Folk

Buddy MacMaster *See* MH Folk

Natalie MacMaster *See* MH Folk

Madeline MacNeil *See* MH Folk

Jeep MacNichol *See* MH Rock

Uncle Dave Macon *See* MH Country, MH Folk

Gordon MacRae *See* MH Lounge

Mad Lion *See* MH R&B

Mad Pudding *See* MH Folk

Madd Skillz *See* MH R&B

Joanie Madden *See* MH Folk

Madder Rose *See* MH Rock

The Maddox Brothers & Rose/Rose Maddox *See* MH Country, MH Folk

Madness *See* MH Rock

Madonna *See* MH Lounge, MH R&B, MH Rock

Magazine *See* MH Rock

Alan Mager *See* MH Folk

Samuel Maghett *See* MH Blues

Magic Sam *See* MH Blues

Magic Slim *See* MH Blues

Magical Strings *See* MH Folk

Magnapop *See* MH Rock

Magnolia Sisters *See* MH Folk

Magpie *See* MH Folk

Taj Mahal *See* MH Blues, MH Folk, MH R&B

Mahavishnu Orchestra *See* MH Jazz

Kevin Mahogany *See* MH Jazz

The Main Ingredient *See* MH R&B

Main Source/Large Professor *See* MH R&B

Mike Maineri *See* MH Jazz

Charlie Major *See* MH Country

Tommy Makem *See* MH Folk

Adam Makowicz *See* MH Jazz

Mac Mall *See* MH R&B

Mallard *See* MH Rock

David Mallett *See* MH Folk

Yngwie Malmsteen *See* MH Rock

Michelle Malone *See* MH Rock

Russell Malone *See* MH Jazz

The Mamas & the Papas *See* MH Folk, MH Rock

Mamou Playboys *See* MH Folk

Man or Astro-Man? *See* MH Lounge, MH Rock

ManBREAK *See* MH Rock

Junior Mance *See* MH Jazz

Melissa Manchester *See* MH Rock

Henry Mancini *See* MH Lounge

Harvey Mandel *See* MH Blues

Mando Mafia *See* MH Folk

Barbara Mandrell *See* MH Country

Mandrill *See* MH R&B

Joe Maneri *See* MH Jazz

Mat Maneri *See* MH Jazz

Albert Mangelsdorff *See* MH Jazz

Chuck Mangione *See* MH Jazz, MH Lounge

Cindy Mangsen *See* MH Folk

The Manhattan Transfer *See* MH Jazz, MH Lounge

The Manhattans *See* MH R&B

Manic Street Preachers *See* MH Rock

Barry Manilow *See* MH Lounge

Manitoba's Wild Kingdom *See* MH Rock

Aimee Mann *See* MH Rock

Carl Mann *See* MH Country

Herbie Mann *See* MH Jazz

Manfred Mann/Manfred Mann's Earth Band *See* MH Rock

Shelly Manne *See* MH Jazz

Mannheim Steamroller *See* MH Lounge

Joseph "Wingy" Manone *See* MH Jazz

Ray Mantilla *See* MH Jazz

Mantovani *See* MH Lounge

Phil Manzanera/801 *See* MH Rock

The Mar-Keys *See* MH R&B

The Marcels *See* MH R&B

Steve Marcus *See* MH Jazz

Rick Margitza *See* MH Jazz

Bob Margolin *See* MH Blues, MH Folk

Kitty Margolis *See* MH Jazz

Tania Maria *See* MH Jazz

Charlie Mariano *See* MH Jazz

Teena Marie *See* MH R&B, MH Rock

Marillion/Fish *See* MH Rock

Marilyn Manson *See* MH Rock

The Mark-Almond Band *See* MH Rock

Marky Mark *See* MH R&B

Ziggy Marley & the Melody Makers *See* MH R&B, MH Rock

Bob Marley & the Wailers *See* MH R&B, MH Rock

Marley Marl *See* MH R&B

Marley's Ghost *See* MH Folk

Marmalade/Dean Ford & the Gaylords/The Gaylords/Dave Dee & Marmalade *See* MH Rock

Dodo Marmarosa *See* MH Jazz

Marry Me Jane *See* MH Rock

Chris Mars *See* MH Rock

Johnny Mars *See* MH Blues

Branford Marsalis *See* MH Jazz

Delfeayo Marsalis *See* MH Jazz

Ellis Marsalis *See* MH Jazz

Wynton Marsalis *See* MH Jazz

Warne Marsh *See* MH Jazz

Amanda Marshall *See* MH Rock

Evan Marshall *See* MH Folk

Mike Marshall *See* MH Folk

The Marshall Tucker Band *See* MH Country, MH Rock

Martha & the Vandellas *See* MH R&B, MH Rock

Claire Martin *See* MH Jazz

Dean Martin *See* MH Lounge

Freddy Martin *See* MH Lounge

Jimmy Martin *See* MH Country, MH Folk

Mel Martin *See* MH Jazz

Tony Martin *See* MH Lounge

Al Martino *See* MH Lounge

Pat Martino *See* MH Jazz

The Marvelettes *See* MH R&B, MH Rock

Richard Marx *See* MH Rock

Masada *See* MH Jazz

Steve Masakowski *See* MH Jazz

Miya Masaoka *See* MH Jazz

Dave Mason *See* MH Folk, MH Rock

Mila Mason *See* MH Country

Nick Mason *See* MH Rock

David Massengill *See* MH Folk

Cal Massey *See* MH Jazz

Zane Massey *See* MH Jazz

Massive Attack/Protection *See* MH R&B, MH Rock

Masta Ace *See* MH R&B

Master P *See* MH R&B

Matchbox 20 *See* MH Rock

Material/Bill Laswell *See* MH Jazz, MH Rock

Material Issue *See* MH Rock

Johnny Mathis *See* MH Lounge, MH R&B

Jas. Mathus & His Knock-Down Society *See* MH Rock

Kathy Mattea *See* MH Country, MH Folk

Eric Matthews *See* MH Lounge, MH Rock

Iain Matthews/Matthews Southern Comfort/Plainsong/Hamilton Pool *See* MH Folk, MH Rock

Dave Matthews Band *See* MH Rock

Matthews Southern Comfort *See* MH Folk

June Maugery *See* MH Folk

The Mavericks *See* MH Country

Maxwell *See* MH R&B

David Maxwell *See* MH Blues

Billy May *See* MH Lounge

Brian May *See* MH Rock

John Mayall *See* MH Blues, MH Rock

Curtis Mayfield *See* MH R&B, MH Rock

Percy Mayfield *See* MH Blues, MH R&B

Maypole *See* MH Rock

Bill Mays *See* MH Jazz

Lyle Mays *See* MH Jazz

Maze *See* MH R&B

Mazzy Star *See* MH Rock

M'Boom *See* MH Jazz

MC Breed & the DFC *See* MH R&B

MC Eiht/Compton's Most Wanted *See* MH R&B

M.C. Hammer *See* MH R&B

MC Lyte *See* MH R&B

MC 900 Ft. Jesus *See* MH R&B, MH Rock

M.C. Shan *See* MH R&B

MC Solaar *See* MH Jazz, MH R&B

Mac McAnally *See* MH Country, MH Folk

Kimberly M'Carver *See* MH Folk

Christian McBride *See* MH Jazz

Martina McBride *See* MH Country

McBride & the Ride/Terry McBride & the Ride *See* MH Country

Jerry McCain *See* MH Blues

Edwin McCain Band *See* MH Rock

Cash McCall *See* MH Blues

C.W. McCall *See* MH Country

Darrell McCall *See* MH Country

Les McCann *See* MH Jazz

Cormac McCarthy *See* MH Folk

Paul McCartney/Wings *See* MH Rock

Kathy McCarty/Glass Eye *See* MH Rock

Mary McCaslin *See* MH Country, MH Folk

Scott McCaughey *See* MH Rock

Charly McClain *See* MH Country

Mighty Sam McClain *See* MH Blues

Debby McClatchy *See* MH Folk

Tommy McClennan *See* MH Blues

Delbert McClinton *See* MH Blues, MH Country, MH Rock

Carol McComb *See* MH Folk

David McComb *See* MH Rock

Billy McComiskey *See* MH Folk

Rob McConnell *See* MH Jazz

Marilyn McCoo *See* MH Lounge

Susannah McCorkle *See* MH Jazz

Maureen McCormick *See* MH Country

The Del McCoury Band/The McCoury Brothers/Ronnie & Rob McCoury *See* MH Country, MH Folk

Neal McCoy *See* MH Country

Van McCoy *See* MH R&B

The McCoy Brothers *See* MH Blues

Jimmy McCracklin *See* MH Blues

Larry McCray *See* MH Blues

Mindy McCready *See* MH Country

Rich McCready *See* MH Country

Ian McCulloch *See* MH Rock

Robert Lee McCullum *See* MH Blues

John McCutcheon *See* MH Folk

Ellas McDaniel *See* MH Blues

Mel McDaniel *See* MH Country

Michael McDermott *See* MH Rock

Country Joe McDonald *See* MH Folk, MH Rock

Michael McDonald *See* MH Rock

Megon McDonough *See* MH Folk

Mississippi Fred McDowell *See* MH Blues, MH Folk

Ronnie McDowell *See* MH Country

Jack McDuff *See* MH Jazz

Reba McEntire *See* MH Country

John McEuen *See* MH Country, MH Folk, MH Rock

Eleanor McEvoy *See* MH Country, MH Folk, MH Rock

McFadden & Whitehead *See* MH R&B

Bobby McFerrin *See* MH Jazz

MC5 *See* MH Rock

Eileen McGann *See* MH Folk

Kate & Anna McGarrigle *See* MH Country, MH Folk, MH Rock

Dennis McGee *See* MH Folk

Sam & Kirk McGee/The Fruit Jar Drinkers/The Dixieliners *See* MH Folk

Sterling McGee *See* MH Blues

Brownie McGhee *See* MH Blues, MH Folk

Howard McGhee *See* MH Jazz

Stick McGhee *See* MH Blues

Maureen McGovern *See* MH Lounge

Tim McGraw *See* MH Country

Jimmy McGriff *See* MH Jazz

Roger McGuinn/McGuinn, Clark & Hillman/McGuinn & Hillman *See* MH Country, MH Folk, MH Rock

Barry McGuire *See* MH Rock

Kalaparusha Maurice McIntyre *See* MH Jazz

Ken McIntyre *See* MH Jazz

Duff McKagan *See* MH Rock

Airto Moreira *See* MH Jazz

Joe Morello *See* MH Jazz

The Morells *See* MH Country, MH Rock

Blake Morgan *See* MH Rock

Frank Morgan *See* MH Jazz

George Morgan *See* MH Country

Lee Morgan *See* MH Jazz

Lorrie Morgan *See* MH Country

Teddy Morgan *See* MH Blues

McKinley Morganfield *See* MH Blues

Ikue Ile Mori *See* MH Rock

Alanis Morissette *See* MH Rock

Morphine *See* MH Rock

Ennio Morricone *See* MH Lounge

Gary Morris *See* MH Country

Joe Morris *See* MH Jazz

Lawrence "Butch" Morris *See* MH Jazz

The Lynn Morris Band *See* MH Country, MH Folk

Van Morrison *See* MH Folk, MH R&B, MH Rock

Morrissey *See* MH Lounge, MH Rock

Bill Morrissey *See* MH Country, MH Folk, MH Rock

Ella Mae Morse *See* MH Lounge

Morse Playboys *See* MH Folk

Jelly Roll Morton *See* MH Jazz

Pete Morton *See* MH Folk

Lisa Moscatiello *See* MH Folk

Bob Moses *See* MH Jazz

Bob Mosley *See* MH Rock

The Motels *See* MH Rock

Bennie Moten *See* MH Jazz

Mother Earth *See* MH Rock

Mother Love Bone *See* MH Rock

Mother's Finest *See* MH R&B, MH Rock

Paul Motian *See* MH Jazz

Mötley Crüe/Vince Neil *See* MH Rock

M.O.T.O./Masters of the Obvious *See* MH Rock

Motorcaster *See* MH Rock

Motörhead *See* MH Rock

The Motors *See* MH Rock

Motown *See* MH R&B

Mott the Hoople *See* MH Rock

Tony Mottola *See* MH Lounge

Bob Mould/Sugar *See* MH Rock

Mountain *See* MH Rock

Nana Mouskouri *See* MH Lounge

Mouth Music *See* MH Folk

Alphonse Mouzon *See* MH Jazz

The Move/Roy Wood *See* MH Rock

Moving Cloud *See* MH Folk

Moving Hearts *See* MH Folk

Moxy Frühvous *See* MH Folk, MH Rock

Famoudou Don Moye *See* MH Jazz

Alison Moyet/Yaz/Yazoo *See* MH R&B, MH Rock

George Mraz *See* MH Jazz

Bheki Mseleku *See* MH Jazz

Mud *See* MH Rock

Mudhoney *See* MH Rock

Karen Mueller *See* MH Folk

The Muffs *See* MH Rock

Ann Mayo Muir *See* MH Folk

Mujician *See* MH Jazz

Maria Muldaur *See* MH Blues, MH Folk, MH R&B

Muleskinner *See* MH Country, MH Folk

Joe Mulholland *See* MH Jazz

Heidi Muller *See* MH Folk

Moon Mullican *See* MH Country

Gerry Mulligan *See* MH Jazz

Peter Mulvey *See* MH Folk

Brendan Mulvihill *See* MH Folk

The Mumps *See* MH Rock

Alan Munde *See* MH Country, MH Folk, MH Rock

Jerry Murad's Harmonicats *See* MH Lounge

Lee Murdock *See* MH Folk

Shirley Murdock *See* MH R&B

The Murmurs *See* MH Rock

Michael Martin Murphey *See* MH Country, MH Folk

Colm Murphy *See* MH Folk

David Lee Murphy *See* MH Country

Eddie Murphy *See* MH R&B

Elliott Murphy *See* MH Folk, MH Rock

Mark Murphy *See* MH Jazz

Matt "Guitar" Murphy *See* MH Blues

Peter Murphy/Dali's Car *See* MH Rock

Turk Murphy *See* MH Jazz

Anne Murray *See* MH Country, MH Lounge

David Murray *See* MH Jazz

Keith Murray *See* MH R&B

Sunny Murray *See* MH Jazz

Music Explosion *See* MH Rock

Music Machine/Bonniwell Music Machine/Friendly Torpedoes *See* MH Rock

Music Revelation Ensemble *See* MH Jazz

Charlie Musselwhite *See* MH Blues

My Bloody Valentine *See* MH Rock

My Drug Hell *See* MH Rock

My Life with the Thrill Kill Kult/The Bomb Gang Girlz *See* MH Rock

Alicia Myers *See* MH R&B

Amina Claudine Myers *See* MH Jazz

Dave Myers *See* MH Blues

Louis Myers *See* MH Blues

Heather Myles *See* MH Country

Mysteries of Life *See* MH Rock

The Mystic Moods Orchestra *See* MH Lounge

Mystikal *See* MH R&B

Jim Nabors *See* MH Lounge

Mark Naftalin *See* MH Blues

Arnie Naiman & Chris Coole *See* MH Folk

Najee *See* MH Jazz

Naked City *See* MH Jazz

Naked Eyes *See* MH Rock

Naked Raygun *See* MH Rock

Ray Nance *See* MH Jazz

Nancy Boy *See* MH Rock

Andy Narell *See* MH Jazz

Nas *See* MH R&B

Milton Nascimento *See* MH Jazz

Graham Nash *See* MH Folk, MH Rock

Johnny Nash *See* MH R&B

Lewis Nash *See* MH Jazz

Ted Nash *See* MH Jazz

The Nashville Bluegrass Band *See* MH Country, MH Folk

The Nashville Mandolin Ensemble *See* MH Country

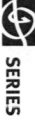

Jay Owens *See* MH Blues

Tony Oxley *See* MH Jazz

The Oyster Band *See* MH Folk, MH Rock

The Ozark Mountain Daredevils *See* MH Country

Makoto Ozone *See* MH Jazz

P *See* MH Rock

Oran "Hot Lips" Page *See* MH Jazz

Patti Page *See* MH Country, MH Lounge

Paul Page *See* MH Lounge

Richard Page *See* MH Rock

Page & Plant/Jimmy Page *See* MH Rock

Cyril Pahinui *See* MH Folk

Gabby Pahinui *See* MH Folk

James "Bla" Pahinui *See* MH Folk

The Pahinui Brothers/Cyril Pahinui/ James "Bla" Pahinui *See* MH Folk

Pailhead *See* MH Rock

Palace/Palace Songs/Palace Music/Palace Brothers *See* MH Rock

Pale Saints *See* MH Rock

Tom Paley *See* MH Folk

Jeff Palmer *See* MH Jazz

Robert Palmer *See* MH R&B, MH Rock

Tena Palmer *See* MH Jazz

Eddie Palmieri *See* MH Jazz

Korla Pandit *See* MH Lounge

The Pandoras *See* MH Rock

Pansy Division *See* MH Rock

Pantera *See* MH Rock

Papas Fritas *See* MH Rock

Paperboy *See* MH R&B

Paris *See* MH R&B

Mica Paris *See* MH R&B

Park Central Squares *See* MH Rock

Billy Parker *See* MH Country

Bobby Parker *See* MH Blues

Caryl Mack Parker *See* MH Country

Charlie Parker *See* MH Jazz, MH Lounge

Evan Parker *See* MH Jazz

Graham Parker/Graham Parker & the Rumor *See* MH Rock

Junior Parker *See* MH Blues

Leon Parker *See* MH Jazz

Maceo Parker *See* MH Jazz, MH R&B

Ray Parker Jr. *See* MH R&B

William Parker *See* MH Jazz

Van Dyke Parks *See* MH Rock

Horace Parlan *See* MH Jazz

Parliament/Parliament-Funkadelic *See* MH Rock

Parlor James *See* MH Country, MH Rock

David Parmley, Scott Vestal & Continental Divide/David Parmley *See* MH Country

Lee Roy Parnell *See* MH Country

Alan Parsons/Alan Parsons Project *See* MH Rock

Gene Parsons *See* MH Country

Gram Parsons *See* MH Country, MH Folk, MH Rock

Niamh Parsons *See* MH Folk

Terry Parsons *See* MH Lounge

Dolly Parton *See* MH Country

Stella Parton *See* MH Country

The Partridge Family *See* MH Rock

Alan Pasqua *See* MH Jazz

Joe Pass *See* MH Jazz

Passengers *See* MH Rock

Passion *See* MH R&B

Deb Pasternak *See* MH Folk

Jaco Pastorius *See* MH Jazz

Mandy Patinkin *See* MH Lounge

John Patitucci *See* MH Jazz

Sandy & Caroline Paton *See* MH Folk

Patrick Street *See* MH Folk

Don Patterson *See* MH Jazz

Charley Patton *See* MH Blues, MH Folk

John Patton *See* MH Jazz

Billy Paul *See* MH R&B

Ellis Paul *See* MH Folk, MH Rock

Gayla Drake Paul *See* MH Folk

Les Paul *See* MH Country, MH Lounge, MH Rock

Pat Paulsen *See* MH Folk

Pavement *See* MH Rock

Mario Pavone *See* MH Jazz

Paw *See* MH Rock

Tom Paxton *See* MH Folk

Johnny Paycheck *See* MH Country

Cecil Payne *See* MH Jazz

Freda Payne *See* MH R&B

Nicholas Payton *See* MH Jazz

Peach Union *See* MH Rock

Peaches & Herb *See* MH R&B

Gary Peacock *See* MH Jazz

Minnie Pearl *See* MH Lounge

Pearl Jam/Mother Love Bone/Green River/Temple of the Dog *See* MH Rock

Duke Pearson *See* MH Jazz

Pebbles *See* MH R&B

Herb Pedersen *See* MH Country, MH Folk

Don Pedi *See* MH Folk

Ann Peebles *See* MH Folk, MH R&B

Peg Leg Sam *See* MH Blues

Bob & Carole Pegg *See* MH Folk

Dave Pegg & Friends *See* MH Rock

George Pegram *See* MH Folk

Dave Pell *See* MH Lounge

Pell Mell *See* MH Rock

Teddy Pendergrass *See* MH R&B

The Penguins *See* MH R&B

CeCe Peniston *See* MH R&B

Michael Penn *See* MH Rock

J.P. Pennington *See* MH Country

Pentangle *See* MH Folk, MH Rock

Tommy Peoples *See* MH Folk

Ken Peplowski *See* MH Jazz

Art Pepper *See* MH Jazz

Pere Ubu *See* MH Rock

Ivo Perelman *See* MH Jazz

Danilo Perez *See* MH Jazz

Perfect *See* MH Rock

Perfect Stranger *See* MH Country

Carl Perkins *See* MH Country, MH Jazz, MH Rock

Larry Perkins *See* MH Country, MH Folk

Pinetop Perkins *See* MH Blues

Ken Perlman *See* MH Folk

Permanent Green Light *See* MH Rock

Tom Peron/Bud Spangler Quartet *See* MH Jazz

Jean-Jacques Perrey *See* MH Lounge

Perrey & Kingsley *See* MH Lounge

Steve Perry *See* MH Rock

Cliff Perry & Laurel Bliss *See* MH Folk

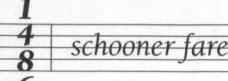

Tar Babies *See* MH Rock

Vladimir Tarasov *See* MH Jazz

Tarheel Slim *See* MH Blues

Al Tariq *See* MH R&B

Tarnation *See* MH Country, MH Rock

Barry & Holly Tashian *See* MH Country, MH Folk

Tasso *See* MH Folk

A Taste of Honey *See* MH R&B

Baby Tate *See* MH Blues

Buddy Tate *See* MH Jazz

Grady Tate *See* MH Jazz

Art Tatum *See* MH Jazz

Tavares *See* MH R&B

Andy Taylor *See* MH Rock

Art Taylor *See* MH Jazz

Billy Taylor *See* MH Jazz

Cecil Taylor *See* MH Jazz

Earl Taylor/The Stoney Mountain Boys *See* MH Country

Eddie Taylor *See* MH Blues

Eric Taylor *See* MH Folk

Hound Dog Taylor *See* MH Blues

James Taylor *See* MH Country, MH Folk, MH Rock

John Taylor *See* MH Rock

Johnnie Taylor *See* MH R&B

Koko Taylor *See* MH Blues, MH R&B

Les Taylor *See* MH Country

Little Johnny Taylor *See* MH Blues

Livingston Taylor *See* MH Folk

Melvin Taylor *See* MH Blues

Roger Taylor *See* MH Rock

S. Alan Taylor *See* MH Country

James Taylor Quartet *See* MH Rock

John Tchicai *See* MH Jazz

The Tea Party *See* MH Rock

Jack Teagarden *See* MH Jazz

Team Dresch *See* MH Rock

The Tearaways *See* MH Rock

The Teardrop Explodes *See* MH Rock

Tears for Fears *See* MH Rock

Teenage Fanclub *See* MH Rock

Richard Teitelbaum *See* MH Jazz

Television *See* MH Rock

Carol Lo Tempio *See* MH Lounge

Johnnie "Geechie" Temple *See* MH Blues

Temple of the Dog *See* MH Rock

The Temptations *See* MH R&B, MH Rock

Ten Foot Pole/Scared Straight *See* MH Rock

10,000 Maniacs/Natalie Merchant *See* MH Rock

Ten Years After *See* MH Blues, MH Rock

10cc *See* MH Rock

Jimi Tenor *See* MH Lounge

Terminator X *See* MH Rock

Jacky Terrasson *See* MH Jazz

Clark Terry *See* MH Jazz

Sonny Terry & Brownie McGhee *See* MH Blues, MH Folk

John Tesh *See* MH Lounge

Tesla *See* MH Rock

Joe Tex *See* MH R&B

Texas *See* MH Rock

The Texas Tornados *See* MH Country, MH Rock

Jimmy Thackery *See* MH Blues

Rosetta Tharpe *See* MH Blues, MH Folk, MH Jazz

that dog. *See* MH Rock

That Petrol Emotion *See* MH Rock

The The *See* MH Rock

Hans Theessink/Blue Groove *See* MH Folk

Thelonious Monster *See* MH Rock

Them *See* MH Folk, MH R&B, MH Rock

Therapy? *See* MH Rock

They Might Be Giants *See* MH Rock

Toots Thielemans/Jean Thielemans *See* MH Jazz

Chris Thile *See* MH Country, MH Folk

Thin Lizzy *See* MH Rock

Thin White Rope *See* MH Rock

3rd Bass *See* MH R&B

Third Eye Blind *See* MH Rock

Third Eye Foundation *See* MH Rock

3rd Party *See* MH Rock

IIIrd Tyme Out *See* MH Country, MH Folk

Third World *See* MH R&B

.38 Special *See* MH Rock

Thirty Ought Six *See* MH Rock

This Mortal Coil *See* MH Rock

Anthony Thistlewaite *See* MH Folk

Beulah Thomas *See* MH Blues

B.J. Thomas *See* MH Country

Buddy Thomas *See* MH Folk

Carla Thomas *See* MH R&B

Gary Thomas *See* MH Jazz

Henry "Ragtime Texas" Thomas *See* MH Blues, MH Folk

Irma Thomas *See* MH Blues, MH R&B

James "Son" Thomas *See* MH Blues

Jesse Thomas *See* MH Blues

Luther Thomas *See* MH Jazz

Mickey Thomas *See* MH Rock

Rufus Thomas *See* MH R&B

Tabby Thomas *See* MH Blues

Linda Thomas & Dan DeLancey *See* MH Folk

Butch Thompson *See* MH Jazz

Carol Thompson *See* MH Folk

Charles W. Thompson *See* MH Blues

Dave Thompson *See* MH Blues

Eric & Suzy Thompson *See* MH Folk

Hank Thompson *See* MH Country

Jimmy Thompson *See* MH Blues

Linda Thompson *See* MH Folk

Lucky Thompson *See* MH Jazz

Malachi Thompson *See* MH Jazz

Richard Thompson/Linda Thompson/Richard & Linda Thompson *See* MH Folk, MH Rock

Sue Thompson *See* MH Country

Sylvester Thompson *See* MH Blues

Tony Thompson *See* MH R&B

The Thompson Brothers Band *See* MH Country

Thompson Twins/Babble *See* MH Rock

Paul Thorn *See* MH Rock

Kathryn Jewel Thorne *See* MH Blues

Claude Thornhill *See* MH Jazz

Bianca Thornton *See* MH Blues

Big Mama Thornton *See* MH Blues, MH R&B

George Thorogood & the Destroyers *See* MH Blues, MH Rock

Roger Thorpe *See* MH Lounge

Thrasher Shiver *See* MH Country

Henry Threadgill *See* MH Jazz

Three Dog Night *See* MH Rock

311 *See* MH Rock

Three Fish *See* MH Rock

The Three O'Clock *See* MH Rock

The Three Suns *See* MH Lounge

Three Times Dope *See* MH R&B

Throbbing Gristle *See* MH Rock

Throwing Muses/Kristin Hersh *See* MH Rock

Rick Thum *See* MH Folk

Thunderclap Newman *See* MH Rock

Kathryn Tickell *See* MH Folk

Tiffany *See* MH Rock

'Til Tuesday *See* MH Rock

Mel Tillis *See* MH Country

Pam Tillis *See* MH Country

Floyd Tillman *See* MH Country

Johnny Tillotson *See* MH Country

Steve Tilston & Maggie Boyle *See* MH Folk

Tim Dog *See* MH R&B

Timbuk 3 *See* MH Folk, MH Rock

The Time *See* MH R&B

Bobby Timmons *See* MH Jazz

Tin Machine *See* MH Rock

Tindersticks *See* MH Lounge, MH Rock

Tiny Tim *See* MH Lounge

Aaron Tippin *See* MH Country

The Billy Tipton Memorial Saxophone Quartet *See* MH Jazz

Wayman Tisdale *See* MH Jazz

T.J. Kirk *See* MH Jazz

Cal Tjader *See* MH Jazz, MH Lounge

TLC *See* MH R&B

Toad the Wet Sprocket *See* MH Rock

Toast String Stretchers *See* MH Folk

Jeremy Toback *See* MH Rock

Toenut *See* MH Rock

The Tokens/The Tokens Featuring Mitch Margo/The Four Winds/The Buddies/The Coeds/Cross Country *See* MH Rock

Tony Toliver *See* MH Country

Charles Tolliver *See* MH Jazz

Tommy Boy *See* MH R&B

Tommy Tutone *See* MH Rock

Tone-Loc *See* MH R&B

Tones on Tail *See* MH Rock

Tonic *See* MH Rock

Tony D *See* MH R&B

Tony! Toni! Tone! *See* MH R&B

Too Much Joy *See* MH Rock

Too $hort *See* MH R&B

Tool/The Replicants *See* MH Rock

Torch Song *See* MH Rock

Mel Tormé *See* MH Jazz, MH Lounge

Tornados *See* MH Rock

Tortoise *See* MH Rock

Peter Tosh *See* MH R&B

Toto *See* MH Rock

Touchstone *See* MH Folk

Allen Toussaint *See* MH R&B, MH Rock

Tower of Power *See* MH R&B, MH Rock

Ralph Towner *See* MH Jazz

Henry Townsend *See* MH Blues

Pete Townshend *See* MH Rock

The Tractors *See* MH Country

The Traditional Grass *See* MH Country

Traffic *See* MH Rock

The Tragically Hip *See* MH Rock

Horace Trahan *See* MH Folk

The Trammps *See* MH R&B

Trance Mission *See* MH Jazz

Tranquility Bass *See* MH Rock

Transglobal Underground *See* MH Rock

Transister *See* MH Rock

Translator *See* MH Rock

Trapezoid *See* MH Folk

Artie Traum *See* MH Folk

Happy Traum/Happy & Artie Traum *See* MH Folk

The Traveling Wilburys *See* MH Rock

Mary Travers *See* MH Folk

Travis *See* MH Rock

Merle Travis *See* MH Country, MH Folk

Randy Travis *See* MH Country

Tre *See* MH Blues

Treadmill Trackstar *See* MH Rock

Treat Her Right *See* MH Rock

Treble Charger *See* MH Rock

The Tremeloes/Brian Poole & the Tremeloes/Chip Hawkes' Tremeloes *See* MH Rock

The Treniers *See* MH Rock

Jackie Trent *See* MH Lounge

Ralph Tresvant *See* MH R&B

Rick Trevino *See* MH Country

Trian *See* MH Folk

Tribal Tech *See* MH Jazz

A Tribe Called Quest *See* MH Jazz, MH R&B

Ed Trickett *See* MH Folk

Tricky *See* MH Rock

The Triffids *See* MH Rock

Trillium *See* MH Folk

Trio *See* MH Rock

Trip Shakespeare *See* MH Rock

Tony Trischka *See* MH Country, MH Folk

Lennie Tristano *See* MH Jazz

Travis Tritt *See* MH Country

Triumph *See* MH Rock

The Troggs *See* MH Rock

Trouble Funk *See* MH R&B

Eva Trout *See* MH Rock

Trout Fishing in America *See* MH Folk

Robin Trower *See* MH Rock

True Believers *See* MH Rock

Frankie Trumbauer *See* MH Jazz

Susan Trump *See* MH Folk

Jennifer Trynin *See* MH Rock

Assif Tsahar *See* MH Jazz

Tsunami *See* MH Rock

Tuatara *See* MH Rock

Ernest Tubb *See* MH Country, MH Folk

Justin Tubb *See* MH Country

The Tubes *See* MH Rock

Tuck & Patti *See* MH Jazz, MH Lounge

Bessie Tucker *See* MH Blues

Leslie Tucker *See* MH Folk

Luther Tucker *See* MH Blues

Maureen Tucker *See* MH Rock

Mickey Tucker *See* MH Jazz

Tanya Tucker *See* MH Country

Tuff Crew *See* MH R&B

XTC/The Dukes of Stratosphear *See* MH Rock

Xymox *See* MH Rock

Yagg Fu Front *See* MH R&B

Yosuke Yamashita *See* MH Jazz

Yamo *See* MH Rock

Frankie Yankovic *See* MH Lounge

Weird Al Yankovic *See* MH Rock

Glenn Yarbrough *See* MH Folk

Yarbrough & Peoples *See* MH R&B

The Yardbirds *See* MH Blues, MH Rock

Peter Yarrow *See* MH Folk

Yaz/Yazoo *See* MH Rock

Trisha Yearwood *See* MH Country

Yello *See* MH Rock

The Yellowjackets *See* MH Jazz

Yes *See* MH Rock

Yo La Tengo *See* MH Rock

Yo Yo *See* MH R&B

Dwight Yoakam *See* MH Country, MH Rock

Asa Yoelson *See* MH Lounge

You Am I *See* MH Rock

Faron Young *See* MH Country

Jesse Colin Young *See* MH Folk, MH Rock

John Young *See* MH Jazz

Johnny Young *See* MH Blues

Johnny Lamar Young *See* MH Blues

Larry Young/Khalid Yasin Abdul Aziz *See* MH Jazz

Lester Young *See* MH Jazz

Mighty Joe Young *See* MH Blues

Neil Young *See* MH Country, MH Folk, MH Rock

Paul Young *See* MH R&B, MH Rock

Rusty Young *See* MH Rock

Snooky Young *See* MH Jazz

Steve Young *See* MH Country, MH Folk

Young Black Teenagers *See* MH R&B

Young Fresh Fellows/Scott McCaughey/The Minus Five *See* MH Rock

Young-Holt Unlimited *See* MH R&B

Young Lay *See* MH R&B

Young Marble Giants *See* MH Rock

Young M.C. *See* MH R&B

The Young Rascals/The Rascals *See* MH R&B, MH Rock

Young Tradition *See* MH Folk

Yum-Yum *See* MH Rock

Z/Dweezil Zappa *See* MH Rock

Rachel Z *See* MH Jazz

Pia Zadora *See* MH Lounge

Zamfir *See* MH Lounge

Robin Zander *See* MH Rock

Dan Zanes *See* MH Rock

Bobby Zankel *See* MH Jazz

Zapp/Zapp & Roger *See* MH R&B

Dweezil Zappa *See* MH Rock

Frank Zappa *See* MH Jazz, MH Rock

Joe Zawinul *See* MH Jazz

Diane Zeigler *See* MH Folk

Denny Zeitlin *See* MH Jazz

Martin Zellar/Gear Daddies *See* MH Rock

Radim Zenkl *See* MH Folk

Warren Zevon *See* MH Rock

Zhane *See* MH R&B

Zimbabwe Legit *See* MH R&B

Rusty Zinn *See* MH Blues

The Zombies *See* MH Rock

Zony Mash *See* MH Jazz

John Zorn *See* MH Jazz

Zumpano *See* MH Rock

Zuzu's Petals *See* MH Rock

Zydeco Force *See* MH Folk

Zydeco Hi-Rollers *See* MH Folk

ZZ Top *See* MH Blues, MH Rock

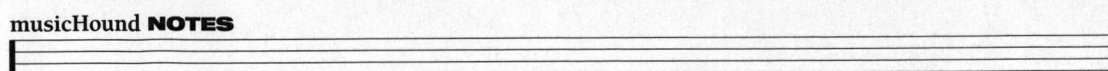

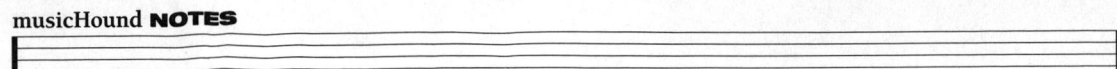

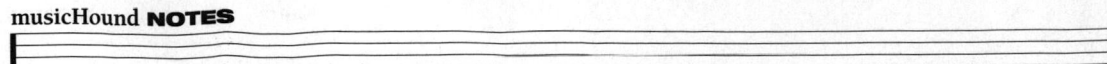

LOOKING TO BUILD A MUSIC COLLECTION?
These helpful guides tell you
what to buy – and why

MusicHound® R&B:
The Essential Album Guide

Rhythm and Blues, today's hottest-selling music category, includes gospel, soul, funk, rap, hip-hop and urban contemporary styles. With this definitive guide to the genre, *MusicHound R&B* reviews the work of more than 1,000 artists and groups, directing fans and collectors to the best buys. The book contains more than 100 photos to highlight the text plus a special resource section which brings the fans closer to the music scene.

Gary Graff, Josh Freedom du Lac and Jim McFarlin • 1997 • paperback with music CD • 766 pp. • ISBN 1-57859-026-4

"An amazingly complete source ... an essential buy!" — Urban Online

MusicHound® Blues:
The Essential Album Guide

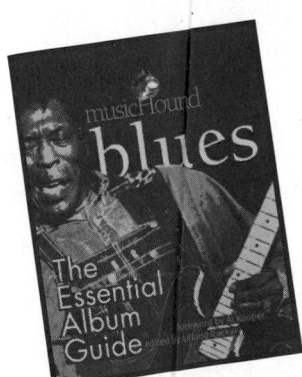

See stunning photos. Listen to great music. Discover hot blues artists — from classic to contemporary. Get all this and more with *MusicHound Blues*. One hundred amazing photographs, a free sampler CD from the House of Blues and more than 600 essays on performers of acoustic and electric blues are included in this indispensable buyer's guide. Pick up advice, reviews and ratings on artists ranging from Robert Johnson to Kenny Wayne Shepherd and Jonny Lang. Become hip to the distinctive sounds of Mississippi, East Texas, Chicago, New Orleans and the West Coast — with *MusicHound Blues*.

Leland Rucker • 1998 • paperback with music CD
511 pp. • ISBN 1-57859-030-2

"One of the most satisfying of books of its type ... discussions supply valuable insights. A very enjoyable and useful guide that hits the spot."
— Cadence (The Review of Jazz & Blues)

MusicHound® Folk: The Essential Album Guide

Folkies span the generations but have one thing in common — they're looking for advice on the best of historic recordings as well as a heads-up on new performers. *MusicHound Folk* is the first and only comprehensive buyer's guide to the entire folk genre, profiling the work of 1,200 artists. Legends like Guthrie, Dylan and Seeger are covered as well as many obscure but inspirational artists like Queen Ida and Spider John Koerner plus current favorites like Mary Chapin Carpenter, Tracy Chapman and Lyle Lovett.

Neal Walters and Brian Mansfield • 1998 • paperback with music CD
1,030 pp. • ISBN 1-57859-037-X

"MusicHound Folk is a tremendous resource, and a volume that I recommend to everyone either as a reference guide for yourself, or as a tool to introduce folk music to your friends."
— Phyllis Barney (Folk Alliance)

VISIBLE INK PRESS

free ROCK music from capitol records

CAPITOL RECORDS delivers!
Want more information on any of the artists on this sampler?
Log on to **hollywoodandvine.com/signmeup** and get press
releases (before they hit the paper), plus advance tour dates,
music, news, and more!
Or write Capitol Records at **mail@hollywoodandvine.com**.

1. **Plastilina Mosh** "Monster Truck" from the album *Aquamosh*

2. **Sonichrome** "Pack Up and Leave" from the album *Breathe the Daylight*

3. **Tommy Hendriksen** "I See the Sun" from the album *Tommy Hendriksen*

4. **Less Than Jake** "Help Save the Youth of America from Exploding" from the album *Hello Rockview*

5. **Second Coming** "Soft" from the album *Second Coming*

6. **Block** "Rhinoceros" from the album *Timing Is Everything*

7. **Kendall Payne** "Honest" from the album *Jordan's Sister*

8. **John Hiatt** "Have a Little Faith in Me" from the album *The Best of John Hiatt, 1973–1998*

9. **Weston** "Bus Stop" from the album *Return to Mono*

10. **Megadeth** "A Secret Place" from the album *Cryptic Writings*

11. **Fat Amy** "Fortunate" from the album *5-way Switch*

12. **The Push Stars** "Everything Shines" from the motion picture soundtrack *There's Something about Mary*